THE WALL STREET JOURNAL.
ALMANAC
1998

THE WALL STREET JOURNAL.
ALMANAC

1998

The Staff of
THE WALL STREET JOURNAL

Ronald J. Alsop
EDITOR

BALLANTINE BOOKS · NEW YORK

Copyright © 1997 by Dow Jones & Company, Inc.

All rights reserved under International and Pan-American
Copyright Conventions. Published in the United States by
Ballantine Books, a division of Random House, Inc., New
York, and simultaneously in Canada by Random House of
Canada Limited, Toronto.

http://www.randomhouse.com

Library of Congress Catalog Card Number: 97-97074

ISBN: 0-345-40521-8

Manufactured in the United States of America

First Edition: November 1997

10 9 8 7 6 5 4 3 2 1

CONTENTS

(This Contents lists articles [in italics] and broad subject categories. For more detail, consult the Index beginning on page 1115.)

Preface

When I took on the challenge of creating *The Wall Street Journal Almanac* in 1996, I knew there were plenty of other almanacs out there and this book would have to be truly distinctive. So I cleared my desk—and my mind—of other almanacs and wrote the outline for the book on a blank slate that I embellished with new features and statistics up until this past summer.

It has been an exciting—at times, exhausting—creation, but the result of the past year and a half, I believe, is a unique almanac tailored to the needs of today's time-pressured consumers. "The almanac for the 21st century," as the writers of the promotional copy for the book put it.

This almanac contains thousands of facts on an array of subjects, all presented in a user-friendly format. What it does *not* contain are dense lists of names and numbers in tiny type. Rather, the information is provided clearly in graphs, charts and tables, most of which are accompanied by a brief description of the trend the numbers illustrate. Statistics on states and foreign countries are presented in a format that makes them easy to locate. The data are arranged so that they flow logically through the entire book, with one subject leading naturally into another. And the articles and essays sprinkled throughout the almanac provide incisive analysis of the data—plus some very fine writing.

Because *The Wall Street Journal* is first and foremost a business and financial newspaper, the almanac naturally provides detailed information on the business world, the economy and the financial markets. Among other things, you can follow the path of the Dow Jones industrials, determine how your mutual fund has performed, check the leading economic indicators, learn about the recent federal tax cuts, and compare home prices in your area with the rest of the country.

But like the *Journal*, the almanac is much more than a business publication. Reflecting the *Journal*'s increasing breadth of coverage in the 1990s, this book also includes the political scene in Washington, travel, entertainment, sports, health and medicine, education, technology and international affairs.

This is an almanac to read, not just to consult when you need to know the name of the twelfth president of the United States or the most active trading day on the New York Stock Exchange. That information is here, but there also are many fascinating facts you might not expect to find in an almanac. How does your job rank on the list of most and least stressful occupations? How does your kid's allowance compare with the national average? Which occupations are expected to grow the most between now and the early part of the 21st century? Which movie is really the box-office champ of all time? Which corporate executives make the most money? It's all here in *The Wall Street Journal Almanac*.

The almanac chronicles the news events of the past year as thoroughly as publishing deadlines would allow. It also takes a look ahead. Four people who make their living predicting the future for major corporations have compiled their list of coming trends exclusively for *The Wall Street Journal Almanac*. In addition, the book provides a forecast of what may happen next in some of the hottest spots around the world and a preview of the millennium.

A major distinguishing feature of this almanac is the collection of essays and stories by *Wall Street Journal* reporters and editors. Journalists who are experts in their fields have written articles that provide interpretation of the top news stories of the year and the most significant issues affecting our lives. Washington bureau chief Alan Murray offers his view of President Clinton's second term. Detroit bureau chief Robert Simison writes about where the auto industry is headed and holds out the possibility that cars may actually get cheaper. Education reporter Steve Stecklow gives parents cautionary advice about the college admissions process, while writer Lisa Miller bemoans the costly and unpleasant state of travel today. And Carol Hymowitz writes about the blurring lines between the workplace and our personal lives. (Appropriately, perhaps, Carol filed her essay to me while on vacation in Massachusetts.)

I want to thank those writers and the many other *Journal* staffers who contributed wonderful essays and stories to the almanac. My appreciation also goes to Paul Steiger and Jim Pensiero, editors at the *Journal*, and to Linda Grey and Ginny Faber at Ballantine Books, for their enthusiastic support of the almanac.

I would like to single out a few people at the *Journal* who helped with the almanac almost from the day I started the project: Suzanne Vranica, Andrea Petersen and Eileen Kinsella. I also received valuable assistance from summer intern Laurie Snyder and the *Journal*'s Washington bureau, statistics department in South Brunswick, N.J., and graphics department in New York.

My appreciation goes to the many people who so generously allowed me to use their proprietary data, including Dun & Bradstreet, NPD Group, Information Resources, Nielsen Media, and DRI/McGraw-Hill. Many government agencies also became very familiar with my name over the last year. Special thanks to Sandy Smith at the National Center for Health Statistics, Larry Moran at the Bureau of Economic Analysis, Kathy Hoyle and her colleagues at the Bureau of Labor Statistics, and the many statisticians at the Census Bureau.

Finally, thanks and love to my wife, Marybeth, who helped me proofread lists of data, and my son, Matthew, for their support and patience—even when I brought the almanac project along with us on vacation.

Enjoy the almanac and consult it often!

Ronald J. Alsop, Editor

KEY ECONOMIC INDICATORS

Real GDP

The real gross domestic product, the measure of all goods and services produced in the U.S., increased at an annual rate of 3.3% in the second quarter of 1997. That was strong growth for the economy, but less than the 4.9% annual rate in the first quarter.

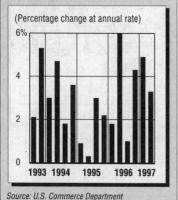

(Percentage change at annual rate)

Source: U.S. Commerce Department

For more on GDP, see pages 154–155.

Unemployment Rate

The job market remained tight into the second half of 1997. Unemployment in August 1997 rose to a seasonally adjusted 4.9% of the labor force from 4.8% in July. But it still was near quarter-century lows.

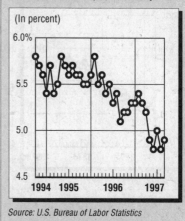

(In percent)

Source: U.S. Bureau of Labor Statistics

For more on Unemployment, see pages 157–158.

Consumer Prices

Inflation was tame through much of 1997. Consumer prices rose 2.2% in the 12-month period ended in August 1997. Excluding the food and energy sectors, the price increase was 2.3%.

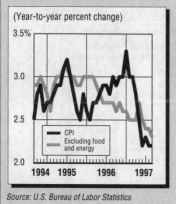

(Year-to-year percent change)

CPI
Excluding food
and energy

Source: U.S. Bureau of Labor Statistics

For more on Consumer Prices, see pages 160–163.

Producer Price Index

Producer prices of finished goods rose a seasonally adjusted 0.3% in August 1997. The increase followed months of declining producer prices. But excluding volatile food and energy prices, producer prices inched up just 0.1% in August from July.

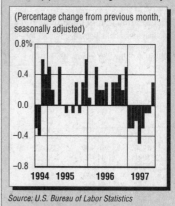

(Percentage change from previous month, seasonally adjusted)

Source: U.S. Bureau of Labor Statistics

For more on Producer Price Index, see pages 164–166.

Retail Sales

Retail sales climbed a moderate 0.4% in August, following a 0.9% spurt in July. Without an 0.8% increase in car sales, retail sales grew just 0.3% in August. The slower growth was expected to keep prices steady.

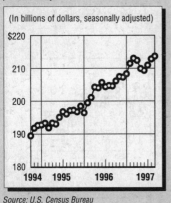

(In billions of dollars, seasonally adjusted)

Source: U.S. Census Bureau

For more on Retail Sales, see page 172.

U.S. Trade Deficit

The U.S trade deficit ballooned to $10.3 billion in July, a 25% jump over June, reflecting substantial increases in deficits with Japan and China.

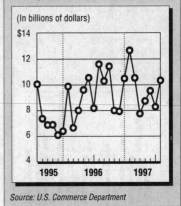

(In billions of dollars)

Source: U.S. Commerce Department

For more on U.S. Trade Deficit, see page 181.

Shares of Household Income

The income gap between the wealthy and the poor grew in 1996. The wealthiest 5% of households received 21.4% of 1996 income, while the bottom fifth claimed only 3.7%.

Year	Lowest fifth	Second fifth	Third fifth	Fourth fifth	Highest fifth	Top 5 percent
1985	4.0%	9.7%	16.3%	24.6%	45.3%	17.0%
1990	3.9	9.6	15.9	24.0	46.6	18.6
1995	3.7	9.1	15.2	23.3	48.7	21.0
1996	3.7	9.0	15.1	23.3	49.0	21.4

Source: U.S. Census Bureau

Median Household Income by Race and Hispanic Origin (Income in 1996 dollars)

Median household income, adjusted for inflation, continued to recover in 1996. For the total population, median household income rose 1.2% to $35,492 from $35,082 in 1995, but it still fell short of the $36,575 of 1989.

Year	All races	White	Black	Asian or Pacific Islander	Hispanic origin
1985	$34,439	$36,320	$21,609	–	$25,467
1986	35,642	37,471	21,588	–	26,272
1987	35,994	37,924	21,646	–	26,706
1988	36,108	38,172	21,760	$42,795	27,002
1989	36,575	38,473	22,881	45,681	27,737
1990	35,945	37,492	22,420	46,158	26,806
1991	34,705	36,367	21,665	41,989	26,140
1992	34,261	36,020	20,974	42,274	25,271
1993	33,922	35,788	21,209	41,638	24,850
1994	34,158	36,026	22,261	42,858	24,796
1995	35,082	36,822	23,054	41,813	23,535
1996	35,492	37,161	23,482	43,276	24,906

Source: U.S. Census Bureau

For more on Household Income, see pages 174–178.

1997 NOBEL LAUREATES

(Winners of the Nobel Prize in all categories since 1901 appear on pages 938–945.)

Physiology or Medicine
Dr. Stanley B. Prusiner of the University of California, San Francisco, for his 1982 discovery of prions. The infectious proteins have been implicated in "mad cow" disease and other brain-wasting ailments.

Literature
Dario Fo, Italian playwright and actor, for his satiric plays. Such works as *Mistero Buffo* and *Accidental Death of an Anarchist* drew condemnation from Rome and the Vatican.

Peace
International Campaign to Ban Landmines and the campaign's coordinator Jody Williams for their work toward the banning and clearing of land mines. The $1 million prize was divided equally.

Economic Sciences
Robert C. Merton of Harvard University and Myron S. Scholes of Stanford University for their pathbreaking research that helped spawn the huge stock-options industry.

Chemistry
One half to Paul D. Boyer of the University of California, Los Angeles, and Dr. John E. Walker of the Medical Research Council Laboratory of Molecular Biology in Britain, for their work on the mechanism underlying the synthesis of adenosine triphosphate (ATP), which functions as a carrier of energy in all living organisms. One half to Jens C. Skou of Aarhus University in Denmark, for the discovery of the enzyme sodium, potassium-stimulated adenosine triphosphatase, which maintains the balance of sodium and potassium ions in the living cell.

Physics
Steven Chu of Stanford University, Claude Cohen-Tannoudji of the College de France and Ecole Normale Superieure in Paris, and Dr. William D. Phillips of the National Institute of Standards and Technology for development of methods to cool and trap atoms with laser light. The prize was awarded jointly.

1998 SOCIAL SECURITY CHANGES

Cost-of-Living Adjustment (COLA)

Based on the increase in the Consumer Price Index (CPI-W) from the third quarter of 1996 through the third quarter of 1997, recipients of Social Security benefits and Supplemental Security Income payments received a 2.1% COLA for 1998.

	1997	**1998**
Tax Rate		
Employee	7.65%*	7.65%*
Self-Employed	15.30%	15.30%

*The Social Security portion is 6.2% on earnings up to the maximum taxable amount; the Medicare portion is 1.45% on all earnings.

Maximum Earnings Taxable

Social Security	$65,400	$68,400
Medicare	No limit	No limit

Retirement Earnings Exempt Amounts

Age 65–69	$13,500/yr. ($1,125/mo)	$14,500/yr ($1,209/mo)
Under age 65	$8,640/yr ($720/mo)	$9,120/yr ($760/mo)

Note: For people 65 through 69, $1 in benefits will be withheld for every $3 in earnings above the limit. For people under 65, $1 will be withheld for every $2 in earnings above the limit.

Maximum Social Security Benefit

(for workers retiring at age 65 in January)	$1,326/mo	$1,342/mo

1998

JANUARY

S	M	T	W	T	F	S
				1	2	3
4	5	6	7	8	9	10
11	12	13	14	15	16	17
18	19	20	21	22	23	24
25	26	27	28	29	30	31

1 New Year's Day
15 Martin Luther King, Jr.'s Birthday
19 Martin Luther King, Jr. Day

FEBRUARY

S	M	T	W	T	F	S
1	2	3	4	5	6	7
8	9	10	11	12	13	14
15	16	17	18	19	20	21
22	23	24	25	26	27	28

12 Lincoln's Birthday
14 Valentine's Day
16 Washington-Lincoln Day
22 Washington's Birthday
25 Ash Wednesday

MARCH

S	M	T	W	T	F	S
1	2	3	4	5	6	7
8	9	10	11	12	13	14
15	16	17	18	19	20	21
22	23	24	25	26	27	28
29	30	31				

17 St. Patrick's Day

APRIL

S	M	T	W	T	F	S
			1	2	3	4
5	6	7	8	9	10	11
12	13	14	15	16	27	18
19	20	21	22	23	24	25
26	27	28	29	30		

5 Palm Sunday
5 Daylight Saving Time begins
10 Good Friday
11 Passover
12 Easter Sunday
22 Professional Secretaries Day

MAY

S	M	T	W	T	F	S
					1	2
3	4	5	6	7	8	9
10	11	12	13	14	15	16
17	18	19	20	21	22	23
24	25	26	27	28	29	30
31						

10 Mother's Day
16 Armed Forces Day
18 Victoria Day (Canada)
25 Memorial Day-Observed
30 Memorial Day

JUNE

S	M	T	W	T	F	S
	1	2	3	4	5	6
7	8	9	10	11	12	13
14	15	16	17	18	19	20
21	22	23	24	25	26	27
28	29	30				

14 Flag Day
21 Father's Day
24 St. Jean (Quebec)

JULY

S	M	T	W	T	F	S
			1	2	3	4
5	6	7	8	9	10	11
12	13	14	15	16	17	18
19	20	21	22	23	24	25
26	27	28	29	30	31	

1 Canada Day (Canada)
4 Independence Day

AUGUST

S	M	T	W	T	F	S
						1
2	3	4	5	6	7	8
9	10	11	12	13	14	15
16	17	18	19	20	21	22
23	24	25	26	27	28	29
30	31					

SEPTEMBER

S	M	T	W	T	F	S
		1	2	3	4	5
6	7	8	9	10	11	12
13	14	15	16	17	18	19
20	21	22	23	24	25	26
27	28	29	30			

7 Labor Day
21 Rosh Hashanah
30 Yom Kippur

OCTOBER

S	M	T	W	T	F	S
				1	2	3
4	5	6	7	8	9	10
11	12	13	14	15	16	17
18	19	20	21	22	23	24
25	26	27	28	29	30	31

12 Columbus Day
12 Thanksgiving Day (Canada)
24 United Nations Day
25 Daylight Saving Time ends
31 Halloween

NOVEMBER

S	M	T	W	T	F	S
1	2	3	4	5	6	7
8	9	10	11	12	13	14
15	16	17	18	19	20	21
22	23	24	25	26	27	28
29	30					

3 Election day
11 Veterans Day
11 Remembrance Day (Canada)
26 Thanksgiving Day

DECEMBER

S	M	T	W	T	F	S
		1	2	3	4	5
6	7	8	9	10	11	12
13	14	15	16	17	18	19
20	21	22	23	24	25	26
27	28	29	30	31		

14 Hanukkah
25 Christmas Day
26 Boxing Day (Canada)

THE YEAR IN REVIEW

Tobacco Peace Talks

It all began on April 14, 1994, with a stark tableau that instantly became an indelible symbol of America's most embattled industry: Seven tobacco chieftains in a lineup, each raising his right hand and intoning to Congress that nicotine wasn't addictive.

"It was the paradigmatic moment," says John Scanlon, a public-relations veteran who has defended the industry for years. "The presentation was so incredible and unbelievable that the industry's traditional arguments—about the whole issue of choice—were tainted even in the eyes of people who wanted to be rational about cigarette companies."

Since that fateful day, cigarette marketers have been forced to drop their smoke screen and start negotiating the terms of their survival. After three months at the bargaining table, the companies—Philip Morris Cos., RJR Nabisco Holdings Corp., B.A.T Industries' Brown and Williamson, and Loews Corp.'s Lorillard—would strike a historic settlement agreement with the attorneys general of 40 states, making an unprecedented host of concessions to wipe away the legal attacks that were depressing their stocks and threatening their very existence.

The companies are now offering to pay $368.5 billion over the next 25 years. They're willing to eliminate billboard advertising, cigarette vending machines, sports promotions, and ads with people and cartoon characters, such as the Marlboro Man and Joe Camel. They would yield to regulation by the Food and Drug Administration and print dire new warning labels such as "Smoking Can Kill You." And they would stop hiding what they know about the deadly effects of smoking—for

the first time, revealing to smokers just how much tar and nicotine they are really inhaling and disclosing the additives believed to make U.S. cigarettes among the world's most hazardous.

For now, it's anyone's guess if the landmark tobacco settlement will survive a bruising fight in the White House and Congress. But regardless of the outcome, the place of cigarettes in American culture and society will never again be the same. Here is a look at the forces that shaped the cigarette controversy and brought the industry to the negotiating table.

Since its beginnings, the tobacco industry has been able to make and market its deadly products free from the kind of government oversight that's borne by virtually every other consumer product in America. But on August 10, 1995, after more than four years of examination, the Food and Drug Administration launched its historic effort to regulate the industry. The FDA's daring move would prove so successful that it ultimately reduced the tobacco industry to haggling over the fine points of how—but not whether—it would be controlled. In the face of an attack that was legally upheld and massively popular, tobacco negotiators say the industry finally concluded that settling was the only way to guarantee that overzealous bureaucrats would never regulate its product out of existence.

The FDA's effort was hinged on nicotine, the addictive chemical in cigarettes. In taking on the industry, the agency would ultimately conclude that cigarette makers not only knew about the addictiveness of nicotine, but they also deliberately relied on it to keep smokers puffing. Once it made that determination, the FDA began looking for a political strategy that would overcome decades of resistance among lawmakers and White House officials alike.

The key came when the FDA Commissioner David Kessler spirited his tobacco team off to Airlie House in Warrenton, Va. for a retreat. There, Dr. Kessler, a pediatrician with a law degree, stumbled on a little-known 1977 study of underage smokers called Project 16. This study, conducted by Imperial Tobacco Ltd., Canada's biggest cigarette seller, explained in part: "However intriguing smoking was around 11, 12, or 13, by the age of 16 or 17 many regretted their use of cigarettes for health reasons and because they feel unable to stop smoking when they want to."

That was it. Forget about all the swirling controversy about smoking and cancer. Who could possibly dispute that cigarettes were a grave threat to the public health of America's children? Henceforth, Dr. Kessler would couch his regulatory ambitions over cigarettes using the morally and politically unimpeachable rationale that smoking was a "pediatric disease."

While the FDA was ruminating about the regulation of cigarettes, a group of Mississippi attorneys was developing a new legal tack that would end up putting tremendous pressure on the $45 billion tobacco industry. Their idea—sue the industry for the Medicaid costs of treating ailing smokers—would end up dramatically increasing the risks of a bankrupting verdict.

Spearheading the effort were two law school buddies who would later emerge at the center of the tobacco industry negotiations. Mississippi Attorney General Michael Moore tapped his old friend Richard Scruggs, a plaintiffs lawyer who had made a fortune from asbestos cases, to sue the industry. Not content merely to represent Mississippi, Mr. Scruggs, with the telegenic and politically ambitious Mr. Moore in tow, crisscrossed the country in his private jet to enlist other state officials to his cause.

By the time the settlement talks were under way in April 1997, more than twenty states had filed copycat suits against the industry, and the companies were braced to lose three or four of the cases. As one negotiator puts it, "The companies were worried that if they lost even one they wouldn't be able to post the bond for appeal."

Both Mississippi and the FDA built their cases with the help of Jeffrey Wigand, a former research chief at Brown & Williamson who later emerged as the highest-ranking defector in industry history. Over the past three years, the scientist revealed the industry's darkest secrets and, in the process, helped a number of government officials and plaintiffs' lawyers. One of his most damaging revelations: Leading tobacco firms add ammonia-based chemicals to cigarettes to convert nicotine into a more potent form called "free nicotine."

"Jeff demonstrated the most blatant examples of nicotine manipulation," Dr. Kessler says. "It all went to the issue of the companies' intent."

Mr. Wigand had come to Brown & Williamson in 1989, lured by the promise that he would lead the development of a safer cigarette. But the company's research chief quickly became frustrated as he came to believe that his efforts were being thwarted by B&W Chief Executive Thomas Sandefur, Jr., who ultimately fired him. His bitterness grew when the company sued him for allegedly breaking his confidentiality agreement and pressured him to sign a more stringent one. But it wasn't until Mr. Sandefur raised his hand before Congress and attested that nicotine wasn't addictive that Mr. Wigand decided to take action.

"That put it over the top," Mr. Wigand says. "When that TV image replayed itself in my mind, I realized that, by my silence, I was not that far removed from the men on my screen."

In March 1996, the industry discovered it had a wholly different breed of enemy within: Bennett S. LeBow, the financier who controls Liggett Group, the industry's smallest and most debt-ridden player. Mr. LeBow, long regarded as an interloper within the tobacco companies' cozy fraternity, unilaterally agreed to settle four state Medicaid suits and other major litigation pending against his firm. The shocking capitulation, at a time when the other tobacco firms were still vowing never to give in, sent the stock prices of his competitors plummeting.

After the shock of his defection wore off, Wall Street started to warm to Mr. LeBow's idea. Although investors roundly rejected the specifics of Mr. LeBow's settlement, they began to signal their support for an industry-wide settlement. This encouraged the bigger tobacco makers to take the idea of settlement a lot more seriously, too.

About a year after Liggett's settlement, Mr. LeBow broke with his brethren again by making stunning admissions about the products he sold. Persuaded that his rivals would soon reach a broad settlement, and determined not to make any payments under such a deal, he effectively turned state's evidence. To settle on favorable terms with all 22 attorneys general then suing the industry, he declared nicotine addictive and pledged to stamp that warning on cigarette packs. He asserted that cigarette marketers target children. He even agreed to turn over privileged documents, including notes about three decades of meetings among lawyers from the leading tobacco firms.

Although the big cigarette makers were by then on the verge of pulling up to the bargaining table anyway, some believe that Mr. LeBow delivered one last prod. Says the attorney, Mr. Scruggs, "He just created more vilification for the industry on the national scene, which was one of their motivations to settle."

Then, on August 9, 1996, the unthinkable happened. Grady Carter, a retired air-traffic controller, shattered the tobacco companies' perfect record in court by winning a $750,000 verdict against Brown & Williamson. His victory intensified the industry's fear that jurors' attitudes were being shaped by the popular culture's relentless hostility toward cigarette makers and that Big Tobacco's blame-the-smoker defense was wearing thin.

The Carter verdict, which is under appeal, also provided evidence that the flood of internal documents that had surfaced from the industry's own files was taking a toll. Jurors cited Brown & Williamson documents—some suggesting that officials there long understood the health risks of smoking—as a key reason they held the company liable for Mr. Carter's illness.

Shortly after the Carter loss, Martin Broughton, the chief executive of London-based B.A.T, made a transatlantic phone call to Geoffrey Bible, the chairman of Philip Morris, to ask whether he had given any thought to settling the tobacco cases once and for all. Mr. Broughton's exploratory phone call emboldened Mr. Bible to contact his counterparts at RJR, Loews and UST Inc., the other major U.S. tobacco firms.

Beginning in September of 1996, Mr. Broughton and the other CEOs held a series of secret meetings at the Plaza, St. Regis and Four Seasons hotels in New York to decide together what they would be willing to give up to make the Grady Carter loss their last as well as their first. On April 3, 1997, negotiations with the anti-tobacco forces began.

Suein L. Hwang and Alix M. Freedman, Wall Street Journal staff reporters who cover the tobacco industry

Campaign-Finance Scandal

With a 1996 national election that broke all previous spending records, it was almost preordained that there would be a national campaign-finance scandal.

Not since Watergate, when huge cash contributions were handed, under the table, to the White House in manila envelopes and black satchels, have the excesses of political fund-raising been so glaring. One of the ironies of the latest imbroglio is that some of the very "reforms" that were enacted in the wake of Watergate have become loopholes that the two political parties exploited in 1996 in order to raise unprecedented sums from large, private interests. In the frenzy to fill campaign coffers, both the Democratic and the Republican parties appear to have transgressed the borders of legality.

The quest for "soft money" is at the root of the fund-raising furor. Altogether, more than $2.6 billion was spent in the 1996 election cycle (January 1, 1995–December 31, 1996) by candidates for federal office, the two major political parties, political-action committees, and other groups. But the most explosive growth came in soft-money contributions, which are made outside the limits of the federal election laws that were enacted after Watergate. These laws, meant to curb the influence of special-interest money, strictly limited individual contributions, outlawed direct corporate and labor union contributions to candidates, and provided some public financing of presidential elections.

But a loophole, spelled out in a Federal Election Commission directive in 1978, allows unlimited contributions for certain party-building activities, such as get-out-the-vote drives, that don't benefit specific candidates. In 1996, this soft-money loophole became a giant money pit, with the two political parties raising six-figure donations from a host of special interests, including labor unions (which also spent $35 million in members' dues to finance an independent advertising blitz), big corporations and shadowy, foreign businessmen.

For example, the Democratic Party raised $123.9 million in soft money, up 242% since the 1992 election. The Republicans raised $138.2 million in soft money, an increase of 178% from four years earlier. The top soft-money contributor to the Republicans was Philip Morris, with $2.5 million, and the top Democratic soft-money contributor was Seagram, with $1.3 million contributed by the company, its subsidiaries and its executives. This flood of soft money was used by both parties to underwrite television advertisements which buttressed the campaign messages of Bill Clinton and Bob Dole. The Democrats and Republicans maintained the ads advocated party, not candidate, agendas and thus were legally paid for. But Common Cause, a group that advocates campaign-finance reform, has challenged the legality of the parties' spending in filings made to the Justice Department and the Federal Election Commission.

The soft money race also intensified after a June 1996 Supreme Court decision that said party organizations could spend an unlimited amount of money to promote their issues, as long as their spending wasn't coor-dinated directly with candidates. The ruling let the parties finance ad campaigns that came perilously close to being outright Clinton and Dole endorsements.

In 1996, the competition between the two parties to raise soft money was akin to a nuclear arms race. The emphasis on these large contributions made the role of professional fund-raisers more important than ever. One of the Democratic Party's most adept fund-raisers was a Democratic National Committee official named John Huang. Exploiting the financial success of the Asian-American community and his many business connections among wealthy Asians with interests in the U.S., Mr. Huang raised more than $3.5 million in 1996. But his unusually aggressive fund-raising drive led to questions about the source of some of these contributions as election day neared. Mr. Huang's job at the Commerce Department, where he was privy to sensitive trade information and his ties to an Indonesian conglomerate, the Lippo Group, also drew scrutiny. Lippo, its executives, and their families contributed nearly $1 million to the Democratic National Committee. Many of its top executives had close ties to President Clinton, dating to his tenure as governor of Arkansas.

It is illegal for foreigners to contribute to U.S. candidates, and it is also illegal to donate money on behalf of someone else. After auditing the contributions raised by Mr. Huang, the DNC found that in many cases it was unable to confirm the legality of the funds raised by Mr. Huang and some of his close allies. In some cases, such as a fund-raising event held at a Buddhist Temple in California, donors had contributed money that was not their own. As for the Lippo-related contributions, the DNC found that some of the individuals who made big donations could not verify that they were legal residents of the U.S. When its audit was completed in early 1997, the DNC promised to return $3 million in contributions from questionable sources.

The DNC was not the only receptacle for suspect foreign funds. A legal defense fund set up by the Clintons to help defray their expenses from lawsuits stemming from the Whitewater affair and the Paula Jones sexual-harassment case was offered more than $600,000 from another Asian-American fund-raiser, Charles Yah Lin Trie. Some of the funds came from a Buddhist sect based in Taiwan. Belatedly, the defense fund disclosed that it had returned the funds raised by Mr. Trie, who worked closely raising money with Mr. Huang.

The campaign-finance scandal also stirred debate about exploiting the trappings of the presidency for financial gain. The Democrats were embarrassed when internal documents shed light on elaborate plans to use the White House for fund-raising. Although President Clinton and his top advisers denied that White House events were organized to raise money (it is illegal to use federal property to solicit money), it became clear that donors were offered various White House perks with explicit price tags, much as an auction house suggests prices for art treasures. Across one fund-raising memo, President Clinton scrawled, "Ready to start overnights right away." He was greenlighting a plan to invite big contributors to spend the night in the White House's venerable Lincoln Bedroom. Other donors were invited to fly on Air Force One. Contributors were also invited to the White House to have coffee with President Clinton. Often, the DNC received large contributions that were closely timed to contributors' White House visits.

Some of the guests who came to sip coffee with the president had questionable backgrounds, including a Chinese businessman whose company was prosecuted for illicit arms-dealings. Other big donors with foreign ties won private audiences with members of the National Security Council staff, including a Thai businesswoman, Pauline Kanchanalak, who once lobbied for Thailand. Roger Tamraz, a Lebanese-American executive who wanted the government's help in putting together a private foreign pipeline project, received special attention from the Energy Department and Central Intelligence Agency after making big donations. He also met with President Clinton. The use of national security policy makers to help donors was considered yet another area where the Clinton White House took fund-raising to new heights. The White House admitted that its vetting process for clearing visitors had broken down and pledged to more strictly scrutinize White House guests.

While major donors have always enjoyed special perks, such brazen use of the White House as a fund-raising vehicle was unprece-

dented. But the controversy over White House perks was largely one of appearances, since no law bars inviting donors to the White House for special events or private meetings with top executive-branch staff. Fund-raising calls that Vice President Al Gore made from his office in the White House complex may have been a technical legal breach, prompting a push for an investigation by an independent counsel.

Much more serious were suggestions of a foreign government's trying to influence the U.S. electoral process. Among the most explosive allegations being investigated by a Federal Bureau of Investigation task force was whether the government of China meddled in U.S. elections. According to news accounts, U.S. intelligence agencies may have intercepted messages from the Chinese embassy in Washington indicating that the Chinese government intended to disperse money to influence the 1996 elections. Whether the money was contributed, and to whom, remained unclear.

Why would China want to influence the U.S. election? One of its rivals, Taiwan, has long maintained one of the most robust lobbies in Washington. Taiwan, in turn, has many friends in the Congress, who have traveled to the small island country on all-expenses paid trips. China has felt pressure to match Taiwan's clout. It is possible, though unproven, that Messrs. Huang, Trie and other DNC fund-raisers attempted to exploit the rivalry between China and Taiwan by raising money from interests in both countries, as well as from wealthy ethnic Chinese in the rest of Asia.

The government of China has repeatedly denied that it was involved in any attempt to influence U.S. elections. If evidence proved otherwise, the fund-raising controversy would become far more serious, possibly even involving intelligence breaches. Sen. Fred Thompson, a Tennessee Republican and chairman of the Senate panel investigating the campain-finance scandal, has said there was evidence of Chinese political meddling in the 1996 U.S. elections.

As criticisms of Democratic fund-raising excesses mounted, the Republicans were embroiled in an Asian money flap of their own. A policy think tank affiliated with the Republican National Committee received a $2.2 million loan guarantee from Young Brothers Development-USA, a Florida company controlled by

Hong Kong magnate Ambrous Tung Young. The RNC and two other GOP organizations also received $122,400 in contributions from Young Bros. Because the company had little or no assets in the United States, the RNC decided to return the donations as foreign funds. The Justice Department was also reviewing the questionable RNC funds from Hong Kong. But GOP officials strongly denied any parallels with the problems of the Democrats. One RNC official called the Young Bros. flap "the equivalent of inadvertently stepping on the out-of-bounds line in a basketball game."

Shortly after the 1994 congressional elections in which the GOP won control of Congress, House Speaker Newt Gingrich and President Clinton shook hands and agreed that the campaign finance laws needed an overhaul. Then nothing happened and record sums were spent on the next election. Now, even with a plethora of scandals touching both Messrs. Gingrich and Clinton, there has been much resistance in Congress to changing the rules of the game, which heavily favor incumbents who are plugged into existing big donor networks. President Clinton has endorsed a bipartisan bill in the Senate that would place voluntary spending limits on candidates, give candidates discounted broadcast time, curb political action committees and close the soft-money loophole, among other things. But the bill faced stiff opposition.

There have been many competing campaign finance bills, including one that would lift all existing contribution limits while strengthening disclosure. Another measure would provide public funding for all federal candidates. Former Senator Bill Bradley of New Jersey endorses another approach: passage of a constitutional amendment that would allow states to set campaign-spending limits. Clearly, there is no consensus on campaign finance in Washington, and every effort to overhaul the election laws since the mid-1970s has ended in failure.

What's more, voters haven't been clamoring for campaign-finance reform. With a strong economy and a deal to balance the budget, the public gave high approval ratings to both Congress and the White House. More and more Americans seem turned off by politics (with lower voter turnouts), and each new disclosure about unethical fund-raising in Washington seems to blur into the next. Rather than public ire, the scandals seem to be inciting boredom. In the post-Watergate era, there have been so many ethics flaps, from Koreagate to Iran-Contra to the Jim Wright affair, that America seems to have a bad case of scandal fatigue.

Jill Abramson, former deputy chief of *The Wall Street Journal*'s Washington bureau

New Rules of the Global Economy

To get an idea of where the world economy is headed, take a look at how far it has come in just the past decade or so.

A new economic order, ushered in by the disintegration of the Soviet bloc and by China's partial abandonment of socialism, has brought property rights and economic freedom to billions of people. The market rules: About 50 countries have set up stock markets in recent years. The state is in retreat: Governments around the world are falling over themselves to cut regulations and sell off state-owned firms. And the buzz about the world economy is positively euphoric.

"We've entered a golden age that will last for decades," Domingo Cavallo, the former

government official who planned Argentina's successful economic restructuring of the early 1990s, told *The Wall Street Journal*. "Historians will come to see the 1990s as the time of its birth."

This is by no means to say that the world is henceforth free of economic ills such as recessions and widespread unemployment. That business will continue to have its ups and downs is recognized even in the giddy United States, where growth is strong, stock prices are flying high and joblessness is at its lowest level in decades.

Nevertheless, the worldwide embrace of market economics has changed the rules of the game. Thanks in part to the freer markets, the annual growth rate of the world economy has risen by nearly one-third in the past three years from the rate of the previous two decades. In the 20 years through 1993, the average gain in economic output was 3% a year; since then, it has been about 4%. The WEFA Group forecasts that world output will continue to grow about 4% a year for the next 20 years. At that rate, the global economy would double in size by the year 2015.

Trade among nations has shifted into overdrive. Between 1985 and 1996, world exports grew 94%, while exports by developing nations surged 217%. Countries that a few years ago were enemies—such as China and South Korea—are now major trading partners. Freer markets in places like China and Mexico, meanwhile, have attracted a torrent of money from the world's fat cats. Total capital flows from rich nations to developing countries, including stock purchases and government aid, grew 20% in 1996 alone, to $285 billion. And today, private companies account for 80% of the money, compared with less than 50% in 1991.

What do all these numbers mean in real terms? Consider one of the biggest turnaround stories, Egypt. For decades, Egypt ran its economy socialist-style, from the top down—and as a result, into the ground. But in the early 1990s, Egypt began adopting free-market policies—opening up to foreign investment, privatizing state companies—and since then, the economy has roared to life. Egypt now sees itself as a model for other Arab states trying to modernize their economies.

"We have always led in the political arena," Youssef Boutros-Ghali, Egypt's minister of state for economic affairs, told *The Wall Street Journal*. "Now we want to lead in economics, too."

Privatization has become a worldwide passion. In Brazil, the government prepared to sell off an electric company that serves a region the size of France. The expected price: $32 billion—more than has been spent on all previous Latin American privatizations to date. It's a worldwide trend, as a look at the business of running airports shows. Governments are putting airports up for sale to alleviate budget deficits and a shortage of flight capacity. Analysts expect tens of billions of dollars worth of airport sell-offs in coming decades. Mexico is selling up to 75 airports, for an estimated asking price of $20 billion. Russia is selling one-third of its airports, and Argentina is leasing out all its airports in a 25-year deal.

Market capitalism has whipped Marxism. But markets don't cure all the world's economic ills. Look at the banking industry. Bad management and poor regulation of lending institutions have spurred banking crises around the world, from Japan and China to Bulgaria and Venezuela. Thailand's financial crisis of 1997, which sent shock waves throughout Southeast Asia, largely stemmed from reckless lending.

In fact, the headlong rush to freer markets seems to be exacerbating financial instability. In many countries, banks haven't expanded their capital bases and haven't learned how to assess risk. Since 1980, 133 of the International Monetary Fund's 181 member nations have had "significant" banking problems, and more are on the way. In China, one-fifth of bank loans are thought to be bad.

And so, no less an authority than the IMF's managing director sounds a note of caution. "I am frequently asked: Where will we have the next international economic crises, the next Mexico?" IMF chief Michael Camdessus said. "I don't know, but I suspect it will begin with a banking crisis."

That's the view from the mountain top. Here's how the new economic order looks from the ground:

The nation that has probably gained the most by embracing free markets is CHINA, its banking mess notwithstanding. Ironic, considering the country is still run by the Communist Party. But China is squarely on the road to becoming a capitalist giant. China has emerged as an export superpower, thanks to foreign companies that have set up Chinese factories. The economy is increasingly run by private business people, not party bosses. In 1978, 78% of industrial output was contributed by state firms; today, the figure is 42%. The country that once denounced the running dogs of capitalism now boasts two of the world's most robust stock markets, in Shanghai and Shenzhen. Beijing's takeover of Hong Kong on July 1, 1997, has given China control of Asia's most dynamic business city. Many people worry that China's meddling will kill this golden goose, but it's just as likely that Hong Kong's hyper-capitalist ways will rub off on the Mainlanders. In the meantime, the Chinese economic juggernaut is rolling on. The country's per-capita income has nearly doubled in the past decade. And the IMF estimates it will take China just 16 years to close half the gap between its per-capita income and the $16,790 income of rich nations, based on China's 1990–1995 growth rates. Reaching that goal will be tough, though. China faces a host of ills that could drag down growth, including its money-losing state enterprises and its banking crisis.

SOUTHEAST ASIA, perhaps the greatest economic success story of the postwar years, fell to earth in 1997. Over the summer, Thailand quit propping up its currency and unleashed the world's worst financial storm since Mexico's near-bankruptcy in 1995. Throughout the region, currencies plunged in value against the dollar, interest rates rose, stock markets sank—and, for the first time in years, these Asian economies suddenly looked vulnerable. The loss of confidence by global financial markets wasn't supposed to happen to the likes of Thailand, Malaysia, Indonesia, Singapore and the Philippines. These economies were envied around the world for their ability to grow rapidly, lift living standards, and avoid the problems that plagued others. But global investors, by selling the region's currencies in hopes of making a quick profit, exposed a grave lack of government economic discipline. That's especially true in Thailand, the worst victim of the crisis, which faces a long and painful restructuring. Still, economists expect the storm to pass. Most of the region's economies were expected to grow in 1997—although at slower rates than before the crisis.

RUSSIA continues to make its painful transition to a market economy. Living standards have fallen sharply since the Soviet Union collapsed in 1991. Unpaid wages in Russia reached $9 billion in mid-1997, and underpaid army officers have resorted to selling blood to get by. But the Russians have nonetheless elected to push ahead with capitalism, as evidenced by the 1996 reelection of pro-reform President Boris Yeltsin. Under his leadership, Russia has freed up prices, privatized state industries, stamped out inflation and held democratic elections. One advantage of the liberalization of economic activity is that people who were once shackled to a specific job are now free to perform a wide range of work. Employees who have gone unpaid by

their companies are supplementing their incomes by growing vegetables, opening small businesses or taking construction jobs. Still, Russia has a long way to go. Only part of the economy runs on a market basis; barter and IOUs are used in many deals between businesses. What's more, the government is failing to collect sufficient taxes and hasn't yet broken up the huge and powerful energy monopolies, such as Gazprom.

In EASTERN EUROPE, two very different fates are befalling the countries that were once stuck behind the Iron Curtain. Poland, Hungary and the Czech Republic have quickly adapted to the West and capitalism. They are thriving by building free markets, attracting investment and privatizing companies. But the southern countries—Albania, Bulgaria, Romania, and most of the former Yugoslavia—seem to be in danger of turning into Europe's backwater. They suffer from ethnic conflict, lingering communist beliefs and autocratic rulers. Bulgaria, for instance, has become Europe's poorest country. Inflation-adjusted wages have fallen below $20 a month from $120 a month in 1996. A quarter of the country's banks have been shut. Gross domestic product fell 10% in 1996. More than four out of five companies remain state-owned—and most of these are losing money.

A little-noted economic miracle may be taking place in sub-Saharan AFRICA. Africa's economic growth reached an estimated 5% last year, according to the International Monetary Fund, the highest rate in two decades. Behind this turnaround is a sweeping change in leadership across the world's poorest continent. In the Cold War days, Africa was dominated by "big men" such as Jomo Kenyatta of Kenya who led their countries to independence—but then ran their economies into the ground by adopting authoritarian government and Marxist policies. Today, a new wave of leaders is championing market economics and democratic reforms. This generation boasts leaders like President Benjamin William Mkapa of Tanzania, who told *The Wall Street Journal*: "The Rubicon of reform has been crossed. Government has no business doing business." Tanzania's economy is now growing about 4% a year. The country is building a stock market and has sold off about one-third of its 400 state-run industries, including a brewery, a tobacco company and a cement factory.

The MIDDLE EAST remains a deeply troubled region, what with the unending Arab-Israeli conflict and the persistence of authoritarian regimes such as Iraq's. There are at least a few economic bright spots, though. There's Egypt, of course: Its foreign reserves are piling up, its budget deficit is now negligible, and inflation has been tamed. Across the Mediterranean, U.S. military ally Turkey has proved a big winner of the Cold War, in spite of its domestic political turmoil. In the Caucasus and Central Asia, the southern tier of the former Soviet Union, Turkish businessmen are cutting deals along the old Silk Road that once linked Europe to China. Istanbul, sidelined for a century by colonial powers and then by the Cold War, is reemerging as the region's business capital, as Western multinationals swarm in to the former Soviet lands to drill for oil and sell soda pop and soap.

LATIN AMERICA, too, has leapt into the new era, led in many cases by technocrats who were schooled in economics in the U.S. In the past, this region has been plagued by intense boom-and-bust cycles. But now, some economists believe that the region's embrace of market reforms and its appointment of wiser macroeconomic managers are smoothing out those cycles. One example is Peru. In 1996, the country acted fast to close a huge deficit in its current account, a broad measure of trade in goods and services, by boosting interest rates and slowing consumption. The country managed to bring its overheated economy in for a soft landing, without a recession. The torrid growth rate of 13% in 1994 fell as a result, to an estimated 2% in 1996. Growth should return to a healthy 4.5% in 1997, predicts Chase Securities Inc.

JAPAN, perhaps the greatest success story of the Cold War system, is having trouble adapting to the new economic order. Until the Iron Curtain fell, Japan left international affairs to its patron, the U.S., and went about manufacturing and exporting its way to ever-rising prosperity. It developed its own brand of capitalism: a mercantilist economy run by an "Iron Triangle" of politicians, powerful bureaucrats and companies flourishing in a hothouse of regulation and protectionism. Those days are over. Japan entered a four-year downturn in 1992, and is suffering from a debilitating banking crisis. The chief culprit is the same "Iron Triangle" that once kept the economy so stable and shielded Japanese companies from foreign competition. Now, the Japanese say they recognize that embracing free markets is the only way out of their rut. At the end of 1996, Prime Minister Ryutaro Hashimoto announced a sweeping plan to deregulate Japan's outdated financial markets by the year 2001. But whatever the outcome of his campaign, it would be unwise to overlook Japan's strengths. In 1996, its economy grew 3.6%—the fastest among the world's seven most advanced economies, and a full point greater than the booming U.S. economy managed.

Michael Williams, assistant foreign editor of
The Wall Street Journal

What Was News
Top National and International News Stories of 1997

THE BALANCED BUDGET PLAN AND TAX CUTS

Two years after their showdown closed the government, President Clinton and Congress's Republican leaders joined on the sunny White House lawn in August for the signing of bills to balance the budget and cut Americans' taxes.

Mr. Clinton hailed the companion measures as "a true milestone for our nation." He celebrated both the promise, in five years, of the first balanced budget since 1969 and the new bipartisanship between two sides that until this year had fought implacably to damn each other's agenda.

The budget-balancing measure would cut projected spending by about $263 billion over five years, with $115 billion of that from Medicare through lower reimbursements to hospitals and other health-care providers and slightly higher premiums for beneficiaries. But both sides emphasized the budget law's new spending and the tax law's $152 billion in cuts over the five years, including the $500-a-child family tax credit, rather than any budget pain.

Republicans, who had doomed Mr. Clinton's universal-health plan in 1994, now acquiesce in the largest expansion of health benefits to uninsured children since Medicaid's creation 32 years ago. And the president, who in 1995 vetoed the GOP's deep tax cuts, has signed their long-sought reductions in capital-gains and estate taxes. It was the first major tax cut since the early days of the Reagan administration.

In fact, for all the self-congratulation about balancing the budget, those spending and tax initiatives force a detour on the government's road to surplus. Given a continued strong economy, internal government projections and private-sector forecasts indicate the budget would be in balance before 2002 without the tax cuts and new spending.

CAMPAIGN FUND-RAISING CONTROVERSY

The controversy over campaign fund-raising continued to unfold throughout 1997, reaching a high point in the summer with the Senate hearings into possible abuses. At the heart of the fund-raising controversy was the aggressive pursuit of so-called "soft money" during the 1996 election campaigns. The Democrats and Republicans raised more than $260 million in soft money, and some of the large, unlimited donations were used on campaign-style television commercials that the parties contended were unregulated issue ads.

The Senate hearings focused heavily on foreign donations, particularly from Asia. In fact, the Senate panel's chairman, Sen. Fred Thompson, a Republican from Tennessee, said at the opening of the hearings that the government of China had concocted an elaborate plan to influence U.S. elections. China has denied the allegations.

A key figure in the investigation was John Huang, a former Democratic National Committee official, who raised $3.5 million for the committee. Some donations proved questionable and had to be returned. Mr. Huang had previously worked for the Lippo Group, an Indonesian conglomerate controlled by a family close to President Clinton. Lippo also has close business ties to China.

Questions also were raised in 1997 about Mr. Clinton's extensive use of the trappings of the presidency to raise money for the 1996 election, particularly the many donors who spent the night in the White House's Lincoln Bedroom and the coffees that he attended with donors.

DEATH OF THE PEOPLE'S PRINCESS

The world was stunned by the violent death of Diana, Princess of Wales, in an automobile crash in Paris at the end of August. People openly expressed both grief over the tragedy and anger over the British royal family's treatment of the Princess of Wales—in life and in death.

Lady Diana, Princess of Wales

The public's ire was so intense that Queen Elizabeth took the highly unusual step of addressing her subjects on television. She praised Diana and talked about the loss suffered by Diana's two sons, Harry and William, the heir to the throne.

The funeral service at Westminster Abbey attracted millions of mourners to London and was watched on television by an estimated two billion people throughout the world. The service itself offered much drama, from Elton John's new version of his song "Candle in the Wind," to the angry eulogy by Diana's brother, Earl Spencer.

Questions persisted about who was to blame for the accident. Police said the driver of the car in which the princess died was legally drunk when, pursued by paparazzi, he crashed in a tunnel near the Seine. The crash also killed Diana's companion, Emad Mohammed al-Fayed, better known as Dodi, and the driver. Only a bodyguard survived.

But many people blamed the photographers for causing the accident in their ruthless quest for pictures of Diana and her new lover. Diana's death stirred an emotional debate over freedom of the press and the lengths to which the paparazzi go to capture the private lives of the rich and famous.

Diana was divorced from Prince Charles in 1996 after a long and bitter separation, during which both acknowledged extramarital affairs. By then, the glamorous 36-year-old princess had become a major celebrity in her own right and the obsession of the tabloids and the public. She frequently appeared at gala charity functions and was praised for her work to help the less fortunate and to seek a ban on land mines. Diana lost the title "Her Royal Highness" in the divorce, but Britain's Prime Minister Tony Blair remembered her more aptly as "the people's princess."

TIMOTHY MCVEIGH'S TRIAL

Timothy McVeigh was found guilty and sentenced to death in June for the bombing of the federal building in Oklahoma City. The federal jury in Denver convicted the 29-year-old Gulf War veteran on all 11 conspiracy and murder charges against him, for the April 19, 1995, attack that killed 168 and injured hundreds, the worst terrorist incident ever on U.S. soil.

Timothy McVeigh

Crowds outside the courthouse and at the bombing site greeted the verdict with cheers. President Clinton called it a "long overdue day" for the survivors and victims' families. The jury of seven men and five women returned the verdict after deliberating 23½ hours over four days following a trial that began April 24. The jurors said they took only one vote to convict Mr. McVeigh, and only one vote to order him executed. Mr. McVeigh became the 14th person on federal death row.

Mr. McVeigh's six-week trial stood in stark contrast to the O.J. Simpson criminal trail that stretched over eight months. Prosecutors, led by Joseph H. Hartzler, rested their case after a swift 18 days of testimony against Mr. McVeigh, while chief defense attorney Stephen Jones and his team wrapped up their case in only three and half days, calling 25 witnesses compared to prosecutors' 137. For the duration of the trial, Judge Richard Matsch ordered that jurors' identities be kept secret and that a controversial gag order be imposed on all participants. Meanwhile, the rule banning television broadcasts of federal criminal proceedings meant that lawyers and witnesses in Denver weren't playing to the camera.

Jury selection began in the trial of Mr. McVeigh's alleged accomplice, Terry Nichols, Sept. 29.

CLONED SHEEP

Researchers in Scotland successfully cloned a grown sheep, the first time scientists have ever used DNA from an adult mammal to produce an exact replica. The breakthrough holds huge potential for animal and drug research and is a major step toward turning science-fiction fantasy into a reality.

The research team at the Roslin Institute in Edinburgh took DNA from a single cell in an adult sheep, inserted it into an unfertilized egg and then implanted the egg into a ewe. In July 1996, a star was born: Dolly, the cloned sheep that is, in effect, a younger identical twin of the DNA donor.

The breakthrough was long thought by biologists to be all but impossible. For the past decade, researchers had been able only to tinker with the genetic code in embryo cells, adding a gene or two to yield desired traits, such as a tendency toward heart disease in lab mice and the capability to produce therapeutic human proteins in animals' milk. Theoretically, there isn't any reason why the new method wouldn't work in other mammals—including humans, Ian Wilmut, the agricultural scientist who led the Roslin team, told *The Wall Street Journal*, although he rejected the notion as "unacceptable." Nobody had tried the technique before because scientists had simply assumed it couldn't work, he said.

The notion of cloning humans stirred debate among ethical experts, who find it both disturbing and fascinating, and immediately set off a storm of controversy among a wide range of special-interest groups, from antiabortion activists to religious leaders to animal-rights groups. The debate, fueled by worries that exact copies of humans could be created, prompted President Clinton to appoint a bioethics panel for some quick advice on cloning issues. In June 1997, the National Bioethics Advisory Commission released its proposal which would bar scientists from implanting a cloned embryo into a woman's uterus. Such a ban, however, wouldn't prevent privately funded scientists from cloning embryos used solely for research and not implanted.

In August, a small company in Wisconsin added to the excitement in the scientific community by announcing that it had developed a cloning method and had used it on cows.

DEATH OF DENG XIAOPING

Deng Xiaoping

Deng Xiaoping died in February, leaving China economically freer but still authoritarian. The blunt-talking 92-year-old revolutionary, who emerged as one of the 20th century's most influential figures by transforming China from a rigidly communist nation into a quasi-capitalist behemoth, died of respiratory failure. His death had been widely anticipated since his last, frail public appearance in early 1994.

But it could scarcely have happened at a more delicate time: China recovered capitalist Hong Kong in 1997, and a number of the country's top leaders will retire soon. Mr. Deng's death also might provide the wild card that jockeying political factions, retired elders and interest groups are looking for to challenge Jiang Zemin, head of China's Communist Party, its military and the state.

One group of people who could benefit from Mr. Deng's death are China's so-called conservatives, who want to slow economic reforms and China's opening to the West. Grumbling is already loud among many Chinese over unemployment and a widening wealth gap spawned by economic restructuring. Yet in China, where information about leaders' positions is as scarce as entrepreneurs now are common, it is equally possible that Mr. Deng's death could unleash a populist wave of pro-Deng feeling and nostalgia.

Mr. Deng's legacy includes both his spectacularly successful economic reforms, encapsulated in his slogan "To get rich is glorious," and the massacre of students demanding democracy on Beijing's Tiananmen Square in 1989, which forever tarnished his image. Although he permitted brief periods of greater freedom during his two-decade rule, he would follow these times with mass jailings of students, intellectuals and anyone else who dared to call for democracy.

Since his official retirement shortly after the massacre, Mr. Deng's influence had waned steadily. Nonetheless, few of the emperors, warlords and ideologues who ruled China for 5,000 years have changed the country as dramatically, from the grass roots to the elite, as Mr. Deng. In his reform-obsessed era, economic progress overrode political movements. Thanks to Mr. Deng, millionaires and stock markets worldwide returned to Communist Party–led China after half a century of civil war and xenophobia. Hundreds of millions of peasants reclaimed land from state collectives, and prospered by selling their own produce on free markets.

HANDOVER OF HONG KONG

China regained sovereignty over Hong Kong in a historic spectacle, amid lingering uncertainty over Beijing's intentions. Britain's handover of Hong Kong to Communist Party–led China on July 1 ended a century and a half of a forced foreign presence in China.

Hong Kong's reversion presents China's business-minded leaders with what could be a defining opportunity and surely will be a decisive challenge: sustaining and drawing benefits from its newest and wealthiest city. With Hong Kong's return, China gains instant expertise in international commerce, some of the world's wealthiest tycoons and the world's fifth-largest stock market.

But maintaining the Hong Kong miracle will be a formidable task for a country more comfortable with authoritarianism than the autonomy it has pledged to Hong Kong for the next 50 years. Although Beijing constantly reiterates a pledge to implement a "one country, two systems" policy in freewheeling Hong Kong, doubts abound that China's top leaders understand what that entails.

The weekend before the handover, Beijing announced it would send 4,000 troops, ships, planes and armored personnel carriers across the border just hours after Britain handed the territory back. While Chinese leaders saw the entry of the People's Liberation Army as a natural exercise of sovereignty, people in Hong Kong and abroad still associate the army with China's bloody crackdown on democracy protests in June 1989.

Chinese leaders witnessed the swearing-in of Hong Kong's new chief executive, Tung Chee Hwa, as well as a new Hong Kong Legislative Council, which quickly abolished British laws China didn't like. The legislature replaced a 60-member elected body that China ordered abolished at midnight. Some of the evicted members protested at the legislative chambers in the heart of Hong Kong's central business district, while the champagne flowed at black-tie parties in nearby restaurants and bars.

MILITARY SEX SCANDALS

The military was shaken in 1997 by a series of problems with sexual conduct and misconduct. The cases highlighted some of the difficulties of integrating more women into the military's male-dominated culture.

The worst cases brought criminal charges of sodomy and rape and complaints of sexual harassment. In May, Army Staff Sgt. Delmar Simpson was sentenced to 25 years in prison following his conviction for raping recruits.

More controversial were cases involving consensual sex in adulterous relationships. Many people in the civilian world felt the military was being too intrusive in the private lives of its members. Air Force Lt. Kelly Flinn, for example, was dismissed from the service for committing adultery and fraternization, and then lying about those matters and disobeying an order to change her behavior. A past adulterous affair also forced Air Force Gen. Joseph Ralston to withdraw as a candidate for chairman of the Joint Chiefs of Staff.

The Army established a hotline for anonymous tips, and in the Pentagon's hallways, officers talked of witch hunts and wondered where it all would end. News reporters chased every tip about decade-old adulterous relationships. The sex scandal even affected Georgia Attorney General Mike Bowers. Mr. Bowers, who was running for governor, said he had once engaged in an adulterous affair and was resigning his commission as a major general in the Georgia Air National Guard.

EUROPE'S TILT LEFT

In a dramatic political shift, voters in Britain and France threw their support behind leftist parties. These elections mean that the left now controls or is part of the governments of 12 of the European Union's 15 nations. The move left portends a greater emphasis on jobs and labor issues and a rejection of major changes in welfare.

Britain's Labor Party won a landslide, regaining power after 18 years. The 43-year-old prime minister, Tony Blair, will govern with a

huge 179-seat House of Commons majority, a bigger cushion even than the 146-seat majority won in Labor's 1945 toppling of Winston Churchill's Conservatives. Mr. Blair moved his party away from its socialist roots in defeating the Tory leader, John Major, who was hurt by squabbles over European integration, scandals within his

Tony Blair

party and the growing number of Brits slipping below the poverty line.

In France, leftist parties triumphed in the June national vote, ushering in a period of political and economic uncertainty. French President Jacques Chirac was forced to name Lionel Jospin prime minister after his Socialists and allied parties won a clear victory in the second-round elections. In particular, the results signaled that the French aren't willing to endure more belt-tightening to be part of Europe's planned common currency. The Socialists and their non-Communist allies won 275 seats in the 577-seat National Assembly, 14 seats short of a majority. They will have to govern with the help of the Communists, who won 39 seats. While Mr. Jospin has expressed support for a common European currency, he says it shouldn't go forward at a cost of more austerity for France.

CLINTON VS. JONES

The U.S. Supreme Court ruled that the sexual-harassment suit filed by Paula Jones can proceed against President Clinton. The court unanimously rejected Mr. Clinton's claim he would be hindered in his duties if the case went forward. The court's opinion, written by Justice John Paul Stevens, noted that sit-

Paula Jones

ting presidents from Grant to Ford have testified in litigation. The justices rejected the notion that litigation imposes an "unacceptable burden on the president's time and energy." Justice Stevens said the case, if properly managed by the trial judge, "appears to us highly unlikely to occupy any substantial amount" of the president's time.

A month after the ruling, Mr. Clinton filed his first formal response in a federal court in Little Rock, Ark. The president "adamantly" denied that in 1991, when he was governor of Arkansas, he propositioned Ms. Jones, a state government employee, in a hotel room. The president also said in the filing that Ms. Jones had intended to hurt him politically. Meanwhile, Mr. Clinton's lawyer Robert Bennett backed off from threats to use Ms. Jones's sexual history as a tactic in defending the president, following complaints by feminists. Mr. Bennett said he would focus instead on the truthfulness of Ms. Jones's claims that Mr. Clinton made improper advances.

There was speculation about a possible out-of-court settlement to avoid what would certainly be an unseemly and expensive trial for both sides. Ms. Jones's attorneys have said that she wants her reputation restored by the president's admitting he remembered meeting her in the hotel room and by paying her some $700,000 in damages. Mr. Bennett has said he might be willing to recommend that the president settle if the funds went to charity.

NATO EXPANSION

The 16 members of the North Atlantic Treaty Organization overcame their differences and in early July agreed to invite the Czech Republic, Poland and Hungary to join their military alliance in 1999. Adding three former communist states of Central Europe marks NATO's most significant enlargement since being founded in 1949. France and eight other NATO members had pushed unsuccessfully to inclue Romania and Slovenia, as well.

Mr. Clinton, the most aggressive proponent of enlarging NATO, called it "a very great day, not only for Europe and the United States, not simply for NATO, but ... for the cause of freedom in the aftermath of the Cold War." The cost of expansion has been pegged from $27 billion to $35 billion over the next 13 years, of which the U.S. will pay at least $150 million annually.

Meanwhile, French President Jacques Chirac insisted no serious conflict remains between France and the U.S., and that all matters of

NATO's evolution remain "open to discussion." The French had argued that including Romania and Slovenia would help bring stability to the Balkans, but President Clinton and his chief ally, British Prime Minister Tony Blair, had insisted that rapid expansion could pose a risk to alliance cohesion and threaten ratification by the U.S. Senate.

In May, Russia and NATO members signed a historic security agreement that cleared the way for the expansion. Russian President Boris Yeltsin, who had earlier bitterly opposed the eastward expansion, also said Russia would no longer target nuclear missiles at the alliance countries. Still, the future of the new NATO–Russia accord remained uncertain as Russia and the U.S. still have not come to clear agreement on such essential issues as how much influence Russia will have over NATO policy.

HEAVEN'S GATE MASS SUICIDE

Thirty-nine members of the Heaven's Gate cult committed suicide in March in their rented mansion in a quiet San Diego suburb. The deaths ranked as the largest mass suicide in the U.S. this century. A medical examiner said the 21 women and 18 men, ages 26 to 72, killed themselves in three groups by taking phenobarbital with vodka. The bodies were draped in purple shrouds, each with a packed bag nearby. Among the dead was the cult's leader, Marshall Applewhite.

The cult, which existed in near isolation for more than 20 years, earned money with an Internet design firm. On videos and a Web site called Heaven's Gate, members said comet Hale-Bopp hid a spacecraft coming for them, and that "graduation" from the "human evolutionary level" was near. Most of the followers had long ago severed ties with family members not in the group.

In May, two other Heaven's Gate followers, who had recently drifted away from the cult, were found in a motel near the San Diego mansion, one dead in a method of suicide similar to that chosen by the 39 other cultists, the other still alive.

The fate of the mansion where the suicides occurred remained uncertain. The sprawling, Spanish-style house had been on the market with a $1.6 million asking price before the suicides, but finding a buyer became much more difficult after the gruesome event. By fall, the house had been cleaned up, but renovations hadn't been started, according to Randall Bell, a California real-estate appraiser. Mr. Bell, who specializes in houses with a tragic past, had taken on the challenge of removing the stigma from the Heaven's Gate mansion.

REBELLION IN CONGO

Laurent-Desire Kabila, the former rebel leader who in seven months drove out Mobutu Sese Seko, Africa's longest-ruling dictator, was sworn in as president of Congo in May. He vowed to hold elections within two years. The 57-year-old Mr. Kabila, a veteran guerrilla leader, is a one-time Marxist who has spent most of his life trying to topple Mr. Mobutu.

His Alliance of Democratic Forces for the Liberation of Congo-Zaire took the capital of the former Zaire, Kinshasa, on May 17. That same day, Mr. Kabila declared himself president and changed the country's name back to its pre-Mobutu appellation, the Democratic Republic of the Congo. At first, Mr. Kabila was hailed as a liberator by the city's residents, but the euphoria faded after he excluded popular opposition leader Etienne Tshisekedi from the government. Then, just a week after Mr. Kabila's inauguration, the government banned all activities by political parties and clamped down on the press.

U.N. investigators in Congo said in July they would stay in the country despite being barred by the new government from sites of alleged massacres of Rwandan refugees. One such massacre happened in mid-May, when the rebel army shot, stabbed and bludgeoned men, women and children to death, witnesses said. Local estimates of the death toll vary from 550 to 2,000. An unknown number of refugees drowned when they jumped off a pier in an escape attempt. The killings were likely the work of special units of mainly Rwandan ethnic Tutsi soldiers, who were instrumental in Mr. Kabila's military campaign.

MURDER OF GIANNI VERSACE

The murder of celebrity fashion designer Gianni Versace in Miami Beach and the hunt for his killer riveted the nation in July. Eventually, Andrew Cunanan, the 27-year-old suspect in the murders of Mr. Versace and four other men, was found shot to death on a houseboat in Miami Beach. He apparently killed himself after being discovered by a caretaker.

The FBI and Miami Beach police department came under criticism because Mr. Cunanan had been moving freely about the area for weeks before Mr. Versace's killing, even though he was on the FBI's list of the most-wanted fugitives.

Mr. Cunanan's death left unanswered questions about the motives behind the murders he was suspected of committing. Police described Mr. Cunanan as a high-class prostitute who catered to older wealthy gay men.

Mr. Versace's death was mourned by such celebrities as Diana, Princess of Wales, Elton John, and Madonna, and it raised questions about the future of his successful Italian fashion company. The maverick designer's fanciful, colorful clothes and flamboyant style had made him an industry star. But fashion-industry insiders voiced little doubt that the Versace empire would live on, in large part because the designer had shifted increasing control to his sister, Donatella, and brother, Santo, who is chief executive of Gianni Versace SpA.

HOSTAGES IN PERU

After a four-month standoff, troops in Peru stormed the home of the Japanese envoy, freeing 71 hostages. Only one of those captured by the leftist Tupac Amaru rebels Dec. 17, 1996, a Peruvian judge, was killed in the lightning raid. Two soldiers died, and all 14 rebels were killed. President Alberto K. Fujimori arrived in a flak jacket soon after the attack by 150 soldiers, reaffirming a tough image. Japan received no warning, which Prime Minister Ryutaro Hashimoto called "regrettable." The U.S. said it played virtually no role.

One hostage, Bolivia's envoy, said the assault began with an explosion in a tunnel under the residence's ballroom. It killed eight rebels playing soccer there. In response to the raid, the White House said Peru's Fujimori acted "in the best interests of his government and his people," a judgment that was generally shared by world leaders.

Soon after the raid, however, accusations began to mount that some of the rebels may have been killed after surrendering and that their bodies had been mutilated, prompting the mother of one rebel to file a request for exhumation of her daughter's body. The Peruvian government denied the reports, and refused to say where the rebels' bodies were buried, reportedly in an unmarked grave.

The day the Tupac Amaru guerrillas staged their assault, they took more than 400 people at a large reception hostage. In exchange for the hostages, the Marxist rebels demanded the release of more than 450 comrades held in Peruvian prisons and called upon the Peruvian government to modify its free-market economic policies. But President Fujimori adamantly refused to negotiate with the group, who nonetheless gradually released many hostages.

Peru charged 19 senior police officials, including two former hostages, with disobedience and negligence that allowed Tupac Amaru rebels to seize the Japanese ambassador's residence. The interior minister said police ignored an intelligence report warning that an attack was possible. Japan also dismissed its ambassador to Peru, Morihisa Aoki, who had become a focus of media criticism in Japan for not providing proper security for the home.

O.J. SIMPSON CIVIL TRIAL

O.J. Simpson

O.J. Simpson was found liable in the deaths of his ex-wife, Nicole Brown Simpson, and her friend Ron Goldman in February. The civil-court verdict, though based on a lower standard of proof, stands in direct contradiction to the former football star's 1995 acquittal on murder charges.

To some, the civil verdict meant justice was finally served. It validated the lingering doubts regarding Mr. Simpson's innocence that continued to swirl after the criminal trial. Race was a major issue in both trials—particularly the criminal trial where the split between whites and blacks became especially divisive. Though the racial tension cooled during the civil trial, polls still showed that the majority of black respondents believed Mr. Simpson is innocent, while the majority of whites believed he is guilty.

After 17 hours of deliberations, the civil trial jury ordered Mr. Simpson to pay $8.5 million in compensatory damages, mostly for loss of companionship to Mr. Goldman's family. Nicole Brown Simpson's family didn't seek such damages. A few days later, the jury ordered Mr. Simpson to pay $25 million in punitive damages for the slayings. The total for both awards is believed to far exceed his holdings.

How much Mr. Simpson is worth remained a matter of contention. Mr. Simpson's attorneys said he's broke, while lawyers for the families accused Mr. Simpson of hiding his wealth and of vastly underestimating his possible future earnings. Judge Hiroshi Fujisaki, who presided over the civil trial, later ordered Mr. Simpson to turn over more than 100 of his belongings that include, among other things, golf clubs, an Andy Warhol silkscreen of Mr. Simpson, and his Heisman Trophy, to help pay the civil damages. The trophy, valued at $400,000, turned up missing, until the sports memorabilia agent who had the trophy, with great reluctance, turned it over to the authorities. But before he did so, the agent pried off the nameplate and vowed to go to jail before relinquishing it.

PROBING THE RED PLANET

The U.S. spacecraft *Pathfinder* landed on Mars on July 4, using a new method involving air bags to cushion the unmanned craft's fall. A small rover vehicle explored the Ares Vallis site, a vast floodplain, and analyzed the rocks.

The Mars rover, called *Sojourner*, inched toward a boulder field where scientists decided to analyze the planet's soil and rocks using an X-ray spectrometer. NASA scientists said the first chemical analysis of a stone by the rover indicated it might be a kind of andesite, a volcanic rock common on Earth. The data surprised geologists, who are studying evidence that huge floods scoured the landscape ages ago. Signs that stable water was left behind would suggest life was possible.

Photos taken by the *Pathfinder*, NASA scientists said, bolstered theories that the landing site is in an area of the now-arid planet that was inundated in a long-ago flood. The photos intrigued the nation. Curious people clogged NASA's World Wide Web site, setting a Web record—45 million visitors in one week.

What Was News
Top Business and Economic News Stories of 1997

ECONOMIC EUPHORIA

Alan Greenspan

The economy maintained a healthy balance through much of the year as consumers saw barely any price increases and factories kept humming along. Federal Reserve Chairman Alan Greenspan was credited with making the right calls as he delicately steered the economy. Early in the summer, for example, the Fed declined to raise interest rates, betting that growth would moderate before sparking inflation.

More than six years into the economic expansion of the 1990s, which officially dates to March 1991, the superlatives were flowing freely. President Clinton declared in June, "America's economy is the healthiest in a generation and the strongest in the world." Steady economic growth, combined with low inflation and low unemployment, caused even economists and corporate executives to wonder if it gets any better than this. In the summer of 1997, unemployment fell to levels not seen in more than 20 years, and inflation seemed well under control.

Yet the U.S. economy wasn't quite as wonderful as the euphoric headlines suggested. A bigger share of Americans were living in poverty than in 1973, and inflation-adjusted wages for many workers were lower than they were 25 years ago. What's more, the gap between the well-off and the rest of America has grown wider.

THE LONG BULL MARKET

The stock market was at its most exuberant and volatile in 1997. But just when stocks took a big dive and it appeared the bull market was ending, they would recover and reach new heights. The higher stocks soared, it seemed, the harder it became for investors to bail out. The combination of bullish corporate earnings and low inflation had even bearish commentators wondering what would derail the market.

The Dow Jones Industrial Average roared past the 8000 milestone for the first time on July 16, adding 63.17 points to reach 8038.88. The industrial average hit that milestone just five months after passing the 7000 benchmark, a little longer than the four months it took to climb to 7000 from 6000. The thousand point gains, however, decline in importance as the market rises—from 7000 to 8000 represents 14.3%, compared with 16.7% for 6000 to 7000—and they no longer awe Wall Street. Yet the broad market push represents a remarkable feat, considering the industrials were at 4000 just 2½ years ago.

"It starts to feel like 'been there, done that, crossed another 1,000,' but it is significant," Joseph McAlinden, chief investment officer at Dean Witter InterCapital, told *The Wall Street Journal.* "It's not a mania or a bubble or irrational exuberance, it is investors reacting to a rapidly improving fundamental environment. Things are changing very quickly. We have a balanced budget in the picture and an economy that stays in a sweet spot and gets better and better."

TOBACCO INDUSTRY SETTLEMENT

An historic tobacco accord, that could require the industry to pay $368.5 billion over 25 years and succumb to sweeping restrictions, sparked a national debate over whether its terms are too easy on cigarette makers.

The deal struck between major tobacco companies and state attorneys general was greeted with strong reservations from the White House, Congress and public-health experts after it was announced in June.

President Clinton declined to endorse the settlement in September and called for a big cigarette-price increase to reduce teenage smoking.

The tobacco companies agreed to yield to regulation by the Food and Drug Administration, sharply limit their marketing, and print dire new warning labels such as "Smoking Can Kill You."

But the pact, put together after nearly three months of fractious negotiations, could help the cigarette industry by spawning a potentially huge new market for "safer" cigarette designs. The settlement also was pockmarked with loopholes that would probably let tobacco companies keep racking up huge profits from addicted smokers, while restricting legal redress in the courtroom. The industry would likely pass along to smokers its massive settlement bill in the form of price increases of 35 to 50 cents a pack.

On paper, the agreement gave the FDA authority to reduce and even eliminate levels of nicotine in cigarettes, but the settlement would create a set of hurdles before the agency could take that step. Among them, the FDA would have to prove that ratcheting down nicotine in cigarettes wouldn't create "significant demand for contraband." Regulators freely conceded they don't have any idea how to prove that.

These limits on the FDA and the penalties that cigarette companies would pay if smoking by youths doesn't decline became major sticking points in the debate. The accord calls for the industry to pay penalties of as much as $2 billion a year if underage smoking doesn't fall 30% in five years from its average level over the past decade, 50% in seven years and 60% in 10 years. But some public health officials wanted the companies to be held accountable sooner and suggested assessing penalties after two years if smoking among teenagers hasn't dropped 15%.

INVESTIGATION OF COLUMBIA/HCA HEALTHCARE

America's largest for-profit hospital chain underwent a major shake-up after it came under intense scrutiny by a number of government agencies in 1997.

Federal investigators were probing Columbia/HCA Heathcare Corp. for possible Medicare and Medicaid fraud, and they significantly expanded their investigation by serving 35 sealed search warrants in mid-July to current or former Columbia facilities in six states, Florida, North Carolina, Tennessee, Texas, Utah, and Oklahoma. Subsequently, three company executives were indicted in Florida on charges they conspired to defraud the government.

Columbia's chairman Richard L. Scott and president David Vandewater resigned under pressure from the board of directors, and Thomas F. Frist, Jr., who took over as chairman and chief executive officer, quickly took steps that might satisfy the company's critics. Among other things, the company said it would "go beyond required disclosure" in its future Medicare cost reports, discontinue offering partnership interests in its hospitals to physicians, and sell its $1.2 billion home health-care operation, which was part of the government investigation.

Government regulators regard home health-care as a field to watch closely. That is partly because home care is one of the fastest-growing parts of the Medicare budget, and also because hospitals with their own home-care subsidiaries have the ability to steer overnight patients into their affiliates after discharge. While home health-care represented just a small slice of Columbia's revenue and profit, it was a fast-growing business and an important part of the company's strategy of offering an integrated health-care delivery system. With more than 570 home-care locations, Columbia was the nation's largest provider of such service.

MERGER WAVE ON WALL STREET

A consolidation wave swept through Wall Street in 1997, starting with the February announcement of a $10.2 billion merger of Morgan Stanley Group and Dean Witter, Discover. Some smaller securities firms were snapped up as the year progressed. Then in late September, another big deal broke: Travelers Group's $9 billion acquisition of investment bank Salomon Inc., whose Salomon Brothers would be combined with Travelers' Smith Barney brokerage firm.

Philip J. Purcell

Wall Street traders and analysts expected more mergers, pushing the stock prices of independent securities firms higher in the fall of 1997. "Because everybody's doing it, it's the right thing to do," John Keefe, an independent brokerage analyst, told *The Wall Street Journal*. "Whether it's truly the right thing to do, we won't know for 10 years."

Driving the Morgan Stanley-Dean Witter deal was a bid to snare the growing assets of small investors, particularly in mutual funds. Dean Witter, Discover's Chairman and CEO Philip J. Purcell emerged as chairman and chief executive of the new powerhouse, Morgan Stanley, Dean Witter, Discover & Co.

As for Salomon Brothers, it gives Smith Barney an overseas presence it was sorely lacking. "This is a terrific time for U.S. firms to expand globally," said Travelers Chairman Sanford Weill.

UPS STRIKE

America's package-delivery system was disrupted in August by a 15-day strike by employees of United Parcel Service of America Inc. But the Teamsters Union strike, which idled 185,000 UPS workers, received public support despite the inconveniences it caused.

Indeed, for the first time in many years, the public at large seemed to be siding with strikers, based on various public opinion polls. It marked a change from strikes of the past couple of decades—from Caterpillar Inc. to McDonnell Douglas Corp.—when labor people felt the country was against them.

What seemed to sway the public was the union's argument that the many UPS part-timers need to work full-time if they are to earn a decent living and get adequate benefits. The union made part-time workers the centerpiece of its position, and in the end, the company agreed to create thousands of full-time jobs. The contract agreement also provided for substantial pay increases for workers. And UPS abandoned its proposal to withdraw from a number of multiemployer pensions plans operated by the union. The Teamsters, in turn, agreed to a five-year contract instead of a three-year pact.

President Clinton declined to order the striking UPS workers back to their jobs, but Labor Secretary Alexis Herman successfully worked to get negotiators for the company and the Teamsters union back to the bargaining table.

BRE-X GOLD MINING FRAUD

As gold-fever outbreaks go, the Bre-X Minerals fiasco is among the worst. And angry investors are still steaming that their promised El Dorado turned out to be filled with fool's gold.

David Walsh

In May, when independent tests finally disclosed that there didn't appear to be gold in any of the 268 holes drilled over the past three years by Calgary-based Bre-X Minerals Ltd. in the Borneo, Indonesia, forests, billions of dollars of wealth had disappeared from the stock market. What only weeks earlier had seemed to be the largest gold find ever had become the biggest mining fraud in history.

In only two years, Bre-X had mushroomed from one of Canada's thousands of speculative mining firms, run by a former bankrupt mining promoter out of the basement of his Calgary home, into Canada's 30th largest corporation. It was courted by companies eager for a piece of its glittering discovery, as investment analysts competed to produce the most glowing description of its prospects; its shareholder list included names like Fidelity Investments and Quebec's Caisse de depot et placement, a giant pension fund.

How the scam worked: Bre-X's own consultants reported that extraneous gold was added to rock samples from the Busang site on Borneo to inflate the claim's value, causing Bre-X's stock to soar on the Toronto and Nasdaq stock exchanges.

So far no physical evidence incriminates any individual as the mastermind behind the scam. The most knowledgeable potential witnesses, the Filipino geologists who ran Bre-X's sampling operations, weren't talking. Bre-X Chairman David Walsh said he's a "victim," with the company itself, of the fraud. He and former vice chairman John Felderhof exercised millions of dollars in Bre-X stock options while the shares were near their peak.

The mysterious death in March of Filipino Michael de Guzman, Bre-X's chief field geologist, added to the intrigue. The Bre-X and Indonesian-police version of Mr. de Guzman's death—that he was despondent over poor health and jumped from a helicopter to his death—was rejected by most Filipinos, who felt convinced Mr. de Guzman was murdered as part of a scheme to pin blame for the Busang fraud on Bre-X's Filipino geologists.

HILTON-ITT TAKEOVER BATTLE

Hilton Hotels Corp. launched a hostile $6.5 billion takeover bid for rival ITT Corp. in January and started a bruising battle between the two big players in the hotel and gambling industries. It marked one of the biggest hostile bids for an independent company in the 1990s.

Soon after the tender offer, ITT began selling off assets, including its share in several New York sports teams and Madison Square Garden and some hotels, to raise cash to fight Hilton's bid. The sales contracts for the hotels contained so-called change-of-control language that gave the new owners the right to cancel management arrangements if Hilton or anyone else took control of ITT. This language immediately raised Hilton's ire and led the company to seek an injunction to prevent ITT from selling hotels under such conditions.

Rand Araskog

ITT made an even bigger move in July: The company said it would split itself into three companies and repurchase a large block of its own stock. Hilton responded by trying to thwart the breakup in court and by raising its bid for ITT to $70 a share, or $8.3 billion. Then in September, a federal judge in Nevada ruled that ITT could not split itself into three pieces without shareholder approval.

Rand V. Araskog, ITT's chairman and chief executive, told *The Wall Street Journal*, "There's a culture difference between our two companies that's recognized by our board that shouldn't put us in the same room." Mr. Araskog insisted that Hilton's bid didn't spur the further breakup of his former conglomerate, which had already split into four companies since 1994. "We were thinking about it—or at least I was—since before the Hilton bid," he said.

Hilton, based in Beverly Hills, Calif., said the combination would create the world's largest gambling and lodging firm, with nearly 230,000 hotel rooms and 30 casinos. Hilton would like to expand its hotel and gambling interests—core areas where the company has been running behind. ITT, based in New York, owns Caesars World Inc. and the Sheraton chain of hotels—a major attraction for Hilton. "We want to own those big full-service hotels," said Hilton's chief Stephen Bollenbach.

CONRAIL SPLIT-UP

It was the railroad coup of the decade. David Goode, chairman of Norfolk Southern, emerged as the victor in a three-way, $10.5 billion takeover fight for Conrail. Mr. Goode forced Conrail to split itself and its lucrative northeast freight business between friendly suitor CSX Corp. and the hostile bidder from Virginia, Norfolk Southern, with Mr. Goode's company taking the lion's share.

David Goode

The breakup of Conrail's routes, announced in March, was the last thing many people expected when the battle over the Philadelphia-based railroad began, especially at the hands of Norfolk's little-known chief executive. But those who know Mr. Goode say he and his tightly run railroad brought an unwavering determination to this fight—as well as a $13 billion war chest—that caught everyone else off guard.

The fight for Conrail began in October 1996 with a surprise announcement by CSX and Conrail that they would merge in a friendly, $8.1 billion deal. Mr. Goode quickly gathered his team to plan an aggressive response, a $9.1 billion all-cash offer. A bitter five-month bidding war ensued, eventually increasing by $2 billion CSX's original offer. Analysts worry that the takeover was too costly and warn that the railroads will have to significantly boost their competitive position with trucks in the East to offset what was the highest purchase price for a railroad in history.

Regulators are expected to approve the merger proposal, but the review could last until the spring or summer of 1998. CSX and Norfolk Southern say their plan will provide vigorous rail competition in major markets such as New York City that haven't had any for more than 20 years. But some small railroads and communities in the Northeast have raised concerns that the Conrail breakup won't be as beneficial as they had hoped.

TRADING IN TEENIES

The New York Stock Exchange, for the first time since its creation in 1792, began offering stocks in increments of one-sixteenths of a dollar, or 6.25 cents, instead of eighths of a dollar, or 12.5 cents. Investors and traders embraced enthusiastically what they have dubbed "teenies."

By reducing the bid-offer spread on stocks,

narrower increments should enable investors to generally buy at lower and sell at higher prices. Traders said that even in stocks that still were quoted in eighths, investors sometimes found themselves getting a price one-sixteenth better than they expected, when specialists filled their orders at the nearest sixteenth instead of the quoted eighth.

The New York Stock Exchange's decision in June to move to sixteenths was an interim step toward trading in decimals, which was expected to begin in as little as a year. The change was viewed in part as a competitive response to other exchanges that had already moved to trade in sixteenths, and to "third market" brokers who had begun trading Big Board stocks in sixteenths.

William Johnston, president of the New York Stock Exchange, said it would take some time to judge the actual impact on investors and the market of trading in the narrower increments. But there have been benefits to investors at both the Nasdaq Stock Market and American Stock Exchange which had earlier allowed trades in sixteenths. A study by the Nasdaq Stock Market found average quoted spreads on stocks it examined fell 10% in the first five trading days after sixteenths were implemented compared with the previous 19 days.

AT&T AND SBC MERGER TALKS

The controversial negotiations aimed at reaching a $50 billion merger agreement between AT&T Corp. and SBC Communications Inc. unraveled in June. Efforts to forge the single biggest deal ever attempted were hobbled by concerns about opposition in Washington, the legal difficulties of getting SBC into the long-distance business, and disarray at AT&T.

Robert Allen

The collapse of the negotiations leaves AT&T apparently set on going it alone in trying to offer local telephone service in the Bells' territories. SBC, instead of teaming up with the leader in long-distance service, may go solo in that hotly competitive market. And the frenzy of telecommunications mergers could cool as compa-

nies sort through the surprisingly virulent opposition to an AT&T–SBC deal.

In the end, the two camps couldn't agree even on the main reasons for ending the courtship. AT&T intimates say SBC quit talking rather than agree to state, in writing, an aggressive plan for opening up the Bell's local phone monopolies. The SBC side says it bailed out because the chances of winning approval for a merger were hurt by AT&T Chairman Robert Allen's unusual public campaign in support of the idea of a Bell merger. First came a speech by Mr. Allen in Boston in which he argued strongly for the freedom to join with a Bell company and that such a combination enhanced competition in the marketplace. When FCC Chairman Reed Hundt countered publicly that such combinations would be "unthinkable," Mr. Allen replied with an opinion piece in *The Wall Street Journal*, arguing further that "a merger between a long-distance company and local service company need not be unthinkable."

That public posture startled SBC executives, who maintained a decidedly low profile throughout the talks, refusing to comment or even acknowledge the possibility of a deal in private discussions with some regulatory officials. SBC Chairman Edward Whitacre was furious, according to executives. They noted that AT&T hadn't even made a public acknowledgment of the talks, and yet Mr. Allen was taking on the White House and the FCC, which had already made clear their opposition to a deal.

Later in the summer, AT&T and Mr. Allen received more unfavorable publicity when John R. Walter, the company's president, resigned after being told he wouldn't become chief executive officer, as planned. He had been hired as the heir apparent to Mr. Allen less than a year before his exit. The company quickly began another search for a successor to Mr. Allen.

STAPLES–OFFICE DEPOT MERGER BLOCKED

A federal judge blocked Staples Inc.'s acquisition of Office Depot Inc. on antitrust grounds, dealing a fatal blow to the $4.3 billion deal. In a period of many big mergers and a friendly regulatory environment, the Staples case showed that the government still tries to stop deals it believes will reduce competition.

The Federal Trade Commission sued in April to block the acquisition, charging that a combination of the two largest office-supply superstores would be anticompetitive and lead to higher prices for consumers. Then in July, Judge Thomas Hogan in Washington granted a preliminary injunction to block the transaction.

"We were looking for our day in court, we got that day ... and we lost," said Thomas Stemberg, chairman and chief executive officer of Staples. He said the 10-month fight to win government approval had been too much of a distraction to the business and too expensive, costing the Westborough, Mass., company at least $25 million in legal and other expenses.

Ruling on narrow grounds, Judge Hogan found a "substantial likelihood" that the FTC would be able to prove its case in an administrative trial and didn't rule on the basic antitrust charges themselves. The FTC had argued that while office supplies were widely available from a variety of companies, the office-superstore market was a distinct segment and that a combination of the two market leaders would lead to higher prices. Using some of the companies' own internal documents, the FTC contended in a five-day hearing in May that the combined company's prices would be 5% to 10% higher. Staples countered that the transaction would allow it to lower prices because of the greater purchasing power and efficiencies that the transaction would bring.

The ruling was particularly damaging to Office Depot, the Delray Beach, Fla., market leader. Its profit and sales growth had been flagging, even as its smaller competitors, Staples and OfficeMax, continued to gain market share at its expense.

Consumer advocates applauded the ruling. James Love of the Center for Responsive Law, a nonprofit group affiliated with Ralph Nader, said: "This means there is still some life in the federal antitrust statutes."

GRAND MET, GUINNESS AND LVMH

Grand Metropolitan PLC and Guinness PLC, two British liquor-industry giants thirsty for growth in a tepid business, announced a $19 billion merger in May that would create a potent new leader in the global spirits marketplace. The proposal was immediately attacked by competitors and appeared to be on the rocks for a while, but the conflict was finally resolved in mid-October.

Bernard Arnault

Behind the proposed merger was a sobering marketplace reality evident in bars, restaurants and living rooms around the world. People aren't knocking back liquor the way they used to. Worldwide sales of spirits, including whisky, gin and rum, were flat in 1996.

The announcement sent shares in both companies soaring, but it drew a swift cry of foul from rival Seagram, which said the merger would pose "serious antitrust problems" by giving the new company control of half the U.S. scotch market. Seagram also cited problems in the gin market, where Grand Met's Bombay and Guinness's Tanqueray would be a formidable combination.

But it was the powerful French luxury-goods company LVMH Moet Hennessy Louis Vuitton SA, which held a substantial interest in both Grand Met and Guinness, that came closest to spoiling the party. LVMH Chairman Bernard Arnault finally relented in his opposition to the merger of his two rivals in October, as LVMH received about $400 million and expanded its existing marketing and distribution joint venture with Guinness to include Grand Met brands.

Mr. Arnault opposed the merger on the grounds that marrying food and beverage groups neither creates synergies nor enhances shareholder value. Instead, he proposed LVMH, Guinness and Grand Met combine their drinks interests into a single, separate entity.

The Grand Met–Guinness combination, which was expected to be dubbed GMG Brands, would be a colossus more than double the size of the next biggest competitor in the liquor business. Grand Met also owns Pillsbury and Burger King.

Major Global Hot Spots in 1997 and 1998

An analysis by *The Wall Street Journal*'s team of foreign correspondents around the world.

CHINA AND TAIWAN

Capping nearly two decades of economic reform and social modernization, China's historic recovery of Hong Kong on July 1, 1997, has fueled nationalist stirrings on the mainland and among its nearly 1.3 billion people.

Nowhere will that resonate more than across a narrow, choppy stretch of water off China's coast, in rugged Taiwan. The prosperous island, the world's largest exporter of laptop computers and a center of Asia's high-tech industry, split from China after a protracted civil war that ended with a Communist Party victory in 1949.

Jiang Zemin

Beijing still claims the island and its 21.5 million people, and President Jiang Zemin is eager to begin the process of reunification.

But Taiwan's strong, democratically elected president, Lee Teng-hui, is more inclined to build Taiwan's international stature than to open talks with China on reunification. Some believe his closet ambition is independence, and his strategy of pushing for wider recognition of Taiwan brought the two sides to the brink of military confrontation in the spring of 1996.

How hard China will seek to corral Taiwan will probably be determined by its own economic and political stability. The mainland's economy has grown at an average of 10% a year over the past two decades, lifting hundreds of millions of Chinese out of agrarian poverty and tens of millions into a genuine consumer class. But it has also forced a tremendous restructuring of once state-run industries and idled millions of workers and farmers.

For now, the momentum of the economy is keeping the populace placated. But popular demonstrations are a recurrent and rising phenomenon in today's China, and Beijing must find ways to mollify its population in order to sustain its growth. That challenge could so preoccupy the leadership that its regional influence will remain limited.

Moreover, the world will be watching how Beijing implements its promise to preserve Hong Kong's way of life for the next half century, and whether or not it interferes in what has been one of Asia's most successful urban dynamos. Any severe meddling by Beijing in Hong Kong's system could bring heavy international pressure and possibly sanctions.

RUSSIA

Russia is led by an aging president, suffers a huge budget deficit, and can't seem to collect taxes or bring a chaotic, poorly regulated stock market under control.

So why is it one of the world's hottest emerging markets?

Boris Yeltsin

The simple answer is that the potential returns on some of the world's biggest and most resource-rich companies are too great to be ignored. Recent political and economic gains have also significantly reduced the risk of investing in Russia. And Russia's growing acceptance of its status as a dismantled superpower that is nonetheless a major world player has helped to allay fears this country has always provoked in the West.

In 1997, for the first time since reforms were launched in 1992, the economy has registered growth: The gross domestic product grew slightly more than 1% in the first six months compared with the same period in 1996, the government said. Inflation was stable at a modest annual rate of about 13%, compared with about 70% a year earlier. Interest rates were falling.

As a result, the stock market was booming at mid-1997, up 128% in dollar terms in the first six months, according to the Moscow Times Index. Mainstream investors have moved in, and significantly: Russia is being included in investment indexes closely followed by major funds.

Also promising are changes in the government, whose market-reform efforts had faltered for years. First Deputy Prime Ministers Anatoly Chubais and Boris Nemtsov, under Prime Minister Viktor Chernomyrdin, are leading an ambitious program of reforms to improve tax collection, break up the country's monopolies, and implement painful but necessary social reforms, such as the removal of housing subsidies. Their mandate is to improve the overall economy and people's lives, enough to ensure a victory for democratic forces in the next presidential election in the year 2000.

Russia also seems to be coming to grips, albeit slowly and discontentedly, with its diminished status on the world stage. Even President Boris

Yeltsin's Communist parliamentary opponents have grudgingly accepted the expansion of the North Atlantic Treaty Organization into the former Soviet bloc as inevitable, though they continue to vehemently oppose expansion of the alliance to include the Baltic republics.

Despite their confidence in Russia, investors remain somewhat guarded. Many wonder how much longer the market will continue to boom, and some observers doubt whether the government will succeed in permanently boosting tax collection to close its budget gap. As Russian discontent with reform remains high, a victory for the democrats two years from now, though a real possibility, is far from assured.

THE MIDDLE EAST

The faltering Middle East peace process and the potential for further violent conflict between the Arabs and the Israelis will continue to dominate the news.

Benjamin Netanyahu

Israeli Prime Minister Benjamin Netanyahu succeeded in getting his hard-line ruling coalition to vote in favor of honoring the Israeli-Palestinian peace agreement and pulling Israeli troops out of the major areas of the West Bank city of Hebron. But the cabinet's subsequent decision to build a new Jewish settlement in the eastern half of Jerusalem triggered massive Palestinian protests and a virtual breakdown in the peace process. Bombing of civilian targets by Palestinian terrorists served only to worsen the situation. Violent confrontations continue to escalate between Israeli soldiers and Palestinian demonstrators in the West Bank, leading one senior U.S. official involved in the peace talks to declare that the peace process is effectively "dead in the water."

Mr. Netanyahu's efforts to revive the stalled peace track with Syria have also failed, and Israeli soldiers remain in Israel's self-declared security zone in southern Lebanon. Syria played a key role in a decision by Arab League members to freeze normalization with Israel, severely curbing economic and political links with the Jewish state, which had been growing.

In addition to the difficulties in the peace process, Mr. Netanyahu is beset by problems at home. After extensive investigation, the police recommended to indict Mr. Netanyahu, his justice minister, and a political ally for their involvement in an influence-peddling scandal stemming from the appointment of a political crony to the post of attorney general. The state attorney general eventually decided not to indict, citing insufficient evidence, and the Israeli Supreme Court upheld the decision. Two cabinet members resigned over political disputes with Mr. Netanyahu, and he faces intense criticism of his policies and actions from within his own party, including calls to replace him as leader of the Likud party in the next elections.

Although elections for prime minister are not slated to be held until 2000, members on both sides of the political spectrum are lobbying for the date to be pushed up, and it's possible that the peace process will suffer another setback if Israel heads into a divisive political campaign. Mr. Netanyahu's domestic troubles have made him more dependent on a small group of hard-line coalition members who oppose territorial compromise with the Palestinians, and Israeli intelligence officials have said the rising anger in the Arab world due to the political stalemate raises the prospects even further of some sort of military confrontation in the region.

MEXICO

Mexico will begin 1998 in a new era of political competitiveness. Countries all over the world are passing through political transitions, but Mexico's could be particularly noisy. Political monopolies never die well, and just how the ruling Institutional Revolutionary Party, or PRI, manages the transition of power remains one of the most important questions of the year.

Ernesto Zedillo

More than 12 years ago, the ruling party began

to adopt free-market policies that were consummated with more than $20 billion in privatizations under former President Carlos Salinas de Gortari and the approval of the North American Free Trade Agreement. By 1994, Mexicans reveled in their seemingly miraculous proximity to First World status. The currency was strong and consumption boomed. Jobs were plentiful. Inflation had fallen into the single digits.

The election of President Ernesto Zedillo that year was a vote of confidence in PRI policies, and a request to continue them. But by December of that year, Mexico plunged into a full-scale economic crisis because of a clumsy devaluation of the peso. The influence of the PRI's technocrats has suffered because of the economic crisis. Corruption scandals have also caused the party to try and distance itself from former President Salinas. Just what will emerge from these pressures remains to be seen.

Mexico's economic model now emphasizes exports and investment, while it disfavors consumption. That model has created an uneven economic recovery, which has resulted in wrenching social strains. Crime is soaring in the nation's gargantuan capital, and the wages of millions of Mexicans have declined in inflation-adjusted terms.

The year 1998 need not be disastrous for Mexico, however. Political competition is exactly what the country needs to break chains of corruption at the state and local levels of government that have kept big foreign investors wary of Mexico for decades. Parties may learn how to share power, and Congress could learn how to act like a democratic watchdog instead of the president's butler.

Whatever Mexico's achievements or failures, they will certainly come bundled in the unique and often folkloric flourishes that have made this nation a joy and a challenge from its founding.

CENTRAL AFRICA

The civil war in the country formerly known as Zaire and the rise to power of rebel chieftain Laurent-Desire Kabila as the president of the renamed Democratic Republic of the Congo have sparked hope of a return to stability in Central Africa for the first time in three decades. Under the corrupt misrule of dictator Mobutu Sese Seko, Zaire meddled in the affairs of many of its nine neighbors.

With Mr. Mobutu gone and Mr. Kabila

Laurent-Desire Kabila

promising to exploit the country's vast riches for the benefit of all while vowing to re-establish democratic rule, many African leaders want to think that the years of turmoil are over. But there are many reasons why the region will likely continue to see political instability for years to come. Competing ethnic rivalries, poverty and misrule still plague the area.

To the east, in tiny Rwanda and Burundi, the conflict between minority Tutsis and majority Hutu communities shows no sign of abating and is likely to continue to be a source of trouble that will spill across borders. To the north of the Congo, the Central African Republic, or CAR, where many years of do-little French rule were followed by three disastrous governments, is continuously on knife's edge. The military is divided along ethnic lines and is mutinous. Only the intervention by French troops based in the capital Bangui has prevented a total breakdown in security. But France is expected to cut back in the next few years, leaving the local authorities to sort out their own troubles. The CAR has also become a base for many members of Mr. Mobutu's defeated Zairean army and could be a staging area for a counter-revolution in the Congo, despite Mr. Mobutu's death from cancer in September 1997.

The Republic of Congo (Brazzaville), Mr. Kabila's smaller similarly named western neighbor, has only 2.5 million people but lots of oil and trouble in the form of a rivalry between the former military leader, Col. Denis Sassou-Nguesso, and current President Pascal Lissouba. The potential for violence, which broke into bloody factional fighting before the 1997 presidential elections, has intensified since Mr. Kabila, an old friend of Mr. Sassou-Nguesso's, came to power. Mr. Lissouba was a close associate of Mr. Mobutu and the Angolan rebel Unita movement, making him an enemy of Mr. Kabila's backers in Luanda, which has been supporting Mr. Sassou-Nguesso with weapons.

Ultimately, Mr. Kabila's Congo holds the key to peace in the whole region. But to ensure stability, Mr. Kabila must first settle things at home and win support from his own people who, while grateful for his ousting of Mr. Mobutu, do not trust him. He must end secessionist tendencies in mineral-rich Katanga and the two Kasai provinces. He must also stop ethnic feuding in the east between Nande, Hunde, Bembe, and other groups that view Mr. Kabila as a front for Rwandan Tutsis. Mr. Kabila's rebel army was lent to him by supporters in Angola, Rwanda and Uganda, and he must now try to build his own to shed his image as a foreign stooge and overcome many of the problems he faces.

EUROPE

For more than a year and likely for the next several years, economic and monetary union, or EMU, will top Europe's agenda. The project is the boldest effort at closer integration attempted by the European Union in its 40-year history—and arguably one of the most audacious economic experiments ever undertaken. Almost overnight, most of the EU's 15 member-states will abandon their moneys and replace them with a common currency, to be called the euro, relinquish independent monetary policy to a common European central bank, and agree to adopt similar, stringent budgetary policies.

The aim of the project, which is slated to begin in 1999, is to turn Europe into a financial superpower, with a currency that will compete internationally with the U.S. dollar and the Japanese yen. At the same time, it aims to bind Europe together and avoid the outbreak of new wars. But these lofty ideals are clashing with cold reality: Many European countries, and particularly France and Germany, the linchpins of European integration, will meet only with great difficulty all the required criteria to qualify for monetary union. This leaves Europe's leaders facing a tough choice: fudge the criteria and go ahead with the project in the name of European unity, or delay it and risk a European crisis.

France's Socialist government basically admitted early on that it was unlikely to meet the deficit ceiling of 3% of gross domestic product that is stipulated in the Maastricht Treaty on monetary union. It also says that with unemployment at a record high of 12.8% of the work force, it doesn't want to impose further austerity to meet the target. Instead, it wants its allies to accept that a downward trend toward the 3% target, rather than strictly meeting it, is sufficient to qualify.

This leaves German Chancellor Helmut Kohl in a bind. Having staked a huge amount of political capital on achieving European monetary union after having reunified Germany, he ardently wants to see EMU get off the ground. But weakened by Germany's own economic problems, he's facing tough pressure from his Bavarian coalition partners and German public opinion, which is loath to trade in the solid German mark for a weak euro, to insist on strict compliance with the criteria.

Accepting that could drive a wedge in the Franco-German alliance and risk a collapse of EMU. But a failure to heed the warnings of his German allies could bring an end to the political career of Germany's iron chancellor, without his having realized his grandest ambition.

NORTH KOREA

North Korea's days are likely numbered, many government officials and political analysts say. The isolated Communist state has seen its economy shrink every year in the 1990s since it lost its main benefactor, the Soviet Union. Since 1995, floods and fuel and fertilizer shortages have sharply reduced supplies of rice, creating near-famine conditions and forcing the government to beg for food donations from other countries. The government, led by Kim Jong Il, the son of the late founder of North Korea, Kim Il Sung, has failed to implement the reforms necessary to reverse North Korea's decline.

Kim Jong Il

A collapse of North Korea could lead to the destabilization of Northeast Asia. Refugees would likely flow into Russia, China and South Korea. The government in Seoul is building refugee camps to prepare. A large sum of money will be needed to resurrect the impoverished country, much of which will likely be raised from South Korea. But doubts exist in many South Koreans' minds about whether Seoul has the economic resources to rebuild North Korea without severely weakening its own economy.

Another fear is that a desperate Pyongyang could launch a war with South Korea in a final attempt to save itself, although some analysts believe that scenario is unlikely. The heavily populated city of Seoul is within close striking distance of the Demilitarized Zone separating North and South Korea, and the resource-poor but large North Korean military could inflict great damage on South Korea before being subdued.

There is still hope that a more peaceful settlement can be reached. Since 1996, the U.S. and South Korea have been trying to lure North Korea into peace talks to resolve the conflict on the peninsula. No peace treaty was signed after the end of hostilities in the 1950–1953 Korean War.

TURKEY

A struggle between Islamists and secularists for control of Turkey both fascinated and alarmed its neighbors in 1997. And the ousting of the modern republic's first tentative Islamist–led government in June convinced nobody that the question had been finally resolved in what is now the regional economic powerhouse bordering Russia, the Mediterranean, Europe and the Middle East.

Massive pressure from the armed forces and other institutions that have led the republic since its foundation on the ruins of the Ottoman Empire in 1923 brought to power a flimsy government, founded in July by 50-year-old Prime Minister Mesut Yilmaz. But all eyes will be on early parliamentary elections that seem inevitable before the spring of 1998. The regular date would be in 2000.

These elections may be the only sure way to see whether more of the 65 million Turks will vote for the highly organized Islamist Welfare Party than the 21.3% who did in 1995, and whether Welfare's 70-year-old leader Necmettin Erbakan is still thought to offer a real alternative after a mixed record in his 11 months in office. Many eyes will also be on the Turkish military, which took a big risk in its high-profile opposition to Mr. Erbakan in 1997. Even stronger military intervention is conceivable if the generals believe that irresponsible government is putting at risk the secular heritage of the republic.

In some ways, however, Turkish society is moving ahead of its ideologues and politicians. The grave political crisis of 1997 damaged Turkey's international standing and macroeconomic management, but had little impact on ordinary people or private business. The economy grew more than 7% in 1995 and 1996 and looked set to increase more than 5% in 1997. Media, the private sector and the commercial and cultural capital of Istanbul are increasingly characterized by dynamic change and diversity. And whether the republican secularists like it or not, Islamist politicians and businessmen who honor Turkey's Ottoman and Muslim past are now firmly part of the country's future.

INDIA AND PAKISTAN

As India and Pakistan celebrate a half-century of independence from Britain, the two rivals are embarking on what may be their best chance for ending the hostility between them that has lasted just as long. If not full peace, at least the new dialogue and thaw in relations will lower tensions between these two threshold nuclear powers in one of the world's poorest and most volatile regions.

After a three-year hiatus, high-level foreign ministry talks resumed in March 1997, followed by a summit between Indian Prime Minister Inder Kumar Gujral and Pakistani Prime Minister Nawaz Sharif and the establishment of a telephone hotline linking the two leaders. The biggest breakthrough came in June, when the two countries agreed on an agenda for peace talks. For the first time in nearly 30 years, India agreed to discuss with Pakistan the divided region of Kashmir. This Himalayan territory—two-thirds held by India and one-third by Pakistan—has been the spark for two of the three Indo-Pakistani wars.

New Delhi maintains that Kashmir, the only Muslim-majority state in India, is an integral part of India. It accuses Pakistan of training guerrillas and fomenting unrest in Kashmir. Islamabad, which wants Kashmiris to decide their future in a referendum, says it gives only moral support to the anti-India insurgents.

The election of new Indian and Pakistani governments in the last year has given impetus to detente. Mr. Gujral, a Hindu refugee from Pakistan, is a moderate whose main foreign policy aim is improving India's relations with its neighbors. Mr. Sharif entered office with the Pakistani economy in shambles. Progress toward peace with India will reduce the burden of defense spending and is likely to increase trade.

But there are considerable hurdles. Both countries have acquired ballistic missiles and nuclear-weapons capability, though neither admits to the latter. Neither is a signatory to the Comprehensive Test Ban Treaty to prevent nuclear proliferation. Progress on these issues is likely to come only after years of so-called confidence-building measures. Also, a revival of guerrilla violence in Kashmir could derail the talks.

Furthermore, political instability could stall, or even reverse, the process. Mr. Gujral leads a minority-coalition government which has already been toppled once, only to be reinstated. Most political analysts believe that fresh Indian elections are likely, perhaps bringing to power the Hindu-nationalist Bharatiya Janata Party, which takes a hard line on Pakistan.

INDONESIA

It has been a tumultuous year for Indonesia and its longtime President Suharto, and the near-term future looks just as rocky. In addition to the chronic problems faced by the world's fourth-most-populous nation—ethnic tensions, overcrowding on the main island of Java, a growing gap between rich and poor—Indonesia has now entered a period of political instability that can't be sorted out until Mr. Suharto's departure from the scene after a long tenure and until a clear successor consolidates power.

President Suharto

The currency turmoil in Southeast Asia in the summer of 1997 also hit Indonesia hard, forcing it to let its currency float and cut spending, with far-reaching economic consequences.

Political analysts offer a bevy of explanations for why, in the past year or so, Indonesia has been rocked by its worst rioting in years. And though the circumstances have varied substantially from outburst to outburst, the common denominator is raw, uncontrolled anger on the part of a public that has apparently grown weary of Mr. Suharto's economically sound but iron-fisted rule. Mr. Suharto and his army are still very much in charge, so all-out chaos appears unlikely. But Indonesia has some difficult times ahead.

Indonesia is proof of the adage that prosperity, rather than poverty, tends to make populations restive. Mr. Suharto, in his 31 years in power, has raised living standards dramatically for nearly all Indonesians. A stalwart practitioner of conservative macroeconomic policies and open markets, he has led Indonesia to 7%–plus annual GDP growth for more than two decades running. Perhaps inevitably in such a poor country, however, prosperity for some—especially for the Suharto family, other ruling-party insiders and the small ethnic-Chinese merchant class anointed by the regime to run the economy—has bred envy and resentment among others. The many disconnected explosions of public unrest in the past year have tended to involve poor, underemployed youth. Their hatred of an economic and political system that they believe is rigged against them has been amply demonstrated in the many shopping malls and government buildings that mobs have looted and burned.

Most at risk, if the authorities do lose control, are Chinese Indonesians, the traditional merchants and scapegoats in ethnically diverse Indonesia. Already, much of the violence in the past year, though invariably sparked by issues unrelated to the small Chinese minority, has targeted Chinese-owned businesses and property, as well as Christian churches associated with the non-Muslim Chinese community.

Though ethnic Chinese business leaders say they're still investing heavily in Indonesia because of the high returns, many ethnic Chinese tycoons are hedging their bets with major investments elsewhere in Southeast Asia.

Mr. Suharto is almost certain to accept another five-year term in May 1998, but the big question is whether he names a clear heir-apparent as his vice president, and if he does, who that person will be. One possible choice is his politically active eldest daughter, a selection that would make many Indonesians hankering for change unhappy. Whoever the person, he or she will have to enjoy the support of Indonesia's powerful military to succeed the aging president. Ultimately, the fact that Indonesians haven't the foggiest idea what Mr. Suharto has in mind for their country is perhaps the most telling commentary on this nation's seething turmoil.

CUBA

Cuba will bear watching in 1998, especially in the hot summer months, the island's traditional season of discontent. So will Cuba's undisputed suzerain, Fidel Castro. He turns 72 in 1998, and with 39 years in power, he is by far the longest-lived of the world's remaining dictators.

Fidel Castro

The island appears to have settled into a resigned, if still desperate stagnation, and watching Cuba these days is a bit like watching paint flake off a wall. This is quite a change from the days immediately following the collapse of the Soviet Union in the early 1990s, a collapse that took most of Cuba's economy with it. For a long while, observers believed the regime's days were numbered.

But despite the decline of the population's living standards and a rash of incidents of public discontent, the regime has masterfully kept a lid on Cuba's simmering pot by following a policy of permitting very modest stop-and-go economic reforms while continuing its unremitting repression.

Most Cubans are hustling to survive and appear to have lost any hope that the country's deep stagnation will soon end. Most feel change will come only after the death of Mr. Castro, who appears to be in good health. Another factor in the island's inertia is the hostile immobility in relations between Cuba and the U.S. That immobility is likely to continue, as many proponents of change have thrown in the towel since the passage of the Helms-Burton bill, which tightened the U.S. trade embargo on the island.

To be sure, the failure of the sugar crop and other signs that the island's much touted economic recovery may well be but a dead man's bounce don't bode well for Cuba's fragile stability. Some well-placed observers believe Havana is laying the groundwork for a seasonal crisis with the U.S., the regime's traditional method of distracting attention from its woes. Witness accusations in 1997 that the U.S. is practicing biological warfare by seeding the island's crops with insect pests, and that the U.S. is behind the explosions that shook up several Havana hotels.

Given the bleak scenario, Cubans are turning to God and eagerly awaiting the visit of Pope John Paul II, scheduled for January.

What Was News
National and International News of 1997

JANUARY

Rivers in the West overflowed as rain and melting snow brought flooding in the Northwestern states, California and Nevada. The floods were blamed for more than 20 deaths, displaced as many as 250,000 people and caused more than $1 billion of property damage.

A presidential panel called for using stocks to bolster Social Security. The advisory council outlined three distinct paths toward putting the system on a more secure financial footing, and each looks to the stock market, instead of bonds, in the hope of generating higher returns to meet the cost of the baby-boom generation's retirement. But the three factions differ markedly on details, such as whether the government or individuals should make investment decisions.

Gulf War syndrome has no single cause such as chemical-arms exposure, a presidential commission said, but combat stress is "an important contributing factor." The report also criticized the Pentagon for slow handling of veterans' health complaints. President Clinton asked the panel to extend its study. Separately, retired General Norman Schwarzkopf told a Senate panel it was possible allied bombing may have caused U.S. troops to be exposed to Iraqi chemical weapons in the Gulf War, but he never received any reports of that.

A commuter airplane crashed on approach to Detroit, killing all 29 aboard. The flight, which originated in Cincinnati with 26 passengers and three crew members, was apparently trying to make an emergency landing during a snowstorm when it nosedived into a field 18 miles short of its destination. The Embraer 120, a twin-turboprop made in Brazil, was operated by Comair, a Delta feeder line. Air-crash investigators said the plane went into a stall 17 seconds before it crashed.

Two female Citadel cadets said they wouldn't return to the South Carolina military school after the holiday break because they feared for their safety. They were among four women admitted after a Supreme Court ruling on admissions policies at all-male academies.

Mexico repaid the remaining $3.5 billion of the $13.5 billion it borrowed from the U.S. to avoid default in the 1994 peso devaluation and resulting financial crisis. The repayment, three years ahead of schedule, reflects Mexico's economic rebound and success in restoring confidence among its foreign investors.

The space shuttle *Atlantis* docked with the Russian space station *Mir* on a mission to pick up U.S. astronaut John Blaha after a four-month stay and drop off Jerry Linenger for the next tour.

China lifted curbs restricting access to Internet sites owned by Western media companies, but will continue to block sites that it considers politically sensitive. Beijing barred access to 100 sites in the fall of 1996, but eased up on curbs after checking their content.

Unions must tell workers how their dues are being spent, the National Labor Relations Board ruled. The setback for organized labor came in a case brought by an Oklahoma man who demanded a refund because he objected to Carpenters Union political donations. The board said workers who pay dues but elect not to join unions are entitled to spending details, but only when demanding the return of funds used for issues unrelated to collective bargaining. The issue stirred debate during the 1996 national elections: The AFL-CIO spent at least $35 million to back Democrats, but nearly 40% of union members vote Republican.

A bomb in Atlanta injured six people who rushed to the scene of an earlier blast in a five-story building housing an abortion clinic. The first bomb wrecked the clinic. The second was in a trash can outside and appeared timed to cause injuries among people drawn by the first.

Israel's parliament approved the accord with the Palestinians on a pullout from Hebron and other areas of the West Bank. Sporadic violence had threatened the accord, but Israeli soldiers made preparations to end their 30 years of rule in a city that is sacred to both Jews and Muslims.

Comedian Bill Cosby's son, Ennis, was shot to death while changing a tire next to the Mulholland Drive ramp off the 405 Freeway in Los Angeles.

President Clinton was sworn in, promising "new government for a new century." The president's second inaugural address was more somber than his first, displaying an acceptance of limits on government's power and offering a mature assessment of the nation's future rather than enthusiastic calls for action on such issues as health care. He asked for an end to partisan bickering. Most of the stirring rhetoric came when he spoke of the need for the nation to come to grips with its racial problems, calling them "America's constant curse."

China said it planned to roll back civil-rights laws after taking control of Hong Kong in July. A panel of Beijing-selected officials preparing for the resumption of Chinese sovereignty over the British colony said they intend to repeal or revise current protections for freedom of speech, press and assembly. Hong Kong's governor blasted China's plans, and London summoned Beijing's envoy to hear a formal protest. The U.S. also urged China to reconsider the decision.

Russian President Boris Yeltsin left a hospital after 12 days of treatment for pneumonia to recuperate for an indefinite period at his dacha. An aide said the president, who had been sidelined by a heart attack and bypass surgery in 1996, intends a gradual return to work. Later in the month, Mr. Yeltsin made an unexpected appearance at the Kremlin and met with Prime Minister Chernomyrdin. The move deflated a Communist push for a nonbinding Duma vote to call on the Russian president to step down and set elections because of his ill health.

Newt Gingrich, who narrowly won reelection as House Speaker, was reprimanded by the House, an unprecedented act that sorely damaged his credibility and political standing. He also was ordered to pay a penalty of $300,000, the severity of which reflects doubts among Republicans themselves about how forthcoming Mr. Gingrich was with the ethics committee, which found he used tax-exempt groups to further his own political agenda.

Bombings and other violence increased in Algeria's five-year-old civil war, following a November 1996 referendum that approved constitutional changes banning Islamic parties.

More than 100 people died in January, including Algeria's top union leader, a vocal critic of the Muslim rebels.

Two earthquakes struck Xinjiang province in far-western China, killing at least 12 people, causing more than 500 buildings to collapse and leaving many homeless. The quakes registered 6.3 and 6.4 on the Richter scale and hit within a minute of each other.

South Korea faced a wave of protests and strikes over a new labor law that makes it easier for companies to impose layoffs. Opposition and union leaders insisted the law, passed in a secret session attended only by ruling-party members, be revoked, and they rejected the president's offer to submit the law to parliament for possible revision.

Attorney General Janet Reno joined FBI Director Louis Freeh in complaining that Saudi Arabia had failed to turn over data about the killing of 19 U.S. servicemen in a Dhahran bombing in 1996. Their criticism marked a shift by U.S. officials, who had in the past made similar complaints in private but praised Riyadh authorities' cooperation in public.

Rwanda's army conducted a weeklong offensive against Hutu militants in a northwestern province, and aid workers and residents said as many as 350 people were killed in attacks mounted as part of the operation. The offensive began after militants were blamed for the killings of three foreign aid workers and 50 other people.

Madeleine Albright was sworn in as secretary of state, the first woman to hold the post. She promised a bipartisan policy and support for the United Nations, urging the financing of "a world-class diplomacy to complement our world-class military."

Canada and Cuba agreed to cooperate more closely in areas from human rights to banking. The accord, made during a visit by Canada's foreign minister, drew mixed U.S. reactions.

A Senate panel approved a $6.5 million year-long investigation of fund-raising during the 1996 presidential campaign. In addition, it was revealed that a comparison of Democratic Party data with Federal Election Commission records showed at least 30 instances in which Clinton guests wrote large checks just before or after White House visits. Democrats denied President Clinton hosted fund-raising events at the White House or that invitations to have coffee with him came with solicitations for donations. Mr. Clinton said at the first news conference of his second term, that campaign contributors received "a respectful hearing" at White House meetings, but not "a guaranteed result." Separately, the Democratic Party set new rules on the campaign funds it will accept, limiting all contributors to $100,000 a year and accepting money only from U.S. citizens.

AIDS deaths in New York fell 30% in 1996, the first significant drop since reporting began in 1983, according to research presented at an AIDS conference. Other papers presented at the meeting bolstered early hopes of new drug therapies' effectiveness, but also pointed out some limitations.

Tupac Amaru guerrillas released nine hostages, leaving 72 at the Japanese ambassador's residence in Lima. The rebels continued to demand the release of jailed comrades as the standoff continued. Peruvian officials, meanwhile, ignored Japan's appeal to limit military maneuvers outside the residence that could inflame the situation.

Albanian troops were deployed outside public buildings to defend them from mobs demanding government reimbursement for losses suffered in the collapse of pyramid investment schemes. Many people lost their life savings in the schemes, two of which were ordered frozen.

A Russia-favored military chief claimed victory in the presidential election in Chechnya. Aslan Maskhadov, a former Soviet artillery colonel and separatist leader who signed the treaty that led to Russian withdrawal and the end of the vicious 21-month war, defeated more hard-line candidates. Moscow reiterated it won't tolerate secession.

Five South African policemen confessed to beating black-power activist Steve Biko to death in 1977 and asked for amnesty, the commission investigating apartheid-era crimes said. Mr. Biko's family continued to press instead for a murder trial in the case.

Protesters in Bulgaria demanded early elections and an end to rule by the former Communists. But

Bulgaria's ruling party said it would form a government under Nikolai Dobrev, the former interior minister, prompting workers to stage antigovernment strikes. In Brussels, President Petar Stoyanov told NATO envoys Bulgaria needed aid to avoid a debt default.

Smokers get higher doses of tar and nicotine than pack labels say, tests showed. Research sponsored by Massachusetts regulators, which is part of a broader effort to force the disclosure of tobacco products' ingredients and health effects, found that most of the 10 brands tested delivered twice as much tar as their makers say, and 46% to 98% more nicotine. The study used methods meant to reflect more realistic smoking conditions than those in tobacco-company tests.

Serbian protesters clashed repeatedly with riot police, and teachers struck at 600 schools, broadening a revolt against the Milosevic government. The strike shut almost all of Belgrade's schools, sending students into the streets to join protesters in their march against the regime. Serb protesters demanded restoration of all opposition victories in municipal elections.

FEBRUARY

President Clinton unveiled his tax package, calling for about $100 billion in cuts through 2002. The big items were a $500 child credit; credits and deductions for higher education; an increase in IRA income limits; and elimination of capital-gains taxes on most home sales.

The American Bar Association voted to seek a moratorium on capital punishment through lobbying efforts in Congress and state legislatures. The delegates called the process of imposing the death penalty in the U.S. "a haphazard maze of unfair practices" and said executions should be halted until the system is fixed. Recommendations include federal review of state prosecutions, efforts to eliminate racial bias, and no executions of mentally retarded or minor defendants.

President Clinton called for a "national crusade" to improve the education system. In his State of the Union address, the president proposed national achievement standards for primary and secondary students, including a voluntary national testing system. White House officials said the

president planned to propose a 20% increase in federal education spending, to $51 billion. Mr. Clinton also criticized the balanced-budget amendment, saying the Republican-supported measure "could cripple our country in time of crisis."

O.J. Simpson was found liable in the deaths of his ex-wife, Nicole Brown Simpson, and her friend, Ron Goldman. The civil-court verdict, though based on a lower standard of proof, stands in direct contrast with the former football star's 1995 acquittal on murder charges. The jury ordered Mr. Simpson to pay $8.5 million in compensatory damages, mostly for loss of companionship to Mr. Goldman's family. Nicole Brown Simpson's family didn't seek such damages. Later in the month, the jury ordered Mr. Simpson to pay an additional $25 million in punitive damages to the two victims' families, but the amount was believed to exceed his holdings.

Bulgaria's ex-Communists backed down after a month of protests, scrapping plans to form a government and setting elections for mid-April. Thousands thronged Sofia, chanting "victory" and cheering President Petar Stoyanov, the recently elected opposition leader who helped engineer the early vote.

Aid agencies in Rwanda held emergency meetings to review the surge in ethnic violence following the return of Hutu refugees from camps in Zaire and Tanzania. The U.N. announced that it had pulled all of its staff out of western Rwanda after five human-rights workers were killed.

President Clinton introduced his budget, kicking off this year's spending debate. The president said he and Congress "have the best chance in a generation" to wipe out deficits. GOP leaders were critical of the $1.69 trillion fiscal 1998 plan, which sees a $120.6 billion deficit, but said the overall blueprint, calling for a $17 billion surplus for 2002, may be the basis for talks. Of Clinton's projected $350 billion in five-year savings, the biggest share, $100.2 billion, is from Medicare. Unspecified cuts of $137 billion would be made from current spending levels, but not Social Security. Republican criticism greeted Mr. Clinton's $21.6 billion package to restore food stamps for immigrants and otherwise soften the blow of the welfare overhaul.

Ecuador's Congress voted to remove President Abdala Bucaram for "mental incapacity" after six months in office. Fabian Alarcon, the legislature's leader, was named president until elections are held in 1998.

The Clinton administration expressed caution on mixing Social Security and stocks. Responding to a bipartisan commission's recommendations in January, the president's economic advisers said such a strategy "raises concerns about risk." Besides the obvious risks for individuals, the advisers said allowing the government to select investments raised the specter of political interference in markets. Their report echoed the argument advanced by Fed Chairman Alan Greenspan that stock investments could drive up borrowing costs for the government.

Bosnian Croat gunmen killed a Bosnian Muslim man and wounded 22 others who were among a crowd of about 200 trying to visit a cemetery in the divided city of Mostar on a religious holiday. It was the worst incident of ethnic violence in the city, nominally run by a Muslim-Croat federation, since the 1995 Dayton peace agreement.

The Army suspended its top-ranking enlisted man pending disposition of sexual-misconduct charges filed against him by a female former colleague. The suspension, initially resisted by the service, came after two senators urged it. Gene C. McKinney, the sergeant major of the Army, earlier left an Army committee on sexual misconduct.

Serbia's parliament voted to restore opposition election victories. The move seals the opposition's victory in a protest campaign that began when the Milosevic regime refused to recognize November 17, 1996, municipal vote results. The president relented, and the legislation gives his opponents control of Belgrade and 13 other cities. Opposition leaders remain wary, and vowed they will continue their efforts to chip away at President Slobodan Milosevic's power.

The FDA planned to crack down on major retail chains under its strategy for enforcing a ban on tobacco sales to teenagers. The agency, working with state and local officials, intends to use computers and other means to track retailers' compliance records and take action against those with a pattern of violations.

The Air Force resumed fighter training flights after a suspension called because of four incidents of warplanes coming too close to commercial jets. The Pentagon said that it has learned airliners' proximity radar is more sensitive than had been believed, and that it will make appropriate changes. Federal safety officials also said a communications failure between military air-traffic controllers and two F-16 pilots apparently led to an incident in February, in which an airliner made several sharp moves when the fighters came too close.

A North Korean official sought asylum in South Korea's Beijing embassy, indicating cracks in the Stalinist regime. Hwang Jang Yop, a top aide to paramount leader Kim Jong Il, would be the highest-ranking defector since the 1960s.

Pakistan's new prime minister was sworn in after winning a parliamentary vote of confidence. Nawaz Sharif's Pakistan Muslim League won 137 of the legislature's 207 seats in February 3 voting; former Prime Minister Benazir Bhutto's party won only 18.

Protests intensified in Albania over the collapse of pyramid investment schemes, and the demonstrators demanded the ouster of the Berisha regime. The government promised residents of the southern town of Lushnje a two-year tax holiday to cope with losses many suffered.

Deng Xiaoping died, leaving China economically freer but still authoritarian. The 91-year-old leader, one of the century's most influential figures, succumbed to respiratory failure after a series of ailments that kept him out of the public eye for years. His death came as China prepares for the recovery of Hong Kong in July and the expected retirement of some top leaders. Deng's legacy includes both his spectacularly successful economic reforms, encapsulated in his slogan "To get rich is glorious," and the massacre of students demanding democracy on Beijing's Tiananmen Square in 1989.

Zaire's government agreed to begin its first face-to-face peace talks with rebels in South Africa, President Nelson Mandela said. The U.N. said it supported Mr. Mandela's efforts to broker a truce in the fighting in Zaire's east.

U.N. officials called for an end to Zaire's arming of Rwandan Hutu militants at an eastern Zaire refugee camp.

Peruvian rebels said they will release no more hostages from the Japanese ambassador's residence in Lima for medical reasons, saying the 72 captives can be treated on site. Meanwhile, a government negotiator and a Tupac Amaru representative began a fresh round of talks on resolving the standoff.

Scottish scientists said they cloned a sheep, the first time researchers have used DNA from an adult mammal to grow an exact replica. Biologists consider the breakthrough by a team at Roslin Institute in Edinburgh both fascinating and disturbing. It holds huge potential for animal and drug research. But the low-tech and cheap procedure theoretically could be used for human cloning, and that possibility arouses deep ethical concerns.

A Palestinian man, Ali Abu Kamal, killed a tourist, wounded six others, and then fatally shot himself on the observation deck of New York's Empire State Building. The shooting spree touched off panic among the tourists, some of whom were trampled in a stampede to escape.

Kenneth Starr reversed his decision to step down from the Whitewater investigation to take an academic post, saying he will stay on as independent counsel until the job is done.

Ordinary birth-control pills can halt pregnancies if taken in sufficient quantities within three days of unprotected sex, the FDA said. The agency, giving details on dosages, said six brands of the pill can safely be used as "morning-after pills." It added that the pills' effectiveness for this use has been known, but kept quiet for some time.

The Mexican government fired at least 36 narcotics agents and said more dismissals will follow. The moves come amid an investigation of the nation's former top drug-enforcement official, arrested on charges he had links to a major drug gang. Nevertheless, President Clinton decided to recertify Mexico as an ally in the war against drugs.

Chemical heir John duPont was found guilty of third-degree murder in the shooting of Olympic wrestler Dave Schultz. The Penn-

sylvania jury decided he was mentally ill at the time. He later received a 13-to-30-year sentence and was being treated in a mental hospital.

The FBI found evidence China may have steered funds to the Democrats. FBI Director Louis Freeh briefed top senators on the inquiry, which could lead him to ask Attorney General Janet Reno for an independent counsel. She continued to resist that, but officials described the FBI investigation as larger than previously reported. Meanwhile, President Clinton said allowing political donors to stay in the Lincoln Bedroom was "entirely appropriate," adding that no funds were solicited on the premises. The guest list suggests the White House was used in a multitude of ways to advance the president's political agenda, not just to court potential contributors.

Israeli Prime Minister Benjamin Netanyahu's cabinet approved the construction of 6,500 homes for Israelis in mostly Arab East Jerusalem. Palestinian leaders immediately denounced the decision as a violation of peace agreements, and said it could spur violence. The U.S., in a rare rebuke, said the proposed project will erode trust between Israel and the Palestinians.

A Swiss Holocaust fund will be started with $103 million in initial contributions and more expected. The fund, set up under intense international criticism of Swiss banks' World War II activities, will aid victims of the Nazis and their families.

The Centers for Disease Control and Prevention said 12% fewer people with AIDS died from the disease in the first half of 1996 than in the year-earlier period, the first marked decline since the disease emerged 15 years ago. New drugs only became available late in the 1996 first half, so experts say other factors, such as growing availability of AIDS-related health care and continuing prevention campaigns, may have played big roles.

Kim Young Sam began what is expected to be a broad shake-up of South Korea's government over the Hanbo Steel bribes-for-loans scandal. Government ministers and ruling-party officials offered to quit after the president made a televised apology. He fired several top aides.

MARCH

Two rhesus monkeys were cloned by scientists in Oregon, but the identical primates were produced from cells taken from embryos, not an adult as in the case of the sheep cloned in Scotland. It was, however, the first cloning within a species so close to humans, adding to evidence that human cloning is possible.

Tornadoes in Arkansas killed an estimated 25 people and injured more than 200 when twisters swept a 260-mile path that included Little Rock and Arkadelphia. At least 15 other people died in four other states as the storm system passed through.

Al Gore defended his active role in Democratic Party fund-raising efforts. The vice president admitted making phone calls, some from the White House, to solicit donations, but added, "Everything that I did I understood to be lawful." He promised, however, not to engage in such activities again. Meanwhile, it was revealed that a top aide of Hillary Clinton's accepted a donation at the White House. The $50,000 check, given by a California businessman during a visit with six Chinese officials, was forwarded to the Democratic National Committee. It was cashed, but recently returned. The incident skirted close to the edge of laws banning fund-raising in government buildings.

A former CIA officer pleaded guilty to espionage and promised to tell the government exactly what secrets he sold to the Russians. Harold Nicholson later received a 23½-year prison term. He had faced life, but his cooperation with investigators resulted in the lighter sentence. The ex-station chief is the highest-ranking CIA official ever convicted on the charge.

Floods drove thousands from their homes in Tennessee, Kentucky, Indiana, Ohio and West Virginia after storms filled the Ohio River and its tributaries to their highest levels in more than 30 years.

A young Russian emigre was charged with the murder of Ennis Cosby, son of the comedian Bill Cosby. Police said the motive was robbery.

The Senate rejected the balanced-budget amendment, again by a single vote. The 66–34 tally marked the second time in as many years that the measure has failed by that margin. All 55 Republicans and 11 Democrats backed it, but a two-thirds majority is required. The measure was a top GOP legislative goal for this year, but President Clinton and Democratic congressional leaders opposed it on grounds it would jeopardize Social Security and tie the government's hands in recessions.

President Clinton banned the use of federal funds for human cloning experiments and called for a voluntary moratorium on private research in the area. The president has asked an expert panel for a report on the implications of such research, following Scottish scientists' cloning of an adult sheep.

President Clinton ordered tighter proof-of-residency requirements for gun purchases following February's shooting attack by a Palestinian visitor on Empire State Building tourists. He also called for a law banning purchases by non-immigrant foreigners.

Suspicions grew about attempts by China to influence politics in the U.S. Senator Dianne Feinstein confirmed the FBI warned her in June 1996 that China might try to funnel money to U.S. lawmakers, but she said she was given no specifics. President Clinton said the FBI kept him in the dark about alleged Chinese political funds. He ordered an inquiry into why White House intelligence aides were alerted to possible Chinese attempts to influence U.S. politics, but were told to keep the information from the president and top aides. The bureau, however, said it placed no limits on disseminating the warning. Beijing denied it tried to funnel money to political campaigns, and said the allegations may hurt ties to the U.S.

President Clinton ordered federal agencies to devise plans within 30 days to hire welfare recipients who will be coming off the rolls as a result of time limits on benefits in the overhaul he signed in 1996. The president's directive relies on a program allowing the hiring of low-skill workers who would be trained to become civil servants. Separately, many states were waiving a provision of the new welfare law cutting food stamps to childless adults after three months if they hadn't found a job or entered a work program.

Boris Yeltsin named Russia's most liberal government since the Soviet breakup, indicating he is serious about implementing deep, painful economic reforms. He appointed his chief of staff, reformer Anatoly Chubais, as first deputy prime minister in charge of the Russian economy. Mr. Chubais, who has had a prickly relationship with the president and colleagues in prior government posts, is now charged with boosting tax receipts and breaking up energy monopolies.

Federal regulators delayed an administration proposal to allow mechanics to disconnect air bags, but moved ahead on rules to reduce their inflation force. The delay came under pressure from automobile and insurance firms. Air bags have been linked to the deaths of a growing number of people, especially children.

South Korea's parliament passed a revised labor law that delays and limits a clause allowing companies to more easily lay off workers and replace strikers. The new law also legalizes an activist union organization. The changes constitute significant concessions and are a response to the worker strikes that were called to protest the original bill.

The Citadel dismissed a male cadet and ordered lesser punishments for nine others accused of harassing two of the formerly all-male military academy's four female cadets into dropping out.

Mexico named a civilian prosecutor as its top drug-fighting official, succeeding an army general who was arrested recently for links to a major drug gang. Mexico also laid out its plans to implement a new law to fight money laundering. Even so, the House of Representatives voted to overrule President Clinton's decision to certify Mexico as a drug-war ally. The president promised a veto, and Senate approval was uncertain.

Senate Republicans agreed to widen the scope of campaign fund-raising hearings. The 99–0 vote was a reversal of the GOP's position that only illegal campaign activities should be scrutinized. The revised mandate gives the investigating panel greater license to challenge the Clinton administration and look at the often unregulated world of "soft money" contributions to both parties.

The U.S. began evacuating Americans as Albania descended into anarchy. Helicopters fer-

ried embassy personnel and dependents out of Tirana to warships in the Ionian Sea. Other countries were taking similar steps as competing mobs armed with looted army weapons clashed in the capital and elsewhere. Italy declared a state of emergency because of the flood of Albanian refugees. The Italian government said it sent back many "undesirables" and would limit the stay of other refugees to three months.

Violence increased in the Middle East as a Jordanian soldier killed seven Israeli schoolgirls on a class trip. The shooting took place on the Jordan River "Island of Peace," which is farmed by Israel but controlled by Jordan. Later in the month, Islamic militants said a suicide bombing in Tel Aviv that killed four people was in retaliation for the construction of an Israeli housing project in East Jerusalem.

Children's health coverage got a significant boost in proposed bipartisan legislation to raise $30 billion over five years through higher cigarette taxes. Of that, $20 billion would subsidize purchase of coverage for uninsured children; the rest would go to cutting deficits.

President Clinton suffered a knee injury in a fall down some steps outside golfer Greg Norman's Florida home. The president returned to the White House following surgery to repair a tendon that ripped from his right kneecap, but the accident delayed briefly a summit meeting with Boris Yeltsin in Helsinki.

President Clinton nominated George Tenet, acting director of the Central Intelligence Agency, to be its new director, after Anthony Lake withdrew. Mr. Lake, former national security adviser, said in a letter to the president that he had "lost patience" after learning the Senate Intelligence panel again planned to delay a vote on his nomination because of a dispute over access to his FBI files and questions about his aides' contacts with campaign donors.

U.N. health officials announced what they called a major breakthrough in tuberculosis treatment, a four-pill, six-month regimen officials predict will save 10 million lives over 10 years worldwide and prevent development of drug-resistant strains. The World Health Organization warned of a surge in cases in former East Bloc nations, but in the U.S., new tuberculosis cases dropped to the lowest level since recordkeeping began in the 1950s. Still, U.S. officials cautioned against relaxing efforts to wipe out the disease, blaming a lack of vigilance for a surge in the late 1980s.

The House passed a ban on certain late-term abortions by a veto-proof margin. The 295–136 vote, in which 77 Democrats joined 218 Republicans, set up a new confrontation with President Clinton, who vetoed a similar bill in 1996. The bill allows the procedure only to save the life of a mother.

At the U.S.–Russian summit in Helsinki, Boris Yeltsin gave grudging endorsement to NATO's expansion, saying the admission of former Warsaw Pact states was a "serious mistake" but agreeing to a new accord between Russia and the Western alliance. Mr. Yeltsin and President Clinton also made progress on arms-control issues.

Vice President Gore said China will take further steps to open markets to U.S. products and seemed more open to discussion of human rights than in the past. The vice president was the highest-ranking U.S. official to visit Beijing since the 1989 Tiananmen Square massacre. During his visit, he assured Chinese officials that the U.S. campaign fund-raising controversy isn't likely to hurt ties between the two countries. He also attended ceremonies at which two U.S. firms secured lucrative business deals: Boeing is to sell at least five 777s to China for about $685 million, while General Motors plans a $1.3 billion joint venture with a Shanghai firm to build Buicks in China.

The hepatitis C death toll is expected to triple in the U.S. in the next 10 to 20 years and will soon kill 24,000 people a year, according to a committee of the National Institutes of Health. The panel called on doctors to treat the disease more aggressively, but conceded doctors currently have few ways to fight it.

Thirty-nine members of a cult committed suicide in a San Diego suburb. A medical examiner said the 21 women and 18 men, ages 26 to 72, killed themselves in three groups by taking phenobarbitol with vodka. The group earned money with an Internet design firm. On videos and a Web site called Heaven's Gate, members said comet Hale-Bopp hid a spacecraft coming for them, and that "graduation" from the "human evolutionary level" was near.

The National Cancer Institute urged women in their 40s to get mammograms every year or two to try to reduce the number of breast-cancer deaths. President Clinton also called on private insurers to cover the costs of the tests. Federal officials hope the new guidelines will quell a controversy over mammography's benefits.

Martin Luther King Jr.'s son met with James Earl Ray at a Tennessee prison. Dexter King asked, "Did you kill my father?" Mr. Ray emphatically denied shooting the civil-rights leader in 1968. "I believe you," Mr. King said. The King family backs a trial for Mr. Ray, 69, who is believed close to death.

India's president gave Prime Minister Deve Gowda's government about 10 days to assemble a parliamentary majority after the Congress Party withdrew support for his center-left coalition.

The Oklahoma City bombing trial began with selection of 18 jurors and alternates from a pool of about 400, a process expected to take several weeks. The judge rejected motions to delay the trial by lawyers for Timothy McVeigh, charged with the April 19, 1995, federal office building bombing that killed 168.

A grenade attack in Cambodia killed 11 people and injured 112 during an opposition political rally in Phnom Penh. The attack wounded the leader of the Khmer National Party and followed predictions that escalating violence could threaten the nation's fragile democracy.

U.N. aid workers in Zaire helped a group of 20,000 Rwandan refugees comply with Zairian rebel orders to move to a site south of Kisangani, the eastern city recently captured in the spreading civil war. Aid workers were trying to get food to the many refugees facing starvation in the area.

A Saudi official said a suspect held in Canada for allegedly serving as a lookout in the 1996 Dhahran bombing that killed 19 U.S. servicemen should be extradited to Saudi Arabia, not the U.S. Separately, Iran denied a U.S. newspaper report that it was sheltering the mastermind of the bombing.

APRIL

The White House acknowledged that several aides to President Clinton, including Thomas

McLarty and Erskine Bowles, asked firms to give work to Webster Hubbell when he left the Justice Department to face Whitewater-related charges. Critics say the jobs may have been hush money to buy silence about the Clintons, but Mr. Clinton said his aides were acting "just out of human compassion."

The FDA said as many as 9,000 people may have been exposed to hepatitis A, a mild form of the liver disease, by eating tainted strawberries grown in Mexico and distributed to schools in six states by a unit of Epitope Inc. The federal government said 175 hepatitis cases had been linked to the berries. The outbreak prompted the Agriculture Department to impose tougher safeguards against foreign-grown food being used in school-lunch programs.

Vietnam will repay the wartime debt of the U.S. client state it defeated in 1975 after a long civil war, according to a pact signed by Treasury Secretary Robert Rubin and leaders of the Hanoi government. Repayment of the $146 million in U.S. loans to the Saigon government would remove an obstacle to improved relations and future economic aid, Mr. Rubin said.

Palestinians rioted in Hebron after two yeshiva students, claiming they had been sprayed with tear gas, shot and killed a youth. Israeli police killed two more Palestinians and wounded dozens in the ensuing unrest. Israeli Prime Minister Benjamin Netanyahu urged cooperation with Palestinian police, but warned that a retaliatory bombing could end the peace process.

A U.S. appeals court upheld California's ban on affirmative action programs, which had been approved as a ballot initiative. The ruling lifted an injunction that blocked implementation of the ban, but opponents were expected to appeal.

A German drug company said it will stop making the RU-486 abortion pill and give its patents and inventory to a company being created by a developer of the drug. The move by Hoechst, which won't affect planned U.S. distribution, came after U.S. antiabortionists called for a boycott of one of its other products.

The space shuttle *Columbia* landed at Cape Canaveral after its mission was cut short by 12 days when one of its three fuel cells, which supply electricity, malfunctioned. Separately, an astronaut and a cosmonaut left the space station *Mir* for a five-hour U.S.–Russian spacewalk to deploy instruments. Russian officials also said most of the space station's malfunctions have been repaired.

A Senate panel issued subpoenas involving both parties' fund-raising tactics. The agreement indicated investigators in that chamber were forging a working relationship. One focus of the Senate inquiry is whether individuals worked with PACs to bypass contribution limits.

The CIA apologized for doing a poor job getting reports to Gulf War commanders about the presence of chemical arms at an Iraqi weapons dump that was blown up by U.S. troops. Some veterans insist ailments they have experienced were caused by their exposure to toxins at the Khamisiyah site.

Republican Richard Riordan won a second term as Los Angeles mayor by a margin of nearly 2–1 over Democrat Tom Hayden, a former Chicago Seven defendant. Turnout was 24% of the city's registered voters.

A U.S. judge struck down line-item veto powers recently given the president. The District Court judge ruled the act violates the separation of powers by allowing presidents to choose which parts of spending bills become law. Such authority "is possessed by Congress alone" under the Constitution, the judge wrote, and "may not be delegated at all." The administration said it would appeal the decision, which was a setback for both GOP leaders and President Clinton.

A German court ruling opened a serious breach between Europe and Iran. The court, in convicting four men in the 1992 killings of four Kurdish opposition leaders in Berlin, found the assassinations were ordered by the "highest state levels" in Tehran. Germany, Iran's biggest trading partner, immediately ordered four Iranian diplomats expelled. European nations also suspended the ministerial meetings that constitute Europe's policy of "critical dialogue" with Tehran. Iran's chief ayatollah said Germany "must pay a high price" for severing ties but didn't elaborate on punishment for what he called a "U.S.–Zionist plot."

President Clinton committed the federal government to hiring over the next four years 10,000 workers who will be coming off the welfare rolls as a result of benefit limits in the welfare overhaul he signed in 1996. The White House will hire six workers, he promised.

Pope John Paul II celebrated Mass at a soccer stadium in Sarajevo, completing a journey he meant to make two years ago but had to cancel because of the Serb siege of the Bosnian capital. Meanwhile, Serbs in Eastern Slavonia took part in local elections, ahead of the area's scheduled reintegration with Croatia in mid-July.

The Justice Department released statistics showing the violent crime rate fell more than 12% in 1995, the steepest drop since the department began compiling the annual survey 24 years ago. The biggest decline occurred in suburban areas, the report said.

Attorney General Janet Reno declined to name an independent counsel in the Democratic campaign fund-raising controversy. Senate Majority Leader Trent Lott called the decision "inexcusable," but the attorney general again said her investigation has failed to turn up evidence that would trigger the special-counsel statute.

James McDougal, the central figure in the long-running Whitewater controversy, drew a relatively light three-year prison term for fraud after prosecutors said the former Clinton business partner's cooperation had given the investigation fresh evidence.

The Justice Department issued a devastating report on the FBI crime lab. The inspector general said lab employees gave testimony distorted to fit prosecutors' needs and produced flawed reports in many cases, including ones as prominent as the Unabomber and World Trade Center bombings. But the report found scientists didn't commit perjury or fabricate evidence. The report recommended structural changes in the lab and disciplinary actions against five of the employees, three of whom already have been transferred.

A suppressed drug study was published after a unit of Germany's BASF agreed not to sue researchers who found the company's Synthroid thyroid medication, which dominates a $600 million market, works no better than cheaper rivals. The study was to have run in January 1995, but was withdrawn due to lawsuit threats.

The cost of the inquiry into the TWA flight 800 crash July 17, 1996, may exceed $100 million, according to the top U.S. transportation-safety official, who called it the largest accident-reconstruction effort in history. The crash killed 230 people.

The U.S. blamed a "failure of will" among European allies for allowing China to block a U.N. Human Rights Commission resolution criticizing Beijing's human-rights record. China said Washington's support for the measure, along with weapons sales to Taiwan, "seriously damaged" bilateral relations.

Saudi Arabia said at least 343 Muslim pilgrims died in a fire that swept a tent city during the annual hajj to Mecca, and the toll was expected to continue climbing because of the condition of some of the injured. The fire was declared an accident, not sabotage.

Former Republican Senator Bob Dole agreed to lend House Speaker Newt Gingrich money to pay his $300,000 in ethics penalties. The loan's terms, which required review by the House ethics panel, would allow the speaker to forgo payments for eight years. If he chooses that option, the accumulated 10% interest will mean a bill of $640,000. Democrats said the loan invites conflicts of interest, given Mr. Dole's job at a law firm with corporate clients, including tobacco firms.

Israeli prosecutors said they wouldn't indict Benjamin Netanyahu in a corruption investigation. Citing insufficient evidence, Israel's attorney general declined to pursue police recommendations that the prime minister be charged with fraud and breach of trust for allegedly participating in a scheme to quash corruption charges against an ally.

Bulgaria's ex-Communists lost parliamentary elections, taking only 19% of the vote to 56% for an opposition alliance, according to exit polls. Protests following the election of an opposition president in November forced the vote two and a half years after the ex-Communists regained power.

A North Korean defector arrived in South Korea from the Philippines under heavy security, ending a 67-day diplomatic tug-of-war that began with his defection in Beijing in February. The former confidant of Pyongyang's leader said North Koreans are starving, the economy is near paralysis and war with the south is a real possibility.

Red River flooding inundated Grand Forks, N.D., with 75% of the city under mandatory evacuation orders and most of the 50,000 residents believed to have left their homes for higher ground. The flooding left the city without drinkable tap water and hampered efforts to fight a downtown fire that destroyed at least six buildings. President Clinton toured the Red River valley and said he would ask Congress for $200 million in emergency funding, representing 100% of the projected costs rather than the usual 75%.

The Justice Department said the FBI "significantly delayed the detection" of CIA spy Aldrich Ames, who gave Moscow the names of agents working for the U.S. The report said the FBI should have been alerted when Moscow moved against U.S. agents in 1985 and 1986, but didn't begin an investigation until 1991. The FBI said it "has strongly taken issue" with many of the conclusions, adding that its relationship with the CIA has improved.

Inder Kumar Gujral took the oath of office as India's prime minister. He kept most of the cabinet, promised to continue peace overtures to Pakistan, and told a business group the economic policies of his predecessor will continue.

Troops in Peru stormed the home of the Japanese envoy, freeing 71 hostages. Only one of those captured by Tupac Amaru rebels on Dec. 17, 1996, a Peruvian judge, was killed in the lightning raid. Two soldiers died, and all 14 rebels were believed killed. The raid boosted domestic support significantly for President Alberto Fujimori and was expected to raise confidence among foreigners, with tourist bookings up and the economy mending.

Whitewater prosecutors said they have gathered "extensive evidence" of possible obstruction of justice, and won a six-month extension of a grand jury investigating the case against the Clintons. The possible offenses under examination included witness tampering, perjury and destroying or concealing documents.

President Clinton banned new U.S. investments in Burma, citing the military regime's harsh treatment of its democratic opposition. The move won't affect an estimated $240 million in existing U.S. investments, and isn't likely to slow Unocal's $1 billion project to pipe natural gas to Thailand in concert with France's Total.

Algerian security forces said suspected Muslim militants hacked 93 people to death and wounded 25 in a village 12 miles south of Algiers. It was the worst massacre in the five-year Islamic fundamentalist revolt. Attacks on Algerian civilians continued, with the death toll rising to more than 420 over the past month.

The Senate ratified an international treaty banning chemical weapons. The 74–26 vote gave President Clinton a major foreign-policy victory. The treaty has been signed by 160 nations and ratified by 75.

Timothy McVeigh went on trial for the April 19, 1995, bombing that killed 168. In its opening statement in Denver, the prosecution said the 29-year-old Gulf War veteran, in the worst act of terrorism on U.S. soil, destroyed the Oklahoma City federal building in order to set off a second American revolution. The defense flatly proclaimed his innocence. It charged the government was trying to twist right-wing views into a motive for mass murder, and accused the FBI lab of slanting evidence.

Russia and China signed a treaty to scale back and redeploy border troops. Leaders of three former Soviet states that share the 4,000-mile frontier also agreed to the pact. Despite the show of rapprochement, mostly driven by trade, analysts say Moscow–Beijing ties aren't as warm as they look.

North Korea clarified its stance on U.S.-proposed negotiations toward a permanent treaty to replace the 1953 Korean War armistice. It said it wanted U.S. recognition, more food aid and an end to sanctions before it would join.

G-7 officials expressed rising concern over the strong dollar and weak yen. The communique from the Washington meeting of leading industrialized nations called for avoiding exchange rates that could lead to big trade imbalances. It gave no hint of plans to intervene, but began to build the case for such action if the dollar climbs much higher. The U.S. used the meeting to press Japan to hold down its global trade surplus.

Former Presidents Bush and Carter joined President Clinton in fixing up dilapidated sections of Philadelphia at the start of a three-day "summit" on volunteerism called by retired Gen. Colin Powell. The dignitaries addressed 5,000 young volunteers, then cleaned graffiti and picked up trash on Germantown Avenue. Former President Ford and former First Lady Nancy Reagan also attended.

A hostage standoff developed in western Texas after members of a militia group captured two people and said they would be held until police free two arrested members of the group. The two hostages were later freed in exchange for a jailed comrade who had been arrested for weapons violations. Another member of the group, which advocates independence for Texas, remained in custody in Austin on contempt charges. The militia members threatened "another Waco" if arrests were attempted.

The Air Force said it found what it believes are remains of the pilot of an A-10 jet who crashed into a Colorado mountain after leaving a training formation over Arizona April 2. The Air Force was investigating the crash but made no comment about the cause.

Aid workers in Zaire said thousands of Rwandan refugees returned to a camp south of Kisangani and told of the massacres of hundreds of fellow Hutus by rebels and villagers. Near the Rwanda border, aid officials said 50 Rwandan children were taken from a hospital by rebel soldiers, and all of them were feared dead.

The Justice Department began an investigation of alleged mismanagement and misconduct by the Immigration and Naturalization Service's citizenship program, which naturalized more than one million people in 1995 and 1996. Some 180,000 were processed before FBI checks were done. Republicans charge the program was rushed to beef up voter rolls in the 1996 elections.

A sergeant was convicted of raping recruits in an Army sex-abuse trial. A military jury found Staff Sgt. Delmar Simpson, who had been a trainer at the Maryland base that is at the center of the scandal, guilty of 18 of 19 rape counts and a host of lesser sexual-misconduct charges. The jury sentenced Mr. Simpson to 25 years in prison.

MAY

The State Department released its annual list of terrorist nations, topped by Iran and including Cuba, Iraq, Libya, North Korea, Sudan and Syria. Meanwhile, Tehran barred the return of the German and Danish envoys, withdrawn after a court blamed Iran for 1992 assassinations in Berlin.

Britain's Labor Party won in a landslide, regaining power after 18 years. Tony Blair, 43 years old, became prime minister, and the Labor Party took a 179-seat majority in the House of Commons. Mr. Blair had moved his party away from its socialist roots in defeating the Tory leader, John Major, who was hurt by squabbles over European integration and scandals within his party. Mr. Blair told the opening session of Parliament his government would focus on health care, education and constitutional reform.

The U.S. sued Boeing for unspecified damages, claiming it knowingly used defective transmission gears in a $1.9 billion contract to rebuild Army helicopters. The U.S. said two crashes resulted, with injuries and damage. Boeing said it "adamantly denies" the allegations.

Energy Secretary Frederico Pena ousted Brookhaven National Laboratory's management, saying it was unresponsive to safety concerns in a recent leak of radioactive tritium. The New York facility was run by a group, including the nation's top universities.

The TWA-crash inquiry was focusing on mechanical failure as the cause of the July 17, 1996, midair explosion that killed 230 off New York, FBI Director Louis Freeh said. Mr. Freeh said evidence was pointing away from a terrorist attack, particularly by a missile.

The FTC proposed letting manufacturers attach "made in the USA" labels to consumer products with only 75% domestic labor and materials, not the 98% that was the unwritten standard for 50 years. The agency said new guidelines reflect U.S. consumers' increasing acceptance of changes in the global marketplace.

Police in Texas killed a secessionist militia leader during a gun battle near the compound he and another man fled when the rest of the group surrendered. Meanwhile, the group's leader was indicted on federal fraud and conspiracy charges for allegedly issuing $1.8 billion in worthless financial warrants to militia members.

President Clinton and Mexican President Ernesto Zedillo announced a raft of accords meant to cement ties. On the first visit to Mexico by a U.S. president in nearly 20 years, drugs and immigration topped the agenda. The two leaders signed a drug-fighting plan calling for more U.S. agents at the border, broader cooperation on money-laundering inquiries and more U.S. funds for aircraft and training of Mexican drug agents. Cabinet-level groups reached 11 other bilateral agreements.

The Army charged its leading enlisted soldier with adultery and assault. Gene McKinney, a 22-year veteran who holds the title of Sergeant Major of the Army but who was suspended in February, will be investigated by a senior officer who will determine whether he should be court-martialed. Three Army women and one sailor have filed 18 charges of sexual misconduct against him, saying they took place between October 1994 and March 1997. "I have done no wrong," Mr. McKinney told reporters.

Switzerland served as the Nazis' main bankers, an official U.S. report said. Eleven federal agencies reviewed 15 million pages of documents on efforts to recover more than $600 million in gold looted by Germany in World War II. The report lashed out at Switzerland's "obdurate" and "legalistic" defense of its wartime dealings, "regardless of the moral issues also at stake." The Swiss government denied it was Nazi Germany's banker or that by trading with the Nazis, the Swiss prolonged World War II.

The death toll reached 1,560 in a northeastern Iran earthquake. The main quake, which registered 7.1 on the Richter scale, hit at midday, and many buildings that survived it were tumbled by more than 155 aftershocks. The quakes were centered on the town of Qaen in a remote region 70 miles from the Afghan border. More than 6,000 people were injured, and about 45,000 villagers were left homeless.

The U.S. Ambassador to Vietnam arrived in Hanoi, Washington's first envoy since the war ended in 1975. Former Rep. Douglas "Pete" Peterson, an airman who spent $6\frac{1}{2}$ years in a Hanoi prison, said an MIA accounting and trade are priorities.

Garry Kasparov lost a six-game chess rematch with IBM's Deep Blue supercomputer. The machine won $3\frac{1}{2}$–$2\frac{1}{2}$, and its victory over the world champion deepened debate on artificial intelligence technology's implications.

Russia and Chechnya signed a treaty formally ending a two-year war. The accord stopped short of granting independence to the tiny Caucasus republic. But Moscow in fact has little control over Chechnya since separatist rebels defeated Russia's military in a bitter conflict. Chechnya remains a source of instability: A local warlord carried out two bombing attacks in

Russia recently, killing four, and hostage-taking is frequent.

Vice President Al Gore unveiled a proposal to tighten the inspection of food imports and seafood as part of a $43.2 million plan to better guard consumers against food poisoning. The administration also requested an additional $16.5 million for new tests to detect pathogens in food.

The airline industry said it won't, after all, oppose a Federal Aviation Administration plan to require installation of fire-suppression equipment on the U.S. commercial fleet. Carriers had balked at the proposal, advanced as a response to the 1996 ValuJet crash.

House Speaker Newt Gingrich paid $50,000 of his $300,000 in ethics penalties from personal funds, and agreed to halve the loan he has arranged with Bob Dole. The concessions cleared the way for House Ethics panel approval of a payment schedule calling for two more $50,000 payments by fall 1998. The full amount is to be paid before the next Congress convenes.

Unabomber prosecutors said they will seek the death penalty against Theodore Kaczynski, who faces trials in California and New Jersey. He is suspected of killing three and injuring 23 with mail bombs. Attorney General Janet Reno cleared the move, saying his actions showed premeditation in two cases.

Rebels seized full control of the capital of Zaire after Mobutu Sese Seko fled, and they renamed the country the Democratic Republic of Congo. Former rebel leader and new president Laurent-Desire Kabila announced the partial formation of a government that placed most power in his own hands and eliminated the post of prime minister. President Kabila's government banned all activities by political parties and clamped down on the press, amid signs that citizens were losing enthusiasm for their new leader.

President Clinton set a target of 10 years for developing an AIDS vaccine but offered no new federal spending. He urged drug companies to put more money into AIDS-vaccine research. Some AIDS activists criticized the plan, citing its ambitious goal and lack of new federal funding.

South Korean officials arrested the president's son on bribery and tax-evasion charges.

The arrest, which was expected, came as President Kim Young Sam was reeling from a scandal surrounding the bankruptcy of Hanbo Steel.

President Clinton recommended a one-year extension of China's "most favored nation" trading status with the U.S. The U.S. has a "huge stake in the continued emergence of China in a way that is open economically and stable politically," Mr. Clinton said. At the same time, he said Washington hopes Beijing will "respect human rights more and the rule of law more, and that China will work with us to secure an international order that is lawful and decent." Opponents of the extension, including the Family Research Council and the National Conference of Catholic Bishops, planned to push for revocation of China's "most favored nation" status.

A former communist was elected president of Mongolia after promising to slow down the transition to capitalism. Natsagiin Bagabandi, who intends to increase spending on social programs, received 60% of the vote to defeat President Ochirbat.

The Senate approved legislation to ban certain late-term abortions. The ban was approved on a 64–36 roll call that came within three votes of a two-thirds, or veto-proof, majority. President Clinton vetoed a similar bill on so-called partial birth abortions in 1996, and White House officials said he would do so again. But the administration is facing a steady erosion of support. Separately, the American Medical Association endorsed the legislation.

The U.S. alleged that two American advisers to Russia abused their positions to profit on the Russian capital markets and misused U.S. funds to pursue private business interests. The U.S. suspended $14 million in funds for two programs run by the Harvard Institute for International Development.

President Clinton imposed economic sanctions on Burma that included prohibiting U.S. citizens from investing in development of its oil resources. He said that he was taking the action because of "serious abuses" by the military regime against political opponents.

The Energy Department invited bids on the Elk Hills oil and natural gas field west of Bakersfield, Calif., initiating what it expects to be one of the largest privatizations of federal property ever.

Bomber pilot Kelly Flinn ended her Air Force career, accepting a general discharge and avoiding a court-martial on charges of adultery, lying and disobeying an order. Air Force Secretary Sheila Widnall said the pilot's "lack of integrity" and her "disobedience to orders" were more important to the Air Force than the adultery charges.

Russian President Boris Yeltsin fired his defense minister and denounced Russia's generals in an address in which he blasted them for resisting cuts in the armed forces. He also fired the country's top commander and said the defense chiefs had ignored his orders to reform the armed forces, which are ill-trained and poorly equipped.

France's unpopular prime minster quit after his coalition suffered election losses. Alain Juppe said he would step down in a bid to revitalize France's center-right legislative majority. The right's lead in opinion polls evaporated when the left and its environment-oriented allies garnered surprisingly strong support in the first round of voting.

Iran elected a moderate cleric, Mohammed Khatami, as president with a stunning 70% of the vote. His upset victory was seen as a sign that voters want a milder form of Islam. The new president declared it is up to the U.S. to take steps leading to improved relations. For his part, President Clinton said he hoped estrangements between the U.S. and Iran "can be bridged."

South Korea agreed to send 50,000 tons of food aid to North Korea. Red Cross officials from the two countries signed an agreement in Beijing that called for delivery of the food by the end of July. U.N. groups have warned that millions of North Koreans face starvation without massive aid.

The Supreme Court said a sexual-harassment suit could proceed against President Clinton. In ruling that Paula Jones could pursue her complaint against the president, the justices unanimously rejected Mr. Clinton's claim he would be hindered in his duties if the case went forward now.

Russia and the 16 NATO members, former Cold War archenemies, signed a pact clearing the way for an expansion of the alliance. Russian President Yeltsin, in an unexpected gesture, said Russia will no longer target nuclear missiles at alliance countries. As Mr. Yeltsin signed the accord, he declared, "This is our joint accomplishment and this is also a victory for reason." President Clinton hailed the lifting of "the veil of hostility between East and West." In the Senate, which must ratify the agreement, questions arose about the wisdom and cost of adding three former Soviet satellites—Poland, Hungary and the Czech Republic—to NATO.

An estimated 28 people were killed and scores more injured as several tornadoes and powerful storms ripped through three central Texas counties from Waco to Austin. Worst-hit was the area around the town of Jarrell, where the deaths occurred, according to police. State troopers described the town as "pretty well flattened."

Mutineers who ousted Sierra Leone's elected government clashed with local militias and seized foreign-owned diamond mines in the eastern town of Koidu. At least 21 people were reported killed. The Pentagon, citing the instability following the coup, said that 250 U.S. citizens would be flown out of the country.

Indonesia's ruling Golkar party headed toward an easy victory in tightly controlled elections aimed at demonstrating public support for President Suharto. Balloting was generally peaceful, except for rebel attacks on troops in East Timor. The election campaign had been marred by violence in which nearly 300 people died.

Independent Counsel Kenneth Starr urged the Supreme Court to reject the White House's assertion that it can withhold notes from a federal grand jury in the Whitewater probe of Hillary Clinton. In court papers, Mr. Starr disputed the White House claim that notes of conversations with Mrs. Clinton are protected by attorney-client privilege.

Angolan troops overran the northeast part of the country, driving thousands of civilians from areas held by the former rebel Unita movement in the biggest military offensive in Angola in two years, military and diplomatic officials said. The action threatened a fragile peace process sponsored by the U.N. and supported by the U.S.

Taliban soldiers lost some crucial military positions in their fight to bring all of Afghanistan under their strict version of Islamic law. Anti-Taliban forces claimed to have driven the religious militia from all northern provinces, though these claims were denied by the Taliban fighters, who firmly control two-thirds of the nation.

JUNE

France's leftist parties won parliamentary elections in a rebuff to President Jacques Chirac. The Socialists and their non-Communist allies won 275 seats in the 577-seat National Assembly, 14 seats short of a majority. They will have to govern with the help of the Communists, who won 39 seats. President Chirac later named Socialist leader Lionel Jospin prime minister.

The U.S. crime rate fell in 1996 for the fifth year in a row, and murders dropped 11%, according to the FBI. Attorney General Janet Reno hailed the numbers as the largest drop in violent crime since 1961. Separately, the Justice Department said the U.S. adult prison population grew 5% to 1.18 million inmates in 1996, continuing a two-year trend of slower growth.

Timothy McVeigh was found guilty in the bombing of the federal building in Oklahoma City in 1995 and was given the death penalty. The Denver federal-court jury convicted the 29-year-old Gulf War veteran on all 11 conspiracy and murder charges against him. The bombing killed 168 people.

Voters gave Canada's Liberal Party only a slim majority of 155 seats in the 301-seat lower house of Parliament. The 51% showing compares with 60% the party won in 1993.

A congressional commission endorsed a plan to make the Internal Revenue Service independent of the Treasury and change the date for filing income-tax returns to May 15. The ideas, part of the most wide-ranging overhaul of the agency since the 1950s, are opposed by the White House but enjoy bipartisan support in Congress.

Algerian President Liamine Zeroual's National Democratic Rally won the most seats in parliamentary elections, strengthening the grip of his military-backed regime as it fights a Muslim insurgency. Opposition parties filed complaints alleging voting fraud.

Air Force Gen. Joseph Ralston withdrew as candidate for chairman of the Joint Chiefs of Staff. The move ended a controversy that began when reports surfaced that he committed adultery years ago. That touched off a debate about equitable treatment of personnel amid a wave of military sex scandals.

Federal investigators said they believe three bombings in Atlanta, including an attack that killed one person during an Olympics concert in 1996, were linked. They extended a reward offer in that bombing to all three, and released sketches of two men whom witnesses said they saw outside an abortion clinic that was bombed Jan. 16, 1997.

The Supreme Court agreed to decide whether U.S. law prohibits workplace sexual harassment by members of the same sex, taking a case in which an offshore oil-rig worker says he was forced to quit out of fear of being raped. Justices also agreed to resolve an important affirmative-action case arising from a New Jersey school board's 1989 dismissal of a white teacher while a black teacher of equal qualifications was retained in an effort to maintain diversity.

Two Turkish hijackers surrendered to police in Germany after commandeering a Maltese jetliner to demand the release of the man who tried to kill Pope John Paul II in 1981. No one was hurt. Separately, the 77-year-old pope wound up a visit to Poland, where he prayed at his family's graves.

President Clinton proposed legislation to ban human cloning for 4½ years, at which time an ethics commission that proposed the ban would make a recommendation on whether to extend it. But the president stopped short of seeking to ban the cloning of animals or some human genes for research purposes.

Medicare made $23 billion in improper payments in 1996, an audit showed. The review by the Health and Human Services Department's inspector-general's office represents a big jump from traditional estimates of medical-spending irregularities, and suggests improper payments to health-care providers accounted for 12% of the fiscal 1996 Medicare budget.

Federal safety officials recommended measures to improve automobile air bags, including using computer sensors similar to airplane data recorders to collect information on crash speeds and air-bag deployment. They also urged states to pass stronger seat-belt laws and require that children under 12 ride in the back seat.

Britain's House of Commons passed a ban on all handguns in a 384–181 vote, and subsequent legislative approvals were all but assured because of Labor's dominance of Parliament. The bill is a response to the 1996 killings of 16 schoolchildren in Scotland.

Congress approved a disaster-aid bill stripped of the riders President Clinton had opposed. The Republican retreat ended an impasse on the $8.9 billion bill, which contains assistance for 30 states damaged in recent storms and floods. The battle was a painful lesson for GOP leaders, who insisted on attaching unrelated conservative-backed items to the bill, and reminded many people of the government shutdowns of 1995.

An Army sergeant was sentenced to five years in prison after being convicted of rape, indecent assault and sodomy involving five female recruits at a base in Darmstadt, Germany. Sgt. Paul Fuller is the second base instructor convicted on sex-abuse charges arising from an Army inquiry on the issue.

IRA gunmen killed two policemen in the Northern Ireland town of Lurgan, southwest of Belfast, prompting Britain to reimpose a recently eased ban on contacts between its officials and the IRA's political wing, Sinn Fein. Signaling that its patience also is nearing an end, the U.S. condemned what it called "an outrageous act of terrorism."

Election monitors in Croatia said the vote, in which more than 61% of the ballots were won by President Franjo Tudjman, did not meet minimum democratic standards. Observers said the judgment was based on media favoritism, vastly unequal campaign resources, disenfranchisement of Serbs and loose absentee-ballot rules.

The FBI said it apprehended the suspected gunman in a 1993 attack that killed two CIA workers outside the agency's headquarters in Virginia. The bureau said Mir Aimal Kansi was turned over by unidentified Afghanis. A Virginia judge ordered him held without bail.

A Walt Disney boycott was approved by the Southern Baptist Convention, the largest U.S. Protestant denomination. The group has been upset over such issues as the holding of gay events at Disney's amusement parks, and said the company has taken an "anti-Christian and antifamily direction."

A Saudi dissident agreed to cooperate with a U.S. investigation of the 1996 Dhahran bombing, which killed 19 Americans. Hani al-Sayegh, suspected of being a lookout in that attack, appeared in court in Washington and was charged with helping plan a bombing that was never carried out.

A government AIDS panel recommended that all people showing symptoms of the disease receive one of the new combination therapies that include protease inhibitors. While the guidelines clarify treatment issues, they raise important questions for insurers and programs that pay for the expensive drugs.

Britain's Conservatives elected William Hague as party leader, succeeding John Major, who quit after May's Labor landslide wiped out much of the Tory hierarchy. At 36, Mr. Hague is the youngest Tory leader since 1783.

Army recruiting efforts are being hurt by the strongest economy since the establishment of an all-volunteer service in 1973, and this fiscal year's enlistment goal of 89,700 may not be met. That hasn't happened since 1979. The shortfall looms even though sign-up bonuses have risen and standards have been lowered.

A G-7 summit ended in Denver, and the presence of Russian president Boris Yeltsin was perhaps the most noteworthy feature of the three-day meeting of the world's richest nations. One concrete result was the admission of Moscow to the Paris Club of creditors, which will make it easier to collect on loans to developing countries. President Clinton had some disputes with his counterparts, the most serious of which concerned curbing environmental damage from development. The eight leaders also threatened to cut off aid to Balkan states if leaders there do not uphold the right of Bosnian war refugees to return to their homes.

The U.N. Security Council voted to warn Iraq it faces further sanctions if it blocks weapons inspectors from searching sensitive sites. The vote came after the U.S. won a deal to avert a Russian veto. The top U.N. arms inspector said Baghdad continues to conceal data on its missile and chemical-weapons programs.

New Jersey jurors said testimony about childhood abuse of Jesse Timmendequas wasn't sufficient to avert the death sentence they imposed for the 1994 rape-murder of seven-year-old Megan Kanka. The case gave rise to many state laws requiring notification of sex offenders' whereabouts.

The Supreme Court handed prosecutors a victory in a Whitewater dispute, refusing to hear an administration challenge to a decision ordering White House lawyers to turn over notes of private conversations with Hillary Clinton.

A former FBI agent was sentenced to 27 years in prison after pleading guilty to spying for Russia. The plea spared Earl Pitts the life sentence he might have received. Once stationed in Moscow, he was charged with taking $224,000 from 1987 to 1996 in return for national security data.

The House backed the renewal of China's favored-nation trade status with the U.S. The 259–173 vote to reject a resolution against renewal came despite pressure from Christian conservatives and represents a victory for business and the White House. But opponents gained 32 votes since the 1996 vote, indicating serious divisions in both parties over the issue. GOP leaders have promised to consider more targeted sanctions and cuts in aid to Beijing's international creditors.

The Senate voted for a Medicare eligibility age of 67, and some higher fees. The age requirement would rise gradually from the current 65, and the higher premiums, to a maximum of $2,145 a year from the current $525, would be charged to the wealthiest 6% of recipients. Chances of the provisions becoming law aren't great, but the bipartisan backing they drew may indicate the shape of battles to come in efforts to overhaul the health-care program serving 38 million.

The House and Senate passed five-year plans to balance the budget. The easy approvals, 73–27 in the Senate and 270–162 in the House, cut projected spending by $137 billion and put the government on course toward erasing deficits for the first time in nearly three decades.

The *Mir* was crippled when a cargo ship punctured the Russian space station. Two Russians and one American aboard managed to seal off a module before it depressurized. The accident occurred during docking maneuvers with the unmanned craft.

Tough new U.S. clean-air standards were approved by President Clinton, but the president sought to ease their impact by giving cities and states several years to implement them. Manufacturers strongly oppose the rules and vow to take their case to Congress, but Republicans have shown they are reluctant to enter the fight.

Cambodia asked the U.N. to set up a tribunal to try Pol Pot for crimes against humanity in the deaths of an estimated 1.7 million people under his regime in the 1970s. The Cambodian government also said it wants Pol Pot removed from the country because it fears the Khmer Rouge leader will be killed if taken to Phnom Penh. Separately, Cambodian officials accused Prince Ranariddh's party of plotting with former Khmer Rouge rebels to overthrow his co-premier, Hun Sen, indicating the breakup of the Communist group continues to pose a threat to political stability. Secretary of State Madeleine Albright canceled a Cambodia visit, citing security concerns.

The Supreme Court found no constitutional right to doctor-assisted suicide. In a pair of unanimous decisions involving New York and Washington bans, the court effectively kept the practice illegal because almost all states have similar laws. The court also ruled, 7–2, that a ban on "indecent" Internet material in the 1996 overhaul of telecommunications laws was an unconstitutional curb on speech. And the court dismissed a challenge to the line-item veto by six members of Congress.

The House approved a $135 billion package of tax cuts by a vote of 253–179. The bill would provide benefits to families with young children and college-bound students, but also cut the capital-gains tax rate for individuals to 20% from 28% and reward big corporations subject to the minimum tax. The administration issued fresh warnings that it views the measure as unfairly skewed to the wealthy.

President Clinton vowed to seek an accord by industry, labor and other groups on steps to cut emissions of carbon dioxide and other gases held responsible for global warming. In a speech to a U.N. conference, he pledged to develop "binding limits," but didn't lay out specific targets as European Union leaders have urged him to do.

The U.S. Persian Gulf commander said Iran is moving closer to nuclear-weapons capability, and is likely to have such arms at or shortly after the turn of the century. Army Gen. Binford Peay said access to fissionable material is the only obstacle to the effort.

Ireland's parliament elected Fianna Fail leader Bertie Ahern prime minister. He will head a center-right coalition government with support from independents including the first Sinn Fein member in recent history.

Japanese police arrested a Kobe schoolboy, 14, who admitted beheading an 11-year-old acquaintance in a case that has riveted the nation. The boy also is suspected in recent knife attacks on two young girls.

Mike Tyson was disqualified in a Las Vegas WBA heavyweight title rematch after biting both of Evander Holyfield's ears. The Nevada Athletic Commission revoked his boxing license and fined him $3 million.

Turkey's president appointed conservative secularist Mesut Yilmaz prime minister after he assembled a governing coalition of four rival parties united only in opposition to the former Islamic government. The former prime minister Necmettin Erbakan quit, yielding to strong military opposition to his pro-Islamic policies.

Albania's Sali Berisha conceded defeat for his Democratic Party in a parliamentary vote, won by the Socialists. The vote was organized by international groups after central authority in the Balkan nation collapsed in the spring over the failure of big pyramid investment schemes.

JULY

China regained sovereignty over Hong Kong. After a speech by Prince Charles and the striking of the British flag, China's president and prime minister presided over the swearing-in of a new chief executive and Legislative Council, which quickly abolished British laws China didn't like. But China took a soft approach to some early challenges in its rule of Hong Kong. Police, continuing a policy of tolerance exhibited at a protest during the handover ceremonies, didn't interfere with a pro-democracy march by more than 3,000 people.

A study of electromagnetic fields found no evidence power lines and appliances can raise children's risk of leukemia. The five-year study by the National Cancer Institute and the University of Minnesota is viewed by experts in the field as one of the most comprehensive yet, and could help resolve a long controversy.

Two freight trains collided in Kansas, killing a crew member and forcing hundreds to evacuate. Two other recent rail accidents prompted federal regulators to order an industrywide safety review. Some experts argue consolidation and cost-cutting have boosted risks.

A federal judge in New York again ruled the "don't ask, don't tell" policy on homosexuals in the military is unconstitutional. For the first time, he found the policy violates equal-protection rights with its ban on homosexual acts.

A Cambodian co-premier said he ousted a rival leader in a coup. Prince Norodom Ranariddh, son of longtime ruler King Sihanouk, fled Phnom Penh after Hun Sen, initially installed by invading Vietnamese forces in 1979, called troops into the capital in a battle that killed at least five people and wounded dozens. In Washington, the State Department said it was pulling most embassy staff and urged the roughly 1,000 Americans in the nation to leave. Hun Sen said he put down nearly all resistance, except for pockets on the Thai border, but Prince Ranariddh's forces insisted they could keep fighting for some months.

The Mars rover began inching toward a boulder field where scientists have decided to begin analysis of the planet's soil and rocks using an X-ray spectrometer. The small solar-powered vehicle rolled off the lander, after a few potential snags were overcome following the craft's air bag-padded arrival.

Japanese maritime officials cleaned up a spill of 400,000 gallons of oil in Tokyo Bay. The government initially estimated the accident at four million gallons, but later found that most of it had ended up in the ship's internal ballast tank.

Mexican opposition parties wrested control of the lower house of Congress from the ruling Institutional Revolutionary Party, or PRI, ending its 68 years of unchallenged rule. The PRI also lost two governorships and the Mexico City mayoralty.

Campaign-finance hearings opened with China accused of a bid to sway U.S. elections. Sen. Fred Thompson, chairman of the Governmental Affairs panel, said Beijing devised an elaborate plan to use funds to influence politics here. Aides said his remarks were based on sensitive intelligence data. John Huang, a former Democratic fund-raiser at the center of many allegations of abuse in the 1996 campaign, offered to testify if given immunity. Meanwhile, investigators were looking into Teamster ties to the Democratic Party.

President Clinton prevailed in limiting NATO expansion to three new members. Russia reiterated its opposition to the move, which will bring in the former Warsaw Pact states of Poland, Hungary and the Czech Republic. France failed in a push to also admit Romania and Slovenia.

Fresh base closings were rejected by the Senate in a 66–33 vote, dealing a blow to one of President Clinton's defense priorities. The House already has omitted base closings from its fiscal 1998 Pentagon spending bill. Defense Secretary William Cohen recommended two rounds of closings in 1999 and 2001 to free some $2.7 billion a year for a weapons modernization.

Kenyan police clashed with hundreds of students and shut down the University of Nairobi in an effort to silence demands for political reforms before elections. Opposition parties and human-rights groups had called for demonstrations to commemorate nine protesters who were killed in battles with security forces. Later in the month, Kenya's ruling party agreed to enact constitutional reforms before elections, Vice President George Saitoti said. The announcement aroused mostly skepticism in opposition parties, which have demanded changes that would effectively reduce the power of President Daniel arap Moi.

An earthquake in Venezuela killed an estimated 59 people, injured hundreds, and leveled buildings, including a school in the town of Cariaco, across the nation's northeast coast. Centered near Trinidad, it was the country's worst quake since 1967. The U.S. Geological Survey measured it at 6.9 on the Richter scale.

Television networks reached a compromise with parents' groups to strengthen the six-month-old ratings system by adding on-screen symbols to warn of violence, sex and harsh language. NBC, however, said it won't sign the agreement, although it will bolster its own advisories.

NATO forces in Bosnia killed a Serb war-crimes suspect and seized a second. The raid near Prijedor ended long inaction by peace-keeping troops. It was carried out by British troops with U.S. support, and the comrade of the man who died resisting arrest was taken to the U.N. tribunal in The Hague. President Clinton, who recently hinted such a move was being planned, called the raid "appropriate." The raid was followed by several bombings and the stabbing of a U.S. soldier in Bosnia.

The House voted 217–216 to terminate funding for the National Endowment for the Arts, bowing to pressure from the Republican leadership.

Supreme Court Justice Ruth Ginsburg's husband said he will sell stock in eight firms after a conservative magazine said the holdings put her in conflict of interest 21 times in recent court cases. *Insight* based its report on 1995 and 1996 financial-disclosure statements.

Malcolm Shabazz pleaded guilty to the juvenile equivalent of manslaughter and arson in the death of his grandmother Betty, the widow of Malcolm X. He was sentenced to at least 18 months in a Massachusetts juvenile detention center.

Cuba blamed two Havana hotel bombings on U.S.-based groups, but Washington demanded proof. The blasts caused minor injuries and appeared aimed at disrupting Cuba's nascent tourist industry. Meanwhile, a Miami exile group mounted a protest flotilla to commemorate the 1994 drownings of 41 refugees fleeing the Communist island.

Russian President Boris Yeltsin said that the inclusion of the Baltic states in NATO's expansion planning is "dangerous" and that Russia is "categorically against this." On a tour of the region, Secretary of State Madeleine Albright told Lithuanian, Latvian and Estonian leaders the U.S. backs their eventual membership.

TWA-crash investigators conducted in-flight testing of the center fuel tank of a chartered 747 off the coast of New York, the first in a series. Each flight was supposed to measure a variable that may have contributed to the July 17, 1996, explosion and crash that killed 230 people.

President Clinton proposed legislation barring health insurers from denying coverage to people on the basis of genetic backgrounds. The president said many people avoid genetic tests for fear of losing insurance.

Millions of Spaniards took part in a brief work stoppage to protest the killing of a young Ermua town councilman by the Basque separatist group ETA. The man's funeral, attended by 15,000, was televised nationwide as anger over the slaying grew.

Gianni Versace was shot and killed outside his Miami Beach villa. There was no sign the 50-year-old fashion designer was robbed, and police named Andrew Cunanan, a suspected serial killer on the FBI's most-wanted list, as the top suspect. Later in the month, Mr. Cunanan was found shot to death aboard a Miami Beach houseboat, an apparent suicide.

U.N. chief Kofi Annan presented his long-awaited reform program. The plan proposes measures to streamline bureaucracy, reduce staff and cut spending, but it is unlikely to satisfy critics on Capitol Hill. No mention is made of the Senate's demand, backed by the White House, that American dues be reduced.

Clinton extended a ban on lawsuits against foreign companies investing in Cuba for another six months. It was the president's third waiver of the provision in the Helms-Burton law. Many allies, including European nations and Canada, are angered by the law, which they say tries to impose American foreign-policy goals on them.

Boris Yeltsin signed a series of decrees aimed at cutting the size of Russia's armed forces by nearly one-third to 1.2 million troops. The steps, which Russian media said also include reorganizations of land, air and missile divisions, are part of Mr. Yeltsin's bid to ease the cash crunch on his government.

North Korean troops fired mortar rounds at a South Korean border post during a heavy exchange of gunfire. The incident, sparked when 14 North Korean soldiers crossed the border, was the most serious since a manhunt in September 1996 for the crew of a grounded North Korean submarine.

Ukraine's parliament confirmed Valery Pustovoitenko as prime minister after the ally of President Leonid Kuchma vowed to work with lawmakers. The appointment may cool fighting between Mr. Kuchma and the legislature, but the premier is considered unlikely to jump-start economic reforms.

U.S. Rep. Bill Paxon said he resigned as chairman of the Republican Party's House leadership team after being implicated in a failed attempt to topple Newt Gingrich as speaker.

President Clinton will seek $350 million to fund minority teaching initiatives. Addressing the NAACP convention in Pittsburgh, the president said his five-year race-relations proposal aims to add 35,000 teachers in rural and inner-city schools. He also urged resistance to calls for segregated schooling.

Russian space officials delayed vital repairs to the *Mir* space station indefinitely after the crew mistakenly pulled a plug that shut down most of the capsule's already disabled power system.

India's lawmakers elected Vice President K.R. Narayanan, 76, as the country's president. He is the first member of Hinduism's lowest class, the Dalits, to hold the post, which is largely ceremonial.

A truce took hold in Northern Ireland, greeted with hope and skepticism. Politicians in both Britain and the Irish Republic welcomed the news of a cease-fire, but reactions in Northern Ireland were muted. Hopes raised by a truce in September 1994 were dashed in February 1996 when the IRA claimed responsibility for a bombing in London's Docklands area. British Prime Minister Tony Blair said Sinn Fein's entry into peace negotiations depends on whether the cease-fire proves "genuine in word and deed." Later, Protestant parties voted down a Northern Ireland disarmament compromise, throwing a roadblock in front of peace talks.

New York City police arrested seven people in a case involving more than 60 Mexicans, most of whom are deaf and mute, who were forced to peddle trinkets on the subway. State and federal charges include smuggling illegal aliens, conspiracy, grand larceny by extortion and assault. City officials said they would look for more victims.

South Korea's ruling party chose Lee Hoi Chang as its presidential candidate for December elections. The move makes the former premier the front-runner to succeed Kim Young Sam.

Swiss banks were publishing the names of 2,000 account holders who may have died in the Holocaust, inviting heirs to step forward. The ads in world newspapers and a posting on the Internet break a long tradition of account secrecy. The Simon Wiesenthal Center called it a small step, long overdue.

Liberian warlord Charles Taylor won Sunday's presidential election by a wide margin, according to official results with most votes counted. Mr. Taylor's 1989 invasion from Ivory Coast precipitated a seven-year civil war that has killed at least 150,000.

Albania's President Berisha quit shortly before the new Socialist-led parliament convened, fulfilling a promise he made before internationally supervised elections to restore a central government in the troubled Balkan nation. The new parliament elected the Socialist Party's secretary, Rexhep Mejdani, as president and lifted a nationwide curfew imposed in March to halt widespread unrest over collapse of pyramid investment schemes.

Serbia's Slobodan Milosevic was sworn in as president of Yugoslavia, now a rump state composed of Serbia and Montenegro. The post gives the authoritarian Belgrade leader a new power base for at least four years; he was barred from seeking re-election in Serbia. Protesters fought police near the ceremony and threw shoes at Mr. Milosevic's car.

Burma and Laos were admitted to Asean, the Southeast Asian trade bloc, but Cambodia was barred until the nation's leadership struggle is settled and the status of Prince Ranariddh, the ousted co-premier, is resolved. Asean said coup leader Hun Sen has now agreed to allow the group a role, if undefined, in settling Cambodia's turmoil.

The Republican Party's former chief defended himself at the Senate campaign hearings. Haley Barbour testified that he thought money used to guarantee a $2.1 million 1994 loan to a Republican think tank came from a U.S. unit of a Hong Kong firm. It actually came from the parent. Mr. Barbour insisted the transaction was "legal and proper." But Sen. Fred Thompson, Republican chairman of the committee, chided Mr. Barbour for getting the GOP financially entangled with an overseas businessman.

Scotland would get its first parliament in nearly 300 years under plans unveiled by the British government, which include a more-limited legislature for Wales. The Edinburgh body would have many powers outside foreign affairs and defense, and would convene in 2000 if it clears a referendum.

A Texas jury ordered the Roman Catholic Diocese of Dallas to pay nearly $120 million in damages for ignoring evidence a priest sexually molested 11 altar boys from 1977 to 1992. The church denied any cover-up and officials, who say the verdict is the largest of its kind ever, plan to appeal.

A former EPA chief was selected by the administration to help resolve a salmon dispute with Canada that led to a blockade of an Alaskan ferry by fishermen. William Ruckleshaus was chosen to negotiate with a Canadian counterpart. Canadian fishermen accuse their U.S. counterparts of catching salmon bound for Canadian rivers.

Federal Medicare regulators aren't adequately policing the home-care program for fraud and waste, according to a GAO report. The budget for home-health activities has risen to $18 billion a year from $2.7 billion in 1989, and the many new companies entering the field aren't being screened well, the report has found.

The Air Force chief quit in what associates say is a disagreement with Defense Secretary William Cohen over sanctions for supposed negligence in the 1996 Saudi Arabia bombing that killed 19 U.S. servicemen. Gen. Ronald Fogleman's move appeared to be the first protest resignation from the Joint Chiefs of Staff.

Pol Pot was tried and sentenced to life in prison at a Khmer Rouge mass meeting near Cambodia's border with Thailand, according to an American journalist who, with a cameraman, witnessed the events. Cambodia's new leader claimed the trial was staged in a Khmer Rouge bid for political legitimacy.

William Weld resigned as Massachusetts governor, saying he wants to work full time on his long-shot bid to be ambassador to Mexico. Sen. Jesse Helms, chairman of the Foreign Relations panel, said Mr. Weld is soft on drugs and refused to schedule a hearing.

The Justice Department said FBI agents made "a major error" by interviewing Atlanta security guard Richard Jewell under the guise of making a training film. Mr. Jewell was suspected, then cleared, in the July 27, 1996, Olympics bombing that killed one.

Two suicide bombers killed 13 people at a crowded market in Jerusalem. The bombs, packed in briefcases and surrounded by nails, also injured more than 150 people at the Mahane Yehuda market. A Hamas leaflet claimed responsibility. Both bombers, dressed as Orthodox Jews, also died. Israel immediately suspended plans to resume peace talks with Palestinians, and the U.S. put off a special envoy's trip. Yasir Arafat condemned the attack, but Israel demanded tougher measures against the militants.

Chinese leaders unveiled a plan to end government ownership of all but a few key industries and broaden the definition of public ownership to include minority government stakes. President Jiang's plan, amounting to privatization in all but name, were due to be adopted at the fall Communist Party conference.

AUGUST

President Clinton lifted the 20-year-old ban on U.S. arms sales to Latin American nations, a move that had been eagerly awaited by Lockheed Martin and Boeing. The administration said Latin nations have made progress toward democracy and civilian control, and such sales would be considered case-by-case.

Montserrat's volcano touched off fires in the capital of the British Caribbean colony when erupting rocks and ash reached Plymouth. The government said 80% of Plymouth, which had been evacuated earlier, had been destroyed or damaged. The volcano came to life in 1995 after four centuries of dormancy. Later in the month, Montserrat's chief minister quit as protests continued over plans to evacuate the island. He said colleagues no longer trusted him to get a better relocation package from Britain.

A Korean Air 747 crashed on Guam with 254 aboard. Only 28 people survived. The flight mostly carried South Korean tourists, including many honeymooners, as well as 13 Americans. The FAA ordered the immediate testing of airport low-altitude warning systems nationwide after it found a software error may have contributed to the crash.

President Clinton signed bills to balance the budget over five years and cut some taxes. The budget measure would cut projected spending by about $263 billion over five years, with $115 billion of that from Medicare through lower reimbursements to hospitals and other care providers, and slightly higher premiums for beneficiaries. The tax measure totals $152 billion in cuts.

Attorney General Janet Reno accused the Republican-led Senate of an "unprecedented slowdown" in confirming nominees for federal judgeships. Ms. Reno told the American Bar Association convention that the president had sent up 62 nominations so far in 1997. Nine had been confirmed, but about 12% of the posts at district and appeals courts were vacant.

Opening arguments began in the trial of Ramzi Yousef, alleged mastermind of the 1993 bombing of New York's World Trade Center, and an accomplice accused of driving the van that carried the bomb. Mr. Yousef "ordered and mixed" chemicals for the attack that killed six, prosecutors said.

Bolivia's Congress elected former dictator Hugo Banzer as president, with support from leftist and populist parties. Banzer pledged to continue efforts to reform the economy, but wants steps to cut poverty.

A Midwest cattle-breeding firm cloned a calf using fetal cells, a technique that may be superior to that used by Scottish scientists who in 1997 disclosed they had cloned an adult sheep.

Cambodia's parliament backed former foreign minister Ung Huot, coup leader Hun Sen's nominee, to succeed ousted co-premier Prince Ranariddh. Earlier, legislators stripped Prince Ranariddh of immunity, meaning he faces arrest if he returns to Cambodia.

The FDA dropped longstanding curbs on TV prescription-drug advertising. A new policy allows pharmaceutical companies to tout specific drugs by name without lengthy warnings and advisories on side effects. Instead, viewers need only be warned about the main risks.

A federal grand jury in Miami indicted a dozen people for allegedly taking part in a $15 million scheme to defraud Medicare. Law-enforcement officials called it one of the nation's biggest home health-care scams. The indictment came as the U.S. was taking more aggressive steps to fight fraud in the big program.

U.S. prison capacity rose substantially from 1990 to 1995, the Justice Department said, with 45 federal and 168 state facilities added. That increased the number of beds 41% to 976,000. But overcrowding persisted as the inmate population grew to 1.02 million from 715,649. State overcapacity is at 3%, while in federal prisons the rate is 24%. Separately, the Justice Department said nearly 3.9 million adults were on probation or parole at the end of 1996, an increase of about 128,000 from 1995. A record 5.5 million adults were under some form of correctional supervision, including incarceration, in 1996.

Iraq was poised to resume limited oil sales after the U.N. approved a pricing plan. The partial lifting of Gulf War-era sanctions is supposed to allow Baghdad to buy civilian supplies. A new U.N. arms-inspection team also arrived in Iraq.

President Clinton crossed out three budget items in the first use of the line-item veto. The president said rejection of the provisions from the recent five-year budget and tax measures will save hundreds of millions of dollars and send the message that "the Washington rules have changed for good." Any such permanence, however, is most likely to be decided by the Supreme Court. The court in June allowed the line-item veto law to stand, but didn't rule on the substance of the new executive power.

New York City police officers were charged with brutally assaulting a Haitian immigrant after he was arrested in a scuffle outside a nightclub and taken to a Brooklyn station house. Some community leaders said the torture of Abner Louima reflected a bigger problem of police brutality against members of minority groups in New York.

President Clinton said he wants testing of drugs on children to establish safeness and dosage. The president proposed new FDA rules meant to address the concerns of children's health experts. Only about 20% of the drugs on the market have been tested on children. While pediatricians routinely prescribe drugs that haven't been studied in children, they often lack important information on precisely how much medication to use and how it will affect patients.

Welfare rolls declined by 1.4 million recipients nationwide in the past year, President Clinton said, claiming credit for the big Republican-crafted overhaul he signed in August 1996. "We now know that welfare reform works," the president said.

The U.S. prepared to sell the nation's two uranium-enrichment facilities, built in the 1950s for weapons production but now the world's leading maker of fuel for nuclear power plants. The transaction is likely to be the largest and most complicated sale of a federally run business ever, eclipsing the 1987 sale of Conrail.

Russia's privatization chief quit amid charges that the recent sales of state-owned telephone and nickel-mining assets were rigged. Alfred Kokh was to be succeeded by Maxim Boiko, who served as President Boris Yeltsin's deputy chief of staff. Both men are allies of economic policy chief Anatoly Chubais.

A new Louisiana law allowed motorists who believe someone is forcibly trying to steal their car while they are inside to shoot the suspect The law makes resulting killings justifiable.

Dow Chemical lost the first round in a class-action suit over breast implants. A New Orleans jury found that the company's silicone research was negligent and that the safety of the substance was misrepresented. Silicone went into the implants manufactured by Dow Corning, which was half-owned by Dow. The verdict was the first of four steps in the suit by 1,800 women, the largest yet to go to trial. Separately, Dow Corning offered $2.4 billion to settle litigation over breast implants, but a plaintiffs group attacked it as "inadequate and unfair." About 200,000 women around the world have filed claims.

Virginia Military Institute registered its first freshman class that includes women, an outcome set in motion when the Supreme Court in 1996 ordered the 158-year-old school to end its men-only policy or stop taking taxpayer funds. School officials expected to have 31 women in a class of 466.

The largest U.S. Lutheran church voted for closer ties to the Presbyterian Church (USA), the United Church of Christ and the Reformed Church in America. The Evangelical Lutheran Church in America, however, rejected closer ties to the Episcopal Church.

Russian President Boris Yeltsin met with the president of Chechnya, and agreed to form a commission to determine the status of the breakaway republic. Both sides agreed not to resort to war to settle disputes. Russia wants limited autonomy, but Chechnya seeks formal independence with international recognition.

Violence flared between Israel and Lebanon, following rocket attacks from Lebanon. Three Israelis were injured and thousands driven to shelters in the heaviest Katyusha barrage in more than a year. Hezbollah claimed responsibility, and the Israeli prime minister demanded that Syria, which controls Lebanon, rein in the guerrillas. The rockets were fired in retaliation for the shelling of the Lebanese city of Sidon by an Israeli-backed militia. Israel reprimanded the militia for that incident.

Federal air-safety investigators issued conclusions about the causes of the 1996 ValuJet crash. Topping the list are maintenance contractor SabreTech's failure to properly package oxygen generators, ValuJet's failure to properly supervise contractors, and the FAA's failure to require systems to fight fires.

Kenya's ruling party rejected opposition demands that constitutional changes to expand civil liberties be made before elections due by the end of 1997. Meanwhile, violence continued in the Mombasa area as more people were killed and a tourist market was torched in Malindi, a resort popular with Italians.

A New Hampshire man killed two state troopers, a local judge and a newspaper editor in a shooting spree that ended when police killed him near the Canadian border. A Vermont deputy and a border guard were wounded. Carl

Drega was believed to have carried a grudge over a tax case.

A U.S. appeals court upheld New Jersey's so-called Megan's law, which requires community notification of sex offenders' whereabouts. The court, however, ordered changes to bolster due-process protections. Most states now have versions of the law.

A federal grand jury indicted 20 people for allegedly smuggling deaf Mexicans into the U.S. and forcing them to sell cheap items on subway trains. The charges, handed up in New York, provided details on a nationwide scheme run out of New York and Chicago.

The U.S. government forced a Nebraska meat plant to close over contamination concerns. The unprecedented action also includes a recall of all of the Hudson Foods plant's production since June, an estimated 25 million pounds of ground beef suspected of being tainted with E. coli. The company destroyed all beef it has yet to ship, and the plant was to stay closed until more stringent safety measures were in place. At least 15 people are known to have fallen ill from June 14 to July 14, according to the Centers for Disease Control and Prevention. Five had to be hospitalized.

The U.S. announced a recall of halogen floor lamps because they pose a fire hazard blamed in 11 deaths since 1992. Some 40 million are on the market. Lamps in stores are to be removed, but current owners were given a guard they can install themselves with low-watt bulbs.

The American Medical Association met resistance from Sunbeam in its effort to pull out of a contract in which the doctors group had agreed to endorse some of the company's products, such as blood-pressure monitors and heating pads, for a fee. The AMA retreated following a public outcry.

Taiwan's president named Vincent Siew, who favors better China ties, to be prime minister.

The Clinton administration shifted its position in a closely watched affirmative-action case, asking the Supreme Court to uphold a ruling striking down a New Jersey town's dismissal of a white teacher. It was the third change in the Justice Department's position in as many years.

The Paula Jones case will go to trial May 27, 1998, a federal judge in Arkansas ruled. The judge refused to dismiss her core claim of being sexually harassed by President Clinton in 1991, but threw out two ancillary charges.

Problems continued throughout August with the Mir space station. A computer temporarily malfunctioned, delaying the docking of an unmanned cargo ship, and later, the ability to make oxygen was lost temporarily when both the primary and backup generators failed. The Mir crew returned to Earth and bitterly denied suggestions they were to blame for the station's recent problems. The former commander instead blamed a general deterioration in the Russian space program.

China executed more people in this decade than the rest of the world combined, putting at least 4,367 people to death in 1996 alone, Amnesty International said. The human-rights group added that capital offenses are rising under a crime crackdown.

The World Bank said poverty in parts of Asia is in a remarkable decline. The international lending agency said nations in East and Southeast Asia reduced the number of poor people to 345.7 million in 1995 from 716.8 million in 1975. The report said South Korea, Taiwan, Hong Kong and Singapore essentially have eliminated absolute poverty as a national concern. Pockets of absolute poverty remain in northwest China, northeast Thailand, the eastern islands of Indonesia and other places, according to the report.

A federal board that oversees the Teamsters began an investigation of the union's top leadership and heard a request for disciplinary action against its president, Ron Carey. Earlier, a federal election officer had thrown out Mr. Carey's January victory after finding that associates of Mr. Carey improperly used funds from the Teamsters to help his campaign.

Union Pacific faced an unprecedented federal review of safety procedures after three train collisions that killed five workers in three months. Some 60 inspectors planned to check the biggest U.S. railroad's work schedules, maintenance, dispatching and operating practices.

Germany said it would seek to renew ties to Iran following the installation of a government viewed as more moderate than its predecessors.

Relations had been frozen since a court in April found Tehran leaders ordered four 1992 assassinations in Berlin.

Former Agriculture Secretary Mike Espy was charged with taking gifts and favors from firms under his purview. A federal grand jury indicted him on 39 counts of accepting such things as trips and sports tickets, valued at $35,000, from such companies as Tyson Foods and Sun-Diamond Growers. The former Mississippi congressman left the Clinton administration in 1994 as the independent counsel's inquiry began. His lawyer argued that "benign activities" had been twisted into crimes. The indictment doesn't allege that Mr. Espy did any favors in return for the companies' gifts. Such a finding isn't required under the gratuities statute.

A top medical journal called for a moratorium on the use of prescription diet drugs Redux and a combination of phentermine and fenfluramine called "phen-fen" because of concerns over side effects. The *New England Journal of Medicine* editorial criticized the FDA's rationale for approving Redux in 1996.

Israel lifted its blockade of Bethlehem, imposed after Jerusalem bombings in July and maintained after restrictions on travel between other West Bank towns had been eased. The blockade led to violent protests by Palestinians and a complaint from the Vatican, but Israel said a change in the security situation led to its decision.

North Korea withdrew from talks with the U.S. on missile proliferation, saying Washington's decision to help two North Korean envoys defect was a "grave insult." The U.S. refused to hand over the two men, who defected with their families.

A federal judge in Florida granted class-action status to a lawsuit alleging that Motel 6 discriminated against blacks by charging them more, segregating them in rear areas and sometimes refusing rooms. The company, owned by Accor of France, said it doesn't condone racial discrimination.

Police in Rome arrested a Libyan man wanted by Germany for the 1986 bombing of a Berlin discotheque that killed two U.S. soldiers and injured hundreds. The attack prompted the U.S. to send warplanes to bomb two Libyan cities, killing at least 15.

For the 1997–1998 winter season, El Niño appeared to be shaping up as the "climate event of the century," an international conference of meteorologists in Geneva said. Weather effects produced by the Pacific current in 1982–83 have been blamed for 2,000 deaths and $13 billion in damage.

A Bosnian Serb mob attacked U.S. troops at a police station in Brcko. The U.S. warned it wouldn't tolerate such violence after two members of the NATO peacekeeping force were injured. The incident began when troops moved into the town, which commands a corridor connecting halves of the Bosnian Serb enclave, to oust police loyal to indicted war criminal Radovan Karadzic. The Pentagon said protesters threw Molotov cocktails and beat soldiers with lumber. Troops fired tear gas and warning shots, but were forced to pull out.

California's affirmative-action ban took effect as the Rev. Jesse Jackson led a protest against the new law in San Francisco. The ban on racial and gender preferences passed as a ballot initiative in 1996, but had been tied up in court. Further legal challenges are certain, and some localities vowed to ignore the law.

Rep. Joseph Kennedy said he won't run for Massachusetts governor, but will seek reelection in 1998. Robert Kennedy's oldest son has been hurt by his ex-wife's critical book and allegations that his brother had an affair with a teenage baby sitter.

Diana, Princess of Wales, was killed in an automobile crash in Paris, along with her companion Emad Mohammed al-Fayed and the car's driver. Police said the driver was legally drunk when he crashed in a tunnel near the Seine. The car was being pursued by paparazzi at the time of the crash, and French authorities were investigating what, if any, role the photographers may have played in the accident.

SEPTEMBER

Attorney General Janet Reno opened a review that could lead to an independent-counsel inquiry into Vice President Gore's campaign fund-raising activities. The attorney general was looking into whether the vice president's admitted fund-raising phone calls were illegal because they were made from federal property. Mr. Gore denies any wrongdoing. Separately, Ms. Reno appointed a new lead prosecutor in the Justice Department campaign inquiry. Charles La Bella, top assistant U.S. attorney in San Diego, was named to succeed Laura Ingersoll. The attorney general also replaced the top FBI agent on the case.

Arizona's governor resigned after he was convicted of lying to secure loans. Fife Symington, a two-term Republican, is the second governor of the state to be forced out by scandal in 10 years. A U.S. jury, after deliberating 17 days, found him guilty on seven fraud counts, acquitted him on three others and deadlocked on 11.

Three suicide bombers killed four people and injured 192 in Jerusalem. Hamas claimed responsibility for sending the three bombers, who also died, in the afternoon attack on busy Ben Yehuda Street. The militant Muslim group promised more bombings unless Israel frees Hamas prisoners.

The Supreme Court refused to block implementation of California's new law barring race and gender preferences in hiring and school admissions. The law took effect after a federal appeals court refused to stay it.

Mother Teresa was mourned by the people of Calcutta, where she devoted her life to comforting the poor. India held a state funeral for the beloved 87-year-old Roman Catholic nun, who died of a heart attack. Her ministry brought her the Nobel Peace Prize in 1979.

Athens won the competition to host the 2004 Summer Olympics. The decision, in which boosters beat off challenges from four other cities, touched off celebrations in the Greek capital.

A Haitian ferry capsized, and about 170 people drowned. The accident occurred when passengers rushed to one side of the overloaded vessel as it approached the wharf at Montrouis, 50 miles northwest of Port-au-Prince, after a trip from the island of La Gonave. Many managed to swim ashore.

Palestinian police arrested 35 suspected militants in the West Bank on the eve of Secretary of State Madeleine Albright's visit to the region. Ms. Albright urged the Palestinians to make

more arrests, and she told Israel's prime minister he should comply with Oslo commitments on West Bank withdrawals, reopen Israel's borders to Palestinian workers and resume payments to the Palestinian authority. Ms. Albright also paid an unannounced visit to Lebanon and urged talks to reduce the recent surge in fighting with Israel.

The Justice Department dropped charges against a Saudi dissident suspected of a role in the 1996 bombing in Dhahran that killed 19 U.S. servicemen, and will seek to extradite him to Saudi Arabia. The charges he faced were unrelated to that bombing, but were part of a proposed plea agreement for him to tell what he knows.

Paula Jones's lawyers were given permission by the judge in her sexual-harassment suit against President Clinton to withdraw from the case. The decision came after Ms. Jones reportedly rejected proposed settlement terms. Meanwhile, State Farm said it would stop paying Mr. Clinton's legal bills after a judge threw out Ms. Jones's defamation claim.

A transit strike in San Francisco caused massive traffic jams, especially at the Bay Bridge, as the 270,000 daily users of the rail system sought other transportation. The strike lasted a week, until unions and management reached a tentative wage agreement.

Air Force Secretary Sheila Widnall said she would quit Oct. 31 to return to teaching at MIT. She was the first woman to have served in the post.

Former Agriculture Secretary Mike Espy pleaded not guilty to charges that he took $35,000 in gifts and favors from companies under his purview. A trial wasn't expected to start until 1998.

The Army released reports showing that sexual discrimination and harassment are more widespread than the service's leaders had believed, and that many in the ranks distrust the complaint system. Improvements were promised as a result of a survey of more than 30,000 soldiers, which was ordered after the sex-abuse scandal at a Maryland base.

Scotland voted overwhelmingly for creation of a separate parliament after 290 years of union with England. The legislature would have authority over domestic matters. Later in the month, Wales approved its own parliament by a narrower margin, but the Welsh body's powers are more limited than Scotland's.

President Clinton nominated Dr. David Satcher, director of the Centers for Disease Control and Prevention, as surgeon general. The post had been vacant since Joycelyn Elders left in late 1994.

China faces a tough task implementing President Jiang's call for privatization of state-run enterprises, made in a speech opening a Communist Party congress. He gave no timetable, but an official said Beijing would begin drafting rules laying out which sectors will stay under state control. Separately, the State Department said China decided to return a Sun Microsystems supercomputer after the U.S. complained it had been diverted from civilian to military use.

Former Massachusetts Governor William Weld ended his bid to become ambassador to Mexico. The opposition of Sen. Jesse Helms, the conservative head of the Foreign Relations panel who refused to schedule a Weld hearing because he considered the nominee soft on drugs, led to the withdrawal. Mr. Weld said he had refused to "go on bended knee" before Mr. Helms. Separately, former Boston Mayor Raymond Flynn quit as envoy to the Vatican to begin a bid to be Massachusetts governor.

The House voted 295–125 to deny funding for President Clinton's national testing plan for students in lower grades, a centerpiece of his education initiatives. The vote came as the House pressed to finish work on a $269 billion spending bill that includes an increase of $2.8 billion for the Education Department.

An Indian group in Colombia made an urgent plea for the government to halt air strikes in a region 185 miles southeast of Bogota, saying tribal communities were being devastated. The army was waging its biggest offensive against leftist rebels since 1990.

North Korea's famine may be the worst since World War II, killing 10,000 children every month, according to the German Red Cross. Another aid agency, World Vision, estimated that one in seven North Koreans have starved to death in northern areas.

The Senate confirmed Army Gen. Henry Shelton to be chairman of the Joint Chiefs of Staff in a voice vote. He succeeded Gen. John Shalikashvili and became the first Green Beret in the post.

President Clinton asked Congress to toughen the proposed tobacco accord by passing legislation to counter teen smoking by raising cigarette prices by as much as $1.50 a pack over 10 years. In addition, tobacco firms would pay penalties based on how popular their brands were among underage smokers under a proposal by Health and Human Services Secretary Donna Shalala. Separately, the FTC sharply criticized the proposed national tobacco accord, saying cigarette makers could reap profits that would far exceed the penalties the pact would impose. An industry spokesman said the FTC report is "based on assumptions that are at best inaccurate."

President Clinton ended U.S. support for an international treaty banning land mines. The move, which opens a split between Washington and its closest allies, came after the president's negotiators in Norway were unable to secure a nine-year exemption for the Korean peninsula, where minefields protect nearly 40,000 U.S. troops. The treaty was approved by 89 countries.

Defense Secretary William Cohen ordered the military to halt training flights for 24 hours, the first safety review to affect all the services at once. Five military aircraft had crashed in recent days, including the collision off Africa of a U.S. C-141 cargo plane with a German plane that killed 33 people.

Three associates of Teamsters union president Ron Carey pleaded guilty in a scheme to raise funds for Mr. Carey's reelection campaign. The three men, who have agreed to cooperate in the inquiry, said the plan involved giving Teamsters funds to the Democrats and the Clinton-Gore campaign, which would then try to find donors for the union chief's now-voided 1996 reelection. Mr. Carey's campaign manager said he broke rules because he felt it necessary to defeat a bid by James Hoffa, son of the longtime Teamsters boss. Mr. Carey's lawyer said his client was unaware of the scheme; the White House issued a similar statement.

Roger Tamraz said he bought White House access over the objections of President Clinton's aides. Testifying before the Senate campaign committee, he said securing meetings with administration officials to promote his Caspian oil-pipeline project was "the only reason" he gave $300,000 to the Democratic Party. Mr. Tamraz said he briefly pitched the proposal to Mr. Clinton himself at a 1996 White House dinner. The president later asked the Energy Department about the project, which hasn't been built.

Ted Turner pledged to give $1 billion in stock over 10 years to a U.N. foundation funding programs to help refugees, battle disease and clear land mines. Mr. Turner, whose cable empire merged with Time Warner in 1996, estimated his net worth at $3.2 billion prior to the gift.

New U.S. cases of AIDS fell 6% to 56,730 in 1996 compared with the year earlier, the first recorded decline in the history of the epidemic, according to the Centers for Disease Control and Prevention. New combination therapies were credited with delaying the onset of full-blown AIDS in those with HIV.

President Clinton addressed the U.N. on arms control and the dues the U.S. owes. The president told the opening session of the 52nd General Assembly that he was sending the Senate the nuclear test-ban treaty for ratification. Mr. Clinton signed the accord in 1996. He also said the U.S. would pay nearly $1 billion in back dues, less than the U.N. says it owes, and expects future assessments to be cut. Secretary-General Kofi Annan called for all member countries to pay what they owe "without conditions."

Solidarity won the most seats of any party in Poland's parliamentary elections. The former trade union won an estimated third of the vote, followed by about 27% for the ex-Communists and about 14% for a pro-market party, the Freedom Union. Solidarity and Freedom Union planned coalition talks.

Thalidomide was on the verge of gaining FDA approval for treating leprosy patients after Celgene Corp. said it saw no surprises in the agency's final conditions, intended to keep the drug away from pregnant women. The U.S.

banned the drug in the 1960s for causing birth deformities.

Montserrat officials evacuated 80 people after two days of eruptions by the island's volcano, and said power and water may be cut to force others to leave. The Caribbean island's abandoned airport was destroyed.

Serbia's Socialists will have to form a coalition government for the first time since the end of the Cold War, according to results of elections. The ultranationalist Radical Party is the most likely partner.

A U.N. report on the Congo Republic said nearly 500,000 people, one-fifth of the population, are now refugees after three months of fighting between rival militias. At least 150,000 have fled the capital, Brazzaville.

The Senate passed a bill to overhaul the FDA in a 98-2 vote. The measure is intended to speed up approvals of new drugs and medical devices.

Protestant parties agreed to join Northern Ireland peace talks despite rejection by Britain and Ireland of their call to expel the IRA's political wing. The two governments also named a Canadian general to oversee efforts to secure an arms surrender during the long-stalled talks.

A grand jury began investigating GOP dealings with a Hong Kong figure. The inquiry stems from Haley Barbour's July testimony at Senate campaign hearings about a 1994 deal that brought $1.6 million to the GOP just before it won control of Congress. Prosecutors were believed to be examining whether the deal broke laws against foreign contributions, and whether the former Republican Party chief testified truthfully.

President Clinton commemorated a crucial early civil-rights victory by holding open the door of Central High School in Little Rock, Ark., for nine African-Americans who braved threats and racial taunts to integrate the school 40 years ago. The president said that while segregation has been outlawed, "too often it is still the rule."

Six former or current IRS workers told a Senate panel the agency is grossly mismanaged and policies from Washington are routinely ignored by field offices. On the final day of the hearings, the acting IRS chief apologized and announced actions he will take in response to the testimony. Separately, President Clinton conceded that the tax-collection agency "has to improve more," but said proposed legislation to take the IRS away from the Treasury and put it under a private-sector board would lead to conflicts of interest.

Smoke from Indonesia fires spurred Westerners in Malaysia to make plans to flee the choking atmosphere, which settled over much of Southeast Asia. The fires had charred about 1.48 million acres, and authorities feared they could burn for months if peat deposits catch.

A U.S. shuttle docked with *Mir*, picking up astronaut Michael Foale after a four and a half month stay and dropping off astronaut David Wolf, who is to spend four months on the Russian space station. NASA is under pressure from Congress to end U.S. *Mir* missions because of safety concerns.

A Garuda Air A-300 crashed near Medan on Sumatra island, killing all 234 aboard. Speculation centered on low visibility caused by the forest fires in the region. But a tower recording showed that the Indonesian airliner's crew engaged in a confused discussion with controllers about location and headings before the crash.

Jury selection began in the trial of Terry Nichols, the alleged accomplice of Timothy McVeigh in the 1995 bombing of the Oklahoma City federal building.

Violence intensified during September in Algeria. At least 200 Algerians were slaughtered in one of the biggest of the frequent massacres that have occurred around the capital. Near the end of the month, Algerian schoolchildren watched as 12 of their teachers had their throats cut in one of the most brutal attacks in the five-year-old war between Muslim militants and the government. The killings took place in a village 260 miles southwest of Algiers.

Israel and the Palestinians agreed at the end of September to resume talks on implementing the Oslo peace accords following a meeting with Secretary of State Madeleine Albright in New York. The agreement would break a six-month deadlock.

An arts-funding compromise was struck by House and Senate negotiators. The National Endowment for the Arts will get $98 million, but it will be distributed more widely, and big states like New York will be capped.

A White House science panel called for an additional $1 billion for energy research over five years, including funds to study whether nuclear plants can be made to work more efficiently and last longer. It also said the U.S. should develop a 100 mpg car by 2010, and equip buildings with solar power.

France's Roman Catholic church asked forgiveness for its silence during the Vichy regime's deportation of 76,000 Jews to World War II Nazi death camps.

Business and Economic News of 1997

JANUARY

Ameritech became the first Baby Bell to ask regulators for permission to offer long-distance services, but it ran into trouble because of errors in its filing with the FCC and withdrew the request in February.

East Coast ports slashed rates up to 30% in a drive to regain market share. The cuts are among the biggest of the decade and will affect more than $80 billion in cargo annually.

Raytheon agreed to buy the missile and defense-electronics holdings of Texas Instru-

ments for $2.95 billion, and later in the month won a bidding contest with Northrop Grumman to acquire the defense business of General Motors' Hughes Electronics unit for $9.5 billion.

Republic Industries reached an agreement to acquire National Car Rental for $600 million in stock, plus the assumption of $1.7 billion of vehicle debt. The move follows Republic's purchase of Alamo and bolsters its plan to use car-rental companies to supply vehicles for its chain of used-car superstores.

General Instrument said it planned to split into three public companies through a tax-free spinoff. The three new entities will focus on telephone and cable equipment, coaxial cable wires and electrical components.

Internal Revenue Service Commissioner Margaret Milner Richardson said she would step down as head of the tax agency. Treasury chief Robert Rubin prompted Ms. Richardson's resignation, signaling his concerns about the state of the tax agency.

American Airlines pilots rejected a contract that offered only modest pay increases and stock options in exchange for higher productivity. The airline warned that the prospects of a strike "are very real" after the National Mediation Board declared an impasse in talks between the carrier and its pilots union.

Volkswagen agreed to pay General Motors $100 million and to buy $1 billion of GM parts over seven years to settle a civil suit alleging trade-secret theft. GM, in turn, agreed to drop the suit in the matter involving former GM purchasing chief Jose Ignacio Lopez de Arriortua, who defected to VW in 1993.

Tyco International proposed acquiring American Standard, a maker of air-conditioning, plumbing and other products, for $50 a share in stock and cash, or about $4 billion, plus assumed debt. American Standard rebuffed the proposal, and Tyco's chairman said the conglomerate would abandon the offer rather than pursue a hostile bid.

ABC was ordered by a federal jury to pay more than $5.5 million in punitive damages to Food Lion for a hidden-camera report accusing the grocery chain of selling tainted food. Separately, ABC's nightly newscast lost the No. 1 slot four of five previous weeks to NBC, a first sign of weakness at the top network newscast since 1989.

The Food and Drug Administration proposed withdrawing its approval for allergy drug Seldane because of its potential side effects. Hoechst Marion Roussel and generic drug maker Ivax vowed to challenge the move.

Ford Motor agreed to sell Budget Rent a Car to Team Rental Group. The pact involves $350 million in cash and stock and assumption of $1.3 billion of vehicle debt.

DuPont didn't have to pay standard benefits to a contract worker, a federal appeals court ruled. The decision was expected to calm corporate America's fears about such benefits.

Boeing canceled plans to build two "super-jumbo" 747 jet models because of spiraling development costs that could have topped $7 billion and insufficient interest in orders from airlines.

Banc One said it agreed to buy First USA for stock valued at $6.65 billion. The pact provides the bank with a long-coveted national consumer-finance business but at a high cost. Stocks of other credit-card firms shot up on news of the purchase of First USA, signaling Wall Street is expecting other deals in the industry.

The FDA approved health claims in advertising for the first time, permitting Quaker Oats and other firms to promote the benefits of oat bran.

ConAgra agreed to pay millions of dollars in penalties to settle the biggest grain-adulteration probe in decades. The criminal inquiry focused on a unit's practice of spraying water on grain stored in its elevators.

The dollar soared to a four-year high against the yen and a 31-month peak against the mark.

PepsiCo said it would spin off its restaurant business and explore the sale of its food-service unit. Pepsi said the new company, which would include Taco Bell, KFC and Pizza Hut, had total sales of $11.3 billion in 1995. The move will return the company to its roots as a soft-drink and snacks concern.

The AFL-CIO backed a drive to unionize Las Vegas hotel, hospital and construction workers in its largest organizing effort nationally in decades.

Publix Super Markets said it would pay $81.5 million to settle a discrimination suit covering about 150,000 current and former female employees.

Hilton launched a hostile takeover bid for rival ITT valued at $55 a share in stock and cash, or $6.5 billion, plus the assumption of debt. Hilton said a merger would create the world's largest gambling and lodging firm, with nearly 230,000 hotel rooms and 30 casinos.

American Express said it would lay off 3,300 employees, or nearly 5% of its work force, in its fourth round of staff cuts since 1991.

Bankruptcy cases in Delaware will be assigned to regular federal judges in addition to bankruptcy court judges, a federal judge ruled. The move was expected to make firms think twice about seeking court protection from creditors in the popular jurisdiction. Delaware's bankruptcy court faced criticism over its reputation for giving firms favorable treatment.

Investors snapped up the federal government's new inflation-indexed bonds. The auction of $7 billion of the 10-year notes, dubbed Treasury Inflation Protection Securities, or TIPS, was far oversubscribed, with investors seeking more than five times the amount offered.

America Online reached a preliminary pact over complaints about its overcrowded network. The pact required it to pay up to $40 to customers who have had difficulty gaining access to the on-line service since it began flat-rate pricing in December 1996. But many America Online users weren't eligible for the refunds.

Mercury Finance said it found phony bookkeeping entries that led it to overstate 1996 profit by over 100% and said its controller has vanished. The company's controller later denied the firm's charges that he inflated its profits and then disappeared. The used-car lender also failed to repay $17 million of commercial-paper debt.

Alan Greenspan called for the creation of an independent commission to set annual cost-of-living adjustment rates for taxes and federal benefits such as Social Security. The Fed chief also endorsed a report by a panel of economists that concluded the Consumer Price Index, the current gauge used to make the adjustments, overstates inflation.

Warner-Lambert's Rezulin won FDA approval. The new type of diabetes drug could reduce, and in some cases even eliminate, the need for insulin shots for about a million diabetics in the U.S., doctors said.

FEBRUARY

The problems of the used-car lending business grew, as Mercury Finance's longtime chief executive officer, John Brincat, resigned amid a deepening investigation of the company's accounting irregularities. His departure came as FBI agents collected records from Mercury's offices. Jayhawk Acceptance, another used-car lender, filed for bankruptcy protection.

Morgan Stanley and Dean Witter, Discover agreed to merge in a deal valued at $10.22 billion

in stock that would create the largest securities firm. Driving the merger was a bid to snare the growing assets of small investors, particularly in mutual funds. The news caused rallies in other brokerage-firm stocks.

CVS agreed to acquire Revco in a $2.9 billion stock swap that would create the nation's No. 2 drugstore chain, behind Walgreen's.

A White House aviation panel called for billions of dollars in spending to boost airport security and accelerate improvement of the air-traffic control system. The report also recommended "replacing the traditional system of excise taxes" on tickets with user fees to pay for system upgrades.

Western Resources reached an agreement to buy Kansas City Power & Light for $2 billion, ending a protracted hostile takeover battle.

CBS's parent Westinghouse Electric said it plans to pay Gaylord Entertainment $1.55 billion in stock for the Nashville Network and the part of Country Music Television it doesn't already own.

Centennial Technologies fired its chairman and CEO and removed its chief financial officer. The maker of computer memory cards also said it was launching an inquiry into the accuracy of its most recent earnings report and prior financial statements. Federal authorities charged Emanuel Pinez, the CEO, with securities fraud.

American General announced an agreement to pay $1.77 billion for USLife. The financial-services firm will also assume $570 million of USLife's debt.

ITT rejected Hilton's hostile $6.5 billion bid and said it plans to sell assets not related to its hotels or casinos. ITT also filed a lawsuit charging that Hilton misused confidential information and failed to disclose important facts to shareholders in its bid.

Mitsubishi's U.S. auto plant, the subject of a major sexual harassment suit, received sweeping recommendations for improving its workplace from former Labor Secretary Lynn Martin.

The Dow Jones Industrial Average closed above 7,000 for the first time, slicing through the fourth 1,000-point mark in just under two years. The index rose 60.81 to 7022.44 on

Feb. 13. The S&P 500 also set a record, rising 9.05 to 811.82.

H.F. Ahmanson, the nation's largest thrift institution, made an unsolicited takeover proposal for rival Great Western Financial valued at $6.59 billion in stock. The combination would create one of the biggest financial institutions in California with assets of $93 billion. The hostile bid came at a time of consolidation in the thrift industry, as well as in the California banking market.

An American Airlines strike was halted by President Clinton after intense lobbying of the White House. Mr. Clinton appointed an emergency board to mediate the contract dispute between the airline and its pilots. Minutes after the president signed his order, American announced a 50%-off fare sale.

Corporate profits jumped 61% in the fourth quarter of 1996 from a year ago, a *Wall Street Journal* tabulation of the results of 690 large firms found. The figures cap a five-year run of growth that could become the longest in postwar history.

A global telecommunications pact was signed by 69 countries. The agreement promises to pry open vast new markets for U.S. and foreign firms.

Stone-Consolidated and Abitibi-Price agreed to merge in a deal valued at about $1.5 billion that would create the world's biggest newsprint maker.

Two Detroit newspapers accepted an unconditional offer by six striking unions to return to work, effectively ending a tumultuous 19-month protest against *The Detroit News* and *Detroit Free Press*. The dailies said they would gradually reinstate workers.

Evergreen Media said it will acquire Chancellor Broadcasting in a $567 million stock swap. The new company will also buy 10 stations from Viacom for $1.08 billion, making it the nation's second-largest radio chain.

The U.S. trade deficit surged to $114.23 billion in 1996, an eight-year high that included a record yearly merchandise imbalance with China.

Levi Strauss said it will cut 20% of its salaried work force over the next 12 months, citing increased competition and slowing demand for jeans.

Johnson Controls reached tentative contract agreements with the UAW for striking workers at two seat-making plants. Ford Motor was without a steady supply of seats for its high-profit Expedition sport-utility vehicle since the strikes began January 28.

AT&T plans to test an electronic box that would tie home telephones directly to the AT&T wireless network. The plan, which uses technology recently patented by the firm, could give AT&T another powerful option for providing local phone services, but at an enormous cost.

Applied Magnetics launched a hostile takeover bid for rival Read-Rite valued at $36 a share in stock, or $1.7 billion. A combination would create a new leader among suppliers of recording heads for PC disk drives. After failing to reach a friendly accord, Applied disclosed the offer and said it would begin a proxy battle to oust the board of Read-Rite.

News Corp. said it would buy 50% of EchoStar Communications in a deal it valued at $1 billion, creating a potent new direct-broadcast satellite competitor out of two fledgling ventures.

New cloning technology was greeted with skepticism on Wall Street, where investors said it could be years before profits accrue from the research. Still, the cloning of a sheep will accelerate the race to create animals designed to produce proteins, drugs and even organs for humans.

McDonald's announced its biggest discounting program ever in a bid to revive the fast-food chain. The company said it would cut the price of selected sandwiches to 55 cents with the purchase of french fries or hash browns and a drink. Competitors said they didn't plan to follow suit.

Some Walt Disney shareholders used the entertainment giant's annual meeting to deliver a strong message of discontent. They complained bitterly about the firm's multimillion-dollar payout to former president Michael Ovitz and a rich new contract for chairman and CEO Michael Eisner.

Two big manufacturers said they planned to sell off parts of their companies to concentrate on their consumer-product businesses. Kimberly-Clark, the marketer of Kleenex tissues and Huggies diapers, said it would get out of the cyclical pulp business by selling three mills, while CPC

International planned to spin off its corn-refining business to focus on its much larger packaged-food brands, including Skippy peanut butter and Hellmann's mayonnaise.

Alan Greenspan made it clear the Federal Reserve is inching closer to boosting interest rates. In congressional testimony, the Fed chief also showed increasing uneasiness about the stock market's ebullience. The Dow Jones industrials quickly fell more than 100 points on the remarks, but recovered to close down 55.03. Bond prices also declined, but the dollar surged.

3Com agreed to buy modem maker U.S. Robotics in a stock deal valued at $6.6 billion, the second-largest technology acquisition ever. Analysts called the deal a bold attempt by 3Com, a network-equipment maker, to challenge Cisco, the leader in that market.

Japanese auto exports to the U.S. surged 75% in January because of a weak yen, strong demand for some models and anemic year-earlier shipments.

Stock mutual funds took in a record $29.39 billion in January. The volume topped expectations and beat the record $28.9 billion of January 1996. Large-company, growth-and-income and index funds were attracting lots of cash, but small-company funds were lagging.

Carl Icahn sold his 7.3% stake in RJR Nabisco for over $730 million, and conceded that winning a proxy fight against the cigarette and food giant would be "exceedingly difficult." Mr. Icahn pocketed an estimated $130 million profit, or a 23% return.

Ford Motor decided to suspend production of its 42-year-old Thunderbird model, choosing to withhold new versions of the slow-selling classic car until after 2000.

The Federal Trade Commission fined a German auto-parts maker a record $5.1 million in the latest sign antitrust enforcers are imposing tougher fines on firms that try to fly beneath their merger radar.

MARCH

Cigna agreed to acquire Healthsource for $1.4 billion, plus $250 million in assumed debt, boosting its managed-care business.

AT&T outlined plans to spend up to $9 billion in 1997 expanding its network to attack new markets. Short-term earnings will be hurt by the spending, which is aimed at positioning AT&T for major earnings gains in five years. Officials also said managers have been told to cut $2.6 billion in costs over two years through already-announced job cuts and other moves.

Toys "R" Us disclosed for the first time that it warned toy makers it might not carry certain lines of their toys if they were also sold to warehouse clubs that sell at a discount. The disclosure came at the start of an administrative law proceeding at the FTC, which has accused the company of illegally boosting prices by working to cut off warehouse clubs. Toys "R" Us maintains that it hasn't done anything illegal.

ITT said it agreed to sell its half of Madison Square Garden, the New York Knicks and New York Rangers, and MSG Cablevision network to its partner, Cablevision Systems, for $650 million in cash and options and $115 million in assumed debt.

China, in a further concession aimed at joining the World Trade Organization, said it would grant Chinese firms the right to trade directly with foreign companies. China pledged to take that action three years after its entry into the WTO.

Major airlines boosted domestic air fares by 4% after an attempt to make consumers pay the reinstated 10% federal ticket tax fell apart.

Conrail's board formally approved a $10.5 billion takeover by CSX. CSX said it will now focus on talks to split up Conrail with Norfolk Southern.

Ronald O. Perelman gave up his fight to maintain control of comic-book publisher Marvel and agreed to hand the company over to a group of dissident bondholders led by Carl Icahn.

The FTC voted to block Staples' $4 billion acquisition of Office Depot, saying a combination of the two office-supply superstores would violate antitrust law and lead to higher consumer prices. Staples reached a last-minute agreement to sell 63 stores to OfficeMax, a moved aimed at averting a federal antitrust challenge.

Newmont won its battle for Santa Fe Pacific Gold, agreeing to acquire its fellow gold producer for stock valued at $2.46 billion, or $18.49 a share. Santa Fe will pay Homestake $65 million to cancel their merger pact.

Marsh & McLennan announced an agreement to acquire insurance-broker Johnson & Higgins for $1.8 billion in cash and stock. The move would restore Marsh to its long-held spot as the world's biggest insurance broker. The deal reflects a consolidation trend sweeping the industry.

Warren Buffett cautioned in an annual letter that stock prices are now so high that it is likely investors are overpaying for "virtually all stocks." The Dow Jones industrials subsequently dropped 81 points.

Apple Computer said it would cut its payroll by 30%, cancel some projects not central to sales of its Macintosh line, and trim research spending. The struggling computer maker also said it expected the current quarter to produce its lowest quarterly revenue in three years. Apple's budget cutting has led to an accelerating exodus of top research scientists.

H.J. Heinz unveiled a restructuring plan, saying it would close or sell 25 plants, cut its work force, and take a $650 million pretax charge.

The FDA approved two protease inhibitors for treating children with AIDS: Abbott's Norvir and Agouron's Viracept.

Applied Magnetics retreated from its hostile takeover bid for Read-Rite, after Read-Rite formally rejected the offer.

Tyco International agreed to merge with ADT in a $5.4 billion deal that tops Western Resources' hostile bid. The deal would create a powerful marketer of fire-protection and home-security services. The transaction is structured so that Tyco winds up as the surviving entity, although ADT is technically the acquirer.

The National Association of Securities Dealers formed an informal task force with the Nasdaq Stock Market to pass on leads to criminal authorities about possible organized-crime activity in the U.S. stock markets.

Texaco and Shell Oil agreed to merge much of their U.S. refining and marketing units. The firms said they would expand the accord if they reach a pact with Saudi Arabia, which owns refining assets with Texaco.

First Bank System agreed to acquire U.S. Bancorp in a stock swap valued at $8.44 billion. The combination would create a banking giant in the Midwest and West.

American Airlines reached a tentative settlement with negotiators for its pilots union, possibly clearing the way for an end to a lengthy and expensive standoff over a new labor contract.

Sprint sought to play down the disclosure that Cable & Wireless may bid for the firm, even as its chairman seemed to leave the door open to a deal if the right suitor came along.

Germany's Krupp suspended its $8 billion hostile takeover bid for rival Thyssen, and the firms agreed to merge their steel businesses, creating the world's fifth largest steel producer.

ConAgra agreed to pay $8.3 million in criminal penalties to settle charges of wire fraud, misgrading crops and adding water to make grain heavier.

Liggett unveiled a settlement with 22 state attorneys general and plaintiffs lawyers calling for it to warn on its cigarettes that smoking is addictive. It will also turn over documents that would help antitobacco forces in litigation with the rest of the industry. Reports that Liggett planned to make the unprecedented concessions sent tobacco stocks plunging.

Dow Jones was ordered by a federal jury in Houston to pay a $223 million libel verdict over a 1993 *Wall Street Journal* article about investment firm MMAR Group. Dow Jones officials said the firm will appeal.

Delta Air Lines agreed to buy planes exclusively from Boeing, including initial firm orders for 106 jets with list prices totaling $6.7 billion. The move prompted an unusually harsh rebuke from Airbus.

The Federal Reserve raised a key short-term interest rate by a quarter of a percentage point. The central bank cited "persisting strength in demand" that "is progressively increasing the risk of inflationary imbalances." The Fed's move, its first since January 1996, brings its target for the federal funds rate, at which banks lend to each other overnight, to 5.5%.

Toyota introduced a hybrid electric-and-gasoline power system for cars that it says doubles fuel efficiency and reduces emissions by 90%.

Bre-X Minerals' Busang gold field contains "insignificant" amounts of gold based on early drilling results, Freeport McMoRan Copper & Gold said. Bre-X had said the Indonesian field contained at least 71 million ounces of gold, valued at over $24 billion. Bre-X's permit to mine the Busang claim was suspended by the Indonesian government, pending an independent analysis of the site's gold reserves. Bre-X also came under investigation by the Ontario Securities Commission after its stock tumbled on the news.

New Era Philanthropy founder John G. Bennett pleaded no contest to federal charges of defrauding hundreds of charities, churches, colleges and philanthropists of $135 million.

Great Western Financial reaffirmed its $6.36 billion sale to Washington Mutual despite receiving a slightly higher offer from hostile bidder H.F. Ahmanson.

Stocks plunged on March 27 as the yield on the 30-year Treasury bond rose to 7.08%, its first close above 7% in six months. Behind the moves were strong economic data that raised fears of further interest-rate increases by the Fed. The Dow Jones industrials tumbled 216.78 points at their low, but recovered to end off 140.11 at 6740.59. The dollar also retreated.

Quaker Oats agreed to sell its Snapple juice and iced-tea business to Triarc for $300 million, a fraction of the $1.7 billion Quaker paid for Snapple in 1994. Quaker will take a pretax charge of $1.4 billion on the sale.

Rental-car companies can't turn away customers solely because of their age, New York state's highest court found, in the first major ruling on a decades-old industry practice.

Intel, Compaq Computer and others teamed up to produce standards for a living-room personal computer dubbed PC Theater.

Ascend agreed to acquire Cascade Communications for $3.7 billion in stock, the latest consolidation move among makers of computer networking gear. The deal comes as networking firms aim to broaden their product lines to provide one-stop shopping for corporations, which are moving to allow employees to share data through computer networks. But investors sent Ascend's stock price down 22%, cutting the deal's value to $2.9 billion.

APRIL

The cable industry lost its Supreme Court challenge of a federal law requiring cable firms to carry local broadcasts. The ruling secures a place for small channels, start-ups and specialty programmers on cable boxes.

SBC's plan to acquire PacTel was approved by California regulators, paving the way for the two Baby Bells to close their $17 billion deal.

ITT sold its remaining stake in France's Alcatel-Alsthom for $530 million, raising more ammunition for its defense against Hilton's hostile bid.

Hokkaido Takushoku Bank and Hokkaido Bank, two troubled Japanese lenders, said they would merge into a new entity in a deal valued at $1.14 billion.

AT&T Chairman Robert E. Allen saw his 1996 bonus cut 18% because of AT&T's "disappointing performance," its proxy statement says. New President John R. Walter was given a $5 million signing bonus, and he will receive $7 million more if he stays five years.

Dow Chemical filed a suit claiming General Electric lured away 14 employees to obtain trade secrets, and won a temporary order prohibiting GE from using any secrets it might have received. The companies settled the suit later in the month.

Atlantic Richfield said it wants to spin off or sell all of its coal-mining operations, months after spending $400 million to acquire additional U.S. coal reserves.

Republic Industries' drive to build a chain of car dealerships hit a roadblock as Toyota moved to stop its purchase of a Texas dealership.

USX's U.S. Steel is scouting prospects for acquisitions, mergers or partnerships, the unit's president told analysts. Such a move would be a big departure for the nation's top steelmaker. Separately, U.S. Steel and Inland Steel confirmed that they had talked about combining operations in 1996 but decided against proceeding with a deal.

Australia's Coca-Cola Amatil said it plans to acquire a unit of the Philippines' San Miguel for stock valued at $2.7 billion. The deal would create Coca-Cola's largest bottler outside the U.S.

Microsoft, Intel and Compaq planned to try to persuade broadcasters to adopt their standards for digital TV, in a bid to ensure PCs play a role in the next generation of home entertainment. Separately, Microsoft agreed to acquire WebTV for $425 million in stock and cash and said it would use the firm's low-cost Internet devices to speed the introduction of digital television.

Bankers Trust said it would buy Alex. Brown in a stock swap valued at about $1.7 billion. The deal would be the biggest purchase of a securities company by a U.S. commercial bank and is the most visible sign yet of the breakdown of the Depression-era Glass-Steagall law separating the commercial and investment banking businesses.

The UAW struck a key General Motors plant in Oklahoma City. The strike halted production of the Chevrolet Malibu amid a dispute over GM's plans to cut hundreds of hourly jobs. Workers went on strike later in the month at GM's truck-assembly plant in Pontiac, Mich., and the company expected more work stoppages at vital parts-making factories.

Knight-Ridder's planned $1.65 billion purchase of four newspapers from Walt Disney marked a reversal of the media company's strategy to diversify.

Allegheny Power agreed to acquire DQE, the parent of Duquesne Light, for $2.51 billion in stock plus the assumption of $1.7 billion in debt and preferred stock. The move continues a trend toward consolidation in a deregulated electricity market.

The FTC expanded its probe of alcohol advertising to include TV ad campaigns aired by Anheuser-Busch and Philip Morris's Miller Brewing.

Procter & Gamble said it would buy Tambrands for $1.85 billion, plus assumed debt. P&G already makes some feminine sanitary-protection products, but the Tambrands acquisition would add tampons to the company's line.

Federal antitrust enforcers set new rules for weighing cost savings and other efficiencies in evaluating mergers. The changes make approval more likely for some combinations that might have been rejected.

The Treasury's second auction of inflation-indexed bonds proved less successful than expected. But market participants caution that it will take some time before the true demand for the novel securities develops.

Polo Ralph Lauren said it intended to raise $600 million in an initial public offering for the fashion company controlled by the designer.

Nippon Credit Bank said it agreed to enter a wide-ranging tie-up with Bankers Trust that would include the U.S. lender's taking over $18 billion of the Japanese bank's overseas assets. The pact could signal new opportunities for U.S. banks in Japan.

Chrysler was forced to shut down four of its profitable light-truck factories by a UAW strike at a key engine plant, even as the No. 3 auto maker posted record first-quarter profit. The company's determination to shed some parts-making jobs was the focus of the strike.

Sears said it used "flawed legal judgment" in collecting debts from some credit-card holders who had sought bankruptcy-court protection. The retailer said resolving the matter could have a "material effect" on 1997 earnings. Separately, Sears was charged in a civil complaint filed by the U.S. attorney in Boston with unfair credit-card collection actions against some consumers.

USA Waste said it agreed to acquire United Waste Systems for stock valued at over $1.5 billion, a move that sent both companies' stocks sliding.

Tobacco companies offered to disclose their research into smoking and health as part of talks to settle the massive legal threat they face for smoking-related illnesses. Although the talks could lead to a settlement of over $300 billion, investors sent tobacco stocks sharply higher. Meanwhile, key tobacco opponents were concerned the proposed pact would be too lenient.

Airtouch said it planned to acquire U S West Media's domestic wireless operations for $2.3 billion in stock, plus $2.2 billion in assumed debt, but a new federal tax proposal appeared to jeopardize that and other possible deals, including America Online's negotiations to acquire H&R Block's CompuServe business. While U S West and AirTouch said they have been discussing a deal for months, they appeared to accelerate the transaction to beat a deadline proposed in legislation aimed at closing a loophole used by corporations to sell assets tax free.

Citicorp shuffled leadership of its consumer-bank unit to streamline management of its worldwide operations and groom possible successors to Citicorp Chairman John S. Reed.

Goodyear Tire was struck by 12,500 United Steelworkers members after the sides failed to reach an agreement by the deadline.

Jayhawk Acceptance said it filed a reorganization plan with a U.S. Bankruptcy Court calling for it to repay $65 million to Fleet Financial, its primary lender, by September 1998.

Fidelity Investments reassigned Gary Burkhead to a new post and named Robert C. Pozen to succeed him as its top investment executive, continuing a year of turmoil at the firm. In the first big move under Mr. Pozen, a new three-person management team was named to oversee Fidelity's stock mutual funds.

ITT Industries agreed to acquire Goulds Pumps for $815 million, or $37 a share, plus $119 million in assumed debt. The deal would make ITT Industries the world's largest pump maker.

Cordiant unveiled a plan to split itself apart, with its two big advertising agency networks, Bates and Saatchi & Saatchi, becoming independent, separately traded companies.

Whirlpool, breaking ranks with other appliance makers, complained that new U.S. energy standards for refrigerators aren't strict enough.

Options markets began experiencing a surge of insider trading. The increase in the number of insider-trading cases came amid a revival of insider trading itself and increased options trading over the past decade.

Hewlett-Packard agreed to buy VeriFone for $1.18 billion in stock, staking a claim in electronic commerce. VeriFone makes credit-card verification products and is moving into Internet-transaction technology.

Quaker Oats posted a quarterly loss of $1.11 billion and said CEO William D. Smithburg would step down. The loss includes a $1.4 billion charge and amounts to a final reckoning of Mr. Smithburg's ill-fated purchase of Snapple.

The International Monetary Fund said it expects worldwide output to grow 4.4% in 1997 and 1998, up from 4% in 1996, and urged the U.S. to continue boosting rates to prevent its economy from overheating.

Bell Atlantic received approval from the Justice Department for its $23 billion acquisition of Nynex, signaling the government is unlikely to block the current telecommunications merger frenzy. Some critics had expected the government to draw a line at the joining of two of the largest former Baby Bells, which would dominate the phone business from Virginia to Maine with revenue of $29 billion a year.

Tobacco foes won new leverage in settlement talks with the industry after a federal judge ruled that the FDA has the authority to regulate cigarettes. Separately, the industry suffered another setback when the Supreme Court refused to hear a challenge to a Baltimore law banning cigarette and liquor ads on many billboards.

Columbia/HCA Healthcare was being scrutinized by federal officials over its physician-referral practices in Miami. Similar to an investigation of the big hospital chain's El Paso, Texas, operations, much of the Miami inquiry focused on referrals of Medicare patients to home health care.

The Treasury planned to pay off $65 billion of the federal debt amid surging tax receipts. The move is only the second cut in the outstanding debt since 1981 and the biggest ever.

Oracle's Lawrence J. Ellison said he wouldn't pursue a bid for Apple Computer, though he said he may "revisit" the decision in the future.

The government said first-quarter GDP surged at an annual rate of 5.6%, fueled by a big inventory build-up, warm weather and the largest rise in consumer spending in nearly 10 years. The figure was later revised to 4.9%.

The Justice Department said it is investigating possible bid-rigging in recent federal auctions of licenses for telephone and communications services.

Time Warner said it planned to unplug its interactive-television network in Orlando, Fla., all but abandoning plans to use its cable systems for a national entertainment and shopping service.

MAY

Lazard Freres and Wasserstein Perella held high-level talks about combining the firms, but senior Lazard partners shot down the idea. Later in the month, Lazard named Steven Rattner deputy chief executive and took other steps to resolve management issues, but didn't name a successor to Chairman Michel David-Weill.

America Online, CompuServe and Prodigy settled FTC charges that they misrepresented the terms of "free-trial" offers and made unauthorized withdrawals from customers' accounts. The FTC consent decrees, among other things, bar the companies from misrepresenting the terms of any trial offers and require them to disclose all charges in advance. Settling the charges isn't an admission of wrongdoing.

Retail coffee prices rose briskly, as heavy rains and labor strife in South and Central America raised concerns about the supply of beans. Late in the month, prices set new 20-year highs as Mexico, a major exporter, said it may need to import beans to satisfy local demand. Several retailers also announced further price boosts.

IBM's pact with the Justice Department to phase out a 1956 consent decree was approved by a federal judge, ending a case that restricted IBM's business practices to curb its power. Also in May, IBM's stock topped its all-time intraday high and nearly beat its closing high of a decade ago, capping the computer maker's recovery from a near-death experience in the early 1990s.

James River agreed to combine with Fort Howard in a transaction valued at about $3.4 billion in stock, plus the assumption of debt. By combining James River's consumer business with Fort Howard's commercial operations, the new company is expected to be a stronger industry player.

Corporate profits rose 18% in the first quarter, according to a *Wall Street Journal* tabulation of the results of 707 large firms.

Bre-X Minerals admitted that its Busang property is a worthless piece of land and a fraud on a scale never seen before in the history of mining. Bre-X shares collapsed to near worthless levels, and the stock was delisted by the Toronto Stock Exchange as Canadian police met to coordinate their inquiry into the firm's Busang property. Bre-X also filed for bankruptcy-court protection from creditors in an attempt to preserve what assets the company and two affiliates may have left.

R.J. Reynolds Tobacco scored a major victory in a Florida state court, where a jury found that the firm wasn't responsible for the death of a three-pack-a-day smoker who died of lung cancer at age 49. The trial had been closely watched as a bellwether for future suits against the industry. Reynolds convinced the jury that the dangers of cigarettes have been common knowledge for years.

The FDA refused to clear generic versions of the menopausal drug Premarin, reinforcing American Home Products' virtual lock on the market for hormone-replacement products.

Unilever agreed to sell its specialty chemicals business to Britain's Imperial Chemical Industries for about $8 billion. The move by the Anglo-Dutch giant is part of an effort to shed noncore operations and concentrate on its consumer-products businesses.

The FTC began looking into pricing of compact disks and asked big recording companies for information on how they enforce pricing policies.

Fuji Photo made plans to begin manufacturing film in the U.S. for the first time, making the Japanese company a more formidable competitor against Eastman Kodak.

US Airways Group, plagued by the industry's highest costs, said it would drop unprofitable routes, ground aircraft, reduce its flying schedule and close excess facilities.

Chrysler engine-plant workers voted to end the firm's longest strike in 30 years, allowing the company to resume light-truck production. The strike cost the company an estimated $430 million.

EchoStar filed a breach-of-contract suit against News Corp., seeking $5 billion over their defunct plan for a satellite-TV venture. EchoStar also said it was seeking a new partner. Later in the month, News Corp. reached an agreement to join PrimeStar Partners, a satellite-dish TV service owned by the nation's largest cable operators.

Dow Chemical won a court ruling that transfers about 10,000 silicone breast-implant cases filed in state and federal courts around the country to a federal court in Detroit. The victory could slow, or even block, the cases.

A Goodyear labor contract was approved by United Steelworkers members, ending an 18-day strike at nine plants that involved 12,500 workers.

Grand Metropolitan agreed to merge with Guinness, in a combination of British liquor-industry giants that values Guinness, the smaller firm, at $19.3 billion. The combined company, GMG Brands, would blend Grand Met's Smirnoff and J&B labels with Guinness's Johnnie Walker and Gordon's into a colossus more than double the size of the next biggest competitor in liquor.

Delta Air Lines' Ronald W. Allen said he would retire as chairman, president and CEO when his 10-year employment contract expired July 31. Delta's board declined to renew his contract in large part because directors felt his drastic cost-cutting program had taken too heavy a toll on employee morale and customer service.

Farmers were expected to harvest bumper corn and soybean crops this fall, replenishing U.S. grain stocks that shrank to precariously low levels in 1996, according to the Agriculture Department.

Digital Equipment filed a sweeping lawsuit claiming that key elements of Intel's flagship Pentium line were built on patented semi-conductor technology stolen from Digital. The suit surprised the computer industry and jolted both firms' shares. Digital is seeking monetary damages and guarantees that Intel will stop producing the line, which is expected to bring in $20 billion in sales in 1997. Intel filed a countersuit and threatened to cut its adversary off from vitally needed new technology and products.

Rupert Murdoch's News Corp. reached a tentative agreement to buy the Los Angeles Dodgers for $350 million.

Prices fell 0.6% at the wholesale level in April, the government said, marking the fourth straight monthly decline and the biggest drop in almost four years. Economists were particularly surprised by the lack of inflationary pressure

since the economy had just completed its most robust quarter in a decade.

Philip Morris disclosed that it was being investigated by the FTC to determine whether the world's largest cigarette maker unfairly restricts the distribution of competing brands.

USX and Ashland said they would combine some of their oil businesses, creating one of the nation's largest refiners and continuing an industry trend to consolidate gas-station operations. Sales of the combined firm would top $13 billion, with over $5 billion in assets.

Glaxo Wellcome's Zyban received FDA approval as the first non-nicotine prescription drug to help smokers wean themselves off cigarettes.

General Motors said it is preparing to build a new small car in Brazil that it plans to offer with one of the lowest sticker prices in the world. The project is expected to give the No. 1 auto maker a competitive advantage in developing markets. Also, experimental techniques GM will use in a new plant for the car could be applied elsewhere.

The Justice Department recommended that the FCC reject SBC Communications' request to sell long-distance service in Oklahoma, where it already offers local phone service. The recommendation means local phone companies face a high hurdle to entering the lucrative market.

A group including Chevron signed a $2 billion pipeline deal in Russia as a law setting rules for Western firms to tap Russia's natural resources received initial legislative clearance.

The Federal Reserve left its target for the federal-funds rate at 5½%, apparently convinced the economy will slow enough to avoid a pickup in inflation. Since the Fed opted to tighten rates by one-quarter percentage point on March 25, economic data have indicated that growth is moderating from its startling first-quarter rate.

Boeing's plan to buy McDonnell Douglas was formally challenged by the European Commission, which argued that Boeing already is abusing its dominance of commercial-jet markets. Boeing's sole-supplier pacts with U.S. airlines are the top concern of the European Commission, which wants them scrapped and other changes to clear Boeing's McDonnell purchase.

The government posted a record $93.94 billion surplus in April, aided by rising revenue from big individual returns. The record may vindicate President Clinton who said a 1993 tax boost would cut the deficit at the expense of the rich.

AT&T was in talks to merge with SBC Communications in a $50 billion-plus deal that would be the largest corporate combination in history. People close to the talks said that numerous issues could block a deal between the nation's biggest long-distance carrier and SBC, owner of the vast Southwestern Bell and Pacific Telesis local-phone systems. The talks would force regulators to decide whether the deal would encourage competition or concentrate too much power in one company.

Swiss drug maker Roche Holding said it would pay $11 billion for Corange, parent of German diagnostics firm Boehringer and controlling holder of U.S. orthopedic-products maker DePuy.

Leading industrial nations agreed to outlaw bribery as a means for companies to win commercial contracts, paving the way for fairer competition among multinational companies. Members of the Organization for Economic Cooperation and Development are expected to negotiate a binding international convention to criminalize bribery of foreign public officials and to put legislation before their parliaments. The objective is to create a "network of laws . . . that will permit effective enforcement and mutual legal assistance" in a campaign against bribery and corruption.

Dow Jones won't have to pay a record $200 million in punitive damages in a libel case brought by defunct brokerage firm MMAR, a federal judge in Houston ruled. But the judge let stand $22.7 million in actual damages.

The Lost World: Jurassic Park shattered box-office records, bringing in $90.1 million over the Memorial Day weekend for Seagram's Universal Studios.

General Motors and the UAW reached a tentative pact to end a 50-day strike by 3,500 workers at GM's Oklahoma City Malibu and Cutlass assembly plant.

CUC International agreed to merge with HFS in a $10.9 billion stock swap that could create a direct-marketing powerhouse through the joining of a huge direct marketer with a growing travel and real-estate franchiser. CUC is best known for its coupon books and traveler and shopper membership clubs. HFS's brands include Ramada Inn, Century 21 Real Estate and Avis.

FCC Chairman Reed Hundt said he planned to step down, winding up a tumultuous four-year tenure overseeing vast changes in the telecommunications industry.

The Conference Board's consumer-confidence index soared to a 27-year high, amid plentiful jobs and the lowest unemployment rate in a quarter century.

The FTC filed an unfair-advertising complaint against R.J. Reynolds Tobacco, alleging that its colorful Joe Camel campaign illegally seeks to entice youngsters to smoke Camels.

The Nasdaq Stock Market said it would allow all of its stocks to be traded in $1/16$-point increments, a milestone that could lead to better prices for small investors.

Over 700,000 Prudential Insurance policy-holders indicated they plan to seek restitution for deceptive sales practices, a response rate that could cost the insurer over $1.6 billion.

The FDA approved the first new treatment for congestive heart failure in 14 years. Coreg will be co-marketed by SmithKline and Boehringer.

JUNE

PepsiCo planned to reorganize its North American beverage business by creating a separate unit for its company-owned bottling operations. The reorganization was viewed by some industry observers as a prelude to an eventual spinoff and public offering of part of the $6 billion-a-year bottling business. But company officials said the new structure is simply a way to give the bottling operations additional autonomy and accountability.

Wal-Mart said it would acquire a majority of the voting stock of Cifra, Mexico's largest retailer, in Wal-Mart's first direct investment in a foreign partner. In addition to a complex share swap,

Wal-Mart planned to spend about $1.2 billion in the transaction.

Viacom named John Antioco to head its troubled Blockbuster video business, just eight months after the executive took the top job at PepsiCo's Taco Bell restaurants subsidiary. Separately, Viacom asked movie studios to cut the prices of the videos they sell to Blockbuster by as much at 15%.

McDonald's said it would drop its rotating 55-cent sandwich offerings except at breakfast, acknowledging it made a major marketing blunder. The promotion had confused consumers and irritated franchisees.

Sears reached a settlement with the FTC over its "flawed" credit-card collection practices. Sears had admitted in April that it made improper collections from people who had filed for bankruptcy protection. The big retailer also said it would pay between $178 million and $265 million and take an undetermined charge, as part of a settlement with lawyers representing consumers and 39 state attorneys general.

H.F. Ahmanson dropped its hostile bid for Great Western Financial, ceding the nation's second largest thrift to Washington Mutual. Ahmanson's decision makes Washington Mutual the nation's largest thrift with assets of nearly $90 billion when combined with Great Western.

The New York Stock Exchange voted to begin trading its stocks in decimals in possibly as little as a year, ending a centuries-old tradition of trading shares in fractions. The exchange began quoting stocks in sixteenths, rather than eighths, in late June, as a first step. The nation's largest stock market, which only recently said it opposed moving to decimals, said the transition would contribute to the globalization of the market.

General Motors officials said the auto maker is speeding up its multibillion-dollar drive to overhaul and consolidate its dealership network. In 1996, the company completed 307 dealer changes, including closings, and in 1997 it expects to complete 500.

Dow Jones agreed to allow three financial markets to offer derivatives based on the Dow Jones Industrial Average. The exchanges would offer options, futures and options on futures, and an exchange-traded fund.

Microsoft said it would spend $1 billion for 11.5% of Comcast, a cable-television company. It was Microsoft's largest investment and the latest in a series of moves in the entertainment industry.

Dakota, Minnesota & Eastern was seeking to finance a $1.2 billion freight line from the Midwest to Wyoming, in a bid to become the first major new U.S. railroad in over 50 years.

The unemployment rate fell to 4.8% in May, the lowest level since November 1973, from 4.9% in April.

IBM prepared to close World Avenue, a Web-based shopping mall the firm unveiled with much fanfare in 1996. The move raised questions about the future of on-line retailing.

News Corp. signed back-to-back deals valued at $2.8 billion designed to give media titan Rupert Murdoch a way into the highly competitive U.S. cable market. News Corp. would sell its satellite assets for a minority stake in the cable industry's direct satellite venture Primestar Partners, and a News Corp. partnership, Fox Kids Worldwide, would acquire control of International Family Entertainment, parent of the Family Channel cable network.

PacifiCorp reached a tentative pact to buy Energy Group of Britain for about $6 billion, plus assumed debt. The merger would create a global energy powerhouse with five million customers and major interests in coal, natural gas, electricity and power trading.

BMW planned an overhaul of its U.S. dealer network in a bid to double its share of the world's largest vehicle market in the next three years. The strategy is to make the buying process simpler for customers and to cut distribution costs by sharply shrinking dealer inventories while allowing for more customization of individual cars.

IBM's chief financial officer, G. Richard Thoman, left the computer maker to take the No. 2 job at Xerox because he will have a chance to run the copier company sooner.

Smith Barney fund executive Jessica Bibliowicz said she was leaving to become president of money manager John Levin, a surprising move for the daughter of Sanford Weill, chairman of Smith Barney parent Travelers Group.

Andrew Lloyd-Webber said he took control of his musical production firm, hoping to stem an estimated loss of up to $16.3 million for the latest fiscal year. He blamed problems on the financially unsuccessful musical *Sunset Boulevard* and said the loss is only temporary. But others in the theater world said the company has fallen out of step with the fast-changing entertainment business.

Motorola planned its third and most ambitious satellite venture yet, a $12.9 billion network designed to deliver very high-speed data and video. Plans for the system confirm Motorola's intent to become a major satellite-systems manufacturer and pose a direct challenge to Craig McCaw's Teledesic, a proposed $9 billion high-speed satellite system.

Lucent Technologies agreed to merge its consumer-phone unit with that of Philips Electronics. The new company would be controlled 60% by the Dutch electronics giant and have annual revenue of $2.5 billion. Lucent, the AT&T equipment spinoff, will hold the remaining stake. Each company would join complementary assets, including product lines and plants.

R.J. Reynolds sued the FTC, accusing it of politically motivated "harassment" and saying the agency didn't follow proper procedures in efforts to ban the Joe Camel cartoon character from cigarette ads. But just a few weeks later, the company announced that it was dropping its Joe Camel campaign, which had long been criticized for its appeal to children and teenagers.

McDonald's was awarded $98,298 in damages by a London judge, ending the restaurant giant's three-year libel case against two vegetarian activists. Among charges deemed false were that the company caused starvation in the Third World and knowingly sold unhealthy food. But the judge said McDonald's was responsible, as alleged, for cruel treatment to some animals and advertising that exploits the susceptibilities of children.

Unisys CEO James Unruh said he would resign after helping to find a successor, who will face a difficult task running the old-line computer maker.

Merrill Lynch agreed to pay $30 million in a settlement that would end Orange County's criminal investigation into Merrill's role in the 1994 collapse of the county's investment pool.

A historic tobacco accord, which could require the industry to pay $368.5 billion over 25 years and succumb to sweeping restrictions, sparked a national debate over whether its terms are too easy on cigarette makers. Public-health groups denounced a provision in the pact they said would cripple FDA regulation of nicotine.

Union Pacific Resources began a hostile takeover bid for Pennzoil valued at $4 billion, plus $2.2 billion of assumed debt. Pennzoil's board urged shareholders to reject the offer.

The House Banking panel cleared a banking overhaul bill. The measure would let banks, securities firms and insurers sell one another's products, acquire one another and combine with nonfinancial firms in some cases.

Stocks plunged on June 23, as traders interpreted comments by Japan's prime minster as a threat that Japanese investors may begin large-scale sales of U.S. stocks and bonds. The Dow Jones industrials tumbled 192.25, or 2.47%, to 7604.26, even as Japanese officials sought to soften the comments. Stocks recouped most of their losses within a few days.

Compaq Computer agreed to pay $3 billion in stock to buy Tandem Computers, a maker of complex systems prized for their reliability. The deal is a big step in the No. 1 PC maker's drive to become a top supplier of machines at all levels of sophistication and power.

Eli Lilly said it would take a $2.4 billion charge against second-quarter earnings to write down by more than half the value of its $4.1 billion investment in PCS Health Systems.

News Corp. and Tele-Communications agreed to buy a 40% stake in Rainbow Media Sports Holdings for $850 million, a transaction that would create the first serious challenge to Walt Disney's ESPN cable sports network.

Wachovia said it would buy Central Fidelity Banks for $2.3 billion in stock. The purchase would catapult the North Carolina-based bank to No. 1 in the Virginia market and marked its biggest acquisition ever.

Walt Disney's ABC television network installed a new executive, Stuart Bloomberg, above

Jamie Tarses, its high-profile but embattled programming chief, in hopes of turning around its ailing prime-time schedule. Mr. Bloomberg was named chairman of ABC Entertainment.

The Supreme Court wiped out a $1.3 billion deal to settle hundreds of thousands of potential personal-injury claims against former asbestos makers. The ruling found that the plaintiffs were too different to be grouped under one settlement.

A key insider trading weapon won Supreme Court approval in a major SEC victory. The justices upheld the misappropriation theory, which has been used since the 1980s to nab traders who use nonpublic information but aren't traditional insiders.

Wireless firms said they can't pay for billions of dollars of licenses won at auction and are threatening to default if the government doesn't restructure the debt. Bidders, including the biggest one, NextWave Telecom, which bid $4.2 billion, hadn't been able to raise enough cash to pay the government and build networks.

Ameritech's bid to offer long-distance service received a negative recommendation from the Justice Department, which said the Bell hasn't done enough to foster local competition. Separately, the FCC, as expected, rejected SBC Communications' bid to sell long-distance service to Oklahoma customers.

Zurich Group of Switzerland said it would buy Scudder Stevens in a pact valued at $2 billion. Scudder said the globalization of the mutual-fund industry drove it into the merger with Zurich.

France's Rhone-Poulenc planned a sweeping corporate overhaul. It would include the spinoff of its chemical, fibers and polymers lines, and a possible $4.3 billion bid for full control of its U.S. drug unit, Rhone-Poulenc Rorer.

AT&T and SBC Communications decided to go it alone as each tries to enter the other's market. SBC Chairman Edward Whitacre called off the talks to forge a $50 billion merger in a phone conversation with AT&T's Robert Allen. The long-distance giant and the regional Bell phone company disagreed over everything from valuations to the correct approach to lobbying officials in Washington. Separately, SBC said it planned charges totaling up to $2.3 billion in 1997 related to its purchase of Pacific Telesis

Group. The charges cover the near-complete shutdown of PacTel's ambitious interactive video effort and the consolidation of network centers, among other costs.

Royal Bank of Canada said it planned to offer $1.74 billion to buy London Insurance, marking the biggest alliance between a bank and a life-insurance firm in North America.

Staples was blocked in its effort to acquire Office Depot by a federal judge citing antitrust grounds. The decision to issue a preliminary injunction dealt a fatal blow to the $4.3 billion merger pact.

Ford Motor and Citicorp said they will discontinue their joint venture offering credit-card users rebates on new cars. Industry observers said the program may have been too generous to survive.

Compaq rolled out two PCs priced below $1,000, in a sign of the fast growth of low-priced computers.

JULY

The Dow Jones industrials closed a turbulent second quarter with a gain of 18.99% for the first half. Meanwhile, sales of new stocks and bonds hit a record $571.9 billion in the half, a 16% increase from a year ago that could pave the way for Wall Street to beat its 1993 peak of $1.16 trillion.

The Big Three automakers added incentives that could total $900 a vehicle in hopes of luring more buyers and boosting weak sales.

Campbell Soup named Dale Morrison, president of international and specialty foods, president and CEO. The company also told financial analysts later in the month that it is considering shedding "nonstrategic" lines with sales of $1.4 billion to concentrate on growth of its core businesses.

Eli Lilly launched an ad campaign to re-energize growth in sales of Prozac, a move that could reopen debate over how widely the drug should be prescribed. Prozac faces increased competition from similar antidepressants.

The Postal Service said it would seek a one-cent increase in the cost of mailing a first-class letter. But the agency proposed cutting by two cents the cost of mailing bill payments when a company provides prepaid envelopes.

The FTC cleared Boeing's purchase of Mc-Donnell Douglas but warned the aerospace giant against signing any more exclusive commercial-jet contracts with major airlines. Boeing also won tentative European approval later in the month for its $14 billion acquisition, after making a number of concessions. The approval headed off a trans-Atlantic trade dispute.

SBC Communications challenged the constitutionality of a key part of the sweeping 1996 telecommunications law, charging it unfairly hinders efforts by the Bells to enter the long-distance business. In a lawsuit filed in federal court, SBC argued that the law makes it harder for the Bells than for independent local-service providers to enter the long-distance market. In June, the FCC rejected the company's bid to offer long-distance service in Oklahoma.

The Federal Reserve left its key short-term interest rate unchanged at 5.5%, amid slowing economic growth and subsiding concerns about inflation. Economists were divided over whether the central bank would have to tighten monetary policy in the coming months to damp growth.

Guinness and Grand Met said they would consider alternatives to their planned $19 billion merger, following talks with LVMH Moët Hennessy.

The U.S. economy will rebound from a sluggish second quarter to post at least one more year of healthy growth, low interest rates and little inflation, according to *The Wall Street Journal*'s semiannual survey of economists.

Lockheed agreed to buy Northrop for $8.26 billion in stock. While the defense-industry combination was expected to win regulators' approval, some U.S. officials may demand divestiture of overlapping operations.

Merger activity rose to $366 billion in announced U.S. deals in the first half of 1997, a record level fueled by a surge in takeovers in financial services, technology and basic industry.

H&R Block was holding out for better offers for its 80% stake in CompuServe despite a lack of interest among potential purchasers of what was once the nation's largest on-line service.

Mississippi became the first state to seal a settlement with the nation's cigarette makers, as the four largest tobacco companies agreed to pay the state $3.6 billion over 25 years and $136 million a year indefinitely thereafter.

Montgomery Ward's parent firm sought bankruptcy-law protection. The retailing unit has been unprofitable, and the parent has been in default on $1.4 billion in obligations.

Federal budget-gap forecasts were slashed again by analysts, following surprisingly strong tax collections in June. This fiscal year's deficit could be under $50 billion, less than a third of the initial projection.

British Telecom's planned $24 billion acquisition of MCI won the approval of the U.S. Justice Department. The deal would be the largest-ever foreign acquisition of a U.S. company.

News Corp. Chief Executive Rupert Murdoch said the company is exploring a "joint venture" with potential partners for its Harper-Collins unit, a move that would reduce its ownership stake in the publisher.

Graduating high-school seniors looking for full-time work faced the best job market in years, as employers struggle to fill the kind of entry-level slots that new, noncollege-bound grads traditionally seek.

ING Group agreed to buy Equitable of Iowa for $2.2 billion in stock and cash, plus $400 million of assumed debt, in a move to double the size of the Dutch financial giant's U.S. life insurance lines. The deal, which is valued at $68 a share, sent Equitable's stock soaring 15% to $65.875. The transaction is the latest in a series of trans-Atlantic acquisitions over the past year by cash-rich European financial firms.

Oil prices should be headed lower, inventory data compiled by the International Energy Agency suggest. The group sees plentiful supplies during the remainder of the year.

Apple Computer ousted Chairman and CEO Gilbert F. Amelio, triggering new turmoil at the embattled computer maker. Apple also said co-founder Steve Jobs, who recently returned as an adviser to Dr. Amelio, will assume a broader role. Apple's chief financial officer said the firm no longer is making a prediction on when it will return to profitability; the firm had said it planned to meet that goal by the quarter ending in September.

McDonald's announced a new team to revitalize its U.S. business and the departure of three top officials in the biggest management shake-up in its history. The fast-food giant said the moves are meant to improve performance as it faces rising competition. Later in July, McDonald's yanked the plum assignment of lead advertising agency from Leo Burnett after 15 years and handed it back to DDB Needham.

President Clinton insisted on changes to the proposed tobacco pact, hoping to fix it rather than kill the chance to reach a historic accord, his aides said. The president stepped up criticism of the part of the proposal that would curtail the FDA regulation of cigarettes.

Falcon Drilling agreed to merge with Reading & Bates in a $2.53 billion stock swap, creating a major force in the booming market for deep-water oil and gas drilling. Falcon has the world's largest fleet of barge rigs, and Reading & Bates is known for its deep-water rigs.

DuPont said it would buy large parts of the industrial chemical business of Britain's ICI for about $3 billion. The deal involves ICI units with annual revenue of about $2.5 billion and includes the group's interests in polyester films, resins and intermediates along with its white-pigments lines in Europe, Asia and Africa. DuPont said the purchase will strengthen the petrochemical firm's position in the $30 billion polyester industry. But analysts wondered how DuPont will squeeze profits from the businesses in the near term.

Marriott International said it has curtailed an effort begun in 1996 in Washington, D.C., to target more disadvantaged welfare recipients in its successful welfare-to-work program.

CalEnergy launched the first stage of a hostile $1.92 billion bid for New York State Electric & Gas. The move came after the New York utility brushed off the Nebraska energy concern's previously undisclosed buyout overtures.

The Dow Jones Industrial Average passed the 8000-point mark on July 16 for the first time, gaining 63.17 points to 8038.88. The rise was fueled by upbeat reports on inflation and earnings. As the industrial average soars, more Wall Street strategists are turning bearish.

AT&T President John Walter resigned after the company's board said it wouldn't name him chief executive as planned by January 1. Mr. Walter's relations with Chairman Robert Allen had grown increasingly strained.

ITT said it is splitting itself into three companies, taking on about $2 billion in new debt, and repurchasing a big block of its own stock. The company hoped the move would be a knockout blow to Hilton Hotels' hostile bid.

The Columbia/HCA Healthcare inquiry by the federal government was significantly expanded, as 35 sealed search warrants were served to facilities of the company in six states. Thomas F. Frist Jr. took over as CEO later in July after the company's board ousted Richard L. Scott. In addition, three Columbia executives were indicted on charges they conspired to defraud the government.

Woolworth said it will close the more than 400 stores of its F.W. Woolworth five-and-dime retail chain in the U.S., marking the end of an American institution. The company said it would terminate the jobs of 9,200 full and part-time employees and record a $223 million charge as a result of the costs of severance, disposing of leases and liquidating inventory.

Lucent Technologies agreed to pay $1.8 billion to acquire voice-mail-systems maker Octel Communications. The move signaled that Lucent wants to plug a hole in its product line and boost sales to phone companies and major corporations.

Burlington Resources agreed to acquire Louisiana Land & Exploration for about $2.44 billion in stock, continuing the trend of combinations among independent energy companies.

Two big German banks announced a merger with a value of $8 billion that will create Europe's second-largest bank. The pact by Bayerische Vereinsbank and Bayerische Hypotheken underscores the consolidation under way in European banking.

First Union agreed to acquire Signet Banking for about $3.25 billion in stock. The rich price for the Virginia bank reflects First Union's desire to beef up its position in the state after smaller rival Wachovia engineered a flurry of Virginia deals.

FCC rules on how local phone companies must open their networks to rivals were thrown out by a federal appeals court. The court's ruling could significantly delay competition in the $90 billion local-telephone market.

Payless Cashways filed for bankruptcy-law protection. The nation's No. 3 home-improvement chain was saddled with debt and under competitive pressure from Home Depot.

Federal Reserve Chairman Alan Greenspan gave no hint that an increase in interest rates is imminent, buoying the financial markets. In congressional testimony, he hailed the current state of the economy as "exceptional" and welcomed the recent slowing of economic growth. Stocks soared in reaction to the remarks, and bond prices took off as well, with the yield on the Treasury's bellwether bond falling to its lowest point since early December.

The fight intensified between Digital Equipment and Intel, as Digital filed antitrust charges against Intel, accusing the chip maker of using "monopoly power" to harm the computer firm by demanding the return of Intel technical documents.

President Clinton planned to nominate William Kennard as chairman of the FCC. Mr. Kennard has served as FCC general counsel for nearly four years.

America Online reversed its stance and said it won't hand over its customers' home phone numbers to telemarketers. The reversal came in the face of customer backlash and pressure from legal authorities.

Donna Karan stepped down as CEO of her namesake firm, in a move to stabilize the floundering fashion house. She ceded the role to John Idol, a Polo Ralph Lauren group president.

Many stocks are expected to gain long-term attractiveness in the wake of the first major federal income-tax-cut package in 16 years, though some investments, such as bonds, may lose some of their shine. Investment advisers say lower capital-gains tax rates will especially help small, high-growth firms that pay little or no dividends. The deal also eliminates capital-gains taxes for most homeowners, and it provides new incentives for retirement and education saving as well as estate-tax relief for individuals, family farms and small businesses.

Smith Barney agreed to pay the government $1,050,000 to settle civil charges connected to the gift of a $2,200 Super Bowl ticket to former Agriculture Secretary Mike Espy. A complaint filed by Independent Counsel Donald Smaltz alleges that Mr. Espy made appeals to high-level federal officials on behalf of a Smith Barney client, Oglethorpe Power, before and after receiving the ticket in 1994. Smith Barney denied the charges, and Mr. Espy has repeatedly denied any wrongdoing.

Sallie Mae managers lost control of the firm as shareholders elected a dissident slate of directors and overwhelmingly approved the privatization of the quasigovernmental student-loan marketer. The votes ended more than two years of feuding at the firm, which has $47 billion in assets.

AUGUST

Corporate profits grew a surprising 5% in the second quarter, as more firms pursued growth plans at home and abroad. The healthy return, based on a tabulation of net income at 698 firms, compared with 19% growth a year ago and an 18% gain in the first quarter.

Barney's said it accepted a bid from Hong Kong-based Dickson Concepts to buy control of the upscale retailer and bring it out of bankruptcy proceedings in a transaction that is valued at $322 million.

U S West, as expected, failed to receive a tax reprieve from Congress to proceed with a plan to sell its wireless business to AirTouch Communications. The two companies said that, for now, they would continue to operate the business as partners.

Wheeling-Pittsburgh reached a pact that would end the longest major steel-industry strike this century, leaving both sides claiming victory.

PacifiCorp's $5.8 billion plan to buy Britain's Energy Group hit a potentially serious roadblock after the Labor government decided to conduct a full-scale regulatory inquiry.

United Parcel Service's 185,000 Teamsters union members staged a 15-day strike against the nation's largest delivery firm. The walkout, which received strong public support, was viewed as a victory for organized labor. The contract agreement satisfied many of the union's demands, including the creation of more full-time jobs for the many part-time UPS workers.

Columbia/HCA Healthcare named Jack Bovender Jr. president and chief operating officer, as new CEO Thomas F. Frist Jr. installed trusted ex-lieutenants at the embattled hospital firm. Separately, prosecutors broadened the criminal investigation into whether Columbia defrauded the federal government, and the company moved to sell some of its businesses.

Mental-health benefits can be capped under group-disability plans without violating the Americans with Disabilities Act, the Sixth U.S. Circuit Court of Appeals in Cincinnati ruled.

General Motors said it would buy back $2.5 billion of its shares, its second such buyback in less than a year and another attempt to boost its lagging stock price.

The Thai government said it would close half the country's finance companies, finally admitting the severity of the nation's financial crisis. Officials said the government had spent at least $16 billion in a desperate attempt to prop up the shaky financial firms and an estimated $20 billion to support the currency. Thailand planned to seek up to $15 billion under an IMF standby credit agreement.

Apple Computer received some breathing room, as Steve Jobs negotiated a surprise deal to win support for the troubled computer company from archrival Bill Gates. Microsoft planned to invest $150 million in Apple, winning the right to place the software giant's Web browser on new Macintosh computers. Mr. Jobs unveiled the pact to boos and gasps of disbelief from the Apple faithful, amid a sweeping overhaul of Apple's board.

Prudential Insurance was told by auditors as early as 1982 of deceptive sales practices by some agents, and officials were later warned that the problems hadn't been resolved. The disclosures, from internal Prudential documents, could have significant legal implications for the firm.

Hilton Hotels raised its bid for ITT Corp. by 27% to $70 a share, or $8.3 billion, hoping to regain momentum in its stalled hostile takeover battle and force ITT to the negotiating table.

DuPont agreed to acquire a 20% stake in seed concern Pioneer Hi-Bred for $1.7 billion, a deal that is likely to heat up the race for genetically engineered crops. DuPont also signed a letter of intent to buy Ralston Purina's soybean-processing unit for $1.5 billion in stock, with plans to use it in the biotech venture with Pioneer Hi-Bred.

Citicorp yanked its $500 million ad account from three incumbent agencies, handing it to Young & Rubicam, as part of an effort to greatly expand the bank's name recognition.

The FCC moved to lower the cost of international calls from the U.S. by an average of 77%, approving a plan it says will double international phone traffic and cut prices worldwide.

Fisher Scientific agreed to be acquired by buyout firm Thomas H. Lee for $1.06 billion, a white-knight deal that tops a tentative proposal from a Bass brothers investment vehicle.

Liggett's tobacco pact was rejected by a federal judge. The decision to throw out the pact, which sought to settle all suits by smokers against the No. 5 tobacco firm, was the first to use a high-court ruling making it harder for big personal-injury suits to be settled through class-action pacts.

Credit Suisse agreed to buy Winterthur Insurance for $9.51 billion. The deal brings together Switzerland's biggest bank and its second-largest insurer to create one of the world's 10 largest financial-services firms.

Hedge funds were seeing money pour into the private investment vehicles for the first time in four years, as investors scrambled to find alternatives to the pricey stock market.

Hicks Muse agreed to buy TV-station operator Lin Television for $1.4 billion. The investment firm also will buy the 46% of Lin owned by AT&T, which acquired the stake as part of its 1994 purchase of McCaw Cellular. Separately, Hicks Muse said its Capstar Broadcasting unit would acquire the SFX Broadcasting radio-station group for $1.2 billion.

Chrysler said the average price of its 1998 vehicle lineup will be 0.6% lower than its comparably equipped 1997 automobiles and light trucks. The announcement marked the first time Chrysler has cut new model-year sticker prices in at least two decades.

Sealed Air agreed to buy the packaging lines of W.R. Grace in a tax-free stock and cash transaction valued at $4.9 billion. The companies said the deal will create the world's top protective and specialty packaging firm. For Grace, the move marks the end of the packaging and chemical firm's year-and-a-half restructuring.

Delta Air Lines named Leo F. Mullin, vice chairman of electric-utility company Unicom, as its president and CEO.

Stocks plunged on August 15 as concerns grew about the continued profit growth of some of the market's largest and most predictable issues. The Dow Jones industrials fell 247.37, or 3.11%, to 7694.66, their second-largest point drop ever. The market recouped most of the losses the next week.

CalEnergy dropped its hostile $1.92 billion bid for New York State Electric after the first phase of its tender for a 9.9% stake in the utility fell flat.

China's central government took direct control of the country's two stock exchanges, signaling tighter management of the country's fast-growing securities industry.

Mexico's economy grew at an explosive 8.8% rate in the second quarter, the fastest pace in 16 years.

Corning said it would sell the majority of its consumer housewares unit for $975 million to a New York-based investment group, shedding a large part of its corporate identity and heritage.

SmithKline Beecham's clinical labs unit was sued by 37 health insurers, which allege it violated federal racketeering laws and overcharged them by hundreds of millions of dollars since 1989. The suit comes six months after SmithKline agreed to pay $325 million to settle similar charges of overbilling involving Medicare and other government health programs. SmithKline denied defrauding any insurance companies.

Cardinal Health and Bergen Brunswig announced a merger agreement valued at about $2.4 billion. Under the agreement, shareholders of Bergen, a pharmaceuticals distributor, would receive 0.775 share of stock in Cardinal, a health-care service provider, for each share of Bergen common stock. Cardinal also planned to assume $386 million in debt.

British Telecom cut $5 billion from its acquisition price for MCI, agreeing to pay about $19 billion, or $34 a share, for the 80% of MCI it doesn't already own. The move underscores the depth of MCI's troubles in the local and long-distance telephone business.

U.S. exports were hitting all-time highs despite the strong dollar as economies overseas showed signs of a pickup and the demand for U.S.-made capital goods was on the rise.

Florida reached a sweeping settlement of its lawsuit against the tobacco industry, with the companies agreeing to pay $11.3 billion, eliminate billboard advertising and support a ban on cigarette vending machines accessible to youths. The major tobacco firms hailed the pact as a sign of the industry's cooperative attitude.

Republic Industries and Toyota said they reached a "framework of an agreement" to settle their dispute over Republic's proposed acquisitions of Toyota auto dealerships in the U.S.

Fidelity Investments said it planned to cut off most new investors from buying shares in Magellan, the world's largest mutual fund. The move was meant to quash criticism that the $62.9 billion pool had grown too big to be managed effectively and was being kept open to generate higher management fees at the expense of current shareholders.

Nine big drug companies remained exposed to potentially far-reaching liability in a civil price-fixing suit filed by thousands of retail drugstores. The U.S. Court of Appeals ruling unexpectedly kept in the case millions of dollars of claims involving drug-company sales through wholesalers.

An Exxon accord that would have allowed the company to tap huge oil deposits in Russia's Far North was scuttled by Kremlin officials. The move was expected to shake investor confidence in Russia's energy sector.

Roche Holding said it was temporarily withdrawing its marketing application for the obesity drug Xenical, citing FDA concerns about a possible link between the drug and breast cancer.

A federal judge reduced the punitive damages award against ABC to $315,000 from $5.5 million in the Food Lion supermarket chain's case against the program "Prime Time Live." The show's hidden-camera report accused Food Lion of selling tainted food.

NationsBank said it would buy Barnett Banks for about $14.6 billion in stock, a move that rocked the banking world. Barnett officials said that after decades of going it alone, they realized they were in danger of being left behind. After

Barnett put itself on the block, it received attractive offers from at least a half-dozen bidders.

SEPTEMBER

Blue-chip stocks soared on Sept. 2, with the Dow Jones industrials rising 257.36 to 7879.78 and marking the average's biggest-ever single-session point advance. The rally's spark was economic data that showed manufacturing growth cooled a bit in August, easing investors' inflation worries.

Doubletree and Promus Hotel agreed to merge in a tax-free stock swap valued at nearly $2 billion. The merger, which comes amid a wave of hotel-industry consolidation, will create the No. 3 U.S. hotel chain.

Apple Computer moved to shut down cloners of its Macintosh line, buying the license and other assets of the biggest cloner and refusing to license new technology to the rest.

Tobacco companies raised wholesale cigarette prices seven cents a pack, as the industry faces the possibility of huge payments to settle litigation. But the industry was dealt a blow late in the month by the Senate, which voted to repeal a controversial credit that would soften the impact of the proposed industry-liability settlement. The provision would have allowed companies to count the cost of new, higher cigarette taxes against their obligations under the $368.5 billion accord.

Hudson Foods agreed to a takeover by poultry rival Tyson Foods in a cash and stock deal valued at about $682 million. The deal came as Hudson was still reeling from a national recall of its ground beef.

General Motors' Saturn division cut output of its cars 17% for the remainder of 1997. The move reflected the U.S. market's shrinking appetite for small cars manufactured by the Big Three.

Malaysia halted several major infrastructure projects, including the controversial $5 billion Bakun dam, and lifted trading restrictions on certain short-selling on the Kuala Lumpur bourse. Meanwhile, Malaysia's prime minister singled out investor George Soros for blame for the nation's currency crisis. But hedge funds run by Mr. Soros were buying, not selling, Malaysia's currency during its fall, the fund firm said.

H&R Block agreed to sell its CompuServe Corp. unit to WorldCom Inc. for about $1.2 bil-

lion in stock, finally putting an end to its involvement in the on-line industry. The real winner may be America Online, which will end up with CompuServe's consumer subscribers.

Levitz Furniture filed for bankruptcy-law protection. The nation's No. 2 home-furniture retailer cited its heavy debt load.

Mutual Life Insurance Co. of New York, one of the oldest and biggest U.S. mutual insurers, said it planned to change its status as a policyholder-owned firm and convert to stock ownership.

Transmitting "roadshows" on the Internet was approved by the SEC for an Atlanta firm, a move that could greatly widen institutional investors' access to corporate presentations.

Three big Wall Street firms—Credit Suisse First Boston, J.P. Morgan and Hambrecht & Quist—arranged to distribute shares of stocks they underwrite to customers of Charles Schwab, a move aimed at selling stock to small investors.

A New Orleans jury awarded $2.5 billion in punitive damages against CSX because of a 1987 chemical-car fire, the largest award ever against a railroad company. The total award was $3.37 billion, including smaller damages assessed against other companies. Analysts said the huge award was likely to be overturned.

Procter & Gamble and nine other leading consumer-product companies consented to pay $4.2 million to settle state antitrust charges that they acted in unison to deprive shoppers of cents-off coupons in western New York.

Campbell Soup said it planned to spin off seven "nonstrategic" business lines, including Vlasic pickles and Swanson frozen foods, to focus on its more-profitable soup, sauce and biscuit lines.

Germany's gross domestic product expanded at a healthy 2.9% annual rate during the second quarter, fueled almost solely by exports.

Five Levi Strauss garment workers were awarded damages of $10.6 million by a Texas jury. The workers alleged that the clothing company retaliated against them for filing costly claims for job-related injuries.

Bank credit-card losses soared in the second quarter to their highest annualized level in more than 14 years, even as insured commercial banks continued to post record earnings, the FDIC said.

The Japanese economy contracted at a startling annualized rate of 11.2% in the second quarter. The data promoted new fears about the staying power of Japan's recovery. Separately, Japan's largest bank moved to write off about $8.4 billion of bad loans. Bank of Tokyo-Mitsubishi's action was expected to push other big Japanese banks to dispose of bad loans faster.

A Venezuelan issue of $4 billion of new 30-year global bonds was snapped up by investors. The eager buying was an indication of how bullish Wall Street has become on Latin America.

Ingersoll-Rand agreed to acquire refrigeration-equipment maker Thermo King from Westinghouse for $2.56 billion, giving the equipment and parts manufacturer another industrial business line. For Westinghouse, the sale clears a major hurdle in the industrial and media concern's effort to reinvent itself.

American Home Products withdrew Redux and its older cousin Pondimin from the market, amid increasing health concerns about the prescription diet drugs.

Sara Lee planned a "fundamental reshaping" of its operations, moving to outsource manufacturing of such goods as L'eggs hosiery, Sara Lee desserts and the Wonderbra. The restructuring will lead to a charge of $1.6 billion, probably erasing earnings for the entire year. Its shares jumped 14 %.

Eastman Kodak said it expected operating earnings for 1997 to be as much as 25% below those of 1996, amid a filmprice war at home and a rising dollar abroad. Separately, Kodak indicated that it would fire more than 200 managers, scale back research and development and trim 10% of its administrative staff in its first major cutbacks since George Fisher become CEO in 1993.

Fleet Financial agreed to acquire Quick & Reilly, the nation's third-largest discount brokerage firm, for about $1.6 billion. The nearly $41-a-share deal came as commercial banks such as Fleet have been scooping up securities and asset-management firms.

Apple Computer named co-founder Steve Jobs interim CEO, formalizing a role he assumed on his return to power at the computer firm two months ago. Industry executives said the move suggests that finding a permanent chief has proved tougher than expected.

The IMF trimmed growth forecasts for Japan, Southeast Asia and most of the developing world, but said the global economy may be entering its best five-year stretch in 25 years.

Adidas agreed to buy French ski and sporting goods maker Salomon for $1.4 billion. The deal by the German shoe concern would create the world's No. 2 sports-gear firm after Nike.

AT&T planned to franchise its name for the first time to wireless and local phone companies, breaking with its tradition of keeping tight control over its network assets. The plan could allow AT&T to hold down its capital spending, saving billions of dollars over several years.

Coopers & Lybrand agreed to merge with Price Waterhouse, creating the world's biggest accounting and consulting firm. No money will change hands in the joining of the two partnerships. The firms' combined annual global revenue is nearly $12 billion, well ahead of the current No. 1 Andersen Worldwide.

Whirlpool said it will cut 10% of its work force amid efforts to revive its European and Asian operations. The appliance maker also said it will sell its financing business to Transamerica for $1.35 billion, boost its Latin American presence and pull out of two ventures in China.

IMF members agreed to chip in about $285 billion to boost the agency's capital base by 45%, in response to the rapidly escalating cost of global financial rescues.

Westinghouse Electric agreed to buy American Radio Systems for $1.6 billion, plus the assumption of $1 billion in debt. The Justice Department said it would do an antitrust review.

IBM said it has become the first company to successfully substitute copper for aluminum in making semiconductors, a vital breakthrough in manufacturing faster and more powerful computer chips.

Viacom agreed to sell its 50% stake in USA Networks to Seagram's Universal Studios for $1.7 billion, giving Universal complete control of the partnership's two cable networks.

B.F. Goodrich agreed to buy Rohr for about $792 million plus the assumption of debt in a stock transaction that ended uncertainty about the future of the maker of parts for the aerospace industry.

Mexico's central bank moved to gradually lower interest rates and decrease investor demand for the peso, indicating concern that the country's currency could become overvalued.

McKesson agreed to buy AmeriSource Health for $1.79 billion in stock, plus the assumption of $532.3 million in debt, in a move to secure its leading position in the drug-distribution business. The acquisition would combine the No. 1 and No. 4 distributors of pharmaceuticals and other health-care products.

Toyota said it plans to build at least one more assembly plant in North America, and Honda is scouting sites for a fourth plant in the U.S. or Canada. The moves represent a heightened aggressiveness toward the Big Three by the Japanese auto makers.

Shell Oil agreed to acquire Tejas Gas for about $1.45 billion. The move is one of the first attempts by a major oil company to tackle the competitive natural-gas marketing business alone.

PepsiCo's Brenda Barnes, one of the highest ranking women in the business world, said she will quit as chief executive of Pepsi's North American beverage business to spend more time with her family. Her successor is Philip Marineau, president of Dean Foods.

Travelers Group agreed to buy Salomon in a $9 billion stock swap. The companies' combined brokerage unit, to be called Salomon Smith Barney Holdings, would be part of a financial-services juggernaut with revenue of over $30 billion and a stock-market value of $55 billion, eclipsing giants Merrill Lynch and Morgan Stanley. The deal was expected to result in job losses for at least 1,500 bankers, traders, analysts and back-office workers.

The FTC launched an inquiry into Intel's dominance of the personal-computer market. The FTC demanded information from key industry players on whether Intel broke the law by trying to monopolize or restrict competition involving microprocessors or other computer components.

The real gross domestic product grew at a 3.3% annual rate in the second quarter, the Commerce Department said. That was down from the 4.9% annual rate in the first quarter, but still showed strong economic growth.

The freight industry struggled to keep up with the booming economy and cope with gridlock at ports that slowed deliveries across the country.

The U.S. International Trade Commission gave final approval to steep antidumping duties on a proposed supercomputer sale by Japan's NEC, effectively shutting the U.S. market to foreign supercomputers.

ITT was dealt a major setback in its fight against Hilton Hotels' hostile takeover. A federal judge ruled that ITT can't split itself into three separate companies without a shareholder vote.

Toyota's Camry was expected to be the No. 1-selling car for the 1997 model year, knocking off Ford's Taurus after four years in the top spot.

Median U.S. household income rose slightly for the second straight year, growing 1.2% to $35,492 in 1996, after falling or stagnating for five years. The Census Bureau also reported that the number of people in poverty remained about the same as in 1995 and that the income gap between the wealthy and the poor grew wider.

US Airways gate, reservations and ticket agents voted to join the Communications Workers of America union in the biggest private-sector organizing victory since 1987.

Raytheon must sell one or more missile-technology units to close its $9.5 billion purchase of the defense lines of Hughes Electronics from General Motors, federal antitrust officials said.

The Federal Reserve left its key short-term interest rate unchanged amid few signs of inflation. But there were growing expectations that if the economy remains strong, the central bank will raise rates later in 1997.

Charges that Toys 'R' Us pressured manufacturers to deny popular toys to warehouse clubs were upheld by an FTC administrative judge.

Cineplex Odeon agreed to merge with a unit of Sony Corp. of America, creating one of the largest movie-theater companies in North America.

WorldCom made a takeover bid, valued at about $30 billion, for MCI Communications, a company more than three times its size. If successful, the offer would tear apart MCI's pending merger with British Telecommunications and turn WorldCom into a telecom titan with an unmatched array of network assets in long-distance, local and Internet services.

What Was News
Notable Deaths in 1997

JANUARY

Harry Helmsley, 87 years old, landlord in big U.S. cities whose vast real-estate holdings included the Empire State Building.

Burton Lane, 84, composer of such Broadway musicals as *Finian's Rainbow* and *On a Clear Day You Can See Forever*.

Paul Tsongas, 55, former Massachusetts senator and a Democratic candidate for president in 1992.

James Dickey, 73, poet and author of the popular novel *Deliverance*.

Curt Flood, 59, former St. Louis Cardinals outfielder who led the fight that established baseball's free-agent system.

Col. Tom Parker, 87, Elvis Presley's manager.

Jeane Dixon, 79, astrologer and self-described psychic.

FEBRUARY

Pamela Harriman, 76, U.S. ambassador to France and Democratic Party doyenne.

Deng Xiaoping, 92, Chinese leader whose legacy included both major economic reforms and the 1989 massacre of students demanding democracy.

Albert Shanker, 68, American Federation of Teachers leader.

Andrei Sinyavsky, 71, Russian novelist whose 1966 trial galvanized anti-Communist dissidence.

MARCH

Stanislav Shatalin, 62, economist and author of a rejected plan for bold economic change in the Soviet Union.

Cheddi Jagan, 78, president of Guyana.

Michael Manley, 72, former Jamaican prime minister.

Edward Mills Purcell, 84, pioneer in nuclear magnetic resonance.

Alfred Sheinwold, 85, authority on the game of bridge.

Fred Zinnemann, 89, Oscar-winning director of such films as *A Man for All Seasons* and *From Here to Eternity*.

Willem de Kooning, 92, Dutch-born U.S. painter who dominated the Abstract Expressionist movement.

V. S. Pritchett, 96, English writer and critic.

Rev. Wilbert Awdry, 85, author of the "Thomas the Tank Engine" books for children.

Lyman Spitzer, 82, astrophysicist who conceived the Hubble telescope and a fusion-research pioneer.

APRIL

Allen Ginsberg, 70, beat poet and counter-culture icon.

Laura Nyro, 49, singer-songwriter whose blend of folk, soul and gospel influenced many artists.

Jack Kent Cooke, 84, owner of football's Washington Redskins.

Michael Dorris, 52, writer whose acclaimed book *The Broken Cord* told of his adopted son's struggle with fetal alcohol syndrome.

Chaim Herzog, 78, former president of Israel.

Emilio Azcarraga Milmo, 66, head of Mexico's Grupo Televisa media empire.

Mike Royko, 64, newspaper columnist in Chicago.

MAY

Virgilio Barco, 75, Colombia's president during one of the country's most difficult periods of drug violence, from 1986 to 1990.

Rose Will Monroe, 77, who as "Rosie the Riveter" urged American women to join the work force during World War II.

JUNE

Nikolai Tikhonov, 92, Soviet prime minister from 1980 to 1985 and one of the last of the Brezhnev-era old guard.

Adolphus "Doc" Cheatham, 91, influential jazz trumpeter over seven decades.

Betty Shabazz, 61, an educator and widow of Malcolm X.

Brian Keith, 75, movie and television actor.

Jacques Cousteau, 87, French oceanographer who helped popularize underseas exploration through numerous TV documentaries.

JULY

Robert Mitchum, 79, actor who specialized in hard-boiled roles in dozens of Hollywood movies.

Jimmy Stewart, 89, actor who starred in many beloved movies, including *Mr. Smith Goes to Washington* and *It's a Wonderful Life*.

Charles Kuralt, 62, CBS newsman best known for his "On the Road" reports.

Dorothy Buffum Chandler, 96, an arts patron and matriarch of Times Mirror's founding family.

Gianni Versace, 50, Italian fashion designer.

Arthur Liman, 64, a trial lawyer and chief counsel of the Senate's Iran-Contra committee.

Sir James Goldsmith, 64, Anglo-French politician and financier.

William J. Brennan, 91, Supreme Court justice whose 1956–1990 career was marked by concern for individual rights and opposition to the death penalty.

Ben Hogan, 84, golfing great who won 63 tournaments over three decades.

Bao Dai, 83, Vietnam's last emperor who was forced to abdicate in 1945.

AUGUST

William S. Burroughs, 83, a writer of the Beat Generation, whose books included the controversial *Naked Lunch*.

Jeanne Calment, 122, French woman believed to be the world's oldest person whose date of birth could be authenticated by records.

Clarence Kelley, 85, director of the FBI from 1973 to 1978.

Brandon Tartikoff, 48, programming chief during NBC's 1980s heyday.

Princess Diana, 36, former wife of Britain's Prince Charles who became an international celebrity and devoted much of her time to charitable causes.

SEPTEMBER

Viktor E. Frankl, 92, eminent psychotherapist and author of *Man's Search for Meaning*.

Sir Rudolf Bing, 95, longtime Metropolitan Opera director in New York City.

Mother Teresa, 87, beloved Roman Catholic nun in Calcutta, India, who devoted her life to comforting the poor and received the Nobel Peace Prize in honor of her ministry.

Mobutu Sese Seko, 66, dictator of the former Zaire from 1965 until his ouster by rebel forces in May 1997.

Sir Georg Solti, 84, conductor who led many of the world's great orchestras, including the Chicago Symphony.

Burgess Meredith, 89, actor whose long career included such roles as George in the film *Of Mice and Men* and the Penguin in TV's *Batman*.

Red Skelton, 84, radio and television comedian known for his pratfalls and buffoonish characters.

Roy Lichtenstein, 73, Pop Art pioneer best known for his paintings resembling comic strip panels.

Countdown to the Millennium

Naysayers relish pointing out that the twenty-first century actually begins in 2001, but it's the year 2000 that's causing all the commotion. Marketers, of course, see money in the millennium, putting the M word on everything from cosmetics to chairs. Over the next three years, a flood of books and movies that tap into a doomsday mood is expected. So many, in fact, that Ted Daniels, director of the Millennium Watch Institute, hopes his new book about millennium folklore "doesn't get drowned in it all." On the Internet, millennium musings abound, as surfers peruse Web pages and participate in on-line chats about what's in store in the coming century. The White House has created its own millennium page on the Internet (www.whitehouse.gov), listing federal projects tied to the new century.

New Year's Eve celebrations are already taking shape: a fund-raising group called the Millennium Society plans a big bash at the foot of the Great Pyramids, and the Pope has declared 2000 a Jubilee Year, a yearlong observance expected to draw about 20 million people to Rome. However, the new millennium sends shivers down some people's spines, as worries of gloom and doom mount.

But rather than raging floods and fires and other apocalyptic mayhem, this millennium meltdown would cause havoc in the virtual world.

Back to the Future

The arrival of the new millennium threatens to throw mainframe computers into chaos. Called variously the "Millennium Problem," "The Millennium Bug" and "Y2K," the problem stems from how some computer programs recognize dates. To save space, the programs, many of which were written in the 1960s, store only the last two digits of a year. To such computers, "1965" becomes "65." If this situation goes uncorrected, the mainframes will read the year 2000 as 00, or 1900.

Such an error would create a rolling wave of data-processing malfunctions that could quickly overwhelm mainframes, impairing or even shutting down companies' operations. The federal government would also suffer a computer freeze, as would state and local governments. Possible results: air-traffic control systems locking up, security systems going on the blink, decades of bank records being wiped out, and prisoners being released prematurely.

Computer programmers had never intended that these programs would still be in use today; rather they thought the programs would be replaced in a few years by better ones. Those few years stretched into decades, and now procrastination has put many businesses in a tight pinch. Fixing the bug is cutting deep into companies pockets: For example, Allstate Corp. has said it will spend about $40 million to avoid any Year 2000 glitches. The return on the investment—the company stays in business. In the end, the total tab to adapt all the world's mainframes could reach $600 billion, says the research firm Gartner Group. Worse, companies and agencies that have put off trying to defuse the ticking time bomb may not have enough time to fix it, no matter how much money they spend.

Correcting the Millennium Problem has spawned an industry of sorts. The programmers hired for the tedious job of combing through millions of lines of code draw hefty salaries, sometimes as high as $200,000. Some insurance companies recently added "bug coverage" to their policy offerings. And with such huge sums of money involved, a throng of lawyers wait ready to file suits from all directions.

Let's Party

Come December 31, 1999, there will be plenty of parties. But if you want to celebrate at a traditional spot you might be out of luck. New York's Rainbow Room stopped taking reservations in 1995 for its millennium bash, but you can still add your name to the 1,000-person-and-counting waiting list. All three floors of the futuristic Space Needle in Seattle were booked in one swoop by a Portland, Ore., woman back in 1991. So that's out. Disney World? Not one hotel room on the grounds is available.

Other ways to ring in the new millennium: Hot-air balloon rides are expected to lift off from Greenwich, England; luxury cruise ships will float across the international dateline; and, for true millennium mavens, one company hopes to charter a Concorde that will zip passengers from one time zone's celebration to the next and the next and the next. Another Concorde trip, pegged the "Journey of a Lifetime" by its sponsor, Intrav, a St. Louis travel company, will take travelers on an 18-day around-the-world-trip that is scheduled to depart on Christmas Eve. But come New Year's Eve, this Concorde will be firmly on the ground, in Hong Kong. "We've found people have much more fun at a luxury hotel rather than on a plane," says Intrav spokesman Richard Hefler.

For the athletically inclined, an around-the-world bicycle trip is slated to leave Los Angeles at the first light of the new year. More than 375 bikers have already signed up. The hit Broadway musical *Chicago* took the bold step of selling tickets in advance for December 31, 1999, and still has seats available. Then there's the old American standby: New York's Times Square, where a megaextravaganza is in the works, including live broadcast of millennium parties from other time zones.

Millennium Marketing

Never ones to ignore a fad, businesses have started capitalizing on the millennium mood. In department stores, Elizabeth Arden hawks its Millenium line of skin-care products and claims the cutting-edge moisturizers will rejuvenate tired end-of-the-century skin. Not to be outdone, Avon Products touts "Brazilian Amazon lilies and ancient temple incense" in its Millenia bath oil. On car lots, Mazda named its high-end model the Millenia, a car you can depend on, perhaps not for a thousand years, but for a long time, the company says.

New York has two Hilton hotels bearing the millennium name but each uses a different spelling: The one downtown is called the Millenium Hilton, and the other, in midtown, is the Millennium Broadway. (Incidentally, millennium has become one of the most frequently misspelled words of the late 20th century, ranking with the likes of minuscule and perseverance.)

The media, too, are getting a head start on 2000. *Newsweek* magazine created a section called, "The Millennium Notebook," for weekly ruminations on twenty-first century subjects. ABC-TV, in cooperation with Hallmark Entertainment, retained 10 playwrights—including David Mamet, August Wilson, Wendy Wasserstein, Arthur Miller and Neil Simon—to write scripts that explore the various "implications of the new century," says Russ Patrick, spokesman for Hallmark Entertainment. The shows are scheduled to be broadcast in late 1999.

And *Time* magazine and CBS News have created yet another millennium project. Called "People of the Century: The *Time* 100," the magazine will release six special issues, with the network producing corresponding one-hour specials, about the "lives and legacies" of the century's most influential people. In the sixth issue, *Time* will announce its person of the century.

Not all businesses view the millennium as a marketing opportunity, however. Some are looking to the past instead. More businesses infuse "the wisdom of the ancients" in their marketing campaigns, says Tom Vierhile of Marketing Intelligence Service Ltd. in Naples, N.Y., a company that monitors new products. Mr. Vierhile believes references to Mayan, Incan and Chinese cultures in marketing natural-foods, teas and bath products are a response to consumers' yearning for a simpler time. It's a backlash against today's computer age filled with ringing cellular phones, buzzing pagers and the hum of fax machines, he says, and where "you can't go anywhere without hearing about the Internet."

What's in a Name?

While some companies are adopting the millennium moniker, the new century puts some businesses in a conundrum over what to do about their names. To avoid being stuck permanently in the past, Twentieth Century Cos., a Kansas City, Mo., mutual-fund company, changed its name to the more timeless, American Century Investments. At this point, Gateway 2000, a computer company, has no plans to abandon its name, but by the time the next century arrives, it has said, it might.

Twentieth Century Fox and 20th Century Draperies, a New York company, intend to stick with their names well past the year 2000. But the movie studio Twentieth Century Fox has filed a patent on Twenty-First Century Fox. Just in case.

Corporate-identity experts urge caution, though. A brand will "transcend the meaning" of the name, says Jonathan Bell of Interbrand Schechter, a consulting firm that assists companies in developing their names. If a company abandons its name, he says, all the "equity" that has been built up will be lost. Instead, he recommends keeping a remnant of the original name intact. So for Gateway 2000, Mr. Bell advises just dropping 2000. "Frankly, it's redundant," he says. "Everyone thinks of it as just Gateway anyway."

Laurie Snyder

Looking to 1998 and Beyond

As 1997 was fading into history, *The Wall Street Journal Almanac* asked four people who make their living spotting trends to do some crystal-ball gazing. Their assignment: to compile a list of the most significant trends as the world heads into the twenty-first century. The researchers, whose clients include such companies as IBM and Nabisco, detect trends in a variety of ways—observing life around them, talking with consumers, reading and watching television and movies, and consulting experts in business, politics, the arts, and other fields. These trend trackers touch on some of the same broad themes—the desire to live longer, healthier lives; unknown health hazards lurking in the environment; and the ability to do more of our work, shopping and learning from home, thanks to technology. But each analyst also offers his or her own distinctive outlook on the world. Here's what they see ahead:

Myra Stark, director of knowledge management and consumer insights at Saatchi & Saatchi Advertising

- **The New Optimism.** Consumers are feeling better. The economy is stronger, and many people have been living with the new realities of work long enough to begin accepting them. America may be building toward a euphoria for the millennium.
- **The Widening Gap in American Life.** As the polarization grows between haves and have-nots, there will be more restlessness among the disadvantaged, and more social concern and desire to restore some balance among the more fortunate. The gap between winners and losers is not only economic, but also intellectual and technological.
- **Home Base.** The home and gardening trend keeps getting stronger as technology makes it possible for more parts of life to be centered in the home. As the home becomes more important, people want to safeguard it, so home security is a growth industry and gated communities and private police forces are spreading.
- **Work: It Ain't What It Used to Be.** Work will continue to be redefined and reorganized, whether it's the virtual office, the disappearance of the secretary or the rise of "knowledge workers." While some baby boomers still reel from the disappearance of secure 9-to-5 jobs, Genera-

tion X is focusing on the accumulation of skills as the only possible security.
- **Entertainment and the Growth of Communiglomerates.** Entertainment is becoming more important to people as they are offered more media options and huge communication/entertainment empires like Disney, Time Warner, and Microsoft battle for their allegiance. Entertainment will be the next arena in which the consumer dilemma of wanting choice but desiring simplicity gets played out.
- **Education, the New Hot Spot.** Education is becoming a bigger concern for people. Technology, home schooling, moves to privatize education, and demands for more accountability in teaching will all change the education establishment.
- **The Mainstreaming of Extreme Sports.** Activities like snowboarding, sky-surfing, free climbing, and street luge are considered "cooler" by kids and teens than traditional sports like baseball and basektball. Among adults, there's rock climbing, eco/adventure travel, and business team-building exercises in the wilderness. The trend may be related to the increased time spent indoors with technology.
- **Holding Back the Hands of Time.** The anti-aging fight of the baby boomers has just begun. Already, people in their fifties and sixties look the way people did in their forties just 15 or 20 years ago. There will be more effective wrinkle treatments and hair-growth products for this generation with its strong need for self-fulfillment.
- **Affluent Kids.** There are more and more doted-on children of older parents, who were so eager to have kids later in life. They are computer literate at an early age, cosmopolitan travelers and privileged in many other ways. They really are different kids, and this is a trend to watch closely.
- **The Rediscovery of Cities.** More money, development and people will be flowing back into cities. This is a counter-trend to the development of exurbs and the fact that many Americans now want to live in rural communities.
- **The Blurring of Product Categories.**

It's going to be an exciting and confusing time for consumers as new products reconfigure traditionally separate categories. Food and health products will merge into "nutraceuticals," and entertainment, communication and information businesses will continue to converge.

- **The Personalization of Technology.** Products will become smaller and more convenient, such as hand-held computers. This will empower consumers and speed the spread and acceptance of technology.
- **The Importance of Advertising in the Attention Economy.** Attention will be the scarce commodity in the information age, and therefore much more valuable. Effective advertising becomes more important because it can command attention, even when people have so little time.

The staff of Inferential Focus, a corporate strategic advisory service in New York

- **Personal Revolution.** At all age levels, people are rethinking their relationships to established institutions and the values that have supported these institutions. Women are the leading indicator of this change, focusing more on cooperation and pragmatic solutions. The "generation apart" (ages 22 to 34) is the primary proponent of new work relationships, such as a demand for personal growth and learning and less loyalty to employers.
- **Communities of Meaning.** The personal revolution is leading people to establish "communities of meaning," in contrast to communities of wealth. The new values include self-reliance, balance, long-term friendships and fairness. Wealth and materialism are being devalued.
- **Information Overload.** The cognitive overload of information can lead to stress and confusion. Some people have tried imposing their own filter on this information barrage.
- **Time Becomes More Precious than Money.** In the workplace and marketplace, companies and institutions that help individuals gain control over their personal lives will connect with them

and develop a relationship. Long-term brand association will be awarded to companies that listen to customers, produce what is desired and offer solutions—not necessarily to the oldest and most pervasive brands.

- **Evolution of Communications Technology.** On-line commerce will change the buyer–seller relationship and undercut loyalty to companies. The ability to gather information and buy products electronically allows consumers to interact with someone other than the big marketers. For example, car buyers will interact more with on-line showrooms, distancing themselves from the traditional dealer and manufacturer.
- **Global Trade.** With the initiation of the World Trade Organization, public rhetoric suggested that free trade would advance around the globe. But there are very early signs of a reversal of the free trade mantra. Some countries are now putting up trade barriers because protectionism is necessary for domestic economic growth.
- **Cheaper Energy.** New sources of oil and economically viable ways to convert oil reserves from nonusable to usable sources will increase supplies. The ensuing battle for market share will lead to lower oil prices.
- **Greater Longevity.** Health-care advances will lengthen life expectancy. Major gains against the most devastating diseases are leading to a much healthier older population.
- **Universities as Corporations.** Universities are operating as corporate institutions in an attempt to gain market share. Outsourcing of teaching staffs results in fewer costly tenured positions, reduced benefit payments and more flexibility in increasing or cutting staff. In addition, on-line classrooms are helping to develop new markets.
- **Investing in Africa.** The continent's ability to attract aid from foreign governments and international institutions has encouraged private investors to fund new projects in South Africa and less-developed countries. Many African economies are showing signs of growth that should encourage further foreign investment.

Faith Popcorn, founder and chairman of BrainReserve, a marketing consultancy in New York, and author of the book Clicking

- **Cocooning.** People increasingly want to protect themselves from the harsh, unpredictable realities of the outside world. When the term was first coined in the 1980s, it meant a "warm and cozy" focus on the home. Now, people are spending more time in their "armored cocoon" for security and relying more on their computers for communication with others.
- **Being Alive.** There's growing awareness that good health not only extends longevity but also leads to a new way of life. There's a lot of trading off of "fitness and fatness," but in general, more people want to be healthier and improve the quality of their lives *now*. That may mean regular exercise, homeopathic medicine, aromatherapy or better diets.
- **Pleasure Revenge.** At the same time, consumers want to cut loose again, whether they eat more fattening food, drink martinis, smoke cigarettes, guzzle coffee or sunbathe. Steakhouses, for instance, are one of the fastest growing types of restaurants. People feel vulnerable and don't know how long they're going to live, so they want to be a little hedonistic.
- **99 Lives.** Too fast a pace and too little time are causing societal schizophrenia and forcing people to assume multiple roles. Cellular phones and drive-through restaurants will continue to grow, and anything else that can help people keep up with their lives and reduce their stress will be a success.
- **Icon Toppling.** The pillars of society are being questioned and rejected. People who are distrustful of doctors are turning to herbal medicine; people who lost their faith in religion are creating their own brand of ritual; and people burned by big business are starting their own companies.
- **The Vigilante Consumer.** Consumers will manipulate marketers and the marketplace through pressure, protest and politics. People are angry and suspicious of marketers of products and services. Those feelings have been exacerbated by the widespread layoffs of the 1990s and are turning into "general corporate hate." One of the obvious characteristics of the 1990s consumer: a high degree of impatience, almost to the boiling point.
- **Egonomics.** In this depersonalized society, consumers crave recognition of their individuality. People will increasingly respond to customized products and sales pitches that make them seem something more than a number or bar code.
- **Female Think.** A new set of values will shift business from a hierarchical model to a more familial one. When women run companies, they often deal from a relationship perspective and believe things will get done if everyone feels good. Women also should be marketed to differently than men because of their desire for relationships and teamwork.
- **Anchoring.** People are looking for spirituality. They are trying to find their roots, whether through genealogy, meditation or religions like Buddhism.
- **Atmosfear.** Consumers are growing more fearful of their immediate atmosphere because of tainted food, water and air. People now have to wonder if they will get sick if they simply eat strawberries. This feeling of vulnerability is causing more people to drink bottled water even when they don't need to and to be more discerning about the food they buy in stores and restaurants.

Gerald Celente, founder and director of the Trends Research Institute, a research organization in Rhinebeck, N.Y., and author of the book Trends 2000

- **New Energy.** There will be a move away from costly oil and gas to a new form of free energy—solar/photovoltaic, cold fusion or a new invention. The ramifications will be great—both for oil producing companies and countries and for consumers who will have more money to spend on other goods and services.

- **Videophones.** As the picture quality improves and they become easier to use, videophones will allow more people to work at home. They also will reduce the number of business trips by enabling people to do product demonstrations from the home or office.

- **Technotribalism.** As people spend more time at home working and using their computers, they will become more interested in local community affairs. Eventually, people may even be able to vote on issues via computer, bypassing elected officials. Call this the techno-tribal town hall.

- **Home Delivery.** With more people working at home, it also will mean the return of old-style home delivery of many products and services, including food, computer repair and health care.

- **Interactive University.** Children will receive their education through computerized learning at home some days and classes in a school building on other days. Higher education will increasingly mean "distance learning" through on-line courses that will bring students the best and brightest teachers in the fields of their choice.

- **Nuclear Calamity.** Whether it comes from the decrepit nuclear facilities in the former Soviet Union, nuclear terrorism or another disaster, the world will be shielding itself from fallout.

- **New Plagues.** Toxins in water, the increasingly unsafe food supply, the threat of new airborne viruses, and the inability of drugs to defeat the new breed of superbugs will mean more illness and death. The elderly, young and generally unhealthy will be most at risk.

- **Longevity Centers.** Part spa and part university, longevity centers will be the place to go to get healthy and feel young. They will offer clean food, clean water and clean air.

- **Healthy Fast Food.** New fast-food outlets will offer chicken certified to be "clean"—free-range, organically fed and brought to market under the strictest controls—burgers that will be free of growth hormones, antibiotics and drug residues, and pesticide-free produce.

- **Communal Living.** The continued growth in single-person households will lead to more shared housing, boarding houses and new types of communes. The trend will be driven both by young people delaying marriage and aging baby boomers facing divorce or spousal death. People will be seeking a personal support system, as well as cheaper housing they can afford.

2

POLITICS & POLICY

I N THE WEEKS FOLLOWING THE ELECTION OF 1996, *President Clinton's aides talked frequently about how a second Clinton term might make a mark on history. It became a White House parlor game. Reform Social Security? Balance the budget? Expand the North American Free Trade Agreement? At one session, domestic policy adviser Bruce Reed jokingly suggested an invasion of Canada might be the best way to ensure a place in the history books.*

The game, however, invariably ended in frustration. Historians were quick to point out to the president's men that second terms seldom make history. That's partly because a second-term president is a lame duck, and the jockeying to replace him begins almost immediately, undercutting his power and influence.

For Mr. Clinton, there was the added problem of a Republican Congress, reelected by a slim margin but nonetheless convinced that it's own mandate was as great as the president's. Then there was the problem of the president himself. In 1993, Mr. Clinton had vowed to be another Franklin Roosevelt, committed to "relentless experimentation" in government. By the beginning of 1997, he had transformed himself into something closer to Dwight Eisenhower. He

was leery of grand initiatives, unwilling to attempt too much at the same time, and committed to small, nonideological and largely symbolic gestures, like advocating school uniforms or educational testing. He was finding a lot of time to play golf.

If Mr. Clinton began the new term showing signs of burnout, he wasn't alone. The previous four years had been a period of enormous and ambitious attempts at change. In 1993 and 1994, Mr. Clinton pushed for a sweeping overhaul of the nation's health-care system that would have restructured one-seventh of the U.S. economy and assured every American quality health care. It failed. In 1995 and 1996, the first GOP-led Congress in two generations promised to follow an equally grand "Contract with America" to roll back three decades worth of growth in the size and scope of government. It, too, failed. As 1997 began, neither political party had the stomach for grand actions.

But what was lacking in energy and ambition in Washington in 1997 was made up for by luck. The economy continued to grow with a vigor that astonished even the president's most optimistic advisers. And most important, it grew without any signs of resurgent inflation, enabling the Federal Reserve to keep interest rates low. The healthy economy had important spillover effects for the Washington agenda.

The welfare reform bill that the president had signed the previous year, over the objections of liberal advisers who felt it too penurious, showed early signs of surprising success. Even before its provisions took hold, the welfare rolls in many states dropped dramatically, as potential welfare recipients were motivated to go to work by both the availability of jobs and the fear of a future cutoff in benefits.

Moreover, the strong economy made the task of balancing the budget a cinch. Tax revenues poured in at a rate far higher than expected in the early months of the year, leading some to predict the budget could be in balance by 1998. After nearly two decades in which deficit politics had dominated economic policy debates in Washington, the deficit suddenly ceased to be a problem. Members of Congress began debating how to spend the surpluses.

With deficits disappearing, efforts by Congress and the president to negotiate a plan to "balance the budget" actually turned into something else. For Republicans, they were an opportunity to deliver some long-promised tax cuts—principally, a cut in the capital-gains tax, a tax credit for middle-class families with children, and a reduction in the estate tax. For President Clinton, they became a means of funding a few of his favorite initiatives—principally health care for children and programs to encourage post-secondary education. The spending cuts included in the plan, the most significant of which were reductions in Medicare and Medicaid payments to hospitals and other health-care providers, largely went to finance these new tax cuts and spending increases. Pain was kept to a minimum.

Advocates of the budget plan argued it would help prevent deficits in the future. But those predictions relied on some questionable assumptions. In particular, the budget called for so-called "discretionary spending" on government programs to continue to grow for the next few years, but then decline in 2001 and 2002—"the Gore years" as some in the administration called them. Cynics doubted those spending cuts would ever occur. And there was little in the budget plan to deal with the biggest problem on the fiscal horizon: the retirement of the baby boomers two decades hence, and the strains that would put on the Social Security and Medicare programs.

Some in the Clinton administration urged the president to tackle the Social Security and Medicare problem. Ensuring a safe retirement for baby boomers, they argued, was a way for the president to gain a spot in the history books. And Mr. Clinton himself insisted in interviews that he was determined to deal with this problem. But not in 1997. That was the problem, he said, for 1998 or 1999.

"One of the things I've learned," the president said in an interview with *Wall Street Journal* reporters midway through the year, "is that you have to be very disciplined in how much the system can absorb. You need to have a rigorous timetable." Attempting to do too much in one year, he argued, would overload the system, as health care had in 1994. He wasn't going to do that in 1997.

With the prospects for domestic policy limited, some administration officials argued that President Clinton should make his mark on history in foreign policy. And at the very beginning of the year, some saw China as the best place to make that mark. The Chinese leaders desperately wanted to be accepted into the club of industrial nations, and, in particular, to gain entry into the World Trade Organization. That gave the U.S. an opportunity to negotiate agreements that would open up the Chinese market to U.S. companies. There was talk of a November U.S.-China summit, punctuated by an agreement to let China into the WTO.

But those hopes faded as intelligence reports surfaced that the Chinese government might have funneled illegal campaign contributions into the American political system. The revelations largely closed off the possibility that Mr. Clinton would make any dramatic gestures toward China. Any such gesture would have been attacked as a sellout for campaign cash.

While the Clinton administration was looking for ways to make history in 1997, the Republicans in Congress risked descending into factional fighting and chaos. In 1995, Newt Gingrich had emerged as the most powerful Speaker of the House to hold that job in many decades. But by 1997, his prominence had also earned him the title of the most unpopular politician in America.

No one was more critical of the speaker's leadership than the rabble-rousing Republicans he helped elect to Congress for the first time in 1994. In mid-summer, a group of them attempted to stage a coup, and managed to enlist some of the speaker's top lieutenants in the effort. But after a few days of almost comical backroom intrigue, the insurrection was quashed. The whole affair left the House leadership badly weakened, and many analysts concluded it was only a matter of time before a new generation of GOP leaders took over.

One of the most interesting developments in Washington during the year got its start elsewhere, when a group of state attorneys general sat down with leaders of the nation's tobacco companies to hammer out a settlement. The administration had already planned to take on big tobacco, with regulations that would limit advertising and marketing to teenagers. But the settlement went far beyond that, committing tobacco companies to pay some $360 billion and to sharply reduce teenage smoking. Both the president and Congress said they planned to put their own mark on the settlement. And as the year went on, it became clear that work would not be completed on the deal in 1997. But it certainly had the potential to be one of the most significant policy changes to come out of Washington in the early part of Mr. Clinton's second term.

None of this was sufficient to alter the public's disaffection and disinterest in Washington. The summer hearings on campaign-finance abuses, which were compared in the press to the Watergate hearings, came and went without causing even a blip on the public's radar screens. Polls showed Americans simply didn't care much about what the federal government was doing. Public anger against the government had turned into indifference. With the Cold War over, and the economy booming, Washington seemed to many Americans to be almost irrelevant.

Alan Murray, Washington bureau chief of *The Wall Street Journal*

WASHINGTON'S MAJOR PLAYERS IN 1997

Madeleine Albright Madeleine Korbel Albright became the first female secretary of state. Appointed by President Clinton with much political fanfare, Secretary Albright, the former U.S. ambassador to the United Nations, already had considerable experience dealing with foreign diplomats and the ponderous international organization that unites them. Just after her confirmation, she had the symbolic honor of welcoming three new European nations into NATO. But the Czech-born secretary's transition to the State Department was not entirely painless. Revelations about her Jewish background, which, she maintained, her parents had kept secret from her after they fled Hitler's invasion, proved embarrassing. The new secretary also traveled to the Middle East in September 1997 to try to revive peace talks between Israelis and Palestinians.

Carol Browner As chief of the Environmental Protection Agency, Carol Browner came into her own in 1997, fighting vigorously for stringent new clean-air standards in spite of opposition from industry and various economic officials in the Clinton administration. Ms. Browner counted on the support of Vice President Al Gore, who has tried to position himself as the environmental candidate for the year 2000 presidential elections. Although her push for tougher standards alienated the moderate Republicans who often support EPA measures, Ms. Browner refused to give in. In the end, the clean-air regulations battle brought both the EPA and its director a much higher profile in Washington.

Newt Gingrich Speaker of the House Newt Gingrich fought off growing discontent among House Republicans over his leadership style. More of his colleagues felt that he might not be the best leader the House had to offer, and Rep. Bill Paxon, the speaker's protege, resigned his House leadership position after a failed coup attempt to oust the longtime Georgia congressman from his position. But the Speaker retained his title and cooperated more and more with his Democratic foes. The bipartisan budget deal was symbolic of this new willingness to work with the administration when a solution seemed in the Republicans' best interest.

Al Gore Amid widespread feeling that the Gore 2000 presidential campaign was already under way, Vice President Al Gore continued to spearhead the White House's technological and environmental initiatives. He worked with the Environmental Protection Agency on more stringent clean-air standards. He also led several administration efforts aimed at encouraging self-regulation on the Internet after the Supreme Court struck down the Communications Decency Act. But Mr. Gore's second term as vice president began under the shadow of the campaign-finance scandal plaguing the Clinton administration. The vice president came under personal attack for his fund-raising efforts, which involved use of his White House office, and for a fund-raising trip to a Buddhist temple where he collected checks from illegal foreign donors.

John Huang At the heart of the Democrats' campaign-finance scandal, John Huang emerged as a pawn of powerful Asian interests seeking to influence American policymaking. In the Senate campaign-finance hearings, Republicans painted Mr. Huang, a former executive with the Indonesian Lippo Group whom President Clinton later awarded a mid-level post in the Commerce Department in gratitude for his prolific fund-raising, as the channel for Chinese government money. Mr. Huang's close ties to Lippo, which in turn had a business relationship with the Beijing government, proved politically embarrassing to the President, especially when investigators discovered that much of Mr. Huang's fund-raising yielded illegal contributions from foreigners and others. Republican senators, however, were unable to prove

that Mr. Huang spied for the Chinese while at Commerce.

John Kasich As chair of the House budget committee, Rep. John Kasich oversaw the groundbreaking balanced-budget accord. The budget deal marked a new spirit of cooperation between the second-term president and the House Republicans, wracked by their own internal leadership intrigues. The bipartisan support that Rep. Kasich mustered for the budget deal revealed his ability to smooth over political differences and bypass hot-button issues. His skillful maneuvering led to speculation that the Ohio Republican might one day emerge as a presidential contender.

Dr. David Kessler As the head of the Food and Drug Administration, Dr. David Kessler helped push tobacco regulation onto the national agenda, sparking debate over such issues as the addictiveness of nicotine and the marketing of cigarettes to youth. Having left the FDA, he once again gained a voice in national policymaking with the proposed tobacco settlement in 1997 between the industry and state attorneys general. Dr. Kessler emerged as one of the most vocal critics of the settlement, which, he asserted, would prevent the FDA from regulating nicotine as a drug. Dr. Kessler's critique punctured the euphoria surrounding the landmark settlement, negotiated behind closed doors in Washington as the tobacco industry sought to limit its liability to reimburse sick smokers.

Trent Lott In a year of increasing bipartisanship and cooperation with the Clinton Administration, Sen. Trent Lott of Mississippi emerged as the key Republican leader and a pragmatic alternative to House Speaker Newt Gingrich and the more ideological House Republicans who had set the agenda in 1995 and 1996. Most notably, Sen. Lott, at the last minute, supported President Clinton on the successful passage of the chemical weapons treaty, which several key conservative legislators in his own party opposed. Having acquired greater leverage with the administration after his support of the treaty, Mr. Lott also helped the GOP negotiate its way through the delicate budget-deal talks, yielding a compromise that won the Republicans a number of important concessions.

Susan Molinari New York Republican Representative Susan Molinari made headlines as she resigned her Congressional seat and took an anchor job with CBS. In her six years as a representative, Ms. Molinari had become an influential young GOP leader, along with her husband, New York Rep. Bill Paxon, and had been invited to give the keynote address at the 1996 Republican National Convention. After she announced her new career plans, some in Washington questioned whether it was appropriate for a former politician to assume the post of a news program anchor, but she and CBS were unapologetic.

Fred Thompson An actor and a former Watergate prosecutor, Sen. Fred Thompson came to prominence as the driving force behind the Senate campaign finance hearings. In a scandal-tinged atmosphere where both Republicans and Democrats accused the other party of opportunistic motives, Sen. Thompson, a Tennessee Republican, tried to maintain a reputation for encouraging bipartisan dialogue at the hearings. Although Sen. Thompson's investigators brought up several embarrassing pieces of evidence suggesting that John Huang's connections to the Lippo Group and his access to sensitive information about China while he was an official at the U.S. Commerce Department were improper, the Republicans on the committee were unable to prove that Mr. Huang in fact spied for the Chinese government.

Chana Schoenberger

1996 Official Presidential Election Results

State	Clinton	Dole	Perot	Electoral vote Clinton	Electoral vote Dole
Alabama	662,165	769,044	92,149	-	9
Alaska	80,380	122,746	26,333	-	3
Arizona	653,288	622,073	112,072	8	-
Arkansas	475,171	325,416	69,884	6	-
California	5,119,835	3,828,380	697,847	54	-
Colorado	671,152	691,848	99,629	-	8
Connecticut	735,740	483,109	139,523	8	-
Delaware	140,355	99,062	28,719	3	-
District of Columbia	158,220	17,339	3,611	3	-
Florida	2,546,870	2,244,536	483,870	25	-
Georgia	1,053,849	1,080,843	146,337	-	13
Hawaii	205,012	113,943	27,358	4	-
Idaho	165,443	256,595	62,518	-	4
Illinois	2,341,744	1,587,021	346,408	22	-
Indiana	887,424	1,006,693	224,299	-	12
Iowa	620,258	492,644	105,159	7	-
Kansas	387,659	583,245	92,639	-	6
Kentucky	636,614	623,283	120,396	8	-
Louisiana	927,837	712,586	123,293	9	-
Maine	312,788	186,378	85,970	4	-
Maryland	966,207	681,530	115,812	10	-
Massachusetts	1,571,763	718,107	227,217	12	-
Michigan	1,989,653	1,481,212	336,670	18	-
Minnesota	1,120,438	766,476	257,704	10	-
Mississippi	394,022	439,838	52,222	-	7
Missouri	1,025,935	890,016	217,188	11	-
Montana	167,922	179,652	55,229	-	3

State	Clinton	Dole	Perot	Electoral vote Clinton	Electoral vote Dole
Nebraska	236,761	363,467	71,278	-	5
Nevada	203,974	199,244	43,986	4	-
New Hampshire	246,214	196,532	48,390	4	-
New Jersey	1,652,329	1,103,078	262,134	15	-
New Mexico	273,495	232,751	32,257	5	-
New York	3,756,177	1,933,492	503,458	33	-
North Carolina	1,107,849	1,225,938	168,059	-	14
North Dakota	106,905	125,050	32,515	-	3
Ohio	2,148,222	1,859,883	483,207	21	-
Oklahoma	488,105	582,315	130,788	-	8
Oregon	649,641	538,152	121,221	7	-
Pennsylvania	2,215,819	1,801,169	430,984	23	-
Rhode Island	233,050	104,683	43,723	4	-
South Carolina	506,283	573,458	64,386	-	8
South Dakota	139,333	150,543	31,250	-	3
Tennessee	909,146	863,530	105,918	11	-
Texas	2,459,683	2,736,167	378,537	-	32
Utah	221,633	361,911	66,461	-	5
Vermont	137,894	80,352	31,024	3	-
Virginia	1,091,060	1,138,350	159,861	-	13
Washington	1,123,323	840,712	201,003	11	-
West Virginia	327,812	233,946	71,639	5	-
Wisconsin	1,071,971	845,029	227,339	11	-
Wyoming	77,934	105,388	25,928	-	3
Total	47,402,357	39,198,755	8,085,402	379	159
	49.24%	40.71%	8.40%	Total electoral vote = 538 Total electoral vote needed to win = 270	

Source: Federal Election Commission and State Elections Offices

National Voter Turnout in Federal Elections

Year	Voting age population	Registration	Turnout	% Turnout of voting age population
1968	120,328,186	81,658,180	73,211,875	60.84%
1970	124,498,000	82,496,747*	58,014,338	46.60
1972	140,776,000	97,328,541	77,718,554	55.21
1974	146,336,000	96,199,020**	55,943,834	38.23
1976	152,309,190	105,037,986	81,555,789	53.55
1978	158,373,000	103,291,265	58,917,938	37.21
1980	164,597,000	113,043,734	86,515,221	52.56
1982	169,938,000	110,671,225	67,615,576	39.79
1984	174,466,000	124,150,614	92,652,680	53.11
1986	178,566,000	118,399,984	64,991,128	36.40
1988	182,778,000	126,379,628	91,594,693	50.11
1990	185,812,000	121,105,630	67,859,189	36.52
1992	189,529,000	133,821,178	104,405,155	55.09
1994	193,650,000	130,292,822	75,105,860	38.78
1996	196,511,000	146,211,960	96,456,345	49.08

*Registrations from Iowa and Missouri not included.
**Registrations from Iowa not included.
Source: Federal Election Commission

Voter Registration and Turnout - 1996

State	1996 voting age population	1996 registered voters	% REG of VAP	Turnout	% T/O of VAP
Alabama	3,220,000	2,470,766	76.73	1,534,349	47.65%
Alaska	425,000	414,815	97.60	241,620	56.85
Arizona	3,145,000	2,244,672	71.37	1,404,405	44.66
Arkansas	1,873,000	1,369,459	73.12	884,262	47.21
California	22,826,000	15,662,075	68.62	10,019,484	43.90
Colorado	2,862,000	2,346,253	81.98	1,510,704	52.78
Connecticut	2,479,000	1,881,323	75.89	1,392,614	56.18
Delaware	548,000	421,710	76.95	270,810	49.42
District of Columbia	422,000	361,419	85.64	185,726	44.01
Florida	11,043,000	8,077,877	73.15	5,300,927	48.00
Georgia	5,418,000	3,811,284	70.34	2,298,899	42.43
Hawaii	890,000	544,916	61.23	360,120	40.46
Idaho	858,000	700,430	81.64	489,481	57.05
Illinois	8,754,000	6,663,301	76.12	4,311,391	49.25
Indiana	4,374,000	3,488,088	79.75	2,135,431	48.82
Iowa	2,138,000	1,776,433	83.09	1,234,075	57.72
Kansas	1,897,000	1,436,418	75.72	1,063,452	56.06
Kentucky	2,928,000	2,396,086	81.83	1,387,999	47.40
Louisiana	3,131,000	2,559,352	81.74	1,783,959	56.98
Maine	945,000	1,001,292*	105.96	679,499	71.90
Maryland	3,820,000	2,587,978	67.75	1,780,870	46.62
Massachusetts	4,649,000	3,459,193	74.41	2,556,459	54.99
Michigan	7,072,000	6,677,079	94.42	3,848,844	54.42
Minnesota	3,422,000	3,067,802	89.65	2,192,640	64.07
Mississippi	1,967,000	1,715,913	87.24	893,857	45.44
Missouri	3,995,000	3,342,849	83.68	2,158,065	54.02
Montana	656,000	590,751	90.05	407,083	62.06
Nebraska	1,211,000	1,015,056	83.82	677,415	55.94
Nevada	1,212,000	778,092	64.20	464,279	38.31
New Hampshire	871,000	754,771	86.66	499,053	57.30
New Jersey	6,034,000	4,320,866	71.61	3,075,860	50.98
New Mexico	1,224,000	851,479	69.57	556,074	45.43
New York	13,564,000	10,162,156	74.92	6,439,129	47.47
North Carolina	5,519,000	4,318,008	78.24	2,515,807	45.58
North Dakota	476,000	N/A	N/A	266,411	55.97
Ohio	8,347,000	6,879,687	82.42	4,534,434	54.32
Oklahoma	2,426,000	1,979,017	81.58	1,206,713	49.74
Oregon	2,411,000	1,962,155	81.38	1,377,760	57.14
Pennsylvania	9,197,000	6,805,612	74.00	4,506,118	49.00
Rhode Island	751,000	602,692	80.25	390,247	51.96
South Carolina	2,771,000	1,814,777	65.49	1,151,689	41.56
South Dakota	535,000	459,971	85.98	323,826	60.53
Tennessee	4,035,000	2,849,910	70.63	1,894,105	46.94
Texas	13,597,000	10,540,678	77.52	5,611,644	41.27
Utah	1,333,000	1,050,452	78.80	665,629	49.93
Vermont	445,000	385,328	86.59	258,449	58.08
Virginia	5,083,000	3,322,135	65.36	2,416,642	47.54
Washington	4,115,000	3,078,128	74.80	2,253,837	54.77
West Virginia	1,417,000	970,745	68.51	636,459	44.92
Wisconsin	3,824,000	N/A	NA	2,196,169	57.43
Wyoming	356,000	240,711	67.62	211,571	59.43
United States	196,511,000	146,211,960	74.40%	96,456,345	49.08%

*Maine's system of election-day registration results in over-representation of registered voters.
Source: Federal Election Commission

The Electoral College

The Electoral College was established by the founding fathers as a compromise between election of the president by Congress and election by popular vote. The electors are a popularly elected body chosen by the states and the District of Columbia on the Tuesday after the first Monday in November. The Electoral College consists of 538 electors (one for each of 435 members of the House of Representatives and 100 Senators; and 3 for the District of Columbia by virtue of the 23rd Amendment). Each state's allotment of electors is equal to the number of House members to which it is entitled plus two Senators. The decennial census is used to reapportion the number of electors allocated among the states.

The electors meet in each state on the first Monday after the second Wednesday in December. A majority of 270 electoral votes is required to elect the President and Vice President. No constitutional provision or federal law requires electors to vote in accordance with the popular vote in their state. But some state laws require electors to cast their votes according to the popular vote.

Source: Office of the Federal Register

States and Electoral College Votes
(Total: 538; Majority Needed to Elect: 270)

Alabama - 9	Montana - 3	Illinois - 22	Rhode Island - 4
Alaska - 3	Nebraska - 5	Indiana - 12	South Carolina - 8
Arizona - 8	Nevada - 4	Iowa - 7	South Dakota - 3
Arkansas - 6	New Hampshire - 4	Kansas - 6	Tennessee - 11
California - 54	New Jersey - 15	Kentucky - 8	Texas - 32
Colorado - 8	New Mexico - 5	Louisiana - 9	Utah - 5
Connecticut - 8	New York - 33	Maine - 4	Vermont - 3
Delaware - 3	North Carolina - 14	Maryland - 10	Virginia - 13
District of Columbia - 3	North Dakota - 3	Massachusetts - 12	Washington - 11
Florida - 25	Ohio - 21	Michigan - 18	West Virginia - 5
Georgia - 13	Oklahoma - 8	Minnesota - 10	Wisconsin - 11
Hawaii - 4	Oregon - 7	Mississippi - 7	Wyoming - 3
Idaho - 4	Pennsylvania - 23	Missouri - 11	

Source: Office of the Federal Register

"Soft Money" Surge

Political Party Fund Raising

	1996	1994	1992
Democratic National Committee			
Receipts	$101,905,186	$43,923,516	$31,356,076
Disbursements	$100,483,977	$45,097,098	$28,388,869
Cash on Hand	$2,007,133	$583,780	$3,302,031
Democratic Senatorial Campaign Committee			
Receipts	$14,176,392	$372,448	$566,111
Disbursements	$14,061,273	$416,743	$506,362
Cash on Hand	$169,327	$74,495	$81,191
Democratic Congressional Campaign Committee			
Receipts	$12,340,824	$5,113,343	$4,368,980
Disbursements	$11,822,790	$5,135,552	$4,017,579
Cash on Hand	$892,164	$418,667	$453,107
Total Democratic			
Receipts	$123,877,924	$49,143,460	$36,256,667
Disbursements	$121,826,562	$50,383,546	$32,878,310
Cash on Hand	$3,068,624	$1,076,942	$3,836,329
Republican National Committee			
Receipts	$113,127,010	$44,870,758	$35,936,945
Disbursements	$114,401,973	$42,413,166	$33,601,431
Cash on Hand	$1,734,081	$3,468,421	$2,766,439
National Republican Senatorial Committee			
Receipts	$29,395,329	$5,582,013	$9,064,167
Disbursements	$29,362,653	$6,527,505	$7,655,641
Cash on Hand	$299,577	$185,845	$1,408,772
National Republican Congressional Committee			
Receipts	$18,530,773	$7,371,097	$6,076,321
Disbursements	$28,746,879	$4,747,525	$6,209,404
Cash on Hand			
Total Republican			
Receipts	$138,199,706	$52,522,763	$49,787,433
Disbursements	$149,658,099	$48,387,091	$46,176,476
Cash on Hand	$2,033,658	$3,654,266	$4,175,211

Note: Totals do not include transfers among the committees.
Source: Federal Election Commission

Biggest Soft Money Donors to Democratic National Party Committees
January 1, 1995 – December 31, 1996

Donor	Soft Money
Communications Workers Of America	$1,128,425
American Federation of State, County & Municipal Employees	1,091,050
Walt Disney	997,050
Joseph E. Seagram & Sons	945,700
United Food & Commercial Workers	714,050
Revlon/MacAndrews & Forbes Holding	673,250
Lazard Freres	617,000
Laborers' Intl Union of North America	610,400
Loral	606,500
MCI Telecommunications	593,603
Association of Trial Lawyers of America	581,300
Integrated Health Services	578,342
Federal Express	577,625
DreamWorks	530,000
Milberg Weiss Bershad Hynes & Lerach	530,000
Arnold Hiatt, Chairman and CEO, Stride-Rite Footwear	500,000
Atlantic Richfield (ARCO)	486,372
Philip Morris	481,518
Time Warner	462,918
American Federation of Teachers	454,400
AFL-CIO	454,135
Goldman Sachs	452,500
AT&T	421,980
National Education Association	408,742
Connell Rice & Sugar	407,000

Biggest Soft Money Donors to Republican National Party Committees
January 1, 1995 – December 31, 1996

Donor	Soft Money
Philip Morris	$2,518,518
RJR Nabisco	1,188,175
American Financial Group	794,000
Atlantic Richfield (ARCO)	766,506
News Corp.	744,700
Union Pacific/Southern Pacific	692,460
Joseph E. Seagram & Sons	685,145
Brown & Williamson Tobacco	635,000
Mariam Cannon Hayes, Concord, NC	600,000
U.S. Tobacco	559,253
AT&T	546,440
Enron	530,690
Eli Lilly	506,825
Larry Fisher/Plaza Cleaning Service	475,000
Glaxo Wellcome	467,245,
Tele-Communications	433,950
Blue Cross & Blue Shield	426,348
Chevron	426,006
Tobacco Institute	424,850
Bristol-Myers Squibb	421,785
NYNEX	415,705
Revlon Group/MacAndrews & Forbes	415,000
Pfizer	409,175
Amway	406,000
Alfa Mutual Insurance	405,000

Source: Common Cause

1996 Presidential Campaign Contributions

Contributions to the Clinton Campaign, by Supporters' Industries/Interest Groups

Lawyers/Law Firms	$3,883,202
Retirees	1,256,840
Real Estate	721,200
Business Services	665,300
Civil Servants/Public Officials	639,470
Securities & Investment	579,941
Health Professionals	567,991
Education	450,510
Media/Entertainment	442,075
Accountants	299,525
Misc. Manufacturing & Distributing	252,600
Lobbyists/Public Relations	233,950
Insurance	228,450
Printing & Publishing	220,331
Misc. Finance	205,945

Contributions to the Dole Campaign, by Supporters' Industries/Interest Groups

Retirees	$1,602,406
Lawyers/Law Firms	1,521,129
Securities & Investment	981,590
Real Estate	668,077
Insurance	606,405
Business Services	590,266
Oil & Gas	541,840
Health Professionals	498,170
Misc. Manufacturing & Distributing	477,060
Misc. Finance	360,300
Accountants	345,352
Lobbyists/Public Relations	306,589
General Contractors	300,760
Commercial Banks	292,822
Automotive	266,205

Top Contributors to Bill Cinton*

Ernst & Young	$135,750
Government of Guam	51,800
U.S. Dept of Agriculture	39,010
Goldman, Sachs & Co.	35,884
Skadden, Arps	32,250
AT&T	31,225
Bear, Stearns & Co.	27,550
Merrill Lynch	27,150
US Sprint	25,500
Jenner & Block	24,650
Time Warner	24,000
Raytheon Co.	23,000
U.S. Dept. of State	22,650
Arnold & Porter	22,300
Future Tech International	22,000
Walt Disney Co.	21,950
Entergy Corp.	21,250
Smith Barney	21,250
U.S. Dept. of Justice	20,600
Holland & Knight	20,550

Top Contributors to Bob Dole**

Ernst & Young	$107,650
Enron Corp.	72,250
Enterprise Rent-a-Car	66,000
PaineWebber	57,340
Goldman, Sachs & Co.	49,000
CSX Corp.	46,100
Price Waterhouse	46,000
Marriott Corp.	45,750
Smith Barney	44,750
Massachusetts Mutual Life Insurance	44,275
Bear, Stearns & Co.	43,250
Union Pacific Railroad	42,202
Mirage Resorts	40,000
Koch Industries	39,700
Arthur Andersen & Co.	39,500
Merrill Lynch	36,300
Skadden, Arps	35,300
U.S. Tobacco Co.	34,250
CS First Boston	32,300
Treasure Island Casino	31,050

*The list above identifies the top financial supporters of the Clinton campaign, based on donations given by company officers or employees and their families through June 30, 1996. The listing does not imply direct contributions by the companies listed, as such contributions are prohibited under federal law.
**The list above identifies the top financial supporters of the Dole campaign, based on PAC contributions and donations given by company officers or employees and their families through June 30, 1996. The listing does not imply direct contributions by the companies listed, as such contributions are prohibited under federal law.
Source: Center for Responsive Politics

Congressional Campaign Finances

Congressional candidates raised $790.5 million and spent $765.3 million in the 1995-96 election cycle, representing increases of 7% in receipts and 5% in expenditures from the record-breaking 1993-94 election cycle, and 20% and 12% over the previous Presidential cycle of 1991-92.

Financial Activity-All Congressional Campaigns (Millions of dollars)

	1981-82	1983-84	1985-86	1987-88	1989-90	1991-92	1993-94	1995-96
Raised	$354.7	$397.2	$472.0	$477.6	$471.7	$659.3	$740.5	$790.5
Spent	$342.4	$374.1	$450.9	$459.0	$446.3	$680.2	$725.2	$765.3
No. of Candidates	2240	2036	1873	1792	1759	2950	2376	2605

Top 10 Senate 1995-96 Receipts

Candidate	State	Party	Net receipts	Candidate	State	Party	Net receipts
1 Mark R. Warner	VA	D L	$11,625,483	6 Harvey Bernard Gantt	NC	D L	$8,128,548
2 John F. Kerry	MA	D W	10,342,115	7 William F. Weld	MA	R L	8,074,417
3 Guy W. Millner	GA	R L	9,917,102	8 Jesse A. Helms	NC	R W	7,808,820
4 Robert G. Torricelli	NJ	D W	9,211,508	9 Carl Levin	MI	D W	6,021,723
5 Dick Zimmer	NJ	R L	8,212,612	10 Paul David Wellstone	MN	DFL* W	5,991,013

Top 10 Senate Contributions From Individuals, 1995-96

Candidate	State	Party	Individual contributions	Candidate	State	Party	Individual contributions
1 John F. Kerry	MA	D W	$7,843,781	6 Dick Zimmer	NJ	R L	$5,525,662
2 Harvey Bernard Gantt	NC	D L	7,619,519	7 Paul David Wellstone	MN	DFL* W	5,288,600
3 William F. Weld	MA	R L	7,062,001	8 Carl Levin	MI	D W	4,937,261
4 Jesse A. Helms	NC	R W	6,614,683	9 Richard J. Durbin	IL	D W	3,394,275
5 Robert G. Torricelli	NJ	D W	6,112,877	10 Tom Harkin	IA	D W	3,390,007

Top 10 Senate Contributions From PACs, 1995-96

Candidate	State	Party	PAC contributions	Candidate	State	Party	PAC contributions
1 John William Warner III	VA	R W	$1,601,460	6 Theodore F. (Ted) Stevens	AK	R W	$1,203,797
2 Larry Pressler	SD	R L	1,513,835	7 Dick Zimmer	NJ	R L	1,197,917
3 Max S. Baucus	MT	D W	1,352,466	8 Pete V. Domenici	NM	R W	1,154,329
4 Mitch McConnell	KY	R W	1,293,151	9 Richard J. Durbin	IL	D W	1,153,210
5 Pat Roberts	KS	R W	1,216,831	10 James M. Inhofe	OK	R W	1,117,944

Top 10 Senate Disbursements, 1995-96

Candidate	State	Party	Net disbursements	Candidate	State	Party	Net disbursements
1 Mark R. Warner	VA	D L	$11,600,424	6 Harvey Bernard Gantt	NC	D L	$8,012,980
2 John F. Kerry	MA	D W	10,962,607	7 William F. Weld	MA	R L	8,002,123
3 Guy W. Millner	GA	R L	9,858,955	8 Jesse A. Helms	NC	R W	7,798,520
4 Robert G. Torricelli	NJ	D W	9,134,854	9 Phil Gramm	TX	R W	6,289,591
5 Dick Zimmer	NJ	R L	8,238,181	10 Paul David Wellstone	MN	DFL* W	5,979,224

*Democrat/Farmer/Labor

Top 10 House Receipts, 1995-96

	Candidate	State	Party	Net receipts		Candidate	State	Party	Net receipts
1	Newton Leroy Gingrich	GA	R W	$6,252,069	6	Joseph P. Kennedy II	MA	D W	$2,414,369
2	Michael J. Coles	GA	D L	3,327,354	7	Victor H. Fazio	CA	D W	2,412,373
3	Charles E. Schumer	NY	D W	3,318,153	8	John Greg Ganske	IA	R W	2,337,935
4	Richard Andrew Gephardt	MO	D W	3,309,642	9	John Eric Ensign	NV	R W	1,989,386
5	Ellen O. Tauscher	CA	D W	2,573,780	10	Jonas Martin Frost III	TX	D W	1,964,330

Top 10 House Contributions From Individuals, 1995-96

	Candidate	State	Party	Individual contributions		Candidate	State	Party	Individual contributions
1	Newton Leroy Gingrich	GA	R W	$5,094,260	6	Thomas J. Campbell	CA	R W	$1,262,932
2	Charles E. Schumer	NY	D W	2,672,010	7	Steve Stockman	TX	R L	1,251,102
3	Joseph P. Kennedy II	MA	D W	2,040,525	8	Richard Andrew Gephardt	MO	D W	1,220,900
4	Ronald E. Paul	TX	R W	1,774,209	9	Martin Rossiter Hoke	OH	R L	1,202,660
5	John R. Kasich	OH	R W	1,388,377	10	William V. Hilleary	TN	R W	1,197,858

Top 10 House Contributions From PACs, 1995-96

	Candidate	State	Party	PAC contributions		Candidate	State	Party	PAC contributions
1	Victor H. Fazio	CA	D W	$1,348,260	6	Kenneth E. Bentsen Jr.	TX	D W	$910,734
2	Richard Andrew Gephardt	MO	D W	1,169,422	7	John D. Dingell	MI	D W	879,060
3	Jonas Martin Frost III	TX	D W	1,112,737	8	David Edward Bonior	MI	D W	862,148
4	Newton Leroy Gingrich	GA	R W	1,098,746	9	Barton Jennings Gordon	TN	D W	742,511
5	Thomas Dale Delay	TX	R W	1,066,875	10	Charles B. Rangel	NY	D W	711,089

Top 10 House Disbursements, 1995-96

	Candidate	State	Party	Net disbursements		Candidate	State	Party	Net disbursements
1	Newton Leroy Gingrich	GA	R W	$5,577,715	6	Victor H. Fazio	CA	D W	$2,320,330
2	Michael J. Coles	GA	D L	3,325,030	7	Jonas Martin Frost III	TX	D W	1,963,529
3	Richard Andrew Gephardt	MO	D W	3,110,509	8	Joseph P. Kennedy II	MA	D W	1,952,906
4	Ellen O. Tauscher	CA	D W	2,571,595	9	Ronald E. Paul	TX	R W	1,927,756
5	John Greg Ganske	IA	R W	2,334,251	10	John Eric Ensign	NV	R W	1,904,413

Source: Federal Election Commission

Growth of Political Action Committee Campaign Contributions

Committee type	Number of committees	Contributions to candidates
Corporate		
1985-86	1,906	$ 49,566,619
1987-88	2,008	56,155,259
1989-90	1,972	58,131,722
1991-92	1,930	68,430,976
1993-94	1,875	69,610,433
1995-96	1,836	78,194,723
Labor		
1985-86	417	31,038,885
1987-88	401	35,495,780
1989-90	372	34,732,029
1991-92	372	41,357,222
1993-94	371	41,867,393
1995-96	358	47,980,492
Non-connected		
1985-86	1,270	19,410,358
1987-88	1,345	20,330,050
1989-90	1,321	15,070,009
1991-92	1,376	18,326,404
1993-94	1,318	18,201,369
1995-96	1,259	23,960,110

Trade/Membership/Health		
1985-86	789	34,551,531
1987-88	848	41,213,596
1989-90	801	44,804,886
1991-92	835	53,870,702
1993-94	852	52,853,630
1995-96	896	60,153,725
Cooperative		
1985-86	57	2,671,545
1987-88	61	2,736,132
1989-90	60	2,950,960
1991-92	61	2,961,140
1993-94	56	3,035,003
1995-96	45	3,006,471
Corporations without Stock		
1985-86	157	2,600,780
1987-88	169	3,312,424
1989-90	151	3,431,890
1991-92	153	3,981,324
1993-94	149	4,063,291
1995-96	134	4,535,098
Total		
1985-86	4,596	139,839,718
1987-88	4,832	159,243,241
1989-90	4,677	159,121,496
1991-92	4,727	188,927,768
1993-94	4,621	189,631,119
1995-96	4,528	217,830,619

Source: Federal Election Commission

Top 10 Corporate PACs, 1995-96

Rank	Name	Contributions to candidates
1	United Parcel Service of America Inc Political Committee	$ 1,788,147
2	American Telephone & Telegraph Company Political Action Committee	1,244,134
3	Lockheed Martin Employees Political Action Committee	1,026,250
4	Federal Express Corporation Political Action Committee	948,000
5	Philip Morris Companies Inc Political Action Committee	850,119
6	Union Pacific Fund for Effective Government	797,357
7	Employees of Northrop Grumman Corporation Political Action Committee	698,175
8	Tenneco Inc. Employees Good Government Fund	658,725
9	RJR Political Action Committee RJR Nabisco Inc	652,150
10	Team Ameritech Political Action Committee	642,285

Top 10 Labor PACs, 1995-96

Rank	Name	Contributions to candidates
1	Democratic Republican Independent Voter Education Committee	$ 2,611,140
2	American Federation of State County & Municipal Employees-People, Qualified	2,505,021
3	UAW-V-CAP (UAW Voluntary Community Action Program)	2,467,319
4	National Education Association Political Action Committee	2,326,830
5	International Brotherhood of Electrical Workers Committee on Political Education	2,080,587
6	Active Ballot Club, A Dept of United Food & Commercial Workers Int'l Union	2,030,795
7	Machinists Non-Partisan Political League	1,999,675
8	Laborers' Political League	1,933,300
9	Committee on Letter Carriers Political Education (Letter Carriers Political Action Fund)	1,715,064
10	American Federation of Teachers Committee on Political Education	1,614,833

Top 10 Non-Connected PACs, 1995-96

Rank	Name	Contributions to candidates
1	National Committee for an Effective Congress	$ 1,108,110
2	Americans for Free International Trade Political Action Committee Inc	936,800
3	Ernst & Young Political Action Committee	880,615
4	Campaign America	819,681
5	Monday Morning Political Action Committee	771,500
6	Majority Leader's Fund	737,558
7	Deloitte and Touche LLP Federal Political Action Committee	593,402
8	National Political Action Committee	590,000
9	Arthur Andersen PAC (FKA) Arthur Andersen/Andersen Consulting PAC	480,301
10	Effective Government Committee	461,095

Top 10 Trade/Membership/Health PACs 1995-96

Rank	Name	Contributions to candidates
1	Association of Trial Lawyers of America Political Action Committee	$ 2,362,938
2	Dealers Election Action Committee of the National Automobile Dealers Association	2,351,925
3	American Medical Association Political Action Committee	2,319,197
4	Realtors Political Action Committee	2,099,683
5	American Institute of Certified Public Accountants Effective Legislation Committee	1,690,925
6	NRA Political Victory Fund	1,565,821
7	Build Political Action Committee of the National Association of Home Builders	1,472,849
8	National Association of Life Underwriters Political Action Committee	1,426,750
9	Nationl Beer Wholesalers' Association Political Action Committee	1,324,992
10	American Bankers Association BankPAC	1,298,850

Source: Federal Election Commission

Annual Salaries of U.S. Government Officials

- The President's salary is $200,000 per year plus expense allowance.
- The Vice President receives a salary of $171,500.
- The Chief Justice of the Supreme Court receives $171,500. The associate justices earn $164,100.

- Cabinet-level officials receive $148,400.
- The Speaker of the House of Representatives receives $171,500. The President Pro Tempore of the Senate earns $148,400. The Majority and Minority Leaders of the House and Senate each receive $148,400. Other Senators and Representatives have a yearly salary of $133,600.

THE EXECUTIVE BRANCH

As required by the U.S. Constitution, the President must be a natural-born citizen and at least 35 years old. The President can serve no more than two four-year terms.

The President of the United States: Bill Clinton of Arkansas, born August 19, 1946.
The Vice President of the United States: Al Gore of Tennessee, born March 31, 1948.

Presidential Staff

COUNSELOR TO THE PRESIDENT AND SPECIAL ENVOY FOR THE AMERICAS: Thomas F. "Mack" McLarty
CHIEF OF STAFF: Erskine Bowles
DEPUTY CHIEF OF STAFF: John Podesta
DEPUTY CHIEF OF STAFF: Sylvia Mathews
COUNSELOR TO THE PRESIDENT: Douglas Sosnik
COUNSEL TO THE PRESIDENT: Charles Ruff
SENIOR ADVISER FOR POLICY DEVELOPMENT: Ira Magaziner
ASSISTANT TO THE PRESIDENT FOR POLICY DEVELOPMENT, DIRECTOR OF DOMESTIC POLICY COUNCIL: Bruce Reed
NATIONAL SECURITY ADVISER: Samuel Berger
ASSISTANT TO THE PRESIDENT FOR ECONOMIC POLICY, DIRECTOR OF NATIONAL ECONOMIC COUNCIL: Gene Sperling
PRESS SECRETARY: Michael McCurry
ASSISTANT TO THE PRESIDENT, COORDINATOR OF STRATEGIC PLANNING: Sidney Blumenthal
ASSISTANT TO THE PRESIDENT, DIRECTOR OF COMMUNICATIONS: Ann Lewis
ASSISTANT TO THE PRESIDENT, LEGISLATIVE AFFAIRS: John Hilley
ASSISTANT TO THE PRESIDENT, MANAGEMENT AND ADMIN- ISTRATION: Virginia Apuzzo
ASSISTANT TO THE PRESIDENT, DIRECTOR OF POLITICAL AFFAIRS: Craig T. Smith
ASSISTANT TO THE PRESIDENT, DIRECTOR OF PRESIDENTIAL PERSONNEL: Bob Nash
ASSISTANT TO THE PRESIDENT, DIRECTOR OF PUBLIC LIAISON: Maria Echaveste
ASSISTANT TO THE PRESIDENT, STAFF SECRETARY: Todd Stern

Executive Agencies

COUNCIL OF ECONOMIC ADVISERS: Janet L. Yellen, chair
COUNCIL OF ENVIRONMENTAL QUALITY: Kathleen McGinty, chair
OFFICE OF ADMINISTRATION: Ada Posey, acting director
OFFICE OF MANAGEMENT AND BUDGET: Franklin D. Raines, director
OFFICE OF NATIONAL DRUG CONTROL POLICY: Barry R. McCaffrey, director
OFFICE OF SCIENCE AND TECHNOLOGY POLICY: John H. Gibbons, director
OFFICE FOR WOMEN'S INITIATIVES AND OUTREACH: Cheri Carter, acting director
FOREIGN INTELIGENCE ADVISORY BOARD: Thomas Foley, chairman
U.S. TRADE REPRESENTATIVE: Charlene Barshefsky

The Cabinet

DEPARTMENT OF AGRICULTURE
Secretary—Dan Glickman
DEPARTMENT OF COMMERCE
Secretary—William Daley
DEPARTMENT OF DEFENSE
Secretary—William Cohen
DEPARTMENT OF EDUCATION
Secretary—Richard Riley
DEPARTMENT OF ENERGY
Secretary—Federico Peña
DEPARTMENT OF HEALTH AND HUMAN SERVICES
Secretary—Donna Shalala

DEPARTMENT OF HOUSING AND URBAN DEVELOPMENT
Secretary—Andrew M. Cuomo
DEPARTMENT OF INTERIOR
Secretary—Bruce Babbitt
DEPARTMENT OF JUSTICE
Attorney General—Janet Reno
DEPARTMENT OF LABOR
Secretary—Alexis Herman

DEPARTMENT OF STATE
Secretary—Madeleine Albright
DEPARTMENT OF TRANSPORTATION
Secretary—Rodney Slater
DEPARTMENT OF THE TREASURY
Secretary—Robert Rubin
DEPARTMENT OF VETERANS' AFFAIRS
Secretary—Hershel Gober (acting)

Heads of Selected U.S. Government Agencies

BUREAU OF ALCOHOL, TOBACCO, AND FIREARMS—John Magaw
BUREAU OF ENGRAVING AND PRINTING—Larry E. Rolufs
CENSUS BUREAU—Martha Farnsworth Riche
CENTERS FOR DISEASE CONTROL AND PREVENTION—David Satcher
CENTRAL INTELLIGENCE AGENCY—George Tenet
COMMODITY FUTURES TRADING COMMISSION—Brooksley Born
CONSUMER PRODUCT SAFETY COMMISSION—Ann Brown
CORPORATION FOR PUBLIC BROADCASTING—No current president; Chief Operating Officer and Executive Vice President, Robert T. Coonrod
DRUG ENFORCEMENT ADMINISTRATION—Thomas Constantine
ENVIRONMENTAL PROTECTION AGENCY—Carol Browner
EQUAL EMPLOYMENT OPPORTUNITY COMMISSION—Gilbert Casellas
EXPORT-IMPORT BANK OF THE UNITED STATES—James A. Harman
FARM CREDIT ADMINISTRATION—Marsha Pyle Martin
FEDERAL AVIATION ADMINISTRATION—Jane Garvey
FEDERAL BUREAU OF INVESTIGATION—Louis Freeh
FEDERAL COMMUNICATIONS COMMISSION—William Kennard (subject to Senate confirmation)
FEDERAL DEPOSIT INSURANCE CORPORATION—Andrew C. Hove, Jr.
FEDERAL ELECTION COMMISSION—John Warren McGarry
FEDERAL EMERGENCY MANAGEMENT AGENCY—James L. Witt
FEDERAL ENERGY REGULATORY COMMISSION SERVICE—James Hoecker
FEDERAL MEDIATION AND CONCILIATION SERVICE—John Calhoun Wells
FEDERAL RESERVE SYSTEM—Alan Greenspan
FEDERAL TRADE COMMISSION—Robert Pitofsky

FOOD AND DRUG ADMINISTRATION—Michael Friedman (lead deputy commissioner)
GENERAL ACCOUNTING OFFICE—James F. Hinchman (acting)
GENERAL SERVICES ADMINISTRATION—David J. Barram
GOVERNMENT PRINTING OFFICE—Michael DiMario
IMMIGRATION AND NATURALIZATION SERVICE—Doris Meissner
INTERNAL REVENUE SERVICE—Michael P. Dolan, acting commissioner
INTERNATIONAL TRADE COMMISSION—Marcia Miller
NATIONAL AERONAUTICS AND SPACE ADMINISTRATION—Daniel Goldin
NATIONAL ENDOWMENT FOR THE ARTS—Scott Shanklin-Peterson (deputy chairman)
NATIONAL HIGHWAY TRAFFIC SAFETY ADMINISTRATION—Dr. Ricardo Martinez
NATIONAL INSTITUTE OF MENTAL HEALTH—Steven Hyman
NATIONAL INSTITUTE OF STANDARDS AND TECHNOLOGY—Robert Hebner (acting)
NATIONAL INSTITUTES OF HEALTH—Dr. Harold Varmus, M.D.
NATIONAL LABOR RELATIONS BOARD—William B. Gould
NATIONAL PARK SERVICE—Robert G. Stanton
NATIONAL TRANSPORTATION SAFETY BOARD—James Hall
NUCLEAR REGULATORY COMMISSION—Shirley Ann Jackson
OCCUPATIONAL SAFETY AND HEALTH ADMINISTRATION—Greg Watchman (acting assistant secretary)
PATENT AND TRADEMARK OFFICE—Bruce Lehman
PEACE CORPS—Mark Gearan
POSTAL SERVICE—Marvin Runyon
SECURITIES AND EXCHANGE COMMISSION—Arthur Levitt
SMALL BUSINESS ADMINISTRATION—Aida Alvarez
SMITHSONIAN INSTITUTION—I. Michael Heyman
SOCIAL SECURITY ADMINISTRATION—Kenneth S. Apfel
SURGEON GENERAL—J. Jarrett Clinton (acting)
U.S. FISH AND WILDLIFE SERVICE—Jamie Rappaport Clark
U.S. FOREST SERVICE—Michael Dombeck

U.S. Presidents and Vice Presidents

	President	Party	Vice President	Years served
1	George Washington	Federalist	John Adams	1789–1797
2	John Adams	Federalist	Thomas Jefferson	1797–1801
3	Thomas Jefferson	Dem.-Rep.	Aaron Burr (1801–1805)	1801–1809
			George Clinton	
4	James Madison	Dem.-Rep.	George Clinton (died 1812)	1809–1817
			Elbridge Gerry (died 1814)	
5	James Monroe	Dem.-Rep.	Daniel D. Tompkins	1817–1825
6	John Quincy Adams	Dem.-Rep.	John C. Calhoun	1825–1829
7	Andrew Jackson	Democratic	John C. Calhoun (resigned 1832)	1829–1837
			Martin Van Buren	
8	Martin Van Buren	Democratic	Richard M. Johnson	1837–1841
9	William Henry Harrison*	Whig	John Tyler	1841
10	John Tyler	Whig	vacant	1841–1845
11	James Knox Polk	Democratic	George M. Dallas	1845–1849
12	Zachary Taylor*	Whig	Millard Fillmore	1849–1850
13	Millard Fillmore	Whig	vacant	1850–1853
14	Franklin Pierce	Democratic	William R. King (died 1853)	1853–1857
15	James Buchanan	Democratic	John C. Breckinridge	1857–1861
16	Abraham Lincoln**	Republican	Hannibal Hamlin (1861–1865)	1861–1865
			Andrew Johnson (1865)	
17	Andrew Johnson	Democratic	vacant	1865–1869
18	Ulysses Simpson Grant	Republican	Schuyler Colfax (1869–1873)	1869–1877
			Henry Wilson (died 1875)	
19	Rutherford Birchard Hayes	Republican	William A. Wheeler	1877–1881
20	James Abram Garfield**	Republican	Chester Alan Arthur	1881
21	Chester Alan Arthur	Republican	vacant	1881–1885
22	Grover Cleveland	Democratic	Thomas A. Hendricks (died 1885)	1885–1889
23	Benjamin Harrison	Republican	Levi P. Morton	1889–1893
24	Grover Cleveland	Democratic	Adlai E. Stevenson	1893–1897
25	William McKinley**	Republican	Garret A. Hobart (died 1899)	1897–1901
			Theodore Roosevelt	
26	Theodore Roosevelt	Republican	Charles W. Fairbanks (1905–1909)	1901–1909
27	William Howard Taft	Republican	James S. Sherman (died 1912)	1909–1913
28	Woodrow Wilson	Democratic	Thomas R. Marshall	1913–1921
29	Warren Gamaliel Harding*	Republican	Calvin Coolidge	1921–1923
30	Calvin Coolidge	Republican	Charles G. Dawes (1925–1929)	1923–1929
31	Herbert Clark Hoover	Republican	Charles Curtis	1929–1933
32	Franklin Delano Roosevelt*	Democratic	John N. Garner (1933–1941)	1933–1945
			Henry A. Wallace (1941–1945)	
			Harry S Truman	
33	Harry S Truman	Democratic	Alben W. Barkley (1949–1953)	1945–1953
34	Dwight David Eisenhower	Republican	Richard M. Nixon	1953–1961
35	John Fitzgerald Kennedy**	Democratic	Lyndon B. Johnson	1961–1963
36	Lyndon Baines Johnson	Democratic	Hubert H. Humphrey (1965–1969)	1963–1969
37	Richard Mihous Nixon†	Republican	Spiro T. Agnew (resigned 1973)	1969–1974
			Gerald R. Ford	
38	Gerald Rudolph Ford	Republican	Nelson A. Rockefeller	1974–1977
39	James Earl Carter	Democratic	Walter F. Mondale	1977–1981
40	Ronald Reagan	Republican	George Bush	1981–1989
41	George Bush	Republican	Dan Quayle	1989–1993
42	Bill Clinton	Democratic	Al Gore	1993–

*Died in office of natural causes.
**Assassinated.
† Resigned.

THE CONGRESS

The Senate is composed of 100 members—two from each state, irrespective of population or area—elected by the people in conformity with the provisions of the 17th Amendment to the Constitution. That amendment changed the former constitutional method under which senators were chosen by the respective state legislatures. A senator must be at least 30 years of age, have been a citizen of the United States for nine years, and, when elected, be a resident of the state for which the senator is chosen. The term of office is six years, and one-third of the total membership of the Senate is elected every second year.

The House of Representatives includes 435 members elected every two years from among the 50 states, apportioned to their total populations. A representative must be at least 25 years of age, have been a citizen of the United States for seven years, and, when elected, be a resident of the state in which the representative is chosen. In addition to the representatives from each of the states, there is a resident commissioner from the Commonwealth of Puerto Rico, as well as delegates from the District of Columbia, American Samoa, Guam and the Virgin Islands. The resident commissioner and the delegates have most of the prerogatives of representatives, with the important exception of the right to vote on matters before the House.

A Congress lasts for two years, commencing in January of the year following the biennial election of members, and is divided into two sessions. Unlike some other parliamentary bodies, both the Senate and the House have equal legislative functions and powers, except that only the House can initiate revenue bills. The chief function of Congress is the making of laws. In addition, the Senate has the function of advising and consenting to treaties and to certain nominations by the President.

Profile of the 105th Congress

Party Breakdown: 227 Republicans, 207 Democrats, and 1 Independent in the House, and 55 Republicans and 45 Democrats in the Senate.
Age: The average age of senators is 58; the average age of representatives is 52.

Representatives must be at least 25 when they take office. The youngest representative is Harold Ford, (D-TN), who is 26. The oldest representative is Sidney Yates, (D-IL), who is 87.

Senators must be at least 30 when they take office. The youngest senator is Rick Santorum (R-PA), who is 38. The oldest senator is Strom Thurmond (R-SC), who is 94.
Occupations: Law is the dominant profession. Other professions include business, journalism, education, agriculture, law enforcement, and public service. There also are:
- 11 doctors, two veterinarians, two nurses, and two pharmacists;
- 14 governors, a federal judge, a state supreme court justice, and an ambassador;
- CIA agent, CIA analyst, FBI agent, three sheriffs, two police officers, a border patrol chief, and two probation officers;
- Six Peace Corps volunteers and a director of the Peace Corps;
- Two actors, two funeral directors, a florist, a librarian, a wine maker, two auctioneers, a volunteer fireman, an automobile assembly line worker, a river boat captain, a hotel bellhop, a jewelry maker, and a taxicab driver.

Education: There are at least 393 representatives and 93 senators with bachelor degrees, 112 representatives and 17 senators with master degrees, 178 representatives and 53 senators with law degrees, 19 representatives and three senators with doctoral degrees, and 11 representatives and two senators with medical degrees.
Congressional Service: The average length of service of representatives is 8 years, or four terms. Representatives are elected for two-year terms. Rep. John Dingell (D-MI) has the longest consecutive service of any representative in the 105th Congress (41 years).

The average length of service of senators in the 105th Congress is 10 years, slightly less than two terms. Senators are elected for six-year terms. Sen. Strom Thurmond (R-SC) has served longer (41 years) in the Senate than any other member.
Women and Minority Members: There is a record number of women (62): 53 in the House, and nine in the Senate.

The 21 Hispanics also are a record number. All are members of the House.

There are 40 black members, one less than the record number of 41 in the 104th Congress. Thirty-nine blacks serve in the House and one black woman serves in the Senate.

There are seven members of Asian/Pacific Island ethnicity, five in the House and two in the Senate.

Finally, two Senators are Native Americans, one an American Indian and the other, Hawaiian.

Number of Women in the U.S. Congress

CONGRESS	YEARS	TOTAL	HOUSE	SENATE
96th	1979–1981	17	16	1
97th	1981–1983	23	21	2
98th	1983–1985	24	22	2
99th	1985–1987	25	23	2
100th	1987–1989	25	23	2
101st	1989–1991	31	29	2
102nd	1991–1993	33	30	3
103rd	1993–1995	55	48	7
104th	1995–1997	58	49	9
105th	1997–1999	62	53	9

Number of Black Members in the U.S. Congress

CONGRESS	YEARS	TOTAL	HOUSE	SENATE
96th	1979–1981	17	17	0
97th	1981–1983	19	19	0
98th	1983–1985	21	21	0
99th	1985–1987	21	21	0
100th	1987–1989	23	23	0
101st	1989–1991	24	24	0
102d	1991–1993	27	27	0
103d	1993–1995	40	39	1
104th	1995–1997	41	40	1
105th	1997–1999	40	39	1

Source: Congressional Research Service

105th U.S. Congress

Senate Leadership

President—Al Gore
  Vice President of the U.S.
President Pro Tempore—Strom Thurmond (R–SC)
Majority Leader—Trent Lott (R–MS)
Majority Whip—Don Nickles (R–OK)
Minority Leader—Thomas A. Daschle (D–SD)
Minority Whip—Wendell Ford (D–KY)

House of Representatives Leadership

Speaker—Newt Gingrich (R–6th GA)
Majority Leader—Richard Armey (R–26th TX)
Majority Whip—Tom DeLay (R–22nd TX)
Minority Leader—Richard Gephardt (D–3rd MO)
Minority Whip—David E. Bonior (D–10th MI)

Senators*

Alabama
Richard C. Shelby (R) 1998
Jeff Sessions (R) 2002

Alaska
Ted Stevens (R) 2002
Frank H. Murkowski (R) 1998

Arizona
John McCain (R) 1998
Jon L. Kyl (R) 2000

Arkansas
Dale Bumpers (D) 1998
Tim Hutchinson (R) 2002

California
Dianne Feinstein (D) 2000
Barbara Boxer (D) 1998

Colorado
Ben Nighthorse Campbell (R) 1998
Wayne Allard (R) 2002

Connecticut
Christopher J. Dodd (D) 1998
Joseph I. Lieberman (D) 2000

Delaware
William V. Roth, Jr. (R) 2000
Joseph R. Biden, Jr. (D) 2002

Florida
Bob Graham (D) 1998
Connie Mack (R) 2000

Georgia
Paul Coverdell (R) 1998
Max W. Cleland (D) 2002

*Year of next reelection follows name.

Hawaii
Daniel K. Inouye (D) 1998
Daniel K. Akaka (D) 2000

Idaho
Larry E. Craig (R) 2002
Dirk Kempthorne (R) 1998

Illinois
Carol Moseley-Braun (D) 1998
Richard J. Durbin (D) 2002

Indiana
Richard G. Lugar (R) 2000
Dan Coats (R) 1998

Iowa
Charles E. Grassley (R) 1998
Tom Harkin (D) 2002

Kansas
Sam Brownback (R) 1998
Pat Roberts (R) 2002

Kentucky
Wendell H. Ford (D) 1998
Mitch McConnell (R) 2002

Louisiana
John B. Breaux (D) 1998
Mary Landrieu (D) 2002

Maine
Olympia J. Snowe (R) 2000
Susan M. Collins (R) 2002

Maryland
Paul S. Sarbanes (D) 2000
Barbara A. Mikulski (D) 1998

Massachusetts
Edward M. Kennedy (D) 2000
John F. Kerry (D) 2002

Michigan
Carl Levin (D) 2002
Spencer Abraham (R) 2000

Minnesota
Paul David Wellstone (D) 2002
Rod Grams (R) 2000

Mississippi
Thad Cochran (R) 2002
Trent Lott (R) 2000

Missouri
Christopher "Kit" S. Bond (R) 1998
John Ashcroft (R) 2000

Montana
Max Baucus (D) 2002
Conrad Burns (R) 2000

Nebraska
J. Robert Kerrey (D) 2000
Chuck Hagel (R) 2002

Nevada
Harry Reid (D) 1998
Richard H. Bryan (D) 2000

New Hampshire
Robert C. Smith (R) 2002
Judd Gregg (R) 1998

New Jersey
Frank R. Lautenberg (D) 2000
Robert G. Torricelli (D) 2002

New Mexico
Pete V. Domenici (R) 2002
Jeff Bingaman (D) 2000

New York
Daniel Patrick Moynihan (D) 2000
Alfonse M. D'Amato (R) 1998

North Carolina
Jesse Helms (R) 2002
Lauch Faircloth (R) 1998

North Dakota
Kent Conrad (D) 2000
Byron L. Dorgan (D) 1998

Ohio
John Glenn (D) 1998
Mike DeWine (R) 2000

Oklahoma
Don Nickles (R) 1998
James M. Inhofe (R) 2002

Oregon
Ron Wyden (D) 1998
Gordon Smith (R) 2002

Pennsylvania
Arlen Specter (R) 1998
Rick Santorum (R) 2000

Rhode Island
John H. Chafee (R) 2000
Jack Reed (D) 2002

South Carolina
Strom Thurmond (R) 2002
Ernest F. Hollings (D) 1998

South Dakota
Thomas A. Daschle (D) 1998
Tim Johnson (D) 2002

Tennessee
Fred Thompson (R) 2002
Bill Frist (R) 2000

Texas
Phil Gramm (R) 2002
Kay Bailey Hutchison (R) 2000

Utah
Orrin G. Hatch (R) 2000
Robert Bennett (R) 1998

Vermont
Patrick J. Leahy (D) 1998
Jim M. Jeffords (R) 2000

Virginia
John W. Warner (R) 2002
Charles S. Robb (D) 2000

Washington
Slade Gorton (R) 2000
Patty Murray (D) 1998

West Virginia
Robert C. Byrd (D) 2000
John D. Rockefeller IV (D) 2002

Wisconsin
Herbert H. Kohl (D) 2000
Russ Feingold (D) 1998

Wyoming
Craig Thomas (R) 2000
Michael B. Enzi (R) 2002

House Members*

Alabama (5 Rep./2 Dem.)
Sonny Callahan (R–1st)
Terry Everett (R–2nd)
Bob Riley (R–3rd)
Robert B. Aderholt (R–4th)
Robert "Bud" E. Cramer, Jr. (D–5th)
Spencer Bachus (R–6th)
Earl Hilliard (D–7th)

Alaska (1 Rep.)
Don Young (R–At Large)

Arizona (5 Rep./1 Dem.)
Matt Salmon (R–1st)
Ed Pastor (D–2nd)
Bob Stump (R–3rd)
John Shadegg (R–4th)
Jim Kolbe (R–5th)
J.D. Hayworth (R–6th)

Arkansas (2 Rep./2 Dem.)
Marion Berry (D–1st)
Vic Snyder (D–2nd)
Asa Hutchinson (R–3rd)
Jay Dickey (R–4th)

California (23 Rep./29 Dem.)
Frank Riggs (R–1st)
Wally Herger (R–2nd)
Vic Fazio (D–3rd)
John Doolittle (R–4th)
Robert T. Matsui (D–5th)

Lynn Woolsey (D–6th)
George Miller (D–7th)
Nancy Pelosi (D–8th)
Ronald V. Dellums (D–9th)
Ellen Tauscher (D–10th)
Richard Pombo (R–11th)
Tom Lantos (D–12th)
Fortney "Pete" Stark (D–13th)
Anna Eshoo (D–14th)
Tom Campbell (R–15th)
Zoe Lofgren (D–16th)
Sam Farr (D–17th)
Gary Condit (D–18th)
George P. Radanovich (R–19th)
Calvin Dooley (D–20th)
William M. Thomas (R–21st)
Walter H. Capps (D–22nd)
Elton Gallegly (R–23rd)
Brad Sherman (D–24th)
Howard "Buck" McKeon (R–25th)
Howard L. Berman (D–26th)
James E. Rogan (R–27th)
David Dreier (R–28th)
Henry A. Waxman (D–29th)
Xavier Becerra (D–30th)
Matthew G. Martinez (D–31st)
Julian C. Dixon (D–32nd)
Lucille Roybal-Allard (D–33rd)
Esteban Edward Torres (D–34th)
Maxine Waters (D–35th)
Jane Harman (D–36th)
Juanita Millender-McDonald (D–37th)

*All House members will be up for reelection in 1998.

Steve Horn (R–38th)
Edward Royce (R–39th)
Jerry Lewis (R–40th)
Jay Kim (R–41st)
George E. Brown, Jr. (D–42nd)
Ken Calvert (R–43rd)
Sonny Bono (R–44th)
Dana Rohrabacher (R–45th)
Loretta L. Sanchez (D–46th)
Christopher Cox (R–47th)
Ron Packard (R–48th)
Brian Bilbray (R–49th)
Bob Filner (D–50th)
Randy Cunningham (R–51st)
Duncan Hunter (R–52nd)

Colorado (4 Rep./2 Dem.)
Diana L. DeGette (D–1st)
David E. Skaggs (D–2nd)
Scott McInnis (R–3rd)
Bob Schaffer (R–4th)
Joel Hefley (R–5th)
Dan Schaefer (R–6th)

Connecticut (2 Rep./4 Dem.)
Barbara B. Kennelly (D–1st)
Sam Gejdenson (D–2nd)
Rosa DeLauro (D–3rd)
Christopher Shays (R–4th)
James H. Maloney (D–5th)
Nancy L. Johnson (R–6th)

Delaware (1 Rep.)
Michael Castle (R–At Large)

Florida (15 Rep./8 Dem.)
Joe Scarborough (R–1st)
F. Allen Boyd, Jr. (D–2nd)
Corrine Brown (D–3rd)
Tillie Fowler (R–4th)
Karen Thurman (D–5th)
Cliff Stearns (R–6th)
John Mica (R–7th)
Bill McCollum (R–8th)
Michael Bilirakis (R–9th)
C.W. "Bill" Young (R–10th)
Jim Davis (D–11th)
Charles Canady (R–12th)
Dan Miller (R–13th)
Porter J. Goss (R–14th)
David Weldon (R–15th)
Mark Foley (R–16th)
Carrie Meek (D–17th)
Ileana Ros-Lehtinen (R–18th)
Robert I. Wexler (D–19th)
Peter Deutsch (D–20th)
Lincoln Diaz-Balart (R–21st)
E. Clay Shaw, Jr. (R–22nd)
Alcee Hastings (D–23rd)

Georgia (8 Rep./3 Dem.)
Jack Kingston (R–1st)
Sanford Bishop (D–2nd)
Michael "Mac" Collins (R–3rd)
Cynthia McKinney (D–4th)
John Lewis (D–5th)
Newt Gingrich (R–6th)
Bob Barr (R–7th)
Saxby Chambliss (R–8th)
Nathan Deal (R–9th)
Charles Norwood (R–10th)
John Linder (R–11th)

Hawaii (2 Dem.)
Neil Abercrombie (D–1st)
Patsy Mink (D–2nd)

Idaho (2 Rep.)
Helen Chenoweth (R–1st)
Michael Crapo (R–2nd)

Illinois (10 Rep./10 Dem.)
Bobby Rush (D–1st)
Jesse Jackson, Jr. (D–2nd)
William O. Lipinski (D–3rd)
Luis Gutierrez (D–4th)
Rod R. Blagojevich (D–5th)
Henry J. Hyde (R–6th)
Danny Davis (D–7th)
Philip M. Crane (R–8th)
Sidney R. Yates (D–9th)
John Edward Porter (R–10th)
Jerry Weller (R–11th)
Jerry F. Costello (D–12th)
Harris W. Fawell (R–13th)
J. Dennis Hastert (R–14th)
Thomas Ewing (R–15th)
Donald Manzullo (R–16th)
Lane Evans (D–17th)
Ray LaHood (R–18th)
Glenn Poshard (D–19th)
John M. Shimkus (R–20th)

Indiana (6 Rep./4 Dem.)
Peter J. Visclosky (D–1st)
David McIntosh (R–2nd)
Tim J. Roemer (D–3rd)
Mark Souder (R–4th)
Steve Buyer (R–5th)
Dan Burton (R–6th)
Edward A. Pease (R–7th)
John N. Hostettler (R–8th)
Lee H. Hamilton (D–9th)
Julia M. Carson (D–10th)

Iowa (4 Rep./1 Dem.)
Jim Leach (R–1st)
Jim Nussle (R–2nd)
Leonard L. Boswell (D–3rd)

Greg Ganske (R–4th)
Tom Latham (R–5th)

Kansas (4 Rep.)
Jerry Moran (R–1st)
Jim R. Ryun (R–2nd)
Vincent K. Snowbarger (R–3rd)
Todd Tiahrt (R–4th)

Kentucky (5 Rep./1 Dem.)
Edward Whitfield (R–1st)
Ron Lewis (R–2nd)
Anne M. Northup (R–3rd)
Jim Bunning (R–4th)
Harold Rogers (R–5th)
Scotty Baesler (D–6th)

Louisiana (5 Rep./2 Dem.)
Bob Livingston (R–1st)
William J. Jefferson (D–2nd)
W.J. "Billy" Tauzin (R–3rd)
Jim McCrery (R–4th)
John C. Cooksey (R–5th)
Richard H. Baker (R–6th)
Chris John (D–7th)

Maine (2 Dem.)
Thomas H. Allen (D–1st)
John E. Baldacci (D–2nd)

Maryland (4 Rep./4 Dem.)
Wayne Gilchrest (R–1st)
Robert Ehrlich, Jr. (R–2nd)
Benjamin L. Cardin (D–3rd)
Albert Wynn (D–4th)
Steny H. Hoyer (D–5th)
Roscoe Bartlett (R–6th)
Elijah Cummings (D–7th)
Constance A. Morella (R–8th)

Massachusetts (10 Dem.)
John W. Olver (D–1st)
Richard E. Neal (D–2nd)
James P. McGovern (D–3rd)
Barney Frank (D–4th)
Marty Meehan (D–5th)
John F. Tierney (D–6th)
Edward J. Markey (D–7th)
Joseph P. Kennedy II (D–8th)
Joe Moakley (D–9th)
William Delahunt (D–10th)

Michigan (6 Rep./10 Dem.)
Bart Stupak (D–1st)
Peter Hoekstra (R–2nd)
Vernon Ehlers (R–3rd)
Dave Camp (R–4th)
James Barcia (D–5th)

Fred Upton (R–6th)
Nick Smith (R–7th)
Debbie Stabenow (D–8th)
Dale E. Kildee (D–9th)
David E. Bonior (D–10th)
Joseph Knollenberg (R–11th)
Sander M. Levin (D–12th)
Lynn Rivers (D–13th)
John Conyers, Jr. (D–14th)
Carolyn C. Kilpatrick (D–15th)
John D. Dingell (D–16th)

Minnesota (2 Rep./6 Dem.)
Gil Gutknecht (R–1st)
David Minge (D–2nd)
Jim Ramstad (R–3rd)
Bruce F. Vento (D–4th)
Martin Olav Sabo (D–5th)
Bill Luther (D–6th)
Collin Peterson (D–7th)
James L. Oberstar (D–8th)

Mississippi (3 Rep./2 Dem.)
Roger Wicker (R–1st)
Bennie G. Thompson (D–2nd)
Charles "Chip" Pickering, Jr. (R–3rd)
Mike Parker (R–4th)
Gene Taylor (D–5th)

Missouri (4 Rep./5 Dem.)
William "Bill" Clay (D–1st)
James Talent (R–2nd)
Richard A. Gephardt (D–3rd)
Ike Skelton (D–4th)
Karen McCarthy (D–5th)
Pat Danner (D–6th)
Roy Blunt (R–7th)
Jo Ann H. Emerson (R–8th)
Kenny C. Hulshof (R–9th)

Montana (1 Rep.)
Rick A. Hill (R–At Large)

Nebraska (3 Rep.)
Doug Bereuter (R–1st)
Jon Christensen (R–2nd)
Bill Barrett (R–3rd)

Nevada (2 Rep.)
John Ensign (R–1st)
James A. Gibbons (R–2nd)

New Hampshire (2 Rep.)
John E. Sununu (R–1st)
Charles Bass (R–2nd)

New Jersey (7 Rep./6 Dem.)
Robert E. Andrews (D–1st)
Frank A. LoBiondo (R–2nd)

Jim Saxton (R–3rd)
Christopher H. Smith (R–4th)
Marge Roukema (R–5th)
Frank Pallone, Jr. (D–6th)
Bob Franks (R–7th)
William J. Pascrell, Jr. (D–8th)
Steven R. Rothman (D–9th)
Donald M. Payne (D–10th)
Rodney Frelinghuysen (R–11th)
Michael Pappas (R–12th)
Robert Menendez (D–13th)

New Mexico (2 Rep./1 Vacant)
Steven Schiff (R–1st)
Joe Skeen (R–2nd)
3rd—Vacant

New York (12 Rep./17 Dem./2 Vacant)
Michael P. Forbes (R–1st)
Rick Lazio (R–2nd)
Peter King (R–3rd)
Carolyn McCarthy (D–4th)
Gary L. Ackerman (D–5th)
6th-Vacant
Thomas J. Manton (D–7th)
Jerrold Nadler (D–8th)
Charles E. Schumer (D–9th)
Edolphus Towns (D–10th)
Major R. Owens (D–11th)
Nydia Velazquez (D–12th)
13th-Vacant
Carolyn Maloney (D–14th)
Charles B. Rangel (D–15th)
Jose Serrano (D–16th)
Eliot Engel (D–17th)
Nita M. Lowey (D–18th)
Sue W. Kelly (R–19th)
Benjamin A. Gilman (R–20th)
Michael R. McNulty (D–21st)
Gerald B.H. Solomon (R–22nd)
Sherwood L. Boehlert (R–23rd)
John McHugh (R–24th)
James T. Walsh (R–25th)
Maurice Hinchey (D–26th)
Bill Paxon (R–27th)
Louise McIntosh Slaughter (D–28th)
John J. LaFalce (D–29th)
Jack Quinn (R–30th)
Amo Houghton, Jr. (R–31st)

North Carolina (6 Rep./6 Dem.)
Eva Clayton (D–1st)
Bob Etheridge (D–2nd)
Walter Jones, Jr. (R–3rd)
David E. Price (D–4th)
Richard M. Burr (R–5th)
Howard Coble (R–6th)
Mike McIntyre (D–7th)
W.G. "Bill" Hefner (D–8th)

Sue Myrick (R–9th)
Cass Ballenger (R–10th)
Charles H. Taylor (R–11th)
Melvin Watt (D–12th)

North Dakota (1 Dem.)
Earl Pomeroy (D–At Large)

Ohio (11 Rep./8 Dem.)
Steve Chabot (R–1st)
Rob Portman (R–2nd)
Tony P. Hall (D–3rd)
Michael G. Oxley (R–4th)
Paul E. Gillmor (R–5th)
Ted Strickland (D–6th)
David Hobson (R–7th)
John A. Boehner (R–8th)
Marcy Kaptur (D–9th)
Dennis J. Kucinich (D–10th)
Louis Stokes (D–11th)
John R. Kasich (R–12th)
Sherrod Brown (D–13th)
Thomas C. Sawyer (D–14th)
Deborah Pryce (R–15th)
Ralph Regula (R–16th)
James A. Traficant, Jr. (D–17th)
Bob Ney (R–18th)
Steven C. LaTourette (R–19th)

Oklahoma (6 Rep.)
Steve Largent (R–1st)
Tom Coburn (R–2nd)
Wes W. Watkins (R–3rd)
J.C. Watts (R–4th)
Ernest Istook, Jr. (R–5th)
Frank D. Lucas (R–6th)

Oregon (1 Rep./4 Dem.)
Elizabeth Furse (D–1st)
Robert F. Smith (R–2nd)
Earl Blumenauer (D–3rd)
Peter A. DeFazio (D–4th)
Darlene Hooley (D–5th)

Pennsylvania (10 Rep./11 Dem.)
Thomas M. Foglietta (D–1st)
Chaka Fattah (D–2nd)
Robert A. Borski (D–3rd)
Ron Klink (D–4th)
John E. Peterson (R–5th)
Tim Holden (D–6th)
Curt Weldon (R–7th)
Jim Greenwood (R–8th)
Bud Shuster (R–9th)
Joseph M. McDade (R–10th)
Paul E. Kanjorski (D–11th)
John P. Murtha (D–12th)
Jon D. Fox (R–13th)
William J. Coyne (D–14th)

Paul McHale (D–15th)
Joseph R. Pitts (R–16th)
George W. Gekas (R–17th)
Mike Doyle (D–18th)
William F. Goodling (R–19th)
Frank R. Mascara (D–20th)
Philip S. English (R–21st)

Rhode Island (2 Dem.)
Patrick J. Kennedy (D–1st)
Robert A. Weygand (D–2nd)

South Carolina (4 Rep./2 Dem.)
Mark Sanford, Jr. (R–1st)
Floyd Spence (R–2nd)
Lindsey Graham (R–3rd)
Bob Inglis (R–4th)
John M. Spratt, Jr. (D–5th)
James Clyburn (D–6th)

South Dakota (1 Rep.)
John R. Thune (R–At Large)

Tennessee (5 Rep./4 Dem.)
William L. Jenkins (R–1st)
John J. Duncan, Jr. (R–2nd)
Zach Wamp (R–3rd)
Van Hilleary (R–4th)
Bob Clement (D–5th)
Bart Gordon (D–6th)
Ed Bryant (R–7th)
John S. Tanner (D–8th)
Harold E. Ford, Jr. (D–9th)

Texas (13 Rep./17 Dem.)
Max A. Sandlin (D–1st)
Jim Turner (D–2nd)
Sam Johnson (R–3rd)
Ralph M. Hall (D–4th)
Pete Sessions (R–5th)
Joe Barton (R–6th)
Bill Archer (R–7th)
Kevin P. Brady (R–8th)
Nicholas V. Lampson (D–9th)
Lloyd Doggett (D–10th)
Chet Edwards (D–11th)
Kay Granger (R–12th)
William "Mac" Thornberry (R–13th)
Ron. E. Paul (R–14th)
Rubén E. Hinojosa (D–15th)
Silvestre Reyes (D–16th)
Charles W. Stenholm (D–17th)
Sheila Jackson Lee (D–18th)
Larry Combest (R–19th)
Henry B. Gonzalez (D–20th)
Lamar S. Smith (R–21st)
Tom DeLay (R–22nd)
Henry Bonilla (R–23rd)
Martin Frost (D–24th)

Ken Bentsen (D–25th)
Richard K. Armey (R–26th)
Solomon P. Ortiz (D–27th)
Ciro Rodriguez (D-28th)
Gene Green (D–29th)
Eddie Bernice Johnson (D–30th)

Utah (3 Rep.)
James V. Hansen (R–1st)
Merrill Cook (R–2nd)
Christopher Cannon (R–3rd)

Vermont (1 Indep.)
Bernard Sanders (I–At Large)

Virginia (5 Rep./6 Dem.)
Herbert H. Bateman (R–1st)
Owen B. Pickett (D–2nd)
Robert "Bobby" C. Scott (D–3rd)
Norman Sisisky (D–4th)
Virgil H. Goode, Jr. (D–5th)
Bob Goodlatte (R–6th)
Thomas. J. Bliley, Jr. (R–7th)
James P. Moran (D–8th)
Rick Boucher (D–9th)
Frank R. Wolf (R–10th)
Thomas M. Davis III (R–11th)

Washington (6 Rep./3 Dem.)
Rick White (R–1st)
Jack Metcalf (R–2nd)
Linda Smith (R–3rd)
Doc Hastings (R–4th)
George R. Nethercutt, Jr. (R–5th)
Norman D. Dicks (D–6th)
Jim McDermott (D–7th)
Jennifer Dunn (R–8th)
Adam Smith (D–9th)

West Virginia (3 Dem.)
Alan B. Mollohan (D–1st)
Robert E. Wise, Jr. (D–2nd)
Nick J. Rahall II (D–3rd)

Wisconsin (4 Rep./5 Dem.)
Mark Neumann (R–1st)
Scott Klug (R–2nd)
Ronald J. Kind (D–3rd)
Jerry Kleczka (D–4th)
Thomas Barrett (D–5th)
Thomas E. Petri (R–6th)
David R. Obey (D–7th)
Jay W. Johnson (D–8th)
F. James Sensenbrenner, Jr. (R–9th)

Wyoming (1 Rep.)
Barbara Cubin (R–At Large)

American Samoa
Eni F.H. Faleomavaega (D)

District of Columbia
Eleanor Holmes Norton (D)

Guam
Robert Underwood (D)

Puerto Rico
Carlos Romero-Barcelo (D)

Virgin Islands
Donna M. Christian-Green (D)

Congressional Committees

Senate

Senate Agriculture, Nutrition and Forestry Committee
Richard G. Lugar, IN, *Chair*
Tom Harkin, IA, *Ranking Democrat*

Senate Appropriations Committee
Ted Stevens, AK, *Chair*
Robert C. Byrd, WV, *Ranking Democrat*

Senate Armed Services Committee
Strom Thurmond, SC, *Chair*
Carl Levin, MI, *Ranking Democrat*

Senate Banking, Housing and Urban Affairs Committee
Alfonse M. D'Amato, NY, *Chair*
Paul S. Sarbanes, MD, *Ranking Democrat*

Senate Budget Committee
Pete V. Domenici, NM, *Chair*
Frank R. Lautenberg, NJ, *Ranking Democrat*

Senate Commerce, Science and Transportation Committee
John McCain, AZ, *Chair*
Ernest F. Hollings, SC, *Ranking Democrat*

Senate Energy and Natural Resources Committee
Frank H. Murkowski, AK, *Chair*
Dale Bumpers, AR, *Ranking Democrat*

Senate Environment and Public Works Committee
John H. Chafee, RI, *Chair*
Max Baucus, MT, *Ranking Democrat*

Senate Finance Committee
William V. Roth, Jr., DE, *Chair*
Daniel Patrick Moynihan, NY, *Ranking Democrat*

Senate Foreign Relations Committee
Jesse Helms, NC, *Chair*
Joseph R. Biden, Jr., DE, *Ranking Democrat*

Senate Governmental Affairs Committee
Fred Thompson, TN, *Chair*
John Glenn, OH, *Ranking Democrat*

Senate Indian Affairs Committee
Ben Nighthorse Campbell, CO, *Chair*
Daniel K. Inouye, HI, *Vice Chair*

Senate Judiciary Committee
Orrin G. Hatch, UT, *Chair*
Patrick J. Leahy, VT, *Ranking Democrat*

Senate Labor and Human Resources Committee
Jim M. Jeffords, VT, *Chair*
Edward M. Kennedy, MA, *Ranking Democrat*

Senate Rules and Administration Committee
John W. Warner, VA, *Chair*
Wendell H. Ford, KY, *Ranking Democrat*

Senate Small Business Committee
Christopher "Kit" S. Bond, MO, *Chair*
John F. Kerry, MA, *Ranking Democrat*

Senate Veterans' Affairs Committee
Arlen Specter, PA, *Chair*
John D. Rockefeller IV, WV, *Ranking Democrat*

Senate Select Committee on Ethics
Robert C. Smith, NH, *Chair*
Harry Reid, NV, *Vice Chair*

Senate Select Committee on Intelligence
Richard C. Shelby, AL, *Chair*
J. Robert Kerrey, NE, *Vice Chair*

Senate Special Committee on Aging
Charles E. Grassley, IA, *Chair*
John B. Breaux, LA, *Ranking Democrat*

House of Representatives

House Agriculture Committee
Robert F. Smith, 2nd-OR, *Chair*
Charles W. Stenholm, 17th-TX, *Ranking Democrat*

House Appropriations Committee
Bob Livingston, 1st-LA, *Chair*
David R. Obey, 7th-WI, *Ranking Democrat*

House Banking and Financial Services Committee
Jim Leach, 1st-IA, *Chair*
Henry B. Gonzalez, 20th-TX, *Ranking Democrat*

House Budget Committee
John R. Kasich, 12th-OH, *Chair*
John M. Spratt, Jr., 5th-SC, *Ranking Democrat*

House Commerce Committee
Thomas J. Bliley, Jr., 7th-VA, *Chair*
John D. Dingell, 16th-MI, *Ranking Democrat*

House Education and the Workforce Committee
William F. Goodling, 19th-PA, *Chair*
William "Bill" Clay, 1st-MO, *Ranking Democrat*

House Government Reform and Oversight Committee
Dan Burton, 6th-IN, *Chair*
Henry A. Waxman, 29th-CA, *Ranking Democrat*

House Oversight Committee
William M. Thomas, 21st-CA, *Chair*
Sam Gejdenson, 2nd-CT, *Ranking Democrat*

House International Relations Committee
Benjamin A. Gilman, 20th-NY, *Chair*
Lee H. Hamilton, 9th-IN, *Ranking Democrat*

House Judiciary Committee
Henry J. Hyde, 6th-IL, *Chair*
John Conyers, Jr., 14th-MI, *Ranking Democrat*

House National Security Committee
Floyd Spence, 2nd-SC, *Chair*
Ronald V. Dellums, 9th-CA, *Ranking Democrat*

House Resources Committee
Don Young, At Large-AK, *Chair*
George Miller, 7th-CA, *Ranking Democrat*

House Rules Committee
Gerald B.H. Solomon, 22nd-NY, *Chair*
Joe Moakley, 9th-MA, *Ranking Democrat*

House Science Committee
F. James Sensenbrenner, Jr., 9th-WI, *Chair*
George E. Brown, Jr., 42nd-CA, *Ranking Democrat*

House Small Business Committee
James Talent, 2nd-MO, *Chair*
John J. LaFalce, 29th-NY, *Ranking Democrat*

House Standards of Official Conduct (Ethics) Committee
James V. Hansen, 1st-UT, *Chair*
Howard L. Berman, 26th-CA, *Ranking Democrat*

House Transportation and Infrastructure Committee
Bud Shuster, 9th-PA, *Chair*
James L. Oberstar, 8th-MN, *Ranking Democrat*

House Veterans' Affairs Committee
Bob Stump, 3rd-AZ, *Chair*
Lane Evans, 17th-IL, *Ranking Democrat*

House Ways and Means Committee
Bill Archer, 7th-TX, *Chair*
Charles B. Rangel, 15th-NY, *Ranking Democrat*

House Permanent Select Committee on Intelligence
Porter J. Gross, 14th-FL, *Chair*
Norman D. Dicks, 6th-WA, *Ranking Democrat*

Joint Committees

Joint Economic Committee
Jim Saxton, 3rd-NJ, *Chair*
Connie Mack, FL, *Vice Chair*

Joint Committee on Printing
John W. Warner, VA, *Chair*
William M. Thomas, 21st-CA, *Vice Chair*

Joint Committee on Taxation
Bill Archer, 7th-TX, *Chair*
William V. Roth, Jr., DE, *Vice Chair*

Major Actions by the Congress in 1997

Budget: The budget bill that President Clinton signed in August represented a bipartisan compromise that promised to balance the federal budget by 2002. The President and Congress cut spending for Medicare by reducing payments to doctors and hospitals and by raising premiums. The bill also increased spending to provide health insurance for uninsured children.

Tax Cuts: Crafted in tandem with the budget bill, the tax bill President Clinton signed in August featured major cuts in the capital gains tax as a concession to Republicans in Congress. The President claimed victory for an array of education and child tax credits. The first major tax cut since 1981, the 1997 tax legislation gave the President his first opportunity to use the line-item veto, testing its constitutionality on several narrowly tailored tax breaks for special interests.

Chemical Weapons Treaty: By a margin of 74 to 26, the Senate voted in April to ratify a treaty curtailing chemical weapons use and storage. The vote, which made the U.S. the 74th nation to ratify the treaty only days before its April 29 enaction date, represented an unusual alliance between President Clinton and Senate Majority Leader Trent Lott, who braved the wrath of GOP conservatives like Sen. Jesse Helms.

Disaster Relief: The $8.9 billion disaster-aid bill to help states hurt by storms and flooding was signed by President Clinton after he won a showdown with the Republicans in Congress. He vetoed the first version of the bill, forcing Congress to strip out the portions that would have withheld new funds for domestic programs and prohibited statistical sampling to adjust Census figures used in drawing House districts.

Late-Term Abortions: Both houses of Congress approved a ban on the controversial late-term abortion procedure known as "partial-birth abortion" or "intact" dilation and extraction. The strict ban would exempt only cases when a mother's life is in danger. President Clinton vetoed the legislation in October because it didn't permit the procedure when the mother's health was in jeopardy.

THE U.S. SUPREME COURT

The Supreme Court is the highest tribunal for all cases and controversies arising under the Constitution or laws of the United States. The court also has "original jurisdiction" in a very small number of cases arising out of disputes between states or between a state and the federal government. When the Supreme Court rules on a constitutional issue, that judgment is virtually final. Its decisions can be altered only by the rarely used procedure of constitutional amendment or by a new ruling of the court. However, when the court interprets a statute, new legislative action can be taken.

A term of the Supreme Court begins, by statute, on the first Monday in October. Usually, court sessions continue until late June or early July. The term is divided between "sittings," when the justices hear cases and deliver opinions, and intervening "recesses," when they consider the business before the court and write opinions. More than 6,500 cases are filed in the Supreme Court each year from the various state and federal courts. Plenary review, with oral arguments by attorneys, is granted in only 120 to 150 cases per term. Formal written opinions are delivered in 115 to 130 cases. About 75 to 100 additional cases are disposed of without granting plenary review.

The nine members of the Supreme Court are appointed by the President, subject to the approval of the U.S. Senate. To ensure an independent judiciary and to protect judges from partisan pressures, the Constitution provides that the justices serve during "good Behaviour," which has generally meant life terms.

HIGHLIGHTS OF THE
1996–97 TERM

Clinton vs. Jones: The court unanimously rebuffed President Clinton's request to delay the Paula Jones sexual-harassment suit until after he leaves office. The president had claimed that exposing a sitting president to civil lawsuits would distract him from his responsibilities and give judges too much power over his schedule.

Washington vs. Glucksberg: Vacco vs. Quill: Ruling in cases from New York and Washington state, the justices unanimously said the Constitution doesn't give terminally ill patients a right to kill themselves with the help of a doctor. The decision allows states to

Justices of the U.S. Supreme Court

Name	Appointed by President	Judicial oath taken
Chief Justice		
William H. Rehnquist (born October 1, 1924)	Reagan	September 26, 1986*
Associate Justices		
John Paul Stevens (born April 20, 1920)	Ford	December 19, 1975
Sandra Day O'Connor (born March 26, 1930)	Reagan	September 25, 1981
Antonin Scalia (born March 11, 1936)	Reagan	September 26, 1986
Anthony M. Kennedy (born July 23, 1936)	Reagan	February 18, 1988
David H. Souter (born September 17, 1939)	Bush	October 9, 1990
Clarence Thomas (born June 23, 1948)	Bush	October 23, 1991
Ruth Bader Ginsburg (born March 15, 1933)	Clinton	August 10, 1993
Stephen G. Breyer (born August 15, 1938)	Clinton	August 3, 1994

*Mr. Rehnquist was appointed to the court by President Nixon and took the oath as an associate justice January 7, 1972.

choose for themselves whether they want to allow or ban physician-assisted suicide.

Printz vs. United States; Mack vs. United States: By a vote of 5–4, the court struck down a key part of the Brady gun-control law. The justices said Congress had no right to force state and local officials to investigate the backgrounds of people who want to buy guns.

City of Boerne vs. Flores: The court threw out the Religious Freedom Restoration Act, which Congress enacted to reverse an earlier Supreme Court decision that had limited religious freedom. In a 6–3 ruling, the justices said Congress overstepped its authority by meddling with the Supreme Court precedent.

Agostini vs. Felton: The justices, voting 5–4, ruled that teachers in a federally funded academic program can go into private religious schools to help troubled students. The decision reversed a 1985 Supreme Court ruling that said allowing publicly paid teachers in religious schools was an unconstitutional mixing of church and state.

Raines vs. Byrd: The court cleared the way for President Clinton to use the line-item veto. In a 7–2 decision, the justices said the members of Congress who challenged the new law hadn't been harmed by it and therefore had no right to sue.

Past Members of the U.S. Supreme Court

Name	Appointed by President	Judicial oath taken	Date service terminated
Chief Justices			
John Jay	Washington	October 19, 1789	June 29, 1795
John Rutledge	Washington	August 12, 1795	December 15, 1795
Oliver Ellsworth	Washington	March 8, 1796	December 15, 1800
John Marshall	John Adams	February 4, 1801	July 6, 1835
Roger Brooke Taney	Jackson	March 28, 1836	October 12, 1864
Salmon Portland Chase	Lincoln	December 15, 1864	May 7, 1873
Morrison Remick Waite	Grant	March 4, 1874	March 23, 1888
Melville Weston Fuller	Cleveland	October 8, 1888	July 4, 1910
Edward Douglass White	Taft	December 19, 1910	May 19, 1921
William Howard Taft	Harding	July 11, 1921	February 3, 1930
Charles Evans Hughes	Hoover	February 24, 1930	June 30, 1941
Harlan Fiske Stone	Franklin D. Roosevelt	July 3, 1941	April 22, 1946
Fred Moore Vinson	Truman	June 24, 1946	September 8, 1953
Earl Warren	Eisenhower	October 5, 1953	June 23, 1969
Warren Earl Burger	Nixon	June 23, 1969	September 26, 1986
Associate Justices			
John Rutledge	Washington	February 15, 1790	March 5, 1791
William Cushing	Washington	February 2, 1790	September 13, 1810
James Wilson	Washington	October 5, 1789	August 21, 1798
John Blair	Washington	February 2, 1790	October 25, 1795
James Iredell	Washington	May 12, 1790	October 20, 1799
Thomas Johnson	Washington	August 6, 1792	January 16, 1793
William Paterson	Washington	March 11, 1793	September 9, 1806
Samuel Chase	Washington	February 4, 1796	June 19, 1811
Bushrod Washington	John Adams	February 4, 1799	November 26, 1829
Alfred Moore	John Adams	April 21, 1800	January 26, 1804
William Johnson	Jefferson	May 7, 1804	August 4, 1834
Henry Brockholst Livingston	Jefferson	January 20, 1807	March 18, 1823
Thomas Todd	Jefferson	May 4, 1807	February 7, 1826
Gabriel Duvall	Madison	November 23, 1811	January 14, 1835
Joseph Story	Madison	February 3, 1812	September 10, 1845
Smith Thompson	Monroe	September 1, 1823	December 18, 1843
Robert Trimble	John Quincy Adams	June 16, 1826	August 25, 1828
John McLean	Jackson	January 11, 1830	April 4, 1861
Henry Baldwin	Jackson	January 18, 1830	April 21, 1844
James Moore Wayne	Jackson	January 14, 1835	July 5, 1867
Philip Pendleton Barbour	Jackson	May 12, 1836	February 25, 1841
John Catron	Van Buren	May 1, 1837	May 30, 1865
John McKinley	Van Buren	January 9, 1838	July 19, 1852
Peter Vivian Daniel	Van Buren	January 10, 1842	May 31, 1860
Samuel Nelson	Tyler	February 27, 1845	November 28, 1872
Levi Woodbury	Polk	September 23, 1845	September 4, 1851
Robert Cooper Grier	Polk	August 10, 1846	January 31, 1870
Benjamin Robbins Curtis	Fillmore	October 10, 1851	September 30, 1857
John Archibald Campbell	Pierce	April 11, 1853	April 30, 1861
Nathan Clifford	Buchanan	January 21, 1858	July 25, 1881
Noah Haynes Swayne	Lincoln	January 27, 1862	January 24, 1881
Samuel Freeman Miller	Lincoln	July 21, 1862	October 13, 1890
David Davis	Lincoln	December 10, 1862	March 4, 1877
Stephen Johnson Field	Lincoln	May 20, 1863	December 1, 1897
William Strong	Grant	March 14, 1870	December 14, 1880
Joseph P. Bradley	Grant	March 23, 1870	January 22, 1892

Name	Appointed by President	Judicial oath taken	Date service terminated
Associate Justices			
Ward Hunt	Grant	January 9, 1873	January 27, 1882
John Marshall Harlan	Hayes	December 10, 1877	October 14, 1911
William Burnham Woods	Hayes	January 5, 1881	May 14, 1887
Stanley Matthews	Garfield	May 17, 1881	March 22, 1889
Horace Gray	Arthur	January 9, 1882	September 15, 1902
Samuel Blatchford	Arthur	April 3, 1882	July 7, 1893
Lucius Quintus C. Lamar	Cleveland	January 18, 1888	January 23, 1893
David Josiah Brewer	Harrison	January 6, 1890	March 28, 1910
Henry Billings Brown	Harrison	January 5, 1891	May 28, 1906
George Shiras, Jr.	Harrison	October 10, 1892	February 23, 1903
Howell Edmunds Jackson	Harrison	March 4, 1893	August 8, 1895
Edward Douglass White	Cleveland	March 12, 1894	December 18, 1910*
Rufus Wheeler Peckham	Cleveland	January 6, 1896	October 24, 1909
Joseph McKenna	McKinley	January 26, 1898	January 5, 1925
Oliver Wendell Holmes	Theodore Roosevelt	December 8, 1902	January 12, 1932
William Rufus Day	Theodore Roosevelt	March 2, 1903	November 13, 1922
William Henry Moody	Theodore Roosevelt	December 17, 1906	November 20, 1910
Horace Harmon Lurton	Taft	January 3, 1910	July 12, 1914
Charles Evans Hughes	Taft	October 10, 1910	June 10, 1916
Willis Van Devanter	Taft	January 3, 1911	June 2, 1937
Joseph Rucker Lamar	Taft	January 3, 1911	January 2, 1916
Mahlon Pitney	Taft	March 18, 1912	December 31, 1922
James Clark McReynolds	Wilson	October 12, 1914	January 31, 1941
Louis Dembitz Brandeis	Wilson	June 5, 1916	February 13, 1939
John Hessin Clarke	Wilson	October 9, 1916	September 18, 1922
George Sutherland	Harding	October 2, 1922	January 17, 1938
Pierce Butler	Harding	January 2, 1923	November 16, 1939
Edward Terry Sanford	Harding	February 19, 1923	March 8, 1930
Harlan Fiske Stone	Coolidge	March 2, 1925	July 2, 1941*
Owen Josephus Roberts	Hoover	June 2, 1930	July 31, 1945
Benjamin Nathan Cardozo	Hoover	March 14, 1932	July 9, 1938
Hugo Lafayette Black	Franklin D. Roosevelt	August 19, 1937	September 17, 1971
Stanley Forman Reed	Franklin D. Roosevelt	January 31, 1938	February 25, 1957
Felix Frankfurter	Franklin D. Roosevelt	January 30, 1939	August 28, 1962
William Orville Douglas	Franklin D. Roosevelt	April 17, 1939	November 12, 1975
Frank Murphy	Franklin D. Roosevelt	February 5, 1940	July 19, 1949
James Francis Byrnes	Franklin D. Roosevelt	July 8, 1941	October 3, 1942
Robert Houghwout Jackson	Franklin D. Roosevelt	July 11, 1941	October 9, 1954
Wiley Blount Rutledge	Franklin D. Roosevelt	February 15, 1943	September 10, 1949
Harold Hitz Burton	Truman	October 1, 1945	October 13, 1958
Tom Campbell Clark	Truman	August 24, 1949	June 12, 1967
Sherman Minton	Truman	October 12, 1949	October 15, 1956
John Marshall Harlan	Eisenhower	March 28, 1955	September 23, 1971
William J. Brennan, Jr.	Eisenhower	October 16, 1956	July 20, 1990
Charles Evans Whittaker	Eisenhower	March 25, 1957	March 31, 1962
Potter Stewart	Eisenhower	October 14, 1958	July 3, 1981
Byron Raymond White	Kennedy	April 16, 1962	June 28, 1993
Arthur Joseph Goldberg	Kennedy	October 1, 1962	July 25, 1965
Abe Fortas	Lyndon Johnson	October 4, 1965	May 14, 1969
Thurgood Marshall	Lyndon Johnson	October 2, 1967	October 1, 1991
Harry A. Blackmun	Nixon	June 9, 1970	August 3, 1994
Lewis F. Powell, Jr.	Nixon	January 7, 1972	June 26, 1987

*Named Chief Justice.

A Disciplinarian Court

The Supreme Court cast itself in the role of disciplinarian during its 1996–1997 term. In a series of unusually high-profile cases, the justices reined in the excesses of everyone from the president of the United States to the local trial judges who oversee complex litigation.

The court struck down legislation on gun control, religious freedom, and the Internet on the grounds that Congress had exceeded its power. It twice denied requests by the Clinton administration to exercise privileges in fighting allegations of scandal. And it repeatedly reversed judges who had read new rights into the Constitution or expanded their own authority to resolve disputes. "They restrained everybody," says Charles Rothfeld, a Supreme Court specialist at Mayer, Brown & Platt in Washington. "They were carefully putting the other branches in the proper boxes."

The Brady Act ruling was one striking example. The law, which required local sheriffs to investigate people who want to buy handguns, passed by solid majorities in Congress and has been credited with substantially reducing the number of guns in the hands of felons. But the court, by a vote of 5–4, said it violated the Constitution by forcing local officials to carry out federal policy. The decision showed how far the high court has shifted from two decades ago, when it was amplifying the federal government's power.

To be sure, the justices sometimes upheld the power of legislators and regulators. They did so narrowly in the term's first case, rejecting a challenge to the federal rules that require cable systems to carry local TV broadcasts. The court also expanded securities regulators' power to prosecute insider traders, and it preserved a government program that sponsors well known advertising campaigns for milk, meat and other farm products. But in historical terms, those cases were drowned out by the chorus of demands for restraint.

Edward Felsenthal

MAJOR BUSINESS CASES OF THE TERM

Turner Broadcasting vs. FCC: The court, in a 5–4 decision, upheld a federal law that requires cable-television systems to carry local broadcast stations. The cable industry had argued that the law violated its free-speech rights.

U.S. vs. O'Hagan: In a 6–3 decision, the court upheld one of the government's most important weapons in fighting insider trading. The ruling allows securities regulators to nab stock traders who obtain nonpublic information but who don't qualify as traditional company insiders.

Reno vs. ACLU: Voting 7–2, the justices struck down the federal law designed to keep "indecent" speech out of cyberspace. The court said the Internet deserves the fullest possible free-speech protection.

Amchem Products vs. Windsor: The court voted 6–2 to throw out a $1.3 billion asbestos settlement on the grounds that the thousands of people covered by it didn't have enough common interests to justify a single comprehensive agreement. Many judges, businesses and plaintiffs lawyers have pushed for such class-action settlements as a way to speed mass litigation through the judicial system.

Glickman vs. Wileman Brothers: The justices, by a 5–4 vote, upheld a Great Depression-era federal program that requires farmers and food distributors to help pay for industry advertising campaigns for products such as fruit, pork, beef and milk. Some farmers and distributors had objected that forcing them to participate violated their free-speech rights.

Supreme Court and Business

A conservative Supreme Court isn't necessarily good for business. Though most of the current justices were appointed by presidents with strong free-market credentials, the 1996–1997 term brought mixed results for business. Of 23 cases where there was a clear business interest on one side, business won

11 and lost 12. In the nine cases where a business was challenging a government enforcement effort or regulation, it won four times and lost five.

The only major win for business was the decision throwing out the federal law designed to keep "indecent" speech out of cyberspace. The ruling, which gave the Internet the fullest possible free-speech protection, will keep the new medium from being hampered by regulation as it develops. Business's biggest defeat was a decision striking down a $1.3 billion asbestos settlement on the grounds that the thousands of people covered by it didn't have enough common interests to justify a single comprehensive agreement. The opinion could make it harder for industry to settle waves of antitrust, consumer-fraud and product-liability cases in one fell swoop.

The court showed a tendency to decide issues on narrow grounds, rather than making sweeping new rules. In some ways, the term was notable "not so much for what they did do as what they didn't do," says Michael Mueller, a Washington lawyer at Akin, Gump, Strauss, Hauer & Feld. "They're leaving lawyers and their clients tied up in knots because nobody knows what the rules are." For example, the justices ducked an opportunity to rein in the use of whistleblower lawsuits against government contractors. And in three cases, they left confusion on an issue that has been litigated thousands of times: the question of whether federal law overrides state rules in the area of employee benefits.

Edward Felsenthal

SEX IN THE MILITARY

Two realities are colliding in the U.S. armed services today: The all-volunteer military can't do without women. But when groups of military women and men live and work in close proximity, some inevitably engage in sexual acts.

The problem with making love, not war, is that it can undermine military order and discipline. Sometimes it violates military rules against "adultery," as Air Force Lt. Kelly Flinn was charged, among other things. It also has veered into being clearly abusive, as happened with several drill sergeants at the Army's training base in Aberdeen Md., and led to a rash of disciplinary actions, including a conviction for rape.

But even when sex is permissible under military rules, it can undermine unit cohesion by provoking jealousies in an institution with far more men than women. "Is it disruptive?" says Gen. William Hartzog, who commands the Army's huge training establishment. "You bet it's disruptive." There is so much consensual sex going on, especially on lengthy deployments, reports one colonel, that the military needs stringent rules just "to keep it to a low roar." But that also means whatever prosecutions do occur—usually after a complaint from a betrayed spouse or unhappy subordinate—inevitably are seen as selective, as many civilians and some service members believe occurred in the case of Lt. Flinn.

Today's generals aren't just being politically correct when they express support for the gender-integrated military. They also would rather command a force of competent volunteers of both sexes than the main alternative—a force of less-trained and sometimes surly male draftees. No modern military has so relied on women, who now constitute 13% of the active-duty force, six times the proportion in place 25 years ago. Consequently, no other military has ever had such opportunities for heterosexual sex to occur between soldiers.

But public dissatisfaction with today's steady-as-she-goes approach, which keeps producing messes such as the Aberdeen sex-abuse scandal and Lt. Flinn's media extravaganza, seems to be mounting—even though the military thinks it handles a difficult issue about as well as can be expected.

Now, outside observers are proposing overhauling how the consensual sex problem is handled. Interestingly, the two most prominent changes being suggested, each from an academic who has advised the Army on personnel issues, are radically different. Duke University law professor Madeline Morris argued recently in a widely noticed law review article that the military should ban all consensual sex within units, making it akin to incest. Such a taboo, she argued, would "mini-

Military Might

Active-Duty Military Personnel Strength Levels

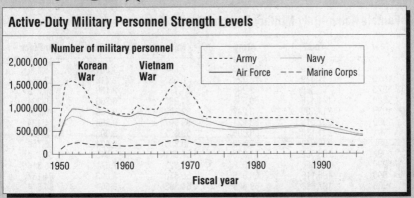

Active-Duty Military Personnel*

Year	Total	Army	Navy	Marine Corps	Air Force
1950	1,459,462	593,167	380,739	74,279	411,277
1955	2,935,107	1,109,296	660,695	205,170	959,946
1960	2,475,438	873,078	616,987	170,621	814,752
1965	2,653,926	969,066	669,985	190,213	824,662
1970	3,064,760	1,322,548	691,126	259,737	791,349
1975	2,128,120	784,333	535,085	195,951	612,751
1980	2,050,627	777,036	527,153	188,469	557,969
1985	2,151,032	780,787	570,705	198,025	601,515
1990	2,043,705	732,403	579,417	196,652	535,233
1991	1,985,555	710,821	570,262	194,040	510,432
1992	1,807,177	610,450	541,883	184,529	470,315
1993	1,705,103	572,423	509,950	178,379	444,351
1994	1,610,490	541,343	468,662	174,158	426,327
1995	1,518,224	508,559	434,617	174,639	400,409
1996	1,471,722	491,103	416,735	174,883	389,001

*Military personnel on extended or continuous active duty. Excludes reserves on active duty for training.
Source: U.S. Defense Department

mize the potential problem of sexual tensions within military units." (But, she adds in an interview, she thinks rules on sex with soldiers from other units might be loosened.)

Many problems of military culture, adds University of Maryland sociologist Mady Wechsler Segal, stem from its historically all-male nature. Prof. Segal, who is a member of the Board of Visitors that oversees the U.S. Military Academy at West Point, argued at an academic meeting that masculine U.S. military culture has become "dysfunctional," and needs to be "attacked," or at least "adapted."

Laura Miller, a sociologist at the University of California at Los Angeles and an expert on gender relations in the enlisted ranks, wholeheartedly supports imposing tough new rules banning consensual sex within units or on military posts. "You can't say it's not going to happen, but I think you should discourage it," she says. "It's like drugs and alcohol—it causes problems, so you should try to minimize it. If you're just going to let people be people, you're going to have all sorts of craziness, fights and indiscipline."

Looking at the same set of facts about the gender-integrated military, Northwestern University Prof. Charles Moskos, the nation's most prominent military sociologist, argues for just the opposite course: easing rules that

Women in Uniform

Female Active-Duty Military Personnel

Year	Total	Army	Navy	Marine Corps	Air Force
1965	30,610	12,326	7,862	1,581	8,841
1970	41,479	16,724	8,683	2,418	13,654
1975	96,868	42,295	21,174	3,186	30,213
1980	171,418	69,338	34,980	6,706	60,394
1985	211,606	79,247	52,603	9,695	70,061
1990	227,018	83,621	59,907	9,356	74,134
1991	221,138	80,306	59,391	9,005	72,436
1992	210,048	73,430	59,305	8,524	68,789
1993	203,506	71,328	57,601	7,845	66,732
1994	199,688	69,878	55,825	7,671	66,314
1995	196,116	68,046	55,830	8,093	64,147
1996	197,693	69,623	54,692	8,564	64,814

Source: U.S. Defense Department

Women and Minority Officers

The percentage of women and minority officers in the military has grown significantly since 1980.

	Army	Navy	Air Force	Marines
1980				
Black	7.1%	2.5%	4.6%	3.9%
Hispanic	1.0	0.7	1.6	1.0
Other minority	2.8	1.6	2.3	0.9
Total minority	11.0	4.9	8.5	5.8
Female	7.7	7.7	8.7	2.7
1996				
Black	11.6%	5.8%	5.8%	6.2%
Hispanic	3.4	3.5	2.1	4.1
Other minority	4.7	3.9	4.2	2.6
Total minority	19.7	13.2	12.0	12.9
Female	13.1	13.7	15.8	4.3

Source: U.S. Defense Department

restrict sexual behavior in the military, even to the extent of allowing some relationships between the ranks. "Loosen up in normal, everyday situations," he recommends, "but tighten up [the rules on consensual sex] on deployments and training." Senate Majority Leader Trent Lott appeared to side with the Moskos approach when, in recent comments to reporters, he said, "the Pentagon isn't in touch with reality on this so-called question of fraternization—I mean, get real."

Prof. Morris's solution—a near-total ban on consensual sex—terrifies many. "Trying to fight biology is the ultimate Vietnam," worries one Army major. "You've got to face the reality that people will have sex." Yet Prof. Moskos's loosening of the rules, which would appear to recognize biological realities, provokes another set of worries, mainly about discipline and unit cohesion.

Military officers generally seem to favor the current approach, which is to wink at consensual sex if it doesn't interfere with the chain of command or disrupt other soldiers' families. Indeed, this ambiguous treatment resembles the "don't ask, don't tell"

America at War

U.S. Military Personnel Serving and Casualties in Principal Wars[a]

War/conflict	Branch of service	Number serving	Battle deaths	Other deaths	Wounds not mortal[b]
			Casualties		
Revolutionary War	Total	–[c]	4,435	–	6,188
1775–1783	Army	–	4,044	–	6,004
	Navy	–	342	–	114
	Marines	–	49	–	70
War of 1812	Total	286,730	2,260	–	4,505
1812–1815	Army	–	1,950	–	4,000
	Navy	–	265	–	439
	Marines	–	45	–	66
Mexican War	Total	78,718	1,733	11,550	4,152
1846–1848	Army	–	1,721	11,550	4,102
	Navy	–	1	–	3
	Marines	–	11	–	47
Civil War	Total	2,213,363	140,414	224,097	281,881
(Union Forces only)	Army	2,128,948	138,154	221,374	280,040
1861–1865[d]	Navy	–	2,112	2,411	1,710
	Marines	84,415	148	312	131
Spanish–American War	Total	306,760	385	2,061	1,662
1898	Army	280,564	369	2,061	1,594
	Navy	22,875	10	–	47
	Marines	3,321	6	–	21
World War I	Total	4,734,991	53,402	63,114	204,002
1917–1918	Army	4,057,101	50,510	55,868	193,663
	Navy	599,051	431	6,856	819
	Marines	78,839	2,461	390	9,520
World War II	Total	16,112,566	291,557	113,842	671,846
1941–1946	Army	11,260,000	234,874	83,400	565,861
	Navy	4,183,466	36,950	25,664	37,778
	Marines	669,100	19,733	4,778	68,207
Korean Conflict	Total	5,720,000	33,651	3,262	103,284
1950–1953	Army	2,834,000	27,709	2,452	77,596
	Navy	1,177,000	475	173	1,576
	Marines	424,000	4,269	339	23,744
	Air Force	1,285,000	1,198	298	368
Vietnam Conflict	Total	8,744,000	47,378	10,799	153,303
1964–1973	Army	4,368,000	30,922	7,273	96,802
	Navy	1,842,000	1,631	931	4,178
	Marines	794,000	13,084	1,753	51,392
	Air Force	1,740,000	1,741	842	931

[a]Data prior to World War I are based on incomplete records in many cases. Casualty data are confined to dead and wounded and, therefore, exclude personnel captured or missing in action who were subsequently returned to military control.

[b]Marine Corps data for World War II, the Spanish–American War, and prior wars represent the number of individuals wounded, whereas all other data in this column represent the total number (incidence) of wounds.

[c]Not known, but estimates range from 184,000 to 250,000.

[d]Authoritative statistics for the Confederate forces are not available. Estimates of the number who served range from 600,000 to 1,500,000. The final report of the Provost Marshal General, 1863–1866, indicated 133,821 Confederate deaths (74,524 battle and 59,297 other) based upon incomplete returns. In addition, an estimated 26,000 to 31,000 Confederate personnel died in Union prisons.

Source: U.S. Defense Department

rule the military now uses for its gay members—a solution in fact devised by Prof. Moskos. This approach doesn't fight biological urges but seeks to channel them through discipline. That's a familiar task in military life, which after all also trains soldiers to overcome the natural urge to flee the battlefield when under fire.

Thomas Ricks

DEFENSE STRATEGY

By steering what appears to be a steady-as-she-goes course, Defense Secretary William Cohen may have rolled the dice on the future of U.S. national security.

Implicit in Mr. Cohen's Quadrennial Defense Review is the gamble that the U.S. can keep a big military of 1.4 million active-duty people and maintain a high pace of overseas operations, yet still boost weapons spending in the coming years by almost 50%—all while the defense budget's real purchasing power slowly declines. The only way to pull that off is by cracking down on expensive support functions in a way that no defense secretary, even those more experienced in the ways of the Pentagon than Mr. Cohen, has ever been able to do.

The review is the most definitive statement available of where the U.S. military is going in terms of strategy, shape of the force and procurement priorities. It remains subject to review not only by Congress but also by the National Defense Panel, created by Congress. Among other things, the review calls for:

- Having the Army retain 10 active-duty divisions, while cutting the active-duty force by 15,000 troops, and also cutting 45,000 personnel from the rolls of the National Guard and Reserve.
- Having the Navy retain 12 carrier battle groups, but reduce the total number of surface combatants in the fleet from 128 to 116.

But defense experts generally are skeptical that these changes will be sufficient to permit an adequate modernization of the military as its Reagan-era gear begins to wear out in the coming years. Without sharply boosting the defense budget, "there is no way to take a force this size, keep it ready and modernize it for tomorrow," said former Pentagon strategist Daniel Goure. "This means essentially the force will rot." He contends that within the next five years, the Pentagon must either increase its budget or cut 500,000 troops and carry out the biggest round of base closings ever. Yet Congress has made it clear that there won't be another round of base closings anytime soon.

Some say the budget crunch will result in a weaker military, while others predict big rounds of cuts in weapons-buying plans or curtailment of U.S. involvement in peacekeeping operations. "I just don't see how they're going to be able to get it all done," said Rep. Ike Skelton, a Missouri Democrat who is one of the most respected voices in Congress on defense issues. He argued that the Cohen review sets the military on course to resemble the post-Vietnam "hollow force," with a shrinking, poorly trained military operating outdated equipment and sinking into demoralization. Worse, he added, today's military is outfitted with high-technology gear that must be operated by well-trained professional soldiers.

Even defense analysts who gave the Pentagon review somewhat better grades said it still doesn't answer the basic budget questions. Steven Kosiak, director of budget studies for the Center for Strategic and Budgetary Assessments, a nonpartisan Washington think tank, estimated that the review's recommended trims to personnel and aircraft programs will save about $5 billion annually. But, he continued, the Pentagon faces an annual shortfall of about two to four times that amount. He predicted another round of troop and procurement cuts within a few years.

Thomas Ricks

Military Spending

U.S. spending for military operations has declined in the post-Cold War era.

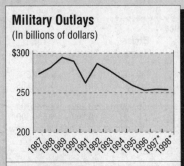

Military Outlays
(In billions of dollars)

Military Outlays
(In millions of dollars)

1987	$273,966
1988	281,935
1989	294,880
1990	289,755
1991	262,389
1992	286,892
1993	278,561
1994	268,622
1995	259,442
1996	253,300
1997*	255,700
1998*	254,300

*Estimate.
Source: Office of Management and Budget

Top Defense Contractors

Companies Receiving the Largest Dollar Volume of Prime Contract Awards From the U.S. Defense Department in 1996

Rank	Contractor	Total (In thousands)
1	Lockheed Martin	$11,998,430
2	McDonnell Douglas	9,938,973
3	General Motors	3,240,326
4	Raytheon	3,011,905
5	General Dynamics	2,670,030
6	Northrop Grumman	2,604,705
7	United Technologies	2,257,695
8	Boeing	1,724,044
9	Litton Industries	1,709,112
10	General Electric	1,530,029
11	Westinghouse Electric	1,440,714
12	Boeing North American	1,287,683
13	Textron	1,193,762
14	Science Applications Intl.	1,066,291
15	United Defense	876,614
16	TRW	786,749
17	Computer Sciences	711,956
18	ITT Industries	670,969
19	GTE	599,073
20	Tracor	580,599
21	Halliburton Energy Services	573,635
22	AT&T	529,037
23	Texas Instruments	528,569
24	AlliedSignal	511,804
25	Rolls-Royce	462,445
26	Alliant Techsystems	456,551
27	Black & Decker	452,589
28	Aetna Services	451,499
29	Exxon	446,735
30	BDM International	407,467
31	Olin	398,459
32	Unisys	381,588
33	DynCorp	379,994
34	Mitre	374,724
35	Standard Missile	372,116
36	Logicon	332,440
37	Avondale Industries	328,065
38	Renco Group	326,446
39	Tenneco	324,550
40	Massachusetts Inst. of Tech.	319,444
41	Nassco Holdings	301,456
42	Chrysler	300,080
43	Motorola	290,091
44	United States Dept. of Energy	284,350
45	IBM	280,096
46	Atlantic Richfield	279,439
47	Longbow	273,786
48	WorldCorp	270,884
49	Harris	268,894
50	Honeywell	263,609

Source: U.S. Defense Department

The United States Budget

Receipts by Source
(In millions of dollars)

Fiscal year	Individual income taxes	Corporate income taxes	Social insurance taxes and contributions	Excise taxes	Other	Total receipts
1987	$392,557	$ 83,926	$303,318	$32,457	$42,137	$ 854,396
1990	466,884	93,507	380,047	35,345	56,186	1,031,969
1996	656,417	171,824	509,414	54,014	61,393	1,453,062
1997*	732,900	187,100	538,500	55,900	63,200	1,577,700
1998*	748,600	192,600	564,800	55,300	70,200	1,631,600

Spending
(In millions of dollars)

	1987	1990	1996	1997*	1998*
National defense	$281,999	$299,331	$265,748	$268,400	$266,400
International affairs	11,648	13,764	13,496	14,000	14,600
General space, science, technology	9,216	14,444	16,709	17,100	16,500
Energy	4,115	3,341	2,836	2,000	2,300
Natural resources and environment	13,363	17,080	21,614	23,200	23,400
Agriculture	26,606	11,958	9,159	10,000	11,900
Commerce and housing credit	6,435	67,600	-10,646	-11,200	2,400
Transportation	26,222	29,485	39,565	39,700	40,200
Community and regional development	5,051	8,498	10,685	12,700	12,100
Education, training, employment, and social services	29,724	38,755	52,001	52,900	56,500
Health	39,967	57,716	119,378	126,400	139,200
Medicare	75,120	98,102	174,225	191,400	199,500
Income security	123,282	147,076	225,989	232,800	244,200
Social security	207,353	248,623	349,676	366,200	383,100
Veterans benefits and services	26,750	29,058	36,985	40,200	41,300
Administration of justice	7,553	9,993	17,548	20,100	24,800
General government	7,565	10,734	11,892	13,200	13,200
Net interest	138,652	184,221	241,090	245,700	248,400
Undistributed offsetting receipts	-36,455	-36,615	-37,620	-49,700	-48,500
Total outlays	1,004,164	1,253,163	1,560,330	1,615,000	1,689,900
Deficit	-149,769	-221,194	-107,268	-37,300	-58,300

*Estimate.
Source: Office of Management and Budget

United States Budget Trend

Government Receipts, Outlays, and Surpluses or Deficits

Year	Total (In millions of dollars)			Year	Total (In millions of dollars)		
	Receipts	Outlays	Surplus or deficit (-)		Receipts	Outlays	Surplus or deficit (-)
1955	65,451	68,444	-2,993	1979	463,302	504,032	-40,729
1956	74,587	70,640	3,947	1980	517,112	590,947	-73,835
1957	79,990	76,578	3,412	1981	599,272	678,249	-78,976
1958	79,636	82,405	-2,769	1982	617,766	745,755	-127,989
1959	79,249	92,098	-12,849	1983	600,562	808,380	-207,818
1960	92,492	92,191	301	1984	666,499	851,888	-185,388
1961	94,388	97,723	-3,335	1985	734,165	946,499	-212,334
1962	99,676	106,821	-7,146	1986	769,260	990,505	-221,245
1963	106,560	111,316	-4,756	1987	854,396	1,004,164	-149,769
1964	112,613	118,528	-5,915	1988	909,303	1,064,489	-155,187
1965	116,817	118,228	-1,411	1989	991,190	1,143,671	-152,481
1966	130,835	134,532	-3,698	1990	1,031,969	1,253,163	-221,194
1967	148,822	157,464	-8,643	1991	1,055,041	1,324,400	-269,359
1968	152,973	178,134	-25,161	1992	1,091,279	1,381,681	-290,402
1969	186,882	183,640	3,242	1993	1,154,401	1,409,414	-255,013
1970	192,807	195,649	-2,842	1994	1,258,627	1,461,731	-203,104
1971	187,139	210,172	-23,033	1995	1,351,830	1,515,729	-163,899
1972	207,309	230,681	-23,373	1996	1,453,062	1,560,330	-107,268
1973	230,799	245,707	-14,908	1997	1,577,700	1,615,000	-37,300
1974	263,224	269,359	-6,135	1998	1,631,600	1,689,900	-58,300
1975	279,090	332,332	-53,242	1999	1,694,300	1,751,800	-57,500
1976	298,060	371,792	-73,732	2000	1,753,900	1,795,300	-41,400
1977	355,559	409,218	-53,659	2001	1,824,800	1,831,800	-7,000
1978	399,561	458,746	-59,186	2002	1,921,900	1,858,800	63,100

The Shrinking U.S. Deficit

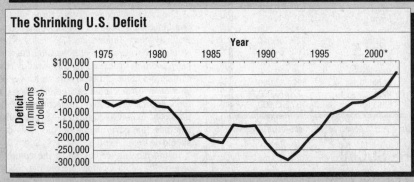

*Estimates, 1997–2002.
Sources: U.S. Treasury Department and Office of Management and Budget

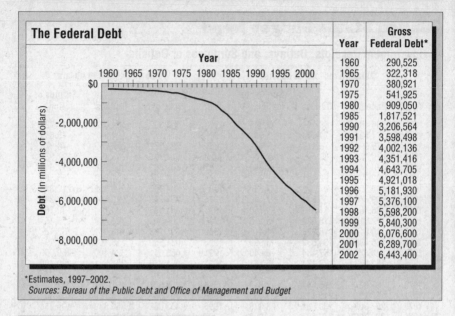

Year	Gross Federal Debt*
1960	290,525
1965	322,318
1970	380,921
1975	541,925
1980	909,050
1985	1,817,521
1990	3,206,564
1991	3,598,498
1992	4,002,136
1993	4,351,416
1994	4,643,705
1995	4,921,018
1996	5,181,930
1997	5,376,100
1998	5,598,200
1999	5,840,300
2000	6,076,600
2001	6,289,700
2002	6,443,400

*Estimates, 1997–2002.
Sources: Bureau of the Public Debt and Office of Management and Budget

Largest Recipients of U.S. Economic and Military Aid in 1996

Israel	$3,000,000,000
Egypt	2,116,603,000
Bosnia	298,012,000
Ukraine	228,243,000
Jordan	182,464,000
India	156,897,000
Russia	148,383,000
South Africa	122,563,000
Haiti	122,470,000
Ethiopia	109,239,000

Source: U.S. Agency for International Development

THE SOCIAL SECURITY DEBATE

From the president to the Congress, the issue of Social Security reform has amounted to all talk, no action. That isn't likely to change anytime soon, despite projections that by 2019 the government's largest and most popular program will be paying out more in benefits than it takes in.

The highlight of the past year was the long-delayed final report in January of a presidential advisory council. While the group of labor, business and think-tank representatives warned that action must be taken "as early as possible," its own sharp divisions signaled the fault lines in what will be a tortuous debate.

The two-year-old panel split three ways in recommending reforms for keeping Social Security fully funded for 75 years while meeting the unprecedented coming costs of baby boomers' retirement. Significantly, the council did unite in raising the controversial idea of investing some retirement assets in the stock market, though the factions differed markedly on how to go about it—in particular, whether the government or the individual should do the investing.

In the months leading up to the council's report, President Clinton and his Republican rival, Robert Dole, avoided taking on the politically charged Social Security issue beyond expressions of concern and a plea for some future bipartisan action. Afterward, the GOP Congress and the president were preoccupied with crafting a bipartisan five-year deal to cut taxes and balance the budget that purposely left Social Security off the table. For the next few years, moreover, policymakers are likely to be distracted by the more immediate and intractable problem of Medicare's looming insolvency; Social Security, by contrast, still could pay three-quarters of all benefits from payroll taxes even if all of its trust funds were exhausted in 2030.

Early in the year's budget negotiations, GOP leaders and top administration officials did consider a proposal to reduce the government's consumer-price index, which is widely held to overstate inflation, as a way to save billions in Social Security cost-of-living payments. But the idea was quickly abandoned amid objections from rank-and-file lawmakers and outside groups of senior citizens and organized labor. Even a slight reduction in the CPI formula would add years to the Social Security system's solvency, and such a step is still considered likely whenever policymakers do tackle the issue. (Separate from the political debate, the Bureau of Labor Statistics is experimenting with a new formula that would slightly reduce the reported inflation rate.)

Despite the lack of legislative action on Social Security, lobbying has begun in earnest, if quietly, given the prospect that any future reform could open the door to investing some of the system's billions in the stock market. Financial industry interests acknowledge they would benefit from millions of dollars in commissions, but they argue that Americans would benefit from higher returns on their savings.

Still, as the advisory council's report made plain, even partial privatization would require higher taxes to cover the costs of current retirees' benefits if workers' payroll taxes were diverted to their own investment accounts. Opponents of privatizing Social Security savings, including a sizable minority on the advisory council, also warn of putting unsophisticated Americans and their retirement savings at the mercy of unpredictable financial markets.

Jackie Calmes

Social Security Faces an Insecure Future

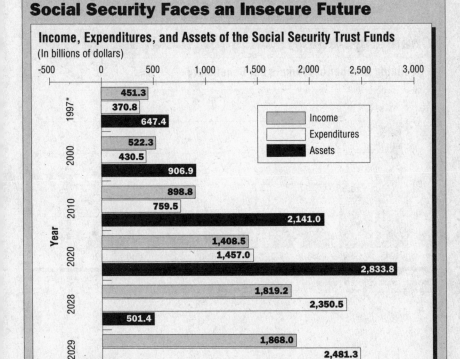

Income, Expenditures, and Assets of the Social Security Trust Funds
(In billions of dollars)

Legend:
- Income
- Expenditures
- Assets

1997*
- Income: 451.3
- Expenditures: 370.8
- Assets: 647.4

2000
- Income: 522.3
- Expenditures: 430.5
- Assets: 906.9

2010
- Income: 898.8
- Expenditures: 759.5
- Assets: 2,141.0

2020
- Income: 1,408.5
- Expenditures: 1,457.0
- Assets: 2,833.8

2028
- Income: 1,819.2
- Expenditures: 2,350.5
- Assets: 501.4

2029
- Income: 1,868.0
- Expenditures: 2,481.3
- Assets: -111.9

*Projections for 1997 and beyond.

Income, Expenditures, and Assets of the Social Security Trust Funds
(In billions of dollars)

Year	Income	Expenditures	Assets (end of year)	Year	Income	Expenditures	Assets (end of year)
1960	$ 12.4	$ 11.8	$ 22.6	1998	$ 470.8	$ 389.1	$ 729.2
1965	17.9	19.2	19.8	1999	495.2	409.3	815.1
1970	37.0	33.1	38.1	2000	522.3	430.5	906.9
1975	67.6	69.2	44.3	2001	552.5	454.3	1,005.1
1980	119.7	123.6	26.5	2002	583.6	479.9	1,108.9
1985	203.5	190.6	42.2	2003	616.8	506.5	1,219.1
1990	315.4	253.1	225.3	2004	651.6	535.6	1,335.1
1991	329.7	274.2	280.7	2005	689.7	566.2	1,458.7
1992	342.6	291.9	331.5	2010	898.8	759.5	2,141.0
1993	355.6	308.8	378.3	2015	1,144.0	1,048.0	2,738.5
1994	381.1	323.0	436.4	2020	1,408.5	1,457.0	2,833.8
1995	399.5	339.8	496.1	2025	1,668.8	1,978.5	1,865.5
1996	424.5	353.6	567.0	2028	1,819.2	2,350.5	501.4
1997*	451.3	370.8	647.4	2029	1,868.0	2,481.3	-111.9

*Projections for 1997 and beyond.
Source: Social Security Administration

Changing Demographics for Social Security

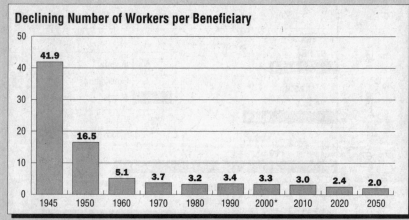

Declining Number of Workers per Beneficiary

*Projections for 2000 and beyond.

Comparison of Covered Workers and Beneficiaries

Year	Covered workers (In thousands)	Beneficiaries (In thousands)	Covered workers per beneficiary	Beneficiaries per 100 covered workers
1945	46,390	1,106	41.9	2
1950	48,280	2,930	16.5	6
1955	65,200	7,563	8.6	12
1960	72,530	14,262	5.1	20
1965	80,680	20,157	4.0	25
1970	93,090	25,186	3.7	27
1975	100,200	31,123	3.2	31
1980	112,212	35,119	3.2	31
1985	120,429	36,650	3.3	30
1990	133,689	39,470	3.4	30
1995	141,436	43,107	3.3	30
1996	143,718	43,498	3.3	30
2000*	148,689	45,628	3.3	31
2005	155,230	49,233	3.2	32
2010	161,023	54,413	3.0	34
2015	164,192	61,143	2.7	37
2020	165,511	68,802	2.4	42
2025	165,956	76,024	2.2	46
2030	167,309	81,616	2.0	49
2035	169,342	84,909	2.0	50
2040	171,393	86,148	2.0	50
2045	172,851	87,412	2.0	51
2050	173,875	89,144	2.0	51

*Projections for 2000 and beyond.
Source: Social Security Administration

Living Longer

People are expected to live longer in the 21st century, putting added pressure on the Social Security and Medicare systems. Here are Census Bureau projections of life expectancy at age 65 and the growing percentage of people over 65.

Life Expectancy at 65

Year	Total	
	Male	Female
1997	15.6	19.3
2000	15.9	19.5
2010	16.8	20.0
2020	17.6	20.6
2030	18.5	21.2
2040	19.3	21.8
2050	20.3	22.4

Elderly Population by Age: 1900 to 2050 (Numbers in thousands)

Census date	65 and over	
	Number	% of total population
1900	3,080	4.1%
1910	3,949	4.3
1920	4,933	4.7
1930	6,634	5.4
1940	9,019	6.8
1950	12,269	8.1
1960	16,560	9.2
1970	19,980	9.8
1980	25,550	11.3
1990	31,235	12.5
2000	34,709	12.6
2010	39,408	13.2
2020	53,220	16.5
2030	69,379	20.0
2040	75,233	20.3
2050	78,859	20.0

Source: U.S. Census Bureau

MEDICARE CHANGES

Congress moved toward curbing the growth of Medicare and making significant structural changes in the health program for the elderly and the disabled. As part of the agreement between Congress and the Clinton administration to balance the budget, lawmakers approved $115 billion in Medicare spending reductions over a five-year period. Most of the cuts, designed to ensure the program's solvency until the year 2007, were drawn from government payments to health-care providers such as hospitals and health maintenance organizations. The rest came from higher payments from beneficiaries, primarily for doctors' visits.

Lawmakers also agreed to major changes in the program to encourage more beneficiaries to join HMOs and other managed-care organizations. The hope was that such health plans, over the long run, would produce savings for the government. For example, under the congressional plans, new types of managed-care plans giving beneficiaries greater freedom in choosing their doctors were approved. And hospital and physician networks—known as provider-sponsored organizations—also were given the green light to offer Medicare plans. To help beneficiaries choose from the expanded menu of managed-care options, all health plans faced new requirements on disclosing information about how their programs work.

Congress also decided to give beneficiaries a third option, beyond the traditional fee-for-service program and managed care plans: medical savings accounts. Beneficiaries would be given a government payment for two purposes: to set up tax-free medical savings accounts to cover routine expenses, such as doctors' visits, and to buy high-deductible insurance policies for illnesses that are expensive to treat. Some consumer advocates worried that beneficiaries using MSAs would end up paying higher portions of their health-care costs. Supporters of the concept, including many Republicans, argued that the accounts would give beneficiaries maximum freedom to make their own medical decisions and encourage them to be prudent purchasers of health services.

In addition, Congress, with the backing of President Clinton, added new preventive benefits to the Medicare program, including colon-cancer screening and diabetes management. Lawmakers also voted to provide $1.5 billion to help low-income beneficiaries pay the premiums for doctors' services.

One of the most important developments on Medicare occurred in the Senate, which voted to gradually raise the eligibility age to 67 from 65, with the change to be fully phased in by 2027. The Senate also voted to charge higher premiums for the most affluent beneficiaries—for example, couples with incomes of over $75,000 a year. Supporters, who were led by Sen. Bob Kerrey, a Nebraska Democrat, argued that the changes were the first of a series of steps needed to maintain Medicare's solvency once the baby-boom generation begins retiring in large numbers around 2010. But the effort failed in the face of opposition in the House and from politically powerful senior citizens' groups such as the American Association of Retired Persons. President Clinton also expressed reluctance to make the changes as part of the 1997 legislation.

Nevertheless, the Senate's approval of such controversial changes suggested that at least some in Congress were prepared to take politically risky steps to tackle the vexing issue of the program's long-term health. These and other difficult questions on how to ensure Medicare's life well into the next century appeared headed for scrutiny by a federal advisory commission.

Laurie McGinley

The Ailing Medicare Program

The Hospital Insurance program, also referred to as Medicare Part A, covers specified inpatient hospital services, skilled nursing care after hospitalization, home health services and hospice care for aged and disabled people. The financially troubled program is funded primarily by payroll taxes paid by workers and employers. These data do not reflect the impact of the Medicare spending reductions in the balanced-budget agreement.

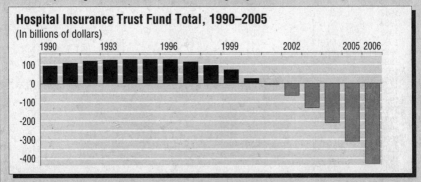

Hospital Insurance Trust Fund Total, 1990–2005
(In billions of dollars)

*Estimates for years 1997 and beyond.
Source: U.S. Health Care Financing Administration

Operations of the Hospital Insurance Trust Fund During Fiscal Years 1970–2006
(In millions)

				Income				
Fiscal year	Payroll taxes	Income from taxation of benefits	Railroad retirement account transfers	Reimbursement for uninsured persons	Premiums from voluntary enrollees	Payments for military wage credits	Interest and other income	Total income
1970	$ 4,785	–	$ 64	$617	–	$ 11	$ 137	$ 5,614
1975	11,291	–	132	481	$ 6	48	609	12,568
1980	23,244	–	244	697	17	141	1,072	25,415
1985	46,490	–	371	766	38	86	3,182	50,933
1986	53,020	–	364	566	40	-714	3,167	56,442
1987	57,820	–	368	447	40	94	3,982	62,751
1988	61,901	–	364	475	42	80	5,148	68,010
1989	67,527	–	379	515	42	86	6,567	75,116
1990	70,655	–	367	413	113	107	7,908	79,563
1991	74,655	–	352	605	367	-1,011	8,969	83,938
1992	80,978	–	374	621	484	86	10,133	92,677
1993	83,147	–	400	367	622	81	12,484	97,101
1994	92,028	$1,639	413	506	852	80	10,676	106,195
1995	98,053	3,913	396	462	998	61	10,963	114,847
1996	106,934	4,069	401	419	1,107	-2,293	10,496	121,135
1997*	111,625	4,001	401	481	1,271	66	9,890	127,735
1998	115,635	4,328	404	34	1,385	64	8,823	130,673
1999	121,296	4,591	400	183	1,514	64	7,095	135,143
2000	127,825	4,975	399	155	1,655	63	4,774	139,846
2001	134,092	5,368	398	150	1,807	63	1,846	143,724
2002	141,081	5,802	409	141	1,974	63	-1,484	147,986
2003	148,298	6,271	421	137	2,150	63	-5,400	151,940
2004	155,719	6,784	435	146	2,343	63	-9,991	155,499
2005	165,585	7,343	451	150	2,538	63	-15,287	160,843
2006	173,464	7,943	468	147	2,752	63	-21,254	163,582

| Fiscal year | Disbursements | | | Trust fund | |
	Benefits payments	Administrative expenses	Total disbursements	Net increase in fund	Fund at end of year
1970	$ 4,804	$ 149	$ 4,953	$ 661	$ 2,677
1975	10,353	259	10,612	1,956	9,870
1980	23,790	497	24,288	1,127	14,490
1985	47,841	813	48,654	4,103	21,277
1986	49,018	667	49,685	17,370	38,648
1987	49,967	836	50,803	11,949	50,596
1988	52,022	707	52,730	15,281	65,877
1989	57,433	805	58,238	16,878	82,755
1990	65,912	774	66,687	12,876	95,631
1991	68,705	934	69,638	14,299	109,930
1992	80,784	1,191	81,974	10,703	120,633
1993	90,738	866	91,604	5,497	126,131
1994	101,535	1,235	102,770	3,425	129,555
1995	113,583	1,300	114,883	-36	129,520
1996	124,088	1,229	125,317	-4,182	125,338
1997*	136,326	1,319	137,645	-9,910	115,428
1998	147,210	1,363	148,573	-17,900	97,528
1999	159,456	1,436	160,892	-25,749	71,779
2000	172,650	1,518	174,168	-34,322	37,457
2001	187,328	1,605	188,933	-45,209	-7,752
2002	203,021	1,696	204,717	-56,731	-64,483
2003	219,751	1,794	221,545	-69,605	-134,088
2004	237,542	1,896	239,438	-83,939	-218,027
2005	256,139	2,003	258,142	-97,299	-315,326
2006	275,934	2,117	278,051	-114,469	-429,795

*Estimates for years 1997 and beyond.
Source: U.S. Health Care Financing Administration

Medicare's Healthier Side

The Supplementary Medical Insurance program, also known as Medicare Part B, covers part of the cost of physicians' services, outpatient hospital care and related services. This program is funded primarily by transfers from the general fund of the U.S. Treasury and by monthly premiums paid by beneficiaries, and is expected to continue to be adequately financed because the law provides for automatic increases in premiums and government contributions to meet expected costs.

Operations of the Supplementary Medical Insurance Trust Fund (Cash Basis) During Fiscal Years 1970–2006
(In millions)

| Fiscal year* | Income | | | | Disbursements | | | Balance at end of year |
	Premium from enrollees	Government contributions	Interest and other income	Total income	Benefit payments	Administrative expenses	Total disbursements	
1970	$ 936	$ 928	$ 12	$ 1,876	$1,979	$ 217	$ 2,196	$ 57
1975	1,887	2,330	105	4,322	3,765	405	4,170	1,424
1980	2,928	6,932	415	10,275	10,144	593	10,737	4,532
1985	5,524	17,898	1,155	24,577	21,808	922	22,730	10,646
1986	5,699	18,076	1,228	25,003	25,169	1,049	26,218	9,432
1987	6,480	20,299	1,018	27,797	29,937	900	30,837	6,392
1988	8,756	25,418	828	35,002	33,682	1,265	34,947	6,447
1989	11,548	30,712	1,022	43,282	36,867	1,450	38,317	11,412
1990	11,494	33,210	1,434	46,138	41,498	1,524	43,022	14,527

Fiscal year*	Income				Disbursements			Balance at end of year
	Premium from enrollees	Government contri-butions	Interest and other income	Total income	Benefit payments	Adminis-trative expenses	Total disburse-ments	
1991	11,807	34,730	1,629	48,166	45,514	1,505	47,019	15,675
1992	12,748	38,684	1,717	53,149	48,627	1,661	50,288	18,535
1993	14,683	44,227	1,889	60,799	54,214	1,845	56,059	23,276
1994	16,895	38,355	2,118	57,368	58,006	1,718	59,724	20,919
1995	19,244	36,988	1,937	58,169	63,491	1,722	65,213	13,874
1996	18,931	61,702	1,392	82,025	67,176	1,771	68,946	26,953
1997*	18,982	59,203	1,896	80,081	73,275	1,863	75,138	31,896
1998	20,125	62,131	1,904	84,160	80,701	1,936	82,637	33,419
1999	21,110	68,721	1,961	91,792	89,298	2,002	91,300	33,911
2000	22,057	76,619	1,990	100,666	98,017	2,078	100,095	34,482
2001	23,037	85,374	2,017	110,428	107,500	2,164	109,664	35,246
2002	24,070	95,367	2,052	121,489	118,384	2,255	120,639	36,096
2003	25,183	106,572	2,077	133,832	130,582	2,351	132,933	36,995
2004	26,382	119,057	2,099	147,538	144,040	2,454	146,494	38,039
2005	27,671	134,274	2,141	164,086	159,200	2,562	161,762	40,363
2006	29,028	151,738	2,276	183,042	176,201	2,675	178,876	44,529

*Estimates for years 1997 and beyond.
Source: U.S. Health Care Financing Administration

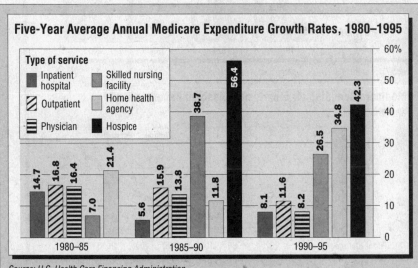

Five-Year Average Annual Medicare Expenditure Growth Rates, 1980–1995

Type of service
- Inpatient hospital
- Outpatient
- Physician
- Skilled nursing facility
- Home health agency
- Hospice

1980–85: 14.7, 16.8, 16.4, 7.0, 21.4
1985–90: 5.6, 15.9, 13.8, 38.7, 11.8, 56.4
1990–95: 8.1, 11.6, 8.2, 26.5, 34.8, 42.3

Source: U.S. Health Care Financing Administration

Medicare Beneficiary Utilization, Services per 1,000 Enrollees

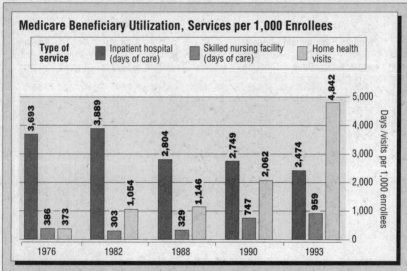

Source: U.S. Health Care Financing Administration

Medicare Spending Trends

Medicare Enrollment: Elderly, Disabled and End-Stage Renal Disease (ESRD)

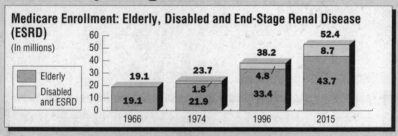

Source: U.S. Health Care Financing Administration

Medicare Spending for Elderly and Disabled Beneficiaries
(In billions of dollars)

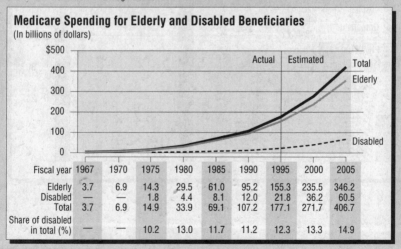

Fiscal year	1967	1970	1975	1980	1985	1990	1995	2000	2005
Elderly	3.7	6.9	14.3	29.5	61.0	95.2	155.3	235.5	346.2
Disabled	—	—	1.8	4.4	8.1	12.0	21.8	36.2	60.5
Total	3.7	6.9	14.9	33.9	69.1	107.2	177.1	271.7	406.7
Share of disabled in total (%)	—	—	10.2	13.0	11.7	11.2	12.3	13.3	14.9

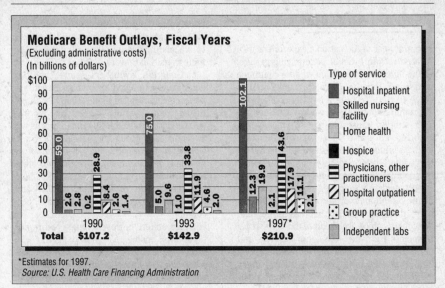

Medicare Benefit Outlays, Fiscal Years
(Excluding administrative costs)
(In billions of dollars)

Type of service
- Hospital inpatient
- Skilled nursing facility
- Home health
- Hospice
- Physicians, other practitioners
- Hospital outpatient
- Group practice
- Independent labs

	1990	1993	1997*
Hospital inpatient	59.0	75.0	102.1
Skilled nursing facility	2.6	5.0	12.3
Home health	2.8	9.6	19.9
Hospice	0.2	1.0	2.1
Physicians, other practitioners	28.9	33.8	43.6
Hospital outpatient	8.4	11.9	17.9
Group practice	2.6	4.6	11.1
Independent labs	1.4	2.0	2.1
Total	**$107.2**	**$142.9**	**$210.9**

*Estimates for 1997.
Source: U.S. Health Care Financing Administration

Medicare Recipients

Growth of Enrollees in Medicare and Annual Spending Per Enrollee (Enrollees in millions)

Year	Enrollees	Spending	Year	Enrollees	Spending	Year	Enrollees	Spending
1969	20.0	$338	1978	27.1	$ 950	1987	32.4	$2,494
1970	20.3	360	1979	27.8	1,079	1988	33.0	2,670
1971	20.7	390	1980	28.4	1,280	1989	33.7	2,971
1972	21.0	422	1981	29.0	1,504	1990	34.3	3,196
1973	21.9	466	1982	29.5	1,736	1991	35.0	3,437
1974	23.7	535	1983	30.0	1,944	1992	35.7	3,791
1975	24.7	636	1984	30.5	2,127	1993	36.4	4,058
1976	25.5	741	1985	31.1	2,259	1994	37.1	4,435
1977	26.4	842	1986	31.7	2,365	1995	37.7	4,882
1978	27.1	950	1987	32.4	2,494			

Source: U.S. Health Care Financing Administration

WELFARE REFORM

The first year of the nation's experiment with welfare reform brought encouraging results, as the number of people on welfare continued to decline. But the gains were attributed as much to the effects of a healthy economy as the requirements of new work mandates.

A subtler cause, state welfare officials reported, was rooted in a fundamental change in the attitude of their clientele. Spurred by the welfare-reform debate, some recipients moved into jobs even before the law required.

Still, evidence remained scarce on the economic condition of former recipients. Preliminary data in states such as Iowa and Wisconsin, which are ahead of most in forcing recipients from the rolls, showed little evidence of homelessness or destitution among former beneficiaries. Instead, many former recipients are reporting incomes that approximate levels they were receiving while on public aid. A primary concern for many, however, remains access to health insurance.

Advocates for the poor continued to predict that former recipients could be forced into homelessness due to the new laws in an economic downturn. At the same time, states continued to struggle to resolve other welfare-related issues. For example, many continued

to develop programs to help provide child care, transportation services and job training to welfare recipients in an effort to smooth their transition to work.

In Congress, lawmakers, spurred by President Clinton, moved to restore benefits to some cut off from aid by the 1996 law. In particular, both parties agreed to increase spending for disabled legal immigrants as well as some adult food stamp recipients. States also acted to mitigate some of effects of the new law. For example, more than 40 states took advantage of food stamp loopholes to continue aid to hundreds of thousands of adults who otherwise would have been cut off.

Other states, however, toughened regulations after finding that some welfare recipients were slow to comply with the new rule. For example, more than a dozen states passed laws that would cut off aid not only to parents, but to their children as well, if the adults refused to comply with job training or other work-related requirements.

The federal government and states also continued reforms in another welfare-related program: Medicaid, the health-care program for the poor. In an effort to help save taxpayer dollars, many states continued to experiment with offering care to poor mothers and

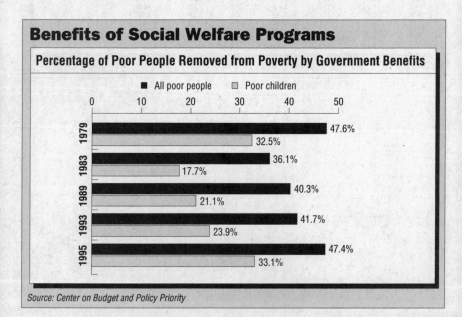

Benefits of Social Welfare Programs

Percentage of Poor People Removed from Poverty by Government Benefits

■ All poor people   ☐ Poor children

Year	All poor people	Poor children
1979	47.6%	32.5%
1983	36.1%	17.7%
1989	40.3%	21.1%
1993	41.7%	23.9%
1995	47.4%	33.1%

Source: Center on Budget and Policy Priority

Major Welfare Programs

Aid to Families with Dependent Children

The AFDC program, which was eliminated under the welfare reform plan of 1996, helped needy families with at least one child under 18 and was financed with both federal and state funds.

Year	Recipients	Federal and state benefits
1975	11,165,185	$ 8,153,448,850
1980	10,597,445	12,061,790,697
1985	10,812,625	14,644,559,007
1990	11,460,382	18,641,562,487
1995	13,652,232	22,031,584,208
1996	12,648,859	20,000,000,000 (est.)

Source: U.S. Health and Human Services Department

Supplemental Security Income

The SSI program, which includes both federal and state funds, pays monthly checks to needy people who are blind, have a disability, or are 65 or older. People who receive SSI also usually receive food stamps and Medicaid.

Year	Recipients	Federal and state payments
1975	4,359,625	$ 5,878,224,000
1980	4,194,100	7,940,734,000
1985	4,200,177	11,060,476,000
1990	4,888,180	16,598,680,000
1995	6,515,753	27,827,658,000
1996	6,676,729	28,791,924,000

Source: Social Security Administration

Food Stamps

Year	Number of Participants	Program cost	Average benefit per person per month
1980	21,100,000	$ 9,100,000,000	$39.47
1985	19,900,000	11,600,000,000	44.99
1986	19,400,000	11,600,000,000	45.59
1987	19,100,000	11,600,000,000	45.49
1988	18,600,000	12,400,000,000	49.83
1989	18,800,000	12,900,000,000	51.85
1990	20,100,000	15,500,000,000	58.91
1991	22,600,000	18,500,000,000	63.86
1992	25,400,000	22,500,000,000	68.57
1993	26,900,000	23,700,000,000	67.96
1994	27,500,000	24,500,000,000	69.01
1995	26,400,000	24,600,000,000	71.27
1996	25,500,000	24,300,000,000	73.24

Source: U.S. Agriculture Department

children through managed care providers, such as health maintenance organizations. Meanwhile, in Washington, both parties agreed to spend billions of dollars more over the next five years to help provide health insurance to hundreds of thousands of the nation's nearly 10 million uninsured children.

Chris Georges

Health Insurance for the Poor

The Medicaid law (Title XIX of the Social Security Act) authorizes federal matching funds to assist the states in providing health care for low-income people. The program has grown considerably, with total medical-assistance payments of about $160 billion a year to nearly 40 million individuals.

Medicaid Medical Assistance Payments*

(Fiscal years; in billions)

	1980	1990	1993	1994	1995	1996
Federal share	$13.3	$38.9	$72.3	$78.8	$86.3	$90.6
States' share	10.7	29.8	53.5	58.8	65.3	69.3
Total	24.0	68.7	125.8	137.6	151.6	159.9

*Excluding state administrative costs.

Medicaid Recipients

(Fiscal years; in millions)

Category*	1975	1980	1985	1990	1995†	1996	1997
Total	22.0	21.6	21.8	25.3	36.2	37.5	38.7
Aged	3.6	3.4	3.1	3.2	4.2	4.4	4.6
Blind	0.1	0.1	0.1	0.1	0.1	0.1	0.1
Disabled	2.4	2.8	2.9	3.6	5.9	6.2	6.5
Children	9.6	9.3	9.8	11.2	17.6	18.2	18.7
Adults	4.5	4.9	5.5	6.0	7.8	8.0	8.3
Other	1.8	1.5	1.2	1.0	0.6	0.6	0.6

*Prior to 1991, recipient categories do not add to total because recipients could be reported in more than one category. Totals after 1990 may not add due to rounding.
†Estimates for years 1995–1997.
Source: Health Care Financing Administration

HOSTILITY TOWARD IMMIGRATION

"Give me your tired, your poor, your huddled masses yearning to breathe free . . ." —inscription on the Statue of Liberty, written by Emma Lazarus

In fact, Lady Liberty's feelings toward the huddled masses are a bit more complex.

The U.S. admitted 916,000 immigrants in 1996—a 27% increase from the year before, according to the U.S. Immigration and Naturalization Service. INS officials played down the increase, saying most of the immigrants were relatives sponsored by a large group of new citizens naturalized five years before.

But the numbers shocked those who hope to restrict immigration, prompting a new round in the debate with those who favor keeping or loosening immigration laws. At the same time, the estimated number of illegal immigrants entering the country is on the rise. The INS estimates that the number of illegal aliens living in the U.S. rose 28% to five million between 1992 and 1996. They now constitute about 2% of the American population.

Many Americans don't like the trend. A 1997 *Wall Street Journal*/NBC News poll found that 49% of Americans feel immigration hurts the country. The same poll last year found that more than 70% of Americans favor tightened restrictions on immigration. "We're now in a period of increased hostile feelings toward immigrants," says Alan M. Kraut, professor of history at American University and vice president of the Immigration History Society.

Popular opinion has stirred government to

action. In 1996, Congress and President Clinton moved to reduce welfare benefits to legal immigrants, although they have since taken steps to restore some of the programs.

Historically, negative feelings toward immigration are strongest when the economy is at its weakest, Dr. Kraut says. But today's economy is strong, and Americans are enjoying low unemployment. Why the hostility?

Certainly, public confusion between legal and illegal immigrants plays a role. A 1993 poll found most Americans believe a majority of immigrants come to the U.S. illegally (though the actual number is estimated to be less than one fifth).

Experts also say the unpopularity of immigrants is rooted in economic concerns. Although studies show that immigrants ultimately contribute more economically to this nation than they require in assistance, they do hurt some groups. For example, they compete for jobs and reduce wages for high-school dropouts, but studies show the impact of immigrants on other income groups is minimal. Indeed, 58% of Americans who make less than $20,000 a year view immigrants negatively, the *Journal*/NBC News poll found, while just 34% of people earning more than $75,000 share such feelings.

A study released in 1997 by the National Research Council argues that both legal and illegal immigrants bring a "modest" net gain of $1 billion to $10 billion a year to the vast national economy. "Since 1980, immigration has only increased the labor supply by 5%. There's a limit to its effect on the overall economy," says James P. Smith, chairman of the panel that compiled the study and a senior economist for Rand Corp. "The New Americans" study says immigration leads to cheaper goods and services for the nation. It doesn't suppress wages for most people, as immigration opponents say, nor does it necessarily cause increases in crime.

But the study does show that a large number of immigrants who arrived in the U.S. over the past 20 years use more in public services than they contribute to the economy. The typical immigrant household has more children than a native-born household, so it makes more extensive use of both public education and medical care. Immigrants also tend to have lower wages, reducing their pur

chasing power and making them more likely to need public assistance.

States like California, New York, Texas and Illinois attract the bulk of immigrants and feel the greatest financial burden. Immigrants in California, for example, caused a net fiscal burden of $1,178 per California household in 1995, according to the New Americans study.

Not surprisingly, Californians have taken the strongest stance against immigrants, particularly illegal immigrants. In 1994, California voters overwhelmingly passed a law forbidding education and medical attention to illegal immigrants. But the law is still tied up in the courts.

Years before that, Gov. Pete Wilson proposed stripping citizenship from the children of illegal immigrants born in the U.S.—a change that would have required an amendment to the U.S. Constitution. "I personally admire the moxie, the gumption of someone bringing their family to a better life from a situation that's not good," says Gov. Wilson, who has since backed participation by illegal immigrants in some social programs as welfare reforms are enacted. "The problem is that there's a limit to what any society, including a relatively well-off society like the United States, can do."

Such feelings aren't limited to California. For many native-born Americans, the changes they see in their communities are disconcerting. "It's a real concern, the stability of a truly multicultural society, in the end," says George Borjas, a Harvard University professor and an influential critic of the nation's immigration policies. "The fact that we've survived these things in the past doesn't mean we will in the future."

Pro-immigrant groups believe the cultural changes will be much less sweeping than people fear. They point out that the descendants of immigrants have traditionally assimilated into American culture after a generation or two. "It's like having a party in a ballroom," says Joel Najar, immigration policy analyst for the National Council of La Raza, an Hispanic civil rights organization. "There's a thousand people, and when three people enter the party, it doesn't have much effect. Then the next year, those three people are part of the thousands."

Carlos Tejada

Coming to America

Immigration Fiscal Years 1820–1996

Years	Number	Years	Number
1820–1996	63,140,227	1901–1910	8,795,386
		1911–1920	5,735,811
1821–1830	143,439	1921–1930	4,107,209
1831–1840	599,125	1931–1940	528,431
1841–1850	1,713,251	1941–1950	1,035,039
1851–1860	2,598,214	1951–1960	2,515,479
1861–1870	2,314,824	1961–1970	3,321,677
1871–1880	2,812,191	1971–1980	4,493,314
1881–1890	5,246,613	1981–1990	7,338,062
1891–1900	3,687,564	1991–1996	6,146,213

Immigration to the U.S. 1981–1996

(In thousands)

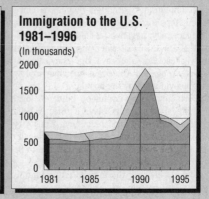

Immigrants Admitted from Top 20 Countries of Birth, Fiscal Year 1995

Country	1994	1995	Change Number	Change Percent
All countries	804,416	720,461	-83,955	-10.4
1. Mexico	111,398	89,932	-21,466	-19.3
2. Philippines	53,535	50,984	-2,551	-4.8
3. Vietnam	41,345	41,752	407	1.0
4. Dominican Republic	51,189	38,512	-12,677	-24.8
5. China, People's Republic	53,985	35,463	-18,522	-34.3
6. India	34,921	34,748	-173	-0.5
7. Cuba	14,727	17,937	3,210	21.8
8. Ukraine	21,010	17,432	-3,578	-17.0
9. Jamaica	14,349	16,398	2,049	14.3
10. Korea	16,011	16,047	36	0.2
11. Russia	15,249	14,560	-689	-4.5
12. Haiti	13,333	14,021	688	5.2
13. Poland	28,048	13,824	-14,224	-50.7
14. Canada	16,068	12,932	-3,136	-19.5
15. United Kingdom	16,326	12,427	-3,899	-23.9
16. El Salvador	17,644	11,744	-5,900	-33.4
17. Colombia	10,847	10,838	-9	-0.1
18. Pakistan	8,698	9,774	1,076	12.4
19. Taiwan	10,032	9,377	-655	-6.5
20. Iran	11,422	9,201	-2,221	-19.4
Other	244,279	242,558	-1,721	-0.7

Source: U.S. Immigration and Naturalization Service

Country of Origin

Immigrants Admitted to the United States from the Top 5 Countries of Last Residence: 1821–1995

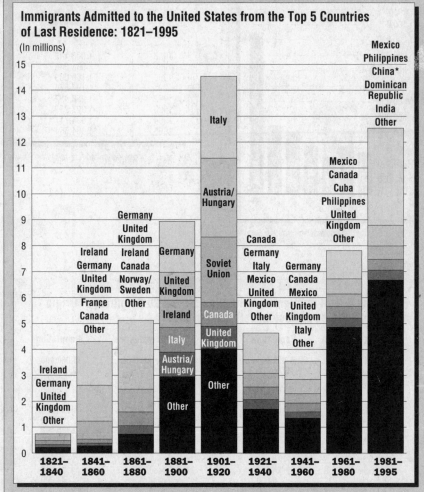

*China includes People's Republic of China and Taiwan.
Source: U.S. Department of Justice, Immigration and Naturalization Service*

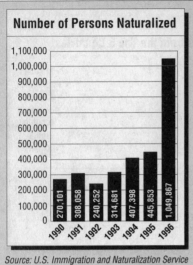

Number of Persons Naturalized

Year	Number
1990	270,101
1991	308,058
1992	240,252
1993	314,681
1994	407,398
1995	445,853
1996	1,049,867

Source: U.S. Immigration and Naturalization Service

Aliens Apprehended

Year	Number of persons apprehended
1988	1,008,145
1989	954,243
1990	1,169,939
1991	1,197,875
1992	1,258,482
1993	1,327,259
1994	1,094,717
1995	1,394,554

Source: U.S. Immigration and Naturalization Service

Estimated Illegal Immigrant Population for Top 20 Countries of Origin and Top 20 States of Residence: October 1996

Country of origin	Population	State of residence	Population
All Countries	5,000,000	All States	5,000,000
1 Mexico	2,700,000	1 California	2,000,000
2 El Salvador	335,000	2 Texas	700,000
3 Guatemala	165,000	3 New York	540,000
4 Canada	120,000	4 Florida	350,000
5 Haiti	105,000	5 Illinois	290,000
6 Philippines	95,000	6 New Jersey	135,000
7 Honduras	90,000	7 Arizona	115,000
8 Poland	70,000	8 Massachusetts	85,000
9 Nicaragua	70,000	9 Virginia	55,000
10 Bahamas	70,000	10 Washington	52,000
11 Colombia	65,000	11 Colorado	45,000
12 Ecuador	55,000	12 Maryland	44,000
13 Dominican Republic	50,000	13 Michigan	37,000
14 Trinidad & Tobago	50,000	14 Pennsylvania	37,000
15 Jamaica	50,000	15 New Mexico	37,000
16 Pakistan	41,000	16 Oregon	33,000
17 India	33,000	17 Georgia	32,000
18 Dominica	32,000	18 District of Columbia	30,000
19 Peru	30,000	19 Connecticut	29,000
20 Korea	30,000	20 Nevada	24,000
Other	744,000	Other	330,000

Fiscal year	Total aliens removed from U.S.	Criminal and narcotics violations		Country	Number of aliens removed in 1995	Percent of total
		Number	Percent			
				All Countries	49,735	100.0%
				Mexico	34,083	68.5
1988	25,829	5,956	23.1%	Honduras	1,878	3.8
1989	34,288	7,801	22.8	El Salvador	1,870	3.8
1990	29,939	11,569	38.6	Guatemala	1,717	3.5
1991	33,087	16,953	51.2	Dominican Republic	1,602	3.2
1992	43,493	24,203	55.6	Colombia	1,393	2.8
1993	42,383	27,683	65.3	Jamaica	1,036	2.1
1994	45,508	30,361	66.7	Canada	867	1.7
1995	49,735	32,029	64.4	Nicaragua	357	0.7
				Haiti	326	0.7

Source: U.S. Immigration and Naturalization Service

3

THE U.S. ECONOMY

AS THE U.S. STRUGGLED *to recover from the recession of the early 1990s, there was plenty of well-justified talk about "the jobless recovery." A majority of Americans, albeit a slim one, told a* Wall Street Journal/NBC News *poll that they didn't expect their kids' standard of living to be better than theirs. With adviser James Carville's slogan as his theme—"It's the economy, stupid!"—Bill Clinton wrested the White House from the Republicans who had held it for 12 years.*

More than six years into the economic expansion of the 1990s, which officially dates to March 1991, giddiness has replaced gloom. As Mr. Clinton welcomed the heads of state of other major industrial powers at their summit in Denver in June 1997, he gloated, "America's economy is the healthiest in a generation and the strongest in the world."

The economy is once again a cover story for news magazines, but the pendulum has swung wildly in the other direction. "The Amazing Economy!" shouts *U.S. News & World Report*. "How Long Can This Last?" asks *Business Week*. "Can This Really Be Happening?" wonders *Time*. And in a startling bit of journalistic hyperbole, *Fortune* asserts: "The U.S. economy is stronger than it's ever been before. These *are* the good old days."

"Another week of data, another opportunity to search the thesaurus for adjectives to describe the incredible performance of the economy," First Union Corp. economist Joel Naroff wrote in his weekly commentary in June 1997. "It is becoming tiresome trying to come up with new accolades." Merrill Lynch & Co's chief economist Bruce Steinberg titled a report: "Paradise Found: The Best of All Possible Economies" and decorated the cover with a Tahitian landscape by Paul Gauguin.

With month after month of economic growth and stock-market records, even seasoned business executives pronounce the business cycle to be dead. "We are in one of the most extraordinary expansions our country has ever seen. There is no natural law that says we have to have a recession," Arthur Martinez, chairman of Sears, Roebuck & Co., told a reporter at a Business Council retreat at Colonial Williamsburg in Virginia. Added H. Laurance Fuller, Amoco Corp.'s chief executive: "I don't see any reason to believe it can't go on until the end of the century."

It's not just executives. Only about a quarter of the academic economists surveyed by *The Wall Street Journal* early in 1997 put the odds of a recession within three years at better than 50%. "There is always some chance of a recession, but it's independent of how long the expansion has lasted. There no reason to think this one is going to end just because we've had six years," says Janet Yellen, the chief White House economist. "It's not obvious what clouds lie on the horizon."

Yikes! Is this euphoria justified? Or is it precisely the sort of "irrational exuberance," to borrow a phrase coined by Federal Reserve Chairman Alan Greenspan, that breeds the excesses in borrowing, spending and business expansion that lead to recession?

The economy is definitely much better than most experts predicted and most Americans expected. In the summer of 1997, unemployment fell to levels not seen since Richard Nixon left the White House, and inflation was hard to find. The stock market was setting one record after another. And the strength of the economy finally seemed to be lifting those at the very bottom of the economic ladder, the Americans with few marketable skills whose inflation-adjusted wages had been falling for years.

Yet the U.S. economy isn't yet as wonderful as some headlines suggest. A bigger share of Americans lived in poverty than in 1973, a year that marked the end of the Golden Age that followed World War II. Inflation-adjusted wages for many workers are lower than they were 25 years ago. National saving and investment, measured against the size of the economy, remain much lower than back in 1973. And by almost any measure the gap between the well-off and the rest of America is much wider than it was back then.

"If you think simply about material standards of living, we are much better off [than a generation ago], not only because we have low unemployment and low inflation, but because we have a generation's worth of technology boosting our total economic prosperity," says economist Bradford DeLong of the University of California at Berkeley, who is writing an economic history of the twentieth century. "If you think about things like long-run productivity growth, it's still a pretty lousy economy. If you think about things like the distribution of income, it's a much worse economy than we had a generation ago."

The enjoyable combination of low unemployment and low inflation, some economists argue, is a pleasant but passing episode. If oil prices may be considered "an adverse supply shock" back in the 1970s, argues Robert Gordon of Northwestern University, then the marked slowing of health-care prices and the rapid decline in computer prices are "a positive supply shock." By this logic, Fed Chairman Greenspan isn't so much skillful or omniscient as he is lucky. And it isn't Mr. Clinton's policies but his good fortune that explains the economy's sterling performance. "It's manna from heaven," Mr. Gordon suggests. And, in his view, it won't last forever.

An alternative explanation is that workers were simply cowed by all the layoffs, downsizing and restructuring, and didn't push for better wages. With unions weakened and executives aware that layoffs seem inevitably to lift a company's stock price, workers chose to press for more job security rather than to demand higher wages. "Capitalism is getting meaner," says Alan Blinder, a Princeton University economist and former vice chairman of the Federal Reserve Board. But this, too, is probably temporary.

Amid the celebrations of the strengths of the U.S. economy in mid-1997, there was a gnawing uneasiness among veteran economists and Federal Reserve officials. Wages were inching up, while prices remained remarkably quiescent. But they feared the old familiar pattern would soon emerge as the economy expanded at an unsustainable pace:

Tight labor markets and higher wages followed by tight product markets and higher prices followed by Fed-engineered increases in interest rates followed by recession.

"Has the business cycle been abolished?" asks Victor Zarnowitz, a retired University of Chicago professor who has been studying business cycles for half a century. "My answer is no, but there are all kinds of qualifications. The business cycle is changing."

Globalization, for instance, changes the dynamics of the economy in ways people are only beginning to appreciate. It makes it far easier for U.S. producers to get supplies from overseas when domestic suppliers can't meet demand, and far easier for exporters to ship to foreign markets when domestic demand is weak. The fear of competition from imports or the fear that one's employer will simply move abroad clearly has contributed to workers' reluctance to take advantage of low unemployment rates to push for big raises, a development that could keep the Fed from slamming on the brakes.

But the 1990s is hardly the first decade to be marked by a comfortably prolonged expansion. To match the 1980s, the U.S. will have to avoid recession into late 1998. To break the post-war record set in the Vietnam War years of the 1960s, expansion will have to go to the end of 1999. No one can know whether that will happen. It's encouraging that the post-war period, so far, has been free of depressions—periods of large declines in prices and economic activity—that occurred not only in the 1930s but five other times in the late nineteenth and early twentieth century, by Mr. Zarnowitz's reckoning.

It's too soon to know how the economic evolution of the 1990s will change the shape of business cycles in the years to come and the amplitude of the cycle. The spread of just-in-time inventory techniques, for instance, could help business avoid an unanticipated and unwelcome buildup of inventories when consumer demand slows. In the past, such inventory buildups have triggered sharp and sudden cutbacks in production that have precipitated recessions. Manufacturing executives are convinced that this will never happen again.

But as recently as 1995, the Federal Reserve was worried about just the opposite effect. With inventories lean, officials feared, the unexpected strength in demand for goods might lead to a sudden surge in orders from manufacturers that suppliers couldn't meet. The result could be a sudden surge in prices followed by a Fed move to increase interest rates, precisely the scenario that has preceded several post-war recessions. It didn't happen in 1995, but that doesn't mean it can't happen.

Still, something does seem to have changed for the better in the U.S. economy. Most important, for the first time in 25 years, there are signs that growth in productivity—

the amount of goods and services produced for each hour of work—is perking up. Nothing would do more to improve American living standards. "Productivity isn't everything, but in the long run, it's almost everything," economist Paul Krugman of the Massachusetts Institute of Technology has written. "To a pretty close approximation, the rate of growth of our living standard equals the rate of growth of our domestic productivity. Period."

Like a once-flabby athlete, the U.S. spent much of the 1980s and early 1990s working out at the health club. It hurt. Millions of American workers lost their jobs, their livelihoods and a way of life. They were steel workers in Pittsburgh, textile and apparel workers in the Carolinas, tellers and middle managers in the consolidating bank industry across the country. But businesses, manufacturers in particular, emerged more efficient. Workers emerged more willing to learn new skills and try new jobs, less wedded to old ways of doing things.

"Computer and telecommunication-based technologies are truly revolutionizing the way we produce goods and service," Fed Chairman Greenspan has said. "This has imparted a substantially increased degree of flexibility into the workplace, which in connection with just-in-time inventory strategies and increased availability of products from around the world, has kept costs in check through increased productivity."

In the past, Mr. Greenspan noted, productivity growth slowed as an expansion matured, partly because employers are forced to hire the least-skilled, less-desirable workers as the unemployment rate falls. But that's not happening this time. "It suggests," Mr. Greenspan reasons, "there may be an undetected delayed bonus from technical and managerial efficiencies coming from the massive advances in computers and telecommunications applications over the last two decades."

If so, that just might justify the euphoria.

David Wessel, chief economics correspondent of *The Wall Street Journal*

Real U.S. Gross Domestic Product

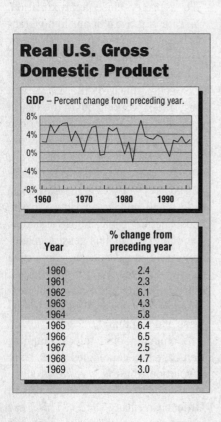

GDP – Percent change from preceding year.

Year	% change from preceding year
1960	2.4
1961	2.3
1962	6.1
1963	4.3
1964	5.8
1965	6.4
1966	6.5
1967	2.5
1968	4.7
1969	3.0

Year	% change from preceding year
1970	0.1
1971	3.3
1972	5.5
1973	5.8
1974	-0.6
1975	-0.4
1976	5.4
1977	4.7
1978	5.4
1979	2.8
1980	-0.3
1981	2.3
1982	-2.1
1983	4.0
1984	7.0
1985	3.6
1986	3.1
1987	2.9
1988	3.8
1989	3.4
1990	1.2
1991	-0.9
1992	2.7
1993	2.3
1994	3.5
1995	2.0
1996	2.8

Source: U.S. Commerce Department, Bureau of Economic Analysis

Real Gross Domestic Product
(Billions of chained 1992 dollars)

Year	GDP	Personal consumption expenditures	Gross private domestic investment	Exports and imports of goods and services		Government	GDP (% change)
				Exports	Imports		
1960	$2,262.9	$1,432.6	$270.5	$86.8	$108.1	$617.2	2.4%
1961	2,314.3	1,461.5	267.6	88.3	107.3	647.2	2.3
1962	2,454.8	1,533.8	302.1	93.0	119.5	686.0	6.1
1963	2,559.4	1,596.6	321.6	100.0	122.7	701.9	4.3
1964	2,708.4	1,692.3	348.3	113.3	129.2	715.9	5.8
1965	2,881.1	1,799.1	397.2	115.6	143.0	737.6	6.4
1966	3,069.2	1,902.0	430.6	123.4	164.2	804.6	6.5
1967	3,147.2	1,958.6	411.8	126.1	176.2	865.6	2.5
1968	3,293.9	2,070.2	433.3	135.3	202.5	892.4	4.7
1969	3,393.6	2,147.5	458.3	142.7	214.0	887.5	3.0
1970	3,397.6	2,197.8	426.1	158.1	223.1	866.8	0.1
1971	3,510.0	2,279.5	474.9	159.2	235.0	851.0	3.3
1972	3,702.3	2,415.9	531.8	172.0	261.0	854.1	5.5
1973	3,916.3	2,532.6	595.5	209.6	272.6	848.4	5.8
1974	3,891.2	2,514.7	546.5	229.8	265.3	862.9	-0.6
1975	3,873.9	2,570.0	446.6	228.2	235.4	876.3	-0.4
1976	4,082.9	2,714.3	537.4	241.6	281.5	876.8	5.4
1977	4,273.6	2,829.8	622.1	247.4	311.6	884.7	4.7
1978	4,503.0	2,951.6	693.4	273.1	338.6	910.6	5.4
1979	4,630.6	3,020.2	709.7	299.0	344.3	924.9	2.8
1980	4,615.0	3,009.7	628.3	331.4	321.3	941.4	-0.3
1981	4,720.7	3,046.4	686.0	335.3	329.7	947.7	2.3
1982	4,620.3	3,081.5	587.2	311.4	325.5	960.1	-2.1
1983	4,803.7	3,240.6	642.1	303.3	366.6	987.3	4.0
1984	5,140.1	3,407.6	833.4	328.4	455.7	1,018.4	7.0
1985	5,323.5	3,566.5	823.8	337.3	485.2	1,080.1	3.6
1986	5,487.7	3,708.7	811.8	362.2	526.1	1,135.0	3.1
1987	5,649.5	3,822.3	821.5	402.0	558.2	1,165.9	2.9
1988	5,865.2	3,972.7	828.2	465.8	580.2	1,180.9	3.8
1989	6,062.0	4,064.6	863.5	520.2	603.0	1,213.9	3.4
1990	6,136.3	4,132.2	815.0	564.4	626.3	1,250.4	1.2
1991	6,079.4	4,105.8	738.1	599.9	622.2	1,258.0	-0.9
1992	6,244.4	4,219.8	790.4	639.4	669.0	1,263.8	2.7
1993	6,389.6	4,343.6	863.6	658.2	728.4	1,252.1	2.3
1994	6,610.7	4,486.0	975.7	712.4	817.0	1,252.3	3.5
1995	6,742.1	4,595.3	991.5	791.2	890.1	1,251.9	2.0
1996	6,928.4	4,714.1	1,069.1	857.0	971.5	1,257.9	2.8

Note: Users of this table are cautioned that for periods before 1982, comparisons across the chained (1992) dollar components of GDP may be misleading.
Source: U.S. Commerce Department, Bureau of Economic Analysis

Boom and Bust Times

Business Cycle Expansions and Contractions

Business cycle reference dates		Duration in months			
				Cycle	
Trough	Peak	Contraction (trough from previous peak)	Expansion (trough to peak)	Trough from previous trough	Peak from previous peak
December 1854	June 1857	—	30	—	—
December 1858	October 1860	18	22	48	40
June 1861	April 1865	8	**46**	30	**54**
December 1867	June 1869	**32**	18	**78**	50
December 1870	October 1873	18	34	36	52
March 1879	March 1882	65	36	99	101
May 1885	March 1887	38	22	74	60
April 1888	July 1890	13	27	35	40
May 1891	January 1893	10	20	37	30
June 1894	December 1895	17	18	37	35
June 1897	June 1899	18	24	36	42
December 1900	September 1902	18	21	42	39
August 1904	May 1907	23	33	44	56
June 1908	January 1910	13	19	46	32
January 1912	January 1913	24	12	43	36
December 1914	August 1918	23	**44**	35	**67**
March 1919	January 1920	**7**	10	**51**	17
July 1921	May 1923	18	22	28	40
July 1924	October 1926	14	27	36	41
November 1927	August 1929	13	21	40	34
March 1933	May 1937	43	50	64	93
June 1938	February 1945	13	**80**	63	**93**
October 1945	November 1948	**8**	37	**88**	45
October 1949	July 1953	11	**45**	48	**56**
May 1954	August 1957	**10**	39	**55**	49
April 1958	April 1960	8	24	47	32
February 1961	December 1969	10	**106**	34	**116**
November 1970	November 1973	**11**	36	**117**	47
March 1975	January 1980	16	58	52	74
July 1980	July 1981	6	12	64	18
November 1982	July 1990	16	92	28	108
March 1991	—	8	—	—	—

Note: Figures printed in bold are the wartime expansions (Civil War, World War I and II, Korean War, and Vietnam War), the postwar contractions, and the full cycles that include the wartime expansions.
Source: National Bureau of Economic Research, Inc., Cambridge, MA

The U.S. Work Force

The labor force grew 92% between 1960 and 1996, reflecting both population growth and a higher percentage of women working.

Civilian Labor Force (Persons 16 Years of Age and Over)
(Numbers in thousands)

Year	Total	Percent of population	Total employed	Total unemployed	Total not in labor force
1960	69,628	59.4%	65,778	3,852	47,617
1965	74,455	58.9	71,088	3,366	52,058
1970	82,771	60.4	78,678	4,093	54,315
1975	93,774	61.2	85,846	7,929	59,377
1980	106,940	63.8	99,302	7,637	60,806
1985	115,461	64.8	107,150	8,312	62,744
1986	117,834	65.3	109,597	8,237	62,752
1987	119,865	65.6	112,440	7,425	62,888
1988	121,669	65.9	114,968	6,701	62,944
1989	123,869	66.5	117,342	6,528	62,523
1990	125,840	66.5	118,793	7,047	63,324
1991	126,346	66.2	117,718	8,628	64,578
1992	128,105	66.4	118,492	9,613	64,700
1993	129,200	66.3	120,259	8,940	65,638
1994	131,056	66.6	123,060	7,996	65,758
1995	132,304	66.6	124,900	7,404	66,280
1996	133,943	66.8	126,708	7,236	66,647

U.S. Unemployment Rate

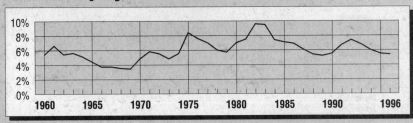

Persons 16 years of age and over

Year	% of labor force unemployed	Year	% of labor force unemployed	Year	% of labor force unemployed	Year	% of labor force unemployed
1960	5.5	1970	4.9	1980	7.1	1990	5.6
1961	6.7	1971	5.9	1981	7.6	1991	6.8
1962	5.5	1972	5.6	1982	9.7	1992	7.5
1963	5.7	1973	4.9	1983	9.6	1993	6.9
1964	5.2	1974	5.6	1984	7.5	1994	6.1
1965	4.5	1975	8.5	1985	7.2	1995	5.6
1966	3.8	1976	7.7	1986	7.0	1996	5.4
1967	3.8	1977	7.1	1987	6.2		
1968	3.6	1978	6.1	1988	5.5		
1969	3.5	1979	5.8	1989	5.3		

Source: U.S. Bureau of Labor Statistics

Age, Color, and Unemployment

Annual Unemployment Rate in the U.S., by Age, Race, and Hispanic Origin

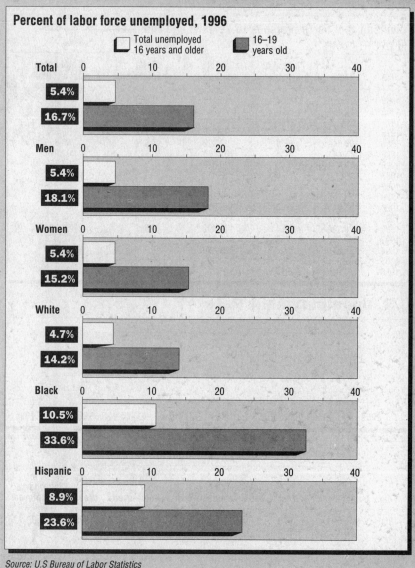

Percent of labor force unemployed, 1996

☐ Total unemployed 16 years and older   ▨ 16–19 years old

Total
- 5.4%
- 16.7%

Men
- 5.4%
- 18.1%

Women
- 5.4%
- 15.2%

White
- 4.7%
- 14.2%

Black
- 10.5%
- 33.6%

Hispanic
- 8.9%
- 23.6%

Source: U.S Bureau of Labor Statistics

The Dwindling Dollar

The purchasing power of the dollar, based on changes in the Consumer Price Index. The base period is 1982–1984, and the data show how much more a dollar would have purchased in earlier years and how much less it would have bought in later years.

Annual Average Purchasing Power of the Dollar as Measured by CPI*
(1982–1984=$1.00)

Year		Year		Year	
1950	$4.151	1966	$3.080	1982	$1.035
1951	3.846	1967	2.993	1983	1.003
1952	3.765	1968	2.873	1984	0.961
1953	3.735	1969	2.726	1985	0.928
1954	3.717	1970	2.574	1986	0.913
1955	3.732	1971	2.466	1987	0.880
1956	3.678	1972	2.391	1988	0.846
1957	3.549	1973	2.251	1989	0.807
1958	3.457	1974	2.029	1990	0.766
1959	3.427	1975	1.859	1991	0.734
1960	3.373	1976	1.757	1992	0.713
1961	3.340	1977	1.649	1993	0.692
1962	3.304	1978	1.532	1994	0.675
1963	3.265	1979	1.380	1995	0.656
1964	3.220	1980	1.215	1996	0.638
1965	3.166	1981	1.098		

*Obtained by dividing the average price index for the 1982–84=100, CPI base period by the price index for a given period and expressing the result in dollars and cents. Annual figures are based on average of monthly data.
Source: U.S. Bureau of Labor Statistics

CHANGING THE CONSUMER PRICE INDEX

The Consumer Price Index may be getting a tune-up.

The index, long maligned for exaggerating the inflation rate, came under even heavier criticism during the past year after a panel of economists appointed by Congress said it overstates annual increases in consumer prices by 1.1 percentage points. The academics say the formula fails to accurately measure changes in consumer behavior when prices rise, and doesn't appropriately reflect the improving quality of goods and services.

Politicians immediately seized on those findings as a way to reduce the federal deficit. That's because the smaller the increase in the consumer price index, the less the government spends on cost-of-living adjustments to Social Security, and the more it collects in income taxes. Even small changes in the index involve billions of dollars. If the index rose a quarter of a percentage point a year less than currently projected, the surplus in 2002 would be about $13 billion bigger, Congressional Budget Office estimates suggest. By 2007, it would be $35 billion bigger.

Shortly after the economists' commission, headed by Stanford University Professor Michael Boskin, released its report in late 1996, President Clinton and congressional Republicans discussed appointing a panel to recommend changes to the index. That notion was shelved—at least for a while. But the politicians are still contemplating the creation of a different index to adjust Social Security benefits and income-tax brackets for inflation. Of course, politicians risk alienating retirees, an important group of voters, if they reduce Social Security payments.

Even if those controversial changes never happen, some modification to the CPI formula is virtually certain. Separate from the political debate, the Bureau of Labor Statistics has begun using an experimental formula for

Consumer Price Index
All Urban Consumers (CPI-U), Annual % Change

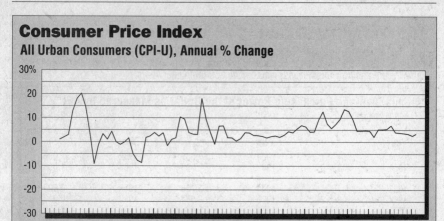

Year	% change	Year	% change	Year	% change	Year	% change
1914	1.0%	1936	1.4%	1958	1.8%	1980	12.5%
1915	2.0	1937	2.9	1959	1.7	1981	8.9
1916	12.6	1938	-2.8	1960	1.4	1982	3.8
1917	18.1	1939	0.0	1961	0.7	1983	3.8
1918	20.4	1940	0.7	1962	1.3	1984	3.9
1919	14.5	1941	9.9	1963	1.6	1985	3.8
1920	2.6	1942	9.0	1964	1.0	1986	1.1
1921	-10.8	1943	3.0	1965	1.9	1987	4.4
1922	-2.3	1944	2.3	1966	3.5	1988	4.4
1923	2.4	1945	2.2	1967	3.0	1989	4.6
1924	0.0	1946	18.1	1968	4.7	1990	6.1
1925	3.5	1947	8.8	1969	6.2	1991	3.1
1926	-1.1	1948	3.0	1970	5.6	1992	2.9
1927	-2.3	1949	-2.1	1971	3.3	1993	2.7
1928	-1.2	1950	5.9	1972	3.4	1994	2.7
1929	0.6	1951	6.0	1973	8.7	1995	2.5
1930	-6.4	1952	0.8	1974	12.3	1996	3.3
1931	-9.3	1953	0.7	1975	6.9		
1932	-10.3	1954	-0.7	1976	4.9		
1933	0.8	1955	0.4	1977	6.7		
1934	1.5	1956	3.0	1978	9.0		
1935	3.0	1957	2.9	1979	13.3		

Source: U.S. Bureau of Labor Statistics

calculating the index that would deal with some of the criticisms raised by the Boskin commission. The bureau said it would decide by the end of 1997 whether to switch to the new formula, one step in its continuing effort to improve the measure, which would reduce the reported inflation rate by as much as a quarter of a percentage point.

The BLS's experimental formula, which isn't likely to be used before January 1999, attempts to better account for consumers'

inclination to adjust their purchases when prices change. Under the current formula, for example, if the price of iceberg lettuce doubles, the BLS assumes that consumers continue to buy the same amount of iceberg lettuce. The experimental index assumes that consumers buy more Romaine lettuce instead.

The BLS calculated the difference in the consumer price index from December 1990 through February 1997 using the current

Consumer Price Index

CPI-U, U.S. City Average, by Commodity and Service Group
(1982–84 = 100, unless otherwise noted)

Commodity and service group	Unadjusted indexes for December								
	1988	1989	1990	1991	1992	1993	1994	1995	1996
All items	120.5	126.1	133.8	137.9	141.9	145.8	149.7	153.5	158.6
Commodities	113.5	118.2	126.0	127.5	130.1	132.0	135.1	137.0	141.4
Food and beverages	120.6	127.2	133.9	137.3	139.5	143.3	147.2	150.3	156.6
Commodities less food and beverages	109.0	112.6	121.1	121.5	124.3	125.1	127.6	128.9	132.1
Nondurables less food and beverages	106.9	112.0	125.8	124.5	127.4	126.5	128.1	128.8	133.7
Apparel products	116.3	117.1	123.0	127.2	128.7	129.7	127.2	127.1	126.5
Nondurables less food, beverages, and apparel	104.5	112.0	130.1	126.0	129.6	127.7	131.5	132.7	140.5
Durables	112.2	113.5	114.5	117.2	120.1	123.3	126.9	129.0	129.9
Services	128.1	134.6	142.3	148.8	154.2	160.0	164.7	170.4	176.1
Rent of shelter*	134.3	140.9	148.4	154.2	158.7	163.5	168.3	174.2	179.3
Household services less rent of shelter*	116.2	119.0	122.2	127.8	131.4	134.9	135.9	138.6	143.4
Transportation services	132.1	138.6	150.0	153.7	159.2	166.9	171.1	176.3	184.1
Medical care services	141.9	154.1	169.3	182.8	195.6	207.1	218.2	227.8	235.0
Other services	136.2	145.1	154.5	164.1	172.8	181.6	188.9	197.3	205.0
Special indexes									
All items less food	120.4	125.8	133.7	138.1	142.5	146.4	150.2	154.2	159.0
Energy	88.7	93.2	110.1	101.9	103.9	102.4	104.7	103.3	112.2
All items less energy	124.8	130.6	137.4	142.8	147.1	151.7	155.7	160.2	164.8
All items less food and energy	126.0	131.5	138.3	144.4	149.2	153.9	157.9	162.7	167.0

Commodity and service group	Percent change from previous December								
	1988	1989	1990	1991	1992	1993	1994	1995	1996
All items	4.4	4.6	6.1	3.1	2.9	2.7	2.7	2.5	3.3
Commodities	3.8	4.1	6.6	1.2	2.0	1.5	2.3	1.4	3.2
Food and beverages	5.1	5.5	5.3	2.5	1.6	2.7	2.7	2.1	4.2
Commodities less food and beverages	3.1	3.3	7.5	0.3	2.3	0.6	2.0	1.0	2.5
Nondurables less food and beverages	3.7	4.8	12.3	-1.0	2.3	-0.7	1.3	0.5	3.8
Apparel products	4.8	0.7	5.0	3.4	1.2	0.8	-1.9	-0.1	-0.5
Nondurables less food, beverages, and apparel	3.0	7.2	16.2	-3.2	2.9	-1.5	3.0	0.9	5.9
Durables	2.5	1.2	0.9	2.4	2.5	2.7	2.9	1.7	0.7
Services	4.8	5.1	5.7	4.6	3.6	3.8	2.9	3.5	3.3
Rent of shelter*	4.5	4.9	5.3	3.9	2.9	3.0	2.9	3.5	2.9
Household services less rent of shelter*	3.5	2.4	2.7	4.6	2.8	2.7	0.7	2.0	3.5
Transportation services	6.0	4.9	8.2	2.5	3.6	4.8	2.5	3.0	4.4
Medical care services	6.9	8.6	9.9	8.0	7.0	5.9	5.4	4.4	3.2
Other services	5.6	6.5	6.5	6.2	5.3	5.1	4.0	4.4	3.9
Special indexes									
All items less food	4.2	4.5	6.3	3.3	3.2	2.7	2.6	2.7	3.1
Energy	0.5	5.1	18.1	-7.4	2.0	-1.4	2.2	-1.3	8.6
All items less energy	4.7	4.6	5.2	3.9	3.0	3.1	2.6	2.9	2.9
All items less food and energy	4.7	4.4	5.2	4.4	3.3	3.2	2.6	3.0	2.6

*Indexes on a December 1982 = 100 base.

Consumer Price Index

CPI-U, U.S. City Average, by Selected Expenditure Categories

Expenditure category	Percent change from previous December								
	1988	1989	1990	1991	1992	1993	1994	1995	1996
Food and beverages	5.1	5.5	5.3	2.5	1.6	2.7	2.7	2.1	4.2
Food	5.2	5.6	5.3	1.9	1.5	2.9	2.9	2.1	4.3
Food at home	5.6	6.2	5.8	1.3	1.5	3.5	3.5	2.0	4.9
Food away from home	4.4	4.6	4.5	2.9	1.4	1.9	1.9	2.2	3.1
Alcoholic beverages	3.9	4.8	4.2	9.9	2.9	1.5	1.0	2.0	3.6
Housing	4.0	3.9	4.5	3.4	2.6	2.7	2.2	3.0	2.9
Shelter	4.5	4.9	5.2	3.9	2.9	3.0	3.0	3.5	2.9
Fuel and other utilities	2.9	3.2	4.0	2.9	2.3	2.5	0.2	1.4	4.6
Household furnishings and operation	3.1	1.0	1.8	2.3	1.6	1.8	0.4	2.5	1.0
Housefurnishings	2.5	-0.4	0.6	0.9	1.5	1.5	0.0	0.7	-0.1
Housekeeping supplies	4.0	5.6	3.2	1.8	-0.2	1.9	0.8	5.2	1.1
Housekeeping services	4.0	1.5	4.0	5.8	3.8	2.2	1.4	4.5	3.3
Apparel and upkeep	4.7	1.0	5.1	3.4	1.4	0.9	-1.6	0.1	-0.2
Apparel products	4.8	0.7	5.0	3.4	1.2	0.8	-1.9	-0.1	-0.5
Apparel services	4.4	3.6	6.8	3.4	3.3	2.7	1.7	0.8	2.4
Transportation	3.0	4.0	10.4	-1.5	3.0	2.4	3.8	1.5	4.4
Private	2.9	3.9	9.8	-1.4	2.7	1.5	4.9	1.3	3.7
New vehicles	2.2	2.4	2.0	3.2	2.3	3.3	3.3	1.9	1.8
Used cars	3.4	-0.4	-2.2	2.6	7.4	8.0	8.8	4.4	-1.6
Motor fuel	-2.1	6.8	36.5	-16.0	1.8	-5.4	5.9	-4.0	12.7
Automobile maintenance and repair	3.9	4.4	4.4	4.5	3.5	3.1	2.8	2.5	3.1
Public transportation	3.6	4.1	17.2	-3.0	5.6	11.6	-6.2	3.1	11.2
Airline fares	3.3	5.3	22.7	-6.0	6.6	17.0	-9.5	1.8	14.7
Other intercity transportation	7.1	1.7	6.6	2.4	0.1	-2.8	2.3	0.8	1.7
Intracity public transportation	2.9	2.1	7.7	3.8	5.0	2.8	1.0	7.6	5.8
Medical care	6.9	8.5	9.6	7.9	6.6	5.4	4.9	3.9	3.0
Medical care products	6.9	8.2	8.4	7.5	5.2	3.1	3.0	1.8	2.6
Prescription drugs	7.8	9.5	9.9	9.4	5.7	3.3	3.3	2.0	3.2
Nonprescription drugs and medical supplies	5.0	5.8	5.5	3.6	3.9	2.7	2.3	1.4	1.3
Medical care services	6.9	8.6	9.9	8.0	7.0	5.9	5.4	4.4	3.2
Professional medical services	6.8	6.5	6.7	6.1	5.7	4.5	4.6	4.0	3.5
Hospital and related services	11.0	11.3	11.3	8.9	8.8	7.6	5.5	4.6	4.1
Entertainment	4.6	5.1	4.3	3.9	2.8	2.8	2.3	3.3	2.9
Entertainment products	4.4	3.5	3.0	3.5	1.8	1.9	1.8	2.9	2.4
Entertainment services	4.6	6.8	5.4	4.4	3.7	3.5	2.7	3.7	3.4
Other goods and services	7.0	8.2	7.6	8.0	6.5	2.7	4.2	4.3	3.6
Tobacco and smoking products	9.4	14.7	10.8	11.1	8.1	-5.9	3.0	2.7	2.7
Personal care	5.1	3.8	4.2	2.5	2.9	2.5	1.9	2.1	1.1
Personal and educational expenses	6.7	7.2	7.5	8.4	6.9	6.5	5.4	5.5	4.6
College tuition	7.7	8.1	8.2	12.1	10.0	7.9	6.3	5.7	5.3

Source: U.S. Bureau of Labor Statistics

CPI Market Basket

Percentage weight given to different goods and services in the Consumer Price Index.

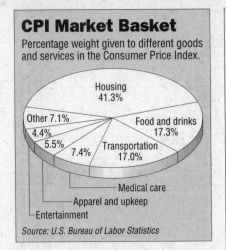

Housing 41.3%

Other 7.1%

4.4%

5.5%

7.4%

Food and drinks 17.3%

Transportation 17.0%

Medical care

Apparel and upkeep

Entertainment

Source: U.S. Bureau of Labor Statistics

A Better Measure?

The maximum impact on the annual change in the consumer price index if the experimental formula had been used in past years

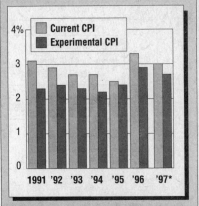

Current CPI
Experimental CPI

1991 '92 '93 '94 '95 '96 '97*

*Percentage change 12 months ended February 1997.
Source: U.S. Bureau of Labor Statistics

measure and the method now under study. Under the current formula, the index rose 18.6%, while under the revised formula, it would have increased 16.2%. The largest gaps were for food and beverages, apparel, medical care and entertainment.

"We are highly likely to do something," said John Greenlees, BLS assistant commissioner for consumer prices and price indexes. But he said it wasn't clear how extensive the changes would be. "This is an experimental index," he stressed. "If we were convinced it were superior to the current index, it would have been implemented already."

Even if the BLS were to make all thechanges contemplated, the index still wouldn't fully account for substitutions con-

sumers make when prices rise, Mr. Greenlees conceded. The new formula would apply only to changes within product groups, such as the shift from one type of lettuce to another. But it wouldn't address wider substitutions—buying more chicken, for example, when beef prices rise. The index also wouldn't reflect consumers' decisions to buy more goods at discount outlets than at department stores. Mr. Greenlees said those types of calculations would be too difficult to complete on a timely basis.

Jacob M. Schlesinger

Producer Price Trend

Year-over-year percentage change in the producer price index for all finished goods and for finished goods (excl. food and energy), monthly data

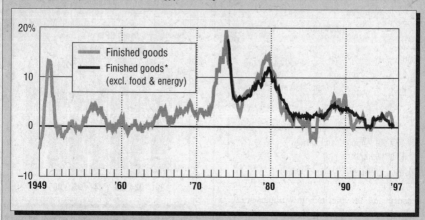

*Available only since 1974
Source: U.S. Bureau of Labor Statistics

Annual Percent Changes for Major Categories of the Producer Price Index, by Stage of Processing

Index	Annual percent changes					
	1991	1992	1993	1994	1995	1996
Finished goods						
Total	-0.1	1.6	0.2	1.7	2.3	2.8
Foods	-1.5	1.6	2.4	1.1	1.9	3.4
Energy	-9.6	-0.3	-4.1	3.5	1.1	11.7
Other	3.1	2.0	0.4	1.6	2.6	0.6
Intermediate materials, supplies, and components						
Total	-2.6	1.0	1.0	4.4	3.3	0.7
Foods	-0.2	-0.5	5.5	-4.5	10.3	2.1
Energy	-11.6	0.7	-4.2	2.9	1.1	11.2
Other	-0.8	1.2	1.6	5.2	3.2	-0.9
Crude materials for further processing						
Total	-11.6	3.3	0.1	-0.5	5.5	14.7
Foods	-5.8	3.0	7.2	-9.4	12.9	-1.0
Energy	-16.6	2.3	-12.3	-0.1	3.7	51.2
Other	-7.6	5.7	10.7	17.3	-4.2	-5.5

Annual Percent Changes in Producer Price Indexes for Selected Finished Goods Other than Foods and Energy

Index	1991	1992	1993	1994	1995	1996
Finished goods other than foods and energy	3.1	2.0	0.4	1.6	2.6	0.6
Consumer goods	-0.9	1.6	-0.2	1.6	2.3	3.6
Passenger cars	3.1	0.6	3.3	2.1	1.7	-0.8
Light trucks	5.4	4.8	4.2	3.3	1.5	0.2
Prescription drugs	7.8	6.4	3.2	3.1	4.2	2.0
Over-the-counter drugs	5.1	5.2	2.7	1.7	1.7	-1.7
Tobacco products	13.2	6.7	-21.4	0.4	3.6	2.6
Books	2.3	5.2	0.6	5.4	6.5	3.2
Periodicals	5.5	4.9	3.1	2.0	3.6	3.3
Newspapers	5.9	5.2	4.8	3.9	8.5	5.4
Household furniture	1.8	1.6	3.7	2.7	2.7	1.4
Capital equipment	2.5	1.7	1.8	2.0	2.2	0.4
Heavy trucks	3.7	3.1	3.1	3.0	4.1	-4.5
Truck trailers	1.3	2.6	3.3	7.7	2.2	-1.4
Metal cutting machine tools	2.9	3.2	0.6	1.8	4.1	3.1
Metal forming machine tools	2.6	1.5	2.6	3.5	2.2	2.6
Computers	-19.4	-14.9	-12.5	-6.8	-12.7	-22.3
Agricultural machinery	3.5	3.0	2.9	2.7	4.7	1.4
Construction machinery	2.8	3.1	1.1	2.0	2.5	1.8

Source: U.S. Bureau of Labor Statistics

Annual Percent Changes in Producer Price Indexes for Selected Food Items

Index	1991	1992	1993	1994	1995	1996
Finished consumer foods	-1.5	1.6	2.4	1.1	1.9	3.4
Pork	-16.9	-0.3	4.3	-11.1	15.3	21.9
Dairy products	6.4	-2.2	3.1	-2.0	5.4	2.4
Fresh fruits and melons	-17.3	-15.7	11.8	-11.2	2.5	37.2
Fresh and dry vegetables	-16.3	67.4	27.7	25.6	-36.0	-24.3
Roasted coffee	-6.2	-6.9	5.5	49.8	-8.2	-8.4
Intermediate foods and feeds	-0.2	-0.5	5.5	-4.5	10.3	2.1
Prepared animal feeds	2.9	0.6	6.0	-10.6	20.6	5.4
Crude vegetable oils	-13.9	5.4	34.3	4.1	-14.1	-9.3
Flour	13.4	0.5	8.6	-1.1	20.1	-9.0
Confectionery materials	4.0	-8.1	10.4	2.2	1.5	2.2
Refined sugar	-1.6	-1.2	-0.6	0.8	0.8	4.2
Crude foodstuffs and feedstuffs	-5.8	3.0	7.2	-9.4	12.9	-1.0
Slaughter hogs	-19.5	7.6	-5.0	-21.3	40.6	23.2
Soybeans	-7.4	3.3	20.1	-18.1	26.7	-3.7
Wheat	37.1	-1.2	18.6	-5.6	29.9	-19.3
Corn	2.2	-10.4	34.7	-22.4	49.4	-21.0
Fluid milk	16.1	-7.2	6.7	-5.2	8.4	1.1

Annual Percent Changes in Producer Price Indexes for Selected Energy Items

Index	1991	1992	1993	1994	1995	1996
Finished energy goods	-9.6	-0.3	-4.1	3.5	1.1	11.7
Gasoline	-25.1	-4.2	-16.8	11.2	2.4	27.1
Home heating oil	-30.5	-5.4	-10.1	6.9	11.9	25.0
Residential electric power	5.1	1.2	0.8	1.5	0.9	0.6
Residential natural gas	0.7	4.6	5.4	-2.6	-2.4	11.2
Intermediate energy goods	-11.6	0.7	-4.2	2.9	1.1	11.2
Residual fuels	-39.0	24.3	-17.8	10.2	-4.7	32.8
Natural gas to electric utilities	2.2	2.7	-13.0	3.4	-1.4	6.1
Diesel fuels	-30.4	-3.8	-15.9	5.9	11.1	26.2
Jet fuels	-32.7	-5.4	-11.7	4.3	6.1	26.1
Commercial power	0.3	1.8	3.2	2.3	0.6	-0.1
Crude energy materials	-16.6	2.3	-12.3	-0.1	3.7	51.2
Natural gas	-4.9	7.5	-3.8	-14.0	-0.3	92.0
Crude petroleum	-30.5	-2.4	-27.7	21.1	10.8	35.8
Coal	-1.6	0.2	1.0	-2.1	-0.8	-1.1

Source: U.S. Bureau of Labor Statistics

Index of Leading Economic Indicators

The index of leading economic indicators is based on 10 different measures and is considered a signal to the direction of the U.S. economy.

Leading Index (1992=100)

	IQ	IIQ	IIIQ	IVQ
1988	100.2	100.5	100.3	100.3
1989	100.0	99.5	99.5	99.6
1990	99.8	99.7	99.2	98.0
1991	98.1	99.1	99.6	99.3
1992	99.7	99.9	99.9	100.5
1993	100.5	100.3	100.3	100.8
1994	101.2	101.4	101.4	101.6
1995	101.1	100.5	100.9	101.0
1996	101.2	102.1	102.4	102.6
1997	103.3	103.7		

Leading Index – Percent change from preceding quarter

	IQ	IIQ	IIIQ	IVQ
1988	0.1	0.3	-0.2	0.0
1989	-0.3	-0.5	0.0	0.1
1990	0.2	-0.1	-0.5	-1.2
1991	0.1	1.0	0.5	-0.3
1992	0.4	0.2	0.0	0.6
1993	0.0	-0.2	0.0	0.5
1994	0.4	0.2	0.0	0.2
1995	-0.5	-0.6	0.4	0.1
1996	0.2	0.9	0.3	0.2
1997	0.7	0.4		

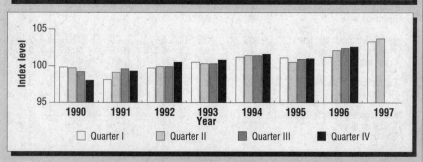

Note: Quarterly data are averages of monthly figures.
Source: Conference Board

Leading Index Components

		Factor
1	Average weekly hours, manufacturing	.222
2	Average weekly initial claims for unemployment insurance	.025
3	Manufacturers' new orders, consumer goods and materials	.047
4	Vendor performance, slower deliveries diffusion index	.026
5	Manufacturers' new orders, nondefense capital goods	.012
6	Building permits, new private housing units	.017
7	Stock prices, 500 common stocks	.031
8	Money supply, M2	.293
9	Interest rate spread, 10-year Treasury bonds less federal funds	.310
10	Index of consumer expectations	.017

Source: Conference Board

Corporate Profits

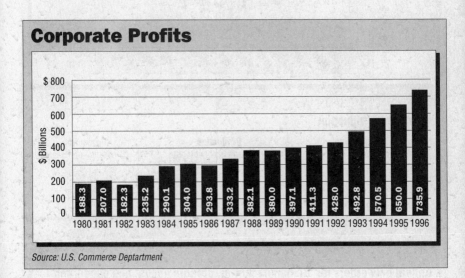

Source: U.S. Commerce Deptartment

Industrial Production and Capacity Utilization

Industrial Production

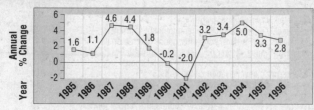

Industrial Capacity Utilization

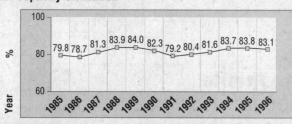

Source: Federal Reserve System

Raw Steel Production

Year	Production (Thousands of net tons)	Year	Production (Thousands of net tons)	Year	Production (Thousands of net tons)
1986	81,606	1990	98,906	1994	100,579
1987	89,151	1991	87,896	1995	104,930
1988	99,924	1992	92,949	1996	105,309
1989	97,943	1993	97,877		

Source: American Iron & Steel Institute

Factory Orders

Annual new orders for all manufacturing, durable goods, and nondurable goods industries ($ billions)

Year	All manufacturing		Durable goods		Nondurable goods	
	Amount	% change	Amount	% change	Amount	% change
1987	$2,512.7	+7.3	$1,329.7	+6.9	$1,183.0	+7.7
1988	2,739.2	+9.0	1,464.9	+10.2	1,274.3	+7.7
1989	2,874.9	+5.0	1,512.7	+3.3	1,362.2	+6.9
1990	2,934.1	+2.1	1,507.0	-0.4	1,427.1	+4.8
1991	2,865.7	-2.3	1,438.2	-4.6	1,427.5	–
1992	2,978.5	+3.9	1,515.7	+5.4	1,462.9	+2.5
1993	3,092.4	+3.8	1,597.0	+5.4	1,495.4	+2.2
1994	3,356.8	+8.6	1,794.5	+12.4	1,562.3	+4.5
1995	3,604.2	+7.4	1,937.6	+8.0	1,666.6	+6.7
1996	3,770.4	+4.6	2,039.6	+5.3	1,730.8	+3.9

Source: U.S. Census Bureau

Capital Spending

Capital Expenditures for Companies with Five or More Employees

	1993		1994		1995	
	$ millions	%	$ millions	%	$ millions	%
Total structures	$144,918	29.6%	$168,101	30.6%	$183,111	30.5%
Total equipment	338,444	69.1	376,340	68.5	417,736	69.5
Other	6,320	1.3	4,833	0.9	277	—
Total	**489,682**	**100**	**549,274**	**100**	**601,123**	**100**

Capital Expenditures for Structures and Equipment by Selected Industry Sectors, 1995 ($ billions)

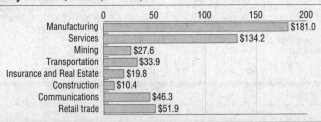

Source: U.S. Census Bureau

Worker Productivity

Changes in Productivity, or Output per Hour Worked, in Nonfarm Businesses

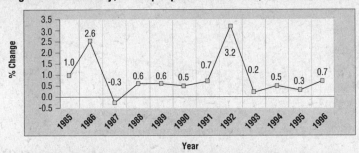

Source: U.S. Census Bureau

Construction Spending

Value of New Construction Put in Place ($ millions)

Type of construction	1985	1986	1987	1988	1989	1990
Private	$323,600	$345,300	$351,000	$360,900	$371,600	$361,100
Residential	158,500	187,100	194,700	198,100	196,600	182,900
Nonresidential buildings and other construction	165,100	158,200	156,300	162,800	175,100	178,200
Public	77,800	84,600	90,600	94,700	98,200	107,500
Total	401,400	429,900	441,600	455,600	469,800	468,500

Type of construction	1991	1992	1993	1994	1995	1996
Private	$314,100	$336,200	$362,688	$399,366	$406,776	$437,079
Residential	157,800	187,800	210,455	238,874	230,688	247,177
Nonresidential buildings and other construction	156,200	148,400	152,233	160,492	176,087	189,902
Public	110,100	115,800	115,960	120,530	127,292	131,506
Total	424,200	452,100	478,648	519,896	534,068	568,585

Source: U.S. Census Bureau

Personal Income: Where It Goes

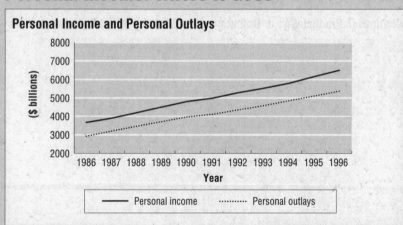

Personal Income and Personal Outlays

Source: U.S. Commerce Department, Bureau of Economic Analysis

U.S. Personal Income

Year	Personal income ($ billions)	Disposable personal income after taxes ($ billions)	Personal outlays ($ billions)	Personal savings ($ billions)
1986	3,658.4	3,198.5	2,991.1	207.4
1987	3,888.7	3,374.6	3,194.7	179.9
1988	4,184.6	3,652.6	3,451.7	200.9
1989	4,501.0	3,906.1	3,706.7	199.4
1990	4,804.2	4,179.4	3,958.1	221.3
1991	4,981.6	4,356.8	4,097.4	259.5
1992	5,277.2	4,626.7	4,341.0	285.6
1993	5,519.2	4,829.2	4,580.7	248.5
1994	5,791.8	5,052.7	4,842.1	210.6
1995	6,150.8	5,355.7	5,101.1	254.6
1996	6,495.2	5,608.3	5,368.8	239.6

Source: U.S. Commerce Department, Bureau of Economic Analysis

Consumer Spending

Personal Consumption Expenditures
(In billions)

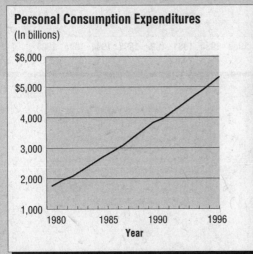

Year	Personal consumption expenditures (In billions)
1980	$1,760.4
1981	1,941.3
1982	2,076.8
1983	2,283.4
1984	2,492.3
1985	2,704.8
1986	2,892.7
1987	3,094.5
1988	3,349.7
1989	3,594.8
1990	3,839.3
1991	3,975.1
1992	4,219.8
1993	4,459.2
1994	4,717.0
1995	4,957.7
1996	5,207.6

Source: U.S. Commerce Department, Bureau of Economic Analysis

Retail Sales

Retail Sales by Type of Business ($ millions)

	1986	1990	1995	1996
Retail sales total	$1,449,636	$1,844,611	$2,324,038	$2,445,296
Durable goods total	540,688	668,835	925,017	993,336
Nondurable goods total	908,948	1,175,776	1,399,021	1,451,960
Kind of business				
Building materials stores	$ 77,104	$ 94,640	$ 125,831	$ 134,485
Automotive dealers	326,138	387,605	551,330	592,919
Furniture stores	75,714	91,545	127,270	133,486
General merchandise stores	169,397	215,514	299,169	312,792
Food stores	297,019	368,333	409,617	423,318
Gasoline service stations	102,093	138,504	146,080	154,967
Apparel and accessory stores	75,626	95,819	110,429	113,668
Eating and drinking places	139,415	190,149	232,060	236,526

Total Retail Sales ($ millions)

Source: U.S. Census Bureau

Consumer Confidence Index

Consumer confidence levels reflect people's feelings about general business conditions, employment opportunities and their own income prospects (1985=100).

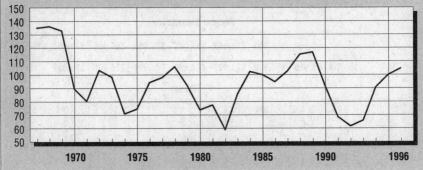

Year	Annual average	Year	Annual average	Year	Annual average
1967	135.0	1977	97.9	1987	102.6
1968	136.1	1978	106.0	1988	115.2
1969	132.9	1979	91.9	1989	116.8
1970	89.6	1980	73.8	1990	91.5
1971	80.4	1981	77.4	1991	68.5
1972	103.3	1982	59.0	1992	61.6
1973	98.3	1983	85.7	1993	65.9
1974	70.9	1984	102.3	1994	90.6
1975	74.5	1985	100.0	1995	100.0
1976	94.3	1986	94.7	1996	104.6

Source: Conference Board

Household Finances

Income Brackets by Race and Hispanic Origin of Householder
(Income in 1995 dollars)

Year	Percent distribution								
	Under $5,000	$5,000 to $9,999	$10,000 to $14,999	$15,000 to $24,999	$25,000 to $34,999	$35,000 to $49,999	$50,000 to $74,999	$75,000 to $99,999	$100,000 and over
All Races									
1970	5.2%	9.1%	8.0%	15.8%	16.9%	21.3%	16.3%	4.6%	2.9%
1975	3.5	10.1	9.1	16.8	15.6	19.8	16.9	5.1	3.2
1980	3.5	9.8	8.7	16.5	14.6	19.3	17.4	6.3	4.0
1985	3.9	9.5	8.3	16.0	14.5	18.1	17.4	7.1	5.3
1990	3.7	8.8	8.1	15.5	14.4	17.7	17.6	7.6	6.6
1991	3.8	9.2	8.5	16.0	14.6	17.1	17.2	7.4	6.3
1992	4.1	9.3	8.8	16.0	14.5	16.8	17.1	7.2	6.2
1993	4.1	9.3	8.8	16.0	14.7	16.2	16.7	7.4	6.7
1994	4.0	9.2	8.9	16.3	14.1	16.3	16.7	7.5	7.1
1995	3.7	8.6	8.7	15.9	14.2	16.9	17.1	7.7	7.1
White									
1970	4.6%	8.4%	7.5%	15.2%	17.0%	22.1%	17.1%	4.9%	3.2%
1975	3.0	9.1	8.6	16.4	15.6	20.5	17.9	5.4	3.4
1980	2.9	8.8	8.1	16.1	14.8	19.9	18.3	6.7	4.4
1985	3.3	8.4	7.9	15.6	14.6	18.7	18.1	7.6	5.8
1990	2.9	7.7	7.7	15.3	14.5	18.2	18.5	8.0	7.1
1991	2.9	8.0	8.3	15.8	14.8	17.5	18.0	8.0	6.7
1992	3.2	8.2	8.3	15.7	14.7	17.2	18.2	7.7	6.7
1993	3.3	8.2	8.4	15.7	14.8	16.9	17.6	7.8	7.2
1994	3.2	8.1	8.6	16.1	14.2	16.7	17.5	7.9	7.7
1995	2.9	7.7	8.4	15.6	14.4	17.3	17.9	8.2	7.7
Black									
1970	10.2%	15.6%	12.7%	21.4%	15.2%	14.2%	8.3%	1.8%	0.6%
1975	7.4	18.9	13.4	19.6	15.4	14.1	8.7	1.9	0.6
1980	8.5	18.2	13.2	20.3	12.9	13.9	9.8	2.5	0.9
1985	8.7	18.3	11.5	19.3	13.4	13.7	10.6	3.1	1.4
1990	10.0	16.8	11.2	17.4	13.5	14.1	10.7	4.0	2.2
1991	10.0	18.2	10.6	17.8	13.5	14.2	10.4	3.2	2.1
1992	10.5	17.6	11.9	18.0	13.4	13.3	9.9	3.3	2.0
1993	9.9	17.6	11.9	18.4	14.0	12.3	10.2	3.4	2.3
1994	9.1	17.0	11.2	18.5	13.0	13.5	10.9	4.0	2.8
1995	8.6	15.4	11.5	18.8	13.6	14.6	11.2	4.0	2.2
Hispanic origin									
1975	5.0%	12.3%	12.3%	22.4%	17.4%	17.9%	9.6%	1.9%	1.2%
1980	5.1	11.9	11.6	21.1	16.2	16.9	12.3	3.3	1.7
1985	5.5	13.5	12.1	19.3	15.6	16.2	11.5	4.3	1.8
1990	5.5	11.9	12.0	18.8	16.2	16.5	12.1	4.3	2.7
1991	5.3	12.2	11.9	20.1	15.6	15.8	12.0	4.0	2.9
1992	5.9	13.2	11.4	20.3	16.3	15.0	11.8	3.5	2.6
1993	5.4	13.7	11.8	20.6	16.9	14.1	11.4	3.5	2.6
1994	6.1	14.0	12.0	19.9	14.9	14.6	11.5	4.1	2.9
1995	6.0	13.9	12.2	21.5	15.4	13.3	11.6	3.7	2.4

Source: U.S. Census Bureau

Making Up Lost Ground

Median household income, adjusted for inflation, is slowly increasing, but is still below the levels of the late 1980s.

Median Household Income by Region: 1994 and 1995

(Income in 1995 dollars)

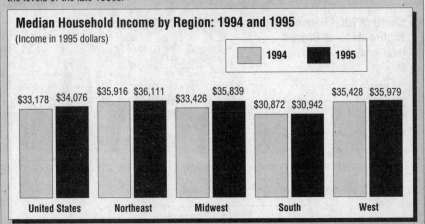

	1994	1995
United States	$33,178	$34,076
Northeast	$35,916	$36,111
Midwest	$33,426	$35,839
South	$30,872	$30,942
West	$35,428	$35,979

Median Household Income in 1995 Dollars, by Race and Hispanic Origin

(Numbers in thousands)

Year	All races	White	Black	Asian and Pacific Islander	Hispanic origin
1967	$29,989	$31,273	$18,158	–	–
1968	31,301	32,590	19,218	–	–
1969	32,449	33,865	20,470	–	–
1970	32,229	33,569	20,432	–	–
1971	31,923	33,390	19,724	–	–
1972	33,284	34,918	20,382	–	$26,351
1973	33,941	35,572	20,939	–	26,295
1974	32,879	34,385	20,449	–	26,152
1975	31,999	33,463	20,089	–	24,040
1976	32,548	34,095	20,274	–	24,551
1977	32,727	34,415	20,309	–	25,674
1978	34,011	35,357	21,248	–	26,649
1979	33,901	35,544	20,868	–	26,859
1980	32,795	34,598	19,932	–	25,278
1981	32,263	34,088	19,129	–	25,879
1982	32,155	33,663	19,079	–	24,196
1983	31,957	33,513	19,018	–	24,338
1984	32,878	34,685	19,759	–	24,924
1985	33,452	35,279	20,989	–	24,737
1986	34,620	36,397	20,969	–	25,519
1987	34,962	36,836	21,025	–	25,940
1988	35,073	37,077	21,136	$41,568	26,227
1989	35,526	37,370	22,225	44,371	26,942
1990	34,914	36,416	21,777	44,834	26,037
1991	33,709	35,324	21,044	40,784	25,390
1992	33,278	34,987	20,373	41,061	24,546
1993	32,949	34,762	20,601	40,443	24,137
1994	33,178	34,992	21,623	41,629	24,085
1995	34,076	35,766	22,393	40,614	22,860

Source: U.S. Census Bureau

The Rich Get Richer...

The top-earning households claim a very large share of the total household income in America.

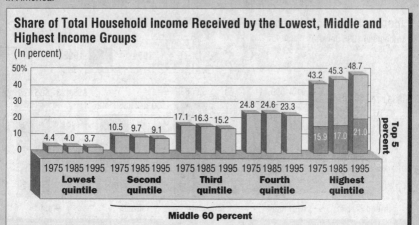

Share of Total Household Income Received by the Lowest, Middle and Highest Income Groups
(In percent)

Share of Total Income Received by Each Fifth and Top 5 Percent of Households
(Income in 1995 dollars)

	Upper limit of each fifth (dollars)				Lower limit of top 5 percent (dollars)	Share of aggregate income					
Year	Lowest	Second	Third	Fourth		Lowest	Second	Third	Fourth	Highest	Top 5 %
1980	$13,992	$26,110	$40,017	$58,701	$95,366	4.3	10.3	16.9	24.9	43.7	15.8
1981	13,802	25,429	39,573	58,524	95,229	4.2	10.2	16.8	25.0	43.8	15.6
1982	13,582	25,522	39,152	58,457	97,413	4.1	10.1	16.6	24.7	44.5	16.2
1983	13,771	25,665	39,352	59,519	98,846	4.1	10.0	16.5	24.7	44.7	16.4
1984	14,081	26,261	40,346	61,019	102,074	4.1	9.9	16.4	24.7	44.9	16.5
1985	14,164	26,701	41,106	62,049	103,767	4.0	9.7	16.3	24.6	45.3	17.0
1986	14,403	27,508	42,487	64,130	108,774	3.9	9.7	16.2	24.5	45.7	17.5
1987	14,489	27,502	42,930	64,881	108,569	3.8	9.6	16.1	24.3	46.2	18.2
1988	14,663	27,697	43,164	65,176	110,326	3.8	9.6	16.0	24.3	46.3	18.3
1989	14,866	28,268	43,446	66,011	112,764	3.8	9.5	15.8	24.0	46.8	18.9
1990	14,575	27,591	42,210	64,371	110,479	3.9	9.6	15.9	24.0	46.6	18.6
1991	14,085	26,855	41,479	63,511	107,866	3.8	9.6	15.9	24.2	46.5	18.1
1992	13,687	26,222	41,169	63,010	107,560	3.8	9.4	15.8	24.2	46.9	18.6
1993	13,676	26,028	40,914	63,597	110,360	3.6	9.0	15.1	23.5	48.9	21.0
1994	13,806	25,914	41,236	64,622	112,933	3.6	8.9	15.0	23.4	49.1	21.2
1995	14,400	26,914	42,002	65,124	113,000	3.7	9.1	15.2	23.3	48.7	21.0

Source: U.S. Census Bureau.

Poverty's Burden

Percentage of All Persons Below Poverty Level

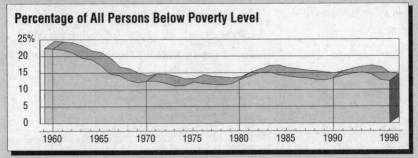

Poverty Rates by Age
(Percent)

Year	Under 18 years of age	18 to 64 years	65 years and over	Year	Under 18 years of age	18 to 64 years	65 years and over
1959	27.3	17.0	35.2	1978	15.9	8.7	14.0
1960	26.9	—	—	1979	16.4	8.9	15.2
1961	25.6	—	—	1980	18.3	10.1	15.7
1962	25.0	—	—	1981	20.0	11.1	15.3
1963	23.1	—	—	1982	21.9	12.0	14.6
1964	23.0	—	—	1983	22.3	12.4	13.8
1965	21.0	—	—	1984	21.5	11.7	12.4
1966	17.6	10.5	28.5	1985	20.7	11.3	12.6
1967	16.6	10.0	29.5	1986	20.5	10.8	12.4
1968	15.6	9.0	25.0	1987	20.3	10.6	12.5
1969	14.0	8.7	25.3	1988	19.5	10.5	12.0
1970	15.1	9.0	24.6	1989	19.6	10.2	11.4
1971	15.3	9.3	21.6	1990	20.6	10.7	12.2
1972	15.1	8.8	18.6	1991	21.8	11.4	12.4
1973	14.4	8.3	16.3	1992	22.3	11.9	12.9
1974	15.4	8.3	14.6	1993	22.7	12.4	12.2
1975	17.1	9.2	15.3	1994	21.8	11.9	11.7
1976	16.0	9.0	15.0	1995	20.8	11.4	10.5
1977	16.2	8.8	14.1	1996	20.5	11.4	10.8

Poverty Rates by Age: 1959-1996

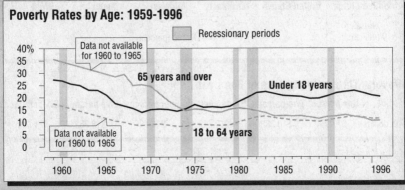

Source: U.S. Census Bureau

Persons Below Poverty Level by Race and Hispanic Origin
(Numbers in thousands)

Year	Total Number	Total Percent	White Number	White Percent	Black Number	Black Percent	Hispanic Origin* Number	Hispanic Origin* Percent
1959	39,490	22.4%	28,484	18.1%	9,927	55.1%	–	–
1960	39,851	22.2	28,309	17.8	–	–	–	–
1965	33,185	17.3	22,496	13.3	–	–	–	–
1966	28,510	14.7	19,290	11.3	8,867	41.8	–	–
1970	25,420	12.6	17,484	9.9	7,548	33.5	–	–
1975	25,877	12.3	17,770	9.7	7,545	31.3	2,991	26.9%
1980	29,272	13.0	19,699	10.2	8,579	32.5	3,491	25.7
1985	33,064	14.0	22,860	11.4	8,926	31.3	5,236	29.0
1990	33,585	13.5	22,326	10.7	9,837	31.9	6,006	28.1
1991	35,708	14.2	23,747	11.3	10,242	32.7	6,339	28.7
1992	38,014	14.8	25,259	11.9	10,827	33.4	7,592	29.6
1993	39,265	15.1	26,226	12.2	10,877	33.1	8,126	30.6
1994	38,059	14.5	25,379	11.7	10,196	30.6	8,416	30.7
1995	36,425	13.8	24,423	11.2	9,872	29.3	8,574	30.3
1996	36,529	13.7	24,650	11.2	9,694	28.4	8,697	29.4

*Persons of Hispanic origin may be of any race.

Persons in Poverty by Region: 1995 and 1996

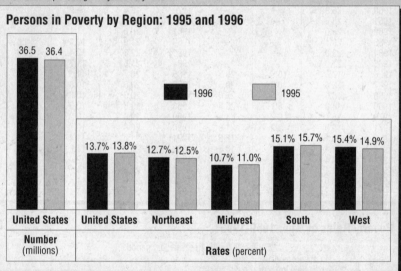

■ 1996   ▢ 1995

36.5 36.4

United States
Number (millions)

13.7% 13.8% 12.7% 12.5% 10.7% 11.0% 15.1% 15.7% 15.4% 14.9%

United States   Northeast   Midwest   South   West

Rates (percent)

Poverty Thresholds by Size of Family in 1996

	One person	Two persons	Three persons	Four persons	Five persons	Six persons
(In dollars)	$7,995	$10,233	$12,516	$16,036	$18,952	$21,389

Source: U.S. Census Bureau

Members of the Board of Governors of the Federal Reserve System

Name	Appointed by President	Term expires
Alan Greenspan, Chairman	Reagan and Bush	January 31, 2006*
Alice Rivlin, Vice Chairman	Clinton	January 31, 2010**
Laurence Meyer	Clinton	January 31, 2002
Susan M. Phillips	Bush	January 31, 1998
Edward W. Kelley Jr.	Reagan and Bush	January 31, 2004
Edward M. Gramlich	Clinton	January 31, 2008†
Roger W. Ferguson	Clinton	January 31, 2000†

*In 1996, Mr. Greenspan was reappointed as chairman until the year 2000, but his term as a Fed governor runs until 2006. **Ms. Rivlin was named vice chairman for a four-year term, ending in 2000, but her term as a Fed governor continues until 2010. †Appointments still awaited Senate approval in early October 1997.

Presidents of the Federal Reserve Banks

District	Head office	President*
First	Boston	Cathy E. Minehan
Second	New York	William J. McDonough
Third	Philadelphia	Edward G. Boehne
Fourth	Cleveland	Jerry L. Jordan
Fifth	Richmond	J. Alfred Broaddus, Jr.
Sixth	Atlanta	Jack Guynn
Seventh	Chicago	Michael H. Moskow
Eighth	St. Louis	Thomas C. Melzer
Ninth	Minneapolis	Gary H. Stern
Tenth	Kansas City, MO	Thomas M. Hoenig
Eleventh	Dallas	Robert D. McTeer, Jr.
Twelfth	San Francisco	Robert T. Parry

*All the presidents are serving five-year terms that end Feb. 28, 2001.

The Money Supply

Money Stock and Liquid Assets
(Billions of dollars, seasonally adjusted)

Year (December)	M1	M2	M3	L
1980	$409.0	$1,601.1	$1,992.3	$2,330.0
1981	436.8	1,756.2	2,240.9	2,601.9
1982	474.7	1,910.9	2,442.3	2,846.0
1983	521.2	2,127.7	2,684.8	3,150.6
1984	552.2	2,312.2	2,979.8	3,518.6
1985	619.9	2,497.6	3,198.3	3,827.0
1986	724.4	2,733.9	3,486.4	4,122.3
1987	749.7	2,832.7	3,672.5	4,339.9
1988	787.0	2,996.3	3,912.9	4,663.5
1989	794.2	3,160.9	4,065.9	4,892.8
1990	825.8	3,279.5	4,125.9	4,976.6

	M1	M2	M3	L
1991	$897.3	$3,379.6	$4,180.4	$5,006.2
1992	1,025.0	3,434.0	4,190.4	5,078.0
1993	1,129.8	3,486.6	4,254.4	5,167.8
1994	1,150.7	3,502.1	4,327.3	5,308.4
1995	1,129.0	3,655.0	4,592.5	5,697.6
1996	1,081.0	3,834.3	4,933.0	6,098.7

M1: Sum of currency, demand deposits, travelers checks, and other checkable deposits.
M2: M1 plus retail money-market mutual fund balances, savings deposits (including money-market deposit accounts) and small time deposits.
M3: M2 plus large time deposits, repurchase agreements, Euro-dollars, and institution-only money-market mutual fund balances.
L: M3 plus other liquid assets.
Source: Federal Reserve System

Key Interest Rates (Average of daily figures)

Year	Discount rate	Federal funds rate	Prime rate
1977	5.46%	5.54%	6.83%
1978	7.46	7.94	9.05
1979	10.29	11.20	12.67
1980	11.77	13.35	15.26
1981	13.42	16.39	18.87
1982	11.01	12.24	14.85
1983	8.50	9.09	10.79
1984	8.80	10.23	12.04
1985	7.69	8.10	9.93
1986	6.32	6.80	8.33
1987	5.66	6.66	8.21
1988	6.20	7.57	9.32
1989	6.93	9.21	10.87
1990	6.98	8.10	10.01
1991	5.45	5.69	8.46
1992	3.25	3.52	6.25
1993	3.00	3.02	6.00
1994	3.60	4.21	7.15
1995	5.21	5.83	8.83
1996	5.02	5.30	8.27

Source: Federal Reserve System

U.S. International Trade

U.S. Balance of Trade (In millions)

Year	Exports		Imports		Balance		
	Goods	Services	Goods	Services	Goods	Services	Total
1980	224,250	47,584	-249,750	-41,491	-25,500	6,093	-19,407
1981	237,044	57,354	-265,067	-45,503	-28,023	11,852	-16,172
1982	211,157	64,079	-247,642	-51,749	-36,485	12,329	-24,156
1983	201,799	64,307	-268,901	-54,973	-67,102	9,335	-57,767
1984	219,926	71,168	-332,418	-67,748	-112,492	3,419	-109,073
1985	215,915	73,155	-338,088	-72,862	-122,173	294	-121,880
1986	223,344	86,312	-368,425	-81,836	-145,081	4,476	-140,605
1987	250,208	98,553	-409,765	-92,349	-159,557	6,204	-153,353
1988	320,230	111,024	-447,189	-99,965	-126,959	11,059	-115,900
1989	362,120	127,142	-477,365	-104,185	-115,245	22,957	-92,288
1990	389,307	147,824	-498,337	-120,019	-109,030	27,805	-81,225
1991	416,913	164,236	-490,981	-121,195	-74,068	43,041	-31,027
1992	440,352	177,154	-536,458	-120,255	-96,106	56,899	-39,207
1993	456,832	186,711	-589,441	-126,403	-132,609	60,308	-72,301
1994	502,398	197,248	-668,590	-135,472	-166,192	61,776	-104,416
1995	575,871	218,739	-749,431	-147,036	-173,560	71,703	-101,857
1996	612,069	236,764	-803,239	-156,634	-191,170	80,130	-111,040

Source: U.S. Commerce Department

Foreign Direct Investment Position in the U.S.
(Historical-cost basis)

Year end — Investment ($ millions)

Year end	Investment ($ millions)
1982	$124,677
1983	$137,061
1984	$164,583
1985	$184,615
1986	$220,414
1987	$263,394
1988	$314,754
1989	$368,924
1990	$394,911
1991	$419,108
1992	$423,131
1993	$467,412
1994	$496,539
1995	$560,850
1996	$630,045

Source: U.S. Commerce Department

U.S. Direct Investment Position Abroad
(Historical-cost basis)

Year end — Investment ($ millions)

Year end	Investment ($ millions)
1982	$207,752
1983	$212,150
1984	$218,093
1985	$238,369
1986	$270,472
1987	$326,253
1988	$347,179
1989	$381,781
1990	$430,521
1991	$467,844
1992	$502,063
1993	$564,283
1994	$640,320
1995	$717,554
1996	$796,494

Source: U.S. Commerce Department

U.S. Direct Investment Position Abroad on a Historical-Cost Basis, by Major Area

Year	All areas	Canada	Europe	Latin America and Other Western Hemisphere	Africa	Middle East	Asia and Pacific	Inter-national
				($ millions)				
1982	207,752	43,511	92,449	28,161	6,487	3,550	28,282	5,314
1985	238,369	47,934	108,664	30,417	6,130	4,554	35,294	5,378
1990	430,521	69,508	214,739	71,413	3,650	3,959	64,718	2,535
1991	467,844	70,711	235,163	77,677	4,427	4,963	72,219	2,684
1992	502,063	68,690	248,744	91,307	4,469	5,759	79,962	3,131
1993	564,283	69,922	285,735	100,482	5,469	6,571	92,671	3,433
1994	640,320	78,018	320,135	115,093	5,606	6,741	111,373	3,355
1995	717,554	85,441	360,994	128,252	6,383	7,669	125,834	2,981
1996	796,494	91,587	399,632	144,209	7,568	8,743	140,402	4,352
				(% total position)				
1982	–	20.9	44.5	13.6	3.1	1.7	13.6	2.6
1985	100.0	20.1	45.6	12.8	2.6	1.9	14.8	2.3
1990	100.0	16.1	49.9	16.6	0.8	0.9	15.0	0.6
1991	100.0	15.1	50.3	16.6	0.9	1.1	15.4	0.6
1992	100.0	13.7	49.5	18.2	0.9	1.1	15.9	0.6
1993	100.0	12.4	50.6	17.8	1.0	1.2	16.4	0.6
1994	100.0	12.2	50.0	18.0	0.9	1.1	17.4	0.5
1995	100.0	11.9	50.3	17.9	0.9	1.1	17.5	0.4
1996	100.0	11.5	50.2	18.1	1.0	1.1	17.6	0.5

Foreign Direct Investment Position in the U.S. on a Historical-Cost Basis, by Major Area

Year	All areas	Canada	Europe	Latin America and Other Western Hemisphere	Africa	Middle East	Asia and Pacific
				($ millions)			
1982	124,677	11,708	83,193	14,229	105	4,401	11,041
1985	184,615	17,131	121,413	16,826	461	4,954	23,830
1990	394,911	29,544	247,320	20,168	505	4,425	92,948
1991	419,108	36,834	256,053	14,546	937	4,864	105,873
1992	423,131	37,515	249,904	19,481	1,209	6,057	108,965
1993	467,412	40,373	285,004	21,908	1,264	6,575	112,289
1994	496,539	41,960	303,649	26,070	1,230	6,674	116,956
1995	560,850	48,258	357,193	25,240	1,164	6,008	122,986
1996	630,045	53,845	410,425	24,627	717	6,177	134,255
				(% total position)			
1982	100.0	9.4	66.7	11.4	0.1	3.5	8.9
1985	100.0	9.3	65.8	9.1	0.2	2.7	12.9
1990	100.0	7.5	62.6	5.1	0.1	1.1	23.5
1991	100.0	8.8	61.1	3.5	0.2	1.2	25.3
1992	100.0	8.9	59.1	4.6	0.3	1.4	25.8
1993	100.0	8.6	61.0	4.7	0.3	1.4	24.0
1994	100.0	8.5	61.2	5.3	0.2	1.3	23.6
1995	100.0	8.6	63.7	4.5	0.2	1.1	21.9
1996	100.0	8.5	65.1	3.9	0.1	1.0	21.3

Source: U.S. Commerce Department

Major U.S. Trading Partners

Top 15 Trading Partners - Exports of Goods in 1996

Rank	Country	($ billions)	% of total
1	Canada	$133.7	21.4%
2	Japan	67.5	10.8
3	Mexico	56.8	9.1
4	United Kingdom	30.9	4.9
5	Korea	26.6	4.3
6	Germany	23.5	3.8
7	Taiwan	18.4	2.9
8	Singapore	16.7	2.7
9	Netherlands	16.6	2.7
10	France	14.4	2.3
11	Hong Kong	14.0	2.2
12	Brazil	12.7	2.0
13	Belgium	12.5	2.0
14	Australia	12.0	1.9
15	China	12.0	1.9

Top 15 Trading Partners - Imports of Goods in 1996

Rank	Country	($ billions)	% of total
1	Canada	$156.5	19.8%
2	Japan	115.2	14.6
3	Mexico	73.0	9.2
4	China	51.5	6.5
5	Germany	38.9	4.9
6	Taiwan	29.9	3.8
7	United Kingdom	28.9	3.7
8	Korea	22.7	2.9
9	Singapore	20.3	2.6
10	France	18.6	2.4
11	Italy	18.2	2.3
12	Malaysia	17.8	2.3
13	Venezuela	12.9	1.6
14	Thailand	11.3	1.4
15	Hong Kong	9.9	1.2

Source: U.S. Census Bureau

BUSINESS & INDUSTRY

MERGER MANIA *is the only way to describe it. Competition was fierce and getting fiercer. Companies were combining with one another in a desperate search for efficiency, market share, and new products and technology. Fueling it all was a strong stock market that made the combinations easier. The result: the formation of some of the biggest and best-known companies the world has ever known. Names like General Electric, United States Steel, DuPont and International Harvester.*

All that took place roughly a century ago. But today's merger-and-acquisition scene is remarkably similar to that of the turn of the last century. Competition, this time from all over the globe, is as tough as it has ever been. That competition has kept a lid on prices, forcing companies in all kinds of businesses to search for efficiency, market share, and new products and technologies. And the Great Bull Stock Market of the 1990s has helped it happen. The result has been a fantastic wave of mergers, both here and abroad, that have created another set of corporate giants that have a good chance of surviving and prospering for another 100 years. Chase Manhattan combines with Chemical Bank to eclipse Citicorp as the nation's largest bank. Boeing and McDonnell-Douglas merge to become a colossus in the aircraft industry. And blue-blood Morgan Stanley marries rough-and-tumble Dean Witter to become a powerhouse in the financial services business.

But those giant combinations are only the surface of what has been happening over the last few years. Consider that in 1996 alone the total volume of all mergers and acquisitions worldwide was a stunning $1 trillion. That included 10,000 deals worth at least $1 million each and 100 transactions worth $1 billion or more in the U.S. alone for a total of $650 billion, twice the dollar volume and the number of deals done at the peak of the last merger boom in the 1980s.

More important than the number and the size of the mergers, though, is the reason for them. These aren't the hostile M&A deals done in the 1980s that typically forced together two companies, laden with debt, that were then milked for quick profits by financial engineers. And they aren't the helter-skelter assemblages of disparate companies thrown together during the 1970s "conglomerate" fad. Rather, these are strategic mergers, the hopefully well-thought-out responses by smart executives to a variety of competitive pressures.

The merger in 1996 of Chemical Banking and Chase Manhattan is a case in point. Where there had been two banks, with two chairmen, two corporate-loan departments, roughly 600 branches and over 75,000 employes, there is today just one bank, one chairman and one loan department. Eventually there will be just 500 branches, and the combined operation will employ 12,000 fewer people. In an industry already plagued by slow-growth and too many players, Chase Manhattan has just grown at the same time it has reduced its costs.

Other mergers reflect variations on the same strategic theme. Gillette paid $7 billion to buy Duracell International, the dominant player in the battery market, because it seems to make sense that Gillette can feed more products through Duracell's existing distribution channel. The combination of Dean Witter, with its huge base of retail brokers serving small investors, and Morgan Stanley, a premier investment banking firm, creates a firm that now has entree to the executive suites of the world's

great companies as well as to the living rooms of ordinary Americans. Boeing, primarily a builder of commercial airliners, now can compete for Pentagon contracts for fighters and bombers through its McDonnell Douglas subsidiary. Even the technology industry, known for disdaining mergers in favor of developing new products and services internally, is getting into the act. Cisco Systems spent $200 million to acquire Granite Systems, a company with few assets beyond an idea for a promising switching technology crucial to setting up computer networks. It was easier—and faster—to simply buy the idea than develop a solution in-house.

A common theme in many modern mergers is sheer size. Tyco International in Exeter, N.H., bought Carlisle Plastics and made it part of its existing Armin plastics unit. The combined entity doubled the volume of its purchases of low-density polyethylene film and gained more clout with suppliers. "There's a general attitude out there that no matter what market you're in, you need to be a gorilla in that market," Tyco Chairman Dennis Kozlowski told *The Wall Street Journal.* "I think virtually every CEO, no matter what size company he's running, has given serious thought to M&A."

Another characteristic of modern mergers is the lack of hostility. The hostile mergers of the 1980s usually ended with the chief executive officer of the acquired company on the street looking for work. Because most of the mergers today are strategic, the two CEOs can more easily work out an accommodation. Frequently the elder of the two gets the top post, sometimes for a designated period, with the understanding that the younger executive will eventually move into the top spot.

Even the occasional fights often end in something close to harmony. When CSX, the big rail company, cut a deal to buy Conrail, CSX's chief rival, Norfolk Southern, launched a hostile bid to try to steal Conrail away from CSX. After months of jockeying for position amid much hissing at one another, CSX and Norfolk Southern agreed to split Conrail between them. Conrail Chairman David LeVan, who had planned to run CSX after the merger, wound up out of a job, albeit with a multimillion-dollar payment for taking a hike.

The merger boom isn't confined to giant companies. The last few years also have seen the emergence of a new kind of entrepreneur, the "consolidator." Rather than create a new business from the ground up, consolidators aim to gather together under a corporate umbrella hundreds of similar small businesses. The point is to provide basic business services—accounting, purchasing, billing—from a central location while letting the people who started and presumably love their businesses concentrate on what they do best. Veterinary Centers of America, for instance, now owns some 150 pet hospitals and plans to buy at least 25 more each year for the foreseeable future. The company needn't worry about running out of veterinary hospitals to buy: At last count there were 16,000, most of them independent. Vets who have sold the pet hospitals they started say they now can focus on what they love best—treating animals—while leaving the details of running a small business to Veterinary Centers. Not everyone is happy, however. Some vets complain about the company's tough standards on cost control and billing. And, of course, consolidation won't be effective for some kinds of small businesses, such as elite restaurants that reflect their owners' abilities and predilections in food preparation. But consolidation makes too much sense to disappear.

Certainly, some of the current couplings won't work out over the long run. But the financial structure of many of today's mergers makes it less likely that a merged company will fall apart. During the 1980s, when stock prices were languishing, the merger mania was fueled by debt, including the issuance of billions of dollars of high-risk bonds, aptly dubbed "junk bonds." A merger of two companies financed through massive issuance of junk bonds had to start working quickly simply to make the installment payments on the vast debt. Today, many more mergers are done with stock and fewer with cash or debt. That reduces the risks to the newly created company because a stagnant or diluted stock isn't nearly as great a threat to the company's existence as a debt that can't be paid. And considering that the Dow Jones Industrial Average has risen nearly 250% since the beginning of the decade, stock is a considerably more valuable currency today than it was back in the 1980s.

The regulatory climate for mergers is much friendlier these days, too. Gone are the trustbusters of old who assumed big was bad and fought mergers tooth-and-nail. They've been replaced by economists who understand that bigger can be more efficient and that more efficient can mean the difference between survival and bankruptcy in the global marketplace. The regulators who staff the Federal Trade Commission and the Justice Department, the two agencies principally concerned with antitrust matters, have recognized that they must look beyond simple questions of market share to consider other circumstances. The domestic bank industry, for example, simply has too many players and must consolidate to remain efficient. Who, after all, wants to deal with an inefficient bank? In industries like telecommunications, technological change is so rapid—hard-wired to cellular to wireless to satellite—that regulators find it virtually impossible to even define what a market is, much less who has what share of it. And, at least so far, there's little evidence even in industries that have undergone consolidation, that the process has resulted in higher prices for consumers. Rather, in many cases—oil services, office products and disk drives, for example—prices have remained unchanged or fallen.

That isn't to say that regulators won't stop a merger they think will result in reduced competition. Witness Staples' effort to buy Office Depot. The government opposed the merger of the two biggest players in the so-called "office supply superstore" business even after Staples offered to sell off more than 60 of its stores to satisfy regulators' objections. Even the third-ranked player in the business, Office Depot, was said to be disappointed by the government's opposition; it had apparently planned to buy some of those Staples stores in a bid to increase its own market share, a move that some experts said would increase competition.

More often, though, regulators take a different tack than outright objections to mergers. Instead, they insist on settlements that give them continuing influence over how the merged company does business. These settlements can be surprisingly intrusive. More than two years after Eli Lilly, the big pharmaceutical concern, bought PCS Health Systems for $4 billion, executives of PCS aren't allowed to discuss some aspects of their business with Lilly executives. The FTC, prodded by drugstore owners and consumer groups, recently supoenaed thousands of pages of Lilly documents as part of an investigation into whether Lilly and PCS are violating any of the terms they agreed to when the FTC permitted the merger to go forward.

"We expect companies to deliver on their commitments, and coming close doesn't cut it," Daniel Ducore, compliance chief at the FTC, told *The Wall Street Journal*.

What could bring all this furious merger activity to a halt? A plunging stock market or a prolonged economic slowdown might. But those don't appear very likely anytime in the foreseeable future. And while lower stock prices might slow the number of mergers done in stock-only deals, they might also spur more all-cash purchases. In short, mergers are likely to just keep rolling along.

Douglas R. Sease, deputy editor, Money and Investing, at *The Wall Street Journal*

Spinoffs Are in Style, Too

While corporations were rushing to the altar in some of the biggest mergers of all time in 1997, many other companies were breaking up.

Corporate spinoffs are clearly in vogue, as more companies hope to maximize profits and stock prices by narrowing their business lines. ITT and American Telephone & Telegraph accomplished two of the biggest breakups in 1995 and 1996, and since then, such companies as Westinghouse Electric, Monsanto, General Instrument, CPC International, Rockwell International, Campbell Soup and PepsiCo have announced spinoffs of parts of their businesses as separate companies.

Books are being written and conferences are being organized, pushing the benefits of spinoffs. The buzzword behind the spinoffs is "focus." Smaller is assumed to be better. And certainly in some cases, unwieldy conglomerates may be better off in smaller pieces. A spinoff, for instance, is likely to help a small subsidiary that hasn't been getting much management attention or financial support.

But some critics question whether spinning off operations to shareholders will really accomplish much in the long run. For example, PepsiCo's restaurant operations haven't been neglected and they will still face a slew of competitors, whether aligned with the company's beverage business or not.

Whatever the wisdom of such deals, the spinoff trend is expected to continue. After all, the merger wave of the 1990s could well lead to a string of divorces that continue into the next century.

Corporate Shopping Spree

Merger and acquisition activity heated up again in the mid-1990s.

Total Value of Mergers and Acquisitions in the U.S.
(In billions)

Value and Number of Mergers and Acquisitions in the U.S.

Announcement date	Value (In millions)	Number of mergers and acquisitions
1985	$203,928.5	2,255
1986	228,222.7	3,147
1987	224,311.8	3,316
1988	352,313.8	3,915
1989	303,238.6	5,451
1990	182,571.6	5,650
1991	138,461.8	5,260
1992	150,067.6	5,504
1993	234,228.8	6,309
1994	340,128.0	7,571
1995	516,704.4	9,149
1996	647,966.1	10,324

The Largest U.S. Corporate Mergers, Acquisitions and Spinoffs

Target name	Acquirer name	Date announced	Value of transaction* (In millions)
MCI Communications Corp.**	WorldCom Inc.	10/01/97	$34,621.8
RJR Nabisco Inc.	Kohlberg Kravis Roberts & Co.	10/24/88	30,598.8
Electronic Data Systems Corp.	Shareholders	08/07/95	27,973.5
Lucent Technologies Inc.	Shareholders	09/20/95	24,067.1
NYNEX Corp.	Bell Atlantic Corp.	04/22/96	21,345.5
MCI Communications Corp.**	British Telecommunications	11/01/96	18,888.5
Capital Cities/ABC Inc.	Walt Disney Co.	07/31/95	18,862.5
Pacific Telesis Group	SBC Communications Inc.	04/01/96	16,490.0
McCaw Cellular Commun Inc.	American Telephone & Telegraph Co.	08/16/93	15,651.7
Warner Communications Inc.	Time Inc.	03/04/89	14,110.0
Barnett Banks, Jacksonville, FL	NationsBank Corp., Charlotte, NC	08/29/97	13,817.7
MFS Communications Co. Inc.	WorldCom Inc.	08/26/96	13,595.7
Kraft Inc.	Philip Morris	10/17/88	13,444.0
Gulf Oil Corp.	Standard Oil Co. of California	03/05/84	13,400.0
McDonnell Douglas Corp.	Boeing Co.	12/17/96	13,359.0
ITT Corp.	Hilton Hotels Corp.	01/27/97	12,365.9
Squibb Corp.	Bristol-Myers Co.	07/27/89	12,094.0
Northrop Grumman Corp.	Lockheed Martin Corp.	07/03/97	11,830.5
Allstate Corp.	Shareholders	11/10/94	11,761.3
Continental Cablevision Inc.	US West Media Group	02/26/96	11,398.0
HFS Inc.	CUC International Inc.	05/27/97	11,342.9
First Interstate Bancorp, CA	Wells Fargo & Co.	10/18/95	10,929.9
Morgan Stanley Group Inc.	Dean Witter Discover & Co.	02/05/97	10,573.0
Conrail Inc.	Investor Group	10/15/96	10,435.9
Getty Oil Co.	Texaco Inc.	01/06/84	10,120.0
Chase Manhattan Corp.	Chemical Banking Corp.	08/28/95	9,883.7
Boatmen's Bancshares, St. Louis	NationsBank Corp., Charlotte, NC	08/30/96	9,667.1
Paramount Communications	Viacom Inc.	09/09/93	9,600.0
American Cyanamid Co.	American Home Products Corp.	08/02/94	9,560.9
Hughes Aircraft Co.	Raytheon Co.	01/16/97	9,500.0

*Securities Data includes assumption of debt in its calculation of the value.
**Two offers had been made for MCI Communications by October 1997.
Source: Securities Data Co.

Largest Announced U.S. Mergers, Acquisitions and Spinoffs in 1997

Target name	Acquirer name	Date announced	Value of transaction* ($ millions)
MCI Communications Corp.	WorldCom Inc.	10/01/97	$34,621.8
Barnett Banks	Nationsbank Corp.	08/29/97	13,817.7
ITT Corp	Hilton Hotels Corp.	01/27/97	12,365.9
Northrop Grumman Corp	Lockheed Martin Corp.	07/03/97	11,830.5
HFS Inc.	CUC International Inc.	05/27/97	11,342.9
Morgan Stanley Group Inc.	Dean Witter Discover & Co.	02/05/97	10,573.0
Hughes Aircraft Co.	Raytheon Co.	01/16/97	9,500.0
US Bancorp, Portland, OR	First Bank Sys., Minneapolis	03/20/97	8,928.9
Salomon Inc.	Travelers Group Inc.	09/24/97	8,852.1
First USA Inc.	BANC ONE Corp., Columbus, OH	01/20/97	7,304.3
Great Western Finl Corp., CA	Washington Mutual Savings, WA	03/06/97	6,847.5
US Robotics Corp.	3Com Corp.	02/26/97	6,510.7
Pennzoil Co.	Union Pacific Resources Group Inc.	06/23/97	6,222.8
Long Island Lighting-Electric	Long Island Power Authority	03/20/97	6,100.0
Fort Howard Corp.	James River Corp. of Virginia	05/05/97	5,682.6
Grace Packaging (W.R. Grace & Co.)	Sealed Air Corp.	08/14/97	4,945.0
US WEST Media Group-US WEST Dex	US WEST Communications Inc.	05/16/97	4,750.0
Rhone-Poulenc Rorer Inc.	Rhone-Poulenc SA (France)	06/26/97	4,464.1
DQE Inc.	Allegheny Power System Inc.	04/07/97	4,088.6
Beacon Properties Corp.	Equity Office Properties Trust	09/15/97	4,049.5
Transamerica-Consumer Finance	Household International Inc.	05/21/97	3,960.0
Revco DS Inc.	CVS Corp.	01/27/97	3,911.7
Cascade Communications Corp.	Ascend Communications Inc.	03/31/97	3,529.3
Signet Banking Corp., Richmond, VA	First Union Corp., Charlotte, NC	07/21/97	3,319.8
Millennium Chemicals-Olefins	Lyondell Petrochemicals-Olefins & Polymers Business	07/28/97	3,250.0
American States Financial Corp.	SAFECO Corp.	06/09/97	3,127.1
Louisiana Land & Exploration	Burlington Resources Inc.	07/17/97	2,954.3
Texas Instruments-Electronics	Raytheon Co.	01/06/97	2,950.0
Bergen Brunswig Corp.	Cardinal Health Inc.	08/25/97	2,876.5
Tandem Computers Inc.	Compaq Computer Corp.	06/23/97	2,780.2

*Securities Data includes assumption of debt in its calculation of the value.
Source: Securities Data Co.

Largest Global Mergers, Acquisitions and Spinoffs

Target name	Acquirer name	Date announced	Value of transaction (in millions)*
MCI Communications**	WorldCom Inc.	10/01/97	$34,621.8
Bank of Tokyo Ltd.	Mitsubishi Bank Ltd.	03/27/95	33,787.7
RJR Nabisco Inc.	Koblberg Kravis Roberts & Co.	10/24/88	30,598.8
Ciba-Geigy AG	Sandoz AG	03/07/96	30,090.2
Electronic Data Systems Corp.	Shareholders	08/07/95	27,973.5
Lucent Technologies Inc.	Shareholders	09/20/95	24,067.1
Taiyo Kobe Bank Ltd.	Mitsui Bank Ltd.	08/28/89	23,016.8
NYNEX Corp.	Bell Atlantic Corp.	04/22/96	21,345.5
MCI Communications**	British Telecommunications PLC	11/01/96	18,888.5
Capital Cities/ABC Inc.	Walt Disney Co.	07/31/95	18,862.5
Pacific Telesis Group	SBC Communications Inc.	04/01/96	16,490.0
Guinness PLC	Grand Metropolitan PLC	05/12/97	15,968.3
McCaw Cellular Communications	American Telephone & Telegraph	08/16/93	15,651.7
Lloyds Bank PLC	TSB Group PLC	10/09/95	15,315.6
Wellcome PLC	Glaxo Holdings PLC	01/20/95	14,284.8
Warner Communications Inc.	Time Inc.	03/04/89	14,110.0
Barnett Banks, Jacksonville, FL	Nationsbank Corp., Charlotte, NC	08/29/97	13,817.7
MFS Communications Co.	WorldCom Inc.	08/26/96	13,595.7
Deutsche Telekom AG	Investors	07/21/92	13,533.8
Kraft Inc.	Philip Morris	10/17/88	13,444.0
Gulf Oil Corp.	Standard Oil Co. of California	03/05/84	13,400.0
McDonnell Douglas Corp.	Boeing Co.	12/17/96	13,359.0
ITT Corp	Hilton Hotels Corp.	01/27/97	12,365.9
Squibb Corp.	Bristol-Myers Co.	07/27/89	12,094.0
Northrop Grumman Corp.	Lockheed Martin Corp.	07/03/97	11,830.5
Allstate Corp.	Shareholders	11/10/94	11,761.3
Continental Cablevision	U.S. West Media Group	02/26/96	11,398.0
HFS Inc.	CUC International Inc.	05/27/97	11,342.9
Corange Ltd.	Roche Holding AG	05/26/97	11,000.0
First Interstate Bancorp, CA	Wells Fargo & Co.	10/18/95	10,929.9

*Securities Data includes assumption of debt in its calculation of the value.
**Two offers had been made for MCI Communications by October 1997.
Source: Securities Data Co.

Total Announced Worldwide Mergers and Acquisitions

Year	Value ($ millions)	Number of deals
1985	$242,994.9	2,806
1986	286,814.4	4,072
1987	340,796.2	5,316
1988	523,786.8	7,864
1989	567,034.0	10,858
1990	453,423.1	11,335
1991	369,581.6	15,977
1992	364,688.6	15,585
1993	455,944.7	16,708
1994	559,022.7	19,128
1995	948,297.0	22,159
1996	1,116,134.6	23,208

Source: Securities Data Co.

Largest Announced Global Mergers, Acquisitions and Spinoffs in 1997

Target name	Acquirer name	Date announced	Value of transaction* ($ millions)
MCI Communications Corp.	WorldCom Inc.	10/01/97	$34,621.8
Guinness PLC	Grand Metropolitan PLC	05/12/97	15,968.3
Barnett Banks, Jacksonville, FL	Nationsbank Corp., Charlotte, NC	08/29/97	13,817.7
ITT Corp.	Hilton Hotels Corp.	01/27/97	12,365.9
Northrop Grumman Corp.	Lockheed Martin Corp.	07/03/97	11,830.5
HFS Inc.	CUC International Inc.	05/27/97	11,342.9
Corange Ltd.	Roche Holding AG	05/26/97	11,000.0
Morgan Stanley Group Inc.	Dean Witter Discover & Co.	02/05/97	10,573.0
Energy Group PLC	PacifiCorp	06/13/97	9,712.0
Hughes Aircraft Co.	Raytheon Co.	01/16/97	9,500.0
US Bancorp, Portland, OR	First Bank Sys., Minneapolis	03/20/97	8,928.9
Winterthur Schweizerische	Credit Suisse Group	08/11/97	8,869.5
Salomon Inc.	Traveler's Group Inc.	09/24/97	8,852.1
Unilever Specialty Chemical Units	ICI PLC	05/07/97	8,000.0
Cie de Suex SA	Lyonnaise des Eaux-Dumez SA	03/17/97	7,445.3
First USA Inc.	Banc One Corp., Columbus, OH	01/20/97	7,304.3
Great Wertern Finl Corp., CA	Washington Mutual Savings, WA	03/06/97	6,847.5
US Robotics Corp.	3Com Corp.	02/26/97	6,510.7
Pennzoil Co.	Union Pacific Resources Group	06/23/97	6,222.8
Long Island Lighting-Electric	Long Island Power Authority	03/20/97	6,100.0
Fort Howard Corp.	James River Corp. of Virginia	05/05/97	5,682.6
Ciba Specialty Chemicals	Shareholders	03/13/97	5,416.8
ADT Ltd.	Tyco International Ltd.	03/17/97	5,269.1
Bayerische Hypotheken	Bayerische Vereinsbank AG	07/21/97	5,132.5
Grace Packaging (W.R. Grace & Co.)	Sealed Air Corp.	08/14/97	4,945.0
US WEST Media Group-US WEST Dex	US WEST Communications Inc.	05/16/97	4,750.0
Rhone-Poulenc Rorer Inc.	Rhone-Poulenc SA (France)	06/26/97	4,464.1
Billiton PLC	Shareholders	06/18/97	4,211.0
DQE Inc.	Allegheny Power System Inc.	04/07/97	4,088.6
Beacon Properties Corp.	Equity Office Properties Trust	09/15/97	4,049.5

*Securities Data includes assumption of debt in its calculation of the value.
Source: Securities Data Co.

Largest U.S. Companies in the Dow Jones Global Indexes

Company Name	Fiscal Year	Sales ($ Millions)	Net Income ($ Millions)
1 General Motors	Dec-96	164,069	4,963
2 Ford Motor	Dec-96	146,991	4,446
3 Exxon	Dec-96	134,249	7,510
4 Wal-Mart Stores	Jan-97	104,859	3,056
5 Mobil	Dec-96	81,503	2,964
6 General Electric	Dec-96	79,179	7,280
7 IBM	Dec-96	75,947	5,429
8 Philip Morris	Dec-96	69,204	6,303
9 Chrysler	Dec-96	61,397	3,529
10 AT&T	Dec-96	52,184	5,908
11 Texaco	Dec-96	45,500	2,018
12 Chevron	Dec-96	43,893	2,607
13 DuPont	Dec-96	43,810	3,636
14 Hewlett-Packard	Oct-96	38,420	2,586
15 Sears, Roebuck	Dec-96	38,236	1,271
16 Amoco	Dec-96	36,112	2,834
17 Procter & Gamble	Jun-96	35,284	3,046
18 Citicorp	Dec-96	32,605	3,788
19 PepsiCo	Dec-96	31,645	1,149
20 Kmart	Jan-97	31,437	(220)
21 American International	Dec-96	28,205	2,897
22 Motorola	Dec-96	27,973	1,154
23 Chase Manhattan	Dec-96	27,421	2,461
24 Lockheed Martin	Dec-96	26,875	1,347
25 Dayton Hudson	Jan-97	25,371	463
26 Kroger	Dec-96	25,171	350
27 Fannie Mae	Dec-96	25,054	2,725
28 Merrill Lynch	Dec-96	25,011	1,619
29 Allstate	Dec-96	24,299	2,075
30 ConAgra	May-97	24,002	615
31 United Technologies	Dec-96	23,512	906
32 Boeing	Dec-96	22,681	1,095
33 J.C. Penney	Jan-97	22,653	565
34 BankAmerica	Dec-96	22,071	2,873
35 Johnson & Johnson	Dec-96	21,620	2,887
36 Travelers	Dec-96	21,345	2,331
37 GTE	Dec-96	21,339	2,798
38 Intel	Dec-96	20,847	5,157
39 Loews	Dec-96	20,442	1,384
40 International Paper	Dec-96	20,100	303
41 Dow Chemical	Dec-96	20,053	1,907
42 Columbia/HCA Healthcare	Dec-96	19,909	1,505
43 Merck	Dec-96	19,829	3,881
44 Costco	Sep-96	19,566	249
45 Home Depot	Jan-97	19,535	938
46 Atlantic Richfield	Dec-96	19,169	1,663
47 BellSouth	Dec-96	19,040	2,863
48 CIGNA	Dec-96	18,950	1,056
49 Walt Disney	Sep-96	18,739	1,214
50 American Stores	Jan-97	18,678	287
51 Sara Lee	Jun-96	18,624	916
52 Coca-Cola	Dec-96	18,546	3,492
53 MCI Communications	Dec-96	18,494	1,202
54 Compaq Computer	Dec-96	18,109	1,313
55 AMR	Dec-96	17,753	1,016
56 NationsBank	Dec-96	17,442	2,452
57 Xerox	Dec-96	17,378	1,206
58 Safeway	Dec-96	17,269	461
59 Supervalu	Feb-97	16,552	175
60 Caterpillar	Dec-96	16,522	1,361
61 UAL	Dec-96	16,362	533
62 USX-Marathon	Dec-96	16,332	664
63 American Express	Dec-96	16,237	1,901
64 Eastman Kodak	Dec-96	15,968	1,288
65 Hughes Electronics	Dec-96	15,918	1,029
66 J.P. Morgan	Dec-96	15,866	1,574
67 Lucent Technologies	Dec-96	15,859	224
68 Phillips Petroleum	Dec-96	15,807	1,303
69 Federated Department Stores	Feb-97	15,229	266
70 Aetna	Dec-96	15,163	651
71 Bristol-Myers Squibb	Dec-96	15,065	2,850
72 Ameritech	Dec-96	14,917	2,134
73 Digital Equipment	Jun-96	14,563	(112)
74 Electronic Data Systems	Dec-96	14,441	432
75 Lehman Brothers	Nov-96	14,260	416

Company Name	Fiscal Year	Sales ($ Millions)	Net Income ($ Millions)
76 3M	Dec-96	14,236	1,526
77 American Home Products	Dec-96	14,088	1,883
78 Sprint	Dec-96	14,045	1,184
79 AlliedSignal	Dec-96	13,971	1,020
80 SBC Communications	Dec-96	13,898	2,101
81 McDonnell Douglas	Dec-96	13,834	788
82 Albertson's	Jan-97	13,767	494
83 NYNEX	Dec-96	13,454	1,477
84 Sysco	Jun-96	13,395	277
85 Archer-Daniels-Midland	Jun-96	13,314	696
86 Enron	Dec-96	13,289	584
87 Ashland	Sep-96	13,285	211
88 Kimberly-Clark	Dec-96	13,149	1,404
89 Alcoa	Dec-96	13,128	515
90 Goodyear Tire & Rubber	Dec-96	13,113	102
91 Bell Atlantic	Dec-96	13,081	1,882
92 Georgia-Pacific	Dec-96	13,024	156
93 Winn-Dixie Stores	Jun-96	12,955	256
94 US West	Dec-96	12,911	1,178
95 McKesson	Mar-97	12,887	134
96 Hartford Financial Services	Dec-96	12,473	(99)
97 Delta Air Lines	Jun-96	12,455	156
98 Raytheon	Dec-96	12,260	761
99 Coastal	Dec-96	12,167	403
100 Viacom	Dec-96	12,084	1,248
101 FHLMC	Dec-96	12,032	1,243
102 May Department Stores	Feb-97	11,650	755
103 First Union	Dec-96	11,950	1,499
104 Walgreen	Aug-96	11,779	372
105 Federal Express	May-97	11,520	361
106 Pfizer	Dec-96	11,306	1,929
107 Sun	Dec-96	11,300	(115)
108 Deere	Oct-96	11,229	817
109 Emerson Electric	Sep-96	11,150	1,019
110 Weyerhaeuser	Dec-96	11,114	463
111 Fluor	Oct-96	11,015	268
112 Abbott Laboratories	Dec-96	11,013	1,882
113 Anheuser-Busch	Dec-96	10,884	1,190
114 McDonald's	Dec-96	10,687	1,573
115 Occidental Petroleum	Dec-96	10,557	668
116 CSX	Dec-96	10,536	855
117 Rockwell International	Sep-96	10,373	726
118 Southern	Dec-96	10,354	1,127
119 Banc One	Dec-96	10,272	1,427
120 Marriott International	Dec-96	10,172	306
121 First Chicago NBD	Dec-96	10,117	1,436
122 United Healthcare	Dec-96	10,074	356
123 Time Warner	Dec-96	10,064	(191)
124 Johnson Controls	Sep-96	10,009	235
125 Texas Instruments	Dec-96	9,940	63
126 Toys 'R' Us	Jan-97	9,931	427
127 Northwest Airlines	Dec-96	9,881	536
128 TRW	Dec-96	9,857	480
129 CPC International	Dec-96	9,844	580
130 Apple Computer	Sep-96	9,833	(816)
131 Gillette	Dec-96	9,698	949
132 PG&E	Dec-96	9,610	755
133 Bankers Trust	Dec-96	9,565	612
134 H.J. Heinz	Apr-97	9,357	302
135 Textron	Dec-96	9,274	253
136 Monsanto	Dec-96	9,262	385
137 Waste Management	Dec-96	9,187	192
138 Nike	May-97	9,187	796
139 Salomon	Dec-96	9,046	617
140 Food Lion	Dec-96	9,006	206
141 Schlumberger	Dec-96	8,956	851
142 Amerada Hess	Dec-96	8,930	660
143 Nabisco	Dec-96	8,889	17
144 Norwest	Dec-96	8,883	1,154
145 Cardinal Health	Jun-96	8,862	112
146 Union Pacific	Dec-96	8,786	904
147 Colgate-Palmolive	Dec-96	8,749	635
148 Wells Fargo	Dec-96	8,723	1,071

Company Name	Fiscal Year	Sales ($ Millions)	Net Income ($ Millions)
149 ITT Industries	Dec-96	8,718	223
150 Whirlpool	Dec-96	8,696	156
151 Microsoft	Jun-96	8,671	2,195
152 Limited	Jan-97	8,645	434
153 Lowe's	Jan-97	8,600	292
154 Seagate Technology	Jun-96	8,588	213
155 Edison International	Sep-96	8,544	717
156 Westinghouse	Dec-96	8,449	30
157 Crown Cork & Seal	Dec-96	8,332	284
158 Equitable	Dec-96	8,305	99
159 General Re	Dec-96	8,296	894
160 Burlington Northern	Dec-96	8,187	889
161 US Airways	Dec-96	8,142	263
162 Woolworth	Jan-97	8,092	169
163 Northrop Grumman	Dec-96	8,071	234
164 Fleet Financial	Dec-96	8,043	1,139
165 Tele-Communications	Dec-96	8,022	278
166 Coca-Cola Enterprises	Dec-96	7,921	114
167 Dell Computer	Jan-97	7,759	518
168 Dana	Dec-96	7,686	306
169 Campbell Soup	Jul-96	7,678	802
170 Circuit City	Feb-97	7,664	137
171 Halliburton	Dec-96	7,385	300
172 Eli Lilly	Dec-96	7,347	1,524
173 Honeywell	Dec-96	7,312	403
174 Pharmacia & Upjohn	Dec-96	7,286	549
175 Warner-Lambert	Dec-96	7,231	787
176 PPG Industries	Dec-96	7,218	744
177 Entergy	Dec-96	7,164	420
178 AFLAC	Dec-96	7,100	394
179 Sun Micro-systems	Jun-96	7,095	476
180 Reynolds Metals	Dec-96	7,016	89
181 Rite Aid	Mar-97	6,970	115
182 Eaton	Dec-96	6,961	349
183 Consolidated Edison	Dec-96	6,960	694
184 Unicom	Dec-96	6,937	666
185 American General	Dec-96	6,887	577
186 Lincoln National	Dec-96	6,721	514
187 Ingersoll-Rand	Dec-96	6,703	358
188 TJX	Jan-97	6,689	363
189 Humana	Dec-96	6,677	12
190 Kellogg	Dec-96	6,677	531
191 R.R. Donnelley & Sons	Dec-96	6,599	(158)
192 ITT	Dec-96	6,597	249
193 Tenneco	Dec-96	6,572	410
194 Dresser Industries	Oct-96	6,562	258
195 Texas Utilities	Dec-96	6,551	754
196 USX-U.S. Steel	Dec-96	6,547	273
197 Arrow Electronics	Dec-96	6,535	203
198 Tyson Foods	Sep-96	6,454	87
199 Unisys	Dec-96	6,371	50
200 PNC Bank	Dec-96	6,333	992
201 Tandy	Dec-96	6,285	(92)
202 Lear	Dec-96	6,249	152
203 Bank Boston	Dec-96	6,237	650
204 Dean Witter	Dec-96	6,230	951
205 Dillard	Jan-97	6,228	239
206 Trans-america	Dec-96	6,228	456
207 Ralston Purina	Sep-96	6,114	360
208 Union Carbide	Dec-96	6,106	593
209 Manpower	Dec-96	6,080	162
210 Office Depot	Dec-96	6,069	129
211 Public Service Enterprise	Dec-96	6,041	612
212 KeyCorp	Dec-96	6,038	783
213 FPL	Dec-96	6,037	579
214 Champion International	Dec-96	5,880	141
215 American Electric Power	Dec-96	5,849	587
216 Browning-Ferris	Sep-96	5,779	(101)
217 Navistar International	Oct-96	5,754	65
218 St. Paul	Dec-96	5,734	450
219 Genuine Parts	Dec-96	5,720	330
220 Bank of New York	Dec-96	5,713	1,020

Company Name	Fiscal Year	Sales ($ Millions)	Net Income ($ Millions)
221 Paine-Webber	Dec-96	5,706	364
222 James River	Dec-96	5,691	157
223 Oracle	May-97	5,684	821
224 Chubb	Dec-96	5,681	513
225 Schering-Plough	Dec-96	5,656	1,213
226 Computer Sciences	Mar-97	5,616	192
227 General Mills	May-97	5,609	445
228 Tenet Healthcare	May-97	5,559	350
229 CVS	Dec-96	5,528	75
230 Ryder System	Dec-96	5,519	(41)
231 AMP	Dec-96	5,468	287
232 Baxter International	Dec-96	5,438	669
233 Case	Dec-96	5,409	316
234 Unocal	Dec-96	5,328	36
235 Cooper Industries	Dec-96	5,316	315
236 Gap	Jan-97	5,284	453
237 Cummins Engine	Dec-96	5,257	160
238 Avnet	Jun-96	5,208	188
239 Quaker Oats	Dec-96	5,199	248
240 Stone Container	Dec-96	5,142	(126)
241 VF	Dec-96	5,137	300
242 Boise Cascade	Dec-96	5,108	9
243 Tyco International	Jun-96	5,090	310
244 FMC	Dec-96	5,081	211
245 Illinois Tool Works	Dec-96	4,997	486
246 Bear Stearns	Jun-96	4,964	491
247 First Data	Dec-96	4,938	637
248 National City	Dec-96	4,928	737
249 Black & Decker	Dec-96	4,914	230
250 Dominion Resources	Dec-96	4,842	472
251 Avon	Dec-96	4,814	318
252 MedPartners	Dec-96	4,814	(159)
253 NorAm Energy	Dec-96	4,788	91
254 Eastman Chemical	Dec-96	4,782	380
255 Norfolk Southern	Dec-96	4,770	770
256 Mellon Bank	Dec-96	4,762	733
257 Duke Energy	Dec-96	4,758	730
258 Mead	Dec-96	4,707	195
259 Bethlehem Steel	Dec-96	4,679	(309)
260 PacifiCare Health Systems	Sep-96	4,637	72
261 Inland Steel	Dec-96	4,584	46
262 Nordstrom	Jan-97	4,453	148
263 Praxair	Dec-96	4,449	282
264 Gannett	Dec-96	4,421	943
265 UNUM	Dec-96	4,403	238
266 CMS Energy	Dec-96	4,333	240
267 Paccar	Dec-96	4,317	201
268 PacifiCorp	Dec-96	4,294	505
269 PECO Energy	Dec-96	4,284	517
270 CoreStates Financial	Dec-96	4,197	649
271 Marsh & McLennan	Dec-96	4,149	459
272 Applied Materials	Oct-96	4,145	600
273 LTV	Dec-96	4,135	109
274 Sherwin-Williams	Dec-96	4,133	229
275 American Financial	Dec-96	4,115	233
276 Ikon Office Solutions	Sep-96	4,100	211
277 Cisco Systems	Jul-96	4,096	913
278 Houston Industries	Dec-96	4,095	405
279 Dover	Dec-96	4,076	390
280 SunTrust Banks	Dec-96	4,064	617
281 Foster Wheeler	Dec-96	4,041	82
282 Computer Associates	Mar-97	4,040	366
283 Comcast	Dec-96	4,038	(54)
284 Union Camp	Dec-96	4,013	85
285 Wachovia	Dec-96	4,011	645
286 Air Products Chemicals	Sep-96	4,008	416
287 Niagara Mohawk Power	Dec-96	3,991	110
288 Hershey Foods	Dec-96	3,989	273
289 Rohm and Haas	Dec-96	3,982	363
290 Staples	Feb-97	3,968	106
291 SAFECO	Dec-96	3,965	439
292 GPU	Dec-96	3,918	298
293 Aon	Dec-96	3,888	335

Company Name	Fiscal Year	Sales ($ Millions)	Net Income ($ Millions)
294 Giant Food	Feb-97	3,881	86
295 Pitney Bowes	Dec-96	3,859	469
296 Owens-Illinois	Dec-96	3,846	191
297 Dole Food	Dec-96	3,840	89
298 First Bank System	Dec-96	3,840	740
299 Owens Corning	Dec-96	3,832	(284)
300 Barnett Banks	Dec-96	3,818	565
301 Allegheny Teledyne	Dec-96	3,816	213
302 Northeast Utilities	Dec-96	3,792	2
303 Phelps Dodge	Dec-96	3,787	462
304 Mattel	Dec-96	3,786	378
305 Centex	Mar-97	3,785	107
306 H.F. Ahmanson	Dec-96	3,767	145
307 CNF Trans-portation	Dec-96	3,662	28
308 Micron Technology	Aug-96	3,654	594
309 Corning	Dec-96	3,652	176
310 Nucor	Dec-96	3,647	248
311 DTE Energy	Dec-96	3,645	309
312 Morton International	Jun-96	3,613	334
313 Litton Industries	Jul-96	3,612	151
314 Sallie Mae	Dec-96	3,590	419
315 Parker Hannifin	Jun-96	3,586	240
316 General Dynamics	Dec-96	3,581	270
317 Universal	Jun-96	3,570	72
318 Automatic Data Processing	Jun-96	3,567	455
319 Great Western Financial	Dec-96	3,553	116
320 W.W. Grainger	Dec-96	3,537	209
321 Williams Cos.	Dec-96	3,531	362
322 USF&G	Dec-96	3,498	261
323 Reebok	Dec-96	3,479	139
324 Progressive	Dec-96	3,478	314
325 Service-Master	Dec-96	3,458	245
326 W.R. Grace	Dec-96	3,454	2,858
327 Willamette Industries	Dec-96	3,425	192
328 Temple-Inland	Dec-96	3,422	133
329 Washington Mutual	Dec-96	3,409	114
330 Southwest Airlines	Dec-96	3,406	207
331 Times Mirror	Dec-96	3,401	206
332 Sonat	Dec-96	3,395	201
333 Columbia Gas System	Dec-96	3,354	222
334 Mapco	Dec-96	3,353	98
335 Kelly Services	Dec-96	3,302	73
336 Harcourt General	Oct-96	3,290	191
337 MBNA	Dec-96	3,279	475
338 CINergy	Dec-96	3,243	335
339 Masco	Dec-96	3,237	295
340 Avery Dennison	Dec-96	3,223	176
341 York International	Dec-96	3,219	148
342 Republic New York	Dec-96	3,203	419
343 Shaw Industries	Dec-96	3,201	34
344 Engelhard	Dec-96	3,184	150
345 Darden Restaurants	May-97	3,172	(91)
346 Brunswick	Dec-96	3,160	186
347 Alumax	Dec-96	3,159	250
348 Baltimore Gas & Electric	Dec-96	3,153	311
349 McDermott International	Mar-97	3,151	(201)
350 Long Island Lighting	Dec-96	3,151	316
351 3Com	May-97	3,147	374
352 Echlin	Aug-96	3,129	142
353 Whitman	Dec-96	3,111	139
354 Hormel Foods	Oct-96	3,099	79
355 Reader's Digest	Jun-96	3,098	81
356 Oxford Health Plans	Dec-96	3,075	100
357 McGraw-Hill	Dec-96	3,075	496
358 Yellow	Dec-96	3,073	(27)
359 Comerica	Dec-96	3,070	417
360 U.S. Bancorp	Dec-96	3,069	479
361 Conseco	Dec-96	3,067	252
362 Westvaco	Oct-96	3,045	212
363 Mercantile Stores	Jan-97	3,031	121
364 Household International	Dec-96	3,031	539

Company Name	Fiscal Year	Sales ($ Millions)	Net Income ($ Millions)
365 Baker Hughes	Sep-96	3,028	176
366 El Paso Natural Gas	Dec-96	3,010	38
367 Hasbro	Dec-96	3,002	200
368 Maytag	Dec-96	3,002	136
369 Intimate Brands	Feb-97	2,997	258
370 Carolina Power & Light	Dec-96	2,996	391
371 IMC Global	Jun-96	2,981	144
372 US West Media Group	Dec-96	2,955	(71)
373 Thermo Electron	Dec-96	2,933	191
374 Silicon Graphics	Jun-96	2,921	115
375 PP&L Resources	Dec-96	2,910	329
376 Harnischfeger	Oct-96	2,894	114
377 Newell	Dec-96	2,873	257
378 Consolidated Natural Gas	Dec-96	2,845	298
379 Cyprus Amax Minerals	Dec-96	2,843	77
380 Longs Drug Stores	Jan-97	2,828	59
381 Solectron	Aug-96	2,817	114
382 Sonoco Products	Dec-96	2,788	171
383 Knight-Ridder	Dec-96	2,775	268
384 Becton Dickinson	Sep-96	2,770	283
385 APL	Dec-96	2,739	70
386 Caliber System	Dec-96	2,718	(165)
387 ASARCO	Dec-96	2,697	138
388 General Instrument	Dec-96	2,690	(2)
389 Stanley Works	Dec-96	2,671	97
390 Northern States Power	Dec-96	2,654	275
391 Omnicom	Dec-96	2,642	176
392 New York Times	Dec-96	2,615	85
393 Golden West Financial	Dec-96	2,597	165
394 USG	Dec-96	2,590	15
395 Western Atlas	Dec-96	2,583	126
396 Pacific Enterprises	Dec-96	2,563	203
397 Centerior Energy	Dec-96	2,553	121
398 Interpublic Group	Dec-96	2,538	205
399 National Semiconductor	May-97	2,507	28
400 Pennzoil	Dec-96	2,487	134
401 Louisiana-Pacific	Dec-96	2,486	(201)
402 Airborne Freight	Dec-96	2,484	27
403 Dow Jones	Dec-96	2,482	190
404 Ohio Edison	Dec-96	2,470	315
405 Leggett & Platt	Dec-96	2,466	141
406 Fruit of the Loom	Dec-96	2,447	151
407 Medtronic	Apr-97	2,438	530
408 Healthsouth	Dec-96	2,437	221
409 Comdisco	Sep-96	2,431	114
410 Tribune	Dec-96	2,406	372
411 Timken	Dec-96	2,395	139
412 Kohl's	Jan-97	2,388	102
413 Pulte	Dec-96	2,384	180
414 Viad	Dec-96	2,361	28
415 Rubbermaid	Dec-96	2,355	152
416 New England Electric	Dec-96	2,351	209
417 CUC International	Jan-97	2,348	164
418 Payless Shoesource	Feb-97	2,334	108
419 Allegheny Power	Dec-96	2,328	210
420 AGCO	Dec-96	2,317	126
421 Service Corp.	Dec-96	2,294	265
422 Provident Companies	Dec-96	2,292	146
423 Polaroid	Dec-96	2,275	(41)
424 EMC	Dec-96	2,274	386
425 Premark	Dec-96	2,268	119
426 Union Electric	Dec-96	2,260	305
427 AirTouch Communications	Dec-96	2,252	179
428 Amgen	Dec-96	2,240	680
429 B.F. Goodrich	Dec-96	2,239	152
430 Trinity Industries	Mar-97	2,234	138
431 Clorox	Jun-96	2,218	222
432 Liz Claiborne	Dec-96	2,218	156
433 Great Lakes Chemical	Dec-96	2,212	250

Company Name	Fiscal Year	Sales ($ Millions)	Net Income ($ Millions)
434 Mallinckrodt	Jun-96	2,210	191
435 Torchmark	Dec-96	2,206	311
436 Ball	Dec-96	2,184	24
437 Public Service of Colorado	Dec-96	2,171	190
438 American Greetings	Feb-97	2,161	167
439 Dun & Bradstreet	Dec-96	2,159	(44)
440 Armstrong	Dec-96	2,156	156
441 Enserch	Dec-96	2,143	19
442 Jefferson-Pilot	Dec-96	2,125	291
443 First of America Bank	Dec-96	2,083	257
444 General Signal	Dec-96	2,065	133
445 Hercules	Dec-96	2,060	325
446 SouthTrust	Dec-96	2,059	255
447 Bay Networks	Jun-96	2,057	206
448 Western Resources	Dec-96	2,047	169
449 Storage Technology	Dec-96	2,040	180
450 Aeroquip-Vickers	Dec-96	2,033	103
451 Ogden	Dec-96	2,031	65
452 Murphy Oil	Dec-96	2,022	138
453 National Service	Aug-96	2,014	101
454 Potomac Electric	Dec-96	2,010	237
455 MCN Energy Group	Dec-96	1,997	150
456 Enova	Dec-96	1,993	231
457 Thomas & Betts	Dec-96	1,985	60
458 Beneficial	Dec-96	1,959	281
459 Advanced Micro Devices	Dec-96	1,953	(69)
460 Tektronix	May-97	1,940	115
461 Kerr-McGee	Dec-96	1,931	220
462 H & R Block	Apr-97	1,930	48
463 Northern Trust	Dec-96	1,929	259
464 Bausch & Lomb	Dec-96	1,927	83
465 Worthington Industries	May-97	1,912	93
466 Freeport-McMoran Copper & Gold	Dec-96	1,905	175
467 Hilton Hotels	Dec-96	1,900	82
468 Tandem Computers	Sep-96	1,900	(23)
469 Crestar Financial	Dec-96	1,900	218
470 Wendy's	Dec-96	1,897	156
471 Deluxe	Dec-96	1,896	66
472 Equitable Resources	Dec-96	1,862	59
473 Cabot	Sep-96	1,856	194
474 Washington Post	Dec-96	1,853	221
475 Charles Schwab	Dec-96	1,851	234
476 NICOR	Dec-96	1,851	136
477 Wm. Wrigley Jr.	Dec-96	1,851	230
478 Crane	Dec-96	1,848	92
479 State Street	Dec-96	1,845	293
480 Brown-Forman	Apr-97	1,841	169
481 Union Pacific Resources	Dec-96	1,831	321
482 Pep Boys	Feb-97	1,829	101
483 Firstar	Dec-96	1,824	250
484 NIPSCO	Dec-96	1,822	177
485 Pinnacle West Capital	Dec-96	1,818	181
486 Danaher	Dec-96	1,812	208
487 Equifax	Dec-96	1,811	178
488 Cincinnati Financial	Dec-96	1,808	224
489 Jacobs Engineering	Sep-96	1,799	40
490 Summit Bancorp	Dec-96	1,798	229
491 Kaufman & Broad	Nov-96	1,787	(61)
492 Huntington Bancshares	Dec-96	1,783	262
493 Wisconsin Energy	Dec-96	1,774	218
494 Fifth Third Bancorp	Dec-96	1,754	335
495 McCormick	Nov-96	1,733	42
496 Adolph Coors	Dec-96	1,732	43
497 Cognizant	Dec-96	1,731	146
498 Cincinnati Milacron	Dec-96	1,730	66
499 Armco	Dec-96	1,724	33
500 Pioneer Hi-Bred	Aug-96	1,721	223
501 Bowater	Dec-96	1,718	200
502 A.G. Edwards	Feb-97	1,700	219
503 Illinova	Dec-96	1,689	191
504 Raychem	Jun-96	1,672	148

Company Name	Fiscal Year	Sales ($ Millions)	Net Income ($ Millions)
505 Bemis	Dec-96	1,655	101
506 Mercantile Bancorporation	Dec-96	1,621	192
507 Cooper Tire & Rubber	Dec-96	1,619	108
508 Harsco	Dec-96	1,609	119
509 Regions Financial	Dec-96	1,607	230
510 Unifi	Jun-96	1,603	72
511 Nine West	Feb-97	1,603	81
512 Varian Associates	Sep-96	1,599	122
513 Lubrizol	Dec-96	1,598	170
514 Alaska Air	Dec-96	1,592	38
515 Harrahs Entertainment	Dec-96	1,588	99
516 Vulcan Materials	Dec-96	1,569	189
517 American National	Dec-96	1,562	216
518 Potlatch	Dec-96	1,554	58
519 Johns Manville	Dec-96	1,552	90
520 Consolidated Papers	Dec-96	1,545	179
521 Harley Davidson	Dec-96	1,531	166
522 Manor Care	May-97	1,527	137
523 Unitrin	Dec-96	1,523	133
524 Franklin Resources	Sep-96	1,523	315
525 Sundstrand	Dec-96	1,521	114
526 Walter Industries	May-97	1,507	37
527 Pittston Burlington	Dec-96	1,500	34
528 Ceridian	Dec-96	1,496	182
529 Ecolab	Dec-96	1,490	113
530 J.B. Hunt	Dec-96	1,487	22
531 Snap-On Tools	Dec-96	1,485	131
532 SunAmerica	Sep-96	1,475	274
533 Marshall & Ilsley	Dec-96	1,475	203
534 First Tennessee National	Dec-96	1,468	180
535 Boston Scientific	Dec-96	1,462	167
536 International Flavors & Fragrances	Dec-96	1,436	190
537 Cabletron Systems	Feb-97	1,407	222
538 UST	Dec-96	1,397	464
539 Oklahoma Gas & Electric	Dec-96	1,387	133
540 Molex	Jun-96	1,383	146
541 DSC Communications	Dec-96	1,381	(8)
542 Novell	Oct-96	1,375	126
543 Tupperware	Dec-96	1,369	175
544 Mirage Resorts	Dec-96	1,368	206
545 AC Nielsen	Dec-96	1,359	16
546 AmSouth	Dec-96	1,354	183
547 Air Express International	Dec-96	1,335	39
548 Circus Circus	Jan-97	1,334	101
549 USFreightways	Dec-96	1,331	31
550 Cablevision Systems	Dec-96	1,315	(332)
551 USA Waste Services	Dec-96	1,313	33
552 Chiron	Dec-96	1,313	55
553 Nalco Chemical	Dec-96	1,304	155
554 Hubbell	Dec-96	1,297	142
555 Burlington Resources	Dec-96	1,293	255
556 Zenith Electronics	Dec-96	1,288	(178)
557 First - Security	Dec-96	1,287	178
558 Landstar System	Dec-96	1,284	19
559 MascoTech	Dec-96	1,281	52
560 DPL	Dec-96	1,256	173
561 Russell	Dec-96	1,244	82
562 Ohio Casualty	Dec-96	1,240	102
563 LSI Logic	Dec-96	1,239	147
564 Alexander & Baldwin	Dec-96	1,233	65
565 DQE	Dec-96	1,225	179
566 Oneok	Aug-96	1,224	53
567 Health Care Property	Dec-96	1,204	61
568 Puget Sound Energy	Dec-96	1,199	135
569 Peoples Energy	Sep-96	1,199	103
570 C.R. Bard	Dec-96	1,194	93
571 Analog Devices	Oct-96	1,194	172
572 Lennar	Nov-96	1,181	88

Company Name	Fiscal Year	Sales ($ Millions)	Net Income ($ Millions)
573 Rayonier	Dec-96	1,178	(98)
574 Stone & Webster	Dec-96	1,165	(11)
575 Brinker International	Jun-96	1,163	34
576 Perkin-Elmer	Jun-96	1,163	14
577 Pacific Century Financial	Dec-96	1,153	133
578 Ethyl	Dec-96	1,150	93
579 E.W. Scripps	Dec-96	1,122	157
580 Signet Banking	Dec-96	1,111	125
581 Dexter	Dec-96	1,100	49
582 360 Communications	Dec-96	1,096	60
583 Intergraph	Dec-96	1,095	(69)
584 America Online	Jun-96	1,094	30
585 Synovus Financial	Dec-96	1,089	140
586 Viking Office Products	Jun-96	1,056	60
587 Guidant	Dec-96	1,049	66
588 Betz Dearborn	Dec-96	1,037	64
589 Sigma-Aldrich	Dec-96	1,035	148
590 Beckman Instruments	Dec-96	1,028	75
591 Sybase	Dec-96	1,012	(79)
592 Union Texas Petroleum	Dec-96	1,008	152
593 Sensormatic Electronics	Jun-96	995	(98)
594 Sunbeam	Dec-96	984	(228)
595 Oakwood Homes	Sep-96	974	68
596 Precision Castparts	Mar-97	973	57
597 Pall	Jul-96	960	139
598 Wheelabrator Technologies	Dec-96	952	7
599 UCAR International	Dec-96	948	152
600 Informix	Dec-96	939	98
601 Adaptec	Mar-97	934	108
602 Clayton Homes	Jun-96	929	107
603 Green Tree Financial	Dec-96	924	309
604 Safety-Kleen	Dec-96	923	61
605 Stryker	Dec-96	910	104
606 Pittston Brink	Dec-96	910	60
607 Star Banc	Dec-96	906	158
608 Kansas City Power	Dec-96	904	108
609 CIPSCO	Dec-96	897	80
610 American Water Works	Dec-96	895	102
611 Noble Affiliates	Dec-96	887	84
612 Louisiana Land & Exploration	Dec-96	873	80
613 Tellabs	Dec-96	869	118
614 Ametek	Dec-96	869	51
615 Valspar	Oct-96	860	56
616 Albemarle	Dec-96	854	156
617 Cintas	May-97	840	91
618 Rouse	Dec-96	832	16
619 A.H. Belo	Dec-96	824	88
620 Questar	Dec-96	818	98
621 St. Jude Medical	Dec-96	809	92
622 Tidewater	Mar-97	803	146
623 HFS	Dec-96	799	170
624 HBO	Dec-96	797	74
625 Donaldson	Jul-96	786	43
626 Adobe Systems	Nov-96	786	153
627 Aztar	Dec-96	777	21
628 Boyd Gaming	Jun-96	776	28
629 Newmont Mining	Dec-96	769	85
630 Homestake Mining	Dec-96	767	30
631 Giddings & Lewis	Dec-96	763	(13)
632 Ipalco Enterprises	Dec-96	763	114
633 Simon DeBartolo Group	Dec-96	748	85
634 Paychex	May-97	735	75
635 International Game Technology	Sep-96	733	118
636 Host Marriott	Dec-96	732	(13)
637 Zeigler Coal Holding	Dec-96	732	58
638 Expeditors	Dec-96	730	24
639 Nabors Industries	Sep-96	720	71
640 Pittston Minerals	Dec-96	697	11

Company Name	Fiscal Year	Sales ($ Millions)	Net Income ($ Millions)
641 Jostens	Jun-96	695	52
642 Global Marine	Dec-96	681	180
643 Keystone International	Dec-96	678	42
644 First Hawaiian	Dec-96	677	80
645 King World	Aug-96	663	150
646 Tambrands	Dec-96	662	46
647 Morrison Knudsen	Nov-96	659	(5)
648 Illinois Central	Dec-96	658	137
649 Symbol Technologies	Dec-96	657	50
650 Dentsply International	Dec-96	657	67
651 Global Industrial Technologies	Oct-96	650	45
652 Werner Enterprises	Dec-96	643	41
653 Rollins	Dec-96	627	23
654 Electronic Arts	Mar-97	625	53
655 Millipore	Dec-96	619	44
656 Nordson	Oct-96	609	53
657 John H. Harland	Dec-96	609	(14)
658 Parametric Technology	Sep-96	600	138
659 Zions Bancorporation	Dec-96	590	101
660 Mercantile Bankshares	Dec-96	588	117
661 Biomet	May-97	580	106
662 Rowan	Dec-96	571	61
663 Anadarko Petroleum	Dec-96	569	101
664 Ascend Communications	Dec-96	549	113
665 Hartford Steam Boiler	Dec-96	549	53
666 MBIA	Dec-96	546	322
667 Wilmington Trust	Dec-96	541	97
668 Cleveland-Cliffs	Dec-96	518	61
669 Rollins Truck Leasing	Sep-96	514	34
670 Autodesk	Jan-97	510	42
671 True North Communications	Dec-96	493	28
672 Grand Casinos	Dec-96	490	(101)
673 ENSCO International	Dec-96	469	95
674 Alza	Dec-96	466	92
675 Overseas Ship-holding	Dec-96	456	3
676 Stride Rite	Nov-96	448	3
677 Lee Enterprises	Sep-96	427	45
678 Battle Mountain Gold	Dec-96	424	(74)
679 Xtra	Sep-96	423	41
680 Washington Federal	Sep-96	410	80
681 CalMat	Dec-96	408	9
682 Handy & Harman	Dec-96	407	16
683 Gartner Group	Sep-96	395	16
684 Helmerich & Payne	Sep-96	393	73
685 Kirby	Dec-96	387	27
686 Linear Technology	Jun-96	378	134
687 Arnold Industries	Dec-96	356	25
688 Zurn Industries	Mar-97	353	5
689 Cracker Barrel Old Country Store	Jul-96	349	64
690 Netscape Communications	Dec-96	346	21
691 Acuson	Dec-96	346	(11)
692 Nextel Communications	Dec-96	333	(556)
693 United Water Resources	Dec-96	332	34
694 Atlas Air	Dec-96	316	38
695 Security Capital Pacific	Dec-96	305	131
696 Fastenal	Dec-96	288	33
697 Regal-Beloit	Dec-96	282	32
698 Biogen	Dec-96	277	41
699 Boston Chicken	Dec-96	265	67
700 Meditrust	Dec-96	254	158
701 Acclaim Entertainment	Aug-96	252	(221)
702 Newhall Land & Farming	Dec-96	220	42

Company Name	Fiscal Year	Sales ($ Millions)	Net Income ($ Millions)	Company Name	Fiscal Year	Sales ($ Millions)	Net Income ($ Millions)
703 California Water Service	Dec-96	183	19	712 Philadelphia Suburban	Dec-96	123	21
704 Federal Realty	Dec-96	179	29	713 Health & Retirement Properties Trust	Dec-96	120	73
705 Kimco Realty	Dec-96	168	74	714 Vornado Realty Trust	Dec-96	117	61
706 New Plan Realty	Jul-96	168	71	715 Amax Gold	Dec-96	108	(34)
707 Hecla Mining	Dec-96	158	(32)	716 Consumers Water	Dec-96	107	6
708 Parker Drilling	Aug-96	157	4	717 Aquarion	Dec-96	95	9
709 Weingarten Realty	Dec-96	151	54	718 Stillwater Mining	Dec-96	56	(5)
710 Catellus Development	Dec-96	138	25	719 Presstek	Dec-96	49	7
711 Centocor	Dec-96	135	(13)	720 Penn Virginia	Dec-96	34	13

Source: Dow Jones Global Indexes

The 250 Largest World Companies in the Dow Jones Global Indexes

	Company Name	Country	Fiscal Year	Sales (US$ Millions)	Net Income (US$ Millions)
1	General Motors	United States	30-Dec-96	$164,069.00	$4,963.00
2	Ford Motor	United States	30-Dec-96	146,991.00	4,446.00
3	Mitsui	Japan	31-Mar-97	142,521.74	316.57
4	Mitsubishi	Japan	31-Mar-97	137,861.86	387.47
5	Exxon	United States	30-Dec-96	134,249.00	7,510.00
6	Itochu Shoji	Japan	31-Mar-97	133,278.11	109.04
7	Marubeni	Japan	31-Mar-97	121,955.24	175.58
8	Sumitomo	Japan	31-Mar-97	117,288.93	−1,271.18
9	Toyota Motor	Japan	31-Mar-97	106,886.34	3,368.96
10	Wal-Mart Stores	United States	30-Jan-97	104,859.00	3,056.00
11	Mobil	United States	30-Dec-96	81,503.00	2,964.00
12	General Electric	United States	30-Dec-96	79,179.00	7,280.00
13	Nissho Iwai	Japan	31-Mar-97	77,602.94	134.62
14	Nippon Telegraph and Telephone	Japan	31-Mar-97	77,012.47	1,308.05
15	IBM	United States	30-Dec-96	75,947.00	5,429.00
16	British Petroleum	United Kingdom	31-Dec-96	74,514.41	4,251.21
17	Hitachi	Japan	31-Mar-97	74,405.04	771.11
18	Philip Morris	United States	30-Dec-96	69,204.00	6,303.00
19	Matsushita Electric Industrial	Japan	31-Mar-97	67,009.25	1,203.43
20	Royal Dutch Petroleum	Netherlands	31-Dec-96	65,925.71	4,879.25
21	Chrysler	United States	31-Dec-96	61,397.00	3,529.00
22	Daimler-Benz	Germany	31-Dec-96	60,942.88	1,582.90
23	Nissan Motor	Japan	31-Mar-97	58,130.32	678.68
24	Volkswagen	Germany	31-Dec-96	57,380.49	377.67
25	Unilever	United Kingdom	31-Dec-96	55,842.08	2,681.99
26	Shell Transport & Trading	United Kingdom	31-Dec-96	54,691.99	3,792.10
27	Siemens	Germany	30-Sep-96	53,974.56	1,590.35
28	AT&T	United States	30-Dec-96	52,184.00	5,908.00
29	Allianz	Germany	31-Dec-96	50,116.84	945.57
30	Sony	Japan	31-Mar-97	49,438.08	1,217.46
31	Toshiba	Japan	31-Mar-97	47,607.12	585.57

	Company Name	Country	Fiscal Year	Sales (US$ Millions)	Net Income (US$ Millions)
32	Honda Motor	Japan	31-Mar-97	46,209.52	1,930.75
33	Tomen	Japan	31-Mar-97	45,729.50	41.51
34	Fiat	Italy	31-Dec-96	45,676.21	1,398.15
35	Texaco	United States	30-Dec-96	45,500.00	2,018.00
36	Unilever	Netherlands	30-Dec-96	44,764.72	2,098.19
37	Tokyo Electric Power	Japan	31-Mar-97	43,987.74	712.37
38	Chevron	United States	30-Dec-96	43,893.00	2,607.00
39	DuPont	United States	30-Dec-96	43,810.00	3,636.00
40	NEC	Japan	31-Mar-97	43,198.91	799.48
41	Nestlé	Switzerland	31-Dec-96	41,375.16	2,326.28
42	Elf Aquitaine	France	31-Dec-96	39,582.75	1,186.77
43	Fujitsu	Japan	31-Mar-97	39,314.47	402.85
44	VEBA	Germany	31-Dec-96	39,025.24	1,408.68
45	Jardine Strategic	Singapore	31-Dec-96	38,963.97	1,839.38
46	Hewlett-Packard	United States	30-Oct-96	38,420.00	2,586.00
47	Sears, Roebuck	United States	30-Dec-96	38,236.00	1,271.00
48	Deutsche Telekom	Germany	31-Dec-96	36,148.28	1,007.51
49	Amoco	United States	30-Dec-96	36,112.00	2,834.00
50	Procter & Gamble	United States	30-Jun-96	35,284.00	3,046.00
51	Philips Electronics	Netherlands	31-Dec-96	35,238.85	−300.47
52	ENI	Italy	30-Dec-96	35,125.47	2,624.71
53	AXA-UAP	France	31-Dec-96	34,170.44	647.90
54	Nichimen	Japan	31-Mar-97	33,967.69	42.94
55	Citicorp	United States	30-Dec-96	32,605.00	3,788.00
56	Mitsubishi Electric	Japan	31-Mar-97	32,520.22	74.40
57	Japan Tobacco	Japan	31-Mar-97	32,278.32	700.10
58	Mitsubishi Motors	Japan	31-Mar-97	32,056.60	101.26
59	Prudential	United Kingdom	31-Dec-96	31,979.01	2,343.83
60	PepsiCo	United States	29-Dec-96	31,645.00	1,149.00
61	Kmart	United States	30-Jan-97	31,437.00	−220.00
62	RWE	Germany	30-Jun-96	31,394.99	685.43
63	Renault	France	31-Dec-96	31,311.11	−892.67
64	Samsung	South Korea	31-Dec-96	31,066.92	58.63
65	Deutsche Bank	Germany	31-Dec-96	30,549.10	1,223.00
66	Kanematsu	Japan	31-Mar-97	30,353.18	−240.35
67	ING	Netherlands	31-Dec-96	30,287.74	1,691.28
68	Total	France	31-Dec-96	30,035.21	969.21
69	BMW	Germany	31-Dec-96	29,953.07	465.93
70	Peugeot	France	31-Dec-96	29,373.70	124.85
71	Hoechst	Germany	31-Dec-96	29,186.26	1,211.53
72	HSBC Holdings	Hong Kong	31-Dec-96	28,814.76	4,852.09
73	American International	United States	30-Dec-96	28,205.27	2,897.26
74	Générale des Eaux	France	31-Dec-96	28,147.59	332.15
75	Motorola	United States	30-Dec-96	27,973.00	1,154.00
76	BASF	Germany	31-Dec-96	27,953.53	1,599.06
77	Bayer	Germany	31-Dec-96	27,857.24	1,561.70
78	Alcatel Alsthom	France	31-Dec-96	27,573.06	463.51
79	Industrial Bank of Japan	Japan	31-Mar-97	27,563.07	111.22
80	Daiei	Japan	28-Feb-97	27,465.22	−103.95
81	Mitsubishi Heavy Industries	Japan	31-Mar-97	27,433.17	1,079.08
82	Chase Manhattan	United States	30-Dec-96	27,421.00	2,461.00
83	Lockheed Martin	United States	30-Dec-96	26,875.00	1,347.00
84	Nippon Steel	Japan	31-Mar-97	26,724.46	30.12
85	Ito-Yokado	Japan	28-Feb-97	26,354.10	648.85
86	Carrefour	France	31-Dec-96	26,348.87	572.89
87	Zurich Insurance	Switzerland	31-Dec-96	25,971.07	778.53

	Company Name	Country	Fiscal Year	Sales (US$ Millions)	Net Income (US$ Millions)
88	Dayton Hudson	United States	30-Jan-97	25,371.00	463.00
89	Kroger	United States	30-Dec-96	25,170.91	349.80
90	Daewoo	South Korea	31-Dec-96	25,074.79	79.67
91	Fannie Mae	United States	30-Dec-96	25,054.00	2,724.70
92	Merrill Lynch	United States	28-Dec-96	25,011.00	1,619.00
93	BT	United Kingdom	31-Mar-97	24,879.23	3,459.94
94	Sanwa Bank	Japan	31-Mar-97	24,379.84	225.70
95	VIAG	Germany	31-Dec-96	24,329.40	457.26
96	Allstate	United States	30-Dec-96	24,299.00	2,075.00
97	ConAgra	United States	30-May-97	24,002.10	615.00
98	STET	Italy	30-Dec-96	23,895.42	1,021.34
99	NatWest	United Kingdom	31-Dec-96	23,663.17	731.30
100	ABN-Amro	Netherlands	31-Dec-96	23,614.28	1,682.11
101	United Technologies	United States	30-Dec-96	23,512.00	906.00
102	CS Holding	Switzerland	31-Dec-96	23,310.72	−1,770.88
103	Nippon Oil	Japan	31-Mar-97	23,224.61	109.77
104	Tesco	United Kingdom	22-Feb-97	23,133.43	866.23
105	Kansai Electric Power	Japan	31-Mar-97	22,791.34	481.63
106	Société Générale	France	31-Dec-96	22,692.81	772.92
107	Boeing	United States	30-Dec-96	22,681.00	1,095.00
108	Peregrine Investments	Hong Kong	31-Dec-96	22,658.44	110.46
109	J.C. Penney	United States	26-Jan-97	22,653.00	565.00
110	Samsung Electronics	South Korea	31-Dec-96	22,389.89	123.51
111	Canon	Japan	31-Dec-96	22,332.84	822.15
112	J. Sainsbury	United Kingdom	08-Mar-97	22,313.84	671.33
113	Thyssen	Germany	30-Sep-96	22,163.38	170.73
114	BankAmerica	United States	30-Dec-96	22,071.00	2,873.00
115	Royal & Sun Alliance Insurance	United Kingdom	31-Dec-96	22,058.97	772.95
116	East Japan Railway	Japan	31-Mar-97	21,944.91	616.86
117	Lloyds TSB Group	United Kingdom	31-Dec-96	21,732.47	2,623.69
118	Johnson & Johnson	United States	30-Dec-96	21,620.00	2,887.00
119	B.A.T. Industries	United Kingdom	31-Dec-96	21,532.57	2,508.75
120	Travelers	United States	30-Dec-96	21,345.40	2,331.00
121	GTE	United States	30-Dec-96	21,339.00	2,798.00
122	Barclays Bank	United Kingdom	31-Dec-96	20,967.85	2,730.30
123	Fuji Bank	Japan	31-Mar-97	20,944.76	951.93
124	Intel	United States	30-Dec-96	20,847.00	5,157.00
125	Munich Reinsurance	Germany	30-Jun-96	20,781.07	285.62
126	Loews	United States	30-Dec-96	20,442.40	1,383.90
127	Sumitomo Bank	Japan	31-Mar-97	20,412.32	297.23
128	BCE	Canada	31-Dec-96	20,396.09	834.18
129	Commercial Union Assurance	United Kingdom	31-Dec-96	20,363.15	661.34
130	Volvo	Sweden	30-Dec-96	20,225.51	1,617.03
131	International Paper	United States	30-Dec-96	20,100.00	303.00
132	Dow Chemical	United States	30-Dec-96	20,053.00	1,907.00
133	Columbia/HCA Healthcare	United States	30-Dec-96	19,909.00	1,505.00
134	Mannesmann	Germany	31-Dec-96	19,876.83	219.50
135	Merck	United States	30-Dec-96	19,828.70	3,881.30
136	Costco	United States	02-Sep-96	19,566.46	248.79
137	Jusco	Japan	20-Feb-97	19,539.72	308.14
138	Home Depot	United States	27-Jan-97	19,535.00	937.74
139	Atlantic Richfield	United States	31-Dec-96	19,169.00	1,663.00
140	BellSouth	United States	30-Dec-96	19,040.00	2,863.00
141	Dai-Ichi Kangyo Bank	Japan	31-Mar-97	18,978.97	−1,548.15
142	Chubu Electric Power	Japan	31-Mar-97	18,950.97	335.09
143	CIGNA	United States	30-Dec-96	18,950.00	1,056.00

	Company Name	Country	Fiscal Year	Sales (US$ Millions)	Net Income (US$ Millions)
144	Walt Disney	United States	29-Sep-96	18,739.00	1,214.00
145	American Stores	United States	01-Feb-97	18,678.13	287.22
146	Sara Lee	United States	30-Jun-96	18,624.00	916.00
147	Ahold	Netherlands	29-Dec-96	18,607.71	322.07
148	Coca-Cola	United States	30-Dec-96	18,546.00	3,492.00
149	MCI Communications	United States	30-Dec-96	18,494.00	1,202.00
150	Kajima	Japan	31-Mar-97	18,338.72	64.12
151	Dresdner Bank	Germany	31-Dec-96	18,307.11	881.03
152	Compaq Computer	United States	30-Dec-96	18,109.00	1,313.00
153	AMR	United States	30-Dec-96	17,753.00	1,016.00
154	LG International	South Korea	31-Dec-96	17,718.06	34.97
155	Paribas	France	31-Dec-96	17,704.71	739.92
156	Tokio Marine & Fire Insurance	Japan	31-Mar-97	17,693.93	229.41
157	Promodès	France	31-Dec-96	17,610.99	212.11
158	Japan Energy	Japan	31-Mar-97	17,587.38	−404.04
159	ICI	United Kingdom	31-Dec-96	17,524.57	458.10
160	Long-Term Credit Bank	Japan	31-Mar-97	17,485.02	170.00
161	Telecom Italia	Italy	31-Dec-96	17,453.39	1,309.72
162	NationsBank	United States	30-Dec-96	17,442.00	2,452.00
163	Sakura Bank	Japan	31-Mar-97	17,379.01	154.92
164	Xerox	United States	30-Dec-96	17,378.00	1,206.00
165	Legal & General	United Kingdom	31-Dec-96	17,345.83	2,999.33
166	Taisei	Japan	31-Mar-97	17,303.92	50.48
167	Safeway	United States	30-Dec-96	17,269.00	460.60
168	Bridgestone	Japan	31-Dec-96	17,093.19	614.00
169	Petrofina	Belgium	31-Dec-96	17,038.42	446.15
170	Isuzu Motors	Japan	31-Mar-97	16,789.76	83.65
171	Commerzbank	Germany	31-Dec-96	16,756.87	681.99
172	Supervalu	United States	27-Feb-97	16,551.90	175.04
173	Mazda Motor	Japan	31-Mar-97	16,536.00	−153.19
174	Caterpillar	United States	30-Dec-96	16,522.00	1,361.00
175	NKK	Japan	31-Mar-97	16,391.57	145.72
176	UAL	United States	30-Dec-96	16,362.00	533.00
177	USX-Marathon	United States	30-Dec-96	16,332.00	664.00
178	American Express	United States	30-Dec-96	16,237.00	1,901.00
179	Sanyo Electric	Japan	31-Mar-97	16,117.23	154.29
180	Ericsson	Sweden	31-Dec-96	16,104.98	921.46
181	Eastman Kodak	United States	30-Dec-96	15,968.00	1,288.00
182	Hughes Electronics	United States	30-Dec-96	15,917.90	1,028.90
183	Union Bank of Switzerland	Switzerland	31-Dec-96	15,869.48	−239.40
184	J.P. Morgan	United States	30-Dec-96	15,866.00	1,574.00
185	Lucent Technologies Inc.	United States	31-Dec-96	15,859.00	224.00
186	Phillips Petroleum	United States	30-Dec-96	15,807.00	1,303.00
187	Toyota Tsusho	Japan	31-Mar-97	15,733.85	54.09
188	Mycal	Japan	28-Feb-97	15,718.75	132.66
189	Sharp	Japan	31-Mar-97	15,631.42	423.80
190	Nippon Express	Japan	31-Mar-97	15,586.88	240.04
191	Lyonnaise des Eaux	France	31-Dec-96	15,584.28	229.46
192	Saint-Gobain	France	31-Dec-96	15,544.14	735.33
193	AGF	France	31-Dec-96	15,430.52	261.27
194	Federated Department Stores	United States	01-Feb-97	15,229.00	265.85
195	Aetna	United States	30-Dec-96	15,163.20	651.00
196	Mitsubishi Chemical	Japan	31-Mar-97	15,122.55	−104.52
197	Compart	Italy	30-Dec-96	15,110.81	56.61
198	Cosmo Oil	Japan	31-Mar-97	15,098.15	77.15
199	Bristol-Myers Squibb	United States	30-Dec-96	15,065.00	2,850.00

	Company Name	Country	Fiscal Year	Sales (US$ Millions)	Net Income (US$ Millions)
200	Bayerische Vereinsbank	Germany	31-Dec-96	15,023.62	465.02
201	Shimizu	Japan	31-Mar-97	14,998.15	46.35
202	Ameritech	United States	30-Dec-96	14,917.00	2,134.00
203	Rhône-Poulenc	France	31-Dec-96	14,597.38	581.73
204	Digital Equipment	United States	30-Jun-96	14,562.78	−111.81
205	Grand Metropolitan	United Kingdom	30-Sep-96	14,537.73	83.29
206	Electronic Data Systems	United States	30-Dec-96	14,441.30	431.50
207	Broken Hill Proprietary	Australia	31-May-96	14,413.76	788.37
208	Preussag	Germany	30-Sep-96	14,352.43	143.74
209	Danone	France	31-Dec-96	14,277.94	575.27
210	Lehman Brothers	United States	29-Nov-96	14,260.00	416.00
211	Electrolux	Sweden	31-Dec-96	14,256.09	239.76
212	3M	United States	30-Dec-96	14,236.00	1,526.00
213	Nippondenso	Japan	31-Mar-97	14,185.12	623.10
214	American Home Products	United States	30-Dec-96	14,088.33	1,883.40
215	Sprint	United States	30-Dec-96	14,044.70	1,183.80
216	BTR	United Kingdom	31-Dec-96	14,014.66	717.97
217	AlliedSignal	United States	30-Dec-96	13,971.00	1,020.00
218	Showa Shell Sekiyu	Japan	31-Dec-96	13,968.28	52.85
219	Kirin Brewery	Japan	31-Dec-96	13,935.88	300.18
220	British Airways	United Kingdom	31-Mar-97	13,924.70	921.21
221	SBC Communications	United States	30-Dec-96	13,898.20	2,101.20
222	Glaxo Wellcome	United Kingdom	31-Dec-96	13,894.72	3,326.67
223	Montedison	Italy	31-Dec-96	13,834.72	175.73
224	McDonnell Douglas	United States	30-Dec-96	13,834.00	788.00
225	Tokai Bank	Japan	31-Mar-97	13,819.40	146.65
226	Karstadt	Germany	31-Dec-96	13,781.35	33.45
227	Albertson's	United States	30-Jan-97	13,766.68	493.78
228	Repsol	Spain	31-Dec-96	13,723.12	809.00
229	Coles Myer	Australia	28-Jul-96	13,698.50	211.34
230	Japan Airlines	Japan	31-Mar-97	13,680.77	−126.39
231	Pinault-Printemps-Redoute	France	31-Dec-96	13,674.78	351.25
232	Telefónica de España	Spain	31-Dec-96	13,612.39	1,087.62
233	Obayashi	Japan	31-Mar-97	13,456.87	118.91
234	NYNEX	United States	30-Dec-96	13,453.80	1,477.00
235	Sysco	United States	29-Jun-96	13,395.10	276.90
236	Kobe Steel	Japan	31-Mar-97	13,386.81	152.82
237	Tohoku Electric Power	Japan	31-Mar-96	13,353.61	340.26
238	Archer-Daniels-Midland	United States	30-Jun-96	13,314.05	695.91
239	Enron	United States	30-Dec-96	13,289.00	584.00
240	Ashland	United States	29-Sep-96	13,285.00	211.00
241	Swiss Bank	Switzerland	31-Dec-96	13,263.44	−1,337.22
242	SmithKline Beecham	United Kingdom	31-Dec-96	13,201.73	1,785.77
243	Kimberly-Clark	United States	30-Dec-96	13,149.10	1,403.80
244	Alcoa	United States	30-Dec-96	13,128.40	514.90
245	Suzuki Motor	Japan	31-Mar-97	13,115.88	293.20
246	Goodyear Tire & Rubber	United States	30-Dec-96	13,112.80	101.70
247	Korea Electric Power	South Korea	31-Dec-96	13,088.59	752.67
248	Bell Atlantic	United States	30-Dec-96	13,081.40	1,881.50
249	Marks & Spencer	United Kingdom	31-Mar-97	13,063.30	1,257.04
250	Georgia-Pacific	United States	30-Dec-96	13,024.00	156.00

Source: Dow Jones Global Indexes

Top 75 Employers With Headquarters in the U.S.

Rank	Name	City	State	Number of Employees
1	U.S. Postal Service	Washington	District of Columbia	700,000
2	Wal-Mart Stores	Bentonville	Arkansas	675,000
3	Kelly Services	Troy	Michigan	669,800
4	General Motors	Detroit	Michigan	647,000
5	Olsten	Melville	New York	568,800
6	PepsiCo	Purchase	New York	480,000
7	Ford Motor	Dearborn	Michigan	346,990
8	United Parcel Service of America	Atlanta	Georgia	332,000
9	Sears Roebuck	Hoffman Estates	Illinois	321,565
10	Kmart	Troy	Michigan	307,000
11	Columbia/HCA Healthcare	Nashville	Tennessee	285,000
12	General Electric	Fairfield	Connecticut	239,000
13	Norrell	Atlanta	Georgia	227,900
14	International Business Machines	Armonk	New York	225,347
15	Dayton Hudson	Minneapolis	Minnesota	214,000
16	McDonald's	Hinsdale	Illinois	212,000
17	Kroger	Cincinnati	Ohio	205,000
18	J.C. Penney	Plano	Texas	202,357
19	Lockheed Martin	Bethesda	Maryland	197,000
20	AccuStaff	Jacksonville	Florida	187,000
21	United Technologies	Hartford	Connecticut	173,800
22	Marriott International	Washington	District of Columbia	161,641
23	Philip Morris	New York	New York	151,000
24	Aramark	Philadelphia	Pennsylvania	150,000
25	Motorola	Schaumburg	Illinois	142,000
26	Sara Lee	Chicago	Illinois	135,200
27	University of California	Oakland	California	131,661
28	Carlson Holdings	Minneapolis	Minnesota	130,000
29	AT&T	New York	New York	128,200
30	Federal Express	Memphis	Tennessee	127,134
31	Boeing	Seattle	Washington	126,000
32	Chrysler	Auburn Hills	Michigan	126,000
33	Winn-Dixie Stores	Jacksonville	Florida	126,000
34	Lucent Technologies	New Providence	New Jersey	124,000
35	City of New York Board of Education	Brooklyn	New York	123,906
36	American Stores	Salt Lake City	Utah	121,000
37	Federated Department Stores	Cincinnati	Ohio	119,100
38	Safeway	Pleasanton	California	114,000
39	Hewlett-Packard	Palo Alto	California	112,000
40	AMR	Fort Worth	Texas	111,300
41	May Department Stores	St. Louis	Missouri	106,000
42	DuPont	Wilmington	Delaware	105,000
43	General Conference of Seventh-Day Adventists	Silver Spring	Maryland	104,000
44	Limited	Columbus	Ohio	104,000
45	Robert Half International	Menlo Park	California	103,100
46	Procter & Gamble	Cincinnati	Ohio	103,000
47	GTE	Stamford	Connecticut	102,000
48	Labor Ready	Tacoma	Washington	100,450
49	Darden Restaurants	Orlando	Florida	100,000
50	Walt Disney	Burbank	California	100,000
51	CVS	Woonsocket	Rhode Island	96,832
52	Eastman Kodak	Rochester	New York	96,600
53	Electronic Data Systems	Plano	Texas	96,000
54	BankAmerica	San Francisco	California	95,300

Rank	Name	City	State	Number of Employees
55	Publix Super Markets	Lakeland	Florida	95,000
56	Woolworth	New York	New York	94,000
57	Flagstar	Spartanburg	South Carolina	93,000
58	Prudential Insurance	Newark	New Jersey	92,966
59	Andersen Worldwide, Societe Cooperative	Chicago	Illinois	91,572
60	ConAgra	Omaha	Nebraska	90,871
61	Home Depot	Atlanta	Georgia	90,000
62	Goodyear Tire & Rubber	Akron	Ohio	88,790
63	International Paper	Purchase	New York	88,000
64	AlliedSignal	Morristown	New Jersey	87,500
65	Seagate Technology	Scotts Valley	California	87,000
66	Emerson Electric	St. Louis	Missouri	86,400
67	Borg-Warner Security	Chicago	Illinois	86,370
68	Citicorp	New York	New York	85,300
69	Xerox	Stamford	Connecticut	85,200
70	UAL	Arlington Heights	Illinois	83,929
71	Beverly Enterprises	Fort Smith	Arkansas	83,000
72	Johnson & Johnson	New Brunswick	New Jersey	82,300
73	Exxon	Irving	Texas	82,000
74	National Amusements	Dedham	Massachusetts	81,700
75	BellSouth	Atlanta	Georgia	81,241

Source: Dun & Bradstreet

Top 75 Employers With Headquarters Outside the U.S.

Rank	Name	Country	Number of Employees
1	Siemens	Germany	378,800
2	Deutsche Bahn	Germany	331,552
3	Daimler-Benz	Germany	321,222
4	Deutsche Post	Germany	308,459
5	Unilever	England	308,000
6	The People's Construction Bank of China	People's Republic of China	307,000
7	Shougang Corporation	People's Republic of China	250,000
8	Volkswagen	Germany	242,285
9	Deutsche Telekom	Germany	231,720
10	Bank of China	Hong Kong	213,767
11	Jardine Matheson Holdings	Hong Kong	200,000
12	Steel Authority of India	India	189,506
13	Nippon Telegraph & Telephone	Japan	185,458
14	Chemins De Fer Francais (Societe Nationale Des)	France	181,114
15	B.A.T Industries	England	173,475
16	Hoechst	Germany	165,928
17	Pakistan Water & Power Development Authority	Pakistan	160,000
18	Robert Bosch	Germany	158,372
19	J. Sainsbury	England	154,661
20	Lefebvre Pascal	France	152,586
21	France Telecom	France	150,403
22	British Telecommunications	England	148,900
23	Bayer	Germany	144,050
24	British Railways Board	England	137,729
25	Hevrat Ha Ovdim	Israel	137,000
26	Pakistan Railways	Pakistan	137,000

Rank	Name	Country	Number of Employees
27	RWE	Germany	135,131
28	Tesco	England	135,037
29	Coles Myer	Australia	135,000
30	Jardine Strategic Holdings	Hong Kong	130,000
31	Ferrovie Dello Stato Societa' Di Trasporti E Servizi	Italy	126,061
32	BTR	England	125,065
33	Thyssen	Germany	123,746
34	Mannesmann	Germany	123,149
35	Veba	Germany	123,046
36	Electricite De France	France	118,000
37	BCE	Canada	116,000
38	Electrolux	Sweden	109,470
39	H.S.B.C. Holdings	England	109,093
40	Compass Group	England	107,843
41	Bayerische Motorenwerke	Germany	106,944
42	Shell Transport & Trading	England	106,000
43	BASF	Germany	105,557
44	Karstadt	Germany	105,129
45	RAG	Germany	103,919
46	Cable & Wireless	Hong Kong	100,000
47	National Westminster Bank	England	96,800
48	Enel	Italy	96,287
49	Genton (Metallerie)	France	96,172
50	Woolworths	Australia	94,600
51	Lonrho	England	93,497
52	Barclays	England	92,400
53	Banco do Brasil	Brazil	91,381
54	Lloyds T S B Group	England	91,044
55	Nippon Life Insurance	Japan	89,690
56	Kamaz	Russian Federation	87,492
57	Bass	England	84,872
58	Viag	Germany	84,544
59	Lukoil Oil Company JSC	Russian Federation	83,100
60	Sprava Post A Telekomunikaci Statni Podnik	Czech Republic	83,000
61	General Electric Co. PLC	England	82,967
62	Boots Co. PLC	England	80,497
63	North East Thames Regional Health Authority	England	80,000
64	Charoen Pokphand Group	Thailand	80,000
65	East Japan Railway	Japan	79,709
66	Chemomorskoye Parokhodstvo	Ukraine	79,200
67	Kingfisher	England	77,436
68	Camellia	England	76,577
69	Anglovaal	South Africa	76,000
70	Hitachi	Japan	75,590
71	PT Astra International	Indonesia	74,955
72	Banco Bradesco	Brazil	74,580
73	Asda Group	England	73,714
74	Coats Viyella	England	73,650
75	McDonald's Co. (Japan) Ltd.	Japan	72,800

Source: Dun & Bradstreet

Number of Insured Banks and Number of Failures, 1980-1996
(Assets in millions of dollars)

Year	Number of insured commercial banks	Total assets	Number of failures	Failed bank assets
1980	14,435	$1,855,695	11	$8,189
1981	14,408	2,029,151	7	104
1982	14,446	2,193,867	34	1,862
1983	14,460	2,341,955	45	4,137
1984	14,483	2,508,871	79	36,394
1985	14,407	2,730,672	118	3,034
1986	14,199	2,940,699	144	7,609
1987	13,703	2,999,949	201	7,538
1988	13,123	3,130,796	221	52,620
1989	12,709	3,299,362	206	28,507
1990	12,343	3,389,490	159	10,739
1991	11,921	3,430,682	108	43,552
1992	11,462	3,505,663	100	16,915
1993	10,958	3,706,164	42	2,588
1994	10,451	4,010,516	11	825
1995	9,940	4,312,680	6	753
1996	9,528	4,578,343	5	186

Number of Insured Savings Institutions and Number of Failures,
1980-1996 (Assets in millions of dollars)

Year	Number of insured savings institutions	Total assets	Number of failures	Failed institution assets
1980	4,328	$ 773,191	11	$ 1,351
1981	4,116	814,388	31	16,332
1982	3,664	854,829	84	32,575
1983	3,477	989,887	57	25,435
1984	3,418	1,144,247	28	6,391
1985	3,626	1,262,654	37	13,100
1986	3,677	1,386,866	52	24,570
1987	3,622	1,502,111	49	12,676
1988	3,438	1,606,489	222	110,761
1989	3,087	1,427,512	330	136,250
1990	2,815	1,259,178	223	134,628
1991	2,561	1,113,002	163	98,545
1992	2,390	1,030,214	81	72,729
1993	2,262	1,000,891	8	6,938
1994	2,152	1,008,568	4	707
1995	2,030	1,025,742	2	456
1996	1,924	1,028,192	1	34

Source: Federal Deposit Insurance Corp.

Top 100 U.S. Commercial Banks in Total Deposits (in thousands)

RANK		TOTAL DEPOSITS 12/31/96
1	Citibank, NA, New York	$171,676,000
2	Chase Manhattan Bank, NA, New York	160,212,000
3	Bank of America NT&SA, San Francisco	131,177,000
4	Wells Fargo Bank, NA, San Francisco	75,855,884
5	Morgan Guaranty Trust Co., New York	53,130,141
6	NationsBank, NA, Charlotte, N.C.	47,606,008
7	Bank of New York	38,782,451
8	NationsBank, NA, South, Atlanta	36,681,610
9	PNC Bank, NA, Pittsburgh	36,393,879
10	Fleet National Bank, Springfield, Mass.	35,206,585
11	CoreStates Bank, NA, Philadelphia	34,647,499
12	Bankers Trust Co., New York	33,604,000
13	Barnett Bank, NA, Jacksonville, Fla.	33,592,449
14	First National Bank, Chicago	32,894,653
15	Republic National Bank of New York	32,042,014
16	First Union National Bank of Florida, Jacksonville	31,589,264
17	NationsBank of Texas, NA, Dallas	28,466,955
18	Mellon Bank, NA, Pittsburgh	28,317,418
19	First National Bank, Boston	27,624,106
20	Union Bank of California, San Francisco	23,200,204
21	First Union National Bank, Avondale, Pa.	21,995,032
22	First Union National Bank of North Carolina, Charlotte	20,133,251
23	State Street Bank & Trust Co., Boston	19,903,820
24	Fleet Bank, NA, Jersey City, N.J.	19,506,330
25	Marine Midland Bank, Buffalo, N.Y.	18,900,209
26	Texas Commerce Bank, NA, Houston	17,810,247
27	KeyBank, NA, Cleveland	17,750,534
28	Bank One, Texas, NA, Dallas	16,653,462
29	NBD Bank, Detroit	$16,485,135
30	Comerica Bank, Detroit	16,429,146
31	Summit Bank (NJ), Princeton	15,972,397
32	Wachovia Bank of North Carolina, NA, Winston-Salem	13,228,456
33	Bank of America NW, NA, Seattle	12,995,000
34	Crestar Bank, Richmond	12,826,561
35	Branch Banking & Trust Co., Winston-Salem, N.C.	11,975,969
36	Bank One, Arizona, NA, Phoenix	11,478,584
37	First Bank NA, Minneapolis	11,402,330
38	Northern Trust Co., Chicago	11,143,250
39	Key Bank of New York, Albany	11,071,003
40	Norwest Bank Minnesota, NA, Minneapolis	10,527,425
41	First of America Bank-Michigan NA, Grand Rapids	10,355,166
42	National City Bank of Pittsburgh	10,317,349
43	MBNA America Bank, NA, Wilmington, Del.	10,304,889

RANK		TOTAL DEPOSITS 12/31/96
44	Banco Popular de Puerto Rico, San Juan	10,096,000
45	Harris Trust & Savings Bank, Chicago	9,738,510
46	United States National Bank, Portland, Ore.	9,693,000
47	Wachovia Bank of Georgia, NA	9,609,066
48	BayBank, NA, Boston	9,488,718
49	Fleet Bank of New York, Albany	9,459,681
50	Regions Bank, Birmingham	9,043,793
51	LaSalle National Bank, Chicago	8,975,557
52	Bank of America Illinois, Chicago	8,667,000
53	SunTrust Bank, Atlanta	8,511,336
54	Old Kent Bank, Grand Rapids, Mich.	8,499,782
55	Huntington National Bank, Columbus, Ohio	8,432,557
56	Manufacturers & Traders Trust Co., Buffalo, N.Y.	8,315,961
57	Boatmen's National Bank, St. Louis	$8,315,520
58	First Tennessee Bank, NA, Memphis	8,201,351
59	Signet Bank, Richmond	8,081,167
60	Central Fidelity National Bank, Richmond	8,071,846
61	Star Bank, NA, Cincinnati	7,920,302
62	Bank of America Arizona, Phoenix	7,875,095
63	NBD Bank, NA, Indianapolis	7,833,149
64	SouthTrust Bank of Alabama, NA, Birmingham	7,809,056
65	First Union National Bank of Georgia, Atlanta	7,777,204
66	Bank of Hawaii, Honolulu	7,761,827
67	Hibernia National Bank, New Orleans	7,606,828
68	Chase Manhattan Bank (USA), NA, Wilmington, Del.	7,551,630
69	U.S. Bank of Washington, NA, Seattle	7,505,463
70	First American National Bank, Nashville, Tenn.	7,333,451
71	First Security Bank of Utah, NA, Salt Lake City	7,291,849
72	Norwest Bank Colorado, NA, Denver	7,186,853
73	European American Bank, New York	7,105,632
74	Michigan National Bank, Farmington Hills	7,042,823
75	Boatmen's National Bank, Kansas City, Mo.	7,008,613
76	Wells Fargo Bank (Texas), NA, Houston	6,929,763
77	First-Citizens Bank & Trust Co., Raleigh, N.C.	6,857,136
78	First National Bank of Maryland, Baltimore	$6,817,469
79	First Union National Bank of Virginia, Roanoke	6,814,336
80	AmSouth Bank of Alabama, Birmingham	6,793,095
81	National City Bank, Cleveland	6,564,845
82	American National Bank & Trust Co., Chicago	6,476,985
83	Key Bank of Washington, Tacoma	6,205,447

RANK		TOTAL DEPOSITS 12/31/96
84	Sanwa Bank California, San Francisco	6,112,911
85	Bank One, Wisconsin, Milwaukee	5,949,652
86	Greenwood Trust Co., New Castle, Del.	5,874,911
87	Fifth Third Bank, Cincinnati	5,788,057
88	Bank One, Columbus, NA, Ohio	5,704,132
89	Bank of America Texas, NA, Irving	5,640,788
90	Wachovia Bank of South Carolina, NA, Columbia	5,594,435
91	First of America Bank-Illinois, NA, Bannockburn	5,303,565
92	Colorado National Bank, Denver	5,131,785

RANK		TOTAL DEPOSITS 12/31/96
93	Firstar Bank, Milwaukee, NA	4,991,700
94	Bank One, Kentucky, NA, Louisville	4,986,297
95	National City Bank, Louisville, Ky.	4,927,400
96	Mercantile Bank, NA. St. Louis, Mo.	4,811,168
97	Centura Bank, Rocky Mount, N.C.	4,756,636
98	Provident Bank, Cincinnati	4,659,806
99	AmSouth Bank of Florida, Pensacola	4,619,481
100	Central Carolina Bank & Trust Co., Durham, N.C.	4,604,030

Source: American Banker

Top 100 U.S. Commercial Banks in Total Assets

In order of total assets on Dec. 31, 1996, compared with Dec. 31, 1995 (dollar amounts in thousands)

RANK DEC. 1996		ASSETS DEC. 31, 1996	DEC. 31, 1995
1	Chase Manhattan Bank, NA, New York	$272,429,000	$147,120,000
2	Citibank, NA, New York	241,006,000	220,110,000
3	Bank of America NT&SA, San Francisco	180,480,000	163,398,000
4	Morgan Guaranty Trust Co., New York	172,562,891	143,397,397
5	Wells Fargo Bank, NA, San Francisco	99,165,167	49,091,757
6	Bankers Trust Co., New York	90,430,000	79,100,000
7	NationsBank, NA, Charlotte, N.C.	80,870,158	79,179,164
8	PNC Bank, NA, Pittsburgh	57,284,961	41,905,459
9	Bank of New York	52,120,460	42,711,907
10	First National Bank, Chicago	51,662,906	49,360,496
11	Republic National Bank of New York	46,952,900	34,579,761
12	NationsBank, NA, South, Atlanta	46,776,149	37,609,624
13	Fleet National Bank, Springfield, Mass.	46,580,793	7,321,413
14	First National Bank, Boston	45,874,949	40,273,929
15	CoreStates Bank, NA, Philadelphia	42,670,362	21,576,881
16	First Union National Bank of Florida, Jacksonville	39,259,452	36,591,486
17	Barnett Bank, NA, Jacksonville, Fla.	39,208,823	3,407,839
18	NationsBank of Texas, NA, Dallas	39,149,395	48,368,452
19	Mellon Bank, NA, Pittsburgh	37,339,293	35,565,119
20	First Union National Bank of North Carolina, Charlotte	32,421,535	27,415,416
21	State Street Bank & Trust Co., Boston	31,389,728	25,558,018
22	Union Bank of California, San Francisco	29,197,382	19,518,095
23	KeyBank, NA, Cleveland	27,812,911	22,307,492
24	First Union National Bank, Avondale, Pa.	27,128,369	32,686,855
25	Comerica Bank, Detroit	27,051,459	28,394,044
26	Wachovia Bank of North Carolina, NA, Winston-Salem	26,751,374	26,865,186
27	Chase Manhattan Bank (USA), NA, Wilmington, Del.	25,310,644	10,889,326
28	Marine Midland Bank, Buffalo, N.Y.	23,345,154	20,342,472
29	Fleet Bank, NA, Jersey City, N.J.	23,116,201	1,580,920
30	Texas Commerce Bank, NA, Houston	22,716,450	19,990,216
31	NBD Bank, Detroit	22,473,845	29,461,639
32	Bank One, Texas, NA, Dallas	20,885,535	18,797,762
33	Summit Bank (NJ), Princeton	19,614,695	13,129,429
34	Wachovia Bank of Georgia, NA	18,918,575	17,345,531
35	Crestar Bank, Richmond	18,264,352	13,557,742
36	Northern Trust Co., Chicago	18,126,874	15,230,538
37	Norwest Bank Minnesota, NA, Minneapolis	17,648,607	18,233,560
38	Bank of America Illinois, Chicago	17,075,000	16,171,000

RANK		ASSETS	
DEC. 1996		DEC. 31, 1996	DEC. 31, 1995
39	First Bank NA, Minneapolis	$17,055,417	$16,376,002
40	Branch Banking & Trust Co., Winston-Salem, N.C.	16,595,684	15,991,534
41	Bank of America NW, NA, Seattle	16,568,000	17,151,000
42	MBNA America Bank, NA, Wilmington, Del.	15,574,852	12,162,767
43	Key Bank of New York, Albany	15,486,227	15,372,762
44	SunTrust Bank, Atlanta	15,015,063	12,459,197
45	Huntington National Bank, Columbus, Ohio	14,405,504	14,424,544
46	Bank One, Arizona, NA, Phoenix	14,310,690	13,080,758
47	United States National Bank, Portland, Ore.	14,290,000	12,126,000
48	Harris Trust & Savings Bank, Chicago	14,263,933	12,247,560
49	Banco Popular de Puerto Rico, San Juan	14,005,000	12,931,000
50	Citibank (South Dakota), NA, Sioux Falls	13,548,951	12,697,891
51	LaSalle National Bank, Chicago	13,386,946	11,216,059
52	National City Bank of Pittsburgh	13,289,468	13,978,565
53	SouthTrust Bank of Alabama, NA, Birmingham	13,272,231	11,121,595
54	First of America Bank-Michigan NA, Grand Rapids	13,022,019	13,338,285
55	First Union National Bank of Georgia, Atlanta	12,877,840	12,116,072
56	Bank of Hawaii, Honolulu	12,458,847	11,827,445
57	Greenwood Trust Co., New Castle, Del.	12,402,034	10,133,809
58	Fleet Bank of New York, Albany	12,257,520	14,621,317
59	First Tennessee Bank, NA, Memphis	12,083,467	11,127,230
60	Citibank (Nevada), NA, Las Vegas	11,986,179	9,369,612
61	Regions Bank, Birmingham	11,922,628	10,280,106
62	Boatmen's National Bank, St. Louis	11,904,565	11,180,056
63	First Security Bank of Utah, NA, Salt Lake City	11,814,743	6,296,988
64	Signet Bank, Richmond	11,670,381	10,727,032
65	BayBank, NA, Boston	11,430,769	11,128,430
66	Manufacturers & Traders Trust Co., Buffalo, N.Y.	11,082,845	10,179,167
67	Bank One, Columbus, NA, Ohio	10,674,509	7,669,198
68	First Union National Bank of Virginia, Roanoke	10,658,980	11,032,717
69	American Express Centurion Bank, Wilmington, Del.	10,597,870	11,173,428
70	Central Fidelity National Bank, Richmond	10,495,512	10,754,999
71	Old Kent Bank, Grand Rapids, Mich.	10,457,094	9,748,228
72	AmSouth Bank of Alabama, Birmingham	10,352,212	9,826,423
73	National City Bank, Cleveland	10,130,561	10,316,756
74	Star Bank, NA, Cincinnati	9,931,600	8,388,681
75	First American National Bank, Nashville, Tenn.	9,732,299	9,009,335
76	Fifth Third Bank, Cincinnati	9,717,256	9,032,357
77	U.S. Bank of Washington, NA, Seattle	9,703,758	7,054,844
78	FCC National Bank, Wilmington, Del.	9,650,287	9,211,572
79	First USA Bank, Wilmington, Del.	9,643,232	7,056,635
80	European American Bank, New York	9,635,381	8,565,808
81	NBD Bank, NA, Indianapolis	9,574,827	10,182,138
82	Boatmen's National Bank, Kansas City, Mo.	9,138,723	4,160,069
83	Michigan National Bank, Farmington Hills	9,091,227	9,385,507
84	Bank of America, NA, Tempe, Ariz.	9,049,659	7,739,750
85	First National Bank of Maryland, Baltimore	8,946,198	8,460,700
86	Hilbernia National Bank, New Orleans	8,928,821	7,192,071
87	Bank of America Arizona, Phoenix	8,905,690	8,716,227
88	Bank One, Wisconsin, Milwaukee	8,798,605	. . . .
89	Wells Fargo Bank (Texas), NA, Houston	8,344,971	6,940,192
90	National City Bank, Louisville, Ky.	8,254,322	6,981,785
91	American National Bank & Trust Co., Chicago	8,208,949	6,617,204
92	Citibank (New York State), Pittsford	8,201,212	7,476,596
93	Key Bank of Washington, Tacoma	8,066,911	7,720,329
94	Norwest Bank Colorado, NA, Denver	7,856,335	6,647,211

RANK DEC. 1996		ASSETS DEC. 31, 1996	DEC. 31, 1995
95	First-Citizens Bank & Trust Co., Raleigh, N.C.	$7,849,661	$6,956,351
96	Sanwa Bank California, San Francisco	7,796,547	7,627,884
97	Household Bank (Nevada), NA, Las Vegas	7,771,506	3,973,629
98	Mercantile Bank, NA, St. Louis, Mo.	7,627,240	6,875,299
99	Wachovia Bank of South Carolina, NA, Columbia	7,326,969	7,127,580
100	Firstar Bank Milwaukee, NA	7,298,875	7,130,385

Source: American Banker

Top 100 World Banking Companies

Based on total assets at year end 1996, or latest fiscal year end, for bank holding companies and commercial and savings banks (dollar amounts in millions)

RANK DEC. 1996		TOTAL ASSETS DEC. 31, 1996	DEC. 31, 1995
1	Bank of Tokyo-Mitsubishi Ltd., Japan (a)	$648,161	$711,300
2	Deutsche Bank AG, Frankfurt, Germany	575,072	502,279
3	Credit Agricole Mutuel, Paris, France	479,963	384,340
4	Dai-Ichi Kangyo Bank Ltd., Tokyo, Japan	434,115	497,612
5	Fuji Bank Ltd., Tokyo, Japan	432,992	486,351
6	Sanwa Bank Ltd., Osaka, Japan	427,689	500,026
7	Sumitomo Bank Ltd., Osaka, Japan	426,103	498,917
8	Sakura Bank Ltd., Tokyo, Japan	423,017	477,079
9	HSBC Holdings, Plc., London, United Kingdom	404,979	351,568
10	Norinchukin Bank, Tokyo, Japan	375,210	428,644
11	Dresdner Bank, Frankfurt, Germany	358,829	332,148
12	Banque Nationale de Paris, France	357,322	323,526
13	Industrial Bank of Japan Ltd., Tokyo, Japan	350,468	360,638
14	ABN-AMRO Bank, N.V., Amsterdam, Netherlands	341,916	339,393
15	Societe Generale, Paris, France	341,867	324,776
16	Chase Manhattan Corp., New York, United States (b)	333,777	302,203
17	Union Bank of Switzerland, Zurich, Switzerland	326,190	335,303
18	NatWest Group, London, United Kingdom	317,295	257,838
19	Credit Lyonnais, Paris, France	311,747	337,595
20	Barclays Plc, London, United Kingdom	308,710	254,485
21	Westdeutsche Landesbank Girozentrale, Duesseldorf, Germany	298,455	290,648
22	Compagnie Financiere de Paribas, Paris, France	292,320	270,771
23	Commerzbank, Frankfurt, Germany	290,300	280,743
24	Mitsubishi Trust & Banking Corp., Tokyo, Japan	284,528	330,076
25	Citicorp, New York, United States	278,941	255,311
26	Tokai Bank Ltd., Nagoya, Japan	273,430	297,705
27	Swiss Bank Corp., Basel, Switzerland	268,519	249,906
28	Bayerische Vereinsbank, Munich, Germany	260,848	247,082
29	Mitsui Trust & Banking Co. Ltd., Tokyo, Japan	254,189	283,711
30	Lloyds TSB Group Inc., London, United Kingdom	252,292	204,213
31	Sumitomo Trust & Banking Co. Ltd., Osaka, Japan	248,418	299,209
32	BankAmerica Corp., San Francisco, United States	247,892	230,151
33	Long-Term Credit Bank of Japan Ltd., Tokyo, Japan	231,761	297,430
34	Asahi Bank Ltd., Tokyo, Japan	230,080	265,969
35	Bayerische Landesbank Girozentrale, Munich, Germany	223,496	211,192
36	J.P. Morgan & Co., Inc., New York, United States	221,814	184,642
37	Bayerische Hypotheken-und Wechsel Bank, Munich, Germany	220,100	207,458

RANK DEC. 1996		TOTAL ASSETS	
		DEC. 31, 1996	DEC. 31, 1995
38	Credit Suisse First Boston, Zurich, Switzerland	$218,870	$212,022
39	Bankgesellschaft Berlin, AG, Berlin, Germany	218,226	194,450
40	Daiwa Bank Ltd., Osaka, Japan	212,967	248,274
41	Abbey National, Plc, London, United Kingdom	212,307	151,302
42	Deutsche Genossenschaftsbank, Frankfurt, Germany	212,061	199,681
43	Yasuda Trust & Banking Co. Ltd., Tokyo, Japan	196,520	224,186
44	Toyo Trust & Banking Co. Ltd., Tokyo, Japan	192,802	189,723
45	NationsBank Corp., Charlotte, N.C., United States	184,886	186,380
46	Rabobank Nederland, Utrecht, Netherlands	180,960	182,273
47	ING Bank, Amsterdam, Netherlands	178,886	153,484
48	Halifax Building Society, Halifax, United Kingdom	175,111	151,302
49	Generale Bank, Brussels, Belgium	174,639	161,131
50	Istituto Bancario San Paolo dI Torino, Italy	172,540	160,389
51	Royal Bank of Canada, Montreal, Canada	157,264	131,595
52	Grupo Santander, Spain	149,881	135,013
53	Canadian Imperial Bank of Commerce, Toronto, Canada	142,160	126,829
54	Norddeutsche Landesbank Girozentrale, Hanover, Germany	140,493	139,425
55	First Union Corp., Charlotte, N.C., United States	139,363	131,400
56	Sudwestdeutsche Landesbank, Stuttgart, Germany	133,452	124,512
57	Banco Bilbao Vizcaya, Bilbao, Spain	132,492	115,910
58	Zenshinren Bank, Tokyo, Japan	130,630	142,527
59	Cassa di Risparmio delle Provincle Lombarde, Milan, Italy	126,808	117,261
60	Shoko Chukin Bank, Tokyo, Japan	125,442	148,752
61	National Australia Bank Ltd, Melbourne, Australia	123,734	98,467
62	Bank of Montreal, Canada	123,580	109,345
63	Bankers Trust New York Corp., United States	119,603	103,502
64	Credit Communal de Belgique, SA, Brussels, Belgium	117,793	119,105
65	Banca Commerciale Italiana, Milan, Italy	116,271	100,062
66	Groupe des Banques Populaires, Paris, France	116,080	111,600
67	Compagnie Financiere de CIC et de L'Union Europeenne, Paris, France	115,975	112,274
68	Credito Itallano, Milan, Italy	115,194	102,485
69	Kredietbank N.V., Brussels, Belgium	114,140	104,587
70	Nippon Credit Bank Ltd., Tokyo, Japan	114,104	146,577
71	Bank Bruxelles Lambert, Brussels, Belgium	113,532	109,650
72	Bank of Nova Scotia, Toronto, Canada	113,033	105,086
73	Deutsche Pfandbriefanstalt -und Hypothekenbank, Wiesbaden, Germany	111,390	104,933
74	Wells Fargo & Co., San Francisco, United States (c)	108,691	108,195
75	First Chicago NBD Bancorp Inc., United States	104,042	121,273
76	Landesbank Hessen Thuringen-Girozentrale, Frankfurt, Germany	103,693	100,075
77	Banc One Corp., Columbus, Ohio, United States	101,813	90,406
78	Chuo Trust & Banking Co. Ltd., Tokyo, Japan	101,271	119,168
79	Royal Bank of Scotland Plc, Edinburgh, United Kingdom	95,341	79,118
80	Toronto Dominion Bank, Canada	93,856	80,734
81	Monte del Paschi di Slena, Italy	93,841	85,712
82	Banca di Roma, Rome, Italy	91,824	133,584
83	Bank of Yokohama Ltd., Japan	91,509	110,190
84	Banca Nazionale del Lavoro, Rome, Italy	90,472	107,523
85	Australia & New Zealand Banking Group Ltd., Melbourne, Australia	89,850	75,455
86	Westpac Banking Corp., Sydney, Australia	87,260	71,105
87	Fleet Financial Group, Inc., Boston, United States	85,468	84,378
88	Bank of Scotland, Edinburgh, United Kingdom	85,095	66,149
89	Corporacion Bancaria de Espana SA (Argentaria), Madrid, Spain	84,742	108,989
90	ASLK-CGER Bank, Brussels, Belgium	82,634	87,436
91	Norwest Corp., Minneapolis, United States	80,136	72,090
92	Skandinaviska Enskilda Banken, Stockholm, Sweden	79,841	65,597
93	Commonwealth Bank of Australia, Sydney, Australia	78,293	70,613
94	Credit Commercial de France, Paris, France	76,504	69,805

RANK DEC. 1996		TOTAL ASSETS DEC. 31, 1996	DEC. 31, 1995
95	Danske Bank, Copenhagen, Denmark	$75,895	$70,198
96	Banco do Brasil, Brasilia, Brazil	75,564	82,091
97	PNC Bank Corp., Pittsburgh, United States	73,198	73,331
98	Hokkaldo Takushoku Bank, Ltd., Sapporo, Japan	72,964	92,880
99	Sparbankernas Sverige, AB, Stockholm, Sweden	72,855	69,869
100	Standard Chartered Bank, London, United Kingdom	72,140	60,348

(a)-1995 pro-forma data for the 4/1/96 merger of Bank of Tokyo and Mitsubishi Bank (b)-1995 pro-forma data for the 3/31/96 merger of Chemical Banking Corp. and Chase Manhattan Corp. (c)-1995 pro-forma data for the 4/1/96 merger of Wells Fargo & Co. and First Interstate Bancorp.

Source: American Banker

The Securities Industry

Securities Industry Profitability

Year	Total revenue (In millions)	Pre-tax profits (In millions)	Pre-tax profit margin (%)
1965	$2,320	$473	20.4%
1966	2,851	578	20.3
1967	3,992	1,022	25.6
1968	5,403	1,328	24.6
1969	4,534	565	12.5
1970	3,972	591	14.9
1971	5,510	1,331	24.2
1972	5,990	789	13.2
1973	4,811	-72	-1.5
1974	4,620	36	0.8
1975	5,867	804	13.7
1976	6,884	979	14.2
1977	6,730	416	6.2
1978	8,832	684	7.7
1979	11,233	1,100	9.8
1980	16,030	2,262	14.1
1981	19,796	2,144	10.8
1982	23,210	3,035	13.1
1983	29,566	3,824	12.9
1984	31,216	1,608	5.2
1985	38,621	4,140	10.7
1986	50,082	5,512	11.0
1987	50,837	1,133	2.2
1988	51,829	2,492	4.8
1989	59,537	1,842	3.1
1990	54,034	-162	-0.3
1991	60,718	5,849	9.6
1992	62,840	6,186	9.8
1993	73,182	8,600	11.8
1994	71,355	1,128	1.6
1995	96,303	7,405	7.7
1996	120,249	11,272	9.4

Source: Securities Industry Association

Largest Securities Firms

Ranking based on each firm's capital, which is the sum of ownership equity and subordinated liabilities unless otherwise noted.

Firm	1997 rank	January 1, 1997 capital rank (000)	1996 rank	January 1, 1996 capital rank (000)
Merrill Lynch & Co., Inc.*	1	$32,994,000	1	$23,481,000
Morgan Stanley Group Inc.*	2	21,901,000[1]	5	15,674,000[2]
Lehman Brothers Holdings Inc.*	3	19,796,000[3]	4	16,463,000[4]
Salomon Inc.*	4	18,992,000	3	17,748,000
Goldman Sachs Group, L.P.*	5	17,685,000	2	18,263,000[5]
Bear Stearns Companies Inc.*	6	9,467,710	6	7,114,084
Paine Webber Group Inc.*	7	4,894,774	8	4,175,085
Smith Barney Inc.	8	3,392,000	9	3,236,000
Donaldson, Lufkin & Jenrette, Inc.*	9	3,388,979	10	2,382,636
Credit Suisse First Boston	10	2,786,474	7	6,176,236
Dean Witter Reynolds Inc.	11	1,770,651	11	1,647,954
UBS Securities LLC	12	1,681,005	14	1,277,518
Chase Securities Inc.*	13	1,560,000	13	1,394,367
Prudential Securities Incorporated	14	1,506,947	12	1,581,521
A.G. Edwards, Inc.	15	1,211,866	15	1,048,913
J.P. Morgan Securities Inc.	16	1,151,637	16	1,014,859
Charles Schwab Corporation	17	1,138,371	20	706,357
Bank of Tokyo-Mitsubishi Trust Company	18	973,288	17	918,163
Nomura Securities International, Inc.	19	932,514	18	885,837
D.E. Shaw & Co.*	20	885,133	21	604,058
Deutsche Morgan Grenfell Inc.	21	865,281	22	595,069
SBC Warburg Inc.	22	819,699	19	880,969
Zurich Kemper Investments, Inc.	23	783,514	–	NA
Greenwich Capital Markets, Inc.	24	641,521	26	464,570
Daiwa Securities America Inc.	25	617,008	28	442,919
Alex. Brown & Sons Incorporated	26	603,945	27	444,160
Citicorp Securities, Inc.	27	584,408	23	586,827
Societe Generale Securities Corporation	28	555,933	39	282,494
Spear, Leeds & Kellogg	29	550,000	24	500,000
Legg Mason, Inc.*	30	505,577	32	352,286
Fidelity Brokerage	31	499,371	29	426,578
CIBC Wood Gundy Securities Corp.	32	488,920	–	NA
Nesbitt Burns Inc.	33	488,819	404	70,319
Edward Jones	34	465,083	33	351,597
ABN AMRO Chicago Corporation	35	444,880	93	81,809
ING Baring (U.S.) Securities, Inc.	36	439,955	25	467,000
Oppenheimer & Co., Inc.	37	398,801	31	361,199
Allen & Company Incorporated	38	362,023	40	280,727
Midland Walwyn Capital Inc.	39	347,313	43	270,022
Raymond James Financial Inc.	40	343,531	41	278,143
Paloma Securities LLC	41	342,240	34	323,921
Paribas Corporation	42	330,647	67	150,930
HSBC Securities, Inc.	43	327,634	80	113,761
TD Securities (USA) Inc.	44	311,870	–	NA
Interra Financial Incorporated	45	303,176	44	263,634
Dillon, Read & Co., Inc.	46	301,010	46	244,706
EVEREN Securities Inc.	47	295,294	45	261,287
Yamaichi International (America), Inc.	48	294,140	36	308,610
American Express Financial Advisors Inc.	49	272,698	54	190,878
John Nuveen Company	50	271,894	35	322,856

NOTE: Rankings do not reflect the securities firm mergers announced in 1997.
[1]Data as of 11/30/96   [2]Data as of 11/30/95   [3]Data as of 11/30/96   [4]Data as of 11/30/95   [5]Data as of 11/24/95
*Firm's capital is the sum of long-term borrowings and ownership equity.
Source: Securities Industry Association

World's Top 20 Advertising Organizations (In millions of U.S. dollars)

Rank 1996	Rank 1995	Ad organization	Headquarters	Worldwide gross income 1996	Worldwide gross income 1995	% change
1	1	WPP Group	London	$3,419.9	$3,125.5	9.4%
2	2	Omnicom Group	New York	3,035.5	2,708.5	12.1
3	3	Interpublic Group of Cos.	New York	2,751.2	2,465.8	11.5
4	4	Dentsu	Tokyo	1,929.9	1,999.1	-3.5
5	6	Young & Rubicam	New York	1,356.4	1,197.5	13.3
6	5	Cordiant	London	1,169.3	1,203.1	-2.8
7	9	Grey Advertising	New York	987.8	896.6	10.2
8	8	Havas Advertising	Levallois-Perret, France	974.3	924.4	5.4
9	7	Hakuhodo	Tokyo	897.7	958.6	-6.3
10	10	True North Communications	Chicago	889.5	805.9	10.4
11	11	Leo Burnett Co.	Chicago	866.3	805.9	7.5
12	12	MacManus Group	New York	754.2	713.9	5.6
13	13	Publicis	Paris	676.8	624.8	8.3
14	14	Bozell, Jacobs, Kenyon & Eckhardt	New York	473.1	404.5	17.0
15	15	GGT/BDDP Group	London	398.1	380.6	4.6
16	16	Daiko Advertising	Osaka, Japan	256.7	263.6	-2.6
17	17	Asatsu Inc.	Tokyo	242.0	254.2	-4.8
18	19	Carlson Marketing Group	Minneapolis	222.0	189.0	17.5
19	18	Tokyu Agency	Tokyo	214.0	231.1	-7.4
20	20	TMP Worldwide	New York	194.6	177.4	9.7

Source: Advertising Age, Crain Communications, Inc.

Largest Accounting Firms

National Accounting Firms

Rank by U.S. revenue	Firm	FY96 U.S. net revenue ($ million)	% change from FY 95	No. of partners	Rev./ partner ($000)	Global revenues FY 96 net revenue ($ million)	Global revenues % change from FY 95
1	Andersen Worldwide*	$4,511	16.9%	1,517	$2,974	$9,500	16.8%
2	Ernst & Young	3,571	20.1	1,933	1,847	7,760	13.0
3	Deloitte & Touche	2,925	13.8	1,556	1,880	6,500	9.5
4	KPMG Peat Marwick	2,310	10.4	1,515	1,525	7,450	8.0
5	Coopers & Lybrand**	2,115	11.1	1,241	1,704	6,800	9.7
6	Price Waterhouse**	2,016	13.9	963	2,093	5,020	12.6
7	Grant Thornton	266	10.8	285	933	1,285	7.1
8	McGladrey & Pullen	251	9.4	386	650	945	8.4
9	BDO Seidman	211	4.2	223	946	1,330	8.1
	National Firms	18,176	14.7	9,619	1,890	46,590	11.4

*Includes Arthur Andersen and Andersen Consulting
**Coopers & Lybrand and Price Waterhouse agreed to merge in September 1997.
Source: Public Accounting Report

Legion of Lawyers

The number of lawyers has nearly tripled in the last 25 years.

Numbers and Percentage of Lawyers by Types of Employment

Year	Total active lawyers
1970	326,842
1975	404,772
1980	574,810
1985	653,686
1990	755,694
1991	777,119
1992	799,760
1993	846,036
1994	862,954
1995	896,140
1996	946,449

Employment setting	1980	1991
Private practice	68.3%	72.9%
Federal judicial department	0.5	0.4
Other federal government	3.7	3.5
State/local judicial department	3.1	2.3
Other state/local government	5.6	4.7
Private industry	10.1	8.8
Private association	0.8	0.7
Legal aid or public defender	1.5	1.1
Education	1.2	1.0
Retired or inactive	5.3	4.6

Sources: American Bar Association and American Bar Foundation

Top Law Firms Ranked by Gross Revenue, 1996

Rank	Firm	Size (Lawyers/Equity partners)	Gross revenue
1	Skadden, Arps, Slate, Meagher & Flom	1,032/243	$ 710,000,000
2	Baker & McKenzie	1,886/506	646,000,000
3	Jones, Day, Reavis & Pogue	1,093/252	450,000,000
4	Latham & Watkins	660/236	363,000,000
5	Davis Polk & Wardwell	430/114	346,000,000
6	Sullivan & Cromwell	395/109	346,000,000
7	Mayer, Brown & Platt	643/254	325,000,000
8	Shearman & Sterling	560/123	324,000,000
9	Weil, Gotshal & Manges	585/160	322,000,000
10	Morgan, Lewis & Bockius	787/307	320,500,000
11	Cleary, Gottlieb, Steen & Hamilton	443/128	310,000,000
12	Sidley & Austin	648/188	303,000,000
13	Gibson, Dunn & Crutcher	560/215	294,000,000
14	White & Case	620/156	282,000,000
15	McDermott, Will & Emery	610/203	281,000,000
16	Simpson Thacher & Bartlett	411/109	279,500,000
17	O'Melveny & Myers	547/193	259,500,000
18	Fulbright & Jaworski	620/283	243,500,000
19	Cravath, Swaine & Moore	323/72	240,000,000
20	Vinson & Elkins	501/234	231,500,000
21	Kirkland & Ellis	463/105	229,000,000
22	Debevoise & Plimpton	355/86	220,500,000
23	Morrison & Foerster	498/155	220,000,000
24	Akin, Gump, Strauss, Hauer & Feld	593/203	218,000,000
25	Pillsbury Madison & Sutro	476/189	212,500,000

Top Law Firms Ranked by Profits Per Partner, 1996

Rank	Firm	Profits per partner	Size (Lawyers/Equity partners)	% change from 1995
1	Cravath, Swaine & Moore	$ 1,515,000	323/72	13.2%
2	Cahill Gordon & Reindel	1,400,000	185/56	12.0
3	Wachtell, Lipton, Rosen & Katz	1,390,000	126/64	-12.8
4	Sullivan & Cromwell	1,330,000	395/109	13.0
5	Simpson Thacher & Bartlett	1,155,000	411/109	4.4
6	Davis Polk & Wardwell	1,125,000	430/114	15.3
7	Debevoise & Plimpton	1,020,000	355/86	15.0
8	Skadden, Arps, Slate, Meagher & Flom	990,000	1,032/243	11.5
9	Cleary, Gottlieb, Steen & Hamilton	975,000	443/128	7.1
10	Willkie Farr & Gallagher	915,000	360/105	20.7
11	Kirkland & Ellis	845,000	463/105	23.0
12	Shearman & Sterling	815,000	560/123	25.0
13	Latham & Watkins	760,000	660/236	20.1
14	Paul, Weiss, Rifkind, Wharton & Garrison	745,000	335/90	10.3
15	Milbank, Tweed, Hadley & McCloy	735,000	315/84	23.8
15	Weil, Gotshal & Manges	735,000	585/160	4.7
17	Dewey Ballantine	650,000	380/111	22.8
18	Cadwalader, Wickersham & Taft	645,000	264/76	14.0
19	Fried, Frank, Harris, Shriver & Jacobson	615,000	361/117	24.1
19	McDermott, Will & Emery	615,000	610/203	9.2
21	Chadbourne & Parke	610,000	293/88	11.2
21	Schulte Roth & Zabel	610,000	201/49	5.5
23	King & Spalding	590,000	336/119	20.7
24	Gibson, Dunn & Crutcher	575,000	560/215	14.3
25	Shook, Hardy & Bacon	565,000	280/70	18.0
25	White & Case	565,000	620/156	-0.2

Source: The American Lawyer, American Lawyer Media, L.P.

Total Gross Revenue of Top 100 Law Firms

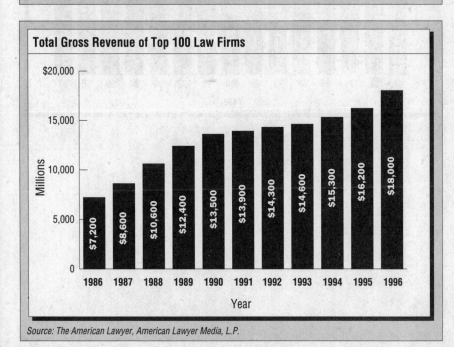

Year	Millions
1986	$7,200
1987	$8,600
1988	$10,600
1989	$12,400
1990	$13,500
1991	$13,900
1992	$14,300
1993	$14,600
1994	$15,300
1995	$16,200
1996	$18,000

Source: The American Lawyer, American Lawyer Media, L.P.

Corporate Name Changes

The number of corporate name changes by publicly traded companies hit a record in the first half of 1997, driven by the flurry of mergers and acquisitions.

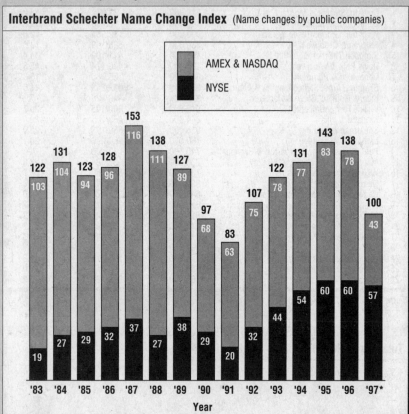

Interbrand Schechter Name Change Index (Name changes by public companies)

AMEX & NASDAQ
NYSE

Year	AMEX & NASDAQ	NYSE	Total
'83	103	19	122
'84	104	27	131
'85	94	29	123
'86	96	32	128
'87	116	37	153
'88	111	27	138
'89	89	38	127
'90	68	29	97
'91	63	20	83
'92	75	32	107
'93	78	44	122
'94	77	54	131
'95	83	60	143
'96	78	60	138
'97*	43	57	100

*First 6 months.
Source: Interbrand Schechter

Corporate Earnings

Year-to-year percentage change in net income for companies in the DJ Global-U.S. Index

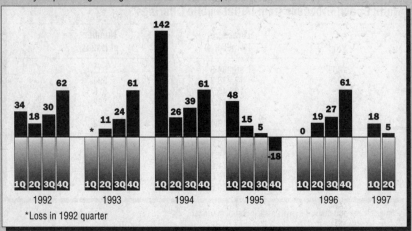

*Loss in 1992 quarter

Stock Buyback Boom

Announced corporate stock repurchases

Announcement date	Value ($ millions)	Number of deals
1983	$ 6,764.9	141
1984	27,346.1	435
1985	20,275.1	195
1986	28,167.1	240
1987	54,993.8	884
1988	37,355.7	327
1989	63,671.7	634
1990	36,087.7	1,009
1991	20,416.2	438
1992	35,623.1	600
1993	38,341.7	606
1994	73,808.8	1,013
1995	99,579.3	1,114
1996	176,577.7	1,474

Source: Securities Data Co.

IPO Volume

Number and Proceeds from Initial Public Offerings*

Year	Proceeds ($ millions)	Number of issues
1985	$6,284.8	332
1986	17,738.8	694
1987	16,745.7	518
1988	6,111.7	222
1989	6,082.0	209
1990	4,519.0	172
1991	16,283.2	366
1992	23,379.8	512
1993	34,461.1	667
1994	22,771.9	571
1995	29,270.8	575
1996	48,789.8	865

*Excludes closed-end funds and real estate investment trusts.
Source: Securities Data Co.

Ranking of IPO Managers, 1996

Rank	Managers	Proceeds ($ millions)	Market share	No. of issues
1	Goldman, Sachs & Co.	$9,793.6	20.1	50
2	Morgan Stanley	6,950.6	14.2	42
3	Merrill Lynch & Co.	3,623.6	7.4	38
4	Smith Barney Inc.	2,857.6	5.9	33
5	Donaldson, Lufkin & Jenrette	2,497.3	5.1	29
6	Alex. Brown & Sons	2,472.2	5.1	51
7	Credit Suisse First Boston	1,906.1	3.9	14
8	Salomon Brothers	1,643.7	3.4	19
9	Lehman Brothers	1,552.6	3.2	26
10	Montgomery Securities	1,302.6	2.7	34
11	Robertson Stephens	1,203.5	2.5	28
12	JP Morgan & Co. Inc.	1,003.2	2.1	13
13	Hambrecht & Quist	964.3	2.0	30
14	Bear, Stearns	846.0	1.7	14
15	Cowen	608.2	1.2	17
16	William Blair	559.9	1.1	11
17	Dillon, Read	510.4	1.0	14
18	NatWest Markets	499.2	1.0	10
19	PaineWebber	438.3	0.9	10
20	Oppenheimer	398.6	0.8	14
21	Prudential Securities	377.1	0.8	7
22	Friedman, Billings, Ramsey & Co.	326.9	0.7	13
23	Furman Selz LLC	317.7	0.7	7
24	UBS	314.6	0.6	9
25	Nesbitt Burns Securities	262.2	0.5	1
—	Top 25 totals	43,229.9	88.6	534
—	Industry totals	48,789.8	100.0	865

Source: Securities Data Co.

Largest U.S. Initial Public Offerings*

Issuer	Offer date	Amount ($ millions)	Offer price (Dollars)
British Petroleum	10/30/87	$2,864.100	$67.950
Lucent Technologies	04/03/96	2,647.000	27.000
Allstate	06/02/93	1,849.500	27.000
Associates First Capital	05/07/96	1,651.550	29.000
Deutsche Telekom	11/17/96	1,605.700	18.890
Consolidated Rail	03/26/87	1,456.000	28.000
YPF Sociedad Anonima	06/28/93	1,235.000	19.000
TeleDanmark	04/27/94	1,219.600	23.526
Henley Group	05/20/86	1,190.000	21.250
Wellcome	07/27/92	1,067.500	15.250
Coca-Cola Enterprises	11/21/86	1,001.385	16.500
PacTel	12/02/93	966.000	23.000
Lyondell Petrochemical	01/18/89	960.000	30.000
Nabisco Holdings	01/19/95	882.000	24.500
Fireman's Fund	10/23/85	824.000	25.750
TIG Holdings	04/20/93	800.472	22.625
Santa Fe International	06/09/97	798.000	28.500
First Data	04/09/92	770.000	22.000
Rockefeller Center Properties	09/12/85	750.000	20.000
New Holland	10/31/96	749.800	21.500

*Excludes closed-end funds.
Source: Securities Data Co.

Largest U.S. Initial Public Offerings of 1997*

Issuer	Offer date	Amount ($ millions)	Offer price (Dollars)
Santa Fe International	06/09/97	$798.0	$28.500
Unibanco Uniao de Bancos Brasilieros SA	05/21/97	695.9	33.750
Security Capital Group	09/18/97	632.0	28.000
Boston Properties	06/17/97	628.0	25.000
Polo Ralph Lauren	06/11/97	611.0	26.000
Galileo International	07/24/97	548.8	24.500
Hartford Life	05/21/97	519.8	28.250
Ispat International	08/07/97	438.8	27.000
Hertz	04/24/97	438.5	24.000
Equity Office Properties Trust	07/07/97	420.0	21.000
CCA Prison Realty Trust	07/15/97	388.5	21.000
Nationwide Financial Services	03/05/97	386.2	23.500
TV Azteca	08/15/97	367.9	18.250
Circuit City Stores-CarMax Group	02/04/97	361.8	20.000
EDP-Electricidade de Portugal	06/16/97	303.6	25.840
Internationale Nederlanden Groep NV	06/12/97	302.1	46.483
Cia Paranaense de Energia	07/29/97	292.8	18.000
J.D. Edwards	09/23/97	290.7	23.000
Kilroy Realty	01/28/97	287.5	23.000
General Cable	05/15/97	283.9	21.000

*Excludes closed-end funds.
Source: Securities Data Co.

American Enterprise

Post-War New Business Incorporations

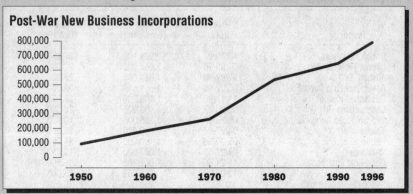

Annual U.S. Business Starts

Year	Starts	% change	Employment	% change
1985	249,770	—	1,657;383	—
1986	253,092	1.3%	1,650,537	-0.4%
1987	233,710	-7.7	1,552,708	-5.9
1988	199,091	-14.8	1,333,426	-14.1
1989	181,645	-8.8	1,212,464	-9.1
1990	158,930	-12.5	827,012	-31.8
1991	155,672	-2.0	731,621	-11.5
1992	164,086	5.4	800,827	9.5
1993	166,154	1.3	780,804	-2.5
1994	188,387	13.4	758,134	-2.9
1995	168,158	-10.7	738,606	-2.6
1996	170,475	1.4	846,973	14.7

Note: Dun & Bradstreet provides two different types of data measuring entrepreneurial activity in the U.S. Incorporations may include "idea" enterprises not yet actively doing business, businesses that have recently begun operation, and existing companies filing for various reasons. Business starts reflect companies that have recently been introduced into Dun & Bradstreet's commercial credit information database.

Annual New Business Incorporations

Year	Number
1946	132,916
1950	93,092
1955	139,915
1960	182,713
1965	203,897
1970	264,209
1975	326,345
1980	533,520
1985	664,235
1986	702,738
1987	685,572
1988	685,095
1989	676,565
1990	647,366
1991	628,604
1992	666,800
1993	706,537
1994	741,657
1995	768,180 *
1996	789,126 *

Source: Dun & Bradstreet

*Estimate.

New Business Incorporations by State and Geographic Regions

	1996	1995	% change 12 months 96 v. 95		1996	1995	% change 12 months 96 v. 95
New England	27,646*	28,582	-3.3%	North Carolina	17,861	16,021	11.5%
Maine	2,873	2,805	2.4	South Carolina	8,049*	7,601	5.9
New Hampshire	3,070	3,095	-0.8	Georgia	26,902	26,990	-0.3
Vermont	1,575	1,630	-3.4	Florida	104,113	98,066	6.2
Massachusetts	12,808*	13,479	-5.0				
Connecticut	4,701	4,830	-2.7	**East South Central**	28,819	28,324*	1.7
Rhode Island	2,619	2,743	-4.5	Kentucky	8,060	7,764*	3.8
				Tennessee	7,785	8,194	-5.0
Middle Atlantic	127,299	128,869	-1.2	Alabama	7,686	7,686	0.0
New York	73,866	72,433	2.0	Mississippi	5,288	4,680	13.0
New Jersey	33,974	37,861	-10.3				
Pennsylvania	19,459	18,575	4.8	**West South Central**	64,684	63,298	2.2
				Arkansas	6,010	6,298	-4.6
East North Central	109,550	107,877	1.6	Louisiana	11,531	11,082	4.1
Ohio	20,517	20,859	-1.6	Oklahoma	8,105	7,796	4.0
Indiana	12,282	12,451	-1.4	Texas	39,038	38,122	2.4
Illinois	36,210	34,495	5.0				
Michigan	31,994	31,254	2.4	**Mountain**	68,457*	61,150	11.9
Wisconsin	8,547	8,818	-3.1	Montana	2,325*	1,767	31.6
				Idaho	2,504	2,622	-4.5
West North Central	37,909	39,128	-3.1	Wyoming	2,167	2,159	0.4
Minnesota	12,639	12,203	3.6	Colorado	16,749	15,309	9.4
Iowa	4,589	5,925	-22.5	New Mexico	3,042	3,584	-15.1
Missouri	10,545	10,743	-1.8	Arizona	12,153	10,866	11.8
North Dakota	925	1,021	-9.4	Nevada	23,222	18,926*	22.7
South Dakota	1,382	1,401	-1.4	Utah	6,295	5,917*	6.42
Nebraska	3,453	3,360	2.8				
Kansas	4,376	4,475	-2.	**Pacific**	71,159*	70,203*	1.4
				Alaska	1,103	1,428*	-22.8
South Atlantic	253,603*	240,749*	5.3	Washington	12,954	13,340	-2.9
Maryland	18,632	18,014	3.4	Oregon	9,267	9,730	-4.8
Delaware	55,122*	50,094	10.0	California	44,043	41,913	5.1
Washington, DC	1,497*	2,256*	-33.6	Hawaii	3,792*	3,792*	0.0
Virginia	19,047	19,172	-0.7				
West Virginia	2,38*	2,535*	-6.1	**Total U.S.**	789,126*	768,180*	2.7

*Includes some or all estimated monthly figures.
Source: Dun & Bradstreet

Business Starts by Industry

	Business starts 1995	Business starts 1996	Change	Employment 1995	Employment 1996	Change
Agriculture, forestry, fishing	2,199	2,295	4.4%	6,146	7,794	26.8%
Mining	564	589	4.4	3,184	4,697	47.5
Construction	16,980	18,624	9.7	53,118	64,478	21.4
Manufacturing	12,172	12,908	6.0	104,660	108,644	3.8
Transportation/ utilities	7,161	7,993	11.6	43,583	50,072	14.9
Wholesale	14,956	16,019	7.1	59,933	69,001	15.1
Retail	36,381	38,407	5.6	176,159	200,354	13.7
Finance/ insurance/ real estate	10,362	11,222	8.3	54,610	61,185	12.0
Services	44,586	50,077	12.3	233,482	278,292	19.2
Nonclassifiable	22,797	12,341	-45.9	3,731	2,456	-34.2
Total	168,158	170,475	1.4	738,606	846,973	14.7

NOTE: This compilation covers all businesses with a 1994, 1995 or 1996 starting date added to the Dun & Bradstreet business data file in December 1996. It includes newly opened establishments. It does not include changes in ownership of previously operating businesses or changes in name, location, legal type or mergers.
Source: Dun & Bradstreet Corp.

Business Starts by State

	Business starts 1995	Business starts 1996	Change	Employment 1995	Employment 1996	Change
New England	9,250	8,960	-3.1%	39,033	45,936	17.7%
Maine	771	712	-7.7	3,161	3,131	-0.9
New Hampshire	908	852	-6.2	3,504	4,079	16.4
Vermont	329	278	-15.5	1,285	1,586	23.4
Massachusetts	4,419	4,351	-1.5	19,083	22,480	17.8
Connecticut	2,273	2,207	-2.9	9,308	12,219	31.3
Rhode Island	550	560	1.8	2,692	2,441	-9.3
Middle Atlantic	30,011	30,137	0.4	109,999	130,404	18.6
New York	15,716	15,174	-3.4	51,805	67,314	29.9
New Jersey	7,462	7,911	6.0	26,592	32,403	21.9
Pennsylvania	6,833	7,052	3.2	31,602	30,687	-2.9
East North Central	23,465	23,280	-0.8	105,083	111,205	5.8
Ohio	5,434	5,468	0.6	25,456	28,875	13.4
Indiana	2,719	2,955	8.7	12,534	13,778	9.9
Illinois	7,245	6,860	-5.3	32,269	32,226	-0.1
Michigan	5,418	5,489	1.3	22,357	23,416	4.7
Wisconsin	2,649	2,508	-5.3	12,467	12,910	3.6

Business Starts by State

	Business starts 1995	Business starts 1996	Change	Employment 1995	Employment 1996	Change
West North Central	8,731	8,390	-3.9%	44,408	46,775	5.3%
Minnesota	2,258	2,286	1.2	10,996	12,632	14.9
Iowa	1,223	1,087	-11.1	6,386	6,795	6.4
Missouri	2,851	2,502	-12.2	14,437	13,102	-9.2
North Dakota	209	233	11.5	1,159	1,448	24.9
South Dakota	252	307	21.8	1,711	1,955	14.3
Nebraska	634	725	14.4	2,947	3,848	30.6
Kansas	1,304	1,250	-4.1	6,772	6,995	3.3
South Atlantic	32,195	32,142	-0.2	146,967	160,654	9.3
Maryland	3,119	3,310	6.1	12,225	15,668	28.2
Delaware	505	534	5.7	2,363	2,675	13.2
District of Columbia	701	595	-15.1	3,701	2,757	-25.5
Virginia	3,542	3,591	1.4	17,570	18,557	5.6
West Virginia	584	569	-2.6	2,010	2,682	33.4
North Carolina	3,975	4,007	0.8	16,806	19,504	16.1
South Carolina	1,954	1,903	-2.6	10,548	10,175	-3.5
Georgia	5,471	5,334	-2.5	25,983	28,627	10.2
Florida	12,344	12,299	-0.4	55,761	60,009	7.6
East South Central	7,643	7,994	4.6	41,534	43,063	3.7
Kentucky	1,534	1,725	12.5	8,552	9,446	10.5
Tennessee	2,894	3,055	5.6	15,708	16,772	6.8
Alabama	2,191	2,138	-2.4	11,616	11,140	-4.1
Mississippi	1,024	1,076	5.1	5,658	5,705	0.8
West South Central	16,435	17,240	4.9	83,966	97,423	16.0
Arkansas	1,155	1,258	8.9	5,401	5,801	7.4
Oklahoma	1,490	1,543	3.6	8,322	8,999	8.1
Louisiana	1,975	2,110	6.8	11,299	11,890	5.2
Texas	11,815	12,329	4.4	58,944	70,733	20.0
Mountain	11,115	12,262	10.3	45,911	60,575	31.9
Montana	485	397	-18.1	1,395	1,510	8.2
Idaho	642	789	22.9	3,026	3,372	11.4
Wyoming	276	281	1.8	907	1,087	19.8
Colorado	3,086	3,424	11.0	12,723	16,892	32.8
New Mexico	1,005	952	-5.3	4,099	4,308	5.1
Arizona	3,061	3,362	9.8	11,940	17,460	46.2
Utah	1,120	1,523	36.0	5,494	7,940	44.5
Nevada	1,440	1,534	6.5	6,327	8,006	26.5
Pacific	29,313	30,070	2.6	121,705	150,938	24.0
Alaska	291	235	-19.2	944	1,303	38.0
Hawaii	645	618	-4.2	2,715	3,470	27.8
Washington	2,926	3,165	8.2	13,108	16,170	23.4
Oregon	1,897	2,065	8.9	8,096	10,097	24.7
California	23,554	23,987	1.8	96,842	119,898	23.8
Total	168,158	170,475	1.4	738,606	846,973	14.7

Note: This compilation covers all businesses with a 1994, 1995 or 1996 starting date added to the Dun & Bradstreet business data file in 1996. It includes newly opened establishments. It does not include changes in ownership of previously operating businesses or changes in name, location, legal type or mergers.
Source: Dun & Bradstreet

Out of Business

Number of Business Failures in the U.S.

Year	Failures
1984	52,078
1985	57,253
1986	61,616
1987	61,111
1988	57,097
1989	50,361
1990	60,747
1991	88,140
1992	97,069
1993	86,133
1994	71,558
1995	71,128
1996*	71,811

*Preliminary.
Source: Dun & Bradstreet

Business Failures by State and Region

	1995 firms	1995 liabilities	1996 firms	1996 liabilities	Firms % change	Liabilities % change
New England	3,395	$2,802,094,173	3,055	$1,532,148,997	-10.0 %	-45.3%
Maine	317	55,444,181	299	45,575,719	-5.7	-17.8
New Hampshire	389	72,879,620	374	74,732,719	-3.9	2.5
Vermont	148	35,103,787	107	207,644,578	-27.7	491.5
Massachusetts	1,927	1,341,563,196	1,607	323,098,417	-16.6	-75.9
Connecticut	485	1,263,546,065	534	827,542,626	10.1	-34.5
Rhode Island	129	33,557,324	134	53,554,938	3.9	59.6
Middle Atlantic	10,595	9,104,321,635	10,297	9,328,198,559	-2.8	2.5
New York	5,060	8,187,277,600	4,931	6,048,122,288	-2.5	-26.1
New Jersey	2,779	262,739,854	2,451	1,865,945,029	-11.8	610.2
Pennsylvania	2,756	654,304,181	2,915	1,414,131,242	5.8	116.1
East North Central	7,456	3,741,231,550	8,167	3,858,578,489	9.5	3.1
Ohio	2,141	708,571,716	2,274	978,387,383	6.2	38.1
Indiana	798	685,587,922	843	1,198,363,518	5.6	74.8
Illinois	1,696	1,057,393,264	2,557	840,721,865	50.8	-20.5
Michigan	1,681	1,099,877,006	1,558	546,258,119	-7.3	-50.3
Wisconsin	1,140	189,801,642	935	294,847,604	-18.0	55.3
West North Central	4,135	$591,074,621	3,817	$770,592,459	-7.7 %	30.4 %
Minnesota	903	186,420,961	593	189,445,287	-34.3	1.6
Iowa	573	51,641,831	453	77,983,272	-20.9	51.0
Missouri	1,109	143,112,423	1,054	159,663,553	-5.0	11.6
North Dakota	98	10,359,385	80	7,187,793	-18.4	-30.6
South Dakota	182	17,643,579	158	14,025,138	-13.2	-20.5
Nebraska	323	17,108,864	390	53,545,331	20.7	213.0
Kansas	947	164,787,578	1,089	268,742,085	15.0	63.1
South Atlantic	9,841	8,240,813,793	8,529	4,744,723,803	-13.3	-42.4
Maryland	1,804	498,817,259	1,620	440,053,821	-10.2	-11.8
Delaware	45	10,510,457	49	140,569,984	8.9	1,237.4
District of Columbia	155	6,020,116,448	123	59,679,799	-20.6	-99.0
Virginia	1,713	609,599,950	1,064	219,798,114	-37.9	-63.9
West Virginia	287	37,459,764	294	51,879,528	2.4	38.5
North Carolina	962	131,611,058	1,041	1,232,442,108	8.2	836.4
South Carolina	490	7,633,836	375	28,535,834	-23.5	273.8
Georgia	1,481	334,724,305	1,308	632,095,098	-11.7	88.8
Florida	2,904	590,340,716	2,655	1,939,669,517	-8.6	228.6

	1995 firms	1995 liabilities	1996 firms	1996 liabilities	Firms % change	Liabilities % change
East South Central	2,429	266,384,410	2,689	276,963,661	10.7%	4.0%
Kentucky	659	149,425,897	638	45,880,515	-3.2	-69.3
Tennessee	991	38,308,826	1,329	60,270,426	34.1	57.3
Alabama	547	40,919,581	538	141,808,946	-1.6	246.6
Mississippi	232	37,730,106	184	29,003,774	-20.7	-23.1
West South Central	8,656	2,179,131,114	8,919	4,411,309,147	3.0	102.4
Arkansas	737	131,617,903	1,003	314,725,032	36.1	139.1
Oklahoma	1,311	161,135,467	1,559	449,818,539	18.9	179.2
Louisiana	456	162,978,849	271	51,858,804	-40.6	-68.2
Texas	6,152	1,723,398,895	6,086	3,594,906,772	-1.1	108.6
Mountain	4,741	1,290,944,203	5,368	2,078,456,635	13.2	61.0
Montana	152	19,254,936	179	15,578,331	17.8	-19.1
Idaho	388	358,645	535	741,648	37.9	106.8
Wyoming	108	127,707	119	154,114	10.2	20.7
Colorado	1,481	367,609,589	2,243	1,882,941,819	51.5	412.2
New Mexico	405	31,487,050	428	48,363,710	5.7	53.6
Arizona	1,410	784,688,462	1,012	48,788,362	-28.2	-93.8
Utah	344	15,367,438	378	22,684,851	9.9	47.6
Nevada	453	72,050,376	474	59,203,800	4.6	-17.8
Pacific	19,880	9,067,555,128	20,970	7,020,147,406	5.5	-22.6
Alaska	124	2,012,025	182	2,406,749	46.8	19.6
Hawaii	270	102,681,697	396	101,376,627	46.7	-1.3
Washington	2,384	652,115,069	2,687	976,381,701	12.7	49.7
Oregon	795	779,506,158	834	119,026,172	4.9	-84.7
California	16,307	7,531,240,179	16,871	5,820,956,157	3.5	-22.7
Total U.S.	71,128	37,283,550,627	71,811	34,021,119,156	1.0	-8.8

Source: Dun & Bradstreet

Business Failures by Industry

Industry	1995 failures	1996 failures	% change	1995 liabilities	1996 liabilities	% change
Agriculture/forestry fishing	2,233	2,714	21.5%	$ 443,288,990	$ 424,415,368	-4.3%
Mining	197	191	-3.0	148,385,363	458,914,300	209.3
Construction	9,170	9,732	6.1	1,827,342,357	1,297,581,260	-29.0
Manufacturing	4,385	4,079	-7.0	2,848,916,489	7,781,908,090	173.2
Transportation/utilities	2,736	3,356	22.7	1,632,571,215	1,695,047,009	3.8
Wholesale	4,154	3,936	-5.2	1,558,284,616	3,074,945,543	97.3
Retail	12,945	13,426	3.7	5,187,692,392	5,176,445,557	-0.2
Finance/insurance/ real estate	4,302	4,126	-4.1	10,592,969,854	8,207,531,241	-22.5
Services	21,831	22,097	4.9	11,642,251,632	4,830,929,479	-58.5
Nonclassifiable	9,175	7,344	-20.0	1,401,847,719	1,073,401,309	-23.4
Total	71,128	71,811	1.0	37,283,550,627	34,021,119,156	-8.8

Source: Dun & Bradstreet

WOMEN IN BUSINESSES OF THEIR OWN

WHEN CAROL WALL QUIT HER JOB at Xerox Corp. to start her own business, she wasn't motivated by the typical entrepreneurial lures of money or power. Instead, the New Yorker says she started Classic Printers Ltd. in 1983 because she wanted to have another baby.

Ms. Wall, now 49, figured owning her own business would give her a relatively flexible child-rearing schedule. She also realized that she would be limiting her career if she took time off to have a baby. "If I got pregnant while working in corporate America, I wouldn't even have had the chance to reach the glass ceiling," says the mother of four. "I wanted to be in charge of my own destiny."

Ms. Wall has plenty of company these days. Women own some 6.4 million businesses—one-third of all U.S. companies, according to the Census Bureau's most recent survey of businesses, taken in 1992.

Furthermore, women-owned businesses are among the fastest-growing segments of the American entrepreneurial economy: Women own 5.9 million sole proprietorships, partnerships and so-called subchapter S companies, according to the 1992 report, up 43% from 4.1 million such concerns in 1987. (Subchapter S companies, which typically are small businesses, enjoy many of the same tax benefits that partnerships do.) Meanwhile, the total number of U.S. small businesses grew just 26% to 17.3 million in 1992, from 13.7 million in 1987, the Census Bureau says.

More than half the women-owned companies—3.8 million—are service businesses, the Census Bureau says. Another 1.1 million, or 18% are retail concerns.

Some women-owned businesses were created to benefit from affirmative-action programs that steer jobs toward such enterprises. And a handful of the nation's largest women-owned concerns, including TLC Beatrice International Holdings Inc., and Raley's, a supermarket chain, were passed on to women by their fathers or spouses. But increasingly, women-owned companies are being formed by corporate refugees who share Carol Wall's desire for more independence and flexibility.

"They're starting businesses because it gives them a feeling of control over their own lives," says Sharon Hadary, executive director of the National Foundation of Women Business Owners, a research group in Silver Spring, Md. "They're saying, 'Boy, I could do my job much better if I went out on my own.'" Many women executives also are leaving companies with "masculine" corporate cultures to form businesses that reflect their values and priorities, she adds. Indeed, it is not unusual to find even small women-owned firms with limited resources offering on-site day care, flexible work schedules and extended maternity leave for employees.

Experts such as Ms. Hadary foresee no slowdown in the trend. In fact, as entrepreneurship grows increasingly popular, future generations of women may bypass corporate careers altogether in favor of business ownership. Still others will take corporate jobs for a few years to learn a business or industry, then use that knowledge to start their own companies. "It is a real tragedy for the big corporations," Ms. Hadary says. "They're losing their best and their brightest women to entrepreneurship."

Despite their growing ranks, however, women-owned businesses accounted for only 11.2% of the revenue produced by all U.S. businesses in 1992. Annual revenues averaged a mere $25,000, a factor that lending experts say largely explains why so many female entrepreneurs have difficulty borrowing money.

To be sure, the growing number of women entrepreneurs has prompted some banks to develop loan programs especially for women. And the U.S. Small Business Administration boasts that in the fiscal year, ended Sept. 30, 1996, 23% of all borrowers in its most popular loan program were women.

But many women entrepreneurs still find money hard to come by, and some attribute their struggle to male control of most business capital. Mary Ann Heathman, who started Lionheart Publishing Inc. in 1994, has had little success attracting outside investors, even though the company is trying to carve out a niche in the romance-novel business—a segment of the publishing world that racks up annual sales of $1 billion. Ms. Heathman attributes their lack of interest to the clearly feminine nature of the business. "They just don't get it," she says.

Other examples of sexism abound: One successful entrepreneur says she brought her

Women Entrepreneurs

Women owned more than 6.4 million businesses in 1992, generating $1.6 trillion in revenues, according to a Census Bureau survey. Here are the metropolitan areas with the most women-owned firms:

Metropolitan area	Number of firms in 1992
Los Angeles-Long Beach	232,723
New York	187,525
Chicago	163,883
Washington, DC	122,007
Philadelphia	95,441
Houston	87,303
Boston	86,133
Atlanta	82,821
Dallas	80,830
Detroit	80,673

Source: U.S. Census Bureau

husband, who knows nothing about her company, to meet her banker; the lender addressed her husband the whole time. Other women say customers and suppliers often assume the business belongs to their fathers or husbands.

Even so, entrepreneurs such as Carol Wall wouldn't have it any other way. Thanks to the flexible hours she set for herself as an entrepreneur, Ms. Wall was able to devote plenty of time to her daughter, who was born shortly after the business was formed. Could the business have grown faster if Ms. Wall worked 60 hours a week? Of course. But, says Ms. Wall, "My husband and kids come first."

Stephanie N. Mehta

Top 20 Women-Owned Businesses

Rank	Name, title	Company, location	Sales ($ million)	Employees	Percent owner-ship
1	Martha Ingram, Chair	Ingram Industries, Nashville	$11,500	13,772	over 50*
2	Loida Nicolas Lewis, Chair, CEO	TLC Beatrice International, New York	2,230	4,700	51
3	Marian Ilitch, Co-founder, Secretary, Treasurer	Little Caesar Enterprises, Detroit	1,800*	8,100	50
4	Maggie Hardy Magerko, President	84 Lumber, Eighty-Four, PA	1,500	4,500	80
5	Lynda Resnick, Co-owner	Roll International, Los Angeles	1,450	7,500	50
6	Antonia Axson Johnson, Chair	Axel Johnson Group (U.S. division), Stockholm	1,300	2,000	100
7	Linda Wachner, Chair, President, CEO	Warnaco Group, New York	1,060	16,400	14.6**
8	Gretchen Minyard Williams, Co-chair	Minyard Food Stores, Coppell, TX	923	7,700	33.3
8	Liz Minyard, Co-chair	Minyard Food Stores, Coppell, TX	923	7,700	33.3
9	Gay Love, Chair	Printpack, Atlanta	805	4,000	over 20
10	Donna Karan, Founder, Chair, Chief Designer	Donna Karan International, New York	613	1,580	24.4**†
11	Ardath Rodale, Chair, CEO	Rodale Press, Emmaus, PA	500	1,400	100
12	Christine Liang, Founder, President, COO	ASI, Fremont, CA	468	400	51
13	Donna Wolf Steigerwaldt, Chair, CEO	Jockey International, Kenosha, WI	450*	5,000	100
14	Helen Copley, Chair, CEO	The Copley Press, La Jolla, CA	421	3,536	100
15	Jenny Craig, Co-founder, Vice Chair	Jenny Craig, La Jolla, CA	401	4,300	67**†
16	Irma Elder, President	Troy Motors, Troy, MI	381	250	100
17	Patricia Gallup, Co-founder, Chair, CEO	PC Connection, Milford, NH	350*	800	50
18	Barbara Levy Kipper, Chair	Chas. Levy Company, Chicago	350	3,000	100
19	Jane O'Dell, Co-owner	Westfall-O'Dell Transportation Services, Kansas City, MO	350	650	50
20	Ellen Gordon, President, COO	Tootsie Roll Industries, Chicago	341	1,750	48**†

*Estimate.
**Public company.
†Owned with husband.
Source: Working Woman magazine, MacDonald Communications Group

MINORITY ENTREPRENEURS

CLARENCE WOOTEN, JR., always knew he wanted to be an entrepreneur. The 26-year-old founder of Metamorphosis Studios Inc., an Internet and CD-ROM development company in Columbia, Md., says he briefly worked for an architecture firm, but didn't like punching a clock or answering to someone else. "I come from an entrepreneurial family; everyone started their own businesses," he says. "I knew that was what I wanted to do."

Mr. Wooten is indeed part of a long tradition of entrepreneurship in the black community in the United States. For decades, black Americans—along with Hispanics, Asians and Native Americans—turned to self-employment because mainstream corporations held few opportunities for minorities.

Today, such opportunities have improved, yet minorities still are starting businesses in droves. Small businesses owned by minorities soared to nearly 2.1 million in 1992, according to the Census Bureau's most recent survey of businesses. That's up 60% from 1.3 million such concerns in 1987. The report counts sole proprietorships, partnerships and Subchapter S corporations, which are typically small companies that enjoy some of the same tax benefits that partnerships do.

In contrast, the total number of U.S. small businesses grew 26% to 17.3 million in 1992, from 13.7 million in 1987, the Census Bureau says.

Why the surge in minority business ownership? Glass ceilings still exist at big institutions. As a result, a growing number of minorities are voluntarily leaving corporate jobs with limited upward mobility in favor of entrepreneurship.

To some degree, minorities also are simply participating in the wave of entrepreneurship that is sweeping the country, says José F. Niño, president and chief executive of the U.S. Hispanic Chamber of Commerce in Washington. Mr. Wooten, for example, is part of the broader wave of young entrepreneurs exploiting technology, especially the Internet, to form new businesses.

Others are taking advantage of the increasingly global economy. For example, some of the biggest beneficiaries of the North American Free Trade Agreement are Hispanic-owned businesses in the U.S. that

Boom in Black-Owned Businesses

Number of Black-Owned Firms in the U.S.

46% Increase

1987 — 424,165
1992 — 620,912

0   200   400   600   800
Scale in thousands

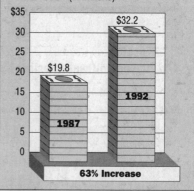

Revenues of Black-Owned Firms in the U.S. (In billions)

1987: $19.8
1992: $32.2

63% Increase

Metropolitan Areas with the Most Black-Owned Firms

Metropolitan area	Number of firms in 1992
New York	39,404
Washington, DC	37,988
Los Angeles-Long Beach	32,645
Chicago	24,644
Atlanta	23,488
Houston	18,840
Philadelphia	13,956
Detroit	13,910
Baltimore	12,492
Dallas	11,395

Source: U.S. Census Bureau

sell goods and services to Mexico, Mr. Niño says. Many of the entrepreneurs benefit from the fact that they share a common background and usually speak the same language as their trading partners.

Similarly, Channel A, a new on-line service based in Los Altos, Calif., tries to match merchants in Asia with customers in the U.S. "We see this huge need," says Peggy Liu, president and chief executive officer of the company. "There are U.S. customers who want access to high-quality Asian products,

Top Black-Owned Companies

Black Enterprise magazine's ranking of the largest industrial and service companies that are at least 51% black-owned.

1996 rank	1995 rank	Company and location	Type of business	Year started	No. of employ-ees	1996 revenues ($ millions)
1	1	TLC Beatrice International Holdings Inc., New York, NY	International food processor and distributor	1987	4,700	$2,230.000
2	2	Johnson Publishing Co., Chicago, IL	Publishing; broadcasting; TV production; cosmetics; hair care	1942	2,702	325.712
3	3	Philadelphia Coca-Cola Bottling Co., Philadelphia, PA	Soft-drink bottling	1985	1,000	325.000
4	5	Pulsar Data Systems Inc., Lanham, MD	Computer systems integration and network design	1982	147	166.000
5	4	H.J. Russell & Co., Atlanta, GA	Construction, property mgt., airport concessions, real estate development	1952	1,416	163.756
6	6	Uniworld Group Inc., New York, NY	Advertising, promotion, event marketing, direct reponse	1969	135	157.865
7	9	Granite Broadcasting Corp., New York, NY	Network TV affiliates	1988	1,035	154.845
8	–	Convenience Corporation of America Inc., West Palm Beach, FL	Convenience stores	1995	300	137.395
9	7	Burrell Communications Group Inc., Chicago, IL	Advertising, PR, consumer promotion, direct response marketing	1971	141	134.700
10	10	BET Holdings Inc., Washington, DC	Cable television network, magazine publishing	1980	500	132.700
11	13	The Bing Group, Detroit, MI	Steel processing and metal stamping distribution	1980	550	129.500
12	12	Envirotest Systems Corp., Sunnyvale, CA	Vehicle emissions testing	1990	4,000	124.472
13	8	Anderson-Dubose Co., Solon, OH	Food, paper products and operating supplies distributor	1991	89	122.200
14	22	Stop Shop Save Food Markets, Baltimore, MD	Supermarkets	1978	800	108.000
15	17	Sylvest Management Systems Corp., Lanham, MD	Computer and network integration solutions	1987	170	107.500
16	16	Midwest Stamping Co., Bowling Green, OH	Automotive metal stamping and assemblies	1993	520	106.800
17	11	Mays Chemical Co., Indianapolis, IN	Industrial chemicals distributor	1980	130	105.300
18	–	Barden Companies Inc., Detroit, MI	Radio broadcasting, real estate development, casino gaming	1981	1,450	93.207
19	18	Essence Communications Inc., New York, NY	Magazine publishing, catalog sales, entertainment	1969	130	92.784
20	15	Soft Sheen Products Inc., Chicago, IL	Hair care products manufacturer	1964	425	91.400

Source: Black Enterprise

and Asian vendors who aren't familiar with American marketing."

Ms. Liu, who co-founded Channel A with Stephen Chin, is exemplary of a new generation of Asian-American entrepreneurs. The daughter of a Chinese immigrant, she says she has a much bigger network of contacts in the Asian-American community than her father did as a newcomer to the United States. "I had access to capital, I had access to mentors, I had all sorts of resources," she says. "My generation is a lot more confident."

Recent waves of immigrants also are contributing to the growth in minority entrepreneurship in the United States. Many of those businesses start and thrive by serving other immigrants, small-business consultants say.

Many minority-owned enterprises remain quite small. Black-owned small businesses, for example, generated $32.2 billion in sales in 1992—an average of about $52,000 per firm. Firms owned by Asian Americans had sales of $104.1 billion in 1992, and Hispanic-owned firms generated $76.9 billion.

Together, these small businesses accounted for less than 2% of total business sales in the U.S. (Critics point out that the Census survey does not capture minority-owned C corporations, which generally have higher sales and more employees.)

Still, minority-owned firms that wish to grow have more financing alternatives than in the past, experts say. A number of banks, credit-card companies and other financiers are now targeting such businesses. A handful of venture capitalists—equity financiers who invest in private, fast-growing companies— have funds that invest specifically in promising minority-owned companies

Of course, minority entrepreneurs these days can turn to one of a growing number of minority-owned financing firms, too: The number of black-owned finance companies, for example, grew to 40,924 in 1992, an increase of more than 50% in five years.

Stephanie N. Mehta

Hispanic-Owned Firms Flourish

Hispanic-Owned Businesses in the U.S.

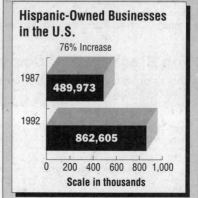

76% Increase

1987	489,973
1992	862,605

0 200 400 600 800 1,000
Scale in thousands

Revenues of Hispanic-Owned Firms in the U.S. (In billions)

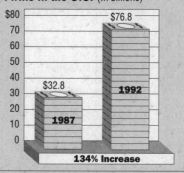

1987 — $32.8
1992 — $76.8

134% Increase

Metropolitan Areas with the Most Hispanic-Owned Firms

Metropolitan area	Number of firms in 1992
Los Angeles-Long Beach	109,104
Miami	77,300
New York	39,175
Houston	33,765
Riverside-San Bernardino, CA	21,380
San Antonio	21,244
Orange County, CA	19,270
San Diego	18,983
Chicago	16,663
Dallas	14,791

Source: U.S. Census Bureau

Hispanic-Owned Business Revenues, by Subgroup, 1992 (In billions)

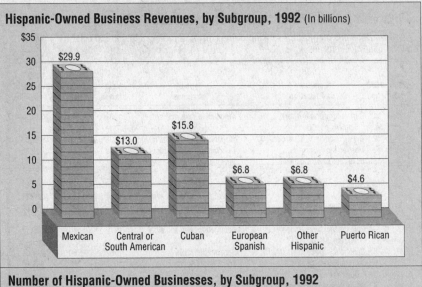

	Mexican	Central or South American	Cuban	European Spanish	Other Hispanic	Puerto Rican
	$29.9	$13.0	$15.8	$6.8	$6.8	$4.6

Number of Hispanic-Owned Businesses, by Subgroup, 1992

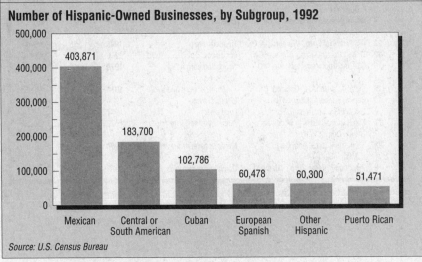

	Mexican	Central or South American	Cuban	European Spanish	Other Hispanic	Puerto Rican
	403,871	183,700	102,786	60,478	60,300	51,471

Source: U.S. Census Bureau

Top Hispanic-Owned Companies

Hispanic Business magazine's ranking of the largest companies that are at least 51% owned by Hispanic U.S. citizens.

1996 rank	1995 rank	Company and location	Type of business	Year started	No. of employ-ees	1996 revenues ($ millions)
1	1	Burt Automotive Network, Englewood, CO	Automotive sales and svcs.	1939	849	$812.97
2	2	Goya Foods, Inc., Secaucus, NJ	Hispanic food mfg. and mktg.	1936	500	602.00
3	11	MasTec Inc., Miami, FL	Telecomm. infrastructure const.	1969	3,200	472.80
4	5	de la Cruz Cos., Miami, FL	Beer whsl./automotive sales and svcs.	1984	950	396.54
5	9	Vincam Group Inc., Coral Gables, FL	Employment svcs.	1984	275	395.62
6	3	Troy Ford, Troy, MI	Automotive sales and svcs.	1967	115	380.99
7	4	Ancira Enterprises Inc., San Antonio, TX	Automotive sales and svcs.	1983	483	377.40
8	–	Galeana Van Dyke Dodge Inc., Warren, MI	Automotive sales and svcs.	1977	460	289.17
9	7	Sedano's Supermarkets, Miami, FL	Supermarket chain	1962	1,750	271.00
10	6	AJ Contracting Co. Inc., New York, NY	Const. mgnt./contracting	1917	218	268.00
11	8	International Bancshares Corp., Laredo, TX	Banking svcs.	1965	1,021	251.97
12	29	IFS Financial Corp., Wilmington, DE	Financial svcs.	1995	1,385	212.00
13	12	United Poultry Corp., Roswell, GA	Food svcs. dist.	1976	275	190.03
14	10	CTA Incorporated, Rockville, MD	Space and comm./info. tech. svcs.	1979	1,210	179.70
15	16	Lloyd A. Wise Cos., Oakland, CA	Automotive sales and svcs.	1914	221	178.00
16	13	Capital Bancorp, Miami, FL	Financial svcs.	1974	765	173.05
17	–	E & G Food Co., Miami, FL	Food dist.	1967	145	165.00
18	17	Mexican Industries in Michigan Inc., Detroit, MI	Automotive soft trim mfg.	1979	1,500	156.00
19	22	Supreme International Corp., Miami, FL	Men's apparel design and whsl.	1967	305	150.00
20	15	Precision Trading Corp., Miami, FL	Consumer electronics whsl.	1979	40	148.00

Source: Hispanic Business Inc., Santa Barbara, CA

Growth of Firms Owned by Asian and Native Americans

Asian– and Pacific Islander–Owned Businesses in the U.S.

56% Increase

1987 386,291

1992 603,439

0 200 400 600 800 1,000
Scale in thousands

American Indian– and Alaska Native–Owned Businesses in the U.S.

93% Increase

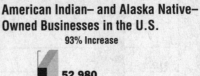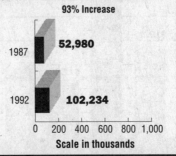

1987 52,980

1992 102,234

0 200 400 600 800 1,000
Scale in thousands

Revenues of Asian– and Pacific Islander–Owned Firms in the U.S. (In billions)

163% Increase

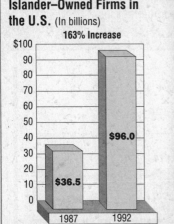

$96.0

$36.5

1987   1992

Revenues of American Indian– and Alaska Native–Owned Firms in the U.S. (In billions)

115% Increase

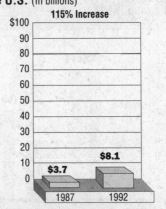

$8.1

$3.7

1987   1992

Metropolitan Areas With the Most Asian–, Pacific Islander–, American Indian–, and Alaska Native–Owned Firms

Metropolitan area	Number of firms, 1992	Metropolitan area	Number of firms, 1992
Los Angeles-Long Beach	92,209	Oakland	19,758
New York	50,283	Washington, DC	19,722
Honolulu	29,940	Chicago	19,706
Orange County, CA	27,252	San Jose	19,113
San Francisco	24,185	Houston	15,010

Source: U.S. Census Bureau

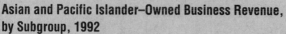

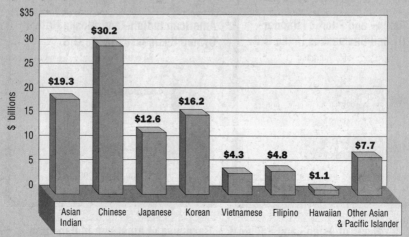

Asian and Pacific Islander–Owned Business Revenue, by Subgroup, 1992

- Asian Indian: $19.3
- Chinese: $30.2
- Japanese: $12.6
- Korean: $16.2
- Vietnamese: $4.3
- Filipino: $4.8
- Hawaiian: $1.1
- Other Asian & Pacific Islander: $7.7

(y-axis: $ billions)

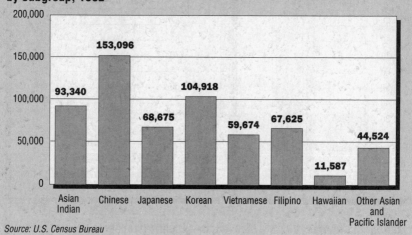

Number of Asian– and Pacific Islander–Owned Buisinesses, by Subgroup, 1992

- Asian Indian: 93,340
- Chinese: 153,096
- Japanese: 68,675
- Korean: 104,918
- Vietnamese: 59,674
- Filipino: 67,625
- Hawaiian: 11,587
- Other Asian and Pacific Islander: 44,524

Source: U.S. Census Bureau

American Indian– and Alaska Native– Owned Business Revenue, by Subgroup, 1992

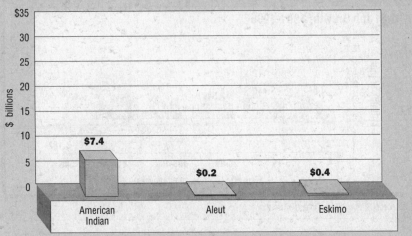

Number of American Indian– and Alaska Native–Owned Businesses, by Subgroup, 1992

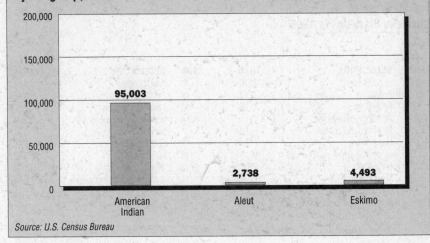

Source: U.S. Census Bureau

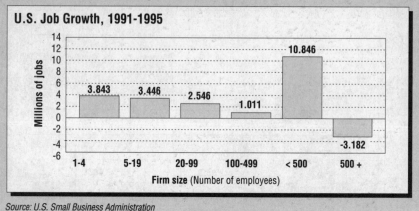

Job Creation by Small Business
Number of Jobs Created, by Size of Business

U.S. Job Growth, 1991-1995

Millions of jobs

- 1-4: 3.843
- 5-19: 3.446
- 20-99: 2.546
- 100-499: 1.011
- < 500: 10.846
- 500 +: -3.182

Firm size (Number of employees)

Source: U.S. Small Business Administration

Entrepreneurial Ventures

Top 20 Types of Business Start-Ups in 1996

RANK	DESCRIPTION	TOTAL
1	Construction	24,787
2	Restaurant	22,781
3	Retail Store	21,081
4	Cleaning Services, Residential & Commercial	19,642
5	Real Estate	17,549
6	Automotive Repairing & Service	16,158
7	Consultant	13,835
8	Beauty Salon	11,762
9	Computer Service & Repair	11,111
10	Management & Business Consulting	9,665
11	Arts & Crafts	9,412
12	Painter	9,156
13	Lawn Maintenance	8,498
14	Marketing Programs & Services	8,314
15	Landscape Contractor	8,268
16	Investment Broker	8,206
17	General Contractor	8,137
18	Communications Consultant	8,022
19	Remodel, Repair-Bldg. Contractor	7,988
20	Audio-Visual Production Service	7,414

Source: County Data Corp.

Venture Dollars and Deals

The number of companies backed by venture capital has continued to rise throughout the 1990s, with the share of venture capital going to information-technology companies increasing to 60% of the total in 1996 from 47% in 1992.

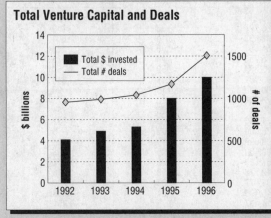

Total Venture Capital and Deals

Source: VentureOne Corp.

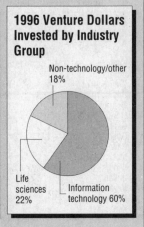

1996 Venture Dollars Invested by Industry Group

Non-technology/other 18%

Life sciences 22%

Information technology 60%

Loans to Small Business

Commercial Bank Loans to Small Business, by Size of Bank, as of June 30, 1996

Total domestic bank assets	Number of banks	Total domestic business lending	Total small business lending	Percent small business of total
Under $1 billion	9,222	$205,092,520,000	$132,600,582,000	64.65 %
1-4.9 billion	268	130,901,764,000	56,909,739,000	43.48
5-9.9 billion	60	93,487,421,000	28,865,904,000	30.88
10-19.9 billion	42	126,627,022,000	32,371,272,000	25.56
20-29.9 billion	14	110,051,725,000	21,182,192,000	19.25
30 billion plus	16	184,435,824,000	30,549,373,000	16.56
Total	**9,622**	**850,596,276,000**	**302,479,062,000**	**35.56**

Source: Wall Street Journal analysis of Call Reports filed with federal banking authorities

SBA 7A Loans

October 1, 1995 – September 30, 1996 (Fiscal 1996)

State	Amount of SBA 7A loans approved*	Percent of total	Number of loans
Alabama	$ 78,870,210	1.02 %	445
Alaska	25,265,720	0.33	189
Arizona	243,490,633	3.14	864
Arkansas	62,151,607	0.80	543
California	1,353,055,753	17.44	5,523
Colorado	201,325,384	2.59	1,050
Connecticut	175,896,737	2.27	846
Delaware	14,406,449	0.19	96
District of Columbia	12,573,538	0.16	73
Florida	329,519,511	4.25	1,766
Georgia	273,871,768	3.53	1,032
Guam	375,000	0.00	5
Hawaii	14,690,699	0.19	130
Idaho	73,462,133	0.95	508
Illinois	224,657,159	2.90	1,647
Indiana	68,312,278	0.88	418
Iowa	79,931,977	1.03	780
Kansas	93,945,495	1.21	766
Kentucky	58,414,437	0.75	351
Louisiana	90,392,378	1.17	602
Maine	33,359,801	0.43	288
Maryland	100,160,032	1.29	759
Massachusetts	174,122,008	2.24	1,295
Michigan	154,787,482	1.99	800
Minnesota	153,918,859	1.98	1,222
Mississippi	59,256,403	0.76	402
Missouri	144,620,617	1.86	1,184
Montana	67,347,240	0.87	549
Nebraska	41,762,709	0.54	331
Nevada	48,499,856	0.63	267
New Hampshire	53,831,077	0.69	435
New Jersey	255,790,478	3.30	1,376
New Mexico	58,496,867	0.75	420
New York	406,360,916	5.24	2,988
North Carolina	115,396,624	1.49	771
North Dakota	38,292,213	0.49	366
Ohio	200,176,618	2.58	1,388
Oklahoma	84,757,311	1.09	675
Oregon	84,511,869	1.09	409
Pennsylvania	216,780,178	2.79	1,601
Puerto Rico	107,608,332	1.39	906
Rhode Island	78,261,180	1.01	473
South Carolina	65,697,115	0.85	351
South Dakota	37,577,333	0.48	275
Tennessee	101,524,469	1.31	558
Texas	771,334,215	9.94	3,990
Utah	74,096,997	0.95	458
Vermont	34,041,517	0.44	319
Virginia	99,769,007	1.29	693
Virgin Islands	1,148,000	0.01	9
Washington	214,375,802	2.76	1,176
West Virginia	26,903,280	0.35	267
Wisconsin	153,790,382	1.98	1,009
Wyoming	26,003,944	0.34	234
Total	**7,758,969,597**	**100.00**	**45,878**

*SBA 7A loans are government-guaranteed loans to small businesses.
Source: Wall Street Journal analysis of data obtained from the Small Business Administration

FRANCHISEE, BEWARE

Franchising is bigger than ever in America, luring thousands of people each year to try running their own fast-food restaurant, dating service, home-cleaning business, bagel shop, or other hot new enterprise. But in fact, buying a franchise is a high-risk proposition with a much greater failure rate than most would-be entrepreneurs realize.

There's no denying that a strong franchise conveys advantages and has turned many people into millionaires. McDonald's outlets have national television advertising behind them, and almost every little kid in America seems hooked, along with a lot of adults. But there are thousands of other franchisers that have much less going for them.

In one study of nearly 1,300 franchises started between 1984 and 1987, only 65% were still operating in 1991. That compared with 72% of nonfranchises, reported economist Timothy Bates of Wayne State University. Franchisers, not just franchisees, are subject to failure. Of 138 companies that began selling franchises in 1983, 104—that is, three of every four—were defunct a decade later, according to a 1995 report by Scott A. Shane, then a researcher at Georgia Institute of Technology.

Still, many people are going the franchise route, eager to be their own boss and strike it rich. But it takes money to make money.

Franchisees pay fees and royalties—a portion of sales—to use the business format of a franchise chain. For example, if you want to sell Davidoff tobacco products, a Swiss brand, you can buy a franchise from Davidoff of Geneva Licensing Corp., a Stamford, Conn. unit of Oettinger Imex A.G. The initial investment in your business will run at least $800,000, and you'll owe the franchiser 5% of gross revenue throughout the life of your business. On the 10th of every month, you'll have to make a royalty payment based on the previous month's results.

Besides paying royalties, franchisees also have less freedom than completely independent entrepreneurs. Many franchisers restrict franchisees' sources of supply, for example, and they generally dictate which products and services the franchise can sell in the first place. Moreover, franchisees often aren't free to sell their businesses whenever, or to whomever, they choose.

In exchange for such limitations, franchisers promise franchisees that they will have a greater chance of success than do most independents. After all, chains often have name recognition and marketing and purchasing power, advantages unmatched by most independents. Franchisers also promise to help franchisees, who often are business neophytes, with many aspects of running the business.

But potential buyers of franchises need to

Franchising Field

Estimated Number of Franchise Establishments in the U.S.

Year	Franchise owned	Total (incl. company owned units)
1981	356,000	442,000
1982	353,000	440,000
1983	355,000	441,000
1984	357,000	444,000
1985	369,000	455,000
1986	374,000	463,000
1987	390,000	479,000
1988	386,844	480,789
1989	404,269	498,780
1990	435,191	532,959
1991	442,000	542,496
1992	465,691	571,574
1993	498,057	611,298
1994	540,342	663,197

Source: International Franchise Association

weigh carefully how much these franchisers really have to offer. The very worst franchises are fraudulent: The sellers want only to collect franchise fees and have no intention of helping people run viable businesses. Sometimes the same people start up four or five different franchise systems, all fraudulent.

Even honest franchisers may lack expertise. Many systems try to sell franchises before they even have a prototype outlet in operation to prove that the business concept can make money. Moreover, not even fran

chisers with proven concepts always deal fairly with franchisees. Some, for example, are quick to set up new franchises in close proximity to existing ones, often hurting the sales of the established franchisees.

Because of such problems, many franchisees have been demanding more state and federal regulation. But for now, "Buyer, beware" remains the best advice for franchise shoppers.

Jeffrey A. Tannenbaum

Office Space

Office Building Vacancy Rates and Rental Rates, First Quarter 1997

Region/ area/ market	Overall vacancy rates		Average rental rates (per square foot)		
	Central business district	Non-central business district	Central business district	Non-central business district	Overall
Atlanta, GA	21.9%	11.2%	$18.54	$21.97	$20.81
Boston, MA	6.0	8.4	33.70	23.10	27.31
Southern NH	*	14.9	*	14.29	14.29
Hartford, CT	22.8	21.6	19.67	16.63	18.01
New Haven, CT	24.1	17.0	23.35	16.77	19.78
New England area totals:	9.1	11.8			
Downtown, NY	17.1	*	29.78	*	29.78
Midtown, NY	10.8	*	37.03	*	37.03
Midtown South, NY	11.1	*	28.64	*	28.64
Brooklyn, NY	8.3	*	25.00	*	25.00
Long Island, NY	*	13.5	*	24.30	24.30
Central NJ	*	15.5	*	22.25	22.25
Northern NJ	*	15.3	*	24.59	24.59
Westchester County, NY	22.9	14.9	24.50	24.14	24.25
Fairfield County, CT	8.4	14.7	27.58	22.30	22.98
New York area totals:	12.6	15.0			
Baltimore, MD	18.1	8.5	21.01	17.82	19.26
Northern VA	*	6.2	*	24.64	24.64
Suburban MD	*	12.1	*	19.49	19.49
Washington, DC	12.7	*	35.09	*	35.09
Philadelphia, PA	14.5	10.5	19.41	19.47	19.44
Mid-Atlantic area totals:	13.7	8.8			
Ft. Lauderdale, FL	11.3	13.5	24.95	21.40	23.28
West Palm Beach, FL	19.7	15.3	27.72	24.37	25.41
Miami, FL	20.0	12.9	25.28	22.42	24.42
Tampa, FL	19.2	9.6	17.02	19.07	17.98
St. Petersburg/Clearwater, FL	*	10.9	*	15.34	15.34
Orlando, FL	7.5	11.2	22.52	17.90	18.89
Florida area totals:	16.4	12.4			

Region/ area/ market	Overall vacancy rates		Average rental rates (per square foot)		
	Central business district	Non-central business district	Central business district	Non-central business district	Overall
Dallas, TX	33.8%	9.6%	$18.01	$20.67	$18.97
Houston, TX	22.6	18.4	15.40	15.86	15.58
Denver, CO	12.0	10.4	16.59	19.14	17.78
Texas/Denver area totals:	23.6	13.4			
Chicago, IL	16.0	12.9	24.04	24.76	24.30
Detroit, MI	20.0	10.3	18.20	21.49	20.39
St. Louis, MO	19.5	8.1	18.11	21.74	19.70
Midwest area totals:	16.7	11.2			
Seattle, WA	6.4	20.5	20.88	15.04	18.18
Bellevue, WA	4.8	5.9	23.75	21.26	21.86
Portland, OR	7.7	6.8	19.62	19.62	19.62
Pacific Northwest area totals:	6.7	9.3			
San Francisco, CA	6.6	8.8	31.42	25.94	29.80
Oakland, CA	15.3	15.7	22.56	23.40	22.68
SF Peninsula, CA	*	2.5	*	30.96	30.96
Contra Costa, CA	*	9.4	*	20.88	20.88
San Jose, CA	9.2	4.5	26.76	26.28	26.40
Northern California area totals:	8.4	7.5			
Los Angeles, CA	24.3	24.3	19.68	19.32	19.44
Los Angeles-North, CA	*	16.3	*	22.08	22.08
Los Angeles-South, CA	*	20.8	*	18.72	18.72
Los Angeles-West, CA	*	15.1	*	26.52	26.52
Ontario, CA	*	24.3	*	18.84	18.84
Orange County, CA	13.9	17.7	21.60	18.84	20.88
Southern California area totals:	18.7	19.0			
Phoenix, AZ	15.9	9.0	18.74	20.54	19.98
National totals:	14.2	12.5			

*Not applicable.
Note: Rental rates are for office space offered through the landlord and are weighted by the amount of available space at each rental rate.
Source: Cushman & Wakefield Inc.

The World's Most Expensive Streets

Rankings of Streets by Rentals Per Square Foot

1996	1995	Street name	City
$575.00	$500.00	Fifth Avenue/49th–57th Streets	New York
500.00	440.00	East 57th Street/5th–Madison Avenues	New York
425.00	350.00	The Ginza (district)	Tokyo
350.00	300.00	Madison Avenue/57th–69th Streets	New York
325.00	275.00	Rue de Rhone	Geneva
310.00	250.00	Place Vendome	Paris
300.00	300.00	Post Street/Stockton Street	San Francisco
290.00	—	Nathan Road	Hong Kong
285.00	280.00	Champs Elysee	Paris
270.00	240.00	Bond Street	London

Source: The Hirschfeld Group Inc.

Malcolm Baldrige National Quality Award Winners

The Malcolm Baldrige National Quality Award, named for the former Secretary of Commerce, was established by Congress in 1987 to recognize companies with strong "quality management" programs and to publicize their successful strategies.

1988

Motorola Inc.
Schaumburg, IL (manufacturing)

Commercial Nuclear Fuel Division
of Westinghouse Electric Corp.
Pittsburgh, PA (manufacturing)

Globe Metallurgical Inc.
Beverly, OH (small business)

1989

Milliken & Co.
Spartanburg, SC (manufacturing)

Xerox Corp.
Business Products and Systems
Rochester, NY (manufacturing)

1990

Cadillac Motor Car Division
Detroit, MI (manufacturing)

IBM Rochester
Rochester, MN (manufacturing)

Federal Express Corp.
Memphis, TN (service)

Wallace Co.
Houston, TX (small business)

1991

Solectron Corp.
Milpitas, CA (manufacturing)

Zytec Corp.
Eden Prairie, MN (manufacturing)

Marlow Industries
Dallas, TX (small business)

1992

AT&T Network Systems Group/
Transmission Systems Business Unit
Morristown, NJ (manufacturing)

Texas Instruments Inc.
Defense Systems & Electronics Group
Dallas, TX (manufacturing)

1992 (continued)

AT&T Universal Card Services
Jacksonville, FL (service)

Ritz-Carlton Hotel Co.
Atlanta, GA (service)

Granite Rock Co.
Watsonville, CA (small business)

1993

Eastman Chemical Co.
Kingsport, TN (manufacturing)

Ames Rubber Corp.
Hamburg, NJ (small business)

1994

AT&T Consumer Communications Services
Basking Ridge, NJ (service)

GTE Directories Corp.
Dallas/Ft. Worth, TX (service)

Wainwright Industries Inc.
St. Peters, MO (small business)

1995

Armstrong World Industries'
Building Products Operation
Lancaster, PA (manufacturing)

Corning Telecommunications
Products Division
Corning, NY (manufacturing)

1996

Dana Commercial Credit Corp.
Toledo, OH (service)

Adac Laboratories
Milpitas, CA (manufacturing)

Custom Research Inc.
Minneapolis, MN (small business)

Trident Precision Manufacturing Inc.
Webster, NY (small business)

Source: U.S. Commerce Department

FARM ECONOMY

The American farm economy cooled to a more sustainable pace in 1997. The record corn and wheat price rallies that swelled farmers' wallets in 1996 triggered a spring planting boom that is now refilling the nation's precariously low granaries. Prices of most crops are skidding as a result. But the prospect for bumper harvests means most farmers will still generate strong incomes in 1997 even as Washington slowly dismantles the decades-old subsidy programs.

Lower crop prices also are reducing the feed costs of livestock producers, and allowing the nation's millers to return their factories to full operation. And food inflation, which spiked in 1996, has fallen back in line with the rest of consumer prices.

Soybeans were the hot crop in 1997, rising to a nine-year high in the spring amid strong demand from China. It is scrambling to build crushing plants to make meal for feeding its growing pig population. Indeed, the U.S. farm sector has been on a roll through most of the 1990s, thanks in large part to swelling world food demand. The value of U.S. agricultural exports have climbed about 40% since 1990, consuming roughly one-third of the grains and oilseeds grown by U.S. farmers.

Surging incomes in Asia and Latin America are allowing hundreds of millions of people to diversify their diets on an unprecedented scale. Baguettes and burgers are replacing rice and beans. Overseas demand for meat is fueling U.S. exports for chicken, pork and beef, as well as for the grain to fatten foreign herds.

The growth of U.S. farm exports slowed slightly in 1997. As in the U.S., the record grain prices of 1996 encouraged farmers across the globe to plant more crops. That armed many exporting nations to better compete against the U.S. But Agriculture Department officials continue to expect the value of U.S. agricultural exports to grow another 16% by the year 2000.

Among other things, an unusually strong El Niño is expected to disrupt growing conditions for some major grain producers, such as Australia and South Africa. El Niño is the nickname for a rapid warming of surface ocean temperatures off Peru, an event that can discombobulate weather patterns in the Southern Hemisphere and Asia while fueling favorable growing conditions in North America.

The strong agricultural economy is making it relatively easy for the government to go through with its plans to slowly wean farmers from Depression-era subsidies. Hoping to save billions of dollars annually, Congress in 1996 repealed price guarantees on major crops such as corn, wheat, cotton and rice. Farmers are getting fixed—but declining—transition payments until the year 2002 to give them time to learn how to play the markets.

Economists expect stress levels to climb in 1998, however, if crop prices continue to slip. That could easily happen because more acreage is going under the plow. When the government offered price guarantees, it required farmers to leave a portion of their land fallow to qualify for them; now the land-idling program is gone along with price guarantees. That means a greater risk of price-depressing gluts.

Scott Kilman

Farmland Erosion

Declining Number of Farms in the U.S.
(In millions)

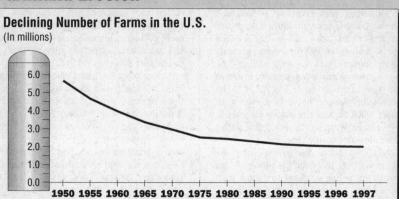

Fewer But Bigger Farms

Year	Number of Farms	Land in Farms (1,000 acres)	Average size (acres)	Year	Number of Farms	Land in Farms (1,000 acres)	Average size (acres)
1950	5,647,800	1,202,019	213	1974	2,795,460	1,084,433	388
1951	5,427,600	1,203,500	222	1975	2,521,420	1,059,420	420
1952	5,197,500	1,204,740	232	1976	2,497,270	1,054,075	422
1953	4,983,600	1,205,740	242	1977	2,455,830	1,047,785	427
1954	4,798,200	1,206,355	251	1978	2,436,250	1,044,790	429
1955	4,653,800	1,201,900	258	1979	2,437,300	1,043,195	428
1956	4,514,100	1,197,070	265	1980	2,439,510	1,038,885	426
1957	4,371,700	1,191,340	273	1981	2,439,920	1,034,190	424
1958	4,232,900	1,184,944	280	1982	2,406,550	1,027,795	427
1959	4,104,520	1,182,563	288	1983	2,378,620	1,023,425	430
1960	3,962,520	1,175,646	297	1984	2,333,810	1,017,803	436
1961	3,825,410	1,167,699	305	1985	2,292,530	1,012,073	441
1962	3,692,410	1,159,383	314	1986	2,249,820	1,005,333	447
1963	3,572,200	1,151,572	322	1987	2,212,960	998,923	451
1964	3,456,690	1,146,106	332	1988	2,200,940	994,423	452
1965	3,356,170	1,139,597	340	1989	2,174,520	990,723	456
1966	3,257,040	1,131,844	348	1990	2,145,820	986,850	460
1967	3,161,730	1,123,456	355	1991	2,116,760	981,736	464
1968	3,070,860	1,115,231	363	1992	2,107,840	978,503	464
1969	3,000,180	1,107,811	369	1993	2,083,430	976,463	469
1970	2,949,140	1,102,371	374	1994	2,064,720	973,403	471
1971	2,902,310	1,096,863	378	1995	2,071,520	972,253	469
1972	2,859,880	1,092,065	382	1996	2,063,910	970,048	470
1973	2,823,260	1,087,923	385	1997	2,058,910	968,338	470

Source: U.S. Agriculture Department

Farm Income (In billions)

	Income of farm operators from farming						
	Gross farm income					Production expenses	Net farm income
		Cash marketing receipts			Value of inventory changes**		
Year	Total*	Total	Livestock and products	Crops			
1945	$25.4	$21.7	$12.0	$ 9.7	$-0.04	$13.1	$12.3
1950	33.1	28.5	16.1	12.4	0.8	19.5	13.6
1955	33.5	29.5	16.0	13.5	0.2	22.2	11.3
1960	38.6	34.0	19.0	15.0	0.4	27.4	11.2
1965	46.5	39.4	21.9	17.5	1.0	33.6	12.9
1970	58.8	50.5	29.5	21.0	0.0	44.5	14.4
1975	100.6	88.9	43.1	45.8	3.4	75.0	25.5
1980	149.3	139.7	68.0	71.7	-6.3	133.1	16.1
1981	166.3	141.6	69.2	72.5	6.5	139.4	26.9
1982	164.1	142.6	70.3	72.3	-1.4	140.3	23.8
1983	153.9	136.8	69.6	67.2	-10.9	139.6	14.2
1984	168.0	142.8	72.9	69.9	6.0	142.0	26.0
1985	161.2	144.1	69.8	74.3	-2.3	132.6	28.6
1986	156.1	135.4	71.6	63.8	-2.2	125.2	30.9
1987	168.4	141.8	76.0	65.8	-2.3	131.0	37.4
1988	177.9	151.2	79.6	71.6	-4.1	139.9	38.0
1989	191.9	160.8	83.9	76.9	3.8	146.7	45.3
1990	198.2	169.5	89.2	80.3	3.3	153.4	44.8
1991	191.9	167.9	85.8	82.1	-0.2	153.3	38.5
1992	200.6	171.3	85.6	85.7	4.2	152.5	48.0
1993	204.2	177.6	90.2	87.5	-4.5	160.5	43.6
1994	215.8	180.8	88.1	92.6	8.2	167.4	48.4
1995	210.4	185.8	86.8	98.9	-3.4	175.6	34.8
1996†	233.0	201.9	92.9	109.1	2.8	183.7	49.3
1997†	231.7	201.1	95.3	105.8	1.1	186.8	44.9

*Cash marketing receipts and inventory changes plus government payments, other farm cash income, and nonmoney income furnished by farms.
**Physical changes in end-of-period inventory of crop and livestock commodities valued at average prices during the period.
†Projections.

Top 15 U.S. Agricultural, Fish and Wood Product Exports, FY 1996

Product	Exports ($ billions)
Coarse grains	$ 9.3
Wheat	6.9
Soybeans	6.3
Red meats	4.6
Cotton	3.0
Poultry meat	2.4
Lumber	2.3
Logs	2.1
Fruit, fresh	2.0
Feeds & fodders	1.9
Fruit, & vegetables, processed	1.9
Hides & skins	1.6
Tobacco	1.4
Tree nuts	1.4
Soybean meal	1.3
Subtotal	48.5
Total U.S. exports	69.7

Top 10 Markets for U.S. Agricultural, Fish, and Wood Products, FY 1996

Market	Exports ($ billions)	% of total U.S. exports
Japan	$ 16.6	23.9%
European Union	10.5	15.0
Canada	7.7	11.0
Mexico	5.3	7.5
South Korea	4.1	6.0
Taiwan	3.1	4.5
China	1.9	2.8
Hong Kong	1.6	2.4
Egypt	1.4	2.0
Russian Federation	1.3	1.8
Subtotal	53.5	
Total U.S. Exports	69.7	

Source: U.S. Agriculture Department

Top 15 U.S. Agricultural, Fish, and Wood Product Imports, FY 1996

Product	Imports ($ billions)
Lumber	$ 6.4
Raw coffee	2.3
Shrimp	2.5
Red meats	2.3
Wine & beer	2.6
Panel products	2.3
Fruit & vegs., processed	1.8
Vegetables, fresh	1.7
Live animals	1.6
Rubber & allied products	1.5
Snack foods	1.4
Sugars & sweeteners	1.3
Bananas	1.2
Fruit, fresh (excl. bananas)	1.2
Nursery products	0.9
Subtotal	30.7
Total U. S. imports	49.8

Top 15 Suppliers of Agricultural, Fish, and Wood Products, FY 1996

Supplier	Imports ($ billions)	% of total U.S. imports
Canada	$ 15.8	31.6%
European Union	6.8	13.6
Mexico	4.5	9.0
Thailand	2.1	4.2
Indonesia	2.1	4.3
Brazil	1.7	3.4
Colombia	1.2	2.4
Chile	1.1	2.3
Ecuador	1.0	2.1
China	1.0	2.1
New Zealand	1.0	1.9
Australia	0.9	1.8
Argentina	0.8	1.6
Costa Rica	0.7	1.5
Philippines	0.7	1.4
Top 15	42.6	
World total	49.8	

Ranking of 10 Leading States in Cash Receipts for Top 10 Commodities, 1995

	Commodity	Value $ millions	State and dollars (In millions)									
			1	2	3	4	5	6	7	8	9	10
1	Cattle & calves	$33,983	$6,296 TX	$4,235 KS	$4,158 NE	$2,081 CO	$1,759 OK	$1,705 IA	$1,290 CA	$1,046 SD	$835 MN	$668 MT
2	Dairy products	19,923	3,078 CA	2,916 WI	1,494 NY	1,456 PA	1,186 MN	792 TX	717 MI	684 WA	599 OH	508 ID
3	Corn	17,400	3,368 IA	3,116 IL	2,021 NE	1,590 IN	1,196 MN	924 OH	623 WI	603 TX	579 KS	526 SD
4	Soybean	13,203	2,334 IL	2,318 IA	1,198 IN	1,168 MN	956 OH	886 MO	651 NE	591 AR	444 SD	352 KS
5	Broilers	11,760	1,772 GA	1,769 AR	1,438 AL	1,162 NC	992 MS	646 TX	474 DE	462 MD	401 VA	383 CA
6	Greenhouse & nursery	10,407	2,172 CA	1,093 FL	858 NC	792 TX	491 OH	425 MI	399 OR	314 PA	264 OK	257 NJ
7	Hogs	10,073	2,550 IA	1,274 NC	865 MN	739 NE	720 IN	664 IL	603 MO	312 SD	298 OH	231 KS
8	Wheat	8,769	1,388 ND	1,262 KS	714 MT	607 WA	458 OK	385 CO	383 ID	362 SD	335 NE	285 TX
9	Cotton	7,566	1,666 TX	1,393 CA	806 MS	767 GA	611 AR	538 LA	387 AZ	314 NC	308 TN	226 MO
10	Chicken eggs	3,958	294 AR	290 GA	288 CA	265 PA	253 OH	236 IN	218 TX	216 AL	203 NC	146 IA
	Livestock & products	86,843	8,454 TX	5,549 CA	5,187 NE	5,068 IA	4,693 KS	3,926 WI	3,735 NC	3,451 MN	3,023 AR	2,789 GA
	Crops	98,906	16,713 CA	6,177 IL	5,891 IA	4,834 TX	4,719 FL	3,564 WA	3,551 MN	3,503 NE	3,251 NC	3,240 IN
	Total	185,750	22,261 CA	13,288 TX	10,959 IA	8,690 NE	7,887 IL	7,521 KS	7,002 MN	6,987 NC	5,849 FL	5,582 WI

Spirit of Generosity

Total amount of money given to different causes in current and inflation-adjusted dollars

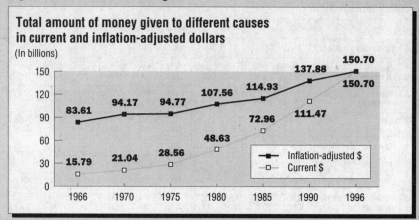

(In billions)

Source: American Association of Fund-Raising Counsel Trust for Philanthropy

50 Largest U.S. Recipients of Private Charitable Contributions, 1995

		Income		Expenses		
		Private support	Total	Program services	Fund raising	Total
1	Salvation Army	$644,267,026	$1,421,005,370	$1,215,397,593	$63,330,926	$1,417,021,194
2	American Red Cross	465,632,246	1,721,200,806	1,661,396,983	66,658,806	1,805,580,053
3	Catholic Charities USA	419,389,526	1,993,985,050	1,661,337,808	27,561,925	1,926,772,086
4	American Cancer Society	381,674,000	420,426,000	271,845,000	83,523,000	387,428,000
5	Second Harvest	369,123,575	371,173,151	370,040,288	642,286	371,102,637
6	United Jewish Appeal (National)	346,649,213	346,784,013	317,929,033	24,681,392	345,288,186
7	Harvard University	323,406,242	1,776,515,791	1,220,783,434	31,393,807	1,317,551,091
8	Boys and Girls Clubs of America	294,892,216	355,734,311	285,707,391	19,862,231	353,427,231
9	YWCA of the USA	283,755,099	569,669,325	477,664,562	9,598,534	554,293,410
10	American Heart Association	256,512,000	317,921,000	236,241,000	43,185,000	302,720,000
11	YMCA of the USA	249,396,104	2,059,863,107	n/a	n/a	1,990,501,158
12	Stanford University	240,832,287	1,577,565,940	1,215,078,172	19,410,815	1,420,194,490
13	World Vision	240,239,000	304,003,311	244,659,324	34,440,866	310,278,479
14	Boy Scouts of America	225,013,000	513,379,000	402,782,000	32,301,000	493,440,000
15	Nature Conservancy	209,535,792	321,613,782	261,600,000	28,641,183	312,462,469
16	Public Broadcasting Service	205,269,398	395,984,506	389,792,815	96,029	392,592,948
17	Habitat for Humanity International	203,911,516	272,222,858	233,525,013	16,458,148	271,846,807
18	Shriners Hospitals for Children	201,085,000	428,842,000	299,472,000	2,784,000	314,327,000
19	Yale University	199,646,606	918,519,812	907,809,619	13,169,889	929,648,296
20	Cornell University	198,736,229	1,541,656,000	1,288,276,000	21,705,000	1,386,146,000
21	Mayo Foundation for Medical Education and Research	191,000,000	2,375,600,000	2,079,200,000	7,300,000	2,086,500,000
22	Fidelity Investments Charitable Gift Fund	185,674,879	191,674,577	70,494,486	645,526	72,592,475
23	Campus Crusade for Christ International	184,755,000	209,107,000	175,827,000	16,659,000	207,367,000
24	Gifts in Kind International	176,651,322	179,011,415	200,497,091	29,563	200,834,384
25	New York Community Trust	168,494,797	350,910,601	62,187,603	n/a	112,807,977

	Income		Expenses		
	Private support	Total	Program services	Fund raising	Total
26 University of Wisconsin at Madison	164,349,458	$1,438,354,383	$1,278,015,202	n/a	$1,386,014,774
27 Duke University	155,164,009	1,424,462,978	1,332,306,472	$12,390,895	1,352,565,681
28 Columbia University	151,800,682	1,473,170,000	1,157,662,000	8,454,000	1,271,914,000
29 United Jewish Appeal–Federation of Jewish Philanthropies of New York	148,852,875	156,237,400	122,276,469	21,147,512	158,662,406
30 University of Michigan	145,757,642	n/a	n/a	n/a	n/a
31 AmeriCares Foundation	145,514,872	145,779,152	141,747,475	1,341,836	144,118,530
32 University of Southern California	138,366,230	1,071,535,000	864,942,000	12,118,000	950,663,000
33 ALSAC/St. Jude's Children's Research Hospital	136,393,181	187,210,997	76,002,320	27,331,041	111,420,910
34 University of Pennsylvania	135,324,761	1,876,330,000	1,744,132,000	19,150,000	1,693,541,000
35 Osmond Foundation (Children's Miracle Network)	132,459,254	136,678,321	119,204,165	16,447,157	135,635,817
36 University of Minnesota	131,638,509	2,078,714,000	1,162,089,000	9,867,181	2,033,984,000
37 University of Washington	127,774,167	n/a	n/a	n/a	n/a
38 March of Dimes Birth Defects Foundation	126,284,620	138,485,018	103,853,529	21,342,371	134,682,868
39 Planned Parenthood Federation of America	122,700,000	504,000,000	385,500,000	24,200,000	477,800,000
40 Larry Jones International Ministries/Feed the Children*	117,412,806	119,535,873	103,063,787	6,008,963	112,319,514
41 University of Illinois	116,578,975	2,317,695,000	2,005,344,000	14,957,000	2,103,452,000
42 Goodwill Industries International	113,400,000	1,037,000,000	852,200,000	4,800,000	974,000,000
43 Indiana University	109,654,739	n/a	n/a	n/a	n/a
44 University of California at San Francisco	108,127,887	1,136,900,000	n/a	n/a	n/a
45 Massachusetts Institute of Technology	107,937,812	1,305,556,000	1,096,670,000	14,130,000	1,182,869,000
46 National Association for the Exchange of Industrial Resources*	107,178,896	116,093,581	94,470,400	n/a	96,393,368
47 American Lung Association	106,578,400	133,223,000	103,100,000	20,071,000	132,997,000
48 MAP International*	105,533,008	108,251,782	100,539,627	2,266,287	103,601,470
49 Princeton University	103,826,392	624,901,000	527,223,000	9,026,000	563,646,000
50 University of California at Berkeley	103,088,570	n/a	n/a	n/a	n/a

n/a: not available.
*Non-cash gifts make up 50 per cent or more of private support.
Source: The Chronicle of Philanthropy

The 50 largest U.S. grantmaking foundations (ranked by total giving)

RANK	NAME	TOTAL GIVING	FISCAL YEAR END DATE
1.	The Ford Foundation	$288,660,188	09/30/95
2.	W.K. Kellogg Foundation	222,691,781	08/31/95
3.	The Pew Charitable Trusts	193,081,614	12/31/95
4.	Soros Humanitarian Foundation	168,359,909	11/30/94
5.	John D. and Catherine T. MacArthur Foundation	123,953,670	12/31/95
6.	The Annenberg Foundation	112,996,033	06/30/95
7.	Lilly Endowment Inc.	111,652,675	12/31/95
8.	The Andrew W. Mellon Foundation	110,606,687	12/31/95
9.	The New York Community Trust	107,795,883	12/31/95
10.	The Rockefeller Foundation	102,008,668	12/31/95
11.	The David and Lucile Packard Foundation	92,862,401	12/31/95
12.	Open Society Institute	86,418,552	12/31/94
13.	The Robert Wood Johnson Foundation	76,893,451	12/31/95
14.	The Kresge Foundation	76,731,005	12/31/95

RANK	NAME	TOTAL GIVING	FISCAL YEAR END DATE
15.	Robert W. Woodruff Foundation, Inc.	72,519,703	12/31/95
16.	The Annie E. Casey Foundation	65,771,718	12/31/95
17.	The McKnight Foundation	55,821,961	12/31/95
18.	Carnegie Corporation of New York	53,508,409	09/30/95
19.	The Harry and Jeanette Weinberg Foundation, Inc.	51,000,000	02/28/95
20.	The Starr Foundation	47,178,974	12/31/95
21.	Arthur S. DeMoss Foundation	44,645,433	12/31/94
22.	Charles Stewart Mott Foundation	43,648,878	12/31/95
23.	The Duke Endowment	41,844,046	12/31/95
24.	Alfred P. Sloan Foundation	40,590,535	12/31/95
25.	Houston Endowment, Inc.	40,401,669	12/31/95
26.	DeWitt Wallace-Reader's Digest Fund, Inc.	39,839,398	12/31/95
27.	The William and Flora Hewlett Foundation	39,802,302	12/31/95
28.	The William Penn Foundation	39,572,493	12/31/95
29.	Lucille P. Markey Charitable Trust	39,119,004	06/30/96
30.	The J. E. and L. E. Mabee Foundation, Inc.	38,862,300	08/31/95
31.	AT&T Foundation	37,244,638	12/31/95
32.	The California Wellness Foundation	37,003,535	12/31/95
33.	Richard King Mellon Foundation	36,097,738	12/31/95
34.	Robert R. McCormick Tribune Foundation	35,988,211	12/31/95
35.	John S. and James L. Knight Foundation	34,756,999	12/31/95
36.	Howard Heinz Endowment	34,680,047	12/31/95
37.	W. M. Keck Foundation	34,293,000	12/31/95
38.	Marin Community Foundation	32,562,000	06/30/95
39.	The Whitaker Foundation	32,535,479	12/31/95
40.	The James Irvine Foundation	32,434,146	12/31/95
41.	The Chicago Community Trust	30,962,680	09/30/95
42.	The Brown Foundation, Inc.	29,254,117	06/30/95
43.	The San Francisco Foundation	28,762,376	06/30/95
44.	Lila Wallace-Reader's Digest Fund, Inc.	28,565,179	12/31/95
45.	Weingart Foundation	28,395,177	06/30/95
46.	The Cleveland Foundation	28,334,085	12/31/95
47.	Ewing Marion Kauffman Foundation	27,557,121	06/30/95
48.	The John W. Kluge Foundation	27,384,340	09/30/95
49.	The Ahmanson Foundation	27,196,888	10/31/95
50.	California Community Foundation	26,687,463	06/30/96

Source: The Foundation Center

The 50 largest U.S. grantmaking foundations (ranked by the market value of their assets)

RANK	NAME	ASSETS	FISCAL YEAR END DATE
1.	The Ford Foundation	$7,503,280,000	09/30/95
2.	J. Paul Getty Trust	6,464,964,495	06/30/95
3.	W. K. Kellogg Foundation	6,034,576,655	08/31/95
4.	Lilly Endowment Inc.	5,296,723,582	12/31/95

RANK	NAME	ASSETS	FISCAL YEAR END DATE
5.	The Robert Wood Johnson Foundation	5,257,995,541	12/31/95
6.	The Pew Charitable Trusts	3,778,481,571	12/31/95
7.	John D. and Catherine T. MacArthur Foundation	3,297,625,923	12/31/95
8.	The Rockefeller Foundation	2,523,653,744	12/31/95
9.	The Andrew W. Mellon Foundation	2,485,168,000	12/31/95
10.	The David and Lucile Packard Foundation	2,354,721,649	12/31/95
11.	Robert W. Woodruff Foundation, Inc.	2,349,578,813	12/31/95
12.	The Kresge Foundation	1,726,799,516	12/31/95
13.	The Duke Endowment	1,653,377,105	12/31/95
14.	Charles Stewart Mott Foundation	1,497,636,406	12/31/95
15.	The Starr Foundation	1,460,488,563	12/31/95
16.	The Annenberg Foundation	1,387,238,383	06/30/95
17.	The William and Flora Hewlett Foundation	1,379,220,267	12/31/95
18.	The McKnight Foundation	1,360,108,000	12/31/95
19.	Richard King Mellon Foundation	1,250,592,027	12/31/95
20.	Carnegie Corporation of New York	1,224,268,188	09/30/95
21.	The New York Community Trust	1,206,806,603	12/31/95
22.	The Annie E. Casey Foundation	1,159,384,313	12/31/95
23.	Donald W. Reynolds Foundation	1,077,979,023	06/30/96
24.	DeWitt Wallace-Reader's Digest Fund, Inc.	1,077,706,815	12/31/95
25.	W. M. Keck Foundation	1,044,818,606	12/31/95
26.	Houston Endowment, Inc.	1,017,856,988	12/31/95
27.	Ewing Marion Kauffman Foundation	995,740,988	06/30/95
28.	The Harry and Jeanette Weinberg Foundation, Inc.	990,900,000	02/28/95
29.	John S. and James L. Knight Foundation	957,491,995	12/31/95
30.	Alfred P. Sloan Foundation	934,961,484	12/31/95
31.	The California Wellness Foundation	917,265,307	12/31/95
32.	The Cleveland Foundation	902,742,052	12/31/95
33.	The James Irvine Foundation	832,679,081	12/31/95
34.	Lila Wallace-Reader's Digest Fund, Inc.	824,564,249	12/31/95
35.	Joseph B. Whitehead Foundation	790,402,293	12/31/95
36.	Robert R. McCormick Tribune Foundation	777,096,506	12/31/95
37.	The Freedom Forum	768,389,014	05/31/95
38.	The William Penn Foundation	755,633,754	12/31/95
39.	Meadows Foundation, Inc.	686,582,223	12/31/95
40.	Howard Heinz Endowment	677,015,120	12/31/95
41.	The Brown Foundation, Inc.	644,391,954	06/30/95
42.	The Ahmanson Foundation	629,235,000	10/31/95
43.	Marin Community Foundation	620,118,000	06/30/95
44.	The Joyce Foundation	587,899,563	12/31/95
45.	The J. E. and L. E. Mabee Foundation, Inc.	585,483,727	08/31/95
46.	The Samuel Roberts Noble Foundation, Inc.	578,644,517	10/31/95
47.	Freeman Foundation	562,822,931	12/31/95
48.	The George Gund Foundation	552,150,413	12/31/95
49.	The Hearst Foundations, Inc.	544,305,010	12/31/95
50.	Weingart Foundation	542,009,793	06/30/95

Source: The Foundation Center

Marketplace

For any sports fan with halfway decent vision, there's no mistaking the players. They have identifiable colors and logos. They show up at every game and compete for the fans' loyalty. And if all goes well, they win.

These players, however, aren't the likes of Michael Jordan or Tiger Woods. They go by the names of Coke, Nike and Tostitos and their muscle and competitive drive are the equal of even the scrappiest ballplayer.

Sports and sponsorship have been inexorably linked ever since the first company noticed there was room on the back of a jersey for a product logo. In days gone by, sponsors were sometimes the only source of funding when a local softball team needed uniforms. The sponsor, usually a neighborhood restaurant or other local business, would buy the team duds in exchange for a little advertising on the back.

Now, marketers have made it into the big leagues, putting their names on entire stadiums and football bowl games. At college football games, corporate logos even pop up like art among the card stunts performed by students during halftime.

Sports-event sponsorship spending has increased steadily in the last 10 years and is expected to reach $3.8 billion in 1997, according to the IEG Sponsorship Report, a Chicago newsletter. That doesn't include the additional millions of dollars spent on individual player endorsements. And these days, sponsors aren't simply paying players to sport their logos; they are giving equity in their companies to sports stars like Michael Jordan, Greg Norman and Cal Ripken Jr.

The growing commercialization of sports comes at a time when advertisers are encroaching more and more into people's lives. Ads are popping up on everything from the Internet to school buses to popcorn bags in movie theaters. Carnegie Hall even renamed its restaurant the Travelers Group Cafe to reward the financial-services firm for its patronage.

But it's the sports world that offers the greatest potential payoff for many companies. They not only reach a huge audience of loyal sports fans, but they also share in the mystique certain teams and players enjoy. Indeed, a study of the most popular celebrity endorsers found that consumers recall athletes over entertainers in television commercials by a two-to-one margin.

"Sports stars, especially professional basketball players, are far more visible on television than entertainers," says David Vadehra, president of Video Storyboard Tests Inc., the New York research firm that conducted the study. "Candice Bergen (the top-ranked entertainment endorser) is on TV half an hour every week, but Michael Jordan (the top-ranked sports endorser) is there several hours each game, several times a week."

The $3.8 billion marketers invest in sports events dwarfs the $2.1 billion spent on all other sponsorships, including concert tours, arts events, festivals, and charitable causes. Such money has become increasingly important in professional sports, where players' and coaches' salaries have been skyrocketing and teams are building expensive new stadiums. Sponsorship funding also helps keep smaller sports events like rodeos and fishing tournaments in business. "Many events wouldn't occur without sponsors," says Lesa Ukman, editor of IEG Sponsorship Report. "NASCAR (stock-car racing) sponsors have communicated to fans that their presence makes it better, not worse. The fan allegiance is high to those sponsors."

(The proposed tobacco settlement between the industry and 40 state attorneys general would eliminate cigarette-brand sponsorships of sports events. That could particularly hurt motor sports that depend heavily on tobacco company support.)

New stadiums are needed partly to accommodate the sponsors and keep the money flowing. In facilities where there isn't sufficient space for sponsorship signage, the venues are in decreasing demand. In contrast, newer sports arenas have corporate signage space that grabs spectators' attention between bleachers, on screens above the scoreboards, and on barriers ringing the field.

With so much competition for fans' attention

at pro games, some sponsors are looking to less cluttered events like high-school sports and skiing. The southern section of the California Interscholastic Federation had gone 82 years without an advertisement or a corporate sponsor. But in 1995, Atlantic Richfield gave the California teams a corporate sponsorship. Arco's a.m./p.m. minimarts, which sell food at the oil company's gas stations, have a three-year contract to support the athletics organization, including championship patches with the minimarket's logo for the lettermen's jackets.

Other marketers are reaching new heights with their sponsorships. At 11,000 feet, *Self* magazine sponsored a slalom race on the ski slopes of Telluride, Colo., giving away Neutrogena body lotions. A Saab sat in the snow, part of another promotion that week on the mountain. And it was a challenge to pick out any skier who wasn't wearing a jacket with a prominent logo.

Golf is becoming more popular with marketers, too, thanks to its increased appeal to weekend athletes. Discount broker Charles Schwab & Co., for example, has signed on as "official investment firm" of the PGA tour. "As the superstars become more well-known, the more well-known are the others in the sport," says Charles Moore, vice president of the golf division at International Management Group, which represents Tiger Woods. "We're just beginning to feel the effect of Tiger Woods since he turned pro."

Of course, there's no guarantee that marketers will score with a particular event sponsorship or player endorsement. But when they do, their brands can gain invaluable exposure. No amount of advertising could equal the impact of news pictures of a jubilant Tiger Woods in Nike shirt and Nike hat when he became the youngest man and first black to win the Masters golf tournament.

Joyce Julius & Associates, an event-marketing analyst in Ann Arbor, Mich., believes the sponsors of the 1996–1997 college bowl games were also big winners. It estimates, for example, that the Tostitos on-field logo received about nine minutes of television exposure during the Fiesta Bowl, which was worth about $1.7 million. FedEx's on-field logo at the Orange Bowl won it nearly eight minutes of TV time, worth about $1.3 million. In addition, the sponsors were frequently mentioned during the televised coverage.

The stakes are high. Nike paid Mr. Woods

Most Valuable Players

Sports stars with the largest estimated annual income from endorsements, as of May 1997.

1	Michael Jordan	$38 million
2	Shaquille O'Neal	23 million
3	Arnold Palmer	16 million
4	Andre Agassi	15.8 million
5	Jack Nicklaus	14.5 million
6	Grant Hill	14 million
7	Tiger Woods	14 million
8	Joe Montana	12 million
9	Wayne Gretzky	8.8 million
10	Dennis Rodman	6 million

Source: Sports Marketing Letter, Westport, CT

about $40 million for an endorsement deal. And Adidas this year negotiated the largest sponsorship pact with a U.S. sports franchise: a 10-year, $93 million deal with the New York Yankees.

The Super Bowl and Olympics remain the premier and priciest sports events. During the 1997 Super Bowl, the most-watched televised event in the world, advertisers shelled out a record $1.2 million for a 30-second commercial. And sponsors of the 1996 Summer Olympic Games in Atlanta paid as much as $250 million for the privilege. Despite the prices, Atlanta wasn't short of corporate sponsors. There were more than 100 licensees, 20 regular sponsors, 10 worldwide sponsors, and 10 Centennial Olympic Partners, contributing to the $1.6 billion Olympic budget.

The Olympics didn't prove to be a golden opportunity for all the marketers, however. A study by Louis Harris & Associates in New York showed that while nearly half of consumers were aware that Coca-Cola Co. was a sponsor of the Atlanta Olympic Games, they had almost no awareness of most other sponsors, including Eastman Kodak Co., General Motors Corp. and *Sports Illustrated*. "It's all how you do it," Robert Leitman, a Louis Harris vice president, told *The Wall Street Journal*. "It involves having a strategy and tracking it, so you know whether you're making an impact."

Some critics believe the commercialization of sports has gone way too far. The Olympics in Atlanta were widely criticized as a sell-out that turned the prestigious sports event into an advertising forum. And fans protested when Candelstick Park, home to the San Francisco Giants, was renamed 3Com Park for the computer-network company. More than half of the respondants in a San Francisco *Examiner* poll hated the new ballpark name, for which 3Com paid a total of $4 million. "The park's identity is a symbol saturated with cultural and psychological ideals," says psychologist and market researcher Carol Moog. "The name is its heritage, and a company who changes it is viewed as a predator."

Ms. Ukman agrees that the Candlestick Park name change was "not well-advised." Sponsorship of a sports venue "has gotten really expensive," she says. "It's more often an ego buy by the CEO based in that market. It's not really about connecting with the fans."

Even so, selling stadium names has spread through the major and the minor leagues. New Jersey's Brendan Byrne Arena, home to the New Jersey Nets, was renamed for Conti-

nental Airlines, which paid $26.4 million to be title sponsor for 12 years. In Los Angeles, cost estimates for renovating the Memorial Coliseum are more than $200 million and mounting. So, selling the stadium's name to a corporate sponsor is one of the financing options, officials say. And in an agreement worth $100,000 a year for 15 years, General Motors provided minor-league baseball with Oldsmobile Park in Lansing, Mich.

There are still a few limits to sports sponsorship. College football's classic Rose Bowl so far has resisted adding a corporate name tag. And New Jersey Gov. Christine Whitman and the New Jersey Sports and Exposition Authority rejected Seagram's bid to put its name on the Meadowlands race track. The liquor company offered $1.5 million, but the governor opposed sponsorship of a sports or cultural center by an alcoholic beverage or cigarette marketer.

Stacy Kravetz,
a *Wall Street Journal* staff reporter

SUPERMARKET SHOPPING BASKET

Billion-Dollar Products

The 50 largest product categories in food stores in 1996 and percentage change from 1995.

CATEGORY	1996 SALES	CHG VS. 1995	CATEGORY	1996 SALES	CHG VS. 1995
Carbonated Beverages	$11,168,362,496	3.0%	Luncheon Meats	$2,914,965,760	2.9%
Milk	9,248,718,848	5.6	Crackers	2,841,129,728	3.8
Cold Cereal	7,461,076,992	−6.1	Dog Food	2,783,039,488	1.1
Fresh Bread & Rolls	6,674,415,616	6.2	Dinners	2,491,810,304	3.0
Cheese	6,271,102,976	5.8	Wine	2,393,794,816	11.0
Chips & Snacks	5,757,186,048	2.7	Toilet Tissue	2,351,292,160	4.0
Cigarettes	5,475,143,680	−3.8	Vegetables	2,046,259,712	1.9
Beer & Ale	5,258,027,008	3.3	Fresh Eggs	2,016,745,728	18.1
Frozen Dinners/Entrees	4,445,155,328	4.5	Baby Formula/ Electrolytes	1,983,646,208	−1.2
Ice Cream	3,710,161,920	1.9	Diapers	1,921,700,096	−7.0
Cookies	3,410,037,504	−1.7	Cat food	1,918,062,336	2.0
Soup	3,359,017,984	2.8	Breakfast Meats	1,913,183,744	12.1
Refrigerated Juice	3,350,999,296	4.0	Frozen Pizza	1,728,949,504	11.8
Coffee	3,167,820,800	−12.5	Frozen Novelties	1,696,186,624	2.5
Candy/Mints	3,087,403,264	6.8	Frozen Plain Vegetables	1,684,563,200	−1.6
Bottled Juices-Shelf Stable	2,993,562,880	1.9	Yogurt	1,667,510,528	3.3
			Paper Towels	1,633,309,184	4.3
Laundry Detergent	2,991,644,672	0.6	Seafood - Shelf Stable	1,565,970,944	0.1
			Shortening & Oil	1,517,004,032	5.3
			Entree/Side Dishes	1,468,775,424	15.9

Spices/Seasonings	$1,455,742,464	2.0%
Canned/Bottled Fruit	1,443,629,568	2.3
Household Cleaner	1,437,971,456	−6.2
Frankfurters	1,428,315,904	2.8
Food & Trash Bags	1,399,925,760	1.5
Bottled Water	1,369,402,112	3.9
Spaghetti/Italian Sauce	1,368,970,752	6.6

Frozen Juices	$1,340,244,992	−2.3%
Pickles/Relish/Olives	1,322,268,928	3.4
Pasta	1,295,086,848	1.5
Margarine/Spreads	1,270,827,520	0.4
Salad Dressings - Shelf Stable	1,246,008,576	2.7
Frozen Poultry	1,210,130,688	14.1

Source: Information Resources Inc.

Sales Leaders and Laggards

Product categories with the greatest increase in dollar sales and the products with the biggest decline in sales. The data include only categories with annual sales of at least $50 million in food stores.

Largest Increase in Sales

CATEGORY	1996 DOLLAR SALES	CHG
Juice/Drink Concentrate - Shelf Stable	$87,180,416	56.1%
Sausage	766,612,480	28.8
Lunches-Refrigerated	498,698,752	27.6
Butter	770,370,304	26.5
Antacids	463,327,232	25.6
Fresh Eggs	2,016,745,728	18.1
Firelogs/Firestarters	91,166,400	17.5
Entree/Side Dishes	1,468,775,424	15.9
All Other Deli	194,417,248	15.5

CATEGORY	1996 DOLLAR SALES	CHG
Frozen Poultry	$1,210,130,688	14.1%
Weight Loss/Protein Supplement	376,527,360	13.4
Creams	687,284,992	12.4
Breakfast Meats	1,913,183,744	12.1
Frozen Pizza	1,728,949,504	11.8
Baking Nuts	292,574,976	11.1
Wine	2,393,794,816	11.0
Flour/Meal	534,140,928	10.7
Hair Coloring	181,312,496	10.5
Pizza-Refrigerated	172,744,144	9.9
Other Frozen Food	50,876,960	9.8

Largest Decrease in Sales

1996 DOLLAR SALES	DOLLAR SALES	% CHG YR AGO
Rice/Popcorn Cakes	$218,863,328	-16.9%
Frozen Egg Substitutes	53,040,304	-14.8
Coffee	3,167,820,800	-12.5
Breadcrumbs/ Batters	220,564,080	-10.3
Hosiery	323,757,568	-9.3
Canned Ham	101,129,344	-9.2
Rug/Upholstery Cleaner	225,900,464	-8.1
Nasal Spray	86,681,744	-7.8
Motor Oil	64,527,024	-7.6
Diapers	1,921,700,096	-7.0
Household Cleaner	1,437,971,456	-6.2

1996 DOLLAR SALES	DOLLAR SALES	% CHG YR AGO
Cold Cereal	$7,461,076,992	-6.1%
Air Fresheners	318,770,944	-5.9
Fragrances— Women's	60,361,792	-5.9
Cold & Sinus Tablets/Cough Drops	663,168,000	-5.7
Tea—Instant Tea Mixes	300,149,504	-5.6
Baby Food	837,434,112	-5.4
Soap	1,064,381,696	-5.3
Baby Needs	119,218,160	-5.1
Hair Spray	191,279,040	-5.0

Source: Information Resources Inc.

Price Check

Price changes in 1996 for some of the largest product categories in food stores.

CATEGORY	AVG PRICE PERCENT CHANGE IN 1996
Fresh Breads & Rolls	6.5%
Cheese	5.4%
Milk	7.8%
Yogurt	3.5%
Refrigerated Juice	5.5%
Breakfast Meats	23.0%
Cold Cereal	-4.6%
Cookies	1.3%
Crackers	4.7%
Chips & Snacks	4.7%
Soup	3.6%
Baby Formula/Electrolytes	8.9%
Coffee	-10.6%

CATEGORY	AVG PRICE PERCENT CHANGE IN 1996
Ice Cream	6.1%
Toothpaste	2.2%
Diapers	1.1%
Laundry Detergent	-2.2%
Toilet Tissue	6.0%
Paper Towels	7.6%
Cat Food	3.7%
Cigarettes	3.5%
Beer & Ale	4.0%
Wine	7.1%
Bottled Water	-0.6%
Carbonated Beverages	-0.3%
Batteries	4.6%

Source: Information Resources Inc.

Clipping Fewer Coupons

After years of steady growth, the number of cents-off coupons issued by marketers has begun to decline, and consumers are redeeming fewer. Some companies are trying other marketing strategies, ranging from price cuts to sponsorships of big events, and devoting less of their budgets to coupon promotions

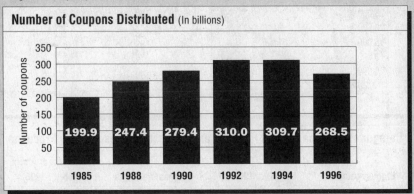

Number of Coupons Distributed (In billions)

1985	1988	1990	1992	1994	1996
199.9	247.4	279.4	310.0	309.7	268.5

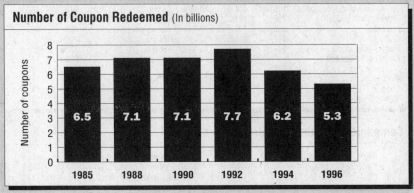

Number of Coupon Redeemed (In billions)

1985	1988	1990	1992	1994	1996
6.5	7.1	7.1	7.7	6.2	5.3

Average Face Value of Redeemed Coupons (In cents)

1985	1988	1990	1992	1994	1996
35	44	50	58	63	69

Source: NCH Promotional Services

Product Proliferation

Total number of new consumer packaged-goods products

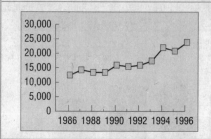

Year	New products
1986	12,436
1987	14,254
1988	13,421
1989	13,382
1990	15,879
1991	15,401
1992	15,886
1993	17,363
1994	21,986
1995	20,808
1996	24,496

Categories with the Largest Increase and Largest Decrease in New Products

Biggest gainers	1995	1996	Biggest decliners	1995	1996
Coffee	440	1,098	Chocolate candies	731	500
Eye makeup and accessories	105	481	Tea	647	492
Vitamins and tonics	790	1,111	Ice cream and ice cream cones	761	630
Lipsticks	399	705	All other baking mixes	286	167
Cheese	112	366	Jams, jellies, marmalades,		
Fingernail products	297	510	sweet butters	270	171
Facial cosmetics and			Sweet toppings	260	176
accessories	227	424	Cigarettes	162	92
Bath products	328	522	Sun-related products	169	115
Soap	344	476	Pickles, relishes, olives	182	129
Milk and non-dairy milk	85	210	Cookies	637	587

Companies With the Most New Products, 1996

1	Avon Products Inc.	649	15	Sumptuous Selections Inc.	157
2	Stella Bella Coffee	600	16	Colgate-Palmolive Co.	150
3	Circle of Beauty Inc.	424	17	Alpha Baking Co., Inc.	130
4	Procter & Gamble Co.	305		General Mills Inc.	130
5	Philip Morris Cos.	264		Le Tropique Inc.	130
6	L'Oreal	261	20	Expanding Horizons Marketing Inc.	126
7	Unilever U.S. Inc.	256	21	ConAgra Inc.	121
8	Coffee Creations Inc.	196		Dial Corp.	121
9	Estee Lauder Inc.	191	23	Campbell Soup Co.	110
10	Tsumura International Inc.	187	24	No Miss Nail Care Products Inc.	109
11	Revlon Inc.	177	25	RJR Nabisco Inc.	106
12	Grand Metropolitan Inc.	170			
13	Wise Woman Herbals Inc.	166		**Total Top 25 Companies**	**5,401**
14	Nestle	165		**% All New Products**	**22.0%**

Source: Marketing Intelligence Service, Ltd.

WHAT'S NEW

Bread that comes already coated with nuggets of honey and butter . . . no-drip glass cleaner . . . a one-step cookie/baking pan that requires no mixing or clean-up.

Those are some of the most innovative new packaged goods of the last year and a half, according to Marketing Intelligence Service Ltd. in Naples, N.Y. The company found that such timesavers were part of a small minority of truly distinctive products among the record 24,500 new packaged goods that hit the market in 1996.

The number of new products rose 18% in 1996 and topped 20,000 for the third year in a row, as marketers continued to seek sales and profit growth through expanded lines of merchandise. It's an expensive and risky marketing strategy. Most new packaged goods are me-too products or minor variations on existing brands, and their chance of survival on crowded store shelves is small. "The fact is that most new products fail simply because

they don't offer the consumer anything really different," says Tom Vierhile, general manager of Marketing Intelligence. The oft quoted failure rate for new products is 80%.

As usual, big companies like Avon Products Inc., Procter & Gamble Co. and Philip Morris Cos. dominated the list of new entries, but small companies, notably coffee marketers and personal-care product makers, also launched a large array of products. In fact, beauty-care items like lipstick, eye makeup and fingernail products were high on the list of categories with the biggest jump in new products. More recently, "fountain of youth" vitamins and nutritional supplements have been very hot, says Mr. Vierhile.

One surprisingly active new-product category is one of the oldest of products: milk. Now, there are carbonated milks and orange-flavored milk for kids and new varieties of fat-free milk for the health-conscious. "The dairy companies are waking up finally," says Mr. Vierhile. "They watched people gravitate for 30 years to soft drinks and other beverages.

The Name Game

Along with the proliferation of new products has come a surge in the number of trademark applications filed with the U.S. Patent and Trademark Office. That is making it harder for companies to think up catchy brand names that haven't already been taken.

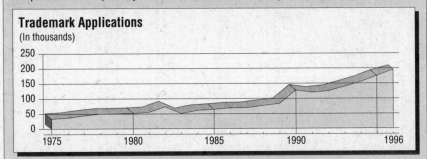

Trademark Applications
(In thousands)

Trademark Applications Filed and Registrations Issued

Year	Applications	Registrations	Year	Applications	Registrations
1975	33,898	27,324	1992	125,237	62,067
1980	52,149	14,614	1993	139,735	74,349
1985	64,677	63,122	1994	155,376	59,797
1990	127,294	56,515	1995	175,307	65,662
1991	120,365	43,152	1996	200,640	78,674

Source: U.S. Patent and Trademark Office

They've been acting like a commodity and letting branded products clean their clock."

Based on the categories with the greatest decline in new products, consumers may be indulging their sweet tooth less. Marketers are concocting significantly fewer new chocolate candies, ice creams, sweet toppings and cookies.

Ronald Alsop

Most Powerful Brands in the World

This ranking of the world's strongest brand names is based on four criteria: dominance over competitors, successful extension into new markets, customer commitment, and broad appeal to many demographic groups and nationalities.

Top 10 Brands

1. McDonald's	6. Gillette
2. Coca-Cola	7. Mercedes-Benz
3. Disney	8. Levi's
4. Kodak	9. Microsoft
5. Sony	10. Marlboro

Source: Interbrand Schechter

Blockbuster Brands

The American consumer's heart still belong's to big-name brands. While people are buying more store brands in some product categories, private-label merchandise accounts for only about 14% of total packaged-goods sales in food, drug, and mass-merchandise stores. Here is an assortment of some of the best-selling consumer products in the U.S.

Top Beverage Brands and Companies, Market Share and Volume

Brands	1995 share	1996 share	1995 cases (millions)	1996 cases (millions)	Volume % change
Coke Classic	20.8 %	20.8 %	1,868.6	1,929.2	+3.2%
Pepsi-Cola	15.0	14.9	1,344.3	1,384.6	+3.0
Diet Coke	8.8	8.7	793.0	811.4	+2.3
Sprite	5.1	5.8	460.3	541.5	+17.6
Dr. Pepper	5.7	5.8	515.0	536.9	+4.3
Mountain Dew	5.7	5.8	509.6	535.6	+5.1
Diet Pepsi	5.8	5.7	521.4	529.8	+1.6
7UP	2.5	2.4	219.9	219.5	-0.2
Caffeine-free Diet Coke	2.0	1.9	182.9	180.1	-1.6
Caffeine-free Diet Pepsi	1.1	1.0	96.5	96.9	+0.4

Companies	1995 share	1996 share	1995 cases (millions)	1996 cases (millions)	Volume % change
Coca-Cola	42.3 %	43.1 %	3,798.0	4,005.1	+5.5%
Pepsi-Cola	30.9	31.0	2,770.7	2,880.8	+4.0
Dr. Pepper/Seven Up	15.3	14.8	1,369.8	1,373.6	+0.3
Cott Corp.	2.7	2.9	245.0	265.0	+8.2
National Beverage	1.9	1.9	170.0	180.0	+5.9
Royal Crown	2.0	1.9	180.2	176.2	-2.2
Monarch	1.7	1.5	148.6	140.5	-5.5
Double Cola	0.3	0.3	31.0	31.2	+0.6
Big Red	0.3	0.3	27.2	28.3	+4.0
Private label/other	2.6	2.3	234.5	214.3	-8.6
Industry totals			**8,975.0**	**9,295.0**	**3.6**

Source: Beverage Digest/Maxwell Report

Top Cereal Brands, Based on 1996 Food Store Sales

Brands	Sales	Dollar market share
Kelloggs Frosted Flakes	$295,844,480	3.93%
General Mills Cheerios	286,388,528	3.80
Kelloggs Corn Flakes	216,370,752	2.87
General Mills Honey Nut Cheerios	211,663,008	2.81
Kelloggs Rice Krispies	188,278,380	2.50
Kelloggs Froot Loops	180,564,064	2.40
Kelloggs Raisin Bran	180,462,336	2.40
General Mills Lucky Charms	164,387,321	2.18
Kelloggs Special K	157,083,093	2.08
Kelloggs Corn Pops	153,257,623	2.03

Top Regular Ground Coffee Brands, Based on 1996 Food Store Sales

Brands	Sales	Dollar market share
Folgers	$504,231,168	27.8%
Maxwell House	394,910,976	21.8
Private Label	135,753,120	7.5
Maxwell House Master Blend	89,546,912	4.9
Hills Brothers	80,678,832	4.4
Chock Full O' Nuts	57,538,560	3.2
Maxwell House Lite	50,276,672	2.8
Folgers Coffee Singles	46,551,184	2.6
Yuban	45,691,056	2.5
MJB	37,965,456	2.1

Top Analgesic Brands, Based on 1996 Sales in Food, Drug and Mass-Merchandise Stores

Brands	Sales	Dollar market share
Tylenol	$586,828,800	23.3%
Private label	552,605,056	22.0
Advil	335,094,848	13.3
Aleve	140,077,520	5.6
Excedrin	131,535,424	5.2
Tylenol PM	113,102,736	4.5
Bayer	103,686,944	4.1
Motrin IB	77,383,024	3.1
Anacin	51,243,468	2.0
Orudis KT	46,613,168	1.9

Top Toothpaste Brands, Based on 1996 Sales in Food, Drug and Mass-Merchandise Stores

Brands	Sales	Dollar market share
Crest	$399,290,112	27.4%
Colgate	277,274,624	19.0
Mentadent	165,806,784	11.4
Aquafresh	152,454,928	10.5
Arm & Hammer	103,479,120	7.1
Sensodyn	49,045,760	3.4
Listerine	44,729,472	3.1
Rembrandt	40,115,392	2.8
Closeup	33,521,328	2.3

Top Laundry Detergent Brands, Based on 1996 Sales in Food, Drug and Mass-Merchandise Stores

Brands	Sales	Dollar market share
Tide	$1,541,733,888	36.6%
Cheer	348,902,400	8.3
Wisk	324,559,360	7.7
All	292,743,424	6.9
Surf	236,544,752	5.6
Purex	230,822,640	5.5
Gain	194,076,096	4.6
Arm & Hammer	175,891,552	4.2
Era	149,151,664	3.5
Private label	121,481,872	2.9

Top Brands of Potato Chips, Based on 1996 Food Store Sales

Brands	Sales	Dollar market share
Lays	$488,000,000	20.9%
Ruffles	407,000,000	17.4
Pringles	194,000,000	8.3
Private label	169,000,000	7.2
Baked Lays	122,000,000	5.2
Pringles Right Crisps	104,000,000	4.5
Wavy Lays	95,000,000	4.1
Frito Lay	89,000,000	3.8
Ruffles Choice	80,000,000	3.4
Wise	53,000,000	2.3

Source: Information Resources, Inc.

Top Brands of Diapers/Training Pants, Based on 1996 Food Store Sales

Brands	Sales	Dollar market share
Huggies	$1,455,000,000	40.5 %
Pampers	894,000,000	24.9
Private label	599,000,000	16.7
Luvs	449,000,000	12.5
Drypers	112,000,000	3.1
Fitti	40,000,000	1.1

Top Brands of Cookies, Based on 1996 Food Store Sales

Brands	Sales	Dollar market share
Private label	$452,000,000	12.7 %
Oreos	327,000,000	9.2
Chips Ahoy	295,000,000	8.2
Snackwells	188,000,000	5.3
Newtons	172,000,000	4.8
Chips Deluxe	124,000,000	3.5
Fudge Shoppe	99,000,000	2.8
Pepperidge Farm Distinctive	97,000,000	2.7
Nilla	72,000,000	2.0
Sandies	59,000,000	1.7

Top Brands of Refrigerated Orange Juice, Based on 1996 Food Store Sales

Brands	Sales	Dollar market share
Tropicana Pure Premium	$671,000,000	30.3%
Private label	533,000,000	24.0
Minute Maid	358,000,000	16.2
Tropicana Seasons Best	163,000,000	7.3
Florida's Natural	150,000,000	6.8
Minute Maid Premium Choice	52,000,000	2.3
Florida Gold	42,000,000	1.9
Tropicana Pure Premium Plus	41,000,000	1.8
Minute Maid Premium	30,000,000	1.4
Citrus World Donald Duck	17,000,000	0.8

Source: Information Resources Inc.

Largest Restaurant Chains

1996 Rank	1995 Rank	Chain	1996 U.S. Sales ($000)	% Sales Change vs. 1995	1996 U.S. Units	% Unit Change vs. 1995
1	1	McDonald's	$16,369,600	2.9%	12,094	6.4%
2	2	Burger King	7,484,645	9.2	7,057	6.9
3	3	Pizza Hut	4,917,000 *	-4.1	8,701	0.1
4	4	Taco Bell	4,419,122	1.0	6,645	6.0
5	5	Wendy's	4,284,046	6.6	4,369	4.1
6	6	KFC	3,900,000	5.4	5,079	-1.2
7	7	Hardee's	2,988,653 *	-7.7	3,225	-5.0
8	8	Subway	2,700,000	3.8	10,848	7.5
9	9	Dairy Queen	2,602,883 *	7.1	5,035	0.7
10	10	Domino's Pizza	2,300,000	2.2	4,300	1.6
11	12	Arby's	1,915,000 *	5.3	2,859	2.5
12	13	Denny's	1,883,832	3.9	1,571	2.7
13	14	Little Caesar	1,800,000 *	0.0	4,810 *	0.4
14	11	Red Lobster	1,776,400	-2.4	683	3.6
15	15	Dunkin' Donuts	1,593,972	10.9	3,200	8.1
16	17	Applebee's	1,464,277 *	22.0	823	22.8

1996 Rank	1995 Rank	Chain	1996 U.S. Sales ($000)	% Sales Change vs. 1995	1996 U.S. Units	% Unit Change vs. 1995
17	19	Jack in the Box	$1,248,738	8.0%	1,251	1.4%
18	18	Olive Garden, The	1,239,000	3.5	475	2.6
19	16	Shoney's	1,209,791	-4.0	844	-4.3
20	27	Boston Market	1,166,591	47.1	1,087	31.1
21	20	Chili's Grill and Bar	1,055,466	12.7	487	11.4
22	24	Cracker Barrel	1,029,548	21.1	283	19.4
23	25	Outback Steakhouse	1,021,220	27.9	372	25.3
24	22	Sonic Drive-Ins	1,012,722	11.4	1,587	6.4
25	23	T.G.I. Friday's	935,361	8.5	319	7.8
26	21	Long John Silver's	893,033	-2.0	1,451	-1.6
27	28	IHoP	756,555 *	11.3	685 *	7.2
28	26	Big Boy	750,000 *	-5.7	700 *	-5.4
29	33	Golden Corral	707,904 *	15.0	438 *	-2.4
30	30	Baskin-Robbins	681,200 *	4.8	2,611	6.3
31	29	Popeyes	666,200	1.5	893	1.7
32	32	Perkins Family Restaurants	659,152	4.0	453	0.7
33	36	Carl's Jr.	629,872	11.5	643	1.6
34	46	Starbucks	621,700 *	45.1	1,009	52.2
35	44	Papa John's	619,196	35.0	1,160	32.1
36	31	Ponderosa	610,000 *	-3.9	521	-10.9
37	37	Ryan's	597,607	7.9	281	12.0
38	34	Friendly Ice Cream	597,000	0.5	707	-3.8
39	35	Bob Evans	590,776	2.2	382	1.3
40	40	Chick-fil-A	569,714	13.6	715	9.2
41	39	Old Country Buffet	545,707 *	4.4	257 *	3.2
42	42	Ruby Tuesday	535,037	8.4	314	4.0
43	41	Churchs	526,200	5.0	990	4.0
44	43	Captain D's	468,264	0.4	598	-1.6
45	47	Luby's Cafeterias	464,078	9.0	222	16.2
46	45	Bennigan's	450,000 *	4.7	221	0.0
47	58	Lone Star	446,258	36.5	205	28.1
48	48	Whataburger	440,000 *	5.5	530 *	1.7
49	49	Waffle House	430,000 *	8.9	1,050	7.7
50	38	Sizzler	430,000 *	-22.0	306	-33.2

*Technomic estimate.

Source: Technomic, Inc.

WHAT'S FOR DINNER?

Percent of Dinner Orders Made at Restaurants that Include Item

Item	% of orders	Item	% of orders
Regular Soft Drink	25%	Diet Soft Drink	8%
French Fries	24%	Tap Water	7%
Pizza	24%	Iced Tea	6%
Side Dish Salad	17%	Fried Chicken	6%
Hamburger/Cheeseburger	16%	Alcohol	6%

Top Toys

Top Selling Toys Ranked by Dollar Sales, December 1996

Rank	Description	Manufacturer	Average retail price
1	Barbie Dream House Playset	Mattel	$89.59
2	Shoppin' Fun Barbie & Kelly Playset	Mattel	18.46
3	Pet Doctor Barbie Doll	Mattel	15.95
4	Sesame Street Tickle Me Elmo	Tyco Preschool	27.63
5	Cabbage Patch Kids-Snacktime Kid	Mattel	36.26
6	'96 Happy Holiday Barbie	Mattel	33.48
7	Hot Wheels 5 Car Gift Set Asst.	Mattel	4.70
8	My Size Dancing Barbie Doll	Mattel	118.44
9	Ocean Magic Barbie Doll	Mattel	14.78
10	Easy Bake Oven & Snack Center	Hasbro Toy Group	18.68
11	Jeep Wrangler	Power Wheels	193.59
12	Kawasaki Ninja ATV	Power Wheels	176.01
13	Wheel of Fortune Handheld	Tiger Electronics	18.92
14	Take Care of Me Twins	Toy Biz	29.48
15	Hot Wheels Super Electronic Garage	Mattel	45.62
16	6.0V Jet Turbo Battery Pack & Charger	Tyco	21.63
17	6.0V Jet Turbo Rebound 4 x 4 Asst.	Tyco	58.32
18	Barbie Beach Patrol	Power Wheels	216.38
19	XRC 9.6V Airdevil	Hasbro Toy Group	73.09
20	All-In-One Kitchen Center	Fisher-Price	66.04

Top Selling Toys Ranked by Dollar Sales, June 1997

Rank	Description	Manufacturer	Average retail price
1	Tamagotchi Virtual Pet Asst.	Bandai America	$15.04
2	The Lost World: Jurassic Park Basic Figure/Dinosaur Asst.	Hasbro Toy Group	5.87
3	Family Swim Center	Intex	42.74
4	Sesame Street Tickle Me Elmo	Tyco Preschool	29.02
5	XP-65 Super Soaker	Hasbro Toy Group	9.53
6	Nano Virtual Pet Asst.	Playmates Toys	14.87
7	Batman & Robin Figure Asst.	Hasbro Toy Group	5.80
8	8" Rainbow Snapset Pool	Intex	16.50
9	Star Wars Figure Asst. 1	Hasbro Toy Group	4.86
10	XP-105 Super Soaker	Hasbro Toy Group	13.57
11	Aquarium Pool	Intex	44.01
12	CPS-2000 Super Soaker	Hasbro Toy Group	30.16
13	10" Jungle Snapset Pool	Intex	36.31
14	Crazy Daisy	Fisher-Price	10.16
15	XXP-175 Super Soaker	Hasbro Toy Group	19.50
16	Super Crocodile Mile	Empire	28.44
17	Sesame Street Tickle Me Elmo Asst. 11"	Tyco Preschool	14.85
18	The Lost World: Jurassic Park Biting-Dino Asst.	Hasbro Toy Group	14.11
19	King Kool Lounge	Intex	8.13
20	Jeep Wrangler	Power Wheels	197.28

Source: NPD Group, Inc.

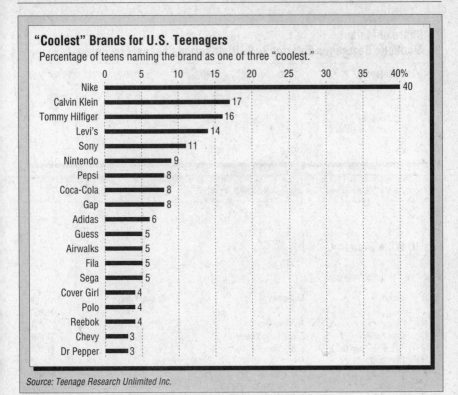

"Coolest" Brands for U.S. Teenagers

Percentage of teens naming the brand as one of three "coolest."

Brand	Percentage
Nike	40
Calvin Klein	17
Tommy Hilfiger	16
Levi's	14
Sony	11
Nintendo	9
Pepsi	8
Coca-Cola	8
Gap	8
Adidas	6
Guess	5
Airwalks	5
Fila	5
Sega	5
Cover Girl	4
Polo	4
Reebok	4
Chevy	3
Dr Pepper	3

Source: Teenage Research Unlimited Inc.

Alcoholic-Beverage Market

The alcoholic-beverage business went flat in the first half of the 1990s, but showed slight growth in 1996.

Alcoholic Beverages Entering U.S. Distribution Channels by Category

(In millions of gallons)

Category	1970	1975	1980	1985	1990	1991	1992	1993	1994	1995	1996
Beer	3,804	4,659	5,515	5,664	5,986	5,854	5,836	5,836	5,803	5,754	5,828
Wine	267	368	478	493	421	410	440	424	437	451	480
Distilled spirits	388	446	452	426	376	347	347	340	333	328	330
Low-alcohol refreshers	–	–	*	98	107	92	90	101	124	108	94
Cider	*	*	*	*	*	*	1	1	1	4	6
Total	4,459	5,473	6,445	6,681	6,890	6,703	6,714	6,702	6,698	6,645	6,738

*Less than 500,000 gallons.

Share of Market
Alcoholic Beverages Entering U.S. Distribution Channels by Category

Category	1970	1980	1990	1996
Beer	85.3%	85.6%	86.9 %	86.5%
Wine	6.0	7.4	6.1	7.1
Distilled spirits	8.7	7.0	5.5	4.9
Low-alcohol refreshers	–	*	1.6	1.4
Cider	*	*	*	0.1
Total	100.0	100.0	100.0	100.0

*Less than 0.05%.
Source: Impact's Annual Beer, Wine and Distilled Spirits Report

Top 10 Wine Brands

(thousands of nine-liter cases)

Rank	Brand	Company	Origin/Type	Depletions 1996
1	Franzia	The Wine Group	California Table	15,800
2	Carlo Rossi	E. & J. Gallo Winery	California Table	11,800
3	Gallo Livingston Cellars	E. & J. Gallo Winery	California Table	11,150
4	The Wine Cellars of Ernest & Julio Gallo	E. & J. Gallo Winery	California Table	9,500
5	Almaden	Canandiagua Wine Co., Inc.	California Table	7,165
6	Inglenook	Canandiagua Wine Co., Inc.	California Table	6,960
7	Sutter Home	Sutter Home Winery, Inc.	California Table	6,255
8	Woodbridge	Robert Mondavi Winery	California Table	4,685
9	Glen Ellen	Heublein Wines Group, Inc. (IDV/Grand Met)	California Table	3,475
10	Vendange	Sebastiani Vineyards	California Table	3,200
	Total Top 10			79,990

Source: Impact Databank

Top 10 Distilled Spirit Brands[1]

(thousands of nine-liter cases)

Rank	Brand	Distiller/Importer	Category	Depletions 1996
1	Bacardi[2]	Bacardi-Martini USA, Inc.	Rum	6,050
2	Smirnoff[3,4]	Heublein, Inc. (IDV/Grand Met)	Vodka	5,950
3	Seagram's Gin	The House of Seagram	Gin	3,625
4	Absolut[3]	The House of Seagram	Vodka	3,330
5	Jim Beam	Jim Beam Brands Co. (American Brands)	Bourbon	3,080
6	Seagram's 7 Crown	The House of Seagram	Blended Whiskey	3,015
7	Jack Daniel's Black	Brown-Forman Beverages Worldwide	Tennessee Whiskey	3,010
8	Canadian Mist	Brown-Forman Beverages Worldwide	Canadian Whiskey	2,885

Rank	Brand	Distiller/Importer	Category	Depletions 1996
9	Popov	Heublein, Inc. (IDV/Grand Met)	Vodka	2,805
10	E & J	E. & J. Gallo Winery	Brandy	2,775
	Total Top 10			36,525

[1] Excludes distilled spirits-based low-alcohol refreshers.
[2] Includes Light, Dark, 151, Black, Reserve, and Anejo.
[3] Includes flavored vodkas.
[4] Excludes Smirnoff Black.

Top 10 Beer Brands*

(millions of barrels)

Rank	Brand	Brewer/Importer	Segment	Shipments 1996
1	Budweiser	Anheuser-Busch, Inc.	Premium	36.3
2	Bud Light	Anheuser-Busch, Inc.	Light	20.7
3	Miller Lite	Miller Brewing Co. (Philip Morris)	Light	15.9
4	Coors Light	Coors Brewing Co.	Light	13.2
5	Busch	Anheuser-Busch, Inc.	Sub-Premium	8.1
6	Natural Light	Anheuser-Busch, Inc.	Light	7.1
7	Miller Genuine Draft	Miller Brewing Co. (Philip Morris)	Premium	5.6
8	Miller High Life	Miller Brewing Co. (Philip Morris)	Sub-Premium	4.4
9	Busch Light	Anheuser-Busch, Inc.	Light	4.3
10	Milwaukee's Best	Miller Brewing Co. (Philip Morris)	Sub-Premium	4.3
	Total Top 10			119.9

* Excludes commercial exports and shipments to Puerto Rico, U.S. possessions and armed forces overseas, including U.S. armed forces post exchanges

Source: Impact Databank

Cigarette Market

A long-term decline in cigarette sales to U.S. consumers ended with an increase in consumption in 1994. Meanwhile, exports of cigarettes are growing fast.

U.S. Consumption of Cigarettes

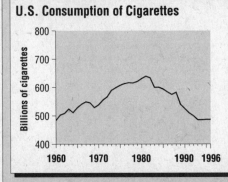

Billions of cigarettes

1960   1970   1980   1990   1996

U.S. Consumption vs. Exports of Cigarettes

Year	U.S. Consumption	Exports
1960	484,400,000,000	20,200,000,000
1970	536,400,000,000	29,200,000,000
1980	631,500,000,000	82,000,000,000
1990	525,000,000,000	164,300,000,000
1991	510,000,000,000	179,200,000,000
1992	500,000,000,000	205,600,000,000
1993	485,000,000,000	195,500,000,000
1994	486,000,000,000	220,200,000,000
1995	487,000,000,000	231,100,000,000
1996	487,000,000,000	243,900,000,000

Source: U.S. Agriculture Department

Top Tobacco Brands

Twelve Month Unit Volume Comparisons for the Leading U.S. Cigarette Brands

	1995			1996			
	Billions of cigarettes	Share	Ranking	Billions of cigarettes	Share	Percent volume change	Ranking
Philip Morris							
Marlboro	144.87	30.1%	1	156.21	32.3%	7.8%	1
Basic	22.66	4.7	6	23.17	4.8	2.2	6
Virginia Slims	11.55	2.4	10	11.57	2.4	0.2	10
Merit	11.44	2.4	11	11.33	2.3	(1.0)	11
Benson & Hedges	11.31	2.4	12	11.11	2.3	(1.8)	12
RJR Nabisco							
Doral	27.54	5.7	4	28.57	5.9	3.7	3
Winston	27.67	5.8	3	25.40	5.3	(8.2)	5
Camel*	21.33	4.4	7	22.47	4.6	5.3	7
Salem	17.88	3.7	8	17.33	3.6	(3.1)	8
Lorillard							
Newport	26.99	5.6	5	29.30	6.1	8.6	2
Brown & Williamson							
GPC	28.11	5.8	2	28.10	5.8	–	4
Kool*	17.14	3.6	9	17.21	3.6	0.4	9
Total leading brands	368.49	76.6		381.77	79.0	3.6	

*Includes filter and non-filter.
Source: The Maxwell Consumer Report, Davenport & Co.

Cigar Revival

Annual Cigar Consumption

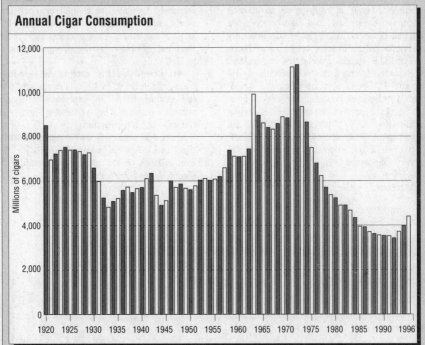

Cigar Consumption in the U.S.

Year	Annual cigar consumption	Per capita cigar consumption		Year	Annual cigar consumption	Total pop.	Male pop.
		Total pop.	Male pop.				
1920	8,502,008,000	80	269	1985	4,335,448,000	18	55
1925	7,391,824,000	64	216	1986	3,948,894,000	16	50
1930	6,583,431,000	53	177	1987	3,919,987,000	16	49
1935	5,215,948,000	41	131	1988	3,706,702,000	15	45
1940	5,709,686,000	43	136	1989	3,620,630,000	15	44
1945	5,114,339,000	39	130	1990	3,553,659,000	14	42
1950	5,607,939,000	37	116	1991	3,530,432,000	14	42
1955	6,077,966,000	37	121	1992	3,518,098,000	14	41
1960	7,103,334,000	39	136	1993	3,423,424,000	13	40
1965	8,948,594,000	46	163	1994	3,718,115,000	14	43
1970	8,881,120,000	44	152	1995	3,970,264,000	15	45
1975	8,645,540,000	41	136	1996	4,396,810,000	17	50
1980	5,374,436,000	24	75				

Source: Cigar Association of America

AGGRESSIVE ADVERTISERS

Madison Avenue is enjoying an advertising boom the likes of which it hasn't seen since the mid-1980s, reflecting the healthy economy and fierce battles in some consumer markets.

Total U.S. spending on advertising in 1997 is expected to rise 6.2% to $186 billion, said Robert J. Coen, McCann-Erickson Worldwide's senior vice president in charge of forecasting. He predicted that 1998 spending would rise 5.6%. "Advertising follows the economy; it does not lead it," Mr. Coen said. "So even if the economy slows a bit, the advertising momentum should continue well into late 1997."

Marketing battles on the automobile, phar-

maceutical and telecommunications fronts helped spur the advertising gains, along with increased spending for computers, beer and mutual funds. Among the media, cable television, magazines, newspapers and radio were expected to enjoy the strongest growth in 1997.

Mr. Coen said the current ad-spending boom, which began in 1993, is reminiscent of the previous 1975–1987 expansion, with one notable exception: "I don't think it's going to last as long," he cautioned.

Mr. Coen predicted that overseas advertising in 1997 would grow 6.3% to $225.5 billion. In 1998, he said, overseas expenditures should increase by 6.6%.

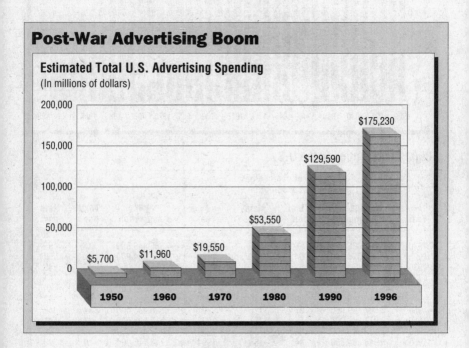

Post-War Advertising Boom

Estimated Total U.S. Advertising Spending
(In millions of dollars)

1950	$5,700
1960	$11,960
1970	$19,550
1980	$53,550
1990	$129,590
1996	$175,230

Estimated Annual U.S. Advertising Expenditures
(In millions of dollars)

	1990	1991	1992	1993	1994	1995	1996
Television	$29,073	$28,189	$30,450	$31,698	$35,435	$37,828	$42,484
Newspapers	32,281	30,409	30,737	32,025	34,356	36,317	38,402
Direct Mail	23,370	24,460	25,391	27,266	29,638	32,866	34,509
Radio	8,726	8,476	8,654	9,457	10,529	11,338	12,269
Yellow Pages	8,926	9,182	9,320	9,517	9,825	10,236	10,849
Magazines	6,803	6,524	7,000	7,357	7,916	8,580	9,010
Other	20,411	20,230	21,098	22,220	23,981	25,765	27,707
Total	129,590	127,470	132,650	139,540	151,680	162,930	175,230

Source: Robert J. Coen, McCann-Erickson

Top 25 Advertisers in 1996
($ in thousands)

Company	Total	Company	Total
1 General Motors Corp.	$1,710,726.5	15 Grand Metropolitan PLC	$579,529.2
2 Procter & Gamble Co.	1,493,456.0	16 News Corp.	573,434.2
3 Philip Morris Cos.	1,236,978.4	17 Toyota Motor Corp.	560,180.1
4 Chrysler Corp.	1,089,153.3	18 General Motors Corp. Dealer Assn.	477,673.5
5 Ford Motor Co.	897,666.1		
6 Johnson & Johnson	840,466.6	19 Nestle SA	477,460.1
7 Walt Disney Co.	773,291.3	20 General Motors Corp. Local Dealers	449,244.9
8 Pepsico Inc.	767,978.2		
9 Time Warner Inc.	747,035.2	21 American Home Products Corp.	446,425.3
10 AT&T Corp.	659,750.2		
11 Ford Motor Co. local dealers	614,007.2	22 Nissan Motor Co.	439,390.7
12 McDonalds Corp.	599,132.9	23 National Amusements Inc.	426,343.4
13 Unilever PLC	593,378.1	24 Sony Corp.	417,875.0
14 Sears Roebuck & Co.	589,469.4	25 Kellogg Co.	410,352.4

Source: Competitive Media Reporting and Publishers Information Bureau

Top 10 Magazine Advertisers in 1996 ($ in thousands)

	Company	Report total
1	General Motors Corp.	$456,433.1
2	Philip Morris Cos.	343,147.8
3	Procter & Gamble Co.	280,194.3
4	Ford Motor Co.	280,152.0
5	Chrysler Corp.	269,451.5
6	Time Warner Inc.	156,415.6
7	Johnson & Johnson	154,612.9
8	Toyota Motor Corp.	126,060.7
9	Unilever PLC	125,246.0
10	Nestle SA	118,911.5

Top 10 Sunday Magazine Advertisers in 1996 ($ in thousands)

	Company	Report total
1	National Syndications Inc.	$97,208.6
2	Roll International Corp.	45,337.4
3	Kaye Elizabeth Inc.	30,841.3
4	Bertelsmann AG	30,559.9
5	Sony Corp.	28,238.2
6	Bradford Exchange	26,884.7
7	Johnson & Johnson	18,823.2
8	Merck & Co.	18,468.7
9	Glaxo Wellcome PLC	18,282.1
10	Chrysler Corp.	17,807.9

Top 10 Newspaper Advertisers in 1996 ($ in thousands)

	Company	Report total
1	Ford Motor Co. Local Dealers	$525,068.7
2	General Motors Corp. Local Dealers	366,887.1
3	Federated Department Stores	339,530.5
4	May Department Stores Co.	326,140.7
5	News Corp. Ltd.	294,135.5
6	Toyota Motor Corp. Local Dealers	272,417.7
7	Circuit City Stores Inc.	250,297.4
8	Valassis Communications Inc.	234,376.9
9	Chrysler Corp. Local Dealers	197,695.3
10	Sears Roebuck & Co.	193,058.1

Top 10 Network TV Advertisers in 1996 ($ in thousands)

	Company	Report total
1	General Motors Corp.	$613,872.7
2	Procter & Gamble Co.	589,467.9
3	Johnson & Johnson	504,776.7
4	PepsiCo Inc.	423,402.5
5	Philip Morris Co.	403,066.9
6	McDonalds Corp.	372,009.6
7	Ford Motor Co.	319,683.5
8	Grand Metropolitan PLC	294,402.4
9	Chrysler Corp.	280,464.9
10	Walt Disney Co.	267,208.8

Top 10 Spot TV Advertisers in 1996 ($ in thousands)

	Company	Report total
1	Chrysler Corp.	$369,672.4
2	General Motors Corp. Dealer Assn.	328,156.4
3	General Motors Corp.	285,233.3
4	Ford Motor Co. Dealer Assn.	260,101.6
5	PepsiCo Inc.	236,739.2
6	Political Advertising	233,126.6
7	Procter & Gamble Co.	198,650.4
8	Philip Morris Cos.	188,646.1
9	General Mills Inc.	185,220.9
10	Toyota Motor Corp	183,120.6

Top 10 Syndicated TV Advertisers in 1996 ($ in thousands)

	Company	Report total
1	Procter & Gamble Co.	$186,777.2
2	Philip Morris Cos. Inc.	100,294.7
3	Kellogg Co.	90,628.3
4	Unilever PLC	86,152.6
5	Johnson & Johnson	73,472.1
6	Grand Metropolitan PLC	61,421.0
7	American Home Products Corp.	59,912.5
8	McDonalds Corp.	52,925.4
9	General Motors Corp.	52,346.0
10	Mars Inc.	47,773.6

Source: Competitive Media Reporting and Publishers Information Bureau

Top 10 Cable TV Advertisers in 1996 ($ in thousands)

	Company	Report total
1	Procter & Gamble Co.	$201,161.3
2	General Motors Corp.	116,649.7
3	AT&T Corp.	98,547.1
4	Time Warner Inc.	94,003.3
5	Sprint Corp.	76,223.7
6	Philip Morris Cos.	74,938.3
7	Grand Metropolitan PLC	72,034.8
8	Unilever PLC	62,616.6
9	Kellogg Co.	61,266.2
10	Hasbro Inc.	60,569.8

Top 10 Network Radio Advertisers in 1996 ($ in thousands)

	Company	Report total
1	Sears Roebuck & Co.	$50,679.8
2	U.S. Government	32,699.5
3	Warner-Lambert Co.	28,717.8
4	Chrysler Corp.	24,836.4
5	Visa International	22,384.8
6	Himmel Group	22,770.2
7	Reading Genius Home Study	21,420.8
8	General Motors Corp.	20,551.8
9	Procter & Gamble Co.	20,256.6
10	AT&T Corp.	17,237.8

Top 10 National Spot Radio Advertisers in 1996 ($ in thousands)

	Company	Report total
1	Political Advertising	$33,224.6
2	News Corp.	30,945.6
3	Chrysler Corp. Dealer Assn.	26,079.0
4	General Motors Corp.	24,335.4
5	Walt Disney Co.	23,721.4
6	CompUSA Inc.	21,012.7
7	National Amusements Inc.	20,380.9
8	U.S. Government	18,628.7
9	US West Inc.	18,188.7
10	AT&T Corp.	16,184.6

Top 10 Outdoor Advertisers in 1996 ($ in thousands)

	Company	Report total
1	Philip Morris Cos.	$81,817.2
2	B.A.T Industries PLC	46,550.2
3	RJR Nabisco Holdings Corp.	29,416.6
4	General Motors Corp.	23,094.9
5	McDonalds Corp.	19,732.2
6	Anheuser-Busch Cos.	15,650.5
7	Loews Corp.	15,458.4
8	Local misc. entertainment - not itemized	11,499.5
9	General Motors Corp. Local Dealers	10,956.2
10	Seagram Co.	10,632.9

Source: Competitive Media Reporting and Publishers Information Bureau

Most Popular Print Ads of 1996

Based on surveys of about 20,000 consumers who were asked to name the most outstanding ad they had seen recently in magazines or newspapers.

1996 rank	1995 rank	Brand	Ad agency
1	2	Absolut	TBWA Chiat/Day
2	9	Nike	Wieden & Kennedy
3	4	Calvin Klein	CRK Advertising
4	1	Milk	Bozell
5	10	Camel	Mezzina/Brown
6	6	Ford	WRG-BDDP and J. Walter Thompson
7	7	Marlboro	Leo Burnett
8	5	Revlon	Tarlow Advertising
9	3	Budweiser	DDB Needham
10	—	Guess	In-house

Source: Video Storyboard Tests Inc.

TV Commercial Stars

Consumers rated these sports and entertainment celebrity endorsers as the most credible stars in television ads in 1996.

Sports Presenters

1. Michael Jordan
2. Shaquille O'Neal
3. Charles Barkley
4. Grant Hill
5. Deion Sanders
6. Larry Bird
7. Arnold Palmer
8. Dennis Rodman
9. George Foreman
10. Wayne Gretzky

Entertainment Presenters

1. Candice Bergen
2. Whoopi Goldberg
3. Bill Cosby
4. Jerry Seinfeld
5. Cindy Crawford
6. Elizabeth Taylor
7. Kate Jackson
8. Rosie O'Donnell
9. Jonathan Pryce
10. Cybill Shepherd

Source: Video Storyboard Tests Inc.

Top 25 Television Advertising Campaigns of 1996

Advertising campaigns that consumers considered the most "outstanding" they had seen. Ranking based on surveys of about 20,000 people, primarily at shopping malls.

1996 rank	1995 rank	Brand (Agency)
1	1	Budweiser (DDB Needham)
2	3	Pepsi (BBDO)
3	2	McDonald's (Leo Burnett)
4	10	Dryer's/Edy's (Goldberg, Moser, O'Neill)
5	5	Coca-Cola (CAA)
6	9	Bud Light (DDB Needham)
7	8	Milk (Goodby, Silverstein)
8	–	Nissan (TBWA/Chiat-Day)
9	4	Little Caesars (Cliff Freeman & Partners)
10	17	Duracell (Ogilvy & Mather)
11	11	Nike (Wieden & Kennedy)
12	21	M&M/Mars (BBDO)
13	–	Old El Paso (Leo Burnett)
14	19	Energizer (TBWA/Chiat-Day)
15	6	Pizza Hut (BBDO)
16	–	Ford (J. Walter Thompson/WRG)
17	–	Polaroid (Goodby, Silverstein)
18	–	Levi's (Foote Cone and Belding)
19	13	Taco Bell (Bozell; Salvati Montgomery)
20	7	AT&T (FCB/Leber Katz, McCann-Erickson, Young & Rubicam)
21	–	Coors Light/Coors (Foote Cone and Belding)
22	15	Jeep (Bozell)
23	–	Burger King (Ammirati Puris Lintas)
24	–	Infinity (TBWA/Chiat-Day)
25	12	Doritos (BBDO)

Source: Video Storyboard Tests Inc.

Marketers Take the Direct Route

Direct marketing is expected to maintain its momentum through the rest of the decade. Business-to-business sales growth will continue to outpace consumer sales increases.

Largest Industries by Direct-Marketing Sales Volume in the Consumer Marketplace (In billions)

	1991	1995	1996*	1997	2001	Compound Annual Growth '91-'96	'96-2001
Non-store retailers	$48.812	$63.769	$67.605	$72.016	$93.455	6.7%	6.7%
Nonprofit organizations	46.032	62.273	65.435	68.697	87.647	7.3	6.0
Auto dealers/service stations	44.989	58.792	63.400	67.054	85.161	7.1	6.1
Food stores	29.955	32.674	33.559	34.530	38.949	2.3	3.0
Food/related products	26.624	31.356	32.611	34.091	42.837	4.1	5.6
Insurance carriers/agents	20.317	27.530	30.181	33.464	55.056	8.2	12.8
Real estate	21.058	27.091	28.810	30.702	40.642	6.5	7.1
Health services	15.952	24.739	27.726	31.705	58.255	11.7	16.0
Specialty retailers	19.931	24.411	25.836	27.147	31.428	5.3	4.0
Personal/repair services	14.244	17.763	18.814	19.963	26.965	5.7	7.5

*Rankings are based on 1996 statistics.
Source: Direct Marketing Association

Direct-Marketing Sales by Medium (In billions)

	1991	1995	1996	1997	2001	Compound Annual Growth '91-'96	'96-2001
Direct Mail	**$263.3**	**$364.4**	**$391.8**	**$421.3**	**$584.9**	**8.3%**	**8.3%**
Consumer	173.9	231.8	246.1	261.6	346.7	7.2	7.1
Business-to-business	89.4	132.7	145.6	159.7	238.2	10.2	10.3
Telephone marketing	**287.5**	**379.3**	**412.9**	**450.8**	**643.5**	**7.5**	**9.3**
Consumer	124.5	157.6	168.8	181.8	248.8	6.3	8.1
Business-to-business	163.0	221.7	244.0	269.1	394.6	8.4	10.1
Newspaper	**103.4**	**131.5**	**141.5**	**151.4**	**206.8**	**6.5**	**7.9**
Consumer	66.8	81.3	86.4	91.5	119.7	5.3	6.7
Business-to-business	36.6	50.1	55.1	60.0	87.1	8.5	9.6
Magazine	**43.6**	**59.7**	**64.7**	**69.8**	**96.7**	**8.2**	**8.4**
Consumer	23.0	30.3	32.4	34.5	45.9	7.1	7.2
Business-to-business	20.6	29.3	32.3	35.3	50.9	9.4	9.5
Television	**49.9**	**72.2**	**79.1**	**86.4**	**127.6**	**9.7**	**10.0**
Consumer	31.3	43.5	47.1	50.8	72.0	8.5	8.9
Business-to-business	18.5	28.7	32.1	35.6	55.6	11.7	11.6
Radio	**18.2**	**26.9**	**29.2**	**31.8**	**45.4**	**9.9**	**9.2**
Consumer	10.6	15.2	16.3	17.6	24.2	9.0	8.2
Business-to-business	7.6	11.7	12.9	14.2	21.2	11.2	10.4
Other	**41.5**	**54.7**	**58.5**	**62.2**	**81.1**	**7.1**	**6.8**
Consumer	28.2	35.5	37.4	39.3	48.8	5.8	5.5
Business-to-business	13.3	19.3	21.0	22.9	32.2	9.6	8.9
Total	**807.4**	**1,088.7**	**1,177.6**	**1,273.8**	**1,785.9**	**7.8**	**8.7**
Consumer	**458.3**	**595.2**	**634.6**	**677.1**	**906.1**	**6.7**	**7.4**
Business-to-business	**349.1**	**493.5**	**543.0**	**596.7**	**879.8**	**9.2**	**10.1**

Source: Direct Marketing Association

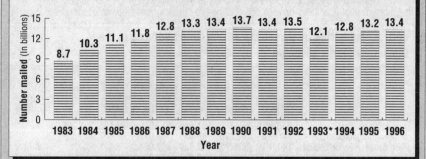

Estimated Number of Catalogs Mailed to Consumers and Businesses

Number mailed (In billions)

Year	1983	1984	1985	1986	1987	1988	1989	1990	1991	1992	1993*	1994	1995	1996
Number mailed	8.7	10.3	11.1	11.8	12.8	13.3	13.4	13.7	13.4	13.5	12.1	12.8	13.2	13.4

*Revision in formula used to calculate catalog volume.

Catalog Sales and Projections (In billions)

Year	Sales	Year	Sales
1990	$47.6	1996	$74.6
1991	49.8	1997	79.8
1992	53.4	1998	85.1
1993	59.2	1999	91.0
1994	65.3	2000	97.1
1995	69.9		

Source: Direct Marketing Association

How to Curtail the Catalogs and Sales Calls

It's impossible to stop all junk mail and telemarketing calls, but frustrated consumers can reduce the volume by contacting the Direct Marketing Association, an industry trade group. To have their names removed from telephone lists, consumers should write to Telephone Preference Service, Direct Marketing Association, P.O. Box 9014, Farmingdale, NY, 11735-9014. To get off mailing lists, people should contact the Mail Preference Service, Direct Marketing Association, P.O. Box 9008, Farmingdale, NY, 11735-9008.

Largest Catalog Marketers

Rank	Company	1995 sales ($ millions)	1996 sales ($ millions)	Market segment
1	Dell Computer Corp.	$5,144.0	$7,554.0	Computer hardware
2	Gateway 2000	3,676.0	5,035.0	Computer hardware
3	J.C. Penney	3,378.0	3,772.0	General merchandise
4	Digital Eqipment	3,000.0*	3,300.0*	Computer hardware
5	Micro Warehouse	1,308.0	1,916.0	Computer hardware, software and peripherals
6	Spiegel	1,760.0	1,681.0	General merchandise
7	Fingerhut	1,782.0	1,638.0	General merchandise
8	Viking Office Products	920.7	1,182.3	Office supplies
9	Lands' End	1,030.0	1,112.0	Apparel
10	Computer Discount Warehouse	634.5	927.9	Computer hardware, software and peripherals
11	Global DirectMail Corp.	634.6	911.9	Computer, office and industrial supplies
12	L.L. Bean	945.0	908.0	Apparel
13	IBM Direct	900.0*	900.0*	Computer hardware
14	Henry Schein	616.2	829.9	Medical, dental and veterinary supplies
15	Brylane	601.1	736.4	Apparel
16	Hanover Direct	749.8	700.3	General merchandise
17	Victoria's Secret	661.0	684.0	Apparel
18	J. Crew Group	640.0*	650.0	Apparel
19	Deluxe Direct	678.5	603.5	Business supplies and stationery
20	Newark Electronics	600.0*	550.0*	Industrial electronics

* Estimate.
Source: Catalog Age

Licensed Merchandise Sales

Whether it's Mickey Mouse or the Olympics, licensed merchandise is a huge business, generating retail sales in 1996 of more than $72 billion.

Licensed Product Retail Sales
U.S. & Canada, by Property Type, 1995-1996
($ in billions)

Property type	1995	1996	% change 1995/1996	% of total 1996
Art	$5.08	$5.20	2%	7%
Celebrities/estates	2.54	2.57	1	4
Entertainment/character	16.19	16.70	3	23
Fashion	12.16	12.60	4	17
Music	1.08	1.03	-5	1
Non-profit	0.69	0.70	–	1
Publishing	1.59	1.64	-1	2
Sports	13.39	13.79	3	19
Trademarks/brands	14.20	15.11	6	21
Toys/games	2.78	2.71	-1	4
Other	0.22	0.23	–	–
Total	69.93	72.28	3	100

Source: The Licensing Letter

Marketing Patrons

More marketers are paying to link their corporate and brand names to sporting and entertainment events, arts programs, and charitable causes.

Sponsorship Spending in North America

*Projected.
Source: IEG Sponsorship Report

Sponsorship Spending by Type of Property (In millions)

	1996	1997*
Sports	$3,540	$3,840
Pop music/entertainment tours	566	650
Festivals, fairs, annual events	512	558
Causes	485	535
Arts	323	354
Total	5,426	5,937

*Projected.
Source: IEG Sponsorship Report

Sponsored By . . .

The 10 Largest Corporate Sponsors in 1996

1. Philip Morris	$120–$125 million
2. Anheuser-Busch	$115–$120 million
3. Coca-Cola	$90–$95 million
4. General Motors	$70–$75 million
5. PepsiCo	$60–$65 million
6. AT&T	$50–$55 million

7. Eastman Kodak	$45–50 million
RJR Nabisco	$45–50 million
9. Chrysler	$40–45 million
IBM	$40–45 million

Source: IEG Sponsorship Report.

Shop Till You Drop

Growth in number of shopping centers, total retailing space, retailing space per capita, and annual sales.

Year	Total square footage	Number of centers	Square feet per capita	Sales
1964*	1,010,000,000	7,600	5.3	$ 78,700,000,000
1972	1,649,972,000	13,174	7.9	123,159,000,000
1976	2,338,210,000	17,523	10.7	211,504,000,000
1980	2,962,701,000	22,050	13.0	385,501,000,000
1984	3,375,632,000	25,508	14.2	475,130,000,000
1988	3,947,025,000	32,563	16.1	641,097,000,000
1991	4,563,800,000	37,975	18.1	716,913,000,000
1992	4,678,527,000	38,966	18.3	768,220,248,000
1993	4,770,700,000	39,633	18.5	806,645,004,000
1994	4,860,920,000	40,368	18.7	851,282,088,000
1995	4,967,160,000	41,235	18.9	893,814,776,000
1996	5,100,000,000	42,130	19.2	933,918,275,000

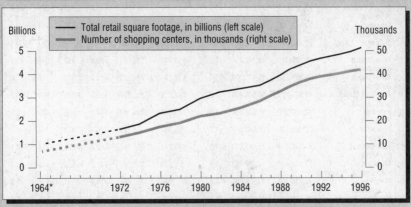

*Estimated.
Source: International Council of Shopping Centers

Ten Largest U.S. Shopping Centers (Gross Leasable Area)

Name & location	Size (square feet)	Name & location	Size (square feet)
Mall of America Bloomington, MN	4,200,000 (2,574,525 retail GLA)	**Sawgrass Mills** Sunrise, FL	2,350,000
Del Amo Fashion Center Torrance, CA	3,000,000	**Roosevelt Field Mall** Garden City, NY	2,100,000
South Coast Plaza/ Crystal Court Costa Mesa, CA	2,918,236	**The Galleria** Houston, TX	2,100,000
Woodfield Mall Schaumburg, IL	2,700,000	**Oak Brook Shopping Center** Oak Brook, IL	2,013,000
		Garden State Plaza Paramus, NJ	1,909,804
		Tysons Corner Center McLean, VA	1,900,000

Source: National Research Bureau and International Council of Shopping Centers

Retail Giants

The nation's largest retailers rang up $716.1 billion in sales in 1996, a 9.2% increase from 1995, according to the National Retail Federation. Drug and discount stores showed continued steady gains, with sales increases of 11% and 7.7% respectively. Apparel and specialty stores bounced back from a difficult year in 1995, with sales growth of nearly 12%. Supermarkets and department stores registered about a 5% sales increase, while home-improvement stores showed a 3.6% gain.

Top 100 Retailers

	Company (Headquarters)	Volume (000)			Earnings (loss) (000)			Units		
		1996	1995	Change	1996	1995	Change	1996	1995	Change
1	Wal-Mart (Bentonville, AR)	$104,859,000	$93,627,000	+20.2%	$3,056,000	$2,740,000	+11.5%	3,054	2,943	+3.8%
2	Sears, Roebuck (Hoffman Estates,IL)	38,236,000	34,995,000	+9.3	1,271,000	1,801,000	-29.4	3,372	2,306	+46.2
3	Kmart (Troy , MI)	31,437,000	31,713,000	-0.9	(220,000)	(571,000)	—	2,419	2,477	-2.3
4	Dayton Hudson (Minneapolis)	25,371,000	23,516,000	+7.9	463,000	311,000	+48.9	1,100	1,029	+6.9
5	Kroger (Cincinnati)	25,170,909	23,937,795	+5.2	349,873	302,813	+15.5	2,187	2,144	+2.0
6	JCPenney (Plano,TX)	22,653,000	20,562,000	+10.2	565,000	838,000	-32.6	3,927	1,883	+108.6
7	Price/Costco (Issaquah, WA)	19,566,456	18,247,286	+7.2	248,793	133,878	+85.8	252	240	+5.0
8	Home Depot (Atlanta)	19,535,503	15,470,358	+26.3	937,739	731,523	+28.2	512	423	+21.0
9	American Stores (Salt Lake City)	18,678,129	18,308,894	+2.0	287,221	316,809	-9.3	1,695	1,650	+2.7
10	Safeway (Pleasanton, CA)	17,269,000	16,397,500	+5.3	460,600	326,300	+41.2	1,052	1,059	-0.7
11	Federated (Cincinnati)	15,228,999	15,048,513	+1.2	265,864	74,553	+256.6	411	412	-0.2
12	Albertsons (Boise, ID)	13,776,678	12,585,034	+9.5	493,779	464,961	+6.2	826	764	+8.1
13	Winn-Dixie (Jacksonville, FL)	12,955,488	11,787,843	+9.9	255,634	232,187	+10.1	1,178	1,175	+0.3
14	Walgreen (Deerfield, IL)	11,778,408	10,395,096	+13.3	371,749	320,791	+15.9	2,193	2,117	+3.6
15	May Dept. Stores (St. Louis)	11,650,000	10,484,000	+11.1	755,000	752,000	+0.4	365	346	+5.5
16	Ahold USA (Atlanta)	11,200,000	8,335,800	+34.4	354,200	222,000	+59.5	895	655	+36.5
17	Publix (Lakeland, FL)	10,400,000	9,360,000	+11.1	265,200	242,300	+9.5	544	492	+10.6
18	A&P (Montvale, NJ)	10,089,014	10,101,356	-0.1	73,032	57,224	+27.6	1,014	973	+4.2
19	Toys "R" Us (Paramus, NJ)	9,932,400	9,426,900	+5.4	427,400	148,100	+188.6	1,372	1,203	+14.0
20	Food Lion (Salisbury, NC)	9,005,932	8,210,884	+9.7	206,070	172,361	+19.6	1,112	1,073	+3.6
21	Limited (Columbus, OH)	8,644,791	7,881,437	+9.7	434,208	961,511	-54.8	3,897	5,298	-26.4
22	Lowe's (N. Wilkesboro, NC)	8,600,241	7,075,442	+21.6	292,150	226,027	+29.3	402	365	+10.1
23	Woolworth (New York)	8,092,000	8,224,000	-1.6	169	(164)	-	7,746	8,178	-5.3
24	Best Buy (Minneapolis)	7,770,683	7,217,448	+7.7	1,748	48,019	-96.4	272	247	+10.1
25	Circuit City (Richmond, VA)	7,663,811	7,029,123	+9.0	136,414	179,375	-24.0	448	383	+17.0

Company (Headquarters)	Volume (000)			Earnings (loss) (000)			Units		
	1996	1995	Change	1996	1995	Change	1996	1995	Change
26 Rite Aid (Camp Hill, PA)	$6,970,201	$5,446,017	+28.0%	$115,377	$158,947	-27.4%	3,623	2,759	+31.3%
27 Southland (Dallas)	6,955,263	6,824,278	+1.9	89,476	270,763	-67.0	5,422	5,424	—
28 TJX (Framingham, MA)	6,689,410	3,975,115	+68.3	363,123	26,261	+1,282.7	1,136	1,116	+1.8
29 Tandy (Fort Worth, TX)	6,285,486	5,839,067	+7.6	(91,571)	211,974	—	6,999	6,952	+0.7
30 Dillard (Little Rock, AR)	6,227,600	5,918,000	+5.2	238,600	167,200	+42.7	250	238	+5.0
31 Meijer (Grand Rapids, MI)	6,100,000	5,600,000	+8.9	NA	NA	—	110	99	+11.1
32 Office Depot (Delray Beach, FL)	6,068,598	5,313,192	+14.2	129,042	132,399	-2.5	570	504	+13.1
33 Montgomery Ward (Chicago)	5,900,000	6,500,000	-9.2	(249,000)	—	—	398	398	—
34 CVS (Woonsocket, RI)	5,528,110	4,865,025	+13.6	75,363	(657,106)	—	1,431	1,366	+4.8
35 Ralphs (Compton, CA)	5,500,000	4,250,000	+29.4	NA	NA	—	410	320	+28.1
36 Vons (El Monte, CA)	5,407,400	5,070,700	+6.6	104,700	68,100	+53.7	325	328	—
37 Gap (San Francisco)	5,284,381	4,395,253	+20.2	452,859	354,039	+27.9	1,854	1,680	+10.4
38 H.E.B. (San Antonio, TX)	5,225,000	5,150,000	+1.5	NA	NA	—	235	230	+2.2
39 Revco (Twinsburg, OH)	5,087,700	4,431,900	+14.8	76,200	61,100	+24.7	2,184	2,118	+3.1
40 Nordstrom (Seattle)	4,453,063	4,113,517	+8.3	147,505	165,112	-10.7	83	78	+6.4
41 Waban (Natick, MA)	4,375,528	3,978,384	+10.0	76,660	72,977	+5.0	165	150	+10.0
42 Supervalu Retail (Eden Prairie, MN)	4,138,000	4,121,500	+0.4	—	—	—	300	285	+5.3
43 Staples (Westborough, MA)	3,967,665	3,068,061	+29.3	106,420	73,705	+44.4	574	460	+24.8
44 Service Merchandise (Nashville, TN)	3,955,016	4,018,525	-1.6	39,330	50,325	-21.8	400	409	-2.2
45 Giant Food (Landover, MD)	3,880,959	3,860,579	+0.5	85,504	102,153	-16.3	174	169	+3.0
46 CompUSA (Dallas)	3,829,786	2,035,901	+88.1	59,665	24,339	+145.1	106	85	+24.7
47 Fred Meyer (Portland, OR)	3,724,839	3,422,718	+8.8	58,545	30,286	+93.3	218	137	+59.1
48 Pathmark (Woodbridge, NJ)	3,710,500	3,971,600	-6.6	(20,800)	32,800	—	145	209	-30.6
49 Fleming Retail (Oklahoma City)	3,627,140	3,850,440	-5.8	—	—	—	310	350	-11.4
50 Penn Traffic (Syracuse, NY)	3,296,462	3,536,642	-6.8	(41,430)	(79,625)	—	265	265	—
51 OfficeMax (Shaker Heights, OH)	3,179,274	2,542,513	+25.0	68,805	125,763	-45.3	574	468	+22.6
52 Mercantile Stores (Fairfield, OH)	3,030,822	2,944,324	+2.9	$121,465	123,248	-1.4	102	101	+1.0
53 Spiegel (Downers Grove, IL)	3,014,620	3,184,184	-5.3	(13,389)	(9,481)	—	489	450	+8.7
54 Menard (Eau Claire, WI)	3,000,000	2,700,000	+11.1	—	—	—	128	115	+11.3
55 Intimate Brands (Columbus, OH)	2,997,340	2,516,555	+19.1	258,210	204,059	+26.5	1,609	—	—
56 Hannaford Bros. (Scarborough, ME)	2,957,559	2,568,061	+15.2	75,205	70,201	+7.1	139	134	+3.7
57 Bruno's (Birmingham, AL)	2,899,044	2,891,076	+0.3	(51,189)	(75,837)	—	218	258	-15.5
58 Smith's Food & Drug (Salt Lake City)	2,889,988	3,083,737	-6.3	(164,166)	(40,512)	—	150	154	-2.6
59 Longs Drug Stores (Walnut Creek, CA)	2,828,338	2,644,376	+7.0	58,612	46,228	+26.8	337	328	+2.7
60 Hy-Vee (W. Des Moines, IA)	2,800,000	2,650,000	+5.7	NA	NA	—	230	185	+24.3

Company (Headquarters)	Volume (000)			Earnings (loss) (000)			Units		
	1996	1995	Change	1996	1995	Change	1996	1995	Change
61 **Consolidated Stores** (Columbus, OH)	$2,647,500	$1,406,000	+88.3%	$83,900	$64,400	+30.3%	1,798	861	+108.8%
62 **Payless Cashways** (Kansas City)	2,642,829	2,680,186	-1.4	(19,078)	(128,549)	—	192	200	-4.0
63 **Caldor** (Norwalk, CT)	2,602,456	2,765,525	-5.9	(185,325)	(301,028)	—	161	170	-5.3
64 **Shaw's** (E. Bridgewater, MA)	2,575,000	2,250,000	+14.4	—	—	—	116	88	+31.8
65 **Dominick's** (Northlake, IL)	2,512,000	2,450,000	+2.5	(7,000)	NA	—	102	97	+5.2
66 **Barnes & Noble** (New York)	2,448,124	1,976,900	+23.8	51,225	(52,976)	—	1,008	997	+1.1
67 **Randalls Markets** (Houston)	2,400,000	2,350,000	+2.1	NA	NA	—	121	125	-3.2
68 **Kohl's** (Menomonee Falls, WI)	2,388,221	1,925,669	+24.0	102,478	72,652	+41.1	150	128	+17.2
69 **Payless Shoesource** (Topeka, KS)	2,333,700	2,330,300	+0.1	107,700	54,000	+99.4	4,236	3,923	+8.0
70 **Shopko Stores** (Green Bay, WI)	2,333,407	1,968,016	+18.6	44,946	38,439	+16.9	130	129	+0.8
71 **Grand Union** (Wayne, NJ)	2,312,673	2,307,810	+0.2	(183,354)	(139,192)	—	226	232	-2.6
72 **Wegman's** (Rochester, NY)	2,250,000	2,100,000	+7.1	—	—	—	66	63	+4.8
73 **Autozone** (Memphis, TN)	2,242,600	1,808,100	+24.0	167,200	138,800	+20.5	1,423	1,143	+24.5
74 **Giant Eagle** (Pittsburgh)	2,200,000	2,100,000	+4.8	—	—	—	136	133	+2.3
75 **Hechinger** (Largo, MD)	2,199,067	2,252,780	-2.4	(25,076)	(77,636)	—	117	118	-0.8
76 **Ames** (Rocky Hill, CT)	2,161,680	2,104,231	+2.7	17,301	(1,618)	—	290	307	-5.5
77 **Dollar General** (Nashville)	2,134,398	1,764,188	+21.0	115,100	87,818	+31.1	2,734	2,416	+13.2
78 **Neiman Marcus** (Chestnut Hill, MA)	2,075,003	1,888,249	+9.9	77,424	55,608	+39.2	32	30	+6.7
79 **Fingerhut Cos.** (Minnetonka, MN)	2,027,356	2,077,344	-2.4	40,159	50,858	-21.0	0	2	-100.0
80 **Borders Group** (Ann Arbor, MI)	1,958,800	1,749,000	+12.0	57,900	(211,100)	—	1,118	1,008	+10.9
81 **Saks** (New York)	1,944,862	1,686,787	+15.3	24,144	(64,095)	—	86	64	+34.4
82 **Raleys** (Sacramento, CA)	1,925,000	1,850,000	+4.1	—	—	—	87	82	+6.1
83 **Bilks** (Charlotte, NC)	1,900,000	1,800,000	+5.6	—	—	—	230	235	-2.1
84 **Proffitt's** (Knoxville, TN)	1,889,779	1,661,056	+13.8	37,399	(1,419)	—	174	135	+28.9
85 **Hills Stores** (Canton, MA)	1,878,477	1,900,104	-1.1	(35,058)	(16,666)	—	165	164	—
86 **Harris-Teeter** (Charlotte, NC)	1,833,042	1,711,813	+7.1	48,459	42,114	+15.1	134	139	-3.6
87 **Pep Boys—MM&J** (Philadelphia)	1,828,539	1,594,340	+14.7	100,824	81,824	+23.2	604	503	+20.1
88 **Musicland** (Minneapolis)	1,821,594	1,722,572	+5.7	(193,738)	(135,750)	—	1,466	1,496	-2.0
89 **Weis Markets** (Sunbury, PA)	1,753,246	1,646,435	+6.5	78,855	79,419	-0.7	155	151	+2.6
90 **Schnuck Markets** (St. Louis)	1,750,000	1,500,000	+16.7	—	—	—	92	85	+8.2
91 **Family Dollar** (Matthews, NC)	1,714,627	1,546,895	+10.8	60,587	58,109	+4.3	2,581	2,416	+6.8
92 **Ross Stores** (Newark, CA)	1,689,810	1,426,397	+18.5	80,905	43,272	+87.0	309	292	+5.8
93 **Stater Brothers** (Colton, CA)	1,650,000	1,625,000	+1.5	—	—	—	112	111	+0.9
94 **Bradlees** (Braintree, MA)	1,619,444	1,840,926	-12.0	(218,759)	(311,946)	—	109	134	-18.7
95 **Burlington Coat Factory** (Burlington, NJ)	1,610,892	1,597,028	+0.9	29,013	14,866	+95.2	244	211	+15.6

	Company (Headquarters)	Volume (000)			Earnings (loss) (000)			Units		
		1996	1995	Change	1996	1995	Change	1996	1995	Change
96	**Heilig-Meyers** (Richmond, VA)	$1,593,119	$1,359,349	+17.2%	$40,185	$41,504	-3.2%	944	716	+31.8%
97	**Petsmart** (Phoenix)	1,501,017	1,168,056	+28.5	20,591	(5,436)	—	397	262	+51.5
98	**Venture** (O'Fallon, MO)	1,485,759	1,928,808	-23.0	(58,478)	(19,855)	—	113	115	-1.7
99	**Ingles Markets** (Asheville, NC)	1,472,578	1,385,127	+6.3	20,731	17,023	+21.8	189	189	—
100	**Marsh Supermarkets** (Indianapolis)	1,451,730	1,390,543	+4.4	(244)	9,033	—	275	271	+1.5

Source: National Retail Federation

Estimated Annual Apparel Sales

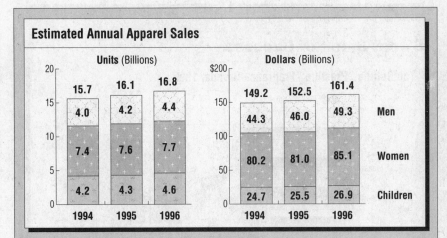

Units (Billions)

1994	1995	1996
15.7	16.1	16.8
4.0	4.2	4.4
7.4	7.6	7.7
4.2	4.3	4.6

Dollars (Billions)

1994	1995	1996	
149.2	152.5	161.4	
44.3	46.0	49.3	Men
80.2	81.0	85.1	Women
24.7	25.5	26.9	Children

Changing Apparel Market Shares, by Type of Retailer

Discount stores have improved their clothing lines and stolen share from other retailers.

	Unit share (%)			Dollar share (%)		
	1994	1995	1996	1994	1995	1996
Department stores	10.1%	9.7%	9.4%	19.5%	19.0%	18.5%
Specialty stores	11.8	11.6	11.4	21.7	22.0	21.3
Major mass merchandise chains	14.7	14.8	14.6	16.8	16.7	16.9
Discount stores	39.3	41.1	42.2	19.2	19.7	19.8
Off-price retailers	5.6	5.4	5.5	6.8	6.3	6.4
Factory outlets	4.3	4.3	4.1	4.0	4.3	4.2
Direct mail	4.0	3.8	3.8	5.7	5.6	6.3
Other outlets	10.2	9.4	9.0	6.3	6.3	6.6

Source: NPD Group Inc.

Loyalty to Levi's

In the fickle world of fashion, shoppers are most loyal to these brands:

Top Men's Brands Ranked by Repurchase Intent

1992	1994	1996
1. Levi's	1. Levi's	1. Levi's
2. Gold Toe	2. Starter	2. Land's End
3. Dockers	3. Dockers	3. L.L. Bean
4. Fruit of the Loom	4. Russell Athletic	4. Nike
5. Reebok	5. Hanes	5. Gold Toe
6. Bugle Boy	5. Gold Toe	5. London Fog
7. Champion	7. Fruit of the Loom	6. Reebok
8. Hanes	8. Lee	8. Champion
9. London Fog	8. Reebok	9. Arizona
9. Nike	10. Champion	9. Disney
		9. Hanes

Top Women's Brands Ranked by Repurchase Intent

1992	1994	1996
1. Levi's	1. Levi's	1. Levi's
2. London Fog	2. London Fog	2. Hanes
3. Liz Claiborne	3. Hanes	3. Reebok
4. Dockers	3. Hanes Her Way	4. Hanes Her Way
5. Lee	4. Hanes	5. L.L. Bean
6. Leslie Fay	5. Reebok	6. Arizona
7. Nike	6. Dockers	7. Fruit of the Loom
8. Reebok	6. Fruit of the Loom	7. Lee
8. Russell Athletic	8. Just My Size	7. London Fog
10. Champion	9. Nike	10. Disney
10. Hanes	10. Lee	

Sources: Kurt Salmon Associates and NPD Group Inc.

Sweet Smell of Success

Top Selling "Prestige" Fragrance Brands, 1996

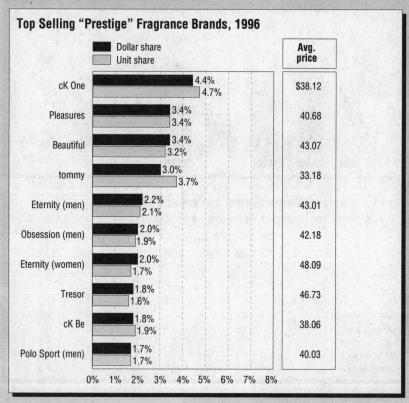

Dollar share / Unit share

Brand	Dollar share	Unit share	Avg. price
cK One	4.4%	4.7%	$38.12
Pleasures	3.4%	3.4%	40.68
Beautiful	3.4%	3.2%	43.07
tommy	3.0%	3.7%	33.18
Eternity (men)	2.2%	2.1%	43.01
Obsession (men)	2.0%	1.9%	42.18
Eternity (women)	2.0%	1.7%	48.09
Tresor	1.8%	1.6%	46.73
cK Be	1.8%	1.9%	38.06
Polo Sport (men)	1.7%	1.7%	40.03

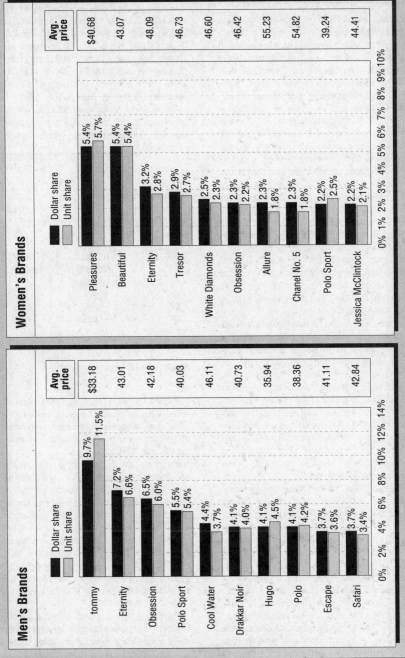

Men's Brands

	Dollar share	Unit share	Avg. price
tommy	9.7%	11.5%	$33.18
Eternity	7.2%	6.6%	43.01
Obsession	6.5%	6.0%	42.18
Polo Sport	5.5%	5.4%	40.03
Cool Water	4.4%	3.7%	46.11
Drakkar Noir	4.1%	4.0%	40.73
Hugo	4.1%	4.5%	35.94
Polo	4.1%	4.2%	38.36
Escape	3.7%	3.6%	41.11
Safari	3.7%	3.4%	42.84

Women's Brands

	Dollar share	Unit share	Avg. price
Pleasures	5.4%	5.7%	$40.68
Beautiful	5.4%	5.4%	43.07
Eternity	3.2%	2.8%	48.09
Tresor	2.9%	2.7%	46.73
White Diamonds	2.5%	2.3%	46.60
Obsession	2.3%	2.2%	46.42
Allure	2.3%	1.8%	55.23
Chanel No. 5	2.3%	1.8%	54.82
Polo Sport	2.2%	2.5%	39.24
Jessica McClintock	2.2%	2.1%	44.41

Source: NPD Group Inc.

SECOND-HAND SHOPPING

WHEN SHE WALKS into a thrift shop, Kate Turner-Walker pauses a moment and takes a deep breath. She's judging the store's aura. If the "feel of fashion" isn't in the sometimes musty mix—that means no Chanel, no Versace, no Ralph Lauren tucked in the racks—the 22-year-old graduate student cruises on.

A self-described "aggressive and highly successful" thrift-store shopper, Ms. Turner-Walker has developed a kind of sixth sense that kicks in as soon as she enters a second-hand store. Once, flipping through a rack of old trench coats, she touched a familiar fabric. "It felt like a Burberry," says the Washington, D.C., resident. Peeling away the edge of the lining, which had been sewn inside-out, she saw the familiar plaid and nabbed the coat for a few dollars. Some of her other recent finds: a Coach bag, minus the strap, for $5 (she got a new strap from Coach for $30), a Ralph Lauren silk skirt for a measly 85 cents, a 1950s vintage black dress with fine-tooled beadwork for $5. "The hunt is very satisfying," she says.

So are the savings. As many consumers see little growth in their disposable income, the thrift business, both upscale and downscale, is hot. Used goods, ranging from clothes and computers to cribs and CDs, are selling briskly. The National Association of Resale and Thrift Shops, a trade group, says its membership jumped 12% during the past year to 1,000. So popular is second-hand shopping in Philadelphia that a company called Thrift Shop Maniac Enterprises offers frequent, all-day "Rackin' 'n Rollin'" bus tours to area thrift shops.

Sales of used goods take many forms. There are, of course, the traditional non-profits like Goodwill Industries and the Salvation Army, and many specialty vintage clothiers. Some chains that sell new merchandise, such as Urban Outfitters Inc., buy used items in bulk from distributors and recast them as "renewal" clothes for a young clientele. Some resellers buy goods outright; others work only on consignment, meaning they pay for the merchandise only if it sells.

Several resale chains and franchises have sprung up in recent years and are reporting strong growth. The aptly named Grow Biz International Inc. of Minneapolis started with a franchise that sells a mix of new and used sporting goods, but in the last 10 years the company has branched into four other areas: new and used CDs, musical instruments, kids' clothes and accessories, and computers. Today, Grow Biz boasts 19 company-owned stores and more than 1,200 franchises; it planned to add another 300 franchises in 1997. At Children's Orchard, a franchise-operation based in Ann Arbor, Mich., that sells all sorts of kids' stuff, 1996 revenues grew nearly 22% from 1995, coming close to the $13 million mark, says president Walt Hamilton.

Goodwill's Growth

Annual retail revenue for Goodwill Industries and percent change

YEAR	RETAIL REVENUE (IN MILLIONS)	PERCENT CHANGE
1996	$598.7	16.6%
1995	513.5	9.2
1994	470.3	11.6
1993	421.6	10.1
1992	382.9	6.6

Source: Goodwill Industries International

Forget the stereotype of a dark shop cluttered with polyester blouses, dented coffee pots and chipped figurines. "Secondhand stores are coming out of church basements," says Susan Whittaker, president of the resale trade group. Instead, she says, many resellers are opening "showplaces" to sell their used name-brand wares, and some traditional thrift stores are improving their image to compete better. "We've upgraded our appearance," says Dave Barringer, director of brand management for Goodwill. The company plans to renovate a slew of its 1,300 stores and is building "bigger and brighter" stores from the ground up. Already, Goodwill's retail sales have taken off, spurting 17% to nearly $600 million in 1996.

Appealing to young professionals and other shoppers who love a bargain, upscale consignment shops have found a profitable niche in fancy neighborhoods. On Manhattan's Upper East Side, in a four block radius, several stores hawk used designer labels, discounted at least 30% off the retail price. Resembling small boutiques, the stores claim to carry only current fashions—usually a year or two old— that have been "gently used." That means the clothes must be spotless, absolutely no stains or snags.

Next to an Eileen Fisher boutique and above a gourmet grocery, Michael's: A Consignment Shop for Women and Brides, targets "women who can afford to buy one Chanel suit a season, but want to buy three," says owner Laura Fluhr, whose father opened the store over 40 years ago. A black Geoffrey Beene evening dress that sold for $875 hangs behind the counter. It would retail for about $4,000, says Ms. Fluhr, as she turns over the hem of the skirt revealing the nicely finished seam. A glass case houses an assortment of pricey handbags, tagged with such names as Hermes, Judith Leiber and Chanel, selling from $250 and up; retail they would go for $400 and up. The most expensive item in the shop: a sable coat for $2,500. The store's sales have doubled since 1991, says Ms. Fluhr, though she declined to disclose exact figures, saying only, "it's in the seven figures."

Consumers shop secondhand for many reasons. The price, of course, can't be beat. "You can give in to whimsy," says Jennifer DeMeritt, 27, of Manhattan, as she holds up a green polyester football jersey. "But you don't have to pay for it by eating frijoles for a week." The shirt's price: $6.

There's also a sense, especially among the younger crowd, that wearing used clothes distinguishes a person from the droves suited in the sedate fashions of Banana Republic and J. Crew. For Joseph D'Amico, the "jeans expert" at Cheap Jack's in New York, it's a matter of quality. He claims that jeans from the 1970s were made with a heavier fabric than they are today. The older fabric, always 100% cotton, holds up as it ages; even better, it softens. "You could sleep in these jeans," says the 27-year old Mr. D'Amico. "I should know; I've done so several times."

Men like Mr. D'Amico are shopping at thrift stores more these days. Typically, men hang onto their clothes longer than women do, the

reason for the historically sluggish sales of used men's clothing. But sales of men's clothes, especially long and short-sleeved shirts, increased 50% in the last year, says Mary Cochran, vice president of operations for Goodwill of Greater New York. For the first time, the demand has outstripped the supply. One New York shop, Gentlemen's Resale specializes in men's designer labels. A black Donna Karan suit sells for $345 (about $1,500 new), and a $120 Hermes tie goes for $60.

Used goods—whether clothing, sports equipment or furniture—especially appeal to parents of growing kids. At a Children's Orchard, tucked in a strip mall in East Hanover, N.J., such trendy brands as Baby Gap and Gymboree sell for as little as 50% of the retail price. And at a Gaithersburg, Md., Toy Traders store, manager Phil Bloom brags he has a matched-set oak crib and changing table for $200 that would fetch $550 new.

"Kids who are seven or eight buy Rollerblades, how long will they be able to wear them?" asks Grow Biz spokesman Richard Brill. Grow Biz's Play It Again Sports, which over the past 15 years has grown into the nation's largest used-sporting goods chain, reported sales in 1996 of $275 million.

There's even a growing secondhand market in the computer industry, which markets every innovation as a must-have. RE-PC, a Seattle company, caters to consumers who shudder at the thought of plunking down $3,000 for cutting-edge technology. A quarter to a third of RE-PC's business comes from first-time users who don't mind buying a computer "one processor shelf down" to save money, says Mark Dabek, part-owner of the store. Its warehouse showroom stocks a wide selection of computer hardware—from high-end Pentium machines to those odd computer parts treasured by computer geeks. Mr. Dabek recalls the time a customer called asking for a 360K floppy drive, an artifact from the 1980s. "I don't know why anybody would want one," he says. "But we had one."

Laurie Snyder

Lost Sales

Shoplifting and employee theft are the two major causes of "inventory shrinkage" for the retailing industry.

Sources of Inventory Shrinkage

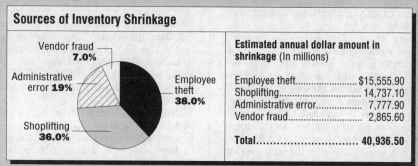

Vendor fraud **7.0%**

Administrative error **19%**

Shoplifting **36.0%**

Employee theft **38.0%**

Estimated annual dollar amount in shrinkage (In millions)

Employee theft	$15,555.90
Shoplifting	14,737.10
Administrative error	7,777.90
Vendor fraud	2,865.60
Total	**40,936.50**

Sources: National Retail Federation and Center for Retailing Education, University of Florida

Customer Dissatisfaction

Better Business Bureaus received about 1.8 million complaints from customers in 1996, with these types of businesses provoking the most gripes. In a sign of the changing times, computer sales and service companies made the top 10 for the first time in 1995.

1995 rank	1996 rank	Type of business	1996 No. of complaints
1	1	Auto dealers, franchised	14,668
2	2	Auto repair shops (mechanical–except transmission)	9,728
4	3	Home furnishing stores (exc. mattress, window, floor cov.)	7,792
5	4	Services, miscellaneous	7,129
3	5	Home remodeling contractors-general	6,829
12	6	Auto dealers, used only	6,164
8	7	Computer sales/services	5,733
15	8	Telephone companies (local and long-distance)	5,682
14	9	Retail stores, other	4,898
6	10	Dry cleaning/laundry companies	4,649

Source: Council of Better Business Bureaus

Workplace

It is 8 p.m. on a weeknight and Dad is on his PC, sending e-mail to employees, while Mom alternates phone calls to the PTA and business clients overseas. Between tasks they help their children with homework and pack tomorrow's school lunches. By bedtime, the couple will have together put in more than 20 hours on their jobs and another 14 hours on childcare and household chores—time that increasingly overlaps and blends together.

Technology, global competition and the ever increasing number of two-income couples are radically altering the boundaries of the workplace. No longer are work and family rigidly separated as they were for most of the past century. PCs, fax machines and voice mail have made it as convenient to work from the family den as the office cubicle—bringing work increasingly into the home and expanding work time far beyond nine-to-five schedules.

For many, the new workplace is more egalitarian and convenient. With 75% of married employees wedded to spouses who also work, men and women are more equally sharing the demands of paid employment and parenting. Gender roles have blurred: Just as more women now are employed as judges, car mechanics and executives, more men are preparing family meals and diapering babies.

Some 30 million U.S. households are equipped with home offices—one third more than in 1992. Although women are still more likely to work entirely from home, according to the U.S. Labor Department, men and women work from home in equal proportions. The trend signals both rapid small-business growth and the desire among parents to be close to their children. Many employees with home offices put in long days doing business—but try to fit their work schedules around family demands, starting work at, say, 6 a.m. but breaking mid-day to pick children up from school or coach them at sports, and then continuing work in the evening.

But such choices are also triggering new kinds of stress. With no clear division between work and home, there is no getting away. Those with professional and managerial jobs, whether they work mostly from home or from corporate offices, increasingly are expected to be on call evenings, weekends, even vacations—to answer phone calls and stay in touch with customers, staff and bosses virtually around the clock. All of which adds up to more time spent at work. According to research by Juliet Schor, an economics professor at Harvard University and author of *The Overworked American*, the average American is working 163 more hours each year—or a month more of full time work—than in 1970.

Underlying some of this heightened load is the rapid pace of technological change, which has created a crisis mentality, a feeling that everything has to be done *now*. Before faxes and e-mail were so readily available, proposals went in the mail and there was a day or two to think about them. But now responses are expected to be instantaneous.

The result is that many employees feel overloaded with tasks that all seem equally pressing. Joanne Spigner, a Madison, N.J., consultant who runs corporate training seminars, says many of the employees she advises are trying to do so much they don't have time "to think or plan or enjoy their work." Instead of prioritizing, they think that everything is urgent.

Moreover, in the reengineered and global workplace, slowing down seems an impossible fantasy. Downsizings have saddled leaner staffs with more work—and workplace paranoia. Among some survivors of downsizings, "there's such gratitude to still have a white-collar job that people develop a masochistic adherence to superhuman demands," says Steven Berglas, director of the Executive Stress Clinic in Chestnut Hill, Mass.

At the same time, global competition means more frequent around-the-clock business negotiating. When a U.S. company goes after a contract with China, some manager is likely to be overseeing the faxes and phones in the middle of the night when it is the middle of the day in Asia. And top executives who a generation ago did much of their dealmaking at the local club now are luring customers on distant continents.

Karl Krapek, president and chief executive of Pratt & Whitney, for example, often starts a workday at his company's headquarters in Connecticut, jets to Paris or Frankfurt for an evening business meeting, then flies on the next morning to Tokyo—a 14-hour flight—for yet another negotiation with a customer. On one recent U.S. to Europe to Asia trip, two of his staff begged off the Asia leg of the journey, insisting they were simply too fatigued to continue, especially since they only planned to be in Tokyo for six hours. But Mr. Krapek went on, convinced the brief stopover was worth it, especially if it increased his chances of clinching an important contract for his company. He didn't slow down on returning home, either—making sure to reserve time for his wife and two sons, while also scheduling meetings with his staff. In today's competitive business climate, he says, the ability to make decisions quickly and swiftly change strategies or direction is critical.

In a 1996 book called *Home and Work*, author Christena Nippert-Eng coined the term "the greedy workplace" to describe an increasingly common type of employer, one that demands so much energy and commit-ment that it limits workers' ability to have a personal life. And a survey of 100 CEOs by Christian & Timbers found that while 85% say they want to spend more time with family, only 7% believe they will.

Other research suggests that as people sink more energy and time into their jobs, they have become consumed with work and have little desire to do much else. Sociologist Arlie Hochschild sees a cultural reversal under way in which the workplace is for some people becoming a retreat and surrogate home, while home is being invaded by the pressures and deadlines of work.

In her study of employees at one company with family-friendly policies—such as part-time and flex-time scheduling—Ms. Hochs-child found that many employees were so attached to their jobs that they didn't take advantage of the policies. Instead, they chose longer hours at work—because they felt more valued and supported by coworkers than by their relatives at home, or because they feared the consequences of appearing uncom-mitted to their jobs.

Ms. Hochschild's findings, reported in her book *The Time Bind: When Work Becomes Home and Home Become Work*, are disputed by many working parents who have sought to adjust their careers in favor of more family time. Consider Doug Tifft, a 40-year-old father of two who has worked part-time and scaled back career aspirations since he and his wife adopted their first child eight years ago. He has changed jobs to attain part-time hours, going backward in income and status to his current job in the production depart-ment of a university publisher. He hopes to get back on a faster track once his younger child starts kindergarten, but for now wants two weekdays free to create "a home life" and share unplanned time with his kids—taking walks in the woods, playing games, or simply talking and listening.

In a similar vein, Gail Heiring Varma, asso-ciate national director of human resources at Deloitte Touche, telecommutes from her New Providence, N.J., home on Mondays and Fri-days and spends midweek at her company's Wilton, Conn., headquarters. She packs in 12-hour days at the office when she is away from her family. But at home, she encourages her two children, ages 11 and 15, to do their homework in her office while she talks with staff on the phone.

Ms. Varma says she no longer strives to achieve a separate but equal balance between work and home, preferring instead to blend the two realms. But that effort often means simultaneously doing a variety of disparate tasks at once. Many mornings, she is out of her house by 5:30 a.m. to take her daughter to ice skating practice. While watching her daughter skate, Ms. Varma power walks around the rink—getting in her daily exer-cising—and simultaneously answers business calls on a cellular phone. "Blending two or three things at once is the only way to get it all done," she says.

Little wonder, then, that psychologists and management consultants say they are seeing many workers who appear to have it all—suc-cessful and lucrative jobs and loving families—yet are stressed and unhappy. In the struggle to juggle the often conflicting demands of work, marriage and parenting, juggling can become an end in itself. "We define ourselves by how much we do rather than what we love or value," putting a premium on proficiency rather than passion, says Carol Farmer, a Boca Raton, Fla., consultant and futurist.

Moreover, as sociologist Ms. Hochschild has observed, home itself is becoming more regimented and professionalized. Even when they don't abandon home for work, many working couples transform their family lives into a workplace of sorts by keeping them-selves and their children perpetually sched-uled. A walk in the park is a workout or not worth the time. Dinner parties are business networking opportunities. And instead of hanging out on the block, playing ball or hide and seek, kids make play dates.

A lot goes by the wayside, including unstructured time to putter or the sheer delight of watching a child play ball instead of simply feeling relief to have made it to the game. "A lot of people seem afraid when they have an unplanned moment and they run from quiet," says Mr. Tifft, who cherishes his part-time schedule precisely because it offers him quiet time.

Still, few families can afford to live on part-time salaries or maintain a strict division between their jobs and family lives. As for the future, it is likely to bring an even greater overlap between work and home. The trend

Changing Complexion of the U.S. Workplace

The shifting racial and ethnic makeup of the U.S. work force: number of workers by race and ethnic origin and their share of the total civilian labor force.

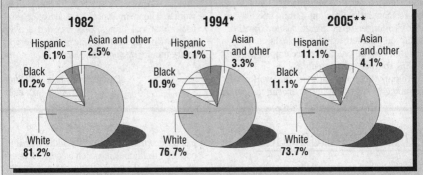

Numbers (thousands)	1982	1994*	2005**	Percent	1982	1994*	2005**
Total	**110,204**	**131,051**	**147,106**	**Total**	**100.0%**	**100.0%**	**100.0%**
Men	62,449	70,814	76,842	Men	56.7	54.0	52.2
Women	47,755	60,238	70,263	Women	43.3	46.0	47.8
White, non-Hispanic	**89,525**	**100,463**	**108,345**	**White, non-Hispanic**	**81.2**	**76.7**	**73.7**
Men	51,075	54,306	56,429	Men	46.4	41.4	38.4
Women	38,450	46,157	51,916	Women	34.9	35.2	35.3
Black, non-Hispanic	**11,230**	**14,304**	**16,392**	**Black, non-Hispanic**	**10.2**	**10.9**	**11.1**
Men	5,744	6,981	7,783	Men	5.2	5.3	5.3
Women	5,486	7,323	8,609	Women	5.0	5.6	5.9
Hispanic origin	**6,734**	**11,974**	**16,330**	**Hispanic origin**	**6.1**	**9.1**	**11.1**
Men	4,148	7,210	9,492	Men	3.8	5.5	6.5
Women	2,586	4,764	6,838	Women	2.3	3.6	4.6
Asian and other, non-Hispanic	**2,714**	**4,310**	**6,039**	**Asian and other, non-Hispanic**	**2.5**	**3.3**	**4.1**
Men	1,481	2,317	3,139	Men	1.3	1.8	2.1
Women	1,233	1,994	2,900	Women	1.1	1.5	2.0

*Data for 1994 are not directly comparable with data for 1982.
**Projected.
Source: U.S. Bureau of Labor Statistics

already is reflected in the 7% annual rise in the number of home-based businesses and growing number of employees who telecommute from home. It also can be seen in the more widespread use of home PCs and cellular phones across industries and job levels. Where a decade ago, evening and weekend work was largely confined to managers and professionals, now even lower-level workers stay in touch with their bosses via cellular phones and PCs.

With this increased overlap, time and flexibility are becoming precious commodities—benefits workers are bargaining for as intently as they once sought pension plans and job security. Already professionals in high demand—from computer programmers to accountants—have made when and how much they work and from where high-priority items when seeking and accepting employment.

While pressure to spend more time at work continues, so does worker demand for more control over job scheduling. The standard convention of having to show up at the office at a prescribed hour is being questioned by many employees who contend they can do a better job when they choose their own hours. Similarly time off—from one day a week to longer-term sabbaticals for travel or study or parental leaves—is an increasingly coveted benefit, one that more employees are willing to trade salary to obtain.

Among the most elite in the workplace, including some high-level executives who once felt a relentless need to prove their career commitment, the new status symbols are unlisted phone numbers and remote and lengthier vacations. Futurists like Ms. Farmer predict a new effort by many to simplify both work and home by consciously choosing less— fewer material things, less frenzied activity, less having to keep in touch with everyone every minute by phone and faxes.

Carol Hymowitz, a *Wall Street Journal* senior editor

SHALLOW LABOR POOL

The U.S. labor market can be summed up in two words: help wanted.

In what has become the tightest labor market in a generation, the national jobless rate plummeted to less than 5% this year—its lowest level since 1973—bolstering the job outlook for millions of workers and sending employers scrambling for qualified help. Unemployment in some parts of the country scraped below the 2% mark, beyond the point at which economists declare "full employment."

The trend has changed the way managers deal with staffing issues. In the Midwest, for instance, where unemployment is lowest, bosses are dangling carrots of all kinds to entice workers to join their ranks. Metro Plastics Technologies Inc., an Indianapolis manufacturer, began offering workers 40 hours pay for 30 hours of work in an attempt to draw candidates for its factory jobs. (The move drew 300 applicants in two days.) Winn-Dixie Stores Inc., the Florida-based grocery chain, began giving vacation and health benefits to part-time workers to keep them from defecting.

Workers, meanwhile, have been blessed with remarkable leverage as they jump from job to job in search of higher pay, better benefits—even better hours. Bosses admit they're afraid to discipline workers for fear of losing them. "We're *extreeeemely* lenient," Rick James, operations manager for Electronic Manufacturing Solutions Inc. in Indianapolis, told *The Wall Street Journal*. "Basically, if you just show up every day, we'll take you."

The trend is a dramatic shift from the past, when unemployment was rising as U.S. companies downsized and sent middle managers packing. In Michigan, which faced 15% unemployment in the early 1980s, workers are so scarce now that it is spending $50,000 to do the unthinkable: advertise in national newspapers to draw people. The Army is struggling to meet its recruiting goals for the first time since 1979, despite increased enlistment bonuses and lower entry standards.

The benefits of the good economy are easy to spot, of course. With a strong labor market, many people who hadn't previously sought work have jumped into the labor force—assured that their search won't be fruitless. Companies also have gone out of their way to train workers whom they wouldn't ordinarily develop. Such a move improves productivity and living standards, most economists agree.

The strong job market has even bolstered the prospects for welfare reform. U.S. firms have hired thousands of workers off the welfare rolls, in part, because of the high demand for help. "There's a window of opportunity here," says Mitchell S. Fromstein, chairman of Manpower Inc., the nation's largest temporary-help business, referring to welfare reform. Manpower has targeted the inner-city population as a new source of labor, setting up recruiting offices in downtown areas.

But there are definite drawbacks to such a tight labor market. The booming economic picture has made for some tough choices for human-resource personnel. With unemployment so low, managers are convinced qualified candidates are already working. So they must decide whether to hang on to profits or raise wages and benefits? Hire temporaries or steal workers from competitors? Train the unskilled or do the work themselves? Manufacturers complain that the labor shortage has hurt their profitability and even increased stress levels. Nearly 40% of companies surveyed by Olsten Corp. in 1997 said understaffing has "increased difficulty in expanding operations." The labor shortage "has got us by the shorts," Mr. James of Electronic Manufacturing Solutions, said.

Not all areas of the country have strong job markets. Northeastern and western states like New York and California continue to suffer from relatively high unemployment

rates of 6% or more. Areas with higher unemployment tend to be those with a large immigrant population because non-citizens have a tougher time finding jobs than U.S. natives.

Still, for those looking for work, it's practically nirvana. College recruiting soared more than 20% in 1997 at some universities, and on-campus recruiting space is at a premium. The University of California at Los Angeles put 150 recruiters on a waiting list and most never got the chance to come. Interviewing rooms at the University of Colorado are so

At Your Service

Jobs in service-producing businesses have grown at a much faster pace than those in the goods-producing industries.

Percentages of Nonfarm Jobs in Service and Goods-Producing Industries

1950 — Goods-producing, **41%** / Service, **59%**

1996 — Goods-producing, **20%** / Service, **80%**

1970 — Goods-producing, **33%** / Service, **67%**

2005* — Goods-producing, **18%** / Service, **82%**

Number of Employees on Nonfarm Payrolls
(In thousands)

	Annual averages				Annual averages		
Year	Total	Goods-producing	Service-producing	Year	Total	Goods-producing	Service-producing
1946	41,652	17,248	54,345	1988	105,210	25,125	80,086
1950	45,197	18,506	64,748	1989	107,895	25,254	82,642
1955	50,641	20,513	72,544	1990	109,419	24,905	84,514
1960	54,189	20,434	74,811	1991	108,256	23,745	84,511
1965	60,763	21,926	24,404	1992	108,604	23,231	85,373
1970	70,880	23,578	26,691	1993	110,730	23,352	87,378
1975	76,945	22,600	30,128	1994	114,172	23,908	90,264
1980	90,406	25,658	33,755	1995	117,203	24,206	92,997
1985	97,387	24,842	38,839	1996	119,554	24,259	95,296
1986	99,344	24,533	47,302	2005*	130,185	22,930	107,256
1987	101,958	24,674	77,284				

*Projection.
Source: U.S. Bureau of Labor Statistics

heavily booked that Gordon Gray, director of career services there, has turned over his own office to recruiters on several occasions.

Many graduating seniors have enjoyed the luxury of pondering multiple job offers. Bryan Kassing, a recent graduate of UCLA, fielded job offers from a dozen employers such as Olsten, GTE, and Pacific Bell. The European studies major settled on Pacific Bell. "I knew I had a good resume," the 23-year-old said, "but I had no idea it would be like this."

Carl Quintanilla

HELP WANTED—
FOR THE 21ST CENTURY

Out of work? Chances are you aren't a home health-care aide, a computer-systems analyst or a high-school teacher. Those are some of the occupations the U.S. Labor Department expects to generate the most new jobs between 1994 and 2005. Health-care employment, technical jobs, teaching and child-care dominate the Labor Department's forecast of occupations with the most growth potential, while farm workers, machine operators, clerks and bank tellers are among the occupations expected to decline the most.

Many of the fast-track occupations reflect demographic trends. The children of the baby-boom generation, for instance, will increase demand for teachers and child-care workers. The growth in the number of elderly Americans will provide more jobs for home health-care aides and physical therapists. On the negative side, the nation's crowded prisons will need more guards and corrections officers, and special-education teaching positions will continue to increase rapidly as more students struggle with learning disabilities.

Some employment experts believe the jobs of the future will require many men to consider doing what was traditionally "women's work." The health-care industry and education, in particular, will attract more men and consequently, will offer higher wages, predicts John A. Challenger, general manager of the outplacement firm Challenger, Gray & Christmas Inc.

Technology, of course, will significantly shape the job landscape. Many of the growth occupations are in the computer and communications industries, while declining occupations include manufacturing and clerical jobs being eliminated by automation. "There's got to be insatiable demand for technicians to fix things that other people, especially older people, don't know how to deal with involving technology and software," says Peter Morrison, a demog-

rapher at Rand Corp. "There will be new ways of connecting with the World Wide Web and other constantly unfolding technologies."

Whatever the industry, employment experts agree, the best jobs of the future will require education and job training. The Labor Department predicts that 34% of the total 17.7 million new jobs created by 2005 will require a bachelor's or more advanced degree, whereas just 21% of all the jobs in 1994 required higher education.

Nuala Beck, a management consultant in Toronto, says the hottest industries will employ a large number of what she calls "knowledge workers," including professionals, senior managers, and technical, engineering and scientific staffs. "Knowledge workers usually have an unemployment rate of around 2%," Ms. Beck adds. "They can be in new jobs before the government even knows they were unemployed."

Of course, not all the growth jobs require great skill and offer such security. Some occupations will likely produce thousands of new jobs simply because they're so large to begin with. Cashiers, janitors and cleaners, retail salespeople, and waiters and waitresses are the occupations with the largest projected numerical increases, although they aren't among the fastest growing occupations on a percentage basis.

Some growth jobs may seem surprising. For example, even though there's been plenty of management pruning in the 1990s, it's still a big growth area because every business, large or small, needs managers. And a few jobs on the Labor Department's lists of hot and cold occupations, such as amusement and recreation attendants and manicurists, defy easy explanation.

"For whatever reason, there's great demand for manicurists," says Neal Rosenthal of the U.S. Bureau of Labor Statistics. "Manicurist shops are popping up everywhere in Washington."

Ronald Alsop

Changing Jobs

Occupations with the Largest Numerical Job Decline, 1994-2005

(Projections in thousands)

	-300 -250 -200 -150 -100 -50 0
Farmers	-273
Typists and word processors	-212
Bookkeeping, accounting, and auditing clerks	-178
Bank tellers	-152
Sewing machine operators, garment	-140
Cleaners and servants, private household	-108
Computer operators, except peripheral equipment	-98
Billing, posting, and calculating machine operators	-64
Duplicating, mail, and other office machine operators	-56
Textile draw-out and winding machine operators and tenders	-47
File clerks	-42
Freight, stock, and material movers, hand	-36
Farm workers	-36
Machine tool cutting operators and tenders, metal and plastic	-34
Central office operators	-34
Central office and PBX installers and repairers	-33
Electrical and electronic assemblers	-30
Station installers and repairers, telephone	-26
Personnel clerks, except payroll and timekeepng	-26
Data entry keyers, except composing	-25
Bartenders	-25
Inspectors, testers, and graders, precision	-25
Directory assistance operators	-24
Lathe and turning machine tool setters and set-up operators, metal and plastic	-22
Custom tailors and sewers	-21
Machine feeders and offbearers	-20
Machinists	-20
Service station attendants	-20
Machine forming operators and tenders, metal and plastic	-19
Communication, transportation, and utilities operations managers	-19

Source: U.S. Bureau of Labor Statistics

Occupations with the Largest Numerical Job Growth, 1994-2005

(Projections in thousands)

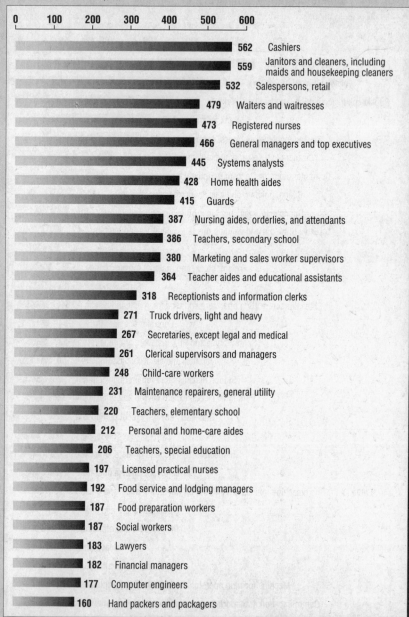

562	Cashiers
559	Janitors and cleaners, including maids and housekeeping cleaners
532	Salespersons, retail
479	Waiters and waitresses
473	Registered nurses
466	General managers and top executives
445	Systems analysts
428	Home health aides
415	Guards
387	Nursing aides, orderlies, and attendants
386	Teachers, secondary school
380	Marketing and sales worker supervisors
364	Teacher aides and educational assistants
318	Receptionists and information clerks
271	Truck drivers, light and heavy
267	Secretaries, except legal and medical
261	Clerical supervisors and managers
248	Child-care workers
231	Maintenance repairers, general utility
220	Teachers, elementary school
212	Personal and home-care aides
206	Teachers, special education
197	Licensed practical nurses
192	Food service and lodging managers
187	Food preparation workers
187	Social workers
183	Lawyers
182	Financial managers
177	Computer engineers
160	Hand packers and packagers

Source: U.S. Bureau of Labor Statistics

Fastest Growing Occupations, 1994-2005
(Projected percentage increase)

0	20	40	60	80	100	120

- 119 Personal and home care aides
- 102 Home health aides
- 92 Systems analysts
- 90 Computer engineers
- 83 Physical and corrective therapy assistants and aides
- 83 Electronic pagination systems workers
- 82 Occupational therapy assistants and aides
- 80 Physical therapists
- 76 Residential counselors
- 75 Human services workers
- 72 Occupational therapists
- 69 Manicurists
- 59 Medical assistants
- 58 Paralegals
- 56 Medical records technicians
- 53 Teachers, special education
- 52 Amusement and recreation attendants
- 51 Correction officers
- 50 Operations research analysts
- 48 Guards
- 46 Speech-language pathologists and audiologists
- 44 Detectives, except public
- 43 Surgical technologists
- 42 Dental hygienists
- 42 Dental assistants
- 40 Adjustment clerks
- 39 Teacher aides and educational assistants
- 38 Data processing equipment repairers
- 37 Nursery and greenhouse managers
- 37 Securities and financial services sales workers

Source: U.S. Bureau of Labor Statistics

Employment Change in Selected Industries, 1994-2005

(Projected annual percentage rate of change)

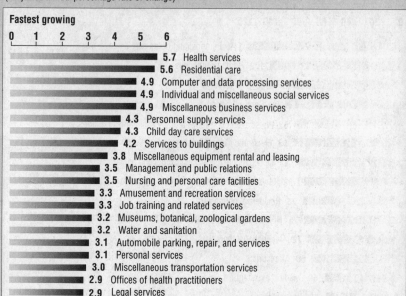

Fastest growing

	Rate	Industry
	5.7	Health services
	5.6	Residential care
	4.9	Computer and data processing services
	4.9	Individual and miscellaneous social services
	4.9	Miscellaneous business services
	4.3	Personnel supply services
	4.3	Child day care services
	4.2	Services to buildings
	3.8	Miscellaneous equipment rental and leasing
	3.5	Management and public relations
	3.5	Nursing and personal care facilities
	3.3	Amusement and recreation services
	3.3	Job training and related services
	3.2	Museums, botanical, zoological gardens
	3.2	Water and sanitation
	3.1	Automobile parking, repair, and services
	3.1	Personal services
	3.0	Miscellaneous transportation services
	2.9	Offices of health practitioners
	2.9	Legal services

Most rapidly declining

Industry	Rate
Footwear, except rubber and plastic	-6.7
Watches, clocks, and parts	-5.3
Coal mining	-4.3
Household audio and video equipment	-4.2
Tobacco products	-4.2
Crude petroleum, natural gas, and gas liquids	-4.2
Metal cans and shipping containers	-3.9
Blast furnaces and basic steel products	-3.9
Luggage, handbags, and leather products	-3.3
Cutlery, hand tools, and hardware	-3.2
Apparel	-2.9
Search and navigation equipment	-2.8
Iron and steel foundries	-2.7
Electrical industrial apparatus	-2.7
Beverages	-2.7
Computer and office equipment	-2.6
Tires and inner tubes	-2.5
Stone, clay, and miscellaneous mineral products	-2.5
Fabricated structural metal products	-2.3
Railroad transportation	-2.3

Source: U.S. Bureau of Labor Statistics

Slower Job Growth

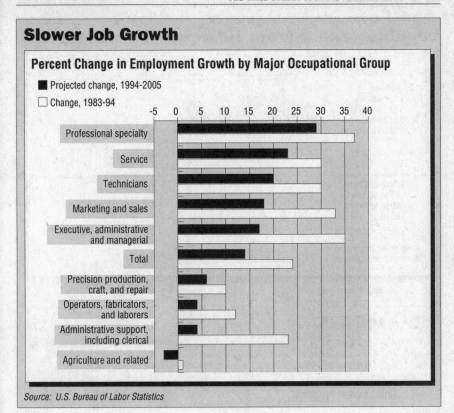

Percent Change in Employment Growth by Major Occupational Group

■ Projected change, 1994-2005
☐ Change, 1983-94

Professional specialty
Service
Technicians
Marketing and sales
Executive, administrative and managerial
Total
Precision production, craft, and repair
Operators, fabricators, and laborers
Administrative support, including clerical
Agriculture and related

Source: U.S. Bureau of Labor Statistics

Work Time

Louis Harris & Associates' surveys of Americans show an increase in the amount of time devoted to work activities and about the same amount of time for leisure as in 1980. Work includes working for pay, keeping house and going to school.

Year	Median number of hours of work per week	Median number of hours of leisure per week
1973	40.6	26.2
1975	43.1	24.3
1980	46.9	19.2
1984	47.3	18.1
1987	46.8	16.6
1989	48.7	18.8
1993	50.0	18.8
1994	50.7	19.5
1995	50.6	19.2
1997	50.8	19.5

Source: Louis Harris & Associates

Percentage of Non-Farm Workers, by Hours on the Job Per Week in 1996

Hours of work	Percent distribution
1 to 34 hours	25.5%
1 to 4 hours	1.0
5 to 15 hours	4.0
15 to 29 hours	12.7
30 to 34 hours	7.7
35 hours and over	74.5
35 to 39 hours	7.2
40 hours	35.9
41 hours and over	31.3
41 to 48 hours	11.7
49 to 59 hours	11.5
60 hours and over	8.1

Average hours, total at work..39.2
Average hours, persons who usually work full time.............43.2

Source: U.S. Bureau of Labor Statistics

Stressed Out

The most and least stressful jobs, based on such factors as quotas and deadlines, long work weeks, the hazards involved, level of competitiveness, physical demands, environmental conditions, contact with the public, need for precision, and amount of stamina required.

Most Stressful Jobs

1. U.S. President
2. Firefighter
3. Senior corporate executive
4. Race car driver (Indy class)
5. Taxi driver
6. Surgeon
7. Astronaut
8. Police officer
9. Football player (NFL)
10. Air traffic controller
11. Highway patrol officer
12. Public relations executive
13. Mayor
14. Jockey
15. Basketball coach (NCAA)
16. Advertising account executive
17. Real estate agent
18. Photojournalist
19. Member of Congress
20. Stockbroker
21. Fisherman
22. Airplane pilot
23. Lumberjack
24. Emergency medical technician
25. Architect

Least Stressful Jobs

1. Medical records technician
2. Janitor
3. Forklift operator
4. Musical instrument repairer
5. Florist
6. Actuary
7. Appliance repairer
8. Medical secretary
9. Librarian
10. Bookkeeper
11. File clerk
12. Piano tuner
13. Photographic process worker
14. Dietitian
15. Paralegal assistant
16. Vending machine repairer
17. Bookbinder
18. Barber
19. Medical laboratory technician
20. Electrical technician
21. Typist/Word processor
22. Broadcast technician
23. Mathematician
24. Dental hygienist
25. Jeweler

Source: The Wall Street Journal, National Business Employment Weekly Jobs Rated Almanac

Where the Jobs Are Moving

Job Migration 1991–1995

	State	Jobs Entering	Jobs Exiting	Net Gain or Loss
1	Georgia	55,667	20,603	35,064
2	Texas	72,129	54,501	17,628
3	Tennessee	42,527	26,537	15,990
4	Colorado	25,239	11,331	13,908
5	Delaware	20,192	6,691	13,501
6	Virginia	45,631	32,187	13,444
7	Ohio	46,630	33,418	13,212
8	New Jersey	74,099	61,209	12,890
9	Florida	54,665	42,163	12,502
10	Maryland	46,305	34,822	11,483
11	Connecticut	35,514	25,729	9,785
12	Massachusetts	33,444	24,566	8,878
13	Arizona	19,480	11,132	8,348
14	North Carolina	27,214	19,575	7,639
15	Nevada	12,432	5,185	7,247
16	South Carolina	17,334	10,577	6,757
17	Utah	9,090	4,497	4,593
18	Indiana	20,203	15,618	4,585
19	Oregon	14,244	9,661	4,583
20	Kansas	16,311	13,983	2,328
21	Arkansas	11,888	9,736	2,152
22	Idaho	5,822	3,879	1,943
23	Washington	14,603	13,157	1,446
24	Missouri	24,293	22,874	1,419
25	New Mexico	4,484	3,107	1,377
26	Alaska	1,443	700	743
27	Alabama	9,025	8,638	387
28	New Hampshire	8,994	8,623	371
29	Nebraska	4,881	4,551	330
30	South Dakota	2,379	2,118	261
31	Kentucky	16,414	16,318	96
32	Virgin Islands	159	158	1
33	Rhode Island	5,568	5,594	-26
34	Montana	1,203	1,332	-129
35	Vermont	1,706	1,853	-147
36	Wyoming	1,697	1,892	-195
37	Puerto Rico	424	945	-521
38	North Dakota	1,223	2,166	-943
39	Hawaii	1,013	2,535	-1,522
40	Oklahoma	9,347	10,904	-1,557
41	Mississippi	4,428	6,128	-1,700
42	Wisconsin	11,244	14,178	-2,934
43	Minnesota	13,283	16,269	-2,986
44	Iowa	5,669	8,885	-3,216
45	Michigan	19,227	22,567	-3,340
46	West Virginia	3,554	7,290	-3,736
47	Maine	1,847	6,663	-4,816
48	Louisiana	6,109	11,517	-5,408
49	Pennsylvania	45,554	52,122	-6,568
50	Illinois	42,795	51,045	-8,250
51	Washington, D.C.	16,749	40,339	-23,590
52	California	48,661	128,499	-79,838
53	New York	62,150	145,619	-83,469
	Total	**1,096,186**	**1,096,186**	**0**

Source: Dun & Bradstreet

Wage and Benefit Growth

The growth of wages, salaries and benefits slowed in the first half of the 1990s, as measured by the Labor Department's Employment Cost Index. But the growth rate for wages rebounded somewhat in 1996.

Annual percent change in wages and salaries and benefit costs for workers in private industry*

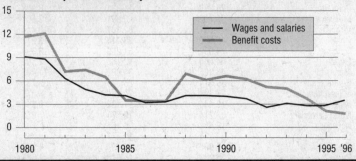

Wages and salaries
Benefit costs

Percent Change in Wages, Salaries, and Benefit Costs of Private Industry Workers Based on Employment Cost Index

Year	Wages and Salaries			Year	Benefit Costs		
	Private industry*	White-collar occupations	Blue-collar occupations		Private industry*	White-collar occupations	Blue-collar occupations
1980	9.1%	8.6%	9.6%	1980	11.7%	12.1%	11.1%
1981	8.8	9.1	8.5	1981	12.1	12.5	11.8
1982	6.3	6.5	5.6	1982	7.2	6.8	7.3
1983	4.9	6.0	3.8	1983	7.4	7.5	7.3
1984	4.2	4.3	3.6	1984	6.5	7.2	5.9
1985	4.1	4.9	3.4	1985	3.5	4.2	2.5
1986	3.2	3.4	2.6	1986	3.4	3.6	3.1
1987	3.3	3.7	3.0	1987	3.4	3.7	3.4
1988	4.1	4.7	3.2	1988	6.9	6.3	7.4
1989	4.1	4.7	3.5	1989	6.1	6.7	5.3
1990	4.0	4.1	3.5	1990	6.6	6.9	6.2
1991	3.7	3.8	3.4	1991	6.2	6.1	6.1
1992	2.6	2.7	2.6	1992	5.2	4.8	5.6
1993	3.1	3.3	2.9	1993	5.0	4.6	5.5
1994	2.8	2.8	2.8	1994	3.7	4.5	2.8
1995	2.8	2.9	2.9	1995	2.2	2.6	1.7
1996	3.4	3.5	3.0	1996	2.0	2.2	1.7

*Excludes farm and household workers.
Source: U.S. Bureau of Labor Statistics

Average Hourly Compensation Costs for Workers in Private Industry, March 1996

Occupational groups	Total compensation	Wages and salaries	Benefit costs
All workers in private industry	$17.49	$12.58	$4.91
White-collar occupations	21.10	15.44	5.66
Executive, administrative, and managerial	33.12	24.07	9.05
Professional	30.80	22.49	8.31
Technical	24.84	17.90	6.94
Administrative support, including clerical	14.93	10.69	4.23
Sales occupations	14.34	11.09	3.25
Blue-collar occupations	17.04	11.61	5.44
Precision production, craft, and repair	22.12	15.10	7.02
Transportation and material moving	16.96	11.62	5.34
Machine operators, assemblers, and inspectors	15.48	10.22	5.27
Handlers, equipment cleaners, helpers, and laborers	12.07	8.48	3.59
Service occupations	8.61	6.53	2.07

Source: U.S. Bureau of Labor Statistics

Benefits Coverage

The percentage of small companies (those with fewer than 500 employees) providing each of the following benefits compared with the percentage of larger concerns

Benefit	Small	Medium & Large
Vacations	86%	97%
Holidays	80	91
Health insurance	62	82
Short-term disability insurance	56	87
Prescription drugs	56	80
Life insurance	54	91
Jury duty with pay	51	90
Sick leave	44	65
Funeral leave	42	83
401(k) plans	29	49
Sickness and accident insurance	24	44
Dental insurance	23	62
Long-term disability insurance	14	41
Personal leave	11	21
Vision care	9	26
Pension plans	9	56

Note: Figures are for 1994, the latest year available, and pertain to benefits both fully paid and partially paid by the employer.

Source: U.S. Bureau of Labor Statistics

Earnings by Occupation

Median Weekly Earnings of Full-Time Workers, 1996

Occupation	Men	Women
Executive, administrative, and managerial	$846	$585
Administrators and officials, public administration	847	638
Financial managers	979	635
Personnel and labor relations managers	1,150	658
Purchasing managers	976	659
Managers, marketing, advertising, and public relations	1,043	674
Accountants and auditors	771	561
Professional specialty	857	647
Engineers	963	793
Mathematical and computer scientists	929	790
Physicians	1,378	802
Registered nurses	729	695
Pharmacists	1,047	931
Social, recreation, and religious workers	577	485
Lawyers	1,261	970
Designers	767	441
Editors and reporters	756	608
Health technologists and technicians	537	470
Computer programmers	797	741
Sales representatives, finance and business services	727	485
Real estate sales	695	510
Securities and financial services sales	977	541
Sales workers, retail and personal services	386	259
Administrative support, including clerical	489	391
Computer equipment operators	538	401
Secretaries, stenographers, and typists	389	404
Bookkeepers, accounting and auditing clerks	450	396
Mail carriers, postal service	684	646
Insurance adjusters, examiners, and investigators	649	458
Police and detectives	616	520
Waiters and waitresses	308	253
Cooks, except short order	279	242
Janitors and cleaners	313	272
Mechanics and repairers, except supervisors	563	502
Construction trades	518	389
Precision metalworking occupations	595	367
Machine operators, assemblers, and inspectors	437	307
Truck drivers	485	359
Farm workers	271	221

Source: U.S. Bureau of Labor Statistics

EARNINGS GAP

Median Weekly Earnings of Full-time Wage and Salary Workers

The gap between men's and women's earnings narrowed through the early 1990s, but widened slightly in recent years. Still, women have made progress, with their earnings averaging 75% of men's in 1996, compared with 69% in 1986. But the gap grew between whites and minorities: the median weekly earnings for backs were 76% of whites' earnings, down from 79% in 1986; Hispanics earned 67% of what whites earned, compared with 75% in 1986.
(Annual averages in current dollars)

	1980	1986	1990	1995	1996
Men	$312.00	$419.00	$485.00	$538.00	$557.00
Women	201.00	290.00	348.00	406.00	418.00
White	268.00	370.00	427.00	494.00	506.00
Black	212.00	291.00	329.00	383.00	387.00
Hispanic	–	277.00	307.00	329.00	339.00

Source: U.S. Bureau of Labor Statistics

Tracking the Minimum Wage

The hourly federal minimum wage and its purchasing power in 1996 dollars

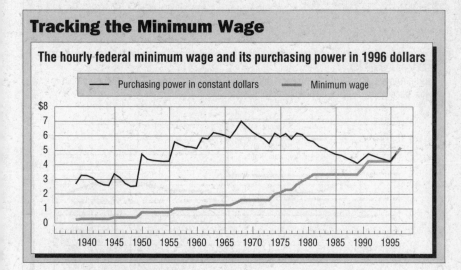

Year	Minimum wage	Purchasing Power in 1996 dollars using CPI-U	Year	Minimum wage	Purchasing Power in 1996 dollars using CPI-U
1938	$0.25	$2.78	1980	$3.10	$5.90
1939	0.30	3.39	1981	3.35	5.78
1940	0.30	3.36	1982	3.35	5.45
1945	0.40	3.49	1983	3.35	5.28
1950	0.75	4.88	1984	3.35	5.06
1955	0.75	4.39	1985	3.35	4.88
1956	1.00	5.77	1986	3.35	4.80
1960	1.00	5.30	1987	3.35	4.63
1961	1.15	6.03	1988	3.35	4.44
1963	1.25	6.41	1989	3.35	4.24
1965	1.25	6.23	1990	3.80	4.56
1967	1.40	6.58	1991	4.25	4.90
1968	1.60	7.21	1992	4.25	4.75
1970	1.60	6.47	1993	4.25	4.61
1974	2.00	6.37	1994	4.25	4.50
1975	2.10	6.12	1995	4.25	4.38
1976	2.30	6.34	1996	4.75	4.75
1977	2.30	5.95	1997	5.15	—
1978	2.65	6.38			
1979	2.90	6.27			

Source: U.S. Bureau of Labor Statistics

Pay Trends

Cash compensation for CEOs rose in 1996 at the slowest rate since 1991, though still at a faster pace than pay for white-collar employees.

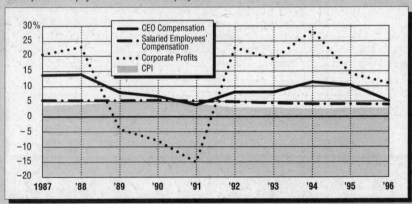

Source: William M. Mercer Inc.

10 Highest Paid CEOs in 1996

Chief executives' zooming cash compensation slowed its skyward ascent in 1996. William M. Mercer Inc., New York compensation consultants, tracked this moderating trend for *The Wall Street Journal* by analyzing 350 proxy statements of the biggest U.S. businesses. Salaries and bonuses of surveyed CEOs rose 5.2%, a noticeably smaller gain than 1995's increase of 10.4%. Nevertheless, the pace in 1996 still exceeded the 4% gain in pay among white-collar employees. In the Mercer study, 166 corporate leaders cashed in stock options during 1996 for a median gain of $1,256,936. That's the biggest treasure chest from stock-option exercises since 1992 and is more than twice the 1995 median gain of $615,058. Median total compensation–including salary, bonuses, gains from exercised options, long-term incentive payouts and the value of restricted stock at the time of grant–vaulted 18% to $2,375,620 in 1996.

Based on an analysis of proxy statements from 350 of the largest U.S. businesses

Company	Executive	Salary & bonus	Gain on option exercise	Restricted stock grants	Long term incentive payouts	Total direct compensation
Travelers Group Inc.	Sanford I. Weill	$8,025,000	$85,232,745	$648,738	$0	$93,906,483
Heinz (H.J.) Co.	Anthony J.F. O'Reilly	2,565,200	61,500,000	0	0	64,065,200
Citicorp	John S. Reed	3,466,667	40,054,875	0	0	43,521,542
Compaq Computer Corp.	Eckhard Pfeiffer	4,250,000	23,546,104	0	0	27,796,104
General Electric Co.	John F. Welch Jr.	6,300,000	6,215,625	0	15,105,000	27,620,625
Lockheed Martin Corp.	Norman R. Augustine	2,737,500	20,324,232	0	0	23,061,732
Mattel Inc.	John W. Amerman	1,470,008	18,503,078	0	420,000	20,393,086
PaineWebber Group Inc.	Donald B. Marron	8,988,097	11,198,361	0	0	20,186,458
American International Group Inc.	Maurice R. Greenberg	4,150,000	5,027,186	0	10,825,000	20,002,186
American Home Products Corp.	John R. Stafford	2,460,000	15,471,563	0	465,780	18,397,343

Source: Study conducted by William M. Mercer Inc. for The Wall Street Journal

Payday for Junior

A survey by *Zillions,* the magazine for kids from *Consumer Reports,* found that 9-to-14 year olds collect the following median weekly income from their parents as allowances, handouts, and payments for chores. The median weekly allowance for 9-and-10 year olds has risen 50 cents since 1994, but it hasn't budged for older kids since 1991. Like many of their elders in the work force, two out of three kids said they asked for an increase but didn't get one.

The Source of Cash for 9-to-14 Year Olds

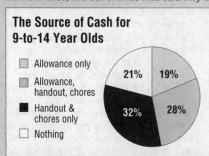

- Allowance only
- Allowance, handout, chores
- Handout & chores only
- Nothing

Median Weekly Income from Parents, by Age

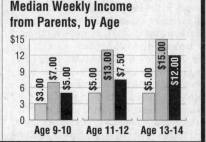

Source: Consumer Reports and Zillions

CRACKS IN THE GLASS CEILING

A growing cadre of women who launched careers in the 1970s are breaking through cracks in the glass ceiling, landing top front-line corporate jobs once monopolized by men.

Among the high-profile promotions in the last year: Jill Barad became chief executive officer of Mattel Inc.; AT&T Corp. named Gail J. McGovern to lead its $26 billion consumer business; and consumer-products behemoth Colgate-Palmolive Co. named Lois Juliber to head operations in North America and Europe.

Of course, none of this means that American corporations have suddenly become level playing fields after years of male domination. The New York research group Catalyst issued a study in late 1996 showing that just 2% of senior executives at large corporations are women. But, at the same time, it would be a mistake to ignore obvious evidence that something important is beginning to happen. The same Catalyst study also found that a "breakthrough generation" of women is beginning to attain power.

The question is: If these women are drawing a road map for other women to the chief executive's office, what does the map look like? They have a remarkable amount in common, aside from their obvious intellectual skills, marketing and motivational abilities and willingness to take risks and work hard. They are nearly all in their 40s and were among the first wave of women admitted to top business schools like Harvard and Stanford as those institutions began striving for diversity in the 1970s. Many have mothers as well as fathers who nurtured their educational and career aspirations. They came up through the ranks of their companies—through the operations side—and, remarkably, often have this in common, too: At some point in their careers, they took over divisions that no one much wanted and turned them around.

They also are committed to making it, whatever the personal sacrifice. When Carol Bartz learned she had breast cancer just two days after taking over as chief executive of Autodesk Inc. in 1992, she had a stopgap lumpectomy but kept working for another month before undergoing a radical mastectomy. She returned to work four weeks after the surgery, rather than the recommended six to eight weeks. Having a "female illness," she later noted, "I thought this could be fodder for anyone inclined to question whether a woman should be doing this job, and I wanted to avoid that at all costs."

For some women, becoming a corporate superstar has meant learning early on how to play men's games. As a math major at Johns Hopkins University, AT&T's Ms. McGovern spent many spring afternoons in the bleachers at Baltimore Orioles' games, immersing herself in baseball to better fit in with her male classmates. "I became an avid sports fan," she says. "It gave me a basis of common interest." Later, she sought out technical jobs and marketing and sales positions—traditionally the provinces of men—to advance her career.

Robert Morrison, chairman and chief executive of Philip Morris Companies' Kraft Foods unit—where five of 11 major operations are run by women—says successful executives of either sex share fundamental qualities: "They are all very smart and have acquired broader and broader experience through their careers, they have a passion to win and an ability to fire up the people who work for them." In effect, corporate women still live in what is largely a man's world where the rules are the same as they ever were: work hard, make the numbers, be a team player.

But to stand out, women have had to do more. They have tackled assignments others shunned as losers and even taken brief career detours to get tough jobs done for their bosses, who almost always are male. Irene Rosenfeld, Kraft Foods executive vice president and president of Kraft Canada, got her big break when she convinced her superiors to name her product manager of the beverage division. "I wasn't on their radar screen" for the job, "even though I'd already done so much work" in the division, she says. "It took a lot for me to raise my hand, and I'm glad I did." She rapidly overhauled the languishing Kool-Aid brand, first by marketing to children with television ads that portrayed a "Kool-Aid man" roller blading to rock 'n' roll music, and then wooing mothers to the drink by making it less sweet. Kool-Aid sales began growing for the first time in years, and the beverage business generated double-digit profit growth. Later, as head of the desserts and snacks division, she revived Jell-O, another declining brand, with an array of new flavors and ads.

Will she and women executives like her attain the big payoffs as chief executives? "I will remain committed to this company as long as I have the opportunity to grow," says Ms. Rosenfeld. Kraft's chief executive, Mr. Morrison, is certain a woman at his company "has a shot at the CEO job," although "whether that happens in three or five or ten years is hard to say."

More CEO's are trying to demonstrate that things are changing, especially in the face of a steady drumbeat of discrimination suits and a continuing exodus of highly talented women and minority managers fed up with corporate good-ol'-boyism. Executive recruiters say corporate clients increasingly expect women

to be in the pool of candidates for any job, and point to the lengthening list of prospects: Christina Gold, senior vice president at Avon Products Inc., in charge of North American operations; Ellen Marram, executive vice president at Seagram Co. and head of the company's $2 billion a year nonalcoholic-beverage business; and Karen Katen, executive vice president of Pfizer Inc.'s pharmaceuticals group.

"Progress is being made," says U.S. Labor Department official Rene Redwood, former executive director of the Federal Glass Ceiling Commission, a bipartisan group that studied diversity in the workplace. "But it's painfully slow."

Joseph B. White and Carol Hymowitz

Women in the Executive and Professional Ranks

Percentage of Employees in Selected Occupations Who Were Women

Occupation	1983	1996
Total work force, 16 years and over	43.7%	46.2%
Executive, administrative, and managerial	32.4	43.8
Officials and administrators, public administration	38.5	47.7
Financial managers	38.6	54.0
Personnel and labor relations managers	43.9	51.6
Purchasing managers	23.6	45.7
Managers, marketing, advertising, and public relations	21.8	37.8
Managers, medicine and health	57.0	75.3
Accountants and auditors	38.7	56.0
Management analysts	29.5	41.1
Professional specialty	48.1	53.3
Architects	12.7	16.7
Engineers	5.8	8.5
Mathematical and computer scientists	29.6	30.6
Natural scientists	20.5	29.3
Physicians	15.8	26.4
Dentists	6.7	13.7
Teachers, college and university	36.3	43.5
Economists	37.9	54.4
Psychologists	57.1	61.4
Lawyers	15.3	29.5
Authors	46.7	54.1
Musicians and composers	28.0	34.2
Editors and reporters	48.4	55.7

*Data for 1983 and 1996 are not strictly comparable.
Source: U.S. Bureau of Labor Statistics

Women and Men in the Work Force

Percent of Population in the Civilian Labor Force

Year	% of population	
	Women	**Men**
1955	35.7%	85.4%
1960	37.7	83.3
1965	39.3	80.7
1970	43.3	79.7
1975	46.3	77.9
1980	51.5	77.4
1985	54.5	76.3
1990	57.5	76.4
1995	58.9	75.0
1996	59.3	74.9
2005*	61.7	72.9

*Projected.
Source: U.S. Bureau of Labor Statistics

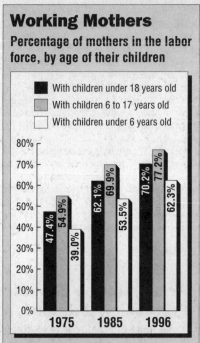

Working Mothers

Percentage of mothers in the labor force, by age of their children

- With children under 18 years old
- With children 6 to 17 years old
- With children under 6 years old

Source: U.S. Bureau of Labor Statistics

THE MYTH OF MR. MOM

When Peter Baylies takes his sons to the playground, mothers completely ignore him as they chat and set up play dates. When he and the boys go on a shopping expedition, storekeepers compliment him for taking a day off work to "babysit." Such treatment irks Mr. Baylies of North Andover, Mass., who has been the children's primary caretaker since he lost his job as a computer software engineer in 1992 and his wife returned to work as a schoolteacher. "It's intimidating going to the playground where all the mothers congregate," he says. "You just don't get much support."

But the reactions aren't surprising because he is still part of a rare breed: at-home dads. Hardly a day goes by that some newspaper, magazine, or television program doesn't trumpet the "Mr. Mom" trend. But demographers say it is far from a trend and that many dads are watching the kids and cleaning the house out of necessity and usually for only a short time. Like Mr. Baylies and the character played by Michael Keaton in the popular 1983 film *Mr. Mom*, many fathers decide to stay home with their children because they've lost their jobs.

Mr. Baylies and others like the arrangement and don't return to the job market immediately, but most seek new jobs right away.

"It's a myth" that more fathers are staying home to care for their children because they want to, says Sandra Hofferth, a research scientist and adjunct professor of sociology at the University of Michigan. "If parents can, they both work to contribute to family income today."

Maternity Leave

Percentage of women, 15 to 44 years of age, by use of maternity leave for the most recent birth

Characteristic of the mother	Not employed	Took maternity leave	Did not take maternity leave		
			Not needed	Not offered	Other reasons
All women	48.0%	37.3%	2.3%	0.9%	11.6%
Age at time of birth					
15–19 years	71.9	14.8	0.7	0.1	12.5
20–24 years	52.8	29.8	1.3	1.3	14.9
25–29 years	44.8	41.1	2.7	0.8	10.5
30–44 years	38.3	48.3	3.5	0.8	9.1
Year of child's birth					
1991–95	43.2	43.5	2.2	0.9	10.3
1981–90	47.4	37.2	2.7	0.8	11.8
1980 and before	61.5	22.0	1.6	0.9	14.0

Source: Centers for Disease Control and Prevention, National Center for Health Statistics

The latest U.S. Census Bureau data show that fathers were the main caretakers for only 16% of the 9.9 million preschool children with working mothers in 1993, down from 20% in 1991 and about the same proportion as in 1988. And most of the men who cared for their children also held down at least a part-time job.

"What many people thought was a social trend in the early '90s was driven more by the economy" and unemployment, says Lynne M. Casper, a statistician and demographer at the Census Bureau. "When the economy improved, men went back to work full-time, and families found other child-care arrangements."

While some men simply don't want to be the full-time caretakers of children, even those who do like such a nurturing role find it financially onerous in the 1990s and worry about a big gap in their resume. "Anybody who's going to stay home four or five years has to expect a setback to their career," says Casey Spencer of La Crescenta, Calif., who cares for his two-year-old daughter, and earns a little money taking wedding photographs and portraits when his wife is home.

Who is really watching most kids? Increasingly, child-care centers. The Census Bureau's latest data show that 30% of pre-schoolers with working moms are being dropped off at day-care centers and nursery schools, up from 23% in 1991. Parents, alarmed by cases of child abuse and neglect by babysitters, view centers as safe and more mentally stimulating for their children than other types of child care. Nonrelatives care for about 21% of the children, either in their home or the child's. And grandparents and other relatives watch about a quarter of the preschoolers.

Despite the statistical trend, some experts on child care and development believe the number of at-home fathers will slowly increase, if for no other reason than it will be more economical to abandon the corporation for the cul-de-sac. As women's wages rise, says Frances Goldscheider, a sociology professor at Brown University, more fathers will become the second-income providers and will voluntarily stay home rather than pay rising child-care costs.

The small minority of dads already at home are developing a sense of fraternity. They communicate by e-mail to fight the feelings of isolation, they have their own newsletter, and nearly 50 dads gathered in November 1996 for the first At-Home Dads Convention in Des Plaines, Ill. "We're trying to make this more socially acceptable," says Robert Frank, who cares for his two children and teaches courses on child development and psychology part-time at colleges in the Chicago area. "The gender stereotype of the male as breadwinner still hasn't been broken. That's really what we're fighting against."

Ronald Alsop

SLOW PROGRESS FOR MINORITY MANAGERS

The management and professional ranks of the American workplace remain overwhelmingly white, reflecting limited progress in recruiting and promoting minorities.

The U.S. Labor Department says blacks accounted for 6.9% of all executive, administrative and managerial positions in 1996, up from 4.7% in 1983, but below their 10.7% representation in the total work force. Similarly, Hispanics held 4.8% of all executive, administrative and managerial jobs, up from 2.8% in 1983, but less than their 9.2% share of the labor force. Blacks claimed 7.9% of professional jobs, while Hispanics held 4.3%.

Some critics blame outright discrimination—or at least lukewarm commitment to diversity—for the slow gains. Earl Graves, publisher of *Black Enterprise* magazine and author of *How to Succeed in Business Without Being White*, believes cultural diversity programs are often mere window dressing that at best create an environment where workers get along and feel appreciated. "It sounds wonderful, but in effect, cultural diversity policies dilute the goals of affirmative action," he says. "They have not translated into jobs for blacks or other minorities. Cultural diversity programs too often are the talk without the walk."

But some executive recruiters contend that the problem is a lack of qualified candidates. "It's basically a numbers game," says John Marra Jr., president of executive-search firm Marra Peters & Partners. "If there are 5,000 CEOs now in the market, and I have to recruit a CEO and only 1% are minority, my chances are pretty slim of getting a minority."

According to an American Management Association survey, managers see fewer obstacles for minorities but feel that past discrimination has deprived minority workers of

Who's Minding the Kids?

Primary Child-Care Arrangements of Preschoolers Under Age 5

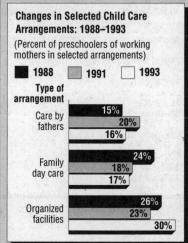

Changes in Selected Child Care Arrangements: 1988–1993

(Percent of preschoolers of working mothers in selected arrangements)

■ 1988   ▨ 1991   ☐ 1993

Type of arrangement	1988	1991	1993
Care by fathers	15%	20%	16%
Family day care	24%	18%	17%
Organized facilities	26%	23%	30%

Type of arrangement 1993	All preschoolers with working mothers	
	Number (Thousands)	Percent
All Preschoolers	9,937	100.0%
Care in child's home	3,054	30.7
By father	1,585	15.9
By grandparent	649	6.5
By other relative	328	3.3
By nonrelative	492	5.0
Care in provider's home	3,184	32.0
By grandparent	996	10.0
By other relative	543	5.5
By nonrelative	1,645	16.6
Organized child care facilities	2,972	29.9
Day/group care center	1,823	18.3
Nursery/preschool	1,149	11.6
Mother cares for child at work*	616	6.2
Other**	111	1.2

*Includes women working at home or away from home.

**Includes preschoolers in kindergarten and school-based activities.

Source: U.S. Census Bureau

the skills and experience needed for many top positions.

"What is missing is leadership skills among blacks and Hispanics," says Angel Martinez, president and chief executive officer of Rockport Co., a subsidiary of Reebok. "Competence isn't the issue; some are extraordinarily competent. The top jobs are about leadership and vision."

To be sure, a few major companies are moving minorities into the executive suite. The most notable recent case was Kenneth Chenault, who was named president and chief operating officer of American Express Co., making him one of the top black business executives in the country and heir apparent to the chairman, Harvey Golub.

Mr. Chenault has consistently played down the issue of discrimination, especially at his current employer. "I believe that at American Express, race has not been a factor one way or the other for me," Mr. Chenault says. "What has been the most important factor is performance."

He does, however, acknowledge the presence of racism. "It would be highly unusual growing up in this society if you did not feel the stain of discrimination," he says. "So yes, I have felt it. Very frankly, my attitude in life as it is in business is that if there are obstacles or barriers in your way, you figure out a way to remove them and what you want to do is really focus on your performance."

Opportunities for minorities vary widely by occupation and industry. In fact, in a few managerial and professional occupations, minorities have seen their representation decline. Blacks, for instance, today account for a smaller share of all purchasing managers, dentists and economists than in 1983.

Employment of Blacks and Persons of Hispanic Origin in Selected Occupations, 1983 and 1996*

(Minorities as a percentage of total employed)

Occupation	Blacks		Hispanic origin	
	1983	1996	1983	1996
Total work force, 16 years and over	9.3%	10.7%	5.3%	9.2%
Executive, administrative, and managerial	4.7	6.9	2.8	4.8
Officials and administrators, public administration	8.3	12.9	3.8	4.9
Financial managers	3.5	6.5	3.1	5.1
Personnel and labor relations managers	4.9	12.9	2.6	4.3
Purchasing managers	5.1	4.6	1.4	6.5
Managers, marketing, advertising, and public relations	2.7	2.9	1.7	2.8
Managers, medicine and health	5.0	8.5	2.0	4.1
Accountants and auditors	5.5	8.8	3.3	4.8
Management analysts	5.3	5.2	1.7	2.3
Professional specialty	6.4	7.9	2.5	4.3
Architects	1.6	2.7	1.5	4.3
Engineers	2.7	4.2	2.2	3.8
Mathematical and computer scientists	5.4	7.2	2.6	2.6
Natural scientists	2.6	3.3	2.1	1.9
Physicians	3.2	4.5	4.5	5.1
Dentists	2.4	1.2	1.0	0.9
Teachers, college and university	4.4	6.5	1.8	4.1
Economists	6.3	3.9	2.7	5.4
Psychologists	8.6	12.2	1.1	3.1
Lawyers	2.6	3.5	0.9	2.8
Authors	2.1	5.4	0.9	0.9
Musicians and composers	7.9	12.8	4.4	10.4
Editors and reporters	2.9	6.5	2.1	3.3

*Data for 1983 and 1996 are not strictly comparable.
Source: U.S. Bureau of Labor Statistics

Blacks, on the other hand, have made a big leap in the government sector, holding 12.9% of all public official and administrative positions.

While the public sector has been the most aggressive in hiring minorities for executive positions, technical service companies, such as engineering consulting firms, have been the least aggressive, according to Mr. Marra, the executive recruiter.

But these days Mr. Marra's clients typically ask to be presented with at least one minority candidate. "Fifteen years ago, I never heard" that request, Mr. Marra says. "Ten years ago, maybe one out of five would ask, maybe worse than that. It's getting better and better."

Barbara Martinez

Displaced Workers

Number of People Who Lost a Job Between January 1993 and December 1995
(In thousands)

Total workers who lost jobs		Industry of job loss	
Total, 20 years and older	9,367	Mining	91
Men	5,315	Construction	974
Women	4,052	Manufacturing	2,166
		Durable goods	1,312
Age		Nondurable goods	854
20 to 24 years	1,117	Transportation and public utilities	607
25 to 54 years	7,310	Wholesale and retail trade	2,042
55 to 64 years	707	Wholasale trade	412
65 years and older	233	Retail trade	1,630
		Finance, insurance, and real estate	599
Occupation		Services	2,012
Managerial and professional specialty	2,021	Agriculture wage and salary workers	132
Technical, sales,		Government workers	498
and administrative support	2,806		
Service occupations	921	**Reason for job loss**	
Precision production, craft, and repair	1,351	Plant or company closed down	
Operators, fabricators, and laborers	2,013	or moved	3,404
Farming, forestry, and fishing	112	Insufficient work	3,500
		Position or shift abolished	2,463

Source: U.S. Bureau of Labor Statistics

White-Collar Blues

A larger percentage of white-collar workers, particularly managers and professionals, lost their jobs in the early 1990s than in the 1980s, while a smaller percentage of blue-collar workers were displaced.

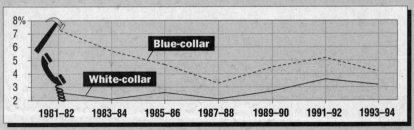

Displacement Rate by Occupation

Occupations	1981–82	1983–84	1985–86	1987–88	1989–90	1991–92	1993–94
White-collar occupations	2.6%	2.1%	2.6%	2.1%	2.7%	3.7%	3.2%
Executive, administrative, and managerial	2.5	2.4	2.8	2.5	3.4	4.8	3.4
Professional specialty	1.7	1.2	1.4	1.1	1.3	2.4	2.3
Technical, sales, and administrative support	3.0	2.4	3.1	2.5	3.1	3.7	3.6
Service occupations	2.0	1.8	1.9	1.5	1.6	2.1	1.7
Blue-collar occupations	7.3	5.7	4.7	3.3	4.5	5.3	4.2
Precision production, craft, and repair	6.2	4.5	3.9	2.7	4.2	5.1	3.3
Operators, fabricators, and laborers	8.2	6.7	5.5	3.8	4.8	5.5	4.9
Farming, forestry, and fishing	0.9	2.1	1.6	0.8	1.5	1.4	0.8

Source: U.S. Bureau of Labor Statistics

Thinning the Management Ranks

The percentage of private-industry jobs that are managerial steadily declined as companies found middle management a ripe area for cutting costs. A larger percentage of women are holding management jobs, while the percentage of men in such positions has declined. Minority groups, however, have shown little if any progress in gaining management jobs.

Year	Managerial jobs	Females who are managers	Males who are managers	Blacks who are managers	Asians who are managers	Hispanics who are managers
1982	12.32%	6.28%	16.81%	4.71%	7.85%	5.43%
1985	12.31	6.85	16.67	4.97	8.25	5.61
1988	12.00	7.21	16.09	4.76	8.16	5.35
1990	11.83	7.45	15.64	4.90	8.25	5.33
1991	11.79	7.53	15.52	4.99	8.10	5.32
1992	11.57	7.52	15.13	4.97	7.90	5.17
1993	11.43	7.65	14.79	4.97	7.87	5.17
1994	11.17	7.62	14.34	4.86	7.67	5.04
1995	11.09	7.73	14.10	4.90	7.62	5.00

Source: The Wall Street Journal and Equal Employment Opportunity Commission

High-Priced Job Seekers

Percentage of people seeking a new job through the Challenger, Gray & Christmas outplacement program who earned more than $60,000 a year in their former jobs.

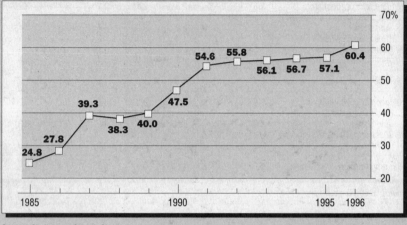

Source: Challenger, Gray & Christmas

The Upside of Downsizing

Many of the companies that laid off the most workers during the first half of the 1990s achieved large gains in productivity, or output per worker, according to an analysis by economists at the Federal Reserve Bank of Dallas

Downsizing and Productivity Among 10 of the Top Job Cutters

Company	Jobs cut 1990–95	Productivity gain or loss (−), 1990–95 (%)
Sears	185,000	−10.3%
IBM	121,601	28.1
Kmart	120,000	31.6
General Electric	76,000	32.2
General Dynamics	70,400	5.6
Digital Equipment	62,300	59.9
McDonnell Douglas	57,578	35.9
Boeing	56,700	−6.8
General Motors	52,400	21.0
GTE	48,000	30.3
Total	**849,979**	**24.7**

Source: Federal Reserve Bank of Dallas

Retirees for Hire

As more men have retired earlier either for personal reasons or because of corporate downsizing, more also have started taking on new jobs to supplement their pensions.

The labor-force participation rate for men 55–64 years old has fallen through the years to about 67% from about 90% just after World War II.

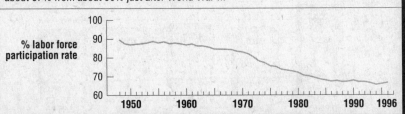

% labor force participation rate

More male pensioners are returning to work, especially those age 50 to 61.

Percent of male pensioners working by age group

Age group	1984	1989	1993
50-54	64	72	73
55-61	37	45	49
62-64	19	20	24
65-69	18	20	19
70 and older	11	11	9

Labor Force Participation Rate For Men, 55–64

Year	% labor force
1948	89.5%
1950	86.9
1955	87.9
1960	86.8
1965	84.6
1970	83.0
1975	75.6
1980	72.1
1985	67.9
1990	67.8
1995	66.0
1996	67.0

Source: U.S. Bureau of Labor Statistics

Corporate Drop-Outs

After corporate downsizing, some former executives and managers are opting to start their own businesses rather than join another large company.

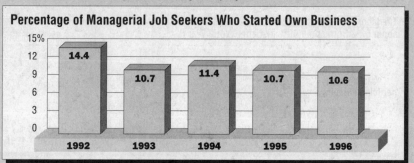

Percentage of Managerial Job Seekers Who Started Own Business

1992	1993	1994	1995	1996
14.4	10.7	11.4	10.7	10.6

Source: Challenger, Gray & Christmas

Employee vs. Employer

Median Compensatory Awards for Wrongful Termination and Constructive Discharge Cases

1990	1991	1992	1993	1994	1995	1996
115,168	152,014	120,736	150,000	150,000	149,385	205,794

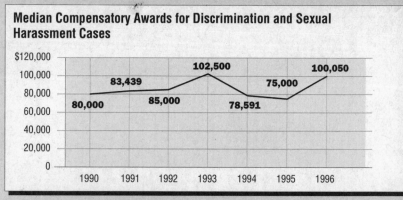

Median Compensatory Awards for Discrimination and Sexual Harassment Cases

1990	1991	1992	1993	1994	1995	1996
80,000	83,439	85,000	102,500	78,591	75,000	100,050

Source: Jury Verdict Research, Horsham, PA

Discrimination Complaints

Number of complaints received, number of cases resolved, and amount of monetary benefits for different types of workplace discrimination.

	1992	1993	1994	1995	1996*
Race					
Complaints received	29,548	31,695	31,656	29,986	26,287
Resolutions	28,497	27,440	25,253	31,674	35,127
Monetary benefits (millions)	$ 31.9	$ 33.3	$ 39.7	$ 30.1	$ 37.2
Sex					
Complaints received	21,796	23,919	25,860	26,181	23,813
Resolutions	20,102	21,606	21,545	26,726	30,965
Monetary benefits (millions)	$ 30.7	$ 44.0	$ 44.1	$ 23.6	$ 47.1
Disabilities					
Complaints received	999**	15,100	18,852	19,782	17,954
Resolutions	28	4,298	12,409	18,874	23,405
Monetary benefits (millions)	$ .018	$ 2.2	$ 30.1	$ 39.3	$ 45.4
Age					
Complaints received	19,264	19,887	19,571	17,401	15,665
Resolutions	19,975	19,761	13,942	19,969	21,253
Monetary Benefits (millions)	$ 57.3	$ 40.7	$ 42.3	$ 34.7	$ 40.9
Sexual Harassment					
Complaints received	10,532	11,908	14,420	15,549	15,342
Resolutions	7,484	9,971	11,478	13,802	15,861
Monetary benefits (millions)	$ 12.7	$ 25.1	$ 22.5	$ 24.3	$ 27.8
National Origin					
Complaints received	7,434	7,454	7,414	7,035	6,687
Resolutions	7,196	6,788	6,453	7,619	9,047
Monetary benefits (millions)	$ 9.5	$ 8.8	$ 15.5	$ 10.5	$ 10.5

*Preliminary.
**EEOC began enforcing Title I of the Americans with Disabilities Act of 1990 on July 26,1992.
Source: U.S. Equal Employment Opportunity Commission

TEMP TREND

Temporary workers, once used mainly as substitutes for sick or vacationing secretaries, have grown into a more significant component of the work force, expanding their repertoire to include even assignments in the professional and executive ranks.

As companies trim full-time positions, they still occasionally need to boost their employment rolls. Consequently, temporary jobs have become an option for a wider range of workers. Indeed, some businesses have even tapped temps who are lawyers or scientists. In 1996, Manpower Inc., the big temporary staffing agency, began a program of finding jobs for physicists with computer and electronics companies. The program was formed through an agreement with the American Institute of Physics. Meantime, Kelly Services Inc., a rival temp agency, began offering scientists for hire as a general category.

Federal statistics indicate temporary work nearly doubled in the first half of the 1990s, growing into a $31 billion industry in 1995 from about $16 billion in 1990. While the industry maintains its core offering of clerical and industrial workers, rapid growth of new technology has pushed information-technology into the forefront. Analysts say revenue in the segment has been increasing recently at a rate of 20% to 25% annually.

Hiring temporary workers—also known as independent contractors and consultants—for certain functions such as accounting, payroll, maintenance and travel services, has proved less expensive and more efficient for many companies than keeping full-time employees on the payroll. Such a strategy allows businesses to avoid certain benefits, including health insurance, stock-ownership programs, paid holidays, and vacations.

As a result, the trend has drawn complaints from labor unions that say companies are hiring temporary workers more in the name of cost cutting than efficiency. Temps have access to unions in some cases, but that requires agreements with both the agency and the client.

Some independent workers shun union membership, finding it intrusive. They say they have chosen temporary employment for its flexibility and actually prefer it to a so-called "regular job."

Companies also find temporary assignments useful for testing prospective employees. They offer full-time positions to about 45% of temporary hires, according to the National Association of Temporary and Staffing Services.

Jonathan Welsh

Alternative Work Styles

About 10% of the American work force is employed under an alternative arrangement, particularly as independent contractors.

Employed Workers with Alternative Work Arrangements by Occupation and Industry, 1995 (Percent distribution)

Characteristic	Workers with alternative arrangements			
	Independent contractors	On-call workers and day laborers	Temporary help agency workers	Workers provided by contract firms
Total, 16 years and over (thousands)	8,309	2,078	1,181	652
Occupation				
Executive, adminisrative, and managerial	18.6	2.9	6.5	5.7
Professional specialty	16.3	20.9	8.3	25.6
Technicians and related support	1.1	1.5	3.7	6.9
Sales occupations	18.8	6.0	2.6	3.2
Administrative support, including clerical	3.8	9.5	30.1	4.8
Service occupations	10.6	19.7	9.0	27.8
Precision production, craft, and repair	19.2	14.3	5.6	14.6
Operators, fabricators, and laborers	6.5	20.5	33.2	10.4
Farming, forestry, and fishing	5.1	4.7	1.0	0.9
Industry				
Agriculture	5.0	4.4	0.4	0.3
Mining	0.2	0.5	0.2	2.4
Construction	21.2	15.2	2.8	8.4
Manufacturing	5.0	5.9	33.4	17.6
Transportation and public utilities	5.0	8.7	7.6	13.4
Wholesale and retail trade	13.2	13.8	8.1	6.0
Finance, insurance, and real estate	9.6	1.8	7.5	6.9
Services	40.6	46.0	38.7	32.3
Public administration	0.3	3.3	1.2	12.6

Because of different survey methodology, the data above on temporary help agency workers do not agree with the numbers in the separate study below of the "temporary help services industry."

The number of workers hired through temporary-help services has risen steadily in the 1980s and 1990s.

Employment, Hours, and Earnings in the Temporary Help Services Industry

Year	Total payroll employment	Total temps	Percent of total	Average hours per week	Average hourly earnings
1982	89,544,000	417,000	0.5%	27.1	$5.97
1986	99,344,000	837,000	0.8	31.1	6.65
1990	109,419,000	1,288,000	1.2	30.8	8.09
1995	117,203,000	2,189,000	1.9	31.8	8.79
1996	119,554,000	2,332,000	2.0	32.1	9.20

Source: U.S. Bureau of Labor Statistics

Contingent Labor

Contingent workers, who do not expect their jobs to last, account for approximately 5% of the U.S. work force. They are disproportionately young and tend to be employed in service jobs.

Employed Contingent Workers by Age, Occupation and Industry, 1995
(Percent distribution)

Characteristic	Percent of contingent work force
Total, 16 years and over (thousands)	6,034
Age	
16 to 19 years	10.7
20 to 24 years	19.8
25 to 34 years	26.3
35 to 44 years	21.0
45 to 54 years	12.6
55 to 64 years	5.9
65 years and over	3.7
Occupation	
Executive, administrative, and managerial	7.6
Professional specialty	20.6
Technicians and related support	2.7
Sales occupations	6.4
Administrative support, including clerical	17.7
Service occupations	16.0
Precision production, craft, and repair	10.0
Operators, fabricators, and laborers	15.8
Farming, forestry, and fishing	3.0
Industry	
Agriculture	2.6
Mining	0.3
Construction	9.8
Manufacturing	10.8
Transportation and public utilities	4.2
Wholesale and retail trade	12.0
Finance, insurance, and real estate	2.6
Services	54.0
Public administration	3.6

Source: U.S. Bureau of Labor Statistics

More Moonlighters

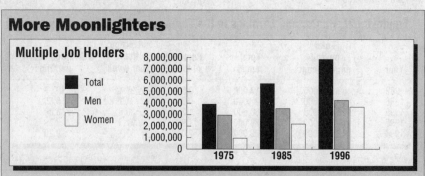

Multiple Job Holders

- ■ Total
- ■ Men
- □ Women

Source: U.S. Bureau of Labor Statistics

Home Work

Most of the people who do job-related work at home aren't compensated for their time, according to 1991 data, the most recent government statistics. Of those who are paid, most are self-employed.

Characteristic	Both sexes Number (thousands)	Percent	Men Number (thousands)	Percent	Women Number (thousands)	Percent
Total, 16 years and older*	19,967	100.0%	10,731	100.0%	9,236	100.0%
Worked at home for pay	7,432	37.2	4,210	39.2	3,222	34.9
Self-employed workers	5,553	27.8	3,439	32.0	2,115	22.9
Wage and salary workers	1,879	9.4	772	7.2	1,107	12.0
Worked 8 hours or more	3,651	18.3	1,894	17.6	1,757	19.0
Self-employed workers	3,078	15.4	1,656	15.4	1,422	15.4
Wage and salary workers	573	2.9	238	2.2	335	3.6
Worked 35 hours or more	1,070	5.4	438	4.1	632	6.8
Self-employed workers	976	4.9	408	3.8	568	6.1
Wage and salary workers	94	0.5	30	0.3	64	0.7
Worked at home, not paid (wage and salary only)	12,165	60.9	6,392	59.6	5,773	62.5

*Groups may not sum to totals because totals include unpaid family workers and wage and salary-workers who did not report their pay status.
Source: U.S. Bureau of Labor Statistics

Top 10 States For Small Offices/Home Offices 1996

	Number of small home offices
1 California	71,266
2 New York	50,101
3 Texas	48,010
4 Pennsylvania	42,142
5 Washington	38,240
6 Illinois	33,700
7 Florida	32,931
8 Ohio	31,026
9 Michigan	30,628
10 New Jersey	28,526

Source: Dun & Bradstreet's Cottage Industry File

Getting Organized

Against the bleak backdrop of dwindling membership, labor unions have pledged a comeback. To do this, recruiters are fishing in new fields.

Three decades ago at the peak of labor's power, unions could net thousands of new members with a single vote at a manufacturing plant. But after decades of downsizing and computerization, high-paying manufacturing jobs are rapidly disappearing. In 1996, union membership was 16.3 million, compared with 17.7 million in 1983. And the percentage of workers in unions fell to 14.5% from 20% in 1983.

But the union movement received a big morale boost in August, when the Teamsters staged a successful strike against United Parcel Service. Not only did the union win many of its contract demands, but it also won strong public support.

To gain new members unions have begun

to focus on small and medium-size employers in lower-paying sectors. Union recruiters show up at nursing homes and in apple orchards. They talk the labor line to workers just off welfare and to blackjack dealers in Las Vegas. They rally both the young and the old to join their cause. The AFL-CIO, for one, added work-family issues to its plate to reach out to women workers, who make up a growing percentage of the labor movement.

To strengthen its ranks, labor is adjusting to the new demographics. For instance, one of the fastest growing sectors in the labor force is elder care, often recognized for low pay and hard work. Only about 10% of the 17,000 nursing homes in the U.S. are unionized. But there is some evidence of change. In 1995 and 1996, the Food and Commercial

Workers targeted eight southern states, winning 25 of 37 union campaigns. This contrasts with the two previous years, when it conducted four union campaigns in the South, winning three. And the Service Employees International Union, also trying to organize nursing-home workers, has won three-quarters of its 232 drives since 1993.

College sudents had a hand in some of that success. The United Food and Commercial Workers union said 32 summer volunteers went on its three-week bus tour of the South and helped spark 15 of its organizing campaigns at nursing homes. Meanwhile, the AFL-CIO tapped into the energies of its retired members by asking them to help with recruiting drives and protests.

The AFL-CIO, under the leadership of John

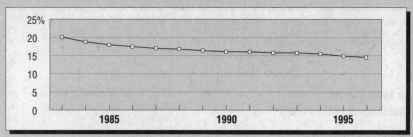

Labor Unions' Waning Influence
Percentage of Wage and Salary Employees Who Were Union or Employee Association Members

Year	Union or employee association members (thousands)	Union or association members as percent of wage and salary employment
1983	17,717	20.1%
1984	17,340	18.8
1985	16,996	18.0
1986	16,975	17.5
1987	16,913	17.0
1988	17,002	16.8
1989	16,960	16.4
1990	16,740	16.1
1991	16,568	16.1
1992	16,390	15.8
1993	16,598	15.8
1994	16,748	15.5
1995	16,360	14.9
1996	16,269	14.5

Source: U.S. Bureau of Labor Statistics

Sweeney, also has made a bid to recruit people recently pushed into the work force because of welfare reform. In Baltimore, for example, the American Federation of State, County and Municipal Employees, voted to target people who are required to work in order to keep their welfare benefits. But critics warn that the union leaders may sabotage welfare reform by driving up wages to artificially high levels.

One of the biggest organizing efforts in years is occurring in Las Vegas. The AFL-CIO launched a three-pronged campaign pursuing hotel, hospital and construction workers. And if the drive, which is expected to last for years and cost millions, is successful, Las Vegas could become the symbol for a revitalized labor movement.

Changing Membership of the 10 Largest Affiliates of the AFL-CIO
(Ranking based on 1995 membership; numbers in thousands)

Organizations	1955	1965	1975	1991	1995
International Brotherhood of Teamsters	—	—	—	1,379	1,285
American Federation of State, County and Municipal Employees	99	237	647	1,191	1,183
Service Employees International Union	—	—	480	881	1,027
United Food and Commercial Workers International Union	—	—	—	997	983
Automobile, Aerospace and Agricultural Implement Workers of America*	1,260	1,150	—	840	751
International Brotherhood of Electrical Workers	460	616	856	730	679
American Federation of Teachers	40	97	396	573	613
Communications Workers of America	249	288	476	492	478
International Association of Machinists and Aerospace Workers	627	663	780	534	448
United Steelworkers of America	980	876	1,062	459	403

*Disaffiliated in 1968 and reaffiliated in 1981.
Source: AFL-CIO

A Striking Trend
Number of Work Stoppages Involving 1,000 or More Workers

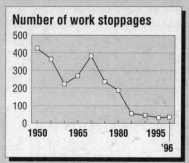

Number of work stoppages

Year	Stoppages		Days Idle
	Number	Workers involved (thousands)	Number (thousands)
1950	424	1,698	30,390
1955	363	2,055	21,180
1960	222	896	13,260
1965	268	999	15,140
1970	381	2,468	52,761
1975	235	965	17,563
1980	187	795	20,844
1985	54	324	7,079
1990	44	185	5,926
1995	31	192	5,771
1996	37	273	4,887

Source: U.S. Bureau of Labor Statistics

Business Trips with Baby

More business travelers are packing diapers in their briefcases.

The number of people bringing kids along on business trips has been exploding, as parents try to save money and spend more time with their children. In 1996, 41 million busi-ness trips included children, a 55% jump from 1990, according to the Travel Industry Association of America. In the process, airlines and hotels have been scrambling to accommodate—and cash in on—this trend with more elaborate programs for kids.

Delta Air Lines, for example, has airport lounges for kids, complete with computer video games, and hotels are making a science out of babysitting kids, offering everything from karaoke contests to desert-survival and computer classes. Parents on business are taking advantage of all this as much as those on vacation. The travel industry sees it as an opportunity to get repeat business when working parents return for vacation.

Hyatt Hotels introduced "Camp Hyatt" as an activity program for kids in 1989, and more and more, the parents using the camp are on business trips. In the summer when school is out, Hyatt officials say, the number of kids on business trips shoots up dramatically. It has been a "big surprise ... completely unexpected," says Ann Lane, director of the camp program, who now occasionally works with corporate-meeting planners to coordinate kid activities with parents' work schedules. For such activities, hotels usually charge $20 to $80 a day, a fee that traveling executives, not their companies, typically pick up.

In New Orleans, Diane Lyons started an on-site child-care company for conventioneers, called Accent on Children's Arrangements Inc., charging $6 to $15 an hour. Her most impressive job: a worldwide convention for McDonald's Corp., in which she organized Cajun dance classes, alligator handlers and crawfish races for 400 children.

Some parents bring kids along on business travel because it's cheaper than hiring a full-time babysitter, especially if the trip doesn't include flying. A few parents even put their kids to work, handing out materials at meetings and putting up posters.

Other parents say they feel too guilty leaving kids at home. Jack Sandner, chairman of the Chicago Mercantile Exchange, says he brings at least one of his seven children along on his business trips. He says he would get lonely and miss his family too much otherwise. But it's not always easy to mix the two. He says he excuses himself during business dinners to do things like stop a food fight among his troop.

Top Transfer Locations

The Top U.S. Cities for Corporate and Government Relocations

	1995				1996		
1.	Houston	6.	Philadelphia	1.	Chicago	6.	Washington D.C.
2.	Chicago	7.	New York	2.	Houston	7.	San Francisco
3.	Atlanta	8.	San Francisco	3.	Atlanta	8.	Philadelphia
4.	Dallas	9.	Denver	4.	Dallas	9.	Denver
5.	Washington D.C.	10.	Los Angeles	5.	New York	10.	Phoenix

The Top Countries for International Transfers

	1995				1996		
1.	Mexico	6.	Hong Kong	1.	England	6.	Japan
2.	Chile	7.	Australia	2.	Mexico	7.	Hong Kong
3.	Belgium	8.	France	3.	Belgium	8.	Singapore
4.	Germany	9.	Netherlands	4.	Germany	9.	France
5.	England	10.	Singapore	5.	Australia	10.	India

Source: PHH Relocation

How Affordable Is Working Abroad?

Worldwide Cost-of-Living Index (Standard City, USA = 100.0)

Expensive Locations		Less Expensive Locations	
Hong Kong, China	412.4	Montreal, Canada	115.2
Tokyo, Japan	397.1	Johannesburg, South Africa	130.0
Seoul, South Korea	389.2	Mexico City, Mexico	139.1
Beijing, China	349.7	Nairobi, Kenya	145.4
Singapore	336.3	Prague, Czech Republic	147.1

The table above is based on a U.S. expatriate family of two with a base salary of $75,000. Total annual costs are based on a combination of housing, transportaion, and goods and services. Taxes are not included.

Annual Housing Costs in Selected Cities

Bombay, India	$70,459
Duesseldorf, Germany	28,868
Hong Kong, China	132,892
London, England	58,770
Madrid, Spain	31,916
New York, NY	61,449
Paris, France	36,985
San Francisco, CA	39,519
Singapore	80,998
Sydney, Australia	34,237
Tokyo, Japan	83,839

The annual rental housing costs are based on a U.S. expatriate family of two earning $75,000 and residing in a four-to-six room unit. Utilities and renter's insurance are included.
Source: Runzheimer International

1997 Business Travel Costs in Selected U.S. Cities

	Per Diem Total
New York (Manhattan)	$342
Chicago	271
Atlanta	206
Nashville	199
Los Angeles	189
Anaheim	176
Las Vegas	170
San Diego	167
Dallas	165
St. Louis	164
Orlando	160

Note: The per diem totals represent average costs for the typical business traveler, and include breakfast, lunch and dinner in business-class restaurants and single-rate lodging in business-class hotels and motels.

Source: Runzheimer International.

1997 Overseas Business Travel Costs

LOCATION	PER DIEM TOTAL
Hong Kong	$474
Tokyo, Japan	440
Moscow, Russia	392
Buenos Aires, Argentina	383
Paris, France	377
Rio de Janeiro, Brazil	286
Edinburgh, Scotland	268
Munich, Germany	247
Cairo, Egypt	238
Johannesburg, S. Africa	161
Penang Island, Malaysia	143
Panama City, Panama	135
Bordeaux, France	133
Monterrey, Mexico	129
Ottawa, Canada	122

Per diem totals shown above represent average costs for the typical business traveler and include breakfast, lunch and dinner in business-class restaurants and single-rate lodging in business-class hotels and motels.

Source: Runzheimer International

HAZARDOUS DUTY

Going to work is getting downright dangerous.

Studies by government agencies and business organizations conclude that workers are in greater jeopardy of being the victims of violence on the job. The Society for Human Resource Management found in a 1996 survey that nearly half of all human-resource managers had seen cases of violence on the job since 1994, compared with 33% in a similar study covering the period 1988 to 1993.

The National Institute for Occupational Safety and Health (NIOSH) says that every week, an average of 20 people are murdered at work. In addition, the U.S. Justice Department reports that more than 1.5 million people a year are the victims of rape, robbery or other assaults on the job.

The increase in violence is widespread, occurring both in offices where coworkers strike out and at commercial establishments like convenience stores and fast-food restaurants where robbers are the aggressors. "Are we ready to accept the murder of 20 workers a week as the cost of doing business?" says Lynn Jenkins, author of the NIOSH study,

"Violence in the Workplace: Risk Factors and Prevention Strategies." "Death or injury should not be an inevitable result of one's chosen occupation." She and other experts on workplace safety believe more precautions must be taken to protect workers, but they say violence still gets too little attention, partly because it often involves low-paying, low-skill jobs.

Indeed, the increase in workplace violence is due primarily to the growth of service businesses. NIOSH found that the riskiest jobs are those in which workers deal with the public, exchange money and deliver goods and services. Being a cab driver is the deadliest occupation, followed by police and security guard; sales-counter clerk, especially at convenience food stores, liquor stores and jewelry shops; and gas-station attendant. In New York City, where taxis reign supreme, picking up fares is an especially scary proposition: A record 45 taxi drivers were killed in the city in 1992. Nationally, the taxi-driver homicide rate per 100,000 workers reached 32.4 in 1995.

Hospitals and nursing homes are particularly hazardous places for nonfatal injuries.

Nursing aides and orderlies are the targets of many nonfatal assaults, which most often include hitting, kicking or beating by patients.

Coworkers can be a threat, too, as job insecurity, sexual harassment and other tensions create more disharmony. The federal government estimates that about 5% of workplace homicides are committed by coworkers. And according to the Society for Human Resource Management's survey, 39% of companies reported verbal threats by workers in the past couple of years, 22% had incidents of pushing and shoving, and 13% said there was a fist fight at the office. The society estimates that personality conflicts are at the root of nearly two-thirds of violent workplace incidents.

Layoffs and firings sometimes spur people to seek revenge. Paul Calden, a then 33-year-old man who lost his job with the Fireman's Fund Insurance Co. in 1992, walked into a cafeteria in a Tampa office building a year later and screamed, "This is what you all get for firing me!" He then proceeded to shoot at five of his former bosses, killing three of them. He later killed himself.

But it doesn't necessarily take a job loss to inspire murderous thoughts. Dorsey Thomas had a spotless record during his 23 years as a postal worker until he entered a mail-sorting plant in Palatine, Ill., and shot two coworkers in the summer of 1995. The U.S. Postal Service has seen more than its share of coworker shootings, and the violence has even spawned the expression "going postal," to mean losing control and turning aggressive with coworkers.

The Postmaster General has established a policy whereby any postal worker bringing a firearm to work would be subject to immediate dismissal. But NIOSH believes the postal service also should add more security devices to post offices, such as metal detectors. "We must begin to change the way work is done to minimize or remove the risk of workplace violence," says Ms. Jenkins of NIOSH. "We must

Violence in the Workplace

Crimes of violence on the job	Number in 1994	Percent of total crimes of this type
Simple assault	1,264,230	20.9%
Aggravated assault	315,520	14.9
Robbery	81,280	6.7
Rape/sexual attack	16,480	3.9
Total	1,677,510	17.1

Source: U.S. Justice Department

Occupations with High Risk of Work-Related Homicides, 1995

Occupation	All fatalities	Number of homicides	Rate of homicides per 100,000 employed
Taxi drivers and chauffeurs	99	69	32.4
Police and detectives	174	81	7.7
Guards	101	59	6.6
Sales counter clerks	10	10	5.0
Gas station attendants	28	8	4.0
Cashiers	116	107	3.9
Managers, food and lodging	58	46	3.6
Sales, supervisors and proprietors	212	133	3.0
Total, all occupations	6,210	1,024	0.8

Source: U.S. Bureau of Labor Statistics

Work-Related Injuries and Illnesses

Number of Nonfatal Occupational Injuries and Illnesses, by Industry Division, 1995

Industry division	Total cases (thousands)		Lost workday cases (thousands)	
	Injury	Illness	Injury	Illness
Private industry	6,080.6	494.8	2,767.6	204.5
Agriculture, forestry, and fishing	115.4	5.4	51.7	1.9
Mining	36.3	1.5	22.8	0.6
Construction	476.2	8.7	217.9	4.0
Manufacturing	1,818.3	304.3	838.1	132.6
Durable goods	1,181.7	188.4	520.4	74.8
Nondurable goods	636.6	115.9	317.7	57.8
Transportation and public utilities	502.0	21.6	289.2	10.1
Wholesale and retail trade	1,583.9	48.2	674.3	19.5
Wholesale trade	445.8	13.1	214.7	6.9
Retail trade	1,138.1	35.1	459.6	12.5
Finance, insurance, and real estate	138.3	17.2	52.2	7.1
Services	1,410.2	87.9	621.4	28.8

Source: U.S. Bureau of Labor Statistics

also change the way we think about workplace violence by shifting the emphasis from reactionary approaches to prevention."

In the private sector, some companies have taken such precautions. Understandably so. Workplace violence is quite costly to the victims and their employers, resulting in 1.8 million lost work days a year and more than $55 million in lost wages. "High levels of stress may lead to violence in the workplace," says Ms. Jenkins, "but a violent incident in the workplace will most certainly lead to stress, perhaps even to post-traumatic stress disorder."

Southland Corp., which owns 7-Eleven Stores, has installed brighter lights, closed-circuit televisions and wider aisles and says its robbery rate dropped significantly. Many human-resource managers also say they have beefed up security to protect their employees.

According to the Society for Human Resource Management, an added check-in desk is the most popular technique, followed by limiting public access, more lighting, access-card entry systems, and employee and visitor identification cards.

While such steps may keep dangerous outsiders out, safety experts say it is extremely difficult to spot potentially violent employees before they lash out. The majority of violent workers are male, lack friends, and exhibit signs of intense anger, but those traits fit a lot of people. Moreover, says James Fox, a professor of criminology at Northeastern University in Boston, trying to weed out such people may provoke an already angry and frustrated person by making him or her feel more isolated. "You may precipitate a blood bath by [singling someone out] or forcing a guy into counseling," he says.

Injury-Prone Businesses

Nonfatal Occupational Injuries: Number of Cases and Incidence Rates per 100 Full-Time Workers, for Industries with 100,000 or More Injury Cases, 1995

Industry	Total cases (Thousands)	Incidence rate
Eating and drinking places	365.6	7.4
Hospitals	268.9	9.0
Nursing and personal care facilities	246.9	17.8
Trucking and courier services, except air	229.0	13.9
Grocery stores	203.1	9.6
Department stores	173.2	10.3
Motor vehicles and equipment	169.4	17.0
Hotels and motels	119.4	9.4

Source: U.S. Bureau of Labor Statistics

Dangerous Occupations

Index of Relative Risk and Number of Occupational Fatalities Resulting from 1995 Injuries, for 10 High-Risk Occupations (Index for All Workers = 1.0)

Occupation	Index of relative risk	Number of fatalities	Major deadly event
Fishers	21.3	48	drowning (81%)
Timber cutters	20.6	98	struck by object (81%)
Airplane pilots	19.9	111	airplane crash (98%)
Structural metal workers	13.1	38	fall (66%)
Taxicab drivers and chauffeurs	9.5	99	homicide (70%)
Construction laborers	8.1	309	vehicular (28%)
Roofers	5.9	60	fall (75%)
Electrical power installers and repairers	5.7	35	electrocution (60%)
Truck drivers	5.3	749	highway crash (68%)
Farm workers	5.1	579	vehicular (50%)

Source: U.S. Bureau of Labor Statistics

Death on the Job

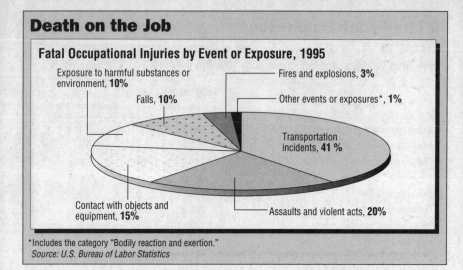

Fatal Occupational Injuries by Event or Exposure, 1995

Exposure to harmful substances or environment, **10%**

Falls, **10%**

Fires and explosions, **3%**

Other events or exposures*, **1%**

Transportation incidents, **41 %**

Contact with objects and equipment, **15%**

Assaults and violent acts, **20%**

*Includes the category "Bodily reaction and exertion."
Source: U.S. Bureau of Labor Statistics

The Corporate Casual Look

Casual dress is gaining greater acceptance in the workplace, boosting morale and saving workers money. The trend is good news for casual clothing makers like Levi Strauss & Co., but sales of dressy apparel have sagged.

Frequency of Casual Dress	1992	1995
Every day of the week	7%	28%
Most days of the week, except when there is contact with customers or clients	12	5
Once a week on a specified "dress down" day	17	42
On special occasions	20	11
On a seasonal basis	4	1
On some other basis	4	3
Total	64	90

Source: Evans Research Associates and Levi Strauss & Co.

Popular Casual Dress	1993 retail sales	1995 retail sales	1996 retail sales
Item of Clothing			
Men's casual pants	$2,300,000,000	$2,800,000,000	$3,000,000,000
Men's knit sport shirts	4,600,000,000	5,700,000,000	6,700,000,000
Women's slacks and pants	4,200,000,000	5,100,000,000	5,500,000,000

Source: NPD Group Inc.

5

MONEY & INVESTING

I T JUST KEEPS ON GOING, *and going, and going. For nearly seven years stock prices have been marching higher. The Dow Jones Industrial Average, far and away the most popular measure of the stock market's health, over that time climbed an astounding 243%, to 8113.44 from 2365.10, as of July 25, 1997. The Great Bull Market of the 1990s, which began on the heels of a modest recession, is the longest in history. During that period the stock market has not experienced even a 10% decline—a "correction" in Wall Street parlance—from the records it has continued to hit. Trading volume on the New York Stock Exchange has climbed to an average daily pace of 515 million shares from 157 million in 1990. Over that period, more than 4,000 companies have entered the glorified ranks of "publicly traded" companies, financing their future growth through the issuance of more than $181 billion of new stock. The total value of all companies listed on the Big Board has burgeoned to $7.6 trillion from $2.8 trillion at the beginning of 1990.*

Fueling the march higher has been an increasing infatuation with stocks by Americans of all stripes. Young Matt Seto, who lives in a suburb of Detroit, began toying with stocks in his early teens. His deep interest and not inconsiderable skill as a stock picker won him a profile on the front page of *The Wall Street Journal* in 1994 while he was still in high school. Since then he has had job offers from major brokerage firms and has penned his own book, *The Whiz Kid of Wall Street's Investment Guide.* At the other extreme is 84-year-old William S. Hall, a lawyer in Indianapolis who spends much of his time exhorting young colleagues to follow his own "buy-and-hold" strategy of investing in stocks.

But the real power that has driven stocks up is the vast bulk of middle America identified by the label "baby boomer." Members of the group— farmers in Iowa, investment bankers on Wall Street, auto workers in Detroit, insurance agents in Los Angeles—have little in common except middle age and their nearly universal concern about retiring without the help of Social Security.

It is that concern, as well as the problems of financing children's educations and meeting other, lesser, financial goals, that has prompted an intense interest in investing, especially in stocks. And their circumstances—usually married, with furniture, cars, and other "necessities" of life already purchased—enable them to do something about it. Today four of every 10 Americans own stock in one form or another, some of them directly and many others through mutual funds. That compares to just two in 10 in the 1980s.

Fortunately for the stock market, the baby boomers' interest in investing coincides with a remarkable economic environment, one that *The Wall Street Journal* has dubbed the Goldilocks Economy—not too strong, not too weak, but just right. That environment—low inflation, low interest rates, and moderate economic growth—is the perfect soil to nurture growing interest in investing and the higher stock prices that result. The environment is the product of several

trends. Some credit can be directly apportioned to specific individuals: Alan Greenspan, the chairman of the Federal Reserve, has, through uncanny skill or just plain luck, used monetary policy to keep the economy in the "slot" between too-fast growth and inflation and no growth or recession. The much-maligned "restructuring" of American industry that resulted in layoffs of hundreds of thousands of blue-collar and white-collar workers during the 1990s has had its benefits, too. American industry is today among the most productive and competitive in the world. Caterpillar's heavy equipment is sold around the world, Microsoft and Intel set the world standards for developments in software and computing, and American financial institutions dominate the globe. Taken together, these industries and this economy have created the values that are reflected by the rise of stock prices for most of this decade.

Of course, the enthusiasm for stocks has occasionally seemed to get out of hand. Remember the

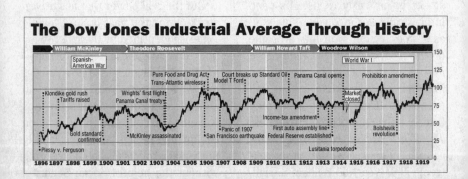

The Dow Jones Industrial Average Through History

public debut of Netscape? The venerable firm of Morgan Stanley & Co. introduced Netscape to the public in August 1995. The frenzy to own a share of the new network browser had people phoning Morgan Stanley begging to be allowed to buy a share of Netscope. Or Netcap. Whatever. While Morgan Stanley judged the stock to be worth $28 a share, the public within minutes of its debut drove the price to a mindboggling $71. Calmer heads eventually prevailed and Netscape early in 1997 was trading at about $25 a share.

Mr. Greenspan, frequently regarded by investors as a sort of demigod, has felt it necessary to discipline his overly enthusiastic admirers like a stern father cautioning a rambunctious offspring to be more careful. Late in 1996, Mr. Greenspan wondered publicly if the stock market was exhibiting "irrational exuberance" as it set one record after another. That and other subtle warnings were largely ignored by investors. The Fed chairman finally decided a spanking of sorts was in order. Late in March, he nudged short-term interest rates moderately higher. That got their attention!

Fears that the Fed would raise rates even further, perhaps putting the economy into a recession that would kill the golden goose of corporate earnings, sent the stock market into a tail spin. In a matter of a few weeks the Dow Jones Industrial Average spiraled down 9.8%, the biggest loss since 1990. But as it hovered just shy of the 10% decline that would officially mark a "correction," companies began reporting their first-quarter profits. One after another, they surprised Wall Street with the strength of their earnings' power and once again, it was off to the races.

Such displays of strength have humbled more than a few Wall Street experts in the past few years. David Shulman is one. The chief stock market strategist for Salomon Brothers was a persistent pessimist for much of the bull market's seven-year run. Only in 1995 did he concede that he had been very wrong. Citing a "paradigm shift" that suddenly made what he had thought was an overvalued market much more reasonable, he finally changed his bearish position and joined the bulls. Elaine Garzarelli, the pundit who claims credit for having

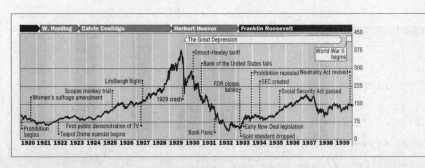

predicted the Stock March Crash of October 1987, predicted in the summer of 1997, a stock market retreat that didn't occur. And Jeffrey Vinik, the mutual-fund meister who was running Fidelity's gigantic and prestigious Magellan Fund back in 1995, got cold feet as stock prices rose and rose and rose. Preparing for the worst, he shifted a huge chunk of Magellan's billions of dollars out of stocks and into what he thought would be the safety of bonds. Sadly for him, it was bonds that weren't safe at that point. Stocks continued their relentless drive higher, leaving the Magellan Fund with a miserable record. Mr. Vinik now works elsewhere. Amid it all, one of the few stock market analysts to get it right consistently has been Goldman Sach's Abbey Joseph Cohen. It is perhaps comforting to note that her recent view called for a continuation of the bull market, albeit at a more stately pace than the rapid growth that investors enjoyed in 1995 and 1996.

Perhaps most humbling of all, however, is the remarkable performance in the last few years of the lowly "index" funds. These funds are designed merely to mimic the performance of some stock market index, usually Standard & Poor's 500-stock index. Because their goal is so simple, it is sometimes said that a monkey could run an index fund. While it isn't quite that simple, it is true that because an index fund requires no highly paid managers or expensive research staff, index funds are very inexpensive compared to funds run by active managers like Mr. Vinik. Yet in 1995 and 1996, the performance of S&P Index funds left the vast majority of active managers in the dust, struggling to justify the high salaries they were paid to do better than the overall market.

And there have been some true disasters among mutual fund managers, especially among the so-called momentum investors, who care little for the true value of a stock, only for the rate at which its price can climb beyond all that is reasonable. While it's difficult to find an investment manager who claims to use the technique, many funds labeled "aggressive growth" enjoyed strong momentum in stock prices in 1995 and early 1996. Money poured

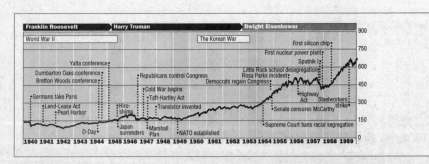

into the funds from investors of every sort. But the summer of 1996 saw a series of disappointing earnings reports among the hot-shot little companies that momentum players favor and the party came to an abrupt end. The funds' prices tumbled and the money flowed back out almost as fast as it had flowed in, as investors decided that perhaps they didn't really want to be *that* aggressive.

Wall Street, of course, never sits still when there is money to be made and the past few years have seen a frenzy of activity as everyone vies to get the little guys' money. The real winners of that competitive frenzy have been the mutual funds. Many small investors have decided that they are better teachers, lawyers or engineers than they are investors and have given the management of their investment portfolio over to the experts. The ability of mutual funds to offer instant diversification and professional management has made them an attractive choice, especially compared to the army of stock brokers who nag clients and make most of their money by persuading customers to trade into and out of indi-

vidual stocks. The popularity of mutual funds as investing instruments has led to a burgeoning number of funds. Indeed, early in 1997 there were more mutual funds than there were individual stocks traded on the New York Stock Exchange.

But the traditional brokerage firms have been fighting back, mostly through the creation of such products as "wrap accounts." These accounts give investors access to several brokerage services—individual stock trades, money market accounts with check-writing privileges, and the firms' proprietary mutual funds—for a single overall fee. That fee, it should be noted, is usually considerably higher than the management expenses charged by mutual funds. At the same time, brokers are being encouraged—sometimes ordered—by their firms to turn themselves into financial advisers offering far more than just stock brokerage advice. The frenzy to get their hands on the small investors' money prompted a wave of deals among mutual funds and investment banks culminating early in 1997 in the decision by one of Wall Street's most prestigious investment banks,

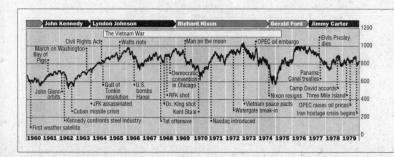

Morgan Stanley, to merge with one of the largest retail brokerage firms, Dean Witter.

Regardless of which camp wins in the long run, the vast amount of money flowing into stocks and other investments has generated record profits on Wall Street. And record profits have, in turn, generated the payment of record bonuses to Wall Street's denizens. Rising sales of expensive sports cars in Manhattan have been just one of the manifestations of money flowing back out of Wall Street. Prices of luxury real estate in Manhattan's coops and condominiums is another. Real estate brokers report happily watching bidding wars erupting among young Wall Streeters for million-dollar residences. And out in the posh Hamptons on Long Island, the really big bonuses are being spent on massive beach houses replete with swimming pools, tennis courts, and the latest mark of ostentation, elevators. All of which leads some of the older, more circumspect observers to conclude that all those young bankers, brokers, and traders who haven't endured even a minor blip in stock prices in six years, are confusing a bull market with their own brainpower.

What will bring it all to a screeching stop? A resurgence of inflation and a punishing crackdown by the Federal Reserve could do the trick. But if Mr. Greenspan continues to be as successful—or lucky—as he has been in managing the economy for the past several years, that isn't very likely to happen. Indeed, that's just the point: The thing that will bring the Great Bull Market of the 1990s to an end and spoil the love affair between investors and the stock market is almost certain to be something that is totally unexpected and unpredictable.

**Douglas R. Sease, deputy editor,
Money and Investing at
*The Wall Street Journal***

The Dow Jones Industrial Average

Dow Milestones

Milestone	Date	Comment
40.94	May 26, 1896	The index of 12 stocks (now 30), is launched by Wall Street Journal co-founder Charles Dow and distributed by hand.
100.00	Jan. 12, 1906	DJIA's first century mark comes 10 years after launch. But the news, greeted with little fanfare, doesn't make the front page of *The Wall Street Journal.*
500.00	March 12, 1956	After taking a quarter century to go from 300 to 400, the average speeds through 500 in little more than a year.
1000.00	Nov. 14, 1972	After near-misses at crossing this mark for the previous six years, the public gapes but reaction is muted in *The Wall Street Journal.* A front-page article attaches "little market significance" to it.
2000.00	Jan. 8, 1987	New Year's rally pushes index past milestone after four years of a bull market.
3000.00	April 17, 1991	Rally after Gulf War propels stocks past milestone, nine months after just missing.
4000.00	Feb. 23, 1995	Optimism about interest rates pushes DJIA ahead, more than a year after first flirting with the mark.
5000.00	Nov. 21, 1995	Just in time for Thanksgiving, DJIA surges past milestone just nine months after breaking 4000.
6000.00	Oct. 14, 1996	Shrugging off a summer pullback that included two 100-point-or-more drops, the DJIA breaks barrier as inflation fears ebb.
7000.00	Feb. 13, 1997	Quickest-ever vault of a 1,000 point milestone continues a long bull market despite increasing warnings about high valuations.
8000.00	July 16, 1997	DJIA recovers from 9.8% plunge in March and April to continue the bull market.

Source: Wall Street Journal research

Defined Bull Markets

Beginning		Ending			
Date	DJIA	Date	DJIA	% Gain	Days
9/24/00	38.80	6/17/01	57.33	47.8	266
11/09/03	30.88	1/19/06	75.45	144.4	802
11/15/07	38.83	11/19/09	73.64	89.7	735
9/25/11	53.43	9/30/12	68.97	29.1	371
12/24/14	53.17	11/21/16	110.15	107.2	698
12/19/17	65.95	11/03/19	119.62	81.4	684
8/24/21	63.90	3/20/23	105.38	64.9	573
10/27/23	85.76	9/03/29	381.17	344.5	2,138
11/13/29	198.69	4/17/30	294.07	48.0	155
7/08/32	41.22	9/07/32	79.93	93.9	61
2/27/33	50.16	2/05/34	110.74	120.8	343
7/26/34	85.51	3/10/37	194.40	127.3	958
3/31/38	98.95	11/12/38	158.41	60.1	226
4/08/39	121.44	9/12/39	155.92	28.4	157
4/28/42	92.92	5/29/46	212.50	128.7	1,492
5/17/47	163.21	6/15/48	193.16	18.4	395
6/13/49	161.60	1/05/53	293.79	81.8	1,302
9/14/53	255.49	4/06/56	521.05	103.9	935
10/22/57	419.79	1/05/60	685.47	63.3	805
10/25/60	566.05	12/13/61	734.91	29.8	414
6/26/62	535.76	2/09/66	995.15	85.7	1,324
10/07/66	744.32	12/03/68	985.21	32.4	788
5/26/70	631.16	4/28/71	950.82	50.6	337
11/23/71	797.97	1/11/73	1051.70	31.8	415
12/06/74	577.60	9/21/76	1014.79	75.7	655
2/28/78	742.12	9/08/78	907.74	22.3	192
4/21/80	759.13	4/27/81	1024.05	34.9	371
8/12/82	776.92	11/29/83	1287.20	65.7	474
7/24/84	1086.57	8/25/87	2722.42	150.6	1,127
10/19/87	1738.74	7/16/90	2999.75	72.5	1,001
10/11/90	2365.10				

A Bull Market requires a 30% rise in the Dow Jones Industrial Average after 50 calendar days or a 13% rise after 155 calendar days. Reversals of 30% in the Value Line Composite since 1965 also qualify. The NYSE was closed from 7/31/14 to 12/11/14 due to World War I. DJIA was then adjusted to reflect the composition change from 12 to 20 stocks.
Source: Ned Davis Research, Inc.

Defined Bear Markets

Beginning		Ending			
Date	DJIA	Date	DJIA	% Decline	Days
6/17/01	57.33	11/09/03	30.88	-46.1	875
1/19/06	75.45	11/15/07	38.83	-48.5	665
11/19/09	73.64	9/25/11	53.43	-27.4	675
9/30/12	68.97	7/30/14	52.32	-24.1	668
11/21/16	110.15	12/19/17	65.95	-40.1	393
11/03/19	119.62	8/24/21	63.90	-46.6	660
3/20/23	105.38	10/27/23	85.76	-18.6	221
9/03/29	381.17	11/13/29	198.69	-47.9	71
4/17/30	294.07	7/08/32	41.22	-86.0	813
9/07/32	79.93	2/27/33	50.16	-37.2	173
2/05/34	110.74	7/26/34	85.51	-22.8	171
3/10/37	194.40	3/31/38	98.95	-49.1	386
11/12/38	158.41	4/08/39	121.44	-23.3	147
9/12/39	155.92	4/28/42	92.92	-40.4	959
5/29/46	212.50	5/17/47	163.21	-23.2	353
6/15/48	193.16	6/13/49	161.60	-16.3	363
1/05/53	293.79	9/14/53	255.49	-13.0	252
4/06/56	521.05	10/22/57	419.79	-19.4	564
1/05/60	685.47	10/25/60	566.05	-17.4	294
12/13/61	734.91	6/26/62	535.76	-27.1	195
2/09/66	995.15	10/07/66	744.32	-25.2	240
12/03/68	985.21	5/26/70	631.16	-35.9	539
4/28/71	950.82	11/23/71	797.97	-16.1	209
1/11/73	1051.70	12/06/74	577.60	-45.1	694
9/21/76	1014.79	2/28/78	742.12	-26.9	525
9/08/78	907.74	4/21/80	759.13	-16.4	591
4/27/81	1024.05	8/12/82	776.92	-24.1	472
11/29/83	1287.20	7/24/84	1086.57	-15.6	238
8/25/87	2722.42	10/19/87	1738.74	-36.1	55
7/16/90	2999.75	10/11/90	2365.10	-21.2	87

A Bear Market requires a 30% drop in the Dow Jones Industrial Average after 50 calendar days or a 13% decline after 145 calendar days. Reversals of 30 % in the Value Line Composite also qualify. This applied to the 1990 high and low. (The table uses corresponding high and low dates and values for DJIA). The NYSE was closed from 7/31/14 to 12/11/14 due to World War I. DJIA was then adjusted to reflect the composition change from 12 to 20 stocks. *Source: Ned Davis Research, Inc.*

Biggest Drops in the Dow Jones Industrial Average

Days with Greatest Net Loss

Rank	Date	Close	Net change	% change
1	10/19/87	1738.74	-508.00	-22.61
2	08/15/97	7694.66	-247.37	-3.11
3	06/23/97	7604.26	-192.25	-2.47
4	10/13/89	2569.26	-190.58	-6.91
5	03/08/96	5470.45	-171.24	-3.04
6	07/15/96	5349.51	-161.05	-2.92
7	03/13/97	6878.89	-160.48	-2.28
8	03/31/97	6583.48	-157.11	-2.33
9	10/26/87	1793.93	-156.83	-8.04
10	08/08/97	8031.22	-156.78	-1.91

Days with Greatest Percentage Loss

Rank	Date	Close	Net change	% change
1	10/19/87	1738.74	-508.00	-22.61
2	10/28/29	260.64	-38.33	-12.82
3	10/29/29	230.07	-30.57	-11.73
4	11/06/29	232.12	-25.55	-9.92
5	12/18/99	58.27	-5.57	-8.72
6	08/12/32	63.11	-5.79	-8.40
7	03/14/07	76.23	-6.89	-8.29
8	10/26/87	1793.93	-156.83	-8.04
9	07/21/33	88.71	-7.55	-7.84
10	10/18/37	125.73	-10.57	-7.75

Biggest Jumps in the Dow Jones Industrial Average

Days with Greatest Net Gain

Rank	Date	Close	Net change	% change
1	09/02/97	7879.78	257.36	3.38
2	10/21/87	2027.85	186.84	10.15
3	04/29/97	6962.00	179.01	2.64
4	09/16/97	7895.92	174.78	2.26
5	04/22/97	6833.59	171.38	2.60
6	07/22/97	8061.65	154.93	1.96
7	06/24/97	7758.06	153.80	2.02
8	05/05/97	7214.50	143.29	2.03
9	06/12/97	7711.47	135.64	1.79
10	04/15/97	6587.16	135.26	2.10

Days with Greatest Percentage Gain

Rank	Date	Close	Net change	% change
1	10/06/31	99.34	12.86	14.87
2	10/30/29	258.47	28.40	12.34
3	09/21/32	75.16	7.67	11.36
4	10/21/87	2027.85	186.84	10.15
5	08/03/32	58.22	5.06	9.52
6	02/11/32	78.60	6.80	9.47
7	11/14/29	217.28	18.59	9.36
8	12/18/31	80.69	6.90	9.35
9	02/13/32	85.82	7.22	9.19
10	05/06/32	59.01	4.91	9.08

Best Years for the Dow Jones Industrial Average

The Dow's Best Years

Rank	Date	Close	% change
1	1915	99.15	81.66
2	1933	99.90	66.69
3	1928	300.00	48.22
4	1908	86.15	46.64
5	1954	404.39	43.96
6	1904	69.61	41.74
7	1935	144.13	38.53
8	1975	852.41	38.32
9	1905	96.20	38.20
10	1958	583.65	33.96

Worst Years for the Dow Jones Industrial Average

The Dow's Worst Years

Rank	Date	Close	% change
1	1931	77.90	-52.67
2	1907	58.75	-37.73
3	1930	164.58	-33.77
4	1920	71.95	-32.90
5	1937	120.85	-32.82
6	1914	54.58	-30.72
7	1974	616.24	-27.57
8	1903	49.11	-23.61
9	1932	59.93	-23.07
10	1917	74.38	-21.71

Source: Dow Jones & Co.

On any given day, the Dow Jones Industrial Average might move quite differently than other indexes because of its focus on blue-chip industrials. But over longer periods of time, the major, popular indexes generally move together. Here is how the DJIA compares for periods ended Dec. 31, 1996.

Index	1 year	3 years	5 years
Dow Jones Industrial Average	26.01%	71.77%	103.49%
Nasdaq Composite	22.71	66.20	120.18
NY Stock Exchange Composite	19.06	51.42	70.89
Russell 2000	14.76	40.23	90.92
Standard & Poor's 500	20.26	58.80	77.60
Wilshire 5000	18.84	54.54	78.13

Source: Dow Jones & Co

The Dow Jones Averages

The Dow Jones Industrial Average is an index of 30 "blue chip" U.S. stocks. At 100 plus years, it is the oldest continuing U.S. market index. It is called an "average" because it originally was computed by adding up stock prices and dividing by the number of stocks. (The very first average price of industrial stocks, on May 26, 1896, was 40.94.) The methodology remains the same today, but the divisor has been changed to preserve historical continuity. The DJIA is the best-known market indicator in the world, partly because it is old enough that many generations of investors have become accustomed to quoting it, and partly because the U.S. stock market is the biggest.

Dow Jones & Co. most recently changed the components of the DJIA, effective with trading on March 17, 1997.

The 30 stocks in the Dow Jones Industrial Average are:

AT&T Corp.	Hewlett-Packard Co.
AlliedSignal Inc.	International Business Machines Corp.
Aluminum Co. of America	International Paper Co.
American Express Co.	Johnson & Johnson
Boeing Co.	McDonald's Corp.
Caterpillar Inc.	Merck & Co.
Chevron Corp.	Minnesota Mining & Manufacturing Co.
Coca-Cola Co.	J.P. Morgan & Co.
Walt Disney Co.	Philip Morris Cos.
DuPont Co.	Procter & Gamble Co.
Eastman Kodak Co.	Sears, Roebuck & Co.
Exxon Corp.	Travelers Group Inc.
General Electric Co.	Union Carbide Corp.
General Motors Corp.	United Technologies Corp.
Goodyear Tire & Rubber Co.	Wal-Mart Stores Inc.

The 20 stocks in the Dow Jones Transportation Average are:

AMR Corp.
Alaska Air Group Inc.
APL Ltd.
CNF Transportation Inc.
Delta Air Lines Inc.
Illinois Central Corp.
Ryder System Inc.
UAL Corp.
US Airways Group Inc.
Xtra Corp.

CSX Corp.
Airborne Freight Corp.
Burlington Northern Santa Fe Corp.
Caliber System Inc.
Federal Express Corp.
Norfolk Southern Corp.
Southwest Airlines Co.
Union Pacific Corp.
USFreightways
Yellow Corp.

The 15 stocks in the Dow Jones Utility Average are:

American Electric Power Co.
Consolidated Edison Co. of New York
Duke Power Co.
Enron Corp.
Peco Corp.
Public Service Enterprise Group
Texas Utilities Co.
Williams Cos.

Columbia Gas System Inc.
Consolidated Natural Gas Co.
Edison International
Houston Industries Inc.
PG&E Corp.
Southern Co.
Unicom Corp.

The Original 12 Stocks in the Dow Jones Industrial Average

American Cotton Oil
American Sugar
American Tobacco
Chicago Gas
Distilling & Cattle Feeding
General Electric

Laclede Gas
National Lead
North American
Tennessee Coal & Iron
U.S. Leather preferred
U.S. Rubber

Long-Term Investment Performance

Average Annual Rates of Return, 1926–1996

Large Company Stocks	10.7%
Small Company Stocks	12.6
Long-Term Corporate Bonds	5.6
Long-Term Government Bonds	5.1
Intermediate-Term Government Bonds	5.2
U.S. Treasury Bills	3.7
Inflation	3.1

Source: Stocks, Bonds, Bills & Inflation 1997 Yearbook, Ibbotson Associates, Chicago

Dow Jones Global Indexes

The Dow Jones Global Indexes are a broad indicator of more than 3,000 companies worldwide, representing more than 80% of the equity capital on 31 stock markets around the globe. The indexes are market capitalization weighted—that is both the stock price and number of shares outstanding enter into the computation. This means a particular stock's effect on the indexes is proportionate to its value in the marketplace. The indexes are broken down by country and region, as well as by nine broad market sectors.

Quarter	World	United States	Americas	Europe	Asia/Pacific
03/31/93	101.34	429.09	108.43	99.72	94.64
06/30/93	106.46	427.84	108.33	98.98	109.55
09/30/93	111.07	436.78	110.28	107.74	114.67
12/31/93	111.08	442.19	112.18	116.08	106.76
03/31/94	111.80	422.69	107.00	113.87	116.43
06/30/94	114.60	420.28	105.93	111.69	127.21
09/30/94	116.11	437.13	110.91	115.39	123.12
12/30/94	113.91	433.07	108.53	115.70	119.39
03/31/95	117.67	472.01	117.07	121.55	116.15
06/30/95	122.21	514.49	127.63	128.66	111.97
09/29/95	127.96	553.41	136.97	132.44	114.95
12/29/95	133.46	581.43	143.61	136.54	119.80
03/29/96	138.01	610.77	150.93	141.40	121.18
06/29/96	141.31	633.63	156.50	143.89	122.91
09/30/96	142.45	653.06	161.08	148.52	118.02
12/31/96	147.57	700.56	173.40	162.41	108.93
03/31/97	146.71	713.69	176.48	168.23	98.23
06/30/97	167.53	831.56	205.34	181.80	115.57

Note: Indexes based on 6/30/82=100 for U.S., 12/31/91 =100 for World.

Country Performance

(In U.S. dollars)

Quarter	Canada	Mexico	U.S.	Austria	Australia	Belgium	France	Germany	Ireland	Italy	Netherlands	Spain	Switzerland	UK	Denmark	Finland
03/31/93	89.29	123.75	429.09	82.02	92.64	102.87	110.55	98.33	96.48	79.07	109.67	88.73	116.85	97.34	79.54	89.38
06/30/93	93.17	115.01	427.84	83.83	89.70	99.93	102.65	92.71	97.01	96.98	106.47	83.80	124.16	97.48	84.40	105.08
09/30/93	89.02	127.80	436.78	96.45	98.10	100.38	113.08	108.59	100.41	105.80	117.66	92.02	137.17	102.65	88.79	124.90
12/31/93	100.36	182.88	442.19	104.82	113.29	111.55	117.78	118.94	111.95	99.11	125.74	94.89	158.28	112.30	95.73	138.66
03/31/94	95.95	159.89	422.69	103.83	110.24	114.78	114.72	116.68	108.36	124.36	123.61	95.99	160.39	104.14	102.07	161.02
06/30/94	90.58	145.45	420.28	106.92	110.88	115.42	108.53	116.24	109.57	121.23	125.05	92.56	159.25	101.64	101.56	162.74
09/30/94	101.37	174.27	437.13	105.52	115.23	113.80	110.35	118.02	121.57	123.75	131.37	94.14	158.85	107.08	97.40	199.34
12/30/94	95.23	107.06	433.07	104.36	114.89	115.75	109.17	122.57	122.90	109.54	133.88	89.33	162.99	107.34	98.16	205.90
03/31/95	97.61	62.02	472.01	105.28	109.26	123.62	120.18	124.92	128.43	100.78	144.11	88.21	180.11	113.44	101.00	195.96
06/30/95	104.38	75.91	514.49	112.90	111.55	133.34	120.73	134.26	141.23	106.92	153.69	100.16	199.43	116.66	107.93	262.19
09/29/95	106.16	81.47	553.41	103.94	126.06	132.83	114.60	135.30	148.34	108.29	157.55	103.54	211.37	121.74	109.73	289.59
12/29/95	108.25	77.96	581.43	101.29	127.90	142.56	120.03	138.24	152.83	103.51	167.30	114.31	232.62	124.49	112.42	202.88
03/29/96	112.71	89.49	610.77	106.64	134.82	140.92	130.05	146.45	157.90	99.76	176.77	119.39	247.62	124.32	115.82	199.22
06/29/96	114.92	94.14	633.63	108.22	136.30	146.54	131.70	145.14	170.23	111.22	183.10	127.32	240.69	126.85	118.40	209.10
09/30/96	121.11	96.31	653.00	104.30	139.32	150.67	131.93	150.42	179.68	108.39	187.57	125.79	240.06	134.50	126.41	241.84
12/31/96	135.41	94.31	700.56	110.00	148.78	158.64	142.38	161.41	196.01	113.62	207.58	149.44	236.03	152.02	137.26	280.72
03/31/97	133.22	103.94	713.69	107.66	147.60	165.15	149.89	177.31	198.40	115.60	220.00	144.51	253.53	151.11	147.02	293.73
06/30/97	149.84	124.82	831.56	108.96	162.08	173.67	152.31	185.66	209.07	129.75	248.32	178.56	299.98	160.45	156.07	324.73

Quarter	Norway	Sweden	South Africa	Hong Kong	Indonesia	Japan	Malaysia	Philippines	Singapore	South Korea	Taiwan	Thailand	New Zealand	World
03/31/93	89.22	80.98	90.21	144.83	132.03	92.43	134.72	155.53	106.76	99.93	105.95	119.04	102.34	101.34
06/30/93	87.00	88.80	98.80	161.55	154.57	108.19	156.26	156.50	117.06	109.97	86.61	122.54	110.67	106.46
09/30/93	97.22	100.46	88.39	172.78	179.69	112.07	190.30	187.48	140.08	103.90	80.48	134.04	133.02	111.07
12/31/93	103.12	104.06	117.70	270.36	233.92	95.71	269.99	350.51	179.22	130.16	139.60	243.90	151.52	111.08
03/31/94	110.08	108.52	116.08	208.88	198.34	112.74	201.17	267.65	144.72	132.41	120.49	182.34	142.92	111.80
06/30/94	107.29	108.70	123.95	199.65	181.67	125.20	218.55	279.18	159.80	144.76	134.58	193.30	148.07	114.60
09/30/94	111.73	114.86	132.58	217.49	190.69	117.90	252.16	322.23	180.26	173.52	167.15	225.31	159.16	116.11
12/30/94	122.41	119.43	139.71	184.08	176.25	116.21	216.69	322.62	178.06	159.71	169.11	207.44	155.86	113.91
03/31/95	118.67	121.30	124.73	192.81	158.01	112.58	221.88	260.59	175.53	151.42	156.39	179.58	167.86	117.67
06/30/95	131.84	139.58	126.51	206.36	186.08	105.77	240.31	305.44	184.54	148.96	132.23	212.88	175.07	117.67
09/29/95	133.16	167.05	129.64	215.95	177.23	108.74	226.36	288.86	181.09	162.36	117.97	198.55	174.72	122.21
12/29/95	129.21	163.14	142.71	223.67	172.48	114.08	223.08	281.48	195.91	145.57	118.99	196.76	176.17	127.96
03/29/96	132.04	179.73	142.50	244.90	185.42	113.43	251.37	309.10	210.17	142.02	117.48	201.08	182.34	133.46
06/29/96	140.51	183.50	133.77	246.00	183.32	115.41	250.35	363.14	199.44	124.01	158.32	193.07	176.94	138.01
09/30/96	137.29	192.33	126.70	266.03	173.27	109.07	248.27	336.56	194.29	113.73	154.22	167.03	187.42	141.31
12/31/96	159.97	213.88	118.64	299.50	187.42	95.63	265.49	342.37	199.84	90.98	160.77	126.66	203.35	142.45
03/31/97	167.23	227.79	134.37	277.06	183.92	83.94	264.20	341.30	180.89	88.07	177.66	105.65	189.41	147.57
06/30/97	168.33	246.00	137.76	331.03	195.18	103.21	226.90	288.81	177.30	99.31	203.64	84.72	208.37	167.53

Market Sector Performance

Basic Materials

Quarter	World	United States	Americas	Europe	Asia/Pacific
03/31/93	100.07	408.20	107.58	99.68	93.05
06/30/93	106.94	412.99	111.31	97.27	109.15
09/30/93	105.80	406.48	107.72	107.06	104.03
12/31/93	109.04	443.38	120.54	116.50	94.05
03/31/94	116.90	448.35	120.86	124.15	109.53
06/30/94	122.48	450.79	120.11	124.91	124.52
09/30/94	131.61	495.23	134.49	132.88	129.42
12/30/94	124.40	456.55	122.37	130.79	123.53
03/31/95	124.80	489.98	128.84	132.65	116.53
06/30/95	126.40	532.95	140.12	140.54	105.44
09/29/95	131.35	546.77	144.12	143.04	112.86
12/29/95	130.91	540.47	142.29	139.82	115.33
03/29/96	142.15	610.04	159.00	155.58	118.91
06/29/96	138.05	572.73	149.76	156.27	117.64
09/30/96	137.01	607.01	155.44	160.96	107.67
12/31/96	136.62	614.63	159.76	175.09	95.66
03/31/97	135.40	625.04	160.00	174.89	88.97
06/30/97	146.19	711.78	176.87	179.91	100.49

Independent

Quarter	World	United States	Americas	Europe	Asia/Pacific
03/31/93	103.30	559.15	118.49	100.42	94.64
06/30/93	111.12	599.98	127.14	98.51	107.07
09/30/93	118.28	609.99	129.26	104.59	117.93
12/31/93	129.80	655.57	138.92	109.95	133.81
03/31/94	125.60	624.39	132.31	112.54	127.16
06/30/94	127.80	586.39	124.26	110.02	138.29
09/30/94	131.18	602.66	127.71	107.61	145.14
12/30/94	127.47	638.07	127.39	107.27	136.92
03/31/95	127.48	686.42	131.99	110.72	131.56
06/30/95	132.09	720.52	141.03	113.27	134.04
09/29/95	138.47	810.07	156.94	112.12	138.63
12/29/95	146.57	891.54	171.54	111.95	147.02
03/29/96	155.56	968.53	188.50	113.50	156.34
06/29/96	160.47	1072.38	208.12	113.08	156.06
09/30/96	162.01	1128.49	220.43	110.45	154.01
12/31/96	171.32	1228.43	239.69	120.42	156.70
03/31/97	166.71	1245.31	243.31	118.81	145.16
06/30/97	192.87	1624.94	314.70	117.47	161.31

Consumer, Cyclical

Quarter	World	United States	Americas	Europe	Asia/Pacific
03/31/93	108.79	556.83	123.73	103.43	98.41
06/30/93	112.10	536.29	119.42	103.28	110.03
09/30/93	120.36	557.91	124.10	114.27	120.35
12/31/93	123.24	596.43	132.71	124.23	115.14
03/31/94	126.45	566.98	125.87	127.93	127.38
06/30/94	128.93	543.79	120.38	124.68	139.61
09/30/94	127.40	544.04	121.08	128.76	133.60
12/30/94	124.27	532.55	116.99	126.99	130.65
03/31/95	125.40	572.78	124.32	130.69	125.16
06/30/95	126.69	609.69	132.32	135.20	119.16
09/29/95	130.83	624.14	135.19	143.31	122.87
12/29/95	135.13	635.01	137.37	141.84	131.00
03/29/96	143.81	691.68	149.60	155.06	134.89
06/29/96	151.19	717.10	155.27	161.79	144.25
09/30/96	147.43	707.89	153.23	160.62	138.10
12/31/96	148.64	711.02	154.81	171.94	134.36
03/31/97	146.77	733.08	159.12	176.44	123.34
06/30/97	162.65	822.66	179.05	179.62	141.92

Consumer, Noncyclical

Quarter	World	United States	Americas	Europe	Asia/Pacific
03/31/93	89.57	681.28	87.07	91.36	97.43
06/30/93	87.82	650.56	83.08	87.66	108.63
09/30/93	88.87	629.37	80.41	90.87	119.56
12/31/93	93.01	684.89	87.39	99.70	102.33
03/31/94	89.77	636.28	81.28	95.89	111.38
06/30/94	90.33	645.17	82.17	94.37	115.40
09/30/94	96.92	723.15	91.97	99.65	112.98
12/30/94	98.64	740.25	93.56	102.47	112.79
03/31/95	106.85	807.49	101.69	115.29	111.56
06/30/95	113.44	877.27	110.64	121.73	110.04
09/29/95	120.15	955.74	120.42	127.56	107.89
12/29/95	130.19	1052.90	132.18	136.69	113.11
03/29/96	135.05	1092.74	136.99	143.34	116.54
06/29/96	141.63	1178.74	147.64	145.25	120.00
09/30/96	144.31	1217.32	152.50	148.02	115.72
12/31/96	152.04	1287.32	161.59	159.80	111.49
03/31/97	156.78	1345.71	168.76	165.43	104.32
06/30/97	183.23	1615.97	202.24	183.63	125.37

Energy

Quarter	World	United States	Americas	Europe	Asia/Pacific
03/31/93	104.10	297.04	111.09	96.04	88.04
06/30/93	107.33	301.88	113.56	97.65	100.61
09/30/93	113.31	316.29	118.58	105.43	106.07
12/31/93	107.82	290.55	109.04	109.88	90.85
03/31/94	105.44	281.84	105.73	105.07	101.73
06/30/94	109.73	286.60	107.26	112.11	112.29
09/30/94	110.79	286.03	107.48	116.17	108.16
12/30/94	110.23	286.70	107.18	115.93	105.20
03/31/95	118.71	315.23	117.72	124.59	101.46
06/30/95	120.97	322.38	120.49	127.88	97.25
09/29/95	121.21	326.95	122.24	127.35	91.42
12/29/95	132.32	358.74	133.90	140.08	96.38
03/29/96	138.48	379.60	141.72	143.29	101.66
06/29/96	144.47	392.48	146.44	151.75	105.46
09/30/96	148.93	396.57	148.35	162.82	100.36
12/31/96	163.27	442.09	165.83	180.43	88.21
03/31/97	167.18	463.17	172.68	184.73	77.22
06/30/97	183.50	502.08	187.27	204.84	89.18

Financial

Quarter	World	United States	Americas	Europe	Asia/Pacific
03/31/93	101.57	447.38	126.79	103.71	90.01
06/30/93	113.23	444.14	126.46	105.18	112.14
09/30/93	119.99	471.88	133.62	116.76	116.41
12/31/93	114.97	436.98	125.19	124.04	106.72
03/31/94	113.75	419.30	119.47	114.41	111.84
06/30/94	118.83	436.79	123.27	110.33	122.34
09/30/94	115.42	428.43	121.67	112.28	115.25
12/30/94	112.75	408.25	115.38	113.44	112.31
03/31/95	114.97	458.30	128.12	117.49	108.47
06/30/95	118.95	510.12	142.46	125.86	105.24
09/29/95	125.06	583.53	162.15	127.20	107.21
12/29/95	134.62	611.76	169.86	138.30	116.48
03/29/96	135.88	658.02	182.33	134.21	115.25
06/29/96	135.48	663.17	184.07	133.85	113.89
09/30/96	139.33	717.06	199.11	141.88	110.39
12/31/96	142.64	809.78	226.06	156.02	96.83
03/31/97	140.16	839.60	234.56	165.95	82.52
06/30/97	163.64	991.84	277.23	181.66	101.18

Industrial

Quarter	World	United States	Americas	Europe	Asia/Pacific
03/31/93	98.21	402.37	109.65	101.55	91.27
06/30/93	104.05	406.15	110.68	99.37	102.28
09/30/93	108.29	413.69	112.37	108.65	106.06
12/31/93	106.00	432.52	117.79	119.17	94.28
03/31/94	112.68	420.08	113.11	122.52	108.80
06/30/94	116.61	406.37	108.87	117.70	120.75
09/30/94	116.48	415.77	114.28	119.99	116.65
12/30/94	112.24	399.79	107.60	118.28	112.64
03/31/95	113.38	438.48	115.20	119.97	110.12
06/30/95	113.40	462.68	122.38	126.09	103.96
09/29/95	117.02	477.70	126.27	128.97	107.72
12/29/95	118.38	499.93	131.64	123.96	109.12
03/29/96	124.54	533.46	140.53	134.18	112.60
06/29/96	127.14	540.93	142.44	137.84	115.47
09/30/96	125.10	555.23	146.13	141.98	108.12
12/31/96	122.31	581.94	153.16	150.92	95.38
03/31/97	117.30	570.07	150.61	152.44	86.22
06/30/97	133.49	675.85	178.14	161.02	99.41

Technology

Quarter	World	United States	Americas	Europe	Asia/Pacific
03/31/93	109.32	340.50	111.29	98.77	109.31
06/30/93	114.65	354.79	115.17	96.25	119.57
09/30/93	116.30	352.31	114.43	108.81	121.71
12/31/93	114.61	361.45	118.08	114.73	108.55
03/31/94	125.19	367.38	119.67	115.48	136.96
06/30/94	128.53	363.00	118.14	115.65	149.81
09/30/94	133.03	393.25	128.31	118.29	145.26
12/30/94	134.91	406.48	132.48	120.32	143.03
03/31/95	142.36	449.60	146.58	128.00	139.07
06/30/95	158.75	531.17	172.70	147.68	136.14
09/29/95	173.04	577.07	187.27	161.36	149.99
12/29/95	168.07	570.55	185.68	147.55	142.55
03/29/96	169.49	589.38	192.06	151.43	133.87
06/29/96	175.80	623.86	203.46	151.18	134.02
09/30/96	184.54	667.17	216.33	163.37	133.41
12/31/96	197.94	730.45	237.57	172.32	127.86
03/31/97	199.00	722.28	235.20	192.69	125.36
06/30/97	238.61	864.51	282.48	215.34	161.01

Utilities

Quarter	World	United States	Americas	Europe	Asia/Pacific
03/31/93	103.29	312.58	110.70	103.24	96.81
06/30/93	108.09	319.81	113.16	106.87	108.79
09/30/93	114.42	337.50	119.14	118.74	111.92
12/31/93	114.42	316.02	112.10	128.75	118.95
03/31/94	106.71	285.12	101.35	126.76	112.54
06/30/94	105.11	277.92	98.38	121.52	117.48
09/30/94	105.98	279.85	99.97	125.90	113.50
12/30/94	101.12	272.82	95.42	124.40	104.44
03/31/95	104.55	285.90	98.35	124.97	112.25
06/30/95	109.67	303.32	104.17	132.80	113.61
09/29/95	114.05	333.97	114.38	135.76	105.84
12/29/95	118.44	362.66	123.74	134.76	104.44
03/29/96	117.09	347.13	118.92	138.09	106.40
06/29/96	118.71	354.21	121.63	141.95	103.55
09/30/96	114.35	332.30	114.42	142.39	100.67
12/31/96	123.90	359.67	124.13	169.31	97.69
03/31/97	120.84	350.00	121.31	172.84	88.82
06/30/97	132.36	377.75	131.82	189.72	98.76

Stock Indexes

Dow Jones Industrials

The Dow Jones Industrial Average is a price-weighted average of 30 actively traded blue-chip stocks. The number of shares outstanding isn't taken into account, so higher-priced issues wield greater influence than lower-priced ones.

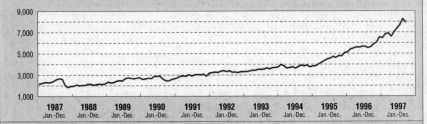

Dow Jones Transportation

The Dow Jones Transportation Average is a price-weighted average of the stocks of 20 large companies in the transportation industry.

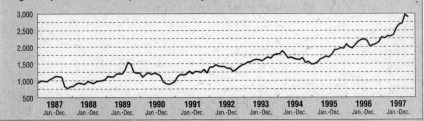

Dow Jones Utilities

The Dow Jones Utilities Average is a price-weighted average composed of 15 utility companies.

Dow Jones Composite

The Dow Jones Composite Average includes the 30 industrial stocks, 20 transportation stocks and 15 utility stocks in the other three averages

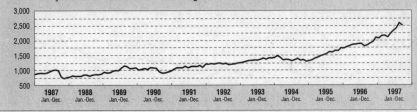

Standard & Poor's 500

The Standard & Poor's 500 Index is a market-value weighted index that includes 500 stocks chosen for market size, liquidity and industry group representation. The stock price is multiplied by the number of shares outstanding so that an issue's weight in the index is proportionate to its market value.

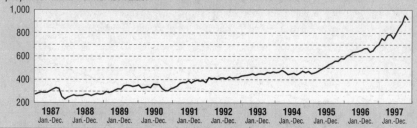

Nasdaq Composite

The Nasdaq Composite Index is a market-value weighted measure of all the common stocks listed on the Nasdaq Stock Market.

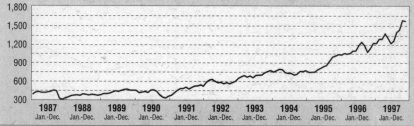

Russell 2000

The Russell 2000 Index represents the smallest two-thirds of the 3,000 largest U.S. companies, based on total market capitalization.

Wilshire 5000

The Wilshire 5000 Index, the broadest stock-market index, includes the equity securities of all U.S.-based companies with readily available price data.

New York Stock Exchange Composite

The New York Stock Exchange Composite Index is a market value-weighted index of all common stocks traded on the Big Board. There are four subgroup indices, shown below.

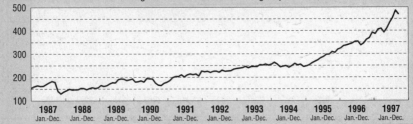

New York Stock Exchange Industrials

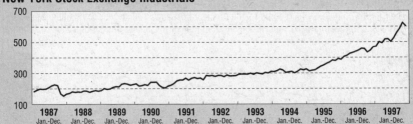

New York Stock Exchange Utilities

New York Stock Exchange Transportation

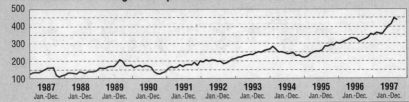

New York Stock Exchange Finance

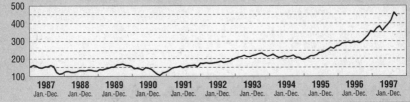

Value-Line Composite
The Value-Line Composite Index follows the performance of about 1,700 common stocks.

London FT-SE 100
The FT-SE 100 Index, which contains the stocks of Britain's 100 largest companies ranked by market capitalization, is the most widely quoted index for tracking the London Stock Exchange.

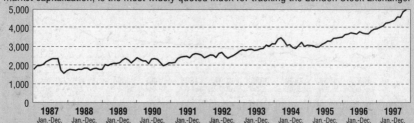

Tokyo Nikkei 225
The Nikkei 225 Index, which tracks 225 major issues, is the main index of the Tokyo Stock Exchange.

Foreign Currency Exchange Data

Japanese Yen
Japanese yen per U.S. dollar

German Mark
German marks per U.S. dollar

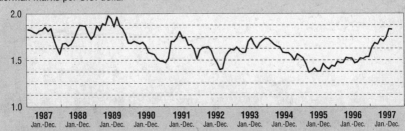

British Pound
British pound in U.S. dollars

Canadian Dollar
Canadian dollar in U.S. dollars

Commodities

Wheat
Price of Kansas City wheat per bushel

Gold
Comex spot price per troy oz.

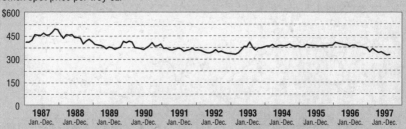

Crude Oil
West Texas intermediate crude, price per barrel

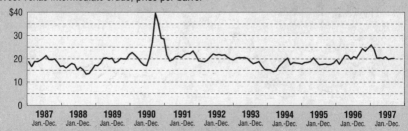

Bond Indexes

Dow Jones 10 Industrial Bonds
Dow Jones 10 Industrial Bonds tracks the bonds of 10 of the largest U.S. industrial companies.

Dow Jones 10 Utility Bonds

Dow Jones 10 Utility Bonds includes the bonds of 10 large utility companies.

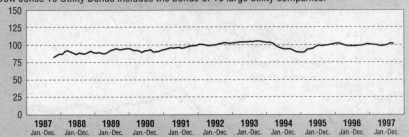

Dow Jones 20 Bond

Dow Jones 20 Bond Average represents the combination of the 10 utility bonds and 10 industrial bonds.

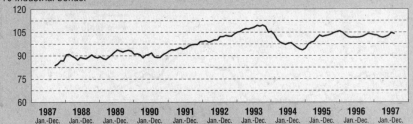

Merrill Lynch Corporate Bond

The Merrill Lynch Corporate Bond Index includes securities issued in the U.S. market with an outstanding face value of at least $100 million and a year or more left to final maturity.

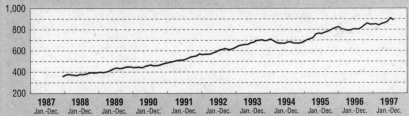

Lehman Long Treasury Bond

The Lehman Brothers Long Treasury Bond Index is a weighted average of all Treasury securities with maturities of 10 years and longer.

Bond Yields and Interest Rates

U.S. Treasury securities

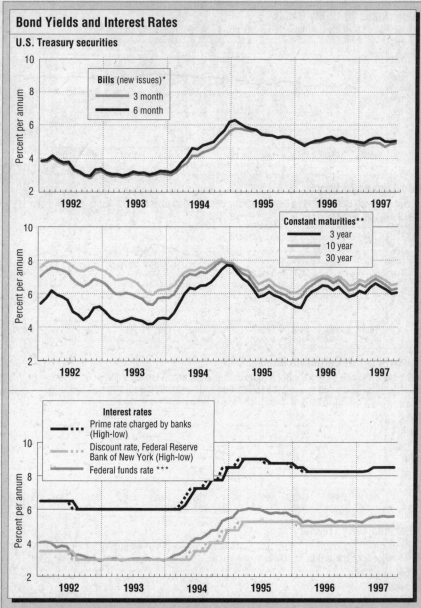

*Rate on new issues within period; bank-discount basis.

**Yields on the more actively traded issues adjusted to constant maturities by the Treasury Department.

***The daily effective rate is an average of the rates on a given day weighted by the volume of transactions at these rates.

Yields on Treasury Securities and Bonds (Percent per annum)

Year	U.S. Treasury securities					Corporate bonds (Moody's)		High-grade municipal bonds (Standard & Poor's)
	Bills (new issues)*		Constant maturities**					
	3-month	6-month	3-yr	10-yr	30-yr	Aaa	Baa	
1980	11.506	11.374	11.55	11.46	11.27	11.94	13.67	8.51
1981	14.029	13.776	14.44	13.91	13.45	14.17	16.04	11.23
1982	10.686	11.084	12.92	13.00	12.76	13.79	16.11	11.57
1983	8.630	8.750	10.45	11.10	11.18	12.04	13.55	9.47
1984	9.580	9.800	11.89	12.44	12.41	12.71	14.19	10.15
1985	7.480	7.660	9.64	10.62	10.79	11.37	12.72	9.18
1986	5.980	6.030	7.06	7.68	7.78	9.02	10.39	7.38
1987	5.820	6.050	7.68	8.39	8.59	9.38	10.58	7.73
1988	6.690	6.920	8.26	8.85	8.96	9.71	10.83	7.76
1989	8.120	8.040	8.55	8.49	8.45	9.26	10.18	7.24
1990	7.510	7.470	8.26	8.55	8.61	9.32	10.36	7.25
1991	5.420	5.490	6.82	7.86	8.14	8.77	9.80	6.89
1992	3.450	3.570	5.30	7.01	7.67	8.14	8.98	6.41
1993	3.020	3.140	4.44	5.87	6.59	7.22	7.93	5.63
1994	4.290	4.660	6.27	7.09	7.37	7.97	8.63	6.19
1995	5.510	5.590	6.25	6.57	6.88	7.59	8.20	5.95
1996	5.020	5.090	5.99	6.44	6.71	7.37	8.05	5.75

Sources: U.S. Treasury Department, Board of Governors of the Federal Reserve System, Federal Housing Finance Board, Moody's Investors Service, and Standard & Poor's Corp.

Stock Positions

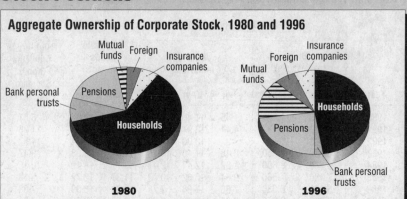

Aggregate Ownership of Corporate Stock, 1980 and 1996

1980

1996

Changing Ownership of Corporate Stock

Year	Households	Bank personal trusts	Pensions	Mutual funds	Foreign	Insurance companies
1955	88.6%	0.0%	2.1%	3.3%	2.2%	3.1%
1960	85.8	0.0	4.0	4.6	2.2	2.9
1965	83.8	0.0	5.9	5.0	2.0	2.9
1970	68.0	10.4	9.2	5.2	3.2	3.3
1975	56.7	11.5	16.5	4.9	4.2	5.2
1980	60.9	8.8	17.4	3.1	4.2	5.1
1985	51.3	7.3	24.8	5.0	5.3	5.5
1990	49.7	5.4	25.1	7.1	6.9	5.0
1995	49.7	2.4	22.6	12.7	6.1	5.9
1996	47.4	2.3	22.7	14.9	6.2	5.8

Source: Federal Reserve Board and New York Stock Exchange

Profile of Stock Owners

Stock ownership has grown dramatically in the 1990s. From 1965 to 1990, stock ownership among Americans doubled from 10.4% to 21.1%. In the next seven years, it doubled again, standing today at about 43% od adult Americans.

Investing in mutual funds has tripled over the past seven years, from 13% of all adults in 1990 tp 40% today. Fully 88% of investors now own shares in one or more mutual funds (up from 60% in 1990). Indeed, nearly half (46%) of all investors investors own all their stock through mutual funds.

Of those who own shares in mutual funds, 69% say their holdings exceed $10,000. Among those who own individual stocks, 59% claim holdings in excess of $10,000. (These groups overlap.) And two-thirds of all investors say that their stock and fund shares make up more than 20% of their total investments. The following is based on a survey of more than 1,200 investors.

Sex

Female 47% Male 53%

Highest Educational Level Reached

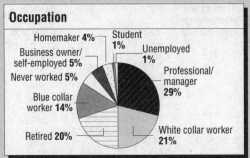

Doctoral/law degree 3%
2-3 years postgraduate work, master's degree 13%
Some high school 2%
High school graduate 23%
Some postgraduate work, no degree 4%
Some college, no degree 13%
4-year college/bachelor's degree 26%
Vocational training, 2-year college 12%

Age

18-24 2%
25-29 6%
65+ 16%
30-34 11%
60-64 6%
35-39 11%
55-59 8%
40-44 13%
50-54 13%
45-49 12%

Occupation

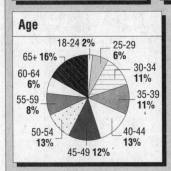

Homemaker 4%
Student 1%
Business owner/self-employed 5%
Unemployed 1%
Never worked 5%
Professional/manager 29%
Blue collar worker 14%
White collar worker 21%
Retired 20%

Race or Ethnic Origin

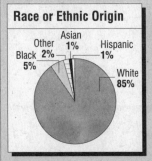

Asian 1%
Other 1%
Hispanic 1%
Black 2%
White 85%
5%

Household Income

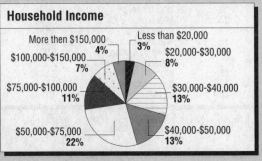

More then $150,000 4%
Less than $20,000 3%
$100,000-$150,000 7%
$20,000-$30,000 8%
$75,000-$100,000 11%
$30,000-$40,000 13%
$50,000-$75,000 22%
$40,000-$50,000 13%

Note: Percentages may not add up to 100% because some survey respondents did not provide all the information or said they were not sure.
Sources: Study by Peter D. Hart Research Associates for the Nasdaq Stock Market

Growth of Investment Clubs

1956	1,967
1960	5,608
1965	7,642
1970	13,678
1975	7,137
1980	3,642
1985	6,065
1990	7,082
1991	7,488
1992	8,639
1993	11,010
1994	12,905
1995	18,203
1996	26,962

Profile of Investment Club Members

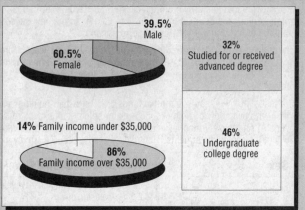

39.5% Male

60.5% Female

32% Studied for or received advanced degree

14% Family income under $35,000

86% Family income over $35,000

46% Undergraduate college degree

Source: National Association of Investment Clubs

Most Popular Stocks with Investment Clubs

Rank by no. of investment clubs holding	Company	Number of clubs holding stock	Rank by total shares held	Number of shares held by NAIC members
1	Motorola	9,334	8	1,867,166
2	PepsiCo	8,812	2	5,604,634
3	Merck	8,106	5	2,615,093
4	McDonald's	7,712	3	4,952,569
5	Intel	6,667	11	1,505,637
6	AFLAC	5,923	1	9,157,606
7	Coca-Cola	5,577	4	2,823,193
8	Lucent Technologies	4,545	29	600,731
9	RPM	4,311	7	2,323,386
10	AT&T	4,017	16	1,126,523
11	Diebold	3,773	25	662,820
12	Walt Disney	3,764	15	1,137,960
13	Microsoft	3,602	13	1,362,409
14	Home Depot	3,157	20	820,416
15	Abbott Laboratories	3,080	10	1,592,438
16	Johnson & Johnson	2,934	6	2,590,391
17	General Electric	2,922	14	1,240,083
18	Wendy's International	2,873	9	1,628,590
19	Cisco Systems	2,634	19	821,777
20	Wal-Mart Stores	2,378	12	1,369,660

Source: National Association of Investment Clubs

The Wall Street Journal Shareholder Scoreboard

Companies ranked by their total return to shareholders, including both change in the stock price and any dividends paid. It is assumed that dividends are reinvested in more shares. Performance is measured over different time periods, ended Dec. 31, 1996.

30 Stocks in the Dow Jones Industrial Average
Ranked on five-year average returns through Dec. 31,1996

Company name	1 year return	3 year average return	5 year average return	10 year average return
Union Carbide Corp	+10.9%	+25.0%	+42.5%	+21.1%
Travelers Group Inc	+46.7	+34.9	+37.9	+18.3
Sears, Roebuck & Co	+20.2	+24.0	+31.3	+17.0
Hewlett-Packard Co	+21.1	+38.0	+30.1	+18.1
Caterpillar Inc	+31.1	+21.2	+29.8	+16.0
American Express Co	+39.8	+31.3	+29.5	+11.9
AlliedSignal Inc	+43.1	+21.3	+27.2	+16.7
General Electric Co	+40.3	+26.8	+24.2	+19.9
United Technologies Corp	+42.4	+32.1	+23.1	+14.8
Coca-Cola Co	+43.3	+35.0	+23.0	+29.9
Procter & Gamble Co	+32.2	+26.3	+20.6	+22.0
Disney, Walt Hldg Co	+19.1	+18.6	+20.3	+21.2
Eastman Kodak Co	+22.3	+25.2	+19.9	+12.5
McDonald's Corp	+ 1.2	+17.6	+19.9	+17.3
Boeing Co	+37.6	+37.4	+19.9	+19.4
DuPont Co	+38.3	+28.8	+18.9	+17.0
Chevron Corp	+28.5	+18.8	+18.3	+16.1
Aluminum Co of America	+23.3	+25.1	+17.2	+17.4
General Motors Corp	+ 8.7	+ 2.9	+17.0	+10.2
Minnesota Mining & Mfg	+33.5	+20.3	+16.2	+15.2
Goodyear Tire & Rubber Co	+15.7	+ 6.2	+16.0	+12.4
Exxon Corp	+26.4	+20.8	+14.9	+15.9
Intl Business Mach	+67.7	+40.7	+14.1	+ 5.8
Johnson & Johnson	+18.1	+33.0	+14.0	+22.2
Philip Morris Companies	+30.7	+33.0	+12.0	+25.1
AT&T Corp	- 4.0	+ 7.5	+11.9	+12.8
Morgan, J.P. & Co Inc	+26.3	+16.8	+11.6	+13.5
Merck & Co	+23.9	+36.0	+10.3	+22.1
Intl Paper Co	+ 9.6	+ 8.7	+ 5.3	+10.9
Wal-Mart Stores Inc	+3.1	-2.3	-4.4	+15.3
Dow Jones Industrials	**+28.2**	**+22.6**	**+18.3**	**+16.6**

Sources: LEK/Alcar Consulting Group, IDD/Tradeline, Media General Financial Services Inc.

The Best Performers in the Shareholder Scoreboard

1 year

Company name	Stock symbol	Average return	Company name	Stock symbol	Average return
Rational Software	RATL	+253.6%	TJX Companies Inc	TJX	+153.6%
Western Digital Corp	WDC	+218.2	Chesapeake Energy Corp	CHK	+151.0
Dell Computer Corp	DELL	+206.9	Global Marine Inc	GLM	+135.7
United Meridian Corp	UMC	+190.6	Rowan Companies Inc	RDC	+135.1
American Power Conversn	APCC	+186.8	Intel Corp	INTC	+131.3
Atlas Air Inc	ATLS	+185.1	Apac Teleservices Inc	APAC	+130.0
Dura Pharmaceuticals Inc	DURA	+174.8	McAfee Associates Inc	MCAF	+125.6
Remedy Corporation	RMDY	+172.2	Interstate Bakeries Corp	IBC	+123.7
Compuware Corp	CPWR	+170.9	Peoplesoft Inc	PSFT	+123.0
CompUSA Inc	CPU	+166.7	Pairgain Technologies	PAIR	+122.4
Ross Stores Inc	ROST	+163.5	Noble Drilling Corp	NE	+120.8
NGC Corp	NGL	+162.8	CDW Computer Ctrs Inc	CDWC	+119.7
Falcon Drilling Co Inc	FLC	+161.7			

5 years

Company name	Stock symbol	Average return	Company name	Stock symbol	Average return
3Com Corp	COMS	+92.0%	Atmel Corp	ATML	+71.7%
Oxford Health Plans Inc	OXHP	+85.2	Aspect Telecommunication	ASPT	+67.5
Western Digital Corp	WDC	+85.0	Oracle Corporation	ORCL	+66.9
HBO & Co	HBOC	+84.2	Acxiom Corp	ACXM	+66.5
Tellabs Inc	TLAB	+83.6	Dell Computer Corp	DELL	+65.6
Clear Channel Comm Inc	CCU	+82.0	Robert Half Intl	RHI	+64.7
Corrections Corp Amer	CXC	+79.6	Wisconsin Central Transp	WCLX	+64.1
Adaptec Inc	ADPT	+78.8	Informix Corp	IFMX	+64.0
U.S. Robotics Corp	USRX	+78.3	Money Store Inc	MONE	+61.8
Glenayre Technologies	GEMS	+75.8	Intel Corp	INTC	+61.1
EMC Corp	EMC	+73.9	Andrew Corp	ANDW	+60.1
Cisco Systems Inc	CSCO	+72.7	Citicorp	CCI	+60.1
Iomega Corp	IOM	+72.6			

10 years

Company name	Stock symbol	Average return	Company name	Stock symbol	Average return
Concord EFS Inc	CEFT	+60.6%	Amgen Inc	AMGN	+40.3%
Oracle Corporation	ORCL	+53.5	Home Depot Inc	HD	+40.2
Microsoft Corp	MSFT	+51.0	Adaptec Inc	ADPT	+39.9
Clear Channel Comm Inc	CCU	+49.4	Sunamerica Inc	SAI	+39.7
Censeco Inc	CNC	+47.3	Intl Game Technology	IGT	+39.0
Nike Inc Cl B	NKE	+46.9	Compaq Computer Corp	CPQ	+36.9
Worldcom Inc	WCOM	+46.3	Iomega Corp	IOM	+36.6
Tellabs Inc	TLAB	+44.3	CUC International Inc	CU	+36.5
Intel Corp	INTC	+43.9	Andrew Corp	ANDW	+36.2
Harley-Davidson Inc	HDI	+43.3	United Healthcare Corp	UNH	+36.0
Micron Technology Inc	MU	+41.8	Linear Technology Corp	LLTC	+35.7
HBO & Co	HBOC	+41.1	Airgas Inc	ARG	+35.6
Applied Materials Inc	AMAT	+40.6			

Sources: LEK/Alcar Consulting Group, IDD/Tradeline, Media General Financial Services Inc.

The Worst Performers in the Shareholder Scoreboard

1 year

Company name	Stock symbol	Average return	Company name	Stock symbol	Average return
Acclaim Entertainment	AKLM	-73.7%	Adobe Systems Inc	ADBE	-39.4%
Ivax Corp	IVX	-64.0	Lam Research Corp	LRCX	-38.5
Intuit Inc	INTU	-59.6	Paging Network Inc	PAGE	-37.4
Sybase Inc	SYBS	-53.6	Medpartners Inc	MDM	-37.1
Caliber System Inc	CBB	-53.0	Bethlehem Steel Corp	BS	-36.0
DSC Communications Corp	DIGI	-51.5	Intergraph Corp	INGR	-34.9
Bay Networks Inc	BAY	-48.9	Apple Computer Inc	AAPL	-34.5
Glenayre Technologies	GEMS	-48.0	Great Lakes Chemical Cp	GLK	-34.4
Cablevision Systems Cl A	CVC	-43.5	Novell Inc	NOVL	-33.6
Digital Equipment Co	DEC	-43.5	Chiron Corp	CHIR	-32.6
Grand Casinos Inc	GND	-41.9	Informix Corp	IFMX	-32.1
Northeast Utilities	NU	-40.9	United Healthcare Corp	UNH	-31.1
C–Cube Microsystems Inc	CUBE	-40.9			

5 years

Company name	Stock symbol	Average return	Company name	Stock symbol	Average return
Ivax Corp	IVX	-23.2%	Intergraph Corp	INGR	-10.4%
Novell Inc	NOVL	-20.6	Yellow Corp	YELL	-9.1
Navistar Intl Hldg	NAV	-19.0	Stone Container Corp	STO	-8.9
United States Surgical	USS	-18.4	Bethlehem Steel Corp	BS	-8.7
Stride Rite Corp	SRR	-17.4	Rubbermaid Inc	RBD	-8.5
Apple Computer Inc	AAPL	-17.3	Digital Equipment Co	DEC	-8.1
Caliber System Inc	CBB	-16.4	Centocor Inc	CNTO	-7.7
Biomet Inc	BMET	-13.1	Bausch & Lomb Inc	BOL	-7.6
Hecla Mining Co	HL	-12.6	Niagara Mohawk Power Corp	NMK	-7.0
KMart Corp	KM	-12.2			
Alza Corporation	AZA	-11.6	Limited Inc (The)	LTD	-7.0
Amax Gold Inc	AU	-11.0	Safety-Kleen Corp	SK	-6.8
Food Lion Cl A	FDLNA	-10.4	RJR Nabisco Hldg Corp	RN	-6.7

10 years

Company name	Stock symbol	Average return	Company name	Stock symbol	Average return
Navistar Intl Hldg	NAV	-15.2%	USF&G Corp	FG	-2.0%
Unisys Corp	UIS	-11.7	Caliber System Inc	CBB	-1.6
Digital Equipment Co	DEC	-10.1	Armco Inc	AS	-1.3
Zenith Electronics Corp	ZE	-6.9	Hunt J.B. Trans Svcs Inc	JBHT	-1.0
Yellow Corp	YELL	-6.5	Dime Bancorp Inc	DME	-0.9
Hecla Mining Co	HL	-6.2	Stone Container Corp	STO	-0.4
Battle Mountain Gold Co	BMG	-4.9	Niagara Mohawk Power Cp	NMK	-0.3
Intergraph Corp	INGR	-4.9	Westinghouse Electric Cp	WX	-0.2
Reading & Bates Corp	RB	-4.2	Consolidated Freight Inc	CFWY	+0.3
U.S. Air Group Inc	U	-4.2	KMart Corp	KM	+0.5
Sun Energy Partners L.p.	SLP	-3.3	Amdahl Corp	AMH	+0.8
Beverly Enterprises Inc	BEV	-2.3	Alaska Air Group Inc	ALK	+1.0
Tandem Computers Inc	TDM	-2.2			

Sources : LEK/Alcar Consulting Group, IDD/Tradeline, Media General Financial Services Inc.

Mutual Funds Review

Largest Stock Funds
Percentage gains for periods ended June 30, 1997; assets as of May 31, 1997

	Assets ($ millions)	Performance 2nd quarter	12 months	5 years
Fidelity Magellan Fund	$56,264.5	+16.55%	+25.91%	+132.12%
Vanguard Index:500 Port	39,055.2	+17.41	+34.56	+144.91
Investment Co Of America	34,842.2	+14.86	+30.54	+120.61
Washington Mutual Inv	30,213.1	+14.44	+32.36	+142.87
Fidelity Growth & Income	29,544.5	+16.75	+29.83	+153.66
Fidelity Contrafund	26,504.1	+12.88	+24.31	+149.72
Fidelity Puritan	20,424.7	+12.34	+24.31	+112.26
Amer Cent:TC Ultra;Inv	20,129.7	+19.13	+21.93	+161.96
Vanguard Windsor	19,336.5	+11.11	+34.82	+138.59
Vanguard Windsor II	19,119.2	+14.70	+31.53	+142.64
Vanguard Wellington Fund	18,375.6	+12.19	+24.97	+107.76
Europacific Growth	18,327.7	+12.21	+24.62	+105.15
Janus Fund	17,554.8	+13.24	+22.37	+109.86
Income Fund of America	17,542.1	+ 7.99	+21.07	+ 93.97
Fidelity Adv Gr Opp;T	17,534.2	+14.42	+28.45	+146.20
Fidelity Equity-Inc	17,164.1	+14.80	+30.37	+146.51
Fidelity Equity-Inc II	15,760.8	+15.93	+26.73	+134.46
Vanguard Instl Index Fd	15,069.6	+17.47	+34.79	+146.47
New Perspective Fund	14,922.9	+11.96	+26.13	+113.03
Putnam Gro & Inc;A	14,775.7	+12.77	+29.23	+132.39
Dean Witter Divid Gro	14,080.0	+15.74	+29.29	+118.55
Templeton Fds:For;I	13,564.4	+ 7.46	+20.33	+ 84.22
AIM Eq:Consteltn;Rtl A	12,644.2	+15.59	+12.92	+156.49
Putnam Gro & Inc;B	11,968.0	+12.59	+28.30	+123.85
Fidelity Asset Manager	11,187.5	+11.28	+20.35	+ 81.71
Fidelity Blue Chip Grow	11,178.4	+16.73	+28.58	+164.13
Templeton Growth;I	11,176.8	+11.60	+26.99	+118.39
Growth Fund of America	10,566.0	+11.88	+22.41	+115.45
T Rowe Price Int:Stock	10,308.4	+11.88	+18.09	+ 89.07
Fidelity Growth Company	10,080.2	+15.70	+19.14	+146.32
T Rowe Price Equ Income	10,049.7	+11.43	+27.72	+134.45
Putnam Voyager;A	9,666.8	+17.32	+12.34	+147.39
Merrill Glbl Alloc;B	9,564.2	+ 7.14	+16.96	+ 85.35
American Mutual	8,701.1	+11.87	+24.92	+111.02
Fundamental Investors	8,586.7	+13.98	+30.65	+146.14
Janus Worldwide	8,296.3	+12.58	+25.72	+160.65
Templeton Fds:World;I	8,045.3	+13.21	+30.40	+131.37
Smallcap World Fund	7,746.7	+12.84	+13.65	+118.16
Brandywine Fund	7,651.0	+11.88	+24.05	+189.62
IDS New Dimensions;A	7,627.4	+15.57	+25.87	+142.68
Fidelity Low-Price	7,547.3	+11.71	+27.46	+160.49
Fidelity Value Fund	7,346.6	+13.67	+24.45	+151.22
Franklin Cust:Inc;I	7,296.9	+ 5.90	+13.19	+ 65.99
Fidelity US Equity Index	7,275.4	+17.38	+34.32	+143.64
Mutual Shares;Z	7,085.0	+ 9.15	+26.93	+148.50
AVERAGE U.S. STOCK FUND	—	+15.37	+22.00	+123.45
S&P 500 (with dividends)	—	+17.47	+34.71	+146.57

Source: Lipper Analytical Services

Total Assets of Mutual Funds (In billions)

Year end	All funds	Equity funds*	Bond & Income funds	Taxable money markets	Tax-exempt money markets
1979	$ 94.5	$ 35.9	$ 13.1	$ 45.2	$ 0.3
1980	134.8	44.4	14.0	74.5	1.9
1981	241.4	41.2	14.0	181.9	4.3
1982	296.7	53.7	23.2	206.6	13.2
1983	292.9	77.0	36.6	162.5	16.8
1984	370.7	83.1	54.0	209.7	23.8
1985	495.5	116.9	134.8	207.5	36.3
1986	716.3	161.5	262.6	228.3	63.8
1987	769.9	180.7	273.1	254.7	61.4
1988	810.3	194.8	277.5	272.3	65.7
1989	982.0	249.0	304.8	358.7	69.4
1990	1,066.9	245.8	322.7	414.7	83.6
1991	1,395.5	411.6	441.4	452.6	89.9
1992	1,646.3	522.8	577.3	451.4	94.8
1993	2,075.4	749.0	761.1	461.9	103.4
1994	2,161.5	866.4	684.0	500.4	110.6
1995	2,820.4	1,269.0	798.3	629.7	123.3
1996	3,539.2	1,750.9	886.5	761.8	140.1

*Equity funds include Aggressive Growth, Growth, Growth & Income, Precious Metals, International, Global-Equity, Income-Equity and Option/Income.

Growing Array of Mutual Funds

Number of funds

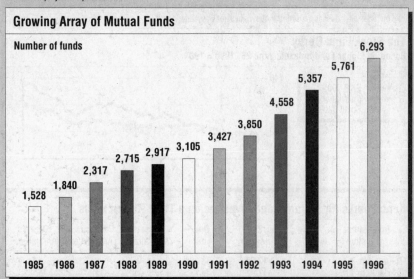

1985	1986	1987	1988	1989	1990	1991	1992	1993	1994	1995	1996
1,528	1,840	2,317	2,715	2,917	3,105	3,427	3,850	4,558	5,357	5,761	6,293

Source: Investment Company Institute

Mutual-Fund Performance Yardsticks
How Fund Categories Stack Up on a Total Return Basis

Investment objective	2nd quarter	One year	3 years (Annualized)	5 years (Annualized)	10 years (Annualized)
Capital Appreciation	+13.57%	+14.30%	+19.62%	+15.94%	+11.44%
Growth	+15.82	+24.39	+23.13	+17.22	+12.83
Small Cap Stock	+16.82	+13.53	+22.24	+18.40	+13.16
Mid-Cap Stock	+15.69	+15.44	+21.64	+17.81	+13.26
Growth & Income	+14.77	+28.98	+24.22	+17.50	+12.79
Equity Income	+13.08	+27.30	+21.75	+16.16	+11.84
Global (can include U.S.)	+11.80	+17.70	+15.10	+13.82	+10.34
International (non U.S.)	+11.02	+16.43	+ 9.80	+12.03	+ 8.08
Stock/Bond Blend	+ 9.68	+18.42	+16.27	+12.79	+10.45
Short-Term Debt	+ 2.20	+ 6.43	+ 6.32	+ 5.40	+ 6.75
Intermediate Corp. Debt	+ 3.31	+ 7.63	+ 7.63	+ 6.43	+ 8.14
Short-Term US Gov't	+ 2.27	+ 6.29	+ 6.18	+ 5.08	+ 6.98
Long-Term Gov't	+ 3.77	+ 7.15	+ 7.45	+ 6.46	+ 7.88
Long-Term Corp	+ 3.80	+ 8.52	+ 8.60	+ 7.46	+ 8.66
High-Yield Taxable	+ 5.15	+14.65	+11.30	+11.08	+ 9.79
General Taxable Bond	+ 4.28	+11.84	+ 9.87	+ 8.70	+ 8.55
Mortgage Bond	+ 3.07	+ 7.84	+ 6.66	+ 5.07	+ 7.94
World Income	+ 3.53	+11.19	+ 9.76	+ 5.77	+ 7.75
General L-T Muni	+ 3.49	+ 7.99	+ 7.18	+ 6.49	+ 7.76
Insured Muni	+ 3.43	+ 7.61	+ 7.18	+ 6.38	+ 7.74
Single State Muni Debt	+ 3.27	+ 7.70	+ 7.02	+ 6.46	+ 7.64

Note: Includes only Nasdaq-reporting funds; data as of 6 PM, July 1.

The Stock Fund Derby
Based on Lipper Fund Indexes; June 28, 1996 = 100

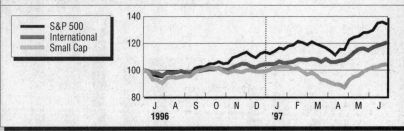

S&P 500
International
Small Cap

Benchmarks for Mutual-Fund Investors on a Total Return Basis

Investment objective	2nd quarter	One year	3 years (Annualized)	5 years (Annualized)	10 years (Annualized)
DJIA (w/divs)	+17.05%	+38.36%	+31.46%	+21.31%	– %
S&P 500 (w/divs)	+17.47	+34.71	+28.86	+19.78	+14.66
Small-Co. Index Fund[1]	+17.33	+18.17	+21.22	+18.61	*
Lipper Index: Europe	+ 7.47	+24.80	+18.56	+13.72	*
Lipper Index: Pacific	+12.29	+ 3.56	+ 2.83	+10.92	*
Lipper L-T Gov't[2]	+ 3.46	+ 7.14	+ 7.07	+ 5.65	+ 7.31
AVG. STOCK FUND	+15.37	+22.00	+22.83	+17.45	+12.90
AVG. BOND FUND[3]	+ 3.38	+ 8.28	+ 7.64	+ 6.70	+ 8.27

*Not applicable
[1]Vanguard's; tracks Russell 2000.   [2]Includes government agency debt.   [3]Taxable; preliminary data.
Source: Lipper Analytical Services

Second-Quarter and 12-Month Winners and Losers

Best- and worst-performing stock funds for the periods ended June 30, 1997; assets are figured as of May 31, 1997. Performance data are total returns, which include both share prices and reinvested dividends.

Second-Quarter Best Performers

Fund name	Assets ($ millions)	2nd quarter	12 months	5 years
			Performance	
Itt Hrtfd:Cap Appr;A	$27.0	+31.91%	* %	* %
Interact Inv:Tech Val	89.0	+31.51	+38.41	*
Morg Stan In:Tech;A	15.0	+29.38	*	*
Transam Prem:Eqty;Inv	46.9	+28.74	+51.38	*
Delaware Gr Aggr Gro;A	*	+28.64	+16.63	*
Stand Ayer Wood:Sm Cp II	1.6	+27.80	*	*
Wasatch:Micro–Cap	74.8	+27.56	+18.28	*
Munder:Micro–Cap Eq;Y	1.5	+26.65	*	*
Santa Barbara:Bender;Y	1.2	+26.63	*	*
Santa Barbara:Bender;C	3.2	+26.33	*	*
PBHG:Limited;PBHG	155.2	+26.08	+14.54	*
Fidelity Sel Brokerage	246.6	+26.01	+50.88	+220.19
TCW/DW Small Cap Gro	279.7	+25.79	− 9.00	*
PBHG:Strat Sm Co;PBHG	73.2	+25.62	*	*
The Japan Fund	478.6	+25.59	+ 0.54	+27.60
Ivy:Glbl Sci & Tech;A	11.2	+25.49	*	*
Morg Stan In:Japan;A	168.9	+25.45	+12.76	*
Flag Inv Emerg Gro;A	59.3	+25.35	+11.84	+108.98
Rydex:Nova Fund	579.0	+25.15	+44.79	*
Munder:Netnet	1.5	+25.15	*	*
Brazos:Jmic Sm Cap Gro	18.3	+25.00	*	*
Overland:Sm Cp Strat;A	2.8	+24.88	*	*
PBHG:Tech & Comm;PBHG	637.6	+24.88	+24.50	*
RCM:Global Small Cap	4.3	+24.87	*	*
Stagecoach:Sm Cap;Inst	32.7	+24.83	*	*
Parkstone:Sm Cap;Inst	527.8	+24.77	−4.39	+203.41
EV Mrthn Greater China	293.0	+24.70	+31.33	*
TCW/DW Mid–Cap Equity	169.3	+24.66	−9.00	*
MFS Strategic Growth;A	8.2	+24.52	+43.05	*
PBHG:Large Cap 20;PBHG	82.0	+24.43	*	*
Stand Ayer Wood:TX Sm Cp	19.7	+24.41	+11.85	*
Keystone Hart Emg Gr;A	74.6	+24.39	+ 8.47	+97.04
Fidelity Sel Telecomm	365.2	+24.32	+14.15	+151.37
Berger Inv:New Generation	102.0	+24.21	+ 6.08	*
Nich–App:Mini–Cap Inst	46.7	+24.15	+10.04	*
Pasadena:Sm&Md Cp Gr;A	13.9	+24.13	+37.36	*
Morg Stan In:Lat Am;A	67.2	+24.11	+59.54	*
Tip:Small Cap	79.7	+24.09	+ 2.57	*
Munder:Sm Co Growth;Y	141.1	+24.09	+19.13	+169.49
Bridgeway:Ultra–Small Co	25.6	+24.06	+26.34	*
Pioneer Growth Shrs;A	370.6	+24.06	+50.03	+171.28
API Trust:Yrktn Cl Val	13.1	+24.06	+40.97	*
Ni Micro Cap Fund	66.6	+24.04	+37.10	*
Ret Sys:Emerg Growth Eq	13.2	+23.92	+ 7.55	+238.04
Amelia Earhrt Eag Eq;A	1.5	+23.83	+33.60	*
Rod Sq Multi–Mgr:Growth	80.9	+23.63	+28.90	+144.11
PBHG:Large Cap Gro;PBHG	133.8	+23.56	+12.62	*
Morg Stan Fds:Latin;A	56.8	+23.51	+57.32	*
Guinness Flght:China	312.0	+23.51	+39.38	*
Dean Witter Japan	239.4	+23.48	− 5.57	*

*Not applicable; fund is too new.
Note: For funds with multiple share classes only the largest is shown.
Source: Lipper Analytical Services

Second-Quarter Worst Performers

Fund name	Assets ($ millions)	2nd quarter	12 months	5 years
Hudson Investors Fund	$ 0.3	−24.90%	−10.06 %	* %
US:Gold Shares	168.0	−22.26	−46.49	−50.16
Bull&Bear Gold Investors	19.0	−21.71	−37.81	−5.83
Lexington Strat Invments	37.3	−20.54	−35.51	+48.95
Midas Fund	173.2	−19.29	−31.94	+83.59
Morg Stan In:Gold;A	27.9	−18.01	−35.02	*
Gabelli Gold Fund	16.4	−17.24	−26.94	*
Lindner Inv:Bulwark;Inv	81.9	−17.18	−18.43	*
Frontier:Equity Fund	0.8	−16.74	−55.34	−59.12
Fontaine:Glbl Growth	4.6	−16.59	−30.68	+22.80
Van Eck:Gold Oppty;A	5.5	−16.29	−28.05	*
PIMCO Prec Metals;C	30.8	−16.04	−30.27	+12.97
Blanchard:Prec Metals	75.9	−15.02	−21.28	+51.44
Fidelity Sel Prec Mtls	226.7	−14.92	−26.65	+40.80
Rydex:Ursa Fund	295.4	−14.10	−20.00	*
INVESCO Strat:Gold	224.7	−13.64	−26.56	+39.19
Capp−Rush:Gold	4.9	−13.33	−29.31	*
Prudent Bear Fund	23.6	−12.64	−14.83	*
Amer Cent:AC Gl Gold	384.7	−12.33	−26.66	+17.76
Van Eck:Intl Gold;A	403.0	−12.15	−28.16	+12.10
Keystone Prec Metals	155.4	−12.07	−21.97	+27.06
Comstock Cap Value;A	148.9	−12.07	−18.36	−22.69
Lexington Goldfund	94.2	−11.93	−25.27	+20.30
Van Eck:Gold/Res;A	111.1	−11.39	−22.94	+21.37
IDS Precious Metals;A	83.2	−11.09	−29.94	+82.09
Monterey:Ocm Gold	1.7	−10.98	−21.35	−47.31
Pioneer Gold Shares;A	32.2	−10.46	−19.10	+23.75
Vanguard Spl:Gold	453.6	−10.29	−20.12	+22.87
Scudder Gold Fund	194.6	−10.26	−17.72	+69.99
MFS Gold & Natl Res;B	17.3	−10.14	−23.52	−8.79
Fidelity Sel Amer Gold	332.1	− 9.17	−18.82	+61.34
US:World Gold	231.5	− 9.06	−20.51	+78.28
Sogen:Gold Fund	48.9	− 8.96	−14.04	*
Dean Witter Prec Mtls	50.6	− 8.48	−22.84	+11.04
Rydex:Precious Metals	32.4	− 8.38	−22.74	*
EV Mrthn WW Dev Res	28.0	− 8.29	+ 1.89	+77.59
USAA Gold Fund	122.1	− 7.97	−22.26	+19.02
Lexington Strat Silver	46.0	− 7.93	−10.76	+43.84
Landmark Em Asia Mkt;A	9.2	− 7.76	−14.64	*
Franklin Gold Fund;I	321.7	− 7.58	−16.87	+18.12
Fidelity Emerging Mkts	1,088.5	− 7.15	− 6.16	+48.84
United Gold & Govt;A	25.6	− 6.41	−13.21	+24.35
Robrtsn Steph:Contr	1,056.0	− 6.01	+ 0.05	*
Oppenheimer Gld & Sp;A	140.2	− 5.16	−10.20	+22.51
Fontaine:Capital Apprec	5.7	− 4.82	−13.62	+32.28
Morgan Grenfell:Euro Sm	10.5	− 3.61	− 3.48	*
Rydex:Juno Fund	16.8	− 3.30	− 0.58	*
DFA Grp:UK Small Company	170.5	− 3.23	+11.93	+55.53
Steadman Amer Industry	1.0	− 2.70	+ 0.00	−43.75
Rightime:Blue Chip Fund	283.4	− 1.90	+ 6.15	+68.16

*Not applicable; fund is too new.
Source: Lipper Analytical Services

12-Month Best Performers

Fund name	Assets ($ millions)	Performance		
		2nd quarter	12 months	5 years
Morg Stan In:Lat Am;A	$ 67.2	+24.11%	+59.54%	* %
Morg Stan Fds:Latin;A	56.8	+23.51	+57.32	*
Fidelity Sel Home Fin	1,045.4	+19.42	+54.14	+309.42
Fidelity Sel Elctronic	2,307.5	+20.13	+52.63	+456.40
Legg Mason Value Tr;Prm	2,685.6	+18.05	+52.16	+198.43
Transam Prem:Eqty;Inv	46.9	+28.74	+51.38	*
Davis:Financial;A	150.8	+17.11	+51.20	+222.01
Fidelity Sel Brokerage	246.6	+26.01	+50.88	+220.19
Offitbank:Lat Am Eq;Sel	57.6	+18.04	+50.28	*
Pioneer Growth Shrs;A	370.6	+24.06	+50.03	+171.28
Fidelity Sel Regl Bnks	882.1	+15.36	+49.71	+214.89
Goldman Eq:Mid Cap;Inst	168.1	+19.64	+48.17	*
Fidelity Sel Enrgy Ser	565.9	+19.87	+48.12	+209.85
SS Research:Aurora;B	24.7	+20.20	+47.78	*
Rembrandt:Lat Am Eq;TR	22.3	+22.73	+47.40	*
INVESCO Strat:Financial	825.9	+18.79	+47.08	+187.65
Fidelity Sel Insurance	90.0	+22.07	+46.09	+165.35
Excelsior:Emerging Amer	90.8	+23.36	+45.98	*
Keystone Fund Amer;B	90.1	+20.84	+45.66	*
Painewbr Finl Svc Gr;A	100.6	+16.49	+45.29	+199.91
J Hancock Reg Bnk;B	3,976.7	+13.35	+45.13	+224.75
Delaware Pld:Real Est	49.0	+ 5.43	+45.00	*
American Heritage Fund	18.1	+20.48	+44.93	+ 16.84
Hudson Cap Apprec;A	20.5	+17.34	+44.85	+143.68
Texas Cap:Value & Growth	4.1	+18.99	+44.83	*
Rydex:Nova Fund	579.0	+25.15	+44.79	*
Titan Financial Svcs	8.2	+17.27	+44.75	*
Century Shares Trust	321.4	+19.89	+44.67	+127.55
Selected American Shares	1,709.2	+18.11	+44.55	+145.21
Federated Lat Am Gr;A	10.7	+21.31	+44.47	*
Fidelity Latin America	966.7	+22.09	+44.39	*
CGM TR:Realty Fund	301.9	+ 3.72	+43.76	*
TCW/DW Latin Amer Gr	325.4	+21.46	+43.58	*
Rydex:OTC Fund	386.5	+21.08	+43.48	*
Sequoia Fund	2,984.3	+21.49	+43.48	+171.17
Dreyfus Midcap Value	.34.4	+17.38	+43.34	*
Grandview Inv:Rlty Gro	1.1	+ 5.83	+43.21	*
MFS Strategic Growth;A	8.2	+24.52	+43.05	*
First Amer:Spec Eq;C	431.7	+17.97	+42.62	*
MAS Fds:Midcap Val;Inst	136.4	+17.56	+42.51	*
Stand Ayer Wood:TX Sn Eq	7.4	+16.70	+42.23	*
Fidelity Sel Financial	461.7	+17.86	+42.22	+205.20
T Rowe Price Int:Lat	405.2	+22.96	+42.21	*
GAM:Global;A	27.8	+16.32	+42.07	+154.02
Merrill Latin Amer;B	622.7	+20.14	+41.79	+ 77.11
Oakmark Small Cap	861.0	+16.03	+41.62	*
Vankamp Am Exchange	68.5	+11.99	+41.45	+153.42
Reynolds:Blue Chip Gro	55.4	+20.58	+41.19	+116.55
API Trust:Yrktn Cl Val	13.1	+24.06	+40.97	*
Franklin Val:Value;I	24.3	+15.16	+40.39	*

*Not applicable; fund is too new.
Source: Lipper Analytical Services

12-Month Worst Performers

Fund name	Assets ($ millions)	Performance 2nd quarter	12 months	5 years
Frontier:Equity Fund	$ 0.8	−16.74%	−55.34%	− 59.12%
US:Gold Shares	168.0	−22.26	−46.49	− 50.16
Bull&Bear Gold Investors	19.0	−21.71	−37.81	− 5.83
Lexington Strat Invments	37.3	−20.54	−35.51	+ 48.95
Morg Stan In:Gold;A	27.9	−18.01	−35.02	*
Steadman Tech & Growth	0.3	+ 4.62	−33.98	− 70.69
Midas Fund	173.2	−19.29	−31.94	+ 83.59
DFA Grp:Japan Small Co	244.0	+16.43	−31.32	+ 3.69
Fontaine:Glbl Growth	4.6	−16.59	−30.68	+ 22.80
PIMCO Prec Metals;C	30.8	−16.04	−30.27	+ 12.97
IDS Precious Metals;A	83.2	−11.09	−29.94	+ 82.09
Capp–Rush:Gold	4.9	−13.33	−29.31	*
Perkins Opportunity Fund	79.7	+11.29	−28.87	*
Van Eck:Intl Gold;A	403.0	−12.15	−28.16	+ 12.10
Van Eck:Gold Oppty;A	5.5	−16.29	−28.05	*
Gabelli Gold Fund	16.4	−17.24	−26.94	*
Amer Cent:AC Gl Gold	384.7	−12.33	−26.66	+ 17.76
Fidelity Sel Prec Mtls	226.7	−14.92	−26.65	+ 40.80
INVESCO Strat:Gold	224.7	−13.64	−26.56	+ 39.19
Govett:Smaller Co;A	162.4	+10.29	−26.38	*
Lexington Goldfund	94.2	−11.93	−25.27	+ 20.30
Fidelity Japan Sm Co	127.7	+22.03	−24.16	*
MFS Gold & Natl Res;B	17.3	−10.14	−23.52	− 8.79
Apex Mid Cap Gro	1.7	− 0.15	−23.29	*
Van Wagoner:Emrg Growth	463.8	+11.23	−23.25	*
Dreyfus Aggr Gro	135.5	+ 8.71	−23.01	*
Van Eck:Gold/Res;A	111.1	−11.39	−22.94	+ 21.37
Dean Witter Prec Mtls	50.6	− 8.48	−22.84	+ 11.04
Rydex:Precious Metals	32.4	− 8.38	−22.74	*
USAA Gold Fund	122.1	− 7.97	−22.26	+ 19.02
Keystone Prec Metals	155.4	−12.07	−21.97	+ 27.06
Monterey:Ocm Gold	1.7	−10.98	−21.35	− 47.31
Blanchard:Prec Metals	75.9	−15.02	−21.28	+ 51.44
Calvert Fd:Strat Gro;A	97.4	+10.63	−20.97	*
Franklin/Temp Japan	9.7	+ 9.95	−20.89	*
US:World Gold	231.5	− 9.06	−20.51	+ 78.28
Vanguard Spl:Gold	453.6	−10.29	−20.12	+ 22.87
Rydex:Ursa Fund	295.4	−14.10	−20.00	*
Japan Alpha Fund	3.8	+14.50	−19.41	*
Pioneer Gold Shares;A	32.2	−10.46	−19.10	+ 23.75
Fidelity Sel Amer Gold	332.1	− 9.17	−18.82	+ 61.34
Warb Pincus JP OTC;Com	82.6	+16.01	−18.52	*
Lindner Inv:Bulwark;Inv	81.9	−17.18	−18.43	*
Comstock Cap Value;A	148.9	−12.07	−18.36	− 22.69
Pioneer India;A	10.6	+12.75	−18.02	*
Scudder Gold Fund	194.6	−10.26	−17.72	+ 69.99
East End:Capital Apprec	2.0	+15.29	−17.40	*
Sm Barney Spec Eqty;B	316.4	+11.17	−16.92	+135.06
Franklin Gold Fund;I	321.7	− 7.58	−16.87	+ 18.12
Van Wagoner:Mid–Cap	100.4	+ 6.16	−16.32	*

*Not applicable; fund is too new.
Source: Lipper Analytical Services

Five-Year and 10-Year Winners and Losers

Best- and worst-performing stock funds for the periods ended June 30, 1997; assets are figured as of May 31, 1997. Performance data are total returns, which include both share prices and reinvested dividends.

Five-Year Best Performers

Fund name	Assets ($ millions)	2nd quarter	12 months	5 years
		Performance		
Fidelity Sel Elctronic	$2,307.5	+20.13%	+52.63%	+456.40%
Seligman Communictn;A	2,689.3	+17.21	+34.84	+325.35
Fidelity Sel Home Fin	1,045.4	+19.42	+54.14	+309.42
Fidelity Sel Computer	614.8	+12.10	+31.23	+301.80
Alliance Technology;A	632.0	+18.74	+17.45	+272.72
AIM Eq:Aggress Gro	2,526.3	+21.21	−0.18	+254.87
PBHG:Growth Fund;PBHG	5,431.0	+17.62	−9.99	+241.57
Ret Sys:Emerg Growth Eq	13.2	+23.92	+7.55	+238.04
T Rowe Price Sci & Tech	3,575.0	+19.21	+10.72	+237.75
Fidelity Sel Technlgy	562.9	+19.47	+31.24	+232.88
J Hancock Reg Bnk;B	3,976.7	+13.35	+45.13	+224.75
FPA Capital	624.8	+6.35	+25.33	+224.64
Putnam New Oppty;A	6,974.5	+19.29	+4.26	+223.02
Davis:Financial;A	150.8	+17.11	+51.20	+222.01
Oakmark Fund	5,361.0	+15.22	+29.89	+221.19
Fidelity Sel Brokerage	246.6	+26.01	+50.88	+220.19
Fidelity Sel Software	459.7	+14.95	+20.09	+219.55
Franklin Str:CA Gro;I	337.1	+11.74	+20.59	+217.91
Fidelity Sel Regl Bnks	882.1	+15.36	+49.71	+214.89
RSI TR:Emerg Growth Eq	80.9	+13.96	+6.59	+213.84
Barr Rosen:Sm Cp;Inst	109.5	+16.27	+29.13	+211.67
Robrtsn Steph:Val+Gro	713.1	+16.36	+30.14	+210.93
Fidelity Sel Enrgy Ser	565.9	+19.87	+48.12	+209.85
Franklin Str:Sm Cap;I	1,342.0	+18.69	+18.23	+208.92
Fidelity Sel Defense	39.1	+13.51	+20.18	+206.57
Fidelity Sel Financial	461.7	+17.86	+42.22	+205.20
INVESCO Strat:Tech	971.3	+17.18	+21.53	+203.55
Parkstone:Sm Cap;Inst	527.8	+24.77	−4.39	+203.41
Oppenheimer Main:I&G;A	4,109.4	+12.86	+22.55	+202.24
Merrill Growth Fund;B	3,699.4	+8.59	+23.69	+200.93
SAFECO Equity;No Ld	1,207.6	+14.20	+30.66	+200.53
Painewbr Finl Svc Gr;A	100.6	+16.49	+45.29	+199.91
Legg Mason Value Tr;Prm	2,685.6	+18.05	+52.16	+198.43
Brandywine Blue Fund	451.2	+14.42	+24.49	+198.41
Amer Cent:TC Giftrust	861.6	+21.08	−10.84	+198.30
Mairs & Power Growth	243.9	+19.03	+35.92	+196.23
Baron Asset Fund	2,066.0	+19.33	+14.01	+195.25
T Rowe Price Mid-Cap Gro	1,285.1	+13.67	+17.23	+194.70
Fidelity Sel Ind Equip	55.5	+19.97	+32.36	+194.29
Spectra Fund	35.9	+18.96	+22.84	+192.26
Kaufmann Fund	5,560.7	+16.51	+8.26	+190.00
Brandywine Fund	7,651.0	+11.88	+24.05	+189.62
SS Research:Gl Res;A	80.6	+7.07	+33.14	+189.52
Vanguard PRIMECAP	5,483.7	+15.60	+31.90	+188.87
INVESCO Strat:Financial	825.9	+18.79	+47.08	+187.65
MFS Emerging Growth;B	4,132.2	+17.15	+12.69	+187.48
Seligman Frontier;A	483.4	+20.34	+6.75	+185.74
Vanguard Spl:Health	3,432.9	+19.14	+32.87	+185.68
CG Cap Mkts:Sm Cap Gro	660.0	+18.35	+1.63	+184.96
MAS Fds:Smcap Val;Inst	700.3	+16.64	+35.64	+184.93

Source: Lipper Analytical Services

Five-Year Worst Performers

Fund name	Assets ($ millions)	Performance 2nd quarter	12 months	5 years
Steadman Tech & Growth	$ 0.3	+ 4.62%	−33.98 %	−70.69 %
Frontier:Equity Fund	0.8	−16.74	−55.34	−59.12
US:Gold Shares	168.0	−22.26	−46.49	−50.16
Monterey:Ocm Gold	1.7	−10.98	−21.35	−47.31
Steadman Amer Industry	1.0	− 2.70	+ 0.00	−43.75
Steadman Investment	1.6	+ 6.25	−2.30	−35.61
Centurion TAA Fund	N.A.	+ 0.88	−5.23	−26.81
Comstock Cap Value;A	148.9	−12.07	−18.36	−22.69
MFS Gold & Natl Res;B	17.3	−10.14	−23.52	−8.79
Bull&Bear Gold Investors	19.0	−21.71	−37.81	−5.83
DFA Grp:Japan Small Co	244.0	+16.43	−31.32	+ 3.69
Mathers Fund	155.5	+ 0.00	+ 2.84	+ 6.91
Dean Witter Prec Mtls	50.6	−8.48	−22.84	+11.04
Van Eck:Intl Gold;A	403.0	−12.15	−28.16	+12.10
PIMCO Prec Metals;C	30.8	−16.04	−30.27	+12.97
American Heritage Fund	18.1	+20.48	+44.93	+16.84
Amer Cent:AC Gl Gold	384.7	−12.33	−26.66	+17.76
Franklin Gold Fund;I	321.7	− 7.58	−16.87	+18.12
USAA Gold Fund	122.1	− 7.97	−22.26	+19.02
Lexington Goldfund	94.2	−11.93	−25.27	+20.30
Van Eck:Gold/Res;A	111.1	−11.39	−22.94	+21.37
Steadman Associated Fd	4.4	+8.45	+10.00	+22.22
Oppenheimer Gld & Sp;A	140.2	− 5.16	−10.20	+22.51
Fontaine:Glbl Growth	4.6	−16.59	−30.68	+22.80
Vanguard Spl:Gold	453.6	−10.29	−20.12	+22.87
Pioneer Gold Shares;A	32.2	−10.46	−19.10	+23.75
United Gold & Govt;A	25.6	− 6.41	−13.21	+24.35
Dreyfus Prem Agg Gro;A	387.9	+15.83	− 1.07	+26.06
T Rowe Price Int:Japan	201.6	+20.39	− 4.20	+26.15
Rea-Graham:Balanced	10.4	+ 3.34	+ 7.56	+26.49
Keystone Prec Metals	155.4	−12.07	−21.97	+27.06
Franklin Mgd:Corp Qual	26.2	+ 1.37	+ 6.58	+27.50
The Japan Fund	478.6	+25.59	+ 0.54	+27.60
UAM:SAMI Prfd Stk;Inst	32.2	+ 1.60	+ 8.60	+28.37
Capstone Nikko Japan	3.0	+22.30	−14.10	+30.24
First Inv Gvt Plus;II	2.0	+ 1.83	+ 4.46	+32.27
Fontaine:Capital Apprec	5.7	− 4.82	−13.62	+32.28
First Inv Gvt Plus;III	0.9	+ 1.24	+ 1.97	+32.31
Permanent Port:Permanent	71.2	+ 3.51	+ 3.43	+35.99
Eagle Growth Shares	3.1	+17.97	+19.01	+38.92
Monterey:Mrphy Tec Cnv	1.5	+ 0.26	+14.08	+38.99
INVESCO Strat:Gold	224.7	−13.64	−26.56	+39.19
INVESCO Strat:Environ	21.7	+ 6.65	+ 6.23	+39.68
GT Global Intl Grow;A	175.4	+ 9.36	+14.03	+39.75
Fidelity Sel Prec Mtls	226.7	−14.92	−26.65	+40.80
DFA Grp:Contl Small Co	310.1	+ 4.65	+13.83	+41.22
Barr Rosen:Japan;Inst	1.2	+21.81	−16.04	+41.54
Alliance Port:Consv;B	28.3	+ 6.39	+11.25	+41.93
GT Global Pacific Gr;A	294.3	− 0.80	+ 5.58	+42.38
GT Global Japan Grow;A	76.2	+14.51	+ 0.61	+42.91

Source: Lipper Analytical Services

10-Year Best Performers

Fund name	Assets ($ millions)	Performance 2nd quarter	12 months	10 years
Fidelity Sel Home Fin	$1,045.4	+19.42%	+54.14%	+700.08%
Fidelity Sel Regl Bnks	882.1	+15.36	+49.71	+618.36
INVESCO Strat:Financial	825.9	+18.79	+47.08	+584.51
Seligman Communictn;A	2,689.3	+17.21	+34.84	+578.38
J Hancock Reg Bnk;B	3,976.7	+13.35	+45.13	+571.05
Kaufmann Fund	5,560.7	+16.51	+8.26	+503.41
Fidelity Adv Eq Gro;Inst	1,107.0	+17.30	+21.77	+495.47
Fidelity Sel Elctronic	2,307.5	+20.13	+52.63	+491.03
Vanguard Spl:Health	3,432.9	+19.14	+32.87	+488.44
FPA Capital	624.8	+6.35	+25.33	+482.90
INVESCO Strat:Health	915.2	+16.36	+18.16	+478.82
Fidelity Sel Health	1,488.8	+21.26	+35.54	+464.61
Painewbr Finl Svc Gr;A	100.6	+16.49	+45.29	+459.43
Fidelity Contrafund	26,504.1	+12.88	+24.31	+443.88
Amer Cent:TC Ultra;Inv	20,129.7	+19.13	+21.93	+440.79
Skyline:Special Eq	314.7	+19.30	+38.08	+440.01
Amer Cent:TC Giftrust	861.6	+21.08	−10.84	+430.77
INVESCO Strat:Tech	971.3	+17.18	+21.53	+425.19
AIM:Value;A	5,815.9	+17.90	+26.34	+423.77
CGM Cap Development	695.5	+16.08	+30.18	+419.38
Fidelity Sel Medical	158.4	+12.77	+17.31	+419.18
AIM Eq:Aggress Gro	2,526.3	+21.21	−0.18	+416.20
Davis NY Venture;A	3,338.0	+16.70	+39.40	+411.42
Baron Asset Fund	2,066.0	+19.33	+14.01	+407.33
Fidelity Sel Software	459.7	+14.95	+20.09	+403.02
Fidelity Destiny II	3,205.4	+14.57	+28.29	+391.24
PBHG:Growth Fund;PBHG	5,431.0	+17.62	−9.99	+385.78
Gabelli Growth	720.8	+19.39	+31.74	+385.48
PIMCO Opportunity;C	613.6	+16.21	−10.24	+383.27
Fidelity Sel Financial	461.7	+17.86	+42.22	+379.06
Fidelity Destiny I	5,409.7	+15.37	+29.37	+376.69
Mairs & Power Growth	243.9	+19.03	+35.92	+376.59
Brandywine Fund	7,651.0	+11.88	+24.05	+375.71
Janus Twenty	4,979.8	+17.77	+34.13	+373.98
Fidelity Growth Company	10,080.2	+15.70	+19.14	+370.90
Founders:Frontier Fund	241.3	+15.42	+5.03	+369.68
Sequoia Fund	2,984.3	+21.49	+43.48	+369.49
Fidelity Sel Telecomm	365.2	+24.32	+14.15	+367.53
MFS Emerging Growth;B	4,132.2	+17.15	+12.69	+366.18
Fidelity Sel Food	258.6	+10.54	+22.07	+366.08
Fidelity Growth & Income	29,544.5	+16.75	+29.83	+363.81
Longleaf Partners Fund	2,517.5	+12.38	+25.67	+360.35
AIM Eq:Consteltn;Rtl A	12,644.2	+15.59	+12.92	+358.41
Putnam Hlth Sciences;A	1,532.7	+20.26	+30.77	+353.30
Fidelity Sel Insurance	90.0	+22.07	+46.09	+351.58
IDS New Dimensions;A	7,627.4	+15.57	+25.87	+349.11
Delaware Value;A	219.9	+15.29	+31.82	+348.22
INVESCO Strat:Leisure	192.7	+12.83	+8.56	+345.96
Berger One Hundred	1,835.9	+12.92	+13.89	+345.66
Janus Fund	17,554.8	+13.24	+22.37	+345.16

Source: Lipper Analytical Services

10-Year Worst Performers

Fund name	Assets ($ millions)	Performance		
		2nd quarter	12 months	10 years
Steadman Tech & Growth	$ 0.3	+ 4.62%	–33.98 %	–89.47%
US:Gold Shares	168.0	–22.26	–46.49	–78.13
Steadman Amer Industry	1.0	– 2.70	+ 0.00	–75.92
Lexington Strat Invments	37.3	–20.54	–35.51	–62.14
Steadman Investment	1.6	+ 6.25	– 2.30	–53.55
USAA Gold Fund	122.1	– 7.97	–22.26	–38.53
Bull&Bear Gold Investors	19.0	–21.71	–37.81	–35.20
Centurion TAA Fund	N.A.	+ 0.88	– 5.23	–33.99
Lexington Strat Silver	46.0	– 7.93	–10.76	–26.90
Van Eck:Gold/Res;A	111.1	–11.39	–22.94	–26.25
INVESCO Strat:Gold	224.7	–13.64	–26.56	–25.47
Van Eck:Intl Gold;A	403.0	–12.15	–28.16	–15.14
Lexington Goldfund	94.2	–11.93	–25.27	– 7.83
US:World Gold	231.5	– 9.06	–20.51	– 4.21
Fidelity Sel Prec Mtls	226.7	–14.92	–26.65	– 0.68
Steadman Associated Fd	4.4	+ 8.45	+10.00	+ 0.98
Keystone Prec Metals	155.4	–12.07	–21.97	+ 2.38
United Gold & Govt;A	25.6	– 6.41	–13.21	+ 2.46
Vanguard Spl:Gold	453.6	–10.29	–20.12	+ 6.07
Sm Barney Nat Res;A	56.3	+ 2.67	+ 1.07	+ 8.91
Comstock Cap Value;A	148.9	–12.07	–18.36	+17.50
Franklin Gold Fund;I	321.7	– 7.58	–16.87	+19.79
US:Global Resources	30.9	+ 6.53	+19.12	+20.74
American Heritage Fund	18.1	+20.48	+44.93	+20.94
Fidelity Sel Amer Gold	332.1	– 9.17	–18.82	+30.78
The Japan Fund	478.6	+25.59	+ 0.54	+32.39
IDS Precious Metals;A	83.2	–11.09	–29.94	+32.82
DFA Grp:Japan Small Co	244.0	+16.43	–31.32	+34.51
Midas Fund	173.2	–19.29	–31.94	+36.09
Fidelity Pacific Basin	320.8	+19.12	+ 2.11	+39.19
BBK Intl:Intl Equity	128.3	+11.09	+18.68	+43.35
INVESCO Intl:Pacific	134.8	+13.99	+ 1.92	+44.48
Cornercap:Growth	14.1	+15.17	+26.53	+46.90
Merrill Glbl Res;B	81.4	+ 4.58	+ 9.23	+47.25
Permanent Port:Permanent	71.2	+ 3.51	+ 3.43	+50.22
Rea-Graham:Balanced	10.4	+ 3.34	+ 7.56	+57.80
DFA Grp:UK Small Company	170.5	– 3.23	+11.93	+61.23
Mathers Fund	155.5	+ 0.00	+ 2.84	+63.58
INVESCO Strat:Energy	200.7	+10.89	+28.84	+65.63
Keystone International	160.0	+11.35	+22.01	+67.92
Oppenheimer Gld & Sp;A	140.2	– 5.16	–10.20	+68.06
Matterhorn Growth	8.9	+ 9.84	+10.65	+75.29
Flag Inv Intl;A	14.3	+11.13	+17.20	+75.66
Federated Intl Eqty;A	131.4	+12.24	+ 9.05	+76.81
PIMCO International;C	167.1	+10.25	+ 9.29	+79.86
Security Ultra;A	73.5	+14.10	+ 7.21	+79.92
Dreyfus Prem Agg Gro;A	387.9	+15.83	– 1.07	+80.11
IDS International;A	909.5	+ 9.55	+ 9.27	+83.33
GT Global Europe;A	432.6	+ 5.29	+14.77	+84.06
Rainbow Fund	1.3	+ 8.67	+30.83	+84.86

Source: Lipper Analytical Services

Largest Taxable Bond Funds
Percentage gains for periods ended June 30, 1997; assets as of May 31, 1997

Fund name	Assets ($ millions)	2nd quarter	12 months	5 years
		Performance		
PIMCO Total Return;Inst	$13,237.0	+4.06%	+ 9.93 %	+49.09 %
Franklin Cust:Govt;I	9,537.0	+3.61	+ 9.27	+37.76
Vanguard Fxd:GNMA Port	7,680.0	+4.01	+ 9.34	+39.62
Bond Fund of America	7,261.0	+4.00	+10.43	+50.70
Dean Witter US Govt	5,843.4	+3.79	+ 8.08	+32.97
Merrill Corp:HI Inc;B	4,985.2	+5.09	+13.71	+65.15
AARP GNMA & US Treas	4,598.9	+3.09	+ 7.69	+31.24
Vanguard Fxd:Sht-Tm Corp	4,536.8	+2.31	+ 6.77	+34.38
Vanguard Idx:Tot Bd;Indv	3,986.2	+3.56	+ 8.03	+40.44
Vanguard Fxd:HI Yld	3,886.3	+4.97	+14.38	+68.07
Oppenheimer Str Inc;A	3,757.9	+4.05	+11.83	+56.11
Kemper US Govt Sec;A	3,679.5	+3.65	+ 8.75	+33.76
Vanguard Fxd:Lg-Tm Corp	3,248.6	+5.28	+ 9.24	+51.80
Putnam High Yield;A	3,202.1	+5.99	+14.95	+66.31
Kemper High Yield;A	3,169.5	+5.35	+14.55	+71.69
Oppenheimer Str Inc;B	3,129.9	+3.85	+10.97	*
Fidelity Intermediate Bd	3,125.3	+2.86	+ 6.85	+36.76
Mainstay:HI Yld Corp;B	2,828.7	+5.55	+14.95	+92.80
GE S&S Prgrm:Lg-Tm Intst	2,817.0	+3.79	+ 8.91	+42.04
PIMCO Low Duration;Inst	2,784.7	+2.88	+ 8.79	+39.27
Stand Ayer Wood:Fxd Inc	2,771.7	+3.76	+10.10	+45.21
MAS Fds:Fxd Inc;Inst	2,732.8	+3.89	+10.38	+50.74
Franklin Age HI Inc;I	2,635.6	+5.21	+16.06	+74.31
Am Exp IDS:Bond;A	2,585.9	+3.78	+10.24	+55.36
Prudential HI Yld;B	2,582.9	+5.53	+14.31	+64.68
IDS Extra Income;A	2,582.5	+5.00	+13.04	+71.63
Sm Barney Dvsd Strat;B	2,402.5	+3.42	+10.08	+42.18
Vankamp Am Govt;A	2,371.3	+3.43	+ 8.28	+33.94
Putnam Dvsfd Income;B	2,275.5	+3.68	+ 9.14	*
Putnam US Govt Inc;A	2,213.9	+3.70	+ 8.74	+33.55
Lord Abbett Inv:Govt;A	2,209.3	+4.08	+ 7.24	+33.21
Fidelity Capital & Inc	2,068.5	+5.30	+12.77	+74.54
Vankamp Am Govt Secs;A	2,012.6	+3.45	+ 7.10	+31.99
Putnam Dvsfd Income;A	1,992.7	+3.86	+ 9.92	+53.99
Fidelity Adv HI Yld;T	1,971.2	+5.59	+13.85	+79.87
Fidelity Sprt HI Inc	1,969.3	+6.16	+15.20	+92.69
American High-Income TR	1,886.8	+6.17	+15.06	+73.56
Lord Abbett Bond-Deb;A	1,883.5	+5.61	+14.40	+65.28
S Bernstein:Intmdt Dur	1,818.6	+3.29	+ 7.90	+40.16
Kemper US Mtge;A	1,768.7	+3.53	+ 8.51	+32.17

*Not Applicable; fund is too new.
Note: Preliminary, data as of 6 PM, July 1.
Source: Lipper Analytical Services

Monitoring Money-Market Funds

A look at consumer-oriented money funds, some of their holdings and the average maturity of their investments at the end of the second quarter. Performance figures are estimated annualized yields, which include earnings from the funds' investments and the effects of compounding. Funds open only to institutions, special-purpose funds and tax-exempt funds are excluded from these tables.

Largest Funds

Fund name	Assets ($ millions)	Performance 2nd quarter	Performance 12 months	Portfolio Comm. paper	Portfolio U.S. Treasury	Avg. mat. (Days)
Merrill Lynch CMA Money Fund	$41,826.2	5.10%	5.06%	48%	6%	76
Smith Barney Cash Port/Cl A	29,769.7	5.04	5.02	46	0	82
Vanguard MMR/Prime Port/Retail	25,037.6	5.32	5.33	29	0	41
Fidelity Cash Reserves	22,676.8	5.25	5.20	34	0	65
Schwab Money Market Fund	19,660.8	4.94	4.93	72	0	62
Dean Witter/Liquid Asset Fund	12,735.8	5.08	5.10	77	1	70
Schwab Value Advantage MF	12,542.0	5.30	5.29	71	0	61
Centennial Money Market Trust	9,102.0	5.00	4.96	71	0	54
Fidelity Spartan MMF	8,994.7	5.27	5.26	34	0	67
Dean Witter/Active Assets MT	8,977.8	5.18	5.20	80	1	65

Highest Second-Quarter Yields

Fund name	Assets ($ millions)	Performance 2nd quarter	Performance 12 months	Portfolio Comm. paper	Portfolio U.S. Treasury	Avg. mat. (Days)
Strategist Money Market Fund	$ 98.8	5.61%	5.57%	0%	0%	26
OLDE Premium Plus MM Series	2,044.6	5.59	5.66	51	1	57
Strong Heritage Money Fund	1,851.3	5.54	5.67	87	3	49
E Fund	20.1	5.44	5.44	92	0	22
Kiewit Mutual Fund/MMP	445.8	5.44	5.43	85	0	36
Transamerica Prem. Cash Res/Inv	41.6	5.40	5.36	84	0	51
Fremont Money Market Fund	401.1	5.35	5.32	88	0	57
John Hancock US Govt Cash Res	58.0	5.35	5.33	0	0	60
Aetna Money Market Fund/Cl A	424.8	5.34	5.37	48	0	49
Marshall MMF/Class A	1,236.8	5.33	5.30	31	0	48
Lake Forest Money Market Fund	6.7	5.33	5.30	0	0	1

Highest 12-Month Yields

Fund name	Assets ($ millions)	Performance 2nd quarter	Performance 12 months	Portfolio Comm. paper	Portfolio U.S. Treasury	Avg. mat. (Days)
Strong Heritage Money Fund	$1,851.3	5.54%	5.67%	87%	3%	49
OLDE Premium Plus MM Series	2,044.6	5.59	5.66	51	1	57
Strategist Money Market Fund	98.8	5.61	5.57	0	0	26
E Fund	20.1	5.44	5.44	92	0	22
Kiewit Mutual Fund/MMP	445.8	5.44	5.43	85	0	36
Aetna Money Market Fund/Cl A	424.8	5.34	5.37	48	0	49
Managers Money Market Fund	39.6	5.31	5.37	33	1	53
Transamerica Prem. Cash Res/Inv	41.6	5.40	5.36	84	0	51
John Hancock US Govt Cash Res	58.0	5.35	5.33	0	0	60
Vanguard MMR/Prime Port	25,037.6	5.32	5.33	29	0	41

Lowest 12-Month Yields

Fund name	Assets ($ millions)	Performance 2nd quarter	Performance 12 months	Portfolio Comm. paper	Portfolio U.S. Treasury	Avg. mat. (Days)
Declaration Cash Account	$ 4.7	2.38%	2.83%	100%	0%	17
State St Research MMF/Cl B	14.2	3.98	3.83	100	0	44
State St Research MMF/Cl D	1.1	3.98	3.83	100	0	44
Sierra US Government MF/Cl S	0.3	3.96	3.88	0	0	23
Sierra US Government MF/Cl B	2.5	3.96	3.88	0	0	23
Sierra Global Money Fund/Cl B	1.3	4.10	4.11	41	0	58
Sierra Global Money Fund/Cl S	6.9	4.10	4.11	41	0	58
Evergreen Money Mkt. Fund/Cl B	12.7	4.23	4.21	87	0	72
First Amer Prime Oblig/Cl B	2.1	4.29	4.22	85	0	36
Pillar Funds US Treas Secs Class A	3.3	4.19	4.24	0	96	44

Average yields		4.87%	4.85%			

Source: IBC's Money Fund Report

Top-Performing Funds in Selected Sectors

Balanced Funds

	Assets ($ millions)	Total return		
		12 months	3 months	5 years
Transam Prem:Bal;Inv	$19.7	+34.50%	+21.75%	* %
IAI Balanced Fund	39.8	+32.63	+14.94	+85.16
Thompson Plumb:Balanced	30.7	+28.89	+12.22	+91.05
Flag Inv Value Bldr;A	315.7	+28.53	+10.45	+120.22
CGM TR:Mutual Fund	1,237.7	+27.87	+ 8.82	+101.71
Chubb Inv:Total Return	32.9	+26.90	+13.29	+103.53
Montag & Caldwell Bal	52.9	+26.47	+14.35	*
Dreyfus Prem Bal;R	131.2	+25.54	+13.67	*
Goldman Eq:Balanced;A	104.2	+25.51	+ 9.92	*
PIMCO Strat Bal;Inst	11.8	+25.51	+12.23	*
Averages & Counts	—	+19.41	+10.19	+84.21

Equity-Income Funds

	Assets ($ millions)	Total return		
		12 months	3 months	5 years
Cutler TR:Equity Income	$58.6	+37.66%	+15.98%	* %
Kemper-Dreman:HI Rtn;A	823.9	+35.07	+14.00	+170.00
Janus Equity Income	47.5	+34.71	+13.17	*
Dreyfus Disc Eq Inc;Rtl	20.2	+34.66	+17.07	*
Strong Equity Income	94.4	+33.90	+15.53	*
Vista:Equity Income;A	29.6	+33.46	+13.49	*
Delaware Decatr Tot;A	757.2	+33.11	+15.30	+134.30
United:Income;A	5,581.5	+32.71	+18.72	+130.71
Stratus:Growth	43.9	+32.64	+16.54	*
Prudential Equ Inc;B	1,058.5	+32.61	+16.25	+119.49
Averages & Counts	—	+26.73	+12.85	+112.25

Capital Appreciation

	Assets ($ millions)	Total return		
		12 months	3 months	5 years
American Heritage Fund	$18.1	+44.93%	+20.48%	+ 16.84%
Rydex:Nova Fund	579.0	+44.79	25.15	*
Rydex:OTC Fund	386.5	+43.48	+21.08	*
Dreyfus Aggr Val	113.0	+37.49	+14.78	*
GAM:North America;A	8.1	+35.47	+17.70	+110.90
Salomon Bros Opportunity	173.6	+34.39	+16.05	+137.98
Berger Sm Cap Val;Inst	39.9	+34.32	+12.13	+163.31
Janus Twenty	4,979.8	+34.13	+17.77	+128.65
PC&J Performance	30.5	+33.64	+19.62	+129.70
First Eagle Fd of Amer	220.7	+33.15	+14.21	+174.22
Averages & Counts	—	+14.44	+13.87	+113.79

Emerging Markets Funds

	Assets ($ millions)	Total return		
		12 months	3 months	5 years
Vontobel:Eastern Euro	$172.2	+31.48%	+ 3.75%	* %
Nich-App:Em Ctry Inst	61.2	+30.88	+15.01	*
Scudder Emrg Mkts Gro	213.0	+29.25	+ 6.11	*
Seligman Hend Em Mkt;A	42.3	+28.09	+16.92	*
Delaware Emerg Mkt;A	9.2	+27.86	+13.45	*
Legg Mason Gl:Em Mkt;Prm	53.3	+27.41	+ 9.55	*
Templeton Dev Mrkts;I	4,252.3	+27.00	+10.77	+109.32
Lazard:Emerg Mkts;Inst	242.9	+26.82	+12.07	*
Piper Glbl:Em Mkt Gr;A	17.0	+26.54	+11.91	*
EV Mrthn Emerging Mkts	9.8	+25.45	+10.27	*
Averages & Counts	—	+18.06	+10.50	+ 74.17

European Region Funds

	Assets ($ millions)	Total return		
		12 months	3 months	5 years
Fidelity Nordic	$78.5	+36.28%	+5.61%	* %
Fidelity Europe Cap Ap	388.2	+33.53	+11.44	*
Vanguard Intl Idx:Euro	1,948.5	+30.25	+ 9.57	+101.88
Kemper Europe;A	6.5	+28.88	+10.60	*
Putnam Europe Growth;A	273.7	+28.49	+ 9.28	+120.02
Excelsior:Pan European	142.2	+28.08	+ 7.40	*
Pioneer Europe;A	134.4	+28.00	+ 7.62	+107.16
Wright Equi:Netherland	14.0	+27.76	+ 8.77	+108.79
JPM Pierpont:Euro Eqty	2.8	+26.82	+ 8.09	*
JPM Instl:European Eqty	10.3	+26.65	+ 8.04	*
Averages & Counts	—	+22.92	+ 6.58	+ 93.02

Financial Services

	Assets ($ millions)	Total return		
		12 months	3 months	5 years
Fidelity Sel Home Fin	$1,045.4	+54.14%	+19.42%	+309.42%
Davis:Financial;A	150.8	+51.20	+17.11	+222.01
Fidelity Sel Brokerage	246.6	+50.88	+26.01	+220.19
Fidelity Sel Regl Bnks	882.1	+49.71	+15.36	+214.89
INVESCO Strat:Financial	825.9	+47.08	+18.79	+187.65
Fidelity Sel Insurance	90.0	+46.09	+22.07	+165.35
Painewbr Finl Svc Gr;A	100.6	+45.29	+16.49	+199.91
J Hancock Reg Bnk;B	3,976.7	+45.13	+13.35	+224.75
Titan Financial Svcs	8.2	+44.75	+17.27	*
Century Shares Trust	321.4	+44.67	+19.89	+127.55
Averages & Counts	—	+43.60	+17.06	+205.91

Flexible Portfolio Funds

	Assets ($ millions)	Total return		
		12 months	3 months	5 years
Muhlenkamp Fund	$69.5	+39.44%	+14.53%	+148.58%
Painewbr Tact Alloc;C	174.6	+32.42	+17.05	*
Maxus Equity	45.1	+31.80	+14.28	+129.37
Stagecoach:Lfpt 2040;A	206.6	+29.03	+16.17	*
Dreyfus Life:Growth;Rtl	42.0	+28.80	+17.04	*
General Securities	48.3	+28.15	+13.17	+102.55
Eastcliff:Total Return	20.9	+28.10	+15.16	+106.80
Enterprise:Managed;A	127.6	+27.33	+13.46	*
Guardian Asset Alloc;A	103.8	+27.19	+12.44	*
Aetna:Ascent;Sel	23.8	+26.62	+10.57	*
Averages & Counts	—	+18.48	+10.56	+ 83.72

Global Funds

	Assets ($ millions)	Total return		
		12 months	3 months	5 years
GAM:Global;A	$27.8	+42.07%	+16.32%	+154.02%
INVESCO Spec:Wrld Cap GD	8.0	+33.83	+21.28	*
Buffalo USA Global	36.9	+32.54	+15.89	*
Dreyfus Prem Growth;B	164.9	+32.08	+14.34	*
Van Eck:Gl Hard Asst;A	52.0	+31.39	+ 8.31	*
Templeton Fds:World;I	8,045.3	+30.40	+13.21	+131.37
Templeton Glbl Opp;I	753.8	+30.02	+11.83	+114.21
Pasadena:Glbl Gro;A	7.1	+29.39	+15.17	*
Atlas:Global Growth;A	22.2	+29.19	+13.13	*
Capital World Gro & Inc	6,283.0	+28.86	+11.44	*
Averages & Counts	—	+19.22	+12.18	+ 91.05

Global Flexible Funds

	Assets ($ millions)	Total return		
		12 months	3 months	5 years
Harris Ins:Hemis;Inst	$12.3	+29.24%	+13.90%	* %
Oppenheimer Gl G&I;A	143.7	+26.07	+ 8.56	+ 99.94
Templeton Cap Accumulatr	157.6	+25.53	+10.49	+131.15
Vontobel:Sand Hill Port	7.7	+21.52	+10.55	*
Putnam Asst:Growth;A	349.1	+21.24	+11.56	*
MAS Fds:Multi Asset;Inst	123.5	+20.96	+11.15	*
Van Eck:Glbl Bal;A	23.9	+20.65	+12.17	*
Merrill Asst:Glbl Op;B	36.4	+20.57	+11.47	*
Merrill Asset Growth;B	8.2	+20.55	+11,12	*
USAA Cornerstone Strat	1,262.5	+20.45	+ 8.50	+ 95.33
Averages & Counts	—	+17.28	+ 8.77	+ 75.87

Gold Oriented Funds

	Assets ($ millions)	Total return		
		12 months	3 months	5 years
Oppenheimer Gld & Sp;A	$140.2	−10.20%	− 5.16%	+22.51%
United Gold & Govt;A	25.6	−13.21	− 6.41	+24.35
Sogen:Gold Fund	48.9	−14.04	− 8.96	*
Franklin Gold Fund;I	321.7	−16.87	− 7.58	+18.12
Scudder Gold Fund	194.6	−17.72	−10.26	+69.99
Fidelity Sel Amer Gold	332.1	−18.82	− 9.17	+61.34
Pioneer Gold Shares;A	32.2	−19.10	−10.46	+23.75
Vanguard Spl:Gold	453.6	−20.12	−10.29	+22.87
US:World Gold	231.5	−20.51	− 9.06	+78.28
Blanchard:Prec Metals	75.9	−21.28	−15.02	+51.44
Averages & Counts	—	−24.36	−12.16	+26.43

Growth & Income Funds

	Assets ($ millions)	Total return		
		12 months	3 months	5 years
Selected American Shares	$1,709.2	+44.55%	+18.11%	+145.21%
Stand Ayer Wood:TX Sn Eq	7.4	+42.23	+16.70	*
Reynolds:Blue Chip Gro	55.4	+41.19	+20.58	+116.55
Franklin Val:Value;I	24.3	+40.39	+15.16	*
Nich-App:Value Inst	3.5	+40.17	+16.43	*
ICAP:Equity	251.8	+39.95	+17.23	*
Excelsior Inst:Val Eq;In	27.4	+39.66	+20.51	*
Goldman Eq:Gro&Inc;A	808.6	+39.45	+15.18	*
Thornburg Value Fund;A	46.6	+39.13	+14.84	*
Nationwide:Fund	1,207.0	+38.92	+18.51	+128.60
Averages & Counts	—	+28.07	+14.30	+122.51

Growth Funds

	Assets ($ millions)	Total return		
		12 months	3 months	5 years
Legg Mason Value Tr;Prm	$2,685.6	+52.16%	+18.05%	+198.43%
Transam Prem:Eqty;Inv	46.9	+51.38	+28.74	*
Pioneer Growth Shrs;A	370.6	+50.03	+24.06	+171.28
Hudson Cap Apprec;A	20.5	+44.85	+17.34	+143.68
Texas Cap:Value & Growth	4.1	+44.83	+18.99	*
Sequoia Fund	2,984.3	+43.48	+21.49	+171.17
MFS Strategic Growth;A	8.2	+43.05	+24.52	*
Vankamp Am Exchange	68.5	+41.45	+11.99	+153.42
API Trust:Yrktn Cl Val	13.1	+40.97	+24.06	*
Papp America-Abroad	101.4	+39.84	+21.49	+166.22
Averages & Counts	—	+23.96	+15.82	+121.62

Japanese Funds

	Assets ($ millions)	Total return		
		12 months	3 months	5 years
Morg Stan In:Japan;A	$168.9	+12.76%	+25.45%	* %
GAM:Japan Capital;A	27.4	+ 8.07	+20.11	*
Colonial Nwprt Japan;B	5.3	+ 6.00	+21.78	*
Warb Pincus JP Gro;Com	21.2	+ 2.24	+21.99	*
Vista:Japan;A	5.0	+ 0.80	+18.84	*
GT Global Japan Grow;A	76.2	+ 0.61	+14.51	+42.91
The Japan Fund	478.6	+ 0.54	+25.59	+27.60
Wright Equi:Japan	15.3	− 0.77	+18.10	*
Fidelity Japan	339.4	− 1.27	+23.45	*
T Rowe Price Int:Japan	201.6	− 4.20	+20.39	+26.15
Averages & Counts	—	− 4.67	+19.99	+31.95

Latin American Funds

	Assets ($ millions)	Total return		
		12 months	3 months	5 years
Morg Stan In:Lat Am;A	$67.2	+59.54%	+24.11%	* %
Morg Stan Fds:Latin;A	56.8	+57.32	+23.51	*
Offitbank:Lat Am Eq;Sel	57.6	+50.28	+18.04	*
Rembrandt:Lat Am Eq;TR	22.3	+47.40	+22.73	*
Excelsior:Emerging Amer	90.8	+45.98	+23.36	*
Keystone Fund Amer;B	90.1	+45.66	+20.84	*
Federated Lat Am Gr;A	10.7	+44.47	+21.31	*
Fidelity Latin America	966.7	+44.39	+22.09	*
TCW/DW Latin Amer Gr	325.4	+43.58	+21.46	*
T Rowe Price Int:Lat	405.2	+42.21	+22.96	*
Averages & Counts	—	+40.95	+19.15	+72.30

Natural Resources Funds

	Assets ($ millions)	Total return		
		12 months	3 months	5 years
Fidelity Sel Enrgy Ser	$565.9	+48.12%	+19.87%	+209.85%
SS Research:Gl Res;A	80.6	+33.14	+ 7.07	+189.52
INVESCO Strat:Energy	200.7	+28.84	+10.89	+102.55
Excelsior:L-T Spply Enrg	37.8	+27.70	+10.51	*
Putnam Gl Ntrl Res;A	224.8	+25.52	+11.01	+ 90.54
Dean Witter Ntrl Res	276.9	+25.21	+11.47	+106.15
Vanguard Spl:Energy	1,009.5	+24.24	+11.37	+133.66
T Rowe Price New Era	1,580.4	+23.99	+10.52	+106.67
US:Global Resources	30.9	+19.12	+ 6.53	+ 58.81
Franklin Str:Nat Res;I	50.9	+19.03	+10.40	*
Averages & Counts	—	+15.78	+ 6.79	+101.78

Pacific (Excluding Japan)

	Assets ($ millions)	Total return		
		12 months	3 months	5 years
Fidelity Hongkong/Chna	$229.8	+40.21%	+18.56%	* %
Guinness Flght:China	312.0	+39.38	+23.51	*
US:China Region Oppty	40.6	+34.38	+12.86	*
Wright Equi:Hong Kong	8.2	+32.06	+19.99	+44.28
EV Mrthn Greater China	293.0	+31.33	+24.70	*
Guinness Flght:Asia SC	207.5	+28.15	+11.28	*
Salomon Inst:Asia Growth	5.2	+27.87	+16.50	*
Salomon Bros:Asia Gr;A	5.7	+27.77	+16.32	*
Lexington Crosby SC Asia	40.2	+26.28	+10.61	*
Ivy:China Region;A	16.7	+24.50	+17.29	*
Averages & Counts	—	+ 8.72	+ 8.88	+73.57

Science & Technology Funds

	Assets ($ millions)	Total return		
		12 months	3 months	5 years
Fidelity Sel Elctronic	$2,307.5	+52.63%	+20.13%	+456.40%
Interact Inv:Tech Val	89.0	+38.41	+31.51	*
Northern Fds:Technology	58.4	+36.55	+22.18	*
Principal Pres:PSE Tech	10.9	+36.01	+16.53	*
Seligman Communictn;A	2689.3	+34.84	+17.21	+325.35
Fidelity Sel Technigy	562.9	+31.24	+19.47	+232.88
Fidelity Sel Computer	614.8	+31.23	+12.10	+301.80
Merrill Technology;B	423.0	+29.91	+14.52	+149.36
Franklin Cust:Dyna;I	144.7	+28.56	+11.31	+117.64
Seligman Hend Gl Tch;A	574.2	+28.42	+14.75	*
Averages & Counts	—	+19.29	+18.32	+216.49

Small-Cap Funds

	Assets ($ millions)	Total return		
		12 months	3 months	5 years
SS Research:Aurora;B	$ 24.7	+47.78%	+20.20%	* %
Oakmark Small Cap	861.0	+41.62	+16.03	*
Skyline:Special Eq	314.7	+38.08	+19.30	+184.79
Lord Abbett Res:S Cp;A	52.7	+37.75	+16.72	*
Schroder:Small Cap Val	81.1	+37.47	+20.45	*
Lazard:Bantam Value;Inst	43.2	+36.04	+18.43	*
MAS Fds:Smcap Val;Inst	700.3	+35.64	+16.64	+184.93
Glenmede:Small Cap Equ	382.9	+35.57	+14.72	+179.58
Longleaf Partners Sm-Cap	414.0	+34.62	+ 9.74	+148.67
Pegasus:Sm Cap Oppty;I	153.4	+34.27	+18.83	*
Averages & Counts	—	+13.71	+17.10	+137.47

Health & Biotechnology Funds

	Assets ($ millions)	Total return		
		12 months	3 months	5 years
Fidelity Sel Health	$1,488.8	+35.54%	+21.26%	+164.69%
Vanguard Spl:Health	3,432.9	+32.87	+19.14	+185.68
Putnam Hlth Sciences;A	1,532.7	+30.77	+20.26	+146.64
Merrill Healthcare;B	189.3	+25.37	+18.10	+ 89.63
GT Global Hlth Care;A	458.1	+18.66	+12.54	+ 91.56
INVESCO Strat:Health	915.2	+18.16	+16.36	+104.40
T Rowe Price Hlth Scienc	242.9	+17.74	+12.48	*
Fidelity Sel Medical	158.4	+17.31	+12.77	+125.19
First Amer:Hlth Sci;C	36.7	+15.64	+11.05	*
EV Trad WW Hlth Sci	77.5	+14.67	+8.49	+171.93
Averages & Counts	—	+18.28	+15.76	+129.01

International Funds

	Assets ($ millions)	Total return		
		12 months	3 months	5 years
GAM:International;A	$1,306.5	+40.15%	+12.98%	+161.13%
Oppenheimer Intl Gro;A	61.5	+35.58	+ 9.00	*
Principal Sp Mkt:Intl	31.6	+30.20	+11.30	*
Waddell&Reed:Intl Gr;B	60.5	+30.17	+ 9.19	*
BT Inv:Intl Equity Fd	354.4	+29.66	+15.30	*
Aetna:Intl Growth;Sel	54.3	+29.64	+11.27	+ 88.04
UAM:Mckee Intl Eqty;Inst	111.6	+29.00	+17.18	*
STI Classic:Int Eq;TR	484.4	+28.99	+12.19	*
Northstar:Intl VI;C	26.7	+28.97	+11.04	*
Harbor:International	4,993.5	+28.60	+13.36	+136.42
Averages & Counts	—	+16.54	+11.05	+ 79.78

Midcap Funds

	Assets ($ millions)	Total return		
		12 months	3 months	5 years
Goldman Eq:Mid Cap;Inst	$168.1	+48.17%	+19.64%	* %
Dreyfus Midcap Value	34.4	+43.34	+17.38	*
First Amer:Spec Eq;C	431.7	+42.62	+17.97	*
MAS Fds:Midcap Val;Inst	136.4	+42.51	+17.56	*
Pasadena:Sm&Md Cp Gr;A	13.9	+37.36	+24.13	*
Chubb Inv:Capital Apprec	10.1	+37.34	+15.91	*
Ni Growth & Value Fund	33.4	+31.96	+19.00	*
Armada:Midcap Regnl;Inst	199.4	+31.25	+16.06	*
Ariel:Appreciation	158.7	+30.97	+14.59	+ 99.37
Dreyfus Disc Midcap;Rtl	27.5	+30.88	+19.39	*
Averages & Counts	—	+15.61	+15.79	+128.62

Real-Estate Funds

	Assets ($ millions)	Total return		
		12 months	3 months	5 years
Delaware Pld:Real Est	$ 49.0	+45.00%	+ 5.43%	* %
CGM TR:Realty Fund	301.9	+43.76	+ 3.72	*
Grandview Inv:Rlty Gro	1.1	+43.21	+ 5.83	*
Columbia Real Estate Eq	103.3	+40.18	+ 4.14	*
Longleaf Partners Realty	419.2	+40.16	+ 9.12	*
Morg Stan In:US RE;A	269.2	+40.01	+ 6.79	*
Davis:Real Estate;A	68.2	+39.56	+ 5.33	*
Evergreen US RE;Y	13.1	+37.64	+15.36	*
Fidelity Real Estate	2,127.0	+37.16	+ 4.98	+113.63
Cohen & Steers Realty	2,706.6	+36.96	+ 4.25	+143.83
Averages & Counts	—	+31.66	+ 5.34	+ 94.67

Utility Funds

	Assets ($ millions)	Total return		
		12 months	3 months	5 years
MFS Utilities;A	$ 77.7	+27.45%	+11.90%	+122.93%
Federated World Util;A	16.0	+24.84	+11.55	*
Colonial Gl Util;A	172.2	+22.26	+ 9.57	+ 73.67
Prudential Utility;B	2,103.6	+22.10	+10.15	+ 86.78
Fidelity Sel Utilities	242.5	+21.49	+13.80	+ 92.82
Franklin Str:Gl UT;I	184.7	+21.32	+12.26	*
AIM:Global Utilities;A	161.9	+19.07	+10.53	+ 71.83
Dean Witter Glbl Util	360.3	+19.05	+11.63	*
Global Utility Fund;B	184.1	+18.67	+ 8.11	+ 76.70
IDS Utilities Income;A	720.6	+18.20	+ 9.34	+ 81.76
Averages & Counts	—	+13.91	+ 8.69	+ 74.74

Note: Group average returns may differ from those in Performance Yardsticks because this table includes non-NASD-reporting funds and a different set of objectives. Data are as of 6 PM, July 1, 1997.
*Not applicable; fund is too new.
Source: Lipper Analytical Services

Bullish on Stocks

As Americans increasingly invest in stocks, the New York Stock Exchange maintains its dominance.

Share and Dollar Volume by Exchanges (In percentage)

Year	Total Share Volume (In thousands)	NYSE	AMEX	CHIC	PSE	PHLX	BSE	CSE	Others
1945	769,018	65.87	21.31	1.77	2.98	1.06	0.66	0.05	6.30
1950	893,320	76.32	13.54	2.16	3.11	0.97	0.65	0.09	3.16
1955	1,321,401	68.85	19.19	2.09	3 .08	0.85	0.48	0.05	5.41
1960	1,441,120	68.47	22.27	2.20	3.11	0.88	0.38	0.04	2.65
1965	2,671,012	69.90	22.53	2.63	2.33	0.81	0.26	0.05	1.49
1970	4,834,887	71.28	19.03	3.16	3.68	1.63	0.51	0.02	0.69
1975	6,376,094	80.99	8.97	3.97	3.26	1.54	0.85	0.13	0.29
1980	15,587,986	79.94	10.78	3.84	2.80	1.54	0.57	0.32	0.21
1985	37,187,567	81.52	5.78	6.12	3.66	1.47	1.27	0.15	0.03
1986	48,580,524	81.12	6.28	5.73	3.68	1.53	1.33	0.30	0.02
1987	64,082,996	83.09	5.57	5.19	3.23	1.30	1.28	0.30	0.04
1988	52,665,654	83.74	4.95	5.26	3.03	1.29	1.32	0.39	0.02
1989	54,416,790	81.33	6.02	5.44	3.34	1.80	1.64	0.41	0.02
1990	53,746,087	81.86	6.23	4.68	3.16	1.82	1.71	0.53	0.01
1991	58,290,641	82.01	5.52	4.66	3.59	1.60	1.77	0.86	0.01
1992	65,705,037	81.34	5.74	4.62	3.19	1.72	1.57	1.83	0.01
1993	83,056,237	82.90	5.53	4.57	2.81	1.55	1.47	1.17	0.00
1994	90,786,603	84.55	4.96	3.88	2.37	1.42	1.39	1.42	0.01
1995	107,069,656	84.49	4.78	3.67	2.56	1.39	1.45	1.66	0.00

Year	Total Dollar Volume ($ in thousands)	NYSE	AMEX	CHIC	PSE	PHLX	BSE	CSE	Others
1945	$ 16,284,552	82.75	0.81	2.00	1.78	0.96	1.16	0.06	0.48
1950	21,808,284	85.91	6.85	2.35	2.19	1.03	1.12	0.11	0.44
1955	38,039,107	86.31	6.98	2.44	1.90	1.03	0.78	0.09	0.47
1960	45,309,825	83.80	9.35	2.72	1.94	1.03	0.60	0.07	0.49
1965	89,549,093	81.78	9.91	3.44	2.43	1.12	0.42	0.08	0.82
1970	131,707,946	78.44	11.11	3.76	3.81	1.99	0.67	0.03	0.19
1975	157,256,676	85.20	3.67	4.64	3.26	1.73	1.19	0.17	0.14
1980	476,500,688	83.53	7.33	4.33	2.27	1.61	0.52	0.40	0.01
1985	1,200,127,848	85.25	2.23	6.59	3.06	1.49	1.20	0.18	0.00
1986	1,707,117,112	85.02	2.56	6.00	3.00	1.57	1.44	0.41	0.00
1987	2,286,902,788	86.79	2.32	5.32	2.53	1.35	1.33	0.35	0.00
1988	1,587,950,769	86.81	1.96	5.46	2.62	1.33	1.34	0.49	0.00
1989	1,847,766,971	85.49	2.35	5.46	2.84	1.77	1.56	0.54	0.00
1990	1,616,798,075	86.15	2.33	4.58	2.77	1.79	1.63	0.74	0.00
1991	1,778,154,074	86.20	2.31	4.34	3.05	1.54	1.72	0.83	0.01
1992	2,032,684,135	86.47	2.07	4.28	2.87	1.70	1.52	1.09	0.00
1993	2,610,504,390	87.21	2.08	4.10	2.38	1.52	1.35	1.37	0.00
1994	2,817,671,150	88.08	2.01	3.49	2.09	1.34	1.31	1.68	0.00
1995	3,507,991,171	87.71	2.10	3.26	2.24	1.27	1.43	1.99	0.00

Key to abbreviations: NYSE, New York Stock Exchange; AMEX, American Stock Exchange; CHIC, Chicago Stock Exchange; PSE, Pacific Stock Exchange; PHLX, Philadelphia Stock Exchange; BSE, Boston Stock Exchange; and CSE, Cincinnati Stock Exchange.

Source: U.S. Securities and Exchange Commission

Sizing Up the Big Board

Daily Average Share Volume on the New York Stock Exchange

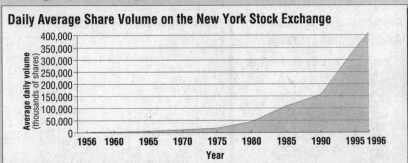

Most Active Trading Days on the NYSE
(Thousands)

Date	Volume
January 23, 1997	684,588
July 16, 1996	680,913
December 20, 1996	654,110
June 20, 1997	652,945
July 16, 1997	652,848
December 15, 1995	652,829
September 24, 1997	645,708
September 16, 1997	642,068
September 19, 1997	630,856
July 17, 1997	629,088

NYSE Membership Prices

Year	High	Low	Year	High	Low
1945	$95,000	$49,000	1988	$820,000	$580,000
1955	90,000	80,000	1989	675,000	420,000
1960	162,000	135,000	1990	430,000	250,000
1965	250,000	190,000	1991	440,000	345,000
1970	320,000	130,000	1992	600,000	410,000
1975	138,000	55,000	1993	775,000	500,000
1980	275,000	175,000	1994	830,000	760,000
1985	480,000	310,000	1995	1,050,000	785,000
1986	600,000	455,000	1996	1,450,000	1,225,000
1987	1,150,000	605,000			

Listings on the NYSE

End of year	Number of companies	Number of issues	Shares listed (millions) Number	Market value
1977	1,575	2,177	26,093	$796,639
1980	1,570	2,228	33,709	1,242,803
1985	1,541	2,298	52,427	1,950,332
1990	1,774	2,284	90,732	2,819,778
1991	1,885	2,426	99,622	3,712,835
1992	2,088	2,658	115,839	4,035,100
1993	2,361	2,904	131,053	4,540,850
1994	2,570	3,060	142,281	4,448,284
1995	2,675	3,126	154,719	6,012,971
1996	2,907	3,285	176,944	17,300,351

Source: New York Stock Exchange

Activity on the Amex

Average Daily Volume on the American Stock Exchange

Year	Average Daily Volume
1970	3,319,355
1975	2,138,079
1980	6,427,165
1985	8,336,568
1990	13,157,780
1991	13,308,784
1992	14,156,651
1993	18,110,724
1994	17,945,357
1995	20,128,255
1996	22,158,216

Most Active Trading Days on the Amex

Date	Volume
October 20, 1987	43,432,760
October 15, 1993	42,940,750
July 16,1996	41,256,875
February 1, 1996	38,538,545
June 27, 1995	38,195,050
September 29, 1994	38,134,000
September 8, 1995	36,928,230
July 27, 1995	36,301,800
September 18, 1997	36,774,665
September 16, 1997	36,378,880

Amex Membership Prices

Year	High	Low	Year	High	Low
1960	$60,000	$51,000	1989	$215,000	$155,000
1965	80,000	55,000	1990	170,000	83,500
1970	185,000	70,000	1991	120,000	80,000
1975	72,000	34,000	1992	110,000	76,000
1980	252,000	95,000	1993	163,000	92,000
1985	160,000	115,000	1994	205,000	155,000
1986	285,000	145,000	1995	152,000	105,000
1987	420,000	265,000	1996	210,000	150,000
1988	280,000	180,000			

Listings on the Amex

Year-end	Number of equity issues	Number of shares outstanding	Total Market Value
1970	1,222	2,857,275,369	$39,535,679,374
1975	1,267	3,180,800,830	29,365,930,815
1980	973	4,179,545,476	82,916,682,074
1985	940	6,339,768,349	87,013,822,402
1990	1,063	9,767,749,621	102,301,457,254
1991	1,055	10,814,101,577	124,454,193,457
1992	943	10,177,908,769	109,354,448,986
1993	1,005	10,611,665,000	135,106,852,386
1994	981	10,924,697,000	113,600,509,489
1995	936	10,493,013,000	137,272,115,187
1996	896	11,011,105,039	135,058,498,619

Source: American Stock Exchange

Trading on Nasdaq

Daily Average Volume on the Nasdaq

Year	Average daily share volume (In millions)	Number of active securities
1985	82.1	4,784
1990	131.9	4,706
1991	163.3	4,684
1992	190.8	4,764
1993	263.0	5,393
1994	295.0	5,761
1995	401.4	5,955
1996	543.7	6,384

Most Active Trading Days on the Nasdaq

Date	Share volume
July 16, 1996	877,329,600
July 16, 1997	836,197,300
May 5, 1997	835,134,600
May 7, 1996	806,501,600
January 23, 1997	795,362,400
August 6, 1997	780,350,500
September 17, 1997	770,015,000
May 23, 1996	757,951,700
May 8, 1996	756,919,400
July 17, 1997	750,891,000

Source: National Association of Securities Dealers

Most Active Stocks on the New York Stock Exchange in 1996

Issue	Reported share volume
Micron Technology	1,070,607,900
AT&T	818,961,200
PepsiCo	757,314,200
Int'l Business Machines	738,603,300
Wal-Mart Stores	731,486,200
Kmart	621,616,700
Compaq Computer	610,361,500
Ford Motor	609,330,200
Motorola	594,376,400
Bay Networks	583,576,000

Source: New York Stock Exchange

Most Active Stocks on the American Stock Exchange in 1996

	Issue	Share volume (In millions)
1	Viacom (Class B)	271.9
2	Trans World Airlines	199.8
3	Echo Bay Mines	198.5
4	IVAX	183.5
5	Ampex (Class A)	179.1
6	XCL	169.1
7	Hasbro	129.3
8	Bema Gold	124.8
9	Royal Oak Mines	117.0
10	Harken Energy	108.5

Source: American Stock Exchange

Most Active Nasdaq National Market Securities in 1996

	Company name	Share volume (In thousands)
1	Intel	2,338,855
2	Cisco Systems	1,789,884
3	Sun Microsystems	1,261,363
4	Microsoft	1,205,766
5	Oracle	1,161,632
6	Applied Materials	1,028,617
7	MCI Communications	944,600
8	Tele-Communications	934,703
9	3Com	907,541
10	Dell Computer	903,925

Source: Nasdaq Stock Market

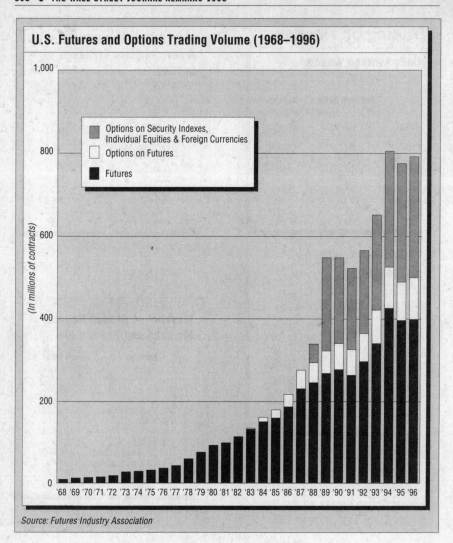

U.S. Futures and Options Trading Volume (1968–1996)

(In millions of contracts)

Legend:
- Options on Security Indexes, Individual Equities & Foreign Currencies
- Options on Futures
- Futures

Source: Futures Industry Association

Total U.S. Futures and Options on U.S. Futures (1972–1990)

Number of contracts

1972	Total U.S. Futures	18,332,055
1973	Total U.S. Futures	25,826,747
1974	Total U.S. Futures	27,733,328
1975	Total U.S. Futures	32,200,106
1976	Total U.S. Futures	36,875,727
1977	Total U.S. Futures	42,847,064
1978	Total U.S. Futures	58,462,172
1979	Total U.S. Futures	75,966,471
1980	Total U.S. Futures	92,096,109
1981	Total U.S. Futures	98,522,371

1982	U.S. Futures	112,400,879
	Options on U.S. Futures	177,350
	(Began trading in 1982)	
	Total	**112,578,229**
1983	U.S. Futures	139,924,940
	Options on U.S. Futures	2,646,865
	Total	**142,571,805**
1984	U.S. Futures	149,372,225
	Options on U.S. Futures	9,928,141
	Total	**159,300,366**
1985	U.S. Futures	158,696,578
	Options on U.S. Futures	20,044,744
	Total	**178,741,322**
1986	U.S. Futures	184,354,496
	Options on U.S. Futures	31,770,613
	Total	**216,125,109**
1987	U.S. Futures	228,876,684
	Options on U.S. Futures	46,185,985
	Total	**275,062,669**
1988	U.S. Futures	245,871,290
	Options on U.S. Futures	49,137,490
	Total	**295,008,780**
1989	U.S. Futures	267,386,263
	Options on U.S. Futures	55,446,130
	Options on U.S. Securities Indexes, Individual Equities & Foreign Currencies	226,657,728
	Total	**549,490,121**
1990	U.S. Futures	276,536,280
	Options on U.S. Futures	64,103,094
	Options on U.S. Securities Indexes, Individual Equities & Foreign Currencies	209,747,484
	Total	**550,386,858**

Source: Futures Industry Association

Total Volume on U.S. Futures, Options on U.S. Futures, and Options on U.S. Securities Indexes and Foreign Currencies (1991–1996)

		Number of contracts
1991	U.S. Futures	262,895,551
	Options on U.S. Futures	62,201,905
	Options on U.S. Securities Indexes, Individual Equities & Foreign Currencies	198,257,932
	Total	**523,355,388**
1992	U.S. Futures	295,292,042
	Options on U.S. Futures	69,244,775
	Options on U.S. Securities Indexes, Individual Equities & Foreign Currencies	201,970,675
	Total	**566,507,492**
1993	U.S. Futures	339,075,626
	Options on U.S. Futures	81,858,635
	Options on U.S. Securities Indexes, Individual Equities & Foreign Currencies	231,377,310
	Total	**652,311,571**
1994	U.S. Futures	426,307,942
	Options on U.S. Futures	100,881,506
	Options on U.S. Securities Indexes, Individual Equities & Foreign Currencies	280,678,941
	Total	**807,868,389**
1995	U.S. Futures	395,313,480
	Options on U.S. Futures	94,208,810
	Options on U.S. Securities Indexes, Individual Equities & Foreign Currencies	287,113,818
	Total	**776,636,108**
1996	U.S. Futures	397,402,153
	Options on U.S. Futures	101,973,807
	Options on U.S. Securities Indexes, Individual Equities & Foreign Currencies	294,256,693
	Total	**793,632,653**

Source: Futures Industry Association

U.S. Futures Volume by Commodity Group

Year	Commodity group by rank	Contracts	Percentage
1995............	Interest rate..	223,587,570	56.56 %
	Ag commodities...................................	63,530,647	16.07
	Energy products..................................	47,166,661	11.93
	Foreign currency/index.........................	23,188,210	5.87
	Equity indexes....................................	20,665,014	5.23
	Precious metals...................................	14,119,753	3.57
	Non-precious metals............................	2,519,414	0.64
	Other..	536,211	0.14
	Total..	**395,313,480**	**100.00**
1996............	Interest rate..	212,546,494	53.48 %
	Ag commodities...................................	74,856,171	18.84
	Energy products..................................	47,181,088	11.87
	Foreign currency/index.........................	22,627,489	5.69
	Equity indexes....................................	22,174,804	5.58
	Precious metals...................................	14,871,995	3.74
	Non-precious metals............................	2,311,919	0.58
	Other..	832,193	0.21
	Total..	**397,402,153**	**100.00**

Source: Futures Industry Association

Options Volume on U.S. Futures & U.S. Securities Exchanges by Commodity Group

Year	Commodity group by rank	Contracts	Percentage
1995............	Interest rate..	58,706,167	62.31 %
	Ag commodities...................................	13,606,295	14.44
	Foreign currency/index.........................	7,387,305	7.84
	Energy Products..................................	6,506,876	6.91
	Equity indexes....................................	4,613,975	4.90
	Precious metals...................................	3,199,966	3.40
	Non-precious metals............................	134,246	0.14
	Other..	53,980	0.06
	Options on futures.........................	**94,208,810**	**100.00**
	Equity indexes....................................	107,823,261	37.55
	Foreign currency/index.........................	4,982,959	1.74
	Interest rate.......................................	65,102	0.02
	Individual equities................................	174,242,496	60.69
	Options on securities indexes individual equities & foreign currencies...............................	**287,113,818**	**100.00**
	Total..	**381,322,628**	

Year	Commodity group by rank	Contracts	Percentage
1996	Interest rate	58,977,452	57.84%
	Ag commodities	19,074,015	18.70
	Foreign currency/index	7,561,909	7.42
	Energy products	8,362,189	8.20
	Equity indexes	4,731,133	4.64
	Precious metals	3,065,975	3.01
	Non-precious metals	150,339	0.15
	Other	50,795	0.05
	Options on futures	**101,973,807**	**100.00**
	Equity indexes	92,422,390	31.41
	Foreign currency/index	3,165,982	1.08
	Interest rate	94,252	0.03
	Individual equities	198,574,069	67.48
	Options on securities indexes individual equities & foreign currencies	**294,256,693**	**100.00**
	Total	**396,230,500**	

Source: Futures Industry Association

Top 20 Futures Contracts Traded in 1996

1996 rank	Futures	1996 contracts	%	1995 contracts	%	1995 rank
1	Eurodollar, CME	88,883,119	22.37	95,730,019	24.22	1
2	T-bonds, CBOT	84,725,128	21.32	86,375,916	21.85	2
3	Crude oil, NYMEX	23,487,821	5.91	23,613,994	5.97	3
4	T-notes (10 year), CBOT	21,939,725	5.52	22,445,356	5.68	4
5	S&P 500 index, CME	19,899,999	5.01	18,852,149	4.77	5
6	Corn, CBOT	19,620,188	4.94	15,105,147	3.82	6
7	Soybeans, CBOT	14,236,295	3.58	10,611,534	2.68	8
8	T-notes (5 year), CBOT	11,463,640	2.88	12,637,054	3.20	7
9	Gold (100 oz.), COMEX Div. of NYMEX	8,902,179	2.24	7,781,596	1.97	11
10	Natural gas, NYMEX	8,813,867	2.22	8,086,718	2.05	10
11	#2 heating oil, NYMEX	8,341,877	2.10	8,266,783	2.09	9
12	Unleaded regular gas, NYMEX	6,312,339	1.59	7,071,787	1.79	13
13	Deutschemark, CME	5,979,464	1.50	7,186,476	1.82	12
14	Soybean meal, CBOT	5,955,977	1.50	5,601,242	1.42	15
15	Wheat, CBOT	5,385,967	1.36	4,955,067	1.25	17
16	Japanese Yen, CME	5,101,819	1.28	5,630,053	1.42	14
17	Silver (5,000 oz.), COMEX Div. of NYMEX	4,870,808	1.23	5,183,236	1.31	16
18	Sugar #11, CSC	4,751,852	1.20	4,711,082	1.19	18
19	Soybean oil, CBOT	4,980,277	1.25	4,611,336	1.17	19
20	Swiss Franc, CME	3,929,225	0.99	4,399,932	1.11	20

Source: Futures Industry Association

U.S. Futures Exchange Volume

1996 rank	Exchange	1996 contracts	%	1995 contracts	%	1995 rank
1	Chicago Board of Trade	171,134,185	43.06	165,616,177	41.89	1
2	Chicago Mercantile Exchange	141,600,469	35.63	146,662,764	37.10	2
3	New York Mercantile Exchange (incl. Comex Division)	64,223,291	16.16	63,636,046	16.10	3
4	Coffee Sugar & Cocoa Exchange	9,102,029	2.29	8,925,205	2.26	4
5	New York Cotton Exchange*	4,967,176	1.25	4,702,985	1.19	5
6	Mid-America Commodity Exchange	3,229,710	0.81	3,047,982	0.77	6
7	Kansas City Board of Trade	2,084,493	0.52	1,747,664	0.44	7
8	Minneapolis Grain Exchange	1,012,598	0.25	936,016	0.24	8
9	Philadelphia Board of Trade	48,202	0.01	38,641	0.01	9
	Total	397,402,153	100.00	395,313,480	100.00	

*The New York Cotton Exchange volume now includes New York Futures Exchange volume.
Source: Futures Industry Association

Volumes of Options Traded on U.S. Futures Exchanges

1996 rank	Exchange	1996 contracts	%	1995 contracts	%	1995 rank
1	Chicago Board of Trade	51,304,320	50.31	45,056,867	47.83	1
2	Chicago Mercantile Exchange	35,421,726	34.74	35,142,349	37.30	2
3	New York Mercantile Exchange (incl. Comex Division)	11,576,001	11.35	9,836,294	10.44	3
4	Coffee Sugar & Cocoa Exchange	2,287,750	2.24	2,390,774	2.54	4
5	New York Cotton Exchange*	1,261,109	1.24	1,645,324	1.75	5
6	Kansas City Board of Trade	68,479	0.07	81,409	0.09	6
7	Mid-America Commodity Exchange	27,531	0.03	23,127	0.02	8
8	Minneapolis Grain Exchange	26,891	0.03	32,666	0.03	7
	Total	101,973,807	100.00	94,208,810	100.00	

Volumes of Options Traded on U.S. Securities Exchanges

1996 rank	Exchange	1996 contracts	%	1995 contracts	%	1995 rank
1	Chicago Board Options Exchange	173,944,877	59.11	178,533,464	62.18	1
2	American Stock Exchange	61,584,845	20.93	52,404,142	18.25	2
3	Pacific Stock Exchange	33,388,258	11.35	30,819,850	10.73	3
4	Philadelphia Stock Exchange	21,949,833	7.46	22,524,134	7.85	4
5	New York Stock Exchange	3,388,880	1.15	2,832,228	0.99	5
	Total	294,256,693	100.00	287,113,818	100.00	

*The New York Cotton Exchange volume now includes New York Futures Exchange volume.
Source: Futures Industry Association

Top 20 Options Contracts Traded in 1996*

1996 rank	Options	1996 contracts	%	1995 contracts	%	1995 rank
1	S&P 100 Index, CBOE	54,929,246	13.86	69,633,460	18.26	1
2	T-bonds, CBOT	25,930,661	6.54	25,639,950	6.72	3
3	S&P 500 Index, CBOE	24,884,808	6.28	26,726,023	7.01	2
4	Eurodollar, CME	22,234,888	5.61	22,363,853	5.86	4
5	T-notes (10 year), CBOT	7,907,650	2.00	6,887,102	1.81	5
6	Corn, CBOT	6,602,010	1.67	3,783,446	0.99	8
7	Crude oil, NYMEX	5,271,456	1.33	3,975,611	1.04	7
8	Soybeans, CBOT	5,135,124	1.30	3,149,635	0.83	10
9	S&P 500 Index, CME	4,636,236	1.17	4,568,232	1.20	6
10	NASDAQ 100, CBOE	3,216,041	0.81	2,082,335	0.55	13
11	British Pound, CME	2,886,041	0.73	1,668,624	0.44	16
12	T-notes (5 year), CBOT	2,723,525	0.69	3,619,462	0.95	9
13	Gold (1,000 oz.), COMEX Div. of NYMEX	2,079,663	0.52	2,006,695	0.53	14
14	Wheat, CBOT	1,886,909	0.48	1,243,567	0.33	18
15	Deutschemark, CME	1,822,649	0.46	2,642,904	0.69	11
16	Japanese Yen, CME	1,734,186	0.44	2,141,043	0.56	12
17	Morgan Stanley High Tech 35 Index, AMEX	1,539,719	0.39	478,954	0.13	36
18	Natural gas, NYMEX	1,234,691	0.31	921,520	0.24	23
19	Semiconducter Index, PHLX	1,132,876	0.29	1,108,474	0.29	21
20	Heating oil, NYMEX	1,108,935	0.28	703,388	0.18	27

*Excludes options on individual equities.
Source: Futures Industry Association

Top 20 International Exchanges Based on Global Futures and Options Volume (Excluding options on individual equities)

1996 rank	1995 rank	Exchange	1995 volume	1996 volume	% change
1	1	Chicago Board of Trade, USA	210,673,044	222,438,505	5.58
2	2	Chicago Mercantile Exchange, USA	181,805,113	177,022,195	-2.63
3	6	LIFFE, U.K.	128,678,388	162,631,867	26.39
4	3	BM&F, Brazil	148,055,778	134,609,876	-9.08
5	7	Chicago Board Options Exchange, USA	101,492,998	85,488,298	-15.77
6	4	Beijing Commodity Exchange, China	141,664,141	81,100,110	-42.75
7	8	New York Mercantile Exchange, USA	73,472,340	75,799,292	3.17
8	9	Matif S.A., France	71,090,512	68,293,238	-3.93
9	10	DTB, Germany	49,407,307	67,290,310	36.20
10	5	BBF, Brazil	128,734,681	50,359,959	-60.88
11	11	London Metal Exchange, U.K.	47,150,330	47,487,007	0.71
12	13	MEFF Renta Variable, Spain	36,276,298	37,883,275	4.43
13	12	TIFFE, Japan	36,722,216	29,970,017	-18.39
14	14	Tokyo Commodity Exchange, Japan	35,125,427	27,560,154	-21.54
15	22	Tokyo Grain Exchange, Japan	14,643,162	27,509,275	87.86
16	15	Sydney Futures Exchange, Australia	25,620,614	25,475,788	-0.57
17	17	MEFF Renta Fija, Spain	19,082,575	23,931,008	25.41
18	19	OM Stockholm, Sweden	18,653,319	22,704,201	21.72
19	16	Singapore Int'l Monetary Exchange, Singapore	24,251,339	22,568,545	-6.94
20	18	Tokyo Stock Exchange, Japan	18,894,835	17,551,142	-7.11

Source: Futures Industry Association

Top Works of Art at Auction

Paintings that sold for the highest prices.

Artist	Title	Sale date	Hammer price	With premium
Vincent van Gogh	Portrait du Dr. Gachet (1890)	05/15/90	$75,000,000	$82,500,000
Pierre-Auguste Renoir	Au Moulin de la Galette (1876)	05/17/90	71,000,000	78,100,000
Pablo Picasso	Les Noces de Pierrette (1905)	11/30/89	49,200,000	49,200,000
Vincent van Gogh	Irises (1889)	11/11/87	49,000,000	53,900,000
Pablo Picasso	Yo Picasso (c.1901)	05/09/89	43,500,000	47,850,000
Pablo Picasso	Au Lapin Agile (1905)	11/15/89	37,000,000	40,700,000
Vincent van Gogh	Sunflowers (1889)	03/30/87	36,292,500	39,921,750
Pablo Picasso	Acrobate et Jeune Arlequin (1905)	11/28/88	34,960,000	38,456,000
Pontormo	Portrait of Duke Cosimo I de Medici	05/31/89	32,000,000	35,200,000
Pablo Picasso	Angel Fernandez de Soto (1903)	05/08/95	26,500,000	29,152,500
Paul Cezanne	Nature Morte: Les Grosses Pommes (c.1890)	05/11/93	26,000,000	28,602,500
Vincent van Gogh	Sous-bois (1890)	11/08/95	24,500,000	26,952,500
Vincent van Gogh	Autoportrait (1888)	05/15/90	24,000,000	26,400,000
Édouard Manet	La Rue Mosnier aux Drapeaux (1878)	11/14/89	24,000,000	26,400,000
Pablo Picasso	Le Miroir (1932)	11/15/89	24,000,000	26,400,000
Pablo Picasso	Maternité (1901)	11/14/88	22,500,000	24,750,000
Claude Monet	Dans la Prairie (1876)	06/28/88	22,230,000	24,453,000
Paul Gauguin	Mata Mua (1892)	05/09/89	22,000,000	24,200,000
Pablo Picasso	Les Tuileries (1901)	06/25/90	21,612,500	23,773,750
Paul Cezanne	Madame Cezanne au Fauteuil Jaune (1888)	05/12/97	21,000,000	23,102,500
John Constable	The Lock	11/14/90	19,230,540	21,153,594
Wassili Kandinsky	Fugue (1914)	05/17/90	19,000,000	20,900,000
Willem de Kooning	Interchange (1955)	11/08/89	18,800,000	20,680,000
Vincent van Gogh	Le Pont de Trinquetaille (1888)	06/29/87	18,515,000	20,366,500
Vincent van Gogh	Le Vieil If (1888)	11/14/89	18,500,000	20,350,000

Source: Sotheby's Holdings Inc.

The Art Market

Sales at the two major auction houses still trail the lofty levels of 1989 and 1990, but they have increased in recent years.

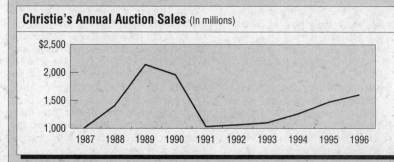

Christie's Annual Auction Sales (In millions)

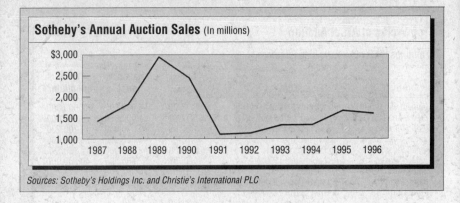

Sotheby's Annual Auction Sales (In millions)

Sources: Sotheby's Holdings Inc. and Christie's International PLC

Personal Finance

CHARGING TOWARD BANKRUPTCY

For Martha Scofield, credit cards filled in the financial holes that her job as a security guard couldn't when her husband was unemployed. Cash advances paid the rent, bought groceries and soothed any anxiety in the days before the next paycheck.

The 38-year-old Cleveland resident says she was also tired of doing without. After years of "mind-numbing" and low-paying jobs, Ms. Scofield saw credit cards as a chance for some finer, though still modest, things. She charged a set of new "not-slept-in" sheets for her queen-size bed. If she saw a blouse she liked at J.C. Penney, she bought it. The high interest rates didn't faze her. When the bills came, Ms. Scofield says, she paid attention only to the remaining available credit, not the steadily rising balances on her 15 cards. "I kept feeling I should use the cards because I deserved some nice stuff," she says. "I was sick of drinking out of Flintstone jelly jars."

Using credit cards to supplement income has become increasingly common—and dangerous. In 1996, a record number of consumers filed for bankruptcy. The 1.1 million filings represent an almost 25% increase from 1995. And the bankruptcies continue to rise: During the second quarter of 1997, there were

353,177 filings, more than in any other quarter, and a 25% increase from the same period in 1996, according to the Administrative Office of the U.S. Courts. The rate of late payments on bank credit cards—an indicator that consumers may be having trouble managing—has also climbed in recent years. In the second quarter of 1997, payments were running late on 3.7% of all bank credit-card accounts, compared with 2.4% in the 1990 second period.

Economists have long maintained that the bankruptcy rate often shoots up when economic conditions deteriorate, a theory that explained the previous spike, in 1992, that came in the wake of a recession. But today's economy is expanding. Unemployment and inflation have been low, and the stock market has reached record heights.

So what's spurring the surge in bankruptcies? "People don't have a safety net," says Norma Haames, a bankruptcy attorney for more than 19 years. Although mortgages and car loans can often get people into trouble, Ms. Haames sees more and more clients carrying heavy credit-card debt. For a while, people's jobs allow them to manage the debt, she says, but if a "triggering event" happens, like the loss of a job, a divorce or an injury, consumers are pushed into bankruptcy. A study by Visa International also found that in a majority of cases, a catastrophic event precedes bankruptcy.

The amount of revolving credit grew

13% in 1996, to $498 billion from $441.9 billion in 1995, according to the Federal Reserve. These days, credit cards pay for textbooks when student loan money is gone, they cover prescription drugs when medical insurance doesn't, they provide a wardrobe for the big job hunt, and they buy holiday presents after the paycheck gives out. Until recently, credit-card issuers made it easy for consumers to stuff their wallets with cards. Mail boxes were filled with credit-card solicitations, offering low introductory interest rates, high credit limits and such perks as frequent-flier miles, free long-distance telephone calls, and price breaks on new cars.

But all that is changing now that credit-card issuers are being stung by bad debts. Personal bankruptcies cost the credit-card industry some $8 billion in 1996, a hit that was passed onto consumers in the form of higher interest rates and service fees.

So after years of encouraging consumers to take record amounts of debt, credit-card issuers recently began to fight the rising tide of bankruptcies. Besides tightening credit standards and starting consumer-education programs, credit-card issuers have launched a major lobbying effort to toughen federal bankruptcy law. The credit-card industry wants to make Chapter 7 filings the exception rather than the rule, arguing that many people who have their unsecured debts totally forgiven could afford to meet at least some of their obligations. "The current law allows debtors to retain more relief than they actually need," says David Sandor, a spokesman for Visa USA.

But consumer advocates and government-appointed bankruptcy trustees maintain that the vast majority of bankrupt people aren't in a position to repay debts and need the relief intended by the Bankruptcy Code. "If credit-card issuers were more careful when the issued credit in the first place," says Ms. Haames. "I think they'd find that they're losses would be minimized." Credit card issuers counter that while the losses are costly, only 1% of bank-card accounts end up in bankruptcy court.

There probably would be even more bankruptcies, if not for the rise in popularity of nonprofit consumer-credit counseling centers. In 1997, the more than 1,300 offices of the National Foundation for Consumer Credit expect to counsel 1.2 million individuals, one third of whom will undertake a "debt management program" with creditors, according to Durant Abernethy, president and chief executive officer of the foundation. The programs, in lieu of bankruptcy, work out voluntary agreements between debtors and creditors that either extend the payment schedule, reduce the burden, or do both. The plans stretch from three to five years; anything longer tends to discourage the clients, Mr. Abernethy says. For its help, the center usually charges the client a nominal fee and asks creditors for a donation.

For Ms. Scofield of Cleveland, the Consumer Credit Counseling Center was a lifesaver. Five years ago, her three-year marriage fell apart. Shortly after that, she lost her job of three months as a receptionist at a law firm. After what she calls years of "stupid decisions," she found she had accumulated more than $15,000 in debts through credit cards and student loans.

She moved in with her parents to cut her expenses. But with no savings, Ms. Scofield wasn't able to make even the minimum payments on her cards. That, in turn, quickly unleashed a flood of "nasty" calls and letters from collection agencies that left her "worn down and traumatized." Although Ms. Scofield soon found a $4.25-an-hour job in the plastics department at a manufacturing plant, she still wasn't able to send her creditors enough money to keep them satisfied. "I sent them three-quarters of my paycheck, and I still got all the calls," she says.

Frustrated, she made an appointment with a credit counselor. She sobbed as she told the counselor what had precipitated her financial woes. "It was humiliating," she says. "I was brought up that your financial stuff is personal." The counselor didn't make her "feel like a loser," and between them they worked out a debt management plan that stopped the calls from collection agencies.

Now, with the help of a small inheritance, Ms. Scofield, who works as a graphic artist, is debt-free. She has her own apartment and, she says, all her bills are paid on time. An invitation for a platinum credit card sits on an end table in her living room, but she doesn't think she'll send in the application. Now, she keeps just one credit card for emergencies, usually to keep her rattling 1986 Mercury Cougar tooling along.

Laurie Snyder

STRATEGIES FOR SAVING

Stop me before I spend again. If you live from paycheck to paycheck, never managing to save any money, it is time for radical action.

But what should you do? Take a look below. Sure, some of the suggestions are a tad unconventional. Yeah, there are smarter ways to manage your money. But the strategies advocated aren't entirely foolish, especially if they get you to spend less and save more.

- While many people fritter away their paychecks, often they are much more careful if they receive a lump sum, like a year-end bonus or an inheritance. "If you have a $100,000 income, but $80,000 is salary and $20,000 is bonus, you won't

raise your lifestyle to $100,000," says Deena Katz, a financial planner in Coral Gables, Fla. "You will see the $20,000 as something separate, and therefore you might invest it rather than spend it."

Many people, of course, don't receive year-end bonuses. But you can simulate the same effect. Suppose you have a youngster in day care and your employer offers a dependent-care reimbursement program, where money is yanked out of your pretax income and set aside to cover child-care costs. With these programs, you can have as much as $5,000 a year withheld from your salary to cover summer camp, day care and after-school programs. The money

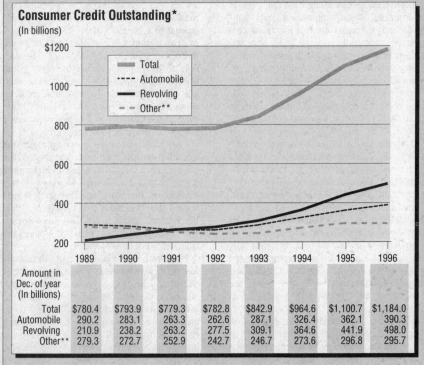

Deeper in Debt

Growth of consumer credit in the 1990s, with revolving credit now accounting for a larger share of the total than auto loans.

Consumer Credit Outstanding*
(In billions)

Amount in Dec. of year (In billions)	1989	1990	1991	1992	1993	1994	1995	1996
Total	$780.4	$793.9	$779.3	$782.8	$842.9	$964.6	$1,100.7	$1,184.0
Automobile	290.2	283.1	263.3	262.6	287.1	326.4	362.1	390.3
Revolving	210.9	238.2	263.2	277.5	309.1	364.6	441.9	498.0
Other**	279.3	272.7	252.9	242.7	246.7	273.6	296.8	295.7

*Covers most short- and intermediate-term consumer credit, excluding loans secured by real estate.
**Loans for mobile homes, education, vacations and other purposes.
Source: Federal Reserve Board

is returned to you when you provide proof that you have incurred dependent-care expenses. It is tempting to reclaim the money as the day-care bills roll in. But if you are an erratic saver, you might wait until the end of the year, empty your dependent-care account all at once and use the cash to buy some stocks or invest in a mutual fund.

You can try the same trick with your taxes. You might arrange to have too much withheld from your paycheck, thereby building up a lump sum that will be returned to you when you file your 1040 and claim your refund. This isn't smart money management because you are effectively making an interest-free loan to Uncle Sam. But the ploy is worthwhile if it helps bolster your savings.

- If you find it difficult to save, you may want to put your investing on autopilot. Consider signing up for an automatic investment plan, where $50 or $100 is plucked from your bank account every month and put directly into a mutual fund. Many fund companies will waive their investment minimum if you sign up for one of these plans. Similarly, arrange to have money deducted from your salary and invested in your employer's 401(k), 403(b), or other retirement-savings plan. With these plans, you will often get the triple benefit of an upfront tax deduction, continuing tax-deferred growth and a matching contribution from your employer.

- If a client is particularly profligate,

investment advisers will take the notion of forced savings one step further. For instance, Eleanor Blayney, a financial planner in McLean, Va., usually recommends that clients opt for a 30-year mortgage rather than a 15-year mortgage. The 30-year mortgage will charge a higher interest rate. But Ms. Blayney likes the flexibility that comes with the lower monthly payment on a 30-year mortgage, and she figures clients can get higher returns by investing the left-over money elsewhere. "But if a client has difficulty saving, sometimes I'll recommend a 15-year mortgage, because it's a forced savings plan," she says.

- Alan Cohn, a financial planner in Bala Cynwyd, Pa., generally avoids cash-value life insurance, which combines a death benefit with an investment account. Instead, he advises clients to buy term insurance, which is far cheaper because it provides only a death benefit, and then stash the extra money in other investments. "You should do better by buying term insurance and investing the difference," Mr. Cohn says. "But that assumes that you have the discipline to invest the difference. For people who don't have any discipline, cash-value life insurance does force them to save."

- Sometimes, investment advisers will even suggest that spendthrift families go into debt to make consumer purchases, rather than pay cash. "If they're going to take $20,000 out of savings to buy a car and then they don't replenish that savings, they're better off taking

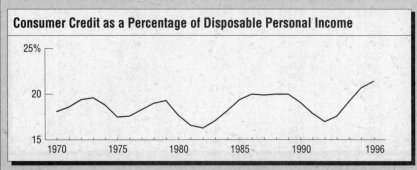

Consumer Credit as a Percentage of Disposable Personal Income

Source: Federal Reserve Board

out a car loan," David Foster, a financial planner in Cincinnati, says. "They have to pay the car loan of $239 a month, but they may never get around to saving the money again."

- The advice can get even more radical. One investment adviser recounts how he sometimes keeps clients in taxable bonds, even if tax-free municipal bonds make more sense, given their tax bracket. His reasoning: With the taxable

bonds, a client's investment account will grow faster because of the higher yield on the taxable bonds. The downside is that the client is taxed on all that interest. But the investment adviser knows that the client will pay Uncle Sam out of his salary. Result? By favoring taxables over munis, the client ends up with more money saved and less spent.

Jonathan Clements

Falling Behind

Percentage of Bank Credit Card Accounts with Payments that are 30 Days or More Overdue

Percentage of Consumer Loans with Payments that are 30 Days or More Overdue

Year, 1st quarter	Bank credit card	Home equity loans	Auto direct	Auto indirect*
1985	2.51%	2.07%	1.63%	2.15%
1986	2.86	1.95	1.82	2.04
1987	2.33	1.66	1.76	2.13
1988	2.54	1.77	1.75	2.04
1989	2.54	1.51	1.73	2.40
1990	2.18	1.47	1.94	2.43
1991	3.34	1.75	2.14	2.66
1992	2.86	1.73	2.37	2.61
1993	2.74	1.48	2.00	2.31
1994	2.54	1.51	1.53	1.64
1995	3.18	1.25	1.45	1.76
1996	3.53	1.44	1.74	2.13
1997	3.51	1.38	2.10	2.55

*Indirect auto loans are originated through car dealers.
Source: American Bankers Association

Bankruptcy Filings

Total, Business, and Consumer Bankruptcy Filings

Calendar year	Total filings	Business cases	Consumer cases
1982	380,251	69,300	310,951
1983	348,880	62,436	286,444
1984	348,521	64,004	284,517
1985	412,510	71,277	341,233
1986	530,438	81,235	449,203
1987	577,999	82,446	495,553
1988	613,465	63,853	549,612
1989	679,461	63,235	616,226
1990	782,960	64,853	718,107
1991	943,987	71,549	872,438
1992	971,517	70,643	900,874
1993	875,202	62,304	812,898
1994	832,829	52,374	780,455
1995	926,601	51,959	874,642
1996	1,178,555	53,549	1,125,006

Bankruptcy Filings by Decade

Decade	Total filings
1900–1909	173,298
1910–1919	215,296
1920–1929	410,475
1930–1939	614,938
1940–1949	296,021
1950–1959	584,272
1960–1969	1,695,416
1970–1979	2,086,189
1980–1989	4,586,432
1990–1996	6,511,651

Bankruptcy Filing Trends by State

State	1984	1996	% change	State	1984	1996	% change
Alaska	433	1,226	183.14	Montana	948	2,805	195.89
Alabama	9,950	31,672	218.31	North Carolina	4,871	22,196	355.68
Arkansas	3,720	13,194	254.68	North Dakota	654	1,688	158.10
Arizona	4,839	20,284	319.18	Nebraska	2,565	5,304	106.78
California	61,882	183,630	196.74	New Hampshire	497	3,692	642.86
Colorado	6,475	16,403	153.33	New Jersey	6,744	34,091	405.50
Connecticut	1,852	11,307	510.53	New Mexico	1,585	5,870	270.35
Washington, D.C.	636	1,950	206.60	Nevada	2,776	10,531	279.36
Delaware	442	2,044	362.44	New York	13,902	62,178	347.26
Florida	8,230	59,354	621.19	Ohio	19,704	44,494	125.81
Georgia	13,090	55,339	322.76	Oklahoma	6,568	18,451	180.92
Hawaii	614	3,092	403.58	Oregon	6,149	16,709	171.74
Iowa	3,913	8,715	122.72	Pennsylvania	9,180	32,502	254.05
Idaho	2,233	5,426	142.99	Rhode Island	713	4,328	507.01
Illinois	24,988	54,498	118.10	South Carolina	2,033	9,778	380.96
Indiana	11,950	29,891	150.13	South Dakota	867	1,912	120.53
Kansas	4,417	11,312	156.10	Tennessee	14,018	48,748	247.75
Kentucky	6,660	18,794	182.19	Texas	14,597	61,515	321.42
Louisiana	6,927	20,437	195.03	Utah	3,583	9,299	159.53
Massachusetts	2,251	17,744	688.27	Virginia	8,531	35,955	321.46
Maryland	3,783	24,347	543.59	Vermont	213	1,368	542.25
Maine	599	3,073	413.02	Washington	10,280	28,630	178.50
Michigan	8,939	31,799	255.73	Wisconsin	7,652	16,137	110.89
Minnesota	5,076	18,236	259.26	West Virginia	1,862	6,013	222.93
Missouri	6,984	22,103	216.48	Wyoming	979	1,783	82.12
Mississippi	4,627	15,743	240.24				

Source: American Bankruptcy Institute

Less Thrift in the '90s

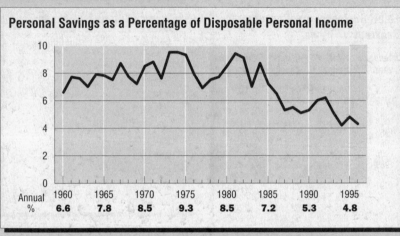

Personal Savings as a Percentage of Disposable Personal Income

Annual %	1960	1965	1970	1975	1980	1985	1990	1995
	6.6	7.8	8.5	9.3	8.5	7.2	5.3	4.8

Source: U.S. Commerce Department, Bureau of Economic Analysis

YOUR RETIREMENT NEST EGG

Am I on track to retire in comfort? Unfortunately, there is no quick and easy answer.

But *The Wall Street Journal* asked T. Rowe Price Associates, the Baltimore mutual-fund company, to put together the accompanying table. It shows the amount you should have saved as a percent of your current annual salary—depending on how far you are from retirement and how aggressively you invest. The table, for instance, indicates that aggressive investors who are 15 years from retirement should have socked away an amount equal to just over three times their pretax salary, while more conservative investors should have a tad more than five times their salary saved.

The table will give you some sense of whether you have put away enough money for retirement so far. But before you read too much into the numbers, be aware of the table's limitations. A fistful of assumptions underlie the numbers. Investors are assumed to save 8% of their pretax salary every year between now and retirement, after which they withdraw an annual amount equal to 75% of their preretirement income. This 75% wouldn't all be spending money; taxes would

have to be paid out of this sum. T. Rowe Price's calculations are based on investors living 25 years in retirement, at which point their savings are exhausted.

What about returns? Aggressive investors are assumed to hold a mix of 80% stocks and 20% bonds before retirement and a combination of 65% stocks and 35% bonds after retirement. Moderate-risk investors, meanwhile, split their money between 65% stocks and 35% bonds until they quit the work force, at which point they switch to a mix of 50% stocks and 50% bonds. As for conservative investors, they maintain a portfolio of 50% stocks and 50% bonds until they retire; thereafter, they hold 35% stocks and 65% bonds.

For stock and bond performance numbers, T. Rowe Price tapped the Ibbotson Associates database to get the average returns over the past 50 years for Standard & Poor's 500-stock index and intermediate-term government bonds. T. Rowe Price further assumed that the salary earned, the amount saved each year, and the annual amount withdrawn in retirement all rise with inflation, which ran at just over 4% a year during the past five decades.

The amount shown for current savings still could prove too high or too low. Suppose your salary rises much faster than inflation and, thus, so does your desired retirement

Enough Already?

Are you on track to retire? Figure out how much you have saved for retirement as a percent of your current annual salary, then compare this number to the appropriate figure in the table. For instance, if you are a conservative investor with 20 years to retirement, you should have amassed a retirement kitty equal to 369% of your salary.

Investment strategy	Years to retirement							
	0	5	10	15	20	25	30	35
Aggressive	957%	675%	463%	307%	193%	109%	48%	3%
Moderate	1,046	773	558	393	268	172	98	42
Conservative	1,148	890	676	505	369	261	174	105

Source: T. Rowe Price Associates

lifestyle. To compensate, you would need either to have more money than the table indicates or to salt away more than the assumed 8% savings rate. On the other hand, if Social Security will make a significant contribution to your retirement income or if you expect a traditional company pension, you probably don't need a nest egg big enough to replace 75% of your salary. For you, the amounts shown in the table will be too high. "Even if you don't think the assumptions apply to you, the table points up the virtues of starting to save early and investing aggressively," notes Steven Norwitz, a T. Rowe Price vice president. "If you delay saving for retirement until the last 10 or 15 years, you've really dug yourself into a hole."

T. Rowe Price's figures are based on projected returns over long periods. To give you a sense for just how iffy such forecasts can be, Minneapolis financial planner Ross Levin ran a "Monte Carlo analysis" focusing on the projected 4% inflation rate. Let's say you are an aggressive investor who is 20 years from retirement. The table suggests you should have 193% of salary saved. But if the average annual inflation rate turns out to be only modestly higher or lower, the right figure might be as much as 258% or as little as 95%. Because returns and inflation may not match your forecasts, "you should look at your portfolio every year," Mr. Levin advises. "You want to monitor your results to make sure you're on track to meet your goal."

What if you seem to have too little currently saved? To catch up, all you may need is a modest boost in your annual savings rate, especially if you are 20 or more years from retirement. Alternatively, you can greatly increase your retirement nest egg by delaying retirement. That has the triple benefit of increasing the time you have to save, lengthening the time over which your nest egg will grow, and shortening the time spent in retirement. You could also, of course, invest more aggressively. Indeed, it is tempting to assume that you will invest heavily in stocks, so that you can then judge yourself by the smaller sums shown in the table for aggressive investors. "Maybe these people are investing too conservatively," Mr. Norwitz says. "But you don't want people to rush out and take more risk than they can live with."

Jonathan Clements

Family Finances

The Federal Reserve System's 1995 Survey of Consumer Finances reveals that consumers' incomes grew from their depressed 1992 levels, but still lagged 1989 levels. Median net worth reported in 1995 returned to a level nearly equal to that in 1989, but mean net worth remained below the 1989 level. Among family assets, stocks and retirement accounts assumed a bigger share. And as for debt, mortgages grew strongly as a share of family debt, while more families used credit cards and reported higher balances outstanding.

Before-tax Family Income for Previous Year, by Selected Characteristics of Families, 1989, 1992, and 1995, and Percentage of Families Who Saved, 1992 and 1995 (Thousands of 1995 dollars except as noted)

Family characteristics	1989			1992				1995			
	Median	Mean	Percentage of families	Median	Mean	Percentage of families who saved	Percentage of families	Median	Mean	Percentage of families who saved	Percentage of families
All families	$31.8	$49.8	100.0%	$29.1	$43.5	57.1%	100.0%	$30.8	$44.3	55.0%	100.0%
Age of head (years)											
Less than 35	25.8	35.4	27.2	26.8	33.1	59.3	25.8	26.7	31.9	56.4	24.8
35–44	46.3	61.8	23.4	39.1	50.8	57.1	22.8	39.1	48.3	54.1	23.2
45–54	45.7	77.4	14.4	45.5	61.5	59.0	16.2	41.1	64.8	57.6	17.8
55–64	32.1	52.7	13.9	31.6	53.3	59.0	13.2	36.0	52.9	58.5	12.5
65–74	19.3	38.6	12.0	19.3	31.4	53.8	12.6	19.5	37.0	49.6	11.9
75 and more	16.7	28.5	9.0	14.9	25.3	49.2	9.4	17.3	27.3	51.5	9.8
Education of head											
No high school diploma	16.7	23.8	24.3	13.4	19.0	38.3	20.4	15.7	21.9	42.7	19.0
High school diploma	27.3	36.2	32.1	25.8	32.7	56.9	29.9	26.7	35.2	50.9	31.6
Some college	36.0	50.3	15.1	30.5	40.3	59.9	17.7	29.8	39.9	54.2	19.0
College degree	51.4	87.0	28.5	48.6	70.8	67.8	31.9	46.3	70.4	67.5	30.5
Current work status of head											
Professional, managerial	55.5	76.6	16.9	50.9	69.8	68.9	16.8	54.4	72.7	67.9	15.9
Technical, sales, clerical	35.2	43.6	13.4	35.8	41.6	64.5	14.8	34.4	46.2	56.3	14.9
Precision production	47.6	50.9	9.6	36.1	43.4	65.6	7.0	41.1	43.8	60.0	8.2
Machine operators and laborers	30.9	35.4	10.6	29.1	34.1	57.6	10.0	32.9	35.6	60.9	13.1
Service occupations	19.3	25.8	6.6	21.3	28.7	51.5	6.2	21.1	27.2	50.2	6.6
Self-employed	48.1	111.0	11.2	48.6	82.2	59.2	10.9	39.0	79.0	62.3	9.7
Retired	17.3	28.4	25.0	16.5	24.9	48.0	26.0	17.5	27.3	46.1	25.0
Other not working	9.0	17.6	6.7	12.3	22.9	41.6	8.2	12.3	19.9	31.4	6.5
Net Worth (1995 dollars)											
Less than 10,000	13.9	19.2	27.8	14.8	19.8	39.3	27.0	15.4	18.9	36.0	25.8
10,000–24,999	27.1	29.5	9.3	26.2	29.5	52.5	10.4	25.7	28.4	54.1	10.0
25,000–49,999	29.6	33.6	10.1	25.8	30.4	50.0	11.4	32.0	33.9	48.2	11.6
50,000–99,999	36.0	39.5	14.6	32.8	35.9	61.3	15.3	35.2	38.2	57.8	16.9
100,000–249,999	42.9	52.2	21.6	40.9	48.0	67.6	20.7	39.4	47.6	64.4	21.3
250,000 and more	72.0	128.4	16.5	70.0	106.5	78.6	15.2	68.4	111.6	78.2	14.4

Source: Federal Reserve System

Family Net Worth, by Selected Characteristics of Families, 1989, 1992, and 1995 (Thousands of 1995 dollars except as noted)

Family characteristics	1989			1992			1995		
	Median	Mean	Percentage of families	Median	Mean	Percentage of families	Median	Mean	Percentage of families
All families	$56.5	$216.7	100.0%	$52.8	$200.5	100.0%	$56.4	$205.9	100.0%
Income (1995 dollars)*									
Less than 10,000	1.6	26.1	15.4	3.3	30.9	15.5	4.8	45.6	16.0
10,000–24,999	25.6	77.9	24.3	28.2	71.2	27.8	30.0	74.6	26.5
25,000–49,999	56.0	121.8	30.3	54.8	124.4	29.5	54.9	119.3	31.1
50,000–99,999	128.1	229.5	22.3	121.2	240.8	20.0	121.1	256.0	20.2
100,000 and more	474.7	1,372.9	7.7	506.1	1,283.6	7.1	485.9	1,435.2	6.1
Age of head (years)									
Less than 35	9.2	66.3	27.2	10.1	50.3	25.8	11.4	47.2	24.8
35–44	69.2	171.3	23.4	46.0	144.3	22.8	48.5	144.5	23.2
45–54	114.0	338.9	14.4	83.4	287.8	16.2	90.5	277.8	17.8
55–64	110.5	334.4	13.9	122.5	358.6	13.2	110.8	356.2	12.5
65–74	88.4	336.8	12.0	105.8	308.3	12.6	104.1	331.6	11.9
75 and more	83.2	250.8	9.0	92.8	231.0	9.4	95.0	276.0	9.8
Education of head									
No high school diploma	28.5	92.1	24.3	21.6	75.8	20.4	26.3	87.2	19.0
High school diploma	43.4	134.4	32.1	41.4	120.6	29.9	50.0	138.2	31.6
Some college	56.4	213.8	15.1	62.6	185.4	17.7	43.2	186.6	19.0
College degree	132.1	416.9	28.5	103.1	363.3	31.9	104.1	361.8	30.5

*For the calendar year preceding the survey.
Source: Federal Reserve System

Family Holdings of Financial Assets, 1995

Family characteristic	Transaction accounts	CDs	Savings bonds	Bonds	Stocks	Mutual funds	Retirement accounts	Life insurance	Other managed	Other financial	Any financial asset
	Percentage of families holding asset										
All families	87.1%	14.1%	22.9%	3.0%	15.3%	12.0%	43.0%	31.4%	3.8%	11.0%	90.8%
Income (1995 dollars)											
Less than 10,000	61.1	7.2	5.9	–	2.5	1.8	5.9	15.8	–	8.9	68.1
10,000–24,999	82.3	16.0	11.8	–	9.2	4.9	24.2	25.2	3.2	8.6	87.6
25,000–49,999	94.7	13.7	27.4	3.2	14.3	12.4	52.6	33.1	4.2	13.2	97.8
50,000–99,999	98.6	15.6	39.9	4.8	26.0	20.9	69.8	42.5	5.3	11.3	99.5
100,000 and more	100.0	21.1	36.3	14.5	45.2	38.0	84.6	54.1	8.0	15.2	100.0
Age of head (years)											
Less than 35	80.8	7.1	21.1	0.5	11.1	8.8	39.2	22.3	1.6	13.5	87.0
35–44	87.4	8.2	31.0	1.6	14.5	10.5	51.5	28.9	3.4	10.5	92.0
45–54	88.9	12.5	25.1	4.6	17.5	16.0	54.3	37.5	2.9	13.0	92.4
55–64	88.2	16.2	19.6	2.9	14.9	15.2	47.2	37.5	7.1	9.0	90.5
65–74	91.9	23.9	17.0	5.1	18.0	13.7	35.0	37.0	5.6	10.4	92.0
75 and more	93.0	34.1	15.3	7.0	21.3	10.4	16.5	35.1	5.7	5.3	93.8
	Median value of holdings for families holding asset (Thousands of 1995 dollars)										
All families	$2.1	$10.0	$1.0	$26.2	$8.0	$19.0	$15.6	$5.0	$30.0	$3.0	$13.0
Income (1995 dollars)											
Less than 10,000	0.7	7.0	0.4	–	2.0	25.0	3.5	1.5	–	2.0	1.2
10,000–24,999	1.4	10.0	0.8	–	5.7	8.0	6.0	3.0	19.7	2.0	5.4
25,000–49,999	2.0	10.0	0.7	29.0	6.9	12.5	10.0	5.0	25.0	2.5	12.1
50,000–99,999	4.5	13.0	1.2	9.4	5.7	15.0	23.0	7.0	35.0	3.0	40.7
100,000 and more	15.8	15.6	1.5	58.0	30.0	48.0	85.0	12.0	62.5	23.0	214.5
Age of head (years)											
Less than 35	1.2	6.0	0.5	2.0	3.7	5.0	5.2	3.4	3.8	1.0	5.3
35–44	2.0	6.0	1.0	11.0	4.0	10.0	12.0	5.0	10.8	2.0	11.6
45–54	2.7	12.0	1.0	17.0	10.0	17.5	25.0	6.5	43.0	5.0	24.8
55–64	3.0	14.0	1.1	10.0	17.0	55.0	32.8	6.0	42.0	9.0	32.3
65–74	3.0	17.0	1.5	58.0	15.0	50.0	28.5	5.0	26.0	9.0	19.1
75 and more	5.0	11.0	4.0	40.0	25.0	50.0	17.5	5.0	100.0	35.0	20.9

Source: Federal Reserve System

Family Holdings of Non-financial Assets, 1995

Family characteristic	Vehicles	Primary residence	Investment real estate	Business	Other non-financial	Any non-financial asset
	Percentage of families holding asset					
All families	84.2%	64.7%	17.5%	11.0%	9.0%	91.1%
Income (1995 dollars)						
Less than 10,000	57.7	37.6	6.9	4.8	3.8	69.8
10,000–24,999	82.7	55.4	11.5	6.2	6.2	89.4
25,000–49,999	92.2	68.4	16.5	9.8	9.6	96.6
50,000–99,999	93.3	84.4	24.9	17.5	11.5	99.1
100,000 and more	90.2	91.1	52.3	32.1	22.6	99.4
Age of head (years)						
Less than 35	83.9	37.9	7.2	9.3	7.6	87.6
35–44	85.1	64.6	14.4	13.9	10.2	90.9
45–54	88.2	75.4	23.9	14.8	10.7	93.7
55–64	88.7	82.1	26.9	11.7	9.8	94.0
65–74	82.0	79.0	26.5	7.9	8.9	92.5
75 and more	72.8	73.0	16.6	3.8	5.4	90.2
	Median value of holdings for families holding asset (thousands of 1995 dollars)					
All families	$10.0	$90.0	$50.0	$41.0	$10.0	$83.0
Income (1995 dollars)						
Less than 10,000	3.6	40.0	16.2	50.6	2.5	13.1
10,000–24,999	6.1	65.0	30.0	30.0	8.0	44.5
25,000–49,999	11.1	80.0	40.0	26.3	6.0	81.5
50,000–99,999	16.2	120.0	57.3	30.0	14.0	145.2
100,000 and more	22.8	200.0	130.0	300.0	20.0	319.3
Age of head (years)						
Less than 35	9.0	80.0	33.5	20.0	5.0	21.5
35–44	10.7	95.0	45.0	35.0	9.0	95.6
45–54	12.4	100.0	55.0	60.0	12.0	111.7
55–64	11.9	85.0	82.5	75.0	10.0	107.0
65–74	8.0	80.0	55.0	100.0	16.0	93.5
75 and more	5.3	80.0	20.0	30.0	15.0	79.0

Source: Federal Reserve System

Family Holdings of Debt, 1995

Family characteristic	Mortgage and home equity	Installment	Other lines of creit	Credit card	Investment real estate	Other debt	Any debt
Percentage of families holding debt							
All families	41.1%	46.5%	1.9%	47.8%	6.3%	9.0%	75.2%
Income (1995 dollars)							
Less than 10,000	8.9	25.9	–	25.4	1.6	6.6	48.5
10,000–24,999	24.8	41.3	1.4	41.9	2.5	8.7	67.3
25,000–49,999	47.3	54.3	2.0	56.7	5.8	8.5	83.9
50,000–99,999	68.7	60.7	3.2	62.8	9.5	10.0	89.9
100,000 and more	73.6	37.0	4.0	37.0	27.9	15.8	86.4
Age of head (years)							
Less than 35	32.9	62.2	2.6	55.4	2.6	7.8	83.8
35–44	54.1	60.7	2.2	55.8	6.5	11.1	87.2
45–54	61.9	54.0	2.3	57.3	10.4	14.1	86.5
55–64	45.8	36.0	1.4	43.4	12.5	7.5	75.2
65–74	24.8	16.7	1.3	31.3	5.0	5.5	54.5
75 and more	7.1	9.6	–	18.3	1.5	3.6	30.1
Median value of holdings for families holding debt (Thousands of 1995 dollars)							
All families	$51.0	$6.1	$3.5	$1.5	$28.0	$2.0	$22.5
Income (1995 dollars)							
Less than 10,000	14.0	2.9	–	0.6	15.0	2.0	2.6
10,000–24,999	26.0	3.9	3.0	1.2	18.3	1.2	9.2
25,000–49,999	46.0	6.6	3.0	1.4	25.0	1.5	23.4
50,000–99,999	68.0	9.0	2.2	2.2	34.0	2.5	65.0
100,000 and more	103.4	8.5	19.5	3.0	36.8	7.0	112.2
Age of head (years)							
Less than 35	63.0	7.0	1.4	1.4	22.8	1.5	15.2
35–44	60.0	5.6	2.0	1.8	30.0	1.7	37.6
45–54	48.0	7.0	5.7	2.0	28.1	2.5	41.0
55–64	36.0	5.9	3.5	1.3	26.0	4.0	25.8
65–74	19.0	4.9	3.8	0.8	36.0	2.0	7.7
75 and more	15.9	3.9	–	0.4	8.0	3.0	2.0

Source: Federal Reserve System

Direct and Indirect Stock Ownership, By Selected Characteristics of Families, 1989, 1992, and 1995 (Percent except as noted)

Family characteristic	Families having direct or indirect stock holdings			Median value, among families with holdings (Thousands of 1995 dollars)			Stock holdings' share of group's financial assets		
	1989	1992	1995	1989	1992	1995	1989	1992	1995
All families	31.7%	37.2%	41.1%	$10.4	$11.5	$13.5	26.3%	34.4%	40.4%
Income (1995 dollars)									
Less than 10,000	2.3	6.9	6.0	35.0	5.9	4.0	10.0	15.2	21.1
10,000–24,999	13.1	19.4	25.3	9.2	4.3	5.0	10.3	18.6	21.6
25,000–49,999	33.1	41.6	47.7	5.5	7.6	8.0	20.3	25.4	33.0
50,000–99,999	54.0	64.1	66.7	10.4	14.6	21.3	25.6	35.1	39.9
100,000 and more	79.7	79.1	83.9	47.9	74.6	90.8	31.4	40.2	47.6
Age of head (years)									
Less than 35	23.3	28.3	38.5	3.7	3.8	5.4	25.4	25.6	32.4
35–44	40.5	42.2	46.7	6.3	8.1	9.0	25.6	30.8	41.4
45–54	40.2	47.3	49.3	12.3	14.4	24.0	29.9	39.4	44.2
55–64	34.2	44.8	41.4	18.6	25.3	20.0	28.4	37.3	45.3
65–74	26.1	31.9	34.0	25.8	21.7	25.0	26.2	34.4	34.3
75 and more	24.7	28.1	28.1	28.2	27.1	28.1	20.7	28.6	39.5

Source: Federal Reserve System

Juggling the Household Budget

How consumers spent their money in 1984 and 1995

Average Annual Expenditures by U.S. Households for Selected Products and Services in 1984 and 1995, and Percentage of Total Budget

Products and services	1984		1995	
	Amount	% of total expenditures	Amount	% of total expenditures
Total expenditures	$21,975	100.0	$32,277	100.0
Food at home	1,970	9.0	2,803	8.7
Food away from home	1,320	6.0	1,702	5.3
Alcoholic beverages	275	1.3	277	0.9
Tobacco and smoking products	228	1.0	269	0.8
Housing	6,674	30.4	10,465	32.4
Utilities, fuels, and public services	1,638	7.5	2,193	6.8
Household furnishings and equipment	926	4.2	1,403	4.3
Apparel products and services	1,319	6.0	1,704	5.3
Transportation	4,304	19.6	6,016	18.6
Health care	1,049	4.8	1,732	5.4
Entertainment	1,055	4.8	1,612	5.0
Education	303	1.4	471	1.5
Personal insurance and pensions	1,897	8.6	2,967	9.2

Source: U.S. Bureau of Labor Statistics

Bringing Up Baby

Estimated Annual Expenditures on a Child by Husband-Wife Families in 1996

Age of child	Total	Housing	Food	Transpor-tation	Clothing	Health care	Child care and education	Miscel-laneous*
Before-tax income: Less than $34,700 (Average = $21,600)								
0–2	$5,670	$2,160	$ 810	$ 720	$370	$390	$660	$560
3–5	5,780	2,140	900	700	360	370	740	570
6–8	5,900	2,060	1,160	810	400	420	440	610
9–11	5,940	1,860	1,380	880	450	460	270	640
12–14	6,740	2,080	1,450	1,000	750	470	190	800
15–17	6,650	1,680	1,570	1,340	670	500	310	580
Before-tax income: $34,700 to $58,300 (Average = $46,100)								
0–2	$7,860	$2,930	$ 960	$1,080	$440	$510	$1,080	$ 860
3–5	8,060	2,900	1,110	1,050	430	490	1,200	880
6–8	8,130	2,830	1,420	1,170	470	560	770	910
9–11	8,100	2,630	1,670	1,240	520	600	500	940
12–14	8,830	2,840	1,680	1,350	880	610	370	1,100
15–17	8,960	2,440	1,870	1,710	780	640	630	890
Before-tax income: More than $58,300 (Average = $87,300)								
0–2	$11,680	$4,650	$1,280	$1,510	$580	$580	$1,630	$1,450
3–5	11,910	4,620	1,450	1,480	560	560	1,780	1,460
6–8	11,870	4,550	1,740	1,600	620	640	1,220	1,500
9–11	11,790	4,350	2,030	1,670	670	690	850	1,530
12–14	12,620	4,570	2,130	1,780	1,110	690	650	1,690
15–17	12,930	4,160	2,240	2,160	1,010	730	1,150	1,480

*Miscellaneous expenses include personal care items, entertainment, and reading materials.

Total Estimated Expenditures on Children Born in 1996 to Age 18, by Income Group

Lowest	Middle	Highest
$178,080	$241,440	$350,920

Source: U.S. Agriculture Department

CD and Money Market Rates (National average)

Date	Money market	Certificates of Deposit				
		3 month CD	6 month CD	1 year CD	2 year CD	5 year CD
August 1997	3.49	4.14	4.78	5.05	5.32	5.56
July 1997	3.51	4.15	4.80	5.08	5.36	5.60
June 1997	3.50	4.17	4.81	5.11	5.39	5.64
May 1997	3.50	4.17	4.82	5.11	5.38	5.64
April 1997	3.47	4.14	4.78	5.06	5.31	5.59
March 1997	3.45	4.08	4.71	4.96	5.18	5.47
February 1997	3.47	4.06	4.71	4.97	5.18	5.47
January 1997	3.48	4.06	4.69	4.95	5.16	5.45
December 1996	3.47	4.06	4.69	4.95	5.15	5.44
November 1996	3.48	4.11	4.73	5.00	5.20	5.49
October 1996	3.48	4.11	4.74	5.01	5.23	5.50
September 1996	3.46	4.10	4.72	4.99	5.23	5.50
August 1996	3.46	4.09	4.70	4.98	5.21	5.49
July 1996	3.47	4.08	4.68	4.95	5.18	5.47
June 1996	3.46	4.06	4.65	4.90	5.11	5.38
May 1996	2.98	4.14	4.46	4.69	4.92	5.31
April 1996	3.00	4.21	4.43	4.59	4.80	5.12

Source: BanxQuote Inc., www.banx.com

Consumer Loan Rates (National average)

Date	Mortgage loans						Car loans					
	Conforming			Jumbo			New			Used		
	15 year	30 year	1 year ARM	15 year	30 year	1 year ARM	36 month	48 month	60 month	1 year old	2 year old	3 year old
August 1997	7.26	7.67	5.91	7.55	7.88	5.96	9.34	9.41	9.47	10.03	10.17	10.38
July 1997	7.24	7.64	5.90	7.44	7.73	5.94	9.34	9.42	9.50	10.03	10.16	10.37
June 1997	7.50	7.88	6.06	7.67	7.99	6.11	9.36	9.43	9.51	10.05	10.19	10.41
May 1997	7.69	8.07	6.24	7.86	8.20	6.26	9.33	9.40	9.46	10.03	10.17	10.37
April 1997	7.89	8.29	6.29	8.07	8.39	6.30	9.26	9.33	9.40	9.96	10.11	10.31
March 1997	7.68	8.11	6.05	7.85	8.21	6.09	9.27	9.33	9.40	9.93	10.10	10.33
February 1997	7.38	7.82	5.83	7.57	7.98	5.91	9.27	9.32	9.40	9.92	10.10	10.33
January 1997	7.57	8.03	5.94	7.78	8.19	6.01	9.27	9.34	9.41	9.92	10.10	10.32
December 1996	7.35	7.81	5.79	7.58	7.98	5.89	9.26	9.34	9.42	9.90	10.10	10.31
November 1996	7.28	7.74	5.81	7.52	7.94	5.88	9.27	9.35	9.43	9.91	10.11	10.31
October 1996	7.56	8.03	6.00	7.79	8.22	6.10	9.28	9.36	9.44	9.92	10.11	10.32
September 1996	7.94	8.40	6.23	8.21	8.62	6.36	9.26	9.33	9.42	9.90	10.10	10.31
August 1996	7.69	8.15	6.12	8.02	8.44	6.22	9.25	9.33	9.42	9.90	10.09	10.31
July 1996	7.93	8.38	6.34	8.25	8.66	6.44	9.25	9.33	9.42	9.91	10.11	10.33
June 1996	7.93	8.41	6.25	8.24	8.73	6.35	9.24	9.32	9.41	9.90	10.09	10.32
May 1996	7.78	8.28	6.12	8.11	8.60	6.23	9.16	9.24	9.33	9.82	10.01	10.24
April 1996	7.62	8.10	6.08	7.94	8.32	6.18	9.07	9.16	9.25	9.74	9.93	10.17

Date	Boat loan	RV loan	Credit cards				Home equity			Unsecured
			Standard		Gold		Loan		Line	Personal loan
	New Rate	New Rate	Fixed rate	Var. rate	Fixed rate	Var. rate	5 year fixed	10 year fixed	Adj. rate	Rate
August 1997	10.46	10.59	16.95	15.82	16.82	15.07	9.57	9.74	9.66	14.14
July 1997	10.50	10.65	16.95	15.80	16.70	15.16	9.62	9.82	9.67	14.16
June 1997	10.55	10.73	16.94	15.72	16.70	15.10	9.64	9.89	9.71	14.16
May 1997	10.53	10.71	16.94	15.76	16.70	15.11	9.59	9.86	9.71	14.16
April 1997	10.49	10.65	16.85	15.72	16.49	14.92	9.54	9.83	9.68	14.07
March 1997	10.47	10.63	16.91	15.66	16.44	14.82	9.55	9.86	9.60	13.91
February 1997	10.46	10.60	16.89	15.69	16.44	14.86	9.62	9.93	9.62	13.85
January 1997	10.45	10.58	16.75	15.66	16.26	14.83	9.61	9.91	9.60	13.88
December 1996	10.44	10.57	16.69	15.69	16.18	14.85	9.59	9.89	9.62	13.89
November 1996	10.46	10.58	16.66	15.67	16.12	14.82	9.60	9.91	9.68	13.88
October 1996	10.48	10.59	16.70	15.69	16.16	14.84	9.58	9.89	9.69	13.88
September 1996	10.45	10.54	16.74	15.68	16.17	14.83	9.57	9.89	9.72	13.65
August 1996	10.45	10.58	17.00	15.64	16.17	14.78	9.58	9.87	9.67	13.93
July 1996	10.44	10.61	16.74	15.61	16.17	14.75	9.57	9.88	9.67	13.90
June 1996	10.43	10.60	16.74	15.61	16.17	14.74	9.53	9.85	9.60	13.89
May 1996	10.39	10.55	16.70	15.60	16.16	14.73	9.50	9.82	9.58	13.84
April 1996	10.35	10.50	16.70	15.60	16.16	14.72	9.61	9.90	9.68	13.80

Source: BanxQuote Inc., www.banx.com

How People Do Their Banking

More customers are using ATMs, but many limit their use to cash withdrawls. Other forms of self-service banking are used by a minority of people.

Usage of Banking Services

	% of surveyed consumers
Self-Service	
ATM	57
Automatic deposit	47
Automatic withdrawl	31
Automated phone system	27
Debit card	17
Banking by mail	15
PC banking	1
Branch Service	
Lobby	72
Drive through	67
Telephone person at bank	27

ATM/Bank Transactions Performed in Past Month by ATM Users

	% of ATM users
ATM	
Withdraw cash	99
Obtain account balance	42
Deposit checks	40
Deposit cash	24
Transfer funds between accounts	16
Didn't use	1
Branch	
Deposit checks	69
Deposit cash	55
Withdraw cash	38
Transfer funds between accounts	20
Obtain account balance	18
Didn't use	19

Source: Consumer study by the Bank Administration Institute of Chicago

Charge It

Consumers are using all of the major credit cards more, but the big winner in the spendfest has been Visa.

Charge Volume and Market Share of Major Credit Card Brands
($ billions charge volume)

Year	Visa	Market share	MasterCard	Market share	American Express	Market share	Discover	Market share	Total
1986	$ 85.2	44.5%	$ 57.3	30.0%	$ 46.8	24.5%	$ 2.0	1.0%	$191.3
1987	98.1	43.4	68.4	30.3	53.5	23.7	5.9	2.6	225.9
1988	116.1	44.5	74.9	28.7	61.2	23.4	8.8	3.4	261.0
1989	128.2	43.3	83.4	28.1	71.9	24.3	12.8	4.3	296.3
1990	151.2	44.7	93.1	27.5	77.6	22.9	16.5	4.9	338.4
1991	163.4	45.3	99.1	27.5	76.7	21.2	21.8	6.0	361.0
1992	180.9	44.9	112.3	27.9	82.4	20.4	27.5	6.8	403.1
1993	215.4	45.2	138.6	29.1	89.8	18.8	32.9	6.9	476.7
1994	273.4	46.8	170.8	29.2	101.2	17.3	39.4	6.7	584.8
1995	343.4	48.4	201.9	28.4	116.7	16.5	47.5	6.7	709.5
1996	408.6	49.4	234.2	28.3	131.0	15.8	53.6	6.5	827.4

Source: RAM Research Group

Projected Growth of Credit and Debit Card Volume in the U.S. ($ billions)

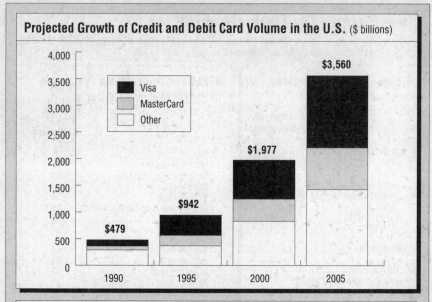

Debit Card Growth in 1996

	Visa		MasterCard		Total	
Cards (In thousands)	46,235	+42%	15,600	+108%	61,835	+54%
Transactions (In millions)	1,237.4	+71%	213.2	+100%	1,450.6	+75%
Total Volume (In billions)	$54.20	+69%	$8.66	+101%	$62.87	+73%

20 Largest Bank Credit Card Issuers in the U.S. – 1996, Ranked by Amount Outstanding

Issuer	'96 rank	'95 rank	Amount outstanding	Change vs. '95	'96 rank	'95 rank	Charge volume	Change vs. '95	'96 rank	'95 rank	Credit cards	Change vs. '95
Citibank	1	1	$47,000,000,000	+5%	1	1	$96,400,000,000	+12%	1	1	38,000,000	0%
MBNA America	2	2	35,274,319,000	+40	2	3	46,718,924,000	+40	3	4	24,100,000	+25
Chase Manhattan	3	7	25,200,000,000	+7	5	7	32,500,000,000	+6	2	7	24,200,000	-2
First USA	4	3	22,196,645,000	+27	8	10	19,968,985,000	+29	7	9	15,946,505	+23
Household Bank	5	6	18,134,492,000	+40	4	4	33,516,251,000	+17	6	5	20,649,000	+20
First Chicago NBD	6	4	18,095,247,563	+5	3	2	45,286,007,536	+9	5	3	22,812,489	-3
AT&T Universal	7	5	13,500,000,000	-4	6	5	25,200,000,000	-6	4	2	23,000,000	-4
Advanta	8	10	12,691,000,000	+27	12	14	14,873,000,000	+34	13	15	7,375,000	+6
Capital One	9	9	12,458,438,000	+19	13	13	14,350,254,000	+8	9	11	12,800,000	+37
Bank of America	10	12	10,126,000,000	+10	9	6	19,787,000,000	+11	10	8	12,314,000	-9
Banc One	11	11	10,102,369,000	+4	11	9	15,789,408,000	+1	8	6	13,502,043	-9
NationsBank	12	14	8,940,326,000	+21	7	8	20,608,312,000	+26	11	12	9,295,000	+9
Providian Bancorp	13	18	6,900,000,000	+53	15	22	8,200,000,000	+61	21	24	4,681,000	+43
First Union Nat'l	14	15	6,640,039,835	+22	19	18	6,659,001,273	+7	15	17	6,422,469	+21
Wells Fargo	15	16	5,592,890,608	+14	14	17	9,570,740,712	+35	16	18	6,413,233	+27
Wachovia Bank	16	17	5,417,428,892	+20	18	20	6,712,289,230	+26	19	21	4,949,666	+20
Bank of New York	17	13	5,302,086,000	-38	16	15	8,043,068,000	-6	17	14	5,201,371	-34
Chevy Chase	18	19	4,902,000,000	+14	21	21	5,878,350,000	+12	24	23	3,691,130	+10
Associates Nat'l	19	20	4,884,568,000	+18	20	19	6,545,031,000	+22	12	13	9,115,000	+11
First Bank Systems	20	21	4,402,956,000	+14	10	11	19,085,279,000	+36	25	26	3,340,018	+23

Source: The Nilson Report

Credit Union Growth

While the number of credit unions has declined, membership, assets, and loans outstanding have all grown during the past decade. Credit unions have also increased their share of auto loans and savings.

Federal Credit Unions (Dollar amounts in millions)

Year	Number	Members	Assets	Loans outstanding
1986	9,758	31,041,142	$ 95,484	$ 55,305
1990	8,511	36,241,607	130,073	83,029
1995	7,329	42,162,627	193,781	120,514
1996	7,152	43,545,541	206,692	134,120

Federally Insured State Credit Unions (Dollar amounts in millions)

Year	Number	Members	Assets	Loans outstanding
1986	4,935	17,362,780	$ 52,244	$ 30,834
1990	4,349	19,453,940	68,133	44,102
1995	4,358	24,926,666	112,861	71,606
1996	4,240	25,665,783	120,176	79,651

Credit Union Household Savings and Auto Loan Market Shares

Year	Household savings	Auto loans
1986	5.9%	15.5%
1990	6.3	16.6
1995	8.1	22.4
1996	8.2	23.8

Sources: National Credit Union Association and the Federal Reserve

Tax Report

Middle-class Americans finally are about to pocket the tax relief that vote-hungry political parties have dangled before them for most of the 1990s. But the wealthy will ultimately reap the greatest rewards.

In the tax-cut compromise between President Clinton and Congress's Republican leaders, many people will benefit from expanded incentives to save for retirement, plus income-tax credits for having children and putting them through college. Childless middle-class taxpayers have less to look forward to, reflecting the politicians' zeal for a pro-family mantle.

In Washington, "middle class" is defined broadly. The tax-compromise benefits begin for single mothers with incomes as low as $12,000 a year, included at Mr. Clinton's behest, to two-parent families making up to $110,000, as Republicans wanted.

At least initially, a big portion of the tax breaks goes to the middle class. But over the long term, when the tax cuts fully take effect, the biggest benefits will go to the richest taxpayers with money to invest and save. They will enjoy a generous capital-gains tax break and expanded savings incentives. In fact, an analysis by the Treasury Department showed that half of the tax cuts would flow to the top 20% of earners by the time the full package

Credit Reports

Consumer advocates urge people to review their credit reports at least once a year to detect any errors and make sure they are up-to-date. Here are the three major credit-reporting agencies:

EQUIFAX P.O. 105873 Atlanta, GA 30348	800-685-1111	Free if credit has been denied; otherwise, $8 per report in most states MA-1st report free GA-two reports free VT-1st report free, additional ones $7.50 MD-1st report free, additional ones $5 CT-$5 ME-$3
Experian (formerly TRW) P.O. BOX 2104 Allen, TX 75013-2104	800-682-7654	Free if credit has been denied; otherwise, $8 per report in most states ME-$2 CO & CT-$5
Trans Union Corp. Consumer Relations Division P.O. Box 390 Springfield, PA 19064-0390	800-888-4213	Free if credit has been denied; otherwise, $8 per report in most states MD,GA,VT,MA,CO-free ME-$2 CT-$5

takes hold in 2007. Nearly 15% of the tax cuts would benefit the top 1% of earners.

Investment advisers and analysts say lower capital-gains tax rates are likely to increase the long-term attractiveness of most types of stocks, especially those of smaller, higher-growth companies that pay little or no dividends. But some types of investments may look less attractive compared with common stocks, financial advisers warn. These include bonds, annuities, stocks with high dividends, preferred stock, art, antiques and collectibles.

Other provisions in the new tax legislation would eliminate capital-gains taxes entirely, as well as record-keeping rules, for most homeowners. And there is estate-tax relief for individuals, as well as for family farms and businesses.

The main features of the tax-relief legislation have been taking shape since 1990, promised in turn, and in various forms, by a Democratic Congress confronting Republican President Bush, by Bill Clinton in his 1992 campaign and finally by the Republicans in their 1994 takeover of Congress.

After nearly seven years of what's been called class warfare, the bipartisan truce has yielded the following highlights:

Child Tax Credit

The new law provides taxpayers with a child tax credit for each qualifying child under 17 years of age. The credit is first available for the 1998 taxable year, and so may be claimed on tax returns to be filed in 1999. For that first year, taxpayers may claim a maximum credit of $400 per qualifying child. The maximum credit increases to $500 for subsequent years. This credit is phased out by $50 for each $1,000 of the taxpayer's modified adjusted gross income ("AGI") in excess of $110,000 for taxpayers filing jointly, $75,000 for single taxpayers, and $55,000 for married taxpayers filing separately. Generally, the credit is limited to tax liability net of credits (other than Earned Income Credit). However, families with three or more children may be entitled to a credit in excess of tax liability.

Education Incentives

HOPE Scholarship and Lifetime Learning Credits

The law provides taxpayers two new nonrefundable tax credits for payments made for qualified tuition and related expenses (tuition and fees, but not books) for post-secondary education—the HOPE Scholarship Credit and the Lifetime Learning Credit.

The **HOPE Scholarship Credit** allows taxpayers to claim a maximum credit of $1,500 (100 percent of the first $1,000 of tuition and fees and 50 percent of the next $1,000 of tuition and fees) for expenses paid on behalf of the taxpayer, the taxpayer's spouse, or a dependent for the first two years of post-secondary education at an eligible institution. The student must be enrolled on at least a half-time basis for at least one academic period during the year for the expenses to be qualified. The HOPE Scholarship Credit applies to expenses paid after December 31, 1997, for education furnished in academic periods beginning after that date.

The **Lifetime Learning Credit** allows taxpayers to claim a maximum credit equal to 20 percent of up to $5,000 of expenses ($10,000 beginning in 2003) incurred during the taxable year for qualified tuition and fees for eligible students for post-secondary education, including any course of instruction to acquire or improve job skills. The Lifetime Learning Credit applies to expenses paid after June 30, 1998, for education furnished in academic periods beginning after that date.

Both credits limit qualified expenses to the expenses of the taxpayer, the taxpayer's spouse, or a dependent of the taxpayer. Additionally, both credits are phased out for taxpayers with modified AGI between $40,000 and $50,000 (between $80,000 and $100,000 for joint filers). For each qualifying student, taxpayers must choose to claim either the HOPE Scholarship Credit, the Lifetime Learning Credit, or the exclusion for certain distributions from an education IRA for the taxable year. They cannot claim more than one of these benefits for a student for any year.

The law also creates a new educational funding vehicle, called an **Education Individual Retirement Account (education IRA)**, for the purpose of paying the qualified higher education expenses of a designated beneficiary. Qualified higher education expenses include tuition, fees, books, supplies and equipment, and room and board. Contributions are non-deductible, and earnings on the amount held in the IRA will be non-taxable until distributed. Annual contributions are limited to $500 per beneficiary under the age of 18. The contribution limit is phased out as a taxpayer's modified AGI

increases from $95,000 to $110,000 ($150,000 to $160,000 for joint returns).

Distributions from an education IRA are excludable from income to the extent the amount does not exceed the qualified higher education expenses of the eligible student during the year. If the distribution from the education IRA exceeds the qualified higher education expenses, only a portion of the distribution is excludable. In addition, distributions not used for higher education are subject to a 10 percent addition to tax. The law requires any balance remaining in an education IRA at the time a beneficiary becomes 30 years of age to be distributed and taxed to the beneficiary (and subject to the 10 percent addition to tax). However, the balance may be rolled over tax free to another education IRA benefiting another family member. This provision is effective for taxable years beginning after December 31, 1997.

Deduction for Interest on Education Loans: The law provides an above-the-line maximum deduction for up to $2,500 of interest paid by taxpayers on qualified education loans. The $2,500 limit is phased in over four years (i.e., the maximum deduction is $1,000 in 1998, $1,500 in 1999, $2,000 in 2000, and $2,500 in 2001). Taxpayers may take a deduction on qualified education loans for the benefit of the taxpayer, the taxpayer's spouse, or any dependent of the taxpayer as of the time the indebtedness was incurred. Deductions are allowed only for the first 60 months that interest payments are required. The deduction is phased out for taxpayers with modified AGI between $40,000 and $55,000 ($60,000 and $75,000 for joint filers). Married taxpayers must file jointly to take the deduction, and the credit may not be claimed on the return of anyone who is claimed as a dependent on another person's return. This provision is effective for interest due and paid after December 31, 1997.

Individual Retirement Accounts (IRAs)

Increased Phase-out Ranges for Deductible IRAs

Under the law, the AGI phase-out ranges for deductible IRAs of active participants in employer-sponsored retirement plans will increase annually beginning in 1998 until they reach double the current phase-out ranges in 2007. In 2007, the phase-out ranges will be between $50,000 and $60,000 for single filers and between $80,000 and $100,000 for married taxpayers filing jointly, double the current ranges of $40,000 to $50,000 for married couples filing jointly, and $25,000 to $35,000 for single filers. An individual is not an active participant in an employer-sponsored retirement plan merely because the individual's spouse is an active participant. However, in such cases, the individual's deductible amount is phased out for married couples with AGI between $150,000 and $160,000.

New Backloaded IRAs

The law provides for a new individual retirement account beginning in 1998 called a "Roth IRA." Key features are:

1. contributions to the account are not deductible,
2. qualified distributions from the account are not taxable, and
3. earnings on the account are taxable only if and when there is a distribution which is not a qualified distribution.

A "qualified distribution" is a distribution:

1. made after the taxpayer attains age 59½;
2. made to a beneficiary after the taxpayer's death;
3. made because the taxpayer is disabled; or
4. used by a first-time home buyer to acquire a principal residence.

No payment can be a qualified distribution unless it is made after the five-taxable-year period beginning with the taxable year in which the taxpayer first contributed to a Roth IRA.

Annual contributions to the Roth IRAs are limited to $2,000 less the taxpayer's deductible IRA contributions. Unlike deductible IRAs, there is no prohibition on making contributions after attaining age 70½. The $2,000 limit is phased out as AGI increases from

1. $150,000 to $160,000 in the case of a married couple filing jointly or
2. $95,000 to $110,000 in the case of a single filer.

Capital Gains
Lower Capital Gains Rates

For individuals, the maximum tax rate on net capital gain from sales or exchanges occurring after May 6, 1997, will be reduced to:

- A maximum tax rate of 20 percent for sales made after May 6, 1997, if the property had been held for more than 18 months at the time of sale. This 20 percent rate also is available for property sold after May 6, 1997, and before July 29, 1997, if the property had been held for more than 12 months (even if it had not been held for 18 months).
- A maximum tax rate of 18 percent for sales of property acquired after December 31, 2000, that had been held for more than 5 years at the time of the sale.
- 25 percent for real estate depreciation recapture treated as capital gain.

The current 28 percent maximum capital gain rate will continue to apply to

1. sales of collectibles,
2. sales before May 7, 1997, and
3. sales after July 28, 1997, of property held for more than one year but not more than 18 months.

Gain from Sale of a Principal Residence The law allows taxpayers to exclude up to $250,000 of gain ($500,000 for married couples filing a joint return) realized on the sale or exchange of a principal residence occurring after May 6, 1997. Unlike the "one time" exclusion provided under prior law, the exclusion is allowed each time a taxpayer sells or exchanges a principal residence, although the exclusion generally may not be claimed more frequently than once every two years. Also unlike prior law, the taxpayer is not required to reinvest the sales proceeds in a new residence to claim the exclusion. To be eligible, the residence must have been owned and used as the taxpayer's principal residence for a combined period of at least two years out of the five years prior to the sale or exchange. The taxpayer must recognize gain to the extent of any depreciation allowable with respect to the rental or business use of such principal residence for periods after May 6, 1997.

Estate Taxes

Beginning in 1998, the unified estate and gift tax credit will increase annually, until the maximum value of estates exempt from tax reaches $1 million in 2006. The current limit is $600,000.

Beginning in 1999, the $10,000 annual exclusion for gifts, the $750,000 ceiling on special use valuation, the $1 million generation-skipping transfer tax exemption, and the $1 million ceiling on the value of a closely-held business eligible for the special low interest rate will all be indexed annually to reflect inflation. The provisions apply to estates of taxpayers dying and to gifts made after December 31, 1997.

Beginning in 1998, executors may elect special estate tax treatment for qualified "family-owned business interests" if these interests comprise more than 50 percent of a decedent's estate and certain other requirements are met. Because the law limits the combined value of this credit and the unified estate and gift tax credit to $1.3 million, the amount of this exclusion that will be available each year will decrease as the value of the unified credit increases during its phase-in period. In 1998, the provision will exclude up to $675,000 of value in qualified family-owned business interests from a decedent's taxable estate (i.e., $1.3 million minus the $625,000 unified credit available in 1998).

Source: Internal Revenue Service

Federal Income Tax Rates

The U.S. tax code requires that federal income tax brackets and other figures be adjusted for inflation annually. The Internal Revenue Service usually releases official numbers in December each year. CCH Inc.'s 1998 tax year projections, which are compared to official 1997 tax year figures, appear below.

MARRIED FILING JOINTLY (& SURVIVING SPOUSE)

1998 Taxable Income	Tax Rate	1997 Taxable Income
$0–$42,350	15%	$0–$41,200
$42,350–$102,300	28%	$41,200–$99,600
$102,300–$155,950	31%	$99,600–$151,750
$155,950–$278,450	36%	$151,750–$271,050
over $278,450	39.6%	over $271,050

MARRIED FILING SEPARATELY

1998 Taxable Income	Tax Rate	1997 Taxable Income
$0–$21,175	15%	$0–$20,600
$21,175–$51,150	28%	$20,600–$49,800
$51,150–$77,975	31%	$49,800–$75,875
$77,975–$139,225	36%	$75,875–$135,525
over $139,225	39.6%	over $135,525

SINGLE FILERS

1998 Taxable Income	Tax Rate	1997 Taxable Income
$0–$25,350	15%	$0–$24,650
$25,350–$61,400	28%	$24,650–$59,750
$61,400–$128,100	31%	$59,750–$124,650
$128,100–$278,450	36%	$124,650–$271,050
over $278,450	39.6%	over $271,050

HEAD OF HOUSEHOLD

1998 Taxable Income	Tax Rate	1997 Taxable Income
$0–$33,950	15%	$0–$33,050
$33,950–$87,700	28%	$33,050–$85,350

1998 Taxable Income	Tax Rate	1997 Taxable Income
$87,700–$142,000	31%	$85,350–$138,200
$142,000–$278,450	36%	$138,200–$271,050
over $278,450	39.6%	over $271,050

STANDARD DEDUCTION AMOUNTS

Filing Status	1998	1997	Increase
Married Filing Jointly			
(& Surviving Spouse)	$7,100	$6,900	$200
Married Filing Separately	$3,550	$3,450	$100
Single	$4,250	$4,150	$100
Head of Household	$6,250	$6,050	$200

STANDARD DEDUCTION FOR DEPENDENTS ("KIDDIE" STANDARD DEDUCTION)

1998	1997	Increase
$700	$650	$50

INCOME LEVEL AT WHICH THREE-PERCENT ITEMIZED DEDUCTION LIMITATION TAKES EFFECT (ADJUSTED GROSS INCOME)

Filing Status	1998	1997	Increase
Married Filing Jointly			
(& Surviving Spouse)	$124,500	$121,200	$3,300
Married Filing Separately	$62,250	$60,600	$1,650
Single	$124,500	$121,200	$3,300
Head of Household	$124,500	$121,200	$3,300

PERSONAL EXEMPTION AMOUNTS

1998	1997	Increase
$2,700	$2,650	$50

THRESHOLD FOR PERSONAL EXEMPTION PHASEOUT

Filing Status	1998	1997	Increase
Married Filing Jointly			
(& Surviving Spouse)	$186,800	$181,800	$5,000
Married Filing Separately	$93,400	$90,900	$2,500
Single	$124,500	$121,200	$3,300
Head of Household	$155,650	$151,500	$4,150

Source: CCH Inc., Riverwoods, Ill.

Federal Tax Collections
(In thousands of dollars)

Fiscal year	Total Internal Revenue collections	Total income and profit taxes	Corporation income and profit taxes	Individual income taxes	Employment taxes	Estate and gift taxes	Excise taxes
1966	$128,879,961	$92,131,794	$30,834,243	$61,297,552	$20,256,133	$3,093,922	$13,398,112
1967	148,374,815	104,288,420	34,917,825	69,370,595	26,958,241	3,014,406	14,113,748
1968	153,636,838	108,148,565	29,896,520	78,252,045	28,085,898	3,081,979	14,320,396
1969	187,919,560	135,778,052	38,337,646	97,440,406	33,068,657	3,530,065	15,542,787
1970	195,722,096	138,688,568	35,036,983	103,651,585	37,449,188	3,680,076	15,904,264
1971	191,647,198	131,072,374	30,319,953	100,752,421	39,918,690	3,784,283	16,871,851
1972	209,855,737	143,804,732	34,925,546	108,879,186	43,714,001	5,489,969	16,847,036
1973	237,787,204	164,157,315	39,045,309	125,112,006	52,081,709	4,975,862	16,572,318
1974	268,952,254	184,648,094	41,744,444	142,903,650	62,093,632	5,100,675	17,109,853
1975	293,822,726	202,146,097	45,746,660	156,399,437	70,140,809	4,688,079	16,847,741
1976	302,519,792	205,751,753	46,782,956	158,968,797	74,202,853	5,307,466	17,399,118
1977	358,139,417	246,805,067	60,049,804	186,755,263	86,076,316	7,425,325	17,832,707
1978	399,776,389	278,438,289	65,380,145	213,058,144	97,291,653	5,381,499	18,664,949
1979	460,412,185	322,993,733	71,447,876	251,545,857	112,849,874	5,519,074	19,049,504
1980	519,375,273	359,927,392	72,379,610	287,547,782	128,330,480	6,498,381	24,619,021
1981	606,799,103	406,583,302	73,733,156	332,850,146	152,885,816	6,910,386	40,419,598
1982	632,240,506	418,599,768	65,990,832	352,608,936	168,717,936	8,143,373	36,779,428
1983	627,246,793	411,407,523	61,779,556	349,627,967	173,847,854	6,225,877	35,765,538
1984	680,475,229	437,071,049	74,179,370	362,891,679	199,210,028	6,176,667	38,017,486
1985	742,871,541	474,072,327	77,412,769	396,659,558	225,214,568	6,579,703	37,004,944
1986	782,251,812	497,406,391	80,441,620	416,964,771	243,978,380	7,194,956	33,672,086
1987	886,290,590	568,311,471	102,858,985	465,452,486	277,000,469	7,667,670	33,310,980
1988	935,106,594	583,349,120	109,682,554	473,666,566	318,038,990	7,784,445	25,934,040
1989	1,013,322,133	632,746,069	117,014,564	515,731,504	345,625,586	8,973,146	25,977,333
1990	1,056,365,652	650,244,947	110,016,539	540,228,408	367,219,321	11,761,939	27,139,445
1991	1,086,851,401	660,475,445	113,598,569	546,876,876	384,451,220	11,473,141	30,451,596
1992	1,120,799,558	675,673,952	117,950,796	557,723,156	400,080,904	11,479,116	33,565,587
1993	1,176,685,625	717,321,668	131,547,509	585,774,159	411,510,516	12,890,965	34,962,476
1994	1,276,466,776	774,023,837	154,204,684	619,819,153	443,831,352	15,606,793	43,004,794
1995	1,375,731,835	850,201,510	174,422,173	675,779,337	465,405,305	15,144,394	44,980,627
1996	1,486,546,674	934,368,068	189,054,791	745,313,276	492,365,178	17,591,817	42,221,611

Source: Internal Revenue Service

Assessing the Tax Burden

Tax Freedom Day

Tax Freedom Day denotes the number of days that the average American must work each year to pay all federal, state and local taxes.

Year	Tax Freedom Day	Year	Tax Freedom Day	Year	Tax Freedom Day
1902	January 31	1940*	March 8	1980*	May 1
1913	January 30	1950	April 3	1990	May 2
1922	February 17	1960*	April 16	1995	May 7
1930	February 13	1970	April 26	1996*	May 7

*Leap year makes Tax Freedom Day appear a day earlier.

Total Taxes as a Percentage of Total Income

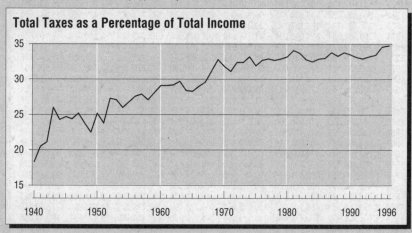

Total Taxes as a Percentage of Total Income

Year	%	Year	%	Year	%
1940	18.3	1970	31.7	1992	32.9
1945	24.7	1975	31.9	1993	33.3
1950	25.2	1980	33.3	1994	33.8
1955	26.8	1985	32.8	1995	34.7
1960	29.2	1990	33.2	1996	34.8
1965	28.3	1991	33.2		

Source: Tax Foundation

Tax Tally

American Family Income Before and After Taxes

	1990		1994		1995		1996	
	Single	Dual	Single	Dual	Single	Dual	Single	Dual
Median family income	$25,878	$42,146	$27,145	$48,970	$27,788	$50,989	$28,447	$53,091
Federal income tax	2,027	4,261	2,002	4,601	2,029	4,863	2,098	5,139
Payroll taxes:								
Employee portion	1,920	3,095	2,014	3,596	2,062	3,745	2,111	3,899
Employer portion	1,920	3,095	2,014	3,596	2,062	3,745	2,111	3,899
Other federal taxes	961	1,565	1,124	2,028	1,214	2,227	1,234	2,303
Total federal taxes	6,829	12,017	7,155	13,822	7,367	14,580	7,554	15,241
Total state/local taxes	3,087	5,028	3,333	6,012	3,419	6,274	3,559	6,643
Total taxes	9,916	17,044	10,488	19,834	10,786	20,853	11,113	21,883
After-tax income	17,883	28,197	18,671	32,732	19,064	33,881	19,444	35,107
Total taxes as a percent of income	35.7%	37.7%	36.0%	37.7%	36.1%	38.1%	36.4%	38.4%
Inflation-adjusted total taxes (1996$)	$11,624	$19,982	$10,948	$20,704	$11,006	$21,279	$11,113	$21,883

Note: The burden of federal and state corporate income taxes are included. After-tax income does not deduct employer's share of payroll taxes because the burden of the payroll tax is assumed to reduce income before the "gross' seen on paychecks. "Total taxes as a percent of income" is calculated by adding the employer's share of the payroll tax to the median family income.
Source: Tax Foundation

State Portions of the Federal Tax Bill

Federal Taxes by State
(In millions of dollars)

State	1985	1996	State	1985	1996	State	1985	1996
Total	$709,400	$1,390,249	Louisiana	$11,522	$17,957	Ohio	$30,657	$57,299
			Maine	2,752	5,365	Oklahoma	9,101	13,278
Alabama	8,996	17,651	Maryland	15,193	30,510	Oregon	7,047	15,515
Alaska	2,355	3,718	Massachusetts	20,451	39,408	Pennsylvania	34,297	65,404
Arizona	8,271	18,395	Michigan	26,213	53,478	Rhode Island	2,896	5,519
Arkansas	5,011	10,000	Minnesota	12,487	25,894	South		
California	86,183	168,387	Mississippi	4,948	9,275	Carolina	7,391	14,989
Colorado	10,178	20,744	Missouri	14,124	26,033	South Dakota	1,641	3,359
Connecticut	13,282	26,990	Montana	2,046	3,636	Tennessee	11,605	24,331
Delaware	1,994	4,461	Nebraska	4,433	8,031	Texas	50,557	88,476
Florida	33,177	75,085	Nevada	3,005	9,054	Utah	3,669	7,494
Georgia	15,395	34,363	New			Vermont	1,286	2,769
Hawaii	2,974	6,446	Hampshire	3,142	6,803	Virginia	17,305	35,807
Idaho	2,179	4,950	New Jersey	29,802	57,643	Washington	13,232	30,277
Illinois	38,475	72,244	New Mexico	3,409	6,626	West Virginia	4,183	6,831
Indiana	14,915	28,262	New York	59,251	117,381	Wisconsin	13,153	26,080
Iowa	8,078	13,442	North			Wyoming	1,537	2,476
Kansas	7,480	12,914	Carolina	15,225	32,304	District		
Kentucky	8,502	15,684	North Dakota	1,889	2,878	of Columbia	2,506	4,333

State Shares of Federal Taxes
(Percent)

State	1960	1970	1980	1990	1996	State	1960	1970	1980	1990	1996
Alabama	1.03	1.11	1.30	1.19	1.27	New Hampshire	0.32	0.35	0.39	0.53	0.49
Alaska	0.12	0.14	0.29	0.28	0.27	New Jersey	4.20	4.27	3.94	4.61	4.15
Arizona	0.57	0.69	0.99	1.21	1.32	New Mexico	0.39	0.36	0.44	0.43	0.48
Arkansas	0.48	0.59	0.69	0.66	0.72	New York	13.22	11.74	8.40	8.89	8.44
California	10.48	11.42	11.61	13.23	12.11	North					
Colorado	0.92	0.95	1.27	1.27	1.49	Carolina	1.46	1.77	2.01	2.19	2.32
Connecticut	2.11	2.11	1.75	2.07	1.94	North Dakota	0.23	0.22	0.26	0.20	0.21
Delaware	0.55	0.36	0.30	0.33	0.32	Ohio	5.82	5.49	5.04	4.08	4.12
Florida	2.46	2.87	3.83	5.22	5.40	Oklahoma	1.02	0.99	1.17	0.98	0.96
Georgia	1.37	1.69	1.89	2.28	2.47	Oregon	0.89	0.95	1.19	1.01	1.12
Hawaii	0.30	0.38	0.44	0.46	0.46	Pennsylvania	7.08	5.95	5.27	4.84	4.70
Idaho	0.27	0.26	0.33	0.29	0.36	Rhode Island	0.52	0.48	0.40	0.43	0.40
Illinois	7.08	6.69	6.16	5.26	5.20	South					
Indiana	2.38	2.45	2.45	1.95	2.03	Carolina	0.64	0.82	1.00	1.00	1.08
Iowa	1.19	1.21	1.32	0.96	0.97	South Dakota	0.23	0.23	0.24	0.21	0.24
Kansas	1.02	1.02	1.07	0.92	0.93	Tennessee	1.20	1.42	1.62	1.62	1.75
Kentucky	1.12	1.10	1.28	1.08	1.13	Texas	4.43	4.78	6.12	6.08	6.36
Louisiana	1.23	1.36	1.54	1.21	1.29	Utah	0.38	0.38	0.48	0.46	0.54
Maine	0.44	0.38	0.37	0.42	0.39	Vermont	0.18	0.18	0.17	0.21	0.20
Maryland	1.90	2.20	2.13	2.29	2.19	Virginia	1.75	1.98	2.31	2.56	2.58
Massachusetts	3.40	3.18	2.62	3.05	2.83	Washington	1.57	1.76	1.95	1.95	2.18
Michigan	4.66	4.78	4.67	3.77	3.85	West Virginia	0.77	0.61	0.69	0.48	0.49
Minnesota	1.68	1.67	1.86	1.76	1.86	Wisconsin	2.07	2.04	1.99	1.82	1.88
Mississippi	0.50	0.59	0.69	0.60	0.67	Wyoming	0.18	0.14	0.23	0.16	0.18
Missouri	2.34	2.19	2.06	1.87	1.87	District					
Montana	0.32	0.28	0.32	0.24	0.26	of Columbia	0.69	0.51	0.39	0.32	0.31
Nebraska	0.64	0.64	0.68	0.55	0.58						
Nevada	0.20	0.27	0.39	0.52	0.65						

Source: Tax Foundation

Taxes Per Capita and as a Percent of Income, 1996

	Per Capita Taxes				Taxes as a Percent of Income		
	Total	Federal	State & local	Per capita income	Total	Federal	State & local
United States	$8,944	$5,910	$3,034	$25,722	34.8%	23.0%	11.8%
Alabama	6,457	4,545	1,912	20,821	31.0	21.8	9.2
Alaska	8,738	6,567	2,162	26,072	33.5	25.2	8.3
Arizona	7,532	4,837	2,695	23,099	32.6	20.9	11.7
Arkansas	6,655	4,435	2,220	19,654	33.9	22.6	11.3
California	8,759	5,769	2,990	25,521	34.3	22.6	11.7
Colorado	8,780	6,124	2,656	26,299	33.4	23.3	10.1
Connecticut	13,580	8,962	4,618	32,773	41.4	27.4	14.1
Delaware	8,572	6,840	1,731	27,109	31.6	25.2	6.4
Florida	8,480	5,777	2,703	25,404	33.4	22.7	10.6
Georgia	7,806	5,252	2,555	23,874	32.7	22.0	10.7
Hawaii	9,708	5,907	3,801	27,013	35.9	21.9	14.1
Idaho	7,396	4,728	2,668	22,042	33.6	21.5	12.1
Illinois	9,631	6,693	2,939	27,565	34.9	24.3	10.7
Indiana	7,887	5,346	2,541	23,829	33.1	22.4	10.7
Iowa	8,103	5,185	2,918	23,735	34.1	21.9	12.3
Kansas	8,257	5,495	2,762	24,097	34.3	22.8	11.5
Kentucky	6,885	4,459	2,426	20,816	33.1	21.4	11.7
Louisiana	6,602	4,543	2,059	20,963	31.5	21.7	9.8
Maine	7,654	4,695	2,959	22,412	34.2	21.0	13.2
Maryland	9,867	6,596	3,271	28,443	34.7	23.2	11.5
Massachusetts	10,454	7,095	3,359	29,559	35.4	24.0	11.4
Michigan	9,243	6,132	3,111	26,088	35.4	23.5	11.9
Minnesota	9,667	6,150	3,517	26,191	36.9	23.5	13.4
Mississippi	5,845	3,778	2,067	18,690	31.3	20.2	11.1
Missouri	7,533	5,360	2,173	24,090	31.3	22.3	9.0
Montana	6,975	4,616	2,360	20,723	33.7	22.3	11.4
Nebraska	8,179	5,388	2,791	24,083	34.0	22.4	11.6
Nevada	9,695	6,603	3,092	28,783	33.7	22.9	10.7
New Hampshire	9,836	6,460	3,377	27,516	35.8	23.5	12.3
New Jersey	12,033	7,925	4,108	31,818	37.8	24.9	12.9
New Mexico	7,311	4,323	2,988	20,184	36.2	21.4	14.8
New York	11,699	7,032	4,668	29,139	40.2	24.1	16.0
North Carolina	7,645	4,942	2,703	23,087	33.1	21.4	11.7
North Dakota	7,616	4,916	2,700	21,622	35.2	22.7	12.5
Ohio	8,289	5,619	2,670	24,355	34.0	23.1	11.0
Oklahoma	6,684	4,428	2,257	20,206	33.1	21.9	11.2
Oregon	8,348	5,442	2,906	24,311	34.3	22.4	12.0
Pennsylvania	9,038	5,912	3,127	25,512	35.4	23.2	12.3
Rhode Island	9,106	6,019	3,087	25,163	36.2	23.9	12.3
South Carolina	6,645	4,429	2,216	20,669	32.2	21.4	10.7
South Dakota	7,213	5,066	2,147	22,804	31.6	22.2	9.4
Tennessee	7,365	5,100	2,266	22,823	32.3	22.3	9.9
Texas	7,736	5,191	2,545	23,044	33.6	22.5	11.1
Utah	6,656	4,233	2,423	20,574	32.4	20.6	11.8
Vermont	8,225	5,178	3,047	22,911	35.9	22.6	13.3
Virginia	8,512	5,906	2,606	26,016	32.7	22.7	10.0
Washington	9,338	6,110	3,228	26,093	35.8	23.4	12.4
West Virginia	6,334	4,099	2,235	19,939	31.8	20.6	11.2
Wisconsin	8,969	5,576	3,393	24,326	36.9	22.9	14.0
Wyoming	7,953	5,663	2,290	23,598	33.7	24.0	9.7
District of Columbia	13,510	8,328	5,182	34,723	38.9	24.0	14.9

Source: Tax Foundation

Tax Bite in the Eight-Hour Day by State, 1996 (Hours:Minutes)

The hours and minutes in an eight hour day devoted to paying taxes.

	Total taxes	Federal taxes	State/ local taxes
United States	2:47	1:50	0:57
Alabama	2:29	1:45	0:44
Alaska	2:41	2:01	0:40
Arizona	2:37	1:41	0:56
Arkansas	2:43	1:48	0:55
California	2:45	1:49	0:56
Colorado	2:41	1:52	0:49
Connecticut	3:19	2:11	1:08
Delaware	2:32	2:01	0:31
Florida	2:41	1:49	0:52
Georgia	2:37	1:46	0:51
Hawaii	2:53	1:45	1:08
Idaho	2:42	1:43	0:59
Illinois	2:48	1:57	0:51
Indiana	2:39	1:48	0:51
Iowa	2:44	1:45	0:59
Kansas	2:45	1:49	0:56
Kentucky	2:39	1:43	0:56
Louisiana	2:32	1:44	0:48
Maine	2:44	1:41	1:03
Maryland	2:47	1:51	0:56
Massachusetts	2:50	1:55	0:55
Michigan	2:51	1:53	0:58
Minnesota	2:58	1:53	1:05
Mississippi	2:31	1:37	0:54
Missouri	2:31	1:47	0:44
Montana	2:42	1:47	0:55
Nebraska	2:44	1:47	0:57
Nevada	2:42	1:50	0:52
New Hampshire	2:52	1:53	0:59
New Jersey	3:02	2:00	1:02
New Mexico	2:54	1:43	1:11
New York	3:13	1:56	1:17
North Carolina	2:39	1:43	0:56
North Dakota	2:50	1:49	1:01
Ohio	2:44	1:51	0:53
Oklahoma	2:39	1:45	0:54
Oregon	2:45	1:47	0:58
Pennsylvania	2:51	1:51	1:00
Rhode Island	2:54	1:55	0:59
South Carolina	2:35	1:43	0:52
South Dakota	2:32	1:47	0:45
Tennessee	2:35	1:47	0:48
Texas	2:42	1:48	0:54
Utah	2:36	1:39	0:57
Vermont	2:53	1:48	1:05
Virginia	2:38	1:49	0:49
Washington	2:52	1:52	1:00
West Virginia	2:33	1:39	0:54
Wisconsin	2:57	1:50	1:07
Wyoming	2:42	1:55	0:47
District of Columbia	3:07	1:55	1:12

Source: Tax Foundation

Balance of Payments

The balance of payments between the federal government and individual states varies widely. In some states, there is a large surplus because the federal government spends significantly more in those states than it collects from them in taxes. On the other hand, some states run big deficits, paying much more in taxes than the federal government returns to them in defense spending, grants, payments to the elderly, disabled, and poor, federal employees' wages, and other expenditures.

Balance of Payments, Fiscal Year 1995
(Per capita)

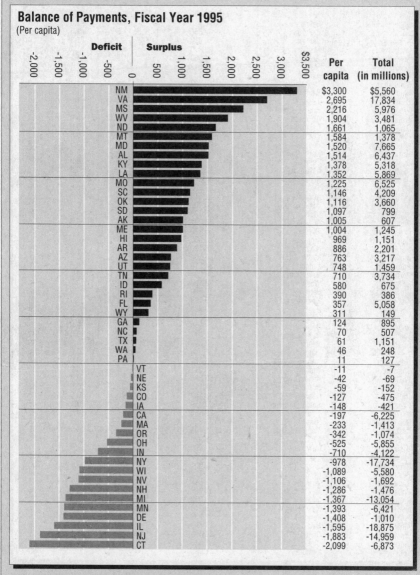

State	Per capita	Total (in millions)
NM	$3,300	$5,560
VA	2,695	17,834
MS	2,216	5,976
WV	1,904	3,481
ND	1,661	1,065
MT	1,584	1,378
MD	1,520	7,665
AL	1,514	6,437
KY	1,378	5,318
LA	1,352	5,869
MO	1,225	6,525
SC	1,146	4,209
OK	1,116	3,660
SD	1,097	799
AK	1,005	607
ME	1,004	1,245
HI	969	1,151
AR	886	2,201
AZ	763	3,217
UT	748	1,459
TN	710	3,734
ID	580	675
RI	390	386
FL	357	5,058
WY	311	149
GA	124	895
NC	70	507
TX	61	1,151
WA	46	248
PA	11	127
VT	-11	-7
NE	-42	-69
KS	-59	-152
CO	-127	-475
IA	-148	-421
CA	-197	-6,225
MA	-233	-1,413
OR	-342	-1,074
OH	-525	-5,855
IN	-710	-4,122
NY	-978	-17,734
WI	-1,089	-5,580
NV	-1,106	-1,692
NH	-1,286	-1,476
MI	-1,367	-13,054
MN	-1,393	-6,421
DE	-1,408	-1,010
IL	-1,595	-18,875
NJ	-1,883	-14,959
CT	-2,099	-6,873

Source: Harvard University, Kennedy School of Government

Odds of Being Audited by the IRS

Odds of IRS District Tax Audit 1995 (Percent is based on individual returns)

District	State	Average adjusted gross income reported	Income rank	Percent audited	Audit rank
United States	–	$33,472	–	0.7%	–
Las Vegas	Nevada	36,490	25	2.0	1
Laguna Niguel	California	36,936	21	1.6	2
San Francisco	California	42,356	5	1.4	3
Los Angeles	California	36,664	23	1.3	4
Jackson	Mississippi	26,993	63	1.2	5
Atlanta	Georgia	34,886	33	1.1	6
Boise	Idaho	32,512	48	1.1	7
Anchorage	Alaska	42,182	6	1.1	8
Manhattan	New York	49,737	1	1.1	8
Sacramento	California	38,845	12	1.1	10
Dallas	Texas	34,531	34	1.0	11
Providence	Rhode Island	35,995	27	1.0	12
Little Rock	Arkansas	28,656	61	0.9	13
San Jose	California	37,799	17	0.9	13
Cheyenne	Wyoming	33,876	38	0.9	13
New Orleans	Louisiana	30,174	55	0.9	16
Fargo	North Dakota	30,513	54	0.9	16
Denver	Colorado	37,401	19	0.9	18
Oklahoma City	Oklahoma	30,060	56	0.8	19
Hartford	Connecticut	47,922	2	0.8	20
Houston	Texas	37,153	20	0.8	20
Birmingham	Alabama	31,516	50	0.7	22
Austin	Texas	28,492	62	0.7	23
Salt Lake City	Utah	35,793	28	0.7	24
Phoenix	Arizona	33,291	40	0.7	25
Ft. Lauderdale	Florida	35,120	31	0.7	26
Helena	Montana	28,866	60	0.7	26
Honolulu	Hawaii	36,126	26	0.7	28
Augusta	Maine	31,504	51	0.7	28
Portland	Oregon	34,918	32	0.7	28
Portsmouth	New Hampshire	38,507	15	0.7	31
Seattle	Washington	38,167	16	0.7	31
Burlington	Vermont	32,600	46	0.6	33
Albuquerque	New Mexico	29,199	59	0.6	34
Aberdeen	South Dakota	29,974	57	0.6	35
Indianapolis	Indiana	35,780	29	0.6	36
Wilmington	Delaware	38,713	13	0.6	37
Brooklyn	New York	38,917	10	0.6	37
St. Paul	Minnesota	38,696	14	0.6	39
Jacksonville	Florida	31,546	49	0.6	40
Greensboro	North Carolina	33,072	43	0.6	40
Chicago	Illinois	42,511	4	0.6	42
Wichita	Kansas	35,305	30	0.6	43
St. Louis	Missouri	34,118	37	0.6	43
Omaha	Nebraska	33,142	42	0.5	45
Columbia	South Carolina	30,859	53	0.5	45
Nashville	Tennessee	32,566	47	0.5	45
Des Moines	Iowa	33,265	41	0.5	48
Boston	Massachusetts	41,408	8	0.5	49
Detroit	Michigan	38,930	9	0.5	50
Buffalo	New York	34,296	36	0.5	50
Parkersburg	West Virginia	29,687	58	0.5	50
Milwaukee	Wisconsin	36,891	22	0.5	50
Baltimore	DC/Maryland	41,497	7	0.5	54
Richmond	Virginia	38,851	11	0.5	54
Philadelphia	Pennsylvania	37,782	18	0.4	56
Springfield	Illinois	33,068	44	0.4	57
Newark	New Jersey	45,348	3	0.4	57
Pittsburgh	Pennsylvania	32,930	45	0.4	59
Albany	New York	36,498	24	0.4	60
Cincinnati	Ohio	34,499	35	0.3	61
Cleveland	Ohio	33,433	39	0.3	61
Louisville	Kentucky	31,223	52	0.3	63

Note: IRS district audits do not include tax audits conducted by IRS service centers.
Source: Transactional Records Access Clearinghouse, Syracuse University

Tax Refunds

The number of federal income-tax refunds issued to individuals and the average amount.

Tax year	Number of refunds (In millions)	Average amount
1990	80.5	$ 970.00
1991	82.4	1,020.00
1992	77.8	1,013.00
1993	79.3	1,069.00
1994	79.3	1,178.00
1995	80.4	1,244.00
1996*	80.6	1,273.00

*As of Sept. 5, 1997.
Source: Internal Revenue Service

Unpaid Taxes

The Internal Revenue Service's most recent estimates of the "gross tax gap," or the amount of individual income taxes that wasn't paid voluntarily and on time.

Gross Tax Gap Estimates and Percentages of "True" Tax Liability
Individual Income Tax
Tax Years 1985, 1988, and 1992

Tax gap components	Gross tax gap (In billions)			Noncompliance as percentage of "true" tax liability		
	1985	1988	1992	1985	1988	1992
Nonfiling	**$9.8**	**$11.2**	**$13.8**	**2.6%**	**2.4%**	**2.5%**
Underpayment	**7.1**	**11.2**	**8.4**	**1.9**	**2.4**	**1.5**
Underreporting	**53.5**	**58.5**	**73.1**	**14.3**	**12.7**	**13.2**
Nonfarm proprietor Income	13.4	14.4	16.9	3.6	3.1	3.1
Informal supplier Income	10.6	10.8	12.3	2.8	2.3	2.2
Other income	5.9	5.0	7.6	1.6	1.1	1.4
Tax credits	2.3	4.1	6.2	0.6	0.9	1.1
Deductions	4.4	4.3	5.1	1.2	0.9	0.9
Rents & royalties	2.0	2.0	3.7	0.5	0.4	0.7
Partnership and small business corporation Income	0.8	2.4	3.6	0.2	0.5	0.7
Farm income	1.9	1.7	3.4	0.5	0.4	0.6
Exemptions	1.6	2.7	2.9	0.4	0.6	0.5
Capital gains	3.6	3.3	2.5	1.0	0.7	0.5
All other items	7.0	7.8	8.9	1.9	1.4	1.6
Total	**70.4**	**80.9**	**95.3**	**18.8**	**17.5**	**17.3**

Source: Internal Revenue Service

State and Local Tax Surge

State and Local Government Taxes, by State (In thousands)

State/year	Total taxes	Property tax	General sales tax	Individual income tax	Corporate net income tax
Alabama					
1980	$2,528,360	$305,953	$ 786,277	$ 425,409	$109,238
1990	5,367,082	658,807	1,625,557	1,173,087	179,833
1994	6,755,333	825,731	2,093,437	1,430,816	218,131
Alaska					
1980	1,675,470	360,002	38,792	100,481 -	565,329
1990	2,237,760	685,358	72,164	0	185,140
1994	1,954,150	644,974	97,161	0	176,070
Arizona					
1980	2,738,160	955,978	976,945	287,498	117,764
1990	7,040,360	2,329,522	2,336,972	1,063,804	179,832
1994	8,873,033	2,726,433	3,067,122	1,408,535	303,239
Arkansas					
1980	1,495,260	305,184	372,733	316,644	83,714
1990	2,993,321	536,465	970,900	739,200	130,300
1994	4,118,336	622,763	1,450,628	958,673	184,281
California					
1980	27,745,541	6,477,533	8,166,479	6,463,736	2,507,183
1990	66,255,664	17,908,070	17,090,084	16,824,356	4,928,377
1994	75,571,146	20,651,778	20,770,002	17,547,763	4,633,449
Colorado					
1980	2,859,274	951,571	873,640	461,325	110,607
1990	6,342,317	2,254,465	1,667,757	1,341,733	123,357
1994	8,207,267	2,652,569	2,266,892	1,925,823	146,042
Connecticut					
1980	3,326,396	1,470,520	802,950	100,953	246,139
1990	8,791,299	3,469,768	2,443,398	610,438	679,726
1994	11,268,961	4,379,497	2,184,139	2,236,725	701,942
Delaware					
1980	629,910	99,581	0	246,240	40,553
1990	1,370,790	202,767	0	480,616	117,802
1994	1,760,893	262,227	0	575,810	155,070
District of Columbia					
1980	940,868	219,395	194,018	342,179	0
1990	2,310,313	727,175	466,557	637,910	140,041
1994	2,523,440	811,009	458,555	650,660	150,208
Florida					
1980	7,381,583	2,184,420	2,252,217	0	371,405
1990	22,593,598	7,916,723	8,211,956	0	698,825
1994	30,499,329	11,000,181	10,343,353	0	950,235
Georgia					
1980	4,206,956	1,087,021	1,147,759	872,073	239,713
1990	11,667,015	3,198,094	3,509,097	2,867,914	478,218
1994	14,923,195	4,405,126	4,375,844	3,580,714	521,399
Hawaii					
1980	1,232,805	186,210	498,293	311,404	50,259
1990	2,875,991	425,552	1,176,687	695,097	94,750
1994	3,755,585	624,723	1,332,248	962,217	68,429
Idaho					
1980	712,036	213,828	137,114	159,138	42,604
1990	1,571,156	416,796	383,088	403,061	72,692
1994	2,219,510	581,231	539,176	564,024	90,061
Illinois					
1980	12,375,201	4,191,522	2,911,981	1,900,676	797,927

State and Local Government Taxes, by State

State/year	Total taxes	Property tax	General sales tax	Individual income tax	Corporate net income tax
1990	24,022,959	8,622,386	5,621,034	4,288,667	939,149
1994	29,080,297	11,204,108	5,723,946	5,054,236	1,229,274
Indiana					
1980	4,083,081	1,348,851	1,331,594	610,406	179,191
1990	9,043,456	2,619,156	2,551,464	2,340,430	340,978
1994	12,189,068	4,253,492	2,505,874	3,394,438	798,600
Iowa					
1980	2,817,577	1,048,298	502,055	602,385	138,564
1990	5,224,732	1,833,512	975,145	1,274,219	199,558
1994	6,496,951	2,236,806	1,440,922	1,528,269	174,285
Kansas					
1980	2,188,423	863,757	443,689	336,061	149,517
1990	4,578,438	1,631,726	1,077,036	856,769	210,462
1994	5,900,338	1,852,141	1,557,554	1,194,329	254,892
Kentucky					
1980	2,709,344	495,923	607,604	686,278	158,846
1990	5,511,001	929,702	1,087,582	1,551,869	279,483
1994	7,385,875	1,219,300	1,560,091	2,151,573	269,067
Louisiana					
1980	3,533,950	466,315	1,304,113	247,438	249,338
1990	6,590,670	1,133,895	2,473,934	737,195	393,978
1994	7,422,331	1,288,048	2,941,790	976,382	219,190
Maine					
1980	965,543	359,405	214,113	142,689	45,086
1990	2,423,966	886,541	509,002	580,562	57,658
1994	2,914,862	1,171,622	617,008	614,654	91,955
Maryland					
1980	4,655,453	1,215,717	712,815	1,857,306	165,857
1990	11,022,141	2,822,266	1,571,866	4,242,060	292,552
1994	13,301,075	3,618,156	1,814,949	4,908,349	320,068
Massachusetts					
1980	7,133,186	3,183,499	745,996	1,860,045	532,383
1990	14,195,746	4,677,758	1,956,467	4,909,728	871,195
1994	17,125,903	5,948,686	2,303,139	5,689,768	1,062,930
Michigan					
1980	9,958,446	3,832,543	1,708,728	2,129,297	910,732
1990	19,219,292	7,617,995	3,187,651	4,316,729	1,815,601
1994	24,234,984	9,961,282	4,538,124	4,865,780	2,174,644
Minnesota					
1980	4,585,508	1,321,712	653,742	1,262,697	381,217
1990	10,082,268	3,100,046	1,883,822	2,876,636	481,854
1994	12,481,181	3,648,824	2,529,144	3,449,331	551,822
Mississippi					
1980	1,629,613	354,296	671,086	150,296	64,369
1990	3,251,536	877,163	1,089,069	430,391	119,985
1994	4,412,512	1,038,328	1,588,018	637,684	167,873
Missouri					
1980	3,734,286	1,058,069	1,024,122	714,557	135,103
1990	7,938,085	1,747,468	2,542,633	1,998,525	221,471
1994	9,843,995	2,303,820	3,011,428	2,381,090	252,392
Montana					
1980	786,757	358,301	0	135,012	45,623
1990	1,434,152	661,950	0	279,643	80,316
1994	1,670,739	714,110	0	345,644	68,872
Nebraska					
1980	1,512,300	629,041	316,816	235,821	57,579
1990	2,864,258	1,202,826	597,784	495,567	71,948

State and Local Government Taxes, by State

State/year	Total taxes	Property tax	General sales tax	Individual income tax	Corporate net income tax
1994	3,716,860	1,369,499	868,667	715,590	113,142
Nevada					
1980	776,761	204,456	211,815	0	0
1990	2,314,513	510,955	809,657	0	0
1994	3,429,936	748,539	1,193,851	0	0
New Hampshire					
1980	681,519	415,033	0	10,474	62,786
1990	1,874,643	1,276,634	0	41,391	126,589
1994	2,489,525	1,640,009	0	35,980	144,157
New Jersey					
1980	8,376,509	3,672,636	1,180,267	1,004,781	497,205
1990	19,472,274	8,879,055	3,291,359	2,952,046	1,123,096
1994	25,421,650	11,723,715	3,778,427	4,499,709	1,085,055
New Mexico					
1980	1,143,006	184,810	431,306	46,846	46,272
1990	2,560,431	331,030	1,023,155	360,971	61,732
1994	3,477,042	435,448	1,407,455	577,290	122,528
New York					
1980	26,245,461	8,791,074	5,113,462	7,481,051	1,235,340
1990	58,764,950	18,399,741	11,074,364	17,868,796	3,560,591
1994	70,029,467	22,639,100	12,077,271	20,121,201	5,597,184
North Carolina					
1980	4,395,222	1,002,658	888,956	1,180,511	291,752
1990	11,103,504	2,336,768	2,651,482	3,390,390	612,388
1994	14,919,242	3,270,465	3,618,770	4,288,148	737,260
North Dakota					
1980	552,964	175,613	124,012	53,346	36,348
1990	1,002,055	304,213	243,791	105,687	46,762
1994	1,295,158	373,277	279,527	136,956	71,461
Ohio					
1980	8,747,727	3,034,301	1,595,860	1,844,109	517,344
1990	19,666,106	5,592,707	4,135,041	5,932,406	643,428
1994	24,472,766	6,978,179	5,214,783	7,316,336	652,543
Oklahoma					
1980	2,500,661	458,001	543,975	361,895	89,869
1990	4,954,384	872,770	1,364,405	1,000,883	95,920
1994	6,014,992	984,636	1,750,674	1,315,068	162,214
Oregon					
1980	2,576,503	1,006,087	0	867,976	177,425
1990	5,496,977	2,425,633	0	1,826,646	147,784
1994	6,992,643	2,519,129	0	2,583,527	263,682
Pennsylvania					
1980	11,605,921	2,957,852	1,995,829	2,656,854	861,682
1990	22,084,607	6,126,406	4,224,983	5,112,729	1,094,778
1994	28,226,143	8,083,822	5,217,990	6,695,580	1,486,299
Rhode Island					
1980	939,862	391,513	169,061	153,912	53,620
1990	2,043,436	807,989	397,426	426,583	68,828
1994	2,490,630	1,048,552	412,820	528,089	79,320
South Carolina					
1980	2,209,084	497,622	576,489	494,789	153,475
1990	5,446,559	1,399,646	1,447,851	1,380,180	150,926
1994	6,597,676	1,887,122	1,713,884	1,530,996	219,052
South Dakota					
1980	544,101	242,013	166,181	0	3,292
1990	1,006,794	405,468	328,815	13	30,714
1994	1,311,422	523,036	441,700	127	36,540

State and Local Government Taxes, by State

State/year	Total taxes	Property tax	General sales tax	Individual income tax	Corporate net income tax
Tennessee					
1980	3,012,262	723,327	1,252,962	30,816	198,222
1990	6,822,965	1,566,790	3,066,549	102,955	332,036
1994	9,103,072	2,071,774	4,014,032	99,124	421,960
Texas					
1980	11,466,322	3,979,559	3,016,421	0	0
1990	28,243,402	11,058,365	9,249,073	160	0
1994	37,247,915	13,881,952	12,067,542	(136)	0
Utah					
1980	1,226,821	342,793	395,454	265,327	40,377
1990	2,725,872	743,614	852,907	646,830	94,167
1994	3,662,780	937,745	1,189,497	925,004	125,191
Vermont					
1980	459,909	192,501	40,836	83,182	22,425
1990	1,130,962	462,775	136,029	250,904	27,128
1994	1,439,727	610,027	175,979	286,108	34,932
Virginia					
1980	4,574,106	1,260,083	802,430	1,103,014	193,847
1990	11,727,662	3,698,150	1,848,960	3,082,207	306,170
1994	14,162,230	4,389,787	2,344,879	3,812,185	306,667
Washington					
1980	4,083,947	1,199,478	1,784,651	0	0
1990	10,332,030	2,841,487	5,085,699	0	0
1994	13,872,522	4,169,235	6,613,301	0	0
West Virginia					
1980	1,551,720	266,766	598,512	252,362	32,889
1990	2,801,478	459,656	764,523	516,858	221,642
1994	3,351,366	655,005	727,192	669,694	184,625
Wisconsin					
1980	4,993,895	1,696,273	853,864	1,430,475	311,321
1990	10,223,151	3,610,402	2,006,578	2,624,896	436,562
1994	13,715,125	5,106,783	2,554,774	3,638,710	541,284
Wyoming					
1980	659,097	259,849	191,602	0	0
1990	1,000,527	409,115	205,241	0	0
1994	1,196,360	447,207	265,740	0	0
U.S. Total					
1980	223,462,640	68,498,743	51,327,616	42,079,764	13,321,331
1990	501,618,648	155,613,321	121,268,594	105,639,737	23,566,322
1994	625,526,527	197,141,008	149,039,299	128,808,562	28,319,516

Source: U.S. Census Bureau

The Home Front

STRONG AND STEADY HOUSING MARKET

As investments go, your house still probably doesn't measure up to your mutual fund.

But home values around the nation, after years of marginal growth, are finally on the rise. The U.S. Office of Federal Housing Enterprise Oversight, which monitors government-sponsored mortgage buyers Fannie Mae and Freddie Mac, said the median price for existing homes rose 3.6% in 1996 nationwide—the second year in a row home appreciation grew faster than the consumer price index, and only the second time since 1989. Meanwhile, the National Association of Home Builders says new home prices in 1996 rose 4.6%, the largest increase in seven years.

Moribund markets like Boston and Washington, D.C., have seen price increases. Even in California, where the value of existing homes has fallen almost 10% since 1992, there's the glimmer of a resurgence. Richard P. Nesbitt, branch manager of a Coldwell Banker Residential Real Estate office in San Diego, predicts homes in his market will appreciate 3% to 5% after six years of flat or falling prices. Home prices "are coming back. It's exciting," he says.

It's not a return to the 1970s, when inflation turned the American home into an investment vehicle. But home values are improving as baby boomers buy their first homes or trade up to bigger, better homes. They put off buying homes during the late 1980s and early 1990s, when concern about home values and economic worries turned many of them into renters. Today, they have more children and improved confidence in the economy. "The baby boomers are hot to trot, and with interest rates the way they are and the good economy, they're moving in in large numbers," says William Apgar, executive director of the Joint Center for Housing Studies at Harvard University.

Homeownership usually tracks employment levels, which are at high levels in many areas of the country. Relatively low mortgage rates in 1996 and 1997 also have spurred homebuyers' interest. Meanwhile, Americans' investments in stocks and mutual funds have paid healthy returns and left many Americans flush with cash.

Trading up in particular is fueling the market. According to Chicago Title and Trust Co., 55.3% of homebuyers in major metropolitan markets in 1996 were previous homeowners, compared with 52.9% in 1994.

How long will the strong market last? For the first half of 1997, sales of both new and existing homes have been brisk, and many housing market experts predict the healthy market will continue. The economy "is close to an even keel," says David Seiders, chief economist with the home builders association. "The housing market is well."

But some have already sounded notes of caution. Paul C. Taylor, senior economist with America's Community Bankers, a Washington, D.C., trade group, warns that inventories of existing homes available for sale are near historic highs and that increases in the median price of homes have been overstated because of trade-up activity among baby boomers. "The trade-up homes skew the data. The homes that are selling are top-dollar homes," he says.

In any case, few predict that homes will appreciate the way they did in the 1970s and 1980s. "It's steady, without big peaks and valleys," says Edward W. Marrs, executive director of the National Home Buying Institute, a consumer group. "It's good for the consumer and good for the industry."

Carlos Tejada

Suburban Sprawl

Metropolitan and Nonmetropolitan Distribution of Housing Units: 1940 and 1990

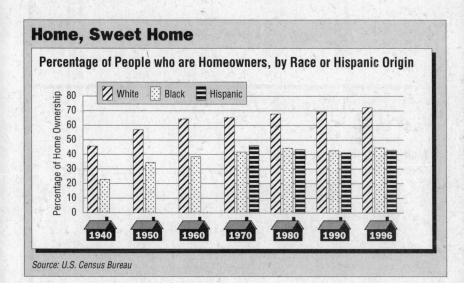

1940*

Central cities
34%

Non-metropolitan
46%

Suburbs
19%

1990

Central cities
32%

Non-metropolitan
24%

Suburbs
44%

*1940 data exclude Alaska and Hawaii.
Source: U.S. Census Bureau

Home, Sweet Home

Percentage of People who are Homeowners, by Race or Hispanic Origin

(Legend: White, Black, Hispanic)

Source: U.S. Census Bureau

The Rise and Fall of Mortgage Rates

Average Annual Interest Rates on 30-Year Fixed-Rate Mortgages

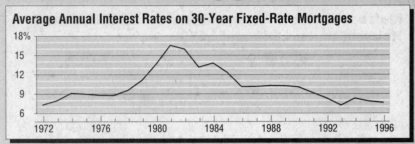

Average Annual Interest Rates

Year	30-year fixed rate	Year	30-year fixed rate	15-year fixed rate	1-year adjustable rate
1972	7.38%	1984	13.88%	—	11.51%
1973	8.04	1985	12.43	—	10.05
1974	9.19	1986	10.19	—	8.43
1975	9.05	1987	10.21	—	7.83
1976	8.87	1988	10.34	—	7.90
1977	8.85	1989	10.32	—	8.80
1978	9.64	1990	10.13	—	8.36
1979	11.20	1991	9.25	—	7.09
1980	13.74	1992	8.39	7.96%	5.62
1981	16.63	1993	7.31	6.83	4.58
1982	16.04	1994	8.38	7.86	5.36
1983	13.24	1995	7.93	7.48	6.06
		1996	7.81	7.32	5.67

Source: Federal Home Loan Mortgage Corp. (Freddie Mac)

Past Due

Mortgage Delinquency Rates

(Percent of loans that were past due in the fourth quarter of each year, seasonally adjusted)

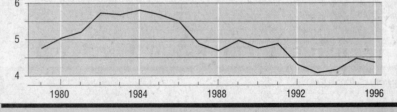

Source: Mortgage Bankers Association of America

Mortgage Payment Table
Principal and interest for a fixed-rate, 15-year loan

Loan amount	5.0%	5.5%	6.0%	6.5%	7.0%	7.5%	8.0%	8.5%	9.0%	9.5%	10.0%
$ 5,000	$ 40	$ 41	$ 42	$ 44	$ 45	$ 46	$ 48	$ 49	$ 51	$ 52	$ 54
10,000	79	82	84	87	90	93	96	98	101	104	107
15,000	119	123	127	131	135	139	143	148	152	157	161
20,000	158	163	169	174	180	185	191	197	203	209	215
25,000	198	204	211	218	225	232	239	246	254	261	269
30,000	237	245	253	261	270	278	287	295	304	313	322
35,000	277	286	295	305	315	324	334	345	355	365	376
40,000	316	327	338	348	360	371	382	394	406	418	430
45,000	356	368	380	392	404	417	430	443	456	470	484
50,000	395	409	422	436	449	464	478	492	507	522	537
55,000	435	449	464	479	494	510	526	542	558	574	591
60,000	474	490	506	523	539	556	573	591	609	627	645
65,000	514	531	549	566	584	603	621	640	659	679	698
70,000	554	572	591	610	629	649	669	689	710	731	752
75,000	593	613	633	653	674	695	717	739	761	783	806
80,000	633	654	675	697	719	742	765	788	811	835	860
85,000	672	695	717	740	764	788	812	837	862	888	913
90,000	712	735	759	784	809	834	860	886	913	940	967
95,000	751	776	802	828	854	881	908	936	964	992	1,021
100,000	791	817	844	871	899	927	956	985	1,014	1,044	1,075

Mortgage Payment Table
Principal and interest for a fixed-rate, 30-year loan

Loan amount	5.0%	5.5%	6.0%	6.5%	7.0%	7.5%	8.0%	8.5%	9.0%	9.5%	10.0%
$ 5,000	$ 27	$ 28	$ 30	$ 32	$ 33	$ 35	$ 37	$ 38	$ 40	$ 42	$ 44
10,000	54	57	60	63	67	70	73	77	80	84	88
15,000	81	85	90	95	100	105	110	115	121	126	132
20,000	107	114	120	126	133	140	147	154	161	168	176
25,000	134	142	150	158	166	175	183	192	201	210	219
30,000	161	170	180	190	200	210	220	231	241	252	263
35,000	188	199	210	221	233	245	257	269	282	294	307
40,000	215	227	240	253	266	280	294	308	322	336	351
45,000	242	256	270	284	299	315	330	346	362	378	395
50,000	268	284	300	316	333	350	367	384	402	420	439
55,000	295	312	330	348	366	385	404	423	443	462	483
60,000	322	341	360	379	399	420	440	461	483	505	527
65,000	349	369	390	411	432	454	477	500	523	547	570
70,000	376	397	420	442	466	489	514	538	563	589	614
75,000	403	426	450	474	499	524	550	577	603	631	658
80,000	429	454	480	506	532	559	587	615	644	673	702
85,000	456	483	510	537	566	594	624	654	684	715	746
90,000	483	511	540	569	599	629	660	692	724	757	790
95,000	510	539	570	600	632	664	697	730	764	799	834
100,000	537	568	600	632	665	699	734	769	805	841	878

Note: For mortgages over $100,000, add the appropriate figures. For example, the principal and interest on a 30-year, $100,000 mortgage at 8 percent is $734 and the principal and interest on a 30-year, $50,000 mortgage at 8 percent is $367, making the total principal and interest payment on a $150,000 mortgage $734 plus $367, or $1,101 per month.
Source: National Association of Home Builders

New Homes

New Privately Owned Housing Units Started
(In thousands)

Year	Total units	Structures with: One unit	2 to 4 units	5 or more units	Region Northeast	Midwest	South	West
1970	1,434	813	85	536	218	294	612	311
1975	1,160	892	64	204	149	294	442	275
1980	1,292	852	110	331	125	218	643	306
1985	1,742	1,072	93	576	252	240	782	468
1990	1,193	895	37	260	131	253	479	329
1991	1,014	840	36	138	113	233	414	254
1992	1,200	1,030	31	139	127	288	497	288
1993	1,288	1,126	29	133	126	298	562	302
1994	1,457	1,198	35	224	138	329	639	351
1995	1,354	1,076	34	244	118	290	615	331
1996	1,475	1,160	45	270	132	321	661	361

New Privately Owned One-Family Houses Sold, by Region
(In thousands)

Year	Total sales	Region Northeast	Midwest	South	West
1970	485	61	100	203	121
1972	718	96	130	305	187
1974	519	69	103	207	139
1976	646	72	128	247	199
1978	817	78	145	331	262
1980	545	50	81	267	145
1982	412	47	48	219	99
1984	639	94	76	309	160
1986	750	136	96	322	196
1988	676	101	97	276	202
1990	534	71	89	225	149
1991	509	57	93	215	144
1992	610	65	116	259	170
1993	666	60	123	295	188
1994	670	61	123	295	191
1995	667	55	125	300	187
1996	758	74	137	338	209

Source: U.S. Census Bureau and U.S. Department of Housing and Urban Development

Dream Homes

Characteristics of New Privately Owned One-Family Houses Completed

(Percent distribution)

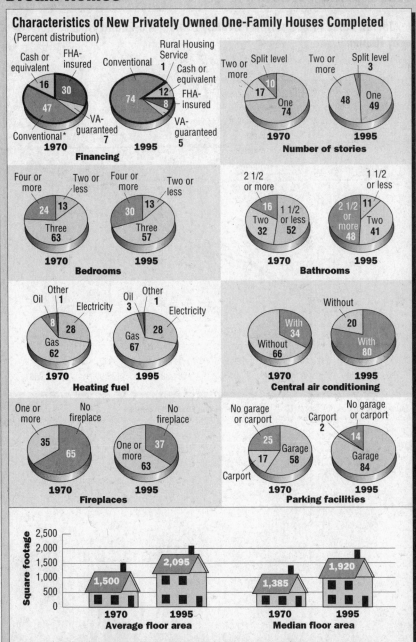

Financing

1970: Cash or equivalent 16, FHA-insured 30, Conventional* 47, VA-guaranteed 7

1995: Conventional 74, Rural Housing Service 1, Cash or equivalent 12, FHA-insured 8, VA-guaranteed 5

Number of stories

1970: Two or more 17, Split level 10, One 74

1995: Two or more 48, Split level 3, One 49

Bedrooms

1970: Four or more 24, Two or less 13, Three 63

1995: Four or more 30, Two or less 13, Three 57

Bathrooms

1970: 2 1/2 or more 16, 1 1/2 or less 52, Two 32

1995: 1 1/2 or less 11, 2 1/2 or more 48, Two 41

Heating fuel

1970: Oil 8, Other 1, Electricity 28, Gas 62

1995: Oil 3, Other 1, Electricity 28, Gas 67

Central air conditioning

1970: With 34, Without 66

1995: Without 20, With 80

Fireplaces

1970: One or more 35, No fireplace 65

1995: No fireplace 37, One or more 63

Parking facilities

1970: No garage or carport 25, Garage 58, Carport 17

1995: Carport 2, No garage or carport 14, Garage 84

Average floor area: 1970: 1,500; 1995: 2,095

Median floor area: 1970: 1,385; 1995: 1,920

(Square footage)

Source: U.S. Census Bureau and U.S. Department of Housing and Urban Development

New Home Prices

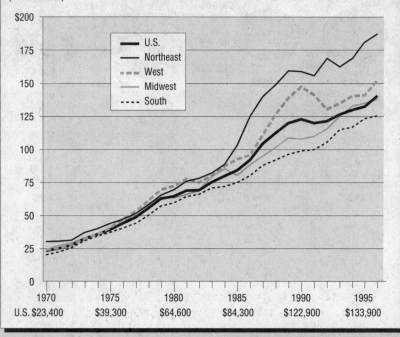

Median Sales Prices of New Privately Owned One-Family Houses Sold, by Region

(In thousands)

Legend:
- **U.S.**
- Northeast
- West
- Midwest
- South

Year	1970	1975	1980	1985	1990	1995
U.S.	$23,400	$39,300	$64,600	$84,300	$122,900	$133,900

Source: U.S. Census Bureau and U.S. Department of Housing and Urban Development

Top 50 Metropolitan Markets Single–Family Building Permits Issued

RANK	AREA	NUMBER OF PERMITS 1995	1996	PCT. CHG.
1	Atlanta GA MSA	34,944	37,523	7.4%
2	Phoenix-Mesa AZ MSA	28,539	29,505	3.4%
3	Chicago IL, PMSA	24,501	24,922	1.7%
4	Washington DC-MD-VA-WV PMSA	22,971	23,184	0.9%
5	Las Vegas NV -N MSA	20,054	20,551	2.5%
6	Dallas TX PMSA	15,735	18,223	15.8%
7	Houston TX PMSA	13,479	16,427	21.9%
8	Detroit MI PMSA	14,425	15,712	8.9%
9	Minneapolis–St. Paul MN-WI MSA	13,902	15,316	10.2%
10	Charlotte-Gastonia-Rock Hill NC-SC MSA	10,056	12,515	24.5%
11	Denver CO PMSA	11,481	12,514	9.0%
12	Philadelphia PA-NJ PMSA	11,845	12,485	5.4%
13	Orlando FL MSA	10,989	12,442	13.2%
14	Portland-Vancouver OR-WA PMSA	10,925	12,176	11.5%
15	Riverside-San Bernardino CA PMSA	10,608	11,690	10.2%
16	Indianapolis IN MSA	10,204	11,459	12.3%
17	Raleigh-Durham—Chapel Hill NC MSA	9,803	10,891	11.1%
18	St. Louis MO-IL MSA	9,998	10,527	5.3%
19	Nashville TN MSA	8,574	10,039	17.1%
20	Tampa-St. Petersburg-Clearwater FL MSA	9,524	10,022	5.2%
21	Kansas City MO-KS MSA	8,292	9,728	17.3%
22	Fort Lauderdale FL PMSA	8,470	9,548	12.7%
23	Baltimore MD PMSA	9,720	9,330	−4.0%
24	Seattle-Bellevue-Everett WA PMSA	8,946	9,057	1.2%
25	Salt Lake City-Ogden UT MSA	7,609	8,901	17.0%
26	West Palm Beach-Boca Raton FL MSA	7,473	8,141	8.9%
27	Austin-San Marcos TX MSA	5,643	8,083	43.2%
28	Columbus OH MSA	6,755	7,622	12.8%
29	Cincinnati OH-KY-IN PMSA	6,275	7,494	19.4%
30	Jacksonville FL MSA	6,567	7,466	13.7%
31	Sacramento CA PMSA	6,931	7,424	7.1%
32	Fort Worth-Arlington TX PMSA	6,463	7,285	12.7%
33	Orange County CA PMSA	5,981	7,023	17.4%
34	Greensboro—Winston/Salem—High Point NC MSA	6,791	7,021	3.4%
35	Norfolk-Virginia Beach-Newport News VA-NC MSA	6,228	6,527	4.8%
36	San Antonio TX MSA	5,937	6,484	9.2%
37	Memphis TN-AR-MS MSA	7,177	6,223	−13.3%
38	Cleveland-Lorain-Elyria OH PMSA	5,660	6,200	9.5%
39	Grand Rapids-Muskegon-Holland MI MSA	5,420	6,076	12.1%
40.	Boston MA- NH PMSA	5,536	5,943	7.4%
41.	Oakland CA PMSA	5,414	5,927	9.5%
42	San Diego CA MSA	4,818	5,821	20.8%
43	Greenville-Spartanburg-Anderson SC MSA	4,943	5,508	11.4%
44	Richmond-Petersburg VA MSA	5,496	5,428	−1.2%
45	Los Angeles-Long Beach CA PMSA	4,839	5,185	7.2%
46	Monmouth-Ocean NJ PMSA	4,651	5,056	8.7%
47	Tucson AZ MSA	4,479	5,035	12.4%
48	Louisville KY -IN MSA	4,674	5,024	7.5%
49	Pittsburgh PA MSA	4,856	4,878	0.5%
50	Albuquerque NM MSA	4,700	4,703	0.1%

Sources: U.S. Census Bureau and National Association of Home Builders

Older Homes

Median Sales Price of Existing Single-Family Homes

Year	United States	Northeast	Midwest	South	West
1970	$23,000	$25,2000	$20,100	$22,200	$24,300
1972	26,700	29,800	23,900	26,400	28,400
1974	32,000	35,800	27,700	32,300	34,800
1976	38,100	41,800	32,900	36,500	46,100
1978	48,700	47,900	42,200	45,100	66,700
1980	62,200	60,800	51,900	58,300	89,300
1982	67,800	63,500	55,100	67,100	98,900
1984	72,400	78,700	57,100	71,300	95,800
1986	80,300	104,800	63,500	78,200	100,900
1988	89,300	143,000	68,400	82,200	124,900
1990	95,500	141,200	74,000	85,900	139,600
1991	100,300	141,900	77,800	88,900	147,200
1992	103,700	140,000	81,700	92,100	143,800
1993	106,800	139,500	85,200	95,100	142,600
1994	109,800	139,100	87,900	96,000	146,700
1995	112,900	136,900	93,600	97,700	147,200
1996	118,000	140,500	100,000	102,500	152,200

Median Sales Price of Existing Homes

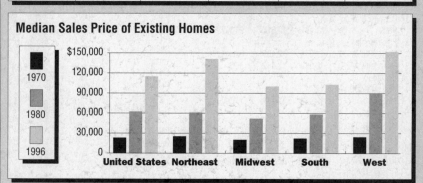

Legend:
- 1970
- 1980
- 1996

United States   Northeast   Midwest   South   West

Existing Single-Family Home Sales
(In thousands)

Year	Total sales	North-east	Mid-west	South	West	Year	Total sales	North-east	Mid-west	South	West
1970	1,612	251	501	568	292	1988	3,513	606	865	1,224	817
1972	2,252	361	630	788	473	1990	3,211	469	831	1,202	709
1974	2,272	354	645	839	434	1991	3,220	479	840	1,199	702
1976	3,064	439	881	1,033	712	1992	3,520	534	939	1,292	755
1978	3,986	516	1,144	1,416	911	1993	3,802	571	1,007	1,416	808
1980	2,973	403	806	1,092	672	1994	3,946	592	1,027	1,464	863
1982	1,990	354	490	780	366	1995	3,802	575	992	1,429	806
1984	2,829	478	720	1,006	624	1996	4,085	612	1,047	1,516	911
1986	3,474	635	922	1,145	773						

Source: National Association of Realtors

Home Values

Median Sales Price of Existing Single-Family Homes for Major Metropolitan Areas

Metropolitan area	1994	1995	1996
Atlanta, GA	$93,600	$97,500	$100,700
Austin/San Marcos, TX	96,200	101,400	108,100
Boston, MA	179,300	179,000	189,300
Buffalo/Niagara Falls, NY	82,300	81,300	82,900
Charlotte/Gastonia/Rock Hill, NC/SC	106,500	107,800	116,800
Chicago, IL	144,100	147,900	153,200
Cincinnati, OH/KY/IN	96,500	100,400	104,800
Cleveland, OH	98,500	104,700	111,900
Columbus, OH	94,800	99,100	108,200
Dallas, TX	95,000	96,400	103,500
Dayton/Springfield, OH	84,200	88,300	95,100
Denver, CO	116,800	127,300	133,400
Detroit, MI	87,000	98,200	111,400
Grand Rapids, MI	76,900	80,600	87,200
Greensboro/Winston-Salem/High Point, NC	96,600	102,500	112,700
Hartford, CT	133,400	133,400	139,200
Houston, TX	80,500	79,200	84,700
Indianapolis, IN	90,700	94,600	98,000
Jacksonville, FL	81,900	83,100	88,400
Kansas City, MO/KS	87,100	91,700	98,800
Las Vegas, NV	110,500	113,500	118,500
Los Angeles Area, CA	189,100	179,900	172,900
Louisville, KY	80,500	86,400	91,300
Memphis, TN/AR/MS	86,300	86,500	96,100
Miami/Hialeah, FL	103,200	107,100	113,200
Milwaukee, WI	109,000	114,700	119,400
Minneapolis/St. Paul, MN/WI	101,500	106,800	113,900
Nashville, TN	96,500	107,300	112,700
New Orleans, LA	76,900	78,000	87,000
New York/N. New Jersey/Long Island, NY/NJ/CT	173,200	169,700	174,500
Bergen/Passaic, NJ	192,700	190,100	199,400
Middlesex/Somerset/Hunterdon, NJ	170,700	171,400	175,900
Monmouth/Ocean, NJ	137,000	137,200	144,700
Nassau/Suffolk, NY	159,300	155,300	159,800
Newark, NJ	187,300	185,100	*
Norfolk/Virginia Beach/Newport News, VA	103,800	104,400	110,200
Oklahoma City, OK	66,700	70,400	74,600
Orlando, FL	90,700	89,200	92,400
Philadelphia, PA/NJ	119,500	118,700	*
Phoenix, AZ	91,400	96,800	105,300
Pittsburgh, PA	80,700	82,100	84,800
Portland, OR	116,900	128,400	141,500
Providence, RI	116,400	115,600	118,100
Raleigh/Durham, NC	115,200	127,000	*
Rochester, NY	85,600	85,000	86,200
Sacramento, CA	124,500	119,500	115,200
Saint Louis, MO/IL	85,000	87,700	91,200
Salt Lake City/Ogden, UT	98,000	113,700	122,700
San Antonio, TX	78,200	80,800	84,900
San Diego, CA	176,000	171,600	174,500
San Francisco Bay Area, CA	255,600	254,400	266,400
Seattle, WA	155,900	159,000	164,600
Tampa/St. Petersburg/Clearwater, FL	76,200	78,300	81,300
Washington, DC/MD/VA	157,900	156,500	160,700
W. Palm Beach/Boca Raton/Delray Beach, FL	117,600	121,300	126,600

*Not available.
Source: National Association of Realtors

Home Price Forecast

Americans are buying homes at a strong pace, but thanks to a spurt of new-home building in the hottest markets, prices aren't spiraling out of control as they did in the housing boom of the mid-1980s. That's the conclusion of a Home Price Forecast prepared for *The Wall Street Journal* by Case Shiller Weiss Inc. of Cambridge, Mass. Here are the firm's projections for 20 major markets:

Percentage Increase in Home Sale Prices

	Projected growth July 1997 to July 1998
Atlanta	+4.4%
Boston	+2.7
Chicago	+3.7
Cleveland-Akron	+4.0
Denver-Boulder-Greeley	+3.5
Detroit	+6.1
Hartford	+0.6
Los Angeles	+0.5
Miami	+3.3
Minneapolis-St. Paul	+2.3
Nashville	+5.8
New York	+3.9
Orlando	+2.9
Philadelphia	+2.6
Phoenix	+4.8
Portland-Salem	+5.0
San Diego	+3.3
San Francisco	+3.7
Seattle-Tacoma-Bremerton	+6.0
Washington, DC	+2.3

Source: Case Shiller Weiss, Inc.

Metros With Greatest Home Price Growth

Quarterly Median Sales Price, Percent Change From Last Year

Metro area	1st qtr. 1996	1st qtr. 1997	% change from last year
Greenville-Spartanburg, SC	$95,900	$111,100	15.8%
Mobile, AL	78,900	89,400	13.3
Aurora-Elgin, IL	131,400	147,100	11.9
Fort Lauderdale-Hollywood- Pompano Beach, FL	110,000	122,100	11.0
Waterloo-Cedar Falls, IA	56,800	62,600	10.2
Bergen-Passaic, NJ	192,000	210,900	9.8
Colorado Springs, CO	117,500	128,500	9.4
Worcester, MA	120,800	132,000	9.3
Indianapolis, IN	97,100	106,000	9.2
Charleston, SC	90,300	98,500	9.1
Akron, OH	91,100	99,000	8.7
Portland, OR	135,800	147,500	8.6
Fort Myers-Cape Coral, FL	76,100	82,600	8.5
Columbia, SC	89,200	96,800	8.5
Houston, TX	80,900	87,600	8.3
Saginaw-Bay City-Midland, MI	62,800	68,000	8.3

Metro area	1st qtr. 1996	1st qtr. 1997	% change from last year
New Orleans, LA	$83,500	$90,400	8.3%
Peoria, IL	68,400	74,000	8.2
Columbus, OH	107,200	115,700	7.9
Detroit, MI	105,800	113,900	7.7
San Francisco, CA area	252,200	271,100	7.5
Albuquerque, NM	122,600	131,700	7.4
Louisville, KY-IN	85,700	92,000	7.4
Phoenix, AZ	102,600	109,500	6.7
Atlanta, GA	98,500	105,100	6.7

Source: National Association of Realtors

Most Expensive Residential Real Estate Markets, According to Coldwell Banker Home Price Comparison Index, 1997

City	Average sale price*
Beverly Hills, CA	$766,250
Greenwich, CT	663,000
Brentwood, CA	599,000
San Francisco, CA	583,325
La Jolla, CA	515,000
Wellesley, MA	510,900
San Mateo, CA	503,000
Newport Beach, CA	500,313
Darien CT	499,062
Palos Verdes, CA	454,250
Chicago/Lincoln Park, IL	450,000
Lexington, MA	443,125
Westport, CT	434,250
Honolulu, HI	430,000
Pasadena, CA	421,500
Monterey Peninsula, CA	396,000
Southern Westchester County, NY	395,375
Fremont, CA	389,833
San Jose, CA	387,488
San Rafael, CA	382,500

*Subject homes are single-family dwellings, approximately 2,200 square feet, 4 bedrooms, 2.5 baths, family room (or equivalent) and two-car garage. Homes and neighborhoods surveyed are typical for corporate middle-management transferees.
Source: Coldwell Banker

Most Expensive New Home Markets in 1996

County name	Average sale price	County name	Average sale price
Marin, CA	$445,720	Montgomery, MD	250,734
Santa Clara, CA	334,910	Norfolk, MA	248,573
Fairfield, CT	334,316	Rockland, NY	247,429
Alameda, CA	311,760	Napa, CA	246,696
San Mateo, CA	307,369	Alexandria City, VA	246,554
Hunterdon, NJ	300,926	Contra Costa, CA	246,239
Arlington, VA	294,202	Fairfax, VA	245,946
Westchester, NY	294,058	Ventura, CA	243,302
San Francisco, CA	285,553	Nantucket, MA	243,026
Bergen, NJ	281,133	North Fulton, GA	242,284
Morris, NJ	270,796	Los Angeles, CA	240,949
Santa Cruz, CA	269,736	Mercer, NJ	237,355
Somerset, NJ	267,083	Chester, PA	233,354
Middlesex, MA	262,895	Monmouth, NJ	232,253
Orange, CA	252,027	Geauga, OH	228,592

Source: Experian

Most and Least Affordable Housing Markets

Ranking of the most and least affordable housing markets, based on the proportion of homes that a family earning the median income in that market could afford to buy. For example, the housing opportunity index in Binghamton, NY, the most affordable market in the fourth quarter of 1996, was 89.5, meaning that families earning the median income could have purchased 89.5% of all the homes sold in the quarter. In contrast, people earning the median income in San Francisco, the least affordable market, could have bought only 22% of the houses sold.

Most Affordable Markets	Housing Opportunity Index		1996 median income	Median sale price			1996 Q4 affordability rank
				Thousands			
Metro area	1995 Q4	1996 Q4	(000s)	1995 Q4	1996 Q4	Percent change	National
Binghamton, NY	82.0	89.5	$40.1	$ 82	$ 65	-20.7%	1
Wilmington, DE-MD	76.9	89.1	55.5	122	110	-9.8	2
Elkhart, IN	85.3	88.3	43.5	92	90	-2.2	3
Lima, OH	86.2	86.2	40.0	67	65	-3.0	4
Elmira, NY	77.9	85.1	37.3	68	63	-7.4	5
Kokomo, IN	NA	83.5	42.7	NA	83	NA	6
Lakeland, FL	79.3	83.4	35.9	70	73	4.3	7
Champaign, IL	82.5	83.0	45.0	85	81	-4.7	8
Kansas City, MO-KS	83.4	82.9	47.7	91	92	1.1	9
Melbourne, FL	83.1	82.5	43.9	78	84	7.7	10
Davenport, IA-IL	79.7	81.8	41.2	66	63	-4.5	11
Baton Rouge, LA	84.7	81.7	39.3	85	85	0.0	12
Pensacola, FL	81.7	81.7	37.2	79	83	5.1	12
Des Moines, IA	75.4	81.4	48.3	89	89	0.0	14
Beaumont, TX	77.2	81.2	37.3	69	70	1.4	15
Peoria, IL	79.5	81.2	43.6	68	74	8.8	15
Syracuse NY,	72.7	80.8	41.8	91	76	-16.5	17
Utica, NY	79.8	80.8	36.2	78	67	-14.1	17
Nashua, NH	80.4	80.5	56.9	115	118	2.6	19
Racine, WI	NA	80.2	46.7	NA	81	NA	20
Jamestown, NY	NA	79.8	34.3	NA	60	NA	21
Springfield, IL	80.8	79.6	47.7	87	91	4.6	22
Minneapolis- St. Paul, MN	79.9	79.5	54.6	104	110	5.8	23
Vineland, NJ	81.7	79.4	41.5	80	81	1.3	24
Dayton, OH	78.2	79.0	44.3	85	88	3.5	25
Duluth, MN-WI	80.2	79.0	38.6	77	78	1.3	25
Least Affordable Markets							
San Francisco, CA	21.4	22.0	$61.3	$276	$285	3.3%	184
Santa Cruz, CA	27.8	28.8	53.1	216	223	3.2	182
Salinas, CA	36.6	28.8	43.0	159	177	11.3	182
Portland, OR-WA	36.5	28.9	44.4	130	144	10.8	181
Santa Rosa, CA	35.7	34.7	49.2	183	183	0.0	180
Provo-Orem, UT	37.5	37.2	40.1	131	142	8.4	179
San Jose, CA	40.7	38.3	67.4	238	255	7.1	178
New York, NY	34.6	40.0	45.8	164	163	-0.6	177
San Luis Obispo, CA	39.7	40.5	43.3	160	155	-3.1	176
Honolulu, HI	39.2	40.7	55.9	221	223	0.9	175
San Diego, CA	45.5	42.0	46.6	159	166	4.4	174
Salem, OR	48.7	42.9	37.8	100	107	7.0	172
Jersey City, NJ	40.9	42.9	43.1	129	130	0.8	172
Greeley, CO	48.8	45.7	39.0	113	119	5.3	171
Santa Barbara, CA	46.8	46.2	48.3	169	173	2.4	170
Salt Lake City, UT	47.9	46.5	45.5	135	144	6.7	169
Oakland, CA	46.3	47.5	58.4	195	198	1.5	168
New Bedford, MA	44.6	47.8	38.8	121	125	3.3	167
Los Angeles, CA	47.3	49.5	46.9	157	158	0.6	166
Austin, TX	45.9	49.6	44.9	129	128	-0.8	165
Lowell, MA-NH	48.1	51.1	55.8	170	174	2.4	164
Chico, CA	52.9	51.3	32.8	100	104	4.0	163
Yuba City, CA	44.9	51.7	32.4	107	103	-3.7	162
Danbury, CT	53.0	53.0	71.4	200	210	5.0	161
Stockton, CA	54.6	54.3	41.5	126	128	1.6	160

Source: National Association of Home Builders

Buying the American Dream

Changing Characteristics of Home Buyers in Major Metropolitan Areas

Characteristics	1976	1989	1996
Median price of home purchased	$43,340	$129,800	$153,200
First-time buyers	37,670	105,200	130,100
Repeat buyers	50,090	144,700	170,700
Average monthly payment	$329	$1,054	$1,087
First-time buyers	313	969	995
Repeat buyers	342	1,118	1,162
Average monthly payment as % of after-tax income	24.0%	31.8%	32.6%
First-time buyers	23.0	34.1	34.9
Repeat buyers	24.9	30.0	30.7
Average age of first-time buyers	28.1	29.6	32.4
Average age of repeat buyers	35.9	39.4	41.1
Down payment as % of sales price			
Average down payment	25.2%	24.4%	19.5%
First-time buyers	18.0	15.8	12.4
Repeat buyers	30.8	30.3	25.3
Median household income	$20,840	$58,700	$63,800
First-time buyers	20,480	50,700	52,000
Repeat buyers	21,080	64,400	73,300

Highs and Lows for Major Metropolitan Housing Markets

Characteristics	Metropolitan market	High	Metropolitan market	Low
Median price of home purchased	San Francisco	$264,800	Memphis	$94,400
First-time buyers	San Francisco	232,200	Memphis	80,800
Repeat buyers	San Francisco	311,700	Memphis	105,000
Average monthly payment	San Francisco	$1,533	Orlando	$814
First-time buyers	San Francisco	1,390	Cleveland	708
Repeat buyers	San Francisco	1,738	Orlando	875
Average monthly payment as % of after-tax income	New York City	37.4%	Minneapolis-St. Paul	21.9%
First-time buyers	New York City	40.5	Minneapolis-St. Paul	29.3
Repeat buyers	Washington, DC	34.9	Phoenix	28.6
Down payment as % of sales price	New York City	27.3%	Washington, DC	16.2%
First-time buyers	New York City	19.1	Orlando	9.5
Repeat buyers	New York City	37.8	Washington, DC	19.3
Average time to save down payment (years)	New York City	5.0	Memphis	1.2
Median household income	Washington, DC	$80,300	Cleveland	$52,900
First-time buyers	San Francisco	74,200	Minneapolis-St. Paul	44,000
Repeat buyers	Washington, DC	89,900	Cleveland	57,700

Source: Chicago Title & Trust Co.

Racial Disparity in Mortgage Approvals

Applications for First Mortgage Loans to Purchase One-to-Four Family Homes

Year	Black applications*	Black approvals	Black denials	Black approval rate (%)	Black denial rate (%)
1990	150,157	100,073	50,080	66.65	33.35
1991	160,536	103,610	56,926	64.54	35.46
1992	176,366	116,158	60,207	65.86	34.14
1993	255,334	175,707	79,621	68.81	31.18
1994	353,238	242,968	110,177	68.78	31.19
1995	430,455	274,941	155,460	63.87	36.12

Year	White applications*	White approvals	White denials	White approval rate (%)	White denial rate (%)
1990	2,070,193	1,765,854	304,271	85.30	14.70
1991	2,262,199	1,842,185	420,008	81.43	18.57
1992	2,540,011	2,118,802	421,167	83.42	16.58
1993	3,212,076	2,714,197	497,808	84.50	15.50
1994	3,649,183	3,038,940	609,746	83.28	16.71
1995	3,783,986	3,016,140	767,499	79.71	20.28

*Approvals and denials may not add to total applications because in some cases applications are withdrawn or files are closed for incompleteness.

Source: Study by The Wall Street Journal of application registers filed by lenders with federal authorities as required by the Home Mortgage Disclosure Act

Biggest Builders

Professional Builder magazine's 1996 ranking of the largest home builders in the U.S., based on the companies' housing revenue.

Rank	Company/Headquarters	Housing revenue	Closings	Starts	Total revenues
1	Pulte Home Corp./Bloomfield Hills, MI	$2,326,462,000	14,673	*14,443	$2,326,462,000
2	Centex Corp./Dallas, TX	2,243,995,000	13,283	12,904	3,658,163,000
3	Kaufman and Broad Home Corp./ Los Angeles, CA	1,673,688,000	11,392	9,944	1,787,041,000
4	Champion Enterprises Inc./Auburn Hills, MI	1,640,000,000	–	**60,000	1,640,000,000
5	The Ryland Group/Columbia, MD	1,456,600,000	8,388	7,867	1,473,200,000
6	Fleetwood Enterprises Inc./Riverside, CA	1,454,018,000	–	**67,615	1,454,018,000
7	U.S. Home Corp./Houston, TX	1,178,938,000	7,099	7,573	1,191,924,000
8	NVR Inc./McLean, VA	1,045,900,000	5,695	*5,690	1,076,900,000
9	Del Webb Corp./Phoenix, AZ	1,011,829,000	5,531	5,800	1,050,733,000
10	Lennar Corp./Miami, FL	894,663,000	5,968	5,795	1,018,029,000
11	M.D.C. Holdings Inc./Denver, CO	880,358,000	4,974	4,882	922,595,000
12	Beazer Homes USA Inc./Atlanta, GA	868,137,000	5,929	5,888	869,481,000
13	Oakwood Homes Corp./Greensboro, NC	862,079,000	–	**25,351	973,922,000
14	A.G. Spanos Cos./Stockton, CA	800,000,000	7,400	10,799	946,500,000
15	Hovnanian Enterprises Inc./Red Bank, NJ	764,682,000	4,134	4,056	807,464,000

Rank	Company/Headquarters	Housing revenue	Closings	Starts	Total revenues
16	**Clayton Homes Inc.**/Knoxville, TN	762,396,000	–	31,049	928,741,000
17	**Toll Brothers Inc.**/Huntingdon Valley, PA	759,303,000	2,109	2,254	760,707,000
18	**Continental Homes Holding Corp.**/				
	Scottsdale, AZ	660,000,000	4,922	4,950	660,000,000
19	**Shea Homes**/Walnut, CA	595,805,000	2,673	2,708	686,723,000
20	**Weyerhaeuser Real Estate Co.**/				
	Federal Way, WA	582,015,000	3,007	3,007	795,513,000
21	**M/I Schottenstein Homes Inc.**/Columbus, OH	575,000,000	3,200	3,200	600,000,000
22	**D.R. Horton Inc.**/Arlington, TX	546,000,000	3,284	3,572	547,000,000
23	**Skyline Corp.**/Elkhart, IN	521,945,000	–	**18,791	637,462,000
24	**Lewis Homes Group of Cos.**/Upland, CA	479,164,870	2,819	2,929	567,947,234
25	**David Weekley Homes**/Houston, TX	473,224,604	2,408	2,549	474,242,827

*Net new orders.
**Factory built units.
Source: Professional Builder's Annual Report of Housing Giants

TOP REAL-ESTATE SELLERS

Real-estate brokerage firms with the largest dollar-volume of closed sales in (Ranking based on number of closed transactions in parantheses)

COMPANY	SALES VOLUME	HEADQUARTERS
Coldwell Banker Residential Brokerage (1)	$22,600,000,000	Mission Viejo, CA
Weichert, Realtors (2)	$11,800,000,000	Morris Plains, NJ
The Prudential Jon Douglas Co. (5)	$10,566,150,506	Los Angeles, CA
Long & Foster Real Estate, Inc. (3)	$7,252,603,000	Fairfax, VA
Burnet Financial Group (4)	$6,080,151,000	Edina, MN
Windermere Real Estate (8)	$5,134,989,000	Seattle, WA
Fred Sands Realtors (14)	$4,810,000,000	Los Angeles, CA
The Prudential Florida Realty (7)	$4,333,000,000	Clearwater, FL
Edina Realty, Inc. (6)	$4,057,630,468	Edina, MN
Cornish & Carey Residential, Inc. (37)	$3,331,000,000	San Mateo, CA
John L. Scott Real Estate (13)	$3,203,944,807	Bellevue, WA
DeWolfe New England (17)	$2,800,000,000	Lexington, MA
Realty Executives (9)	$2,757,617,253	Phoenix, AZ
Coldwell Banker Hunneman & Co. (26)	$2,747,578,353	Boston, MA
Realty One Inc. (10)	$2,582,258,639	Cleveland, OH
Century 21 Contempo Realty (42)	$2,483,432,217	Campbell, CA
O'Conor, Piper & Flynn (11)	$2,436,576,832	Timonium, MD
Gundaker Realtors Better Homes & Gardens (12)	$2,344,377,000	St. Louis, MO
Baird & Warner Inc. (27)	$2,200,000,000	Chicago, IL
The Prudential Carolinas Realty (15)	$2,160,668,717	Charlotte, NC
Coldwell Banker Premier Van Schaack Inc. (18)	$1,886,311,099	Salt Lake City, UT
Ebby Halliday, Realtors (21)	$1,885,090,373	Dallas, TX
Smythe, Cramer Co. (19)	$1,853,462,814	Seven Hills, OH
Crye-Leike Inc. (16)	$1,827,913,381	Memphis, TN
Henry S. Miller Co. Realtors (22)	$1,778,024,024	Dallas, TX

Source: REAL Trends, Dallas, TX

Modern Conveniences

Percent of U.S. Households with Appliances and Equipment in 1993

Central air conditioner	43.5%	Waterbed heater	12.3%	Range	99.4%
Clothes washer	77.1	Office equipment	24.2	Refrigerator	99.8
Clothes dryer	71.2	Fax machine	3.0	Microwave oven	84.1
Dishwasher	45.2	Laser printer	5.5	Outdoor grill	28.5
Freezer	34.5	Personal computer	23.3		
		Photocopier	1.6		

Usage of Home Appliances (Percent of U.S. households in 1993)

Loads of laundry washed each week
1 to 5 loads	37.8%
6 to 10 loads	25.8
11 to 15 loads	8.9
16 or more loads	4.5
No washing machine	22.9

Dishwasher use
Less than once a week	2.4
A few times a week	22.0
Several times a week	12.2
Every day	7.5
More than every day	1.1
No dishwasher	54.8

Number of hot meals cooked in the home
2 or more a day	35.9%
1 a day	44.3
A few per week	15.9
About 1 a week	2.1
Less than 1 a week	1.9

Amount of food cooked in microwave oven
Most or all	4.9
About half	13.6
Some or very little	23.0
Only for defrosting, reheating, or snacks	42.7
No microwave oven	15.9

Source: U.S. Energy Department, Energy Information Administration

Fixing Up

Because much of the U.S. housing stock was built before 1940, the remodeling industry is expected to remain strong. However, the rate of growth has slowed. The remodeling market is expected to grow just 4% to 5% per year through the rest of the 1990s.

Residential Remodeling (In billions of dollars)

Year	Total	Maintenance/repair	Improvements
1980	$ 46.3	$ 15.2	$ 31.2
1985	80.3	35.4	44.9
1990	106.8	51.3	55.5
1991	97.5	49.8	47.7
1992	103.7	45.2	58.6
1993	108.3	41.7	66.6
1994	115.0	42.9	72.1
1995	112.6	42.3	70.3
Projected			
1996	118.5	43.5	75.1
1997	125.3	45.3	80.0
2000	143.0	53.4	89.7

The Age of Homes in the U.S.

Year built	Total housing units Number built (In thousands)	%	Owner occupied Number built (In thousands)	%	Renter occupied Number built (In thousands)	%
Before 1920	10,252	10	5,178	8	3,808	11
1920–1949	20,953	20	10,808	18	7,631	23
1950–1969	29,703	28	18,337	30	8,428	25
1970–1979	23,474	22	13,290	22	7,528	22
1980–1989	17,094	16	9,917	16	5,224	16
1990–1994	5,134	5	3,720	6	855	3
Total	**106,610**	**100**	**61,250**	**100**	**33,474**	**100**
Median Age	**28 years**		**27 years**		**29 years**	

Sources: U.S. Census Bureau and National Association of Home Builders

Apartment Living

Average Monthly Apartment Rent*

Some of the most expensive apartment rents in the U.S. (New York City is not included in the survey.)

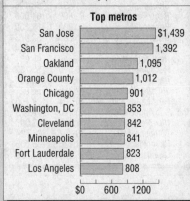

Top metros

San Jose	$1,439
San Francisco	1,392
Oakland	1,095
Orange County	1,012
Chicago	901
Washington, DC	853
Cleveland	842
Minneapolis	841
Fort Lauderdale	823
Los Angeles	808

*First quarter 1997.
Source: M/PF Research, Inc.

Apartment Residents

(Number of U.S. apartment households in millions)

1970	1975	1980	1985	1990	1995
8.5	9.9	10.8	12.9	14.2	14.5

Sources: U.S. Census Bureau and National Multi Housing Council

Apartment Resident Demographics

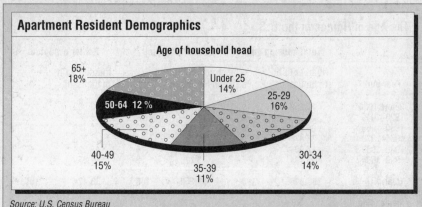

Age of household head

- 65+ 18%
- Under 25 14%
- 25-29 16%
- 50-64 12%
- 30-34 14%
- 40-49 15%
- 35-39 11%

Source: U.S. Census Bureau

20 Largest U.S. Multifamily Housing Owners as of Jan. 1, 1997

1997 rank	1996 rank	Company	Headquarters	1997 apts.	1996 apts.
1	1	Insignia Financial Group, Inc.	Greenville, SC	131,219	135,163
2	2	NHP Partners, Inc.	Washington, DC	127,972	127,428
3	3	Related Capital Company	New York, NY	120,384	109,988
4	4	Boston Capital Partners, Inc.	Boston, MA	81,642	74,569
5	5	Boston Financial	Boston, MA	71,500	66,000
6	8	Equity Residential Properties Trust	Chicago, IL	71,497	58,176
7	7	Lefrak Organization Inc.	Rego Park, NY	61,000	61,000
8	6	Winthrop Financial Associates	Boston, MA	60,900	61,100
9	11	National Partnership Investments Corp.	Beverly Hills, CA	56,899	52,973
10	20	United Dominion Realty Trust	Richmond, VA	55,559	34,224
11	14	Sentinel Real Estate Corp.	New York, NY	54,841	44,631
12	10	CRI, Inc.	Rockville, MD	49,599	53,753
13	13	Lincoln Property Company	Dallas, TX	44,792	46,090
14	9	Security Capital Pacific Trust	El Paso, TX	42,702	56,021
15	16	Edward Rose Building Enterprises	Farmington Hills, MI	40,704	39,706
16	25	Sunamerica Affordable Housing Partners, Inc.	Los Angeles, CA	40,120	26,023
17	16	Milstein Properties	New York, NY	37,000	37,000
18	17	Oxford Realty Financial Group, Inc.	Bethesda, MD	36,292	36,624
19	18	Cardinal Realty Services, Inc.	Reynoldsburg, OH	34,435	35,035
20	21	Forest City Residential Group	Cleveland, OH	33,063	31,829

20 Largest U.S. Multifamily Housing Managers as of Jan. 1, 1997

1997 rank	1996 rank	Company	Headquarters	1997 apts.	1996 apts.
1	1	Insignia Financial Group, Inc.	Greenville, SC	244,689	272,071
2	2	NHP Incorporated	Vienna, VA	133,044	133,667
3	3	Lincoln Property Company	Dallas, TX	107,989	92,070
4	5	Equity Residential Properties Trust	Chicago, IL	84,355	74,108
5	4	Pinnacle Realty Management Company	Seattle, WA	80,323	77,300
6	6	Trammell Crow Residential	Atlanta, GA	68,586	60,099
7	16	United Dominion Realty Trust	Richmond, VA	56,719	34,224
8	7	SCG Realty Services Incorporated	El Paso, TX	56,210	50,212
9	44	Lexford Properties	Irving, TX	55,191	21,418
10	8	Sentinel Real Estate Corporation	New York, NY	54,841	44,631
11	17	Conam Management Corporation	San Diego, CA	47,250	33,000
12	12	Apartment Investment and Management Company	Denver, CO	42,804	35,447
13	28	Sentry Management Inc.	Longwood, FL	42,010	27,274
14	9	Milstein Properties	New York, NY	42,000	42,000
15	14	Jupiter Western National	Irvine, CA	39,438	34,861
16	33	Ledic Management Group, Inc.	Memphis, TN	38,612	25,232
17	11	Edward Rose Building Enterprises	Farmington Hills, MI	38,521	37,544
18	20	Wentworth Group	Philadelphia, PA	35,437	31,400
19	15	Boston Financial	Boston, MA	34,000	34,333
20	10	R&B Realty Group	Los Angeles, CA	33,001	40,000

Source: National Multi Housing Council

Business and Economy Glossary

arbitrage The practice of simultaneously buying and selling a security in separate markets to take advantage of slight differences in price. Arbitrage is a high-volume undertaking: Because any discrepancy in price is usually razor-thin, a transaction must involve a great number of shares to generate significant profit. The term also refers to the activities of those who speculate in the stocks of companies thought to be takeover targets; they are said to engage in "risk arbitrage."

balance of payments A statistical record of economic transactions between one country and the rest of the world, which represents the flow of money into and out of the nation. No single figure represents an overall balance.

Current Account Balance: Also known as the current balance or balance of payments on current account, it is the most widely used figure. It is the net balance on trade in goods and services plus remittances (which are unilateral transfers such as Social Security payments to a recipient outside the country) and government grants to other countries. It doesn't include long-term loans.

Balance on Goods and Services: This is the difference between the value of imports of goods and services and exports.

Balance of Trade: Also known as the balance of merchandise trade, this is the difference between the value of imports of goods only and exports.

Bankruptcy Code The U.S. Bankruptcy Code is divided into chapters that provide different types of relief to debtors:

Chapter 7 governs liquidation, rather than reorganization. A debtor can voluntarily file for Chapter 7, or creditors can file an involuntary petition against a debtor to force the debtor into bankruptcy proceedings. A trustee, elected by the creditors, collects and liquidates all the debtor's property and examines creditors' claims against the property. If the debtor has not been guilty of any misconduct, the federal bankruptcy court will grant a discharge releasing the debtor from most or all pre-bankruptcy petition debts. Once the debtor obtains the discharge, a creditor is forbidden from taking any steps to collect the discharged debt.

Chapter 9 provides for municipal debt adjustments. To obtain relief under Chapter 9, the municipality must be insolvent or unable to meet its debts, and it ordinarily must show some prior efforts to negotiate a settlement with its various creditors. A municipality may not liquidate under Chapter 7; it must attempt to formulate a plan under Chapter 9 and then, only if the state involved allows, resort to federal bankruptcy law.

Chapter 11 relief is generally available to individuals, partnerships and corporations. It is not necessary that a company be insolvent to qualify for Chapter 11. The absence of an insolvency requirement has enabled debtors having problems other than an inability to meet current obligations—such as a massive potential liability—to seek relief under the bankruptcy code. Chapter 11 is the provision under which most corporate reorganizations occur. Ordinarily, the debtor will continue to operate its business as a "debtor in possession" after filing under Chapter 11. The filing automatically stays unilateral action by any creditor to enforce or secure a lien on the debtor's property. A secured creditor is given assurance under the code that the value of its collateral will be maintained and that at the end of the proceedings it will receive the value of its interest in the collateral. The proceeding culminates in a plan of reorganization that classifies the claims against the debtor and provides for satisfaction of those claims, as far as possible. A plan of reorganization must be approved by the court.

bond A certificate issued by a corporation or a government that states the amount of a loan, the interest to be paid, the time for repayment and the collateral pledged if payment cannot be made. In the case of a bond, repayment generally isn't due for a long period, generally seven years or more—as distinguished from a note, which has a shorter life span.

bond rating A rating is an assessment of the stability and strength of an issue. The rating is made by an independent agency such as Moody's Investors Service or Standard & Poor's Ratings Group. The agency, which is hired by the issuer, investigates the risk of default.

For a bond investor, a lower rating generally means greater risk and a higher yield, while a higher rating offers more security and usually a lower yield. An issuer with a sturdy reputation and higher bond rating can offer lower interest rates and still find customers for its debt. Ratings agencies periodically reevaluate their assessments, either issuing "upgrades" or "downgrades," or "affirming" a debt rating. An agency may also put a company's ratings under review.

book-to-bill ratio A measure of sales trends in a company or industry. For the North American semiconductor industry, for example, the monthly figure is used as the leading economic indicator. A figure above 1 indicates an expanding market, and a number below 1 is a contracting market. For example, a book-to-bill ratio of 1.03 means that for every $100 of products shipped, $103 in new orders was received.

book value The difference between a company's assets and its liabilities, usually expressed in per-share terms. It takes into account all money invested in the company since its founding, as well as retained earnings. Book value is also referred to as stockholders' equity and is calculated by subtracting liabilities from assets and dividing the result by the number of shares outstanding.

Bundesbank Germany's central bank. It controls monetary policy and money supply. Its U.S. counterpart is the Federal Reserve System.

capital gains tax A tax levied on the difference between the purchase price and the sale price of an asset—including real estate, stocks, bonds and other securities—when the asset is sold for a profit.

commercial paper The document that describes the details of a short-term corporate loan with a maturity typically between 30 and 90 days.

common stock An investment in common stock represents an ownership stake in a company. Dividends may be paid to common stock holders, and they may be increased or lowered as the company's earnings rise and fall. When preferred or preference classes of stock are also outstanding, the common stock holders are the last to receive dividends and the last to receive payments if the company is dissolved.

composite trading Composite trading figures, which appear in *The Wall Street Journal*'s stock tables and articles, take into account a stock's action on exchanges other than its primary one. For instance, a stock listed on the New York Stock Exchange may also be traded on regional stock exchanges, such as those in Boston or Cincinnati.

Comptroller of the Currency An office of the U.S. government that charters and overseas nationally chartered banks. It also has the power to declare an institution insolvent and to liquidate it. The comptroller is appointed by the President.

consumer confidence This closely watched statistic, generated by the Conference Board, a private research organization, measures consumers' feelings about the economy. It is based on their responses to questions about current and future business conditions, employment opportunities and family income.

consumer prices, Consumer Price Index (CPI) The CPI is a measure of change in prices of consumer goods, and therefore a main gauge of inflation. The figures, released monthly by the U.S. Labor Department, are based on a list of specific goods and services as purchased in urban areas. Components include food, housing, apparel, transportation, medical care and entertainment. The change in consumer prices is usually reported in terms of a percentage increase or decrease. The reason: The actual index is in the form of a number, but the figure by itself is abstract and makes sense only when compared with a previous period's CPI. Because it is an important indicator of the presence or absence of inflation, the CPI is often used as a benchmark for cost-of-living adjustments in retirement benefits and employment contracts.

currency depreciation, currency devaluation A nation's money depreciates when its value falls in relation to the currencies of other nations or in relation to its own prior value. A nation's money is devalued when its government deliberately reduces its value in relation to the currencies of other nations. When a country devalues its currency, the goods it imports become more expensive, while its exports become less costly abroad and thus more competitive.

deflation The opposite of inflation, deflation is an actual decline in prices.

derivatives Financial instruments with returns that move in response to some underlying asset or index. Futures contracts, for instance, "derive" their value from an underlying commodity such as gold or pork bellies. Other derivatives are based variously on bonds, currencies or intricate formulas that take into account changes in the prime rate or certain benchmark indexes.

discount rate The interest rate at which banks are able to borrow money from a central bank to loan to their customers. It is one of the key tools in a central bank's role as traffic cop for a nation's money supply; the higher the rate, the more expensive it becomes for businesses and individuals to borrow, and therefore spend money.

disinflation This slowing of price increases usually occurs during a recession when retailers are unable to pass higher prices along to consumers.

disposable personal income This is the income that a person retains after income taxes, Social Security deductions, property taxes and other payments to the various levels of government.

dividend The amount paid per share to holders of common stock. Payouts are generally made in quarterly installments. The dividend usually amounts to a portion of earnings. However, if a company shows no profit during a given period, it may be able to use earnings retained from profitable periods to pay its dividend on schedule.

Dow Jones Averages The Dow Jones Industrial, Transportation, Utilities and Composite Averages are widely used indicators of stock-market performance and sentiment. The industrial average is based on 30 major industrial issues listed on the New York Stock Exchange. The stocks are selected by

editors of *The Wall Street Journal*, and the average is found by adding the stocks' closing prices and dividing by an adjusted denominator. The average is price-weighted—that is, number of shares outstanding isn't taken into account, so higher-priced issues wield greater influence than lower-priced ones. It was first calculated in 1884 by Charles Dow, a founder of *The Wall Street Journal*.

The Dow Jones transportation, utilities and composite averages are calculated by the same method as the industrial average. The transportation average tracks 20 stocks, while the utilities average includes 15.

The Dow Jones Composite Average reflects the 65 stocks that together constitute the industrials, transportation and utilities averages.

The four averages are published daily in the *Journal*.

Dow Jones U.S. Index A broad indicator of movement in the stock market based on stocks in more than 120 industry groups in nine industry sectors: basic materials, consumer cyclical, consumer noncyclical, energy, financial, industrial, technology, utilities and independent (large companies with wide-ranging interests). Altogether, the stocks in the index represent about 80% of U.S. market capitalization. The index includes more than 700 issues that trade on the New York Stock Exchange, the American Stock Exchange and the Nasdaq Stock Market. The index is market-capitalization weighted—that is, both the stock price and number of shares outstanding enter into the computation. The effect is that a given stock's influence on the index is proportionate to its value in the market. The index's base date is June 30, 1982, which is equal to 100.

Dow Jones Global Indexes A broad indicator of more than 3,000 companies worldwide, representing more than 80% of the equity capital on 31 stock markets around the globe. The indexes are market-capitalization weighted—that is, both the stock price and number of shares outstanding enter into the computation. This means a particular stock's effect on the indexes is proportionate to its value in the marketplace. The indexes are structured to make adjustments for mergers, acquisitions, spinoffs, corporate restructurings, noncash distributions and other out-of-the-ordinary events. Companies are selected to represent about 80% of a country's market capitalization. The Dow Jones U.S. Index is the U.S. component of the Global Indexes, which are broken down by country and region, as well as by nine broad economic sectors and more than 120 industry groups. The base date is Dec. 31, 1991, which is equal to 100.

Export-Import Bank of the U.S. The Ex-Im Bank assists in the financing, insuring and guaranteeing of certain aspects of the import-export business, its general goal being to encourage international trade with the U.S. The bank itself, which is independent of the government but was federally chartered in 1934, finances its workings by borrowing from the U.S. Treasury.

federal-funds rate The interest rate charged for the overnight loans banks make to one another. It is named for federal funds—the money banks are required by the Federal Reserve to keep on hand to back up deposits. A bank that has more federal funds than necessary may lend the excess to a bank that needs it to meet requirements. The Fed sets a recommended federal-funds rate, but the rate itself is negotiated daily by the parties to a particular loan. That's why it is regarded as an important gauge of interest-rate trends.

Federal Home Loan Bank System This network of regional Federal Home Loan Banks provides loans to savings banks, savings and loans and other institutions that are important providers of mortgage loans. The FHLB's role is much like the Federal Reserve's among larger, commercial banks.

Federal Home Loan Mortgage Corp. Known as Freddie Mac, it helps to provide banks and other lenders with money for home loans by buying from them the mortgages they issue. It pools the mortgages, then sells securities backed by the interest and principal payments produced by those mortgage pools. Freddie Mac was chartered by the U.S. government but is now publicly owned; its shares trade on the New York Stock Exchange.

Federal National Mortgage Association Known as Fannie Mae, it buys mortgages from banks and lenders and repackages them as investment securities. Its purpose is to improve liquidity in the secondary market for such mortgages. Fannie Mae was chartered by the U.S. government but is now publicly owned; its shares trade on the New York Stock Exchange.

Federal Open Market Committee The policy-making arm of the Federal Reserve Board, this committee sets monetary policy geared to achieving the larger objectives of the Fed as regulator of money supply and credit. The FOMC's chief tool is the purchase and sale of government securities to increase or decrease the money supply, respectively. It also sets key interest rates, such as the discount rate and the federal-funds rate. The FOMC, which meets monthly, is made up of Federal Reserve governors and the presidents of several Federal Reserve Banks.

Federal Reserve System/Bank/Board The Federal Reserve System is the nation's central bank. It is responsible for regulating banking and credit in the U.S. economy. It was formed in 1913 by an act of Congress in the wake of a financial scare and a severe run on banks. The Fed controls the money supply, holds the federal government's savings accounts and acts as examiner for national-chartered and state-chartered banks. (Other institutions, such as savings banks and savings and loans, are regulated by the Federal Home Loan Bank System.)

The Federal Reserve System includes the 12 regional Federal Reserve Banks, and its policies are established by the Federal Reserve Board. That panel's seven members are appointed by the President to 14-year, staggered terms.

Financial Accounting Standards Board Chief rule-making body for U.S. accountants.

futures contract A futures contract is an agreement to buy or sell an asset—such as pork bellies or U.S. Treasury bonds—at a set time in the future at an agreed-upon price. Futures contracts may also be based on other types of financial instruments or on certain stock-market indexes.

Activity in the futures market is an important measure of market sentiment because it indicates the direction investors believe prices of real commodities, financial instruments and other assets are headed.

Government National Mortgage Association Known as Ginnie Mae, it is a middleman in residential mortgages, particularly those for low-income housing. It is owned by the Department of Housing and Urban Development and has a two-part role: It helps to provide lenders with money for home loans by buying mortgages they issue, and it guarantees interest and principal payments on certain mortgage-backed securities.

gross domestic product The total value of goods and services produced by a nation. In the U.S., the GDP is calculated by the Commerce Department, and it is the main measure of U.S. economic output.

hedge An investment strategy designed to limit the risk of loss. It can be as simple as putting money in a bank account instead of a mattress; by earning interest, the investor hedges against losses of purchasing power due to inflation. More complex strategies take the form of a series of investments set up so that one balances another. For example, an investor might buy some stock while simultaneously investing in a "put option" for the same stock. (The option grants its holder the right but not the obligation to sell shares at a specified price by a certain date.) As a result, the investor makes money if his shares rise in value. However, the option can be exercised to limit losses if the share price falls. Hedging is also a driving force behind the commodities futures market.

hedge fund A little-regulated, private investment partnership that invests huge sums in global currency, bond and stock markets in search of profit. To avoid regulation as a mutual fund in the U.S., such funds must have 99 or fewer U.S. investors. Therefore, they are private investment clubs for the well-to-do—although some hedge funds trade publicly abroad. Hedge funds typically require minimum investments that start in the hundreds of thousands of dollars. Despite the name, many hedge funds don't necessarily hedge. Indeed, the spectacular returns for which they are known and mighty tumbles often result from mammoth, leveraged one-way bets in the market. They got the name because the funds often are pitched as producing high returns and—courtesy of sophisticated strategies that are rarely revealed—little risk of loss.

historical cost A valuation method for direct investment that values assets and liabilities at their book value.

housing starts An estimate of the number of houses on which construction began in a certain period, such as a month or a year. It is one of the leading gauges of the health and direction of the U.S. economy and the level of consumer confidence. The figure also indicates the pace of future sales of lumber and materials, and of big-ticket consumer items such as furnishings and appliances.

inflation A rise in prices. Inflation may be caused by an increase in the money supply; when there are more dollars available to spend, each dollar buys less. It may also be caused by rising manufacturing costs, a decrease in supply of goods or a combination of factors.

initial public offering (IPO) The first offering of stock that a company makes to the public.

International Monetary Fund The IMF makes loans and provides other services intended to stabilize world currencies and foster orderly and balanced trade. Its pool of money is funded and supported by subscriptions of member nations, and IMF aid typically comes with conditions that a recipient country take certain steps to stabilize its economy by reducing inflation or its trade deficit.

junk bonds Debt issues that are considered risky investments. To attract investors, they typically offer higher yields than bonds with investment-grade ratings. If a junk bond carries a rating at all, it is set below triple-B by Standard & Poor's Ratings Group and below Baa by Moody's Investors Service Inc.

leading economic indicators A composite index of important economic measures used to forecast likely changes in the economy as a whole. Some of the factors taken into consideration: length of work week, unemployment claims, orders for consumer goods, building permits, plant and equipment orders, stock prices, money supply and consumer expectations. The monthly index is compiled by the Conference Board.

leveraged buyout The purchase of a company that is financed largely by borrowed money. Ultimately, the debt is paid with funds generated by the acquired company's operations or by the sale of its assets.

limited partnership A type of partnership in which general partners are responsible for the running of the firm, while limited partners have no say in its operation. However, general partners carry the burden of full liability. The limited partners' liability is no greater than the capital they contributed to the venture.

loss In corporate reports, the excess of expenses over revenue during a company's fiscal period.

money-supply measures There are three basic categories for measuring the supply of money in the U.S. economy.

The basic money-supply gauge is M1. It consists of funds that are readily available for spending, including cash and checking accounts. (M1 is sometimes broken down into M1-A and M1-B. M1-A is the total private checking-account deposits at commercial banks plus cash in public hands. M1-B is cash plus checking-type deposits at all financial institutions, including credit unions and savings-and-loan associations.)

M2 consists of cash and private deposits, such as CDs, but not large ones that tie up funds for a length of time. It also includes certain short-term assets, such as the amounts held in money-market mutual funds.

M3 includes cash and all private deposits, as well as other financial instruments, such as large-denomination time deposits.

most-favored nation A status bestowed by the U.S. on trading partners with which it has a good relationship. Most-favored nation standing gives a country the same privileges and tariff levels that the U.S. grants to the vast majority of its trading partners. Considering this, the term is somewhat misleading. Rather than being a special, select status, MFN is actually the term for a normal trading relationship between countries.

mutual fund A fund run by an investment company that provides a way for small investors to pool their money so that together they can afford to hire a professional money manager. Though a fund is owned by its shareholders, it is usually established, managed and distributed by the fund's invest-

ment adviser and its affiliated companies. Among the many types of mutual funds are these:

Balanced Fund: This fund invests in a combination of stocks and bonds, with a typical combination being 60% stocks and 40% bonds.

Closed-End Fund: Mutual fund that sells a limited number of shares, after which the fund is closed to investors and the shares are listed on a stock exchange. After that, the only way new investors can get in is to buy some of the exchange-traded shares.

Index Fund: A fund that tries to mimic the performance of a stock-market or bond-market index by buying all or many of the securities that make up the index. However, because of fund-management fees, its returns never quite match those of the index. But fees for index funds are typically much lower than for "actively managed" funds.

Money-Market Fund: A type of mutual fund that invests in stable, short-term securities. Money funds are designed to be easily converted into cash, and are structured to maintain an unchanging value of $1 a share. The yield fluctuates.

Nasdaq Stock Market A system set up for the trading of so-called over-the-counter stocks, those not listed on major exchanges. Unlike the New York Stock Exchange and other major markets, there is no Nasdaq trading floor. All trading takes place on a computer network. "Nasdaq" began as an acronym for National Association of Securities Dealers Automated Quotations, but now doesn't stand for anything but itself, Nasdaq insists. The system is operated by the National Association of Securities Dealers.

National Association of Securities Dealers A membership organization for securities brokers and underwriters in the U.S. that promise to abide by association rules. It sets guidelines for ethics and standardized industry practices, and has a disciplinary structure for looking into allegations of rules violations. The NASD also operates the Nasdaq Stock Market.

net asset value For a mutual fund, the NAV is the value of all investments held by the fund, usually expressed in per-share terms. The NAV is calculated daily at the close of markets in a process called "marking to market," or the valuing of all a fund's investments at current market prices.

net income, profit, earnings The amount left after a company pays taxes and all other expenses. A portion may be committed to pay preferred dividends. Some of what remains may, at the company's discretion, be paid in dividends to holders of common stock. The rest may be invested to obtain interest revenue or spent to acquire new buildings or equipment to increase the company's ability to make a future profit.

North American Free Trade Agreement, NAFTA Nafta phases out tariffs among the U.S., Canada and Mexico over 15 years and greatly eases investment across borders. Passed by Congress in late 1993, it took effect Jan. 1, 1994.

note A certificate issued by a corporation or a government that states the amount of a loan, the interest to be paid, the time for repayment and the collateral pledged if payment cannot be made. The repayment date is generally more than a year after issue but not more than seven or eight years later. This is the primary distinction between a note and a bond, which has a longer life span.

operating profit/loss Net income excluding income derived from sources other than the company's regular activities. It is calculated before income deductions, including taxes. Also called net operating income/loss.

option This agreement allows an investor to buy or sell something—such as shares of stock—within a specified period and at a set price. Options can be bought and sold as investments, but they are also important to some companies' executive-compensation plans.

Purchasers of options speak in terms of "calls" and "puts"—which are options to buy and sell, respectively. They may be purchased either to hedge against stock-market risks or to speculate in the market. Because calls can rise more sharply than an underlying stock's price, some investors expecting a stock to jump will use them to maximize returns. Similarly, puts often appreciate quickly as a stock falls. Options may also be based on the value of certain stock indexes, and on futures contracts.

As for executive compensation: By paying executives in stock options, a company can argue it is giving its management an incentive to boost corporate performance. If the stock price rises, executives get to cash in. Their options let them purchase shares at a lower-than-market price, which they can turn around and sell for a gain.

Organization for Economic Cooperation and Development Founded in 1961 to replace the Organization for European Economic Cooperation, which was set up in connection with the Marshall Plan, the OECD is a forum for its members to discuss and attempt to coordinate economic policies. The 29 members of the Paris-based group include Australia, Austria, Belgium, Canada, Czech Republic, Denmark, Finland, France, Germany, Greece, Hungary, Iceland, Ireland, Italy, Japan, Luxembourg, Mexico, Netherlands, New Zealand, Norway, Poland, Portugal, South Korea, Spain, Sweden, Switzerland, Turkey, the United Kingdom and the U.S.

Organization of Petroleum Exporting Countries Established in 1960 to link countries whose main source of export earnings is petroleum, it is based in Vienna. The 11 members of OPEC: Algeria, Indonesia, Iran, Iraq, Kuwait, Libya, Nigeria, Qatar, Saudi Arabia, United Arab Emirates and Venezuela.

prime rate The interest rate banks use as a base for a wide range of loans to businesses and to individuals. Changes in the prime typically don't have an immediate effect on consumer rates, such as mortgages and personal loans.

producer prices, producer price index The producer price index is a measure of change in prices paid by producers of goods. Actually there are three producer price indexes. The main one is the index for finished goods. As its name implies, it tracks prices of goods that are ready for sale to consumers. The other two are for intermediate materials and for crude materials. The indexes are based on specific "baskets" of goods as purchased by producers.

The three indexes are considered guides to future inflation because they chart the production costs of goods that will reach the consumer market a few months later.

proxy fight A battle for control of a company in which several groups seek proxies from the company's shareholders. (A proxy is an authorization for someone else to vote on behalf of a shareholder.) The winner is the one who collects enough proxies to guarantee it can vote the majority of shares outstanding in its own favor.

purchasing power parity A calculation method for other countries' gross domestic product that involves the use of international dollar price weights, which are applied to the quantities of goods and services produced in a given economy. This is an alternative to using conversions at official currency exchange rates and is considered a better way to compare the economic well-being of countries.

recession A downturn in economic activity, it is defined broadly by many economists as at least two consecutive quarters of decline in a nation's gross domestic product.

recovery In a business cycle, it is the period after a downturn or recession when economic activity picks up and the gross domestic product grows. It leads into the expansion phase of the business cycle.

revenue The amount of money a company took in during a fiscal period. The figure includes interest earned and receipts from services provided, sales, rents and royalties.

revenue passenger mile A calculation used by airlines to measure traffic. It is one paying passenger carried one mile.

revolving credit line A line of credit that may be used repeatedly up to a specific total, with periodic full or partial repayment.

sales In a corporate report, the money a company received in a fiscal period for goods and services sold.

Securities and Exchange Commission The SEC enforces securities laws and sets standards for disclosure about publicly traded securities, including mutual funds. It was created in 1934 and is made up of five commissioners, who are appointed by the President to staggered terms.

short sale, cover A short sale is a bet that the price of a stock will fall. A short seller bor-

rows stock he thinks is overvalued, then sells it, hoping that before long other investors will see what he has seen and sell their shares, driving down the price. The short seller will then "short cover," or buy back shares to replace the borrowed ones, and pocket the difference between the higher selling price and the lower repurchase price.

Standard & Poor's 500 index The S&P 500 is made up of large-capitalization stocks and leading companies within major industries in the U.S. economy. The index is market-value weighted. That is, a stock price is multiplied by number of shares outstanding so that an issue's weight in the index is proportionate to its market value. The main criteria for a stock's inclusion in the index are market value and industry-group representation, along with liquidity, operating condition and proportion of closely held ownership. The S&P 500 includes issues traded in the three major U.S. markets, the New York Stock Exchange, the American Stock Exchange and Nasdaq Stock Market

Student Loan Marketing Association Known as Sallie Mae, it is a middleman in student loans. It helps to provide money for such loans by buying them from lenders. It then repackages the loans and sells them on a secondary market, and provides related services to financial and educational institutions. Sallie Mae was chartered by the U.S. government, but now its shares are traded on the New York Stock Exchange.

tariff A tax levied on imported goods that makes them more expensive and less appealing to consumers. Tariffs are sometimes imposed on imports that are hurting a domestic industry's sales.

tender offer An offer to acquire stock of a company for cash, stock of another company, bonds, other types of securities or a combination of these. A tender offer can be used to obtain control of a company.

Treasury bill/note/bond A Treasury bill is a certificate representing a short-term loan to the federal government that matures in three, six or 12 months. A Treasury note matures in two to 10 years. A Treasury bond matures in more than 10 years. Among bonds, the 30-year issue is considered a key indicator of trends in long-term interest rates, so its performance is regularly cited.

The yield on Treasury issues fluctuates—if their prices rise, yields fall. It works this way: A given bond pays a set interest rate and carries a set face value. But once it begins to trade, its price is set by market conditions. If the market expects interest rates to rise, the bond's price will fall because the rate it pays is less desirable.

underwriter An underwriter is a company that—for a fee—brings an issue of stocks, bonds or other securities to market. The underwriter buys all or most of the issue, then resells it to individual investors or other buyers. It makes money by purchasing the securities at one price and reselling them at a higher price (a difference known as the "underwriting spread.") Issuers turn to underwriters to minimize the risk of taking a security to market and to benefit from an underwriter's sales and marketing staff. Underwriting is an important source of income for investment banks and securities firms.

unemployment rate The unemployment rate is the percentage of people in the work force who aren't working and are looking for jobs. The numbers are compiled monthly by the Labor Department.

World Bank An organization created to make loans primarily in developing countries, with the stipulation that the country's government must guarantee the loan. The full name is International Bank for Reconstruction and Development.

6

TECHNOLOGY & SCIENCE

I

T'S BEEN 20 YEARS *since the mass-market personal computer caught fire, and in that brief time it has surely become one of the most influential inventions in modern history, putting tremendous power into the hands of hundreds of millions of ordinary people. But, as the PC enters its third decade, its primacy in the digital world is being challenged by whole new categories of fledgling digital devices, aimed at simplifying and spreading the power of computing even more than the PC has been able to do.*

Until the Apple II took off in 1977, along with a few lesser-known competitors, the notion that a computer could be a personal device was considered ludicrous. A computer was something so huge it occupied whole rooms, and so complex and fragile it required the ministrations of teams of scientists and technicians.

Not only that, but computers were used to do only big, serious jobs for big, serious institutions—like compiling the Census, or keeping vital business records or calculating missile trajectories. Movies and television shows often employed mockups of huge computer rooms, with blinking lights and spinning tape drives the size of refrigerators, to stage scenes where good guys were trying to crack hellish scientific problems, or bad guys were harnessing technology to take over the world. The computer had both great power and great mystery.

Now, millions of 14-year-old kids routinely master personal computers vastly more powerful than those early behemoths, and command them to do things far more varied and audacious than anything attempted by all the squadrons of white-coated computer technicians in the 1950s and 1960s. As many as 200 million PCs are out there, in businesses, homes and schools, and they have become an integral part of life in the developed world. The personal computer is not only the main means for producing documents, but an important entertainment and education device, and the vital component in the world's emerging new digital communication and information system, the Internet.

This very proliferation has been

part of the PC's secret of success. From the start, it was cheap enough and easy enough to use to be adopted not merely by big organizations, but by individuals, families and very small businesses. As a result, millions took to tinkering with the machines, writing software, designing hardware add-ons and launching small businesses to promote these products. Apple Computer Inc., which launched the revolution, promised to make computers "for the rest of us." And Microsoft Corp., whose software propelled the PC wave, called for "a PC on every desktop and in every home."

But, in recent years, it's become clear that the general-purpose PC, whether based on Microsoft's software or Apple's design, won't come close anytime soon to universal adoption in homes. In the United States, about 40% of homes own a personal computer, a figure that has barely budged for several years, after surging in the early 1990s. While retail PC sales continue to post healthy annual growth rates, most of the new computers are being sold to people who already own one. In other developed countries, home penetration is even lower—surprisingly low in some very rich countries, such as France. And in most of the world, the PC has barely arrived.

In mid-1997, Microsoft finally admitted that, despite its corporate goal, the U.S. home penetration number wasn't likely to increase dramatically over the next few years. The figure is likely to climb a little, because PC makers are slashing prices to entice new buyers, establishing a new entry-level price point of around $1,000 for a basic machine. But price cuts alone aren't likely to drive the PC to the 90%-plus penetration levels of the TV and telephone, a status many once assumed it would inexorably achieve. For many people, the PC is just too much trouble. It is still too complex to master easily and it fails so often, to one degree or another, that it's the least reliable machine in the home.

This stagnation of home PC penetration is especially worrisome for the future of the Internet, including both the content-rich World Wide Web and electronic mail. Despite frequent predictions that Internet use will sweep the world, its proliferation is largely dependent on PC penetration, because one needs a PC to use the Internet. Only about half the households which own PCs are connected to the Internet, even intermittently.

So a new generation of home computers is on the drawing boards, and is gingerly entering the marketplace. Unlike the PC, which promises to run just about any kind of software and drive just about any peripheral device (even if such promises are often broken), these are specialized digital devices, purposely limited to only a few core tasks. The idea is that, by narrowly targeting their functions they can be made surprisingly good at doing those tasks, for very little money. Also, they needn't carry the burden of operating systems and user interfaces designed to support a multitude of features. That means they can be made simpler to use. And they stand a good chance of working all the time, like a TV set and not like a PC.

These home devices, called info appliances, are different from another challenger to the PC, the Network Computer. The latter, mainly applicable in large corporations, is a terminal on a fast local network, which draws its software and data from a central computer. The concept of the NC is based on the notion that an average worker linked to a company network doesn't need the power and complexity of a PC at his or her desk. It's a throwback to the old, pre-PC idea of a huge computer driving dumb terminals and is being pushed by companies that make servers, the central computers that control networks.

By contrast, info appliances for the home must be tuned to work without the aid of a fast, constantly available network and an army of computer technicians. They must store much of their software and data locally, because homes are typically connected to a network—the Internet—only occasionally, and at slow speeds.

The first of these new info appliances are small, cheap devices that make the World Wide Web and e-mail available via a TV set. A small

startup firm called WebTV—begun by three ex-Apple engineers—developed such a system in 1995, and it was brought to market starting in 1996 by two consumer electronics giants, Sony and Phillips, for about $300.

WebTV is a slim, sleek black box, resembling a small videotape recorder, that sits atop the set and is run via a remote control and wireless keyboard. It connects to the Internet via a phone line and modem, but uses a bright, simple interface that is far easier for novices to master than a PC.

Though the first version of WebTV had only modest sales, Microsoft bought the company in 1997 for $425 million, and planned to use it as the basis for a massive drive to reach the majority of households that have shunned the PC. Other companies are racing to market similar devices, either in the form of set-top boxes or circuitry built into high-end TV sets. The next generation will not only receive the Internet, but will also add some degree of interactivity to regular TV programming and be able to use fast cable modems and other higher-speed forms of data transmission.

Another type of info appliance is a mini-laptop computer that weighs only about half as much as the lightest regular laptops and costs well under $1,000. These machines will use a stripped-down, simplified version of Microsoft's Windows operating system, and will only do a handful of tasks—word processing, spreadsheets, e-mail, Web browsing, and calendar and address-book listings. They will be able to swap and synchronize data with PCs, but can also be used alone.

A third category of info appliances is the e-mail telephone. This is a $500 phone with a laptop-type screen and a pull-out keyboard that combines standard phone functions with both voice-mail and e-mail.

It's too soon to know if these initial info appliances will take off. It may require several years before the high-tech industry finds just the right combination of design, function and price to entice the public to buy the new computers. But the search is on to replace, or at least augment, the PC in the home, and to make the Internet available on simpler, cheaper hardware.

Walt Mossberg,
The Wall Street Journal's
Personal Technology Columnist

The Technology Culture

A Gadget Generation
Share of U.S. households with the following:

Television	98%
Radio	98
Cordless phone	66
Telephone answering device	65
Stereo component system	54
Home CD player	49
Personal computer	40
Computer printer	38
Cellular phone	34
Pager	28
Electric car alarm	27
Camcorder	26
Computer with CD-ROM	21
Modem or fax/modem	19
Caller-ID equipment	18
Direct-view satellite dish	10
Fax machine	9

Note: Figures are for January 1997
Source: Consumer Electronics Manufacturers Assn.

The Speed of Change
How many years it took each of these technologies to spread to 25% of the U.S. population*

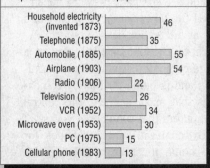

Household electricity (invented 1873)	46
Telephone (1875)	35
Automobile (1885)	55
Airplane (1903)	54
Radio (1906)	22
Television (1925)	26
VCR (1952)	34
Microwave oven (1953)	30
PC (1975)	15
Cellular phone (1983)	13

*Defined as 25% of households, except for airplane, automobile and cell phone. Airplane: 25% of the 1996 level of air miles traveled per capita. Automobile: The number of motor vehicles reached 25% of the number of people age 16 and older. Cellular phone: The number of cellular phones reached 25% of the number of registered passenger automobiles.
Source: Dallas Federal Reserve Bank

SHAKEOUT IN CYBERSPACE

With more than 50 million people online, 1997 can be called the year that the Internet grew up.

It can also be called the year of the great shakeout: Gone is the excuse "It'll work, as soon as enough people come on-line." Now, companies are ready for their big investments in the World Wide Web to pay off. Some Web sites, like Wired Ventures Inc.'s Hotwired, are revamping, streamlining, and refocusing. Others, like Politics Now and on-line magazines *Spiv* and *Out*, shut down all together.

Consolidation has also increased, particularly among the Internet service providers. Going into 1997, flat-rate pricing for on-line services became king, as giant America Online Inc. offered unlimited access for $19.95. AOL, with more than nine million subscribers, led the rest of the pack; smaller Internet service providers were left out in the cold, leaving the market to the big players. One of the more visible signs of the consolidation: WorldCom Inc. agreed to buy CompuServe from H&R Block and to transfer CompuServe's 2.6 million subscribers to AOL.

Those Web players who stuck it out took marketing and advertising to a new extreme on the Internet. Once, Net denizens scorned even banner ads; in 1997, boxy banner ads started being ignored and drawing fewer click-through rates. The result: More intrusive—and more obnoxious—forms of advertising were tested on the Web. One of the most invasive forms is the robot program that hangs out in chat rooms, listening for key words like "messy house." The right phrase might lead the robot to join in the conversa-

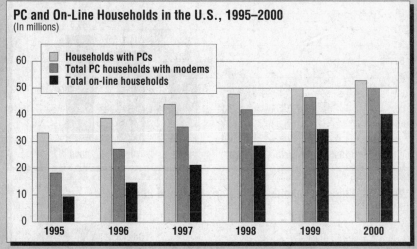

Going On-Line

The projected number of U.S. households with personal computers, modems and on-line services.

PC and On-Line Households in the U.S., 1995–2000
(In millions)

Legend:
- Households with PCs
- Total PC households with modems
- Total on-line households

	1995	1996	1997	1998	1999	2000
Households in the U.S.	97.7	98.9	100.0	101.0	102.1	103.2
Households with PCs	33.2	38.7	44.0	47.8	50.2	52.8
Households with PCs and modems	18.3	27.2	35.5	42.1	46.5	50.2
On-line households	9.4	15.2	21.8	28.7	34.9	40.8

Source: Jupiter Communications

tion and throw in a sales pitch for, say, the Black & Decker Dustbuster. Other Web sites, like the Riddler.com game site, grew bold enough to force visitors to download entire full-screen ads before getting to the content, a time-consuming ordeal. And, in the ultimate sign of desperation, some Web marketers even will pay viewers to look at their ads. One such company, CyberGold, offered viewers the prospect of either cold, hard cash or frequent-flier miles in exchange for looking at ads.

Some Web sites had no problem turning a profit: those that require an XXX rating. Cyberporn is the envy of the Internet; adult sites can take in millions of dollars a month. In cyberspace, things operate just as they do in the real world: Sex sells. And, as an added advantage, the Internet lets viewers download racy pictures in the privacy of their own homes. Beyond that, sex sites on the Web have taken up savvy targeted marketing techniques and advanced technology tactics that mainstream sites would do well to imitate.

As the Internet moves from its educational, nonprofit roots into a commercial entity, growing pains are inevitable. One problem that arose in 1997 was the dispute over domain names—Internet addresses like wsj.com that help readers locate Web pages. One company, Network Solutions Inc., has been responsible for doling out all names that end in ".com," the most popular Internet suffix. The company has raised more than $40

The World On-Line Market

The estimated number of on-line households around the world and the changing regional breakdown.

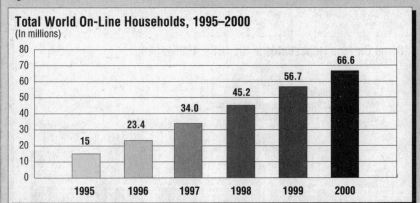

Total World On-Line Households, 1995–2000
(In millions)

1995	1996	1997	1998	1999	2000
15	23.4	34.0	45.2	56.7	66.6

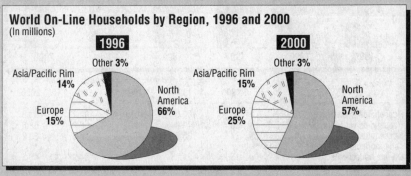

World On-Line Households by Region, 1996 and 2000
(In millions)

1996
- Other 3%
- Asia/Pacific Rim 14%
- Europe 15%
- North America 66%

2000
- Other 3%
- Asia/Pacific Rim 15%
- Europe 25%
- North America 57%

Source: Jupiter Communications

Cyberspace Demographics

Demographic Characteristics of On-Line Users, or "Cybercitizens"

Gender		Income	
Male	60%	Under $50,000	48%
Female	40	$50,000 or more	52
Age		**Number in household**	
16-29	31	2 or fewer	33
30-49	52	3 or more	67
50 +	17		
Education		**Employment**	
High school or less	31	Employed	76
Beyond high school	69	Not employed	24
Marital status		**Race**	
Married	52	White	76
Not married	48	Non-white	24

Source: Yankelovich Partners Inc.

million since 1995 by charging $50 a year to register and maintain an address. But Network Solutions' contract with the National Science Foundation expires in March 1998, and the NSF has said it won't issue a new contract; it is leaving the problem up to the Internet community to figure out.

Several competing plans have emerged, but none has unilateral support. The problem focuses the spotlight on an even bigger problem: There's no central authority in charge of the Internet. The Internet—a series of computer networks linked together—has always been run by consensus; without that consensus, the fragile network could fray. Now, every area of the U.S. government—from the White House to Congress, from the Commerce Department to the Justice Department—is trying to determine its role in governing the Internet.

Rebecca Quick

On-Line Advertising

Jupiter Communications, a New York research firm, estimates that advertisers spent $300 million on-line in the U.S. in 1996, $260 million of which went to Web sites and the rest to non-Web publishers such as America Online and PointCast. That represents more than a fivefold increase over 1995 spending, but is still just a tiny fraction of marketers' budgets. What's more, most of the largest on-line advertisers are major web publishers themselves.

Top On-Line Advertisers in 1996

1996 rank	Advertiser	Spending (in millions)
1	Microsoft	$13.0
2	AT&T	7.3
3	Excite	6.9
4	IBM	5.9
5	Netscape Communications	5.7
6	Infoseek	5.1
7	NYNEX	4.0
8	Yahoo!	3.9
9	Lycos	3.9
10	CNET	2.7

Web Publishers with the Greatest 1996 Advertising Revenue

1996 rank	Publisher	Ad Revenue (in millions)
1	Netscape	$27.7
2	Yahoo!	20.6
3	Infoseek	18.1
4	Lycos	12.8
5	Excite	12.2
6	CNET	11.4
7	ZD Net	10.2
8	WebCrawler	7.3
9	ESPNET Sports Zone	6.5
10	Pathfinder	5.8

Source: Jupiter Communications

POWER PLAYERS IN THE PC MARKET

The big keep getting bigger in the booming U.S. personal-computer market.

The two biggest PC-research firms, International Data Corp. and Dataquest Inc., reported that U.S. unit sales grew 19% and 21.9% in the second quarter of 1997, respectively, and that worldwide unit sales rose 15% and 17%, respectively. In addition, both research firms said the top four PC suppliers—Compaq Computer Corp., International Business Machines Corp., Hewlett-Packard Co. and Dell Computer Corp.—control nearly 38% of the computer market, up from 34% a year earlier.

The biggest PC suppliers continued to see sales gains that outstripped those of the overall market. Unit sales at Dell, for example, grew 52%, according to IDC, and 61.4%, according to Dataquest; both outfits reported a 42% surge for Compaq. H-P also saw a big gain, leaping to the No. 3 spot from No. 6, on sales increases of between 48% and 58%.

Analysts said the leading PC makers used the economies of scale gained from their size to take market share away from such second-tier players as AST Research Inc. and Digital Equipment Corp., as well as from third-tier direct-sales companies. The trend appears even more pronounced in the business market, where the top four companies now control almost half the market, IDC said.

Analysts said the consolidation is very likely to accelerate, portending a major shift of strategic power in high technology. One result could be that the top PC makers will gain leverage with the industry's two key suppliers, Intel Corp. and Microsoft Corp., on such issues as technology direction and pricing.

Both surveys showed that Apple Computer Inc. continued to wither, dropping to No. 9 on IDC's list from No. 4 a year ago, on a 21% decline in unit sales.

The booming economy in the U.S. made it the healthiest computer market, much more robust than Japan and Europe. Indeed, IDC and Dataquest said the U.S. market was strong in both businesses and homes.

The overall figures showed the PC industry's worldwide sales growth rate in the second quarter either holding steady or advancing slightly from earlier quarters. Dataquest's estimated 17% growth rate represents an increase from the 16% it reported for each of the previous two quarters, while IDC's 15% is identical to its figure for the first quarter. While neither firm's numbers are anywhere near the 25% growth rates seen in 1995, they at least indicate that the PC market hasn't cooled as much as technology bears had feared.

But even as the big PC companies ring up sales, they must deal with a problem: prices. According to IDC, the average computer price in 1997 will be $1,878, down 10% from $2,068 in 1996.

Analysts cite several reasons for falling prices. Most of the big PC companies have brought out a new line of $999 machines that have been a hit at computer stores. In addi-

tion, the prices of PC components, such as memory chips, continue to fall. Further, traditional vendors are being forced to match the lower prices of direct sellers like Dell, if not in their official price lists then in the negotiations leading up to a big business sale. Big companies "are being very aggressive behind closed doors," said Scott Miller at Dataquest.

While the two studies agreed on most topics, they differed in outlook. Mr. Miller expected unit sales over the rest of 1997 to grow at a more rapid rate than the first half, largely because of the increased availability of Intel's Pentium II microprocessor. IDC's Kevin Hause, however, said he expected growth rates for the rest of the year to remain near those seen in the first two quarters.

Lee Gomes

Information-Technology Industry

Worldwide sales estimates and projections for the information-technology industry, including computer and data-communications equipment, packaged software, and such services as consulting, operations management, maintenance and training. Projections and growth rate are based on 1996 currency conversion rates.

Information Technology Sales and Percent Change From Previous Year
(Dollars in billions)

Year	Hardware Sales	Hardware Change	Software Sales	Software Change	Services Sales	Services Change	Total Sales	Total Change
1995	$277	–	$93	–	$170	–	$540	–
1996	318	15%	107	15%	185	9%	610	13%
1997	360	13	121	13	201	9	682	12
1998	398	10	137	13	220	9	755	11
1999	434	9	155	13	241	10	830	10
2000	469	8	176	14	264	9	910	10

Source: International Data Corp.

Top Companies in the PC Market

Apple Computer and IBM, the leading personal-computer makers in the U.S. market in 1992, have seen their shares fall and have lost their dominant positions to Compaq and Packard Bell NEC.

Top 10 Marketers of Personal Computers (U.S. Shipments)

		1992			1995			1996	
Rank	Vendor	Shipments	Market share	Vendor	Shipments	Market share	Vendor	Shipments	Market share
1	Apple	1,550,000	13.2%	Compaq	2,665,000	11.6%	Compaq	3,467,000	13.1%
2	IBM	1,374,600	11.7	Packard Bell	2,486,000	10.8	Packard Bell NEC	3,031,000	11.4
3	Compaq	675,820	5.7	Apple	2,446,000	10.6	IBM	2,219,000	8.4
4	Packard Bell	623,500	5.3	IBM	1,812,000	7.9	Dell	1,791,000	6.8
5	Dell	438,994	3.7	Gateway 2000	1,182,000	5.1	Apple	1,691,000	6.4
6	Gateway 2000	428,180	3.6	Dell	1,130,000	4.9	Gateway 2000	1,615,000	6.1
7	Tandy	330,000	2.8	Hewlett-Packard	867,000	3.8	Hewlett-Packard	1,405,000	5.3
8	AST	320,000	2.7	Acer	821,000	3.6	Toshiba	1,335,000	5.0
9	Toshiba	242,950	2.1	Toshiba	739,000	3.2	Acer	891,000	3.4
10	NEC	173,450	1.5	NEC	552,000	2.4	AST	633,000	2.4
	Others	5,603,538	47.6	Others	8,331,000	36.2	Others	8,407,000	31.7
	All Vendors	11,761,032	100.0	All Vendors	23,030,000	100.0	All Vendors	26,484,000	100.0

Top 10 Marketers of Personal Computers (Worldwide Shipments)

		1992			1995			1996	
Rank	Vendor	Shipments	Market share	Vendor	Shipments	Market share	Vendor	Shipments	Market share
1	IBM	3,210,153	10.4%	Compaq	5,757,000	9.8%	Compaq	7,036,000	10.2%
2	Apple	2,780,055	9.0	IBM	4,785,000	8.1	IBM	6,143,000	8.9
3	Compaq	1,555,510	5.1	Apple	4,627,000	7.9	Packard Bell NEC	4,267,000	6.2
4	NEC	1,375,700	4.5	NEC	3,042,000	5.2	Apple	3,587,000	5.2
5	Packard Bell	700,000	2.3	Packard Bell	3,031,000	5.2	Hewlett-Packard	2,972,000	4.3
6	Dell	697,523	2.3	Hewlett-Packard	2,040,000	3.5	Dell	2,837,000	4.1
7	Toshiba	629,557	2.0	Acer	1,872,000	3.2	Toshiba	2,682,000	3.9
8	AST	594,052	1.9	Dell	1,834,000	3.1	NEC (Japan)	2,658,000	3.9
9	Olivetti	551,857	1.8	Fujitsu/ICL	1,617,000	2.8	Fujitsu/ICL	2,559,000	3.7
10	Groupe Bull/ZDS	499,081	1.6	Toshiba	1,480,000	2.5	Acer	2,246,000	3.3
	Others	18,159,512	59.0	Others	28,675,000	48.8	Others	31,792,000	46.2
	All Vendors	30,753,000	100.0	All Vendors	58,760,000	100.0	All Vendors	68,779,000	100.0

Source: International Data Corp.

Growth of the Personal Computer

U.S. and Worldwide Shipments of Personal Computers

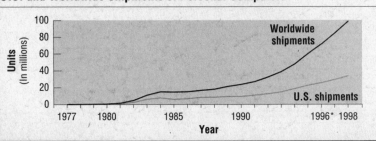

*Estimates 1996–1998.

Personal Computer Shipments and Revenues

	Worldwide shipments (Thousands)	Worldwide revenue (Millions of U.S. $)	U.S. shipments (Thousands)	U.S. revenue (Millions of U.S. $)
Pre 1977	17		16.3	
1977	48		43	
1978	189		158	
1979	350		274	
1980	609		490	
1981	1,631		764	
1982	4,893		2,567	
1983	11,123	$11,019	6,199	$6,497
1984	15,044	18,496	7,768	10,683
1985	14,705	22,765	6,072	11,980
1986	15,064	22,968	6,814	12,092
1987	16,676	24,975	8,391	13,821
1988	18,061	33,367	8,616	17,361
1989	21,327	40,435	9,330	19,700
1990	23,738	46,000	9,430	18,898
1991	26,966	57,580	10,903	24,589
1992	32,411	64,095	12,544	25,858
1993	38,851	73,561	14,775	29,663
1994	47,894	94,457	18,605	37,339
1995	60,171	123,643	22,583	47,749
1996*	70,850	150,712	25,650	60,113
1997*	84,278	177,337	29,900	71,178
1998*	98,377	217,357	34,600	81,885

*Estimates 1996–1998.
Source: Dataquest

Total Worldwide Semiconductor Market Share

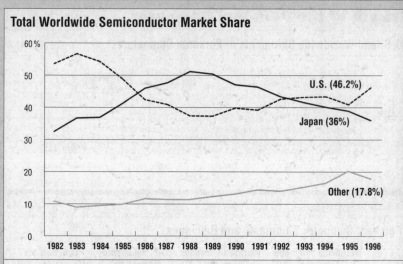

World Semiconductor Market Sales and Shares
(In millions of dollars)

Mkt	1982	1983	1984	1985	1986	1987	1988	1989	1990	1991	1992	1993	1994	1995	1996
U.S.	6,259	7,763	11,599	8,091	8,607	10,359	13,768	15,049	14,445	15,376	18,410	24,744	33,562	46,998	42,679
Europe	2,998	3,319	4,738	4,541	5,373	6,214	8,253	9,040	9,599	10,114	11,470	14,599	19,736	28,199	27,561
Japan	3,985	5,534	8,034	7,598	10,695	13,031	18,658	19,575	19,563	20,934	19,396	23,798	29,406	39,667	34,175
Asia/ Pacific	920	1,326	1,824	1,530	2,291	3,756	5,624	5,997	6,911	8,181	10,588	14,168	19,174	29,540	27,550
Total	**14,162**	**17,942**	**26,195**	**21,760**	**26,966**	**33,360**	**46,303**	**49,661**	**50,518**	**54,605**	**59,864**	**77,309**	**101,878**	**144,404**	**131,966**
U.S	56.7%	54.3%	53.6%	48.9%	42.4%	40.9%	37.4%	37.3%	39.8%	39.2%	42.6%	43.2%	43.4%	40.9%	46.2%
Japan	32.5	36.7	36.9	41.2	46.0	47.7	51.2	50.4	47.1	46.4	43.4	41.6	40.1	38.9	36.0
Other	10.8	9.0	9.5	9.9	11.6	11.4	11.4	12.3	13.1	14.4	14.0	15.2	16.5	20.2	17.8

Source: Semiconductor Industry Association

Top Software Publishers

Total software sales jumped more than 12% to $4.6 billion in 1996 from $4.1 billion in 1995, with 20 companies controlling about two-thirds of the market.

Publishers, Ranked by Dollar Sales

Publisher	1996 $	1996 units	Mkt share $	Mkt share units
Microsoft	$929,749,431	10,375,133	20.37%	10.16%
CUC Software	310,183,384	9,545,182	6.80	9.35
Intuit	238,510,457	4,585,324	5.23	4.49
Symantec	190,830,779	2,304,093	4.18	2.26
Broderbund	174,346,681	4,304,885	3.82	4.22
Learning Co.	156,509,234	5,807,929	3.43	5.69
Corel	139,777,604	1,784,553	3.06	1.75
GT Interactive	133,000,491	5,417,542	2.91	5.31
Electronic Arts	121,239,843	3,349,740	2.66	3.28
Adobe	118,050,424	578,060	2.59	0.57
Disney	78,584,789	2,561,953	1.72	2.51
Virgin	62,894,373	1,745,149	1.38	1.71
Quarterdeck	60,996,422	1,260,187	1.34	1.23
LucasArts	57,234,467	1,629,398	1.25	1.60
MicroProse	49,494,055	1,334,355	1.08	1.31
Activision	49,168,924	1,306,505	1.08	1.28
Interplay	47,592,531	1,337,384	1.04	1.31
Maxis	43,124,844	1,243,480	0.94	1.22
Mindscape	42,101,420	1,487,189	0.92	1.46
Netscape	39,278,393	917,953	0.86	0.90
	$3,042,668,548	62,875,993	66.66%	61.61%
Total Software Sales	$4,585,812,710	103,121,600		

Source: PC Data

Most Popular CD-ROM Titles

Top Selling CD-ROMs Ranked by Unit Sales, in 1996

No.	Title	Publisher	Unit sales	Dollar sales	Avg. price
1	Microsoft Windows 95 Upgrade	Microsoft	1,264,133	$110,586,286	$87.48
2	Warcraft II	CUC (Sierra/Davidson)	797,567	32,840,119	41.18
3	Myst	Broderbund	765,538	24,987,766	32.64
4	Duke Nukem 3D	GT Interactive	620,791	24,998,291	40.27
5	Quicken Deluxe	Intuit	519,795	30,261,553	58.22
6	Corel Printhouse	Corel	511,631	11,180,421	21.85
7	Toy Story Animated Storybook	Disney	490,016	16,011,769	32.68
8	Civilization 2	MicroProse	482,522	21,074,429	43.68
9	Netscape Navigator Personal Edition 3.0	Netscape	463,647	19,028,146	41.04
10	Microsoft Plus	Microsoft	418,244	18,202,209	43.52
11	Turbo Tax Deluxe-Final	Intuit	412,740	18,069,425	43.78
12	Quake Shareware	Id Software	393,575	3,005,519	7.64
13	Barbie Fashion Designer	Mattel	351,945	14,044,994	39.91
14	Microsoft Encarta Encyclopedia	Microsoft	350,595	15,851,876	45.21
15	Command & Conquer Red Alert	Virgin	347,844	16,498,346	47.43
16	Microsoft Flight Simulator	Microsoft	340,005	16,131,449	47.44
17	Print Shop Ensemble III	Broderbund	326,778	17,001,595	52.03
18	Command and Conquer	Virgin	322,893	14,670,797	45.44
19	Family Tree Maker Deluxe	Broderbund	303,684	20,036,032	65.98
20	Math Blaster: In Search of Spot	CUC (Sierra/Davidson)	300,738	10,050,614	33.42

Source: PC Data

STATIC ON THE LINE

Whoever thought the simple telephone would turn out to be so complicated?

Unprecedented change is sweeping the telecommunications industry. New legislation passed in the last year in the U.S. and some overseas markets should finally begin to pry open local phone markets to competition. Meanwhile, AT&T Corp. and others are struggling to build vast networks offering ever more sophisticated services, even as they must contend with price wars and eroding profits in their core businesses.

Customers are telling market researchers that they want a simplified package of services from one carrier and on one monthly statement. But the costs of providing such services, including local, long-distance, wireless, Internet, and even entertainment fare, are enormous. AT&T might have to spend more than $30 billion just to enter the Bells' local phone business if it can't find partners to help it set up. The Bells face a similarly expensive marketing war if they are ever going to lure lucrative long-distance customers away from AT&T and MCI.

Smaller players that can't keep up financially will be forced into mergers or will be absorbed by the giants. Numerous wireless players that spent billions in federal auctions to go up against the national networks of AT&T, Sprint and others, now are finding that they can't pay for the rights. Many of these smallfry haven't even begun to build their networks yet.

Already, some players are girding for the competitive battle by joining forces. Two Bell mergers were announced in the past year. Southwest regional Bell giant SBC Communications Inc. completed its $18 billion purchase of Pacific Telesis Group, while Bell Atlantic Corp. combined with Nynex Corp. in a $23 billion merger to form a Northeast Bell giant.

It looked as if U.K. titan British Telecommunications PLC had its acquisition of MCI Communications Corp. all sewn up until upstart long-distance carrier WorldCom Inc. made an unsolicited offer in early October to acquire MCI for $30 billion, about $10 billion more than BT planned to pay. BT and MCI had hoped to set the pace in international alliances and knock AT&T off its perch by creating a transatlantic powerhouse with networks in the U.S. and Europe. MCI could accept WorldCom's offer and still manage to keep BT as part of the team, although any talks aimed at such a broad partnership would be difficult and take months to complete.

But the story on the minds of most telecommunications experts remains the crisis at AT&T. Under attack in every one of its markets—from long-distance to wireless services—and falling behind to its rivals, AT&T has lost two presidents in a year and lacks a clear succession plan. The company's embattled chairman, Robert E. Allen, came under increasing fire for pushing out an heir apparent that he himself chose in October 1996. Now, Mr. Allen is facing early retirement as AT&T's directors search for a new CEO.

The global consolidation that is under way could aid their search. AT&T might seek a big merger with another telecommunications giant, preferably in local services, that would also give AT&T the management team and the new CEO it needs.

The Telephone's Reach

The percentage of U.S. households with telephones has increased, but phone service still isn't universal primarily because many low-income people cannot afford it.

Year	Percentage of households with telephones
1920	35.0%
1930	40.9
1940	36.9
1950	61.8
1960	78.3
1970	90.5
1980	92.9
1990	94.8
1996	93.9

Source: U.S. Census Bureau and Federal Communications Commission

Mr. Allen has already tried this route. Early in 1997, he attempted to merge AT&T with SBC, a $50 billion-plus deal that would have been the biggest business combination ever. However, disclosure of the plan brought a firestorm of protest from regulators, politicians and consumer activists, who accused AT&T of trying to reconstruct its Bell monopoly—a big stretch, considering that five other Bells wouldn't have taken part.

Still, the complaints helped to put the kibosh on AT&T's plan and make it tough for the company to ever do a Bell deal. The talks also broke off over SBC's refusal to commit to AT&T's demand that it adhere to a strict time-frame for opening its local network to rivals. AT&T felt it was the only way to enhance competition and to convince regulators to let the deal proceed. SBC said forget it.

The failed merger talks highlight the battle lines in the coming war between local and long-distance players. Current law says the Bells can't get into long-distance services until they set up their local networks so that rivals can connect easily to Bell lines, phone numbers and databases, and sell services to Bell customers. The long-distance players are reluctant to push too quickly into the Bell markets, lest their advance trigger a Bell entry into long-distance. It isn't that AT&T, MCI and others never expect to compete head-on with Bells. They just want to be certain that the Bells will give them equitable terms for connecting to their networks.

This standoff was recently reinforced by a federal appeals court, which threw out guidelines of the Federal Communications Commission under which the Bells would have had to lease their facilities to rivals such as AT&T at a discount. The FCC now plans to take its case to the Supreme Court.

All of this will eventually be settled. Experts say it could take another year. But when the final terms are set, they will pave the way for a new kind of phone competition in which global carriers will offer all services on one bill.

Get ready for more interruptions from telemarketers at dinnertime.

John J. Keller

Telecommunications Industry Revenue

Telecommunications Industry Revenue Reached Nearly $200 Billion in 1995 and Grew 8.8% from 1994 (Amounts in millions)

	1992	1993	1994	1995
Local service				
Local exchange	$39,235	$40,176	$42,245	$45,188
Local private line	1,049	1,088	1,138	1,226
Cellular, PCS, paging & other mobile	7,285	10,237	14,293	18,698
Other local	7,687	8,002	8,302	10,428
Total local service	55,256	59,503	65,977	75,540
Interstate & intrastate access service	29,353	30,832	32,759	33,895
Long distance service				
Operator (including pay telephone & card)	9,465	10,772	10,539	11,164
Non-operator switched toll	54,300	58,294	60,819	64,385
Long distance private line	7,783	8,067	9,043	9,718
Other long distance	4,196	5,392	4,078	4,303
Total long distance	75,744	82,525	84,478	89,570
Total reported revenue	160,353	172,860	183,214	199,005

Source: Federal Communications Commission

The Long-Distance Market

The fourth-quarter market shares of the major long-distance telephone companies, based on their quarterly shareholder reports.

Market Share

	AT&T	MCI	SPRINT	WORLDCOM	Others
4Q84	87.7%	4.9%	3.0%	–	4.4%
4Q85	85.7	6.3	3.2	–	4.8
4Q86	81.5	7.9	5.1	–	5.6
4Q87	78.3	9.0	6.2	–	6.5
4Q88	73.9	11.7	7.2	0.1%	7.1
4Q89	69.0	13.7	8.9	0.2	8.2
4Q90	66.5	15.1	9.1	0.3	9.0
4Q91	63.9	15.9	8.8	1.2	10.2
4Q92	60.6	17.2	9.3	1.3	11.6
4Q93	57.5	18.1	9.3	2.3	12.8
4Q94	57.6	17.3	8.7	2.9	13.4
4Q95	54.8	17.8	8.8	4.3	14.3
4Q96	53.8	17.7	8.9	5.1	15.4

Source: Federal Communications Commission

The Baby Bells

COMPANY	1996 REVENUE (In billions $)	1996 NET INCOME (LOSS) (In billions $)	LOCAL TELEPHONE SERVICE AREA	HEADQUARTERS
Ameritech	$14.92	$2.13	Illinois, Indiana, Michigan, Ohio, Wisconsin	Chicago, Ill.
Bell Atlantic*	13.08	1.88	Delaware, Maryland, New Jersey, Pennsylvania, Virginia, Washington, DC, West Virginia	Philadelphia, Pa.
BellSouth	19.04	2.86	Alabama, Florida, Georgia, Kentucky, Louisiana, Mississippi, North Carolina, South Carolina, Tennessee	Atlanta, Ga.
NYNEX*	13.45	1.48	Connecticut, Massachusetts, Maine, New York, New Hampshire, Vermont, Rhode Island	New York, N.Y.
SBC Communications (combined results of SBC and Pacific Telesis, which merged 4/1/97)	23.49	3.25	Texas, Oklahoma, Missouri, Arkansas, Kansas, California, Nevada	San Antonio, Texas
US West	12.9	1.18	Arizona, Colorado, Idaho, Iowa, Minnesota, Montana, Nebraska, New Mexico, North Dakota, Oregon, South Dakota, Utah, Washington, Wyoming	Englewood, Colo.
Communications Group	10.08	1.25		
Media Group	2.96	(-0.071)		

*Merger of Bell Atlantic and NYNEX completed in August 1997

Telephone Bills

Monthly Telephone Service Expenditures

Year	Basic local service charge*	Toll and other telephone expenditures**	Total telephone expenditures
1980	$8.74	$21	$30
1985	14.54	27	41
1990	17.79	35	53
1991	18.66	36	55
1992	18.70	37	55
1993	18.94	39	58
1994	19.07	42	61
1995	19.49	42	62

*Monthly service charges for unlimited local service, taxes and subscriber line charges.
**The "Toll and other" category is primarily toll, but also includes charges for equipment, additional access lines, connection, touch-tone, call waiting, 900 service and directory listings.
Source: Federal Communications Commission

Phone Prices

Percent Change From December of Previous Year Through December of the Year Shown

Year	Telephone services	Local services	Interstate toll service	Intrastate toll service
1980	4.6%	7.0%	3.4%	-0.6%
1981	11.7	12.6	14.6	6.2
1982	7.2	10.8	2.6	4.2
1983	3.6	3.1	1.5	.7.4
1984	9.2	17.2	-4.3	3.6
1985	4.7	8.9	-3.7	0.6
1986	2.7	7.1	-9.4	0.3
1987	-1.3	3.3	-12.4	-3.0
1988	1.3	4.5	-4.2	-4.2
1989	-0.3	0.6	-1.3	-2.6
1990	-0.4	1.0	-3.7	-2.2
1991	3.5	5.1	1.3	-1.5
1992	-0.3	0.5	-1.3	-2.4
1993	1.8	1.0	6.5	0.2
1994	0.7	-0.3	5.4	-1.0
1995	1.2	2.6	0.1	-3.8
1996	2.1	0.9	3.7	6.1

Source: U.S. Bureau of Labor Statistics

Cell Phone Callers

As the number of people using cell phones has soared, the average local monthly bill has declined.

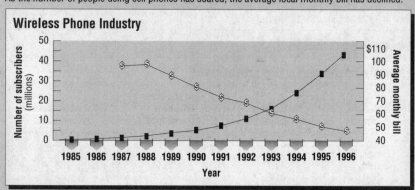

Wireless Phone Industry

Source: Cellular Telecommunications Industry Association

Year	Subscribers	Annual revenues	Average local monthly bill
1985	340,213	$482,428,000	–
1986	681,825	823,052,000	–
1987	1,230,855	1,151,519,000	$96.83
1988	2,069,441	1,959,548,000	98.02
1989	3,508,944	3,340,595,000	89.30
1990	5,283,055	4,548,820,000	80.90
1991	7,557,148	5,708,522,000	72.74
1992	11,032,753	7,822,726,000	68.68
1993	16,009,461	10,892,165,000	61.48
1994	24,134,421	14,229,920,000	56.21
1995	33,785,661	19,071,966,000	51.00
1996	44,000,000	23,634,971,000	47.70

Source: Cellular Telecommunications Industry Association

Research Report

U.S. Expenditures for Research & Development by Source of Funds and Performer

	Total	Source of funds - Millions of current dollars			
		Federal Government	Industry	Universities & colleges*	Other nonprofits
1970	26,134	14,891	10,444	462	337
1975	35,213	18,109	15,820	749	535
1980	62,596	29,455	30,912	1,326	903
1985	113,818	52,127	57,978	2,369	1,344
1990	151,544	61,493	83,380	4,329	2,342
1995	171,000	60,700	101,650	5,500	3,150

	Total	Source of funds - Millions of constant 1987 dollars			
		Federal Government	Industry	Universities & colleges*	Other nonprofits
1970	74,597	42,622	29,673	1,335	966
1975	72,237	37,396	32,162	1,574	1,105
1980	87,649	41,385	43,118	1,878	1,268
1985	120,599	55,245	61,418	2,512	1,425
1990	134,135	54,587	73,604	3,865	2,079
1995	132,078	46,989	78,381	4,270	2,437

	Performer - Millions of current dollars				
	Federal Government	Industry	Universities & colleges	Univ. & college FFRDCs**	Other nonprofits
1970	4,079	18,067	2,335	737	916
1975	5,354	24,187	3,409	987	1,276
1980	7,632	44,505	6,063	2,246	2,150
1985	12,945	84,239	9,686	3,523	3,425
1990	16,002	109,727	16,283	4,832	4,700
1995	16,700	121,400	21,600	5,300	6,000
	Performer - Millions of constant 1987 dollars				
	Federal Government	Industry	Universities & colleges	Univ. & college FFRDCs**	Other nonprofits
1970	11,789	51,327	6,749	2,130	2,602
1975	11,248	49,161	7,162	2,074	2,593
1980	10,810	62,071	8,588	3,181	2,999
1985	13,727	89,236	10,271	3,736	3,628
1990	14,288	96,846	14,538	4,314	4,148
1995	12,966	93,601	16,770	4,115	4,626

*Includes state and local government funds to universities and colleges.
**FFDRC = federally funded research and development center; FFRDCs are administered by individual universities and colleges and by university consortia.
Source: National Science Foundation

Top Patent Recipients

Corporations Receiving the Most Patents for Inventions 1969–1996

	Total 1969–1996	1996
General Electric	23,776	819
International Business Machines	19,202	1,867
Hitachi	16,048	963
AT&T	14,363	510
Canon	13,680	1,541
Toshiba	13,649	914
Eastman Kodak	13,121	768
DuPont	12,693	395
U.S. Philips	12,642	477
Westinghouse Electric	11,806	132
Siemens	11,522	418
Bayer	11,110	323
General Motors	10,803	297
Mitsubishi	10,381	934
Motorola	10,026	1,064
Fuji Photo Film	9,848	510
Xerox	9,598	703
Dow Chemical	9,568	196
Matsushita Electric Industrial	8,950	841
Ciba-Geigy	8,289	271

Foreign Countries Receiving the Most Patents for Inventions 1963–1996

	Total 1963–1996	1996
Japan	336,319	23,053
Germany	195,645	6,818
United Kingdom	88,295	2,453
France	74,945	2,788
Canada	45,293	2,233
Switzerland	39,667	1,112
Italy	28,118	1,200
Sweden	24,793	854
Netherlands	23,406	797
Taiwan	11,127	1,897

Source: U.S. Patent and Trademark Office

Increasing Innovation

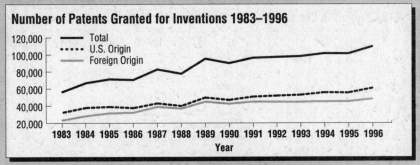

Number of Patents Granted for Inventions 1983–1996

- Total
- U.S. Origin
- Foreign Origin

Number of Patents Granted by Type of Recipient 1983–1996

Recipients	1983	1985	1988	1991	1994	1995	1996
U.S. Corporations	25,677	31,181	31,437	39,133	44,036	44,035	48,741
U.S. Government	1,048	1,139	733	1,183	1,258	1,028	923
U.S. Individuals	7,574	9,265	10,122	13,207	12,805	12,885	13,729
Foreign Corporations	19,246	25,957	30,960	37,594	38,788	38,688	41,476
Foreign Government	339	483	453	472	296	245	259
Foreign Individuals	2,976	3,636	4,219	4,924	4,493	4,538	4,518
Total	56,860	71,661	77,924	96,513	101,676	101,419	109,646

Source: U.S. Patent and Trademark Office

Space Program Spending

NASA Budget in Current Year and Constant Year 1996 Dollars (In millions)

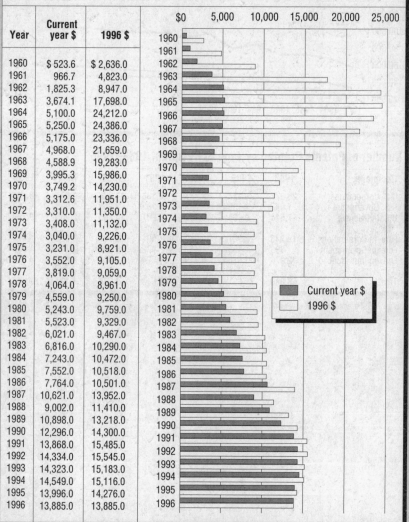

Year	Current year $	1996 $
1960	$ 523.6	$ 2,636.0
1961	966.7	4,823.0
1962	1,825.3	8,947.0
1963	3,674.1	17,698.0
1964	5,100.0	24,212.0
1965	5,250.0	24,386.0
1966	5,175.0	23,336.0
1967	4,968.0	21,659.0
1968	4,588.9	19,283.0
1969	3,995.3	15,986.0
1970	3,749.2	14,230.0
1971	3,312.6	11,951.0
1972	3,310.0	11,350.0
1973	3,408.0	11,132.0
1974	3,040.0	9,226.0
1975	3,231.0	8,921.0
1976	3,552.0	9,105.0
1977	3,819.0	9,059.0
1978	4,064.0	8,961.0
1979	4,559.0	9,250.0
1980	5,243.0	9,759.0
1981	5,523.0	9,329.0
1982	6,021.0	9,467.0
1983	6,816.0	10,290.0
1984	7,243.0	10,472.0
1985	7,552.0	10,518.0
1986	7,764.0	10,501.0
1987	10,621.0	13,952.0
1988	9,002.0	11,410.0
1989	10,898.0	13,218.0
1990	12,296.0	14,300.0
1991	13,868.0	15,485.0
1992	14,334.0	15,545.0
1993	14,323.0	15,183.0
1994	14,549.0	15,116.0
1995	13,996.0	14,276.0
1996	13,885.0	13,885.0

Source: National Aeronautics and Space Administration

Principal NASA Contractors

The 50 contractors that received the largest dollar value of NASA direct awards to business firms during fiscal year 1996

Contractor	(In thousands)	(Percent)
Total awards to businesses	**$9,800,819**	**100.00%**
Boeing Co.	1,607,774	16.40
Lockheed Martin Corp.	833,387	8.50
Rockwell International Corp.	756,319	7.72
United Space Alliance LLC	544,424	5.55
Thiokol Corp.	396,184	4.04
McDonnell Douglas Corp.	388,587	3.96
Rockwell Space Operations Inc.	292,423	2.98
TRW Inc.	287,339	2.93
AlliedSignal Technical Services	285,084	2.91
Computer Sciences Corp.	213,543	2.18
EG&G Florida Inc.	175,147	1.79
Lockheed Martin Engineering & Science Co.	165,571	1.69
United Technologies Corp.	162,456	1.66
Lockheed Martin Aerospace Corp.	160,630	1.64
USBI Booster Production Co.	157,096	1.60
Hughes Aircraft Co.	152,864	1.56
Hughes Information Tech. Corp.	133,486	1.36
Boeing Commercial Airplane Group	83,045	.85
Johnson Controls World Services	68,806	.70
Bamsi Inc.	59,322	.61
General Electric Co.	58,383	.60
Grumman Aerospace Corp.	57,729	.59
Orbital Sciences Corp.	56,204	.57
Sterling Software US inc.	55,433	.57
Santa Barbara Research Center	53,707	.55
Space Systems Loral Inc.	50,018	.51
Ball Aerospace & Tech. Corp.	47,347	.48
Hughes STX Corp.	46,966	.48
Cortez III Service Corp.	45,527	.46
Spacehab Inc.	44,831	.46
Hughes Training Inc.	43,629	.45
Calspan Corp.	39,939	.41
Raytheon Service Co.	39,508	.40
Teledyne Industries Inc.	35,988	.37
Aerojet General Corp.	35,439	.36
Lockheed Martin Services Inc.	35,262	.36
Lockheed Space Operations Co.	33,825	.35
Jackson & Tull Inc.	33,683	.34
Swales & Associates Inc.	33,450	.34
NYMA Inc.	31,787	.32
Cray Research Inc.	31,677	.32
Silicon Graphics Inc.	30,925	.32
Science Application International Corp.	30,426	.31
Krug Life Sciences Inc.	30,387	.31
General Electric UTC JV	29,900	.31
CTA Inc.	28,331	.29
Dyncorp	28,319	.29
Johnson Engineering Corp.	28,058	.29
Government Micro Resources	27,989	.29
Sverdrup Technology Inc.	26,500	.27

Source: National Aeronautics and Space Administration

7

THE WORLD

DIPLOMACY HAS LONG BEEN *a game of peacemaking and mapmaking. Think diplomacy and what comes to mind is Churchill, Roosevelt, and Stalin plotting Europe's future at Yalta, or more recently, Clinton and Yeltsin agreeing to the expansion of NATO eastward into the former Soviet bloc.*

But now that superpower military confrontation has ended with the Cold War, statecraft is increasingly dominated by a different kind of envoy: the trade negotiator. The most important diplomatic undertakings of our age are the creation and expansion of bodies that are writing new rules of international commerce. Instead of redrawing borders, today's cutting-edge statesmen are easing the passage of goods, capital, and sometimes workers across national frontiers.

"Commercial interaction has more and more become a force that shapes relations among nations," Renato Ruggiero, director general of the World Trade Organization, told *The Wall Street Journal*. In the past year, the 130 countries in the WTO lowered tariffs and trade barriers on high-tech goods and telecommunication services. And the 15 nations of the European Union are aiming to achieve the ultimate free-trade grail by 1999—a common currency.

The growing impact of trade blocs and rule-making bodies doesn't mean, however, that truly free global trade is at hand. The growing openness of the world economy troubles many people, and resistance to free trade may be spreading. For instance, the U.S. government, sensing opposition to the idea, isn't pushing very hard for the Free Trade Area of the Americas, a trading zone that all nations of the Western Hemisphere except Cuba have agreed to negotiate by 2005.

The creation of a pan-European currency, to be called the euro, has broad support among the continent's elites—but it is by no means a done deal. French and German citizens have begun balking at the social price, including lower welfare benefits, that they'll have to pay for the currency. So concerned are the

French, in fact, that in June 1997 they voted out their conservative prime minister, a staunch advocate of the single currency, in favor of a Socialist with a go-slow attitude.

And many Europeans fear that closer integration of the EU will lead to dominance by Germany, Europe's greatest economic power. Former French defense minister Jean-Pierre Chevenement put it this way: "What Germany couldn't obtain in two world wars—continental preponderance—it's well on its way to obtaining through finance and peace, in the name of a free-market and technocratic conception of Europe."

Is this anxiety overblown? Many of Europe's business leaders and government officials insist it is. Monetary union is critical to Europe's prosperity, they argue. Unifying the continent's currencies, goes the conventional wisdom in high places, will make the European economy more efficient.

Maybe. A single currency undoubtedly would cut certain costs, most notably the commissions on foreign-exchange trades. But no one has *proven* the case that the euro would increase the continent's wealth. Monetary union, then, is essentially a shot in the dark.

In Washington, in fact, U.S. government officials worry that monetary union could make things worse. Their reasoning: Europe already has an effective continental financial authority in the Bundesbank, the German central bank, which protects the soundness of Germany's

mighty mark, the continent's most widely used currency. But as of January 1, 1999, the Bundesbank and the monetary authorities of other participating nations are scheduled to be replaced by a new continental body, the European Central Bank. Problem is, there is no guarantee this entity will work. Even the plan's architects aren't sure whether the bank will favor a strong currency, to resist inflation, or a weak one, to boost exports and jobs.

Around the world, people worry that free-trade pacts will undermine a nation's ability to protect the public welfare, by, for instance, threatening legitimate regulations on food and drugs. Senator Robert Byrd of West Virginia has called the World Trade Organization a "Tyrannosaurus rex about to ransack its way around decades of statutes."

Over the top, perhaps, but the senator has a point. Placing primacy on free trade can sometimes undermine national sovereignty. Many people in Europe fear that meat from hormone-treated cattle is unhealthy, and so in 1989, the European Union banned the import of such meat. But the WTO, siding with the U.S. in May 1997, ruled that the ban violated global trade rules. That ruling means the European Union may have to remove its ban. In this instance, the ruling was good news for the American economy: The U.S. said the ban cost it $250 million a year in lost beef exports. But in the future, the U.S. could just as easily find its own health safeguards challenged by the WTO.

So free trade brings pain. But it also brings tremendous gains. The share of trade in world economic activity has risen to 21% from just 7% at the end of World War II, according to the WTO. For the U.S., international trade now makes up 24% of America's gross domestic product. The volume of world trade has increased 15-fold in the past 40 years, outpacing the sixfold rise in overall economic output. Greater trade clearly has been driving world growth.

So which is free trade, a panacea or a disaster? One battleground in the debate is the North American Free Trade Agreement, or Nafta, the customs union among the U.S., Mexico and Canada that began in 1994. Ross Perot warned us to brace for a "giant sucking sound" as American jobs drained south to Mexico. Nafta boosters promised that for each billion dollars of extra exports yielded by the pact, America would generate an additional 15,000 jobs.

Both sides were wrong.

Nafta's impact on American jobs has been "near zero" or only barely positive, concludes a U.S. government study released at the end of 1996. The pact created 49,000 U.S. jobs through greater exports to Mexico, and wiped out 38,000 U.S. jobs through rising imports from Mexico. Net, Nafta created 11,000 U.S. jobs, the study found, a blip in the U.S. market of 125 million jobs. And an April 1996 report by the National Bureau of Economic Research found that "maquiladora" plants, built by U.S. companies just south of the U.S.–Mexico border and blamed by Nafta's enemies for killing American jobs, actually create employment on both sides of the border.

And so, many economists are concluding that one clear winner of the free-trade pacts is the U.S. In most of the trade pacts it enters, Washington is for the most part simply lowering the trade barriers of other nations. Because the U.S. economy is already one of the world's most open, the U.S. often gives up less in these deals than it gets. The two recent world accords on trade in technology and telecommunications should help dismantle obstacles to commerce in industries dominated by American businesses.

That would mean more business abroad for U.S. companies and eventually, higher wages for Americans who work in export-related businesses. In the end, this positive calculation is the one that's likely to prevail in politicians' thinking, keeping up support in America for creating stronger free-trade rules and institutions.

Michael Williams,
assistant foreign editor of
The Wall Street Journal

THE BIG GUYS

*Major Trading Blocs
and Trade Organizations*

WORLD TRADE ORGANIZATION (WTO)

The WTO includes 130 countries that agree to rules that govern a set of global trade and economic policies. Twenty-eight more countries, including China and Russia, have applied to join. The organization has a dispute-settlement body that has emerged as the leading international arbiter of trade spats. The WTO netted two big trade pacts in the past year, on information-technology products such as computers, and on telecommunications services, opening up markets worth $1 trillion a year in sales. But beyond these coups, the WTO has largely been bogged down in the role of fair-trade referee, settling arguments over imports of bananas and Costa Rican underwear. Small potatoes in the grand scheme of things, but somebody's got to do the job.

EUROPEAN UNION (EU)

A free-trade and economic-policy bloc of 15 European nations: Austria, Belgium, Denmark, Finland, France, Germany, Greece, Ireland, Italy, Luxembourg, Netherlands, Portugal, Spain, Sweden, and the United Kingdom. It was launched as the European Economic Community in 1958. Next on the EU's agenda is a step that would take it far further than any trade group has gone before: a unified common currency, which is supposed to go into effect by 1999. The impact on business—including American firms operating in Europe—would be profound: Currency-exchange markets would probably be decimated; export-transaction costs should fall; psychological price barriers between nations would vanish; contracts would have to be rewritten. But Economic and Monetary Union, as the initiative is called, isn't a done deal yet.

NORTH AMERICAN FREE TRADE AGREEMENT (NAFTA)

A free-trade bloc grouping the U.S., Canada, and Mexico, begun in 1994. Nafta has led to a big increase in trade between the U.S. and Mexico, but the pact's scope is less ambitious than the EU's—no common currency here. The countries of the Western Hemisphere, except Cuba, have agreed to negotiate an even bigger trade zone, the Free Trade Area of the Americas, by 2005.

ASIA-PACIFIC ECONOMIC COOPERATION (APEC)

Eighteen countries in a consultative body, begun in 1993, that tries to promote cooperation on trade and investment. A smaller, weaker, Asian version of the WTO. Members: Australia, Brunei, Canada, Chile, China, Hong Kong, Indonesia, Japan, South Korea, Malaysia, Mexico, New Zealand, Papua New Guinea, Philippines, Singapore, Taiwan, Thailand, and the U.S.

ASSOCIATION OF SOUTHEAST ASIAN NATIONS (ASEAN)

Set up in 1967 to promote stability and economic growth in Southeast Asia. Functions as a trade group, and though trade by the individual members has been greater with the U.S. and Japan, intra-Asean trade is growing fast. Members are Brunei, Indonesia, Malaysia, Philippines, Singapore, Thailand, Vietnam and Burma.

SOUTHERN COMMON MARKET (MERCOSUR)

Mercosur, established in 1991, groups four South American trading partners in a free-trade zone: Argentina, Brazil, Paraguay, and Uruguay. Chile and Bolivia have signed free-trade deals with the group.

GROUP OF SEVEN (G-7)

The members are the U.S., Japan, Germany, France, Italy, Britain, and Canada. The group tries to coordinate macroeconomic policy, which mainly involves talking up or down the dollar's value against other currencies—with limited success.

North American Trade After Nafta

Overall, U.S. Trade Is Increasing, With Imports Outpacing Exports
U.S.-Mexico and U.S.-Canada merchandise trade

(In billions of dollars)

Legend: U.S. exports — U.S. imports

MEXICO chart (years 1990, '91, '92, '93, '94, '95[1], '96)

CANADA chart (years 1990, '91, '92, '93, '94, '95, '96)

[1]Shows effect of peso devaluation.
Sources: U.S. Department of Commerce, Bureau of Economic Analysis

World Population Growth

Population by Country or Area (In thousands)

Region and country or area	1996	2020*	Region and country or area	1996	2020*
World	5,772,351	7,600,071	**North Africa**	137,225	207,152
Less Developed Countries	4,601,370	6,351,222	Algeria	29,183	44,783
More Developed Countries	1,170,981	1,248,849	Egypt	63,575	92,350
Africa	731,538	1,230,003	Libya	5,445	12,391
Sub-Saharan Africa	594,313	1,022,851	Morocco	29,779	44,519
Angola	10,343	19,272	Tunisia	9,020	12,751
Benin	5,710	11,920	Western Sahara	223	357
Bostwana	1,478	1,553	**Near East**	157,333	276,264
Burkina Faso	10,623	16,569	Bahrain	590	870
Burundi	5,943	10,197	Cyprus	745	936
Cameroon	14,262	25,896	Gaza Strip	929	2,452
Cape Verde	449	812	Iraq	21,422	46,260
Central African Republic	3,274	4,780	Israel	5,215	6,935
Chad	6,977	12,831	Jordan	4,212	7,529
Comoros	569	1,249	Kuwait	1,950	3,560
Congo	2,528	3,817	Lebanon	3,776	5,748
Côte d'Ivoire	14,762	24,634	Oman	2,187	4,731
Djibouti	428	751	Qatar	548	735
Equatorial Guinea	431	783	Saudi Arabia	19,409	43,255
Eritrea	3,910	7,674	Syria	15,609	28,926
Ethiopia	57,172	100,813	Turkey	62,484	85,643
Gabon	1,173	1,675	United Arab Emirates	3,057	6,080
Gambia, The	1,020	2,073	West Bank	1,717	3,135
Ghana	17,698	26,516	Yemen	13,483	29,469
Guinea	7,412	11,849	**Asia**	3,270,944	4,218,889
Guinea-Bissau	1,151	1,925	Afghanistan	22,664	43,050
Kenya	28,177	35,236	Bangladesh	123,063	172,041
Lesotho	1,971	2,693	Bhutan	1,823	3,035
Liberia	2,110	5,991	Brunei	300	490
Madagascar	13,671	25,988	Burma	45,976	67,501
Malawi	9,453	10,719	Cambodia	10,861	20,208
Mali	9,653	20,427	China	1,231,471	1,438,406
Mauritania	2,336	4,859	Mainland	1,210,005	1,413,251
Mauritius	1,139	1,428	Taiwan	21,466	25,155
Mayotte	101	233	Hong Kong	6,305	7,967
Mozambique	17,878	30,810	India	952,108	1,289,473
Namibia	1,677	3,267	Indonesia	206,612	276,017
Niger	9,113	17,983	Iran	66,094	104,282
Nigeria	103,912	205,160	Japan	125,450	123,620
Reunion	679	962	Laos	4,976	8,923
Rwanda	6,853	11,040	Macau	497	570
Saint Helena	7	7	Malaysia	19,963	29,830
Sao Tome and Principe	144	232	Maldives	271	554
Senegal	9,093	19,497	Mongolia	2,497	3,393
Seychelles	78	89	Nepal	22,094	37,767
Sierra Leone	4,793	9,716	North Korea	23,904	30,969
Somalia	9,639	18,955	Pakistan	129,276	198,722
South Africa	41,743	52,264	Philippines	74,481	112,963
Sudan	31,065	58,545	Singapore	3,397	4,330
Swaziland	999	2,128	South Korea	45,482	53,451
Tanzania	29,058	40,102	Sri Lanka	18,553	22,877
Togo	4,571	10,146	Thailand	58,851	69,298
Uganda	20,158	30,872	Vietnam	73,977	99,153
Zaire	46,499	91,548	**Latin America and**	488,608	643,058
Zambia	9,159	13,022	**the Caribbean**		
Zimbabwe	11,271	11,344	Anguilla	7	8

*Projection.

Population by Country or Area (In thousands)

Region and country or area	1996	2020*	Region and country or area	1996	2020*
Antigua and Barbuda	66	80	Greece	10,719	10,689
Argentina	34,673	43,190	Guernsey	65	76
Aruba	66	74	Iceland	268	306
Bahamas, The	259	314	Ireland	3,563	4,034
Barbados	257	284	Isle of Man	73	87
Belize	219	356	Italy	57,460	55,665
Bolivia	7,165	10,246	Jersey	87	95
Brazil	162,661	194,246	Liechtenstein	31	36
British Virgin Islands	13	18	Luxembourg	407	436
Cayman Islands	35	81	Malta	372	420
Chile	14,333	17,535	Monaco	32	34
Colombia	36,813	49,266	Netherlands	15,532	16,222
Costa Rica	3,463	5,044	Norway	4,346	4,446
Cuba	11,007	12,266	Portugal	9,865	10,005
Dominica	83	96	San Marino	25	27
Dominican Republic	8,089	11,152	Spain	38,853	35,444
Ecuador	11,466	16,546	Sweden	8,861	9,469
El Salvador	5,829	8,473	Switzerland	7,125	7,696
French Guiana	151	251	United Kingdom	58,490	59,289
Grenada	95	141	**Eastern Europe**	**120,190**	**122,218**
Guadeloupe	408	492	Albania	3,249	4,257
Guatemala	11,278	18,131	Bosnia and	2,656	2,966
Guyana	712	685	Herzegovina		
Haiti	6,732	10,252	Bulgaria	8,613	8,777
Honduras	5,605	9,042	Croatia	5,004	4,821
Jamaica	2,594	3,208	Czech Republic	10,321	10,271
Martinique	399	474	Hungary	10,003	9,103
Mexico	95,772	136,096	Macedonia, The	2,104	2,296
Montserrat	13	13	Former Yugoslav		
Netherlands Antilles	209	246	Republic of		
Nicaragua	4,272	6,973	Montenegro	635	679
Panama	2,655	3,625	Poland	38,643	40,833
Paraguay	5,504	9,474	Romania	21,657	20,135
Peru	24,523	33,226	Serbia	9,979	10,388
Puerto Rico	3,819	4,227	Slovakia	5,374	5,837
Saint Kitts and Nevis	41	57	Slovenia	1,951	1,856
Saint Lucia	158	202	**New Independent**	**292,799**	**317,547**
Saint Vincent and	118	146	**States**		
the Grenadines			Baltics	7,574	7,228
Suriname	436	598	Estonia	1,459	1,370
Trinidad and Tobago	1,272	1,409	Latvia	2,469	2,212
Turks and Caicos Islands	14	18	Lithuania	3,646	3,646
Uruguay	3,239	3,811	Commonwealth of	285,225	310,318
Venezuela	21,983	30,876	Independent States		
Virgin Islands	97	111	Armenia	3,464	3,665
Europe and the New	**799,589**	**833,550**	Azerbaijan	7,677	9,007
Independent States			Belarus	10,416	11,059
Western Europe	**386,600**	**393,786**	Georgia	5,220	5,205
Andorra	68	78	Kazakstan	16,916	18,408
Austria	8,014	8,329	Kyrgyzstan	4,530	6,257
Belgium	10,098	10,015	Moldova	4,464	5,000
Denmark	5,211	5,307	Russia	148,190	149,652
Faroe Islands	49	57	Tajikistan	5,916	10,019
Finland	5,100	5,283	Turkmenistan	4,149	6,380
France	58,317	61,334	Ukraine	50,864	49,038
Germany	83,536	88,870	Uzbekistan	23,418	36,628
Gibraltar	32	36			

*Projection.

Population by Country or Area (In thousands)

Region and country or area	1996	2020*	Region and country or area	1996	2020*
North America	**295,424**	**361,226**	Kiribati	81	98
Bermuda	62	74	Marshall Islands	58	144
Canada	28,821	34,753	Nuaru	10	12
Greenland	58	69	New Caledonia	188	255
Saint Pierre and Miquelon	7	8	New Zealand	3,548	4,326
United States	266,476	326,322	Northern Mariana Islands	52	86
Oceania	**28,915**	**37,080**	Palau	17	21
American Samoa	60	86	Papua New Guinea	4,395	7,044
Australia	18,261	21,696	Solomon Islands	413	767
Cook Islands	20	24	Tonga	106	128
Federated States of Micronesia	125	143	Tuvalu	10	15
Fiji	782	1,037	Vanuatu	178	266
French Polynesia	225	343	Wallis and Futuna	15	18
Guam	157	230	Western Samoa	214	341

Distribution of World Population

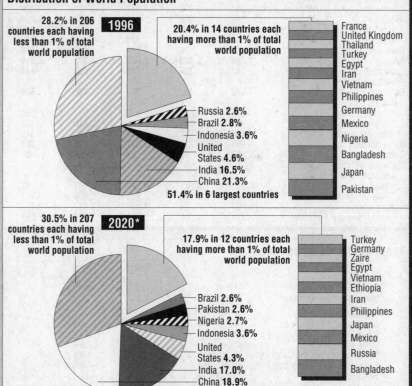

1996

28.2% in 206 countries each having less than 1% of total world population

20.4% in 14 countries each having more than 1% of total world population

France
United Kingdom
Thailand
Turkey
Egypt
Iran
Vietnam
Philippines
Germany
Mexico
Nigeria
Bangladesh
Japan
Pakistan

Russia 2.6%
Brazil 2.8%
Indonesia 3.6%
United States 4.6%
India 16.5%
China 21.3%
51.4% in 6 largest countries

2020*

30.5% in 207 countries each having less than 1% of total world population

17.9% in 12 countries each having more than 1% of total world population

Turkey
Germany
Zaire
Egypt
Vietnam
Ethiopia
Iran
Philippines
Japan
Mexico
Russia
Bangladesh

Brazil 2.6%
Pakistan 2.6%
Nigeria 2.7%
Indonesia 3.6%
United States 4.3%
India 17.0%
China 18.9%
51.7% in 7 largest countries

NOTE: China includes mainland China and Taiwan.
*Projection.
Source: U.S. Census Bureau

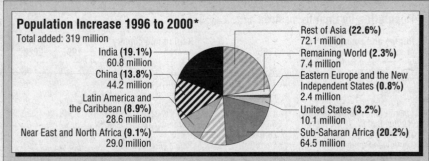

Population Increase 1996 to 2000*
Total added: 319 million

India **(19.1%)**
60.8 million

China **(13.8%)**
44.2 million

Latin America and
the Caribbean **(8.9%)**
28.6 million

Near East and North Africa **(9.1%)**
29.0 million

Rest of Asia **(22.6%)**
72.1 million

Remaining World **(2.3%)**
7.4 million

Eastern Europe and the New
Independent States **(0.8%)**
2.4 million

United States **(3.2%)**
10.1 million

Sub-Saharan Africa **(20.2%)**
64.5 million

NOTE: Percentages are of population added from 1996 to 2000. China includes Mainland China and Taiwan.

World Population by Region and Development Category (In millions)

Region	1950	1970	1990	1996	2020*
World	**2,556**	**3,706**	**5,282**	**5,772**	**7,600**
Less Developed Countries	1,749	2,703	4,139	4,601	6,351
More Developed Countries	807	1,003	1,142	1,171	1,249
Africa	**229**	**360**	**624**	**732**	**1,230**
Sub-Saharan Africa	185	289	504	594	1,023
North Africa	44	71	120	137	207
Near East	**43**	**74**	**134**	**157**	**276**
Asia	**1,368**	**2,039**	**2,989**	**3,271**	**4,219**
Latin America and the Caribbean	**166**	**285**	**443**	**489**	**643**
Europe and the New Independent States	**572**	**703**	**789**	**800**	**834**
Western Europe	304	352	377	387	394
Eastern Europe	88	108	122	120	122
New Independent States	180	242	289	293	318
North America	**166**	**226**	**277**	**295**	**361**
Oceania	**12**	**19**	**27**	**29**	**37**
Excluding China (Mainland and Taiwan):					
World	1,985	2,871	4,128	4,541	6,162
Less Developed Countries	1,179	1,868	2,985	3,370	4,913
Asia	797	1,204	1,835	2,039	2,780
Less Developed Countries	714	1,099	1,711	1,914	2,657

Share of World Population (Percent)

Region	1996	2020*
Less Developed Countries	79.7%	83.6%
More Developed Countries	20.3	16.4
Sub-Saharan Africa	10.3	13.5
Near East and North Africa	5.1	6.4
China (Mainland and Taiwan)	21.3	18.9
Other Asia	33.2	35.0
Latin America and the Caribbean	8.5	8.5
Eastern Europe and the New Independent States	7.2	5.8
Rest of the World	14.5	12.0

NOTE: Other Asia excludes China and Japan. Rest of the World includes Western Europe, North America, Japan, and Oceania.
*Projection
Source: U.S. Census Bureau

Distribution of World Births by Country

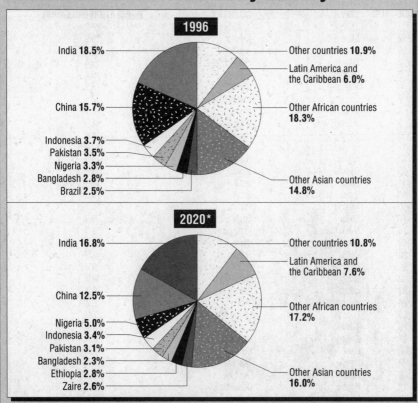

1996

- India **18.5%**
- China **15.7%**
- Indonesia **3.7%**
- Pakistan **3.5%**
- Nigeria **3.3%**
- Bangladesh **2.8%**
- Brazil **2.5%**
- Other countries **10.9%**
- Latin America and the Caribbean **6.0%**
- Other African countries **18.3%**
- Other Asian countries **14.8%**

2020*

- India **16.8%**
- China **12.5%**
- Nigeria **5.0%**
- Indonesia **3.4%**
- Pakistan **3.1%**
- Bangladesh **2.3%**
- Ethiopia **2.8%**
- Zaire **2.6%**
- Other countries **10.8%**
- Latin America and the Caribbean **7.6%**
- Other African countries **17.2%**
- Other Asian countries **16.0%**

NOTE: China includes Mainland China and Taiwan.
*Projection.
Source: U.S. Census Bureau

World's 50 Largest Urban Areas in 1996

RANK	CITY	COUNTRY	POPULATION (MILLIONS)
1	Tokyo	Japan	27.2
2	Mexico City	Mexico	16.9
3	Sao Paulo	Brazil	16.8
4	New York	United States	16.4
5	Bombay	India	15.7
6	Shanghai	China	13.7
7	Los Angeles	United States	12.6
8	Calcutta	India	12.1
9	Buenos Aires	Argentina	11.9
10	Seoul	Republic of Korea	11.8
11	Beijing	China	11.4
12	Lagos	Nigeria	10.9
13	Osaka	Japan	10.6
14	Delhi	India	10.3
15	Rio de Janeiro	Brazil	10.3
16	Karachi	Pakistan	10.1
17	Cairo	Egypt	9.9
18	Metro Manila	Philippines	9.6
19	Tianjin	China	9.6
20	Paris	France	9.6
21	Moscow	Russian Federation	9.3
22	Dhaka	Bangladesh	9.0
23	Jakarta	Indonesia	8.8
24	Istanbul	Turkey	8.2
25	London	United Kingdom	7.6
26	Teheran	Iran	6.9
27	Chicago	United States	6.9
28	Lima	Peru	6.8
29	Bangkok	Thailand	6.7
30	Essen	Germany	6.5
31	Bogotá	Colombia	6.2
32	Madras	India	6.1
33	Hong Kong	China	5.9
34	Hyderabad	India	5.7
35	Shenyang	China	5.2
36	Lahore	Pakistan	5.2
37	St. Petersburg	Russian Federation	5.1
38	Santiago	Chile	5.0
39	Bangalore	India	5.0
40	Harbin	China	4.7
41	Guangzhou	China	4.6
42	Hangzhou	China	4.6
43	Chengdu	China	4.5
44	Changchun	China	4.4
45	Baghdad	Iraq	4.4
46	Toronto	Canada	4.4
47	Kinshasa	Zaire	4.4
48	Wuhan	China	4.3
49	Philadelphia	United States	4.3
50	Milan	Italy	4.2

Source: United Nations

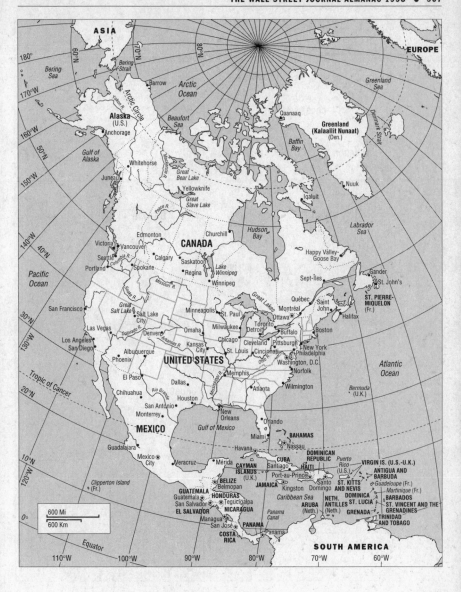

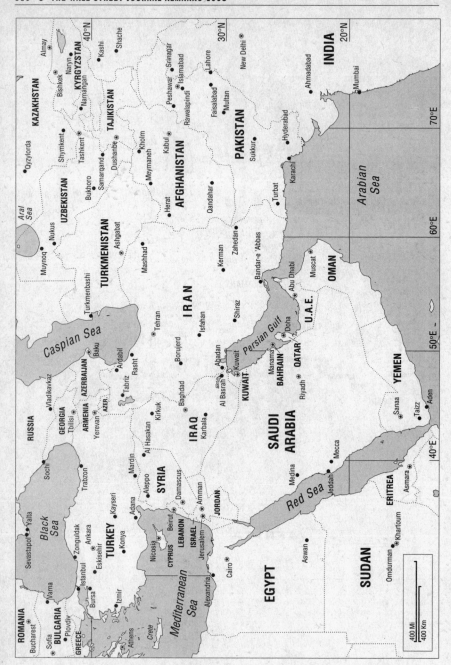

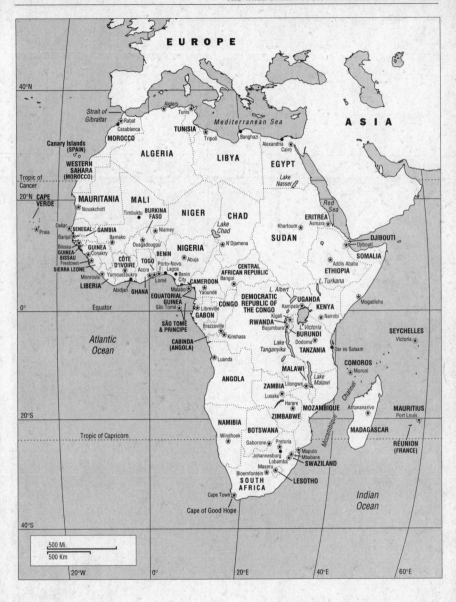

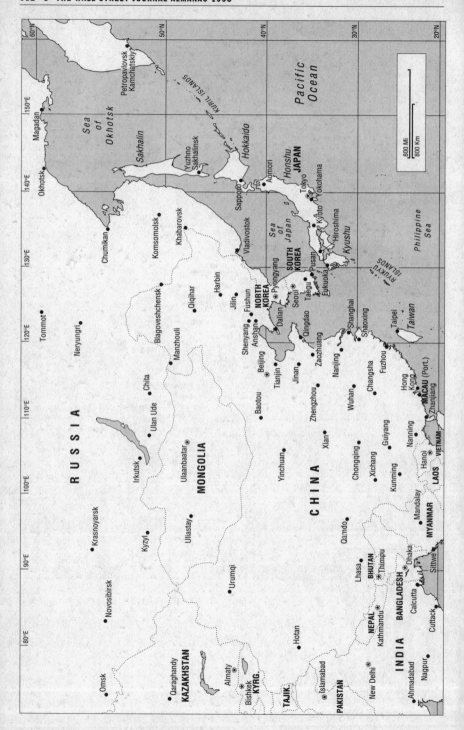

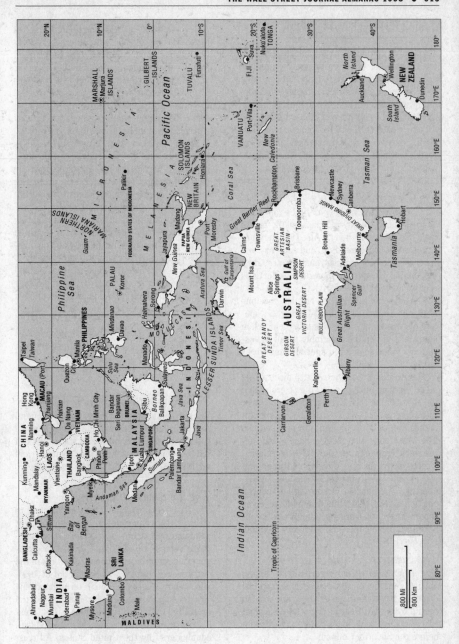

THE UNITED NATIONS

The United Nations is an organization of sovereign nations, not a world government. It provides the machinery to help find solutions to disputes or problems, and to deal with virtually any matter of concern to humanity.

The U.N. has six main organs, listed below. All are based at U.N. Headquarters in New York, except the International Court of Justice, which is located at The Hague, Netherlands.

The General Assembly

The General Assembly, sometimes called the nearest thing to a world parliament, is the main deliberative body. All 185 member states are represented in it, and each has one vote. Decisions on ordinary matters are taken by simple majority. Important questions require a two-thirds majority.

The Assembly holds its regular sessions from mid-September to mid-December; special or emergency sessions are held when necessary. When the Assembly is not in session, its work goes on in special committees and bodies.

The Assembly has the right to discuss and make recommendations on all matters within the scope of the U.N. Charter. It has no power to compel action by any state, but its recommendations carry the weight of world opinion. The Assembly also sets policies and determines programs for the U.N. Secretariat, directs activities for development and approves the U.N. budget, including peacekeeping operations. Occupying a central position in the U.N., the Assembly receives reports from other organs, admits new members and appoints the U.N. Secretary-General.

The Security Council

The *U.N. Charter*, an international treaty, obligates states to settle their international disputes by peaceful means. They are to refrain from the threat or use of force against other states, and may bring any dispute before the Security Council.

The Council is the organ to which the Charter gives primary responsibility for maintaining peace and security. It can be convened at any time, whenever peace is threatened. Member states are obligated to carry out its decisions.

The Council has 15 members. Five of these—China, France, the Russian Federation, the United Kingdom and the United States—are permanent members. The other 10 are elected by the Assembly for two-year terms. Decisions require nine votes; except in votes on procedural questions, a decision cannot be taken if there is a negative vote by a permanent member (known as the "veto").

When a threat to international peace is brought before the Council, it usually first asks the parties to reach agreement by peaceful means. The Council may undertake mediation or set forth principles for a settlement. It may deploy peace-keepers to prevent the outbreak of conflict. If fighting breaks out, the Council tries to secure a cease-fire. It may send peace-keeping missions to troubled areas, with the consent of the parties involved, to reduce tension and keep opposing forces apart. It has the power to enforce its decisions by imposing economic sanctions and by ordering collective military action.

The Council also makes recommendations to the Assembly on a candidate for Secretary-General and on the admission of new members to the U.N.

The Economic and Social Council

Working under the authority of the General Assembly, the Economic and Social Council coordinates the economic and social work of the U.N. and its specialized agencies and institutions. The Council has 54 members.

The Trusteeship Council

The Trusteeship Council was established to ensure that governments responsible for administering trust territories take adequate steps to prepare them for self-government or independence. The task of the Trusteeship System was completed in 1994, when the Security Council terminated the Trusteeship Agreement for the last of the original 11 U.N. Trusteeships—the Trust Territory of the Pacific Islands (Palau), administered by the United States. All trust territories have attained self-government or independence, either as separate states or by joining neighboring independent countries. The trusteeship Council, by amending its rules of procedure, will now meet as and where occasion may require.

The International Court of Justice

The International Court of Justice (also known as the World Court) is the main judicial organ of the U.N. It consists of 15 judges elected by the General Assembly and the Security Council. Only countries may be parties in cases brought before the Court. If a country does not wish to take part in a proceeding it does not have to do so (unless required by special treaty provisions), but if it accepts, it is obligated to comply with the Court's decision.

The Secretariat

The Secretariat works for all the other organs of the U.N. and administers their programs. With a staff of some 9,000, working at headquarters and all over the world, it carries out the day-to-day work of the U.N. At its head is the Secretary-General. Staff members are drawn from some 170 countries.

The Specialized Agencies

Fourteen specialized agencies work for development and international cooperation in their areas of expertise:

1. *International Labour Organization* (ILO)
2. *Food and Agriculture Organization of the U.N.* (FAO)
3. *U.N. Educational, Scientific and Cultural Organization* (UNESCO)
4. *World Health Organization* (WHO)
5. *World Bank*
6. *International Monetary Fund* (IMF)
7. *International Civil Aviation Organization* (ICAO)
8. *Universal Postal Union* (UPU)
9. *International Telecommunication Union* (ITU)
10. *World Meteorological Organization* (WMO)
11. *International Maritime Organization* (IMO)
12. *World Intellectual Property Organization* (WIPO)
13. *International Fund for Agricultural Development* (IFAD)
14. *U.N. Industrial Development Organization* (UNIDO)

Although not a specialized agency, the *International Atomic Energy Agency* (IAEA) is an autonomous intergovernmental organization under the aegis of the U.N. The *World Trade Organization* (WTO) cooperates with some U.N. bodies, although it does not have the formal status of a specialized agency.

Budget

The U.N. regular budget ($1.3 billion in 1996) is paid through assessed contributions from member states. But most of its assistance programs are funded through voluntary contributions.

UNITED NATIONS MEMBER STATES

With the admission of Palau, there are now 185 member states of the United Nations. The member states and the dates on which they joined the organization are listed below:

Afghanistan—*(Nov. 19 1946)*
Albania—*(Dec. 14 1955)*
Algeria—*(Oct. 8 1962)*
Andorra—*(July 28 1993)*
Angola—*(Dec. 1 1976)*
Antigua and Barbuda—*(Nov. 11 1981)*
Argentina—*(Oct. 24 1945)*
Armenia—*(Mar. 2 1992)*
Australia—*(Nov. 1 1945)*
Austria—*(Dec. 14 1955)*
Azerbaijan—*(Mar. 9 1992)*
Bahamas—*(Sep. 18 1973)*
Bahrain—*(Sep. 21 1971)*
Bangladesh—*(Sep. 17 1974)*
Barbados—*(Dec. 9 1966)*
Belarus—*(Oct. 24 1945)* On September 19, 1991, Byelorussia informed the United Nations that it had changed its name to Belarus.
Belgium—*(Dec. 27 1945)*
Belize—*(Sep. 25 1981)*
Benin—*(Sep. 20 1960)*
Bhutan—*(Sep. 21 1971)*
Bolivia—*(Nov. 14 1945)*
Bosnia and Herzegovina—*(May 22 1992)*
Botswana—*(Oct. 17 1966)*
Brazil—*(Oct. 24 1945)*
Brunei Darussalam—*(Sep. 21 1984)*

Bulgaria—*(Dec. 14 1955)*
Burkina Faso—*(Sep. 20 1960)*
Burundi—*(Sep. 18 1962)*
Cambodia—*(Dec. 14 1955)*
Cameroon—*(Sep. 20 1960)*
Canada—*(Nov. 9 1945)*
Cape Verde—*(Sep. 16 1975)*
Central African Republic—*(Sep. 20 1960)*
Chad—*(Sep. 20 1960)*
Chile—*(Oct. 24 1945)*
China—*(Oct. 24 1945)*
Colombia—*(Nov. 5 1945)*
Comoros—*(Nov. 12 1975)*
Congo—*(Sep. 20 1960)*
Costa Rica—*(Nov. 2 1945)*
Côte d'Ivoire—*(Sep. 20 1960)*
Croatia—*(May 22 1992)*
Cuba—*(Oct. 24 1945)*
Cyprus—*(Sep. 20 1960)*
Czech Republic—*(Jan. 19 1993)* Czechoslovakia was an original member of the United Nations from October 24, 1945. In a letter dated December 10, 1992, its permanent representative informed the Secretary-General that the Czech and Slovak Federal Republic would cease to exist on December 31, 1992 and that the Czech Republic and the Slovak Republic, as successor states, would apply for membership in the United Nations. Following the receipt of its application, the Security Council, on January 8, recommended to the General Assembly that the Czech Republic be admitted to United Nations membership. The Czech Republic was thus admitted on January 19, as a member state.

Democratic People's Republic of Korea—*(Sep. 17 1991)*
Denmark—*(Oct. 24 1945)*
Djibouti—*(Sep. 20 1977)*
Dominica—*(Dec. 18 1978)*
Dominican Republic—*(Oct. 24 1945)*
Ecuador—*(Dec. 21 1945)*
Egypt—*(Oct. 24 1945)* Egypt and Syria were original members of the United Nations from October 24, 1945. Following a plebiscite on February 21, 1958, the United Arab Republic was established by a union of Egypt and Syria and continued as a single member. On October 13, 1961, Syria, having resumed its status as an independent state, resumed its separate membership in the United Nations. On September 2, 1971, the United Arab Republic changed its name to the Arab Republic of Egypt.

El Salvador—*(Oct. 24 1945)*

Equatorial Guinea—*(Nov. 12 1968)*
Eritrea—*(May 28 1993)*
Estonia—*(Sep. 17 1991)*
Ethiopia—*(Nov. 13 1945)*
Federated States of Micronesia—*(Sep. 17 1991)*
Fiji—*(Oct. 13 1970)*
Finland—*(Dec. 14 1955)*
France—*(Oct. 24 1945)*
Gabon—*(Sep. 20 1960)*
Gambia—*(Sep. 21 1965)*
Georgia—*(July 31 1992)*
Germany—*(Sep. 18 1973)* The Federal Republic of Germany and the German Democratic Republic were admitted to membership in the United Nations on September 18, 1973. Through the accession of the German Democratic Republic to the Federal Republic of Germany, effective from October 3, 1990, the two German states have united to form one sovereign state.

Ghana—*(Mar. 8 1957)*
Greece—*(Oct. 25 1945)*
Grenada—*(Sep. 17 1974)*
Guatemala—*(Nov. 21 1945)*
Guinea—*(Dec. 12 1958)*
Guinea-Bissau—*(Sep. 17 1974)*
Guyana—*(Sep. 20 1966)*
Haiti—*(Oct. 24 1945)*
Honduras—*(Dec. 17 1945)*
Hungary—*(Dec. 14 1955)*
Iceland—*(Nov. 19 1946)*
India—*(Oct. 30 1945)*
Indonesia—*(Sep. 28 1950)* By letter of January 20, 1965, Indonesia announced its decision to withdraw from the United Nations "at this stage and under the present circumstances." By telegram of September 19, 1966, it announced its decision "to resume full cooperation with the United Nations and to resume participation in its activities." On September 28, 1966, the General Assembly took note of this decision and the President invited representatives of Indonesia to take seats in the Assembly.

Iran—*(Oct. 24 1945)*
Iraq—*(Dec. 21 1945)*
Ireland—*(Dec. 14 1955)*
Israel—*(May 11 1949)*
Italy—*(Dec. 14 1955)*
Jamaica—*(Sep. 18 1962)*
Japan—*(Dec. 18 1956)*
Jordan—*(Dec. 14 1955)*
Kazakstan—*(Mar. 2 1992)*
Kenya—*(Dec. 16 1963)*

Kuwait—*(May 14 1963)*
Kyrgyzstan—*(Mar. 2 1992)*
Laos —*(Dec. 14 1955)*
Latvia—*(Sep. 17 1991)*
Lebanon—*(Oct. 24 1945)*
Lesotho—*(Oct. 17 1966)*
Liberia—*(Nov. 2 1945)*
Libya—*(Dec. 14 1955)*
Liechtenstein—*(Sep. 18 1990)*
Lithuania—*(Sep. 17 1991)*
Luxembourg—*(Oct. 24 1945)*
Madagascar—*(Sep. 20 1960)*
Malawi—*(Dec. 1 1964)*
Malaysia—*(Sep. 17 1957)* The Federation of Malaya joined the United Nations on September 17, 1957. On September 16, 1963, its name was changed to Malaysia, following the admission to the new federation of Singapore, Sabah (North Borneo) and Sarawak. Singapore became an independent state on August 9, 1965 and a member of the United Nations on September 21, 1965.
Maldives—*(Sep. 21 1965)*
Mali—*(Sep. 28 1960)*
Malta—*(Dec. 1 1964)*
Marshall Islands—*(Sep. 17 1991)*
Mauritania—*(Oct. 7 1961)*
Mauritius—*(Apr. 24 1968)*
Mexico—*(Nov. 7 1945)*
Monaco—*(May 28 1993)*
Mongolia—*(Oct. 27 1961)*
Morocco—*(Nov. 12 1956)*
Mozambique—*(Sep. 16 1975)*
Myanmar—*(Apr. 19 1948)*
Namibia—*(Apr. 23 1990)*
Nepal—*(Dec. 14 1955)*
Netherlands—*(Dec. 10 1945)*
New Zealand—*(Oct. 24 1945)*
Nicaragua—*(Oct. 24 1945)*
Niger—*(Sep. 20 1960)*
Nigeria—*(Oct. 7 1960)*
Norway—*(Nov. 27 1945)*
Oman—*(Oct. 7 1971)*
Pakistan—*(Sep. 30 1947)*
Palau—*(Dec. 15 1994)*
Panama—*(Nov. 13 1945)*
Papua New Guinea—*(Oct. 10 1975)*
Paraguay—*(Oct. 24 1945)*
Peru—*(Oct. 31 1945)*
Philippines—*(Oct. 24 1945)*
Poland—*(Oct. 24 1945)*
Portugal—*(Dec. 14 1955)*
Qatar—*(Sep. 21 1971)*
Republic of Korea—*(Sep. 17 1991)*
Republic of Moldova—*(Mar. 2 1992)*

Romania—*(Dec. 14 1955)*
Russian Federation—*(Oct. 24 1945)* The Union of Soviet Socialist Republics was an original member of the United Nations from October 24, 1945. In a letter dated December 24, 1991, Boris Yeltsin, the President of the Russian Federation, informed the Secretary-General that the membership of the Soviet Union in the Security Council and all other United Nations organs was being continued by the Russian Federation with the support of the 11 member countries of the Commonwealth of Independent States.
Rwanda—*(Sep. 18 1962)*
Saint Kitts and Nevis—*(Sep. 23 1983)*
Saint Lucia—*(Sep. 18 1979)*
Saint Vincent and the Grenadines—*(Sep. 16 1980)*
Samoa—*(Dec. 15 1976)*
San Marino—*(Mar. 2 1992)*
Sao Tome and Principe—*(Sep. 16 1975)*
Saudi Arabia—*(Oct. 24 1945)*
Senegal—*(Sep. 28 1960)*
Seychelles—*(Sep. 21 1976)*
Sierra Leone—*(Sep. 27 1961)*
Singapore—*(Sep. 21 1965)*
Slovak Republic—*(Jan. 19 1993)* Czechoslovakia was an original member of the United Nations from October 24, 1945. In a letter dated December 10, 1992, its permanent representative informed the Secretary-General that the Czech and Slovak Federal Republic would cease to exist on December 31, 1992 and that the Czech Republic and the Slovak Republic, as successor states, would apply for membership in the United Nations. Following the receipt of its application, the Security Council, on January 8, recommended to the General Assembly that the Slovak Republic be admitted to United Nations membership. The Slovak Republic was thus admitted on January 19, as a member state.
Slovenia—*(May 22 1992)*
Solomon Islands—*(Sep. 19 1978)*
Somalia—*(Sep. 20 1960)*
South Africa—*(Nov. 7 1945)*
Spain—*(Dec. 14 1955)*
Sri Lanka—*(Dec. 14 1955)*
Sudan—*(Nov. 12 1956)*
Suriname—*(Dec. 4 1975)*
Swaziland—*(Sep. 24 1968)*
Sweden—*(Nov. 19 1946)*
Syria—*(Oct. 24 1945)* Egypt and Syria were original members of the United Nations from October 24, 1945. Following a plebiscite on

February 21, 1958, the United Arab Republic was established by a union of Egypt and Syria and continued as a single member. On October 13, 1961, Syria, having resumed its status as an independent state, resumed its separate membership in the United Nations.

Tajikistan—*(Mar. 2 1992)*
Thailand—*(Dec. 16 1946)*

The former Yugoslav Republic of Macedonia—*(Apr. 8 1993)* The General Assembly decided on April 8, 1993 to admit to United Nations membership the state being provisionally referred to for all purposes within the United Nations as "the former Yugoslav Republic of Macedonia" pending settlement of the difference that had arisen over its name.

Togo—*(Sep. 20 1960)*
Trinidad and Tobago—*(Sep. 18 1962)*
Tunisia—*(Nov. 12 1956)*
Turkey—*(Oct. 24 1945)*
Turkmenistan—*(Mar. 2 1992)*
Uganda—*(Oct. 25 1962)*
Ukraine—*(Oct. 24 1945)*
United Arab Emirates—*(Dec. 9 1971)*
United Kingdom—*(Oct. 24 1945)*
United Republic of Tanzania—*(Dec. 14 1961)*

Tanganyika was a member of the United Nations from December 14, 1961 and Zanzibar was a member from December 16, 1963. Following the ratification on April 26, 1964 of Articles of Union between Tanganyika and Zanzibar, the United Republic of Tanganyika and Zanzibar continued as a single member, changing its name to the United Republic of Tanzania on November 1, 1964.

United States—*(Oct. 24 1945)*
Uruguay—*(Dec. 18 1945)*
Uzbekistan—*(Mar. 2 1992)*
Vanuatu—*(Sep. 15 1981)*
Venezuela—*(Nov. 15 1945)*
Vienam—*(Sep. 20 1977)*
Yemen—*(Sep. 30 1947)* Yemen was admitted to membership in the United Nations on September 30, 1947 and Democratic Yemen on December 14, 1967. On May 22, 1990, the two countries merged and have since been represented as one member with the name "Yemen."

Yugoslavia—*(Oct. 24 1945)*
Zambia—*(Dec. 1 1964)*
Zimbabwe—*(Aug. 25 1980)*

Source: United Nations

Selected Countries

AFGHANISTAN

GEOGRAPHY:
Location: Southern Asia
Area:
  total area: 647,500 sq km
  land area: 647,500 sq km
Capital city: Kabul
Natural Resources: Natural gas, petroleum, coal, copper, talc, barites, sulphur, lead, zinc, iron ore, salt, precious and semi-precious stones

PEOPLE:
Population: 22,664,136
Population growth rate: 4.78%
Age structure:
  0–14 years: 43%
  15–64 years: 54%
  65 years & over: 3%
Literacy rate: *(age 15 and over can read and write)*
31.5% *of total population,*
  (males: 47.2%, *females:* 15%)
Languages: Pastu, Afghan Persian (*Dari*), Turk languages (*primarily Uzbek and Turkmen*), minor languages (*primarily Balochi and Pashai*)
Religions: 84%- Sunni Muslim, 15%-Shi'a Muslim, 1%-Other

VITAL STATISTICS:
Birth rate: 43.04 *(per 1,000 population)*
Death rate: 18.16 *(per 1,000 population)*
Infant mortality rate: 149.7 *(deaths per 1,000 live births)*
Fertility rate: 6.14 *(per woman)*
Life expectancy at birth:
  total population: 45.85
    (*males:* 46.43, *females:* 45.24)

GOVERNMENT:
Type of government: Transitional government
Independence: August 19, 1919 *(from UK)*

Leaders:
chief of state: President Burhanuddin Rabbani
head of government: Prime Minister Gulbuddin Hekmatyar

ECONOMY:
GDP: purchasing power parity - $12.8 billion
GDP real growth rate: NA%
GDP per capita: $600
Inflation Rate (consumer prices): NA%
National budget:
revenues: $NA
expenditures: $NA
External debt: $2.3 billion
Currency: 1 Afghani = 100 puls
Labor Force: 4.98 million
Unemployment rate: NA%
Agriculture: Wheat, fruit, nuts, karakul pelts; wool, mutton
Industries: Small-scale production of textiles, soap, furniture, shoes, fertilizer, cement; handwoven carpets; natural gas, oil, coal, copper
Exports: $188.2 million
commodities: Fruits and nuts, hand-woven carpets, wool, cotton, hides and pelts, precious and semi- precious gems
Imports: $616.4 million
commodities: Food and petroleum products; most consumer goods

DEFENSE:
Defense expenditures: $NA, NA% of GDP

ALBANIA

GEOGRAPHY:
Location: Southeastern Europe
Area:
total area: 28,750 sq km
land area: 27,400 sq km
Capital city: Tirana
Natural Resources: Petroleum, natural gas, coal, chromium, copper, timber, nickel

PEOPLE:
Population: 3,249,136
Population growth rate: 1.34%
Age structure:
0–14 years: 34%
15–64 years: 60%
65 years & over: 6%
Literacy rate: 72% *of total population,* (*males:* 80%, *females:* 63%)
Languages: Albanian (*Tosk is the official dialect*), Greek

Religions: 70%-Muslim, 20%-Albanian Orthodox, 10%-Roman Catholic

VITAL STATISTICS:
Birth rate: 22.21 *(per 1,000 population)*
Death rate: 7.64 *(per 1,000 population)*
Infant mortality rate: 49.2 *(deaths per 1,000 live births*
Fertility rate: 2.65 *(per woman)*
Life expectancy at birth:
total population: 67.92
(*males:* 64.91, *females:* 71.17)

GOVERNMENT:
Type of government: Emerging Democracy
Independence: November 28, 1912 *(from Ottoman Empire)*
Leaders:
chief of state: President of the Republic Rexhep Mejdani
head of government: Prime Minister of the Council of Ministers Fatos Nano

ECONOMY:
GDP: purchasing power parity - $4.1 billion
GDP real growth rate: 6%
GDP per capita: $1,210
Inflation Rate *(consumer prices):* 16%
National budget:
revenues: $486.3 million
expenditures: $550.4 million
External debt: $977 million
Currency: 1 lek = 100 qintars
Labor Force: 1.692 million
Unemployment rate: 19%
Agriculture: Wide range of temperate-zone crops, livestock
Industries: Food processing, textiles and clothing; lumber, oil, cement, chemicals, mining, basic metals, hydropower
Exports: $141 million
commodities: Asphalt, metals and metallic ores, electricity, crude oil, vegetables, fruits, tobacco
Imports: $601 million
commodities: Machinery, consumer goods, grains

DEFENSE:
Defense expenditures: *exchange rate conversion -* $45 *million,* 2.5% *of GDP*

ALGERIA

GEOGRAPHY:
Location: Northern Africa

Area:
  total area: 2,381,740 sq km
  land area: 2,381,740 sq km
Capital city: Algiers
Natural Resources: Petroleum, natural gas, iron ore, phosphates, uranium, lead, zinc

PEOPLE:
Population: 29,183,032
Population growth rate: 2.21%
Age structure:
  0–14 years: 40%
  15–64 years: 56%
  65 years & over: 4%
Literacy rate: 61.6% *of total population,*
  (males: 73.9%, *females:* 49%)
Languages: Arabic *(official),* French, Berber dialects
Religions: 99%- Sunni Muslim *(state religion),* 1%-Christian and Jewish

VITAL STATISTICS:
Birth rate: 28.51 *(per 1,000 population)*
Death rate: 5.9 *(per 1,000 population)*
Infant mortality rate: 48.7 *(deaths per 1,000 live births*
Fertility rate: 3.59 *(per woman)*
Life expectancy at birth:
  total population: 68.31
    (males: 67.22, *females:* 69.46)

GOVERNMENT:
Type of government: Republic
Independence: July 5, 1962 *(from France)*
Leaders:
  chief of state: President General Liamine Zeroual
  head of government: Prime Minister Ahmed Ouyahia

ECONOMY:
GDP: purchasing power parity - $108.7 billion
  GDP real growth rate: 3.5%
  GDP per capita: $3,800
Inflation Rate *(consumer prices):* 28%
National budget:
  revenues: $14.3 billion
  expenditures: $17.9 billion
External debt: $26 billion
Currency: 1 Algerian dinar = 100 centimes
Labor Force: 6.2 million
Unemployment rate: 25%
Agriculture: Wheat, barley, oats, grapes, olives, citrus, fruits; cattle, sheep
Industries: Petroleum, light industries, natural gas, mining, electrical, petrochemical, food processing
Exports: $9.5 billion
  commodities: Petroleum and natural gas

Imports: $10.6 billion
  commodities: Capital goods, food and beverages, consumer goods

DEFENSE:
Defense expenditures: *exchange rate conversion -* $1.3 *billion,* 2.7% *of GDP*

ANGOLA

GEOGRAPHY:
Location: Southern Africa
Area:
  total area: 1,246,700 sq km
  land area: 1,246,700 sq km
Capital city: Luanda
Natural Resources: Petroleum, diamonds, iron ore, phosphates, copper, feldspar, gold, bauxite, uranium

PEOPLE:
Population: 10,342,899
Population growth rate: 2.68%
Age structure:
  0–14 years: 45%
  15–64 years: 53%
  65 years & over: 2%
Literacy rate: 42% *of total population,*
  (males: 56%, *females:* 28%)
Languages: Portuguese *(official),* Bantu and other African Languages
Religions: 47%- indigenous beliefs, 38%-Roman Catholic, 15%-Protestant

VITAL STATISTICS:
Birth rate: 44.58 *(per 1,000 population)*
Death rate: 17.66 *(per 1,000 population)*
Infant mortality rate: 138.9 *(deaths per 1,000 live births)*
Fertility rate: 6.35 *(per woman)*
Life expectancy at birth:
  total population: 46.8
    (males: 44.65, *females:* 49.06)

GOVERNMENT:
Type of government: Transitional government nominally a multiparty democracy with strong presidential system
Independence: November 11, 1975 *(from Portugal)*
Leaders:
  chief of state: President Jose Eduardo Dos Santos
  head of government: Prime Minister M. Fernando Jose de Franca Dias Van-Dunem

ECONOMY:
GDP: purchasing power parity - $7.4 billion
 GDP real growth rate: 4%
 GDP per capita: $700
Inflation Rate *(consumer prices):* 20%
National budget:
 revenues: $928 million
 expenditures: $2.5 billion
External debt: $12 billion
Currency: 1 new kwanza = 100 lwei
Labor Force: 2.783 million
Unemployment rate: 24% *(with extensive underemployment)*
Agriculture: Bananas, sugarcane, coffee, sisal, corn, cotton, manioc(tapioca), tobacco, vegetables, plantains; livestock; forest products; fish
Industries: Petroleum; diamonds, iron ore, phosphates, feldspar, bauxite, uranium, and gold; fish processing; food processing; brewing; tobacco; sugar; textiles; cement; basic metal products
Exports: $3 billion
 commodities: Oil, diamonds, refined petroleum products, gas, coffee, sisal, fish and fish products, timber, cotton
Imports: $1.6 billion
 commodities: Capital equipment *(machinery and elecrical equipment)*, food, vehicles and spare parts, textiles and clothing, medicines, substantial military deliveries

DEFENSE:
Defense expenditures: *exchange rate conversion -* $1.1 *billion*, 31% *of GDP*

ARGENTINA

GEOGRAPHY:
Location: Southern South America
Area:
 total area: 2,766,890 sq km
 land area: 2,736,690 sq km
Capital city: Buenos Aires
Natural Resources: Fertile plains of the pampas, lead, zinc, tin, copper, iron ore, manganese, petroleum, uranium

PEOPLE:
Population: 34,672,997
Population growth rate: 1.1%
Age structure:
 0–14 years: 28%
 15–64 years: 63%
 65 years & over: 9%
Literacy rate: 96.2% *of total population,* *(males:* 96.2%, *females:* 96.2%)
Languages: Spanish *(official),* English, Italian, German, French
Religions: 90%-Roman Catholic *(less than 20% practicing),* 2%- Protestant, 2%-Jewish, 6%-other

VITAL STATISTICS:
Birth rate: 19.41 *(per 1,000 population)*
Death rate: 8.62 *(per 1,000 population)*
Infant mortality rate: 28.3 *(deaths per 1,000 live births)*
Fertility rate: 2.62 *(per woman)*
Life expectancy at birth:
 total population: 71.66
 (males: 68.37, *females:* 75.12)

GOVERNMENT:
Type of government: Republic
Independence: July 9, 1816 *(from Spain)*
Leaders:
 chief of state & head of government: President Carlos Saul Menem

ECONOMY:
GDP: purchasing power parity - $278.5 billion
 GDP real growth rate: -4.4%
 GDP per capita: $8,100
Inflation Rate *(consumer prices):* 1.7%
National budget:
 revenues: $48.46 billion
 expenditures: $46.5 billion
External debt: $90 billion
Currency: 1 nuevo peso Argentino = 100 centavos
Labor Force: 10.9 million
Unemployment rate: 16%
Agriculture: Wheat, corn, sorghum, soybeans, sugar beets; livestock
Industries: Food processing, motor vehicles, consumer durables, textiles, chemicals and petrochemicals, printing, metallurgy, steel
Exports: $20.7 billion
 commodities: Meat, wheat, corn, oilseed, manufactured goods
Imports: $19.5 billion
 commodities: Machinery and equipment, chemicals, metals, fuels and lubricants, agricultural products

DEFENSE:
Defense expenditures: *exchange rate conversion -* $4.7 *billion*, 1.5% *of GDP*

ARMENIA

GEOGRAPHY:
Location: Southwestern Asia

Area:
  total area: 29,800 sqkm
  land area: 28,400 sqkm
Capital city: Yerevan
Natural Resources: Small deposits of gold, copper, molybdenum, zinc, alumina

PEOPLE:
Population: 3,463,574
Population growth rate: 0.02%
Age structure:
  0–14 years: 28%
  15–64 years: 64%
  65 years & over: 8%
Literacy rate: 99% *of total population,* (*males:* 99%, *females:* 98%)
Languages: Armenian, Russian, other
Religions: 94%- Armenian Orthodox

VITAL STATISTICS:
Birth rate: 16.27 *(per 1,000 population)*
Death rate: 7.73 *(per 1,000 population)*
Infant mortality rate: 38.9 *(deaths per 1,000 live births)*
Fertility rate: 2.06 *(per woman)*
Life expectancy at birth:
  total population: 69.06
    (*males:* 64.44, *females:* 73.92)

GOVERNMENT:
Type of government: Republic
Independence: May 28, 1918 *(from First Armenian Republic)* September 23, 1991 *(from Soviet Union)*
Leaders:
  chief of state: President Levon Ter-Petrossian
  head of government: Prime Minister Robert Kocharian

ECONOMY:
GDP: purchasing power parity - $9.1 billion
  GDP real growth rate: 5.2%
  GDP per capita: $2,560
Inflation Rate *(consumer prices):* 32.2%
National budget:
  revenues: $NA
  expenditures: $NA
External debt: $850 million
Currency: 1 dram = 100 luma
Labor Force: 1.012 million
Unemployment rate: 8% *(officially registered unemployed, large numbers of underemployed)*
Agriculture: Fruit *(especially grapes)*, vegetables; brandy, liqueurs; minor livestock sector
Industries: Much of industry is shut down; metal-cutting machine tools, forging-pressing machines, electric motors, tires, knitted wear, hoisery, shoes, silk fabric, washing machines, chemicals, trucks, watches, instruments, microelectronics
Exports: $248 million
  commodities: Gold and jewlery, aluminum, transport equipment, electrical equipment scrap metal
Imports: $661 million
  commodities: Grain, other foods, fuel, other energy

DEFENSE:
Defense expenditures: *exchange rate conversion -* $75 *million*, NA% *of GDP*

AUSTRALIA

GEOGRAPHY:
Location: Oceania
Area:
  total area: 7,686,850 sq km
  land area: 7,617,930 sq km
Capital city: Canberra
Natural Resources: Bauxite, coal, iron ore, copper, tin, silver, uranium, nickel, tungsten, mineral sands, lead, zinc, diamonds, natural gas, petroleum

PEOPLE:
Population: 18,260,863
Population growth rate: 0.99%
Age structure:
  0–14 years: 21%
  15–64 years: 66%
  65 years & over: 13%
Literacy rate: 100% *of total population*
Languages: English, Native Languages
Religions: 26.1%- Anglican, 26%-Roman Catholic, 24.3%-Other Christian

VITAL STATISTICS:
Birth rate: 13.99 *(per 1,000 population)*
Death rate: 6.88 *(per 1,000 population)*
Infant mortality rate: 5.5 *(deaths per 1,000 live births)*
Fertility rate: 1.84 *(per woman)*
Life expectancy at birth:
  total population: 79.39
    (*males:* 76.44, *females:* 82.5)

GOVERNMENT:
Type of government: Federal Parliamentary State
Independence: January 1, 1901 *(federation of UK colonies)*

Leaders:
chief of state: Queen Elizabeth II, represented by Governor General Sir William Deane
head of government: Prime Minister John Winston Howard

ECONOMY:
GDP: purchasing power parity - $405.4 billion
GDP real growth rate: 3.3%
GDP per capita: $22,100
Inflation Rate *(consumer prices):* 4.75%
National budget:
revenues: $95.69 billion
expenditures: $95.15 billion
External debt: $147.2 billion
Currency: 1 Australian dollar = 100 cents
Labor Force: 8.63 million
Unemployment rate: 8.1%
Agriculture: Wheat, barley, sugarcane, fruits; cattle sheep, poultry
Industries: Mining, industrial and transportation equipment, food processing, chemicals, steel
Exports: $51.57 billion
commodities: Coal, gold, meat, wool, alumina, wheat, machinery and transport equipment
Imports: $57.41 billion
commodities: Machinery and transport equipment, computers and office machines, crude oil and petroleum products

DEFENSE:
Defense expenditures: *exchange rate conversion - 7.3 billion,* 2.0% *of GDP*

AUSTRIA

GEOGRAPHY:
Location: Central Europe
Area:
total area: 83,850 sq km
land area: 82,730 sq km
Capital city: Vienna
Natural Resources: Iron ore, oil, timber, magnesite, lead, coal, lignite, copper, hydropower

PEOPLE:
Population: 8,023,244
Population growth rate: 0.41%
Age structure:
0–14 years: 18%
15–64 years: 67%
65 years & over: 15%
Literacy rate: 99% *of total population*
Languages: German
Religions: 85%-Roman Catholic, 6%- Protestant, 9%- other

VITAL STATISTICS:
Birth rate: 11.19 *(per 1,000 population)*
Death rate: 10.43 *(per 1,000 population)*
Infant mortality rate: 6.2 *(deaths per 1,000 live births)*
Fertility rate: 1.49 *(per woman)*
Life expectancy at birth:
total population: 76.53
(males: 73.38, *females:* 79.84)

GOVERNMENT:
Type of government: Federal Republic
Independence: November 12, 1918 *(from Austro-Hungarian Empire)*
Leaders:
chief of state: President Thomas Klestil
head of government: Chancellor Viktor Klima

ECONOMY:
GDP: purchasing power parity - $152 billion
GDP real growth rate: 2.4%
GDP per capita: $19,000
Inflation Rate *(consumer prices):* 2.3%
National budget:
revenues: $65 billion
expenditures: $75.8 billion
External debt: $28.7 billion
Currency: 1 Austrian schilling = 100 groschen
Labor Force: 3.47 million
Unemployment rate: 4.6%
Agriculture: Grains, fruits, potatoes, sugar beets; cattle, pigs, poultry; sawn wood
Industries: Food, iron and steel, machines, textiles, chemicals, electrical, paper and pulp, tourism, mining, motor vehicles
Exports: $45.2 billion
commodities: Machinery and equipment, iron and steel, lumber, textiles, paper products, chemicals
Imports: $55.3 billion
commodities: Petroleum, foodstuffs, machinery and equipment, vehicles, chemicals, textiles and clothing, pharmaceuticals

DEFENSE:
Defense expenditures: *exchange rate conversion - $2.1 billion,* 1.0% *of GDP*

AZERBAIJAN

GEOGRAPHY:
Location: Southwestern Asia
Area:
total area: 86,600 sq km
land area: 86,100 sq km

Capital city: Baku (Baki)
Natural Resources: Petroleum, natural gas, iron ore, nonferrous metals, alumina

PEOPLE:
Population: 7,676,953
Population growth rate: 0.78%
Age structure:
  0–14 years: 32%
  15–64 years: 61%
  65 years & over: 7%
Literacy rate: 97%, *of total population*
  (*males:* 99%, *females:* 96%)
Languages: Azeri, Russian, Armenian, other
Religions: 93.4%-Muslim, 2.5%-Russian Orthodox, 2.3%-Armenian Orthodox, 1.8%-other *(note— religious affiliation is still nominal in Azerbaijan; actual practicing adherents are much lower)*

VITAL STATISTICS
Birth rate: 22.28 *(per 1,000 population)*
Death rate: 8.69 *(per 1,000 population)*
Infant mortality rate: 74.5 *(deaths per 1,000 live births)*
Fertility rate: 2.64 *(per woman)*
Life expectancy at birth:
  total population: 64.84,
    (*males:* 60.13, *females:* 69.78)

GOVERNMENT:
Type of government: Republic
Independence: August 30, 1991 *(from Soviet Union)*
Leaders:
  chief of state: President Heydar Aliyev
  head of government: Prime Minister Artur Razizade

ECONOMY:
GDP: purchasing power parity-$11.5 billion
  GDP real growth rate: −17%
  GDP per capita: $1,480
Inflation Rate *(consumer prices):* 85%
National budget:
  revenues: $465 million
  expenditures: $488 million
External debt: $100 million
Currency: 1 manat = 100 gopik
Labor Force: 2.789 million
Unemployment rate: 2.3% *(registered unemployed); (large numbers of unregistered unemployed and underemployed workers)*
Agriculture: Cotton, grain, rice, grapes, fruit, vegetables, tea, tobacco; cattle, pigs, sheep, goats
Industries: Petroleum and natural gas, petroleum products, oilfield equipment; steel, iron ore, cement; chemicals and petrochemicals; textiles
Exports: $549.9 million

  commodities: Oil and gas, chemicals, oilfield equipment, textiles, cotton
Imports: $681.5 million
  commodities: Machinery and parts, consumer durables, foodstuffs, textiles

DEFENSE:
Defense expenditures: 33.5 *billion manats*, NA% *of GDP; (note—conversion of defense expenditures into US dollars using the current exchange rate could produce misleading results)*

BAHRAIN

GEOGRAPHY:
Location: Middle East
Area:
  total area: 620 sq km
  land area: 620 sq km
Capital city: Manama
Natural Resources: Oil, associated and nonassociated natural gas, fish

PEOPLE:
Population: 590,042
Population growth rate: 2.27%
Age structure:
  0–14 years: 31%
  15–64 years: 67%
  65 years & over: 2%
Literacy rate: 85.2%, *of total population*,
  (*males:* 89.1%, *females:* 79.4%)
Languages: Arabic, English, Farsi, Urdu
Religions: 75%-Shi'a Muslim, 25%-Sunni Muslim

VITAL STATISTICS:
Birth rate: 23.58 *(per 1,000 population)*
Death rate: 3.29 *(per 1,000 population)*
Infant mortality rate: 17.1 *(deaths per 1,000 live births)*
Fertility rate: 3.08 *(per woman)*
Life expectancy at birth:
  total population: 74.27,
    (*males:* 71.78, *females:* 76.83)

GOVERNMENT:
Type of government: Traditional Monarchy
Independence: August 15, 1971 *(from UK)*
Leaders:
  chief of state: Amir Isa bin Salman Al Khalifa
  head of government: Prime Minister Khalifa bin Salman Al Khalifa

ECONOMY:
GDP: purchasing power parity-$7.3 billion

GDP real growth rate: −2%
GDP per capita: $12,000
Inflation Rate *(consumer prices):* 3%
National budget:
  revenues: $1.38 billion
  expenditures: $1.7 billion
External debt: $2.6 billion
Currency: 1 Bahraini dinar = 1,000 fils
Labor Force: 140,000
Unemployment rate: 25%
Agriculture: Fruit, vegetables; poultry, dairy products; shrimp, fish
Industries: Petroleum processing and refining, aluminum smelting, offshore banking, ship repairing
Exports: $3.2 billion
  commodities: Petroleum and petroleum products, aluminum
Imports: $3.29 billion

DEFENSE:
Defense expenditures: *exchange rate conversion-* $247 *million,* 5.5% *of GDP*

BANGLADESH

GEOGRAPHY:
Location: Southern Asia
Area:
  total area: 144,000 sq km
  land area: 133,910 sq km
Capital city: Dhaka
Natural Resources: Natural gas, arable land, timber

PEOPLE:
Population: 123,062,800
Population growth rate: 1.85%
Age structure:
  0–14 years: 39%
  15–64 years: 58%
  65 years & over: 3%
Literacy rate: 38.1% *of total population,*
  (*males:* 49.4%, *females:* 26.1%)
Languages: Bangla *(official),* English
Religions: 83%- Muslim, 16%-Hindu, Buddhist, Christian, other

VITAL STATISTICS:
Birth rate: 30.5 *(per 1,000 population)*
Death rate: 11.21 *(per 1,000 population)*
Infant mortality rate: 102.3 *(deaths per 1,000 live births)*
Fertility rate: 3.57 *(per woman)*
Life expectancy at birth:
  total population: 55.86
    (*males:* 56.02, *females:* 55.69)

GOVERNMENT:
Type of government: Republic
Independence: December 16, 1971 *(from Pakistan)*
Leaders:
  chief of state: President Shahabuddin Ahmed
  head of government: Prime Minister Skeikh Hasina

ECONOMY:
GDP: purchasing power parity - $144.5 billion
  GDP real growth rate: 4.6%
  GDP per capita: $1,130
Inflation Rate *(consumer prices):* 4.5%
National budget:
  revenues: $2.8 billion
  expenditures: $4.1 billion
External debt: $15.7 billion
Currency: 1 taka = 100 poiska
Labor Force: 50.1 million
Unemployment rate: NA %
Agriculture: Jute, rice, wheat, tea, sugarcane, potatoes; beef, milk, poultry
Industries: Jute manufacturing, cotton textiles, food processing, steel, fertilizer
Exports: $2.7 billion
  commodities: Garments, jute and jute goods, leather shrimp
Imports: $4.7 billion
  commodities: Capital goods, petroleum, food, textiles

DEFENSE:
Defense expenditures: *exchange rate conversion -* $481 *million,* 1.7% *of GDP*

BELARUS

GEOGRAPHY:
Location: Eastern Europe
Area:
  total area: 207,600 sq km
  land area: 207,600 sq km
Capital city: Minsk
Natural Resources: Forests, peat deposits, small quantities of oil and natural gas

PEOPLE:
Population: 10,415,973
Population growth rate: 0.2%
Age structure:
  0–14 years: 21%
  15–64 years: 66%
  65 years & over: 13%
Literacy rate: 98% *of total population,*
  (*males:* 99%, *females:* 97%)
Languages: Byelorussian, Russian, other

Religions: 60%- Eastern Orthodox, 40%-other
(*Including Roman Catholic and Muslim*)

VITAL STATISTICS:
Birth rate: 12.15 *(per 1,000 population)*
Death rate: 13.64 *(per 1,000 population)*
Infant mortality rate: 13.4 *(deaths per 1,000 live births)*
Fertility rate: 1.69 *(per woman)*
Life expectancy at birth:
  total population: 68.57
    (*males:* 63.2, *females:* 74.21)

GOVERNMENT:
Type of government: Republic
Independence: August 25, 1991 *(from Soviet Union);* the Belarussian Supreme Soviet issued a proclamation of independence; on July 17, 1990 Belarus issued a declaration of sovereignty
Leaders:
  chief of state: President Aleksandr Lukashenko
  head of government: Prime Minister Syargei Ling

ECONOMY:
GDP: purchasing power parity - $49.2 billion
  GDP real growth rate: −10%
  GDP per capita: $4,700
Inflation Rate *(consumer prices):* 244%
National budget:
  revenues: $4.95 billion
  expenditures: $5.47 billion
External debt: $2 billion
Currency: Belarusian rubel
Labor Force: 4.259 million
Unemployment rate: 2.6% *(large number of underemployed workers)*
Agriculture: Grain, potatoes, vegetables; meat, milk
Industries: Tractors, metal-cutting machine tools, off-highway dump trucks, wheel type earth movers for construction and mining, eight-wheel-drive, high-flotation trucks for use in tundra and roadless areas, equipment for animal husbandry and livestock feeding, motorcycles, television sets, chemical fibers, fertilizer, linen fabric, wool fabric, radios, refrigerators, other consumer goods
Exports: $4.2 billion
  commodities: Machinery and transport equipment, chemicals, foodstuffs
Imports: $4.6 billion
  commodities: Fuel, natural gas, industrial raw materials, textiles, sugar

DEFENSE:
Defense expenditures: 892 *billion rubels*, 1% *of GDP (note-Conversion of defense expenditures into US dollars could produce misleading results)*

BELGIUM

GEOGRAPHY:
Location: Western Europe
Area:
  total area: 30,510 sq km
  land area: 30,230 sq km
Capital city: Brussels
Natural Resources: Coal, natural gas

PEOPLE:
Population: 10,170,241
Population growth rate: 0.33%
Age structure:
  0–14 years: 18%
  15–64 years: 66%
  65 years & over: 16%
Literacy rate: 99% *of total population*
Languages: Dutch, French, German
Religions: 75%-Roman Catholic, 25%-Protestant and other

VITAL STATISTICS:
Birth rate: 12 *(per 1,000 population)*
Death rate: 10.3 *(per 1,000 population)*
Infant mortality rate: 6.4 *(deaths per 1,000 live births)*
Fertility rate: 1.69 *(per woman)*
Life expectancy at birth:
  total population: 77.09
    (*males:* 73.86, *females:* 80.51)

GOVERNMENT:
Type of government: Constitutional Monarchy
Independence: October 4, 1830 *(from the Netherlands)*
Leaders:
  chief of state: King Albert II
  head of government: Prime Minister Jean-Luc Dehaene

ECONOMY:
GDP: purchasing power parity - $197 billion
  GDP real growth rate: 2.3%
  GDP per capita: $19,500
Inflation Rate *(consumer prices):* 1.6%
National budget:
  revenues: $97.8 billion
  expenditures: $109.3 billion
External debt: $31.3 billion
Currency: 1 Belgian franc = 100 centimes
Labor Force: 4.126 million
Unemployment rate: 14%
Agriculture: Sugar beets, fresh vegetables, fruits, grain, tobacco; beef, veal, pork, milk
Industries: Engineering and metal products, motor

vehicle assembly, processed food and beverages, chemicals, basic metals, textiles, glass, petroleum, coal

Exports: $108 billion

commodities: Iron and steel, transportation equipment, tractors, diamonds, petroleum products

Imports: $140 billion

commodities: Fuels, grains, chemicals, foodstuffs

DEFENSE:

Defense expenditures: *exchange rate conversion -* $4.6 *billion,* 1.7% *of GDP*

BOLIVIA

GEOGRAPHY:

Location: Central South America

Area:

total area: 1,098,580 sq km

land area: 1,084,390 sq km

Capital city: Sucre *(judicial),* La Paz *(administrative)*

Natural Resources: Tin, natural gas, petroleum, zinc, tungsten, antimony, silver, iron, lead, gold, timber

PEOPLE:

Population: 7,165,257

Population growth rate: 1.82%

Age structure:

0–14 years: 39%

15–64 years: 56%

65 years & over: 5%

Literacy rate: 83.1% *of total population,* (*males:* 90.5%, *females:* 76%)

Languages: Spanish*(official),* Quechua*(official),* Aymara*(official)*

Religions: 95%- Roman Catholic; Protestant*(Evangelical Methodist)*

VITAL STATISTICS:

Birth rate: 32.37 *(per 1,000 population)*

Death rate: 10.75 *(per 1,000 population)*

Infant mortality rate: 67.5 *(deaths per 1,000 live births)*

Fertility rate: 4.25 *(per woman)*

Life expectancy at birth:

total population: 59.81

(*males:* 56.94, *females:* 62.82)

GOVERNMENT:

Type of government: Republic

Independence: August 6, 1825 *(from Spain)*

Leaders:

chief of state & head of government: President Hugo Banzer

ECONOMY:

GDP: purchasing power parity - $20 billion

GDP real growth rate: 3.7%

GDP per capita: $2,530

Inflation Rate *(consumer prices)*: 12%

National budget:

revenues: $3.75 billion

expenditures: $3.75 billion

External debt: $4.4 billion

Currency: 1 boliviano = 100 centavos

Labor Force: 3.54 million

Unemployment rate: urban rate 8%

Agriculture: Coffee, coca, cotton, corn, sugarcane, rice, potatoes; timber

Industries: Mining, smelting, petroleum, food and beverages, tobacco, handicrafts, clothing

Exports: $1.1 billion

commodities: Metals, natural gas, soybeans, jewlery, wood

Imports: $1.21 billion

commodities: Capital goods, chemicals, petroleum food

DEFENSE:

Defense expenditures: *exchange rate conversion -* $145 *million,* 1.9% *of GDP*

BOSNIA AND HERZEGOVINA

GEOGRAPHY:

Location: Southeastern Europe

Area:

total area: 51,233 sq km

land area: 51,233 sq km

Capital city: Sarajevo

Natural Resources: Coal, iron, bauxite, manganese, forests, copper, chromium, lead, zinc

PEOPLE:

Population: 2,656,240

Population growth rate: -2.84%

Age structure:

0–14 years: 20%

15–64 years: 68%

65 years & over: 12%

Literacy rate: NA%

Languages: Serbo-Croatian

Religions: 40%-Muslim, 31%- Orthodox, 15%- Catholic, 4%- Protestant, 10%-other

VITAL STATISTICS:
Birth rate: 6.34 *(per 1,000 population)*
Death rate: 15.92 *(per 1,000 population)*
Infant mortality rate: 43.2 *(deaths per 1,000 live births)*
Fertility rate: 1 *(per woman)*
Life expectancy at birth:
   total population: 56.11
      (males: 51.16, *females:* 61.39)

GOVERNMENT:
Type of government: Emerging Democracy
Independence: April 1992 *(from Yugoslavia)*
Leaders:
   chief of state: President Alija Izetbegovic
   head of government: Prime Minister Haris Silajdzic
                    Prime Minister Boro Bosic

ECONOMY:
GDP: purchasing power parity - $1 billion
   GDP real growth rate: NA%
   GDP per capita: $300
Inflation Rate *(consumer prices):* NA%
National budget:
   revenues: $NA
   expenditures: $NA
External debt: $NA
Currency: 1 dinar = 100 para *(Croatian dinar used in Croat-held area, presumably to be replaced by new Croatian kuna; old and new Serbian dinars used in Serb-held area; hard currencies probably supplanting local currencies in areas held by Bosnian Government)*
Labor Force: 1,026,254
Unemployment rate: NA%
Agriculture: Wheat, corn, fruits, vegetables; livestock
Industries: Steel, coal, iron ore, lead, zinc, manganese, bauxite, vehicle assembly, textiles, tobacco products, wooden furniture, tank and aircraft assembly, domestic appliances, oil refining; much of capacity damaged or shut down
Exports: $NA
   commodities: NA
Imports: $NA
   commodities: NA

DEFENSE:
Defense expenditures: $NA, NA% of GDP

B R A Z I L

GEOGRAPHY:
Location: Eastern South America

Area:
   total area: 8,511,965 sq km
   land area: 8,456,510 sq km
Capital city: Brasilia
Natural Resources: Bauxite, gold, iron ore, manganese, nickel, phosphate, platinum, tin, uranium, petroleum, hydropower timber

PEOPLE:
Population: 162,661,214
Population growth rate: 1.16%
Age structure:
   0–14 years: 31%
   15–64 years: 65%
   65 years & over: 4%
Literacy rate: 83.3% *of total population,*
   (males: 83.3%, *females:* 83.2%)
Languages: Portuguese*(official)*, Spanish, English, French
Religions: 70%-Roman Catholic *(nominal)*

VITAL STATISTICS:
Birth rate: 20.8 *(per 1,000 population)*
Death rate: 9.19 *(per 1,000 population)*
Infant mortality rate: 55.3 *(deaths per 1,000 live births)*
Fertility rate: 2.34 *(per woman)*
Life expectancy at birth:
   total population: 61.62
      (males: 56.67, *females:* 66.81)

GOVERNMENT:
Type of government: Federal Republic
Independence: September 7, 1822 *(from Portugal)*
Leaders:
   chief of state & head of government:
      President Fernando Henrique Cardoso

ECONOMY:
GDP: purchasing power parity - $976.8 billion
   GDP real growth rate: 4.2%
   GDP per capita: $6,100
Inflation Rate *(consumer prices):* 23%
National budget:
   revenues: $58.7 billion
   expenditures: $54.9 billion
External debt: $94 billion
Currency: 1 real = 100 centavos
Labor Force: 57 million
Unemployment rate: 5%
Agriculture: Coffee, soybeans, wheat, rice, corn, sugarcane, cocoa, citrus; beef
Industries: Textiles, shoes, chemicals, cement, lumber, iron ore, tin, steel, aircraft, motor vehicles and parts, other machinery and equipment
Exports: $46.5 billion
   commodities: Iron ore, soybean bran, orange juice, footwear, coffee, motor vehicle parts

Imports: $49.7 billion
commodities: Crude oil, capital goods, chemical products, foodstuffs, coal

DEFENSE:
Defense expenditures: *exchange rate conversion -* $6.736 *billion*, 1.1% *of GDP*

B R U N E I

GEOGRAPHY:
Location: Southeastern Asia
Area:
  total area: 5,770 sq km
  land area: 5,270 sq km
Capital city: Bandar Seri Begawan
Natural Resources: Petroleum, natural gas, timber

PEOPLE:
Population: 299,939
Population growth rate: 2.56%
Age structure:
  0–14 years: 33%
  15–64 years: 62%
  65 years & over: 5%
Literacy rate: 88.2%, *of total population,*
  (*males:* 92.6%, *females:* 83.4%)
Languages: Malay *(official)*, English, Chinese
Religions: 63%-Muslim *(official)*, 14%-Buddhism, 8%-Christian, 15%-indigenous beliefs and other

VITAL STATISTICS:
Birth rate: 25.5 *(per 1,000 population)*
Death rate: 5.1 *(per 1,000 population)*
Infant mortality rate: 24.2 *(deaths per 1,000 live births)*
Fertility rate: 3.39 *(per woman)*
Life expectancy at birth:
  total population: 71.39
  (*males:* 69.82, *females:* 73.04)

GOVERNMENT:
Type of government: constitutional sultanate
Independence: January 1, 1984 *(from UK)*
Leaders:
  chief of state & head of government: Sultan Haji Hassanal Bolkiah

ECONOMY:
GDP: purchasing power parity-$4.6 billion
  GDP real growth rate: 2%
  GDP per capita: $15,800
Inflation Rate *(consumer prices):* 2.4%

National budget:
  revenues: $2.1 billion
  expenditures: $2.1 billion
External debt: 0
Currency: 1 Bruneian dollar = 100 cents
Labor Force: 119,000
Unemployment rate: 4.8%
Agriculture: Rice cassava *(tapioca)*, bananas; water buffalo, pigs
Industries: Petroleum, petroleum refining, liquefied natural gas, construction
Exports: $2.4 billion
  commodities: Crude oil, liquefied natural gas, petroleum products
Imports: $1.8 billion
  commodities: Machinery and transport equipment, manufactured goods, food, chemicals

DEFENSE:
Defense expenditures: *exchange rate conversion-* $312 *million*, 6.2% *of GDP*

B U L G A R I A

GEOGRAPHY:
Location: Southeastern Europe
Area:
  total area: 110,910 sq km
  land area: 110,550 sq km
Capital city: Sofia
Natural Resources: Bauxite, copper, lead, zinc, coal, timber, arable land

PEOPLE:
Population: 8,612,757
Population growth rate: 0.46%
Age structure:
  0–14 years: 17%
  15–64 years: 68%
  65 years & over: 15%
Literacy rate: 98% *of total population,*
  (*males:* 99%, *females:* 97%)
Languages: Bulgarian
Religions: 85%- Bulgarian Orthodox, 13% - Muslim, 0.8%-Jewish, 0.5%-Roman Catholic, 0.2%-uniate Catholic

VITAL STATISTICS:
Birth rate: 8.33 *(per 1,000 population)*
Death rate: 13.55 *(per 1,000 population)*
Infant mortality rate: 15.7 *(deaths per 1,000 live births)*
Fertility rate: 1.17 *(per woman)*

Life expectancy at birth:
total population: 71
   (*males:* 67.07, *females:* 75.12)

GOVERNMENT:
Type of government: Emerging Democracy
Independence: September 22, 1908 *(from Ottoman Empire)*
Leaders:
   chief of state: President Petar Stoyanov
   head of government: Chairman of the Council of Ministers (Prime Minister) Ivan Kostov

ECONOMY:
GDP: purchasing power parity - $43.2 billion
   GDP real growth rate: 2.4%
   GDP per capita: $4,920
Inflation Rate *(consumer prices)*: 35%
National Budget:
   revenues: $3.8 billion
   expenditures: $4.4 billion
External debt: $10.4 billion
Currency: 1 lev = 100 stotinki
Labor Force: 3.1 million
Unemployment rate: 11.9%
Agriculture: Grain, oilseed, vegetables, fruits, tobacco; livestock
Industries: Machine building and metal working, food processing, chemicals, textiles, construction materials, ferrous and nonferrous metals
Exports: $4.2 billion
   commodities: Machinery and equipment, agriculture and food, textiles and apparel, metals and ores, chemicals, minerals and fuels
Imports: $4 billion
   commodities: Fuels, minerals, raw materials, machinery and equipment, textiles and apparel, agricultural products, metals and ores, chemicals

DEFENSE:
Defense expenditures: *exchange rate conversion -* $352 *million,* 2.5% *of GDP*

BURMA

GEOGRAPHY:
Location: Southeastern Asia
Area:
   total area: 678,500 sq km
   land area: 657,740 sq km
Capital city: Rangoon *(regime refers to the capital as* Yangon*)*
Natural Resources: Petroleum, timber, tin, copper, antimony, zinc, tungsten, lead, coal, some marble, limestone, precious stones, natural gas

PEOPLE:
Population: 45,975,625
Population growth rate: 1.84%
Age structure:
   0–14 years: 37%
   15–64 years: 59%
   65 years & over: 4%
Literacy rate: 83.1% *of total population,*
   (*males:* 88.7%, *females:* 77.7%)
Languages: Burmese, minority ethnic groups have their own languages
Religions: 89%- Buddhist, 4% -Christian (3%-Baptist, 1%-Roman Catholic), 4%-Muslim, 1%-animist beliefs, 2%-Other

VITAL STATISTICS:
Birth rate: 30.01 *(per 1,000 population)*
Death rate: 11.66 *(per 1,000 population)*
Infant mortality rate: 80.7 *(deaths per 1,000 live births)*
Fertility rate: 3.83 *(per woman)*
Life expectancy at birth:
   total population: 56.14
   (*males:* 54.46, *females:* 57.92)

GOVERNMENT:
Type of government: Military Regime
Independence: January 4, 1948 *(from UK)*
Leaders:
   chief of state & head of government: Prime Minister and Chairman of the State Law and Order Restoration Council General Than Shwe
   State Law and Order Restoration Council: Military junta which assumed power September 18, 1988

ECONOMY:
GDP: purchasing power parity - $47 billion
   GDP real growth rate: 6.8%
   GDP per capita: $1,000
Inflation Rate *(consumer prices)*: 38%
National budget:
   revenues: $5.3 billion
   expenditures: $10 billion
External debt: $5.5 billion
Currency: 1 kyat = 100 pyas
Labor Force: 16.007 million
Unemployment rate: NA%
Agriculture: Paddy rice, corn, oilseed, sugarcane, pulses; hardwood
Industries: Agricultural processing; textiles and footwear; wood and wood products; petroleum refining; copper, tin, tungsten, iron; construction materials; pharmeceuticals; fertilizer
Exports: $879 million
   commodities: Pulses and beans, teak, rice, hardwood
Imports: $1.5 billion

commodities: Machinery, transport equipment, construction materials, food products, consumer goods

DEFENSE:
Defense expenditures: *exchange rate conversion -* $135 *million*, NA% *of GDP*

CAMBODIA

GEOGRAPHY:
Location: Southeastern Asia
Area:
total area: 181,040 sq km
land area: 176,520 sq km
Capital city: Phnom Penh
Natural Resources: Timber, gemstones, some iron ore, manganese, phosphates, hydropower potential

PEOPLE:
Population: 10,861,218
Population growth rate: 2.77%
Age structure:
0–14 years: 45%
15–64 years: 51%
65 years & over: 4%
Literacy rate: 35% *of total population,* (*males:* 48%, *females:* 22%)
Languages: Khemer *(official)*, French
Religions: 95%- Theravada Buddhism, 5%-other

VITAL STATISTICS:
Birth rate: 43.5 *(per 1,000 population)*
Death rate: 15.78 *(per 1,000 population)*
Infant mortality rate: 107.8 *(deaths per 1,000 live births)*
Fertility rate: 5.81 *(per woman)*
Life expectancy at birth:
total population: 49.86
(*males:* 48.39, *females:* 51.39)

GOVERNMENT:
Type of government: Multiparty liberal democracy under a constitutional monarchy established in September 1993
Independence: November 9, 1949 *(from France)*
Leaders:
chief of state: King Norodom Sihanouk
head of government: (Shared Power) First Prime Minister Ung Huot and Second Prime Minister Hun Sen

ECONOMY:
GDP: purchasing parity - $7 billion
GDP real growth rate: 6.7%
GDP per capita: $660

Inflation Rate *(consumer prices):* 6%
National budget:
revenues: $210 million
expenditures: $346 million
External debt: $383 million
Currency: 1 new riel = 100 sen
Labor Force: 2.5–3 million
Unemployment rate: NA%
Agriculture: Rice, rubber, corn, vegetables
Industries: Rice milling, fishing, wood and wood products, rubber, cement, gem mining
Exports: $240.7 million
commodities: Timber, rubber, soybeans, sesame
Imports: $630.5 million
commodities: Cigarettes, construction materials, petroleum products, machinery, motor vehicles

DEFENSE:
Defense expenditures: *exchange rate conversion -* $85 *million*, 1.4% *of GDP*

CANADA

GEOGRAPHY:
Location: Northern North America
Area:
total area: 9,976,140 sq km
land area: 9,220,970 sq km
Capital city: Ottawa
Natural Resources: Nickel, zinc, copper, gold, lead, molybdenum, potash, silver, fish, timber, wildlife, coal, petroleum, natural gas

PEOPLE:
Population: 28,820,671
Population growth rate: 1.06%
Age structure:
0–14 years: 21%
15–64 years: 67%
65 years & over: 12%
Literacy rate: 97% *of total population*
Languages: English *(official)*, French *(official)*
Religions: 45%-Roman Catholic, 12%-United Church, 8%-Anglican, 35%-other

VITAL STATISTICS:
Birth rate: 13.33 *(per 1,000 population)*
Death rate: 7.17 *(per 1,000 population)*
Infant mortality rate: 6.1 *(deaths per 1,000 live births)*
Fertility rate: 1.81 *(per woman)*
Life expectancy at birth:
total population: 79.07
(*males:* 75.67, *females:* 82.65)

GOVERNMENT:
Type of government: Confederation with parliamentary democracy
Independence: July 1, 1867 *(from UK)*
Leaders:
chief of state: Queen Elizabeth II represented by Governor General Romeo Le Blanc
head of government: Prime Minister Jean Chretien

ECONOMY:
GDP: purchasing power parity - $694 billion
GDP real growth rate: 2.1%
GDP per capita: $24,400
Inflation Rate *(consumer prices):* 2.4%
National budget:
revenues: $90.4 billion
expenditures: $114.1 billion
External debt: $233 billion
Currency: 1 Canadian dollar = 100 cents
Labor Force: 13.38 million
Unemployment rate: 9.5%
Agriculture: Wheat, barley, oilseed, tobacco, fruits, vegetables; dairy products; forest products, commercial fisheries *(provide annual catch of 1.5 million metric tons)*
Industries: Processed and unprocessed minerals, food products, wood and paper products, transportation equipment, chemicals, fish products, petroleum and natural gas
Exports: $185 billion
commodities: Newsprint, wood pulp, timber, crude petroleum, machinery, natural gas, aluminum, motor vehicles and parts; telecommunications equipment
Imports: $166.7 billion
commodities: Crude oil, chemicals, motor vehicles and parts, durable consumer goods, electronic computers; telecommunications equipment and parts

DEFENSE:
Defense expenditures: *exchange rate conversion - $9.0 billion,* 1.6% *of GDP*

CHILE

GEOGRAPHY:
Location: Southern South America
Area:
total area: 756,950 sq km
land area: 748,800 sq km
Capital city: Santiago
Natural Resources: Copper, timber, iron ore, nitrates, precious metals, molybdenum

PEOPLE:
Population: 14,333,258
Population growth rate: 1.24%
Age structure:
0–14 years: 29%
15–64 years: 65%
65 years & over: 6%
Literacy rate: 95.2% *of total population,* *(males:* 95.4%, *females:* 95%)
Languages: Spanish
Religions: 89%-Roman Catholic, 11%-Protestant, Jewish

VITAL STATISTICS:
Birth rate: 18.09 *(per 1,000 population)*
Death rate: 5.68 *(per 1,000 population)*
Infant mortality rate: 13.6 *(deaths per 1,000 live births)*
Fertility rate: 2.23 *(per woman)*
Life expectancy at birth:
total population: 74.49
(males: 71.26, *females:* 77.72)

GOVERNMENT:
Type of government: Republic
Independence: September 18, 1810 *(from Spain)*
Leaders:
chief of state & head of government: President Eduardo Frei Ruiz-Tagle

ECONOMY:
GDP: purchasing power parity - $113.2 billion
GDP real growth rate: 8.5%
GDP per capita: $8,000
Inflation Rate *(consumer prices):* 8.1%
National budget:
revenues: $17 billion
expenditures: $17 billion
External debt: $21.1 billion
Currency: 1 Chilean Peso = 100 centavos
Labor Force: 4.728 million
Unemployment rate: 5.4%
Agriculture: Wheat, corn, grapes, beans, sugar beets, potatoes, fruit; beef, poultry, wool; timber; fish *(catch of 6.6 million metric tons)*
Industries: Copper, other minerals, foodstuffs, fish processing, iron and steel, wood and wood products, transport equipment, cement, textiles
Exports: $15.9 billion
commodities: Copper, other metals and minerals, wood products, fish and fishmeal, fruits
Imports: $14.3 billion
commodities: Capital goods, spare parts, raw materials, petroleum, foodstuffs

DEFENSE:
Defense expenditures: *exchange rate conversion - $970 million,* 2.0% *of GDP*

CHINA

GEOGRAPHY:
Location: Eastern Asia
Area:
total area: 9,596,960 sq km
land area: 9,326,410 sq km
Capital city: Beijing
Natural Resources: Coal, iron ore, petroleum, mercury, tin, tungsten, antimony, manganese, molybdenum, vanadium, magnetite, aluminum, lead, zinc, uranium, hydropower potential *(world's largest)*

PEOPLE:
Population: 1,210,004,956
Population growth rate: 0.98%
Age structure:
0–14 years: 26%
15–64 years: 67%
65 years & over: 7 %
Literacy rate: 81.5% *of total population,* (*males:* 89.9%, *females:* 72.7%)
Languages: Standard Chinese or Mandarin *(putonghua, based on the Beijing dialect),* Yue *(Cantonese),* Wu *(Shanghaise),* Minbei *(Fuzhou),* Minnan *(Hokkien-Taiwanese),* Xiang, Gan, Hakka dialects
Religions: Daoism (Taoism), Buddhism; 2%-3%-Muslim, 1%-Christian

VITAL STATISTICS:
Birth rate: 17.01 *(per 1,000 population)*
Death rate: 6.92 *(per 1,000 population)*
Infant mortality rate: 39.6 *(deaths per 1,000 live births)*
Fertility rate: 1.81 *(per woman)*
Life expectancy at birth:
total population: 69.62
(*males:* 68.33, *females:* 71.06)

GOVERNMENT:
Type of government: Communist State
Independence: 221 BC *(unification under the Qin or Ch'in Dynasty 221 BC; Qing or Ch'ing Dynasty replaced by the Republic on February 12, 1912; People's Republic established October 1, 1949)*
Leaders:
chief of state: President Jiang Zemin
head of government: Premier Li Peng

ECONOMY:
GDP: purchasing power parity - $3.5 Trillion
GDP real growth rate: 10.3%
GDP per capita: $2,900
Inflation Rate *(consumer prices):* 10.1%

National budget:
revenues: $NA
expenditures: $NA
External debt: $92 billion
Currency: 1 yuan = 10 jiao
Labor Force: 583.6 million
Unemployment rate: 5.2% *(substantial underemployment)*
Agriculture: Rice, potatoes, sorghum, peanuts, tea, millet, barley, cotton, other fibers, oilseed; pork and other livestock products; fish
Industries: Steel, coal, machine building, armaments, textiles and apparel, petroleum, cement, chemicals, fertilizers, consumer durables, food processing, autos, consumer electronics, telecommunications
Exports: $148.8 billion
commodities: Garments, textiles, footwear, toys, machinery and equipment
Imports: $132.1 billion
commodities: Industrial machinery, textiles, plastics, telecommunications equipment, steel bars, aircraft

DEFENSE:
Defense expenditures: *The officially announced but suspect figures are:* 70.2 *billion yuan, NA% of GDP. (note-Conversion of defense budget into dollars using the current exchange rate could produce misleading results)*

COLOMBIA

GEOGRAPHY:
Location: Northern South America
Area:
total area: 1,138,910 sq km
land area: 1,038,700 sq km
Capital city: Bogota
Natural Resources: Petroleum, natural gas, coal, iron ore, nickel, gold, copper, emeralds

PEOPLE:
Population: 36,813,161
Population growth rate: 1.66%
Age structure:
0–14 years: 32%
15–64 years: 64%
65 years & over: 4%
Literacy rate: 91.3% *of total population,* (*males:* 91.2%, *females:* 91.4%)
Languages: Spanish
Religions: 95%-Roman Catholic

VITAL STATISTICS:
Birth rate: 21.34 *(per 1,000 population)*
Death rate: 4.65 *(per 1,000 population)*

Infant mortality rate: 25.8 *(deaths per 1,000 live births)*
Fertility rate: 2.35 *(per woman)*
Life expectancy at birth:
   total population: 72.81
      (*males:* 69.97, *females:* 75.73)

GOVERNMENT:
Type of government: Republic; executive branch dominates government stucture
Independence: July 20, 1810 *(Spain)*
Leaders:
   chief of state & head of government: President Ernesto Samper

ECONOMY:
GDP: purchasing power parity - $192.5 billion
   GDP real growth rate: 5.3%
   GDP per capita: $5,300
Inflation Rate *(consumer prices)*: 19.5%
National budget:
   revenues: $NA
   expenditures: $24 billion
External debt: $14 billion
Currency: 1 Colombian peso = 100 centavos
Labor Force: 12 million
Unemployment rate: 9.5%
Agriculture: Coffee, cut flowers, bananas, rice, tobacco, corn, sugarcane, cocoa beans, oilseed, vegetables; forest products, shrimp farming
Industries: Textiles, food processing, oil, clothing and footwear, beverages, chemicals, cement; gold, coal, emeralds
Exports: $10.5 billion
   commodities: Petroleum, coffee, coal, bananas, fresh cut flowers
Imports: $13.5 billion
   commodities: Industrial equipment, transportation equipment, consumer goods, chemicals, paper products

DEFENSE:
Defense expenditures: *exchange rate conversion -* $2 *billion*, 2.8% *of GDP*

COSTA RICA

GEOGRAPHY:
Location: Central America
Area:
   total area: 51,100 sq km
   land area: 50,660 sq km
Capital city: San Jose
Natural Resources: Hydropower potential

PEOPLE:
Population: 3,463,083
Population growth rate: 2.06%
Age structure:
   0–14 years: 35%
   15–64 years: 61%
   65 years & over: 4%
Literacy rate: 94.8% *of total population,*
   (*males:* 94.7%, *females:* 95%)
Languages: Spanish *(official)*, English spoken around Puerto Limon
Religions: 95%-Roman Catholic

VITAL STATISTICS:
Birth rate: 23.84 *(per 1,000 population)*
Death rate: 4.14 *(per 1,000 population)*
Infant mortality rate: 13.5 *(deaths per 1,000 live births)*
Fertility rate: 2.9 *(per woman)*
Life expectancy at birth:
   total population: 75.72
      (*males:* 73.31, *females:* 78.24)

GOVERNMENT:
Type of government: Democratic Republic
Independence: September 15, 1821 *(from Spain)*
Leaders:
   chief of state & head of government: President Jose Maria Figueres Olsen

ECONOMY:
GDP: purchasing power parity- $18.4 billion
   GDP real growth rate: 2.5%
   GDP per capita: $5,400
Inflation Rate 22.5% *(consumer prices)*
National budget:
   revenues: $1.1 billion
   expenditures: $1.34 billion
External debt: $4 billion
Currency: 1 Costa Rican colon = 100 centimos
Labor Force: 868,300
Unemployment rate: 5.2% *(much underemployment)*
Agriculture: Coffee, bananas, sugar, corn, rice, beans, potatoes; beef; timber *(depletion of forest resources has resulted in declining timber output)*
Industries: Food processing, textiles and clothing, construction materials, fertilizer, plastic products
Exports: $2.4 billion
   commodities: Coffee, bananas, textiles, sugar
Imports: $3 billion
   commodities: Raw materials, consumer goods, capital equipment, petroleum

DEFENSE:
Defense expenditures: *exchange rate conversion -* $55 *million*, 2.0% *of GDP*

COTE D'IVOIRE

GEOGRAPHY:
Location: Western Africa
Area:
total area: 322, 460 sq km
land area: 318,000 sq km
Capital city: Yamoussoukro
Natural Resources: Petroleum, diamonds, manganese, iron ore, cobalt, bauxite, copper

PEOPLE:
Population: 14,762,445
Population growth rate: 2.92%
Age structure:
0–14 years: 48%
15–64 years: 50%
65 years & over: 2%
Literacy rate: 40.1% *of total population,*
(*males:* 49.9%, *females:* 30%)
Languages: French *(official),* 60 native dialects with Dioula the most widely spoken
Religions: 60%-Muslim, 25%-indigenous, 12%-Christian

VITAL STATISTICS:
Birth rate: 42.48 *(per 1,000 population)*
Death rate: 15.7 *(per 1,000 population)*
Infant mortality rate: 82.4 *(deaths per 1,000 live births)*
Fertility rate: 6.15 *(per woman)*
Life expectancy at birth:
total population: 46.73
(*males:* 46.23, *females:* 47.25)

GOVERNMENT:
Type of government: Republic; multiparty presidential regime established 1960
Independence: August 7, 1960 *(from France)*
Leaders:
chief of state: President Henri Konan Bedie
head of government: Prime Minister Daniel Kablan Duncan

ECONOMY:
GDP: purchasing power parity-$21.9 billion
GDP real growth rate: 5%
GDP per capita: $1,500
Inflation Rate *(consumer prices):* 10%
National budget:
revenues: $1.9 billion
expenditures: $3.4 billion
External debt: $19 billion
Currency: 1 Communaute Financiere Africaine franc = 100 centimes
Labor Force: 5.718 million

Unemployment rate: NA%
Agriculture: Coffee, cocoa beans, bananas, palm kernels, corn, rice, manioc, sweet potatoes, sugar; cotton, rubber; timber
Industries: Foodstuffs, beverages; wood products, oil refining, automobile assembly, textiles, fertilizer, construction materials, electricity
Exports: $2.9 billion
commodities: Cocoa, coffee, tropical woods, petroleum, cotton, bananas, pineapples, palm oil; fish
Imports: $1.6 billion
commodities: Food, capital gods, consumer goods, fuel

DEFENSE:
Defense expenditures: *exchange rate conversion -* $140 *million,* 1.4% *of GDP*

CROATIA

GEOGRAPHY:
Location: Southeastern Europe
Area:
total area: 56,538 sq km
land area: 56,410 sq km
Capital city: Zagreb
Natural Resources: Oil, some coal, bauxite, low-grade iron ore, calcium, natural asphalt, silica, mica, clays, salt

PEOPLE:
Population: 5,004,112
Population growth rate: 0.58%
Age structure:
0–14 years: 18%
15–64 years: 69%
65 years & over: 13%
Literacy rate: 97% *of total population,*
(*males:* 99%, *females:* 95%)
Languages: Serbo-Croation and Other
Religions: 76.5%-Catholic, 11.1%-Orthodox, 1.2% Slavic Muslim, 0.4%-Protestant, 10.8%- others and unknown

VITAL STATISTICS:
Birth rate: 9.83 *(per 1,000 population)*
Death rate: 11.33 *(per 1,000 population)*
Infant mortality rate: 10.2 *(deaths per 1,000 live births)*
Fertility rate: 1.4 *(per woman)*
Life expectancy at birth:
total population: 72.81
(*males:* 69.13, *females:* 76.72)

GOVERNMENT:
Type of government: Parlimentary Democracy

Independence: June 25, 1991 *(from Yugoslavia)*
Leaders:
chief of state: President Franjo Tudjman
head of government: Prime Minister Zlatko
Matesa

ECONOMY:
GDP: purchasing power parity - $20.1 billion
GDP real growth rate: 1.5%
GDP per capita: $4,300
Inflation Rate *(consumer prices):* 3.7%
National budget:
revenues: $3.86 billion
expenditures: $3.72 billion
External debt: $3.15 billion
Currency: 1 Croatian kuna = 100 paras
Labor Force: 1.444 million
Unemployment rate: 18.1%`
Agriculture: Wheat, corn, sugar beets, sunflower
seed, alfalfa, clover, olives, citrus, grapes, vegetables; livestock breeding, dairy farming
Industries: Chemicals and plastic, machine tools,
fabricated metals, electronics, pig iron and rolled
steel products, aluminum, paper, wood products, construction materials, textiles, shipbuilding, petroleum and petroleum refining, food
and beverages
Exports: $4.3 billion
commodities: Machinery and transport equipment, miscellaneous manufactures, chemicals, food and live animals, raw materials,
fuels and lubricants, beverages and tobacco
Imports: $5.2 billion
commodities: Machinery and transport equipment, fuels and lubricants, food and live animals, chemicals, miscellaneous manufactured
articles, raw materials, beverages and tobacco

DEFENSE:
Defense expenditures: 337 - 393 *billion dinars,
NA% of GDP. (note-conversion of defense
expenditures into US dollars using current
exchange rate could prodeuce misleading
results)*

C U B A

GEOGRAPHY:
Location: Caribbean
Area:
total area: 110,860 sq km
land area: 110,860 sq km
Capital city: Havana
Natural Resources: Cobalt, nickel, iron ore, copper,
manganese, salt, timber, silica, petroleum

PEOPLE:
Population: 10,951,334
Population growth rate: 0.44%
Age structure:
0–14 years: 22%
15–64 years: 68%
65 years & over: 10%
Literacy rate: 95.7% *of total population,*
(males: 96.2%, *females:* 95.3%)
Languages: Spanish
Religions: 85%-Roman Catholic *(prior to Castro's
assuming power),* Protestant, Jehovah's Witnesses, Jews and Santeria are also represented

VITAL STATISTICS:
Birth rate: 13.37 *(per 1,000 population)*
Death rate: 7.39 *(per 1,000 population)*
Infant mortality rate: 9 *(deaths per 1,000 live
births)*
Fertility rate: 1.52 *(per woman)*
Life expectancy at birth:
total population: 75.05
(males: 72.71, *females:* 77.54)

GOVERNMENT:
Type of government: Communist State
Independence: May 20, 1902 *(from Spain December 10, 1898; administered by the US from 1898
to 1902)*
Leaders:
chief of state & head of government: President of
the Council of State and President of the
Council of Ministers Fidel Castro

ECONOMY:
GDP: purchasing power parity - $14.7 billion
GDP real growth rate: 2.5%
GDP per capita: $1,300
Inflation Rate *(consumer prices):* NA%
National budget:
revenues: $NA
expenditures: $NA
External debt: $9.1 billion
Currency: 1 Cuban peso = 100 centavos
Labor Force: 4.71 million
Unemployment rate: NA%
Agriculture: Sugarcane, tobacco, citrus, coffee,
rice, potatoes, and other tubers, beans; livestock
Industries: Sugar, petroleum, food, tobacco, tex-
tiles, chemicals, paper and wood products,
metals(particularly nickel), cement, fertilizer,
consumer goods, agricultural machinery
Exports: $1.6 billion
commodities: Sugar, nickel, shellfish, tobacco,
medical products, citrus, coffee
Imports: $2.4 billion
commodities: Petroleum, food, machinery,
chemicals

DEFENSE:
Defense expenditures: *exchange rate conversion -*
$NA, 4% of GDP roughly (note-Moscow,
for decades the key military supporter and
supplier of Cuba, cut off almost all military aid
by 1993)

CYPRUS

GEOGRAPHY:
Location: Middle East
Area:
  total area: 9,250 sq km
  land area: 9,240 sq km
Capital city: Nicosia
Natural Resources: Copper, pyrites, asbestos,
  gypsum, timber, salt, marble, clay earth pigment

PEOPLE:
Population: 744,609
Population growth rate: 1.11%
Age structure:
  0–14 years: 25%
  15–64 years: 64%
  65 years & over: 11%
Literacy rate: 94%, *of total population,*
  (*males:* 98%, *females:* 91%)
Languages: Greek, Turkish, English
Religions: 78%-Greek Orthodox, 18%-Muslim,
  4%-Maronite, Armenian Apostolic and other

VITAL STATISTICS:
Birth rate: 15.39 *(per 1,000 population)*
Death rate: 7.66 *(per 1,000 population)*
Infant mortality rate: 8.4 *(deaths per 1,000 live*
  births)
Fertility rate: 2.19 *(per woman)*
Life expectancy at birth:
  total population: 76.26
  (*males:* 74.11, *females:* 78.52)

GOVERNMENT:
Type of government: Republic
Independence: August 16, 1960 (*from UK*)
  (note - Turkish area proclaimed self-rule in Feb-
  ruary 1975 from Republic of Cyprus)
Leaders:
  chief of state & head of government: President
    Glafcos Clerides

ECONOMY:
GDP: purchasing power parity:
  Greek area: $7.8 billion
  Turkish area: $520 million
  GDP real growth rate:
    Greek area: 5%
    Turkish area: 0.5%
  GDP per capita:

  Greek area: $13,000
  Turkish area: $3,900
Inflation Rate *(consumer prices)*:
  Greek area: 3%
  Turkish area: 215%
National budget:
  revenues:
    Greek area: $2.3 billion
    Turkish area: $246 million
  expenditures:
    Greek area: $3.4 billion
    Turkish area: $350 million
External debt:
  Greek area: $1.4 billion
Currency: 1 Cypriot pound = 100 cents
  1 Turkish lira = 100 kurus
Labor Force:
  Greek area: 294,000
  Turkish area: 75,320
Unemployment rate:
  Greek area: 2.7%
  Turkish area: 1.6%
Agriculture: Potatoes, vegetables, barley, grapes,
  olives, citrus
Industries: Food, beverages, textiles, chemicals,
  metal products, tourism, wood products
Exports:
  Greek area: $968 million
    commodities: Citrus, potatoes, grapes, wine
      cement, clothing and shoes
  Turkish area: $59 million
    commodities: Citrus, potatoes, textiles
Imports:
  Greek area: $2.7 billion
    commodities: Consumer goods, petroleum and
      lubricants, food and feed grains, machinery
  Turkish area: $330 million
    commodities: food, minerals, chemicals,
      machinery

DEFENSE:
Defense expenditures: *exchange rate conversion -*
$493 *million, 5.6% of GDP*

CZECH REPUBLIC

GEOGRAPHY:
Location: Central Europe
Area:
  total area: 78,703 sq km
  land area: 78,645 sq km
Capital city: Prague
Natural Resources: Hard coal, soft coal, kaolin,
  clay, graphite

PEOPLE:
Population: 10,321,120

Population growth rate: -0.03%
Age structure:
0–14 years: 18%
15–64 years: 68%
65 years & over: 14%
Literacy rate: 99% *of total population*
Languages: Czech, Slovak
Religions: 39.8%-atheist, 39.2%-Roman Catholic, 4.6%-Protestant, 3%-Orthodox, 13.4%-other

VITAL STATISTICS:

Birth rate: 10.39 *(per 1,000 population)*
Death rate: 10.89 *(per 1,000 population)*
Infant mortality rate: 8.4 *(deaths per 1,000 live births)*
Fertility rate: 1.38 *(per woman)*
Life expectancy at birth:
total population: 73.76
(males: 70.08, *females:* 77.65)

GOVERNMENT:

Type of government: Parlimentary Democracy
Independence: January 1, 1993 *(from Czechoslovakia)*
Leaders:
chief of state: President Vaclav Havel
head of government: Prime Minister Vaclav Klaus

ECONOMY:

GDP: purchasing power parity - $106.2 billion
GDP real growth rate: 5%
GDP per capita: $10,200
Inflation Rate *(consumer prices):* 9.1%
National budget:
revenues: $16.5 billion
expenditures: $16.2 billion
External debt: $14.9 billion
Currency: 1 koruna = 100 haleru
Labor Force: 5.389 million
Unemployment rate: 2.9%
Agriculture: Grains, potatoes, sugar beets, hops, fruit; pigs, cattle, poultry; forest products
Industries: Fuels, ferrous metallurgy, machinery and equipment, coal, motor vehicles, glass, armaments
Exports: $17.4 billion
commodities: Manufactured goods, machinery and transport equipment, chemicals, fuels, minerals, metals, agricultural products
Imports: $21.3 billion
commodities: Machinery and transport equipment, manufactured goods, chemicals, fuels and lubricants, raw materials, agricultural products

DEFENSE:

Defense expenditures: *exchange rate conversion -* $931 *million,* 2.5% *of GDP*

DEMOCRATIC REPUBLIC OF CONGO (FORMERLY ZAIRE)

GEOGRAPHY:

Location: Central Africa
Area:
total area: 2,345,410 sq km
land area: 2,267,600 sq km
Capital city: Kinshasa
Natural Resources: Cobalt, copper, cadmium, petroleum, industrial and gem diamonds, gold, silver, zinc, manganese, tin, germanium, uranium, radium, bauxite, iron ore, coal, hydropower potential

PEOPLE:

Population: 46,498,539
Population growth rate: 1.67%
Age structure:
0–14 years: 48%
15–64 years: 49%
65 years & over: 3%
Literacy rate: 77.3% *of total population,*
(*males:* 86.6%, *females:* 67.7%)
Languages: French *(official),* Lingala *(a lingua franca trade language),* Kingwana *(a dialect of Kiswahili or Swahili),* Kikongo, Tshiluba
Religions: 50%-Roman Catholic, 20%-Protestant, 10%-Kimbanguist, 10%-Muslim, 10%-other syncretic sects and traditional beliefs

VITAL STATISTICS:

Birth rate: 48.1 *(per 1,000 population)*
Death rate: 16.9 *(per 1,000 population)*
Infant mortality rate: 108 *(deaths per 1,000 live births)*
Fertility rate: 6.64 *(per woman)*
Life expectancy at birth:
total population: 46.7
(*males:* 44.97, *females:* 48.47)

GOVERNMENT:

Type of government: Transitional government— Civil war
Independence: June 30, 1960 *(from Belgium)*
Leaders:
chief of state & head of government: Laurent Kabila

ECONOMY:

GDP: purchasing power parity - $16.5 billion
GDP real growth rate: −7.4%
GDP per capita: $400
Inflation Rate *(consumer prices):* 12%

National budget:
  revenues: $479 million
  expenditures: $479 million
External debt: $11.3 billion
Currency: 1 zaire = 100 makuta
Labor Force: 14.51 million
Unemployment rate: NA%
Agriculture: Coffee, sugar, palm oil, rubber, tea, quinine, cassava (tapioca), palm oil, bananas, root crops, corn, fruits; wood products
Industries: Mining, mineral processing, consumer products *(including textiles, footwear, cigarettes, processed foods and beverages)*, cement, diamonds
Exports: $419 million
  commodities: Copper, coffee, diamonds, cobalt, crude oil
Imports: $382 million
  commodities: Consumer goods, foodstuffs, mining and other machinery, transport equipment, fuels

DEFENSE:
Defense expenditures: *exchange rate conversion -* $46 *million*, 1.5% *of GDP*

DENMARK

GEOGRAPHY:
Location: Northern Europe
Area:
  total area: 43,070 sq km
  land area: 42,370 sq km
Capital city: Copenhagen
Natural Resources: Petroleum, natural gas, fish, salt, limestone

PEOPLE:
Population: 5,249,632
Population growth rate: 0.38%
Age structure:
  0–14 years: 17%
  15–64 years: 67%
  65 years & over: 16%
Literacy rate: 99% *of total population*
Languages: Danish, Faroese, Greenlandic *(an Eskimo dialect)*, German *(small minority)*
Religions: 91%-Evangelical Lutheran, 2%-Protestant and Roman Catholic, 7%-other

VITAL STATISTICS:
Birth rate: 12.24 *(per 1,000 population)*
Death rate: 10.42 *(per 1,000 population)*
Infant mortality rate: 4.8 *(deaths per 1,000 live births)*
Fertility rate: 1.67 *(per woman)*

Life expectancy at birth:
  total population: 77.3
    (*males:* 73.78, *females:* 81.01)

GOVERNMENT:
Type of government: Constitutional Monarchy
Independence: 10th Century first organized as a unified state; in 1849 became a constitutional monarchy
Leaders:
  chief of state: Queen Margrethe II
  head of government: Prime Minister Poul Nyrup Rasmussen

ECONOMY:
GDP: purchasing power parity - $112.8 billion
  GDP real growth rate: 3.1%
  GDP per capita: $21,700
Inflation Rate *(consumer prices):* 2.4%
National budget:
  revenues: $56.5 billion
  expenditures: $64.4 billion
External debt: $40.9 billion
Currency: 1 Danish krone = 100 oere
Labor Force: 2,553,900
Unemployment rate: 9.5%
Agriculture: Grain, potatoes, rape, sugar beets; meat, dairy products; fish
Industries: Food processing, machinery and equipment, textiles and clothing, chemical products, electronics, construction, furniture, and other wood products, shipbuilding
Exports: $39.6 billion
  commodities: Meat and meat products, dairy products, transport equipment (shipbuilding), fish, chemicals, industrial machinery
Imports: $34 billion
  commodities: Petroleum, machinery and equipment, chemicals, grain and foodstuffs, textiles, paper

DEFENSE:
Defense expenditures: *exchange rate conversion -* $3.2 *billion*, 1.8% *of GDP*

DOMINICAN REPUBLIC

GEOGRAPHY:
Location: Caribbean
Area:
  total area: 48,730 sq km
  land area: 48,380 sq km
Capital city: Santo Domingo
Natural Resources: Nickel, bauxite, gold, silver

PEOPLE:
Population: 8,088,881

Population growth rate: 1.73%
Age structure:
0–14 years: 34%
15–64 years: 62%
65 years & over: 4%
Literacy rate: 82.1% *of total population,*
(males: 82%*, females:* 82.2%*)*
Languages: Spanish
Religions: 95%-Roman Catholic

VITAL STATISTICS:
Birth rate: 23.51 *(per 1,000 population)*
Death rate: 5.66 *(per 1,000 population)*
Infant mortality rate: 47.7 *(deaths per 1,000 live*
births)
Fertility rate: 2.66 *(per woman)*
Life expectancy at birth:
total population: 69.06
(males: 66.89*, females:* 71.34*)*

GOVERNMENT:
Type of government: Republic
Independence: February 27, 1844 *(from Haiti)*
Leaders:
chief of state & head of government: President
Leonel Fernandez

ECONOMY:
GDP: purchasing power parity - $26.8 billion
GDP real growth rate: 3.5%
GDP per capita: $3,400
Inflation Rate *(consumer prices)*: 9.5%
National budget:
revenues: $1.8 billion
expenditures: $2.2 billion
External debt: $4.6 billion
Currency: 1 Dominican peso = 100 centavos
Labor Force: 2.3–2.6 million
Unemployment rate: 30%
Agriculture: Sugarcane, coffee, cotton, cocoa,
tobacco, rice, beans, potatoes, corn, bananas;
cattle, pigs, dairy products, meat, eggs
Industries: Tourism, sugar processing, ferronickel
and gold mining, textiles, cement, tobacco
Exports: $837.7 million
commodities: Ferronickel, sugar, gold, coffee,
cocoa
Imports: $2.867 billion
commodities: Foodstuffs, petroleum, cotton and
fabrics, chemicals and pharmaceuticals

DEFENSE:
Defense expenditures: *exchange rate conversion -*
$116 *million*, 1.4% *of GDP*

ECUADOR

GEOGRAPHY:
Location: Western South America
Area:
total area: 283,560 sq km
land area: 276,840 sq km
Capital city: Quito
Natural Resources: Petroleum, fish, timber

PEOPLE:
Population: 11,466,291
Population growth rate: 1.96%
Age structure:
0–14 years: 35%
15–64 years: 60%
65 years & over: 5%
Literacy rate: 90.1% *of total population,*
(males: 92% *and females:* 88.2%*)*
Languages: Spanish *(official)*, Indian languages
(especially Quechua)
Religions: 93%-Roman Catholic

VITAL STATISTICS:
Birth rate: 25.06 *(per 1,000 population)*
Death rate: 5.5 *(per 1,000 population)*
Infant mortality rate: 34.8 *(deaths per 1,000 live*
births)
Fertility rate: 2.89 *(per woman)*
Life expectancy at birth:
total population: 71.09
(males: 68.49*, females:* 73.82*)*

GOVERNMENT:
Type of government: Republic
Independence: May 24, 1822 *(from Spain)*
Leaders:
chief of state & head of government: President
Fabian Alaracon Rivera

ECONOMY:
GDP: purchasing power parity - $44.6 billion
GDP real growth rate: 2.3%
GDP per capita: $4,100
Inflation Rate *(consumer prices)*: 25%
National budget:
revenues: $3.3 billion
expenditures: $3.3 billion
External debt: $12.6 billion
Currency: 1 sucre = 100 centavos
Labor Force: 2.8 million
Unemployment rate: 7.1%
Agriculture: Bananas, coffee, cocoa, rice, potatoes,
manioc, plantains, sugarcane, cattle, sheep, pigs,
beef, pork, dairy products; balsa wood; fish, shrimp
Industries: Petroleum, food processing, texties,

metal work, paper products, wood products,
chemcials, plastics, fishing, lumber
Exports: $4 billion
  commodities: Petroleum, bananas, shrimp,
  cocoa, coffee
Imports: $3.7 billion
  commodities: Transport equipment, consumer
  goods, vehicles, machinery, chemicals

DEFENSE:
Defense expenditures: *exchange rate conversion -*
$386 *million*, 2.1 % *of GDP*

EGYPT

GEOGRAPHY:
Location: Northern Africa
Area:
  total area: 1,001,450 sq km
  land area: 995,450 sq km
Capital city: Cairo
Natural Resources: Petroleum, natural gas, iron
  ore, phosphates, maganese, limestone, gypsum,
  talc, asbestos, lead, zinc

PEOPLE:
Population: 63,575,107
Population growth rate: 1.91%
Age structure:
  0–14 years: 37%
  15–64 years: 60%
  65 years & over: 3%
Literacy rate: 51.4% *of total population,*
  (*males:* 63.6%, *females:* 38.8%)
Languages: Arabic *(official),* English and French
  (widely understood by educated classes)
Religions: 94%-Muslim *(mostly Sunni) (official*
  estimate), 6%-Coptic Christian and other

VITAL STATISTICS:
Birth rate: 28.18 *(per 1,000 population)*
Death rate: 8.7 *(per 1,000 population)*
Infant mortality rate: 72.8 *(deaths per 1,000 live*
  births)
Fertility rate: 3.58 *(per woman)*
Life expectancy at birth:
  total population: 61.43
  (*males:* 59.51, *females:* 63.46)

GOVERNMENT:
Type of government: Republic
Independence: February 28, 1922 *(from UK)*
Leaders:
  chief of state: President Mohammed Hosni
  Mubarak
  head of government: Prime Minister Kamal
  Ganzouri

ECONOMY:
GDP: purchasing power parity - $171 billion
  GDP real growth rate: 4%
  GDP per capita: $2,760
Inflation Rate *(consumer prices):* 9.4%
National budget:
  revenues: $18 billion
  expenditures: $19.4 billion
External debt: $33.6 billion
Currency: 1 Egyptian pound = 100 piasters
Labor Force: 16 million
Unemployment rate: 20%
Agriculture: Cotton, rice, corn, wheat, beans, fruits,
  vegetables; cattle, water buffalo, sheep, goats; fish
  (catch about 14,000 metric tons)
Industries: Textiles, food processing,tourism,
  chemicals, petroleum, construction, cement,
  metals
Exports: $5.4 billion
  commodities: Crude oil and petroleum products,
  cotton yarn, raw cotton, textiles, metal products, chemicals
Imports: $15.2 billion
  commodities: Machinery and equipment, foods,
  fertilizers, wood products, durable consumer
  goods, capital goods

DEFENSE:
Defense expenditures: *exchange rate conversion -*
  $3.5 *billion*, 8.2% *of GDP*

EL SALVADOR

GEOGRAPHY:
Location: Central America
Area:
  total area: 21,040 sq km
  land area: 20,720 sq km
Capital city: San Salvador
Natural Resources: Hydropower, geothermal
  power, petroleum

PEOPLE:
Population: 5,828,987
Population growth rate: 1.81%
Age structure:
  0–14 years: 38%
  15–64 years: 57%
  65 years & over: 5%
Literacy rate: 71.5% *of total population,*
  (*males:* 73.5%, *females:* 69.8 %)
Languages: Spanish, Nahua *(among some Indians)*
Religions: 75%-Roman Catholic

VITAL STATISTICS:
Birth rate: 28.3 *(per 1,000 population)*
Death rate: 5.81 *(per 1,000 population)*
Infant mortality rate: 31.9 *(deaths per 1,000 live births)*
Fertility rate: 3.2 *(per woman)*
Life expectancy at birth:
  total population: 68.88
    (males: 65.44, *females:* 72.5)

GOVERNMENT:
Type of government: Republic
Independence: September 15, 1821 *(from Spain)*
Leaders:
  chief of state & head of government: Preisdent Armando Calderon Sol

ECONOMY:
GDP: purchasing power parity - $11.4 billion
  GDP real growth rate: 6.3%
  GDP per capita: $1,950
Inflation Rate *(consumer prices):* 11.4%
National budget:
  revenues: $846 million
  expenditures: $890 million
External debt: $2.6 billion
Currency: 1 Salvadoran colones = 100 centavos
Labor Force: 1.7 milion
Unemployment rate: 6.7%
Agriculture: Coffee, sugarcane, corn, rice, beans, oilseed; beef, dairy products; shrimp
Industries: Food processing, beverages, petroleum, tobacco, chemicals, textiles, furniture
Exports: $1.6 billion
  commodities: Coffee, sugarcane, shrimp
Imports: $3.3 billion
  commodities: Raw materials, consumer goods, capital goods

DEFENSE:
Defense expenditures: *exchange rate conversion -* $100 *million,* 1% *of GDP*

ESTONIA

GEOGRAPHY:
Location: Eastern Europe
Area:
  total area: 45,100 sq km
  land area: 43,200 sq km
Capital city: Tallinn
Natural Resources: Shale oil, peat, phosphorite, amber

PEOPLE:
Population: 1,459,428
Population growth rate: −1.13%

Age structure:
  0–14 years: 20%
  15–64 years: 66%
  65 years & over: 14%
Literacy rate: 100% *of total population*
Languages: Estonian *(official)*, Latvian, Lithuanian, Russian, other
Religions: Lutheran, Orthodox Christian

VITAL STATISTICS:
Birth rate: 10.74 *(per 1,000 population)*
Death rate: 14.12 *(per 1,000 population)*
Infant mortality rate: 17.4 *(deaths per 1,000 live births)*
Fertility rate: 1.55 *(per woman)*
Life expectancy at birth:
  total population: 68.13
    (males: 62.5, *females:* 74.05)

GOVERNMENT:
Type of government: Republic
Independence: September 6, 1991 *(from Soviet Union)*
Leaders:
  chief of state: President Lennart Meri
  head of government: Prime Minister Mart Siimann

ECONOMY:
GDP: purchasing power parity - $12.3 billion
  GDP real growth rate: 6%
  GDP per capita: $7,600
Inflation Rate *(consumer prices):* 29%
National budget:
  revenues: $620 million
  expenditures: $582 million
External debt: $270 million
Currency: 1 Estonian kroon = 100 cents *(introduced in August 1992)*
Labor Force: 750,000
Unemployment rate: 8%
Agriculture: Potatoes, fruits, vegetables; livestock and dairy products; fish
Industries: Oil shale, shipbuilding, phosphates, electric motors, excavators, cement, furniture, clothing, textiles, paper, shoes, apparel
Exports: $1.8 billion
  commodities: Textile, food products, vehicals, metals
Imports: $2.5 billion
  commodities: Machinery, fuels, vehicles, textiles

DEFENSE:
Defense expenditures: *exchange rate conversion -* $35 *million,* 1.5% *of GDP*

E T H I O P I A

GEOGRAPHY:
Location: Eastern Africa
Area:
total area: 1,127,127 sq km
land area: 1,119,683 sq km
Capital city: Addis Ababa
Natural Resources: Small reserves of gold, platinum, copper, potash

PEOPLE:
Population: 57,171,662
Population growth rate: 2.72%
Age structure:
0–14 years: 46%
15–64 years: 51%
65 years & over: 3%
Literacy rate: 35.5% *of total population,*
(*males:* 45.5%, *females:* 25.3%)
Languages: Amharic *(official)*, Tigrinya, Orominga, Guaraginga, Somali, Arabic, English *(major foreign language taught in schools)*
Religions: 45–50%-Muslim, 35–40%-Ethiopian Orthodox, 12%-animist, 5%-other

VITAL STATISTICS:
Birth rate: 46.05 *(per 1,000 population)*
Death rate: 17.53 *(per 1,000 population)*
Infant mortality rate: 122.8 *(deaths per 1,000 live births)*
Fertility rate: 7 *(per woman)*
Life expectancy at birth:
total population: 46.85
(*males:* 45.71, *females:* 48.02)

GOVERNMENT:
Type of government: Federal Republic
Independence: Oldest independent country in Africa and one of the oldest in the world - at least 2,000 years
Leaders:
chief of state: President Negasso Ghidada
head of government: Prime Minister Meles Zenawi

ECONOMY:
GDP: purchasing power parity - $24.2 billion
GDP real growth rate: 2.7%
GDP per capita: $400
Inflation Rate *(consumer prices)*: 10%
National budget:
revenues: $1.2 billion
expenditures: $1.7 billion
External debt: $3.7 billion
Currency: 1 birr = 100 cents

Labor Force: 18 million
Unemployment rate: NA%
Agriculture: Cereals, pulses, coffee, oilseed, sugarcane, potatoes, other vegetables; hides, cattle, sheep, goats
Industries: Food processing, beverages, textiles, chemicals, metals processing, cement
Exports: $296 million
commodities: Coffee, leather products, gold
Imports: $972 million
commodities: Capital goods, consumer goods, fuel

DEFENSE:
Defense expenditures: *exchange rate conversion -* $140 *million,* 4.1% *of GDP*

F I J I

GEOGRAPHY:
Location: Oceania
Area:
total area: 18,270 sq km
land area: 18,270 sq km
Capital city: Suva
Natural Resources: Timber, fish, gold, copper, offshore oil potential

PEOPLE:
Population: 782,381
Population growth rate: 1.28%
Age structure:
0–14 years: 35%
15–64 years: 62%
65 years & over: 3%
Literacy rate: 91.6% *of total population,*
(*males:* 93.8%, *females"* 89.3%)
Languages: English *(official)*, Fijian, Hindustani
Religions: 52%-Christian, (37%-*Methodist*, 9%-*Roman Catholic*), 38%-Hindu, 8%-Muslim, 2%-other

VITAL STATISTICS:
Birth rate: 23.37 *(per 1,000 population)*
Death rate: 6.35 *(per 1,000 population)*
Infant mortality rate: 17.4 *(deaths per 1,000 live births)*
Fertility rate: 2.83 *(per woman))*
Life expectancy at birth:
total population: 65.71
(*males:* 63.39, *females:* 68.14)

GOVERNMENT:
Type of government: Republic
Independence: October 10, 1970 *(from UK)*
Leaders:
chief of state: President Ratu Sir Kamisese Mara

head of government: Prime Minister Sitiveni Ligamamada Rabuka

ECONOMY:
GDP: purchasing power parity - $4.7 billion
GDP real growth rate: 2.2%
GDP per capita: $6,100
Inflation Rate *(consumer prices):* 2%
National budget:
revenues: $495.6 million
expenditures: $591.2 million
External debt: $670 million
Currency: 1 Fijian dollar = 100 cents
Labor Force: 235,000
Unemployment rate: 5.4%
Agriculture: Sugarcane, coconuts, cassava (tapioca), rice, sweet potatoes, bananas; cattle, pigs, horses, goats; fish *(catch nearly 33,000 tons)*
Industries: Sugar, tourism, copra, gold, silver, clothing, lumber, small cottage industries
Exports: $571.8 million
commodities: Sugar, clothing, gold, processed fish, lumber
Imports: $864.3 million
commodities: Machinery and transport equipment, petroleum products, food, consumer goods, chemicals

DEFENSE:
Defense expenditures: *exchange rate conversion - $28 million, 2.5% of GDP*

F I N L A N D

GEOGRAPHY:
Location: Northern Europe
Area:
total area: 337,030 sq km
land area: 305,470 sq km
Capital city: Helsinki
Natural Resources: Timber, copper, zinc, iron ore, silver

PEOPLE:
Population: 5,105,230
Population growth rate: 0.1%
Age structure:
0–14 years: 19%
15–64 years: 67%
65 years & over: 14%
Literacy rate: 100% *of total population*
Languages: Finnish *(official)*, Swedish *(official)*, small Lapp- and Russian-speaking minorities
Religions: 89%-Evangelical Lutheran, 1%-Greek Orthodox, 9%-none, and 1% other

VITAL STATISTICS:
Birth rate: 11.32 *(per 1,000 population)*
Death rate: 10.92 *(per 1,000 population)*
Infant mortality rate: 4.9 *(deaths per 1,000 live births)*
Fertility rate: 1.68 *(per woman)*
Life expectancy at birth:
total population: 75.47
(males: 73.82, *females:* 77.18)

GOVERNMENT:
Type of government: Republic
Independence: December 6, 1917 *(from Soviet Union)*
Leaders:
chief of state: President Martti Ahtisaari
head of government: Prime Minister Paavo Tapio Lipponen

ECONOMY:
GDP: purchasing power parity - $92.4 billion
GDP real growth rate: 5%
GDP per capita: $18,200
Inflation Rate *(consumer prices):* 2%
National budget:
revenues: $21.7 billion
expenditures: $31.7 billion
External debt: $30 billion
Currency: 1 markka or finmark = 100 pennia
Labor Force: 2.533 million
Unemployment rate: 17%
Agriculture: Cereals, sugar beet, potatoes; dairy cattle; fish *(annual catch about 160,000 metric tons)*
Industries: Metal products, shipbuilding, pulp and paper, copper refining, foodstuffs, chemicals, textiles, clothing
Exports: $29.7 billion
commodities: Paper and pulp, machinery, chemicals, metals timber
Imports: $23.2 billion
commodities: Foodstuffs, petroleum and petroleum products, chemicals, transport equipment, iron and steel, machinery, textile yarn and fabrics, fodder grains

DEFENSE:
Defense expenditures: *exchange rate conversion - $1.9 billion, 1.6% of GDP*

F R A N C E

GEOGRAPHY:
Location: Western Europe
Area:
total area: 547,030 sq km
land area: 545,630 sq km

Capital city: Paris
Natural Resources: Coal, iron ore, bauxite, fish, timber, zinc, potash

PEOPLE:
Population: 58,317,450
Population growth rate: 0.34%
Age structure:
0–14 years: 19.04%
15–64 years: 65.62%
65 years & over: 15.34%
Literacy rate: 99% *of total population*
Languages: French 100%, rapidly declining regional dialects and languages *(Provencal, Breton, Alsatian, Corsican, Catalan, Basque, Flemish)*
Religions: 90%-Roman Catholic, 2%-Protestant, 1%-Jewish, 1%-Muslim *(North African workers),* and 6%-unaffiliated

VITAL STATISTICS:
Birth rate: 10.82 *(per 1,000 population)*
Death rate: 9.27 *(per 1,000 population)*
Infant mortality rate: 5.3 *(deaths per 1,000 live births)*
Fertility rate: 1.49 *(per woman)*
Life expectancy at birth:
total population: 77.93
(males: 73.98, *females:* 82.11)

GOVERNMENT:
Type of government: Republic
Independence: 486 *(unified by Clovis)*
Leaders:
chief of state: President Jacques Chirac
head of government: Prime Minister Lionel Jospin

ECONOMY:
GDP: purchasing power parity - $1.173 trillion
GDP real growth rate: 2.4%
GDP per capita: $20,200
Inflation Rate *(consumer prices):* 1.7%
National budget:
revenues: $220.5 billion
expenditures: $249.1 billion
External debt: $300 billion
Currency: 1 French franc = 100 centimes
Labor Force: 24.17 million
Unemployment rate: 11.7%
Agriculture: Wheat, cereals, sugar beets, potatoes, wine grapes; beef, dairy products; fish *(catch of 850,000 metric tons rank among world's top 20 countries and is all used domestically)*
Industries: Machinery, chemicals, automobiles, metallurgy, aircraft, electronics, mining, textiles, food processing, tourism
Exports: $235.5 billion

commodities: Machinery and transportation equipment, chemicals, foodstuffs, agricultural products, iron and steel products, textiles and clothing
Imports: $229.3 billion
commodities: Crude oil, machinery and equipment, agricultural products, chemicals, iron and steel products

DEFENSE:
Defense expenditures: *exchange rate conversion - $47.7 billion, 2.5% of GDP*

GERMANY

GEOGRAPHY:
Location: Central Europe
Area:
total area: 356,910 sq km
land area: 349,520 sq km
Capital city: Berlin
Natural Resources: Iron ore, coal, potash, timber, lignite, uranium, copper, natural gas, salt, nickel

PEOPLE:
Population: 83,536,115
Population growth rate: 0.67%
Age structure:
0–14 years: 16.15%
15–64 years: 68.52%
65 years & over: 15.33%
Literacy rate: 99% *of total population*
Languages: German
Religions: 45%- Protestant, 37%-Roman Catholic, 18%-unaffiliated or other

VITAL STATISTICS:
Birth rate: 9.66 *(per 1,000 population)*
Death rate: 12.21 *(per 1,000 population)*
Infant mortality rate: 6 *(deaths per 1,000 live births)*
Fertility rate: 1.3 *(per woman)*
Life expectancy at birth:
total population: 75.95
(males: 72.8, *females:* 79.27)

GOVERNMENT:
Type of government: Federal Republic
Independence: January 18, 1871 *(German Empire unification);* divided into four zones of occupation *(UK, US, USSR, and later, France)* in 1945 following the WWII; Federal Republic of Germany *(FRG or West Germany)* proclaimed May 23, 1949 and included the former UK, US and French zones; German Democratic Republic (GDR or East Germany) proclaimed October 7, 1949 and included the former USSR zone; unifi-

cation of West Germany and East Germany took place October 3, 1990; all four power rights formally relinquished March 15, 1991

Leaders:
chief of state: President Roman Herzog
head of government: Chancellor Helmut Kohl

ECONOMY:
GDP: purchasing power parity -
(Germany) $1.4522 trillion
(western) $1.3318 trillion
(eastern) $120.4 billion
GDP real growth rate:
(Germany) 1.8%
(western) 1.5%
(eastern) 6.3%
GDP per capita:
(Germany) $17,900
(western) $21,100
(eastern) $6,600
Inflation Rate *(consumer prices)*:
(western) 2%
(eastern) 2%
National budget;
revenues: $690 billion
expenditures: $780 billion
External debt: $NA
Currency: 1 deutsche mark = 100 pfennige
Labor Force: 36.75 million
Unemployment rate:
(western) 8.7%
(eastern) 14.9%
Agriculture:
(western)- Potatoes, wheat, barley, sugar beets, fruit, cabbage; cattle, pigs, poultry
(eastern)- Wheat, rye, barley, potatoes, sugar beets, fruit; pork, beef, chicken, milk, hides
Industries:
(western:)- Among the world's largest and most technologically advanced producers of iron, steel, coal, cement, chemicals, machinery, vehicles, machine tools, electronics, food and beverages
(eastern)- Metal fabrication, chemicals. brown coal, shipbuilding, machine building, food and beverages, textiles, petroleum refining
Exports: $437 billion
commodities: Manufactured goods *(including machines and machine tools, chemicals, motor vehicles, iron and steel products)*, agricultural products, raw materials, fuels
Imports: $362 billion
commodities: Manufactured goods, agricultural products, fuels, raw material

DEFENSE:
Defense expenditures: *exchange rate conversion -* $42.8 *billion,* 1.5% *of GDP*

GHANA

GEOGRAPHY:
Location: Western Africa
Area:
total area: 238,540 sq km
land area: 230,020 sq km
Capital city: Accra
Natural Resources: Gold, timber, industrial diamonds, bauxite, maganese, fish, rubber

PEOPLE:
Population: 17,698,271
Population growth rate: 2.29%
Age structure:
0–14 years: 43%
15–64 years: 54%
65 years & over: 3%
Literacy rate: 64.5%, *of total population,*
(*males:* 64.5%, *females:* 53.5%)
Languages: English *(official),* African languages *(including Akan, Moshi-Dagomba, Ewe, and Ga)*
Religions: 38%-indigenous beliefs, 30%-Muslim, 24%-Christian, 8%-other

VITAL STATISTICS:
Birth rate: 35 *(per 1,000 population)*
Death rate: 11.15 *(per 1,000 population)*
Infant mortality rate: 80.3 *(deaths per 1,000 live births)*
Fertility rate: 4.59 *(per woman)*
Life expectancy at birth:
total population: 56.17
(*males:* 54.18, *females:* 58.22)

GOVERNMENT:
Type of government: Constitutional Democracy
Independence: March 6, 1957 *(from UK)*
Leaders:
chief of state & head of government: President Jerry John Rawlings

ECONOMY:
GDP: purchasing power parity - $25.1 billion
GDP real growth rate: 5%
GDP per capita: $1,400
Inflation Rate *(consumer prices):* 69%
National budget:
revenues: $1.05 billion
expenditures: $1.2 billion
External debt: $4.6 billion
Currency: 1 new cedi = 100 pesewas
Labor Force: 3.7 million
Unemployment rate: 10%
Agriculture: Cocoa, rice, coffee, cassava *(tapioca),* peanuts, corn, shea nuts, bananas; timber

Industries: mining, lumbering, light manufacturing, aluminum, food processing
Exports: $1 billion
  commodities: Cocoa, gold, timber, tuna, bauxite, aluminum, manganese ore, diamonds
Imports: $1.7 billion
  commodities: Petroleum, consumer goods, intermediate goods, capital equipment

DEFENSE:
Defense expenditures: *exchange rate conversion -* $30 *million,* 0.8% *of GDP*

```
GREECE
```

GEOGRAPHY:
Location: Southern Europe
Area:
  total area: 131,940 sq km
  land area: 130,800 sq km
Capital city: Athens
Natural Resources: Bauxite, lignite, magnesite, petroleum, marble

PEOPLE:
Population: 10,538,594
Population growth rate: 0.42%
Age structure:
  0–14 years: 16%
  15–64 years: 68%
  65 years & over: 16%
Literacy rate: 95% *of total population,* (*males:* 98%, *females:* 93%)
Languages: Greek *(official),* English, French
Religions: 98%-Greek Orthodox, 1.3%-Muslim, 0.7%-other

VITAL STATISTICS:
Birth rate: 9.78 *(per 1,000 population)*
Death rate: 9.53 *(per 1,000 population)*
Infant mortality rate: 7.4 *(deaths per 1,000 live births)*
Fertility rate 1.37 *(per woman)*
Life expectancy at birth:
  total population: 78.1
    (*males:* 75.6, *females:* 80.78)

GOVERNMENT:
Type of government: Parlimentary republic; monarchy rejected by referendum December 8, 1974
Independence: 1829 (*from the Ottoman Em*pire)
Leaders:
  chief of state: President Constantinos (Kostis) Stephanopoulos
  head of government: Prime Minister Konstantine Simitis

ECONOMY:
GDP: purchasing power parity - $101.7 billion
  GDP real growth rate: 1.7%
  GDP per capita: $9,500
Inflation Rate *(consumer prices):* 8.1%
National budget:
  revenues: $43.2 billion
  expenditures: $47 billion
External debt: $31.2 billion
Currency: 1 drachma = 100 lepta
Labor Force: 4.077 million
Unemployment rate: 9.6%
Agriculture: Wheat, corn, barley, sugar beets, olives, tomatoes, wine, tobacco, potatoes; meat, dairy products
Industries: Tourism; food and tobacco processing; textiles; chemicals, metal products, mining, petroleum
Exports: $8.8 billion
  commodities: Manufactured goods, foodstuffs, fuels
Imports: $21.9 billion
  commodities: Manufactured goods, foodstuffs, fuels

DEFENSE:
Defense expenditures: *exchange rate conversion -* $4.9 *billion,* 4.6% *of GDP*

```
GREENLAND
```

GEOGRAPHY:
Location: Northern North America
Area:
  total area: 2,175,600 sq km
  land area: 383,600 *(ice free)* sq km
Capital city: Nuuk (Godthab)
Natural Resources: Zinc, lead, iron ore, coal, molybdenum, cryolite, uranium, fish

PEOPLE:
Population: 58,203
Population growth rate: 1%
Age structure:
  0–14 years: 27%
  15–64 years: 68%
  65 years & over: 5%
Literacy rate: NA
Languages: Eskimo dialects, Danish
Religions: Evangelical Lutheran

VITAL STATISTICS:
Birth rate: 17.06 *(per 1,000 population)*
Death rate: 7.11 *(per 1,000 population)*
Infant mortality rate: 23.8 *(deaths per 1,000 live births)*
Fertility rate: 2.22 *(per woman)*

Life expectancy at birth:
total population: 68.24
(*males:* 63.97, *females:* 72.53)

GOVERNMENT:

Type of government: Part of the Danish realm; self-governing overseas administrative division
Independence: None
Leaders:
chief of state: Queen Margrethe II, represented by High Commissioner Steen Spore
head of government: Prime Minister Lars Emil Johansen

ECONOMY:

GDP: purchasing power parity - $892 million
GDP real growth rate: NA%
GDP per capita: $15,500
Inflation Rate: *(consumer prices)* 1.3%
National budget:
revenues: $667 million
expenditures: $635 million
External debt: $297.1 million
Currency: 1 Danish krone = 100 oere
Labor Force: 22,800
Unemployment rate: 6.6%
Agriculture: Forage crops, small garden vegetables; sheep; fish *(catch of 133,500 metric tons)*
Industries: Fish processing *(mainly shrimp)*, lead, zinc, handicrafts, small shipyards
Exports: $330.5 million
commodities: Fish and fish products
Imports: $369.6 million
commodities: Manufactured goods, machinery and transport equipment, food and live animals, petroleum products

DEFENSE:

Defense expenditures: *Defense is the responsibility of Denmark*

GUATEMALA

GEOGRAPHY:

Location: Central America
Area:
total area: 108,890 sq km
land area: 108,430 sq km
Capital city: Guatemala City
Natural Resources: Petroleum, nickel, rare wood, fish, chicle

PEOPLE:

Population: 11,277,614
Population growth rate: 2.48%
Age structure:
0–14 years: 43%

15–64 years: 54%
65 years & over: 3%
Literacy rate: 55.6% *of total population,* (*males:* 62.5%, *females:* 48.6%)
Languages: Spanish, Indian language *(23 Indian dialects, including Quiche, Cakchiquel, Kekchi)*
Religions: Roman Catholic, Protestant, traditional Mayan

VITAL STATISTICS:

Birth rate: 33.96 *(per 1,000 population)*
Death rate: 7.15 *(per 1,000 population)*
Infant mortality rate: 50.7 *(deaths per 1,000 live births)*
Fertility rate: 4.5 *(per woman)*
Life expectancy at birth:
total population: 65.24
(*males:* 62.64, *females:* 67.97)

GOVERNMENT:

Type of government: Republic
Independence: September 15, 1821 *(from Spain)*
Leaders:
chief of state & head of government: President Alvaro Enrique Arzu Irigoyen

ECONOMY:

GDP: purchasing power parity - $36.7 billion
GDP real growth rate: 4.9%
GDP per capita: $3,300
Inflation Rate *(consumer prices):* 9%
National budget:
revenues: $1.6 billion
expenditures: $1.88 billion
External debt: $3.1 billion
Currency: 1 quetzal = 100 centavos
Labor Force: 3.2 million
Unemployment rate: 4.9% *(Underemployment 30–40%)*
Agriculture: Sugarcane, corn, bananas, coffee, beans, cardamom; cattle, sheep, pigs, chickens
Industries: Sugar, textiles and clothing, furniture, chemicals, petroleum, metals rubber, tourism
Exports: $2.3 billion
commodities: Coffee, sugar, bananas, cardamom, beef
Imports: $2.85 billion
commodities: Fuel and petroleum products, machinery, grain, fertilizers, motor vehicles

DEFENSE:

Defense expenditures: *exchange rate conversion -* $130 *million,* 1% *of GDP*

HAITI

GEOGRAPHY:
Location: Caribbean
Area:
total area: 27,750 sq km
land area: 27,560 sq km
Capital city: Port-au-Prince
Natural Resources: Bauxite

PEOPLE:
Population: 6,731,539
Population growth rate: 1.77%
Age structure:
0–14 years: 46%
15–64 years: 50%
65 years & over: 4%
Literacy rate: 45% *of total population,*
(males: 48%, *females:* 42.2%)
Languages: French *(official),* Creole
Religions: 80%-Roman Catholic *(of which an over-whelming majority also practice Voodoo),* 16%-Protestant (10%-*Baptist, 4%- Pentecostal, 1%-Adventist, and 1%- other),* 1%-none, 3%-other

VITAL STATISTICS:
Birth rate: 38.15 *(per 1,000 population)*
Death rate: 15.96 *(per 1,000 population)*
Infant mortality rate: 103.8 *(deaths per 1,000 live births)*
Fertility rate: 5.69 *(per woman)*
Life expectancy at birth:
total population: 49.26
(males: 47.26, *females:* 51.35)

GOVERNMENT:
Type of government: Republic
Independence: January 1, 1804 *(from France)*
Leaders:
chief of state: President Rene Garcia Preval
head of government: Prime Minister (vacant)

ECONOMY:
GDP: purchasing power parity - $6.5 billion
GDP real growth rate: 4.5%
GDP per capita: $1,000
Inflation Rate *(consumer prices):* 14.5%
National budget:
revenues: $242 million
expenditures: $299.4 million
External debt: $827 million
Currency: 1 gourde = 100 centimes
Labor Force: 2.3 million
Unemployment rate: 60%

Agriculture: Coffee, mangoes, sugarcane, rice, corn, sorghum; wood
Industries: Sugar refining, flour milling, textiles, cement, tourism, light assembly industries based on imported parts
Exports: $161 million
commodities: Light manufactured goods, coffee, other agriculture
Imports: $537 million
commodities: Machines and manufactured goods, food and beverages, petroleum products, chemicals, fats and oils

DEFENSE:
Defense expenditures: $NA, NA% of GDP

HONDURAS

GEOGRAPHY:
Location: Central America
Area:
total area: 112,090 sq km
land area: 111,890 sq km
Capital city: Tegucigalpa
Natural Resources: Timber, gold, silver, copper, lead, zinc, iron ore, antimony, coal, fish

PEOPLE:
Population: 5,605,193
Population growth rate: 2.6%
Age structure:
0–14 years: 43%
15–64 years: 54%
65 years & over: 3%
Literacy rate: 72.7%, *of total population,*
(males: 72.6%, *females:* 72.7%)
Languages: Spanish, Indian dialects
Religions: 97%-Roman Catholic, Protestant minority

VITAL STATISTICS:
Birth rate: 33.38 *(per 1,000 population)*
Death rate: 5.83 *(per 1,000 population)*
Infant mortality rate: 41.8 *(deaths per 1,000 live births)*
Fertility rate: 4.41 *(per woman)*
Life expectancy at birth:
total population: 68.42
(males: 66.01, *females:* 70.96)

GOVERNMENT:
Type of government: Republic
Independence: September 15, 1821 *(from Spain)*
Leaders:
chief of state & head of government: President Carlos Roberto Reina Idiaquez

ECONOMY:
GDP: purchasing power parity - $10.8 billion
GDP real growth rate: 4%
GDP per capita: $1,980
Inflation Rate *(consumer prices):* 30%
National budget:
revenues: $527 million
expenditures: $668 million
External debt: $3.7 billion
Currency: 1 lempira = 100 centavos
Labor Force: 1.3 million
Unemployment rate: 10% *(30–40%-Underemployed)*
Agriculture: Bananas, coffee, citrus; beef; timber, shrimp
Industries: Sugar, coffee, textiles, clothing, wood products
Exports: $843 million
commodities: Bananas, coffee, shrimp, lobster, minerals, meat, lumber
Imports: $1.1 billion
commodities: Machinery and transport equipment, chemical products, manufactured goods, fuel and oil, foodstuffs

DEFENSE:
Defense expenditures: *exchange rate conversion -* $41 *million*, 0.4% *of GDP*

H U N G A R Y

GEOGRAPHY:
Location: Central Europe
Area:
total area: 93,030 sq km
land area: 92,340 sq km
Capital city: Budapest
Natural Resources: Bauxite, coal, natural gas, fertile soils

PEOPLE:
Population: 10,002,541
Population growth rate: -0.68%
Age structure:
0–14 years: 18%
15–64 years: 68%
65 years & over: 14%
Literacy rate: 99% *of total population*, (*males:* 99%, *females:* 98%)
Languages: Hungarian, other
Religions: 67.5%-Roman Catholic, 20%-Calvinist, 5%-Lutheran, 7.5%-atheist and other

VITAL STATISTICS:
Birth rate: 10.72 *(per 1,000 population)*

Death rate: 15.06 *(per 1,000 population)*
Infant mortality rate: 12.3 *(deaths per 1,000 live births)*
Fertility rate: 1.51 *(per woman)*
Life expectancy at birth:
total population: 69.02
(*males:* 64.23, *females:* 74.04)

GOVERNMENT:
Type of government: Republic
Independence: 1001 *(unification by King Stephen I)*
Leaders:
chief of state: President Arpad Goncz
head of government: Prime Minister Gyula Horn

ECONOMY:
GDP: purchasing power parity - $72.5 billion
GDP real growth rate: 1.5%
GDP per capita: $7,000
Inflation Rate *(consumer prices)*: 28.3%
National budget:
revenues: $12.6 billion
expenditures: $13.8 billion
External debt: 32.7 billion
Currency: 1 forint = 100 filler
Labor Force: 4.8 million
Unemployment rate: 10.4%
Agriculture: Wheat, corn, sunflower seed, potatoes, sugar beets; pigs, cattle, poultry, dairy products
Industries: Mining, metallurgy, construction materials, processed foods, textiles, chemicals *(especially pharmaceuticals)*, motor vehicles
Exports: $13 billion
commodities: Raw material and semi-finished goods, consumer goods, food and agriculture, capital goods, fuels and energy
Imports: $15 billion
commodities: Fuel and energy, raw materials and semi-finished goods, capital goods, consumer goods, food and agriculture

DEFENSE:
Defense expenditures: *exchange rate conversion -* $620 *million*, 1.7 *of GDP*

I C E L A N D

GEOGRAPHY:
Location: Northern Europe
Area:
total area: 103,000 sq km
land area: 100,250 sq km
Capital city: Reykjavik
Natural Resources: Fish, hydropower, geothermal power, diatomite

PEOPLE:
Population: 270,292
Population growth rate: 0.83%
Age structure:
0–14 years: 24%
15–64 years: 64%
65 years & over: 12%
Literacy rate: 100% *of total population*
Languages: Icelandic
Religions: 96%- Evangelical Lutheran, 3%-other
Protestant and Roman Catholic, and 1%-none

VITAL STATISTICS:
Birth rate: 16.94 *(per 1,000 population)*
Death rate: 6.17 *(per 1,000 population)*
Infant mortality rate: 4.3 *(deaths per 1,000 live births)*
Fertility rate: 2.24 *(per woman)*
Life expectancy at birth:
total population: 80.08
(males: 77.68, *females:* 82.6)

GOVERNMENT:
Type of government: Republic
Independence: June 17, 1944 *(from Denmark)*
Leaders:
chief of state: President Olafur Ragnar Grimsson
head of government: Prime Minister David Oddsson

ECONOMY:
GDP: purchasing power parity - $5 billion
GDP real growth rate: 3.2%
GDP per capita: $18,800
Inflation Rate *(consumer prices):* 2.5%
National budget:
revenues: $1.9 billion
expenditures: $2.1 billion
External debt: $2.5 billion
Currency: 1 Icelandic krona = 100 aurar
Labor Force: 127,900
Unemployment rate: 3.9%
Agriculture: Potatoes, turnips; cattle, sheep; fish
(catch of about 1.1 million metric tons in 1992)
Industries: Fish processing, aluminum smelting, ferrosilicon production, geothermal power
Exports: $1.6 billion
commodities: Fish and fish products, animal products, aluminum, ferrosilicon, diatomite
Imports: $1.5 billion
commodities: Machinery and transportation equipment, petroleum products, food stuffs, textiles

DEFENSE:
Defense expenditures: $NA, NA% of GDP

I N D I A

GEOGRAPHY:
Location: Southern Asia
Area:
total area: 3,287,590 sq km
land area: 2,973,190 sq km
Capital city: New Delhi
Natural Resources: Coal, iron ore, maganese, mica, bauxite, titanium, ore, chromite, natural gas, diamonds, petroleum, limestone

PEOPLE:
Population: 952,107,694
Population growth rate: 1.64%
Age structure:
0–14 years: 34%
15–64 years: 62%
65 years & over: 4%
Literacy rate: 52% *of total population,*
(males: 65.5%, *females:* 37.7%)
Languages: English enjoys associate status but is the most important language for national, political, and commercial communication, Hindi the national language and primary tongue of 30% of the people, Bengali*(official)*, Telugu *(official)*, Marathi *(official)*, Tamil *(official)*, Urdu *(official)*, Gujarati *(official)*, Malayalam *(official)*, Kannada *(official)*, Oriya *(official)*, Punjabi *(official)*, Assamese *(official)*, Kashmiri *(official)*, Sindhi *(official)*, Sanskrit *(official)*, Hindustani a popular variant of Hindu/Urdu, is spoken widely throughout northern India; (note-24 languages each spoken by a million or more persons; numerous other languages and dialects, for the most part mutually unintelligible)
Religions: 80%-Hindu, 14%-Muslim, 2.4%-Christian, 2%-Sikh, 0.7%-Buddhist, 0.5%-Jains, 0.4%-other

VITAL STATISTICS:
Birth rate: 25.94 *(per 1,000 population)*
Death rate: 9.61 *(per 1,000 population)*
Infant mortality rate: 71.1 *(deaths per 1,000 live births)*
Fertility rate: 3.2 *(per woman)*
Life expectancy at birth:
total population: 59.71
(males: 59.12, *females:* 60.32)

GOVERNMENT:
Type of government: Federal Republic
Independence: August 15, 1947 *(from the UK)*
Leaders:
Chief of State: President K. R. Narayanan

Head of government: Prime Minister Inder Kumar Gujral

ECONOMY:
GDP: purchasing power parity - $1.4087 trillion
GDP real growth rate: 5.5%
GDP per capita: $1,500
Inflation Rate *(consumer prices):* 9%
National budget:
revenues: $36.5 billion
expenditures: $54.9 billion
External debt: $97.9 billion
Currency: Indian rupee = 100 paise
Labor Force: 314.751 million
Unemployment rate: NA
Agriculture: Rice, wheat, oilseed, cotton, jute, tea, sugarcane, potatoes; cattle, water buffalo, sheep, goats, poultry; fish *(catch of about 3 million metric tons ranks India among the world's top 10 fishing nations)*
Industries: Textiles, chemicals, food processing, steel, transportation equipment, cement, mining, petroleum, machinery
Exports: $29.96 billion
commodities: Clothing, gems and jewelry, engineering goods, chemicals, leather manufactures, cotton yarn, fabric
Imports: $33.5 billion
commodities: Crude oil and petroleum products, machinery, gems, fertilizers, chemicals

DEFENSE:
Defense expenditures: *exchange rate conversion -* $8.0 billion, 2.7% *of GDP*

INDONESIA

GEOGRAPHY:
Location: Southeastern Asia
Area:
total area: 1,919,440 sq km
land area: 1,826,440 sq km
Capital city: Jakarta
Natural Resources: Petroleum, tin, natural gas, nickel, timber, bauxite, copper, fertile soils, coal, gold, silver

PEOPLE:
Population: 206,611,600
Population growth rate: 1.53%
Age structure:
0–14 years: 32%
15–64 years: 64%
65 years & over: 4%
Literacy rate: 83.8% *of total population,* (*males:* 89.6%, *females:* 78%)
Languages: Bahasa Indonesian, *(official, modified form of Malay),* English, Dutch, local dialects the most widely spoken of which is Javanese
Religions: 87%-Muslim, 6%-Protestant, 3%-Roman Catholic, 2%-Hindu, 1%-Buddhist, 1%-other

VITAL STATISTICS:
Birth rate: 23.67 *(per 1,000 population)*
Death rate: 8.38 *(per 1,000 population)*
Infant mortality rate: 63.1 *(deaths per 1,000 live births)*
Fertility rate: 2.7 *(per woman)*
Life expectancy at birth:
total population: 61.64
(*males:* 59.51, *females:* 63.88)

GOVERNMENT:
Type of government: Republic
Independence: August 17, 1945 *(proclaimed independence; on December 27, 1949, Indonesia became legally independent from the Netherlands)*
Leaders:
Chief of State and head of government: President Suharto

ECONOMY:
GDP: purchasing power parity - $710.9 billion
GDP real growth rate: 7.5%
GDP per capita: $3,500
Inflation Rate *(consumer prices):* 8.6%
National budget:
revenues: $38.1 billion
expenditures: $38.1 billion
External debt: $97.6 billion
Currency: Inonesian rupiah
Labor Force: 67 million
Unemployment rate: 3% official rate; Underemployment 40%
Agriculture: Rice, cassava (tapioca), peanuts, rubber, cocoa, coffee, palm oil, copra, other tropical products; poultry, beef, pork, eggs
Industries: Petroleum and natural gas, textiles, mining, cement, chemical fertilizers, plywood, food, rubber
Exports: $39.9 billion
commodities: Manufactured goods, fuels, foodstuffs, raw materials
Imports: $32 billion
commodities: Manufactured goods, raw materials, foodstuffs, fuels

DEFENSE:
Defense expenditures: *exchange rate conversion -* $2.7 billion, 1.4% *of GNP*

IRAN

GEOGRAPHY:
Location: Middle East
Area:
total area: 1.648 million sq km
land area: 1.636 million sq km
Capital city: Tehran
Natural Resources: Petroleum, natural gas, coal, chromium, copper, iron ore, lead, manganese, zinc, sulfur

PEOPLE:
Population: 66,094,264
Population growth rate: 2.21%
Age structure:
0–14 years: 45%
15–64 years: 52%
65 years & over: 3%
Literacy rate: 72.1% *of total population,* (*males:* 78.4%, *females:* 65.8%)
Languages: Persian and Persian dialects, Turkic and Turkic dialects, Kurdish, Arabic, Turkish
Religions: 89%-Shi'a Muslim, 10%-Sunni Muslim, 1%-Zoroastrian, Jewish, Christian and Baha'i

VITAL STATISTICS:
Birth rate: 33.67 *(per 1,000 population)*
Death rate: 6.61 *(per 1,000 population)*
Infant mortality rate: 52.7 *(deaths per 1,000 live births)*
Fertility rate: 4.72 *(per woman)*
Life expectancy at birth:
total population: 67.39
(*males:* 66.12, *females:* 68.72)

GOVERNMENT:
Type of government: Theocratic Republic
Independence: April 1, 1979 *(Islamic Republic of Iran proclaimed)*
Leaders:
chief of state & head of government: President Mohammed Khatami

ECONOMY:
GDP: purchasing power parity - $323.5 billion
GDP real growth rate: -2%
GDP per capita: $4,700
Inflation Rate *(consumer prices):* 60%
National budget:
revenues: $NA
expenditures: $NA
External debt: $30 billion
Currency: 10 Iranian rials = 1 toman
Labor Force: 15.4 million
Unemployment rate: over 30%

Agriculture: Wheat, rice, other grains, sugar beets, fruits, nuts, cotton; dairy products, wool; caviar
Industries: Petroleum, petrochemicals, textiles, cement and other construction materials, food processing *(particularly sugar refining and vegetable oil production)*, metal fabrication, armaments
Exports: $16 billion
commodities: Petroleum, carpets, fruits, nuts, hides, iron, steel
Imports: $13 billion
commodities: Machinery, military supplies, metal works, foodstuffs, pharmaceuticals, technical services, refined oil products

DEFENSE:
Defense expenditures: *According to official Iranian data, Iran in 1994 budgeted 4,377 billion rials and in 1993 spent 2,182 billion rials, including $850 million in hard currency; (note- conversion of defense expenditures into US dollars using current exchange rates could produce misleading results)*

IRAQ

GEOGRAPHY:
Location: Middle East
Area:
total area: 437,072 sq km
land area: 432,162 sq km
Capital city: Baghdad
Natural Resources: Petroleum, natural gas, phosphates, sulfur

PEOPLE:
Population: 21,422,292
Population growth rate: 3.69%
Age structure:
0–14 years: 48%
15–64 years: 49%
65 years & over: 3%
Literacy rate: 58% *of total population,* (*males:* 70.7%, *females:* 45%)
Languages: Arabic, Kurdish *(official in Kurdish regions)*, Assyrian, Armenian
Religions: 97%-Muslim *(60–65% -Shi'a, 32–37%-Sunni)*, 3%-Christian or other

VITAL STATISTICS:
Birth rate: 43.07 *(per 1,000 population)*
Death rate: 6.57 *(per 1,000 population)*
Infant mortality rate: 60 *(deaths per 1,000 live births)*
Fertility rate: 6.41 *(per woman)*

Life expectancy at birth:
total population: 66.95
(*males:* 65.92, *females:* 68.03)

GOVERNMENT:
Type of government: Republic
Independence: October 3, 1932 *(from League of Nations mandate under British administration)*
Leaders:
chief of state & head of government: President Saddam Hussein

ECONOMY:
GDP: purchasing power parity - $41.1 billion
GDP real growth rate: NA%
GDP per capita: $2,000
Inflation Rate *(consumer prices):* NA%
National budget:
revenues: $NA
expenditures: $NA
External debt: $50 billion
Currency: 1 Iraqi dinar = 1,000 fils
Labor Force: 4.4 million
Unemployment rate: NA%
Agriculture: Wheat, barley, rice, vegetables, dates, other fruit, cotton; cattle, sheep
Industries: Petroleum. chemicals, textiles, construction materials, food processing
Exports: $NA
commodities: Crude oil and refined products, fertilizer, sulfur
Imports: $NA
commodities: Manufactured goods, food

DEFENSE:
Defense expenditures: $NA, NA% of GDP

IRELAND

GEOGRAPHY:
Location: Western Europe
Area:
total area: 70,280 sq km
land area: 68,890 sq km
Capital city: Dublin
Natural Resources: Zinc, lead, natural gas, petroleum, barite, copper, gypsum, limestone, dolomite, peat, silver

PEOPLE:
Population: 3,566,833
Population growth rate: -0.22%
Age structure:
0–14 years: 23%
15–64 years: 65%
65 years & over: 12%
Literacy rate: 98% *of total population*

Languages: Irish *(Gaelic)*, spoken mainly in areas located along the western seaboard, English is the language generally used
Religions: 93%-Roman Catholic, 3%-Anglican, 1%-none, 2%-unknown, 1%-other

VITAL STATISTICS:
Birth rate: 13..22 *(per 1,000 population)*
Death rate: 8.93 *(per 1,000 population)*
Infant mortality rate: 6.4 *(deaths per 1,000 live births)*
Fertility rate: 1.83 *(per woman)*
Life expectancy at birth:
total population: 75.58
(*males:* 72.88, *females:* 78.46)

GOVERNMENT:
Type of government: Republic
Independence: December 6, 1921 *(from UK)*
Leaders:
chief of state: President Mary Bourke Robinson
head of government: Prime Minister Bertie Ahern

ECONOMY:
GDP: purchasing power parity - $54.6 billion
GDP real growth rate: 7%
GDP per capita: $15,400
Inflation Rate: *(consumer prices)* 2.8%
National budget:
revenues: $19.3 billion
expenditures: $20.3 billion
External debt: $19.5 billion
Currency: 1 Irish pound = 100 pence
Labor Force: 1.37 million
Unemployment rate: 13.5%
Agriculture: Turnips, barley, potatoes, sugar beets, wheat; meat and dairy products
Industries: Food products, brewing, textiles, clothing, chemicals, pharmaceuticals, machinery, transportation equipment, glass and crystal
Exports: $29.9 billion
commodities: Chemicals, data processing equipment, industrial machinery, live animals, animal products
Imports: $25.3 billion
commodities: Food, animal feed, data processing equipment, pertroleum and petroleum products, machinery, textiles, clothing

DEFENSE:
Defense expenditures: *exchange rate conversion* - $618 *million*, 1.3% *of GDP*

ISRAEL

GEOGRAPHY:
Location: Middle East
Area:
total area: 20,770 sq km
land area: 20,330 sq km
Capital city: Jerusalem
Natural Resources: Copper, phosphates, bromide, potash, clay, sand, sulfur, asphalt, manganese, small amounts of natural gas and crude oil

PEOPLE:
Population: 5,421,995
Population growth rate: 2.11%
Age structure:
0–14 years: 29%
15–64 years: 62%
65 years & over: 9%
Literacy rate: 95% *of total population,*
(males: 97%, *females:* 93%)
Languages: Hebrew *(official),* Arabic used officially for Arab minority, English most commonly used foreign language
Religions: 82%-Judaism, 14%-Islam *(mostly Sunni Muslim),* 2%-Christian, 2%-Druze and other

VITAL STATISTICS:
Birth rate: 20.31 *(per 1,000 population)*
Death rate: 6.26 *(per 1,000 population)*
Infant mortality rate: 8.5 *(deaths per 1,000 live births)*
Fertility rate: 2.77 *(per woman)*
Life expectancy at birth:
total population: 78.01
(males: 76.16, *females:* 79.96)

GOVERNMENT:
Type of government: Republic
Independence: May 14, 1948 *(from League of Nations mandate under British administration)*
Leaders:
chief of state: President Ezer Weizman
head of government: Prime Minister Benjamin Netanyahu

ECONOMY:
GDP: purchasing power parity - $80.1 billion
GDP real growth rate: 7.1%
GDP per capita: $15,500
Inflation Rate*(consumer prices):* 10.1%
National budget:
revenues: $41 billion
expenditures: $53 billion
External debt: $18.5 billion

Currency: 1 new Israeli shekel = 100 new agorot
Labor Force: 1.9 million
Unemployment rate: 6.3%
Agriculture: Citrus and other fruits, vegetables, cotton; beef, poultry, dairy products
Industries: Food processing, diamond cutting and polishing, textiles and apparel, chemicals, metal products, military equipment, transport equipment, electrical equipment, potash mining, high-technology, electronics, tourism
Exports: $28.4 billion
commodities: Machinery and equipment, cut diamonds, chemicals, textiles and apparel, agricultural products
Imports: $40.1 billion
commodities: Military equipment, investment goods, rough diamonds, oil, other productive inputs, consumer goods

DEFENSE:
Defense expenditures: *exchange rate conversion -* $9.2 *billion,* 9.8% *of GDP*

ITALY

GEOGRAPHY:
Location: Southern Europe
Area:
total area: 301,230 sq km
land area: 294,020 sq km
Capital city: Rome
Natural Resources: Mercury, potash, marble, sulfur, dwindling natural gas and crude oil reserves, fish, coal

PEOPLE:
Population: 57,460,274
Population growth rate: 0.13%
Age structure:
0–14 years: 15%
15–64 years: 68%
65 years & over: 17%
Literacy rate: 97% *of total population,*
(males: 98%, *females:* 96%)
Languages: Italian, German *(parts of Trentino-Alto Adige region are predominantly German speaking),* French *(small French-speaking minority in Valle d'Aosta region),* Slovene *(Slovene-speaking minority in the Trieste-Gorizia area)*
Religions: 98%-Roman Catholic, 2%-other

VITAL STATISTICS:
Birth rate: 9.87 *(per 1,000 population)*
Death rate: 9.82 *(per 1,000 population)*

Infant mortality rate: 6.9 *(deaths per 1,000 live births)*
Fertility rate: 1.27 *(per woman)*
Life expectancy at birth:
  total population: 78.06
    (males: 74.85, *females:* 81.48)

GOVERNMENT:
Type of government: Republic
Independence: March 17, 1861 *(Kingdom of Italy proclaimed)*
Leaders:
  chief of state: President Oscar Luigi Scalfaro
  head of government: Prime Minister *(referred to in Italy as the President of the Council of Ministers)* Romano Prodi *(announced resignation October 1997)*

ECONOMY:
GDP: purchasing power parity - $1.0886 trillion
  GDP real growth rate: 3.2%
  GDP per capita: $18,700
Inflation Rate *(consumer prices):* 5.4%
National budget:
  revenues: $339 billion
  expenditures: $431 billion
External debt: $67 billion
Currency: 1 Italian lira = 100 centesimi
Labor Force: 23.988 million
Unemployment rate: 12.2%
Agriculture: Fruits, vegetables, grapes, potatoes, sugar beets, soybeans, grains, olives; meats and dairy products, fish *(catch of 525,000 metric tons)*
Industries: Tourism, machinery, iron and steel, food processing, textiles, motor vehicles, clothing, footwear, ceramics
Exports: $190.8 billion
  commodities: Metals, textiles and clothing, production machinery, motor vehicles, transportation equipment, chemicals
Imports: $168.7 billion
  commodities: Industrial machinery, chemicals, transport equipment, petroleum, metals, food, agricultural products

DEFENSE:
Defense expenditures: *exchange rate conversion -* $20.4 *billion,* 1.9% *of GDP*

JAMAICA

GEOGRAPHY:
Location: Caribbean
Area:
  total area: 10,990 sq km
  land area: 10,830 sq km

Capital city: Kingston
Natural Resources: Bauxite, gypsum, limestone

PEOPLE:
Population: 2,595,275
Population growth rate: 0.8%
Age structure:
  0–14 years: 32%
  15–64 years: 61%
  65 years & over: 7%
Literacy rate: 85% *of total population,*
  (males: 80.8%, *females:* 89.1%)
Languages: English, Creole
Religions: 55.9%-Protestant, (18.4%-Church of God, 10%-Baptist, 7.1%-Anglican, 6.9%-Seventh-Day Adventist, 5.2%-Pentecostal, 3.1%-Methodist, 2.7%-United Church, 2.5%-other), 5%-Roman Catholic, 39.1%-other, including spiritual cults

VITAL STATISTICS:
Birth rate: 22.19 *(per 1,000 population)*
Death rate: 5.57 *(per 1,000 population)*
Infant mortality rate: 15.6 *(deaths per 1,000 live births)*
Fertility rate: 2.45 *(per woman)*
Life expectancy at birth:
  total population: 74.88
    (males: 72.6, *females:* 77.29)

GOVERNMENT:
Type of government: Parliamentary Democracy
Independence: August 6, 1962 *(from UK)*
Leaders:
  chief of state: Queen Elizabeth II, represented by Sir Howard Cooke
  head of government: Prime Minister Percival James Patterson

ECONOMY:
GDP: purchasing power parity - $8.2 billion
  GDP real growth rate: 0.8%
  GDP per capita: $3,200
Inflation Rate *(consumer prices):* 25.5%
National budget:
  revenues: $1.45 billion
  expenditures: $2 billion
External debt: $3.6 billion
Currency: 1 Jamaican dollar = 100 cents
Labor Force: 1,062,100 million
Unemployment rate: 15.4%
Agriculture: Sugarcane, bananas, coffee, citrus, potatoes, vegetables; poultry, goats, milk
Industries: Bauxite, tourism, textiles, food processing, light manufactures
Exports: $2 billion
  commodities: Alumina, bauxite, sugar, bananas, rum
Imports: $2.7 billion

commodities: Machinery and transport equipment, construction materials, fuel, food, chemicals

DEFENSE:
Defense expenditures: *exchange rate conversion -* $30 *million,* NA% *of GDP*

JAPAN

GEOGRAPHY:
Location: Eastern Asia
Area:
total area: 377,835 sq km
land area: 374,744 sq km
Capital city: Tokyo
Natural Resources: Negligible mineral resources, fish

PEOPLE:
Population: 125,449,703
Population growth rate: 0.21%
Age structure:
0–14 years: 16%
15–64 years: 69%
65 years & over: 15%
Literacy rate: 99% *of total population*
Languages: Japanese
Religions: 84%-observe both Shinto and Buddhist, 16%-other (*including* 0.7%-Christian)

VITAL STATISTICS:
Birth rate: 10.19 *(per 1,000 population)*
Death rate: 7.71 *(per 1,000 population)*
Infant mortality rate: 4.4 *(deaths per 1,000 live births)*
Fertility rate: 1.46 *(per woman)*
Life expectancy at birth:
total population: 79.55
(*males:* 76.57, *females:* 82.68)

GOVERNMENT:
Type of government: Constitutional Monarchy
Independence: 660 BC *(traditional founding by Emperor Jimmu)*
Leaders:
chief of state: Emperor Akihito
head of government: Prime Minister Ryutaro Hashimoto

ECONOMY:
GDP: purchasing power parity - $2.6792 trillion
GDP real growth rate: 0.3%
GDP per capita: $21,300
Inflation Rate *(consumer prices):* −0.1%

National budget:
revenues: $595 billion
expenditures: $829 billion
External debt: $NA
Currency: Yen
Labor Force: 65.87 million
Unemployment rate: 3.1%
Agriculture: Rice, sugar beets, vegetables, fruit; pork, poultry, dairy products, eggs; fish *(catch of 10 million metric tons)*
Industries: Among world's largest and technologically advanced producers of steel and non-ferrous metallurgy, heavy electrical equipment, construction and mining equipment, motor vehicles and parts, electronic and telecommunication equipment, machine tools, automated production systems, locomotives and railroad rolling stock, ships, chemicals; textiles, processed foods
Exports: $442.84 billion
commodities: Manufactured goods (including machinery, motor vehicles, consumer electronics)
Imports: $336.09 billion
commodities: Manufactured goods, fossil fuels, foodstuffs and raw materials

DEFENSE:
Defense expenditures: *exchange rate conversion -* $50.2 *billion,* 1% *of GDP*

JORDAN

GEOGRAPHY:
Location: Middle East
Area:
total area: 89,213 sq km
land area: 88,884 sq km
Capital city: Amman
Natural Resources: phosphates, potash, shale oil

PEOPLE:
Population: 4,212,152
Population growth rate: 2.65%
Age structure:
0–14 years: 44%
15–64 years: 53%
65 years & over: 3%
Literacy rate: 86.6% *of total population,* (*males:* 93.4%, *females:* 79.4%)
Languages: Arabic *(official)*, English widely understood among upper and middle classes
Religions: 92%-Sunni Muslim, 8%-Christian

VITAL STATISTICS:
Birth rate: 36.67 *(per 1,000 population)*
Death rate: 3.95 *(per 1,000 population)*

Infant mortality rate: 31.5 *(deaths per 1,000 live births)*
Fertility rate: 5.1 *(per woman)*
Life expectancy at birth:
total population: 72.48
    (males: 70.62, *females:* 74.45)

GOVERNMENT:
Type of government: Constitutional Monarchy
Independence: May 25, 1946 *(from League of Nations mandate under British administration)*
Leaders:
chief of state: King Hussein
head of government: Prime Minister Abdul-Salam Majali

ECONOMY:
GDP: purchasing power parity - $19.3 billion
GDP real growth rate: 6.5%
GDP per capita: $4,700
Inflation Rate *(consumer prices):* 3%
National budget:
revenues: $2.5 billion
expenditures: $2.5 billion
External debt: $6.9 billion
Currency: 1 Jordanian dinars = 1,000 fils
Labor Force: 600,000
Unemployment rate: 16%
Industries: Phosphate mining, petroleum refining, cement, potash, light manufacturing
Agriculture: Wheat, barley, citrus, tomatoes, melons, olives; sheep, goats, poultry
Exports: $1.7 billion
commodities: Phosphates, fertilizers, potash, agricultural products, manufactured goods
Imports: $3.8 billion
commodities: Crude oil, machinery, transport equipment, food, live animals, manufactured goods

DEFENSE:
Defense expenditures: *exchange rate conversion -* $589 *million,* 8.2% *of GDP*

KAZAKSTAN

GEOGRAPHY:
Location: Central Asia
Area:
total area: 2,717,300 sq km
land area: 2,669,800 sq km
Capital city: Almaty
Natural Resources: Major deposits of petroleum, coal, iron ore, manganese, chrome ore, nickel, cobalt, copper, molybdenum, lead, zinc, bauxite, gold, uranium

PEOPLE:
Population: 16,916,463
Population growth rate: −0.15%
Age structure:
0–14 years: 30%
15–64 years: 63%
65 years & over: 7%
Literacy rate: 98% *of total population,* *(males:* 99%, *females:* 96%)
Languages: Kazak (Qazaqz) *(official language spoken by over 40% of the population)* Russian *(language of interethnic communication spoken by two-thirds of population and used in everyday business)*
Religions: 47%-Muslim, 44%-Russian Orthodox, 2%-Protestant, 7%-other

VITAL STATISTICS:
Birth rate: 19.02 *(per 1,000 population)*
Death rate: 9.65 *(per 1,000 population)*
Infant mortality rate: 63.2 *(deaths per 1,000 live births)*
Fertility rate: 2.36 *(per woman)*
Life expectancy at birth:
total population: 64.09
    (males: 58.56, *females:* 69.9)

GOVERNMENT:
Type of government: Republic
Independence: December 16, 1991 *(from the Soviet Union)*
Leaders:
chief of state: President Nursultan A. Nazarbayev
head of government: Premier Nurlan Balgimbayev

ECONOMY:
GDP: purchasing power parity - $46.9 billion
GDP real growth rate: −8.9%
GDP per capita: $2,700
Inflation Rate *(consumer prices):* 60.3%
National budget:
revenues: $NA
expenditures: $NA
External debt: $2.5 billion
Currency: Tenge
Labor Force: 7.356 million
Unemployment rate: 1.4%; *(large number of underemployed workers)*
Agriculture: Grain, mostly spring wheat, cotton; wool, meat
Industries: Oil, coal, iron ore, manganese, chromite, lead, zinc, copper, titanium, bauxite, gold, silver, phosphates, sulfur, iron and steel, nonferrous metal, tractors and other agricultural machinery, electric motors, construction materials; much of industrial capacity is shut down and/or is in need of repair

Exports: $5.1 billion
  commodities: Oil, ferrous and nonferrous metals, chemicals, grain, wool, meat, coal
Imports: $3.9 billion
  commodities: Machinery and parts, industrial materials, oil and gas

DEFENSE:
Defense expenditures: $18.9 billion tenges, NA% of GDP; (*note - conversion of defense expenditures into US dollars using the current exchange rate could produce misleading results*)

K E N Y A

GEOGRAPHY:
Location: Eastern Africa
Area:
  total area: 582,650 sq km
  land area: 569,250 sq km
Capital city: Nairobi
Natural Resources: Gold, limestone, soda ash, salt barytes, rubies, fluorspar, garnets, wildlife

PEOPLE:
Population: 28,176,686
Population growth rate: 2.27%
Age structure:
  0–14 years: 45%
  15–64 years: 53%
  65 years & over: 2%
Literacy rate: 78.1% *of total population* (*males:* 86.3% *females:* 70%)
Languages: English (*official*), Swahili (*official*), numerous indigenous languages
Religions: 38%-Protestant (*including Anglican*), 28%-Roman Catholic, 26%-indigenous beliefs, 8%-other

VITAL STATISTICS:
Birth rate: 33.38 (*per 1,000 population*)
Death rate: 10.3 (*per 1,000 population*)
Infant mortality rate: 55.3 (*deaths per 1,000 live births*)
Fertility rate: 4.45 (*per woman*)
Life expectancy at birth:
  total population: 55.61
    (*males:* 55.53, *females:* 55.69)

GOVERNMENT:
Type of government: Republic
Independence: December 12, 1963 (*from UK*)
Leaders:
  chief of state & head of government: President Daniel Toroitich arap Moi

ECONOMY:
GDP: purchasing power parity - $36.8 billion

  GDP real growth rate: 5%
  GDP per capita: $1,300
Inflation Rate (*consumer prices*): 1.7%
National budget:
  revenues: $2.4 billion
  expenditures: $2.8 billion
External debt: $ 7 billion
Currency: 1 Kenyan shilling = 100 cents
Labor Force: NA
Unemployment rate: 35%
Agriculture: Coffee, tea, corn, wheat, sugarcane, fruit, vegetables; dairy products, beef, pork, poultry, eggs
Industries: small-scale consumer goods (*plastic, furniture, batteries, textiles, soap, cigarettes, flour*), agricultural processing; oil refining, cement; tourism
Exports: $1.6 billion
  commodities: Tea, coffee, petroleum products
Imports: $2.2 billion
  commodities: Machinery and transportation equipment, petroleum and petroleum products, iron and steel, raw materials, food and consumer goods

DEFENSE:
Defense expenditures: *exchange rate conversion -* $136 *million,* 1.9% *of GDP*

N O R T H   K O R E A

GEOGRAPHY:
Location: Eastern Asia
Area:
  total area: 120,540 sq km
  land area: 120,410 sq km
Capital city: Pyongyang
Natural Resources: Coal, lead, tungsten, zinc, graphite, magnesite, iron ore, copper, gold, pyrites, salt, fluorspar, hydropower

PEOPLE:
Population: 23,904,124
Population growth rate: 1.74%
Age structure:
  0–14 years: 30%
  15–64 years: 66%
  65 years & over: 4%
Literacy rate: 99% *of total population*, (*males:* 99%, *females:* 99%)
Languages: Korean
Religions: Buddism and Confucianism, some Christianity and syncretic Chondogyo (*note: Autonomous religious activities now almost nonexistant; government-sponsored religious groups exist to provide illusion of religious freedom*)

VITAL STATISTICS:
Birth rate: 22.86 *(per 1,000 population)*
Death rate: 5.45 *(per 1,000 population)*
Infant mortality rate: 25.9 *(deaths per 1,000 live births)*
Fertility rate: 2.31 *(per woman)*
Life expectancy at birth:
   total population: 70.32
      (males: 67.23, *females:* 73.57)

GOVERNMENT:
Type of government: Communist State; Stalinist dictatorship
Independence: September 9, 1948
Leaders:
   chief of state: Kim Jong II

ECONOMY:
GDP: purchasing power parity - $21.5 billion
   GDP real growth rate: -5%
   GDP per capita: $920
Inflation Rate *(consumer prices)*: NA%
National budget:
   revenues: $19.3 billion
   expenditures: $19.3 billion
External debt: $8 billion
Currency: 1 North Korean won = 100 chon
Labor Force: 9.615 million
Unemployment rate: NA%
Agriculture: Rice, corn, potatoes, soybeans, pulses; cattle, pigs, pork, eggs
Industries: Military products; machine building, electric power, chemicals; mining *(coal, iron ore, magnesite, graphite, copper, zinc, lead, and precious metals)*, metallurgy; textiles, food processing
Exports: $840 million
   commodities: Minerals, metallurgical products, agricultural and fishery products, manufactured goods *(including armaments)*
Imports: $1.27 billion
   commodities: Petroleum, grain, coking coal, machinery and equipment, consumer goods

DEFENSE:
Defense expenditures: *exchange rate conversion -* $5–$7 *billion*, 25%–33% *of GDP*

SOUTH KOREA

GEOGRAPHY:
Location: Eastern Asia
Area:
   total area: 98,480 sq km
   land area: 98,190 sq km
Capital city: Seoul

Natural Resources: Coal, tungsten, graphite, molybdenum, lead, hydropower

PEOPLE:
Population: 45,482,291
Population growth rate: 1.02%
Age structure:
   0–14 years: 23%
   15–64 years: 71%
   65 years & over: 6%
Literacy rate: 98% *of total population,*
   (male: 99.3%, *female:* 96.7%)
Languages: Korean, English widely taught in high school
Religions: 48.6%-Christianity, 47.4%-Buddhism, 3%-Confucianism, pervasive folk religion *(shamanism),* 0.2%-Chondogyo *(religion of the Heavenly Way)*

VITAL STATISTICS:
Birth rate: 16.24 *(per 1,000 population)*
Death rate: 5.66 *(per 1,000 population)*
Infant mortality rate: 8.2 *(deaths per 1,000 live births)*
Fertility rate: 1.77 *(per woman)*
Life expectancy at birth:
   total population: 73.26
      (males: 69.65, *females:* 77.39)

GOVERNMENT:
Type of government: Republic
Independence: August 15, 1948
Leaders:
   chief of state: President Kim Young-sam
   head of government: Prime Minister Koh Kun

ECONOMY:
GDP: purchasing power parity - $590.7 billion
   GDP real growth rate: 9%
   GDP per capita: $13,000
Inflation Rate *(consumer prices)*: 4.3%
National budget:
   revenues: $69 billion
   expenditures: $67 billion
External debt: $77 billion
Currency: 1 South Korean won = 100 chun (theoretical)
Labor Force: 20 million
Unemployment rate: 2%
Agriculture: Rice, root crops, barley, vegetables, fruit; cattle, pigs, chickens, milk, eggs; fish *(catch of 2.9 million metric tons, seventh largest in the world)*
Industries: Electronics, automobile production, chemicals, shipbuilding, steel, textiles, clothing, footwear, food processing
Exports: $125.4 billion
   commodities: Electronics and electrical equipment, machinery, steel, automobiles, ships;

textiles, clothing, footwear; fish
Imports: $135.1 billion
commodities: Machinery, electronics and electrical equipment, oil, steel, transport equipment, textiles, organic chemicals, grains

DEFENSE:
Defense expenditures: *exchange rate conversion -* $17.4 *billion,* 3.3% *of GDP*

KUWAIT

GEOGRAPHY:
Location: Middle East
Area:
total area: 17,820 sq km
land area: 17,820 sq km
Capital city: Kuwait
Natural Resources: Petroleum, fish shrimp, natural gas

PEOPLE:
Population: 1,950,047
Population growth rate: 6.65%
Age structure:
0–14 years: 33%
15–64 years: 65%
65 years & over: 2%
Literacy rate: 78.6% *of total population,*
(males: 82.2%, *females:* 74.9%)
Languages: Arabic *(official)*, English widely spoken
Religions: 85%-Muslim (30%-*Shi'a,* 45%-*Sunni,* 10%-*other*), 15%-Christian, Hindu, Parsi, other

VITAL STATISTICS:
Birth rate: 20.28 *(per 1,000 population)*
Death rate: 2.2 *(per 1,000 population)*
Infant mortality rate: 11.1 *(deaths per 1,000 live births)*
Fertility rate: 2.82 *(per woman)*
Life expectancy at birth:
total population: 75.92
(males: 73.59, *females:* 78.38)

GOVERNMENT:
Type of government: Nominal Constitutional Monarchy
Independence: June 19, 1961 *(from UK)*
Leaders:
chief of state: Amir Sheikh Jabar
head of government: Acting Prime Minister and Crown Prince Sheikh Al-Abdullah Al-Sabah

ECONOMY:
GDP: purchasing power parity - $30.8 billion

GDP real growth rate: 3%
GDP per capita: $17,000
Inflation Rate *(consumer prices):* 5%
National budget:
revenues: $9.7 billion
expenditures: $14.2 billion
External debt: NA
Currency: 1 Kuwaiti dinar = 1,000 fils
Labor Force: 1 million
Unemployment rate: NEGL%
Agriculture: Practically no crops; extensive fishing in territorial waters
Industries: Petroleum, petrochemicals, desalination, food processing, construction materials, salt, construction
Exports: $11.9 billion
commodities: Oil
Imports: $6.7 billion
commodities: Food, construction materials, vehicles and parts, clothing

DEFENSE:
Defense expenditures: *exchange rate conversion -* $3.5 *billion,* 12.8% *of GDP*

KYRGYZSTAN

GEOGRAPHY:
Location: Central Asia
Area:
total area: 198,500 sq km
land area: 191,300 sq km
Capital city: Bishkek
Natural Resources: Abundant hydroelectric potential; significant deposits of gold and rare earth metals; locally exploitable coal, oil, and natural gas; other deposits of nepheline, mercury, bismuth, lead, zinc

PEOPLE:
Population: 4,529,648
Population growth rate: 0.07%
Age structure:
0–14 years: 37%
15–64 years: 57%
65 years & over: 6%
Literacy rate: 97%, *of total population,*
(males: 99%, *females:* 96%)
Languages: Kirghiz *(Kyrgyz) (official)*, Russian *(official) (note—in March 1996, the Kyrgyz legislature amended the constitution to make Russian an official language, along with Kyrgyz, in territories and work places where Russian-speaking citizens predominate)*
Religions: Muslim, Russian Orthodox

VITAL STATISTICS:
Birth rate: 26.02 *(per 1,000 population)*
Death rate: 8.83 *(per 1,000 population)*
Infant mortality rate: 77.8 *(deaths per 1,000 live births)*
Fertility rate: 3.22 *(per woman)*
Life expectancy at birth:
  total population: 63.86
    (males: 59.18, *females:* 68.77)

GOVERNMENT:
Type of government: Republic
Independence: August 31, 1991 *(from Soviet Union)*
Leaders:
  chief of state: President Askar Akayev
  head of government: Prime Minister Apas Dzhumagulov ·

ECONOMY:
GDP: purchasing power parity - $5.4 billion
  GDP real growth rate: −6%
  GDP per capita: $1,140
Inflation Rate *(consumer prices):* 32%
National budget:
  revenues: $NA
  expenditures: $NA
External debt: $480 million
Currency: introduced national currency, the som *(May 10, 1993)*
Labor Force: 1.836 million
Unemployment rate: 4.8% *(large number of underemployed)*
Agriculture: Wool, tobacco, cotton, potatoes, vegetables, grapes, fruits and berries; sheep, goats, cattle
Industries: Small machinery, textiles, food processing, cement, shoes, sawn logs, refrigerators, furniture, electric motors, gold, rare earth metals
Exports: $380 million
  commodities: Cotton, wool, meat, tobacco; gold, mercury, uranium, hydropower; machinery; shoes
Imports: $439 million
  commodities: Grain, lumber, industrial products, ferrous metals, fuel, machinery, textiles, footwear

DEFENSE:
Defense expenditures: 151 million soms, NA% of GDP *(note - conversion of defense expenditures into US dollars using the current exchange rate could produce misleading results)*

LAOS

GEOGRAPHY:
Location: Southeastern Asia
Area:
  total area: 236,800 sq km
  land area: 230,800 sq km
Capital city: Vientiane
Natural Resources: Timber, hydropower, gypsum, tin, gold, gemstones

PEOPLE:
Population: 4,975,772
Population growth rate: 2.81%
Age structure:
  0–14 years: 45%
  15–64 years: 51%
  65 years & over: 4%
Literacy rate: 56.6% *of total population,*
  (males: 69.4%, *females:* 44.4%)
Languages: Lao *(official)*, French, English, and various ethnic languages
Religions: 60%-Buddhist, 40%-animist and other

VITAL STATISTICS:
Birth rate: 41.94 *(per 1,000 population)*
Death rate: 13.83 *(per 1,000 population)*
Infant mortality rate: 96.8 *(deaths per 1,000 live births)*
Fertility rate: 5.87 *(per woman)*
Life expectancy at birth:
  total population: 52.69
    (males: 51.14, *females:* 54.31)

GOVERNMENT:
Type of government: Communist State
Independence: July 19, 1949 *(from France)*
Leaders:
  chief of state: President Nouhak Phoumsavanh
  head of government: Prime Minister General Khamtay Siphandone

ECONOMY:
GDP: purchasing power parity - $5.2 billion
  GDP real growth rate: 8%
  GDP per capita: $1,100
Inflation Rate *(consumer prices):* 20%
National budget:
  revenues: $198 million
  expenditures: $351 million
External debt: $2 billion
Currency: 1 new kip = 100 at
Labor Force: 1–1.5 million
Unemployment rate: 21%
Agriculture: Sweet potatoes, vegetables, corn,

coffee, sugarcane, cotton; water buffalo, pigs, cattle, poultry

Industries: Tin and gypsum mining, timber, electric power, agricultural processing, construction

Exports: $278 million
commodities: electricity, wood products, coffee, tin, garments

Imports: $486 million
commodities: Food, fuel oil, consumer goods, manufactured goods

DEFENSE:
Defense expenditures: *exchange rate conversion -* $105 *million*, 8.1% *of GDP*

LATVIA

GEOGRAPHY:
Location: Eastern Europe
Area:
total area: 64,100 sq km
land area: 64,100 sq km
Capital city: Riga
Natural Resources: Minimal; amber, peat, limestone, dolomite

PEOPLE:
Population: 2,468,982
Population growth rate: -1.39%
Age structure:
0-14 years: 20%
15-64 years: 66%
65 years & over: 14%
Literacy rate: 100% *of total population,*
(*males:* 100%, *females:* 99%)
Languages: Lettish*(official)*, Lithuanian, Russian, other
Religions: Lutheran, Roman Catholic, Russian Orthodox

VITAL STATISTICS:
Birth rate: 10.94 *(per 1,000 population)*
Death rate: 15.19 *(per 1,000 population)*
Infant mortality rate: 21.2 *(deaths per 1,000 live births)*
Fertility rate: 1.62 *(per woman)*
Life expectancy at birth:
total population: 66.91
(*males:* 60.84, *females:* 73.27)

GOVERNMENT:
Type of government: Republic
Independence: September 6, 1991 *(from Soviet Union)*
Leaders:
chief of state: President Guntis Ulmanis
head of government: Prime Minister Guntars Krasts

ECONOMY:
GDP: purchasing power parity - $14.7 billion
GDP real growth rate: -1.5%
GDP per capita: $5,300
Inflation Rate *(consumer prices):* 20%
National budget:
revenues: $NA
expenditures: $NA
External debt: $NA
Currency: 1 lat = 100 cents *(introduced March 1993)*
Labor Force: 1.407 million
Unemployment rate: 6.5%
Agriculture: Grain, sugar beets, potatoes, vegetables; meat, milk, eggs; fish
Industries: Buses, vans, street and railroad cars, synthetic fibers, agricultural machinery, fertilizers, washing machines, radios, electronics, pharmaceuticals, processed foods, textiles; dependent on imports for energy, raw materials, and intermediate products
Exports: $1.3 billion
commodities: Timber, textiles, dairy products
Imports: $1.7 billion
commodities: Fuels, cars, chemicals

DEFENSE:
Defense expenditures: 176 million rubles, 3% to 5% of the GDP *(note-conversion of defense expenditures into US dollars using prevailing exchange rate could produce misleading results)*

LEBANON

GEOGRAPHY:
Location: Middle East
Area:
total area: 10,400 sq km
land area: 10,230 sq km
Capital city: Beirut
Natural Resources: Limestone, iron ore, salt, water-surplus state in a water deficit region

PEOPLE:
Population: 3,776,317
Population growth rate: 2.16%
Age structure:
0-14 years: 36%
15-64 years: 59%
65 years & over: 5%
Literacy rate: 92.4% *of total population,*
(*males:* 94.7%, *females:* 90.3%)
Languages: Arabic *(official)*, French *(official)*, Armenian, English
Religions: 70%-Islam *(5 legally recognized Islamic groups-Alawite or Nusayri, Druze, Isma'ilite, Shi'a, Sunni)*, 30% Christian *(11 legally recog-*

nized Christian groups-4 Orthodox Christian, 6
Catholic, 1 Protestant), Judaism

VITAL STATISTICS:
Birth rate: 27.93 *(per 1,000 population)*
Death rate: 6.35 *(per 1,000 population)*
Infant mortality rate: 36.7 *(deaths per 1,000 live
births)*
Fertility rate: 3.24 *(per woman)*
Life expectancy at birth:
total population: 69.99
(males: 67.49, *females:* 72.62)

GOVERNMENT:
Type of government: Republic
Independence: November 22, 1943 *(from the
League of Nations mandate under French admin-
istration)*
Leaders:
chief of state: President Elias Hrawi
head of government: Prime Minister Rafiq
Hariri

ECONOMY:
GDP: purchasing power parity - $18.3 billion
GDP real growth rate: 6.5%
GDP per capita: $4,900
Inflation Rate *(consumer prices)*: 9%
National budget:
revenues: $1.4 billion
expenditures: $3.2 billion
External debt: $1.2 billion
Currency: 1 Lebanese pound = 100 piasters
Labor Force: 650,000
Unemployment rate: 30%
Agriculture: Citrus, vegetable, potatoes, olives,
tobacco, hemp (hashish); sheep, goats
Industries: Banking, food processing, textiles,
cement, oil refining, chemicals, jewelry, some
metal fabricating
Exports: $1 billion
commodities: Agricultural products, chemicals,
textiles, precious and semiprecious metals
and jewelry, metals and metal products
Imports: $7.3 billion
commodities: Consumer goods, machinery and
transport equipment, petroleum products

DEFENSE:
Defense expenditures: *exchange rate conversion -*
$278 million, 5.5% of *GDP*

LIBERIA

GEOGRAPHY:
Location: Western Africa
Area:
total area: 111,370 sq km
land area: 96,320 sq km
Capital city: Monrovia
Natural Resources: Iron ore, timber, diamonds,
gold

PEOPLE:
Population: 2,109,789
Population growth rate: 2.13%
Age structure:
0–14 years: 45%
15–64 years: 52%
65 years & over: 3%
Literacy rate: 38.3% *of total population,*
(males: 53.9%, *females:* 22.4%)
Languages: English *(official)*, Niger-Congo lan-
guage group about 20 local languages come
from this group
Religions: 70%- traditional, 20%-Muslim, 10%-
Christian

VITAL STATISTICS:
Birth rate: 42.72 *(per 1,000 population)*
Death rate: 11.95 *(per 1,000 population)*
Infant mortality rate: 108.1 *(deaths per 1,000 live
births)*
Fertility rate: 6.23 *(per woman)*
Life expectancy at birth:
total population: 58.59
(males: 56.05, *females:* 61.21)

GOVERNMENT:
Type of government: Republic
Independence: July 26, 1847
Leaders:
chief of state & head of government: President
Charles G. Taylor

ECONOMY:
GDP: purchasing power parity - $2.3 billion
GDP real growth rate: 0%
GDP per capita: $770
Inflation Rate *(consumer prices):* 50%
National budget:
revenues: $225 million
expenditures: $285 million
External debt: $1.9 billion
Currency: 1 Liberian dollar = 100 cents
Labor Force: 510,000
Unemployment rate: NA%
Agriculture: Rubber, coffee, cocoa, rice,

cassava *(tapioca)*, palm oil, sugarcane, bananas; sheep, goats; timber
Industries: Rubber processing, food processing, construction materials, furniture, palm oil processing, iron ore, diamonds
Exports: $530 million
commodities: Iron ore, rubber, timber, coffee
Imports: $NA
commodities: Mineral fuels, chemicals, machinery, transporation equipment, manufactured goods; rice and other foodstuffs

DEFENSE:
Defense expenditures: *exchange rate conversion -* $14 *million*, 2.9% *of GDP*

LIBYA

GEOGRAPHY:
Location: Northern Africa
Area:
total area: 1,759,540 sq km
land area: 1,759,540 sq km
Capital city: Tripoli
Natural Resources: Petroleum, natural gas, gypsum

PEOPLE:
Population: 5,445,436
Population growth rate: 3.67%
Age structure:
0–14 years: 48%
15–64 years: 49%
65 years & over: 3%
Literacy rate: 76.2% *of total population,* (*males:* 87.9%, *females:* 63%)
Languages: Arabic, Italian, English, all are widely undersood in the major cities
Religions: 97%-Sunni Muslim

VITAL STATISTICS:
Birth rate: 44.42 *(per 1,000 population)*
Death rate: 7.7 *(per 1,000 population)*
Infant mortality rate: 59.5 *(deaths per 1,000 live births)*
Fertility rate: 6.26 *(per woman)*
Life expectancy at birth:
total population: 64.67
(*males:* 62.48, *females:* 66.97)

GOVERNMENT:
Type of government: Jamahiriya *(a state of the masses)* in theory, governed by the populace through local councils; in fact, a military dictatorship
Independence: December 24, 1951 *(from Italy)*

Leaders:
chief of state: Revolutionary Leader Col. Muammar Gadhafi
head of government: Secretary of the General People's Committee *(Premier)* Abdal Majid al-Qaud

ECONOMY:
GDP: purchasing power parity - $32.9 billion
GDP real growth rate: −0.9%
GDP per capita: $6,510
Inflation Rate *(consumer prices)*: 25%
National budget:
revenues: $8.1 billion
expenditures: $9.8 billion
External debt: $3.5 billion
Currency: 1 Libyan dinar = 100 dirhams
Labor Force: 1 million
Unemployment rate: NA
Agriculture: Wheat, barley, olives, dates, citrus, vegetables, peanuts; meat, eggs
Industries: Petroleum, food processing, textiles, handicrafts, cement
Exports: $7.2 billion
commodities: Crude oil, refined petroleum products, natural gas
Imports: $6.9 billion
commodities: Machinery, transport equipment, food, manufactured goods

DEFENSE:
Defense expenditures: *exchange rate conversion -* $1.4 billion, 6.1% *of GDP*

LIECHTENSTEIN

GEOGRAPHY:
Location: Central Europe
Area:
total area: 160 sq km
land area: 160 sq km
Capital city: Vaduz
Natural Resources: Hydroelectric potential

PEOPLE:
Population: 31,122
Population growth rate: 1.08%
Age structure:
0–14 years: 19%
15–64 years: 70%
65 years & over: 11%
Literacy rate: 100% *of total population*
Languages: German *(official)*, Alemannic dialect
Religions: 87.3%- Roman Catholic, 8.3%-Protestant, 1.6%-unknown, 2.8%-other

VITAL STATISTICS:
Birth rate: 11.47 *(per 1,000 population)*
Death rate: 6.81 *(per 1,000 population)*
Infant mortality rate: 5.3 *(deaths per 1,000 live births)*
Fertility rate: 1.37 *(per woman)*
Life expectancy at birth:
  total population: 78.84
    (*males:* 75.92, *females:* 82.17)

GOVERNMENT:
Type of government: Hereditary Constitutional Monarchy
Independence: January 23, 1719 *(Imperial Principality of Liechtenstein established)*
Leaders:
  chief of state: Prince Hans Adam II
  head of government: Mario Frick

ECONOMY:
GDP: purchasing power parity - $630 million
  GDP real growth rate: NA%
  GDP per capita: $22,300
Inflation Rate *(consumer prices):* 5.4%
National budget:
  revenues: $455 million
  expenditures: $442 million
External debt: $NA
Currency: 1 Swiss franc, franken, or franco = 100 centimes, rappen, or centesimi
Labor Force: 20,000 *(12,000 of which are foreigners)*
Unemployment rate: 0.9%
Agriculture: Vegetables, corn, wheat, potatoes, grapes, livestock
Industries: Electronics, metal manufacturing, textiles, ceramics, pharmaceuticals, food products, precision instruments
Exports: $1.636 billion
  commodities: Small specialty machinery, dental products, stamps, hardware, pottery
Imports: $NA
  commodities: Machinery, metal goods, textiles, foodstuffs, motor vehicles

DEFENSE:
Defense expenditures: *defense is the responsibility of Switzerland*

LITHUANIA

GEOGRAPHY:
Location: Eastern Europe
Area:
  total area: 65,200 sq km
  land area: 65,200 sq km

Capital city: Vilnius
Natural Resources: Peat

PEOPLE:
Population: 3,646,041
Population growth rate: -0.35%
Age structure:
  0–14 years: 22%
  15–64 years: 66%
  65 years & over: 12%
Literacy rate: 98% *of total population,*
  (*males:* 99%, *females:* 98%)
Languages: Lithuanian *(official)*, Polish, Russian
Religions: Roman Catholic, Lutheran, Other

VITAL STATISTICS:
Birth rate: 12.93 *(per 1,000 population)*
Death rate: 13.33 *(per 1,000 population)*
Infant mortality rate: 17 *(deaths per 1,000 live births)*
Fertility rate: 1.78 *(per woman)*
Life expectancy at birth:
  total population: 68.03
    (*males:* 62.15, *females:* 74.21)

GOVERNMENT:
Type of government: Republic
Independence: Sepetember 6, 1991 *(from Soviet Union)*
Leaders:
  chief of state: President Algirdas Mykolas Brauskas
  head of government: Prime Minister Gediminas Vagnorius

ECONOMY:
GDP: purchasing power parity - $13.3 billion
  GDP real growth rate: 1%
  GDP per capita: $3,400
Inflation Rate *(consumer prices):* 35%
National budget:
  revenues: $NA
  expenditures: $NA
External debt: $895 million
Currency: Introduced the convertible litas in June 1993
Labor Force: 1.836 million
Unemployment rate: 6.1%
Agriculture: Grain, potatoes, sugar beets, vegetables; meat, milk, eggs; fish
Industries: Metal-cutting machine tools, electric motors, television sets, refrigerators and freezers, petroleum refining, shipbuilding *(small ships)*, furniture making, textiles, food processing, fertilizers, agricultural machinery, optical equipment, electronic components, computers, amber
Exports: $2.2 billion

commodities: Electronics, food, chemicals,
  petroleum products
Imports: $2.7 billion
  commodities: Oil, machinery, chemicals, grain

DEFENSE:
Defense expenditures: exchange rate conversion -
$31.7 million, 1% of GDP

```
        LUXEMBOURG
```

GEOGRAPHY:
Location: Western Europe
Area:
  total area: 2,586 sq km
  land area: 2,586 sq km
Capital city: Luxembourg
Natural Resources: Iron ore (no longer exploited)

PEOPLE:
Population: 415,870
Population growth rate: 1.57%
Age structure:
  0–14 years: 18%
  15–64 years: 68%
  65 years & over: 14%
Literacy rate: 100% of total population
Languages: Luxembourgisch, German, French,
  English
Religions: 97%-Roman Catholic, 3%-Protestant
  and Jewish

VITAL STATISTICS:
Birth rate: 13.14 (per 1,000 population)
Death rate: 8.32 (per 1,000 population)
Infant mortality rate: 4.7 (deaths per 1,000 live
  births)
Fertility rate: 1.76 (per woman)
Life expectancy at birth:
  total population: 78.26
    (males: 75.24, females: 81.56)

GOVERNMENT:
Type of government: Constitutional Monarchy
Independence: 1839
Leaders:
  chief of state: Grand Duke Jean
  head of government: Prime Minister Jean-Claude
    Juncker

ECONOMY:
GDP: purchasing power parity - $10 billion
  GDP real growth rate: 2.6%
  GDP per capita: $24,800
Inflation Rate (consumer prices): 3.6%

National budget:
  revenues: $4 billion
  expenditures: $4.05 billion
External debt: $800 million
Currency: 1 Luxembourg frac = 100 centimes
Labor Force: 200,400
Unemployment rate: 2.5%
Agriculture: Barley, oats, potatoes, wheat, fruits,
  wine grapes; livestock products
Industries: Banking, iron and steel, food pro-
  cessing, chemicals, metal products, engineering,
  tires, glass, aluminum
Exports: $5.9 million
  commodities: Finished steel products, chemi-
    cals, rubber products, glass, aluminum, other
    industrial products
Imports: $7.5 million
  commodities: Minerals, metals, foodstuffs,
    quality consumer goods

DEFENSE:
Defense expenditures: exchange rate conversion -
$142 million, 0.8% of GDP

```
        MALAYSIA
```

GEOGRAPHY:
Location: Southeastern Asia
Area:
  total area: 329,750 sq km
  land area: 328,550 sq km
Capital city: Kuala Lumpur
Natural Resources: Tin, petroleum, timber, copper,
  iron ore, natural gas, bauxite

PEOPLE:
Population: 19,962,893
Population growth rate: 2.07%
Age structure:
  0–14 years: 36%
  15–64 years: 60%
  65 years & over: 4%
Literacy rate: 83.5% of total population,
  (males: 89.1%, females: 78.1%)
Languages: Peninsular Malaysia: Maylay (official),
  English, Chinese dialects, Tamil
  Sabah: English, Malay, numerous tribal dialects,
    Chinese (Mandarin and Hakka dialects pre-
    dominate)
  Sarawak: English, Malay, Mandarin, numerous
    tribal languages
Religions:
  Peninsular Malaysia: Muslim (Malays), Buddhist
    (Chinese), Hindu (Indians)
  Sabah: 38%-Muslim, 17%-Christian, 45%-other

Sarawak: 35%-Tribal Religion, 24%-Buddhist and Confucianist, 20%-Muslim, 16%-Christian, 5%-other

VITAL STATISTICS:
Birth rate: 26.2 *(per 1,000 population)*
Death rate: 5.49 *(per 1,000 population)*
Infant mortality rate: 24 *(deaths per 1,000 live births)*
Fertility rate: 3.27 *(per woman)*
Life expectancy at birth:
total population: 69.75
(males: 66.82, *females:* 72.89)

GOVERNMENT:
Type of government: Constitutional Monarchy
Independence: August 31, 1957 *(from UK)*
Leaders:
chief of state: Paramount Ruler Tuanku Ja'afar
head of government: Prime Minister Mahathir Mohamad

ECONOMY:
GDP: purchasing power parity - $193.6 billion
GDP real growth rate: 9.5%
GDP per capita: $9,800
Inflation Rate *(consumer prices):* 5.3%
National budget:
revenues: $20.2 billion
expenditures: $19.9 billion
External debt: $27.4 million
Currency: 1 ringgit = 100 sen
Labor Force: 7.627 million
Unemployment rate: 2.8%
Agriculture:
Peninsular: Natural Rubber, Palm oil, rice
Sabah: Subsistence crops, rubber, timber, coconut, rice
Sarawak: Rubber, pepper; timber
Industries:
Peninsular: Rubber and oil palm processing and manufacturing, light manufacturing industry, electronics, tin, mining and smelting, logging and processing timber
Sabah: Logging, petroleum production
Sarawak: Agriculture processing, petroleum production and refining, logging
Exports: $72 billion
commodities: Electronic equipment, petroleum and petroleum products, palm oil, wood and wood products, rubber, textiles
Imports: $72.2 billion
commodities: Machinery and equipment, chemicals, food, petroleum products

DEFENSE:
Defense expenditures: *exchange rate conversion -* $2.4 billion, 2.9% of GDP

MALTA

GEOGRAPHY:
Location: Southern Europe
Area:
total area: 320 sq km
land area: 320 sq km
Capital city: Valletta
Natural Resources: Limestone, salt

PEOPLE:
Population: 375,576
Population growth rate: 1.01%
Age structure:
0–14 years: 22%
15–64 years: 67%
65 years & over: 11%
Literacy rate: 84% *of total population,*
(males: 86%, *females:* 82%)
Languages: Maltese *(official)*, English *(official)*
Religions: 98%-Roman Catholic

VITAL STATISTICS:
Birth rate: 14.79 *(per 1,000 population)*
Death rate: 6.83 *(per 1,000 population)*
Infant mortality rate: 6.9 *(deaths per 1,000 live births)*
Fertility rate: 2.17 *(per woman)*
Life expectancy at birth:
total population: 78.11
(males: 75.77, *females:* 80.6)

GOVERNMENT:
Type of government: Parliamentary Democracy
Independence: September 21, 1964 *(from UK)*
Leaders:
chief of state: President Ugo Mifsud Bonnici
head of government: Prime Minister Alfred Sant

ECONOMY:
GDP: purchasing power parity - $4.4 billion
GDP real growth rate: 5%
GDP per capita: $12,000
Inflation Rate *(consumer prices):* 5%
National budget:
revenues: $1.4 billion
expenditures: $1.4 billion
External debt: $603 million
Currency: 1 Maltese lira = 100 cents
Labor Force: 139,600
Unemployment rate: 3.4%
Agriculture: Potatoes, cauliflower, grapes, wheat, barley, tomatoes, citrus, cut flowers, green pep-

pers; pork, milk, poultry, eggs
Industries: Tourism, electronics, ship repair yard, construction, food manufacturing, textiles, footwear, clothing, beverages, tobacco
Exports: $1.5 billion
  commodities: Machinery and transport equipment, clothing and footwear, printed matter
Imports: $2.5 billion
  commodities: Food, petroleum, machinery, semi-manufactured goods

DEFENSE:
Defense expenditures: *exchange rate conversion -* $21.0 *million*, 1.0% *of GDP*

M E X I C O

GEOGRAPHY:
Location: Central America
Area:
  total area: 1,972,550 sq km
  land area: 1,923,040 sq km
Capital city: Mexico City
Natural Resources: Petroleum, silver, copper, gold, lead, zinc, natural gas, timber

PEOPLE:
Population: 95,772,462
Population growth rate: 1.87%
Age structure:
  0–14 years: 36%
  15–64 years: 59%
  65 years & over: 5%
Literacy rate: 89.6% *of total population,* (*males:* 91.8%, *females:* 87.4%)
Languages: Spanish, varian Mayan dialects
Religions: 89%-Roman Catholic, 6%-Protestant

VITAL STATISTICS:
Birth rate: 26.24 *(per 1,000 population)*
Death rate: 4.58 *(per 1,000 population)*
Infant mortality rate: 25 *(deaths per 1,000 live births)*
Fertility rate: 3.03 *(per woman)*
Life expectancy at birth:
  total population: 73.67
  (*males:* 70.07, *females:* 77.45)

GOVERNMENT:
Type of government: Federal Republic operating under centralized government
Independence: September 16, 1810 *(from Spain)*
Leaders:
  chief of state & head of government: President Ernesto Zedillo

ECONOMY:
GDP: purchasing power parity - $721.4 billion
  GDP real growth rate: −6.9%
  GDP per capita: $7,700
Inflation Rate *(consumer prices):* 52%
National budget:
  revenues: $56 billion
  expenditures: $54 billion
External debt: $155 billion
Currency: 1 New Mexican peso = 100 centavos
Labor Force: 33.6 million
Unemployment rate: 10%
Agriculture: Corn, wheat, soybeans, rice, beans, cotton, coffee, fruit, tomatoes; beef, poultry, dairy products; wool
Industries: Food and beverages, tobacco, chemicals, iron and steel, petroleum, mining, textiles, clothing, motor vehicles, consumer durables, tourism
Exports: $80 billion
  commodities: Crude oil, oil products, coffee, silver, engines, motor vehicles, cotton, consumer electronics
Imports: $72 billion
  commodities: Metal-working machines, steel mill products, agricultural machinery, electrical equipment, cars parts for assembly, repair parts for motor vehicles, aircraft, and aircraft parts

DEFENSE:
Defense expenditures: *exchange rate conversion -* $2.24 *billion*, 0.9% *of GDP*

M O N A C O

GEOGRAPHY:
Location: Western Europe
Area:
  total area: 1.9 sq km
  land area: 1.9 sq km
Capital city: Monaco
Natural Resources: None

PEOPLE:
Population: 31,719
Population growth rate: 0.59%
Age structure:
  0–14 years: 17%
  15–64 years: 63%
  65 years & over: 20%
Literacy rate: NA%
Languages: French *(official)*, English, Italian, Monegasque
Religions: 95%-Roman Catholic

VITAL STATISTICS:
Birth rate: 10.66 *(per 1,000 population)*
Death rate: 12.11 *(per 1,000 population)*
Infant mortality rate: 6.9 *(deaths per 1,000 live births)*
Fertility rate: 1.7 *(per woman)*
Life expectancy at birth:
total population: 78.07
(males: 74.38, *females:* 81.93)

GOVERNMENT:
Type of government: Constitutional Monarchy
Independence: 1419 *(rule by the House of Grimaldi)*
Leaders:
chief of state: Prince Rainier III
head of government: Minister of State Paul Dijoud

ECONOMY:
GDP: purchasing power parity - $788 million
GDP real growth rate: NA%
GDP per capita: $25,000
Inflation Rate *(consumer prices)*: NA%
National budget:
revenues: $660 million
expenditures: $586 million
External debt: NA%
Currency: 1 French franc = 100 centimes
Labor Force: NA
Unemployment rate: 3.1%
Agriculture: None
Industries: None
Exports: $NA; full customs integration with France, which collects and rebates Monacan trade duties; also participating in EU market system through customs union with France
Imports: $NA; full customs integration with France, which collects and rebates Monacan trade duties; also participating in EU market system through customs union with France

DEFENSE:
Defense expenditures: *defense is the responsibility of France*

MONGOLIA

GEOGRAPHY:
Location: Northern Asia
Area:
total area: 1.565 million sq km
land area: 1.565 million sq km
Capital city: Ulaanbaatar
Natural Resources: Oil, coal, copper, molybdenum, tungsten, phosphates, tin, nickel, zinc, wolfram, fluorspar, gold

PEOPLE:
Population: 2,496,617
Population growth rate: 1.69%
Age structure:
0–14 years: 38%
15–64 years: 58%
65 years & over: 4%
Literacy rate: 82.9% *of total population,*
(males: 88.6%, *females:* 77.2%)
Languages: Khalkha Mongol, Turkic, Russian, Chinese
Religions: Tibetan Buddhist, 4%-Muslim

VITAL STATISTICS:
Birth rate: 25.55 *(per 1,000 population)*
Death rate: 8.65 *(per 1,000 population)*
Infant mortality rate: 69.7 *(deaths per 1,000 live births)*
Fertility rate: 3.04 *(per woman)*
Life expectancy at birth:
total population: 60.75
(males: 58.8, *females:* 62.8)

GOVERNMENT:
Type of government: Republic
Independence: March 13, 1921 *(from China)*
Leaders:
chief of state: President Natsagiin Bagabandi
head of government: Prime Minister Mendsaikhany Engkhsaikan

ECONOMY:
GDP: purchasing power parity - $4.9 billion
GDP real growth rate: 6%
GDP per capita: $1,970
Inflation Rate *(consumer prices)*: 53%
National budget:
revenues: $1.5 billion
expenditures: $1.3 billion
External debt: $473.7 million
Currency: 1 tughrik = 100 mongos
Labor Force: 1.115 million
Unemployment rate: 15%
Agriculture: Wheat, barley, potatoes, forage crops; sheep, goats, cattle, camels, horses
Industries: Copper, construction material, mining *(particularly coal)*, food and beverage, processing of animal products
Exports: $400 million
commodities: Copper, livestock, animal products, cashmere, wool, hides, fluorspar, other nonferrous metals
Imports: $223 million
commodities: Machinery and equipment, fuels, food products, industrial consumer goods, chemicals, building materials, sugar, tea

DEFENSE:
Defense expenditures: *exchange rate conversion -* $22.8 *million*, 1% *of GDP*

MOROCCO

GEOGRAPHY:
Location: Northern Africa
Area:
  total area: 446,550 sq km
  land area: 446,300 sq km
Capital city: Rabat
Natural Resources: phosphates, iron ore, manganese, lead, zinc, fish, salt

PEOPLE:
Population: 29,779,156
Population growth rate: 2.05%
Age structure:
  0–14 years: 38%
  15–64 years: 58%
  65 years & over: 4%
Literacy rate: 43.7% *of total population*,
  (*males:* 56.6%, *females:* 31%)
Languages: Arabic *(official)*, Berber dialects,
French the language of business, government,
and diplomacy
Religions: 98.7%- Muslim, 1.1%-Christian, 0.2%-Jewish

VITAL STATISTICS:
Birth rate: 27.39 *(per 1,000 population)*
Death rate: 5.77 *(per 1,000 population)*
Infant mortality rate: 43.2 *(deaths per 1,000 live births)*
Fertility rate: 3.58 *(per woman)*
Life expectancy at birth:
  total population: 69.52
    (*males:* 67.53, *females:* 71.61)

GOVERNMENT:
Type of government: Constitutional Monarchy
Independence: March 2, 1956 *(from France)*
Leaders:
  chief of state: King Hassan II
  head of government: Prime Minister Abdellatif
  Filali

ECONOMY:
GDP: purchasing power parity - $87.4 billion
  GDP real growth rate: -6.5%
  GDP per capita: $3,000
Inflation Rate *(consumer prices)*: 5.4%
National budget:
  revenues: $8.1 billion
  expenditures: $8.9 billion
External debt: $20.5 billion

Currency: 1 Moroccan dirham = 100 centimes
Labor Force: 7.4 million
Unemployment rate: 16%
Agriculture: Barley, wheat, citrus, wine, vegetables, olives; livestock
Industries: Phosphate rock mining and processing, food processing, leather goods, textiles, construction, tourism
Exports: $4 billion
  commodities: Food and beverages, semi-processed foods, consumer goods, phospates
Imports: $7.2 billion
  commodities: Capital goods, semiprocessed goods, raw materials, fuel and lubricants, food and beverages, consumer goods

DEFENSE:
Defense expenditures: *exchange rate conversions -* $1.38 *billion*, 4.1% *of GDP*

NEPAL

GEOGRAPHY:
Location: Southern Asia
Area:
  total area: 140,800 sq km
  land area: 136,800 sq km
Capital city: Katmandu
Natural Resources: Quartz, water, timber, hydropower potential, scenic beauty, small deposits of lignite, copper, cobalt, iron ore

PEOPLE:
Population: 22,094,033
Population growth rate: 2.45%
Age structure:
  0–14 years: 42%
  15–64 years: 55%
  65 years & over: 3%
Literacy rate: 27.5% *of total population*,
  (*males:* 40.9%, *females:* 14%)
Languages: Nepali *(official)*, 20 other languages divided into numerous dialects
Religions: 90%- Hindu, 5%-Buddhist, 3%-Muslim, and 2%-Other

VITAL STATISTICS:
Birth rate: 37 *(per 1,000 population)*
Death rate: 12.56 *(per 1,000 population)*
Infant mortality rate: 79 *(deaths per 1,000 live births)*
Fertility rate: 5.06 *(per woman)*
Life expectancy at birth:
  total population: 53.63
    (*males:* 53.35, *females:* 53.93)

GOVERNMENT:

Type of government: Parliamentary Democracy as
of May 12, 19991

Independence: 1768 *(unified by Prithvi Narayan
Shan)*

Leaders:
chief of state: King Birendra Bir Bikram Shah Debv
head of government: Prime Minister Surya
Bahadur Thapa

ECONOMY:

GDP: purchasing power parity - $25.2 billion
GDP real growth rate: 2.3%
GDP per capita: $1200

Inflation Rate: 6.7% *(consumer prices)*

National budget:
revenues: $645 million
expenditures: $1.05 billion

External debt: $2.3 billion

Currency: 1 Nepalese rupee = 100 paisa

Labor Force: 8.5 million

Unemployment rate: NA%

Agriculture: Rice, corn, wheat, sugarcane, root
crops; milk, water buffalo meat

Industries: Tourism, carpets, textiles; small rice,
jute sugar, and oilseed mills; cigarette; cement,
brick production

Exports: $430 million
commodities: Carpets, clothing, leather goods,
jute goods, grain

Imports: $1.4 billion
commodities: Petroleum products, fertilizer,
machinery

DEFENSE:

Defense expenditures: *exchange rate conversion -*
$36 *million,* 1.2% *of GDP*

NETHERLANDS

GEOGRAPHY:

Location: Western Europe

Area:
total area: 37,330 sq km
land area: 33,920 sq km

Capital city: Amsterdam; The Hague is the seat of
government

Natural Resources: Natural gas, petroleum, fertile
soil

PEOPLE:

Population: 15,568,034

Population growth rate: 0.56%

Age structure:
0–14 years: 18%
15–64 years: 68%
65 years & over: 14%

Literacy rate: 99% *of total population*

Languages: Dutch

Religions: 34%- Roman Catholic, 25%-Protestant,
3%-Muslim, 2%-other, 36%-unaffiliated

VITAL STATISTICS:

Birth rate: 12.08 *(per 1,000 population)*

Death rate: 8.7 *(per 1,000 population)*

Infant mortality rate: 4.9 *(deaths per 1,000 live
births)*

Fertility rate: 1.51 *(per woman)*

Life expectancy at birth:
total population: 77.73
(males: 74.91, *females:* 80.68)

GOVERNMENT:

Type of government: Constitutional Monarchy

Independence: 1579 *(from Spain)*

Leaders:
chief of state: Queen Beatrix, Queen of the
Netherlands
head of government: Prime Minister Wim
Kok

ECONOMY:

GDP: purchasing power parity - $301.9 billion
GDP real growth rate: 2.5%
GDP per capita: $19,500

Inflation Rate *(consumer prices)*: 2.25%

National budget:
revenues: $109.9 billion
expenditures: $122.1 billion

External debt: $0

Currency: 1 Netherlands guilder, gulden, or florin
= 100 cents

Labor Force: 6.4 million

Unemployment rate: 7.1%

Agriculture: Grains, potatoes, sugar beets, fruits,
vegetables; livestock

Industries: Agroindustries, metal and engineering
products, electrical machinery and equipment,
chemicals, petroleum, fishing, construction,
microelectronics

Exports: $146 billion
commodities: Metal products, chemicals,
processed food and tobacco, agricultural
products

Imports: $133 billion
commodities: Raw materials and semifinished
products, consumer goods, transportation
equipment, crude oil, food products

DEFENSE:

Defense expenditures: *exchange rate conversion -*
$8.2 *billion,* 2.1% *of GDP*

NEW ZEALAND

GEOGRAPHY:
Location: Oceania
Area:
  total area: 268,680 sq km
  land area: 268,670 sq km
Capital city: Wellington
Natural Resources: Natural gas, iron ore, sand, timber, hydropower, gold, limestonel

PEOPLE:
Population: 3,547,983
Population growth rate: 1.12%
Age structure:
  0–14 years: 23%
  15–64 years: 65%
  65 years & over: 12%
Literacy rate: 99% *of total population*
Languages: English *(official)*, Maori
Religions: 24%-Anglican, 18%-Presbyterian, 15%-Roman Catholic, 5%-Methodist, 2%-Baptist, and 3%-other Protestant, 33%-unspecified or none

VITAL STATISTICS:
Birth rate: 15.78 *(per 1,000 population)*
Death rate: 7.72 *(per 1,000 population)*
Infant mortality rate: 6.7 *(deaths per 1,000 live births)*
Fertility rate: 2.01 *(per woman)*
Life expectancy at birth:
  total population: 77.01
    (males: 73.96, *females:* 80.21)

GOVERNMENT:
Type of government: Parlimentary Democracy
Independence: September 26, 1907 *(from UK)*
Leaders:
  chief of state: Queen Elizabeth II, represented by Dame Catherine Tizard
  head of government: Prime Minister Jim Bolger

ECONOMY:
GDP: purchasing power parity - $62.3 billion
  GDP real growth rate: 5.5%
  GDP per capita: $18,300
Inflation Rate *(consumer prices):* 2%
National budget:
  revenues: $22.18 billion
  expenditures: $20.28 billion
External debt: $38.5 billion
Currency: 1 New Zealand dollar = 100 cents
Labor Force: 1,634,500
Unemployment rate: 6.1%
Agriculture: Wheat, barley, potatoes, pulses, fruits, vegetables; wool, meat, dairy products; fish *(catch reached a record 503,000 metric tons in 1988)*
Industries: Food processing, wool and paper products, textiles, machinery, transportation equipment, banking and insurance, tourism, mining
Exports: $13.41 billion
  commodities: Wool, lamb, mutton, beef, fish, vegetables, cheese, chemicals, forestry products, fruits and vegetables, manufactured goods
Imports: $13.62 billion
  commodities: Machinery and equipment, vehicles and aircraft, petroleum, consumer goods

DEFENSE:
Defense expenditures: *exchange rate conversion -* $556 *million,* 1% *of GDP*

NICARAGUA

GEOGRAPHY:
Location: Central America
Area:
  total area: 129,494 sq km
  land area: 120,254 sq km
Capital city: Managua
Natural Resources: Gold, silver, copper, tungsten, lead, zinc, timber, fish

PEOPLE:
Population: 4,272,352
Population growth rate: 2.67%
Age structure:
  0–14 years: 44%
  15–64 years: 53%
  65 years & over: 3%
Literacy rate: 65.7% *of total population,*
    (males: 64.6%, *females:* 66.6%)
Languages: Spanish *(official)*
Religions: 95%-Roman Catholic, 5%-Protestant

VITAL STATISTICS:
Birth rate: 33.83 *(per 1,000 population)*
Death rate: 6.01 *(per 1,000 population)*
Infant mortality rate: 45.8 *(deaths per 1,000 live births)*
Fertility rate: 4.03 *(per woman)*
Life expectancy at birth:
  total population: 65.72
    (males: 63.41, *females:* 68.1)

GOVERNMENT:
Type of government: Republic
Independence: September 15, 1821 *(from Spain)*

Leaders:
chief of state & head of government: President
Arnoldo Aleman

ECONOMY:
GDP: purchasing power parity - $7.1 billion
GDP real growth rate: 4.2%
GDP per capita: $1,700
Inflation Rate *(consumer prices):* 11.4%
National budget:
revenues: $389 million
expenditures: $551 million
External debt: $11.7 billion
Currency: 1 gold cordoba = 100 centavos
Labor Force: 1.086 million
Unemployment rate: 20%
Agriculture: Coffee, bananas, sugarcane, cotton,
rice, corn, cassava (tapioca), citrus, beans; beef,
veal, pork, poultry, dairy products
Industries: Food processing, chemicals, metal
products, textiles, clothing, petroleum refining
and distribution, beverages, footwear
Exports: $525.5 million
commodities: Meat, coffee, cotton, sugar,
seafood, gold, bananas
Imports: $870 million
commodities: Consumer goods, machinery and
equipment, petroleum products

DEFENSE:
Defense expenditures: *exchange rate conversion -*
$28.1 *million*, NA% *of GDP*

NIGERIA

GEOGRAPHY:
Location: Western Africa
Area:
total area: 923,770 sq km
land area: 910,770 sq km
Capital city: Abuja
Natural Resources: Petroleum, tin, columbite, iron
ore, coal, limestone, lead, zinc, natural gas

PEOPLE:
Population: 103,912,489
Population growth rate: 3.05%
Age structure:
0–14 years: 45%
15–64 years: 52%
65 years & over: 3%
Literacy rate: 57.1% *of total population,*
(*males:* 67.3%, *females:* 47.3%)
Languages: English *(Official),* Hausa, Yoruba, Ibo,
Fulani
Religions: 50%- Muslim, 40%-Christian, 10%-
indigenous beliefs

VITAL STATISTICS:
Birth rate: 42.89 *(per 1,000 population)*
Death rate: 12.71 *(per 1,000 population)*
Infant mortality rate: 72.4 *(deaths per 1,000 live
births)*
Fertility rate: 6.24 *(per woman)*
Life expectancy at birth:
total population: 54.34
(*males:* 53.06, *females:* 55.65)

GOVERNMENT:
Type of government: Military government; Nigeria
has been ruled by one military regime after
another since December 31, 1983; on October 1,
1995, the present military government
announced it will turn power over to democratically elected civilian authorities in October 1998
Independence: October 1, 1960 *(from UK)*
Leaders:
chief of state & head of government: Chairman
of the Provisional Ruling Council and Commander in Chief of Armed Forces and Defense
Minister Gen. Sani Abacha

ECONOMY:
GDP: purchasing power parity - $135.9 billion
GDP real growth rate: 2.6%
GDP per capita: $1,300
Inflation Rate *(consumer prices):* 57%
National budget:
revenues: $2.7 billion
expenditures: $6.4 billion
External debt: $32.5 billion
Currency: 1 naira = 100 kobo
Labor Force: 42.844 million
Unemployment rate: 28%
Agriculture: Cocoa, peanuts, palm oil, rubber, corn,
rice, sorghum, millet, cassava (tapioca), yams;
cattle, sheep, goat, pigs; fishing and forest
resources extensively exploited
Industries: Crude oil, coal, tin, columbite, palm oil,
peanuts, cotton, rubber, wood, hides and skins,
textiles, cement and other construction materials, food products, footwear, chemicals,
ceramics, fertilizer, ceramics, steel
Exports: $9.9 billion
commodities: Oil, cocoa, rubber
Imports: $7.5 billion
commodities: Machinery, transportation equipment, manufactured goods, chemicals, food
and animals

DEFENSE:
Defense expenditures: *exchange rate conversion -*
$172 *million*, 1% *of GDP*

NORWAY

GEOGRAPHY:
Location: Northern Europe
Area:
total area: 324,220 sq km
land area: 307,860 sq km
Capital city: Oslo
Natural Resources: Petroleum, copper, natural gas, pyrites, nickel, iron ore, zinc, lead, fish, timber, hydropower

PEOPLE:
Population: 4,383,807
Population growth rate: 0.48%
Age structure:
0-14 years: 19%
15-64 years: 65%
65 years & over: 16%
Literacy rate: 99% *of total population*
Languages: Norwegian *(official)*
Religions: 87.8%-Evangelical Lutheran *(state church)*, 3.8%-other Protestant and Roman Catholic, 3.2%-none

VITAL STATISTICS:
Birth rate: 11.96 *(per 1,000 population)*
Death rate: 10.68 *(per 1,000 population)*
Infant mortality rate: 4.9 *(deaths per 1,000 live births)*
Fertility rate: 1.63 *(per woman)*
Life expectancy at birth:
total population: 77.53
 (males: 74.63, *females:* 80.61)

GOVERNMENT:
Type of government: Constitutional Monarchy
Independence: October 26, 1905 *(from Sweden)*
Leaders:
chief of state: King Harald V
head of government: Prime Minister Thorbjoern Jagland

ECONOMY:
GDP: purchasing power parity - $106.2 billion
GDP real growth rate: 4.5%
GDP per capita: $24,500
Inflation Rate *(consumer prices):* 2.5%
National budget:
revenues: $48.6 billion
expenditures: $53 billion
External debt: $NA
Currency: 1 Norwegian krone = 100 oere
Labor Force: 2.13 million
Unemployment rate: 8%
Agriculture: Oats, other grains; beef milk; livestock

output exceeds value of crop; fish *(among the world's top 10 fishing nations, fish catch of 1.76 million metric tons in 1989)*
Industries: Petroleum and gas, food processing, shipbuilding, pulp and paper products, metal, chemicals, timber, mining, textiles, fishing
Exports: $34.7 billion
commodities: Petroleum and petroleum products, metals and products, foodstuffs *(mostly fish)*, chemicals and raw materials, natural gas, ships
Imports: $27.3 billion
commodities: Machinery and equipment and manufactured consumer goods, chemicals and other industrial inputs, foodstuffs

DEFENSE:
Defense expenditures: *exchange rate conversion -* $3.7 *billion*, 2.9% *of GDP*

OMAN

GEOGRAPHY:
Location: Middle East
Area:
total area: 212,460 sq km
land area: 212,460 sq km
Capital city: Muscat
Natural Resources: Petroleum, copper, asbestos, some marble, limestone, chromium, gypsum, natural gas

PEOPLE:
Population: 2,186,548
Population growth rate: 3.53%
Age structure:
0–14 years: 46%
15–64 years: 51%
65 years & over: 3%
Literacy rate: NA%
Languages: Arabic *(official)*, English, Baluchi, Urdu, Indian dialects
Religions: 75%- Ibadhi Muslim, Sunni Muslim, Shi'a Muslim, Hindu

VITAL STATISTICS:
Birth rate: 37.86 *(per 1,000 population)*
Death rate: 4.44 *(per 1,000 population)*
Infant mortality rate: 27.3 *(deaths per 1,000 live births)*
Fertility rate: 6.09 *(per woman)*
Life expectancy at birth:
total population: 70.53
 (males: 68.59, *females:* 72.57)

GOVERNMENT:
Type of government: Monarchy

Independence: 1650 *(expulsion of the Portuguese)*
Leaders:
  chief of state & head of government: Sultan
  Qaboos

ECONOMY:
GDP: purchasing power parity - $19.1 billion
  GDP real growth rate: 3.5%
  GDP per capita: $10,800
Inflation Rate *(consumer prices):* -0.7%
National budget:
  revenues: $4.7 billion
  expenditures: $5.6 billion
External debt: $3 billion
Currency: 1 Omani rial = 1000 baiza
Labor Force: 454,000
Unemployment rate: NA%
Agriculture: Dates, limes, bananas, alfalfa, vege-
  tables; camels, cattle; fish *(annual fish catch
  averages 100,000 metric tons)*
Industries: Crude oil production and refining,
  natural gas production, construction, cement,
  copper
Exports: $4.8 billion
  commodities: Petroleum, fish, processed copper,
  textile
Imports: $4 billion
  commodities: Machinery and transportation
  equipment, manufactured goods, food, livestock, lubricants

DEFENSE:
Defense expenditures: *exchange rate conversion -*
  $1.82 *billion*, 13.7% *of GDP*

PAKISTAN

GEOGRAPHY:
Location: Southern Asia
Area:
  total area: 803,940 sq km
  land area: 778,720 sq km
Capital city: Islamabad
Natural Resources: Land, extensive natural gas
  reserves, limited petroleum, poor quality coal,
  iron ore, copper, salt, limestone

PEOPLE:
Population: 129,275,660
Population growth rate: 2.24%
Age structure:
  0–14 years: 42%
  15–64 years: 53%
  65 years & over: 5%
Literacy rate: 37.8% *of total population,*
  (*males:* 50%, *females:* 24.4%)
Languages: Punjabi, Sindhi, Siraiki *(a Punjabi*

variant), Pashtu, Urdu, Balochi, Hindko, Brahui,
  English *(official and lingua franca of Pakistani
  elite and most government ministries)*,
  Burushaski, other
Religions: 97%- Muslim (77%-Sunni, 20%-Shi'a),
  Christian, Hindu, and 3% Other

VITAL STATISTICS:
Birth rate: 36.16 *(per 1,000 population)*
Death rate: 11.22 *(per 1,000 population)*
Infant mortality rate: 96.8 *(deaths per 1,000 live
  births)*
Fertility rate: 5.25 *(per woman)*
Life expectancy at birth:
  total population: 58.46
    (*males:* 57.7, *females:* 59.25)

GOVERNMENT:
Type of government: Republic
Independence: August 14, 1947 *(from UK)*
Leaders:
  chief of state: President Sardar Farooq Ahmed
  Leghari
  head of government: Prime Minister Mohammad
  Nawaz Sharif

ECONOMY:
GDP: purchasing power parity - $274.2 billion
  GDP real growth rate: 4.7%
  GDP per capita: $2,100
Inflation Rate *(consumer prices):* 13%
National budget:
  revenues: $11.9 billion
  expenditures: $12.4 billion
External debt: $26 billion
Currency: 1 Pakistani rupee = 100 paisa
Labor Force: 36 million
Unemployment rate: NA%
Agriculture: Cotton, wheat, rice sugarcane, fruits
  vegetables; milk, beef, mutton, eggs
Industries: Textiles, food processing, beverages,
  construction materials, clothing, paper products,
  shrimp
Exports: $8.7 billion
  commodities: Cotton, textiles, clothing, rice,
  leather, carpets
Imports: $10.7 billion
  commodities: Petroleum and petroleum products, machinery and transportation equipment, vegetable oils, animal fats, chemicals

DEFENSE:
Defense expenditures: *exchange rate conversion -*
  $3.1 *billion*, 5.3% *of GDP*

PANAMA

GEOGRAPHY:
Location: Central America
Area:
 total area: 78,200 sq km
 land area: 75,990 sq km
Capital city: Panama City
Natural Resources: Copper, mahogany forests, shrimp

PEOPLE:
Population: 2,655,094
Population growth rate: 1.64%
Age structure:
 0–14 years: 33%
 15–64 years: 62%
 65 years & over: 5%
Literacy rate: 90.8% *of total population,* (*males:* 91.4%, *females:* 90.2%)
Languages: Spanish *(official)*, English
Religions: 85%- Roman Catholic, 15% Protestant

VITAL STATISTICS:
Birth rate: 23.2 *(per 1,000 population)*
Death rate: 5.42 *(per 1,000 population)*
Infant mortality rate: 29.7 *(deaths per 1,000 live births)*
Fertility rate: 2.71 *(per woman)*
Life expectancy at birth:
 total population: 73.92
 (*males:* 71.19, *females:* 76.75)

GOVERNMENT:
Type of government: Constitutional Republic
Independence: November 3, 1903 *(from Columbia)*
November 28, 1821 *(from Spain)*
Leaders:
 chief of state & head of government: President Ernesto Perez Balladares

ECONOMY:
GDP: purchasing power parity - $13.6 billion
 GDP real growth rate: 2.8%
 GDP per capita: $5,100
Inflation Rate *(consumer prices):* 1.1%
National budget:
 revenues: $1.86 billion
 expenditures: $1.86 billion
External debt: $6.7 billion
Currency: 1 balboa = 100 centesimos
Labor Force: 979,000
Unemployment rate: 13.8%
Agriculture: Bananas, rice, corn, coffee, sugarcane, vegetables; livestock, fishing *(shrimp)*

Industries: Construction, petroleum refining, brewing, cement, and other construction materials, sugar milling
Exports: $548 million
 commodities: Bananas, shrimp, sugar, clothing, coffee
Imports: $2.45 billion
 commodities: Capital goods, crude oil, foodstuffs, consumer goods, chemicals

DEFENSE:
Defense expenditures: *exchange rate conversions -* $78 *million,* NA% *of GDP*

PAPUA NEW GUINEA

GEOGRAPHY:
Location: Southeasten Asia
Area:
 total area: 461,690 sq km
 land area: 451,710 sq km
Capital city: Port Moresby
Natural Resources: Gold, silver, copper, natural gas, timber, oil potential

PEOPLE:
Population: 4,394,537
Population growth rate: 2.29%
Age structure:
 0–14 years: 40%
 15–64 years: 57%
 65 years & over: 3%
Literacy rate: 72.2% *of total population,* (*males:* 81%, *females:* 62.7%)
Languages: English, pidgin English, Motu, 715 indigenous languages
Religions: 22%- Roman Catholic, 16%-Lutheran, 8%-Presbyterian/Methodist/London Missionary Society, 5%-Anglican, 4%-Evangelican Alliance, 1%-Seventh-Day Adventist, 10%-other Protestant sects, 34%-indigenous beliefs

VITAL STATISTICS:
Birth rate: 32.93 *(per 1,000 population)*
Death rate: 10.01 *(per 1,000 population)*
Infant mortality rate: 60.1 *(deaths per 1,000 live births)*
Fertility rate: 4.45 *(per woman)*
Life expectancy at birth:
 total population: 57.25
 (*males:* 56.4, *females:* 58.15)

GOVERNMENT:
Type of government: Parliamentary Democracy
Independence: September 16, 1975 *(from the Australian-administered UN trusteeship)*

Leaders:
chief of state: Queen Elizabeth II represented by
Governor General Wiwa Korowi
head of government: Prime Minister Bill Skates

ECONOMY:
GDP: purchasing power parity - $10.2 billion
GDP real growth rate: -3%
GDP per capita: $2,400
Inflation Rate *(consumer prices):* 15%
National budget:
revenues: $1.86 billion
expenditures: $1.9 billion
External debt: $3.2 billion
Currency: 1 kina = 100 toea
Labor Force: 1.941 million
Unemployment rate: NA%
Agriculture: Coffee, cocoa, coconuts, palm kernals,
tea, rubber, sweet potatoes, fruit, vegetables;
poultry, pork
Industries: Copra crushing, palm oil processing,
plywood production, wood chip production;
mining of gold, silver, copper; construction,
tourism
Exports: $2.4 billion
commodities: Gold, copper ore, oil, logs, palm
oil, coffee, cocoa, lobster
Imports: $1.4 billion
commodities: Machinery and transport equipment, manufactured goods, food, fuels,
chemicals

DEFENSE:
Defense expenditures: *Exchange rate conversion -*
$40 *million,* 0.9% *of GDP*

PARAGUAY

GEOGRAPHY:
Location: Central South America
Area:
total area: 406,750 sq km
land area: 397,300 sq km
Capital city: Asuncion
Natural Resources: Hydropower, timber, iron ore,
manganese, limestone

PEOPLE:
Population: 5,504,146
Population growth rate: 2.67%
Age structure:
0–14 years: 41%
15–64 years: 55%
65 years & over: 4%
Literacy rate: 92.1% *of total population,*
(males: 93.5%, *females:* 90.6%)
Languages: Spanish *(official),* Guarani

Religions: 90%- Roman Catholic, Mennonite and
other Protestant denominations

VITAL STATISTICS:
Birth rate: 30.97 *(per 1,000 population)*
Death rate: 4.31 *(per 1,000 population)*
Infant mortality rate: 23.2 *(deaths per 1,000 live
births)*
Fertility rate: 4.15 *(per woman)*
Life expectancy at birth:
total population: 73.84
(males: 72.33, *females:* 75.43)

GOVERNMENT:
Type of government: Republic
Independence: May 14, 1811 *(from Spain)*
Leaders:
chief of state & head of government: President
Juan Carlos Wasmosy

ECONOMY:
GDP: purchasing power parity - $17 billion
GDP real growth rate: 4.2%
GDP per capita: $3,200
Inflation Rate *(consumer prices):* 10.5%
National budget:
revenues: $1.25 billion
expenditures: $1.66 billion
External debt: $1.38 billion
Currency: 1 guarani = 100 centimos
Labor Force: 1.692 million
Unemployment rate: 12%
Agriculture: Cotton, sugarcane, soybeans, corn,
wheat, tobacco, cassava (tapioca), fruits, vege-
tables; beef, pork, eggs, milk; timber
Industries: Meat packing, oilseed crushing, milling,
brewing, textiles, other light consumer goods,
cement, construction
Exports: $819.5 million
commodities: Cotton, soybeans, timber, vegetable oils, meat packing, coffee, tung oil
Imports: $2.871 billion
commodities: Capital goods, foodstuffs, consumer goods, raw materials, fuels

DEFENSE:
Defense expenditures: *exchange rate conversion -*
$94 *million,* 0.6% *of GDP*

PERU

GEOGRAPHY:
Location: Western South America
Area:
total area: 1,285,220 sq km
land area: 1.28 million sq km

Capital city: Lima
Natural Resources: Copper, silver, gold, petroleum, timber, fish, iron ore, coal, phosphate, potash

PEOPLE:
Population: 24,523,408
Population growth rate: 1.74%
Age structure:
 0–14 years: 35%
 15–64 years: 61%
 65 years & over: 4%
Literacy rate: 88.7% *of total population,*
 (*males:* 94.5%, *females:* 83%)
Languages: Spanish *(official)*, Quechua *(official)*, Aymara
Religions: Roman Catholic

VITAL STATISTICS:
Birth rate: 24.33 *(per 1,000 population)*
Death rate: 6.13 *(per 1,000 population)*
Infant mortality rate: 52.2 *(deaths per 1,000 live births)*
Fertility rate: 3.04 *(per woman)*
Life expectancy at birth:
 total population: 69.13
 (*males:* 66.97, *females:* 71.39)

GOVERNMENT:
Type of government: Republic
Independence: July 28, 1821 *(from Spain)*
Leaders:
 chief of state & head government: President Alberto Kenyo Fujimori

ECONOMY:
GDP: purchasing power parity - $87 billion
 GDP real growth rate: 6.8%
 GDP per capita: $3,600
Inflation Rate *(consumer prices):* 10.2%
National budget:
 revenues: $8.5 billion
 expenditures: $9.3 billion
External debt: $22.4 billion
Currency: 1 nuevo sol = 100 centimos
Labor Force: 8 million
Unemployment rate: 10.2%
Agriculture: Coffee, cotton, sugarcane, rice, wheat, potatoes, plantains, cocoa; poultry, red meats, dairy products, wool; fish *(catch of 6.9 million tons in 1990)*
Industries: Mining of metals, petroleum, fishing, textiles, clothing, food processing, cement, auto assembly, steel, shipbuilding, metal fabrication
Exports: $5.6 billion
 commodities: Copper, zinc, fishmeal, crude petroleum and byproducts, lead, refined silver, coffee, cotton

Imports: $7.4 billion
 commodities: Machinery, transport equipment, foodstuffs, petroleum, iron and steel, chemicals, pharmaceuticals

DEFENSE:
Defense expenditures: *exchange rate conversion -* $998 *million*, 1.6% *of GDP*

PHILIPPINES

GEOGRAPHY:
Location: Southeastern Asia
Area:
 total area: 300,000 sq km
 land area: 298,170 sq km
Capital city: Manila
Natural Resources: Timber, petroleum, nickel, cobalt, silver, gold, salt, copper

PEOPLE:
Population: 74,480,848
Population growth rate: 2.18%
Age structure:
 0–14 years: 38%
 15–64 years: 58%
 65 years & over: 4%
Literacy rate: 94.6% *of total population,*
 (*males:* 95%, *females:* 94.3%)
Languages: Philipino *(official, based on Tagalog)*, English *(official)*
Religions: 83%-Roman Catholic, 9%-Protestant, 5%-Muslim, 3%-Buddhist and other

VITAL STATISTICS:
Birth rate: 29.51 *(per 1,000 population)*
Death rate: 6.66 *(per 1,000 population)*
Infant mortality rate: 35.9 *(deaths per 1,000 live births)*
Fertility rate: 3.69 *(per woman)*
Life expectancy at birth:
 total population: 65.91
 (*males:* 63.14, *females:* 68.83)

GOVERNMENT:
Type of government: Republic
Independence: July 4, 1946 *(from US)*
Leaders:
 chief of state & head of government: President Fidel Valdes Ramos

ECONOMY:
GDP: purchasing power parity - $179.7 billion
 GDP real growth rate: 4.8%
 GDP per capita: $2,530
Inflation Rate *(consumer prices):* 8.1%

National budget:
revenues: $14.1 billion
expenditures: $13.6 billion
External debt: $41 billion
Currency: 1 Philippine peso = 100 centavos
Labor Force: 24.12 million
Unemployment rate: 9.5%
Agriculture: Rice, coconuts, corn, sugarcane, bananas, pineapples, mangoes; pork, eggs, beef; fish *(catch of 2 million metric tons annually)*
Industries: Textiles, pharmaceuticals, chemicals, wood products, food processing, electronics assembly, petroleum refining fishing
Exports: $17.4 billion
commodities: Electronics, textiles, coconut products, copper, fish
Imports: $26.5 billion
commodities: Raw materials, capital goods, petroleum products

DEFENSE:
Defense expenditures: *exchange rate conversion -* $1 *billion*, 1.4% *of GDP*

P O L A N D

GEOGRAPHY:
Location: Central Europe
Area:
total area: 312,683 sq km
land area: 304,510 sq km
Capital city: Warsaw
Natural Resources: Coal, sulfur, copper, natural gas, silver, lead, salt

PEOPLE:
Population: 38,642,565
Population growth rate: 0.14%
Age structure:
0–14 years: 22%
15–64 years: 66%
65 years & over: 12%
Literacy rate: 99% *of total population,*
(*males:* 99%, *females:* 98%)
Languages: Polish
Religions: 95%-Roman Catholic *(about 75% practicing)*, 5%-Eastern Orthodox, Protestant and other

VITAL STATISTICS:
Birth rate: 11.92 *(per 1,000 population)*
Death rate: 10.08 *(per 1,000 population)*
Infant mortality rate: 12.4 *(deaths per 1,000 live births)*
Fertility rate: 1.69 *(per woman)*
Life expectancy at birth:

total population: 72.1
(*males:* 68.02, *females:* 76.41)

GOVERNMENT:
Type of government: Democratic State
Independence: November 11, 1918 *(independent republic proclaimed)*
Leaders:
chief of state: President Aleksander Kwasniewski
head of government: Prime Minister Wlodzimierz Cimoszewicz

ECONOMY:
GDP: purchasing power parity - $226.7 billion
GDP real growth rate: 6.5%
GDP per capita: $5,800
Inflation Rate *(consumer prices)*: 21.6%
National budget:
revenues: $34.5 billion
expenditures: $37.8 billion
External debt: $42.1 billion
Currency: 1 zloty = 100 groszy
Labor Force: 17.743 million
Unemployment rate: 14.9%
Agriculture: Potatoes, milk, fruits, vegetables, wheat; poultry, and eggs, pork, beef
Industries: Machine building, iron and steel, coal mining, chemicals, shipbuilding, food processing, glass, beverages, textiles
Exports: $22.2 billion
commodities: Intermediate goods, machinery and transport equipment, miscellaneous manufactured goods
Imports: $23.4 billion
commodities: Machinery and transport equipment, intermediate goods, chemicals, fuels, miscellaneous manufactured goods

DEFENSE:
Defense expenditures: *exchange rate conversion -* $2.4 *billion*, 2.4% *of GDP*

P O R T U G A L

GEOGRAPHY:
Location: Southwestern Europe
Area:
total area: 92,080 sq km
land area: 91,640 sq km
Capital city: Lisbon
Natural Resources: Fish, forest (cork), tungsten, iron ore, uranium ore, marble

PEOPLE:
Population: 9,865,114
Population growth rate: 0.02%

Age structure:
  0–14 years: 18%
  15–64 years: 68%
  65 years & over: 14%
Literacy rate: 85% *of total population,*
  (*males:* 89%, *females:* 82%)
Languages: Potuguese
Religions: 97%-Roman Catholic, 1%-Protestant
  denominations, 2%- other

VITAL STATISTICS:
Birth rate: 10.53 *(per 1,000 population)*
Death rate: 10.2 *(per 1,000 population)*
Infant mortality rate: 7.6 *(deaths per 1,000 live
  births)*
Fertility rate: 1.36 *(per woman)*
Life expectancy at birth:
  total population: 75.31
    (*males:* 71.52, *females:* 79.31)

GOVERNMENT:
Type of government: Republic
Independence: 1140 *(independent republic proclaimed October 5, 1910)*
Leaders:
  chief of state: President Jorge Sampaio
  head of government: Prime Minister Antonio
    Guterres

ECONOMY:
GDP: purchasing power parity - $116.2 billion
  GDP real growth rate: 2.8%
  GDP per capita: $11,000
Inflation Rate *(consumer prices):* 4.6%
National budget:
  revenues: $31 billion
  expenditures: $41 billion
External debt: $11.8 billion
Currency: 1 Portuguese escudo = 100 centavos
Labor Force: 4.24 million
Unemployment rate: 7.1%
Agriculture: Grain, potatoes, olives, grapes; sheep,
  cattle, goats, poultry, meat, dairy products
Industries: Textiles and footwear; wood pulp, paper
  and cork; metalworking; oil refining; chemicals;
  fish canning; wine; tourism
Exports: $18.9 billion
  commodities: Clothing and footwear, machinery,
    cork and paper products, hides
Imports: $24.1 billion
  commodities: Machinery and transport equip-
    ment, agricultural products, chemicals, petro-
    leum, textiles

DEFENSE:
Defense expenditures: *exchange rate conversion -*
  $1.9 *billion,* 2.4% *of GDP*

ROMANIA

GEOGRAPHY:
Location: Southeastern Europe
Area:
  total area: 237,500 sq km
  land area: 230,340 sq km
Capital city: Bucharest
Natural Resources: Petroleum, timber, natural gas,
  coal, iron ore, salt

PEOPLE:
Population: 21,657,162
Population growth rate: -1.21%
Age Structure:
  0-14 years: 20%
  15-64 years: 68%
  65 years & over: 12%
Literacy rate: 97% *of total population,*
  (*males:* 98%, *females:* 95%)
Languages: Romanian, Hungarian, German
Religions: 70%-Romanian Orthodox, 6%-Roman
  Catholic *(of which 3% are Uniate),* 6%-Protes-
  tant, 18%-unaffiliated

VITAL STATISTICS:
Birth rate: 9.77 *(per 1,000 population)*
Death rate: 12.27 *(per 1,000 population)*
Infant mortality rate: 23.2 *(deaths per 1,000 live
  births)*
Fertility rate: 1.25 *(per woman)*
Life expectancy at birth:
  total population: 69.42
    (*males:* 65.51, *females:* 73.57)

GOVERNMENT:
Type of government: Republic
Independence: 1881 *(from Turkey; republic proclaimed December 30, 1947)*
Leaders:
  chief of state: President Emil Constantinescu
  head of government: Prime Minister Victor
    Ciorbea

ECONOMY:
GDP: purchasing power parity - $105.7 billion
  GDP real growth rate: 5.4%
  GDP per capita: $4,600
Inflation Rate*(consumer prices):* 25%
National budget:
  revenues: $5.35 billion
  expenditures: $6.6 billion
External debt: $4.7 billion
Currency: 1 leu = 100 bani
Labor Force: 11.3 million
Unemployment rate: 8.9%

Agriculture: Wheat, corn, sugar beets, sunflower seed, potatoes, grapes; milk, eggs, meat

Industries: Mining, timber, construction materials, metallurgy, chemicals, machine building, food processing, petroleum production and refining

Exports: $6.2 billion

commodities: Textiles and footwear, metals and metal products, fuels and mineral products, machinery and transport equipment, chemicals, food and agricultural goods

Imports: $7.1 billion

commodities: Fuels and minerals, machinery and transport equipment, textiles and footwear, food and agricultural goods, chemicals

DEFENSE:

Defense expenditures: *exchange rate conversion -* $885 *million*, 3% *of GDP*

RUSSIA

GEOGRAPHY:

Location: Northern Asia

Area:

total area: 17,075,200 sq km

land area: 16,995,800 sq km

Capital city: Moscow

Natural Resources: Wide natural resource base including major deposits of oil, natural gas, coal, and many strategic minerals, timber

PEOPLE:

Population: 148,178,487

Population growth rate: -0.07%

Age structure:

0-14 years: 21%

15-64 years: 67%

65 years & over: 12%

Literacy rate: 98% *of total population,* (*males:* 100%, *females:* 97%)

Languages: Russian, other

Religions: Russian Orthodox, Muslim, other

VITAL STATISTICS:

Birth rate: 10.15 *(per 1,000 population)*

Death rate: 16.34 *(per 1,000 population)*

Infant mortality rate: 24.7 *(deaths per 1,000 live births)*

Fertility rate: 1.42 *(per woman)*

Life expectancy at birth:

total population: 63.24

(*males:* 56.51, *females:* 70.31)

GOVERNMENT:

Type of government: Federation

Independence: August 24, 1991 *(from Soviet Union)*

Leaders:

chief of state: President Boris Yeltsin

head of government: Premier and Chairman of the Russian Federation Government Viktor S. Chernomyrdin

ECONOMY:

GDP: purchasing power parity - $769 billion

GDP real growth rate: -4%

GDP per capita: $5,300

Inflation Rate *(consumer prices)*: 7%

National budget:

revenues: $NA

expenditures: $NA

External debt: $130 billion

Currency: 1 ruble = 100 kopeks

Labor Force: 85 million

Unemployment rate: 8.2% *(with considerable additional underemployment)*

Agriculture: Grain, sugar beets, sunflower seed, vegetables, fruits; meat, milk

Industries: Complete range of mining and extractive industries producing coal, oil, gas, chemicals, and metals; all forms of machine building from rolling mills to high-performance aircraft and space vehicles; shipbuilding; road and rail transportation equipment; communication equipment; agricultural machinery, tractors, and construction equipment; electric power generating and transmitting equipment; medical and scientific instruments; consumer durables, textiles, foodstuffs, handicrafts

Exports: $77.8 billion

commodities: Petroleum and petroleum products, natural gas, wood and wood products, metal, chemicals, and a wide variety of civilian military manufactured goods

Imports: $57.9 billion

commodities: Machinery and equipment, consumer goods, medicines, meat, grain, sugar, semifinished metal products

DEFENSE:

Defense expenditures: $NA, NA % *of GDP. (note - The Intelligence Community estimates that defense spending in Russia fell by 20% in real terms in 1995, reducing Russian defense outlays to about one-fifth of peak Soviet levels in the late 1980s)*

RWANDA

GEOGRAPHY:

Location: Central Africa

Area:
total area: 26,340 sq km
land area: 24,950 sq km
Capital city: Kigali
Natural Resources: Gold, cassiterite *(tin ore)*, wolframite *(tungsten ore)*, natural gas, hydropower

PEOPLE:
Population: 6,853,359
Population growth rate: 16.49%
Age structure:
0-14 years: 46%
15-64 years: 51%
65 years & over: 3%
Literacy rate: 60.5% *of total population,*
(*males:* 69.8%, *females:* 51.6%)
Languages: Kinyarwanda *(official)*, French *(official)*, Kiswahili *(Swahili)*, used in commercial centers
Religions: 65%-Roman Catholic, 9%-Protestant, 1%-Muslim, 25%-indigenous beliefs and other

VITAL STATISTICS:
Birth rate: 38.83 *(per 1,000 population)*
Death rate: 20.33 *(per 1,000 population)*
Infant mortality rate: 118.8 *(deaths per 1,000 live births)*
Fertility rate: 5.99 *(per woman)*
Life expectancy at birth:
total population: 40.12
(*males:* 39.72, *females:* 40.53)

GOVERNMENT:
Type of government: Republic; presidential system
Independence: July 1, 1962 *(from Belgium-administered UN trusteeship)*
Leaders:
chief of state: President Pasteur Bizimungu
head of government: Prime Minister Pierre Celestine Rwigema

ECONOMY:
GDP: purchasing power parity - $3.8 billion
GDP real growth rate: -2.7%
GDP per capita: $400
Inflation Rate *(consumer prices):* 64%
National budget:
revenues: $NA
expenditures: $NA
External debt: $873 million
Currency: 1 Rwandan franc = 100 centimes
Labor Force: 3.6 million
Unemployment rate: NA%
Agriculture: Coffee, tea, pyrethrum *(insecticide made from chrysanthemums)*, bananas, beans, sorghum, potatoes; livestock
Industries: Mining of cassiterite *(tin ore)*, and wolframite *(tungsten ore)*, tin, cement, agricultural

processing, small-scale beverage production, soap, furniture, shoes, plastic goods, textiles, cigarettes
Exports: $52 million
commodities: Coffee, tea, cassiterite, wolframite, pyrethrum
Imports: $37 million
commodities: Textiles, foodstuffs, machines and equipment, capital goods, steel, petroleum products, cement and construction material

DEFENSE:
Defense expenditures: *exchange rate conversion -* $112.5 *million,* 7% of GDP

SAUDI ARABIA

GEOGRAPHY:
Location: Middle East
Area:
total area: 1,960,582 sq km
land area: 1,960,582 sq km
Capital city: Riyadh
Natural Resources: Petroleum, natural gas, iron ore, gold, copper

PEOPLE:
Population: 19,409,058
Population growth rate: 3.45%
Age structure:
0-14 years: 43%
15-64 years: 55%
65 years & over: 2%
Literacy rate: 62.8% *of total population,*
(*males:* 71.5%, *females:* 50.2%)
Languages: Arabic
Religions: 100%-Muslim

VITAL STATISTICS:
Birth rate: 38.32 *(per 1,000 population)*
Death rate: 5.36 *(per 1,000 population)*
Infant mortality rate: 46.4 *(deaths per 1,000 live births)*
Fertility rate: 6.45 *(per woman)*
Life expectancy at birth:
total population: 69
(*males:* 67.25, *females:* 70.84)

GOVERNMENT:
Type of government: Monarchy
Independence: September 23, 1932 *(unification)*
Leaders:
chief of state & head of government: King Fahd

ECONOMY:
GDP: purchasing power parity - $189.3 billion

GDP real growth rate: 0%
GDP per capita: $10,100
Inflation Rate *(consumer prices):* 5%
National budget:
  revenues: $35.1 billion
  expenditures: $40 billion
External debt: $18.9 billion
Currency: 1 Saudi riyal = 100 halalah
Labor Force: 6 million - 7 million
Unemployment rate: 6.5%
Agriculture: Wheat, barley, tomatoes, melons, dates, citrus; mutton, chickens, eggs, milk
Industries: Crude oil production, petroleum refining, basic petrochemicals, cement, two small steel-rolling mills, construction, fertilizer, plastics
Exports: $41.7 billion
  commodities: Petroleum and petroleum products
Imports: $21.3 billion
  commodities: Machinery and equipment, chemicals, foodstuffs, motor vehicles, textiles

DEFENSE:
Defense expenditures: *exchange rate conversion -* $12.1 *billion,* 8.5% *of GDP*

SERBIA AND MONTENEGRO

GEOGRAPHY:
Location: Southeastern Europe
Area:
  total area: 102,350 sq km
  land area: 102,136 sq km
Capital city: Belgrade
Natural Resources: Oil, gas, coal, antimony, copper, lead, zinc, nickel, gold, pyrite, chrome

PEOPLE:
Population:
  Total: 10,614,588
  Montenegro: 635,442
  Serbia: 9,979,116
Population growth rate:
  Montenegro: 0.39%
  Serbia: 0.39%
Age structure:
  Montenegro: 0-14 years: 22%
  Montenegro: 15-64 years: 67%
  Montenegro: 65 years & over: 11%
  Serbia: 0-14 years: 21%
  Serbia: 15-64 years: 66%
  Serbia: 65 years & over: 13%
Literacy rate: NA%
Languages: Serbo-Croatian, Albanian

Religions: 65%-Orthodox, 19%-Muslim, 4%-Roman Catholic, 1%-Protestant, 11%-other

VITAL STATISTICS:
Birth rate:
  Montenegro: 11.86 *(per 1,000 population)*
  Serbia: 13.98 *(per 1,000 population)*
Death rate:
  Montenegro: 7.76 *(per 1,000 population)*
  Serbia: 10.25 *(per 1,000 population)*
Infant mortality rate:
  Montenegro: 27.5 *(deaths per 1,000 live births)*
  Serbia: 22.9 *(deaths per 1,000 live births)*
Fertility rate:
  Montenegro: 1.53 *(per woman)*
  Serbia: 2 *(per woman)*
Life expectancy at birth:
  Montenegro: total population: 74.88
    (males: 70.86, *females:* 79.11)
  Serbia: total population: 71.98
    (males: 68.97, *females:* 75.22)

GOVERNMENT:
Type of government: Republic
Independence: April 11, 1992 *(Federal Republic of Yugoslavia formed as self-proclaimed successor to the Socialist Federal Republic of Yugoslavia—SFRY)*
Leaders:
  chief of state: President Zoran Lilic
  head of government: Prime Minister Radoje Kontic

ECONOMY:
GDP: purchasing power parity - $20.6 billion
  GDP real growth rate: 4%
  GDP per capita: $2,000
Inflation Rate *(consumer prices):* 20%
National budget:
  revenues: $NA
  expenditures: $NA
External debt: $4.2 billion
Currency: 1 Yugoslav New Dinar = 100 paras
Labor Force: 2,640,909
Unemployment rate: more than 40%
Agriculture: Cereals, fruits, vegetables, tobacco, olives; cattle, sheep, goats
Industries: Machine building *(aircraft, trucks, and automobiles; armored vehicles and weapons; electrical equipment; agricultural machinery),* metallurgy *(steel, aluminum, copper, lead, zinc, chromium, antimony, bismuth, cadmium),* mining *(coal, bauxite, nonferrous ore, iron ore, limestone),* consumer goods *(textiles, footwear, foodstuffs, appliances),* electronics, petroleum products, chemicals, pharmaceuticals
Exports: $NA
  commodities: prior to the breakup of the federa-

tion, Yugoslavia exported machinery and transport equipment, manufactured goods, chemicals, food and live animals, raw materials

Imports: $NA

commodities: prior to the breakup of the federation, Yugoslavia imported machinery and transport equipment, fuels, and lubricants, manufactured goods, chemicals, food and live animals, raw materials including coking coal for the steel industry

DEFENSE:

Defense expenditures: 245 billion dinars, 4% to 6% of GDP; *(note - conversion of defense expenditures into US dollars using current exchange rate could produce misleading results)*

S I N G A P O R E

GEOGRAPHY:

Location: Southeastern Asia

Area:
total area: 632.6 sq km
land area: 622.6 sq km

Capital city: Singapore

Natural Resources: Fish, deepwater ports

PEOPLE:

Population: 3,396,924

Population growth rate: 1.9%

Age structure:
0-14 years: 22%
15-64 years: 72%
65 years & over: 6%

Literacy rate: 91.1% *of total population,* *(males:* 95.9%, *females:* 86.3%)

Languages: Chinese *(official)*, Malay, *(official and national)*, Tamil *(official)*, English *(official)*

Religions: Buddhist *(Chinese)*, Muslim *(Malays)*, Christian, Hindu, Sikh, Taoist, Confucianist

VITAL STATISTICS:

Birth rate: 16.28 *(per 1,000 population)*

Death rate: 4.56 *(per 1,000 population)*

Infant mortality rate: 4.7 *(deaths per 1,000 live births)*

Fertility rate: 1.65 *(per woman)*

Life expectancy at birth:
total population: 78.13
(males: 75.07, *females:* 81.39)

GOVERNMENT:

Type of government: Republic within Commonwealth

Independence: August 9, 1965 *(from Malaysia)*

Leaders:
chief of state: President Ong Teng Cheong
head of government: Prime Minister Goh Chok Tong

ECONOMY:

GDP: purchasing power parity - $66.1 billion
GDP real growth rate: 8.9%
GDP per capita: $22,900

Inflation Rate *(consumer prices)*: 1.7%

National budget:
revenues: $17.3 billion
expenditures: $12.9 billion

External debt: $3.2 million

Currency: 1 Singapore dollar = 100 cents

Labor Force: 1.649 million

Unemployment rate: 2.6%

Agriculture: Rubber, copra, fruit, vegetables; poultry

Industries: Petroleum refining, electronics, oil drilling equipment, rubber processing and rubber products, processed food and beverages, ship repair, entrepot trade, financial services, biotechnology

Exports: $119.6 billion
commodities: Computer equipment, rubber and rubber products, petroleum products, telecommunications equipment

Imports: $125.9 billion
commodities: Aircraft, petroleum, chemicals, foodstuffs

DEFENSE:

Defense expenditures: *exchange rate conversion -* $3.9 *billion,* 4.3% *of GDP*

S L O V A K I A

GEOGRAPHY:

Location: Central Europe

Area:
total area: 48,845 sq km
land area: 48,800 sq km

Capital city: Bratislava

Natural Resources: Brown coal and lignite; small amounts of iron ore, copper and manganese ore; salt

PEOPLE:

Population: 5,374,362

Population growth rate: 0.34%

Age structure:
0-14 years: 22%
15-64 years: 67%
65 years & over: 11%

Literacy rate: NA%

Languages: Slovak *(official)*, Hungarian

Religions: 60.3%-Roman Catholic, 9.7%-atheist, 8.4%-Protestant, 4.1%-Orthodox, 17.5%-other

VITAL STATISTICS:
Birth rate: 12.62 *(per 1,000 population)*
Death rate: 9.35 *(per 1,000 population)*
Infant mortality rate: 10.7 *(deaths per 1,000 live births)*
Fertility rate: 1.65 *(per woman)*
Life expectancy at birth:
total population: 73.01
(males: 69.01, *females:* 77.21)

GOVERNMENT:
Type of government: Parliamentary Democracy
Independence: January 1, 1993 *(from Czechoslovakia)*
Leaders:
chief of state: President Michal Kovac
head of government: Prime Minister Vladimir Meciar

ECONOMY:
GDP: purchasing power parity - $39 billion
GDP real growth rate: 6%
GDP per capita: $7,200
Inflation Rate *(consumer prices):* 7.5%
National budget:
revenues: $6.1 billion
expenditures: $6.4 billion
External debt: $4.6 billion *(hard currency indebtness)*
Currency: 1 koruna = 100 halierov
Labor Force: 2.484 million
Unemployment rate: 13%
Agriculture: Grains, potatoes, sugar beets, hops, fruits; hogs, cattle, poultry; forest products
Industries: Metal and metal products; food and beverages; electricity, gas, coke, oil, nuclear fuel; chemicals and manmade fibers; machinery; paper and printing; earthenware and ceramics; transport vehicles; textiles; electrical and optical apparatus; rubber products
Exports: $8.8 billion
commodities: Machinery and transport equipment; chemicals; fuels, minerals, metals; agricultural products
Imports: $8.7 billion
commodities: Machinery and transport equipment, fuels and lubricants; manufactured goods; raw materials; chemicals; agricultural products

DEFENSE:
Defense expenditures: *exchange rate conversion -* $430 billion, 3.0% of GDP

SLOVENIA

GEOGRAPHY:
Location: Southeastern Europe
Area:
total area: 20,256 sq km
land area: 20,256 sq km
Capital city: Ljubljana
Natural Resources: Lignite, coal, lead, zinc, mercury, uranium, silver

PEOPLE:
Population: 1,951,443
Population growth rate: -0.27%
Age structure:
0-14 years: 17%
15-64 years: 70%
65 years & over: 13%
Literacy rate: NA%
Languages: Slovenian, Serbo-Croatian, other
Religions: 96%-Roman Catholic (including 2%-uniate), 1%-Muslim, 3%-other

VITAL STATISTICS:
Birth rate: 8.27 *(per 1,000 population)*
Death rate: 9.4 *(per 1,000 population)*
Infant mortality rate: 7.3 *(deaths per 1,000 live births)*
Fertility rate: 1.13 *(per woman)*
Life expectancy at birth:
total population: 75.09
(males: 71.4, *females:* 79)

GOVERNMENT:
Type of government: Emerging Democracy
Independence: June 25, 1991 *(from Yugoslavia)*
Leaders:
chief of state: President Milan Kucan
head of government: Prime Minister Janez Drnovsek

ECONOMY:
GDP: purchasing power parity - $22.6 billion
GDP real growth rate: 4.8%
GDP per capita: $11,000
Inflation Rate *(consumer prices):* 8%
National budget:
revenues: $6.6 billion
expenditures: $6.6 billion
External debt: $2.9 billion
Currency: 1 tolar = 100 stotins
Labor Force: 786,036
Unemployment rate: 8%
Agriculture: Potatoes, hops, wheat, sugar beets, corn, grapes; cattle, sheep, poultry
Industries: Ferrous metallurgy and rolling mill

products, aluminum reduction and rolled products, lead and zinc smelting, electronics *(including military electronics)*, trucks, electric power equipment, wood products, textiles, chemicals, machine tools
Exports: $8.3 billion
  commodities: Machinery and transport equipment; intermediate manufactured goods, chemicals; food, raw materials, consumer goods
Imports: $9.1 billion
  commodities: Machinery and transport equipment, intermediate manufactured goods, chemicals, raw materials, fuels and lubricants, food

DEFENSE:
Defense expenditures: 13.5 *billion tolars, 3.6% of GDP (note-conversion of military budget into US dollars using current exchange rate could produce misleading results)*

SOMALIA

GEOGRAPHY:
Location: Eastern Africa
Area:
  total area: 637,660 sq km
  land area: 627,340 sq km
Capital city: Mogadishu
Natural Resources: Uranium and largely unexploited reserves of iron ore, tin, gypsum, bauxite, copper, salt

PEOPLE:
Population: 9,639,151
Population growth rate: 3.1%
Age structure:
  0–14 years: 44%
  15–64 years: 52%
  65 years & over: 4%
Literacy rate: 24% *of total population,* (*males:* 36%, *females:* 14%)
Languages: Somali *(official),* Arabic, Italian, English
Religions: Sunni Muslim

VITAL STATISTICS:
Birth rate: 44.17 *(per 1,000 population)*
Death rate: 13.22 *(per 1,000 population)*
Infant mortality rate: 121.1 deaths *(per 1,000 live births)*
Fertility rate: 7.01 *(per woman)*
Life expectancy at birth:
  total population: 55.49
  (*males:* 55.18, *females:* 55.8)

GOVERNMENT:
Type of government: None
Independence: July 1, 1960 *(from a merger of British Somaliland, which became independent from the UK on June 26, 1960, and Italian Somaliland, which became independent from the Italian-administered UN trusteeship on July 1, 1960, to form the Somali Republic)*
Leaders:
  Somalia has no functioning government; the United Somali Congress (USC) ousted the regime of Major General Mohamed Siad Barre on January 27, 1991; the present political situation is one of anarchy, marked by inter-clan fighting and random banditry

ECONOMY:
GDP: purchasing power parity - $3.6 billion
  GDP real growth rate: 2%
  GDP per capita: $500
Inflation Rate *(consumer prices):* NA%
National budget:
  revenues: $NA
  expenditures: $NA
External debt: $1.9 billion
Currency: 1 Somali shilling = 100 cents
Labor Force: 3.7 million *(very few are skilled laborers)*
Unemployment rate: NA%
Agriculture: Bananas, sorghum, corn, mangoes, sugarcane; cattle, sheep, goats; fishing potential largely unexploited
Industries: A few small industries, including sugar refining, textiles, petroleum refining *(mostly shut down)*
Exports: $100 million
  commodities: Bananas, live animals, fish, hides
Imports: $249 million
  commodities: Petroleum products, foodstuffs, construction materials

DEFENSE:
Defense expenditures: $NA, NA% *of GDP*

SOUTH AFRICA

GEOGRAPHY:
Location: Southern Africa
Area:
  total area: 1,219,912 sq km
  land area: 1,219,912 sq km
Capital city: Pretoria *(administrative)*; Cape Town *(legislative)*; Bloemfontein *(judicial)*
Natural Resources: Gold, chromium, antimony, coal, iron ore, manganese, nickel, phosphates, tin, uranium, gems, diamonds, platinum, copper, vanadium, salt, natural gas

PEOPLE:
Population: 41,743,459
Population growth rate: 1.76%
Age structure:
0-14 years: 36%
15-64 years: 60%
65 years & over: 4%
Literacy rate: 81.8% *of total population,*
(males: 81.9%, *females:* 81.7%)
Languages: 11 official languages, including
Afrikaans, English, Ndebele, Pedi, Sotho, Swazi,
Tsonga, Tswana, Venda, Xhosa, Zulu
Religions: Christians *(most whites and coloreds*
and about 60% of blacks), Hindu *(60% of*
Indians), 2%-Muslim

VITAL STATISTICS:
Birth rate: 27.91 *(per 1,000 population)*
Death rate: 10.32 *(per 1,000 population)*
Infant mortality rate: 48.8 *(deaths per 1,000 live*
births)
Fertility rate: 3.43 *(per woman)*
Life expectancy at birth:
total population: 59.47
(males: 57.21, *females:* 61.8)

GOVERNMENT:
Type of government: Republic
Independence: May 31, 1910 *(from UK)*
Leaders:
chief of state & head of government: President
Nelson R. Mandela

ECONOMY:
GDP: purchasing power parity - $215 billion
GDP real growth rate: 3.3%
GDP per capita: $4,800
Inflation Rate *(consumer prices):* 8.7%
National budget:
revenues: $30.5 billion
expenditures: $38 billion
External debt: $22 billion
Currency: 1 rand = 100 cents
Labor Force: 14.2 million
Unemployment rate: 32.6% economically active
(an additional 11% underemployment)
Agriculture: Corn, wheat, sugarcane, fruits, vege-
tables; cattle, poultry, sheep, wool, milk, beef
Industries: Mining *(world's largest producer of*
platinum, gold, chromium), automobile
assembly, metalworking, machinery, textiles,
iron and steel, chemicals, fertilizer, foodstuffs
Exports: $27.9 billion
commodities: Gold, other minerals and metals,
food, chemicals
Imports: $27 billion
commodities: Machinery, transport equipment,
chemicals, oil, textiles, scientific instruments

DEFENSE:
Defense expenditures: *exchange rate conversion -*
$2.9 *billion,* 2.2% *of GDP*

SPAIN

GEOGRAPHY:
Location: Southwestern Europe
Area:
total area: 504,750 sq km
land area: 499,400 sq km
Capital city: Madrid
Natural Resources: Coal, lignite, iron ore, uranium,
mercury, pyrites, fluorspar, gypsum, zinc, lead,
tungsten, copper, kaolin, potash, hydropower

PEOPLE:
Population: 39,181,114
Population growth rate: 0.16%
Age structure:
0-14 years: 16%
15-64 years: 68%
65 years & over: 16%
Literacy rate: 96% *of total population,*
(males: 98%, *females:* 94%)
Languages: Castilian Spanish, Catalan, Galician,
Basque
Religions: 99%-Roman Catholic, 1%-other sects

VITAL STATISTICS:
Birth rate: 10.04 *(per 1,000 population)*
Death rate: 8.86 *(per 1,000 population)*
Infant mortality rate: 6.3 *(deaths per 1,000 live*
births)
Fertility rate: 1.26 (per woman)
Life expectancy at birth:
total population: 78.26
(males: 74.95, *females:* 81.81)

GOVERNMENT:
Type of government: Parliamentary Monarchy
Independence: 1492 *(expulsion of the Moors and*
unification)
Leaders:
chief of state: King Juan Carlos I
head of government: Prime Minister Jose Maria
Aznar

ECONOMY:
GDP: purchasing power parity - $565 billion
GDP real growth rate: 3%
GDP per capita: $14,300
Inflation Rate *(consumer prices):* 4.3%
National budget:
revenues: $96.8 billion
expenditures: $122.5 billion
External debt: $90 billion

Currency: 1 peseta = 100 centimos
Labor Force: 11.837 million
Unemployment rate: 22.8%
Agriculture: Grain, vegetables, olives, wine grapes, sugar beets, citrus; beef, pork, poultry, dairy products; fish *(catch of 1.4 million metric tons is among top 20 nations)*
Industries: Textiles and apparel *(including footwear)*, food and beverages, metals and metal manufactures, chemicals, shipbuilding, automobiles, machine tools, tourism
Exports: $85 billion
commodities: Cars and trucks, semifinished manufactured goods, foodstuffs, machinery
Imports: $110 billion
commodities: Machinery, transport equipment fuels, semifinished goods, foodstuffs, consumer goods, chemicals

DEFENSE:
Defense expenditures: *exchange rate conversion -* $6.3 *billion,* 1.4% *of GDP*

SRI LANKA

GEOGRAPHY:
Location: Southern Asia
Area:
total area: 65,610 sq km
land area: 64,740 sq km
Capital city: Colombo
Natural Resources: Limestone, graphite, mineral sands, gems, phosphates, clay

PEOPLE:
Population: 18,553,074
Population growth rate: 1.13%
Age structure:
0-14 years: 28%
15-64 years: 66%
65 years & over: 6%
Literacy rate: 90.2% *of total population,* (*males:* 93.4%, *females:* 87.2%)
Languages: Sinhala *(official and national language)*, Tamil *(national language)*, English *(commonly used in government and spoken by 10% of population)*
Religions: 69%-Buddhist, 15%-Hindu, 8%-Christian, 8%-Muslim

VITAL STATISTICS:
Birth rate: 17.89 *(per 1,000 population)*
Death rate: 5.8 *(per 1,000 population)*
Infant mortality rate: 20.8 *(deaths per 1,000 live births)*
Fertility rate: 2.05 *(per woman)*

Life expectancy at birth:
total population: 72.35
(*males:* 69.77, *females:* 75.06)

GOVERNMENT:
Type of government: Republic
Independence: February 4, 1948 *(from UK)*
Leaders:
chief of state & head of government: President Chandrika Bandaranaike Kumaratunga

ECONOMY:
GDP: purchasing power parity - $65.6 billion
GDP real growth rate: 5%
GDP per capita: $3,600
Inflation Rate *(consumer prices)*: 8.4%
National budget:
revenues: $2.7 billion
expenditures: $3.7 billion
External debt: $8.8 billion
Currency: 1 Sri Lankan rupee = 100 cents
Labor Force: 6.1 million
Unemployment rate: 13%
Agriculture: Rice, sugarcane, grains, pulses, oilseed, roots, spices, tea, rubber, coconuts; milk, eggs, hides, meat
Industries: Processing of rubber, tea, coconuts, and other agricultural commodities; clothing, cement, petroleum refining, textiles, tobacco
Exports: $3.2 billion
commodities: Garments and textiles, teas, diamonds, other gems, petroleum products, rubber products, other agricultural products, marine products, graphite
Imports: $4.8 billion
commodities: Textiles and textile materials, machinery and equipment, transport equipment, food, petroleum, building material

DEFENSE:
Defense expenditures: *exchange rate conversion -* $640 *million,* 4.4% *of GDP*

SUDAN

GEOGRAPHY:
Location: Northern Africa
Area:
total area: 2,505,810 sq km
land area: 2.376 million sq km
Capital city: Khartoum
Natural Resources: Petroleum; small reserves of iron ore, copper, chromium ore, zinc, tungsten, mica, silver, gold

PEOPLE:
Population: 31,547,543

Population growth rate: 3.48%
Age structure:
0–14 years: 46%
15–64 years: 52%
65 years & over: 2%
Literacy rate: 46.1% *of total population,*
(*males:* 57.7%, *females:* 34.6%)
Languages: Arabic *(official),* Nubian, Ta Bedawie,
diverse dialects of Nilotic, Nilo-Hamitic, Sudanic
languages, English
Religions: 70%-Sunni Muslim *(in North),* 25%-
indigenous beliefs, 5%- Christian *(mostly in the
south and Khartoum)*

VITAL STATISTICS:
Birth rate: 41.08 *(per 1,000 population)*
Death rate: 11.46 *(per 1,000 population)*
Infant mortality rate: 76 *(deaths per 1,000 live births)*
Fertility rate: 5.89 *(per woman)*
Life expectancy at birth:
total population: 55.12
(*males:* 54.2, *females:* 56.09)

GOVERNMENT:
Type of government: Transitional- previously ruling
military junta; presidential and National
Assembly elections held in March 1996; new
constitution to be drafted by the National
Assembly
Independence: January 1, 1956 *(from Egypt and
UK)*
Leaders:
chief of state and head of government: President
Lt. General Omar Hassan Ahmed el-Bashir

ECONOMY:
GDP: purchasing power parity - $25 billion
GDP real growth rate: 0%
GDP per capita: $800
Inflation Rate *(consumer prices):* 66%
National budget:
revenues: $382 million
expenditures: $1.06 billion
External debt: $18 billion
Currency: 1 Sudanese pound = 100 piastres
Labor Force: 8.9 million
Unemployment rate: 30%
Agriculture: Cotton, oilseed, sorghum, millet,
wheat, gum arabic; sheep
Industries: Cotton ginning, textiles, cement, edible
oils, sugar, soap distilling, shoes, petroleum
refining
Exports: $535 million
commodities: Cotton, livestock/meat, gum arabic
Imports: $1.1 billion
commodities: Foodstuffs, petroleum products,
manufactured goods, machinery and equipment, medicines and chemicals, textiles

DEFENSE:
Defense expenditures: $NA, NA% *of GDP*

SWEDEN

GEOGRAPHY:
Location: Northern Europe
Area:
total area: 449,964 sq km
land area: 410,928 sq km
Capital city: Stockholm
Natural Resources: Zinc, iron ore, lead, copper,
silver, timber, uranium, hydropower potential

PEOPLE:
Population: 8,900,954
Population growth rate: 0.56%
Age structure:
0-14 years: 19%
15-64 years: 64%
65 years & over: 17%
Literacy rate: 99% *of total population*
Languages: Swedish
Religions: 94%-Evangelical Lutheran, 1.5%-
Roman Catholic, 1%-Pentecostal, 3.5%-other

VITAL STATISTICS:
Birth rate: 11.55 *(per 1,000 population)*
Death rate: 11.43 *(per 1,000 population)*
Infant mortality rate: 4.5 *(deaths per 1,000 live
births)*
Fertility rate: 1.72 *(per woman)*
Life expectancy at birth:
total population: 78.06
(*males:* 75.62, *females:* 80.63)

GOVERNMENT:
Type of government: Constitutional Monarchy
Independence: June 6, 1523 *(Gustav Vasa was
elected king);* June 6, 1809 *(a constitutional
monarchy was established)*
Leaders:
chief of state: King Carl XVI Gustaf
head of government: Prime Minister Goeran
Persson

ECONOMY:
GDP: purchasing power parity - $177.3 billion
GDP real growth rate: 3.5%
GDP per capita: $20,100
Inflation Rate *(consumer prices):* 2.6%
National budget:
revenues: $109.4 billion
expenditures: $146.1 billion
External debt: $66.5 billion
Currency: 1 Swedish krona = 100 oere

Labor Force: 4.552 million
Unemployment rate: 7.8% *(plus about 6% in training programs)*
Agriculture: Grains, sugar beets, potatoes; meat, milk
Industries: Iron and steel, precision equipment *(bearings, radio and telephone parts, armaments)*, wood pulp and paper products, processed food, motor vehicles
Exports: $61.2 billion
commodities: Machinery, motor vehicles, paper products, pulp and wood, iron and steel products, chemicals, petroleum and petroleum products
Imports: $51.8 billion
commodities: Machinery, petroleum and petroleum products, chemicals, motor vehicles, foodstuffs, iron and steel, clothing

DEFENSE:
Defense expenditures: *exchange rate conversion -* $5.8 billion, 2.5% *of GDP*

S W I T Z E R L A N D

GEOGRAPHY:
Location: Central Europe
Area:
total area: 41,290 sq km
land area: 39,770 sq km
Capital city: Bern
Natural Resources: Hydropower potential, timber, salt

PEOPLE:
Population: 7,207,060
Population growth rate: 0.59%
Age structure:
0-14 years: 17%
15-64 years: 68%
65 years & over: 15%
Literacy rate: 99% *of total population*
Languages: German, French, Italian, Romansch, other
Religions: 47.6%-Roman Catholic, 44.3%-Protestant, 8.1%-other

VITAL STATISTICS:
Birth rate: 11.35 *(per 1,000 population)*
Death rate: 9.64 *(per 1,000 population)*
Infant mortality rate: 5.4 *(deaths per 1,000 live births)*
Fertility rate: 1.47 *(per woman)*
Life expectancy at birth:
total population: 77.62
(males: 74.58, *females:* 80.82)

GOVERNMENT:
Type of government: Federal Republic
Independence: August 1, 1291
Leaders:
chief of state & head of government: President Arnold Koller

ECONOMY:
GDP: purchasing power parity - $158.5 billion
GDP real growth rate: 1.2%
GDP per capita: $22,400
Inflation Rate *(consumer prices)*: 1.8%
National budget:
revenues: $31 billion
expenditures: $36.9 billion
External debt: $NA
Currency: 1 Swiss franc, franken, or franco = 100 centimes, rappen, or centesimi
Labor Force: 3.48 million *(900,000 foreign workers, mostly Italian)*
Unemployment rate: 3.3%
Agriculture: Grains, fruits, vegetables; meat, eggs
Industries: Machinery, chemicals, watches, textiles, precision instruments
Exports: $69.6 billion
commodities: Machinery and equipment, precision instruments, metal products, foodstuffs, textiles and clothing
Imports: $68.2 billion
commodities: Agricultural products, machinery and transportation equipment, chemicals, textiles, construction materials

DEFENSE:
Defense expenditures: *exchange rate conversion -* $3.74 *billion,* 1.4% *of GDP*

S Y R I A

GEOGRAPHY:
Location: Middle East
Area:
total area: 185,180 sq km
land area: 184,050 sq km
Capital city: Damascus
Natural Resources: Petroleum, phosphates, chrome and manganese ores, asphalt, iron ore, rock salt, marble, gypsum

PEOPLE:
Population: 15,608,648
Population growth rate: 3.37%
Age structure:
0-14 years: 47%
15-64 years: 50%
65 years & over: 3%

Literacy rate: 70.8% *of total population,*
(males: 85.7%, *females:* 55.8%)
Languages: Arabic *(official)*, Kurdish, Armenian,
Aramaic, Circassian, French widely understood
Religions: 74%-Sunni Muslim, 16%-Alawite,
Druze, and other Muslim sects, 10%-Christian
(various sects), Jewish

VITAL STATISTICS:
Birth rate: 39.56 *(per 1,000 population)*
Death rate: 5.86 *(per 1,000 population)*
Infant mortality rate: 40 *(deaths per 1,000 live
births)*
Fertility rate: 5.91 *(per woman)*
Life expectancy at birth:
total population: 67.13
(males: 65.94, *females:* 68.38)

GOVERNMENT:
Type of government: Republic under military
regime since March 1963
Independence: April 17, 1946 *(from League of
Nations mandate under French administration)*
Leaders:
chief of state: President Hafez al-Assad
head of government: Prime Minister Mahmoud
Zoubi

ECONOMY:
GDP: purchasing power parity - $91.2 billion
GDP real growth rate: 4.4%
GDP per capita: $5,900
Inflation Rate *(consumer prices):* 15.1%
National budget:
revenues: $2.5 billion
expenditures: $3.4 billion
External debt: $21.2 billion
Currency: 1 Syrian pound = 100 piastres
Labor Force: 4.7 million
Unemployment rate: 8%
Agriculture: Wheat, barley, cotton, lentils, chick-
peas; beef, lamb, eggs, poultry, milk
Industries: Textiles, food processing, beverages,
tobacco, phosphate rock mining, petroleum
Exports: $3.5 billion
commodities: Petroleum, cotton, fruits and vegetables, textiles, animal products, industrial
products
Imports: $5.4 billion
commodities: Machinery, metal products, transport equipment, foodstuffs, textiles

DEFENSE:
Defense expenditures: *exchange rate conversion -
$875 million, 8% of GDP. (Note-based on offi-
cial budget data that understate actual spending)*

TAIWAN

GEOGRAPHY:
Location: Eastern Asia
Area:
total area: 35,980 sq km
land area: 32,260 sq km
Capital city: Taipei
Natural Resources: Small deposits of coal, natural
gas, limestone, marble, asbestos

PEOPLE:
Population: 21,465,881
Population growth rate: 0.89%
Age structure:
0-14 years: 23%
15-64 years: 69%
65 years & over: 8%
Literacy rate: 86% *of total population,*
(males: 93%, *females:* 79%)
Languages: Mandarin Chinese *(official)*, Taiwanese
(Min), Hakka dialects
Religions: 93%-Mixture of Buddhist, Confucian,
and Taoist, 4.5%-Christian, 2.5%-other

VITAL STATISTICS:
Birth rate: 15.01 *(per 1,000 population)*
Death rate: 5.52 *(per 1,000 population)*
Infant mortality rate: 7 *(deaths per 1,000 live
births)*
Fertility rate: 1.76 *(per woman)*
Life expectancy at birth:
total population: 76.02
(males: 73.43, *females:* 78.82)

GOVERNMENT:
Type of government: Multiparty democratic
regime; opposition political parties legalized in
March 1989
Leaders:
chief of state: President Lee Teng-hui
head of government: Premier Vincent Siew

ECONOMY:
GDP: purchasing power parity - $290.5 billion
GDP real growth rate: 6%
GDP per capita: $13,510
Inflation Rate *(consumer prices):* 4%
National budget:
revenues: $30.3 billion
expenditures: $30.1 billion
External debt: $620 million
Currency: 1 New Taiwan dollar = 100 cents
Labor Force: 8.874 million
Unemployment rate: 1.6%
Agriculture: Rice, wheat, corn, soybeans, vege-

tables, fruit, tea; pigs, poultry, beef, milk; fish *(catch increasing, reached 1.4 million metric tons)*

Industries: Electronics, textiles, chemicals, clothing food processing, plywood, sugar milling, cement, shipbuilding, petroleum refining

Exports: $93 billion
commodities: Electrical machinery, electronic products, textiles, footwear, foodstuffs, plywood and wood products

Imports: $85.1 billion
commodities: Machinery and equipment, electronic products, chemicals, iron and steel, crude oil, foodstuffs

DEFENSE:
Defense expenditures: *exchange rate conversion - $11.5 billion, and 3.6% of GDP*

TAJIKISTAN

GEOGRAPHY:
Location: Central Asia
Area:
total area: 143,100 sq km
land area: 142,700 sq km
Capital city: Dushanbe
Natural Resources: Significant hydropower potential, some petroleum, uranium, mercury, brown coal, lead, zinc, antimony, tungsten

PEOPLE:
Population: 5,916,373
Population growth rate: 1.54%
Age structure:
0–14 years: 43%
15–64 years: 53%
65 years & over: 4%
Literacy rate: 98% *of total population,* (*males:* 99%, *females:* 97%)
Languages: Tajik *(official)*, Russian widely used in government and business
Religions: 80%-Sunni Muslim, 5%-Shi'a Muslim

VITAL STATISTICS:
Birth rate: 33.78 *(per 1,000 population)*
Death rate: 8.43 *(per 1,000 population)*
Infant mortality rate: 113.1 *(deaths per 1,000 live births)*
Fertility rate: 4.38 *(per woman)*
Life expectancy at birth:
total population: 64.45
(*males:* 60.84, *females:* 68.24)

GOVERNMENT:
Type of government: Republic

Independence: September 9, 1991 *(from Soviet Union)*
Leaders:
chief of state: President Emomali Rakhmonov
head of government: Prime Minister Yahyo Azimov

ECONOMY:
GDP: purchasing power parity - $6.4 billion
GDP real growth rate: -12.4%
GDP per capita: $1,040
Inflation Rate *(consumer prices):* 28%
National budget:
revenues: $NA
expenditures: $NA
External debt: $635 million
Currency: introduced its own currency, the Tajik ruble, in May 1995
Labor Force: 1.95 million
Unemployment rate: 3.3% *(includes only officially registered unemployed; large number of underemployed and unregistered unemployed)*
Agriculture: Cotton, grain, fruits, grapes, vegetables; cattle, sheep, goats
Industries: Aluminum, zinc, lead, chemicals and fertilizers, cement vegetable oil, metal-cutting machine tools, refrigerators and freezers
Exports: $707 million
commodities: Cotton, aluminum, fruits, vegetable oil, textiles
Imports: $690 million
commodities: Fuel, chemicals, machinery and transport equipment, textiles, foodstuffs

DEFENSE:
Defense expenditures: 180 *billion rubles, 3.4% of GDP (note - conversion of defense expenditures into US dollars could produce misleading results)*

TANZANIA

GEOGRAPHY:
Location: Eastern Africa
Area:
total area: 945,090 sq km
land area: 886,040 sq km
Capital city: Dar es Salaam
Natural Resources: Hydropower potential, tin, phosphates, iron ore, coal, diamonds, gemstones, gold, natural gas, nickel

PEOPLE:
Population: 29,058,470
Population growth rate: 1.15%
Age structure:
0–14 years: 45%
15–64 years: 52%
65 years & over: 3%

Literacy rate: 67.8% *of total population,* (*males:* 79.4%, *females:* 56.8%) *(note-age 15 and over can read and write Kiswahili(Swahili), English, or Arabic)*

Languages: Kiswahili or Swahili *(official),* Kiunguju*(name for Swahili in Zanzibar),* English*(official, primary language of commerce, administration, and higher education),* Arabic*(widely spoken in Zanzibar),* many local languages *(note: Kiswahili (Swahili) is the mother tongue of Bantu people living in Zanzibar and nearby coastal Tanzania; although Kiswahili is Bantu in structure and origin, its vocabulary draws on a variety of sources, including Arabic and English, and it has become the lingua franca of central and eastern Africa; the first language of most people is one of the local languages)*

Religions:
-*Mainland:* 45%-Christian, 35%-Muslim, 20%-indigenous beliefs
-*Zanzibar:* 99%-Muslim

VITAL STATISTICS:
Birth rate: 41.31 *(per 1,000 population)*
Death rate: 19.47 *(per 1,000 population)*
Infant mortality rate: 105.9 *(deaths per 1,000 live births)*
Fertility rate: 5.67 *(per woman)*
Life expectancy at birth:
 total population: 42.34
  (*male:* 40.95, *female:* 43.78)

GOVERNMENT:
Type of government: Republic
Independence: April 26, 1964; Tanganyika became independent December 9, 1961 *(from UK-administered UN trusteeship);* Zanzibar became independent December 19, 1963 *(from UK)* Tanganyika united with Zanzibar April 26, 1964 to form the United Republic of Tanganyika and Zanzibar; renamed United Republic of Tanzania October 29, 1964
Leaders:
 chief of state: President Benjamin William Mkapa
 head of government: Prime Minister Frederick Sumaye

ECONOMY:
GDP: purchasing power parity - $23.1 billion
 GDP real growth rate: 2.7%
 GDP per capita: $800
Inflation Rate *(consumer prices):* 25%
National budget:
 revenues: $495 million
 expenditures: $631 million
External debt: $6.7 billion
Currency: 1 Tanzanian shilling = 100 cents
Labor Force: 13.495 million

Unemployment rate: NA%
Agriculture: Coffee, sisal, tea, cotton, pyrethrum*(insecticide made from chrysanthemums),* cashews, tobacco, cloves *(Zanzibar),* corn, wheat, cassava*(tapioca),* bananas, fruits, vegetables; cattle, sheep, goats
Industries: Primarily agricultural processing (sugar, beer, cigarettes, sisal twine), diamond and gold mining, oil refining, shoes, cement, textiles, wood products, fertilizer
Exports: $462 million
 commodities: Coffee, cotton, tobacco, tea, cashew nuts, sisal
Imports: $1.4 billion
 commodities: Manufactured goods, machinery and transporation equipment, cotton piece goods, crude oil, foodstuffs

DEFENSE:
Defense expenditures: *exchange rate conversion -* $69 *million,* NA% *of GDP*

THAILAND

GEOGRAPHY:
Location: Southeastern Asia
Area:
 total area: 514,000 sq km
 land area: 511,770 sq km
Capital city: Bangkok
Natural Resources: Tin rubber, natural gas, tungsten, tantalum, timber, lead, fish, gypsum, lignite, flourite

PEOPLE:
Population: 58,851,357
Population growth rate: 1.03%
Age structure:
 0-14 years: 25%
 15-64 years: 69%
 65 years & over: 6%
Literacy rate: 93.8% *of total population,* (*males:* 96%, *females:* 91.6%)
Languages: Thai, English the secondary language of the elite, ethnic and regional dialects
Religions: 95%-Buddhism, 3.8%-Muslim, 0.5%-Christianity, 0.1%-Hinduism, 0.6%-other

VITAL STATISTICS:
Birth Rate: 17.29 *(per 1,000 population)*
Death rate: 7 *(per 1,000 population)*
Infant mortality rate: 33.4 *(deaths per 1,000 live births)*
Fertility rate: 1.89 *(per woman)*
Life expectancy at birth:
 total population: 68.6
  (*males:* 64.89, *females:* 72.49)

GOVERNMENT:

Type of government: Constitutional Monarchy
Independence: 1238 *(traditional founding date: never colonized)*
Leaders:
chief of state: King Bhumibol Adulyadej
head of government: Prime Minister Chavalit Yongchaiyudh

ECONOMY:

GDP: purchasing power parity - $416.7 billion
GDP real growth rate: 8.6%
GDP per capita: $6,900
Inflation Rate *(consumer prices):* 5.8%
National budget:
revenues: $28.4 billion
expenditures: $28.4 billion
External debt: $53.7 billion
Currency: 1 baht = 100 satang
Labor Force: 32,152,600
Unemployment rate: 2.7%
Agriculture: Rice, cassava *(tapioca)*, rubber, corn, sugarcane, coconuts, soybeans
Industries: Tourism; textiles and garments, agricultural processing, beverages, tobacco, cement, light manufacturing (such as jewelry); electric appliances and components, integrated circuits, furniture, plastics; world's second-largest tungsten producer and third-largest tin producer
Exports: $45.1 billion
commodities: Manufactured goods, agricultural products and fisheries, raw materials, fuels
Imports: $53.9 billion
commodities: Manufactured goods, fuels, raw materials, foodstuffs

DEFENSE:

Defense expenditures: *exchange rate conversion -* $4.0 *billion, and* 2.5% *of GDP*

TUNISIA

GEOGRAPHY:

Location: Northern Africa
Area:
total area: 163,610 sq km
land area: 155,360 sq km
Capital city: Tunis
Natural Resources: Petroleum, phosphates, iron ore, lead, zinc, salt

PEOPLE:

Population: 9,019,687
Population growth rate: 1.81%
Age structure:
0–14 years: 34%

15–64 years: 61%
65 years & over: 5%
Literacy rate: 66.7% *of total population,*
(males: 78.6%, *females:* 54.6%)
Languages: Arabic*(official and one of the languages of commerce)*, French*(commerce)*
Religions: 98%-Muslim, 1%-Christian, 1%-Jewish

VITAL STATISTICS:

Birth rate: 24.03 *(per 1,000 population)*
Death rate: 5.18 *(per 1,000 population)*
Infant mortality rate: 35.1 *(deaths per 1,000 live births)*
Fertility rate: 2.92 *(per woman)*
Life expectancy at birth:
total population: 72.6
(males: 71.27, *females:* 74.03)

GOVERNMENT:

Type of government: Republic
Independence: March 20, 1956 *(from France)*
Leaders:
chief of state: President Zine El Abidine Ben Ali
head of government: Prime Minister Hamed Karoui

ECONOMY:

GDP: purchasing power parity - $37.1 billion
GDP real growth rate: 4.4%
GDP per capita: $4,250
Inflation Rate *(consumer prices):* 5.5%
National budget:
revenues: $4.3 billion
expenditures: $5.5 billion
External debt: $7.7 billion
Currency: 1 Tunisian dinar = 1,000 millimes
Labor Force: 2.917 million
Unemployment rate: 16.2%
Agriculture: Olives, dates, oranges, almonds, grain, sugar beets, grapes; poultry, beef, dairy products
Industries: Petroleum, mining*(particularly phosphate and iron ore)*, tourism, textiles, footwear, food, beverages
Exports: $4.7 billion
commodities: Hydrocarbons, agricultural products, phosphates and chemicals
Imports: $6.6 billion
commodities: Industrial goods and equipment, hydrocarbons, food, consumer goods

DEFENSE:

Defense expenditures: *exchange rate conversion -* $535 *million,* 2.8% *of GDP*

TURKEY

GEOGRAPHY:
Location: Southwestern Asia
Area:
total area: 780,580 sq km
land area: 770,760 sq km
Capital city: Ankara
Natural Resources: Antimony, coal, chromium, mercury, copper, borate, sulfur, iron ore

PEOPLE:
Population: 62,484,478
Population growth rate: 1.67%
Age structure:
0-14 years: 32%
15-64 years: 62%
65 years & over: 6%
Literacy rate: 82.3% *of total population,* (*males:* 91.7%, *females:* 72.4%)
Languages: Turkish *(official)*, Kurdish, Arabic
Religions: 99.8%-Muslim *(mostly Sunni)*, 0.2%-other *(Christians and Jews)*

VITAL STATISTICS:
Birth rate: 22.26 *(per 1,000 population)*
Death rate: 5.52 *(per 1,000 population)*
Infant mortality rate: 43.2 *(deaths per 1,000 live births)*
Fertility rate: 2.58 *(per woman)*
Life expectancy at birth:
total population: 71.92
(*males:* 69.53, *females:* 74.43)

GOVERNMENT:
Type of government: Republican Parliamentary Democracy
Independence: October 29, 1923 *(successor state to the Ottoman Empire)*
Leaders:
chief of state: President Suleyman Demirel
head of government: Prime Minister A. Mesut Yilmaz

ECONOMY:
GDP: purchasing power parity - $345.7 billion
GDP real growth rate: 6.8%
GDP per capita: $5,500
Inflation Rate: *(consumer prices):* 94%
National budget:
revenues: $30.2 billion
expenditures: $35 billion
External debt: $73.8 billion
Currency: Turkish lira
Labor Force: 20.9 million
Unemployment rate: 10.2%

Agriculture: Tobacco, cotton, grain, olives, sugar beets, pulses, citrus; livestock
Industries: Textiles, food processing, mining *(coal, chromite, copper, boron)*, steel, petroleum, construction, lumber, paper
Exports: $20.7 billion
commodities: Textiles and apparel, steel products, fruits and vegetables
Imports: $32.6 billion
commodities: Machinery, fuels, raw materials, foodstuffs

DEFENSE:
Defense expenditures: *exchange rate conversion - $6.0 billion, and 4% of GDP (note - figures do not include about $7 billion for the government's counterinsurgency effort against the separatist Kurdistan Workers' Party (PKK))*

TURKMENISTAN

GEOGRAPHY:
Location: Central Asia
Area:
total area: 488,100 sq km
land area: 488,100 sq km
Capital city: Ashgabat
Natural Resources: Petroleum, natural gas, coal, sulfur, salt

PEOPLE:
Population: 4,149,283
Population growth rate: 1.82%
Age structure:
0–14 years: 39%
15–64 years: 56%
65 years & over: 5%
Literacy rate: 98% *of total population,* (*males:* 99%, *females:* 97%)
Languages: Turkmen, Russian, Uzbek, other
Religions: 87%-Muslim, 11%-Eastern Orthodox, 2%-unknown

VITAL STATISTICS:
Birth rate: 29.12 *(per 1,000 population)*
Death rate: 8.89 *(per 1,000 population)*
Infant mortality rate: 81.6 *(deaths per 1,000 live births)*
Fertility rate: 3.62 *(per woman)*
Life expectancy at birth:
total population: 61.48
(*males:* 56.68, *females:* 66.52)

GOVERNMENT:
Type of government: Republic
Independence: October 27, 1991 *(from the Soviet Union)*

Leaders:
chief of state: President Saparmyrat Niyazov
head of government: Prime Minister Elly Gurban-
muradov

ECONOMY:
GDP: purchasing power parity - $11.5 billion
GDP real growth rate: -10%
GDP per capita: $2,820
Inflation Rate *(consumer prices):* 25%
National budget:
revenues: $NA
expenditures: $NA
External debt: $400 million
Currency: Turkmenistan introduced its national
currency, the manat, on November 1, 1993
Labor Force: 1.642 million
Unemployment rate: NA%
Agriculture: Cotton, grain; livestock
Industries: Natural gas, oil, petroleum products,
textiles, food processing
Exports: $1.9 billion
commodities: Natural gas, cotton, petroleum
products, electricity, textiles, carpets
Imports: $777 million
commodities: Machinery and parts, grain and
food, plastics and rubber, consumer durables,
textiles

DEFENSE:
Defense expenditures: 4.5 billion manats, 3.0% of
GDP *(note-conversion of defense expenditures
into US dollars using current exchange rate
could produce misleading results)*

UGANDA

GEOGRAPHY:
Location: Eastern Africa
Area:
total area: 236,040 sq km
land area: 199,710 sq km
Capital city: Kampala
Natural Resources: Copper, cobalt, limestone, salt

PEOPLE:
Population: 20,158,176
Population growth rate: 2.24%
Age structure:
0-14 years: 50%
15-64 years: 48%
65 years & over: 2%
Literacy rate: 61.8% *of total population,
(males: 73.7%, females: 50.2%)*
Languages: English *(official),* Luganda, Swahili,
Bantu languages, Nilotic languages

Religions: 33%-Roman Catholic, 33%-Protestant,
16%-Muslim, 18%-indigenous beliefs

VITAL STATISTICS:
Birth rate: 45.92 *(per 1,000 population)*
Death rate: 20.72 *(per 1,000 population)*
Infant mortality rate: 99.4 *(deaths per 1,000 live
births)*
Fertility rate: 6.61 *(per woman)*
Life expectancy at birth:
total population: 40.29
(males: 39.98, *females:* 40.6)

GOVERNMENT:
Type of government: Republic
Independence: October 9, 1962 *(from UK)*
Leaders:
chief of state: President Lt. General Yoweri
Kaguta Museveni
head of government: Prime Minister Kintu
Musoke

ECONOMY:
GDP: purchasing power parity - $16.8 billion
GDP real growth rate: 7.1%
GDP per capita: $900
Inflation Rate *(consumer prices):* 6.1%
National budget:
revenues: $574 million
expenditures: $1.07 billion
External debt: $3.2 billion
Currency: 1 Ugandan shilling = 100 cents
Labor Force: 8.361 million
Unemployment rate: NA%
Agriculture: Coffee, tea, cotton, tobacco, cassava
(tapioca), potatoes, corn, millet, pulses; beef,
goat meat, milk, poultry
Industries: Sugar, brewing, tobacco, cotton tex-
tiles, cement
Exports: $424 million
commodities: Coffee, cotton, tea
Imports: $870 million
commodities: Petroleum products, machinery,
cotton piece goods, metals, transportation
equipment, food

DEFENSE:
Defense expenditure: *exchange rate conversion -
$56 million,* 1.7% of budget

UKRAINE

GEOGRAPHY:
Location: Eastern Europe
Area:
total area: 603,700 sq km
land area: 603,700 sq km

Capital city: Kiev
Natural Resources: Iron ore, coal, manganese, natural gas, oil, salt, graphite, titanium, magnesium, kaolin, nickel, mercury, timber

PEOPLE:
Population: 50,864,009
Population growth rate: -0.4%
Age structure:
  0-14 years: 20%
  15-64 years: 66%
  65 years & over: 14%
Literacy rate: 98% *of total population,*
  (males: 100%, *females:* 97%)
Languages: Ukrainian, Russian, Romanian, Polish, Hungarian
Religions: Ukranian Orthodox-Moscow Patriarchate, Ukrainian Orthodox-Kiev Patriarchate, Ukrainian Autocephalous Orthodox, Ukrainian Catholic (Uniate), Protestant, Jewish

VITAL STATISTICS:
Birth rate: 11.17 *(per 1,000 population)*
Death rate: 15.16 *(per 1,000 population)*
Infant mortality rate: 22.5 *(deaths per 1,000 live births)*
Fertility rate: 1.6 *(per woman)*
Life expectancy at birth:
  total population: 66.8
    (males: 61.54, *females:* 72.32)

GOVERNMENT:
Type of government: Republic
Independence: December 1, 1991 *(from Soviet Union)*
Leaders:
  chief of state: President Leonid D. Kuchma
  head of government: Prime Minister Valery Pustovoitenko

ECONOMY:
GDP: purchasing power parity - $174.6 billion
  GDP real growth rate: -4%
  GDP per capita: $3,370
Inflation Rate *(consumer prices):* 9%
National budget:
  revenues: $NA
  expenditures: $NA
External debt: $8.8 billion
Currency: hryvnis = 100 hryvni
Labor Force: 23.55 million
Unemployment rate: 0.7% *(officially registered; large numbers of underemployed)*
Agriculture: Grain, sugar beets, vegetables; meat, milk
Industries: Coal, electric power, ferrous and nonferrous metals, machinery and transport equipment, chemicals, food-processing *(especially sugar)*

Exports: $11.3 billion
  commodities: Coal, electric power, ferrous and nonferrous metals, chemicals, machinery and transport equipment, grain, meat
Imports: $10.7 billion
  commodities: Energy, machinery and parts, transportation equipment, chemicals, textiles

DEFENSE:
Defense expenditures: 1.35 billion hryvni, less than 2% of GDP *(Ukrainian Government's forecast for 1996); (note-conversion of defense expenditures into US dollars using the current exchange rate could produce misleading results)*

UNITED ARAB EMIRATES

GEOGRAPHY:
Location: Middle East
Area:
  total area: 75,581 sq km
  land area: 75,581 sq km
Capital city: Abu Dhabi
Natural Resources: Petroleum, natural gas

PEOPLE:
Population: 3,057,337
Population growth rate: 4.33%
Age structure:
  0-14 years: 35%
  15-64 years: 64%
  65 years & over: 1%
Literacy rate: 79.2% *of total population,*
  (males: 78.9%, *females:* 79.8%)
Languages: Arabic *(official)*, Persian, English, Hindu, Urdu
Religions: 96%-Muslim *(Shi' a 16%)*, 4%-Christian, Hindu, other

VITAL STATISTICS:
Birth rate: 26.43 *(per 1,000 population)*
Death rate: 3.03 *(per 1,000 population)*
Infant mortality rate: 20.4 *(deaths per 1,000 live births)*
Fertility rate: 4.46 *(per woman)*
Life expectancy at birth:
  total population: 72.74
    (males: 70.64, *females:* 74.94)

GOVERNMENT:
Type of government: Federation with specified powers delegated to the UAE central government and other powers reserved to member emirates

Independence: December 2, 1971 *(from UK)*
Leaders:
chief of state: Sheik Zayed bin Sultan
Al-Nahyan
head of government: Prime Minister Maktoum
bin Rashid Al-Maktoum

ECONOMY:
GDP: purchasing power parity - $70.1 billion
GDP real growth rate: 3.3%
GDP per capita: $24,000
Inflation Rate *(consumer prices):* 4.6%
National budget:
revenues: $4.6 billion
expenditures: $4.9 billion
External debt: $11.6 billion
Currency: 1 Emirian dirham = 100 fils
Labor Force: 794,400
Unemployment rate: NEGL%
Agriculture: Dates, vegetables, watermelons;
poultry, eggs, dairy products; fish
Industries: Petroleum, fishing, petrochemicals,
construction materials, some boat buildings,
handicrafts, pearling
Exports: $25.3 billion
commodities: Crude oil, natural gas, reexports,
dried fish, dates
Imports: $21.7 billion
commodities: Manufactured goods, machinery
and transport equipment, food

DEFENSE:
Defense expenditures: *exchange rate conversion -*
$1.59 *billion,* 4.3% *of GDP*

UNITED KINGDOM

GEOGRAPHY:
Location: Western Europe
Area:
total area: 244,820 sq km
land area: 241,590 sq km
Capital city: London
Natural Resources: Coal, petroleum, natural gas,
tin, limestone, iron ore, salt, clay, chalk, gypsum,
lead, silica

PEOPLE:
Population: 58,489,975
Population growth rate: 0.22%
Age structure:
0-14 years: 20%
15-64 years: 65%
65 years & over: 15%
Literacy rate: 99% *of total population*
Languages: English, Welsh *(about 26% of the
population of Wales),* Scottish form of Gaelic

(about 60,000 in Scotland)
Religions: 27-million Anglican, 9 million-Roman
Catholic, 1 million-Muslim, 800,000-
Presbyterian, 760,000-Methodist, 400,000-Sikh,
350,000-Hindu, 300,000-Jewish

VITAL STATISTICS:
Birth rate: 13.12 *(per 1,000 population)*
Death rate: 11.24 *(per 1,000 population)*
Infant mortality rate: 6.4 *(deaths per 1,000 live
births)*
Fertility rate: 1.82 *(per woman)*
Life expectancy at birth:
total population: 76.41
(males: 73.78, *females:* 79.17)

GOVERNMENT:
Type of government: Constitutional Monarchy
Independence: January 1, 1801 *(United Kingdom
Established)*
Leaders:
chief of state: Queen Elizabeth II
head of government: Prime Minister Tony Blair

ECONOMY:
GDP: purchasing power parity - $1.1384 trillion
GDP real growth rate: 2.7%
GDP per capita: $19,500
Inflation Rate *(consumer prices):* 3.1%
National budget:
revenues: $388.9 billion
expenditures: 447.6 billion
External debt: $16.2 billion
Currency: 1 British pound = 100 pence
Labor Force: 28.048 million
Unemployment rate: 8%
Agriculture: Cereals, oilseed, potatoes, vegetables;
cattle, sheep, poultry, fish
Industries: Production machinery including
machine tools, electric power equipment,
automation equipment, railroad equipment, shipbuilding, aircraft, motor vehicles and parts, electronics and communication equipment, metals,
chemicals, coal, petroleum, paper and paper
products, food processing, textiles, clothing and
other consumer goods
Exports: $200.4 billion
commodities: Manufactured goods, machinery,
fuels, chemicals, semifinished goods, transportation equipment
Imports: $221.9 billion
commodities: Manufactured goods, machinery,
semifinished goods, foodstuffs, consumer
goods

DEFENSE:
Defense expenditures: *exchange rate conversion -*
$35.1 *billion,* 3.1% *of GDP*

UNITED STATES

GEOGRAPHY:
Location: North America
Area:
total area: 9,372,610 sq km
land area: 9,166,600 sq km
Capital city: Washington D.C.
Natural Resources: Coal, copper, lead, molybdenum, phosphates, uranium, bauxite, gold, iron, mercury, nickel, potash, silver, tungsten, zinc, petroleum, natural gas, timber

PEOPLE:
Population: 265,284,000
Population growth rate: 0.91%
Age structure:
0-14 years: 22%
15-64 years: 65%
65 years & over: 13%
Literacy rate: 97% *of total population,*
(males: 97%, *females:* 97%)
Languages: English, Spanish *(spoken by a sizable minority)*
Religions: 56%-Protestant, 28%-Roman Catholic, 2%-Jewish, 4%-other, 10%-none

VITAL STATISTICS:
Birth rate: 14.8 *(per 1,000 population)*
Death rate: 8.8 *(per 1,000 population)*
Infant mortality rate: 7.2 *(deaths per 1,000 live births)*
Fertility rate: 2.06 *(per woman)*
Life expectancy at birth:
total population: 76.1
(males: 73.0, *females:* 79.0)

GOVERNMENT:
Type of government: Federal Republic; strong democratic tradition
Independence: July 4, 1776 *(from England)*
Leaders:
chief of state & head of government: President Bill Clinton

ECONOMY:
GDP: purchasing power parity - $7.2477 trillion
GDP real growth rate: 2.8%
GDP per capita: $27,500
Inflation Rate *(consumer prices):* 3.3%
National budget:
revenues: $1.258 trillion
expenditures: $1.461 trillion
Currency: 1 United States dollar = 100 cents
Labor Force: 133.943 million *(includes unemployed)*

Unemployment rate: 5.4%
Agriculture: Wheat, other grains, corn, fruits, vegetables, cotton; beef, pork, poultry, dairy products; forest products; fish
Industries: Leading industrial power in the world, highly diversified and technologically advanced; petroleum, steel, motor vehicles, aerospace, telecommunications, chemicals, electronics, food processing, consumer goods, lumber, mining
Exports: $578 billion
commodities: Capital goods, automobiles, industrial supplies and raw materials, consumer goods, agricultural products
Imports: $751 billion
commodities: Crude oil and refined petroleum products, machinery, automobiles, consumer goods, industrial raw materials, food and beverages

DEFENSE:
Defense expenditures: *exchange rate conversion -* $272.2 *billion,* 3.8% *of GDP*

URUGUAY

GEOGRAPHY:
Location: Southern South America
Area:
total area: 176,220 sq km
land area: 173,620 sq km
Capital city: Montevideo
Natural Resources: Fertile soil, hydropower potential, minor minerals

PEOPLE:
Population: 3,238,952
Population growth rate: 0.7%
Age structure:
0-14 years: 24%
15-64 years: 63%
65 years & over: 13%
Literacy rate: 97.3% *of total population,*
(males: 96.9%, *females:* 97.7%)
Languages: Spanish, Brazilero *(Portuguese-Spanish mix on the Brazilian frontier)*
Religions: 66%-Roman Catholic *(less than one-half of the adult population attends church regularly),* 2%-Protestant, 2%-Jewish, 30%-nonprofessing or other

VITAL STATISTICS:
Birth rate: 17.02 *(per 1,000 population)*
Death rate: 9.05 *(per 1,000 population)*
Infant mortality rate: 15.4 *(deaths per 1,000 live births)*

Fertility rate: 2.32 *(per woman)*
Life expectancy at birth:
total population: 74.94
(males: 71.8, *females:* 78.25)

GOVERNMENT:
Type of government: Republic
Independence: August 25, 1828 *(from Brazil)*
Leaders:
chief of state & head of government: President Julio Maria Sanguinetti

ECONOMY:
GDP: purchasing power parity - $24.4 billion
GDP real growth rate: -2.4%
GDP per capita: $7,600
Inflation Rate *(consumer prices):* 35.4%
National budget:
revenues: $3.03 billion
expenditures: $3.37 billion
External debt: $4.95 billion
Currency: 1 Uruguayan peso = 100 centesimos
Labor Force: 1.355 million
Unemployment rate: 11%
Agriculture: Wheat, rice, corn, sorghum; livestock; fishing
Industries: Meat processing, wool and hides, sugar, textiles, footwear, leather apparel, tires, cement, petroleum refining, wine
Exports: $2.3 billion
commodities: Wool and textiles manufactured goods, beef and other animal products, leather, rice
Imports: $3.1 billion
commodities: Machinery and equipment, vehicles, chemicals, minerals, plastics

DEFENSE:
Defense expenditures: *exchange rate conversion* - $256 *million*, 1.5% *of GDP*

U Z B E K I S T A N

GEOGRAPHY:
Location: Central Asia
Area:
total area: 447,400 sq km
land area: 425,400 sq km
Capital city: Tashkent
Natural Resources: Natural gas, petroleum, coal, gold, uranium, silver, copper, lead and zinc, tungsten, molybdenum

PEOPLE:
Population: 23,418,381
Population growth rate: 1.87%

Age structure:
0-14 years: 40%
15-64 years: 55%
65 years & over: 5%
Literacy rate: 97%, *of total population*,
(males: 98%, *females:* 96%)
Languages: Uzbek, Russian, Tajik, other
Religions: 88%-Muslim *(mostly Sunnis)*, 9%- Eastern Orthodox, 3%-other

VITAL STATISTICS:
Birth rate: 29.86 *(per 1,000 population)*
Death rate: 8.02 *(per 1,000 population)*
Infant mortality rate: 79.6 *(deaths per 1,000 live births)*
Fertility rate: 3.69 *(per woman)*
Life expectancy at birth:
total population: 64.6
(males: 60.44, *females:* 68.97)

GOVERNMENT:
Type of government: Republic
Independence: August 31, 1991 *(from Soviet Union)*
Leaders:
chief of state: President Islam A. Karimov
head of government: Prime Minister Otkir T. Sultanov

ECONOMY:
GDP: purchasing power parity - $54.7 billion
GDP real growth rate: -1%
GDP per capita: $2,370
Inflation Rate *(consumer prices):* 7.7%
National budget:
revenues: $NA
expenditures: $NA
External debt: $1.285 billion
Currency: introduced provisional som-coupons November 10, 1993 which circulated parallel to the Russian rubles; became the sole legal currency January 31, 1994; was replaced in July 1994 by the som currency
Labor Force: 8.234 million
Unemployment rate: 0.4% *(includes only officially registered unemployed; large numbers of underemployed workers)*
Agriculture: Cotton, vegetable, fruits, grains; livestock
Industries: Textiles, food processing, machine building, metallurgy, natural gas
Exports: $3.1 billion
commodities: Cotton, gold, natural gas, mineral fertilizers, ferrous metals, textiles, food products
Imports: $2.9 billion
commodities: Grain, machinery and parts, consumer durables, other foods

DEFENSE:
Defense expenditures: 164 *million soms*, 3.7% *of GDP (note - conversion of defense expenditures into US dollars using the current exchange rate could produce misleading results)*

V E N E Z U E L A

GEOGRAPHY:
Location: Northern South America
Area:
  total area: 912,050 sq km
  land area: 882,050 sq km
Capital city: Caracas
Natural Resources: Petroleum, natural gas, iron ore, gold, bauxite, other minerals, hydropower, diamonds

PEOPLE:
Population: 21,983,188
Population growth rate: 1.89%
Age structure:
  0-14 years: 35%
  15-64 years: 61%
  65 years & over: 4%
Literacy rate: 91.1% *of total population*, (*males:* 91.8%, *females:* 90.3%)
Languages: Spanish *(official), native dialects spoken by about 200,000 Amerindians in the remote interior*
Religions: 96%-Roman Catholic *(nominally)*, 2%-Protestant

VITAL STATISTICS:
Birth rate: 24.39 *(per 1,000 population)*
Death rate: 5.09 *(per 1,000 population)*
Infant mortality rate: 29.5 *(deaths per 1,000 live births)*
Fertility rate: 2.87 *(per woman)*
Life expectancy at birth:
  total population: 72.09
    (*males:* 69.11, *females:* 75.29)

GOVERNMENT:
Type of government: Republic
Independence: July 5, 1811 *(from Spain)*
Leaders:
  chief of state & head of government: President Rafael Caldera

ECONOMY:
GDP: purchasing power parity - $195.5 billion
  GDP real growth rate: 2.2%
  GDP per capita: $9,300
Inflation Rate *(consumer prices):* 57%
National budget:
  revenues: $7.25 billion

  expenditures: $9.8 billion
External debt: $40.1 billion
Currency: 1 bolivar = 100 centimos
Labor Force: 7.6 million
Unemployment rate: 11.7%
Agriculture: Corn, sorghum, sugarcane, rice, bananas, vegetables, coffee; beef, pork, milk, eggs; fish
Industries: Petroleum, iron ore mining, construction materials, food processing, textiles, steel, aluminum, motor vehicle assembly
Exports: $18.3 billion
  commodities: Petroleum, bauxite and aluminum, steel, chemicals, agricultural products, basic manufactured goods
Imports: $11.6 billion
  commodities: Raw materials, machinery and equipment, transport equipment, construction materials

DEFENSE:
Defense expenditures: *exchange rate conversion -* $902 *million*, 1.4% *of GDP*

V I E T N A M

GEOGRAPHY:
Location: Southeastern Asia
Area:
  total area: 329,560 sq km
  land area: 325,360 sq km
Capital city: Hanoi
Natural Resources: Phosphates, coal, manganese, bauxite, chromate, offshore oil deposits, forests

PEOPLE:
Population: 73,976,973
Population growth rate: 1.57%
Age structure:
  0-14 years: 36%
  15-64 years: 59%
  65 years & over: 5%
Literacy rate: 93.7% *of total population*, (*males:* 96.5%, *females:* 91.2%)
Languages: Vietnamese *(official)*, French, Chinese, English, Khmer, tribal language *(Mon-Khmer and Malayo-Polynesian)*
Religions: Buddhist, Taoist, Roman Catholic, indigenous beliefs, Islam, Protestant

VITAL STATISTICS:
Birth rate: 23 *(per 1,000 population)*
Death rate: 6.95 *(per 1,000 population)*
Infant mortality rate: 38.4 *(deaths per 1,000 live births)*
Fertility rate: 2.69 *(per woman)*

Life expectancy at birth:
total population: 67.02
(*males:* 64.69, *females:* 69.48)

GOVERNMENT:
Type of government: Communist State
Independence: September 2, 1945 *(from France)*
Leaders:
chief of state: President Tran Duc Luong
head of government: Prime Minister Phan Van Khai

ECONOMY:
GDP: purchasing power parity - $97 billion
GDP real growth rate: 9.5%
GDP per capita: $1,300
Inflation Rate *(consumer prices):* 14%
National budget:
revenues: $4.67 billion
expenditures: $5 billion
External debt: $7.3 billion
Currency: 1 new dong = 100 xu
Labor Force: 32.7 million
Unemployment rate: 25%
Agriculture: Paddy rice, corn, potatoes, rubber, soybeans, coffee, tea, bananas; poultry, pigs; fish *(catch of 943,100 metic tons)*
Industries: Food processing, textiles, machine building, mining, cement, chemical fertilizer, glass, tires, oil
Exports: $5.3 billion
commodities: Crude oil, rice, marine products, coffee, rubber, tea; garments
Imports: $7.5 billion
commodities: Petroleum products, machinery and equipment, steel products, fertilizer, raw cotton, grain

DEFENSE:
Defense expenditures: *exchange rate conversions -* $544 *million,* 2.7% *of GDP*

YEMEN

GEOGRAPHY:
Location: Middle East
Area:
total area: 527,970 sq km
land area: 527,970 sq km
Capital city: Sanaa
Natural Resources: Petroleum, fish, rock salt, marble, small deposits of coal, gold, lead, nickel, copper, fertile soil in west

PEOPLE:
Population: 13,483,178
Population growth rate: 3.56%

Age structure:
0–14 years: 48%
15–64 years: 50%
65 years & over: 2%
Literacy rate: 38% *of total population,*
(*males:* 53%, *females:* 26%)
Languages: Arabic
Religions: Muslim including Sha'fi *(Sunni)* and Zaydi *(Shi'a)*, small numbers of Jewish, Christian, and Hindu

VITAL STATISTICS:
Birth rate: 45.22 *(per 1,000 population)*
Death rate: 9.59 *(per 1,000 population)*
Infant mortality rate: 71.5 *(deaths per 1,000 live births)*
Fertility rate: 7.29 *(per woman)*
Life expectancy at birth:
total population: 59.58
(*males:* 58.23, *females:* 60.99)

GOVERNMENT:
Type of government: Republic
Independence: May 22, 1990 Republic of Yemen was established with the merger of the Yemen Arab Republic {Yemen *(Sanaa)* or North Yemen} and the Marxist-dominated People's Democratic Republic of Yemen {Yemen *(Aden)* or South Yemen}; previously North Yemen had become independent in November 1918 *(from the Ottoman Empire)* and South Yemen had become independent on November 30, 1967 *(from the UK)*
Leaders:
chief of state: President Lt. Gen. Ali Abdallah Salih
head of government: Prime Minister Faraj Bin Ghanem

ECONOMY:
GDP: purchasing power parity - $37.1 billion
GDP real growth rate: 3.6%
GDP per capita: $2,520
Inflation Rate *(consumer prices):* 71.3%
National budget:
revenues: $1.4 billion
expenditures: $1.2 billion
External debt: $8 billion
Currency: Yameni rial *(new currency)*
Labor Force: *(no reliable estimates exist)*
Unemployment rate: 30%
Agriculture: Grain, fruits, vegetables, qat*(mildly narcotic shrub)*, coffee, cotton; dairy products, poultry, meat; fish
Industries: Crude oil production and petroleum refining; small-scale production of cotton textiles and leather goods; food processing; handicrafts; small aluminum products factory; cement
Exports: $1.1 billion

commodities: Crude oil, cotton, coffee, hides, vegetables, dried and salted fish

Imports: $1.8 billion

commodities: Textiles and other manufactured consumer goods, petroleum products, sugar, grain, flour, other foodstuffs, cement, machinery, chemicals

DEFENSE:
Defense expenditures: $NA, NA% of GDP

ZAMBIA

GEOGRAPHY:
Location: Southern Africa
Area:
total area: 752,610 sq km
land area: 740,720 sq km
Capital city: Lusaka
Natural Resources: Copper, cobalt, zinc, lead, coal, emeralds, gold, silver, uranium, hydropower potential

PEOPLE:
Population: 9,159,072
Population growth rate: 2.11%
Age structure:
0–14 years: 49%
15–64 years: 48%
65 years & over: 3%
Literacy rate: 78.2% *of total population,* (*males:* 85.6%, *females:* 71.3%)
Languages: English*(official)*, major vernaculars-Bemba, Kaonda, Lozi, Lunda, Luvale, Nyanja, Tonga, and about 70 other indigenous languages
Religions: 50%–75%-Christian, 24%–49%-Muslim and Hindu, 1%-indigenous beliefs

VITAL STATISTICS:
Birth rate: 44.73 *(per 1,000 population)*
Death rate: 23.65 *(per 1,000 population)*
Infant mortality rate: 96.1 *(deaths per 1,000 live births)*
Fertility rate: 6.55 *(per woman)*
Life expectancy at birth:
total population: 36.31
(*males:* 36.15, *females:* 36.46)

GOVERNMENT:
Type of government: Republic
Independence: October 24, 1964 *(from UK)*
Leaders:
chief of state & head of government: President Frederick Chiluba

ECONOMY:
GDP: purchasing power parity - $8.9 billion

GDP real growth rate: NA%
GDP per capita: $900
Inflation Rate *(consumer prices):* 55%
National budget:
revenues: $665 million
expenditures: $767 million
External debt: $7 billion
Currency: 1 Zambian kwacha = 100 ngwee
Labor Force: 3.4 million
Unemployment rate: 22%
Agriculture: Corn, sorghum, rice, peanuts, sunflower seed, tobacco, cotton, sugarcane, cassava*(tapioca)*; cattle, goats, beef, eggs
Industries: Copper mining and processing, construction, foodstuffs, beverages, chemicals, textiles, fertilizer
Exports: $1.075 billion
commodities: Copper, zinc, cobalt, lead, tobacco
Imports: $845 million
commodities: Machinery, transportation equipment, foodstuffs, fuels, manufactures

DEFENSE:
Defense expenditures: *exchange rate conversion -* $96 million, 2.7% of GDP

ZIMBABWE

GEOGRAPHY:
Location: Southern Africa
Area:
total area: 390,580 sq km
land area: 386,670 sq km
Capital city: Harare
Natural Resources: Coal, chromium ore, asbestos, gold, nickel, copper, iron ore, vanadium, lithium, tin, platinum group metals

PEOPLE:
Population: 11,271,314
Population growth rate: 1.41%
Age structure:
0-14 years: 44%
15-64 years: 53%
65 years & over: 3%
Literacy rate: 85% *of total population,* (*males:* 90%, *females:* 80%)
Languages: English *(official)*, Shona, Sindebele *(the language of the Ndebele, sometimes called Ndebele)*, numerous but minor tribal dialects
Religions: 50%-syncretic *(part Christan, part indigenous beliefs)*, 25%-Christian, 24%-indigenous beliefs, 1%-Muslim and other

VITAL STATISTICS:
Birth rate: 32.34 *(per 1,000 population)*

Death rate: 18.2 *(per 1,000 population)*
Infant mortality rate: 72.8 *(deaths per 1,000 live births)*
Fertility rate: 4.09 *(per woman)*
Life expectancy at birth:
total population: 41.85
(males: 41.91, *females:* 41.78)

GOVERNMENT:
Type of government: Parliamentary Democracy
Independence: April 18, 1980 *(from UK)*
Leaders:
chief of state & head of government: Executive President Robert Gabriel Mugabe

ECONOMY:
GDP: purchasing power parity - $18.1 billion
GDP real growth rate: -2.4%
GDP per captia: $1,620
Inflation Rate *(consumer prices):* 25.8%
National budget:
revenues: $1.7 billion
expenditures: $2.2 billion

External debt: $4.4 billion
Currency: 1 Zimbabwean dollar = 100 cents
Labor Force: 4.228 million
Unemployment rate: at least 45%
Agriculture: Corn, cotton, tobacco, wheat, coffee, sugarcane, peanuts; cattle, sheep, goats, pigs
Industries: Mining, steel, clothing and footwear, chemicals, foodstuffs, fertilizer, beverage, transportation equipment, wood products
Exports: $2.2 billion
commodities: Agricultural *(tobacco and other),* manufactured goods, gold, ferrochrome, textiles
Imports: $1.8 billion
commodities: Machinery and transportation equipment, other manufactured goods, chemicals, fuels

DEFENSE:
Defense expenditures: *exchange rate conversion -* $236 *million, 3.4% of GDP*

Sources: CIA World Factbook, *U.S. Census Bureau and the U.S. embassies of the countries.*

Compiled by Suzanne Vranica

GLOBAL ECONOMY

Top 20 Economies Ranked by Real 1996 GDP (Billions of 1990 U.S. $)

	1995	1996
United States	6,309.204	6,462.928
Japan	3,182.895	3,291.659
Germany	1,786.991	1,811.591
France	1,264.028	1,280.998
Italy	1,156.511	1,165.577
United Kingdom	1,036.732	1,059.799
China	652.235	715.196
Canada	618.123	627.219
Spain	527.689	538.811
Brazil	500.770	515.261
Korea	363.873	388.617
India	361.581	382.131
Australia	336.032	350.593
Netherlands	314.961	323.736
Mexico	254.643	267.623
Sweden	234.378	236.942
Taiwan	220.526	232.764
Switzerland	225.972	224.483
Belgium	205.933	209.426
Argentina	182.421	190.409

Top 20 Economies Ranked by Real 1996 GDP per Capita (1990 U.S. $)

	1995	1996
Norway	31,250.7	32,466.0
Switzerland	32,097.8	31,732.1
Denmark	27,305.0	27,706.5
Sweden	26,226.1	26,448.9
Japan	25,414.9	26,183.4
Finland	25,442.6	26,014.5
United States	23,936.8	24,267.9
Germany	21,940.4	22,184.4
France	21,728.4	21,915.6
Austria	21,757.3	21,859.9
Canada	20,782.7	20,858.0
Belgium	20,302.9	20,587.1
Netherlands	20,188.8	20,538.3
Italy	20,246.5	20,418.7
Singapore	18,876.2	19,729.7
Australia	18,618.5	18,773.3
United Kingdom	17,689.9	18,031.0
Ireland	16,097.9	17,061.2
Hong Kong	15,801.9	16,062.8
Israel	13,503.9	13,865.5

Top 20 Economies Ranked by Real GDP % Growth in 1996

	1995	1996
China	10.5%	9.7%
Albania	13.4%	8.7%
Malaysia	9.6%	8.2%
Indonesia	8.1%	7.4%
Turkey	7.3%	6.9%
Korea	9.0%	6.8%
Ireland	10.3%	6.7%
Chile	8.6%	6.7%
Singapore	8.8%	6.5%
Philippines	4.8%	6.5%
Thailand	8.6%	6.5%
Iran	2.8%	6.1%
Slovakia	7.4%	6.0%
Pakistan	5.7%	6.0%
Poland	7.0%	5.9%
India	6.2%	5.7%
Taiwan	6.0%	5.5%
Romania	7.4%	5.2%
Israel	7.1%	4.9%
Algeria	1.3%	4.7%

Top 20 Economies Ranked by Real GDP per Capita (% Growth in 1996)

	1995	1996
China	9.4%	8.1%
Albania	11.7%	7.1%
Ireland	9.8%	6.0%
Korea	8.0%	5.8%
Poland	7.0%	5.8%
Indonesia	6.4%	5.7%
Malaysia	7.1%	5.7%
Slovakia	7.0%	5.5%
Romania	7.5%	5.3%
Chile	7.0%	5.1%
Turkey	5.1%	4.7%
Singapore	6.6%	4.5%
Thailand	7.9%	4.5%
Taiwan	5.1%	4.4%
Philippines	2.7%	4.3%
Czech Republic	4.9%	4.2%
Norway	2.8%	3.9%
India	4.3%	3.8%
Iran	0.6%	3.8%
Japan	1.0%	3.0%

10 Countries with Largest 1996 Trade Deficit (U.S. $ billions)

	1995	1996
United States	-105.3	-119.1
Korea	-8.4	-23.7
Brazil	-18.0	-21.1
Australia	-20.2	-15.9
Thailand	-14.0	-15.7
Greece	-11.8	-12.6
Turkey	-6.6	-11.4
Israel	-11.1	-10.5
Indonesia	-7.9	-9.8
Malaysia	-11.2	-8.3

10 Countries with Largest 1996 Trade Surplus (U.S. $ billions)

	1995	1996
Japan	119.0	77.7
Italy	46.5	70.4
France	46.3	49.0
Netherlands	30.1	28.5
Germany	21.4	23.3
Kuwait	18.2	20.9
Sweden	14.5	18.6
Saudi Arabia	16.6	18.5
South Africa	16.4	17.7
Singapore	16.0	15.8

10 Countries with Largest 1996 Government Deficit (U.S. $ billions)

	1995	1996
Japan	-209.0	-228.6
United States	-161.7	-132.0
Germany	-89.1	-105.2
Italy	-77.0	-85.6
France	-81.0	-69.7
United Kingdom	-55.4	-45.4
Colombia	18.9	-31.9
Brazil	-19.7	-22.8
India	-19.8	-20.7
Turkey	-6.9	-19.4

10 Countries with Largest 1996 Government Surplus (U.S. $ billions)

	1995	1996
Singapore	9.8	9.8
Norway	4.5	6.0
Thailand	5.4	5.9
Indonesia	1.0	2.5
Chile	2.3	2.0
Romania	-1.5	1.5
Malaysia	3.1	1.1
New Zealand	0.1	0.9
Philippines	0.4	0.8
Venezuela	-6.7	0.7

Source: DRI/McGraw-Hill

Country Risk Assessment May 1997

Dun & Bradstreet's analysis of risk is a composite index of the following categories: socio-political, economic, external debt, and commercial. Variables within each group are assessed, scored, weighted and ranked globally to give an assessment of the risk of doing business in a country. Risk assessment should cover such issues as the ability of a country to generate sufficient foreign exchange to service its payment obligations; the willingness of the country to create an enabling environment for trade and foreign investment; and the resilience of an economy to withstand domestic and external shocks.

Riskiest Countries With Which to Do Business:

- Democratic Republic of the Congo
- Albania
- Myanmar (Burma)
- Yugoslavia
- Belarus
- Tajikistan
- Ukraine
- Nigeria
- Sierra Leone
- Nicaragua

Least Risky Countries With Which To Do Business:

- United States
- Denmark
- Luxembourg
- France
- Germany
- United Kingdom
- Japan
- Netherlands
- Austria
- Switzerland

Source: International Risk and Payment Review, Dun & Bradstreet UK Ltd.

Financing Development

Where the Money Comes From

Net long-term flow of money to developing countries, in billions of dollars

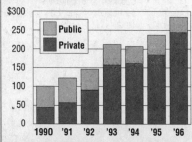

Where the Money Goes

12 countries get 75% of the private capital flowing to developing world

Country	'96 Inflow ($ billions)	Country	'96 Inflow ($ billions)
China	$52.0	Argentina	$11.3
Mexico	28.1	India	8.0
Indonesia	17.9	Turkey	4.7
Malaysia	16.0	Chile	4.6
Brazil	14.7	Russia	3.6
Thailand	13.3	Hungary	2.5

Source: World Bank's "Global Development Finance 1997"

EUROPE'S POLITICAL SHIFT

Europe has turned left.

With Lionel Jospin's appointment as French prime minister following the Socialist Party's stunning electoral victory in June, the left is clearly Europe's dominant political force at a crucial time in the continent's race toward a common currency. Coming one month after Tony Blair's resounding triumph in Britain, left-wing parties control or are part of 12 governments out of the 15 in the European Union. Only Ireland, Germany and Spain are holdouts—and many say Mr. Jospin's victory further weakens embattled Chancellor Helmut Kohl ahead of German elections in 1998.

The leftward lean portends a shift in Europe's political and economic agenda toward an emphasis on jobs and labor issues, which could weaken European countries' resolve to tackle deep change in their welfare states. "This slows down the main topic on the agenda: the EU's adaptation to the rules of tomorrow's world," says Sergio Romano, a professor of international relations at Milan's Bocconi University. "There is undoubtedly uneasiness in European societies about moving toward greater competitiveness."

But this appearance of a uniform changeover is deceptive, as many leftists openly embrace the free market. Moreover, while European Socialists may now hold the levers of political power, their ability to bring substantial economic change is limited by two key factors: economic globalization and Europe's drive to forge a common currency, which the Socialists support in most of Europe and which force governments to adhere to strict budgetary and fiscal criteria. "There's a political turn to the left, but not an economic one," says Philippe Moreau Defarges, head of European studies at the French Institute for International Relations.

Leaning Left

Twelve of the 15 countries in the European Union are headed by a center-left government or a coalition that includes the center-left.

COUNTRY	HEAD OF GOVT.	PARTY	PARTY RULING SINCE
France	Lionel Jospin	Center-left	June '97
Italy	Romano Prodi	Coalition led by center-left	April '96
United Kingdom	Tony Blair	Center-left	May '97
Belgium	Jean-Luc Dehaene	Coalition led by center-left	March '92
Greece	Costas Simitis	Center-left	Sept. '96
Netherlands	Wim Kok	Coalition led by center-left	Sept. '94
Portugal	Antonio Guterres	Center-left	Oct. '95
Austria	Viktor Klima	Coalition led by center-left	Jan. '97
Sweden	Goeran Persson	Center-left	Oct. '94
Denmark	Poul Nyrup Rasmussen	Coalition led by center-left	Jan. '93
Finland	Paavo Lipponen	Coalition led by center-left	April '95
Luxembourg	Jean-Claude Juncker	Center-left	Jan. '95

Top Countries for Tourism

World's Top 25 Tourism Destinations, 1996
International tourist arrivals (excluding same-day visitors)
(Thousands of arrivals)

Country	Arrivals 1996	% change 1995/96	% of total 1996	Country	Arrivals 1996	% change 1995/96	% of total 1996
1 France	61,500	2.3%	10.4%	14 Russian Federation	14,587	57.5%	2.5%
2 United States	44,791	3.2	7.5	15 Hong Kong	11,703	14.7	2.0
3 Spain	41,295	5.0	7.0	16 Switzerland	11,097	-3.5	1.9
4 Italy	32,853	5.8	5.5	17 Portugal	9,900	2.0	1.7
5 United Kingdom	26,025	8.4	4.4	18 Greece	8,987	-11.3	1.5
6 China	22,765	13.6	3.8	19 Turkey	7,966	12.5	1.3
7 Mexico	21,732	7.8	3.7	20 Malaysia	7,742	3.7	1.3
8 Hungary	20,670	-0.1	3.5	21 Thailand	7,201	3.6	1.2
9 Poland	19,420	1.1	3.3	22 Singapore	6,608	2.9	1.1
10 Canada	17,345	2.7	2.9	23 Netherlands	6,546	-0.4	1.1
11 Austria	17,090	-0.5	2.9	24 Belgium	5,753	3.5	1.0
12 Czech Republic	17,000	3.0	2.9	25 Ireland	5,280	9.5	0.9
13 Germany	15,205	2.4	2.6				

World's Top 25 Tourism Earners, 1996
International tourism receipts (excluding transport)
(US$ million)

Country	Receipts 1996	% change 1995/96	% of total 1996	Country	Receipts 1996	% change 1995/96	% of total 1996
1 United States	$ 64,373	5.3%	15.1%	14 Thailand	$ 8,600	12.2%	2.0%
2 Spain	28,428	10.6	6.7	15 Poland	8,400	25.4	2.0
3 France	28,241	2.6	6.6	16 Mexico	6,898	11.9	1.6
4 Italy	27,349	-0.4	6.4	17 Netherlands	6,256	8.6	1.5
5 United Kingdom	19,738	3.5	4.6	18 Turkey	6,000	21.0	1.4
6 Germany	15,815	-2.5	3.7	19 Belgium	5,893	3.0	1.4
7 Austria	15,095	3.3	3.6	20 Indonesia	5,662	8.3	1.3
8 Hong Kong	10,836	12.8	2.5	21 Korea Republic	5,419	-3.0	1.3
9 China	10,200	16.8	2.4	22 Russian Federation	5,166	19.8	1.2
10 Singapore	9,410	14.6	2.2	23 Argentina	4,572	6.2	1.1
11 Canada	8,727	8.9	2.1	24 Malaysia	4,409	12.8	1.0
12 Australia	8,690	22.4	2.0	25 Portugal	4,260	-3.2	1.0
13 Switzerland	8,661	-7.5	2.0				

Source: World Tourism Organization

World Geography: Earth's Extremes

The Earth

Mass:	5,974,000,000,000,000,000,000 metric tons
Area:	510,066,000 sq km
Land:	148,429,000 sq km (29.1%)
Water:	361,637,000 sq km (70.9%)

The Continents

	Area (sq km)	Percent of Earth's Land
Asia	44,579,000	30.0
Africa	30,065,000	20.3
North America	24,256,000	16.3
South America	17,819,000	12.0
Antarctica	13,209,000	8.9
Europe	9,938,000	6.7
Australia	7,687,000	5.2

Highest Point on Each Continent

		Meters
1	Everest, *Asia*	8,848
2	Aconcagua, *South America*	6,960
3	McKinley (Denali), *North America*	6,194
4	Kilimanjaro, *Africa*	5,895
5	El'brus, *Europe*	5,642
6	Vinson Massif, *Antarctica*	4,897
7	Kosciusko, *Australia*	2,228

Lowest Surface Point on Each Continent

		Meters
1	Dead Sea, *Asia*	-408
2	Lake Assal, *Africa*	-156
3	Death Valley, *North America*	-86
4	Valdés Peninsula, *South America*	-40
5	Caspian Sea, *Europe*	-28
6	Lake Eyre, *Australia*	-16
7	Antarctica (Ice covered)	-2,538

The Oceans

	Area (sq km)	Percent of Earth's Water Area
Pacific	166,241,000	46.0
Atlantic	86,557,000	23.9
Indian	73,427,000	20.3
Arctic	9,485,000	2.6

Deepest Point in Each Ocean

		Meters
1	Challenger Deep, Mariana Trench, *Pacific*	10,920
2	Puerto Rico Trench, *Atlantic*	8,605
3	Java Trench, *Indian*	7,125
4	Eurasia Basin, *Arctic*	5,122

Major Seas

		Area (sq km)	Average Depth (meters)
1	South China	2,974,600	1,464
2	Caribbean	2,515,900	2,575
3	Mediterranean	2,510,000	1,501
4	Bering	2,261,100	1,491
5	Gulf of Mexico	1,507,600	1,615
6	Sea of Okhotsk	1,392,100	973
7	Sea of Japan	1,012,900	1,667
8	Hudson Bay	730,100	93
9	East China	664,600	189
10	Andaman	564,900	1,118
11	Black	507,900	1,191
12	Red	453,000	538

Major Islands

		Area (sq km)
1	Greenland	2,175,600
2	New Guinea	792,500
3	Borneo	725,500
4	Madagascar	587,000
5	Baffin	507,500
6	Sumatra	427,300
7	Honshu	227,400
8	Great Britain	218,100
9	Victoria	217,300
10	Ellesmere	196,200
11	Celebes	178,700
12	South (New Zealand)	151,000
13	Java	126,700
14	North (New Zealand)	114,000
15	Newfoundland	108,900

Major Lakes

		Area (sq km)	Greatest Depth (meters)
1	Caspian Sea, *Europe-Asia*	371,000	1,025
2	Superior, *North America*	82,100	406
3	Victoria, *Africa*	69,500	82
4	Huron, *North America*	59,600	229
5	Michigan, *North America*	57,800	281
6	Tanganyika, *Africa*	32,900	1,470
7	Baikal, *Asia*	31,500	1,637
8	Great Bear, *North America*	31,300	446
9	Aral Sea, *Asia*	30,700	51
10	Malawi, *Africa*	28,900	695

Longest Rivers

		Length (km)
1	Nile, *Africa*	6,825
2	Amazon, *South America*	6,437
3	Chang Jiang (Yangtze), *Asia*	6,380
4	Mississippi-Missouri, *North America*	5,971
5	Yenisey-Angara, *Asia*	5,536
6	Huang (Yellow), *Asia*	5,464
7	Ob-Irtysh, *Asia*	5,410
8	Amur, *Asia*	4,416
9	Lena, *Asia*	4,400
10	Congo (Zaire), *Africa*	4,370
11	MacKenzie-Peace, *North America*	4,241
12	Mekong, *Asia*	4,184
13	Niger, *Africa*	4,170

Other Superlatives

Highest Waterfall: Angel, Venezuela; 979 m

Largest Canyon: Grand Canyon, Colorado River, Arizona; 446 km long along river, 549m to 29 km wide, about 1.6 km deep

Most Predictable Geyser: Old Faithful, Wyoming; annual average interval 60 to 79 minutes

Longest Reef: Great Barrier Reef, Australia; 2,012 km

Greatest Tides: Bay of Fundy, Nova Scotia; 16m

Largest Desert: Sahara, Africa; 9,000,000 sq km

Biggest Cave: Mammoth-Flint Ridge cave system, Kentucky; more than 531 km of passageways

Source: National Geographic Society

Man-Made Marvels

Highest Bridge
Royal Gorge, Arkansas River, CO, U.S.; 1,053 feet (321 m) above water

Longest Bridge Span
Humber Estuary, Hull, England; 4,626 feet (1,410 m)

Longest Big Ship Canal
Suez Canal, Egypt, links the Red Sea and the Mediterranean; 100.6 miles (162 km)

Biggest Dam (Concrete)
Grand Coulee, Columbia River, WA, U.S.; 10,585,000 cubic yards (8,093,000 cu m)

Biggest Dam (Earthfill)
Pati Pavana River, Argentina; 311,527,000 cubic yards (238,193,544 cu m)

Tallest Dam
Nurek, Tajikistan; 984 feet (300 m)

Great Pyramid of Cheops
Giza, Egypt; 450 feet (137 m) high; base covers 13.1 acres (5.3 ha)

Great Wall of China
3,930 miles (6,325 km) long; averages 25 feet (7.6 m) high; 15 feet (4.6 m) wide at top;
25 feet (7.6 m) wide at base

Largest Artificial Lake
Lake Volta, formed by the Akosombo Dam on the Volta River, Ghana; 3,500 square miles
(9,065 sq km)

Tallest Office Building
Petronas Towers, Kuala Lumpur, Malaysia; 1,483 feet (452 m); 88 stories

Longest Railroad
Trans-Siberian Railroad, Moscow to Nakhodka, near Vladivostok, Russia; 5,864 miles (9,437 km)

Tallest Tower (Freestanding)
Canadian National Railroad Tower, Toronto, Canada; 1,815.5 feet (553.3 m)

Longest Rail Tunnel
Seikan Undersea Tunnel, from Honshu to Hokkaido, Japan; 33.46 miles (53.85 km)

Longest Road Tunnel
St. Gotthard, from Göschenen to Airolo, Switzerland; 10.1 miles (16.3 km)

Longest Artificial Waterway
St. Lawrence Seaway, on the St. Lawrence River from Montreal, Canada, to Lake Ontario;
189 miles (304 km)

Deepest Water Well
Stensvad Well 11-W1, Rosebud County, MT, U.S.; 7,320 feet (2,231 m)

Source: National Geographic Society

8

LIVING IN AMERICA

"I'm so glad I'm livin' in the U.S.A.
Anything you want we got it right here in the U.S.A."

THOSE LYRICS *from Chuck Berry's 1959 rock 'n' roll classic never seemed truer. The good news about life in America just kept on coming in 1997: a near perfect economy . . . a roaring stock market . . . jobs aplenty . . . a balanced U.S. budget in sight . . . a falling crime rate . . . fewer AIDS deaths . . . the first major federal tax cut since the early days of the Reagan administration . . . a drop in teenage pregnancies . . . the lowest infant mortality rate ever, thanks to fewer cases of sudden infant death syndrome.*

Does it get any better than this? A lot of people certainly hope so.

Despite the flood of feel-good news, pollsters and consumer researchers, pyschotherapists and sociologists all say they detect deep anxiety coursing through the country on the eve of the next millennium. America, it seems, really is a Prozac nation.

Such melancholy appears to be at odds with the fact that a large majority of Americans say they are satisfied with their current jobs and standard of living. But remember: Money can't buy happiness.

People are worried about bigger things than the size of this week's paycheck: personal safety, job security, the quality and affordability of education, health-care costs, their children's future, retirement finances, the country's moral decline. "The fault lines in our society really bother people," says Jean Johnson, senior vice president at Public Agenda, a research organization in New York. "A lot of the real alarm we pick up is dissatisfaction with the moral trend of the country. There's concern that the values and traditions that made our country strong are being challenged."

When consumer behavior expert Faith Popcorn coined the term cocooning more than 10 years ago, she was describing the growing number of people embracing their homes and spending more time there. It was a positive trend. No longer. Ms. Popcorn still sees a cocooning trend, but this one is an attempt to create an armored fortress against the threatening outside world.

"To me, the essential issue families face in the '90s is how to protect themselves from what is noxious in our culture, which is often the media," says Mary Pipher, a psychologist and author of *The Shelter of Each Other—Rebuilding Our Families*. "You have to have walls to protect your family—things like family vacations and meals together. If you just let American culture happen to you, you end up stressed, addicted, fat and broke."

People are particularly scared of America's violent side. Never mind that the national crime rate has declined. Home and car alarms and other security devices are selling briskly despite the statistics. Crimes in the '90s seem more random and more horrific: the new phenomenon of carjackings ... the bombings of New York's World Trade Center, the federal building in Oklahoma City and the Olympics site in Atlanta ... Polly Klaas snatched from a slumber party in her California home and then murdered ... two pizza deliverymen shot to death in rural New Jersey by teenagers wanting to experience the feeling of killing someone ... a transient man's murder of a young librarian in Lincoln, Neb., while she was on her regular evening walk in the neighborhood. Such random crimes make people feel very uncomfortable, very vulnerable.

In fact, some parents worry so much about their children becoming crime victims that they have altered the experience of childhood, keeping their kids near home and not even letting them ride their bikes alone. It's understandable. The notorious Megan Kanka and Polly Klaas cases aren't isolated incidents. The number of murder victims under the age of 18 totaled 2,428 in 1995, compared with 1,573 in 1985, according to the U.S. Justice Department.

"People now are staying home for security," says Ms. Popcorn, chairman of BrainReserve, a consulting firm in New York. "Computers allow them to communicate and work from their cocoons."

Americans fear the water they drink and the food they eat, too. The bacterial contamination of ground beef in the summer of 1997, which forced a massive recall and the closing of a meat plant, heightened people's apprehension about the nation's food supply. "If you eat a hamburger or some strawberries, you might die," says Ms. Popcorn. "People are getting up in the morning already on edge and feeling very vulnerable before the day even begins."

Then they head off to another anxiety producer: the workplace. People remain insecure about their jobs, despite the healthy labor market in 1997. The psychological impact of the corporate job slashing of the early 1990s won't fade easily. Nearly three-quarters of Americans polled by Princeton Survey Research Associates in the summer of 1997 said workers are subject to more on-the-job stress than in the past, while about 60% believed people have to work harder to earn a decent living and 70% felt there is less job security.

Exacerbating the job insecurity are people's precarious personal finances. Consumer debt and bankruptcy filings are at all-time highs. College costs scare parents. And many people know they have been lax in preparing for retirement, especially given the likelihood that Social Security and Medicare benefits will be less generous in the future.

Americans' concerns aren't just personal. They also realize that broader social problems have proved more persistent than the country's economic ills. Indeed, the glowing economic indicators of 1997 invite comparisons with the early 1970s, the last time the unemployment rate had dropped below 5%. Indicators of social health in the mid-1990s, however, compare quite poorly with the early 1970s.

The Fordham Institute for Social Policy regularly tracks 16 indicators of social health and finds them lagging near their lowest point in the 27 years since the study began. The latest Index of Social Health shows a score of 40 points out of a possible 100, down 46% from the peak of 74 points in 1973.

Among the most enduring problems: child abuse and child poverty, the wide gap between the rich and the poor, inadequate health-insurance coverage and teenage suicide. On the other hand, progress has been made in reducing the number of elderly in poverty and increasing the proportion of high-school graduates. "The Index of Social Health helps explain why things aren't as rosy as the economy suggests," says Marc Miringoff, director of the Fordham Institute. "We need to fly the plane with more gauges than the GDP and the stock market."

The economy and social health of the country improved in tandem in the past, but that hasn't been the case in recent years. Mr. Miringoff suspects that two-income households help explain the divergence of the GDP and the Index of Social Health. The need—or desire—for two paychecks has radically altered family life. Too many children are being raised by babysitters and television these days. In fact, a significant number of Americans say they find work more rewarding than home and in cases of time conflict, would choose to work even if their home life suffers.

Parents themselves readily concede it's harder giving children a proper upbringing today and they aren't doing a great job of it. Citing time pressures and disciplinary challenges, fully half of all mothers of children under 18 say they are doing a worse job than their own mothers did. That, according to a recent survey by the Pew Research Center for the People and the Press in Washington.

Parents especially come in for criticism for failing to instill values in their children. Many children are swearing like sailors, young women are hiding their pregnancies and then killing their newborn babies, and many teenagers are turning to drugs and suicide. "Only about one in five Americans thinks that it's very common for parents to be good role models and teach kids right from wrong," says Ms. Johnson of Public Agenda. "They believe parents give kids material things instead of spending time with them and teaching them values. There are a lot of spoiled kids out there with the 'gimmes.' " When asked to describe today's teenagers in surveys, people use words like "rude" and "wild."

A *Wall Street Journal*/NBC News poll in late 1996 found that nearly two-thirds of respondents believe America's morals are "pretty bad and getting worse." That compared with only 41% who felt morals were bad and growing worse in 1964.

Drug abuse and chaotic public schools also receive some of the blame for America's sinking values. Studies show that nearly one in 20 high school seniors is a daily marijuana smoker, and more than a third of high-school students have seen drugs sold at school.

That's symptomatic of bigger problems with discipline, violence and inadequate teachers in the schools. A *Wall Street Journal*/NBC News poll in 1997, yielded some of the most negative ratings of education in years. Overall, school safety and student conduct worry people more than mediocre or poor academic achievement. Undisciplined children and lack of parental involvement were cited as "very important"

reasons schools don't work. "There is much concern about schools being lax, tolerating bad behavior and not making kids be responsible," says Ms. Johnson. "They don't make kids show up on time, and grades don't mean what they used to."

Nevertheless, schools may offer the best hope for reversing the nation's moral decline. "People aren't optimistic about changing the media messages kids receive," Ms. Johnson says. "But they feel schools can be changed to help keep kids out of trouble and away from drugs through more discipline and after-school activities." A study reported in the Journal of the American Medical Association in September 1997 found that the closer teenagers are to their parents and the more connected they feel to classmates and teachers, the less likely they are to smoke, use drugs and alcohol, engage in violence, commit suicide, or have sex at a young age.

Ms. Pipher, the psychologist and author, believes too that people will find relief from their anxieties only within their own families, neighborhoods and schools. Washington is too removed from people's lives, and many Americans showed their alienation from the federal government by ignoring the last presidential election. The turnout of only 49% of the voting-age population was among the lowest ever. "The fact of the matter is that most people don't see Washington as affecting their lives very much in a positive way," says Ms. Pipher. "But people are becoming more interested in their communities, as they feel the costs of living in an isolated world. I recommend that people form parent groups because they can't raise children alone; it takes an extended family and the community."

But to ease their anxieties, people also will have to change their priorities and do some hard work of a different sort. It seems hypocritical for people to fret about America's values at the same time they are using the office as a refuge from the complexities of family life. Tagging along on a field trip with a pack of wiggly preschoolers may be less exciting and more exhausting than jetting to London to clinch a big deal. But people may find that living in America is a happier experience if once in awhile they join a field trip to the zoo or the pumpkin patch.

Ronald Alsop

Growth Chart

States Ranked by Percentage Population Change Between 1990 and 1996

State	% change	State	% change
Nevada	33.41%	Mississippi	5.46%
Arizona	20.81	Indiana	5.35
Idaho	18.13	Kentucky	5.34
Utah	16.12	South Dakota	5.23
Colorado	16.03	Oklahoma	4.94
Washington	13.69	New Hampshire	4.80
Georgia	13.51	Missouri	4.73
New Mexico	13.09	Nebraska	4.67
Oregon	12.71	Vermont	4.60
Texas	12.61	Kansas	3.82
Florida	11.30	Illinois	3.64
North Carolina	10.41	New Jersey	3.33
Alaska	10.36	Michigan	3.22
Montana	10.05	Louisiana	3.09
Tennessee	9.07	Ohio	3.00
Delaware	8.81	Iowa	2.70
Virginia	7.86	West Virginia	1.80
California	7.12	Pennsylvania	1.46
Hawaii	6.81	Massachusetts	1.26
Arkansas	6.77	Maine	1.25
Minnesota	6.45	New York	1.08
Wyoming	6.13	North Dakota	0.74
South Carolina	6.09	Connecticut	-0.39
Maryland	6.08	Rhode Island	-1.32
Alabama	5.76	District of Columbia	-10.49
Wisconsin	5.48		

Source: U.S. Census Bureau

Regional and State Population (In thousands)

U.S. region, state	Population, April 1, 1990 (Census)	Population, July 1, 1996 (Estimate)	% change
Total	**249,398***	**265,284**	**6.4 %**
Northeast	50,811	51,580	1.5
New England	13,207	13,351	1.1
Middle Atlantic	37,604	38,229	1.7
Midwest	59,669	62,082	4.0
East North Central	42,009	43,614	3.8
West North Central	17,660	18,468	4.6
South	85,454	93,098	8.9
South Atlantic	43,571	47,616	9.3
East South Central	15,180	16,193	6.7
West South Central	26,703	29,290	9.7
West	52,784	58,523	10.9
Mountain	13,659	16,118	18.0
Pacific	39,125	42,406	8.4
Alabama	4,040	4,273	5.8
Alaska	550	607	10.4
Arizona	3,665	4,428	20.8
Arkansas	2,351	2,510	6.8
California	29,758	31,878	7.1
Colorado	3,294	3,823	16.0
Connecticut	3,287	3,274	-0.4
Delaware	666	725	8.8
District of Columbia	607	543	-10.5
Florida	12,938	14,400	11.3
Georgia	6,478	7,353	13.5
Hawaii	1,108	1,184	6.8
Idaho	1,007	1,189	18.1
Illinois	11,431	11,847	3.6
Indiana	5,544	5,841	5.3
Iowa	2,777	2,852	2.7
Kansas	2,478	2,572	3.8
Kentucky	3,687	3,884	5.3
Louisiana	4,220	4,351	3.1
Maine	1,228	1,243	1.3
Maryland	4,781	5,072	6.1
Massachusetts	6,016	6,092	1.3
Michigan	9,295	9,594	3.2
Minnesota	4,376	4,658	6.4
Mississippi	2,575	2,716	5.5
Missouri	5,117	5,359	4.7
Montana	799	879	10.1
Nebraska	1,578	1,652	4.7
Nevada	1,202	1,603	33.4
New Hampshire	1,109	1,162	4.8
New Jersey	7,730	7,988	3.3
New Mexico	1,515	1,713	13.1
New York	17,991	18,185	1.1
North Carolina	6,632	7,323	10.4
North Dakota	639	644	0.7
Ohio	10,847	11,173	3.0
Oklahoma	3,146	3,301	4.9
Oregon	2,842	3,204	12.7
Pennsylvania	11,883	12,056	1.5
Rhode Island	1,003	990	-1.3
South Carolina	3,486	3,699	6.1
South Dakota	696	732	5.2
Tennessee	4,877	5,320	9.1
Texas	16,986	19,128	12.6
Utah	1,723	2,000	16.1
Vermont	563	589	4.6
Virginia	6,189	6,675	7.9
Washington	4,867	5,533	13.7
West Virginia	1,793	1,826	1.8
Wisconsin	4,892	5,160	5.5
Wyoming	454	481	6.1

*U.S. Total for 1990 has been revised, but not the state and regional totals.
Source: *U.S. Census Bureau*

State Population Projections (Numbers in thousands)

State	2000	2010	2015	2020	2025
New England					
Maine	1,259	1,323	1,362	1,396	1,423
New Hampshire	1,224	1,329	1,372	1,410	1,439
Vermont	617	651	662	671	678
Massachusetts	6,199	6,431	6,574	6,734	6,902
Rhode Island	998	1,038	1,070	1,105	1,141
Connecticut	3,284	3,400	3,506	3,621	3,739
Middle Atlantic					
New York	18,146	18,530	18,916	19,359	19,830
New Jersey	8,178	8,638	8,924	9,238	9,558
Pennsylvania	12,202	12,352	12,449	12,567	12,683
East North Central					
Ohio	11,319	11,505	11,588	11,671	11,744
Indiana	6,045	6,318	6,404	6,481	6,546
Illinois	12,051	12,515	12,808	13,121	13,440
Michigan	9,679	9,836	9,917	10,002	10,078
Wisconsin	5,326	5,590	5,693	5,788	5,867
West North Central					
Minnesota	4,830	5,147	5,283	5,406	5,510
Iowa	2,900	2,968	2,994	3,019	3,040
Missouri	5,540	5,864	6,005	6,137	6,250
North Dakota	662	690	704	717	729
South Dakota	777	826	840	853	866
Nebraska	1,705	1,806	1,850	1,892	1,930
Kansas	2,668	2,849	2,939	3,026	3,108
South Atlantic					
Delaware	768	817	832	847	861
Maryland	5,275	5,657	5,862	6,071	6,274
District of Columbhia	523	560	594	625	655
Virginia	6,997	7,627	7,921	8,204	8,466
West Virginia	1,841	1,851	1,851	1,850	1,845
North Carolina	7,777	8,552	8,840	9,111	9,349
South Carolina	3,858	4,205	4,369	4,517	4,645
Georgia	7,875	8,824	9,200	9,552	9,869
Florida	15,233	17,363	18,497	19,634	20,710
East South Central					
Kentucky	3,995	4,170	4,231	4,281	4,314
Tennessee	5,657	6,180	6,365	6,529	6,665
Alabama	4,451	4,798	4,956	5,100	5,224
Mississippi	2,816	2,974	3,035	3,093	3,142
West South Central					
Arkansas	2,631	2,840	2,922	2,997	3,055
Louisiana	4,425	4,683	4,840	4,991	5,133
Oklahoma	3,373	3,639	3,789	3,930	4,057
Texas	20,119	22,857	24,280	25,729	27,183
Mountain					
Montana	950	1,040	1,069	1,097	1,121
Idaho	1,347	1,557	1,622	1,683	1,739
Wyoming	525	607	641	670	694
Colorado	4,168	4,658	4,833	5,012	5,188
New Mexico	1,860	2,155	2,300	2,454	2,612
Arizona	4,798	5,522	5,808	6,111	6,412
Utah	2,207	2,551	2,670	2,781	2,883
Nevada	1,871	2,131	2,179	2,241	2,312
Pacific					
Washington	5,858	6,658	7,058	7,446	7,808
Oregon	3,397	3,803	3,992	4,177	4,349
California	32,521	37,644	41,373	45,278	49,285
Alaska	653	745	791	838	885
Hawaii	1,257	1,440	1,553	1,677	1,812

Source: U.S. Census Bureau

Changing State Demographics

Percent ot Total Population 65 Years and Over

Region, division, and state	Persons 65 and over				Region, division, and state	Persons 65 and over			
	1990	2000	2010	2020		1990	2000	2010	2020
United States	12.5%	12.6%	13.2%	16.5%					
Northeast	13.7	14.1	14.3	16.9	South Atlantic	13.3%	14.3%	15.5%	19.2%
New England	13.3	14.0	14.4	17.5	Delaware	12.1	13.1	13.8	16.7
Middle Atlantic	13.8	14.1	14.2	16.7	Maryland	10.8	11.3	12.1	14.8
Midwest	12.9	13.1	13.4	16.2	District of Columbia	12.7	13.5	12.5	13.7
East North Central	12.6	12.8	13.2	15.9	Virginia	10.7	11.4	12.5	15.7
West North Central	13.8	13.7	14.0	17.1	West Virginia	14.9	15.1	15.2	18.5
South	12.5	13.1	14.0	17.5	North Carolina	12.1	13.1	14.4	18.1
South Atlantic	13.3	14.3	15.5	19.2	South Carolina	11.3	12.3	13.3	16.8
East South Central	12.7	12.9	13.7	17.0	Georgia	10.0	10.5	11.7	15.0
West South Central	11.0	11.2	11.8	14.9	Florida	18.2	19.6	21.0	25.6
West	10.9	10.9	11.6	14.6	East South Central	12.7	12.9	13.7	17.0
Mountain	11.1	11.4	12.4	16.0	Kentucky	12.6	12.8	13.5	16.9
Pacific	10.8	10.8	11.4	14.1	Tennessee	12.6	12.9	14.0	17.6
New England	13.3	14.0	14.4	17.5	Alabama	12.9	13.2	13.8	16.7
Maine	13.3	14.2	14.6	18.3	Mississippi	12.4	12.7	13.4	16.6
Vermont	11.7	12.2	13.1	16.8	West South Central	11.0	11.2	11.8	14.9
New Hampshire	11.2	12.1	13.0	16.9	Arkansas	14.8	14.9	15.7	19.3
Massachusetts	13.5	14.1	14.5	17.4	Louisiana	11.1	11.5	11.8	14.3
Rhode Island	14.9	15.1	14.8	17.9	Oklahoma	13.4	13.4	13.6	16.5
Connecticut	13.5	14.4	14.8	2.6	Texas	10.1	10.3	11.1	14.2
Middle Atlantic	13.8	14.1	14.2	16.7	Mountain	11.1	11.4	12.4	16.0
New York	13.0	13.3	13.6	15.8	Montana	13.3	12.8	13.0	16.2
New Jersey	13.3	13.7	13.9	16.3	Idaho	12.0	11.1	11.9	15.4
Pennsylvania	15.3	15.6	15.3	18.2	Wyoming	10.4	9.7	9.0	11.2
East North Central	12.6	12.8	13.2	15.9	Colorado	10.0	10.2	11.4	15.3
Ohio	12.9	13.5	13.9	2.3	New Mexico	10.7	11.2	11.9	15.0
Indiana	12.5	12.8	13.3	16.2	Arizona	13.0	14.0	15.4	19.6
Illinois	12.5	12.4	12.6	14.8	Utah	8.7	8.7	9.3	12.1
Michigan	11.9	12.4	12.7	15.2	Nevada	10.5	10.8	12.0	15.5
Wisconsin	13.3	13.2	13.8	17.3	Pacific	10.8	10.8	11.4	14.1
West North Central	13.8	13.7	14.0	17.1	Washington	11.8	11.1	11.9	15.6
Minnesota	12.5	12.5	13.3	16.9	Oregon	13.7	12.7	13.0	16.6
Iowa	15.3	15.0	15.0	18.0	California	10.5	10.6	11.2	13.8
Missouri	14.0	14.1	14.5	17.5	Alaska	4.0	4.4	4.8	6.2
North Dakota	14.2	14.5	13.7	16.2	Hawaii	11.2	11.9	12.3	14.4
South Dakota	14.7	14.0	13.6	16.4					
Nebraska	14.1	13.8	13.9	16.8					
Kansas	13.8	13.5	13.5	16.5					

Source: U.S. Census Bureau

Top Five States with the Largest Population, Ranked by Race and Hispanic Origin: 1995 and 2025 (In thousands)

YEAR AND RANK	WHITE		NON-HISPANIC BLACK		AMERICAN INDIAN		ASIAN		HISPANIC ORIGIN*	
	State	Pop.	State	Pop.	State	Pop.	State.	Pop.	State.	Pop.
1995										
1	California	16,630	New York	2,635	Oklahoma	257	California	3,380	California	9,206
2	New York	12,082	Texas	2,189	Arizona	217	New York	825	Texas	5,173
3	Texas	10,891	California	2,184	California	189	Hawaii	704	New York	2,541
4	Pennsylvania	10,474	Georgia	2,004	New Mexico	140	Texas	412	Florida	1,955
5	Florida	10,010	Florida	1,964	Arkansas	90	New Jersey	357	Illinois	1,090
2025										
1	California	16,626	Texas	3,466	Oklahoma	363	California	8,564	California	21,232
2	Texas	12,501	Georgia	3,292	Arizona	292	New York	1,807	Texas	10,230
3	Florida	12,196	Florida	3,067	New Mexico	257	Hawaii	1,179	Florida	4,944
4	New York	10,585	New York	3,065	California	183	New Jersey	960	New York	4,309
5	Pennsylvania	10,181	California	2,680	Washington	136	Texas	911	Illinois	2,275

*Persons of Hispanic origin may be of any race.

Source: U.S. Census Bureau

States of the Union

ALABAMA

GEOGRAPHY:
Area:
total area: 52,237 sq mi
land area: 50,750 sq mi
Capital: Montgomery, (population: 195,471)
Statehood: December 14, 1819 (22nd state)
Postal abbreviation: AL
State symbols:
State motto: Audemus jura nostra defendere (We dare defend our rights)
State song: "Alabama"
State bird: Yellowhammer
State flower: Camellia
State tree: Southern Pine

PEOPLE:
Population: 4,273,084
Change since 1990: 5.8%

Population density: 83.8 per sq mi
% population 65 years and over: 12.9 (1990), 16.7 (2020 est.)

VITAL STATISTICS:
Birth rate: 14.8 *(per 1,000 population)*
Death rate: 10.0 *(per 1,000 population)*
Infant mortality rate: 10.3 *(deaths per 1,000 live births)*

GOVERNMENT:
Governor: Fob James, Jr. (Republican)
Regular term: 4 years
Current term began: January 1995
Salary: $87,643
Lt. Governor: Don Siegelman (Democrat)

STATE ECONOMY:
Gross state product: $88.661 billion
State budget: *(in thousands)*
State revenues: $12,279,726

Total expenditures: $11,541,881
Debt at end of fiscal year: $3,758,726
Cash and security holdings: $17,373,025
Chief products:
Agriculture: Poultry, beef cattle, soybeans, eggs, peanuts, hogs, corn, cotton, forest products
Fishing Industry: Shrimp and oysters
Manufacturing: Primary metals, paper products, chemicals, textiles, fabricated metal products, clothing, food products, rubber and plastics products
Minerals: Coal, petroleum, natural gas, stone, iron-ore, steel, limestone

PERSONAL FINANCES:
Per capita personal income: $19,181
Median household income: $25,991
Average annual pay: $23,616
Percent of persons in poverty: 20.1%
Homeownership rate: 71.0%

EMPLOYMENT:
Labor force: 2,088,000
Unemployment rate: 5.1%
Total number of businesses: 227,119
Total number of women owned businesses: 71,466
Total number of minority owned businesses: 17,432

CRIME:
Crime rate: 4,848.1 *(per 100,000 people)*
Violent crime: 632.4 (per 100,000)
Property crime: 4,215.7 (per 100,000)
Total prisoners in custody: 17,039
Prison capacity occupied: 98.5%

HEALTH CARE:
Persons without health insurance coverage: 13.5%
Occupancy rate in community hospitals: 60.7%

EDUCATION:
Current high school completion rate: 83.3%
High school graduates: 29.4%
Some college: 16.8%
Associate degree: 5.0%
Bachelor degree: 10.1%
Advanced degree: 5.5%
Estimated pubic elementary and secondary school finances (*in millions*):
Revenues: $3,265
Expenditures: $3,486

ALASKA

GEOGRAPHY:
Area:
total area: 615,230 sq mi
land area: 507,374 sq mi
Capital: Juneau, (population: 26,751)
Statehood: January 3, 1959 (49th state)
Postal abbreviation: AK
State symbols:
State motto: North to the future
State song: "Alaska's Flag"
State bird: Willow Ptarmigan
State flower: Forget-Me-Not
State tree: Sitka Spruce

PEOPLE:
Population: 607,007
Change since 1990: 10.4%
Population density: 1.1 per sq mi
% population 65 years and over: 4.0 (1990), 6.2 (2020 est.)

VITAL STATISTICS:
Birth rate: 18.5 *(per 1,000 population)*
Death rate: 4.0 *(per 1,000 population)*
Infant mortality rate: 8.2 *(deaths per 1,000 live births)*

GOVERNMENT:
Governor: Tony Knowles (Democrat)
Regular term: 4 years
Current term began: December 1994
Salary: $81,648
Lt. Governor: Fran Ulmer (Democrat)

STATE ECONOMY:
Gross state product: $22.720 billion
State budget: *(in thousands)*
State revenues: $8,288,036
Total expenditures: $5,599,033
Debt at end of fiscal year: $3,232,262
Cash and security holdings: $28,233,430
Chief products:
Agriculture: Greenhouse products, dairy products, potatoes, poultry, cattle, barley
Fishing Industry: Salmon, crab, shrimp, groundfish
Manufacturing: Food products, petroleum, coal products, lumber and wood products, areospace industries
Minerals: Petroleum, natural gas, sand and gravel, gold, silver, lead, zinc, coal

PERSONAL FINANCES:
Per capita personal income: $24,002

Median household income: $47,954
Average annual pay: $32,657
Percent of persons in poverty: 7.1%
Homeownership rate: 62.9

EMPLOYMENT:
Labor force: 316,000
Unemployment rate: 7.8%
Total number of businesses: 58,898
   Total number of women owned businesses:
    19,380
   Total number of minority owned businesses:
    5,382

CRIME:
Crime rate: 5,753.8 *(per 100,000 people)*
   Violent crime: 770.9 (per 100,000)
   Property crime: 4,982.9 (per 100,000)
Total prisoners in custody: 2,791
Prison capacity occupied: 104.6%

HEALTH CARE:
Persons without health insurance coverage:
   12.5%
Occupancy rate in community hospitals: 52.8%

EDUCATION:
Current high school completion rate: 89.8%
High school graduates: 28.7%
Some college: 27.6%
Associate degree: 7.2%
Bachelor degree: 15.0%
Advanced degree: 8.0%
Estimated pubic elementary and secondary
   school finances (*in millions*):
   Revenues: $1,183
   Expenditures: $1,163

A R I Z O N A

GEOGRAPHY:
Area:
   total area: 114,006 sq mi
   land area: 113,642 sq mi
Capital: Phoenix, (population: 1,048,949)
Statehood: February 14, 1912 (48th state)
Postal abbreviation: AZ
State symbols:
   State motto: Ditat Deus (God enriches)
   State songs: "Arizona March Song" and "Arizona"
   State bird: Cactus Wren
   State flower: Saguaro Cactus Blossom
   State tree: Palo Verde

PEOPLE:
Population: 4,428,068

Change since 1990: 20.8%
Population density: 37.1 per sq mi
% population 65 years and over: 13.0 (1990), 19.6
   (2020 est.)

VITAL STATISTICS:
Birth rate: 17.5 *(per 1,000 population)*
Death rate: 8.5 *(per 1,000 population)*
Infant mortality rate: 7.6 *(deaths per 1,000 live*
   births)

GOVERNMENT:
Governor: Jane Dee Hull (Republican)*
   Regular term: 4 years
   Current term began: January 1995
   Salary: $75,000
Lt. Governor: (vacant)

STATE ECONOMY:
Gross State Product: $94.093 billion
State budget: *(in thousands)*
   State revenues: $12,593,371
   Total expenditures: $11,162,452
   Debt at end of fiscal year: $3,037,066
   Cash and security holdings: $18,430,585
Chief products:
   Agriculture: Wheat, cotton, soybeans, cattle,
    poultry, hogs
   Manufacturing: Transportation equipment, aero-
    space, electronics, printers and publishers,
    communications
   Mineral products: Coal, copper ore

PERSONAL FINANCES:
Per capita personal income: $20,489
Median household income: $30,863
Average annual pay: $24,276
Percent of persons in poverty: 16.1%
Homeownership rate: 62.0%

EMPLOYMENT:
Labor Force: 2,249,000
Unemployment Rate: 5.5%
Total number of businesses: 248,337
   Total number of women owned businesses:
    93,300
   Total number of minority owned businesses:
    26,185

CRIME:
Crime rate: 8,213.6 *(per 100,000 people)*
   Violent crime: 713.5 *(per 100,000)*
   Property crime: 7,500.1 *(per 100,000)*
Total prisoners in custody: 19,582
Prison capacity occupied: 105.9%

---

*Assumed governorship in September 1997, due to resigna-
tion of Fife Symington.

HEALTH CARE:
Persons without health insurance coverage:
  20.4%
Occupancy rate in community hospitals: 57.1%

EDUCATION:
Current high school completion rate: 83.7%
High school graduates: 26.1%
Some college: 25.4 %
Associate degree: 6.8%
Bachelor degree: 13.3%
Advanced degree: 7.0%
Estimated pubic elementary and secondary
  school finances (in millions):
  Revenues: $4,201
  Expenditures: $3,899

ARKANSAS

GEOGRAPHY:
Area:
  total area: 53,182 sq mi
  land area: 52,075 sq mi
Capital: Little Rock, (population: 178,136)
Statehood: June 15, 1836 (25th state)
Postal abbreviation: AR
State symbols:
  State motto: Regnat Populus (The people rule)
  State songs: "Arkansas (You Run Deep in Me)"
    "Oh, Arkansas"
  State bird: Mockingbird
  State flower: Apple Blossom
  State tree: Pine

PEOPLE:
Population: 2,509,793
Change since 1990: 6.8%
Population density: 47.7 per sq mi
% population 65 years and over: 14.8 (1990), 19.3
  (2020 est.)

VITAL STATISTICS:
Birth rate: 14.1 (per 1,000 population)
Death rate: 10.9 (per 1,000 population)
Infant mortality rate: 10.0 (deaths per 1,000 live
  births)

GOVERNMENT:
Governor: Mike Huckabee* (Republican)
  Regular term: 4 years
  Current term began: July 1996
  Salary: $65,182
Lt. Governor: Winthrop Rockefeller (Republican)

STATE ECONOMY:
Gross state product: $50.575 billion
State budget: (in thousands)
  State revenues: $7,368,193
  Total expenditures: $6,616,119
  Debt at end of fiscal year: $1,982,537
  Cash and security holdings: $9,239,768
Chief products:
  Agriculture: Wheat, barley, cotton, hay, vege-
    tables, cattle, poultry
  Manufacturing: Consumer goods, food products,
    paper products, textiles, fabricated metal
    products, clothing, rubber and plastics prod-
    ucts, lumber, electrical and nonelectrical
    machinery
  Minerals: Bauxite (aluminum ore) coal, petro-
    leum, natural gas, stone

PERSONAL FINANCES:
Per capita personal income: $18,101
Median household income: $25,814
Average annual pay: $20,898
Percent of persons in poverty: 14.9%
Homeownership rate: 66.6%

EMPLOYMENT:
Labor force: 1,234,000
Unemployment rate: 5.4%
Total number of businesses: 159,820
  Total number of women owned businesses:
    50,440
  Total number of minority owned businesses:
    7,594

CRIME:
Crime rate: 4,690.9 (per 100,000 people)
  Violent crime: 553.2 (per 100,000)
  Property crime: 4,137.7 (per 100,000)
Total prisoners in custody: 8,806
Prison capacity occupied: 109.5%

HEALTH CARE:
Persons without health insurance coverage:
  17.9%
Occupancy rate in community hospitals: 58.3%

EDUCATION:
Current high school completion rate: 87.5%
High school graduates: 32.7%
Some college: 16.6%
Associate degree: 3.7%
Bachelor degree: 8.9%

---

*Governor Huckabee, as lieutenant governor, became governor
after Governor Jim Guy Tucker resigned. After Mr. Huckabee
completes his term, he is eligible to serve two more terms.

Advanced degree: 4.5%
Estimated pubic elementary and secondary school finances (*in millions*):
Revenues: $2,236
Expenditures: $2,062

CALIFORNIA

GEOGRAPHY:
Area:
total area: 158,869 sq mi
land area: 155,973 sq mi
Capital: Sacramento, (population: 373,964)
Statehood: September 9, 1850 (31st state)
Postal abbreviation: CA
State symbols:
State motto: Eureka (I have found it)
State song: "I Love You California"
State bird: California Valley Quail
State flower: Golden Poppy
State tree: California Redwood

PEOPLE:
Population: 31,878,234
Change since 1990: 7.1%
Population density: 202.5 per sq mi
% population 65 years and over: 10.5 (1990), 13.8 (2020 est.)

VITAL STATISTICS:
Birth rate: 18.8 *(per 1,000 population)*
Death rate: 7.1 *(per 1,000 population)*
Infant mortality rate: 6.8 *(deaths per 1,000 live births)*

GOVERNMENT:
Governor: Pete Wilson (Republican)
Regular term: 4 years
Current term began: January 1995
Salary: $126,000*
Lt. Governor: Gray Davis (Democrat)

STATE ECONOMY:
Gross state product: $875.697 billion
State budget: *(in thousands)*
State revenues: $118,303,386
Total expenditures: $109,231,147
Debt at end of fiscal year: $48,197,317
Cash and security holdings: $182,653,289
Chief products:
Agriculture: Dairy products, grapes, almonds, artichokes, dates, figs, kiwi, olives, oranges, pistachios, prunes, raisins, walnuts, cattle, livestock, hogs
Manufacturing: Aerospace-defense, electric and electronic equipment, transportation equipment, machinery, processed food
Minerals: Petroleum, natural gas, boron, cement, sand, gravel

PERSONAL FINANCES:
Per capita personal income: $24,073
Median household income: $37,009
Average annual pay: $29,878
Percent of persons in poverty: 16.7%
Homeownership rate: 55.0%

EMPLOYMENT:
Labor force: 15,596,000
Unemployment rate: 7.2%
Total number of businesses: 2,259,327
Total number of women owned businesses: 801,487
Total number of minority owned businesses: 541,414

CRIME:
Crime rate: 5,831.1 *(per 100,000 people)*
Violent crime: 966.0 *(per 100,000)*
Property crime: 4,865.1 *(per 100,000)*
Total prisoners in custody: 125,605**
Prison capacity occupied: 175.3%

HEALTH CARE:
Persons without health insurance coverage: 20.6%
Occupancy rate in community hospitals: 61.1%

EDUCATION:
Current high school completion rate: 78.9%
High school graduates: 22.3%
Some college: 22.6%
Associate degree: 7.9%
Bachelor degree: 15.3%
Advanced degree: 8.1%
Estimated pubic elementary and secondary school finances (*in millions*):
Revenues: $29,492
Expenditures: $28,176

---

*Governor accepts only $114,000.
**Includes institutional camps, community-based facilities, and state mental hospitals

COLORADO

GEOGRAPHY:
Area:
total area: 104,100 sq mi
land area: 103,729 sq mi
Capital: Denver, (population: 493,559)
Statehood: August 1, 1876 (38th state)

Postal abbreviation: CO
State symbols:
  State motto: Nil Sine Numine
    (Nothing without the deity)
  State song: "Where the Columbines Grow"
  State bird: Lark Bunting
  State flower: White and Lavender Columbine
  State tree: Colorado Blue Spruce

PEOPLE:
Population: 3,822,676
Change since 1990: 16.0%
Population density: 36.1 per sq mi
% population 65 years and over: 10.0 (1990), 15.3
  (2020 est.)

VITAL STATISTICS:
Birth rate: 15.2 *(per 1,000 population)*
Death rate: 6.7 *(per 1,000 population)*
Infant mortality rate: 7.9 *(deaths per 1,000 live
  births)*

GOVERNMENT:
Governor: Roy Romer (Democrat)
  Regular term: 4 years
  Current term began: January 1995
  Salary: $70,000
Lt. Governor: Gail Schoettler (Democrat)

STATE ECONOMY:
Gross state product: $99.767 billion
State budget: *(in thousands)*
  State revenues: $11,554,711
  Total expenditures: $9,801,852
  Debt at end of fiscal year: $3,368,181
  Cash and security holdings: $18,294,511
Chief products:
  Agriculture: Alfalfa, wheat, corn, cattle, sheep,
    livestock, sorghum
  Manufacturing: Food products, military ord-
    nance, machinery equipment
  Minerals: Molybdenum, petroleum, coal

PERSONAL FINANCES:
Per capita personal income: $23,961
Median household income: $40,706
Average annual pay: $26,155
Percent of persons in poverty: 8.8%
Homeownership rate: 64.5%

EMPLOYMENT:
Labor force: 2,102,000
Unemployment rate: 4.2%
Total number of businesses: 323,147
  Total number of women owned businesses:
    121,659
  Total number of minority owned businesses:
    23,463

CRIME:
Crime rate: 5,396.3 *(per 100,000 people)*
  Violent crime: 440.2 *(per 100,000)*
  Property crime: 4,956.1 *(per 100,000)*
Total prisoners in custody: 8,037*
Prison capacity occupied: 101.0%

HEALTH CARE:
Persons without health insurance coverage:
  14.8%
Occupancy rate in community hospitals: 58.6%

EDUCATION:
Current high school completion rate: 87.6%
High school graduates: 26.5%
Some college: 24.0%
Associate degree: 6.9%
Bachelor degree: 18.0%
Advanced degree: 9.0%
**Estimated pubic elementary and secondary
  school finances** (*in millions*):
  Revenues: $3,708
  Expenditures: $3,907

---

*Includes off-grounds inmates

CONNECTICUT

GEOGRAPHY:
Area:
  total area: 5,544 sq mi
  land area: 4,845 sq mi
Capital: Hartford, (population: 124,196)
Statehood: January 9, 1788 (5th state)
Postal abbreviation: CT
State symbols:
  State motto: Qui Transtulit Sustinet
    (He who transplanted still sustains)
  State song: "Yankee Doodle"
  State bird: American Robin
  State flower: Mountain Laurel
  State tree: White Oak

PEOPLE:
Population: 3,274,238
Change since 1990: −0.4%
Population density: 675.9 per sq mi
% population 65 years and over: 13.5 (1990), 2.6
  (2020 est.)

VITAL STATISTICS:
Birth rate: 14.2 *(per 1,000 population)*
Death rate: 8.7 *(per 1,000 population)*
Infant mortality rate: 7.1 *(deaths per 1,000 live
  births)*

GOVERNMENT:
Governor: John G. Rowland (Republican)
Regular term: 4 years
Current term began: January 1995
Salary: $78,000
Lt. Governor: M. Jodi Rell (Republican)

STATE ECONOMY:
Gross state product: $110.449 billion
State budget: *(in thousands)*
State revenues: $13,717,638
Total expenditures: $13,575,807
Debt at end of fiscal year: $15,456,310
Cash and security holdings: $17,189,049
Chief products:
Agriculture: Dairy products, tobacco, livestock
Fishing Industry: Oysters
Manufacturing: Transportation equipment, helicopters, submarines, aircraft engines, guns and ammunition, chemicals
Minerals: Sand, gravel, stone, limestone, feldspar, clay, mica

PERSONAL FINANCES:
Per capita personal income: $31,776
Median household income: $40,243
Average annual pay: $33,811
Percent of persons in poverty: 9.7%
Homeownership rate: 69.0%

EMPLOYMENT:
Labor force: 1,720,000
Unemployment rate: 5.7%
Total number of businesses: 237,705
Total number of women owned businesses: 79,931
Total number of minority owned businesses: 13,435

CRIME:
Crime rate: 4,503.2 *(per 100,000 people)*
Violent crime: 405.9 *(per 100,000)*
Property crime: 4,097.3 *(per 100,000)*
Total prisoners in custody: 14,246
Prison capacity occupied: 90.6%

HEALTH CARE:
Persons without health insurance coverage: 8.8%
Occupancy rate in community hospitals: 74.5%

EDUCATION:
Current high school completion rate: 92.6%
High school graduates: 29.5%
Some college: 15.9%
Associate degree: 6.6%
Bachelor degree: 16.2%
Advanced degree: 11.0%

Estimated pubic elementary and secondary school finances *(in millions)*:
Revenues: $4,462
Expenditures: $4,462

DELAWARE

GEOGRAPHY:
Area:
total area: 2,396 sq mi
land area: 1,955 sq mi
Capital: Dover, (population: 27,630)
Statehood: December 7, 1787, (1st state)
Postal abbreviation: DE
State symbols:
State motto: Liberty and Independence
State song: "Our Delaware"
State bird: Blue Hen Chicken
State flower: Peach Blossom
State tree: American Holly

PEOPLE:
Population: 724,842
Change since 1990: 8.8%
Population density: 366.9 per sq mi
% population 65 years and over: 12.1 (1990), 16.7 (2020 est.)

VITAL STATISTICS:
Birth rate: 15.1 *(per 1,000 population)*
Death rate: 8.8 *(per 1,000 population)*
Infant mortality rate: 8.8 *(deaths per 1,000 live births)*

GOVERNMENT:
Governor: Tom Carper (Democrat)
Regular term: 4 years
Current term began: January 1997
Salary: $112,000
Lt. Governor: Ruth Ann Minner (Democrat)

STATE ECONOMY:
Gross state product: $26.697 billion
State budget: *(in thousands)*
State revenues: $3,441,210
Total expenditures: $2,980,188
Debt at end of fiscal year: $3,524,495
Cash and security holdings: $6,278,994
Chief products:
Agriculture: Broilers, soybeans, corn, milk
Fishing Industry: Crabs and clams
Manufacturing: Chemicals, food products, paper and rubber products, primary metals, printed materials

Mining: Sand, gravel, magnesium
  compounds

PERSONAL FINANCES:
Per capita personal income: $26,273
Median household income: $34,928
Average annual pay: $27,952
Percent of persons in poverty: 10.3%
Homeownership rate: 71.5%

EMPLOYMENT:
Labor force: 382,000
Unemployment rate: 5.2%
Total number of businesses: 42,228
  Total number of women owned businesses:
  14,904
  Total number of minority owned businesses:
  3,301

CRIME:
Crime rate: 5,158.7 *(per 100,000 people)*
  Violent crime: 725.0 *(per 100,000)*
  Property crime: 4,433.8 *(per 100,000)*
Total prisoners in custody: 4,388
Prison capacity occupied: 145.1%

HEALTH CARE:
Persons without health insurance coverage: 15.7%
Occupancy rate in community hospitals: 70.9%

EDUCATION:
Current high school completion rate: 93.7%
High school graduates: 32.7%
Some college: 16.9%
Associate degree: 6.5%
Bachelor degree: 13.7%
Advanced degree: 7.7%
Estimated pubic elementary and secondary
  school finances (*in millions*):
  Revenues: $822
  Expenditures: $780

DISTRICT OF COLUMBIA

GEOGRAPHY:
Area:
  total area: 68 sq mi
  land area: 61 sq mi
Postal abbreviation: DC
Symbols:
  Motto: Justitia omnibus (Justice for all)
  Bird: Wood Thrush
  Flower: American Beauty Rose
  Tree: Scarlet Oak

PEOPLE:
Population: 543,213

Change since 1990: −10.5%
Population density: 9,086.2 per sq mi
% population 65 years and over: 12.7 (1990), 13.7
  (2020 est.)

VITAL STATISTICS:
Birth rate: 18.4 *(per 1,000 population)*
Death rate: 12.1 *(per 1,000 population)*
Infant mortality rate: 17.4 *(deaths per 1,000 live births)*

GOVERNMENT:
Mayor: Marion Barry (Democrat)
  Regular term: 4 years
  Salary: $90,705

ECONOMY:
Gross product: $48.028 billion
Chief products:
  Manufacturing: Printing and publishing, food
    products, stone and glass products

PERSONAL FINANCES:
Per capita personal income: $33,452
Median household income: $30,748
Average annual pay: $40,919
Persons below poverty level: 22.2%
Homeownership rate: 40.4%

EMPLOYMENT:
Labor force: 272,000
Unemployment rate: 8.5%
Total number of businesses: 35,344
  Total number of women owned businesses:
  14,599
  Total number of minority owned businesses:
  12,669

CRIME:
Crime rate: 12,173.5 *(per 100,000 people)*
  Violent crime: 2,661.4 *(per 100,000)*
  Property crime: 9,512.1 *(per 100,000)*
Total prisoners in custody: 10,621
Prison capacity occupied: 95.8%

HEALTH CARE:
Persons without health insurance coverage:
  17.3%
Occupancy rate in community hospitals: 73.2%

EDUCATION:
Current high school completion rate: 86.4%
High school graduates: 21.2%
Some college: 15.6%
Associate degree: 3.1%
Bachelor degree: 16.1%
Advanced degree: 17.2%

Estimated pubic elementary and secondary
 school finances (*in millions*):
 Revenues: $595
 Expenditures: $616

FLORIDA

GEOGRAPHY:
Area:
 total area: 59,928 sq mi
 land area: 53,937 sq mi
Capital: Tallahassee, (population: 133,718)
Statehood: March 3, 1845 (27th state)
Postal abbreviation: FL
State symbols:
 State motto: "In God We Trust"
 State song: "The Swanee River"
 State bird: Mockingbird
 State flower: Orange Blossom
 State tree: Sabal Palm

PEOPLE:
Population: 14,399,985
Change since 1990: 11.3%
Population density: 262.3 per sq mi
% population 65 years and over: 18.2 (1990), 25.6 (2020 est.)

VITAL STATISTICS:
Birth rate: 14.0 (*per 1,000 population*)
Death rate: 10.6 (*per 1,000 population*)
Infant mortality rate: 8.6 (*deaths per 1,000 live births*)

GOVERNMENT:
Governor: Lawton Chiles (Democrat)
 Regular term: 4 years
 Current term began: January 1995
 Salary: $107,961
Lt. Governor: Buddy MacKay (Democrat)

STATE ECONOMY:
Gross state product: $317.829 billion
State budget: (*in thousands*)
 State revenues: $37,359,429
 Total expenditures: $34,749,505
 Debt at end of fiscal year: $15,369,609
 Cash and security holdings: $52,464,253
Chief products:
 Agriculture: Citrus fruit, nuts, berries, vegetables, livestock
 Manufacturing: Electronics, aerospace, food products, chemicals, rubber and plastic
 Minerals: Phosphate, titanium, zircon, petroleum

PERSONAL FINANCES:
Per capita personal income: $23,061
Median household income: $29,745
Average annual pay: $23,918
Percent of persons in poverty: 16.2%
Homeownership rate: 67.1%

EMPLOYMENT:
Labor force: 6,938,000
Unemployment rate: 5.1%
Total number of businesses: 1,000,542
 Total number of women owned businesses: 352,048
 Total number of minority owned businesses: 173,287

CRIME:
Crime rate: 7,701.5 (*per 100,000 people*)
 Violent crime: 1,071.0 (*per 100,000*)
 Property crime: 6,630.6 (*per 100,000*)
Total prisoners in custody: 57,139
Prison capacity occupied: 99.2%

HEALTH CARE:
Persons without health insurance coverage: 18.3%
Occupancy rate in community hospitals: 60.2%

EDUCATION:
Current high school completion rate: 83.2%
High school graduates: 30.1%
Some college: 19.4%
Associate degree: 6.6%
Bachelor degree: 12.0%
Advanced degree: 6.3%
Estimated pubic elementary and secondary school finances (*in millions*):
 Revenues: $13,502
 Expenditures: $13,747

GEORGIA

GEOGRAPHY:
Area:
 total area: 58,977 sq mi
 land area: 57,919 sq mi
Capital: Atlanta, (population: 396,052)
Statehood: January 2, 1788 (4th state)
Postal abbreviation: GA
State symbols:
 State motto: "Wisdom, Justice, and Moderation."
 State song: "Georgia On My Mind"
 State bird: Brown Thrasher
 State flower: Cherokee Rose
 State tree: Live Oak

PEOPLE:
Population: 7,353,225
Change since 1990: 13.5%
Population density: 124.3 per sq mi
% population 65 years and over: 10.0 (1990), 15.0 (2020 est.)

VITAL STATISTICS:
Birth rate: 16.0 *(per 1,000 population)*
Death rate: 8.0 *(per 1,000 population)*
Infant mortality rate: 10.4 *(deaths per 1,000 live births)*

GOVERNMENT:
Governor: Zell Miller (Democrat)
  Regular term: 4 years
  Current term began: January 1995
  Salary: $107,200
Lt. Governor: Pierre Howard (Democrat)

STATE ECONOMY:
Gross state product: $183.042 billion
State budget: *(in thousands)*
  State revenues: $20,283,513
  Total expenditures: $19,154,482
  Debt at end of fiscal year: $5,621,662
  Cash and security holdings: $28,648,157
Chief products:
  Agriculture: Peanuts, cotton, wheat, tobacco, soybeans, poultry, cattle, pigs
  Manufacturing: Textiles, airplane and automobile assembly, mobile homes, chemicals, food processing, lumber
  Minerals: Marble, granite, kaolin

PERSONAL FINANCES:
Per capita personal income: $21,741
Median household income: $34,099
Average annual pay: $25,313
Percent of persons in poverty: 12.1%
Homeownership rate: 69.3%

EMPLOYMENT:
Labor force: 3,753,000
Unemployment rate: 4.6%
Total number of businesses: 425,118
  Total number of women owned businesses: 143,045
  Total number of minority owned businesses: 52,131

CRIME:
Crime rate: 6,003.6 *(per 100,000 people)*
  Violent crime: 657.1 *(per 100,000)*
  Property crime: 5,346.5 *(per 100,000)*
Total prisoners in custody: 33,383
Prison capacity occupied: 101.4%

HEALTH CARE:
Persons without health insurance coverage: 17.9%
Occupancy rate in community hospitals: 63.4%

EDUCATION:
Current high school completion rate: 79.4%
High school graduates: 29.6%
Some college: 17.0%
Associate degree: 5.0%
Bachelor degree: 12.9%
Advanced degree: 6.4%
Estimated pubic elementary and secondary school finances *(in millions)*:
  Revenues: $7,310
  Expenditures: $7,222

HAWAII

GEOGRAPHY:
Area:
  total area: 6,459 sq mi
  land area: 6,423 sq mi
Capital: Honolulu, (population: 385,881)
Statehood: August 21, 1959 (50th state)
Postal abbreviation: HI
State symbols:
  State motto: Ua mau ke ea o ka aina i ka pono (The life of the land is perpetuated in righteousness.)
  State song: "Hawaii Ponoi"
  State bird: Nene (Hawaiian Goose)
  State flower: Yellow Hibiscus
  State tree: KuKui (Candlenut)

PEOPLE:
Population: 1,183,723
Change since 1990: 6.8%
Population density: 184.8 per sq mi
% Population 65 years and over: 11.2 (1990), 14.4 (2020 est.)

VITAL STATISTICS:
Birth rate: 16.8 *(per 1,000 population)*
Death rate: 6.1 *(per 1,000 population)*
Infant mortality rate: 7.2 *(deaths per 1,000 live births)*

GOVERNMENT:
Governor: Benjamin J. Cayetano (Democrat)
  Regular term: 4 years
  Current term began: December 1994
  Salary: $94,780
Lt. Governor: Mazie Hirono (Democrat)

STATE ECONOMY:
Gross state product: $36.718 billion

State budget: *(in thousands)*
  State revenues: $5,777,523
  Total expenditures: $6,014,741
  Debt at end of fiscal year: $5,195,820
  Cash and security holdings: $8,948,617
Chief products:
  Agriculture: Sugarcane, sorghum, corn,
    pineapple, macadamia nuts
  Manufacturing: Sugar, canned pineapple, oil-
    refining, steelmilling, printing and publishing
  Minerals: Stone, cement, sand, gravel

PERSONAL FINANCES:
Per capita personal income: $24,590
Median household income: $42,851
Average annual pay: $26,746
Percent of persons in poverty: 10.3%
Homeownership rate: 50.6%

EMPLOYMENT:
Labor force: 591,000
Unemployment rate: 6.4%
Total number of businesses: 79,050
  Total number of women owned businesses:
    29,743
  Total number of minority owned businesses:
    41,111

CRIME:
Crime rate: 7,198.6 *(per 100,000 people)*
  Violent crime: 295.6 *(per 100,000)*
  Property crime: 6,902.9 *(per 100,000)*
Total prisoners in custody: 2,905
Prison capacity occupied: 171.5%

HEALTH CARE:
Persons without health insurance coverage: 8.9%
Occupancy rate in community hospitals: 82.6%

EDUCATION:
Current high school completion rate: 90.7%
High school graduates: 28.7%
Some college: 20.1%
Associate degree: 8.3%
Bachelor degree: 15.8%
Advanced degree: 7.1%
Estimated pubic elementary and secondary
  school finances *(in millions)*:
  Revenues: $1,192
  Expenditures: $1,173

IDAHO

GEOGRAPHY:
Area:
  total area: 83,574 sq mi
  land area: 82,751 sq mi
Capital: Boise, (population: 145,987)
Statehood: July 3, 1890 (43rd state)
Postal abbreviation: ID
State symbols:
  State motto: Esto Perpetua (It is perpetual)
  State song: "Here We Have Idaho"
  State bird: Mountain Bluebird
  State flower: Syringa
  State tree: Western White Pine

PEOPLE:
Population: 1,189,251
Change since 1990: 18.1%
Population density: 14.1 per sq mi
% Population 65 years and over: 12.0 (1990),
  15.4 (2020 est.)

VITAL STATISTICS:
Birth rate: 15.8 *(per 1,000 population)*
Death rate: 7.5 *(per 1,000 population)*
Infant mortality rate: 7.2 *(deaths per 1,000 live
  births)*

GOVERNMENT:
Governor: Philip E. Batt (Republican)
  Regular term: 4 years
  Current term began: January 1995
  Salary: $85,000
Lt. Governor: C.L. "Butch" Otter (Republican)

STATE ECONOMY:
Gross state product: $24.185 billion
State budget: *(in thousands)*
  State revenues: $3,845,325
  Total expenditures: $3,360,314
  Debt at end of fiscal year: $1,302,540
  Cash and security holdings: $6,193,287
Chief products:
  Agriculture: Potatoes, wheat, sugar beets, cattle,
    livestock, sheep, forestry
  Manufacturing: Food processing, machinery,
    electronic equipment, chemicals
  Minerals: Silver, lead, antimony, molybdenum,
    semiprecious stones

PERSONAL FINANCES:
Per capita personal Income: $18,906
Median household income: $32,676
Average annual pay: $21,938

Percent of persons in poverty: 14.0%
Homeownership rate: 71.4%

EMPLOYMENT:
Labor force: 619,000
Unemployment rate: 5.2%
Total number of businesses: 88,712
  Total number of women owned businesses: 29,946
  Total number of minority owned businesses:
   2,747

CRIME:
Crime rate: 4,401.5 *(per 100,000 people)*
  Violent crime: 322.0 *(per 100,000)*
  Property crime: 4,079.4 *(per 100,00)*
Total prisoners in custody: 2,253
Prison capacity occupied: 106.3%

HEALTH CARE:
Persons without health insurance coverage:
  14.0%
Occupancy rate in community hospitals: 55.5%

EDUCATION:
Current high school completion rate: 86.7%
High school graduates: 30.4%
Some college: 24.2%
Associate degree: 7.5%
Bachelor degree: 12.4%
Advanced degree: 5.3%
Estimated pubic elementary and secondary
  school finances *(in millions)*:
  Revenues: $1,112
  Expenditures: $1,112

I L L I N O I S

GEOGRAPHY:
Area:
  total area: 57,918 sq mi
  land area: 55,593 sq mi
Capital: Springfield, (population: 105,938)
Statehood: December 3, 1818 (21st state)
Postal abbreviation: IL
State symbols:
  State motto: State Sovereignty, National Union
  State song: "Illinois"
  State bird: Cardinal
  State flower: Violet
  State tree: White oak

PEOPLE:
Population: 11,846,544
Change since 1990: 3.6%
Population density: 212.8 per sq mi
% population 65 years and over: 12.5 (1990), 14.8
  (2020 est.)

VITAL STATISTICS:
Birth rate: 16.3 *(per 1,000 population)*
Death rate: 9.2 *(per 1,000 population)*
Infant mortality rate: 9.9 *(deaths per 1,000 live*
  births)

GOVERNMENT:
Governor: Jim Edgar (Republican)
  Regular term: 4 years
  Current term began: January 1995
  Salary: $123,022
Lt. Governor: Bob Kustra (Republican)

STATE ECONOMY:
Gross state product: $332.853 billion
State budget: *(in thousands)*
  State revenues: $34,689,103
  Total expenditures: $32,991,313
  Debt at end of fiscal year: $21,950,300
  Cash and security holdings: $45,333,845
Chief products:
  Agriculture: Soybean, wheat, corn, pork, dairy
   products, beef
  Manufacturing: Fabricated metals, food prod-
   ucts, rubber products, electrical and nonelec-
   trical machinery, chemicals
  Minerals: Fluorite, coal, sulfur, lead, zinc, lime-
   stone, silica, florite

PERSONAL FINANCES:
Per capita personal income: $25,225
Median household income: $38,071
Average annual pay: $29,107
Percent of persons in poverty: 12.4%
Homeownership rate: 68.2%

EMPLOYMENT:
Labor force: 6,100,000
Unemployment rate: 5.3%
Total number of businesses: 726,974
  Total number of women owned businesses:
   250,613
  Total number of minority owned businesses:
   67,603

CRIME:
Crime rate: 5,455.7 *(per 100,000)*
  Violent crime: 996.1 *(per 100,000)*
  Property crime: 4,459.6 *(per 100,000)*
Total prisoners in custody: 36,531
Prison capacity occupied: 138.5%

HEALTH CARE:
Persons without health insurance coverage:
  11.0%
Occupancy rate in community hospitals: 63.5%

EDUCATION:
Current high school completion rate: 86.7%
High school graduates: 30.0%
Some college: 19.4%
Associate degree: 5.8%
Bachelor degree: 13.6%
Advanced degree: 7.5%
Estimated pubic elementary and secondary school finances (*in millions*):
Revenues: $12,894
Expenditures: $10,719

INDIANA

GEOGRAPHY:
Area:
total area: 36,420 sq mi
land area: 35,870 sq mi
Capital: Indianapolis, (population: 752,279)
Statehood: December 11, 1816 (19th state)
Postal abbreviation: IN
State symbols:
State motto: The Crossroads of America
State song: "On the Banks of the Wabash, Far Away"
State bird: Cardinal
State flower: Peony
State tree: Tulip Tree

PEOPLE:
Population: 5,840,528
Change since 1990: 5.3%
Population density: 161.8 per sq mi
% Population 65 years and over: 12.5 (1990), 16.2 (2020 est.)

VITAL STATISTICS:
Birth rate: 14.7 *(per 1,000 population)*
Death rate: 9.3 *(per 1,000 population)*
Infant mortality rate: 9.2 *(deaths per 1,000 live births)*

GOVERNMENT:
Governor: Frank O'Bannon (Democrat)
Regular term: 4 years
Current term began: January 1997
Salary: $77,194*
Lt. Governor: Joe Kernan (Democrat)

STATE ECONOMY:
Gross state product: $138.190 billion
State budget: *(in thousands)*
State revenues: $16,260,515
Total expenditures: $15,284,083
Debt at end of fiscal year: $5,456,751
Cash and security holdings: $19,549,771

Chief products:
Agriculture: Corn, soybeans, wheat, tomatoes, cattle, hogs
Manufacturing: Transportation equipment, steel, musical instruments, diamond cutting tools, chemicals
Minerals: Coal, quarry stone

PERSONAL FINANCES:
Per capita personal income: $21,433
Median household income: $33,385
Average annual pay: $24,908
Percent of persons in poverty: 9.6%
Homeownership rate: 74.2%

EMPLOYMENT:
Labor force: 3,072,000
Unemployment rate: 4.1%
Total number of businesses: 364,253
Total number of women owned businesses: 125,411
Total number of minority owned businesses: 13,865

CRIME:
Crime rate: 4,631.5 *(per 100,000 people)*
Violent crime: 524.7 *(per 100,000)*
Property crime: 4,106.8 *(per 100,000)*
Total prisoners in custody: 14,111
Prison capacity occupied: 114.6%

HEALTH CARE:
Persons without health insurance coverage: 12.6%
Occupancy rate in community hospitals: 58.7%

EDUCATION:
Current high school completion rate: 88.4%
High school graduates: 38.2%
Some college: 16.6%
Associate degree: 5.3%
Bachelor degree: 9.2%
Advanced degree: 6.4%
Estimated pubic elementary and secondary school finances (*in millions*):
Revenues: $6,359
Expenditures: $6,293

---

*Accepts $66,000

IOWA

GEOGRAPHY:
Area:
total area: 56,276 sq mi
land area: 55,875 sq mi

Capital: Des Moines, (population: 194,965)
Statehood: December 28, 1846 (29th state)
Postal abbreviation: IA
State symbols:
State motto: Our Liberties We Prize, Our Rights
We Will Maintain
State song: "Song of Iowa"
State bird: Eastern Goldfinch
State flower: Wild Rose
State tree: Oak

PEOPLE:
Population: 2,851,792
Change since 1990: 2.7%
Population density: 50.9 per sq mi
% population 65 years and over: 15.3 (1990), 18.0
(2020 est.)

VITAL STATISTICS:
Birth rate: 13.4 *(per 1,000 population)*
Death rate: 9.3 *(per 1,000 population)*
Infant mortality rate: 6.9 *(deaths per 1,000 live
births)*

GOVERNMENT:
Governor: Terry E. Branstad (Republican)
Regular term: 4 years
Current term began: January 1995
Salary: $101,312
Lt. Governor: Joy Corning (Republican)

STATE ECONOMY:
Gross state product: $68.298 billion
State budget: *(in thousands)*
State revenues: $9,268,151
Total expenditures: $8,585,952
Debt at end of fiscal year: $2,110,974
Cash and security holdings: $11,582,094
Chief Products:
Agriculture: Corn, soybean,oats, grain, beef, pork
Manufacturing: Food processing, agricultural
machinery, refrigeration equipment
Minerals: Cement and gypsum

PERSONAL FINANCES:
Per capita personal income: $20,921
Median household income: $35,519
Average annual pay: $22,189
Percent of persons in poverty: 12.2%
Homeownership rate: 72.8%

EMPLOYMENT:
Labor force: 1,599,000
Unemployment rate: 3.8%
Total number of businesses: 206,840
Total number of women owned businesses:
71,040

Total number of minority owned businesses:
2,939

CRIME:
Crime rate: 4,101.9 *(per 100,000 people)*
Violent crime: 354.4 *(per 100,000)*
Property crime: 3,747.5 *(per 100,000)*
Total prisoners in custody: 5,437
Prison capacity occupied: 117.6%

HEALTH CARE:
Persons without health insurance coverage:
11.3%
Occupancy rate in community hospitals: 57.9%

EDUCATION:
Current high school completion rate: 94.2%
High school graduates: 38.5%
Some college: 17.0%
Associate degree: 7.7%
Bachelor degree: 11.7%
Advanced degree: 5.2%
**Estimated pubic elementary and secondary
school finances** *(in millions)*:
Revenues: $3,168
Expenditures: $3,314

KANSAS

GEOGRAPHY:
Area:
total area: 82,282 sq mi
land area: 81,823 sq mi
Capital: Topeka, (population: 120,646)
Statehood: January 29, 1861 (34th state)
Postal abbreviation: KS
State symbols:
State motto: Ad Astra Per Aspera
(To the stars through difficulties)
State song: "Home on the Range"
State bird: Western Meadowlark
State flower: Wild Native Sunflower
State tree: Cottonwood

PEOPLE:
Population: 2,572,150
Change since 1990: 3.8%
Population density: 31.4 per sq mi
% population 65 years and over: 13.8 (1990), 16.5
(2020 est.)

VITAL STATISTICS:
Birth rate: 14.8 *(per 1,000 population)*
Death rate: 9.2 *(per 1,000 population)*

Infant mortality rate: 8.8 *(deaths per 1,000 live births)*

GOVERNMENT:
Governor: Bill Graves (Republican)
Regular term: 4 years
Current term began: January 1995
Salary: $74,000
Lt. Governor: Gary Sherrer (Republican)

STATE ECONOMY:
Gross state product: $61.758 billion
State budget: *(in thousands)*
State revenues: $7,374,389
Total expenditures: $7,116,429
Debt at end of fiscal year: $1,145,493
Cash and security holdings: $7,434,544
Chief products:
Agriculture: Wheat, corn, sorghum, tobacco, soybeans, beef, veal, hogs
Manufacturing: Meat-packing, grain-milling, aviation aircraft, the assembly of machinery, printing and publishing
Minerals: Petroleum and natural gas

PERSONAL FINANCES:
Per capita personal income: $21,841
Median household income: $30,341
Average annual pay: $22,907
Percent of persons in poverty: 10.8%
Homeownership rate: 67.5%

EMPLOYMENT:
Labor force: 1,340,000
Unemployment rate: 4.5%
Total number of businesses: 191,262
Total number of women owned businesses: 66,429
Total number of minority owned businesses: 7,244

CRIME:
Crime rate: 4,886.9 *(per 100,000 people)*
Violent crime: 420.7 *(per 100,000)*
Property crime: 4,466.2 *(per 100,000)*
Total prisoners in custody: 6,299
Prison capacity occupied: 94.7%

HEALTH CARE:
Persons without health insurance coverage: 12.4%
Occupancy rate in community hospitals: 54.5%

EDUCATION:
Current high school completion rate: 92.2%
High school graduates: 32.8%
Some college: 21.9%
Associate degree: 5.4%

Bachelor degree: 14.1%
Advanced degree: 7.0%
Estimated pubic elementary and secondary school finances (*in millions*)
Revenues: $2,991
Expenditures: $2,673

KENTUCKY

GEOGRAPHY:
Area:
total area: 40,411 sq mi
land area: 39,732 sq mi
Capital: Frankfort, (population: 41,302)
Statehood: June 1, 1792 (15th state)
Postal abbreviation: KY
State symbols:
State motto: United We Stand, Divided We Fall
State song: "My Old Kentucky Home, Good Night!"
State bird: Cardinal
State flower: Goldenrod
State tree: Tulip poplar

PEOPLE:
Population: 3,883,723
Change since 1990: 5.3%
Population density: 97.2 per sq mi
% population 65 years and over: 12.6 (1990), 16.9 (2020 est.)

VITAL STATISTICS:
Birth rate: 14.0 *(per 1,000 population)*
Death rate: 9.8 *(per 1,000 population)*
Infant mortality rate: 8.2 *(deaths per 1,000 live births)*

GOVERNMENT:
Governor: Paul E. Patton (Democrat)
Regular term: 4 years
Current term began: December 1995
Salary: $93,904
Lt. Governor: Stephen Henry, M.D. (Democrat)

STATE ECONOMY:
Gross state product: $86.485 billion
State budget: *(in thousands)*
State revenues: $12,845,822
Total expenditures: $11,395,067
Debt at end of fiscal year: $7,097,496
Cash and security holdings: $16,636,630
Chief products:
Agriculture: Tobacco farming, wheat, soybeans, corn, hogs, livestock, cattle
Manufacturing: Bourbon whiskey, thoroughbred horses, transportation equipment, chemicals

Minerals: Bituminous coal, coal, natural gas, petroleum, asphalt, iron ore

PERSONAL FINANCES:
Per capita personal income: $18,849
Median household income: $29,810
Average annual pay: $22,747
Percent of persons in poverty: 14.7%
Homeownership rate: 73.2%

EMPLOYMENT:
Labor force: 1,867,000
Unemployment rate: 5.6%
Total number of businesses: 236,525
  Total number of women owned businesses: 74,280
  Total number of minority owned businesses: 7,421

CRIME:
Crime rate: 3,351.7 *(per 100,000 people)*
  Violent crime: 364.7 *(per 100,000)*
  Property crime: 2,987.0 *(per 100,000)*
Total prisoners in custody: 9,097
Prison capacity occupied: 99.2%

HEALTH CARE:
Persons without health insurance coverage: 14.6%
Occupancy rate in community hospitals: 62.2%

EDUCATION:
Current high school completion rate: 83.3%
High school graduates: 31.8%
Some college: 15.2%
Associate degree: 4.1%
Bachelor degree: 8.1%
Advanced degree: 5.5%
Estimated pubic elementary and secondary school finances *(in millions)*:
  Revenues: $3,717
  Expenditures: $3,507

LOUISIANA

GEOGRAPHY:
Area:
  total area: 49,651 sq mi
  land area: 43,566 sq mi
Capital: Baton Rouge, (population: 227,482)
Statehood: April 30, 1812 (18th state)
Postal abbreviation: LA
State symbols:
  State motto: Union, Justice, Confidence

State song: "Give Me Louisiana" and "You Are My Sunshine"
State bird: Eastern Brown Pelican
State flower: Magnolia
State tree: Bald Cypress

PEOPLE:
Population: 4,350,579
Change since 1990: 3.1%
Population density: 99.7 per sq mi
% population 65 years and over: 11.1 (1990), 14.3 (2020 est.)

VITAL STATISTICS:
Birth rate: 16.2 *(per 1,000 population)*
Death rate: 9.4 *(per 1,000 population)*
Infant mortality rate: 10.8 *(deaths per 1,000 live births)*

GOVERNMENT:
Governor: Mike Foster (Republican)
  Regular term: 4 years
  Current term began: January 1996
  Salary: $95,000
Lt. Governor: Kathleen Blanco (Democrat)

STATE ECONOMY:
Gross state product: $101.101 billion
State budget: *(in thousands)*
  State revenues: $13,956,017
  Total expenditures: $14,461,235
  Debt at end of fiscal year: $8,520,442
  Cash and security holdings: $24,227,662
Chief products:
  Agriculture: Soybeans, cotton, beef cattle, poultry, dairy products, tree-farming, sugarcane
  Fishing Industry: Shrimp
  Manufacturing: Chemicals, refined petroleum, paper, transportation equipment, processed food
  Minerals: Natural gas, petroleum, sulfur, salt

PERSONAL FINANCES:
Per capita personal income: $18,981
Median household income: $27,949
Average annual pay: $23,178
Percent of persons in poverty: 19.7%
Homeownership rate: 64.9%

EMPLOYMENT:
Labor Force: 1,997,000
Unemployment rate: 6.7%
Total number of businesses: 236,589
  Total number of women owned businesses: 76,849
  Total number of minority owned businesses: 29,784

CRIME:
Crime rate: 6,676.0 *(per 100,000 people)*
    Violent crime: 1,007.4 *(per 100,000)*
    Property crime: 5,668.6 *(per 100,000)*
Total prisoners in custody: 15,623
Prison capacity occupied: 97.4%

HEALTH CARE:
Persons without health insurance coverage: 20.5%
Occupancy rate in community hospitals: 57.0%

EDUCATION:
Current high school completion rate: 83.9%
High school graduates: 31.7%
Some college: 17.2%
Associate degree: 3.3%
Bachelor degree: 10.5%
Advanced degree: 5.6%
**Estimated pubic elementary and secondary
    school finances** *(in millions)*:
    Revenues: $4,101
    Expenditures: $3,733

MAINE

GEOGRAPHY:
Area:
    total area: 33,741 sq mi
    land area: 30,865 sq mi
Capital: Augusta,(population: 21,325)
Statehood: March 15, 1820 (23rd state)
Postal abbreviation: ME
State symbols:
    State motto: Dirigo (I lead)
    State song: "State of Maine Song"
    State bird: Chickadee
    State flower: White Pine Cone and Tassel
    State tree: White Pine

PEOPLE:
Population: 1,243,316
Change since 1990: 1.3%
Population density: 40.2 per sq mi
% population 65 years and over: 13.3 (1990), 18.3
    (2020 est.)

VITAL STATISTICS:
Birth rate: 12.2 *(per 1,000 population)*
Death rate: 9.2 *(per 1,000 population)*
Infant mortality rate: 6.8 *(deaths per 1,000 live
    births)*

GOVERNMENT:
Governor: Angus S. King, Jr. (Independent)
    Regular term: 4 years

    Current term began: January 1995
    Salary: $70,000
Senate President: Mark Lawrence (Democrat)

STATE ECONOMY:
Gross state product: $26.069 billion
State budget: *(in thousands)*
    State revenues: $4,207,954
    Total expenditures: $4,179,160
    Debt at end of fiscal year: $3,041,348
    Cash and security holdings: $6,841,397
Chief products:
    Agriculture: Potatoes, oats, apples, blueberries,
        poultry, dairy products
    Fishing Industry: Shellfish
    Manufacturing: Paper and pulp products
    Minerals: Sand, gravel, limestone, building stone

PERSONAL FINANCES:
Per capita personal income: $20,105
Median household income: $33,858
Average annual pay: $22,389
Percent of persons in poverty: 11.2%
Homeownership rate: 76.5%

EMPLOYMENT:
Labor force: 669,000
Unemployment rate: 5.1%
Total number of businesses: 109,360
    Total number of women owned businesses: 35,260
    Total number of minority owned businesses:
        1,099

CRIME:
Crime rate: 3,284.7 *(per 100,000 people)*
    Violent crime: 131.4 *(per 100,000)*
    Property crime: 3,153.3 *(per 100,000)*
Total prisoners in custody: 1,386
Prison capacity occupied: 85.4%

HEALTH CARE:
Persons without health insurance coverage:
    13.5%
Occupancy rate in community hospitals: 68.0%

EDUCATION:
Current high school completion rate: 94.0%
High school graduates: 37.1%
Some college: 16.1%
Associate degree: 6.9%
Bachelor degree: 12.7%
Advanced degree: 6.1%
**Estimated pubic elementary and secondary
    school finances** *(in millions)*:
    Revenues: $1,376
    Expenditures: $1,376

MARYLAND

GEOGRAPHY:
Area:
total area: 12,297 sq mi
land area: 9,775 sq mi
Capital: Annapolis, (population: 33,187)
Statehood: April 28, 1788 (7th state)
Postal abbreviation: MD
State symbols:
State motto: Fatti Mashii, Parole Femine
(Manly deeds, womanly words)
State song: "Maryland, My Maryland"
State bird: Baltimore Oriole
State flower: Black-Eyed Susan
State tree: White Oak

PEOPLE:
Population: 5,071,604
Change since 1990: 6.1%
Population density: 515.9 per sq mi
% population 65 years and over: 10.8 (1990), 14.8 (2020 est.)

VITAL STATISTICS:
Birth rate: 15.1 *(per 1,000 population)*
Death rate: 8.1 *(per 1,000 population)*
Infant mortality rate: 9.8 *(deaths per 1,000 live births)*

GOVERNMENT:
Governor: Parris N. Glendening (Democrat)
Regular term: 4 years
Current term began: January 1995
Salary: $120,000
Lt. Governor: Kathleen Kennedy Townsend (Democrat)

STATE ECONOMY:
Gross state product: $132.703 billion
State budget: *(in thousands)*
State revenues: $16,429,739
Total expenditures: $15,069,402
Debt at end of fiscal year: $9,438,060
Cash and security holdings: $25,478,485
Chief products:
Agriculture: Chicken, corn, soybeans, tobacco
Fishing Industry: Crab and finfish
Manufacturing: Primary metals, electronic and electrical equipment, food products, transportation equipment
Minerals: Sand, gravel, bituminous coal

PERSONAL FINANCES:
Per capita personal income: $26,333

Median household income: $41,041
Average annual pay: $28,416
Percent of persons in poverty: 10.1%
Homeownership rate: 66.9%

EMPLOYMENT:
Labor force: 2,786,000
Unemployment rate: 4.9%
Total number of businesses: 328,403
Total number of women owned businesses: 121,777
Total number of minority owned businesses: 55,587

CRIME:
Crime rate: 6,294.8 *(per 100,000 people)*
Violent crime: 986.9 *(per 100,000)*
Property crime: 5,307.9 *(per 100,000)*
Total prisoners in custody: 20,256
Prison capacity occupied: 164.7%

HEALTH CARE:
Persons without health insurance coverage: 15.3%
Occupancy rate in community hospitals: 75.2%

EDUCATION:
Current high school completion rate: 92.9%
High school graduates: 28.1%
Some college: 18.6%
Associate degree: 5.2%
Bachelor degree: 15.6%
Advanced degree: 10.9%
Estimated pubic elementary and secondary school finances *(in millions)*:
Revenues: $5,497
Expenditures: $5,452

MASSACHUSETTS

GEOGRAPHY:
Area:
total area: 9,241 sq mi
land area: 7,838 sq mi
Capital: Boston, (population: 547,725)
Statehood: February 6, 1788, (6th state)
Postal abbreviation: MA
State symbols:
State motto: Ense Petit Placidam Sub Libertate Quietem (By the sword we seek peace, but peace only under liberty)
State song: "All Hail to Massachusetts"
State bird: Chickadee
State flower: Mayflower
State tree: American Elm

PEOPLE:
Population: 6,092,352
Change since 1990: 1.3%
Population density: 774.9 per sq mi
% population 65 years and over: 13.5 (1990), 17.4 (2020 est.)

VITAL STATISTICS:
Birth rate: 14.1 *(per 1,000 population)*
Death rate: 9.0 *(per 1,000 population)*
Infant mortality rate: 6.2 *(deaths per 1,000 live births)*

GOVERNMENT:
Governor: Argeo Paul Cellucci* (Republican)
Regular term: 4 years
Current term began: January 1995
Salary: $90,000
Lt. Governor: (vacant)

STATE ECONOMY:
Gross state product: $186.199 billion
State budget: *(in thousands)*
State revenues: $24,100,544
Total expenditures: $24,282,382
Debt at end of fiscal year: $27,734,128
Cash and security holdings: $29,474,541
Chief products:
Agriculture: Cranberries, greenhouse and nursery products, potatoes, dairy products
Manufacturing: Electronic and electrical equipment, watches, cutlery, guns, leather goods
Minerals: Babingtonite

PERSONAL FINANCES:
Per capita personal income: $28,021
Median household income: $38,574
Average annual pay: $31,024
Percent of persons in poverty: 11.0%
Homeownership rate: 61.7%

EMPLOYMENT:
Labor force: 3,189,000
Unemployment rate: 4.3%
Total number of businesses: 442,848
Total number of women owned businesses: 147,572
Total number of minority owned businesses: 20,749

CRIME:
Crime rate: 4,341.6 *(per 100,000 people)*
Violent crime: 687.2 *(per 100,000)*
Property crime: 3,654.4 *(per 100,000)*
Total prisoners in custody: 10,591
Prison capacity occupied: 164.5%

HEALTH CARE:
Persons without health insurance coverage: 11.1%
Occupancy rate in community hospitals: 71.5%

EDUCATION:
Current high school completion rate: 91.2%
High school graduates: 29.7%
Some college: 15.8%
Associate degree: 7.2%
Bachelor degree: 16.6%
Advanced degree: 10.6%
Estimated pubic elementary and secondary school finances *(in millions)*:
Revenues: $6,531
Expenditures: $6,370

---

*Formerly Lt. Governor, Mr. Cellucci became governor on July 29, 1997, when William Weld resigned the post.

MICHIGAN

GEOGRAPHY:
Area:
total area: 96,705 sq mi
land area: 56,809 sq mi
Capital: Lansing, (population: 119,590)
Statehood: January 26, 1837 (26th state)
Postal abbreviation: MI
State symbols:
State motto: Si Quaeris Peninsulam Amoenam Circumspice (If you seek a pleasant peninsula, look about you)
State song: "Michigan, My Michigan"
State bird: Robin
State flower: Apple Blossom
State tree: White Pine

PEOPLE:
Population: 9,594,350
Change since 1990: 3.2%
Population density: 168.1 per sq mi
% Population 65 years and over: 11.9 (1990), 15.2 (2020 est.)

VITAL STATISTICS:
Birth rate: 14.8 *(per 1,000 population)*
Death rate: 8.8 *(per 1,000 population)*
Infant mortality rate: 9.5 *(deaths per 1,000 live births)*

GOVERNMENT:
Governor: John Engler (Republican)
Regular term: 4 years
Current term began: January 1995
Salary: $124,195
Lt. Governor: Connie Binsfeld (Republican)

STATE ECONOMY:
Gross state product: $240.390 billion
State budget: *(in thousands)*
  State revenues: $35,328,334
  Total expenditures: $34,668,698
  Debt at end of fiscal year: $12,535,217
  Cash and security holdings: $39,872,130
Chief products:
  Agriculture: Dairy products, grains, potatoes,
    fruit, corn
  Manufacturing: Automobiles, machinery, fabri-
    cated metals, rubber and plastic products,
    chemicals
  Minerals: Copper and iron ore

PERSONAL FINANCES:
Per capita personal income: $23,915
Median household income: $36,426
Average annual pay: $29,541
Percent of persons in poverty: 12.2%
Homeownership rate: 73.3%

EMPLOYMENT:
Labor force: 4,807,000
Unemployment rate: 4.9%
Total number of businesses: 551,091
  Total number of women owned businesses:
    193,820
  Total number of minority owned businesses:
    31,740

CRIME:
Crime rate: 5,182.8 *(per 100,000 people)*
  Violent crime: 687.8 *(per 100,000)*
  Property crime: 4,495.0 *(per 100,000)*
Total prisoners in custody: 40.352
Prison capacity occupied: 104.5%

HEALTH CARE:
Persons without health insurance coverage: 9.7%
Occupancy rate in community hospitals: 64.6%

EDUCATION:
Current high school completion rate: 89.2%
High school graduates: 32.3%
Some college: 20.4%
Associate degree: 6.7%
Bachelor degree: 10.9%
Advanced degree: 6.4%
Estimated pubic elementary and secondary
  school finances *(in millions)*:
  Revenues: $12,368
  Expenditures: $12,002

MINNESOTA

GEOGRAPHY:
Area:
  total area: 86,943 sq mi
  land area: 79,617 sq mi
Capital: St. Paul, (population: 262,071)
Statehood: May 11, 1858 (32th state)
Postal abbreviation: MN
State symbols:
  State motto: L'Etoile du Nord
    (The star of the north)
  State song: "Hail! Minnesota"
  State bird: Common Loon
  State flower: Pink & White Lady Slipper
  State tree: Norway Pine

PEOPLE:
Population: 4,657,758
Change since 1990: 6.4%
Population density: 57.9 per sq mi
% Population 65 years and over: 12.5 (1990),
  16.9 (2020 est.)

VITAL STATISTICS:
Birth rate: 14.3 *(per 1,000 population)*
Death rate: 8.0 *(per 1,000 population)*
Infant mortality rate: 7.5 *(deaths per 1,000 live
  births)*

GOVERNMENT:
Governor: Arne H. Carlson (Republican)
  Regular term: 4 years
  Current term began: January 1995
  Salary: $117,000
Lt. Governor: Joanne Benson (Republican)

STATE ECONOMY:
Gross state product: $124.641 billion
State budget: *(in thousands)*
  State revenues: $18,329,240
  Total expenditures: $16,379,809
  Debt at end of fiscal year: $4,494,029
  Cash and security holdings: $26,654,673
Chief products:
  Agriculture: Dairy products, grain, cattle,
    livestock
  Manufacturing: Processed food, pulp and paper
    products, electrical and electronic equipment
  Minerals: Iron ore, taconite, granite,
    limestone

PERSONAL FINANCES:
Per capita personal income: $23,971
Median household income: $37,933
Average annual pay: $26,422

Percent of persons in poverty: 9.2%
Homeownership rate: 75.4%

EMPLOYMENT:
Labor force: 2,609,000
Unemployment rate: 4.0%
Total number of businesses: 358,921
   Total number of women owned businesses: 124,143
   Total number of minority owned businesses: 7,449

CRIME:
Crime rate: 4,497.3 *(per 100,000 people)*
   Violent crime: 356.1 *(per 100,000)*
   Property crime: 4,141.2 *(per 100,000)*
Total prisoners in custody: 4,488
Prison capacity occupied: 108.3%

HEALTH CARE:
Persons without health insurance coverage: 8.0%
Occupancy rate in community hospitals: 65.9%

EDUCATION:
Current high school completion rate: 93.2%
High school graduates: 33.0%
Some college: 19.0%
Associate degree: 8.6%
Bachelor degree: 15.6%
Advanced degree: 6.3%
Estimated pubic elementary and secondary school finances *(in millions)*:
   Revenues: $6,641
   Expenditures: $5,682

MISSISSIPPI

GEOGRAPHY:
Area:
   total area: 48,286 sq mi
   land area: 46,914 sq mi
Capital: Jackson, (population: 193,097)
Statehood: December 10, 1817 (20th state)
Postal abbreviation: MS
State symbols:
   State motto: "*Virtute et Armis*" By Valor & Arms
   State song: "Go Mississippi"
   State bird: Northern Mockingbird
   State flower: Southern Magnolia
   State tree: Southern Magnolia

PEOPLE:
Population: 2,716,115
Change since 1990: 5.5%
Population density: 57.5 per sq mi

% population 65 years and over: 12.4 (1990), 16.6 (2020 est.)

VITAL STATISTICS:
Birth rate: 16.0 *(per 1,000 population)*
Death rate: 10.1 *(per 1,000 population)*
Infant mortality rate: 11.5 *(deaths per 1,000 live births)*

GOVERNMENT:
Governor: Kirk Fordice (Republican)
   Regular term: 4 years
   Current term began: January 1996
   Salary: $83,160
Lt. Governor: Ronnie Musgrove (Democrat)

STATE ECONOMY:
Gross state product: $50.587 billion
State budget: *(in thousands)*
   State revenues: $8,300,728
   Total expenditures: $7,413,908
   Debt at end of fiscal year: $1,924,051
   Cash and security holdings: $12,547,784
Chief products:
   Agriculture: Cotton, Soybeans, wheat, rice, corn, poultry, cattle
   Manufacturing: Processed food, pulp and paper products, primary metals, electrical equipment, apparel and textiles, lumber and wood products
   Minerals: Petroleum, natural gas, iron ore, bauxite

PERSONAL FINANCES:
Per capita personal income: $16,683
Median household income: $26,538
Average annual pay: $20,382
Percent of persons in poverty: 23.5%
Homeownership rate: 73.0%

EMPLOYMENT:
Labor force: 1,262,000
Unemployment rate: 6.1%
Total number of businesses: 135,497
   Total number of women owned businesses: 40,879
   Total number of minority owned businesses: 16,386

CRIME:
Crime rate: 4,514.5 *(per 100,000 people)*
   Violent crime: 502.8 *(per 100,000)*
   Property crime: 4,011.7 *(per 100,000)*
Total prisoners in custody: 9,746
Prison capacity occupied: 100.7%

HEALTH CARE:
Persons without health insurance coverage:
19.7%
Occupancy rate in community hospitals: 59.0%

EDUCATION:
Current high school completion rate: 88.8%
High school graduates: 27.5%
Some college: 16.9%
Associate degree: 5.2%
Bachelor degree: 9.7%
Advanced degree: 5.1%
Estimated pubic elementary and secondary
school finances (*in millions*):
Revenues: $2,275
Expenditures: $2,187

MISSOURI

GEOGRAPHY:
Area:
total area: 69,709 sq mi
land area: 68,898 sq mi
Capital: Jefferson City, (population: 35,481)
Statehood: August 10, 1821 (24th state)
Postal abbreviation: MO
State symbols:
State motto: Salus populi Suprema lex esto (Let
the good of the people be the Supreme Law)
State song: "Missouri Waltz"
State bird: Bluebird
State flower: Blossom of the Hawthorn
State tree: Dogwood

PEOPLE:
Population: 5,358,692
Change since 1990: 4.7%
Population density: 77.3 per sq mi
% Population 65 years and over: 14.0 (1990),
17.5 (2020 est.)

VITAL STATISTICS:
Birth rate: 14.4 *(per 1,000 population)*
Death rate: 10.6 *(per 1,000 population)*
Infant mortality rate: 8.4 *(deaths per 1,000 live
births)*

GOVERNMENT:
Governor: Mel Carnahan (Democrat)
Regular term: 4 years
Current term began: January 1997
Salary: $107,269
Lt. Governor: Roger B. Wilson (Democrat)

STATE ECONOMY:
Gross state product: $128.216 billion
State budget: *(in thousands)*
State revenues: $15,586,334
Total expenditures: $12,482,046
Debt at end of fiscal year: $6,714,353
Cash and security holdings: $27,125,007
Chief products:
Agriculture: Soybeans, corn, wheat, cattle, sheep
Manufacturing: Processed food, aerospace
and transportation equipment, rubber,
chemicals
Minerals: Lead, iron ore, limestone

PERSONAL FINANCES:
Per capita personal income: $21,819
Median household income: $34,825
Average annual pay: $24,628
Percent of persons in poverty: 9.4%
Homeownership rate: 70.2%

EMPLOYMENT:
Labor force: 2,898,000
Unemployment rate: 4.6%
Total number of businesses: 348,978
Total number of women owned businesses:
117,885
Total number of minority owned businesses:
15,437

CRIME:
Crime rate: 5,120.5 *(per 100,000 people)*
Violent crime: 663.8 *(per 100,000)*
Property crime: 4,456.8 *(per 100,000)*
Total prisoners in custody: 17,334
prison capacity occupied: 95.4%

HEALTH CARE:
Persons without health insurance coverage:
14.6%
Occupancy rate in community hospitals: 58.7%

EDUCATION:
Current high school completion rate: 90.0%
High school graduates: 33.1%
Some college: 18.4%
Associate degree: 4.5%
Bachelor degree: 11.7%
Advanced degree: 6.1%
Estimated pubic elementary and secondary
school finances (*in millions*):
Revenues: $5,069
Expenditures: $4,646

MONTANA

GEOGRAPHY:
Area:
total area: 147,046 sq mi
land area: 145,556 sq mi
Capital: Helena, (population: 24,569)
Statehood: November 8, 1889 (41st state)
Postal abbreviation: MT
State symbols:
State motto: Oro y Plata (Gold and Silver)
State song: "Montana"
State bird: Western Meadowlark
State flower: Bitterroot
State tree: Ponderosa Pine

PEOPLE:
Population: 879,372
Change since 1990: 10.1%
Population density: 6.0 per sq mi
% population 65 years and over: 13.3 (1990), 16.2 (2020 est.)

VITAL STATISTICS:
Birth rate: 13.5 *(per 1,000 population)*
Death rate: 8.6 *(per 1,000 population)*
Infant mortality rate: 7.4 *(deaths per 1,000 live births)*

GOVERNMENT:
Governor: Marc Racicot (Republican)
Regular term: 4 years
Current term began: January 1997
Salary: $78,245
Lt Governor: Judy Martz (Republican)

STATE ECONOMY:
Gross state product: $16.862 billion
State budget: *(in thousands)*
State revenues: $3,292,673
Total expenditures: $2,987,807
Debt at end of fiscal year: $2,209,910
Cash and security holdings: $6,642,064
Chief products:
Agriculture: Oats, barley, wheat, sugar beets, livestock, cattle
Manufacturing: Lumber and wood products, petroleum, food products
Minerals: Coal, petroleum, natural gas, copper, phosphates, vermiculite, bentonite, sand, gravel, gypsum

PERSONAL FINANCES:
Per capita personal income: $18,445
Median household income: $27,757
Average annual pay: $20,218

Percent of persons in poverty: 15.3%
Homeownership rate: 68.6%

EMPLOYMENT:
Labor force: 447,000
Unemployment rate: 5.3%
Total number of businesses: 76,331
Total number of women owned businesses: 25,310
Total number of minority owned businesses: 1,498

CRIME:
Crime rate: 5,304.9 *(per 100,000 people)*
Violent crime: 170.6 *(per 100,000)*
Property crime: 5,134.4 *(per 100,000)*
Total prisoners in custody: 1,700
Percent of prison capacity occupied: 182.4%

HEALTH CARE:
Persons without health insurance coverage: 12.7%
Occupancy rate in community hospitals: 64.1%

EDUCATION:
Current high school completion rate: 91.6%
High school graduates: 33.5%
Some college: 22.1%
Associate degree: 5.6%
Bachelor degree: 14.1%
Advanced degree: 5.7%
Estimated pubic elementary and secondary school finances (*in millions*):
Revenues: $932
Expenditures: $952

NEBRASKA

GEOGRAPHY:
Area:
total area: 77,358 sq mi
land area: 76,878 sq mi
Capital: Lincoln, (population: 203,076)
Statehood: March 1, 1867 (37th state)
Postal abbreviation: NE
State symbols:
State motto: Equality Before the Law
State song: "Beautiful Nebraska"
State bird: Western Meadowlark
State flower: Goldenrod
State tree: Cottonwood

PEOPLE:
Population: 1,652,093
Change since 1990: 4.7%
Population density: 21.3 per sq mi

% population 65 years and over: 14.1 (1990), 16.8 (2020 est.)

VITAL STATISTICS:
Birth rate: 14.4 *(per 1,000 population)*
Death rate: 9.1 *(per 1,000 population)*
Infant mortality rate: 9.1 *(deaths per 1,000 live births)*

GOVERNMENT:
Governor: E. Benjamin Nelson (Democrat)
Regular term: 4 years
Current term began: January 1995
Salary: $65,000
Lt. Governor: Kim Robak (Democrat)

STATE ECONOMY:
Gross state product: $41.357 billion
State budget: *(in thousands)*
State *revenues:* $4,614,629
Total expenditures: $4,250,378
Debt at end of fiscal year: $1,367,815
Cash and security holdings: $5,521,258
Chief products:
Agriculture: Corn, hay, wheat, sorghum, soybeans, sugar beets, cattle, hogs
Manufacturing: Food processing, machinery, chemicals, printing and publishing, electronic, transportation equipment, metals
Minerals: Petroleum

PERSONAL FINANCES:
Per capita personal income: $21,477
Median household income: $32,929
Average annual pay: $21,500
Persons below poverty level: 9.6%
Homeownership rate: 66.8%

EMPLOYMENT:
Labor force: 913,000
Unemployment rate: 2.9%
Total number of businesses: 124,212
Total number of women owned businesses: 43,637
Total number of minority owned businesses: 3,138

CRIME:
Crime rate: 4,544.5 *(per 100,000 people)*
Violent crime: 382.0 *(per 100,000)*
Property crime: 4,162.5 *(per 100,000)*
Total prisoners in custody: 2,686
Prison capacity occupied: 127.7%

HEALTH CARE:
Persons without health insurance coverage: 9.0%
Occupancy rate in community hospitals: 55.2%

EDUCATION:
Current high school completion rate: 95.9%
High school graduates: 34.7%
Some college: 21.1%
Associate degree: 7.1%
Bachelor degree: 13.1%
Advanced degree: 5.9%
Estimated pubic elementary and secondary school finances (*in millions*):
Revenues: $1,502
Expenditures: $1,593

NEVADA

GEOGRAPHY:
Area:
total area: 110,567 sq mi
land area: 109,806 sq mi
Capital: Carson City, (population: 40,443)
Statehood: October 31, 1864 (36th state)
Postal abbreviation: NV
State symbols:
State motto: All For Our Country
State song: "Home Means Nevada"
State bird: Mountain Bluebird
State flower: Sagebrush
State tree: Pinon Pine and Bristlecone Pine

PEOPLE:
Population: 1,603,163
Change since 1990: 33.4%
Population density: 13.9 per sq mi
% population 65 years and over: 10.5 (1990), 15.5 (2020 est.)

VITAL STATISTICS:
Birth rate: 16.2 *(per 1,000 population)*
Death rate: 8.1 *(per 1,000 population)*
Infant mortality rate: 6.7 *(deaths per 1,000 live births)*

GOVERNMENT:
Governor: Bob Miller (Democrat)
Regular term: 4 years
Current term began: January 1995
Salary: $90,000
Lt. Governor: Lonnie Hammargren, M.D. (Republican)

STATE ECONOMY:
Gross state product: $43.958 billion
State budget: *(in thousands)*
State revenues: $5,477,926
Total expenditures: $4,581,276
Debt at end of fiscal year: $1,996,136
Cash and security holdings: $8,838,965

Chief products:
Agriculture: Hay, dairy products, potatoes, onions, cattle
Manufacturing: Gaming devices, printing and publishing
Minerals: Gold, silver, barite, mercury

PERSONAL FINANCES:
Per capita personal income: $24,390
Median household income: $36,084
Average annual pay: $25,700
Percent of persons in poverty: 11.1%
Homeownership rate: 61.1%

EMPLOYMENT:
Labor force: 844,000
Unemployment rate: 5.4%
Total number of businesses: 87,786
Total number of women owned businesses: 32,430
Total number of minority owned businesses: 8,223

CRIME:
Crime rate: 6,579.3 *(per 100,000 people)*
Violent crime: 945.2 *(per 100,000)*
Property crime: 5,634.2 *(per 100,000)*
Total prisoners in custody: 6,909
Prison capacity occupied: 107.0%

HEALTH CARE:
Persons without health insurance coverage: 18.7%
Occupancy rate in community hospitals: 67.8%

EDUCATION:
Current high school completion rate: 83.4%
High school graduates: 31.5%
Some college: 25.8%
Associate degree: 6.2%
Bachelor degree: 10.1%
Advanced degree: 5.2%
Estimated pubic elementary and secondary school finances (*in millions*):
Revenues: $1,427
Expenditures: $1,403

NEW HAMPSHIRE

GEOGRAPHY:
Area:
total area: 9,283 sq mi
land area: 8,969 sq mi
Capital: Concord, (population: 36,006)
Statehood: June 21, 1788 (9th state)
Postal abbreviation: NH

State symbols:
State motto: Live Free or Die
State song: "Old New Hampshire."
State bird: Purple Finch
State flower: Purple Lilac
State tree: White Birch

PEOPLE:
Population: 1,162,481
Change since 1990: 4.8%
Population density: 128.0 per sq mi
% population 65 years and over: 11.2 (1990), 16.9 (2020 est.)

VITAL STATISTICS:
Birth rate: 13.7 *(per 1,000 population)*
Death rate: 7.8 *(per 1,000 population)*
Infant mortality rate: 5.6 *(deaths per 1,000 live births)*

GOVERNMENT:
Governor: Jeanne Shaheen (Democrat)
Regular term: 2 years
Current term began: January 1997
Salary: $86,235
Senate President: Joseph Delahunty (Republican)

STATE ECONOMY:
Gross state product $29.393 billion
State budget: *(in thousands)*
State revenues: 3,269,799
Total expenditures: $3,095,874
Debt at end of fiscal year: $5,781,281
Cash and security holdings: $8,227,929
Chief products:
Agriculture: Dairy products, sugar, fruits, and vegtables, maple syrup and sugar
Manufacturing: Lumber, paper, pulp, maple syrup, electrical and electric goods
Minerals: Granite

PERSONAL FINANCES:
Per capita personal income: $25,587
Median household income: $39,171
Average annual pay: $25,555
Persons below poverty level: 5.3%
Homeownership rate: 65.0%

EMPLOYMENT:
Labor force: 624,000
Unemployment rate: 4.2%
Total number of businesses: 97,772
Total number of women owned businesses: 31,492
Total number of minority owned businesses: 1,463

CRIME:
Crime rate: 2,655.4 *(per 100,000 people)*

Violent crime: 114.5 *(per 100,000)*
Property crime: 2,540.9 *(per 100,000)*
Total prisoners in custody: 2,066
Prison capacity occupied: 115.6%

HEALTH CARE:
Persons without health insurance coverage: 10.0%
Occupancy rate in community hospitals: 63.7%

EDUCATION:
Current high school completion rate: 86.6%
High school graduates: 31.7%
Some college: 18.0%
Associate degree: 8.1%
Bachelor degree: 16.4%
Advanced degree: 7.9%
Estimated pubic elementary and secondary school finances (*in millions*):
Revenues: $1,224
Expenditures: $1,149

NEW JERSEY

GEOGRAPHY:
Area:
total area: 8,215 sq mi
land area: 7,419 sq mi
Capital: Trenton, (population: 88,675)
Statehood: December 18, 1787 (3rd state)
Postal abbreviation: NJ
State symbols:
State motto: Liberty & Prosperity
State song: "New Jersey Loyalty" (unofficial)
State bird: Eastern Goldfinch
State flower: Purple Violet
State tree: Red Oak

PEOPLE:
Population: 7,987,933
Change since 1990: 3.3%
Population density: 1,070.9 per sq mi
% population 65 years and over: 13.3 (1990), 16.3 (2020 est.)

VITAL STATISTICS:
Birth rate: 15.0 *(per 1,000 population)*
Death rate: 9.2 *(per 1,000 population)*
Infant mortality rate: 8.3 *(deaths per 1,000 live births)*

GOVERNMENT:
Governor: Christine T. Whitman (Republican)

Regular term: 4 years
Current term began: January 1994
Salary: $130,000*
Senate President: Donald T. DiFrancesco (Republican)

STATE ECONOMY:
Gross state product: $254.945 billion
State budget: *(in thousands)*
State revenues: $32,675,210
Total expenditures: $32,605,483
Debt at end of fiscal year: $24,357,951
Cash and security holdings: $51,888,015
Chief products:
Agriculture: Fruits and vegtables, nursery and greenhouse products
Manufacturing: Chemicals, electronic and electrical equipment, clothing, toys, sporting goods, glass and stone products
Minerals: Stone, glass, clay

PERSONAL FINANCES:
Per capita personal income: $29,848
Median household income: $43,924
Average annual pay: $33,439
Percent of persons in poverty: 7.8%
Homeownership rate: 64.6%

EMPLOYMENT:
Labor force: 4,124,000
Unemployment rate: 6.2%
Total number of businesses: 517,204
Total number of women owned businesses: 164,798
Total number of minority owned businesses: 64,074

CRIME:
Crime rate: 4,703.7 *(per 100,000 people)*
Violent crime: 599.8 *(per 100,000)*
Property crime: 4,103.9 *(per 100,000)*
Total prisoners in custody: 19,241
Prison capacity occupied: 138.7%

HEALTH CARE:
Persons without health insurance coverage: 14.2%
Occupancy rate in community hospitals: 77.0%

EDUCATION:
Current high school completion rate: 91.0%
High school graduates: 31.1%
Some college: 15.5%
Associate degree: 5.2%
Bachelor degree: 16.0%
Advanced degree: 8.8%
Estimated public elementary and secondary school finances (*in millions*):

Revenues: $11,705
Expenditures: $11,272

---

*Governor accepts only $85,000

NEW MEXICO

GEOGRAPHY:
Area:
total area: 121,598 sq mi
land area: 121,364 sq mi
Capital: Santa Fe, (population: 55,859)
Statehood: January 6, 1912 (47th state)
Postal abbreviation: NM
State symbols:
State motto: Crescit Eundo (It grows as it goes)
State song: "O, Fair New Mexico"
State bird: Roadrunner
State flower: Yucca
State tree: Pine

PEOPLE:
Population: 1,713,407
Change since 1990: 13.1%
Population density: 13.9 per sq mi
% population 65 years and over: 10.7 (1990), 15.0 (2020 est.)

VITAL STATISTICS:
Birth rate: 17.2 *(per 1,000 population)*
Death rate: 7.4 *(per 1,000 population)*
Infant mortality rate: 8.4 *(deaths per 1,000 live births)*

GOVERNMENT:
Governor: Gary E. Johnson (Republican)
Regular term: 4 years
Current term began: January 1995
Salary: $90,000
Lt. Governor: Walter Bradley (Republican)

STATE ECONOMY:
Gross state product: $37.832 billion
State budget: *(in thousands)*
State revenues: $6,634,459
Total expenditures: $6,363,127
Debt at end of fiscal year: $1,824,098
Cash and security holdings: $15,252,467
Chief products:
Agriculture: Beef, milk, hay
Manufacturing: Food processing, petroleum refining, smelting, construction materials, electronics, precision instruments
Minerals: Oil, natural gas, potash, uranium, coal

PERSONAL FINANCES:
Per capita personal income: $18,206
Median household income: $25,991

Average annual pay: $22,351
Percent of persons in poverty: 25.3%
Homeownership rate: 67.1%

EMPLOYMENT:
Labor force: 800,000
Unemployment rate: 8.1%
Total number of businesses: 107,377
Total number of women owned businesses: 40,636
Total number of minority owned businesses: 26,729

CRIME:
Crime rate: 6,428.0 *(per 100,000 people)*
Violent crime: 819.2 *(per 100,000)*
Property crime: 5,608.8 *(per 100,000)*
Total prisoners in custody: 3,868
Prison capacity occupied: 95.2%

HEALTH CARE:
Persons without health insurance coverage: 25.6%
Occupancy rate in community hospitals: 53.8%

EDUCATION:
Current high school completion rate: 83.7%
High school graduates: 28.7%
Some college: 20.9%
Associate degree: 5.0%
Bachelor degree: 12.1%
Advanced degree: 8.3%
Estimated public elementary and secondary school finances *(in millions)*:
Revenues: $2,106
Expenditures: $1.911

NEW YORK

GEOGRAPHY:
Area:
total area: 53,989 sq mi
land area: 47,224 sq mi
Capital: Albany, (population: 104,828)
Statehood: July 26, 1788, (11th state)
Postal abbreviation: NY
State symbols:
State motto: Excelsior (Ever Upward)
State song: "I Love New York"
State bird: Red-breasted Bluebird
State flower: Rose
State tree: Sugar Maple

PEOPLE:
Population: 18,184,774
Change since 1990: 1.1%
Population density: 384.0 per sq mi

% population that is 65 years and over: 13.0 (1990), 15.8 (2020 est.)

VITAL STATISTICS:
Birth rate: 15.6 *(per 1,000 population)*
Death rate: 9.2 *(per 1,000 population)*
Infant mortality rate: 8.4 *(deaths per 1,000 live births)*

GOVERNMENT:
Governor: George E. Pataki (Republican)
Regular term: 4 years
Current term began: January 1995
Salary: $130,000
Lt. Governor: Betsy McCaughey Ross (Republican)

STATE ECONOMY:
Gross state product: $570.994 billion
State budget: *(in thousands)*
State revenues: $90,997,110
Total expenditures: $81,371,988
Debt at end of fiscal year: $68,465,667
Cash and security holdings: $129,845,301
Chief products:
Agriculture: Dairy Products, cattle, hay, corn, apples, potatoes
Manufacturing: Photographic and optical equipment, primary metals, machinery, paper products
Minerals: Stone, sand, gravel, zinc, salt

PERSONAL FINANCES:
Per capita personal income: $27,678
Median household income: $33,028
Average Annual Pay: $33,439
Percent of persons in poverty: 16.5%
Homeownership rate: 52.7%

EMPLOYMENT:
Labor Force: 8,639,000
Unemployment rate: 6.2%
Total number of businesses: 1,159,700
Total number of women owned businesses: 395,944
Total number of minority owned businesses: 160,751

CRIME:
Crime rate: 4,560.1 *(per 100,000 people)*
Violent crime: 841.9 *(per 100,000)*
Property crime: 3,718.3 *(per 100,000)*
Total prisoners in custody: 66,758
Prison capacity occupied: 130.8%

HEALTH CARE:
Persons without health insurance coverage: 15.2%

Occupancy rate in community hospitals: 82.8%

EDUCATION:
Current high school completion rate: 87.5%
High school graduates: 29.5%
Some college: 15.7%
Associate degree: 6.5%
Bachelor degree: 13.2%
Advanced degree: 9.9%
Estimated public elementary and secondary school finances (*in millions*):
Revenues: $27,302
Expenditures: $25,945

NORTH CAROLINA

GEOGRAPHY:
Area:
total area: 52,672 sq mi
land area: 48,718 sq mi
Capital: Raleigh, (population: 236,707)
Statehood: November 21, 1789 (12th state)
Postal abbreviation: NC
State symbols:
State motto: Esse Quam Videri
(To be rather than to seem)
State song: "The Old North State"
State bird: Cardinal
State flower: Dogwood
State tree: Pine

PEOPLE:
Population: 7,322,870
Change since 1990: 10.4%
Population density: 147.7 per sq mi
% population 65 years and over: 12.1 (1990), 18.1 (2020 est.)

VITAL STATISTICS:
Birth rate: 14.6 *(per 1,000 population)*
Death rate: 9.1 *(per 1,000 population)*
Infant mortality rate: 10.5 *(deaths per 1,000 live births)*

GOVERNMENT:
Governor: James B. Hunt, Jr. (Democrat)
Regular term: 4 years
Current term began: January 1997
Salary: $107,132
Lt. Governor: Dennis A. Wicker (Democrat)

STATE ECONOMY:
Gross state product: $181.521 billion
State budget: *(in thousands)*
State revenues: $22,091,333
Total expenditures: $20,436,613

Debt at end of fiscal year: $4,547,541
Cash and security holdings: $35,305,857
Chief products:
Agriculture: Tobacco, corn, soybeans, sweet
potatoes, peanuts
Manufacturing: Textiles, tobacco, furniture, pulp
and paper products, chemicals, metal
working, plastics, food processing
Minerals: Phosphate, kaolin, mica, feldspar,
granite, copper, limestone, marl

PERSONAL FINANCES:
Per capita personal income: $21,103
Median household income: $31,979
Average annual pay: $23,460
Percent of persons in poverty: 12.6%
Homeownership rate: 70.4%

EMPLOYMENT:
Labor force: 3,796,000
Unemployment rate: 4.3%
Total number of businesses: 439,301
Total number of women owned businesses:
142,516
Total number of minority owned businesses:
37,670

CRIME:
Crime rate: 5,639.5 *(per 100,000 people)*
Violent crime: 646.4 *(per 100,000)*
Property crime: 4,993.1 *(per 100,000)*
Total prisoners in custody: 22,653
Prison capacity occupied: 103.1%

HEALTH CARE:
Persons without health insurance coverage:
14.3%
Occupancy rate in community hospitals: 69.5%

EDUCATION:
Current high school completion rate: 85.3%
High school graduates: 29.0%
Some college: 16.8%
Associate degree: 6.8%
Bachelor degree: 12.0%
Advanced degree: 5.4%
**Estimated public elementary and secondary
school finances** (*in millions*):
Revenues: $6,086
Expenditures: $5,759

NORTH DAKOTA

GEOGRAPHY:
Area:
total area: 70,704 sq mi
land area: 68,994 sq mi

Capital: Bismarck, (population: 49,256)
Statehood: November 2, 1889 (39th state)
Postal abbreviation: ND
State symbols:
State motto: "Liberty and Union Now and For-
ever, One and Inseparable"
State song: North Dakota Hymn
State bird: Western Meadowlark
State flower: Wild Prairie Rose
State tree: American Elm

PEOPLE:
Population: 643,539
Change since 1990: 0.7%
Population density: 9.3 per sq mi
% population 65 years and over: 14.2 (1990), 16.2
(2020 est.)

VITAL STATISTICS:
Birth rate: 13.6 *(per 1,000 population)*
Death rate: 9.6 *(per 1,000 population)*
Infant mortality rate: 7.9 *(deaths per 1,000 live
births)*

GOVERNMENT:
Governor: Edward T. Schafer (Republican)
Regular term: 4 years
Current term began: December 1996
Salary: $73,176
Lt. Governor: Rosemarie Myrdal (Republican)

STATE ECONOMY:
Gross state product: $13.494 billion
State budget: *(in thousands)*
State revenues: $2,448,480
Total expenditures: $2,212,660
Debt at end of fiscal year: $855,350
Cash and security holdings: $3,182,891
Chief products:
Agriculture: Wheat, cattle, grains, sunflower,
seeds, flaxseed, rye, potatoes
Manufacturing: Farm equipment, processed
food
Minerals: Oil, lignite coal, natural gas

PERSONAL FINANCES:
Per capita personal income: $18,625
Median household income: $29,089
Average annual pay: $19,893
Percent of persons in poverty: 12.0%
Homeownership rate: 68.2%

EMPLOYMENT:
Labor force: 343,000
Unemployment rate: 3.1%
Total number of businesses: 48,368

Total number of woman owned businesses:
15,355
Total number of minority owned businesses: 613

CRIME:
Crime rate: 2,866.3 *(per 100,000 people)*
Violent crime: 86.7 *(per 100,000)*
Property crime: 2,779.6 *(per 100,000)*
Total prisoners in custody: 526
Prison capacity occupied: 87.7%

HEALTH CARE:
Persons without health insurance coverage: 8.3%
Occupancy rate in community hospitals: 64.2%

EDUCATION:
Current high school completion rate: 96.6%
High school graduates: 28.0%
Some college: 20.5%
Associate degree: 10.0%
Bachelor degree: 13.5%
Advanced degree: 4.5%
Estimated public elementary and secondary school finances (*in millions*):
Revenues: $626
Expenditures: $569

OHIO

GEOGRAPHY:
Area:
total area: 44,828 sq mi
land area: 40,953 sq mi
Capital: Columbus, (population: 635,913)
Statehood: March 1, 1803 (17th state)
Postal abbreviation: OH
State symbols:
State motto: With God, All Things Are Possible
State song: "Beautiful Ohio"
State bird: Cardinal
State flower: Scarlet Carnation
State tree: Buckeye Tree

PEOPLE:
Population: 11,172,782
Change since 1990: 3.0%
Population density: 272.3 per sq mi
% population 65 years and over: 12.9 (1990), 2.3 (2020 est.)

VITAL STATISTICS:
Birth rate: 14.4 *(per 1,000 population)*
Death rate: 9.5 *(per 1,000 population)*
Infant mortality rate: 9.2 *(deaths per 1,000 live births)*

GOVERNMENT:
Governor: George V. Voinovich (Republican)
Regular term: 4 years
Current term began: January 1995
Salary: $115,752
Lt. Governor: Nancy Hollister (Republican)

STATE ECONOMY:
Gross state product: $274.844 billion
State budget: *(in thousands)*
State revenues: $41,306,049
Total expenditures: $34,990,296
Debt at end of fiscal year: $12,295,305
Cash and security holdings: $100,479,601
Chief products:
Agriculture: Corn, soybeans, wheat, oats, fruit, feed, livestock, poultry
Manufacturing: Rubber products, porcelain, electrical machinery and apparatus, pumps and plumbing equipment
Minerals: Coal, petroleum, natural gas, limestone, sandstone, clays, shales, gypsum, peat, salt

PERSONAL FINANCES:
Per capita personal income: $22,514
Median household income: $34,941
Average annual pay: $26,134
Percent of persons in poverty: 11.5%
Homeownership rate: 69.2%

EMPLOYMENT:
Labor force: 5,643,000
Unemployment rate: 4.9%
Total number of businesses: 666,183
Total number of women owned businesses:
224,693
Total number of minority owned businesses:
33,844

CRIME:
Crime rate: 4,405.2 *(per 100,000 people)*
Violent crime: 482.5 *(per 100,000)*
Property crime: 3,922.7 *(per 100,000)*
Total prisoners in custody: 41,718
Prison capacity occupied: 170.1%

HEALTH CARE:
Persons without health insurance coverage:
11.9%
Occupancy rate in community hospitals: 60.5%

EDUCATION:
Current high school completion rate: 89.6%
High school graduates: 36.3%
Some college: 17.0%
Associate degree: 5.3%
Bachelor degree: 11.1%

Advanced degree: 5.9%
Estimated public elementary and secondary school finances (*in millions*):
Revenues: $11,479
Expenditures: $11,192

OKLAHOMA

GEOGRAPHY:
Area:
total area: 69,903 sq mi
land area: 68,679 sq mi
Capital: Oklahoma City, (population: 463,201)
Statehood: November 16, 1907 (46th state)
Postal abbreviation: OK
State symbols:
State motto: Labor Omnia Vincit
(Labor Conquers All Things)
State song: "Oklahoma"
State bird: Scissor-tailed Flycatcher
State flower: Mistletoe
State tree: Redbud

PEOPLE:
Population: 3,300,902
Change since 1990: 4.9%
Population density: 47.7 per sq mi
% population 65 years and over: 13.4 (1990), 16.5 (2020 est.)

VITAL STATISTICS:
Birth rate: 14.3 *(per 1,000 population)*
Death rate: 10.0 *(per 1,000 population)*
Infant mortality rate: 8.8 *(deaths per 1,000 live births)*

GOVERNMENT:
Governor: Frank Keating (Republican)
Regular term: 4 years
Current terms began: January 1995
Salary: $70,000
Lt. Governor: Mary Fallin (Republican)

STATE ECONOMY:
Gross state product: $66.189 billion
State budget: *(in thousands)*
State revenues: $9,159,948
Total expenditures: $8,989,785
Debt at end of fiscal year: $3,735,682
Cash and security holdings: $12,761,525
Chief products:
Agriculture: Livestock, cattle, wheat, hay, sorghum, peanuts
Manufacturing: Transportation equipment, machinery, fabricated metal products, rubber, and plastic products

Minerals: Natural gas, coal, petroleum, stone, timber

PERSONAL FINANCES:
Per capita personal income: $18,580
Median household income: $26,311
Average annual pay: $22,293
Percent of persons in poverty: 17.1%
Homeownership rate: 68.4%

EMPLOYMENT:
Labor force: 1,577,000
Unemployment rate: 4.1%
Total number of businesses: 246,936
Total number of women owned businesses: 82,894
Total number of minority owned businesses: 12,865

CRIME:
Crime rate: 5,596.8 *(per 100,000 people)*
Violent crime: 664.1 *(per 100,000)*
Property crime: 4,932.7 *(per 100,000)*
Total prisoners in custody: 13,398
Prison capacity occupied: 106.4%

HEALTH CARE:
Persons without health insurance coverage: 19.2%
Occupancy rate in community hospitals: 54.3%

EDUCATION:
Current high school completion rate: 83.1%
High school graduates: 30.5%
Some college: 21.3%
Associate degree: 5.0%
Bachelor degree: 11.8%
Advanced degree: 6.0%
Estimated public elementary and secondary school finances (*in millions*):
Revenues: $3,039
Expenditures: $2,952

OREGON

GEOGRAPHY:
Area:
total area: 97,132 sq mi
land area: 96,002 sq mi
Capital: Salem, (population: 115,912)
Statehood: February 14, 1859 (33rd state)
Postal abbreviation: OR
State symbols:
State motto: She Flies With Her Own Wings
State song: "Oregon, My Oregon"

State bird: Western Meadowlark
State Flower: Oregon Grape
State tree: Douglas Fir

PEOPLE:
Population: 3,203,735
Change since 1990: 12.7%
Population density: 32.7 per sq mi
% population 65 years and over: 13.7 (1990), 16.6 (2020 est.)

VITAL STATISTICS:
Birth rate: 13.7 *(per 1,000 population)*
Death rate: 8.8 *(per 1,000 population)*
Infant mortality rate: 7.2 *(deaths per 1,000 live births)*

GOVERNMENT:
Governor: John A. Kitzhaber (Democrat)
Regular term: 4 years
Current term began: January 1995
Salary: $88,300
Secretary of State: Phil Keisling (Democrat)

STATE ECONOMY:
Gross state product: $74.366 billion
State budget: *(in thousands)*
State revenues: $12,985,916
Total expenditures: $11,029,980
Debt at end of fiscal year: $5,481,572
Cash and security holdings: $17,285,860
Chief products:
Agriculture: Livestock, cattle, wheat, barley, vegetables, fruit
Manufacturing: Lumber, plywood and hardwood, pulp and paper, metals related industries, aluminum
Fishing Industry: Salmon and shellfish
Minerals: Nickel, sand, gravel, cement, pumice

PERSONAL FINANCES:
Per capita personal income: $21,611
Median household income: $36,374
Average annual pay: $24,780
Percent of persons in poverty: 11.2%
Homeownership rate: 63.1%

EMPLOYMENT:
Labor force: 1,721,000
Unemployment rate: 5.9%
Total number of businesses: 238,967
Total number of women owned businesses: 87,970
Total number of minority owned businesses: 10,160

CRIME:
Crime rate: 6,563.9 *(per 100,000 people)*
Violent crime: 522.4 *(per 100,000)*
Property crime: 6,041.5 *(per 100,000)*
Total prisoners in custody: 6,915
Prison capacity occupied: 102.5%

HEALTH CARE:
Persons without health insurance coverage: 12.5%
Occupancy rate in community hospitals: 54.6%

EDUCATION:
Current high school completion rate: 82.9%
High school graduates: 28.9%
Some college: 25.0%
Associate degree: 6.9%
Bachelor degree: 13.6%
Advanced degree: 7.0%
Estimated public elementary and secondary school finances (*in millions*):
Revenues: $3,384
Expenditures: $3,452

PENNSYLVANIA

GEOGRAPHY:
Area:
total area: 46,058 sq mi
land area: 44,820 sq mi
Capital: Harrisburg, (population: 52,376)
Statehood: December 12, 1787 (2nd state)
Postal abbreviation: PA
State symbols:
State motto: Virtue, Liberty, and Independence
State song: "Pennsylvania"
State bird: Ruffed Grouse
State flower: Mountain Laurel
State tree: Hemlock

PEOPLE:
Population: 12,056,112
Change since 1990: 1.5%
Population density: 269.3 per sq mi
% population 65 years and over: 15.3 (1990), 18.2 (2020 est.)

VITAL STATISTICS:
Birth rate: 13.4 *(per 1,000 population)*
Death rate: 10.6 *(per 1,000 population)*
Infant mortality rate: 8.6 *(deaths per 1,000 live births)*

GOVERNMENT:
Governor: Tom Ridge (Republican)

Regular term: 4 years
Current term began: January 1995
Salary: $105,000
Lt. Governor: Mark Schweiker (Republican)

STATE ECONOMY:
Gross state product: $294.431 billion
State budget: *(in thousands)*
State revenues: $40,015,395
Total expenditures: $39,394,469
Debt at end of fiscal year: $14,294,000
Cash and security holdings: $54,888,739
Chief products:
Agriculture: Dairy products, oats, mushrooms, corn, hay, apples, grapes, poultry
Manufacturing: Steel, food processing, chemicals, machinery, electrical and electronic equipment
Minerals: Coal, natural gas, iron ore, limestone, silver, gold, copper, cobalt, zinc, salt

PERSONAL FINANCES:
Per capita personal income: $23,558
Median household income: $34,524
Average annual pay: $26,950
Percent of persons in poverty: 12.2%
Homeownership rate: 71.7%

EMPLOYMENT:
Labor force: 5,903,000
Unemployment rate: 5.3%
Total number of businesses: 728,063
Total number of women owned businesses: 227,500
Total number of minority owned businesses: 32,712

CRIME:
Crime rate: 3,364.9 *(per 100,000 people)*
Violent crime: 427.3 *(per 100,000)*
Property crime: 2,937.6 *(per 100,000)*
Total prisoners in custody: 27,522
Percent of prison capacity occupied: 121.7%

HEALTH CARE:
Persons without health insurance coverage: 9.9%
Occupancy rate in community hospitals: 72.6%

EDUCATION:
Current high school completion rate: 89.7%
High school graduates: 38.6%
Some college: 12.9%
Associate degree: 5.2%
Bachelor degree: 11.3%
Advanced degree: 6.6%
Estimated public elementary and secondary school finances *(in millions):*

Revenues: $13,716
Expenditures: $12,367

PUERTO RICO

GEOGRAPHY:
Area:
total area: 3,508 sq mi
land area: 3,427 sq mi
Capital city: San Juan, (population 437,745)

PEOPLE:
Population: 3,819,023
Population growth rate: 0.18%

VITAL STATISTICS:
Birth rate: 18.0 *(rate per 1,000 population)*
Death rate: 7.8 *(rate per 1,000 population)*
Infant mortality rate: 12.4 *(deaths per 1,000 live births)*
Life expectancy: 73.9

GOVERNMENT:
Type of government: Commonwealth associated with the U.S.
Governor: Governor Pedro Rossello (Democrat and New Progressive Party)
Regular term: 4 years
Current term began: January 1997
Salary: $70,000
Secretary of State: Norma Burgos (New Progressive Party)

ECONOMY:
GDP: $29.7 billion
GDP real growth rate: 4.3%
GDP per capita: $7,800
Inflation Rate *(consumer prices):* 2.9%
National budget:
revenues: $5.1 billion
expenditures: $5.1 billion
Chief Products:
Agriculture: Sugarcane, coffee, pineapples, plantains, bananas; cattle, chickens
Industries: Pharmaceuticals, electronics, apparel, food products, instruments, tourism

PERSONAL FINANCES:
Per capita personal income: $7,296
Average family income: $24,337

EMPLOYMENT:
Average labor force: 1,201,000
Average umemployment rate: 16.8%

RHODE ISLAND

GEOGRAPHY:
Area:
total area: 1,231 sq mi
land area: 1,045 sq mi
Capital: Providence, (population: 150,639)
Statehood: May 29, 1790 (13th state)
Postal abbreviation: RI
State symbols:
State motto: Hope
State song: "Rhode Island"
State bird: Rhode Island Red
State flower: Violet
State tree: Red Maple

PEOPLE:
Population: 990,225
Change since 1990: −1.3%
Population density: 947.2 per sq mi
% population 65 years and over: 14.9 (1990), 17.9 (2020 est.)

VITAL STATISTICS:
Birth rate: 14.0 *(per 1,000 population)*
Death rate: 9.4 *(per 1,000 population)*
Infant mortality rate: 7.3 *(deaths per 1,000 live births)*

GOVERNMENT:
Governor: Lincoln Almond (Republican)
Regular term: 4 years
Current term began: January 1995
Salary: $69,900
Lt. Governor: Bernard Jackvony (Republican)

STATE ECONOMY:
Gross state product: $23.867 billion
State budget: *(in thousands)*
State revenues: $4,156,437
Total expenditures: $4,265,140
Debt at end of fiscal year: $5,515,554
Cash and security holdings: $7,191,691
Chief products:
Agriculture: Nursery and greenhouse products, potatoes, dairy products, poultry
Manufacturing: Jewelry and silverware, textile and clothing, electrical machinery and electronics, ships
Fishing Industry: Shellfish and finfish
Minerals: Granite, limestone, sand, gravel; cumberlandite, bowenite

PERSONAL FINANCES:
Per capita personal income: $23,844
Median household income: $35,359
Average annual pay: $25,454
Percent of persons in poverty: 10.6%
Homeownership rate: 56.6%

EMPLOYMENT:
Labor force: 496,000
Unemployment rate: 5.1%
Total number of businesses: 67, 641
Total number of women owned businesses: 21,353
Total number of minority owned businesses: 3,047

CRIME:
Crime rate: 4,244.5 *(per 100,000 people)*
Violent crime: 368.0 *(per 100,000)*
Property crime: 3,876.6 *(per 100,000)*
Total prisoners in custody: 2,938
Prison capacity occupied: 110.7%

HEALTH CARE:
Persons without health insurance coverage: 12.9%
Occupancy rate in community hospitals: 73.3%

EDUCATION:
Current high school completion rate: 90.7%
High school graduates: 29.5%
Some college: 15.0%
Associate degree: 6.3%
Bachelor degree: 13.5%
Advanced degree: 7.8%
Estimated public elementary and secondary school finances *(in millions)*:
Revenues: $1.061
Expenditures: $1,036

SOUTH CAROLINA

GEOGRAPHY:
Area:
total area: 31,189 sq mi
land area: 30,111 sq mi
Capital: Columbia, (population: 104,104)
Statehood: May 23, 1788 (8th state)
Postal abbreviation: SC
State symbols:
State mottos: Animis Opibusque Parati (Ready In Soul & Resource) *Dum Spiro Spero* (While I Breathe I Hope)
State songs: "Carolina" and "South Carolina on My Mind"
State bird: Carolina Wren
State flower: Carolina Yellow Jessamine
State tree: Palmetto

PEOPLE:
Population: 3,698,746
Change since 1990: 6.1%
Population density: 122.0 per sq mi
% population 65 years and over: 11.3 (1990), 16.8 (2020 est.)

VITAL STATISTICS:
Birth rate: 14.8 *(per 1,000 population)*
Death rate: 8.6 *(per 1,000 population)*
Infant mortality rate: 10.1 *(deaths per 1,000 live births)*

GOVERNMENT:
Governor: David M. Beasley (Republican)
Regular term: 4 years
Current term began: January 1995
Salary: $106,078
Lt. Governor: Bob Peeler (Republican)

STATE ECONOMY:
Gross state product: $79.925 billion
State budget: *(in thousands)*
State revenues: $12,067,916
Total expenditures: $11,623,103
Debt at end of fiscal year: $5,019,617
Cash and security holdings: $16,213,107
Chief products:
Agriculture: Tobacco, soybeans, peaches, wheat, peanuts, watermelon, poultry, cattle
Manufacturing: Textiles, chemicals, apparel
Fishing Industries: Shrimp, crabs, oysters
Minerals: Clay, cement, stone, gravel

PERSONAL FINANCES:
Per capita personal income: $18,998
Median household income: $29,071
Average annual pay: $22,477
Percent of persons in poverty: 19.9%
Homeownership rate: 72.9%

EMPLOYMENT:
Labor force: 1,848,000
Unemployment rate: 6.0%
Total number of businesses: 197,330
Total number of women owned businesses: 64,812
Total number of minority owned businesses: 21,127

CRIME:
Crime rate: 6,063.8 *(per 100,000 people)*
Violent crime: 981.9 *(per 100,000)*
Property crime: 5,081.8 *(per 100,000)*
Total prisoners in custody: 17,359
Prison capacity occupied: 106.4%

HEALTH CARE:
Persons without health insurance coverage: 14.6%
Occupancy rate in community hospitals: 67.3%

EDUCATION:
Current high school completion rate: 87.0%
High school graduates: 29.5%
Some college: 15.8%
Associate degree: 6.3%
Bachelor degree: 11.2%
Advanced degree: 5.4%
Estimated public elementary and secondary school finances (*in millions*):
Revenues: $3,594
Expenditures: $3,287

SOUTH DAKOTA

GEOGRAPHY:
Area:
total area: 77,121 sq mi
land area: 75,896 sq mi
Capital: Pierre, (population: 12,906)
Statehood: November 2, 1889 (40th state)
Postal abbreviation: SD
State symbols:
State motto: Under God the People Rule
State song: "Hail, South Dakota"
State bird: Chinese Ring-Neck Pheasant
State flower: Pasque
State tree: Black Hills Spruce

PEOPLE:
Population: 732,405
Change since 1990: 5.2%
Population density: 9.6 per sq mi
% population 65 years and over: 14.7 (1990), 16.4 (2020 est.)

VITAL STATISTICS:
Birth rate: 15.0 *(per 1,000 population)*
Death rate: 9.5 *(per 1,000 population)*
Infant mortality rate: 9.5 *(deaths per 1,000 live births)*

GOVERNMENT:
Governor: William J. Janklow (Republican)
Regular term: 4 years
Current term began: January 1995
Salary: $84,739
Lt. Governor: Carole Hillard (Republican)

STATE ECONOMY:
Gross state product: $17.250 billion
State budget: *(in thousands)*

State revenues: $2,089,882
Total expenditures: $1,879,678
Debt at end of fiscal year: $1,663,499
Cash and security holdings: $4,705,624
Chief products:
Agriculture: Grains, sunflower seed, livestock,
  cattle, hogs
Manufacturing: Meat processing, industrial
  machinery
Minerals: Rose quartz, gold

PERSONAL FINANCES:
Per capita personal income: $19,576
Median household income: $29,578
Average annual pay: $19,255
Percent of persons in poverty: 14.5%
Homeownership rate: 67.8%

EMPLOYMENT:
Labor force: 390,000
Unemployment rate: 3.2%
Total number of businesses: 57,084
  Total number of women owned businesses:
  18,215
  Total number of minority owned businesses:
  891

CRIME:
Crime rate: 3,060.6 *(per 100,000 people)*
  Violent crime: 207.5 *(per 100,000)*
  Property crime: 2,853.1 *(per 100,000)*
Total prisoners in custody: 1,661
Prison capacity occupied: 109.6%

HEALTH CARE:
Persons without health insurance coverage: 9.4%
Occupancy rate in community hospitals: 60.7%

EDUCATION:
Current high school completion rate: 93.2%
High school graduates: 33.7%
Some college: 18.8%
Associate degree: 7.4%
Bachelor degree: 12.3%
Advanced degree: 4.9%
Estimated public elementary and secondary
  school finances (*in millions*):
  Revenues: $712
  Expenditures: $695

TENNESSEE

GEOGRAPHY:
Area:
  total area: 42,146 sq mi
  land area: 41,219 sq mi
Capital: Nashville, (population: 504,505)
Statehood: June 1, 1796 (16th state)
Postal abbreviation: TN
State symbols:
  State motto: Agriculture and Commerce
  State song: "The Tennessee Waltz"
  State bird: Mockingbird
  State flower: Iris
  State tree: Tulip Popular

PEOPLE:
Population: 5,319,654
Change since 1990: 9.1%
Population density: 127.5 per sq mi
% population that is 65 years and over: 12.6
  (1990), 17.6 (2020 est.)

VITAL STATISTICS:
Birth rate: 14.3 *(per 1,000 population)*
Death rate: 9.6 *(per 1,000 population)*
Infant mortality rate: 9.4 *(deaths per 1,000 live*
  births)

GOVERNMENT:
Governor: Don Sundquist (Republican)
  Regular term: 4 years
  Current term began: January 1995
  Salary: $85,000
Lt. Governor: John S. Wilder (Democrat)

STATE ECONOMY:
Gross state product: $126.539 billion
State budget: *(in thousands)*
  State revenues: $12,899,912
  Total expenditures: $13,432,374
  Debt at end of fiscal year: $2,821,948
  Cash and security holdings: $14,604,755
Chief products:
  Agriculture: Cotton, tobacco, poultry, fruits and
    vegetables, hogs, pigs, soybeans, corn
  Manufacturing: Chemicals, food processing,
    transportation equipment, lumber
  Minerals: Zinc

PERSONAL FINANCES:
Per capita personal income: $21,038
Median household income: $29,015
Average annual pay: $24,106
Percent of persons in poverty: 15.5%
Homeownership rate: 68.8%

EMPLOYMENT:
Labor force: 2,751,000
Unemployment rate: 5.2%
Total number of businesses: 325,371
  Total number of women owned businesses:
  101,134
  Total number of minority owned businesses:
  19,382

CRIME:
Crime rate: 5,362.7 *(per 100,000 people)*
  Violent crime: 771.5 *(per 100,000)*
  Property crime: 4,591.2 *(per 100,000)*
Total prisoners in custody: 12,421
Prison capacity occupied: 95.6%

HEALTH CARE:
Persons without health insurance coverage:
  14.8%
Occupancy rate in community hospitals: 60.7%

EDUCATION:
Current high school completion rate: 82.3%
High school graduates: 30.0%
Some college: 16.9%
Associate degree: 4.2%
Bachelor degree: 10.5%
Advanced degree: 5.4%
Estimated public elementary and secondary
  school finances (*in millions*):
  Revenues: $3,909
  Expenditures: $3,829

TEXAS

GEOGRAPHY:
Area:
  total area: 267,277 sq mi
  land area: 261,914 sq mi
Capital: Austin, (population: 514,013)
Statehood: December 29, 1845 (28th state)
Postal abbreviation: TX
State symbols:
  State motto: Friendship
  State song: "Texas, Our Texas"
  State bird: Mockingbird
  State flower: Bluebonnet
  State tree: Pecan

PEOPLE:
Population: 19,128,261
Change since 1990: 12.6%
Population density: 71.5 per sq mi
% population 65 years and over: 10.1 (1990),
  14.2 (2020 est.)

VITAL STATISTICS:
Birth rate: 17.9 *(per 1,000 population)*
Death rate: 7.5 *(per 1,000 population)*
Infant mortality rate: 7.5 *(deaths per 1,000 live*
  births)

GOVERNMENT:
Governor: George W. Bush, Jr. (Republican)
  Regular term: 4 years
  Current term began: January 1995
  Salary: $99,122
Lt. Governor: Bob Bullock (Democrat)

STATE ECONOMY:
Gross state product: $479.774 billion
State budget: *(in thousands)*
  State revenues: $49,421,533
  Total expenditures: $44,643,310
  Debt at end of fiscal year: $9,921,999
  Cash and security holdings: $80,649,800
Chief products:
  Agriculture: Cotton, sorghum, grains, beef cattle,
    sheep
  Manufacturing: Petroleum, sulfur, petrochemi-
    cals, electronic and electrical machinery
  Minerals: Oil, natural gas

PERSONAL FINANCES:
Per capita personal income: $21,206
Median household income: $32,039
Average annual pay: $25,959
Percent of persons in poverty: 17.4%
Homeownership rate: 61.8%

EMPLOYMENT:
Labor force: 9,748,000
Unemployment rate: 5.6%
Total number of businesses: 1,256,121
  Total number of women owned businesess:
  414,179
  Total number of minority owned businesses:
  241,334

CRIME:
Crime rate: 5,684.3 *(per 100,000 people)*
  Violent crime: 663.9 *(per 100,000)*
  Property crime: 5,020.5 *(per 100,000)*
Total prisoners in custody: 97,650
Prison capacity occupied: 94.6%

HEALTH CARE:
Persons without health insurance coverage:
  24.5%
Occupancy rate in community hospitals: 55.1%

EDUCATION:
Current high school completion rate: 80.5%

High school graduates: 25.6%
Some college: 21.1%
Associate degree: 5.2%
Bachelor degree: 13.9%
Advanced degree: 6.5%
Estimated public elementary and secondary school finances (*in millions*):
  Revenues: $21,584
  Expenditures: $21,120

U T A H

GEOGRAPHY:
Area:
  total area: 84,904 sq mi
  land area: 82,168 sq mi
Capital: Salt Lake City, (population: 171,849)
Statehood: January 4, 1896 (45th state)
Postal abbreviation: UT
State symbols:
  State motto: Industry
  State song: "Utah, We Love Thee"
  State bird: California Gull (Seagull)
  State flower: Sego Lily
  State tree: Blue Spruce

PEOPLE:
Population: 2,000,494
Change since 1990: 16.1%
Population density: 23.7 per sq mi
% population 65 years and over: 8.7 (1990), 12.1 (2020 est.)

VITAL STATISTICS:
Birth rate: 20.0 *(per 1,000 population)*
Death rate: 5.5 *(per 1,000 population)*
Infant mortality rate: 6.0 *(deaths per 1,000 live births)*

GOVERNMENT:
Governor: Michael O. Leavitt (Republican)
  Regular term: 4 years
  Current term began: January 1997
  Salary: $87,600
Lt. Governor: Olene S. Walker (Republican)

STATE ECONOMY:
Gross state product: $41.657 billion
State budget: *(in thousands)*
  State revenues: $6,324,604
  Total expenditures: $5,780,232
  Debt at end of fiscal year: $2,061,145
  Cash and security holdings: $10,798,006
Chief products:
  Agriculture: Livestock, hay, wheat, barley, corn

Manufacturing: Printing and publishing, food processing, rocket engines, fabricated metals, petroleum refining, transportation equipment, computer software and hardware
Minerals: Cooper, beryllium, gold, silver, lead, uranium, coal, petroleum, molybdenum

PERSONAL FINANCES:
Per capita personal income: $18,232
Median household income: $36,480
Average annual pay: $22,811
Percent of persons in poverty: 8.4%
Homeownership rate: 72.7%

EMPLOYMENT:
Labor force: 998,000
Unemployment rate: 3.5%
Total number of businesses: 129,202
  Total number of women owned businesses: 45,626
  Total number of minority owned businesses: 4,352

CRIME:
Crime rate: 6,090.8 *(per 100,000 people)*
  Violent crime: 328.8 *(per 100,000)*
  Property crime: 5,762.0 *(per 100,000)*
Total prisoners in custody: 3,239
Prison capacity occupied: 99.8%

HEALTH CARE:
Persons without health insurance coverage: 11.7%
Occupancy rate in community hospitals: 53.4%

EDUCATION:
Current high school completion rate: 93.9%
High school graduates: 27.2%
Some college: 27.9%
Associate degree: 7.8%
Bachelor degree: 15.4%
Advanced degree: 6.8%
Estimated public elementary and secondary school finances (*in millions*):
  Revenues: $2,100
  Expenditures: $2,146

V E R M O N T

GEOGRAPHY:
Area:
  total area: 9,615 sq mi
  land area: 9,249 sq mi
Capital: Montpelier, (population: 8,392)
Statehood: March 4, 1791, (14th state)

Postal abbreviation: VT
State symbols:
State motto: Freedom and Unity
State song: "Hail, Vermont"
State bird: Hermit Thrush
State flower: Red Clover
State tree: Sugar Maple

PEOPLE:
Population: 588,654
Change since 1990: 4.6%
Population density: 63.2 per sq mi
% population 65 years and over: 11.7 (1990), 16.8 (2020 est.)

VITAL STATISTICS:
Birth rate: 13.0 *(per 1,000 population)*
Death rate: 7.9 *(per 1,000 population)*
Infant mortality rate: 6.7 *(deaths per 1,000 live births)*

GOVERNMENT:
Governor: Howard Dean, M.D. (Democrat)
Regular term: 2 years
Current term began: January 1997
Salary: $80,725
Lt. Governor: Douglas Racine (Democrat)

STATE ECONOMY:
Gross state product: $13.282 billion
State budget: *(in thousands)*
State revenues: $2,073,665
Total expenditures: $2,013,565
Debt at end of fiscal year: $1,667,649
Cash and security holdings: $2,584,566
Chief products:
Agriculture: Dairy products, corn
Manufacturing: Wood and paper products, printing
Minerals: Marble, granite, and slate

PERSONAL FINANCES:
Per capita personal income: $21,231
Median household income: $33,824
Average Annual Pay: $22,964
Percent of persons in poverty: 10.3%
Homeownership rate: 70.3%

EMPLOYMENT:
Labor force: 324,000
Unemployment rate: 4.6%
Total number of businesses: 58,924
Total number of women owned businesses: 21,033
Total number of minority owned businesses: 747

CRIME:
Crime rate: 3,433.7 *(per 100,000 people)*
Violent crime: 118.3 *(per 100,000)*
Property crime: 3,315.4 *(per 100,000)*
Total prisoners in custody: 976
Prison capacity occupied: 99.1%

HEALTH CARE:
Persons without health insurance coverage: 13.2%
Occupancy rate in community hospitals: 64.3%

EDUCATION:
Current high school completion rate: 89.8%
High school graduates: 34.6%
Some college: 14.7%
Associate degree: 7.2%
Bachelor degree: 15.4%
Advanced degree: 8.9%
Estimated public elementary and secondary school finances (*in millions*):
Revenues: $769
Expenditures: $734

VIRGINIA

GEOGRAPHY:
Area:
total area: 42,326 sq mi
land area: 39,589 sq mi
Capital: Richmond, (population: 201,108)
Statehood: June 25, 1788 (10th state)
Postal abbreviation: VA
State symbols:
State motto: Sic Semper Tyrannis (Thus Always to Tyrants)
State song: "Carry Me Back to Old Virginia"
State bird: Cardinal
State flower: Dogwood
State tree: Dogwood

PEOPLE:
Population: 6,675,451
Change since 1990: 7.9%
Population density: 167.1 per sq mi
% population 65 years and over: 10.7 (1990), 15.7 (2020 est.)

VITAL STATISTICS:
Birth rate: 14.7 *(per 1,000 population)*
Death rate: 8.2 *(per 1,000 population)*
Infant mortality rate: 8.7 *(deaths per 1,000 live births)*

GOVERNMENT:
Governor: George Allen (Republican)
Regular term: 4 years
Current term began: January 1994
Salary: $110,000*
Lt. Governor: Donald S. Beyer, Jr (Democrat)

STATE ECONOMY:
Gross state product: $177.708 billion
State budget: *(in thousands)*
State revenues: $18,992,594
Total expenditures: $17,040,384
Debt at end of fiscal year: $8,716,051
Cash and security holdings: $28,745,099
Chief products:
Agriculture: Tobacco, dairy products, vegetables, apples, peaches
Manufacturing: Food processing, tobacco products, textiles, apparel, chemicals, pine timber
Minerals: Coal, stone, clay, sand, gravel

PERSONAL FINANCES:
Per capita personal income: $23,974
Median household income: $36,222
Average annual pay: $26,035
Percent of persons in poverty: 10.2%
Homeownership rate: 68.5%

EMPLOYMENT:
Labor force: 3,389,000
Unemployment rate: 4.4%
Total number of businesses: 391,451
Total number of women owned businesses: 138,494
Total number of minority owned businesses: 46,666

CRIME:
Crime rate: 3,989.2 *(per 100,000 people)*
Violent crime: 361.5 *(per 100,000)*
Property crime: 3,627.7 *(per 100,000)*
Total prisoners in custody: 20,893
Percent of prison capacity occupied: 139.8%

HEALTH CARE:
Persons without health insurance coverage: 13.5%
Occupancy rate in community hospitals: 64.2%

EDUCATION:
Current high school completion rate: 88.6%
High school graduates: 26.6%
Some college: 18.5%

---

*Governor returns 10 percent of his salary.

Associate degree: 5.5%
Bachelor degree: 15.4%
Advanced degree: 9.1%
Estimated public elementary and secondary school finances *(in millions)*:
Revenues: $6,093
Expenditures: $6,435

WASHINGTON

GEOGRAPHY:
Area:
total area: 70,637 sq mi
land area: 66,581 sq mi
Capital: Olympia, (population: 15,003)
Statehood: November 11, 1889 (42nd state)
Postal abbreviation: WA
State symbols:
State motto: Alki (Bye and bye)
State song: "Washington, My Home"
State bird: Willow Goldfinch
State flower: Western Rhododendron
State tree: Western Hemlock

PEOPLE:
Population: 5,532,939
Change since 1990: 13.7%
Population density: 81.6 per sq mi
% population 65 years and over: 11.8 (1990), 15.6 (2020 est.)

VITAL STATISTICS:
Birth rate: 15.0 *(per 1,000 population)*
Death rate: 7.4 *(per 1,000 population)*
Infant mortality rate: 6.4 *(deaths per 1,000 live births)*

GOVERNMENT:
Governor: Gary Locke (Democrat)
Regular term: 4 years
Current term began: January 1997
Salary: $121,000
Lt. Governor: Brad Owen (Democrat)

STATE ECONOMY:
Gross state product: $143.867 billion
State budget: *(in thousands)*
State revenues: $23,575,810
Total expenditures: $21,200,290
Debt at end of fiscal year: $8,820,118
Cash and security holdings: $35,502,317
Chief products:
Agriculture: Wheat, timber, apples, potatoes
Manufacturing: Aircraft and aircraft parts, lumber and wood products, processed food, paper

and allied products, primary metals (aluminum), nonelectrical machinery
Fishing industry: Shrimp, oysters, clams, tuna, halibut, red snapper
Minerals: Lead, zinc, magnesium, gold, coal, sand, gravel

PERSONAL FINANCES:
Per capita personal income: $23,774
Median household income: $35,568
Average annual pay: $26,362
Percent of persons in poverty: 12.5%
Homeownership rate: 63.1%

EMPLOYMENT:
Labor force: 2,887,000
Unemployment rate: 6.5%
Total number of businesses: 372,975
Total number of women owned businesses: 136,377
Total number of minority owned businesses: 25,935

CRIME:
Crime rate: 6,269.8 *(per 100,000 people)*
Violent crime: 484.3 *(per 100,000)*
Property crime: 5,785.5 *(per 100,000)*
Total prisoners in custody: 10,847
Prison capacity occupied: 134.4%

HEALTH CARE:
Persons without health insurance coverage: 12.4%
Occupancy rate in community hospitals: 57.6%

EDUCATION:
Current high school completion rate: 87.3%
High school graduates: 27.9%
Some college: 25.0%
Associate degree: 7.9%
Bachelor degree: 15.9%
Advanced degree: 7.0%
Estimated public elementary and secondary school finances *(in millions)*:
Revenues: $6,301
Expenditures: $6,316

WEST VIRGINIA

GEOGRAPHY:
Area:
total area: 24,231 sq mi
land area: 24,087 sq mi
Capital: Charleston, (population: 57,256)
Statehood: June 20, 1863 (35th state)
Postal abbreviation: WV

State symbols:
State motto: Montani Semper Liberty
(Mountaineers are always free)
State songs: "West Virginia, My Home Sweet Home," "The West Virginia Hills," and "This Is My West Virginia"
State bird: Cardinal
State flower: Big Rhododendron
State tree: Sugar Maple

PEOPLE:
Population: 1,825,754
Change since 1990: 1.8%
Population density: 75.9 per sq mi
% population 65 years and over: 14.9 (1990), 18.5 (2020 est.)

VITAL STATISTICS:
Birth rate: 12.0 *(per 1,000 population)*
Death rate: 11.1 *(per 1,000 population)*
Infant mortality rate: 8.6 *(deaths per 1,000 live births)*

GOVERNMENT:
Governor: Cecil Underwood (Republican)
Regular term: 4 years
Current term began: January 1997
Salary: $70,000
Senate President: Earl Ray Tomblin (Democrat)

STATE ECONOMY:
Gross state product: $34.654 billion
State budget: *(in thousands)*
State revenues: $6,629,138
Total expenditures: $6,261,769
Debt at end of fiscal year: $2,585,972
Cash and security holdings: $6,863,952
Chief products:
Agriculture: Greenhouse products, cattle, poultry
Manufacturing: Chemicals, primary and fabricated metals, transportation equipment
Minerals: Bituminous coal, natural gas, petroleum, limestone, rock-salt

PERSONAL FINANCES:
Per capita personal income: $17,687
Median household income: $24,880
Average annual pay: $22,959
Percent of persons in poverty: 16.7%
Homeownership rate: 74.3%

EMPLOYMENT:
Labor force: 808,000
Unemployment rate: 7.5%
Total number of businesses: 94,912
Total number of women owned businesses: 30,644

Total number of minority owned businesses:
2,070

CRIME:
Crime rate: 2,458.2 *(per 100,000 people)*
  Violent crime: 210.2 *(per 100,000)*
  Property crime: 2,248.0 *(per 100,000)*
Total prisoners in custody: 1,865
Prison capacity occupied: 88.8%

HEALTH CARE:
Persons without health insurance coverage:
  15.3%
Occupancy rate in community hospitals: 62.0%

EDUCATION:
Current high school completion rate: 85.6%
High school graduates: 36.6%
Some college: 13.2%
Associate degree: 3.8%
Bachelor degree: 7.5%
Advanced degree: 4.8%
Estimated public elementary and secondary
  school finances (*in millions*):
  Revenues: $2,115
  Expenditures: $2,088

W I S C O N S I N

GEOGRAPHY:
Area:
  total area: 65,499 sq mi
  land area: 54,314 sq mi
Capital: Madison, (population: 194,586)
Statehood: May 29, 1848 (30th state)
Postal abbreviation: WI
State symbols:
  State motto: Forward
  State song: "On, Wisconsin!"
  State bird: Robin
  State flower: Wood Violet
  State tree: Sugar Maple

PEOPLE:
Population: 5,159,795
Change since 1990: 5.5%
Population density: 94.3 per sq mi
% population 65 years and over: 13.3 (1990), 17.3
  (2020 est.)

VITAL STATISTICS:
Birth rate: 13.8 *(per 1,000 population)*
Death rate: 8.8 *(per 1,000 population)*
Infant mortality rate: 7.9 *(deaths per 1,000 live*
  births)

GOVERNMENT:
Governor: Tommy G. Thompson (Republican)
  Regular term: 4 years
  Current term began: January 1995
  Salary: $101,861
Lt. Governor: Scott McCallum (Republican)

STATE ECONOMY:
Gross state product: $125.321 billion
State budget: *(in thousands)*
  State revenues: $16,826,271
  Total expenditures: $16,301,863
  Debt at end of fiscal year: $8,235,991
  Cash and security holdings: $37,784,496
Chief products:
  Agriculture: Dairy products, livestock
  Manufacturing: Food products, industrial
    machinery and equipment, paper products,
    printing and publishing
  Minerals: Stone, sand/gravel, lime

PERSONAL FINANCES:
Per capita personal income: $22,261
Median household income: $40,955
Average annual pay: $24,324
Percent of persons in poverty: 8.5%
Homeownership rate: 68.2%

EMPLOYMENT:
Labor force: 2,918,000
Unemployment rate: 3.5%
Total number of businesses: 300,348
  Total number of women owned businesses:
    99,357
  Total number of minority owned businesses:
    7,619

CRIME:
Crime rate: 3,885.7 *(per 100,000 people)*
  Violent crime: 281.1 *(per 100,000)*
  Property crime: 3,604.6 *(per 100,000)*
Total prisoners in custody: 10,020
Prison capacity occupied: 147.8%

HEALTH CARE:
Persons without health insurance coverage: 7.3%
Occupancy rate in community hospitals:
  63.4%

EDUCATION:
Current high school completion rate: 93.4%
High school graduates: 37.1%
Some college: 16.7%
Associate degree: 7.1%
Bachelor degree: 12.1%
Advanced degree: 5.6%
Estimated public elementary and secondary
  school finances (*in millions*):

Revenues: $6,498
Expenditures: $6,009

WYOMING

GEOGRAPHY:
Area:
total area: 97,818 sq mi
land area: 97,105 sq mi
Capital: Cheyenne, (population: 5,839)
Statehood: July 10, 1890 (44th state)
Postal abbreviation: WY
State symbols:
State motto: Equal Rights
State song: "Wyoming"
State bird: Meadowlark
State flower: Indian Paintbrush
State tree: Plains Cottonwood

PEOPLE:
Population: 481,400
Change since 1990: 6.1%
Population density: 4.9 per sq mi
% population 65 years and over: 10.4 (1990), 11.2 (2020 est.)

VITAL STATISTICS:
Birth rate: 14.0 *(per 1,000 population)*
Death rate: 7.4 *(per 1,000 population)*
Infant mortality rate: 7.9 *(deaths per 1,000 live births)*

GOVERNMENT:
Governor: Jim Geringer (Republican)
Regular term: 4 years
Current term began: January 1995
Salary: $92,000
Secretary of State: Diana Ohman (Republican)

STATE ECONOMY:
Gross state product: $15.660 billion
State budget: *(in thousands)*
State revenues: $2,239,881
Total expenditures: $2,045,221
Debt at end of fiscal year: $788,132
Cash and security holdings: $6,057,934
Chief products:
Agriculture: Barley, wheat, corn, hay, oats, sugar beets, dry beans, potatoes

Manufacturing: Wool, petroleum refining, chemicals, fertilizer, glass, electrical energy
Minerals: Coal, petroleum, natural-gas, uranium, bentonite, trona, iron-ore

PERSONAL FINANCES:
Per capita personal income: $20,684
Median household income: $31,529
Average annual pay: $22,054
Percent of persons in poverty: 12.2%
Homeownership rate: 68.0%

EMPLOYMENT:
Labor force: 258,000
Unemployment rate: 5.0%
Total number of businesses: 40,696
Total number of women owned businesses: 14,617
Total number of minority owned businesses: 1,195

CRIME:
Crime rate: 4,320.2 *(per 100,000 people)*
Violent crime: 254.2 *(per 100,000)*
Property crime: 4,066.0 *(per 100,000)*
Total prisoners in custody: 1,065
Prison capacity occupied: 106.2%

HEALTH CARE:
Persons without health insurance coverage: 15.9%
Occupancy rate in community hospitals: 48.5%

EDUCATION:
Current high school completion rate: 91.6%
High school graduates: 33.2%
Some college: 24.2%
Associate degree: 6.9%
Bachelor degree: 13.1%
Advanced degree: 5.7%
Estimated public elementary and secondary school finances (*in millions*):
Revenues: $693
Expenditures: $628

Sources: U.S. Census Bureau, U.S. Bureau of Economic Analysis. National Center for Health Statistics, Council of State Governments, Bureau of Justice Statistics, National Governors' Association and individual states

Compiled by Suzanne Vranica

Population of U.S. Metropolitan Areas

Resident Population and Change for Metropolitan Areas in the U.S. April 1, 1990 to July 1, 1994

Metropolitan area	April 1, 1990 census	July 1, 1994 estimate	Change 1990–94 Number	Change 1990–94 %	CMSA/MSA rank Population 1990	CMSA/MSA rank Population 1994	CMSA/MSA rank % change 1990–94
Abilene, TX MSA	119,655	121,904	2,249	1.9%	221	225	208%
Albany, GA MSA	112,571	116,970	4,399	3.9	232	235	163
Albany-Schenectady-Troy, NY MSA	861,623	875,240	13,617	1.6	49	52	218
Albuquerque, NM MSA	589,131	645,533	56,402	9.6	66	62	51
Alexandria, LA MSA	131,556	126,480	(5,076)	-3.9	202	219	271
Allentown-Bethlehem-Easton, PA MSA	595,208	611,765	16,557	2.8	64	66	194
Altoona, PA MSA	130,542	131,820	1,278	1.0	207	212	229
Amarillo, TX MSA	187,514	197,039	9,525	5.1	157	157	127
Anchorage, AK MSA	226,338	253,649	27,311	12.1	141	138	23
Anniston, AL MSA	116,032	116,874	842	0.7	227	236	235
Appleton-Oshkosh-Neenah, WI MSA	315,121	332,186	17,065	5.4	113	115	113
Asheville, NC MSA	191,772	203,544	11,772	6.1	153	153	90
Athens, GA MSA	126,262	133,325	7,063	5.6	212	210	109
Atlanta, GA MSA	2,959,500	3,330,997	371,497	12.6	13	12	18
Augusta-Aiken, GA-SC MSA	415,220	448,434	33,214	8.0	85	83	66
Austin-San Marcos, TX MSA	846,227	963,981	117,754	13.9	52	48	14
Bakersfield, CA MSA	544,981	609,332	64,351	11.8	70	68	25
Bangor, ME MSA	91,629	90,306	(1,323)	-1.4	258	258	263
Barnstable-Yarmouth, MA MSA	134,954	142,640	7,686	5.7	198	197	104
Baton Rouge, LA MSA	528,261	558,145	29,884	5.7	71	71	107
Beaumont-Port Arthur, TX MSA	361,218	372,735	11,517	3.2	101	102	183
Bellingham, WA MSA	127,780	145,409	17,629	13.8	210	196	15
Benton Harbor, MI MSA	161,378	161,737	359	0.2	171	177	245
Billings, MT MSA	113,419	122,765	9,346	8.2	231	221	62
Biloxi-Gulfport-Pascagoula, MS MSA	312,368	339,144	26,776	8.6	115	114	58
Binghamton, NY MSA	264,497	261,962	(2,535)	-1.0	127	135	260
Birmingham, AL MSA	839,942	872,222	32,280	3.8	53	55	165
Bismarck, ND MSA	83,831	88,155	4,324	5.2	263	261	123
Bloomington, IN MSA	108,978	113,833	4,855	4.5	237	240	147
Bloomington-Normal, IL MSA	129,180	137,579	8,399	6.5	209	206	86
Boise City, ID MSA	295,851	347,773	51,922	17.6	117	109	5
Boston-Worcester-Lawrence, MA-NH-ME-CT CMSA	5,455,403	5,497,284	41,881	0.8	7	7	233
Boston, MA-NH MSA	3,227,707	3,240,150	12,443	0.4	–	–	–
Brockton, MA PMSA	236,409	239,073	2,664	1.1	–	–	–
Fitchburg-Leominster, MA PMSA	138,165	135,889	(2,276)	-1.6	–	–	–
Lawrence, MA-NH PMSA	353,232	364,425	11,193	3.2	–	–	–

Metropolitan area	April 1, 1990 census	July 1, 1994 estimate	Change 1990–94		CMSA/MSA rank		
					Population		% change
			Number	%	1990	1994	1990–94
Lowell, MA-NH PMSA	280,578	285,110	4,532	1.6%	–	–	–%
Manchester, NH PMSA	173,783	177,470	3,687	2.1	–	–	–
Nashua, NH PMSA	168,233	175,805	7,572	4.5	–	–	–
New Bedford, MA PMSA	175,641	172,234	(3,407)	-1.9	–	–	–
Portsmouth-Rochester, NH-ME PMSA	223,271	221,954	(1,317)	-0.6	–	–	–
Worcester, MA-CT PMSA	478,384	485,174	6,790	1.4	–	–	–
Brownsville-Harlingen-San Benito, TX MSA	260,120	299,594	39,474	15.2	131	122	7
Bryan-College Station, TX MSA	121,862	130,389	8,527	7.0	217	214	79
Buffalo-Niagara Falls, NY MSA	1,189,340	1,189,237	(103)	0.0	33	34	247
Burlington, VT MSA	151,506	158,096	6,590	4.3	178	182	151
Canton-Massillon, OH MSA	394,106	402,465	8,359	2.1	93	95	203
Casper, WY MSA	61,226	63,886	2,660	4.3	270	270	152
Cedar Rapids, IA MSA	168,767	176,814	8,047	4.8	168	166	138
Champaign-Urbana, IL MSA	173,025	167,487	(5,538)	-3.2	165	171	270
Charleston, WV MSA	250,454	254,756	4,302	1.7	136	137	215
Charleston-North Charleston, SC MSA	506,877	522,274	15,397	3.0	73	73	186
Charlotte-Gastonia-Rock Hill, NC-SC MSA	1,162,140	1,260,390	98,250	8.5	34	35	61
Charlottesville, VA MSA	131,373	140,675	9,302	7.1	204	201	78
Chattanooga, TN-GA MSA	424,347	439,189	14,842	3.5	83	88	170
Cheyenne, WY	73,142	78,039	4,897	6.7	269	269	83
Chicago-Gary-Kenosha, IL-IN-WI CMSA	8,239,820	8,526,804	286,984	3.5	3	3	171
Chicago, IL PMSA	7,410,858	7,667,826	256,968	3.5	–	–	–
Gary, IN PMSA	604,526	619,880	15,354	2.5	–	–	–
Kankakee, IL PMSA	96,255	101,288	5,033	5.2	–	–	–
Kenosha, WI PMSA	128,181	137,810	9,629	7.5	–	–	–
Chico-Paradise, CA MSA	182,120	192,253	10,133	5.6	160	162	110
Cincinnati-Hamilton, OH-KY-IN CMSA	1,817,569	1,894,071	76,502	4.2	22	23	157
Cincinnati, OH-KY-IN PMSA	1,526,090	1,581,228	55,138	3.6	–	–	–
Hamilton-Middletown, OH PMSA	291,479	312,843	21,364	7.3	–	–	–
Clarksville-Hopkinsville, TN-KY MSA	169,439	186,017	16,578	9.8	167	164	47
Cleveland-Akron, OH CMSA	2,859,644	2,898,855	39,211	1.4	14	14	220
Akron, OH PMSA	657,575	676,815	19,240	2.9	–	–	–
Cleveland-Lorain-Elyria, OH PMSA	2,202,069	2,222,040	19,971	0.9	–	–	–
Colorado Springs, CO MSA	397,014	452,424	55,410	14.0	91	81	13
Columbia, MO MSA	112,379	121,478	9,099	8.1	233	226	63
Columbia, SC MSA	453,932	486,339	32,407	7.1	79	78	77

Metropolitan area	April 1, 1990 census	July 1, 1994 estimate	Change 1990–94		CMSA/MSA rank		
					Population		% change
			Number	%	1990	1994	1990–94
Columbus, GA-AL MSA	260,862	274,134	13,272	5.1%	130	134	125%
Columbus, OH MSA	1,345,450	1,422,875	77,425	5.8	29	30	103
Corpus Christi, TX MSA	349,894	375,686	25,792	7.4	104	101	73
Cumberland, MD-WV MSA	101,643	101,107	(536)	-0.5	246	250	255
Dallas-Fort Worth, TX CMSA	4,037,282	4,362,483	325,201	8.1	9	9	65
Dallas, TX PMSA	2,676,248	2,898,169	221,921	8.3	–	–	–
Fort Worth-Arlington, TX PMSA	1,361,034	1,464,314	103,280	7.6	–	–	–
Danville, VA MSA	108,728	109,961	1,233	1.1	238	242	226
Davenport-Moline-Rock Island, IA-IL MSA	350,855	357,775	6,920	2.0	103	107	207
Dayton-Springfield, OH MSA	951,270	956,382	5,112	0.5	43	49	238
Daytona Beach, FL MSA	399,438	440,495	41,057	10.3	88	87	40
Decatur, AL MSA	131,556	138,617	7,061	5.4	202	205	116
Decatur, IL MSA	117,206	116,588	(618)	-0.5	224	237	254
Denver-Boulder-Greeley, CO CMSA	1,980,140	2,189,994	209,854	10.6	21	20	33
Boulder-Langmont, CO PMSA	225,339	249,625	24,286	10.8	–	–	–
Denver, CO PMSA	1,622,980	1,796,255	173,275	10.7	–	–	–
Greeley, CO PMSA	131,821	144,114	12,293	9.3	–	–	–
Des Moines, IA	392,928	416,485	23,557	6.0	94	92	94
Detroit-Ann Arbor-Flint, MI CMSA	5,187,171	5,255,700	68,529	1.3	8	8	221
Ann Arbor, MI PMSA	490,058	515,295	25,237	5.1	–	–	–
Detroit, MI PMSA	4,266,654	4,307,109	40,455	0.9	–	–	–
Flint, MI PMSA	430,459	433,296	2,837	0.7	–	–	–
Dothan, AL MSA	130,964	134,498	3,534	2.7	206	209	196
Dover, DE MSA	110,993	119,952	8,959	8.1	235	231	64
Dubuque, IA MSA	86,403	88,215	1,812	2.1	261	260	204
Duluth-Superior, MN-WI MSA	239,971	240,919	948	0.4	139	141	240
Eau Claire, WI MSA	137,543	141,945	4,402	3.2	196	199	180
El Paso, TX MSA	591,610	664,813	73,203	12.4	65	60	21
Elkhart-Goshen, IN MSA	156,198	163,995	7,797	5.0	174	174	132
Elmira, NY MSA	95,195	94,528	(667)	-0.7	254	256	258
Enid, OK MSA	56,735	56,932	197	0.3	271	271	241
Erie, PA MSA	275,572	280,320	4,748	1.7	125	131	214
Eugene-Springfield, OR MSA	282,912	298,999	16,087	5.7	123	123	105
Evansville-Henderson, IN-KY MSA	278,990	286,628	7,638	2.7	124	127	195
Fargo-Moorhead, ND-MN MSA	153,296	161,644	8,348	5.4	176	178	112
Fayetteville, NC MSA	274,713	286,372	11,659	4.2	126	128	155
Fayetteville-Springdale-Rogers, AR MSA	210,908	242,468	31,560	15.0	148	140	8
Flagstaff, AZ-UT MSA	101,760	114,092	12,332	12.1	245	239	22
Florence, AL MSA	131,327	135,688	4,361	3.3	205	207	177

Metropolitan area	April 1, 1990 census	July 1, 1994 estimate	Change 1990–94		CMSA/MSA rank		
					Population		% change
			Number	%	1990	1994	1990–94
Florence, SC MSA	114,344	121,167	6,823	6.0%	230	227	96%
Fort Collins-Loveland, CO MSA	186,136	212,352	26,216	14.1	158	150	11
Fort Myers-Cape Coral, FL MSA	335,113	367,436	32,323	9.6	110	104	50
Fort Pierce-Port St. Lucie, FL MSA	251,071	278,281	27,210	10.8	135	132	32
Fort Smith, AR-OK MSA	175,911	185,124	9,213	5.2	163	165	120
Fort Walton Beach, FL MSA	143,777	160,812	17,035	11.8	190	179	24
Fort Wayne, IN MSA	456,281	469,065	12,784	2.8	78	79	193
Fresno, CA MSA	755,580	834,663	79,083	10.5	56	56	37
Gadsden, AL MSA	99,840	100,427	587	0.6	248	251	236
Gainesville, FL MSA	181,596	193,054	11,458	6.3	161	161	89
Glens Falls, NY MSA	118,539	122,124	3,585	3.0	223	224	188
Goldsboro, NC MSA	104,666	109,255	4,589	4.4	242	243	149
Grand Forks, ND-MN MSA	103,272	103,619	347	0.3	244	248	242
Grand Junction, CO MSA	93,145	103,633	10,488	11.3	257	247	27
Grand Rapids-Muskegon-Holland, MI MSA	937,891	984,990	47,099	5.0	45	44	130
Great Falls, MT MSA	77,691	81,167	3,476	4.5	267	267	146
Green Bay, WI MSA	194,594	207,269	12,675	6.5	150	152	85
Greensboro-Winston-Salem-High Point, NC MSA	1,050,304	1,107,051	56,747	5.4	39	38	114
Greenville, NC MSA	108,480	116,342	7,862	7.2	239	238	74
Greenville-Spartanburg-Anderson, SC MSA	830,539	873,356	42,817	5.2	55	54	124
Harrisburg-Lebanon-Carlisle, PA MSA	587,986	609,715	21,729	3.7	67	67	167
Hartford, CT MSA	1,157,585	1,151,413	(6,172)	-0.5	35	36	256
Hattiesburg, MS MSA	98,738	103,676	4,938	5.0	249	246	131
Hickory-Morganton-Lenoir, NC MSA	292,405	305,779	13,374	4.6	120	121	144
Honolulu, HI MSA	836,231	847,330	38,099	4.6	54	53	145
Houma, LA MSA	182,842	187,271	4,429	2.4	159	163	200
Houston-Galveston-Brazoria, TX CMSA	3,731,029	4,098,776	367,747	9.9	10	10	46
Brazoria, TX PMSA	191,707	211,526	19,819	10.3	–	–	–
Galveston-Texas City, TX PMSA	217,396	234,688	17,292	8.0	–	–	–
Houston, TX PMSA	3,321,926	3,652,562	330,636	10.0	–	–	–
Huntington-Ashland, WV-KY-OH MSA	312,529	316,466	3,937	1.3	114	116	225
Huntsville, AL MSA	293,047	316,134	23,087	7.9	118	118	67
Indianapolis, IN MSA	1,380,491	1,461,693	81,202	5.9	28	28	99
Iowa City, IA MSA	96,119	100,003	3,884	4.0	253	252	161
Jackson, MI MSA	149,756	153,290	3,534	2.4	183	188	202
Jackson, MS MSA	395,396	411,868	16,472	4.2	92	93	158
Jackson, TN MSA	77,982	82,557	4,575	5.9	266	266	100
Jacksonville, FL MSA	906,727	971,829	65,102	7.2	46	46	76
Jacksonville, NC MSA	149,838	146,326	(3,512)	-2.3	182	194	268

| Metropolitan area | April 1, 1990 census | July 1, 1994 estimate | Change 1990–94 | | CMSA/MSA rank | | |
			Number	%	Population 1990	1994	% change 1990–94
Jamestown, NY MSA	141,895	142,170	275	0.2%	193	198	246%
Janesville-Beloit, WI MSA	139,510	145,959	6,449	4.6	194	195	143
Johnson City-Kingsport-Bristol, TN-VA MSA	436,047	450,641	14,594	3.3	80	82	176
Johnstown, PA MSA	241,280	239,765	(1,515)	-0.6	138	142	257
Joplin, MO MSA	134,910	141,743	6,833	5.1	199	200	128
Kalamazoo-Battle Creek, MI MSA	429,453	442,637	13,184	3.1	82	86	185
Kansas City, MO-KS MSA	1,582,874	1,647,241	64,367	4.1	25	24	160
Killeen-Temple, TX MSA	255,299	287,171	31,872	12.5	133	126	19
Knoxville, TN MSA	585,960	631,107	45,147	7.7	69	64	69
Kokomo, IN MSA	96,946	99,343	2,397	2.5	252	253	199
La Crosse, WI-MN MSA	116,401	120,120	3,719	3.2	226	229	182
Lafayette, IN MSA	161,572	166,737	5,165	3.2	170	172	181
Lafayette, LA MSA	345,053	361,338	16,285	4.7	105	105	140
Lake Charles, LA MSA	168,134	173,337	5,203	3.1	169	169	184
Lakeland-Winter Haven, FL MSA	405,382	429,578	24,196	6.0	87	91	95
Lancaster, PA MSA	422,822	442,687	19,865	4.7	84	85	141
Lansing-East Lansing, MI MSA	432,674	436,129	3,455	0.8	81	89	232
Laredo, TX MSA	133,239	163,066	29,827	22.4	201	175	2
Las Cruces, NM MSA	135,510	155,469	19,959	14.7	197	187	9
Las Vegas, NV-AZ MSA	852,646	1,076,267	223,621	26.2	51	40	1
Lawrence, KS MSA	81,798	88,032	6,234	7.6	264	262	71
Lawton, OK MSA	111,486	117,627	6,141	5.5	234	234	111
Lewiston-Auburn, ME MSA	93,679	91,723	(1,956)	-2.1	256	257	267
Lexington, KY MSA	405,936	430,845	24,909	6.1	86	90	91
Lima, OH MSA	154,340	155,856	1,516	1.0	175	186	228
Lincoln, NE MSA	213,641	225,746	12,105	5.7	147	146	106
Little Rock-North Little Rock, AR MSA	513,026	537,544	24,518	4.8	72	72	137
Longview-Marshall, TX MSA	193,801	201,336	7,535	3.9	152	155	164
Los Angeles-Riverside-Orange County, CA CMSA	14,531,529	15,302,275	770,746	5.3	2	2	119
Los Angeles-Long Beach, CA PMSA	8,863,052	9,149,812	286,760	3.2	–	–	–
Orange County, CA PMSA	2,410,668	2,543,164	132,496	5.5	–	–	–
Riverside-San Bernardino, CA PMSA	2,588,793	2,906,558	317,765	12.3	–	–	–
Ventura, CA PMSA	669,016	702,741	33,725	5.0	–	–	–
Louisville, KY-IN MSA	949,012	980,855	31,843	3.4	44	45	175
Lubbock, TX MSA	222,636	230,527	7,891	3.5	144	144	169
Lynchburg, VA MSA	193,928	202,894	8,966	4.6	151	154	142
Macon, GA MSA	291,079	307,420	16,341	5.6	121	120	108
Madison, WI MSA	367,085	390,262	23,177	6.3	99	98	88
Mansfield, OH MSA	174,007	175,570	1,563	0.9	164	168	231
McAllen-Edinburg-Mission, TX MSA	383,545	461,025	77,480	20.2	95	80	3
Medford-Ashland, OR MSA	146,387	162,370	15,983	10.9	188	176	31

Metropolitan area	April 1, 1990 census	July 1, 1994 estimate	Change 1990–94		CMSA/MSA rank		
			Number	%	Population 1990	1994	% change 1990–94
Melbourne-Titusville-Palm Bay, FL MSA	398,978	443,498	44,520	11.2%	90	84	28%
Memphis, TN-AR-MS MSA	1,007,306	1,056,096	48,790	4.8	40	42	134
Merced, CA MSA	178,403	196,851	18,448	10.3	162	158	39
Miami-Fort Lauderdale, FL CMSA	3,192,725	3,408,038	215,313	6.7	11	11	82
Fort Lauderdale, FL PMSA	1,255,531	1,382,991	127,460	10.2	–	–	–
Miami, FL PMSA	1,937,194	2,025,047	87,853	4.5	–	–	–
Milwaukee-Racine, WI CMSA	1,607,183	1,637,278	30,095	1.9	24	25	210
Milwaukee-Waukesha, WI PMSA	1,432,149	1,455,575	23,426	1.6	–	–	–
Racine, WI PMSA	175,034	181,703	6,669	3.8	–	–	–
Minneapolis-St. Paul, MN-WI MSA	2,538,776	2,688,455	149,679	5.9	15	15	97
Mobile, AL MSA	476,923	512,150	35,227	7.4	77	76	72
Modesto, CA MSA	370,522	406,765	36,243	9.8	97	94	48
Monroe, LA MSA	142,191	146,446	4,255	3.0	192	193	190
Montgomery, AL MSA	292,517	312,020	19,503	6.7	119	119	84
Muncie, IN MSA	119,659	119,244	(415)	-0.3	220	232	252
Myrtle Beach, SC MSA	144,053	152,877	8,824	6.1	189	189	92
Naples, FL MSA	152,099	176,422	24,323	16.0	177	167	6
Nashville, TN MSA	985,026	1,069,648	84,622	8.6	41	41	57
New London-Norwich, CT-RI MSA	290,734	285,029	(5,705)	-2.0	122	129	266
New Orleans, LA MSA	1,285,262	1,308,904	23,642	1.8	31	32	211
New York-Northern New Jersey-Long Island, NY-NJ-CT-PA CMSA	19,549,649	19,796,430	246,781	1.3	1	1	223
Bergen-Passaic, NJ PMSA	1,278,682	1,304,165	25,483	2.0	–	–	–
Bridgeport, CT PMSA	443,722	442,681	(1,041)	-0.2	–	–	–
Danbury, CT PMSA	193,597	198,868	5,271	2.7	–	–	–
Dutchess County, NY PMSA	259,462	261,481	2,019	0.8	–	–	–
Jersey City, NJ PMSA	553,099	552,387	(712)	-0.1	–	–	–
Middlesex-Somerset-Hunterdon, NJ PMSA	1,019,858	1,068,756	48,898	4.8	–	–	–
Monmouth-Ocean, NJ PMSA	986,296	1,035,024	48,728	4.9	–	–	–
Nassau-Suffolk, NY PMSA	2,609,212	2,651,743	42,531	1.6	–	–	–
New Haven-Meriden, CT PMSA	530,180	522,871	(7,309)	-1.4	–	–	–
New York, NY PMSA	8,546,846	8,586,281	39,435	0.5	–	–	–
Newark, NJ PMSA	1,915,694	1,933,712	18,018	0.9	–	–	–
Newburgh, NY-PA PMSA	335,613	355,999	20,386	6.1	–	–	–
Stamford-Norwalk, CT PMSA	329,935	331,835	1,900	0.6	–	–	–
Trenton, NJ PMSA	325,824	329,431	3,607	1.1	–	–	–
Waterbury, CT PMS	221,629	221,196	(433)	-0.2	–	–	–
Norfolk-Virginia Beach-Newport News, VA-NC MSA	1,444,710	1,529,207	84,497	5.8	27	27	101
Ocala, FL MSA	194,835	219,808	24,973	12.8	149	149	17
Odessa-Midland, TX MSA	225,545	237,295	11,750	5.2	142	143	121
Oklahoma City, OK MSA	958,839	1,007,302	48,463	5.1	42	43	129
Omaha, NE-IA MSA	639,580	662,811	23,231	3.6	60	61	168
Orlando, FL MSA	1,224,844	1,361,489	136,645	11.2	32	31	29

Metropolitan area	April 1, 1990 census	July 1, 1994 estimate	Change 1990–94		CMSA/MSA rank		
			Number	%	Population		% change
					1990	1994	1990–94
Owensboro, KY MSA	87,189	90,140	2,951	3.4%	260	259	174%
Panama City, FL MSA	126,994	139,919	12,925	10.2	211	203	42
Parkersburg-Marietta, WV-OH MSA	149,169	151,560	2,391	1.6	185	190	216
Pensacola, FL MSA	344,406	370,761	26,355	7.7	106	103	70
Peoria-Pekin, IL MSA	339,172	343,531	4,359	1.3	108	112	222
Philadelphia-Wilmington-Atlantic City, PA-NJ-DE-MD CMSA	5,893,019	5,959,301	66,282	1.1	6	6	227
Atlantic City-May, MJ PMSA	319,416	330,002	10,586	3.3	–	–	–
Philadelphia, PA-NJ PMSA	4,922,257	4,949,202	26,945	0.5	–	–	–
Vineland-Millville-Bridgeton, NJ PMSA	138,053	138,803	750	0.5	–	–	–
Wilmington-Newark, DE-MD PMSA	513,293	541,294	28,001	5.5	–	–	–
Phoenix-Mesa, AZ MSA	2,238,498	2,473,384	234,886	10.5	19	18	36
Pine Bluff, AR MSA	85,487	84,032	(1,455)	-1.7	262	265	265
Pittsburgh, PA MSA	2,394,811	2,402,012	7,201	0.3	18	19	243
Pittsfield, MA MSA	88,695	86,171	(2,524)	-2.8	259	264	269
Portland, ME MSA	221,095	225,477	4,382	2.0	145	147	206
Portland-Salem, OR-WA CMSA	1,793,476	1,982,238	188,762	10.5	23	22	35
Portland-Vancouver, OR-WA PMSA	1,515,452	1,676,449	160,997	10.6	–	–	–
Salem, OR PMSA	278,024	305,789	27,765	10.0	–	–	–
Providence-Fall River-Warwick, RI-MA MSA	1,134,350	1,129,172	(5,178)	-0.5	36	37	253
Provo-Orem, UT MSA	263,590	290,989	27,399	10.4	129	124	38
Pueblo, CO MSA	123,051	127,666	4,615	3.8	215	217	166
Punta Gorda, FL MSA	110,975	126,492	15,517	14.0	236	218	12
Raleigh-Durham-Chapel Hill, NC MSA	858,485	965,127	106,642	12.4	50	47	20
Rapid City, SD MSA	81,343	86,585	5,242	6.4	265	263	87
Reading, PA MSA	336,523	347,629	11,106	3.3	109	110	179
Redding, CA MSA	147,036	160,021	12,985	8.8	187	180	55
Reno, NV MSA	254,667	282,936	28,269	11.1	134	130	30
Richland-Kennewick-Pasco, WA MSA	150,033	172,010	21,977	14.6	181	170	10
Richmond-Petersburg, VA MSA	865,640	916,674	51,034	5.9	47	51	98
Roanoke, VA MSA	224,592	228,602	4,010	1.8	143	145	212
Rochester, MN MSA	106,470	112,910	6,440	6.0	241	241	93
Rochester, NY MSA	1,062,470	1,090,596	28,126	2.6	38	39	197
Rockford, IL MSA	329,676	346,714	17,038	5.2	111	111	122
Rocky Mount, NC MSA	133,369	139,694	6,325	4.7	200	204	139
Sacramento-Yolo, CA CMSA	1,481,220	1,587,898	106,678	7.2	26	26	75
Sacramento, CA PMSA	1,340,010	1,441,476	101,466	7.6	–	–	–
Yolo, CA PMSA	141,210	146,422	5,212	3.7	–	–	–
Saginaw-Bay City-Midland, MI MSA	399,320	402,306	2,986	0.7	89	96	234
Salinas, CA MSA	355,660	351,928	(3,732)	-1.0	102	108	261
Salt Lake City-Ogden, UT MSA	1,072,227	1,178,338	106,111	9.9	37	35	45
San Angelo, TX MSA	98,458	101,244	2,786	2.8	250	249	192

Metropolitan area	April 1, 1990 census	July 1, 1994 estimate	Change 1990–94		CMSA/MSA rank		
			Number	%	Population		% change
					1990	1994	1990–94
San Antonio, TX MSA	1,324,749	1,437,306	112,557	8.5%	30	29	59%
San Diego, CA MSA	2,498,016	2,632,078	134,062	5.4	16	16	117
San Francisco-Oakland- San Jose, CA CMSA	6,249,881	6,513,322	263,441	4.2	5	5	156
Oakland, CA PMSA	2,080,434	2,182,416	101,982	4.9	–	–	–
San Francisco, CA PSMA	1,603,678	1,645,952	42,274	2.6	–	–	–
San Jose, CA PMSA	1,497,577	1,557,235	59,658	4.0	–	–	–
Santa Cruz-Watsonville, CA PMSA	229,734	234,973	5,239	2.3	–	–	–
Santa Rosa, CA PMSA	388,222	410,192	21,970	5.7	–	–	–
Vallejo-Fairfield-Napa, CA PMSA	450,236	482,554	32,318	7.2	–	–	–
San Luis Obispo-Atascadero- Paso Robles, CA MSA	217,162	223,708	6,546	3.0	146	148	189
Santa Barbara-Santa Maria- Lompoc, CA MSA	369,608	380,495	10,887	2.9	98	99	191
Santa Fe, NM MSA	117,043	130,761	13,718	11.7	225	213	26
Sarasota-Bradenton, FL MSA	489,483	517,934	28,451	5.8	74	75	102
Savannah, GA MSA	257,899	275,656	17,757	6.9	132	133	80
Scranton–Wilkes-Barre–Hazleton, PA MSA	638,524	636,993	(1,531)	-0.2	61	63	251
Seattle-Tacoma-Bremerton, WA CMSA	2,970,300	3,225,517	255,217	8.6	12	13	56
Bremerton, WA PMSA	189,731	220,395	30,664	16.2	–	–	–
Olympia, WA PMSA	161,238	187,241	26,003	16.1	–	–	–
Seattle-Bellevue-Everett, WA PMSA	2,033,128	2,179,543	146,415	7.2	–	–	–
Tacoma, WA PMSA	586,203	638,338	52,135	8.9	–	–	–
Sharon, PA MSA	121,003	122,161	1,158	1.0	218	223	230
Sheboygan, WI MSA	103,877	107,032	3,155	3.0	243	244	187
Sherman-Denison, TX MSA	95,019	97,267	2,248	2.4	255	255	201
Shreveport-Bossier City, LA MSA	376,330	378,374	2,044	0.5	96	100	237
Sioux City, IA-NE MSA	115,018	119,016	3,998	3.5	229	233	172
Sioux Falls, SD MSA	139,236	151,540	12,304	8.8	195	191	54
South Bend, IN MSA	247,052	255,435	8,383	3.4	137	136	173
Spokane, WA MSA	361,333	395,882	34,549	9.6	100	97	52
Springfield, IL MSA	189,550	195,835	6,285	3.3	154	159	178
Springfield, MA MSA	587,884	579,905	(7,979)	-1.4	68	70	262
Springfield, MO MSA	264,346	288,990	24,644	9.3	128	125	53
St. Cloud, MN MSA	149,509	156,912	7,403	5.0	184	185	133
St. Joseph, MO MSA	97,715	97,990	275	0.3	251	254	244
St. Louis, MO-IL MSA	2,492,348	2,536,080	43,732	1.8	17	17	213
State College, PA MSA	124,812	129,837	5,025	4.0	213	215	162
Steubenville-Weirton, OH-WV MSA	142,523	140,260	(2,263)	-1.6	191	202	264
Stockton-Lodi, CA MSA	480,628	518,167	37,539	7.8	76	74	68
Sumter, SC MSA	101,276	106,700	5,424	5.4	247	245	118
Syracuse, NY MSA	742,237	753,980	11,743	1.6	57	57	217
Tallahassee, FL MSA	233,609	253,367	19,758	8.5	140	139	60

Metropolitan area	April 1, 1990 census	July 1, 1994 estimate	Change 1990–94		CMSA/MSA rank		
					Population		% change
			Number	%	1990	1994	1990–94
Tampa-St. Petersburg-Clearwater, FL MSA	2,067,959	2,156,546	88,587	4.3%	20	21	153%
Terre Haute, IN MSA	147,585	149,656	2,071	1.4	186	192	219
Texarkana, TX-Texarkana, AR MSA	120,132	122,647	2,515	2.1	219	222	205
Toledo, OH MSA	614,128	613,945	(183)	0.0	62	65	248
Topeka, KS MSA	160,976	165,123	4,147	2.6	172	173	198
Tucson, AZ MSA	666,957	731,523	64,566	9.7	59	59	49
Tulsa, OK MSA	708,954	743,107	34,153	4.8	58	58	136
Tuscaloosa, AL MSA	150,522	157,090	6,568	4.4	180	184	150
Tyler, TX MSA	151,309	158,999	7,690	5.1	179	181	126
Utica-Rome, NY MSA	316,645	316,368	(277)	-0.1	112	117	250
Victoria, TX MSA	74,361	79,438	5,077	6.8	268	268	81
Visalia-Tulare-Porterville, CA MSA	311,921	343,257	31,336	10.0	116	113	43
Waco, TX MSA	189,123	197,171	8,048	4.3	155	156	154
Washington-Baltimore, DC-MD-VA-WV CMSA	6,726,395	7,051,495	325,100	4.8	4	4	135
Baltimore, MD PMSA	2,382,172	2,458,424	76,252	3.2	–	–	–
Hagerstown, MD PMSA	121,393	126,601	5,208	4.3	–	–	–
Washington, DC-MD-VA-WV PMSA	4,222,830	4,466,470	243,640	5.8	–	–	–
Waterloo-Cedar Falls, IA MSA	123,798	123,703	(95)	-0.1	214	220	249
Wausau, WI MSA	115,400	120,110	4,710	4.1	228	230	159
West Palm Beach-Boca Raton, FL MSA	863,503	954,539	91,036	10.5	48	50	34
Wheeling, WV-OH MSA	159,301	157,878	(1,423)	-0.9	173	183	259
Wichita Falls, TX MSA	130,351	131,996	1,645	1.3	208	211	224
Wichita, KS MSA	485,270	506,831	21,561	4.4	75	77	148
Williamsport, PA MSA	118,710	120,940	2,230	1.9	222	228	209
Wilmington, NC MSA	171,269	193,419	22,150	12.9	166	160	16
Yakima, WA MSA	188,823	207,683	18,860	10.0	156	151	44
York, PA MSA	339,574	357,812	18,238	5.4	107	106	115
Youngstown-Warren, OH MSA	600,895	604,123	3,228	0.5	63	69	239
Yuba City, CA MSA	122,643	135,185	12,542	10.2	216	208	41
Yuma, AZ MSA	106,895	127,680	20,785	19.4	240	216	4

Note: Areas defined by Office of Management and Budget, June 30, 1995. Primary MSAs (PMSAs) appear under their consolidated MSA (CMSA))
Source: U.S. Census Bureau

Population of U.S. Cities

Resident Population for Cities with 1994 Population Greater Than 100,000

City	April 1, 1990 census	July 1, 1994	Number	% change	Rank 4/90 pop.	Rank 7/94 pop.
New York, NY	7,322,564	7,333,253	10,689	0.1%	1	1
Los Angeles, CA	3,485,557	3,448,613	-36,944	-1.1	2	2
Chicago, IL	2,783,726	2,731,743	-51,983	-1.9	3	3
Houston, TX	1,630,864	1,702,086	71,222	4.4	4	4
Philadelphia, PA	1,585,577	1,524,249	-61,328	-3.9	5	5
San Diego, CA	1,110,623	1,151,977	41,354	3.7	6	6
Phoenix, AZ	984,309	1,048,949	64,640	6.6	9	7
Dallas, TX	1,007,618	1,022,830	15,212	1.5	8	8
San Antonio, TX	935,393	998,905	63,512	6.8	10	9
Detroit, MI	1,027,974	992,038	-35,936	-3.5	7	10
San Jose, CA	782,224	816,884	34,660	4.4	11	11
Indianapolis, IN	731,311	752,279	20,968	2.9	13	12
San Francisco, CA	723,959	734,676	10,717	1.5	14	13
Baltimore, MD	736,014	702,979	-33,035	-4.5	12	14
Jacksonville, FL	635,230	665,070	29,840	4.7	15	15
Columbus, OH	632,945	635,913	2,968	0.5	16	16
Milwaukee, WI	628,088	617,044	-11,044	-1.8	17	17
Memphis, TN	618,652	614,289	-4,363	-0.7	18	18
El Paso, TX	515,342	579,307	63,965	12.4	22	19
Washington, DC	606,900	567,094	-39,806	-6.6	19	20
Boston, MA	574,283	547,725	-26,558	-4.6	20	21
Seattle, WA	516,259	520,947	4,688	0.9	21	22
Austin, TX	465,648	514,013	48,365	10.4	27	23
Nashville-Davidson, TN	488,366	504,505	16,139	3.3	25	24
Denver, CO	467,610	493,559	25,949	5.5	26	25
Cleveland, OH	505,616	492,901	-12,715	-2.5	23	26
New Orleans, LA	496,938	484,149	-12,789	-2.6	24	27
Oklahoma City, OK	444,724	463,201	18,477	4.2	29	28
Fort Worth, TX	447,619	451,814	4,195	0.9	28	29
Portland, OR	438,802	450,777	11,975	2.7	30	30
Kansas City, MO	434,829	443,878	9,049	2.1	31	31
Charlotte, NC	395,934	437,797	41,863	10.6	35	32
Tucson, AZ	408,754	434,726	25,972	6.4	33	33
Long Beach, CA	429,321	433,852	4,531	1.1	32	34
Virginia Beach, VA	393,089	430,295	37,206	9.5	37	35
Albuquerque, NM	384,619	411,994	27,375	7.1	38	36
Atlanta, GA	393,929	396,052	2,123	0.5	36	37
Fresno, CA	354,091	386,551	32,460	9.2	47	38
Honolulu CDP, HI	377,059	385,881	8,822	2.3	39	39
Tulsa, OK	367,302	374,851	7,549	2.1	44	40
Sacramento, CA	369,365	373,964	4,599	1.2	42	41
Miami, FL	358,648	373,024	14,376	4.0	46	42
St. Louis, MO	396,685	368,215	-28,470	-7.2	34	43
Oakland, CA	372,242	366,926	-5,316	-1.4	40	44
Pittsburgh, PA	369,879	358,883	-10,996	-3.0	41	45
Cincinnati, OH	364,114	358,170	-5,944	-1.6	45	46
Minneapolis, MN	368,383	354,590	-13,793	-3.7	43	47
Omaha, NE	335,719	345,033	9,314	2.8	48	48
Las Vegas, NV	258,204	327,878	69,674	27.0	63	49
Toledo, OH	332,943	322,550	-10,393	-3.1	49	50
Colorado Springs, CO	280,430	316,480	36,050	12.9	54	51
Mesa, AZ	289,199	313,649	24,450	8.5	53	52
Buffalo, NY	328,175	312,965	-15,210	-4.6	50	53
Wichita, KS	304,017	310,236	6,219	2.0	51	54

City	April 1, 1990 census	July 1, 1994	Number	% change	Rank 4/90 pop.	Rank 7/94 pop.
Santa Ana, Ca	293,827	290,827	-3,000	-1.0%	52	55
Arlington, TX	261,717	286,922	25,205	9.6	61	56
Tampa, FL	280,015	285,523	5,508	2.0	55	57
Anaheim, CA	266,406	282,133	15,727	5.9	59	58
Corpus Christi, TX	257,453	275,419	17,966	7.0	64	59
Louisville, KY	269,555	270,308	753	0.3	58	60
Birmingham, AL	265,347	264,527	-820	-0.3	60	61
St. Paul, MN	272,235	262,071	-10,164	-3.7	57	62
Newark, NJ	275,221	258,751	-16,470	-6.0	56	63
Anchorage, AK	226,338	253,649	27,311	12.1	69	64
Aurora, CO	222,103	250,717	28,614	12.9	72	65
Riverside, CA	226,546	241,644	15,098	6.7	68	66
Norfolk, VA	261,250	241,426	-19,824	-7.6	62	67
St. Petersburg, FL	240,318	238,585	-1,733	-0.7	65	68
Lexington-Fayette, KY	225,366	237,612	12,246	5.4	70	69
Raleigh, NC	212,092	236,707	24,615	11.6	74	70
Rochester, NY	230,356	231,170	814	0.4	66	71
Baton Rouge, LA	219,531	227,482	7,951	3.6	73	72
Jersey City, NJ	228,517	226,022	-2,495	-1.1	67	73
Stockton, CA	210,943	222,633	11,690	5.5	75	74
Akron, OH	223,019	221,886	-1,133	-0.5	71	75
Mobile, AL	196,263	204,490	8,227	4.2	79	76
Lincoln, NE	191,972	203,076	11,104	5.8	81	77
Richmond, VA	202,798	201,108	-1,690	-0.8	76	78
Shreveport, LA	198,525	196,982	-1,543	-0.8	77	79
Greensboro, NC	183,894	196,167	12,273	6.7	89	80
Montgomery, AL	187,543	195,471	7,928	4.2	86	81
Madison, WI	190,766	194,586	3,820	2.0	82	82
Lubbock, TX	186,206	194,467	8,261	4.4	87	83
Garland, TX	180,635	194,218	13,583	7.5	92	84
Hialeah, FL	188,008	194,120	6,112	3.3	85	85
Des Moines, IA	193,189	193,965	776	0.4	80	86
Jackson, MS	196,637	193,097	-3,540	-1.8	78	87
Spokane, WA	177,165	192,781	15,616	8.8	95	88
Bakersfield, CA	174,978	191,060	16,082	9.2	98	89
Grand Rapids, MI	189,126	190,395	1,269	0.7	83	90
Huntington Beach, CA	181,519	189,220	7,701	4.2	91	91
Columbus, GA	178,683	186,470	7,787	4.4	94	92
Fremont, CA	173,339	183,575	10,236	5.9	99	93
Yonkers, NY	188,082	183,490	-4,592	-2.4	84	94
Fort Wayne, IN	184,221	183,359	-862	-0.5	88	95
Tacoma, WA	176,664	183,060	6,396	3.6	96	96
San Bernardino, CA	164,164	181,718	17,554	10.7	106	97
Chesapeake, VA	151,982	180,577	28,595	18.8	115	98
Newport News, VA	171,439	179,127	7,688	4.5	100	99
Dayton, OH	182,005	178,540	-3,465	-1.9	90	100
Glendale, CA	180,038	178,481	-1,557	-0.9	93	101
Little Rock, AR	175,727	178,136	2,409	1.4	97	102
Orlando, FL	164,674	176,948	12,274	7.5	105	103
Modesto, CA	164,746	176,357	11,611	7.0	104	104
Arlington CDP, VA	170,897	174,603	3,706	2.2	101	105
Salt Lake City, UT	159,928	171,849	11,921	7.5	109	106
Knoxville, TN	165,039	169,311	4,272	2.6	103	107
Glendale, AZ	147,864	168,439	20,575	13.9	119	108
Worcester, MA	169,759	165,387	-4,372	-2.6	102	109
Amarillo, TX	157,571	165,036	7,465	4.7	111	110

City	April 1, 1990 census	July 1, 1994	Number	% change	Rank 4/90 pop.	Rank 7/94 pop.
Irving, TX	155,037	164,917	9,880	6.4%	113	111
Fort Lauderdale, FL	149,238	162,842	13,604	9.1	118	112
Huntsville, AL	159,880	160,325	445	0.3	110	113
Syracuse, NY	163,860	159,895	-3,965	-2.4	107	114
Plano, TX	127,885	157,394	29,509	23.1	142	115
Winston-Salem, NC	150,958	155,128	4,170	2.8	116	116
Scottsdale, AZ	130,075	152,439	22,364	17.2	140	117
Chattanooga, TN	152,393	152,259	-134	-0.1	114	118
Providence, RI	160,728	150,639	-10,089	-6.3	108	119
Laredo, TX	122,899	149,914	27,015	22.0	148	120
Springfield, MO	140,494	149,727	9,233	6.6	127	121
Chula Vista, CA	135,160	149,255	14,095	10.4	132	122
Springfield, MA	156,983	149,164	-7,819	-5.0	112	123
Garden Grove, CA	142,965	147,958	4,993	3.5	121	124
Oceanside, CA	128,090	146,229	18,139	14.2	141	125
Boise City, ID	125,551	145,987	20,436	16.3	146	126
Oxnard, CA	142,560	145,863	3,303	2.3	122	127
Reno, NV	133,850	145,029	11,179	8.4	133	128
Tempe, AZ	141,993	144,289	2,296	1.6	123	129
Ponoma, CA	131,700	143,870	12,170	9.2	137	130
Durham, NC	136,612	143,439	6,827	5.0	131	131
Rockford, IL	140,003	143,263	3,260	2.3	128	132
Kansas City, KS	149,800	142,630	-7,170	-4.8	117	133
Warren, MI	144,864	142,625	-2,239	-1.5	120	134
Savannah, GA	137,812	140,597	2,785	2.0	130	135
Hampton, VA	133,811	139,628	5,817	4.3	134	136
Moreno Valley, CA	118,779	139,311	20,532	17.3	152	137
Paterson, NJ	140,891	138,290	-2,601	-1.8	126	138
Torrance, CA	133,107	138,219	5,112	3.8	136	139
Flint, MI	140,925	138,164	-2,761	-2.0	125	140
Ontario, CA	133,179	134,825	1,646	1.2	135	141
Pasadena, CA	131,586	134,170	2,584	2.0	138	142
Tallahassee, FL	124,773	133,718	8,945	7.2	147	143
Bridgeport, CT	141,686	132,919	-8,767	-6.2	124	144
Evansville, IN	126,272	129,452	3,180	2.5	145	145
Pasadena, TX	119,604	129,292	9,688	8.1	151	146
Lakewood, CO	126,475	126,031	-444	-0.4	144	147
Irvine, CA	110,330	125,624	15,294	13.9	168	148
Overland Park, KS	111,790	125,225	13,435	12.0	163	149
Hollywood, FL	121,720	124,992	3,272	2.7	149	150
Hartford, CT	139,739	124,196	-15,543	-11.1	129	151
Santa Clarita, CA	118,142	123,676	5,534	4.7	153	152
Topeka, KS	119,883	120,646	763	0.6	150	153
Salinas, CA	108,777	119,814	11,037	10.1	174	154
New Haven, CT	130,474	119,604	-10,870	-8.3	139	155
Lansing, MI	127,321	119,590	-7,731	-6.1	143	156
Sunnyvale, CA	117,324	119,584	2,260	1.9	155	157
Sterling Heights, MI	117,810	119,505	1,695	1.4	154	158
Chandler, AZ	89,862	119,227	29,365	32.7	205	159
Lancaster, CA	97,300	119,186	21,886	22.5	201	160
Eugene, OR	112,733	118,122	5,389	4.8	161	161
Santa Rosa, CA	113,261	116,962	3,701	3.3	160	162
Fullerton, CA	114,144	116,863	2,719	2.4	158	163
Orange, CA	110,658	116,785	6,127	5.5	167	164
Escondido, CA	108,648	116,349	7,701	7.1	177	165
Salem, OR	107,793	115,912	8,119	7.5	179	166

City	April 1, 1990 census	July 1, 1994	Number	% change	Rank 4/90 pop.	Rank 7/94 pop.
Hayward, CA	111,343	115,590	4,247	3.8%	164	167
Beaumont, TX	114,323	115,022	699	0.6	157	168
Rancho Cucamonga, CA	101,409	114,799	13,390	13.2	191	169
Gary, IN	116,646	114,256	-2,390	-2.0	156	170
Mesquite, TX	101,484	113,631	12,147	12.0	190	171
Cedar Rapids, IA	108,772	113,438	4,666	4.3	175	172
Brownsville, TX	98,962	112,904	13,942	14.1	198	173
Alexandria, VA	111,182	112,879	1,697	1.5	166	174
Peoria, IL	113,513	112,878	-635	-0.6	159	175
Aurora, IL	99,556	112,313	12,757	12.8	197	176
Concord, CA	111,308	111,889	581	0.5	165	177
Independence, MO	112,301	111,669	-632	-0.6	162	178
Vallejo, CA	109,199	111,484	2,285	2.1	172	179
Thousand Oaks, CA	104,381	110,981	6,600	6.3	186	180
Inglewood, CA	109,602	110,085	438	0.4	171	181
Abilene, TX	106,707	110,034	3,327	3.1	181	182
Macon, GA	107,365	109,191	1,826	1.7	180	183
Sioux Falls, SD	100,836	109,174	8,338	8.3	193	184
Grand Prairie, TX	99,606	108,908	9,302	9.3	196	185
Ann Arbor, MI	109,608	108,817	-791	-0.7	170	186
Erie, PA	108,718	108,398	-320	-0.3	176	187
Stamford, CT	108,056	107,199	-857	-0.8	178	188
Simi Valley, CA	100,218	106,949	6,731	6.7	194	189
Elizabeth, NJ	110,002	106,298	-3,704	-3.4	169	190
Springfield, IL	105,417	105,938	521	0.5	184	191
Waco, TX	103,590	105,892	2,302	2.2	188	192
Allentown, PA	105,301	105,339	38	0.0	185	193
South Bend, IN	105,511	105,092	-419	-0.4	183	194
Albany, NY	100,031	104,828	4,797	4.8	195	195
El Monte, CA	106,162	104,661	-1,501	-1.4	182	196
Columbia, SC	103,477	104,101	624	0.6	189	197
Fontana, CA	87,535	103,737	16,202	18.5	206	198
Waterbury, CT	108,961	103,523	-5,438	-5.0	173	199
Portsmouth, VA	103,910	103,464	-446	-0.4	187	200
Palmdale, CA	70,262	103,423	33,161	47.2	208	201
West Covina, CA	96,226	103,298	7,072	7.3	203	202
Green Bay, WI	96,466	102,708	6,242	6.5	202	203
Lafayette, LA	97,416	102,281	4,865	5.0	200	204
Henderson, NV	64,948	101,997	37,049	57.0	209	205
Naperville, IL	85,806	101,163	15,357	17.9	207	206
Norwalk, CA	94,279	100,744	6,465	6.9	204	207
Pueblo, CO	98,640	100,471	1,831	1.9	199	208
Livonia, MI	100,850	100,415	-435	-0.4	192	209

Source: U.S. Census Bureau

Mayors of Major U.S. Cities

CITY	NAME	SALARY	CITY	NAME	SALARY
New York City, NY	Rudolph Giuliani	$165,000	Jacksonville, FL	John A. Delaney	$110,922
Los Angeles, CA	Richard Riordan	$1	Columbus, OH	Gregory S. Lashutka	$103,968
Chicago, IL	Richard M. Daley	$170,000	Milwaukee, WI	John O. Norquist	$108,978
Houston, TX	Bob Lanier	$133,000	Memphis, TN	Willie W. Herenton	$110,000
Philadelphia, PA	Edward Rendell	$110,000	El Paso, TX	Carlos Ramirez	$27,562
San Diego, CA	Susan Golding	$68,239	Washington, DC	Marion Barry, Jr.	$90,705
Phoenix. AZ	Skip Rimsza	$37,500	Boston, MA	Thomas Menino	$110,000
Detroit, MI	Dennis W. Archer	$143,000	Seattle, WA	Norman B. Rice	$112,731
Dallas, TX	Ronald Kirk	$50*	Austin, TX	Kirk Watson	$35,600
San Antonio, TX	Howard Peak	$50*	Nashville, TN	Philip N. Bredesen	$75,000
San Jose, CA	Susan Hammer	$85,000	Denver, CO	Wellington E. Webb	$99,612
Indianapolis, IN	Stephen Goldsmith	$83,211			
San Francisco, CA	Willie L. Brown, Jr.	$140,862			
Baltimore, MD	Kurt Schmoke	$95,000			

*Per council meeting

Source: U.S. Conference of Mayors

Where Most Minorities Live
Number of Minorities and Their Share of the Total 1990 Population in Cities of 200,000 or More People

Cities with the Most Blacks

Rank	City	Black population	%	Rank	City	Black population	%
1	New York, NY	2,102,512	28.7	11	Dallas, TX	296,994	29.5
2	Chicago, IL	1,087,711	39.1	12	Atlanta, GA	264,262	67.1
3	Detroit, MI	777,916	75.7	13	Cleveland, OH	235,405	46.6
4	Philadelphia, PA	631,936	39.9	14	Milwaukee, WI	191,255	30.5
5	Los Angeles, CA	487,674	14.0	15	St. Louis, MO	188,408	47.5
6	Houston, TX	457,990	28.1	16	Birmingham, AL	168,277	63.3
7	Baltimore, MD	435,768	59.2	17	Indianapolis, IN	165,570	22.6
8	Washington, DC	399,604	65.8	18	Oakland, CA	163,335	43.9
9	Memphis, TN	334,737	54.8	19	Newark, NJ	160,885	58.5
10	New Orleans, LA	307,728	61.9	20	Jacksonville, FL	160,283	25.2

Cities with the Most Hispanics

Rank	City	Hispanic population	%	Rank	City	Hispanic population	%
1	New York, NY	1,783,511	24.4	11	Phoenix, AZ	197,103	20.0
2	Los Angeles, CA	1,391,411	39.9	12	Santa Ana, CA	191,383	65.2
3	Chicago, IL	545,852	19.6	13	Albuquerque, NM	132,706	34.5
4	San Antonio, TX	520,282	55.6	14	Corpus Christi, TX	129,708	50.4
5	Houston, TX	450,483	27.6	15	Tucson, AZ	118,595	29.3
6	El Paso, TX	355,669	69.0	16	Denver, CO	107,382	23.0
7	San Diego, CA	229,519	20.7	17	Austin, TX	106,868	23.0
8	Miami, FL	223,964	62.5	18	Fresno, CA	105,787	29.9
9	Dallas, TX	210,240	20.9	19	Long Beach, CA	101,419	23.6
10	San Jose, CA	208,388	26.6	20	San Francisco, CA	100,717	13.9

Cities with the Most Asians or Pacific Islanders

Rank	City	Asian or Pacific Islander population	%	Rank	City	Asian or Pacific Islander population	%
1	New York, NY	512,719	7.0	11	Sacramento, CA	55,426	15.0
2	Los Angeles, CA	341,807	9.8	12	Oakland, CA	54,931	14.8
3	Honolulu, HI	257,552	70.5	13	Stockton, CA	48,087	22.8
4	San Francisco, CA	210,876	29.1	14	Fresno, CA	44,358	12.5
5	San Jose, CA	152,815	19.5	15	Philadelphia, PA	43,522	2.7
6	San Diego, CA	130,945	11.8	16	Boston, MA	30,388	5.3
7	Chicago, IL	104,118	3.7	17	Santa Ana, CA	28,585	9.7
8	Houston, TX	67,113	4.1	18	Jersey City, NJ	25,959	11.4
9	Seattle, WA	60,819	11.8	19	Anaheim, CA	25,018	9.4
10	Long Beach, CA	58,266	13.6	20	Portland, OR	23,185	5.3

Source: U.S. Census Bureau

Metropolitan Area Job Growth

(Total employment and job gain are in thousands)

Rank % change 1Q '96–'97	Metro area	Total employment 1Q '97	Job gain 1Q '96–'97	% change 1Q '96–'97	Rank job gain 1Q '96–'97
1	Las Vegas, NV	619.6	50.9	8.94%	8
2	Orlando, FL	777.2	44.6	6.09	11
3	Phoenix, AZ	1,359.3	75.9	5.91	2
4	Sarasota, FL	235.5	12.8	5.73	49
5	Seattle, WA	1,250.8	59.9	5.03	6
6	Santa Rosa-Petaluma, CA	159.4	6.9	4.55	72
7	Baton Rouge, LA	283.1	12.0	4.41	51
8	San Jose, CA	897.1	37.8	4.40	15
9	Salt Lake City-Ogden, UT	652.4	27.4	4.38	25
10	Portland, OR	894.3	37.0	4.31	16
11	Boise City, ID	188.9	7.8	4.31	65
12	Norfolk-Virginia Beach, VA	651.9	26.7	4.27	26
13	West Palm Beach-Boca Raton, FL	432.8	17.3	4.16	41
14	Colorado Springs, CO	209.4	8.3	4.13	63
15	Tulsa, OK	367.2	14.5	4.10	44
16	Dallas, TX	1,681.1	64.1	3.96	5
17	Wilmington, DE-NJ-MD	291.1	10.7	3.82	55
18	Indianapolis, IN	823.9	29.9	3.76	22
19	San Francisco, CA	965.9	34.7	3.73	18
20	Bakersfield, CA	178.1	6.4	3.71	75
21	Riverside-San Bernardino, CA	825.4	29.3	3.68	23
22	Jacksonville, FL	506.8	17.7	3.63	40
23	Fort Lauderdale, FL	623.4	21.7	3.61	29
24	Atlanta, GA	1,917.7	65.6	3.54	3
25	Oklahoma City, OK	500.3	17.1	3.53	42
26	Grand Rapids, MI	538.9	18.2	3.49	38
27	Kansas City, KS/MO	888.2	29.0	3.38	24
28	Mobile, AL	216.3	6.8	3.26	73
29	Sacramento, CA	614.5	19.4	3.26	34

Rank % change 1Q '96–'97	Metro area	Total employment 1Q '97	Job gain 1Q '96–'97	% change 1Q '96–'97	Rank job gain 1Q '96–'97
30	Fort Worth-Arlington, TX	685.4	21.4	3.22%	31
31	Middlesex-Somerset-Hunterdon, NJ	585.8	18.2	3.21	37
32	McAllen-Edinburg-Mission, TX	130.7	4.0	3.19	83
33	Madison, WI	262.6	8.1	3.18	64
34	Tampa-St. Petersburg, FL	1,046.6	32.3	3.18	19
35	Ventura, CA	243.0	7.4	3.14	69
36	Charlotte-Gastonia-Rock Hill, NC-SC	737.3	22.2	3.10	28
37	Gary-Hammond, IN	258.8	7.7	3.05	66
38	Harrisburg-Lebanon-Carlisle, PA	344.9	9.9	2.97	58
39	Tucson, AZ	313.9	8.7	2.84	62
40	St. Louis, MO-IL	1,273.4	34.9	2.82	17
41	Orange County, CA	1,197.1	31.2	2.68	20
42	Boston, MA	1,853.9	47.1	2.60	10
43	Los Angeles-Long Beach, CA	3,836.3	95.3	2.55	1
44	Fort Myers, FL	153.4	3.8	2.54	85
45	Louisville, KY-IN	536.9	13.0	2.48	48
46	Detroit, MI	2,058.1	49.1	2.44	9
47	Oakland, CA	922.5	21.6	2.40	30
48	Raleigh-Durham, NC	583.2	13.5	2.37	46
49	Greenville-Spartanburg, SC	451.3	10.4	2.37	56
50	Columbus, OH	799.1	18.1	2.31	39
51	Denver, CO	1,007.6	22.7	2.30	27
52	Austin, TX	542.4	12.1	2.28	50
53	Houston, TX	1,816.2	38.8	2.18	14
54	Miami-Hialeh, FL	955.6	20.0	2.14	32
55	El Paso, TX	237.5	4.8	2.08	79
56	Charleston, SC	211.9	4.3	2.06	82
57	Monmouth-Ocean, NJ	345.5	6.8	2.01	74
58	Omaha, NE-IA	385.6	7.5	1.98	67
59	Minneapolis-St. Paul, MN	1,577.8	30.4	1.96	21
60	San Diego, CA	1,006.7	19.3	1.95	35
61	Bergen-Passaic, NJ	622.9	11.3	1.84	53
62	Philadelphia, PA-NJ	2,207.6	39.6	1.83	13
63	Washington, DC-MD-VA	2,420.2	43.3	1.82	12
64	Baltimore, MD	1,128.1	19.8	1.79	33
65	Cincinnati, OH-KY-IN	817.3	14.0	1.75	45
66	Albuquerque, NM	325.6	5.6	1.74	76
67	Little Rock, AR	297.4	5.1	1.73	78
68	Des Moines, IA	266.8	4.5	1.73	80
69	Memphis, TN-AR-MS	546.5	9.1	1.69	61
70	Cleveland, OH	1,114.3	18.4	1.68	36
71	Chicago, IL	3,946.6	64.4	1.66	4
72	Nashville, TN	608.4	9.8	1.64	59
73	San Antonio, TX	634.0	10.2	1.63	57
74	Springfield, MA	242.6	3.9	1.62	84
75	Greensboro–Winston-Salem, NC	615.5	9.8	1.61	60
76	Nassau-Suffolk, NY	1,084.9	16.7	1.57	43
77	Dayton-Springfield, OH	467.6	7.1	1.55	71
78	New York, NY	3,848.9	55.9	1.47	7
79	Toledo, OH	312.2	4.5	1.47	81
80	Newark, NJ	929.3	13.4	1.46	47
81	Richmond-Petersburg, VA	505.8	7.3	1.46	70
82	Milwaukee, WI	811.8	11.1	1.38	54

Rank % change 1Q '96–'97	Metro area	Total employment 1Q '97	Job gain 1Q '96–'97	% change 1Q '96–'97	Rank job gain 1Q '96–'97
83	Fresno, CA	267.7	3.6	1.36%	86
84	Scranton–Wilkes-Barre, PA	268.3	3.5	1.33	88
85	Birmingham, AL	450.2	5.6	1.25	77
86	New Orleans, LA	602.7	7.4	1.24	68
87	Pittsburgh, PA	1,047.8	11.9	1.15	52
88	Akron, OH	314.9	3.3	1.05	89
89	Knoxville, TN	309.4	3.1	1.00	90
90	Syracuse, NY	328.6	2.0	0.61	92
91	Hartford, CT	581.3	3.5	0.61	87
92	Rochester, NY	521.7	2.7	0.51	91
93	Albany-Schenectady- Troy, NY	420.7	1.4	0.33	93
94	Buffalo, NY	527.9	-0.5	-0.09	94
95	Providence, RI	487.2	-0.8	-0.16	95

Source: M/PF Research Inc.

Major Metro Area Incomes

	Income per capita	
Metropolitan area	1996	2006*
Los Angeles-Long Beach, CA PMSA	$24,223.66	$38,033.43
New York, NY PMSA	32,893.32	54,846.52
Chicago, IL PMSA	28,828.30	46,191.43
Boston, MA-NH-ME-CT NECMA	30,024.46	53,037.48
Philadelphia, PA-NJ-DE-MD PMSA	28,000.67	45,231.33
Washington, DC-MD-VA-WV PMSA	31,888.54	50,816.32
Detroit, MI PMSA	27,813.87	45,245.11
Houston, TX PMSA	25,542.17	40,536.99
Atlanta, GA MSA	26,326.39	38,684.71
Dallas, TX PMSA	27,596.86	42,992.30
Riverside-San Bernardino, CA PMSA	19,593.54	31,664.34
Minneapolis-St. Paul, MN-WI MSA	28,567.40	45,690.73
Nassau-Suffolk, NY PMSA	32,927.16	59,439.11
San Diego, CA MSA	24,335.75	38,130.38
Orange County, CA MSA	28,725.74	46,416.04
Phoenix-Mesa, AZ MSA	23,150.36	33,548.94
St. Louis, MO-IL MSA	26,540.21	43,746.18
Baltimore, MD PMSA	26,520.39	43,604.35
Pittsburgh, PA PMSA	25,198.42	41,232.37
Cleveland-Lorain-Elyria, OH PMSA	26,304.45	43,686.88
Seattle-Bellevue-Everett, WA PMSA	30,125.06	50,693.56
Oakland, CA PMSA	29,946.70	48,435.26
Tampa-St. Petersburg-Clearwater, FL MSA	23,948.78	39,910.18
Miami, FL PMSA	23,156.12	36,394.39
Newark, NJ PMSA	33,121.02	54,866.43
Denver, CO PMSA	27,600.80	43,347.07
Portland-Vancouver, OR-WA PMSA	25,350.69	37,461.60
Kansas City, MO-KS MSA	25,126.99	39,939.48
San Francisco, CA PMSA	39,008.86	61,690.03
New Haven-Bridgeport-Stamford-Danbury, CT MSA	36,656.51	62,015.74
Cincinnati, OH-KY-IN PMSA	25,037.95	40,410.36

Metropolitan area	Income per capita	
	1996	2006*
San Jose, CA PMSA	32,335.18	51,909.64
Norfolk-Virginia Beach-Newport News, VA-NC MSA	20,823.21	31,478.78
Fort Worth-Arlington, TX PMSA	23,473.58	35,377.97
Indianapolis, IN MSA	25,582.13	40,045.29
San Antonio, TX MSA	21,154.39	32,134.30
Milwaukee-Waukesha, WI PMSA	26,754.52	42,854.83
Sacramento, CA PMSA	24,653.03	37,524.68
Columbus, OH MSA	24,290.48	38,188.34
Fort Lauderdale, FL PMSA	27,647.85	40,290.98
Orlando, FL MSA	21,865.23	36,301.95
New Orleans, LA MSA	22,268.79	37,397.33
Bergen-Passaic, NJ PMSA	35,055.42	58,805.50
Charlotte-Gastonia-Rock Hill, NC-SC MSA	25,041.38	41,023.06
Salt Lake City-Ogden, UT MSA	20,942.42	34,548.93
Buffalo-Niagara Falls, NY MSA	23,509.25	39,534.39
Las Vegas, NV-AZ MSA	23,566.08	34,920.98
Greensboro–Winston-Salem–High Point, NC	24,785.02	41,403.78
Hartford, CT NECMA	30,490.75	51,922.10
Nashville, TN MSA	25,458.90	39,077.17
Rochester, NY MSA	24,891.65	42,106.00

*Projected.
Source: Regional Financial Associates

City Cost Comparisons

Cost of Living Values in Selected U.S. Locations, 1997

Location	Total annual cost	Index
San Francisco, CA	$80,574	134.3
New York, NY	74,037	123.4
Boston, MA	72,102	120.2
Washington, DC	70,183	117.0
Chicago, IL	67,511	112.5
Los Angeles, CA	67,167	111.9
Minneapolis, MN	63,831	106.4
Milwaukee, WI	62,768	104.6
Denver, CO	62,144	103.6
Atlanta, GA	62,138	103.6
Madison, WI	61,902	103.2

Location	Total annual cost	Index
Iowa City, IA	61,591	102.7
Columbus, OH	60,698	101.2
St. Louis, MO	60,154	100.3
Racine, WI	60,151	100.3
Standard City, USA	**60,000**	**100.0**
Des Moines, IA	59,377	99.0
Kansas City, MO	58,057	96.8
Dallas, TX	57,587	96.0
Indianapolis, IN	57,257	95.4

NOTE: The table above is based on a family of four with a $60,000 annual income. Annual cost of living includes housing, transportation, taxes, and goods and services, plus a portion set aside for investments and savings. The family resides in a 2,200 sq. ft. home which carries a current mortgage and incurs all normal home ownership and maintenance costs. They own two cars, a late model driven 14,000 miles per year and a 4-year-old model driven 6,000 miles yearly. Taxes include federal, state, and local income taxes. They purchase goods and services typical for a family in their income bracket at that location.
Source: Runzheimer International

The Smartest Towns

The towns with the highest percentage of adults with college degrees, based on an analysis of 1990 U.S. census results.

Rank	Place	Population aged 25 and older	Percent with Bachelor's degree or higher
1	Stanford. CA	6,090	90.9%
2	Chevy Chase, MD (town)	1,879	80.2
3	Winnetka, IL	8,030	79.2
4	Scarsdale, NY	10,969	74.7
5	Portola Valley, CA	3,203	74.1
6	Mission Hills, KS	2,487	73.7
7	Princeton, NJ (township)	9,585	73.6
8	University Heights, VA	1,204	73.1
9	Hanover, NH	4,072	73.0
10	University Park, TX	13,334	72.9
11	Kensington, CA	3,957	72.6
12	Bunker Hill Village, TX	2,370	72.3
13	Glencoe, IL	5,821	72.1
14	Fox Chapel, PA	3,604	71.5
	Mountain Lakes, NJ	2,480	71.5
16	Chapel Hill, NC	19,230	71.2
	East Lansing, MI	16,425	71.2
	Piedmont, CA	7,263	71.2
19	Ann Arbor, MI (township)	2,784	70.3
20	Potomac, MD	30,406	70.2
21	Bloomfield Hills, MI	3,118	69.8
22	Cherry Hills Village, CO	3,455	69.6
23	Bronxville, NY	4,018	69.5
	Ottawa Hills, OH	3,066	69.5
25	Kingston, RI	922	69.4

Source: American Demographics

Normal Daily Maximum and Minimum Temperatures for 50 Major U.S. Cities (°F)

City	January Max.	January Min.	February Max.	February Min.	March Max.	March Min.	April Max.	April Min.	May Max.	May Min.	June Max.	June Min.
New York, NY	37.6	25.3	40.3	26.9	50.0	34.8	61.2	43.8	71.1	53.7	80.1	63.0
Los Angeles, CA	65.7	47.8	65.9	49.3	65.5	50.5	67.4	52.8	69.0	56.3	71.9	59.5
Chicago, IL	29.0	12.9	33.5	17.2	45.8	28.5	58.6	38.6	70.1	47.7	79.6	57.5
Houston, TX	61.0	39.7	65.3	42.6	71.1	50.0	78.4	58.1	84.6	64.4	90.1	70.6
Philadelphia, PA	37.9	22.8	41.0	24.8	51.6	33.2	62.6	42.1	73.1	52.7	81.7	61.8
San Diego, CA	65.9	48.9	66.5	50.7	66.3	52.8	68.4	55.6	69.1	59.1	71.6	61.9
Phoenix, AZ	65.9	41.2	70.7	44.7	75.5	48.8	84.5	55.3	93.6	63.9	103.5	72.9
Dallas, TX	54.1	32.7	58.9	36.9	67.8	45.6	76.3	54.7	82.9	62.6	91.9	70.0
San Antonio, TX	60.8	37.9	65.7	41.3	73.5	49.7	80.3	58.4	85.3	65.7	91.8	72.6
Detroit, MI	30.3	15.6	33.3	17.6	44.4	27.0	57.7	36.8	69.6	47.1	78.9	56.3
San Jose, CA	58.2	40.6	62.5	43.9	65.3	45.4	70.0	47.1	74.6	50.9	79.6	54.6
Indianapolis, IN	33.7	17.2	38.3	20.9	50.9	31.9	63.3	41.5	73.8	51.7	82.7	61.0
San Francisco, CA	55.6	41.8	59.4	45.0	60.8	45.8	63.9	47.2	66.5	49.7	70.3	52.6
Baltimore, MD	40.2	23.4	43.7	25.9	54.0	34.1	64.3	42.5	74.2	52.6	83.2	61.8
Jacksonville, FL	64.2	40.5	67.0	43.3	73.0	49.2	79.1	54.9	84.7	62.1	89.3	69.1
Columbus, OH	34.1	18.5	38.0	21.2	50.5	31.2	62.0	40.0	72.3	50.1	80.4	58.0
Milwaukee, WI	26.1	11.6	30.1	15.9	40.4	26.2	52.9	35.8	64.3	44.8	74.9	55.0
Memphis, TN	48.5	30.9	53.5	34.8	63.2	43.0	73.3	52.4	81.0	61.2	89.3	68.9
El Paso, TX	56.1	29.4	62.2	33.9	69.9	40.2	78.7	48.0	87.1	56.5	96.5	64.3
Washington, DC	42.3	26.8	45.9	29.1	56.5	37.7	66.7	46.4	76.2	56.6	84.7	66.5
Boston, MA	35.7	21.6	37.5	23.0	45.8	31.3	55.9	40.2	66.6	49.8	76.3	59.1
Seattle, WA	45.0	35.2	49.5	37.4	52.7	38.5	57.2	41.2	63.9	46.3	69.9	51.9
Austin, TX	58.9	38.6	63.4	42.1	71.9	51.1	79.4	59.8	84.7	66.5	91.1	71.5
Nashville-Davidson, TN	45.9	26.5	50.8	29.9	61.2	39.1	70.8	47.5	78.8	56.6	86.5	64.7
Denver, CO	43.2	16.1	46.6	20.2	52.2	25.8	61.8	34.5	70.8	43.6	81.4	52.4
Cleveland, OH	31.9	17.6	35.0	19.3	46.3	28.2	57.9	37.3	68.6	47.3	78.3	56.8
New Orleans, LA	60.8	41.8	64.1	44.4	71.6	51.6	78.5	58.4	84.4	65.2	89.2	70.8
Oklahoma City, OK	46.7	25.2	52.1	29.6	62.0	38.5	71.9	48.8	79.1	57.7	87.3	66.1
Fort Worth, TX	54.1	32.7	58.9	36.9	67.8	45.6	76.3	54.7	82.9	62.6	91.9	70.0
Portland, OR	45.4	33.7	51.0	36.1	56.0	38.6	60.6	41.3	67.1	47.0	74.0	52.9
Kansas City, MO	34.7	16.7	40.6	21.8	52.8	32.6	65.1	43.8	74.3	53.9	83.3	63.1
Charlotte, NC	49.0	29.6	53.0	31.9	62.3	39.4	71.2	47.5	78.3	56.4	85.8	65.6
Tucson, AZ	63.9	38.6	67.8	41.0	72.8	44.6	81.2	50.4	89.9	58.0	99.6	67.9
Long Beach, CA	66.8	44.9	67.7	46.9	68.0	49.0	71.5	51.8	73.3	56.3	77.0	59.8
Albuquerque, NM	46.8	21.7	53.5	26.4	61.4	32.2	70.8	39.6	79.7	48.6	90.0	58.3
Atlanta, GA	50.4	31.5	55.0	34.5	64.3	42.5	72.7	50.2	79.6	58.7	85.8	66.2
Fresno, CA	54.1	37.4	61.7	40.5	66.6	43.4	75.1	47.3	84.2	53.7	92.7	60.4
Honolulu, HI	80.1	65.6	80.5	65.4	81.6	67.2	82.8	68.7	84.7	70.3	86.5	72.2
Tulsa, OK	45.4	24.9	51.0	29.5	62.1	39.1	73.0	49.9	79.7	58.8	87.7	67.7
Sacramento, CA	52.7	37.7	60.0	41.1	64.0	43.2	71.1	45.5	80.3	50.3	87.8	55.3
Miami, FL	75.2	59.2	76.5	60.4	79.1	64.2	82.4	67.8	85.3	72.1	87.6	75.1
St. Louis, MO	37.7	20.8	42.6	25.1	54.6	35.5	66.9	46.4	76.1	56.0	85.2	65.7
Pittsburgh, PA	33.7	18.5	36.9	20.3	49.0	29.8	60.3	38.8	70.6	48.4	78.9	56.9
Minneapolis, MN	20.7	2.8	26.6	9.2	39.2	22.7	56.5	36.2	69.4	47.6	78.8	57.6
Omaha, NE	31.3	10.9	37.1	16.7	49.4	27.7	63.8	39.9	74.0	50.9	83.7	60.4
Las Vegas, NV	57.3	33.6	63.3	38.8	68.8	43.8	77.5	50.7	87.8	60.2	100.3	69.4
Toledo, OH	30.2	14.9	33.4	17.0	45.5	26.8	58.8	36.4	70.5	46.7	79.8	56.0
Colorado Springs, CO	41.1	16.1	44.6	19.3	50.0	24.6	59.8	33.0	68.7	42.1	79.0	51.1
Buffalo, NY	30.2	17.0	31.6	17.4	41.7	25.9	54.2	36.2	66.1	47.0	75.3	56.5
Wichita, KS	39.8	19.2	45.9	23.7	57.2	33.6	68.3	44.5	76.9	54.3	86.8	64.6

City	July Max.	July Min.	August Max.	August Min.	September Max.	September Min.	October Max.	October Min.	November Max.	November Min.	December Max.	December Min.
New York, NY	85.2	68.4	83.7	67.3	76.2	60.1	65.3	49.7	54.0	41.1	42.5	30.7
Los Angeles, CA	75.3	62.8	76.6	64.2	76.6	63.2	74.4	59.2	70.3	52.8	65.9	47.9
Chicago, IL	83.7	62.6	81.8	61.6	74.8	53.9	63.3	42.2	48.4	31.6	34.0	19.1
Houston, TX	92.7	72.4	92.5	72.0	88.4	67.9	81.6	57.6	72.4	49.6	64.7	42.2
Philadelphia, PA	86.1	67.2	84.6	66.3	77.6	58.7	66.3	46.4	55.1	37.6	43.4	28.1
San Diego, CA	76.2	65.7	77.8	67.3	77.1	65.6	74.6	60.9	69.9	53.9	66.1	48.8
Phoenix, AZ	105.9	81.0	103.7	79.2	98.3	72.8	88.1	60.8	74.9	48.9	66.2	41.8
Dallas, TX	96.5	74.1	96.2	73.6	87.8	66.9	78.5	55.8	66.8	45.4	57.5	36.3
San Antonio, TX	95.0	75.0	95.3	74.5	89.3	69.2	81.7	58.8	71.9	48.8	63.5	40.8
Detroit, MI	83.3	61.3	81.3	59.6	73.9	52.5	61.5	40.9	48.1	32.2	35.2	21.4
San Jose, CA	82.4	56.6	82.0	56.6	80.6	55.8	74.5	51.6	64.4	45.5	57.5	40.7
Indianapolis, IN	85.5	65.2	83.6	62.8	77.6	55.6	65.8	43.5	51.9	34.1	38.5	23.2
San Francisco, CA	71.6	53.9	72.3	55.0	73.6	55.2	70.1	51.8	62.4	47.1	56.1	42.7
Baltimore, MD	87.2	66.8	85.4	65.7	78.5	58.4	67.3	45.9	56.4	37.1	45.2	28.2
Jacksonville, FL	91.4	71.9	90.7	71.8	87.2	69.0	80.2	59.3	73.6	50.2	66.8	43.4
Columbus, OH	83.7	62.7	82.1	60.8	76.2	54.8	64.5	42.9	51.4	34.3	39.2	24.6
Milwaukee, WI	79.9	62.0	77.8	60.8	70.6	52.8	58.7	41.8	44.7	30.7	31.2	17.5
Memphis, TN	92.3	72.9	90.8	71.1	83.9	64.5	74.3	51.9	62.3	42.7	52.5	34.8
El Paso, TX	96.1	68.4	93.5	66.6	87.1	61.6	78.4	49.6	66.4	38.4	57.5	30.7
Washington, DC	88.5	71.4	86.9	70.0	80.1	62.5	69.1	50.3	58.3	41.1	47.0	31.7
Boston, MA	81.8	65.1	79.8	64.0	72.8	56.8	62.7	46.9	52.2	38.3	40.4	26.7
Seattle, WA	75.2	55.2	75.2	55.7	69.3	51.9	59.7	45.8	50.5	40.1	45.1	35.8
Austin, TX	95.0	73.9	95.5	73.9	90.5	69.8	82.1	60.0	71.8	49.9	62.0	41.2
Nashville-Davidson, TN	89.5	68.9	88.4	67.7	82.5	61.1	72.5	48.3	60.4	39.6	50.2	30.9
Denver, CO	88.2	58.6	85.8	56.9	76.9	47.6	66.3	36.4	52.5	25.4	44.5	17.4
Cleveland, OH	82.4	61.4	80.5	60.3	73.6	54.2	62.1	43.5	50.0	35.0	37.4	24.5
New Orleans, LA	90.6	73.1	90.2	72.8	86.6	69.5	79.4	58.7	71.1	51.1	64.3	44.8
Oklahoma City, OK	93.4	70.6	92.5	69.6	83.8	62.2	73.6	50.4	60.4	38.6	49.9	28.6
Fort Worth, TX	96.5	74.1	96.2	73.6	87.8	66.9	78.5	55.8	66.8	45.4	57.5	36.3
Portland, OR	79.9	56.5	80.3	56.9	74.6	52.0	64.0	44.9	52.6	39.5	45.6	34.8
Kansas City, MO	88.7	68.2	86.4	65.7	78.1	56.9	67.5	45.7	52.6	33.6	38.8	21.9
Charlotte, NC	88.9	69.6	87.7	68.9	81.9	62.9	72.0	50.6	62.6	41.5	52.3	32.8
Tucson, AZ	99.4	73.6	96.8	72.1	93.3	67.5	84.3	56.6	72.7	45.6	64.3	39.8
Long Beach, CA	82.7	63.4	84.0	64.8	82.1	62.7	78.4	57.8	72.1	50.4	67.0	45.0
Albuquerque, NM	92.5	64.4	89.0	62.6	81.9	55.2	71.0	43.0	57.3	31.2	47.5	23.1
Atlanta, GA	88.0	69.5	87.1	69.0	81.8	63.5	72.7	51.9	63.4	42.8	54.0	35.0
Fresno, CA	98.6	65.1	96.7	63.8	90.1	58.8	79.7	50.7	64.7	42.5	53.7	37.1
Honolulu, HI	87.5	73.5	88.7	74.2	88.5	73.5	86.9	72.3	84.1	70.3	81.2	67.0
Tulsa, OK	93.7	72.8	92.5	70.6	83.6	63.0	73.8	50.7	60.3	39.5	48.8	28.9
Sacramento, CA	93.2	58.1	92.1	58.0	87.3	55.7	77.9	50.4	63.1	43.4	52.7	37.8
Miami, FL	89.0	76.2	89.0	76.7	87.8	75.9	84.5	72.1	80.4	66.7	76.7	61.5
St. Louis, MO	89.3	70.4	87.3	67.9	79.9	60.5	68.5	48.3	54.7	37.7	41.7	26.0
Pittsburgh, PA	82.6	61.6	80.8	60.2	74.3	53.5	62.5	42.3	50.4	34.1	38.6	24.4
Minneapolis, MN	84.0	63.1	80.7	60.3	70.7	50.3	58.8	38.8	41.0	25.2	25.5	10.2
Omaha, NE	87.9	65.9	85.2	62.9	76.5	53.6	65.6	41.2	49.3	28.7	34.6	15.6
Las Vegas, NV	105.9	76.2	103.2	74.2	94.7	66.2	82.1	54.3	67.4	42.6	57.5	33.9
Toledo, OH	83.4	60.6	81.3	58.4	74.4	51.5	62.4	40.0	48.5	31.5	35.2	20.5
Colorado Springs, CO	84.4	57.1	81.3	55.2	73.6	47.1	63.5	36.3	50.7	24.9	42.2	17.4
Buffalo, NY	80.2	61.9	77.9	60.1	70.8	53.0	59.4	42.7	47.1	33.9	35.3	22.9
Wichita, KS	92.8	69.9	90.7	67.9	81.4	59.2	70.6	46.6	55.3	33.9	43.0	23.0

Source: National Oceanic and Atmospheric Administration

Weather Report

The record-setting cities in different weather categories in the 48 contiguous states:

10 Hottest Cities (Mean temp °F)

1	Key West, FL	77.8
2	Miami, FL	75.9
3	West Palm Beach, FL	74.7
4	Fort Myers, FL	74.4
5	Yuma, AZ	74.2
6	Brownsville, TX	73.8
7	Phoenix, AZ	72.6
8	Vero Beach, FL	72.4
9	Orlando, FL	72.3
9	Tampa, FL	72.3

10 Coldest Cities (Mean temp °F)

1	International Falls, MN	36.8
2	Duluth, MN	38.5
3	Caribou, ME	38.8
4	Marquette, MI	39.1
5	Sault Ste. Marie, MI	39.7
6	Fargo, ND	41.0
7	Alamosa, CO	41.1
8	St. Cloud, MN	41.5
8	Williston, ND	41.5
10	Bismarck, ND	41.6

10 Driest Cities (Precip. in inches)

1	Yuma, AZ	3.17
2	Las Vegas, NV	4.13
3	Bishop, CA	5.37
4	Bakersfield, CA	5.72
5	Reno, NV	7.53
6	Alamosa, CO	7.57
7	Phoenix, AZ	7.66
8	Yakima, WA	7.97
9	Winslow, AZ	8.04
10	Winnemucca, NV	8.23

10 Wettest Cities (Precip. in inches)

1	Quillayute, WA	105.18
2	Astoria, OR	66.40
3	Tallahassee, FL	65.71
4	Mobile, AL	63.96
5	Pensacola, FL	62.25
6	New Orleans, LA	61.88
7	Baton Rouge, LA	60.89
8	West Palm Beach, FL	60.75
9	Meridian, MS	56.71
10	Tupelo, MS	55.87

10 Windiest Cities (Mean speed mph)

1	Blue Hill, MA	15.4
2	Dodge City, KS	13.9
3	Amarillo, TX	13.5
4	Rochester, MN	13.1
5	Cheyenne, WY	12.9
6	Casper, WY	12.8
7	Great Falls, MT	12.6
8	Goodland, KS	12.5
9	Boston, MA	12.5
10	Lubbock, TX	12.4

10 Snowiest Cities (Snowfall in inches)

1	Marquette, MI	130.6
2	Sault Ste, Marie, MI	117.1
3	Syracuse, NY	114.7
4	Caribou, ME	110.7
5	Lander, WY	102.2
6	Flagstaff, AZ	100.3
7	Muskegon, MI	97.9
8	Buffalo, NY	91.8
9	Rochester, NY	90.3
10	Erie, PA	86.5

10 Sunniest Cities (% of possible)

1	Yuma, AZ	90
2	Redding, CA	88
3	Phoenix, AZ	86
4	Tucson, AZ	85
5	Las Vegas, NV	85
6	El Paso, TX	84
7	Fresno, CA	79
7	Reno, NV	79
9	Flagstaff, AZ	78
9	Sacramento, CA	78

10 Cloudiest Cities (No. of cloudy days)

1	Quillayute, WA	239
1	Astoria, OR	239
3	Olympia, WA	228
4	Seattle, WA	226
5	Portland. OR	222
6	Kalispell, MT	214
7	Binghamton, NY	212
7	Elkins, WV	212
9	Beckley, WV	210
10	Eugene, OR	209

Source: National Oceanic and Atmospheric Administration

The 10 Most Costly U.S. Civil Disorders

Date	Location	Estimated insured losses
April 29-May 4, 1992	Los Angeles	$775,000,000
Aug. 11-17, 1965	Los Angeles	44,000,000
July 23, 1967	Detroit	41,500,000
May 17-19, 1980	Miami	65,250,000
April 4-9, 1968	Washington, D.C.	24,000,000
July 13-14, 1977	New York City	28,000,000
July 12, 1967	Newark	15,000,000
April 6-9, 1968	Baltimore	14,000,000
April 4-11, 1968	Chicago	13,000,000
April 4-11, 1968	New York City	4,200,000

Sources: Property Claim Services division of American Insurance Services Group, and Insurance Information Institute

People Patterns

From the Pepsi Generation of the 1960s to the have-it-all yuppies of the 1980s, the baby boomers have been the most sought after consumers ever. Now, as they enter a new stage of life, they may become even more desirable to marketers.

Many of the 78 million baby boomers born between 1946 and 1964 are starting to reach what has traditionally been the pinnacle of household income and buying power—the period between ages 45 and 54. People in this age group typically spend 17% more than the average household, according to the U.S. Bureau of Labor Statistics, while those between 55 and 64 spend 15% more.

"While people age 50 and older account for only 27% of the population, they represent 43% of total consumer demand, 65% of total net worth and 74% of all personal financial assets," says Ken Dychtwald, president of Age Wave Inc., a consulting firm in Emeryville, Calif., that specializes in demographic issues. "These figures will continue to increase with the aging of the boomers."

There is some question, however, about whether middle-aged boomers will be quite as lucrative a target market as expected. Many of them delayed having children and will face high college costs into their 50s and even 60s. Some research studies also indicate that they may turn more frugal, realizing that they are woefully unprepared for their retirement years. Many boomers have failed to save much, and they may not be able to count on as much support from the precarious Social Security system as previous generations. "The idea that boomers need to grow up and take responsibility while there's still time is pervasive," says Judith Langer, president of Langer Associates Inc., a market-research and consulting firm in New York. "It's not easy to predict what will happen, but it's clear that many aren't going to save enough and will wind up in trouble."

Financial-services companies, of course, hope boomers change their ways and are trying to convert the big spenders into savers. Fidelity Investment Co. created an "It's Time" promotional campaign that admonished consumers to stop putting off their investment plans. A Fidelity spokeswoman said many of its regular customers are boomers who have long-term savings strategies, but company surveys indicate many people, even those within a few years of retirement age, haven't saved enough.

The campaign was designed to attract new and younger customers, particulary the baby boomers. So the commercials were set to the Chambers Brothers' song "Time Has Come Today," a rock 'n' roll hit that was performed at the 1969 Woodstock concert, a landmark event and subject of nostalgia for many boomers.

Meanwhile, other marketers are betting boomers will remain as self-indulgent as ever and are gearing up to sell expensive toys to the yuppies in midlife. They are changing their approach to the traditional mature market because they expect boomers to redefine the middle and golden years much as they revolutionized society in their younger years. Boomers are generally better educated and more sophisticated consumers who will be more demanding of businesses, such as the health-care and financial-services industries that cater to older people.

General Motors' Cadillac division has changed the appearance and marketing of its lineup as boomers move into the auto maker's target age group. One of the most striking marketing changes is the recent ad campaign for the DeVille, a large, four-door sedan with a stodgy history. The DeVille has long been viewed as grandfather's car, and with good reason: Cadillac says the bulk of DeVille drivers are 65 and over. But a recent television commercial opened with a jazzy tune and a photographic timeline that follows a couple from their hippie days through the present. Another shows a group of fiftyish people who have stuck together through the years. The ad looks like *The Big Chill* 15 years later—but without the whining. Presumably, the folks in the ad have enjoyed rewarding careers, raised families, and made sacrifices along the way. Now it's time to splurge a bit. The company's advertising theme, "For the time of your life," promotes the idea that boomers have earned a midlife reward.

Janet Eckhoff, brand manager for DeVille, says the company knows boomers are growing into a huge potential market, but they won't be looking for the same qualities as yesterday's DeVille buyer. "Most of these people will be considering a Cadillac for the first time, so we have given the car a more youthful appeal," she says. "The mid-50s is the beginning of an interesting new life stage. In many cases the nest is empty, and people may have taken early retirement."

Cadillac began pursuing younger buyers with the introduction a few years ago of its performance-oriented Seville and Eldorado models. Now the DeVille has joined its siblings with improvements in its engine, suspension, and other components to boost performance and compete with popular European and Japanese high-performance luxury models.

It's no coincidence that a flurry of expensive convertibles debuted as the oldest boomers reached 50 in 1996. Cars like the Porsche Boxter, Mercedes-Benz SLK, and BMW Z3, all costing in the neighborhood of $40,000, clearly are aimed at affluent boomers. The ragtops are reminiscent of older models that have tempted boomers for years and play to their desire to have just what they've always wanted. (Cadillac has no pint-sized convertibles on deck, in part, it says, because much of the over-50 crowd, including boomers, want more size, comfort, and practicality.)

Even Winnebago Industries, the maker of recreational vehicles, has begun targeting boomers. It says the group will be a huge potential market within the next several years. But skeptics aren't convinced boomers will buy into the recreational-vehicle lifestyle.

"Companies can't use their tired old approach when trying to attract the boomers," says Cheryl Russell, editor-in-chief of *New Strategist*, a demographic publication. In some cases, companies that cater to older age groups may have to split their marketing programs to cover today's 60-plus consumers and the vastly different midlife group that will be replacing them in the coming decades. For instance, the American Association of Retired Persons is considering a second edition of its magazine, *Modern Maturity*, to appeal to the next wave of seniors.

Some marketing experts even say the boomers will never develop into a mature market—at least as it is now defined. Instead, they will form a new mid-life market that will share certain traits with the youth culture that boomers created in the 1960s. Already, there is a strong market for products that help boomers hold on to their youth. From skin treatments, hair coloring, and other cosmetics, to nutritional aids to sports cars, products that enhance the aging population's sense of vitality are being snapped up.

"By 2020, a new adult life stage characterizing the period from 40 to 60 years old will become the marketing epicenter in the United States," says Mr. Dychtwald, the California consultant, "with aging-friendly products and services transforming consumer activities during the next 25 years."

What puzzles consumer researchers is the fact that many marketers still haven't addressed the aging boomers. "They jumped on the youth-market bandwagon and they're still hanging on, essentially ignoring the growing midlife market," says Ms. Russell. "It's so obvious, but marketers don't seem to realize that boomers will continue to be their biggest market. Businesses catering to youth and abandoning the boom are making a big mistake." For example, she says her research shows women from 55 to 64 spend an average of $100 more annually on clothes than those in their 20s.

Some marketers may feel that it's premature to make a major marketing shift for the aging boomers. They won't all even be considered middle-aged until 2005. At that point, boomers will range in age from 41 to 59. By 2010, the oldest boomers will be on the verge of retirement age and the whole generation will have crossed the bridge—chronologically, at least—to retirement by 2030.

Marketers may also believe the boomers will finally rein in their spending and save, as their elders have been exhorting them to do for years. Economists say boomers will have to drastically boost their rate of savings to avoid a financial crisis following retirement, especially given the uncertainties about Social Security. The huge boomer population will be drawing financial support from a much smaller base of contributors to Social Security. The number of working taxpayers supporting each Social Security recipient has fallen to just over three today from more than five in 1960. By 2040, when the youngest boomers will be in their 70s, it is estimated there will be two or fewer workers per Social Security recipient.

There are some early signs that boomers are increasing their financial assets. A survey completed in February 1997 by the National Association of Securities Dealers showed a surge in investment during the 1990s. According to the NASD's findings, about 43% of American adults own shares in public companies, compared with 21% in 1990. The majority of investors are under 50, the survey found, leaving no doubt that boomers were driving the increase. The survey also found boomers more often prefer to make their own investment decisions rather than rely on advisers, and a growing number consider themselves savvy about the financial markets, giving themselves a grade of "A" or "B" in investment knowledge. These findings refute the argument that boomers are in a state of denial, avoiding the issue of their financial future and showing little initiative.

"It's clear that boomers will have to do more if they are to fulfill their retirement plans, but they also have to deal with the burden of generational prejudice of critics who say they've been irresponsible," Ms. Russell, the demographics expert, says. "There's a certain self-righteousness among older people toward the baby-boom generation. Just because they lived through the Great Depression and World War II, they feel no one else knows about suffering and sacrifice."

Jonathan Welsh, a *Wall Street Journal* staff reporter

Demographic Trends

U.S. Population: 1790–1996

Year	Number	% increase over preceding census	Year	Number	% increase over preceding census
1790	3,929,214	–	1900	75,994,575	20.7
1800	5,308,483	35.1	1910	91,972,266	21.0
1810	7,239,881	36.4	1920	105,710,620	14.9
1820	9,638,453	33.1	1930	122,775,046	16.1
1830	12,866,020	33.5	1940	131,669,275	7.2
1840	17,069,453	32.7	1950	150,697,361	14.5
1850	23,191,876	35.9	1960	179,323,175	18.5
1860	31,443,321	35.6	1970	203,302,031	13.5
1870	39,818,449	26.6	1980	226,546,000	11.4
1880	50,155,783	26.0	1990	249,398,000	10.1
1890	62,947,714	25.5	1996	265,284,000	6.4

U.S. Population Projections: 2000–2050

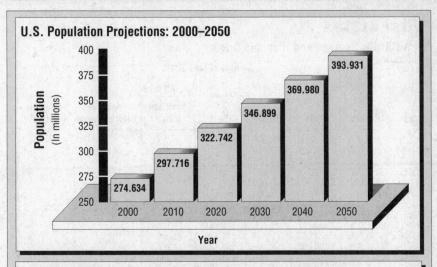

Percent Distribution of the U.S. Population By Age: 1995–2050

Year	Total	Under 5 years	5–13 years	14–17 years	18–24 years	25–34 years	35–44 years	45–64 years	65 years and over	85 years and over	100 years and over
1995	100.0	7.4	13.0	5.6	9.6	15.5	16.2	19.9	12.8	1.4	0.0
2000	100.0	6.9	13.1	5.7	9.6	13.6	16.3	22.2	12.6	1.6	0.0
2005	100.0	6.7	12.5	5.9	9.9	12.7	14.7	24.9	12.6	1.7	0.0
2010	100.0	6.7	12.0	5.7	10.1	12.9	12.9	26.5	13.2	1.9	0.0
2020	100.0	6.8	12.0	5.3	9.3	13.3	12.3	24.6	16.5	2.0	0.1
2030	100.0	6.6	12.0	5.4	9.2	12.3	12.8	21.7	20.0	2.4	0.1
2040	100.0	6.8	11.9	5.4	9.3	12.4	11.9	22.0	20.3	3.7	0.1
2050	100.0	6.9	12.1	5.4	9.2	12.5	12.0	21.8	20.0	4.6	0.2

Source: U.S. Census Bureau

Vital Stats

Birth Rate Per 1,000*

Fertility Rate Per 1,000*

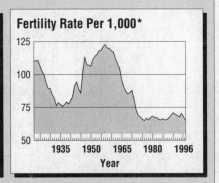

*Birth rates are live births per 1,000 population. Fertility rates are live births per 1,000 women aged 15-44 years.
Source: National Center for Health Statistics

Vital Stats

Live Births by Race and Hispanic Origin

			Number of Live Births				
				All other			
Year	All races	White	Total	Black	American Indian	Asian or Pacific Islander	Hispanic origin[†]
1923	2,910,000	2,531,000	380,000	–	–	–	–
1925	2,909,000	2,506,000	403,000	–	–	–	–
1930	2,618,000	2,274,000	344,000	–	–	–	–
1935	2,377,000	2,042,000	334,000	–	–	–	–
1940	2,559,000	2,199,000	360,000	–	–	–	–
1945	2,858,000	2,471,000	388,000	–	–	–	–
1950	3,632,000	3,108,000	524,000	–	–	–	–
1955	4,097,000	3,485,000	613,000	–	–	–	–
1960	4,257,850	3,600,744	–	602,264	21,114	–	–
1965	3,760,358	3,123,860	–	581,126	24,066	–	–
1970	3,731,386	3,109,956	–	561,992	22,264	–	–
1975	3,144,198	2,576,818	–	496,829	22,690	–	–
1980	3,612,258	2,936,351	–	568,080	29,389	74,355	307,163
1981	3,629,238	2,947,679	–	564,955	29,688	84,553	321,954
1982	3,680,537	2,984,817	–	568,506	32,436	93,193	337,390
1983	3,638,933	2,946,468	–	562,624	32,881	95,713	336,833
1984	3,669,141	2,967,100	–	568,138	33,256	98,926	346,986
1985	3,760,561	3,037,913	–	581,824	34,037	104,606	372,814
1986	3,756,547	3,019,175	–	592,910	34,169	107,797	389,048
1987	3,809,394	3,043,828	–	611,173	35,322	116,560	406,153
1988	3,909,510	3,102,083	–	638,562	37,088	129,035	449,604
1989	4,040,958	3,192,355	–	673,124	39,478	133,075	532,249
1990	4,158,212	3,290,273	–	684,336	39,051	141,635	595,073
1991	4,110,907	3,241,273	–	682,602	38,841	145,372	623,085
1992	4,065,014	3,201,678	–	673,633	39,453	150,250	643,271
1993	4,000,240	3,149,833	–	658,875	38,732	152,800	654,418
1994	3,952,767	3,121,004	–	636,391	37,740	157,632	665,026
1995	3,699,589	3,096,865	–	603,139	37,278	160,287	679,768
1996	3,914,953	3,113,014		596,039	38,456	167,444	697,829

[†]Persons of Hispanic origin may be of any race.

Birth Rates by Race and Hispanic Origin

Year	All races	White	Birth Rate* All other Total	Black	American Indian	Asian or Pacific Islander	Hispanic origin
1923	26.0	25.2	33.2	–	–	–	–
1925	25.1	24.1	34.2	–	–	–	–
1930	21.3	20.6	27.5	–	–	–	–
1935	18.7	17.9	25.8	–	–	–	–
1940	19.4	18.6	26.7	–	–	–	–
1945	20.4	19.7	26.5	–	–	–	–
1950	24.1	23.0	33.3	–	–	–	–
1955	25.0	23.8	34.5	–	–	–	–
1960	23.7	22.7	–	31.9	–	–	–
1965	19.4	18.3	–	27.7	–	–	–
1970	18.4	17.4	–	25.3	–	–	–
1975	14.6	13.6	–	20.7	–	–	–
1980	15.9	15.1	–	21.3	20.7	19.9	23.5
1981	15.8	15.0	–	20.8	20.0	20.1	24.1
1982	15.9	15.1	–	20.7	21.1	20.3	23.9
1983	15.6	14.8	–	20.2	20.6	19.5	22.8
1984	15.6	14.8	–	20.1	20.1	18.8	22.7
1985	15.8	15.0	–	20.4	19.8	18.7	23.3
1986	15.6	14.8	–	20.5	19.2	18.0	23.3
1987	15.7	14.9	–	20.8	19.1	18.4	23.3
1988	16.0	15.0	–	21.5	19.3	19.2	24.1
1989	16.4	15.4	–	22.3	19.7	18.7	26.2
1990	16.7	15.8	–	22.4	18.9	19.0	26.7
1991	16.3	15.4	–	21.9	18.3	18.2	26.7
1992	15.9	15.0	–	21.3	18.4	18.0	26.5
1993	15.5	14.7	–	20.5	17.8	17.7	26.0
1994	15.2	14.4	–	19.5	17.1	17.5	25.5
1995	14.8	14.2	–	18.2	16.6	17.3	25.2
1996	14.8	–	–	–	–	–	–

*Birth rates are live births per 1,000 population in specified groups.

Fertility Rates by Race and Hispanic Origin

Year	All races	White	Fertility rate* All other Total	Black	American Indian	Asian or Pacific Islander	Hispanic origin
1923	110.5	108.0	130.5	–	–	–	–
1925	106.6	103.3	134.0	–	–	–	–
1930	89.2	87.1	105.9	–	–	–	–
1935	77.2	74.5	98.4	–	–	–	–
1940	79.9	77.1	102.4	–	–	–	–
1945	85.9	83.4	106.0	–	–	–	–
1950	106.2	102.3	137.3	–	–	–	–
1955	118.3	113.7	154.3	–	–	–	–
1960	118.0	113.2	–	153.5	–	–	–
1965	96.3	91.3	–	133.2	–	–	–
1970	87.9	84.1	–	115.4	–	–	–
1975	66.0	62.5	–	87.9	–	–	–
1980	68.4	65.6	–	84.7	82.7	73.2	95.4
1981	67.3	64.8	–	82.0	79.6	73.7	97.5
1982	67.3	64.8	–	80.9	83.6	74.8	96.1
1983	65.7	63.4	–	78.7	81.8	71.7	91.8
1984	65.5	63.2	–	78.2	79.8	69.2	91.5
1985	66.3	64.1	–	78.8	78.6	68.4	94.0
1986	65.4	63.1	–	78.9	75.9	66.0	93.9
1987	65.8	63.3	–	80.1	75.6	67.1	93.0
1988	67.3	64.5	–	82.6	76.8	70.2	96.4
1989	69.2	66.4	–	86.2	79.0	68.2	104.9
1990	70.9	68.3	–	86.8	76.2	69.6	107.7
1991	69.6	67.0	–	85.2	75.1	67.6	108.1
1992	68.9	66.5	–	83.2	75.4	67.2	108.6
1993	67.6	65.4	–	80.5	73.4	66.7	106.9
1994	66.7	64.9	–	76.9	70.9	66.8	105.6
1995	65.6	64.4	–	72.3	69.1	66.4	105.0
1996	65.7	–	–	–	–	–	–

*Fertility rates are live births per 1,000 women aged 15-44 years in specified group.
Source: National Center for Health Statistics

Marriage Rates Per 1,000 Population Over 15 Years of Age by Sex

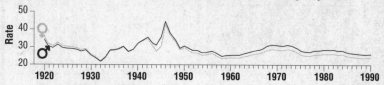

Marriages and Marriage Rates

Year	Number	Total population	Rate per 1,000 population Men 15 years of age and over	Women 15 years of age and over
1920	1,274,476	12.0	34.2	36.0
1925	1,188,334	10.3	29.2	30.3
1930	1,126,856	9.2	25.6	26.2
1935	1,327,000	10.4	28.4	28.8
1940	1,595,879	12.1	32.3	32.3
1945	1,612,992	12.2	35.8	30.5
1950	1,667,231	11.1	30.7	29.8
1955	1,531,000	9.3	27.2	25.8
1960	1,523,000	8.5	25.4	24.0
1965	1,800,000	9.3	27.9	26.0
1970	2,158,802	10.6	31.1	28.4
1975	2,152,662	10.0	27.9	25.6
1980	2,390,252	10.6	28.5	26.1
1985	2,412,625	10.1	27.0	24.9
1986	2,407,099	10.0	26.6	24.5
1987	2,403,378	9.9	26.3	24.3
1988	2,395,926	9.8	26.0	24.0
1989	2,403,268	9.7	25.8	23.9
1990	2,443,489	9.8	26.0	24.1
1991	2,371,000	9.4	–	–
1992	2,362,000	9.3	–	–
1993	2,334,000	9.0	–	–
1994	2,362,000	9.1	–	–
1995	2,336,000	8.9	–	–
1996	2,334,000	8.8	–	–

Source: National Center for Health Statistics

Divorce and Annulment Rate Per 1,000 Population

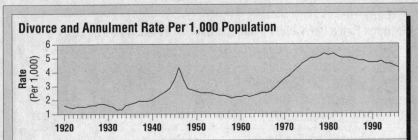

Divorces and Annulments and Rates Per 1,000 Population

Year	Divorces and annulments	Rate per 1,000 population	Year	Divorces and annulments	Rate per 1,000 population
1920	170,505	1.6	1983	1,158,000	5.0
1925	175,449	1.5	1984	1,169,000	5.0
1930	195,961	1.6	1985	1,190,000	5.0
1935	218,000	1.7	1986	1,178,000	4.9
1940	264,000	2.0	1987	1,166,000	4.8
1945	485,000	3.5	1988	1,167,000	4.8
1950	385,000	2.6	1989	1,157,000	4.7
1955	377,000	2.3	1990	1,175,000	4.7
1960	393,000	2.2	1991	1,187,000	4.7
1965	479,000	2.5	1992	1,215,000	4.8
1970	708,000	3.5	1993	1,187,000	4.6
1975	1,036,000	4.8	1994	1,191,000	4.6
1980	1,189,000	5.2	1995	1,169,000	4.4
1981	1,213,000	5.3	1996	1,150,000	4.3
1982	1,170,000	5.1			

Source: National Center for Health Statistics

Death Rates Per 1,000 Population

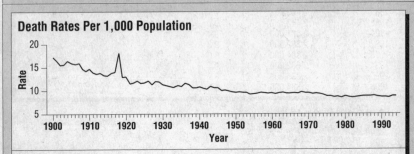

Death Rates*
(Per 1,000 population)

Year	Rate	Total deaths	Year	Rate	Total deaths
1940	10.8	1,417,269	1991	8.6	2,169,518
1950	9.6	1,452,454	1992	8.5	2,175,613
1960	9.5	1,711,982	1993	8.8	2,268,553
1970	9.5	1,921,031	1994	8.8	2,278,994
1980	8.8	1,989,841	1995	8.8	2,312,132
1985	8.8	2,086,440	1996	8.8	2,322,421
1990	8.6	2,148,463			

Source: National Center for Health Statistics

Infant Mortality Rate, 1919–1996*
(Per 1,000 live births)

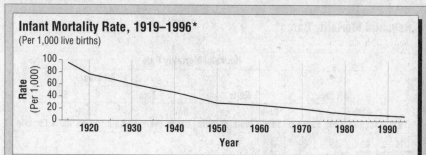

Infant Mortality Rates*
(Per 1,000 live births)

	Infant Mortality Rate										
	All races			White			All other				
							Total			Black		
Year	Both sexes	Male	Female	Both sexes	Male	Female	Both sexes	Male	Female	Both sexes	Male	Female
1915-19	95.7	–	–	92.8	–	–	149.7	–	–	150.4	–	–
1920-24	76.7	–	–	73.3	–	–	115.3	–	–	117.4	–	–
1925-29	69.0	–	–	65.0	–	–	105.4	–	–	105.3	–	–
1930-34	60.4	–	–	55.2	–	–	98.6	–	–	90.5	–	–
1935-39	53.2	–	–	49.2	–	–	81.3	–	–	80.1	–	–
1940	47.0	52.5	41.3	43.2	48.3	37.8	73.8	82.2	65.2	72.9	81.1	64.6
1950	29.2	32.8	25.5	26.8	30.2	23.1	44.5	48.9	39.9	43.9	48.3	39.4
1960	26.0	29.3	22.6	22.9	26.0	19.6	43.2	47.9	38.5	44.3	49.1	39.4
1970	20.0	22.4	17.5	17.8	20.0	15.4	30.9	34.2	27.5	32.6	36.2	29.0
1975	16.1	17.9	14.2	14.2	15.9	12.3	24.2	26.2	22.2	26.2	28.3	24.0
1980	12.6	13.9	11.2	10.9	12.1	9.5	20.2	21.9	18.4	22.2	24.2	20.2
1985	10.6	11.9	9.3	9.2	10.4	7.9	16.8	18.3	15.3	19.0	20.8	17.2
1986	10.4	11.5	9.1	8.8	9.9	7.7	16.7	18.5	14.9	18.9	20.9	16.8
1987	10.1	11.2	8.9	8.5	9.5	7.5	16.5	18.1	14.8	18.8	20.6	16.8
1988	10.0	11.0	8.9	8.4	9.4	7.3	16.1	17.3	14.8	18.5	20.0	17.0
1989	9.8	10.8	8.8	8.1	9.0	7.1	16.3	17.6	15.0	18.6	20.0	17.2
1990	9.2	10.3	8.1	7.6	8.5	6.6	15.5	17.0	14.0	18.0	19.6	16.2
1991	8.9	10.0	7.8	7.3	8.3	6.3	15.1	16.5	13.6	17.6	19.4	15.7
1992	8.5	9.4	7.6	6.9	7.7	6.1	14.4	15.7	13.1	16.8	18.4	15.3
1993	8.4	9.3	7.4	6.8	7.6	6.0	14.1	15.6	12.5	16.5	18.3	14.7
1994	8.0	8.8	7.2	6.6	7.2	5.9	13.5	14.8	12.1	15.8	17.5	14.1
1995	7.6	8.3	6.8	6.3	7.0	5.6	12.6	13.5	11.6	15.1	16.3	13.9
1996	7.2	–	–	6.0	–	–	–	–	–	14.2	–	–

*Rates are infant (under 1 year) deaths per 1,000 live births in specified group. Beginning in 1980, race for live births is tabulated according to race of mother.
Source: National Center for Health Statistics

Neonatal Mortality Rates*
(Per 1,000 live births)

	Neonatal Mortality Rate											
	All races			White			All other					
							Total			Black		
Year	Both sexes	Male	Female	Both sexes	Male	Female	Both sexes	Male	Female	Both sexes	Male	Female
1915-19	43.4	–	–	42.3	–	–	58.1	–	–	67.9	–	–
1920-24	39.7	–	–	38.7	–	–	51.1	–	–	52.1	–	–
1925-29	37.2	–	–	36.0	–	–	47.9	–	–	48.2	–	–
1930-34	34.4	–	–	32.5	–	–	48.2	–	–	45.8	–	–
1935-39	31.0	–	–	29.5	–	–	41.4	–	–	41.5	–	–
1940	28.8	32.6	24.7	27.2	30.9	23.3	39.7	44.9	34.5	39.9	44.8	34.9
1950	20.5	23.3	17.5	19.4	22.2	16.4	27.5	30.8	24.2	27.8	31.1	24.4
1960	18.7	21.2	16.1	17.2	19.7	14.7	26.9	30.0	23.6	27.8	31.1	24.5
1970	15.1	17.0	13.1	13.8	15.5	11.9	21.4	23.9	18.9	22.8	25.4	20.1
1975	11.6	12.9	10.2	10.4	11.7	9.0	16.8	18.2	15.3	18.3	19.8	16.8
1980	8.5	9.3	7.6	7.4	8.2	6.5	13.2	14.3	12.1	14.6	15.9	13.3
1985	7.0	7.8	6.1	6.0	6.8	5.2	11.0	12.0	10.0	12.6	13.8	11.4
1986	6.7	7.4	6.0	5.7	6.3	5.1	10.8	11.8	9.7	12.3	13.6	11.0
1987	6.5	7.1	5.8	5.4	6.0	4.8	10.7	11.7	9.6	12.3	13.5	11.1
1988	6.3	6.9	5.7	5.3	5.8	4.7	10.3	11.2	9.4	12.1	13.1	10.9
1989	6.2	6.8	5.6	5.1	5.7	4.6	10.3	11.1	9.5	11.9	12.8	11.0
1990	5.8	6.5	5.2	4.8	5.4	4.2	9.9	10.8	8.9	11.6	12.7	10.4
1991	5.6	6.2	5.0	4.5	5.0	4.0	9.5	10.5	8.5	11.2	12.6	9.9
1992	5.4	5.8	4.9	4.3	4.7	4.0	9.2	10.0	8.3	10.8	11.8	9.8
1993	5.3	5.7	4.8	4.3	4.6	3.9	9.0	9.9	8.1	10.7	11.8	9.6
1994	5.1	5.6	4.6	4.2	4.5	3.8	8.6	9.5	7.7	10.2	11.3	9.1
1995	4.9	5.4	4.4	4.1	4.5	3.6	8.1	8.7	7.5	9.8	10.6	9.0
1996	4.7	—	—	3.9	—	—	—	—	—	9.2	—	—

*Rates are neonatal (under 28 days) deaths per 1,000 live births in specified group. Beginning in 1980, race for live births is tabulated according to race of mother.
Source: National Center for Health Statistics

STIRRING THE MELTING POT

America has long prided itself on being a cultural "melting pot," but the mix will be more varied and volatile than ever in the 21st century.

The Census Bureau predicts that through a combination of immigration and higher birth rates among some minority groups, the U.S. population in 2050 will be substantially more diverse than it is today. In fact, some demographers predict that, by 2060 non-Hispanic whites will no longer be a majority. While whites will still be the largest racial group, their share of the total population will steadily decline to 53% by 2050 and will likely fall below 50% a few years later. That's a steep drop from their nearly 75% share in 1995.

"What you think is unimaginable today could be the status quo in the future," says David Word, a demographer at the Census Bureau.

The changing face of America is already evident in many ways as more minorities integrate cities and suburbs, move into the workplace, and begin to show their muscle at the voting booth. But in the next century, the changes will be more dramatic. Businesses will face the challenge of creating an even more diverse workplace and selling to a much more fragmented consumer market. For government, demographers say, the increased diversity will mean greater demand for public education, welfare benefits, and other social services.

All of the groups measured by the Census Bureau are expected to have more babies, but the Asian and Hispanic populations will experience the most dramatic increases. By 2050, the number of births for each group is expected to be triple the number of babies born in 1995.

At the same time, the Census Bureau estimates that immigration will total about 820,000 annually, with Hispanics accounting for the largest share—about 350,000—and Asians in second place with about 226,000. By the middle of the next century, it is expected that the population will include "80 million, post-1994 immigrants and their descendants, or 25% of the total population," according to the Census Bureau.

By 2050, Hispanics are expected to be the second largest ethnic group at 24.5% of the total population of 394 million, compared with about 10% of the 265 million Americans today. The percentage of blacks will be relatively stable, increasing from 12% to 13.6% in 2050. And Asians will make a big jump to 8.2% in 2050 from 3.3%.

The Census Bureau notes that its projections are based on assumptions that may have to be revised over time, but it is unlikely that there will be drastic changes in immigration patterns or birth and death rates. Despite moves to limit immigration, Mark Krikorian, chairman for the Center for Immigration Studies in Washington, D.C., says it would be "a number of years before any changes in legal immigration would have an impact on the demographics of the population."

In light of the inevitable demographic shifts, some businesses are already trying to master the skills of selling to ethnic groups. The Asian market is now attracting the kind of attention the Hispanic market started getting in the 1980s. For example, Mosaica, a division of Young and Rubicam, Inc., was formed four years ago when the advertising agency realized more clients wanted to target the Asian-American market. Denise Leo, senior vice president of Mosaica, says demographics of the Asian-American community, such as high education levels, median household income and savings rates, make it particularly attractive to marketers. "Four to five years ago, few large multinational companies were targeting this market," says Ms. Leo, "but after telecommunication companies and banks first began to understand the long-term value of these customers, others soon followed."

Similarly, in the workplace, some companies are embracing diversity. Inland Steel Industries, Inc., in Chicago, for example, has a support group, Hispanics Initiating Progress (HIP), that promotes the advancement of Hispanics. The members meet periodically with management to provide information about issues of concern to the Hispanic community. "The relationship benefits the workers as well as the company which uses the group's feedback to better understand the Hispanic market," says Teresa Villarreal, who heads the group.

But not everyone is so amenable to diversity. The Federation for American Immigration Reform advocates more limits on immigration and rails against "cultural fragmentation." Other critics complain about efforts to create a multicultural curriculum in schools at the expense of traditional teachings. And U.S. English, a citizens' action group, has helped push through legislation in about half the states declaring English the official language.

"Calling for lower levels of immigration is not xenophobia; it is a reasonable response to a growing problem," says Mr. Krikorian of the Center for Immigration Studies, who cites the high costs of educating so many children who won't be able to speak English and the problem of so many people seeking a limited pool of welfare and medical benefits. "It is inappropriate," he declares, "to develop assistance programs for citizens, and then import people with similar needs."

Much of the debate about diversity focuses on Hispanics because they represent such a high percentage of immigrants and are projected to be the second largest ethnic group by 2050. Charles Kamasaki, vice president of the National Council of La Raza, a Hispanic civil-rights group based in Washington, complains that the focus on immigration helps to perpetuate a negative image of "a brown horde sneaking across the border," and that little attention is paid to the employment and education problems of Hispanics. Historically, the poverty rate for Hispanics has fallen between the rates for whites and blacks, but recently the rate for Hispanics has surpassed that for blacks. And while blacks have practically caught up to whites with 87% of teenagers finishing high school, Hispanics lag far behind with only a 57% completion rate.

Although these statistics would seem to paint a grim picture, there's a growing group of middle-class Hispanics. Richard Tobin, president of Strategy Research Corp. in Miami, estimates Hispanic buying power in the United States at $228 billion in 1996. He notes that Hispanic Americans are already moving into positions of political and business power and creating opportunities for other Hispanics. "Hispanics have already been here for one generation, and they know the system well," says Mr. Tobin. "They will continue to move into positions of political power. As a result, we will see that increasing diversity reflected in policymaking in the next generation."

The growing influence of Hispanics in the political sphere was visible in the most recent presidential election when the number of Hispanic voters grew by 30% to a record high of five million voters. Their strong turnout at the polls resulted in a heavily Democratic vote and the success of a number of Hispanic candidates. Perhaps the most surprising upset was the defeat of Rep. Robert Dornan (R., Calif.) by Hispanic businesswoman Loretta Sanchez in traditionally conservative Orange County, Calif.

The increased participation of Hispanics was due in part to anger and fear about harsh immigration and social policy proposals. "Latinos are mobilized to register and to vote as never before because of the negative environment," says Cecilia Muñoz, deputy vice president for policy at La Raza. "They are angry and they used their vote to register that anger."

Eileen Kinsella

White Minority?

U.S. Resident Population by Race and Hispanic Origin

(In thousands)

Year	Total number	Hispanic origin*	Not of Hispanic origin			
			White	Black	American Indian, Eskimo, Aleut	Asian, Pacific Islander
1980	226,546	14,609	180,906	26,142	1,326	3,563
1985	237,924	18,368	184,945	27,738	1,558	5,315
1990	249,398	22,558	188,583	29,374	1,802	7,080
1995	262,890	27,277	193,281	31,565	1,931	8,836
1996	265,284	28,269	193,978	31,912	1,954	9,171
2000	274,634	31,366	197,061	33,568	2,054	10,584
2010	297,716	41,139	202,390	37,466	2,320	14,402
2020	322,742	52,652	207,393	41,538	2,601	18,557
2030	346,899	65,570	209,998	45,448	2,891	22,993
2040	369,980	80,164	209,621	49,379	3,203	27,614
2050	393,931	96,508	207,901	53,555	3,534	32,432

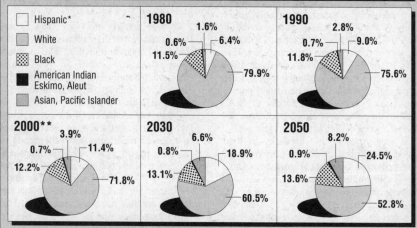

Legend:
- ☐ Hispanic*
- White
- ▥ Black
- ■ American Indian Eskimo, Aleut
- Asian, Pacific Islander

1980: 1.6%, 0.6%, 6.4%, 11.5%, 79.9%

1990: 2.8%, 0.7%, 9.0%, 11.8%, 75.6%

2000**: 3.9%, 0.7%, 11.4%, 12.2%, 71.8%

2030: 6.6%, 0.8%, 18.9%, 13.1%, 60.5%

2050: 8.2%, 0.9%, 24.5%, 13.6%, 52.8%

*Persons of Hispanic origin can be of any race.
**Data for years 1995 and beyond are estimates.
Source: U.S. Census Bureau

FORGOTTEN AMERICANS

A small but growing group of Americans live between this nation's narrow racial lines. Their controversial campaign for recognition by the federal government has ignited a debate that could change the way Americans think about race and identity.

An estimated 1% to 2% of the U.S. population considers itself "multiracial," and many of them have lobbied the U.S. Office of Management and Budget to add a biracial or multiracial category to the year 2000 Census. A bill with a similar intent—nicknamed the Tiger Woods bill, after the golfer of African, Asian and European descent—has been proposed in the U.S. House of Representatives.

By late summer, the OMB hadn't ruled on the issue, but a federal task force recommended against a multiracial category and suggested instead that the next Census allow Americans to check off more than one racial category.

Currently, biracial and multiracial people are encouraged by the U.S. Census Bureau to pick the race with which they most identify or, if they prefer, the race of their mothers. They end up being counted as white; black; American Indian, Eskimo, Aleut; Asian or Pacific Islander; or "other race"—choices that some feel don't include them or their children. "You're putting a child in a position where they're choosing one parent over another, one side over another," says Gayle M. Montgomery, a training coordinator in Monrovia, Calif., who is white. Genetically, her daughter is majority white, but her blond-haired young grandson is majority black. "We're supposed to be a melting pot," she says. "It's rather ludicrous to assume we're not going to be some combination of things."

If demographic trends are any indication, such questions of interracial identity aren't likely to fade. The Census Bureau found in 1995 that about 3% of the nation's 54.9 million couples were interracial. By comparison, less than 1% of the 44.6 million couples in 1970 were interracial, even though laws against interracial marriages had been ruled unconstitutional three years before. As of 1990, 4.1% of the nation's 47.1 million children differed from one or both parents in race.

In addition, about 3% of couples in 1990 included one Hispanic person. Currently, the Census Bureau considers Hispanics an ethnic group who can be of any race. However, many consider themselves their own racial group, so children with one Hispanic parent and one non-Hispanic parent—an estimated two million children—could be tempted to check the "multiracial" category as well.

Some mixed-race people embrace one of their cultures. Some, ostracized by both cultures, seek their own identity. "I always just tried to fit in," says Raina Carpio Bell, a Georgia State University law school student who is black, American Indian, white and Filipino. "But the harder I tried, the more obvious it became that I didn't fit in anywhere." When she saw that her law school application offered multiracial as a category, "I couldn't wait to check that box," she says.

The children of Richard and Vesta Pellegrino vary in coloration from very dark—what most Americans would instinctively call black—to a light color that most Americans consider white. For Mr. Pellegrino, his children's multiple heritages are given short shrift by the "other" category. "We always create our own category," says the Atlanta-based counselor and marketing consultant, who is white. Ms. Pellegrino, a homemaker, is black, of Caribbean descent. "We draw in a line (on the form) and write out their real description. Sometimes, we just write 'human.' "

But the proposed multiracial category faces considerable opposition. Members of civil rights groups like the National Association for the Advancement of Colored People, the League of United Latin American Citizens, and the National Asian Pacific American Legal Consortium have spoken out against the measure, fearing a multiracial category will draw from their ranks. Reduced numbers of blacks, Hispanic Americans, and Asians in the Census count could reduce their political power and gut affirmative action programs, they say.

To test that possibility, a 1996 Census Bureau survey put the multiracial question to almost 112,000 households. The numbers calling themselves white or black didn't change significantly. However, the number of respondents calling themselves Asian or American Indian fell slightly.

Critics of the multiracial category contend that racism depends less on what a person considers himself than on how others see him. A black person isn't denied a job because he *thinks* he's black, but because he looks black to others. "I have an African father and a British mother, and I usually check 'black,' " says K. Anthony Appiah, a professor at Harvard University's Afro-American Studies department. "I could check 'white,' I suppose . . . but nobody reacts to me as a white person. Nobody." Adds Harold McDougall, Washington bureau chief of the NAACP, "Checking that box isn't going to change the way people think of you."

The multiracial classification also awakens fears that people will try to deny the non-white part of their heritage because white is seen by some as superior. Indeed, one study of the 1990 Census found that one-quarter of Californians with some Asian background were both white and Asian, but they were more likely to consider themselves "white."

Many people of varied racial background feel caught in the middle of the debate.

Joycelyn Damita, a Philadelphia adoption agency volunteer who is white and black, was told by her black relatives several years ago that she wasn't "black" enough to be one of them. "It was a wake-up call," says Ms. Damita, who founded her own organization to encourage use of a multiracial category among cities and states. "It was time for me to say, 'Let's do something, and be proud of who I am.' "

Such groups have had success in seven states, including Georgia, Illinois and Michigan, which use the multiracial category to tabulate some data. Efforts are also under way in Texas and California, the two most populous states, to mandate use of the category. So far, response has been limited. For example, the state of Georgia says public school students calling themselves multiracial make up less than half of one percent—next to American Indians, the smallest of any racial group in the state by far.

The new organizations of multiracial people can be partially credited to the Internet. World Wide Web sites with names like InterRace and Interracial Voice encourage lobbying and provide information on meetings and parades. Newsgroups dedicated to the subject offer a glimpse of how controversial the multi-racial category is even among multiracial people. One on-line reader castigates others for "passing" as something other than black. One partially Asian man laments that he would pass for white if he could. A third posting encourages mixed-race Hollywood stars to own up to their backgrounds.

Whether or not the multiracial category is approved by the federal government, multiracial people are no longer invisible. Hip, urban-oriented advertising is experimenting with models whose faces and builds defy easy-categorization: caramel skin and curly hair, a pair of almond-shaped blue eyes. Says Peter Ferraro, advertising director for *The Source*, a rap and hip-hop magazine, "We're not just black, white or Asian anymore."

Carlos Tejada

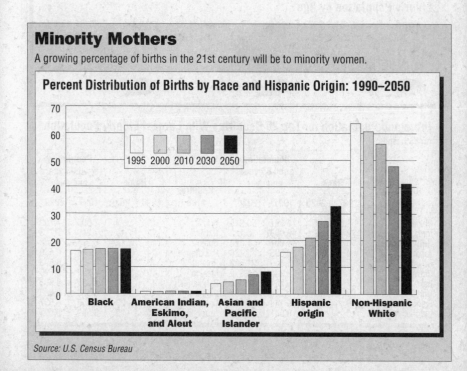

Minority Mothers

A growing percentage of births in the 21st century will be to minority women.

Percent Distribution of Births by Race and Hispanic Origin: 1990–2050

Legend: 1995 2000 2010 2030 2050

Source: U.S. Census Bureau

An Aging America

The elderly will represent a growing share of the population well into the 21st century.

Elderly Population by Age (In thousands)

Census date	Total, all ages	Age in years			
		65 and over		85 and over	
		Number	%	Number	%
1900	75,995	3,080	4.1	122	0.2
1910	91,972	3,949	4.3	167	0.2
1920	105,711	4,933	4.7	210	0.2
1930	122,775	6,634	5.4	272	0.2
1940	131,669	9,019	6.8	365	0.3
1950	150,697	12,269	8.1	577	0.4
1960	179,323	16,560	9.2	929	0.5
1970	203,302	19,980	9.8	1,409	0.7
1980	226,546	25,550	11.3	2,240	1.0
1990	249,398	31,235	12.5	3,059	1.2
1996*	265,284	33,861	12.8	3,762	1.4
2000	274,634	34,709	12.6	4,259	1.6
2010	297,716	39,408	13.2	5,671	1.9
2020	322,742	53,220	16.5	6,460	2.0
2030	346,899	69,379	20.0	8,455	2.4
2040	369,980	75,233	20.3	13,552	3.7
2050	393,931	78,859	20.0	18,223	4.6

Elderly Population by Age

1900 65–84, **3.9%** 85+, **0.2%**

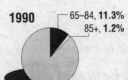

1990 65–84, **11.3%** 85+, **1.2%**

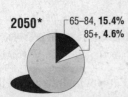

2050* 65–84, **15.4%** 85+, **4.6%**

Projected Population for Top 20 Countries With Largest Elderly Population
(In thousands)

Country/ area	Rank		Population aged 65 years and over		Country/ area	Rank		Population aged 65 years and over	
	1997	2020	1997	2020*		1997	2020	1997	2020*
China	1	1	77,891	169.925	Brazil	11	8	7,895	17,702
India	2	2	40,063	88,140	Ukraine	12	18	7,210	7,773
United States	**3**	**3**	34,097	53,220	Spain	13	16	6,298	8,243
Japan	4	4	19,385	32,226	Pakistan	14	13	5,338	9,439
Russia	5	5	18,019	21,582	Poland	15	22	4,455	6,573
Germany	6	7	12,908	18,532	Mexico	16	12	4,352	10,625
Italy	7	10	9,764	12,846	Bangladesh	17	14	4,051	8,731
United Kingdom	8	11	9,226	11,667	Vietnam	18	21	3,920	6,643
France	9	9	9,144	13,121	Canada	19	23	3,655	6,537
Indonesia	10	6	8,041	19,476	Argentina	20	25	3,589	5,591

*Estimate for 1996 and beyond.
Source: U.S. Census Bureau

America's Generations

Age Range of Selected Birth Cohorts, 1997–2010

Year	GI generation pre-1930	Depression generation 1939-39	War babies 1940-45	Baby boom 1946-64	Baby bust 1965-76	Baby boomlet 1977-94	Echo bust 1995-?
1997	68+	58-67	52-57	33-51	21-32	3-20	0-2
2000	71+	61-70	55-60	36-54	24-35	6-23	0-5
2005	76+	66-75	60-65	41-59	29-40	11-28	0-10
2010	81+	71-80	65-70	46-64	34-45	16-33	0-15

Source: American Demographics

JUNIOR BOOMERS

The baby boomers' babies are growing up.

Although the baby-boom echo may be fading as boomers move out of their child-bearing years, they have produced a new generation of children that promises to dominate the first half of the 21st century.

Just what have the boomers begot? Although not expected to be quite as formidable as their parents, who have been shaking up American society since the sexual revolution of the 1960s, the baby boomers' children are a very large, influential group in their own right. They are nearly 70 million strong and range from infants to teens.

Already, they have made their mark in many ways. Among them are the first test-tube babies, part of the revolution in medical technology sparked by infertile couples who delayed childbearing and found conception harder than they had bargained for. They have stirred debate over balancing career and family life because so many of the children have two working parents. They have been a boon to such businesses as day-care centers, the Nickelodeon cable-television channel and Baby Gap stores. And they have influenced political discourse over everything from family values in movies to the methods for teaching reading in elementary school.

"This is the generation for the 21st century," says Susan Mitchell, author of *The Official Guide to the Generations*. "It is more racially and ethnically diverse than other generations. And it's diverse in other ways because it's more likely to live in arrangements other than the traditional nuclear family."

The baby boomers' children resemble their parents in some ways, such as their receptivity to new technology and their rejection of authority figures. But unlike their parents, who have often been criticized for feeling they should have it all, the second baby boom may turn out to be much more pragmatic and flexible.

On the positive side, the second baby boom is resilient and less likely to be devastated by career and financial setbacks. "Baby boomers were born into post–World War II affluence and security and were made to feel that the world was theirs for the taking," says Lillian Maresch, president of Generation Insights, a marketing consulting firm in Minneapolis. "But children and teens today live in more of a state of flux, having witnessed their parents' career upheavals and the emotional upheaval of divorce. They have had to learn to fend for themselves very early with their parents out of the home so much."

Demographers have defined the second baby boom as those children born between 1977 and 1994. The number of births was especially high in the second half of the 1980s and early 1990s, rising above four million in 1989 for the first time since 1964 and peaking at 4,158,212 in 1990. Since then, the number of new babies has been on a slow, steady decline, falling below four million again in 1994. The infant population will bottom out around the year 2000, according to the U.S. Census Bureau, before starting to climb again.

The second baby boom follows the "baby bust" generation (1965 to 1976), which came after the first baby boom (1946 to 1964). Baby Boom II has roughly 69 million members, compared with about 78 million in Baby Boom I and about 45 million in the Baby Bust (also called Generation X), according to *American Demographics* magazine. While baby boomers still dominate, demographers predict that sometime around 2020, the second baby boom will outnumber the first.

When the biggest part of the second baby-boom grows into the teenage years, it will be the first time since the 1960s that America has seen such a wave of adolescents. "Generation X was so small, there was no sense of the menace of youth," says Ms. Mitchell. "I think we're going to be blindsided by this new generation, confronted by a swell of teenagers with all that exuberance, rebellion, and vitality."

Because they will grow up with classrooms full of whites, blacks, Hispanics, and Asians, teenagers of the second baby boom are expected to be more tolerant of cultural differences than previous generations. Conflict between the sexes also is expected to be less intense because this generation has grown up with mothers working and fathers sharing home responsibilities as the norm. In fact, some marketing experts believe unisex products, like Calvin Klein's hit fragrance CK One for men and women, will have growing appeal.

The members of the second baby boom also are likely to be one of the best educated, most sophisticated generation ever. They are embracing the Internet and other computer technology—often helping their parents stay on the cutting edge. Moreover, the baby boomers are providing the best education they can afford and making sure their kids get the most from their schools. "Baby boomers are very investment oriented, and they want a high return from their children's education just as they do from their stock portfolio," says Ms. Maresch of Generation Insights. "They are adapting their work schedules to spend time at their children's day-care centers and schools."

The new generation is sharply divided in its economic status: Many children live in comfortable, two-income families, while a large number are growing up in low-income and single-parent households. But to varying degrees, both the haves and have-nots are feeling the financial jitters of the 1990s. Children in low-income homes are always on tight budgets, while middle-class kids are seeing their parents and relatives hurt by the corporate downsizing of the 1990s and the loss of many professional and managerial jobs. Some population experts even believe the second baby boom may turn out to be another financially insecure Depression generation.

Some consumer-product marketers are playing to the demographics and values of this new generation. Mattel and Little Tikes produce more toys that feature people of color, Nike runs ads that portray the growing number of women in competitive sports, and Mountain Dew soft drink created a high-tech promotion using beepers.

But they're the exceptions. Many consumer-product marketers are still fixated on young adults, even though marketing consultants say their clients should get ready for the second baby boom, which looks like a tricky target. "They are more diverse in their tastes than other generations and with the exception of Nike and Levi's, there aren't those strong arbiters of taste, products you must have," says Irma Zandl, president of the Zandl Group in New York, a consulting firm specializing in the youth market. "They're also really educated consumers and are very marketing savvy. They're on to us."

Ronald Alsop

Baby Boomers and Their Babies

The baby-boom generation, born between 1946 and 1964, produced their own smaller boom between 1977 and 1994.

Number of U.S. Births, 1946 through 1964 and 1977 through 1994
(In millions)

Source: National Center for Health Statistics

THE SINGLES SCENE

MORE AMERICANS are going it alone.

It used to be that the most common American household consisted of married couples with children, reminiscent of the days of *Ozzie and Harriet* when people usually moved straight from their parents' homes into their own life-long marriages. Many of the people back then who lived alone were poor and on the fringe of society.

But today, a quarter of American households—or roughly 25 million—include just one person. That compares with a mere 7.4% of households 50 years ago, according to the Census Bureau. And the proportion of single-person households is expected to continue to climb into the next century. The Census Bureau projects that 27% of households will consist of a single person by 2010, outnumbering households with married couples and children.

The increase in single-person households is being driven by two primary forces: delayed marriage and lifestyle changes among the elderly. In 1995, the median age for marriage was 26.9 for men and 24.5 for women, compared with 22.8 for men and 20.3 for women in 1950. At the same time, elderly Americans, particularly women, are wealthier, more independent, and living longer than ever before.

It's also less of a taboo to be alone. "Society has accepted the single lifestyle," says Michael S. Broder, a psychologist in Philadelphia and author of *The Art of Living Single*. Prime-time television shows like *Seinfeld* and *Friends* are loaded with images of young adults having problems finding the right mate and preferring to stay single. Nowadays, people are more likely to end their bad relationships and marriages, striking out on their own, says Dr. Broder. "There also are more broken engagements than there used to be."

In fact, a growing number of people are adjusting to the idea that they could be single for life, some researchers say. "I hear more and more people saying 'I may be single forever.' Some of them want it that way," says Judith Langer, president of Langer Associates

Slower Household Growth

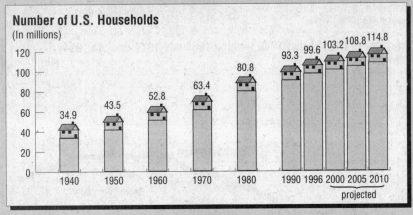

Number of U.S. Households
(In millions)

Source: U.S. Census Bureau

Inc., a market-research and consulting company in New York.

Lisa Skriloff, a self-employed marketing consultant and newsletter editor in New York, doesn't want it that way. Ms. Skriloff, 42 years old, says she'd like to marry some day, but like so many other singles, she's delayed marriage because she feels she simply hasn't met the right match. So, Ms. Skriloff, who is childless, has been putting her energy and money into building her small business—a three-year-old enterprise. "In a way, my business is kind of my parents' grandchild," she says.

Marketers of many stripes have taken note of the single-household trend, targeting consumers with products that defy the stereotypes of the swinging bachelor or the old maid. For example, *Singles In Sight,* a fledgling magazine in Phoenix, features the typical personal-ad fare with photos and profiles of people looking for mates, but it also includes personal-finance information. The magazine draws ads that range from real estate to retail, plastic surgery to health insurance.

"It used to be that you lived with orange crates as bookcases until you got married," Ms. Langer says. Not anymore. Many singles are "nesting," purchasing homes, furniture and cars, and making more use of financial services. "People are satisfying their lifestyle in every way," says Delia Passi, publisher of *Single Living*, a national magazine aimed at unmarried adults that has lured ads from the automotive and travel industries. Single adults are "a very valuable consumer."

Marketers also are benefiting from the fact that single living is becoming more common among the elderly. The trend is particularly evident among women who tend to outlive their older husbands but are choosing not to move in with their adult children. The "assisted living" industry, for example, is expanding fast, offering alternative housing to the elderly who need some support, but not nursing-home care. "Most of these companies are adding anywhere between 20 and 40 facilities a year," says Peter Sidoti, an industry analyst at Schroder & Co.. in New York. Compared with nursing homes, assisted-living centers "are superior in terms of life-style in that the resident still has independence."

The number of single elderly is expected to increase, both because of the aging of the large baby-boom generation and the steady increase in life expectancy. At birth today, females are expected to live close to 80 years, compared with about 73 years for men, according to George P. Moschis, director of the Center for Mature Consumer Studies at Georgia State University in Atlanta. That's a dramatic increase from a life expectancy of 71 for women and 66 for men in 1950. "The socioeconomic status of women in particular has been increasing," Prof. Moschis says. "There is less of a need to remarry and be supported by a husband."

That was the case with Minnie R. Combs of Oxford, Miss., who has no children and has lived on her own since her husband died in 1981. The 86-year-old moved from her own home in 1996 into a retirement community called Azalea Gardens that offers both "independent" and "assisted" living arrangements. Ms. Combs chose an independent option: a two-bedroom apartment and one meal a day in the center's dining room. "I still drive; I'm very independent," says Ms. Combs, who also enjoys cooking for herself in her apartment's kitchen.

Lisa Brownlee

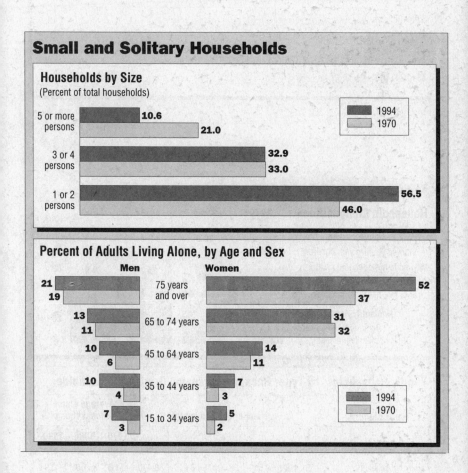

Small and Solitary Households

Households by Size
(Percent of total households)

1994 / 1970

5 or more persons: 10.6 / 21.0
3 or 4 persons: 32.9 / 33.0
1 or 2 persons: 56.5 / 46.0

Percent of Adults Living Alone, by Age and Sex

Men / Women

75 years and over: Men 21 / 19, Women 52 / 37
65 to 74 years: Men 13 / 11, Women 31 / 32
45 to 64 years: Men 10 / 6, Women 14 / 11
35 to 44 years: Men 10 / 4, Women 7 / 3
15 to 34 years: Men 7 / 3, Women 5 / 2

1994 / 1970

Projected Number of Persons Living Alone by Age
(In millions)

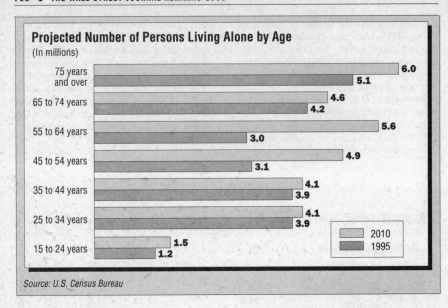

Age	2010	1995
75 years and over	6.0	5.1
65 to 74 years	4.6	4.2
55 to 64 years	5.6	3.0
45 to 54 years	4.9	3.1
35 to 44 years	4.1	3.9
25 to 34 years	4.1	3.9
15 to 24 years	1.5	1.2

Source: U.S. Census Bureau

Fewer Traditional Families

Household Composition

	1970	1980	1990	1994
Family Households				
Married couples with children	40.3	30.9	26.3	25.8
Married couples without children	30.3	29.9	29.8	29.0
Other families with children		7.5	8.3	9.2
Other families without children	5.0	5.4	6.5	6.6
Nonfamily Households	5.6			
Persons living alone	17.1	22.7	24.6	24.3
Other nonfamily households	1.7%	3.6%	4.6%	5.2%

Family Households, by Type, Race, and Hispanic Origin of Householder

Type of family	Number (in thousands)					Average annual percent change		
	1970	1980	1990	1993	1994	1970–1980	1980–1990	1990–1994
All Races								
Family households	51,456	59,550	66,090	68,216	68,490	1.5	1.0	0.9
Married-couple families	44,728	49,112	52,317	53,090	53,171	0.9	0.6	0.4
Male householder, no wife present	1,228	1,733	2,884	3,065	2,913	3.4	5.1	0.3
Female householder, no husband present	5,500	8,705	10,890	12,061	12,406	4.6	2.2	3.3

Type of family	Number (in thousands)					Average annual percent change		
	1970	1980	1990	1993	1994	1970–1980	1980–1990	1990–1994
White								
Family households	46,166	52,243	56,590	57,669	57,870	1.2	0.8	0.6
Married-couple families	41,029	44,751	46,981	47,383	47,443	0.9	0.5	0.2
Male householder, no wife present	1,038	1,441	2,303	2,418	2,297	3.3	4.7	-0.1
Female householder, no husband present	4,099	6,052	7,306	7,868	8,130	3.9	1.9	2.7
Black								
Family households	4,856	6,184	7,470	7,982	7,989	2.4	1.9	1.7
Married-couple families	3,317	3,433	3,750	3,777	3,714	0.3	0.9	-0.2
Male householder, no wife present	181	256	446	467	450	3.5	5.6	0.2
Female householder, no husband present	1,358	2,495	3,275	3,738	3,825	6.1	2.7	3.9
Asian or Pacific Islander								
Family households	(NA)	818	1,531	1,760	1,737	(NA)	6.3	3.2
Married-couple families	(NA)	691	1,256	1,409	1,426	(NA)	6.0	3.2
Male householder, no wife present	(NA)	39	86	106	79	(NA)	7.9	-2.1
Female householder, no husband present	(NA)	88	188	245	232	(NA)	7.6	5.3
Hispanic								
Family households	2,004	3,029	4,840	5,733	5,940	4.1	4.7	5.1
Married-couple families	1,615	2,282	3,395	3,940	4,033	3.5	4.0	4.3
Male householder, no wife present	82	138	329	445	410	5.2	8.7	5.5
Female householder, no husband present	307	610	1,116	1,348	1,498	6.9	6.0	7.4

Source: U.S. Census Bureau

Changing Family Composition

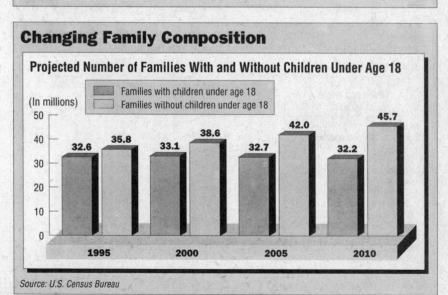

Projected Number of Families With and Without Children Under Age 18

(In millions)

- Families with children under age 18
- Families without children under age 18

	1995	2000	2005	2010
With children	32.6	33.1	32.7	32.2
Without children	35.8	38.6	42.0	45.7

Source: U.S. Census Bureau

The State of Matrimony

Marital Status of Persons 18 Years and Over, by Race and Hispanic Origin

(In percent)

☐ Married   ☐ Divorced   ☐ Widowed   ■ Never married

Total Population
	Married	Divorced	Widowed	Never married
1995	60.9	9.2	7.0	22.9
1970	71.7	3.2	8.9	16.2

White
	Married	Divorced	Widowed	Never married
1995	63.2	9.1	7.0	20.6
1970	72.6	3.1	8.7	15.6

Black
	Married	Divorced	Widowed	Never married
1995	43.2	10.7	7.6	38.4
1970	64.1	4.4	11.0	20.6

Hispanic Origin
	Married	Divorced	Widowed	Never married
1995	59.3	7.9	4.2	28.8
1970	71.8	3.9	5.6	18.6

Median Age at First Marriage, by Sex

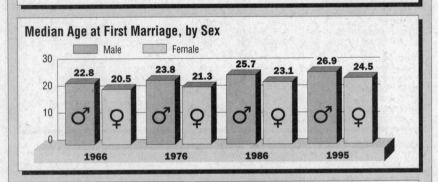

■ Male   ☐ Female

Year	Male	Female
1966	22.8	20.5
1976	23.8	21.3
1986	25.7	23.1
1995	26.9	24.5

Married Couples of Same and Mixed Races and Origins

(Numbers in thousands)

Race and origin of spouses	1980 Number	1980 Percent	1990 Number	1990 Percent	1995 Number	1995 Percent
Race						
Same race married couples	48,264	97.1	50,889	95.6	51,733	94.2
White/White	44,910	90.3	47,202	88.6	48,030	87.4
Black/Black	3,354	6.7	3,687	6.9	3,703	6.7
Interracial married couples	651	1.2	964	1.8	1,392	2.5
Black/White	167	0.3	211	0.4	328	0.6
Black husband/White wife	122	0.2	150	0.3	206	0.4
White husband/Black wife	45	0.1	61	0.1	122	0.2
White/other race (excl. White and Black)	450	0.9	720	1.4	988	1.8
Black/other race (excl. White and Black)	34	0.1	33	0.1	76	0.1
Hispanic Origin						
Hispanic/Hispanic married couples	1,906	3.8	3,085	5.8	3,857	7.0
Hispanic/not Hispanic married couples	891	1.8	1,193	2.2	1,434	2.6

Source: U.S. Census Bureau

Single Mothers

Percentage of Births to Unmarried Women

Year	All	Whites	Blacks
1940	3.8	–	–
1950	4.0	–	–
1955	4.5	–	–
1960	5.3	–	–
1965	7.7	–	–
1970	10.7	5.5	37.5
1975	14.3	7.1	49.5
1980	18.4	11.2	56.1
1985	22.0	14.7	61.2
1986	23.4	15.9	62.4
1987	24.5	16.9	63.4
1988	25.7	18.0	64.7
1989	27.1	19.2	65.7
1990	28.0	20.4	66.5
1991	29.5	21.8	67.9
1992	30.1	22.6	68.1
1993	31.0	23.6	68.7
1994	32.6	25.4	70.4
1995	32.2	25.3	69.9
1996	32.4	25.7	69.8

Source: National Center for Health Statistics

Percentage of Births to Unmarried Women by Race

Percentage of Births to Unmarried Women by Country, 1992

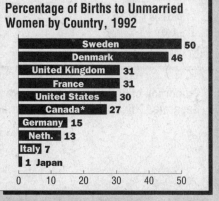

Country	Value
Sweden	50
Denmark	46
United Kingdom	31
France	31
United States	30
Canada*	27
Germany	15
Neth.	13
Italy	7
Japan	1

*1991 data.
Source: Department of Health and Human Services

More Parents Without Partners

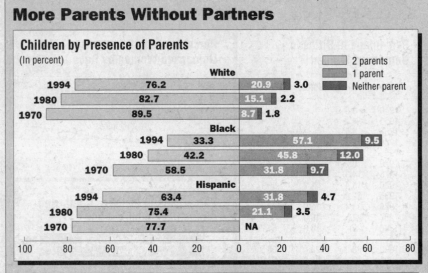

Children by Presence of Parents
(In percent)

Legend: 2 parents / 1 parent / Neither parent

White
- 1994: 76.2 | 20.9 | 3.0
- 1980: 82.7 | 15.1 | 2.2
- 1970: 89.5 | 8.7 | 1.8

Black
- 1994: 33.3 | 57.1 | 9.5
- 1980: 42.2 | 45.8 | 12.0
- 1970: 58.5 | 31.8 | 9.7

Hispanic
- 1994: 63.4 | 31.8 | 4.7
- 1980: 75.4 | 21.1 | 3.5
- 1970: 77.7 | NA

Scale: 100 80 60 40 20 0 20 40 60 80

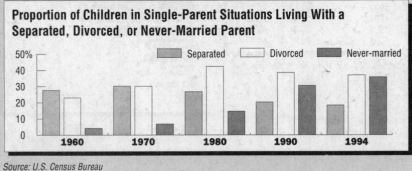

Proportion of Children in Single-Parent Situations Living With a Separated, Divorced, or Never-Married Parent

Legend: Separated / Divorced / Never-married

Scale: 50% 40 30 20 10 0

Years: 1960 1970 1980 1990 1994

Source: U.S. Census Bureau

Homeless People in Shelters and on the Streets

Count of Persons in Selected Locations Where Homeless Persons Are Found:1990 Census of Population*

Shelter and Street Enumeration

State	Emergency shelters		Shelters for runaway, neglected and homeless youth		Visible in street locations		Shelters for abused women	
	Number	Percent	Number	Percent	Number	Percent	Number	Percent
United States	168,309	100.0	10,329	100.0	49,734	100.0	11,768	100.0
Alabama	1,367	0.8	163	1.6	364	0.7	127	1.1
Alaska	402	0.2	45	0.4	79	0.2	157	1.3
Arizona	2,600	1.5	135	1.3	1,697	3.6	279	2.4
Arkansas	398	0.2	91	0.9	62	0.1	105	0.9
California	29,930	17.7	976	9.4	18,081	36.4	1,257	10.7
Colorado	2,444	1.5	110	1.1	393	0.8	167	1.4
Connecticut	3,965	2.4	229	2.2	221	0.4	155	1.3
Delaware	302	0.2	11	0.1	19	0.0	36	0.3
District of Columbia	4,419	2.6	263	2.5	131	0.3	49	0.4
Florida	6,275	3.7	835	8.1	3,189	6.4	601	5.1
Georgia	3,697	2.2	233	2.3	450	0.9	192	1.6
Hawaii	773	0.5	81	0.8	1,071	2.2	73	0.6
Idaho	390	0.2	71	0.7	19	0.0	78	0.7
Illinois	7,002	4.2	479	4.6	1,755	3.5	536	4.6
Indiana	1,902	1.1	349	3.4	268	0.5	279	2.4
Iowa	780	0.5	209	2.0	148	0.3	164	1.4
Kansas	797	0.5	143	1.4	158	0.3	60	0.5
Kentucky	1,127	0.7	157	1.5	118	0.2	190	1.6
Louisiana	1,321	0.8	238	2.3	184	0.4	244	2.1
Maine	389	0.2	30	0.3	7	0.0	43	0.4
Maryland	2,365	1.4	142	1.4	523	1.1	199	1.7
Massachusetts	5,948	3.5	259	2.5	674	1.4	269	2.3
Michigan	3,442	2.0	342	3.3	262	0.5	506	4.3
Minnesota	2,152	1.3	101	1.0	138	0.3	230	2.0
Mississippi	223	0.1	160	1.5	83	0.2	125	1.1
Missouri	2,154	1.3	122	1.2	215	0.4	117	1.0
Montana	419	0.2	26	0.3	17	0.0	49	0.4
Nebraska	719	0.4	45	0.4	20	0.0	41	0.3
Nevada	978	0.6	35	0.3	436	0.9	49	0.4
New Hampshire	334	0.2	43	0.4	8	0.0	27	0.2
New Jersey	7,299	4.3	171	1.7	1,639	3.3	255	2.2
New Mexico	642	0.4	25	0.2	164	0.3	108	0.9
New York	31,436	18.7	1,036	10.0	10,732	21.6	756	6.4
North Carolina	2,453	1.5	184	1.8	259	0.5	315	2.7
North Dakota	279	0.2	0	0.0	30	0.1	36	0.3
Ohio	3,814	2.3	463	4.5	188	0.4	496	4.2
Oklahoma	2,025	1.2	197	1.9	340	0.7	113	1.0
Oregon	3,170	1.9	84	0.8	564	1.1	251	2.1
Pennsylvania	7,815	4.6	422	4.1	1,312	2.6	603	5.1
Rhode Island	433	0.3	36	0.3	44	0.1	33	0.3
South Carolina	814	0.5	159	1.5	102	0.2	87	0.7
South Dakota	329	0.2	67	0.6	71	0.1	41	0.3
Tennessee	1,644	1.0	220	2.1	357	0.7	230	2.0
Texas	7,082	4.2	734	7.1	1,442	2.9	1,049	8.9
Utah	894	0.5	31	0.3	276	0.6	49	0.4
Vermont	232	0.1	0	0.0	16	0.0	29	0.2
Virginia	2,544	1.5	113	1.1	319	0.6	185	1.6
Washington	4,493	2.7	72	0.7	772	1.6	297	2.5
West Virginia	404	0.2	47	0.5	33	0.1	128	1.1
Wisconsin	1,464	0.9	91	0.9	71	0.1	258	2.2
Wyoming	129	0.1	54	0.5	13	0.0	45	0.4

*Includes persons counted the evening of March 20th in sites listed as shelters for the homeless; women and children counted the evening of March 20th in shelters and safe houses for abused women; persons counted during the early morning hours of March 21st at pre-identified street sites, abandoned buildings and open public locations where homeless persons were likely to congregate.
Source: U.S. Census Bureau

CHILDREN IN CRISIS

"Dear Lord, please be good to me. The sea is so wide and my boat is so small."

Those lines from an old seafarer's poem appeared in the literature of the Children's Defense Fund some 20 years ago. But the words seem more timely than ever in the 1990s, when statistics show that millions of American children live in poverty, suffer from abuse and neglect, and lack proper health care. At the same time, drug and alcohol abuse, violence, and suicide have become all too common among older children and adolescents.

"The problems are very revealing of how children are experiencing life in this country. It is quite a crisis, one that has enormous implications for the future," says Marc Miringoff, director of the Fordham Institute for Social Policy in Tarrytown, N.Y. The center, which publishes an annual "Index of Social Health" examining the status of 16 social problems, finds that young people are among America's most needy, with high rates of poverty, physical abuse, suicide and drug use.

The nearly 15 million people under age 18 who are living in poverty are particularly troubling to social workers and child psychologists because they see poverty as a precursor of other trouble to come. "There is a whole package of problems associated with growing up poor, including an increased risk of child abuse, inadequate education, teen pregnancy and crime," says John O'Hare, coordinator of "Kids Count," a project of the Annie E. Casey Foundation in Baltimore.

The Department of Health and Human Services reported a 25% rise in the number of victims of child maltreatment between 1990 and 1995. And one needn't look any further than the nightly news to see that shootings and stabbings among young people have become a common occurrence. One study found that between 1992 and 1994, 105 children died violently in or near secondary schools, with most of the deaths ruled homicides, usually as a result of an argument, gang-related activity, or involvement with drugs.

The statistics on juvenile crime and violence appear even more startling when compared with those of other industrialized countries. The Centers for Disease Control

and Prevention in Atlanta recently reported that the child homicide rate in the U.S. was five times higher than 25 other countries combined, between 1950 and 1993. Etienne Krug, author of the study, says it is too early to fully explain the U.S. statistics, though he cites the social acceptability of violence, economic stress, and high divorce rates as contributing factors.

The number of children in poverty declined during the 1960s and 1970s, but began climbing again in the 1980s. The percentage of poor children hit 22.7% in 1993, but dropped back to 20.8% in 1995. Still, that's far higher than the 14% to 16% rate from the late-1960s to the end of the 1970s, and there is a disproportionate number of poor children. The Census Bureau recently reported that children under 18 account for about 40% of all poor people, though they make up just a little more than a quarter of the population.

It isn't just a "welfare mother" problem. The National Center for Children in Poverty at the Columbia School of Public Health in New York, recently reported that 6.1 million children under the age of six live in poverty, compared with 3.5 million in 1974. Of those children, 62% lived with at least one parent or relative who worked part or full time.

The center's study reported other statistics that defy conventional wisdom. The child poverty rate has risen two times faster among whites than blacks, though the problem remains more entrenched in black communities. "People associate poverty with minorities and the inner city, but the study may break some of those stereotypes by demonstrating that no region of America is an island when it comes to child poverty," says Julian Palmer, a spokesman for the center.

The increase in the number of working poor families is particularly significant amid current changes being made to the welfare system, particularly the emphasis on moving recipients into the work force. A job alone may not be enough to sustain families who will eventually have to move off public assistance. "There are many people willing to work who do not always get the pay they need to get out of poverty," says Deborah Weinstein, director of the family income division at the Children's Defense Fund.

Even in families above the poverty line, the affordability of proper health care is a growing concern. Since 1989, the number of children without private health insurance has increased by an average of 1.2 million a year, or 3,300 per day, according to the Children's Defense Fund. Many children are ineligible for Medicaid because their parents earn too much to qualify. The Children's Defense Fund says more than half of uninsured children with asthma and one third of children with recurring ear infections never see a doctor, often resulting in serious but preventable illnesses. A bright spot for the millions of uninsured children is the $24 billion that will go to the states to provide health-care for youngsters, as part of the federal budget agreement reached in the summer of 1997. The funding, which will come partly from cigarette tax increases, marks the largest expansion in child health-care since the creation of Medicaid in 1965.

But all too often, child-welfare advocates say, juvenile issues slip down the priority list. "Most social policy is conducted on a fiscal basis, and that is putting it kindly," says Mr. Miringoff of the Fordham Institute.

Some concerned groups are disturbed that more people aren't trying to help kids. Because of the many children in crisis in America, the Advertising Council in New York has decided to focus 80% of its public-service ad campaigns on youth issues, under a comprehensive program entitled, "Commitment 2000: Raising a Better Tomorrow." In preparation for the campaign, the Ad Council conducted research with consumer focus groups to explore the puzzling question: "Why does the American public seem to ignore the plight of children?"

The answers were discouraging: People say they do care about children but are

Starting Life in Poverty

The percentage of young people living below the poverty level declined in the 1960s, but in the 1980s and 1990s the number shot above 20% again.

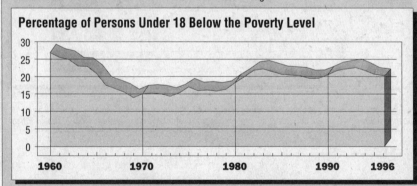

Percentage of Persons Under 18 Below the Poverty Level

Year	Percent	Year	Percent
1960	26.9%	1991	21.8%
1965	21.0	1992	22.3
1970	15.1	1993	22.7
1975	17.1	1994	21.8
1980	18.3	1995	20.8
1985	20.7	1996	20.5
1990	20.6		

Source: U.S. Census Bureau

unwilling or unable to act on their behalf. The findings revealed that many felt the problems of children were a result of parents' corrupt moral values, as well as symptomatic of society's problems as a whole. Many also believed that the problems mirrored an irreversible pattern of moral and economic decay, adding to feelings of powerlessness about the ability to make a difference. Furthermore, people who are in a position to help often don't feel that they know of seriously troubled families and children, nor do they interact with them on a regular basis.

Thus the Ad Council's campaign has as its central theme the question, "Whose side are you on?," raising the provocative point that unless people actively try to improve the lot of children, they are, in effect, acting against them.

Eileen Kinsella

Children Without Coverage

Many children lack health insurance, and many of those with insurance rely on Medicaid rather than private plans.

Health Care Insurance for Persons Under 15, According to Type of Coverage (In percent)

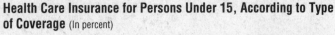
Private insurance | Medicaid | Not covered

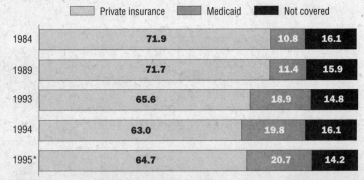

Year	Private insurance	Medicaid	Not covered
1984	71.9	10.8	16.1
1989	71.7	11.4	15.9
1993	65.6	18.9	14.8
1994	63.0	19.8	16.1
1995*	64.7	20.7	14.2

*Preliminary.
Note: Percentages do not add up to 100 because persons with other types of health insurance are not included.
Sources: Centers for Disease Control and Prevention, National Center for Health Statistics, and U.S. Census Bureau

Crimes Against Children

Number of Murders of Victims Under Age 18 Reported to the Police

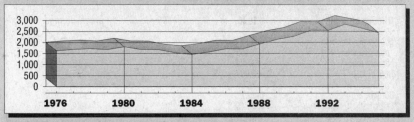

Murders of Persons Under Age 18

Year	Number	Percent committed with a handgun*	Murdered by: Child	Murdered by: Adult	Murdered by: Unknown
1976	1,629	28.5%	327	986	316
1980	1,813	29.6	277	1,107	429
1985	1,573	29.0	246	1,026	300
1990	2,295	41.7	432	1,252	611
1991	2,574	44.7	463	1,407	704
1992	2,564	48.8	489	1,350	724
1993	2,841	49.9	553	1,446	841
1994	2,660	47.6	567	1,345	749
1995	2,428	NA	NA	NA	NA

*Percentages are based on all cases, including those in which the type of weapon was not reported.

Violent Child Victimizers in State Prisons, by Age of Victim, 1991*

Violent offense	Prisoners serving time for crimes against children — All	Victims age 12 or younger	Victims age 13 to 17	Percent with victims age 12 or younger
Total	60,285	33,287	26,998	55.2%
Homicide	5,792	3,006	2,787	51.9
Murder	4,677	2,279	2,399	48.7
Negligent manslaughter	1,115	727	388	65.2
Kidnapping	1,508	682	826	45.2
Rape and sexual assault	42,993	25,102	17,892	58.4
Forcible rape	8,908	3,893	5,015	43.7
Forcible sodomy	1,729	1,039	690	60.1
Statutory rape	984	611	373	62.1
Lewd acts with children	10,370	7,175	3,195	69.2
Other sexual assault	21,002	12,384	8,619	59.0
Robbery	3,656	1,051	2,605	28.7
Assault	6,035	3,215	2,818	53.3
Aggravated assault	3,933	1,623	2,309	41.3
Child abuse	1,694	1,513	181	89.3
Simple assault	408	79	328	19.4
Other violent offense	301	231	70	76.7

*Excludes 752 cases for which the specific age of the victim was not reported. Detail may not add to total because of rounding.
Source: U.S. Justice Department

Juvenile Crime Spree

Arrests of Persons Under 18 Years of Age

Offense charged	1986	1995	Percent change
Murder and non-negligent manslaughter	1,255	2,383	+89.9%
Forcible rape	3,994	3,853	-3.5
Robbery	25,607	41,841	+63.4
Aggravated assault	32,598	58,113	+78.3
Burglary	113,921	93,484	-17.9
Larceny-theft	309,746	353,667	+14.2
Motor vehicle theft	44,675	57,209	+28.1
Arson	5,095	7,137	+40.1
Violent crimes	63,454	106,190	+67.3
Property crimes	473,437	511,497	+8.0

Source: U.S. Justice Department, Federal Bureau of Investigation

Damaged Kids

Estimated Number of Victims of child abuse and neglect

Year	
1990	798,318
1991	857,968
1992	1,002,288
1993	1,018,692
1994	1,011,595
1995	1,000,502

Source: U.S. Health and Human Services Department

Perpetrators in Cases of Child Abuse and Neglect, 1994

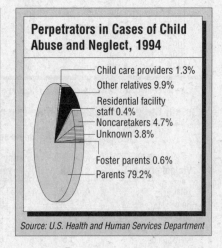

Child care providers 1.3%
Other relatives 9.9%
Residential facility staff 0.4%
Noncaretakers 4.7%
Unknown 3.8%
Foster parents 0.6%
Parents 79.2%

Source: U.S. Health and Human Services Department

How Americans Eat

Sources of Sustenance

Annual Main Meals Per Person by Source*

Prepared & eaten in-home	690 (-6)
Carried from home	55 (+7)
Skipped/missed	113 (-4)
Commercial restaurants (includes take-out)	115 (+10)
Non-commercial eating places	34 (+4)
Supermarkets & convenience stores	5 (+1)
Vending	2
Other person's home	29 (-5)

*Increase or decrease since 1990 noted in parentheses.
Source: NPD Group's National Eating Trends and CREST service

Eating Out

Annual Meals (Including Snacks) Purchased at Commercial Restaurants Per Person

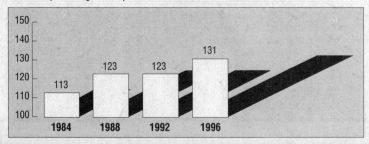

1984	1988	1992	1996
113	123	123	131

Source: NPD Group's CREST service

Take-Out Takes Off

Number of Take-Out and On-premise Meals Purchased at Commercial Restaurants Per Person Annually

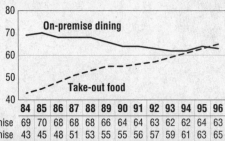

	84	85	86	87	88	89	90	91	92	93	94	95	96
On-Premise	69	70	68	68	68	66	64	64	63	62	62	64	63
Off-Premise	43	45	48	51	53	55	55	56	57	59	61	63	65

Source: NPD Group's CREST service

Changing Tastes

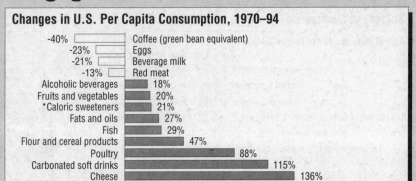

Changes in U.S. Per Capita Consumption, 1970–94

- -40% Coffee (green bean equivalent)
- -23% Eggs
- -21% Beverage milk
- -13% Red meat
- Alcoholic beverages 18%
- Fruits and vegetables 20%
- *Caloric sweeteners 21%
- Fats and oils 27%
- Fish 29%
- Flour and cereal products 47%
- Poultry 88%
- Carbonated soft drinks 115%
- Cheese 136%

*Includes caloric sweeteners used in soft drinks.

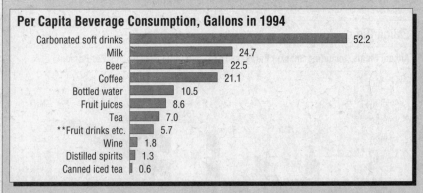

Per Capita Beverage Consumption, Gallons in 1994

- Carbonated soft drinks 52.2
- Milk 24.7
- Beer 22.5
- Coffee 21.1
- Bottled water 10.5
- Fruit juices 8.6
- Tea 7.0
- **Fruit drinks etc. 5.7
- Wine 1.8
- Distilled spirits 1.3
- Canned iced tea 0.6

**Includes fruit cocktails and ades
Source: U.S. Agriculture Department

Reality Check

NPD Group Inc., a market-research firm that monitors Americans' eating habits, has created an anvil that it says reflects people's actual diets, heavy on the fats and sweets. The anvil contrasts sharply with the U.S. Agriculture Department's pyramid, which recommends a daily diet rich in grains, fruits, and vegetables.

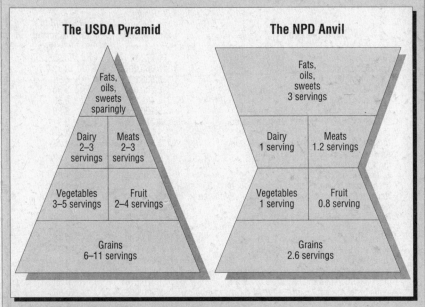

The USDA Pyramid

Fats, oils, sweets sparingly

Dairy 2–3 servings | Meats 2–3 servings

Vegetables 3–5 servings | Fruit 2–4 servings

Grains 6–11 servings

The NPD Anvil

Fats, oils, sweets 3 servings

Dairy 1 serving | Meats 1.2 servings

Vegetables 1 serving | Fruit 0.8 serving

Grains 2.6 servings

Sources: U.S. Agriculture Department and NPD Group Inc.

Belief in God

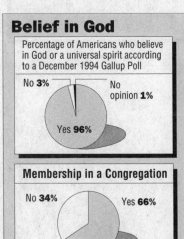

Percentage of Americans who believe in God or a universal spirit according to a December 1994 Gallup Poll

No **3%**
No opinion **1%**
Yes **96%**

Membership in a Congregation

No **34%**   Yes **66%**

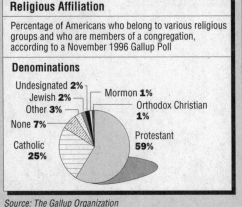

Religious Affiliation

Percentage of Americans who belong to various religious groups and who are members of a congregation, according to a November 1996 Gallup Poll

Denominations

Undesignated **2%**
Jewish **2%**
Other **3%**
None **7%**
Catholic **25%**
Mormon **1%**
Orthodox Christian **1%**
Protestant **59%**

Source: The Gallup Organization

U.S. Christian Church Membership

Ranking of the largest denominations that reported membership data. The list includes most of the denominations with more than 400,000 members, but does not contain three large organizations, the Greek Orthodox Archdiocese of North and South America, the Christian Methodist Episcopal Church and the United Pentecostal Church International.

Denomination	Membership	Percent of total reported
Roman Catholic Church	60,280,454	38.93%
Southern Baptist Convention	15,663,296	10.12
United Methodist Church	8,538,662	5.51
National Baptist Convention, U.S.A., Inc.	8,200,000	5.30
Church of God in Christ	5,499,875	3.55
Evangelical Lutheran Church in America	5,190,489	3.35
Church of Jesus Christ of Latter-day Saints	4,711,500	3.04
Presbyterian Church (U.S.A.)	3,669,489	2.37
National Baptist Convention of America, Inc.	3,500,000	2.26
African Methodist Episcopal Church	3,500,000	2.26
Lutheran Church - Missouri Synod	2,594,555	1.68
Episcopal Church	2,536,550	1.64
Progressive National Baptist Convention, Inc.	2,500,000	1.61
National Missionary Baptist Convention of America	2,500,000	1.61
Assemblies of God	2,387,982	1.54
Orthodox Church in America	2,000,000	1.29
Churches of Christ	1,655,000	1.07
American Baptist Churches in the U.S.A.	1,517,400	0.98
Baptist Bible Fellowship International	1,500,000	0.97
United Church of Christ	1,472,213	0.95
African Methodist Episcopal Zion Church	1,230,842	0.79
Christian Churches and Churches of Christ	1,070,616	0.69
Pentecostal Assemblies of the World	1,000,000	0.65
Jehovah's Witnesses	966,243	0.62
Christian Church (Disciples of Christ)	929,725	0.60
Seventh-day Adventist Church	790,731	0.51
Church of God (Cleveland, Tennessee)	753,230	0.49
Church of the Nazarene	601,900	0.39
Salvation Army	453,150	0.29
Wisconsin Evangelical Lutheran Synod	412,478	0.27

Source: National Council of the Churches of Christ in the U.S.A.

THE COLLECTION PLATE

Church contributions vary widely among some of the major denominations, according to a study funded by the Lilly Endowment.

Average Congregation Size

	ASSEMBLIES OF GOD	SOUTHERN BAPTIST CONVENTION	ROMAN CATHOLIC	EVANGELICAL LUTHERAN CHURCH IN AMERICA	PRESBYTERIAN CHURCH (U.S.A.)
Number of members*	266	318	2,723	319	303
Number of households	105	167	1,041	183	173
Average worship attendance on a typical weekend, all worship services	168	161	1,255	146	155

*For Assemblies of God, members plus frequent attenders on the mailing list.

Average Contributions per Member and Household

	ASSEMBLIES OF GOD	SOUTHERN BAPTIST CONVENTION	ROMAN CATHOLIC	EVANGELICAL LUTHERAN CHURCH IN AMERICA	PRESBYTERIAN CHURCH (U.S.A.)
Average contribution per member	$628	$550	$160	$415	$611
Average contribution per household	1,696	1,154	386	746	1,085

Pet Population

Americans love their pets: Market Statistics Inc. of New York estimates that people spend about $21.3 billion a year on their animals. Here are the estimated number of pets and percentages of households with different types of pets:

	Pet population (In millions)		Percent of households	
	1991	1998*	1991	1998*
Cats	57.0	61.1	30.9%	31.4%
Dogs	52.5	53.6	36.5	34.3
Birds	11.7	–	5.7	–
Horses	4.9	–	2.0	–

*Projected.   Source: American Veterinary Medical Association

Health and Medicine

It's hard to summon up much sympathy for members of a profession whose average annual incomes approach $200,000. But the nation's 720,000 physicians are being battered by the most significant economic upheaval to hit medicine since the federal Medicare program for the elderly was launched in the mid-1960s.

Evidence of bloodshed is everywhere. In many regions of the country, physician income—especially among specialists—is falling. Doctors are merging their solo practices with large medical groups or selling out in record numbers to hospital systems and new for-profit enterprises called physician-management companies. Anesthesiologists, who have long enjoyed one of medicine's most lucrative and lifestyle-friendly specialties, can't find jobs, while cardiologists and psychiatrists are being forced to leave some specialist-saturated markets to make a living.

Renowned academic centers such as Johns Hopkins Medical Institutions and Duke University Medical School are trimming the slots they have available to train the next generation of physicians. A union movement among doctors is beginning to take hold. And some doctors are even selling Amway soap on the side to help make up for lost income.

"Physicians are practicing in a turbulent environment few anticipated at the time they entered the profession," understates a recent report from the Commonwealth Fund, a health-care research philanthropy. The report, based on a survey of 1,700 doctors around the U.S., found high levels of stress and dissatisfaction over changes in the health-care system.

Indeed, after sitting atop the medical world for decades, doctors are now being blamed for its foibles, particularly its expensive ones. Physician fees and salaries account for about 20% of the nation's trillion-dollar health-care bill, but the procedures, tests, and treatments that doctors alone prescribe make up another 60%. This influence over the use of medical resources has prompted more than one observer to remark that among the nation's vaunted arsenal of medical technology, the most expensive tool of all is the physician's ordering pen.

Not surprisingly then, as managed care has emerged as the leading weapon of America's employers in the vigorous decade-long war on health-care costs, targeting doctors has become blood sport. Many are reeling as a result.

One recent study, based on a rigorous survey by the American Medical Association, found that inflation-adjusted income for the average physician *fell* by 4% to $186,600 in 1994, though more recent data indicate incomes bounced back in 1995. Still, there is little doubt managed-care is having an impact: In the 1994 survey, doctors with the highest proportion of income from managed-care patients suffered the biggest income declines. In popular urban markets, a glut of such specialists as psychiatrists, cardiologists, dermatologists, and orthopedists makes these physicians particularly vulnerable to fee reductions by health-maintenance organizations and other managed-care plans that recruit only a limited number of these groups for their physician rosters.

But it isn't only the raid on their wallets that is frustrating doctors. It is the challenge to their autonomy. HMOs have imposed an avalanche of rules, guidelines, and protocols on medical practice that many physicians regard as usurping their authority. Trained to exercise their own judgment in the advocacy of their patients—regardless of costs—physicians now find they must consult a list of approved drugs before writing a prescription or call an 800-number to get permission to do a diagnostic test or refer a patient to a specialist.

"Once you do that, you don't need a doctor to make individual clinical decisions," says John D. Lantos, a pediatrician and bioethicist at the University of Chicago. "You just need somebody who can follow the algorithm."

Compounding the problem, doctors are now subject to new systems of evaluation, including public report cards on their performance. They are graded not only on death rates of their surgical patients, but on efficiency, on how many tests and surgeries they prescribe, and on how happy their patients are. Often these categories can cause conflicts.

"Primary-care doctors in an efficiently managed health-delivery system get 10 to 12 minutes to spend with a patient," says Dr. Lantos. If doctors rush patients through the examining room, they risk a poor report on patient satisfaction. But if they spend too much time with patients, they risk a black mark on their efficiency score card.

Many physicians are convinced these annoyances serve not the medical needs of patients but the economic interests of health plans, which can often abruptly fire—or "deselect" in industry jargon—any doctor who fails to go along. "Doctors are being left with all the accountability and none of the authority," Dr. Lantos laments. All of this prompted him to write a book published in 1997 with a title that captures both the frustration and fear that is reverberating through the medical community: *Do We Still Need Doctors?*

To be sure, doctors brought much of this turmoil on themselves, and their complaints come with a heavy dose of self-interest. After all, they were willing co-conspirators in an almost blank-check health-care system in which the more tests and procedures they ordered, the more money they made. In addition, the medical literature is surprisingly thin on professional consensus on the most effective ways to treat hundreds of illnesses, a phenomenon that has led to wide variation in treatments provided to patients with similar maladies and in the cost of such care. The managed-care industry is championing efforts to develop more clinical and economic data to reduce this variation, a move leaders say will improve the quality of care as well.

Meantime, doctors are responding to the assault on their turf with an eclectic array of strategies that underscores their concerns and their confusion. Selling practices is one major option. In suburban Cleveland, for instance, one group of pediatricians decided to sell their practice to a major university-based medical system after cuts in reimbursements meant the group couldn't meet payroll. Others are being scooped up by a new crop of entrepreneurs who operate physician-management companies that acquire the assets of doctor practices, handle the administrative chores and let doctors concentrate on practicing medicine.

Sentiment for unionizing is also growing among doctors, whose characteristic high incomes, entrepreneurialism, and fierce independence would seem to make them unlikely candidates for picket lines. Because most doctors are considered independent contractors and not employees, it isn't clear that any managed-care company will be compelled to bargain with them. But a group of podiatrists, non-M.D. physicians who treat foot problems, have mounted an effort they maintain will prompt some 10,000 of their specialty to join unions. Though the actual number of union-card carrying MDs is still very small, some highly trained doctors are seeking to organize as well.

Doctors also are using their political clout to fuel and take advantage of a backlash that is prompting a flurry of legislative activity across the country aimed at curbing alleged abuses by managed-care providers. More than 1,000 bills have been debated in state legislatures in recent sessions. Those enacted into law include measures banning so-called gag clauses in managed-care contracts that doctors assert may restrict them from fully informing patients of options for treatment; forbidding health plans from firing doctors "without cause"; and promising patients the option of going directly to specialists without having to get approval from a primary-care doctor.

But the new conventional wisdom for doctors who want to regain control of medical decisions is that, much like an insurance company, they will have to accept financial risk for those decisions. One result is that in an "if you can't beat 'em, join 'em" tactic, doctors have tried setting up their own broad-based HMOs. Results so far have been mixed at best. Two physician-launched HMOs in Connecticut and another in New Jersey, for instance, recently sold out to larger managed-care companies in the belief that they would be unable to thrive as stand-alone concerns.

But smaller, aggressively managed physician practices in the managed-care battle-ground of Southern California may be having more success. A recent study by researchers at the University of California at Berkeley found that doctors in six large medical groups in California who share in the profits of managed-care practices turn out to be more efficient than the HMOs they complain about, especially by reducing use of hospitals by their patients. What this means for quality of care is the question that will nag doctors and patients alike as economic turbulence continues to rattle the world of medicine.

All this change is affecting the nation's new crop of doctors as well. An increasing share of physicians completing their training are choosing primary-care, instead of the traditionally more lucrative sub-specialties for their careers. And an annual survey of final-year residents by Merritt, Hawkins & Associates, a physician placement company, revealed that new doctors these days are much more concerned about finding a job and managing their medical school debt than about dealing with managed care.

Ron Winslow, a *Wall Street Journal* staff reporter who covers the health-care industry

More Doctors on Call

Total Number of U.S. Physicians

Year	Total physicians	Physicians per 100,000 population
1950	219,997	142
1955	241,711	144
1960	260,484	142
1965	292,088	148
1970	334,028	161
1975	393,742	180
1980	467,679	202
1985	552,716	228
1990	615,421	244
1994	684,414	263
1995	720,325	274

States with Largest Number of Private Physicians

State	Total private physicians	Private physicians per 100,000 population
1980		
California	58,368	248
New York	49,105	280
Pennsylvania	23,347	197
Texas	22,571	159
Illinois	21,740	191
Florida	20,374	208
Ohio	18,342	170
Massachusetts	16,342	285
Michigan	15,347	166
New Jersey	14,799	201
1995		
California	86,317	275
New York	70,751	391
Texas	38,352	206
Florida	37,964	269
Pennsylvania	36,266	301
Illinois	31,304	265
Ohio	26,974	242
Massachusetts	25,467	420
New Jersey	23,970	302
Michigan	22,149	232

Source: American Medical Association

Fields of Medicine

Number of Physicians in Selected Specialties

Specialty	1975 Number	%	1985 Number	%	1995 Number	%
Total	393,742		552,716		720,325	
Anesthesiology	12,861	3.3	22,021	4.0	32,853	4.6
Family practice	12,183	3.1	40,021	7.2	59,345	8.2
General practice	42,374	10.8	27,030	4.9	16,867	2.3
General surgery	31,562	8.0	38,169	6.9	37,569	5.2
Ob/Gyn	21,731	5.4	30,867	5.6	37,652	5.2
Pediatrics	22,192	5.6	36,026	6.5	50,620	7.0
Psychiatry	23,922	6.1	32,255	5.8	38,098	5.3

Women in Medicine

Physicians Under 35, by Sex
(In percent)

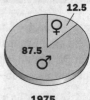

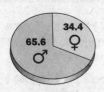

1975 1985 1995

Male and Female Physicians

	1975 Number	%	1980 Number	%	1985 Number	%	1990 Number	%	1995 Number	%
Total	393,742		467,679		552,716		615,421		720,325	
Male	358,106	90.9	413,395	88.4	471,991	85.4	511,227	83.1	570,921	79.3
Female	35,636	9.1	54,284	11.6	80,725	14.6	104,194	16.9	149,404	20.7

Female Physicians in Selected Specialties

Specialty	1975 Number	%	1985 Number	%	1995 Number	%
Total	35,636		80,725		149,404	
Family practice	590	1.7	5,657	7.0	13,971	9.4
Internal medicine	4,006	11.2	14,716	18.2	27,609	18.5
Ob/Gyn	1,777	5.0	5,597	6.9	11,231	7.5
Pediatrics	5,135	14.4	12,440	15.4	22,646	15.2
Psychiatry	3,144	8.8	6,539	8.1	10,392	7.0

Source: American Medical Association

Physicians' Financial Health

Median Fees for Selected Surgical Procedures, for Private Physicians, 1995
(In dollars)

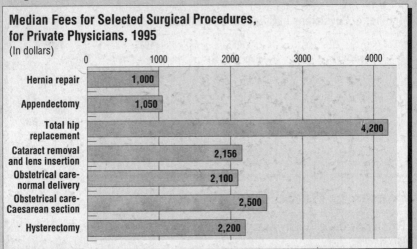

Hernia repair	1,000
Appendectomy	1,050
Total hip replacement	4,200
Cataract removal and lens insertion	2,156
Obstetrical care– normal delivery	2,100
Obstetrical care– Caesarean section	2,500
Hysterectomy	2,200

Median Physician Income after Expenses, before Taxes
(In thousands of dollars)

Specialty	1985	1995
All physicians	94	160
General/Family practice	70	124
Internal medicine	90	150
Surgery	129	225
Pediatrics	70	129
Obstetrics/Gynecology	120	200
Radiology	135	230
Psychiatry	80	124
Anesthesiology	133	203
Pathology	115	185

Average Annual Percentage Change in Median Income after Expenses before Taxes, for Private Physicians, for Selected Specialties, 1985–1995

Specialty	Percentage
All physicians	5.5
General/Family practice	5.9
Internal medicine	5.2
Surgery	5.7
Pediatrics	6.3
Obstetrics/Gynecology	5.2
Radiology	5.5
Psychiatry	4.5
Anesthesiology	4.3
Pathology	4.9

Source: American Medical Association

Doctor's Fees

Percentage Change in Average Fees for Selected Types of Visits for All Physicians, 1985–1996

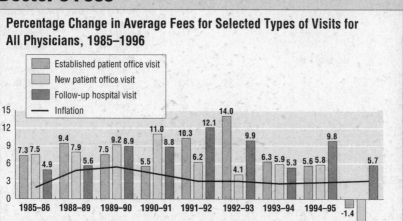

Legend:
- Established patient office visit
- New patient office visit
- Follow-up hospital visit
- — Inflation

	Established	New	Follow-up
1985–86	7.3	7.5	4.9
1988–89	9.4	7.9	5.6
1989–90	7.5	9.2	8.9
1990–91	5.5	11.0	8.8
1991–92	10.3	6.2	12.1
1992–93	14.0	4.1	9.9
1993–94	6.3	5.9	5.3
1994–95	5.6	5.8	9.8
1995–96	-1.4	-5.3	5.7

Average Fees
(In dollars)

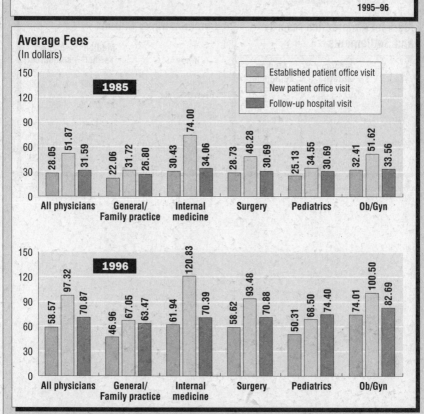

Legend:
- Established patient office visit
- New patient office visit
- Follow-up hospital visit

1985

	Established	New	Follow-up
All physicians	28.05	51.87	31.59
General/Family practice	22.06	31.72	26.80
Internal medicine	30.43	74.00	34.06
Surgery	28.73	48.28	30.69
Pediatrics	25.13	34.55	30.69
Ob/Gyn	32.41	51.62	33.56

1996

	Established	New	Follow-up
All physicians	58.57	97.32	70.87
General/Family practice	46.96	67.05	63.47
Internal medicine	61.94	120.83	70.39
Surgery	58.62	93.48	70.88
Pediatrics	50.31	68.50	74.40
Ob/Gyn	74.01	100.50	82.69

Source: American Medical Association

Income for Other Health-Care Providers

Nursing Pay*

1990	$29,900
1991	$32,300
1992	$33,600
1993	$34,900
1994	$35,800
1995	$37,000
1996	$37,500

*Staff Nurse, RN
Source: Watson Wyatt Worldwide

Dentist Income

Average Income from a Primary Private Practice

Year	Independent General Practioner	Independent Specialist
1990	$88,530	$142,910
1991	$92,030	$143,160
1992	$98,140	$153,410
1993	$107,780	$159,430
1994	$117,610	$177,590

Source: American Dental Association

Medical Malpractice

Medical Malpractice Awards and Settlements

Year	Median award	Median settlement
1990	$431,125	$318,500
1991	415,544	481,250
1992	350,000	350,000
1993	500,000	400,000
1994	362,500	300,000
1995	500,000	401,500
1996	568,000	455,000

Common Injury Claims

Injury	Median verdict	Median settlement
Death	$ 600,000	$ 350,000
Severe mental deficiency	5,950,000	1,850,000
Mild/moderate brain damage	1,439,200	675,000
Spinal nerve injuries	700,000	500,000
Visual impairment	510,000	312,000
Paraplegia/quadriplegia	4,037,807	1,250,000

Source: Jury Verdict Research, Horsham, PA

Health Care and the Economy

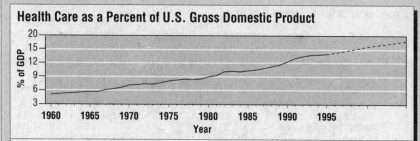

Health Care as a Percent of U.S. Gross Domestic Product

National Health Expenditures

Year	Amount (In billions)	% GDP	Amount Per Capita	Year	Amount (In billions)	% GDP	Amount Per Capita
1960	$26.9	5.1	$141	1990	$697.5	12.1	$2,683
1965	41.1	5.7	202	1991	761.7	12.9	2,901
1970	73.2	7.1	341	1992	834.2	13.4	3,145
1975	130.7	8.0	582	1993	892.1	13.6	3,330
				1994	937.1	13.5	3,465
1980	247.2	8.9	1,052	1995	988.5	13.6	3,621
1985	428.2	10.2	1,733				
1986	460.9	10.4	1,847	1997*	1,173.5	14.8	4,218
1987	500.1	10.7	1,984	2000	1,481.7	15.9	5,198
1988	559.6	11.1	2,198	2005	2,173.7	17.9	7,352
1989	622.0	11.4	2,418				

*Projections for years 1997 and beyond.
Source: U.S. Health Care Financing Administration

Total Health Expenditures as a Percent of GDP and Per Capita* Health Expenditures for Selected Countries

	1960 % GDP	1960 Per Capita	1970 % GDP	1970 Per Capita	1980 % GDP	1980 Per Capita	1990 % GDP	1990 Per Capita	1996 % GDP	1996 Per Capita
Australia	4.9	$98	5.7	$212	7.3	$669	8.2	$1,316	8.4	$1,776
Austria	4.4	67	5.4	166	7.9	697	7.1	1,160	7.9	1,681
Belgium	3.4	53	4.1	131	6.6	588	7.6	1,247	7.9	1,693
Canada	5.5	105	7.1	255	7.3	729	9.2	1,691	9.2	2,002
Denmark	3.6	67	6.1	215	6.8	595	6.5	1,069	6.4	1,430
Finland	3.9	55	5.7	165	6.5	521	8.0	1,292	7.5	1,389
France	4.2	73	5.8	208	7.6	716	8.9	1,539	9.6	1,978
Germany**	4.3	91	5.7	230	8.1	860	8.2	1,642	10.5	2,222
Greece	2.4	16	3.3	60	3.6	190	4.2	389	5.9	748
Iceland	3.3	50	5.0	139	6.2	637	8.0	1,375	7.9	1,839
Ireland	3.8	37	5.3	98	8.8	468	6.6	748	4.9	923
Italy	3.6	50	5.2	157	7.0	591	8.1	1,322	7.6	1,520
Japan	–	27	4.4	132	6.4	535	6.0	1,082	–	–
Luxembourg	–	–	3.7	150	6.2	617	6.6	1,499	–	–
Netherlands	3.8	68	5.9	205	7.9	693	8.3	1,325	8.6	1,756
New Zealand	4.3	92	5.2	177	6.0	463	7.0	937	7.2	1,251
Norway	3.0	47	4.6	135	7.0	639	7.8	1,365	7.9	1,937
Portugal	–	–	2.8	45	5.8	264	6.5	616	8.2	1,077
Spain	1.5	14	3.7	83	5.7	332	6.9	813	7.7	1,131
Sweden	4.7	90	7.1	274	9.4	867	8.8	1,492	7.3	1,405
Switzerland	3.3	93	5.2	270	7.3	850	8.4	1,782	–	–
Turkey	–	–	2.4	23	3.3	77	2.5	119	–	–
United Kingdom	3.9	77	4.5	149	5.6	453	6.0	957	6.9	1,304
United States	5.1	141	7.1	341	8.9	1,052	12.1	2,683	14.2	3,708

*Per capita health expenditures adjusted to U.S. dollars using GDP purchasing power parities for each year.
**There is a change between the 1990 and 1996 Germany figures. Up to 1990, the figures represent the former West Germany. Starting in 1996, the figures are for the united Germany.
Sources: Organization for Economic Cooperation and Development and U.S. Health Care Financing Administration

Annual Spending for Different Types of Health Care

Type of Expenditure	Amount in billions (average annual % increase from previous year shown)				
	1970	**1975**	**1980**	**1985**	**1990**
Personal Health Care	$63.8 10.5%*	$114.5 12.4%	$217.0 13.6%	$376.4 11.6%	$614.7 10.3%
Hospital Care	28.0 11.7	52.6 13.4	102.7 14.3	168.3 10.4	256.4 8.8
Physician Services	13.6 9.9	23.9 12.0	45.2 13.6	83.6 13.1	146.3 11.8
Dental Services	4.7 9.1	8.0 11.2	13.3 10.9	21.7 10.2	31.6 7.8
Other Professional Services	1.4 8.8	2.7 14.2	6.4 18.4	16.6 21.2	34.7 15.8
Home Health Care	0.2 14.5	0.6 23.2	2.4 30.7	5.6 18.9	13.1 18.4
Drugs and Other Medical Non-Durables	8.8 7.6	13.0 8.1	21.6 10.7	37.1 11.4	59.9 10.1
Vision Products and Other Medical Durables	1.6 9.6	2.5 9.5	3.8 8.1	6.7 12.4	10.5 9.2
Nursing Home Care	4.2 17.4	8.7 15.5	17.6 15.3	30.7 11.7	50.9 10.7
Other Personal Health Care	1.3 6.5	2.5 13.8	4.0 10.2	6.1 8.8	11.2 12.9
	1991	**1992**	**1993**	**1994**	**1995**
Personal Health Care	$676.6 10.1%	$740.5 9.5%	$786.9 6.3%	$827.9 5.2%	$878.8 6.1%
Hospital Care	282.3 10.1	305.4 8.2	323.3 5.9	335.0 3.6	350.1 4.5
Physician Services	159.2 8.8	175.7 10.4	182.7 4.0	190.6 4.4	201.6 5.8
Dental Services	33.3 5.6	37.0 11.0	39.2 6.0	42.1 7.3	45.8 8.9
Other Professional Services	38.3 10.4	42.1 10.0	46.3 10.0	49.1 6.1	52.6 7.0
Home Health Care	16.1 22.4	19.6 22.3	23.0 17.1	26.3 14.4	28.6 8.6
Drugs and Other Medical Non-Durables	65.6 9.4	71.2 8.6	75.0 5.4	77.7 3.6	83.4 7.3
Vision Products and Other Medical Durables	11.2 7.0	11.9 6.3	12.5 5.1	12.9 2.8	13.8 7.2
Nursing Home Care	57.2 12.2	62.3 9.0	67.0 7.6	72.4 8.1	77.9 7.5
Other Personal Health Care	13.6 20.7	15.4 13.3	17.9 16.4	21.7 21.6	25.0 14.9

*Average annual percent change since 1960.
Source: U.S. Health Care Financing Administration

Health Benefit Costs

Health benefit costs moderated in the mid-1990s, after years of much larger increases. But the benefits consultant firm Foster Higgins predicts that employers' health-plan costs may be headed up again, with an increase of about 4% possible in 1997.

Total Health Benefit Cost Per Employee for Active and Retired Workers, 1992–1996

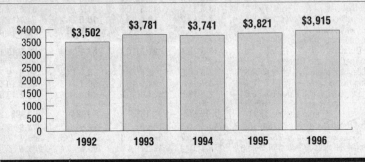

Decline in Percentage of Large Employers Offering Retiree Medical Coverage, 1993–1996

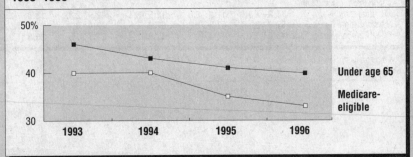

Source: Foster Higgins

Health-Care Safety Net

Insurance Status of People Under Age 65

	1984	1989	1993	1994	1995*
% not covered	15.4	15.7	17.3	17.8	16.5
% under Medicaid	6.0	6.4	9.7	10.2	10.9
% with private insurance	76.9	76.6	71.3	70.1	71.0

Health-Care Coverage Status for Persons Age 65 and Over, According to Type of Coverage and Selected Characteristics (Percent of each group)

Characteristic	Medicare and private insurance					Medicare and Medicaid					Medicare only				
	'84	'89	'93	'94	'95*	'84	'89	'93	'94	'95*	'84	'89	'93	'94	'95*
Total	70.9	73.5	75.5	75.1	72.0	5.4	5.7	5.2	5.3	7.0	20.0	16.8	15.3	14.8	16.2
Age															
65–74 years	73.3	74.2	76.0	74.9	71.6	4.5	5.0	4.6	4.5	6.1	17.7	15.5	14.2	14.4	16.3
75 years and over	66.8	72.3	74.5	75.3	72.8	7.0	6.8	6.4	6.9	8.6	24.1	19.0	17.2	15.4	16.0
75–84 years	69.2	74.1	76.5	77.3	74.1	6.5	6.4	5.8	5.8	8.1	22.0	17.4	15.6	14.4	15.0
85 years and over	56.2	64.8	66.7	67.4	68.2	9.3	8.5	8.5	11.0	10.3	33.4	26.1	23.7	19.5	19.2
Sex															
Male	71.6	73.9	76.5	75.8	72.5	3.3	4.0	3.0	3.0	4.6	20.8	17.2	15.7	15.8	17.3
Female	70.5	73.4	74.7	74.7	71.8	6.9	6.8	6.9	7.0	8.8	19.4	16.4	15.0	13.9	15.3
Race/Ethnic origin															
White	74.4	77.3	79.1	78.8	75.6	4.0	4.5	4.2	4.4	5.5	18.5	14.7	13.2	12.9	14.8
Black	38.1	39.3	43.6	42.4	40.1	19.9	16.5	13.3	14.9	22.2	35.4	37.9	36.2	34.5	31.3
Hispanic	39.4	38.8	38.1	49.2	33.8	19.6	20.4	23.6	19.5	27.9	31.3	24.1	31.7	23.2	28.4
Family income															
Less than $14,000	57.5	64.8	58.3	59.0	54.9	12.3	11.4	14.1	15.0	19.6	27.3	21.5	24.3	22.8	23.1
$14,000–24,999	79.8	81.2	82.8	82.5	79.5	1.8	2.6	1.6	2.0	3.4	15.1	13.4	13.1	12.3	13.7
$25,000–34,999	80.3	80.0	85.7	83.5	80.6	2.2	2.4	1.5	1.4	2.1	13.7	12.5	9.4	9.5	12.1
$35,000–49,999	81.0	80.3	83.6	83.9	80.9	2.3	1.9	2.1	2.0	1.4	11.9	10.2	9.4	9.3	11.4
$50,000 or more	78.5	76.5	81.3	79.1	78.4	1.8	1.1	2.4	1.4	2.0	14.4	12.6	8.5	8.4	10.4

*Preliminary.
Source: Centers for Disease Control and Prevention, National Center for Health Statistics

America's Uninsured

Percentage of People Under Age 65 Not Covered Under Any Insurance Plan, by Race and Sex

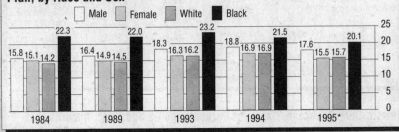

Legend: ☐ Male ▨ Female ▨ White ■ Black

	1984	1989	1993	1994	1995*
Male	15.8	16.4	18.3	18.8	17.6
Female	15.1	14.9	16.3	16.9	15.5
White	14.2	14.5	16.2	16.9	15.7
Black	22.3	22.0	23.2	21.5	20.1

Percentage of People Not Covered Under Any Insurance Plan, by Age

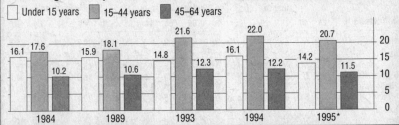

Legend: ☐ Under 15 years ▨ 15–44 years ▨ 45–64 years

	1984	1989	1993	1994	1995*
Under 15 years	16.1	15.9	14.8	16.1	14.2
15–44 years	17.6	18.1	21.6	22.0	20.7
45–64 years	10.2	10.6	12.3	12.2	11.5

Percentage of People Under Age 65 Not Covered Under Any Insurance Plan, by Family Income

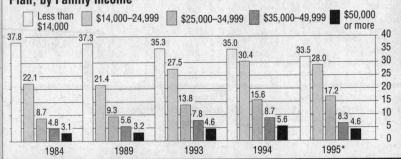

Legend: ☐ Less than $14,000 ▨ $14,000–24,999 ▨ $25,000–34,999 ▨ $35,000–49,999 ■ $50,000 or more

	1984	1989	1993	1994	1995*
Less than $14,000	37.8	37.3	35.3	35.0	33.5
$14,000–24,999	22.1	21.4	27.5	30.4	28.0
$25,000–34,999	8.7	9.3	13.8	15.6	17.2
$35,000–49,999	4.8	5.6	7.8	8.7	8.3
$50,000 or more	3.1	3.2	4.6	5.6	4.6

*Preliminary.
Sources: National Center for Health Statistics and U.S. Census Bureau

Prescription for Health Insurance

Bigger incomes and bigger companies generally mean health insurance coverage.

As Income Rises, Chances of Being Uninsured Generally Decline

Percent of all persons in these household income brackets never covered by health insurance during the year, 1995.

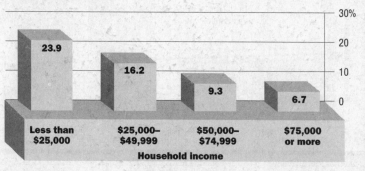

23.9	Less than $25,000
16.2	$25,000–$49,999
9.3	$50,000–$74,999
6.7	$75,000 or more

Household income

Workers in Large Firms Are the Most Likely to Have Employment-Based Insurance

Percent of workers (aged 15 and older) with employment-based health insurance policies in their own name, by size of firm they worked for: 1995

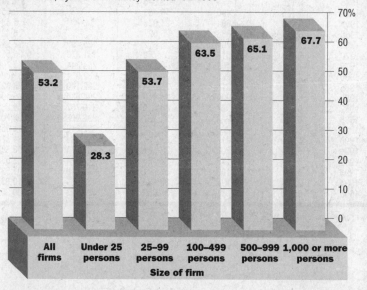

53.2	All firms
28.3	Under 25 persons
53.7	25–99 persons
63.5	100–499 persons
65.1	500–999 persons
67.7	1,000 or more persons

Size of firm

Source: U.S. Census Bureau

Hospital Industry's Vital Signs

Total Number of Hospital Admissions and Outpatient Visits, 1965–1995
(In millions)

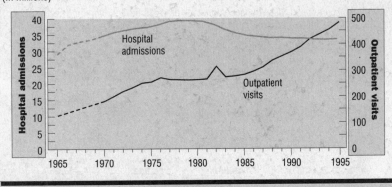

Number of Hospitals, Beds, Admissions, and Outpatient Visits, and Total Expenses in the U.S.

Year	Hospitals	Beds (In thousands)	Admissions (In thousands)	Outpatient Visits (In thousands)	Total Expenses (In millions)
1946	6,125	1,436	15,675	–	$ 1,963
1950	6,788	1,456	18,483	–	3,651
1955	6,956	1,604	21,073	–	5,594
1960	6,876	1,658	25,027	–	8,421
1965	7,123	1,704	28,812	125,793	12,948
1970	7,123	1,616	31,759	181,370	25,556
1975	7,156	1,466	36,157	254,844	48,706
1980	6,965	1,365	38,892	262,951	91,886
1985	6,872	1,318	36,304	282,140	153,327
1986	6,841	1,290	35,219	294,634	165,194
1987	6,821	1,267	34,439	310,707	178,662
1988	6,780	1,248	34,107	336,208	196,704
1989	6,720	1,226	33,742	352,248	214,886
1990	6,649	1,213	33,774	368,184	234,870
1991	6,634	1,202	33,567	387,675	258,508
1992	6,539	1,178	33,536	417,874	282,531
1993	6,467	1,163	33,201	435,619	301,538
1994	6,374	1,128	33,125	453,584	310,834
1995	6,291	1,081	33,282	483,195	320,252

Source: American Hospital Association

The Move to Managed Care

The Number of People Receiving Care in HMOs*

(Millions of members)

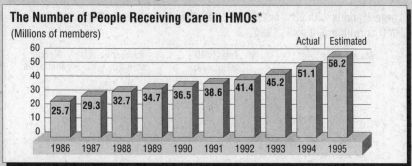

	1986	1987	1988	1989	1990	1991	1992	1993	1994	1995
	25.7	29.3	32.7	34.7	36.5	38.6	41.4	45.2	51.1	58.2

Actual | Estimated

*Includes POS enrollment, excludes employer self-insured enrollment.
Source: American Association of Health Plans

The Number of People Receiving Care through PPOs (Millions of members)

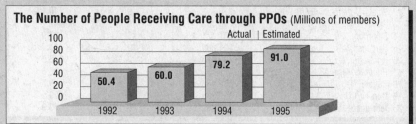

Actual | Estimated

1992	1993	1994	1995
50.4	60.0	79.2	91.0

Source: American Association of Health Plans

Average Cost Per Employee

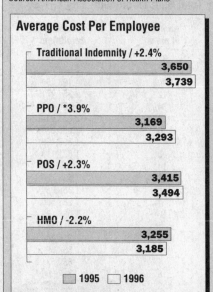

Traditional Indemnity / +2.4%
3,650
3,739

PPO / *3.9%
3,169
3,293

POS / +2.3%
3,415
3,494

HMO / -2.2%
3,255
3,185

■ 1995 □ 1996

Source: Foster Higgins

Type of Health Plan

Traditional indemnity plan
Fee-for-service health insurance. Plan participants or providers are reimbursed following submission of a claim. Participants have no restrictions on which hospitals or doctors they may use.

Preferred provider plan (PPO)
An indemnity plan in which a group of health-care providers offer their services under defined financial arrangements. Plan participants usually have incentives to use the "preferred provider" network. A participant's access to specialists in the network is *not* controlled by a primary care physician.

Point-of-service plan (POS)
A "managed care" plan in which a participant's access to a provider network (usually an HMO) is controlled by a primary care physician. Participants retain the option to seek care outside the network, but at reduced coverage levels. Includes open-ended HMOs.

Health Maintenance Organization (HMO)
A prepaid health plan in which participants may obtain care only from a specified list of providers. No benefits are available outside the HMO network. Includes Exclusive Provider Organizations (EPOs).

Top HMO Markets and Marketers

Large Markets with 25% or Greater HMO Penetration Ranked by HMO Enrollment, July 1, 1995

	Metropolitan area	Total HMO enrollment	Number of HMOs	Market penetration
1	Los Angeles-Long Beach, CA	3,833,749	22	39.2%
2	Philadelphia, PA-NJ	1,592,011	12	29.3
3	Boston, MA	1,555,606	14	42.1
4	Washington, DC-MD-VA-WV	1,271,694	17	27.3
5	Oakland, CA	1,187,804	12	51.7
6	Minneapolis-St. Paul, MN-WI	1,176,794	8	42.0
7	Anaheim-Santa Ana, CA	1,010,144	15	38.0
8	Riverside-San Bernardino, CA	1,001,440	13	35.0
9	Miami, FL	932,911	18	43.6
10	San Diego, CA	896,934	12	32.5
11	Sacramento, CA	894,477	12	60.5
12	Portland-Vancouver, OR-WA	770,913	9	46.1
13	San Francisco, CA	746,052	15	42.1
14	Baltimore, MD	707,471	16	26.9
15	San Jose, CA	691,254	12	41.8
16	Rochester, NY	662,675	2	56.5
17	Phoenix-Mesa, AZ	649,139	10	26.3
18	Buffalo, NY	532,287	3	49.8
19	Denver, CO	522,254	10	29.1
20	Milwaukee-Waukesha, WI	472,400	8	29.9

National Managed Care Firms Ranked by Total HMO Enrollment, July 1, 1996

	National managed care firm	Number of plans	Reported total enrollment
1	The Blue Cross and Blue Shield System	81	10,610,983
2	Kaiser Foundation Health Plans, Inc.	12	7,074,778
3	United HealthCare Corporation	40	4,193,894
4	U.S. HealthCare, Inc.	12	2,364,271
5	CIGNA Health Plans, Inc.	34	2,268,010
6	Prudential Health Care Plan, Inc.	34	2,243,884
7	PacifiCare Health Systems, Inc.	6	1,996,370
8	FHP, Inc.	11	1,898,466
9	Health Systems International, Inc.	8	1,821,114
10	Humana Inc.	14	1,792,536
11	Aetna Health Plans	21	1,583,750
12	Foundation Health Corporation	8	1,353,950
13	Oxford Health Plans, Inc.	4	1,281,500
14	NYLCare Health Plans, Inc.	10	1,086,192
15	Health Insurance Plan of Greater New York	4	1,016,169
16	Harvard Pilgrim Health Plan	1	958,406
17	Healthsource, Inc.	15	883,692
18	Mid-Atlantic Medical Services, Inc.	4	830,831
19	Principal Health Care, Inc.	18	717,806
20	Group Health Cooperative of Puget Sound	3	655,623

Source: InterStudy Publications

Pharmaceutical Prices

The Weighed Average Price Change for Pharmaceuticals

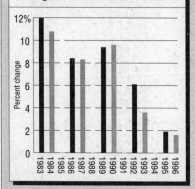

Source: IMS America

World's Largest Pharmaceutical Companies

Worldwide Pharmaceutical Sales by Market Share

Corporations	1996 ranked by sales	1995 market share %	1996 market share %
Novartis (Ciba-Geigy/ Sandoz)	1	4.4 %	4.4 %
Glaxo Wellcome	2	4.4	4.4
Merck & Co.	3	3.5	4.0
Hoechst Marion Roussel	4	3.5	3.3
Bristol-Myers Squibb	5	3.1	3.2
Johnson & Johnson	6	2.8	3.1
American Home	7	3.0	3.1
Pfizer	8	2.8	3.1
SmithKline Beecham	9	2.5	2.7
Roche	10	2.6	2.7
Leading 10 corporations	–	**32.6**	**34.0**
Bayer	11	2.2	2.1
Astra	12	1.9	2.1
Eli Lilly	13	2.0	2.1
Rhone Poulenc	14	2.1	2.1
Abbott	15	1.8	2.0
Schering Plough	16	1.8	2.0
Pharmacia & Upjohn	17	1.8	1.8
Boehringer Ingelheim	18	1.5	1.5
Takeda	19	1.5	1.5
Warner-Lambert	20	1.3	1.4
Leading 20 corporations	–	**50.5**	**52.4**

Source: IMS International

Prescription Payments

More prescriptions are being paid for by insurance companies, managed-care organizations and other third parties.

% of Retail Prescriptions Paid

Year	Cash	3rd party
1991	63.1%	36.8%
1992	59.2	40.8
1993	55.6	44.4
1994	50.5	49.5
1995	44.7	55.3
1996*	38.2	61.8

*Estimate.
Source: IMS America

Faster Drug Approval

The Food and Drug Administration, criticized by both consumers and the pharmaceutical industry for taking too long to clear beneficial new drugs, has speeded up the approval process in recent years. Drug makers now pay fees to the government to help cover the cost of additional drug reviewers. Here are the number of new drugs, which the FDA calls new molecular entities because they contain a new active substance, and the median time to approval.

Number and Median Times of Approval for New Drugs Referred to as New Molecular Entities

Calendar year	Number	Median time to approval (months)
1986	20	32.9
1987	21	29.9
1988	20	27.2
1989	23	29.3
1990	23	24.3
1991	30	22.1
1992	26	22.6
1993	25	23.0
1994	22	17.5
1995	28	15.9
1996	53	14.3

Source: Food and Drug Administration

Pharmaceutical Companies, Ranked by 1996 U.S. Sales

Rank	Company	Total sales (Thousands)	Percent change vs. '95
1	Glaxo Wellcome	$ 5,802,973	+10%
2	Johnson & Johnson	5,275,107	+18
3	American Home Products	5,250,868	+12
4	Bristol-Myers Squibb	5,159,772	+9
5	Merck	5,025,825	+20
6	Pfizer	4,511,169	+16
7	Novartis	3,785,898	+8
8	SmithKline Beecham	3,588,645	+17
9	Eli Lilly	3,567,019	+9
10	Abbott	3,423,143	+12
11	Schering-Plough	3,271,916	+17
12	Hoechst-Marion	2,473,567	-11
13	Hoffman-LaRoche	2,315,541	+9
14	Amgen	1,860,364	+19
15	Bayer	1,853,548	+4
16	Astra Merck	1,832,786	+45
17	Pharmacia & Upjohn	1,593,779	-2
18	Warner-Lambert	1,313,673	+14
19	Zeneca	1,288,506	+15
20	Searle	1,142,390	+12
	Total all companies	**85,348,593**	**+10**

Top 25 Prescription Drugs, Based on 1996 U.S. Sales

Rank	Drug	Total sales (Thousands)	Percent change vs. '95
1	Zantac (ulcer medicine)	$ 1,760,726	-18
2	Prilosec (ulcer medicine)	1,741,898	+46
3	Prozac (antidepressant	1,685,345	+14
4	Epogen (anemia)	1,183,595	+23
5	Zoloft (antidepressant)	1,097,819	+23
6	Zocor (cholesterol drug)	1,015,003	+78
7	Procardia (blood pressure drug)	961,936	-13
8	Vasotec (blood pressure drug)	865,512	+1
9	Mevacor (cholesterol drug)	791,972	- 7
10	Premarin (estrogen)	768,224	+8
11	Biaxin (antibiotic)	760,432	+23
12	Cardizem (blood pressure drug)	734,388	-3
13	Lupron Depot (prostate cancer treatment)	725,077	+21
14	Norvasc (blood pressure drug)	722,673	+45
15	Paxil (antidepressant)	695,611	+43
16	Cipro (antibiotic)	684,407	+4
17	Neupogen (anti-infective)	676,768	+13
18	Augmentin (antibiotic)	672,451	+11
19	Claritin(antihistamine)	657,013	+48
20	Pepcid (ulcer medicine)	650,716	+8
21	Imitrex (migraine headache drug)	580,351	+72
22	Pravachol (cholesterol drug)	564,733	+42
23	Risperdal (antipsychotic)	542,099	+49
24	Tylenol (analgesic)	540,231	-4
25	Rocephin (antibiotic)	431,736	-2
	Total all products	**85,348,593**	**+10**

Top 25 Drugs, Based on Number of Prescriptions Dispensed in U.S. in 1996

Rank	Drug	Total prescriptions (Thousands)	Percent change vs. '95
1	Premarin (estrogen)	44,791	+1%
2	Trimox (antibiotic)	35,388	+16
3	Synthroid (thyroid treatment)	33,272	+12
4	Lanoxin (cardiac treatment)	25,743	-1
5	Zantac (ulcer medicine)	23,064	-17
6	Vasotec (blood pressure drug)	21,622	-1
7	Prozac (antidepressant)	20,705	+10
8	Procardia (blood pressure drug)	18,837	-13
9	Hydrocodone (analgesic)	18,810	+52
10	Coumadin Sodium (anticoagulant)	17,453	+17
11	Zoloft (antidepressant)	17,104	+20
12	Prilosec (ulcer medicine)	16,082	+43
13	Norvasc (blood pressure drug)	15,607	+42
14	Cardizem (blood pressure drug)	15,539	- 4
15	Albuterol (asthma treatment)	15,466	+232
16	Biaxin (antibiotic)	14,731	+14
17	Amoxil (antibiotic)	14,097	-41
18	Triamterene (diuretic)	13,607	+10
19	Zestril (blood pressure drug)	13,586	+8
20	Claritin (antihistamine)	13,463	+35
21	Zocor (cholesterol drug)	13,357	+68
22	Furosemide (diuretic)	12,319	+23
23	Augmentin (antibiotic)	12,216	0
24	Paxil (antidepressant)	11,982	+33
25	Cipro (antibiotic)	11,710	+1
	Total all products	**2,413,082**	**+ 4**

Source: IMS America

Health News of 1997
The Good News

Medical researchers showed for the first time that it may be possible to slow the progression of Alzheimer's disease in patients suffering from moderate symptoms. A study found that high doses of vitamin E or standard doses of a drug used to treat Parkinson's disease can delay such consequences as the onset of severe dementia or the need to be admitted to a nursing home by as much as seven months, compared with patients who don't receive the treatment.

The risk of Alzheimer's can be cut by long-term use of anti-inflammatory drugs such as ibuprofen, research by the National Institute on Aging and Johns Hopkins University found. The study, involving 1,600 patients over 15 years, found the risk could be cut in half.

An estrogen study found the use of the hormone reduced the death rate in older women by 37%, chiefly by cutting heart attack risk. The Harvard study, the most extensive yet, found women with high risk factors, such as obesity or smoking, benefited most from estrogen therapy. Healthy women, however, reduced their mortality rate by a more modest 11% when they took the hormone. The study indicates that healthy women might be better off avoiding the long-term hormone therapy because women on estrogen for 10 years or more were 43% more likely to die of breast cancer than women who didn't take the hormone.

A new minimally invasive method to perform coronary-artery bypass surgery without breaking open a patient's chest leads to shorter hospital stays, fewer complications and lower costs than the traditional procedure, researchers said.

Heart researchers found that a new drug being developed by Merck can cut deaths, heart attacks and other complications by one-third in patients with severe chest pain. The studies suggest that the drug could prevent as many as 10,000 deaths a year in the U.S.

A major study found that seven ounces of fish a week can cut the risk of heart attack by 60% in men. And other research shows that middle-aged men who had two to six drinks a day sliced their risk of developing heart disease by half, compared to those who abstained. For men, drinking does not seem to increase cancer risk, researchers noted.

The cancer drug Taxol increased survival of women with advanced ovarian cancer by more than 50% when combined with standard chemotherapy, according to a study. The findings represent the first time in 15 years that a new drug used in initial treatment of ovarian cancer led to significant improvement in survival. Doctors recommended that Taxol in combination with cisplatin be considered standard therapy for advanced ovarian cancer.

Women who exercise at least four hours a week have a 37 percent lower risk of developing breast cancer than sedentary women, a study found. This was one of a string of studies that have shown a correlation between exercise and a lower incidence of breast cancer.

Ordinary birth-control pills can halt pregnancies if taken in sufficient quantities within three days of unprotected sex, the FDA said. The agency, giving details on dosages, said six brands of the pill can safely be used as "morning-after pills." It added that the pills' effectiveness for this use has been known, but kept quiet for some time.

Antidepressant pills can help smokers stop the habit. Wellbutrin has helped hundreds of smokers quit in chemical trials by manipulating some of the same brain chemicals that are involved in nicotine addiction.

New nerve-regenerating drugs are showing promise in treating spinal injuries and diseases such as Alzheimer's and Parkinson's. Guilford Pharmaceuticals researchers said they have found medicines that, unlike those used now, needn't be injected into the brain.

The FDA approved Warner-Lamber Co.'s diabetes drug Rezulin, a new type of medication that doctors said could greatly reduce—and in some cases eliminate—the need for insulin shots for about a million diabetics in the U.S.

Keeping a patient warm—with something as revolutionary as a blanket—during surgery can cut the risk of a postoperative heart attack by half. In an operation, a patient's body temperature drops, and the cold often increases the level of stress hormones, causes blood vessels to constrict, and raises blood pressure.

A medical version of Super Glue is proving superior to stitches in closing many types of wounds. Gluing wounds shut was faster, less painful, and resulted in healed skin that looks just as good as stitched wounds, a study of 130 emergency-room patients found. Also, gluing seems to avert some of the infections that occur in stitched wounds.

Mayo Clinic researchers are developing a new blood test that can detect the genetic marker for prostate cancer. The test, researchers say, should improve screening for prostate cancer, helping to avoid unnecessary biopsies.

Strap on your safety glasses and open wide: Painless drilling may be coming to a dentist near you. The FDA approved the first laser device for hard-tissue dental procedures like removing decayed tissue and filling cavities.

Researchers at Boston University discovered that one shot of the antibiotic Rocephin is nearly as effective in treating childhood ear infections as 10 days of oral antibiotics.

British scientists said they have found evidence that bacterial infections can cause heart attacks, and that antibiotics may emerge as an important weapon against them. The findings, in a study of 213 patients, bolster new theories about heart disease that could redraw the cardiovascular-drug landscape.

Government researchers said a new nasal spray vaccine for the influenza virus prevented flu in a large test in children, possibly paving the way for a new class of easily administered vaccines for large numbers of patients.

U.S. researchers have unraveled the complete genetic structure of a bacterium that causes stomach ulcers, a major advance promising better drugs and tests. Surprising evidence emerged a few years ago implicating the micro-be, Helicobacter pylori, in ulcers.

Estrogen researchers have developed a compound that appears to provide the benefits of the hormone therapy without the cancer risks. If borne out in human tests, the Duke University-Glaxo Wellcome compound could become a potent weapon for fighting breast cancer, osteo-porosis and heart disease in women.

The Bad News

The American Cancer Society urged women to start getting annual mammograms at age 40, instead of waiting until they turn 50. The guide-lines were issued amid an emotional debate over the best method to prevent breast cancer. Ear-lier, the National Cancer Institute found evi-dence of mammography's benefits before age 50 inconclusive; however, a few months later, under growing political pressure, the panel backed off its decision and urged women in their 40s to get mammograms every year or two. President Clinton also called on private insurers to cover the costs of the tests.

Drinking alcohol appears to sharply raise estrogen levels in women who take estrogen-replacement therapy, according to researchers. The early-stage research raises questions about possible adverse effects, such as an increased breast-cancer risk, in women who consume more than three drinks a week and take estrogen.

A strategy routinely used to treat thousands of heart-attack patients with coronary bypass surgery or other aggressive procedures may do more harm than good. Heart researchers said a study involving 920 patients who suffered small heart attacks found that those given early aggressive treatment were more than twice as likely to die or suffer a second heart attack in the hospital as patients who were treated more conservatively.

Women with heart disease should get much more aggressive treatment to lower cholesterol than they do now, researchers said. A study of 2,763 women, many already taking cholesterol drugs, found only 10% met U.S. guidelines.

Arterial inflammation may be an important cause of heart attacks and strokes, according to a Harvard study that could spur new treatment approaches. Researchers found that men who had chronic low-grade inflammation, possibly caused by a virus or bacteria, had three times as many attacks as those who didn't.

A federal study confirmed that air bags are effective in reducing fatalities during head-on collisions, even when the driver is unbelted. But it also revealed that air bags increase the risk of death in passengers 12 years old or younger and drivers more than 70 years old.

In a landmark study, two teams of scientists identified the last link in the chain of evidence showing how cigarettes cause cancer. They demonstrated precisely how a chemical in ciga-rette smoke can damage a gene that suppresses the haywire cell growth of cancer.

Smokers get higher doses of tar and nicotine than pack labels say, tests showed. Research sponsored by Massachusetts regulators found that most of the 10 brands tested delivered twice as much tar as their makers say, and 46% to 98% more nicotine. The study used methods meant to reflect more realistic smoking conditions than those in tobacco-company tests.

A study of 32,000 nurses found that regular exposure to secondhand smoke appears to almost double the risk of heart disease in women who don't smoke. The study, published in the American Heart Association journal *Circulation*, looked at total exposure to secondhand smoke at home and at work.

Babies born to mothers who smoke during pregnancies, or even babies exposed to second-hand smoke, are more likely to have lungs that don't function properly, a study found. Recent studies have linked secondhand smoke to a host of ailments from bronchitis and pneumonia to sudden infant death syndrome.

Cockroaches are a major cause of a surge in asthma cases among inner-city children, a feder-ally sponsored study indicated. Researchers found that children who are allergic and exposed to the insects are three times more likely to be hospitalized than children who aren't.

The National Institutes of Health said new diabetes guidelines, calling for universal testing by age 45, could help identify many of the eight million Americans who have the disease but don't know it. The guidelines, drafted by an international panel, lower the blood-sugar diagnostic standard and list high-risk ethnic groups.

The FDA proposed stringent limits on the manufacturing and marketing of ephedrine-based dietary supplements that would effectively ban a wide array of body-building and weight-loss products. Since 1994, more than 800 adverse reactions, including seizures, strokes, and heart attacks, and 18 deaths, have been linked to ephedrine capsules, tablets and teas.

In the past year, several studies drew a clearer connection between emotions and health. One study found that clinically depressed adults face a 50% increased risk of dying from a stroke; the researchers said depression may alter blood platelet activity in such a way that it triggers clot formation. Other studies found that people who feel tense, sad, or anxious for a prolonged period of time are at greater risk of developing heart disease and hypertension.

Nearly 35,000 blood donors, or 2% of donors, failed to acknowledge that they had engaged in high-risk behaviors, such as unprotected gay male sex or intravenous drug use, a study found. Although the study determined the nation's blood supply is safe, it suggested that donor screening procedures should be reviewed.

Nearly one in four women with breast implants suffered local complications serious enough to warrant reoperation within five years, according to a study. The results could shift the debate over silicone away from immune-system illnesses and toward such chest-area ailments as abnormal tissue growth and chronic pain.

Two marijuana studies said it affects the brain in the same way drugs such as heroin and cocaine do, and produces symptoms of emotional withdrawal. The findings come as research shows marijuana use is soaring in the U.S., especially among teenagers.

A large-scale study of newborns found babies discharged within 30 hours of birth were 28% more likely to require rehospitalization within a week than those who stayed longer. The findings, based on an analysis of 310,000 Washington births, are likely to add to debate over so-called drive-through deliveries.

Calcium is lacking in U.S. diets, leading to an "alarming" increase in osteoporosis, an Institute of Medicine panel said. The panel said average intake is less than 75% of the more than 1,000 milligrams a day needed. It urged more dairy consumption, which has fallen due to concerns about fat.

American Home Products withdrew Redux and its older cousin Pondimin from the market, amid increasing health concerns about the prescription diet drugs. The decision ended a two-year saga in which Redux and Pondimin, the "fen" in the popular fen-phen combination, had been linked to brain damage in animals and heart problems in humans. The next generation of fat-fighting drugs could be years away.

The Changing Face of Death

Life Expectancy in the U.S. at Birth

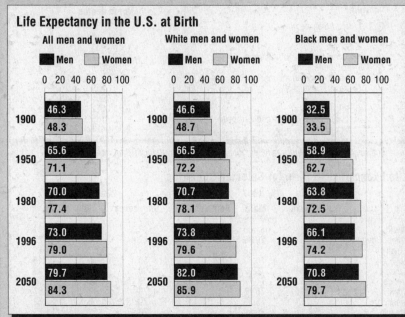

	All men and women	White men and women	Black men and women
	■ Men ☐ Women	■ Men ☐ Women	■ Men ☐ Women
1900	Men 46.3 / Women 48.3	Men 46.6 / Women 48.7	Men 32.5 / Women 33.5
1950	Men 65.6 / Women 71.1	Men 66.5 / Women 72.2	Men 58.9 / Women 62.7
1980	Men 70.0 / Women 77.4	Men 70.7 / Women 78.1	Men 63.8 / Women 72.5
1996	Men 73.0 / Women 79.0	Men 73.8 / Women 79.6	Men 66.1 / Women 74.2
2050	Men 79.7 / Women 84.3	Men 82.0 / Women 85.9	Men 70.8 / Women 79.7

*Estimates for years 1997 and beyond.
Source: National Center for Health Statistics, U.S. Census Bureau

Leading Causes of Death

1900

	No. of deaths
1. Pneumonia and influenza	40,362
2. Tuberculosis	38,820
3. Diarrhea, enteritis, and ulceration of the intestines	28,491
4. Heart disease	27,427
5. Stroke	21,353
6. Nephritis	17,699
7. All accidents	14,429
8. Cancer	12,769
9. Senility	10,015
10. Diphtheria	8,056
All causes	**343,217**

1940

1. Heart disease	385,191
2. Cancer	158,335
3. Stroke	119,753
4. Nephritis	107,351
5. Pneumonia and influenza	92,525
6. Accidents, excluding motor-vehicle	62,384
7. Tuberculosis	60,428
8. Diabetes mellitus	35,015
9. Motor-vehicle accidents	34,501
10. Premature birth	32,346
All causes	**1,417,269**

Leading Causes of Death

1996	No. of deaths
1. Heart disease	733,834
2. Cancer	544,278
3. Stroke	160,431
4. Chronic respiratory diseases	106,146
5. Accidents	93,874
6. Pneumonia and influenza	82,579
7. Diabetes mellitus	61,559
8. HIV	32,655
9. Suicide	30,862
10. Chronic liver disease and cirrhosis	25,135
All causes	**2,322,421**

Sources: Centers for Disease Control and Prevention, National Center for Health Statistics

Life Expectancy at Birth for Selected Countries

	1997			2000 projected		
	Both sexes	Male	Female	Both sexes	Male	Female
World	62.67	61.00	64.43	63.39	61.57	65.31
China, Hong Kong	82.35	79.06	85.84	82.84	79.61	86.25
Japan	79.66	76.68	82.79	80.00	77.03	83.12
Australia	79.64	76.69	82.74	80.41	77.49	83.48
Canada	79.30	75.92	82.86	80.01	76.69	83.49
France	78.56	74.72	82.62	79.19	75.47	83.11
Spain	78.47	75.17	81.99	79.10	75.86	82.57
Singapore	78.40	75.33	81.67	79.22	76.12	82.52
Greece	78.31	75.80	81.01	78.97	76.40	81.73
Israel	78.21	76.34	80.18	78.82	76.89	80.84
Italy	78.20	75.00	81.60	78.64	75.49	81.99
Sweden	78.18	75.74	80.74	78.54	76.12	81.08
Netherlands	77.85	75.05	80.79	78.23	75.47	81.13
Switzerland	77.75	74.72	80.93	78.14	75.16	81.26
United Kingdom	76.58	73.96	79.34	77.13	74.52	79.87
China, Taiwan	76.33	73.72	79.14	77.27	74.62	80.14
Germany	76.13	73.00	79.44	76.70	73.62	79.96
Ireland	75.74	73.06	78.61	76.24	73.60	79.05
Cuba	75.20	72.83	77.71	75.64	73.21	78.22
Chile	74.73	71.50	77.95	75.45	72.25	78.65
Mexico	74.00	70.39	77.78	75.02	71.39	78.83
Czech Republic	73.87	70.18	77.78	74.21	70.48	78.16
South Korea	73.60	70.01	77.69	74.66	71.13	78.65
Colombia	73.14	70.28	76.09	74.15	71.20	77.20
Turkey	72.37	69.95	74.91	73.75	71.25	76.38
Poland	72.22	68.14	76.55	72.61	68.49	76.99
China, Mainland	69.98	68.61	71.50	71.08	69.48	72.85
Saudi Arabia	69.51	67.72	71.40	71.09	69.16	73.11
Thailand	68.80	65.12	72.66	69.41	65.81	73.19
Iran	67.82	66.47	69.23	69.12	67.55	70.78
Vietnam	67.38	65.03	69.86	68.47	66.06	71.03
Philippines	66.13	63.35	69.05	66.80	64.01	69.73
Russia	63.77	57.20	70.68	65.36	59.37	71.65
Indonesia	62.06	59.89	64.34	63.36	61.06	65.77
Egypt	61.75	59.80	63.80	62.71	60.69	64.83
Brazil	61.42	56.78	66.30	60.87	57.09	64.84
India	60.15	59.52	60.81	61.51	60.73	62.32
South Africa	58.88	56.64	61.19	57.17	54.98	59.43
Pakistan	58.77	57.97	59.61	59.67	58.75	60.64
Nigeria	54.65	53.32	56.03	55.61	54.10	57.17

Source: U.S. Census Bureau

Incidence of Heart Attacks and Strokes

Estimated Annual Number of Americans, by Age and Sex, Experiencing Heart Attack

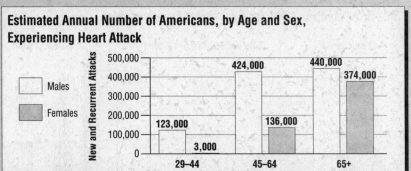

Sources: American Heart Association and Framingham Heart Study, 26-year follow-up

Estimated Annual Number of Americans, by Age and Sex, Experiencing Stroke

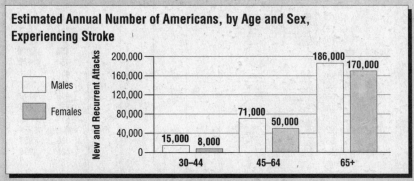

Sources: American Heart Association and Framingham Heart Study, 24-year follow-up

Death Rates for Cardiovascular Diseases and All Causes in Selected Countries, 1994 (or most recent year available)

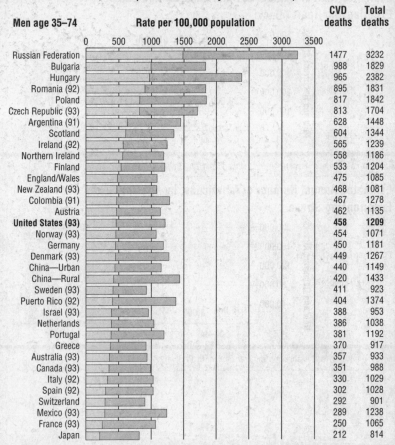

Men age 35–74	Rate per 100,000 population	CVD deaths	Total deaths
Russian Federation		1477	3232
Bulgaria		988	1829
Hungary		965	2382
Romania (92)		895	1831
Poland		817	1842
Czech Republic (93)		813	1704
Argentina (91)		628	1448
Scotland		604	1344
Ireland (92)		565	1239
Northern Ireland		558	1186
Finland		533	1204
England/Wales		475	1085
New Zealand (93)		468	1081
Colombia (91)		467	1278
Austria		462	1135
United States (93)		**458**	**1209**
Norway (93)		454	1071
Germany		450	1181
Denmark (93)		449	1267
China—Urban		440	1149
China—Rural		420	1433
Sweden (93)		411	923
Puerto Rico (92)		404	1374
Israel (93)		388	953
Netherlands		386	1038
Portugal		381	1192
Greece		370	917
Australia (93)		357	933
Canada (93)		351	988
Italy (92)		330	1029
Spain (92)		302	1028
Switzerland		292	901
Mexico (93)		289	1238
France (93)		250	1065
Japan		212	814

Source: World Health Organization and the American Heart Association

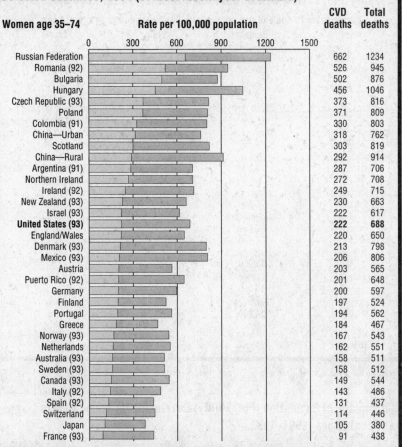

Death Rates for Cardiovascular Diseases and All Causes in Selected Countries, 1994 (or most recent year available)

Women age 35–74   Rate per 100,000 population

Country	CVD deaths	Total deaths
Russian Federation	662	1234
Romania (92)	526	945
Bulgaria	502	876
Hungary	456	1046
Czech Republic (93)	373	816
Poland	371	809
Colombia (91)	330	803
China—Urban	318	762
Scotland	303	819
China—Rural	292	914
Argentina (91)	287	706
Northern Ireland	272	708
Ireland (92)	249	715
New Zealand (93)	230	663
Israel (93)	222	617
United States (93)	**222**	**688**
England/Wales	220	650
Denmark (93)	213	798
Mexico (93)	206	806
Austria	203	565
Puerto Rico (92)	201	648
Germany	200	597
Finland	197	524
Portugal	194	562
Greece	184	467
Norway (93)	167	543
Netherlands	162	551
Australia (93)	158	511
Sweden (93)	158	512
Canada (93)	149	544
Italy (92)	143	486
Spain (92)	131	437
Switzerland	114	446
Japan	105	380
France (93)	91	438

Source: World Health Organization and the American Heart Association

Cancer Targets

Leading Sites of New Cancer Cases and Deaths — 1997 Estimates*

Cancer cases by site and sex		Cancer deaths by site and sex	
Male	**Female**	**Male**	**Female**
Prostate 334,500	Breast 180,200	Lung 94,400	Lung 66,000
Lung 98,300	Lung 79,800	Prostate 41,800	Breast 43,900
Colon & rectum 66,400	Colon & rectum 64,800	Colon & rectum 27,000	Colon & rectum 27,900
Urinary bladder 39,500	Corpus uteri 34,900	Pancreas 13,500	Pancreas 14,600
Non-Hodgkin's lymphoma 30,300	Ovary 26,800	Non-Hodgkin's lymphoma 12,400	Ovary 14,200
Melanoma of the skin 22,900	Non-Hodgkin's lymphoma 23,300	Leukemia 11,770	Non-Hodgkin's lymphoma 11,400
Oral cavity 20,900	Melanoma of the skin 17,400	Esophagus 8,700	Leukemia 9,540
Kidney 17,100	Urinary bladder 15,000	Stomach 8,300	Corpus uteri 6,000
Leukemia 15,900	Cervix 14,500	Urinary bladder 7,800	Brain 6,000
Stomach 14,000	Pancreas 14,200	Liver 7,500	Stomach 5,700
All sites 785,800	All sites 596,600	All sites 294,100	All sites 265,900

*Excluding basal and squamous cell skin cancer and in situ carcinomas except bladder.

Percentage of Population (Probability) Developing Invasive Cancers at Certain Ages, 1991–1993

		Birth to 39	40–59	60–79	Birth to death
All sites*	Male	1.71 (1 in 58)	8.27 (1 in 12)	37.79 (1 in 3)	48.17 (1 in 2)
	Female	1.96 (1 in 51)	9.12 (1 in 11)	22.48 (1 in 4)	38.33 (1 in 3)
Breast	Female	0.46 (1 in 217)	3.92 (1 in 26)	6.94 (1 in 14)	12.61 (1 in 8)
Colon & rectum	Male	0.06 (1 in 1,667)	0.92(1 in 109)	4.27 (1 in 23)	6.02 (1 in 17)
	Female	0.05 (1 in 2,000)	0.70 (1 in 143)	3.24 (1 in 31)	5.77 (1 in 17)
Lung	Male	0.04 (1 in 2,500)	1.46 (1 in 68)	6.82 (1 in 15)	8.60 (1 in 12)
	Female	0.03 (1 in 3,333)	1.05 (1 in 95)	3.83 (1 in 26)	5.48 (1 in 18)
Prostate	Male	Less than 1 in 10,000	1.58 (1 in 63)	17.04 (1 in 6)	19.84 (1 in 5)

*Excludes basal and squamous cell skin cancers and in situ carcinomas except bladder.
Sources: American Cancer Society, National Cancer Institute

20 Year Trends in Cancer Death Rates* per 100,000 Population, 1971–1973 to 1991–1993

Sites	Sex	Rates in 1971–73	Rates in 1991–93	% changes	Number of deaths 1973	Number of deaths 1993
All sites	Male	204.5	219.0	7%	190,487	279,375
	Female	132.0	142.0	8%	159,110	250,529
Brain	Male	4.7	5.1	9%	4,650	6,551
	Female	3.2	3.5	9%	3,661	5,442
Breast	Male	0.3	0.2	-33%	293	355
	Female	26.8	26.4	-1%	31,850	43,555
Cervix	Female	5.6	2.9	-48%	6,041	4,583
Colon & rectum	Male	25.3	22.3	-12%	22,680	28,199
	Female	20.0	15.1	-25%	24,823	29,206
Corpus uteri	Female	4.7	3.4	-28%	5,686	6,098
Esophagus	Male	5.0	6.2	24%	4,768	7,813
	Female	1.4	1.5	7%	1,723	2,637
Hodgkin's disease	Male	1.9	0.7	-63%	1,732	900
	Female	1.1	0.4	-64%	1,188	674
Kidney	Male	4.3	5.1	19%	4,004	6,358
	Female	1.9	2.3	21%	2,330	3,964
Larynx	Male	2.8	2.5	-11%	2,656	3,163
	Female	0.3	0.5	67%	388	818
Leukemia	Male	8.9	8.4	-6%	8,262	10,873
	Female	5.3	4.9	-8%	6,216	8,834
Liver	Male	3.4	4.6	35%	3,013	6,068
	Female	1.8	2.1	17%	2,116	3,995
Lung	Male	61.3	73.5	20%	59,082	92,493
	Female	12.7	32.9	159%	15,706	56,234
Melanoma	Male	2.0	3.2	60%	1,964	4,128
	Female	1.3	1.5	15%	1,465	2,584
Multiple myeloma	Male	2.8	3.8	36%	2,579	4,902
	Female	1.9	2.6	37%	2,389	4,939
Non-Hodgkin's lymphoma	Male	5.8	8.1	40%	5,473	10,458
	Female	3.9	5.3	36%	4,747	10,028
Oral cavity	Male	5.9	4.4	-25%	5,553	5,515
	Female	1.9	1.6	-16%	2,269	2,726
Ovary	Female	8.6	7.8	-9%	9,885	12,870
Pancreas	Male	11.1	10.0	-10%	10,380	12,669
	Female	6.7	7.3	9%	8,273	13,776
Prostate	Male	21.4	26.8	25%	18,830	34,865
Stomach	Male	10.4	6.6	-37%	9,178	8,229
	Female	5.0	3.0	-40%	6,020	5,621
Testis	Male	0.7	0.2	-71%	798	374
Thyroid	Male	0.4	0.3	-25%	315	398
	Female	0.5	0.4	-20%	657	732
Urinary bladder	Male	7.2	5.7	-21%	6,481	7,474
	Female	2.2	1.7	-23%	2,855	3,488

*Adjusted to the age distribution of the 1970 U.S. census population.
Note: Even though death rates declined or remained stable, the number of deaths increased because the population over 65 has become larger and older.
Source: American Cancer Society

A TURNING POINT FOR AIDS

The number of AIDS-related deaths in the U.S. dropped in 1996, at least partly because of the effectiveness of the new drug therapy using protease inhibitors. The Centers for Disease Control and Prevention said the number of deaths fell 23% to 38,780 from 50,140 in 1995.

It was the first sustained decline in AIDS-related deaths since the epidemic began in the early 1980s, marking a turning point in the history of the illness. "We have entered a new era in the HIV epidemic—both in terms of treatment and prevention," Helene Gayle, a CDC AIDS expert, said. The government also said the number of new AIDS cases fell 6% to 56,730 in 1996, compared with the year before, the first recorded decline ever.

Now, the federal government hopes to spread use of the protease inhibitors—the breakthrough drugs that are combined with older AIDS drugs to make potent three-drug "cocktails" to beat back HIV, the virus that causes AIDS. A government panel in 1997 recommended a relatively aggressive approach in treating people with HIV, giving much-needed guidance to physicians and patients but raising important issues for insurers and public programs that pay for the pricey drugs. The long-awaited clinical guidelines—the first ones from the government on how to use the protease inhibitors that have revolutionized AIDS treatment over the past two years—are likely to result in more people being treated with more drugs at an earlier stage of infection, AIDS doctors and activists say.

The guidelines were drafted by a 32-member panel made up of some of the nation's most prominent AIDS researchers, physicians, and activists. The committee, co-headed by Anthony Fauci, director of the National Institute of Allergy and Infectious Diseases and John Bartlett of Johns Hopkins University's School of Medicine, was convened by the Department of Health and Human Services and the Kaiser Family Foundation, a philanthropic organization that funds health-care research.

The panel strongly recommended that all individuals with AIDS symptoms, regardless of the level of virus in their blood, receive combination antiretroviral therapy—preferably one protease inhibitor and two other drugs called nucleoside analogs. It urged doctors to avoid treating patients with a single drug, except in the cases of pregnant women who are given AZT to cut the transmission of the virus to the fetuses. Treatment with two drugs, the group said, was "less than optimal."

On the important question of when to start treatment for patients who show no symptoms, the group gave several guideposts but didn't provide a hard-and-fast rule, saying that the decision depended heavily on doctors' judgments and patients' preferences. Once treatment is begun, however, it should constitute a full-scale assault aimed at driving HIV below detectable limits, with all three drugs begun at the same time, the panel said. If a particular combination doesn't work, two or three drugs should be changed.

Dr. Fauci said the recommendations are needed because rapid changes in the treatment of HIV—and the availability of 11 antiretrovirals and an array of possible combinations—have left some physicians confused about how to administer the complicated new therapies. Doctors, he said, are grappling with such difficult questions as, "When do you start [drug therapy]? What do you start with? How do you know if you're being successful?"

AIDS activist David Barr was appalled by what he heard at a meeting to discuss new drugs for people with HIV. A newly diagnosed woman was taking only AZT, a decade-old drug that's largely ineffective when used alone. A young man, following his doctor's advice, was taking Merck's Crixivan with meals; in fact, the new protease inhibitor should be taken an hour before or after eating. Miscalculations in administering the new drugs can lead to the rapid development of a resistant form of the virus that disarms even the most powerful treatment arsenal.

AIDS groups applauded the guidelines, but expressed concern that people without generous private insurance may have trouble getting treatments because of the expense involved. The new drug therapies can cost between $10,000 and $15,000 a year per patient. "I don't know where the resources are going to come from to give people the standard of care outlined in this document," said Richard Jefferys, access project director for AIDS Treatment Data Network. Of special concern, he said, are federally funded state programs—many already low on funds—that offer AIDS drug assistance for the uninsured and underinsured.

Caught in a severe cash crunch, 22 states imposed emergency restrictions to limit either the number of people enrolled in their AIDS-drug assistance programs or the availability of the drugs themselves, a report in the summer of 1997 said. Some of the states capped the number of people with AIDS and HIV, who can enroll in the programs. Others limited the number of people who may receive protease inhibitors. And some states set ceilings on the amount spent for each patient's drug costs. The study was conducted for the Kaiser Family Foundation by the National Alliance of State and Territorial AIDS Directors and the AIDS Treatment Data Network.

The state drug-assistance programs, which receive federal funding under the Ryan White Care Act, are designed to help uninsured patients; generally these are people who don't have private insurance and don't qualify for Medicaid. The money crunch comes even as the funding for AIDS-drug programs has risen sharply. For 1997, the amount from all sources—federal and state governments, and company rebates—was expected to rise 86% to $385 million from $207.5 million.

As for private health plans, many cover at least some of the new HIV therapies, but some have limits on the number of prescriptions that can be filled each month. Clinton administration officials hope that the guidelines—by essentially establishing a government-backed standard of care—will prod insurers to remove obstacles to treatment.

Laurie McGinley

AIDS in America

AIDS Cases, Case-Fatality Rates, and Deaths, by Half-Year and Age Group, Through June 1997*

Half-year	Adults/adolescents			Children under 13 years old		
	Cases diagnosed during interval	Case-fatality rate**	Deaths occurring during interval	Cases diagnosed during interval	Case-fatality rate**	Deaths occurring during interval
Before 1981	85	91.8	29	8	75.0	1
1981 Jan.–June	107	88.8	37	10	80.0	2
July–Dec.	206	93.7	83	6	100.0	6
1982 Jan.–June	437	92.9	151	14	92.9	10
July–Dec.	727	92.3	296	17	82.4	4
1983 Jan.–June	1,352	94.3	527	33	100.0	14
July–Dec.	1,717	94.2	949	44	93.2	16
1984 Jan.–June	2,691	93.8	1,428	53	86.8	27
July–Dec.	3,513	94.2	2,026	66	86.4	24
1985 Jan.–June	5,175	92.9	2,875	113	82.3	47
July–Dec.	6,552	93.4	3,979	140	87.1	72
1986 Jan.–June	8,702	92.4	5,203	144	85.4	70
July–Dec.	10,254	92.9	6,729	199	80.9	98
1987 Jan.–June	13,556	91.8	7,813	229	80.3	121
July–Dec.	14,908	90.6	8,285	269	77.3	173
1988 Jan.–June	17,419	88.8	9,716	265	69.8	140
July–Dec.	17,887	88.9	11,070	347	70.0	179
1989 Jan.–June	21,039	86.2	12,755	367	69.5	175
July–Dec.	21,341	85.5	14,653	348	71.3	192
1990 Jan.–June	24,372	83.4	15,068	392	65.3	196
July–Dec.	23,749	82.2	16,052	408	60.0	199
1991 Jan.–June	28,462	79.6	17,129	409	60.6	174
July–Dec.	30,575	77.5	19,046	394	56.6	220
1992 Jan.–June	37,250	72.3	19,681	488	54.7	194
July–Dec.	40,169	69.0	20,906	448	57.1	226
1993 Jan.–June	42.367	59.8	21,309	439	51.9	254
July–Dec.	35,204	55.1	22,460	442	51.6	268
1994 Jan.–June	36,660	47.5	23,388	418	47.4	295
July–Dec.	32,786	40.4	24,275	351	44.4	253
1995 Jan.–June	34,505	31.5	23,806	303	32.7	263
July–Dec.	29,292	24.0	23,474	291	26.8	236
1996 Jan.–June	28,453	16.9	19,658	232	20.7	214
July–Dec.	21,341	12.1	13,852	150	12.7	159
1997 Jan.–June	11,323	6.4	5,551	65	10.8	71
Total*	**604,176**	**62.0**	**374,656**	**7,902**	**58.2**	**4,602**

*Recent year data are incomplete because of a long lag in reporting cases and deaths.
**Case-fatality rates are calculated for each half-year by date of diagnosis. Each 6-month case-fatality rate is the number of deaths ever reported among cases diagnosed in that period (regardless of the year of death), divided by the number of total cases diagnosed in that period, multiplied by 100. For example, during the interval January through June 1982, AIDS was diagnosed in 437 adults/adolescents. Through June 1997, 406 of these 437 were reported as dead. Therefore, the case fatality rate is 92.9 (406 divided by 437, multiplied by 100). The case-fatality rates shown here may be underestimates because of incomplete reporting of deaths. Reported deaths are not necessarily caused by HIV-related disease.
***Death totals include 397 adults/adolescents and 9 children known to have died, but whose dates of death are unknown.
Source: Centers for Disease Control and Prevention

AIDS Cases and Annual Rates per 100,000 Population, by State, Reported in 1995 and 1996; and Cumulative Totals Through December 1996

State of residence	1995 No.	1995 Rate	1996 No.	1996 Rate	Cumulative totals Adults/ adolescents	Cumulative totals Children under 13 years of age	Total
Alabama	637	15.0	607	14.2	4,203	63	4,266
Alaska	69	11.5	36	5.9	358	5	363
Arizona	675	15.7	594	13.4	5,017	21	5,038
Arkansas	277	11.1	269	10.7	2,128	30	2,158
California	11,054	35.0	9,610	30.1	97,623	534	98,157
Colorado	672	17.9	522	13.7	5,728	27	5,755
Connecticut	1,645	50.3	1,112	34.0	8,347	170	8,517
Delaware	316	44.1	285	39.3	1,764	13	1,777
District of Columbia	1,027	185.2	1,262	232.3	9,272	142	9,414
Florida	7,979	56.3	7,330	50.9	57,678	1,233	58,911
Georgia	2,310	32.0	2,411	32.8	16,829	175	17,004
Hawaii	258	21.9	198	16.7	1,979	14	1,993
Idaho	48	4.1	39	3.3	364	2	366
Illinois	2,215	18.8	2,199	18.6	18,355	216	18,571
Indiana	523	9.0	596	10.2	4,391	33	4,424
Iowa	116	4.1	112	3.9	975	8	983
Kansas	304	11.9	239	9.3	1,836	10	1,846
Kentucky	296	7.7	401	10.3	2,205	19	2,224
Louisiana	1,079	24.9	1,470	33.8	9,016	110	9,126
Maine	129	10.4	50	4.0	747	8	755
Maryland	2,567	50.9	2,253	44.4	15,037	261	15,298
Massachusetts	1,438	23.7	1,307	21.5	11,880	187	12,067
Michigan	1,193	12.5	965	10.1	8,300	86	8,386
Minnesota	365	7.9	304	6.5	2,980	19	2,999
Mississippi	440	16.3	450	16.6	2,820	41	2,861
Missouri	786	14.8	858	16.0	7,209	50	7,259
Montana	25	2.9	34	3.9	225	2	227
Nebraska	115	7.0	100	6.1	780	9	789
Nevada	494	32.2	427	26.6	3,047	21	3,068
New Hampshire	110	9.6	93	8.0	705	7	712
New Jersey	4,400	55.3	3,613	45.2	32,256	670	32,926
New Mexico	164	9.7	205	12.0	1,437	5	1,442
New York	12,369	68.0	12,379	68.1	104,961	1,936	106,897
North Carolina	1,000	13.9	895	12.2	7,210	103	7,313
North Dakota	5	0.8	12	1.9	78	–	78
Ohio	1,101	9.9	1,161	10.4	8,637	106	8,743
Oklahoma	295	9.0	272	8.2	2,708	23	2,731
Oregon	458	14.5	463	14.5	3,848	14	3,862
Pennsylvania	2,370	19.7	2,348	19.5	17,190	233	17,423
Rhode Island	221	22.3	178	18.0	1,574	16	1,590
South Carolina	976	26.6	869	23.5	6,207	66	6,273
South Dakota	18	2.5	14	1.9	114	4	118
Tennessee	892	17.0	826	15.5	5,492	44	5,536
Texas	4,456	23.7	4,830	25.3	39,572	299	39,871
Utah	164	8.4	196	9.8	1,365	20	1,385
Vermont	43	7.4	25	4.2	295	3	298
Virginia	1,605	24.3	1,195	17.9	8,960	144	9,104
Washington	882	16.2	804	14.5	7,563	28	7,591
West Virginia	125	6.8	121	6.6	737	8	745
Wisconsin	349	6.8	270	5.2	2,762	24	2,786
Wyoming	18	3.8	7	1.5	140	–	140
Subtotal	**71,073**	**27.0**	**66,816**	**25.2**	**554,904**	**7,262**	**562,166**
Guam	–	–	4	2.8	17	–	17
Pacific Islands, U.S.	–	–	1	0.4	3	–	3
Puerto Rico	2,578	68.7	2,243	59.0	18,230	353	18,583
Virgin Islands, U.S.	39	37.4	18	17.2	266	12	278
Total*	**73,767**	**27.6**	**69,151**	**25.6**	**573,800**	**7,629**	**581,429**

*Death totals include 382 whose state of residence is unknown.
Source: Centers for Disease Control and Prevention

AIDS Cases in 1996 by Exposure Category and Sex

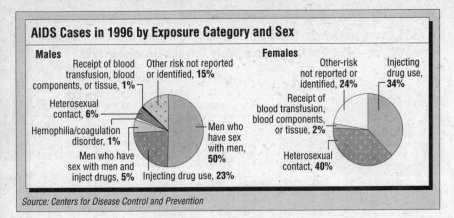

Males

Receipt of blood transfusion, blood components, or tissue, **1%**

Heterosexual contact, **6%**

Hemophilia/coagulation disorder, **1%**

Men who have sex with men and inject drugs, **5%**

Other risk not reported or identified, **15%**

Men who have sex with men, **50%**

Injecting drug use, **23%**

Females

Other-risk not reported or identified, **24%**

Injecting drug use, **34%**

Receipt of blood transfusion, blood components, or tissue, **2%**

Heterosexual contact, **40%**

Source: Centers for Disease Control and Prevention

The Global HIV/AIDS Pandemic

The Joint United Nations Programme on HIV/AIDS estimates that 22.5 million people are infected with human immunodeficiency virus (HIV) throughout the world, including those who have AIDS and those who have not yet developed AIDS. By 2000, the U.N. group projects that 30 million to 40 million people will have been infected.

Prevalence of HIV, by region of the world:

Sub-Saharan Africa: 14 million
Asia and Pacific: 5.3 million
Latin America and the Caribbean: 1.6 million
North America: 750,000
Western Europe: 510,000
North Africa and the Middle East: 200,000
Eastern Europe and Central Asia: 50,000

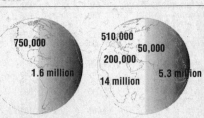

750,000

1.6 million

510,000

50,000

200,000

14 million

5.3 million

Adult AIDS Deaths by Region, 1996

Sub-Saharan Africa	783,700
Asia and Pacific	145,900
Latin America and the Caribbean	85,400
North America	61,300
Western Europe	21,000
North Africa and the Middle East	10,800
Eastern Europe and Central Asia	1,000

MALADIES OF THE 1990S

A look at some of the diseases and other ailments that have received increased attention in the 1990s.

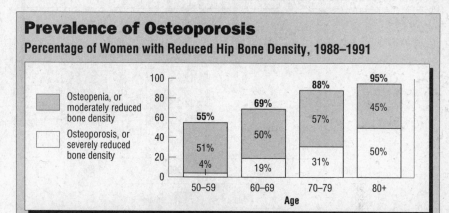

Prevalence of Osteoporosis
Percentage of Women with Reduced Hip Bone Density, 1988–1991

Osteopenia, or moderately reduced bone density

Osteoporosis, or severely reduced bone density

Age	
50–59	55% (51% / 4%)
60–69	69% (50% / 19%)
70–79	88% (57% / 31%)
80+	95% (45% / 50%)

Source: Centers for Disease Control and Prevention, National Center for Health Statitics

Second-Hand Smoke Exposure

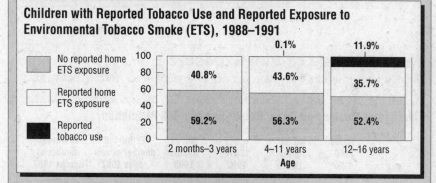

Children with Reported Tobacco Use and Reported Exposure to Environmental Tobacco Smoke (ETS), 1988–1991

No reported home ETS exposure

Reported home ETS exposure

Reported tobacco use

Age	2 months–3 years	4–11 years	12–16 years
No reported home ETS exposure	40.8%	43.6%	11.9%
		0.1%	35.7%
Reported home/tobacco	59.2%	56.3%	52.4%

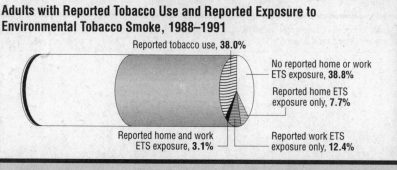

Adults with Reported Tobacco Use and Reported Exposure to Environmental Tobacco Smoke, 1988–1991

Reported tobacco use, **38.0%**

No reported home or work ETS exposure, **38.8%**

Reported home ETS exposure only, **7.7%**

Reported home and work ETS exposure, **3.1%**

Reported work ETS exposure only, **12.4%**

Source: Centers for Disease Control and Prevention

Alzheimer's Disease

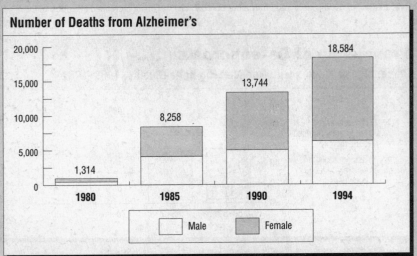

Number of Deaths from Alzheimer's

NOTE: The increase in deaths from Alzheimer's disease at least partly reflects improvements in reporting and diagnosis of the condition.
Source: Centers for Disease Control and Prevention, National Center for Health Statistics

The Dark Side of Sun Exposure

The most serious skin cancer is melanoma. Since 1973, the incidence rate of melanoma has increased about 4% a year.

Melanoma Deaths and Death Rates* per 100,000 Population

Sex	Rates 1960–1962	No. of deaths 1962	Rates 1991–1993	No. of deaths 1993	Estimated number of new cases 1997	Estimated number of deaths 1997
Male	1.5	1,285	3.2	4,128	22,900	4,600
Female	1.1	1,054	1.5	2,584	17,400	2,700

*Adjusted to the age distribution of the 1970 U.S. census population.
Source: American Cancer Society

U.S. Cases of Lyme Disease

State	'80	'82	'83	'84	'85	'86	'87	'88	'89	'90	'91	'92	'93	'94	'95	'96	Total
Alabama	0	0	0	0	0	1	1	1	25	33	13	10	4	6	12	9	117
Alaska	0	0	0	0	0	–	–	–	–	–	–	–	–	–	–	–	
Arizona	0	0	0	0	0	0	0	0	0	0	1	0	0	0	1	0	2
Arkansas	0	0	1	4	0	0	0	16	10	22	31	20	8	15	11	23	161
California	0	0	11	24	70	107	182	200	250	345	265	231	134	68	84	74	2,052
Colorado	0	0	0	0	0	0	0	2	1	0	1	0	0	1	0	0	5
Connecticut	52	135	73	483	699	0	215	362	774	704	1,192	1,760	1,350	2,030	1,548	2,937	14,314
Delaware	0	1	4	1	0	0	6	4	25	54	73	219	143	106	56	105	797
District of Columbia	0	0	0	0	0	0	0	0	0	5	5	3	2	9	3	3	34
Florida	0	0	0	0	2	0	1	0	6	7	35	24	30	28	17	45	205
Georgia	1	0	0	1	1	2	4	53	715	161	25	48	44	127	14	1	1,198
Hawaii	0	0	0	0	0	0	0	0	1	2	0	2	1	0	0	1	7
Idaho	0	0	0	0	0	0	0	1	42	1	2	2	2	3	0	2	55
Illinois	0	0	0	0	2	0	6	5	79	30	51	41	19	24	18	3	278
Indiana	0	0	0	1	0	1	3	0	8	15	16	22	32	19	19	29	168
Iowa	0	0	0	0	1	1	4	15	27	16	22	33	8	17	16	20	180
Kansas	0	0	0	0	0	0	1	0	15	14	22	18	54	17	23	37	201
Kentucky	0	0	0	0	0	0	3	5	21	18	44	28	16	24	16	25	201
Louisiana	0	0	0	0	0	0	0	2	2	3	6	7	3	4	9	8	45
Maine	0	0	0	0	1	4	0	1	3	9	15	16	18	33	45	55	202
Maryland	1	1	5	11	20	15	27	66	138	238	282	183	180	341	454	445	2,449
Massachusetts	11	15	13	33	69	163	95	80	129	117	265	223	148	247	189	342	2,173
Michigan	0	0	1	0	1	0	4	21	165	134	46	35	23	33	5	0	468
Minnesota	8	22	55	86	64	94	94	67	92	70	84	197	141	208	208	126	1,623
Mississippi	0	0	0	0	0	0	0	6	7	7	8	0	0	0	17	21	77
Missouri	0	0	0	2	1	1	4	5	108	205	207	150	108	102	53	37	983
Montana	–	–	–	–	–	–	–	–	–	–	–	–	–	–	–	–	
Nebraska	0	0	0	0	0	0	0	0	0	0	25	22	6	3	6	5	69
Nevada	1	0	0	0	0	0	0	0	7	2	5	1	5	1	6	2	30
New Hampshire	0	0	1	0	0	7	0	8	3	4	38	44	15	30	28	48	230
New Jersey	10	57	70	155	175	219	257	500	680	1,074	915	688	786	1,533	1,703	1,916	10,845
New Mexico	0	0	0	0	0	0	0	0	5	0	3	2	2	5	1	1	19
New York	7	170	267	466	1,235	482	877	2,673	3,224	3,244	3,944	3,448	2,818	5,200	4,438	4,968	37,474
North Carolina	0	0	1	16	14	6	2	19	61	87	73	67	86	77	84	66	661
North Dakota	0	0	0	0	0	0	0	1	12	3	2	1	2	0	0	1	22
Ohio	0	0	0	3	2	2	14	39	99	36	112	32	30	45	30	53	508
Oklahoma	0	0	0	0	0	2	2	4	16	13	29	27	19	99	63	25	300
Oregon	0	0	1	10	5	10	19	4	5	11	5	13	8	6	20	19	141
Pennsylvania	1	2	0	5	29	31	65	306	626	553	718	1,173	1,085	1,438	1,562	1,621	9,517
Rhode Island	3	29	20	20	41	57	74	121	415	101	142	275	272	471	345	537	2,950
South Carolina	0	0	0	1	3	3	3	10	18	7	10	2	9	7	17	9	100
South Dakota	0	0	0	0	0	0	2	2	3	2	1	1	0	0	0	0	11
Tennessee	0	0	1	1	4	1	1	13	30	28	35	31	20	13	28	21	231
Texas	0	0	1	18	172	8	33	18	82	44	57	113	48	56	77	65	793
Utah	0	1	1	0	0	1	0	2	3	1	2	6	2	3	1	1	24
Vermont	0	0	0	0	0	0	0	1	1	11	7	9	12	16	9	16	84
Virginia	0	0	0	1	2	7	27	25	54	129	151	123	95	131	55	53	853
Washington	0	0	0	0	0	0	8	9	33	30	7	14	9	4	10	18	142
West Virginia	0	0	0	0	0	0	0	5	15	11	43	14	50	29	26	12	205
Wisconsin	25	58	69	176	135	162	358	246	762	337	424	525	401	409	369	–	4,456
Wyoming	0	0	0	0	0	0	0	0	6	5	11	5	9	5	4	2	47
Unknown	106			4	2	2											114
Total	226	491	595	1,518	2,752	1,389	2,394	4,882	8,803	7,943	9,470	9,908	8,257	13,043	11,700	13,807	97,821

Source: Lyme Disease Foundation

Incidence and Cost of Uncured Disease in the U.S.

Uncured disease	Approximate 1995 incidence	Approximate 1995 economic cost (Billions)
Heart disease	60,340,000	$128
Cancer	1,359,000	104
Alzheimer's Disease	4,000,000	100
Diabetes	16,000,000	92
Arthritis	37,000,000	65
Depression	26,000,000*	44
Stroke	550,000	30
Osteoporosis	25,000,000	10

*Extrapolation based on 10.3 percent active prevalence of major depression in U.S. population.
Source: Pharmaceutical Research and Manufacturers of America

Slowing the Spread of Disease

Selected Disease Rates in the U.S.

Disease	1950	1960	1970	1980	1990	1991	1992	1993	1994	1995
	Cases per 100,000 population									
Diphtheria	3.83	0.51	0.21	0.00	0.00	0.00	0.00	–	0.00	–
Hepatitis A	–	–	27.87	12.84	12.64	9.67	9.06	9.40	10.29	12.13
Hepatitis B	–	–	4.08	8.39	8.48	7.14	6.32	5.18	4.81	4.19
Mumps	–	–	55.55	3.86	2.17	1.72	1.03	0.66	0.60	0.35
Pertussis (whooping cough)	79.82	8.23	2.08	0.76	1.84	1.08	1.60	2.55	1.77	1.97
Poliomyelitis, total	22.02	1.77	0.02	0.00	0.00	0.00	0.00	0.00	0.00	0.00
Paralytic	–	1.40	0.02	0.00	0.00	0.00	0.00	0.00	0.00	0.00
Rubella (German measles)	–	–	27.75	1.72	0.45	0.56	0.06	0.07	0.09	0.05
Rubeola (measles)	211.01	245.42	23.23	5.96	11.17	3.82	0.88	0.12	0.37	0.12
Salmonellosis, excluding typhoid fever	–	3.85	10.84	14.88	19.54	19.10	16.04	16.15	16.64	17.66
Shigellosis	15.45	6.94	6.79	8.41	10.89	9.34	9.38	12.48	11.44	12.32
Tuberculosis	80.45	30.83	18.28	12.25	10.33	10.42	10.46	9.82	9.36	8.70
Varicella (chicken pox)	–	–	–	96.69	120.06	135.82	176.54	118.54	135.76	118.11
Sexually transmitted diseases										
Syphilis	146.02	68.78	45.26	30.51	54.30	51.00	44.20	39.30	31.40	26.20
Gonorrhea	192.45	145.33	297.22	444.99	278.00	247.10	196.70	171.90	165.10	149.50

Disease	1950	1960	1970	1980	1990	1991	1992	1993	1994	1995
	Number of cases									
Diphtheria	5,796	918	435	3	4	5	4	–	2	–
Hepatitis A	–	–	56,797	29,087	31,441	24,378	23,112	24,238	29,796	31,582
Hepatitis B	–	–	8,310	19,015	21,102	18,003	16,126	13,361	12,517	10,805
Mumps	–	–	104,953	8,576	5,292	4,264	2,572	1,692	1,537	906
Pertussis (whooping cough)	120,718	14,809	4,249	1,730	4,570	2,719	4,083	6,586	4,617	5,137
Poliomyelitis, total	33,300	3,190	33	9	6	9	6	3	–	2
Paralytic	–	2,525	31	8	6	9	6	3	–	2
Rubella (German measles)	–	–	56,552	3,904	1,125	1,401	160	192	227	128
Rubeola (measles)	319,124	441,703	47,351	13,506	27,786	9,643	2,237	312	963	281
Salmonellosis, excluding typhoid fever	–	6,929	22,096	33,715	48,603	48,154	40,912	41,641	43,323	45,970
Shigellosis	23,367	12,487	13,845	19,041	27,077	23,548	23,931	32,198	29,769	32,080
Tuberculosis	121,742	55,494	37,137	27,749	25,701	26,283	26,673	25,313	24,361	22,860
Varicella (chicken pox)	–	–	–	190,894	173,099	147,076	158,364	134,722	151,219	120,624
Sexually transmitted diseases										
Syphilis	217,558	122,538	91,382	68,832	135,043	128,637	112,816	101,333	81,696	68,953
Gonorrhea	286,746	258,933	600,072	1,004,029	691,368	623,009	501,777	443,278	418,068	392,848

Source: Centers for Disease Control and Prevention

Selected Major Infectious Diseases Identified, 1975–1994

Year	Agent	Disease
1976	Cryptosporidium parvum	Acute enterocolitis
1977	Ebola virus	Ebola hemorrhagic fever
1977	Legionella pneumophila	Legionnaire's disease
1977	Hantaan virus	Hemorrhagic fever with renal syndrome (HFRS)
1980	Human T-cell lymphotropic virus	T-cell lymphoma leukemia
1981	Staphylococcus toxin	Toxic shock syndrome associated with tampon use
1982	Escherichia coli 0157:H7	Hemorrhagic colitis; hemolytic uremic syndrome
1982	HTLV II	Hairy cell leukemia
1982	Borrelia burgdorferi	Lyme disease
1983	Human immunodeficiency virus (HIV)	Acquired immunodeficiency syndrome (AIDS)
1989	Ehrlichia chaffeensis	Human ehrlichiosis
1989	Hepatitis C	Parenterally transmitted non-A, non-B hepatitis
1991	Guanarito virus	Venezuelan hemorrhagic fever
1992	Bartonella	Cat-scratch disease; bacillary angiomatosis
1993	Hantavirus	Hantavirus pulmonary syndrome
1994	Sabia virus	Brazilian hemorrhagic fever

Source: Centers for Disease Control and Prevention

The State of Mental Health in America

Number of U.S. Adults With Mental Disorders, 1990*

Disorders	In a one-month period — Number (millions)	In a one-month period — Percent	In a one-year period — Number (millions)	In a one-year period — Percent
Any mental disorder and substance use disorder covered in survey	28.7	15.7%	51.3	28.1%
Any mental disorder except substance use disorders	23.7	13.0	40.4	22.1
Schizophrenia/schizophreniform disorders	1.3	0.7	2.0	1.1
Depressive (affective) disorders	9.5	5.2	17.4	9.5
Manic-depressive illness (Bipolar disorder)	1.1	0.6	2.2	1.2
Major depression	3.3	1.8	9.1	5.0
Dysthymia	6.0	3.3	9.9	5.4
Anxiety disorders	13.3	7.3	23.0	12.6
Phobia	11.5	6.3	19.9	10.9
Panic disorder	0.9	0.5	2.4	1.3
Obsessive-compulsive disorder	2.4	1.3	3.8	2.1
Somatization disorder**	0.2	0.1	0.4	0.2
Antisocial personality disorder	0.9	0.5	2.7	1.5
Severe cognitive impairment	3.1	1.7	4.9	2.7
Substance use disorders	6.9	3.8	17.3	9.5
Alcohol abuse/dependence	5.1	2.8	13.5	7.4
Drug abuse/dependence	2.4	1.3	5.7	3.1

*Number of affected adults is based on estimates of the U.S. resident population from the 1990 census of 182.6 million persons aged 18 and over. Some people have more than one mental disorder. Therefore, the numbers for each type of disorder, if added together, will be more than the total number for all individuals with mental disorders.

**Somatization disorder is a chronic psychiatric condition characterized by multiple physical complaints for which there is no apparent physical cause.

Source: National Institute of Mental Health

Mental Health Organization Expenditures in the U.S.

(In millions)

Year	Expenditure
1969	3,293
1975	6,564
1979	8,764
1983	14,432
1986	18,458
1988	23,028
1990	28,410
1992	29,765

Source: U.S. Center for Mental Health Services

Accidental Deaths

Someone dies from an unintentional injury every six minutes, according to the National Safety Council. Here are the major types of accidents and the number of deaths in 1995:

Type of accident	Number of deaths	Percent change since 1994
Motor-vehicle accidents	43,900	3 %
Falls	12,600	-1
Poisoning by solids and liquids	10,000	11
Drowning	4,500	7
Fires, burns and deaths associated with fires	4,100	-2
Suffocation by ingested object	2,800	-7
Firearms	1,400	-7
Poisoning by gases and vapors	600	-14
Other	13,400	0
Total	**93,300**	**2**

Source: National Safety Council

Household Hazards

The estimated number of deaths and injuries treated at hospital emergency rooms that were associated with the use of these consumer products.

Product group	Total injuries Oct. 1, 1995– Sept. 30, 1996	Total deaths Oct. 1, 1993– Sept. 30, 1994
Sports and recreational activities and equipment	4,044,701	1,131
Home structures and construction materials	3,313,330	365
Home furnishings and fixtures	1,940,288	874
Housewares	780,170	25
Personal use items	393,077	238
Home workshop apparatus, tools and attachments	338,255	131
Packaging and containers for household products	333,417	120
Yard and garden equipment	255,906	357
Miscellaneous	200,496	78
Space heating, cooling and ventilating appliances	151,380	177
General household appliances	147,625	70
Toys	138,097	19
Home and family maintenance products	125,411	49
Home communication, entertainment and hobby equipment	98,687	34
Child nursery equipment and supplies	88,056	73

Source: U.S. Consumer Product Safety Commission

In the Operating Room

Some of the Most Common Surgeries for Men and Women

	Operations in thousands				Operations per 1,000 population			
Both sexes	1985	1990	1994	1995	1985	1990	1994	1995
Total..	24,109	23,051	22,629	22,530	102.1	93.0	87.4	86.2
Male								
All ages..	8,737	8,538	8,369	8,388	76.5	71.1	66.5	66.0
Under 15 years...	827	598	507	518	31.4	21.6	17.3	17.5
Reduction of fracture (excluding skull and facial)..........................	52	37	37	29	2.0	1.3	1.2	1.0
Appendectomy..	41	40	38	31	1.6	1.4	1.3	1.0
Tonsillectomy, with or without adenoidectomy.....................................	97	33	14	15	3.7	1.2	0.5	0.5
Myringotomy..	53	30	16	15	2.0	1.1	0.5	0.5
15–44 years...	2,705	2,257	1,980	1,899	49.1	39.1	33.9	32.4
Excision or destruction of intervertebral disc and spinal fusion............	119	147	131	130	2.2	2.5	2.2	2.2
Reduction of fracture (excluding skull and facial)..........................	160	137	119	121	2.9	2.4	2.0	2.1
Appendectomy..	88	80	90	80	1.6	1.4	1.5	1.4
Cardiac catheterization..............................	58	68	62	62	1.0	1.2	1.1	1.1
Cholecystectomy.......................................	33	34	27	27	0.6	0.6	0.5	0.5
Excision of semilunar cartilage of knee...........	48	25	21	19	0.9	0.4	0.4	0.3
Coronary angioplasty.................................	10	17	26	23	0.2	0.3	0.4	0.4
45–64 years...	2,482	2,499	2,516	2,541	116.7	112.5	102.5	100.9
Cardiac catheterization..............................	241	306	286	294	11.4	13.8	11.7	11.7
Direct heart revascularization (coronary bypass)..................................	102	132	165	192	4.8	6.0	6.7	7.6
Coronary angioplasty.................................	34	111	138	141	1.6	5.0	5.6	5.6
Excision or destruction of intervertebral disc and spinal fusion...........	60	80	94	87	2.8	3.6	3.8	3.4
Prostatectomy..	81	80	61	55	3.8	3.6	2.5	2.2
Cholecystectomy.......................................	53	50	51	46	2.5	2.2	2.1	1.8
Reduction of fracture (excluding skull and facial)..........................	47	41	51	53	2.2	1.9	2.1	2.1
65–74 years...	1,546	1,849	1,889	1,900	210.7	233.1	227.8	227.8
Cardiac catheterization..............................	102	170	184	196	13.9	21.4	22.2	23.4
Prostatectomy..	150	159	117	102	20.4	20.0	14.1	12.3
Direct heart revascularization (coronary bypass)..................................	45	100	127	151	6.1	12.6	15.3	18.1
Coronary angioplasty.................................	11	58	82	78	1.5	7.3	9.9	9.3
Pacemaker insertion or replacement.............	37	38	46	39	5.0	4.8	5.6	4.7
Cholecystectomy.......................................	34	33	37	37	4.6	4.2	4.4	4.4
Reduction of fracture (excluding skull and facial).......................	16	20	22	20	2.1	2.6	2.6	2.4
Arthroplasty and replacement of hip...............	20	24	20	29	2.7	3.0	2.4	3.4
Carotid endarterectomy...............................	26	14	27	35	3.5	1.8	3.2	4.2
75 years and over......................................	1,177	1,335	1,477	1,531	290.4	288.5	284.9	286.3
Prostatectomy..	134	125	83	81	33.2	27.0	16.1	15.2
Cardiac catheterization..............................	24	66	93	102	5.9	14.3	18.0	19.1
Pacemaker insertion or replacement.............	45	62	79	82	11.1	13.4	15.3	15.3
Direct heart revascularization (coronary bypass)..................................	12	37	55	67	3.0	8.1	10.7	12.5
Coronary angioplasty.................................	–	15	33	44	–	3.2	6.4	8.1
Cholecystectomy.......................................	27	30	32	30	6.6	6.5	6.2	5.5
Reduction of fracture (excluding skull and facial)..........................	26	29	33	33	6.3	6.3	6.3	6.1
Arthroplasty and replacement of hip..............	20	27	26	33	4.9	5.8	5.1	6.2
Carotid endarterectomy...............................	15	11	18	24	3.6	2.3	3.6	4.6

Female	Operations in thousands				Operations per 1,000 population			
	1985	1990	1994	1995	1985	1990	1994	1995
All ages	15,372	14,513	14,260	14,142	126.0	113.7	107.1	105.3
Under 15 years	548	413	366	362	21.8	15.6	13.1	12.9
Appendectomy	28	26	25	22	1.1	1.0	0.9	0.8
Reduction of fracture (excluding skull and facial)	32	18	18	17	1.3	0.7	0.7	0.6
Tonsillectomy, with or without adenoidectomy	100	41	15	12	4.0	1.6	0.5	0.4
Myringotomy	36	22	13	10	1.4	0.8	0.5	0.3
15–44 years	8,777	8,129	7,430	7,235	155.2	138.9	125.7	122.0
Procedures to assist delivery	2,221	2,480	2,400	2,282	39.3	42.4	40.6	38.5
Cesarean section	875	940	856	784	15.5	16.1	14.5	13.2
Repair of current obstetrical laceration	546	793	907	961	9.7	13.5	15.3	16.2
Bilateral destruction or occlusion of fallopian tubes	461	418	360	326	8.1	7.1	6.1	5.5
Hysterectomy	421	349	298	325	7.4	6.0	5.0	5.5
Cholecystectomy	134	172	124	134	2.4	2.9	2.1	2.3
Excision or destruction of intervertebral disc and spinal fusion	65	86	100	69	1.1	1.5	1.7	1.2
Reduction of fracture (excluding skull and facial)	71	60	59	63	1.3	1.0	1.0	1.1
Appendectomy	86	77	74	59	1.5	1.3	1.2	1.0
Cardiac catheterization	22	32	27	26	0.4	0.5	0.4	0.4
Mastectomy	17	13	14	13	0.3	0.2	0.2	0.2
Excision of semilunar cartilage of knee	12	10	9	8	0.2	0.2	0.1	0.1
45–64 years	2,879	2,586	2,635	2,566	123.6	107.6	100.2	95.1
Hysterectomy	190	184	188	191	8.2	7.7	7.1	7.1
Cardiac catheterization	108	151	158	144	4.7	6.3	6.0	5.3
Excision or destruction of intervertebral disc and spinal fusion	48	67	84	69	2.1	2.8	3.2	2.6
Cholecystectomy	104	118	97	95	4.4	4.9	3.7	3.5
Reduction of fracture (excluding skull and facial)	66	53	56	60	2.8	2.2	2.1	2.2
Coronary angioplasty	12	37	55	53	0.5	1.6	2.1	2.0
Direct heart revascularization (coronary bypass)	24	37	52	45	1.0	1.5	2.0	1.7
Mastectomy	49	52	42	41	2.1	2.1	1.6	1.5
Carotid endarterectomy	14	7	11	12	0.6	0.3	0.4	0.4
65–74 years	1,631	1,679	1,814	1,832	171.3	165.2	174.0	175.9
Cardiac catheterization	76	126	130	127	8.0	12.4	12.5	12.2
Cholecystectomy	49	48	53	47	5.2	4.7	5.1	4.5
Direct heart revascularization (coronary bypass)	23	40	52	63	2.4	3.9	5.0	6.1
Reduction of fracture (excluding skull and facial)	49	46	47	43	5.1	4.5	4.5	4.2
Coronary angioplasty	9	31	51	48	0.9	3.1	4.8	4.6
Arthroplasty and replacement of hip	36	42	47	43	3.7	4.1	4.5	4.2
Hysterectomy	43	38	48	45	4.5	3.7	4.6	4.3
Excision or destruction of intervertebral disc and spinal fusion	12	23	27	30	1.2	2.2	2.6	2.9
Pacemaker insertion or replacement	27	32	44	40	2.8	3.1	4.2	3.8
Mastectomy	28	31	29	23	3.0	3.0	2.7	2.3
Carotid endarterectomy	20	13	17	23	2.1	1.2	1.7	2.3
75 years and over	1,537	1,706	2,015	2,147	204.9	200.6	217.6	227.7
Reduction of fractrue (excluding skull and facial)	112	122	127	138	15.0	14.4	13.7	14.6
Cardiac catheterization	26	59	95	105	3.4	6.9	10.3	11.1
Arthroplasty and replacement of hip	73	86	93	94	9.7	10.1	10.1	9.9
Pacemaker insertion or replacement	59	67	105	94	7.9	7.9	11.4	10.0
Cholecystectomy	40	36	39	52	5.3	4.2	4.2	5.5
Direct heart revascularization (coronary bypass)	8	27	31	38	1.1	3.1	3.3	4.1
Mastectomy	20	25	22	24	2.6	2.9	2.4	2.5
Coronary angioplasty	–	12	36	40	–	1.4	3.9	4.2

Source: Centers for Disease Control and Prevention, National Center for Health Statistics

FAT OF THE LAND

Snackwell's reduced-fat cookies and Baked Lay's low-fat potato crisps have been a mammoth marketing success. But you'd never know it from measuring Americans' mammoth waistlines.

Despite greater awareness of the benefits of physical activity and the dangers of fat intake, people are eating more and exercising less. One-third of adult Americans are now considered overweight, up from one-quarter in 1980. And among certain demographic groups, the weight problem is even worse: About half of all black and Mexican-American women are overweight according to the standards set by the U.S. Centers for Disease Control and Prevention.

Worse yet, Americans look even fatter when judged by more stringent international health standards. Using World Health Organization guidelines, the National Center for Health Statistics says more than half of all Americans are overweight. "With all the emphasis on thinness and the knowledge we have about exercise, it's strange that this is happening," says Bonnie Liebman, a nutritionist at the Center for Science in the Public Interest, a consumer-interest group in Washington.

Perhaps not. The film and fashion worlds may be obsessed with thin thighs and washboard stomachs, but most Americans are more tolerant of flab. NPD Group Inc., a market-research firm based in Port Washington, N.Y., says the percentage of Americans who believe being overweight makes a person less attractive has fallen—from 55% in 1985 to 28% in 1996.

The American diet isn't all bad, of course. People are in fact eating less fat and steadily reducing their cholesterol levels, thanks to the profusion of low-fat products. Whereas 31.8% of adult Americans had high levels of cholesterol in 1962, now about 19% do. The incidence of hypertension also has fallen, along with salt consumption. Less than a quarter of Americans have elevated blood pressure, compared with 39% in 1980.

So why aren't the low-fat products also helping people whittle away extra pounds? Unfortunately, consumers tend to wolf down low-fat products, forgetting that they're still loaded with calories. "People are snacking more, eating on the run, and eating out, all contributing to overall weight gain," explains Dr. Jim Marks, director of the National Center for

Chronic Disease Prevention and Health Promotion in Atlanta.

Indeed, the big enemy in America's battle of the bulge, some nutrition experts say, is restaurant cuisine. The American diet includes an ever-increasing number of pizzas, tacos, and burgers; for many people, the only vegetable of the day is a bag of french fries. Restaurants—fast-food outlets in particular—have become cheaper and more convenient.

"Many Americans are eating out six or seven meals in a week," especially at lunchtime, says Ms. Liebman, who published a study on the nutritional and caloric content of restaurant food. She found that a restaurant meal often has double the number of calories and fat as a similar home-cooked meal. A serving of kung pao chicken, for instance, contains a hefty 1,620 calories and 76 grams of fat. That's a colossal amount, considering that in an entire day, a moderately active adult should consume only 2,000 calories and a maximum of 30 grams of fat. In contrast to the Chinese food, Ms. Liebman says, an average home-cooked dinner of chicken breast, potatoes and vegetable weighs in at 700 to 800 calories.

The failure of McDonald's McLean Deluxe sandwich speaks volumes about today's consumers. Most people still let their taste buds, not their bathroom scales, be their guide. The McLean Deluxe was introduced in the early 1990s with great fanfare, but the reduced-fat burger, laced with a seaweed derivative, wasn't juicy enough to satisfy most palates. It died a slow death, finally disappearing from McDonald's menu boards in 1996.

Burgers and fries are only partly to blame, however, for the increase in weight. Nearly 30% of Americans say they get no physical activity whatsoever in their leisure time; only 14% get regular, vigorous activity. The television and computer age and a less physically active workforce certainly contributed to the trend. "Our balance between physical activity and intake is off," says Dr. Marks. "And it's going in the wrong direction. Fewer people are exercising, even moderately so."

The future doesn't look any healthier. There is a growing number of overweight children and adolescents, and fat children tend to become fat adults. A study at the Harvard School of Public Health tracked a group of 740 children ages 6 through 11 and found that a child at a healthy weight who views more than five hours of television shows a day is five times more likely to get fat than a child who watches two hours or less. "Kids aren't running outside to play after dinner anymore," says Dr. Marks. "They're meandering over to the TV."

Many truly obese people turned to the weight-loss drug Redux when it hit the market in April 1996—the first new diet drug approved by the Food and Drug Administration since 1973. Redux and Pondimin, a similar drug, work by increasing the levels of the neurotransmitter serotonin in the brain, which creates a sense of being satisfied and feeling full.

But after research suggested the drugs produce potentially severe heart problems, they were pulled from store shelves in September 1997. Dieters who depended on the drugs suddenly felt stranded. American Home Products,

Tipping the Scales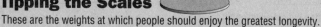

These are the weights at which people should enjoy the greatest longevity.

Height and Weight Tables for Men and Women According to Frame, Ages 25–59
(Weight in pounds, in indoor clothing*)

Height (in shoes)		Small frame	Medium frame	Large frame
Feet	**Inches**	**Men**		
5	2	128–134	131–141	138–150
5	3	130–136	133–143	140–153
5	4	132–138	135–145	142–156
5	5	134–140	137–148	144–160
5	6	136–142	139–151	146–164
5	7	138–145	142–154	149–168
5	8	140–148	145–157	152–172
5	9	142–151	148–160	155–176
5	10	144–154	151–163	158–180
5	11	146–157	154–166	161–184
6	0	149–160	157–170	164–188
6	1	152–164	160–174	168–192
6	2	155–168	164–178	172–197
6	3	158–172	167–182	176–202
6	4	162–176	171–187	181–207
		Women		
4	10	102–111	109–121	118–131
4	11	103–113	111–123	120–134
5	0	104–115	113–126	122–137
5	1	106–118	115–129	125–140
5	2	108–121	118–132	128–143
5	3	111–124	121–135	131–147
5	4	114–127	124–138	134–151
5	5	117–130	127–141	137–155
5	6	120–133	130–144	140–159
5	7	123–136	133–147	143–163
5	8	126–139	136–150	146–167
5	9	129–142	139–153	149–170
5	10	132–145	142–156	152–173
5	11	135–148	145–159	155–176
6	0	138–151	148–162	158–179

*Indoor clothing weighing 5 pounds for men and 3 pounds for women. Shoes with 1-inch heels.
Source: Metropolitan Life Insurance Co.

the drugs' marketer, said its toll-free information line received calls from more than 100,000 people in just its first four days. A week later, new evidence emerged that the research that led to the recall may have been flawed, and scientists rushed to untangle the web.

Beyond the problem of side effects, such diet drugs aren't a panacea for obesity. "Redux, like all the other anti-obesity drugs, is a quick-fix, and quick-fixes don't work on a grand scale," says Dr. Sidney Wolfe, director of Public Citizens' Health Research Group in Washington, who opposed the FDA's approval of Redux. "The only way to turn the trend around is by convincing the population to eat less and exercise more. It's that simple."

Tamar Hausman

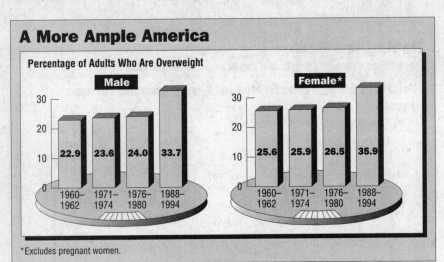

A More Ample America

Percentage of Adults Who Are Overweight

Male

1960–1962	1971–1974	1976–1980	1988–1994
22.9	23.6	24.0	33.7

Female*

1960–1962	1971–1974	1976–1980	1988–1994
25.6	25.9	26.5	35.9

*Excludes pregnant women.

Fat City

Metropolitan Areas Ranked by Percentage of Adults Who Are Overweight

	City	Total %		City	Total %
1	New Orleans	37.55%	16	Portland	27.15%
2	Norfolk	33.94	17	Chicago	27.13
3	San Antonio	32.96	18	New York	27.05
4	Kansas City	31.66	19	Miami	26.95
5	Cleveland	31.50	20	Baltimore	26.43
6	Detroit	31.01	21	Boston	26.17
7	Columbus	30.75	22	Seattle	25.87
8	Cincinnati	30.71	23	Indianapolis	25.77
9	Pittsburgh	29.99	24	Atlanta	25.49
10	Houston	29.19	25	Los Angeles	25.22
11	Philadelphia	29.05	26	San Francisco	25.16
12	Milwaukee	28.79	27	Tampa	24.91
13	Buffalo	28.43	28	St. Louis	24.78
14	Sacramento	28.15	29	Phoenix	24.36
15	Dallas-Ft. Worth	27.46	30	Washington, DC	23.84

Source: Centers for Disease Control and Prevention, and Coalition for Excess Weight Risk Education

Cholesterol Count

Serum Cholesterol Levels Among Adults

	% of population with high serum cholesterol*				Mean serum cholesterol level, mg/dL			
	1960–1962	1971–1974	1976–1980	1988–1994	1960–1962	1971–1974	1976–1980	1988–1994
Male								
20–34 years	15.1	12.4	11.9	8.2	198	194	192	186
35–44 years	33.9	31.8	27.9	19.4	227	221	217	206
45–54 years	39.2	37.5	36.9	26.6	231	229	227	216
55–64 years	41.6	36.2	36.8	28.0	233	229	229	216
65–74 years	38.0	34.7	31.7	21.9	230	226	221	212
75 years and over	–	–	–	20.4	–	–	–	205
Female								
20–34 years	12.4	10.9	9.8	7.3	194	191	189	184
35–44 years	23.1	19.3	20.7	12.3	214	207	207	195
45–54 years	46.9	38.7	40.5	26.7	237	232	232	217
55–64 years	70.1	53.1	52.9	40.9	262	245	249	235
65–74 years	68.5	57.7	51.6	41.3	266	250	246	233
75 years and over	–	–	–	38.2	–	–	–	229

*High serum cholesterol is defined as greater than or equal to 240 mg/dL.
Source: Centers for Disease Control and Prevention, National Center for Health Statistics

Blood Pressure Check

Percentage of Adults with Hypertension*

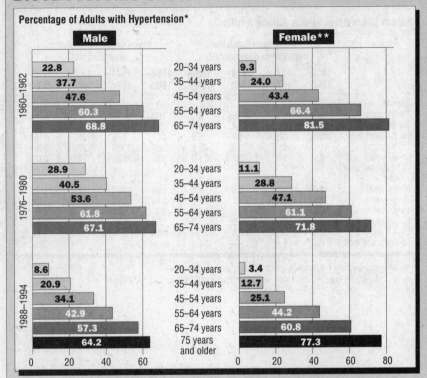

*A person with hypertension is defined by either having elevated blood pressure (systolic pressure of at least 140 mmHg or diastolic pressure of at least 90 mmHg) or taking antihypertensive medication.

**Excludes pregnant women.

Source: Centers for Disease Control and Prevention, National Center for Health Statistics

Languor and Vigor

Adults Who Participate in Regular, Vigorous Physical Activity, and Those Who Don't
(Percentage)

Demographic group	No physical activity	Vigorous physical activity	Demographic group	No physical activity	Vigorous physical activity
Overall	28.7	14.4	Age (years)		
Sex			Females		
Males	26.5	12.9	18–29	25.4	11.4
Females	30.7	15.8	30–44	26.9	18.0
Race/Ethnicity			45–64	32.1	17.7
White, non-Hispanic	26.8	15.3	65–74	36.6	16.5
Males	25.3	13.3	75+	50.5	12.8
Females	28.2	17.1	Education (years)		
Black, non-Hispanic	38.5	9.4	Less than 12	46.5	8.2
Males	33.1	9.5	12	32.8	11.5
Females	42.7	9.4	Some college (13–15)	22.6	14.9
Hispanic	34.8	11.9	College (16 or more)	17.8	21.9
Males	30.2	12.4	Income		
Females	39.0	11.4	Less than $10,000	41.5	9.0
Age (years)			$10,000–19,999	34.6	10.8
Males			$20,000–34,999	26.9	14.2
18–29	18.9	8.0	$35,000–49,999	23.0	16.3
30–44	25.0	11.1	$50,000 or more	17.7	20.5
45–64	32.0	16.3			
65–74	33.2	20.6			
75+	38.2	20.6			

Source: Centers for Disease Control and Prevention, National Center for Chronic Disease Prevention and Health Promotion

Adults Reporting Participation in Selected Common Physical Activities in the Prior 2 Weeks, by Sex and Age
(Percentage)

Activity category	Males	Females	Activity category	Males	Females
Walking for exercise	39.4	48.3	Bowling	4.7	3.6
Gardening or yard work	34.2	25.1	Golf	8.2	1.8
Stretching exercises	25.0	26.0	Baseball or softball	5.8	1.4
Weight lifting or other exercise to increase muscle strength	20.0	8.8	Handball, racquetball, or squash	2.7	0.5
Jogging or running	12.8	5.7	Skiing	0.9	0.5
Aerobics or aerobic dance	2.8	11.1	Cross-country skiing	0.4	0.4
Riding a bicycle or exercise bike	16.2	14.6	Water skiing	0.7	0.4
			Basketball	10.5	1.5
Stair climbing	9.9	11.6	Volleyball	3.1	1.8
Swimming for exercise	6.9	6.2	Soccer	1.4	0.4
Tennis	3.5	2.0	Football	2.7	0.3
			Other sports	7.3	4.1

Source: Centers for Disease Control and Prevention, National Center for Health Statistics

Youth and Exercise

Young People (Grades 9–12) Who Participate in Regular, Moderate, or Vigorous Physical Activity, and Those Who Don't
(Percentage)

Demographic group	No physical activity	Moderate or vigorous activity	Demographic group	No physical activity	Moderate or vigorous activity
Overall	10.4	63.7	Grade in school		
Sex			Males		
Males	7.3	74.4	9	6.0	80.8
Females	13.8	52.1	10	5.2	75.9
Race/Ethnicity			11	7.9	70.2
White, non-Hispanic	9.3	67.0	12	10.0	66.9
Males	7.3	76.0	Females		
Females	11.6	56.7	9	8.7	60.9
Black, non-Hispanic	15.3	53.2	10	9.2	54.4
Males	8.1	68.1	11	17.8	44.7
Females	21.4	41.3	12	18.5	41.0
Hispanic	11.3	57.3			
Males	7.5	69.7			
Females	15.0	45.2			

Source: Centers for Disease Control and Prevention, National Center for Chronic Disease Prevention and Health Promotion

Young People Reporting Participation in Selected Physical Activities in the Prior Week
(Percentage)

Activity	Males	Females
Aerobics or dancing	22.6	53.9
Baseball, softball, or Frisbee	27.2	17.5
Basketball, football, or soccer	61.7	29.7
Housecleaning or yardwork (30 minutes or more)	78.1	87.5
Running, jogging, or swimming	57.6	53.0
Skating, skiing, or skateboarding	15.9	10.6
Tennis, racquetball, or squash	11.7	9.3

Source: Centers for Disease Control and Prevention, National Center for Health Statistics

Look, Ma, No Cavities!

Not quite, but more people are getting preventive dental care, such as cleanings and fluoride treatments, and a smaller percentage need fillings and tooth extractions.

Percentage of Patients Receiving Selected Dental Services from Private Practitioners

Procedure	1959	1969	1979	1990
Oral examination	20.1%	27.8%	30.1%	42.8%
X-rays	18.1	23.9	21.0	25.3
Prophylaxis (teeth cleaning)	19.9	25.5	24.9	38.6
Fluoride treatment	0.9	4.0	6.8	9.8
Amalgam, 1 surface (filling)	20.1	15.9	8.5	5.3
Amalgam, 2 surface (filling)	20.6	16.4	9.6	7.2
Crown	1.6	2.9	5.2	5.3
Root canal	1.7	2.9	3.2	2.6
Extraction	13.0	9.8	5.4	4.9
Periodontal treatment	3.2	2.5	3.3	4.1
Orthodontic treatment	3.7	6.5	6.8	3.6

Source: American Dental Association

America's Addictions

Percentage of People Age 12 and Older Reporting Past Month Use of Alcohol or Any Illicit Drug, by Race and Sex, 1996

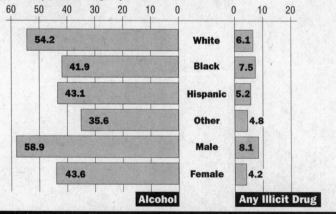

	Alcohol	Any Illicit Drug
White	54.2	6.1
Black	41.9	7.5
Hispanic	43.1	5.2
Other	35.6	4.8
Male	58.9	8.1
Female	43.6	4.2

Estimated Past-Year Users of Illicit Drugs and Alcohol in the U.S. Age 12 and Older and Their Percentage of the Population

(Numbers in thousands)

Drug	1985 No.	1985 %	1990 No.	1990 %	1992 No.	1992 %	1995 No.	1995 %	1996 No.	1996 %
Any illicit drug*	31,488	16.3	23,449	11.7	20,046	9.7	22,662	10.7	23,182	10.8
Marijuana and hashish	26,145	13.6	18,931	9.4	16,322	7.9	17,755	8.4	18,398	8.6
Cocaine	9,839	5.1	5,442	2.7	4,332	2.1	3,664	1.7	4,033	1.9
Crack	–	–	1,463	0.7	1,144	0.6	1,018	0.5	1,375	0.6
Inhalants	2,657	1.4	2,212	1.1	1,889	0.9	2,308	1.1	2,427	1.1
Hallucinogens	3,198	1.7	2,350	1.2	2,530	1.2	3,416	1.6	3,602	1.7
PCP	455	0.2	136	0.1	207	0.1	322	0.2	382	0.2
LSD	–	–	–	–	–	–	2,108	1.0	2,104	1.0
Heroin	347	0.2	443	0.2	304	0.1	428	0.2	455	0.2
Nonmedical use of any psychotherapeutic**	11,988	6.2	6,878	3.4	6,260	3.0	6,166	2.9	6,652	3.1
Stimulants	5,637	2.9	2,319	1.2	1,478	0.7	1,656	0.8	1,896	0.9
Sedatives	2,209	1.1	991	0.5	802	0.4	666	0.3	678	0.3
Tranquilizers	6,181	3.2	2,376	1.2	2,851	1.4	2,210	1.0	2,430	1.1
Analgesics	6,921	3.6	4,986	2.5	4,871	2.4	4,102	1.9	4,510	2.1
Alcohol	140,394	72.9	132,859	66.0	133,090	64.7	138,314	65.4	138,912	64.9

*Any illicit drug indicates use at least once of marijuana or hashish, cocaine (including crack), inhalants, hallucinogens (including PCP and LSD), heroin, or any prescription-type psychotherapeutic used nonmedically.
**Nonmedical use of any prescription-type stimulant, sedative, tranquilizer, or analgesic; does not include over-the-counter drugs.
Source: Substance Abuse and Mental Health Services Administration

Percentages Reporting Past-Month Use of Alcohol by Age

Age group	Any		Binge*		Heavy**	
	1995	1996	1995	1996	1995	1996
Total	52.2	51.0	15.8	15.5	5.5	5.4
12–17	21.1	18.8	7.9	7.2	2.8	2.9
18–25	61.3	60.0	29.9	32.0	12.0	12.9
26–34	63.0	61.6	24.0	22.8	7.9	7.1
35 and older	52.6	51.7	11.8	11.3	3.9	3.8

*Binge alcohol use is defined as drinking five or more drinks on the same occasion on at least one day in the past 30 days. By "occasion" is meant at the same time or within a couple hours of each other.
**Heavy alcohol use is defined as drinking five or more drinks on the same occasion on each of five or more days in the past 30 days; all heavy alcohol users are also binge alcohol users.

Percentages Reporting Past-Year Use of Illicit Drugs by Age

Age group	Any*		Marijuana		Cocaine	
	1995	1996	1995	1996	1995	1996
Total	10.7	10.8	8.4	8.6	1.7	1.9
12–17	18.0	16.7	14.2	13.0	1.7	1.4
18–25	25.5	26.8	21.8	23.8	4.3	4.7
26–34	14.6	14.6	11.8	11.3	3.1	3.5
35 and older	5.0	5.3	3.4	3.8	0.8	0.9

*Any illicit drug indicates use at least once of marijuana or hashish, cocaine (including crack), inhalants, hallucinogens (including PCP and LSD), heroin, or any prescription-type psychotherapeutic used nonmedically.
Source: Substance Abuse and Mental Health Services Administration

Youth and Addictive Substances

Percentages of Eighth, Tenth, and Twelfth Graders Who Used Drugs or Consumed Alcohol in the Past Year

Type of drug	1992	1993	1994	1995	1996
Any illicit drug					
8th graders	12.9	15.1	18.5	21.4	23.6
10th graders	20.4	24.7	30.0	33.3	37.5
12th graders	27.1	31.0	35.8	39.0	40.2
Marijuana/hashish					
8th graders	7.2	9.2	13.0	15.8	18.3
10th graders	15.2	19.2	25.2	28.7	33.6
12th graders	21.9	26.0	30.7	34.7	35.8
Inhalants					
8th graders	9.5	11.0	11.7	12.8	12.2
10th graders	7.5	8.4	9.1	9.6	9.5
12th graders	6.2	7.0	7.7	8.0	7.6
Hallucinogens					
8th graders	2.5	2.6	2.7	3.6	4.1
10th graders	4.3	4.7	5.8	7.2	7.8
12th graders	5.9	7.4	7.6	9.3	10.1
Cocaine					
8th graders	1.5	1.7	2.1	2.6	3.0
10th graders	1.9	2.1	2.8	3.5	4.2
12th graders	3.1	3.3	3.6	4.0	4.9
Heroin					
8th graders	0.7	0.7	1.2	1.4	1.6
10th graders	0.6	0.7	0.9	1.1	1.2
12th graders	0.6	0.5	0.6	1.1	1.0
Stimulants					
8th graders	6.5	7.2	7.9	8.7	9.1
10th graders	8.2	9.6	10.2	11.9	12.4
12th graders	7.1	8.4	9.4	9.3	9.5
Alcohol*					
8th graders	53.7	45.4	46.8	45.3	46.5
10th graders	70.2	63.4	63.9	63.5	65.0
12th graders	76.8	72.7	73.0	73.7	72.5
Been drunk					
8th graders	18.3	18.2	18.2	18.4	19.8
10th graders	37.0	37.8	38.0	38.5	40.1
12th graders	50.3	49.6	51.7	52.5	51.9

Note: Two of the major sources of data on drug and alcohol abuse conduct different types of surveys and produce results that are not comparable. The University of Michigan's Monitoring the Future Study focuses on eighth, tenth, and twelfth graders, while the Substance Abuse and Mental Health Services Administration's National Household Survey on Drug Abuse includes a sample of all Americans, age twelve and older.

*In 1993, the survey was changed to indicate that a "drink" meant "more than a few sips".

Source: The Monitoring the Future Study, University of Michigan

Learning About Drugs

Percentage of students who say their school is not drug-free, meaning that some students keep drugs, use drugs, or sell drugs on school grounds, and students who know a drug dealer and can buy marijuana within a day.

Percentage of Students Who Say Their School Is Not Drug-Free

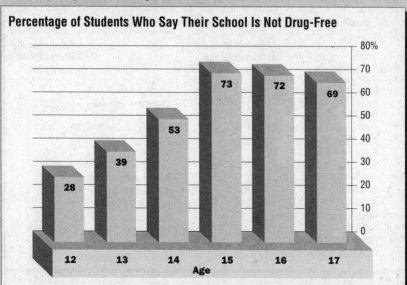

Percentage of Youth Who Know a Drug Dealer and Can Buy Marijuana Within a Day

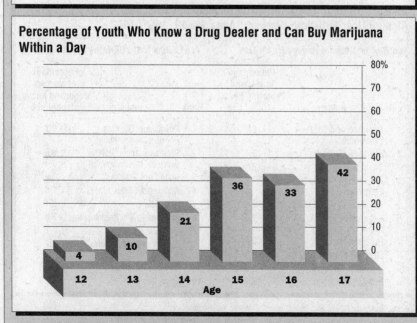

Source: National Center on Addiction and Substance Abuse

Drugs and Drinking on the Job

Businesses and Professions with the Highest and Lowest Rates of Illicit Drug Use, Full-time Workers, Ages 18–49, 1991–1993

	Ten Highest Rates of Illicit Drug Use			Ten Lowest Rates of Illicit Drug Use	
Rank	Industry	Percentage of workers reporting drug use	Rank	Industry	Percentage of workers reporting drug use
1	Eating and Drinking Places	16.3	1	Child-Care Services	1.3
2	Furniture and Appliance Retail Sales	14.4	2	Physicians, Dentists, Chiropractors Offices	1.5
3	Entertainment and Recreation	13.7	3	Administration of Programs	1.8
4	Advertising, Business Management, and Consulting	13.1	4	Elementary and Secondary Schools	2.2
5	Telegraph and Miscellaneous Communications	12.3	5	Justice and Public Order	2.2
			6	Rubber and Plastic Products	2.5
6	Construction	12.2	7	Air Transportation	3.2
7	Automotive Service and Repair	12.0	8	National Security	3.4
8	Other Business and Repair Services	11.9	9	Telephone	3.4
9	Printing and Publishing	11.7	10	Agricultural	3.6
10	Auto Supply and Gas Stations	11.2		Chemical Products	3.6
				Colleges and Universities	3.6

Businesses and Professions with the Highest and Lowest Rates of Heavy Alcohol Use, Full-time Workers, Ages 18–49, 1991–1993

	Ten Highest Rates of Heavy Alcohol Use			Ten Lowest Rates of Heavy Alcohol Use	
Rank	Industry	Percentage of workers reporting heavy alcohol use	Rank	Industry	Percentage of workers reporting heavy alcohol use
1	Computer and Data Processing	16.2	1	Physicians, Dentists, Chiropractors Offices	0.1
2	Eating and Drinking Places	15.4	2	Professional and Related Services, miscellaneous	0.6
3	Construction	13.4	3	Child-Care Services	0.9
4	Auto Supply and Gas Stations	13.2	4	Apparel and Shoe Stores	1.5
5	Lumber and Wood Products	12.0	5	Hospitals	2.1
6	Automotive Service and Repair	11.4	6	Accounting and Bookkeeping	2.3
7	Horticultural	10.8	7	Electrical Machinery	2.7
8	Electrical Machinery	10.0	8	Elementary and Secondary Schools	2.7
9	Wholesale Grocery	9.8	9	Private Household	2.8
10	Hotel and Motel	9.6	10	Legal Services	3.0

Source: Substance Abuse and Mental Health Services Administration

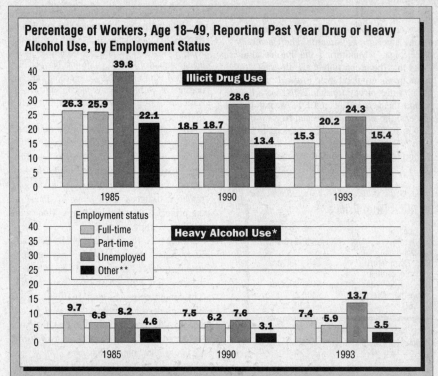

Percentage of Workers, Age 18–49, Reporting Past Year Drug or Heavy Alcohol Use, by Employment Status

Illicit Drug Use

- 1985: 26.3, 25.9, 39.8, 22.1
- 1990: 18.5, 18.7, 28.6, 13.4
- 1993: 15.3, 20.2, 24.3, 15.4

Employment status
- Full-time
- Part-time
- Unemployed
- Other**

Heavy Alcohol Use*

- 1985: 9.7, 6.8, 8.2, 4.6
- 1990: 7.5, 6.2, 7.6, 3.1
- 1993: 7.4, 5.9, 13.7, 3.5

*Heavy alcohol use is defined as drinking 5 or more drinks on 5 or more occasions during the previous 30 days.
**Retired, disabled, homemakers, students, and others
Source: Substance Abuse and Mental Health Services Administration

Teen Drug Abuse

Illicit drug use continued to rise in 1996 among American adolescents. The University of Michigan's Monitoring the Future study found that the proportion of eighth-grade students using any illicit drug in the 12 months prior to the survey reached 24%, more than double the percentage in 1991. Among 10th graders, the proportion jumped to 38% from 20% in 1992, and among 12th graders, to 40% from 27% in 1992.

Marijuana use accounted for much of the overall increase, and the study's authors were particularly concerned to see the continuing rise in daily marijuana use. Nearly one in 20 of today's high-school seniors is a daily marijuana smoker. Indeed, 42% of 17-year-olds say they know a drug dealer and can buy marijuana within a day, according to the National Center on Addiction and Substance Abuse.

The substantial increase in cigarette smoking by young people may be contributing to their progression into drug use, particularly marijuana. "Learning to smoke cigarettes is excellent training for learning to smoke marijuana," says Lloyd D. Johnston, the principal investigator for the Monitoring the Future study.

Meanwhile, the University of Michigan's study found that alcohol use among high-school students has remained fairly stable in recent years, although at rates many parents consider unacceptably high. In 1996, 16% of eighth graders, a quarter of 10th graders, and 30% of 12th graders reported that they had consumed five or more drinks in a row during the two weeks before the survey.

Illicit Drug Prices*	
Cocaine	$300-$2,200/oz.
Heroin	$800-$18,000/oz.
Marijuana	
Commercial	$40-$400/oz.
Sensemilla	
(higher potency)	$100-$900/oz.
Methamphetamine	$400-$2,700/oz.
LSD	$0.65-$20.00/hit

*U.S. domestic retail price range.
Source: U.S. Drug Enforcement Administration

Smoker Profile

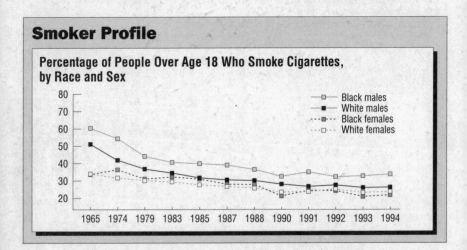

Percentage of People Over Age 18 Who Smoke Cigarettes, by Race and Sex

Percentage of People Over Age 18 Who Smoke, by Age and Sex

	1965	1974	1979	1983	1985	1988	1990	1991	1992	1993	1994
All persons											
18 years and older	42.4	37.1	33.5	32.1	30.1	28.1	25.5	25.6	26.5	25.0	25.5
Males											
18 years and older	51.9	43.1	37.5	35.1	32.6	30.8	28.4	28.1	28.6	27.7	28.2
18–24 years	54.1	42.1	35.0	32.9	28.0	25.5	26.6	23.5	28.0	28.8	29.8
25–34 years	60.7	50.5	43.9	38.8	38.2	36.2	31.6	32.8	32.8	30.2	31.4
35–44 years	58.2	51.0	41.8	41.0	37.6	36.5	34.5	33.1	32.9	32.0	33.2
45–64 years	51.9	42.6	39.3	35.9	33.4	31.3	29.3	29.3	28.6	29.2	28.3
65 years and older	28.5	24.8	20.9	22.0	19.6	18.0	14.6	15.1	16.1	13.5	13.2
Females											
18 years and older	33.9	32.1	29.9	29.5	27.9	25.7	22.8	23.5	24.6	22.5	23.1
18–24 years	38.1	34.1	33.8	35.5	30.4	26.3	22.5	22.4	24.9	22.9	25.2
25–34 years	43.7	38.8	33.7	32.6	32.0	31.3	28.2	28.4	30.1	27.3	28.8
35–44 years	43.7	39.8	37.0	33.8	31.5	27.8	24.8	27.6	27.3	27.4	26.8
45–64 years	32.0	33.4	30.7	31.0	29.9	27.7	24.8	24.6	26.1	23.0	22.8
65 years and older	9.6	12.0	13.2	13.1	13.5	12.8	11.5	12.0	12.4	10.5	11.1

Percentage of People Age 25 and Over Who Smoke, by Level of Education

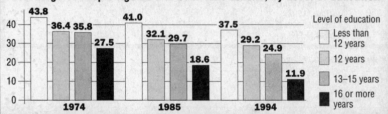

Level of education
- Less than 12 years
- 12 years
- 13–15 years
- 16 or more years

Note: Data for 1992 and beyond are not strictly comparable with data for earlier years.
Sources: Centers for Disease Control and Prevention, National Center for Health Statistics

Percentage of Eighth, Tenth, and Twelfth Graders Who Smoked Cigarettes in the Last 30 Days

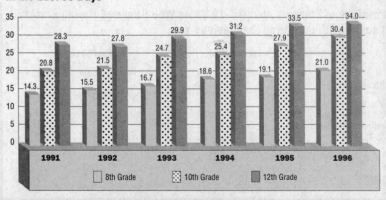

8th Grade   10th Grade   12th Grade

Source: The Monitoring the Future Study, University of Michigan

Tobacco Smoking Rates in Selected Countries

Estimated smoking prevalence among men and women 15 years of age and over, by country, latest available year.

Country (year of survey)	Men	Women
Russian Federation (1993)	67.0%	30.0%
China (1984)	61.0	7.0
Japan (1994)	59.0	14.8
Poland (1993)	51.0	29.0
Thailand (1995)	49.0	4.0
Spain (1993)	48.0	25.0
Israel (1989)	45.0	30.0
Czech Republic (1994)	43.0	31.0
Argentina (1992)	40.0	23.0
France (1993)	40.0	27.0
India (1980s)	40.0	3.0
Brazil (1989)	39.9	25.4
Egypt (1986)	39.8	1.0
Mexico (1990)	38.3	14.4
Italy (1994)	38.0	26.0
Germany (1992)	36.8	21.5
Singapore (1995)	31.9	2.7
Australia (1993)	29.0	21.0
United Kingdom (1994)	28.0	26.0
Sweden (1994)	22.0	24.0

Source: World Health Organization

Young Cigar Smokers

The cigar-smoking trend among adults, which sparked the creation of cigar bars and magazines about stogies, has filtered down to young people. A recent study by the Centers for Disease Control and Prevention found that an estimated six million teenagers, or more than a quarter of people 14 to 19 years old, reported having smoked at least one cigar in the previous year.

Percentage of Students Aged 14–19 Years Who Reported Having Smoked at Least One Cigar During the Previous Year

Characteristic	At least one cigar			At least 50 cigars		
	Female %	Male %	Total %	Female %	Male %	Total %
Race/ethnicity						
White, non-Hispanic	16.0	41.6	28.9	1.2	3.4	2.3
Black, non-Hispanic	13.4	25.2	19.3	1.6	5.6	3.6
Hispanic	20.0	32.3	26.2	1.8	3.2	2.5
Age group (yrs.)						
14–16	16.8	32.1	24.4	1.3	2.9	2.1
17–18	14.9	43.9	29.8	1.1	5.2	3.2
19	14.9	35.5	27.5	3.1	4.9	4.2

Source: Centers for Disease Control and Prevention

Sex, Fertility and Family Planning

Percentage of Women 20–44 Years of Age and Cumulative Percent Who Have Ever Had Sexual Intercourse After Menarche and Before Reaching Selected Ages, 1995

Characteristic	Exact age in years			Mean age at first intercourse
Age	15	18	20	
All women	9.2%	52.3%	75.0%	17.3
20–24 years	13.6	62.2	80.2	16.6
25–29 years	10.9	54.9	75.0	17.5
30–34 years	10.1	53.1	75.8	17.8
35–39 years	7.6	52.2	75.2	18.0
40–44 years	4.6	40.6	69.2	18.6
Education				
No high school diploma or GED	20.4%	73.0%	87.1%	16.5
High school diploma or GED	11.2	59.8	83.1	17.3
Some college, no Bachelor's degree	7.0	49.5	73.6	17.9
Bachelor's degree or higher	2.2	31.7	56.6	19.3
Race and Hispanic origin				
Hispanic	7.6%	42.2%	66.7%	18.4
Non-Hispanic white	8.3	52.8	76.0	17.7
Non-Hispanic black	16.1	65.9	85.6	16.8
Non-Hispanic other	8.1	28.4	48.1	20.0

Source: Centers for Disease Control and Prevention, National Center for Health Statistics

Number of Women 15–44 Years of Age and Percent Distribution by Number of Pregnancies, According to Selected Characteristics, 1995

Characteristic		Number of pregnancies				
Characteristic	Number in thousands	None	1	2	3	4 or more
		Percent distribution				
All women	60,201	33.4%	16.4%	20.3%	14.2%	15.7%
Age						
15–19 years	8,961	84.0	12.3	3.2	0.6	0.1
20–24 years	9,041	55.2	20.2	14.0	5.0	5.6
25–29 years	9,693	31.1	24.1	19.4	13.1	12.3
30–34 years	11,065	17.4	16.8	26.3	18.9	20.7
35–39 years	11,211	12.5	12.6	27.6	22.4	24.8
40–44 years	10,230	12.1	13.4	26.9	21.3	26.3
Education[2]						
No high school diploma or GED[3]	5,424	3.2%	10.7%	22.8%	23.3%	40.0%
High school diploma or GED	18,169	13.9	17.6	27.4	20.2	21.0
Some college, no bachelor's degree	12,399	25.7	17.6	22.9	15.9	17.9
Bachelor's degree or higher	11,748	37.9	18.1	21.1	12.7	10.2
Race and Hispanic origin						
Hispanic	6,702	26.8%	16.6%	19.1%	15.2%	22.2%
Non-Hispanic white	42,522	34.9	16.2	21.0	14.1	13.7
Non-Hispanic black	8,210	28.1	17.8	18.1	14.8	21.2
Non-Hispanic other	2,767	41.2	15.2	17.7	11.2	14.8

Number of Women 15–44 Years of Age and Percent Distribution by Number of Children Ever Born, According to Selected Characteristics, 1995

Characteristic	Number in thousands	Number of children ever born				
		None	1	2	3	4 or more
		Percent distribution				
All women	60,201	41.9%	17.8%	23.0%	11.6%	5.7%
Age						
15–19 years	8,961	91.6	7.6	0.5	0.2	–
20–24 years	9,041	65.3	20.2	10.2	3.6	0.8
25–29 years	9,693	43.5	23.2	20.2	9.0	4.1
30–34 years	11,065	26.4	21.0	30.4	15.1	7.1
35–39 years	11,211	19.6	16.8	35.5	19.0	9.1
40–44 years	10,230	17.5	17.0	35.2	19.0	11.2
Education[2]						
No high school diploma or GED[3]	5,424	7.9%	15.3%	29.2%	27.2%	20.5%
High school diploma or GED	18,169	21.1	21.4	32.6	16.8	8.1
Some college, no bachelor's degree	12,399	35.6	21.0	27.6	11.4	4.5
Bachelor's degree or higher	11,748	49.1	17.6	22.9	8.1	2.4
Race and Hispanic origin						
Hispanic	6,702	34.8%	17.9%	20.3%	16.3%	10.7%
Non-Hispanic white	42,522	43.5	17.2	24.2	10.9	4.1
Non-Hispanic black	8,210	37.3	20.7	20.5	12.3	9.2
Non-Hispanic other	2,767	48.4	17.2	19.5	8.3	6.7

Number of Currently Married Women 15–44 Years of Age and Percent Distribution by Infertility Status, According to Selected Characteristics, 1995

Characteristic	Surgically sterile	Infertile	Fecund
	Percent distribution		
All women	41.0%	7.1%	52.0%
Age			
15–24 years	6.2	4.4	89.4
25–34 years	27.3	6.6	66.1
35–44 years	59.1	8.0	32.9
0 births			
15–44 years	13.1	17.1	69.8
15–24 years	2.5	6.0	91.6
25–34 years	6.5	13.5	80.0
35–44 years	31.1	30.3	38.6
1 or more births			
15–44 years	47.6	4.7	47.7
15–24 years	8.8	3.3	87.8
25–34 years	33.5	4.5	62.0
35–44 years	62.9	5.0	32.2

Number of Women 15–44 Years of Age, Percent Who Have Received Any Infertility Services, and Percent Who Have Ever Received the Specified Infertility Services, by Selected Characteristics, 1995

Characteristic	Any services[4]	Advice	Tests on woman or man	Ovulation drugs	Surgery or treatment for blocked tubes	Assisted reproductive technology[5]
All women	15.4%	6.4%	4.2%	3.0%	1.5%	1.0%
Age						
15–24 years	4.4	1.1	0.2	0.3	0.1	0.0
25–34 years	17.1	6.3	3.7	3.1	1.2	0.8
35–44 years	22.9	10.9	8.1	5.2	2.9	2.1
0 births	6.4	4.6	3.7	2.2	1.1	1.2
15–24 years	1.2	0.5	0.2	0.2	0.1	0.1
25–34 years	8.7	6.5	4.6	3.0	1.0	1.1
35–44 years	20.7	15.5	14.5	8.0	4.8	5.3
1 or more births	21.8	7.7	4.6	3.6	1.8	0.9
15–24 years	16.1	3.3	0.3	0.6	0.5	–
25–34 years	21.5	6.2	3.1	3.1	1.3	0.6
35–44 years	23.4	9.8	6.7	4.6	2.4	1.4

[1]Mean ages are based only on women who ever had intercourse after menarche.
[2]Limited to women 22–44 years of age at time of interview.
[3]GED is general equivalency dilploma.
[4]Includes services to help get pregnant as well as to prevent miscarriages.
[5]Includes artificial insemination, in vitro fertilization (IVF), gamete intrafallopian transfer (GIFT), and other techniques not shown separately.
Source: Centers for Disease Control and Prevention, National Center for Health Statistics

Infertility Treatment

The number of babies born through assisted reproductive technology, such as invitro fertilization, has grown steadily in the 1990s.

Year	Number of live deliveries
1989	3,472
1990	3,951
1991	5,699
1992	7,355
1993	8,741
1994	9,573

Source: American Society for Reproductive Medicine

Multiple Births

The number of babies born as twins, triplets, and other multiples has increased rapidly both because women are having children after they reach the age of 30, when chances of such births increase, and because more are using fertility drugs.

Year	Twins	Triplets	Quads	Quintuplets and larger multiples
1989	90,118	2,529	229	40
1990	93,865	2,830	185	13
1991	94,779	3,121	203	22
1992	95,372	3,547	310	26
1993	96,445	3,834	277	57
1994	97,064	4,233	315	46
1995	96,736	4,551	365	57

Source: National Center for Health Statistics

Birth Control

Nearly 60% of women 15 to 44 years of age used contraception in 1990, up from about 56% in 1982. Here are the percentage of women using contraception who choose these methods:

	1982	1988	1990
Female sterilization	23.2	27.5	29.5
Male sterilization	10.9	11.7	12.6
Birth control pill	28.0	30.7	28.5
Intrauterine device	7.1	2.0	1.4
Diaphragm	8.1	5.7	2.8
Condom	12.0	14.6	17.7

Source: National Center for Health Statistics

BITTER ABORTION DEBATE

THE ABORTION DEBATE remains as rancorous as ever on the eve of the 25th anniversary of the U.S. Supreme Court ruling that legalized abortion.

Late-term abortions became a major issue in 1997, with politicians in Washington and some state capitals trying to outlaw them. Even the American Medical Association took the unusual step of declaring so-called "partial-birth" abortions "bad medicine." Both houses of Congress again passed a ban on late-term abortions, though the president threatened a second veto. Meanwhile, on the front lines, demonstrations and violence continued, with the bombing of an abortion clinic in Atlanta.

Why is abortion still so divisive? It's an issue, both sides agree, with no middle ground, no room for compromise. "We do not want a place at the negotiating table" with abortion-rights advocates, says the Rev. Flip Benham, national director of Operation Rescue, an anti-abortion group that considers the procedure murder. "We want to kick the table over." Operation Rescue focused on protests outside high schools in 1997, displaying signs that graphically depicted aborted fetuses and handing out literature to students getting off buses.

The number of abortions has declined slightly over the last few years. According to the latest statistics, 1.4 million abortions were performed in 1994, down from 1.5 million in 1993. Abortion rights advocates aren't certain how to interpret the decrease—is it because of better preventive measures or is it the result of fewer abortion providers? For their part, abortion opponents see the decrease as a sign that their demonstrations and "sidewalk counseling" tactics work and that popular opinion is shifting in their direction.

But according to a 1996 Gallup poll, about 75% of American adults believe abortion, in some form, should be legal, a percentage that has held fairly steady over the last 10 years. However, the same poll found that 57% of Americans would support a law prohibiting the partial-birth abortions performed in the last six months of pregnancy.

The decline in abortions could continue over the next few years because of developments in the medical world. After a protracted journey, "the abortion pill" mifepristone, commonly known as RU-486, is on the cusp of Food and Drug Administratrion approval; the agency says it just needs information about how the drug will be manufactured and labeled. That could take a while, however. The nonprofit group that holds the U.S. patent rights to the drug is having trouble finding a company willing to manufacture it.

In the meantime, prodded by reproductive-health groups to act, the FDA announced that the use of birth-control pills for "emergency contraception" is safe and effective, if taken in sufficient quantities within three days of unprotected sex. The FDA rarely makes such decisions without first being petitioned by private industry, but in this case no companies asked the FDA for such a ruling. In the announcement, the FDA conceded that the pills' effectiveness as a "morning-after pill" has been known, but kept quiet for some time. Abortion opponents immediately denounced the practice as a "chemical abortion."

Such reactions cause some pro-choice groups to dismiss abortion opponents as hypo-critical. "For many, it's not about reducing

the need for abortion," says Kate Michelman, president of the National Abortion and Repro-ductive Rights Action League. Because they also want to restrict access to contraceptives and sex education, she adds, "they want to deny women the right to self-determination."

Laurie Snyder

Number of Reported Abortions, Rate per 1,000 Women Aged 15–44 and Ratio of Abortions per 100 Pregnancies Ending in Abortions or Live Births

Year	Abortions (in 000s)	Rate	Ratio	Year	Abortions (in 000s)	Rate	Ratio
1973	744.6	16.3	19.3	1985	1,588.6	28.0	29.7
1974	898.6	19.3	22.0	1986	(1,574.0)	(27.4)	(29.4)
1975	1,034.2	21.7	24.9	1987	1,559.1	26.9	28.8
1976	1,179.3	24.2	26.5	1988	1,590.8	27.3	28.6
1977	1,316.7	26.4	28.6	1989	(1,566.9)	(26.8)	(27.5)
1978	1,409.6	27.7	29.2	1990	(1,608.6)	(27.4)	(28.0)
1979	1,497.7	28.8	29.6	1991	1,556.5	26.3	27.4
1980	1,553.9	29.3	30.0	1992	1,528.9	25.9	27.5
1981	1,577.3	29.3	30.1	1993*	1,500.0	25.4	27.4
1982	1,573.9	28.8	30.0	1994*	1,430.0	24.1	26.7
1983	(1,575.0)	(28.5)	(30.4)				
1984	1,577.2	28.1	29.7				

Note: Figures in parentheses are estimated by interpolation of numbers of abortions.
*Estimate.

Stage at Which Abortions Were Performed, 1992

	Number
<9 weeks	798,850
9-10 weeks	377,570
11-12 weeks	181,960
13-15 weeks	94,060
16-20 weeks	60,040
>20 weeks	16,450
21-22 weeks	10,340
23-24 weeks	4,940
25-26 weeks	850
>26 weeks	320

When Women Have Abortions (In weeks)

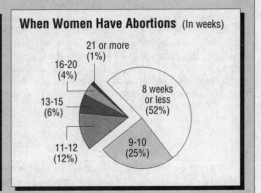

21 or more (1%)
16-20 (4%)
13-15 (6%)
11-12 (12%)
8 weeks or less (52%)
9-10 (25%)

Number of Abortion Providers, by Type of Facility

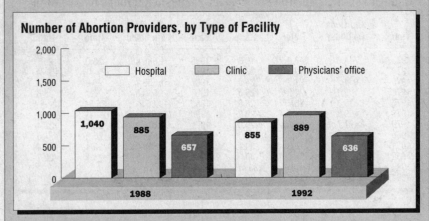

Hospital　Clinic　Physicians' office

1988: 1,040, 885, 657
1992: 855, 889, 636

Source: Alan Guttmacher Institute

Education

Picture a business in which the most well-to-do customers pay the product's full price. Most everyone else receives a discount, which varies so greatly, no one really knows what the next person's paying. And those who haggle—or better yet, have a relative in the business—often get the best deal.

A new car showroom? The airline industry? A Mexican souvenir stand?

Try the American system of higher education. In terms of quality, the system is still considered the finest in the world. But radical changes in pricing and admissions policies at many schools—particularly private ones a notch or two below the Ivy League—have caused many parents of college-age children to come to view the system with skepticism, even scorn.

Who can blame them?

At Johns Hopkins University in Baltimore, administrators, with the help of a consultant, created a statistical model to predict, down to the dollar, how much financial aid it would take to convince a prospective freshman to enroll. The model—which officials say they never fully implemented—suggested slashing aid to some prospects who attend on-campus interviews because statistically they are more likely to come anyway. Hopkins' literature, by the way, urges all applicants to do such interviews.

At Carnegie Mellon University in Pittsburgh, accepted students are invited to fax the school any better financial–aid offers they receive from other colleges, an open invitation to haggle. Though financial-aid officers universally despise such practices, an increasing number are doing it. An administrator at Chestnut Hill College in Philadelphia recently told his colleagues at other schools, "Last year, I felt like Monty Hall."

At Franklin and Marshall College in Lancaster, Pa., officials have used the list of wait-listed students—that mysterious netherworld in which students are neither accepted nor rejected—to weed out the wealthiest ones. Students who indicated they needed financial aid had no chance of getting in. In fact, an increasing number of colleges have quietly abandoned policies that guaranteed equal admissions consideration and tuition help for needy students. "Need-blind" admissions policies have given way to such euphemisms as "need-conscious" or "need-aware" policies. The bottom line: The more affluent candidate often has a leg up on the equally qualified, but poorer applicant.

Parents of prospective students aren't aware of many of these practices, and that's no accident. The colleges deliberately don't advertise them. At a gathering of financial-aid administrators in San Antonio, Texas, two years ago, two top Hopkins aid officials conceded that if word leaked out about their statistical model, the public-relations consequences could be "scarifying." Parents and students "don't need to know the specifics of, 'If you come for an interview you're not going to get financial aid,' for example," one said.

How did colleges, for so long viewed with respect, even reverence, suddenly gain reputations as rip-off artists? ("How Colleges Are Gouging U," reads the headline on a recent *Time* magazine cover.)

To a large degree, the colleges have brought it upon themselves. A recent U.S. General Accounting Office report documented that between 1980 and 1994, tuition at four-year public colleges and universities jumped 234 percent, while median household income rose 82 percent. Private schools have boosted prices similarly; annual costs at many top schools, including tuition, room and board, have surpassed $30,000—saddling some graduates with as much debt as a home mortgage.

The GAO study determined that much of the increase was due to rising college expenses. Faculty salaries jumped 97 percent. (The average full professor at a private research university last year earned $92,112.) Costs for such generous higher education perks as subsidizing the college tuition of employees' children—even at other institutions—soared. So did the cost of physical upkeep of ever-expanding campuses.

The colleges initially figured they could jack up their prices because many parents and students view a college degree as a worthy and necessary investment toward a comfortable future. But the tuition increases eventually got out of hand. As Moody's Investors Service recently said of the phenomenon, "College pricing has seemingly defied the fundamental laws of supply and demand: Prices began to rise faster when demand appeared to drop. Tuition charged by private higher education started to rise faster than both inflation and incomes in the early 1980s, just at the time that the traditional source of demand for higher education—high school graduates—began to drop as the 'baby boom' generation aged and passed through their early twenties."

To increase demand, colleges could have frozen or even reduced tuition across the board. But if they did that, they worried, applicants might respond the wrong way— and assume quality must be going down, especially if competitors didn't follow suit. So instead, many schools began to mimic the travel industry—offering large discounts to certain customers. Just as airlines offer bargain fares to budget travelers willing to stay over a Saturday night, while charging business fliers the full fare, the colleges began offering tuition cuts—in the form of grants— to all but the most affluent, or least desirable students, who were charged the full sticker price.

Unfortunately, the discount strategy created a vicious cycle. The more colleges charged, the more pressure there was to increase financial aid. The federal government didn't pick up the slack; for years, its contributions have been shifting from direct grants to loans. So the colleges, facing ballooning financial-aid budgets, found themselves under ever more pressure to raise prices.

The truth is, the unlucky students who end up paying full freight actually are subsidizing those receiving discounts. This pricing strategy, known as leveraging, is now prevalent in private colleges and represents a sea change in the original intent of financial aid. In the past, colleges mostly used aid to subsidize needy, but qualified students who couldn't otherwise attend. Remember the word scholarship? But once colleges began to price themselves beyond the reach of most American families, widespread discounting— through grants—became the norm, especially at schools without huge endowments.

So did the use of consultants. Many colleges, like Hopkins, have hired consultants to measure applicants' "price sensitivity" to college costs, using such factors as a student's home state, ethnic background, area of study, and who initiated the first contact with the school. It all adds up to one thing: how anxious the student is to attend. The more eager the student, the less aid he or she can expect to get. Some colleges have been known to offer less aid to applicants who apply early because the schools know these students desperately want to come.

Given such tactics, parents have resorted to a number of defensive measures. Some hire their own financial-aid consultants, who coach them through the intricacies of the process, and provide advice on how to maximize assistance. In the *Princeton Review Student Advantage Guide for Paying for College*, consultant Kalman A. Chany suggests setting up a money-losing business on the side, becoming an independent contractor, or even requesting a pay cut. ("Is this fair?" he asks. "No. But lots of things in life aren't fair.")

To the dismay of college officials, families coached by consultants come prepared to do battle. "Families have read that if they don't negotiate their financial–aid awards, if they don't deal with the financial-aid office the same way as if they were dealing with someone they were buying a used car from, then they're saps," says Don Sala, dean of admissions and financial aid at Cornell University in Ithaca, NY.

Other families resort to outright fraud. The U.S. Education Department recently found that 4.4% of 2.3 million Pell grant recipients understated their family income in their applications. Among the cheaters—a student who reported earning $1.3 million on his federal tax return, but claimed zero income on his aid application. The student was awarded a federal Pell grant, which is intended to provide tuition relief for the poor.

Some colleges also have been guilty of dishonesty. Two years ago, *The Wall Street Journal* documented how dozens of schools, including Harvard University, fudged test scores, graduation rates, and other data to make themselves look better than they were in college guidebooks, like *U.S. News & World Report's America's Best Colleges*. Colleges loathe being ranked like automobiles and toaster-ovens. But instead of not participating in the surveys, some chose to cheat.

Where are costs and admissions procedures headed? At the moment, the colleges are on the defensive. On the matter of pricing, they argue quite accurately that the vast majority of colleges don't charge anywhere near $30,000 a year (the average four-year public institution charged $2,966 for tuition and fees in 1996; the average private school cost $12,823). They also say that the places that do charge $30,000 actually spend more than that to educate their students, and that

even at full price, it's worth it. "College is still a bargain," declared a recent report on college costs by the American Council on Education.

Even so, in response to widespread criticism, many schools have begun to shrink their tuition increases. The average 5% hike in 1996 was the lowest rate of increase in at least 20 years, according to the College Board. And institutions are making a more

Baby Boom Echo

The baby-boom generation's children have caused a resurgence in elementary and secondary school enrollment that will continue into the 21st century.

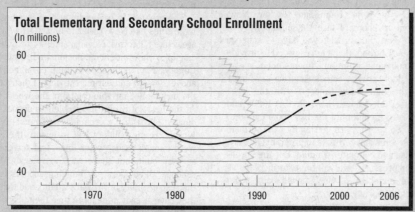

Total Elementary and Secondary School Enrollment
(In millions)

Elementary and Secondary School Enrollment
(In thousands)

Year	Total	Public	Private*	Year	Total	Public	Private*
1964	47,716	41,416	6,300	1990	46,448	41,217	5,232
1966	49,239	43,039	6,200	1992	48,198	42,823	5,375
1968	50,744	44,944	5,800	1993	48,936	43,465	5,471
1970	51,257	45,894	5,363	1994	49,705	44,109	5,596
1972	50,726	45,726	5,000	1995	50,528	44,840	5,688
1974	50,073	45,073	5,000		Projected		
1976	49,478	44,311	5,167				
1978	47,637	42,551	5,086	1996	51,484	45,700	5,784
1980	46,208	40,877	5,331	1997	52,217	46,353	5,863
1982	45,166	39,566	5,600	1998	52,725	46,806	5,920
1984	44,908	39,208	5,700	1999	53,132	47,170	5,963
1986	45,205	39,753	5,452	2000	53,465	47,467	5,998
1988	45,430	40,189	5,241	2006	54,388	48,318	6,070

*Beginning in fall 1980, data include estimates for an expanded universe of private schools.
Source: U.S. Education Department

serious effort to control expenses, especially in the area of health care and other employee benefits. A few colleges even have announced tuition freezes or reductions, although such cases remain rare.

But the issue goes beyond cost. It comes down to trust. Many college administrators consider the gritty world of business to be beneath them. But whether they like it or not, higher education is a service business that relies on customers who want to be treated fairly and pay a fair price.

Steve Stecklow,
The Wall Street Journal's
national education writer

BACK TO SCHOOL— IN DROVES

Many baby boomers remember the overcrowded classrooms of the 1950s and 1960s. It wasn't uncommon for 30 to 40 children to share the same room and teacher. Now, grown-up boomers face the possibility that their own children also will have to squeeze into a classroom that's too crowded to provide the individual attention students need.

School districts across America have been caught unprepared to cope with the large number of children born in the 1980s and 1990s to members of the baby-boom generation. So far, they are getting by with portable classrooms and cutbacks in programs like art, music, and computer training. But the enrollment pressures will continue to increase as more members of this second baby boom reach school age.

"Ten straight years of record enrollments are going to be difficult to deal with just with portables," says Pascal D. Forgione Jr., commissioner of education statistics at the U.S. Education Department. "What's most alarming is the tremendous influx into secondary schools, which are more expensive to build."

Enrollment in elementary and secondary schools hit a record 52.2 million in the 1997–98 school year, and the education department projects it will reach 54.4 million in 2006. "What makes this growth trend different from the surge in the late 1960s is that this current growth trend is a long, slow, rising wave, and we see no immediate fall-off," says Richard Riley, the U.S. Secretary of Education. In addition to the children of baby boomers, a growing number of immigrant children are helping swell enrollments.

Many demographers are amazed that school planners did not see the wave of children coming and start preparing for their arrival years ago. Indeed, many communities that built schools for the baby boomers in the 1960s converted the buildings into senior-centers or condos in the 1970s and 1980s, and now can't easily reclaim them as schools.

The problem is especially severe in some large cities like New York and in fast-growing areas like California, Nevada, and Florida. For example, the student explosion in Broward County, Fla., has pushed total enrollment above 200,000 and earned the school district the nickname "portable capital of the world." At the heart of Broward's problem is uncoordinated growth, a common affliction in Florida. Home builders had to ensure there were enough roads, water lines, and sewers as they built, but there was no rule about schools. Developers say building schools is the responsibility of Broward County and that they have already done more than their share.

Adjustments are being made—at the expense of the kids. At some schools trying to fit in more students, children board buses as early as 6:30 a.m., and lunch shifts start at 10:30 a.m. Rooms for art, music, speech, Spanish, science, and computer training have been turned into regular classrooms at other schools, so teachers of special subjects must push their materials from room to room on carts.

The big concern among parents and educators is the possible increase in class size. In the early 1990s, the national average was about 25 students per elementary class and about 23 per secondary-school class. Possible solutions include more double-shift school days and more year-round schools to maximize the use of teachers and facilities.

"Many local school boards will face the task of finding the resources to build new schools and recruit additional well-trained teachers to

School Enrollment Growth

Fifteen States with the Largest Projected Enrollment Increases in Public Elementary and Secondary Schools: Fall 1997 to Fall 2007

State	Projected enrollment (In thousands)		Number of additional students, 1997 to 2007
	1997	2007	
California	5,860	6,780	920
Texas	3,900	4,314	414
Georgia	1,358	1,502	144
North Carolina	1,240	1,332	92
Arizona	832	922	90
Virginia	1,115	1,198	83
Florida	2,300	2,372	72
New York	2,902	2,965	63
Tennessee	923	984	61
Utah	488	543	55
Colorado	684	727	43
New Mexico	352	393	41
Alabama	748	789	41
Indiana	989	1,023	34
New Jersey	1,248	1,280	32

Fifteen States with the Largest Projected Percent Increases in Public Elementary and Secondary Enrollment: Fall 1997 to Fall 2007

State	Projected enrollment (In thousands)		Percent change, 1997 to 2007
	1997	2007	
California	5,860	6,780	15.7
Hawaii	204	228	11.8
New Mexico	352	393	11.6
Utah	488	543	11.3
Idaho	255	283	11.0
Arizona	832	922	10.8
Texas	3,900	4,314	10.6
Georgia	1,358	1,502	10.6
Alaska	133	145	9.0
Nevada	295	321	8.8
Virginia	1,115	1,198	7.4
North Carolina	1,240	1,332	7.4
Tennessee	923	984	6.6
Colorado	684	727	6.3
Alabama	748	789	5.5

Source: U.S. Education Department

keep class size down," says Mr. Riley. To maintain current services in 2006, the U.S. will need an additional 190,000 teachers, more than 6,000 schools and about $15 billion more in annual operating expenditures. "Col-

lege education departments need to get the message out to freshmen about the teaching opportunities," says Mr. Forgione.

Ronald Alsop

Classroom Costs

As School Revenues Climb...
Revenues for Public Elementary and Secondary Schools
(In billions)

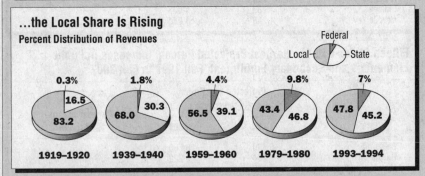

School Year

...the Local Share Is Rising
Percent Distribution of Revenues

Federal
Local— —State

0.3%	1.8%	4.4%	9.8%	7%
16.5	30.3	39.1	43.4 46.8	47.8 45.2
83.2	68.0	56.5		
1919–1920	**1939–1940**	**1959–1960**	**1979–1980**	**1993–1994**

Total Expenditures for Public Elementary and Secondary Education
(In thousands)

School year	Total expenditures	Expenditure per pupil	
		Current $	Constant 1996–97 $
1919–20	$ 1,036,151	$64	$ 533
1929–30	2,316,790	108	1,007
1939–40	2,344,049	106	1,202
1949–50	5,837,643	260	1,747
1959–60	15,613,255	471	2,547
1969–70	40,683,429	955	4,017
1979–80	95,961,561	2,491	5,098
1989–90	212,473,108	5,550	6,946
1990–91	229,429,715	5,885	6,983
1991–92	241,062,373	6,075	6,984
1992–93	252,934,872	6,281	7,003
1993–94	265,285,370	6,492	7,055
1994–95	278,965,657	6,724	7,104

Source: U.S. Education Department

Growth of Special Education

The number of students in special-education programs has increased significantly, largely because more are being classified as learning disabled.

Children in Federally Supported Programs for the Disabled

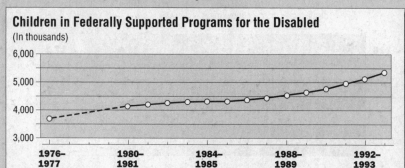

(In thousands)

Number of disabled children (In thousands)

Type of disability	1976–1977	1980–1981	1985–1986	1990–1991	1991–1992	1992–1993	1993–1994
All disabilities	3,692	4,142	4,317	4,762	4,949	5,125	5,318
Specific learning disabilities	796	1,462	1,862	2,130	2,234	2,354	2,424
Speech or language impairments	1,302	1,168	1,125	985	997	996	1,005
Mental retardation	959	829	660	534	538	519	536
Serious emotional disturbance	283	346	375	390	399	401	413
Hearing impairments	87	79	66	58	60	60	63
Orthopedic impairments	87	58	57	49	51	52	56
Other health impairments	141	98	57	55	58	65	82
Visual impairments	38	31	27	23	24	23	24
Multiple disabilities	–	68	86	96	97	102	108
Deaf-blindness	–	3	2	1	1	1	1
Autism and other	–	–	–	–	5	19	24
Preschool disabled	–	–	–	441	484	531	582

Number served as a percent of total enrollment

Type of disability	1976–1977	1980–1981	1985–1986	1990–1991	1991–1992	1992–1993	1993–1994
All disabilities	8.33%	10.13%	10.95%	11.55%	11.77%	11.97%	12.23%
Specific learning disabilities	1.80	3.58	4.72	5.17	5.31	5.50	5.57
Speech or language impairments	2.94	2.86	2.85	2.39	2.37	2.33	2.31
Mental retardation	2.16	2.03	1.68	1.30	1.28	1.21	1.23
Serious emotional disturbance	0.64	0.85	0.95	0.95	0.95	0.94	0.95
Hearing impairments	0.20	0.19	0.17	0.14	0.14	0.14	0.15
Orthopedic impairments	0.20	0.14	0.14	0.12	0.12	0.12	0.13
Other health impairments	0.32	0.24	0.14	0.13	0.14	0.15	0.19
Visual impairments	0.09	0.08	0.07	0.06	0.06	0.05	0.06
Multiple disabilities	–	0.17	0.22	0.23	0.23	0.24	0.25
Deaf-blindness	–	0.01	0.01	0.00	0.00	0.00	0.00
Autism and other	–	–	–	–	0.01	0.04	0.05
Preschool disabled	–	–	–	1.07	1.15	1.24	1.34

Source: U.S. Education Department

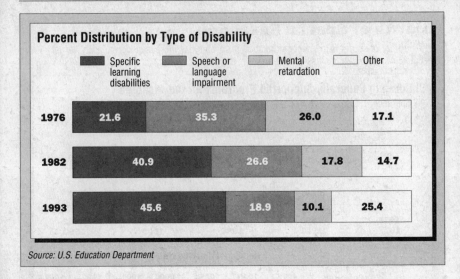

Percent Distribution by Type of Disability

Legend:
- Specific learning disabilities
- Speech or language impairment
- Mental retardation
- Other

Year	Specific learning disabilities	Speech or language impairment	Mental retardation	Other
1976	21.6	35.3	26.0	17.1
1982	40.9	26.6	17.8	14.7
1993	45.6	18.9	10.1	25.4

Source: U.S. Education Department

Public School Alternatives

More parents are turning away from the public schools because of concern about the quality of instruction, lack of discipline, and increasing violence. Many are choosing taxpayer-funded charter schools, Catholic schools and other private schools. There's also a small but growing contingent of parents teaching their own children at home.

The dissatisfaction with public schools came through loud and clear in a *Wall Street Journal*/NBC News poll in 1997. Only 18% of Americans surveyed said the public primary and secondary schools are doing B-or-better work, while 28% gave schools a D or F. In fact, a quarter of the people rated improving education as the top priority for government attention, ranking it ahead of Social Security and the budget deficit.

Yet the public is still divided over letting parents use taxpayer funds to send their children to private schools. In the *Journal*/NBC poll, 73% said they favor free choice in sending children to any public school in their district, but only 45% endorsed such free choice when it involves using public funds in private schools.

Taking Attendance in Catholic Schools

Enrollment in Catholic schools reversed course in the 1990s, ending about 25 years of decline. At the same time, non-Catholics account for a growing share of the students.

Enrollment in Catholic Schools: 1920–1997

(In thousands)

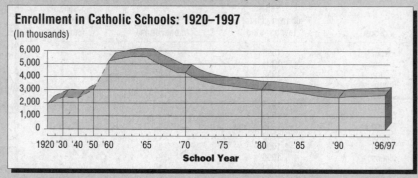

School Year

Enrollment in Catholic Schools

School year	Total enrollment	School year	Total enrollment	School year	Total enrollment
1920	1,926,000	1970–1971	4,363,000	1992–1993	2,567,630
1930	2,465,000	1975–1976	3,415,000	1993–1994	2,576,845
1940	2,396,000	1980–1981	3,106,000	1994–1995	2,618,567
1950	3,067,000	1985–1986	2,821,000	1995–1996	2,635,218
1960	5,253,000	1990–1991	2,475,439	1996–1997	2,645,462
1965	5,574,000	1991–1992	2,550,863		

Percentage of Catholic School Students Who Are Non-Catholic

School year	Percent
1982–1983	10.6%
1990–1991	11.9
1991–1992	12.0
1992–1993	12.3
1993–1994	12.8
1994–1995	13.0
1995–1996	13.2
1996–1997	13.5

Source: National Catholic Educational Association

Catholic Schools: Tuition and Per-Pupil Expenditures

School year	Tuition	Per-pupil expenditure
Elementary schools*		
1988–1989	$ 924	$1,476
1990–1991	969	1,819
1992–1993	1,152	2,044
1994–1995	1,303	2,145
Secondary schools**		
1987–1988	$1,875	$2,690
1991–1992	2,700	3,700
1993–1994	3,100	4,120

*Average reported tuition/expenditure.
**Median reported tuition/expenditure.

Total and Current Expenditures* Per Pupil in Public Elementary and Secondary Schools

School year	Current	Total
1988–1989	$4,645	$5,109
1989–1990	4,972	5,542
1990–1991	5,258	5,885
1991–1992	5,421	6,075
1992–1993	5,584	6,281
1993–1994	5,767	6,491
1994–1995**	5,986	6,738
1995–1996**	6,213	6,993

*Current expenditures exclude capital outlays and interest on school debt.
**Estimates.
Source: U.S. Education Department

Charter School Movement

Charter Schools Operating or Approved to Open, September 1997

State	Year charter school law adopted	Schools in operation	Schools approved to open
Alaska	1995	15	-
Arizona	1994	247	7
California	1992	128	7
Colorado	1993	49	-
Connecticut	1996	12	-
Delaware	1995	3	4
District of Columbia	1996	3	1
Florida	1996	34	6
Georgia	1993	21	-
Hawaii	1994	2	-
Illinois	1996	8	-
Kansas	1994	1	6
Louisiana	1995	6	-
Massachusetts	1993	23	2
Michigan	1993	110	25
Minnesota	1991	29	3
New Jersey	1996	13	3
New Mexico	1993	5	-
North Carolina	1996	34	-
Pennsylvania	1997	6	-
Rhode Island	1995	1	1
South Carolina	1996	1	2
Texas	1995	19	1
Wisconsin	1993	17	-
23 states and D.C.		**787**	**68**

Note: States with charter legislation but no charter schools in operation include Arkansas, Mississippi, Nevada, New Hampshire, Ohio and Wyoming.
Source: Center for Education Reform

Number of Children Home Educated in the U.S. (Estimated)

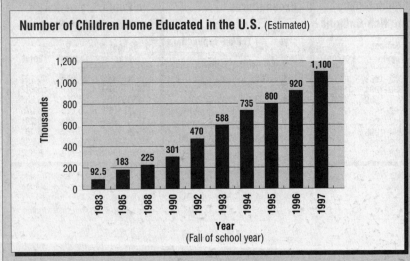

Source: National Home Education Research Institute, Salem, OR

High-Tech Teaching

Percentage of Students Using Computers at School and at Home

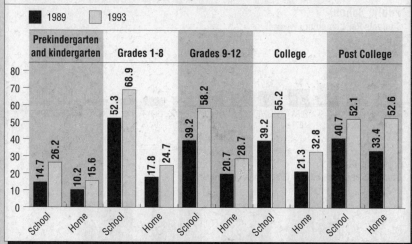

■ 1989 □ 1993

	Prekindergarten and kindergarten		Grades 1-8		Grades 9-12		College		Post College	
	School	Home	School	Home	School	Home	School	Home	School	Home
1989	14.7	10.2	52.3	17.8	39.2	20.7	39.2	21.3	40.7	33.4
1993	26.2	15.6	68.9	24.7	58.2	28.7	55.2	32.8	52.1	52.6

Percentage of Students Using Computers at School and at Home
(Percentage of Prekindergarten through Post College)

Student and school characteristics	October 1993 At school	October 1993 At home
Total	59.0%	27.0%
Race/ethnicity		
White, non-Hispanic	61.6	32.8
Black, non-Hispanic	51.5	10.9
Hispanic	52.3	10.4
Other	59.0	28.7
Household income		
Less than $5,000	51.2	9.7
$5,000 to 9,999	53.3	8.0
$10,000 to 14,999	56.4	11.4
$15,000 to 19,999	58.1	15.1
$20,000 to 24,999	56.4	16.8
$25,000 to 29,999	60.0	21.1
$30,000 to 34,999	59.1	24.1
$35,000 to 39,999	60.7	27.1
$40,000 to 49,999	59.3	32.2
$50,000 to 74,999	62.6	43.0
$75,000 or more	64.6	56.1
Control of school		
Public	60.2	25.3
Private	52.1	37.4

Sources: U.S. Census Bureau and Education Department

Computers in the Schools

The ratio of students per computer has dropped from 125:1 in 1983-84 to 10:1 in 1995-96.

Public School
Students Per Computer (Average)

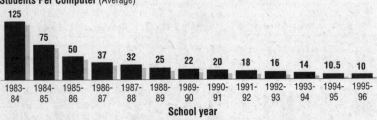

1983-84	1984-85	1985-86	1986-87	1987-88	1988-89	1989-90	1990-91	1991-92	1992-93	1993-94	1994-95	1995-96
125	75	50	37	32	25	22	20	18	16	14	10.5	10

School year

Public School
Students Per Computer by Grade Level (Average)

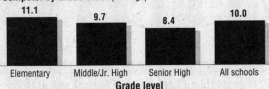

Elementary	Middle/Jr. High	Senior High	All schools
11.1	9.7	8.4	10.0

Grade level

Public School
Students Per Multimedia Capable Computer (Average)

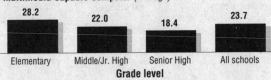

Elementary	Middle/Jr. High	Senior High	All schools
28.2	22.0	18.4	23.7

Grade level

Public Schools with CD-ROM
(Percent of schools)

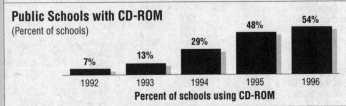

1992	1993	1994	1995	1996
7%	13%	29%	48%	54%

Percent of schools using CD-ROM

Public Schools with Online Access by Grade Level
(Percent of schools)

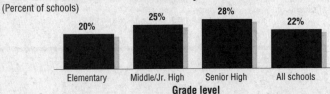

Elementary	Middle/Jr. High	Senior High	All schools
20%	25%	28%	22%

Grade level

Source: Quality Education Data

Public-School Teacher Salaries

The average U.S. public-school teacher salary rose 3% between 1994 and 1995 to $37,685, slightly ahead of the inflation rate, according to the National Education Association. Between 1985 and 1995, the average salary rose about 5% after adjusting for inflation.

Average Salaries of Public School Teachers, 1995–96

Connecticut	$50,254	Indiana	$37,677	West Virginia	$32,155
Alaska	49,620	Minnesota	36,937	Texas	32,000
New York	48,115	Vermont	36,295	South Carolina	31,622
New Jersey	47,910	Nevada	36,167	Wyoming	31,571
Pennsylvania	46,087	Hawaii	35,807	Nebraska	31,496
Michigan	44,796	New Hampshire	35,792	Alabama	31,313
District of Columbia	43,700	Colorado	35,364	Idaho	30,891
California	43,114	Kansas	35,134	Utah	30,588
Massachusetts	42,882	Virginia	35,037	North Carolina	30,411
Rhode Island	42,160	Georgia	34,087	New Mexico	29,632
Maryland	41,215	Missouri	33,341	Montana	29,364
Illinois	40,919	Florida	33,330	Arkansas	29,322
Delaware	40,533	Tennessee	33,126	Oklahoma	28,404
Oregon	39,575	Kentucky	33,080	Mississippi	27,692
Wisconsin	38,182	Maine	32,869	North Dakota	26,969
Washington	38,025	Arizona	32,484	Louisiana	26,800
Ohio	37,835	Iowa	32,372	South Dakota	26,346

Percent Change in Average Salaries of Public School Teachers, 1985–86 to 1995–96

(Constant dollars)

Connecticut	32.7%	California	4.0%
Pennsylvania	25.3	Georgia	3.9
New Hampshire	24.1	Idaho	3.5
New Jersey	23.9	South Carolina	2.9
Vermont	22.6	South Dakota	2.3
Maine	18.0	Washington	2.0
Delaware	15.7	Wisconsin	1.8
Massachusetts	13.7	Rhode Island	0.5
Kentucky	11.0	Nevada	-0.8
New York	10.9	Hawaii	-2.6
West Virginia	9.5	Colorado	-4.0
Kansas	9.0	North Carolina	-4.3
Tennessee	8.9	Utah	-4.7
Indiana	8.8	Alabama	-4.7
Ohio	8.4	Minnesota	-5.1
Oregon	8.4	New Mexico	-5.3
Maryland	8.1	Oklahoma	-6.8
Illinois	6.9	Louisiana	-7.2
Missouri	6.8	Arizona	-7.5
Virginia	6.6	District of Columbia	-7.5
Nebraska	5.7	Texas	-8.1
Arkansas	5.6	Montana	-8.2
Mississippi	5.4	North Dakota	-9.0
Florida	5.3	Alaska	-10.9
Iowa	5.0	Wyoming	-18.5
Michigan	4.7	**United States**	**5.1**

Source: National Education Association

Average Salaries for Full-time Teachers in Public and Private Elementary and Secondary Schools, 1993–94

	Public school	Private school
Elementary	$33,517	$19,977
Secondary	34,815	24,896

Source: U.S. Education Department

Earnings in Higher Education

Academic year and sex	All faculty	Professor	Associate professor	Assistant professor	All faculty	Professor	Associate professor	Assistant professor
Total	**Current dollars**				**Constant 1994–95 dollars**			
1970–71	$12,710	$17,958	$13,563	$11,176	$48,121	$67,991	$51,354	$42,315
1972–73	13,856	19,191	14,580	12,032	48,684	67,427	51,228	42,274
1974–75	15,622	21,277	16,146	13,295	45,367	61,790	46,890	38,609
1975–76	16,659	22,649	17,065	13,986	45,180	61,427	46,283	37,932
1976–77	17,560	23,792	17,905	14,662	45,002	60,971	45,884	37,575
1977–78	18,709	25,133	18,987	15,530	44,927	60,356	45,596	37,295
1978–79	19,820	26,470	20,047	16,374	43,520	58,122	44,019	35,954
1979–80	21,348	28,388	21,451	17,465	41,360	55,000	41,559	33,837
1980–81	23,302	30,753	23,214	18,901	40,460	53,397	40,307	32,818
1981–82	25,449	33,437	25,278	20,608	40,674	53,441	40,401	32,937
1982–83	27,196	35,540	26,921	22,056	41,676	54,463	41,255	33,799
1984–85	30,447	39,743	29,945	24,668	43,298	56,517	42,584	35,080
1985–86	32,392	42,268	31,787	26,277	44,773	58,423	43,936	36,320
1987–88	35,897	47,040	35,231	29,110	46,608	61,076	45,744	37,796
1989–90	40,133	52,810	39,392	32,689	47,540	62,555	46,662	38,722
1990–91	42,165	55,540	41,414	34,434	47,358	62,379	46,513	38,675
1991–92	43,851	57,433	42,929	35,745	47,722	62,503	46,718	38,901
1992–93	44,714	58,788	43,945	36,625	47,187	62,039	46,375	38,650
1993–94	46,364	60,649	45,278	37,630	47,693	62,387	46,575	38,709
1994–95*	47,811	62,709	46,713	38,756	47,811	62,709	46,713	38,756
Men								
1972–73	14,422	19,414	14,723	12,193	50,673	68,213	51,731	42,841
1974–75	16,303	21,532	16,282	13,458	47,344	62,530	47,283	39,084
1975–76	17,414	22,902	17,209	14,174	47,228	62,112	46,672	38,442
1976–77	18,378	24,029	18,055	14,851	47,096	61,578	46,270	38,059
1977–78	19,575	25,370	19,133	15,726	47,008	60,924	45,947	37,765
1978–79	20,777	26,727	20,221	16,602	45,620	58,686	44,399	36,453
1979–80	22,394	28,672	21,651	17,720	43,386	55,550	41,947	34,331
1980–81	24,499	31,082	23,451	19,227	42,538	53,968	40,718	33,384
1981–82	26,796	33,799	25,553	21,025	42,827	54,019	40,840	33,603
1982–83	28,664	35,956	27,262	22,586	43,926	55,100	41,777	34,611
1984–85	32,182	40,269	30,392	25,330	45,765	57,265	43,220	36,021
1985–86	34,294	42,833	32,273	27,094	47,402	59,204	44,608	37,450
1987–88	38,112	47,735	35,823	30,086	49,484	61,978	46,512	39,064
1989–90	42,763	53,650	40,131	33,781	50,655	63,551	47,537	40,015
1990–91	45,065	56,549	42,239	35,636	50,615	63,513	47,440	40,024
1991–92	46,848	58,494	43,814	36,969	50,983	63,657	47,682	40,232
1992–93	47,866	59,972	44,855	37,842	50,513	63,289	47,336	39,935
1993–94	49,579	61,857	46,229	38,794	51,000	63,630	47,554	39,906
1994–95*	51,228	64,046	47,705	39,923	51,228	64,046	47,705	39,923
Women								
1972–73	$11,925	$17,123	$13,827	$11,510	$41,898	$60,161	$48,581	$40,440
1974–75	13,471	19,012	15,481	12,858	39,120	55,212	44,959	37,340
1975–76	14,308	20,308	16,364	13,522	38,804	55,077	44,380	36,673
1976–77	15,100	21,536	17,189	14,225	38,695	55,189	44,050	36,455
1977–78	16,159	22,943	18,325	15,109	38,804	55,096	44,006	36,283
1978–79	17,080	24,143	19,300	15,914	37,503	53,011	42,378	34,942
1979–80	18,396	25,910	20,642	16,974	35,641	50,200	39,992	32,885
1980–81	19,996	27,959	22,295	18,302	34,719	48,546	38,711	31,778
1981–82	21,802	30,438	24,271	19,866	34,845	48,647	38,791	31,751
1982–83	23,261	32,221	25,738	21,130	35,646	49,376	39,442	32,380
1984–85	25,941	35,824	28,517	23,575	36,890	50,944	40,553	33,525
1985–86	27,576	38,252	30,300	24,966	38,116	52,872	41,881	34,508
1987–88	30,499	42,371	33,528	27,600	39,600	55,014	43,532	35,836
1989–90	34,183	47,663	37,469	31,090	40,491	56,459	44,384	36,827
1990–91	35,881	49,728	39,329	32,724	40,299	55,852	44,173	36,754
1991–92	37,534	51,621	40,766	34,063	40,847	56,178	44,364	37,070
1992–93	38,385	52,755	41,861	35,032	40,508	55,673	44,176	36,970
1993–94	40,058	54,746	43,178	36,169	41,207	56,315	44,415	37,206
1994–95*	41,369	56,555	44,626	37,352	41,369	56,555	44,626	37,352

*Preliminary data.
Source: U.S. Education Department

SAT Scorecard

Past SAT scores have been recalculated to reflect revisions in the test's 200–800 scoring scale.

Mean SAT Scores for College-Bound Seniors

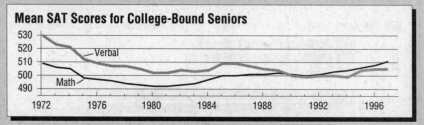

Mean SAT Scores for Males and Females

Year	Verbal			Math		
	Male	Female	Total	Male	Female	Total
1975	515	509	512	518	479	498
1980	506	498	502	515	473	492
1985	514	503	509	522	480	500
1990	505	496	500	521	483	501
1991	503	495	499	520	482	500
1992	504	496	500	521	484	501
1993	504	497	500	524	484	503
1994	501	497	499	523	487	504
1995	505	502	504	525	490	506
1996	507	503	505	527	492	508
1997	507	503	505	530	494	511

Average SAT Scores for Ethnic Groups, 1987 and 1997

Ethnic group	Verbal			Math		
	1987	1997	Difference	1987	1997	Difference
American Indian	471	475	+4	463	475	+12
Asian American	479	496	+17	541	560	+19
Black	428	434	+6	411	423	+12
Mexican American	457	451	-6	455	458	+3
Puerto Rican	436	454	+18	432	447	+15
Other Hispanic	464	466	+2	462	468	+6
White	524	526	+2	514	526	+12
Other	480	512	+32	482	514	+32
All Students	507	505	-2	501	511	+10

Source: College Board

Making the Grade

Educational Attainment by Race and Ethnicity

Completed 4 years of high school or more ■ **Completed 4 years of college or more** ▨

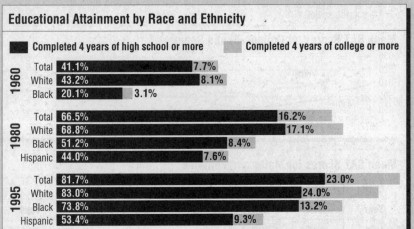

1960
- Total 41.1% / 7.7%
- White 43.2% / 8.1%
- Black 20.1% / 3.1%

1980
- Total 66.5% / 16.2%
- White 68.8% / 17.1%
- Black 51.2% / 8.4%
- Hispanic 44.0% / 7.6%

1995
- Total 81.7% / 23.0%
- White 83.0% / 24.0%
- Black 73.8% / 13.2%
- Hispanic 53.4% / 9.3%

Source: U.S. Census Bureau

Higher Education Population by Race or Ethnic Origin

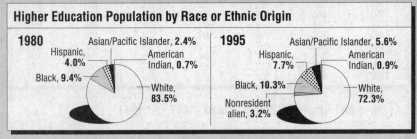

1980
- Asian/Pacific Islander, 2.4%
- American Indian, 0.7%
- Hispanic, 4.0%
- Black, 9.4%
- White, 83.5%

1995
- Asian/Pacific Islander, 5.6%
- American Indian, 0.9%
- Hispanic, 7.7%
- Black, 10.3%
- Nonresident alien, 3.2%
- White, 72.3%

Source: U.S. Department of Education

Educational Attainment by Race, Ethnicity, and Sex

Year	All races		White		Black		Hispanic	
Completed four years of high school or more	Male	Female	Male	Female	Male	Female	Male	Female
1960	39.5%	42.5%	41.6%	44.7%	18.2%	21.8%	(NA)	(NA)
1970	51.9	52.8	54.0	55.0	30.1	32.5	37.9	34.2
1980	67.3	65.8	69.6	68.1	50.8	51.5	67.3	65.8
1990	77.7	77.5	79.1	79.0	65.8	66.5	50.3	51.3
1995	81.7	81.6	83.0	83.0	73.4	74.1	52.9	53.8
Completed four years of college or more	Male	Female	Male	Female	Male	Female	Male	Female
1960	9.7%	5.8%	10.3%	6.0%	2.8%	3.3%	(NA)	(NA)
1970	13.5	8.1	14.4	8.4	4.2	4.6	7.8	4.3
1980	20.1	12.8	21.3	13.3	8.4	8.3	9.4	6.0
1990	24.4	18.4	25.3	19.0	11.9	10.8	9.8	8.7
1995	26.0	20.2	27.2	21.0	13.6	12.9	10.1	8.4

Source: U.S. Census Bureau

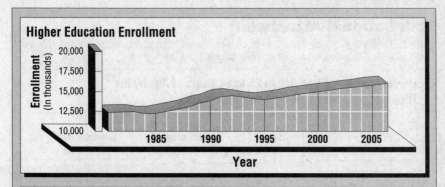

Higher Education Enrollment

(In thousands)

Year	Total	Year	Projected Total*
1985	12,247	1997	14,085
1990	13,819	2000	14,800
1995	14,262	2006	15,896
1996	13,917		

*Projections are based on data through 1994.
Source: U.S. Education Department

Educational Attainment

The U.S ranks high among major foreign countries in educational attainment, according to a study by the Organization for Economic Cooperation and Development.

Percentage of the Population 25 to 64 Years of Age by the Highest Completed Level of Education (1994)

	Secondary education	Non-university post-secondary education	University-level education
North America			
Canada	28	29	17
United States	**53**	**8**	**24**
Pacific Area			
Australia	27	10	13
New Zealand	34	14	9
European Union			
Austria	60	2	6
Belgium	27	12	10
Denmark	40	6	14
Finland	44	9	11
France	50	8	9
Germany	62	10	13
Greece	27	6	12
Ireland	27	10	9
Italy	26	–	8
Netherlands	38	–	21
Portugal	8	3	7
Spain	11	4	11
Sweden	46	14	12
United Kingdom	54	9	12
Other OECD countries			
Czech Republic	63	–	10
Norway	53	11	16
Switzerland	61	13	8
Turkey	13	–	7

Source: Organization for Economic Cooperation and Development

Total Fall Enrollment in Institutions of Higher Education by Sex and Race/Ethnic Origin

Sex and race/ethnicity of student	Number (In thousands)							% distribution					
	1976	1980	1984	1988	1990	1994	1995	1976	1980	1988	1990	1994	1995
Total	10,985.6	12,086.8	12,233.0	13,043.1	13,818.6	14,278.8	14,261.8	100.0	100.0	100.0	100.0	100.0	100.0
White, non-Hispanic	9,076.1	9,833.0	9,814.7	10,283.2	10,722.5	10,427.0	10,311.2	84.3	83.5	81.1	79.9	75.4	72.3
Total minority	1,690.8	1,948.8	2,083.8	2,398.8	2,704.7	3,395.9	3,496.2	15.7	16.5	18.9	20.1	24.6	24.5
Black, non-Hispanic	1,033.0	1,106.8	1,075.8	1,129.6	1,247.0	1,448.6	1,473.7	9.6	9.4	8.9	9.3	10.5	10.3
Hispanic	383.8	471.7	534.9	680.0	782.4	1,045.6	1,093.8	3.6	4.0	5.4	5.8	7.6	7.7
Asian or Pacific Islander	197.9	286.4	389.5	496.7	572.4	774.3	797.4	1.8	2.4	3.9	4.3	5.6	5.6
American Indian/Alaskan Native	76.1	83.9	83.6	92.5	102.8	127.4	131.3	0.7	0.7	0.7	0.8	0.9	0.9
Nonresident alien	218.7	305.0	334.6	361.2	391.5	455.9	454.4	–	–	–	–	–	–
Men	5,794.4	5,868.1	5,858.3	5,998.2	6,283.9	6,371.9	6,342.5	52.4	48.0	45.4	45.0	44.1	44.5
White, non-Hispanic	4,813.7	4,772.9	4,689.9	4,711.6	4,861.0	4,650.7	4,594.1	44.7	40.5	37.2	36.2	33.6	32.2
Total minority	826.6	884.4	937.9	1,051.3	1,176.6	1,451.7	1,484.2	7.7	7.5	8.3	8.8	10.5	10.4
Black, non-Hispanic	469.9	463.7	436.8	442.7	484.7	549.7	555.9	4.4	3.9	3.5	3.6	4.0	3.9
Hispanic	209.7	231.6	253.8	310.3	353.9	464.0	480.2	1.9	2.0	2.4	2.6	3.4	3.4
Asian or Pacific Islander	108.4	151.3	210.0	259.2	294.9	385.0	393.3	1.0	1.3	2.0	2.2	2.8	2.8
American Indian/Alaskan Native	38.5	37.8	37.4	39.1	43.1	53.0	54.8	0.4	0.3	0.3	0.3	0.4	0.4
Nonresident alien	154.1	210.8	230.4	235.3	246.3	269.5	264.3	–	–	–	–	–	–
Women	5,191.2	6,218.7	6,374.7	7,044.9	7,534.7	7,906.9	7,919.2	47.6	52.0	54.6	55.0	55.9	55.5
White, non-Hispanic	4,262.4	5,060.1	5,124.7	5,571.6	5,861.5	5,776.3	5,717.2	39.6	42.9	43.9	43.7	41.8	40.1
Total minority	864.2	1,064.4	1,145.8	1,347.4	1,528.1	1,944.2	2,012.0	8.0	9.0	10.6	11.4	14.1	14.1
Black, non-Hispanic	563.1	643.0	639.0	686.9	762.3	898.9	917.8	5.2	5.5	5.4	5.7	6.5	6.4
Hispanic	174.1	240.1	281.2	369.6	428.5	581.6	613.7	1.6	2.0	2.9	3.2	4.2	4.3
Asian or Pacific Islander	89.4	135.2	179.5	237.5	277.5	389.3	404.1	0.8	1.1	1.9	2.1	2.8	2.8
American Indian/Alaskan Native	37.6	46.1	46.1	53.4	59.7	74.4	76.5	0.3	0.4	0.4	0.4	0.5	0.5
Nonresident alien	64.6	94.2	104.1	125.9	145.2	186.4	190.1	–	–	–	–	–	–

Source: U.S. Education Department

College Costs Outlook

The worst is over.

That's the message from colleges about the steep rise in tuition and other costs. They say double-digit percentage increases are a thing of the past and the recent trend of about 5% annual growth in tuition rates is expected to continue, with even smaller boosts possible. "Anecdotal evidence is for continued moderation" in tuition price increases, says David Merkowitz, director of public affairs for the American Council on Education. According to the Consumer Price Index, college tuition rose 5.3% in 1996, a significant drop from the 12.1% increase in 1991, but still higher than the overall 3.3% increase for all goods and services.

David L. Warren, president of the National Association of Independent Colleges and Universities, believes future increases will be within a percentage point of the overall Consumer Price Index. And "where the increase is greater, there will be a good reason," he says, such as a building program or major technological upgrade.

Even with smaller increases, college costs already have reached a level that is out of reach for many people. The College Board Annual Survey of Colleges found that average costs for a student to attend college in the 1997–1998 school year ranged from $6,196 for someone living at home and commuting to a two-year college, to $21,424 for someone living on campus at a four-year private college. The costs include tuition, fees, room and board, books, transportation, and other expenses.

To try to make college more affordable, President Clinton and Congress included tuition tax credits for middle-income families and new IRAs for education in the 1997 tax bill. The credits could total up to $1,500 a year the first two years of college and up to $1,000 annually for later years. In addition, parents under certain income limits will be able to contribute up to $500 per child annually to an education IRA. Contributions won't be tax-deductible, but the earnings will be tax-free.

Stuart Ferguson

Higher Prices for Higher Education

Average Undergraduate Tuition and Fees and Room and Board Rates

Year and control of institution	Total tuition, room, and board					Tuition and required fees (in-state)				
		4-year institutions					4-year institutions			
	All institutions	All 4-year	Universities	Other 4-year	2-year	All institutions	All 4-year	Universities	Other 4-year	2-year
All institutions										
1976–77	$2,275	$2,577	$2,647	$2,527	$1,598	$924	$1,218	$1,210	$1,223	$346
1977–78	2,411	2,725	2,777	2,685	1,703	984	1,291	1,269	1,305	378
1978–79	2,587	2,917	2,967	2,879	1,828	1,073	1,397	1,370	1,413	411
1979–80	2,809	3,167	3,223	3,124	1,979	1,163	1,513	1,484	1,530	451
1980–81	3,101	3,499	3,535	3,469	2,230	1,289	1,679	1,634	1,705	526
1981–82	3,489	3,951	4,005	3,908	2,476	1,457	1,907	1,860	1,935	590
1982–83	3,877	4,406	4,466	4,356	2,713	1,626	2,139	2,081	2,173	675
1983–84	4,167	4,747	4,793	4,712	2,854	1,783	2,344	2,300	2,368	730
1984–85	4,563	5,160	5,236	5,107	3,179	1,985	2,567	2,539	2,583	821
1985–86*	4,885	5,504	5,597	5,441	3,367	2,181	2,784	2,770	2,793	888
1986–87**	5,206	5,964	6,124	5,857	3,295	2,312	3,042	3,042	3,042	897
1987–88	5,494	6,272	6,339	6,226	3,263	2,458	3,201	3,168	3,220	809
1988–89	5,869	6,725	6,801	6,673	3,573	2,658	3,472	3,422	3,499	979
1989–90	6,207	7,212	7,347	7,120	3,705	2,839	3,800	3,765	3,819	978
1990–91	6,562	7,602	7,709	7,528	3,930	3,016	4,009	3,958	4,036	1,087
1991–92	7,074	8,252	8,389	8,164	4,089	3,282	4,399	4,366	4,417	1,186
1992–93	7,452	8,758	8,934	8,648	4,207	3,517	4,752	4,665	4,795	1,276
1993–94	7,931	9,296	9,495	9,186	4,449	3,827	5,119	5,104	5,127	1,399
1994–95	8,306	9,728	9,863	9,646	4,633	4,044	5,391	5,287	5,441	1,488
1995–96+	8,774	10,315	10,551	10,177	4,730	4,312	5,771	5,725	5,794	1,518

Year and control of institution	Total tuition, room, and board				Tuition and required fees				
		4-year institutions				4-year institutions			
	All insti-tutions	All 4-year	Univer-sities	Other 4-year	2-year	All insti-tutions	All 4-year	Univer-sities	Other 4-year	2-year

Year and control of institution	All insti-tutions	All 4-year	Univer-sities	Other 4-year	2-year	All insti-tutions	All 4-year	Univer-sities	Other 4-year	2-year
Public institutions										
1964–65	$950	–	$1,051	$867	$638	$243	–	$298	$224	$99
1965–66	983	–	1,105	904	670	257	–	327	241	109
1966–67	1,026	–	1,171	947	710	275	–	360	259	121
1967–68	1,064	–	1,199	997	789	283	–	366	268	144
1968–69	1,117	–	1,245	1,063	883	295	–	377	281	170
1969–70	1,203	–	1,362	1,135	951	323	–	427	306	178
1970–71	1,287	–	1,477	1,206	998	351	–	478	332	187
1971–72	1,357	–	1,579	1,263	1,073	376	–	526	354	192
1972–73	1,458	–	1,668	1,460	1,197	407	–	566	455	233
1973–74	1,517	–	1,707	1,506	1,274	438	–	581	463	274
1974–75	1,563	–	1,760	1,558	1,339	432	–	599	448	277
1975–76	1,666	–	1,935	1,657	1,386	433	–	642	469	245
1976–77	1,789	$1,935	2,067	1,827	1,491	479	$617	689	564	283
1977–78	1,888	2,038	2,170	1,931	1,590	512	655	736	596	306
1978–79	1,994	2,145	2,289	2,027	1,691	543	688	777	622	327
1979–80	2,165	2,327	2,487	2,198	1,822	583	738	840	662	355
1980–81	2,373	2,550	2,712	2,421	2,027	635	804	915	722	391
1981–82	2,663	2,871	3,079	2,705	2,224	714	909	1,042	813	434
1982–83	2,945	3,196	3,403	3,032	2,390	798	1,031	1,164	936	473
1983–84	3,156	3,433	3,628	3,285	2,534	891	1,148	1,284	1,052	528
1984–85	3,408	3,682	3,899	3,518	2,807	971	1,228	1,386	1,117	584
1985–86*	3,571	3,859	4,146	3,637	2,981	1,045	1,318	1,536	1,157	641
1986–87**	3,805	4,138	4,469	3,891	2,989	1,106	1,414	1,651	1,248	660
1987–88	4,050	4,403	4,619	4,250	3,066	1,218	1,537	1,726	1,407	706
1988–89	4,274	4,678	4,905	4,526	3,183	1,285	1,646	1,846	1,515	730
1989–90	4,504	4,975	5,324	4,723	3,299	1,356	1,780	2,035	1,608	756
1990–91	4,757	5,243	5,585	5,004	3,467	1,454	1,888	2,159	1,707	824
1991–92	5,135	5,695	6,051	5,459	3,623	1,624	2,119	2,410	1,933	937
1992–93	5,379	6,020	6,442	5,740	3,799	1,782	2,349	2,604	2,192	1,025
1993–94	5,694	6,365	6,710	6,146	3,996	1,942	2,537	2,820	2,360	1,125
1994–95	5,965	6,670	7,077	6,409	4,137	2,057	2,681	2,977	2,499	1,192
1995–96†	6,252	7,013	7,451	6,727	4,236	2,176	2,848	3,151	2,661	1,245
Private institutions										
1964–65	$1,907	–	$2,202	$1,810	$1,455	$1,088	–	$1,297	$1,023	$702
1965–66	2,005	–	2,316	1,899	1,557	1,154	–	1,369	1,086	768
1966–67	2,124	–	2,456	2,007	1,679	1,233	–	1,456	1,162	845
1967–68	2,205	–	2,545	2,104	1,762	1,297	–	1,534	1,237	892
1968–69	2,321	–	2,673	2,237	1,876	1,383	–	1,638	1,335	956
1969–70	2,530	–	2,920	2,420	1,993	1,533	–	1,809	1,468	1,034
1970–71	2,738	–	3,163	2,599	2,103	1,684	–	1,980	1,603	1,109
1971–72	2,917	–	3,375	2,748	2,186	1,820	–	2,133	1,721	1,172
1972–73	3,038	–	3,512	2,934	2,273	1,898	–	2,226	1,846	1,221
1973–74	3,164	–	3,717	3,040	2,410	1,989	–	2,375	1,925	1,303
1974–75	3,403	–	4,076	3,156	2,591	2,117	–	2,614	1,954	1,367
1975–76	3,663	–	4,467	3,385	2,711	2,272	–	2,881	2,084	1,427
1976–77	3,906	$3,977	4,715	3,714	2,971	2,467	$2,534	3,051	2,351	1,592
1977–78	4,158	4,240	5,033	1,967	3,148	2,624	2,700	3,240	2,520	1,706
1978–79	4,514	4,609	5,403	4,327	3,389	2,867	2,958	3,487	2,771	1,831
1979–80	4,912	5,013	5,891	4,700	3,751	3,130	3,225	3,811	3,020	2,062
1980–81	5,470	5,594	6,569	5,249	4,303	3,498	3,617	4,275	3,390	2,413
1981–82	6,166	6,330	7,443	5,947	4,746	3,953	4,113	4,887	3,853	2,605
1982–83	6,920	7,126	8,536	6,646	5,364	4,439	4,639	5,583	4,329	3,008
1983–84	7,508	7,759	9,308	7,244	5,571	4,851	5,093	6,217	4,726	3,099
1984–85	8,202	8,451	10,243	7,849	6,203	5,315	5,556	6,843	5,135	3,485
1985–86*	8,885	9,228	11,034	8,551	6,512	5,789	6,121	7,374	5,641	3,672
1986–87**	9,676	10,039	12,278	9,276	6,384	6,316	6,658	8,118	6,171	3,684
1987–88	10,512	10,659	13,075	9,854	7,078	6,988	7,116	8,771	6,574	4,161
1988–89	11,189	11,474	14,073	10,620	7,967	7,461	7,722	9,451	7,172	4,817
1989–90	12,018	12,284	15,098	11,374	8,670	8,147	8,396	10,348	7,778	5,196
1990–91	12,910	13,237	16,503	12,220	9,302	8,772	9,083	11,379	8,389	5,570
1991–92	13,907	14,273	17,779	13,189	9,631	9,434	9,775	12,192	9,053	5,752
1992–93	14,634	15,009	18,898	13,882	9,903	9,942	10,294	13,055	9,533	6,059
1993–94	15,496	15,904	20,097	14,640	10,406	10,572	10,952	13,874	10,100	6,370
1994–95	16,207	16,602	21,041	15,363	11,170	11,111	11,481	14,537	10,653	6,914
1995–96†	17,207	17,613	22,470	16,203	11,502	11,858	12,239	15,581	11,294	7,039

Year and control of institution	Dormitory rooms					Board (7-day basis)				
	All insti-tutions	4-year institutions				All insti-tutions	4-year institutions			
		All 4-year	Univer-sities	Other 4-year	2-year		All 4-year	Univer-sities	Other 4-year	2-year
All institutions										
1976–77	$603	$611	$649	$584	$503	$748	$748	$788	$719	$750
1977–78	645	654	691	628	525	781	780	818	752	801
1978–79	688	696	737	667	575	826	825	860	800	842
1979–80	751	759	803	729	628	895	895	936	865	900
1980–81	836	846	881	821	705	976	975	1,020	943	1,000
1981–82	950	961	1,023	919	793	1,083	1,082	1,121	1,055	1,094
1982–83	1,064	1,078	1,150	1,028	873	1,187	1,189	1,235	1,155	1,165
1983–84	1,145	1,162	1,211	1,130	916	1,239	1,242	1,282	1,214	1,208
1984–85	1,267	1,282	1,343	1,242	1,058	1,310	1,311	1,353	1,282	1,301
1985–86*	1,338	1,355	1,424	1,309	1,107	1,356	1,365	1,403	1,339	1,372
1986–87**	1,405	1,427	1,501	1,376	1,034	1,489	1,495	1,581	1,439	1,364
1987–88	1,488	1,516	1,576	1,478	1,017	1,549	1,555	1,596	1,529	1,437
1988–89	1,575	1,609	1,665	1,573	1,085	1,636	1,644	1,715	1,601	1,509
1989–90	1,638	1,675	1,732	1,638	1,105	1,730	1,737	1,850	1,663	1,622
1990–91	1,743	1,782	1,848	1,740	1,182	1,802	1,811	1,903	1,751	1,660
1991–92	1,874	1,921	1,998	1,874	1,210	1,918	1,931	2,026	1,873	1,692
1992–93	1,939	1,991	2,104	1,926	1,240	1,996	2,015	2,165	1,927	1,692
1993–94	2,057	2,111	2,190	2,068	1,332	2,047	2,067	2,201	1,992	1,718
1994–95	2,145	2,200	2,281	2,155	1,396	2,116	2,138	2,295	2,049	1,750
1995–96+	2,263	2,317	2,423	2,259	1,476	2,199	2,226	2,404	2,124	1,735
Public institutions										
1964–65	$271	–	$291	$241	$178	$436	–	$462	$402	$361
1965–66	281	–	304	255	194	445	–	474	408	367
1966–67	294	–	321	271	213	457	–	490	417	376
1967–68	313	–	337	292	243	468	–	496	437	402
1968–69	337	–	359	318	278	485	–	509	464	435
1969–70	369	–	395	346	308	511	–	540	483	465
1970–71	401	–	431	375	338	535	–	568	499	473
1971–72	430	–	463	400	366	551	–	590	509	515
1972–73	476	–	500	455	398	575	–	602	550	566
1973–74	480	–	505	464	409	599	–	621	579	591
1974–75	506	–	527	497	424	625	–	634	613	638
1975–76	544	–	573	533	442	689	–	720	655	699
1976–77	582	$592	614	572	465	728	$727	763	692	742
1977–78	621	631	649	616	486	755	752	785	720	797
1978–79	655	664	689	641	527	796	793	823	764	837
1979–80	715	725	750	703	574	867	865	898	833	893
1980–81	799	811	827	796	642	940	936	969	904	994
1981–82	909	925	970	885	703	1,039	1,036	1,067	1,006	1,086
1982–83	1,010	1,030	1,072	993	755	1,136	1,134	1,167	1,103	1,162
1983–84	1,087	1,110	1,131	1,092	801	1,178	1,175	1,213	1,141	1,205
1984–85	1,196	1,217	1,237	1,200	921	1,241	1,237	1,276	1,201	1,302
1985–86*	1,242	1,263	1,290	1,240	960	1,285	1,278	1,320	1,240	1,380
1986–87**	1,301	1,323	1,355	1,295	979	1,398	1,401	1,464	1,348	1,349
1987–88	1,378	1,410	1,410	1,409	943	1,454	1,456	1,482	1,434	1,417
1988–89	1,457	1,496	1,483	1,506	965	1,533	1,536	1,576	1,504	1,488
1989–90	1,513	1,557	1,561	1,554	962	1,635	1,638	1,728	1,561	1,581
1990–91	1,612	1,657	1,658	1,655	1,050	1,691	1,698	1,767	1,641	1,594
1991–92	1,731	1,785	1,789	1,782	1,074	1,780	1,792	1,852	1,745	1,612
1992–93	1,756	1,816	1,856	1,787	1,106	1,841	1,854	1,982	1,761	1,668
1993–94	1,873	1,934	1,897	1,958	1,190	1,880	1,895	1,993	1,828	1,681
1994–95	1,959	2,023	1,992	2,044	1,232	1,949	1,967	2,108	1,866	1,712
1995–96†	2,057	2,121	2,107	2,130	1,303	2,019	2,045	2,193	1,936	1,688

Year and control of institution	Dormitory rooms					Board (7-day basis)				
	All insti-tutions	4-year institutions			2-year	All insti-tutions	4-year institutions			2-year
		All 4-year	Univer-sities	Other 4-year			All 4-year	Univer-sities	Other 4-year	
Private institutions										
1964–65	$331	–	$390	$308	$289	$488	–	$515	$479	$464
1965–66	356	–	418	330	316	495	–	529	483	473
1966–67	385	–	452	355	347	506	–	548	490	487
1967–68	392	–	455	366	366	516	–	556	501	504
1968–69	404	–	463	382	391	534	–	572	520	529
1969–70	436	–	503	409	413	561	–	608	543	546
1970–71	468	–	542	434	434	586	–	641	562	560
1971–72	494	–	576	454	449	603	–	666	573	565
1972–73	524	–	622	490	457	616	–	664	598	595
1973–74	533	–	622	502	483	642	–	720	613	624
1974–75	586	–	691	536	564	700	–	771	666	660
1975–76	636	–	753	583	572	755	–	833	718	712
1976–77	649	$651	783	604	607	790	$791	882	759	772
1977–78	698	702	850	648	631	836	838	943	800	811
1978–79	758	761	916	704	700	889	890	1,000	851	858
1979–80	827	831	1,001	768	766	955	957	1,078	912	923
1980–81	918	921	1,086	859	871	1,054	1,056	1,209	1,000	1,019
1981–82	1,038	1,039	1,229	970	1,022	1,175	1,178	1,327	1,124	1,119
1982–83	1,181	1,181	1,453	1,083	1,177	1,300	1,306	1,501	1,234	1,179
1983–84	1,278	1,279	1,531	1,191	1,253	1,380	1,387	1,559	1,327	1,219
1984–85	1,426	1,426	1,753	1,309	1,424	1,462	1,469	1,647	1,405	1,294
1985–86*	1,553	1,557	1,940	1,420	1,500	1,542	1,551	1,720	1,490	1,340
1986–87**	1,658	1,673	2,097	1,518	1,266	1,702	1,708	2,063	1,587	1,434
1987–88	1,748	1,760	2,244	1,593	1,380	1,775	1,783	2,060	1,687	1,537
1988–89	1,849	1,863	2,353	1,686	1,540	1,880	1,889	2,269	1,762	1,609
1989–90	1,923	1,935	2,411	1,774	1,663	1,948	1,953	2,339	1,823	1,811
1990–91	2,063	2,077	2,654	1,889	1,744	2,074	2,077	2,470	1,943	1,989
1991–92	2,221	2,241	2,860	2,038	1,789	2,252	2,257	2,727	2,098	2,090
1992–93	2,348	2,362	3,018	2,151	1,970	2,344	2,354	2,825	2,197	1,875
1993–94	2,490	2,506	3,277	2,261	2,067	2,434	2,445	2,946	2,278	1,970
1994–95	2,587	2,601	3,469	2,347	2,233	2,509	2,520	3,035	2,362	2,023
1995–96†	2,739	2,753	3,672	2,475	2,363	2,610	2,622	3,216	2,434	2,100

*Room and board data are estimated.
**Because of revisions in data collection procedures, figures are not entirely comparable with those for previous years.
†Preliminary data.
Source: U.S. Education Department

Academic Aid

Total financial aid for college students continues to increase, but the federal share has shifted more to loans in recent years.

Aid Awarded to Postsecondary Students in Constant 1995 Dollars (In millions)

	Academic Year						
	1963-64	1970-71	1975-76	1980-81	1985-86	1990-91	1995-96
Total Federal Aid	1,142	12,886	23,787	25,272	22,272	24,116	36,859
State Grant Programs	277	905	1,346	1,409	1,836	2,115	2,980
Institutional and Other Grants	1,332	3,210	3,211	2,858	4,149	6,552	9,828
Total Federal, State, and Institutional Aid	2,752	17,002	28,345	29,539	28,258	32,783	49,667

The Shifting Balance of Federal Student Aid, 1975 to 1995

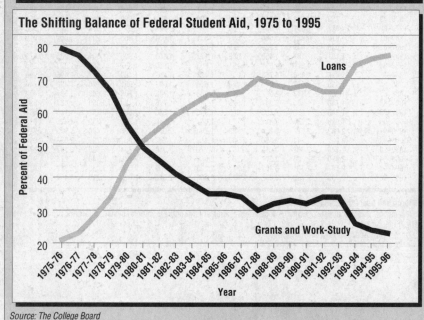

Source: The College Board

100 Largest Four-Year Colleges, Ranked by Undergraduate and Graduate Student Enrollment

Name and campus	State	Total 1995 enrollment	1996-97 undergrad tuition and fees
University of Texas, Austin	Texas	48,776	$2,754
Ohio State University, Columbus	Ohio	45,969	3,468
Texas A&M University	Texas	43,223	2,361
Penn State University, University Park	Pennsylvania	38,992	5,624
Arizona State University	Arizona	38,783	2,009
University of Florida	Florida	38,686	1,795
Michigan State University	Michigan	37,865	4,921
University of Illinois, Urbana	Illinois	36,465	4,186
University of Wisconsin, Madison	Wisconsin	36,045	3,030
Purdue University	Indiana	33,602	3,208
University of Michigan	Michigan	33,125	5,710
University of California, Los Angeles	California	33,071	4,007
University of Washington	Washington	33,021	3,136
University of Minnesota, Twin Cities	Minnesota	32,828	4,099
Indiana University, Bloomington	Indiana	32,525	3,683
University of Arizona	Arizona	32,510	2,009
San Diego State University	California	31,326	1,902
New York University	New York	30,893	20,756
University of Maryland, College Park	Maryland	30,646	4,169
Wayne State University	Michigan	30,450	3,255
Brigham Young University	Utah	30,378	2,530
University of South Florida	Florida	30,196	1,961
University of California, Berkeley	California	29,630	4,355
Florida State University	Florida	28,835	1,882
University of Georgia	Georgia	28,722	2,688
University of Houston	Texas	27,883	1,726
University of Southern California	California	26,887	19,516
North Carolina State University	North Carolina	26,829	2,162
Cal State University, Fullerton	California	26,566	1,928
Western Michigan University	Michigan	26,540	3,332
University of Iowa	Iowa	26,386	2,646
Florida International University	Florida	26,352	1,875
University of Tennessee, Knoxville	Tennessee	26,085	2,220
San Francisco State University	California	26,043	1,982
University of Utah	Utah	26,025	2,514
San Jose State University	California	25,997	1,942
Louisiana State University A&M	Louisiana	25,594	2,663
Kent State University	Ohio	25,364	4,288
Temple University	Pennsylvania	25,291	5,828
California State University, Northridge	California	25,015	1,970
California State University, Long Beach	California	24,723	1,816
University of Central Florida	Florida	24,603	1,924
University of Kansas	Kansas	24,535	2,310
University of Colorado, Boulder	Colorado	24,443	2,834
Virginia Tech	Virginia	24,406	4,131
Iowa State University	Iowa	24,271	2,666
Georgia State University	Georgia	24,236	2,388
University of North Texas	Texas	24,121	2,044
University of South Carolina	South Carolina	24,081	3,432
University of Akron	Ohio	23,709	3,486
Boston University	Massachusetts	23,623	20,864
University of Pittsburgh	Pennsylvania	23,610	5,870
Texas Tech University	Texas	23,562	2,326
University of Nebraska, Lincoln	Nebraska	23,341	2,638

Name and campus	State	Total 1995 enrollment	1996-97 undergrad tuition and fees
Eastern Michigan University	Michigan	23,142	3,300
University of Texas, Arlington	Texas	23,036	2,170
University of Massachusetts, Amherst	Massachusetts	22,916	5,413
University of Kentucky	Kentucky	22,509	2,676
University of Wisconsin, Milwaukee	Wisconsin	22,342	3,100
Indiana University/Purdue University, Indianapolis	Indiana	22,335	3,301
SUNY, Buffalo	New York	22,197	4,190
Auburn University	Alabama	22,101	2,355
University of Illinois, Chicago	Illinois	21,635	4,194
Colorado State University	Colorado	21,543	2,855
California State University, Sacramento	California	21,445	1,950
University of Toledo	Ohio	21,278	3,778
University of North Carolina, Chapel Hill	North Carolina	21,248	2,110
Southern Illinois University, Carbondale	Illinois	20,979	3,522
University of New Mexico	New Mexico	20,905	2,071
University of California, Davis	California	20,842	4,230
University of Missouri, Columbia	Missouri	20,764	4,121
Northern Illinois University	Illinois	20,490	3,948
Kansas State University	Kansas	20,476	2,373
Southwest Texas State University	Texas	20,202	2,388
University of Oklahoma	Oklahoma	19,995	2,216
University of Nevada, Las Vegas	Nevada	19,865	1,920
Utah State University	Utah	19,861	2,088
University of Cincinnati	Ohio	19,671	4,152
George Mason University	Virginia	19,627	4,248
Regents College	New York	19,428	595
West Virginia University	West Virginia	19,141	2,262
Ball State University	Indiana	19,115	3,286
Washington State University	Washington	19,105	3,136
Northern Arizona University	Arizona	18,937	2,009
University of Puerto Rico, Rio Piedras	Puerto Rico	18,738	970
Ohio University	Ohio	18,724	4,080
University of Louisville	Kentucky	18,724	2,570
Illinois State University	Illinois	18,714	3,720
University of Memphis	Tennessee	18,436	2,180
University of California, Santa Barbara	California	18,213	4,098
California State University, Los Angeles	California	18,170	1,758
Cornell University	New York	18,048	20,974
University of Alabama	Alabama	17,930	2,470
University of Hawaii, Manoa	Hawaii	17,858	2,422
University of Delaware	Delaware	17,771	4,475
Eastern Kentucky University	Kentucky	17,729	1,970
Oklahoma State University	Oklahoma	17,714	2,038
CUNY Queens College	New York	17,522	3,393
Middle Tennessee State University	Tennessee	17,424	2,012
University of Texas, San Antonio	Texas	17,389	2,392

Source: College Entrance Examination Board

Top College Endowment Funds

Colleges and Universities Ranked by June 30, 1996, Market Value of Endowment Assets (In thousands)

	Institution	Endowment assets as of 6/30/96
1	Harvard University	$8,811,785
2	University of Texas System	5,697,150
3	Yale University	4,853,010
4	Princeton University	4,467,000
5	Stanford University	3,779,420
6	Emory University	3,013,112
7	University of California	2,572,492
8	Columbia University	2,558,090
9	Massachusetts Institute of Technology	2,476,630
10	The Texas A&M University System and Foundations	2,458,043
11	Washington University	2,305,686
12	University of Pennsylvania	2,108,961
13	Rice University	1,850,312
14	Cornell University	1,829,185
15	Northwestern University	1,763,000
16	University of Chicago	1,675,559
17	University of Michigan	1,624,349
18	University of Notre Dame	1,227,256
19	Dartmouth College	1,082,934
20	University of Southern California	1,022,339

Source: Survey by National Association of College & University Business Officers

The Value of Education

Median Weekly Earnings of Full-time Wage and Salary Workers 25 Years and Over, by Educational Attainment

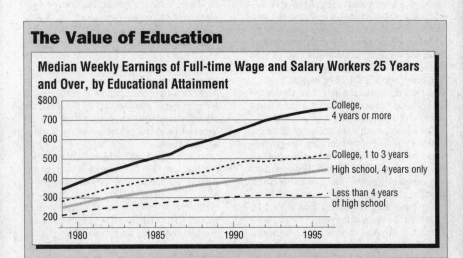

Year	Less than 4 years of high school*	High school, 4 years only*	College, 1 to 3 years*	College, 4 years or more*
1980	$222	$266	$304	$376
1982	248	302	351	438
1984	263	323	382	486
1986	278	344	409	525
1988	288	368	430	585
1990	304	386	476	639
1992	312	404	485	697
1994	307	421	499	733
1995	309	432	508	747
1996	317	443	518	758

*Since 1992, data on educational attainment have been based on the "highest diploma or degree received" rather than the "number of years of school completed." Data for 1994 and beyond are not directly comparable with data from earlier years.
Source: U.S. Bureau of Labor Statistics

THE JUSTICE SYSTEM

If nothing else, the American legal system has always been a source of good theater.

Take a suit filed in 1997 against the producers of the Broadway musical *Cats*. It began when a cast member pulled an unemployed office worker from her orchestra seat during a performance and tried to get her to dance. The result was a $12 million lawsuit for emotional distress, which when it hit the newspapers, was panned by critics as the latest example of American litigiousness.

But what do such suits really say about the justice system? For two decades, the conventional wisdom has been that justice operates like a game of Trivial Pursuit. Huge verdicts are common. People file gratuitous suits. Lawyers clean up.

Yet the reality is that few people, in fact, can afford the costs of lawyers these days. As a result, a growing number aren't bothering to go to court even if they have legitimate gripes. Half of all people in households with incomes of up to $60,000 have reason to seek out a lawyer each year but usually don't, in part because of the cost involved, says the American Bar Association.

Some people attempt to handle disputes on their own without a lawyer. But "they cannot effectively represent themselves," says Alan Houseman, the director of the Washington, D.C.–based Center for Law and Social Policy, an advocacy group. "People with real needs who may have just causes are unable to participate in the system." These days, it's more likely that the public will be represented by proxy in huge "class action" suits, where the plaintiffs may end up getting coupons for boxes of breakfast cereal, while the lawyers feast on steak.

So, this is the paradox of the justice system on the eve of the twenty-first century.—a projected million by the year 2000—the system is increasingly out of reach for most people. "The complaints of litigiousness and overuse of the legal system are really missing what are more fundamental problems," says Deborah Rhode, a legal ethics specialist at Stanford Law School. A large "percentage of the population is priced out of the system. Litigation has become a sort of spectator sport for that group. They simply don't have a realistic option for justice on the terms we are currently providing."

The price of admission can certainly be steep. In Texas, for example, the typical general practice lawyer charges about $150 an hour, a state bar survey shows. Figuring in every phone call, letter, and court appearance, and the possibility of a lengthy appeal, the fees add up in a hurry.

In California, "you can't do a contested case of any size with lawyers involved for less than $25,000," says Ralph Warner, co-founder of Nolo Press, a Berkeley, Calif., firm that publishes do-it-yourself wills and other self-help legal materials. Some of the most common legal problems, such as divorces, can take on a life of their own. "That is why people come away hating the legal system," he adds.

Personal-injury lawyers usually charge a percentage of anything they recover, which is supposed to make the system more accessible to people who can't afford big upfront fees. But those lawyers often end up turning away potential clients because they deem the work too risky or not lucrative enough. Lawyers who advertise on television, for example, reject up to 90% of the calls they receive, says Herbert Kritzer, professor at the University of Wisconsin.

If justice has become a bad joke for average citizens, it is even worse for the poor. Most criminal defendants, of course, cannot afford the dream team of O. J. Simpson fame; in a growing number of cases, they are lucky to afford a team at all. Recent cuts in the budget of the federally funded Legal Services Corp., which was set up to help families at or below the poverty line with everyday legal problems, left the program with fewer than half the lawyers it had in its 1981 peak year.

In murder cases, notwithstanding the Simpson case and Oklahoma City bombing trials, lawyers are also doing a disappearing act, reflecting cuts in federal assistance and new limits on post-conviction appeals. And funding cuts for lawyers for death-row inmates have had the desired effect of quickening the pace of executions, which at mid-year 1997 were headed for a record in any year since the Supreme Court restored capital punishment in 1976.

"Interest in making sure that people are not wrongly sentenced or wrongly executed seems to be at an all-time low," asserts Bryan Stevenson, director of the Equal Justice Initiative, a Montgomery, Ala., nonprofit firm that represents death-row inmates. Court-appointed lawyers in capital cases in Alabama are currently paid $1,000 per trial; Mr. Stevenson says the system doesn't attract very many qualified lawyers, although the proceedings tend to have the advantage of being short and predictable. "People get the death penalty not for committing the worst crime but for getting the worst lawyer," he adds.

Besides cost barriers, the public also is finding itself more constrained in what it can sue for, as corporate-sponsored "tort reform" initiatives sail through state legislatures. Starting in January, for example, people in Ohio began facing tough new limits on what they can recover for the "pain and suffering" caused by accidents, as well as restrictions on the time they have to bring suits against negligent doctors and manufacturers of defective products.

So-called frivolous suits against businesses are getting the boot, meanwhile, including a high school biology teacher's attempt to hold the perfume industry accountable for sinus and brain damage. Judges are being much more aggressive about dismissing such suits before they get to juries, meaning the *Cats* suit could have a short run. Certainly, the dairy industry is highly confident about a suit filed against it in Seattle federal court in May 1997 by a man who claimed that a lifetime of drinking whole milk contributed to his clogged arteries and a minor stroke.

The irony is that while pushing for tort reform, business itself has been using the courts more than ever. Legal expenditures by business have grown much more rapidly than those by individuals in recent years, to the point where they now account for more than half of lawyers' income, a reversal from the 1960s and 1970s, Census Bureau statistics show.

Damage awards may be getting out of hand, but the biggest are tending to involve business as plaintiffs rather than defendants. Recently, a funeral home operator in Mississippi won a $500 million judgment in an unfair competition suit against a Canadian firm; it was more than twice as large as the highest won in a personal-injury case in 1996, according to Jury Verdict Research, a Horsham, Pa., research firm. Among the biggest of 1997 is a $125 million verdict handed down by a Colorado jury in April over a cable-television deal gone bad.

While consumers are filing more class-action suits, most have the look of being cooked up by enterprising lawyers. Who else would think of filing suit against computer makers for deceiving people over the size of monitors they buy, as did a group of about 40 law firms, which proposed a settlement under which they would pocket a $5.8 million fee while consumers would receive a cash rebate of $13 each. Meanwhile, a group of lawyers settled a case with General Motors Corp. over some trucks with supposedly defective gas tanks on terms that give the vehicle owners coupons that most probably will never use—and the lawyers $24 million. Another lawyer group went a step further, settling a suit on behalf of some customers of a Boston bank, some of whom actually lost money in a settlement over mortgage escrow accounts.

Defendants have been catching on and even initiating cozy deals in some cases, turning the whole concept of the class-action, which was set up to give some leverage to the common man, on its head. The tobacco industry settlement talks in 1997 are symptomatic of how companies are trying to use large class-action suits to resolve legal problems and protect themselves from punitive damages, which are supposed to deter wrongful conduct. That corporate strategy is being tested in other cases from arsenic poisoning to wood siding. "You dump it all, and pay some lawyers off," says Susan Koniak, a professor at Boston University's law school, who believes companies are finding a neat solution to their liability woes using the class action.

Is there any hope? There are, in fact, a few who still soldier on in the public interest. Lawrence Schonbrun, a retired Berkeley, Calif., legal-services lawyer, has been flying around the country in an effort to challenge what he views as abusive class-action fees. A

Washington, D.C., firm known as HALT is celebrating its 20th anniversary of trying to push bar associations into letting nonlawyers offer certain limited legal services, such as drafting wills.

On the other hand, Mr. Schonbrun was himself attacked in court by the lawyers he goes after on the theory that he was drumming up specious litigation, and HALT's membership is less than half its peak of 150,000 a decade ago, with its mission still unaccomplished. "Nobody has done anything, anywhere," says William Fry, executive director.

Some private lawyers are trying to pick up the slack, adopting poor neighborhoods for free to help them with community legal problems; some courts are trying to make themselves user-friendly, opening self-serve kiosks where people file divorces just as they deposit money in an automatic cash machine. But the performance is spotty.

In a promising move, Congress got into the act in 1990 with the "Civil Justice Reform Act," in the hope of speeding up the flow of cases through the federal system by encouraging arbitration and other cost-saving measures. In 1997, the verdict came in, in an analysis done by Rand Corp., a Santa Monica, Calif., think tank, which found that the act was largely ineffectual because judges were ignoring its mandates or lawyers were continuing to run up the hours.

"For those who hoped that passing the CJRA statute would bring about substantial change in the federal courts, the results . . . may be disappointing," the researchers concluded, adding that the experience provided much food for thought. "The next step . . . is to engage with the bench, the bar, and other experts in what will surely be an extended and spirited discussion."

Meanwhile, sit back and enjoy the show.

Richard B. Schmitt, *Wall Street Journal* staff reporter

The Cost of Crime

Justice System Expenditures in the U.S.
(In billions of dollars)

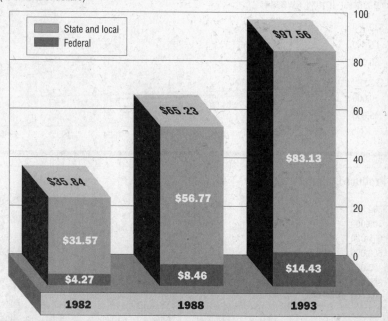

State and local
Federal

	1982	1988	1993
Total	$35.84	$65.23	$97.56
State and local	$31.57	$56.77	$83.13
Federal	$4.27	$8.46	$14.43

Justice System Expenditures by Level of Government and Type of Activity
(In millions of dollars)

Fiscal year	Total justice system	Level of government*		Type of activity		
		Federal	State and local	Police protection	Judicial and legal	Corrections
1982	$35,842	$4,269	$31,573	$19,022	$7,771	$9,049
1983	39,680	4,844	34,836	20,648	8,621	10,411
1984	43,943	5,787	38,156	22,686	9,463	11,794
1985	48,563	6,279	42,284	24,399	10,629	13,535
1986	53,500	6,430	47,070	26,255	11,485	15,759
1987	58,871	7,231	51,640	28,768	12,555	17,549
1988	65,231	8,464	56,767	30,961	13,971	20,299
1989	70,949	9,204	61,745	32,794	15,589	22,567
1990	79,434	10,219	69,215	35,923	17,357	26,154
1991	87,567	12,106	75,461	38,971	19,298	29,297
1992	93,777	13,529	80,248	41,327	20,989	31,461
1993	97,556	14,429	83,127	44,007	21,575	31,974

*Data show direct expenditures by level of government and do not include duplicated intergovernmental expenditures.
Source: U.S. Justice Department

Personal-Injury Verdicts

The median compensatory award for all types of personal-injury claims and the median award for product-liability cases:

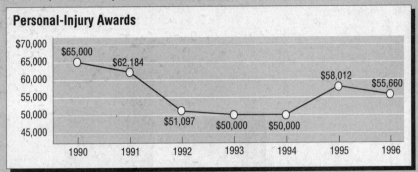

Personal-Injury Awards

$65,000 — 1990
$62,184 — 1991
$51,097 — 1992
$50,000 — 1993
$50,000 — 1994
$58,012 — 1995
$55,660 — 1996

Product-Liability Awards

$300,000 — 1990
$468,139 — 1991
$420,621 — 1992
$500,600 — 1993
$401,328 — 1994
$536,149 — 1995
$773,500 — 1996

Source: Jury Verdict Research, Horsham, PA

Federal Court Caseload

The number of cases filed increased throughout the federal judiciary in 1996, with the number of appeals and the number of bankruptcy petitions reaching all-time highs. Civil appeals grew primarily because of increases in prisoner petitions and employment civil rights cases, while criminal appeals were spurred by cases involving fraud and drugs.

Judicial caseload	Fiscal years			
	1991	1994	1995	1996
U.S. Courts of Appeals*				
Cases filed	43,027	48,322	50,072	51,991
Cases terminated	41,640	49,184	49,805	50,413
Cases pending	33,428	37,269	37,310	38,888
U.S. District Courts				
Civil				
Cases filed	210,890	236,391	248,335	269,132
Cases terminated	220,262	228,361	229,820	250,387
Cases pending	226,234	223,759	234,008	252,753

Judicial caseload	Fiscal years			
	1991	1994	1995	1996
Criminal (includes transfers)				
Cases filed	47,123	45,484	45,788	47,889
Cases terminated	43,073	45,129	41,527	45,499
Cases pending	39,562	26,328	28,738	31,128
U.S. Bankruptcy Courts				
Cases filed	918,988	837,797	883,457	1,111,964
Cases terminated	751,992	869,771	892,796	1,005,025
Cases pending	1,147,765	1,110,428	1,086,453	1,193,392
Federal Probation System				
Persons under supervision**	83,012	89,103	85,822	88,966
Presentence reports	44,226	44,434	43,151	48,372
Pretrial Services				
Pretrial service cases activated	54,654	56,070	60,020	63,497
Total released on supervision	22,185	27,507	28,671	30,502

*Excludes data for the U.S. Court of Appeals for the Federal Circuit.
**The decrease in persons under supervision in 1995 resulted from a review of the probation statistical database, which identified and closed case records that had been coded incorrectly.
Source: Administrative Office of the U.S. Courts

State Court Caseload

State courts have seen an increase in most types of cases filed over the last decade. The decline in traffic cases filed reflects the decriminalization of less serious offenses, and the shift of some of the caseload to traffic bureaus or agencies.

	1985	1990	1995
Juvenile	1,202,555	1,489,183	1,871,147
Traffic	63,888,938	67,643,673	50,926,093
Domestic	3,077,352	3,938,575	4,901,214
Criminal	10,647,755	12,982,996	13,264,432
Civil	12,055,176	14,440,150	14,754,589

Source: National Center for State Courts

CRIME STATISTICS AND PERCEPTIONS

Crime is down. Preliminary 1996 statistics from the Federal Bureau of Investigation show that the total number of crimes fell 3%, while violent crime decreased 7% and homicides declined by 11%. By all appearances, good news.

Yet consumer surveys indicate that people are more afraid than ever of going shopping after dark, and sales of home and personal-security products are higher than ever. Nearly a quarter of single-family homes had security systems in 1995, up from 14.9% in 1990, according to Specialists in Business Information. The firm forecasts an increase to about 30% by the year 2000.

Clearly, many people still don't feel safe, despite the FBI statistics. "The people we're doing business with are convinced that crime is a very serious problem," says Peter A. Michel, president and chief executive officer of Brink's Home Security, whose sales of alarm systems have been steadily increasing. Mr. Michel says people's insecurity often stems from crimes they experienced indirectly, hearing stories from friends, neighbors, and coworkers.

The fear also comes from watching crime news on television and personal observations, such as seeing neighbors put bars on their windows or patrol cars roaming the streets. "The growing concern about crime is accelerated by exposure to crime through the media," says Cheryl Maxson, director at the Center on Crime and Social Control at the University of Southern California. "People get a terrific amount of the information they have about crime from TV."

Some people also believe that the much quoted FBI statistics are flawed and may overstate the decline in crime. Critics note that some crimes are left out. For instance, the FBI's counting method, called hierarchical counting, records only the most serious crime committed by one person in one night's crime spree. If the same burglar robs a house but then commits a more heinous crime down the street, the FBI counts only one crime. Similarly, if more than one crime is committed against someone on the same evening, only the most serious gets counted in the FBI's methodology. Philadelphia, for example, shows higher burglary and larceny rates because police include every crime reported to them.

"You're missing part of the picture," says Anne Morrison Piehl, associate professor at Harvard University's Kennedy School of Government. "When you start cutting the data, you start missing things."

There also are many crimes that are never reported to the authorities. According to one study on rape in America by the National Victim Center and the Crime Victims Research and Treatment Center, 84% of rape survivors did not report the crime to police. Despite the greater public awareness that rape and battery are crimes, "a lot of women who are raped or battered do not report it," says Ellen Okamoto, a counselor at the Los Angeles Commission on Assault Against Women. The organization's rape and battery hotline received an increase in calls after the O.J. Simpson case brought the issue into the public eye, she says. But "from the work we do, I do not have the sense that crime has been reduced."

Still, most crime experts believe that the FBI statistics point in the correct direction. Indeed, a separate victimization study from the Bureau of Justice Statistics showed a 9% drop in violent crimes during the same 1995 period in which the FBI showed a 3% decrease. The Bureau of Justice Statistics' data include rapes, assaults, robberies, thefts and burglaries, which decreased to 9.9 million in 1995 from 10.9 million in 1994. They also include unreported crimes, based on interviews with 100,000 people over age 12 who discussed crimes, excluding murder, that they had experienced in the previous six months. "The victimization study comes closest to capturing the actual level of crime," says Ms. Maxson of the Center on Crime and Social Control.

Stacy Kravetz

Crime in America

Estimated Rate (per 100,000 Inhabitants) of Offenses Known to Police

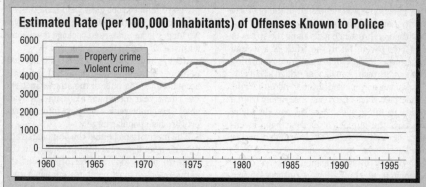

Year	Total crime index	Violent crime	Property crime	Murder and non-negligent man-slaughter	Forcible rape	Robbery	Aggravated assault	Burglary	Larceny-theft	Motor vehicle theft
				Rate per 100,000 inhabitants						
1960	1,887.2	160.9	1,726.3	5.1	9.6	60.1	86.1	508.6	1,034.7	183.0
1965	2,449.0	200.2	2,248.8	5.1	12.1	71.7	111.3	662.7	1,329.3	256.8
1970	3,984.5	363.5	3,621.0	7.9	18.7	172.1	164.8	1,084.9	2,079.3	456.8
1975	5,298.5	487.8	4,810.7	9.6	26.3	220.8	231.1	1,532.1	2,804.8	473.7
1980	5,950.0	596.6	5,353.3	10.2	36.8	251.1	298.5	1,684.1	3,167.0	502.2
1985	5,207.1	556.6	4,650.5	7.9	37.1	208.5	302.9	1,287.3	2,901.2	462.0
1986	5,480.4	617.7	4,862.6	8.6	37.9	225.1	346.1	1,344.6	3,010.3	507.8
1987	5,550.0	609.7	4,940.3	8.3	37.4	212.7	351.3	1,329.6	3,081.3	529.4
1988	5,664.2	637.2	5,027.1	8.4	37.6	220.9	370.2	1,309.2	3,134.9	582.9
1989	5,741.0	663.7	5,077.9	8.7	38.1	233.0	383.4	1,276.3	3,171.3	630.4
1990	5,820.3	731.8	5,088.5	9.4	41.2	257.0	424.1	1,235.9	3,194.8	657.8
1991	5,897.8	758.1	5,139.7	9.8	42.3	272.7	433.3	1,252.0	3,228.8	659.0
1992	5,660.2	757.5	4,902.7	9.3	42.8	263.6	441.8	1,168.2	3,103.0	631.5
1993	5,484.4	746.8	4,737.6	9.5	41.1	255.9	440.3	1,099.2	3,032.4	606.1
1994	5,373.5	713.6	4,660.0	9.0	39.3	237.7	427.6	1,042.0	3,026.7	591.3
1995	5,275.9	684.6	4,591.3	8.2	37.1	220.9	418.3	987.1	3,043.8	560.4
1996	5,078.9	634.1	4,444.8	7.4	36.1	202.4	388.2	943.0	2,975.9	525.9
				Number of offenses						
1960	3,384,200	288,460	3,095,700	9,110	17,190	107,840	154,320	912,100	1,855,400	328,200
1965	4,739,400	387,390	4,352,000	9,960	23,410	138,690	215,330	1,282,500	2,572,600	496,900
1970	8,098,000	738,820	7,359,200	16,000	37,990	349,860	334,970	2,205,000	4,225,800	928,400
1975	11,292,400	1,039,710	10,252,700	20,510	56,090	470,500	492,620	3,265,300	5,977,700	1,009,600
1980	13,408,300	1,344,520	12,063,700	23,040	82,990	565,840	672,650	3,795,200	7,136,900	1,131,700
1985	12,431,400	1,328,800	11,102,600	18,980	88,670	497,870	723,250	3,073,300	6,926,400	1,102,900
1986	13,211,900	1,489,170	11,722,700	20,610	91,460	542,780	834,320	3,241,400	7,257,200	1,224,100
1987	13,508,700	1,484,000	12,024,700	20,100	91,110	517,700	855,090	3,236,200	7,499,900	1,288,700
1988	13,923,100	1,566,220	12,356,900	20,680	92,490	542,970	910,090	3,218,100	7,705,900	1,432,900
1989	14,251,400	1,646,040	12,605,400	21,500	94,500	578,330	951,710	3,168,200	7,872,400	1,564,800
1990	14,475,600	1,820,130	12,655,500	23,440	102,560	639,270	1,054,860	3,073,900	7,945,700	1,635,900
1991	14,872,900	1,911,770	12,961,100	24,700	106,590	687,730	1,092,740	3,157,200	8,142,200	1,661,700
1992	14,438,200	1,932,270	12,505,900	23,760	109,060	672,480	1,126,970	2,979,900	7,915,200	1,610,800
1993	14,144,800	1,926,020	12,218,800	24,530	106,010	659,870	1,135,610	2,834,800	7,820,900	1,563,100
1994	13,989,500	1,857,670	12,131,900	23,330	102,220	618,950	1,113,180	2,712,800	7,879,800	1,539,300
1995	13,862,700	1,798,790	12,063,900	21,610	97,470	580,510	1,099,210	2,593,800	7,997,700	1,472,400
1996	13,473,600	1,682,280	11,791,300	19,650	95,770	537,050	1,029,810	2,501,500	7,894,600	1,395,200

Source: U.S. Justice Department, Federal Bureau of Investigation

Bomb Alert

A wave of bombings is shaking up America.

A pipe bomb was detonated in the doorway of city hall in Spokane, Wash., killing no one but blasting three-inch nails along the street. A pipe bomb went off in the truck of a federal mine inspector in California, seriously injuring him and his wife. A mail bomb killed a 37-year-old woman and injured three children in Fort Lauderdale, Fla. That's just a sampling from a typical month in 1996. Over the past decade in the U.S., the number of explosive and incendiary devices—planted by disgruntled people of all sorts—has steadily increased. The Federal Bureau of Investigation reported 2,577 bombing incidents (24% were unsuccessful) in 1995, up from 847 in 1985.

The bombing of the federal building in Oklahoma City in 1995, the explosion at the World Trade Center in 1993, and other bombings and bomb threats have rattled government agencies, businesses and the news media—all of which have stepped up security. At airports, nary a luggage locker can be found, and cars left unoccupied at the terminal are more likely to be towed, and towed quickly, than ticketed. In many abortion clinics, receptionists now work behind thick plates of bullet-proof glass, and armed bodyguard escort doctors who perform abortions. No longer is an unmarked package a welcome surprise, thanks to the Unabomber.

Bombs hidden in mailboxes and other corners of private and commercial property accounted for the bulk of the attacks in 1995, the latest year for which FBI data are available. Cars, universities and government property are also popular targets.

The motivations behind the bombings vary, ranging from domestic disputes and gang violence to bored kids and terrorists. But the perpetrators of most bombings remain a mystery. Indeed, it's still unknown who planted the recent spate of bombs in Atlanta: the 1996 bombing at Centennial Olympic Park and the separate bombings of an abortion clinic and a gay nightclub. Federal agents have said that all three incidents may be the work of the same person or persons—a serial bomber who, investigators say, will likely strike again.

Laurie Snyder

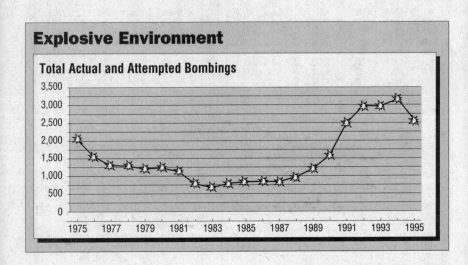

Explosive Environment

Total Actual and Attempted Bombings

Bombing Incidents Known to Police

Year	Total actual and attempted bombings	Persons injured	Deaths
1975	2,074	326	69
1976	1,570	212	50
1977	1,318	162	22
1978	1,301	135	18
1979	1,220	173	22
1980	1,249	160	34
1981	1,142	133	30
1982	795	99	16
1983	687	100	12
1984	803	112	6
1985	847	144	28
1986	858	185	14
1987	848	107	21
1988	977	145	20
1989	1,208	202	11
1990	1,582	222	27
1991	2,499	230	29
1992	2,989	349	26
1993	2,980	1,323*	49*
1994	3,163	308	31
1995	2,577	744**	193**

Terrorist Incidents, by Type of Incident and Target, 1982–95

	Number
Total	178
Type of incident	
Bombing attacks	143
Malicious destruction of property	4
Acts of sabotage	2
Hostile takeovers	4
Arson	8
Kidnapping; assaults; alleged assassinations; assassinations	11
Robbery; attempted robbery	5
Hijacking	1
Type of target	
Private residence/vehicle	18
Military personnel/establishments	33
Educational establishments	6
Commercial establishments	72
State and U.S. government buildings/property	32
Diplomatic establishments	17

*Includes 1,042 injuries and 6 deaths in the World Trade Center bombing in New York.
**Includes 518 injuries and 168 deaths in the Oklahoma City federal building bombing.
Source: U.S. Justice Department

CAPITAL PUNISHMENT

The executioner has been busy.

By mid-September, 52 inmates had been executed, and it appeared that 1997 would set a record for the most people put to death in a single year since the Supreme Court reinstated capital punishment in 1976.

Executions are becoming so common many people have begun to view them as an almost mundane event. Fewer news reporters, demonstrators and curiosity seekers gather outside prison gates on the night of an execution, and some state legislatures have bumped up the time of executions from midnight to the early evening to better accommodate prison officials.

Critics, who say the death penalty is applied disproportionately to poor and minority defendants, call the increased pace of executions dangerous because it increases the chance that innocent people will be put to death. The American Bar Association agrees

and asked in 1997 for a moratorium on capital punishment, calling the entire process of imposing the death penalty in the U.S. "a haphazard maze of unfair practices."

But many judges, lawmakers, and citizens don't see it that way. In 1996, the Supreme Court upheld a federal law that limited death row inmates' appeals, and since then, many states have passed similar laws. Such laws are expected to cut the average stay on death row—about nine years—by half. In addition, Congress eliminated the funding for resource centers that provided experienced legal counsel to inmates who could not afford their own attorneys, a category nearly all of the approximately 3,100 prisoners on death row fit.

Capital punishment also seems to enjoy growing public support. A 1996 Gallup poll found that 79% of respondents favored the death penalty for persons convicted of murder, while only 18% said they were opposed. But in 1978 just two years after reinstatement of capital punishment, only

Prison Population Surge

Number of Sentenced Prisoners in State and Federal Institutions

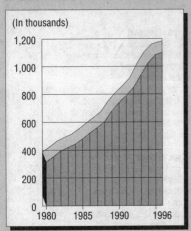

(In thousands)

Year	Total	Male	Female
1980	315,974	303,643	12,331
1981	353,167	338,940	14,227
1982	394,374	378,045	16,329
1983	419,820	402,391	17,429
1984	443,398	424,193	19,205
1985	480,568	458,972	21,296
1986	522,084	497,540	24,544
1987	560,812	533,990	26,822
1988	603,732	573,587	30,145
1989	680,907	643,643	37,264
1990	739,980	699,416	40,564
1991	789,610	745,808	43,802
1992	846,277	799,776	46,501
1993	932,074	878,037	54,037
1994	1,016,691	956,566	60,125
1995	1,085,363	1,021,463	63,900
1996	1,138,187	1,068,573	69,614

Source: U.S. Justice Department

62% were in favor. Experts say there's no conclusive proof that capital punishment deters crime, but for many, the death penalty is about justice. That belief was reinforced in two widely publicized cases in 1997: the convictions and death sentences for Timothy McVeigh in the Oklahoma City bombing trial and for Jesse Timmendequas, who raped and murdered 7-year-old Megan Kanka in New Jersey.

Thirty-eight states have adopted the death penalty, the latest being New York in 1995. But the rate of executions varies widely. Since 1976, more than 80% have taken place in southern states. Texas alone has executed more than a third of the prisoners put to death since 1976; it also holds the record for the most prisoners put to death in one month— eight in both May and June 1997. New Jersey, on the other hand, has not executed an inmate since its death penalty was reinstated in 1982, and the federal government hasn't done so since John F. Kennedy was president.

Some death penalty opponents believe executions would be less common if more juries could sentence defendants to prison with little if any chance of parole. According to a poll commissioned by the Death Penalty Information Center, an anti–death penalty group in Washington, D.C., public support of capital punishment drops below 50% when respondents are given the option of life imprisonment for at least 25 years and mandatory restitution, as an alternative to execution. Juries seem to feel more comfortable taking this "middle ground," says Lisa Bartle, a spokeswoman for the Death Penalty Information Center. But a quarter of the states still don't have "sentencing for life" laws on their books, she says, adding, "Texas is one of those states that doesn't give juries that option."

Laurie Snyder

Crowding on Death Row

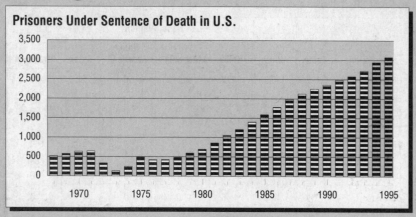

Prisoners Under Sentence of Death in U.S.

Prisoners Executed, by Race

Year	Under sentence of death on Dec. 31	Executions Total	White	Black	Other	Year	Under sentence of death on Dec. 31	Executions Total	White	Black	Other
1968	517	0	0	0	0	1982	1,050	2	1	1	0
1969	575	0	0	0	0	1983	1,209	5	4	1	0
1970	631	0	0	0	0	1984	1,405	21	13	8	0
1971	642	0	0	0	0	1985	1,591	18	11	7	0
1972	334	0	0	0	0	1986	1,781	18	11	7	0
1973	134	0	0	0	0	1987	1,984	25	13	12	0
1974	244	0	0	0	0	1988	2,124	11	6	5	0
1975	488	0	0	0	0	1989	2,250	16	8	8	0
1976	420	0	0	0	0	1990	2,356	23	16	7	0
1977	423	1	1	0	0	1991	2,482	14	7	7	0
1978	482	0	0	0	0	1992	2,575	31	19	11	1
1979	593	2	2	0	0	1993	2,716	38	23	14	1
1980	691	0	0	0	0	1994	2,890	31	20	11	0
1981	856	1	1	0	0	1995	3,054	56	33	22	1

Source: U.S. Justice Department

Prisoners Under Sentence of Death by Race, Ethnicity, and Jurisdiction, on April 30, 1996

Jurisdiction	Total	Race, ethnicity					
		White	Black	Hispanic	Native American	Asian	Unknown
United States	3,122	1,493	1,272	236	50	22	49
Federal statutes	8	2	5	1	0	0	0
U.S. military	8	1	6	0	0	1	0
Alabama	144	79	56	1	0	1	7
Arizona	121	80	16	21	4	0	0
Arkansas	37	20	15	1	1	0	0
California	444	179	158	61	13	7	26
Colorado	4	2	1	1	0	0	0
Connecticut	5	3	2	0	0	0	0
Delaware	11	5	6	0	0	0	0
Florida	351	192	122	35	1	1	0
Georgia	108	61	46	0	0	0	1
Idaho	19	18	0	1	0	0	0
Illinois	164	54	104	5	0	0	1
Indiana	50	32	17	1	0	0	0
Kansas	0	0	0	0	0	0	0
Kentucky	28	21	7	0	0	0	0
Louisiana	53	13	33	5	0	0	2
Maryland	17	3	14	0	0	0	0
Mississippi	54	21	32	0	0	0	1
Missouri	92	49	38	1	1	1	2
Montana	6	5	0	0	1	0	0
Nebraska	10	7	2	0	1	0	0
Nevada	85	41	33	10	0	1	0
New Hampshire	0	0	0	0	0	0	0
New Jersey	14	6	7	1	0	0	0
New Mexico	3	1	0	2	0	0	0
New York	0	0	0	0	0	0	0
North Carolina	154	73	74	1	4	0	2
Ohio	150	70	74	3	2	0	1
Oklahoma	119	68	34	1	13	3	0
Oregon	22	19	1	1	1	0	0
Pennsylvania	200	62	124	12	0	2	0
South Carolina	71	33	37	0	1	0	0
South Dakota	2	2	0	0	0	0	0
Tennessee	102	66	32	1	2	1	0
Texas	394	165	147	68	5	3	6
Utah	10	7	2	1	0	0	0
Virginia	54	26	27	1	0	0	0
Washington	13	10	2	0	0	1	0
Wyoming	0	0	0	0	0	0	0

*Detail will not add to total because prisoners sentenced to death in more than one state are listed in the respective state totals, but each is counted only once at the national level.
Sources: NAACP Legal Defense and Educational Fund, U.S. Justice Department

Energy

Robert L. Olson wasn't a big fan of his local electric utility, Public Service Co. of New Hampshire. The 60-year-old says he got tired of paying rates well above the national average.

So, when state regulators offered 17,000 customers a chance to choose their own power supplier as part of a deregulation pilot-program, he signed up. Soon, he was deluged with phone calls and fliers from 30 energy companies that wanted to sell him cut-rate electricity.

Granite State Electric Co. advertised guaranteed low rates and threw in a free bird feeder. Green Mountain Energy Partners of Vermont, which touted its environmentally friendly practices, attached tree seedlings to its brochures. Houston-based energy giant Enron Corp. went further, courting whole towns with parties and development funds and offering individual customers a $50 sign-up bonus.

In the end, Mr. Olson went with Green Mountain. "They were nuclear free and very environmentally concerned, which I liked," he says. They were also cheaper than Public Service: Mr. Olson says his monthly electric bill is about $15 less than before.

Mr. Olson's story is a harbinger of things to come as parts of the $200 billion electricity industry—one of the country's last great monopolies—are opened to competition. Besides New Hampshire, California, Pennsylvania, Rhode Island, Oklahoma, Montana, Maine and Nevada also have started deregulating their electric utilities. Other states are planning to follow suit. And Congress is considering laws that would set a date—2001 is a popular choice—by which full retail competition must begin nationally.

That means consumers will get to pick their electric company much as they now decide who provides their long-distance phone service. Like Mr. Olson, they will have to choose among a bewildering variety of companies and payment plans. The promised reward: lower electric bills.

But while Mr. Olson's case shows some of the promise deregulation holds for consumers, it also shows some of the limitations. The Manchester, N.H., homeowner says that for a recent month he paid Green Mountain

just $12.90 for electricity. But he had to pay an additional $58 to Public Service, including fees for the use of the local utility's wires and a surcharge to help pay off debts it had run up making unprofitable investments.

Mr. Olson says he figured buying cheaper power would translate into greater savings than it did. "There are so many hidden charges people don't know about," he complains.

The savings may be even less in 1998, when New Hampshire plans to open up the entire state to free competition. That's because the state is giving customers in the pilot program a temporary rebate on their bills. And many of the energy marketers who participated in the pilot program sliced their profit margins thin in order to win customers, something they won't be able to continue indefinitely.

Electric companies, which have been sheltered from the free market by the government, also have lessons to learn from the pilot program. Many hope to be selling power to customers around the country, which will require them to be more efficient and cost competitive. Only 12 of the 31 entrants, for example, survived the marketing melee in New Hampshire. "The industry is being turned on its head," says Mitchell S. Diamond, a consultant at Booz-Allen & Hamilton Inc.

It isn't just the utility industry that will be shaken by the changes. Investors will have to rethink their portfolios. Utility stocks, whose consistent dividend yields and steady performance have made them a favorite of the risk-averse, may not be such a sure bet anymore. And local governments and school districts will be faced with finding new sources of revenue if utilities close down unprofitable power-generating stations and pay less in taxes.

Electric utilities have always operated as monopolies, starting with inventor Thomas Edison's Edison Electric Light Co., which started the first electricity generation and distribution network in New York City in 1882. It was widely believed that such a system, with rates set by state regulators, would be the surest and most efficient way to deliver electricity for a reasonable price.

But many politicians, businesses and

residential consumers—frustrated by high power costs—now disagree. All have been fighting to open electricity markets to more competition, something they say should mean lower utility bills.

But untying the Gordian knot of regulation won't be easy. Many conservationists, consumer groups and some utilities oppose the deregulation plans. And many argue that new laws to protect consumers and the environment will need to be put on the books before the electricity market is opened up.

Just who will gain from deregulation and by how much is still unclear. "It's not going to be the panacea that it's being made out to be," cautions Sarkis Soultanian, president of National Utility Service Inc., an energy consultancy. Indeed, Mr. Soultanian says, many residential customers won't see any dramatic change in the near term.

People in Idaho, Wyoming, Utah and Kentucky—where ready supplies of hydropower and coal help keep power costs low—are not likely to see their bills fall. The biggest rate cuts are expected where rates are now the highest: the Northeast, California and parts of the Midwest. In those areas, large industrial users are likely to benefit the most. Because they purchase large amounts of electricity, they will have more bargaining power with suppliers. They also have the support of politicians worried that high electric rates will drive business—and jobs—away from their states.

In New York, for example, Consolidated Edison says that as it prepares for deregulation, it will give its industrial customers an immediate 25% rate cut. Residential users will see their bills fall by just 10% over five years. But some analysts say that neighborhoods or whole municipalities may band together to strengthen their hand with power companies. That's what happened in New Hampshire, where some towns chose "preferred suppliers." Peterborough went with Enron; Manchester chose Green Mountain.

Choosing a utility will require careful shopping. Matthew D. Vesci, another participant in New Hampshire's pilot program, says he chose Granite State Electric because the company promised to lock in its low price for two years, something others did not. Gary R. Schreiber, another program participant, decided to stick with his old utility, Public Service Co. of New Hampshire. The 44-year-old facilities controller at an Internet access

company, says he was most concerned about reliability. "If there was a power outage, would we get the same service if we weren't a PSNH customer?" he asks.

One of the most important issues facing utilities and their customers is how to deal with the mountains of debt some companies have run up building nuclear power plants and making other unprofitable investments. All told, the industry has somewhere between $50 billion and $250 billion of these liabilities on its books.

Regulators generally have allowed utilities to recoup these expenses by raising the rates they charge their customers. In a competitive market, however, this would put them at a disadvantage and could drive some into bankruptcy. Utilities have argued that since their investments were made with the blessing of regulators, they should be able to recover their so-called "stranded costs" before deregulation takes place.

So far, most states have agreed. That means that customers will have to pay a surcharge on their bills to pay off the utility's debt, even if they are buying electricity from someone else.

In New Hampshire, however, state utility regulators decided utilities should not be allowed to recover all of their stranded costs. Northeast Utilities, a New England utility company, says the plan could bankrupt its New Hampshire Public Service subsidiary and has sued to block it.

California and Pennsylvania have both passed laws that would allow utilities to lower the financing costs for this debt by issuing asset-backed securities. Other states are considering similar legislation, which allows utilities to use the cash flow from utility-bill surcharges as collateral for bonds that offer better interest rates than bank loans.

Clearing their books of these white-elephant investments will help utility companies. But there are many other adjustments that will have to be made. Utilities must decide whether to focus on electricity generation or power transmission and distribution, or both. These stodgy monopolists are also having to learn business skills such as marketing for the first time.

New England Electric System, an electric-utility holding company based in Westborough, Mass., for example, has decided to sell its electricity-generating plants and concentrate on transmission and distribution. Boston Edison in Massachusetts and Edison International and Pacific Gas & Electric Co. in California, also plan to auction off power plants.

Other companies are positioning themselves as generators, including Enron, Duke Power Co. of Charlotte, N.C., Cal-Energy of Omaha, Neb., and Southern Co. of Atlanta. These companies are already moving to establish themselves as national brand names for electric power with big advertising campaigns. Enron even advertised during the Super Bowl, the most expensive commercial time on television. And some utilities are already signing power-supply contracts for the future, even before electricity markets are actually deregulated.

The impending changes in the electricity marketplace have also touched off a round of mergers and acquisitions as companies try to strengthen themselves by joining forces. It is a trend that is expected to continue in coming years.

Enron is joining hands with Portland Electric Co. in Oregon, while Duke and PanEnergy have merged. Allegheny Power is acquiring neighboring utility DQE Inc. in a $2.6 billion deal that will create a power company stretching from western Pennsylvania to Virginia. Similarly, Western Resources has agreed to buy Kansas City Power & Light for $2 billion in stock.

Many electric companies are also trying to diversify. They hope to make the most of their customer base by selling a bundle of consumer services. In the future, the local utility may provide everything from electricity and natural gas to telephones, Internet connections, cable television and home

Energy Levels

U.S. energy consumption, production, imports, and exports

Energy Overview (Quadrillion BTUs)

	Production	Consumption*	Imports	Exports	Net imports
1973	62.060	74.282	14.731	2.051	12.680
1975	59.860	70.546	14.111	2.359	11.752
1980	64.761	75.955	15.971	3.723	12.247
1985	64.871	73.981	12.103	4.231	7.872
1990	67.853	81.265	18.987	4.910	14.077
1991	67.484	81.116	18.577	5.220	13.357
1992	66.853	82.144	19.650	5.017	14.633
1993	65.163	83.863	21.530	4.350	17.180
1994	67.448	85.587	22.695	4.125	18.570
1995	67.759	87.193	22.454	4.571	17.884
1996	69.006	89.814	23.699	4.687	19.012

*The sum of domestic energy production and net imports of energy does not equal domestic energy consumption. The difference is attributed to stock changes; losses and gains in conversion, transportation, and distribution; the addition of blending compounds; shipments of anthracite to U.S. Armed Forces in Europe; and adjustments to account for discrepancies between reporting systems.

Energy Production by Source

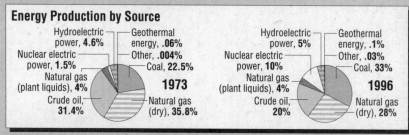

1973: Hydroelectric power, 4.6%; Geothermal energy, .06%; Nuclear electric power, 1.5%; Other, .004%; Coal, 22.5%; Natural gas (plant liquids), 4%; Crude oil, 31.4%; Natural gas (dry), 35.8%

1996: Hydroelectric power, 5%; Geothermal energy, .1%; Nuclear electric power, 10%; Other, .03%; Coal, 33%; Natural gas (plant liquids), 4%; Crude oil, 20%; Natural gas (dry), 28%

Source: U.S. Energy Department

Petroleum Supply
(Million barrels per day)

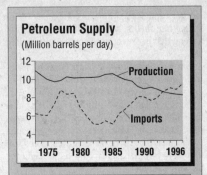

U.S. Production vs. Imports
(Million barrels per day)

	Production	Imports
1973	10.95	6.26
1975	10.01	6.06
1978	10.27	8.36
1980	10.17	6.91
1982	10.20	5.11
1984	10.51	5.44
1986	10.23	6.22
1988	9.76	7.40
1990	8.91	8.02
1991	9.08	7.63
1992	8.87	7.89
1993	8.58	8.62
1994	8.39	9.00
1995	8.32	8.83
1996	8.30	9.40

Source: U.S. Energy Department

Investors, like electric customers, will soon have to study each utility before deciding which best meets their needs. Energy companies that stick to power transmission and distribution as their primary business will, from an investor's point of view, behave more like utilities of old. Since these businesses aren't being deregulated, companies will continue to have steady earnings streams, guaranteed by government rate-setting programs.

Companies that move more into electricity generation and consumer services will be more risky, but also could eventually offer higher returns. Electricity generators will essentially be producing a commodity, meaning that their earnings could prove highly volatile. And dividends are likely to be low as companies invest in their restructuring efforts. Ipalco Enterprises, the parent of Indianapolis Power & Light, cut its common-stock dividend by a third, saying it needed to retain more earnings to prepare for deregulation.

Electricity deregulation is definitely coming, though the exact shape of the new marketplace is still being worked out by state regulators and the federal government. Utilities and other players with a stake in deregulation are spending huge sums of money to lobby legislators and guide the process. And politicians will have to tread a fine line balancing the differing and sometimes conflicting interests of utility investors, residential customers and businesses. If the politicians achieve that balance, utility industry experts say, the forces of the market should mean stronger, more efficient power suppliers and less expensive electricity for all.

Gordon Fairclough,
Wall Street Journal
staff reporter

security. Brooklyn Union Gas Co. of New York, for instance, has formed a joint venture with Metricom, a Los Gatos, Calif., wireless Internet-services company, to build and operate data-communications networks in 16 Midwestern and Northeastern states.

Energy Powers

World's Major Producers of Primary Energy,* 1995 (Quadrillion Btu)

1	United States	69.10	14	United Arab Emirates	6.19
2	Russia	39.91	15	South Africa	6.08
3	China	35.49	16	Germany	5.42
4	Saudi Arabia	20.34	17	France	4.92
5	Canada	16.81	18	Algeria	4.89
6	United Kingdom	10.57	19	Kuwait	4.81
7	Iran	9.35	20	Brazil	4.55
8	Norway	8.35	21	Nigeria	4.50
9	India	8.33	22	Japan	3.98
10	Venezuela	8.22	23	Poland	3.74
11	Mexico	8.15	24	Ukraine	3.34
12	Australia	7.29	25	Libya	3.23
13	Indonesia	6.65		**World Total**	**361.02**

World's Major Consumers of Primary Energy,* 1995 (Quadrillion Btu)

1	United States	88.28	14	Mexico	5.59
2	China	35.67	15	South Africa	5.51
3	Russia	26.75	16	Spain	4.46
4	Japan	21.42	17	Australia	4.43
5	Germany	13.71	18	Iran	3.90
6	Canada	11.72	19	Netherlands	3.77
7	India	10.50	20	Poland	3.75
8	United Kingdom	9.85	21	Saudi Arabia	3.72
9	France	9.43	22	Indonesia	3.06
10	Italy	7.42	23	Taiwan	2.69
11	Brazil	6.76	24	Venezuela	2.53
12	Ukraine	6.32	25	Turkey	2.53
13	South Korea	6.28		**World Total**	**362.24**

*Primary energy production and consumption include petroleum, natural gas, coal, and net hydroelectric, nuclear, geothermal, solar and wind electric power. Data for the U.S. also include electricity generated from wood and waste.
Source: U.S. Energy Department

Outside Sources of Petroleum

Petroleum Imports by Country of Origin (Thousand barrels per day)

Year	Persian Gulf nations	Selected OPEC countries					Selected non-OPEC countries					Total imports	Imports from Persian Gulf nations as share of total imports	Imports from OPEC as share of total imports
		Algeria	Nigeria	Saudi Arabia	Venezuela	Total OPEC	Canada	Mexico	United Kingdom	Virgin Islands and Puerto Rico	Total non-OPEC			
1960	NA	NA	0	84	911	1,314	120	16	—	36	500	1,815	NA	72.4%
1965	NA	NA	15	158	994	1,476	323	48	—	47	992	2,468	NA	59.8
1970	NA	NA	50	30	989	1,343	766	42	11	271	2,076	3,419	NA	39.3
1975	1,165	282	762	715	702	3,601	846	71	14	496	2,454	6,056	19.2%	59.5
1980	1,519	488	857	1,261	481	4,300	455	533	176	476	2,609	6,909	22.0	62.2
1985	312	187	293	168	605	1,830	770	816	310	275	3,237	5,067	6.1	36.1
1990	1,966	280	800	1,339	1,025	4,296	934	755	189	315	3,721	8,018	24.5	53.6
1995	1,573	234	627	1,344	1,480	4,002	1,332	1,068	383	293	4,833	8,835	17.8	45.3
1996*	1,604	256	614	1,363	1,657	4,188	1,415	1,240	298	333	5,211	9,399	17.1	44.6

* Preliminary.
Source: U.S. Energy Department

ENERGY PRICE TRENDS

Energy prices skyrocketed in 1996, while 1997 has proven a more slippery slope for oil and its byproducts. But both years illustrate the roller-coaster quality of energy commodity prices.

In the first half of 1997, crude-oil futures prices had fallen 26%, to $19.27 a barrel from $25.92, while crude's two main byproducts, heating oil and gasoline, declined 28% and 15% respectively. Heating oil futures fell to 52.55 cents a gallon from 72.84 cents, and gasoline futures dropped to 60.15 cents a gallon from 70.67 cents.

This after 1996, when crude prices soared 33%, gasoline 11%, and heating oil 24%. Energy prices, said Nizam Sharief, director of energy research at Hornsby & Co. in Houston, are "quite a yo-yo thing."

The reason for the downward shift after such a steep climb?

In part, simple supply and demand. In 1996 oil refiners, who convert crude into its useful products, sought to shave costs in their low-margin business by keeping gasoline and heating-oil inventories lean. With less of these key products available, prices for them soared. Gasoline futures, for example, climbed above 78 cents a gallon in May 1996. (Compare this with 1994, before so-called "just-in-time" inventories were common, when gasoline traded as low as 37 cents a gallon.)

Meanwhile, world politics, as always, played a major role in crude's ups and downs. Uncertainty surrounding Iraq's negotiations with the United Nations over whether it could begin exporting oil again and thus raise the volume of crude available to world markets fueled speculation, sending prices up one day and forcing them down the next.

The overall trend for crude prices, however, was upward thanks to strong product demand. The trend continued even after Iraq, which had been banned from selling its oil since the Persian Gulf war, reached its agreement with the U.N. to sell oil, provided it use the proceeds for food and humanitarian purposes. The war-torn but oil-rich Middle Eastern nation began exporting in December 1996, but was allowed to ship just $2 billion worth of crude oil over six months. Because the maximum was set in terms of dollars and not volume, the market's fears that a flood of Iraqi oil would overwhelm world markets were assuaged.

The weather, always a wild card, also con-

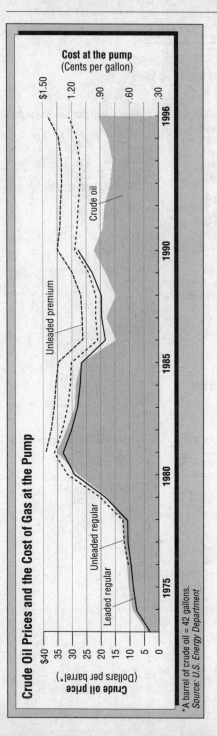

Crude Oil Prices and the Cost of Gas at the Pump

Cost at the pump
(Cents per gallon)

Crude oil

Unleaded premium

Unleaded regular

Leaded regular

Crude oil price
(Dollars per barrel*)

*A barrel of crude oil = 42 gallons.
Source: U.S. Energy Department

tributed to uncertainty in 1996, especially in the heating-oil pit. Prices were pushed above 76 cents a gallon when fears arose that a cold winter would deplete the already-tight supplies hoarded by refiners.

The volatility continued in 1997, though the overall trend has been down. After a brief surge in January, crude prices fell again as fears about an undersupply faded. Instead, traders began reacting to reports of an oversupply, a trend that is expected to continue. The International Energy Agency, a Paris-based industry group, issued a report in July suggesting "oil markets in the second half of 1997 are expected to soften appreciably." One factor cited in the study is a decision made in June by the Organization of Petroleum Exporting Countries (OPEC) not to decrease crude output despite the recent slip in prices.

Contributing to the lower-price trend on the domestic front, imports, particularly those from South America and the Carribbean, are up "substantially" in 1997, says Robert Boslego, president of consulting firm Boslego Corp. He and other analysts also say 1997 crude prices include a discount reflecting the oil-for-food deal with Iraq, which was renewed in June. However, disagreements between the United Nations and Iraq delayed shipments until early August, contributing to speculation about world supplies. Mr. Boslego expects crude prices to sit at around $20 a barrel for the rest of 1997.

Because heating oil and gasoline prices depend in part on crude's lead, customers concerned about heating bills and prices at the pump can relax a bit. But longer-term, many traders see energy prices bolstered by growing world demand for crude and its products, particularly in China and other developing countries.

Terzah Ewing

WORLD'S LARGEST ENERGY COMPANIES

Largest Producers of Crude Oil and Other Liquids in 1995

Rank	Company	Ownership Status	Production (1,000 barrels per day)
1.	Saudi Arabian Oil Co.	State-owned	8,585
2.	National Iranian Oil Co.	State-owned	3,720
3.	China National Petroleum Corp.	State-owned	2,796
3.	Petroleos de Venezuela	State-owned	2,796
5.	Petroleos Mexicanos (Pemex)	State-owned	2,722
6.	Royal Dutch/Shell	Private	2,254
7.	Kuwait Petroleum Corp.	State-owned	2,100
8.	Exxon	Private	1,726
9.	Libya National Oil Co.	State-owned	1,345
10.	Abu Dhabi National Oil Co.	State-owned	1,300
11.	Sonatrach	State-owned (Algeria)	1,283
12.	British Petroleum	Private	1,213
13.	Nigerian National Petroleum Corp.	State-owned	1,200
14.	Lukoil	45% state-owned (Russia)	1,159
15.	Pertamina	State-owned (Indonesia)	1,065
16.	Chevron	Private	1,001
17.	Mobil	Private	810
18.	Texaco	Private	765
19.	Elf Aquitaine	Private	764
20.	Yukos	51% state-owned (Russia)	722

Companies With Largest Worldwide Reserves of Crude Oil and Other Liquids, 1995

Rank	Company	Ownership Status	Reserves (Millions of barrels)
1.	Saudi Arabian Oil Co.	State-owned	261,450
2.	Iraq National Oil Co.	State-owned	100,000
3.	Kuwait Petroleum Corp.	State-owned	97,000
4.	National Iranian Oil Co.	State-owned	93,700
5.	Petroleos de Venezuela	State-owned	66,328
6.	Abu Dhabi National Oil Co.	State-owned	64,452
7.	Petroleos Mexicanos (Pemex)	State-owned	49,027
8.	Libya National Oil Co.	State-owned	27,590
9.	China National Petroleum Corp.	State-owned	21,000
10.	Nigerian National Petroleum Corp.	State-owned	12,000
11.	Lukoil	45% state-owned (Russia)	10,400
12.	Sonatrach	State-owned (Algeria)	9,979
13.	Royal Dutch/Shell	Private	8,846
14.	Yukos	51% state-owned (Russia)	7,300
15.	Gazprom	40% state-owned (Russia)	7,055
16.	Sidanko	49% state-owned (Russia)	6,935
17.	Exxon	Private	6,670
18.	British Petroleum	Private	6,577
19.	Rosneft	51% state-owned (Russia)	5,840
20.	Oil & Natural Gas Commission	State-owned (India)	5,336

Largest Producers of Natural Gas in 1995

Rank	Company	Ownership status	Production (million cubic feet per day)
1.	Gazprom	40% state-owned (Russia)	54,095
2.	Royal Dutch/Shell	Private	7,624
3.	Sonatrach	State-owned (Algeria)	6,039
4.	Exxon	Private	6,013
5.	Mobil	Private	4,554
6.	Amoco	Private	4,239
7.	Pertamina	State-owned (Indonesia)	4,238
8.	Saudi Arabian Oil Co.	State-owned	3,920
9.	National Iranian Oil Co.	State-owned	3,814
10.	Petroleos Mexicanos (Pemex)	State-owned	3,759
11.	Petroleos de Venezuela	State-owned	3,392
12.	Chevron	Private	2,433
13.	Ente Nazionale Idrocarburi	State-owned (Italy)	2,118
14.	Texaco	Private	1,992
15.	Abu Dhabi National Oil Co.	State-owned	1,765
15.	Unocal	Private	1,765
17.	Oil & Natural Gas Commission	State-owned (India)	1,624
18.	Arco	Private	1,556
19.	China National Petroleum Corp.	State-owned	1,554
20.	Phillips	Private	1,481

Companies With Largest Worldwide Reserves of Natural Gas, 1995

Rank	Company	Ownership status	Reserves (billion cubic feet)
1.	Gazprom	40% state-owned (Russia)	1,161,041
2.	National Iranian Oil Co.	State-owned	682,616
3.	Qatar General Petroleum Corp.	State-owned	249,410
4.	Saudi Arabian Oil Co.	State-owned	195,613
5.	Petroleos de Venezuela	State-owned	143,542
6.	Iraq National Oil Co.	State-owned	118,532
7.	Abu Dhabi National Oil Co.	State-owned	111,195
8.	Sonatrach	State-owned (Algeria)	103,539
9.	Nigerian National Petroleum Corp.	State-owned	76,023
10.	Petroleos Mexicanos (Pemex)	State-owned	66,317
11.	Pertamina	State-owned (Indonesia)	62,088
12.	Surgutneftegaz	51% state-owned (Russia)	57,537
13.	Rosneft	51% state-owned (Russia)	53,727
14.	Kuwait Petroleum Corp.	State-owned	53,000
15.	Royal Dutch/Shell	Private	47,607
16.	Libya National Oil Co.	State-owned	45,860
17.	Sidanko	49% state-owned (Russia)	44,696
18.	Exxon	Private	42,036
19.	China National Petroleum Corp.	State-owned	39,652
20.	Petronas	State-owned (Malaysia)	38,265

Companies With the Largest Oil Refining Capacity, 1995

Rank	Company	Ownership status	Capacity (1,000 barrels per day)
1.	Exxon	Private	4,241
2.	Royal Dutch/Shell	Private	4,137
3.	China Petrochemical Corp.	State-owned (China)	2,850
4.	Petroleos de Venezuela	State-owned	2,370
5.	Mobil	Private	2,256
6.	Saudi Arabian Oil Co.	State-owned	2,000
6.	British Petroleum	Private	2,000
8.	Chevron	Private	1,723
9.	Texaco	Private	1,602
10.	Petroleo Braziliero	51% state-owned	1,540
11.	Petoleos Mexicanos (Pemex)	State-owned	1,520
12.	National Iranian Oil Co.	State-owned	1,092
13.	Ente Nazionale Idrocarburi	State-owned	1,080
14.	Amoco	Private	998
15.	Pertamina	State-owned (Indonesia)	986
16.	Kuwait Petroleum Corp.	State-owned	949
17.	Total	Private	919
18.	Idemitsu	Private	872
19.	Elf Aquitaine	Private	870
20.	Sidanko	49% state-owned (Russia)	793

Source: Ranking the World's Top Oil Companies—1997. Petroleum Intelligence Weekly and Price Waterhouse

Fill 'Er Up

Americans are driving more miles and using more gasoline, in total and per household.

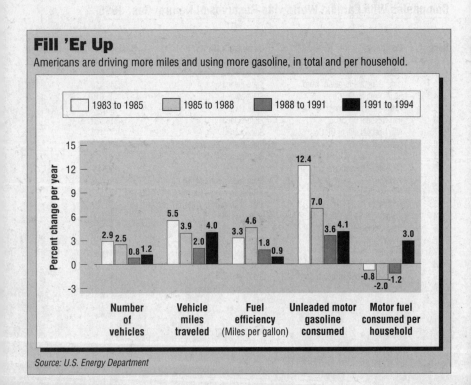

Source: U.S. Energy Department

U.S. Residential End-Use Consumption of Electricity, 1993

End Use/Appliance	Households (millions)	Annual kWh Consumption per Household
Total Households	96.6	9,965
Central Air-Conditioning System	41.0	2,667
Room Air Conditioners*	33.1	738
Water Heating	37.0	2,671
Main Space-Heating System	25.0	4,541
Secondary Space-Heating	12.1	400
Refrigerator*	115.7	1,155
Appliances (total of list below)	96.6	4,933
Lighting (indoor and outdoor)	96.6	940
TV*	198.3	360
Clothes Dryer	54.7	875
Freezer	33.4	1,204
Range/Oven	58.3	458
Microwave Oven	81.3	191
Waterbed Heater*	14.6	960
Dishwasher	43.7	299
Swimming Pool Pump	4.6	2,022
Clothes Washer	74.5	99
Dehumidifier	9.1	370
Well Pump	13.0	228
Personal Computer	22.6	77
Hot Tub/Spa Heater	1.9	482
Residual	96.6	1,364

*Count of individual units within household.
Source: U.S. Energy Information Administration

Households With Selected Appliances, 1993

Appliance	Percent of Households 1993
Total Households	100
Type of Appliances	
Electric Appliances	
Television Set (Color)	98
Television Set (B/W)	20
Clothes Washer	77
Range (Stove-Top Burner)	61
Oven, Regular or Microwave	91
Oven, Microwave	84
Clothes Dryer	57
Separate Freezer	35
Dishwasher	45
Dehumidifier	9
Waterbed Heaters	12
Window or Ceiling Fan	60
Whole House Fan	4
Evaporative Cooler	3
Personal Computer	23
Pump for Well Water	13
Swimming-Pool Pump	5
Gas Appliances	
Range (Stove-Top or Burner)	38
Oven	36
Clothes Dryer	15
Outdoor Gas Grill	29
Outdoor Gas Light	1
Swimming Pool Heater	1
Refrigerators	
One	85
Two or More	15
Air Conditioning (A/C)	
Central	44
Individual Room Units	25
None	32
Portable Kerosene Heaters	2

Source: U.S. Energy Information Administration

Home Heating Trend

Types of Heating in Occupied Housing Units, 1950 and 1995

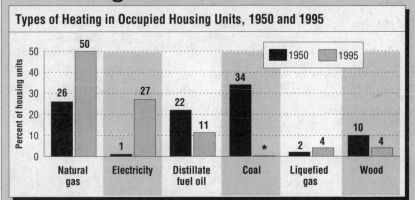

*Less than 0.5.
Source: U.S. Energy Department

America's Nuclear Generation

The nuclear industry's share of America's electricity generation rose steadily in the 1980s, then leveled off at about 22% in the 1990s. But the amount of nuclear power is expected to drop considerably in the early part of the next century, according to the U.S. Energy Department.

Nuclear Portion of Domestic Electricity Net Generation

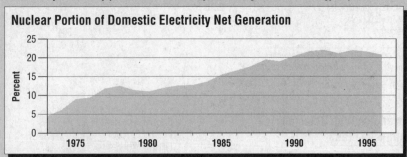

Nuclear Power Plant Operations

	Operable units (Number)	Nuclear electricity net generation (Million kilowatt-hours)	Nuclear portion of domestic electricity net generation (Percent)
1973	39	83,479	4.5
1975	54	172,505	9.0
1980	70	251,116	11.0
1985	95	383,691	15.5
1990	111	576,862	20.5
1991	111	612,565	21.7
1992	109	618,776	22.1
1993	109	610,291	21.2
1994	109	640,440	22.0
1995	109	673,402	22.5
1996	110	674,729	21.9

Source: U.S. Energy Department, Nuclear Regulatory Commission

Global Nuclear Energy Rankings

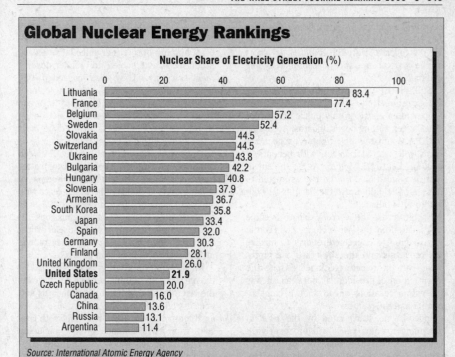

Nuclear Share of Electricity Generation (%)

Lithuania	83.4
France	77.4
Belgium	57.2
Sweden	52.4
Slovakia	44.5
Switzerland	44.5
Ukraine	43.8
Bulgaria	42.2
Hungary	40.8
Slovenia	37.9
Armenia	36.7
South Korea	35.8
Japan	33.4
Spain	32.0
Germany	30.3
Finland	28.1
United Kingdom	26.0
United States	**21.9**
Czech Republic	20.0
Canada	16.0
China	13.6
Russia	13.1
Argentina	11.4

Source: International Atomic Energy Agency

The Environment

The Environmental Protection Agency, which has a long, stormy tradition of butting heads with industry over the Clean Air Act, stirred up another battle royal in 1997 over proposals to tighten air-pollution rules.

Oil companies, car makers, utilities, small businesses, and even other government agencies joined the fight against the agency's harsher emissions standards for ozone, or smog, and particulates, fine dust and soot pieces released into the air by cars, factories and other sources.

EPA representatives say their statistics show serious health hazards will be reduced by the tougher rules, which were scheduled to take effect in September. Industry officials counter that the data are inconclusive and that rule tightening will prove much more costly than EPA is estimating. Mobil Corp.'s ads proclaimed, "EPA: Let science do its job,"

and attacked the scientific basis for the agency's new standards.

"Should there be more research into these issues? Yes," says Mike Shanahan, a spokesman for the American Petroleum Institute, a Washington, D.C.-based industry trade group. "But we think [EPA is] putting the cart way before the horse."

Representatives of the auto industry agree. In a summary of its stance on the proposals, the American Automobile Manufacturers Association said the scientific studies backing the EPA's new particulate rule have "serious problems" and called the benefits of the more stringent ozone standard "truly minimal."

The new regulations lower the acceptable level for urban ozone to 0.08 parts per million cubic feet of air from 0.12 parts per million, and impose limitations, for the first time, on particulates 2.5 microns in diameter or smaller. Under the previous rules, 134 counties nationwide weren't in compliance with EPA standards. But 411 counties fall short of the stricter measures, according to one estimate.

Still, the EPA doesn't think the new rules are extreme. Under the Clean Air Act, the agency must consider only public health, not costs, when setting new standards. According to EPA estimates, the tighter ozone standards will cost $1.1 billion with benefits of $400 million to $2.1 billion. As for the small-particle regulations, the cost is estimated to be about $8.6 billion and the benefits $19 billion to $104 billion.

So bitter did the current debate become that in late May the White House entered the fray, hoping to coordinate efforts to finalize the proposals and thereby reach a compromise. But the debate continued despite the intervention of presidential aides, and it was rife with accusations of bad science, bad economics and bad politics.

Indeed, one study cited by the EPA in defending its new rules will be reanalyzed during the next two years by an impartial research group. The study, conducted by Harvard University, concluded that particulates can be fatal. Industry representatives have criticized the university for refusing to release the data that have caused the confusion over the study.

Unlike past disputes over clean air issues, however, industry this time didn't question the necessity of the Clean Air Act itself. Indeed, industry representatives agreed that breathing has been easier since factories and products became subject to tougher government scrutiny. They also conceded that there's still work to do in achieving compliance with the old rules, especially in urban areas. But, says the American Petroleum Institute's Mr. Shanahan, "we've done most of the heavy lifting in cleaning up the air."

Some EPA statistics bear him out. Between 1970 and 1994, emissions of particulate matter have decreased 72%, while emissions of volatile organic compounds, which react with sunlight to create ozone, decreased 24% over the same period. Though emissions of nitrogen oxides, the other root cause of ozone, have increased, national ozone concentrations in 1995 were 6% lower than in 1986.

But EPA officials, citing health trends like the increase in asthma-related deaths over the last 20 years, contend that standards still need to be stricter. The agency also has a legal motivation: In 1996, it was hit with lawsuits from environmental groups, including the Sierra Club, which claimed the EPA wasn't doing enough to clean up smog in certain cities, and the American Lung Association, which charged that the agency wasn't protecting asthmatics. "Air pollution has been cut," says Mike Casey of the Environmental Information Center, "but what's still there aggravates respiratory conditions."

Terzah Ewing

Monitoring Air Pollution

National Emissions of Major Air Pollutants

(In thousand short tons, except lead; 1.1 million short tons equal 1 million metric tons)

Year	Carbon monoxide	Nitrogen oxides	Volatile organic compounds	Sulfur dioxide	Particulate matter	Lead (short tons)
1900	NA	2,611	8,503	9,988	NA	NA
1905	NA	3,314	8,850	13,959	NA	NA
1910	NA	4,102	9,117	17,275	NA	NA
1915	NA	4,672	9,769	20,290	NA	NA
1920	NA	5,159	10,004	21,144	NA	NA
1925	NA	7,302	14,257	23,264	NA	NA
1930	NA	8,018	19,451	21,106	NA	NA
1935	NA	6,639	17,208	16,978	NA	NA
1940	93,615	7,374	17,161	19,953	15,956	NA
1945	98,112	9,332	18,140	26,373	16,545	NA
1950	102,609	10,093	20,936	22,358	17,133	NA
1955	106,177	11,667	23,249	21,453	16,346	NA
1960	109,745	14,140	24,459	22,227	15,558	NA
1965	118,912	17,424	30,247	26,380	14,198	NA
1970	128,079	20,625	30,646	31,161	13,044	219,471
1975	115,110	21,889	25,677	28,011	7,617	158,541
1980	115,625	23,281	25,893	25,905	7,050	74,956
1984	114,262	23,172	25,572	23,470	6,220	42,217
1985	114,690	22,860	25,798	23,230	4,094	20,124
1986	109,199	22,348	24,991	22,442	3,890	7,296
1987	108,012	22,403	24,778	22,204	3,931	6,857
1988	115,849	23,618	25,719	22,647	4,750	6,513
1989	103,144	23,222	23,935	22,785	3,927	6,034
1990	100,650	23,038	23,599	22,433	3,882	5,666
1991	97,376	22,672	22,877	22,068	3,594	5,279
1992	94,043	22,847	22,420	21,836	3,485	4,899
1993	94,133	23,276	22,575	21,517	3,409	4,938
1994	98,017	23,615	23,174	21,118	3,705	4,956
1995	92,099	21,779	22,865	18,319	42,636	4,986
2000**	81,461	20,545	19,551	17,382	56,882	*
2005**	83,100	20,769	19,881	16,693	62,180	*
2010**	87,169	21,643	20,256	15,659	66,440	*

Carbon Monoxide (CO) Two-thirds of all emissions of carbon monoxide, a colorless, odorless, poisonous gas, are caused by motor-vehicle exhaust. In cities, automobiles account for almost 95 percent of emissions. Exposure to high levels of CO can lead to eyesight problems, poor learning ability, reduced manual dexterity, and difficulty in performing complex tasks.

Lead (Pb) Lead in the air is caused primarily by smelters and battery plants. Lead can also be found in food, paint, water, soil, or dust. Exposure to lead can cause anemia, kidney disease, and reproductive and neurological problems.

Nitrogen Oxides Motor-vehicle exhaust and the byproducts of electric utilities and industrial boilers are the primary sources of nitrogen oxides. Nitrogen dioxide (NO_2) can cause respiratory problems.

Ozone (O_3) Ozone is the major component of smog. It is formed by sunlight acting on NO and VOC (Volatile Organic Compounds) gasses that can be emitted from gas stations, factories, and dry cleaners, among other sources. Exposure to ozone can cause respiratory problems.

Particulate Matter (PM-10) Particulate matter consists of solid or liquid airborne particles that can originate from any number of sources, including power plants and diesel trucks. Exposure can cause respiratory problems and cancer.

Sulfur Dioxide (SO_2) Sulfur dioxide is formed when sulfur-containing fuels are burned. Exposure can cause respiratory problems and exacerbate heart disease.

*Lead levels are expected to diminish at such a rate that they will be minimal by the year 2000.
**Projections.
Source: U.S Environmental Protection Agency

Water Quality in Lakes and Rivers

The following charts illustrate water quality in the nation's rivers, lakes, and the Great Lakes, which, according to the EPA, contain one-fifth of the world's fresh surface water. A good rating describes bodies of water that have attained the water quality standards of states and other jurisdictions. Those with a bad rating have fallen short of those standards.

Impaired River Miles

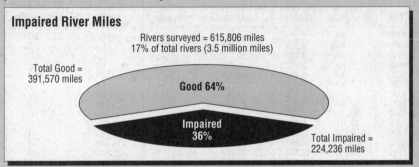

Rivers surveyed = 615,806 miles
17% of total rivers (3.5 million miles)

Total Good = 391,570 miles

Good 64%

Impaired 36%

Total Impaired = 224,236 miles

Impaired Lake Acres

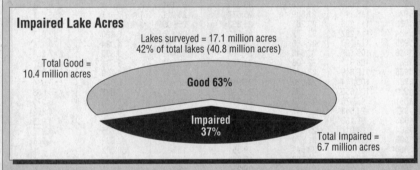

Lakes surveyed = 17.1 million acres
42% of total lakes (40.8 million acres)

Total Good = 10.4 million acres

Good 63%

Impaired 37%

Total Impaired = 6.7 million acres

Impaired Great Lakes Shoreline

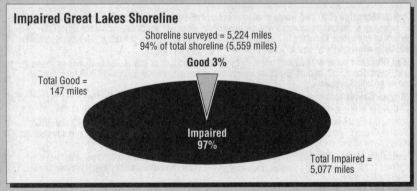

Shoreline surveyed = 5,224 miles
94% of total shoreline (5,559 miles)

Good 3%

Total Good = 147 miles

Impaired 97%

Total Impaired = 5,077 miles

Source: U.S. Environmental Protection Agency

Municipal Waste

Municipal solid waste includes materials such as containers and packaging, food scraps, yard trimmings, and durable and nondurable goods (including appliances, automobile tires, and newspapers).

Generation of Municipal Solid Waste (Thousands of tons)

Year	Total	Per capita*	Year	Total	Per capita*	Year	Total	Per capita*	Year	Total	Per capita*
1960	88,120	2.67	1980	151,640	3.67	1994	209,630	4.40	2000	221,670	4.42
1970	121,060	3.29	1990	197,300	4.33	1995	208,050	4.34	2010	253,000	4.66

*Pounds per person per day.

Materials Generated in the Municipal Waste Stream (Millions of tons)

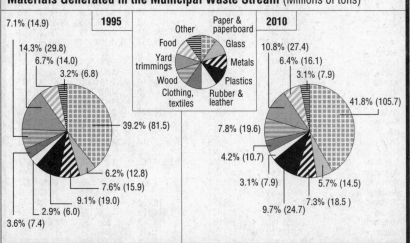

1995

7.1% (14.9)
14.3% (29.8)
6.7% (14.0)
3.2% (6.8)
39.2% (81.5)
6.2% (12.8)
7.6% (15.9)
9.1% (19.0)
2.9% (6.0)
3.6% (7.4)

Other
Paper & paperboard
Food
Glass
Yard trimmings
Metals
Wood
Plastics
Clothing, textiles
Rubber & leather

2010

10.8% (27.4)
6.4% (16.1)
3.1% (7.9)
41.8% (105.7)
7.8% (19.6)
4.2% (10.7)
3.1% (7.9)
5.7% (14.5)
7.3% (18.5)
9.7% (24.7)

Percentage of Municipal Solid Waste Recovered

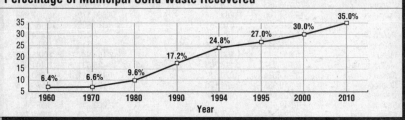

6.4% 1960
6.6% 1970
9.6% 1980
17.2% 1990
24.8% 1994
27.0% 1995
30.0% 2000
35.0% 2010

Year

What Happens to Municipal Waste?

Landfill
Recycled
Composted
Combusted

1960: 63.0% 30.6% 6.4%
1995: 56.9% 22.4% 4.6% 16.1%
2000: 53.7% 24.8% 5.3% 16.2%
2010: 49.6% 29.1% 5.9% 15.4%

Source: U.S. Environmental Protection Agency

States, Ranked by Total Release of Toxic Chemicals, 1995

State	Total air emissions (Pounds)	Surface water discharges (Pounds)	Underground injection (Pounds)	Releases to land (Pounds)	Total releases (Pounds)
Texas	128,694,945	23,413,945	118,850,176	12,973,077	283,932,143
Louisiana	84,841,485	28,268,576	54,494,533	4,654,598	172,259,192
Ohio	73,749,306	3,433,797	14,469,938	30,217,526	121,870,567
Tennessee	103,130,070	1,549,615	1,174,570	5,328,644	111,182,899
Alabama	91,867,818	3,589,626	16	7,307,586	102,765,046
Illinois	70,935,342	5,779,855	365	23,037,696	99,753,258
North Carolina	65,805,573	2,622,401	0	17,732,509	86,160,483
Florida	32,028,305	821,305	25,343,332	25,779,920	83,972,862
Indiana	70,573,627	2,357,535	3,398	6,843,418	79,777,978
Utah	69,215,983	16,236	0	7,089,515	76,321,734
Michigan	62,996,379	653,999	7,566,827	4,046,748	75,263,953
Mississippi	44,048,247	8,373,840	82,251	4,250,916	56,755,254
Georgia	47,606,516	6,345,066	0	1,572,312	55,523,894
South Carolina	51,850,487	1,747,320	0	741,224	54,339,031
Pennsylvania	47,232,633	5,487,942	0	1,539,478	54,260,053
Virginia	50,856,146	872,506	0	1,184,680	52,913,332
Missouri	31,778,685	3,282,973	0	14,585,208	49,646,866
Montana	4,374,595	96,659	0	39,420,586	43,891,840
California	36,819,632	2,641,665	478,974	2,786,805	42,727,076
Kentucky	40,703,729	432,680	0	788,794	41,925,203
New York	30,045,576	5,334,499	5	1,192,979	36,573,059
Arizona	7,306,986	4,829	14	28,520,806	35,832,635
Iowa	29,600,556	3,783,443	0	1,381,081	34,765,080
Arkansas	29,792,097	916,093	2,637,068	1,336,719	34,681,977
Wisconsin	28,534,060	2,094,078	5	549,601	31,177,744
West Virginia	18,393,929	8,665,922	1,000	296,542	27,357,393
Washington	24,025,989	2,367,757	0	57,224	26,450,970
Oklahoma	23,563,664	718,224	10,238	661,337	24,953,463
Kansas	19,450,900	394,121	1,674,129	1,297,174	22,816,324
Minnesota	21,559,433	375,055	0	525,136	22,459,624
Oregon	18,949,703	597,554	0	1,647,454	21,194,711
New Mexico	1,892,903	1,153	0	16,812,196	18,706,252
New Jersey	12,728,407	1,632,366	5	284,578	14,645,356
Maryland	8,868,815	1,881,350	0	2,571,728	13,321,893
Wyoming	2,786,865	8,984	8,168,366	38,347	11,002,562
Nebraska	10,014,706	283,104	0	660,179	10,957,989
Maine	9,242,209	610,781	0	314,865	10,167,855
Puerto Rico	9,397,960	22,262	0	4,456	9,424,678
Connecticut	7,179,523	1,489,456	0	95,110	8,764,089
Idaho	4,689,903	1,390,186	0	2,107,947	8,188,036
Massachusetts	7,996,222	116,200	0	28,631	8,141,053
Alaska	5,405,584	1,070,617	193	483,911	6,960,305
Colorado	4,159,933	294,179	0	121,314	4,575,426
Delaware	4,209,960	286,148	0	14,327	4,510,435
Nevada	1,349,667	0	0	2,209,741	3,559,408
Rhode Island	2,734,284	48,475	0	40	2,782,799
New Hampshire	2,472,394	79,718	0	10,960	2,563,072
North Dakota	2,538,973	21,589	0	1,275	2,561,837
South Dakota	1,911,132	1,487	0	387	1,913,006
Virgin Islands	1,403,451	30,876	0	2,461	1,436,788
Vermont	547,459	2,712	0	2,674	552,845
Hawaii	443,607	1,510	24,306	545	469,968
District of Columbia	10,460	255	0	19,000	29,715
American Samoa	5,300	0	0	0	5,300
Guam	0	3,100	0	0	3,100
Total	1,562,322,113	136,315,624	234,979,709	275,131,965	2,208,749,411

Source: U.S. Environmental Protection Agency

Industries With Largest Total Release of Toxic Chemicals, 1995

Industry	Total release (Pounds)
Chemicals	787,752,210
Primary metals	331,199,802
Paper	233,225,214
Plastics	112,218,977
Transportation equipment	110,017,733
Food	86,012,864
Fabricated metals	82,585,482
Petroleum	59,943,433
Furniture	40,961,204

Parent Companies With the Largest Releases of Toxic Chemicals, 1995

Industry	Total air emissions (Pounds)	Surface water discharges (Pounds)	Underground injection (Pounds)	Releases to land (Pounds)	Total releases (Pounds)
DuPont Co.	32,403,067	3,951,895	48,833,965	592,959	85,781,886
Renco Group Inc.	64,975,116	8,757	0	8,508,400	73,492,273
Asarco Inc.	2,104,053	9,477	175,855	62,732,872	65,022,257
General Motors Corp.	22,418,901	51,881	0	16,429,428	38,900,210
Monsanto Co.	4,083,006	666,772	32,143,357	60,426	36,953,561
Courtaulds United States Inc.	35,182,207	51,870	0	529,400	35,763,477
International Paper Co.	30,475,130	1,107,445	0	53,003	31,635,578
Cytec Industries	2,139,355	459,832	26,387,958	19,236	29,006,381
BP America Inc.	1,440,916	141,524	26,055,630	12,563	27,650,633
Arcadian Corp.	11,240,914	15,841,216	5	442,297	27,524,432

20 Facilities With the Largest Total Release of Toxic Chemicals, 1995

Facility name	City	State	Total release (Pounds)
Magnesium Corp. of America	Rowley	UT	64,339,080
Asarco Inc.	East Helena	MT	39,517,514
Courtaulds Fibers Inc.	Axis	AL	34,018,200
Cytec Industries	Westwego	LA	27,034,568
DuPont Co.	Victoria	TX	25,488,181
Lenzing Fibers Corp.	Lowland	TN	23,231,860
DuPont Co.	Beaumont	TX	21,763,320
BASF Corp.	Freeport	TX	19,324,697
Asarco Inc.	Hayden	AZ	18,310,475
Monsanto Co.	Cantonment	FL	18,058,737
Arcadian Fertilizer L.P.	Geismar	LA	16,780,139
Northwestern Steel & Wire Co.	Sterling	IL	15,759,052
Sterling Chemicals Inc.	Texas City	TX	15,720,998
Elkem Metals Co.	Marietta	OH	15,632,648
General Motors Corp.	Defiance	OH	14,730,020
Hoechst-Celanese Chemical	Pasadena	TX	13,660,060
BP Chemicals Inc.	Lima	OH	13,566,795
PCS Phosphate Co.	Aurora	NC	13,481,075
BP Chemicals Inc.	Port Lavaca	TX	13,105,950
Lafarge Corp.	Alpena	MI	12,746,262

Source: U.S. Environmental Protection Agency

Hazardous-Waste Sites

States Ranked by Final and Proposed Hazardous-Waste Sites for the National Priorities List

These are uncontrolled hazardous-waste sites that warrant further investigation to determine if long-term clean-up and other remedial action are needed under the Superfund program.

State	Total	State	Total
New Jersey	108	Tennessee	15
Pennsylvania	101	Alabama	13
California	94	Arkansas	12
New York	79	Maine	12
Michigan	75	Rhode Island	12
Florida	53	Kansas	11
Washington	50	Oklahoma	11
Illinois	40	Oregon	11
Wisconsin	40	Arizona	10
Ohio	38	Idaho	10
Indiana	31	Nebraska	10
Massachusetts	30	New Mexico	10
Minnesota	30	Puerto Rico	10
Texas	27	Montana	9
South Carolina	26	Vermont	8
Virginia	25	Alaska	7
North Carolina	23	West Virginia	7
Missouri	22	Hawaii	4
Delaware	18	Mississippi	3
Louisiana	18	South Dakota	3
New Hampshire	18	Wyoming	3
Colorado	17	Guam	2
Iowa	17	Virgin Islands	2
Kentucky	16	Nevada	1
Utah	16	North Dakota	1
Connecticut	15	District of Columbia	0
Georgia	15		
Maryland	15	**Total**	**1,254**

Source: U.S. Environmental Protection Agency

Global Warming

The nations of the world are attempting to negotiate a treaty to reduce emissions of gases that create the problem of global warming. The focus is on carbon dioxide, which has been accumulating in the earth's atmosphere and trapping heat from the sun. Here are the world's biggest emitters of carbon dioxide, in millions of metric tons* per year:

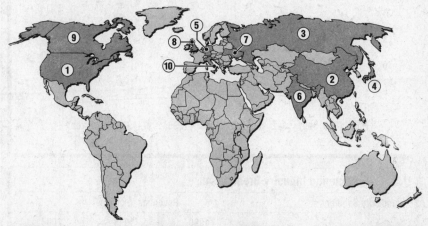

1	U.S.	4.80
2	China	2.60
3	Russian Federation	2.10
4	Japan	1.06
5	Germany	0.87

6	India	0.76
7	Ukraine	0.61
8	United Kingdom	0.56
9	Canada	0.41
10	Italy	0.41

*Equal to 2,204.62 lbs.

Source: U.S. State Department

Cleaning Up

A large environmental services industry has developed in the U.S., but its growth rate has slowed during the 1990s.

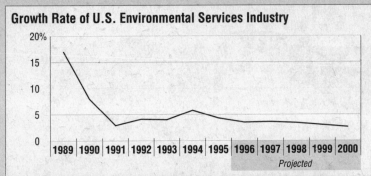

Growth Rate of U.S. Environmental Services Industry

Projected

U.S. Environmental Industry Breakdown

Industry Segment	Revenues ($ billions)		
	1990	1995	2000*
Services			
Analytical Services	1.5	1.5	1.5
Wastewater Treatment Works	19.8	27.3	33.6
Solid Waste Management	26.1	32.5	37.3
Hazardous Waste Management	6.3	6.2	5.3
Remediation/Industrial Services	8.5	8.5	9.0
Consulting and Engineering	12.5	15.5	17.7
Equipment			
Water Equipment and Chemicals	13.5	16.5	20.8
Instruments and Information Systems	2.0	3.0	3.8
Air Pollution Control Equipment	10.7	11.9	12.9
Waste Management Equipment	10.4	11.7	12.1
Process and Prevention Technology	0.4	0.8	1.6
Resources			
Water Utilities	19.8	25.3	30.4
Resource Recovery	13.1	16.9	21.5
Environmental Energy Sources	1.8	2.3	3.3
Total Industry:	**146.4**	**180.0**	**210.7**

*Projected.
Source: Environmental Business International, Inc.

America's Deadliest Disasters*

Type and Location	No. of deaths	Date
Floods:		
Galveston tidal wave	6,000	Sept. 8, 1900
Johnstown, PA	2,209	May 31, 1889
Ohio and Indiana	732	Mar. 28, 1913
St. Francis, CA, dam burst	450	Mar. 13, 1928
Ohio and Mississippi River valleys	380	Jan. 22, 1937
Hurricanes:		
Florida	1,833	Sept. 16–17, 1928
New England	657	Sept. 21, 1938
Louisiana	500	Sept. 29, 1915
Florida	409	Sept. 1–2, 1935
Louisiana and Texas	395	June 27–28, 1957
Tornadoes:		
Illinois	606	Mar. 18, 1925
Mississippi, Alabama, Georgia	402	Apr. 2-7, 1936
Southern and Midwestern states	307	Apr. 3, 1974
Indiana, Ohio, Michigan, Illinois, Wisconsin	272	April 11, 1965
Arkansas, Tennessee, Missouri, Mississippi, Alabama	229	Mar. 21–22, 1952
Earthquakes:		
San Francisco earthquake and fire	452	Apr. 18, 1906
Alaskan earthquake-tsunami hit Hawaii, California	173	Apr. 1, 1946
Long Beach, CA, earthquake	120	Mar. 10, 1933
Alaskan earthquake and tsunami	117	Mar. 27, 1964
San Fernando–Los Angeles, CA, earthquake	64	Feb. 9, 1971
Marine:		
Sultana exploded - Mississippi River	1,547	Apr. 27, 1865
General Slocum burned - East River	1,030	June 15, 1904
Empress of Ireland ship collision - St. Lawrence River	1,024	May 29, 1914
Eastland capsized - Chicago River	812	July 24, 1915
Morro-Castle burned - off New Jersey coast	135	Sept. 8, 1934
Aircraft:		
Crash of scheduled plane near O'Hare Airport, Chicago	273	May 25, 1979
Explosion and crash of scheduled plane off Long Island, NY	230	July 17, 1996
Crash of scheduled plane, Detroit, MI	156	Aug. 16, 1987
Crash of scheduled plane in Kenner, LA	154	July 9, 1982
Two-plane collision over San Diego, CA	144	Sept. 25, 1978
Railroad:		
Two-train collision near Nashville, TN	101	July 9, 1918
Two-train collision, Eden, CO	96	Aug. 7, 1904
Avalanche hit two trains near Wellington, WA	96	Mar. 1, 1910
Bridge collapse under train, Ashtabula, OH	92	Dec. 29, 1876
Rapid transit train derailment, Brooklyn, NY	92	Nov. 1, 1918
Fires:		
Peshtigo, WI, and surrounding area, forest fire	1,152	Oct. 9, 1871
Iroquois Theatre, Chicago	603	Dec. 30, 1903
Northeastern Minnesota, forest fire	559	Oct. 12, 1918
Cocoanut Grove nightclub, Boston	492	Nov. 28, 1942
North German Lloyd Steamships, Hoboken, NJ	326	June 30, 1900
Explosions:		
Texas City, TX, ship explosion	552	Apr. 16, 1947
Port Chicago, CA, ship explosion	322	July 18, 1944
New London, TX, school explosion	294	Mar. 18, 1937
Oakdale, PA, munitions plant explosion	158	May 18, 1918
Eddystone, PA, munitions plant explosion	133	Apr. 10, 1917
Mines:		
Monongha, WV, coal mine explosion	361	Dec. 6, 1907
Dawson, NM, coal mine fire	263	Oct. 22, 1913
Cherry, IL, coal mine fire	259	Nov. 13, 1909
Jacobs Creek, PA, coal mine explosion	239	Dec. 19, 1907
Scofield, UT, coal mine explosion	200	May 1, 1900

*Based on unintentional accidents or disasters.
Source: National Safety Council

Costliest Catastrophes

Total Insured Losses for Catastrophes (In millions)

Year	Estimated loss payment	No. of catastrophes	Year	Estimated loss payment	No. of catastrophes
1985	$2,816	34	1991	$4,723	36
1986	872	26	1992	22,970	36
1987	946	24	1993	5,620	36
1988	1,409	32	1994	17,010	38
1989	7,642	34	1995	8,325	34
1990	2,825	32	1996	7,735	41

The 10 Most Costly Insured Catastrophes

Month/Year	Catastrophe	Estimated insured loss
Aug. 1992	Hurricane Andrew	$13–20,000,000,000
Jan. 1994	Northridge, CA earthquake, fire	12,500,000,000
Sept. 1989	Hurricane Hugo	4,195,000,000
Oct. 1995	Hurricane Opal	2,100,000,000
March 1993	Multi-state winter storm	1,750,000,000
Oct. 1991	Oakland, CA fire	1,700,000,000
Sept. 1992	Hurricane Iniki	1,600,000,000
Sept. 1996	Hurricane Fran	1,600,000,000
May 1995	Texas and New Mexico: wind, hail, flooding	1,135,000,000
Oct. 1989	Loma Prieta, CA earthquake	960,000,000

Sources: Property Claim Services division of American Insurance Services Group and Insurance Information Institute

The 10 Most Costly U.S. Earthquakes*

Year	Locality	Estimated property damage
1994	Northridge, CA	$13–20,000,000,000
1989	San Francisco Bay area (Loma Prieta quake)	7,000,000,000
1971	San Fernando, CA	553,000,000
1964	Alaska and west coast of United States (tsunami damage from earthquake near Anchorage, AK)	500,000,000
1987	Southern California; primarily in Los Angeles-Pasadena-Whittier area	358,000,000
1992	Southern California; Landers, Joshua Tree, Big Bear	92,000,000
1992	Northern California coast; Petrolia, Eureka	66,000,000
1952	Kern County, CA	60,000,000
1933	Long Beach, CA	40,000,000
1983	Central California (Coalinga)	31,000,000

*One of history's most catastrophic occurrences, the San Francisco earthquake-fire of 1906 caused direct quake losses of some $24 million, plus fire losses of $350 million to $500 million, for a total loss in current dollars of nearly $6.0 billion.

Sources: National Geophysical Data Center, National Oceanic and Atmospheric Administration, and Insurance Information Institute

The 10 Most Costly Insured Hurricanes

Dates	Place	Hurricane	Estimated insured loss
Aug. 1992	FL, LA	Andrew	$15,500,000,000
Sept. 1989	U.S. Virgin Islands, PR, GA, SC, NC, VA	Hugo	4,195,000,000
Oct. 1995	FL, AL, GA, SC, NC, TN	Opal	2,100,000,000
Sept. 1992	Kauai and Oahu, HI	Iniki	1,600,000,000
Sept. 1996	NC, SC, VA, MD, WV, PA, OH	Fran	1,600,000,000
Sept. 1995	VI, PR	Marilyn	875,000,000
Sept. 1979	MS, AL, FL, LA, TN, KY, WV, OH, PA, NY	Frederic	752,510,000
Aug. 1983	TX	Alicia	675,520,000
Aug. 1991	NC, NY, CT, RI, MA, ME	Bob	620,000,000
Aug. 1985	FL, AL, MS, LA	Elena	543,000,000

Sources: Property Claim Services division of American Insurance Services Group and Insurance Information Instute

Travel

Pity the poor frequent traveler.

Airplanes are more crowded than they've been at any time in the history of commercial aviation. Business travelers are increasingly stuck in the middle seat, between a crying child and a vacationer with raw oysters in his luggage. Airlines are replacing full-fledged meals with bag lunches, snack baskets and peanuts. And they're taking movies off flights and charging more for lost tickets and for changing tickets.

The travel experience isn't much better on the ground. Hotel rooms in major cities are scarcer than they've ever been, and rental cars are older, grimier and harder to come by. Then there's the price: Air fares, hotel rates, and rental-car rates are at or close to all-time highs. "Anybody planning a vacation now is going to get hammered," says Dave Orr, who owns Ticket to Ride, a travel agency in Chicago.

Blame the situation on the travel industry's new prosperity. In 1996, it generated revenues of a whopping $467 billion: $75 billion by

the airlines, $75 billion by the hotels, and the remainder by travel agents, tour operators and rental-car companies.

But as the industry's revenues grow, so does customer dissatisfaction. The major airlines are "squeezing more people into smaller spaces," says Tim Zagat, publisher of the famous restaurant guide who also does a biannual consumer travel survey. "They're so efficient, they have smaller staffs, smaller planes, smaller everything." The U.S. Transportation Department received more than 7,000 complaints about the airlines in 1996, up nearly 20% from 1993.

Back then, travelers may have been happier, but airline executives were miserable. Travel, always closely tied to consumer confidence and general economic prosperity, fell off in the early 1990s, requiring the airlines to slash prices dramatically to keep their planes full. Virgin Atlantic was offering $89 fares from Newark to London; America West was flying people across the country for $99. With prices like those, the airlines were losing money on every seat. Between 1989 and 1994, the U.S. airline industry lost $12 billion.

Now, the airlines have hit upon a winning formula—one that derives from Economics 101. They've squelched "capacity"—industry jargon for the number of seats in the air—as demand has risen. Their stated goal has been to have slightly fewer seats than they have customers who want them. The strategy has been a resounding success. In 1994, the airlines increased capacity by 1.3%, while traffic rose 5.8%. And in 1996, they boosted capacity by just 3.4%, while traffic jumped 7%.

Capacity can be constrained in several ways. You can fly fewer planes. And you can fly smaller planes. Nearly every major airline has started swapping glorious old 747s and L1011s—planes that, in the words of one airline consultant, "were like a theater with wings"—for skinnier, more cramped 757s. These are the planes that make airline passengers complain that their knees are embedded in their rib cage. Ed Perkins, editor of *Consumer Reports Travel Letter*, characterizes 757s as planes "only an airline treasurer could like."

Further inflaming airline passengers are refinements in the airline's "yield management" systems: software that helps the airline anticipate demand and thus sell each seat for the highest possible price. The most far-reaching result of this technology has been the airline's ability to crank up prices to business travelers—the ones who travel the most, pay the highest prices, and keep coming back again and again. According to a monthly survey by American Express Travel Related Services, business travelers paid 24% more in April 1997 than they did in April 1996. For example, business fares in and out of Atlanta rose 27% to $406, while those in and out of Dallas surged 37% to $517.

Hotels have used a similar supply-demand equation. At the beginning of this decade, the hotel industry had just completed the biggest building boom ever, adding 500,000 rooms in five years. Because of tax incentives, hotels were an attractive investment in the 1980s, and "many projects were built solely for the purpose of being tax writeoffs," says Mark Lomanno, of Smith Travel Research in Hendersonville, Tenn. When travel slacked, the hotel industry took a bath, losing $14 billion between 1986 and 1991.

So in the early 1990s, the hotel industry put a lid on new building projects, creating fewer rooms than the number of people who wanted them. Suddenly, hotel rates skyrocketed. In major cities, business travelers began complaining there wasn't a room to be found. In San Francisco, for instance, average occupancy in 1996 was 78%. In Honolulu, occupancy was 81%. And in New York City, the problem grew so dire that business travelers were forced to sleep on friends' floors and in welfare hotels. Andy Popell, a San Francisco software executive, had to pay $260 a night in Manhattan for a tiny room with itty-bitty beds. And he only got the room for one night. After that, he had to crash with friends.

But while high-end hotel companies resisted building new properties in voguish downtowns, other companies took the opportunity to expand like wildfire in the suburbs and other underdeveloped parts of the country. New building reached an all-time high in 1996 in the center of the country. Now there are 300,000 economy-level rooms in the U.S., three times as many as in 1987.

These new properties are unlike anything that came before. They're low-cost, high-value business hotels, such as Residence Inns, Courtyard by Marriott, Studio Plus. They're targeted especially at the mid-level business travelers away from home for long stretches. They are utterly standardized, so a Studio Plus property in Evansville, Ind., is a clone of a Studio Plus property in Birmingham, Ala. They have few amenities. Gone is the restaurant, the bar, the room service, the turn-down service. Instead, they have perks that make travelers feel at home—and make it easier to work on the road. Standard equipment includes washers and dryers down the hall and data ports near the desk.

Only the car-rental companies have so far been unable to take full advantage of the healthy economy and the rise in U.S. travel. In 1995, the seven major car-rental companies, as a group, broke even on revenues of about $14 billion. The companies made money in 1996, but barely. Industry insiders say total profits amounted to less than $100 million.

With too many cars and not enough customers, the companies have been famously unable to raise prices. "You can rent a car cheaper than you can rent a tuxedo," says Henry R. Silverman, chief executive officer of HFS Inc., the franchise company that owns

30% of Avis Inc. Indeed, over the past 20 years, car-rental rates have barely increased at all, averaging $35 a day.

Over the past year, however, most of the major car-rental companies have changed hands—and now, for the first time in decades, the car-rental companies are either publicly traded or have a publicly traded parent. The new owners say they'll start paying more attention to the bottom line, which would mean the car-rental industry should start to resemble the airline industry: higher prices, scarcer cars and a lot more customer frustration. Already, the rental companies are figuring out as many ways as they can to pass on their costs to the consumer: raising gas prices, passing through state fees and charges, and stocking their print advertisements with paragraphs of small print.

The big question: Will there be a consumer backlash? Will high prices and scarce airline seats finally stop Americans from traveling? Already, there are small signs of softening. Leisure air fares for summer 1997 were slightly lower than in 1996, a sign that customers may be refusing to pay the sky-high prices of recent years. And rental-car customers are expressing their dissatisfaction: In Zagat's travel survey, they were less satisfied than two years ago in every category—service, convenience and availability.

"What other industry treats its best customers worst?" asks Sam Buttrick, airline analyst at Paine Webber. "I'll answer that for you: none."

Lisa Miller, a *Wall Street Journal* staff reporter

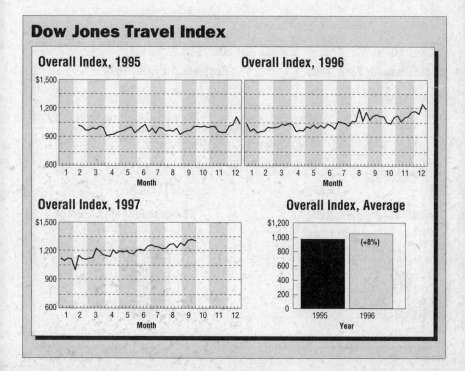

Dow Jones Travel Index

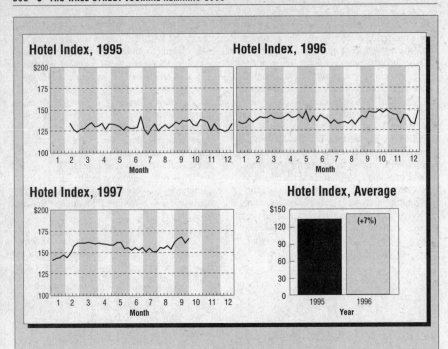

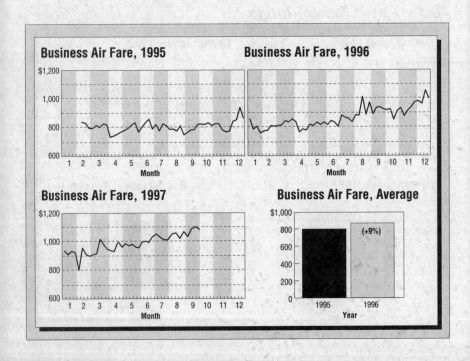

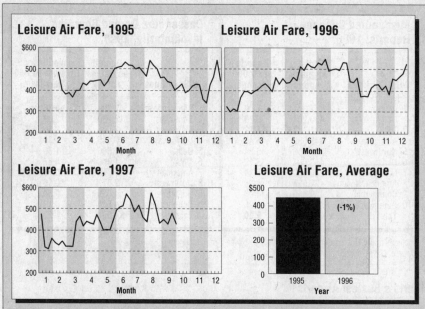

Leisure Air Fare, 1995

Leisure Air Fare, 1996

Leisure Air Fare, 1997

Leisure Air Fare, Average

Note: The overall index——reflecting the average cost of an overnight business trip— tracks the cost of business fares on 20 major routes plus hotel and car-rental rates in 20 cities. Hotel data based on daily rates from 10 leading hotel chains. Business fares based on refundable fares on 20 major routes. Leisure fares based on advance-purchace-fares on the same routes.

Airline Performance Rankings*

Percentage of Reported Flights Arriving on Time

U.S. Airlines	1996 %	Sept. 87– Dec. 96 %
1 Southwest	81.8%	84.8%
2 Continental	76.6	78.7
3 Northwest	76.6	81.7
4 US Airways	75.7	79.1
5 United	73.8	77.4
6 American	72.2	80.0
7 Delta	71.2	77.7
8 America West	70.8	82.4
9 Alaska	68.6	79.3
10 TWA	68.5	77.2
Total	74.5	79.4

Air Travel Consumer Complaint Report, 1996

U.S. Airlines	Complaints	Complaints per 100,000 passengers
1 TWA	293	1.25
2 America West	221	1.22
3 American	741	0.93
4 Northwest	446	0.85
5 United	606	0.74
6 Delta	701	0.72
7 US Airways	388	0.68
8 Continental	210	0.58
9 Alaska	60	0.51
10 Southwest	117	0.21
Total	3,783	0.74

Mishandled Baggage Reports, 1996

U.S. Airlines	Total baggage reports	Reports per 1,000 passengers
1 Alaska	77,371	7.00
2 United	480,204	6.73
3 TWA	131,477	6.12
4 American	343,039	5.47
5 Northwest	233,458	5.34
6 Delta	482,004	5.19
7 US Airways	285,139	5.14
8 America West	77,999	4.38
9 Continental	130,546	4.05
10 Southwest	219,252	3.96
Total	2,460,487	5.30

Passengers Denied Boarding Involuntarily, 1996

U.S. Airlines	Denied boardings (DB's)	Involuntary DB's per 10,000 persons
1 America West	7,896	4.36
2 Southwest	13,230	2.39
3 Alaska	2,651	2.25
4 US Airways	7,445	1.34
5 Delta	11,586	1.30
6 TWA	1,943	0.87
7 American	5,718	0.79
8 Northwest	2,677	0.56
9 United	4,055	0.54
10 Continental	636	0.19
Total	57,837	1.20

*Includes major U.S. carriers with more than $1 billion of annual revenue.
Source: U.S. Transportation Department

World's Busiest Airports

RANK	CITY (AIRPORT)	1996 TOTAL PASSENGERS
1	Chicago (O'Hare Int'l)	69,133,189
2	Atlanta (Hartsfield Atlanta Int'l)	63,344,730
3	Dallas/Ft. Worth Airport, (Dallas/Fort Worth Int'l)	58,034,503
4	Los Angeles (Los Angeles Int'l))	57,974,559
5	London (Heathrow)	56,037,813
6	Tokyo (Haneda)	46,631,475
7	San Francisco (San Francisco Int'l)	39,247,308
8	Frankfurt/Main (Rheim/Main)	38,761,174
9	Seoul (Kimpo Int'l)	34,707,549
10	Miami (Miami Int'l)	33,504,579
11	Denver (Denver Int'l)	32,264,312
12	Paris (Charles de Gaulle)	31,823,741
13	New York (J.F. Kennedy Int'l)	31,015,239
14	Detroit (Metro Wayne County)	30,614,038
15	Las Vegas (McCarran Int'l)	30,470,957
16	Phoenix (Sky Harbor Int'l)	30,376,584
17	Hong Kong (Hong Kong Int'l)	30,212,327
18	Minneapolis/St. Paul (Minneapolis/St. Paul Int'l)	29,612,167
19	Newark (Newark Int'l)	29,072,591
20	Amsterdam (Schiphol)	27,753,088
21	Paris (Orly)	27,364,985
22	St. Louis (Lambert-St. Louis Int'l)	27,274,846
23	Houston (Intercontinental)	26,475,801
24	Orlando (Orlando Int'l)	25,548,773
25	Tokyo (Narita)	25,408,196

Source: Airports Council International

Top 30 Domestic Airline Markets*

			Number of Passengers (outbound plus inbound)
1	New York	Los Angeles	3,149,020
2	New York	Chicago	2,996,460
3	New York	Miami	2,777,610
4	Honolulu	Kahului, Maui	2,750,020
5	New York	Boston	2,400,920
6	New York	San Francisco	2,282,480
7	New York	Orlando	2,234,940
8	Dallas/Ft. Worth	Houston	2,205,080
9	Los Angeles	Las Vegas	2,102,850
10	New York	Washington	2,087,370
11	Los Angeles	San Francisco	2,034,980
12	New York	Atlanta	1,978,680
13	Honolulu	Lihue, Kauai	1,832,820
14	New York	Ft. Lauderdale	1,768,430
15	Los Angeles	Oakland	1,710,310
16	New York	San Juan	1,673,790
17	Chicago	Los Angeles	1,511,120
18	Chicago	Detroit	1,506,680
19	Los Angeles	Phoenix	1,474,500
20	New York	West Palm Beach	1,453,700
21	Honolulu	Kona, Hawaii	1,391,420
22	Los Angeles	Honolulu	1,371,240
23	Honolulu	Hilo, Hawaii	1,281,090
24	Chicago	Minneapolis	1,275,160
25	Los Angeles	Seattle/Tacoma	1,259,130
26	Boston	Washington	1,218,870
27	Chicago	Atlanta	1,216,750
28	New York	Dallas/Ft. Worth	1,168,750
29	New York	Tampa	1,153,880
30	San Francisco	San Diego	1,139,240

*Twelve months ended September 1996. Includes all commercial airports in a metropolitan area. Does not include connecting passengers.

Sources: Air Transport Association, U.S. Transportation Department

The Soaring Airline Industry

The U.S. airline industry achieved record profits in 1996 of $2.82 billion and set records for both the number of passengers and the amount of cargo carried. Passenger traffic increased 7% to 578.4 billion revenue passenger miles, while cargo traffic rose 4.6% to 17.7 billion revenue ton miles.

Individual Airlines

Airline	Number of aircraft	Employees	Aircraft departures	Passengers (Thousands)	Revenue passenger miles (Thousands)	Passenger revenues (Thousands)	Cargo revenues (Thousands)	Total operating revenues (Thousands)	Operating profit/ (loss) (Thousands)	Net profit/ (loss) (Thousands)
Alaska	74	7,440	153,094	11,758	9,793,978	$ 1,105,883	$ 78,528	$ 1,306,621	$ 80,691	$ 45,609
Aloha	17	1,894	77,534	5,059	695,716	187,665	31,233	232,671	6,171	4,335
America West	99	9,357	206,509	18,130	15,275,989	1,625,460	46,519	1,751,813	68,666	8,505
American	642	82,571	787,415	79,324	104,521,123	13,631,844	672,343	15,136,003	1,330,845	573,819
American Trans Air	45	4,480	31,180	3,431	4,914,897	385,556	—	716,123	(39,825)	(30,969)
Continental	317	29,199	442,944	35,743	37,344,225	4,885,152	177,647	5,487,150	394,421	319,551
Delta	544	58,935	942,988	97,201	93,876,999	11,980,514	525,798	13,317,693	571,113	249,024
DHL	27	8,036	67,427	—	—	—	632,092	1,085,360	30,787	27,504
Emery*	74	864	47,750	—	—	—	211,007	213,088	23,654	16,562
Evergreen*	21	388	8,456	—	—	—	160,128	213,029	19,165	(11,408)
Federal Express	563	97,809	310,996	—	—	—	4,723,166	10,950,187	646,985	318,495
Hawaiian	23	2,262	58,683	5,338	3,297,979	326,266	18,771	384,473	1,911	(1,533)
Kiwi	8	855	14,063	1,205	900,064	172,644	1,433	182,749	2,199	2,022
Midwest Express	22	1,430	34,954	1,489	1,239,147	239,172	11,118	270,599	31,442	19,541
Northwest	399	45,320	585,924	52,682	68,626,530	8,598,293	745,787	9,751,383	1,107,926	578,817
Polar Air Cargo	5	409	4,084	—	—	—	231,215	260,181	6,523	3,377
Reeve Aleutian	15	297	4,148	73	40,025	16,403	7,848	27,259	(3,086)	(1,930)
Southwest	243	21,863	748,374	55,372	27,085,489	3,269,240	80,004	3,407,361	349,728	207,337
Trans World	192	24,731	284,416	23,281	27,110,708	3,077,905	153,076	3,554,407	(199,297)	(284,816)
United	564	79,205	785,158	81,863	116,554,641	14,246,992	772,324	16,316,749	1,130,224	533,744
United Parcel Service*	197	4,129	116,725	—	—	—	341,908	1,792,199	76,125	30,135
US Airways	390	39,417	737,628	56,639	38,942,794	6,799,420	158,899	7,704,057	368,668	183,232
Associate Members										
Air Canada	136	19,868	NA	12,600	19,199,000	3,980,000	347,000	4,880,000	215,000	149,000
Canadian	80	15,464	NA	8,578	16,145,000	2,570,700	227,200	3,096,400	91,400	187,100
KLM-Royal Dutch	109	25,033	NA	NA	31,286,000	3,554,000	914,000	5,433,000	47,000	223,000

* Includes non-scheduled service.
Source: AirTransport Association

Total U.S Scheduled Airlines

	1986	1987	1988	1989	1990	1991	1992	1993	1994	1995	1996
Traffic–Scheduled Service											
Revenue passengers enplaned (Thousands)	418,946	447,678	454,614	453,692	465,560	452,301	475,108	488,520	528,848	547,773	581,201
Revenue passenger miles (Thousands)	366,545,855	404,471,484	423,301,559	432,714,309	457,926,286	447,954,829	478,553,708	489,684,421	519,381,688	540,656,211	578,408,509
Available seat miles (Thousands)	607,435,847	648,720,938	676,802,328	684,375,876	733,374,893	715,199,140	752,772,435	771,640,648	784,330,936	807,077,839	834,688,294
Revenue passenger load factor (%)	60.3	62.3	62.5	63.2	62.4	62.6	63.6	63.5	66.2	67.0	69.3
Average passenger trip length (Miles)	875	903	931	954	984	990	1,007	1,002	982	987	995
Freight and express ton miles (Thousands)	7,344,054	8,260,278	9,632,219	10,275,002	10,546,329	10,225,199	11,129,712	11,943,595	13,792,157	14,577,522	15,244,952
Aircraft departures	6,426,970	6,581,309	6,699,564	6,622,080	6,923,593	6,782,782	7,050,633	7,245,395	7,531,026	8,061,521	8,227,938
Financial											
Passenger revenues ($ thousands)	40,056,093	44,940,391	50,295,686	53,802,067	58,453,215	57,091,675	59,828,487	63,945,223	65,421,539	69,594,423	75,315,600
Freight and express revenues ($ thousands)	5,627,996	6,398,156	7,477,731	6,892,754	5,431,627	5,508,572	5,915,650	6,662,389	7,283,927	8,616,169	9,795,068
Mail revenues ($ thousands)	838,278	923,022	971,807	955,455	970,475	957,077	1,184,205	1,211,631	1,183,268	1,265,522	1,279,721
Charter revenues ($ thousands)	1,268,899	1,611,673	1,697,793	2,051,883	2,876,581	3,717,358	2,801,163	3,081,990	3,548,428	3,484,645	3,444,198
Total operating revenues ($ thousands)	50,524,933	56,985,709	63,748,886	69,315,854	76,141,739	75,158,493	78,140,243	84,559,213	88,313,425	94,577,657	101,918,628
Total operating expenses ($ thousands)	49,201,832	54,516,820	60,312,383	67,504,587	78,054,094	76,943,234	80,584,703	83,121,041	85,599,970	88,718,139	95,693,889
Operating profit ($ thousands)	1,323,101	2,468,889	3,436,503	1,811,267	(1,912,355)	(1,784,741)	(2,444,460)	1,438,172	2,713,455	5,859,518	6,224,739
Interest expense ($ thousands)	1,692,548	1,695,388	1,845,762	1,944,388	1,978,163	1,776,994	1,742,641	2,026,793	2,347,478	2,423,877	1,972,589
Net profit ($ thousands)	(234,909)	593,398	1,685,599	127,902	(3,921,002)	(1,940,157)	(4,791,284)	(2,135,626)	(344,115)	2,313,591	2,824,328
Revenue per passenger mile (Cents)	10.9	11.1	11.9	12.4	12.8	12.7	12.5	13.1	12.6	12.9	13.0
Rate of return on investment (%)	4.9	7.2	10.8	6.3	(6.0)	(0.5)	(9.3)	(0.4)	5.2	11.9	11.5
Operating profit margin (%)	2.6	4.3	5.4	2.6	(2.5)	(2.4)	(3.1)	1.7	3.1	6.2	6.1
Net profit margin (%)	(0.5)	1.0	2.6	0.2	(5.1)	(2.6)	(6.1)	(2.5)	(0.4)	2.4	2.8
Employees	421,686	457,349	480,553	506,728	545,809	533,565	540,413	537,111	539,759	546,987	564,425

U.S. Aviation Accidents

	Year	Accidents		Fatalities		Accident rates per 100,000 aircraft hours	
		Total	Fatal	Total	Aboard	Total	Fatal
Large Commercial Carriers	1985	17	4	197	196	0.206	0.048
	1986	21	2	5	4	0.211	0.011
	1987	32	4	231	229	0.306	0.030
	1988	28	3	285	274	0.257	0.019
	1989	24	8	131	130	0.226	0.075
	1990	22	6	39	12	0.191	0.052
	1991	25	4	62*	49	0.224	0.036
	1992	16	4	33	31	0.136	0.034
	1993	22	1	1	0	0.184	0.008
	1994	19	4	239	237	0.146	0.033
	1995	34	2	166	160	0.266	0.016
	1996	32	3	342	342	0.248	0.023
Commuter Carriers	1985	21	7	37	36	1.209	0.403
	1986	15	2	4	4	0.870	0.116
	1987	33	10	59	57	1.695	0.514
	1988	19	2	21	21	0.908	0.096
	1989	19	5	31	31	0.848	0.223
	1990	16	4	7	5	0.683	0.171
	1991	22	8	99*	77	0.960	0.349
	1992	23	7	21	21	0.931	0.269
	1993	16	4	24	23	0.606	0.151
	1994	10	3	25	25	0.359	0.108
	1995	11	2	9	9	0.444	0.081
	1996	11	1	14	12	0.445	0.040
Unscheduled Air Taxis	1985	154	35	76	75	5.99	1.36
	1986	117	31	65	61	4.35	1.15
	1987	96	30	65	63	3.61	1.13
	1988	101	28	59	55	3.84	1.06
	1989	110	25	83	81	3.64	0.83
	1990	106	28	50	48	4.71	1.24
	1991	87	27	70	66	3.88	1.20
	1992	76	24	68	65	3.78	1.19
	1993	69	19	42	42	3.81	1.05
	1994	85	26	63	62	4.26	1.30
	1995	75	24	52	52	3.93	1.26
	1996	87	27	59	59	4.57	1.42
General Aviation**	1985	2,739	498	955	944	9.66	1.75
	1986	2,582	474	967	878	9.54	1.75
	1987	2,495	447	838	823	9.25	1.65
	1988	2,385	460	800	792	8.69	1.68
	1989	2,232	431	768	765	7.98	1.53
	1990	2,215	442	766	761	7.77	1.55
	1991	2,175	432	786	772	7.98	1.58
	1992	2,073	446	857	855	8.71	1.87
	1993	2,039	398	736	732	9.05	1.76
	1994	1,994	404	730	723	9.11	1.84
	1995	2,054	411	733	726	8.72	1.74
	1996	1,907	358	631	614	8.06	1.51

*Includes 12 persons killed aboard a Skywest commuter plane and 22 persons killed aboard a US Airways plane when the aircraft collided.

**Private planes.

Source: National Transportation Safety Board

Danger in the Skies

Accidents and Fatalities: Worldwide Scheduled Air Services

| Year | Excluding the Commonwealth of Independent States | | | Including the Commonwealth of Independent States | |
	Aircraft accidents involving passenger fatalities	Passengers killed	Fatal accidents per 100,000 aircraft hours	Aircraft accidents	Passengers killed
1975	21	467	0.17	–	–
1976	20	734	0.15	–	–
1977	24	516	0.18	–	–
1978	25	754	0.18	–	–
1979	31	877	0.21	–	–
1980	22	814	0.15	–	–
1981	21	362	0.14	–	–
1982	26	764	0.18	–	–
1983	20	809	0.13	–	–
1984	16	223	0.10	–	–
1985	22	1,066	0.13	–	–
1986	17	331	0.09	22	546
1987	24	890	0.12	26	901
1988	25	699	0.12	28	729
1989	27	817	0.12	27	817
1990	22	440	0.09	25	495
1991	25	510	0.11	30	653
1992	25	990	0.10	29	1,097
1993	31	801	0.12	34	936
1994	24	732	0.09	28	941
1995	22	557	0.08	26	710
1996	22	1,132	0.07	23	1,135

Hijackings and Sabotage

| Year | Number of acts of unlawful interference | Number of acts of unlawful seizure | | Number of acts of sabotage | Other acts* | Number of persons injured or killed during acts of unlawful interference | |
		Attempted seizures	Actual seizures			Injured	Killed
1975	47	11	12	24	–	217	92
1976	54	13	13	28	–	215	218
1977	65	16	18	31	–	71	133
1978	37	13	13	11	–	22	59
1979	37	10	16	11	–	194	64
1980	54	17	29	8	–	39	72
1981	53	14	24	15	–	39	8
1982	36	11	19	6	–	119	14
1983	45	17	21	7	–	70	15
1984	41	7	21	13	–	249	68
1985	40	7	20	13	–	243	473
1986	14	6	5	3	–	235	112
1987	13	6	4	3	–	121	166
1988	12	3	7	2	–	21	300
1989	14	4	8	2	–	38	278
1990	36	12	20	1	3	145	137
1991	15	5	7	0	3	2	0
1992	10	2	6	0	2	123	10
1993	30	4	21	0	5	2	28
1994	37	5	20	2	10	53	36
1995	14	2	9	0	3	3	0
1996	14	2	10	0	2	53	126

*Includes missile and facility attacks.
Source: International Civil Aviation Organization

Changing Modes of Travel

Market share of different means of intercity transportation, based on number of passengers carried.

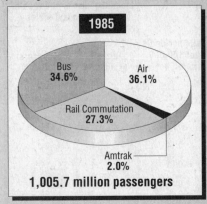

1985

Bus 34.6%
Air 36.1%
Rail Commutation 27.3%
Amtrak 2.0%

1,005.7 million passengers

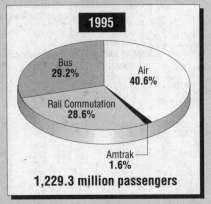

1995

Bus 29.2%
Air 40.6%
Rail Commutation 28.6%
Amtrak 1.6%

1,229.3 million passengers

Source: Eno Transportation Foundation Inc.

Amtrak's Shaky Ride

Increasing Losses (In millions of dollars)

Fiscal year	Revenue	Expenses	Operating loss	Federal subsidies	Net loss
1990	$1,308	$2,012	-$703	$520	-$183
1991	1,359	2,081	-722	488	-234
1992	1,325	2,037	-712	481	-231
1993	1,403	2,134	-731	498	-233
1994	1,413	2,490	-834	502	-332
1995	1,497	2,305	-808	542	-266
1996	1,555	2,318	-764	441	-322

Decreasing Ridership (In millions of passenger trips)

Fiscal year	Northeast corridor	Intercity*	Amtrak West	Total
1990	11.2	11.0	–	22.2
1991	10.9	11.1	–	22.0
1992	10.1	11.2	–	21.3
1993	10.3	11.8	–	22.1
1994	11.7	6.3	3.1	21.2
1995	11.6	6.1	3.0	20.7
1996	11.0	5.4	3.3	19.7

*For years 1990-1993, this number includes Amtrak West Ridership.
Source: Amtrak

The Shifting Rental-Car Market

The major rental-car companies have changed hands at a rapid pace over the last couple of years. Here is a look at the rental-car market before and after the many ownership changes.

Top Rental Car Players Before Ownership Changes
Share of 1996 Rental Car Days (U.S. Travel)

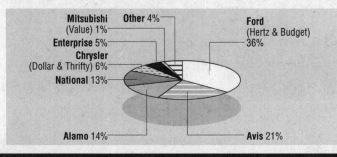

Mitsubishi (Value) 1%
Other 4%
Enterprise 5%
Ford (Hertz & Budget) 36%
Chrysler (Dollar & Thrifty) 6%
National 13%
Alamo 14%
Avis 21%

Top Rental Car Players After Ownership Changes
Share of 1996 Rental Car Days (U.S. Travel)

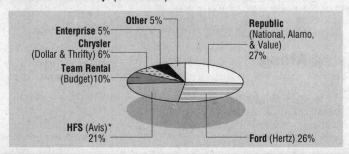

Other 5%
Enterprise 5%
Chrysler (Dollar & Thrifty) 6%
Republic (National, Alamo, & Value) 27%
Team Rental (Budget) 10%
HFS (Avis)* 21%
Ford (Hertz) 26%

Note: The rental car sample was drawn from a total of 300,000 questionaires, which are mailed out each year to a Census-based, representative sample of U.S. households. Market share figures are in "Car-Days" (total number of days cars were rented from all locations) for both business and leisure travel.
*After a public stock offering in 1997, HFS retained about a 30% interest in Avis.
Source: D.K. Shifflet & Associates Ltd., McLean, VA.

Top Car-Rental Companies In 1996

Company	U.S. cars in service (average) 1996	# U.S. locations	U.S. rental revenue* ($ millions) 1995	U.S. rental revenue* ($ millions) 1996 (est.)
Enterprise	315,100	2,636	$ 2,060.0	$ 2,610.0
Hertz	250,000	1,200	2,400.0	2,700.0
Avis	190,000	1,130	1,500.0	1,800.0
Alamo	130,000	171	1,180.0	1,300.0
Budget	126,000	1,052	1,500.0	1,500.0
National	135,000	935	1,200.0	1,350.0
Dollar	63,500	450	560.0	592.0
FRCS (Ford)	55,250	1,784	312.5	325.0
Thrifty	34,000	480	340.0	350.0
PROP (Chrysler)	27,000	1,500	160.0	165.0
Value	18,000	45	150.1	182.1
Snappy	15,500	259	85.0	100.0
Payless	15,000	100	47.0	50.0
U-Save	13,500	500	95.0	115.0
Rent-A-Wreck	10,942	460	78.0	85.4
Total market	**1,588,217**	**22,188**	**13,030.0 million**	**14,620 million**

*Revenue comes from car rental operations only, including ancillary counter sales. Revenue represents the entire system, including corporate and franchise revenue.
Source: Auto Rental News

Cruising Along

More vacationers are taking a sea cruise, a trend that has prompted Walt Disney Co. to launch its own ships.

Annual Number of Cruise Ship Passengers

(On cruises originating in the U.S. and Canada)

1970	0.5 million
1980	1.4 million
1990	3.6 million
1995	4.4 million
1996	4.7 million

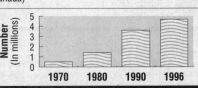

Source: Cruise Lines International Association

Most Popular Cruise Routes

Percentage of cruise ship capacity for 1996

Caribbean, Western Caribbean and Bahamas	50.3%	Europe	3.3
Mediterranean	9.3	Bermuda	2.7
Alaska	9.5	Trans-Atlantic	1.6
Panama	7.0	Hawaii	1.9
Mexico	5.2	South Pacific	0.8

Source: Cruise Lines International Association

Checking In

The top 25 hotel markets in the U.S. and their average occupancy rates and room rates for 1996.

Largest U.S. Hotel Markets Based on Room Count 1996 Year End

Rank	Market	Number of hotels	Rooms	Occupancy percent	Average room rate
1	Las Vegas, NV	249	101,500	84.8 %	$ 72.42
2	Orlando, FL	310	85,800	80.2	73.19
3	Los Angeles-Long Beach, CA	630	78,900	67.9	75.91
4	Chicago, IL	384	69,000	72.0	92.04
5	Washington, DC-Metro Area	360	68,400	68.4	94.42
6	Atlanta, GA	454	67,300	67.7	81.69
7	New York, NY	237	63,300	80.2	150.26
8	Dallas, TX	388	46,500	69.5	74.76
9	San Diego, CA	290	44,700	68.7	80.86
10	Anaheim-Santa Ana, CA	352	44,500	69.5	70.04
11	San Francisco, CA	302	42,800	78.7	106.47
12	Houston, TX	242	40,400	62.0	66.11
13	Miami-Hialeah, FL	215	38,200	71.2	85.83
14	Oahu Island, HI	232	36,300	80.7	107.11
15	Phoenix, AZ	117	36,200	71.4	95.34
16	Boston, MA	219	34,500	73.5	105.51
17	Tampa-St. Petersburg, FL	272	33,100	63.4	67.45
18	Norfolk-Virginia Beach, VA	299	32,100	58.1	61.83
19	Detroit, MI	244	30,800	68.7	64.79
20	Riverside-San Bernardino, CA	344	30,700	57.6	75.93
21	Philadelphia, PA	203	29,300	70.1	83.56
22	Nashville, TN	209	26,800	67.1	70.12
23	Seattle, WA	226	25,800	73.4	82.60
24	Minneapolis-St.Paul, MN	195	25,700	69.8	73.64
25	New Orleans, LA	133	25,700	70.6	99.00

Source: Smith Travel Research

Where America Sleeps

Both the average occupancy rate and room rate for the U.S. lodging industry have been rising, following a slump in the early 1990s.

Average U.S. Hotel Occupancy and Daily Room Rates

Year	Occupancy rate	Room rate	Year	Occupancy rate	Room rate
1987	63.2 %	$ 52.58	1992	62.6 %	$ 58.91
1988	63.5	54.47	1993	63.5	60.53
1989	64.3	56.35	1994	64.7	62.86
1990	63.5	57.96	1995	65.1	65.81
1991	61.8	58.08	1996	65.2	69.66

The Largest Hotel and Motel Chains in the U.S., Ranked by Total Number of Rooms, December 1996

Chain	Number of rooms	Number of properties	Chain	Number of rooms	Number of properties
1. Holiday Inn	225,342	1,196	6. Marriott	95,202	226
2. Best Western	182,045	1,991	7. Super 8	88,565	1,450
3. Days Inn	151,576	1,657	8. Motel 6	83,971	742
4. Ramada	102,422	660	9. Hampton Inn	66,997	617
5. Comfort Inn	100,271	1,213	10. Sheraton Hotel	59,160	153

Source: Smith Travel Research

Vacations off the Beaten Path

When Rayne Pollack plans her summer vacations, Walt Disney World and Las Vegas don't even make her list.

Instead, the 34-year-old legislative assistant to Sen. James Jeffords of Vermont is more likely to hop on her bike for a week-long cycling tour of the Irish countryside, go climbing in the Pyrenees and ride horses in France's Loire Valley. "I love my job, but its very sedentary," she explains. "I love to be active and athletic."

So do thousands of other Americans. Although theme parks and beaches are still a huge draw, more travelers crave adventure and exotic experiences. They're turning to mountain biking, canoeing, and white-water rafting or heading to the far corners of the world—places like the Amazon jungle and Nepal. For some people, such trips are a status symbol; for others, they satisfy a personal interest.

"Most of their [travelers'] lives are so predictable, they want to be a little stretched," says Richard Weiss, president of Mountain Travel-Sobek in El Cerrito, Calif., which offers vacations to Kilimanjaro, visits to nomadic tribes in China and Pakistan, and a sea-kayaking trip off the coast of Greenland.

Jerry Mallett, president of the Adventure Travel Society, says there are 10,000 adventure-travel outfits in the United States, up from about 7,000 five years ago. The Society estimates that between 75 and 100 million adventure trips are taken each year—from half-day canoeing excursions to three-week African safaris.

One thriving tour operator is Bill Dvorak's Kayak and Rafting Expeditions in Nathrop, Colo., which takes about 3,000 people a year on river trips in five western states. Mr. Dvorak has seen his business grow 5% to 10% a year during the last decade. Twice a year, Mr. Dvorak even runs an eight-day trip with a string quartet from famous orchestras around the country that serenades travelers on the banks of the Dolores River in Colorado ($1,660 per person) or the Green River in Utah ($1,705). The trip is for "people who want to combine a wilderness adventure with a little culture," says Mr. Dvorak, who has constructed a special "splash-proof" box to house the $150,000 worth of instruments he carries in his raft.

Among the affluent, cruises in Antarctica, treks in the mountains of Nepal, and beach vacations in Thailand are all on the rise. "These are people who have pretty much been everywhere.... They're looking for something new," says Rosalie Maniscalco, a field marketing manager for American Express Co. Even young people with more modest travel budgets are seeking out the unconventional. While a post-college jaunt to Europe is still popular, many Generation Xers are flocking to spots off the beaten track, such as Turkey, Poland, Thailand and Vietnam.

Jerry Useem, a 26-year-old magazine writer from Boston, is well traveled for his age. He studied in France during his junior year in college, traveled through Europe during school vacations, and has trekked across America more than once. So he and his girlfriend headed to Indonesia for eight days of snorkeling, hiking and climbing volcanoes. "I guess it really depresses me when I find it hard to get anywhere in the world that feels really foreign," Mr. Useem says. Indonesia "is still one place in the world that hasn't fallen prey to the homogenization of world culture and western norms."

Armed with volumes of travel information available over the Internet, some travelers are combining their interests and hobbies with their vacations, whether it be a passion for wine or concern for the environment. The EcoTourism Society estimates that 43 million Americans took a nature trip to places like the rain forests of Costa Rica or the rivers of Antarctica between 1992 and 1995. People on these expeditions learn about different

ecosystems and often plant trees and visit schools in the local towns.

Such trips teach "global awareness, that not all parts of the world are exactly like the U.S.," says Amy Bonanata, president of Costa Rica Experts in Chicago, which promotes a 10-day trip to Costa Rica for $1,600. "It used to be naturalists, biologists, botanists, and birders" who went to the rain forests she adds. "Now, it's honeymooners and yuppies. They've heard it's a nice place to go."

Andrea Petersen

Top Summer Travel Destinations

1995
1. Disneyland/Walt Disney World
2. Las Vegas
3. Europe
4. Caribbean
5. Florida
6. Mexico
7. Other
8. Hawaii
9. California
10. Alaska

1996
1. Disneyland/Walt Disney Word
2. Florida
3. Las Vegas
4. Caribbean
5. Mexico
6. Europe
7. Hawaii
8. Alaska
9. California
10. Canada

Source: Carlson Wagonlit Travel

How I Spent My Summer Vacation

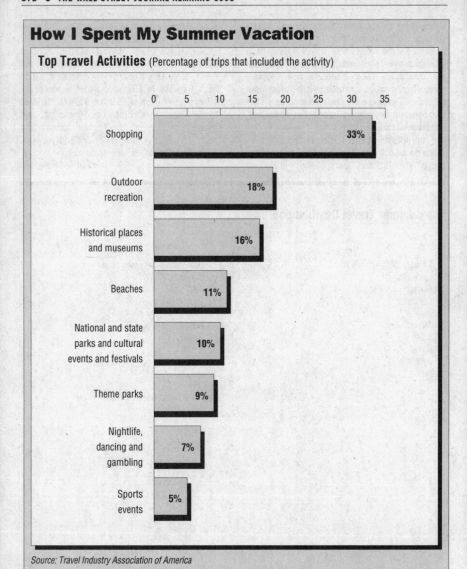

Top Travel Activities (Percentage of trips that included the activity)

- Shopping — 33%
- Outdoor recreation — 18%
- Historical places and museums — 16%
- Beaches — 11%
- National and state parks and cultural events and festivals — 10%
- Theme parks — 9%
- Nightlife, dancing and gambling — 7%
- Sports events — 5%

Source: Travel Industry Association of America

Animals, Aquariums and Amusements

Annual Attendance Figures

Year	Zoos	Aquariums	Amusement Parks
1990	80,385,123	24,520,550	253,000,000
1991	75,598,685	24,750,410	260,000,000
1992	77,917,025	30,734,641	267,000,000
1993	79,850,529	35,485,101	275,000,000
1994	81,415,327	34,289,580	267,000,000
1995	85,045,542	34,770,315	280,000,000
1996	85,504,189	34,738,589	290,000,000

Sources: American Zoo and Aquarium Association and
International Association of Amusement Parks and Attractions

Attendance at Top 10 Amusement/Theme Parks*

Name	1994	1995	1996
Disneyland Anaheim, CA	10.3 million	14.1 million	15.0 million
The Magic Kingdom at Walt Disney World Lake Buena Vista, FL	11.2 million	12.9 million	13.8 million
Epcot at Walt Disney World Lake Buena Vista, FL	9.7 million	10.7 million	11.2 million
Disney-MGM Studios at Walt Disney World Lake Buena Vista, FL	8.0 million	9.5 million	10.0 million
Universal Studios Florida Orlando, FL	7.7 million	8.0 million	8.4 million
Universal Studios Hollywood Universal City, CA	4.6 million	4.7 million	5.4 million
Sea World of Florida Orlando, FL	4.6 million	5.0 million	5.1 million
Busch Gardens Tampa Tampa, FL	3.7 million	3.8 million	4.2 million
Six Flags Great Adventure Jackson, NJ	3.2 million	4.0 million	4.0 million
Sea World of California San Diego, CA	3.7 million	3.75 million	3.9 million

*Top 10 designation derived from 1996 attendance ranking.
Source: Amusement Business

Fun With Physics

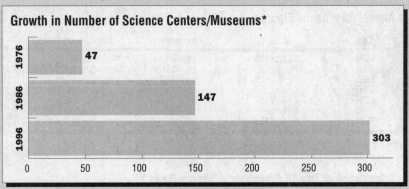

Growth in Number of Science Centers/Museums*

Year	Value
1976	47
1986	147
1996	303

*Figures include members of the association only.
Source: Association of Science-Technology Centers

Visiting America's National Parks

Annual Attendance

National Park	1993	1994	1995	1996
Acadia	2,656,000	2,710,700	2,845,400	2,704,800
Badlands	1,179,500	1,130,500	1,075,600	1,024,700
Bryce Canyon	1,108,000	1,028,100	944,500	1,269,600
Death Valley	998,500	971,500	1,109,400	1,189,200
Everglades	973,700	886,500	820,500	890,200
Glacier	2,141,700	2,153,000	1,839,500	1,720,800
Grand Canyon	4,575,600	4,364,300	4,557,600	4,537,700
Grand Teton	2,568,700	2,540,700	2,731,000	2,733,400
Great Smoky Mountains	9,283,800	8,628,200	9,080,400	9,265,700
Haleakala	1,317,400	1,527,300	1,594,600	1,553,300
Hawaii Volcanoes	1,143,700	1,174,300	1,175,000	1,231,600
Hot Springs	1,477,300	1,618,800	1,617,100	1,538,100
Joshua Tree	1,252,400	1,184,900	1,235,700	1,095,000
Kings Canyon	636,500	725,900	832,800	506,700
Mammoth Cave	2,396,200	2,009,900	1,935,700	1,896,800
Mesa Verde	666,100	685,000	663,800	617,400
Mount Rainier	1,365,200	1,426,200	1,438,200	1,339,000
Olympic	2,679,600	3,381,600	3,658,600	3,348,700
Petrified Forest	936,400	922,900	935,100	829,500
Redwood	421,000	475,000	552,500	426,900
Rocky Mountain	2,780,300	2,968,500	2,878,200	2,923,800
Sequoia	1,066,600	1,034,100	844,600	838,100
Shenandoah	1,951,400	1,926,900	1,757,800	1,571,000
Yellowstone	2,912,200	3,046,100	3,125,300	3,012,200
Yosemite	3,839,600	3,962,100	3,958,400	4,046,200
Zion	2,392,600	2,270,900	2,430,200	2,498,000

Source: National Park Service

ANNUAL VACATION COST SURVEY
(For a Family of Two Adults and Two Children)

State	Avg. Daily Meal Costs*	Avg. Nightly Lodging Rate**	Total
Alabama	$107	$62	$169
Alaska	$113	$104	$217
Arizona	$112	$118	$230
Arkansas	$89	$73	$162
California	$124	$134	$258
Colorado	$104	$132	$236
Connecticut	$116	$89	$205
Delaware	$135	$111	$246
Florida	$110	$142	$252
Georgia	$100	$115	$215
Hawaii	$141	$270	$411
Idaho	$94	$84	$178
Illinois	$111	$114	$225
Indiana	$90	$63	$153
Iowa	$84	$62	$146
Kansas	$84	$63	$147
Kentucky	$100	$65	$165
Louisiana	$122	$135	$257
Maine	$103	$74	$177
Maryland	$121	$123	$244
Massachusetts	$111	$183	$294
Michigan	$91	$76	$167
Minnesota	$99	$53	$152
Mississippi	$107	$67	$174
Missouri	$92	$83	$175
Montana	$94	$61	$155
Nebraska	$82	$55	$137
Nevada	$124	$88	$212
New Hampshire	$100	$88	$188
New Jersey	$131	$141	$272
New Mexico	$105	$65	$170
New York	$140	$172	$312
North Carolina	$98	$96	$194
North Dakota	$80	$49	$129
Ohio	$99	$74	$173
Oklahoma	$89	$71	$160
Oregon	$112	$81	$193
Pennsylvania	$111	$107	$218
Rhode Island	$108	$98	$208
South Carolina	$98	$56	$154
South Dakota	$78	$62	$140
Tennessee	$97	$72	$169
Texas	$105	$79	$184
Utah	$106	$85	$191
Vermont	$105	$103	$208
Virginia	$110	$88	$198
Washington	$102	$93	$195
West Virginia	$93	$82	$175
Wisconsin	$94	$85	$179
Wyoming	$91	$90	$181
National Average	$104	$95	$199

Most Expensive States	Least Expensive States
1. Hawaii ($411)	1. North Dakota ($129)
2. New York ($312)	2. Nebraska ($137)
3. New Jersey ($272)	3. South Dakota ($140)
4. California ($258)	4. Iowa ($146)
5. Louisiana ($257)	5. Kansas ($147)

* excludes beverages, taxes and gratuity
** 2 person/2 beds rate plus $12 for two children

Source: American Automobile Association

International Travelers to the U.S.
(Estimates in Thousands)

RANK IN 1996	1996	% CHANGE 96/95	1997	% CHANGE 97/96
Canada	15,301	4%	15,884	4%
Mexico	8,530	6%	8,960	5%
Japan	5,047	10%	5,471	8%
United Kingdom	3,105	8%	3,313	7%
Germany	1,973	7%	2,057	4%
France	990	7%	1,056	7%
Brazil	891	6%	963	8%
South Korea	796	34%	954	20%
Italy	552	5%	575	4%
Australia	461	9%	494	7%
Venezuela	456	-11%	461	1%
Netherlands	434	6%	457	5%
Taiwan	427	3%	456	7%
Argentina	426	12%	456	7%
Switzerland	412	4%	429	4%
Spain	321	6%	337	5%

Source: Tourism Industries, International Trade Administration

On the Go

Total Number of Trips Taken by Americans

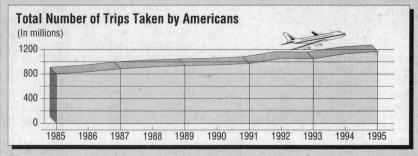

(In millions)

Type of Trip (In millions)

Year	Pleasure	Business	Total*
1985	540	196	808
1986	576	200	841
1987	603	218	894
1988	621	224	925
1989	633	246	945
1990	649	222	956
1991	667	224	980
1992	736	278	1,063
1993	740	275	1,058
1994	781	247	1,139
1995	810	275	1,173

*Includes other types of trips, such as for funerals or other personal reasons.
Source: Travel Industry Association of America

Foreign Invasion

International Travel to the United States

Year	Foreign visitors (millions)	Trade surplus (billions)
1986	26.0	$ -6.5
1987	29.5	-6.0
1988	34.1	-1.4
1989	36.6	5.2
1990	39.5	10.4
1991	43.0	18.9
1992	47.3	22.3
1993	45.7	22.5
1994	45.5	21.6
1995	43.5	19.5
1996	46.3	21.1

Tourist Dollars

Growth in Travel Receipts Over the Past Decade

Year	Expenditures (billions) Domestic	International
1986	$216	$26
1987	235	31
1988	258	38
1989	273	47
1990	291	58
1991	296	64
1992	308	71
1993	322	75
1994	339	78
1995	352	78

Economic Impact of Travel and Tourism in the United States in 1996

Expenditures: $467 billion   Payroll: $116 billion   Jobs: 6.6 million   Tax revenue: $64 billion

Source: Travel Industry Association of America

Transportation

Not long ago, a headline in a computer trade publication asked, "What if General Motors Sold Computers?" Here are a few answers posted by wags on the Internet:

- A lot of hoopla would accompany the introduction of each year's new models, even though they would be pretty much the same as the previous year's.
- When a computer crashed, it would bounce across the room out of control, destroying three other computers.
- Every computer available in 1997 would have the same capacity and performance as in 1987—but would cost twice as much.
- Right after the salesman finished telling you how reliable your new computer is, you would be pressured to buy an extended computer warranty.

Americans' contempt for the car business is about as strong as their love affair with cars. But as the U.S. auto industry embarks on its second century, the people who make and sell cars are trying to shake some of the industry's more contemptible aspects. The ultimate consumer-product industry is showing signs of catching up with other, more nimble consumer-product sectors.

Among the indications is that Detroit is shedding its old arrogance and starting to listen to customers. Auto makers are overhauling how they decide what to make, packing new cars with more high-tech, user-friendly capabilities, and whacking cost-bloating waste out of the way they make, distribute, and sell vehicles. Cars, vans, pickups, and sport-utility vehicles are becoming safer, easier to maintain, and longer-lasting.

In many ways, the auto business is thus starting to act more like, well, the computer business. New technology—including computers themselves—are making new cars and trucks substantially different from their predecessors, and the pace of change is picking up. Alternative engines are appearing. Retailing is turning into a free-for-all, with new, "big-box" participants jumping in and stiffening the competition. "I've never seen a period of such rapid change on so many fronts," declares Robert L. Rewey, Ford Motor Co.'s group vice president for marketing and sales.

Perhaps most surprisingly the automatic annual price increase for virtually the same car as last year's seems to be dying. The Japanese have already proved it possible to offer a new, improved Toyota Camry at a lower price than the old one without giving up profits. Now the Big Three are racing to cut thousands of dollars out of the cost of each vehicle, knowing that the competition is likely to force them to pass some of the reductions on to consumers, just as computer makers do.

"It's very unlikely that we will get a price increase out of the American consumer any time in the next several years," concedes Alex Trotman, the chairman of Ford. "The challenge for us is to offer a vehicle so attractive to the consumer that we can still improve our margins." This strategy relies on Ford's determination to reduce its total costs for the first time in its 94-year history.

For an industry that always thought it knew what Americans wanted, the last quarter of the twentieth century has been humbling. When high-quality, low-priced competition from the Japanese gave consumers more choices, Detroit's old ways of making product decisions based on financial formulas and executives' tastes quit working. When increases in auto prices outpaced growth in personal incomes, the industry learned how high was too high. And when consumers started choosing between a new car and a new computer system, or a new electronic entertainment center, or a Mediterranean cruise, auto moguls realized their products needed to inspire more enthusiasm and loyalty.

So auto makers started taking a harder look at what they were doing and why. GM hired Vince Barabba, a former director of the U.S. Census Bureau, to help it understand the vehicle needs of different demographic groups. It later hired Ronald Zarrella, a consumer marketer with experience at Proctor & Gamble and at Bausch & Lomb, to teach engineers how to think about brand management. Ford and Chrysler Corp. have similarly put extensive demographic and consumer-needs analysis at the center of new-product development, and they are bringing in new marketing blood.

When GM started developing the 1997

Chevrolet Malibu five years ago, it hired a cultural anthropologist to help determine what customers really wanted. Developers learned that exterior styling wasn't as important as they had thought. "People tend to look at their car as more of a tool today," says Pat Henyon, a member of the Malibu team. "Customers just want their cars to work right and last long. They don't want it to make a statement about themselves."

Such realizations have led to a wholesale reversal of how auto makers design new cars and trucks. Functionality and comfort are more important than ever. Designers exhaustively study just where to place vehicle controls, sound-system knobs, cup holders and electrical outlets for video games, CD players and computers. There are compartments everywhere. Another top priority is durability. Several new engine families now are designed to run 100,000 miles without a tuneup—more than three times as long as previously. With more sophisticated use of sheet metal, rust has become virtually a nonissue.

Computers are bringing a raft of new capabilities to autos—besides such gimmicks as satellite-based navigation systems. The most important have to do with helping drivers to better maintain control of their vehicles and avoid accidents. Already, some luxury cars are offering computerized systems that help keep a vehicle from skidding by integrating engine, steering and brake controls with sensors that detect wheel speeds, steering-wheel orientation and whether the vehicle itself is spinning out. All this enables ordinary drivers to pull off avoidance maneuvers that only those with special training and practice can handle in conventional autos. It probably won't be long before mass-market vehicles have something similar.

Other advances that once sounded far-out already are being driven on test vehicles and could go into production within the next half-dozen years. For example, Japan's Toyota Motor Corp. showed off in 1997 an experimental car loaded with sensors that work with 15 safety systems. These include cameras in the front bumper to see around blind corners, an airbag on the hood to protect a pedestrian hit by the car and a seat with a vibrator to awaken a drowsy driver. The car also uses radar and video cameras to detect slower-moving or stopped objects, warn the driver and then automatically stop the car if the driver doesn't take evasive action.

Several auto makers and components suppliers have been developing "smart" cruise control systems. These use lasers or radar to detect slower-moving vehicles and then adjust a car's speed to avoid accidents or too-close following. And then there are experiments that would free motorists from the trouble of driving altogether—by turning the job over to sensors and computers. That development may be a little further in the future.

For the first time in several decades, consumers may soon have a choice besides conventional internal combustion engines for powering their vehicle. In response to regulatory pressure, several auto makers have started selling electric vehicles in California, although their range is still limited and recharging batteries is time-consuming. In Japan in 1997, Toyota planned to start selling a midsized car powered by a so-called "hybrid" system combining a small conventional engine with an electric motor. It is expected to get 70 miles to a gallon, and Toyota is contemplating selling it in the U.S.

After struggling for years to catch up with their Japanese rivals, the U.S. auto makers appear to be on the verge of making real progress on cutting manufacturing and distribution costs. In the 1990s, all the auto makers have been shifting more and more components design, engineering and manufacturing to lower-cost, more specialized suppliers. Now, in Latin America, GM is experimenting with futuristic factory schemes that would hand off significant portions of vehicle assembly to the suppliers of major components. Germany's Volkswagen AG and others are pursuing similar ideas.

While that particular development may not come to the U.S. right away, Ford in 1997 started rolling out what may be the industry's first comprehensive attempt to gain efficiencies all the way from supplier factories to the dealer showroom floor. The complex scheme involves efforts to cut parts inventories by ordering components only as they are needed to build specific vehicles, to cut vehicle inventories by building only what is ordered by dealers and by squeezing transit times, and to maximize profits by building more cars that precisely fit what customers want. Ford thinks the program will wring billions of dollars of waste and added costs out of its system, and rivals are pursuing similar ends.

For consumers, gaining distribution

efficiencies holds big potential. Distribution costs—including advertising, transportation, inventory carrying costs and other outlays—account for about 25% of vehicle sticker prices, or about $5,000 for a $20,000 car. Industry marketers believe they can cut $1,000 to $2,000 of those costs, which would help hold down price increases or give auto makers leeway to reduce prices. In addition, each of the Big Three hopes to cut the amount of time it takes to fill a customer's order to two weeks from the present two months. This would encourage consumers to custom-order vehicles rather than settle for whatever is available on a dealer lot.

Such initiatives tie in with the revolution that is taking place in auto retailing. Thanks to pressure from new entries in the vehicle-selling business, such as Republic Industries Inc.'s AutoNation unit and Circuit City Stores Inc.'s CarMax, the American way of buying a car is rapidly changing. The auto makers themselves have started pressing harder to consolidate and make more uniform the operations of their own dealer networks.

As a result of all this, buying a car will become more like buying a computer or another major appliance. Big chains of auto dealers and the manufacturers themselves are determined to cut the average time it takes to complete a car-purchase transaction to 90 minutes or less from around six hours spread over two or more days. New technology is making financing a car about as easy as pulling out your Visa card to charge the groceries. And getting the best price no longer requires a lot of haggling. The Internet and various buying services already have taken most of the mystery out of new-car price tags, and some auto dealers have taken to offering rock-bottom prices on their Web pages.

Will there be big automotive department stores offering Chevies next to Fords next to Toyotas? Perhaps, if CarMax and AutoNation have their way, but that isn't the auto makers' idea of brand management. What seems more likely, marketing experts say, is that the Internet will become even more of a virtual marketplace than it already has become, providing car shoppers a place to make comparisons, look for the best prices and even customize the car they want. More and more, dealers will be simply closing the transaction, delivering vehicles and servicing them.

Robert L. Simison,
Detroit bureau chief of
The Wall Street Journal

America Keeps on Truckin'

Americans are buying more sport-utility vehicles and other types of trucks, reducing passenger cars' share of the total vehicle market.

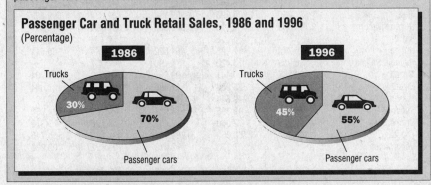

Passenger Car and Truck Retail Sales, 1986 and 1996
(Percentage)

1986 — Trucks 30%, Passenger cars 70%
1996 — Trucks 45%, Passenger cars 55%

Annual U.S. Motor Vehicle Retail Sales
(In thousands)

Year	Passenger cars			Trucks			Motor vehicles		
	Domestic	Import	Total	Domestic	Import	Total	Domestic	Import	Total
1931	1,903	NA	1,903	328	NA	328	2,231	NA	2,231
1941	3,763	NA	3,763	902	NA	902	4,665	NA	4,665
1951	5,143	21	5,164	1,111	NA	1,111	6,254	21	6,275
1961	5,556	379	5,935	908	29	937	6,464	408	6,872
1971	8,681	1,561	10,242	2,011	85	2,096	10,693	1,646	12,338
1981	6,209	2,327	8,536	1,809	451	2,260	8,018	2,778	10,796
1982	5,759	2,224	7,982	2,146	414	2,560	7,905	2,637	10,542
1983	6,795	2,387	9,182	2,658	471	3,129	9,454	2,858	12,312
1984	7,952	2,439	10,390	3,475	618	4,093	11,427	3,057	14,484
1985	8,205	2,838	11,042	3,902	779	4,682	12,107	3,617	15,724
1986	8,215	3,245	11,460	3,921	941	4,863	12,136	4,186	16,322
1987	7,081	3,196	10,277	4,055	858	4,912	11,136	4,053	15,189
1988	7,526	3,004	10,530	4,508	641	5,149	12,034	3,645	15,679
1989	7,073	2,699	9,772	4,403	538	4,941	11,476	3,237	14,713
1990	6,897	2,403	9,300	4,215	631	4,846	11,112	3,034	14,146
1991	6,137	2,038	8,175	3,813	551	4,365	9,950	2,589	12,539
1992	6,277	1,937	8,213	4,481	422	4,903	10,758	2,359	13,116
1993	6,742	1,776	8,518	5,287	394	5,681	12,029	2,170	14,199
1994	7,255	1,735	8,991	5,995	426	6,421	13,251	2,161	15,411
1995	7,129	1,506	8,635	6,064	417	6,481	13,193	1,923	15,116
1996	7,254	1,273	8,527	6,478	452	6,930	13,731	1,725	15,456

Source: American Automobile Manufacturers Association

U.S. Auto Market

U.S. Retail Sales of Passenger Cars

	Domestic sales				
	1992	1993	1994	1995	1996
Chrysler	617,412	766,144	782,975	771,357	827,941
Ford	1,731,250	1,836,508	1,899,156	1,732,034	1,699,893
General Motors	2,749,943	2,851,818	3,052,686	2,930,568	2,755,995
BMW	–	–	–	6,194	20,508
Honda	475,718	417,928	464,622	511,044	665,511
Hyundai Sonata	16,985	15,420	1,190	7	–
Mazda	79,267	100,441	109,165	105,852	85,904
Mitsubishi	64,592	75,980	117,485	101,033	125,634
Nissan	144,588	249,844	313,058	299,884	308,891
Subaru Legacy	55,116	49,395	55,938	74,151	94,950
Suzuki Swift	188	2,960	2,907	4,126	3,379
Toyota	341,498	368,053	384,048	498,635	555,746
Volkswagen	–	7,176	72,073	93,822	109,230
Total	6,276,557	6,741,667	7,255,303	7,128,707	7,253,582

	Import sales				
	1992	1993	1994	1995	1996
Chrysler	62,174	67,988	28,849	14,823	4,692
Ford	46,385	41,641	39,685	59,191	37,359
General Motors	93,917	56,871	5,186	51	1,676
Alfa Romeo	2,828	1,325	565	414	–
BMW	65,693	78,010	84,501	87,115	85,253
Daihatsu	5,030	–	–	–	–
Honda	293,127	298,512	297,620	229,443	120,643
Hyundai	91,564	93,376	124,905	107,371	108,468
Isuzu	7,823	1,762	109	16	1
Jaguar	8,681	12,734	15,195	18,085	17,878
Mazda	169,007	159,449	173,634	117,859	95,071
Mercedes-Benz	63,315	61,899	73,002	76,752	90,844
Mitsubishi	90,980	92,222	83,518	74,234	45,548
Nissan	273,382	232,802	224,170	220,374	191,486
Porsche	4,133	3,714	5,824	5,771	7,152
Saab	26,451	18,784	21,679	25,592	28,439
Subaru	49,698	54,784	44,627	26,256	25,798
Suzuki	6,098	3,648	4,229	4,385	7,009
Toyota	418,661	373,773	381,095	295,339	237,846
Volkswagen/Audi	87,949	49,251	32,870	37,956	53,061
Volvo	67,916	72,955	81,788	88,505	88,581
Other imports	1,743	692	12,163	16,725	26,366
Total	1,936,555	1,776,192	1,735,214	1,506,257	1,273,171
Total passenger car sales	8,213,112	8,517,859	8,990,517	8,634,964	8,526,753

Top 20 Selling Passenger Cars in the U.S.*

	1994			1995			1996	
1	Ford Taurus	397,037	1	Ford Taurus	366,266	1	Ford Taurus	401,049
2	Honda Accord	367,615	2	Honda Accord	341,384	2	Honda Accord	382,298
3	Ford Escort	336,967	3	Toyota Camry	328,595	3	Toyota Camry	359,433
4	Toyota Camry	321,979	4	Honda Civic	289,435	4	Honda Civic	286,350
5	Saturn	286,003	5	Saturn	285,674	5	Ford Escort	284,644
6	Honda Civic	267,023	6	Ford Escort	285,570	6	Saturn	278,574
7	Pontiac Grand Am	262,310	7	Dodge/Plymouth Neon	240,189	7	Chevrolet Cavalier	277,222
8	Chevrolet Corsica/ Beretta	222,129	8	Pontiac Grand Am	234,226	8	Chevrolet Lumina	237,973
9	Toyota Corolla	210,926	9	Chevrolet Lumina	214,595	9	Pontiac Grand Am	222,477
10	Chevrolet Cavalier	187,263	10	Toyota Corolla	213,636	10	Toyota Corolla	209,048
11	Nissan Sentra	172,148	11	Chevrolet Cavalier	212,767	11	Ford Contour	174,187
12	Nissan Altima	163,138	12	Chevrolet Corsica/ Beretta	192,361	12	Chevrolet Corsica/ Beretta	149,117
13	Buick LeSabre	159,500	13	Ford Contour	174,214	13	Nissan Altima	147,910
14	Ford Mustang	158,421	14	Nissan Altima	148,172	14	Dodge Intrepid	145,402
15	Oldsmobile Ciera	141,100	15	Dodge Intrepid	147,576	15	Dodge Neon	139,831
16	Buick Century	138,948	16	Buick LeSabre	141,410	16	Buick LeSabre	131,316
17	Dodge Intrepid	133,475	17	Ford Mustang	136,962	17	Nissan Sentra	129,596
18	Ford Thunderbird	130,713	18	Nissan Sentra	134,854	18	Nissan Maxima	128,395
19	Cadillac DeVille	124,804	19	Pontiac Grand Prix	131,747	19	Ford Mustang	122,674
20	Chevrolet Lumina	122,314	20	Oldsmobile Ciera	128,860	20	Mercury Sable	114,164

Source: American Automobile Manufacturers Association and Ward's Automotive Reports

Top 10 Selling Trucks in the U.S.*

	1994			1995			1996	
1	Ford F Series	646,039	1	Ford F Series	691,452	1	Ford F Series	780,838
2	Chevrolet C/K	580,445	2	Chevrolet C/K	536,901	2	Chevrolet C/K	549,167
3	Ford Ranger	344,744	3	Ford Explorer	395,227	3	Ford Explorer	402,663
4	Ford Explorer	278,065	4	Ford Ranger	309,085	4	Dodge Ram Pickup	383,960
5	Dodge Caravan	268,013	5	Dodge Ram Pickup	271,501	5	Dodge Caravan	300,117
6	Chevrolet S10 Pickup	250,991	6	Dodge Caravan	264,937	6	Ford Ranger	288,393
7	Jeep Grand Cherokee	238,512	7	Jeep Grand Cherokee	252,186	7	Jeep Grand Cherokee	279,195
8	Dodge Ram Pickup	232,092	8	Ford Windstar	222,147	8	Chevrolet Blazer	246,307
9	Plymouth Voyager	211,494	9	Chevrolet Blazer	214,661	9	Ford Windstar	209,033
10	Toyota Compact Pickup	204,212	10	Chevrolet S10 Pickup	207,193	10	Chevrolet S10 Pickup	190,178

*Includes domestic and imported vehicles.

Automotive Paint Color Popularity for Full-Size/Intermediate Cars, 1996 Model Year

Color	Percent	Color	Percent	Color	Percent
Dark green	18.8	Silver	5.7	Purple	3.9
White	17.5	Medium blue	5.2	Teal/aqua	3.3
Light brown	10.3	Dark red	4.7	Medium gray	3.0
Medium red	9.5	Bright red	4.0	Other	6.8
Black	7.3				

Sources: DuPont Automotive Products and American Automobile Manufacturers Association

Global Car Market

World Motor Vehicle Production
(In thousands)

Year	United States	Canada	Europe	Japan	Other	World total	U.S. as percent of world total
1950	8,006	388	1,991	32	160	10,577	75.7
1960	7,905	398	6,837	482	866	16,488	47.9
1970	8,284	1,160	13,049	5,289	1,637	29,419	28.2
1980	8,010	1,324	15,496	11,043	2,692	38,565	20.8
1990	9,783	1,928	18,866	13,487	4,496	48,554	20.1
1991	8,811	1,888	17,804	13,245	5,180	46,928	18.8
1992	9,729	1,961	17,628	12,499	6,269	48,088	20.2
1993	10,898	2,246	15,208	11,228	7,205	46,785	23.3
1994	12,263	2,321	16,195	10,554	8,167	49,500	24.8
1995	11,985	2,420	17,001	10,196	8,405	50,008	24.0
1996	11,799	2,397	17,728	10,346	9,244	51,513	22.9

Top 25 Manufacturers Ranked by 1994 Worldwide Production

		1993	1994
1	General Motors - U.S.	6,841,916	7,423,381
2	Ford - U.S.	5,964,872	6,619,082
3	Toyota - Japan	4,273,986	4,288,299
4	Volkswagen - Germany	2,799,345	2,884,081
5	Chrysler - U.S.	2,299,271	2,632,705
6	Nissan - Japan	2,787,272	2,578,677
7	PSA- France	2,069,472	2,417,852
8	Renault - France	1,897,053	2,129,021
9	Fiat - Italy	1,533,364	1,888,363
10	Honda - Japan	1,655,245	1,604,744
11	Mitsubishi - Japan	1,574,666	1,551,138
12	Mazda - Japan	1,248,224	1,232,825
13	Hyundai - S. Korea	974,642	1,134,611
14	Daimler-Benz - Germany	706,881	868,414
15	Suzuki - Japan	832,321	797,962
16	Kia - S. Korea	599,904	619,875
17	Fuji - Japan	564,482	587,974
18	BMW - Germany	510,112	550,636
19	VAZ - Russia	660,275	530,876
20	Rover Group - U.K.	426,744	486,828
21	Daihatsu - Japan	560,320	482,242
22	Volvo - Sweden	355,543	438,758
23	Isuzu - Japan	397,793	376,788
24	Daewoo - S. Korea	300,094	340,707
25	FSM - Poland	192,239	247,973

Source: American Automobile Manufacturers Association

New Car Ratings Top Three Vehicles Per Segment In Initial Quality

Car Segments

Compact Car
BEST: SATURN SL (tie)
BEST: TOYOTA TERCEL (tie)
Honda Civic

Entry Midsize Car
BEST: NISSAN ALTIMA
Buick Skylark
Chrysler Cirrus

Premium Midsize Car
BEST: HONDA ACCORD
Toyota Camry
Chevrolet Lumina

Sporty Car
BEST: ACURA INTEGRA
Honda Prelude
Nissan 200SX

Entry Luxury Car
BEST: INFINITI I30
Acura TL
Lexus ES300

Premium Luxury Car
BEST: LEXUS LS400
Lexus SC300/400
Acura RL

Truck Segments

Compact Pickup
BEST: TOYOTA TACOMA
Ford Ranger
Nissan pickup

Full-Size Pickup
BEST: FORD F-SERIES
Chevrolet C/K
Toyota T100

Compact Van
BEST: HONDA ODYSSEY
Ford Windstar
Toyota Previa

Compact Sport Utility Vehicle
BEST: INFINITI QX4
Toyota 4 Runner
Chevrolet Blazer

Full-Size Sport Utility Vehicle
BEST: LEXUS LX450
Toyota Landcruiser
Chevrolet Suburban

Note: Rankings are based on surveys of new-vehicle owners about any problems during the first 90 days of ownership.

Source: J.D. Power and Associates 1997 Initial Quality Study

J.D. Power's 1997 Customer Satisfaction Study

Customer Satisfaction Index Performance
(Rankings reflect customers' experience with vehicle reliability after one year and the quality of treatment during dealer service or repair visits)

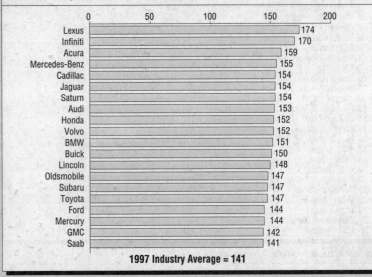

Lexus	174
Infiniti	170
Acura	159
Mercedes-Benz	155
Cadillac	154
Jaguar	154
Saturn	154
Audi	153
Honda	152
Volvo	152
BMW	151
Buick	150
Lincoln	148
Oldsmobile	147
Subaru	147
Toyota	147
Ford	144
Mercury	144
GMC	142
Saab	141

1997 Industry Average = 141

Note: Finishing below industry average in alphabetical order are: Chevrolet, Chrysler, Dodge, Eagle, Geo, Hyundai, Isuzu, Jeep, Kia, Land Rover, Mazda, Mitsubishi, Nissan, Plymouth, Pontiac, Porsche, Suzuki and Volkswagen.
Source: J.D. Power & Associates

Corporate Average Fuel Economy Trend
for the Automotive Industry (miles per gallon)

MODEL YEAR	TOTAL FLEET	PASSENGER CARS	DOMESTIC	IMPORT	LIGHT TRUCKS	DOMESTIC	IMPORT
78	19.9	19.9	18.7	27.3	—	—	—
79	20.1	20.3	19.3	26.1	18.2	17.7	20.8
80	23.1	24.3	22.6	29.6	18.5	16.8	24.3
81	24.6	25.9	24.2	31.5	20.1	18.3	27.4
82	25.1	26.6	25.0	31.1	20.5	19.2	27.0
83	24.8	26.4	24.4	32.4	20.7	19.6	27.1
84	25.0	26.9	25.5	32.0	20.6	19.3	26.7
85	25.4	27.6	26.3	31.5	20.7	19.6	26.5
86	25.9	28.2	26.9	31.6	21.5	20.0	25.9
87	26.2	28.5	27.0	31.2	21.7	20.5	25.2
88	26.0	28.8	27.4	31.5	21.3	20.6	24.6
89	25.6	28.4	27.2	30.8	20.9	20.4	23.5
90	25.4	28.0	26.9	29.9	20.8	20.3	23.0
91	25.6	28.4	27.3	30.1	21.3	20.9	23.0
92	25.1	27.9	27.0	29.2	20.8	20.5	22.7
93	25.2	28.4	27.8	29.6	21.0	20.7	22.8
94	24.7	28.3	27.5	29.6	20.7	20.5	22.0
95	24.9	28.6	27.7	30.3	20.5	20.3	21.5
*96	24.9	28.7	28.3	29.7	20.7	20.5	22.1
*97	24.5	28.6	27.9	30.1	20.4	20.2	22.2

*Preliminary Estimates

Source: National Highway Traffic Safety Administration

Fuel Efficiency Ratings

MANUFACTURER	Vehicle Type	MODEL YEAR 1997 Corporate Average Fuel Economy (miles per gallon)
BMW	IP	25.5
Chrysler	DP	27.9
Chrysler	DT	20.2
Chrysler	IP	27.3
Fiat	IP	13.4
Ford	DP	27.2
Ford	DT	19.9
Ford	IP	31.9
General Motors	DP	28.1
General Motors	DT	20.4
General Motors	IP	31.5
Honda	DP	29.2
Honda	IP	34.8
Honda	IT	27.2
Hyundai	IP	30.9
Isuzu	IT	19.4
Kia	IP	30.8
Kia	IT	23.7
Mazda	DP	29.9
Mazda	IP	31.4
Mazda	IT	20.8
Mercedes	IP	24.9
Mitsubishi	IP	29.9
Mitsubishi	IT	21.3

MANUFACTURER	Vehicle Type	MODEL YEAR 1997 Corporate Average Fuel Economy (miles per gallon)
Nissan	IP	30.1
Nissan	IT	22.9
Porsche	IP	22.0
Rover	IT	17.2
Subaru	IP	28.3
Suzuki	IP	33.9
Suzuki	IT	27.6
Toyota	DP	28.8
Toyota	IP	30.3
Toyota	IT	22.6
Volvo	IP	25.8
Volkswagen	IP	28.9
Volkswagen	IT	18.5

IP=Import Passenger Car
DP=Domestic Passenger Car
IT=Import Light Truck
DT=Domestic Light Truck
Note: The government standard for passenger car fuel economy is 27.5 miles per gallon, and the standard for light trucks is 20.7 miles per gallon.

Source: National Highway Traffic Safety Administration

Largest Auto Recalls

MANUFACTURER	Number of Vehicles	RECALL	SUBJECT
Ford	7,900,000	6-1-96	Ignition switch
General Motors	6,682,084	12-10-71	Engine mounts
General Motors	5,821,160	2-20-81	Single axle-rear control arm
Chrysler	4,300,000	3-27-95	Minivan latches
Ford	4,072,000	6-28-72	Shoulder belts
General Motors	3,707,064	1-19-73	Power brake booster shield
Volkswagen	3,700,000	10-12-72	Windshield wiper arm
Honda	3,700,000	4-16-95	Seat belts
Ford	3,600,000	9-01-87	Fuel line coupling
General Motors	3,100,000	12-17-84	Axle shaft separation
General Motors	2.,966,979	3-25-69	Throttle linkage
Nissan	2,730,462	4-16-95	Seat belts
General Motors	2,570,914	3-25-69	Exhaust system
General Motors	2,216,325	9-11-95	Seat belt anchorage
General Motors	2,200,000	4-28-77	Hydraulic power assist

Source: National Highway Traffic Safety Administration

Private Passenger Automobile Insurance State Average Expenditures, 1995

Rank	State	Average expenditure
1	New Jersey	$1,013.47
2	Hawaii	963.08
3	District of Columbia	958.58
4	New York	905.90
5	Massachusetts	898.21
6	Connecticut	880.53
7	Rhode Island	869.80
8	California	830.98
9	Louisiana	787.44
10	Delaware	783.74
11	Nevada	758.82
12	Florida	739.41
13	Maryland	732.10
14	Alaska	729.50
15	Arizona	727.24
16	Colorado	721.93
17	Texas	710.52
18	Pennsylvania	667.23
19	Washington	649.55
20	West Virginia	646.14
21	Michigan	645.49
22	New Mexico	639.15
23	Minnesota	630.02
24	Illinois	612.27

Rank	State	Average expenditure
25	New Hampshire	$609.14
26	Georgia	596.41
27	South Carolina	582.26
28	Mississippi	579.24
29	Missouri	572.20
30	Oregon	564.86
31	Kentucky	555.42
32	Virginia	552.91
33	Alabama	549.09
34	Utah	547.49
35	Indiana	542.35
36	Ohio	532.29
37	Oklahoma	526.17
38	Tennessee	519.29
39	Vermont	511.76
40	Wisconsin	505.55
41	North Carolina	500.50
42	Arkansas	499.87
43	Kansas	473.77
44	Maine	472.05
45	Montana	468.46
46	Nebraska	451.87
47	Idaho	446.81
48	Wyoming	432.89
49	Iowa	428.67
50	South Dakota	428.64
51	North Dakota	380.98
	U.S. Average	**665.52**

Source: National Association of Insurance Commissioners

Hot Cars

The 25 Vehicles Stolen Most Often in 1996

Rank	Model year	Make	Model name	Rank	Model year	Make	Model name
1	'94	Honda	Accord EX	14	'84	Oldsmobile	Cutlass Supreme
2	'88	Honda	Accord LX	15	'95	Toyota	Corolla
3	'92	Honda	Accord LX	16	'87	Chevrolet	Caprice
4	'87	Oldsmobile	Cutlass Supreme	17	'86	Cadillac	Deville
5	'95	Ford	Mustang	18	'85	Oldsmobile	Cutlass Supreme
6	'86	Oldsmobile	Cutlass Supreme	19	'90	Toyota	Camry
7	'95	Honda	Accord EX	20	'88	Toyota	Camry
8	'90	Honda	Accord EX	21	'91	Acura	Legend
9	'89	Toyota	Camry	22	'95	Toyota	Camry LE
10	'92	Honda	Accord EX	23	'91	Honda	Civic
11	'89	Honda	Accord LX	24	'94	Honda	Accord LX
12	'91	Honda	Accord EX	25	'90	Honda	Accord LX
13	'91	Honda	Accord LX				

Source: CCC Information Services Inc.

Highway Death Toll

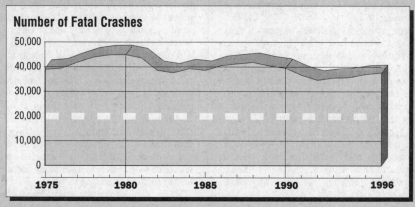

Number of Fatal Crashes

Automobile Fatalities

Year	Number of persons killed	Fatality rate per 100,000 population	Year	Number of persons killed	Fatality rate per 100,000 population	Year	Number of persons killed	Fatality rate per 100,000 population
1966	50,894	26.02	1977	47,878	21.79	1988	47,087	19.26
1967	50,724	25.69	1978	50,331	22.66	1989	45,582	18.47
1968	52,725	26.44	1979	51,093	22.75	1990	44,599	17.88
1969	53,543	26.59	1980	51,091	22.48	1991	41,508	16.46
1970	52,627	25.80	1981	49,301	21.49	1992	39,250	15.39
1971	52,542	25.40	1982	43,945	18.97	1993	40,150	15.57
1972	54,589	26.08	1983	42,589	18.22	1994	40,716	15.64
1973	54,052	25.57	1984	44,257	18.77	1995	41,817	15.91
1974	45,196	21.18	1985	43,825	18.42	1996	41,907	15.80
1975	44,525	20.66	1986	46,087	19.19			
1976	45,523	20.92	1987	46,390	19.15			

Source: National Highway Traffic Safety Administration

DRIVING DRUNK

Are drunks getting back in the driver's seat?

A decade-long decline in the number of drunk-driving fatalities on U.S. highways ended abruptly in 1995, to the surprise and dismay of transportation safety experts and anti-alcohol activists. Although it's hard to pinpoint the cause, experts blame the sudden reversal on public complacency, less vigorous law enforcement, and an increase in the number of miles Americans drive.

Data for 1996 show that the number of alcohol-related fatalities fell slightly from 1995 to 17,126, but that is still more than in 1994. Jim Wright, manager of the youth alcohol program at the National Highway Traffic Safety Administration, notes a disturbing development in the latest data: a 5% increase in the number of fatalities among 15 to 20 year olds. "This is a reversal of the 1995 trend, when the youth fatality rate actually decreased," he says, "as other age groups' were increasing."

The long-term trend is still encouraging. The latest data represent a substantial reduction from the 25,165 alcohol-related deaths recorded in 1982, when drinking accounted for 57% of all traffic fatalities. And Stephanie Faul, a spokeswoman for the AAA Foundation for Traffic Safety, says, "People are simply driving more" and the increase in fatalities may be a natural result of that. She points to the fatality rate per 100 million vehicle miles traveled, which has remained unchanged at 1.7 since 1992.

But as far as Mothers Against Drunk Driving (MADD) and other highway safety advocates are concerned, any increase in the actual number of alcohol-related deaths is cause for alarm. The biggest obstacle to further reducing the number of fatalities may be the public misperception that intoxicated drivers are no longer an urgent problem. "Over the past decade, we have made so much progress that people think the problem is solved, and that contributes to a general sense of complacency," says Jo Marie Alexander, president of the Minnesota chapter of MADD.

Moreover, other issues such as AIDS and violent crime have received increased media attention in recent years, elbowing drunk driving from the forefront of public consciousness. Alan Rodgers, a research analyst at the Minnesota Department of Public Safety, says anti–drunk driving sentiment was at it its height in the late 1980s. "Concern was widespread and everyone was talking about it. As a result, behavior changed," he says. He recalls attending a wedding in the mid-1980s, where friends checked up on each other's level of sobriety throughout the evening and especially at the end of the affair. But that's not the case nowadays. Aside from a question or glance at friends, people no longer focus as much attention on drinking and driving, Mr. Rodgers says. "It is difficult to sustain that type of interest on a prolonged basis."

The reduced interest isn't because of lack of publicity. According to Paula Veale, a spokeswoman for the Advertising Council in New York, in 1995 a record $59 million was donated in advertising time and space to the "Friends Don't Let Friends Drive Drunk" campaign. Of that amount, radio was the largest contributor of air time, with a total of $31 million, followed by cable television, with $15 million, and network television with $6.6 million. Even so, says Ms. Faul, "After a while you end up with 'issue fatigue' where people begin to tune out a message."

Another worrisome trend is a decline in law enforcement attention. According to Mr. Wright of NHTSA, there has been a marked decrease in police time devoted to intoxicated drivers because violent crime has received so much emphasis. "Police departments only have so many resources to devote to a particular issue," says Mr. Wright. But "when police do stop people for sobriety checks, word gets out very quickly and it certainly effects a change in behavior."

Although police may be less vigilant, they are meting out stiffer penalties to the intoxicated drivers they do catch. Some states have passed administrative license suspension laws, whereby a driver loses his license on the spot for failing or refusing a breathalyzer test. This method is quicker and much more effective than revocation or suspension through a judicial process. States that have enacted such laws have seen an average 6% decline in drunk driving fatalities, according to NHTSA.

While fear of arrest may change the behavior of social drinkers, it doesn't always work with chronic offenders, however. Katherine Prescott, president of MADD, says chronic offenders usually have an addiction problem, and fear of arrest is unlikely to stop them from getting behind the wheel after drinking. So some states have come up with special methods to try to deter repeat offenders, such as the stigma of conspicuous license plates that will alert police officers and other drivers to a potential hazard. Some states are also experimenting with ignition interlock systems that would require drivers to breathe into a device that locks the ignition if any alcohol is detected.

And in Minnesota, about 50 counties have adopted a home-video electronic monitoring system to deal with drunk drivers. The system is used during pre-trial periods in lieu of bail, for repeat offenders, who must pay an $8-per-day fee. The monitor (which contains a Breathalyzer) is hooked up to the participant's telephone, which must be answered daily at three set times. A breath sample is then tested. If a participant misses a telephone call or if results reveal any alcohol, the offender is placed in police custody within an average of two hours. While this system may sound intrusive, it has been effective in forcing offenders to remain sober, and for many of them it is a desirable alternative to spending the time before their trial in jail.

One deterrent for teenagers is the "zero-tolerance" law passed by Congress and enacted in 37 states and the District of Columbia. The law sets substantially lower limits of blood alcohol concentration (BAC) for drivers under the age of 21 to be declared legally drunk. BAC limits range from 0 to 0.08 under the zero-tolerance laws; the most common limit is 0.02, which can usually be reached with one drink. Before these laws were passed, offenders younger than 21 were treated as adults, with no extra consideration or stiffer penalty given because they were below the legal drinking age.

Ms. Faul of the AAA Foundation believes that bringing the traffic laws more in line with drinking laws has sent out the right message to young people. "There is an inherent hypocrisy," says Ms. Faul, "in telling those under 21 that it is illegal for them to consume alcohol, while simultaneously setting a separate standard for driving." A study by Ralph Hinckson of Boston University's School of Public Affairs found that states with a zero-tolerance law had a 16% decline in fatalities among drivers under 21, compared with a 1% increase in the states without such a law. States that do not adopt a zero-tolerance law risk the loss of some federal highway construction funds.

While such progress is encouraging, "the easiest gains are the ones we've already made," says Ms. Prescott of MADD. "There is still a long way to go."

Eileen Kinsella

Traffic Deaths Linked to Alcohol

Number of Persons Killed, by Highest Blood Alcohol Concentration (BAC) in the Crash

Year	BAC = 0.00 Number	%	BAC = 0.01–0.09 Number	%	BAC = 0.10+ Number	%	Total fatalities in alcohol-related crashes Number	%
1982	18,780	42.7	4,809	10.9	20,356	46.3	25,165	57.3
1984	20,499	46.3	4,766	10.8	18,992	42.9	23,758	53.7
1986	22,042	47.8	5,109	11.1	18,936	41.1	24,045	52.2
1988	23,461	49.8	4,895	10.4	18,731	39.8	23,626	50.2
1990	22,515	50.5	4,434	9.9	17,650	39.6	22,084	49.5
1991	21,621	52.1	3,957	9.5	15,930	38.4	19,887	47.9
1992	21,392	54.5	3,625	9.2	14,234	36.3	17,859	45.5
1993	22,677	56.5	3,496	8.7	13,977	34.8	17,473	43.5
1994	24,136	59.3	3,480	8.5	13,100	32.2	16,580	40.7
1995	24,570	58.8	3,746	9.0	13,501	32.3	17,247	41.2
1996	24,781	59.1	3,732	8.9	13,395	32.0	17,126	40.9

Total Fatalities in Alcohol-Related Crashes

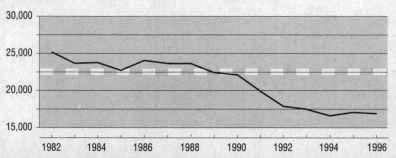

Source: National Highway Traffic Safety Administration

Journey to Work

Commuters are doing less to help the environment and conserve energy, according to the latest government data. People in car pools, riders of public transportation, bicyclists, and pedestrians make up a smaller share of the work force, as more Americans drive to work alone. One positive sign for gasoline conservation: more people working from home.

Means of Transportation	1980		1990	
	Number	Percent	Number	Percent
Total workers	96,617,296	100.0%	115,070,274	100.0%
⇒ Private vehicle	81,258,496	84.1	99,592,932	86.5
Drove alone	62,193,449	64.4	84,215,298	73.2
Carpooled	19,065,047	19.7	15,377,634	13.4
⇒ Public transportation	6,175,061	6.4	6,069,589	5.3
Bus or trolley bus*	3,924,787	4.1	3,445,000	3.0
Streetcar or trolley car*	NA	NA	78,130	0.1
Subway or elevated	1,528,852	1.6	1,755,476	1.5
Railroad	554,089	0.6	574,052	0.5
Ferryboat	NA	NA	37,497	0.0
Taxicab	167,133	0.2	179,434	0.2
⇒ Motorcycle	419,007	0.4	237,404	0.2
⇒ Bicycle	468,348	0.5	466,856	0.4
⇒ Walked only	5,413,248	5.6	4,488,886	3.9
⇒ Worked at home	2,179,863	2.3	3,406,025	3.0
⇒ All other means	703,273	0.7	808,582	0.7
Average travel time (minutes)	21.7		22.4	

*This category was "Bus or streetcar" in 1980.
Source: U.S. Census Bureau

Cities with Highest Percentage of Workers Using Public Transportation, 1990

CITY	PERCENT USING PUBLIC TRANSPORTATION	CITY	PERCENT USING PUBLIC TRANSPORTATION
New York, NY	53.4	Evanston, IL	20.9
Hoboken, NJ	51.0	Atlanta, GA	20.0
Jersey City, NJ	36.7	White Plains, NY	19.1
Washington, DC	36.6	Camden, NJ	18.1
San Francisco, CA	33.5	Oakland, CA	17.9
Boston, MA	31.5	Hartford, CT	17.1
Chicago, IL	29.7	New Orleans, LA	16.9
Philadelphia, PA	28.7	Idaho Falls, ID	16.5
Atlantic City, NJ	26.2	Minneapolis, MN	16.0
Arlington, VA	25.4	Seattle, WA	15.9
Newark, NJ	24.6	Berkeley, CA	15.2
Cambridge, MA	23.5	Albany, NY	15.1
Pittsburgh, PA	22.2		
Baltimore, MD	22.0	Source: U.S. Census Bureau	

Transit Ridership Trend

From 1900 to 1929, transit ridership grew steadily; first due to technical innovation and investment opportunities during the early development of street railways and then due to the economic boom of World War I and the post-war period. The Great Depression caused a steep decline in ridership between 1929 and 1939 as people made fewer work trips and often could not afford to take pleasure trips. World War II caused motor fuel rationing and an economic boom that led to a new rapid growth cycle in transit ridership. Ridership quickly declined from artificially high war levels as people fled to suburbs. In 1973, the ridership cycle reversed again and transit showed modest growth.

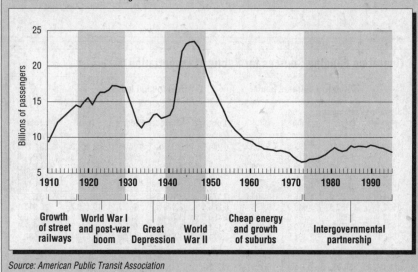

Source: American Public Transit Association

20 Largest Transit Agencies, Fiscal Year 1995, Ranked by Number of Unlinked Passenger Trips*

RANK	TRANSIT AGENCY	URBANIZED AREA	RANK	TRANSIT AGENCY	URBANIZED AREA
1	Metropolitan Transportation Authority (Includes MTA New York City Transit, MTA Long Island Rail Road, MTA Metro-North Railroad, MTA Long Island Bus, and MTA Staten Island Railway)	New York, NY	4	Washington Metropolitan Area Transit Authority	Washington, DC
			5	Southeastern Pennsylvania Transportation Authority	Philadelphia, PA
			6	Massachusetts Bay Transportation Authority	Boston, MA
			7	New Jersey Transit Corporation	New York, NY
			8	San Francisco Municipal Railway	San Francisco, CA
2	Regional Transportation Authority (Includes Chicago Transit Authority, Northeast Illinois Regional Commuter Railroad Corporation, and PACE Suburban Bus)	Chicago, IL	9	Metropolitan Atlanta Rapid Transit Authority	Atlanta, GA
			10	Mass Transit Administration, Maryland Department of Transportation	Baltimore, MD
			11	New York City Department of Transportation	New York, NY
3	Los Angeles County Metropolitan Transportation Authority	Los Angeles, CA	12	King County Department of Transportation	Seattle, WA

RANK	TRANSIT AGENCY	URBANIZED AREA
13	Metro-Dade Transit Agency	Miami, FL
14	Metropolitan Transit Authority of Harris County	Houston, TX
15	San Francisco Bay Area Rapid Transit District	San Francisco, CA
16	Port Authority of Allegheny County	Pittsburgh, PA
17	City & County of Honolulu Department of Transportation Services	Honolulu, HI

RANK	TRANSIT AGENCY	URBANIZED AREA
18	Regional Transit Authority of Orleans and Jefferson	New Orleans, LA
19	Regional Transportation District	Denver, CO
20	Port Authority of New York and New Jersey	New York, NY

*Excludes commuter-type services operated independently by Amtrak.

Source: American Public Transit Association

Operating Funding Sources for Public Transportation (Millions of dollars)

Calendar year	Directly generated funds			Government funds				Total
	Passenger fares*	Other	Total	Local**	State	Federal	Total	
1986	$ 5,113.1	$ 737.3	$ 5,850.4	$ 4,244.5	$ 2,305.6	$ 941.2	$ 7,491.3	$ 13,341.7
1987	5,114.1	776.6	5,890.7	4,680.6	2,564.6	955.1	8,200.3	14,091.0
1988	5,224.6	840.7	6,065.3	4,893.1	2,677.1	905.1	8,471.3	14,536.6
1989	5,419.9	836.7	6,256.6	4,995.4	2,796.3	936.6	8,728.3	14,984.9
1990	5,890.8	895.0	6,785.8	5,326.8	2,970.6	970.0	9,267.4	16,053.2
1991	6,037.2	766.8	6,804.0	5,373.4	3,199.5	955.9	9,728.8	16,532.8
1992 †	6,152.5	645.9	6,798.4	5,268.1	3,879.5	969.1	10,116.7	16,915.1
1993	6,350.9	764.0	7,114.9	5,490.6	3,704.2	966.5	10,161.3	17,276.2
1994	6,756.0	2,270.6	9,026.6	4,171.2	3,854.4	915.6	8,941.2	17,967.8
1995 P	6,850.3	2,361.5	9,211.8	3,871.4	3,812.1	734.9	8,418.4	17,630.2
1995 % of total	38.9%	13.4%	52.3%	22.0%	21.6%	4.2%	47.8%	100.0%

P=Preliminary
*Includes fares retained by contractors; beginning 1991 includes fare subsidies formerly included in "other."
**"Local" includes taxes levied directly by transit agency and other subsidies from local government such as bridge and tunnel tolls and non-transit parking lot funds. Beginning 1994, such funds reclassified from "local" to "other."
†Beginning 1992, "local" and "other" declined by about $500 million due to change in accounting procedures at New York City Transit Authority.
Source: American Public Transit Association

TOP TRUCKERS

25 Largest U.S. Motor Carriers by Revenue
United Parcel Service
Atlanta, GA
$22,368,000,000

Roadway Express
Akron, OH
$2,372,718,000

Yellow Freight System
Shawnee Mission, KS
$2,323,710,000

Consolidated Freightways Corp.
Menlo Park, CA
$2,146,172,000

J.B. Hunt Transport Inc.
Lowell, AR
$1,486,748,000

RPS, Inc.
Pittsburgh, PA
$1,340,000,000

Schneider National, Inc.
Green Bay, WI
$1,306,894,000 (1995)

Con-Way Transportation Svcs.
Menlo Park, CA
$1,292,082,000

ABF Freight System
Fort Smith, AR
$1,199,437,000

Ryder Integrated Logistics
Miami, FL
$1,100,000,000

Viking Freight System*
San Jose, CA
$965,800,000

Overnite Transportation Co.
Richmond, VA
$961,000,000
American Freightways
Harrison, AR
$729,042,000

United Van Lines
Fenton, MO
$682,612,000

North American Van Lines
Fort Wayne, IN
$669,758,000

Werner Enterprises
Omaha, NE
$643,274,000

USF Holland Motor Express
Holland, MI
$598,378,000

Swift Transportation Co.
Phoenix, AZ
$562,259,000

Watkins Motor Lines
Lakeland, FL
$531,135,004

Commercial Carriers, Inc.
Troy, MI
$481,693,186

Allied Van Lines
Naperville, IL
$449,603,000

NationsWay Transport Service
Commerce City, CO
$435,155,000 (1995)

Preston Trucking Co.
Preston, MD
$414,734,674

M.S. Carriers
Memphis, TN
$340,236,000

Landstar Ranger
Jacksonville, FL
$338,477,000

1996 revenue, unless otherwise specified.
*This is a one-time only slot for this company. Prior to 1996, it was a single entity. In 1996, it was merged with several other subsidiaries of Caliber System. Now, it has been pared down to a very small size.

Source: American Trucking Associations, 1996 Motor Carrier Annual Report

Freight Bill

Spending for freight transportation in the U.S., and changing market shares of the different modes of delivery.

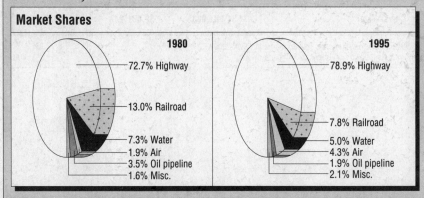

Market Shares

1980: 72.7% Highway, 13.0% Railroad, 7.3% Water, 1.9% Air, 3.5% Oil pipeline, 1.6% Misc.

1995: 78.9% Highway, 7.8% Railroad, 5.0% Water, 4.3% Air, 1.9% Oil pipeline, 2.1% Misc.

Freight Costs

| Type of Carrier | Expenditures (In millions) | |
	1980	1995
Highway	$155,331	$348,109
Railroad	27,858	34,360
Water	15,498	22,236
Oil pipeline	7,548	8,288
Air	4,013	18,869
Other carriers	1,056	4,956
Other shipper costs	2,432	4,316
Total	213,736	441,134
% of GNP	7.79%	6.10%

Source: Eno Transportation Foundation

Freight Railroads

| Railroad | Operating revenue | | |
	1995 (Thousands)	1996 (Thousands)	Change %
Conrail	$ 3,586,490	$ 3,597,248	0.3%
CSX	4,818,961	4,909,073	1.9
Grand Trunk Western	323,686	363,168	12.2
Illinois Central	643,766	617,264	-4.1
Norfolk Southern	4,011,814	4,101,038	2.2
Total East	13,384,717	13,587,791	1.5
Burlington Northern Santa Fe	8,179,376	8,184,191	0.1
Kansas City Southern	502,134	491,635	-2.1
Soo Line	679,680	668,961	-1.6
Southern Pacific*	2,940,731	3,030,194	3.0
Union Pacific*	6,195,345	6,728,470	8.6
Total West	18,497,266	19,103,451	3.3
Class I Total	31,881,983	32,691,242	2.5

*Union Pacific and Southern Pacific merged in September 1996
Source: Association of American Railroads

9

MEDIA & ENTERTAINMENT

I**N A MOVE** *that made the Raisinets suddenly seem like a bargain, Sony Theatres raised its ticket prices in 1997 to a record $9 at its Lincoln Square cineplex in Manhattan.*

But there were no protests, no boycotts. The only crowd, in fact, was the line for *Liar, Liar,* the hit comedy starring Jim Carey. "People," said a ticket agent on a recent afternoon, "will pay just about anything to see a good movie."

Consumers are spending more than ever on media and entertainment, and they aren't showing signs of slowing down. The average American household spent $1,612 in 1995 on entertainment, including books, TV, movies and theater— almost as much as for health care, according to a survey by the U.S. Labor Department.

If anything, people want more and they want it faster. Entertainment and consumer-electronics companies are obliging with a cascade of new and usually more expensive choices. Consumers can now watch television on their computer and surf the Internet on their TV. And a viewer who misses a movie at the theater can catch it later on a pay-per-view movie channel, rent it in a video store, wait till it hits HBO or Showtime, or watch it free on network TV.

Americans' voracious appetite for entertainment can make leisure time look exhausting. "A lot of people have argued we're entertaining ourselves to death," says Geoffrey Godbey, professor of leisure studies at Pennsylvania State University. "When someone asks, 'How many Broadway plays have you seen?' it becomes a game of one-upsmanship." Never mind that the best seats on Broadway now cost $75. "Leisure," says Prof. Godbey, "is what drives the economy."

Many people have adapted to this massive infusion of TV, video games, Web sites and magazines by taking in more at the same time. Whereas once families huddled around the radio to hear the daring exploits of *The Shadow* in the 1940s, today teenagers watch TV while playing hand-held video games.

Others listen to the radio as they read the newspaper. "We're 'multi-tasking,' in the same way computers do," says Gary Arlen, president of Arlen Communications Inc., a Bethesda, Md., research company specializing in interactive media. "I time household chores around a video I want to watch. Is that work or leisure?"

Prof. Godbey calls this phenomenon "time deepening"—squeezing more activities into a set amount of time. In their recent book *Time for Life*, Prof. Godbey and co-author John P. Robinson, a professor of sociology at the University of Maryland, argue that Americans have more free time now than they did in the 1960s. We just *feel* more rushed. Most of our free time is broken up in tiny blocks scattered across the work week. "It's 20 minutes here, 45 minutes there," says Prof. Godbey. "Long enough to channel surf, but not enough for deep relaxation and leisure of the sort that we enjoy during vacations."

For advertisers, the fragmentation of consumers' time means that any single medium will be less effective than in the past. But there's also a silver lining: With a wider array of niche media-buying opportunities, advertisers can more precisely target their audience. For media companies, people's quest for entertainment means fabulous growth opportunities. But the competition is brutal. Like hungry dogs feeding from the same bowl, each media company is trying to take a bite out of the next company's business.

Cable companies are stealing "eyeballs" from the broadcast networks with a growing array of programming, from the Adam and Eve Channel, an adult home-shopping network, to Z Music, a Christian rock-music channel. Satellite-dish companies, meantime, are taking from cable with their 200-channel package of crystal-clear images and CD-quality sound. And the Internet is starting to steal time from reading, TV watching and other leisure pursuits. "There's a lot more competition for the same entertainment dollars," says Michael Wolf, head of the media and entertainment division of Booz-Allen & Hamilton. "And people will make the trade-offs on a product-by-product basis."

Consumers say the choices are overwhelming. "It's more a matter of time than money when it comes to entertainment," says Cherry Arnold, a marketing director for Avalanche Systems, an interactive ad agency. "On any given week, there's 20 other things I'd rather be doing," says Ms. Arnold, who spends an hour on weekends on her computer checking electronic mail and reading electronic newspapers.

The Internet is by far the hottest new toy for American media mavens. About 40% of the nation's households own a computer, and about 20% subscribe to an on-line service. With the cost of computers and on-line services decreasing, predicts Veronis Suhler & Associates Inc., an investment banking firm, the number of on-line subscribers will reach 34 million by 2001. The Internet is making the transition from an "over-hyped curiosity to a communications and information utility on which millions of Americans now rely," says Thomas Miller, a vice president at Find/SVP, a media research firm. Not bad, he says, for a medium that didn't exist five years ago.

Paul Tutundgy, a part owner of the Trilogy Bar & Grill in Manhattan, says TV still gets the biggest cut of his time, but he now spends about an hour a day surfing the Internet instead of watching TV. "The choices are great," he says, but admits "there are limits."

Indeed, the Internet isn't quite ready for prime-time. Grandiose promises of shopping, entertainment and games haven't panned out. And the marketing is sometimes way ahead of the technology. In a modern-day traffic jam on the Info-Highway in December 1996, thousands of paying America Online customers couldn't log onto the service after the company offered a flat $19.95 rate. Frustrated users were met with busy signals, slow response times and disconnected calls because of the heavy volume.

The big winners in the leisure-time marketplace continue to be movies and television. In fact, one of the most provocative findings by time researchers Robinson and Godbey—who drew from three decades of research from the Americans' Use of Time Project—is that the gains in leisure time over the last 30 years have been "spent on the couch in front of the tube." Time

in front of the TV, according to the authors, has cut into everything else in our lives—especially activities outside the home. Watching the boob-tube takes up 40% of the free time of the average American adult.

Americans also are flocking to movie theaters. In 1996, theaters sold $5.9 billion of tickets, a 7.6% increase from 1995. While there still are many big-budget flops and critics and patrons alike decry the lack of depth and quality in many movies, films that deliver two hours of pure escape are really pulling in the crowds. Just consider the reissue of the *Star Wars* trilogy, which raked in about $250 million in 1997, and the dinosaur adventure *The Lost World: Jurassic Park*, with its record box-office take of $90 million over the 1997 Memorial Day weekend.

The strong movie attendance has spurred the big theater chains to erect "megaplexes" or "ultraplexes." While the average multiplex theater in America boasts about five screens, theater owners such as Cineplex Odeon, National Amusements, and Cinemark USA are racing to build theaters with as many as 30 screens. The one segment of the film industry that is dying—albeit a slow death— is the drive-in theater. Drive-ins have dropped to 826 screens, a third of the total just 10 years ago.

While Americans are spending more time and money on movies and television, they are showing less interest in reading and listening to music. Newspaper circulation continues to drop, while magazine circulation and unit sales of books are flat or even down in some categories. The music industry, meanwhile, is still looking for the next hot trend, as CD sales plateaued and new releases from major stars fell flat.

One stark sign of how deparate the industry is for new hits is that half of the 10 best-selling albums of 1996—including Alanis Morissette's 7.4 million selling *Jagged Little Pill* at No. 1—were released in 1995. More troubling for record companies is the fact that 1996 was supposed to be a hot year, with eagerly awaited new albums from R.E.M., Hootie and the Blowfish, and George Michael. A sign of the music industry's desperation: The No. 1 hit on the 1996 Billboard Hot 100 Singles Chart, based on radio air play and sales data, was the comical, if catchy dance tune "Macarena" by Los Del Rio.

Despite the gluttony for entertainment, media experts believe there are limits to how much consumers will spend—and that ceiling may not be much higher. Already consumers are howling about cable-TV rates, which have continued to rise more than the rate of inflation. Cable giant TCI lost a million pay-TV subscribers in one quarter in 1996, many of whom were frustrated with rate increases.

What's more, the consumer-electronics graveyard is littered with pricey products that failed to fill a niche or find a market. To date, consumers haven't shown a compelling need for digital audio tapes or compact mini-disks, for example, two formats whose superior sound were touted as the next generation of audio products. And some highly hyped Internet products have an uncertain future. For example, Web TV, which allows a person to surf the Net on the TV using a fancy remote control, is still struggling to get into American homes.

But don't bet on Americans' hunger for media and entertainment slowing down anytime soon. Says Booz-Allen's Mr. Wolf: "Think about it—*Seinfeld* is a reference point in our conversation now. It's a huge part of our culture. Entertainment for most people has become a necessity in life."

Mark Robichaux, a *Wall Street Journal* staff reporter

Favorite Leisure Pursuits

Percentage of people in 1997 who consider these activities their favorite ways to spend leisure time:

Activity	All adults	Men	Women
Reading	28%	15%	41%
TV watching	19	19	20
Fishing	12	21	4
Spending time with family/kids	12	13	12
Gardening	11	8	13
Team sports	9	15	4
Golf	8	14	2
Walking	8	6	10
Going to movies	7	4	9
Swimming	6	6	6
Renting movies	5	6	5
Traveling	5	4	5
Sewing/crocheting	4	–	8
Exercise	4	4	4
Hunting	4	7	–
Church/church activities	4	3	5

Source: Louis Harris & Associates

SPENDTHRIFT SUMMER IN HOLLYWOOD

When Hollywood began rolling out an unprecedented lineup of big-budget action/adventure movies in the summer of 1997, industry insiders predicted the biggest disaster of all would be the financial fallout from studios plowing too much money into lookalike productions.

Yet by the time Labor Day arrived, Hollywood and moviegoers had surprised the skeptics. The movie industry set a box-office record for the 17-week period ended Sept. 1, grossing $2.374 billion, compared with $2.367 billion the summer before, according to Exhibitor Relations Co. in Los Angeles. Attendance, however, was only slightly higher than 1996, with ticket price increases producing most of the added revenue.

While there were the anticipated big-budget flops like *Speed 2: Cruise Control*, some smaller films proved highly popular and even some of the blockbusters exceeded expectations. The big summer successes included Sony Corp.'s *Men in Black*, the highest grossing movie with $235.1 million in revenue, and Steven Spielberg's *Lost World: Jurassic Park*, which took in $227.9 million.

My Best Friend's Wedding, one of the only big-budget romantic comedies in the summer of 1997, did well, grossing $119.5 million. And Walt Disney had a dark-horse surprise in *George of the Jungle*, which grossed $95 million and proved a stronger box-office draw than Disney's other muscleman, Hercules. *Hercules,* with a gross of $91.2 million, didn't measure up to some of Disney's other animated films of the 1990s, such as *The Lion King*.

But a record box office isn't what it used to be. Pulling in $100 million in revenue doesn't mean as much these days when production budgets are at least as much. In March 1997, the Motion Picture Association of America announced that the average cost of making a film had risen 9.5% to $39.8 million in 1996. Add in marketing costs, and the average shoots up to $60 million.

This was "a difficult summer to show a profit," says Harold Vogel, entertainment industry analyst at Cowen & Co. "There are simply too many expensive films around, and the audience seems to move on to the next one faster and faster." Case in point: Warner Bros.' *Batman and Robin*, with a production budget of more than $100 million, had a promising opening, racking up more than $40 million in revenue, but then the box-office gross plunged nearly 65% the following week.

Twentieth Century Fox, too, was disappointed by its *Speed 2: Cruise Control*, the sequel to the 1994 summer hit. The film, which had a production budget estimated at more than $140 million, grossed only about $50 million. "Ordinarily this would be a blockbuster," says Jill Krutick, entertainment analyst at Smith Barney. But, she adds, the big budgets and tough competition have resulted in a "double whammy" for the movie industry.

When independent films like *Fargo* and *The English Patient* won major awards at the Oscar ceremonies in 1997, studios took notice, and in some cases, purchased independent films to fill out their schedules. But if independents made an impression on the big studios, it wasn't very deep or lasting.

"It's difficult to resist the lure of blockbusters, after seeing the success of those movies, even when the price tags are so high," says Jim Kozak, a spokesman for the National Association of Theater Owners, a trade association. Indeed, the 1996 record movie industry revenue of $5.9 billion came disproportionately from a handful of blockbuster films, most notably *Twister* and *Independence Day*. Those two movies alone

Movie Ticket Costs

U.S. movie ticket prices seem like a bargain compared with the average charge in some major countries.

Movie Ticket Prices Around the World

Japan	$17.19
Switzerland	13.15
Germany	8.93
France	8.85
Australia	8.77
Brazil	7.95
U.K.	7.84
Russia	7.83
Hong Kong	7.55
U.S.	7.07
Singapore	5.30
South Africa	4.15

Source: Business Traveler International

accounted for nearly $548 million in ticket sales, while the average film's revenue declined by 3% in 1996.

Movies that weren't big hits at the box office in the U.S. could still recoup their costs because of the home-video market and the growth in foreign markets in recent years. Hit U.S. movies can increase their revenue by 50% or more when they are marketed abroad. "The domestic market can be very important as a branding process since it often sets the tone for how a film will be received abroad," says Ms. Krutick of Smith Barney.

"Budgets and genres tend to be cyclical," she adds, suggesting there will likely be a trend of belt-tightening to come. "It would appear that egos got out of control in 1997."

Eileen Kinsella

At the Movies

The Cost of Making Movies
(In thousands)

Year	Average production costs	Average marketing costs
1980	$9,383	$4,329
1981	11,336	4,407
1982	11,850	4,936
1983	11,885	5,205
1984	14,413	6,651
1985	16,779	6,454
1986	17,455	6,673
1987	20,051	8,257
1988	18,061	8,509
1989	23,454	9,248
1990	26,783	11,967
1991	26,136	12,064
1992	28,858	13,456
1993	29,910	14,066
1994	34,288	16,060
1995	36,370	17,737
1996	39,836	19,838

NOTE: These figures are for MPAA members which include Disney, Paramount, Universal, Warner Brothers, MGM, Fox, Sony, and Turner.
Source: Motion Picture Association of America

Movie Box-Office Gross and Attendance (In millions)

Year	Box office gross	Attendance/ admissions
1950	$1,379.0	3,017.5
1960	984.4	1,304.5
1970	1,429.2	920.6
1980	2,748.5	1,021.5
1981	2,965.6	1,067.0
1982	3,452.7	1,175.4
1983	3,766.0	1,196.9
1984	4,030.6	1,199.1
1985	3,749.4	1,056.1
1986	3,778.0	1,017.2
1987	4,252.9	1,088.5
1988	4,458.4	1,084.8
1989	5,033.4	1,262.8
1990	5,021.8	1,188.6
1991	4,803.2	1,140.6
1992	4,871.0	1,173.2
1993	5,154.2	1,244.0
1994	5,396.2	1,291.7
1995	5,493.5	1,262.6
1996	5,911.5	1,338.6

Source: Motion Picture Association of America

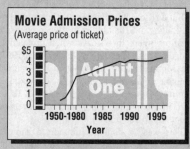

Movie Admission Prices
(Average price of ticket)

Note: 1989–1996 based on National Association of Theater Owners Average Ticket Prices. 1980–1988 based on CPI-W Index.
Source: Motion Picture Association of America

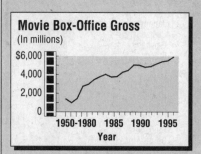

Movie Box-Office Gross
(In millions)

Source: Motion Picture Association of America

THE SILVER SCREEN

Top Movies that Opened in 1996, ranked by total box-office receipts.

	Title	Distributor	1996 Gross	Total Gross	Estimated Production Cost
1.	Independence Day	20th-Fox	$306,153,456	$306,153,456	$75,000,000
2.	Twister	Warner Bros	$241,717,524	$241,717,524	$82,000,000
3.	Mission: Impossible	Paramount	$180,943,675	$180,943,675	$65,000,000
4.	Jerry Maguire	Sony	$60,351,092	$153,620,822	$50,000,000
5.	Ransom	Buena Vista	$124,641,941	$136,485,602	$54,000,000
6.	101 Dalmations	Buena Vista	$104,111,652	$136,182,161	$66,000,000
7.	The Rock	Buena Vista	$134,067,443	$134,067,443	$75,000,000
8.	The Nutty Professor	Universal	$128,810,418	$128,810,418	$45,000,000
9.	The Birdcage	MGM/UA	$123,986,682	$123,986,682	$42,000,000
10.	A Time to Kill	Warner Bros	$108,706,165	$108,706,165	$38,000,000
11.	The First Wives Club	Paramount	$103,368,736	$105,480,706	$37,400,000
12.	Phenomenon	Buena Vista	$104,464,977	$104,632,573	$42,000,000
13.	Scream	Miramax	$21,253,204	$103,001,286	$15,000,000
14.	Eraser	Warner Bros	$101,283,031	$101,283,031	$100,000,000
15.	The Hunchback of Notre Dame	Paramount	$99,843,665	$100,138,851	$48,000,000
16.	Michael	New Line	$27,629,196	$95,345,070	$30,000,000
17.	Star Trek: First Contact	Paramount	$85,122,152	$92,017,585	$82,000,000
18.	Space Jam	Warner Bros	$81,926,334	$90,443,603	$105,000,000
19.	The English Patient	Miramax	$22,758,252	$78,467,151	$35,000,000
20.	Broken Arrow	20th-Fox	$70,646,997	$70,646,997	$61,000,000

Source: Baseline

Top Movies that Opened in 1997, ranked by total box-office receipts.

(As of September 1, 1997)

	Title	Distributor	1997 Gross	Estimated Production Cost
1.*	Men in Black	Sony	$235,057,188	$90,000,000
2.*	The Lost World: Jurassic Park	Universal	$227,881,749	$70,000,000
3.*	Liar Liar	Universal	$180,551,970	$65,000,000
4.*	Air Force One	Sony	$154,240,266	$90,000,000
5.	Star Wars	20th-Fox	$138,195,523	$7,000,000
6.*	My Best Friend's Wedding	Sony	$119,454,579	$42,000,000
7.*	Face/Off	Paramount	$109,380,852	$90,000,000
8.*	Batman & Robin	Warner Bros	$106,712,335	$100,000,000**
9.*	Con Air	Buena Vista	$99,504,802	$80,000,000
10.*	Contact	Warner Bros	$94,977,242	$90,000,000
11.*	George of the Jungle	Buena Vista	$94,974,307	$50,000,000
12.*	Hercules	Buena Vista	$91,187,796	$85,000,000
13.	The Empire Strikes Back	20th - Fox	$67,484,485	$32,000,000
14.	Dante's Peak	Universal	$67,155,742	$100,000,000
15.*	Anaconda	Sony	$65,557,989	$50,000,000
16.	The Fifth Element	Sony	$63,125,637	$95,000,000
17.*	Conspiracy Theory	Columbia	$62,969,824	$80,000,000
18.	The Saint	Warner Bros	$61,355,436	$70,000,000

	Title	Distributor	1997 Gross Production Cost	Estimated
19.*	Jungle 2 Jungle	Buena Vista	$59,925,026	N/A
20.*	Austin Powers	New Line	$53,705,042	$16,000,000

*Indicates a movie is still being tracked.
**Published estimates range from $80,000,000 to $175,000,000

Source: Baseline

THE REAL BOX-OFFICE CHAMPS

Top 25 Films of All-Time (adjusted for inflation)*

RANK	FILM	ADMISSIONS	OPENED	DOMESTIC GROSS	ADJUSTED GROSS
1	Gone With the Wind	197,548,731	1939	$193,597,756	$869,214,415
2	Star Wars	176,063,374	5/25/77	$460,935,665	$774,992,216
3	E.T.	135,987,938	6/11/82	$399,804,539	$598,346,929
4	The Ten Commandments	131,000,000	1956	$ 65,500,000	$576,400,000
5	The Sound of Music	130,571,429	1965	$163,214,286	$574,514,287
6	Jaws	128,078,818	6/20/75	$260,000,000	$563,546,798
7	Doctor Zhivago	124,135,456	1965	$111,721,910	$546,196,004
8	Jungle Book	111,045,538	1967	$135,475,556	$488,600,366
9	Snow White	109,000,000	1937	$184,925,486	$479,600,000
10	Ben-Hur	107,692,308	1959	$ 70,000,000	$473,846,154
11	101 Dalmations	105,207,663	1961	$152,551,111	$462,913,716
12	The Empire Strikes Back	98,049,707	5/21/80	$290,020,125	$431,571,424
13	The Exorcist	94,285,714	12/26/73	$165,000,000	$414,857,143
14	Return of the Jedi	93,796,001	5/25/83	$308,146,508	$412,803,112
15	The Sting	91,209,330	12/25/73	$159,616,327	$401,321,051
16	Raiders of the Lost Ark	87,185,055	6/12/81	$242,374,454	$383,614,244
17	Jurassic Park	86,193,170	6/11/93	$356,839,725	$379,249,949
18	The Graduate	85,571,393	1967	$104,397,100	$376,514,131
19	Fantasia	83,043,478	1940	$ 76,400,000	$365,391,304
20	Forrest Gump	78,873,439	7/6/94	$329,690,974	$347,043,131
21	The Godfather	78,646,424	3/15/72	$133,698,921	$346,044,266
22	Mary Poppins	78,181,818	1964	$ 86,000,000	$344,000,000
23	The Lion King	74,845,828	6/15/94	$312,855,561	$329,321,643
24	Close Encounters of the Third Kind	74,439,462	11/16/77	$166,000,000	$327,533,632
25	Sleeping Beauty	72,676,056	1959	$51,600,000	$319,774,646

*Grosses through 5/4/97; includes reissues

Source: Exhibitor Relations Co.

Top 25 Films of All-Time
(in current dollars)*

RANK	FILM	DOMESTIC GROSS	OPENED	RANK	FILM	DOMESTIC GROSS	OPENED
1	Star Wars	$460,935,665	5/25/77	16	Mrs. Doubtfire	$219,194,773	11/24/93
2	E.T.	$399,804,539	6/11/82	17	Ghost	$217,631,306	7/13/90
3	Jurassic Park	$356,839,725	6/11/93	18	Aladdin	$217,350,219	11/11/92
4	Forrest Gump	$329,690,974	7/6/94	19	Back to the Future	$210,609,762	7/3/85
5	The Lion King	$312,855,561	6/15/94	20	Terminator 2	$204,446,562	7/3/91
6	Return of the Jedi	$308,146,508	5/25/83	21	Indiana Jones	$197,171,806	5/24/89
7	Independence Day	$306,169,255	7/3/96		and the Last		
8	The Empire	$290,020,125	5/21/80		Crusade		
	Strikes Back			22	Gone With	$193,597,756	1939
9	Home Alone	$285,016,000	11/16/90		the Wind		
10	Jaws	$260,000,000	6/20/75	23	Toy Story	$191,773,049	11/22/95
11	Batman	$251,188,924	6/23/89	24	Snow White	$184,925,486	1937
12	Raiders of	$242,374,454	6/12/81	25	Dances With	$184,208,848,	11/9/90
	the Lost Ark				Wolves		
13	Twister	$241,708,908	5/10/96				
14	Beverly Hills Cop	$234,760,478	12/5/84				
15	Ghostbusters	$220,858,490	7/8/84				

*Grosses through 5/4/97; includes reissues

Entertainment Favorites

Television shows, performers (excluding soap opera actors), and cartoon characters that received the highest Q scores in recent studies by Marketing Evaluations Inc.

Television Program Q Scores

	Familiarity	Score		Familiarity	Score
E.R.	60%	54	Seinfeld	66%	37
Touched by an Angel	54	46	Millennium	25	36
Home Improvement	82	46	King of the Hill	27	36
The X-Files	46	43	New America's Most Wanted	45	36
Promised Land	28	43	High Incident	22	35
New York Undercover	28	42	Living Single	29	34
Friends	49	39	Party of Five	28	34
Walker, Texas Ranger	58	38			

Performer Q Scores

	Familiarity	Score		Familiarity	Score
Tom Hanks	87%	53	Chuck Norris	80%	40
Tim Allen	92	46	Richard Karn	76	39
Bill Cosby	86	45	David Duchovny	49	38
James Earl Jones	78	44	Patricia Richardson	77	38
Tom Cruise	92	42	Malik Yoba	28	37
Roma Downey	46	42	Anthony Edwards	53	37
Whoopi Goldberg	89	41	Della Reese	63	36
Michael Richards	62	41			

Cartoon Character Q Scores

	Familiarity	Score		Familiarity	Score
Bugs Bunny	95%	51	Wile E. Coyote	83%	39
Mickey Mouse	97	49	Winnie the Pooh	90	39
Minnie Mouse	96	44	Donald Duck	95	39
Road Runner	90	42	Tommy (from Rugrats)	44	38
Tweety Bird	93	42	Frosty the Snowman	90	37
Charlie Brown	92	40	Tom & Jerry	93	36
Snoopy	90	40	Woody Woodpecker	93	34
Garfield	94	40			

Q Score = % of those who are familiar with program, performer or character and rate it "One Of My Favorites."

Source: Marketing Evaluations Inc.

ZAPPING THE NETWORKS

LONG GONE are the days when the big broadcast networks reigned over television. First came the threat from cable television. Then the VCR and home videos diverted viewers' attention. More recently, satellite TV and even the Internet have been blamed for the broadcast networks' loss of viewers, which continued in the 1996–1997 season.

About 1.7 million fewer homes watched the four big networks in the season that ended in May 1997 than in the year-earlier season. Nielsen Media Research said prime-time viewing of CBS, NBC, ABC, and Fox dropped to 62% of all U.S. households from 65% the season before. The decline marks a record low for the big television networks. For the entire day, the networks fare even worse—with only about 53% of the audience, compared with 72% just 15 years ago.

Broadcast network declines ranged from a 13% drop in household viewing at Walt Disney Co.'s ABC, which slipped from second to third place during the year, and a 10% drop at NBC, the General Electric Co. unit that nevertheless remained television's top-rated network. Second-ranked CBS, a unit of Westinghouse Electric Corp., ended the year up slightly in total household viewership, while Fox Broadcasting Co., a News Corp. unit, was the big gainer, up about 5% for the season.

While a number of cable networks have seen ratings decline similar to those at the broadcast networks, overall cable viewership is up. During the 1996–1997 season, for instance, prime-time viewership for basic cable totaled 32.4% of U.S. households, up from 29.5% a year earlier.

Cable's gains have been especially strong in certain markets, such as news, sports and kids programming. Among children, for example, Nickelodeon, with its irreverent programs such as *Rugrats*, has muscled the broadcast networks aside. "Kids programming on the networks was limited to Saturday or Sunday morning," says Jack Loftus, vice president of communications for Nielsen. "Now kids can just flick Nickelodeon on and watch their programs whenever they want to."

Of course, no single cable channel can rival the broadcast networks in their ability to reach tens of millions of viewers. That's why the networks can still command advertising rate increases, despite lower audience ratings.

Some network television executives attack the messenger in trying to explain the audience erosion. They complain that the Nielsen ratings system is flawed and doesn't accurately show the broadcast networks' share of the audience.

Broadcast Television Networks' Average Prime-Time Audience Ratings

	1996–97 TV SEASON	1995–96 TV SEASON
ABC	9.2%	10.6%
CBS	9.6	9.6
NBC	10.5	11.7
FOX	7.7	7.3
WB	2.6	3.1
UPN	3.2	2.4

Note: The audience rating is the percentage of all 97 million U.S. households with TV sets.

Source: Nielsen Media Research

But that doesn't entirely explain away the networks' loss of viewers. Some media officials say the network's obsession with courting young adults—the cohort most desired by advertisers—with shows like *Friends*, is partly to blame for audience defection. "We've been doing a lot of programming targeting the same group," says David Poltrack, executive vice president of planning

and research at CBS Television Network. "We're leaving a substantial part of the audience unserved." With dramas like *Touched by an Angel*, Mr. Poltrack says, CBS is focusing on an older audience to try to reach viewers it says its competitors are ignoring.

Leslie Moonves, president of CBS Entertainment, blames the overall broadcast decline on a glut of choices—not all of them

Tuned In

The percentage of homes with television sets grew quickly, from 10% in 1950 to 67% in 1955 to 87% by 1960. The ownership rate reached 98% in 1980 and has held steady since then.

Percentage of U.S. TV Households with Various Products and Services

Year	Multiple sets	Color	Cable	VCR	Remote control	Pay cable
1955	4	–	–	–	–	–
1960	12	–	–	–	–	–
1965	22	7	–	–	–	–
1970	35	41	7	–	–	–
1975	43	74	12	–	–	–
1980	50	83	20	–	–	–
1985	57	91	43	14	29	26
1990	65	98	56	66	77	29
1996	74	99	65	81	94	34

Average Weekly Hours and Minutes of Viewing per TV Household

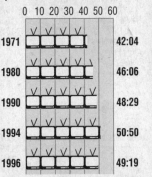

1971	42:04
1980	46:06
1990	48:29
1994	50:50
1996	49:19

Source: Nielsen Media Research

Changing Channels

Shifting Share of the Television Audience as More Homes Receive Cable Programming*

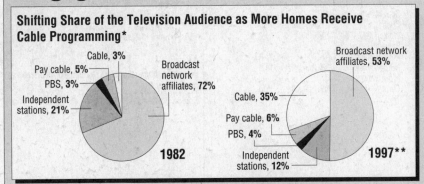

1982: Cable, 3%; Pay cable, 5%; PBS, 3%; Independent stations, 21%; Broadcast network affiliates, 72%

1997**: Broadcast network affiliates, 53%; Cable, 35%; Pay cable, 6%; PBS, 4%; Independent stations, 12%

*Shares don't add to 100% because of viewing of multiple TV sets in some households.
**Independent stations include all superstations except TBS; broadcast network affiliates include Fox; cable includes TBS.
Source: Nielsen Media Research

good. "There is too much product on television and a little bit of it is too watered down," he says. A *Wall Street Journal*/NBC News poll in 1997 found that more than half of people cited lack of interesting programs as the reason for watching fewer shows on the major networks. Many people said they would like to see more history and arts programs, documentaries, movies and news and information shows, and fewer talk shows, soap operas and game shows.

Some media experts wonder if people may be tempted to just turn off the set as they continue to be flooded with an ever expanding menu of television choices. "In five years, you may have 1,000 channels to choose from," says Mr. Loftus. "Will you become much more selective and watch television less?"

Top Rated Network Television Shows, 1996-1997 TV Season

RANK	PROGRAM NAME	NETWORK	AVERAGE AUDIENCE RATING
1	E.R.	NBC	21.2%
2	Seinfeld	NBC	20.5
3	Suddenly Susan	NBC	17.0
4	Friends	NBC	16.8
4	Naked Truth	NBC	16.8
6	Fired Up	NBC	16.5
7	NFL Monday Night Football	ABC	16.2
8	Single Guy	NBC	14.1
9	Home Improvement	ABC	14.0
10	Touched By An Angel	CBS	13.6
11	60 Minutes	CBS	13.3
12	20/20	ABC	12.8
13	NYPD Blue	ABC	12.5
14	CBS Sunday Movie	CBS	12.1
15	Primetime Live	ABC	11.9
16	Frasier	NBC	11.8
17	Spin City	ABC	11.7
18	NBC Sunday Night Movie	NBC	11.5
18	Drew Carey Show	ABC	11.5
20	X-Files	FOX	11.4
20	Dateline NBC-Tue.	NBC	11.4
22	Soul Man	ABC	11.2
22	Cosby	CBS	11.2
24	Walker, Texas Ranger	CBS	11.0
24	Mad About You	NBC	11.0
24	NBC Monday Night Movies	NBC	11.0
24	Caroline In The City	NBC	11.0

RANK	PROGRAM NAME	NETWORK	AVERAGE AUDIENCE RATING
28	3rd Rock From The Sun	NBC	10.8
28	Law And Order	NBC	10.8
30	Ellen	ABC	10.6
31	Dateline NBC-Fri.	NBC	10.5
31	Cybill	CBS	10.5
31	Chicago Hope	CBS	10.5
34	Murphy Brown	CBS	10.4
35	Roseanne	ABC	10.1
36	CBS Tuesday Movie	CBS	10.0
37	Ink	CBS	9.6
38	Life's Work	ABC	9.5
38	Something So Right	NBC	9.5
40	ABC Sunday Night Movie	ABC	9.4
41	Sabrina-Teenage Witch	ABC	9.3
41	CBS Wednesday Movie	CBS	9.3
43	King Of The Hill	FOX	9.2
43	Practice, The	ABC	9.2
45	Grace Under Fire	ABC	9.1
45	Nanny	CBS	9.1
45	Pearl	CBS	9.1
45	Diagnosis Murder	CBS	9.1
49	Early Edition	CBS	9.0
50	Family Matters	ABC	8.8

Note: The audience rating is the percentage of all U.S. households with TV sets

Source: Nielsen Media Research

Top Ranking Network Series Programs (Sept-April)

Season	Program	Network	Rating*
1950-51	Texaco Star Theatre	NBC	61.6
1951-52	Godfrey's Talent Scouts	CBS	53.8
1952-53	I Love Lucy	CBS	67.3
1953-54	I Love Lucy	CBS	58.8
1954-55	I Love Lucy	CBS	49.3
1955-56	$64,000 Question	CBS	47.5
1956-57	I Love Lucy	CBS	43.7
1957-58	Gunsmoke	CBS	43.1
1958-59	Gunsmoke	CBS	39.6
1959-60	Gunsmoke	CBS	40.3
1960-61	Gunsmoke	CBS	37.3
1961-62	Wagon Train	NBC	32.1
1962-63	Beverly Hillbillies	CBS	36.0
1963-64	Beverly Hillbillies	CBS	39.1
1964-65	Bonanza	NBC	36.3
1965-66	Bonanza	NBC	31.8
1966-67	Bonanza	NBC	29.1
1967-68	Andy Griffith	CBS	27.6
1968-69	Rowan & Martin Laugh-In	NBC	31.8
1969-70	Rowan & Martin Laugh-In	NBC	26.3
1970-71	Marcus Welby, MD	ABC	29.6
1971-72	All In The Family	CBS	34.0
1972-73	All In The Family	CBS	33.3
1973-74	All In The Family	CBS	31.2
1974-75	All In The Family	CBS	30.2
1975-76	All In The Family	CBS	30.1
1976-77	Happy Days	ABC	31.5
1977-78	Laverne & Shirley	ABC	31.6
1978-79	Laverne & Shirley	ABC	30.5
1979-80	60 Minutes	CBS	28.2
1980-81	Dallas	CBS	31.2
1981-82	Dallas	CBS	28.4
1982-83	60 Minutes	CBS	25.5
1983-84	Dallas	CBS	25.7
1984-85	Dynasty	ABC	25.0
1985-86	Bill Cosby Show	NBC	33.8
1986-87	Bill Cosby Show	NBC	34.9
1987-88	Bill Cosby Show	NBC	27.8
1988-89	Roseanne	ABC	25.5
1989-90	Roseanne	ABC	23.4
1990-91	Cheers	NBC	21.6
1991-92	60 Minutes	CBS	21.7
1992-93	60 Minutes	CBS	21.6
1993-94	Home Improvement	ABC	21.9
1994-95	Seinfeld	NBC	20.5
1995-96	E.R.	NBC	22.0
1996-97	E.R.	NBC	21.2

*Each rating point represents 1% of all U.S. households with television sets.
Source: Nielsen Media Research

TV Programs With the Largest Audience Ratings of All Time

Rank	Program	Telecast date	Network	Average audience rating (%)	Share (%)	Average audience (in thousands)
1	M*A*S*H Special	Feb. 28, 1983	CBS	60.2	77	50,150
2	Dallas	Nov. 21, 1980	CBS	53.3	76	41,470
3	Roots Pt. VIII	Jan. 30, 1977	ABC	51.1	71	36,380
4	Super Bowl XVI Game	Jan. 24, 1982	CBS	49.1	73	40,020
5	Super Bowl XVII Game	Jan. 30, 1983	NBC	48.6	69	40,480
6	XVII Winter Olympics	Feb. 23, 1994	CBS	48.5	64	45,690
7	Super Bowl XX Game	Jan. 26, 1986	NBC	48.3	70	41,490
8	Gone with the Wind Pt. 1 (Big Event - Pt.1)	Nov. 7, 1976	NBC	47.7	65	33,960
9	Gone with the Wind Pt. 2 (NBC Monday Movie)	Nov. 8, 1976	NBC	47.4	64	33,750
10	Super Bowl XII Game	Jan. 15, 1978	CBS	47.2	67	34,410
11	Super Bowl XIII Game	Jan. 21, 1979	NBC	47.1	74	35,090
12	Bob Hope Christmas Show	Jan. 15, 1970	NBC	46.6	64	27,260
13	Super Bowl XVIII Game	Jan. 22, 1984	CBS	46.4	71	38,800
13	Super Bowl XIX Game	Jan. 20, 1985	ABC	46.4	63	39,390
15	Super Bowl XIV Game	Jan. 20, 1980	CBS	46.3	67	35,330
16	Super Bowl XXX Game	Jan. 28, 1996	NBC	46.0	68	44,150
16	ABC Theater (The Day After)	Nov. 20, 1983	ABC	46.0	62	38,550
18	Roots Pt. VI	Jan. 28, 1977	ABC	45.9	66	32,680
18	The Fugitive	Aug. 29, 1967	ABC	45.9	72	25,700
20	Super Bowl XXI Game	Jan. 25, 1987	CBS	45.8	66	40,030
21	Roots Pt. V	Jan. 27, 1977	ABC	45.7	71	32,540
22	Super Bowl XXVIII Game	Jan. 29, 1994	NBC	45.5	66	42,860
22	Cheers	May 20, 1993	NBC	45.5	64	42,360
24	Ed Sullivan	Feb. 9, 1964	CBS	45.3	60	23,240
25	Super Bowl XXVII	Jan. 31, 1993	NBC	45.1	66	41,990
26	Bob Hope Christmas Show	Jan. 14, 1971	NBC	45.0	61	27,050
27	Roots Pt. III	Jan. 25, 1977	ABC	44.8	68	31,900
28	Super Bowl XI Game	Jan. 9, 1977	NBC	44.4	73	31,610
28	Super Bowl XV Game	Jan. 25, 1981	NBC	44.4	63	34,540
30	Super Bowl VI Game	Jan. 16, 1972	CBS	44.2	74	27,450
31	XVII Winter Olympics	Feb. 25, 1994	CBS	44.1	64	41,540
31	Roots Pt. II	Jan. 24, 1977	ABC	44.1	62	31,400
33	Beverly Hillbillies	Jan. 8, 1964	CBS	44.0	65	22,570
34	Roots Pt. IV	Jan. 26, 1977	ABC	43.8	66	31,190
34	Ed Sullivan	Feb. 16, 1964	CBS	43.8	60	22,445
36	Super Bowl XXIII Game	Jan. 22, 1989	NBC	43.5	68	39,320
37	Academy Awards	Apr. 7, 1970	ABC	43.4	78	25,390
38	Super Bowl XXXI Game	Jan. 26, 1997	Fox	43.3	65	42,000
39	Thorn Birds Pt. III	Mar. 29, 1983	ABC	43.2	62	35,990
40	Thorn Birds Pt. IV	Mar. 30, 1983	ABC	43.1	62	35,900
41	CBS NFC Championship Game	Jan. 10, 1982	CBS	42.9	62	34,960
42	Beverly Hillbillies	Jan. 15, 1964	CBS	42.8	62	21,960
43	Super Bowl VII Game	Jan. 14, 1973	NBC	42.7	72	27,670
44	Thorn Birds Pt. II	Mar. 28, 1983	ABC	42.5	59	35,400
45	Super Bowl IX Game	Jan. 12, 1975	NBC	42.4	72	29,040
45	Beverly Hillbillies	Feb. 26, 1964	CBS	42.4	60	21,750
47	Super Bowl X Game	Jan. 18, 1976	CBS	42.3	78	29,440
47	Airport (Movie Specials)	Nov. 11, 1973	ABC	42.3	63	28,000
47	Love Story (Sun. Night Mov.)	Oct. 1, 1972	ABC	42.3	62	27,410
47	Cinderella	Feb. 22, 1965	CBS	42.3	59	22,250
47	Roots Pt. VII	Jan. 29, 1977	ABC	42.3	65	30,120

Note: The rating is the percentage of all TV households; the share is the percentage of all TVs in use at the time.
Source: Nielsen Media Research

RATING THE TV RATINGS

When Frank Baker's two sons aged 10 and 12 asked to watch *Clueless*, an ABC sitcom, their father took note of the TV-G rating and figured the general-audience label was a safe bet. But Mr. Baker soon felt clueless himself.

"Right out of the starting gate, I heard the word 'naked,' " says Mr. Baker of Longwood, Fla. And that was followed almost immediately by the use of the word "privates" as an anatomical reference. Mr. Baker says he doesn't find the words shocking or offensive, nor does he naively believe his sons have never heard them before. But he was disturbed by the fact that a show with a G rating—described as content that "most parents would find suitable for all ages"—contained such language.

Similar scenes have been played out in dozens of households across the country since the TV ratings system was introduced in January 1997. Like Mr. Baker, many parents and concerned viewers attempting to make sense of the ratings were baffled about who exactly is making these judgments and what criteria they are using. Some parents simply dismissed the existing system as a "farce" and "joke," while others said they have little or no idea what the ratings mean when they appear on screen at the beginning of programs.

The ratings controversy started soon after Congress passed the Telecommunications Act of 1996, which included the provision that a so-called V-chip allowing parents to block out unacceptable shows be installed in all television sets manufactured after mid-1998. The law also required the creation of a ratings system to classify program content and serve as a guide for parents. Six age-based ratings—two for children's shows and four for other programs—were ultimately developed by industry groups, including television networks and stations, the National Association of Broadcasters, and the Motion Picture Association of America.

Many parents cheered the ratings idea at first, but the applause quickly turned to confusion, disappointment, and, in some cases, downright anger. The most common complaint was that the ratings were age, not content-based, so that a logo simply gave parents an idea of the approximate age group for which the show may be appropriate. But it left them in the dark about the nature of the show's content. For instance a TV-PG rating meant that a show "may contain some material that parents would find unsuitable for younger children," but did not make clear whether the questionable material was of a violent or sexual nature or simply included foul language.

In July, the industry yielded to pressure from Capitol Hill and various advocacy groups and agreed to strengthen the system by including more content specific rating symbols. The revised ratings include the symbols, V, S, and L, for violence, sex, and language that may be viewed as offensive. A letter D is used to denote suggestive dialogue to warn parents of language with sexual innuendo.

The ratings, which also use larger icons, are displayed in addition to the age-based system already in place. For the rating category TV-Y7 which applies to children 7 years of age and older, FV indicates intense fantasy violence.

ABC, CBS, Fox and the major cable networks have agreed to the modified ratings. The one exception has been NBC, which, citing constitutional concerns, has indicated it will adhere to the original system and add content specific symbols on a case-by-case basis.

"With more permutations, you run the risk of adding some confusion. We still believe the original system is adequate since it would have theoretically used the V-chip in its simplest form," says Rich Taylor of the Motion Picture Association. Even so, he concedes, "the revised system will essentially accomplish its original goal if people give it a chance to work."

But some critics still argue that allowing the networks to rate their own shows is like letting the fox into the hen house. "It stinks!" says Lee Wells, a father and physician in Duxbury, Mass. "They hope that you make a mistake and end up watching the wrong show. Especially when a child sees a violent scene, you don't want to immediately switch and leave it unresolved."

Parents complain that too many shows fall into the so-called "black hole" of the TV-PG rating, despite content that merits the stronger TV-14 rating. For example, a few weeks into the ratings system, NBC aired a PG-rated episode of the popular sitcom *Friends*, in which one cast member was overheard having sex and another was drunk. The show prompted some media critics to question the network's judgment. For its part, NBC says, "Overall, we feel the ratings system is very effective, but they are still relatively new and will most likely be further refined as time goes on."

Not surprisingly, the networks have avoided the mature audience (TV-MA) rating, knowing it will scare away some advertisers and viewers. One of the rare shows with a TV-MA rating is the new, explicitly violent CBS series *Brooklyn South.*

"Nobody wants to censor the networks or stop them from conducting business as usual, but let it be labeled for what it is," says Jeff Chester, executive director of the Center for Media Education in Washington.

Some media critics believe the debate is an important wake-up call. "The ratings system is not so important because of what it covers," says Elizabeth Tholman, executive director of the Center for Media Literacy. "What is important is that the national debate has focused attention on a critical fact: Families need to be involved in what their children watch."

Eileen Kinsella

Television Program Ratings

The following categories apply to programs designed solely for children:

TV-Y All Children *This program is designed to be appropriate for all children.* Whether animated or live-action, the themes and elements in this program are specifically designed for a very young audience, including children from ages 2–6. This program is not expected to frighten younger children.

TV-Y7 Directed to Older Children *This program is designed for children age 7 and above.* It may be more appropriate for children who have acquired the developmental skills needed to distinguish between make-believe and reality. Themes and elements in this program may include mild fantasy violence or comedic violence, or may frighten children under the age of 7. Therefore, parents may wish to consider the suitability of this program for their very young children. Note: For those programs where fantasy violence may be more intense or more combative than other programs in this category, such programs will be designated **TV-Y7-FV**.

The following categories apply to programs designed for the entire audience:

TV-G General Audience *Most parents would find this program suitable for all ages.* Although this rating does not signify a program designed specifically for children, most parents may let younger children watch this program unattended. It contains little or no violence, no strong language and little or no sexual dialogue or situations.

TV-PG Parental Guidance Suggested *This program contains material that parents may find unsuitable for younger children.* Many parents may want to watch it with their younger children. The theme itself may call for parental guidance and/or the program contains one or more of the following: moderate violence (V), some sexual situations (S), infrequent coarse language (L), or some suggestive dialogue (D).

TV-14 Parents Strongly Cautioned *This program contains some material that many parents would find unsuitable for children under 14 years of age.* Parents are strongly urged to exercise greater care in monitoring this program and are cautioned against letting children under the age of 14 watch unattended. This program contains one or more of the following: intense violence (V), intense sexual situations (S), strong coarse language (L), or intensely suggestive dialogue (D).

TV-MA Mature Audience Only *This program is specifically designed to be viewed by adults and therefore may be unsuitable for children under 17.* This program contains one or more of the following: graphic violence (V), explicit sexual activity (S), or crude, indecent language (L).

Top Cable Networks by Number of Subscribers

The cable-television networks that reached the largest number of subscribers in 1996.

1.	CNN	69,950,000
2.	TBS	69,920,000
3.	ESPN	69,800,000
4.	USA Network	69,677,000
5.	Discovery Channel	69,499,000
6.	TNT	69,075,000
7.	C-SPAN	68,700,000
8.	TNN: The Nashville Network	67,000,000
9.	The Family Channel	66,900,000
10.	A&E	66,880,000
11.	Lifetime	66,000,000
12.	Nickelodeon/Nick at Nite	66,000,000
13.	MTV: Music Television	65,900,000
14.	The Weather Channel	64,700,000
15.	Headline News	62,619,000
16.	AMC (American Movie Classics)	61,000,000
17.	CNBC	60,000,000
18.	QVC	57,017,455
19.	VH1 (Music First)	56,230,000
20.	The Learning Channel	52,000,000

Source: National Cable Television Association

Rising Cable-TV Rates

Average Monthly Cable Rates

YEAR	BASIC RATE
1980	$7.69
1981	7.99
1982	8.30
1983	8.61
1984	8.98
1985	9.73
1986	10.67
1987	12.18
1988	13.86
1989	15.21
1990	16.78
1991	18.10
1992	19.08
1993	19.39
1994	21.62
1995	23.07
1996	24.41
1997*	26.00

Note: As of year-end 1994, the basic and expanded basic rates are combined as regulated basics.
*Estimate
Source: Paul Kagan Associates, Inc.,

Satellite TV's Reach

System operator	June 30, 1994	June 30, 1995	June 30, 1996	July 1997
DIRECTV	0	650,000	1,650,000	2,730,000
USSB #1*	0	321,000	918,000	1,480,000
USSB #2**	0	28,000	75,000	133,000
Primestar	65,000	479,000	1,280,000	1,899,500
Echostar	0	0	70,000	640,000
Totals	65,000	1,157,000	3,075,000	5,402,500

*USSB numbers in this row are for subscribers who are taking both the USSB and DIRECTV services (these numbers are not included in the totals because they are included in the totals for DIRECTV).
**USSB estimates in this row are for USSB subscribers who are taking only USSB's service and not DIRECTV (these numbers are included in the totals).
Source: Carmel Group

Digital TV Preview

Digital television, hailed as the biggest thing to hit broadcasting since color TV, will offer movie-quality pictures and the sharp sound of compact disks. But so far, consumers have reacted with a yawn. The promise of a new generation of television sets hasn't caused people to put off buying conventional tubes, and TV retailers say they've heard few questions about the new technology. Though the government has started to back off of an aggressive timetable for high-definition television, some form of advanced TV is coming. Here's what consumers may want to know.

What's different about digital TV? Broadcasters will be able to send more data over the airwaves using a digital signal that can handle more information. That produces a more detailed picture, with clearer images, brighter colors and sharper sound. The set themselves will be flatter, like the screens at movie theaters.

As TV makers race to put out new sets, technology companies including Microsoft, Compaq and Intel say they are teaming up to develop digital computer screens that will carry TV programs. Sports fans especially will appreciate the wider angle and zippier images of high-definition TV. Imagine, for instance, a close-up of a quarterback that includes a much wider view of the field around him and the coaches on the sidelines.

Viewers also could get more choice in programs. Some broadcasters will use their ability to compress digital data to offer a single, high-definition TV channel; others will offer several different channels that may not be as super-sharp, but will be sharper than what viewers receive now. Broadcasters also could use the channels to offer paging or other data services, or to combine conventional programming with chunks of data. A basketball game, for instance, would be accompanied by a stream of data containing team statistics and player bios, called up at a viewer's whim.

How much will digital sets cost? TV makers estimate the earliest sets will be available in the fall of 1998 at a starting price of between $2,500 and $5,000, making them a likely purchase only for gadget freaks and videophiles. But high-definition set prices are expected to tumble as more people buy sets and makers cut manufacturing costs. Still, nobody expects the majority of Americans to own high-definition sets until well after 2010.

When will digital service be available? As soon as fall 1998 in many metropolitan areas, though not for several years in smaller markets. Broadcasters now must install transmitters and production equipment that will enable them to broadcast a digital signal.

Must people buy a new TV set? Not for a long time. Local stations will continue to broadcast their current analog signals for as long as another decade while they launch the digital service. While current TVs can't receive a digital signal, consumers will be able to buy a converter box, which will cost $100 to $200 and look like the boxes provided by cable operators. Reception over the converter will be better than what viewers currently get— but not as crisp as over a digital unit. The Federal Communications Commission had hoped that by 2006, traditional broadcast feeds would end; many in Congress, though, don't expect that deadline to stick, so TV buyers could have several more years to switch over.

Will people still be able to get cable or satellite-dish service? Yes, without any noticeable difference. Digital TV sets will enhance reception for satellite customers because satellite carriers already broadcast in digital. That will also be true for cable customers as the cable industry converts to a digital feed over the next several years.

Will viewers still be able to watch their favorite old programs? Yes, all the programs in the networks' current libraries will be reformatted for the digital standard. Some shows, like movies and some filmed dramas shot in high-quality film, already work digitally. Production of other programs, though, will have to be completely revamped to comply with the digital standard. News and sports programming, for instance, will require new sets, new cameras and even new makeup to look right on a sharper digital screen.

Home Video: A Buyer's Market

Growth of the home-video industry is slowing, and in a major shift, video buyers are expected to start generating more revenue than renters.

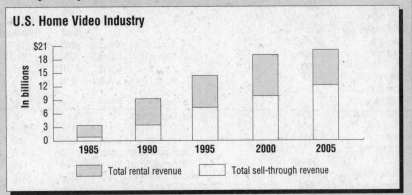

U.S. Home Video Industry

Total rental revenue / Total sell-through revenue

Year	Total rental revenue (In billions)	% change* rental	Total sell-through revenue (In billions)	% change* sell-through	Total revenue (In billions)	% change* total
1985	$2.55	—	$0.86	—	$3.41	—
1990	6.63	160%	3.18	272%	9.81	188%
1995	7.49	13	7.34	131	14.83	51
2000	8.26	10	9.92	35	18.18	23
2005	8.48	3	12.04	21	20.53	13

*Percent change is over five-year period.
Source: Paul Kagan Associates Inc.

Top Video Rentals for 1996

Rank	Title	Video label	Weeks in release	Turns (In millions)	Revenues (In millions)
1	Braveheart	Paramount	42	20.766	$54.85
2	Seven	New Line	40	19.979	53.30
3	The Net	Columbia TriStar	51	16.469	42.98
4	Twister	Warner	13	15.292	41.07
5	The Nutty Professor	Universal	7	14.445	39.04
6	Ace Ventura: When Nature Calls	Warner	42	14.670	38.56
7	Jumanji	Columbia TriStar	33	14.704	38.30
8	Under Siege 2: Dark Territory	Warner	47	13.984	36.86
9	Get Shorty	MGM/UA	31	13.553	36.35
10	Executive Decision	Warner	21	13.401	36.02
11	Dangerous Minds	BV/Hollywood	46	13.690	35.94
12	Independence Day	20th Century Fox	6	13.386	35.85
13	Mission: Impossible	Paramount	7	13.261	35.59
14	Copycat	Warner	45	13.360	35.55
15	Heat	Warner	28	13.032	34.95
16	The American President	Columbia TriStar	33	13.097	34.74
17	Babe	Universal	41	13.167	34.04
18	GoldenEye	MGM/UA	32	12.106	32.24
19	Assassins	Warner	42	12.174	32.21
20	Money Train	Columbia TriStar	35	11.965	31.82

Source: Video Software Dealers Association

Top Selling Videos in 1996

	Title	Studio	Units Sold (mil.)
1	Independence Day	Fox	22.0
2	Toy Story	Disney	21.0
3	Pocahontas	Disney	17.0
4	The Aristocats	Disney	12.8
5	Hunchback of Notre Dame	Disney	12.5
6	Aladdin and the King of Thieves	Disney	10.0
7	Oliver & Co.	Disney	10.0
8	Twister	Warner	9.5
9	Muppett Treasure Island	Disney	8.0
10	All Dogs Go to Heaven 2	MGM	6.0

Source: Paul Kagan Associates Inc.

Home Video's Greatest Hits: Top 10 Selling Videos of All Time

	Title	Studio	Date	Units Sold (in millions)
1	The Lion King	Disney	03/95	30.0
2	Snow White	Disney	10/94	28.0
3	Aladdin	Disney	10/93	24.0
4	Jurassic Park	Universal	10/92	24.0
5	Beauty & the Beast	Disney	10/92	22.0
6	Independence Day	Fox	11/96	22.0
7	Toy Story	Disney	10/96	21.0
8	Pocahontas	Disney	02/96	17.0
9	Forrest Gump	Paramount	04/95	16.0
10	Mrs. Doubtfire	Fox	03/94	14.0

Source: Paul Kagan Associates Inc.

Top Video-Game Players

Top 10 Publishers Ranked by Interactive Entertainment Software Units Sold, 1996

		Publisher's sales mix		
		Percent of entertainment software units sold		
Rank	Publisher	Video game console	vs.	Computer
1	Nintendo of America	100%		0%
2	Electronic Arts	62		38
3	Sega of America	98		2
4	Acclaim*	95		5
5	CUC International*	2		98
6	GT Interactive*	0		100
7	Sony*	87		13
8	Midway Home Entertainment	100		0
9	Interplay	20		80
10	Virgin Interactive	29		71

*Corporate.
Source: NPD Group Inc.

Sour Note

Sales of recorded music have turned sluggish after years of solid growth.

Record Manufacturers' Unit Shipments and Dollar Value
(In millions, net after returns)

	1987	1988	1989	1990	1991	1992	1993	1994	1995	% change 1994–1995	1996	% change 1995–1996
(Units shipped)	102.1	149.7	207.2	286.5	333.3	407.5	495.4	662.1	722.9	9.2%	778.9	7.7%
(Dollar value) CD	$1,593.6	$2,089.9	$2,587.7	$3,451.6	$4,337.7	$5,326.5	$6,511.4	$8,464.5	$9,377.4	10.8	$9,934.7	5.9
CD single	–	1.6	-0.1	1.1	5.7	7.3	7.8	9.3	21.5	131.2	43.2	100.9
	–	9.8	-0.7	6.0	35.1	45.1	45.8	56.1	110.9	97.7	184.1	66.0
Cassette	410.0	450.1	446.2	442.2	360.1	366.4	339.5	345.4	272.6	-21.1	225.3	-17.4
	2,959.7	3,385.1	3,345.8	3,472.4	3,019.6	3,116.3	2,915.8	2,976.4	2,303.6	-22.6	1,905.3	-17.3
Cassette single	5.1	22.5	76.2	87.4	69.0	84.6	85.6	81.1	70.7	-12.8	59.9	-15.3
	14.3	57.3	194.6	257.9	230.4	298.8	298.5	274.9	236.3	-14.0	189.3	-19.9
LP/EP	107.0	72.4	34.6	11.7	4.8	2.3	1.2	1.9	2.2	15.8	2.9	31.8
	793.1	532.2	220.3	86.5	29.4	13.5	10.6	17.8	25.1	41.0	36.8	46.6
Vinyl single	82.0	65.6	36.6	27.6	22.0	19.8	15.1	11.7	10.2	-12.8	10.1	-1.0
	203.3	180.4	116.4	94.4	63.9	66.4	51.2	47.2	46.7	-1.1	47.5	1.7
Music video	–	–	6.1	9.2	6.1	7.6	11.0	11.2	12.6	12.5	16.9	34.1
	–	–	115.4	172.3	118.1	157.4	213.3	231.1	220.3	-4.7	236.1	7.2
Total units	706.8	761.9	806.7	865.7	801.0	895.5	955.6	1,122.7	1,112.7	-0.9	1,137.2	2.2
Total value	$5,567.5	$6,254.8	$6,579.4	$7,541.1	$7,834.2	$9,024.0	$10,046.6	$12,068.0	$12,320.3	2.1	$12.533.8	1.7

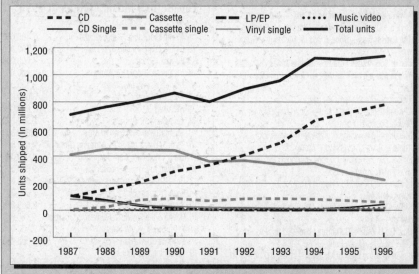

Source: Recording Industry Association of America

Changing the Tune

Market shares of different types of recorded music in 1986 and 1996 show America's changing musical tastes.

	1987	1996
Rock	45.5%	32.6%
Country	10.6	14.7
R&B	9.0	12.1
Pop	13.5	9.3
Rap	3.8	8.9
Gospel	2.9	4.3
Classical	3.9	3.4
Jazz	3.8	3.3
Oldies	0.7	0.8
Soundtracks	0.2	0.8
New Age	NA	0.7
Children's	0.5	0.7
Other	4.8	5.2

Source: Recording Industry Association of America.

Top 40 Singles of 1996

1. Macarena (Bayside Boys Mix)—*Los Del Río*—RCA
2. One Sweet Day—*Mariah Carey & Boyz II Men*—Columbia
3. Because You Loved Me (From Up Close & Personal)—*Celine Dion*—550 Music
4. Nobody Knows—*The Tony Rich Project*—LaFace
5. Always Be My Baby—*Mariah Carey*—Columbia
6. Give Me One Reason—*Tracy Chapman*—Elektra
7. Tha Crossroads—*Bone Thugs-N-Harmony*—Ruthless
8. I Love You Always Forever—*Donna Lewis*—Atlantic
9. You're Making Me High/Let IT Flow—*Toni Braxton*—LaFace
10. Twistred—*Keith Sweat*—Elektra
11. C'mon N' Ride It (The Train)—*Quad City DJ's*—QuadraSound/Big Beat
12. Missing—*Everything But The Girl*—Atlantic
13. Ironic—*Alanis Morissette*—Maverick
14. Exhale (Shoop Shoop) (From Waiting to Exhale)—*Whitney Houston*—Arista
15. Follow You Down/Til I Hear It From You—*Gin Blossoms*—A&M
16. Sittin' Up In My Room (From Waiting To Exhale)—*Brandy*—Arista
17. How Do U Want It/California Love—*2Pac (Featuring KC & JoJo)*—Death Row
18. It's All Coming Back to Me Know—*Celine Dion*—550 Music
19. Change The World (From Phenomenon)—*Eric Clapton*—Reprise
20. Hey Lover—*LL Cool J*—Def Jam
21. Lougin—*LL Cool J*—Def Jam
22. Insensitive (From Bed of Roses)—*Jann Arden*—A&M
23. Be My Lover—*La Bouche*—RCA
24. Name—*Goo Goo Dolls*—Warner Bros.
25. Who Will Save Your Soul—*Jewel*—Atlantic
26. Where Do You Go—*No Mercy*—Arista
27. I Can't Sleep Baby (If I)—*R. Kelly*—Jive
28. Counting Blue Cars—*Dishwalla*—A&M
29. You Learn/You Oughta Know—*Alanis Morissette*—Maverick
30. One of Us—*Joan Osborne*—Blue Gorilla
31. Wonder—*Natalie Merchant*—Elektra
32. Not Gon' Cry (From Waiting to Exhale)—*Mary J. Blige*—Arista
33. Gangsta's Paradise (From Dangerous Minds)—*Coolio Featuring L.V.*—MCA Soundtracks
34. Only You—*112 Featuring The Notorious B.I.G.*—Bad Boy
35. Down Low (Nobody Has To Know)—*R. Kelly Featuring Ronald Isley*—Jive
36. You're The One—*SWV*—RCA
37. Sweet Dreams—*LA Bouche*—RCA
38. Before You Walk Out Of My Life/Like This And Like That—*Monica*—Rowdy
39. Breakfast At Tiffany's—*Deep Blue Something*—Rain-Maker
40. 1, 2, 3, 4 (Sumpin' New)—*Coolio*—Tommy Boy

Source: Billboard Hot 100 Singles Chart for 1996, which is based on amount of radio air play and sales data

Top-Selling Music Albums of 1996

1. Alanis Morissette, *Jagged Little Pill*		7,400,000
2. Celine Dion, *Falling Into You*		6,100,000
3. Fugees, *Score*		4,500,000
4. No Doubt, *Tragic Kingdom*		4,400,000
5. Mariah Carey, *Daydream*		3,100,000
6. 2 Pac, *All Eyez On Me*		3,000,000
7. Metallica, *Load*		3,000,000
8. Toni Braxton, *Secrets*		2,900,000
9. Shania Twain, *Woman In Me*		2,800,000
10. Oasis, *What's the Story Morning Glory*		2,600,000
11. Tracy Chapman, *New Beginning*		2,600,000
12. *Waiting to Exhale*, Soundtrack		2,600,000
13. Bone Thugs N Harmony, *East 1999 Eternal*		2,500,000
14. Leann Rimes, *Blue*		2,500,000
15. Bush, *Sixteen Stone*		2,300,000
16. Hootie & the Blowfish, *Fairweather Johnson*		2,100,000
17. Keith Sweat, *Keith Sweat*		2,100,000
18. Dave Matthews Band, *Crash*		2,000,000
19. Smashing Pumpkins, *Mellon Collie & Infinite*		1,900,000
20. Hootie & the Blowfish, *Cracked Rear View*		1,700,000

Source: SoundScan Inc.

Top-Selling Music Albums of All Time

24,000,000
TITLE: *Thriller*
ARTIST: Michael Jackson
LABEL: Epic

TITLE: *Eagles—Their Greatest Hits 1971–1975*
ARTIST: Eagles
LABEL: Elektra

17,000,000
TITLE: *Rumours*
ARTIST: Fleetwood Mac
LABEL: Warner Bros.

16,000,000
TITLE: *Led Zeppelin IV*
ARTIST: Led Zeppelin
LABEL: Swan Song

TITLE: *Boston*
ARTIST: Boston
LABEL: Epic

TITLE: *The Bodyguard* (Soundtrack)
ARTIST: Whitney Houston, et al.
LABEL: Arista

15,000,000
TITLE: *Born in the U.S.A.*
ARTIST: Bruce Springsteen
LABEL: Columbia

TITLE: *Jagged Little Pill*
ARTIST: Alanis Morissette
LABEL: Maverick

TITLE: *Cracked Rear View*
ARTIST: Hootie & The Blowfish
LABEL: Atlantic

14,000,000
TITLE: *Hotel California*
ARTIST: Eagles
LABEL: Elektra

TITLE: *Appetite for Destruction*
ARTIST: Guns 'N Roses
LABEL: Geffen

13,000,000
TITLE: *No Fences*
ARTIST: Garth Brooks
LABEL: Liberty

TITLE: *Greatest Hits*
ARTIST: Elton John
LABEL: Rockett

TITLE: *The Dark Side of the Moon*
ARTIST: Pink Floyd
LABEL: Capitol

TITLE: *Purple Rain* (Soundtrack)
ARTIST: Prince & The Revolution
LABEL: Warner Bros.

TITLE: *Bat Out of Hell*
ARTIST: Meat Loaf
LABEL: Epic

12,000,000
TITLE: *Back in Black*
ARTIST: AC/DC
LABEL: ATCO

TITLE: *Slippery When Wet*
ARTIST: Bon Jovi
LABEL: Mercury

TITLE: *II*
ARTIST: Boyz II Men
LABEL: Motown

TITLE: *Whitney Houston*
ARTIST: Whitney Houston
LABEL: Arista

TITLE: *Bruce Springsteen & E Street Band Live 1975–'85*
ARTIST: Bruce Springsteen
LABEL: Columbia

11,000,000
TITLE: *Saturday Night Fever* (Soundtrack)
ARTIST: Bee Gees
LABEL: RSO

TITLE: *Ropin' the Wind*
ARTIST: Garth Brooks
LABEL: Liberty

TITLE: *Hysteria*
ARTIST: Def Leppard
LABEL: Mercury

TITLE: *Breathless*
ARTIST: Kenny G
LABEL: Arista

TITLE: *Dirty Dancing*
ARTIST: Soundtrack
LABEL: RCA

TITLE: *James Taylor's Greatest Hits*
ARTIST: James Taylor
LABEL: Warner Bros.

TITLE: *Abbey Road*
ARTIST: The Beatles
LABEL: Capitol

TITLE: *Sgt. Pepper's Lonely Hearts Club Band*
ARTIST: The Beatles
LABEL: Capitol

10,000,000

TITLE: *Unplugged*
ARTIST: Eric Clapton
LABEL: Reprise

TITLE: *Best of the Doobies*
ARTIST: Doobie Brothers
LABEL: Warner Bros.

TITLE: *Please Hammer Don't Hurt 'em*
ARTIST: Hammer
LABEL: Capitol

TITLE: *Tapestry*
ARTIST: Carole King
LABEL: Ode

TITLE: *The Wall*
ARTIST: Pink Floyd
LABEL: Columbia

TITLE: *Can't Slow Down*
ARTIST: Lionel Richie
LABEL: Motown

TITLE: *The Lion King*
ARTIST: Soundtrack
LABEL: Walt Disney

TITLE: *Crazy, Sexy,Cool*
ARTIST: TLC
LABEL: LaFace

TITLE: *The Joshua Tree*
ARTIST: U2
LABEL: Island

TITLE: *Van Halen*
ARTIST: Van Halen
LABEL: Warner Bros.

TITLE: *Eliminator*
ARTIST: ZZ Top
LABEL: Warner Bros.

TITLE: *Ten*
ARTIST: Pearl Jam
LABEL: Epic

TITLE: *Faith*
ARTIST: George Michael
LABEL: Columbia

Source: Recording Industry Association of America

Making Music—and Money

Major Concert Ticket Sales in North America

Top Concert Tours of All Time

Rank	Performer	Year	Gross revenues
1	Rolling Stones	1994	$121,200,000
2	Pink Floyd	1994	103,500,000
3	Rolling Stones	1989	98,000,000
4	Eagles	1994	79,400,000
5	New Kids On The Block	1990	74,100,000
6	U2	1992	67,000,000
7	Eagles	1995	63,300,000
8	Barbra Streisand	1994	58,900,000
9	Grateful Dead	1994	52,400,000
10	Elton John/Billy Joel	1994	47,800,000

Source: Pollstar

1996 Concert Tours with the Largest Ticket Revenues

Rank	Gross	Artist
1	$43,600,000	Kiss
2	34,500,000	Garth Brooks
3	32,200,000	Neil Diamond
4	29,100,000	Rod Stewart
5	26,300,000	Bob Seger
6	26,200,000	Jimmy Buffett
7	26,100,000	Reba McEntire
8	23,200,000	Alanis Morissette
9	21,400,000	Hootie & the Blowfish
10	21,300,000	Ozzy Osbourne
11	21,100,000	AC/DC
12	20,600,000	Dave Matthews Band
13	20,300,000	George Strait
14	18,900,000	Sting
15	18,400,000	The Smashing Pumpkins
16	18,100,000	"The H.O.R.D.E. Festival"
17	17,300,000	The Who
18	16,500,000	Phish
19	15,900,000	"Lollapalooza '96"
20	15,800,000	Alan Jackson
21	15,600,000	Brooks & Dunn
22	15,500,000	Vince Gill
23	15,400,000	Tim McGraw
24	14,000,000	Gloria Estefan
25	11,700,000	Bush

Source: Pollstar

FUN AND GAMES
ON THE NET

The Internet is a great place to goof off.

That's the sentiment of thousands of on-line users who are whiling away the hours playing games, chatting with friends, listening to music, even watching soap operas. In fact, adult Internet users say 48% of their time on the World Wide Web is for personal entertainment, according to Find/SVP, a market-research firm in New York.

"It's something to do when I'm home," says Beverly Hughes, a mother of three young children in Beaufort, S.C., who communicates with other parents and plays bingo on-line. "I can have fun and I don't even need to get a babysitter."

One of the most popular forms of on-line entertainment is chat, where people meet in an on-line space and electronically "talk." Often, chat rooms focus on a specific subject. There are chat rooms for parents, sports fans and wine connoisseurs. While most chat still is purely text, it is getting more sophisticated. Participants in Microsoft's Comic Chat appear as cartoon characters. In Microsoft's V-chat, participants create their own avatars—characters that represents their on-line selves. "You can stand around in a circle like you would at a party," says Linda Stone, director of Microsoft's virtual worlds group.

And forget traditional board games. According to Find/SVP, 37% of adult World Wide Web users say they play games on-line. The Bingo Zone (www.bingozone.com) runs 54 free bingo games a day. In each game, more than 800 players vie for prizes of $3 to $20. The site has few bells and whistles—the games are straightforward and the graphics are elementary, so downloading time is limited. "It's simple, easy, immediate gratification," says Steven Kane, president of Boston's nineCo Inc., which produces BingoZone. Meanwhile, Interactive Imagination's Riddler.com has given away more than $500,000 in prizes, including cars, books, computers and compact disks to winners of its games. Participants, who must register but play for free, can choose from 13 different games. They include Mental Floss, a single-player trivia game, and Checkered Flag, in which three players vie in real time to complete crossword puzzles.

When The Spot debuted in June of 1995, a new form of cyber-entertainment was born—original dramatic programming on-line. Using still photographs and text, The Spot follows the lives, loves and neuroses of a group of young Californians living in a group house. Dozens of other cyber-soaps followed. At The Couch (www.thecouch.com), a set of young New Yorkers attending group therapy in the city's Flatiron building deal with marriage, career and infidelity in daily vignettes and journal entries. In Marinex Multimedia Corp.'s East Village (www.eastvillage.com), artists, musicians and hustlers survive in the edgy New York neighborhood.

Interactivity is a large part of cyber-soaps. Fans can chat with characters and send advice through e-mail. At The Couch, fans and characters discuss the latest storyline, dish on characters, and sometimes move onto more serious topics, such as the rights of HIV-infected individuals. Some cyber-serials are hoping to land deals in traditional entertainment media to help pay the bills. For example, the creators of the East Village have formed a film production company, Miscellaneous Films, and have produced a compact disk (on sale on the site) featuring East Village bands.

Creators of on-line entertainment face a number of challenges. Although on-line advertising revenue is increasing, it's difficult for smaller entertainment players to get a piece of the pie. And asking participants to pay for on-line fun is still pretty much taboo. While 36% of World Wide Web users read entertainment magazines on-line, only 13% of those would pay to subscribe, according to market-research firm NPD Group Inc.

There are technical limitations, too. Slick sound and video have been a problem, for instance, because they take so long to download. But as the technology improves and modem speeds increase, on-line producers hope to become more sophisticated. Riddler.com plans to start an on-line version of Name That Tune, with more advanced sound effects. And Entertainment Asylum, a subsidiary of America Online Inc.'s Greenhouse Networks, is developing an entertainment network with four hours of programming each day. Scott Zakarin, creator of The Spot and Entertainment Asylum's president of programming, envisions a 24-hour video and audio channel—television where you can e-mail the stars. "We're taking baby steps toward interactive television," he says. "We're Neil Armstrong stepping onto the moon."

Andrea Petersen

Radio Industry Consolidation

The radio industry has experienced major consolidation since federal legislation allowed companies to own as many stations as they want nationwide and as many as eight stations in a single market. The new law spurred a shopping spree in 1996 and 1997. Since then, advertising rates and revenues have risen, sparking concern among marketers and their ad agencies that some radio markets now will be controlled by only two companies.

Radio Station Transaction Volume

Year	No. of stations sold	Value of transactions (In millions)
1987	1,021	$2,254
1988	1,082	3,315
1989	1,205	2,248
1990	1,059	773
1991	1,009	807
1992	1,194	1,412
1993	1,410	2,829
1994	1,255	2,650
1995	1,259	5,371
1996	2,157	14,336

Note: Based on dates announced, not approved.

10 Largest Radio Groups

	1996				1995		
Owner rank	Owner	Total stations	Revenues (In $000)	Owner rank	Owner	Total stations	Revenues (In $000)
1	CBS Corp.	79	$1,013,700	1	CBS Radio Station Group	39	$495,750
2	Jacor Communications Inc.	112	407,125	2	Infinity Broadcasting Corp.	34	403,750
3	Evergreen Media Corp.	42	399,850	3	Evergreen Media Corp.	35	274,500
4	American Radio Systems	93	376,850	4	Walt Disney Co.	21	269,800
5	ABC Inc. (Disney)	21	295,350	5	Chancellor Broadcasting	33	177,950
6	Clear Channel	101	291,675	6	Cox Enterprises	18	138,300
7	Chancellor Broadcasting	51	272,350	7	Clear Channel	36	137,200
8	SFX Broadcasting Inc.	75	270,450	8	Jacor Communications Inc.	20	124,250
9	Cox Enterprises	41	197,675	9	Viacom International Inc.	12	121,500
10	Heftel Broadcasting Corp.	37	131,350	10	Bonneville International	17	119,400
	Top 10 Radio Owners	652	3,656,375		Top 10 Radio Owners	265	2,262,400
	Total Industry		11,230,000		Total Industry		10,450,000

Note: Proforma revenues for entire year based on all stations owned or under contract at the end of the year.
Source: BIA Research Inc.

On the Radio Dial

While the number of radio stations continues to grow, traditional formats like Top-40 and Adult Contemporary are being replaced by more rock, religion, and news.

Number of Radio Stations by Format

Commercial format	1989	1996	Noncommercial format	1989	1996
Country	2,448	2,525	Religion (Teaching & Music)	302	556
Adult Contemporary	2,058	1,572	Variety	387	377
News, Talk, Business, Sports	308	1,272	Rock (Album, Modern, Classic)	226	287
Religion (Teaching & Music)	696	1,020	News, Talk, Business, Sports	11	410
Rock (Album, Modern, Classic)	365	879	Classical, Fine Arts	306	130
Oldies	545	738	Jazz & New Age	37	78
Spanish & Ethnic	313	527	Top-40	71	41
Adult Standards	332	499	Spanish & Ethnic	34	47
Urban, Black	284	348	Urban, Black	32	30
Top-40	951	333	Adult Contemporary	16	20
Jazz & New Age	64	89	Easy Listening	7	8
Easy Listening	328	57	Country	8	12
Variety	134	54	Adult Standards	0	4
Classical, Fine Arts	49	41	Oldies	0	4
Pre-Teen	0	33	**Total**	**1,566**	**2,034**
Comedy	1	0			
Total	**9,254**	**10,261**			

Source: M Street Corp.

BROADWAY AND BUSINESS

In a meeting of power suits and sequins, corporate America has landed a leading role on Broadway.

With the Great White Way churning out mega-hits such as *Rent* and long-running shows like *Phantom of the Opera* still attracting crowds, major companies are sharing the spotlight through cross-promotions and sponsorships. For example, MasterCard International and American Express Co. are creating advertising featuring their brands alongside Broadway stars and promoting shows in mailings to their customers. And Ford Motor Co. and Walt Disney Co. have gone one step further: They have invested millions of dollars in their own theaters.

"Everybody wants to be a star on Broadway, and that includes companies," says Scott Walton of Boneau/Bryan-Brown, a marketing firm that represents 10 Broadway and Off-Broadway shows including *Tap Dogs* and *Smokey Joe's Cafe*.

Marketers are attracted to the stage because of its glitzy image and rising popularity. Broadway also is appealing because it gives companies access to an affluent and edu-

cated group of consumers. Almost three-quarters of theatergoers have a household income of more than $50,000, says the League of American Theatres and Producers Inc., an industry trade organization.

"Now that Broadway is less of a gamble and more of a business, corporate America is getting interested," says Nancy Coyne, a co-founder of New York advertising firm Serino, Coyne Inc., which represents Broadway shows. Indeed, Broadway is performing quite well financially. In the 1996–1997 season, 10.6 million people attended Broadway shows, and the industry grossed $499 million. That compares with 7.3 million people and $267 million in 1990–1991. Touring companies grossed an additional $781.8 million in 1996–1997.

While sports teams, rock concerts, and the Olympics have turned to corporations for promotions and sponsorships for years, the idea is still relatively new on Broadway. Industry officials say that only in the last decade or so, since the advent of the mega-musicals, has Broadway had enough mainstream appeal and national recognition to attract much corporate interest. "Broadway was considered elite. Now it's considered a family event," says Mr. Walton.

Corporate support is increasingly important as the cost of staging a Broadway show keeps rising and ticket prices of as much as $75 already are beyond the reach of many people. Today, the most expensive shows cost $9 million to $12 million to produce; 10 years ago, the price tag was $3 million to $4 million. "The need for other revenue streams is critical," says Jed Bernstein, executive director of the League of American Theatres and Producers. "There is some sort of theoretical ceiling of how much you can charge for a ticket."

On Broadway

Box Office Gross and Attendance on Broadway

Season	Gross	Attendance
1957-58	$38 million	7.2 million
1960-61	44 million	7.7 million
1965-66	54 million	9.6 million
1970-71	55 million	7.4 million
1975-76	71 million	7.3 million
1980-81	197 million	11.0 million
1985-86	189,517,166	6,511,591
1990-91	266,823,321	7,316,095
1991-92	293,014,578	7,379,506
1992-93	327,740,483	7,856,793
1993-94	356,065,697	8,102,927
1994-95	406,121,744	9,038,977
1995-96	436,000,000	9,455,284
1996-97	499,000,000	10,600,000

Broadway Road Tours

Season	Box office gross	Number of shows
1992-93	$626.0 million	52
1993-94	705.0 million	42
1994-95	702.0 million	44
1995-96	810.0 million	47
1996-97	781.8 million	46

Longest Running Broadway Shows

Show	Opening date	Closing date
Cats	9/23/82	currently running
A Chorus Line	7/25/75	4/28/90
Oh Calcutta	9/24/76	8/06/89
Les Miserables	2/28/87	currently running
Phantom of the Opera	1/09/88	currently running
42nd Street	8/25/80	1/08/89
Grease	2/14/72	4/13/80
Fiddler on the Roof	9/22/64	7/01/72
Life With Father	11/08/39	7/12/47
Tobacco Road	12/04/33	5/31/41

Average Ticket Prices on Broadway

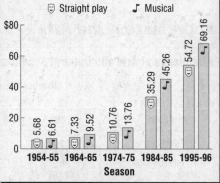

Broadway Box Office Gross

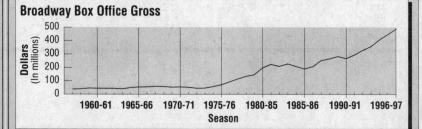

Source: League of American Theatres and Producers

The financial assistance can come in many forms. Virgin Atlantic Airways provided the $6.5 million production of *Jeckyl and Hyde* with cash, free airline tickets and promotion in the carrier's magazine. In return, the company is included on every piece of advertising the show does.

Bloomingdale's created a major promotion with the edgy musical *Rent*, running full-page newspaper ads featuring the show's cast and selling an entire line of clothing inspired by the show in *"Rent* boutiques" in its department stores. "The musical hit a chord for Bloomingdale's," says Kal Ruttenstein, the company's senior vice president. "It happened to be financially successful as well as an emotionally productive experience for all involved."

Walt Disney and Ford have taken the biggest leap onto the Broadway stage. The musical *Ragtime*, produced by Canada's Livent Inc., will open at the newly christened Ford Center for the Performing Arts this winter. The reason for the new name? The automobile company's "significant" cash investment in Livent's new 42nd Street theater. "It's a

good way to extend the Ford name," says Ford spokeswoman Brenda Hines.

Disney, meanwhile, has renovated the New Amsterdam Theater, where it introduced the new musical *King David* and plans to present the stage version of *The Lion King*. Disney made its Broadway debut in 1994, when it produced a musical version of its animated film, *Beauty and the Beast*, whose New York success spawned international touring companies, including ones in Australia, Canada, Japan, and Austria. Ms. Coyne believes New York's efforts to clean up Times Square and the close involvement of Ford and Disney will lure more companies to Broadway. "Once Disney made the commitment to Broadway, people said, 'It must be good to do business on Broadway,'" she says.

The League of American Theatres and Producers is trying to increase corporate support further by attracting industry-wide sponsors, not just single-show tie-ins. The League recently unveiled a logo titled "Live Broadway" for official sponsors, who would contribute "seven or eight figures." Continental Airlines became the first official corporate sponsor. Its

Appreciating the Arts ♫ ♪

Attendance at Arts and Cultural Activities

Art Form	Number attending (In millions)		Percentage change
	1982	1992	1982-92
Art/craft fairs	63.9	75.6	18.3
Historic parks	60.6	64.1	5.8
Art museums	36.2	49.6	37.0
Musicals	30.5	32.3	5.9
Plays	19.5	25.1	28.7
Classical music	21.3	23.2	8.9
Jazz	15.7	19.7	25.5
Ballet	6.9	8.7	26.1
Other dance	NA	13.2	NA
Opera	4.5	6.1	35.6

Source: National Endowment for the Arts

multimillion dollar five-year sponsorship will fund a Broadway telephone information line, free concerts, and marketing programs.

Whether it's in the form of official sponsorships or catchy promotions, Margery Singer, a New York entertainment-marketing consultant for such shows as *Titanic*, says blue-chip names like American Express and Blooming-

dale's give a show something intangible but infinitely valuable—a seal of approval. "When Saks Fifth Avenue does a *Titanic*-themed window," she says, "it almost says Saks thinks the show is good."

Andrea Petersen

The Printed Word

Fewer Dailies, Fewer Readers

During the 1990s, the number of daily morning newspapers has increased, but the number of evening papers and total daily circulation have dropped. The number of Sunday papers and Sunday circulation have remained more stable.

Number of Newspapers and Their Circulation

Year	Morning	Evening	Total*	Total circulation	Sunday	Sunday circulation
1920	437	1,605	2,042	27,790,656	522	17,083,604
1930	388	1,554	1,942	39,589,172	521	26,413,047
1940	380	1,498	1,878	41,131,611	525	32,371,092
1950	322	1,450	1,772	53,829,072	549	46,582,348
1960	312	1,459	1,763	58,881,746	563	47,698,651
1970	334	1,429	1,748	62,107,527	586	49,216,602
1980	387	1,388	1,747	62,201,840	736	54,676,173
1985	482	1,220	1,676	62,766,232	798	58,825,978
1990	559	1,084	1,611	62,327,962	863	62,634,512
1991	571	1,042	1,586	60,687,125	875	66,093,415
1992	596	996	1,570	60,164,499	891	62,159,971
1993	623	954	1,556	59,811,594	884	62,565,574
1994	635	935	1,548	59,305,436	886	62,294,799
1995	656	891	1,533	58,193,391	888	61,529,296
1996	686	846	1,520	56,983,290	890	63,732,708

*Morning and Evening do not equal Total because some papers have both morning and evening editions.
Source: Editor & Publisher

Top 50 Daily Newspapers in the U.S. According to Circulation
(Sept. 30,1996)

New York (NY) *Wall Street Journal*	(m)	1,783,532
Arlington (VA) *USA Today*	(m)	1,591,629
New York (NY) *Times*	(m)	1,071,120
Los Angeles (CA) *Times*	(m)	1,029,073
Washington (DC) *Post*	(m)	789,198
New York (NY) *Daily News*	(m)	734,277
Chicago (IL) *Tribune*	(m)	680,535
Long Island (NY) *Newsday*	(m)	564,754
Houston (TX) *Chronicle*	(m)	545,348
Chicago (IL) *Sun-Times*	(m)	496,030
San Francisco (CA) *Chronicle*	(m)	486,977
Dallas (TX) *Morning News*	(m)	478,181
Boston (MA) *Globe*	(m)	471,024
New York (NY) *Post*	(m)	429,642
Philadelphia (PA) *Inquirer*	(m)	427,175
Newark (NJ) *Star -Ledger*	(m)	405,869
Minneapolis (MN) *Star Tribune*	(m)	393,740
Cleveland (OH) *Plain Dealer*	(m)	386,256
Phoenix (AZ) *Arizona Republic*	(m)	382,122
San Diego (CA) *Union-Tribune*	(all day)	372,081
Detroit (MI) *Free Press*	(m)	363,385
Miami (FL) *Herald*	(m)	361,279
Orange County (CA) *Register*	(m)	353,812
St. Petersburg (FL) *Times*	(m)	340,878
Portland (WA) *Oregonian*	(all day)	338,586
Denver (CO) *Post*	(m)	334,436
St. Louis (MO) *Post-Dispatch*	(m)	321,461
Denver (CO) *Rocky Mountain News*	(m)	316,910
Atlanta (GA) *Constitution*	(m)	308,301
Baltimore (MD) *Sun*	(m)	304,412
Milwaukee (WI) *Journal Sentinel*	(m)	287,673
San Jose (CA) *Mercury News*	(m)	285,735
Boston (MA) *Herald*	(m)	284,794
Kansas City (MO) *Star*	(m)	279,305
Sacramento (CA) *Bee*	(m)	276,758
Orlando (FL) *Sentinel*	(all day)	262,802
Buffalo (NY) *News*	(all day)	262,045
New Orleans (LA) *Times-Picayune*	(m)	259,577
Tampa (FL) *Tribune*	(m)	255,142
Fort Lauderdale (FL) *Sun-Sentinel*	(m)	255,050
Columbus (OH) *Dispatch*	(m)	253,549
Pittsburgh (PA) *Post-Gazette*	(m)	240,992
Detroit (MI) *News*	(e)	237,917
Charlotte (NC) *Observer*	(m)	236,050
Louisville (KY) *Courier-Journal*	(m)	232,539
Indianapolis (IN) *Star*	(m)	230,095
Omaha (NE) *World-Herald*	(all day)	227,721
Seattle (WA) *Times*	(e)	226,287
Los Angeles (CA)		
Investor's Business Daily	(m)	222,972
Fort Worth (TX) *Star-Telegram*	(m)	221,860

Top 50 Sunday Newspapers in the U.S. According to Circulation
(Sept. 30,1996)

New York (NY) *Times*	1,652,800
Los Angeles (CA) *Times*	1,349,889
Washington (DC) *Post*	1,122,276
Chicago (IL) *Tribune*	1,046,777
New York (NY) *Daily News*	888,759
Philadelphia (PA) *Inquirer*	876,669
Detroit (MI) *Free Press and News*	789,666
Dallas (TX) *Morning News*	785,934
Boston (MA) *Sunday Globe*	763,135
Houston (TX) *Chronicle*	748,082
Atlanta (GA) *Journal and Constitution*	687,297
Minneapolis (MN) *Star Tribune*	678,001
Long Island (NY) *Newsday*	656,895
San Francisco (CA) *Examiner and Chronicle*	633,513
Newark (NJ) *Star-Ledger*	605,627
Phoenix (AZ) *Arizona Republic*	553,192
St. Louis (MO) *Post-Dispatch*	538,743
Cleveland (OH) *Plain Dealer*	518,196
Seattle (WA) *Post Intelligencer & Times*	502,395
Miami (FL) *Herald*	483,339
Baltimore (MD) *Sunday Sun*	476,001
Denver (CO) *Post*	461,837
Milwaukee (WI) *Journal Sentinel*	461,710
San Diego (CA) *Union-Tribune*	450,984
Chicago (IL) *Sun-Times*	442,905
St. Petersburg (FL) *Times*	436,669
Pittsburgh (PA) *Post-Gazette*	421,026
Kansas City (MO) *Star*	416,812
Orange County (CA) *Register*	415,553
Denver (CO) *Rocky Mountain News*	406,473
Indianapolis (IN) *Star*	403,956
Columbus (OH) *Dispatch*	391,919
Fairfax (VA) *Journal Newspapers*	386,000
Orlando (FL) *Sentinel*	385,098
San Antonio (TX) *Express-News*	374,425
Fort Lauderdale (FL) *Sun-Sentinel*	370,519
Buffalo (NY) *News*	355,900
Tampa (FL) *Tribune*	353,366
Cincinnati (OH) *Enquirer*	346,279
Sacramento (CA) *Bee*	346,261
San Jose (CA) *Mercury News*	344,356
Fort Worth (TX) *Star-Telegram*	337,525
Louisville (KY) *Courier-Journal*	319,112
New Orleans (LA) *Times-Picayune*	304,361
Hartford (CT) *Courant*	302,188
Charlotte (NC) *Observer*	301,412
Oklahoma City (OK) *Sunday Oklahoman*	300,941
New York (NY) *Post*	291,497
Omaha (NE) *World-Herald*	290,367
Des Moines (IA) *Register*	288,987

Source: Editor and Publisher Yearbook

Top 50 Daily Newspapers in the World, 1996 Circulation

Yomiuri Shimbun (Japan)	14,485,393	Xin Min Wan Bao (China)	1,625,789
Asahi Shimbun (Japan)	12,660,066	USA Today (United States)	1,591,629
Sichuan Ribao (China)	8,000,000	Sports Nippon (Japan)	1,560,204
Guangming Ribao (China)	6,000,000	Joong-Ang Daily News (South Korea)	1,550,000
Mainichi Shimbun (Japan)	5,865,571	Economic Daily (China)	1,500,000
O Diario (Portugal)	5,666,915	Kyung-Hyang Daily News (South Korea)	1,478,000
Bild (Germany)	5,567,100	Shizuoka Shimbun (Japan)	1,428,488
News of The World (England)	4,607,189	NRZ (Germany)	1,332,800
Chunichi Shimbun (Japan)	4,323,142	West Deutsche Allgemeine (Germany)	1,313,400
Nihon Keizai Shimbun (Japan)	4,176,095	United Daily News (Taiwan)	1,300,000
Sun (England)	4,057,668	China Times (Taiwan)	1,270,000
Renmin Ribao (China)	3,000,000	Daily Express (England)	1,257,880
Sankei Shimbun (Japan)	2,876,351	O Estado de Sao Paulo (Brazil)	1,230,160
Chosun Ilbo (South Korea)	2,505,700	Jang Daily (Pakistan)	1,200,000
Gongren Ribao (China)	2,500,000	Jang Lahore (Pakistan)	1,200,000
Daily Mirror (England)	2,484,238	Akhbar El Yom/Al Akhbar (Egypt)	1,159,339
Dong-A Ilbo (South Korea)	2,150,000	Hankook Ilbo (South Korea)	1,156,000
The People (England)	2,064,439	Nishi Nippon Shimbun (Japan)	1,128,345
Daily Mail (England)	2,049,100	Tokyo Shimbun (Japan)	1,128,345
Al Ahram (Egypt)	2,000,000	Hochi Shimbun (Japan)	1,079,500
Hokkaido Shimbun (Japan)	1,975,949	New York Times (United States)	1,071,120
Eleftherotypia (Greece)	1,858,316	Tokyo Sports (Japan)	1,055,600
Wall Street Journal (United States)	1,783,532	Yediot Ahranot (Israel)	1,050,000
Kerala Kaumudi (India)	1,720,000	Daily Telegraph (England)	1,040,316
Wen Hui Bao Daily (China)	1,700,000	Los Angeles Times (United States)	1,029,073

Source: Editor and Publisher Yearbook

Magazine Spread

Annual Combined Magazine Circulation

Year	No. of magazines	Single copy sales	Subscription sales	Total
1950	250	62,804,448	84,170,060	146,974,508
1960	271	61,669,550	127,503,181	189,172,731
1965	277	65,230,878	148,342,267	213,573,145
1970	302	70,231,003	174,504,070	244,735,073
1975	325	83,935,424	166,048,037	249,983,461
1980	407	90,895,454	189,846,505	280,741,959
1985	477	81,076,776	242,810,339	323,887,115
1990	561	73,667,773	292,444,099	366,111,872
1995	591	65,846,048	299,050,282	364,896,329
1996	605	65,984,883	299,532,710	365,517,593

Sources: Audit Bureau of Circulations and Magazine Publishers of America

Leading U.S. Magazines Ranked by Advertising Revenue in 1996

Rank	Publication	Advertising revenue 1996*	% change from 1995	1996 Ad pages	% change from 1995
1	People Weekly	$525,563,737	20.1	3,708.27	11.4
2	Sports Illustrated	522,173,037	19.8	2,870.06	9.2
3	Time	439,623,516	8.7	2,392.92	3.0
4	TV Guide	402,973,357	-1.0	3,038.87	-5.9
5	Newsweek	383,767,258	15.6	2,533.30	10.2
6	Better Homes & Gardens	335,490,904	22.2	1,809.93	9.4
7	PC Magazine	318,057,411	-3.9	6,089.80	-8.5
8	Business Week	298,813,422	11.7	3,885.10	1.8
9	U.S. News & World Report	227,545,016	2.3	2,083.59	-4.0
10	Forbes	222,447,221	8.1	4,548.18	0.1
11	Woman's Day	216,908,112	9.8	1,664.77	-2.4
12	Reader's Digest	201,592,101	8.0	1,071.14	-2.6
13	Fortune	198,875,040	10.8	3,336.59	4.8
14	Good Housekeeping	184,812,233	-22.6	1,165.76	-24.9
15	Family Circle	175,362,534	6.9	1,341.52	-2.6
16	Ladies' Home Journal	159,527,008	0.7	1,452.60	-0.1
17	Cosmopolitan	158,327,519	-2.1	1,687.05	-8.8
18	Vogue	132,902,947	14.1	2,545.91	3.9
19	Entertainment Weekly	124,188,639	38.6	1,847.92	18.8
20	Money	117,198,522	11.3	1,303.13	3.7
21	Glamour	116,758,193	12.6	1,669.15	2.8
22	Southern Living	112,871,496	12.4	1,523.92	2.3
23	Rolling Stone	107,481,835	8.9	1,825.12	-2.4
24	McCall's	102,974,274	-1.1	1,000.70	-0.6
25	Golf Digest	101,217,645	7.4	1,252.56	-4.1
26	Redbook	99,848,782	-11.3	1,130.93	-14.6
27	PC Computing	98,724,792	-2.5	2,665.15	-11.0
28	Car and Driver	97,993,131	15.4	1,382.50	1.6
29	Parents	89,738,473	20.5	1,391.42	10.5
30	New Yorker	84,555,820	6.9	2,038.62	-4.4
31	Vanity Fair	84,480,713	19.2	1,516.11	7.4
32	Elle	84,084,587	18.9	1,841.04	10.2
33	Inc.	77,722,705	7.3	1,379.69	-0.8
34	Country Living	75,456,883	-12.4	1,089.87	-18.4
35	Bride's	75,341,247	5.6	3,082.18	4.5
36	Harper's Bazaar	71,130,313	8.5	1,499.38	-2.4
37	Golf Magazine	71,014,863	8.7	1,131.54	-3.4
38	Windows Magazine	70,683,440	5.3	2,788.25	-18.1
39	Travel & Leisure	66,048,993	22.7	1,279.16	10.4
40	Martha Stewart Living	65,577,525	87.1	855.43	42.9
41	W	63,332,181	42.8	1,586.41	14.0
42	Modern Bride	63,212,902	6.3	2,723.84	-0.4
43	Gentlemen's Quarterly	61,608,643	22.4	1,558.70	11.9
44	Seventeen	61,512,081	19.2	1,218.40	7.5
45	Road & Track	61,331,008	7.0	1,314.30	-1.3
46	Parenting	61,058,221	24.5	1,171.68	1.4
47	National Geographic	60,671,984	16.0	374.70	7.0
48	Modern Maturity	59,460,589	-8.1	239.27	-7.4
49	Self	58,220,275	9.1	1,155.90	0.2
50	Mademoiselle	56,828,554	22.3	1,223.15	11.8

*Based on the published ad rates provided by each magazine.
Sources: Publishers Information Bureau

50 Leading Magazines By Average Total Paid Circulation Per Issue For Second Six Months of 1996

Rank	Publication name	Avg. total circ. for July-Dec. 1996	Avg. total circ. for July-Dec. 1995	Percent change
1	NRTA/AARP Bulletin	20,567,352	21,100,610	-2.53 %
2	Modern Maturity	20,528,786	21,064,030	-2.54
3	Reader's Digest	15,072,260	15,103,830	-0.21
4	TV Guide	13,013,938	13,175,549	-1.23
5	National Geographic	9,025,003	8,987,830	+0.41
6	Better Homes and Gardens	7,605,325	7,603,207	+0.03
7	Family Circle	5,239,074	5,007,542	+4.62
8	Good Housekeeping	4,951,240	5,372,786	-7.85
9	Ladies' Home Journal	4,544,416	5,045,644	-9.93
10	Woman's Day	4,317,604	4,707,330	-8.28
11	McCall's	4,290,216	4,520,186	-5.09
12	Time	4,102,168	4,083,105	+0.47
13	People Weekly	3,449,852	3,321,198	+3.87
14	Prevention	3,311,244	3,252,115	+1.82
15	Playboy	3,236,517	3,277,783	-1.26
16	Newsweek	3,194,769	3,150,872	+1.39
17	Sports Illustrated	3,173,639	3,157,303	+0.52
18	Redbook	2,926,702	3,173,313	-7.77
19	The American Legion Magazine	2,777,351	2,852,332	-2.63
20	Home & Away	2,719,931	2,204,014	+23.41
21	Avenues	2,549,695	2,776,787	-8.18
22	Southern Living	2,490,542	2,471,170	+0.78
23	Cosmopolitan	2,486,393	2,569,186	-3.22
24	National Enquirer	2,480,349	2,613,647	-5.10
25	Seventeen	2,442,090	2,172,923	+12.39
26	Motorland	2,376,974	2,334,938	+1.80
27	U.S. News & World Report	2,260,857	2,220,327	+1.83
28	Star	2,220,711	2,375,575	-6.52
29	NEA Today	2,168,447	2,156,098	+0.57
30	YM	2,153,815	2,165,079	-0.52
31	Glamour	2,115,488	2,125,495	-0.47
32	Smithsonian	2,095,819	2,151,172	-2.57
33	Martha Stewart Living	2,025,182	1,449,744	+39.69
34	Money	1,993,119	1,922,737	+3.66
35	V.F.W. Magazine	1,980,947	2,013,258	-1.60
36	Ebony	1,803,566	1,879,221	-4.03
37	Popular Science	1,793,192	1,805,525	-0.68
38	Field & Stream	1,750,180	1,995,725	-12.30
39	Parents	1,737,249	1,848,008	-5.99
40	Country Living	1,674,925	1,837,429	-8.84
41	Life	1,601,069	1,556,189	+2.88
42	American Rifleman	1,545,242	1,666,397	-7.27
43	Golf Digest	1,515,829	1,501,525	+0.95
44	Woman's World	1,504,067	1,363,240	+10.33
45	Soap Opera Digest	1,468,333	1,381,080	+6.32
46	Sunset	1,431,549	1,451,846	-1.40
47	Popular Mechanics	1,428,356	1,586,137	-9.95
48	Cooking Light	1,379,055	1,213,158	+13.67
49	Men's Health	1,373,817	1,314,802	+4.49
50	Outdoor Life	1,353,061	1,359,602	-0.48
	Total for top 50 magazines	**195,247,305**	**197,438,599**	**-1.11**

Source: Audit Bureau of Circulations and Magazine Publishers of America

Getting a Reading on Book Sales

The number of books sold is increasing very slowly, but price increases keep dollar sales rising about 5% a year.

Book Publishers' Net Dollar Sales and Net Unit Sales*

*Includes trade, mass market, professional, educational, and university press publishers.
Source: Book Industry Study Group

What People Are Reading

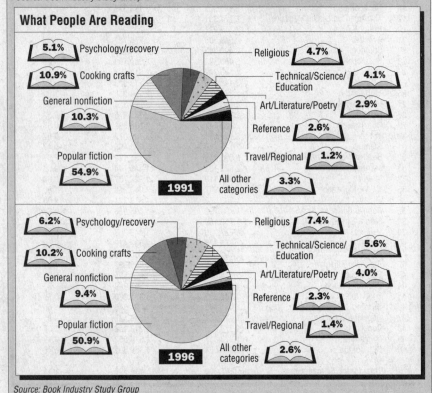

1991

- 5.1% Psychology/recovery
- 10.9% Cooking crafts
- General nonfiction 10.3%
- Popular fiction 54.9%
- Religious 4.7%
- Technical/Science/Education 4.1%
- Art/Literature/Poetry 2.9%
- Reference 2.6%
- Travel/Regional 1.2%
- All other categories 3.3%

1996

- 6.2% Psychology/recovery
- 10.2% Cooking crafts
- General nonfiction 9.4%
- Popular fiction 50.9%
- Religious 7.4%
- Technical/Science/Education 5.6%
- Art/Literature/Poetry 4.0%
- Reference 2.3%
- Travel/Regional 1.4%
- All other categories 2.6%

Source: Book Industry Study Group

Where Book Buyers Shop

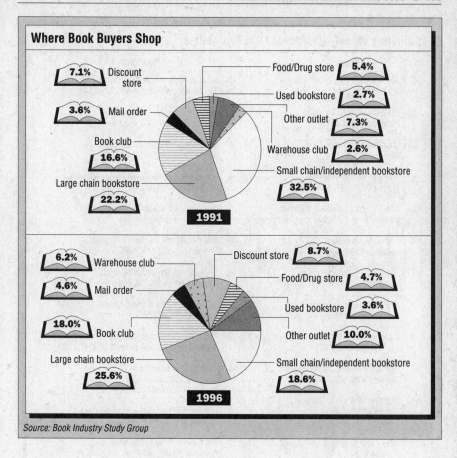

1991

- Discount store **7.1%**
- Mail order **3.6%**
- Book club **16.6%**
- Large chain bookstore **22.2%**
- Food/Drug store **5.4%**
- Used bookstore **2.7%**
- Other outlet **7.3%**
- Warehouse club **2.6%**
- Small chain/independent bookstore **32.5%**

1996

- Warehouse club **6.2%**
- Mail order **4.6%**
- Book club **18.0%**
- Large chain bookstore **25.6%**
- Discount store **8.7%**
- Food/Drug store **4.7%**
- Used bookstore **3.6%**
- Other outlet **10.0%**
- Small chain/independent bookstore **18.6%**

Source: Book Industry Study Group

Publishers Weekly Hardcover 1996 Bestsellers

Fiction	Nonfiction
1 *The Runaway Jury.* John Grisham. Doubleday (5/96) **2,775,000	1 *Make the Connection.* Oprah Winfrey & Bob Greene. Hyperion (9/96) 2,302,697
2 *Executive Orders.* Tom Clancy. Putnam (8/96) 2,371,602	2 *Men Are from Mars...* John Gray. HarperCollins (4/93) 1,485,089
3 *Desperation.* Stephen King Viking (9/96) 1,542,077	3 *The Dilbert Principle.* Scott Adams. HarperBusiness (3/96) 1,319,507
4 *Airframe.* Michael Crichton. Knopf (12/96) 1,487,494	4 *Simple Abundance.* Sarah Ban Breathnach. Warner (11/95) 1,087,149
5 *The Regulators.* Richard Bachman Dutton (9/96) 1,200,000	5 *The Zone.* Barry Sears with Bill Lawren. ReganBooks (5/95) 930,311
6 *Malice.* Danielle Steel. Delacorte (5/96) **1,150,000	6 *Bad As I Wanna Be.* Dennis Rodman. Delacorte. (6/96) **800,000
7 *Silent Honor.* Danielle Steel. Delacorte (12/96)**1,150,000	7 *In Contempt.* Christopher Darden. ReganBooks (3/96) 752,648
8 *Primary Colors.* Anonymous. Random House (2/96) 972,385	8 *A Reporter's Life.* Walter Cronkite. Knopf (12/96) 673,591
9 *Cause of Death.* Patricia Cornwell. Putnam (7/96) 920,403	9 *Dogbert's Top Secret Management Handbook.* Scott Adams. HarperBusiness (9/96) 652,085
10 *The Tenth Insight.* James Redfield. Warner (4/96) 892,687	10 *My Sergei: A Love Story.* Ekaterina Gordeeva with E.M. Swift. Warner (11/95) 563,567
11 *The Deep End of the Ocean.* Jacquelyn Mitchard. Viking (4/96) 840,263	11 *Gift and Mystery.* Pope John Paul II. Doubleday (12/96) **500,000
12 *How Stella Got Her Groove Back.* Terry McMillan. Viking (4/96) 782,699	12 *I'm Not Really Here.* Tim Allen. Hyperion (11/96) 508,015
13 *Moonlight Becomes You.* Mary Higgins Clark. Simon & Schuster (10/96) **750,000	13 *Rush Limbaugh is a Big Fat Idiot and Other Observations.* Al Franken. Delacorte. (2/96) **500,000
14 *My Gal Sunday.* Mary Higgins Clark. Simon & Schuster (10/96) **750,000	14 *James Herriot's Favorite Dog Stories.* James Herriot. St. Martin's (9/96) **500,000
15 *The Celestine Prophecy.* James Redfield. Warner (3/94) *718,000	15 *My Story.* The Duchess of York. Simon & Schuster (11/96) **450,000

Note: Rankings are determined by sales figures provided by publishers; the numbers generally reflect reports of copies "shipped and billed" in calendar year 1996 and publishers were instructed to adjust sales figures to include returns through Feb., 24, 1997. Publishers did not at that time know what their total returns would be—indeed, the majority of returns occur later in the year. So none of these figures should be regarded as final net sales. (Dates in parentheses indicate month and year of publication.)
*Sales figures reflect only books sold in calendar year 1996.
**Sales figures were submitted to *PW* in confidence, for use in placing titles on the lists. Numbers shown are rounded down to the nearest 25,000 to indicate relationship to sales figures of other titles.
Source: Publishers Weekly

Trade Paperbacks

1 *A 3rd Serving of Chicken Soup for the Soul.* Jack Canfield and Mark Victor Hansen. Orig. Health Communications (1,602,439)

2 *Snow Falling on Cedars.* David Guterson. Rep. Vintage (1,490,590)

3 *It's a Magical World: A Calvin and Hobbes Collection.* Bill Waterson. Orig. Andrews & McMeel (1,250,000)

4 *There's Treasure Everywhere: A Calvin & Hobbes Collection.* Bill Watterson. Orig. Andrews & McMeel (1,100,000)

5 *Chicken Soup for the Woman's Soul.* Jack Canfield, Mark Victor Hansen, Jennifer Read Hawthorne and Marci Shimoff. Orig. Health Communications (1,069,402)

6 *A Journal of Daily Renewal: The Companion to Make the Connection.* Bob Greene and Oprah Winfrey. Orig. Hyperion (1,034,160)

7 *Windows '95 for Dummies.* Andy Rathbone. Orig. IDG (1,000,000)

8 *Fugitive from the Cubicle Police: A Dilbert Book.* Scott Adams. Orig. Andrews & McMeel (663,123)

9 *The Last Chapter and Worse: A Far Side Collection.* Gary Larson. Orig. Andrews & McMeel (605,000)

10 *The English Patient (movie tie-in).* Michael Ondaatje. Rep. Vintage (575,630)

11 *Reviving Ophelia.* Mary Pipher. Rep. Ballantine (556,347)

12 *Microsoft Windows '95 Resource Kit.* Microsoft. Rep. Microsoft (468,337)

13 *Still Pumped from Using the Mouse: A Dilbert Book.* Scott Adams. Orig. Andrews & McMeel (451,023)

14 *SSN: A Strategy Guide to Submarine Warfare.* Tom Clancy. Orig. Berkley (450,000)

15 *Dr. Atkin's New Diet Revolution.* Robert Atkins, M.D. Rep. M. Evans (427,148)

Mass Market Paperbacks

1 *The Rainmaker.* John Grisham. Rep. Dell (5,110,613)

2 *The Green Mile, Part 1: The Two Dead Girls.* Stephen King. Orig. Signet (3,865,447)

3 *The Green Mile, Part 2: The Mouse on the Mile.* Stephen King. Orig. Signet (3,655,547)

4 *The Green Mile, Part 3: Coffey's Hands.* Stephen King. Orig. Signet (3,515,141)

5 *The Green Mile, Part 5: Night Journey.* Stephen King. Orig. Signet (3,480,382)

6 *The Green Mile, Part 4: The Bad Death of Eduard Delacroix.* Stephen King. Orig. Signet (3,475,145)

7 *The Green Mile, Part 6: Coffey on the Mile.* Stephen King. Orig. Signet (3,475,036)

8 *The Gift.* Danielle Steel. Rep. Dell (3,093,781)

9 *Lightning.* Danielle Steel. Rep. Dell (3,092,532)

10 *The Lost World.* Michael Crichton. Rep. Ballantine (2,738,561)

11 *Let Me Call You Sweetheart.* Mary Higgins Clark. Rep. Pocket

12 *The Horse Whisperer.* Nicholas Evans. Rep. Dell (2,384,141)

13 *Rose Madder.* Stephen King. Rep. Signet (2,330,508)

14 *Tom Clancy's Op-Center (III): Games of State.* Tom Clancy and Steve Pieczenik. Orig. Berkley (2,300,000)

15 *From Potter's Field.* Patricia Cornwell. Rep. Berkley (2,200,000)

Source: Publishers Weekly

Children's Hardcover Frontlist

1 *Falling Up*. Shel Silverstein. Harper-Collins

2 *The Hunchback of Notre Dame (Classic)*. Disney/Mouse Works (1,204,600)

3 *Disney's Hunchback of Notre Dame*. Adapted by Justine Korman, illus. by Don Williams. Golden (603,600)

4 *My Many Colored Days*. Dr. Seuss, illus. by Steve Johnson and Lou Fancher (496,833)

5 *Disney's Hunchback of Notre Dame: Quasimodo the Hero*. Barbara Bazaldua, illus. by Don Williams. Golden (485,100)

6 *Disney's 101 Dalmatians: Snow Puppies* Barbara Bazaldua, illus. by Don Williams. Golden (455,555)

7 *Disney's Winnie the Pooh: The Sweetest Christmas*. Ann Braybrooks, illus. by Josie Yee. Golden (441,200)

8 *Guess How Much I Love You (board book)*. Sam Mc Bratney, illus. by Anita Jeram. Candlewick (434,018)

9 *The Hunchback of Notre Dame (Little Library)*. Disney/Mouse Works (315,200)

10 *Djall's Jolly Day (Squeeze Me)*. Disney/Mouse Works (305,100)

11 *Forever Free (Sturdy Tab Book)*. Disney/Mouse Works (296,600)

12 *Muppets Treasure Island*. Ellen Weiss, illus. by Tom Brannon. Golden (287,400)

13 *Sesame Street: Elmo's Twelve Days of Christmas*. Sarah Albee, illus. by Maggie Swanson. Golden (253,600)

14 *The Rainbow Fish (board book)*. Marcus Pfister. North-South. (250.781)

15 *Dr. Seuss's ABC (board book)*. Random House (241,412)

Children's Hardcover Backlist

1 *Oh, the Places You'll Go!* Dr. Seuss. Random House, 1990 (395,594)

2 *Guess How Much I Love You*. Sam McBratney, illus. by Anita Jeram. Candlewick, 1995 (384,016)

3 *Barney's Farm Animals*. Kimberly Kearns and Marie O'Brien, illus. by Karen Malzeke-McDonald. Lyrick/Barney, 1993 (383,603)

4 *Green Eggs and Ham*. Dr. Seuss. Random House, 1966 (373,484)

5 *Disney's Winnie the Pooh: Grand and Wonderful Day*. Mary Packard, illus. by Darrell Baker. Golden, 1995 (371,100)

6 *Disney's 101 Dalmations*. Adapted by Justine Korman, illus. by Bill Langley and Ron Dias. Golden. 1988 (365,300)

7 *Goodnight Moon (board book)*. Margaret Wise Brown, .illus. by Clement Hurd HarperFestival, 1991

8 *The Giving Tree*. Shel Silverstein. HarperCollins, 1964

9 *The Very Hungry Caterpillar (board book)*. Eric Carle. Philomel, 1994 (335,811)

10 *Baby Animals on the Farm*. James Shooter, illus. by J. Ellen Dolee. Golden, 1990 (335,700)

11 *A Day with Barney*. Mary Ann Dudko and Margie Larsen, illus. by Larry Daste. Lyrick/Barney, 1994 (317,197)

12 *Winnie the Pooh (Classic)*. Disney/Mouse Works, 1994 (306,300)

13 *Disney's Winnie the Pooh: Eeyore, Be Happy*. Don Ferguson. Golden, 1991 (300,800)

14 *Disney's Pocahontas: Into the Forest*. Mary Packard, illus. by Darrell Baker. Golden, 1995 (297,100)

15 *Disney's Baby Mickey's Book of Shapes*. Golden, 1986 (292,600)

Source: Publishers Weekly

GAMBLING BACKLASH

Gambling has been on a roll in America for the last decade, but its hot streak is finally cooling.

Although people are betting more than ever and the gambling industry's take continues to increase, the growth rate slowed markedly in 1996. Gambling industry gross revenues rose just 5.6%, less than half the growth rate in 1995. At the same time, attempts to legalize casinos in such states as Ohio, Washington, and New York have failed, as have moves to start lotteries in Oklahoma and Arkansas. And gambling in cyberspace is under attack in Congress.

What's more, psychologists are becoming more concerned about the number of compulsive gamblers in the United States, and a federal commission is conducting a two-year study to assess gambling's impact, the first such review since 1976.

"There's been a backlash against gambling— no doubt," says Charles Anderer, editorial director of International Gaming & Wagering Business, a trade publication. "But gambling has become our culture, and I don't think it's going away."

Indeed, gambling is still a booming industry, providing entertainment to millions of people and enriching both companies and state governments: In 1996, Americans wagered $586.5 billion, up from $125 billion in 1982. From that pool of money, casino-hotel operators, state lotteries, Indian reservations and other gambling concerns reaped a ponderous stack of chips—$47.6 billion in total revenue. About 40% came from casinos on land and on riverboats, 34% from lotteries, 11% from Indian gambling facilities, 8% from parimutuel venues, and 7% from such activities as bookmaking and bingo.

"Gambling's expansion has been rapid, occurring in a very short time," says Shannon Bybee, executive director of the International Gaming Institute, which is affiliated with the University of Nevada, Las Vegas. True enough. In 1963, New Hampshire introduced the first U.S. lottery; today 37 states run lotteries. In 1988, there were legalized casinos in only Nevada and New Jersey; today 26 states operate several hundred casinos that attract 125 million visitors a year.

This fast growth has stirred opposition, pri-marily among religious groups and mental-health experts. With the zeal of a politician out on the hustings, the Rev. Thomas Grey of Hanover, Ill., has led many of the insurgents. The founder of the National Coalition Against Legalized Gambling rails against the evils of crime and compulsive gambling and accuses the casino developers of "cannibalizing" small businesses with their lavish hotels and restaurants. But he insists he isn't a prohibitionist and that his crusade is merely about "whether gambling belongs on Main Street or on the other side of the tracks."

"Five years ago I stood up in a little town expecting I'd get beat," declares Rev. Grey. "Now I'm dangerous." Since 1994, he says, gambling referendums have been defeated on 32 ballots and approved on only three. And in Louisiana, voters even outlawed an existing form of gambling—video poker. This, according to Mark Edwards, Jr., of State Capital Strategies, an organization that monitors state legislation, marked the first actual rolling back of gambling during the current wave.

For its part, the gambling industry points to the economic benefits it provides through job creation. Frank Fahrenkopf, president of the American Gaming Association, says he hopes the federal commission will finally "put to rest" the perception that legalizing gambling is tantamount to creating a new source of crime. Mr. Fahrenkopf also is quick to assert that his industry's recent lobbying setbacks are in no way connected to the National Coalition Against Legalized Gambling. Rather, he attributes the defeats to a stronger economy that makes people less inclined to approve gambling to generate new tax revenues and provide new jobs.

One problem that can't be easily dismissed is compulsive gambling. While there's disagreement over how widespread such addiction is, gambling's increased availability is widely believed to cause more people to get hooked. Rachel Volberg, president of Gemini Research, a company in Roaring Springs, Pa., that assesses compulsive gambling in the U.S. and Canada, conducted 17 state studies of "problem and pathological gambling" and found that its incidence in New York state jumped from 4.2% of adults in 1986 to 7.3% in 1996, and in Iowa, from 1.7% in 1989 to 5.4% in 1995. According to Ms. Volberg, the rise in Iowa is "very clearly associated with the introduction of riverboat gambling and the availability of slots at race tracks."

The American Gaming Association recently established the National Center for Responsible Gaming, whose board includes both industry officials and compulsive-gambling experts. The group will funnel $1 million dollars annually into research grants. Yet, critics such as Valerie Lorenz, executive director of the Compulsive Gambling Center in Baltimore, have dismissed the center as a smoke screen. She asks: "Why would they want to do away with their best customer?" Mr. Fahrenkopf responds that her charge is "an insult to the interests who care about abuses in gaming."

Joshua Harris Prager

Gambling Fever

Americans are gambling more of their money than ever, as revenue-hungry states have legalized more types of wagering and Indians have opened more casinos. But the industry's revenue growth rate slowed in 1996 from the heated pace of the early 1990s.

Gross Gambling Revenues (Dollars in millions)

	1982 gross revenues	1995 gross revenues	1996 gross revenues	1982-96 increase/ decrease in gross revenues (Dollars)	1982-96 increase/ decrease in gross revenues (Percent)	Average annual rate 1982-1996 (Percent)
Horses	$2,250.0	$3,079.5	$3,151.3	$901.3	40.1%	2.4%
Greyhounds	430.0	593.2	504.7	74.7	17.4	1.2
Jai Alai	112.0	66.4	54.0	-58.0	-51.8	-5.1
Lotteries	2,170.0	15,343.0	16,219.8	14,049.8	647.5	15.5
Casinos	4,200.0	18,014.4	19,140.9	14,940.9	355.7	11.4
Legal Bookmaking	25.8	101.6	86.5	60.8	235.9	9.0
Card Rooms	50.0	668.9	679.3	629.3	1,258.6	20.5
Charitable Bingo	780.0	980.8	952.2	172.2	22.1	1.4
Charitable Games	396.0	1,460.8	1,475.3	1,079.3	272.5	9.8
Indian Reservations	–	4,774.1	5,358.8	5,358.8	–	–
Grand Total	**$10,413.8**	**$45,082.7**	**$47,622.7**	**37,209.0**	**357.3**	**11.5**

Sources: International Gaming & Wagering Business and Christiansen/Cummings Associates

More Players Sharing the Pot

With increased competition from riverboat and Indian casinos, both Las Vegas and Atlantic City are experiencing a slowdown in the growth of gambling revenues. The gambling win rose less than 2% in 1996 in both casino meccas.

Atlantic City	Casino gambling revenues	Number of visitors	Las Vegas and the rest of Clark County	Casino gambling revenues	Number of Las Vegas visitors
1990	$ 2,951,580,214	31,812,733	1990	$ 4,104,001,000	20,954,420
1991	2,991,561,232	30,788,400	1991	4,152,407,000	21,315,116
1992	3,215,968,867	30,705,332	1992	4,381,710,000	21,886,865
1993	3,301,365,943	30,224,968	1993	4,727,424,000	23,522,593
1994	3,422,615,117	31,321,500	1994	5,430,651,000	28,214,362
1995	3,726,581,413	33,271,808	1995	5,717,567,000	29,002,122
1996	3,789,350,761	34,041,548	1996	5,783,735,000	29,636,631

Sources: New Jersey Casino Control Commission and South Jersey Transportation Authority; Las Vegas Convention and Visitor's Authority

Casinos in Cyberspace

As any gambler will tell you, there are no sure things. Gambling on the Internet is no exception.

A few dozen small on-line betting parlors have set up shop in the past year. These sites—many of which try to re-create the feel of a real casino with digital slot machine and roulette, blackjack, and poker games—hope to become playgrounds for risk-hungry couch potatoes. But the would-be gambling moguls will have to clear myriad obstacles before they can cash in.

First among them is the issue of trust: Sending hundreds or thousands of dollars to set up a gambling account with a company you have never heard of requires a huge leap of faith. The prospect of a federal ban of on-line gambling also looms. And even if they can sidestep that, the entrepreneurs could get squashed if the business someday draws such deep-pocketed players as the major casino operators.

The key to success, experts say, is regulation. That is, the industry needs it. "Consumers won't gamble unless they have assurances that the game is fair," says Sebastian Sinclair, an analyst for Christiansen/Cummings Associates Inc., a management-consulting firm in New York. "One scandal could potentially destroy this entire industry."

But thus far, some federal authorities seem intent on banning, rather than regulating, on-line gambling. Legislation introduced in the Senate in March 1997 seeks to ban all gambling over the Internet by extending a law from the 1930s that prohibits sports gambling over telegraph wires or phone lines. Along with pushing the ban into a new medium, the legislation also expands the pool of people held responsible for breaking the law. Existing law makes it illegal only to operate a gambling venture; this legislation targets the gamblers themselves with a maximum fine of $5,000 and up to one year in jail.

Sen. Jon Kyl, an Arizona Republican who wrote the bill, says that making it illegal for people to place bets is a natural extension of the law and is only fair. Vincent Sollitto, a spokesman for Sen. Kyl, says, "We thought it would be inconsistent if we only prosecute the providers and not the gamblers." Even if this legislation were to become law, enforcing it could be all but impossible. Most Internet gambling sites are run by offshore companies; foreign governments that have legalized gam-

bling aren't likely to take kindly to intervention attempts from the U.S.

Tracking down illegal operations based in the U.S. could be tricky because programmers can disguise a site's true origins. And going so far as to track down gamblers in their homes could prove to be prohibitively expensive and impractical—not to mention an invasion of privacy. "It conjures up visions of [law officials] knocking down front doors because people are sitting in their underwear placing bets from their living rooms," says Frank Fahrenkopf, head of the American Gaming Association, a trade association. (Still, the American Gaming Association—reflecting the views of the legal gaming establishment—supports the overall goal of banning Internet gambling.)

The Justice Department says it hasn't taken a stand on the Kyl bill, but admits that "transnational enforcement issues" would make a ban on Internet gambling difficult to impose. "We're waiting to see what happens with the legislation," says a Justice spokesman.

The fate of the Kyl bill is far from certain; similar legislation introduced in the Senate in 1996 was never acted upon. In light of the U.S. efforts, most on-line operators prefer not to risk setting up shop in this country. Instead, many are heading for Antigua, where gambling is entirely legal. Another plus: Antigua is one of only two Caribbean islands with an undersea fiber-optic link directly to the United States, ensuring a strong Internet link even in a hurricane. "Every hour someone calls us looking for a license," says Gyneth McAllister, the Antigua official in charge of gaming.

Getting a handle on the size of Web-based gambling is pretty much impossible because the sites don't report their figures to regulatory authorities, as U.S. casinos do. The biggest site, Intertops, run by Intertops GmbH of Austria, claims to have signed up 40,000 on-line accounts in just six months, boosted by a telephone-betting business that has operated since 1982.

For now, the entrepreneurs have the on-line gambling market to themselves. Most of the larger casinos have declined to start gambling Web sites of their own. The big casinos would be risking their existing U.S. licenses if they were involved in unregulated gaming, analysts say.

Rebecca Quick

Awards

Nobel Laureates

Alfred Nobel, a nineteenth-century Swedish industrialist and the inventor of dynamite, created the Nobel Prizes to recognize and reward outstanding achievements in physics, chemistry, physiology or medicine, literature, and the peace process. His will stipulated that the bulk of his estate, more than 31 million Swedish kronor, should be invested, with the income awarded to "those who during the preceding year shall have conferred the greatest benefit on mankind." The prize in economics was established in 1968 by the Bank of Sweden.

Physics

1901	Röntgen, Wilhelm Conrad (Germany)	1932‡	Heisenberg, Werner (Germany)
1902*	Lorentz, Hendrik Antoon (The Netherlands)	1933*	Schrödinger, Erwin (Austria)
	Zeeman, Pieter (The Netherlands)		Dirac, Paul Adrien Maurice (Great Britain)
1903**	Becquerel, Antoine Henri (France)	1934†	–
	Curie, Pierre (France) and	1935	Chadwick, Sir James (Great Britain)
	Curie, Marie, (France)*	1936**	Hess, Victor Franz (Austria)
1904	Rayleigh, Lord (John William Strutt) (Great Britain)		Anderson, Carl David (USA)
1905	Lenard, Philipp Eduard Anton (Germany)	1937*	Davisson, Clinton Joseph (USA)
1906	Thomson, Sir Joseph John (Great Britain)		Thomson, Sir George Paget (Great Britain)
1907	Michelson, Albert Abraham (USA)	1938	Fermi, Enrico (Italy)
1908	Lippmann, Gabriel (France)	1939	Lawrence, Ernest Orlando (USA)
1909*	Marconi, Guglielmo (Italy)	1940–42†	–
	Braun, Carl Ferdinand (Germany)	1943‡	Stern, Otto (USA)
1910	Van Der Waals, Johannes Diderik (The Netherlands)	1944	Rabi, Isidor Isaac (USA)
1911	Wien, Wilhelm (Germany)	1945	Pauli, Wolfgang (Austria)
1912	Dalén, Nils Gustaf (Sweden)	1946	Bridgman, Percy Williams (USA)
1913	Kamerlingh-Onnes, Heike (The Netherlands)	1947	Appleton, Sir Edward Victor (Great Britain)
1914	Von Laue, Max (Germany)	1948	Blackett, Lord Patrick Maynard Stuart (Great Britain)
1915*	Bragg, Sir William Henry (Great Britain)		
	Bragg, Sir William Lawrence (Great Britain)	1949	Yukawa, Hideki (Japan)
1916†	–	1950	Powell, Cecil Frank (Great Britain)
1917‡	Barkla, Charles Glover (Great Britain)	1951*	Cockcroft, Sir John Douglas (Great Britain)
1918‡	Planck, Max Karl Ernst Ludwig (Germany)		Walton, Ernest Thomas Sinton (Ireland)
1919	Stark, Johannes (Germany)		
1920	Guillaume, Charles Edouard (Switzerland)	1952*	Bloch, Felix (USA)
1921‡	Einstein, Albert (Germany and Switzerland)		Purcell, Edward Mills (USA)
1922	Bohr, Niels (Denmark)	1953	Zernike, Frits (Frederik) (The Netherlands)
1923	Millikan, Robert Andrews (USA)		
1924‡	Siegbahn, Karl Manne Georg (Sweden)	1954**	Born, Max (Great Britain)
1925‡*	Franck, James (Germany)		Bothe, Walther (Germany)
	Hertz, Gustav (Germany)	1955**	Lamb, Willis Eugene (USA)
1926	Perrin, Jean Baptiste (France)		Kusch, Polykarp (USA)
1927**	Compton, Arthur Holly (USA)	1956*	Shockley, William (USA)
	Wilson, Charles Thomson Rees (Great Britain)		Bardeen, John (USA)
1928‡			Brattain, Walter Houser (USA)
	Richardson, Sir Owen Willans (Great Britain)	1957*	Yang, Chen Ning (China)
1929			Lee, Tsung-Dao (China)
1930	De Broglie, Prince Louis-Victor (France)	1958*	Cherenkov, Pavel Alekseyevich (USSR)
	Raman, Sir Chandrasekhara Venkata (India)		Frank, Il'ja Mikhailovich (USSR)
1931†	–		Tamm, Igor Yevgenyevich (USSR)

Physics

1959*	Segré, Emilio Gino (USA)
	Chamberlain, Owen (USA)
1960	Glaser, Donald A. (USA)
1961**	Hofstadter, Robert (USA)
	Mössbauer, Rudolf Ludwig (Germany)
1962	Landau, Lev Davidovich (USSR)
1963**	Wigner, Eugene P. (USA)
	Goeppert-Mayer, Maria (USA) and
	Jensen, J. Hans D. (Germany)*
1964**	Townes, Charles H. (USA)
	Basov, Nicolay Gennadiyevich
	(USSR) and
	Prokhorov, Aleksandr Mikhailovich
	(USSR)*
1965*	Tomonaga, Sin-Itiro (Japan)
	Schwinger, Julian (USA)
	Feynman, Richard P. (USA)
1966	Kastler, Alfred (France)
1967	Bethe, Hans Albrecht (USA)
1968	Alvarez, Luis W. (USA)
1969	Gell-Mann, Murray (USA)
1970**	Alfvén, Hannes (Sweden)
	Néel, Louis (France)
1971	Gabor, Dennis (Great Britain)
1972*	Bardeen, John (USA)
	Cooper, Leon N. (USA)
	Schrieffer, J. Robert (USA)
1973**	Esaki, Leo (Japan) and
	Giaever, Ivar (USA)
	Josephson, Brian D. (Great Britain)
1974*	Ryle, Sir Martin (Great Britain)
	Hewish, Antony (Great Britain)
1975*	Bohr, Aage (Denmark)
	Mottelson, Ben (Denmark)
	Rainwater, James (USA)
1976**	Richter, Burton (USA)
	Ting, Samuel C. C. (USA)
1977**	Anderson, Philip W. (USA)
	Mott, Sir Nevill F. (Great Britain)
	Van Vleck, John H. (USA)
1978**	Kapitsa, Pyotr Leonidovich (USSR)
	Penzias, Arno A. (USA) and
	Wilson, Robert W. (USA)
1979**	Glashow, Sheldon L. (USA)
	Salam, Abdus (Pakistan)
	Weinberg, Steven (USA)
1980**	Cronin, James, W. (USA)
	Fitch, Val L. (USA)
1981**	Bloembergen, Nicolaas (USA) and
	Schawlow, Arthur L. (USA)
	Siegbahn, Kai M. (Sweden)
1982	Wilson, Kenneth G. (USA)
1983**	Chandrasekhar, Subramanyan (USA)
	Fowler, William A. (USA)
1984*	Rubbia, Carlo (Italy)
	Van Der Meer, Simon (The Netherlands)
1985	Von Klitzing, Klaus
	(Federal Republic of Germany)
1986**	Ruska, Ernst
	(Federal Republic of Germany)

	Binnig, Gerd and
	(Federal Republic of Germany)
	Rohrer, Heinrich (Switzerland)*
1987*	Bednorz, J. Georg
	(Federal Republic of Germany)
	Müller, K. Alexander (Switzerland)
1988*	Lederman, Leon M. (USA)
	Schwartz, Melvin (USA)
	Steinberger, Jack (USA)
1989**	Ramsey, Norman F. (USA)
	Dehmelt, Hans G. (USA) and
	Paul, Wolfgang
	(Federal Republic of Germany)
1990*	Friedman, Jerome I. (USA)
	Kendall, Henry W. (USA)
	Taylor, Richard E. (Canada)
1991	de Gennes, Pierre-Gilles (France)
1992	Charpak, Georges (France)
1993*	Hulse, Russell A. (USA)
	Taylor Jr., Joseph H. (USA)
1994**	Brockhouse, Bertram N. (Canada)
	Shull, Clifford G. (USA)
1995**	Perl, Martin L. (USA)
	Reines, Frederick (USA)
1996*	Lee, David M. (USA),
	Osheroff, Douglas D. (USA), and
	Richardson, Robert C. (USA)

Chemistry

1901	Van't Hoff, Jacobus Henricus
	(The Netherlands)
1902	Fischer, Hermann Emil (Germany)
1903	Arrhenius, Svante August (Sweden)
1904	Ramsay, Sir William (Great Britain)
1905	Von Baeyer, Johann Friedrich
	Wilhelm Adolf (Germany)
1906	Moissan, Henri (France)
1907	Buchner, Eduard (Germany)
1908	Rutherford, Lord Ernest (Great Britain)
1909	Ostwald, Wilhelm (Germany)
1910	Wallach, Otto (Germany)
1911	Curie, Marie (France)
1912**	Grignard, Victor (France)
	Sabatier, Paul (France)
1913	Werner, Alfred (Switzerland)
1914‡	Richards, Theodore William (USA)
1915	Willstätter, Richard Martin (Germany)
1916†	–
1917†	–
1918‡	Haber, Fritz (Germany)
1919†	–
1920‡	Nernst, Walther Hermann (Germany)
1921‡	Soddy, Frederick (Great Britain)
1922	Aston, Francis William (Great Britain)
1923	Pregl, Fritz (Austria)
1924†	–
1925‡	Zsigmondy, Richard Adolf (Germany)
1926	Svedberg, The (Theodor) (Sweden)
1927‡	Wieland, Heinrich Otto (Germany)

Chemistry

1928	Windaus, Adolf Otto Reinhold (Germany)		Norrish, Ronald George Wreyford (Great Britain) and
1929**	Harden, Sir Arthur (Great Britain)		Porter, Lord (George) (Great Britain)
	Von Euler-Chelpin, Hans Karl August Simon (Sweden)	1968	Onsager, Lars (USA)
		1969**	Barton, Sir Derek H. R. (Great Britain)
1930	Fischer, Hans (Germany)		Hassel, Odd (Norway)
1931*	Bösch, Carl (Germany)	1970	Leloir, Luis F. (Argentina)
	Bergius, Friedrich (Germany)	1971	Herzberg, Gerhard (Canada)
1932	Langmuir, Irving (USA)	1972**	Anfinsen, Christian B. (USA)
1933†	–		Moore, Stanford (USA)
1934	Urey, Harold Clayton (USA)		Stein, William (USA)
1935*	Joliot, Frédéric (France)	1973**	Fischer, Ernst Otto (Federal Republic of Germany)
	Joliot-Curie, Irene (France)		Wilkinson, Sir Geoffrey (Great Britain)
1936	Debye, Petrus (Peter) Josephus Wilhelmus (The Netherlands)	1974	Flory, Paul J. (USA)
1937**	Haworth, Sir Walter Norman (Great Britain)	1975**	Cornforth, Sir John Warcup (Australia and Great Britain)
	Karrer, Paul (Switzerland)		Prelog, Vladimir (Switzerland)
1938‡	Kuhn, Richard (Germany)	1976	Lipscomb, William N. (USA)
1939**	Butenandt, Adolf Friedrich Johann (Germany)	1977	Prigogine, Ilya (Belgium)
		1978	Mitchell, Peter D. (Great Britain)
	Ruzicka Leopold (Switzerland)	1979**	Brown, Herbert C. (USA)
1940–42†	–		Wittig, Georg (Federal Republic of Germany)
1943‡	De Hevesy, George (Hungary)		
1944‡	Hahn, Otto (Germany)	1980**	Berg, Paul (USA)
1945	Virtanen, Artturi Ilmari (Finland)		Gilbert, Walter (USA) and
1946**	Sumner, James Batcheller (USA)		Sanger, Frederick (Great Britain)
	Northrop, John Howard (USA) and	1981*	Fukui, Kenichi (Japan)
	Stanley, Wendell Meredith (USA)		Hoffmann, Roald (USA)
1947	Robinson, Sir Robert (Great Britain)	1982	Klug, Sir Aaron (Great Britain)
1948	Tiselius, Arne Wilhelm Kaurin (Sweden)	1983	Taube, Henry (USA)
1949	Giauque, William Francis (USA)	1984	Merrifield, Robert Bruce (USA)
1950*	Diels, Otto, Paul Hermann (Germany)	1985*	Hauptman, Herbert A. (USA)
	Alder, Kurt (Germany)		Karle, Jerome (USA)
1951*	McMillan, Edwin Mattison (USA)	1986*	Herschbach, Dudley R. (USA)
	Seaborg, Glenn Theodore (USA)		Lee, Yuan T. (USA)
1952*	Martin, Archer John Porter (Great Britain)		Polanyi, John C. (Canada)
	Synge, Richard Laurence Millington (Great Britain)	1987*	Cram, Donald J. (USA)
			Lehn, Jean-Marie (France)
1953	Staudinger, Hermann (Germany)		Pedersen, Charles J. (USA)
1954	Pauling, Linus Carl (USA)	1988*	Deisenhofer, Johann (Federal Republic of Germany)
1955	Du Vigneaud, Vincent (USA)		Huber, Robert (Federal Republic of Germany)
1956*	Hinshelwood, Sir Cyril Norman (Great Britain)		Michel, Hartmut (Federal Republic of Germany)
	Semenov, Nikolay Nikolaevich (USSR)	1989*	Altman, Sidney (USA)
1957	Todd, Lord Alexander R. (Great Britain)		Cech, Thomas R. (USA)
1958	Sanger, Frederick (Great Britain)	1990	Corey, Elias James (USA)
1959	Heyrovsky, Jaroslav (Czechoslovakia)	1991	Ernst, Richard R. (Switzerland)
1960	Libby, Willard Frank (USA)	1992	Marcus, Rudolph A. (USA)
1961	Calvin, Melvin (USA)	1993**	Mullis, Kary B. (USA)
1962**	Perutz, Max Ferdinand (Great Britain)		Smith, Michael (Canada)
	Kendrew, Sir John Cowdery (Great Britain)	1994	Olah, George A. (USA)
		1995*	Rowland, F. Sherwood (USA)
1963**	Ziegler, Karl (Germany)		Molina, Mario (USA)
	Natta, Giulio (Italy)		Crutzen, Paul (The Netherlands)
1964	Hodgkin, Dorothy Crowfoot (Great Britain)	1996*	Curl, Robert F., Jr. (USA)
1965	Wooward, Robert Burns (USA)		Kroto, Sir Harold W. (Great Britain)
1966	Mulliken, Robert S. (USA)		Smalley, Richard E. (USA)
1967**	Eigen, Manfred (Federal Republic of Germany)		

Physiology or Medicine

1901	Von Behring, Emil Adolf (Germany)
1902	Ross, Sir Ronald (Great Britain)
1903	Finsen, Niels Ryberg (Denmark)
1904	Pavlov, Ivan Petrovich (Russia)
1905	Koch, Robert (Germany)
1906*	Golgi, Camillo (Italy)
	Ramon y Cajal, Santiago (Spain)
1907	Laveran, Charles Louis Alphonse (France)
1908*	Mechnikov, Ilya Ilyich (Russia)
	Ehrlich, Paul (Germany)
1909	Kocher, Emil Theodor (Switzerland)
1910	Kossel, Albrecht (Germany)
1911	Gullstrand, Allvar (Sweden)
1912	Carrel, Alexis (France)
1913	Richet, Charles Robert (France)
1914	Bárány, Robert (Austria)
1915–1918†	–
1919‡	Bordet, Jules (Belgium)
1920	Krogh, Schack August Steenberger (Denmark)
1921†	–
1922‡**	Hill, Sir Archibald Vivian
	Meyerhof, Otto Fritz (Germany)
1923*	Banting, Sir Frederick Grant (Canada)
	Macleod, John James Richard (Canada)
1924	Einthoven, Willem (The Netherlands)
1925†	–
1926‡	Fibiger, Johannes Andreas Grib (Denmark)
1927	Wagner-Jauregg, Julius (Austria)
1928	Nicolle, Charles Jules Henri (France)
1929**	Eijkman, Christiaan (The Netherlands)
	Hopkins, Sir Frederick Gowland (Great Britain)
1930	Landsteiner, Karl (Austria)
1931	Warburg, Otto Heinrich (Germany)
1932*	Sherrington, Sir Charles Scott (Great Britain)
	Adrian, Lord (Edgar Douglas) (Great Britain)
1933	Morgan, Thomas Hunt (USA)
1934*	Whipple, George Hoyt (USA)
	Minot, George Richards (USA)
	Murphy, William Parry (USA)
1935	Spemann, Hans (Germany)
1936*	Dale, Sir Henry Hallett (Great Britain)
	Loewi, Otto (Austria)
1937	Szent-Györgyi Von Nagyrapolt, Albert (Hungary)
1938‡	Heymans, Corneille Jean François (Belgium)
1939	Domagk, Gerhard (Germany)
1940–1942†	–
1943‡**	Dam, Henrik Carl Peter (Denmark)
	Doisy, Edward Adelbert (USA)
1944*	Erlanger, Joseph (USA)
	Gasser, Herbert Spencer (USA)
1945*	Fleming, Sir Alexander (Great Britain)

	Chain, Sir Ernst Boris (Great Britain)
	Florey, Lord (Howard Walter) (Great Britain)
1946	Muller, Hermann Joseph (USA)
1947**	Cori, Carl Ferdinand (USA) and
	Cori, Gerty Theresa (USA)*
	Houssay, Bernardo Alberto (Argentina)
1948	Müller, Paul Hermann (Switzerland)
1949**	Hess, Walter Rudolf (Switzerland)
	Moniz, Antonio Caetano de Abreu Freire Egas (Portugal)
1950*	Kendall, Edward Calvin (USA)
	Reichstein, Tadeus (Switzerland)
	Hench, Philip Showalter (USA)
1951	Theiler, Max (Union of South Africa)
1952	Waksman, Selman Abraham (USA)
1953**	Krebs, Sir Hans Adolf (Great Britain)
	Lipmann, Fritz Albert (USA)
1954*	Enders, John Franklin (USA)
	Weller, Thomas Huckle (USA)
	Robbins, Frederick Chapman (USA)
1955	Theorell, Axel Hugo Theodor (Sweden)
1956*	Cournand, André Frédéric (USA)
	Forssmann, Werner (Germany)
	Richards, Dickinson W. (USA)
1957	Bovet, Daniel (Italy)
1958**	Beadle, George Wells (USA) and
	Tatum, Edward Lawrie (USA)
	Lederberg, Joshua (USA)
1959*	Ochoa, Severo (USA)
	Kornberg, Arthur (USA)
1960*	Burnet, Sir Frank MacFarlane (Australia)
	Medawar, Sir Peter Brian (Great Britain)
1961	Von Békésy, Georg (USA)
1962*	Crick, Francis Harry Compton (Great Britain)
	Watson, James Dewey (USA)
	Wilkins, Maurice Hugh Frederick (Great Britain)
1963*	Eccles, Sir John Carew (Australia)
	Hodgkin, Sir Alan Lloyd (Great Britain)
	Huxley, Sir Andrew Fielding (Great Britain)
1964*	Bloch, Konrad (USA)
	Lynen, Feodor (Germany)
1965*	Jacob, François (France)
	Lwoff, André (France)
	Monod, Jacques, (France)
1966**	Rous, Peyton (USA)
	Huggins, Charles Brenton (USA)
1967*	Granit, Ragnar (Sweden)
	Hartline, Haldan Keffer (USA)
	Wald, George (USA)
1968*	Holley, Robert W. (USA)
	Khorana, Har Gobind (USA)
	Nirenberg, Marshall W. (USA)
1969*	Delbrück, Max (USA)
	Hershey, Alfred D. (USA)

Physiology or Medicine

Luria, Salvador E. (USA)
1970* Katz, Sir Bernard (Great Britain)
Von Euler, Ulf (Sweden)
Axelrod, Julius (USA)
1971 Sutherland, Earl W. Jr. (USA)
1972* Edelman, Gerald M. (USA)
Porter, Rodney R. (Great Britain)
1973* Von Frisch, Karl (Federal Republic
of Germany)
Lorenz, Konrad (Austria)
Tinbergen, Nikolaas (Great Britain)
1974* Claude, Albert (Belgium)
De Duve, Christian (Belgium)
1975* Palade, George E. (USA)
Baltimore, David (USA)
Dulbecco, Renato (USA)
1976* Temin, Howard Martin (USA)
Blumberg, Baruch S. (USA)
1977** Gajdusek, D. Carleton (USA)
Guillemin, Roger (USA) and
Schally, Andrew V. (USA)
1978* Yalow, Rosalyn (USA)
Arber, Werner (Switzerland)
Nathans, Daniel (USA)
1979* Smith, Hamilton O. (USA)
Cormack, Alan M. (USA)
Hounsfield, Sir Godfrey N.
1980* (Great Britain)
Benacerraf, Baruj (USA)
Dausset, Jean (France)
1981** Snell, George D. (USA)
Sperry, Roger W. (USA)
Hubel, David H. (USA) and
1982* Wiesel, Torsten N. (Sweden)
Bergström, Sune K. (Sweden)
Samuelsson, Bengt I. (Sweden)
1983 Vane, Sir John R. (Great Britain)
1984* McClintock, Barbara (USA)
Jerne, Niels K. (Denmark)
Köhler, Georges J. F. (Federal Republic
of Germany)
Milstein, César (Great Britain and
1985* Argentina)
Brown, Michael S. (USA)
1986* Goldstein, Joseph L. (USA)
Cohen, Stanley (USA)
1987 Levi-Montalcini, Rita (Italy and USA)
1988* Tonegawa, Susumu (Japan)
Black, Sir James W. (Great Britain)
Elion, Gertrude B. (USA)
1989* Hitchings, George H. (USA)
Bishop, J. Michael (USA)
1990* Varmus, Harold E. (USA)
Murray, Joseph E. (USA)
1991* Thomas, E. Donnall (USA)
Neher, Erwin (Germany) and
1992* Sakmann, Bert (Germany)
Fischer, Edmond H. (USA) and
1993* Krebs, Edwin G. (USA)
Roberts, Richard J. (England)

Sharp, Phillip A. (USA)
1994* Gilman, Alfred G. (USA) and
Rodbell, Martin (USA)
1995* Wieschaus, Eric F. (USA)
Lewis, Edward B. (USA)
Nuesslein-Volhard, Christiane (Germany)
1996* Doherty, Peter C. (Australia)
Zinkernagel, Rolf M. (Switzerland)
Prudhomme, René François Armand)
(France)

Literature

1901 Sully, Prudhomme (pen-name of
1902 Mommsen, Christian Matthias Theodor
(Germany)
Bjørnson, Bjørnstjerne Martinus
1903 (Norway)
1904** Mistral, Frédéric (France)
Echegaray y Eizaguirre, José (Spain)
1905 Sienkiewicz, Henryk (Poland)
1906 Carducci, Giosuè (Italy)
1907 Kipling, Rudyard (Great Britain)
1908 Eucken, Rudolf Christoph (Germany)
1909 Lagerlöf, Selma Ottilia Lovisa (Sweden)
1910 Heyse, Paul Johann Ludwig (Germany)
1911 Maeterlinck, Count, Maurice (Mooris)
Polidore Marie Bernhard (Belgium)
1912 Hauptmann, Gerhart Johann Robert
(Germany)
1913 Tagore, Rabindranath (India)
1914† –
1915‡ Rolland, Romain (France)
1916 Von Heidenstam, Carl Gustaf Verner
(Sweden)
1917** Gjellerup, Karl Adolph (Denmark)
Pontoppidan, Henrik (Denmark)
1918† –
1919‡ Spitteler, Carl Friedrich Georg
(Switzerland)
1920 Hamsun, Knut Pedersen (Norway)
1921 Anatole France (pen-name of Thibault,
Jacques Anatole) (France)
1922 Benavente, Jacinto (Spain)
1923 Yeats, William Butler (Ireland)
1924 Reymont, (pen-name of Reyment),
Wladyslaw Stanislaw (Poland)
1925‡ Shaw, George Bernard (Great Britain)
1926‡ Grazia Deledda (pen-name of
Madesani, Grazia) (Italy)
1927‡ Bergson, Henri (France)
1928 Undset, Sigrid (Norway)
1929 Mann, Thomas (Germany)
1930 Lewis, Sinclair (USA)
1931 Karlfeldt, Erik Axel (Sweden)
1932 Galsworthy, John (Great Britain)
1933 Bunin, Ivan Alekseyevich (stateless
domicile in France)
1934 Pirandello, Luigi (Italy)
1935† –
1936 O'Neill, Eugene Gladstone (USA)

Literature

1937	Martin du Gard, Roger (France)	1986	Soyinka, Wole (Nigeria)
1938	Pearl Buck (pen-name of Walsh,	1987	Brodsky, Joseph (USA)
	Pearl) (USA)	1988	Mahfouz, Naguib (Egypt)
1939	Sillanpää, Frans Eemil (Finland)	1989	Cela, Camilo José (Spain)
1940–43†	–	1990	Paz, Octavio (Mexico)
1944	Jensen, Johannes Vilhelm (Denmark)	1991	Gordimer, Nadine (South Africa)
1945	Gabriela Mistral (pen-name of Godoy y	1992	Walcott, Derek (Saint Lucia)
	Alcayaga, Lucila) (Chile)	1993	Morrison, Toni (USA)
1946	Hesse, Hermann (Switzerland)	1994	Oe, Kenzaburo (Japan)
1947	Gide, André Paul Guillaume (France)	1995	Seamus, Heaney (Ireland)
1948	Eliot, Thomas Stearns (Great Britain)	1996	Szymborska, Wislawa (Poland)
1949‡	Faulkner, William (USA)		
1950	Russell, Earl (Bertrand Arthur William)		

Peace

	(Great Britain)	1901**	Dunant, Jean Henri (Switzerland)
1951	Lagerkvist, Pär Fabian (Sweden)		Passy, Frédéric (France)
1952	Mauriac, François (France)	1902**	Ducommun, Élie (Switzerland)
1953	Churchill, Sir Winston Leonard		Gobat, Charles Albert (Switzerland)
	Spencer (Great Britain)	1903	Cremer, Sir William Randal
1954	Hemingway, Ernest Miller (USA)		(Great Britain)
1955	Laxness, Halldór Kiljan (Iceland)	1904	Institut de Droit International (Institute of
1956	Jiménez, Juan Ramón (Spain)		International Law) (Ghent)
1957	Camus, Albert (France)	1905	Von Suttner, Baroness Bertha Sophie
1958	Pasternak, Boris Leonidovich (USSR)		Felicita (Austria)
1959	Quasimodo, Salvatore (Italy)	1906	Roosevelt, Theodore (USA)
1960	Saint-John Perse (pen-name of Léger,	1907**	Moneta, Ernesto Teodoro (Italy)
	Alexis) (France)		Renault, Louis (France)
1961	Andríc, Ivo (Yugoslavia)	1908**	Arnoldson, Klas Pontus (Sweden)
1962	Steinbeck, John (USA)		Bajer, Fredrik (Denmark)
1963	Seferis, Giorgos (pen-name of	1909**	Beernaert, Auguste Marie François
	Seferiadis, Giorgos) (Greece)		(Belgium)
1964	Sartre, Jean-Paul (France)		D'Estournelles de Constant, Paul Henri
	(declined the prize)		Benjamin Balluet, Baron de Constant
1965	Sholokhov, Michail Aleksandrovich		de Rebecque (France)
	(USSR)	1910	Bureau International Permanent de la Paix
1966**	Agnon, Shmuel Yosef (Israel)		(Permanent International Peace Bureau)
	Sachs, Nelly (Sweden)		(Berne)
1967	Asturias, Miguel Angel (Guatemala)	1911**	Asser, Tobias Michael Carel
1968	Kawabata, Yasunari (Japan)		(The Netherlands)
1969	Beckett, Samuel (Ireland)		Fried, Alfred Hermann (Austria)
1970	Solzhenitsyn, Aleksandr Isaevich	1912	Root, Elihu (USA)
	(USSR)	1913	La Fontaine, Henri (Belgium)
1971	Neruda, Pablo (Chile)	1914–16†	–
1972	Böll, Heinrich (Federal Republic	1917	Comité International de la Croix Rouge
	of Germany)		(International Committee of the Red
1973	White, Patrick (Australia)		Cross) (Geneva)
1974**	Johnson, Eyvind (Sweden)	1918†	–
	Martinson, Harry (Sweden)	1919‡	Wilson, Thomas Woodrow (USA)
1975	Montale, Eugenio (Italy)	1920	Bourgeois, Léon Victor Auguste
1976	Bellow, Saul (USA)		(France)
1977	Aleixandre, Vicente (Spain)	1921**	Branting, Karl Hjalmar (Sweden)
1978	Singer, Isaac Bashevis (USA)		Lange, Christian Lous (Norway)
1979	Elytis Odysseus (pen-name of	1922	Nansen, Fridtjof (Norway)
	Alepoudhelis, Odysseus) (Greece)	1923†	–
1980	Milosz, Czeslaw, (USA and Poland)	1924†	–
1981	Canetti, Elias (Great Britain)	1925‡*	Chamberlain, Sir Austen (Great Britain)
1982	García Márquez, Gabriel		Dawes, Charles Gates (USA)
	(Colombia)	1926*	Briand, Aristide (France)
1983	Golding, Sir William (Great Britain)		Stresemann, Gustav (Germany)
1984	Seifert, Jaroslav (Czechoslovakia)	1927**	Buisson, Ferdinand (France)
1985	Simon, Claude (France)		Quidde, Ludwig (Germany)

Peace

1928[+]	–
1929[‡]	Kellogg, Frank Billings (USA)
1930	Söderblom, Lars Olof Nathan (Jonathan) (Sweden)
1931**	Addams, Jane (USA)
	Butler, Nicholas Murray (USA)
1932[†]	–
1933[‡]	Angell (Ralph Lane), Sir Norman (Great Britain)
1934	Henderson, Arthur (Great Britain)
1935[‡]	Von Ossietzky, Carl (Germany)
1936	Saavedra Lamas, Carlos (Argentina)
1937	Cecil of Chelwood, Viscount, (Lord Edgar Algernon Robert Gascoyne Cecil) (Great Britain)
1938	Office International Nansen pour les Réfugiés (Nansen International Office for Refugees) (Geneva)
1939–43[†]	–
1944[‡]	Comité International de la Croix-Rouge (International Committee of the Red Cross) (Geneva)
1945[‡]	Hull, Cordell (USA)
1946**	Balch, Emily Greene (USA)
	Mott, John Raleigh (USA)
1947*	The Friends Service Council (The Quakers) (London)
	The American Friends Service Committee (The Quakers) (Washington)
1948[†]	–
1949	Boyd Orr of Brechin, Lord (John) (Great Britain)
1950	Bunche, Ralph (USA)
1951	Jouhaux, Léon (France)
1952[‡]	Schweitzer, Albert (France)
1953	Marshall, George Catlett (USA)
1954[‡]	Office of the United Nations High Commissioner for Refugees (Geneva)
1955[†]	–
1956[†]	–
1957	Pearson, Lester Bowles (Canada)
1958	Pire, Georges (Belgium)
1959	Noel-Baker, Philip J. (Great Britain)
1960*	Lutuli, Albert John (South Africa)
1961	Hammarskjöld, Dag Hjalmar Agne Carl (Sweden)
1962[‡]	Pauling, Linus Carl (USA)
1963**	Comité International de la Croix-Rouge (International Committee of the Red Cross) (Geneva)
	Ligue des Sociétés de la Croix-Rouge (League of Red Cross Societies) (Geneva)
1964	King Jr., Martin Luther (USA)
1965	United Nations Children's Fund (UNICEF) (New York)
1966[†]	–
1967[†]	–
1968	Cassin, René (France)
1969	International Labour Organization (I.L.O.) (Geneva)

1970	Borlaug, Norman (USA)
1971	Brandt, Willy (Federal Republic of Germany)
1972[†]	–
1973*	Kissinger, Henry, A. (USA)
	Le Duc Tho (Democratic Republic of Viet Nam (declined the prize)
1974**	Mac Bride, Seán (Ireland)
	Sato, Eisaku (Japan)
1975	Sakharov, Andrei Dmitrievich (USSR)
1976[‡]	Williams, Betty (Northern Ireland)
1977	Corrigan, Mairead (Northern Ireland)
	Amnesty International (Great Britain)
1978**	El Sadat, Mohamed Anwar (Egypt)
	Begin, Menachem (Israel)
1979	Mother Teresa (India)
1980	Perez Esquivel, Adolfo (Argentina)
1981	Office of the United Nations High Commissioner for Refugees (Geneva)
1982*	Myrdal, Alva (Sweden)
	García Robles, Alfonso (Mexico)
1983	Walesa, Lech (Poland)
1984	Tutu, Desmond Mpilo (South Africa)
1985	International Physicians for the Prevention of Nuclear War, Inc. (USA)
1986	Wiesel, Elie (USA)
1987	Arias Sanchez, Oscar (Costa Rica)
1988	The United Nations Peace-Keeping Forces, New York, USA)
1989	The 14th Dalai Lama (Tenzin Gyatso) (Tibet)
1990	Gorbachev, Mikhail Sergeyevich (USSR)
1991	Aung San Suu Kyi (Burma)
1992	Menchu Tum, Rigoberta (Guatemala)
1993*	Mandela, Nelson (South Africa)
	de Klerk, Fredrik Willem (South Africa)
1994*	Arafat, Yasser (Palestine)
	Peres, Shimon (Israel)
	Rabin, Yitzhak (Israel)
1995	Rotblat, Joseph (Great Britain)
	Pugwash Conferences on Science and World Affairs (Canada)
1996**	Belo, Carlos Filipe Ximenes (East Timor)
	Ramos Horta, José (East Timor)

Economic Sciences

1969*	Frisch, Ragnar (Norway)
	Tinbergen, Jan (The Netherlands)
1970	Samuelson, Paul A. (USA)
1971	Kuznets, Simon (USA)
1972*	Hicks, Sir John R. (Great Britain)
	Arrow, Kenneth J. (USA)
1973	Leontief, Wassily (USA)
1974**	Myrdal, Gunnar (Sweden)
	Von Hayek, Friedrich August (Great Britain)
1975*	Kantorovich, Leonid Vitaliyevich (USSR)
	Koopmans, Tjalling C. (USA)

Economic Sciences

1976	Friedman, Milton (USA)		1988	Allais, Maurice (France)
1977**	Ohlin, Bertil (Sweden) and		1989	Haavelmo, Trygve (Norway)
	Meade, James E. (Great Britain)		1990**	Markowitz, Harry M. (USA)
1978	Simon, Herbert A. (USA)			Miller, Merton M. (USA)
1979**	Shultz, Theodore W. (USA)			Sharpe, William F. (USA)
	Lewis, Sir Arthur (United Kingdom)		1991	Coase, Ronald H. (Great Britain)
1980	Klein, Lawrence R. (USA)		1992	Becker, Gary S. (USA)
1981	Tobin, James (USA)		1993*	Fogel, Robert W. (USA)
1982	Stigler, George J. (USA)			North, Douglass C. (USA)
1983	Debreu, Gerard (USA)		1994*	Harsanyi, John C. (USA)
1984	Stone, Sir Richard (Great Britain)			Nash, John F. (USA)
1985	Modigliani, Franco (USA)			Selten, Reinhard (Germany)
1986	Buchanan, Jr., James M. (USA)		1995	Lucas, Robert E. (USA)
1987	Solow, Robert M. (USA)		1996*	Mirrlees, James A. (Great Britain)
				Vickrey, William (USA)

*Awarded jointly.
**Award divided.
†Award reserved.
‡Award reserved and awarded the following year.
 Source: Nobel Foundation

Pulitzer Prize Awards, 1997

Prizes in Journalism

Meritorious Public Service
The Times-Picayune, New Orleans, LA, for its comprehensive series analyzing the conditions that threaten the world's supply of fish.

Spot News Reporting
The staff of Newsday, Long Island, NY, for its enterprising coverage of the crash of TWA Flight 800 and its aftermath.

Investigative Reporting
Eric Nalder, Deborah Nelson and Alex Tizon of The Seattle Times for their investigation of widespread corruption and inequities in the federally sponsored housing program for Native Americans, which inspired much-needed reforms.

Explanatory Journalism
Michael Vitez, reporter, and April Saul and Ron Cortes, photographers, of The Philadelphia Inquirer for a series on the choices that confronted critically ill patients who sought to die with dignity.

Beat Reporting
Byron Acohido of The Seattle Times for his coverage of the aerospace industry, notably an exhaustive investigation of rudder control problems on the Boeing 737, which contributed to new FAA requirements for major improvements.

National Reporting
The Wall Street Journal staff for its coverage of the struggle against AIDS in all of its aspects, the human, the scientific and the business, in light of promising treatments for the disease.

International Reporting
John F. Burns of The New York Times for his courageous and insightful coverage of the harrowing regime imposed on Afghanistan by the Taliban.

Feature Writing
Lisa Pollak of The Baltimore Sun for her compelling portrait of a baseball umpire who endured the death of a son while knowing that another son suffers from the same deadly genetic disease.

Commentary
Eileen McNamara of The Boston Globe for her many-sided columns on Massachusetts people and issues.

Criticism
Tim Page of The Washington Post for his lucid and illuminating music criticism.

Editorial Writing
Michael Gartner of The Daily Tribune, Ames, Iowa, for his common sense editorials about issues deeply affecting the lives of people in his community.

Editorial Cartooning
Walt Handelsman of The Times-Picayune, New Orleans, LA

Spot News Photography
Annie Wells of The Press Democrat, Santa Rosa, CA, for her dramatic photograph of a local firefighter rescuing a teenager from raging floodwaters.

Feature Photography
Alexander Zemlianichenko of the Associated Press for his photograph of Russian President Boris Yeltsin dancing at a rock concert during his campaign for re-election.

Letters and Drama Prizes

Fiction

Martin Dressler: The Tale of an American Dreamer, Steven Millhauser.

Drama

No Award

History

Original Meanings: Politics and Ideas in the Making of the Constitution, Jack N. Rakove.

Biography

Angela's Ashes: A Memoir, Frank McCourt.

Poetry

Alive Together: New and Selected Poems, Lisel Mueller.

General Non-Fiction

Ashes to Ashes: America's Hundred-Year Cigarette War, the Public Health, and the Unabashed Triumph of Philip Morris, Richard Kluger.

Prize in Music

Blood on the Fields by Wynton Marsalis, premiered on January 28, 1997, at Woolsey Hall, Yale University, New Haven, Conn.

Pulitzer Prizes, 1917–1996

Journalism

Meritorious Public Service

1917	–
1918	*The New York Times*
1919	*Milwaukee Journal*
1920	–
1921	*Boston Post*
1922	*New York World*
1923	*Memphis Commercial Appeal*
1924	*New York World*
1925	–
1926	*Columbus* (GA) *Enquirer Sun*
1927	*Canton* (OH) *Daily News*
1928	*Indianapolis Times*
1929	*New York Evening World*
1930	–
1931	*Atlanta Constitution*
1932	*Indianapolis News*
1933	*New York World-Telegram*
1934	*Medford* (OR) *Mail Tribune*
1935	*The Sacramento* (CA) *Bee*
1936	*The Cedar Rapids* (IA) *Gazette*
1937	*St. Louis Post-Dispatch*
1938	*The Bismarck* (ND) *Tribune*
1939	*The Miami Daily News*
1940	*Waterbury* (CT) *Republican & American*
1941	*St. Louis Post-Dispatch*
1942	*Los Angeles Times*
1943	*Omaha* (NE) *World-Herald*
1944	*The New York Times*
1945	*The Detroit Free Press*
1946	*Scranton Times*
1947	*Baltimore Sun*
1948	*St. Louis Post-Dispatch*
1949	*Nebraska State Journal*
1950	*Chicago Daily News* and *St. Louis Post-Dispatch*
1951	*The Miami Herald* and *Brooklyn Eagle*
1952	*St. Louis Post-Dispatch*
1953	*Whiteville* (NC) *News Reporter* and *Tabor City* (NC) *Tribune*
1954	*Newsday* (Garden City, NY)
1955	*Columbus* (GA) *Ledger* and *Sunday Ledger-Enquirer*
1956	*Watsonville* (CA) *Register-Pajaronian*
1957	*Chicago Daily News*
1958	*Arkansas Gazette*
1959	*Utica* (NY) *Observer-Dispatch* and *The Utica Daily Press*
1960	*Los Angeles Times*
1961	*Amarillo* (TX) *Globe-Times*
1962	*Panama City* (FL) *News-Herald*
1963	*Chicago Daily News*
1964	*St. Petersburg* (FL) *Times*
1965	*Hutchinson* (KS) *News*
1966	*The Boston Globe*
1967	*The Louisville Courier-Journal* *The Milwaukee Journal*
1968	*The Riverside* (CA) *Press-Enterprise*
1969	*Los Angeles Times*
1970	*Newsday* (Garden City, NY)
1971	*The Winston-Salem* (NC) *Journal and Sentinel*
1972	*The New York Times*
1973	*The Washington Post*
1974	*Newsday* (Garden City, NY)
1975	*The Boston Globe*
1976	*Anchorage Daily News*
1977	*The Lufkin* (TX) *News*
1978	*The Philadelphia Inquirer*
1979	*Point Reyes* (CA) *Light*
1980	*Gannett News Service*
1981	*Charlotte* (NC) *Observer*
1982	*The Detroit News*
1983	*The Jackson* (MS) *Clarion-Ledger*
1984	*Los Angeles Times*
1985	*The Fort Worth* (TX) *Star-Telegram*
1986	*The Denver Post*
1987	*The Pittsburgh Press*
1988	*The Charlotte Observer*
1989	*Anchorage Daily News*
1990	*The Philadelphia Inquirer* *The Washington* (NC) *Daily News*
1991	*The Des Moines Register*
1992	*The Sacramento* (CA) *Bee*
1993	*The Miami Herald*
1994	*Akron Beacon Journal*
1995	*The Virgin Islands Daily News* (St. Thomas)
1996	*The News & Observer* (Raleigh, NC)

Reporting

1917 Herbert Bayard Swope, *New York World*
1918 Harold A. Littledale, *New York Evening Post*
1919 –
1920 John J. Leary, Jr., *New York World*
1921 Louis Seibold, *New York World*
1922 Kirke L. Simpson, Associated Press
1923 Alva Johnston, *The New York Times*
1924 Magner White, *San Diego Sun*
1925 James W. Mulroy and Alvin H. Goldstein, *Chicago Daily News*
1926 William Burke Miller, *Louisville Courier-Journal*
1927 John T. Rogers, *St. Louis Post-Dispatch*
1928 –
1929 Paul Y. Anderson, *St. Louis Post-Dispatch*
1930 Russell D. Owen, *The New York Times*
1931 A. B. MacDonald, *Kansas City* (MO) *Star*
1932 W. C. Richards, D. D. Martin, J. S. Pooler, F. D. Webb, and J. N. W. Sloan, *Detroit Free Press*
1933 Francis A. Jamieson, Associated Press
1934 Royce Brier, *San Francisco Chronicle*
1935 William H. Taylor, *New York Herald Tribune*
1936 Lauren D. Lyman, *The New York Times*
1937 John J. O'Neill, *New York Herald Tribune*; William L. Laurence, *The New York Times*; Howard W. Blakeslee, AP; Gobind Behari Lal, Universal Service; and David Dietz, Scripps-Howard
1938 Raymond Sprigle, *Pittsburgh Post-Gazette*
1939 Thomas Lunsford Stokes, Scripps-Howard Newspaper Alliance
1940 S. Burton Heath, *New York World-Telegram*
1941 Westbrook Pegler, *New York World-Telegram*
1942 Stanton Delaplane, *San Francisco Chronicle*
1943 George Weller, *Chicago Daily News*
1944 Paul Schoenstein and associates, *New York Journal-American*
1945 Jack S. McDowell, *San Francisco Call-Bulletin*
1946 William Leonard Laurence, *The New York Times*
1947 Frederick Woltman, *New York World-Telegram*

Local Reporting

1948 George E. Goodwin, *Atlanta Journal*
1949 Malcolm Johnson, *New York Sun*
1950 Meyer Berger, *The New York Times*
1951 Edward S. Montgomery, *San Francisco Examiner*
1952 George De Carvalho, *San Francisco Chronicle*

Local Reporting, Edition Time

1953 *Providence* (RI) *Journal* and *Evening Bulletin*
1954 *Vicksburg* (MS) *Sunday Post-Herald*
1955 Mrs. Caro Brown, *Alice* (TX) *Daily Echo*
1956 Lee Hills, *Detroit Free Press*
1957 *Salt Lake* (UT) *Tribune*
1958 *Fargo* (ND) *Forum*
1959 Miss Mary Lou Werner, *The Evening Star* (Washington, DC)
1960 Jack Nelson, *Atlanta Constitution*
1961 Sanche De Gramont, *New York Herald Tribune*
1962 Robert D. Mullins, *Deseret News,* (Salt Lake City)

1963 Sylvan Fox, Anthony Shannon, and William Longgood, *New York World-Telegram and Sun*

Local General Spot News Reporting

1964 Norman C. Miller, Jr., *The Wall Street Journal*
1965 Melvin H. Ruder, *The Hungry Horse News* (Columbia Falls, MT)
1966 *Los Angeles Times* staff
1967 Robert V. Cox, *Chambersburg* (PA) *Public Opinion*
1968 *The Detroit Free Press*
1969 John Fetterman, *Louisville Times* and *Courier-Journal*
1970 Thomas Fitzpatrick, *Chicago Sun-Times*
1971 The staff of the *Akron* (OH) *Beacon Journal*
1972 Richard Cooper and John Machacek, *Rochester* (NY) *Times-Union*
1973 *Chicago Tribune*
1974 Arthur M. Petacque and Hugh F. Hough, *Chicago Sun-Times*
1975 The staff of the *Xenia* (OH) *Daily Gazette*
1976 Gene Miller, *The Miami Herald*
1977 Margo Huston, *The Milwaukee Journal*
1978 Richard Whitt, *The Louisville Courier-Journal*
1979 *The San Diego* (CA) *Evening Tribune*
1980 The staff of *The Philadelphia Inquirer*
1981 *The Longview* (WA) *Daily News* staff
1982 *The Kansas City Star* and *The Kansas City Times*
1983 *The Fort Wayne* (IN) *News-Sentinel* editorial staff
1984 *Newsday* (Long Island, NY) team of reporters

General News Reporting

1985 Thomas Turcol, *The Virginian-Pilot and Ledger-Star* (Norfolk, VA)
1986 Edna Buchanan, *The Miami Herald*
1987 *Akron Beacon Journal* staff
1988 The staff of *The Alabama Journal* (Montgomery, AL) *Lawrence* (MA) *Eagle-Tribune* staff
1989 *The Louisville Courier-Journal* staff
1990 *San Jose* (CA) *Mercury News* staff

Spot News Reporting

1991 *The Miami Herald* staff
1992 *New York Newsday* staff
1993 *Los Angeles Times* staff
1994 *The New York Times* staff
1995 *Los Angeles Times* staff
1996 Robert D. McFadden, *The New York Times*

Local Reporting, No Edition Time

1953 Edward J. Mowery, *New York World-Telegram & Sun*
1954 Alvin Scott McCoy, *Kansas City* (MO) *Star*
1955 Roland Kenneth Towery, *Cuero* (TX) *Record*

1956 Arthur Daley, *The New York Times*
1957 Wallace Turner and William Lambert, *Portland Oregonian*
1958 George Beveridge, *The Evening Star*, (Washington, DC)
1959 John Harold Brislin, *Scranton* (PA) *Tribune* and *The Scrantonian*
1960 Miriam Ottenberg, *The Evening Star* (Washington, DC)
1961 Edgar May, *Buffalo* (NY) *Evening News*
1962 George Bliss, *Chicago Tribune*
1963 Oscar Griffin, Jr., *Pecos* (TX) *Independent and Enterprise*

Local Investigative Specialized Reporting

1964 James V. Magee, Albert V. Gaudiosi, and Frederick A. Meyer, *Philadelphia Bulletin*
1965 Gene Goltz, *The Houston Post*
1966 John Anthony Frasca, *Tampa* (FL) *Tribune*
1967 Gene Miller, *The Miami Herald*
1968 J. Anthony Lukas, *The New York Times*
1969 Albert L. Delugach and Denny Walsh, *St. Louis Globe-Democrat*
1970 Harold Eugene Martin, *Montgomery Advertiser* and *Alabama Journal*
1971 William Jones, *Chicago Tribune*
1972 Timothy Leland, Gerard M. O'Neill, Stephen A. Kurkjian, and Ann Desantis, *The Boston Globe*
1973 Sun Newspapers of Omaha
1974 William Sherman, *New York Daily News*
1975 *Indianapolis Star*
1976 Chicago Tribune staff members
1977 Acel Moore and Wendell Rawls Jr., *The Philadephia Inquirer*
1978 Anthony R. Dolan, *Stamford* (CT) *Advocate*
1979 Gilbert M. Gaul and Elliot G. Jaspin, *Pottsville* (PA) *Republican*
1980 Stephen A. Kurkjian, Alexander B. Hawes Jr., Nils Bruzelius, Joan Vennochi, and Robert M. Porterfield, *The Boston Globe Spotlight* team
1981 Clark Hallas and Robert B. Lowe, *Arizona Daily Star*
1982 Paul Henderson, *The Seattle Times*
1983 Loretta Tofani, *The Washington Post*
1984 Kenneth Cooper, Joan Fitz Gerald, Jonathan Kaufman, Norman Lockman, Gary McMillan, Kirk Scharfenberg, and David Wessel, *The Boston Globe*

Investigative Reporting

1985 William K. Marimow, *The Philadelphia Inquirer*;
Lucy Morgan and Jack Reed, *St. Petersburg* (FL) *Times*
1986 Jeffrey A. Marx and Michael M. York, *Lexington* (KY) *Herald-Leader*
1987 Daniel R. Biddle, H. G. Bissinger, and Frederic N. Tulsky, *The Philadelphia Inquirer* John Woestendiek, *The Philadelphia Inquirer*
1988 Dean Baquet, William Gaines, and Ann Marie Lipinski, *Chicago Tribune*
1989 Bill Dedman, *Atlanta Journal and Constitution*
1990 Lou Kilzer and Chris Ison, *Star Tribune* (Minneapolis-St. Paul, MN)
1991 Joseph T. Hallinan and Susan M. Headden, *The Indianapolis Star*
1992 Lorraine Adams and Dan Malone, *The Dallas Morning News*
1993 Jeff Brazil and Steve Berry, *The Orlando Sentinel*
1994 *The Providence Journal-Bulletin*
1995 Brian Donovan and Stephanie Saul, *Newsday* (Long Island, NY)
1996 *Orange County Register* (Santa Ana, CA)

Explanatory Journalism

1985 Jon Franklin, *The Baltimore Evening Sun*
1986 *The New York Times* staff
1987 Jeff Lyon and Peter Gorner, *Chicago Tribune*
1988 Daniel Hertzberg and James B. Stewart, *The Wall Street Journal*
1989 David Hanners, William Snyder, and Karen Blessen, *The Dallas Morning Star*
1990 David A. Vise and Steve Coll, *The Washington Post*
1991 Susan C. Faludi, *The Wall Street Journal*
1992 Robert S, Capers and Eric Lipton, *The Hartford* (CT) *Courant*
1993 Mike Toner, *The Atlanta Journal-Constitution*
1994 Ronald Kotulak, *Chicago Tribune*
1995 Leon Dash and Lucian Perkins, *The Washington Post*
1996 Laurie Garrett, *Newsday* (Long Island, NY)

Specialized Reporting

1985 Randall Savage and Jackie Crosby, *Macon* (GA) *Telegraph and News*
1986 Andrew Schneider and Mary Pat Flaherty, *The Pittsburgh Press*
1987 Alex S. Jones, *The New York Times*
1988 Walt Bogdanich, *The Wall Street Journal*
1989 Edward Humes, *The Orange County Register*
1990 Tamar Stieber, *Albuquerque Journal*

Beat Reporting

1991 Natalie Angier, *The New York Times*
1992 Deborah Blum, *The Sacramento Bee*
1993 Paul Ingrassia and Joseph B. White, *The Wall Street Journal*
1994 Eric Freedman and Jim Mitzelfeld, *The Detroit News*
1995 David Shribman, *The Boston Globe*
1996 Bob Keeler, *Newsday* (Long Island, NY)

Correspondence

1929 Paul Scott Mowrer, *Chicago Daily News*
1930 Leland Stowe, *New York Herald Tribune*
1931 H. R. Knickerbocker, *Philadelphia Public Ledger* and *New York Evening Post*
1932 Walter Duranty, *The New York Times* Charles G. Ross, *St. Louis Post-Dispatch*
1933 Edgar Ansel Mowrer, *Chicago Daily News*

1934 Frederick T. Birchall, *The New York Times*
1935 Arthur Krock, *The New York Times*
1936 Wilfed C. Barber, *Chicago Tribune*
1937 Anne O'Hare McCormick, *The New York Times*
1938 Arthur Krock, *The New York Times*
1939 Louis P. Lochner, Associated Press
1940 Otto D. Tolischus, *The New York Times*
1941 Group Award—American news reporters in the war zones of Europe, Asia, and Africa.
1942 Carlos P. Romulo, *Philippines Herald*
1943 Hanson W. Baldwin, *The New York Times*
1944 Ernest Taylor Pyle, Scripps-Howard Newspaper Alliance
1945 Harold V. (Hal) Boyle, Associated Press
1946 Arnaldo Cortesi, *The New York Times*
1947 Brooks Atkinson, *The New York Times*

Telegraphic Reporting (National)

1942 Louis Stark, *The New York Times*
1943 –
1944 Dewey L. Fleming, *The Baltimore Sun*
1945 James B. Reston, *The New York Times*
1946 Edward A. Harris, *St. Louis Post-Dispatch*
1947 Edward T. Folliard, *The Washington Post*

National Reporting

1948 Bert Andrews, *New York Herald Tribune*
    Nat S. Finney, *Minneapolis Tribune*
1949 C. P. Trussel, *The New York Times*
1950 Edwin O. Guthman, *Seattle Times*
1951 –
1952 Anthony Leviero, *The New York Times*
1953 Don Whitehead, Associated Press
1954 Richard Wilson, *Des Moines Register & Tribune*
1955 Anthony Lewis, *Washington Daily News*
1956 Charles L. Bartlett, *Chattanooga Times*
1957 James Reston, *The New York Times*
1958 Relman Morin, Associated Press
    Clark Mollenhoff, *Des Moines Register and Tribune*
1959 Howard Van Smith, *Miami* (FL) *News*
1960 Vance Trimble, Scripps-Howard Newspaper Alliance
1961 Edward R. Cony, *The Wall Street Journal*
1962 Nathan G. Caldwell and Gene S. Graham, *Nashville Tennessean*
1963 Anthony Lewis, *The New York Times*
1964 Merriman Smith, United Press International
1965 Louis M. Kohlmeier, *The Wall Street Journal*
1966 Haynes Johnson, *Washington Evening Star*
1967 Stanley Penn and Monroe Karmin, *The Wall Street Journal*
1968 Howard James, *Christian Science Monitor*
    Nathan K. (Nick) Kotz, *The Des Moines Register* and *Minneapolis Tribune*
1969 Robert Cahn, *Christian Science Monitor*
1970 William J. Eaton, *Chicago Daily News*
1971 Lucinda Franks and Thomas Powers, United Press International
1972 Jack Anderson, syndicated columnist

1973 Robert Boyd and Clark Hoyt, the Knight Newspapers
1974 James R. Polk, *Washington Star-News*
    Jack White, *Providence* (RI) *Journal and Evening Bulletin*
1975 Donald L. Barlett and James B. Steele, *The Philadelphia Inquirer*
1976 James Risser, *The Des Moines Register*
1977 Walter Mears, Associated Press
1978 Gaylord D. Shaw, *Los Angeles Times*
1979 James Risser, *The Des Moines Register*
1980 Bette Swenson Orsini and Charles Stafford, *St. Petersburg* (FL) *Times*
1981 John M. Crewdson, *The New York Times*
1982 Rick Atkinson, *The Kansas City Times*
1983 *The Boston Globe*
1984 John Noble Wilford, *The New York Times*
1985 Thomas J. Knudson, *The Des Moines Register*
1986 Arthur Howe, *The Philadelphia Inquirer*
    Craig Flournoy and George Rodrigue, *The Dallas Morning News*
1987 *The Miami Herald* staff
    The New York Times staff
1988 Tim Weiner, *The Philadelphia Inquirer*
1989 Donald L. Barlett and James B. Steele, *The Philadelphia Inquirer*
1990 Ross Anderson, Bill Dietrich, Mary Ann Gwinn and Eric Nalder, *The Seattle Times*
1991 Marjie Lundstrom and Rochelle Sharpe, Gannett News Service
1992 Jeff Taylor and Mike McGraw, *The Kansas City Star*
1993 David Maraniss, *The Washington Post*
1994 Eileen Welsome, *The Albuquerque Tribune*
1995 Tony Horwitz, *The Wall Street Journal*
1996 Alix M. Freedman, *The Wall Street Journal*

Telegraphic Reporting (International)

1942 Laurence Edmund Allen, Associated Press
1943 Ira Wolfert, North American Newspaper Alliance Inc.
1944 Daniel De Luce, Associated Press
1945 Mark S. Watson, *Baltimore Sun*
1946 Homer William Bigart, *New York Herald Tribune*
1947 Eddy Gilmore, Associated Press

International Reporting

1948 Paul W. Ward, *Baltimore Sun*
1949 Price Day, *Baltimore Sun*
1950 Edmund Stevens, *Christian Science Monitor*
1951 Keyes Beech, *Chicago Daily News*; Homer Bigart, *New York Herald Tribune*; Marguerite Higgins, *New York Herald Tribune*; Relman Morin, Associated Press; Fred Sparks, *Chicago Daily News*; and Don Whitehead, Associated Press

1952 John M. Hightower, Associated Press
1953 Austin Wehrwein, *Milwaukee Journal*
1954 Jim G. Lucas, Scripps-Howard Newspapers
1955 Harrison E. Salisbury, *The New York Times*
1956 William Randolph Hearst Jr., J. Kingsbury-
     Smith, and Frank Conniff, International
     News Service
1957 Russell Jones, United Press
1958 *The New York Times*
1959 Joseph Martin and Philip Santora,
     The New York Daily News
1960 A. M. Rosenthal, *The New York Times*
1961 Lynn Heinzerling, Associated Press
1962 Walter Lippmann, *New York Herald Tribune*
     Syndicate
1963 Hal Hendrix, *Miami* (FL) *News*
1964 Malcolm W. Browne, Associated Press,
     David Halberstam, *The New York Times*
1965 J. A. Livingston, *Philadelphia Bulletin*
1966 Peter Arnett, Associated Press
1967 R. John Hughes, *Christian Science Monitor*
1968 Alfred Friendly, *The Washngton Post*
1969 William Tuohy, *Los Angeles Times*
1970 Seymour M. Hersh, Dispatch News Service
     (Washington, DC)
1971 Jimmie Lee Hoagland, *The Washington Post*
1972 Peter R. Kann, *The Wall Street Journal*
1973 Max Frankel, *The New York Times*
1974 Hedrick Smith, *The New York Times*
1975 William Mullen and Ovie Carter, *Chicago
     Tribune*
1976 Sydney H. Schanberg, *The New York Times*
1977 –
1978 Henry Kamm, *The New York Times*
1979 Richard Ben Cramer, *The Philadelphia Inquirer*
1980 Joel Brinkley and Jay Mather, *The Louisville
     Courier-Journal*
1981 Shirley Christian, *The Miami Herald*
1982 John Darnton, *The New York Times*
1983 Thomas L. Friedman, *The New York Times*
     and Loren Jenkins, *The Washington Post*
1984 Karen Elliott House, *The Wall Street Journal*
1985 Josh Friedman and Dennis Bell, and Ozier
     Muhammad, *Newsday* (Long Island, NY)
1986 Lewis M. Simons, Pete Carey and Katherine
     Ellison, *San Jose* (CA) *Mercury News*
1987 Michael Parks, *Los Angeles Times*
1988 Thomas L. Friedman, *The New York Times*
1989 Glenn Frankel, *The Washington Post*
     Bill Keller, *The New York Times*
1990 Nicholas D. Kristof and Sheryl Wu Dunn,
     The New York Times
1991 Caryle Murphy, *The Washington Post*
     Serge Schmemann, *The New York Times*
1992 Patrick J. Sloyan, *Newsday* (Long Island, NY)
1993 John F. Burns, *The New York Times* and
     Roy Gutman, *Newsday* (Long Island, NY)
1994 *The Dallas Morning News* team
1995 Mark Fritz, Associated Press
1996 David Rohde, *Christian Science Monitor*

Feature Writing

1979 Jon D. Franklin, *The Baltimore Evening Sun*
1980 Madeleine Blais, *The Miami Herald*
1981 Teresa Carpenter, *The Village Voice*
1982 Saul Pett, Associated Press
1983 Nan Robertson, *The New York Times*
1984 Peter Mark Rinearson, *The Seattle Times*
1985 Alice Steinbach, *The Baltimore Sun*
1986 John Camp, *St. Paul Pioneer Press
     and Dispatch*
1987 Steve Twomey, *The Philadelphia Inquirer*
1988 Jacqui Banaszynski, *St. Paul Pioneer
     Press Dispatch*
1989 David Zucchino, *The Philadelphia Inquirer*
1990 Dave Curtin, *Colorado Springs Gazette
     Telegraph*
1991 Sheryl James, *St. Petersburg* (FL) *Times*
1992 Howell Raines, *The New York Times*
1993 George Lardner, Jr., *The Washington Post*
1994 Isabel Wilkerson, *The New York Times*
1995 Ron Suskind, *The Wall Street Journal*
1996 Rick Bragg, *The New York Times*

Commentary

1970 Marquis W. Childs, *St. Louis Post-Dispatch*
1971 William A. Caldwell, *The Record*
     (Hackensack, NJ)
1972 Mike Royko, *Chicago Daily News*
1973 David S. Broder, *The Washington Post*
1974 Edwin A. Roberts Jr., *National Observer*
1975 Mary McGrory, *Washington Star*
1976 Walter Wellesley (Red) Smith, *The
     New York Times*
1977 George F. Will, *Washington Post*
     Writer's Group
1978 William Safire, *The New York Times*
1979 Russell Baker, *The New York Times*
1980 Ellen H. Goodman, *The Boston Globe*
1981 Dave Anderson, *The New York Times*
1982 Art Buchwald, *Los Angeles Times Syndicate*
1983 Claude Sitton, *Raleigh* (NC) *News & Observer*
1984 Vermont Royster, *The Wall Street Journal*
1985 Murray Kempton, *Newsday* (Long Island, NY)
1986 Jimmy Breslin, *New York Daily News*
1987 Charles Krauthammer, *Washington Post*
     Writer's Group
1988 Dave Barry, *The Miami Herald*
1989 Clarence Page, *Chicago Tribune*
1990 Jim Murray, *Los Angeles Times*
1991 Jim Hoagland, *The Washington Post*
1992 Anna Quindlen, *The New York TImes*
1993 Liz Balmaseda, *The Miami Herald*
1994 William Raspberry, *The Washington Post*
1995 Jim Dwyer, *Newsday* (Long Island, NY)
1996 E. R. Shipp, *New York Daily News*

Criticism

1970 Ada Louise Huxtable, *The New York Times*
1971 Harold C. Schonberg, *The New York Times*
1972 Frank Peters Jr., *St. Louis Post-Dispatch*
1973 Ronald Powers, *Chicago Sun-Times*
1974 Emily Genauer, *Newsday* Syndicate

1975 Roger Ebert, *Chicago Sun-Times*
1976 Alan M. Kriegsman, *The Washington Post*
1977 William McPherson, *The Washington Post*
1978 Walter Kerr, *The New York Times*
1979 Paul Gapp, *Chicago Tribune*
1980 William A. Henry III, *The Boston Globe*
1981 Jonathan Yardley, *The Washington Star*
1982 Martin Bernheimer, *Los Angeles Times*
1983 Manuela Hoelterhoff, *The Wall Street Journal*
1984 Paul Goldberger, *The New York Times*
1985 Howard Rosenberg, *Los Angeles Times*
1986 Donal Henahan, *The New York Times*
1987 Richard Eder, *Los Angeles Times*
1988 Tom Shales, *The Washington Post*
1989 Michael Skube, *The News and Observer* (Raleigh, NC)
1990 Allan Temko, *San Francisco Chronicle*
1991 David Shaw, *Los Angeles Times*
1992 –
1993 Michael Dirda, *The Washington Post*
1994 Lloyd Schwartz, *The Boston Phoenix*
1995 Margo Jefferson, *The New York Times*
1996 Robert Campbell, *The Boston Globe*

Editorial Writing

1917 *New York Tribune*
1918 *Louisville Courier Journal*
1919 –
1920 Harvey E. Newbranch, *Evening World Herald* (Omaha, NE)
1921 –
1922 Frank M. O'Brien, *New York Herald*
1923 William Allen White, *Emporia* (KS) *Gazette*
1924 *Boston Herald*
1925 *Charleston* (SC) *News and Courier*
1926 *The New York Times,* Edward M. Kingsbury
1927 *Boston Herald,* F. Lauriston Bullard
1928 Grover Cleveland Hall, *Montgomery* (AL) *Advertiser*
1929 Louis Isaac Jaffe, *Norfolk Virginian-Pilot*
1930 –
1931 Charles S. Ryckman, *Fremont* (NE) *Tribune*
1932 –
1933 *Kansas City* (MO) *Star*
1934 E. P. Chase, *Atlantic* (IA) *News -Telegraph*
1935 –
1936 Felix Morley, *The Washington Post*, and George B. Parker, Scripps-Howard Newspapers
1937 John W. Owens, *The Baltimore Sun*
1938 William Wesley Waymack, *The Register & Tribune* (Des Moines, IA)
1939 Ronald G. Callvert, *The Oregonian*
1940 Bart Howard, *St. Louis Post-Dispatch*
1941 Reuben Maury, *New York Daily News*
1942 Geoffrey Parsons, *New York Herald Tribune*
1943 Forrest W. Seymour, *Register & Tribune* (Des Moines, IA)
1944 *Kansas City* (MO) *Star*, Henry J. Haskell
1945 George W. Potter, *Providence* (RI) *Journal-Bulletin*
1946 Hodding Carter, *Delta Democrat-Times*

(Greenville, MS)
1947 William H. Grimes, *The Wall Street Journal*
1948 Virginius Dabney, *Richmond Times-Dispatch*
1949 John H. Crider, *Boston Herald*, and Herbert Elliston, *The Washington Post*
1950 Carl M. Saunders, *Jackson* (MI) *Citizen Patriot*
1951 William Harry Fitzpatrick, *New Orleans States*
1952 Louis LaCoss, *St. Louis Globe Democrat*
1953 Vermont Connecticut Royster, *The Wall Street Journal*
1954 *Boston Herald*, Don Murray
1955 *Detroit Free Press*, Royce Howes
1956 Lauren K. Soth, *Register and Tribune* (Des Moines, IA)
1957 Buford Boone, *Tuscaloosa* (AL) *News*
1958 Harry S. Ashmore, *Arkansas Gazette*
1959 Ralph McGill, *Atlanta* (GA) *Constitution*
1960 Lenoir Chambers, *Norfolk Virginian-Pilot*
1961 William J. Dorvillier, *San Juan* (PR) *Star*
1962 Thomas M. Storke, *Santa Barbara* (CA) *News-Press*
1963 Ira B. Harkey, Jr., *Pascagoula* (MS) *Chronicle*
1964 Hazel Brannon Smith, *Lexington* (MS) *Advertiser*
1965 John R. Harrison, *Gainesville* (FL) *Sun*
1966 Robert Lasch, *St. Louis Post-Dispatch*
1967 Eugene Patterson, *Atlanta Constitution*
1968 John S. Knight, Knight Newspapers
1969 Paul Greenberg, *Pine Bluff* (AR) *Commercial*
1970 Philip L. Geyelin, *The Washington Post*
1971 Horance G. Davis Jr., *Gainesville* (FL) *Sun*
1972 John Strohmeyer, *Bethlehem* (PA) *Globe-Times*
1973 Roger B. Linscott, *Berkshire Eagle* (Pittsfield, MA)
1974 F. Gilman Spencer, *Trentonian* (Trenton, NJ)
1975 John Daniell Maurice, *Charleston* (WV) *Daily Mail*
1976 Philip P. Kerby, *Los Angeles Times*
1977 Warren L. Lerude, Foster Church, and Norman F. Cardoza, *Reno* (NV) *Evening Gazette* and *Nevada State Journal*
1978 Meg Greenfield, *The Washington Post*
1979 Edwin M. Yoder Jr., *The Washington Star*
1980 Robert L. Bartley, *The Wall Street Journal*
1981 –
1982 Jack Rosenthal, *The New York Times*
1983 *The Miami Herald* editorial board
1984 Albert Scardino, *The Georgia Gazette* (Savannah)
1985 Richard Aregood, *The Philadelphia Daily News*
1986 Jack Fuller, *Chicago Tribune*
1987 Jonathan Freedman, *The Tribune* (San Diego, CA)
1988 Jane Healy, *The Orlando Sentinel*
1989 Lois Wille, *Chicago Tribune*
1990 Thomas J. Hylton, *The Pottstown* (PA) *Mercury*
1991 Ron Casey, Harold Jackson, and Joey Kennedy, *The Birmingham* (AL) *News*

1992 Maria Henson, *Lexington* (KY) *Herald-Leader*
1993 –
1994 R. Bruce Dold, *Chicago Tribune*
1995 Jeffrey Good, *St. Petersburg* (FL) *Times*
1996 Robert B. Semple, Jr., *The New York Times*

Cartoons

1922 Rollin Kirby, *New York World*
1923 –
1924 Jay Norwood Darling, *Des Moines Reigister & Tribune*
1925 Rollin Kirby, *The New York World*
1926 D. R. Fitzpatrick, *St. Louis Post-Dispatch*
1927 Nelson Harding, *Brooklyn Daily Eagle*
1928 Nelson Harding, *Brooklyn Daily Eagle*
1929 Rollin Kirby, *The New York World*
1930 Charles R. Macauley, *Brooklyn Daily Eagle*
1931 Edmund Duffy, *The Baltimore Sun*
1932 John T. McCutcheon, *Chicago Tribune*
1933 H. M. Talburt, *Washington Daily News*
1934 Edmund Duffy, *The Baltimore Sun*
1935 Ross A. Lewis, *Milwaukee Journal*
1936 –
1937 C. D. Batchelor, *New York Daily News*
1938 Vaughn Shoemaker, *Chicago Daily News*
1939 Charles G. Werner, *Daily Oklahoman*
1940 Edmund Duffy, *The Baltimore Sun*
1941 Jacob Burck, *Chicago Times*
1942 Herbert Lawrence Block (Herblock), NEA Service
1943 Jay Norwood Darling, *Des Moines Register & Tribune*
1944 Clifford K. Berryman, *The Evening Star* (Washington, DC)
1945 Sergeant Bill Mauldin, United Feature Syndicate, Inc.
1946 Bruce Alexander Russell, *Los Angeles Times*
1947 Vaughn Shoemaker, *Chicago Daily News*
1948 Reuben L. Goldberg, *New York Sun*
1949 Lute Pease, *Newark Evening News*
1950 James T. Berryman, *The Evening Star* (Washington, DC)
1951 Reg (Reginald W.) Manning, *Arizona Republic*
1952 Fred L. Packer, *New York Mirror*
1953 Edward D. Kuekes, *Cleveland Plain Dealer*
1954 Herbert L. Block (Herblock), *Washington Post & Times-Herald*
1955 Daniel R. Fitzpatrick, *St. Louis Post-Dispatch*
1956 Robert York, *Louisville* (KY) *Times*
1957 Tom Little, *Nashville Tennessean*
1958 Bruce M. Shanks, *Buffalo* (NY) *Evening News*
1959 William H. (Bill) Mauldin, *St. Louis Post-Dispatch*
1960 –
1961 Carey Orr, *Chicago Tribune*
1962 Edmund S. Valtman, *Hartford Times*
1963 Frank Miller, *The Des Moines Register*
1964 Paul Conrad, *The Denver Post*
1965 –
1966 Don Wright, *Miami News*
1967 Patrick B. Oliphant, *Denver Post*

1968 Eugene Gray Payne, *Charlotte Observer*
1969 John Fischetti, *Chicago Daily News*
1970 Thomas F. Darcy, *Newsday* (Garden City, NY)
1971 Paul Conrad, *Los Angeles Times*
1972 Jeffrey K. MacNelly, *Richmond News-Leader*
1973 –
1974 Paul Szep, *The Boston Globe*
1975 Garry Trudeau
1976 Tony Auth, *The Philadelphia Inquirer*
1977 Paul Szep, *The Boston Globe*
1978 Jeffrey K. MacNelly, *The Richmond News-Leader*
1979 Herbert L. Block, *The Washington Post*
1980 Don Wright, *The Miami News*
1981 Mike Peters, *Dayton* (OH) *Daily News*
1982 Ben Sargent, *The Austin* (TX) *American-Statesman*
1983 Richard Locher, *Chicago Tribune*
1984 Paul Conrad, *Los Angeles Times*
1985 Jeff MacNelly, *Chicago Tribune*
1986 Jules Feiffer, *The Village Voice* (New York, NY)
1987 Berke Breathed, *The Washington Post Writers Group*
1988 Doug Marlette, *The Atlanta Constitution* and *The Charlotte Observer*
1989 Jack Higgins, *Chicago Sun-Times*
1990 Tom Toles, *The Buffalo News*
1991 Jim Borgman, *The Cincinnati Enquirer*
1992 Signe Wilkinson, *Philadelphia Daily News*
1993 Stephen R. Benson, *The Arizona Republic*
1994 Michael P. Ramirez, *The Commercial Appeal* (Memphis, TN)
1995 Mike Luckovich, *The Atlanta Constitution*
1996 Jim Morin, *The Miami Herald*

Photography

1942 Milton Brooks, *Detroit News*
1943 Frank Noel, Associated Press
1944 Frank Filan, Associated Press
     Earle L. Bunker, *World-Herald* (Omaha, NE)
1945 Joe Rosenthal, Associated Press
1946 –
1947 Arnold Hardy
1948 Frank Cushing, *Boston Traveler*
1949 Nathaniel Fein, *New York Herald-Tribune*
1950 Bill Crouch, *Oakland* (CA) *Tribune*
1951 Max Desfor, Associated Press
1952 John Robinson and Don Ultang, *Des Moines Register and Tribune*
1953 William M. Gallagher, *Flint* (MI) *Journal*
1954 Mrs. Walter M. Schau
1955 John L. Gaunt, Jr., *Los Angeles Times*
1956 *New York Daily News*
1957 Harry A. Trask, *Boston Traveler*
1958 William C. Beall, *Washington* (DC) *Daily News*
1959 William Seaman, *Minneapolis Star*
1960 Andrew Lopez, United Press International
1961 Yasushi Nagao, *Mainichi* (Tokyo)
1962 Paul Vathis, Associated Press
1963 Hector Rondon, *La Republica*

(Caracas, Venezuela)
1964 Robert H. Jackson, *Dallas Times-Herald*
1965 Horst Faas, Associated Press
1966 Kyoichi Sawada, United Press International
1967 Jack R. Thornell, Associated Press

Spot News Photography

1968 Rocco Morabito, *Jacksonville* (FL) *Journal*
1969 Edward T. Adams, Associated Press
1970 Steve Starr, Associated Press
1971 John Paul Filo, *Valley Daily News and Daily Dispatch* (Tarentum and New Kensington, PA)
1972 Horst Faas and Michel Laurent, Associated Press
1973 Huynh Cong Ut, Associated Press
1974 Anthony K. Roberts, freelance photographer (Beverly Hills, CA)
1975 Gerald H. Gay, *The Seattle Times*
1976 Stanley Forman, *Boston Herald American*
1977 Neal Ulevich, Associated Press
     Stanley Forman, *Boston Herald American*
1978 John H. Blair, United Press International
1979 Thomas J. Kelly III, *The Pottstown* (PA) *Mercury*
1980 An unnamed photographer, United Press International
1981 Larry C. Price, *Fort Worth* (TX) *Star-Telegram*
1982 Ron Edmonds, Associated Press
1983 Bill Foley, Associated Press
1984 Stan Grossfeld, *The Boston Globe*
1985 The photo staff of *The Register* (Santa Ana, CA)
1986 Carol Guzy and Michel duCille, *The Miami Herald*
1987 Kim Komenich, *San Francisco Examiner*
1988 Scott Shaw, *The Odessa* (TX) *American*
1989 Ron Olshwanger, freelance photographer
1990 The photo staff of *The Tribune* (Oakland, CA)
1991 Greg Marinovich, Associated Press
1992 The Associated Press staff
1993 Ken Geiger and William Snyder, *The Dallas Morning News*
1994 Paul Watson, *The Toronto Star*
1995 Carol Guzy, *The Washington Post*
1996 Charles Porter IV, freelance photographer

Feature Photography

1968 Toshio Sakai, United Press International
1969 Moneta Sleet Jr., *Ebony*
1970 Dallas Kinney, *Palm Beach Post*
1971 Jack Dykinga, *Chicago Sun-Times*
1972 Dave Kennerly, United Press International
1973 Brian Lanker, *Topeka Capital-Journal*
1974 Slava Veder, Associated Press
1975 Matthew Lewis, *The Washington Post*

1976 *The Louisville Courier-Journal and Times* photo staff
1977 Robin Hood, *Chattanooga News-Free Press*
1978 J. Ross Baughman, Associated Press
1979 Staff photographers of *The Boston Herald American*
1980 Erwin H. Hagler, *Dallas Times Herald*
1981 Taro M. Yamasaki, *Detroit Free Press*
1982 John H. White, *Chicago Sun-Times*
1983 James B. Dickman, *Dallas Times Herald*
1984 Anthony Suau, *The Denver Post*
1985 Stan Grossfeld, *The Boston Globe*
     Larry C. Price, *The Philadelphia Inquirer*
1986 Tom Gralish, *The Philadelphia Inquirer*
1987 David Peterson, *The Des Moines Register*
1988 Michel duCille, *The Miami Herald*
1989 Manny Crisostomo, *Detroit Free Press*
1990 David C. Turnley, *Detroit Free Press*
1991 William Snyder, *The Dallas Morning News*
1992 John Kaplan, Block Newspapers (Toledo, OH)
1993 The Associated Press staff
1994 Kevin Carter, freelance photographer
1995 The Associated Press staff
1996 Stephanie Welsh, freelance photographer

Newspaper History Award

1918 Minna Lewinson and Henry Beetle Hough

Special Awards and Citations

1930 William O. Dapping, *The Auburn* (NY) *Citizen*
1938 *Edmonton* (Alberta) *Journal*
1941 *The New York Times*
1944 Byron Price
     Mrs. William Allen White
1945 The cartographers of the American press
1947 (Pulitzer centennial year) Columbia University and the Graduate School of Journalism
1948 Dr. Frank Diehl Fackenthal
1951 Cyrus L. Sulzberger, *The New York Times*
1952 Max Kase, *New York Journal-American*
     Kansas City (MO) *Star*
1953 *The New York Times*
1958 Walter Lippmann, *The New York Herald Tribune*
1964 Gannett Newspapers
1976 Professor John Hohenberg
1978 Richard Lee Strout
1987 Joseph Pulitzer Jr.
1996 Herb Caen, *San Francisco Chronicle*

Letters

Fiction

1917 –
1918 *His Family*, Ernest Poole
1919 *The Magnificent Ambersons*, Booth Tarkington
1920 –
1921 *The Age of Innocence*, Edith Wharton
1922 *Alice Adams*, Booth Tarkington
1923 *One of Ours*, Willa Cather
1924 *The Able McLaughlins*, Margaret Wilson
1925 *So Big*, Edna Ferber
1926 *Arrowsmith*, Sinclair Lewis
1927 *Early Autumn*, Louis Bromfield
1928 *The Bridge of San Luis Rey*, Thornton Wilder
1929 *Scarlet Sister Mary*, Julia Peterkin
1930 *Laughing Boy*, Oliver LaFarge
1931 *Years of Grace*, Margaret Ayer Barnes
1932 *The Good Earth*, Pearl S. Buck
1933 *The Store*, T. S. Stribling
1934 *Lamb in His Bosom*, Caroline Miller
1935 *Now in November*, Josephine Winslow Johnson
1936 *Honey in the Horn*, Harold L. Davis
1937 *Gone With the Wind*, Margaret Mitchell
1938 *The Late George Apley*, John Phillips Marquand
1939 *The Yearling*, Marjorie Kinnan Rawlings
1940 *The Grapes of Wrath*, John Steinbeck
1941 –
1942 *In This Our Life*, Ellen Glasgow
1943 *Dragon's Teeth*, Upton Sinclair
1944 *Journey in the Dark*, Martin Flavin
1945 *A Bell for Adano*, John Hersey
1946 –
1947 *All the King's Men*, Robert Penn Warren
1948 *Tales of the South Pacific*, James A. Michener
1949 *Guard of Honor*, James Gould Cozzens
1950 *The Way West*, A. B. Guthrie, Jr.
1951 *The Town*, Conrad Richter
1952 *The Caine Mutiny*, Herman Wouk
1953 *The Old Man and the Sea*, Ernest Hemingway
1954 –
1955 *A Fable*, William Faulkner
1956 *Andersonville*, MacKinlay Kantor
1957 –
1958 *A Death in the Family*, James Agee
1959 *The Travels of Jaimie McPheeters*, Robert Lewis Taylor
1960 *Advise and Consent*, Allen Drury
1961 *To Kill a Mockingbird*, Harper Lee
1962 *The Edge of Sadness*, Edwin O'Connor
1963 *The Reivers*, William Faulkner
1964 –
1965 *The Keepers of the House*, Shirley Ann Grau
1966 *Collected Stories*, Katherine Anne Porter
1967 *The Fixer*, Bernard Malamud
1968 *The Confessions of Nat Turner*, William Styron
1969 *House Made of Dawn*, N. Scott Momaday
1970 *Collected Stories*, Jean Stafford

1971 –
1972 *Angle of Repose*, Wallace Stegner
1973 *The Optimist's Daughter*, Eudora Welty
1974 –
1975 *The Killer Angels*, Michael Shaara
1976 *Humboldt's Gift*, Saul Bellow
1977 –
1978 *Elbow Room*, James Alan McPherson
1979 *The Stories of John Cheever*, John Cheever
1980 *The Executioner's Song*, Norman Mailer
1981 *A Confederacy of Dunces*, John Kennedy Toole
1982 *Rabbit Is Rich*, John Updike
1983 *The Color Purple*, Alice Walker
1984 *Ironweed*, William Kennedy
1985 *Foreign Affairs*, Alison Lurie
1986 *Lonesome Dove*, Larry Mc Murtry
1987 *A Summons to Memphis*, Peter Taylor
1988 *Beloved*, Toni Morrison
1989 *Breathing Lessons*, Anne Tyler
1990 *The Mambo Kings Play Songs of Love*, Oscar Hijuelos
1991 *Rabbit at Rest*, John Updike
1992 *A Thousand Acres*, Jane Smiley
1993 *A Good Scent from a Strange Mountain*, Robert Olen Butler
1994 *The Shipping News*, E. Annie Proulx
1995 *The Stone Diaries*, Carol Shields
1996 *Independence Day*, Richard Ford

Drama

1917 –
1918 *Why Marry?*, Jesse Lynch Williams
1919 –
1920 *Beyond the Horizon*, Eugene O'Neill
1921 *Miss Lulu Bett*, Zona Gale
1922 *Anna Christie*, Eugene O'Neill
1923 *Icebound*, Owen Davis
1924 *Hell-Bent fer Heaven*, Hatcher Hughes
1925 *They Knew What They Wanted*, Sidney Howard
1926 *Craig's Wife*, George Kelly
1927 *In Abraham's Bosom*, Paul Green
1928 *Strange Interlude*, Eugene O'Neill
1929 *Street Scene*, Elmer L. Rice
1930 *The Green Pastures*, Marc Connelly
1931 *Alison's House*, Susan Glaspell
1932 *Of Thee I Sing*, George S. Kaufman, Morrie Ryskind, and Ira Gershwin
1933 *Both Your Houses*, Maxwell Anderson
1934 *Men in White*, Sidney Kingsley
1935 *The Old Maid*, Zoe Akins
1936 *Idiot's Delight*, Robert E. Sherwood
1937 *You Can't Take It With You*, Moss Hart and George S. Kaufman
1938 *Our Town*, Thornton Wilder
1939 *Abe Lincoln in Illinois*, Robert E. Sherwood
1940 *The Time of Your Life*, William Saroyan
1941 *There Shall Be No Night*, Robert E. Sherwood
1942 –
1943 *The Skin of Our Teeth*, Thornton Wilder
1944 –
1945 *Harvey*, Mary Chase

1946 *State of the Union*, Russel Crouse and
    Howard Lindsay
1947 –
1948 *A Streetcar Named Desire*, Tennessee
    Williams
1949 *Death of a Salesman*, Arthur Miller
1950 *South Pacific*, Richard Rodgers,
    Oscar Hammerstein II, and Joshua Logan
1951 –
1952 *The Shrike*, Joseph Kramm
1953 *Picnic*, William Inge
1954 *The Teahouse of the August Moon*,
    John Patrick
1955 *Cat on a Hot Tin Roof*, Tennessee Williams
1956 *Diary of Anne Frank*, Albert Hackett and
    Frances Goodrich
1957 *Long Day's Journey Into Night*,
    Eugene O'Neill
1958 *Look Homeward*, Angel, Ketti Frings
1959 *J. B.*, Archibald MacLeish
1960 *Fiorello!*, book by Jerome Weidman and
    George Abbott, music by Jerry Bock, and
    lyrics by Sheldon Harnick
1961 *All the Way Home*, Tad Mosel
1962 *How To Succeed In Business Without Really
    Trying*, Frank Loesser and Abe Burrows
1963 –
1964 –
1965 *The Subject Was Roses*, Frank D. Gilroy
1966 –
1967 *A Delicate Balance*, Edward Albee
1968 –
1969 *The Great White Hope*, Howard Sackler
1970 *No Place to Be Somebody*, Charles Gordone
1971 *The Effect of Gamma Rays on Man-in-the-
    Moon Marigolds*, Paul Zindel
1972 –
1973 *That Championship Season*, Jason Miller
1974 –
1975 *Seascape*, Edward Albee
1976 *A Chorus Line*, conceived, choreographed
    and directed by Michael Bennett, with
    book by James Kirkwood and Nicholas
    Dante, music by Marvin Hamlisch, and
    lyrics by Edward Kleban
1977 *The Shadow Box*, Michael Cristofer
1978 *The Gin Game*, Donald L. Coburn
1979 *Buried Child*, Sam Shepard
1980 *Talley's Folly*, Lanford Wilson
1981 *Crimes of the Heart*, Beth Henley
1982 *A Soldier's Play*, Charles Fuller
1983 *'Night, Mother*, Marsha Norman
1984 *Glengarry Glen Ross*, David Mamet
1985 *Sunday in the Park With George*, music
    and lyrics by Stephen Sondheim
1986 –
1987 *Fences*, August Wilson
1988 *Driving Miss Daisy*, Alfred Uhry
1989 *The Heidi Chronicles*, Wendy Wasserstein
1990 *The Piano Lesson*, August Wilson
1991 *Lost in Yonkers*, Neil Simon
1992 *The Kentucky Cycle*, Robert Schenkkan

1993 *Angels in America: Millennium Approaches*,
    Tony Kushner
1994 *Three Tall Women*, Edward Albee
1995 *The Young Man From Atlanta*, Horton Foote
1996 *Rent*, Jonathan Larson

History

1917 *With Americams of Past and Present Days*,
    His Excellency J. J. Jusserand
1918 *A History of the Civil War, 1861-1865*,
    James Ford Rhodes
1919 –
1920 *The War with Mexico*, 2 vols.,
    Justin H. Smith
1921 *The Victory at Sea*, William Sowden Sims
    in collaboration with Burton J. Hendrick
1922 *The Founding of New England*, James
    Truslow Adams
1923 *The Supreme Court in United States
    History*, Charles Warren
1924 *The American Revolution—A Constitutional
    Interpretation*, Charles Howard McIlwain
1925 *History of the American Frontier*,
    Frederic L. Paxson
1926 *A History of the United States*,
    Edward Channing
1927 *Pinckney's Treaty*, Samuel Flagg Bemis
1928 *Main Currents in American Thought*, 2 vols.,
    Vernon Louis Parrington
1929 *The Organization and Administration of
    the Union Army, 1861-1865*, Fred
    Albert Shannon
1930 *The War of Independence*, Claude H. Van Tyne
1931 *The Coming of the War 1914*, Bernadotte
    E. Schmitt
1932 *My Experiences in the World War*,
    John J. Pershing
1933 *The Significance of Sections in American
    History*, Frederick J. Turner
1934 *The People's Choice*, Herbert Agar
1935 *The Colonial Period of American History*,
    Charles McLean Andrews
1936 *A Constitutional History of the United States*,
    Andrew C. McLaughlin
1937 *The Flowering of New England 1815-1865*,
    Van Wyck Brooks
1938 *The Road to Reunion, 1865-1900*,
    Paul Herman Buck
1939 *A History of American Magazines*,
    Frank Luther Mott
1940 *Abraham Lincoln: The War Years*,
    Carl Sandburg
1941 *The Atlantic Migration, 1607-1860*,
    Marcus Lee Hansen
1942 *Reveille in Washington, 1860-1865*,
    Margaret Leech
1943 *Paul Revere and the World He Lived In*,
    Esther Forbes
1944 *The Growth of American Thought*, Merle Curti
1945 *Unfinished Business*, Stephen Bonsal
1946 *The Age of Jackson*, Arthur Meier
    Schlesinger, Jr.

1947 *Scientists Against Time*, James Phinney Baxter 3rd
1948 *Across the Wide Missouri*, Bernard DeVoto
1949 *The Disruption of American Democracy*, Roy Franklin Nichols
1950 *Art and Life in America*, Oliver W. Larkin
1951 *The Old Northwest, Pioneer Period 1815-1840*, R. Carlyle Buley
1952 *The Uprooted*, Oscar Handlin
1953 *The Era of Good Feelings*, George Dangerfield
1954 *A Stillness at Appomattox*, Bruce Catton
1955 *Great River: The Rio Grande in North American History*, Paul Horgan
1956 *The Age of Reform*, Richard Hofstadter
1957 *Russia Leaves the War: Soviet-American Relations, 1917-1920*, George F. Kennan
1958 *Banks and Politics in America*, Bray Hammond
1959 *The Republican Era: 1869-1901*, Leonard D. White, with the assistance of Miss Jean Schneider
1960 *In the Days of McKinley*, Margaret Leech
1961 *Between War and Peace: The Potsdam Conference*, Herbert Feis
1962 *The Triumphant Empire: Thunder-Clouds Gather in the West 1763-1766*, Lawrence H. Gipson
1963 *Washington, Village and Capital, 1800-1878*, Constance McLaughlin Green
1964 *Puritan Village: The Formation of a New England Town*, Sumner Chilton Powell
1965 *The Greenback Era*, Irwin Unger
1966 *The Life of the Mind in America*, Perry Miller
1967 *Exploration and Empire: The Explorer and the Scientist in the Winning of the American West*, William H. Goetzmann
1968 *The Ideological Origins of the American Revolution*, Bernard Bailyn
1969 *Origins of the Fifth Amendment*, Leonard W. Levy
1970 *Present at the Creation: My Years in the State Department*, Dean Acheson
1971 *Roosevelt: The Soldier of Freedom*, James MacGregor Burns
1972 *Neither Black Nor White*, Carl N. Degler
1973 *People of Paradox: An Inquiry Concerning the Origins of American Civilization*, Michael Kammen
1974 *The Americans: The Democratic Experience*, Daniel J. Boorstin
1975 *Jefferson and His Time*, vols. I-V, Dumas Malone
1976 *Lamy of Santa Fe*, Paul Horgan
1977 *The Impending Crisis, 1841-1861*, David M. Potter, manuscript finished by Don E. Fehrenbacher
1978 *The Visible Hand: The Managerial Revolution in American Business*, Alfred D. Chandler, Jr.
1979 *The Dred Scott Case*, Don E. Fehrenbacher
1980 *Been in the Storm So Long*, Leon F. Litwack

1981 *American Education: The National Experince, 1783-1876*, Lawrence A. Cremin
1982 *Mary Chesnut's Civil War*, edited by C. Vann Woodward
1983 *The Transformation of Virginia, 1740-1790*, Rhys L. Isaac
1984 –
1985 *Prophets of Regulation*, Thomas K. McCraw
1986 *...the Heavens and the Earth*, Walter A. McDougall
1987 *Voyagers to the West*, Bernard Bailyn
1988 *The Launching of Modern American Science 1846-1876*, Robert V. Bruce
1989 *Parting the Waters*, Taylor Branch
       Battle Cry of Freedom, James M. McPherson
1990 *In Our Image*, Stanley Karnow
1991 *A Midwife's Tale*, Laurel Thatcher Ulrich
1992 *The Fate of Liberty: Abraham Lincoln and Civil Liberties*, Mark E. Neely, Jr.
1993 *The Radicalism of the American Revolution*, Gordon S. Wood
1994 –
1995 *No Ordinary Time: Franklin and Eleanor Roosevelt: The Home Front in World War II*, Doris Kearns Goodwin
1996 *William Cooper's Town: Power and Persuasion on the Frontier of the Early American Republic*, Alan Taylor

Biography or Autobiography

1917 *Julia Ward Howe*, Laura E. Richards and Maude Howe Elliott, assisted by Florence Howe Hall
1918 *Benjamin Franklin, Self-Revealed*, William Cabell Bruce
1919 *The Education of Henry Adams*, Henry Adams
1920 *The Life of John Marshall*, 4 vols., Albert J. Beveridge
1921 *The Americanization of Edward Bok*, Edward Bok
1922 *A Daughter of the Middle Border*, Hamlin Garland
1923 *The Life and Letters of Walter H. Page*, Burton J. Hendrick
1924 *From Immigrant to Inventor*, Michael Idvorsky Pupin
1925 *Barrett Wendell and His Letters*, M. A. DeWolfe Howe
1926 *The Life of Sir William Osler*, 2 vols., Harvey Cushing
1927 *Whitman*, Emory Holloway
1928 *The American Orchestra and Theodore Thomas*, Charles Edward Russell
1929 *The Training of an American. The Earlier Life and Letters of Walter H. Page*, Burton J. Hendrick
1930 *The Raven*, Marquis James
1931 *Charles W. Eliot*, Henry James
1932 *Theodore Roosevelt*, Henry F. Pringle
1933 *Grover Cleveland*, Allan Nevins
1934 *John Hay*, Tyler Dennett
1935 *R. E. Lee*, Douglas S. Freeman

1936 *The Thought and Character of William James*, Ralph Barton Perry
1937 *Hamilton Fish*, Allan Nevins
1938 *Pedlar's Progress*, Odell Shepard *Andrew Jackson*, 2 vols., Marquis James
1939 *Benjamin Franklin*, Carl Van Doren
1940 *Woodrow Wilson, Life and Letters*, vols. VII and VIII, Ray Stannard Baker
1941 *Jonathan Edwards*, Ola Elizebeth Winslow
1942 *Crusader in Crinoline*, Forrest Wilson
1943 *Admiral of the Ocean Sea*, Samuel Eliot Morison
1944 *The American Leonardo: The Life of Samuel F. B. Morse*, Carleton Mabee
1945 *George Bancroft: Brahmin Rebel*, Russell Blaine Nye
1946 *Son of the Wilderness*, Linnie Marsh Wolfe
1947 *The Autobiography of William Allen White*
1948 *Forgotten First Citizen: John Bigelow*, Margaret Clapp
1949 *Roosevelt and Hopkins*, Robert E. Sherwood
1950 *John Quincy Adams and the Foundations of American Foreign Policy*, Samuel Flagg Bemis
1951 *John C. Calhoun: American Portrait*, Margaret Louise Coit
1952 *Charles Evans Hughes*, Merlo J. Pusey
1953 *Edmund Pendleton 1721-1803*, David J. Mays
1954 *The Spirit of St. Louis*, Charles A. Lindbergh
1955 *The Taft Story*, William S. White
1956 *Benjamin Henry Latrobe*, Talbot Faulkner Hamlin
1957 *Profiles in Courage*, John F. Kennedy
1958 *George Washington*, vols. I-VI, Douglas Southall Freeman, and vol. VII, written by John Alexander Carroll and Mary Wells Ashworth after Dr. Freeman's death in 1953
1959 *Woodrow Wilson, American Prophet*, Arthur Walworth
1960 *John Paul Jones*, Samuel Eliot Morison
1961 *Charles Sumner and the Coming of the Civil War*, David Donald
1962 –
1963 *Henry James*, Leon Edel
1964 *John Keats*, Walter Jackson Bate
1965 *Henry Adams*, 3 vols., Ernest Samuels
1966 *A Thousand Days*, Arthur M. Schlesinger, Jr.
1967 *Mr. Clemens and Mark Twain*, Justin Kaplan
1968 *Memoirs*, George F. Kennan
1969 *The Man From New York: John Quinn and His Friends*, Benjamin Lawrence Reid
1970 *Huey Long*, T. Harry Williams
1971 *Robert Frost: The Years of Triumph, 1915-1938*, Lawrance Thompson
1972 *Eleanor and Franklin*, Joseph P. Lash
1973 *Luce and His Empire*, W. A. Swanberg
1974 *O'Neill, Son and Artist*, Louis Sheaffer
1975 *The Power Broker: Robert Moses and the Fall of New York*, Robert Caro
1976 *Edith Wharton: A Biography*, R. W. B. Lewis
1977 *A Prince of Our Disorder, The Life of T. E. Lawrence*, John E. Mack
1978 *Samuel Johnson*, Walter Jackson Bate

1979 *Days of Sorrow and Pain: Leo Baeck and the Berlin Jews*, Leonard Baker
1980 *The Rise of Theodore Roosevelt*, Edmund Morris
1981 *Peter the Great: His Life and World*, Robert K. Massie
1982 *Grant: A Biography*, William McFeely
1983 *Growing Up*, Russell Baker
1984 *Booker T. Washington*, Louis R. Harlan
1985 *The Life and Times of Cotton Mather*, Kenneth Silverman
1986 *Louise Bogan: A Portrait*, Elizabeth Frank
1987 *Bearing the Cross*, David J. Garrow
1988 *Look Homeward: A Life of Thomas Wolfe*, David Herbert Donald
1989 *Oscar Wilde*, Richard Ellmann
1990 *Machiavelli in Hell*, Sebastian de Grazia
1991 *Jackson Pollock*, Steven Naifeh and Gregory White Smith
1992 *Fortunate Son: The Healing of a Vietnam Vet*, Lewis B. Puller, Jr.
1993 *Truman*, David McCullough
1994 *W. E. B. Du Bois: Biography of a Race 1868-1919*, David Levering Lewis
1995 *Harriet Beecher Stowe: A Life*, Joan D. Hedrick
1996 *God: A Biography*, Jack Miles

Poetry*

1918* *Love Songs*, Sara Teasdale
1919* *Old Road to Paradise*, Margaret Widdemer *Corn Huskers*, Carl Sandburg
1922 *Collected Poems*, Edwin Arlington Robinson
1923 *The Ballad of the Harp-Weaver; A Few Figs from Thistles; Eight Sonnets in American Poetry, 1922, A Miscellany*, Edna St. Vincent Millay
1924 *New Hampshire: A Poem with Notes and Grace Notes*, Robert Frost
1925 *The Man Who Died Twice*, Edwin Arlington Robinson
1926 *What's O'Clock*, Amy Lowell
1927 *Fiddler"s Farwell*, Leonora Speyer
1928 *Tristram*, Edwin Arlington Robinson
1929 *John Brown's Body*, Stephen Vincent Benét
1930 *Selected Poems*, Conrad Aiken
1931 *Collected Poems*, Robert Frost
1932 *The Flowering Stone*, George Dillon
1933 *Conquistador*, Archibald MacLeish
1934 *Collected Verse*, Robert Hillyer
1935 *Bright Ambush*, Audrey Wurdemann
1936 *Strange Holiness*, Robert P. Tristram Coffin
1937 *A Further Range*, Robert Frost
1938 *Cold Morning Sky*, Marya Zaturenska
1939 *Selected Poems*, John Gould Fletcher
1940 *Collected Poems*, Mark Van Doren
1941 *Sunderland Capture*, Leonard Bacon
1942 *The Dust Which Is God*, William Rose Benét

*Previous to the establishment of this prize in 1922, these awards had been made from gifts provided by the Poetry Society.

1943 *A Witness Tree*, Robert Frost
1944 *Western Star*, Stephen Vincent Benét
1945 *V-Letter and Other Poems*, Karl Shapiro
1946 –
1947 *Lord Weary's Castle*, Robert Lowell
1948 *The Age of Anxiety*, W. H. Auden
1949 *Terror and Decorum*, Peter Viereck
1950 *Annie Allen*, Gwendolyn Brooks
1951 *Complete Poems*, Carl Sandburg
1952 *Collected Poems*, Marianne Moore
1953 *Collected Poems 1917-1952*,
        Archibald MacLeish
1954 *The Waking*, Theodore Roethke
1955 *Collected Poems*, Wallace Stevens
1956 *Poems—North & South*, Elizabeth Bishop
1957 *Things of This World*, Richard Wilbur
1958 *Promises: Poems 1954-1956*, Robert
        Penn Warren
1959 *Selected Poems 1928-1958*, Stanley Kunitz
1960 *Heart's Needle*, W. D. Snodgrass
1961 *Times Three: Selected Verse From Three
        Decades*, Phyllis McGinley
1962 *Poems*, Alan Dugan
1963 *Pictures from Breughel*, William
        Carlos Williams
1964 *At the End of the Open Road*, Louis
        Simpson
1965 *77 Dream Songs*, John Berryman
1966 *Selected Poems*, Richard Eberhart
1967 *Live or Die*, Anne Sexton
1968 *The Hard Hours*, Anthony Hecht
1969 *Of Being Numerous*, George Oppen
1970 *Untitled Subjects*, Richard Howard
1971 *The Carrier of Ladders*, William S. Merwin
1972 *Collected Poems*, James Wright
1973 *Up Country*, Maxine Kumin
1974 *The Dolphin*, Robert Lowell
1975 *Turtle Island*, Gary Snyder
1976 *Self-Portrait in a Convex Mirror*,
        John Ashbery
1977 *Divine Comedies*, James Merrill
1978 *Collected Poems*, Howard Nemerov
1979 *Now and Then*, Robert Penn Warren
1980 *Selected Poems*, Donald Justice
1981 *The Morning of the Poem*, James Schuyler
1982 *The Collected Poems*, Sylvia Plath
1983 *Selected Poems*, Galway Kinnell
1984 *American Primitive*, Mary Oliver
1985 *Yin*, Carolyn Kizer
1986 *The Flying Change*, Henry Taylor
1987 *Thomas and Beulah*, Rita Dove
1988 *Partial Accounts*, William Meredith
1989 *New and Collected Poems*, Richard Wilbur
1990 *The World Doesn't End*, Charles Simic
1991 *Near Changes*, Mona Van Duyn
1992 *Selected Poems*, James Tate
1993 *The Wild Iris*, Louise Glück
1994 *Neon Vernacular: New and Selected
        Poems*, Yusef Komunyakaa
1995 *The Simple Truth*, Philip Levine
1996 *The Dream of the Unified Field*,
        Jorie Graham

General Non-Fiction

1962 *The Making of the President 1960*,
        Theodore H. White
1963 *The Guns of August*, Barbara W. Tuchman
1964 *Anti-Intellectualism in American Life*,
        Richard Hofstadter
1965 *O Strange New World*, Howard
        Mumford Jones
1966 *Wandering Through Winter*, Edwin Way Teale
1967 *The Problem of Slavery in Western Culture*,
        David Brion Davis
1968 *Rousseau and Revolution*, the tenth and
        concluding volume of *The Story of
        Civilization*, Will and Ariel Durant
1969 *So Human an Animal*, René Jules Dubos
        The Armies of the Night, Norman Mailer
1970 *Gandhi's Truth*, Erik K. Erikson
1971 *The Rising Sun*, John Toland
1972 *Stilwell and the American Experience in China,
        1911-1945*, Barbara W. Tuchman
1973 *Children of Crisis*, vols. II and III, Robert Coles
        *Fire in the Lake: The Vietnamese and the
        Americans in Vietnam*, Frances FitzGerald
1974 *The Denial of Death*, Ernest Becker
1975 *Pilgrim at Tinker Creek*, Annie Dillard
1976 *Why Survive? Being Old in America*,
        Robert N. Butler
1977 *Beautiful Swimmers*, William W. Warner
1978 *The Dragons of Eden*, Carl Sagan
1979 *On Human Nature*, Edward O. Wilson
1980 *Gödel, Escher, Bach: an Eternal Golden Braid*,
        Douglas R. Hofstadter
1981 *Fin-de Siécle Vienna: Politics and Culture*,
        Carl E. Schorske
1982 *The Soul of a New Machine*, Tracy Kidder
1983 *Is There No Place on Earth for Me?*
        Susan Sheehan
1984 *The Social Transformation of American
        Medicine*, Paul Starr
1985 *The Good War*, Studs Terkel
1986 *Move Your Shadow*, Joseph Lelyveld
        Common Ground, J. Anthony Lukas
1987 *Arab and Jew*, David K. Shipler
1988 *The Making of the Atomic Bomb*,
        Richard Rhodes
1989 *A Bright Shining Lie*, Neil Sheehan
1990 *And Their Children After Them*, Dale Maharidge
        and Michael WIlliamson
1991 *The Ants*, Bert Hölldobler and Edward O. Wilson
1992 *The Prize: The Epic Quest for Oil, Money
        & Power*, Daniel Yergin
1993 *Lincoln at Gettysburg: The Words that
        Remade America*, Garry Wills
1994 *Lenin's Tomb: The Last Days of the Soviet
        Empire*, David Remnick
1995 *The Beak of the Finch: A Story of Evolution
        in Our Time*, Jonathan Weiner
1996 *The Haunted Land: Facing Europe's Ghosts
        After Communism*, Tina Rosenberg

Music

1943 William Schuman for his *Secular Cantata No. 2, A Free Song*
1944 Howard Hanson, *Symphony No. 4, Opus 34*
1945 Aaron Copland, *Appalachian Spring*
1946 Leo Sowerby, *The Canticle of the Sun*
1947 Charles Ives, *Symphony No. 3*
1948 Walter Piston, *Symphony No. 3*
1949 Virgil Thomson, music for the film *Louisiana Story*
1950 Gian-Carlo Menotti, music in *The Consul*
1951 Douglas S. Moore, music in *Giants in the Earth*
1952 Gail Kubik, *Symphony Concertante*
1953 –
1954 Quincy Porter, *Concerto for Two Pianos and Orchestra*
1955 Gian-Carlo Menotti, *The Saint of Bleecker Street*
1956 Ernst Toch, *Symphony No. 3*
1957 Norman Dello Joio, *Meditations on Ecclesiastes*
1958 Samuel Barber, *Vanessa*, an opera in four acts, Libretto by Gian-Carlo Menotti
1959 John LaMontaine, *Concerto for Piano and Orchestra*
1960 Elliott Carter, *Second String Quartet*
1961 Walter Piston, *Symphony No. 7*
1962 Robert Ward, *The Crucible*, an opera in three acts, Libretto by Bernard Stambler, based on the play by Arthur Miller
1963 Samuel Barber, *Piano Concerto No. 1*
1964 –
1965 –
1966 Leslie Bassett, *Variations for Orchestra*
1967 Leon Kirchner, *Quartet No. 3*
1968 George Crumb, orchestral suite, *Echoes of Time and the River*
1969 Karel Husa, *String Quartet No. 3*
1970 Charles Wuorinen, *Time's Encomium*
1971 Mario Davidovsky, *Synchronisms No. 6 for Piano and Electronic Sound (1970)*
1972 Jacob Druckman, *Windows*
1973 Elliott Carter, *Spring Quartet No. 3*
1974 Donald Martino, *Notturno*
1975 Dominick Argento, *From the Diary of Virginia Woolf*, for medium voice and piano
1976 Ned Rorem, *Air Music* (Ten Etudes for Orchestra)
1977 Richard Wernick, *Visions of Terror and Wonder* for mezzo-soprano and orchestra
1978 Michael Colgrass, *Deja Vu for Percussion Quartet and Orchestra*
1979 Joseph Schwantner, *Aftertones of Infinity*
1980 David Del Tredici, *In Memory of a Summer Day*, a work for soprano solo and orchestra
1981 –
1982 Roger Sessions, *Concerto for Orchestra*
1983 Ellen Taaffe Zwilich, *Symphony No. 1* (Three Movements for Orchestra)
1984 Bernard Rands, *"Canti del Sole"* for Tenor and Orchestra
1985 Stephen Albert for *Symphony, RiverRun*
1986 George Perle, *Wind Quintet IV*
1987 John Harbison, *The Flight Into Egypt*
1988 William Bolcom, *12 New Etudes for Piano*
1989 Roger Reynolds, *Whispers Out of Time*
1990 Mel Powell, *"Duplicates": A Concerto for Two Pianos and Orchestra*
1991 Shulamit Ran, *Symphony*
1992 Wayne Peterson, *The Face of the Night, The Heart of the Dark*
1993 Christopher Rouse, *Trombone Concerto*
1994 Gunther Schuller, *Of Reminiscences and Reflections*
1995 Morton Gould, *Stringmusic*
1996 George Walker, *Lilacs*

Special Awards and Citations

1974 A special citation to Roger Sessions for his life's work as a distinguished American composer.
1976 A special award bestowed posthumously on Scott Joplin for his contributions to American music.
1982 A special citation to Milton Babbitt for his life's work as a distinguished and seminal American composer.
1985 A special citation to William Schuman for more than half a century of contribution to American music as composer and educational leader.

Source: Columbia University

Academy Award Winners

Awards No. year	Date awarded	Best picture	Actor in a leading role*	Actress in a leading role**	Actor in a supporting role	Actress in a supporting role	Directing
1 1927–1928	May 16, 1929	Wings	Emil Jannings, The Way of All Flesh	Janet Gaynor 7th Heaven	–	–	Comedy Picture: Lewis Milestone, Two Arabian Knights Dramatic Picture: Frank Borzage, 7th Heaven
2 1928–1929	April 3, 1930	The Broadway Melody	Warner Baxter, In Old Arizona	Mary Pickford, Coquette	–	–	Frank Lloyd, The Divine Lady
3 1929–1930	Nov. 5, 1930	All Quiet on the Western Front	George Arliss, Disraeli	Norma Shearer, The Divorcée	–	–	Lewis Milestone, All Quiet on the Western Front
4 1930–1931	Nov. 10, 1931	Cimarron	Lionel Barrymore, A Free Soul	Marie Dressler, Min and Bill	–	–	Norman Taurog, Skippy
5 1931–1932	Nov. 18, 1932	Grand Hotel	†Fredric March, Dr. Jeckyll and Mr. Hyde †Wallace Beery, The Champ	Helen Hayes, The Sin of Madelon Claudet	–	–	Frank Borzage, Bad Girl
6 1932–1933	March 16, 1934	Cavalcade	Charles Laughton, The Private Life of Henry VIII	Katharine Hepburn, Morning Glory	–	–	Frank Lloyd, Cavalcade
7 1934	Feb. 27, 1935	It Happened One Night	Clark Gable, It Happened One Night	Claudette Colbert, It Happened One Night	–	–	Frank Capra, It Happened One Night
8 1935	March 5, 1936	Mutiny on the Bounty	Victor McLaglen, The Informer	Bette Davis, Dangerous	–	–	John Ford, The Informer
9 1936	March 4, 1937	The Great Ziegfeld	Paul Muni, The Story of Louis Pasteur	Luise Rainer, The Great Ziegfeld	Walter Brennan, Come and Get It	Gale Sondergaard, Anthony Adverse	Frank Capra, Mr. Deeds Goes to Town
10 1937	March 10, 1938	The Life of Emile Zola	Spencer Tracy, Captains Courageous	Luise Rainer, The Good Earth	Joseph Schildkraut, The Life of Emile Zola	Alice Brady, In Old Chicago	Leo McCarey, The Awful Truth
11 1938	Feb. 23, 1939	You Can't Take It With You	Spencer Tracy, Boys Town	Bette Davis, Jezebel	Walter Brennan, Kentucky	Fay Bainter, Jezebel	Frank Capra, You Can't Take it With You
12 1939	Feb. 29, 1940	Gone With the Wind	Robert Donat, Goodbye, Mr. Chips	Vivien Leigh, Gone With the Wind	Thomas Mitchell, Stagecoach	Hattie McDaniel, Gone With the Wind	Victor Fleming, Gone With the Wind

*Prior to the 1976 (49th) Awards, this category was known as "Actor."

**Prior to the 1976 (49th) Awards, this category was known as "Actress."

†Tie

Awards No.	year	Date awarded	Best picture	Actor in a leading role*	Actress in a leading role**	Actor in a supporting role	Actress in a supporting role	Directing
13	1940	Feb. 27, 1941	Rebecca	James Stewart, The Philadelphia Story	Ginger Rogers, Kitty Foyle	Walter Brennan, The Westerner	Jane Darwell, The Grapes of Wrath	John Ford, The Grapes of Wrath
14	1941	Feb. 26, 1942	How Green Was My Valley	Gary Cooper, Sergeant York	Joan Fontaine, Suspicion	Donald Crisp, How Green Was My Valley	Mary Astor, The Great Lie	John Ford, How Green Was My Valley
15	1942	March 4, 1943	Mrs. Miniver	James Cagney, Yankee Doodle Dandy	Greer Garson, Mrs. Miniver	Van Heflin, Johnny Eager	Teresa Wright, Mrs. Miniver	William Wyler, Mrs. Miniver
16	1943	March 2, 1944	Casablanca	Paul Lukas, Watch on the Rhine	Jennifer Jones, The Song of Bernadette	Charles Coburn, The More the Merrier	Katina Paxinou, For Whom the Bell Tolls	Michael Curtiz, Casablanca
17	1944	March 15, 1945	Going My Way	Bing Crosby, Going My Way	Ingrid Bergman, Gaslight	Barry Fitzgerald, Going My Way	Ethel Barrymore, None But the Lonely Heart	Leo McCarey, Going My Way
18	1945	March 7, 1946	The Lost Weekend	Ray Milland, The Lost Weekend	Joan Crawford, Mildred Pierce	James Dunn, A Tree Grows in Brooklyn	Anne Revere, National Velvet	Billy Wilder, The Lost Weekend
19	1946	March 13, 1947	The Best Years of Our Lives	Fredric March, The Best Years of Our Lives	Olivia de Havilland, To Each His Own	Harold Russell, The Best Years of Our Lives	Anne Baxter, The Razor's Edge	William Wyler, The Best Years of Our Lives
20	1947	March 20, 1948	Gentleman's Agreement	Ronald Colman, A Double Life	Loretta Young, The Farmer's Daughter	Edmund Gwenn, Miracle on 34th Street	Celeste Holm, Gentleman's Agreement	Elia Kazan, Gentleman's Agreement
21	1948	March 24, 1949	Hamlet	Laurence Olivier, Hamlet	Jane Wyman, Johnny Belinda	Walter Huston, The Treasure of the Sierra Madre	Claire Trevor, Key Largo	John Huston, The Treasure of the Sierra Madre
22	1949	March 23, 1950	All the King's Men	Broderick Crawford, All the King's Men	Olivia de Havilland, The Heiress	Dean Jagger, Twelve O'Clock High	Mercedes McCambridge, All the King's Men	Joseph L. Mankiewicz, A Letter to Three Wives
23	1950	March 29, 1951	All About Eve	José Ferrer, Cyrano de Bergerac	Judy Holliday, Born Yesterday	George Sanders, All About Eve	Josephine Hull, Harvey	Joseph L. Mankiewicz, All About Eve
24	1951	March 20, 1952	An American in Paris	Humphrey Bogart, The African Queen	Vivien Leigh, A Streetcar Named Desire	Karl Malden, A Streetcar Named Desire	Kim Hunter, A Streetcar Named Desire	George Stevens, A Place in the Sun
25	1952	March 19, 1953	The Greatest Show on Earth	Gary Cooper, High Noon	Shirley Booth, Come Back, Little Sheba	Anthony Quinn, Viva Zapata!	Gloria Grahame, The Bad and the Beautiful	John Ford, The Quiet Man
26	1953	March 25, 1954	From Here to Eternity	William Holden, Stalag 17	Audrey Hepburn, Roman Holiday	Frank Sinatra, From Here to Eternity	Donna Reed, From Here to Eternity	Fred Zinnemann, From Here to Eternity

*Prior to the 1976 (49th) Awards, this category was known as "Actor."

**Prior to the 1976 (49th) Awards, this category was known as "Actress."

Awards No.	year	Date awarded	Best picture	Actor in a leading role*	Actress in a leading role**	Actor in a supporting role	Actress in a supporting role	Directing
27	1954	March 30, 1955	On the Waterfront	Marlon Brando, On the Waterfront	Grace Kelly, The Country Girl	Edmond O'Brien, The Barefoot Contessa	Eva Marie Saint, On the Waterfront	Elia Kazan, On the Waterfront
28	1955	March 21, 1956	Marty	Ernest Borgnine, Marty	Anna Magnani, The Rose Tattoo	Jack Lemmon, Mister Roberts	Jo Van Fleet, East of Eden	Delbert Mann, Marty
29	1956	March 27, 1957	Around the World in 80 Days	Yul Brynner, The King and I	Ingrid Bergman, Anastasia	Anthony Quinn, Lust for Life	Dorothy Malone, Written on the Wind	George Stevens, Giant
30	1957	March 26, 1958	The Bridge on the River Kwai	Alec Guinness, The Bridge on the River Kwai	Joanne Woodward, The Three Faces of Eve	Red Buttons, Sayonara	Miyoshi Umeki, Sayonara	David Lean, The Bridge on the River Kwai
31	1958	April 6, 1959	Gigi	David Niven, Separate Tables	Susan Hayward, I Want to Live!	Burl Ives, The Big Country	Wendy Hiller, Separate Tables	Vincente Minnelli, Gigi
32	1959	April 4, 1960	Ben-Hur	Charlton Heston, Ben-Hur	Simone Signoret, Room at the Top	Hugh Griffith, Ben-Hur	Shelley Winters, The Diary of Anne Frank	William Wyler, Ben-Hur
33	1960	April 17, 1961	The Apartment	Burt Lancaster, Elmer Gantry	Elizabeth Taylor, Butterfield 8	Peter Ustinov, Spartacus	Shirley Jones, Elmer Gantry	Billy Wilder, The Apartment
34	1961	April 9, 1962	West Side Story	Maximilian Schell, Judgment at Nuremberg	Sophia Loren, Two Women	George Chakiris, West Side Story	Rita Moreno, West Side Story	Robert Wise, Jerome Robbins, West Side Story
35	1962	April 8, 1963	Lawrence of Arabia	Gregory Peck, To Kill a Mockingbird	Anne Bancroft, The Miracle Worker	Ed Begley, Sweet Bird of Youth	Patty Duke, The Miracle Worker	David Lean, Lawrence of Arabia
36	1963	April 13, 1964	Tom Jones	Sidney Poitier, Lilies of the Field	Patricia Neal, Hud	Melvyn Douglas, Hud	Margaret Rutherford, The V.I.P.s	Tony Richardson, Tom Jones
37	1964	April 5, 1965	My Fair Lady	Rex Harrison, My Fair Lady	Julie Andrews, Mary Poppins	Peter Ustinov, Topkapi	Lila Kedrova, Zorba the Greek	George Cukor, My Fair Lady
38	1965	April 18, 1966	The Sound of Music	Lee Marvin, Cat Ballou	Julie Christie, Darling	Martin Balsam, A Thousand Clowns	Shelley Winters, A Patch of Blue	Robert Wise, The Sound of Music
39	1966	April 10, 1967	A Man for All Seasons	Paul Scofield, A Man for All Seasons	Elizabeth Taylor, Who's Afraid of Virginia Woolf?	Walter Matthau, The Fortune Cookie	Sandy Dennis, Who's Afraid of Virginia Woolf?	Fred Zinnemann, A Man for All Seasons
40	1967	April 10, 1968	In the Heat of the Night	Rod Steiger, In the Heat of the Night	Katharine Hepburn, Guess Who's Coming to Dinner?	George Kennedy, Cool Hand Luke	Estelle Parsons, Bonnie and Clyde	Mike Nichols, The Graduate

*Prior to the 1976 (49th) Awards, this category was known as "Actor."
**Prior to the 1976 (49th) Awards, this category was known as "Actress."

No.	Awards year	Date awarded	Best picture	Actor in a leading role*	Actress in a leading role**	Actor in a supporting role	Actress in a supporting role	Directing
41	1968	April 14, 1969	Oliver!	Cliff Robertson, Charly	†Katharine Hepburn, The Lion in Winter, †Barbra Streisand, Funny Girl	Jack Albertson, The Subject Was Roses	Ruth Gordon, Rosemary's Baby	Carol Reed, Oliver!
42	1969	April 7, 1970	Midnight Cowboy	John Wayne, True Grit	Maggie Smith, The Prime of Miss Jean Brodie	Gig Young, They Shoot Horses, Don't They?	Goldie Hawn, Cactus Flower	John Schlesinger, Midnight Cowboy
43	1970	April 15, 1971	Patton	George C. Scott, Patton	Glenda Jackson, Women in Love	John Mills, Ryan's Daughter	Helen Hayes, Airport	Franklin J. Schaffner, Patton
44	1971	April 10, 1972	The French Connection	Gene Hackman, The French Connection	Jane Fonda, Klute	Ben Johnson, The Last Picture Show	Cloris Leachman, The Last Picture Show	William Friedkin, The French Connection
45	1972	March 27, 1973	The Godfather	Marlon Brando, The Godfather	Liza Minnelli, Cabaret	Joel Grey, Cabaret	Eileen Heckart, Butterflies Are Free	Bob Fosse, Cabaret
46	1973	April 2, 1974	The Sting	Jack Lemmon, Save the Tiger	Glenda Jackson, A Touch of Class	John Houseman, The Paper Chase	Tatum O'Neal, Paper Moon	George Roy Hill, The Sting
47	1974	April 8, 1975	The Godfather Part II	Art Carney, Harry and Tonto	Ellen Burstyn, Alice Doesn't Live Here Anymore	Robert De Niro, The Godfather Part II	Ingrid Bergman, Murder on the Orient Express	Francis Ford Coppola, The Godfather Part II
48	1975	March 29, 1976	One Flew Over the Cuckoo's Nest	Jack Nicholson, One Flew Over the Cuckoo's Nest	Louise Fletcher, One Flew Over the Cuckoo's Nest	George Burns, The Sunshine Boys	Lee Grant, Shampoo	Milos Forman, One Flew Over the Cuckoo's Nest
49	1976	March 28, 1977	Rocky	Peter Finch, Network	Faye Dunaway, Network	Jason Robards, All the President's Men	Beatrice Straight, Network	John G. Avildsen, Rocky
50	1977	April 3, 1978	Annie Hall	Richard Dreyfuss, The Goodbye Girl	Diane Keaton, Annie Hall	Jason Robards, Julia	Vanessa Redgrave, Julia	Woody Allen, Annie Hall
51	1978	April 9, 1979	The Deer Hunter	Jon Voight, Coming Home	Jane Fonda, Coming Home	Christopher Walken, The Deer Hunter	Maggie Smith, California Suite	Michael Cimino, The Deer Hunter
52	1979	April 14, 1980	Kramer vs. Kramer	Dustin Hoffman, Kramer vs. Kramer	Sally Field, Norma Rae	Melvyn Douglas, Being There	Meryl Streep, Kramer vs. Kramer	Robert Benton, Kramer vs. Kramer
53	1980	March 31, 1981	Ordinary People	Robert De Niro, Raging Bull	Sissy Spacek, Coal Miner's Daughter	Timothy Hutton, Ordinary People	Mary Steenburgen, Melvin and Howard	Robert Redford, Ordinary People

*Prior to the 1976 (49th) Awards, this category was known as "Actor."
**Prior to the 1976 (49th) Awards, this category was known as "Actress."
†Tie

Awards No.	year	Date awarded	Best picture	Actor in a leading role	Actress in a leading role	Actor in a supporting role	Actress in a supporting role	Directing
54	1981	March 29, 1982	Chariots of Fire	Henry Fonda, On Golden Pond	Katharine Hepburn, On Golden Pond	John Gielgud, Arthur	Maureen Stapleton, Reds	Warren Beatty, Reds
55	1982	April 11, 1983	Gandhi	Ben Kingsley, Gandhi	Meryl Streep, Sophie's Choice	Louis Gossett, Jr., An Officer and a Gentleman	Jessica Lange, Tootsie	Richard Attenborough, Gandhi
56	1983	April 9, 1984	Terms of Endearment	Robert Duvall, Tender Mercies	Shirley MacLaine, Terms of Endearment	Jack Nicholson, Terms of Endearment	Linda Hunt, The Year of Living Dangerously	James L. Brooks, Terms of Endearment
57	1984	March 25, 1985	Amadeus	F. Murray Abraham, Amadeus	Sally Field, Places in the Heart	Haing S. Ngor, The Killing Fields	Peggy Ashcroft, A Passage to India	Milos Forman, Amadeus
58	1985	March 24, 1986	Out of Africa	William Hurt, Kiss of the Spider Woman	Geraldine Page, The Trip to Bountiful	Don Ameche, Cocoon	Anjelica Huston, Prizzi's Honor	Sydney Pollack, Out of Africa
59	1986	March 30, 1987	Platoon	Paul Newman, The Color of Money	Marlee Matlin, Children of a Lesser God	Michael Caine, Hannah and Her Sisters	Dianne Wiest, Hannah and Her Sisters	Oliver Stone, Platoon
60	1987	April 11, 1988	The Last Emperor	Michael Douglas, Wall Street	Cher, Moonstruck	Sean Connery, The Untouchables	Olympia Dukakis, Moonstruck	Bernardo Bertolucci, The Last Emperor
61	1988	March 29, 1989	Rain Man	Dustin Hoffman, Rain Man	Jodie Foster, The Accused	Kevin Kline, A Fish Called Wanda	Geena Davis, The Accidental Tourist	Barry Levinson, Rain Man
62	1989	March 26, 1990	Driving Miss Daisy	Daniel Day Lewis, My Left Foot	Jessica Tandy, Driving Miss Daisy	Denzel Washington, Glory	Brenda Fricker, My Left Foot	Oliver Stone, Born on the Fourth of July
63	1990	March 25, 1991	Dances With Wolves	Jeremy Irons, Reversal of Fortune	Kathy Bates, Misery	Joe Pesci, Good Fellas	Whoopi Goldberg, Ghost	Kevin Costner, Dances With Wolves
64	1991	March 30, 1992	The Silence of the Lambs	Anthony Hopkins, The Silence of the Lambs	Jodie Foster, The Silence of the Lambs	Jack Palance, City Slickers	Mercedes Ruehl, The Fisher King	Jonathan Demme, The Silence of the Lambs
65	1992	March 29, 1993	Unforgiven	Al Pacino, Scent of a Woman	Emma Thompson, Howards End	Gene Hackman, Unforgiven	Marisa Tomei, My Cousin Vinny	Clint Eastwood, Unforgiven
66	1993	March 21, 1994	Schindler's List	Tom Hanks, Philadelphia	Holly Hunter, The Piano	Tommy Lee Jones, The Fugitive	Anna Paquin, The Piano	Steven Spielberg, Schindler's List
67	1994	March 27, 1995	Forrest Gump	Tom Hanks, Forrest Gump	Jessica Lange, Blue Sky	Martin Landau, Ed Wood	Dianne Wiest, Bullets Over Broadway	Robert Zemeckis, Forrest Gump
68	1995	March 25, 1996	Braveheart	Nicolas Cage, Leaving Las Vegas	Susan Sarandon, Dead Man Walking	Kevin Spacey, The Usual Suspects	Mira Sorvino, Mighty Aphrodite	Mel Gibson, Braveheart
69	1996	March 24, 1997	The English Patient	Geoffrey Rush, Shine	Frances McDormand, Fargo	Cuba Gooding, Jr., Jerry Maguire	Juliette Binoche, The English Patient	Anthony Minghella, The English Patient

Source: Academy of Motion Picture Arts and Sciences

Emmy Awards

1948
Most Popular Television Program
Pantomime Quiz. KTLA.
Best Film Made for Television
The Necklace (*Your Show Time* series), Marshall Grant-Realm Productions.

1949
Best Live Show
The Ed Wynn Show. KTTV (CBS).
Best Kinescope Show
Texaco Star Theater. KNBH (NBC).

1950
Best Dramatic Show
Pulitzer Prize Playhouse. KECA-TV (ABC).
Best Variety Show
The Alan Young Show. KTTV (CBS).

1951
Best Dramatic Show
Studio One. CBS
Best Comedy Show
Red Skelton Show. NBC.

1952
Best Dramatic Program
Robert Montgomery Presents. NBC.
Best Situation Comedy
I Love Lucy. CBS.

1953
Best Dramatic Program
U.S. Steel Hour. ABC.
Best Situation Comedy
I Love Lucy. CBS.

1954
Best Dramatic Series
U.S. Steel Hour. ABC.
Best Situation Comedy Series
Make Room for Daddy. ABC.

1955
Best Dramatic Series
Producers' Showcase. NBC.
Best Comedy Series
The Phil Silvers Show. CBS.

1.956
Best Series—One Hour or More
Caesar's Hour. NBC.
Best Series—Half Hour or Less
The Phil Silvers Show. CBS.

1957
Best Dramatic Series with Continuing Characters
Gunsmoke. CBS
Best Comedy Series
The Phil Silvers Show. CBS.

1958–59
Best Dramatic Series—One Hour or Longer
Playhouse 90. CBS.
Best Dramatic Series—Less Than One Hour
The Alcoa Hour/Goodyear Playhouse. NBC.
Best Comedy Series
The Jack Benny Show. CBS.

1959–60
Outstanding Program Achievement in the Field of Drama
Playhouse 90. CBS.
Outstanding Program Achievement in the Field of Humor
Art Carney Special. NBC.

1960–61
Outstanding Program Achievement in the Field of Drama
Macbeth, Hallmark Hall of Fame. NBC.
Outstanding Program Achievement in the Field of Humor
The Jack Benny Show. CBS.

1961–62
Outstanding Program Achievement in the Field of Drama
The Defenders. CBS.
Outstanding Program Achievement in the Field of Humor
The Bob Newhart Show. NBC.

1962–63
Outstanding Program Achievement in the Field of Drama
The Defenders. CBS.
Outstanding Program Achievement in the Field of Humor
The Dick Van Dyke Show. CBS.

1963–64
Outstanding Program Achievement in the Field of Drama
The Defenders. CBS.

Outstanding Program Achievement
in the Field of Comedy
The Dick Van Dyke Show. CBS.

1964–65
Outstanding Program Achievements
in Entertainment
The Dick Van Dyke Show. CBS.
The Magnificent Yankee, Hallmark Hall of Fame. NBC.
My Name is Barbra. CBS.
"What is Sonata Form?," *New York Philharmonic Young People's Concerts with Leonard Bernstein.* CBS.

1965–66
Outstanding Dramatic Series
The Fugitive. ABC.
Outstanding Comedy Series
The Dick Van Dyke Show. CBS.

1966–67
Outstanding Dramatic Series
Mission: Impossible. CBS.
Outstanding Comedy Series
The Monkees. NBC.

1967–68
Outstanding Dramatic Series
Mission: Impossible. CBS.
Outstanding Comedy Series
Get Smart. NBC.

1968–69
Outstanding Dramatic Series
NET Playhouse. NET.
Outstanding Comedy Series
Get Smart. NBC.

1969–70
Outstanding Dramatic Series
Marcus Welby, M.D. ABC.
Outstanding Comedy Series
My World and Welcome To It. NBC.

1970–71
Outstanding Series—Drama
The Senator, The Bold Ones. NBC.
Outstanding Series—Comedy
All in the Family. CBS.

1971–72
Outstanding Series—Drama
Elizabeth R, Masterpiece Theatre. PBS.
Outstanding Series—Comedy
All in the Family. CBS.

1972–73
Outstanding Drama Series
The Waltons. CBS.

Outstanding Comedy Series
All in the Family. CBS.

1973–74
Outstanding Drama Series
Upstairs, Downstairs, Masterpiece Theatre. PBS.
Outstanding Comedy Series
*M*A*S*H.* CBS.

1974–75
Outstanding Drama Series
Upstairs, Downstairs, Masterpiece Theatre. PBS.
Outstanding Comedy Series
The Mary Tyler Moore Show. CBS.

1975–76
Outstanding Drama Series
Police Story. NBC.
Outstanding Comedy Series
The Mary Tyler Moore Show. CBS.

1976–77
Outstanding Drama Series
Upstairs, Downstairs, Masterpiece Theatre. PBS.
Outstanding Comedy Series
The Mary Tyler Moore Show. CBS.

1977–78
Outstanding Drama Series
The Rockford Files. NBC.
Outstanding Comedy Series
All in the Family. CBS.

1978–79
Outstanding Drama Series
Lou Grant. CBS.
Outstanding Comedy Series
Taxi. ABC.

1979–80
Outstanding Drama Series
Lou Grant. CBS.
Outstanding Comedy Series
Taxi. ABC.

1980–81
Outstanding Drama Series
Hill Street Blues. NBC.
Outstanding Comedy Series
Taxi. ABC.

1981–82
Outstanding Drama Series
Hill Street Blues. NBC.
Outstanding Comedy Series
Barney Miller. ABC.

1982–83
Outstanding Drama Series
Hill Street Blues. NBC.
Outstanding Comedy Series
Cheers. NBC.

1983–84
Outstanding Drama Series
Hill Street Blues. NBC.
Outstanding Comedy Series
Cheers. NBC.

1984–85
Outstanding Drama Series
Cagney & Lacey. CBS.
Outstanding Comedy Series
The Cosby Show. NBC.

1985–86
Outstanding Drama Series
Cagney & Lacey. CBS.
Outstanding Comedy Series
The Golden Girls. NBC.

1986–87
Outstanding Drama Series
L.A. Law. NBC.
Outstanding Comedy Series
The Golden Girls. NBC.

1987–88
Outstanding Drama Series
thirtysomething. ABC.
Outstanding Comedy Series
The Wonder Years. ABC.

1988–89
Outstanding Drama Series
L.A. Law. NBC.
Outstanding Comedy Series
Cheers. NBC.

1989–90
Outstanding Drama Series
L.A. Law. NBC.
Outstanding Comedy Series
Murphy Brown. CBS.

1990–91
Outstanding Drama Series
L.A. Law. NBC.
Outstanding Comedy Series
Cheers. NBC.

1991–92
Outstanding Drama Series
Northern Exposure. CBS.
Outstanding Comedy Series
Murphy Brown. CBS.

1992–93
Outstanding Drama Series
Picket Fences. CBS.
Outstanding Comedy Series
Seinfeld. NBC.

1993–94
Outstanding Drama Series
Picket Fences. CBS.
Outstanding Comedy Series
Frasier. NBC.

1994–95
Outstanding Drama Series
NYPD Blue. ABC.
Outstanding Comedy Series
Frasier. NBC.

1995–96
Outstanding Drama Series
E.R. NBC.
Outstanding Comedy Series
Frasier. NBC.

1996–97
Outstanding Drama Series
Law and Order. NBC.
Outstanding Comedy Series
Frasier. NBC.

Source: Academy of Television Art and Sciences

Grammy Award Winners

Year	Record of the year	Album of the year	Song of the year
1958	*Nel Blu Dipinto Di Blu (Volare)* Domenico Modugno	*The Music from Peter Gunn* Henry Mancini	*Nel Blu Dipinto Di Blu (Volare)* Domenico Modugno
1959	*Mack the Knife* Bobby Darin	*Come Dance with Me* Frank Sinatra	*The Battle of New Orleans* Composer: Jimmy Driftwood
1960	*Theme from A Summer Place* Percy Faith	*Button Down Mind* Bob Newhart	*Theme from Exodus* Composer: Ernest Gold
1961	*Moon River* Henry Mancini	*Judy at Carnegie Hall* Judy Garland	*Moon River* Comps: Henry Mancini and Johnny Mercer
1962	*I Left My Heart in San Francisco* Tony Bennett	*The First Family* Vaughn Meader	*What Kind of Fool Am I* Comps: Leslie Bricusse and Anthony Newley
1963	*The Days of Wine and Roses* Henry Mancini	*The Barbra Streisand Album* Barbra Streisand	*The Days of Wine and Roses* Comps: Henry Mancini and Johnny Mercer
1964	*The Girl from Ipanema* Stan Getz, Astrud Gilberto	*Getz/Gilberto* Stan Getz, Joao Gilberto	*Hello, Dolly!* Composer: Jerry Herman
1965	*A Taste of Honey* Herb Albert & the Tijuana Brass	*September of My Years* Frank Sinatra	*The Shadow of Your Smile (Love Theme from The Sandpiper)* Comps: Paul Francis Webster and Johnny Mandel
1966	*Strangers in the Night* Frank Sinatra	*Sinatra: a Man & His Music* Frank Sinatra	*Michelle* Songwriters: John Lennon and Paul McCartney
1967	*Up, Up and Away* 5th Dimension	*Sgt. Pepper's Lonely Hearts Club Band* The Beatles	*Up, Up and Away* Songwriter: Jimmy L. Webb
1968	*Mrs. Robinson* Simon & Garfunkel	*By the Time I Get to Phoenix* Glen Campbell	*Little Green Apples* Songwriter: Bobby Russell
1969	*Aquarius/Let the Sunshine In* 5th Dimension	*Blood, Sweat & Tears* Blood, Sweat & Tears	*Games People Play* Songwriter: Joe South
1970	*Bridge Over Troubled Water* Simon & Garfunkel	*Bridge Over Troubled Water* Simon & Garfunkel	*Bridge Over Troubled Water* Songwriter: Paul Simon
1971	*It's Too Late* Carole King	*Tapestry* Carole King	*You've Got a Friend* Songwriter: Carole King
1972	*The First TIme Ever I Saw Your Face* Roberta Flack	*The Concert for Bangladesh* Various artists	*The First TIme Ever I Saw Your Face* Songwriter: Ewan MacColl
1973	*Killing Me Softly with His Song* Roberta Flack	*Innervisions* Stevie Wonder	*Killing Me Softly with His Song* Songwriters: Norman Gimbel and Charles Fox

Year	Record of the year	Album of the year	Song of the year
1974	*I Honestly Love You* Olivia Newton-John	*Fulfillingness' First Finale* Stevie Wonder	*The Way We Were* Songwriters: Marylyn and Alan Bergman, Marvin Hamlisch
1975	*Love Will Keep Us Together* Captain & Tennille	*Still Crazy After All* *These Years* Paul Simon	*Send in the Clowns* Songwriter: Stephen Sondheim
1976	*This Masquerade* George Benson	*Songs in the Key of Life* Stevie Wonder	*I Write the Songs* Songwriter: Bruce Johnston
1977	*Hotel California* Eagles	*Rumours* Fleetwood Mac	*Love Theme from* *A Star Is Born (Evergreen)** Songwriters: Barbra Streisand and Paul Williams *You Light Up My Life** Songwriter: Joe Brooks
1978	*Just the Way You Are* Billy Joel	*Saturday Night Fever* Various artists	*Just the Way You Are* Songwriter: Billy Joel
1979	*What a Fool Believes* The Doobie Brothers	*52nd Street* Billy Joel	*What a Fool Believes* Songwriters: Kenny Loggins and Michael McDonald
1980	*Sailing* Christopher Cross	*Christopher Cross* Christopher Cross	*Sailing* Songwriter: Christopher Cross
1981	*Bette Davis Eyes* Kim Carnes	*Double Fantasy* John Lennon/Yoko Ono	*Bette Davis Eyes* Songwriters: Donna Weiss and Jackie DeShannon
1982	*Rosanna* Toto	*Toto IV* Toto	*Always on My Mind* Songwriters: Johnny Christopher, Mark James, and Wayne Carson
1983	*Beat It* Michael Jackson	*Thriller* Michael Jackson	*Every Breath You Take* Songwriter: Sting
1984	*What's Love Got to Do with It* Tina Turner	*Can't Slow Down* Lionel Richie	*What's Love Got to Do with It* Songwriters: Graham Lyle and Terry Britten
1985	*We Are the World* USA for Africa	*No Jacket Required* Phil Collins	*We Are the World* Songwriters: Michael Jackson and Lionel Richie
1986	*Higher Love* Steve Winwood	*Graceland* Paul Simon	*That's What Friends Are For* Songwriters: Burt Bacharach and Carole Bayer Sager
1987	*Graceland* Paul Simon	*Joshua Tree* U2	*Somewhere Out There* Songwriters: James Horner, Barry Mann, Cynthia Weil

*Tie

Year	Record of the year	Album of the year	Song of the year
1988	*Don't Worry Be Happy* Bobby McFerrin	*Faith* George Michael	*Don't Worry Be Happy* Songwriter: Bobby McFerrin
1989	*Wind Beneath My Wings* Bette Midler	*Nick of Time* Bonnie Raitt	*Wind Beneath My Wings* Songwriters: Larry Henley and Jeff Silbar
1990	*Another Day in Paradise* Phil Collins	*Back on the Block* Quincy Jones	*From a Distance* Songwriter: Julie Gold
1991	*Unforgettable* Natalie Cole (with Nat King Cole)	*Unforgettable* Natalie Cole	*Unforgettable* Songwriter: Irving Gordon
1992	*Tears in Heaven* Eric Clapton	*Unplugged* Eric Clapton	*Tears in Heaven* Songwriters: Eric Clapton and Will Jennings
1993	*I Will Always Love You* Whitney Houston	*The Bodyguard -* *Original Soundtrack Album* Various artists	*A Whole New World (Aladdin's Theme)* Songwriters: Alan Menken and Tim Rice
1994	*All I Wanna Do* Sheryl Crow	*MTV Unplugged:* *Tony Bennett* Tony Bennett	*Streets of Philadelphia* Songwriter: Bruce Springsteen
1995	*Kiss from a Rose* Seal	*Jagged Little Pill* Alanis Morissette	*Kiss from a Rose* Songwriter: Seal
1996	*Change the World* Eric Clapton	*Falling Into You* Celine Dion	*Change the World* Songwriters: Gordon Kennedy, Wayne Kirkpatrick, and Tommy Sims

Source: National Academy of Recording Arts and Sciences

Tony Award Winners

Year	Best Play	Best Musical
1949	Death of a Salesman	Kiss Me Kate
1950	The Cocktail Party	South Pacific
1951	The Rose Tattoo	Guys and Dolls
1952	The Fourposter	The King & I
1953	The Crucible	Wonderful Town
1954	The Teahouse of the August Moon	Kismet
1955	The Desperate Hours	The Pajama Game
1956	The Diary of Ann Frank	Damn Yankees
1957	Long Day's Journey Into Night	My Fair Lady
1958	Sunrise at Campobello	The Music Man
1959	J.B.	Redhead
1960	The Miracle Worker	The Sound of Music; Fiorello!
1961	Becket	Bye, Bye Birdie
1962	A Man for All Seasons	How to Succeed in Business Without Really Trying
1963	Who's Afraid of Virginia Woolf?	A Funny Thing Happened on the Way to the Forum
1964	Luther	Hello, Dolly!
1965	The Subject Was Roses	Fiddler on the Roof
1966	Marat/Sade	Man of La Mancha
1967	The Homecoming	Cabaret
1968	Rosencrantz and Guildenstern Are Dead	Hallelujah, Baby!
1969	The Great White Hope	1776
1970	Borstal Boy	Applause
1971	Sleuth	Company
1972	Sticks and Bones	Two Gentlemen of Verona
1973	That Championship Season	A Little Night Music
1974	The River Niger	Raisin
1975	Equus	The Wiz
1976	Travesties	A Chorus Line
1977	The Shadow Box	Annie
1978	Da	Ain't Misbehavin'
1979	The Elephant Man	Sweeney Todd
1980	Children of a Lesser God	Evita
1981	Amadeus	42nd Street
1982	The Life and Adventures of Nicholas Nickleby	Nine
1983	Torch Song Trilogy	Cats
1984	The Real Thing	La Cage aux Folles
1985	Biloxi Blues	Big River
1986	I'm Not Rappaport	The Mystery of Edwin Drood
1987	Fences	Les Miserables
1988	M. Butterfly	The Phantom of the Opera
1989	The Heidi Chronicles	Jerome Robbins' Broadway
1990	The Grapes of Wrath	City of Angels
1991	Lost in Yonkers	The Will Rogers Follies
1992	Dancing at Lughnasa	Crazy for You
1993	Angels in America: Millennium Approaches	Kiss of the Spider Woman
1994	Angels in America: Perestroika	Passion
1995	Love! Valour! Compassion!	Sunset Boulevard
1996	Master Class	Rent
1997	The Last Night of Ballyhoo	Titanic

Sources: The League of American Theatres and Producers and the American Theatre Wing

1997 National Magazine Awards

(Sponsored by the American Society of Magazine Editors and administered by the Graduate School of Journalism, Columbia University)

GENERAL EXCELLENCE
(over 1,000,000 circulation)
Vanity Fair

GENERAL EXCELLENCE
(400,000 to 1,000,000 circulation)
Outside

GENERAL EXCELLENCE
(100,000 to 400,000 circulation)
Wired

GENERAL EXCELLENCE
(under 100,000 circulation)
I.D. Magazine

REPORTING
Outside

PUBLIC INTEREST
Fortune

SPECIAL INTERESTS
Smithsonian

FEATURE WRITING
Sports Illustrated

PERSONAL SERVICE
Glamour

SPECIAL AWARD FOR GENERAL EXCELLENCE IN NEW MEDIA
Money

FICTION
The New Yorker

DESIGN
I.D. Magazine

PHOTOGRAPHY
National Geographic

ESSAYS & CRITICISM
The New Yorker

SINGLE-TOPIC ISSUE
Scientific American

National Book Award Winners

Year	Fiction	Nonfiction
1984	Ellen Gilchrist, *Victory Over Japan: A Book of Stories*	Robert V. Remini, *Andrew Jackson & the Course of American Democracy, 1833–1845*
1985	Don DeLillo, *White Noise*	J. Anthony Lukas, *Common Ground: A Turbulent Decade in the Lives of Three American Families*
1986	E.L. Doctorow, *World's Fair*	Barry Lopez, *Arctic Dreams*
1987	Larry Heinemann, *Paco's Story*	Richard Rhodes, *The Making of the Atom Bomb*
1988	Pete Dexter, *Paris Trout*	Neil Sheehan, *A Bright Shining Lie: John Paul Vann and America in Vietnam*
1989	John Casey, *Spartina*	Thomas L. Friedman, *From Beruit to Jerusalem*
1990	Charles Johnson, *Middle Passage*	Ron Chernow, *The House of Morgan: An American Banking Dynasty and the Rise of Modern Finance*

Year	Fiction	Nonfiction	Poetry
1991	Norman Rush, *Mating*	Orlando Patterson, *Freedom*	Philip Levin, *What Work Is*
1992	Cormac McCarthy, *All the Pretty Horses*	Paul Monette, *Becoming a Man: Half a Life Story*	Mary Oliver, *New & Selected Poems*
1993	E. Annie Proulx, *The Shipping News*	Gore Vidal, *United States: Essays 1952–1992*	A.R. Ammons, *Garbage*
1994	William Gaddis, *A Frolic of His Own*	Sherwin B. Nuland, *How We Die: Reflections on Life's Final Chapter*	James Tate, *A Worshipful Company of Fletchers*
1995	Philip Roth, *Sabbath's Theater*	Tina Rosenberg, *The Haunted Land: Facing Europe's Ghosts After Communism*	Stanley Kunitz, *Passing Through: The Later Poems, New & Selected*
1996	Andrea Barrett, *Ship Fever and Other Stories*	James Carroll, *An American Requiem: God, My Father, and the War that Came Between Us*	Hayden Carruth, *Scrambled Eggs and Whiskey, Poems 1991–1995*

Source: National Book Foundation

The National Book Critics Circle Awards

1976
FICTION: John Gardner, *October Light*
GENERAL NONFICTION: Maxine Hong Kingston, *The Woman Warrior: Memoirs of a Girlhood Among Ghosts*
POETRY: Elizabeth Bishop, *Geography III*
CRITICISM: Bruno Bettelheim, *The Uses of Enchantment: The Meaning and Importance of Fairy Tales*

1977
FICTION: Toni Morrison, *Song of Solomon*
GENERAL NONFICTION: Walter Jackson Bate, *Samuel Johnson*
POETRY: Robert Lowell, *Day by Day*
CRITICISM: Susan Sontag, *On Photography*

1978
FICTION: John Cheever, *The Stories of John Cheever*
GENERAL NONFICTION: Maureen Howard, *Facts of Life*
POETRY: (Edited by Peter Davison), *Hello, Darkness: The Collected Poems of L.E. Sissman*
CRITICISM: Meyer Schapiro, *Modern Art: 19th & 20th Centuries, Selected Papers*

1979
FICTION: Thomas Flanagan, *The Year of the French*
GENERAL NONFICTION: Telford Taylor, *Munich: The Price of Peace*
POETRY: Philip Levine, *Ashes* and *7 Years from Somewhere*
CRITICISM: Elaine Pagels, *The Gnostic Gospels*
IVAN SANDROF/BOARD AWARD: Flannery O'Connor

1980
FICTION: Shirley Hazzard, *The Transit of Venus*
GENERAL NONFICTION: Ronald Steel, *Walter Lippmann and the American Century*
POETRY: Frederick Seidel, *Sunrise*
CRITICISM: Helen Vendler, *Part of Nature, Part of Us: Modern American Poets*

1981
FICTION: John Updike, *Rabbit is Rich*
GENERAL NONFICTION: Stephen Jay Gould, *The Mismeasure of Man*
POETRY: A.R. Ammons, *A Coast of Trees*
CRITICISM: Virgil Thomson, *A Virgil Thomson Reader*

1982
FICTION: Stanley Elkin, *George Mills*
GENERAL NONFICTION: Robert A. Caro, *The Path of Power: The Years of Lyndon Johnson*
POETRY: Katha Pollitt, *Antarctic Traveler*
CRITICISM: Gore Vidal, *The Second American Revolution and Other Essays, 1976–82*
IVAN SANDROF/BOARD AWARD: Leslie A. Marchand

1983
FICTION: William Kennedy, *Ironweed*
GENERAL NONFICTION: Seymour M. Hersh, *The Price of Power: Kissinger in the Nixon White House*
BIOGRAPHY/AUTOBIOGRAPHY: Joyce Johnson, *Minor Characters*
POETRY: James Merrill, *The Changing Light at Sandover*

CRITICISM: John Updike, *Hugging the Shore: Essays and Criticism*

1984

FICTION: Louise Erdrich, *Love Medicine*
GENERAL NONFICTION: Freeman Dyson, *Weapons and Hope*
BIOGRAPHY/AUTOBIOGRAPHY: Joseph Frank, *Dostoevsky: The Years of Ordeal, 1850–1859*
POETRY: Sharon Olds, *The Dead and the Living*
CRITICISM: Robert Hass, *Twentieth Century Pleasures: Prose on Poetry*
IVAN SANDROF/BOARD AWARD: The Library of America

1985

FICTION: Anne Tyler, *The Accidental Tourist*
GENERAL NONFICTION: J. Anthony Lukas, *Common Ground: A Turbulent Decade in the Lives of Three American Families*
BIOGRAPHY/AUTOBIOGRAPHY: Leon Edel, *Henry James: A Life*
POETRY: Louise Gluck, *The Triumph of Achilles*
CRITICISM: William H. Gass, *Habitations of the Word: Essays*

1986

FICTION: Reynolds Price, *Kate Vaiden*
GENERAL NONFICTION: John W. Dower, *War Without Mercy: Race and Power in the Pacific War*
BIOGRAPHY/AUTOBIOGRAPHY: Theodore Rosengarten, *Tombee: Portrait of a Cotton Planter*
POETRY: Edward Hirsch, *Wild Gratitude*
CRITICISM: Joseph Brodsky, *Less Than One: Selected Essays*

1987

FICTION: Philip Roth, *The Counterlife*
GENERAL NONFICTION: Richard Rhodes, *The Making of the Atomic Bomb*
BIOGRAPHY/AUTOBIOGRAPHY: Donald R. Howard, *Chaucer: His Life, His Works, His World*
POETRY: C.K. Williams, *Flesh and Blood*
CRITICISM: Edwin Denby, (Edited by Robert Cornfield and William MacKay), *Dance Writings*
IVAN SANDROF/BOARD AWARD: Robert Giroux

1988

FICTION: Bharati Mukherjee, *The Middleman and Other Stories*
GENERAL NONFICTION: Taylor Branch, *Parting the Waters: America in the King Years, 1954–63*
BIOGRAPHY/AUTOBIOGRAPHY: Richard Ellman, *Oscar Wilde*
POETRY: Donald Hall, *The One Day*
CRITICISM: Clifford Geertz, *Works and Lives: The Anthropologist as Author*

1989

FICTION: E. L. Doctorow, *Billy Bathgate*
GENERAL NONFICTION: Michael Dorris, *The Broken Cord*
BIOGRAPHY/AUTOBIOGRAPHY: Geoffrey C. Ward, *A First-Class Temperament: The Emergence of Franklin Roosevelt*
POETRY: Rodney Jones, *Transparent Gestures*
CRITICISM: John Clive, *Not by Fact Alone: Essays on the Writing and Reading of History*
IVAN SANDROF/BOARD AWARD: James Laughlin

1990

FICTION: John Updike, *Rabbit at Rest*
GENERAL NONFICTION: Shelby Steele, *The Content of Our Character: A New Vision of Race in America*
BIOGRAPHY/AUTOBIOGRAPHY: Robert A. Caro, *Means of Ascent: The Years of Lyndon Johnson, Vol. II*
POETRY: Amy Gerstler, *Bitter Angel*
CRITICISM: Arthur C. Danto, *Encounters and Reflections: Art in the Historical Present*
IVAN SANDROF/BOARD AWARD: Donald Keene

1991

FICTION: Jane Smiley, *A Thousand Acres*
GENERAL NONFICTION: Susan Faludi, *Backlash: The Undeclared War Against American Women*
BIOGRAPHY/AUTOBIOGRAPHY: Philip Roth, *Patrimony: A True Story*
POETRY: Albert Goldbarth, *Heaven and Earth: A Cosmology*
CRITICISM: Lawrence L. Langer, *Holocaust Testimonies: The Ruins of Memory*
NONA BALAKIAN EXCELLENCE IN REVIEWING AWARD: George Scialabba

1992

FICTION: Cormac McCarthy, *All the Pretty Horses*
GENERAL NONFICTION: Norman Maclean, *Young Men and Fire*
BIOGRAPHY/AUTOBIOGRAPHY: Carol Brightman, *Writing Dangerously: Mary McCarthy and Her World*
POETRY: Hayden Carruth, *Collected Shorter Poems 1946–1991*
CRITICISM: Garry Wills, *Lincoln at Gettysburg: The Words That Remade America*
IVAN SANDROF/BOARD AWARD: Gregory Rabassa
NONA BALAKIAN EXCELLENCE IN REVIEWING AWARD: Elizabeth Ward

1993

FICTION: Ernest J. Gaines, *A Lesson Before Dying*
GENERAL NONFICTION: Alan Lomax, *The Land Where the Blues Began*
BIOGRAPHY/AUTOBIOGRAPHY: Edmund White, *Genet*
POETRY: Mark Doty, *My Alexandria*
CRITICISM: John Dizikes, *Opera in America: A Cultural History*
NONA BALAKIAN EXCELLENCE IN REVIEWING AWARD: Brigitte Frase

1994

FICTION: Carol Shields, *The Stone Diaries*
GENERAL NONFICTION: Lynn H. Nicholas, *The Rape of*

Europa: The Fate of Europe's Treasures in the Third Reich and the Second World War

BIOGRAPHY/AUTOBIOGRAPHY: Mikal Gilmore, *Shot in the Heart*

POETRY: Mark Rudman, *Rider*

CRITICISM: Gerald Early, *The Culture of Bruising: Essays on Prizefighting, Literature and Modern American Culture*

NONA BALAKIAN EXCELLENCE IN REVIEWING AWARD: JoAnn C. Gutin, Berkeley, CA

IVAN SANDROF AWARD FOR LIFETIME ACHIEVEMENT IN PUBLISHING: William Maxwell

1995

FICTION: Stanley Elkin, *Mrs. Ted Bliss*

GENERAL NONFICTION: Jonathan Harr, *A Civil Action*

BIOGRAPHY/AUTOBIOGRAPHY: Robert Polito, *Savage Art: A Biography of Jim Thompson*

POETRY: William Matthews, *Time & Money*

CRITICISM: Robert Darnton, *The Forbidden Bestsellers of Pre-Revolutionary France*

1996

FICTION: Gina Berriault, *Women in Their Beds*

GENERAL NONFICTION: Jonathan Raban, *Bad Land*

BIOGRAPHY/AUTOBIOGRAPHY: Frank McCourt, *Angela's Ashes*

POETRY: Robert Hass, *Sun Under Wood*

CRITICISM: William Gass, *Finding a Form*

Source: The National Book Critics Circle Journal

Booker Prize Winners

1969: P.H. Newby, *Something to Answer For*
1970: Bernice Rubens, *The Elected Member*
1971: V.S. Naipaul, *In a Free State*
1972: John Berger, *G*
1973: J.G. Farrell, *The Seige of Krishnapur*
1974: *Nadine Gordimer, *The Conservationist*
      Stanley Middleton, *Holiday*
1975: Ruth Prawer Jhabvala, *Heat and Dust*
1976: David Storey, *Saville*
1977: Paul Scott, *Staying On*
1978: Irish Murdoch, *The Sea, The Sea*
1979: Penelope Fitzgerald, *Offshore*
1980: William Golding, *Rites of Passage*
1981: Salman Rushdie, *Midnight's Children*
1982: Thomas Keneally, *Schindler's Ark*
1983: J.M. Coetzee, *Life & Times of Michael K*

1984: Anita Brookner, *Hotel du Lac*
1985: Keri Hulme, *The Bone People*
1986: Kingsley Amis, *The Old Devils*
1987: Penelope Lively, *Moon Tiger*
1988: Peter Carey, *Oscar and Lucinda*
1989: Kazuo Ishiguro, *The Remains of the Day*
1990: A.S. Byatt, *Possession*
1991: Ben Okri, *The Famished Road*
1992:* Michael Ondaatje, *The English Patient*
      Barry Unsworth, *Sacred Hunger*
1993: Roddy Doyle, *Paddy Clarke Ha Ha Ha*
1994: James Kelman, *How Late it Was, How Late*
1995: Pat Barker, *The Ghost Road*
1996: Graham Swift, *The Last Orders*

*Joint winners.

10

SPORTS

WHEN LOS ANGELES DODGERS PRESIDENT *Peter O'Malley announced in early 1997 that he was selling the baseball team his father had moved to the West Coast 40 years earlier, he insisted on making a point: Owning a professional sports franchise just isn't a viable family business anymore.*

Mr. O'Malley's resigned declaration said a lot about the changing sports landscape in America. The cozy if omnipotent paternalism of dynastic sports families such as the O'Malleys, Griffiths and Yawkeys in baseball, or the Maras, Irsays and Halases in football seems quaintly outdated. In its place is a tacit understanding that the high-stakes business of professional sports is more realistically left to tycoons who have made their money elsewhere or, increasingly these days, corporations able to "leverage" team ownership with network-television contracts and sponsorship deals.

In turn-of-the-century America, sports are no longer merely a form of entertainment but a business worthy of public scrutiny. Today's fans are as familiar with salary caps, arbitration hearings, franchise relocations and stadium referendums as they are with touchdowns, home runs, slam dunks and slap shots.

Pick a day, any day, and the volume of news about the business side of sports is overwhelming. Here, for instance, is just a small sample of what was happening on May 19, 1997, not a special day for any reason in the sports world: American Express signed golfing phenom Tiger Woods to a five-year promotional contract worth well over $20 million. The CART auto-racing circuit said it was producing its first TV advertisements. National Football League owners meeting in San Diego examined a proposal to bring a team back to the vacant Los Angeles market. Bankers for the Formula One racing circuit planned an initial public stock offering valued at up to $3.2 billion. Anheuser-Busch announced a sponsorship deal with the San Jose Sharks of the National Hockey League. A proposal for a new baseball stadium in Minneapolis suffered a setback, while the cost of a new football stadium in Cleveland was raised to $247 million. The Interpublic Group acquired Advantage International and API Group, two sports marketing and management companies with billings of around $550 million.

And on and on and on. How big has the business of sports become? Those news items and others were chronicled by a newsletter called, simply enough, *The Sports Business Daily* that is faxed or e-mailed to hundreds of journalists and executives. The statistically obsessive Society for American Baseball Research not long ago formed a business of baseball committee. Newspapers and magazines continued to add reporters who cover nothing but the sports business; even *The Wall Street Journal*, in 1995, began a weekly sports page.

The coverage of sports business news wouldn't be justifiable if the content weren't compelling, and in 1997, the numbers kept escalating and stakes kept rising for leagues, players, companies, and fans. And if sports are a temple of the familiar for fans, nothing has become more familiar than what athletes make. Newspapers routinely publish the salaries of every player in the four big sports leagues. And the latest signing is fodder for hours of griping on sports talk radio and teeth-gnashing by cranky columnists; the Chicago White Sox's decision to pay Albert Belle $11 million a year for five years, combining what was then baseball's biggest salary with one of its most disliked superstars, was a

cause celebre for weeks. The question is always the same: Are athletes worth the money?

It is, of course, an absurd question. Athletes, like movie stars, truck drivers, teachers or accountants, are worth what someone is willing to pay them for their services. Nonetheless, tongue firmly planted in cheek, *The Wall Street Journal* calculated the "worth" of National Basketball Association players through a statistical combination of salary and performance. While the grid had its flaws—Michael Jordan, with a $30.14 million salary for the 1996–1997 season, tops in pro sports, naturally delivered the least statistical bang for the buck—it was surprisingly revealing. Led by the San Antonio Spurs' Dominique Wilkins, who earned minimum salary, a handful of lower-paid players having productive seasons topped the ratings index. But the true value in the NBA came in the middle of the earnings pack; players such as the Seattle SuperSonics' Shawn Kemp and the Charlotte Hornets' Anthony Mason looked like bargains at $3.3 million and $2.8 million, respectively.

After a dramatic 20-year run-up in salaries, fans not only are accustomed to money talk but are expert at it. They know that, in the NBA, trades are contingent on salaries matching up so that each participating team remains within the constraints of the league's "salary cap," or payroll maximum. In the NFL, fans understand that ridiculous-sounding upfront bonuses are used to help skirt that sport's salary cap, and that clubs employ "capologists," whose job is to manage complicated payroll rules. In baseball, the public knows that teams are broken down into small, medium and large markets and spend accordingly, and that front offices focus on when players are due for salary arbitration or free agency in planning rosters.

To wit: Few blinked when the Atlanta Braves swapped star outfielders David Justice and Marquis Grissom for star outfielder Kenny Lofton of the Cleveland Indians during 1997 spring training. On the surface, it was a rare trade involving great players—rare because salaries so often are impediments to trades these days. But this was a business deal plain and simple: Mr. Lofton was due to become a free agent at the end of the season and the Indians believed he would leave town, so they wanted to get something in return. Atlanta, which reduced its salary commitments by $15.9 million via the trade, wanted to clear space to sign one or both of its ace pitchers, Greg Maddux and Tom Glavine. In the press, the deal was reported for what it was: a money transaction. (Cleveland soon after signed Messrs. Justice and Grissom to long-term contracts worth $53 million. Atlanta committed $34 million to Mr. Glavine.)

While nothing appeared on the horizon to stem salary inflation—Mr. Belle's pay was soon surpassed by an $11.45-million-a-year contract extension for San Francisco Giants outfielder Barry Bonds—mechanisms introduced by leagues and their unions began reshuffling the deck.

The NBA's new collective-bargaining agreement, with a more stringent salary cap, saw the creation of a class of megastars such as Shaquille O'Neal, Alonzo Mourning, and Juwan Howard, who signed seven-year deals worth more than $100 million apiece. But there was a trickle-down effect. Numerous mid-level veterans found teams were unwilling to offer even the average NBA pay of $2.3 million. Some took drastic cuts, like Phoenix guard Rex Chapman, who went from $2 million to the league minimum of $247,500; others, like 11-year NBA veteran Spud Webb, couldn't find a job at all.

It was the same story in baseball: Top salaries soared, pulling total salary spending by the 30 teams up 18% in 1997 to $1.06 billion and the league average to $1.4 million. But the median salary slipped to under $300,000 from $450,000 in 1994.

In the NFL, teams traded away high draft picks in exchange for lower—and cheaper—ones. And coaches jumped on the salary express with blockbuster deals led by Rick Pitino's reported $7-million-a-year contract to coach and run the Boston Celtics.

Such salary inflation has made television the puppet-master of pro sports. All eyes were on the leagues in 1997 as it came time to renegotiate TV contracts for football, basketball and golf. The NFL was likely to get a four-year deal worth more than $6 billion, up from the current $4.4 billion package. The NBA expected to perhaps double its $1.1 billion, four-year network and cable contract that expires in 1998. Golf capitalized on the public's fascination with Tiger Woods's startling debut. CBS's broadcast of the final day of Mr. Woods's win at the Masters in Augusta, Ga., for instance, drew 44 million viewers, a 53% increase over a year earlier. The aftermath: The Professional Golfers Association Tour sold domestic TV rights starting in 1999 for what could total close to $200 million a year by 2002, double the current level.

The NHL was also thinking TV, though its network contract with Fox and ESPN does not expire until 1999. Unimpressive ratings have fueled concern over whether the NHL will be able to attract more TV money than the current $43 million-a-year deal, and it needs more money to sustain continuing growth that has seen the league add new Sun Belt markets, boost salaries and expand its marketing and promotion. Only Major League Baseball could relax a bit; its five-year contract with Fox, ESPN, and NBC also doesn't expire until 1999, but it's worth a total of $1.7 billion.

While the major sports can always bank on their lush television deals and loyal fans to pay rising player salaries, the economic perils of the salary boom gave other leagues pause. In fact, a group of smaller sports leagues had to adapt to survive in the competitive sports environment. Major League Soccer led a

parade of new leagues built from the inside out: business plan first, sports plan second. MLS, which played its second season in 1997, was structured specifically to avoid the chronic pitfalls of the major sports leagues, namely lofty player expenses, musical franchises and, most important, a wide gulf between revenue-rich and revenue-challenged teams. To do so, the soccer league created a "single-entity" organization, meaning its 10 teams are owned collectively by a group of investors—including three billionaires. The investors operate the individual clubs. Players are signed to league contracts to avoid frantic bidding wars for international talent, and player salaries are kept low. (Top stars supplemented their income with league-arranged marketing deals.) Just to get on national television, the league charged ABC and ESPN nothing for broadcast rights. Attendance targets were modest. Sponsorships were a bargain. MLS expected to lose money for three years. But in seeking to control its destiny, the league ran into a problem: an antitrust lawsuit filed by players claiming the structure unfairly restricted salaries.

Two women's basketball leagues adopted the same central-ownership philosophy. The underdog was the American Basketball League, which attracted more than half of the 1996 U.S. Olympic hoopsters. Its competition: the behemoth NBA, which unveiled the Women's National Basketball Association, with play beginning in June 1997. The NBA's clout— and about $50 million in seed money—helped attract big sponsors. NBC, ESPN and Lifetime Television agreed to telecast games, and, as with MLS, the networks didn't pay a rights fee but agreed to share advertising revenue. The WNBA kept salaries relatively low—a $37,500 average— but the ABL attracted several top Americans by paying six figures.

Television and salaries, television and influence, television and growth. In such an environment, only the deepest pockets stand a chance of surviving. In that light, Mr. O'Malley's decision to sell the Dodgers to media baron Rupert Murdoch's News Corp. for a sports-industry record $350 million (the price including Dodger Stadium and training camps in Florida and the Dominican Republic) made eminent sense. After all, Walt Disney Co. had ABC and ESPN, baseball's Anaheim Angels, and hockey's Anaheim Mighty Ducks. Time Warner had Turner Broadcasting, Time magazine, Warner Bros. studios, baseball's Atlanta Braves and basketball's Atlanta Hawks. Mr. Murdoch *needed* the Dodgers: as programming for Fox's growing cable efforts, as real estate on which to consider building a new football stadium for an NFL team, as a way to leverage Fox's national football and baseball broadcast contracts, as a symbol of his status as a player on par with his entertainment-industry rivals.

Mr. O'Malley understood that he was better off on the sidelines because the playing field wasn't level anymore. Whether the sports themselves are better off in this big-money age is an open question. But the turnstiles keep spinning. Like it or not, fans finally seem to understand that the sports business is all business.

Stefan Fatsis,
Wall Street Journal staff reporter
who writes on the business of sports

Take Me Out to the Ball Game

The cost of attending professional sporting events has been outpacing the national inflation rate in recent years.

Professional sports league average ticket prices and Fan Cost Index*

MLB Season	Average ticket price	Ticket % change	FCI	FCI % change
1991	$ 8.64	–	$ 77.40	–
1992	9.30	7.6%	86.24	11.4%
1993	9.60	3.2	90.84	5.3
1994	10.45	8.9	95.80	5.5
1995	10.55	1.0	96.83	1.1
1996	11.19	6.1	102.58	5.9
1997	11.98	7.1	105.63	3.0

NFL Season	Average ticket price	Ticket % change	FCI	FCI % change
1991	$25.21	–	$151.55	–
1992	27.19	7.8%	163.19	7.6%
1993	28.68	5.5	173.33	6.2
1994	30.56	6.6	182.72	5.4
1995	33.52	9.7	199.09	9.0
1996	35.74	6.6	208.45	4.7
NHL Season‡	**Average ticket price**	**Ticket % change**	**FCI**	**FCI % change**
1994-95	$32.75	–	$193.10	–
1995-96	34.75	6.1%	203.46	5.4%
1996-97	38.16	9.8	219.74	8.0
NBA Season	**Average ticket price**	**Ticket % change**	**FCI**	**FCI % change**
1991-92	$23.24	–	$144.10	–
1992-93	25.16	8.3%	158.17	9.8%
1993-94	27.12	7.8	168.68	6.6
1994-95	28.63	5.6	177.12	5.0
1995-96	31.56	10.2	191.31	8.0
1996-97	34.08	8.0	203.38	6.3

*The Fan Cost Index (FCI) includes the cost of four average-price tickets, four small soft drinks, two small beers, four hot dogs, parking for one car, two game programs and two souvenir caps.
‡No NHL surveys were conducted prior to 1994-95.
Source: Team Marketing Report, Chicago

TOP SPORTS PERSONALITIES OF 1997

Paul Allen: Stadium lust continued to infect owners of professional sports teams, and perhaps no one had a worse case than Paul Allen, the billionaire co-founder of Microsoft. In 1996, the Seattle Seahawks came this close to bolting the rainy Pacific Northwest for sunny Southern California. A search for a new owner eventually led to Mr. Allen, who agreed to buy the team, but with one condition: A new stadium be built to get the Seahawks out of the Kingdome, where pieces of ceiling tile have been known to come plummeting out of the sky. The state legislature passed a $425 million stadium and exhibition-hall measure, funded by various public monies and $100 million from Mr. Allen. From there, the measure went to a public vote—paid for by Mr. Allen. All told, he spent more than $12 million on the referendum, including about $2 million to get it on the ballot, $4 million to finance the election itself and another $6 million or so campaigning to get the measure passed. It did: 51% to 49%.

The 72,000-seat, open-air facility is expected to be ready by 2002. With the stadium in hand, Mr. Allen then made good on his promise to buy the team, for around $200 million. In one of his first acts as owner, he slashed the ticket price of 7,000 seats at the Kingdome for the 1997 season to $10, lowest in the National Football League.

Brett Favre: Talk about having a lot to prove. When Brett Favre of the Green Bay Packers started the 1996 season, with an eye toward the Super Bowl in January 1997, the then 26-year-old Mississippi native was the National Football League's reigning Most Valuable Player (can he do it again?) and he was the quarterback of a team that had lost to eventual Super Bowl champion Dallas Cowboys in the National Conference title game (can he win the Big One?). The answers, as provided by Mr. Favre, were a resounding Yes and Yes. In the regular season he completed 325 of 543 passes (59.9%) for 3,899 yards, with an NFC record 39 touchdowns against just 13 interceptions. In doing so he became just the second player to win back-to-back MVP titles. Then in the playoffs he led the Pack to a 4–0 record and a 35–21 Super Bowl win over the New England Patriots, passing for 246 yards and two touchdowns, plus a third on a run. But that was just the half of it, or maybe even less. When Mr. Favre started the '96 season, he was fresh off a 46-day stay in a rehab center after admitting he was addicted to a painkiller—used to ease the rigors of 16 Sundays as an NFL quarterback.

Martina Hingis: How quickly we forget. Seems as if it was only a year ago we were wringing our hands, fretting over the fact that for too many too-young girls, tennis had become a killing field. Then in 1997, along came 16-year-old Martina Hingis, who in the space of nine months won the Australian Open to become the youngest Grand Slam winner ever, won a Steffi Graf-free Wimbledon to become the youngest All-England women's winner since 1887, and then took a surging 17-year-old Venus Williams to school, 6–0, 6–4, in winning the U.S. Open title in September. In between, she ran her record to an astounding 62–2, became the youngest ever top-ranked women's tennis player and, refreshingly, acted like a teenager when not holding a tennis racket. Her mother is her coach (never a good sign), but she's allowed to go Rollerblading and horseback riding (and tear her anterior cruciate ligament in the process, a good sign in a round about way). So keep your fingers crossed. It appears Ms. Hingis has the head to go with her game. Said she after dispatching Jana Novotna, 2–6, 6–3, 6–3, to win Wimbledon: "It may be that I am too young to win this tournament." Wise and innocent, the observation spoke volumes.

Michael Jordan: His face was ashen, his legs wobbly, his eyes sunken. It hardly mattered. It was Game Five of the National Basketball Association Finals, the Chicago Bulls and Utah Jazz were tied at two games apiece entering the third and final game being played on Utah's home court, and hanging in the balance was the right to return to Chicago leading the series three games to two. And so Michael Jordan played, despite a flu that had him vomiting in the locker room before the game. At times he appeared on the verge of collapse. During breaks he would fall into a chair, immovable. He still scored 38 points, including a 3-pointer with 25 seconds remaining to seal the 90–88 win.

Two nights later the Bulls would win their fifth NBA title in seven years, on a shot by Steve Kerr—off a pass from a triple-teamed Michael Jordan. It was all vintage Airness, more stuff to add to the crowded legend that already is Michael Jordan. So forget, if just for a moment, his salary, his endorsements, the "Space Jam" movie with Bugs Bunny, the Michael Jordan fragrance, his new "Jordan Brand" Nike-backed apparel company. Forget, even, the five NBA titles in five trips, plus the five Finals MVP trophies. His Airness does what the very best have always done through the first 50 years of the NBA: He comes to play, every day. It's enough to make his opponents sick.

Rebecca Lobo: Talk about coming up big. A year ago Rebecca Lobo, arguably the most recognized name in U.S. women's basketball, was a little-used and very obvious end-of-the-bencher on the U.S. women's gold-medal basketball team at the Atlanta Olympic Games. The championship glory at the University of Connecticut was but a memory. She was only 22, and playing with and against women with years of international experience, she looked it. But she still had the name, so when she joined the WNBA, the new women's pro league bankrolled by the National Basketball Association, Rebecca Lobo, icon, was front and center in the league's push for recognition, respect and revenue. There was just one problem: Did Rebecca Lobo, ball player, have, uh, you know, *the game* to go with the hype? Cynthia Cooper of the Houston Comets would win the regular-season and championship-game most valuable player awards, but Ms. Lobo, slimmer and more powerful than in Atlanta, showed that the WNBA had made no mistake in giving her the promotional ball and asking for a big shot. The Liberty dominated the first half of the 28-game summer league and made it to the championship game, where it lost to Cooper's Comets, 65–61. The WNBA, meanwhile, surpassed virtually all expectations. "We Got Next," Ms. Lobo promised in commercials and public appearances, mouthing the league's playground-savvy slogan. Then she delivered. Good thing, too.

Rupert Murdoch: Baseball traditionalists surely shed a few tears when they heard that

News Corp., the international media giant controlled by Rupert Murdoch, was going to be the next owner of the Los Angeles Dodgers, the storied baseball franchise. But the move made sense. Gone are the days when a single family (in the Dodgers' case, the O'Malleys) could own and operate a sports team and expect it to come anywhere near profitability. Synergy is today's watch word, and it is not by accident that Time Warner Inc., Tribune Co. and Walt Disney Co. already own pro teams. Stadium deals! Cable-TV contracts! Sports programming! The Dodgers were said to cost about $350 million. For News Corp. and Mr. Murdoch, it would have been a bargain at twice the price.

Rachel Robinson: The widow of Jackie Robinson, the man who broke baseball's color barrier in 1947, proved herself as skillful at orchestrating the event's 50th anniversary commemoration as her husband had been on the base paths for the old Brooklyn Dodgers. Artfully balancing the commercial demands of 1997 with the historical significance of 1947, Mrs. Robinson brought to the task a quiet dignity, an even surehandedness and an appealing self-effacement that reminded a nation of how far it has come while gently suggesting that it still has a long, long way to go.

Pete Sampras: Don't blame Pete because he's beautiful. Or because by midsummer the 28-year-old Mr. Sampras had added two Grand Slam championships—the Australian and Wimbledon—to go along with the eight he already has in his trophy case. Don't blame Pete because he dominated men's tennis so completely and appeared to do it so effortlessly—despite an early exit at the U.S. Open—that few outside the hardcore tennis establishment seemed to notice, or care. A great champion (which Mr. Sampras most assuredly is) needs great competition (which men's tennis today most decidedly does not have). Andre, where are you? Boris, don't retire! Here's a thought, and a sad one at that: Better enjoy the man many are already calling the best tennis player ever while we can. All that winning is bound to grow tiresome even-

tually, and should he quit, we'll never know how good he really might have been.

Mike Tyson: Quick, name any sports events in 1997 that garnered more water-cooler talk the day after than the Mike Tyson-Evander Holyfield heavyweight championship bout at the MGM Grand in Las Vegas at the end of June. Mr. Tyson bit off a piece of Holyfield's right ear, then, duly warned by referee Mills Lane that another such chomp would cost him the fight, promptly tried to do the same to the left lobe. It was repulsive and disgusting, compelling and utterly fascinating. Once again Iron Mike—child of the streets, convicted rapist, former heavyweight champion—proved his ability to show us the dark side. And we again demonstrated our inclination to be titillated by the peek inside. Mr. Tyson was fined $3 million dollars by the Nevada State Athletic Commission and his license to fight was revoked for a year. "I'll be back," he said. We can hardly wait.

Tiger Woods: He is Tiger Woods. Midway through 1997 the 21-year-old Mr. Woods had been a professional golfer for less than a year, and already he had won six tournaments in 23 starts, captured his first "major," the Masters, bagged nearly $2 million in prize money to lead his fellow (and sometimes envious) pros and made millions more in endorsements. He also led a charge of twenty-something golfers to the forefront of the game—U.S. Open champion Ernie Els was 27, British Open champ Justin Leonard 25. On the course Mr. Woods was a genius, capable of winning any tournament he entered—and stirring fierce debates as to what happened when he didn't. Off the course he was usually gracious and accommodating, but he could sometimes still act his age. It was obvious, too, that at other times all the attention that comes with being a walking commercial-icon was beginning to wear. Fame has its price, after all, but that's not always a bad thing. Tiger, of mixed African-American, Asian and Native American heritage, single-handedly raised the consciousness of a polyglot nation that claims to take pride in its spicy ethnic stew.

Steve McKee

Most Popular Sports Personalities

	March 1997 familiarity	Q score*
Michael Jordan	93%	53%
Harlem Globetrotters	85	53
Joe Montana	90	47
Willie Mays	83	43
Nolan Ryan	80	42
Jerry Rice	71	41
Cal Ripken Jr.	76	41
Walter Payton	67	41
Tiger Woods	73	41
John Madden	76	40
Reggie White	74	39
Ken Griffey Jr.	76	38
Julius "Dr. J" Erving	79	38
Grant Hill	68	38
Scott Hamilton	80	38

*Q score = % of those who are familiar with personality and rate "One of My Favorites."
Source: Marketing Evaluations Inc.

10 Highest-Paid Athletes by Sport

National Football League (1996 season)

1. Troy Aikman, Dallas Cowboys, quarterback, $5.37 million
2. Dan Marino, Miami Dolphins, quarterback, $5.33 million
3. Steve Young, San Francisco 49ers, quarterback, $4.98 million
4. Troy Vincent, Philadelphia Eagles, cornerback, $4.6 million
5. Barry Sanders, Detroit Lions, running back, $4.35 million
6. Scott Mitchell, Detroit Lions, quarterback, $4.32 million
7. John Elway, Denver Broncos, quarterback, $4.23 million
8. Brett Favre, Green Bay Packers, quarterback, $4.18 million
9. Drew Bledsoe, New England Patriots, quarterback, $4.09 million
10. Emmitt Smith, Dallas Cowboys, running back, $4.0 million

Major League Baseball (1997 season)

1. Albert Belle, Chicago White Sox, outfielder, $10 million
2. Cecil Fielder, New York Yankees, designated hitter, $9.24 million
3. Barry Bonds, San Francisco Giants, outfielder, $8.67 million
4. Roger Clemens, Toronto Blue Jays, pitcher, $8.25 million
5. Jeff Bagwell, Houston Astros, first baseman, $8.02 million
6. Ken Griffey Jr., Seattle Mariners, outfielder, $7.48 million
7. Juan Gonzalez, Texas Rangers, outfielder, $7.4 million
8. Frank Thomas, Chicago White Sox, first baseman, $7.15 million
9. Mark McGwire, Oakland Athletics, first baseman, $7.1 million
10. Cal Ripken Jr., Baltimore Orioles, third baseman, $7.08 million

National Basketball Association (1996–97 season)

1. Michael Jordan, Chicago Bulls, guard, $30.14 million
2. Horace Grant, Orlando Magic, forward, $17.86 million
3. Reggie Miller, Indiana Pacers, guard, $11.25 million
4. Shaquille O'Neal, Los Angeles Lakers, center, $10.71 million
5. Gary Payton, Seattle SuperSonics, guard, $10.21 million
6. David Robinson, San Antonio Spurs, center, $9.95 million
7. Hakeem Olajuwon, Houston Rockets, center, $9.66 million
8. Alonzo Mourning, Miami Heat, center, $9.38 million
9. Juwan Howard, Washington Bullets, forward, $9.375 million
10. Dennis Rodman, Chicago Bulls, forward, $9.0 million

National Hockey League (1996–97 season)

1. Mario Lemieux, Pittsburgh Penguins, center, $11.32 million
2. Mark Messier, New York Rangers, center, $6.0 million
3. Wayne Gretzky, New York Rangers, center, $5.05 million
4. Pavel Bure, Vancouver Canucks, right wing, $5.0 million
5. Pat LaFontaine, Buffalo Sabres, center, $4.6 million
6. Steve Yzerman, Detroit Red Wings, center, $4.49 million
7. Patrick Roy, Colorado Avalanche, goaltender, $4.46 million
8. Brett Hull, St. Louis Blues, right wing, $4.4 million
9. (tie) Dominik Hasek, Buffalo Sabres, goaltender, $4.2 million
    Sergei Fedorov, Detroit Red Wings, center, $4.2 million

Average Major-League Player Salaries

Major League Baseball Salaries

Year	Minimum Salary	Average Salary
1980	$ 30,000	$ 143,756
1981	32,500	185,651
1982	33,500	241,497
1983	35,000	289,194
1984	40,000	329,408
1985	60,000	371,157
1986	60,000	412,520
1987	62,500	412,454
1988	62,500	438,729
1989	68,000	497,254
1990	100,000	597,537
1991	100,000	851,492
1992	109,000	1,028,667
1993	109,000	1,076,089
1994	109,000	1,168,263
1995	109,000	1,110,766
1996	109,000	1,119,981

Source: Major League Baseball Players Association

National Hockey League Average Salaries

1970	$ 25,000
1975	74,000
1976	86,000
1977	96,000
1978	92,000
1979	101,000
1980	108,000
1981–82	120,000
1982–83	110,000*
1983–84	118,000*
1984–85	120,000*
1985–86	144,000
1986–87	158,000
1987–88	172,000
1988–89	188,000
1989–90	211,000
1990–91	271,000
1991–92	368,000
1992–93	467,000
1993–94	562,000
1994–95	733,000
1995–96	892,500
1996–97	981,000

*These figures represent not the average salary, but the median salary.
Source: National Hockey League Players Association

National Football League
Average Salaries (In thousands of dollars)

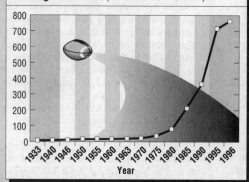

Year

Average Salary for NFL Quarterbacks

1990	$ 660,000
1991	803,000
1992	911,000
1993	1,523,000
1994	1,138,000
1995	1,307,000
1996	1,336,000

Source: NFL Players Association

NBA Average Salaries and Salary Caps

Season	Average salary (per player)	Salary cap (per team)
1976–77	$ 130,000	
1977–78	139,000	
1978–79	148,000	
1979–80	170,000	
1980–81	171,000	
1981–82	212,000	
1982–83	249,000	
1983–84	275,000	
1984–85	325,000	$ 3,600,000
1985–86	375,000	4,233,000
1986–87	440,000	4,945,000
1987–88	510,000	6,164,000
1988–89	600,000	7,232,000
1989–90	750,000	9,802,000
1990–91	900,000	11,871,000
1991–92	1,100,000	12,500,000
1992–93	1,300,000	14,000,000
1993–94	1,700,000	15,125,000
1994–95	1,900,000	15,900,000
1995–96	2,100,000	23,000,000
1996–97	2,300,000	24,300,000

Source: National Basketball Association

FOOTBALL

NFL 1996–97 SEASON

The Green Bay Packers won the Super Bowl in January, beating a game New England Patriots team, 35–21. "Winning is the only thing," as a former Packers' coach once said, so any recap of the 1996 National Football League season must begin there. But if you're looking for a theme, try this: "Sometimes, youth isn't wasted on the young." And if you want a poster boy, try this: John Elway, the grand old man of the 13–3 Denver Broncos, and his look of utter disbelief as the realization struck that probably the best Bronco team he had ever played on was being denied a trip to the Super Bowl by the two-year-old, 9–7, *expansion* Jacksonville Jaguars in the America Football Conference divisional playoff. Final score: 30–27. Life is indeed not fair. But it sure makes for a heck of a story.

Of the top 11 passers in 1996, six were under 30: Brett Favre, Brad Johnson, Mark Brunell, Drew Bledsoe, Ty Detmer and Jeff Blake. These young guns threw for three or more touchdowns in 36 games. They tossed 27 of the season's 50 300-yard games.

And they were throwing to a cadre of young receivers. Make that *really* young receivers. *Rookie* receivers—maybe the best class of first-round new hands ever. Terry Glenn, Marvin Harrison, Keyshawn Johnson, Eddie Kenniston, and Eric Moulds caught 291 passes for 4,015 yards and 33 touchdowns. The best numbers of any receiver class of the 1990s. Mr. Glenn, with 90 catches, broke the NFL rookie mark of 83 set back in 1980.

What's-a-matter with kids today? In the NFL, apparently, not much.

Not that the old guard didn't have its moments. Take Mr. Elway. The 14-year quarterback played in his 126th win, beating Fran Tarkenton's record. He reached 45,000 career passing yards to rank No. 3, and threw his 251st touchdown pass to take over the ninth spot. And he ran the ball for the 687th time, breaking Randall Cunningham's mark of 677.

In other old-guy news: Dan Marino reached the 50,000-yard passing plateau with a 36-yard toss to O.J. McDuffie on Nov. 10. One week earlier Jerry Rice caught his 1,000th

pass—a nine-yarder from Steve Young. Nick Lowery, who had begun his career in the *seventies*, kicked his 383rd field goal, surpassing Jan Stenerud's 373 career mark. And 15-year pro Marcus Allen played in his 206th game, most ever by a running back.

Still, it was Kid's Day in the NFL.

Both expansion teams, Jacksonville and the Carolina Panthers (12–4), made the playoffs in just their second year. They also both made it to their conference championship games before falling, to, respectively, the New England Patriots (20–8) and the Packers (30–13).

"Wait!" you say. The Patriots and Packers? They're two of the old-time greats. The Patriots of the original American Football Conference, the Packers of the original NFL. Well, yes. But they both were quarterbacked by young guns: Mr. Bledsoe and league Most Valuable Player Favre.

Carolina and Jacksonville, by the way, inflicted some other damage on some old-guard teams. Carolina took out the Dallas Cowboys in the second round of the playoffs, 26–17. Meanwhile, in the first round, the Jags traveled to Buffalo to play the Bills—the never-lost-a-home-playoff-game Bills—and beat their hosts, 30–27. It would prove to be the last game for Bills quarterback Jim Kelly, the original four-Super Bowl warhorse. He retired—wisely, it was generally agreed—after the season.

Super Bowl XXXI at first threatened to be overwhelmed by the will-he-won't-he machinations of New England coach Bill Parcells. Would he leave the Patriots for the hapless New York Jets? Turned out he did, for those who just have to know.

But the Big Game itself turned on a pair of legs that had rediscovered their youth. Desmond Howard, the 1991 Heisman Trophy winner who had languished as a receiver with the Washington Redskins, found a home as a kick-return specialist with the Packers, and he made the biggest game of his life special indeed. In the first half, he returned punts for 32 and 34 yards that set up 10 Packer points. Then in the third quarter, after the Patriots had closed to within six at 27–21, Mr. Howard returned the ensuing kickoff 99 yards for a

Final 1996 NFL Regular-Season Standings

	American Football Conference						National Football Conference					
	W	L	T	Pct.	Pts.	OP		W	L	T	Pct.	Pts.	OP

Eastern Division

	W	L	T	Pct.	Pts.	OP		W	L	T	Pct.	Pts.	OP
New England	11	5	0	.688	418	313	Dallas	10	6	0	.625	286	250
Buffalo*	10	6	0	.625	319	266	Philadelphia*	10	6	0	.625	363	341
Indianapolis*	9	7	0	.563	317	334	Washingtoin	9	7	0	.563	364	312
Miami	8	8	0	.500	339	325	Arizona	7	9	0	.438	300	397
New York Jets	1	15	0	.063	279	454	New York Giants	6	10	0	.375	242	297

Central Division

	W	L	T	Pct.	Pts.	OP		W	L	T	Pct.	Pts.	OP
Pittsburgh	10	6	0	.625	344	257	Green Bay	13	3	0	.813	456	210
Jacksonville*	9	7	0	.563	325	335	Minnesota*	9	7	0	.563	298	315
Cincinnati	8	8	0	.500	372	369	Chicago	7	9	0	.438	283	305
Houston	8	8	0	.500	345	319	Tampa Bay	6	10	0	.375	221	293
Baltimore	4	12	0	.250	371	441	Detroit	5	11	0	.313	302	368

Western Division

	W	L	T	Pct.	Pts.	OP		W	L	T	Pct.	Pts.	OP
Denver	13	3	0	.813	391	275	Carolina	12	4	0	.750	367	218
Kansas City	9	7	0	.563	297	300	San Francisco*	12	4	0	.750	398	257
San Diego	8	8	0	.500	310	376	St. Louis	6	10	0	.375	303	409
Oakland	7	9	0	.438	340	293	Atlanta	3	13	0	.188	309	461
Seattle	7	9	0	.438	317	376	New Orleans	3	13	0	.188	229	339

*Wild Card qualifier for playoffs.

NFL Post Season

Wild Card Playoffs

American Football Conference
Jacksonville 30, Buffalo 27
Pittsburgh 42, Indianapolis 14

National Football Conference
Dallas 40, Minnesota 15
San Francisco 14, Philadelphia 0

Divisional Playoffs

American Football Conference
Jacksonville 30, Denver 27
New England 28, Pittsburgh 3

National Football Conference
Green Bay 35, San Francisco 14
Carolina 26, Dallas 17

Championship Games

American Football Conference
New England 20, Jacksonville 6

National Football Conference
Green Bay 30, Carolina 13

Super Bowl XXXI

Green Bay (NFC) 35, New England (AFC) 21, at Louisiana Superdome, New Orleans, LA

AFC-NFC Pro Bowl

AFC 26, NFC 23 (OT), at Aloha Stadium, Honolulu, HI

Source: National Football League

Super Bowl Results

Season	Date	Winner	Loser	Score	Site	Attendance
I	Jan. 15,1967	Green Bay	Kansas City	35-10	Los Angeles, CA	61,946
II	Jan. 14,1968	Green Bay	Oakland	33-14	Miami, FL	75,546
III	Jan. 12,1969	N.Y. Jets	Baltimore	16-7	Miami, FL	75,389
IV	Jan. 11,1970	Kansas City	Minnesota	23-7	New Orleans, LA	80,562
V	Jan. 17,1971	Baltimore	Dallas	16-13	Miami, FL	79,204
VI	Jan. 16,1972	Dallas	Miami	24-3	New Orleans, LA	81,023
VII	Jan. 14,1973	Miami	Washington	14-7	Los Angeles, CA	90,182
VIII	Jan. 13,1974	Miami	Minnesota	24-7	Houston, TX	71,882
IX	Jan. 12,1975	Pittsburgh	Minnesota	16-6	New Orleans, LA	80,997
X	Jan. 18,1976	Pittsburgh	Dallas	21-17	Miami, FL	80,187
XI	Jan. 09,1977	Oakland	Minnesota	32-14	Pasadena, CA	103,438
XII	Jan. 15,1978	Dallas	Denver	27-10	New Orleans, LA	75,583
XIII	Jan. 21,1979	Pittsburgh	Dallas	35-31	Miami, FL	79,484
XIV	Jan. 20,1980	Pittsburgh	Los Angeles	31-19	Pasadena, CA	103,985
XV	Jan. 25,1981	Oakland	Philadelphia	27-10	New Orleans, LA	76,135
XVI	Jan. 24,1982	San Francisco	Cincinnati	26-21	Pontiac, MI	81,270
XVII	Jan. 30,1983	Washington	Miami	27-17	Pasadena, CA	103,667
XVIII	Jan. 22,1984	L.A. Raiders	Washington	38-9	Tampa, FL	72,920
XIX	Jan. 20,1985	San Francisco	Miami	38-16	Stanford, CA	84,059
XX	Jan. 26,1986	Chicago	New England	46-10	New Orleans, LA	73,818
XXI	Jan. 25,1987	N.Y. Giants	Denver	39-20	Pasadena, CA	101,063
XXII	Jan. 31,1988	Washington	Denver	42-10	San Diego, CA	73,302
XXIII	Jan. 22,1989	San Francisco	Cincinnati	20-16	Miami, FL	75,129
XXIV	Jan. 28,1990	San Francisco	Denver	55-10	New Orleans, LA	72,919
XXV	Jan. 27,1991	N.Y. Giants	Buffalo	20-19	Tampa, FL	73,813
XXVI	Jan. 26,1992	Washington	Buffalo	37-24	Minneapolis, MN	63,130
XXVII	Jan. 31,1993	Dallas	Buffalo	52-17	Pasadena, CA	98,374
XXVIII	Jan. 30,1994	Dallas	Buffalo	30-13	Atlanta, GA	72,817
XXIX	Jan. 29,1995	San Francisco	San Diego	49-26	Miami, FL	74,107
XXX	Jan. 28,1996	Dallas	Pittsburgh	27-17	Tempe, AZ	76,347
XXXI	Jan. 26, 1997	Green Bay	New England	35-21	New Orleans, LA	72,301

Source: National Football League

Super Bowl Composite Standings

Team	W	L	Pct.	Pts.	OP	Team	W	L	Pct.	Pts.	OP
San Francisco 49ers	5	0	1.000	188	89	Kansas City Chiefs	1	1	.500	33	42
Green Bay Packers	3	0	1.000	103	45	Miami Dolphins	2	3	.400	74	103
New York Giants	2	0	1.000	59	39	Los Angeles Rams	0	1	.000	19	31
Chicago Bears	1	0	1.000	46	10	Philadelphia Eagles	0	1	.000	10	27
New York Jets	1	0	1.000	16	7	San Diego Chargers	0	1	.000	26	49
Pittsburgh Steelers	4	1	.800	120	100	Cincinnati Bengals	0	2	.000	37	46
Oakland/L.A. Raiders	3	1	.750	111	66	New England Patriots	0	2	.000	31	81
Dallas Cowboys	5	3	.625	221	132	Buffalo Bills	0	4	.000	73	139
Washington Redskins	3	2	.600	122	103	Denver Broncos	0	4	.000	50	163
Baltimore Colts	1	1	.500	23	29	Minnesota Vikings	0	4	.000	34	95

Source: National Football League

back-breaking touchdown. Packer Favre, who had termed the season "Super Bowl or Bust," threw for 246 yards on 14 of 27 passes, passed for two long touchdowns and ran for another, but Mr. Howard's electrifying moment of youth-reclaimed earned him the game's Most Valuable Player Award.

After 29 years, the Super Bowl trophy—the Vince Lombardi Trophy—was back home in Packer Town. And, suddenly, everything old seemed young again.

Steve McKee

Super Bowl Most Valuable Player

Super Bowl I	— QB Bart Starr, Green Bay
Super Bowl II	— QB Bart Starr, Green Bay
Super Bowl III	— QB Joe Namath, N.Y. Jets
Super Bowl IV	— QB Len Dawson. Kansas City
Super Bowl V	— LB Chuck Howley, Dallas
Super Bowl VI	— QB Roger Staubach, Dallas
Super Bowl VII	— S Jake Scott, Miami
Super Bowl VIII	— RB Larry Csonka, Miami
Super Bowl IX	— RB Franco Harris, Pittsburgh
Super Bowl X	— WR Lynn Swann, Pittsburgh
Super Bowl XI	— WR Fred Biletnikoff, Oakland
Super Bowl XII	— DT Randy White and
	DE Harvey Martin, Dallas
Super Bowl XIII	— QB Terry Bradshaw, Pittsburgh
Super Bowl XIV	— QB Terry Bradshaw, Pittsburgh
Super Bowl XV	— QB Jim Plunkett, Oakland
Super Bowl XVI	— QB Joe Montana, San Francisco
Super Bowl XVII	— RB John Riggins, Washington
Super Bowl XVIII	— RB Marcus Allen, L.A. Raiders
Super Bowl XIX	— QB Joe Montana, San Francisco
Super Bowl XX	— DE Richard Dent, Chicago
Super Bowl XXI	— QB Phil Simms, N.Y. Giants
Super Bowl XXII	— QB Doug Williams, Washington
Super Bowl XXIII	— WR Jerry Rice, San Francisco
Super Bowl XXIV	— QB Joe Montana, San Francisco
Super Bowl XXV	— RB Ottis Anderson, N.Y. Giants
Super Bowl XXVI	— QB Mark Rypien, Washington
Super Bowl XXVII	— QB Troy Aikman, Dallas
Super Bowl XXVIII	— RB Emmitt Smith, Dallas
Super Bowl XXIX	— QB Steve Young, San Francisco
Super Bowl XXX	— CB Larry Brown, Dallas
Super Bowl XXXI	— KR-PR Desmond Howard, Green Bay

Source: National Football League

The Super Bowl of Selling

The cost of 30 seconds of advertising time has soared on the annual Super Bowl telecast, which has become a showcase for marketers' splashiest commercials.

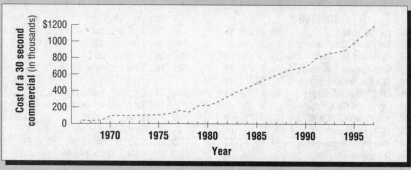

Source: McCann-Erickson Worldwide

Super Bowl TV Ratings

While advertisers pay more each year for commercial time on the Super Bowl, television ratings have been erratic.

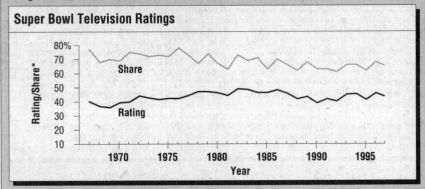

Super Bowl Television Ratings

*The rating represents the percentage of all U.S. households with television sets watching the program. The share represents the percentage of all television sets in use at the time that were tuned to the program.
Source: Nielsen Media Research

From the NFL Records Book
ANNUAL STATISTICAL LEADERS

SCORING

YEAR	PLAYER, TEAM	TD	FG	PAT	TP
1932	Earl (Dutch) Clark, Portsmouth	6	3	10	55
1933	Ken Strong, N.Y. Giants	6	5	13	64
	Glenn Presnell, Portsmouth	6	6	10	64
1934	Jack Manders, Chi. Bears	3	10	31	79
1935	Earl (Dutch) Clark, Detroit	6	1	16	55
1936	Earl (Dutch) Clark, Detroit	7	4	19	73
1937	Jack Manders, Chi. Bears	5	8	15	69
1938	Clarke Hinkle, Green Bay	7	3	7	58
1939	Andy Farkas, Washington	11	0	2	68
1940	Don Hutson, Green Bay	7	0	15	57
1941	Don Hutson, Green Bay	12	1	20	95
1942	Don Hutson, Green Bay	17	1	33	138
1943	Don Hutson, Green Bay	12	3	36	117
1944	Don Hutson, Green Bay	9	0	31	85
1945	Steve Van Buren, Philadelphia	18	0	2	110
1946	Ted Fritsch, Green Bay	10	9	13	100
1947	Pat Harder, Chi. Cardinals	7	7	39	102
1948	Pat Harder, Chi. Cardinals	6	7	53	110
1949	Pat Harder, Chi. Cardinals	8	3	45	102
	Gene Roberts, N.Y. Giants	17	0	0	102
1950	*Doak Walker, Detroit	11	8	38	128
1951	Elroy (Crazylegs) Hirsch, Los Angeles	17	0	0	102
1952	Gordy Soltau, San Francisco	7	6	34	94
1953	Gordy Soltau, San Francisco	6	10	48	114
1954	Bobby Walston, Philadelphia	11	4	36	114
1955	Doak Walker, Detroit	7	9	27	96
1956	Bobby Layne, Detroit	5	12	33	99

YEAR	PLAYER, TEAM	TD	FG	PAT	TP
1957	Sam Baker, Washington	1	14	29	77
	Lou Groza, Cleveland	0	15	32	77
1958	Jim Brown, Cleveland	18	0	0	108
1959	Paul Hornung, Green Bay	7	7	31	94
1960	Paul Hornung, Green Bay, NFL	15	15	41	176
	*Gene Mingo, Denver, AFL	6	18	33	123
1961	Gino Cappelletti, Boston, AFL	8	17	48	147
	Paul Hornung, Green Bay, NFL	10	15	41	146
1962	Gene Mingo, Denver, AFL	4	27	32	137
	Jim Taylor, Green Bay, NFL	19	0	0	114
1963	Gino Cappelletti, Boston, AFL	2	22	35	113
	Don Chandler, N.Y. Giants, NFL	0	18	52	106
1964	Gino Cappelletti, Boston, AFL	7	25	36	155
	Lenny Moore, Baltimore, NFL	20	0	0	120
1965	*Gale Sayers, Chicago, NFL	22	0	0	132
	Gino Cappelletti, Boston, AFL	9	17	27	132
1966	Gino Cappelletti, Boston, AFL	6	16	35	119
	Bruce Gossett, Los Angeles, NFL	0	28	29	113
1967	Jim Bakken, St. Louis, NFL	0	27	36	117
	George Blanda, Oakland, AFL	0	20	56	116
1968	Jim Turner, N.Y. Jets, AFL	0	34	43	145
	Leroy Kelly, Cleveland, NFL	20	0	0	120
1969	Jim Turner, N.Y. Jets, AFL	0	32	33	129
	Fred Cox, Minnesota, NFL	0	26	43	121
1970	Fred Cox, Minnesota, NFC	0	30	35	125
	Jan Stenerud, Kansas City, AFC	0	30	26	116
1971	Garo Yepremian, Miami, AFC	0	28	33	117
	Curt Knight, Washington, NFC	0	29	27	114
1972	*Chester Marcol, Green Bay, NFC	0	33	29	128

YEAR	PLAYER, TEAM				
	Bobby Howfield, N.Y. Jets, AFC	0	27	40	121
1973	David Ray, Los Angeles, NFC	0	30	40	130
	Roy Gerela, Pittsburgh, AFC	0	29	36	123
1974	Chester Marcol, Green Bay, NFC	0	25	19	94
	Roy Gerela, Pittsburgh, AFC	0	20	33	93
1975	O.J. Simpson, Buffalo, AFC	23	0	0	138
	Chuck Foreman, Minnesota, NFC	22	0	0	132
1976	Toni Linhart, Baltimore, AFC	0	20	49	109
	Mark Moseley, Washington, NFC	0	22	31	97
1977	Errol Mann, Oakland, AFC	0	20	39	99
	Walter Payton, Chicago, NFC	16	0	0	96
1978	*Frank Corral, Los Angeles, NFC	0	29	31	118
	Pat Leahy, N.Y. Jets, AFC	0	22	41	107
1979	John Smith, New England, AFC	0	23	46	115
	Mark Moseley, Washington, NFC	0	25	39	114
1980	John Smith, New England, AFC	0	26	51	129
	*Ed Murray, Detroit, NFC	0	27	35	116
1981	Ed Murray, Detroit, NFC	0	25	46	121
	Rafael Septien, Dallas, NFC	0	27	40	121
	Jim Breech, Cincinnati, AFC	0	22	49	115
	Nick Lowery, Kansas City, AFC	0	26	37	115
1982	*Marcus Allen, L.A. Raiders, AFC	14	0	0	84
	Wendell Tyler, L.A. Rams, NFC	13	0	0	78
1983	Mark Moseley, Washington, NFC	0	33	62	161
	Gary Anderson, Pittsburgh, AFC	0	27	38	119
1984	Ray Wersching, San Francisco, NFC	0	25	56	131
	Gary Anderson, Pittsburgh, AFC	0	24	45	117
1985	*Kevin Butler, Chicago, NFC	0	31	51	144
	Gary Anderson, Pittsburgh, AFC	0	33	40	139
1986	Tony Franklin, New England, AFC	0	32	44	140
	Kevin Butler, Chicago, NFC	0	28	36	120
1987	Jerry Rice, San Francisco, NFC	23	0	0	138
	Jim Breech, Cincinnati, AFC	0	24	25	97
1988	Scott Norwood, Buffalo, AFC	0	32	33	129
	Mike Cofer, San Francisco, NFC	0	27	40	121
1989	Mike Cofer, San Francisco, NFC	0	29	49	136
	*David Treadwell, Denver, AFC	0	27	39	120
1990	Nick Lowery, Kansas City, AFC	0	34	37	139
	Chip Lohmiller, Washington, NFC	0	30	41	131
1991	Chip Lohmiller, Washington, NFC	0	31	56	149
	Pete Stoyanovich, Miami, AFC	0	31	28	121
1992	Pete Stoyanovich, Miami, AFC	0	30	34	124
	Morten Andersen, New Orleans, NFC	0	29	33	120
	Chip Lohmiller, Washington, NFC	0	30	30	120
1993	Jeff Jaeger, L.A. Raiders, AFC	0	35	27	132
	Jason Hanson, Detroit, NFC	0	34	28	130
1994	John Carney, San Diego, AFC	0	34	33	135
	Fuad Reveiz, Minnesota, NFC	0	34	30	132
1995	Emmitt Smith, Dallas, NFC	25	0	0	150
	Norm Johnson, Pittsburgh, AFC	0	34	39	141
1996	John Kasay, Carolina, NFC	0	37	34	145
	Cary Blanchard, Indianapolis, AFC	0	36	27	135

*First season of professional football.

TOUCHDOWNS

YEAR	PLAYER, TEAM	TD	RUSH	PASS	RET.
1932	Earl (Dutch) Clark, Portsmouth	6	3	3	0
	Red Grange, Chi. Bears	6	3	3	0
1933	*Charlie (Buckets) Goldenberg, Green Bay	7	4	1	2
	John (Shipwreck) Kelly, Brooklyn	7	2	3	2
	*Elvin (Kink) Richards, N.Y. Giants	7	4	3	0
1934	*Beattie Feathers, Chi. Bears	9	8	1	0
1935	*Don Hutson, Green Bay	7	0	6	1
1936	Don Hutson, Green Bay	9	0	8	1
1937	Cliff Battles, Washington	7	5	1	1
	Clarke Hinkle, Green Bay	7	5	2	0
	Don Hutson, Green Bay	7	0	7	0
1938	Don Hutson, Green Bay	9	0	9	0
1939	Andrew Farkas, Washington	11	5	5	1
1940	John Drake, Cleveland	9	9	0	0
	Richard Todd, Washington	9	4	4	1
1941	Don Hutson, Green Bay	12	2	10	0
	George McAfee, Chi. Bears	12	6	3	3
1942	Don Hutson, Green Bay	17	0	17	0
1943	Don Hutson, Green Bay	12	0	11	1
	*Bill Paschal, N.Y. Giants	12	10	2	0
1944	Don Hutson, Green Bay	9	0	9	0
	Bill Paschal, N.Y. Giants	9	9	0	0
1945	Steve Van Buren, Philadelphia	18	15	2	1
1946	Ted Fritsch, Green Bay	10	9	1	0
1947	Steve Van Buren, Philadelphia	14	13	0	1
1948	Mal Kutner, Chi. Cardinals	15	1	14	0
1949	Gene Roberts, N.Y. Giants	17	9	8	0
1950	Bob Shaw, Chi. Cardinals	12	0	12	0
1951	Elroy (Crazylegs) Hirsch, Los Angeles	17	0	17	0
1952	Cloyce Box, Detroit	15	0	15	0
1953	Joseph Perry, San Francisco	13	10	3	0
1954	*Harlon Hill, Chi. Bears	12	0	12	0
1955	*Alan Ameche, Baltimore	9	9	0	0
	Harlon Hill, Chi. Bears	9	0	9	0
1956	Rick Casares, Chi. Bears	14	12	2	0
1957	Lenny Moore, Baltimore	11	3	7	1
1958	Jim Brown, Cleveland	18	17	1	0
1959	Raymond Berry, Baltimore	14	0	14	0
	Jim Brown, Cleveland	14	14	0	0
1960	Paul Hornung, Green Bay, NFL	15	13	2	0

	Sonny Randle, St. Louis, NFL	15	0	15	0
	Art Powell, N.Y. Titans, AFL	14	0	14	0
1961	Bill Groman, Houston, AFL	18	1	17	0
	Jim Taylor, Green Bay, NFL	16	15	1	0
1962	Abner Haynes, Dallas, AFL	19	13	6	0
	Jim Taylor, Green Bay, NFL	19	19	0	0
1963	Art Powell, Oakland, AFL	16	0	16	0
	Jim Brown, Cleveland, NFL	15	12	3	0
1964	Lenny Moore, Baltimore, NFL	20	16	3	1
	Lance Alworth, San Diego, AFL	15	2	13	0
1965	*Gale Sayers, Chicago, NFL	22	14	6	2
	Lance Alworth, San Diego, AFL	14	0	14	0
	Don Maynard, N.Y. Jets, AFL	14	0	14	0
1966	Leroy Kelly, Cleveland, NFL	16	15	1	0
	Dan Reeves, Dallas, NFL	16	8	8	0
	Lance Alworth, San Diego, AFL	13	0	13	0
1967	Homer Jones, N.Y. Giants, NFL	14	1	13	0
	Emerson Boozer, N.Y. Jets, AFL	13	10	3	0
1968	Leroy Kelly, Cleveland, NFL	20	16	4	0
	Warren Wells, Oakland, AFL	12	1	11	0
1969	Warren Wells, Oakland, AFL	14	0	14	0
	Tom Matte, Baltimore, NFL	13	11	2	0
	Lance Rentzel, Dallas, NFL	13	0	12	1
1970	Dick Gordon, Chicago, NFC	13	0	13	0
	MacArthur Lane, St. Louis, NFC	13	11	2	0
	Gary Garrison, San Diego, AFC	12	0	12	0
1971	Duane Thomas, Dallas, NFC	13	11	2	0
	Leroy Kelly, Cleveland, AFC	12	10	2	0
1972	Emerson Boozer, N.Y. Jets, AFC	14	11	3	0
	Ron Johnson, N.Y. Giants, NFC	14	9	5	0
1973	Larry Brown, Washington, NFC	14	8	6	0
	Floyd Little, Denver, AFC	13	12	1	0
1974	Chuck Foreman, Minnesota, NFC	15	9	6	0
	Cliff Branch, Oakland, AFC	13	0	13	0
1975	O.J. Simpson, Buffalo, AFC	23	16	7	0
	Chuck Foreman, Minnesota, NFC	22	13	9	0
1976	Chuck Foreman, Minnesota, NFC	14	13	1	0
	Franco Harris, Pittsburgh, AFC	14	14	0	0
1977	Walter Payton, Chicago, NFC	16	14	2	0
	Nat Moore, Miami, AFC	13	1	12	0
1978	David Sims, Seattle, AFC	15	14	1	0
	Terdell Middleton, Green Bay, NFC	12	11	1	0
1979	Earl Campbell, Houston, AFC	19	19	0	0
	Walter Payton, Chicago, NFC	16	14	2	0
1980	*Billy Sims, Detroit, NFC	16	13	3	0
	Earl Campbell, Houston, AFC	13	13	0	0
	Curtis Dickey, Baltimore, AFC	13	11	2	0
	John Jefferson, San Diego, AFC	13	0	13	0
1981	Chuck Muncie, San Diego, AFC	19	19	0	0
	Wendell Tyler, Los Angeles, NFC	17	12	5	0
1982	*Marcus Allen, L.A. Raiders, AFC	14	11	3	0
	Wendell Tyler, L.A. Rams, NFC	13	9	4	0
1983	John Riggins, Washington, NFC	24	24	0	0
	Pete Johnson, Cincinnati, AFC	14	14	0	0
	*Curt Warner, Seattle, AFC	14	13	1	0
1984	Marcus Allen, L.A. Raiders, AFC	18	13	5	0
	Mark Clayton, Miami, AFC	18	0	18	0
	Eric Dickerson, L.A. Rams, NFC	14	14	0	0
	John Riggins, Washington, NFC	14	14	0	0
1985	Joe Morris, N.Y. Giants, NFC	21	21	0	0
	Louis Lipps, Pittsburgh, AFC	15	1	12	2
1986	George Rogers, Washington, NFC	18	18	0	0
	Sammy Winder, Denver, AFC	14	9	5	0
1987	Jerry Rice, San Francisco, NFC	23	1	22	0
	Johnny Hector, N.Y. Jets, AFC	11	11	0	0
1988	Greg Bell, L.A. Rams, NFC	18	16	2	0
	Eric Dickerson, Indianapolis, AFC	15	14	1	0
	*Ickey Woods, Cincinnati, AFC	15	15	0	0
1989	Dalton Hilliard, New Orleans, NFC	18	13	5	0
	Christian Okoye, Kansas City, AFC	12	12	0	0
	Thurman Thomas, Buffalo, AFC	12	6	6	0
1990	Barry Sanders, Detroit, NFC	16	13	3	0

	Derrick Fenner, Seattle, AFC	15	14	1	0
1991	Barry Sanders, Detroit, NFC	17	16	1	0
	Mark Clayton, Miami, AFC	12	0	12	0
	Thurman Thomas, Buffalo, AFC	12	7	5	0
1992	Emmitt Smith, Dallas, NFC	19	18	1	0
	Thurman Thomas, Buffalo, AFC	12	9	3	0
1993	Jerry Rice, San Francisco, NFC	16	1	15	0
	Marcus Allen, Kansas City, AFC	15	12	3	0
1994	Emmitt Smith, Dallas, NFC	22	21	1	0
	*Marshall Faulk, Indianapolis, AFC	12	11	1	0
	Natrone Means, San Diego, AFC	12	12	0	0
1995	Emmitt Smith, Dallas, NFC	25	25	0	0
	Carl Pickens, Cincinnati, AFC	17	0	17	0
1996	Terry Allen, Washington, NFC	21	21	0	0
	Curtis Martin, New England, AFC	17	14	3	0

*First season of professional football.

MOST FIELD GOALS MADE

YEAR	PLAYER, TEAM	ATT.	MADE	PCT.
1932	Earl (Dutch) Clark, Portsmouth		3	
1933	*Jack Manders, Chi. Bears		6	
	Glenn Presnell, Portsmouth		6	
1934	Jack Manders, Chi. Bears		10	
1935	Armand Niccolai, Pittsburgh		6	
	Bill Smith, Chi. Cardinals		6	
1936	Jack Manders, Chi. Bears		7	
	Armand Niccolai, Pittsburgh		7	
1937	Jack Manders, Chi. Bears		8	
1938	Ward Cuff, N.Y. Giants	9	5	55.6
	Ralph Kercheval, Brooklyn	13	5	38.5
1939	Ward Cuff, N.Y. Giants	16	7	43.8
1940	Clarke Hinkle, Green Bay	14	9	64.3
1941	Clarke Hinkle, Green Bay	14	6	42.9
1942	Bill Daddio, Chi. Cardinals	10	5	50.0
1943	Ward Cuff, N.Y. Giants	9	3	33.3
	Don Hutson, Green Bay	5	3	60.0
1944	Ken Strong, N.Y. Giants	12	6	50.0
1945	Joe Aguirre, Washington	13	7	53.8
1946	Ted Fritsch, Green Bay	17	9	52.9
1947	Ward Cuff, Green Bay	16	7	43.8
	Pat Harder, Chi. Cardinals	10	7	70.0
	Bob Waterfield, Los Angeles	16	7	43.8
1948	Cliff Patton, Philadelphia	12	8	66.7
1949	Cliff Patton, Philadelphia	18	9	50.0
	Bob Waterfield, Los Angeles	16	9	56.3
1950	Lou Groza, Cleveland	19	13	68.4
1951	Bob Waterfield, Los Angeles	23	13	56.5
1952	Lou Groza, Cleveland	33	19	57.6
1953	Lou Groza, Cleveland	26	23	88.5
1954	Lou Groza, Cleveland	24	16	66.7
1955	Fred Cone, Green Bay	24	16	66.7
1956	Sam Baker, Washington	25	17	68.0
1957	Lou Groza, Cleveland	22	15	68.2
1958	Paige Cothren, Los Angeles	25	14	56.0
	*Tom Miner, Pittsburgh	28	14	50.0
1959	Pat Summerall, N.Y. Giants	29	20	69.0
1960	Tommy Davis, San Francisco, NFL	32	19	59.4
	*Gene Mingo, Denver, AFL	28	18	64.3
1961	Steve Myhra, Baltimore, NFL	39	21	53.8
	Gino Cappelletti, Boston, AFL	32	17	53.1
1962	Gene Mingo, Denver, AFL	39	27	69.2
	Lou Michaels, Pittsburgh, NFL	42	26	61.9
1963	Jim Martin, Baltimore, NFL	39	24	61.5
	Gino Cappelletti, Boston, AFL	38	22	57.9
1964	Jim Bakken, St. Louis, NFL	38	25	65.8
	Gino Cappelletti, Boston, AFL	39	25	64.1
1965	Pete Gogolak, Buffalo, AFL	46	28	60.9
	Fred Cox, Minnesota, NFL	35	23	65.7
1966	Bruce Gossett, Los Angeles, NFL	49	28	57.1
	Mike Mercer, Oakland-Kansas City, AFL	30	21	70.0
1967	Jim Bakken, St. Louis, NFL	39	27	69.2
	Jan Stenerud, Kansas City, AFL	36	21	58.3
1968	Jim Turner, N.Y. Jets, AFL	46	34	73.9
	Mac Percival, Chicago, NFL	36	25	69.4
1969	Jim Turner, N.Y. Jets, AFL	47	32	68.1
	Fred Cox, Minnesota, NFL	37	26	70.3
1970	Jan Stenerud, Kansas City, AFC	42	30	71.4
	Fred Cox, Minnesota, NFC	46	30	65.2
1971	Curt Knight, Washington, NFC	49	29	59.2
	Garo Yepremian, Miami, AFC	40	28	70.0
1972	*Chester Marcol, Green Bay, NFC	48	33	68.8
	Roy Gerela, Pittsburgh, AFC	41	28	68.3
1973	David Ray, Los Angeles, NFC	47	30	63.8
	Roy Gerela, Pittsburgh, AFC	43	29	67.4
1974	Chester Marcol, Green Bay, NFC	39	25	64.1
	Roy Gerela, Pittsburgh, AFC	29	20	69.0
1975	Jan Stenerud, Kansas City, AFC	32	22	68.8
	Toni Fritsch, Dallas, NFC	35	22	62.9
1976	Mark Moseley, Washington, NFC	34	22	64.7
	Jan Stenerud, Kansas City, AFC	38	21	55.3
1977	Mark Moseley, Washington, NFC	37	21	56.8
	Errol Mann, Oakland, AFC	28	20	71.4
1978	*Frank Corral, Los Angeles, NFC	43	29	67.4
	Pat Leahy, N.Y. Jets, AFC	30	22	73.3
1979	Mark Moseley, Washington, NFC	33	25	75.8
	John Smith, New England, AFC	33	23	69.7
1980	*Ed Murray, Detroit, NFC	42	27	64.3
	John Smith, New England, AFC	34	26	76.5
	Fred Steinfort, Denver, AFC	34	26	76.5
1981	Rafael Septien, Dallas, NFC	35	27	77.1
	Nick Lowery, Kansas City, AFC	36	26	72.2
1982	Mark Moseley, Washington, NFC	21	20	95.2
	Nick Lowery, Kansas City, AFC	24	19	79.2
1983	*Ali-Haji-Sheikh, N.Y. Giants, NFC	42	35	83.3

	*Raul Allegre, Baltimore, AFC	35	30	85.7
1984	*Paul McFadden,			
	Philadelphia, NFC	37	30	81.1
	Gary Anderson, Pittsburgh, AFC	32	24	75.0
	Matt Bahr, Cleveland, AFC	32	24	75.0
1985	Gary Anderson, Pittsburgh, AFC	42	33	78.6
	Morten Andersen,			
	New Orleans, NFC	35	31	88.6
	*Kevin Butler, Chicago, NFC	37	31	83.8
1986	Tony Franklin, New England, AFC	41	32	78.0
	Kevin Butler, Chicago, NFC	41	28	68.3
1987	Morten Andersen,			
	New Orleans, NFC	36	28	77.8
	Dean Biasucci, Indianapolis, AFC	27	24	88.9
	Jim Breech, Cincinnati, AFC	30	24	80.0
1988	Scott Norwood, Buffalo, AFC	37	32	86.5
	Mike Cofer, San Francisco, NFC	38	27	71.1
1989	Rich Karlis, Minnesota, NFC	39	31	79.5
	*David Treadwell, Denver, AFC	33	27	81.8
1990	Nick Lowery, Kansas City, AFC	37	34	91.9
	Chip Lohmiller, Washington, NFC	40	30	75.0
1991	Pete Stoyanovich, Miami, AFC	37	31	83.8
	Chip Lohmiller, Washington, NFC	43	31	72.1
1992	Pete Stoyanovich, Miami, AFC	37	30	81.1
	Chip Lohmiller, Washington, NFC	40	30	75.0
1993	Jeff Jaeger, L.A. Raiders, AFC	44	35	79.5
	Jason Hanson, Detroit, NFC	43	34	79.1
1994	John Carney, San Diego, AFC	38	34	89.5
	Fuad Reveiz, Minnesota, NFC	39	34	87.2
1995	Norm Johnson, Pittsburgh, AFC	41	34	82.9
	Morten Andersen, Atlanta, NFC	37	31	83.8
1996	John Kasay, Carolina, NFC	45	37	82.2
	Cary Blanchard, Indianapolis, AFC	40	36	90.0

*First season of professional football.

RUSHING

YEAR	PLAYER, TEAM	ATT.	YARDS	AVG.	TD
1932	*Cliff Battles, Boston	148	576	3.9	3
1933	Jim Musick, Boston	173	809	4.7	5
1934	*Beattie Feathers, Chi. Bears	119	1,004	8.4	8
1935	Doug Russell,				
	Chi. Cardinals	140	499	3.6	0
1936	*Alphonse (Tuffy) Leemans,				
	N.Y. Giants	206	830	4.0	2
1937	Cliff Battles, Washington	216	874	4.0	5
1938	*Byron (Whizzer) White,				
	Pittsburgh	152	567	3.7	4
1939	*Bill Osmanski, Chicago	121	699	5.8	7
1940	Byron (Whizzer) White,				
	Detroit	146	514	3.5	5
1941	Clarence (Pug) Manders,				
	Brooklyn	111	486	4.4	5
1942	*Bill Dudley, Pittsburgh	162	696	4.3	5
1943	*Bill Paschal, N.Y. Giants	147	572	3.9	10
1944	Bill Paschal, N.Y. Giants	196	737	3.8	9
1945	Steve Van Buren,				
	Philadelphia	143	832	5.8	15

YEAR	PLAYER, TEAM	ATT.	YARDS	AVG.	TD
1946	Bill Dudley, Pittsburgh	146	604	4.1	3
1947	Steve Van Buren,				
	Philadelphia	217	1,008	4.6	13
1948	Steve Van Buren,				
	Philadelphia	201	945	4.7	10
1949	Steve Van Buren,				
	Philadelphia	263	1,146	4.4	11
1950	Marion Motley, Cleveland	140	810	5.8	3
1951	Eddie Price, N.Y. Giants	271	971	3.6	7
1952	Dan Towler, Los Angeles	156	894	5.7	10
1953	Joe Perry, San Francisco	192	1,018	5.3	10
1954	Joe Perry, San Francisco	173	1,049	6.1	8
1955	*Alan Ameche, Baltimore	213	961	4.5	9
1956	Rick Casares, Chi. Bears	234	1,126	4.8	12
1957	*Jim Brown, Cleveland	202	942	4.7	9
1958	Jim Brown, Cleveland	257	1,527	5.9	17
1959	Jim Brown, Cleveland	290	1,329	4.6	14
1960	Jim Brown,				
	Cleveland, NFL	215	1,257	5.8	9
	*Abner Haynes,				
	Dall. Texans, AFL	156	875	5.6	9
1961	Jim Brown,				
	Cleveland, NFL	305	1,408	4.6	8
	Billy Cannon, Houston, AFL	200	948	4.7	6
1962	Jim Taylor, Green Bay, NFL	272	1,474	5.4	19
	Cookie Gilchrist,				
	Buffalo, AFL	214	1,096	5.1	13
1963	Jim Brown, Cleveland, NFL	291	1,863	6.4	12
	Clem Daniels,				
	Oakland, AFL	215	1,099	5.1	3
1964	Jim Brown, Cleveland, NFL	280	1,446	5.2	7
	Cookie Gilchrist,				
	Buffalo, AFL	230	981	4.3	6
1965	Jim Brown,				
	Cleveland, NFL	289	1,544	5.3	17
	Paul Lowe, San Diego, AFL	222	1,121	5.0	7
1966	Jim Nance, Boston, AFL	299	1,458	4.9	11
	Gale Sayers, Chicago, NFL	229	1,231	5.4	8
1967	Jim Nance, Boston, AFL	269	1,216	4.5	7
	Leroy Kelly,				
	Cleveland, NFL	235	1,205	5.1	11
1968	Leroy Kelly,				
	Cleveland, NFL	248	1,239	5.0	16
	*Paul Robinson,				
	Cincinnati, AFL	238	1,023	4.3	8
1969	Gale Sayers, Chicago, NFL	236	1,032	4.4	8
	Dickie Post,				
	San Diego, AFL	182	873	4.8	6
1970	Larry Brown,				
	Washington, NFC	237	1,125	4.7	5
	Floyd Little, Denver, AFC	209	901	4.3	3
1971	Floyd Little, Denver, AFC	284	1,133	4.0	6
	*John Brockington,				
	Green Bay, NFC	216	1,105	5.1	4
1972	O.J. Simpson, Buffalo, AFC	292	1,251	4.3	6
	Larry Brown,				
	Washington, NFC	285	1,216	4.3	8
1973	O.J. Simpson, Buffalo, AFC	332	2,003	6.0	12

		ATT	YARDS	AVG	TD
	John Brockington, Green Bay, NFC	265	1,144	4.3	3
1974	Otis Armstrong, Denver, AFC	263	1,407	5.3	9
	Lawrence McCutcheon, Los Angeles, NFC	236	1,109	4.7	3
1975	O.J. Simpson, Buffalo, AFC	329	1,817	5.5	16
	Jim Otis, St. Louis, NFC	269	1,076	4.0	5
1976	O.J. Simpson, Buffalo, AFC	290	1,503	5.2	8
	Walter Payton, Chicago, NFC	311	1,390	4.5	13
1977	Walter Payton, Chicago, NFC	339	1,852	5.5	14
	Mark van Eeghen, Oakland, AFC	324	1,273	3.9	7
1978	*Earl Campbell, Houston, AFC	302	1,450	4.8	13
	Walter Payton, Chicago, NFC	333	1,395	4.2	11
1979	Earl Campbell, Houston, AFC	368	1,697	4.6	19
	Walter Payton, Chicago, NFC	369	1,610	4.4	14
1980	Earl Campbell, Houston, AFC	373	1,934	5.2	13
	Walter Payton, Chicago, NFC	317	1,460	4.6	6
1981	*George Rogers, New Orleans, NFC	378	1,674	4.4	13
	Earl Campbell, Houston, AFC	361	1,376	3.8	10
1982	Freeman McNeil, N.Y. Jets, AFC	151	786	5.2	6
	Tony Dorsett, Dallas, NFC	177	745	4.2	5
1983	*Eric Dickerson, L.A. Rams, NFC	390	1,808	4.6	18
	*Curt Warner, Seattle, AFC	335	1,449	4.3	13
1984	Eric Dickerson, L.A. Rams, NFC	379	2,105	5.6	14
	Earnest Jackson, San Diego, AFC	296	1,179	4.0	8
1985	Marcus Allen, L.A. Raiders, AFC	380	1,759	4.6	11
	Gerald Riggs, Atlanta, NFC	397	1,719	4.3	10
1986	Eric Dickerson, L.A. Rams, NFC	404	1,821	4.5	11
	Curt Warner, Seattle, AFC	319	1,481	4.6	13
1987	Charles White, L.A. Rams, NFC	324	1,374	4.2	11
	Eric Dickerson, Indianapolis, AFC	223	1,011	4.5	5
1988	Eric Dickerson, Indianapolis, AFC	388	1,659	4.3	14
	Herschel Walker, Dallas, NFC	361	1,514	4.2	5
1989	Christian Okoye, Kansas City, AFC	370	1,480	4.0	12
	*Barry Sanders, Detroit, NFC	280	1,470	5.3	14
1990	Barry Sanders, Detroit, NFC	255	1,304	5.1	13
	Thurman Thomas, Buffalo, AFC	271	1,297	4.8	11
1991	Emmitt Smith, Dallas, NFC	365	1,563	4.3	12
	Thurman Thomas, Buffalo, AFC	288	1,407	4.9	7
1992	Emmitt Smith, Dallas, NFC	373	1,713	4.6	18
	Barry Foster, Pittsburgh, AFC	390	1,690	4.3	11
1993	Emmitt Smith, Dallas, NFC	283	1,486	5.3	9
	Thurman Thomas, Buffalo, AFC	355	1,315	3.7	6
1994	Barry Sanders, Detroit, NFC	331	1,883	5.7	7
	Chris Warren, Seattle, AFC	333	1,545	4.6	9
1995	Emmitt Smith, Dallas, NFC	377	1,773	4.7	25
	Curtis Martin, New England, AFC	368	1,487	4.0	14
1996	Barry Sanders, Detroit, NFC	307	1,553	5.1	11
	Terrell Davis, Denver, AFC	345	1,538	4.5	13

*First season of professional football.

PASSING

(Current rating system implemented in 1973)

YEAR PLAYER, TEAM	ATT	COMP	YARDS	TD	INT	RATING
1932 Arnie Herber, Green Bay	101	37	639	9	9	
1933 *Harry Newman, N.Y. Giants	136	53	973	11	17	
1934 Arnie Herber, Green Bay	115	42	799	8	12	
1935 Ed Danowski, N.Y. Giants	113	57	794	10	9	
1936 Arnie Herber, Green Bay	173	77	1,239	11	13	
1937 *Sammy Baugh, Washington	171	81	1,127	8	14	
1938 Ed Danowski, N.Y. Giants	129	70	848	7	8	
1939 *Parker Hall, Cleveland	208	106	1,227	9	13	
1940 Sammy Baugh, Washington	177	111	1,367	12	10	
1941 Cecil Isbell, Green Bay	206	117	1,479	15	11	
1942 Cecil Isbell, Green Bay	268	146	2,021	24	14	

Year / Player / Team	Att	Comp	Yards	TD	Int	Rating
1943 Sammy Baugh, Washington	239	133	1,754	23	19	
1944 Frank Filchock, Washington	147	84	1,139	13	9	
1945 Sammy Baugh, Washington	182	128	1,669	11	4	
Sid Luckman, Chi. Bears	217	117	1,725	14	10	
1946 Bob Waterfield, Los Angeles	251	127	1,747	18	17	
1947 Sammy Baugh, Washington	354	210	2,938	25	15	
1948 Tommy Thompson, Philadelphia	246	141	1,965	25	11	
1949 Sammy Baugh, Washington	255	145	1,903	18	14	
1950 Norm Van Brocklin, Los Angeles	233	127	2,061	18	14	
1951 Bob Waterfield, Los Angeles	176	88	1,566	13	10	
1952 Norm Van Brocklin, Los Angeles	205	113	1,736	14	17	
1953 Otto Graham, Cleveland	258	167	2,722	11	9	
1954 Norm Van Brocklin, Los Angeles	260	139	2,637	13	21	
1955 Otto Graham, Cleveland	185	98	1,721	15	8	
1956 Ed Brown, Chi. Bears	168	96	1,667	11	12	
1957 Tommy O'Connell, Cleveland	110	63	1,229	9	8	
1958 Eddie LeBaron, Washington	145	79	1,365	11	10	
1959 Charlie Conerly, N.Y. Giants	194	113	1,706	14	4	
1960 Milt Plum, Cleveland, NFL	250	151	2,297	21	5	
Jack Kemp, L.A. Chargers, AFL	406	211	3,018	20	25	
1961 George Blanda, Houston, AFL	362	187	3,330	36	22	
Milt Plum, Cleveland, NFL	302	177	2,416	18	10	
1962 Len Dawson, Dall. Texans, AFL	310	189	2,759	29	17	
Bart Starr, Green Bay, NFL	285	178	2,438	12	9	
1963 Y.A. Tittle, N.Y. Giants, NFL	367	221	3,145	36	14	
Tobin Rote, San Diego, AFL	286	170	2,510	20	17	
1964 Len Dawson, Kansas City, AFL	354	199	2,879	30	18	
Bart Starr, Green Bay, NFL	272	163	2,144	15	4	
1965 Rudy Bukich, Chicago, NFL	312	176	2,641	20	9	
John Hadl, San Diego, AFL	348	174	2,798	20	21	
1966 Bart Starr, Green Bay, NFL	251	156	2,257	14	3	
Len Dawson, Kansas City, AFL	284	159	2,527	26	10	
1967 Sonny Jurgensen, Washington, NFL	508	288	3,747	31	16	
Daryle Lamonica, Oakland, AFL	425	220	3,228	30	20	
1968 Len Dawson, Kansas City, AFL	224	131	2,109	17	9	
Earl Morrall, Baltimore, NFL	317	182	2,909	26	17	
1969 Sonny Jurgensen, Washington, NFL	442	274	3,102	22	15	
*Greg Cook, Cincinnati, AFL	197	106	1,854	15	11	
1970 John Brodie, San Francisco, NFC	378	223	2,941	24	10	
Daryle Lamonica, Oakland, AFC	356	179	2,516	22	15	
1971 Roger Staubach, Dallas, NFC	211	126	1,882	15	4	
Bob Griese, Miami, AFC	263	145	2,089	19	9	
1972 Norm Snead, N.Y. Giants, NFC	325	196	2,307	17	12	
Earl Morrall, Miami, AFC	150	83	1,360	11	7	
1973 Roger Staubach, Dallas, NFC	286	179	2,428	23	15	94.6
Ken Stabler, Oakland, AFC	260	163	1,997	14	10	88.5
1974 Ken Anderson, Cincinnati, AFC	328	213	2,667	18	10	95.9
Sonny Jurgensen, Washington, NFC	167	107	1,185	11	5	94.6
1975 Ken Anderson, Cincinnati, AFC	377	228	3,169	21	11	94.1
Fran Tarkenton, Minnesota, NFC	425	273	2,994	25	13	91.7
1976 Ken Stabler, Oakland, AFC	291	194	2,737	27	17	103.4
James Harris, Los Angeles, NFC	158	91	1,460	8	6	89.8
1977 Bob Griese, Miami, AFC	307	180	2,252	22	13	88.0
Roger Staubach, Dallas, NFC	361	210	2,620	18	9	87.1
1978 Roger Staubach, Dallas, NFC	413	231	3,190	25	16	84.9
Terry Bradshaw, Pittsburgh, AFC	368	207	2,915	28	20	84.8
1979 Roger Staubach, Dallas, NFC	461	267	3,586	27	11	92.4
Dan Fouts, San Diego, AFC	530	332	4,082	24	24	82.6

1980 Brian Sipe,
      Cleveland, AFC 554 337 4,132 30 14 91.4
      Ron Jaworski,
      Philadelphia, NFC 451 257 3,529 27 12 90.9
1981 Ken Anderson,
      Cincinnati, AFC 479 300 3,754 29 10 98.5
      Joe Montana, San
      Francisco, NFC 488 311 3,565 19 12 88.2
1982 Ken Anderson,
      Cincinnati, AFC 309 218 2,495 12 9 95.5
      Joe Theismann,
      Washington, NFC 252 161 2,033 13 9 91.3
1983 Steve Bartkowski,
      Atlanta, NFC 432 274 3,167 22 5 97.6
      *Dan Marino,
      Miami, AFC 296 173 2,210 20 6 96.0
1984 Dan Marino,
      Miami, AFC 564 362 5,084 48 17 108.9
      Joe Montana, San
      Francisco, NFC 432 279 3,630 28 10 102.9
1985 Ken O'Brien,
      N.Y. Jets, AFC 488 297 3,888 25 8 96.2
      Joe Montana, San
      Francisco, NFC 494 303 3,653 27 13 91.3
1986 Tommy Kramer,
      Minnesota, NFC 372 208 3,000 24 10 92.6
      Dan Marino,
      Miami, AFC 623 378 4,746 44 23 92.5
1987 Joe Montana, San
      Francisco, NFC 398 266 3,054 31 13 102.1
      Bernie Kosar,
      Cleveland, AFC 389 241 3,033 22 9 95.4
1988 Boomer Esiason,
      Cincinnati, AFC 388 223 3,572 28 14 97.4
      Wade Wilson,
      Minnesota, NFC 332 204 2,746 15 9 91.5
1989 Joe Montana, San
      Francisco, NFC 386 271 3,521 26 8 112.4
      Boomer Esiason,
      Cincinnati, AFC 455 258 3,525 28 11 92.1
1990 Jim Kelly,
      Buffalo, AFC 346 219 2,829 24 9 101.2
      Phil Simms, N.Y.
      Giants, NFC 311 184 2,284 15 4 92.7
1991 Steve Young, San
      Francisco, NFC 279 180 2,517 17 8 101.8
      Jim Kelly,
      Buffalo, AFC 474 304 3,844 33 17 97.6
1992 Steve Young, San
      Francisco, NFC 402 268 3,465 25 7 107.0
      Warren Moon,
      Houston, AFC 346 224 2,521 18 12 89.3
1993 Steve Young, San
      Francisco, NFC 462 314 4,023 29 16 101.5
      John Elway,
      Denver, AFC 551 348 4,030 25 10 92.8
1994 Steve Young, San
      Francisco, NFC 461 324 3,969 35 10 112.8

      Dan Marino,
      Miami, AFC 615 385 4,453 30 17 89.2
1995 Jim Harbaugh,
      Indianapolis, AFC 314 200 2,575 17 5 100.7
      Brett Favre,
      Green Bay, NFC 570 359 4,413 38 13 99.5
1996 Steve Young, San
      Francisco, NFC 316 214 2,410 14 6 97.2
      John Elway,
      Denver, AFC 466 287 3,328 26 14 89.2

---

*First season of professional football.

NFL ALL-TIME RECORDS

POINTS

MOST POINTS, CAREER

2,002   George Blanda, Chi. Bears, 1949, 1950–58; Balti-
        more, 1950; Houston, 1960–66; Oakland,
        1967–75 (9-td, 943-pat, 335-fg)

1,711   Nick Lowery, New England, 1978; Kansas City,
        1980–93; N.Y. Jets, 1994–96 (562-pat, 383-fg)

1,699   Jan Stenerud, Kansas City, 1967–79; Green Bay,
        1980–83; Minnesota, 1984–85 (580-pat, 373-fg)

MOST POINTS, SEASON

176   Paul Hornung, Green Bay, 1960 (15-td, 41-pat,
      15-fg)

161   Mark Moseley, Washington, 1983 (62-pat, 33-fg)

155   Gino Cappelletti, Boston, 1964 (7-td, 38-pat,
      25-fg)

TOUCHDOWNS

MOST TOUCHDOWNS, CAREER

165   Jerry Rice, San Francisco, 1985–96 (10-r, 154-p,
      1 ret)

134   Marcus Allen, L.A. Raiders, 1982–92; Kansas City,
      1993–96 (112-r, 21-p, 1-ret)

126   Jim Brown, Cleveland, 1957–65 (106-r, 20-p)

MOST TOUCHDOWNS, SEASON

25   Emmitt Smith, Dallas, 1995 (25-r)

24   John Riggins, Washington, 1983 (24-r)

23   O.J. Simpson, Buffalo, 1975 (16-r, 7-p)
     Jerry Rice, San Francisco, 1987 (1-r, 22-p)

FIELD GOALS

MOST FIELD GOALS, CAREER

383   Nick Lowery, New England, 1978; Kansas City,
      1980–93; N.Y. Jets, 1994–96

373   Jan Stenerud, Kansas City, 1967–79; Green Bay,
      1980–83; Minnesota, 1984–85

356   Gary Anderson, Pittsburgh, 1982–94; Philadelphia,
      1995–96

MOST FIELD GOALS, SEASON
37   John Kasay, Carolina, 1996
36   Cary Blanchard, Indianapolis, 1996
35   Ali Haji-Sheikh, N.Y. Giants, 1983
      Jeff Jaeger, L.A. Raiders, 1993

RUSHING

MOST YARDS GAINED, CAREER
16,726   Walter Payton, Chicago, 1975–87
13,259   Eric Dickerson, L.A. Rams, 1983–87; India-napolis, 1987–91; L.A. Raiders, 1992; Atlanta, 1993
12,739   Tony Dorsett, Dallas, 1977–87; Denver, 1988

MOST YARDS GAINED, SEASON
2,105   Eric Dickerson, L.A. Rams, 1984
2,003   O.J. Simpson, Buffalo, 1973
1,934   Earl Campbell, Houston, 1980

PASSING

MOST PASSES COMPLETED, CAREER
4,134 Dan Marino, Miami, 1983–96

3,686   Fran Tarkenton, Minnesota, 1961–66, 1972–78; N.Y. Giants, 1967–71
3,633   John Elway, Denver, 1983–96

MOST PASSES COMPLETED, SEASON
404   Warren Moon, Houston, 1991
400   Drew Bledsoe, New England, 1994
385   Dan Marino, Miami, 1994

MOST TOUCHDOWN PASSES, CAREER
369   Dan Marino, Miami, 1983–96
342   Fran Tarkenton, Minnesota, 1961–66, 1972–78; N.Y. Giants, 1967–71
290   Johnny Unitas, Baltimore, 1956–72; San Diego, 1973

MOST TOUCHDOWN PASSES, SEASON
48 Dan Marino, Miami, 1984
44 Dan Marino, Miami, 1986
39 Brett Favre, Green Bay, 1996

Basketball

NBA 1996–97 SEASON

If you want to talk about the 1996–97 National Basketball Association season, there's only one place to start. And it's not with the NBA's celebration of its 50th anniversary. Or Michael Jordan and the Chicago Bulls winning their fifth championship in the '90s. Or John Stockton and Karl Malone of the Utah Jazz finally getting a chance to play in the NBA Finals.

No. You start with the money. Shaquille O'Neal moved from the Orlando Magic to the Los Angeles Lakers for $120 million. Alonzo Mourning stayed with the Miami Heat for $112 million. Juwan Howard almost went from the Washington Bullets to the Heat for about $100 million but, after the NBA said "No deal!" to the deal, ended up back with the Bullets for the same (though someone else's) $100 million. It got to where a $50 million contract—and there were a bunch of those, too—wasn't worth the mention.

But the spending came with a price, and it was paid for mostly by the midlevel, service-able veteran. NBA economics demanded that the superstars be paid their due, but that left most teams cash poor, forcing them to fill out their rosters with rookies grateful for the work or experienced players willing to take huge paycuts. For rookie Matt Maloney, the Ivy Leaguer from Penn who caught on with the Houston Rockets and wound up a starter, it was a dream come true. But scoring machine Dominique Wilkens wound up in San Antonio playing for the league minimum, as did Rex Chapman, late of the Heat, in Phoenix. For some vets these brave new economics proved the end of the line: Spud Webb, the 5'7" fireplug with 11 solid NBA years on his resume, didn't get to an even dozen.

But there was a method to the madness, maybe. The Chicago Bulls were coming off a 72–10 season and their fourth NBA title. Matching up with Chicago's trinity of Mr. Jordan, Scottie Pippen, and Dennis Rodman became the league's latest challenge. And so the Houston Rockets added Charles Barkley to their superstar duo of Hakeem Olajuwan and Clyde Drexler. And the New York Knicks signed on Chris Childs, Allan Houston, and Larry Johnson.

But in the end, of course, none of it mattered.

Not that there weren't teams that didn't make it interesting, at least for a while. Pat Riley, who had escaped from the Knicks just the year before, pushed and shoved his Heat to a 61–21 record and the Atlantic Division title. The Phoenix Suns got off to an 0–13 start, fired Cotton Fitzsimmons and hired Danny Ainge, who brought his team out of the ashes and into the playoffs. Shaquille hurt his knee, missed a long stretch of games and the Lakers kept on winning at almost the same clip.

The Boston Celtics were awful, finishing at 15–67, much to the delight of many. The Knicks spent virtually the entire season telling everyone that it was going to take some time to blend their three new players with Patrick Ewing, their reigning superstar and No. 1 offensive option. The Utah Jazz did the nearly unthinkable: They played so well through the second half of the season that Karl Malone beat out Michael Jordan for the Most Valuable Player Award and people started to believe that there really was someone out there who could beat the Bulls. The Bulls, meanwhile, kept on winning, dealing with Dennis Rodman (among other things, he was suspended for 11 games for kicking a courtside cameraman), and providing endless speculation as to what would happen to Mr. Jordan, Scottie Pippen and coach Phil Jackson once the season finally ended.

In the playoffs leading up to the Finals you need to remember two things: Out West,

John Stockton destroyed the Houston Rockets with a last second shot to win Game six, 103–100, and propel the Jazz into the Finals for the first time ever. In the East, a bench clearing brawl between the Knicks and Heat in the conference semifinal resulted in five Knicks serving one-game suspensions in Games six and seven (there were so many Knicks suspended they had to take turns sitting out). They lost both games.

In the Finals, Bulls vs. Jazz, Chicago won the first two at home, 84–82 and 97–85, and looked unbeata-bull. But out in Salt Lake City, the Jazz rebounded, winning the first two of the three-game set, 104–93 and 78–73, with Game Four won on a full court one-handed flick from Mr. Stockton to Mr. Malone, over the outstretched hands of Mr. Jordan himself. Had the Jazz gone on from there to win the series, "The Pass," as it was quickly dubbed, would have entered the annals of all-time NBA Finals lore, right up there with "Havlicek stole the ball!" Instead, it became merely the signature moment of Mr. Stockton to Mr. Malone, perhaps the NBA's best-ever guard-forward combination.

And then there was Game Five. Mr. Jordan—suffering the flu, dehydrated and weak—willed himself to perhaps his greatest championship performance ever: 38 points, including the game winning 3-pointer with 25 seconds remaining. Game Six back in Chicago was just a formality. Steve Kerr sunk a shot from the top of the key off a pass from his Air-ness to clinch a 90–86 victory. Five trips to the Finals. Five championship trophies. Not a bad way to spend the '90s.

Steve McKee

1996-97 NBA Regular Season Statistics

Eastern Conference

Atlantic Division

	W	L	Pct.	GB	Home	Road	Last-10	Streak
Miami	61	21	.744	–	29-12	32-9	7-3	Won 1
New York	57	25	.695	4	31-10	26-15	6-4	Won 3
Orlando	45	37	.549	16	26-15	19-22	5-5	Lost 3
Washington	44	38	.537	17	25-16	19-22	7-3	Won 4
New Jersey	26	56	.317	35	16-25	10-31	3-7	Won 2
Philadelphia	22	60	.268	39	11-30	11-30	1-9	Lost 2
Boston	15	67	.183	46	11-30	4-37	2-8	Lost 1

Central Division

	W	L	Pct.	GB	Home	Road	Last-10	Streak
Chicago	69	13	.841	–	39 - 2	30-11	6-4	Lost 2
Atlanta	56	26	.683	13	36 - 5	20-21	6-4	Lost 1
Charlotte	54	28	.659	15	30-11	24-17	8-2	Lost 2
Detroit	54	28	.659	15	30-11	24-17	4-6	Won 1
Cleveland	42	40	.512	27	25-16	17-24	5-5	Lost 1
Indiana	39	43	.476	30	21-20	18-23	4-6	Lost 3
Milwaukee	33	49	.402	36	20-21	13-28	4-6	Won 1
Toronto	30	52	.366	39	18-23	12-29	5-5	Won 2

Western Conference

Midwest Division

	W	L	Pct.	GB	Home	Road	Last-10	Streak
Utah	64	18	.780	–	38 - 3	26-15	9-1	Won 4
Houston	57	25	.695	7	30-11	27-14	8-2	Won 4
Minnesota	40	42	.488	24	25-16	15-26	5-5	Lost 1
Dallas	24	58	.293	40	14-27	10-31	2-8	Lost 2
Denver	21	61	.256	43	12-29	9-32	1-9	Won 1
San Antonio	20	62	.244	44	12-29	8-33	2-8	Lost 6
Vancouver	14	68	.171	50	8-33	6-35	2-8	Won 1

Pacific Division

	W	L	Pct.	GB	Home	Road	Last-10	Streak
Seattle	57	25	.695	–	31-10	26-15	7-3	Won 3
LA Lakers	56	26	.683	1	31-10	25-16	7-3	Lost 1
Portland	49	33	.598	8	29-12	20-21	7-3	Won 4
Phoenix	40	42	.488	17	25-16	15-26	7-3	Lost 1
LA Clippers	36	46	.439	21	21-20	15-26	5-5	Lost 3
Sacramento	34	48	.415	23	22-19	12-29	5-5	Lost 1
Golden State	30	52	.366	27	18-23	12-29	4-6	Lost 2

1997 NBA Playoffs

First Round - Eastern Conference

Chicago vs. Washington

April 25	Washington	86	at	Chicago	98
April 27	Washington	104	at	Chicago	109
April 30	Chicago	96	at	Washington	95

(Bulls won series 3-0)

Miami vs. Orlando

April 24	Orlando	64	at	Miami	99
April 27	Orlando	87	at	Miami	104
April 29	Miami	75	at	Orlando	88
May 1	Miami	91	at	Orlando	99
May 4	Orlando	83	at	Miami	91

(Heat won series 3-2)

New York vs. Charlotte

April 24	Charlotte	99	at	New York	109
April 26	Charlotte	93	at	New York	100
April 28	New York	104	at	Charlotte	95

(Knicks won series 3-0)

Atlanta vs. Detroit

April 25	Detroit	75	at	Atlanta	89
April 27	Detroit	93	at	Atlanta	80
April 29	Atlanta	91	at	Detroit	99
May 2	Atlanta	94	at	Detroit	82
May 4	Detroit	79	at	Atlanta	84

(Hawks won series 3-2)

First Round - Western Conference

Utah vs. LA Clippers

April 24	LA Clippers	86	at	Utah	106
April 26	LA Clippers	99	at	Utah	105
April 28	Utah	104	at	LA Clippers	92

(Jazz won series 3-0)

Seattle vs. Phoenix

April 25	Phoenix	106	at	Seattle	101
April 27	Phoenix	78	at	Seattle	122
April 29	Seattle	103	at	Phoenix	110
May 1	Seattle	122	at	Phoenix	115 OT
May 3	Phoenix	92	at	Seattle	116

(SuperSonics won series 3-2)

Houston vs. Minnesota

April 24	Minnesota	95	at	Houston	112
April 26	Minnesota	84	at	Houston	96
April 29	Houston	125	at	Minnesota	120

(Rockets won series 3-0)

LA Lakers vs. Portland

April 25	Portland	77	at	LA Lakers	95
April 27	Portland	93	at	LA Lakers	107
April 30	LA Lakers	90	at	Portland	98
May 2	LA Lakers	95	at	Portland	91

(LA Lakers won series 3-1)

Conference Semifinals - Eastern Conference

Chicago vs. Atlanta

May 6	Atlanta	97	at	Chicago	100
May 8	Atlanta	103	at	Chicago	95
May 10	Chicago	100	at	Atlanta	80
May 11	Chicago	89	at	Atlanta	80
May 13	Atlanta	92	at	Chicago	107

(Bulls won series 4-1)

Miami vs. New York

May 7	New York	88	at	Miami	79
May 9	New York	84	at	Miami	88
May 11	Miami	73	at	New York	77
May 12	Miami	76	at	New York	89
May 14	New York	81	at	Miami	96
May 16	Miami	95	at	New York	90
May 18	New York	90	at	Miami	101

(Heat won series 4-3)

Conference Semifinals - Western Conference

Utah vs. LA Lakers

May 4	LA Lakers	77	at	Utah	93
May 6	LA Lakers	101	at	Utah	103
May 8	Utah	84	at	LA Lakers	104
May 10	Utah	110	at	LA Lakers	95
May 12	LA Lakers	93	at	Utah	98

(Jazz won series 4-1)

Houston vs. Seattle

May 5	Seattle	102	at	Houston	112
May 7	Seattle	106	at	Houston	101
May 9	Houston	97	at	Seattle	93
May 11	Houston	110	at	Seattle	106
May 13	Seattle	100	at	Houston	94
May 15	Houston	96	at	Seattle	99
May 17	Seattle	91	at	Houston	96

(Rockets won series 4-3)

Conference Finals - Eastern Conference

Miami vs. Chicago

May 20	Miami	77	at	Chicago	84
May 22	Miami	68	at	Chicago	75
May 24	Chicago	98	at	Miami	74
May 26	Chicago	80	at	Miami	87
May 28	Miami	87	at	Chicago	100

(Bulls won series 4-1)

Conference Finals - Western Conference

Houston vs. Utah

May 19	Houston	86	at	Utah	101
May 21	Houston	92	at	Utah	104
May 23	Utah	100	at	Houston	118
May 25	Utah	92	at	Houston	95
May 27	Houston	91	at	Utah	96
May 29	Utah	103	at	Houston	100

(Jazz won series 4-2)

NBA Finals

Utah vs. Chicago

June 1	Utah	82	at	Chicago	84
June 4	Utah	85	at	Chicago	97
June 6	Chicago	93	at	Utah	104
June 8	Chicago	73	at	Utah	78
June 11	Chicago	90	at	Utah	88
June 13	Utah	86	at	Chicago	90

(Bulls won series 4-2)

National Basketball Association Champions

Season	Champion	Eastern Div./Conf. (W-L)	Western Div./Conf. (W-L)
1946-47	Philadelphia	Philadelphia (35-25)	Chicago (39-22)
1947-48	Baltimore	Philadelphia (27-21)	Baltimore (28-20)
1948-49	Minneapolis	Washington (38-22)	Minneapolis (44-16)
1949-50	Minneapolis	Syracuse (51-13)	Minneapolis (51-17)
1950-51	Rochester	New York (36-30)	Rochester (41-27)
1951-52	Minneapolis	New York (37-29)	Minneapolis (40-26)
1952-53	Minneapolis	New York (47-23)	Minneapolis (48-22)
1953-54	Minneapolis	Syracuse (42-30)	Minneapolis (46-26)
1954-55	Syracuse	Syracuse (43-29)	Fort Wayne (43-29)
1955-56	Philadelphia	Philadelphia (45-27)	Fort Wayne (37-35)
1956-57	Boston	Boston (44-28)	St. Louis (34-38)
1957-58	St. Louis	Boston (49-23)	St. Louis (41-31)
1958-59	Boston	Boston (52-20)	Minneapolis (33-39)
1959-60	Boston	Boston (59-16)	St. Louis (46-29)
1960-61	Boston	Boston (57-22)	St. Louis (51-28)
1961-62	Boston	Boston (60-20)	Los Angeles (54-26)
1962-63	Boston	Boston (58-22)	Los Angeles (53-27)
1963-64	Boston	Boston (59-21)	San Francisco (48-32)
1964-65	Boston	Boston (62-18)	Los Angeles (49-31)
1965-66	Boston	Boston (54-26)	Los Angeles (45-35)
1966-67	Philadelphia	Philadelphia (68-13)	San Francisco (44-37)
1967-68	Boston	Boston (54-28)	Los Angeles (52-30)
1968-69	Boston	Boston (48-34)	Los Angeles (55-27)
1969-70	New York	New York (60-22)	Los Angeles (46-36)
1970-71	Milwaukee	Baltimore (42-40)	Milwaukee (66-16)
1971-72	Los Angeles	New York (48-34)	Los Angeles (69-13)
1972-73	New York	New York (57-25)	Los Angeles (60-22)
1973-74	Boston	Boston (56-26)	Milwaukee (59-23)
1974-75	Golden State	Washington (60-22)	Golden State (48-34)
1975-76	Boston	Boston (54-28)	Phoenix (42-40)
1976-77	Portland	Philadelphia (50-32)	Portland (49-33)
1977-78	Washington	Washington (44-38)	Seattle (47-35)
1978-79	Seattle	Washington (54-28)	Seattle (52-30)
1979-80	Los Angeles	Philadelphia (59-23)	Los Angeles (60-22)
1980-81	Boston	Boston (62-20)	Houston (40-42)
1981-82	Los Angeles	Philadelphia (58-24)	Los Angeles (57-25)
1982-83	Philadelphia	Philadelphia (65-17)	Los Angeles (58-24)
1983-84	Boston	Boston (62-20)	Los Angeles (54-28)
1984-85	L.A. Lakers	Boston (63-19)	L.A. Lakers (62-20)
1985-86	Boston	Boston (67-15)	Houston (51-31)
1986-87	L.A. Lakers	Boston (59-23)	L.A. Lakers (65-17)
1987-88	L.A. Lakers	Detroit (54-28)	L.A. Lakers (62-20)
1988-89	Detroit	Detroit (63-19)	L.A. Lakers (57-25)
1989-90	Detroit	Detroit (59-23)	Portland (59-23)
1990-91	Chicago	Chicago (61-21)	L.A.Lakers (58-24)
1991-92	Chicago	Chicago (67-15)	Portland (57-25)
1992-93	Chicago	Chicago (57-25)	Phoenix (62-20)
1993-94	Houston	New York (57-25)	Houston (58-24)
1994-95	Houston	Orlando (57-25)	Houston (47-35)
1995-96	Chicago	Chicago (72-10)	Seattle (64-18)
1996-97	Chicago	Chicago (69-13)	Utah (64-18)

Source: National Basketball Association

From the NBA Records Book

NBA Most Valuable Player*

1955-56	Bob Pettit, St. Louis	1976-77	Kareem Abdul-Jabbar, Los Angeles
1956-57	Bob Cousy, Boston	1977-78	Bill Walton, Portland
1957-58	Bill Russell, Boston	1978-79	Moses Malone, Houston
1958-59	Bob Pettit, St. Louis	1979-80	Kareem Abdul-Jabbar, Los Angeles
1959-60	Wilt Chamberlain, Philadelphia	1980-81	Julius Erving, Philadelphia
1960-61	Bill Russell, Boston	1981-82	Moses Malone, Houston
1961-62	Bill Russell, Boston	1982-83	Moses Malone, Philadelphia
1962-63	Bill Russell, Boston	1983-84	Larry Bird, Boston
1963-64	Oscar Robertson, Cincinnati	1984-85	Larry Bird, Boston
1964-65	Bill Russell, Boston	1985-86	Larry Bird, Boston
1965-66	Wilt Chamberlain, Philadelphia	1986-87	Magic Johnson, L.A. Lakers
1966-67	Wilt Chamberlain, Philadelphia	1987-88	Michael Jordan, Chicago
1967-68	Wilt Chamberlain, Philadelphia	1988-89	Magic Johnson, L.A. Lakers
1968-69	Wes Unseld, Baltimore	1989-90	Magic Johnson, L.A. Lakers
1969-70	Willis Reed, New York	1990-91	Michael Jordan, Chicago
1970-71	Kareem Abdul-Jabbar, Milwaukee	1991-92	Michael Jordan, Chicago
1971-72	Kareem Abdul-Jabbar, Milwaukee	1992-93	Charles Barkley, Phoenix
1972-73	Dave Cowens, Boston	1993-94	Hakeem Olajuwon, Houston
1973-74	Kareem Abdul-Jabbar, Milwaukee	1994-95	David Robinson, San Antonio
1974-75	Bob McAdoo, Buffalo	1995-96	Michael Jordan, Chicago
1975-76	Kareem Abdul-Jabbar, Los Angeles	1996-97	Karl Malone, Utah

NBA Yearly Scoring Leaders in Regular Season Play

Season	Pts.	Scoring	Season	Pts.	Scoring
1946-47	1,389	Joe Fulks, Philadelphia	1979-80	33.1†	George Gervin, San Antonio
1947-48	1,007	Max Zaslofsky, Chicago	1980-81	30.7†	Adrian Dantley, Utah
1948-49	1,698	George Mikan, Minneapolis	1981-82	32.3†	George Gervin, San Antonio
1949-50	1,865	George Mikan, Minneapolis	1982-83	28.4†	Alex English, Denver
1950-51	1,932	George Mikan, Minneapolis	1983-84	30.6†	Adrian Dantley, Utah
1951-52	1,674	Paul Arizin, Philadelphia	1984-85	32.9†	Bernard King, New York
1952-53	1,564	Neil Johnston, Philadelphia	1985-86	30.3†	Dominique Wilkins, Atlanta
1953-54	1,759	Neil Johnston, Philadelphia	1986-87	37.1†	Michael Jordan, Chicago
1954-55	1,631	Neil Johnston, Philadelphia	1987-88	35.0†	Michael Jordan, Chicago
1955-56	1,849	Bob Pettit, St. Louis	1988-89	32.5†	Michael Jordan, Chicago
1956-57	1,817	Paul Arizin, Philadelphia	1989-90	33.6†	Michael Jordan, Chicago
1957-58	2,001	George Yardley, Detroit	1990-91	31.5†	Michael Jordan, Chicago
1958-59	2,105	Bob Pettit, St. Louis	1991-92	30.1†	Michael Jordan, Chicago
1959-60	2,707	Wilt Chamberlain, Philadelphia	1992-93	32.6†	Michael Jordan, Chicago
1960-61	3,033	Wilt Chamberlain, Philadelphia	1993-94	29.8†	David Robinson, San Antonio
1961-62	4,029	Wilt Chamberlain, Philadelphia	1994-95	29.3†	Shaquille O'Neal, Orlando
1962-63	3,586	Wilt Chamberlain, San Francisco	1995-96	30.4†	Michael Jordan, Chicago
1963-64	2,948	Wilt Chamberlain, San Francisco	1996-97	29.6†	Michael Jordan, Chicago
1964-65	2,534	Wilt Chamberlain, S.F.-Phi.			
1965-66	2,649	Wilt Chamberlain, Philadelphia			
1966-67	2,775	Rick Barry, San Francisco			
1967-68	2,142	Dave Bing, Detroit			
1968-69	2,327	Elvin Hayes, San Diego			
1969-70	31.2†	Jerry West, Los Angeles			
1970-71	31.7†	Kareem Abdul-Jabbar, Milwaukee			
1971-72	34.8†	Kareem Abdul-Jabbar, Milwaukee			
1972-73	34.0†	Nate Archibald, K.C./Omaha			
1973-74	30.6†	Bob McAdoo, Buffalo			
1974-75	34.5†	Bob McAdoo, Buffalo			
1975-76	31.1†	Bob McAdoo, Buffalo			
1976-77	31.1†	Pete Maravich, New Orleans			
1977-78	27.2†	George Gervin, San Antonio			
1978-79	29.6†	George Gervin, San Antonio			

Top 10 NBA Career Scoring Leaders

Player	Yrs.	Pts.
Kareem Abdul-Jabbar	20	38,387
Wilt Chamberlain	14	31,419
Moses Malone	19	27,409
Elvin Hayes	16	27,313
Michael Jordan	14	26,710
Oscar Robertson	16	26,395
Dominique Wilkins	15	25,613
John Havlicek	13	25,389
Alex English	14	25,192
Karl Malone	15	23,177

*Selected by vote of NBA players until 1979–80; by writers and broadcasters since 1980–81.
†Based on average per game.
Source: National Basketball Association

NBA Career Leaders

Scoring Average (minimum 400 games or 10,000 points)

	G	FGM	FTM	Pts.	Avg.
Michael Jordan	848	10,081	6,233	26,920	31.7
Wilt Chamberlain	1,045	12,681	6,057	31,419	30.1
Elgin Baylor	846	8,693	5,763	23,149	27.4
Jerry West	932	9,016	7,160	25,192	27.0
Bob Pettit	792	7,349	6,182	20,880	26.4
George Gervin	791	8,045	4,541	20,708	26.2
Karl Malone	980	9,510	6,505	25,592	26.1
Oscar Robertson	1,040	9,508	7,694	26,710	25.7
David Robinson	563	5,087	4,168	14,366	25.5
Dominique Wilkins	1,047	9,913	6,002	26,534	25.3

Field Goal Percentage (minimum 2,000 made)

	FGA	FGM	Pct.
Artis Gilmore	9,570	5,732	.599
Mark West	4,264	2,491	.584
Shaquille O'Neal	6,513	3,760	.577
Steve Johnson	4,965	2,841	.572
Darryl Dawkins	6,079	3,477	.572
James Donaldson	5,442	3,105	.571
Jeff Ruland	3,734	2,105	.564
Kareem Abdul-Jabbar	28,307	15,837	.559
Kevin McHale	12,334	6,830	.554
Otis Thorpe	11,155	6,154	.552

Free Throw Percentage (minimum 1,200 made)

	FTA	FTM	Pct.
Mark Price	2,259	2,048	.907
Rick Barry	4,243	3,818	.900
Calvin Murphy	3,864	3,445	.892
Scott Skiles	1,741	1,548	.889
Larry Bird	4,471	3,960	.886
Bill Sharman	3,559	3,143	.883
Reggie Miller	4,597	4,034	.878
Ricky Pierce	3,819	3,346	.876
Kiki Vandeweghe	3,997	3,484	.872
Jeff Malone	3,383	2,947	.871

Assists

John Stockton	12,170
Magic Johnson	10,141
Oscar Robertson	9,887
Isiah Thomas	9,061
Maurice Cheeks	7,392
Len Wilkens	7,211
Bob Cousy	6,955
Guy Rodgers	6,917
Mark Jackson	6,825
Nate Archibald	6,476

Steals

John Stockton	2,531
Maurice Cheeks	2,310
Michael Jordan	2,165
Alvin Robertson	2,112
Clyde Drexler	2,081
Isiah Thomas	1,861
Derek Harper	1,841
Hakeem Olajuwon	1,811
Magic Johnson	1,724
Scottie Pippen	1,692

Personal Fouls

Kareem Abdul-Jabbar	4,657
Robert Parish	4,443
Elvin Hayes	4,193
Buck Williams	4,174
James Edwards	4,042
Jack Sikma	3,879
Hal Greer	3,855
Tom Chambers	3,740
Hakeem Olajuwon	3,695
Dolph Schayes	3,664

Field Goals

Kareem Abdul-Jabbar	15,837
Wilt Chamberlain	12,681
Elvin Hayes	10,976
Alex English	10,659
John Havlicek	10,513
Michael Jordan	10,081
Dominique Wilkins	9,913
Robert Parish	9,614
Karl Malone	9,510
Oscar Robertson	9,508

Free Throws

Moses Malone	8,531
Oscar Robertson	7,694
Jerry West	7,160
Dolph Schayes	6,979
Adrian Dantley	6,832
Kareem Abdul-Jabbar	6,712
Karl Malone	6,505
Michael Jordan	6,233
Bob Pettit	6,182
Wilt Chamberlain	6,057

Rebounds

Wilt Chamberlain	23,924
Bill Russell	21,620
Kareem Abdul-Jabbar	17,440
Elvin Hayes	16,279
Moses Malone	16,212
Robert Parish	14,715
Nate Thurmond	14,464
Walt Bellamy	14,241
Wes Unseld	13,769
Jerry Lucas	12,942

Source: National Basketball Association

Women's National Basketball Association

1997 Regular Season Standings

Eastern Conference	W	L	Pct.	GB	Western Conference	W	L	Pct.	GB
Houston	18	10	.643	–	Phoenix	16	12	.571	–
New York	17	11	.607	1	Los Angeles	14	14	.500	2
Cleveland	15	13	.536	3	Sacramento	10	18	.357	6
Charlotte	15	13	.536	3	Utah	7	21	.250	9

Semifinals	Finals
Houston 70, Charlotte 54 New York 59, Phoenix 41	Houston 65, New York 51

American Basketball League

1996-97 Regular Season Standings

Eastern Conference	W	L	Pct.	GB	Western Conference	W	L	Pct.	GB
Colorado	25	15	.625	–	Columbus	31	9	.775	–
San Jose	18	22	.450	7	Richmond	21	19	.525	7
Seattle	17	23	.425	8	Atlanta	18	22	.450	8
Portland	14	26	.350	11	New England	16	24	.350	11

Semifinals	Finals
Richmond 80, Colorado 77 Columbus 94, San Jose 69 Richmond 82, Colorado 66 Columbus 81, San Jose 69 (Columbus won series 2–0) (Richmond won series 2–0)	Columbus 90, Richmond 89 Richmond 75, Columbus 62 Richmond 72, Columbus 67 Columbus 95, Richmond 84 Columbus 77, Richmond 64 (Columbus won series 3–2)

Baseball

As Major League Baseball weathered the August Dog Days, there was plenty of good news—the kind baseball has needed for years, and especially since the disastrous 1994 players strike that canceled that season's World Series and delayed the start of the next season.

First and foremost, of course, was that the 1997 season celebrated the 50th anniversary of Jackie Robinson's taking the field with the Brooklyn Dodgers and thereby breaking the game's vaunted color barrier. Rachel Robinson, Jackie's widow, served as the nation's Mistress of Ceremonies, combining an easy grace with understated dignity. Yes, we have come a long way since April 15, 1947, she said in one breath, and then reminded us in the next that we still had a long, long way to go.

In the stands, attendance was up across the board. The first-ever interleague games proved a huge hit with fans. On the field, Ken Griffey, Jr., Mark McGwire and Tino Martinez had people dreaming, if not exactly outright believing, that Roger Maris's single-season homerun record of 61 dingers could be broken, or at least approached. Tony Gwynn and Larry Walker had spent enough time flirting with the magical .400 batting-average mark that there was much talk (most of it fanciful) that we would be seeing our first .400 hitter since Ted Williams in 1941. And Hideki Irabu, late of Japan and currently of the New York Yankees combined with—who else?—Yankees owner George Steinbrenner to produce the season's longest-running drama.

Mr. Irabu, whose rights belonged to the San Diego Padres, made it quite clear that he wanted to pitch only for the Yankees. Mr. Steinbrenner, bidding against himself, essentially, procured Mr. Irabu's rights and promptly paid him $12.3 million. In his first start, against the Detroit Tigers in early July, in a packed Yankee Stadium, Mr. Irabu made Mr. Steinbrenner look like a genius, striking out nine and displaying some of the fastball that had earned him the sobriquet "The Nolan Ryan of Japan." It was one of baseball's great nights of the season.

The rest has been . . . not so great. Mr. Irabu's earned-run average soared, so did his temper on occasion, and after falling to 2–2 he was returned to the minors. Back with the big club a few weeks later he won his first "restart" unimpressively. Still, no one denied Mr. Irabu gave baseball what it needed most: a real BASEBALL story.

That said, the business of baseball remains business. The year started off on a hopeful note when the players and owners buried the hatchet and settled their differences with a labor deal through the millennium. But then Chicago White Sox owner Jerry Reinsdorf, king of the hard-liners, went out and spent $55 million to pay Albert Belle and take him away from the Cleveland Indians. But, midway through the season, Mr. Reinsdorf proclaimed his Sox couldn't catch the Indians in the American League's Central Division, so in a cost-cutting move he got rid of four players (though not Mr. Belle).

As August moved into September "realignment" became the latest buzzword. Baseball, that supposedly leaderless entity, was moving swiftly toward a restructuring. One plan was to move a couple of teams around between the leagues. The radical plan, dubbed 16–14, would essentially split the country in two, east and west, creating such regional rivalries as Yankees vs. New York Mets and Los Angeles Dodgers vs. the Anaheim Angels. At least that's what baseball was saying. Detractors were saying this was a grand scheme to keep East Coast teams from playing late-night West Coast games—which kill TV and radio ratings. Reverting to leaderless form, baseball postponed the realignment vote until the fall of 1997.

One final note: Early in the year Dodger owner Peter O'Malley caught the world by surprise when he announced he was selling the family-owned team. Baseball traditionalists wept bitter tears. Brooklynites shouted with unrealistic joy, thinking somehow the Dodgers could be returned home. Meanwhile, Rupert Murdoch smiled. His News Corp. media empire was slated to buy the team for about $350 million.

Steve McKee

World Series Results

Year	Winner		Loser		Attendance
1903	Boston (AL)	5	Pittsburgh (NL)	3	100,429
1904		No World Series played			
1905	New York (NL)	4	Philadelphia (AL)	1	91,723
1906	Chicago (AL)	4	Chicago (NL)	2	99,845
1907	Chicago (NL)	4	Detroit (AL)	0 1 tie	78,068
1908	Chicago (NL)	4	Detroit (AL)	1	62,232
1909	Pittsburgh (NL)	4	Detroit (AL)	3	145,205
1910	Philadelphia (AL)	4	Chicago (NL)	1	124,222
1911	Philadelphia (AL)	4	New York (NL)	2	179,851
1912	Boston (AL)	4	New York (NL)	3 1 tie	252,037
1913	Philadelphia (AL)	4	New York (NL)	1	151,000
1914	Boston (NL)	4	Philadelphia (AL)	0	111,009
1915	Boston (AL)	4	Philadelphia (NL)	1	143,351
1916	Boston (AL)	4	Brooklyn (NL)	1	162,859
1917	Chicago (AL)	4	New York (NL)	2	186,654
1918	Boston (AL)	4	Chicago (NL)	2	128,483
1919	Cincinnati (NL)	5	Chicago (AL)	3	236,928
1920	Cleveland (AL)	5	Brooklyn (NL)	2	178,737
1921	New York (NL)	5	New York (AL)	3	269,976
1922	New York (NL)	4	New York (AL)	0 1 tie	185,947
1923	New York (AL)	4	New York (NL)	2	301,430
1924	Washington (AL)	4	New York (NL)	3	283,665
1925	Pittsburgh (NL)	4	Washington (AL)	3	282,848
1926	St. Louis (NL)	4	New York (AL)	3	328,051
1927	New York (AL)	4	Pittsburgh (NL)	0	201,705
1928	New York (AL)	4	St. Louis (NL)	0	199,072
1929	Philadelphia (AL)	4	Chicago (NL)	1	190,490
1930	Philadelphia (AL)	4	St. Louis (NL)	2	212,619
1931	St. Louis (NL)	4	Philadelphia (AL)	3	231,567
1932	New York (AL)	4	Chicago (NL)	0	191,998
1933	New York (NL)	4	Washington (AL)	1	163,076
1934	St. Louis (NL)	4	Detroit (AL)	3	281,510
1935	Detroit (AL)	4	Chicago (NL)	2	286,672
1936	New York (AL)	4	New York (NL)	2	302,924
1937	New York (AL)	4	New York (NL)	1	238,142
1938	New York (AL)	4	Chicago (NL)	0	200,833
1939	New York (AL)	4	Cincinnati (NL)	0	183,849
1940	Cincinnati (NL)	4	Detroit (AL)	3	281,927
1941	New York (AL)	4	Brooklyn (NL)	1	235,773
1942	St. Louis (NL)	4	New York (AL)	1	277,101
1943	New York (AL)	4	St. Louis (NL)	1	277,312
1944	St. Louis (NL)	4	St. Louis (AL)	2	206,708
1945	Detroit (AL)	4	Chicago (NL)	3	333,457
1946	St. Louis (NL)	4	Boston (AL)	3	250,071
1947	New York (AL)	4	Brooklyn (NL)	3	389,763
1948	Cleveland (AL)	4	Boston (NL)	2	358,362
1949	New York (AL)	4	Brooklyn (NL)	1	236,716

Year	Winner		Loser		Attendance
1950	New York (AL)	4	Philadelphia (NL)	0	196,009
1951	New York (AL)	4	New York (NL)	2	341,977
1952	New York (AL)	4	Brooklyn (NL)	3	340,706
1953	New York (AL)	4	Brooklyn (NL)	2	307,350
1954	New York (NL)	4	Cleveland (AL)	0	251,507
1955	Brooklyn (NL)	4	New York (AL)	3	362,310
1956	New York (AL)	4	Brooklyn (NL)	3	345,903
1957	Milwaukee (NL)	4	New York (AL)	3	394,712
1958	New York (AL)	4	Milwaukee (NL)	3	393,909
1959	Los Angeles (NL)	4	Chicago (AL)	2	420,784
1960	Pittsburgh (NL)	4	New York (AL)	3	349,813
1961	New York (AL)	4	Cincinnati (NL)	1	223,247
1962	New York (AL)	4	San Francisco (NL)	3	376,864
1963	Los Angeles (NL)	4	New York (AL)	0	247,279
1964	St. Louis (NL)	4	New York (AL)	3	321,807
1965	Los Angeles (NL)	4	Minnesota (AL)	3	364,326
1966	Baltimore (AL)	4	Los Angeles (NL)	0	220,791
1967	St. Louis (NL)	4	Boston (AL)	3	304,085
1968	Detroit (AL)	4	St. Louis (NL)	3	379,670
1969	New York (NL)	4	Baltimore (AL)	1	272,378
1970	Baltimore (AL)	4	Cincinnati (NL)	1	253,183
1971	Pittsburgh (NL)	4	Baltimore (AL)	3	351,091
1972	Oakland (AL)	4	Cincinnati (NL)	3	363,149
1973	Oakland (AL)	4	New York (NL)	3	358,289
1974	Oakland (AL)	4	Los Angeles (NL)	1	260,004
1975	Cincinnati (NL)	4	Boston (AL)	3	308,272
1976	Cincinnati (NL)	4	New York (AL)	0	223,009
1977	New York (AL)	4	Los Angeles (NL)	2	337,708
1978	New York (AL)	4	Los Angeles (NL)	2	337,304
1979	Pittsburgh (NL)	4	Baltimore (AL)	3	367,597
1980	Philadelphia (NL)	4	Kansas City (AL)	2	324,516
1981	Los Angeles (NL)	4	New York (AL)	2	338,081
1982	St. Louis (NL)	4	Milwaukee (AL)	3	348,570
1983	Baltimore (AL)	4	Philadelphia (NL)	1	304,139
1984	Detroit (AL)	4	San Diego (NL)	1	271,820
1985	Kansas City (AL)	4	St. Louis (NL)	3	327,494
1986	New York (NL)	4	Boston (AL)	3	321,774
1987	Minnesota (AL)	4	St. Louis (NL)	3	387,178
1988	Los Angeles (NL)	4	Oakland (AL)	1	259,984
1989	Oakland (AL)	4	San Francisco (NL)	0	222,843
1990	Cincinnati (NL)	4	Oakland (AL)	0	208,544
1991	Minnesota (AL)	4	Atlanta (NL)	3	373,160
1992	Toronto (AL)	4	Atlanta (NL)	2	311,460
1993	Toronto (AL)	4	Philadelphia (NL)	2	344,394
1994		No World Series played			
1995	Atlanta (NL)	4	Cleveland (AL)	2	286,385
1996	New York (AL)	4	Atlanta (NL)	2	324,685

Source: Office of the Commissioner of Baseball

World Series Most Valuable Player

1955	Johnny Podres, Brooklyn	1977	Reggie Jackson, New York (AL)
1956	Don Larsen, New York (AL)	1978	Bucky Dent, New York (AL)
1957	Lew Burdette, Milwaukee	1979	Willie Stargell, Pittsburgh
1958	Bob Turley, New York (AL)	1980	Mike Schmidt, Philadelphia
1959	Larry Sherry, Los Angeles	1981	Ron Cey, Pedro Guerrero, Steve Yeager,
1960	Bobby Richardson, New York (AL)		Los Angeles
1961	Whitey Ford, New York (AL)	1982	Darrell Porter, St. Louis
1962	Ralph Terry, New York (AL)	1983	Rick Dempsey, Baltimore
1963	Sandy Koufax, Los Angeles	1984	Alan Trammell, Detroit
1964	Bob Gibson, St. Louis	1985	Bret Saberhagen, Kansas City
1965	Sandy Koufax, Los Angeles	1986	Ray Knight, New York (NL)
1966	Frank Robinson, Baltimore	1987	Frank Viola, Minnesota
1967	Bob Gibson, St. Louis	1988	Orel Hershiser, Los Angeles
1968	Mickey Lolich, Detroit	1989	Dave Stewart, Oakland
1969	Donn Clendenon, New York (NL)	1990	Jose Rijo, Cincinnati
1970	Brooks Robinson, Baltimore	1991	Jack Morris, Minnesota
1971	Roberto Clemente, Pittsburgh	1992	Pat Borders, Toronto
1972	Gene Tenace, Oakland	1993	Paul Molitor, Toronto
1973	Reggie Jackson, Oakland	1994	No World Series played
1974	Rollie Fingers, Oakland	1995	Tom Glavine, Atlanta
1975	Pete Rose, Cincinnati	1996	John Wetteland, New York (AL)
1976	Johnny Bench, Cincinnati		

Source: Office of the Commissioner of Baseball

All-Star Game Results

Date	Winner	Score	Date	Winner	Score
July 6, 1933	American	4-2	July 8, 1952	National	3-2
July 10, 1934	American	9-7	July 14, 1953	National	5-1
July 8, 1935	American	4-1	July 13, 1954	American	11-9
July 7, 1936	National	4-3	July 12, 1955	National	6-5*
July 7, 1937	American	8-3	July 10, 1956	National	7-3
July 6, 1938	National	4-1	July 9, 1957	American	6-5
July 11, 1939	American	3-1	July 8, 1958	American	4-3
July 9, 1940	National	4-0	July 7, 1959	National	5-4
July 8, 1941	American	7-5	Aug. 3, 1959	American	5-3
July 6, 1942	American	3-1	July 11, 1960	National	5-3
July 13, 1943	American	5-3	July 13, 1960	National	6-0
July 11, 1944	National	7-1	July 11, 1961	National	5-4*
1945	No game played		July 31, 1961	Tie	1-1**
July 9, 1946	American	12-0	July 10, 1962	National	3-1
July 8, 1947	American	2-1	July 30, 1962	American	9-4
July 13, 1948	American	5-2	July 9, 1963	National	5-3
July 12, 1949	American	11-7	July 7, 1964	National	7-4
July 11, 1950	National	4-3*	July 13, 1965	National	6-5
July 10, 1951	National	8-3	July 12, 1966	National	2-1

Date	Winner	Score	Date	Winner	Score
July 11, 1967	National	2-1*	July 6, 1983	American	13-3
July 9, 1968	National	1-0*	July 10, 1984	National	3-1
July 23, 1969	National	9-3	July 16, 1985	National	6-1
July 14, 1970	National	5-4	July 15, 1986	American	3-2
July 13, 1971	American	6-4*	July 14, 1987	National	2-0
July 25, 1972	National	4-3	July 12, 1988	American	2-1*
July 24, 1973	National	7-1*	July 11, 1989	American	5-3
July 23, 1974	National	7-2	July 10, 1990	American	2-0
July 15, 1975	National	6-3	July 9, 1991	American	4-2
July 13, 1976	National	7-1	July 14, 1992	American	13-6
July 19, 1977	National	7-5	July 13, 1993	American	9-3
July 11, 1978	National	7-3	July 12, 1994	National	8-7
July 17, 1979	National	7-6	July 11, 1995	National	3-2*
July 8, 1980	National	4-2	July 9, 1996	National	6-0
Aug. 9, 1981	National	5-4	July 8, 1997	American	3-1
July 13, 1982	National	4-1			

Note: From 1959 to 1962, two all-star games were played.
*Extra innings.
**Game called because of rain after nine innings.
Source: Office of the Commissioner of Baseball

All-Star Game Most Valuable Player

Year	Player, team	Position	Year	Player, team	Position
1962 (1)	Maury Wills, L.A. (NL)	SS	1979	*Dave Parker, Pit.	RF
1962 (2)	*Leon Wagner, L.A. (AL)	LF	1980	Ken Griffey, Cin.	LF
1963	*Willie Mays, S.F.	CF	1981	*Gary Carter, Mon.	C
1964	Johnny Callison, Phi.	RF	1982	*Dave Concepcion, Cin.	SS
1965	*Juan Marichal, S.F.	P	1983	*Fred Lynn, CA	CF
1966	*Brooks Robinson, Bal.	3B	1984	*Gary Carter, Mon.	C
1967	Tony Perez, Cin.	3B	1985	*LaMarr Hoyt, S.D.	P
1968	*Willie Mays, S.F.	CF	1986	*Roger Clemens, Bos.	P
1969	*Willie McCovey, S.F.	1B	1987	Tim Raines, Mon.	LF
1970	*Carl Yastrzemski, Bos.	CF-1B	1988	*Terry Steinbach, Oak.	C
1971	*Frank Robinson, Bal.	RF	1989	*Bo Jackson, K.C.	LF
1972	*Joe Morgan, Cin.	2B	1990	Julio Franco, TX	2B
1973	Bobby Bonds, S.F.	RF	1991	*Cal Ripken, Bal.	SS
1974	*Steve Garvey, L.A.	1B	1992	*Ken Griffey, Jr., Sea.	CF
1975	Bill Madlock, Chi. (NL)	3B	1993	*Kirby Puckett, MN	LF
	Jon Matlack, N.Y. (NL)	P	1994	Fred McGriff, Atl.	1B
1976	*George Foster, Cin.	CF-RF	1995	Jeff Conine, FL	OF
1977	*Don Sutton, L.A.	P	1996	*Mike Piazza, L.A.	C
1978	*Steve Garvey, L.A.	1B	1997	Sandy Alomar, Jr., Cleve	C

*Started game.
Source: Office of the Commissioner of Baseball

Major League Baseball Regular Season Yearly Leaders

Batting Average

American League

1901: Nap Lajoie, Philadelphia	.422
1902: Ed Delahanty, Washington	.376
1903: Nap Lajoie, Cleveland	.355
1904: Nap Lajoie, Cleveland	.381
1905: Elmer Flick, Cleveland	.308
1906: George Stone, St. Louis	.358
1907: Ty Cobb, Detroit	.350
1908: Ty Cobb, Detroit	.324
1909: Ty Cobb, Detroit	.377
1910: Ty Cobb, Detroit	.385
1911: Ty Cobb, Detroit	.420
1912: Ty Cobb, Detroit	.410
1913: Ty Cobb, Detroit	.390
1914: Ty Cobb, Detroit	.368
1915: Ty Cobb, Detroit	.369
1916: Tris Speaker, Cleveland	.386
1917: Ty Cobb, Detroit	.383
1918: Ty Cobb, Detroit	.382
1919: Ty Cobb, Detroit	.384
1920: George Sisler, St. Louis	.407
1921: Harry Heilmann, Detroit	.394
1922: George Sisler, St. Louis	.420
1923: Harry Heilmann, Detroit	.403
1924: Babe Ruth, New York	.378
1925: Harry Heilmann, Detroit	.393
1926: Heinie Manush, Detroit	.378
1927: Harry Heilmann, Detroit	.398
1928: Goose Goslin, Washington	.379
1929: Lew Fonseca, Cleveland	.369
1930: Al Simmons, Philadelphia	.381
1931: Al Simmons, Philadelphia	.390
1932: Dale Alexander, Detroit/Boston	.367
1933: Jimmie Foxx, Philadelphia	.356
1934: Lou Gehrig, New York	.363
1935: Buddy Myer, Washington	.349
1936: Luke Appling, Chicago	.388
1937: Charlie Gehringer, Detroit	.371
1938: Jimmie Foxx, Boston	.349
1939: Joe DiMaggio, New York	.381
1940: Joe DiMaggio, New York	.352
1941: Ted Williams, Boston	.406
1942: Ted Williams, Boston	.356
1943: Luke Appling, Chicago	.328
1944: Lou Boudreau, Cleveland	.327
1945: George Stirnweiss, New York	.309
1946: Mickey Vernon, Washington	.353
1947: Ted Williams, Boston	.343
1948: Ted Williams, Boston	.369
1949: George Kell, Detroit	.343
1950: Billy Goodman, Boston	.354
1951: Ferris Fain, Philadelphia	.344
1952: Ferris Fain, Philadelphia	.327
1953: Mickey Vernon, Washington	.337
1954: Bobby Avila, Cleveland	.341
1955: Al Kaline, Detroit	.340
1956: Mickey Mantle, New York	.353
1957: Ted Williams, Boston	.388
1958: Ted Williams, Boston	.328
1959: Harvey Kuenn, Detroit	.353
1960: Pete Runnels, Boston	.320
1961: Norm Cash, Detroit	.361
1962: Pete Runnels, Boston	.326
1963: Carl Yastrzemski, Boston	.321
1964: Tony Oliva, Minnesota	.323
1965: Tony Oliva, Minnesota	.321
1966: Frank Robinson, Baltimore	.316
1967: Carl Yastrzemski, Boston	.326
1968: Carl Yastrzemski, Boston	.301
1969: Rod Carew, Minnesota	.332
1970: Alex Johnson, California	.329
1971: Tony Oliva, Minnesota	.337
1972: Rod Carew, Minnesota	.318
1973: Rod Carew, Minnesota	.350
1974: Rod Carew, Minnesota	.364
1975: Rod Carew, Minnesota	.359
1976: George Brett, Kansas City	.333
1977: Rod Carew, Minnesota	.388
1978: Rod Carew, Minnesota	.333
1979: Fred Lynn, Boston	.333
1980: George Brett, Kansas City	.390
1981: Carney Lansford, Boston	.336
1982: Willie Wilson, Kansas City	.332
1983: Wade Boggs, Boston	.361
1984: Don Mattingly, New York	.343
1985: Wade Boggs, Boston	.368
1986: Wade Boggs, Boston	.357
1987: Wade Boggs, Boston	.363
1988: Wade Boggs, Boston	.366
1989: Kirby Puckett, Minnesota	.339
1990: George Brett, Kansas City	.329
1991: Julio Franco, Texas	.341
1992: Edgar Martinez, Seattle	.343
1993: John Olerud, Toronto	.363
1994: Paul O'Neill, New York	.359
1995: Edgar Martinez, Seattle	.356
1996: Alex Rodriguez, Seattle	.358

National League

1876: Ross Barnes, Chicago	.404
1877: Deacon White, Boston	.385
1878: Abner Dalrymple, Milwaukee	.356
1879: Cap Anson, Chicago	.407
1880: George Gore, Chicago	.365
1881: Cap Anson, Chicago	.399
1882: Dan Brouthers, Buffalo	.367

1883: Dan Brouthers, Buffalo	.371
1884: Jim O'Rourke, Buffalo	.350
1885: Roger Connor, New York	.371
1886: King Kelly, Chicago	.388
1887: Cap Anson, Chicago	.421
1888: Cap Anson, Chicago	.343
1889: Dan Brouthers, Boston	.373
1890: Jack Glasscock, New York	.336
1891: Billy Hamilton, Philadelphia	.338
1892: Dan Brouthers, Brooklyn	.335
Cupid Childs, Cleveland	.335
1893: Hugh Duffy, Boston	.378
1894: Hugh Duffy, Boston	.438
1895: Jesse Burkett, Cleveland	.423
1896: Jesse Burkett, Cleveland	.410
1897: Willie Keeler, Baltimore	.432
1898: Willie Keeler, Baltimore	.379
1899: Ed Delahanty, Philadelphia	.408
1900: Honus Wagner, Pittsburgh	.381
1901: Jesse Burkett, St. Louis	.382
1902: Ginger Beaumont, Pittsburgh	.357
1903: Honus Wagner, Pittsburgh	.355
1904: Honus Wagner, Pittsburgh	.349
1905: Cy Seymour, Cincinnati	.377
1906: Honus Wagner, Pittsburgh	.339
1907: Honus Wagner, Pittsburgh	.350
1908: Honus Wagner, Pittsburgh	.354
1909: Honus Wagner, Pittsburgh	.339
1910: Sherry Magee, Philadelphia	.331
1911: Honus Wagner, Pittsburgh	.334
1912: Heine Zimmerman, Chicago	.372
1913: Jake Daubert, Brooklyn	.350
1914: Jake Daubert, Brooklyn	.329
1915: Larry Doyle, New York	.320
1916: Hal Chase, Cincinnati	.339
1917: Edd Roush, Cincinnati	.341
1918: Zack Wheat, Brooklyn	.335
1919: Edd Roush, Cincinnati	.321
1920: Rogers Hornsby, St. Louis	.370
1921: Rogers Hornsby, St. Louis	.397
1922: Rogers Hornsby, St. Louis	.401
1923: Rogers Hornsby, St. Louis	.384
1924: Rogers Hornsby, St. Louis	.424
1925: Rogers Hornsby, St. Louis	.403
1926: Bubbles Hargrave, Cincinnati	.353
1927: Paul Waner, Pittsburgh	.380
1928: Rogers Hornsby, Boston	.387
1929: Lefty O'Doul, Philadelphia	.398
1930: Bill Terry, New York	.401
1931: Chick Hafey, St. Louis	.349
1932: Lefty O'Doul, Brooklyn	.368
1933: Chuck Klein, Philadelphia	.368
1934: Paul Waner, Pittsburgh	.362
1935: Arky Vaughan, Pittsburgh	.385
1936: Paul Waner, Pittsburgh	.373
1937: Joe Medwick, St. Louis	.374
1938: Ernie Lombardi, Cincinnati	.342
1939: Johnny Mize, St. Louis	.349
1940: Debs Garms, Pittsburgh	.355
1941: Pete Reiser, Brooklyn	.343
1942: Ernie Lombardi, Boston	.330
1943: Stan Musial, St. Louis	.357
1944: Dixie Walker, Brooklyn	.357
1945: Phil Cavarretta, Chicago	.355
1946: Stan Musial, St. Louis	.365
1947: Harry Walker, St. Louis/Philadelphia	.363
1948: Stan Musial, St. Louis	.376
1949: Jackie Robinson, Brooklyn	.342
1950: Stan Musial, St. Louis	.346
1951: Stan Musial, St. Louis	.355
1952: Stan Musial, St. Louis	.336
1953: Carl Furillo, Brooklyn	.344
1954: Willie Mays, New York	.345
1955: Richie Ashburn, Philadelphia	.338
1956: Hank Aaron, Milwaukee	.328
1957: Stan Musial, St. Louis	.351
1958: Richie Ashburn, Philadelphia	.350
1959: Hank Aaron, Milwaukee	.355
1960: Dick Groat, Pittsburgh	.325
1961: Roberto Clemente, Pittsburgh	.351
1962: Tommy Davis, Los Angeles	.346
1963: Tommy Davis, Los Angeles	.326
1964: Roberto Clemente, Pittsburgh	.339
1965: Roberto Clemente, Pittsburgh	.329
1966: Matty Alou, Pittsburgh	.342
1967: Roberto Clemente, Pittsburgh	.357
1968: Pete Rose, Cincinnati	.335
1969: Pete Rose, Cincinnati	.348
1970: Rico Carty, Atlanta	.366
1971: Joe Torre, St. Louis	.363
1972: Billy Williams, Chicago	.333
1973: Pete Rose, Cincinnati	.338
1974: Ralph Garr, Atlanta	.353
1975: Bill Madlock, Chicago	.354
1976: Bill Madlock, Chicago	.339
1977: Dave Parker, Pittsburgh	.338
1978: Dave Parker, Pittsburgh	.334
1979: Keith Hernandez, St. Louis	.344
1980: Bill Buckner, Chicago	.324
1981: Bill Madlock, Pittsburgh	.341
1982: Al Oliver, Montreal	.331
1983: Bill Madlock, Pittsburgh	.323
1984: Tony Gwynn, San Diego	.351
1985: Willie McGee, St. Louis	.353
1986: Tim Raines, Montreal	.334
1987: Tony Gwynn, San Diego	.370
1988: Tony Gwynn, San Diego	.313
1989: Tony Gwynn, San Diego	.336
1990: Willie McGee, St. Louis	.335
1991: Terry Pendleton, Atlanta	.319
1992: Gary Sheffield, San Diego	.330
1993: Andres Galarraga, Colorado	.370
1994: Tony Gwynn, San Diego	.394
1995: Tony Gwynn, San Diego	.368
1996: Tony Gwynn, San Diego	.353

Note—Bases on balls counted as hits in 1887.

Slugging Average

American League

1901: Nap Lajoie, Philadelphia	.635
1902: Ed Delahanty, Washington	.589
1903: Nap Lajoie, Cleveland	.533
1904: Nap Lajoie, Cleveland	.549
1905: Elmer Flick, Cleveland	.466
1906: George Stone, St. Louis	.496
1907: Ty Cobb, Detroit	.473
1908: Ty Cobb, Detroit	.475
1909: Ty Cobb, Detroit	.517
1910: Ty Cobb, Detroit	.554
1911: Ty Cobb, Detroit	.621
1912: Ty Cobb, Detroit	.586
1913: Joe Jackson, Cleveland	.551
1914: Ty Cobb, Detroit	.513
1915: Jack Fournier, Chicago	.491
1916: Tris Speaker, Cleveland	.502
1917: Ty Cobb, Detroit	.571
1918: Babe Ruth, Boston	.555
1919: Babe Ruth, Boston	.657
1920: Babe Ruth, New York	.847
1921: Babe Ruth, New York	.846
1922: Babe Ruth, New York	.672
1923: Babe Ruth, New York	.764
1924: Babe Ruth, New York	.739
1925: Ken Williams, St. Louis	.613
1926: Babe Ruth, New York	.737
1927: Babe Ruth, New York	.772
1928: Babe Ruth, New York	.709
1929: Babe Ruth, New York	.697
1930: Babe Ruth, New York	.732
1931: Babe Ruth, New York	.700
1932: Jimmie Foxx, Philadelphia	.749
1933: Jimmie Foxx, Philadelphia	.703
1934: Lou Gehrig, New York	.706
1935: Jimmie Foxx, Philadelphia	.636
1936: Lou Gehrig, New York	.696
1937: Joe DiMaggio, New York	.673
1938: Jimmie Foxx, Boston	.704
1939: Jimmie Foxx, Boston	.694
1940: Hank Greenberg, Detroit	.670
1941: Ted Williams, Boston	.735
1942: Ted Williams, Boston	.648
1943: Rudy York, Detroit	.527
1944: Bobby Doerr, Boston	.528
1945: George Stirnweiss, New York	.476
1946: Ted Williams, Boston	.667
1947: Ted Williams, Boston	.634
1948: Ted Williams, Boston	.615
1949: Ted Williams, Boston	.650
1950: Joe DiMaggio, New York	.585
1951: Ted Williams, Boston	.556
1952: Larry Doby, Cleveland	.541
1953: Al Rosen, Cleveland	.613
1954: Ted Williams, Boston	.635
1955: Mickey Mantle, New York	.611
1956: Mickey Mantle, New York	.705
1957: Ted Williams, Boston	.731
1958: Rocky Colavito, Cleveland	.620
1959: Al Kaline, Detroit	.530
1960: Roger Maris, New York	.581
1961: Mickey Mantle, New York	.687
1962: Mickey Mantle, New York	.605
1963: Harmon Killebrew, Minnesota	.555
1964: Boog Powell, Baltimore	.606
1965: Carl Yastrzemski, Boston	.536
1966: Frank Robinson, Baltimore	.637
1967: Carl Yastrzemski, Boston	.622
1968: Frank Howard, Washington	.552
1969: Reggie Jackson, Oakland	.608
1970: Carl Yastrzemski, Boston	.592
1971: Tony Oliva, Minnesota	.546
1972: Dick Allen, Chicago	.603
1973: Reggie Jackson, Oakland	.531
1974: Dick Allen, Chicago	.563
1975: Fred Lynn, Boston	.566
1976: Reggie Jackson, Baltimore	.502
1977: Jim Rice, Boston	.593
1978: Jim Rice, Boston	.600
1979: Fred Lynn, Boston	.637
1980: George Brett, Kansas City	.664
1981: Bobby Grich, California	.543
1982: Robin Yount, Milwaukee	.578
1983: George Brett, Kansas City	.563
1984: Harold Baines, Chicago	.541
1985: George Brett, Kansas City	.585
1986: Don Mattingly, New York	.573
1987: Mark McGwire, Oakland	.618
1988: Jose Canseco, Oakland	.569
1989: Ruben Sierra, Texas	.543
1990: Cecil Fielder, Detroit	.592
1991: Danny Tartabull, Kansas City	.593
1992: Mark McGwire, Oakland	.585
1993: Juan Gonzalez, Texas	.632
1994: Frank Thomas, Chicago	.729
1995: Albert Belle, Cleveland	.690
1996: Mark McGwire, Oakland	.730

National League

1900: Honus Wagner, Pittsburgh	.572
1901: Jimmy Sheckard, Brooklyn	.541
1902: Honus Wagner, Pittsburgh	.467
1903: Fred Clarke, Pittsburgh	.532
1904: Honus Wagner, Pittsburgh	.520
1905: Cy Seymour, Cincinnati	.559
1906: Harry Lumley, Brooklyn	.477
1907: Honus Wagner, Pittsburgh	.513
1908: Honus Wagner, Pittsburgh	.542
1909: Honus Wagner, Pittsburgh	.489
1910: Sherry Magee, Philadelphia	.507
1911: Frank Schulte, Chicago	.534
1912: Heinie Zimmerman, Chicago	.571
1913: Gavvy Cravath, Philadelphia	.568
1914: Sherry Magee, Philadelphia	.509

1915: Gavvy Cravath, Philadelphia	.510		1973: Willie Stargell, Pittsburgh	.646
1916: Zack Wheat, Brooklyn	.461		1974: Mike Schmidt, Philadelphia	.546
1917: Rogers Hornsby, St. Louis	.484		1975: Dave Parker, Pittsburgh	.541
1918: Edd Roush, Cincinnati	.455		1976: Joe Morgan, Cincinnati	.576
1919: Hy Myers, Brooklyn	.436		1977: George Foster, Cincinnati	.631
1920: Rogers Hornsby, St. Louis	.559		1978: Dave Parker, Pittsburgh	.585
1921: Rogers Hornsby, St. Louis	.659		1979: Dave Kingman, Chicago	.613
1922: Rogers Hornsby, St. Louis	.722		1980: Mike Schmidt, Philadelphia	.624
1923: Rogers Hornsby, St. Louis	.627		1981: Mike Schmidt, Philadelphia	.644
1924: Rogers Hornsby, St. Louis	.696		1982: Mike Schmidt, Philadelphia	.547
1925: Rogers Hornsby, St. Louis	.756		1983: Dale Murphy, Atlanta	.540
1926: Cy Williams, Philadelphia	.569		1984: Dale Murphy, Atlanta	.547
1927: Chick Hafey, St. Louis	.590		1985: Pedro Guerrero, Los Angeles	.577
1928: Rogers Hornsby, Boston	.632		1986: Mike Schmidt, Philadelphia	.547
1929: Rogers Hornsby, Chicago	.679		1987: Jack Clark, St. Louis	.597
1930: Hack Wilson, Chicago	.723		1988: Darryl Strawberry, New York	.545
1931: Chuck Klein, Philadelphia	.584		1989: Kevin Mitchell, San Francisco	.635
1932: Chuck Klein, Philadelphia	.646		1990: Barry Bonds, Pittsburgh	.565
1933: Chuck Klein, Philadelphia	.602		1991: Will Clark, San Francisco	.536
1934: Rip Collins, St. Louis	.615		1992: Barry Bonds, Pittsburgh	.624
1935: Arky Vaughan, Pittsburgh	.607		1993: Barry Bonds, San Francisco	.677
1936: Mel Ott, New York	.588		1994: Jeff Bagwell, Houston	.750
1937: Joe Medwick, St. Louis	.641		1995: Dante Bichette, Colorado	.620
1938: Johnny Mize, St. Louis	.614		1996: Ellis Burks, Colorado	.639
1939: Johnny Mize, St. Louis	.626			
1940: Johnny Mize, St. Louis	.636		**Runs**	
1941: Pete Reiser, Brooklyn	.558			
1942: Johnny Mize, New York	.521		**American League**	
1943: Stan Musial, St. Louis	.562		1901: Nap Lajoie, Philadelphia	145
1944: Stan Musial, St. Louis	.549		1902: Dave Fultz, Philadelphia	110
1945: Tommy Holmes, Boston	.577		1903: Patsy Dougherty, Boston	108
1946: Stan Musial, St. Louis	.587		1904: Patsy Dougherty, Boston/New York	113
1947: Ralph Kiner, Pittsburgh	.639		1905: Harry Davis, Philadelphia	92
1948: Stan Musial, St. Louis	.702		1906: Elmer Flick, Cleveland	98
1949: Ralph Kiner, Pittsburgh	.658		1907: Sam Crawford, Detroit	102
1950: Stan Musial, St. Louis	.596		1908: Matty McIntyre, Detroit	105
1951: Ralph Kiner, Pittsburgh	.627		1909: Ty Cobb, Detroit	116
1952: Stan Musial, St. Louis	.538		1910: Ty Cobb, Detroit	106
1953: Duke Snider, Brooklyn	.627		1911: Ty Cobb, Detroit	147
1954: Willie Mays, New York	.667		1912: Eddie Collins, Philadelphia	137
1955: Willie Mays, New York	.659		1913: Eddie Collins, Philadelphia	125
1956: Duke Snider, Brooklyn	.598		1914: Eddie Collins, Philadelphia	122
1957: Willie Mays, New York	.626		1915: Ty Cobb, Detroit	144
1958: Ernie Banks, Chicago	.614		1916: Ty Cobb, Detroit	113
1959: Hank Aaron, Milwaukee	.636		1917: Donie Bush, Detroit	112
1960: Frank Robinson, Cincinnati	.595		1918: Ray Chapman, Cleveland	84
1961: Frank Robinson, Cincinnati	.611		1919: Babe Ruth, Boston	103
1962: Frank Robinson, Cincinnati	.624		1920: Baby Ruth, New York	158
1963: Hank Aaron, Milwaukee	.586		1921: Babe Ruth, New York	177
1964: Willie Mays, San Francisco	.607		1922: George Sisler, St. Louis	134
1965: Willie Mays, San Francisco	.645		1923: Babe Ruth, New York	151
1966: Dick Allen, Philadelphia	.632		1924: Babe Ruth, New York	143
1967: Hank Aaron, Atlanta	.573		1925: Johnny Mostil, Chicago	135
1968: Willie McCovey, San Francisco	.545		1926: Babe Ruth, New York	139
1969: Willie McCovey, San Francisco	.656		1927: Babe Ruth, New York	158
1970: Willie McCovey, San Francisco	.612		1928: Babe Ruth, New York	163
1971: Hank Aaron, Atlanta	.669		1929: Charlie Gehringer, Detroit	131
1972: Billy Williams, Chicago	.606		1930: Al Simmons, Philadelphia	152

1931: Lou Gehrig, New York	163
1932: Jimmie Foxx, Philadelphia	151
1933: Lou Gehrig, New York	138
1934: Charlie Gehringer, Detroit	134
1935: Lou Gehrig, New York	125
1936: Lou Gehrig, New York	167
1937: Joe DiMaggio, New York	151
1938: Hank Greenberg, Detroit	144
1939: Red Rolfe, New York	139
1940: Ted Williams, Boston	134
1941: Ted Williams, Boston	135
1942: Ted Williams, Boston	141
1943: George Case, Washington	102
1944: George Stirnweiss, New York	125
1945: George Stirnweiss, New York	107
1946: Ted Williams, Boston	142
1947: Ted Williams, Boston	125
1948: Tommy Henrich, New York	138
1949: Ted Williams, Boston	150
1950: Dom DiMaggio, Boston	131
1951: Dom DiMaggio, Boston	113
1952: Larry Doby, Cleveland	104
1953: Al Rosen, Cleveland	115
1954: Mickey Mantle, New York	129
1955: Al Smith, Cleveland	123
1956: Mickey Mantle, New York	132
1957: Mickey Mantle, New York	121
1958: Mickey Mantle, New York	127
1959: Eddie Yost, Detroit	115
1960: Mickey Mantle, New York	119
1961: Mickey Mantle, New York	132
Roger Maris, New York	132
1962: Albie Pearson, Los Angeles	115
1963: Bob Allison, Minnesota	99
1964: Tony Oliva, Minnesota	109
1965: Zoilo Versalles, Minnesota	126
1966: Frank Robinson, Baltimore	122
1967: Carl Yastrzemski, Boston	112
1968: Dick McAuliffe, Detroit	95
1969: Reggie Jackson, Oakland	123
1970: Carl Yastrzemski, Boston	125
1971: Don Buford, Baltimore	99
1972: Bobby Murcer, New York	102
1973: Reggie Jackson, Oakland	99
1974: Carl Yastrzemski, Boston	93
1975: Fred Lynn, Boston	103
1976: Roy White, New York	104
1977: Rod Carew, Minnesota	128
1978: Ron LeFlore, Detroit	126
1979: Don Baylor, California	120
1980: Willie Wilson, Kansas City	133
1981: Rickey Henderson, Oakland	89
1982: Paul Molitor, Milwaukee	136
1983: Cal Ripken, Baltimore	121
1984: Dwight Evans, Boston	121
1985: Rickey Henderson, New York	146
1986: Rickey Henderson, New York	130
1987: Paul Molitor, Milwaukee	114

1988: Wade Boggs, Boston	128
1989: Wade Boggs, Boston	113
Rickey Henderson, New York/Oakland	113
1990: Rickey Henderson, Oakland	119
1991: Paul Molitor, Milwaukee	133
1992: Tony Phillips, Detroit	114
1993: Rafael Palmeiro, Texas	124
1994: Frank Thomas, Chicago	106
1995: Albert Belle, Cleveland	121
Edgar Martinez, Seattle	121
1996: Alex Rodriguez, Seattle	141

National League

1900: Roy Thomas, Philadelphia	131
1901: Jesse Burkett, St. Louis	139
1902: Honus Wagner, Pittsburgh	105
1903: Ginger Beaumont, Pittsburgh	137
1904: George Browne, New York	99
1905: Mike Donlin, New York	124
1906: Honus Wagner, Pittsburgh	103
Frank Chance, Chicago	103
1907: Spike Shannon, New York	104
1908: Fred Tenney, New York	101
1909: Tommy Leach, Pittsburgh	126
1910: Sherry Magee, Philadelphia	110
1911: Jimmy Sheckard, Chicago	121
1912: Bob Bescher, Cincinnati	120
1913: Tommy Leach, Chicago	99
Max Carey, Pittsburgh	99
1914: George J. Burns, New York	100
1915: Gavvy Cravath, Philadelphia	89
1916: George J. Burns, New York	105
1917: George J. Burns, New York	103
1918: Heinie Groh, Cincinnati	88
1919: George J. Burns, New York	86
1920: George J. Burns, New York	115
1921: Rogers Hornsby, St. Louis	131
1922: Rogers Hornsby, St. Louis	141
1923: Ross Youngs, New York	121
1924: Frankie Frisch, New York	121
Rogers Hornsby, St. Louis	121
1925: Kiki Cuyler, Pittsburgh	144
1926: Kiki Cuyler, Pittsburgh	113
1927: Lloyd Waner, Pittsburgh	133
Rogers Hornsby, New York	133
1928: Paul Waner, Pittsburgh	142
1929: Rogers Hornsby, Chicago	156
1930: Chuck Klein, Philadelphia	158
1931: Bill Terry, New York	121
Chuck Klein, Philadelphia	121
1932: Chuck Klein, Philadelphia	152
1933: Pepper Martin, St. Louis	122
1934: Paul Waner, Pittsburgh	122
1935: Augie Galan, Chicago	133
1936: Arky Vaughan, Pittsburgh	122
1937: Joe Medwick, St. Louis	111

1938: Mel Ott, New York		116
1939: Bill Werber, Cincinnati		115
1940: Arky Vaughan, Pittsburgh		113
1941: Pete Reiser, Brooklyn		117
1942: Met Ott, New York		118
1943: Arky Vaughan, Brooklyn		112
1944: Bill Nicholson, Chicago		116
1945: Eddie Stanky, Brooklyn		128
1946: Stan Musial, St. Louis		124
1947: Johnny Mize, New York		137
1948: Stan Musial, St. Louis		135
1949: Pee Wee Reese, Brooklyn		132
1950: Earl Torgeson, Boston		120
1951: Stan Musial, St. Louis		124
Ralph Kiner, Pittsburgh		124
1952: Stan Musial, St. Louis		105
Solly Hemus, St. Louis		105
1953: Duke Snider, Brooklyn		132
1954: Stan Musial, St. Louis		120
Duke Snider, Brooklyn		120
1955: Duke Snider, Brooklyn		126
1956: Frank Robinson, Cincinnati		122
1957: Hank Aaron, Milwaukee		118
1958: Willie Mays, San Francisco		121
1959: Vada Pinson, Cincinnati		131
1960: Billy Bruton, Milwaukee		112
1961: Willie Mays, San Francisco		129
1962: Frank Robinson, Cincinnati		134
1963: Hank Aaron, Milwaukee		121
1964: Dick Allen, Philadelphia		125
1965: Tommy Harper, Cincinnati		126
1966: Felipe Alou, Atlanta		122
1967: Hank Aaron, Atlanta		113
Lou Brock, St. Louis		113
1968: Glenn Beckert, Chicago		98
1969: Bobby Bonds, San Francisco		120
Pete Rose, Cincinnati		120
1970: Billy Williams, Chicago		137
1971: Lou Brock, St. Louis		126
1972: Joe Morgan, Cincinnati		122
1973: Bobby Bonds, San Francisco		131
1974: Pete Rose, Cincinnati		110
1975: Pete Rose, Cincinnati		112
1976: Rose Rose, Cincinnati		130
1977: George Foster, Cincinnati		124
1978: Ivan DeJesus, Chicago		104
1979: Keith Hernandez, St. Louis		116
1980: Keith Hernandez, St. Louis		111
1981: Mike Schmidt, Philadelphia		78
1982: Lonnie Smith, St. Louis		120
1983: Tim Raines, Montreal		133
1984: Ryne Sandberg, Chicago		114
1985: Dale Murphy, Atlanta		118
1986: Tony Gwynn, San Diego		107
Von Hayes, Philadelphia		107
1987: Tim Raines, Montreal		123
1988: Brett Butler, San Francisco		109

1989: Will Clark, San Francisco		104
Howard Johnson, New York		104
Ryne Sandberg, Chicago		104
1990: Ryne Sandberg, Chicago		116
1991: Brett Butler, Los Angeles		112
1992: Barry Bonds, Pittsburgh		109
1993: Lenny Dykstra, Philadelphia		143
1994: Jeff Bagwell, Houston		104
1995: Craig Biggio, Houston		123
1996: Ellis Burks, Colorado		142

Hits

American League

1901: Nap Lajoie, Philadelphia		229
1902: Charles Hickman, Boston/Cleveland		194
1903: Patsy Dougherty, Boston		195
1904: Nap Lajoie, Cleveland		211
1905: George Stone, St. Louis		187
1906: Nap Lajoie, Cleveland		214
1907: Ty Cobb, Detroit		212
1908: Ty Cobb, Detroit		188
1909: Ty Cobb, Detroit		216
1910: Nap Lajoie, Cleveland		227
1911: Ty Cobb, Detroit		248
1912: Ty Cobb, Detroit		227
1913: Joe Jackson, Cleveland		197
1914: Tris Speaker, Boston		193
1915: Ty Cobb, Detroit		208
1916: Tris Speaker, Cleveland		211
1917: Ty Cobb, Detroit		225
1918: George H. Burns, Philadelphia		178
1919: Ty Cobb, Detroit		191
Bobby Veach, Detroit		191
1920: George Sisler, St. Louis		257
1921: Harry Heilmann, Detroit		237
1922: George Sisler, St. Louis		246
1923: Charlie Jamieson, Cleveland		222
1924: Sam Rice, Washington		216
1925: Al Simmons, Philadelphia		253
1926: George H. Burns, Cleveland		216
Sam Rice, Washington		216
1927: Earle Combs, New York		231
1928: Heinie Manush, St. Louis		241
1929: Dale Alexander, Detroit		215
Charlie Gehringer, Detroit		215
1930: Johnny Hodapp, Cleveland		225
1931: Lou Gehrig, New York		211
1932: Al Simmons, Philadelphia		216
1933: Heinie Manush, Washington		221
1934: Charlie Gehringer, Detroit		214
1935: Joe Vosmik, Cleveland		216
1936: Earl Averill Sr., Cleveland		232
1937: Beau Bell, St. Louis		218
1938: Joe Vosmik, Boston		201
1939: Red Rolfe, New York		213

1940: Rip Radcliff, St. Louis	200	
Barney McCosky, Detroit	200	
Doc Cramer, Boston	200	
1941: Cecil Travis, Washington	218	
1942: Johnny Pesky, Boston	205	
1943: Dick Wakefield, Detroit	200	
1944: George Stirnweiss, New York	205	
1945: George Stirnweiss, New York	195	
1946: Johnny Pesky, Boston	208	
1947: Johnny Pesky, Boston	207	
1948: Bob Dillinger, St. Louis	207	
1949: Dale Mitchell, Cleveland	203	
1950: George Kell, Detroit	218	
1951: George Kell, Detroit	191	
1952: Nellie Fox, Chicago	192	
1953: Harvey Kuenn, Detroit	209	
1954: Nellie Fox, Chicago	201	
Harvey Kuenn, Detroit	201	
1955: Al Kaline, Detroit	200	
1956: Harvey Kuenn, Detroit	196	
1957: Nellie Fox, Chicago	196	
1958: Nellie Fox, Chicago	187	
1959: Harvey Kuenn, Detroit	198	
1960: Minnie Minoso, Chicago	184	
1961: Norm Cash, Detroit	193	
1962: Bobby Richardson, New York	209	
1963: Carl Yastrzemski, Boston	183	
1964: Tony Oliva, Minnesota	217	
1965: Tony Oliva, Minnesota	185	
1966: Tony Oliva, Minnesota	191	
1967: Carl Yastrzemski, Boston	189	
1968: Bert Campaneris, Oakland	177	
1969: Tony Oliva, Minnesota	197	
1970: Tony Oliva, Minnesota	204	
1971: Cesar Tovar, Minnesota	204	
1972: Joe Rudi, Oakland	181	
1973: Rod Carew, Minnesota	203	
1974: Rod Carew, Minnesota	218	
1975: George Brett, Kansas City	195	
1976: George Brett, Kansas City	215	
1977: Rod Carew, Minnesota	239	
1978: Jim Rice, Boston	213	
1979: George Brett, Kansas City	212	
1980: Willie Wilson, Kansas City	230	
1981: Rickey Henderson, Oakland	135	
1982: Robin Yount, Milwaukee	210	
1983: Cal Ripken, Baltimore	211	
1984: Don Mattingly, New York	207	
1985: Wade Boggs, Boston	240	
1986: Don Mattingly, New York	238	
1987: Kirby Puckett, Minnesota	207	
Kevin Seitzer, Kansas City	207	
1988: Kirby Puckett, Minnesota	234	
1989: Kirby Puckett, Minnesota	215	
1990: Rafael Palmeiro, Texas	191	
1991: Paul Molitor, Milwaukee	216	
1992: Kirby Puckett, Minnesota	210	
1993: Paul Molitor, Toronto	211	

1994: Kenny Lofton, Cleveland	160
1995: Lance Johnson, Chicago	186
1996: Paul Molitor, Minnesota	225

National League

1900: Willie Keeler, Brooklyn	208
1901: Jesse Burkett, St. Louis	228
1902: Ginger Beaumont, Pittsburgh	194
1903: Ginger Beaumont, Pittsburgh	209
1904: Ginger Beaumont, Pittsburgh	185
1905: Cy Seymour, Cincinnati	219
1906: Harry Steinfeldt, Chicago	176
1907: Ginger Beaumont, Boston	187
1908: Honus Wagner, Pittsburgh	201
1909: Larry Doyle, New York	172
1910: Honus Wagner, Pittsburgh	178
Bobby Byrne, Pittsburgh	178
1911: Doc Miller, Boston	192
1912: Heinie Zimmerman, Chicago	207
1913: Gavvy Cravath, Philadelphia	179
1914: Sherry Magee, Philadelphia	171
1915: Larry Doyle, New York	189
1916: Hal Chase, Cincinnati	184
1917: Heinie Groh, Cincinnati	182
1918: Charlie Hollocher, Chicago	161
1919: Ivy Olson, Brooklyn	164
1920: Rogers Hornsby, St. Louis	218
1921: Rogers Hornsby, St. Louis	235
1922: Rogers Hornsby, St. Louis	250
1923: Frankie Frisch, New York	223
1924: Rogers Hornsby, St. Louis	227
1925: Jim Bottomley, St. Louis	227
1926: Eddie Brown, Boston	201
1927: Paul Waner, Pittsburgh	237
1928: Fred Lindstrom, New York	231
1929: Lefty O'Doul, Philadelphia	254
1930: Bill Terry, New York	254
1931: Lloyd Waner, Pittsburgh	214
1932: Chuck Klein, Philadelphia	226
1933: Chuck Klein, Philadelphia	223
1934: Paul Waner, Pittsburgh	217
1935: Billy Herman, Chicago	227
1936: Joe Medwick, St. Louis	223
1937: Joe Medwick, St. Louis	237
1938: Frank McCormick, Cincinnati	209
1939: Frank McCormick, Cincinnati	209
1940: Stan Hack, Chicago	191
Frank McCormick, Cincinnati	191
1941: Stan Hack, Chicago	186
1942: Enos Slaughter, St. Louis	188
1943: Stan Musial, St. Louis	220
1944: Stan Musial, St. Louis	197
Phil Cavarretta, Chicago	197
1945: Tommy Holmes, Boston	224
1946: Stan Musial, St. Louis	228
1947: Tommy Holmes, Boston	191
1948: Stan Musial, St. Louis	230
1949: Stan Musial, St. Louis	207

1950: Duke Snider, Brooklyn	199
1951: Richie Ashburn, Philadelphia	221
1952: Stan Musial, St. Louis	194
1952: Richie Ashburn, Philadelphia	205
1954: Don Mueller, New York	212
1955: Ted Kluszewski, Cincinnati	192
1956: Hank Aaron, Milwaukee	200
1957: Red Schoendienst, New York/Milwaukee	200
1958: Richie Ashburn, Philadelphia	215
1959: Hank Aaron, Milwaukee	223
1960: Willie Mays, San Francisco	190
1961: Vada Pinson, Cincinnati	208
1962: Tommy Davis, Los Angeles	230
1963: Vada Pinson, Cincinnati	204
1964: Roberto Clemente, Pittsburgh	211
Curt Flood, St. Louis	211
1965: Pete Rose, Cincinnati	209
1966: Felipe Alou, Atlanta	218
1967: Roberto Clemente, Pittsburgh	209
1968: Felipe Alou, Atlanta	210
Pete Rose, Cincinnati	210
1969: Matty Alou, Pittsburgh	231
1970: Pete Rose, Cincinnati	205
Billy Williams, Chicago	205
1971: Joe Torre, St. Louis	230
1972: Pete Rose, Cincinnati	198
1973: Pete Rose, Cincinnati	230
1974: Ralph Garr, Atlanta	214
1975: Dave Cash, Philadelphia	213
1976: Pete Rose, Cincinnati	215
1977: Dave Parker, Pittsburgh	215
1978: Steve Garvey, Los Angeles	202
1979: Garry Templeton, St. Louis	211
1980: Steve Garvey, Los Angeles	200
1981: Pete Rose, Philadelphia	140
1982: Al Oliver, Montreal	204
1983: Jose Cruz, Houston	189
Andre Dawson, Montreal	189
1984: Tony Gwynn, San Diego	213
1985: Willie McGee, St. Louis	216
1986: Tony Gwynn, San Diego	211
1987: Tony Gwynn, San Diego	218
1988: Andres Galarraga, Montreal	184
1989: Tony Gwynn, San Diego	203
1990: Brett Butler, San Francisco	192
Lenny Dykstra, Philadelphia	192
1991: Terry Pendleton, Atlanta	187
1992: Terry Pendleton, Atlanta	199
Andy Van Slyke, Pittsburgh	199
1993: Lenny Dykstra, Philadelphia	194
1994: Tony Gwynn, San Diego	165
1995: Dante Bichette, Colorado	197
Tony Gwynn, San Diego	197
1996: Lance Johnson, New York	227

Home Runs

American League

1901: Nap Lajoie, Philadelphia	14
1902: Socks Seybold, Philadelphia	16
1903: Buck Freeman, Boston	13
1904: Harry Davis, Philadelphia	10
1905: Harry Davis, Philadelphia	8
1906: Harry Davis, Philadelphia	12
1907: Harry Davis, Philadelphia	8
1908: Sam Crawford, Detroit	7
1909: Ty Cobb, Detroit	9
1910: Jake Stahl, Boston	10
1911: Home Run Baker, Philadelphia	11
1912: Home Run Baker, Philadelphia	10
Tris Speaker, Boston	10
1913: Home Run Baker, Philadelphia	12
1914: Home Run Baker, Philadelphia	9
1915: Braggo Roth, Chicago/Cleveland	7
1916: Wally Pipp, New York	12
1917: Wally Pipp, New York	9
1918: Babe Ruth, Boston	11
Tilly Walker, Philadelphia	11
1919: Babe Ruth, Boston	29
1920: Babe Ruth, New York	54
1921: Babe Ruth, New York	59
1922: Ken Williams, St. Louis	39
1923: Babe Ruth, New York	41
1924: Babe Ruth, New York	46
1925: Bob Meusel, New York	33
1926: Babe Ruth, New York	47
1927: Babe Ruth, New York	60
1928: Babe Ruth, New York	54
1929: Babe Ruth, New York	46
1930: Babe Ruth, New York	49
1931: Babe Ruth, New York	46
Lou Gehrig, New York	46
1932: Jimmie Foxx, Philadelphia	58
1933: Jimmie Foxx, Philadelphia	48
1934: Lou Gehrig, New York	49
1935: Jimmie Foxx, Philadelphia	36
Hank Greenberg, Detroit	36
1936: Lou Gehrig, New York	49
1937: Joe DiMaggio, New York	46
1938: Hank Greenberg, Detroit	58
1939: Jimmie Foxx, Boston	35
1940: Hank Greenberg, Detroit	41
1941: Ted Williams, Boston	37
1942: Ted Williams, Boston	36
1943: Rudy York, Detroit	34
1944: Nick Etten, New York	22
1945: Vern Stephens, St. Louis	24
1946: Hank Greenberg, Detroit	44
1947: Ted Williams, Boston	32
1948: Joe DiMaggio, New York	39
1949: Ted Williams, Boston	43
1950: Al Rosen, Cleveland	37
1951: Gus Zernial, Chicago/Philadelphia	33

1952: Larry Doby, Cleveland	32
1953: Al Rosen, Cleveland	43
1954: Larry Doby, Cleveland	32
1955: Mickey Mantle, New York	37
1956: Mickey Mantle, New York	52
1957: Roy Sievers, Washington	42
1958: Mickey Mantle, New York	42
1959: Rocky Colavito, Cleveland	42
Harmon Killebrew, Washington	42
1960: Mickey Mantle, New York	40
1961: Roger Maris, New York	61
1962: Harmon Killebrew, Minnesota	48
1963: Harmon Killebrew, Minnesota	45
1964: Harmon Killebrew, Minnesota	49
1965: Tony Conigilaro, Boston	32
1966: Frank Robinson, Baltimore	49
1967: Harmon Killebrew, Minnesota	44
Carl Yastrzemski, Boston	44
1968: Frank Howard, Washington	44
1969: Harmon Killebrew, Minnesota	49
1970: Frank Howard, Washington	44
1971: Bill Melton, Chicago	33
1972: Dick Allen, Chicago	37
1973: Reggie Jackson, Oakland	32
1974: Dick Allen, Chicago	32
1975: Reggie Jackson, Oakland	36
George Scott, Milwaukee	36
1976: Graig Nettles, New York	32
1977: Jim Rice, Boston	39
1978: Jim Rice, Boston	46
1979: Gorman Thomas, Milwaukee	45
1980: Reggie Jackson, New York	41
Ben Oglivie, Milwaukee	41
1981: Tony Armas, Oakland	22
Dwight Evans, Boston	22
Bobby Grich, California	22
Eddie Murray, Baltimore	22
1982: Reggie Jackson, California	39
Gorman Thomas, Milwaukee	39
1983: Jim Rice, Boston	39
1984: Tony Armas, Boston	43
1985: Darrell Evans, Detroit	40
1986: Jesse Barfield, Toronto	40
1987: Mark McGwire, Oakland	49
1988: Jose Canseco, Oakland	42
1989: Fred McGriff, Toronto	36
1990: Cecil Fielder, Detroit	51
1991: Jose Canseco, Oakland	44
Cecil Fielder, Detroit	44
1992: Juan Gonzalez, Texas	43
1993: Juan Gonzalez, Texas	46
1994: Ken Griffey, Jr., Seattle	40
1995: Albert Belle, Cleveland	50
1996: Mark McGwire, Oakland	52

National League

1876: George Hall, Philadelphia	5
1877: George Shaffer, Louisville	3
1878: Paul Hines, Providence	4
1879: Charley Jones, Boston	9
1880: Jim O'Rourke, Boston	6
Harry Stovey, Worcester	6
1881: Dan Brouthers, Buffalo	8
1882: George Wood, Detroit	7
1883: Buck Ewing, New York	10
1884: Ned Williamson, Chicago	27
1885: Abner Dalrymple, Chicago	11
1886: Hardy Richardson, Detroit	11
1887: Roger Connor, New York	17
Billy O'Brien, Washington	17
1888: Roger Connor, New York	14
1889: Sam Thompson, Philadelphia	20
1890: Walt Wilmot, Chicago	14
1891: Harry Stovey, Boston	16
Mike Tiernan, New York	16
1892: Bug Holliday, Cincinnati	13
1893: Ed Delahanty, Philadelphia	19
1894: Hugh Duffy, Boston	18
Bobby Lowe, Boston	18
1895: Bill Joyce, Washington	17
1896: Ed Delahanty, Philadelphia	13
Sam Thompson, Philadelphia	13
1897: Nap Lajoie, Philadelphia	10
1898: Jimmy Collins, Boston	14
1899: Buck Freeman, Washington	25
1900: Herman Long, Boston	12
1901: Sam Crawford, Cincinnati	16
1902: Tommy Leach, Pittsburgh	6
1903: Jimmy Sheckard, Brooklyn	9
1904: Harry Lumley, Brooklyn	9
1905: Fred Odwell, Cincinnati	9
1906: Tim Jordan, Brooklyn	12
1907: Dave Brain, Boston	10
1908: Tim Jordan, Brooklyn	12
1909: Red Murray, New York	7
1910: Fred Beck, Boston	10
Frank Schulte, Chicago	10
1911: Frank Schulte, Chicago	21
1912: Heinie Zimmerman, Chicago	14
1913: Gavvy Cravath, Philadelphia	19
1914: Gavvy Cravath, Philadelphia	19
1915: Gavvy Cravath, Philadelphia	24
1916: Dave Robertson, New York	12
Cy Williams, Chicago	12
1917: Dave Robertson, New York	12
Gavvy Cravath, Philadelphia	12
1918: Gavvy Cravath, Philadelphia	8
1919: Gavvy Cravath, Philadelphia	12
1920: Cy Williams, Philadelphia	15
1921: George Kelly, New York	23
1922: Rogers Hornsby, St. Louis	42
1923: Cy Williams, Philadelphia	41
1924: Jack Fournier, Brooklyn	27
1925: Rogers Hornsby, St. Louis	39
1926: Hack Wilson, Chicago	21
1927: Hack Wilson, Chicago	30

Cy Williams, Philadelphia	30
1928: Hack Wilson, Chicago	31
Jim Bottomley, St. Louis	31
1929: Chuck Klein, Philadephia	43
1930: Hack Wilson, Chicago	56
1931: Chuck Klein, Philadelphia	31
1932: Chuck Klein, Philadelphia	38
Mel Ott, New York	38
1933: Chuck Klein, Philadelphia	28
1934: Rip Collins, St. Louis	35
Mel Ott, New York	35
1935: Wally Berger, Boston	34
1936: Mel Ott, New York	33
1937: Mel Ott, New York	31
Joe Medwick, St. Louis	31
1938: Mel Ott, New York	36
1939: Johnny Mize, St. Louis	28
1940: Johnny Mize, St. Louis	43
1941: Dolf Camilli, Brooklyn	34
1942: Mel Ott, New York	30
1943: Bill Nicholson, Chicago	29
1944: Bill Nicholson, Chicago	33
1945: Tommy Holmes, Boston	28
1946: Ralph Kiner, Pittsburgh	23
1947: Ralph Kiner, Pittsburgh	51
Johnny Mize, New York	51
1948: Ralph Kiner, Pittsburgh	40
Johnny Mize, New York	40
1949: Ralph Kiner, Pittsburgh	54
1950: Ralph Kiner, Pittsburgh	47
1951: Ralph Kiner, Pittsburgh	42
1952: Ralph Kiner, Pittsburgh	37
Hank Sauer, Chicago	37
1953: Eddie Mathews, Milwaukee	47
1954: Ted Kluszewski, Cincinnati	49
1955: Willie Mays, New York	51
1956: Duke Snider, Brooklyn	43
1957: Hank Aaron, Milwaukee	44
1958: Ernie Banks, Chicago	47
1959: Eddie Mathews, Milwaukee	46
1960: Ernie Banks, Chicago	41
1961: Orlando Cepeda, San Francisco	46
1962: Willie Mays, San Francisco	49
1963: Hank Aaron, Milwaukee	44
Willie McCovey, San Francisco	44
1964: Willie Mays, San Francisco	47
1965: Willie Mays, San Francisco	52
1966: Hank Aaron, Atlanta	44
1967: Hank Aaron, Atlanta	39
1968: Willie McCovey, San Francisco	36
1969: Willie McCovey, San Francisco	45
1970: Johnny Bench, Cincinnati	45
1971: Willie Stargell, Pittsburgh	48
1972: Johnny Bench, Cincinnati	40
1973: Willie Stargell, Pittsburgh	44
1974: Mike Schmidt, Philadelphia	36
1975: Mike Schmidt, Philadelphia	38
1976: Mike Schmidt, Philadelphia	38

1977: George Foster, Cincinnati	52
1978: George Foster, Cincinnati	40
1979: Dave Kingman, Chicago	48
1980: Mike Schmidt, Philadelphia	48
1981: Mike Schmidt, Philadelphia	31
1982: Dave Kingman, New York	37
1983: Mike Schmidt, Philadelphia	40
1984: Dale Murphy, Atlanta	36
Mike Schmidt, Philadelphia	36
1985: Dale Murphy, Atlanta	37
1986: Mike Schmidt, Philadelphia	37
1987: Andre Dawson, Chicago	49
1988: Darryl Strawberry, New York	39
1989: Kevin Mitchell, San Francisco	47
1990: Ryne Sandberg, Chicago	40
1991: Howard Johnson, New York	38
1992: Fred McGriff, San Diego	35
1993: Barry Bonds, San Francisco	46
1994: Matt Williams, San Francisco	43
1995: Dante Bichette, Colorado	40
1996: Andres Galarraga, Colorado	47

Runs Batted In

American League

1907: Ty Cobb, Detroit	116
1908: Ty Cobb, Detroit	101
1909: Ty Cobb, Detroit	115
1910: Sam Crawford, Detroit	115
1911: Ty Cobb, Detroit	144
1912: Home Run Baker, Philadelphia	133
1913: Home Run Baker, Philadelphia	126
1914: Sam Crawford, Detroit	112
1915: Sam Crawford, Detroit	116
1916: Wally Pipp, New York	99
1917: Bobby Veach, Detroit	115
1918: George H. Burns, Philadelphia	74
Bobby Veach, Detroit	74
1919: Babe Ruth, Boston	112
1920: Babe Ruth, New York	137
1921: Babe Ruth, New York	171
1922: Ken Williams, St. Louis	155
1923: Babe Ruth, New York	131
1924: Goose Goslin, Washington	129
1925: Bob Meusel, New York	138
1926: Babe Ruth, New York	145
1927: Lou Gehrig, New York	175
1928: Babe Ruth, New York	142
Lou Gehrig, New York	142
1929: Al Simmons, Philadelphia	157
1930: Lou Gehrig, New York	174
1931: Lou Gehrig, New York	184
1932: Jimmie Foxx, Philadelphia	169
1933: Jimmie Foxx, Philadelphia	163
1934: Lou Gehrig, New York	165
1935: Hank Greenberg, Detroit	170
1936: Hal Trosky, Cleveland	162
1937: Hank Greenberg, Detroit	183

1938: Jimmie Foxx, Boston	175
1939: Ted Williams, Boston	145
1940: Hank Greenberg, Detroit	150
1941: Joe DiMaggio, New York	125
1942: Ted Williams, Boston	137
1943: Rudy York, Detroit	118
1944: Vern Stephens, St. Louis	109
1945: Nick Etten, New York	111
1946: Hank Greenberg, Detroit	127
1947: Ted Williams, Boston	114
1948: Joe DiMaggio, New York	155
1949: Ted Williams, Boston	159
Vern Stephens, Boston	159
1950: Walt Dropo, Boston	144
Vern Stephens, Boston	144
1951: Gus Zernial, Chicago-Philadelphia	129
1952: Al Rosen, Cleveland	105
1953: Al Rosen, Cleveland	145
1954: Larry Doby, Cleveland	126
1955: Ray Boone, Detroit	116
Jackie Jensen, Boston	116
1956: Mickey Mantle, New York	130
1957: Roy Sievers, Washington	114
1958: Jackie Jensen, Boston	122
1959: Jackie Jensen, Boston	112
1960: Roger Maris, New York	112
1961: Roger Maris, New York	142
1962: Harmon Killebrew, Minnesota	126
1963: Dick Stuart, Boston	118
1964: Brooks Robinson, Baltimore	118
1965: Rocky Colavito, Cleveland	108
1966: Frank Robinson, Baltimore	122
1967: Carl Yastrzemski, Boston	121
1968: Ken Harrelson, Boston	109
1969: Harmon Killebrew, Minnesota	140
1970: Frank Howard, Washington	126
1971: Harmon Killebrew, Minnesota	119
1972: Dick Allen, Chicago	113
1973: Reggie Jackson, Oakland	117
1974: Jeff Burroughs, Texas	118
1975: George Scott, Milwaukee	109
1976: Lee May, Baltimore	109
1977: Larry Hisle, Minnesota	119
1978: Jim Rice, Boston	139
1979: Don Baylor, California	139
1980: Cecil Cooper, Milwaukee	122
1981: Eddie Murray, Baltimore	78
1982: Hal McRae, Kansas City	133
1983: Cecil Cooper, Milwaukee	126
Jim Rice, Boston	126
1984: Tony Armas, Boston	123
1985: Don Mattingly, New York	145
1986: Joe Carter, Cleveland	121
1987: George Bell, Toronto	134
1988: Jose Canseco, Oakland	124
1989: Ruben Sierra, Texas	119
1990: Cecil Fielder, Detroit	132
1991: Cecil Fielder, Detroit	133

1992: Cecil Fielder, Detroit	124
1993: Albert Belle, Cleveland	129
1994: Kirby Puckett, Minnesota	112
1995: Albert Belle, Cleveland	126
Mo Vaughn, Boston	126
1996: Albert Belle, Cleveland	148

National League

1907: Honus Wagner, Pittsburgh	91
1908: Honus Wagner, Pittsburgh	106
1909: Honus Wagner, Pittsburgh	102
1910: Sherry Magee, Philadelphia	116
1911: Frank Schulte, Chicago	121
1912: Heinie Zimmerman, Chicago	98
1913: Gavvy Cravath, Philadelphia	118
1914: Sherry Magee, Philadelphia	101
1915: Gavvy Cravath, Phildadelphia	118
1916: Hal Chase, Cincinnati	84
1917: Heinie Zimmerman, New York	100
1918: Fred Merkle, Chicago	71
1919: Hy Myers, Brooklyn	72
1920: George Kelly, New York	94
Rogers Hornsby, St. Louis	94
1921: Rogers Hornsby, St. Louis	126
1922: Rogers Hornsby, St. Louis	152
1923: Irish Meusel, New York	125
1924: George Kelly, New York	136
1925: Rogers Hornsby, St. Louis	143
1926: Jim Bottomley, St. Louis	120
1927: Paul Waner, Pittsburgh	131
1928: Jim Bottomley, St. Louis	136
1929: Hack Wilson, Chicago	159
1930: Hack Wilson, Chicago	190
1931: Chuck Klein, Philadelphia	121
1932: Don Hurst, Philadelphia	143
1933: Chuck Klein, Philadelphia	120
1934: Mel Ott, New York	135
1935: Wally Berger, Boston	130
1936: Joe Medwick, St. Louis	138
1937: Joe Medwick, St. Louis	154
1938: Joe Medwick, St. Louis	122
1939: Frank McCormick, Cincinnati	128
1940: Johnny Mize, St. Louis	137
1941: Dolf Camilli, Brooklyn	120
1942: Johnny Mize, New York	110
1943: Bill Nicholson, Chicago	128
1944: Bill Nicholson, Chicago	122
1945: Dixie Walker, Brooklyn	124
1946: Enos Slaughter, St. Louis	130
1947: Johnny Mize, New York	138
1948: Stan Musial, St. Louis	131
1949: Ralph Kiner, Pittsburgh	127
1950: Del Ennis, Philadelphia	126
1951: Monte Irvin, New York	121
1952: Hank Sauer, Chicago	121
1953: Roy Campanella, Brooklyn	142
1954: Ted Kluszewski, Cincinnati	141
1955: Duke Snider, Brooklyn	136

1956: Stan Musial, St. Louis	109
1957: Hank Aaron, Milwaukee	132
1958: Ernie Banks, Chicago	129
1959: Ernie Banks, Chicago	143
1960: Hank Aaron, Milwaukee	126
1961: Orlando Cepeda, San Francisco	142
1962: Tommy Davis, Los Angeles	153
1963: Hank Aaron, Milwaukee	130
1964: Ken Boyer, St. Louis	119
1965: Deron Johnson, Cincinnati	130
1966: Hank Aaron, Atlanta	127
1967: Orlando Cepeda, St. Louis	111
1968: Willie McCovey, San Francisco	105
1969: Willie McCovey, San Francisco	126
1970: Johnny Bench, Cincinnati	148
1971: Joe Torre, St. Louis	137
1972: Johnny Bench, Cincinnati	125
1973: Willie Stargell, Pittsburgh	119
1974: Johnny Bench, Cincinnati	129
1975: Greg Luzinski, Philadelphia	120
1976: George Foster, Cincinnati	121
1977: George Foster, Cincinnati	149
1978: George Foster, Cincinnati	120
1979: Dave Winfield, San Diego	118
1980: Mike Schmidt, Philadelphia	121
1981: Mike Schmidt, Philadelphia	91
1982: Dale Murphy, Atlanta	109
Al Oliver, Montreal	109
1983: Dale Murphy, Atlanta	121
1984: Gary Carter, Montreal	106
Mike Schmidt, Philadelphia	106
1985: Dave Parker, Cincinnati	125
1986: Mike Schmidt, Philadelphia	119
1987: Andre Dawson, Chicago	137
1988: Will Clark, San Francisco	109
1989: Kevin Mitchell, San Francisco	125
1990: Matt Williams, San Francisco	122
1991: Howard Johnson, New York	117
1992: Darren Daulton, Philadelphia	109
1993: Barry Bonds, San Francisco	123
1994: Jeff Bagwell, Houston	116
1995: Dante Bichette, Colorado	128
1996: Andres Galarraga, Colorado	150

Note—Not compiled prior to 1907; officially adopted in 1920.

Pitching

Winning Percentage

American League

1901: Clark Griffith, Chicago	.774
1902: Bill Bernhard, Philadelphia/Cleveland	.783
1903: Cy Young, Boston	.757
1904: Jack Chesbro, New York	.759
1905: Jesse Tannehill, Boston	.710
1906: Eddie Plank, Philadephia	.760
1907: Bill Donovan, Detroit	.862

1908: Ed Walsh, Sr., Chicago	.727
1909: George Mullin, Detroit	.784
1910: Chief Bender, Philadelphia	.821
1911: Chief Bender, Philadelphia	.773
1912: Joe Wood, Boston	.872
1913: Walter Johnson, Washington	.837
1914: Chief Bender, Philadelphia	.850
1915: Joe Wood, Boston	.750
1916: Ed Cicotte, Chicago	.682
1917: Reb Russell, Chicago	.750
1918: Sam Jones, Boston	.762
1919: Ed Cicotte, Chicago	.806
1920: Jim Bagby, Sr., Cleveland	.721
1921: Carl Mays, New York	.750
1922: Joe Bush, New York	.788
1923: Herb Pennock, New York	.760
1924: Walter Johnson, Washington	.767
1925: Stan Coveleski, Washington	.800
1926: George Uhle, Cleveland	.711
1927: Waite Hoyt, New York	.759
1928: Alvin Crowder, St. Louis	.808
1929: Lefty Grove, Philadephia	.769
1930: Lefty Grove, Philadephia	.848
1931: Lefty Grove, Philadephia	.886
1932: Johnny Allen, New York	.810
1933: Lefty Grove, Philadephia	.750
1934: Lefty Gomez, New York	.839
1935: Eldon Auker, Detroit	.720
1936: Monte Pearson, New York	.731
1937: Johnny Allen, Cleveland	.938
1938: Red Ruffing, New York	.750
1939: Lefty Grove, Boston	.789
1940: Schoolboy Rowe, Detroit	.842
1941: Lefty Gomez, New York	.750
1942: Tiny Bonham, New York	.808
1943: Spud Chandler, New York	.833
1944: Tex Hughson, Boston	.783
1945: Hal Newhouser, Detroit	.735
1946: Boo Ferriss, Boston	.806
1947: Allie Reynolds, New York	.704
1948: Jack Kramer, Boston	.783
1949: Ellis Kinder, Boston	.793
1950: Vic Raschi, New York	.724
1951: Bob Feller, Cleveland	.733
1952: Bobby Shantz, Philadelphia	.774
1953: Eddie Lopat, New York	.800
1954: Sandy Consuegra, Chicago	.842
1955: Tommy Byrne, New York	.762
1956: Whitey Ford, New York	.760
1957: Dick Donovan, Chicago	.727
Tom Sturdivant, New York	.727
1958: Bob Turley, New York	.750
1959: Bob Shaw, Chicago	.750
1960: Jim Perry, Cleveland	.643
1961: Whitey Ford, New York	.862
1962: Ray Herbert, Chicago	.690
1963: Whitey Ford, New York	.774
1964: Wally Bunker, Baltimore	.792

1965: Mudcat Grant, Minnesota	.750
1966: Sonny Siebert, Cleveland	.667
1967: Joe Horlen, Chicago	.731
1968: Denny McLain, Detroit	.838
1969: Jim Palmer, Baltimore	.800
1970: Mike Cuellar, Baltimore	.750
1971: Dave McNally, Baltimore	.808
1972: Catfish Hunter, Oakland	.750
1973: Catfish Hunter, Oakland	.808
1974: Mike Cuellar, Baltimore	.688
1975: Mike Torrez, Baltimore	.690
1976: Bill Campbell, Minnesota	.773
1977: Paul Splittorff, Kansas City	.727
1978: Ron Guidry, New York	.893
1979: Mike Caldwell, Milwaukee	.727
1980: Steve Stone, Baltimore	.781
1981: Pete Vuckovich, Milwaukee	.778
1982: Pete Vuckovich, Milwaukee	.750
1983: Rich Dotson, Chicago	.759
1984: Doyle Alexander, Toronto	.739
1985: Ron Guidry, New York	.786
1986: Roger Clemens, Boston	.857
1987: Roger Clemens, Boston	.690
1988: Frank Viola, Minnesota	.774
1989: Bret Saberhagen, Kansas City	.793
1990: Bob Welch, Oakland	.818
1991: Scott Erickson, Minnesota	.714
1992: Mike Mussina, Baltimore	.783
1993: Jimmy Key, New York	.750
1994: Jason Bere, Chicago	.857
1995: Randy Johnson, Seattle	.900
1996: Charles Nagy, Cleveland	.773

National League

1876: Al Spalding, Chicago	.783
1877: Tommy Bond, Boston	.646
1878: Tommy Bond, Boston	.678
1879: Monte Ward, Providence	.710
1880: Fred Goldsmith, Chicago	.880
1881: Hoss Radbourn, Providence	.694
1882: Larry Corcoran, Chicago	.675
1883: Jim McCormick, Cleveland	.675
1884: Hoss Radbourn, Providence	.833
1885: Mickey Welch, New York	.800
1886: Jocko Flynn, Chicago	.800
1887: Charlie Getzien, Detroit	.690
1888: Tim Keefe, New York	.745
1889: John Clarkson, Boston	.721
1890: Tom Lovett, Brooklyn	.744
1891: John Ewing, New York	.733
1892: Cy Young, Cleveland	.766
1893: Frank Killen, Pittsburgh	.773
1894: Jouett Meekin, New York	.791
1895: Bill Hoffer, Baltimore	.811
1896: Bill Hoffer, Baltimore	.788
1897: Fred Klobedanz, Boston	.788
1898: Ted Lewis, Boston	.765
1899: Jim Hughes, Brooklyn	.824
1900: Joe McGinnity, Brooklyn	.763
1901: Jack Chesbro, Pittsburgh	.700
1902: Jack Chesbro, Pittsburgh	.824
1903: Sam Leever, Pittsburgh	.781
1904: Joe McGinnity, New York	.814
1905: Sam Leever, Pittsburgh	.800
1906: Ed Reulbach, Chicago	.826
1907: Ed Reulbach, Chicago	.810
1908: Ed Reulbach, Chicago	.774
1909: Christy Mathewson, New York	.806
Howie Camnitz, Pittsburgh	.806
1910: King Cole, Chicago	.833
1911: Rube Marquard, New York	.774
1912: Claude Hendrix, Pittsburgh	.727
1913: Bert Humphries, Chicago	.800
1914: Bill James, Boston	.788
1915: Grover Alexander, Philadelphia	.756
1916: Tom Hughes, Boston	.842
1917: Ferdie Schupp, New York	.750
1918: Claude Hendrix, Chicago	.741
1919: Dutch Ruether, Cincinnati	.760
1920: Burleigh Grimes, Brooklyn	.676
1921: Bill Doak, St. Louis	.714
1922: Pete Donohue, Cincinnati	.667
1923: Dolf Luque, Cincinnati	.771
1924: Emil Yde, Pittsburgh	.842
1925: Willie Sherdel, St. Louis	.714
1926: Ray Kremer, Pittsburgh	.769
1927: Larry Benton, Boston/New York	.708
1928: Larry Benton, New York	.735
1929: Charlie Root, Chicago	.760
1930: Freddie Fitzsimmons, New York	.731
1931: Paul Derringer, St. Louis	.692
1932: Lon Warneke, Chicago	.786
1933: Ben Cantwell, Boston	.667
1934: Dizzy Dean, St. Louis	.811
1935: Bill Lee, Chicago	.769
1936: Carl Hubbell, New York	.813
1937: Carl Hubbell, New York	.733
1938: Bill Lee, Chicago	.710
1939: Paul Derringer, Cincinnati	.781
1940: Freddie Fitzsimmons, Brooklyn	.889
1941: Elmer Riddle, Cincinnati	.826
1942: Larry French, Brooklyn	.789
1943: Mort Cooper, St. Louis	.724
1944: Ted Wilks, St. Louis	.810
1945: Harry Brecheen, St. Louis	.789
1946: Murry Dickson, St. Louis	.714
1947: Larry Jansen, New York	.808
1948: Harry Brecheen, St. Louis	.741
1949: Preacher Roe, Brooklyn	.714
1950: Sal Maglie, New York	.818
1951: Preacher Roe, Brooklyn	.880
1952: Hoyt Wilhelm, New York	.833
1953: Carl Erskine, Brooklyn	.769
1954: Johnny Antonelli, New York	.750
1955: Don Newcombe, Brooklyn	.800
1956: Don Newcombe, Brooklyn	.794

1957: Bob Buhl, Milwaukee	.720	
1958: Warren Spahn, Milwaukee	.667	
Lew Burdette, Milwaukee	.667	
1959: Roy Face, Pittsburgh	.947	
1960: Ernie Broglio, St. Louis	.700	
1961: Johnny Podres, Los Angeles	.783	
1962: Bob Purkey, Cincinnati	.821	
1963: Ron Perranoski, Los Angeles	.842	
1964: Sandy Koufax, Los Angeles	.792	
1965: Sandy Koufax, Los Angeles	.765	
1966: Juan Marichal, San Francisco	.806	
1967: Dick Hughes, St. Louis	.727	
1968: Steve Blass, Pittsburgh	.750	
1969: Tom Seaver, New York	.781	
1970: Bob Gibson, St. Louis	.767	
1971: Don Gullett, Cincinnati	.727	
1972: Gary Nolan, Cincinnati	.750	
1973: Tommy John, Los Angeles	.696	
1974: Andy Messersmith, Los Angeles	.769	
1975: Don Gullett, Cincinnati	.789	
1976: Steve Carlton, Philadelphia	.741	
1977: John Candelaria, Pittsburgh	.800	
1978: Gaylord Perry, San Diego	.778	
1979: Tom Seaver, Cincinnati	.727	

1980: Jim Bibby, Pittsburgh	.760
1981: Tom Seaver, Cincinnati	.875
1982: Phil Niekro, Atlanta	.810
1983: John Denny, Philadelphia	.760
1984: Rick Sutcliffe, Chicago	.941
1985: Orel Hershiser, Los Angeles	.864
1986: Bob Ojeda, New York	.783
1987: Dwight Gooden, New York	.682
1988: David Cone, New York	.870
1989: Mike Bielecki, Chicago	.720
1990: Doug Drabek, Pittsburgh	.786
1991: John Smiley, Pittsburgh	.714
Jose Rijo, Cincinnati	.714
1992: Bob Tewksbury, St. Louis	.762
1993: Mark Portugal, Houston	.818
1994: Marvin Freeman, Colorado	.833
1995: Greg Maddux, Atlanta	.905
1996: John Smoltz, Atlanta	.750

Note—Based on 15 or more victories.

Note—1981 and 1994 percentages based on 10 or more victories.

Source: Society for American Baseball Research

From Major League Baseball's Records Book
All-Time Leaders Through 1996 Season

Runs

1.	Ty Cobb	2,246
2.	Hank Aaron	2,174
	Babe Ruth	2,174
4.	Pete Rose	2,165
5.	Willie Mays	2,062
6.	Stan Musial	1,949
7.	Lou Gehrig	1,888
8.	Tris Speaker	1,882
9.	Mel Ott	1,859
10.	Frank Robinson	1,829
	Rickey Henderson	1,829

Walks

1.	Babe Ruth	2,056
2.	Ted Williams	2,019
3.	Joe Morgan	1,865
4.	Carl Yastrzemski	1,845
5.	Mickey Mantle	1,733
6.	Mel Ott	1,708
7.	Rickey Henderson	1,675
8.	Eddie Yost	1,614
9.	Darrell Evans	1,605
10.	Stan Musial	1,599

Home Runs

1.	Hank Aaron	755
2.	Babe Ruth	714
3.	Willie Mays	660

4.	Frank Robinson	586
5.	Harmon Killebrew	573
6.	Reggie Jackson	563
7.	Mike Schmidt	548
8.	Mickey Mantle	536
9.	Jimmie Foxx	534
10.	Ted Williams	521
	Willie McCovey	521

Grand Slam Home Runs

1.	Lou Gehrig	23
2.	Eddie Murray	19
3.	Willie McCovey	18
4.	Jimmie Foxx	17
	Ted Williams	17
6.	Hank Aaron	16
	Babe Ruth	16
	Dave Kingman	16
9.	Gil Hodges	14
10.	Joe DiMaggio	13
	Ralph Kiner	13
	George Foster	13

Runs Batted In (RBI)

1.	Hank Aaron	2,297
2.	Babe Ruth	2,213
3.	Lou Gehrig	1,995
4.	Stan Musial	1,951
5.	Ty Cobb	1,937

6.	Jimmie Foxx	1,922
7.	Willie Mays	1,903
8.	Eddie Murray	1,899
9.	Cap Anson	1,879
10.	Mel Ott	1,860

Stolen Bases

1.	Rickey Henderson	1,186
2.	Lou Brock	938
3.	Billy Hamilton	912
4.	Ty Cobb	892
5.	Tim Raines	787
6.	Vince Coleman	752
7.	Eddie Collins	744
8.	Arlie Latham	739
9.	Max Carey	738
10.	Honus Wagner	722

Strikeouts

1.	Reggie Jackson	2,597
2.	Willie Stargell	1,936
3.	Mike Schmidt	1,883

4.	Tony Perez	1,867
5.	Dave Kingman	1,816
6.	Bobby Bonds	1,757
7.	Dale Murphy	1,748
8.	Lou Brock	1,730
9.	Mickey Mantle	1,710
10.	Harmon Killebrew	1,699

At Bats

1.	Pete Rose	14,053
2.	Hank Aaron	12,364
3.	Carl Yastrzemski	11,988
4.	Ty Cobb	11,434
5.	Eddie Murray	11,169
6.	Robin Yount	11,008
7.	Dave Winfield	11,003
8.	Stan Musial	10,972
9.	Willie Mays	10,881
10.	Brooks Robinson	10,654

Source: Total Baseball, the Official Encyclopedia of Major League Baseball

Hockey

NHL 1996–97 SEASON

IN DETROIT—Hockeytown, USA!—it was the best of times. And then, all too suddenly, it was the worst of times.

The city's Red Wings had gone 42 years in the National Hockey League without winning a Stanley Cup, the league's longest current futility streak. But it came to an abrupt end on June 7 when the Red Wings beat the Philadelphia Flyers 2–1 in Game Four to complete a 4–0 sweep and send all of Detroit into absolute paroxysms of joy. Instrumental in the Wings victory were five Russian Red Wings who had at one time played for the old Soviet Union national team. Russians winning at Canada's national game in a city that produced the automobile, the very symbol of U.S. capitalism: The irony was too delicious.

And then it was the worst of times. Just days after the Red Wings paraded the Stanley Cup through the streets of Detroit, the limousine in which the Red Wings' Vladimir Konstantinov, Vyacheslav Fetisov and team masseur Sergei Mnatsakanov were riding slammed into a tree on a Detroit street at 55 miles an hour. Mr. Fetisov suffered severe chest injuries. Mr. Konstantinov and Mr. Mnatsakanov sustained severe head injuries. They both slipped into comas.

It was a sobering end to what had been an eventful season of hockey.

The inaugural World Cup of Hockey in late August and early September kicked off the season with a three-game final between Canada and the U.S. The Americans, playing Game 3 in Montreal, overcame a 2–1 deficit with four unanswered goals to stun their neighbor to the north, 5–2. It was easily the biggest win for U.S. hockey since the 1980 Olympic team beat the old Soviet powerhouse. The tournament, featuring, among others, Dream Teamers from Russia, Canada, the U.S., and Sweden, proved a huge success and presaged an exciting Olympics in Nagano, Japan, in February 1998, when NHL players will be competing for gold for the first time.

The NHL season itself began on an equally heartwarming note when San Jose left wing Tony Granato skated onto the ice for his team's opener. He had earlier had surgery to remove an intracranial hematoma. Other opening nights of note: Wayne Gretzky wearing a New York Rangers' uniform, and the Phoenix Coyotes, formerly the Winnipeg Jets, bringing ice hockey to the Arizona desert.

Notable achievements:

Dec. 1: The Great One notches his 3,000th point (playoffs included), the most ever in the NHL, with one goal and one assist in a 6–2 win over the Montreal Canadiens.

February 8: Coach Scottie Bowman of the Red Wings captures his 1,000th regular-season win with a 6–5 overtime victory over the Pittsburgh Penguins.

March 14: Joe Mullen of Pittsburgh gets his 500th career goal, the first American to reach that milestone.

March 27: Boston Bruin defenseman Ray Bourque records his 1,000th career assist to become only the fifth player—and second defensemen—to turn the trick.

April 11: Martin Brodeur, the Jersey Devil's goalie, stops 26 shots in a 2–0 win over the Bruins to collect his 10th shutout, the most in 20 years; his goals against average of 1.88 is the lowest in 25 years.

April 26: Mario Lemieux, Pittsburgh's center nonpareil, plays his final regular-season NHL game, a 7–3 loss to the Boston Bruins. Finishing the season with 122 points, Mr. Lemieux wins the Art Ross Trophy as the NHL scoring leader for the sixth time.

The NHL's "real" season, the Playoffs, dropped the puck with a number of firsts. Both the Ottawa Senators and the Mighty Ducks of Anaheim made it to the tournament for the first time, where they both proved they belonged. The Senators fell in seven games to the Buffalo Sabres, while the Ducks made it to the second round before being swept by eventual Stanley Cup winner Detroit. Even in defeat the Ducks took flight: Three of the four games went into overtime, with the deciding contest a marathon affair that needed all but 2:57 of a second OT before the Wings prevailed.

The Rangers gave their fans hope that the combination of Mr. Gretzky and Mark Messier could work some magic from their long-gone Edmonton Oilers glory days when they beat the defending Eastern Conference champion Florida Panthers four games to one. But those hopes lasted only long enough for the Rangers to get eliminated in the Conference finals by the Eric Lindros–led Flyers in five games.

Meanwhile, out West, the Red Wings and Colorado Avalanche, the defending Stanley Cup Champions, found themselves in a rematch of the previous year's conference final. The Red Wings used three straight wins at home to reverse 1996 and advance to the finals for the second time in three years.

In the finals, it was all Detroit. The Red Wings swept the Flyers 4–2, 4–2, 6–1, 2–1. Goaltender Mike Vernon won the Conn Smythe Trophy as the playoffs MVP. He finished with a 16–4 record and a 1.76 goals-against average. Much to the delight of their Hockeytown USA fans, the Red Wings posted a daunting 9–1 playoffs record on their home ice at Joe Louis Arena.

And then the cheering stopped. By mid-summer defenseman Vyacheslav Fetisov had recovered enough from his chest injuries to leave the hospital. Masseur Sergei Mnatsakanov emerged from his coma and was reportedly making progress. Defenseman Vladimir Konstantinov, meanwhile, had come out of his coma but was not yet fully awake. He was scheduled to be moved to a rehabilitation unit, where months of intense physical therapy awaited him. His Russian teammates on the Red Wings, following the hallowed Stanley Cup tradition of each player on the winning team taking the Cup to his hometown, took Lord Stanley's silver trophy back to the Motherland without him.

Steve McKee

National Hockey League Regular Season 1996-97

Team Standings

Eastern Conference

Northeast Division

	GP	W	L	T	GF	GA	Pts.	Pct.*
Buffalo	82	40	30	12	237	208	92	.561
Pittsburgh	82	38	36	8	285	280	84	.512
Ottawa	82	31	36	15	226	234	77	.470
Montreal	82	31	36	15	249	276	77	.470
Hartford	82	32	39	11	226	256	75	.457
Boston	82	26	47	9	234	300	61	.372

Atlantic Division

	GP	W	L	T	GF	GA	Pts.	Pct.*
New Jersey	82	45	23	14	231	182	104	.634
Philadelphia	82	45	24	13	274	217	103	.628
Florida	82	35	28	19	221	201	89	.543
NY Rangers	82	38	34	10	258	231	86	.524
Washington	82	33	40	9	214	231	75	.457
Tampa Bay	82	32	40	10	217	247	74	.451
NY Islanders	82	29	41	12	240	250	70	.427

Western Conference

Central Division

	GP	W	L	T	GF	GA	Pts.	Pct.*
Dallas	82	48	26	8	252	198	104	.634
Detroit	82	38	26	18	253	197	94	.573
Phoenix	82	38	37	7	240	243	83	.506
St. Louis	82	36	35	11	236	239	83	.506
Chicago	82	34	35	13	223	210	81	.494
Toronto	82	30	44	8	230	273	68	.415

Pacific Division

	GP	W	L	T	GF	GA	Pts.	Pct.*
Colorado	82	49	24	9	277	205	107	.652
Anaheim	82	36	33	13	245	233	85	.518
Edmonton	82	36	37	9	252	247	81	.494
Vancouver	82	35	40	7	257	273	77	.470
Calgary	82	32	41	9	214	239	73	.445
Los Angeles	82	28	43	11	214	268	67	.409
San Jose	82	27	47	8	211	278	62	.378

*Percentage of actual points vs. possible points.

Results of All Playoff Series

Conference Quarterfinals (Best-of-seven series)

Eastern Conference

Series 'A'

April 17	Montreal	2	at	New Jersey	5
April 19	Montreal	1	at	New Jersey	4
April 22	New Jersey	6	at	Montreal	4
April 24	New Jersey	3	at	Montreal	4
April 26	Montreal	0	at	New Jersey	4

(New Jersey won series 4-1)

Series 'B'

April 17	Ottawa	1	at	Buffalo	3
April 19	Ottawa	3	at	Buffalo	1
April 21	Buffalo	3	at	Ottawa	2
April 23	Buffalo	0	at	Ottawa	1
April 25	Ottawa	4	at	Buffalo	1
April 27	Buffalo	3	at	Ottawa	0
April 29	Ottawa	2	at	Buffalo	3

(Buffalo won series 4-3)

Series 'C'

April 17	Pittsburgh	1	at	Philadelphia	5
April 19	Pittsburgh	2	at	Philadelphia	3
April 21	Philadelphia	5	at	Pittsburgh	3
April 23	Philadelphia	1	at	Pittsburgh	4
April 26	Pittsburgh	3	at	Philadelphia	6

(Philadelphia won series 4-1)

Series 'D'

April 17	NY Rangers	0	at	Florida	3
April 20	NY Rangers	3	at	Florida	0
April 22	Florida	3	at	NY Rangers	4
April 23	Florida	2	at	NY Rangers	3
April 25	NY Rangers	3	at	Florida	2

(NY Rangers won series 4-1)

Western Conference

Series 'E'

April 16	Chicago	0	at	Colorado	6
April 18	Chicago	1	at	Colorado	3
April 20	Colorado	3	at	Chicago	4
April 22	Colorado	3	at	Chicago	6
April 24	Chicago	0	at	Colorado	7
April 26	Colorado	6	at	Chicago	3

(Colorado won series 4-2)

Series 'F'

April 16	Edmonton	3	at	Dallas	5
April 18	Edmonton	4	at	Dallas	0
April 20	Dallas	3	at	Edmonton	4
April 22	Dallas	4	at	Edmonton	3
April 25	Edmonton	1	at	Dallas	0
April 27	Dallas	3	at	Edmonton	2
April 29	Edmonton	4	at	Dallas	3

(Edmonton won series 4-3)

Series 'G'

April 16	St. Louis	2	at	Detroit	0
April 18	St. Louis	1	at	Detroit	2
April 20	Detroit	3	at	St. Louis	2
April 22	Detroit	0	at	St. Louis	4
April 25	St. Louis	2	at	Detroit	5
April 27	Detroit	3	at	St. Louis	1

(Detroit won series 4-2)

Series 'H'

April 16	Phoenix	2	at	Anaheim	4
April 18	Phoenix	2	at	Anaheim	4
April 20	Anaheim	1	at	Phoenix	4
April 22	Anaheim	0	at	Phoenix	2
April 24	Phoenix	5	at	Anaheim	2
April 27	Anaheim	3	at	Phoenix	2
April 29	Phoenix	0	at	Anaheim	3

(Anaheim won series 4-3)

Conference Semifinals (Best-of-seven series)

Eastern Conference

Series 'I'

May 2	NY Rangers	0	at	New Jersey	2
May 4	NY Rangers	2	at	New Jersey	0
May 6	New Jersey	2	at	NY Rangers	3
May 8	New Jersey	0	at	NY Rangers	3
May 11	NY Rangers	2	at	New Jersey	1

(NY Rangers won series 4-1)

Series 'J'

May 3	Philadelphia	5	at	Buffalo	3
May 5	Philadelphia	2	at	Buffalo	1
May 7	Buffalo	1	at	Philadelphia	4
May 9	Buffalo	5	at	Philadelphia	4
May 11	Philadelphia	6	at	Buffalo	3

(Philadelphia won series 4-1)

Western Conference

Series 'K'

May 2	Edmonton	1	at	Colorado	5
May 4	Edmonton	1	at	Colorado	4
May 7	Colorado	3	at	Edmonton	4
May 9	Colorado	3	at	Edmonton	2
May 11	Edmonton	3	at	Colorado	4

(Colorado won series 4-1)

Series 'L'

May 2	Anaheim	1	at	Detroit	2
May 4	Anaheim	2	at	Detroit	3
May 6	Detroit	5	at	Anaheim	3
May 8	Detroit	3	at	Anaheim	2

(Detroit won series 4-0)

Conference Finals (Best-of-seven series)

Eastern Conference

Series 'M'

May 16	NY Rangers	1	at	Philadelphia	3
May 18	NY Rangers	5	at	Philadelphia	4
May 20	Philadelphia	6	at	NY Rangers	3
May 23	Philadelphia	3	at	NY Rangers	2
May 25	NY Rangers	2	at	Philadelphia	4

(Philadelphia won series 4-1)

Western Conference

Series 'N'

May 15	Detroit	1	at	Colorado	2
May 17	Detroit	4	at	Colorado	2
May 19	Colorado	1	at	Detroit	2
May 22	Colorado	0	at	Detroit	6
May 24	Detroit	0	at	Colorado	6
May 26	Colorado	1	at	Detroit	3

(Detroit won series 4-2)

Stanley Cup Finals (Best-of-seven series)

Series 'O'

May 31	Detroit	4	at	Philadelphia	2
June 3	Detroit	4	at	Philadelphia	2
June 5	Philadelphia	1	at	Detroit	6
June 7	Philadelphia	1	at	Detroit	2

(Detroit won series 4-0)

Stanley Cup Winners

Year*	Winner		Finalist		Year	Winner		Finalist	
1918	Tor. Arenas	3	Van. Millionaires	2	1956	Montreal	4	Detroit	1
1919	No decision - series between Montreal				1957	Montreal	4	Boston	1
	and Seattle cancelled due to influenza				1958	Montreal	4	Boston	2
	epidemic; series tied 2-2 and 1 tie.				1959	Montreal	4	Toronto	1
1920	Ottawa	3	Seattle	2	1960	Montreal	4	Toronto	3
1921	Ottawa	3	Van. Millionaires	2	1961	Chicago	4	Detroit	2
1922	Tor. St. Pats	3	Van. Millionaires	2	1962	Toronto	4	Chicago	2
1923	Ottawa	2	Edm. Eskimos	0	1963	Toronto	4	Detroit	1
	Ottawa	2	Van. Maroons	1	1964	Toronto	4	Detroit	3
1924	Montreal	2	Calgary Tigers	0	1965	Montreal	4	Chicago	3
	Montreal	2	Van. Maroons	0	1966	Montreal	4	Detroit	2
1925	Victoria	3	Montreal	1	1967	Toronto	4	Montreal	2
1926	Mtl. Maroons	3	Victoria	1	1968	Montreal	4	St. Louis	0
1927	Ottawa	2	Boston	0**	1969	Montreal	4	St. Louis	0
1928	N.Y. Rangers	3	Mtl. Maroons	2	1970	Boston	4	St. Louis	0
1929	Boston	2	N.Y. Rangers	0	1971	Montreal	4	Chicago	3
1930	Montreal	2	Boston	0	1972	Boston	4	N.Y. Rangers	2
1931	Montreal	3	Chicago	2	1973	Montreal	4	Chicago	2
1932	Toronto	3	N.Y. Rangers	0	1974	Philadelphia	4	Boston	2
1933	N.Y. Rangers	3	Toronto	1	1975	Philadelphia	4	Buffalo Sabres	2
1934	Chicago	3	Detroit	1	1976	Montreal	4	Philadelphia	0
1935	Mtl. Maroons	3	Toronto	0	1977	Montreal	4	Boston	0
1936	Detroit	3	Toronto	1	1978	Montreal	4	Boston	2
1937	Detroit	3	N.Y. Rangers	2	1979	Montreal	4	N.Y. Rangers	1
1938	Chicago	3	Toronto	1	1980	N.Y. Islanders	4	Philadelphia	2
1939	Boston	4	Toronto	1	1981	N.Y. Islanders	4	Minnesota	1
1940	N.Y. Rangers	4	Toronto	2	1982	N.Y. Islanders	4	Vancouver	0
1941	Boston	4	Detroit	0	1983	N.Y. Islanders	4	Edmonton	0
1942	Toronto	4	Detroit	3	1984	Edmonton	4	N.Y. Islanders	1
1943	Detroit	4	Boston	0	1985	Edmonton	4	Philadelphia	1
1944	Montreal	4	Chicago	0	1986	Montreal	4	Calgary Flames	1
1945	Toronto	4	Detroit	3	1987	Edmonton	4	Philadelphia	3
1946	Montreal	4	Boston	1	1988	Edmonton	4	Boston	0
1947	Toronto	4	Montreal	2	1989	Calgary	4	Montreal	2
1948	Toronto	4	Detroit	0	1990	Edmonton	4	Boston	1
1949	Toronto	4	Detroit	0	1991	Pittsburgh	4	Minnesota	2
1950	Detroit	4	N.Y. Rangers	3	1992	Pittsburgh	4	Chicago	0
1951	Toronto	4	Montreal	1	1993	Montreal	4	Los Angeles	1
1952	Detroit	4	Montreal	0	1994	N.Y. Rangers	4	Vancouver	3
1953	Montreal	4	Boston	1	1995	New Jersey	4	Detroit	0
1954	Detroit	4	Montreal	3	1996	Colorado	4	Florida	0
1955	Detroit	4	Montreal	3	1997	Detroit	4	Philadelphia	0

*The National Hockey League assumed control of Stanley Cup Competition after 1926.
**There were also 2 ties.
Source: National Hockey League

Selling Hockey

The National Hockey League has billed itself as the Coolest Game on Earth for so long it could be called the National Hype League.

But it has reason to crow. Four seasons after embarking on a major makeover, the NHL is skating rings around its stodgy old Canadian-dominated self. The league has staged an impressive recovery from a 103-day lockout during the 1994–95 season. In its latest season, the NHL played to 93% of capacity, drawing a record 17.6 million fans. Licensing revenue has doubled in five years to $1.2 billion, while more games than ever are being televised nationally.

Nontraditional markets like Phoenix, Denver, Dallas, and Miami have become new hockey hotbeds, and the league is reaping $80 million apiece from expansion teams in Nashville, Tenn., which will begin play in 1998; Atlanta and Columbus, Ohio, in 1999; and Minneapolis-St. Paul, in 2000 The current 26 teams are still posting big combined losses, but they're now less than $50 million, a 40% drop from 1996. And league sponsors—which now include IBM, Nike, Campbell Soup, and Norelco—are spending around $150 million a year, up from $20 million in 1994.

All is not rosy, though. The NHL's vaunted return to national U.S. television three years ago has been less than rousing. Ratings for regular-season games on Fox Sports fell 11% in 1997 and were flat or down slightly on ESPN and ESPN2. Playoff ratings also were down slightly, though viewership rose on both Fox and ESPN for the Stanley Cup finals between Detroit and Philadelphia, when both networks posted their second-highest ratings ever for a single hockey game. Executives also happily noted that the key viewer demographic of men over 18 years old posted sharp gains during the playoffs.

Fox and ESPN have two years left on five-year contracts paying the league a combined $43 million a year, while the NHL gets $45 million annually from Canadian television. That's a pittance compared with the National Basketball Association's more than $275 million in annual broadcast revenue. With expansion diluting each team's take and player payrolls escalating, the NHL will need fatter deals to meet its goal of all teams breaking even or making money by 2000, compared with about half now.

The league hopes to create a buzz around its new stars and profit from their celebrity. The NBA exploited the presence of Magic Johnson, Larry Bird, and Michael Jordan in the 1980s, while the NHL mostly missed the chance to ride the coattails of Wayne Gretzky, who is nearing the end of his career, or Mario Lemieux, who retired after this past season. But officials were cheered when young Dallas Stars standout Mike Modano was profiled in *People* magazine. "This game has been underexposed," says NHL Commissioner Gary Bettman, who has engineered the league's dramatic leap forward since arriving from the NBA in 1992. "Basketball was never underexposed. We've got to sell the game and the stars."

Stefan Fatsis

The Olympics

The 1998 Winter Olympic Games

The games will be played between Feb. 7 and Feb. 22, with more than 60 national Olympic committees and about 3,000 athletes expected to participate. The host city is Nagano, Japan, about 90 minutes from Tokyo by bullet train. It is the most southern location ever for the winter games. The torch relay will begin with the kindling of the Olympic flame in Greece in December 1997.

Winter Olympic Games

Year	Site	Attending Nations	Most Medals Won	# of Male Athletes	# of Female Athletes
1924	Chamonix, France	16	Norway (17)	281	13
1928	St. Moritz, Switzerland	25	Norway (15)	366	27
1932	Lake Placid, NY, USA	17	USA (12)	277	30
1936	Garmish-Partenkirchen, Germany	28	Norway (15)	680	76
1940	Canceled	–	–	–	–
1944	Canceled	–	–	–	–
1948	St. Moritz, Switzerland	28	Norway, Sweden, Switzerland (10)	636	77
1952	Oslo, Norway	30	Norway (16)	624	108
1956	Cortina d'Ampezzo, Italy	32	USSR (16)	687	132
1960	Squaw Valley, CA, USA	30	USSR (21)	521	144
1964	Innsbruck, Austria	36	USSR (25)	986	200
1968	Grenoble, France	37	Norway (14)	1,063	230
1972	Sapporo, Japan	35	USSR (16)	927	218
1976	Innsbruck, Austria	37	USSR (27)	1,013	218
1980	Lake Placid, NY, USA	37	East Germany (23)	1,012	271
1984	Sarajevo, Yugoslavia	49	USSR (25)	1,127	283
1988	Calgary, Canada	57	USSR (29)	1,270	364
1992	Albertville, France	64	Germany (26)	1,318	490
1994	Lillehammer, Norway	67	Norway (26)	1,302	542

Gold Medalists

Biathlon–Men's 10 Kilometers

1980: Frank Ullrich, East Germany
1984: Eirik Kvalfoss, Norway
1988: Frank-Peter Roetsch, East Germany
1992: Mark Kirchner, Germany
1994: Serguei Tchepikov, Russia

Biathlon–Men's 20 Kilometers

1960: Klas Lestander, Sweden
1964: Vladimir Melanin, USSR
1968: Magnar Solberg, Norway
1972: Magnar Solberg, Norway
1976: Nikolai Kruglov, USSR
1980: Anatoli Alyabiev, USSR

1984: Peter Angerer, West Germany
1988: Frank-Peter Roetsch, East Germany
1992: Yevgeny Redkine, Unified Team
1994: Serguei Tchepikov, Russia

Biathlon–Men's 4 × 7.5-Kilometer Relay

1968: USSR
1972: USSR
1976: USSR
1980: USSR
1984: USSR
1988: USSR
1992: Germany
1994: Germany

Biathlon–Women's 7.5 Kilometers
1992: Anfissa Restzova, Unified Team
1994: Myriam Bedard, Canada

Biathlon–Women's 15 Kilometers
1992: Antje Misersky, Germany
1994: Myriam Bedard, Canada

Biathlon–Women's 3 × 7.5-Kilometer Relay
1992: France

Biathlon–Women's 30-Kilometer Relay
1994: Russia.

Bobsled–Two-Man
1932: USA, Hubert Stevens, Curtis Stevens
1936: USA, Ivan Brown, Alan Washbound
1948: Switzerland, Felix Endrich, Friedrich Waller
1952: Germany, Andreas Ostler, Lorenz Nieberl
1956: Italy, Lamberto Dalla Costa, Giacomo Conti
1960:*
1964: Great Britain, Anthony Nash, Robin Dixon
1968: Italy, Eugenio Monti, Luciano De Paolis
1972: West Germany, Wolfgang Zimmerer, Peter
    Utzschneider
1976: East Germany, Meinhard Nehmer, Bernhard
    Germeshausen
1980: Switzerland, Erich Schaerer, Josef Benz
1984: East Germany, Wolfgang Hoppe, Dietmar Schauer-
    hammer
1988: USSR, Ianis Kipours, Vladimir Kozlov
1992: Switzerland, Gustav Weder, Donat Acklin
1994: Switzerland, Gustav Weber, Donat Acklin

*Event not held.

Bobsled–Four-Man
1924: Switzerland
1928: USA
1932: USA
1936: Switzerland
1948: USA
1952: Germany
1956: Switzerland
1960:*
1964: Canada
1968: Italy
1972: Switzerland
1976: East Germany
1980: East Germany
1984: East Germany
1988: Switzerland
1992: Austria
1994: Germany

*Event not held.

Figure Skating–Men's Singles**
1908: Ulrich Salchow, Sweden

1920: Gillis Grafström, Sweden
1924: Gillis Grafström, Sweden
1928: Gillis Grafström, Sweden
1932: Karl Schafer, Austria
1936: Karl Schafer, Austria
1948: Richard Button, USA
1952: Richard Button, USA
1956: Hayes Alan Jenkins, USA
1960: David Jenkins, USA
1964: Manfred Schnelldörfer, West Germany
1968: Wolfgang Schwarz, Austria
1972: Ondrej Nepela, Czechoslovakia
1976: John Curry, Great Britain
1980: Robin Cousins, Great Britain
1984: Scott Hamilton, USA
1988: Brian Boitano, USA
1992: Viktor Petrenko, Unified Team
1994: Aleksei Urmanov, Russia

**Before 1924 (the first separate Winter Games), figure skating
events were held when a rink was available.

Figure Skating–Women's Singles**
1908: Madge Syers, Great Britain
1920: Magda Julin-Mauroy, Sweden
1924: Herma Planck-Szabó, Austria
1928: Sonja Henie, Norway
1932: Sonja Henie, Norway
1936: Sonja Henie, Norway
1948: Barbara Ann Scott, Canada
1952: Jeannette Altwegg, Great Britain
1956: Tenley Albright, USA
1960: Carol Heiss, USA
1964: Sjoukje Dijkstra, Netherlands
1968: Peggy Fleming, USA
1972: Beatrix Schuba, Austria
1976: Dorothy Hamill, USA
1980: Anett Potzsch, East Germany
1984: Katarina Witt, East Germany
1988: Katarina Witt, East Germany
1992: Kristi Yamaguchi, USA
1994: Oksana Baiul, Ukraine

**Before 1924 (the first separate Winter Games), figure skating
events were held when a rink was available.

Figure Skating–Pairs**
1908: Germany, Anna Hubler, Heinrich Burger
1920: Finland, Ludovika Jakobsson-Eilers, Walter
    Jakobsson
1924: Austria, Helene Engelmann, Alfred Berger
1928: France, Andree Joly, Pierre Brunet
1932: France, Andree Brunet-Joly, Pierre Brunet
1936: Germany, Maxi Herber, Ernst Baier
1948: Belgium, Micheline Lannoy, Pierre Baugniet
1952: West Germany, Ria Falk, Paul Falk
1956: Austria, Elisabeth Schwarz, Kurt Oppelt

1960: Canada, Barbara Wagner, Robert Paul
1964: USSR, Lyudmila Belousova, Oleg Protopopov
1968: USSR, Lyudmila Belousova, Oleg Protopopov
1972: USSR, Irina Rodnina, Aleksei Ulanov
1976: USSR, Irina Rodnina, Aleksandr Zaitsev
1980: USSR, Irina Rodnina, Aleksandr Zaitsev
1984: USSR, Elena Valova, Oleg Vassiliev
1988: USSR, Ekaterina Gordeeva, Sergei Grinkov
1992: Unified Team, Natalia Michkouteniok, Artur Dmitriev
1994: Russia, Ekaterina Gordeeva, Sergei Grinkov

**Before 1924 (the first separate Winter Games), figure skating events were held when a rink was available.

Figure Skating–Ice Dancing
1976: USSR, Ljudmila Pakhomova, Alexandr Gorshkov
1980: USSR, Natalia Linichuk, Gennadi Karponosov
1984: Great Britain, Jayne Torvill, Christopher Dean
1988: USSR, Natalia Bestemianova, Andrei Boukin
1992: Unified Team, Marina Klimova, Sergei Ponomarenko
1994: Russia, Oksana Grichtchuk, Yevgeny Platov

Ice Hockey
1920: Canada
1924: Canada
1928: Canada
1932: Canada
1936: Great Britain
1948: Canada
1952: Canada
1956: USSR
1960: USA
1964: USSR
1968: USSR
1972: USSR
1976: USSR
1980: USA
1984: USSR
1988: USSR
1992: Unified Team
1994: Sweden

Luge–Men's Singles
1964: Thomas Kohler, East Germany
1968: Manfred Schmid, Austria
1972: Wolfgang Scheidl, East Germany
1976: Detlef Guenther, East Germany
1980: Bernhard Glass, East Germany
1984: Paul Hildgartner, Italy
1988: Jens Mueller, East Germany
1992: Georg Hackl, Germany
1994: Georg Hackl, Germany

Luge–Men's Doubles
1964: Austria, Josef Feistmantl, Manfred Stengl
1968: East Germany, Klaus-M. Bonsack, Thomas Kohler
1972: Italy, Paul Hildgartner, Walter Plaikner
1976: East Germany, Hans Rinn, Norbert Hahn
1980: East Germany, Hans Rinn, Norbert Hahn

1984: West Germany, Hans Stangassinger, Franz Wembacher
1988: East Germany, Joerg Hoffmann, Jochen Pietzsch
1992: Germany, Stefan Krausse, Jan Behrendt
1994: Italy, Kurt Brugger, Wilfried Huber

Luge–Women's Singles
1964: Ortrun Enderlein, East Germany
1968: Erica Lechner, Italy
1972: Anna-Maria Muller, East Germany
1976: Margit Schumann, East Germany
1980: Vera Zozulia, USSR
1984: Steffi Martin, East Germany
1988: Steffi Walter-Martin, East Germany
1992: Doris Neuner, Austria
1994: Gerda Weissensteiner, Italy

Alpine Skiing–Men's Downhill
1948: Henri Oreiller, France
1952: Zeno Colo, Italy
1956: Toni Sailer, Austria
1960: Jean Vuarnet, France
1964: Egon Zimmermann, Austria
1968: Jean-Claude Killy, France
1972: Bernhard Russi, Switzerland
1976: Franz Klammer, Austria
1980: Leonhard Stock, Austria
1984: William Johnson, USA
1988: Pirmin Zurbriggen, Switzerland
1992: Patrick Ortlieb, Austria
1994: Tommy Moe, USA

Alpine Skiing–Men's Slalom
1948: Edi Reinalter, Switzerland
1952: Othmar Schneider, Austria
1956: Toni Sailer, Austria
1960: Ernst Hinterseer, Austria
1964: Pepi Stiegler, Austria
1968: Jean-Claude Killy, France
1972: Francisco Fernandez Ochoa, Spain
1976: Piero Gros, Italy
1980: Ingemar Stenmark, Sweden
1984: Phil Mahre, USA
1988: Alberto Tomba, Italy
1992: Finn Christian Jagge, Norway
1994: Thomas Stangassinger, Austria

Alpine Skiing–Men's Giant Slalom
1952: Stein Eriksen, Norway
1956: Toni Sailer, Austria
1960: Roger Staub, Switzerland
1964: François Bonlieu, France
1968: Jean-Claude Killy, France
1972: Gustav Thoni, Italy
1976: Heini Hemmi, Switzerland
1980: Ingemar Stenmark, Sweden
1984: Max Julen, Switzerland
1988: Alberto Tomba, Italy

1992: Alberto Tomba, Italy
1994: Markus Wasmeier, Germany

Alpine Skiing–Men's Super Giant Slalom
1988: Franck Piccard, France
1992: Kjetil Andre Aamodt, Norway
1994: Markus Wasmeier, Germany

Alpine Skiing–Men's Combined
(Downhill and Slalom)
1936: Franz Pfnur, Germany
1940-1944:*
1948: Henri Oreiller, France
1952-1984:*
1988: Hubert Strolz, Austria
1992: Josef Polig, Italy
1994: Lasse Kjus, Norway

*Event not held.

Alpine Skiing–Women's Downhill
1948: Hedy Schlunegger, Switzerland
1952: Trude Jochum-Beiser, Austria
1956: Madeleine Berthod, Switzerland
1960: Heidi Biebl, West Germany
1964: Christl Haas, Austria
1968: Olga Pall, Austria
1972: Marie-Theres Nadig, Switzerland
1976: Rosi Mittermaier, West Germany
1980: Annemarie Moser-Pröll, Austria
1984: Michela Figini, Switzerland
1988: Marina Kiehl, West Germany
1992: Kerrin Lee-Gartner, Canada
1994: Katja Seizinger, Germany

Alpine Skiing–Women's Slalom
1948: Gretchen Fraser, USA
1952: Andrea Mead Lawrence, USA
1956: Renée Colliard, Switzerland
1960: Anne Heggtveit, Canada
1964: Christine Goitschel, France
1968: Marielle Goitschel, France
1972: Barbara Cochran, USA
1976: Rosi Mittermaier, West Germany
1980: Hanni Wenzel, Liechtenstein
1984: Paoletta Magoni, Italy
1988: Vreni Schneider, Switzerland
1992: Petra Kronberger, Austria
1994: Vreni Schneider, Switzerland

Alpine Skiing–Women's Giant Slalom
1952: Andrea Mead Lawrence, USA
1956: Ossi Reichert, West Germany
1960: Yvonne Ruegg, Switzerland
1964: Marielle Goitschel, France
1968: Nancy Greene, Canada
1972: Marie-Theres Nadig, Switzerland
1976: Kathy Kreiner, Canada
1980: Hanni Wenzel, Liechtenstein

1984: Debbie Armstrong, USA
1988: Vreni Schneider, Switzerland
1992: Pernilla Wiberg, Sweden
1994: Deborah Compagnoni, Italy

Alpine Skiing–Women's Super Giant Slalom
1988: Sigrid Wolf, Austria
1992: Deborah Campagnoni, Italy
1994: Diann Roffe-Steinrotter, USA

Alpine Skiing–Women's Combined
(Downhill and Slalom)
1936: Christl Cranz, Germany
1940–1944:*
1948: Trude Beiser, Austria
1952–1984:*
1988: Anita Wachter, Austria
1992: Petra Kronberger, Austria
1994: Pernilla Wiberg, Sweden

*Event not held.

Freestyle Skiing–Men's Moguls
1992: Edgar Grospiron, France
1994: Jean-Luc Brassard, Canada

Freestyle Skiing–Women's Moguls
1992: Donna Weinbrecht, USA
1994: Stine Lise Hattestad, Norway

Men's Aerials
1994: Andreas Schoenbaechler, Switzerland

Women's Aerials
1994: Lina Tcherjazova, Uzbekistan

Nordic Skiing–Men's 10-Kilometer Cross Country
1992: Vegard Ulvang, Norway
1994: Bjorn Daehlie, Norway

Nordic Skiing–Men's 15-Kilometer Cross Country
1924: Thorleif Haug, Norway
1928: Johan Grottumsbraaten, Norway
1932: Sven Utterstrom, Sweden
1936: Erik-August Larsson, Sweden
1948: Martin Lundstrom, Sweden
1952: Hallgeir Brenden, Norway
1956: Hallgeir Brenden, Norway
1960: Haakon Brusveen, Norway
1964: Eero Mantyranta, Finland
1968: Harald Gronningen, Norway
1972: Sven-Ake Lundbäck, Sweden
1976: Nikolai Bazhukov, USSR
1980: Thomas Wassberg, Sweden
1984: Gunde Anders Svan, Sweden
1988: Mikhail Deviatyarov, USSR
1992: Bjorn Daehlie, Norway
1994: Bjorn Daehlie, Norway

Nordic Skiing—Men's 30-Kilometer Cross Country
1956: Veikko Hakulinen, Finland
1960: Sixten Jernberg, Sweden
1964: Eero Mantyranta, Finland
1968: Franco Nones, Italian
1972: Vyacheslav Vedenine, USSR
1976: Sergei Saveliev, USSR
1980: Nikolai Zimiatov, USSR
1984: Nikolai Zimiatov, USSR
1988: Alexei Prokurorov, USSR
1992: Vegard Ulvang, Norway
1994: Thomas Alsgaard, Norway

Nordic Skiing—Men's 50-Kilometer Cross Country
1924: Thorleif Haug, Norway
1928: Per-Erik Hedlund, Sweden
1932: Veli Saarinen, Finland
1936: Elis Wiklund, Sweden
1948: Nils Karlsson, Sweden
1952: Veikko Hakulinen, Finland
1956: Sixten Jernberg, Sweden
1960: Kalevi Hamalainen, Finland
1964: Sixten Jernberg, Sweden
1968: Ole Ellefsaeter, Norway
1972: Pal Tyldum, Norway
1976: Ivar Formo, Norway
1980: Nikolai Zimiatov, USSR
1984: Thomas Wassberg, Sweden
1988: Gunde Anders Svan, Sweden
1992: Bjorn Daehlie, Norway
1994: Vladimir Smirnov, Kazakhstan

Nordic Skiing—Men's 4 × 10-Kilometer Relay
1936: Finland
1948: Sweden
1952: Finland
1956: USSR
1960: Finland
1964: Sweden
1968: Norway
1972: USSR
1976: Finland
1980: USSR
1984: Sweden
1988: Sweden
1992: Norway
1994: Italy

Nordic Skiing—Women's 5-Kilometer Cross Country
1964: Claudia Boyarskikh, USSR
1968: Toini Gustafsson, Sweden
1972: Galina Kulakova, USSR
1976: Helena Takalo, Finland
1980: Raisa Smetanina, USSR
1984: Marja-L. Haemaelainen, Finland
1988: Marjo Matikainen, Finland

1992: Marjut Lukkarinen, Finland
1994: Lyubov Egorova, Russia

Nordic Skiing—Women's 10-Kilometer Cross Country
1952: Lydia Wideman, Finland
1956: Lyubov Kosyreva, USSR
1960: Maria Gusakova, USSR
1964: Claudia Boyarskikh, USSR
1968: Toini Gustafsson, Sweden
1972: Galina Kulakova, USSR
1976: Raisa Smetanina, USSR
1980: Barbara Petzold, East Germany
1984: Marja-L. Haemaelainen, Finland
1988: Vida Ventsene, USSR
1992: Lyubov Egorova, Unified Team
1994: Lyubov Egorova, Russia

Nordic Skiing—Women's 15-Kilometer Cross Country
1992: Lyubov Egorova, Unified Team
1994: Manuela Di Centa, Italy

Nordic Skiing—Women's 20–30-Kilometer Cross Country
1984: Marja-L. Haemaelainen, Finland
1988: Tamara Tikhonova, USSR
1992: Stefania Belmondo, Italy
1994: Manuela Di Centa, Italy

Nordic Skiing—Women's 4 3 5-Kilometer Relay
1956: Finland
1960: Sweden
1964: USSR
1968: Norway
1972: USSR
1976: USSR
1980: East Germany
1984: Norway
1988: USSR
1992: Unified Team
1994: Russia

Nordic Skiing—Men's 70-Meter Ski Jumping
1924: Jacob Tullin Thams, Norway
1928: Alf Andersen, Norway
1932: Birger Ruud, Norway
1936: Birger Ruud, Norway
1948: Petter Hugsted, Norway
1952: Arnfinn Bergmann, Norway
1956: Antti Hyvarinen, Finland
1960: Helmut Recknagel, East Germany
1964: Veikko Kankkonen, Finland
1968: Jiri Raska, Czechoslovakia
1972: Yukio Kasaya, Japan
1976: Hans-Georg Aschenbach, East Germany
1980: Anton Innauer, Austria
1984: Jens Weissflog, East Germany

1988: Matti Nykänen, Finland
1992: Ernst Vettori, Austria
1994: Espen Bredesen, Norway

Nordic Skiing–Men's 90-Meter Ski Jumping

1964: Toralf Engan, Norway
1968: Vladimir Beloussov, USSR
1972: Wojciech Fortuna, Poland
1976: Karl Schnabl, Austria
1980: Jouko Tormanen, Finland
1984: Matti Nykänen, Finland
1988: Matti Nykänen, Finland
1992: Toni Nieminen, Finland
1994: Jens Weissflog, Germany

Nordic Skiing–Men's 90-Meter Team Ski Jumping

1988: Finland
1992: Finland
1994: Germany

Nordic Skiing–Men's Combined
(70m Jump, 15km)

1924: Thorleif Haug, Norway
1928: Johan Grottumsbraaten, Norway
1932: Johan Grottumsbraaten, Norway
1936: Oddbjorn Hagen, Norway
1948: Heikki Hasu, Finland
1952: Simon Slattvik, Norway
1956: Sverre Stenersen, Norway
1960: Georg Thoma, West Germany
1964: Tormod Knutsen, Norway
1968: Franz Keller, West Germany
1972: Ulrich Wehling, East Germany
1976: Ulrich Wehling, East Germany
1980: Ulrich Wehling, East Germany
1984: Tom Sandberg, Norway
1988: Hippolyt Kempf, Switzerland
1992: Fabrice Guy, France
1994: Fred Barre Lundberg, Norway

Nordic Skiing–Men's Team Combined
(70m Jump, 3×10km Relay)

1988: West Germany
1992: Japan
1994: Japan

Long Track Speedskating–Men's 500 Meters

1924: Charles Jewtraw, USA
1928: Bernt Evensen, Norway
 Clas Thunberg, Finland [tie]
1932: John A. Shea, USA
1936: Ivar Ballangrud, Norway
1948: Finn Helgesen, Norway
1952: Kenneth Henry, USA
1956: Yevgeny Grishin, USSR
1960: Yevgeny Grishin, USSR
1964: Richard McDermott, USA
1968: Erhard Keller, West Germany

1972: Erhard Keller, West Germany
1976: Yevgeny Kulikov, USSR
1980: Eric Heiden, USA
1984: Sergei Fokitchev, USSR
1988: Jens-Uwe Mey, East Germany
1992: Jens-Uwe Mey, Germany
1994: Aleksandr Golubev, Russia

Long Track Speedskating–Men's 1,000 Meters

1976: Peter Mueller, USA
1980: Eric Heiden, USA
1984: Gaétan Boucher, Canada
1988: Nikolai Gouliaev, USSR
1992: Olaf Zinke, Germany
1994: Dan Jansen, USA

Long Track Speedskating–Men's 1,500 Meters

1924: Clas Thunberg, Finland
1928: Clas Thunberg, Finland
1932: John A. Shea, USA
1936: Charles Mathiesen, Norway
1948: Sverre Farstad, Norway
1952: Hjalmar Andersen, Norway
1956: Yevgeny Grishin, USSR
1960: Roald Aas, Norway
1964: Ants Antson, USSR
1968: Cornelis Verkerk, Netherlands
1972: Ard Schenk, Netherlands
1976: Jan-Egil Storholt, Norway
1980: Eric Heiden, USA
1984: Gaétan Boucher, Canada
1988: Andre Hoffmann, East Germany
1992: Johann Koss, Norway
1994: Johann Koss, Norway

Long Track Speedskating–Men's 5,000 Meters

1924: Clas Thunberg, Finland
1928: Ivar Ballangrud, Norway
1932: Irving Jaffee, USA
1936: Ivar Ballangrud, Norway
1948: Reidar Liaklev, Norway
1952: Hjalmar Andersen, Norway
1956: Boris Shilkov, USSR
1960: Viktor Kosichkin, USSR
1964: Knut Johannesen, Norway
1968: Fred Anton Maier, Norway
1972: Ard Schenk, Netherlands
1976: Sten Stensen, Norway
1980: Eric Heiden, USA
1984: Sven Tomas Gustafson, Sweden
1988: Sven Tomas Gustafson, Sweden
1992: Geir Karlstad, Norway
1994: Johann Koss, Norway

Long Track Speedskating–Men's 10,000 Meters

1924: Julius Skutnabb, Finland

1928: Event called off in the fifth race because of the bad condition of the ice.
1932: Irving Jaffee, USA
1936: Ivar Ballangrud, Norway
1948: Ake Seyffarth, Sweden
1952: Hjalmar Andersen, Norway
1956: Sigvard Ericsson, Sweden
1960: Knut Johannesen, Norway
1964: Jonny Nilsson, Sweden
1968: Johnny Hoglin, Sweden
1972: Ard Schenk, Netherlands
1976: Piet Kleine, Netherlands
1980: Eric Heiden, USA
1984: Igor Malkov, USSR
1988: Sven Tomas Gustafson, Sweden
1992: Bart Veldkamp, Netherlands
1994: Johann Koss, Norway

Short Track Speedskating–Men's 1,000 Meters
1992: Kim Ki-Hoon, South Korea
1994: Kim Ki-Hoon, South Korea

Short Track Speedskating–Men's 5 Kilometers Relay
1992: South Korea
1994: Italy

Long Track Speedskating–Women's 500 Meters
1932: Jean Wilson, Canada
1936-1956:*
1960: Helga Haase, East Germany
1964: Lydia Skoblikova, USSR
1968: Lyudmila Titova, USSR
1972: Anne Henning, USA
1976: Sheila Young, USA
1980: Karin Enke, East Germany
1984: Christa Rothenburger, East Germany
1988: Bonnie Blair, USA
1992: Bonnie Blair, USA
1994: Bonnie Blair, USA

_____
*Event not held.

Long Track Speedskating–Women's 1,000 Meters
1932: Elizabeth Dubois, USA
1936-1956:*
1960: Klara Guseva, USSR

_____
*Event not held.

1964: Lydia Skoblikova, USSR
1968: Carolina Geijssen, Netherlands
1972: Monika Pflug, West Germany
1976: Tatiana Averina, USSR
1980: Natalia Petruseva, USSR
1984: Karin Kania-Enke, East Germany
1988: Christa Rothenburger, East Germany
1992: Bonnie Blair, USA
1994: Bonnie Blair, USA

Long Track Speedskating–Women's 1,500 Meters
1932: Kit Klein, USA
1936-1956:*
1960: Lydia Skoblikova, USSR
1964: Lydia Skoblikova, USSR
1968: Kaija Mustonen, Finland
1972: Dianne Holum, USA
1976: Galina Stepanskaya, USSR
1980: Annie Borckink, Netherlands
1984: Karin Kania-Enke, East Germany
1988: Yvonne van Gennip, Netherlands
1992: Jacqueline Boerner, Germany
1994: Emese Hunyady, Austria

_____
*Event not held.

Long Track Speedskating–Women's 3,000 Meters
1960: Lydia Skoblikova, USSR
1964: Lydia Skoblikova, USSR
1968: Johanna Schut, Netherlands
1972: Christina Baas-Kaiser, Netherlands
1976: Tatiana Averina, USSR
1980: Bjorg-Eva Jensen, Norway
1984: Andrea Schoene, East Germany
1988: Yvonne van Gennip, Netherlands
1992: Gunda Niemann, Germany
1994: Svetlana Bazhanova, Russia

Long Track Speedskating–Women's 5,000 Meters
1988: Yvonne van Gennip, Netherlands

Short Track Speedskating–Women's 500 Meters
1992: Cathy Turner, USA
1994: Cathy Turner, USA

Short Track Speedskating–Women's 3-Kilometer Relay
1992: Canada
1994: South Korea

Summer Olympic Games

Year	Site	Attending Nations	Most Medals Won	# of Male Athletes	# of Female Athletes
1896	Athens, Greece	13	Greece (47)	311	0
1900	Paris, France	22	France (102)	1,319	11
1904	St. Louis, MO, USA	12	USA (238)	681	6
1906	Athens, Greece	20	France (40)	877	7
1908	London, England	23	Britain (145)	1,999	36
1912	Stockholm, Sweden	28	Sweden (65)	2,490	57
1916	Canceled	–	–	–	–
1920	Antwerp, Belgium	29	USA (96)	2,453	64
1924	Paris, France	44	USA (99)	2,956	136
1928	Amsterdam, Netherlands	46	USA (56)	2,724	290
1932	Los Angeles, CA, USA	37	USA (104)	1,281	127
1936	Berlin, Germany	49	Germany (89)	3,738	328
1940	Canceled	–	–	–	–
1944	Canceled	–	–	–	–
1948	London, England	59	USA (84)	3,714	385
1952	Helsinki, Finland	69	USA (76)	4,407	518
1956	Melbourne, Australia	67	USSR (98)	2,958	384
1960	Rome, Italy	83	USSR (103)	4,738	610
1964	Tokyo, Japan	93	USA (90)	4,457	683
1968	Mexico City, Mexico	112	USA (107)	4,750	781
1972	Munich, West Germany	122	USSR (99)	5,848	1,299
1976	Montreal, Canada	92	USSR (125)	4,834	1,251
1980	Moscow, USSR	81	USSR (195)	4,265	1,088
1984	Los Angeles, CA, USA	141	USA (174)	5,458	1,620
1988	Seoul, South Korea	159	USSR (132)	6,983	2,438
1992	Barcelona, Spain	172	The Unified Team (former Soviet Union republics) (112)	7,555	3,008
1996	Atlanta, GA, USA	197	USA (101)	6,596	3,785

Gold Medalists

Archery–Men's Individual

1972: John Williams, USA
1976: Darrell Pace, USA
1980: Tomi Poikolainen, Finland
1984: Darrell Pace, USA
1988: Jay Barrs, USA
1992: Sebastian Flute, France (70-meter)
1996: Justin Huish, USA

Archery–Men's Team

1988: South Korea
1992: Spain
1996: USA

Archery–Women's Individual

1972: Doreen Wilber, USA
1976: Luann Ryon, USA
1980: Keto Losaberidze, USSR
1984: Hyang-Soon Seo, South Korea
1988: Soo-Nyung Kim, South Korea

1992: Cho Youn-Jeong, South Korea (70 meter)
1996: Kim Kyung-Wook, South Korea

Archery–Women's Team

1988: South Korea
1992: South Korea
1996: South Korea

Badminton–Men's Singles

1992: Alan Budi Kusuma, Indonesia
1996: Poul-Erik Hoyer-Larsen, Denmark

Badminton–Men's Doubles

1992: South Korea, Kim Moon-Soo and Park Joo-Bong
1996: Indonesia, Ricky Subagja and Rexy Mainaky

Badminton–Women's Singles

1992: Susi Susanti, Indonesia
1996: Soo-Hyun Bang, South Korea

Badminton–Women's Doubles

1992: South Korea, Huang Hye Young, Chung So-Young
1996: China, Jun Gu and Fei Ge

Badminton–Mixed Doubles

1996: South Korea, Young-Ah Gil and Dung-Moon Kim

Baseball

1992: Cuba
1996: Cuba

Basketball–Men's Team

1904: USA
1936: USA
1948: USA
1952: USA
1956: USA
1960: USA
1964: USA
1968: USA
1972: USSR
1976: USA
1980: Yugoslavia
1984: USA
1988: USSR
1992: USA
1996: USA

Basketball–Women's Team

1976: USSR
1980: USSR
1984: USA
1988: USA
1992: Unified Team
1996: USA

Boxing–106 lbs. (Light Flyweight)

1968: Francisco Rodriguez, Venezuela
1972: Gyorgy Gedo, Hungary
1976: Jorge Hernandez, Cuba
1980: Shamil Sabyrov, USSR
1984: Paul Gonzales, USA
1988: Ivalio Hristov, Bulgaria
1992: Rogelio Marcelo, Cuba
1996: Daniel Petrov Bojilov, Bulgaria

Boxing–112 lbs. (Flyweight)

1904: George Finnegan, USA
1906–1912:*
1920: Frank Genaro, USA
1924: Fidel LaBarba, USA
1928: Antal Kocsis, Hungary
1932: Istvan Enekes, Hungary
1936: Willy Kaiser, West Germany
1948: Pascual Perez, Argentina
1952: Nathan Brooks, USA

*Event not held.

1956: Terence Spinks, Great Britain
1960: Gyula Torok, Hungary
1964: Fernando Atzori, Italy
1968: Ricardo Delgado, Mexico
1972: Georgi Kostadinov, Bulgaria
1976: Leo Randolph, USA
1980: Petr Lesov, Bulgaria
1984: Steven McCrory, USA
1988: Kwang-Sun Kim, South Korea
1992: Su-Choi-Chol, North Korea
1996: Maikro Romero, Cuba

Boxing–119 lbs. (Bantamweight)

1904: Oliver Kirk, USA
1906:*
1908: A. Henry Thomas, Great Britain
1912:*
1920: Clarence Walker, South Africa
1924: William Smith, South Africa
1928: Vittorio Tamagnimi, Italy
1932: Horace Gwynne, Canada
1936: Ulderico Sergo, Italy
1948: Tibor Csik, Hungary
1952: Pentti Hamalainen, Finland
1956: Wolfgang Behrendt, East Germany
1960: Oleg Grigoryev, USSR
1964: Takao Sakurai, Japan
1968: Valeri Sokolov, USSR
1972: Orlando Martinez, Cuba
1976: Yong-Jo Gu, North Korea
1980: Juan Hernandez, Cuba
1984: Maurizio Stecca, Italy
1988: Kennedy McKinney, USA
1992: Joel Casamayor, Cuba
1996: Istvan Kovacs, Hungary

*Event not held.

Boxing–125 lbs. (Featherweight)

1904: Oliver Kirk, USA
1906:*
1908: Richard Gunn, Great Britain
1912:*
1920: Paul Fritsch, France
1924: John "Jackie" Fields, USA
1928: Lambertus "Bep" van Klaveren, Netherlands
1932: Carmelo Robledo, Argentina
1936: Oscar Casanovas, Argentina
1948: Ernesto Formenti, Italy
1952: Jan Zachara, Czechoslovakia
1956: Valdimir Safronov, USSR
1960: Francesco Musso, Italy
1964: Stanislav Stepashkin, USSR
1968: Antonio Roldan, Mexico
1972: Boris Kuznetsov, USSR

*Event not held.

1976: Angel Herrera, Cuba
1980: Rudi Fink, East Germany
1984: Meldrick Taylor, USA
1988: Giovanni Parisi, Italy
1992: Andreas Tews, Germany
1996: Somluck Kamsing, Thailand

Boxing—132 lbs. (Lightweight)
1904: Harry Spanger, USA
1906:*
1908: Frederick Grace, Great Britain
1912:*
1920: Samuel Mosberg, USA
1924: Hans Nielsen, Denmark
1928: Carlo Orlandi, Italy
1932: Lawrence Stevens, South Africa
1936: Imre Harangi, Hungary
1948: Gerald Dreyer, South Africa
1952: Aureliano Bolognesi, Italy
1956: Richard McTaggart, Great Britain
1960: Kazimierz Pazdzior, Poland
1964: Jozef Grudzien, Poland
1968: Ronald Harris, USA
1972: Jan Szczepanski, Poland
1976: Howard Davis, USA
1980: Angel Herrera, Cuba
1984: Pernell Whitaker, USA
1988: Andreas Zuelow, East Germany
1992: Oscar De La Hoya, USA
1996: Hocine Soltani, Algeria

*Event not held.

Boxing—139 lbs. (Light Welterweight)
1952: Charles Adkins, USA
1956: Vladimir Yengibaryan, USSR
1960: Bohumil Nemecek, Czechoslovakia
1964: Jerzy Kulej, Poland
1968: Jerzy Kulej, Poland
1972: Ray Seales, USA
1976: "Sugar" Ray Leonard, USA
1980: Patrizio Oliva, Italy
1984: Jerry Page, USA
1988: Viatcheslav Janovski, USSR
1992: Hector Vinent, Cuba
1996: Hector Vinent, Cuba

Boxing—147 lbs. (Welterweight)
1904: Albert Young, USA
1906–1912:*
1920: Albert "Bert" Schneider, Canada
1924: Jean Delarge, Belgium
1928: Edward Morgan, New Zealand
1932: Edward Flynn, USA
1936: Sten Suvio, Finland
1948: Julius Torma, Czechoslovakia
1952: Zygmunt Chychla, Poland

*Event not held.

1956: Nicolae Linca, Romania
1960: Giovanni Benvenuti, Italy
1964: Marian Kasprzyk, Poland
1968: Manfred Wolke, East Germany
1972: Emilio Correa, Cuba
1976: Jochen Bachfeld, East Germany
1980: Andres Aldama, Cuba
1984: Mark Breland, USA
1988: Robert Wangila, Kenya
1992: Michael Carruth, Ireland
1996: Oleg Saitov, Russia

Boxing—156 lbs. (Light Middleweight)
1952: Laszlo Papp, Hungary
1956: Laszlo Papp, Hungary
1960: Wilbert McClure, USA
1964: Boris Lagutin, USSR
1968: Boris Lagutin, USSR
1972: Dieter Kottysch, West Germany
1976: Jerzy Rybicki, Poland
1980: Armando Martinez, Cuba
1984: Frank Tate, USA
1988: Si-Hun Park, South Korea
1992: Juan Lemus, Cuba
1996: David Reid, USA

Boxing—165 lbs. (Middleweight)
1904: Charles Mayer, USA
1906:*
1908: John Douglas, Great Britain
1912:*
1920: Harry Mallin, Great Britain
1924: Harry Mallin, Great Britain
1928: Piero Toscani, Italy
1932: Carmen Barth, USA
1936: Jean Despeaux, France
1948: Laszlo Papp, Hungary
1952: Floyd Patterson, USA
1956: Gennady Schatkov, USSR
1960: Edward Crook, USA
1964: Valeri Popenchenko, USSR
1968: Christopher Finnegan, Great Britain
1972: Vyacheslav Lemeschev, USSR
1976: Michael Spinks, USA
1980: Jose Gomez, Cuba
1984: Joon-Sup Shin, South Korea
1988: Henry Maske, East Germany
1992: Ariel Hernandez, Cuba
1996: Ariel Hernandez, Cuba

*Event not held.

Boxing—178 lbs. (Light Heavyweight)
1920: Edward Eagan, USA
1924: Harry Mitchell, Great Britain
1928: Victor Avendano, Argentina
1932: David Carstens, South Africa
1936: Roger Michelot, France

1948: George Hunter, South Africa
1952: Norvel Lee, USA
1956: James Boyd, USA
1960: Cassius Clay, USA
1964: Cosimo Pinto, Italy
1968: Dan Posnyak, USSR
1972: Mate Parlov, Yugoslavia
1976: Leon Spinks, USA
1980: Slobodan Kacar, Yugoslavia
1984: Anton Josipovic, Yugoslavia
1988: Andrew Maynard, USA
1992: Torsten May, Germany
1996: Vasilii Jirov, Kazakhkstan

Boxing–201 lbs. (Heavyweight)
1904: Samuel Berger, USA
1906:*
1908: A. L. Oldham, Great Britain
1912:*
1920: Ronald Rawson, Great Britain
1924: Ott von Porat, Norway
1928: Arturo Rodriguez Jurado, Argentina
1932: Santiago Lovell, Argentina
1936: Herbert Runge, Germany
1948: Rafael Iglesias, Argentina
1952: H. Edward Sanders, USA
1956: Peter Rademacher, USA
1960: Franco De Piccolo, Italy
1964: Joe Frazier, USA
1968: George Foreman, USA
1972: Teofilo Stevenson, Cuba
1976: Teofilo Stevenson, Cuba
1980: Teofilo Stevenson, Cuba
1984: Henry Tillman, USA
1988: Ray Mercer, USA
1992: Felix Savon, Cuba
1996: Felix Savon, Cuba

_____
*Event not held.

Boxing–over 201 lbs. (Super Heavyweight)
1984: Tyrell Biggs, USA
1988: Lennox Lewis, Canada
1992: Roberto Balado, Cuba
1996: Vladimir Klichko, Ukraine

Canoe/Kayak–Men's Canadian Singles, 500 Meters
1976: Aleksandr Rogov, USSR
1980: Sergei Postrekhin, USSR
1984: Larry Cain, Canada
1988: Olaf Heukrodt, East Germany
1992: Nikolai Boukhalov, Bulgaria
1996: Martin Doktor, Czech Republic

Canoe/Kayak–Men's Canadian Singles, 1,000 Meters
1936: Francis Amyot, Canada

1948: Josef Holecek, Czechoslovakia
1952: Josef Holecek, Czechoslovakia
1956: Leon Rotman, Romania
1960: Janos Parti, Hungary
1964: Jurgen Eschert, East Germany
1968: Tibor Tatai, Hungary
1972: Ivan Patzaichin, Romania
1976: Matija Ljubek, Yugoslavia
1980: Liubomir Liubenov, Bulgaria
1984: Ulrich Eicke, West Germany
1988: Ivan Klementiev, USSR
1992: Nikolai Boukhalov, Bulgaria
1996: Martin Doktor, Czech Republic

Canoe/Kayak–Men's Canadian Singles, Slalom
1992: Lukas Pollert, Czechoslovakia
1996: Michael Martikan, Slovakia

Canoe/Kayak–Men's Canadian Pairs, 500 Meters
1976: USSR, Sergei Petrenko, Aleksandr Vonogradov
1980: Hungary, Laszlo Fultan, Istvan Vaskuti
1984: Yugoslavia, Matija Ljub, Mirko Nisovic
1988: USSR, Victor Reneiski, Nikolai Jouravski
1992: Unified Team, Alexandre Masseikov, Dmitri Dovgalenok
1996: Hungary, Csba Horvath, Gyorgy Kolonics

Canoe/Kayak–Men's Canadian Pairs, 1,000 Meters
1936: Czechoslovakia, Vladimir Syrovatka, Jan-Felix Brzak
1948: Czechoslovakia, Jan-Felix Brzak, Bohumil Kudrna
1952: Denmark, Bent Peder Rasch, Finn Haunstoft
1956: Romania, Alexe Dumitru, Simion Ismailciuc
1960: USSR, Leonid Geischtor, Sergei Makarenko
1964: USSR, Andrei Khimich, Stepan Oschepkov
1968: Romania, Ivan Patzaichin, Serahei Covaliov
1972: USSR, Vladas Chessyunas, Yuri Lobanov
1976: USSR, Sergei Petrenko, Aleksandr Vinogradov
1980: Romania, Ivan Patzaichin, Toma Simionov
1984: Romania, Ivan Potzaichin, Toma Simionov
1988: USSR, Victor Reneiski, Nikolai Jouravski
1992: Germany, Ulrich Papke, Ingo Spelly
1996: Germany, Andreas Dittmer, Gunar Kirchbach

Canoe/Kayak–Men's Canadian Pairs, Slalom
1992: USA, Scott Strausbaugh, Joe Jacobi
1996: France, Franck Adisson, Wilfrid Forgues

Canoe/Kayak–Men's Kayak Singles, 500 Meters
1976: Vasile Diba, Romania
1980: Vladimir Parfenovich, USSR
1984: Ian Ferguson, New Zealand
1988: Zsolt Gyulay, Hungary
1992: Mikko Yrjoe Kolehmainen, Finland
1996: Antonio Rossi, Italy

Canoe/Kayak–Men's Kayak Singles, 1,000 Meters
1936: Gregor Hradetzky, Austria

1948: Gert Fredriksson, Sweden
1952: Gert Fredriksson, Sweden
1956: Gert Fredriksson, Sweden
1960: Erik Hansen, Denmark
1964: Rolf Peterson, Sweden
1968: Mihaly Hesz, Hungary
1972: Aleksandr Shaparenko, USSR
1976: Rudiger Helm, East Germany
1980: Rudiger Helm, East Germany
1984: Alan Thompson, New Zealand
1988: Greg Barton, USA
1992: Clint Robinson, Australia
1996: Knut Holmann, Norway

Canoe/Kayak–Men's Kayak Singles, Slalom
1992: Pierpaolo Ferrazzi, Italy
1996: Oliver Fix, Germany

Canoe/Kayak–Men's Kayak Pairs, 500 Meters
1976: East Germany, Bernd Olbricht, Joachim Mattern
1980: USSR, Vladimir Parfenovich, Sergei Chukhrai
1984: New Zealand, Ian Ferguson, Paul McDonald
1988: New Zealand, Ian Ferguson, Paul MacDonald
1992: Germany, Kay Bluhm, Torsten Rene Gutsche
1996: Germany, Kay Bluhm, Torsten Rene Gutsche

Canoe/Kayak–Men's Kayak Pairs, 1,000 Meters
1936: Austria, Adolf Kainz, Alfons Dorfner
1948: Sweden, Hans Berglund, Lennart Klingstrom
1952: Finland, Kurt Wires, Yrjo Hietanen
1956: West Germany, Michel Scheuer, Meinrad Miltenberger
1960: Sweden, Gert Fredriksson, Sven-Olov Sjodelius
1964: Sweden, Sven-Olov Sjodelius, Gunnar Utterberg
1968: USSR, Aleksandr Shaparenko, Vladimir Morozov
1972: USSR, Nikolai Gorbachev, Viktor Kratassyuk
1976: USSR, Sergei Nagorny, Vladimir Romanovsky
1980: USSR, Vladimir Parfenovich, Sergei Chukhrai
1984: Canada, Hugh Fisher, Alwyn Morris
1988: USA, Greg Barton, Norman Bellingham
1992: Germany, Kay Bluhm, Torsten Rene Gutsche
1996: Italy, Antonio Rossi, Daniele Scarpa

Canoe/Kayak–Men's Kayak Pairs, 1,000 Meters
1964: USSR
1968: Norway
1972: USSR
1976: USSR
1980: East Germany
1984: New Zealand
1988: Hungary
1992: Germany
1996: Germany

Canoe/Kayak–Women's Kayak Singles, 500 Meters
1948: Karen Hoff, Denmark
1952: Sylvi Saimo, Finland
1956: Yelisaveta Dementyeva, USSR
1960: Antonina Seredina, USSR

1964: Lyudmila Khvedosyuk, USSR
1968: Lyudmila Pinayeva-Khvedosyuk, USSR
1972: Yulia Ryabchinskaya, USSR
1976: Carola Drechsler-Zirzow, East Germany
1980: Birgit Fischer, East Germany
1984: Agneta Andersson, Sweden
1988: Vania Guecheva, Bulgaria
1992: Birgit Schmidt, Germany
1996: Rita Koban, Hungary

Canoe/Kayak–Women's Kayak Singles, Slalom
1992: Elisabeth Micheler, Germany
1996: Stepanka Hilgertova, Czech Republic

Canoe/Kayak–Women's Kayak Pairs, 500 Meters
1960: USSR, Maria Chubina, Antonina Seredina
1964: West Germany, Roswitha Esser, Annemarie Zimmermann
1968: West Germany, Roswitha Esser, Annemarie Zimmermann
1972: USSR, Lyudmila Pinayeva-Khvedosyuk, Jekaterina Kuryshko
1976: USSR, Nina Popova, Galina Kreft
1980: East Germany, Carsta Genauss, Martina Bischof
1984: Sweden, Agneta Anderson, Anna Olsson
1988: East Germany, Birgit Schmidt, Anke Nothnagel
1992: Germany, Ramona Portwich, Anke Von Seck
1996: Sweden, Agneta Andersson, Susanne Gunnarsson

Canoe/Kayak–Women's Kayak Fours, 500 Meters
1984: Romania
1988: East Germany
1992: Hungary
1996: Germany

Cycling–Men's Individual Cross Country Mountain Biking
1996: Bart Jan Brentjens, Netherlands

Cycling–Men's 100-Kilometer Team Time Trial
1960: Italy
1964: Netherlands
1968: Netherlands
1972: USSR
1976: USSR
1980: USSR
1984: Italy
1988: East Germany
1992: Germany
1996:*

---

*Event not held.

Cycling–Men's Individual Time Trial
1996: Miguel Indurain, Spain

Cycling–Men's One-Kilometer Time Trial
1896: Paul Masson, France

1900–1904:*
1906: Francesco Verri, Italy
1908–1924:*
1928: Willy Falck Hansen, Denmark
1932: Edgar Gray, Australia
1936: Arie van Vliet, Netherlands
1948: Jacques Dupont, France
1952: Russell Mockridge, Australia
1956: Leandro Faggin, Italy
1960: Sante Gaiardoni, Italy
1964: Patrick Sercu, Belgium
1968: Pierre Trentin, France
1972: Niels Fredborg, Denmark
1976: Klaus Juergen Gruenke, East Germany
1980: Lothar Thoms, East Germany
1984: Fredy Schmidtke, West Germany
1988: Alexander Kirichenko, USSR
1992: Jose Moreno Perinan, Spain
1996: Florian Rousseau, France

*Event not held.

Cycling–Men's 4,000-Meter Individual Pursuit
1964: Jiri Daler, Czechoslovakia
1968: Daniel Rebillard, France
1972: Knut Knudsen, Norway
1976: Gregor Braun, West Germany
1980: Robert Dill-Bundi, Switzerland
1984: Steve Hegg, USA
1988: Gintaoutas Umaras, USSR
1992: Chris Boardman, Britain
1996: Andrea Collinelli, Italy

Cycling–Men's 4,000-Meter Team Pursuit
1908: Great Britain
1912:*
1920: Italy
1924: Italy
1928: Italy
1932: Italy
1936: France
1948: France
1952: Italy
1956: Italy
1960: Italy
1964: West Germany
1968: Denmark
1972: West Germany
1976: West Germany
1980: USSR
1984: Australia
1988: USSR
1992: Germany
1996: France

*Event not held.

Cycling–Men's Match Sprint
1896: Paul Masson, France
1900: Georges Taillandier, France
1904:*
1906: Francesco Verri, Italy
1908: Final was declared void because the time limit was exceeded.
1912:*
1920: Maurice Peeters, Netherlands
1924: Lucien Michard, France
1928: Roger Beaufrand, France
1932: Jacobus van Egmond, Netherlands
1936: Toni Merkens, Germany
1948: Mario Ghella, Italy
1952: Enzo Sacchi, Italy
1956: Michel Rousseau, France
1960: Sante Gaiardoni, Italy
1964: Giovanni Pettenella, Italy
1968: Daniel Morelon, France
1972: Daniel Morelon, France
1976: Anton Tkac, Czechoslovakia
1980: Lutz Hesslich, East Germany
1984: Mark Gorski, USA
1988: Lutz Hesslich, East Germany
1992: Jens Fiedler, Germany
1996: Jens Fiedler, Germany

*Event not held.

Cycling–Men's Individual Points Race
1984: Rogers Ilegems, Belgium
1988: Dan Frost, Denmark
1992: Giovanni Lombardi, Italy
1996: Silvio Martinello, Italy

Cycling–Men's Individual Road Race
1896: Aristidis Konstantinidis, Greece
1900–1904:*
1906: B. Vast, France
1908:*
1912: Rudolph Lewis, South Africa
1920: Harry Stenqvist, Sweden
1924: Armand Blanchonnet, France
1928: Henry Hansen, Denmark
1932: Attilio Pavesi, Italy
1936: Robert Charpentier, France
1948: Jose Beyaert, France
1952: Andre Noyelle, Belgium
1956: Ercole Baldini, Italy
1960: Viktor Kapitonov, USSR
1964: Mario Zanin, Italy
1968: Pierfranco Vianelli, Italy
1972: Hennie Kuiper, Netherlands
1976: Bernt Johansson, Sweden
1980: Sergei Sukhoruchenkov, USSR

*Event not held.

1984: Alexi Grewal, USA
1988: Olaf Ludwig, East Germany
1992: Fabio Casartelli, Italy
1996: Pascal Richard, Switzerland

Cycling–Women's Individual Cross Country Mountain Biking
1996: Paola Pezzo, Italy

Cycling–Women's Match Sprint
1988: Erika Salumae, USSR
1992: Erika Salumae, Estonia
1996: Felicia Ballanger, France

Cycling–Women's Individual Road Race
1984: Connie Carpenter-Phinney, USA
1988: Monique Knol, Netherlands
1992: Kathryn Watt, Australia
1996: Jeannie Longo-Ciprelli, France

Cycling–Women's 3,000-Meter Individual Pursuit
1992: Petra Rossner, Germany
1996: Antonella Bellutti, Italy

Cycling–Women's Individual Time Trial
1996: Zulfiya Zabirova, Russia

Cycling–Women's Individual Points Race
1996: Nathalie Lancien, France

Diving–Men's Platform
1904: George Sheldon, USA
1906: Gottlob Walz, Germany
1908: Hjalmar Johansson, Sweden
1912: Erik Adlerz, Sweden
1920: Clarence Pinkston, USA
1924: Albert White, USA
1932: Harold Smith, USA
1936: Marshall Wayne, USA
1948: Samuel Lee, USA
1952: Samuel Lee, USA
1956: Joaquin Capilla Perez, Mexico
1960: Robert Webster, USA
1964: Robert Webster, USA
1968: Klaus Dibiasi, Italy
1972: Klaus Dibiasi, Italy
1976: Klaus Dibiasi, Italy
1980: Falk Hoffmann, East Germany
1984: Gregory Louganis, USA
1988: Gregory Louganis, USA
1992: Sun Shuwei, China
1996: Dmitri Sautin, Russia

Diving–Men's Springboard
1908: Albert Zurner, Germany
1912: Paul Gunther, Germany
1920: Louis Kuehn, USA
1924: Albert White, USA

1928: Peter Desjardins, USA
1932: Michael Galitzen, USA
1936: Richard Degener, USA
1948: Bruce Harlan, USA
1952: David Browning, USA
1956: Robert Clotworthy, USA
1960: Gary Tobian, USA
1964: Kenneth Sitzberger, USA
1968: Bernie Wrightson, USA
1972: Vladimir Vasin, USSR
1976: Philip G. Boggs, USA
1980: Aleksandr Portnov, USSR
1984: Gregory Louganis, USA
1988: Gregory Louganis, USA
1992: Mark Lenzi, USA
1996: Xiong Ni, China

Diving–Women's Platform
1912: Greta Johanson, Sweden
1920: Stefani Fryland-Clausen, Denmark
1924: Caroline Smith, USA
1928: Elizabeth Pinkston-Becker, USA
1932: Dorothy Poynton, USA
1936: Dorothy Hill-Poynton, USA
1948: Victoria Draves, USA
1952: Patricia McCormick, USA
1956: Patricia McCormick, USA
1960: Ingrid Kramer, East Germany
1964: Lesley Bush, USA
1968: Milena Duchkova, Czechoslovakia
1972: Ulrika Knape, Sweden
1976: Elena Vaytsekhovskaya, USSR
1980: Martina Jaschke, East Germany
1984: Jihong Zhou, China
1988: Yanmei Xu, China
1992: Fu Mingxia, China
1996: Fu Mingxia, China

Diving–Women's Springboard
1920: Aileen Riggin, USA
1924: Elizabeth Becker, USA
1928: Helen Meany, USA
1932: Georgia Coleman, USA
1936: Marjorie Gestring, USA
1948: Victoria Draves, USA
1952: Patricia McCormick, USA
1956: Patricia McCormick, USA
1960: Ingrid Kramer, East Germany
1964: Ingrid Engel-Kramer, East Germany
1968: Sue Gossick, USA
1972: Micki King, USA
1976: Jennifer Chandler, USA
1980: Irina Kalinina, USSR
1984: Sylvie Bernier, Canada
1988: Min Gao, China
1992: Gao Min, China
1996: Fu Mingxia, China

Equestrian–Individual Dressage
1996: Isabell Werth, Germany

Equestrian–Team Dressage
1996: Germany

Equestrian–Individual Show Jumping
1900: Aime Haegeman, Belgium
1904–1908:*
1912: Jean Cariou, France
1920: Tommaso Lequio, Italy
1924: Alphonse Gemuseus, Switzerland
1928: Frantisek Ventura, Czechoslovakia
1932: Takeichi Nishi, Japan
1936: Kurt Hasse, Germany
1948: Humberto Mariles, Cortes, Mexico
1952: Pierre Jonqueres d'Oriola, France
1956: Hans-Gunter Winkler, West Germany
1960: Raimondo D'Inzeo, Italy
1964: Pierre Jonqueres d'Oriola, France
1968: William Steinkraus, USA
1972: Graziano Mancinelli, Italy
1976: Alwin Schockemoehle, West Germany
1980: Jan Kowalczyk, Poland
1984: Joe Fargis, USA
1988: Pierre Durand, France
1992: Ludger Beerbaum, Germany
1996: Ulrich Kirchhoff, Germany

---

*Event not held.

Equestrian–Team Show Jumping
1912: Sweden
1920: Sweden
1924: Sweden
1928: Spain
1932: No nation completed the course with three riders.
1936: Germany
1948: Mexico
1952: Great Britain
1956: West Germany
1960: West Germany
1964: West Germany
1968: Canada
1972: West Germany
1976: France
1980: USSR
1984: USA
1988: West Germany
1992: Netherlands
1996: Germany

Equestrian–Individual Three-Day Event
1912: Axel Nordlander, Sweden
1920: Helmer Morner, Sweden
1924: Adolph van der Voort van Zijp, Netherlands

1928: Charles F. Pahud de Mortanges, Netherlands
1932: Charles F. Pahud de Mortanges, Netherlands
1936: Ludwig Stubbendorf, Germany
1948: Bernard Chevallier, France
1952: Hans von Blixen-Finecke, Jr., Sweden
1956: Petrus Kastenman, Sweden
1960: Lawrence Morgan, Australia
1964: Mauro Checcoli, Italy
1968: Jean-Jacques Guyon, France
1972: Richard Meade, Great Britain
1976: Edmund Coffin, USA
1980: Federico Euro Roman, Italy
1984: Mark Todd, New Zealand
1988: Mark Todd, New Zealand
1992: Matthew Ryan, Australia
1996: Blyth Tait, New Zealand

Equestrian–Team Three-Day Event
1912: Sweden
1920: Sweden
1924: Netherlands
1928: Netherlands
1932: USA
1936: Germany
1948: USA
1952: Sweden
1956: Great Britain
1960: Australia
1964: Italy
1968: Great Britain
1972: Great Britain
1976: USA
1980: USSR
1984: USA
1988: West Germany
1992: Australia
1996: Australia

Fencing–Men's Individual Épée
1900: Ramon Fonst, Cuba
1904: Ramon Fonst, Cuba
1906: Georges de la Falaise, France
1908: Gaston Alibert, France
1912: Paul Anspach, Belgium
1920: Armand Massard, France
1924: Charles Delporte, Belgium
1928: Lucien Gaudin, France
1932: Giancarlo Cornaggia-Medici, Italy
1936: Franco Riccardi, Italy
1948: Luigi Cantone, Italy
1952: Edoardo Mangiarotti, Italy
1956: Carlo Pavesi, Italy
1960: Giuseppe Delfino, Italy
1964: Grigori Kriss, USSR
1968: Gyozo Kulcsar, Hungary
1972: Csaba Fenyvesi, Hungary
1976: Alexander Pusch, West Germany

1980: Johan Harmenberg, Sweden
1984: Philippe Boisse, France
1988: Arnd Schmitt, West Germany
1992: Eric Srecki, France
1996: Aleksandr Beketov, Russia

Fencing–Men's Team Épée
1906: France
1908: France
1912: Belgium
1920: Italy
1924: France
1928: Italy
1932: France
1936: Italy
1948: France
1952: Italy
1956: Italy
1960: Italy
1964: Hungary
1968: Hungary
1972: Hungary
1976: Sweden
1980: France
1984: West Germany
1988: France
1992: Germany
1996: Italy

Fencing–Men's Individual Foil
1896: Emile Gravelotte, France
1900: Emile Coste, France
1904: Ramon Fonst, Cuba
1906: Georges Dillon-Kavanagh, France
1912: Nedo Nadi, Italy
1920: Nedo Nadi, Italy
1924: Roger Ducret, France
1928: Lucien Gaudin, France
1932: Gustavo Marzi, Italy
1936: Giulio Gaudini, Italy
1948: Jehan Buhan, France
1952: Christian d'Oriola, France
1956: Christian d'Oriola, France
1960: Viktor Zhdanovich, USSR
1964: Egon Franke, Poland
1968: Ion Drimba, Romania
1972: Witold Woyda, Poland
1976: Fabio dal Zotto, Italy
1980: Vladimir Smirnov, USSR
1984: Mauro Numa, Italy
1988: Stefano Cerioni, Italy
1992: Philippe Omnes, France
1996: Alessandro Puccini, Italy

Fencing–Men's Team Foil
1904: Cuba
1906–1912:*

*Event not held.

1920: Italy
1924: France
1928: Italy
1932: France
1936: Italy
1948: France
1952: France
1956: Italy
1960: USSR
1964: USSR
1968: France
1972: Poland
1976: West Germany
1980: France
1984: Italy
1988: USSR
1992: Germany
1996: Russia

Fencing–Men's Individual Sabre
1896: Jean Georgiadis, Greece
1900: Georges de la Falaise, France
1904: Manuel Diaz, Cuba
1906: Jean Georgiadis, Greece
1908: Jeno Fuchs, Hungary
1912: Jeno Fuchs, Hungary
1920: Nedo Nadi, Italy
1924: Sandor Posta, Hungary
1928: Odon Terstyanszky, Hungary
1932: Gyorgy Piller, Hungary
1936: Endre Kabos, Hungary
1948: Aladar Gerevich, Hungary
1952: Pal Kovacs, Hungary
1956: Rudolf Karpati, Hungary
1960: Rudolf Karpati, Hungary
1964: Tibor Pezsa, Hungary
1968: Jerzy Pawlowski, Poland
1972: Viktor Sidiak, USSR
1976: Viktor Krovopuskov, USSR
1980: Viktor Krovopuskov, USSR
1984: Jean-Francois Lamour, France
1988: Jean-Francois Lamour, France
1992: Bence Szabo, Hungary
1996: Stanislav Pozdnyakov, Russia

Fencing–Men's Team Sabre
1906: West Germany
1908: Hungary
1912: Hungary
1920: Italy
1924: Italy
1928: Hungary
1932: Hungary
1936: Hungary
1948: Hungary

1952: Hungary
1956: Hungary
1960: Hungary
1964: USSR
1968: USSR
1972: Italy
1976: USSR
1980: USSR
1984: Italy
1988: Hungary
1992: Unified Team
1996: Russia

Fencing–Women's Individual Épée
1996: Laurel Flessel, France

Fencing–Women's Team Épée
1996: France

Fencing–Women's Individual Foil
1924: Ellen Osiier, Denmark
1928: Helene Mayer, Germany
1932: Ellen Preis, Austria
1936: Ilona Elek, Hungary
1948: Ilona Elek, Hungary
1952: Irene Camber, Italy
1956: Gillian Sheen, Great Britain
1960: Heidi Schmid, West Germany
1964: Ildiko Ujlaki-Rejto, Hungary
1968: Yelena Novikova, USSR
1972: Antonella Lonzi-Ragno, Italy
1976: Ildiko Schwarzenberger-Tordasi, Hungary
1980: Pascale Trinquet-Hachin, France
1984: Jujie Luan, China
1988: Anja Fichtel, West Germany
1992: Giovanna Trillini, Italy
1996: Laura Badea, Romania

Fencing–Women's Team Foil
1960: USSR
1964: Hungary
1968: USSR
1972: USSR
1976: USSR
1980: France
1984: West Germany
1988: West Germany
1992: Italy
1996: Italy

Field Hockey–Men's Team
1908: Great Britain
1912:*
1920: Great Britain
1924:*

_____
*Event not held.

1928: India
1932: India
1936: India
1948: India
1952: India
1956: India
1960: Pakistan
1964: India
1968: Pakistan
1972: West Germany
1976: New Zealand
1980: India
1984: Pakistan
1988: Great Britain
1992: Germany
1996: Netherlands

Field Hockey–Women's Team
1980: Zimbabwe
1984: Netherlands
1988: Australia
1992: Spain
1996: Australia

Gymnastics, Artistic–Men's Individual All-Around
(Combined Exercises)
1900: Gustave Sandras, France
1904: Julius Lenhart, Austria
1906: Pierre Paysse, France
1908: Alberto Braglia, Italy
1912: Alberto Braglia, Italy
1920: Georgio Zampori, Italy
1924: Leon Stukelj, Yugoslavia
1928: Georges Miez, Switzerland
1932: Romeo Neri, Italy
1936: Alfred Schwarzmann, Germany
1948: Veikko Huhtanen, Finland
1952: Viktor Chukarin, USSR
1956: Viktor Chukarin, USSR
1960: Boris Shakhlin, USSR
1964: Yukio Endo, Japan
1968: Sawao Kato, Japan
1972: Sawao Kato, Japan
1976: Nikolai Andrianov, USSR
1980: Aleksandr Dityatin, USSR
1984: Koji Gushiken, Japan
1988: Vladimir Artemov, USSR
1992: Vitali Chtcherbo, Belarus
1996: Li Xiaoshuang, China

Gymnastics, Artistic–Men's Team
(Combined Exercises)
1904: Philadelphia
1906: Norway
1908: Sweden
1912: Italy
1920: Italy

1924: Italy
1928: Switzerland
1932: Italy
1936: Germany
1948: Finland
1952: USSR
1956: USSR
1960: Japan
1964: Japan
1968: Japan
1972: Japan
1976: Japan
1980: USSR
1984: USA
1988: USSR
1992: Unified Team
1996: Russia

Gymnastics, Artistic–Men's Floor Exercise
1932: Istvan Pelle, Hungary
1936: Georges Miez, Switzerland
1948: Ferenc Pataki, Hungary
1952: William Thoresson, Sweden
1956: Valentin Muratov, USSR
1960: Nobuyuki Aihara, Japan
1964: Franco Menichelli, Italy
1968: Sawao Kato, Japan
1972: Nikolai Andrianov, USSR
1976: Nikolai Andrianov, USSR
1980: Roland Bruckner, East Germany
1984: Ning Li, China
1988: Serguei Kharikov, USSR
1992: Li Xiaoshuang, China
1996: Ioannis Melissanidis, Greece

Gymnastics, Artistic–Men's Horizontal Bar
1896: Hermann Weingartner, Germany
1900:*
1904: Anton Heida, USA
1906–1920: *
1924: Leon Stukelj, Yugoslavia
1928: Georges Miez, Switzerland
1932: Dallas Bixler, USA
1936: Aleksanteri Saarvala, Finland
1948: Josef Stalder, Switzerland
1952: Jack Gunthard, Switzerland
1956: Takashi Ono, Japan
1960: Takashi Ono, Japan
1964: Boris Shakhlin, USSR
1968: Akinori Nakayama, Japan
1972: Mitsuo Tsukahara, Japan
1976: Mitsuo Tsukahara, Japan
1980: Stoian Delchev, Bulgaria
1984: Shinji Morisue, Japan
1988: Vladimir Artemov, USSR
1992: Trent Dimas, USA
1996: Andreas Wecker, Germany

---

*Event not held.

Gymnastics, Artistic–Men's Parallel Bars
1896: Alfred Flatow, Germany
1900:*
1904: George Eyser, USA
1908–1920:*
1924: August Guttinger, Switzerland
1928: Ladislav Vacha, Czechoslovakia
1932: Romeo Neri, Italy
1936: Konrad Frey, Germany
1948: Michael Reusch, Switzerland
1952: Hans Eugster, Switzerland
1956: Viktor Chukarin, USSR
1960: Boris Shakhlin, USSR
1964: Yukio Endo, Japan
1968: Akinori Nakayama, Japan
1972: Sawao Kato, Japan
1976: Sawao Kato, Japan
1980: Aleksandr Tkachyov, USSR
1984: Bart Conner, USA
1988: Vladimir Artemov, USSR
1992: Vitali Chtcherbo, Belarus
1996: Rustam Sharipov, Ukraine

---

*Event not held.

Gymnastics, Artistic–Men's Pommel Horse
1896: Louis Zutter, Switzerland
1900:*
1904: Anton Heida, USA
1906–1920:*
1924: Josef Wilhelm, Switzerland
1928: Hermann Hanggi, Switzerland
1932: Istvan Pelle, Hungary
1936: Konrad Frey, Germany
1948: Paavo Aaltonen, Finland
1952: Viktor Chukarin, USSR
1956: Boris Shakhlin, USSR
1960: Eugen Ekman, Finland
1964: Miroslav Cerar, Yugoslavia
1968: Miroslav Cerar, Yugoslavia
1972: Viktor Klimenko, USSR
1976: Zoltan Magyar, Hungary
1980: Zoltan Magyar, Hungary
1984: Ning Li, China
1988: Dmitri Bilozertchev, USSR
1992: Vitali Chtcherbo, Belarus
1996: Donghua Li, Switzerland

---

*Event not held.

Gymnastics, Artistic–Men's Still Rings
1896: Ioannis Metropoulos, Greece
1900:*
1904: Hermann Glass, USA
1906–1920:*
1924: Francesco Martino, Italy

---

*Event not held.

1928: Leon Stukelj, Yugoslavia
1932: George Gulack, USA
1936: Alois Hudec, Czechoslovakia
1948: Karl Frei, Switzerland
1952: Grant Shaginyan, USSR
1956: Albert Azaryan, USSR
1960: Albert Azaryan, USSR
1964: Takuji Hayata, Japan
1968: Akinori Nakayama, Japan
1972: Akinori Nakayama, Japan
1976: Nikolai Andrianov, USSR
1980: Aleksandr Dityatin, USSR
1984: Koji Gushiken, Japan
1988: Holger Behrendt, East Germany
1992: Vitali Chtcherbo, Belarus
1996: Yuri Chechi, Italy

Gymnastics, Artistic–Men's Horse Vault
1896: Carl Schuhmann, Germany
1900:*
1904: George Eyser, USA
1906–1920:*
1924: Frank Kriz, USA
1928: Eugen Mack, Switzerland
1932: Savino Guglielmetti, Italy
1936: Alfred Schwarzmann, Germany
1948: Paavo Aaltonen, Finland
1952: Viktor Chukarin, USSR
1956: Helmut Bantz, West Germany
1960: Takashi Ono, Japan
1964: Haruhiro Yamashita, Japan
1968: Mikhail Voronin, USSR
1972: Klaus Koste, East Germany
1976: Nikolai Andrianov, USSR
1980: Nikolai Andrianov, USSR
1984: Yun Lou, China
1988: Yun Lou, China
1992: Vitali Chtcherbo, Belarus
1996: Alexei Nemov, Russia

*Event not held.

Gymnastics, Artistic–Women's Individual All-Around (Combined Exercises)
1952: Maria Gorokhovskaya, USSR
1956: Larissa Latynina, USSR
1960: Larissa Latynina, USSR
1964: Vera Caslavska, Czechoslovakia
1968: Vera Caslavska, Czechoslovakia
1972: Lyudmila Tourischeva, USSR
1976: Nadia Comaneci, Romania
1980: Yelena Davydova, USSR
1984: Mary Lou Retton, USA
1988: Elena Shoushounova, USSR
1992: Tatiana Goutsou, Ukraine
1996: Lilia Podkopayeva, Ukraine

Gymnastics, Artistic–Women's Team (Combined Exercises)
1928: Netherlands
1932:*
1936: Germany
1948: Czechoslovakia
1952: USSR
1956: USSR
1960: USSR
1964: USSR
1968: USSR
1972: USSR
1976: USSR
1980: USSR
1984: Romania
1988: USSR
1992: Unified Team
1996: USA

*Event not held.

Gymnastics, Artistic–Women's Balance Beam
1952: Nina Bocharova, USSR
1956: Agnes Keleti, Hungary
1960: Eva Bosakova, Czechoslovakia
1964: Vera Caslavska, Czechoslovakia
1968: Natalia Kutschinskaya, USSR
1972: Olga Korbut, USSR
1976: Nadia Comaneci, Romania
1980: Nadia Comaneci, Romania
1984: Simona Pauca, Romania
1988: Daniela Silivas, Romania
1992: Tatiana Lyssenko, Ukraine
1996: Shannon Miller, USA

Gymnastics, Artistic–Women's Floor Exercise
1952: Agnes Keleti, Hungary
1956: Agnes Keleti, Hungary
1960: Larissa Latynina, USSR
1964: Larissa Latynina, USSR
1968: Vera Caslavska, Czechoslovakia
1972: Olga Korbut, USSR
1976: Nelli Kim, USSR
1980: Nelli Kim, USSR
1984: Ecaterina Szabo, Romania
1988: Daniela Silivas, Romania
1992: Lavinia Milosovici, Romania
1996: Lilia Podkopayeva, Ukraine

Gymnastics, Artistic–Women's Uneven Bars
1952: Margit Korondi, Hungary
1956: Agnes Keleti, Hungary
1960: Polina Astakhova, USSR
1964: Polina Astakhova, USSR
1968: Vera Caslavska, Czechoslovakia
1972: Karin Janz, East Germany

1976: Nadia Comaneci, Romania
1980: Maxi Gnauck, East Germany
1984: Yanhong Ma, China
1988: Daniela Silivas, Romania
1992: Lu Li, China
1996: Svetlana Chorkina, Russia

Gymnastics, Artistic–Women's Horse Vault

1952: Yekaterina Kalinchuk, USSR
1956: Larissa Latynina, USSR
1960: Margarita Nikolayeva, USSR
1964: Vera Caslavska, Czechoslovakia
1968: Vera Caslavska, Czechoslovakia
1972: Karin Janz, East Germany
1976: Nelli Kim, USSR
1980: Natalia Shaposhnikova, USSR
1984: Ecaterina Szabo, Romania
1988: Svetlana Boguinskaia, USSR
1992: Henrietta Onodi, Hungary
1996: Simona Amanar, Romania

Gymnastics, Rhythmic–Women's Individual All-Around

1984: Lori Fung, Canada
1988: Marina Lobatch, USSR
1992: Alexandra Timoshenko, Ukraine
1996: Ekaterina Serebryanskaya, Ukraine

Gymnastics, Rhythmic–Women's Group All-Around

1996: Spain

Judo–Men's Extra Lightweight (Up to 60 kg)

1980: Thierry Rey, France
1984: Shinji Hosokawa, Japan
1988: Jae-Yup Kim, South Korea
1992: Nazim Gousseinov, Azerbaijan
1996: Tadahiro Nomura, Japan

Judo–Men's Half Lightweight (Up to 65 kg)

1980: Nikolai Solodukhin, USSR
1984: Yoshiyuki Matsuoka, Japan
1988: Kyung-Keun Lee, South Korea
1992: Rogerio Cardoso, Brazil
1996: Udo Quellmalz, Germany

Judo–Men's Lightweight (Up to 71 kg)

1964: Takehide Nakatani, Japan
1968:*
1972: Takao Kawaguchi, Japan
1976: Hector Rodriguez, Cuba
1980: Ezio Gamba, Italy
1984: Byeng-Keun Ahn, South Korea
1988: Marc Alexandre, France
1992: Toshihiko Koga, Japan
1996: Kenzo Nakamura, Japan

---

*Event not held.

Judo–Men's Half Middleweight (Up to 78 kg)

1972: Toyokazu Nomura, Japan
1976: Vladimir Nevzorov, USSR
1980: Shota Khabareli, USSR
1984: Frank Wieneke, West Germany
1988: Waldemar Legien, Poland
1992: Hidehiko Yoshida, Japan
1996: Djamel Bouras, France

Judo–Men's Middleweight (Up to 86 kg)

1964: Isao Okano, Japan
1968:*
1972: Shinobu Sekine, Japan
1976: Isamu Sonoda, Japan
1980: Jurg Rothlisberger, Switzerland
1984: Peter Seisenbacher, Austria
1988: Peter Seisenbacher, Austria
1992: Waldemar Legien, Poland
1996: Jeon Ki-Young, South Korea

---

*Event not held.

Judo–Men's Half Heavyweight (Up to 95 kg)

1972: Schota Chochoshvili, USSR
1976: Kazuhiro Ninomiya, Japan
1980: Robert van de Walle, Belgium
1984: Hyoung-Zoo Ha, South Korea
1988: Aurelio Miguel, Brazil
1992: Antal Kovacs, Hungary
1996: Pawel Nastula, Poland

Judo–Men's Heavyweight (Over 95 kg)

1964: Isao Inokuma, Japan
1968:*
1972: Wim Ruska, Netherlands
1976: Sergei Novikov, USSR
1980: Angelo Parisi, France
1984: Hitoshi Saito, Japan
1988: Hitoshi Saito, Japan
1992: David Khakhaleichvili, Georgia
1996: David Douillet, France

---

*Event not held.

Judo–Men's Open Category

1964: Antonius Geesink, Netherlands
1968:*
1972: Wim Ruska, Netherlands
1976: Haruko Uemura, Japan
1980: Dietmar Lorenz, East Germany
1984: Yasuhiro Yamashita, Japan
1988–1996:*

---

*Event not held.

Judo–Women's Extra Lightweight (Up to 48kg)
1992: Cécile Nowak, France
1996: Sun Hi Kye, North Korea

Judo–Women's Half Lightweight (Up to 52kg)
1992: Almudena Martinez, Spain
1996: Marie-Claire Restoux, France

Judo–Women's Lightweight (Up to 56kg)
1992: Miriam Blasco Soto, Spain
1996: Driulis Gonzalez, Cuba

Judo–Women's Half Middleweight (Up to 61kg)
1992: Catherine Fleury, France
1996: Yuko Emoto, Japan

Judo–Women's Middleweight (Up to 66kg)
1992: Odalis Reve Jimenez, Cuba
1996: Cho Min Sun, South Korea

Judo–Women's Half Heavyweight (Up to 72kg)
1992: Kim Mi-Jung, South Korea
1996: Ulla Werbrouck, Belgium

Judo–Women's Heavyweight (Over 72kg)
1992: Zhuang Xiaoyan, China
1996: Fuming Sun, China

Modern Pentathlon–Individual
1912: Gosta Lilliehook, Sweden
1920: Gustaf Dyrssen, Sweden
1924: Bo Lindman, Sweden
1928: Sven Thofelt, Sweden
1932: Johan Oxenstierna, Sweden
1936: Gotthard Handrick, Germany
1948: William Grut, Sweden
1952: Lars Hall, Sweden
1956: Lars Hall, Sweden
1960: Ferenc Nemeth, Hungary
1964: Ferenc Torok, Hungary
1968: Bjorn Ferm, Sweden
1972: Andras Balczo, Hungary
1976: Janusz Pyciak-Peciak, Poland
1980: Anatoli Starostin, USSR
1984: Daniele Masala, Italy
1988: Janos Martinek, Hungary
1992: Arkadiusz Skrzypaszek, Poland
1996: Aleksandr Parygin, Kazakhstan

Modern Pentathlon–Team
1952: Hungary
1956: USSR
1960: Hungary
1964: USSR
1968: Hungary
1972: USSR
1976: Great Britain
1980: USSR

1984: Italy
1988: Hungary
1992: Poland
1996:*

---

*Event not held.

Rowing–Men's Single Sculls
1900: Henri Barrelet, France
1904: Frank Greer, USA
1906: Gaston Delaplane, France
1908: Harry Blackstaffe, Great Britain
1912: William Kinnear, Great Britain
1920: John Kelly, Sr., USA
1924: Jack Beresford, Jr., Great Britain
1928: Henry Pearce, Australia
1932: Henry Pearce, Australia
1936: Gustav Schafer, Germany
1948: Mervyn Wood, Australia
1952: Yuri Tyukalov, USSR
1956: Vyacheslav Ivanov, USSR
1960: Vyacheslav Ivanov, USSR
1964: Vyacheslav Ivanov, USSR
1968: Henri Jan Wienese, Netherlands
1972: Yuri Malishev, USSR
1976: Pertti Karppinen, Finland
1980: Pertti Karppinen, Finland
1984: Pertti Karppinen, Finland
1988: Thomas Lange, East Germany
1992: Thomas Lange, Germany
1996: Xeno Mueller, Switzerland

Rowing–Men's Double Sculls
1904: USA, John Mulcahy, William Varley
1906–1912:*
1920: USA, John Kelly, Sr., Paul Costello
1924: USA, Paul Costello, John Kelly, Sr.
1928: USA, Paul Costello, Charles McIlvaine
1932: USA, Kenneth Myers, William E. Garrett Gilmore
1936: Great Britain, Jack Beresford, Jr., Leslie Southwood
1948: Great Britain, Richard Burnell, B. Herbert Bushnell
1952: Argentina, Tranquilo Cappozzo, Eduardo Guerrero
1956: USSR, Aleksandr Berkutov, Yuri Tyukalov
1960: Czechoslovakia, Vaclav Kozak, Pavel Schmidt
1964: USSR, Oleg Tyurin, Boris Dubrovski
1968: USSR, Anatoli Sass, Aleksandr Timoschinin
1972: USSR, Aleksandr Timoshinin, Gennady Korshikikov
1976: Norway, Frank Hansen, Alf Hansen
1980: East Germany, Joachim Dreifke, Kroppelien Klaus
1984: USA, Bradley Lewis, Paul Enquist
1988: Netherlands, Ronald Florijn, Nicolaas Rienks
1992: Australia, Stephen Hawkins, Peter Antonie
1996: Italy, Davide Tizzano, Agostino Abbagnale

---

*Event not held.

Rowing–Men's Lightweight Double Sculls
1996: Switzerland, Markus Gier, Michael Gier

Rowing–Men's Coxless Pairs
1908: Great Britain, J. R. K. Fenning, Gordon Thomson
1912–1920:*
1924: Netherlands, Antonie C. Beijnen, Wilhelm H. Rosingh
1928: Germany, Bruno Muller, Kurt Moeschter
1932: Great Britain, H.R. Arthur Edwards, Lewis Clive
1936: Germany, Willi Eichhorn, Hugo Strauss
1948: Great Britain, John Wilson, W. George Laurie
1952: USA, Charles Logg, Thomas Price
1956: USA, James Fifer, Duvall Hecht
1960: USSR, Valentin Boreiko, Oleg Golovanov
1964: Canada, George Hungerford, Roger Ch. Jackson
1968: East Germany, Jorg Lucke, Heinz-Jurgen Bothe
1972: East Germany, Siegfried Brietzke, Wolfgang Meyer
1976: East Germany, Jurgen Landvoigt, Bernd Landvoigt
1980: East Germany, Bernd Landvoigt, Jurgen Landvoigt
1984: Romania, Petru Iosub, Valer Toma
1988: Great Britain, Andrew Holmes, Steven Redgrave
1992: Great Britain, Steven Redgrave, Matthew Pinsent
1996: Great Britain, Steven Redgrave, Matthew Pinsent

*Event not held.

Rowing–Men's Coxed Pairs
1900: Netherlands
1904:*
1906: Italy
1908–1912:*
1920: Italy
1924: Switzerland
1928: Switzerland
1932: USA
1936: Germany
1948: Denmark
1952: France
1956: USA
1960: West Germany
1964: USA
1968: Italy
1972: East Germany
1976: East Germany
1980: East Germany
1984: Italy
1988: Italy
1992: Great Britain
1996:*

*Event not held.

Rowing–Men's Quadruple Sculls
1976: East Germany
1980: East Germany
1984: West Germany
1988: Italy
1992: Germany
1996: Germany

Rowing–Men's Coxless Fours
1904: USA
1906:*
1908: Great Britain
1912–1920:*
1924: Great Britain
1928: Great Britain
1932: Great Britain
1936: Germany
1948: Italy
1952: Yugoslavia
1956: Canada
1960: USA
1964: Denmark
1968: East Germany
1972: East Germany
1976: East Germany
1980: East Germany
1984: New Zealand
1988: East Germany
1992: Australia
1996: Australia

*Event not held.

Rowing–Men's Coxed Fours
1900: France
1904:*
1906: Italy
1908:*
1912: Germany
1920: Switzerland
1924: Switzerland
1928: Italy
1932: Germany
1936: Germany
1948: USA
1952: Czechoslovakia
1956: Italy
1960: West Germany
1964: West Germany
1968: New Zealand
1972: West Germany
1976: USSR
1980: East Germany
1984: Great Britain
1988: East Germany
1992: Romania
1996:*

*Event not held.

Rowing–Men's Lightweight Coxless Fours
1996: Denmark

Rowing–Men's Eight Oars

1900: USA
1904: USA
1906:*
1908: Great Britain
1912: Great Britain
1920: USA
1924: USA
1928: USA
1932: USA
1936: USA
1948: USA
1952: USA
1956: USA
1960: West Germany
1964: USA
1968: West Germany
1972: New Zealand
1976: East Germany
1980: East Germany
1984: Canada
1988: West Germany
1992: Canada
1996: Netherlands

---

*Event not held.

Rowing–Women's Single Sculls

1976: Christine Scheiblich, East Germany
1980: Sanda Toma, Romania
1984: Valeria Racila, Romania
1988: Jutta Behrendt, East Germany
1992: Elisabeta Lipa, Romania
1996: Yekaterina Khodotovich, Belarus

Rowing–Women's Double Sculls

1976: Bulgaria, Svetla Ozetova, Zdravko Yordanova-
    Barboulova
1980: USSR, Yelena Khloptseva, Larissa Popova
1984: Romania, Manoara Popescu, Elisabeta Oleniuc
1988: East Germany, Birgit Peter, Martina Schroeter
1992: Germany, Kerstin Koeppen, Kathrin Boron
1996: Canada, Marnie McBean, Kathleen Heddle

Rowing–Women's Coxless Pairs

1976: Bulgaria, Siika Kelbecheva-Barboulova, Stoyanka
    Grouicheva
1980: East Germany, Ute Steindorf, Cornelia Klier
1984: Romania, Rodica Arba, Elena Horvat
1988: Romania, Rodica Arba, Olga Homeghi
1992: Canada, Marnie McBean, Kathleen Heddle
1996: Australia, Megan Still, Kate Slatter

Rowing–Women's Coxless Fours

1992: Canada
1996:*

---

*Event not held.

Rowing–Women's Lightweight Double Sculls

1996: Romania, Constanta Burcica, Camelia Macoviciuc

Rowing–Women's Quadruple Sculls

1976: East Germany
1980: East Germany
1984: Romania
1988: East Germany
1992: Germany
1996: Germany

Rowing–Women's Coxed Fours

1976: East Germany
1980: East Germany
1984: Romania
1988: East Germany
1992–1996:*

---

*Event not held.

Rowing–Women's Eight Oars

1976: East Germany
1980: East Germany
1984: USA
1988: East Germany
1992: Canada
1996: Romania

Shooting–Men's Air Pistol

1988: Taniou Kiriakov, Bulgaria
1992: Wang Yifu, China
1996: Roberto DiDonna, Italy

Shooting–Men's Free Pistol

1896: Sumner Paine, USA
1900: Conrad Roderer, Switzerland
1904:*
1906: Georgios Orphanidis, Greece
1908:*
1912: Alfred Lane, USA
1920: Karl Frederick, USA
1924–1932:*
1936: Torsten Ullman, Sweden
1948: Edwin Vasquez Cam, Peru
1952: Huelet Benner, USA
1956: Pentti Linnosvuo, Finland
1960: Aleksei Gustchin, USSR
1964: Vaino Markkanen, Finland
1968: Grigori Kossykh, USSR
1972: Ragnar Skanaker, Sweden
1976: Uwe Potteck, East Germany
1980: Aleksandr Melentiev, USSR
1984: Haifeng Xu, China
1988: Sorin Babii, Romania
1992: Konstantine Loukachik, Belarus
1996: Boris Kokorev, Russia

---

*Event not held.

Shooting–Men's Rapid-Fire Pistol
1896: Jean Phrangoudis, Greece
1900: Marice Larrouy, France
1904:*
1906: Maurice Lecoq, France
1908: Paul Van Asbroeck, Belgium
1912: Alfred Lane, USA
1920: Guilherme Paraense, Brazil
1924: H. M. Bailey, USA
1928:*
1932: Renzo Morigi, Italy
1936: Cornelius Van Oyen, Germany
1948: Karoly Takacs, Hungary
1952: Karoly Takacs, Hungary
1956: Stefan Petrescu, Romania
1960: William McMillan, USA
1964: Pentti Linnosvuo, Finland
1968: Jozef Zapedzki, Poland
1972: Jozef Zapedzki, Poland
1976: Norbert Klaar, East Germany
1980: Corneliu Ion, Romania
1984: Takeo Kamachi, Japan
1988: Afanasi Kouzming, USSR
1992: Ralf Schumann, Germany
1996: Ralf Schumann, Germany

*Event not held.

Shooting–Men's Running Game Target
1900: Louis Debray, France
1904–1968:*
1972: Yakov Zhelezniak, USSR
1976: Aleksandr Gazov, USSR
1980: Igor Sokolov, USSR
1984: Yuwei Li, China
1988: Tor Heiestad, Norway
1992: Michael Jakosits, Germany
1996: Yang Ling, China

*Event not held.

Shooting–Men's Air Rifle
1984: Philippe Heberle, France
1988: Goran Maksimovic, Yugoslavia
1992: iouri Fedkine, Russia
1996: Artem Khadzhibekov, Russia

Shooting–Men's Smallbore Free Rifle, Prone
1908: A. A. Carnell, Great Britain
1912: Frederick Hird, USA
1920: Lawrence A. Nuesslein, USA
1924: Pierre Coquelin De Lisle, France
1928:*
1932: Bertil Ronnmark, Sweden
1936: Willy Rogeberg, Norway
1948: Arthur Cook, USA

*Event not held.

1952: Iosif Sirbu, Romania
1956: Gerald R. Ouellette, Canada
1960: Peter Kohnke, West Germany
1964: Laszlo Hammerl, Hungary
1968: Jan Kurka, Czechoslovakia
1972: Ho-Jun Li, North Korea
1976: Karlheinz Smieszek, West Germany
1980: Karoly Vargo, Hungary
1984: Edward Etzel, USA
1988: Miroslav Varga, Czechoslovakia
1992: Eun-Chul Lee, South Korea
1996: Christian Klees, Germany

Shooting–Men's Smallbore Rifle, Three-Position
1952: Erling Kongshaug, Norway
1956: Anatoli Bogdanov, USSR
1960: Viktor Shamburkin, USSR
1964: Lones Wigger, USA
1968: Bernd Klingner, West Germany
1972: John Writer, USA
1976: Lanny Bassham, USA
1980: Viktor Vlasov, USSR
1984: Malcolm Cooper, Great Britain
1988: Malcolm Cooper, Great Britain
1992: Gratchia Petikian, Armenia
1996: Jean-Pierre Amat, France

Shooting–Olympic Trap (Open)
1900: Roger De Barbarin, France
1904:*
1906: Gerald Merlin, Great Britain, Sidney Merlin, Great Britain
1908: Walter H. Ewing, Canada
1912: James Graham, USA
1920: Mark Arie, USA
1924: Gyula Halasy, Hungary
1928–1948:*
1952: George P. Genereux, Canada
1956: Galliano Rossini, Italy
1960: Ion Dumitrescu, Romania
1964: Ennio Mattarelli, Italy
1968: John R. Braithwaite, Great Britain
1972: Angelo Scalzone, Italy
1976: Donald Haldeman, USA
1980: Luciano Giovannetti, Italy
1984: Luciano Giovannetti, Italy
1988: Dmitri Monakov, USSR
1992: Petr Hrdlicka, Czechoslovakia
1996: Michael Diamond, Australia

*Event not held.

Shooting–Men's Olympic Double Trap (Open)
1996: Russell Mark, Australia

Shooting–Olympic Skeet (Open)

1968: Yevgeny Petrov, USSR
1972: Konrad Wirnhier, West Germany
1976: Josef Panacek, Czechoslovakia
1980: Hans Kjeld Rasmussen, Denmark
1984: Matthew Dryke, USA
1988: Axel Wegner, East Germany
1992: Zhang Shan, China
1996: Ennio Falco, Italy

Shooting–Women's Air Pistol

1988: Jasna Sekaric, Yugoslavia
1992: Marina Logvinenko, Russia
1996: Olga Klochneva, Russia

Shooting–Women's Sport Pistol

1984: Linda Thom, Canada
1988: Nino Salukvadze, USSR
1992: Marina Logvinenko, Russia
1996: Li Duihong, China

Shooting–Women's Air Rifle

1984: Pat Spurgin, USA
1988: Irina Chilova, USSR
1992: Kab-Soon Yeo, South Korea
1996: Renata Mauer, Poland

Shooting–Women's Smallbore Rifle, Three-Position

1984: Xiao Xuan Wu, China
1988: Silvia Sperber, West Germany
1992: Launi Meili, USA
1996: Aleksandra Ivosev, Yugoslavia

Shooting–Women's Olympic Double Trap (Open)

1996: Kim Rhode, USA

Men's Soccer

1900: Great Britain
1904: Canada
1906: Denmark
1908: Great Britain
1912: Great Britain
1920: Belgium
1924: Uruguay
1928: Uruguay
1932:*
1936: Italy
1948: Sweden
1952: Hungary
1956: USSR
1960: Yugoslavia
1964: Hungary
1968: Hungary

*Event not held.

1972: Poland
1976: East Germany
1980: Czechoslovakia
1984: France
1988: USSR
1992: Spain
1996: Nigeria

Women's Soccer

1996: USA

Softball

1996: USA

Swimming–Men's 50-Meter Freestyle

1904: Zoltan von Halmay, Hungary
1906–1984:*
1988: Matthew Biondi, USA
1992: Aleksandr Popov, Russia
1996: Aleksandr Popov, Russia

_____
*Event not held.

Swimming–Men's 100-Meter Freestyle

1896: Alfred Hajos, Hungary
1900:*
1904: Zoltan von Halmay, Hungary
1906: Charles Daniels, USA
1908: Charles Daniels, USA
1912: Duke Paoa Kahanamoku, USA
1920: Duke Paoa Kahanamoku, USA
1924: John Weissmuller, USA
1928: John Weissmuller, USA
1932: Yasuji Miyazaki, Japan
1936: Ferenc Csik, Hungary
1948: Walter Ris, USA
1952: Clarke Scholes, USA
1956: Jon Henricks, Australia
1960: John Devitt, Australia
1964: Don Schollander, USA
1968: Michael Wenden, Australia
1972: Mark Spitz, USA
1976: Jim Montgomery, USA
1980: Jorg Woithe, East Germany
1984: Ambrose Gaines, USA
1988: Matthew Biondi, USA
1992: Aleksandr Popov, Russia
1996: Aleksandr Popov, Russia

_____
*Event not held.

Swimming–Men's 200-Meter Freestyle

1900: Frederick C. V. Lane, Australia
1904: Charles Daniels, USA
1906–1964:*

_____
*Event not held.

1968: Michael Wenden, Australia
1972: Mark Spitz, USA
1976: Bruce Furniss, USA
1980: Sergei Kopliakov, USSR
1984: Michael Gross, West Germany
1988: Duncan Armstrong, Australia
1992: Evgueni Sadovyi, Russia
1996: Danyon Loader, New Zealand

Swimming–Men's 400-Meter Freestyle
1896: Paul Neumann, Australia
1900:*
1904: Charles Daniels, USA
1906: Otto Scheff, Austria
1908: Henry Taylor, Great Britain
1912: George Hodgson, Canada
1920: Norman Ross, USA
1924: John Weissmuller, USA
1928: Alberto Zorilla, Argentina
1932: Clarence Crabbe, USA
1936: Jack Medica, USA
1948: William Smith, USA
1952: Jean Boiteux, France
1956: Murray Rose, Australia
1960: Murray Rose, Australia
1964: Don Schollander, USA
1968: Michael Burton, USA
1972: Bradford Cooper, Australia
1976: Brian Goodell, USA
1980: Vladimir Salnikov, USSR
1984: George Dicarlo, USA
1988: Uwe Dassler, East Germany
1992: Evgueni Sadovyi, Russia
1996: Danyon Loader, New Zealand

*Event not held

Swimming–Men's 1,500-Meter Freestyle
1896: Alfred Hajos, Hungary
1900: John Jarvis, Great Britain
1904: Emil Rausch, Germany
1906: Henry Taylor, Great Britain
1908: Henry Taylor, Great Britain
1912: George Hodgson, Canada
1920: Norman Ross, USA
1924: Andrew Charlton, Australia
1928: Arne Borg, Sweden
1932: Kusuo Kitamura, Japan
1936: Noboru Terada, Japan
1948: James McLane, USA
1952: Ford Konno, USA
1956: Murray Rose, Australia
1960: John Konrads, Australia
1964: Robert Windle, Australia
1968: Michael Burton, USA
1972: Michael Burton, USA
1976: Brian Goodell, USA
1980: Vladimir Salnikov, USSR

1984: Michael O'Brien, USA
1988: Vladimir Salnikov, USSR
1992: Kieren Perkins, Australia
1996: Kieren Perkins, Australia

Swimming–Men's 100-Meter Backstroke
1904: Walter Brack, Germany
1906:*
1908: Arno Bieberstein, Germany
1912: Harry Hebner, USA
1920: Warren Paoa Kealoha, USA
1924: Warren Paoa Kealoha, USA
1928: George Kojac, USA
1932: Masaji Kiyokawa, Japan
1936: Adolf Kiefer, USA
1948: Allen Stack, USA
1952: Yoshinobu Oyakawa, USA
1956: David Theile, Australia
1960: David Theile, Australia
1964:*
1968: Roland Matthes, East Germany
1972: Roland Matthes, East Germany
1976: John Naber, USA
1980: Bengt Baron, Sweden
1984: Richard Carey, USA
1988: Daichi Suzuki, Japan
1992: Mark Tewksbury, Canada
1996: Jeff Rouse, USA

*Event not held.

Swimming–Men's 200-Meter Backstroke
1900: Ernst Hoppenberg, Germany
1904–1960:*
1964: Jed Graef, USA
1968: Roland Matthes, East Germany
1972: Roland Matthes, East Germany
1976: John Naber, USA
1980: Sandor Wladar, Hungary
1984: Richard Carey, USA
1988: Igor Polianski, USSR
1992: Martin Lopez-Zubero, Spain
1996: Brad Bridgewater, USA

*Event not held.

Swimming–Men's 100-Meter Breaststroke
1968: Donald McKenzie, USA
1972: Nobutaka Taguchi, Japan
1976: John Hencken, USA
1980: Dunkan Goodhew, Great Britain
1984: Steve Lundquist, USA
1988: Adrian Moorhouse, Great Britain
1992: Nelson Diebel, USA
1996: Fred DeBurghgraeve, Belgium

Swimming–Men's 200-Meter Breaststroke
1908: Frederick Holman, Great Britain

1912: Walther Bathe, Germany
1920: Hakan Malmroth, Sweden
1924: Robert Skelton, USA
1928: Yoshiyuki Tsuruta, Japan
1932: Yoshiyuki Tsuruta, Japan
1936: Tetsuo Hamuro, Japan
1948: Joseph Verdeur, USA
1952: John Davies, Australia
1956: Masaru Furukawa, Japan
1960: William Mulliken, USA
1964: Ian O'Brien, Australia
1968: Felipe Munoz, Mexico
1972: John Hencken, USA
1976: David Wilkie, Great Britain
1980: Robertas Zulpa, USSR
1984: Victor Davis, Canada
1988: Jozsef Szabo, Hungary
1992: Mike Barrowman, USA
1996: Norbert Rozsa, Hungary

Swimming–Men's 100-Meter Butterfly
1968: Douglas Russell, USA
1972: Mark Spitz, USA
1976: Matt Vogel, USA
1980: Par Arvidsson, Sweden
1984: Michael Gross, West Germany
1988: Anthony Nesty, Suriname
1992: Pablo Morales, USA
1996: Denis Pankratov, Russia

Swimming–Men's 200-Meter Butterfly
1956: William Yorzyk, USA
1960: Michael Troy, USA
1964: Kevin Berry, Australia
1968: Carl Robie, USA
1972: Mark Spitz, USA
1976: Mike Bruner, USA
1980: Sergei Fesenko, USSR
1984: Jon Sieben, Australia
1988: Michael Gross, West Germany
1992: Mel Stewart, USA
1996: Denis Pankratov, Russia

Swimming–Men's 200-Meter Individual Medley
1968: Charles Hickcox, USA
1972: Gunnar Larsson, Sweden
1976–1980:*
1984: Alex Baumann, Canada
1988: Tamas Darnyi, Hungary
1992: Tamas Darnyi, Hungary
1996: Attila Czene, Hungary

*Event not held.

Swimming–Men's 400-Meter Individual Medley
1964: Richard Roth, USA
1968: Charles Hickcox, USA
1972: Gunnar Larsson, Sweden

1976: Rod Strachan, USA
1980: Aleksandr Sidorenko, USSR
1984: Alex Baumann, Canada
1988: Tamas Darnyi, Hungary
1992: Tamas Darnyi, Hungary
1996: Tom Dolan, USA

Swimming–Men's 4 × 100-Meter Freestyle Relay
1964: USA
1968: USA
1972: USA
1976–1980:*
1984: USA
1988: USA
1992: USA
1996: USA

*Event not held.

Swimming–Men's 4 × 100-Meter Medley Relay
1960: USA
1964: USA
1968: USA
1972: USA
1976: USA
1980: Australia
1984: USA
1988: USA
1992: USA
1996: USA

Swimming–Men's 4 × 200-Meter Freestyle Relay
1906: Hungary
1908: Great Britain
1912: Australia
1920: USA
1924: USA
1928: USA
1932: Japan
1936: Japan
1948: USA
1952: USA
1956: Australia
1960: USA
1964: USA
1968: USA
1972: USA
1976: USA
1980: USSR
1984: USA
1988: USA
1992: Unified Team
1996: USA

Swimming–Women's 50-Meter Freestyle
1988: Kristin Otto, East Germany
1992: Yang Wenyi, China
1996: Amy Van Dyken, USA

Swimming–Women's 100-Meter Freestyle
1912: Fanny Durack, Australia
1920: Ethelda Bleibtrey, USA
1924: Ethel Lackie, USA
1928: Albina Osipowich, USA
1932: Helene Madison, USA
1936: Hendrika Mastenbroek, Netherlands
1948: Greta Andersen, Denmark
1952: Katalin Szoke, Hungary
1956: Dawn Fraser, Australia
1960: Dawn Fraser, Australia
1964: Dawn Fraser, Australia
1968: Jan Henne, USA
1972: Sandra Neilson, USA
1976: Kornelia Ender, East Germany
1980: Barbara Krause, East Germany
1984: Nancy Hogshead, USA
1988: Kristin Otto, East Germany
1992: Zhuang Yong, China
1996: Jingyi Le, China

Swimming–Women's 200-Meter Freestyle
1968: Debbie Meyer, USA
1972: Shane Gould, Australia
1976: Kornelia Ender, East Germany
1980: Barbara Krause, East Germany
1984: Mary Wayte, USA
1988: Heike Friedrich, East Germany
1992: Nicole Haislett, USA
1996: Claudia Poll, Costa Rica

Swimming–Women's 400-Meter Freestyle
1920: Ethelda Bleibtrey, USA
1924: Martha Norelius, USA
1928: Martha Norelius, USA
1932: Helene Madison, USA
1936: Hendrika Mastenbroek, Netherlands
1948: Ann Curtis, USA
1952: Valeria Gyenge, Hungary
1956: Lorraine Crapp, Australia
1960: Christine Von Saltza, USA
1964: Virginia Duenkel, USA
1968: Debbie Meyer, USA
1972: Shane Gould, Australia
1976: Petra Thuemer, East Germany
1980: Ines Diers, East Germany
1984: Tiffany Cohen, USA
1988: Janet Evans, USA
1992: Dagmar Hase, Germany
1996: Michelle Smith, Ireland

Swimming–Women's 800-Meter Freestyle
1968: Debbie Meyer, USA
1972: Keena Rothhammer, USA
1976: Petra Thuemer, East Germany
1980: Michelle Ford, Australia
1984: Tiffany Cohen, USA
1988: Janet Evans, USA

1992: Janet Evans, USA
1996: Brooke Bennett, USA

Swimming–Women's 100-Meter Backstroke
1924: Sybil Bauer, USA
1928: Maria Johanna Braun, Netherlands
1932: Eleanor Holm, USA
1936: Dina W. Senff, Netherlands
1948: Karen Margrete Harup, Denmark
1952: Joan Harrison, South Africa
1956: Judith Grinham, Great Britain
1960: Lynn Burke, USA
1964: Cathy Ferguson, USA
1968: Kaye Hall, USA
1972: Melissa Belote, USA
1976: Ulrike Richter, East Germany
1980: Rica Reinisch, East Germany
1984: Theresa Andrews, USA
1988: Kristin Otto, East Germany
1992: Kirsztina Egerszegi, Hungary
1996: Beth Botsford, USA

Swimming–Women's 200-Meter Backstroke
1968: Pokey Watson, USA
1972: Melissa Belote, USA
1976: Ulrike Richter, East Germany
1980: Rica Reinisch, East Germany
1984: Jolanda De Rover, Netherlands
1988: Krisztina Egerszegi, Hungary
1992: Krisztina Egerszegi, Hungary
1996: Krisztina Egerszegi, Hungary

Swimming–Women's 100-Meter Breaststroke
1968: Djurdjica Bjedov, Yugoslavia
1972: Catherine Carr, USA
1976: Hannelore Anke, East Germany
1980: Ute Geweniger, East Germany
1984: Petra Van Staveren, Netherlands
1988: Tania Dangalakova, Bulgaria
1992: Elena Roudkovskaïa, Belarus
1996: Penelope Heyns, South Africa

Swimming–Women's 200-Meter Breaststroke
1924: Lucy Morton, Great Britain
1928: Hilde Schrader, Germany
1932: Claire Dennis, Australia
1936: Hideko Maehata, Japan
1948: Petronella van Vliet, Netherlands
1952: Eva Szekely, Hungary
1956: Ursula Happe, West Germany
1960: Anita Lonsbrough, Great Britain
1964: Galina Prozumenshikova, USSR
1968: Sharon Wichman, USA
1972: Beverly Whitfield, Australia
1976: Marina Koshevaia, USSR
1980: Lina Kochushite, USSR
1984: Anne Ottenbrite, Canada

1988: Silke Hoerner, East Germany
1992: Kyoko Iwasaki, Japan
1996: Penelope Heyns, South Africa

Swimming–Women's 100-Meter Butterfly
1956: Shelley Mann, USA
1960: Carolyn Schuler, USA
1964: Sharon Stouder, USA
1968: Lynette McClements, Australia
1972: Mayumi Aoki, Japan
1976: Kornelia Ender, East Germany
1980: Caren Metschuck, East Germany
1984: Mary T. Meagher, USA
1988: Kristin Otto, East Germany
1992: Qian Hong, China
1996: Amy Van Dyken, USA

Swimming–Women's 200-Meter Butterfly
1968: Ada Kok, Netherlands
1972: Karen Moe, USA
1976: Andrea Pollack, East Germany
1980: Ines Geissler, East Germany
1984: Mary T. Meagher, USA
1988: Kathleen Nord, East Germany
1992: Summer Sanders, USA
1996: Susan O'Neill, Australia

Swimming–Women's 200-Meter Individual Medley
1968: Claudia Kolb, USA
1972: Shane Gould, Australia
1976-1980*
1984: Tracy Caulkins, USA
1988: Daniela Hunger, East Germany
1992: Lin Li, China
1996: Michelle Smith, Ireland

---
*Event not held.

Swimming–Women's 400-Meter Individual Medley
1964: Donna De Varona, USA
1968: Claudia Kolb, USA
1972: Gail Neall, Australia
1976: Ulrike Tauber, East Germany
1980: Petra Schneider, East Germany
1984: Tracy Caulkins, USA
1988: Janet Evans, USA
1992: Krisztina Egerszegi, Hungary
1996: Michelle Smith, Ireland

Swimming–Women's 4 × 100-Meter Freestyle Relay
1912: Great Britain
1920: USA
1924: USA
1928: USA
1932: USA
1936: Netherlands
1948: USA
1952: Hungary
1956: Australia
1960: USA
1964: USA
1968: USA
1972: USA
1976: USA
1980: East Germany
1984: USA
1988: East Germany
1992: USA
1996: USA

Swimming–Women's 4 × 100-Meter Medley Relay
1960: USA
1964: USA
1968: USA
1972: USA
1976: East Germany
1980: East Germany
1984: USA
1988: East Germany
1992: USA
1996: USA

Swimming–Women's 4 × 200-Meter Freestyle Relay
1996: USA

Synchronized Swimming–Solo
1984: Tracie Ruiz, USA
1988: Carolyn Waldo, Canada
1992: Kristen Babb-Sprague, USA
1996*

---
*Event not held.

Synchronized Swimming–Duet
1984: USA, Candy Costie, Tracie Ruiz
1988: Canada, Michelle Cameron, Carolyn Waldo
1992: USA, Karen Josephson, Sarah Josephson
1996*

---
*Event not held.

Synchronized Swimming–Team
1996: USA

Table Tennis–Men's Singles
1988: Nam-Kyu Yoo, South Korea
1992: Jan Waldner, Sweden
1996: Guoliang Liu, China

Table Tennis–Men's Doubles
1988: China, Longcan Chen, Qingguang Wei
1992: China, Lu Lin, Wang Tao
1996: China, Linghui Kung, Guoliang Liu

Table Tennis–Women's Singles
1988: Jing Chen, China
1992: Deng Yaping, China
1996: Deng Yaping, China

Table Tennis–Women's Doubles
1988: South Korea, Jung-Hwa Hyun, Young-Ja Yang
1992: China, Deng Yaping, Qiao Hong
1996: China, Deng Yaping, Qiao Hong

Team Handball–Men's Team
1936: Germany
1948:*
1952: Demonstration game only.
1956-1968:*
1972: Yugoslavia
1976: USSR
1980: East Germany
1984: Yugoslavia
1988: USSR
1992: Unified Team
1996: Croatia

_____
*Event not held.

Team Handball–Women's Team
1976: USSR
1980: USSR
1984: Yugoslavia
1988: South Korea
1992: South Korea
1996: Denmark

Tennis–Men's Singles
1896: John Boland, Great Britain
1900: Hugh Doherty, Great Britain
1904: Beals Wright, USA
1906: Max Decugis, France
1908: Josiah Ritchie, Great Britain, outdoor; Wentworth
  Gore, Great Britain, indoor
1912: Charles Winslow, South Africa, outdoor, Andre
  Govert, France, indoor
1920: Louis Raymond, South Africa
1924: Vincent Richards, USA
1928-1984:*
1988: Miloslav Mecir, Czechoslovakia
1992: Marc Rosset, Switzerland
1996: Andre Agassi, USA

_____
*Event not held.

Tennis–Men's Doubles
1896: Great Britain/Germany

1900: Great Britain
1904: USA
1906: France
1908: Great Britain, outdoor, Great Britain, indoor
1912: South Africa, outdoor, France, indoor
1920: Great Britain
1924: USA
1928-1984:*
1988: USA, Ken Flach, Robert Seguso
1992: Germany, Boris Becker, Michael Stich
1996: Australia, Todd Woodbridge, Mark Woodforde

_____
*Event not held.

Tennis–Women's Singles
1900: Charlotte Cooper, Great Britain
1904:*
1906: Esmee Simiriotou, Greece
1908: Dorothea Chambers, Great Britain, outdoor, Gwen
  Eastlake-Smith, Great Britain, indoor
1912: Maarguerite Broquedis, France, outdoor, Ethel
  Hannam, Great Britain, indoor
1920: Suzanne Lenglen, France
1924: Helen Wills, USA
1928-1984:*
1988: Steffi Graf, West Germany
1992: Jennifer Capriati, USA
1996: Lindsay Davenport, USA

_____
*Event not held.

Tennis–Women's Doubles
1920: Great Britain
1924: USA
1928-1984:*
1988: USA. Zina Garrison, Pam Shriver
1992: USA. Gigi Fernandez, Mary Joe Fernandez
1996: USA. Mary Joe Fernandez, Gigi Fernandez

_____
*Event not held.

Track and Field–Men's High Jump
1896: Ellery Clark, USA
1900: Irving Baxter, USA
1904: Samuel Jones, USA
1906: Con Leahy, Great Britain/Ireland
1908: Harry Porter, USA
1912: Alma Richards, USA
1920: Richmond Landon, USA
1924: Harold Osborn, USA
1928: Robert King, USA
1932: Duncan McNaughton, Canada
1936: Cornelius Johnson, USA
1948: John Winter, Australia
1952: Walter Davis, USA
1956: Charles Dumas, USA
1960: Robert Shavlakadze, USSR

1964: Valeri Brumel, USSR
1968: Dick Fosbury, USA
1972: Yuri Tarmak, USSR
1976: Jacek Wzsola, Poland
1980: Gerd Wessig, East Germany
1984: Dietmar Moegenburg, West Germany
1988: Guennadi Avdeenko, USSR
1992: Javier Sotomayor Sanabria, Cuba
1996: Charles Austin, USA

Track and Field–Men's Pole Vault

1896: William Hoyt, USA
1900: Irving Baxter, USA
1904: Charles Dvorak, USA
1906: Fernand Gonder, France
1908: Edward Cooke, USA, Alfred Gilbert, USA
1912: Harry Babcock, USA
1920: Frank Foss, USA
1924: Lee Barnes, USA
1928: Sabin Carr, USA
1932: William Miller, USA
1936: Earle Meadows, USA
1948: Guinn Smith, USA
1952: Robert Richards, USA
1956: Robert Richards, USA
1960: Donald Bragg, USA
1964: Fred Hansen, USA
1968: Bob Seagren, USA
1972: Wolfgang Nordwig, East Germany
1976: Tadeusz Slusarski, Poland
1980: Wladyslaw Kazakiewicz, Poland
1984: Pierre Quinon, France
1988: Sergei Bubka, USSR
1992: Maxim Tarassov, Russia
1996: Jean Galfione, France

Track and Field–Men's Long Jump

1896: Ellery Clark, USA
1900: Alvin Kraenzlein, USA
1904: Meyer Prinstein, USA
1906: Meyer Prinstein, USA
1908: Francis Irons, USA
1912: Albert Gutterson, USA
1920: William Petersson, Sweden
1924: William DeHart Hubbard, USA
1928: Edward Hamm, USA
1932: Edward Gordon, USA
1936: Jesse Owens, USA
1948: Willie Steele, USA
1952: Jerome Biffle, USA
1956: Greg Bell, USA
1960: Ralph Boston, USA
1964: Lynn Davies, Great Britain
1968: Bob Beamon, USA
1972: Randy Williams, USA
1976: Arnie Robinson, USA

1980: Lutz Dombrowski, East Germany
1984: Carl Lewis, USA
1988: Carl Lewis, USA
1992: Carl Lewis, USA
1996: Carl Lewis, USA

Track and Field–Men's Triple Jump

1896: James Connolly, USA
1900: Meyer Prinstein, USA
1904: Meyer Prinstein, USA
1906: Peter O'Connor, Great Britain/Ireland
1908: Timothy Ahearne, Great Britain/Ireland
1912: Gustaf Lindblom, Sweden
1920: Vilho Tuulos, Finland
1924: Anthony Winter, Australia
1928: Mikio Oda, Japan
1932: Chuhei Nambu, Japan
1936: Naoto Tajima, Japan
1948: Arne Ahman, Sweden
1952: Adhemar Ferreira da Silva, Brazil
1956: Adhemar Ferreira da Silva, Brazil
1960: Jozef Schmidt, Poland
1964: Jozef Schmidt, Poland
1968: Viktor Saneyev, USSR
1972: Viktor Saneyev, USSR
1976: Viktor Saneyev, USSR
1980: Jaak Uudmae, USSR
1984: Al Joyner, USA
1988: Hristo Markov, Bulgaria
1992: Mike Conley, USA
1996: Kenny Harrison, USA

Track and Field–Women's High Jump

1928: Ethel Catherwood, Canada
1932: Jean Shiley, USA
1936: Ibolya Csak, Hungary
1948: Alice Coachman, USA
1952: Esther Brand, South Africa
1956: Mildred McDaniel, USA
1960: Iolanda Balas, Romania
1964: Iolanda Balos, Romania
1968: Miloslava Rezkova, Czechoslovakia
1972: Ulrike Meyfarth, West Germany
1976: Rosemarie Ackermann, East Germany
1980: Sara Simeoni, Italy
1984: Ulrike Mayfarth, West Germany
1988: Louise Ritter, USA
1992: Heike Henkel, Germany
1996: Stefka Kostadinova, Bulgaria

Track and Field–Women's Long Jump

1948: Olga Gyarmati, Hungary
1952: Yvette Williams, New Zealand
1956: Elzbieta Krzesinska, Poland
1960: Vyera Krepkina, USSR
1964: Mary Rand, Great Britain
1968: Viorica Viscopoleanu, Romania

1972: Heidemarie Rosendahl, West Germany
1976: Angela Voigt, East Germany
1980: Tatiana Kolpakova, USSR
1984: Anisoara Cusmir-Stanciu, Romania
1988: Jackie Joyner-Kersee, USA
1992: Heike Dreschsler, Germany
1996: Chioma Ajunwa, Nigeria

Track and Field–Women's Triple Jump
1996: Inessa Kravets, Ukraine

Track and Field–Men's 100 Meters
1896: Thomas Burke, USA
1900: Francis Jarvis, USA
1904: Archie Hahn, USA`
1906: Archie Hahn, USA
1908: Reginald Walker, South Africa
1912: Ralph Craig, USA
1920: Charles Paddock, USA
1924: Harold Abrahams, Great Britain
1928: Percy Williams, Canada
1932: Eddie Tolan, USA
1936: Jesse Owens, USA
1948: Harrison Dillard, USA
1952: Lindy Remigino, USA
1956: Robert Morrow, USA
1960: Armin Hary, West Germany
1964: Robert Hayes, USA
1968: Jim Hines, USA
1972: Valery Borsov, USSR
1976: Hasely Crawford, Trinidad and Tobago
1980: Allan Wells, Great Britain
1984: Carl Lewis, USA
1988: Carl Lewis, USA
1992: Linford Christie, Britain
1996: Donovan Bailey, Canada

Track and Field–Men's 200 Meters
1900: John Walter Tewksbury, USA
1904: Archie Hahn, USA
1906:*
1908: Robert Kerr, Canada
1912: Ralph Craig, USA
1920: Allen Woodring, USA
1924: Jackson Scholz, USA
1928: Percy Williams, Canada
1932: Eddie Tolan, USA
1936: Jesse Owens, USA
1948: Mel Patton, USA
1952: Andrew Stanfield, USA
1956: Robert Morrow, USA
1960: Livio Berruti, Italy
1964: Henry Carr, USA
1968: Tommie Smith, USA
1972: Valery Borsov, USSR
1976: Donald Quarrie, Jamaica

1980: Pietro Mennea, Italy
1984: Carl Lewis, USA
1988: Joe DeLoach, USA
1992: Mike Marsh, USA
1996: Michael Johnson, USA

Track and Field–Men's 400 Meters
1896: Thomas Burke, USA
1900: Maxwell Long, USA
1904: Harry Hillman, USA
1906: Paul Pilgrim, USA
1908: Wyndham Halswelle, Great Britain
1912: Charles Reidpath, USA
1920: Bevil Rudd, South Africa
1924: Eric Liddell, Great Britain
1928: Raymond Barbuti, USA
1932: William Carr, USA
1936: Archie Williams, USA
1948: Arthur Wint, Jamaica
1952: George Rhoden, Jamaica
1956: Charles Jenkins, USA
1960: Otis Davis, USA
1964: Michael Larrabee, USA
1968: Lee Evans, USA
1972: Vincent Matthews, USA
1976: Alberto Juantorena, Cuba
1980: Viktor Markin, USSR
1984: Alonzo Babers, USA
1988: Steven Lewis, USA
1992: Quincy Watts, USA
1996: Michael Johnson, USA

Track and Field–Men's 800 Meters
1896: Edwin Flack, Australia
1900: Alfred Tysoe, Great Britain
1904: James Lightbody, USA
1906: Paul Pilgrim, USA
1908: Melvin Sheppard, USA
1912: James Meredith, USA
1920: Albert Hill, Great Britain
1924: Douglas Lowe, Great Britain
1928: Douglas Lowe, Great Britain
1932: Thomas Hampson, Great Britain
1936: John Woodruff, USA
1948: Malvin Whitfield, USA
1952: Malvin Whitfield, USA
1956: Tom Courtney, USA
1960: Peter Snell, New Zealand
1964: Peter Snell, New Zealand
1968: Ralph Doubell, Australia
1972: David Wottle, USA
1976: Alberto Juantorena, Cuba
1980: Steven Ovett, Great Britain
1984: Joaquim Cruz, Brazil
1988: Paul Ereng, Kenya
1992: William Tanui, Kenya
1996: Vebjoern Rodal, Norway

*Event not held.

Track and Field–Men's 1,500 Meters

1896: Edwin Flack, Australia
1900: Charles Bennett, Great Britain
1904: James Lightbody, USA
1906: James Lightbody, USA
1908: Melvin Sheppard, USA
1912: Arnold Jackson, Great Britain
1920: Albert Hill, Great Britain
1924: Poavo Nurmi, Finland
1928: Harri Larva, Finland
1932: Luigi Beccali, Italy
1936: John Lovelock, New Zealand
1948: Henry Eriksson, Sweden
1952: Josef Barthel, Luxembourg
1956: Ron Delany, Ireland
1960: Herbert Elliott, Australia
1964: Peter Snell, New Zealand
1968: Kipchoge Keino, Kenya
1972: Kipchoge Keino, Kenya
1976: John Walker, New Zealand
1980: Sebastian Coe, Great Britain
1984: Sebastian Coe, Great Britain
1988: Peter Rono, Kenya
1992: Fermin Cacho Ruiz, Spain
1996: Noureddine Morceli, Algeria

Track and Field–Men's 5,000 Meters

1912: Johannes Kolehmainen, Finland
1920: Joseph Guillemot, France
1924: Paavo Nurmi, Finland
1928: Ville Ritola, Finland
1932: Lauri Lehtinen, Finland
1936: Gunnar Hockert, Finland
1948: Gaston Reiff, Belgium
1952: Emil Zatopek, Czechoslovakia
1956: Vladimir Kuts, USSR
1960: Murray Halberg, New Zealand
1964: Robert Schul, USA
1968: Mohamed Gammoudi, Tunisia
1972: Lasse Viren, Finland
1976: Lasse Viren, Finland
1980: Miruts Yifter, Ethiopia
1984: Said Aouita, Morocco
1988: John Ngugi, Kenya
1992: Dieter Baumann, Germany
1996: Venuste Niyongabo, Burundi

Track and Field–Men's 10,000 Meters

1912: Johannes Kolehmainen, Finland
1920: Paavo Nurmi, Finland
1924: Ville Ritola, Finland
1928: Paavo Nurmi, Finland
1932: Janusz Kusocinski, Poland
1936: Ilmari Salminen, Finland
1948: Emil Zatopek, Czechoslovakia
1952: Emil Zatopek, Czechoslovakia
1956: Vladmir Kuts, USSR
1960: Pyotr Bolotnikov, USSR

1964: William Mills, USA
1968: Naftali Temu, Kenya
1972: Lasse Viren, Finland
1976: Lasse Viren, Finland
1980: Miruts Yifter, Ethiopia
1984: Alberto Cova, Italy
1988: Brahim Boutaib, Morocco
1992: Khalid Skah, Morocco
1996: Haile Gebrselassie, Ethiopia

Track and Field–Men's Marathon

1896: Spyridon Louis, Greece
1900: Michel Theato, France
1904: Thomas Hicks, USA
1906: W. John Sherring, Canada
1908: John Hayes, USA
1912: Kenneth McArthur, South Africa
1920: Johannes Kolehmainen, Finland
1924: Albin Stenroos, Finland
1928: Boughera El Ouafi, France
1932: Juan Zabala, Argentina
1936: Kitei Son, Japan/South Korea
1948: Delfo Cabrera, Argentina
1952: Emil Zatopek, Czechoslovakia
1956: Alain Mimoun O'Kacha, France
1960: Abebe Bikila, Ethiopia
1964: Abebe Bikila, Ethiopia
1968: Mamo Wolde, Ethiopia
1972: Frank Shorter, USA
1976: Waldemar Cierpinski, East Germany
1980: Waldemar Cierpinski, East Germany
1984: Carlos Lopez, Portugal
1988: Gelindo Bordin, Italy
1992: Hwang Young-Cho, South Korea
1996: Josia Thugwane, South Africa

Track and Field–Men's 110-Meter Hurdles

1896: Thomas Curtis, USA
1900: Alvin Kraenzlein, USA
1904: Frederick Schule, USA
1906: Robert Leavitt, USA
1908: Forest Smithson, USA
1912: Frederick Kelly, USA
1920: Earl Thomson, Canada
1924: Daniel Kinsey, USA
1928: Sydney Atkinson, South Africa
1932: George Saling, USA
1936: Forrest Towns, USA
1948: William Porter, USA
1952: Harrison Dillard, USA
1956: Lee Calhoun, USA
1960: Lee Calhoun, USA
1964: Hayes Jones, USA
1968: Willie Davenport, USA
1972: Rod Milburn, USA
1976: Guy Drut, France
1980: Thomas Munkelt, East Germany
1984: Roger Kingdom, USA

1988: Roger Kingdom, USA
1992: Mark McKoy, Canada
1996: Allen Johnson, USA

Track and Field–Men's 400-Meter Hurdles
1900: John Walter Tewksbury, USA
1904: Harry Hillman, USA
1906:*
1908: Charles Bacon, USA
1912:*
1920: Frank Loomis, USA
1924: F. Morgan Taylor, USA
1928: David Burghley, Great Britain
1932: Robert Tisdall, Ireland
1936: Glenn Hardin, USA
1948: Roy Cochran, USA
1952: Charles Moore, USA
1956: Glenn Davis, USA
1960: Glenn Davis, USA
1964: Warren Cawley, USA
1968: David Hemery, Great Britain
1972: John Akii-Bua, Uganda
1976: Edwin Moses, USA
1980: Volker Beck, East Germany
1984: Edwin Moses, USA
1988: Andre Phillips, USA
1992: Kevin Young, USA
1996: Derrick Adkins, USA

*Event not held.

Track and Field–3,000 Meter Steeplechase
1900: George Orton, Canada
1904: James Lightbody, USA
1906:*
1908: Arthur Russell, Great Britain
1912:*
1920: Percy Hodge, Great Britain
1924: Ville Ritola, Finland
1928: Toivo Loukola, Finland
1932: Volmari Iso-Hollo, Finland
1936: Volmari Iso-Hollo, Finland
1948: Thore Sjostrand, Sweden
1952: Horace Ashenfelter, USA
1956: Christopher Brasher, Great Britain
1960: Zdzislaw Krzyszkowiak, Poland
1964: Gaston Roelants, Belgium
1968: Amos Biwott, Kenya
1972: Kipchoge Keino, Kenya
1976: Anders Garderud, Sweden
1980: Bronislav Malinovski, Poland
1984: Julius Korir, Kenya
1988: Julius Kariuki, Kenya
1992: Matthew Birir, Kenya
1996: Joseph Keter, Kenya

*Event not held.

Track and Field–Men's 4 × 100-Meter Relay
1912: Great Britain
1920: USA
1924: USA
1928: USA
1932: USA
1936: USA
1948: USA
1952: USA
1956: USA
1960: East Germany
1964: USA
1968: USA
1972: USA
1976: USA
1980: USSR
1984: USA
1988: USSR
1992: USA
1996: Canada

Track and Field–Men's 4 × 400-Meter Relay
1908: USA
1912: USA
1920: Great Britain
1924: USA
1928: USA
1932: USA
1936: Great Britain
1948: USA
1952: Jamaica
1956: USA
1960: USA
1964: USA
1968: USA
1972: Kenya
1976: USA
1980: USSR
1984: USA
1988: USA
1992: USA
1996: USA

Track and Field–Men's 20-Kilometer Walk
1956: Leonid Spirin, USSR
1960: Vladimir Golubnichi, USSR
1964: Kenneth Matthews, Great Britain
1968: Vladimir Golubnichi, USSR
1972: Peter Frenkel, East Germany
1976: Daniel Bautista, Mexico
1980: Maurizio Damilano, Italy
1984: Ernesto Canto, Mexico
1988: Jozef Pribilinec, Czechoslovakia
1992: Daniel Plaza Montero, Spain
1996: Jefferson Perez, Ecuador

Track and Field–Men's 50-Kilometer Walk

1932: Thomas Green, Great Britain
1936: H. Harold Whitlock, Great Britain
1948: John Ljunggren, Sweden
1952: Giuseppe Dordoni, Italy
1956: Norman Read, New Zealand
1960: Donald Thompson, Great Britain
1964: Abdon Pamich, Italy
1968: Christoph Hohne, East Germany
1972: Bernd Kannenberg, West Germany
1976:*
1980: Hartwig Gauder, East Germany
1984: Raul Gonzalez, Mexico
1988: Viacheslav Ivanenka, USSR
1992: Andrey Perlov, Russia
1996: Robert Korzeniowski, Poland

_____
*Event not held.

Track and Field–Women's 100 Meters

1928: Elizabeth Robinson, USA
1932: Stanislawa Walasiewicz, Poland
1936: Helen Stephens, USA
1948: Francina Blankers-Koen, Netherlands
1952: Marjorie Jackson, Australia
1956: Betty Cuthbert, Australia
1960: Wilma Rudolph, USA
1964: Wyomia Tyus, USA
1968: Wyomia Tyus, USA
1972: Renate Stecher, East Germany
1976: Annegret Richter, West Germany
1980: Lyudmila Kondratyeva, USSR
1984: Evelyn Ashford, USA
1988: Florence Griffith Joyner, USA
1992: Gail Devers, USA
1996: Gail Devers, USA

Track and Field–Women's 200 Meters

1948: Francina Blankers-Koen, Netherlands
1952: Marjorie Jackson, Australia
1956: Betty Cuthbert, Australia
1960: Wilma Rudolph, USA
1964: Edith McGuire, USA
1968: Irena Szewinska-Kirszenstein, Poland
1972: Renate Stecher, East Germany
1976: Barbel Eckert, East Germany
1980: Barbel Eckert Wockel, East Germany
1984: Valerie Brisco-Hooks, USA
1988: Florence Griffith Joyner, USA
1992: Gwen Torrence, USA
1996: Marie-José Pérec, France

Track and Field–Women's 400 Meters

1964: Betty Cuthbert, Australia
1968: Colette Besson, France
1972: Monika Zehrt, East Germany
1976: Irena Szewinska-Kirszenstein, Poland
1980: Marita Koch, East Germany
1984: Valerie Brisco-Hooks, USA
1988: Olga Bryzguina, USSR
1992: Marie-José Pérec, France
1996: Marie-José Pérec, France

Track and Field–Women's 800 Meters

1928: Lina Radke, Germany
1932–1956:*
1960: Lyudmila Shevtsova, USSR
1964: Ann Packer, Great Britain
1968: Madeline Manning, USA
1972: Hildegard Falck, West Germany
1976: Tatyana Kazankina, USSR
1980: Nadezhda Olizarenko, USSR
1984: Doina Melinte, Romania
1988: Sigrun Wodars, East Germany
1992: Ellen Van Langen, Netherlands
1996 Svetlana Masterkova, Russia

_____
*Event not held.

Track and Field–Women's 1,500 Meters

1972: Ljudmila Bragina, USSR
1976: Tatyana Kazankina, USSR
1980: Tatyana Kazankina, USSR
1984: Gabriella Dorio, Italy
1988: Paula Ivan, Romania
1992: Hassiba Boulmerka, Algeria
1996: Svetlana Masterkova, Russia

Track and Field–Women's 3,000 Meters

1984: Maricica Puica, Romania
1988: Tatiana Samolenko, USSR
1992: Elena Romanova, Russia
1996:*

_____
*Event not held.

Track and Field–Women's 5,000 Meters

1996: Wang Junxia, China

Track and Field–Women's 10,000 Meters

1988: Olga Bondarenko, USSR
1992: Derartu Tulu, Ethiopia
1996: Fernanda Ribeiro, Portugal

Track and Field–Women's Marathon

1984: Joan Benoit, USA
1988: Rosa Mota, Portugal
1992: Valentina Yegorova, Russia
1996: Fatuma Roba, Ethiopia

Track and Field–Women's 100-Meter Hurdles†

1932: Mildred "Babe" Didrikson, USA
1936: Trebisonda Valla, Italy

_____
†80-meter hurdles, 1932–1968.

1948: Francina Blankers-Koen, Netherlands
1952: Shirley De La Hunty-Strickland, Australia
1956: Shirley De La Hunty-Strickland, Australia
1960: Irina Press, USSR
1964: Karin Balzer, East Germany
1968: Maureen Caird, Australia
1972: Annelie Ehrhardt, East Germany
1976: Johanna Schaller, East Germany
1980: Vera Komisova, USSR
1984: Benita Fitzgerald-Brown, USA
1988: Jordanka Donkova, Bulgaria
1992: Paraskevi Patoulidou, Greece
1996: Ludmila Engquist, Sweden

Track and Field–Women's 400-Meter Hurdles
1984: Nawal El Moutawakel, Morocco
1988: Debra Flintoff-King, Australia
1992: Sally Gunnell, Britain
1996: Deon Hemmings, Jamaica

Track and Field–Women's 4 × 100-Meter Relay
1928: Canada
1932: USA
1936: USA
1948: Netherlands
1952: USA
1956: Australia
1960: USA
1964: Poland
1968: USA
1972: West Germany
1976: East Germany
1980: East Germany
1984: USA
1988: USA
1992: USA
1996: USA

Track and Field–Women's 4 × 400-Meter Relay
1972: East Germany
1976: East Germany
1980: USSR
1984: USA
1988: USSR
1992: Unified Team
1996: USA

Track and Field–Women's 10-Kilometer Walk
1992: Chen Yueling, China
1996: Yelena Nikolayeva, Russia

Track and Field–Men's Shot Put
1896: Robert Garrett, USA
1900: Richard Sheldon, USA
1904: Ralph Rose, USA
1906: Martin Sheridan, USA
1908: Ralph Rose, USA
1912: Patrick McDonald, USA

1920: Ville Porhola, Finland
1924: Clarence Houser, USA
1928: John Kuck, USA
1932: Leo Sexton, USA
1936: Hans Woellke, Germany
1948: Wilbur Thompson, USA
1952: Parry O'Brien, USA
1956: Parry O'Brien, USA
1960: William Nieder, USA
1964: Dallas Long, USA
1968: Randy Matson, USA
1972: Wladyslaw Komar, Poland
1976: Udo Beyer, East Germany
1980: Vladimir Kiselyov, USSR
1984: Alessandro Andrei, Italy
1988: Ulf Timmerman, East Germany
1992: Michael Stulce, USA
1996: Randy Barnes, USA

Track and Field–Men's Discus Throw
1896: Robert Garrett, USA
1900: Rudolf Bauer, Hungary
1904: Martin Sheridan, USA
1906: Martin Sheridan, USA
1908: Martin Sheridan, USA
1912: Armas Taipale, Finland
1920: Elmer Niklander, Finland
1924: Clarence Houser, USA
1928: Clarence Houser, USA
1932: John Anderson, USA
1936: Kenneth Carpenter, USA
1948: Adolfo Consolini, Italy
1952: Sim Iness, USA
1956: Al Oerter, USA
1960: Al Oerter, USA
1964: Al Oerter, USA
1968: Al Oerter, USA
1972: Ludvik Danek, Czechoslovakia
1976: Mac Wilkins, USA
1980: Viktor Rashchupkin, USSR
1984: Rolf Danneberg, West Germany
1988: Jurgen Schult, East Germany
1992: Robert Ubartas, Lithuania
1996: Lars Riedel, Germany

Track and Field–Men's Hammer Throw
1900: John Flanagan, USA
1904: John Flanagan, USA
1906:*
1908: John Flanagan, USA
1912: Matthew McGrath, USA
1920: Patrick Ryan, USA
1924: Frederick Tootell, USA
1928: Patrick O'Callaghan, Ireland
1932: Patrick O'Callaghan, Ireland

---

*Event not held.

1936: Karl Hein, Germany
1948: Imre Nemeth, Hungary
1952: Jozsef Csermak, Hungary
1956: Harold Connolly, USA
1960: Vasily Rudenkov, USSR
1964: Romuald Klim, USSR
1968: Gyula Zsivotzky, Hungary
1972: Anatoli Bondarchuk, USSR
1976: Yuriy Sedykh, USSR
1980: Yuriy Sedykh, USSR
1984: Juha Tiainen, Finland
1988: Serguei Litvinov, USSR
1992: Andrey Abduvaliyev, Tadzhikstan
1996: Balazs Kiss, Hungary

Track and Field–Men's Javelin Throw
1906: Eric Lemming, Sweden
1908: Eric Lemming, Sweden
1912: Eric Lemming, Sweden
1920: Jonni Myyra, Finland
1924: Jonni Myyra, Finland
1928: Erik Lundkvist, Sweden
1932: Matti Jarvinen, Finland
1936: Gerhard Stock, Great Britain
1948: Tapio Rautavaara, Finland
1952: Cyrus Young, USA
1956: Egil Danielsen, Norway
1960: Viktor Tsibulenko, USSR
1964: Pauli Nevala, Finland
1968: Janis Lusis, USSR
1972: Klaus Wolfermann, West Germany
1976: Miklos Nemeth, Hungary
1980: Dainis Kula, USSR
1984: Arto Harkonen, Finland
1988: Tapio Korjus, Finland
1992: Jan Zelezny, Czechoslovakia
1996: Jan Zelezny, Czech Republic

Track and Field–Men's Decathlon
1904: Thomas Kiely, Great Britain/Ireland
1906–1908:*
1912: James Thorpe, USA (previously disqualified, Jim Thorpe's medals were restored in 1982)
1920: Helge Lovland, Norway
1924: Harold Osborn, USA
1928: Paavo Yrjola, Finland
1932: James Bausch, USA
1936: Glenn Morris, USA
1948: Robert B. Mathias, USA
1952: Robert B. Mathias, USA
1956: Milton Campbell, USA
1960: Rafer Johnson, USA
1964: Willi Holdorf, West Germany
1968: Bill Toomey, USA
1972: Nikolai Avilov, USSR
1976: Bruce Jenner, USA

*Event not held

1980: Daley Thompson, Great Britain
1984: Daley Thompson, Great Britain
1988: Christian Schenk, East Germany
1992: Robert Zmelik, Czechoslovakia
1996: Dan O'Brien, USA

Track and Field–Women's Shot Put
1948: Micheline Ostermeyer, France
1952: Galina Zybina, USSR
1956: Tamara Tyshkevich, USSR
1960: Tamara Press, USSR
1964: Tamara Press, USSR
1968: Margitta Gummel-Helmbolt, East Germany
1972: Nadezhda Chizhova, USSR
1976: Ivanka Hristova, Bulgaria
1980: Ilona Slupianek, East Germany
1984: Claudia Losch, West Germany
1988: Natalia Lisovskaya, USSR
1992: Svetlana Kriveleva, Russia
1996: Astrid Kumbernuss, Germany

Track and Field–Women's Discus
1928: Halina Konopacka, Poland
1932: Lillian Copeland, USSR
1936: Gisela Mauermeyer, Germany
1948: Micheline Ostermeyer, France
1952: Nina Romaschkova, USSR
1956: Olga Fikotova, Czechoslovakia
1960: Nina Ponomaryeva-Romaschkova, USSR
1964: Tamara Press, USSR
1968: Lia Manoliu, Romania
1972: Faina Melnik, USSR
1976: Evelin Schlaak, East Germany
1980: Evelin Jahl-Schlaak, East Germany
1984: Ria Stalman, Netherlands
1988: Martina Hellmann, East Germany
1992: Maritza Marten Garcia, Cuba
1996: Ilke Wyludda, Germany

Track and Field–Women's Javelin
1932: Mildred "Babe" Didrikson, USA
1936: Tilly Fleischer, Germany
1948: Herma Bauma, Austria
1952: Dana Zatopkova, Czechoslovakia
1956: Inese Jaunzeme, USSR
1960: Elvira Ozolina, USSR
1964: Mihaela Penes, Romania
1968: Angela Nemeth, Hungary
1972: Ruth Fuchs, East Germany
1976: Ruth Fuchs, East Germany
1980: Maria Colon, Cuba
1984: Tessa Sanderson, Great Britain
1988: Petra Felke, East Germany
1992: Silke Renk, Germany
1996: Helia Rantanen, Finland

Track and Field–Women's Pentathlon
1964: Irina Press, USSR
1968: Ingrid Becker, West Germany

1972: Mary Peters, Great Britain
1976: Siegrun Siegl, East Germany
1980: Nadezhda Tkachenko, USSR
1984–1996:*

---

*Event not held

Track and Field–Women's Heptathlon
1984: Glynis Nunn, Australia
1988: Jackie Joyner-Kersee, USA
1992: Jackie Joyner-Kersee, USA
1996: Ghada Shouaa, Syria

Water Polo
1900: Great Britain
1904: USA
1906:*
1908: Great Britain
1912: Great Britain
1920: Great Britain
1924: France
1928: Germany
1932: Hungary
1936: Hungary
1948: Italy
1952: Hungary
1956: Hungary
1960: Italy
1964: Hungary
1968: Yugoslavia
1972: USSR
1976: Hungary
1980: USSR
1984: Yugoslavia
1988: Yugoslavia
1992: Italy
1996: Spain

---

*Event not held.

Weightlifting–52 kg
1972: Zygmunt Smalcerz, Poland
1976: Alexander Voronin, USSR
1980: Kanybek Osmonaliev, USSR
1984: Guoqiang Zeng, China
1988: Sevdalin Marinov, Bulgaria
1992: Ivan Ivanov, Bulgaria
1996: Halil Mutlu, Turkey (54 kg)

Weighlifting–56 kg
1948: Joseph De Pietro, USA
1952: Ivan Udodov, USSR
1956: Charles Vinci, USA
1960: Charles Vinci, USA
1964: Aleksei Vakhonin, USSR
1968: Mohammad Nassiri, Iran
1972: Imre Foldi, Hungary
1976: Norair Nourikian, Bulgaria
1980: Daniel Nunez, Cuba

1984: Shude Wu, China
1988: Oxen Mirzoian, USSR
1992: Chun Byung-Kwan, South Korea
1996: Tang Ningsheng, China (59 kg)

Weightlifting–60 kg
1920: Frans De Haes, Belgium
1924: Pierino Gabetti, Italy
1928: Franz Andrysek, Austria
1932: Raymond Suvigny, France
1936: Anthony Terlazzo, USA
1948: Mahmoud Fayad, Egypt
1952: Rafael Chimishkyan, USSR
1956: Isaac Berger, USA
1960: Yevgeny Minayev, USSR
1964: Yoshinobu Miyake, Japan
1968: Yoshinobu Miyake, Japan
1972: Norair Nurikjan, Bulgaria
1976: Nikolai Kolesnikov, USSR
1980: Viktor Mazin, USSR
1984: Weiqiang Chen, China
1988: Naim Suleymanoglu, Turkey
1992: Naim Suleymanoglu, Turkey
1996: Naim Suleymanoglu, Turkey (64 kg)

Weightlifting–67.5 kg
1920: Alfred Neuland, Estonia
1924: Edmond Decottignies, France
1928: Hans Haas, Austria
1932: Rene Duverger, France
1936: Robert Fein, Austria
1948: Ibrahim H. Shams, Egypt
1952: Tamio "Tommy" Kono, USA
1956: Igor Rybak, USSR
1960: Viktor Buschuyev, USSR
1964: Waldemar Baszanowski, Poland
1968: Waldemar Baszanowski, Poland
1972: Muckarbi Kirzhinov, USSR
1976: Zbigniew Kaczmarek, Poland
1980: Yanko Rusev, Bulgaria
1984: Yao Jingyuan, China
1988: Joachim Kunz, East Germany
1992: Israel Militossian, Armenia
1996: Xugang Zhan, China (70 kg)

Weightlifting–75 kg
1920: Henri Gance, France
1924: Carlo Galimberti, Italy
1928: Roger Francois, France
1932: Rudolf Ismayr, Germany
1936: Khadr Sayed El Touni, Egypt
1948: Frank Spellman, USA
1952: Peter George, USA
1956: Fyodor Bogdanovsky, USSR
1960: Aleksandr Kurynov, USSR
1964: Hans Zdazila, Czechoslovakia
1968: Viktor Kurentsov, USSR
1972: Yordan Bikow, Bulgaria

1976: Yordan Mitkov, Bulgaria
1980: Assen Zlatev, Bulgaria
1984: Karl-Heinz Radschinsky, West Germany
1988: Borislav Guidikov, Bulgaria
1992: Fedor Kassapu, Moldavia
1996: Pablo Lara, Cuba (76 kg)

Weightlifting–82.5 kg

1920: Ernest Cadine, France
1924: Charles Rigoulot, France
1928: El Sayed Nosseir, Egypt
1932: Louis Hostin, France
1936: Louis Hostin, France
1948: Stanley Stanczyk, USA
1952: Trofim Lomakin, USSR
1956: Tamio "Tommy" Kono, USA
1960: Ireneusz Palinski, Poland
1964: Rudolf Plukfelder, USSR
1968: Boris Selitsky, USSR
1972: Leif Jenssen, Norway
1976: Valeri Shary, USSR
1980: Yurik Vardanjan, USSR
1984: Petre Becheru, Romania
1988: Israil Arsamakov, USSR
1992: Pyrros Dimas, Greece
1996: Pyrros Dimas, Greece (83 kg)

Weightlifting–90 kg

1952: Norbert Schemansky, USA
1956: Arkadi Vorobyov, USSR
1960: Arkadi Vorobyov, USSR
1964: Vladimir Golovanov, USSR
1968: Kaarlo Kangasniemi, Finland
1972: Andon Nikolov, Bulgaria
1976: David Rigert, USSR
1980: Peter Baczaka, Hungary
1984: Nicu Vlad, Romania
1988: Anatoli Khrapatyi, USSR
1992: Kakhi Kakhiachvili, Russia
1996: Aleksey Petrov, Russia (91 kg)

Weightlifting–100 kg

1980: Ota Zaremba, Czechoslovakia
1984: Rolf Milser, West Germany
1988: Pavel Kouznetsov, USSR
1992: Victor Tregoubov, Russia
1996: Akakide Kakhiashvilis, Greece (99 kg)

Weightlifting–110 kg

1896: Launceston Elliott, Great Britain (one-hand lift),
   Viggo Jensen, Denmark (two-hand lift)
1900:*
1904: Oscar Paul Osthoff, USA (one-hand lift), Perikles
   Kakousis, Greece (two-hand lift)
1906: Josef Steinbach, Austria (one-hand lift), Dimitrios
   Tofalos, Great Britain (two-hand lift)
1908–1912:*

*Event not held.

1920: Filippo Bottino, Italy
1924: Giuseppe Tonani, Italy
1928: Josef Strassberger, Germany
1932: Jaroslav Skobla, Czechoslovakia
1936: Josef Manger, Germany
1948: John Davis, USA
1952: John Davis, USA
1956: Paul Anderson, USA
1960: Yuri Vlassov, USSR
1964: Leonid Zhabotinsky, USSR
1968: Leonid Schabotinski, USSR
1972: Jan Talts, USSR
1976: Valentin Khristov, Bulgaria
1980: Leonid Taranenko, USSR
1984: Norberto Oberburger, Italy
1988: Yuri Zakharevitch, USSR
1992: Ronny Weller, Germany
1996: Timur Taimazov, Ukraine (108 kg)

Weightlifting–Over 110 kg

1972: Vassili Alekseyev, USSR
1976: Vassili Alekseyev, USSR
1980: Sultan Rakhmanov, USSR
1984: Dean "Dinko" Lukin, Australia
1988: Alexandre Kourlovitch, USSR
1992: Alexandre Kourlovitch, Belarus
1996: Andrey Chemerkin, Russia (over 108 kg)

Wrestling, Freestyle–48 kg

1904: Robert Curry, USA
1906–1968:*
1972: Roman Dmitriev, USSR
1976: Hassan Issaev, Bulgaria
1980: Claudio Pollio, Italy
1984: Robert Weaver, USA
1988: Takashi Kobayashi, Japan
1992: Kim Il, North Korea
1996: Kim Il, North Korea

*Event not held.

Wrestling, Freestyle–52 kg

1904: George Mehnert, USA
1906–1936:*
1948: Lennart Viitala, Finland
1952: Hasan Gemici, Turkey
1956: Mirian Tsalkalamanidze, USSR
1960: Ahmet Bilek, Turkey
1964: Yoshikatsu Yoshida, Japan
1968: Shigeo Nakata, Japan
1972: Kiyomi Kato, Japan
1976: Yuji Takada, Japan
1980: Anatoli Beloglazov, USSR
1984: Saban Trstena, Yugoslavia
1988: Mitsuru Sato, Japan
1992: Li Hak-Son, South Korea
1996: Valentin Jordanov, Bulgaria

*Event not held.

Wrestling, Freestyle–57 kg
1904: Isaac Niflot, USA
1906:*
1908: George Mehnert, USA
1912–1920:*
1924: Kustaa Pihlajamaki, Finland
1928: Kaarlo Makinen, Finland
1932: Robert Pearce, USA
1936: Odon Zombori, Hungary
1948: Nasuh Akar, Turkey
1952: Shohachi Ishii, Japan
1956: Mustafa Dagistanli, Turkey
1960: Terrence McCann, USA
1964: Yojiro Uetake, Japan
1968: Yojiro Uetake, Japan
1972: Hideaki Yanagida, Japan
1976: Vladimir Umin, USSR
1980: Sergei Beloglazov, USSR
1984: Hideaki Tomiyama, Japan
1988: Sergei Beloglazov, USSR
1992: Alejandro Puerto, Cuba
1996: Kendall Cross, USA

*Event not held.

Wrestling, Freestyle–62 kg
1904: Benjamin Bradshaw, USA
1906:*
1908: George Dole, USA
1912:*
1920: Charles E. Ackerly, USA
1924: Robin Reed, USA
1928: Allie Morrison, USA
1932: Hermanni Pihlajamaki, Finland
1936: Kustaa Pihlajamaki, Finland
1948: Gazanfer Bilge, Turkey
1952: Bayram Sit, Turkey
1956: Shozo Sasahara, Japan
1960: Mustafa Dagistanli, Turkey
1964: Osamu Watanabe, Japan
1968: Masaaki Kaneko, Japan
1972: Sagalav Abdulbekov, USSR
1976: Yang Mo Yang, South Korea
1980: Magomedgasan Abushev, USSR
1984: Randy Lewis, USA
1988: John Smith, USA
1992: John Smith, USA
1996: Tom Brands, USA

*Event not held.

Wrestling, Freestyle–68 kg
1904: Otto Roehm, USA
1906:*
1908: George de Relwyskow, Great Britain
1912:*

*Event not held.

1920: Kalle Anttila, Finland
1924: Russell Vis, USA
1928: Osvald Kapp, Estonia
1932: Charles Pacome, France
1936: Karoly Karpati, Hungary
1948: Celal Atik, Turkey
1952: Olle Anderberg, Sweden
1956: Emamali Habibi, Iran
1960: Shelby Wilson, USA
1964: Enyu Waltschev, Bulgaria
1968: Abdollah Movahed Ardabili, Iran
1972: Dan Gable, USA
1976: Pavel Pinegin, USSR
1980: Saipulla Absaidov, USSR
1984: In-Tak Youh, South Korea
1988: Arsen Fadzaev, USSR
1992: Arsen Fadzaev, Russia
1996: Vadim Bogiyev, Russia

Wrestling, Freestyle–74 kg
1904: Charles Erickson, USA
1906–1920:*
1924: Hermann Gehri, Switzerland
1928: Arvo Haavisto, Finland
1932: Jack Van Bebber, USA
1936: Frank Lewis, USA
1948: Yasar Dogu, Turkey
1952: William Smith, USA
1956: Mitsuo Ikeda, Japan
1960: Douglas Blubaugh, USA
1964: Ismail Ogan, Turkey
1968: Mahmut Atalay, Turkey
1972: Wayne Wells, USA
1976: Ijichiro Date, Japan
1980: Valentin Raitchev, Bulgaria
1984: David Schultz, USA
1988: Kenneth Monday, USA
1992: Park Jang-Soon, South Korea
1996: Buvaysa Saytyev, Russia

*Event not held.

Wrestling, Freestyle–82 kg
1908: Stanley Bacon, Great Britain
1912:*
1920: Eino Leino, Finland
1924: Firtz Hagmann, Switzerland
1928: Ernst Kyburz, Switzerland
1932: Ivar Johansson, Sweden
1936: Emile Poilve, France
1948: Glen Brand, USA
1952: David Tsimakuridze, USSR
1956: Nikola Stantchev, Bulgaria
1960: Hasan Gungor, Turkey
1964: Prodan Gardschev, Bulgaria

*Event not held.

1968: Boris Gurevitch, USSR
1972: Levan Tediashvili, USSR
1976: John Peterson, USA
1980: Ismail Abilov, Bulgaria
1984: Mark Schultz, USA
1988: Myung-Woo Han, South Korea
1992: Kevin Jackson, USA
1996: Khadzhimurad Magomedov, Russia

Wrestling, Freestyle–90 kg
1920: Anders Larsson, Sweden
1924: John Spellman, USA
1928: Thure Sjostedt, Sweden
1932: Peter Mehringer, USA
1936: Knut Fridell, Sweden
1948: Henry Wittenberg, USA
1952: Wiking Palm, Sweden
1956: Gholam-Reza Takhti, Iran
1960: Ismet Atli, Turkey
1964: Aleksandr Medved, USSR
1968: Ahmet Ayik, Turkey
1972: Ben Peterson, USA
1976: Levan Tediashvili, USSR
1980: Sanasar Oganesyan, USSR
1984: Ed Banach, USA
1988: Makharbek Khadartsev, USSR
1992: Makharbek Khadartsev, Russia
1996: Rasull Khadem Azghadi, Iran

Wrestling, Freestyle–100 kg
1904: B. Hansen, USA
1906:*
1908: George C. O'Kelly, Great Britain/Ireland
1912:*
1920: Robert Roth, Switzerland
1924: Harry Steele, USA
1928: Johan Richtoff, Sweden
1932: Johan Richtoff, Sweden
1936: Kristjan Palusalu, Estonia
1948: Gyula Bobis, Hungary
1952: Arsen Mekokischvili, USSR
1956: Hamit Kaplan, Turkey
1960: Wilfried Dietrich, West Germany
1964: Aleksandr Ivanitsky, USSR
1968: Aleksandr Medved, USSR
1972: Ivan Yarygin, USSR
1976: Ivan Yarygin, USSR
1980: Ilya Mate, USSR
1984: Lou Banach, USA
1988: Vasile Puscasu, Romania
1992: Leri Khabelov, Georgia
1996: Kurt Angle, USA

*Event not held.

Wrestling, Freestyle–130 kg
1972: Aleksandr Medved, USSR
1976: Soslan Andiev, USSR
1980: Soslan Andiev, USSR
1984: Bruce Baumgartner, USA
1988: David Gobedjichvili, USSR
1992: Bruce Baumgartner, USA
1996: Mahmut Demir, Turkey

Wrestling, Greco-Roman–48 kg
1972: Gheorghe Berceanu, Romania
1976: Aleksei Shumakov, USSR
1980: Zaksylik Ushkempirov, USSR
1984: Vincenzo Maenza, Italy
1988: Vincenzo Maenza, Italy
1992: Oleg Koutherenko, Ukraine
1996: Sim Kwon Ho, South Korea

Wrestling, Greco-Roman–52 kg
1948: Pietro Lombardi, Italy
1952: Boris Gurevitch, USSR
1956: Nikolai Solovyov, USSR
1960: Dumitru Pirvulescu, Romania
1964: Tsutomu Hanahara, Japan
1968: Petar Kirov, Bulgaria
1972: Petar Kirov, Bulgaria
1976: Vitali Konstantinov, USSR
1980: Vakhtang Blagidze, USSR
1984: Atsuji Miyahara, Japan
1988: Jon Ronningen, Norway
1992: Jon Ronningen, Norway
1996: Armen Nazaryan, Armenia

Wrestling, Greco-Roman–57 kg
1924: Eduard Putsep, Estonia
1928: Kurt Leucht, Germany
1932: Jakob Brendel, Germany
1936: Marton Lorincz, Hungary
1948: Kurt Pettersen, Sweden
1952: Imre Hodos, Hungary
1956: Konstantin Vyrupayev, USSR
1960: Oleg Karavayev, USSR
1964: Masamitsu Ichiguchi, Japan
1968: Janos Varga, Hungary
1972: Rustem Kazakov, USSR
1976: Pertti Ukkola, Finland
1980: Shamil Serikov, USSR
1984: Pasquale Passarelli, West Germany
1988: Andras Sike, Hungary
1992: An Han-Bong, South Korea
1996: Yuriy Melnichenko, Kazakhstan

Wrestling, Greco-Roman–62 kg
1912: Kaarlo Koskelo, Finland
1920: Oskari Friman, Finland
1924: Kalle Anttila, Finland
1928: Voldemar Vali, Estonia
1932: Giovanni Gozzi, Italy

1936: Yasar Erkan, Turkey
1948: Mehmet Oktav, Turkey
1952: Jakov Punkin, USSR
1956: Rauno Makinen, Finland
1960: Muzahir Sille, Turkey
1964: Imre Polyak, Hungary
1968: Roman Rurua, USSR
1972: Georgi Markow, Bulgaria
1976: Kazimierz Lipien, Poland
1980: Stilianos Migiakis, Greece
1984: Weon-Kee Kim, South Korea
1988: Kamander Madjidov, USSR
1992: M. Akif Pirim, Turkey
1996: Wlodzimierz Zawadski, Poland

Wrestling, Greco-Roman–68 kg
1906: Rudolf Watzl, Austria
1908: Enrico Porro, Italy
1912: Eemil Vare, Finland
1920: Eemil Vare, Finland
1924: Oskari Friman, Finland
1928: Lajos Keresztes, Hungary
1932: Erik Malmberg, Sweden
1936: Lauri Koskela, Finland
1948: Gustav Freij, Sweden
1952: Schasam Safin, USSR
1956: Kyosti Lehtonen, Finland
1960: Avtandil Koridze, USSR
1964: Kazim Ayvaz, Turkey
1968: Munji Mumemura, Japan
1972: Schamil Khisamutdinov, USSR
1976: Suren Nalbandyan, USSR
1980: Stefan Rusu, Romania
1984: Vlado Lisjak, Yugoslavia
1988: Levon Djoulfalakian, USSR
1992: Attila Repka, Hungary
1996: Ryszard Wolny, Poland

Wrestling, Greco-Roman–74 kg
1932: Ivar Johansson, Sweden
1936: Rudolf Svedberg, Sweden
1948: Gosta Andersson, Sweden
1952: Mikos Szilvasi, Hungary
1956: Mithat Bayrak, Turkey
1960: Mithat Bayrak, Turkey
1964: Anatoli Kolesov, USSR
1968: Rudolf Vesper, East Germany
1972: Vitezslav Macha, Czechoslovakia
1976: Anatoli Bykov, USSR
1980: Ferenc Kocsis, Hungary
1984: Jouko Salomaki, Finland
1988: Young-Nam Kim, South Korea
1992: Mnatsakan Iskandarian, Armenia
1996: Feliberto Ascuy Aguilera, Cuba

Wrestling, Greco-Roman–82 kg
1906: Verner Weckman, Finland
1908: Frithiof Martensson, Sweden

1912: Claes Johanson, Sweden
1920: Carl Westergren, Sweden
1924: Edvard Westerlund, Finland
1928: Vaino Kokkinen, Finland
1932: Vaino Kokkinen, Finland
1936: Ivar Johansson, Sweden
1948: Axel Gronberg, Sweden
1952: Axel Gronberg, Sweden
1956: Givi Kartoziya, USSR
1960: Dimiter Dobrev, Bulgaria
1964: Branislav Simic, Yugoslavia
1968: Lothar Metz, East Germany
1972: Csaba Hegedus, Hungary
1976: Momir Petkovic, Yugoslavia
1980: Gennady Korban, USSR
1984: Ion Draica, Romania
1988: Mikhail Mamiachvili, USSR
1992: Peter Earkas, Hungary
1996: Humza Yerlikaya, Turkey

Wrestling, Greco-Roman–90 kg
1908: Verner Weckman, Finland
1912: no gold medalist
1920: Claes Johanson, Sweden
1924: Carl Westergren, Sweden
1928: Ibrahim Moustafa, Egypt
1932: Rudolf Svensson, Sweden
1936: Axel Cadier, Sweden
1948: Karl-Erik Nilsson, Sweden
1952: Kaelpo Grondahl, Finland
1956: Valentin Nikolayev, USSR
1960: Tevfik Kis, Turkey
1964: Bojan Radev, Bulgaria
1968: Bojan Radev, Bulgaria
1972: Valeri Rezantsev, USSR
1976: Valeri Rezantsev, USSR
1980: Norbert Noevenyi, Hungary
1984: Steven Fraser, USA
1988: Atanas Komchev, Bulgaria
1992: Maik Bullmann, Germany
1996: Vyacheslav Oleynyk, Ukraine

Wrestling, Greco-Roman–100 kg
1896: Carl Schuhmann, Germany
1900–1904:*
1906: Soren M. Jensen, Denmark
1908: Richard Weisz, Hungary
1912: Yrjo Saarela, Finland
1920: Adolf Lindfors, Finland
1924: Henri Deglane, France
1928: Rudolf Svensson, Sweden
1932: Carl Westergren, Sweden
1936: Kristjan Palusalu, Estonia
1948: Ahmet Kirecci, Turkey
1952: Johannes Kotkas, USSR
1956: Anatoli Parfenov, USSR

---

*Event not held.

1960: Ivan Bogdan, USSR
1964: Istvan Kozma, Hungary
1968: Istvan Kozma, Hungary
1972: Nicolae Martinescu, Romania
1976: Nikolai Bolboshin, USSR
1980: Georgi Raikov, Bulgaria
1984: Vasile Andrei, Romania
1988: Andrzej Wronski, Poland
1992: Hector Milian Perez, Cuba
1996: Andrzej Wronski, Poland

Wrestling, Greco-Roman–130 kg

1972: Anatoli Roshin, USSR
1976: Aleksandr Kolchinsky, USSR
1980: Aleksandr Kolchinsky, USSR
1984: Jeffrey Blatnick, USA
1988: Alexandre Karelin, USSR
1992: Alexander Karelin, Russia
1996: Aleksandr Karelin, Russia

Yachting–Men's 470

1976: West Germany, Frank Huebner, Harro Bode
1980: Brazil, Marcos Pinto Rizzo Soares, Eduardo Henrique Penido
1984: Spain, Jose Luis Doreste, Roberto Molina
1988: France, Thierry Peponnet, Luc Pillot
1992: Spain, Jordi Calafat, Francisco Sanchez
1996: Ukraine, Yevhen Braslavets, Ihor Matviyenko

Yachting–Women's 470

1988: USA, Allison Jolly, Lynne Jewell
1992: Spain, Theresa Zabell, Patricia Guerra
1996: Spain, Begona Via Dufresne, Theresa Zabell

Yachting–Finn

1924: Leon Huybrechts, Belgium
1928: Sven Thorell, Sweden
1932: Jacques Lebrun, France
1936: Daniel M. J. Kagchelland, Netherlands
1948: Paul Elvstrom, Denmark
1952: Paul Elvstrom, Denmark
1956: Paul Elvstrom, Denmark
1960: Paul Elvstrom, Denmark
1964: Wilhelm Kuhweide, West Germany
1968: Valentin Mankin, USSR
1972: Serge Maury, France
1976: Jochen Schumann, East Germany
1980: Esko Rechardt, Finland
1984: Russell Coutts, New Zealand
1988: Jose Luis Doreste, Spain
1992: Jose Van Der Ploeg, Spain
1996: Mateusz Kusznierewicz, Poland

Yachting–Europe

1992: Linda Anderson, Norway
1996: Kristine Roug, Denmark

Yachting–Flying Dutchman

1960: Norway, Peder Lunde Jr., Bjorn Bergvall
1964: New Zealand, Helmer Pedersen, Earle Wells
1968: Great Britain, Rodney Pattison, Iain S. MacDonald-Smith
1972: Great Britain, Rodney Pattison, Christopher Davies
1976: West Germany, Jorg Diesch, Eckart Diesch
1980: Spain, Alesandro Abascal, Miguel Noguer
1984: USA, Jonathan McKee, William Carl Buchan
1988: Denmark, Jorgen Bojsen-Moller, Christian Gronborg
1992: Spain, Luis Doreste, Domingo Manrique
1996:*

---

*Event not held.

Yachting–Division II Sailboard (Windgliding)

1984: Stephan Van Den Berg, Netherlands
1988: Bruce Kendall, New Zealand
1992: Franck David, France
1996:*

---

*Event not held.

Yachting–Women's Sailboard

1992: Barbara Kendall, New Zealand
1996:*

---

*Event not held.

Yachting–Soling

1972: USA
1976: Denmark
1980: Denmark
1984: USA
1988: East Germany
1992: Denmark
1996: Germany

Yachting–Star

1932: USA, Gilbert Gray, Andrew Libano
1936: Germany, Peter Bischoff, Hans-Joachim Weise
1948: USA, Hilary Smart, Paul Smart
1952: Italy, Agostino Straulino, Nicolo Rode
1956: USA, Herbert Williams, Lawrence Low
1960: USSR, Timir Pinegin, Fyodor Shutkov
1964: Bahamas, Durward Knowles, C. Cecil Cooke
1968: USA, Lowell North, Peter Barrett
1972: Australia, David Forbes, John Anderson
1976:*
1980: USSR, Valentin Mankin, Aleksandr Muzychenko
1984: USA, William E. Buchan, Stephen Erikson
1988: Great Britain, Michael McIntyre, Bryn Vaile
1992: USA, Mark Reynolds, Hal Haenel
1996: Brazil, Torben Grael, Marcelo Ferreira

---

*Event not held.

Yachting–Tornado
1976: Great Britain, Reginald White, John Osborn
1980: Brazil, Alexandre Welter, Lars Sigurd Bjorkstrom
1984: New Zealand, Rex Sellers, Christopher Timms
1988: France, Jean-Yves Le Deroff, Nicolas Henard
1992: France, Yves Loday, Nicolas Henard
1996: Spain, Jose Luis Ballester, Fernando Leon

Yachting–Tempest
1972: USSR, Valentin Mankin, Vitali Dyrdyra
1976: Sweden, John Albrechtson, Ingvar Hansson

Yachting–Laser
1996: Robert Scheidt, Brazil

Yachting–Women's Mistral
1996: Lai Shan Lee, Hong Kong

Yachting–Men's Mistral
1996: Nikolaos Kaklamanakis, Greece

Source: *The Olympic Factbook: A Spectator's Guide to the Winter Games* and *The Olympic Factbook: A Spectator's Guide to the Summer Games*, published by Visible Ink Press in Detroit, an official licensee of the U.S. Olympic Committee.

Olympic Gold

The Olympic Games increasingly rely on the television networks and major corporate sponsors to pay the bills. The cost of television rights continues to surge, as does the price of a global sponsorship.

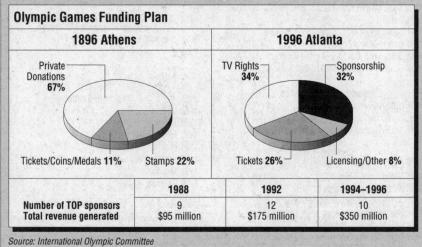

Olympic Games Funding Plan

1896 Athens

Private Donations **67%**
Tickets/Coins/Medals **11%**   Stamps **22%**

1996 Atlanta

TV Rights **34%**   Sponsorship **32%**
Tickets **26%**   Licensing/Other **8%**

	1988	1992	1994–1996
Number of TOP sponsors	9	12	10
Total revenue generated	$95 million	$175 million	$350 million

Source: *International Olympic Committee*

Olympic Games U.S. Broadcast Rights

Summer Games

1980: Moscow	NBC	$87,000,000
1984: Los Angeles	ABC	225,600,000
1988: Seoul	NBC	300,000,000
1992: Barcelona	NBC	401,000,000
1996: Atlanta	NBC	456,000,000
2000: Sydney	NBC	715,000,000*
2004: Athens	NBC	793,000,000*
2008:	NBC	894,000,000*

Winter Games

1980: Lake Placid	ABC	$15,500,000
1984: Sarajevo	ABC	91,600,000
1988: Calgary	ABC	309,000,000
1992: Albertville	CBS	243,000,000
1994: Lillehammer	CBS	295,000,000
1998: Nagano	CBS	375,000,000
2002: Salt Lake City	NBC	555,000,000*
2006:	NBC	613,000,000*

*Plus profit sharing.
Source: International Olympic Committee

Olympic Games Global TV Revenues

Summer Games

1980: Moscow	$101,000,000
1984: Los Angeles	287,000,000
1988: Seoul	403,000,000
1992: Barcelona	636,000,000
1996: Atlanta	900,000,000
2000: Sydney	1,396,000,000*
2004: Athens	1,238,000,000*
2008:	1,400,000,000*

Winter Games

1980: Lake Placid	$21,000,000
1984: Sarajevo	103,000,000
1988: Calgary	325,000,000
1992: Albertville	292,000,000
1994: Lillehammer	353,000,000
1998: Nagano	513,000,000*
2002: Salt Lake City	677,000,000*
2006:	763,000,000*

*To date. Other TV rights still to be negotiated.
Source: International Olympic Committee

Olympics TV Ratings

Winter Olympics—Prime Time

Year	Site	Network	Average rating/share*	Number of households
1968	Grenoble	ABC	13.4/22	7,594,000
1972	Sapporo	NBC	17.2/28	10,681,000
1976	Innsbruck	ABC	21.7/34	15,103,000
1980	Lake Placid	ABC	23.6/37	18,007,000
1984	Sarajevo	ABC	18.2/28	15,252,000
1988	Calgary	ABC	19.3/30	17,100,000
1992	Albertville	CBS	18.7/29	17,260,000
1994	Lillehammer	CBS	27.8/42	26,187,600

Summer Olympics—Prime Time

Year	Site	Network	Average rating/share*	Number of households
1968	Mexico City	ABC	14.3/26	8,104,000
1972	Munich	ABC	25.0/45	15,525,000
1976	Montreal	ABC	24.8/48	17,260,000
1980	Moscow	U.S. Boycott	–	–
1984	Los Angeles	ABC	23.2/44	19,440,000
1988	Seoul	NBC	16.9/30	14,975,000
1992	Barcelona	NBC	17.5/34	16,130,000
1996	Atlanta	NBC	21.6/41	20,714,400

*The rating represents the percentage of all U.S. households with television sets watching the program. The share represents the percentage of all television sets in use at the time that were tuned to the program.
Source: Nielsen Media Research

College Sports

Football Bowl Games

Rose Bowl
Pasadena, CA

Jan. 1, 1902	Michigan 49, Stanford 0
Jan. 1, 1916	Washington St. 14, Brown 0
Jan. 1, 1917	Oregon 14, Pennsylvania 0
Jan. 1, 1918	Mare Island 19, Camp Lewis 7
Jan. 1, 1919	Great Lakes 17, Mare Island 0
Jan. 1, 1920	Harvard 7, Oregon 6
Jan. 1, 1921	California 28, Ohio St. 0
Jan. 2, 1922	California 0, Wash. & Jeff. 0
Jan. 1, 1923	Southern Cal 14, Penn St. 3
Jan. 1, 1924	Navy 14, Washington 14
Jan. 1, 1925	Notre Dame 27, Stanford 10
Jan. 1, 1926	Alabama 20, Washington 19
Jan. 1, 1927	Alabama 7, Stanford 7
Jan. 2, 1928	Stanford 7, Pittsburgh 6
Jan. 1, 1929	Georgia Tech 8, California 7
Jan. 1, 1930	Southern Cal 47, Pittsburgh 14
Jan. 1, 1931	Alabama 24, Washington St. 0
Jan. 1, 1932	Southern Cal 21, Tulane 12
Jan. 2, 1933	Southern Cal 35, Pittsburgh 0
Jan. 1, 1934	Columbia 7, Stanford 0
Jan. 1, 1935	Alabama 29, Stanford 13
Jan. 1, 1936	Stanford 7, Southern Methodist 0
Jan. 1, 1937	Pittsburgh 21, Washington 0
Jan. 1, 1938	California 13, Alabama 0
Jan. 2, 1939	Southern Cal 7, Duke 3
Jan. 1, 1940	Southern Cal 14, Tennessee 0
Jan. 1, 1941	Stanford 21, Nebraska 13
Jan. 1, 1942	Oregon St. 20, Duke 16
Jan. 1, 1943	Georgia 9, UCLA 0
Jan. 1, 1944	Southern Cal 29, Washington 0
Jan. 1, 1945	Southern Cal 25, Tennessee 0
Jan. 1, 1946	Alabama 34, Southern Cal 14
Jan. 1, 1947	Illinois 45, UCLA 14
Jan. 1, 1948	Michigan 49, Southern Cal 0
Jan. 1, 1949	Northwestern 20, California 14
Jan. 2, 1950	Ohio St. 17, California 14
Jan. 1, 1951	Michigan 14, California 6
Jan. 1, 1952	Illinois 40, Stanford 7
Jan. 1, 1953	Southern Cal 7, Wisconsin 0
Jan. 1, 1954	Michigan St. 28, UCLA 20
Jan. 1, 1955	Ohio St. 20, Southern Cal 7
Jan. 2, 1956	Michigan St. 17, UCLA 14
Jan. 1, 1957	Iowa 35, Oregon St. 19
Jan. 1, 1958	Ohio St. 10, Oregon 7
Jan. 1, 1959	Iowa 38, California 12
Jan. 1, 1960	Washington 44, Wisconsin 8
Jan. 2, 1961	Washington 17, Minnesota 7
Jan. 1, 1962	Minnesota 21, UCLA 3
Jan. 1, 1963	Southern Cal 42, Wisconsin 37
Jan. 1, 1964	Illinois 17, Washington 7
Jan. 1, 1965	Michigan 34, Oregon St. 7
Jan. 1, 1966	UCLA 14, Michigan St. 12
Jan. 2, 1967	Purdue 14, Southern Cal 13
Jan. 1, 1968	Southern Cal 14, Indiana 3
Jan. 1, 1969	Ohio St. 27, Southern Cal 16
Jan. 1, 1970	Southern Cal 10, Michigan 3
Jan. 1, 1971	Stanford 27, Ohio St. 17
Jan. 1, 1972	Stanford 13, Michigan 12
Jan. 1, 1973	Southern Cal 42, Ohio St. 17
Jan. 1, 1974	Ohio St. 42, Southern Cal 21
Jan. 1, 1975	Southern Cal 18, Ohio St. 17
Jan. 1, 1976	UCLA 23, Ohio St. 10
Jan. 1, 1977	Southern Cal 14, Michigan 6
Jan. 2, 1978	Washington 27, Michigan 20
Jan. 1, 1979	Southern Cal 17, Michigan 10
Jan. 1, 1980	Southern Cal 17, Ohio St. 16
Jan. 1, 1981	Michigan 23, Washington 6
Jan. 1, 1982	Washington 28, Iowa 0
Jan. 1, 1983	UCLA 24, Michigan 14
Jan. 2, 1984	UCLA 45, Illinois 9
Jan. 1, 1985	Southern Cal 20, Ohio St. 17
Jan. 1, 1986	UCLA 45, Iowa 28
Jan. 1, 1987	Arizona St. 22, Michigan 15
Jan. 1, 1988	Michigan St. 20, Southern Cal 17
Jan. 2, 1989	Michigan 22, Southern Cal 14
Jan. 1, 1990	Southern Cal 17, Michigan 10
Jan. 1, 1991	Washington 46, Iowa 34
Jan. 1, 1992	Washington 34, Michigan 14
Jan. 1, 1993	Michigan 38, Washington 31
Jan. 1, 1994	Wisconsin 21, UCLA 16
Jan. 2, 1995	Penn St. 38, Oregon 20
Jan. 1, 1996	Southern Cal 41, Northwestern 32
Jan. 1, 1997	Ohio St. 20, Arizona St. 17

Orange Bowl
Miami, FL

Jan. 1, 1935	Bucknell 26, Miami (FL) 0
Jan. 1, 1936	Catholic 20, Mississippi 19
Jan. 1, 1937	Duquesne 13, Mississippi St. 12
Jan. 1, 1938	Auburn 6, Michigan St. 0
Jan. 2, 1939	Tennessee 17, Oklahoma 0
Jan. 1, 1940	Georgia Tech 21, Missouri 7
Jan. 1, 1941	Mississippi St. 14, Georgetown 7
Jan. 1, 1942	Georgia 40, Texas Christian 26
Jan. 1, 1943	Alabama 37, Boston College 21
Jan. 1, 1944	LSU 19, Texas A&M 14
Jan. 1, 1945	Tulsa 26, Georgia Tech 12
Jan. 1, 1946	Miami (FL) 13, Holy Cross 6
Jan. 1, 1947	Rice 8, Tennessee 0
Jan. 1, 1948	Georgia Tech 20, Kansas 14
Jan. 1, 1949	Texas 41, Georgia 28

Jan. 2, 1950	Santa Clara 21, Kentucky 13	Jan. 1, 1944	Georgia Tech 20, Tulsa 18
Jan. 1, 1951	Clemson 15, Miami (FL) 14	Jan. 1, 1945	Duke 29, Alabama 26
Jan. 1, 1952	Georgia Tech 17, Baylor 14	Jan. 1, 1946	Oklahoma St. 33, St. Mary's (CA) 13
Jan. 1, 1953	Alabama 61, Syracuse 6	Jan. 1, 1947	Georgia 20, North Carolina 10
Jan. 1, 1954	Oklahoma 7, Maryland 0	Jan. 1, 1948	Texas 27, Alabama 7
Jan. 1, 1955	Duke 34, Nebraska 7	Jan. 1, 1949	Oklahoma 14, North Carolina 6
Jan. 2, 1956	Oklahoma 20, Maryland 6	Jan. 2, 1950	Oklahoma 35, LSU 0
Jan. 1, 1957	Colorado 27, Clemson 21	Jan. 1, 1951	Kentucky 13, Oklahoma 7
Jan. 1, 1958	Oklahoma 48, Duke 21	Jan. 1, 1952	Maryland 28, Tennessee 13
Jan. 1, 1959	Oklahoma 21, Syracuse 6	Jan. 1, 1953	Georgia Tech 24, Mississippi 7
Jan. 1, 1960	Georgia 14, Missouri 0	Jan. 1, 1954	Georgia Tech 42, West Virginia 19
Jan. 2, 1961	Missouri 21, Navy 14	Jan. 1, 1955	Navy 21, Mississippi 0
Jan. 1, 1962	LSU 25, Colorado 7	Jan. 2, 1956	Georgia Tech 7, Pittsburgh 0
Jan. 1, 1963	Alabama 17, Oklahoma 0	Jan. 1, 1957	Baylor 13, Tennessee 7
Jan. 1, 1964	Nebraska 13, Auburn 7	Jan. 1, 1958	Mississippi 39, Texas 7
Jan. 1, 1965	Texas 21, Alabama 17	Jan. 1, 1959	LSU 7, Clemson 0
Jan. 1, 1966	Alabama 39, Nebraska 28	Jan. 1, 1960	Mississippi 21, LSU 0
Jan. 2, 1967	Florida 27, Georgia Tech 12	Jan. 2, 1961	Mississippi 14, Rice 6
Jan. 1, 1968	Oklahoma 26, Tennessee 24	Jan. 1, 1962	Alabama 10, Arkansas 3
Jan. 1, 1969	Penn St. 15, Kansas 14	Jan. 1, 1963	Mississippi 17, Arkansas 13
Jan. 1, 1970	Penn St. 10, Missouri 3	Jan. 1, 1964	Alabama 12, Mississippi 7
Jan. 1, 1971	Nebraska 17, LSU 12	Jan. 1, 1965	LSU 13, Syracuse 10
Jan. 1, 1972	Nebraska 38, Alabama 6	Jan. 1, 1966	Missouri 20, Florida 18
Jan. 1, 1973	Nebraska 40, Notre Dame 6	Jan. 2, 1967	Alabama 34, Nebraska 7
Jan. 1, 1974	Penn St. 16, LSU 9	Jan. 1, 1968	LSU 20, Wyoming 13
Jan. 1, 1975	Notre Dame 13, Alabama 11	Jan. 1, 1969	Arkansas 16, Georgia 2
Jan. 1, 1976	Oklahoma 14, Michigan 6	Jan. 1, 1970	Mississippi 27, Arkansas 22
Jan. 1, 1977	Ohio St. 27, Colorado 10	Jan. 1, 1971	Tennessee 34, Air Force 13
Jan. 2, 1978	Arkansas 31, Oklahoma 6	Jan. 1, 1972	Oklahoma 40, Auburn 22
Jan. 1, 1979	Oklahoma 31, Nebraska 24	Dec. 31, 1972	Oklahoma 14, Penn St. 0
Jan. 1, 1980	Oklahoma 24, Florida St. 7	Dec. 31, 1973	Notre Dame 24, Alabama 23
Jan. 1, 1981	Oklahoma 18, Florida St. 17	Dec. 31, 1974	Nebraska 13, Florida 10
Jan. 1, 1982	Clemson 22, Nebraska 15	Dec. 31, 1975	Alabama 13, Penn St. 6
Jan. 1, 1983	Nebraska 21, LSU 20	Jan. 1, 1977	Pittsburgh 27, Georgia 3
Jan. 2, 1984	Miami (FL) 31, Nebraska 30	Jan. 2, 1978	Alabama 35, Ohio St. 6
Jan. 1, 1985	Washington 28, Oklahoma 17	Jan. 1, 1979	Alabama 14, Penn St. 7
Jan. 1, 1986	Oklahoma 25, Penn St. 10	Jan. 1, 1980	Alabama 24, Arkansas 9
Jan. 1, 1987	Oklahoma 42, Arkansas 8	Jan. 1, 1981	Georgia 17, Notre Dame 10
Jan. 1, 1988	Miami (FL) 20, Oklahoma 14	Jan. 1, 1982	Pittsburgh 24, Georgia 20
Jan. 2, 1989	Miami (FL) 23, Nebraska 3	Jan. 1, 1983	Penn St. 27, Georgia 23
Jan. 1, 1990	Notre Dame 21, Colorado 6	Jan. 2, 1984	Auburn 9, Michigan 7
Jan. 1, 1991	Colorado 10, Notre Dame 9	Jan. 1, 1985	Nebraska 28, LSU 10
Jan. 1, 1992	Miami (FL) 22, Nebraska 0	Jan. 1, 1986	Tennessee 35, Miami (FL) 7
Jan. 1, 1993	Florida St. 27, Nebraska 14	Jan. 1, 1987	Nebraska 30, LSU 15
Jan. 1, 1994	Florida St. 18, Nebraska 16	Jan. 1, 1988	Auburn 16, Syracuse 16
Jan. 1, 1995	Nebraska 24, Miami (FL) 17	Jan. 2, 1989	Florida St. 13, Auburn 7
Jan. 1, 1996	Florida St. 31, Notre Dame 26	Jan. 1, 1990	Miami (FL) 33, Alabama 25
Dec. 31, 1996	Nebraska 41, Virginia Tech 21	Jan. 1, 1991	Tennessee 23, Virginia 22
		Jan. 1, 1992	Notre Dame 39, Florida 28
Sugar Bowl		Jan. 1, 1993	Alabama 34, Miami (FL) 13
New Orleans, LA		Jan. 1, 1994	Florida 41, West Virginia 7
		Jan. 2, 1995	Florida St. 23, Florida 17
Jan. 1, 1935	Tulane 20, Temple 14	Dec. 31, 1995	Virginia Tech 28, Texas 10
Jan. 1, 1936	Texas Christian 3, LSU 2	Jan. 2, 1997	Florida 52, Florida St. 20
Jan. 1, 1937	Santa Clara 21, LSU 14		
Jan. 1, 1938	Santa Clara 6, LSU 0	**Cotton Bowl**	
Jan. 2, 1939	Texas Christian 15,	Dallas, TX	
	Carnegie Mellon 7	Jan. 1, 1937	Texas Christian 16, Marquette 6
Jan. 1, 1940	Texas A&M 14, Tulane 13	Jan. 1, 1938	Rice 28, Colorado 14
Jan. 1, 1941	Boston College 19, Tennessee 13	Jan. 2, 1939	St. Mary's (CA) 20,
Jan. 1, 1942	Fordham 2, Missouri 0		Texas Tech 13
Jan. 1, 1943	Tennessee 14, Tulsa 7		

Jan. 1, 1940	Clemson 6, Boston College 3
Jan. 1, 1941	Texas A&M 13, Fordham 12
Jan. 1, 1942	Alabama 29, Texas A&M 21
Jan. 1, 1943	Texas 14, Georgia Tech 7
Jan. 1, 1944	Randolph Field 7, Texas 7
Jan. 1, 1945	Oklahoma St. 34, Texas Christian 0
Jan. 1, 1946	Texas 40, Missouri 27
Jan. 1, 1947	Arkansas 0, LSU 0
Jan. 1, 1948	Penn St. 13, Southern Methodist 13
Jan. 1, 1949	Southern Methodist 21, Oregon 13
Jan. 2, 1950	Rice 27, North Carolina 13
Jan. 1, 1951	Tennessee 20, Texas 14
Jan. 1, 1952	Kentucky 20, Texas Christian 7
Jan. 1, 1953	Texas 16, Tennessee 0
Jan. 1, 1954	Rice 28, Alabama 6
Jan. 1, 1955	Georgia Tech 14, Arkansas 6
Jan. 2, 1956	Mississippi 14, Texas Christian 13
Jan. 1, 1957	Texas Christian 28, Syracuse 27
Jan. 1, 1958	Navy 20, Rice 7
Jan. 1, 1959	Air Force 0, Texas Christian 0
Jan. 1, 1960	Syracuse 23, Texas 14
Jan. 2, 1961	Duke 7, Arkansas 6
Jan. 1, 1962	Texas 12, Mississippi 7
Jan. 1, 1963	LSU 13, Texas 0
Jan. 1, 1964	Texas 28, Navy 6
Jan. 1, 1965	Arkansas 10, Nebraska 7
Jan. 1, 1966	LSU 14, Arkansas 7
Dec. 31, 1966	Georgia 24, Southern Methodist 9
Jan. 1, 1968	Texas A&M 20, Alabama 16
Jan. 1, 1969	Texas 36, Tennessee 13
Jan. 1, 1970	Texas 21, Notre Dame 17
Jan. 1, 1971	Notre Dame 24, Texas 11
Jan. 1, 1972	Penn St. 30, Texas 6
Jan. 1, 1973	Texas 17, Alabama 13
Jan. 1, 1974	Nebraska 19, Texas 3
Jan. 1, 1975	Penn St. 41, Baylor 20
Jan. 1, 1976	Arkansas 31, Georgia 10
Jan. 1, 1977	Houston 30, Maryland 21
Jan. 2, 1978	Notre Dame 38, Texas 10
Jan. 1, 1979	Notre Dame 35, Houston 34
Jan. 1, 1980	Houston 17, Nebraska 14
Jan. 1, 1981	Alabama 30, Baylor 2
Jan. 1, 1982	Texas 14, Alabama 12
Jan. 1, 1983	Southern Methodist 7, Pittsburgh 3
Jan. 2, 1984	Georgia 10, Texas 9
Jan. 1, 1985	Boston College 45, Houston 28
Jan. 1, 1986	Texas A&M 36, Auburn 16
Jan. 1, 1987	Ohio St. 28, Texas A&M 12
Jan. 1, 1988	Texas A&M 35, Notre Dame 10
Jan. 2, 1989	UCLA 17, Arkansas 3
Jan. 1, 1990	Tennessee 31, Arkansas 27
Jan. 1, 1991	Miami (FL) 46, Texas 3
Jan. 1, 1992	Florida St. 10, Texas A&M 2
Jan. 1, 1993	Notre Dame 28, Texas A&M 3
Jan. 1, 1994	Notre Dame 24, Texas A&M 21
Jan. 2, 1995	Southern Cal 55, Texas Tech 14
Jan. 1, 1996	Colorado 38, Oregon 6
Jan. 1, 1997	Brigham Young 19, Kansas St. 15

Gator Bowl
Jacksonville, FL

Jan. 1, 1946	Wake Forest 26, South Carolina 14
Jan. 1, 1947	Oklahoma 34, North Carolina St. 13
Jan. 1, 1948	Georgia 20, Maryland 20
Jan. 1, 1949	Clemson 24, Missouri 23
Jan. 2, 1950	Maryland 20, Missouri 7
Jan. 1, 1951	Wyoming 20, Wash. & Lee 7
Jan. 1, 1952	Miami (FL) 14, Clemson 0
Jan. 1, 1953	Florida 14, Tulsa 13
Jan. 1, 1954	Texas Tech 35, Auburn 13
Dec. 31, 1954	Auburn 33, Baylor 13
Dec. 31, 1955	Vanderbilt 25, Auburn 13
Dec. 29, 1956	Georgia Tech 21, Pittsburgh 14
Dec. 28, 1957	Tennessee 3, Texas A&M 0
Dec. 27, 1958	Mississippi 7, Florida 3
Jan. 2, 1960	Arkansas 14, Georgia Tech 7
Dec. 31, 1960	Florida 13, Baylor 12
Dec. 30, 1961	Penn St. 30, Georgia Tech 15
Dec. 29, 1962	Florida 17, Penn St. 7
Dec. 28, 1963	North Carolina 35, Air Force 0
Jan. 2, 1965	Florida St. 36, Oklahoma 19
Dec. 31, 1965	Georgia Tech 31, Texas Tech 21
Dec. 31, 1966	Tennessee 18, Syracuse 12
Dec. 30, 1967	Florida St. 17, Penn St. 17
Dec. 28, 1968	Missouri 35, Alabama 10
Dec. 27, 1969	Florida 14, Tennessee 13
Jan. 2, 1971	Auburn 35, Mississippi 28
Dec. 31, 1971	Georgia 7, North Carolina 3
Dec. 30, 1972	Auburn 24, Colorado 3
Dec. 29, 1973	Texas Tech 28, Tennessee 19
Dec. 30, 1974	Auburn 27, Texas 3
Dec. 29, 1975	Maryland 13, Florida 0
Dec. 27, 1976	Notre Dame 20, Penn St. 9
Dec. 30, 1977	Pittsburgh 34, Clemson 3
Dec. 29, 1978	Clemson 17, Ohio St. 15
Dec. 28, 1979	North Carolina 17, Michigan 15
Dec. 29, 1980	Pittsburgh 37, South Carolina 9
Dec. 28, 1981	North Carolina 31, Arkansas 27
Dec. 30, 1982	Florida St. 31, West Virginia 12
Dec. 30, 1983	Florida 14, Iowa 6
Dec. 28, 1984	Oklahoma St. 21, South Carolina 14
Dec. 30, 1985	Florida St. 34, Oklahoma St. 23
Dec. 27, 1986	Clemson 27, Stanford 21
Dec. 31, 1987	LSU 30, South Carolina 13
Jan. 1, 1989	Georgia 34, Michigan St. 27
Dec. 30, 1989	Clemson 27, West Virginia 7
Jan. 1, 1991	Michigan 35, Mississippi 3
Dec. 29, 1991	Oklahoma 48, Virginia 14
Dec. 31, 1992	Florida 27, North Carolina St. 10
Dec. 31, 1993	Alabama 24, North Carolina 10
Dec. 30, 1994	Tennessee 45, Virginia Tech 23
Jan.1, 1996	Syracuse 41, Clemson 0
Jan. 1, 1997	North Carolina 20, West Virginia 13

Florida Citrus Bowl
Orlando, FL

Jan. 1, 1947	Catawba 31, Maryville (TN) 6
Jan. 1, 1948	Catawba 7, Marshall 0

Jan. 1, 1949	Murray St. 21, Sul Ross St. 21	Jan. 1, 1988	Clemson 35, Penn St. 10
Jan. 2, 1950	St. Vincent 7, Emory & Henry 6	Jan. 2, 1989	Clemson 13, Oklahoma 6
Jan. 1, 1951	Morris Harvey 35, Emory & Henry 14	Jan. 1, 1990	Illinois 31, Virginia 21
Jan. 1, 1952	Stetson 35, Arkansas St. 20	Jan. 1, 1991	Georgia Tech 45, Nebraska 21
Jan. 1, 1953	East Texas St. 33, Tennessee Tech 0	Jan. 1, 1992	California 37, Clemson 13
		Jan. 1, 1993	Georgia 21, Ohio St. 14
Jan. 1, 1954	Arkansas St. 7, East Texas St. 7	Jan. 1, 1994	Penn St. 31, Tennessee 13
Jan. 1, 1955	Nebraska-Omaha 7, Eastern Ky. 6	Jan. 2, 1995	Alabama 24, Ohio St. 17
Jan. 2, 1956	Juniata 6, Missouri Valley 6	Jan. 1, 1996	Tennessee 20, Ohio St. 14
Jan. 1, 1957	West Texas A&M 20, Southern Miss. 13	Jan. 1, 1997	Tennessee 48, Northwestern 28

Jan. 1, 1958	East Texas St. 10, Southern Miss. 9
Jan. 1, 1960	Middle Tenn. St. 21, Presbyterian 12
Dec. 30, 1960	Citadel 27, Tennessee Tech 0
Dec. 29, 1961	Lamar 21, Middle Tenn. St. 14
Dec. 22, 1962	Houston 49, Miami (OH) 21
Dec. 28, 1963	Western Ky. 27, Coast Guard 0
Dec. 12, 1964	East Carolina 14, Massachusetts 13
Dec. 11, 1965	East Carolina 31, Maine 0
Dec. 10, 1966	Morgan St. 14, West Chester 6
Dec. 16, 1967	Tenn.-Martin 25, West Chester 8
Dec. 27, 1968	Richmond 49, Ohio 42
Dec. 26, 1969	Toledo 56, Davidson 33
Dec. 28, 1970	Toledo 40, William & Mary 12
Dec. 28, 1971	Toledo 28, Richmond 3
Dec. 29, 1972	Tampa 21, Kent 18
Dec. 22, 1973	Miami (OH) 16, Florida 7
Dec. 21, 1974	Miami (OH) 21, Georgia 10
Dec. 20, 1975	Miami (OH) 20, South Caro. 7
Dec. 18, 1976	Oklahoma St. 49, Brigham Young 21
Dec. 23, 1977	Florida St. 40, Texas Tech 17
Dec. 23, 1978	North Carolina St. 30, Pittsburgh 17
Dec. 22, 1979	LSU 34, Wake Forest 10
Dec. 20, 1980	Florida 35, Maryland 20
Dec. 19, 1981	Missouri 19, Southern Miss. 17
Dec. 18, 1982	Auburn 33, Boston College 26
Dec. 17, 1983	Tennessee 30, Maryland 23
Dec. 22, 1984	Florida St. 17, Georgia 17
Dec. 28, 1985	Ohio St. 10, Brigham Young 7
Jan. 1, 1987	Auburn 16, Southern Cal 7

Fiesta Bowl

Tempe, AZ

Dec. 27, 1971	Arizona St. 45, Florida St. 38
Dec. 23, 1972	Arizona St. 49, Missouri 35
Dec. 21, 1973	Arizona St. 28, Pittsburgh 7
Dec. 28, 1974	Oklahoma St. 16, Brigham Young 6
Dec. 26, 1975	Arizona St. 17, Nebraska 14
Dec. 25, 1976	Oklahoma 41, Wyoming 7
Dec. 25, 1977	Penn St. 42, Arizona St. 30
Dec. 25, 1978	Arkansas 10, UCLA 10
Dec. 25, 1979	Pittsburgh 16, Arizona 10
Dec. 26, 1980	Penn St. 31, Ohio St. 19
Jan. 1, 1982	Penn St. 26, Southern Cal 10
Jan. 1, 1983	Arizona St. 32, Oklahoma 21
Jan. 2, 1984	Ohio St. 28, Pittsburgh 23
Jan. 1, 1985	UCLA 39, Miami (FL) 37
Jan. 1, 1986	Michigan 27, Nebraska 23
Jan. 2, 1987	Penn St. 14, Miami (FL) 10
Jan. 1, 1988	Florida St. 31, Nebraska 28
Jan. 2, 1989	Notre Dame 34, West Virginia 21
Jan. 1, 1990	Florida St. 41, Nebraska 17
Jan. 1, 1991	Louisville 34, Alabama 7
Jan. 1, 1992	Penn St. 42, Tennessee 17
Jan. 1, 1993	Syracuse 26, Colorado 22
Jan. 1, 1994	Arizona 29, Miami (FL) 0
Jan. 2, 1995	Colorado 41, Notre Dame 24
Jan. 2, 1996	Nebraska 62, Florida 24
Jan. 1, 1997	Penn St. 38, Texas 15

Source: National Collegiate Athletic Association

Heisman Trophy Winners

Year	Heisman winner, Team, Position
1935	Jay Berwanger, Chicago, HB
1936	Larry Kelley, Yale, E
1937	Clint Frank, Yale, HB
1938	Davey O'Brien, Texas Christian, QB
1939	Nile Kinnick, Iowa, HB
1940	Tom Harmon, Michigan, HB
1941	Bruce Smith, Minnesota, HB
1942	Frank Sinkwich, Georgia, HB
1943	Angelo Bertelli, Notre Dame, QB
1944	Les Horvath, Ohio St., QB
1945	Doc Blanchard, Army, FB
1946	Glenn Davis, Army, HB
1947	Johnny Lujack, Notre Dame, QB
1948	Doak Walker, Southern Methodist, HB
1949	Leon Hart, Notre Dame, E
1950	Vic Janowicz, Ohio St., HB
1951	Dick Kazmeier, Princeton, HB
1952	Billy Vessels, Oklahoma, HB
1953	John Lattner, Notre Dame, HB
1954	Alan Ameche, Wisconsin, FB
1955	Howard Cassady, Ohio St., HB
1956	Paul Hornung, Notre Dame, QB
1957	John David Crow, Texas A&M, HB
1958	Pete Dawkins, Army, HB
1959	Billy Cannon, LSU, HB
1960	Joe Bellino, Navy, HB
1961	Ernie Davis, Syracuse, HB
1962	Terry Baker, Oregon St., QB
1963	Roger Staubach, Navy, QB
1964	John Huarte, Notre Dame, QB
1965	Mike Garrett, Southern Cal, HB
1966	Steve Spurrier, Florida, QB
1967	Gary Beban, UCLA, QB
1968	O.J. Simpson, Southern Cal, HB
1969	Steve Owens, Oklahoma, HB
1970	Jim Plunkett, Stanford, QB
1971	Pat Sullivan, Auburn, QB
1972	Johnny Rodgers, Nebraska, FL
1973	John Cappelletti, Penn St., HB
1974	Archie Griffin, Ohio St., HB
1975	Archie Griffin, Ohio St., HB
1976	Tony Dorsett, Pittsburgh, HB
1977	Earl Campbell, Texas, HB
1978	Billy Sims, Oklahoma, HB
1979	Charles White, Southern Cal, HB
1980	George Rogers, South Carolina, HB
1981	Marcus Allen, Southern Cal, HB
1982	Herschel Walker, Georgia, HB
1983	Mike Rozier, Nebraska, HB
1984	Doug Flutie, Boston College, QB
1985	Bo Jackson, Auburn, HB
1986	Vinny Testaverde, Miami (FL), QB
1987	Tim Brown, Notre Dame, WR
1988	Barry Sanders, Oklahoma St., RB
1989	Andre Ware, Houston, QB
1990	Ty Detmer, Brigham Young, QB
1991	Desmond Howard, Michigan, WR
1992	Gino Torretta, Miami (FL), QB
1993	Charlie Ward, Florida St., QB
1994	Rashaan Salaam, Colorado, RB
1995	Eddie George, Ohio St., RB
1996	Danny Wuerffel, Florida, QB

Source: National Collegiate Athletic Association

NCAA Basketball Tournament Most Outstanding Player Award

Year	Winner, team
1939	none selected
1940	Marvin Huffman, Indiana
1941	John Kotz, Wisconsin
1942	Howard Dallmar, Stanford
1943	Ken Sailors, Wyoming
1944	Arnold Ferrin, Utah
1945	Bob Kurland, Oklahoma St.
1946	Bob Kurland, Oklahoma St.
1947	George Kaftan, Holy Cross
1948	Alex Groza, Kentucky
1949	Alex Groza, Kentucky
1950	Irwin Dambrot, CCNY
1951	none selected
1952	Clyde Lovellette, Kansas
1953	B. H. Born, Kansas
1954	Tom Gola, La Salle
1955	Bill Russell, San Francisco
1956	Hal Lear, Temple
1957	Wilt Chamberlain, Kansas
1958	Elgin Baylor, Seattle
1959	Jerry West, West Virginia
1960	Jerry Lucas, Ohio St.
1961	Jerry Lucas, Ohio St.
1962	Paul Hogue, Cincinnati
1963	Art Heyman, Duke
1964	Walt Hazzard, UCLA
1965	Bill Bradley, Princeton
1966	Jerry Chambers, Utah
1967	Lew Alcindor, UCLA
1968	Lew Alcindor, UCLA
1969	Lew Alcindor, UCLA
1970	Sidney Wicks, UCLA
1971	Howard Porter, Villanova*
1972	Bill Walton, UCLA
1973	Bill Walton, UCLA
1974	David Thompson, N. Carolina St.
1975	Richard Washington, UCLA
1976	Kent Benson, Indiana
1977	Butch Lee, Marquette
1978	Jack Givens, Kentucky
1979	Earvin Johnson, Michigan St.
1980	Darrell Griffith, Louisville
1981	Isiah Thomas, Indiana
1982	James Worthy, North Carolina
1983	Akeem Olajuwon, Houston
1984	Patrick Ewing, Georgetown
1985	Ed Pinckney, Villanova
1986	Pervis Ellison, Louisville
1987	Keith Smart, Indiana
1988	Danny Manning, Kansas
1989	Glen Rice, Michigan
1990	Anderson Hunt, UNLV
1991	Christian Laettner, Duke
1992	Bobby Hurley, Duke
1993	Donald Williams, North Carolina
1994	Corliss Williamson, Arkansas
1995	Ed O'Bannon, UCLA
1996	Tony Delk, Kentucky
1997	Miles Simon, Arizona

*Later vacated because player declared ineligible.
Source: National Collegiate Athletic Association

NCAA Basketball Championship Results

Year	Winner	Loser	Score	Championship total attendance
1939	Oregon	Ohio St.	46-33	15,025
1940	Indiana	Kansas	60-42	36,880
1941	Wisconsin	Washington St.	39-34	48,055
1942	Stanford	Dartmouth	53-38	24,372
1943	Wyoming	Georgetown	46-34	56,876
1944	Utah	Dartmouth	42-40*	59,369
1945	Oklahoma St.	New York U.	49-45	67,780
1946	Oklahoma St.	North Carolina	43-40	73,116
1947	Holy Cross	Oklahoma	58-47	72,959
1948	Kentucky	Baylor	58-42	72,523
1949	Kentucky	Oklahoma St.	46-36	66,077
1950	CCNY	Bradley	71-68	75,464
1951	Kentucky	Kansas St.	68-58	110,645
1952	Kansas	St. John's (NY)	80-63	115,712
1953	Indiana	Kansas	69-68	127,149
1954	La Salle	Bradley	92-76	115,391
1955	San Francisco	La Salle	77-63	116,983
1956	San Francisco	Iowa	83-71	132,513
1957	North Carolina	Kansas	54-53**	108,891
1958	Kentucky	Seattle	84-72	176,878
1959	California	West Virginia	71-70	161,809
1960	Ohio St.	California	75-55	155,491
1961	Cincinnati	Ohio St.	70-65*	169,520
1962	Cincinnati	Ohio St.	71-59	177,469
1963	Loyola (IL)	Cincinnati	60-58*	153,065
1964	UCLA	Duke	98-83	140,790
1965	UCLA	Michigan	91-80	140,673
1966	UTEP	Kentucky	72-65	140,925
1967	UCLA	Dayton	79-64	159,570
1968	UCLA	North Carolina	78-55	160,888
1969	UCLA	Purdue	92-72	165,712
1970	UCLA	Jacksonville	80-69	146,794
1971	UCLA	+Villanova	68-62	207,200
1972	UCLA	Florida St.	81-76	147,304
1973	UCLA	Memphis	87-66	163,160
1974	North Carolina St.	Marquette	76-64	154,112
1975	UCLA	Kentucky	92-85	183,857
1976	Indiana	Michigan	86-68	202,502
1977	Marquette	North Carolina	67-59	241,610
1978	Kentucky	Duke	94-88	227,149
1979	Michigan St.	Indiana St.	75-64	262,101
1980	Louisville	+UCLA	59-54	321,260
1981	Indiana	North Carolina	63-50	347,414
1982	North Carolina	Georgetown	63-62	427,251
1983	North Carolina St.	Houston	54-52	364,356
1984	Georgetown	Houston	84-75	397,481
1985	Villanova	Georgetown	66-64	422,519
1986	Louisville	Duke	72-69	499,704
1987	Indiana	Syracuse	74-73	645,744
1988	Kansas	Oklahoma	83-79	558,998
1989	Michigan	Seton Hall	80-79*	613,242
1990	UNLV	Duke	103-73	537,138
1991	Duke	Kansas	72-65	665,707
1992	Duke	Michigan	71-51	580,462
1993	North Carolina	Michigan	77-71	707,719
1994	Arkansas	Duke	76-72	578,007
1995	UCLA	Arkansas	89-78	539,440
1996	Kentucky	Syracuse	76-67	634,584
1997	Arizona	Kentucky	84-79	643,290

*Overtime.
**Three overtimes.
+Later vacated because of ineligibility.
Source: National Collegiate Athletic Association

NCAA Women's Basketball Championship Results

Year	Winner	Score	Loser
1982	Louisiana Tech	76-62	Cheyney
1983	Southern Cal	69-67	Louisiana Tech
1984	Southern Cal	72-61	Tennessee
1985	Old Dominion	70-65	Georgia
1986	Texas	97-81	Southern Cal
1987	Tennessee	67-44	Louisiana Tech
1988	Louisiana Tech	56-54	Auburn
1989	Tennessee	76-60	Auburn
1990	Stanford	88-81	Auburn
1991	Tennessee	70-67*	Virginia
1992	Stanford	78-62	Western Kentucky
1993	Texas Tech	84-82	Ohio State
1994	North Carolina	60-59	Louisiana Tech
1995	Connecticut	70-64	Tennessee
1996	Tennessee	83-65	Georgia
1997	Tennessee	68-59	Old Dominion

NCAA Women's Basketball Most Outstanding Player Award

1982	—	Janice Lawrence, Louisiana Tech
1983	—	Cheryl Miller, Southern Cal
1984	—	Cheryl Miller, Southern Cal
1985	—	Tracy Claxton, Old Dominion
1986	—	Clarissa Davis, Texas
1987	—	Tonya Edwards, Tennessee
1988	—	Erica Westbrooks, Louisiana Tech
1989	—	Bridgette Gordon, Tennessee
1990	—	Jennifer Azzi, Stanford
1991	—	Dawn Staley, Virginia
1992	—	Molly Goodenbour, Stanford
1993	—	Sheryl Swoopes, Texas Tech
1994	—	Charlotte Smith, North Carolina
1995	—	Rebecca Lobo, Connecticut
1996	—	Michelle Marciniak, Tennessee
1997	—	Chamique Holdsclaw, Tennessee

*Overtime.
Source: National Collegiate Athletic Association

Tennis

U.S. Open Champions—Men's Singles

YEAR	CHAMPION	RUNNER-UP	YEAR	CHAMPION	RUNNER-UP
1881	Richard D. Sears (U.S.)	William E. Glyn (U.S.)	1911	William A. Larned (U.S.)	Maurice E. McLoughlin (U.S.)
1882	Richard D. Sears (U.S.)	Clarence M. Clark (U.S.)	1912	Maurice E. McLoughlin (U.S.)	Wallace F. Johnson (U.S.)
1883	Richard D. Sears (U.S.)	James Dwight (U.S.)	1913	Maurice E. McLoughlin (U.S.)	Richard N. Williams (U.S.)
1884	Richard D. Sears (U.S.)	Howard A. Taylor (U.S.)	1914	Richard N. Williams (U.S.)	Maurice E. McLoughlin (U.S.)
1885	Richard D. Sears (U.S.)	Godfrey M. Brinley (U.S.)	1915	William M. Johnston (U.S.)	Maurice E. McLoughlin (U.S.)
1886	Richard D. Sears (U.S.)	R. Livingston Beeckman (U.S.)	1916	Richard N. Williams (U.S.)	William M. Johnston (U.S.)
1887	Richard D. Sears (U.S.)	Henry W. Slocum, Jr. (U.S.)	1917	R. Lindley Murray (U.S.)	Nathaniel Niles (U.S.)
1888	Henry W. Slocum, Jr. (U.S.)	Howard A. Taylor (U.S.)	1918	R. Lindley Murray (U.S.)	William T. Tilden (U.S.)
1889	Henry W. Slocum, Jr. (U.S.)	Quincy Shaw (U.S.)	1919	William M. Johnston (U.S.)	William T. Tilden (U.S.)
1890	Oliver S. Campbell (U.S.)	Henry W. Slocum, Jr. (U.S.)	1920	William T. Tilden (U.S.)	William M. Johnston (U.S.)
1891	Oliver S. Campbell (U.S.)	Clarence Hobart (U.S.)	1921	William T. Tilden (U.S.)	Wallace J. Johnson (U.S.)
1892	Oliver S. Campbell (U.S.)	Fred H. Hovey (U.S.)	1922	William T. Tilden (U.S.)	William M. Johnston (U.S.)
1893	Robert D. Wrenn (U.S.)	Fred H. Hovey (U.S.)	1923	William T. Tilden (U.S.)	William M. Johnston (U.S.)
1894	Robert D. Wrenn (U.S.)	Manliffe Goodbody (Great Britain)	1924	William T. Tilden (U.S.)	William M. Johnston (U.S.)
1895	Fred H. Hovey (U.S.)	Robert D. Wrenn (U.S.)	1925	William T. Tilden (U.S.)	William M. Johnston (U.S.)
1896	Robert D. Wrenn (U.S.)	Fred H. Hovey (U.S.)	1926	Rene Lacoste (France)	Jean Borotra (France)
1897	Robert D. Wrenn (U.S.)	Wilberforce Eaves (Great Britain)	1927	Rene Lacoste (France)	William T. Tilden (U.S.)
1898	Malcolm D. Whitman (U.S.)	Dwight F. Davis (U.S.)	1928	Henri Cochet (France)	Francis T. Hunter (U.S.)
1899	Malcolm D. Whitman (U.S.)	J. Parmly Paret (U.S.)	1929	William T. Tilden (U.S.)	Francis T. Hunter (U.S.)
1900	Malcolm D. Whitman (U.S.)	William A. Larned (U.S.)	1930	John H. Doeg (U.S.)	Francis X. Shields (U.S.)
1901	William A. Larned (U.S.)	Beals C. Wright (U.S.)	1931	H. Ellsworth Vines (U.S.)	George M. Lott, Jr. (U.S.)
1902	William A. Larned (U.S.)	Reginald F. Doherty (Great Britain)	1932	H. Ellsworth Vines (U.S.)	Henri Cochet (France)
1903	Hugh L. Doherty (Great Britain)	William A. Larned (U.S.)	1933	Fred Perry (Great Britain)	John H. Crawford (Australia)
1904	Holcombe Ward (U.S.)	William J. Clothier (U.S.)	1934	Fred Perry (Great Britain)	Wilmer L. Allison (U.S.)
1905	Beals C. Wright (U.S.)	Holcombe Ward (U.S.)	1935	Wilmer L. Allison (U.S.)	Sidney B. Wood (U.S.)
1906	William J. Clothier (U.S.)	Beals C. Wright (U.S.)	1936	Fred Perry (Great Britain)	J. Donald Budge (U.S.)
1907	William A. Larned (U.S.)	Robert LeRoy (U.S.)	1937	J. Donald Budge (U.S.)	Gottfried von Cramm (Germany)
1908	William A. Larned (U.S.)	Beals C. Wright (U.S.)	1938	J. Donald Budge (U.S.)	C. Gene Mako (U.S.)
1909	William A. Larned (U.S.)	William J. Clothier (U.S.)	1939	Robert Riggs (U.S.)	S. Welby van Horn (U.S.)
1910	William A. Larned (U.S.)	Thomas C. Bundy (U.S.)			

YEAR	CHAMPION	RUNNER-UP
1940	Donald McNeill (U.S.)	Robert Riggs (U.S.)
1941	Robert Riggs (U.S.)	Francis Kovacs, 2d (U.S.)
1942	Frederick Schroeder (U.S.)	Frank Parker (U.S.)
1943	Lt. Joseph R. Hunt (U.S.)	Seaman Jack Kramer (U.S.)
1944	Sgt. Frank Parker (U.S.)	William F. Talbert (U.S.)
1945	Sgt. Frank Parker (U.S.)	William F. Talbert (U.S.)
1946	Jack Kramer (U.S.)	Tom Brown, Jr. (U.S.)
1947	Jack Kramer (U.S.)	Frank Parker (U.S.)
1948	Richard A. Gonzalez (U.S.)	Eric W. Sturgess (South Africa)
1949	Richard A. Gonzalez (U.S.)	Fredrick Schroeder (U.S.)
1950	Arthur Larsen (U.S.)	Herbert Flam (U.S.)
1951	Frank Sedgman (Australia)	E. Victor Seixas, Jr. (U.S.)
1952	Frank Sedgman (Australia)	Gardnar Mulloy (U.S.)
1953	Tony Trabert (U.S.)	E. Victor Seixas, Jr. (U.S.)
1954	E. Victor Seixas, Jr. (U.S.)	Rex Hartwig (Australia)
1955	Tony Trabert (U.S.)	Ken Rosewall (Australia)
1956	Ken Rosewall (Australia)	Lewis Hoad (Australia)
1957	Malcolm J. Anderson (Australia)	Ashley J. Cooper (Australia)
1958	Ashley J. Cooper (Australia)	Malcolm J. Anderson (Australia)
1959	Neale Fraser (Australia)	Alejandro Olmedo (Peru)
1960	Neale Fraser (Australia)	Rod Laver (Australia)
1961	Roy Emerson (Australia)	Rod Laver (Australia)
1962	Rod Laver (Australia)	Roy Emerson (Australia)
1963	Rafael Osuna (Mexico)	Frank Froehling, III (U.S.)
1964	Roy Emerson (Australia)	Fred Stolle (Australia)
1965	Manuel Santana (Spain)	Cliff Drysdale (South Africa)
1966	Fred Stolle (Australia)	John Newcombe (Australia)
1967	John Newcombe (Australia)	Clark Graebner (U.S.)
1968	Arthur Ashe (U.S.)	Tom Okker (Netherlands)

YEAR	CHAMPION	RUNNER-UP
1969	Rod Laver (Australia)	Tony Roche (Australia)
1970	Ken Rosewall (Australia)	Tony Roche (Australia)
1971	Stan Smith (U.S.)	Jan Kodes (Czechoslovakia)
1972	Ilie Nastase (Romania)	Arthur Ashe (U.S.)
1973	John Newcombe (Australia)	Jan Kodes (Czechoslovakia)
1974	Jimmy Connors (U.S.)	Ken Rosewall (Australia)
1975	Manuel Orantes (Spain)	Jimmy Connors (U.S.)
1976	Jimmy Connors (U.S.)	Bjorn Borg (Sweden)
1977	Guillermo Villas (Argentina)	Jimmy Connors (U.S.)
1978	Jimmy Connors (U.S.)	Bjorn Borg (Sweden)
1979	John McEnroe (U.S.)	Vitas Gerulaitis (U.S.)
1980	John McEnroe (U.S.)	Bjorn Borg (Sweden)
1981	John McEnroe (U.S.)	Bjorn Borg (Sweden)
1982	Jimmy Connors (U.S.)	Ivan Lendl (Czechoslovakia)
1983	Jimmy Connors (U.S.)	Ivan Lendl (Czechoslovakia)
1984	John McEnroe (U.S.)	Ivan Lendl (Czechoslovakia)
1985	Ivan Lendl (Czechoslovakia)	John McEnroe (U.S.)
1986	Ivan Lendl (Czechoslovakia)	Miloslav Mecir (Czechoslovakia)
1987	Ivan Lendl (Czechoslovakia)	Mats Wilander (Sweden)
1988	Mats Wilander (Sweden)	Ivan Lendl (Czechoslovakia)
1989	Boris Becker (West Germany)	Ivan Lendl (Czechoslovakia)
1990	Pete Sampras (U.S.)	Andre Agassi (U.S.)
1991	Stefan Edberg (Sweden)	Jim Courier (U.S.)
1992	Stefan Edberg (Sweden)	Pete Sampras (U.S.)
1993	Pete Sampras (U.S.)	Cedric Pioline (France)
1994	Andre Agassi (U.S.)	Michael Stich (Germany)
1995	Pete Sampras (U.S.)	Andre Agassi (U.S.)
1996	Pete Sampras (U.S.)	Michael Chang (U.S.)
1997	Patrick Rafter (Australia)	Greg Rusedski (Great Britain)

Source: U.S. Open

U.S. Open Champions—Women's Singles

YEAR	CHAMPION	RUNNER-UP
1887	Ellen Hansell (U.S.)	Laura Knight (U.S.)
1888	Bertha L. Townsend (U.S.)	Ellen Hansell (U.S.)
1889	Bertha L. Townsend (U.S.)	Lida D. Voorhes (U.S.)
1890	Ellen C. Roosevelt (U.S.)	Bertha L. Townsend (U.S.)

YEAR	CHAMPION	RUNNER-UP
1891	Mabel Cahill (U.S.)	Ellen C. Roosevelt (U.S.)
1892	Mabel Cahill (U.S.)	Elisabeth Moore (U.S.)
1893	Aline Terry (U.S.)	Augusta Schultz (U.S.)
1894	Helen Hellwig (U.S.)	Aline Terry (U.S.)

YEAR	CHAMPION	RUNNER-UP
1895	Juliette Atkinson (U.S.)	Helen Hellwig (U.S.)
1896	Elisabeth Moore (U.S.)	Juliette Atkinson (U.S.)
1897	Juliette Atkinson (U.S.)	Elisabeth Moore (U.S.)
1898	Juliette Atkinson (U.S.)	Marion Jones (U.S.)
1899	Marion Jones (U.S.)	Maud Banks (U.S.)
1900	Myrtle McAteer (U.S.)	Edith Parker (U.S.)
1901	Elisabeth Moore (U.S.)	Myrtle McAteer (U.S.)
1902	Marion Jones (U.S.)	Elisabeth Moore (U.S.)
1903	Elisabeth Moore (U.S.)	Marion Jones (U.S.)
1904	May Sutton (U.S.)	Elisabeth Moore (U.S.)
1905	Elisabeth Moore (U.S.)	Helen Homans (U.S.)
1906	Helen Homans (U.S.)	Maud Barger-Wallach (U.S.)
1907	Evelyn Sears (U.S.)	Carrie Neely (U.S.)
1908	Maud Barger-Wallach (U.S.)	Evelyn Sears (U.S.)
1909	Hazel Hotchkiss (U.S.)	Maud Barger-Wallach (U.S.)
1910	Hazel Hotchkiss (U.S.)	Louise Hammond (U.S.)
1911	Hazel Hotchkiss (U.S.)	Florence Sutton (U.S.)
1912	Mary K. Browne (U.S.)	Eleonora Sears (U.S.)
1913	Mary K. Browne (U.S.)	Dorothy Green (U.S.)
1914	Mary K. Browne (U.S.)	Marie Wagner (U.S.)
1915	Molla Bjurstedt (Norway)	Hazel Hotchkiss Wightman (U.S.)
1916	Molla Bjurstedt (Norway)	Louise Hammond Raymond (U.S.)
1917	Molla Bjurstedt (Norway)	Marion Vanderhoef (U.S.)
1918	Molla Bjurstedt (Norway)	Eleanor E. Goss (U.S.)
1919	Hazel Hotchkiss Wightman (U.S.)	Marion Zinderstein (U.S.)
1920	Molla B. Mallory (U.S.)	Marion Zinderstein (U.S.)
1921	Molla B. Mallory (U.S.)	Mary K. Browne (U.S.)
1922	Molla B. Mallory (U.S.)	Helen Wills (U.S.)
1923	Helen Wills (U.S.)	Molla B. Mallory (U.S.)
1924	Helen Wills (U.S.)	Molla B. Mallory (U.S.)
1925	Helen Wills (U.S.)	Kathleen McKane (Great Britain)
1926	Molla B. Mallory (U.S.)	Elizabeth Ryan (U.S.)
1927	Helen Wills (U.S.)	Betty Nuthall (Great Britain)
1928	Helen Wills (U.S.)	Helen H. Jacobs (U.S.)
1929	Helen Wills (U.S.)	Phoebe Holcroft Watson (Great Britain)
1930	Betty Nuthall (Great Britain)	Anna McCune Harper (U.S.)
1931	Helen Wills Moody (U.S.)	Eileen Bennett Whitingstall (Great Britain)
1932	Helen H. Jacobs (U.S.)	Carolin A. Babcock (U.S.)
1933	Helen H. Jacobs (U.S.)	Helen Wills Moody (U.S.)
1934	Helen H. Jacobs (U.S.)	Sarah H. Palfrey (U.S.)
1935	Helen H. Jacobs (U.S.)	Sarah Palfrey Fabyan (U.S.)
1936	Alice Marble (U.S.)	Helen H. Jacobs (U.S.)
1937	Anita Lizana (Chile)	Jadwiga Jedrzejowska (Poland)
1938	Alice Marble (U.S.)	Nancye Wynne (Australia)
1939	Alice Marble (U.S.)	Helen H. Jacobs (U.S.)
1940	Alice Marble (U.S.)	Helen H. Jacobs (U.S.)
1941	Sarah Palfrey Cooke (U.S.)	Pauline Betz (U.S.)
1942	Pauline Betz (U.S.)	A. Louise Brough (U.S.)
1943	Pauline Betz (U.S.)	A. Louise Brough (U.S.)
1944	Pauline Betz (U.S.)	Margaret Osborne (U.S.)
1945	Sarah Palfrey Cooke (U.S.)	Pauline Betz (U.S.)
1946	Pauline Betz (U.S.)	Patricia Canning (U.S.)
1947	A. Louise Brough (U.S.)	Margaret Osborne (U.S.)
1948	Margaret Osborne duPont (U.S.)	A. Louise Brough (U.S.)
1949	Margaret Osborne duPont (U.S.)	Doris Hart (U.S.)
1950	Margaret Osborne duPont (U.S.)	Doris Hart (U.S.)
1951	Maureen Connolly (U.S.)	Shirley J. Fry (U.S.)
1952	Maureen Connolly (U.S.)	Doris Hart (U.S.)
1953	Maureen Connolly (U.S.)	Doris Hart (U.S.)
1954	Doris Hart (U.S.)	A. Louise Brough (U.S.)
1955	Doris Hart (U.S.)	Patricia Ward (Great Britain)
1956	Shirley J. Fry (U.S.)	Althea Gibson (U.S.)
1957	Althea Gibson (U.S.)	A. Louise Brough (U.S.)
1958	Althea Gibson (U.S.)	Darlene R. Hard (U.S.)
1959	Maria Bueno (Brazil)	Christine Truman (Great Britain)
1960	Darlene R. Hard (U.S.)	Maria Bueno (Brazil)
1961	Darlene R. Hard (U.S.)	Ann Haydon (Great Britain)
1962	Margaret Smith (Australia)	Darlene R. Hard (U.S.)
1963	Maria Bueno (Brazil)	Margaret Smith (Australia)
1964	Maria Bueno (Brazil)	Carole Caldwell Graebner (U.S.)
1965	Margaret Smith (Australia)	Billie Jean Moffitt (U.S.)
1966	Maria Bueno (Brazil)	Nancy Richey (U.S.)
1967	Billie Jean Moffitt King (U.S.)	Ann Haydon Jones (Great Britain)
1968	Virginia Wade (Great Britain)	Billie Jean King (U.S.)
1969	Margaret Smith Court (Australia)	Nancy Richey (U.S.)
1970	Margaret Smith Court (Australia)	Rosemary Casals (U.S.)
1971	Billie Jean King (U.S.)	Rosemary Casals (U.S.)
1972	Billie Jean King (U.S.)	Kerry Melville (Australia)

YEAR	CHAMPION	RUNNER-UP
1973	Margaret Smith Court (Australia)	Evonne Goolagong (Australia)
1974	Billie Jean King (U.S.)	Evonne Goolagong (Australia)
1975	Chris Evert (U.S.)	Evonne Goolagong (Australia)
1976	Chris Evert (U.S.)	Evonne Goolagong (Australia)
1977	Chris Evert (U.S.)	Wendy Turnbull (Australia)
1978	Chris Evert (U.S.)	Pam Shriver (U.S.)
1979	Tracy Austin (U.S.)	Chris Evert Lloyd (U.S.)
1980	Chris Evert Lloyd (U.S.)	Hana Mandlikova (Czechoslovakia)
1981	Tracy Austin (U.S.)	Martina Navratilova (U.S.)
1982	Chris Evert Lloyd (U.S.)	Hana Mandikova (Czechoslovakia)
1983	Martina Navratilova (U.S.)	Chris Evert Lloyd (U.S.)
1984	Martina Navratilova (U.S.)	Chris Evert Lloyd (U.S.)
1985	Hana Mandlikova (Czechoslovakia)	Martina Navratilova (U.S.)
1986	Martina Navratilova (U.S.)	Helena Sukova (Czechoslovakia)

YEAR	CHAMPION	RUNNER-UP
1987	Martina Navratilova (U.S.)	Steffi Graf (West Germany)
1988	Steffi Graf (West Germany)	Gabriela Sabatini (Argentina)
1989	Steffi Graf (West Germany)	Martina Navratilova (U.S.)
1990	Gabriela Sabatini (Argentina)	Steffi Graf (West Germany)
1991	Monica Seles (Yugoslavia)	Martina Navratilova (U.S.)
1992	Monica Seles (Yugoslavia)	Arantxa Sanchez Vicario (Spain)
1993	Steffi Graf (Germany)	Helena Sukova (Czech Republic)
1994	Arantxa Sanchez Vicario (Spain)	Steffi Graf (Germany)
1995	Steffi Graf (Germany)	Monica Seles (U.S.)
1996	Steffi Graf (Germany)	Monica Seles (U.S.)
1997	Martina Hingis (Switzerland)	Venus Williams (U.S.)

Source: U.S. Open

U.S. Open Doubles Champions

Men's

1881: Clarence M. Clark–Fred W. Taylor
1882: Richard D. Sears–James Dwight
1883: Richard D. Sears–James Dwight
1884: Richard D. Sears–James Dwight
1885: Richard D. Sears–Joseph S. Clark
1886: Richard D. Sears–James Dwight
1887: Richard D. Sears–James Dwight
1888: Oliver S. Campbell–Valentine G. Hall
1889: Henry W. Slocum, Jr.–Howard A. Taylor
1890: Valentine G. Hall–Clarence Hobart
1891: Oliver S. Campbell–Robert Huntington, Jr.
1892: Oliver S. Campbell–Robert Huntington, Jr.
1893: Clarence Hobart–Fred H. Hovey
1894: Clarence Hobart–Fred H. Hovey
1895: Malcolm G. Chace–Robert D. Wrenn
1896: Carr B. Neel–Samuel R. Neel
1897: Leo E. Ware–George P. Sheldon, Jr.
1898: Leo E. Ware–George P. Sheldon, Jr.
1899: Holcombe Ward–Dwight F. Davis
1900: Holcombe Ward–Dwight F. Davis
1901: Holcombe Ward–Dwight F. Davis
1902: Reginald F. Doherty–Hugh L. Doherty
1903: Reginald F. Doherty–Hugh L. Doherty
1904: Holcombe Ward–Beals C. Wright
1905: Holcombe Ward–Beals C. Wright
1906: Holcombe Ward–Beals C. Wright
1907: Fred B. Alexander–Harold H. Hackett
1908: Fred B. Alexander–Harold H. Hackett

1909: Fred B. Alexander–Harold H. Hackett
1910: Fred B. Alexander–Harold H. Hackett
1911: Raymond D. Little–Gustave Touchard
1912: Maurice E. McLoughlin–Thomas C. Bundy
1913: Maurice E. McLoughlin–Thomas C. Bundy
1914: Maurice E. McLoughlin–Thomas C. Bundy
1915: William Johnston–Clarence Griffin
1916: William Johnston–Clarence Griffin
1917: Fred Alexander–Harold Throckmorton
1918: William Tilden, 2nd–Vincent Richards
1919: Norman E. Brookes–Gerald Patterson
1920: William Johnston–Clarence Griffin
1921: William Tilden, 2nd–Vincent Richards
1922: William Tilden, 2nd–Vincent Richards
1923: William Tilden, 2nd–Brian I.C. Norton
1924: Howard Kinsey–Robert Kinsey
1925: Richard Williams, 2nd–Vincent Richards
1926: Richard Williams, 2nd–Vincent Richards
1927: William Tilden, 2nd–Francis T. Hunter
1928: George M. Lott, Jr–John Hennessey
1929: George M. Lott, Jr.–John H. Doeg
1930: George M. Lott, Jr.–John H. Doeg
1931: Wilmer L. Allison–John Van Ryn
1932: H. Ellsworth Vines, Jr.–Keith Gledhill
1933: George M. Lott, Jr.–Lester R. Stoefen
1934: George M. Lott, Jr.–Lester R. Stoefen
1935: Wilmer L. Allison–John Van Ryn
1936: J. Donald Budge–C. Gene Mako
1937: Gottfried von Cramm–Henner Henkel

1938: J. Donald Budge–C. Gene Mako
1939: Adrian K. Quist–John E. Bromwich
1940: Jack Kramer–Frederick R. Schroeder, Jr.
1941: Jack Kramer–Frederick R. Schroeder, Jr.
1942: Lt. Gardnar Mulloy–William F. Talbert
1943: Jack Kramer–Frank A. Parker
1944: Lt. W. Donald McNeill–Robert Falkenburg
1945: Lt. Gardnar Mulloy–William F. Talbert
1946: Gardnar Mulloy–William F. Talbert
1947: Jack Kramer–Frederick R. Schroeder, Jr.
1948: Gardnar Mulloy–William F. Talbert
1949: John Bromwich–William Sidwell
1950: John Bromwich–Frank Sedgman
1951: Kenneth McGregor–Frank Sedgman
1952: Mervyn Rose–E. Victor Seixas, Jr.
1953: Rex Hartwig–Mervyn Rose
1954: E. Victor Seixas, Jr.–Tony Trabert
1955: Kosei Kamo–Atushi Miyagi
1956: Lewis Hoad–Kenneth Rosewall
1957: Ashley J. Cooper–Neale Fraser
1958: Alex Olmedo–Hamilton Richardson
1959: Neale Fraser–Roy Emerson
1960: Neale Fraser–Roy Emerson
1961: Charles McKinley–Dennis Ralston
1962: Rafael Osuna–Antonio Palafox
1963: Charles McKinley–Dennis Ralston
1964: Charles McKinley–Dennis Ralston
1965: Roy Emerson–Fred Stolle
1966: Roy Emerson–Fred Stolle
1967: John Newcombe–Tony Roche
1968: Robert Lutz–Stan Smith
1969: Ken Rosewall–Fred Stolle
1970: Pierre Barthes–Nikki Pilic
1971: John Newcombe–Roger Taylor
1972: Cliff Drysdale–Roger Taylor
1973: Owen Davidson–John Newcombe
1974: Robert Lutz–Stan Smith
1975: Jimmy Connors–Ilie Nastase
1976: Marty Riessen–Tom Okker
1977: Bob Hewitt–Frew McMillan
1978: Robert Lutz–Stan Smith
1979: John McEnroe–Peter Fleming
1980: Robert Lutz–Stan Smith
1981: John McEnroe–Peter Fleming
1982: Kevin Curren–Steve Denton
1983: John McEnroe–Peter Fleming
1984: John Fitzgerald–Tomas Smid
1985: Ken Flach–Robert Seguso
1986: Andres Gomez–Slobodan Zivojinovic
1987: Stefan Edberg–Anders Jarryd
1988: Sergio Casal–Emilio Sanchez
1989: John McEnroe–Mark Woodforde
1990: Pieter Aldrich–Danie Visser
1991: John Fitzgerald–Anders Jarryd
1992: Jim Grabb–Richey Reneberg
1993: Ken Flach–Rick Leach
1994: Jacco Eltingh–Paul Haarhuis

1995: Todd Woodbridge–Mark Woodforde
1996: Todd Woodbridge–Mark Woodforde
1997: Yevgeny Kafelnikov–Daniel Vacek

Women's

1889: Bertha Townsend–Margarette Ballard
1890: Ellen C. Roosevelt–Grace W. Roosevelt
1891: Mabel Cahill–Mrs. W. Fellowes Morgan
1892: Mabel E. Cahill–Adeline McKinlay
1893: Aline M. Terry–Hattie Butler
1894: Helen Hellwig–Juliette P. Atkinson
1895: Helen Hellwig–Juliette P. Atkinson
1896: Elisabeth H. Moore–Juliette P. Atkinson
1897: Juliette P. Atkinson–Kathleen Atkinson
1898: Juliette P. Atkinson–Kathleen Atkinson
1899: Jane W. Craven–Myrtle McAteer
1900: Edith Parker–Hallie Champlin
1901: Juliette P. Atkinson–Myrtle McAteer
1902: Juliette P. Atkinson–Marion Jones
1903: Elisabeth H. Moore–Carrie B. Neely
1904: May G. Sutton–Miriam Hall
1905: Helen Homans–Carrie B. Neely
1906: Mrs. L.S. Coe–Mrs. D.S. Platt
1907: Marie Wimer–Carrie B. Neely
1908: Evelyn Sears–Margaret Curtis
1909: Hazel V. Hotchkiss–Edith E. Rotch
1910: Hazel V. Hotchkiss–Edith E. Rotch
1911: Hazel V. Hotchkiss–Eleanora Sears
1912: Dorothy Green–Mary K. Browne
1913: Mary K. Browne–Mrs. R.H. Williams
1914: Mary K. Browne–Mrs. R.H. Williams
1915: Hazel Hotchkiss Wightman–Eleonora Sears
1916: Molla Bjurstedt–Eleanora Sears
1917: Molla Bjurstedt–Eleanora Sears
1918: Marion Zinderstein–Eleanor Goss
1919: Marion Zinderstein–Eleanor Goss
1920: Marion Zinderstein–Eleanor Goss
1921: Mary K. Browne–Mrs. R. H. Williams
1922: Marion Zinderstein Jessup–Helen N. Wills
1923: Kathleen McKane–Phyllis H. Covell
1924: Hazel Hotchkiss Wightman–Helen N. Wills
1925: Mary K. Browne–Helen N. Wills
1926: Elizabeth Ryan–Eleanor Goss
1927: Kathleen Godfree–Ermyntrude Harvey
1928: Hazel Hotchkiss Wightman–Helen N. Wills
1929: Phoebe Watson–Peggy S. Michell
1930: Betty Nuthall–Sarah Palfrey
1931: Betty Nuthall–Eileen B. Whitingstall
1932: Helen Jacobs–Sarah Palfrey
1933: Betty Nuthall–Freda James
1934: Helen Jacobs–Sarah Palfrey
1935: Helen Jacobs–Sarah Palfrey Fabyan
1936: Marjorie G. Van Ryn–Carolin Babcock
1937: Sarah Palfrey Fabyan–Alice Marble
1938: Sarah Palfrey Fabyan–Alice Marble
1939: Sarah Palfrey Fabyan–Alice Marble
1940: Sarah Palfrey Fabyan–Alice Marble
1941: Sarah Palfrey Fabyan–Margaret E. Osborne

1942: A. Louise Brough–Margaret E. Osborne
1943: A. Louise Brough–Margaret E. Osborne
1944: A. Louise Brough–Margaret E. Osborne
1945: A. Louise Brough–Margaret E. Osborne
1946: A. Louise Brough–Margaret E. Osborne
1947: A. Lousie Brough–Margaret E. Osborne
1948: A. Louise Brough–Margaret O. duPont
1949: A. Louise Brough–Margaret O. duPont
1950: A. Louise Brough–Margaret O. duPont
1951: Shirley Fry–Doris Hart
1952: Shirley Fry–Doris Hart
1953: Shirley Fry–Doris Hart
1954: Shirley Fry–Doris Hart
1955: A. Louise Brough–Margaret O. duPont
1956: A. Louise Brough–Margaret O. duPont
1957: A. Louise Brough–Margaret O. duPont
1958: Jeanne M. Arth–Darlene R. Hard
1959: Jeanne M. Arth–Darlene R. Hard
1960: Maria Bueno–Darlene R. Hard
1961: Darlene R. Hard–Lesley Turner
1962: Darlene R. Hard–Maria Bueno
1963: Robyn Ebbern–Margaret Smith

1964: Billie Jean Moffitt–Karen H. Susman
1965: Carole Caldwell Graebner–Nancy Richey
1966: Maria Bueno–Nancy Richey
1967: Rosemary Casals–Billie Jean King
1968: Maria Bueno–Margaret Smith Court
1969: Francoise Durr–Darlene R. Hard
1970: Margaret Smith Court–Judy Tegart Dalton
1971: Rosemary Casals–Judy Tegart Dalton
1972: Francoise Durr–Betty Stove
1973: Margaret Smith Court–Virginia Wade
1974: Rosemary Casals–Billie Jean King
1975: Margaret Smith Court–Virginia Wade
1976: Delina Boshoff–Ilana Kloss
1977: Martina Navratilova–Betty Stove
1978: Billie Jean King–Martina Navratilova
1979: Betty Stove–Wendy Turnbull
1980: Billie Jean King–Martina Navratilova
1981: Anne Smith–Kathy Jordan
1982: Rosemary Casals–Wendy Turnbull
1983: Pam Shriver–Martina Navratilova
1984: Pam Shriver–Martina Navratilova
1985: Claudia Kohde-Kilsch–Helena Sukova

U.S. Open Winners' Prize Money

	Singles		Doubles (per team)		
	Men	Women	Men	Women	Mixed
1968	$14,000	$6,000	$4,200	$1,750	–
1969	16,000	6,000	3,000	2,000	$2.000
1970	20,000	7,500	3,000	2,000	2,000
1971	15,000	5,000	2,000	1,000	1,000
1972	25,000	10,000	3,000	2,000	2,000
1973	25,000	25,000	4,000	4,000	2,000
1974	22,500	22,500	4,500	4,500	2,000
1975	25,000	25,000	4,500	4,500	2,000
1976	30,000	30,000	12,000	12,000	6,500
1977	33,000	33,000	13,125	13,125	6,500
1978	38,000	38,000	15,500	15,500	6,500
1979	39,000	39,000	15,750	15,750	7,100
1980	46,000	46,000	18,500	18,500	7,100
1981	66,000	66,000	26,400	26,400	9,680
1982	90,000	90,000	36,000	36,000	14,000
1983	120,000	120,000	48,000	48,000	17,000
1984	160,000	160,000	64,000	64,000	17,000
1985	187,500	187,500	65,000	65,000	19,000
1986	210,000	210,000	72,800	72,800	21,800
1987	250,000	250,000	86,667	86,667	26,160
1988	275,000	275,000	95,333	95,333	28,800
1989	300,000	300,000	104,000	104,000	34,000
1990	350,000	350,000	142,861	142,861	42,500
1991	400,000	400,000	163,500	163,500	46,500
1992	500,000	500,000	184,000	184,000	46,500
1993	535,000	535,000	200,000	200,000	46,500
1994	550,000	550,000	200,000	200,000	46,500
1995	575,000	575,000	210,000	210,000	50,000
1996	600,000	600,000	240,000	240,000	60,000
1997	650,000	650,000	300,000	300,000	100,000

Source: U.S. Open

1986: Martina Navratilova–Pam Shriver
1987: Martina Navratilova–Pam Shriver
1988: Gigi Fernandez–Robin White
1989: Hana Mandlikova–Martina Navratilova
1990: Gigi Fernandez–Martina Navratilova
1991: Pam Shriver–Natalia Zvereva

1992: Gigi Fernandez–Natalia Zvereva
1993: Arantxa Sanchez Vicario–Helena Sukova
1994: Jana Novotna–Arantxa Sanchez Vicario
1995: Gigi Fernandez–Natasha Zvereva
1996: Gigi Fernandez–Natasha Zvereva
1997: Lindsay Davenport–Jana Novotna

U.S. Open "Triple Crowns"

Thirty times in the history of the national championships, a player has accomplished the feat of winning all three possible titles in the same year—singles, doubles, and mixed doubles. This has been done by 21 players, 15 women and 6 men. Here are the three-championship winners:

1892: Mabel Cahill
1895: Juliette P. Atkinson
1909: Hazel Hotchkiss Wightman
1910: Hazel Hotchkiss Wightman
1911: Hazel Hotchkiss Wightman
1912: Mary K. Browne
1913: Mary K. Browne
1914: Mary K. Browne
1917: Molla Bjurstedt
1922: Bill Tilden
1923: Bill Tilden
1924: Helen N. Wills
1928: Helen N. Wills
1934: Helen H. Jacobs

1938: Don Budge, Alice Marble*
1939: Alice Marble
1940: Alice Marble
1941: Sarah Palfrey (Fabyan) Cooke
1947: Louise Brough
1950: Margaret O. duPont
1951: Frank Sedgman
1954: Vic Seixas, Doris Hart*
1956: Ken Rosewall
1959: Neale Fraser
1960: Neale Fraser
1967: Billie Jean King
1970: Margaret Smith Court
1987: Martina Navratilova

*Only twice have two players combined on a championship mixed doubles team and also won both of their own titles in singles and doubles, 1938 (Budge and Marble) and 1954 (Seixas and Hart).

Source: U.S. Open

Wimbledon Champions

YEAR	Men's	Women's	YEAR	Men's	Women's
1877	Spencer Gore		1897	Reggie Doherty	Blanche Bingley Hillyard
1878	Frank Hadow				
1879	John Hartley		1898	Reggie Doherty	Charlotte Cooper
1880	John Hartley		1899	Reggie Doherty	Blanche Bingley Hillyard
1881	William Renshaw				
1882	William Renshaw		1900	Reggie Doherty	Blanche Bingley Hillyard
1883	William Renshaw				
1884	William Renshaw	Maud Watson	1901	Arthur Gore	Charlotte Cooper Sterry
1885	William Renshaw	Maud Watson			
1886	William Renshaw	Blanche Bingley	1902	Laurie Doherty	Muriel Robb
1887	Herbert Lawford	Charlotte Dod	1903	Laurie Doherty	Dorothea Douglass
1888	Ernest Renshaw	Charlotte Dod	1904	Laurie Doherty	Dorothea Douglass
1889	William Renshaw	Blanche Bingley Hillyard	1905	Laurie Doherty	May Sutton
			1906	Laurie Doherty	Dorothea Douglass
1890	William Hamilton	Lena Rice	1907	Norman Brookes	May Sutton
1891	Wilfred Baddeley	Charlotte Dod	1908	Arthur Gore	Charlotte Cooper Sterry
1892	Wilfred Baddeley	Charlotte Dod			
1893	Joshua Pim	Charlotte Dod	1909	Arthur Gore	Dora Boothby
1894	Joshua Pim	Blanche Bingley Hillyard	1910	Anthony Wilding	Dorothea Lambert Chambers
1895	Wilfred Baddeley	Charlotte Cooper	1911	Anthony Wilding	Dorothea Lambert Chambers
1896	Harold Mahoney	Charlotte Cooper			

YEAR	Men's	Women's	YEAR	Men's	Women's
1912	Anthony Wilding	Ethel Thomson Larcombe	1959	Alex Olmedo	Maria Bueno
1913	Anthony Wilding	Dorothea Lambert Chambers	1960	Neale Fraser	Maria Bueno
1914	Norman Brookes	Dorothea Lambert Chambers	1961	Rod Laver	Angela Mortimer
			1962	Rod Laver	Karen Hantze Susman
1915–1918	no tournament		1963	Chuck McKinley	Margaret Smith
1919	Gerald Patterson	Suzanne Lenglen	1964	Roy Emerson	Maria Bueno
1920	Bill Tilden	Suzanne Lenglen	1965	Roy Emerson	Margaret Smith
1921	Bill Tilden	Suzanne Lenglen	1966	Manuel Santana	Billie Jean King
1922	Gerald Patterson	Suzanne Lenglen	1967	John Newcombe	Billie Jean King
1923	William Johnston	Suzanne Lenglen	1968	Rod Laver	Billie Jean King
1924	Jean Borotra	Kathleen McKane	1969	Rod Laver	Ann Haydon Jones
1925	Rene Lacoste	Suzanne Lenglen	1970	John Newcombe	Margaret Smith Court
1926	Jean Borotra	Kathleen McKane Godfree	1971	John Newcombe	Evonne Goolagong
1927	Henri Cochet	Helen Wills	1972	Stan Smith	Billie Jean King
1928	Rene Lacoste	Helen Wills	1973	Jan Kodes	Billie Jean King
1929	Henri Cochet	Helen Wills	1974	Jimmy Connors	Chris Evert
1930	Bill Tilden	Helen Wills Moody	1975	Arthur Ashe	Billie Jean King
1931	Sidney Wood	Cilly Aussem	1976	Bjorn Borg	Chris Evert
1932	Ellsworth Vines	Helen Wills Moody	1977	Bjorn Borg	Virginia Wade
1933	Jack Crawford	Helen Wills Moody	1978	Bjorn Borg	Martina Navratilova
1934	Fred Perry	Dorothy Round	1979	Bjorn Borg	Martina Navratilova
1935	Fred Perry	Helen Wills Moody	1980	Bjorn Borg	Evonne Goolagong Cawley
1936	Fred Perry	Helen Jacobs	1981	John McEnroe	Chris Evert Lloyd
1937	Don Budge	Dorothy Round	1982	Jimmy Connors	Martina Navratilova
1938	Don Budge	Helen Wills Moody	1983	John McEnroe	Martina Navratilova
1939	Bobby Riggs	Alice Marble	1984	John McEnroe	Martina Navratilova
1940–1945	no tournament		1985	Boris Becker	Martina Navratilova
1946	Yvon Petra	Pauline Betz	1986	Boris Becker	Martina Navratilova
1947	Jack Kramer	Margaret Osborne	1987	Pat Cash	Martina Navratilova
1948	Bob Falkenburg	Louise Brough	1988	Stefan Edberg	Steffi Graf
1949	Ted Schroeder	Louise Brough	1989	Boris Becker	Steffi Graf
1950	Budge Patty	Louise Brough	1990	Stefan Edberg	Martina Navratilova
1951	Dick Savitt	Doris Hart	1991	Michael Stich	Steffi Graf
1952	Frank Sedgman	Maureen Connolly	1992	Andre Agassi	Steffi Graf
1953	Vic Seixas	Maureen Connolly	1993	Pete Sampras	Steffi Graf
1954	Jaroslav Drobny	Maureen Connolly	1994	Pete Sampras	Conchita Martinez
1955	Tony Trabert	Louise Brough	1995	Pete Sampras	Steffi Graf
1956	Lew Hoad	Shirley Fry	1996	Richard Krajicek	Steffi Graf
1957	Lew Hoad	Althea Gibson	1997	Pete Sampras	Martina Hingis
1958	Ashley Cooper	Althea Gibson			

Source: Wimbledon Compendium

ATP Tour Prize Money Leaders

1968: Tony Roche	$63,504	1978: Eddie Dibbs	$575,273
1969: Rod Laver	$124,000	1979: Bjorn Borg	$1,008,742
1970: Rod Laver	$201,453	1980: John McEnroe	$972,369
1971: Rod Laver	$292,717	1981: John McEnroe	$991,000
1972: Ilie Nastase	$176,000	1982: Ivan Lendl	$2,028,850
1973: Ilie Nastase	$228,750	1983: Ivan Lendl	$1,747,128
1974: Jimmy Connors	$285,490	1984: John McEnroe	$2,026,109
1975: Arthur Ashe	$326,750	1985: Ivan Lendl	$1,971,074
1976: Raul Ramirez	$484,343	1986: Ivan Lendl	$1,987,537
1977: Guillermo Vilas	$766,065	1987: Ivan Lendl	$2,003,656

1988: Mats Wilander	$1,726,731	1994: Pete Sampras	$4,857,812
1989: Ivan Lendl	$2,344,367	1995: Pete Sampras	$5,415,066
1990: Pete Sampras	$2,900,057	1996: Boris Becker	$4,313,007
1991: David Wheaton	$2,479,239		
1992: Michael Stich	$2,777,411		
1993: Pete Sampras	$4,579,325	*Source: ATP Tour*	

WTA Tour Prize Money Leaders

1974: Chris Evert	$107,485	1987: Steffi Graf	$1,063,785
1975: Chris Evert	$347,227	1988: Steffi Graf	$1,378,128
1976: Chris Evert	$319,565	1989: Steffi Graf	$1,963,905
1977: Chris Evert	$316,045	1990: Steffi Graf	$1,921,853
1978: Chris Evert	$454,486	1991: Monica Seles	$2,457,758
1979: Martina Navratilova	$618,698	1992: Monica Seles	$2,622,352
1980: Martina Navratilova	$749,250	1993: Steffi Graf	$2,821,337
1981: Martina Navratilova	$865,437	1994: Arantxa Sanchez Vicario	$2,943,665
1982: Martina Navratilova	$1,475,055	1995: Steffi Graf	$2,538,620
1983: Martina Navratilova	$1,456,030	1996: Steffi Graf	$2,665,706
1984: Martina Navratilova	$2,173,556		
1985: Martina Navratilova	$1,328,829		
1986: Martina Navratilova	$1,905,841	*Source: Women's Tennis Association*	

Golf

U.S. Open Championship

1895: Horace Rawlins	1920: Edward Ray
1896: James Foulis	1921: James M. Barnes
1897: Joe Lloyd	1922: Gene Sarazen
1898: Fred Herd	1923: Robert T. Jones, Jr.
1899: Willie Smith	1924: Cyril Walker
1900: Harry Vardon	1925: William Macfarlane
1901: Willie Anderson	1926: Robert T. Jones, Jr.
1902: Laurence Auchterlonie	1927: Tommy Armour
1903: Willie Anderson	1928: Johnny Farrell
1904: Willie Anderson	1929: Robert T. Jones, Jr.
1905: Willie Anderson	1930: Robert T. Jones, Jr.
1906: Alex Smith	1931: Billy Burke
1907: Alex Ross	1932: Gene Sarazen
1908: Fred McLeod	1933: John Goodman
1909: George Sargent	1934: Olin Dutra
1910: Alex Smith	1935: Sam Parks, Jr.
1911: John J. McDermott	1936: Tony Manero
1912: John J. McDermott	1937: Ralph Guldahl
1913: Francis Ouimet	1938: Ralph Guldahl
1914: Walter Hagen	1939: Byron Nelson
1915: Jerome D. Travers	1940: Lawson Little
1916: Charles Evans, Jr.	1941: Craig Wood
1917–18: *	1942–45: *
1919: Walter Hagen	1946: Lloyd Mangrum

1947: Lew Worsham
1948: Ben Hogan
1949: Cary Middlecoff
1950: Ben Hogan
1951: Ben Hogan
1952: Julius Boros
1953: Ben Hogan
1954: Ed Furgol
1955: Jack Fleck
1956: Cary Middlecoff
1957: Dick Mayer
1958: Tommy Bolt
1959: Bill Casper, Jr.
1960: Arnold Palmer
1961: Gene Littler
1962: Jack Nicklaus
1963: Julius Boros
1964: Ken Venturi
1965: Gary Player
1966: Bill Casper, Jr.
1967: Jack Nicklaus
1968: Lee Trevino
1969: Orville Moody
1970: Tony Jacklin
1971: Lee Trevino
1972: Jack Nicklaus
1973: John Miller

1974: Hale Irwin
1975: Lou Graham
1976: Jerry Pate
1977: Hubert Green
1978: Andy North
1979: Hale Irwin
1980: Jack Nicklaus
1981: David Graham
1982: Tom Watson
1983: Larry Nelson
1984: Fuzzy Zoeller
1985: Andy North
1986: Raymond Floyd
1987: Scott Simpson
1988: Curtis Strange
1989: Curtis Strange
1990: Hale Irwin
1991: Payne Stewart
1992: Tom Kite
1993: Lee Janzen
1994: Ernie Els
1995: Corey Pavin
1996: Steve Jones
1997: Ernie Els

*No championships.

Source: U.S. Golf Association

U.S. Women's Open Championship

1946: Patty Berg
1947: Betty Jameson
1948: Babe Didrikson Zaharias
1949: Louise Suggs
1950: Babe Didrikson Zaharias
1951: Betsy Rawls
1952: Louise Suggs
1953: Betsy Rawls
1954: Babe Didrikson Zaharias
1955: Fay Crocker
1956: Kathy Cornelius
1957: Betsy Rawls
1958: Mickey Wright
1959: Mickey Wright
1960: Betsy Rawls
1961: Mickey Wright
1962: Murle Lindstrom
1963: Mary Mills
1964: Mickey Wright
1965: Carol Mann
1966: Sandra Spuzich
1967: Catherine Lacoste
1968: Susie Maxwell Berning
1969: Donna Caponi
1970: Donna Caponi
1971: JoAnne Gunderson Carner
1972: Susie Maxwell Berning

1973: Susie Maxwell Berning
1974: Sandra Haynie
1975: Sandra Palmer
1976: JoAnne Gunderson Carner
1977: Hollis Stacy
1978: Hollis Stacy
1979: Jerilyn Britz
1980: Amy Alcott
1981: Pat Bradley
1982: Janet Alex
1983: Jan Stephenson
1984: Hollis Stacy
1985: Kathy (Baker) Guadagnino
1986: Jane Geddes
1987: Laura Davies
1988: Liselotte Neumann
1989: Betsy King
1990: Betsy King
1991: Meg Mallon
1992: Patty Sheehan
1993: Lauri Merten
1994: Patty Sheehan
1995: Annika Sorenstam
1996: Annika Sorenstam
1997: Alison Nicholas

Source: U.S. Golf Association

U.S. Senior Open Championship

1980: Roberto de Vicenzo
1981: Arnold Palmer
1982: Miller Barber
1983: Billy Casper
1984: Miller Barber
1985: Miller Barber
1986: Dale Douglass
1987: Gary Player
1988: Gary Player
1989: Orville Moody

1990: Lee Trevino
1991: Jack Nicklaus
1992: Larry Laoretti
1993: Jack Nicklaus
1994: Simon Hobday
1995: Tom Weiskopf
1996: Dave Stockton
1997: Graham Marsh

Source: U.S. Golf Association

Masters Tournament Winners

Year Winner
1934: Horton Smith
1935: Gene Sarazen
1936: Horton Smith
1937: Byron Nelson
1938: Henry Picard
1939: Ralph Guldahl
1940: Jimmy Demaret
1941: Craig Wood
1942: Byron Nelson
1943:-1945:*
1946: Herman Keiser
1947: Jimmy Demaret
1948: Claude Harmon
1949: Sam Snead
1950: Jimmy Demaret
1951: Ben Hogan
1952: Sam Snead
1953: Ben Hogan
1954: Sam Snead
1955: Cary Middlecoff
1956: Jack Burke, Jr.
1957: Doug Ford
1958: Arnold Palmer
1959: Art Wall, Jr.
1960: Arnold Palmer
1961: Gary Player
1962: Arnold Palmer
1963: Jack Nicklaus
1964: Arnold Palmer
1965: Jack Nicklaus

1966: Jack Nicklaus
1967: Gay Brewer, Jr.
1968: Bob Goalby
1969: George Archer
1970: Billy Casper
1971: Charles Coody
1972: Jack Nicklaus
1973: Tommy Aaron
1974: Gary Player
1975: Jack Nicklaus
1976: Ray Floyd
1977: Tom Watson
1978: Gary Player
1979: Fuzzy Zoeller
1980: Seve Ballesteros
1981: Tom Watson
1982: Craig Stadler
1983: Seve Ballesteros
1984: Ben Crenshaw
1985: Bernhard Langer
1986: Jack Nicklaus
1987: Larry Mize
1988: Sandy Lyle
1989: Nick Faldo
1990: Nick Faldo
1991: Ian Woosnam
1992: Fred Couples
1993: Bernhard Langer
1994: Jose Maria Olazabal
1995: Ben Crenshaw
1996: Nick Faldo
1997: Tiger Woods

*No championship

Source: 1997 PGA Tour Media Guide

PGA Championship

Year   Winner
1916: James M. Barnes
1917-1918: *

*No Championship

1919: James M. Barnes
1920: Jock Hutchison
1921: Walter Hagen
1922: Gene Sarazen
1923: Gene Sarazen

1924: Walter Hagen
1925: Walter Hagen
1926: Walter Hagen
1927: Walter Hagen
1928: Leo Diegel
1929: Leo Diegel
1930: Tommy Armour
1931: Tom Creavy
1932: Olin Dutra
1933: Gene Sarazen
1934: Paul Runyan
1935: Johnny Revolta
1936: Denny Shute
1937: Denny Shute
1938: Paul Runyan
1939: Henry Picard
1940: Byron Nelson
1941: Vic Ghezzi
1942: Sam Snead
1943: *
1944: Bob Hamilton
1945: Byron Nelson
1946: Ben Hogan
1947: Jim Ferrier
1948: Ben Hogan
1949: Sam Snead
1950: Chandler Harper
1951: Sam Snead
1952: Jim Turnesa
1953: Walter Burkemo
1954: Chick Harbert
1955: Doug Ford
1956: Jack Burke
1957: Lionel Hebert
1958: Dow Finsterwald
1959: Bob Rosburg
1960: Jay Hebert

1961: Jerry Barber
1962: Gary Player
1963: Jack Nicklaus
1964: Bobby Nichols
1965: Dave Marr
1966: Al Geiberger
1967: Don January (69)
1968: Julius Boros
1969: Raymond Floyd
1970: Dave Stockton
1971: Jack Nicklaus
1972: Gary Player
1973: Jack Nicklaus
1974: Lee Trevino
1975: Jack Nicklaus
1976: Dave Stockton
1977: Lanny Wadkins
1978: John Mahaffey
1979: David Graham
1980: Jack Nicklaus
1981: Larry Nelson
1982: Raymond Floyd
1983: Hal Sutton
1984: Lee Trevino
1985: Hubert Green
1986: Bob Tway
1987: Larry Nelson
1988: Jeff Sluman
1989: Payne Stewart
1990: Wayne Grady
1991: John Daly
1992: Nick Price
1993: Paul Azinger
1994: Nick Price
1995: Steve Elkington
1996: Mark Brooks
1997: Davis Love III

British Open

1860: Willie Park
   (The first event was open only to professional golfers)
1861: Tom Morris, Sr.
   (The second Open was open to amateurs also)
1862: Tom Morris, Sr.
1863: Willie Park
1864: Tom Morris, Sr.
1865: Andrew Strath
1866: Willie Park
1867: Tom Morris, Sr.
1868: Tom Morris, Jr.
1869: Tom Morris, Jr.
1870: Tom Morris, Jr.
1871: *
1872: Tom Morris, Jr.
1873: Tom Kidd
1874: Mungo Park
1875: Willie Park

1876: Bob Martin
1877: Jamie Anderson
1878: Jamie Anderson
1879: Jamie Anderson
1880: Robert Ferguson
1881: Robert Ferguson
1882: Robert Ferguson
1883: Willie Fernie
1884: Jack Simpson
1885: Bob Martin
1886: David Brown
1887: Willie Park, Jr.
1888: Jack Burns
1889: Willie Park, Jr.
1890: John Ball, Jr.
1891: Hugh Kirkaldy
1892: Harold H. Hilton
1893: William Auchterlonie

1894: John H. Taylor	1950: Bobby Locke
1895: John H. Taylor	1951: Max Faulkner
1896: Harry Vardon	1952: Bobby Locke
1897: Harold H. Hilton	1953: Ben Hogan
1898: Harry Vardon	1954: Peter Thomson
1899: Harry Vardon	1955: Peter Thomson
1900: John H. Taylor	1956: Peter Thomson
1901: James Braid	1957: Bobby Locke
1902: Alexander Herd	1958: Peter Thomson
1903: Harry Vardon	1959: Gary Player
1904: Jack White	1960: Kel Nagle
1905: James Braid	1961: Arnold Palmer
1906: James Braid	1962: Arnold Palmer
1907: Arnaud Massy	1963: Bob Charles
1908: James Braid	1964: Tony Lema
1909: John H. Taylor	1965: Peter Thomson
1910: James Braid	1966: Jack Nicklaus
1911: Harry Vardon	1967: Roberto De Vicenzo
1912: Edward (Ted) Ray	1968: Gary Player
1913: John H. Taylor	1969: Tony Jacklin
1914: Harry Vardon	1970: Jack Nicklaus
1915-1919: *	1971: Lee Trevino
1920: George Duncan	1972: Lee Trevino
1921: Jock Hutchison	1973: Tom Weiskopf
1922: Walter Hagen	1974: Gary Player
1923: Arthur G. Havers	1975: Tom Watson
1924: Walter Hagen	1976: Johnny Miller
1925: James M. Barnes	1977: Tom Watson
1926: Robert T. Jones, Jr.	1978: Jack Nicklaus
1927: Robert T. Jones, Jr.	1979: Seve Ballesteros
1928: Walter Hagen	1980: Tom Watson
1929: Walter Hagen	1981: Bill Rogers
1930: Robert T. Jones, Jr.	1982: Tom Watson
1931: Tommy D. Armour	1983: Tom Watson
1932: Gene Sarazen	1984: Seve Ballesteros
1933: Denny Shute	1985: Sandy Lyle
1934: Henry Cotton	1986: Greg Norman
1935: Alfred Perry	1987: Nick Faldo
1936: Alfred Padgham	1988: Seve Ballesteros
1937: Henry Cotton	1989: Mark Calcavecchia
1938: R. A. Whitcombe	1990: Nick Faldo
1939: Richard Burton	1991: Ian Baker-Finch
1940-1945: *	1992: Nick Faldo
1946: Sam Snead	1993: Greg Norman
1947: Fred Daly	1994: Nick Price
1948: Henry Cotton	1995: John Daly
1949: Bobby Locke	1996: Tom Lehman
	1997: Justin Leonard

*No Championship

Professional Golf Association: Leading Money-Winners

1934: Paul Runyan	$6,767	1939: Henry Picard	$10,303
1935: Johnny Revolta	9,543	1940: Ben Hogan	10,655
1936: Horton Smith	7,682	1941: Ben Hogan	18,358
1937: Harry Cooper	14,138	1942: Ben Hogan	13,143
1938: Sam Snead	19,534	1943: No Statistics Compiled	

1944: Byron Nelson (War Bonds)	$37,967	1972: Jack Nicklaus	$320,542
1945: Byron Nelson (War Bonds)	63,335	1973: Jack Nicklaus	308,362
1946: Ben Hogan	42,556	1974: Johnny Miller	353,021
1947: Jimmy Demaret	27,936	1975: Jack Nicklaus	298,149
1948: Ben Hogan	32,112	1976: Jack Nicklaus	266,438
1949: Sam Snead	31,593	1977: Tom Watson	310,653
1950: Sam Snead	35,758	1978: Tom Watson	362,428
1951: Lloyd Mangrum	26,088	1979: Tom Watson	462,636
1952: Julius Boros	37,032	1980: Tom Watson	530,808
1953: Lew Worsham	34,002	1981: Tom Kite	375,698
1954: Bob Toski	65,819	1982: Craig Stadler	446,462
1955: Julius Boros	63,121	1983: Hal Sutton	426,668
1956: Ted Kroll	72,835	1984: Tom Watson	476,260
1957: Dick Mayer	65,835	1985: Curtis Strange	542,321
1958: Arnold Palmer	42,607	1986: Greg Norman	653,296
1959: Art Wall	53,167	1987: Curtis Strange	925,941
1960: Arnold Palmer	75,262	1988: Curtis Strange	1,147,644
1961: Gary Player	64,540	1989: Tom Kite	1,395,278
1962: Arnold Palmer	81,448	1990: Greg Norman	1,165,477
1963: Arnold Palmer	128,230	1991: Corey Pavin	979,430
1964: Jack Nicklaus	113,284	1992: Fred Couples	1,344,188
1965: Jack Nicklaus	140,752	1993: Nick Price	1,478,557
1966: Billy Casper	121,944	1994: Nick Price	1,499,927
1967: Jack Nicklaus	188,998	1995: Greg Norman	1,654,959
1968: Billy Casper	205,168	1996: Tom Lehman	1,780,159
1969: Frank Beard	164,707		
1970: Lee Trevino	157,037		
1971: Jack Nicklaus	244,490	*Source: PGA*	

Ladies Professional Golf Association: Leading Money Winners

1950: Babe Zaharias	$14,800	1975: Sandra Palmer	$76,374
1951: Babe Zaharias	15,087	1976: Judy Rankin	150,734
1952: Betsy Rawls	14,505	1977: Judy Rankin	122,890
1953: Louise Suggs	19,816	1978: Nancy Lopez	189,814
1954: Patty Berg	16,011	1979: Nancy Lopez	197,489
1955: Patty Berg	16,492	1980: Beth Daniel	231,000
1956: Marlene Hagge	20,235	1981: Beth Daniel	206,998
1957: Patty Berg	16,272	1982: JoAnne Carner	310,400
1958: Beverly Hanson	12,639	1983: JoAnne Carner	291,404
1959: Betsy Rawls	26,774	1984: Betsy King	266,771
1960: Louise Suggs	16,892	1985: Nancy Lopez	416,472
1961: Mickey Wright	22,236	1986: Pat Bradley	492,021
1962: Mickey Wright	21,641	1987: Ayako Okamoto	466,034
1963: Mickey Wright	31,269	1988: Sherri Turner	350,851
1964: Mickey Wright	29,800	1989: Betsy King	654,132
1965: Kathy Whitworth	28,658	1990: Beth Daniel	863,578
1966: Kathy Whitworth	33,517	1991: Pat Bradley	763,118
1967: Kathy Whitworth	32,937	1992: Dottie Mochrie	693,335
1968: Kathy Whitworth	48,379	1993: Betsy King	595,992
1969: Carol Mann	49,152	1994: Laura Davies	687,201
1970: Kathy Whitworth	30,235	1995: Annika Sorenstam	666,533
1971: Kathy Whitworth	41,181	1996: Karrie Webb	1,002,000
1972: Kathy Whitworth	65,063		
1973: Kathy Whitworth	82,864		
1974: JoAnne Carner	87,094	*Source: LPGA*	

Horse Racing

Winners of the Kentucky Derby

YEAR	HORSE	JOCKEY	YEAR	HORSE	JOCKEY
1875	Aristides	O. Lewis	1923	Zev	E. Sande
1876	Vagrant	B. Swim	1924	Black Gold	J. D. Mooney
1877	Baden-Baden	W. Walker	1925	Flying Ebony	E. Sande
1878	Day Star	J. Carter	1926	Bubbling Over	A. Johnson
1879	Lord Murphy	C. Shauer	1927	Whiskery	L. McAtee
1880	Fonso	G. Lewis	1928	Reigh Count	C. Lang
1881	Hindoo	J. McLaughlin	1929	Clyde Van Dusen	L. McAtee
1882	Apollo	B. Hurd	1930	Gallant Fox	E. Sande
1883	Leonatus	W. Donohue	1931	Twenty Grand	C. Kurtsinger
1884	Buchanan	I. Murphy	1932	Burgoo King	E. James
1885	Joe Cotton	E. Henderson	1933	Brokers Tip	D. Meade
1886	Ben Ali	P. Duffy	1934	Cavalcade	M. Garner
1887	Montrose	I. Lewis	1935	Omaha	W. Saunders
1888	Macbeth II	G. Covington	1936	Bold Venture	I. Hanford
1889	Spokane	T. Kiley	1937	War Admiral	C. Kurtsinger
1890	Riley	I. Murphy	1938	Lawrin	E. Arcaro
1891	Kingman	I. Murphy	1939	Johnstown	J. Stout
1892	Azra	A. Clayton	1940	Gallahadion	C. Bierman
1893	Lookout	E. Kunze	1941	Whirlaway	E. Arcaro
1894	Chant	F. Goodale	1942	Shut Out	W. Wright
1895	Halma	J. Perkins	1943	Count Fleet	J. Longden
1896	Ben Brush	W. Simms	1944	Pensive	C. McCreary
1897	Typhoon II	F. Garner	1945	Hoop Jr	E. Arcaro
1898	Plaudit	W. Simms	1946	Assault	W. Mehrtens
1899	Manuel	F. Taral	1947	Jet Pilot	E. Guerin
1900	Lieut. Gibson	J. Boland	1948	Citation	E. Arcaro
1901	His Eminence	J. Winkfield	1949	Ponder	S. Brooks
1902	Alan-a-Dale	J. Winkfield	1950	Middleground	W. Boland
1903	Judge Himes	H. Booker	1951	Count Turf	C. McCreary
1904	Elwood	F. Prior	1952	Hill Gail	E. Arcaro
1905	Agile	J. Martin	1953	Dark Star	H. Moreno
1906	Sir Huon	R. Troxler	1954	Determine	R. York
1907	Pink Star	A. Minder	1955	Swaps	W. Shoemaker
1908	Stone Street	A. Pickens	1956	Needles	D. Erb
1909	Wintergreen	V. Powers	1957	Iron Liege	B. Hartack
1910	Donau	F. Herbert	1958	Tim Tam	I. Valenzuela
1911	Meridian	G. Archibald	1959	Tomy Lee	W. Shoemaker
1912	Worth	C. H. Shilling	1960	Venetian Way	B. Hartack
1913	Donerail	R. Goose	1961	Carry Back	J. Sellers
1914	Old Rosebud	J. McCabe	1962	Decidedly	B. Hartack
1915	Regret	J. Notter	1963	Chateaugay	B. Baeza
1916	George Smith	J. Loftus	1964	Northern Dancer	B. Hartack
1917	Omar Khayyam	C. Borel	1965	Lucky Debonair	W. Shoemaker
1918	Exterminator	W. Knapp	1966	Kauai King	D. Brumfield
1919	Sir Barton	J. Loftus	1967	Proud Clarion	B. Ussery
1920	Paul Jones	T. Rice	1968	Forward Pass	I. Valenzuela
1921	Behave Yourself	C. Thompson	1969	Majestic Prince	B. Hartack
1922	Morvich	A. Johnson	1970	Dust Commander	M. Manganello

YEAR	HORSE	JOCKEY	YEAR	HORSE	JOCKEY
1971	Canonero II	G. Avila	1986	Ferdinand	W. Shoemaker
1972	Riva Ridge	R. Turcotte	1987	Alysheba	C. McCarron
1973	Secretariat	R. Turcotte	1988	Winning Colors	G. Stevens
1974	Cannonade	A. Cordero, Jr.	1989	Sunday Silence	P. Valenzuela
1975	Foolish Pleasure	J. Vasquez	1990	Unbridled	C. Perret
1976	Bold Forbes	A. Cordero, Jr.	1991	Strike the Gold	C. Antley
1977	Seattle Slew	J. Cruguet	1992	Lil E. Tee	P. Day
1978	Affirmed	S. Cauthen	1993	Sea Hero	J. Bailey
1979	Spectacular Bid	R. Franklin	1994	Go for Gin	C. McCarron
1980	Genuine Risk	J. Vasquez	1995	Thunder Gulch	G. Stevens
1981	Pleasant Colony	J. Velasquez	1996	Grindstone	J.D. Bailey
1982	Gato Del Sol	E. Delahoussaye	1997	Silver Charm	G. Stevens
1983	Sunny's Halo	E. Delahoussaye			
1984	Swale	L. Pincay, Jr.			
1985	Spend a Buck	A. Cordero, Jr.			

Source: Kentucky Derby Media Guide

Winners of the Preakness Stakes

YEAR	HORSE	JOCKEY	YEAR	HORSE	JOCKEY
1873	Survivor	G. Barbee	1913	Buskin	J. Butwell
1874	Culpepper	W. Donohue	1914	Holiday	A Schuttinger
1875	Tom Ochiltree	L. Hughes	1915	Rhine Maiden	D. Hoffman
1876	Shirley	G. Barbee	1916	Damrosch	L. McAtee
1877	Cloverbrook	C. Holloway	1917	Kalitan	Ev. Haynes
1878	Duke of Magenta	C. Holloway	1918	War Cloud	J. Loftus
1879	Harold	L. Hughes	1918	Jack Hare, Jr.	C. Peak
1880	Grenada	L. Hughes	1919	Sir Barton	J. Loftus
1881	Saunterer	T. Costello	1920	Man o' War	C. Kummer
1882	Vanguard	T. Costello	1921	Broomspun	F. Coltiletti
1883	Jacobus	G. Barbee	1922	Pillory	L. Morris
1884	Knight of Ellerslie	S. Fisher	1923	Vigil	B. Marinelli
1885	Tucumseh	J. McLaughlin	1924	Nellie Morse	J. Merimee
1886	The Bard	S. Fisher	1925	Coventry	C. Kummer
1887	Dunboyne	W. Donohue	1926	Display	J. Maiben
1888	Refund	F. Littlefield	1927	Bostonian	A. Abel
1889	Buddhist	W. Anderson	1928	Victorian	R. Workman
1890	Montague	W. Martin	1929	Dr. Freeland	L. Schaefer
1894	Assignee	F. Taral	1930	Gallant Fox	E Sande
1895	Belmar	F. Taral	1931	Mate	G. Ellis
1896	Margrave	H. Griffin	1932	Burgoo King	E. James
1897	Paul Kauvar	Thorpe	1933	Head Play	C. Kurtsinger
1898	Sly Fox	W. Simms	1934	High Quest	R. Jones
1899	Half Time	R. Clawson	1935	Omaha	W. Saunders
1900	Hindus	H. Spencer	1936	Bold Venture	G. Woolf
1901	The Parader	Landry	1937	War Admiral	C. Kurtsinger
1902	Old England	L. Jackson	1938	Dauber	M. Peters
1903	Flocarline	W. Gannon	1939	Challedon	G. Seabo
1904	Bryn Mawr	E. Hildebrand	1940	Bimelech	F. A. Smith
1905	Cairngorm	W Davis	1941	Whirlaway	E. Arcaro
1906	Whimsical	W. Miller	1942	Alsab	B. James
1907	Don Enrique	G. Mountain	1943	Count Fleet	J. Longden
1908	Royal Tourist	E. Dugan	1944	Pensive	C. McCreary
1909	Effendi	W. Doyle	1945	Polynesian	W. D. Wright
1910	Layminster	R. Estep	1946	Assault	W. Mehrtens
1911	Watervale	E. Dugan	1947	Faultless	D. Dobson
1912	Colonel Holloway	C.Turner	1948	Citation	E. Arcaro

YEAR	HORSE	JOCKEY			
1949	Capot	T. Atkinson	1973	Secretariat	Ron Turcotte
1950	Hill Prince	E. Arcaro	1974	Little Current	M. A. Rivera
1951	Bold	E. Arcaro	1975	Master Derby	D. G. McHargue
1952	Blue Man	C. McCreary	1976	Elocutionist	John Lively
1953	Native Dancer	E. Guerin	1977	Seattle Slew	Jean Cruguet
1954	Hasty Road	J. Adams	1978	Affirmed	Steve Cauthen
1955	Nashua	E. Arcaro	1979	Spectacular Bid	Ron Franklin
1956	Fabius	W. Hartack	1980	Codex	Angel Cordero, Jr.
1957	Bold Ruler	E. Arcaro	1981	Pleasant Colony	Jorge Velasquez
1958	Tim Tam	I. Valenzuela	1982	Aloma's Ruler	Jack Kaenel
1959	Royal Orbit	W. Harmatz	1983	Deputed Testamony	Donald Miller, Jr.
1960	Bally Ache	R. Ussery	1984	Gate Dancer	Angel Cordero, Jr.
1961	Carry Back	J. Sellers	1985	Tank's Prospect	Pat Day
1962	Greek Money	J. L. Rotz	1986	Snow Chief	Alex Solis
1963	Candy Spots	W. Shoemaker	1987	Alysheba	Chris J. McCarron
1964	Northern Dancer	W. Hartack	1988	Risen Star	Eddie Delahoussaye
1965	Tom Rolfe	R. Turcotte	1989	Sunday Silence	Patrick Valenzuela
1966	Kauai King	D. Brumfield	1990	Summer Squall	Patrick Day
1967	Damascus	W. Shoemaker	1991	Hansel	Jerry Bailey
1968	Forward Pass	I. Valenzuela	1992	Pine Bluff	Chris J. McCarron
1969	Majestic Prince	W. Hartack	1993	Prairie Bayou	Mike Smith
1970	Personality	E. Belmonte	1994	Tabasco Cat	Pat Day
1971	Canonero II	G. Avila	1995	Timber Country	Pat Day
1972	Bee Bee Bee	Eldon Nelson	1996	Louis Quatorze	Pat Day
			1997	Silver Charm	Gary Stevens

Winners of the Belmont Stakes

YEAR	HORSE	JOCKEY	YEAR	HORSE	JOCKEY
1867	Ruthless	J. Gilpatrick	1895	Belmar	F. Taral
1868	General Duke	R. Swim	1896	Hastings	H. Griffin
1869	Fenian	C. Miller	1897	Scottish Chieftain	J. Scherrer
1870	Kingfisher	E. Brown	1898	Bowling Brook	F. Littlefield
1871	Harry Basset	W. Miller	1899	Jean Bereaud	R.R. Clawson
1872	Joe Daniels	J. Rowe	1900	Ildrim	N. Turner
1873	Springbok	J. Rowe	1901	Commando	H. Spencer
1874	Saxon	G. Barbee	1902	Masterman	J. Bullman
1875	Calvin	R. Swim	1903	Africander	J. Bullman
1876	Algerine	W. Donohue	1904	Delhi	G. Odom
1877	Cloverbrook	C. Holloway	1905	Tanya	E. Hildebrand
1878	Duke of Magenta	L. Hughes	1906	Burgomaster	L. Lyne
1879	Spendthrift	S. Evans	1907	Peter Pan	G. Mountain
1880	Grenada	L. Hughes	1908	Colin	J. Notter
1881	Saunterer	T. Costello	1909	Joe Madden	E. Dugan
1882	Forester	J. McLaughlin	1910	Sweep	J. Butwell
1883	George Kinney	J. McLaughlin	1911	no race	
1884	Panique	J. McLaughlin	1912	no race	
1885	Tyrant	P. Duffy	1913	Price Eugene	R. Troxler
1886	Inspector B.	J. McLaughlin	1914	Luke McLuke	M. Buxton
1887	Hanover	J. McLaughlin	1915	The Finn	G. Byrne
1888	Sir Dixon	J. McLaughlin	1916	Friar Rock	E. Haynes
1889	Eric	W. Hayward	1917	Hourless	J. Butwell
1890	Burlington	S. Barnes	1918	Johren	F. Robinson
1891	Foxford	E. Garrison	1919	Sir Barton	J. Loftus
1892	Patron	W. Hayward	1920	Man o' War	C. Kummer
1893	Commanche	W.Simms	1921	Grey Lag	E. Sande
1894	Henry of Navarre	W. Simms	1922	Pillory	C. H. Miller

YEAR	HORSE	JOCKEY	YEAR	HORSE	JOCKEY
1923	Zev	E. Sande	1961	Sherluck	B. Baeza
1924	Mad Play	E. Sande	1962	Jaipur	W. Shoemaker
1925	American Flag	A. Johnson	1963	Chateaugay	B. Baeza
1926	Crusader	A. Johnson	1964	Quadrangle	M. Ycaza
1927	Chance Shot	E. Sande	1965	Hail to All	J. Sellers
1928	Vito	C. Kummer	1966	Amberoid	W. Boland
1929	Blue Larkspur	M. Garner	1967	Damascus	W. Shoemaker
1930	Gallant Fox	E. Sande	1968	Stage Door Johnny	H. Gustines
1931	Twenty Grand	C. Kurtsinger	1969	Arts and Letters	B. Baeza
1932	Faireno	T. Malley	1970	High Echelon	J. L. Rotz
1933	Hurryoff	M. Garner	1971	Pass Catcher	W. Blum
1934	Peace Chance	W. D. Wright	1972	Riva Ridge	R. Turcotte
1935	Omaha	W. Saunders	1973	Secretariat	R. Turcotte
1936	Granville	J. Stout	1974	Little Current	M. A. Rivera
1937	War Admiral	C. Kurtsinger	1975	Avatar	W. Shoemaker
1938	Pasteurized	J. Stout	1976	Bold Forbes	A. Cordero Jr.
1939	Johnstown	J. Stout	1977	Seattle Slew	J. Cruguet
1940	Bimelech	F.A. Smith	1978	Affirmed	S. Cauthen
1941	Whirlaway	E. Arcaro	1979	Coastal	R. Hernandez
1942	Shut Out	E. Arcaro	1980	Temperence Hill	E. Maple
1943	Count Fleet	J. Longden	1981	Summing	G. Martens
1944	Bounding Home	G.L. Smith	1982	Conquistador Cielo	L. Pincay Jr.
1945	Pavot	E. Arcaro	1983	Caveat	L. Pincay Jr.
1946	Assault	W. Mehrtens	1984	Swale	L. Pincay Jr.
1947	Phalanx	R. Donoso	1985	Creme Fraiche	E. Maple
1948	Citation	E. Arcaro	1986	Danzig Connection	C. J. McCarron
1949	Capot	T. Atkinson	1987	Bet Twice	C. Perret
1950	Middleground	W. Boland	1988	Risen Star	E. Delahoussaye
1951	Counterpoint	D. Gorman	1989	Easy Goer	P. Day
1952	One Count	E. Arcaro	1990	Go and Go	J.J. Kinane
1953	Native Dancer	E. Guerin	1991	Hansel	J.D. Bailey
1954	High Gun	E. Guerin	1992	A.P. Indy	E. Delahoussaye
1955	Nashua	E. Arcaro	1993	Colonial Affair	J. A. Krone
1956	Needles	D. Erb	1994	Tabasco Cat	P. Day
1957	Gallant Man	W. Shoemaker	1995	Thunder Gulch	G. L. Stevens
1958	Cavan	P. Anderson	1996	Editor's Note	R. Douglas
1959	Sword Dancer	W. Shoemaker	1997	Touch Gold	C. McCarron
1960	Celtic Ash	W. Hartack			

Triple Crown Winners

YEAR	HORSE	JOCKEY	TRAINER	OWNER	YEAR	HORSE	JOCKEY	TRAINER	OWNER
1919	Sir Barton	John Loftus	H. G. Bedwell	J. K. L. Ross	1946	Assault	Warren Mehrtens	Max Hirsch Hirsch	King Ranch
1930	Gallant Fox	Earl Sande	James Fitzsimmons	Belair Stud	1948	Citation	Eddie Arcaro	Ben A Jones	Calumet Farm
1935	Omaha	William Saunders	James Fitzsimmons	Belair Stud	1973	Secretariat	Ron Turcotte	Lucien Laurin	Meadow Stable
1937	War Admiral	Charley Kurtsinger	George Conway	Samuel D. Riddle	1977	Seattle Slew	Jean Cruget	William Turner, Jr.	Karen L. Taylor
1941	Whirlaway	Eddie Arcaro	Ben A. Jones	Calumet Farm	1978	Affirmed	Steve Cauthen	Lazaro S. Barrera	Harbor View Farm
1943	Count Fleet	John Longden	Don Cameron	Mrs. J.D. Hertz					

Top Money-Winning Jockeys

Year	Jockey	Amt. Won	Year	Jockey	Amt. Won
1908	J. Notter	$464,322	1954	W. Shoemaker	1,876,760
1909	E. Dugan	166,355	1955	E. Arcaro	1,864,796
1910	C.H. Shilling	176,030	1956	W. Hartack	2,343,955
1911	T. Koerner	88,308	1957	W. Hartack	3,060,501
1912	J. Butwell	79,843	1958	W. Shoemaker	2,961,693
1913	M. Buxton	82,552	1959	W. Shoemaker	2,843,133
1914	J. McCahey	121,845	1960	W. Shoemaker	2,123,961
1915	M. Garner	96,628	1961	W. Shoemaker	2,690,819
1916	J. McTaggart	155,055	1962	W. Shoemaker	2,916,844
1917	F. Robinson	148,057	1963	W. Shoemaker	2,526,925
1918	L. Luke	201,864	1964	W. Shoemaker	2,649,553
1919	J. Loftus	252,707	1965	B. Baeza	2,582,702
1920	C. Kummer	292,376	1966	B. Baeza	2,951,022
1921	E. Sande	263,043	1967	B. Baeza	3,088,888
1922	A. Johnson	345,054	1968	B. Baeza	2,835,108
1923	E. Sande	569,394	1969	J. Velasquez	2,542,315
1924	I. Parke	290,395	1970	L. Pincay, Jr.	2,626,526
1925	L. Fator	305,775	1971	L. Pincay, Jr.	3,784,377
1926	L. Fator	361,435	1972	L. Pincay, Jr.	3,225,827
1927	E. Sande	277,877	1973	L. Pincay, Jr.	4,093,492
1928	L. McAtee	301,295	1974	L. Pincay, Jr.	4,251,060
1929	M. Garner	314,975	1975	B. Baeza	3,674,398
1930	R. Workman	420,438	1976	A. Cordero, Jr.	4,709,500
1931	C. Kurtsinger	392,095	1977	S. Cauthen	6,151,750
1932	R. Workman	385,070	1978	D.G. McHargue	6,188,353
1933	R. Jones	226,285	1979	L. Pincay, Jr.	8,183,535
1934	W.D. Wright	287,185	1980	C.J. McCarron	7,666,100
1935	S. Coucci	319,760	1981	C.J. McCarron	8,397,604
1936	W.D. Wright	264,000	1982	A. Cordero, Jr.	9,702,520
1937	C. Kurtsinger	384,202	1983	A. Cordero, Jr.	10,116,807
1938	N. Wall	385,161	1984	C.J. McCarron	12,038,213
1939	B. James	353,333	1985	L. Pincay, Jr.	13,415,049
1940	E. Arcaro	343,661	1986	J.A. Santos	11,329,297
1941	D. Meade	398,627	1987	J.A. Santos	12,407,355
1942	E. Arcaro	481,949	1988	J.A. Santos	14,877,298
1943	J. Longden	573,276	1989	J.A. Santos	13,847,003
1944	T. Atkinson	899,101	1990	G.L. Stevens	13,881,198
1945	J. Longden	981,977	1991	C.J. McCarron	14,456,073
1946	T. Atkinson	1,036,825	1992	K.J. Desormeaux	14,193,006
1947	D. Dodson	1,429,949	1993	M.E. Smith	14,008,148
1948	E. Arcaro	1,686,230	1994	M.E. Smith	9,985,703
1949	S. Brooks	1,316,817	1995	J. Bailey	16,308,230
1950	E. Arcaro	1,410,160	1996	J. Bailey	17,064,409
1951	W. Shoemaker	1,329,890			
1952	E. Arcaro	1,859,591			
1953	W. Shoemaker	1,784,187			

Source: Daily Racing Form

Auto Racing

Indianapolis 500 Winners

Year	Winner	Speed (mph)	Year	Winner	Speed (mph)
1911	Ray Harroun	74.602	1957	Sam Hanks	135.601
1912	Joe Dawson	78.719	1958	Jimmy Bryan	133.791
1913	Jules Goux	75.933	1959	Rodger Ward	135.857
1914	Rene Thomas	82.474	1960	Jim Rathmann	138.767
1915	Ralph DePalma	89.840	1961	A. J. Foyt	139.131
1916	Dario Resta	84.001	1962	Rodger Ward	140.293
1917–18	Race not held due to World War I		1963	Parnelli Jones	143.137
1919	Howard Wilcox	88.050	1964	A. J. Foyt	147.350
1920	Gaston Chevrolet	88.618	1965	Jimmy Clark	150.686
1921	Tommy Milton	89.621	1966	Graham Hill	144.317
1922	Jimmy Murphy	94.484	1967	A. J. Foyt	151.207
1923	Tommy Milton	90.954	1968	Bobby Unser	152.882
1924	L. L. Corum, Joe Boyer	98.234	1969	Mario Andretti	156.867
1925	Pete DePaolo	101.127	1970	Al Unser	155.749
1926	Frank Lockhart	95.904	1971	Al Unser	157.735
1927	George Souders	97.545	1972	Mark Donohue	162.962
1928	Louis Meyer	99.482	1973	Gordon Johncock	159.036
1929	Ray Keech	97.585	1974	Johnny Rutherford	158.589
1930	Billy Arnold	100.448	1975	Bobby Unser	149.213
1931	Louis Schneider	96.629	1976	Johnny Rutherford	148.725
1932	Fred Frame	104.144	1977	A. J. Foyt	161.331
1933	Louis Meyer	104.162	1978	Al Unser	161.363
1934	Bill Cummings	104.863	1979	Rick Mears	158.899
1935	Kelly Petillo	106.240	1980	Johnny Rutherford	142.862
1936	Louis Meyer	109.069	1981	Bobby Unser	139.084
1937	Wilbur Shaw	113.580	1982	Gordon Johncock	162.029
1938	Floyd Roberts	117.200	1983	Tom Sneva	162.117
1939	Wilbur Shaw	115.035	1984	Rick Mears	163.612
1940	Wilbur Shaw	114.277	1985	Danny Sullivan	152.982
1941	Floyd Davis, Mauri Rose	115.117	1986	Bobby Rahal	170.722
1942–45	Race not held due to World War II		1987	Al Unser	162.175
1946	George Robson	114.820	1988	Rick Mears	144.809
1947	Mauri Rose	116.338	1989	Emerson Fittipaldi	167.581
1948	Mauri Rose	119.814	1990	Arie Luyendyk	185.981
1949	Bill Holland	121.327	1991	Rick Mears	176.457
1950	Johnnie Parsons	124.002	1992	Al Unser, Jr.	134.479
1951	Lee Wallard	126.244	1993	Emerson Fittipaldi	157.207
1952	Troy Ruttman	128.922	1994	Al Unser, Jr.	160.872
1953	Bill Vukovich	128.740	1995	Jacques Villeneuve	153.616
1954	Bill Vukovich	130.840	1996	Buddy Lazier	147.956
1955	Bob Sweikert	128.209	1997	Arie Luyendyk	145.857
1956	Pat Flaherty	128.490			

Source: Indianapolis Motor Speedway

Speedway Money

Year	Purse	Winner	Year	Purse	Winner
1911	$27,550	$14,000	1957	$300,252	$103,844
1912	55,225	35,000	1958	305,217	111,327
1913	55,875	35,000	1959	338,100	105,805
1914	51,675	39,750	1960	369,150	110,000
1915	51,200	22,600	1961	400,000	117,975
1916	31,350	12,000	1962	426,152	125,015
1917–18	Race not held due to World War I		1963	494,030	148,513
1919	55,275	20,000	1964	506,575	153,650
1920	93,550	36,300	1965	628,399	186,621
1921	86,650	36,000	1966	691,808	156,297
1922	70,575	33,700	1967	734,634	171,227
1923	83,425	28,500	1968	712,269	177,523
1924	86,850	20,500	1969	805,127	205,727
1925	87,750	27,800	1970	1,000,002	271,697
1926	88,100	29,500	1971	1,001,604	238,454
1927	89,850	25,100	1972	1,011,848	218,767
1928	90,750	28,500	1973	1,006,105	236,022
1929	95,150	24,600	1974	1,015,686	245,031
1930	96,250	36,900	1975	1,001,321	214,031
1931	81,800	29,500	1976	1,037,755	256,121
1932	93,900	32,050	1977	1,116,807	259,791
1933	54,450	18,000	1978	1,145,225	290,383
1934	83,775	29,075	1979	1,271,954	270,401
1935	78,575	30,600	1980	1,503,225	318,819
1936	82,525	31,300	1981	1,609,375	299,124
1937	92,135	35,075	1982	2,067,475	290,609
1938	91,075	31,950	1983	2,411,450	385,886
1939	87,050	27,375	1984	2,795,899	434,061
1940	85,525	31,875	1985	3,271,025	517,662
1941	90,925	29,735	1986	4,001,450	581,062
1942–45	Race not held due to World War II		1987	4,490,375	526,762
1946	115,450	42,550	1988	5,025,400	809,853
1947	137,425	31,450	1989	5,723,725	1,001,604
1948	171,075	42,800	1990	6,325,803	1,090,940
1949	179,050	51,575	1991	7,009,150	1,219,704
1950	201,135	57,458	1992	7,527,450	1,244,184
1951	207,650	63,612	1993	7,681,300	1,155,304
1952	230,100	61,743	1994	7,864,800	1,373,813
1953	246,300	89,496	1995	8,063,550	1,312,019
1954	269,375	74,934	1996	8,114,600	1,367,854
1955	270,400	76,138	1997	8,642,450	1,568,150
1956	282,052	93,819			

Source: Indianapolis Motor Speedway

Top Indianapolis 500 Winners

Winner	Years
A. J. Foyt	1961, 1964, 1967, 1977
Rick Mears	1979, 1984, 1988, 1991
Al Unser, Sr.	1970, 1971, 1978, 1987
Louis Meyer	1928, 1933, 1936
Mauri Rose	1941, 1947, 1948
Johnny Rutherford	1974, 1976, 1980
Wilbur Shaw	1937, 1939, 1940
Bobby Unser	1968, 1976, 1981

Source: Indianapolis Motor Speedway

NASCAR Winston Cup Champions

Year	Driver
1949	Red Byron
1950	Bill Rexford
1951	Herb Thomas
1952	Tim Flock
1953	Herb Thomas
1954	Lee Petty
1955	Tim Flock
1956	Buck Baker
1957	Buck Baker
1958	Lee Petty
1959	Lee Petty
1960	Rex White
1961	Ned Jarrett
1962	Joe Weatherly
1963	Joe Weatherly
1964	Richard Petty
1965	Ned Jarrett
1966	David Pearson
1967	Richard Petty
1968	David Pearson
1969	David Pearson
1970	Bobby Isaac
1971	Richard Petty
1972	Richard Petty
1973	Benny Parsons
1974	Richard Petty
1975	Richard Petty
1976	Cale Yarborough
1977	Cale Yarborough
1978	Cale Yarborough
1979	Richard Petty
1980	Dale Earnhardt
1981	Darrel Waltrip
1982	Darrel Waltrip
1983	Bobby Allison
1984	Terry Labonte
1985	Darrel Waltrip
1986	Dale Earnhardt
1987	Dale Earnhardt
1988	Bill Elliott
1989	Rusty Wallace
1990	Dale Earnhardt
1991	Dale Earnhardt
1992	Alan Kulwicki
1993	Dale Earnhardt
1994	Dale Earnhardt
1995	Jeff Gordon
1996	Terry Labonte

Heavyweight Boxing Champions

	Winner	Opponent	Site of Championship
Aug. 29, 1885	John L. Sullivan (Wins Vacant World Title)	Dominick McCaffrey	Cincinnati
Sept. 7, 1892	James J. Corbett	John L. Sullivan	New Orleans
March 17, 1897	Bob Fitzsimmons	James J. Corbett	Carson City, NV
June 9, 1899	James J. Jeffries	Bob Fitzsimmons	Brooklyn, NY
July 3, 1905	Marvin Hart (Wins Vacant World Title)	Jack Root	Reno
Feb. 23, 1906	Tommy Burns	Marvin Hart	Los Angeles
Dec. 26, 1908	Jack Johnson	Tommy Burns	Sydney
April 5, 1915	Jess Willard	Jack Johnson	Havana
July 4, 1919	Jack Dempsey	Jess Willard	Toledo, OH
Sept. 23, 1926	Gene Tunney	Jack Dempsey	Philadelphia
June 12, 1930	Max Schmeling (Wins Vacant World Title)	Jack Sharkey	Bronx, NY
June 21, 1932	Jack Sharkey	Max Schmeling	Long Island City, NY
June 29, 1933	Primo Carnera	Jack Sharkey	Long Island City, NY
June 14, 1934	Max Baer	Primo Carnera	Long Island City,NY
June 13, 1935	James J. Braddock	Max Baer	Long Island City, NY
June 22, 1937	Joe Louis	James J. Braddock	Chicago
June 22, 1949	Ezzard Charles (Wins Vacant World Title)	Jersey Joe Walcott	Chicago
July 18, 1951	Jersey Joe Walcott	Ezzard Charles	Pittsburgh
Sept. 23, 1952	Rocky Marciano	Jersey Joe Walcott	Philadelphia
Nov. 30, 1956	Floyd Patterson (Wins Vacant World Title)	Archie Moore	Chicago
June 26, 1959	Ingemar Johansson	Floyd Patterson	Bronx, NY
June 20, 1960	Floyd Patterson	Ingemar Johansson	New York City
Sept. 25, 1962	Sonny Liston	Floyd Patterson	Chicago
Feb. 25, 1964	Cassius Clay*	Sonny Liston	Miami Beach
March 5, 1965	Ernie Terrell (Wins Vacant World Boxing Association Title)	Eddie Machen	Chicago
Feb. 6, 1967	Muhammad Ali (Unifies World Title)	Ernie Terrell	Houston
March 4, 1968	Joe Frazier (Wins Vacant New York World Title)	Buster Mathis	New York City
April 27, 1968	Jimmy Ellis (Wins Vacant WBA Title)	Jerry Quarry	Oakland, CA
Feb. 16, 1970	Joe Frazier (Unifies World Title)	Jimmy Ellis	New York City
Jan. 22, 1973	George Foreman	Joe Frazier	Kingston, Jamaica
Oct. 30, 1974	Muhammad Ali	George Foreman	Kinshasa, Zaire
Feb. 15, 1978	Leon Spinks	Muhammad Ali	Las Vegas
June 9, 1978	Larry Holmes (Wins World Boxing Council Title)	Ken Norton**	Las Vegas
Sept. 15, 1978	Muhammad Ali (Regains WBA Title)	Leon Spinks	New Orleans
Oct. 20, 1979	John Tate (Wins Vacant WBA Title)	Gerrie Coetzee	Pretoria, South Africa
March 31, 1980	Mike Weaver (Wins WBA Title)	John Tate	Knoxville, TN
Dec. 10, 1982	Michael Dokes (Wins WBA Title)	Mike Weaver	Las Vegas
Sept. 23, 1983	Gerrie Coetzee (Wins WBA Title)	Michael Dokes	Richfield, OH

	Winner	Opponent	Site of Championship
March 9, 1984	Tim Witherspoon (Wins Vacant WBC Title)	Greg Page	Las Vegas
Aug. 31, 1984	Pinklon Thomas (Wins WBC Title)	Tim Witherspoon	Las Vegas
Dec. 1, 1984	Greg Page (Wins WBA Title)	Gerrie Coetzee	Sun City
April 29, 1985	Tony Tubbs (Wins WBA Title)	Greg Page	Buffalo
Sept. 21, 1985	Michael Spinks (Wins International Boxing Federation Title)	Larry Holmes†	Las Vegas
Jan. 17, 1986	Tim Witherspoon (Wins WBA Title)	Tony Tubbs	Atlanta
March 22, 1986	Trevor Berbick (Wins WBC Title)	Pinklon Thomas	Las Vegas
Nov. 22, 1986	Mike Tyson (Wins WBC Title)	Trevor Berbick	Las Vegas
Dec. 12, 1986	Bonecrusher Smith (Wins WBA Title)	Tim Witherspoon	New York City
March 7, 1987	Mike Tyson (Wins WBA Title)	Bonecrusher Smith	Las Vegas
May 30, 1987	Tony Tucker (Wins Vacant IBF Title)	Buster Douglas	Las Vegas
Aug. 1, 1987	Mike Tyson (Wins IBF Title; Unifies World Title)	Tony Tucker	Las Vegas
Feb. 11, 1990	Buster Douglas (Wins World Title)	Mike Tyson	Tokyo
Oct. 25, 1990	Evander Holyfield (Wins World Title)	Buster Douglas	Las Vegas
Nov. 13, 1992	Riddick Bowe (Wins World Title)	Evander Holyfield	Las Vegas
Nov. 6, 1993	Evander Holyfield (Regains WBA, IBF Titles)	Riddick Bowe	Las Vegas
April 22, 1994	Michael Moorer (Wins WBA, IBF Titles)	Evander Holyfield	Las Vegas
Sept. 24, 1994	Oliver McCall (Wins WBC Title)	Lennox Lewis‡	London
Nov. 5, 1994	George Foreman (Regains WBA Title; Wins IBF Title)	Michael Moorer	Las Vegas
April 8, 1995	Bruce Seldon (Wins Vacant WBA Title)	Tony Tucker	Las Vegas
Sept. 2, 1995	Frank Bruno (Wins WBC Title)	Oliver McCall	London
Dec. 9, 1995	Frans Botha (Wins Vacant IBF Title)	Axel Schulz	Stuttgart, Germany
March 16, 1996	Mike Tyson (Regains WBC Title)	Frank Bruno	Las Vegas
June 22, 1996	Michael Moorer (Regains Vacant IBF Title)	Axel Schulz	Dortmund, Germany
Sept. 7, 1996	Mike Tyson (Regains WBA Title)	Bruce Seldon	Las Vegas
Nov. 9, 1996	Evander Holyfield (Regains WBA Title)	Mike Tyson	Las Vegas
Feb. 7, 1997	Lennox Lewis (Regains WBC title)	Oliver McCall	Las Vegas

*Immediately after winning the title, Clay changed his name to Muhammad Ali
**Norton had been named WBC champion following his victory over Jimmy Young in November 1977
†After vacating the WBC title, Holmes had been named IBF champion following his November 1983 victory over Marvis Frazier
‡Lewis had been named WBC champion following his victory over Razor Ruddock in October 1992

Source: The Ring Magazine

The 1998 World Cup ⚽

The 64 soccer matches of the 16th World Cup competition will be played in 10 French cities between June 10 and July 12,1998. A record 172 countries participated in the preliminary competition in 1996 and 1997, with 32 countries qualifying for the final competition.

Year	Champion	Runner-up	Score
1930	Uruguay	Argentina	4-2
1934	Italy	Czechoslovakia	2-1 (in overtime)
1938	Italy	Hungary	4-2
1950	Uruguay	Brazil	2-1
1954	West Germany	Hungary	3-2
1958	Brazil	Sweden	5-2
1962	Brazil	Czechoslovakia	3-1
1966	England	West Germany	4-2 (in overtime)
1970	Brazil	Italy	4-1
1974	West Germany	Holland	2-1
1978	Argentina	Holland	3-1 (in overtime)
1982	Italy	West Germany	3-1
1986	Argentina	West Germany	3-2
1990	West Germany	Argentina	1-0
1994	Brazil	Italy	0-0 (decided by penalty kicks, 3-2)

Source: FIFA-Féderation Internationale de Football Association

Running Marathons

New York City Marathon Winners

Men	Time	Women	Time
1970: Gary Muhrche	2:31:38	NO WINNER	
1971: Norman Higgins	2:22:54	Beth Bonner	2:55:22
1972: Sheldon Karlin	2:27:52	Nina Kuscsik	3:08:41
1973: Tom Fleming	2:21:54	Nina Kuscsik	2:57:07
1974: Norbert Sander	2:26:30	Kathrine Switzer	3:07:29
1975: Tom Fleming	2:19:27	Kin Merritt	2:46:14
1976: Bill Rodgers	2:10:10	Miki Gorman	2:39:11
1977: Bill Rodgers	2:11:38	Miki Gorman	2:43:10
1978: Bill Rodgers	2:12:12	Grete Waitz	2:32:30
1979: Bill Rodgers	2:11:42	Grete Waitz	2:27:33
1980: Alberto Salazar	2:09:41	Grete Waitz	2:25:42
1981: Alberto Salazar	2:08:13	Allison Roe	2:25:29
1982: Alberto Salazar	2:09:29	Grete Waitz	2:27:14
1983: Rod Dixon	2:08:59	Grete Waitz	2:27:00
1984: Orlando Pizzolato	2:14:53	Grete Waitz	2:29:30
1985: Orlando Pizzolato	2:11:34	Grete Waitz	2:28:34
1986: Gianni Poli	2:11:06	Grete Waitz	2:28:06
1987: Ibrahim Hussein	2:11:01	Priscilla Welch	2:30:17
1988: Steve Jones	2:08:20	Grete Waitz	2:28:07
1989: Juma Ikangaa	2:08:01	Ingrid Kristiansen	2:25:30

Men	Time	Women	Time
1990: Douglas Wakiihuri	2:12:39	Wenda Panfil	2:30:45
1991: Salvador Garcia	2:09:28	Liz McColgan	2:27:00
1992: Willie Mtolo	2:09:29	Lisa Ondieki	2:24:40
1993: Andres Espinosa	2:10:04	Uta Pippig	2:26:24
1994: German Silva	2:11:21	Tegla Loroupe	2:27:37
1995: German Silva	2:10:00	Tegla Loroupe	2:28:06
1996: Giacomo Leone	2:09:54	Anuta Catuna	2:28:18

Source: New York Road Runners Club

Boston Marathon Champions

Men's Open	Time		Time
1897: John J. McDermott	2:55:10	1940: Gerard Cote	2:28:28
1898: Ronald J. MacDonald	2:42:00	1941: Leslie S. Pawson	2:30:38
1899: Lawrence J. Brignolia	2:54:38	1942: Bernard Joseph Smith	2:26:51
1900: John Peter Caffery	2:39:44	1943: Gerard Cote	2:28:25
1901: John Peter Caffery	2:29:23	1944: Gerard Cote	2:31:50
1902: Sammy Mellor	2:43:12	1945: John A. Kelley	2:30:40
1903: John C. Lorden	2:41:29	1946: Stylianos Kyriakides	2:29:27
1904: Michael Spring	2:38:04	1947: Yun Bok	2:25:39
1905: Fred Lorz	2:38:25	1948: Gerard Cote	2:31:02
1906: Timothy Ford	2:45:45	1949: Karl Gosta Leandersson	2:31:50
1907: Tom Longboat	2:24:24	1950: Kee Yong Ham	2:32:39
1908: Thomas Morrissey	2:25:43	1951: Shigeki Tanaka	2:27:45
1909: Henri Renaud	2:53:36	1952: Doroteo Flores	2:31:53
1910: Fred S. Cameron	2:28:52	1953: Keizo Yamada,	2:18:51
1911: Clarence H. DeMar	2:21:39	1954: Veikko Karvonen	2:20:39
1912: Mike Ryan	2:21:18	1955: Hideo Hamamura	2:18:22
1913: Fritz Carlson	2:25:14	1956: Antti Viskari	2:14:14
1914: James Duffy	2:25:01	1957: John J. Kelley	2:20:05
1915: Edouard Fabre	2:31:41	1958: Franjo Mihalic	2:25:54
1916: Arthur Roth	2:27:16	1959: Eino Oksanen	2:22:42
1917: Bill Kennedy	2:28:37	1960: Paavo Kotil	2:20:54
1918: Camp DevenA	2:24:53	1961: Eino Oksanen	2:23:39
1919: Carl Linde	2:29:13	1962: Eino Oksanen	2:23:48
1920: Peter Trivoulides	2:29:31	1963: Aurele Vandendriessche	2:18:58
1921: Frank Zuna	2:18:57	1964: Aurele Vandendriessche	2:19:59
1922: Clarence H. DeMar	2:18:10	1965: Morio Shigematsu	2:16:33
1923: Clarence H. DeMar	2:23:37	1966: Kenji Kimihara	2:17:11
1924: Clarence H. DeMar	2:29:40	1967: David C. McKenzie	2:15:45
1925: Charles Mellor	2:33:00	1968: Amby Burfoot	2:22:17
1926: Johnny Miles	2:25:40	1969: Yoshiaki Unetani	2:13:49
1927: Clarence H. DeMar	2:40:22	1970: Ron Hill, Cheshird	2:10:30
1928: Clarence H. DeMar	2:37:07	1971: Alvaro Mejia	2:18:45
1929: Johnny Miles	2:33:08	1972: Olavi Suomalainend	2:15:39
1930: Clarence H. DeMar	2:34:48	1973: Jon P. Andersonn	2:16:03
1931: James P. Henigan	2:46:45	1974: Neil Cusack	2:13:39
1932: Paul deBruyn	2:33:36	1975: Bill Rodgers	2:09:55
1933: Leslie S. Pawso	2:31:01	1976: Jack Fultz	2:20:19
1934: Dave Komonen	2:32:53	1977: Jerome P. Drayton	2:14:46
1935: John A. Kelley	2:32:07	1978: Bill Rodgers	2:10:13
1936: Ellison M. Brown	2:33:40	1979: Bill Rodgers	2:09:27
1937: Walter Young	2:33:20	1980: Bill Rodgers	2:12:11
1938: Leslie S. Pawson	2:35:34	1981: Toshihiko Seko	2:09:26
1939: Ellison M. Brown	2:28:51	1982: Alberto B. Salazar	2:08:52
		1983: Gregory A. Meyer	2:09:00

1984: Geoff Smith	2:10:34		1974: Miki Gorman	2:47:11
1985: Geoff Smith	2:14:05		1975: Liane Winte	2:42:24
1986: Robert de Castella	2:07:51		1976: Kim Merritt	2:47:10
1987: Toshihiko Seko	2:11:50		1977: Miki Gorman	2:48:33
1988: Ibrahim Hussein	2:08:43		1978: Gayle Barron	2:44:52
1989: Abebe Mekonnen	2:09:06		1979: Joan Benoi	2:35:15
1990: Gelindo Bordin	2:08:19		1980: Jacqueline Gareau	2:34:28
1991: Ibrahim Hussein	2:11:06		1981: Allison Roe	2:26:46
1992: Ibrahim Hussein	2:08:14		1982: Charlotte Tesk	2:29:33
1993: Cosmas Ndet	2:09:33		1983: Joan Benoit	2:22:43
1994: Cosmas Ndet	2:07:15		1984: Lorraine Moller	2:29:28
1995: Cosmas Ndeti	2:09:22		1985: Lisa Larsen Weidenbach	2:34:06
1996: Moses Tanui	2:09:15		1986: Ingrid Kristiansen	2:24:55
1997: Lameck Aguta	2:10:34		1987: Rosa Mota	2:25:21
			1988: Rosa Mota	2:24:30
Women's Open	**Time**		1989: Ingrid Kristiansen	2:24:33
1966: Roberta Gibb—Unofficial	3:21:40		1990: Rosa Mota	2:25:24
1967: Roberta Gibb—Unofficial	3:27:17		1991: Wanda Panfil	2:24:18
1968: Roberta Gibb—Unofficial	3:30:00		1992: Olga Markova	2:23:43
1969: Sara Mae Berman—Unofficial	3:22:46		1993: Olga Markova	2:25:27
1970: Sara Mae Berman—Unofficial	3:05:07		1994: Uta Pippig	2:21:45
1971: Sara Mae Berman—Unofficial	3:08:30		1995: Uta Pippig	2:25:11
1972: Nina L. Kuscsik	3:10:26		1996: Uta Pippig	2:27:12
1973: Jacqueline A. Hansen	3:05:59		1997: Fatuma Roba	2:26:23

Fastest Marathons

Men

Time	Runner, Country	Site	Date
2:06:50	Belayneh Dinsamo, Ethiopia	Rotterdam	April 17, 1988
2:07:02	Sammy Lelei, Kenya	Berlin	Sept. 24, 1995
2:07:07	Ahmed Salah, Djibouti	Rotterdam	April 17, 1988
2:07:12	Carlos Lopes, Portugal	Rotterdam	April 20, 1985
2:07:13	Steve Jones, Great Britain	Chicago	Oct. 20, 1985
2:07:15	Cosmos Ndeti, Kenya	Boston	April 18, 1994
2:07:19	Andreas Espinosa, Mexico	Boston	April 18, 1994
2:07:20	Vincent Rousseau, Belgium	Berlin	Sept. 24, 1995
2:07:35	Taisuke Kodama, Japan	Beijing	Oct. 19, 1986
2:07:35	Abebe Mekonnen, Ethiopia	Beijing	Oct. 16, 1988

Women

Time	Runner, Country	Site	Date
2:21:06	Ingrid Kristiansen, Norway	London	April 21, 1985
2:21:21	Joan Benoit Samuelson, USA	Chicago	Oct. 20, 1985
2:21:45	Uta Pippig, Germany	Boston	April 18, 1994
2:22:43	Joan Benoit, Samuelson, USA	Boston	April 18, 1983
2:22:48	Ingrid Kristiansen, Norway	London	May 10, 1987
2:23:05	Ingrid Kristiansen, Norway	Chicago	Oct. 20, 1985
2:23:29	Rosa Mota, Portugal	Chicago	Oct. 20, 1985
2:23:33	Valentina Yegorova, Russia	Boston	April 18, 1994
2:23:43	Olga Markova, Russia	Boston	April 20, 1992
2:23:51	Lisa Ondieki, Australia	Osaka	Jan. 31, 1988

Source: NYC Marathon Media Guide

Most Popular Participation Sports

Number of Persons Who Participated More Than Once, Seven Years of Age and Older (In millions)

	Sport	1985	1990	1995	1996
1	Exercise Walking	41.5	71.4	70.3	73.3
2	Swimming	73.3	67.5	61.5	60.2
3	Bicycle Riding	50.7	55.3	56.3	53.3
4	Exercising with Equipment	32.1	35.3	44.3	47.8
5	Fishing	–	46.9	44.2	45.6
6	Camping	46.4	46.2	42.8	44.7
7	Bowling	35.7	40.1	41.9	42.9
8	Billiards/Pool	23.0	28.1	31.1	34.5
9	Basketball	19.5	26.3	30.1	33.3
10	Boating (Motor/Power)	26.6	28.6	26.8	28.8
11	Hiking	21.1	22.0	25.0	26.5
12	Inline Skating	–	3.6	23.9	25.5
13	Aerobic Exercises	23.9	23.3	23.1	24.1
14	Golf	18.5	23.0	24.0	23.1
15	Running/Jogging	26.3	23.8	20.6	22.2
16	Dart Throwing	9.4	16.4	19.8	21.3
17	Softball	21.6	20.1	17.6	19.9
18	Hunting with Firearms	–	18.5	17.4	19.3
19	Volleyball	20.1	23.2	18.0	18.5
20	Target Shooting	–	12.8	13.9	15.7
21	Roller Skating—2x2	18.1	18.0	14.4	15.1
22	Baseball	12.8	15.6	15.7	14.8
23	Soccer	8.6	10.9	12.0	13.9
24	Football	–	–	12.1	11.6
25	Tennis	19.0	18.4	12.6	11.5

Source: National Sporting Goods Association

Sales of Sporting Goods
(In billions)

	1991	1994	1997*
Equipment	$13.4	$16.7	$18.1
Footwear	11.8	11.1	13.4
Clothing	10.7	9.5	11.4

*Projections.
Source: National Sporting Goods Association

WOMEN IN SPORTS

Is it good or bad to throw like a girl? Even with women's sports on the upswing, that can be a tough question to answer.

Twenty-five years after a federal statute called Title IX formally prohibited sex discrimination in sports, the country has seen female athletes flock to fields, courts, and tracks. One in three girls played some sort of sport in high school in 1996, up from one in 27 in 1971, according to the Women's Sports Foundation. Just in the past year, women's teams in gymnastics and basketball triumphed at the Olympics (and posed on Wheaties boxes), and two new professional basketball leagues "of their own" hit the hardwood.

But even though women jocks, known as Title IX babies, have come a long way, they still feel like the minor leagues. A recent

Boys and Girls in High-School Sports

Girls account for a growing percentage of high-school athletes, 39% in the 1995–96 school year, compared with 35% a decade earlier.

Year	Boys	Girls
1975–76	4,109,021	1,645,039
1980–81	3,503,124	1,853,789
1985–86	3,344,275	1,807,121
1990–91	3,406,355	1,892,316
1995–96	3,634,052*	2,367,936*

*Total does not include a portion total of 17,901 participants in coeducational sports.

Most Popular Boys Programs 1995–96

Sport	Number of athletes
Football	957,573
Basketball	545,596
Track & Field (outdoor)	454,645
Baseball	444,476
Soccer	283,728
Wrestling	221,162
Cross Country	168,203
Golf	140,011
Tennis	136,534
Swimming & Diving	81,000

Most Popular Girls Programs 1995–96

Sport	Number of athletes
Basketball	445,869
Track & Field (outdoor)	379,060
Volleyball	357,576
Softball (fast pitch)	305,217
Soccer	209,287
Tennis	146,573
Cross Country	140,187
Swimming & Diving	111,360
Field Hockey	56,142
Golf	39,634

Source: National Federation of State High School Associations

Men and Women in College Sports

Total NCAA Sports Participation

Year	Men	Women
1982–83	180,235	80,040
1985–86	200,031	95,351
1990–91	184,593	92,778
1995–96*	199,556	123,936

*Data for 1995-96 are not strictly comparable with earlier years because they include provisional members of the NCAA.

study on "gender equity" by the National Collegiate Athletic Association found that a bias in favor of men's sports persists. The biggest sports universities, classified by the NCAA as Division I, spend almost three times as much money recruiting for men's teams as for women's teams. And nearly twice as much scholarship money in Division I goes to the guys. "We're not really making up much ground," says Patty Viverito, chair of the NCAA's Committee on Women's Athletics.

Such inequities mean women athletes sometimes must fight their battles in court. In April 1997, for instance, the Supreme Court decided not to review a lower-court ruling that Brown University, which in 1991 attempted to eliminate its women's gymnastics and volleyball teams, was in violation of Title IX.

Women coaches also note that they haven't seen the employment opportunities they had hoped for. Sandra Scott, executive director of the New York State Public High School Athletic Association, says that when boys' and girls' athletic programs merged after the law's passage, women competing with men for coaching or administrative jobs often lost out. Women's Sports Foundation statistics bear her out: Only 13% of high school athletic directors are women.

Nevertheless, some big players are betting that women's sports will continue to grow. Magazine publishers are planning and testing new books on women's sports, including a female version of *Sports Illustrated*. And officials at the two new women's professional basketball leagues say their timing has been perfect in drawing media and marketing support.

"Media interest is heightened, corporate and television interest is heightened, and there's finally acceptance of what women can do, whether it's in the workplace or on the athletic field," says Val Ackerman, president of the Women's National Basketball Association. Adds Anne Cribbs, a co-founder of the American Basketball League, "We're only just now seeing the positive results of Title IX."

Both leagues have landed big name sponsors. The WNBA has lined up seven, including Anheuser-Busch's Bud Light, Nike, and Sears, while the ABL has Reebok, Nissan, and four others. Networks are interested too: The WNBA's games were shown on NBC, ESPN, and Lifetime, while ABL games were carried on several cable television networks. And the number of fans, though still small, is growing. The ABL, with one season already under its belt, saw average attendance running 20% above its pre-season projections of 3,000 a game. "You can hear the little girls in the stands saying they want to be like the big girls on the court," Ms. Cribbs says.

Not everyone believes the U.S. is ready to support two women's professional basketball leagues. Their seasons and geography don't yet overlap, but already they're competing for players and sponsors. Ms. Cribbs concedes that rounding up sponsors has been difficult and notes that "our entire budget still is less than what Michael Jordan gets paid."

Still, there's no doubt girl jocks have gained ground. Dorothy McIntyre, associate director of the Minnesota State High School League, recalls having to get a bus driver's license herself because the school where she worked at the time wouldn't hire anyone to drive girls' teams. "Asking me if we've made progress since the '60s," she says, "is like asking the Wright brothers if they'd like a ride on the Concorde."

Terzah Ewing

1995–1996 Participation in NCAA Men's Sports

Sport	Number of athletes
Baseball	24,332
Basketball	15,160
Cross Country	10,113
Fencing	731
Football	53,900
Golf	7,163
Gymnastics	457
Ice Hockey	3,554
Lacrosse	5,592
Rifle	481
Skiing	504
Soccer	16,885
Swimming	7,580
Tennis	7,961
Track, indoor	15,680
Track, outdoor	19,246
Volleyball	1,053
Water Polo	877
Wrestling	6,385
Crew	1,693
Squash	302
Total	**199,556**

Note: Provisional NCAA members are included in these numbers.

1995–1996 Participation in NCAA Women's Sports

Sport	Number of athletes
Basketball	13,343
Cross Country	9,949
Fencing	575
Field Hockey	4,828
Golf	2,083
Gymnastics	1,323
Lacrosse	3,635
Skiing	455
Soccer	13,394
Softball	12,606
Swimming	8,499
Tennis	8,156
Track, indoor	12,827
Track, outdoor	15,427
Volleyball	12,122
Rowing	3,569
Ice Hockey	416
Squash	364
Water Polo	365
Total	**123,936**

Note: Provisional NCAA members are included in these numbers.
Source: National Collegiate Athletic Association

INDEX

Coming in March 1998

THE WALL STREET JOURNAL GUIDE TO WHO'S WHO AND WHAT'S WHAT ON WALL STREET
By the Editors of *The Wall Street Journal*

From the ultimate source for investing, the definitive guide to the people, the corporations, and the agencies that govern Wall Street today, including . . .

THE FULL-SERVICE FIRMS
Wall Street's giants—the biggest and most diversified companies
• Merrill Lynch • Salomon Smith Barney • Prudential
• Morgan Stanley, Dean Witter • PaineWebber

THE TRADING POWERHOUSES
The gunslingers—rough and tumble risk-takers with the fattest paychecks
• Bear Stearns • Lehman Brothers

THE INVESTMENT BANKS
The white shoe firms—prestigious but powerful, they live by their brains, not their brawn
• Goldman Sachs • First Boston

THE COMMERCIAL BANKS
The new breed of creative financiers—trading in traditional banking roles for a piece of the wheeling and dealing securities industry
• J. P. Morgan • Bankers Trust

THE EXCHANGES
The Street's most venerable venues—locked in mortal combat for more than a decade
• The New York Stock Exchange • The NASD

THE REGULATORS
Wall Street's watchdogs—policemen of the nation's financial system
• The Securities and Exchange Commission • The Federal Reserve

Filled with privileged accounts and illuminating personality profiles of major Wall Street players, this book is the definitive guide for anyone who invests, works on the Street, or simply wants to know about the state of the financial world today and its prospects for tomorrow.